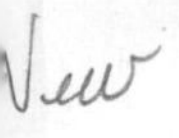

W9-BYQ-401

AMERICAN NATIONAL BIOGRAPHY

AMERICAN NATIONAL BIOGRAPHY

Published under the auspices of the
AMERICAN COUNCIL OF LEARNED SOCIETIES

General Editors

John A. Garraty
Mark C. Carnes

VOLUME 23

OXFORD UNIVERSITY PRESS
New York 1999 Oxford

OXFORD UNIVERSITY PRESS

Oxford New York
Athens Auckland Bangkok Bogotá
Buenos Aires Calcutta Cape Town Chennai
Dar es Salaam Delhi Florence Hong Kong Istanbul
Karachi Kuala Lumpur Madrid Melbourne Mexico City
Mumbai Nairobi Paris São Paulo Singapore
Taipei Tokyo Toronto Warsaw
and associated companies in
Berlin Ibadan

Published by Oxford University Press, Inc.,
198 Madison Avenue, New York, New York 10016
http://www.oup-usa.org

Funding for this publication was provided in part by
the Andrew W. Mellon Foundation, the Rockefeller Foundation,
and the National Endowment for the Humanities,
a federal agency.

Library of Congress Cataloging-in-Publication Data

American national biography / general editors, John A. Garraty, Mark C. Carnes
p. cm.
"Published under the auspices of the American Council of Learned Societies."
Includes bibliographical references and index.
1. United States—Biography—Dictionaries. I. Garraty, John Arthur,
1920– . II. Carnes, Mark C. (Mark Christopher), 1950– .
III. American Council of Learned Societies.
CT213.A68 1998 98-20826 920.073—dc21 CIP
ISBN 0-19-520635-5 (set)
ISBN 0-19-512802-8 (vol. 23)

Printing (last digit): 9 8 7 6 5 4 3 2 1

Printed in the United States of America
on acid-free paper

CONTINUED

WELLEK, René (22 Aug. 1903–10 Nov. 1995), literary theorist and historian of modern literary criticism, was born in Vienna, Austria, the son of Bronislaw Wellek, a lawyer in the Finance Ministry of the Austrian government, and Gabriele von Zelewski. Wellek's father was a Czech nationalist, of a patriotic family with peasant roots, who later held a post in the newly proclaimed Czech republic; he was also a talented singer, opera reviewer, and translator of modern poetry. Wellek's mother, born in Rome, was the cosmopolitan, multilingual daughter of a prosperous family with ties to West Prussian nobility. Young Wellek received a classical education emphasizing Greek, Latin, and history; he read voraciously and cherished "well-illustrated encyclopedic books." In January 1919 the family moved from Vienna to Prague, and Wellek entered a Czech high school whose mechanical pedagogy he learned to despise, later recalling, "It was learning by rote of the worst tradition."

In 1922 Wellek enrolled in Germanic philology at Prague's Charles University, later shifting to English and working under the noted scholar Vilém Mathesius. He received a Ph.D. in English literature in June 1926 and did postgraduate work at Princeton University (1927–1928); he then taught German at Smith College (1928–1929) and Princeton (1929–1930) before returning to Prague. While doing research at the British Museum, Wellek discovered manuscript evidence showing that Coleridge had paraphrased and even translated large passages from Kant's *Critique of Pure Reason*. His view, incorporated in *Immanuel Kant in England: 1793–1838* (1931), that Coleridge was "an unoriginal eclectic philosopher who put doctrines compatible with Anglican theology on top of an edifice freely adapted" from Kant and Schelling outraged many Coleridge scholars and launched a continuing debate ("My Early Life," p. 221).

Living in Prague from 1930 to 1935, Wellek taught elementary English, wrote an essay on a medieval poem, *The Pearl*, collaborated on translations of D. H. Lawrence and Joseph Conrad, gave lectures for the near-blind Mathesius, and participated actively in the Prague Linguistic Circle, which Mathesius had founded in 1929. The Circle's concern for system, wholeness, and theoretical rather than narrowly historical approaches appealed to him. Here he met theoreticians Roman Jakobson and Jan Mukarovsky, gave lectures on literary theory and methodology, and reported on recent books. In 1932 he met his future wife, an elementary school teacher from Eastern Moravia named Olga Brodská; they were married on 22 December despite Wellek's bout that summer with apparent tuberculosis. They had one child. In 1935 Wellek accepted a lectureship in Czech language and literature funded by the Czech government at the University of London's School of Slavonic Studies. From 1937 to 1939 he gave over eighty talks to British societies to help counteract German propaganda. When Hitler invaded Czechoslovakia in March 1939, the Germans immediately cut off Wellek's stipend. Luckily, he was able to secure a position as lecturer in Norman Foerster's English department at the University of Iowa and sailed for America with his wife in June 1939. He became a naturalized citizen in 1946.

At Iowa Wellek found an English department bitterly divided between "scholars" and "critics": historical scholarship and Foerster's New Humanism. Wellek was associated with the neohumanists, and he revised a 1936 Prague Circle essay, "Theory of Literary History," for Foerster's 1941 collection, *Literary Scholarship: Its Aims and Methods*. His own goal, however, was to introduce to America "the insights gained from a knowledge of Russian formalism, of the Prague Linguistic Circle . . . of the phenomenology of Roman Ingarden, and of the massive movements of German *Geistesgeschichte* and stylistics" (*Teacher and Critic*, p. 72). With his colleague Austin Warren, he began work on *Theory of Literature* (1949); Wellek wrote the more theoretical chapters and, when Warren's wife became ill, completed the rest of the book himself. Reviewers singled out concepts that harmonized with recent New Critical approaches: the (Kantian) idea of the autonomy of the work of art, the literary work as an object of study in its own right (a "monument," not a "document"), the opposition of "intrinsic" and "extrinsic" analysis, and the work's identity as a "complex organization . . . of multiple meanings and interrelationships" (*Theory*, p. 27). The book, immensely influential and translated into twenty-two languages, soon became known as the philosophical basis for American New Criticism. The first edition concluded with a call to reform "The Study of Literature in the Graduate School" by hiring "professors of literature" rather than narrow specialists.

In 1946 Wellek moved to New Haven, where he became professor of Slavic and comparative literature at Yale University, chair of the department in 1948, and Sterling Professor in 1952. Influential in the development of American comparative literature studies, he provoked decades of controversy in a 1955 lecture, "The Crisis of Comparative Literature," that described prevailing American and French approaches as a choice between literary theory, criticism, and textual analysis, and the "dead hand of nineteenth-century factualism, scientism, and historical relativism" (*Concepts of Criticism*, p. 282).

A founding editor of *Norton World Masterpieces* (1956–), he instituted conceptual divisions, such as

"Romanticism" and "Realism and Naturalism" to replace then-current century divisions. Wellek considered his monumental analytic survey, *A History of Modern Criticism: 1750–1950* (8 vols., 1955–1992), his chief contribution to scholarship, continuing work on it after his retirement and dictating the last two volumes while confined to a nursing-home bed. Several important essay collections also gathered his theoretical positions, from *Concepts of Criticism* (1963) to *The Attack on Literature* (1982), in which he upheld a "perspectivist" approach and defended concepts of aesthetic value and critical judgment against deconstructionist relativism. An early reviewer welcomed Wellek's ability to lead readers through the most complicated questions, noting that he brought "floods of light and fresh air into the dustiest corners of contemporary literary criticism" (*Comparative Literature Studies*, June 1964).

He held posts in various professional organizations, from the Modern Language Association to the Czechoslovakia Society of Arts and Sciences in America, and received honors and awards in both Europe and America. In his own discipline he was president of the International Comparative Literature Association (1961–1964) and the American Comparative Literature Association (1962–1965) and a founding member of the editorial board of *Comparative Literature*. A year after Olga Wellek's death in 1967, he married Nonna Dolodarenko Shaw, a Russian émigré and professor of Russian literature. Wellek retired in 1972 but maintained an active professional life. His papers are housed in a special collection in the University of California at Irvine. Called "the most erudite man in America" and a "walking encyclopedia," Wellek became a constant reference point for generations of theorists, teachers, and literary critics. Both revered and attacked, he was in Aldo Scaglione's words "the leading figure in the field of comparative literary studies on both sides of the Atlantic" and also, in American letters, a prominent example of the intellectual émigré, "part of the stuff of which this country has been formed" (*Romance Philology* [Feb. 1964]).

• Wellek's personal library, including books, periodicals, manuscripts, and archived material, is housed in a special collection at the library of the University of California, Irvine. In addition to the works mentioned previously, see *The Rise of English Literary History* (1941), *Essays on Czech Literature* (1963), *Confrontations: Studies in the Intellectual and Literary Relations between Germany, England, and the United States during the Nineteenth Century* (1965), *The Literary Theory and Aesthetics of the Prague School* (1969), *Discriminations: Further Concepts of Criticism* (1970), and *Four Critics: Croce, Valéry, Lukács, and Ingarden* (1981). Autobiographical remarks are found in his "Collaborating with Austin Warren on *Theory of Literature*," in *Teacher and Critic: Essays by and about Austin Warren*, ed. Myron Simon and Harvey Gross (1976); "My Early Life," in *Contemporary Authors Autobiography Series*, vol. 7 (1988), pp. 205–26; "Prospect and Retrospect," *Yale Review* 69 (1980): 301–12; and "Respect for Tradition," *TLS*, 10 Dec. 1982. Martin Bucco's detailed biography *René Wellek* (1981) also presents a bibliography through 1980. See in addition Peter Demetz, "Interview with René Wellek," *Cross Currents* 9 (1990): 135–45; Sarah Lawall, "René Wellek and Modern Literary Criticism," *Comparative Literature* 40, no. 1 (Winter 1988): 3–24; and "René Wellek: In Memoriam," *Yearbook of Comparative and General Literature* 44 (1997): 7–48. An obituary is in the *New York Times*, 16 Nov. 1995.

SARAH LAWALL

WELLER, John Brown (22 Feb. 1812–17 Aug. 1875), U.S. senator and governor of California, was born on a small farm in Montgomery, Hamilton County, Ohio, the son of Lodowick Weller and Lydia Miller. In 1827 the family moved to Oxford, Butler County. John grew up without any religious faith. He attended a few sessions at Miami University and then moved to Hamilton to study law under Jesse Corwin, a brother of Thomas Corwin.

Weller's four marriages illustrate his ambition. In 1834 he wed Ann E. Ryan, daughter of a Hamilton merchant and sister of his future law partner, Michael C. Ryan, but she died in 1836. His second wife, a daughter of state auditor John A. Bryan, bore a son during their brief marriage from 1839 to 1841, when she died. In 1845 Congressman Weller married Susan P. McDowell Taylor, daughter of Virginia congressman William Taylor (1788–1846) and niece of Missouri senator Thomas Hart Benton (1782–1858). Her death during a cholera epidemic on 22 December 1848 occurred shortly before Weller left Ohio for California. Six years later Senator Weller married Lizzie Brocklebank Stanton; they had one son, and she outlived him.

An 1882 Butler County history declared that Weller "filled more important public stations than any one else who ever lived in this county," and until 1861 his life was, as one paper noted, "an almost uninterrupted course of political success and advancement."

In 1833 Democrat Weller defeated his Whig mentor Jesse Corwin to become Butler County district attorney, serving until 1836. From 4 March 1839 to 3 March 1845 he represented the Second Congressional District of Ohio, gaining a reputation as an ardent partisan. Strongly supporting the Mexican War, Lieutenant Colonel Weller bravely commanded the Second Ohio Regiment of Volunteers at the battle of Monterrey. True to southern principles migration patterns allied southern Ohio with the South, and a cardinal Democratic party principle stressed black inferiority—he wanted the new territories to be open to slavery. In 1848 Weller ran for governor, speaking in 78 of 88 counties, but the Whigs carried Ohio by a mere 345 votes among 300,000 cast.

On 16 January 1849 President James K. Polk asked Weller to head the boundary commission. The rush of gold seekers delayed his arrival in California until 1 June, but he worked well with his Mexican counterpart, running the boundary line from the Pacific Ocean to the Gila River. Weller was a lame duck appointment, however, and virulent Whig opposition hampered his work, fostered rumors, and froze federal funds.

Replaced at last in February 1850, Weller moved to San Francisco, where he practiced law and sought office. At the first Democratic State Convention on 20 May 1851, he stood fifth among the candidates for the gubernatorial nomination. Weller was campaigning in Downieville on 5 July when angry miners hanged a local woman known through history only by her first name, Juanita—though contemporary accounts call her Josepha—for knifing Fred Cannon. Weller was a candidate for U.S. senator, and foes charged him with cowardice for not protesting the Downieville hanging. However, California's dominant senator, William M. Gwin, preferred to have the more pliant Weller rather than northern Democrat David C. Broderick occupying California's second seat. The legislature elected Weller on 30 January 1852, and he served until 3 March 1857.

In the Senate Weller spoke for the Pacific Railroad, homesteads, and the proslavery Lecompton constitution for Kansas. Two significant bills of his became law. One authorized the Interior Department to build wagon roads over the Central Overland Route, while the second provided for semiweekly mail to California along the Southern Overland Road commencing in September 1858.

Weller's proclivities to defend political cronies led to continual trouble. Washingtonians became upset at his defense of defaulting House clerk C. J. McNulty, while Californians grew angry over his defense of Congressman Philemon T. Herbert, who shot a waiter at Willard's Hotel when he could not get a late morning breakfast. At Sonora, miner John Paul Dart summarized outraged feelings when he wrote, "Weller has d——d himself."

On 14 July 1857 the Democrats nominated Weller for governor rather than a second term as senator. Easily elected, he served uneasily from 8 January 1858 to 9 January 1860. Commentators then and later noted his apologetic manner. On leaving office, Weller admitted, "I came into the executive office wholly unacquainted with its duties and with but little knowledge of State affairs."

When Weller spoke on national matters, he defended slavery. In his inaugural address, he asked that the territories be open to immigrants "with their different species of property." Two years later Weller denounced the "wild spirit of fanaticism" in the North and followed Senator Gwin in declaring that, if the Union broke up, an independent California would "found a mighty republic."

Governor Weller spoke loudly for law and order and in 1859 followed words with deeds. When Shasta County miners began expelling Chinese on 4 March, Weller quickly sent 113 rifles to the sheriff to put down "this spirit of mobocracy." Echoing a feeling widespread in California and Oregon that U.S. troops would do "no good whatever" in suppressing American Indian strife in Tehama and Mendocino counties, Weller authorized Walter S. Jarboe and Adjutant General William C. Kibbe to raise companies of citizen volunteers. Though Weller felt the campaigns were "eminently successful," Congress in 1860 documented some of the most heinous atrocities on record.

Prison reform attracted the governor. On 1 March 1858 Weller took personal control of San Quentin state prison from the venal lessee and spent several months directing it. He denounced harsh sentences, recommended imprisoning juvenile offenders apart from adult criminals, and urged job assistance for released convicts.

Defeated in a bid for renomination in 1859 when the more astute and ambitious Milton S. Latham shoved him aside, Weller retired to his farm in Alameda County. In 1860 he actively campaigned for the proslavery presidential candidate. On 17 November, having been appointed by President James Buchanan, Weller became minister to Mexico, his last public office. He followed Robert McLane, who in 1859 had negotiated the McLane-Ocampo Treaty authorizing a U.S. protectorate under certain circumstances, and Weller agreed with these views. He served until 14 May 1861, when Republican Thomas Corwin replaced him.

During the Civil War, Weller, though born in a free state, supported southern independence. In a political speech he gave as a congressional candidate on 6 June 1863, he prayed for "peaceful separation with a view to future re-construction"—but would leave that reunion to "the next generation." Similarly, declaring that he owed "no allegiance to Abraham Lincoln," Weller refused to take the California attorney's oath.

In October 1863 the defeated congressional candidate went to Austin, Nevada. Weller returned to California to preside over the Democratic State Convention on 10 May 1864 and was named a delegate to the national convention. He then visited Oregon, Idaho, Utah, California again, and Washington, D.C., before deciding to settle in New Orleans in early 1867 to practice law. Weller died there of smallpox but was buried in Lone Mountain Cemetery in San Francisco.

Weller had the ability to hold high office and the ambition to gain it. However, after he became senator and then governor, his lack of vision, his slavish political loyalty, his perceived absence of ethics, and Gwin's dominance of California Democratic politics hampered him. Weller remained wedded to southern political beliefs, and the Civil War ended his political career.

• Weller's public speeches are available in the *Congressional Globe* and the California *Assembly Journals*. Some appeared as pamphlets, in the San Francisco *Alta California*, or in the Sacramento *Union*. The *Alta* of 4 Aug. 1857 contains a column-length biography probably written with Weller's help. Another contemporary view, plus a portrait, is in *Hutchings' California Magazine*, Mar. 1858, pp. 386–87. The *Speech of Ex-Governor John B. Weller Delivered before the Democratic Club at Petaluma, Cal., June 6, 1863* gave his views on the Civil War. Family background is in the sketch of his brother, Charles Locke Weller, in *Contemporary Biography of California's Representative Men*, ed. Alonzo Phelps (1881). Biographical sketches of Weller tend to be bland. H. Brett Melendy and Benjamin F. Gilbert, *The Governors of California*

(1965), contains the most current. Democrat Oscar T. Shuck concentrated on Weller's pre-California years in *Representative and Leading Men of the Pacific* (1870), while Republican Theodore H. Hittell described Weller's term as governor in vol. 4 of his *History of California* (1897). *A History and Biographical Cyclopedia of Butler County, Ohio* (1882) celebrated a native son. Lewis P. Lesley praised Weller in "The International Boundary Survey from San Diego to the Gila River, 1849–50," *California Historical Society Quarterly* 9 (Mar. 1930): 2–15, while William H. Goetzmann placed Weller's work in context in *Army Exploration in the American West, 1803–1863* (1959). A thorough account of the Downieville tragedy is William B. Secrest, *Juanita* (1967). Hubert Howe Bancroft detailed the Downieville hanging and Herbert affair in *Popular Tribunals*, vol. 2 (1887). Ward M. McAfee covered Weller's role in "San Quentin: The Forgotten Issue of California's Political History in the 1850s," *Southern California Quarterly* 72 (Fall 1990): 235–54, and settler actions are in "Majority and Minority Reports of the Select Joint Committee on the Mendocino War," appendix to California Senate *Journal* (1860).

ROBERT J. CHANDLER

WELLES, Charles Bradford (9 Aug. 1901–8 Oct. 1969), ancient historian, epigraphist, and papyrologist, was born in Old Saybrook, Connecticut, the son of Charles Thomas Welles, a Hartford banker, and Edith Smith. He was educated at public high school in Hartford, Phillips Exeter Academy for a postgraduate year, and Yale (B.A., 1924; Ph.D. in classics, 1928). The decisive event of his career occurred with the arrival at Yale in 1925 of Michael I. Rostovtzeff, the great Russian émigré ancient historian who led Welles to direct his talents from philological to historical pursuits. Welles's dissertation, *Royal Correspondence in the Hellenistic Period* (1934), a study of the language in letters of Hellenistic kings, thus became a corpus with historical and philological commentary of those letters. Welles became like a son to the childless Michael and Sophie Rostovtzeff and was later named the executor of Sophie's estate.

Welles was appointed instructor at Yale in 1927; in 1930–1931 a Sterling Fellowship allowed him to travel throughout Turkey, Syria, Egypt, and Europe to do much of the work on his first book and to meet many European scholars, including his contemporary Louis Robert, the great French epigraphist, who played an important part in his scholarly life. On his return to Yale in 1931, he was named assistant professor; after a year as associate professor in 1939–1940, he was appointed professor of ancient history. During the 1930s he was much involved with Rostovtzeff's excavations at Dura-Europos, a Hellenistic and Roman town in Syria that yielded many important and well-preserved inscriptions, graffiti, and papyri, many of which Welles published.

During these years he also joined the Army Field Artillery Reserve. He went on active duty in the spring of 1941, the first Yale faculty member to do so, training an all-black regiment in Louisiana before returning to Yale for two years as assistant professor of military science and tactics (1942–1944); a nickname of "the iron major" probably dates to these years. He was then posted in Cairo as head of X-2, the counterintelligence unit of the Office of Strategic Services. His work earned him promotion to lieutenant colonel and the rank of honorary officer in the Order of the British Empire (1946). He returned to Yale in 1946 and plunged into scholarly activity, including editing an archaeological digest in the *American Journal of Archaeology*. But he also had a continuing role in military intelligence and was brought back to active service in 1950 for two more years, this time in G-2 in the Pentagon with the rank of colonel. He remained in the reserves until his death. Welles liked the military and its discipline, but military service required long absences from his wife, Eleanor Bogert, whom he had married in 1926, and their two young children. A lasting consequence of his service in Cairo was Welles's interest in the Middle East and his sympathy for Arab (and particularly Egyptian) views, as well as his keen appreciation of topography.

After Welles's final return to Yale in 1952, he entered an enormously productive period that lasted until his death, during which he produced with colleagues the monumental edition of the papyri from Dura and a first volume of Yale papyri, along with numerous articles. He served as general editor of the Dura publications for many years, devoting much time to the work of others. He was also active in scholarly organizations, serving a term (1956–1957) as president of the American Philological Association and, most importantly, founding the American Society of Papyrologists in 1961, serving as its first president, and launching a series of summer seminars to train students in papyrology. He was honored with a volume of essays published as the first number of the society's monograph series. Despite an often austere outer demeanor, he was a good mentor to his students, whom he treated seriously as junior colleagues and warmly as friends, and who responded with great affection. Many colleagues at a distance experienced this same generosity through his wide correspondence.

Welles's last years were shadowed by turmoil in the Yale classics department, brought on by the determination of a new chairman to emphasize the study of ancient literature at the expense of archaeology. The chairman dismissed several younger faculty and forced Welles into academic exile in another university building. A year at the Institute for Advanced Study was some solace, but the effective destruction of the multigenerational ancient history enterprise at Yale was a bitter blow. Welles died of a heart attack in a taxi in New Haven on his way to take a train to New York for a meeting of the Ancient Civilization Group.

Welles was highly productive, despite his military intermissions, publishing, in addition to *Royal Correspondence* and the two volumes of papyri, an edition and translation of part of Diodorus Siculus for the Loeb Classical Library and a textbook on Hellenistic history entitled *Alexander and the Hellenistic World* (1970), along with more than seventy articles (some of book length) and 110 book reviews. His editions of documents matched textual precision with profound historical and philological commentaries. They and his Diodorus volume remain standard, frequently cited works. The articles of his later years took on increasingly broad historical themes. Teaching remained central, however, for Welles was profoundly concerned for younger scholars and for the transmission of his discipline, training many of the next generation's ancient historians.

• Welles's professional correspondence, books, and scholarly offprints, including a vast amount inherited from Rostovtzeff, are in the Duke University Library. Some personal papers are in the hands of his son David W. Welles in New York, who provided important information for this article. For a listing of his writings up to 1966, see K. J. Rigsby, "Bibliography of the Works of C. Bradford Welles," in *Essays in Honor of C. Bradford Welles*, ed. A. E. Samuel (1966), pp. ix–xxii. A frontispiece is also printed in that volume; an earlier photograph appears in the 1942 *Yale Banner*. On Welles's OSS service, see R. W. Winks, *Cloak and Gown* (1987), pp. 136–38. Obituaries include A. E. Samuel, *Bulletin of the American Society of Papyrologists* 6 (1969): 59–60; Anna Swiderek, *Journal of Juristic Papyrology* 18 (1974): 7–8; Fritz Uebel, *Archiv für Papyrusforschung* 21 (1971): 216; the *New York Times*, 9 Oct. 1969; and A. E. Samuel, *Proceedings of the American Philological Association* 100 (1969): xix–xxi.

ROGER S. BAGNALL

WELLES, Clara (4 Aug. 1868–14 Mar. 1965), silversmith and designer, was born Clara Pauline Barck in New York City, the daughter of John Barck and Margaret Bowman, both of Scandinavian descent. After Clara's birth the Barcks moved to Oregon. In the late 1890s she left the Pacific Northwest to enroll in the Department of Decorative Design at the School of the Art Institute of Chicago. Influenced by C. R. Ashbee and the English Arts and Crafts movement, she graduated from the school in 1900, and in September of that year she opened the Kalo Shop ("Kalo" derives from the Greek word for beautiful) at 175 Dearborn Avenue in Chicago. Staffed by young women known as the Kalo girls, the shop produced a variety of craft wares including burnt-leather and base-metal goods. In 1902 the Kalo Shop displayed their wares at the first annual arts and crafts exhibition of the Chicago Art Institute. The firm continued to exhibit there until 1921.

Clara Barck's marriage in 1905 to George S. Welles, a coal businessman and amateur metalworker, marked a watershed in her career. Husband and wife both shared an interest in silver, and they established the Kalo Art-Craft Community, a school and workshop that operated until 1914 in their suburban house in Park Ridge and sold its wares in downtown Chicago. In those years the Welleses practiced the somewhat utopian ideals of the Arts and Crafts movement to their fullest extent. In 1914, however, Clara and George were divorced, and Clara Welles merged the Kalo workshop with the retail operation and moved them to 32 North Michigan Avenue in Chicago. Once back in the city, Kalo became primarily a business venture, losing much of its identity as a community of craftspeople and students. The firm moved in 1918 to the Fine Arts Building at 416 South Michigan Avenue, a prime location that served as a meeting place for artists and women's clubs. By 1925 Welles had moved the establishment to 152 East Ontario, a less accessible location that was not advantageous for business. In 1936 Welles moved the Kalo Shop back to the Railway Exchange Building at 222 South Michigan Avenue, where it would remain. She also maintained a retail shop in New York City at 130 West Fifty-fourth Street from 1914 to 1918.

Welles's Kalo Shop was one of the most important of the several enterprises that helped revitalize silversmithing in Chicago in the arts and crafts style. Under Welles's artistic direction and management it became one of the leading silver shops in America, notable for its large size, its employment of women, and its encouragement of Scandinavian immigrant artists. Kalo objects were distinguished by their purity and simplicity, exhibiting clean lines, restrained ornament, and superb handcraftsmanship. Early designs tended to be angular and geometric, but the Kalo Shop soon adopted a soft, curvilinear style for which it became best known. The shop produced a full line of pitchers, bowls, and hollowware, as well as fine flatware and jewelry. Welles was praised for her fairness toward her employees and for her advocacy of women silversmiths. As many as twenty five craftspeople, many of them Scandinavian immigrants, worked in the Kalo Shop at one time, including Julius Randahl, Matthias Hanck, Emery Todd, and Esther Meacham. The Metropolitan Museum of Art included Kalo silver in a 1937 exhibition of contemporary design, and the high praise it received established the reputation of Welles as an important twentieth-century silversmith.

Welles continued to operate the Kalo Shop in Chicago until 1940. She lectured frequently in the Chicago area and led a vigorous public life; she was active in the Cordon Club, an association of professional women in the arts, the Municipal Art League, and the Improvement Society. In 1940 she retired to Mission Hills, near San Diego, California. In retirement she was active in the Travelers Aid Society and the American Red Cross. In 1959 she gave the Kalo Shop to its then-current four employees—Robert R. Bower, Daniel P. Pederson, Yngve Olsson, and Arne Myhre. She died in Mission Hills. The Kalo Shop remained in business until 31 July 1970, producing many of the same traditional designs that it had issued for more than half a century. Today, Kalo silver is represented in many public and private collections.

• Some three hundred Kalo Shop drawings, many by Welles or annotated by her, are on deposit in the Prints and Photographs Department of the Chicago Historical Society. The Decorative and Industrial Arts Department of the same institution has files on the Kalo Shop. Pertinent information on Welles is also included in the transcript of a 1976 interview with Robert R. Bower, a longtime Kalo employee, also at the Chicago Historical Society. Biographical profiles are by Kristan H. McKinsey in the *Historical Encyclopedia of Chicago Women* (1996) and by R. Tripp Evans, "A Profitable Partnership," *Chicago History* 24, no. 2 (Summer 1995): 5–21.

Welles and Kalo are discussed in Sharon S. Darling with Gail Farr Casterline, *Chicago Metalsmiths: An Illustrated History* (1977). See also the relevant entries by W. Scott Braznell in Wendy Kaplan, ed., *"The Art That Is Life": The Arts and Crafts Movement in America, 1875–1920* (1987). An obituary is in the *San Diego Union*, 17 Mar. 1965.

GERALD W. R. WARD

WELLES, Gideon (1 July 1802–11 Feb. 1878), journalist, diarist, and secretary of the navy, was born in Glastonbury, Connecticut, the son of Samuel Welles, a shipbuilder and merchant in the West Indies trade, and Anne Hale. Welles studied law with William W. Ellsworth in Hartford, Connecticut, but never practiced. In 1835 he married his cousin Mary Jane Hale. They had nine children, three of whom survived to adulthood.

In 1825 Welles became acquainted with John M. Niles, editor and proprietor of the *Hartford Times and Weekly Advertizer*, who espoused Andrew Jackson as the coming political figure in the nation. His opinion on states' rights, banking corporations, free trade, and hard money appealed to Welles, who joined Niles's publishing venture and soon gained a reputation for his support of Jackson and his attacks on the John Quincy Adams administration. He was elected to the Connecticut General Assembly in 1825 and served another term in 1835. That year he was elected state comptroller.

In 1846 Welles became the first civilian bureau chief in the Navy Department, responsible for the department's supply of provisions and clothing during the Mexican-American War. Though an honest and capable administrator, the Whig triumph of 1848 resulted in his dismissal.

Welles and Niles became involved in the antislavery movement that gained renewed impetus after the Wilmot Proviso debates in Congress, which made a resounding political statement for free soil in the Mexican cession after the peace treaty of Guadalupe Hidalgo. Both men supported Martin Van Buren and the Free Soil ticket in 1848, Niles openly and Welles, still a jobholder in Washington, covertly.

Under pen names Welles wrote editorials or public letters for such journals as the *New York Evening Post* and the antislavery *National Era* in Washington. An opponent of the Compromise of 1850, he denounced the Fugitive Slave Act in the compromise on constitutional, political, and moral grounds. Nevertheless, he supported Franklin Pierce, the Democratic party nominee in 1852, and hoped that Pierce, if elected, would not adhere strictly to the party platform that accepted the compromise. As president, Pierce did not oppose the expansion of slavery. When the Kansas-Nebraska Act of 1854 threw the territories open to popular sovereignty and the *Hartford Times* along with the Democratic organization in the state supported that legislation, Welles and Niles broke with the party and the paper and joined the new Republican party.

To give wider currency to the new party, Welles and Niles established the *Hartford Evening Press*. Welles became its first editor. He also ran for governor of the state on the Republican ticket in 1856 but was defeated.

After the election of James Buchanan as president, Welles condemned his administration for its Kansas policy, the Dred Scott decision, and the upsurgence of nativism, whose intolerance he had opposed over many years. Appointed a member of the Republican party's executive committee, he devoted himself to planning for the campaign of 1860. He advocated the publication and distribution at the party's expense of Hinton Helper's antislavery tract, *The Impending Crisis of the South* (1857).

By now Welles had gained a large following among Republican party leaders, especially in New England. As a result, he was pushed for a cabinet position when the party won the election of 1860. President Abraham Lincoln appointed him secretary of the navy on 4 March 1861.

When Welles took over the Navy Department, he was immediately faced with the loss of more than half of the officer corps, 300 of whom resigned or were dismissed for disloyalty. The Union fleet consisted of forty-five ships, most of which were obsolete. Only twelve vessels were ready for service. The navy was, therefore, unprepared to implement Lincoln's blockade of the southern ports. To make matters worse, Lincoln's attempt to placate Virginia before Fort Sumter resulted in the loss of the Union's best-equipped naval base at Norfolk, Virginia.

Welles moved rapidly to expand the navy. He initiated development of a river fleet that would assist the Treasury Department's internal blockade of the Confederacy as well as cooperate with the army in joint operations. Before northern shipyards could begin to build new vessels, Welles sought merchant shipping that could be quickly converted into gunboats and other auxiliary vessels. He dealt with his brother-in-law George D. Morgan, a New York merchant who purchased ninety vessels, and the Massachusetts magnate John Murray Forbes (1813–1898), who acquired ten more. Morgan drove hard bargains with ship owners and no doubt saved the department large sums, but he received commissions that amounted to $70,000 and that prompted a congressional investigation. Welles was not accused of any wrongdoing, but the unfavorable image fixed on him of a sleepy Rip Van Winkle was long the subject of cartoons.

Welles was fortunate to have associated with him a dynamic former naval officer, Gustavus Vasa Fox, first as chief clerk and ultimately assistant secretary. His staff also included a capable administrator, William Faxon, a business associate on the *Press*. In all, the navy purchased or had constructed 313 vessels, about one-half of its fleet, and bought or leased another 184 ships from private parties and the War and Treasury Departments. Personnel increased from 7,600 officers and men to 51,500 in 1865.

Welles complemented the navy's expansion program with a comprehensive study of naval strategy, setting up what was called the "Committee of Conference." The committee produced four "Memoirs" that analyzed the blockade problem, divided the southern Atlantic Coast into operational theaters, and recommended where specific lodgments be made. The job required the blockade of the outer coastline and inner bays from the Virginia capes to the Rio Grande.

First fruits of the committee's recommendations were the army-navy capture of the Hatteras forts on 28 August 1861 and Admiral Samuel F. Du Pont's seizure of the harbor of Port Royal, South Carolina, on 7 November 1861. On 6 February 1862 the navy silenced the batteries of Fort Henry on the Tennessee River. Two days later a joint army-navy expedition seized Roanoke Island, which dominated Albemarle Sound. On 16 February the army and navy cooperated in the capture of Fort Donelson on the Cumberland River in Tennessee, and they captured Island Number 10 in the Mississippi on 7 April 1862. The Union navy now controlled most of the inland waterways off the Confederacy's Atlantic Coast, the Tennessee River, the Cumberland River, and much of the Mississippi River. Although the blockade was never completely effective, it did cut off a major source of foreign munitions and other contraband supplies.

The committee also recommended that a squadron already operating in the Gulf of Mexico be made the core of another joint army navy assault on New Orleans. By the end of 1861 the Navy Department had completed planning for this operation. Welles selected David G. Farragut to head the expedition. On 25 April 1862 Farragut ran the forts that guarded the approaches to New Orleans and captured the city. The army then took control. After the successes of the Port Royal, Fort Henry, and New Orleans expeditions, public and political criticism of Welles diminished, though it never completely ended.

The engagement between the Union ironclad *Monitor* and the Confederate ironclad *Virginia* on 9 March 1862 that ended the threat posed to the wooden Union fleet also solidified Welles's status within the Lincoln administration. However, the failure of the ironclads to capture Charleston in 1863 led to attacks on his department in Congress.

By the war's end Welles had been primarily responsible for building a navy second only to that of Great Britain. He had also reorganized the department, improved significantly contract administration, and established an academy of science, the forerunner of all government-sponsored research agencies.

As a cabinet member, Welles gave complete support and loyalty to Lincoln on broad policy measures. He retained, however, much of his Democratic political views. Though he backed emancipation, he was decidedly conservative on extending full civil rights to the former slaves. An ardent believer in states' rights, he insisted such legislation must be left to the states. His views on Reconstruction were similar to those of Andrew Johnson. Welles consulted on many of Johnson's veto messages and consistently approved of his stand against Congressional Reconstruction.

Welles is best known as a diarist. His voluminous journal, kept from 10 August 1861 until 6 June 1869, is the most comprehensive account available for the Lincoln and Johnson administrations. This document and the essays he wrote in retirement present a vivid though intensely personal record of the Civil War and Reconstruction. At the close of Johnson's administration, on 4 March 1869, Welles returned to Hartford, where he resided until his death there.

• The Library of Congress has the major collection of Welles's papers, but significant additional collections are at the Connecticut Historical Society, primarily in the John M. Niles Papers; the New York Public Library; and the E. Huntington Library, San Marino, Calif., which has portions of Welles's manuscript diaries for 1846, 1848, and 1860. The manuscript Welles diary, 1862–1869, is at the Library of Congress. First published as *Diary of Gideon Welles, Secretary of the Navy under Lincoln and Johnson* under the direction of John T. Morse (3 vols., 1911), it has been published and edited by Howard K. Beale and Alan Brownsword in a critical edition with the same title (3 vols., 1960). Welles's essays are available in published form in the *Galaxy* 10–14 (1870–1877); and in his *Lincoln and Seward* (1874). Two modern biographies of Welles are Richard West, Jr., *Gideon Welles: Lincoln's Navy Department* (1943), and John Niven, *Gideon Welles: Lincoln's Secretary of the Navy* (1973). A shorter version of Welles's career is in Paolo E. Coletta, ed., *American Secretaries of the Navy*, vol. 1, *1775–1913* (1980). Valuable material on Welles's administration of the Navy Department may also be found in Charles O. Paullin, "Half Century of Naval Administration in America: The Navy Department during the Civil War," *U.S. Naval Institute Proceedings (Dec. 1912)*, no. 1, no. 2, Mar. 1913. Substantive obituaries are in the *Hartford Times* and the *New York Tribune*, both 12 Feb. 1878, which may be supplemented by Gustavus Vasa Fox, Manuscript Diary, 12 Feb. 1878, in the New-York Historical Society.

JOHN NIVEN

WELLES, Orson (6 May 1915–10 Oct. 1985), director and actor, was born George Orson Welles in Kenosha, Wisconsin, the son of Richard Hodgon Welles, an inventor and businessman, and Beatrice Ives, a talented amateur musician. Welles was precocious, his pampered childhood abruptly ending after his mother's death when he was nine. At eleven he was enrolled in the progressive Todd School in Woodstock, Illinois, where he directed and acted in classics by Shakespeare and Shaw. After graduation in 1930, he spent a summer at the Chicago Art Institute.

His father died in late December 1930, and the following August Welles set out for a walking and painting tour of Ireland. Although he lacked professional experience, he talked his way into a position with the Gate Theater in Dublin, where he made his stage debut at the age of sixteen. Welles remained in Dublin until March 1933 when he returned to the United States. Although he received respectable notices abroad, he was at first unable to get theatrical work at home. In September 1933 he was offered a place in Katharine Cornell's touring company, in which Welles made his American professional debut that year in *The Barretts of Wimpole Street*. He married socialite Virginia Nicholson in 1934 and moved to New York. He divorced Nicholson in 1940; they had one child. In New York, with John Houseman, a young theatrical producer, he formed one of the most important partnerships in the American arts. Houseman was running the Negro section of the Works Progress Administration's Federal Theater Project, for which Welles mounted in 1936 a "voodoo version of *Macbeth*," with an all-black cast plus dancers and drummers. The opening night attracted a crowd of thousands outside the Lafayette Theater in Harlem, and the innovative dynamism of the production as well as the publicity surrounding it launched Welles as a major figure in the American theater.

Over the next three years Welles and Houseman produced a remarkable array of theatrical events, including a striking version of Marlowe's *Dr. Faustus*, a politically styled production of Shakespeare's *Julius Caesar*, and Marc Blitzstein's controversial opera, *The Cradle Will Rock*. In 1937 Welles and Houseman founded the Mercury Theater, which attracted a talented ensemble of actors, many of whom later followed Welles to Hollywood. In addition to his stage career, Welles appeared regularly on radio, playing the Shadow in a weekly adventure drama. He soon had the Mercury Theater on the air, experimenting with the possibilities of radio drama. His best-known Mercury radio play was an updated version of H. G. Wells's science fiction tale, *The War of the Worlds*, broadcast on Halloween night. Simulating news coverage of a Martian invasion of the United States, the production created panic along the eastern seaboard. The broadcast received widespread publicity and won Welles a contract with RKO Radio Pictures. In July 1939 he went to Hollywood to begin his career in films, the medium that would largely occupy him for the rest of his life.

Welles's unprecedented contract to direct, star in, write, and edit a motion picture was the envy of the movie industry. After some false starts, he settled on an idea developed with Houseman and veteran scriptwriter Herman Mankiewicz, loosely based on the life of newspaper magnate William Randolph Hearst. *Citizen Kane*, Welles's first feature-length film, so outraged Hearst that he tried to buy the negative and, failing that, banned any mention of the movie in his newspapers. The film, released on 1 May 1941, fared only moderately well at the box office. However, *Citizen Kane* was directed with such stylistic verve and with such innovative use of cinematography, sound, and music and within such a daring narrative structure that it became one of the most celebrated films ever made.

Welles next directed a costly and ambitious movie based on Booth Tarkington's bestselling novel, *The Magnificent Ambersons*. Welles had not finished its editing when he went to Brazil to begin shooting a film for the U.S. Office of the Coordinator of Inter-American Affairs. The project was designed to help strengthen relationships among nations of the Western Hemisphere and to counter Nazi influence in South America. Although he shot miles of film, *It's All True* was never completed. In Welles's absence, the studio severely edited *The Magnificent Ambersons* and released it without fanfare during the summer of 1942. Although Welles complained throughout his life about the butchering of the release print, critics have regarded *The Magnificent Ambersons* as one of his greatest films. Welles's last venture at RKO was the 1943 movie version of Eric Ambler's thriller *Journey into Fear*, which Welles starred in, cowrote, and without credit did much of the direction. In September 1943 he married Hollywood star Rita Hayworth; they had one child and were divorced in 1947. Although he continued to be heard on radio, Welles spent the remaining war years working for the government in various capacities and writing political journalism, mostly essays and editorials.

During the postwar years Welles assumed a frantic pace: acting on radio and in movies, directing and producing for both stage and screen, and giving speeches, making radio broadcasts, and writing editorials and newspaper columns in support of progressive political causes. In 1946 he completed, as director, costar, and coscenarist, a film melodrama, *The Stranger*; staged an innovative version of Cole Porter's musical *Around the World in Eighty Days* in New York; and began work as director and costar with Hayworth on *The Lady from Shanghai*, which was released after much studio revision in 1948. In 1947 Welles prepared another stage version of *Macbeth* for the Utah Centennial Festival in Salt Lake City. Later that year he directed a film version of the play for Republic Pictures in twenty-one days on a small budget to prove that classics could be made cheaply and be accessible to the average moviegoer; it was released in 1948.

At the end of the 1940s Welles moved to Europe, where for years he acted in films. Among the most celebrated of the roles he created was Harry Lime in Carol Reed's *The Third Man* (1949). Also in 1949 he began work on a film version of *Othello*, which received widespread critical acclaim from the European press when it was released in 1952. To make this film, Welles established a pattern he would often repeat, using his earnings as an actor to underwrite his work as a director, for increasingly he was forced to rely on his own intermittent financing to produce his films.

By the 1950s Welles was recognized, at least by European critics, as one of America's most important filmmakers. He next directed *Mr. Arkadin*, a film based on his own script. Released in 1955, the film was not shown in the United States until 1962. In 1955 he married Paola Mori; they had one child. That same year Welles also appeared in a dramatic version of *Moby Dick* in London, and the next year he played King Lear on the New York stage. At the insistence of Charlton Heston, who was to star in the film, Welles returned to Hollywood to direct the offbeat and suspenseful *Touch of Evil* (1958), in which he also played the lead. In Europe in 1962 he began filming his version of Franz Kafka's labyrinthine novel *The Trial*, which was released in 1963.

During the early 1960s Welles initiated work on a long-standing project about Shakespeare's Falstaff, primarily using material from the two Henry IV plays. The majestic but uneven *Chimes at Midnight* was released in 1966. Another film, *The Immortal Story*, based on an Isak Dinesen tale, appeared in 1968. Although Welles continued to work on his own films, *Don Quixote, The Deep*, and *The Other Side of the Wind*, none was completed, and he spent his later years acting in films and appearing on the celebrity circuit, making television guest appearances and doing voice-overs for commercials. His last released film, *F for Fake* (1975), about art forgeries, was premiered at film festivals in New York and San Sebastián.

During the final years of his life Welles received increasing recognition for the quality and originality of his film work. In 1970 the Academy of Motion Picture Arts and Sciences awarded him a special Oscar, and he was presented with a Life Achievement Award by the American Film Institute in 1975. He assisted in a number of documentaries about his career, cooperated in the writing of two books about himself, and continued to trade on his magnificent voice by recording readings of literary works. Until the end, his prodigality stayed with him. Just before his death, financing of his film version of *King Lear* fell through because of its inflated budget and extremely difficult production requirements. Welles died in Hollywood.

Welles's bold experimentation as a director and actor, on the stage, on radio, and in films, established him as one of the great artists of the twentieth century. However, he will probably be best remembered as a filmmaker of international reputation. *Citizen Kane* appears on virtually every film critic's list of ten best movies and is regarded by many as the singular achievement of one hundred years of American films. The great French critic André Bazin noted that through his distinctive style Welles had achieved a major breakthrough in the evolution of film language.

• Welles's personal papers, scripts, letters, and other miscellany are housed in the Lilly Library of Indiana University. Other libraries with material on Welles are the Federal Theater Collection, George Mason University; the British Film Institute, London; the Academy of Motion Picture Arts and Sciences, Los Angeles; and the Museum of Broadcasting, New York City.

The initial critical assessment of Welles's films was André Bazin's *Orson Welles* (1950), and most of Bazin's judgments still hold up. The best critical monograph is James Naremore's *The Magic World of Orson Welles* (1978; rev. ed., 1989). Robert Carringer's *The Making of Citizen Kane* (1985) traces in detail the elements that went into the making of Welles's first film. Richard France's *The Theater of Orson Welles* (1977) contains the most thorough analysis of Welles's contribution to the theater, and *Orson Welles on the Air: The Radio Years* (1988) examines his career on radio. Howard Koch, who wrote the radio play for the "War of the Worlds" broadcast, published an account of the event in *The Panic Broadcast* (1971). Frank Brady's *Citizen Welles* (1989) and a long interview book by Peter Bogdanovich, *This Is Orson Welles* (1992), contain the best and most accurate accounts of his life and work. Bret Wood's *Orson Welles: A Bio-Bibliography* (1990) provides the most comprehensive bibliography of materials by and about Welles. A *New York Times* obituary appeared on 11 Oct. 1985.

CHARLES L. P. SILET

WELLES, Sumner (14 Oct. 1892–24 Sept. 1961), diplomat and author, was born Benjamin Sumner Welles in New York City, the son of Benjamin Welles and Frances Swan. The Welles family was socially prominent and wealthy, and the young man preferred to be called Sumner, reflecting the relationship to his famous ancestor, Charles Sumner, an abolitionist senator from Massachusetts. The Welles family was close to the Roosevelts, and when Sumner went off to boarding school, he roomed with the brother of Eleanor Roosevelt. At Eleanor's wedding to her distant cousin Franklin Delano Roosevelt, Sumner carried the bride's wedding gown train. Welles attended Groton, where headmaster Endicott Peabody was a great influence on his development. A thin, frail adolescent, Welles eschewed sports and social activities. He was a brilliant student, however, and graduated from Harvard University in 1914 after spending the previous year abroad. He briefly considered studying art in Paris but decided on a career in diplomacy, following the advice of Franklin D. Roosevelt, then assistant secretary of the navy. Welles scored the highest marks on the Foreign Service exam in 1915 and won a choice assignment to Tokyo. That year, prior to departing for his diplomatic post, he married Esther Slater, whose family owned the Slater Mills in Massachusetts. They had two sons.

In 1917, after two years in Japan, Welles decided to specialize in Latin American affairs, an unusual decision for an ambitious young Foreign Service officer. Assigned to Buenos Aires in 1919, he became fluent in Spanish and impressed his superiors with his quick grasp of Latin American issues. In 1920 he returned to the United States, where he was appointed assistant chief of the Division of Latin American Affairs and focused his attention on the Caribbean and Central America. He monitored the Cuban elections in 1920 and traveled to Haiti to review the possibility of ending U.S. military occupation in that country. In 1922 Welles resigned from the State Department, upset with Republican tariff policies and the inefficiencies of the bureaucracy. However, within months he was lured back to government service by Secretary of State Charles Evans Hughes, who asked Welles to serve as a special commissioner to the Dominican Republic with the rank of minister and with direct access to the secretary. Welles remained in this post for three years but failed to end U.S. control of the nation's economy or to bring about the withdrawal of American troops from that country.

Welles was thin, above average in height, and a fastidious dresser. Intelligent and urbane, he was seen by his admirers as a superb diplomat. Others viewed him as pompous and self-centered. Many found him overbearing and possessing a strange temperament. Welles seemed to delight in punishing those he thought had crossed him. In 1923 his marriage ended in divorce, and Esther was awarded custody of their two sons. In 1925 he married Mathilde Townsend Gerry, who had recently divorced her husband, Rhode Island senator Peter Gerry. They had no children. Rumors circulated around Washington that an affair between Welles and Gerry had wrecked both their marriages. Eleven years older than Welles, Mathilde was a wealthy and attractive socialite. Throughout their marriage, which ended with Mathilde's death in 1949, the two appeared completely supportive of each other, and her great wealth allowed the couple to live an extravagant lifestyle, which included mansions in Washington, D.C., and rural Maryland and a 38-room "cottage" in Bar Harbor, Maine.

Following Welles's second marriage, President Calvin Coolidge refused his secretary of state's nomination of Welles to a panel of the Central American court. Welles resigned immediately. It was clear that the president's disapproval of Welles's marriage and lifestyle had forced the resignation. By this time Welles's behavior had already irritated members of the diplomatic corps. Of Welles's departure, Under Secretary of State William Castle commented, "I cannot but applaud the move although I think it should have come before rather than after he married the woman" (Gellman, p. 63). Following his abrupt separation from the State Department, Welles devoted himself to writing *Naboth's Vineyard: The Dominican Republic 1844–1924* (1928), in which he viewed the history of the Dominican Republic as analogous to the biblical story of Naboth, murdered at the instigation of Jezebel, who desired his fine vineyard. Welles saw the Dominican Republic as Naboth and the United States as Jezebel and concluded his study with an appeal for a more cooperative and enlightened American policy toward Latin America. Franklin D. Roosevelt found the book of great interest and made Welles his principal adviser on Latin American affairs. Following his election to the presidency, Roosevelt in 1933 named Welles assistant secretary of state, and Welles immediately became a principal architect for the new administration's "Good Neighbor" policy toward Latin America.

Political instability in Cuba provided an immediate challenge to the Good Neighbor policy. On 21 April 1933 Welles was assigned as a special presidential ambassador to Havana, where he mediated between President Gerardo Machado, a reactionary dictator, and his political rivals. Welles applied pressure on Machado to step aside in favor of a more representative caretaker government headed by Dr. Carlos Manuel de Céspedes y Quesada. Because Céspedes was known to be favorably disposed to Washington, the emergence of the new regime made Welles a hero among American policy makers in Havana and Washington. However, Céspedes lacked broad support among the Cuban population, and on 5 September his government was overthrown in the "Sergeants' Rebellion" by a coalition of noncommissioned officers and student radicals. Welles called for U.S. marines to restore Céspedes, but his appeal was rejected by Roosevelt and Secretary of State Cordell Hull. Welles considered the revolutionary government, headed by Dr. Ramon Grau San Martín to be comprised of "either self-seeking small caliber politicians or fuzzy-minded theorists who have neither the training, the experience nor the capacity to govern" (Gellman, p. 80). He concurred with Washington's policy of nonrecognition of the government of San Martín, and when the coalition eventually collapsed and one of the sergeants, Fulgencio Batista, emerged as Cuba's new military strongman, San Martín stated, "I fell because Washington willed it" (Alexander DeConde, *History of American Foreign Policy*, 2d ed. [1971], p. 540).

Welles's mission to Cuba was seen by most State Department insiders as a disaster, and Welles returned to Washington and his duties as assistant secretary for Western Hemisphere policy a dejected diplomat in December 1933. As assistant secretary, in 1934 he negotiated with Cuba a treaty discarding the Platt Amendment, which had given the United States the right to interfere militarily to restore order in Cuba. Welles also negotiated with Panama for a new treaty to correct imbalances of the 1903 canal treaty. Negotiations for a new agreement were completed in 1936, but a skeptical U.S. Senate did not approve the treaty for three years. In 1936 Welles convinced Roosevelt to organize a special inter-American peace conference in Buenos Aires to end the Chaco War between Paraguay and Bolivia. At the conference Welles was instrumental in generating the principle of collective consultation to maintain peace in the Americas.

In 1937 Roosevelt made Welles under secretary of state, despite the misgivings of Secretary Hull about the close relationship between the president and the new under secretary. Hull and Welles were never close, and their relationship deteriorated as Hull's health declined, forcing long absences from his post, during which Welles stepped in to serve as acting secretary. In 1943 Assistant Secretary Adolf Berle stated, "The antagonism between Secretary Hull and Mr. Welles makes a good deal of difficulty; the Secretary resents Sumner going to the White House too much but as he does not go very much himself, this leaves the President at the mercy of unskilled advisors" (Gellman, p. 309). Nevertheless, Welles was an effective administrator and helped shape the planning for postwar international cooperation.

When war broke out in Europe in 1939, Welles attended an inter-American conference in Panama that established a neutrality zone in most of the Western Hemisphere. In February 1940 President Roosevelt sent Welles to Rome, Berlin, Paris, and London to meet with European leaders and explore possibilities for peace. At this point the possibility of negotiating for peace in Europe was unrealistic, and Roosevelt seems to have understood this. The president's more immediate goals in the controversial Welles mission seem to have been to stall an anticipated Nazi attack on the Allies and to demonstrate to the American public that the administration had done everything possible in seeking peace. Welles returned to Washington with solid information on the situation in Europe and with the personal views of the European leaders. Even Hull was impressed with Welles's report.

Beginning in 1942 Welles chaired a State Department committee that planned for postwar international cooperation and in this capacity drafted proposals that were later used, in modified form, as a basis for the United Nations. In August 1941 Welles attended the conference between President Roosevelt and Sir Winston Churchill aboard the battleship *Prince of Wales* off the coast of Newfoundland, where he participated in writing the Atlantic Charter. After the United States entered World War II, Welles in 1942 represented the country at a meeting of foreign ministers of the nations of North and South America in Rio de Janeiro. At this gathering only Argentina and Chile refused to support an immediate break in diplomatic relations with Germany, Japan, and Italy. To preserve unity among the nations of the Western Hemisphere, the conference issued a compromise joint declaration that merely recommended a break with the Axis nations. Hull, who was not consulted about the compromise wording, accused Welles of selling out American interests and expressed his disapproval of the under secretary's actions. Roosevelt supported the under secretary's position, thus exacerbating the conflict between Hull and Welles.

Rumors of Welles's homosexuality and reckless sexual behavior eventually led to his dismissal from the State Department. Cuban officials had reported on Welles's homosexual adventures in 1933, and one diplomat reported that at that time the department had "enough on Welles to blow him out of the water" (Gellman, p. 83). Hull had heard rumors of Welles's homosexuality and referred to his under secretary as "my fairy" (Gellman, p. 308). Welles was reported to be a heavy drinker who, while intoxicated, propositioned cabdrivers, hotel attendants, and train porters. Several members of Congress were aware of reports of Welles's behavior, and it appeared that a hearing by a Senate committee was likely in 1944, an election year. In the summer of 1943 Hull met with Director of the Federal Bureau of Investigation J. Edgar Hoover to discuss the bureau's file on Welles. At a luncheon meeting with the president at the White House on 15 August, Hull insisted on Welles's dismissal. The president met with his longtime friend later in the day and offered him a post as a roving ambassador to Latin America in return for his resignation as under secretary. Welles resigned formally the next day, refusing to accept another position in the department. His resignation became effective 30 September.

In retirement, Welles devoted his energies to writings and broadcast commentaries on foreign affairs. He enjoyed a reputation as an authority on international relations and remained a respected spokesman for active U.S. involvement in world affairs and international organizations. In 1944 he authored *Time for Decision*, an appraisal of Roosevelt's diplomacy and the origins of World War II. In 1946 he authored *Where Are We Heading?*, an insider's view of World War II diplomacy and the Atlantic Charter meeting that presents Roosevelt as taking the first steps toward postwar cooperation with the Soviet Union. This book also advocates support for the United Nations. Other books include *We Need Not Fail* (1948) and *Seven Decisions That Shaped History* (1951). From 1949 to 1953 he edited a series of books, the American Foreign Policy Library, for Harvard University Press. In 1952 Welles married a woman he had known since childhood, Harriette Post, the daughter of the founder of the New York Stock Exchange. They had no children. Welles died at his wife's family home in Bernardsville, New Jersey.

• Welles's papers (approximately 105 linear feet) are in the Franklin D. Roosevelt Library at Hyde Park, N.Y. His official activities are documented in the records of the Department of State in the National Archives, and much of his material is published in the *Foreign Relations of the United States* (1920–1925, 1933–1943). Also see Irwin F. Gellman, *Secret Affairs: Franklin Roosevelt, Cordell Hull and Sumner Welles* (1995); Frank Warren Graff, *Strategy of Involvement: A Diplomatic Biography of Sumner Welles* (1988); Stanley E. Hilton, "Welles Mission to Europe, February–March 1940: Illusion or Realism," *Journal of American History* 58 (1971): 93–120; Warren Kimball, *The Juggler: Franklin Roosevelt as Wartime Statesman* (1991); and Cordell Hull, *The Memoirs of Cordell Hull* (2 vols., 1948). An obituary is in the *New York Times*, 25 Sept. 1961.

MICHAEL J. DEVINE

WELLMAN, Walter (3 Nov. 1858–31 Jan. 1934), journalist and adventurer, was born in Mentor, Ohio, the son of Alonzo Wellman and Minerva Graves. Educated in local schools in Michigan, Wellman's formal education ended when he was fourteen years old. He recalled that his most important childhood possession had been a dictionary, which helps to explain his later literary talent.

As a teenager, Wellman started a weekly newspaper in Sutton, Nebraska. He founded the *Cincinnati Evening Post* before his twenty-first birthday. On 24 December 1878 he married Laura McCann. The union, which ended for unknown reasons, produced one child. He later married Belgljat Bergerson; they had three children.

In 1884 Wellman went to Washington, D.C., as political reporter for the *Chicago Herald* (subsequently, the *Record-Herald*), a position he would hold for the next twenty-seven years. In 1891 Wellman embarked on the first of a series of adventures when he led a *Herald*-sponsored expedition in search of the location where Christopher Columbus first landed in the New World. Visiting the Bahamas, he claimed to have identified the exact spot of Columbus's landing and erected a monument on San Salvador, or Watlings Island. This feat brought Wellman the first public recognition that he came to prize. Three years later, he embarked on an overland expedition to reach the North Pole but was forced back at 81 degrees north latitude. A second attempt in 1898–1899 fared no better.

A talented fund-raiser, Wellman in 1905 persuaded Victor Lawson, owner of the *Record-Herald*, to finance a new attempt to reach the Pole, this time by using a powered balloon. Wellman contracted with Louis Godard of Paris, France, to build an airship with a lifting capacity of eight tons. Driven by dual propellers that were turned by two gasoline engines with a total horsepower of seventy-five, plus a 5-horsepower engine to inflate the balloon, the *America* departed Spitzbergen on 2 September 1907, carrying Wellman, two crew members, and ten dogs for the 717-mile journey to the Pole. Two hours later, however, a bad storm forced down the airship and caused Wellman to abandon the voyage. Undaunted, he tried again in 1909, but without success. Wellman gave up plans for a third attempt after learning that Admiral Robert E. Peary had reached the Pole on April 6 1909.

Wellman's most ambitious aerial adventure came in 1910 when he attempted to cross the Atlantic Ocean in an enlarged version of the *America*. Again, Wellman, who contributed $10,000 of his own to the project, demonstrated his ability to raise money by securing $40,000 from the *Record-Herald*, the *New York Times*, and the *London Daily Telegraph*. He also persuaded the Aero Club of Atlantic City to build a $12,000 hangar for the *America*, now enlarged so that its hydrogen-filled envelope could lift twelve tons. Powered by two eighty-horsepower gasoline engines that drove four propellers, the giant airship featured a 156-foot car, suspended by cables below the envelope, with a 27-foot lifeboat hanging below the car. The most distinctive feature of the *America* was its "tail" of thirty cylindrical steel tanks, each weighing 100 pounds and containing reserve gasoline, trailing from the airship by a 300-foot steel cable. At the end of the "tail" were forty wooden blocks that were designed to float. Wellman termed this an "equilibrator." It was supposed to keep the airship at a uniform height of 200 feet above the surface of the ocean by automatically compensating for variations in buoyancy due to changes in pressure and temperature.

The *America* got underway from Atlantic City on 15 October 1910, with Wellman, five crew members, and supplies for a ten-day aerial voyage. The airship also carried a wireless radio. The first message ever from an airship to a shore station took place shortly before the *America* departed when a crew member's cat, Kiddo, was discovered on board. At that point, a less-than-memorable historic transmission was broadcast: "Roy, come and get this goddamn cat!" The attempt to retrieve the feline was unsuccessful, and Kiddo headed out into the Atlantic with the rest of the crew at 8 A.M.

The dangerously overloaded airship managed to stay aloft for seventy-one-and-one-half hours and cover 1,000 miles in an elliptical course. Finally, after one of its engines failed, the *America* set down at sea next to the steamer *Trent*, some 375 miles east of Cape Hatteras. All on board were rescued.

Wellman never again entered an airship or an airplane. In 1911 he published an account of his adventures under the title *The Aerial Age*. His other writings included an exposé of Dr. Frederick Cook's claim to have reached the North Pole before Peary; he later called for the American people to lead the way toward world peace through participation in the League of Nations. During the 1920s Wellman became interested in the problem of rapid transit in New York City. He told reporters that he was working on an invention that would reduce the cost of building rapid transit cars by 50 percent while extending their running life. This invention never appeared. A story in the *New York Times* in 1926 suggested that Wellman had fallen on hard times. Jailed for a debt of $280, he was released after an admirer of his earlier exploits sent in a check to cover the debt.

Prior to his death in New York City, Wellman had seen airships cross the Atlantic (in 1919) and reach the North Pole (in 1926). Wellman's adventurous spirit anticipated the triumphs that followed his abortive early efforts, although he contributed little to the technological success of the later voyages.

• Wellman's personal papers apparently have not survived. Material on his airship adventures can be found in the papers of A. Louis Loud, a crew member on the *America*, at the Illinois State Historical Library, Springfield. See *The Aerial Age* (1911) for Wellman's account of his voyages. Edward Mabley, *The Motor Balloon "America"* (1969), covers the voyages and contains biographical information on Wellman. An obituary is in the *New York Times*, 1 Feb. 1934.

WILLIAM M. LEARY

WELLMAN, William Augustus (29 Feb. 1896–9 Dec. 1975), American film director, was born in Brookline, Massachusetts, the son of Arthur Gouverneur and Cecelia Guiness McCarthy. A profane, iconoclastic, and rugged individualist both professionally and personally, Wellman committed a series of petty crimes in his youth, and one arrest for car theft resulted in probation. He went to public elementary school in Brookline and attended Newton High School, Newton Highlands, Massachusetts, from 1910 until 1914.

Dropping out of high school, he drifted into playing for a professional minor league ice hockey team. In April 1917 he joined the Norton-Harjes Ambulance Corps in New York City, which was being sent to France to assist in the war effort. In June 1917 he joined the French Foreign Legion. When the United States entered World War I, Wellman became a member of the Lafayette Flying Corps (Escadrille No. 87) and saw combat as a pursuit pilot. Shot down by enemy planes, he sustained a serious back injury that plagued him for the rest of his life. He returned to the United States, and in December 1917 he was made a lieutenant in the U.S. Aviation Service, Rockwell Field, California. When Armistice was declared, he was awarded the Croix de Guerre with four gold palm leaves by the French government as well as five citations from the United States.

A civilian again, Wellman became a retail wool trade salesman in Boston. He also found time to write a book, *Go, Get 'Em*, published in 1918. That same year he married Helene Chadwick. They divorced in 1920, the marriage producing one child. Wellman briefly joined a cross-country touring air show, performing acrobatic stunts. During one of his exhibitions he made an emergency landing on property owned by Douglas Fairbanks, Sr., the motion picture star. The two men hit it off, and Fairbanks offered Wellman a role in the film *Knickerbocker Buckaroo* (1919). Wellman accepted, made his sole acting screen appearance, and decided he wanted to direct movies instead. Subsequently, he accepted a job as a messenger at the Goldwyn Studios, and by 1920 he was an assistant director. In 1920 he directed his first feature film, *The Twins of Suffering Creek*, a Dustin Farnum western, although he did not receive credit. In 1923 he made his credited directorial debut with *The Man Who Won*, another Farnum western.

Also in 1920 Wellman began a series of three additional marriages, none of which produced children. The details of these marriages have been thoroughly suppressed. Wellman considered them disastrous, and he despaired of finding a compatible wife. Then in 1933 he married Dorothy Coonan (whom he promptly nicknamed "Mommy"), after directing her in *Wild Boys of the Road* (1933); this marriage lasted until his death. The couple had six children.

There followed an undistinguished series of Buck Jones program westerns, such as *Second-Hand Love* (1923), *Big Dan* (1923), *Cupid's Fireman* (1923), *The Vagabond Trail* (1924), and others, before Wellman directed a young Lucille Le Sueur (Joan Crawford) in *The Boob* (1926). He then got his break with the classic aviation drama *Wings* (1927). Wellman won an Academy Award for his direction. This gritty, realistic look at the perils of war starred Clara Bow, Charles (Buddy) Rogers, Richard Arlen, and Richard Tucker, as well as introducing to wider audiences a young Gary Cooper in a prominent bit part. Many critics feel that the aerial combat sequences in *Wings* have seldom been equaled. The film was reissued with an added sound track in 1929.

The solid critical and commercial success of *Wings* led to a series of prestige "A" budget films, including *The Legion of the Condemned* (1928), in which Gary Cooper now received second billing after Fay Wray; *Ladies of the Mob* (1928), another Clara Bow vehicle; *Beggars of Life* (1928), with Wallace Beery and Louise Brooks; and *Chinatown Nights* (1929), a story of the tong wars, again starring Wallace Beery. Wellman left Paramount for Warner Bros. in 1930. After two forgettable films at Warner's (*Maybe It's Love* [1930], a weak campus comedy with Joan Bennett and Joe E. Brown; and *Other Men's Women* [1931], starring Grant Withers, Regis Toomey, and Mary Astor), Wellman clicked with his second major hit, *The Public Enemy* (1931), the film that established James Cagney as one of the screen's most effective tough guys. Wellman followed this film with a series of fast-paced dramas, including *Night Nurse* (1931) with Barbara Stanwyck and Clark Gable; *The Star Witness* (1931) with Walter Huston and Chic Sale; and *The Hatchet Man* (1932) with Edward G. Robinson and Loretta Young.

Wellman earned a reputation as a speedy, reliable director who worked his crews relentlessly to get the job done. In 1931–1932 alone, he directed ten feature films, working from 6 A.M. until late at night in the days before unions had any say in motion picture production. Wellman often printed the first take of a scene, compelling his actors to give their all in every performance; he also carried a loaded gun on the set, which he would brandish in a threatening manner when things were not going his way. When difficulties arose, Wellman's temper was legendary; he hurled invective, one observer wrote, "like a poet." A heavy drinker, Wellman also was contemptuous of studio authority. All of these characteristics gave him a reputation as a cantankerous but talented maverick. He continued on in the 1930s with a variety of films, including the first version of Edna Ferber's *So Big* (1932) with Barbara Stanwyck and George Brent; *The Conquerors* (1932) with Richard Dix; *Central Airport* (1933) with Richard Barthelmess; and the memorable *Wild Boys of the Road* (1933), a rough-and-tumble story of young men and women forced into vagrancy as a result of the depression. After directing the bizarre political allegory *The President Vanishes* (1934) for Paramount, Wellman landed at MGM with *Call of the Wild* (1935), a watered-down adaptation of Jack London's novel featuring Clark Gable and Loretta Young.

In 1937 Wellman made two excellent films with producer David O. Selznick, for whom he had the profoundest respect: the first version of *A Star Is Born* (1937), featuring an Academy Award-winning script that Wellman coauthored; and *Nothing Sacred* (1937) with Carole Lombard and Fredric March. Now firmly entrenched as an "A" category director, Wellman entered a new phase of his career with the big-budget, action-adventure *Beau Geste* (1939) with Gary Cooper and Ray Milland, followed by his adaptation of Rudyard Kipling's *The Light That Failed* (1939), starring Ronald Colman and Ida Lupino. In 1943 Wellman directed *The Ox-Bow Incident*, a compelling tract against mob violence, as well as *Lady of Burlesque* with Barbara Stanwyck, which was based on Gypsy Rose Lee's mystery novel (actually written by Craig Rice) *The G-String Murders*.

Wellman's politics, always inclined toward the military, swung strongly to the right after the end of World War II; in the closing days of that conflict, he directed *The Story of G.I. Joe* (1945), based on war correspondent Ernie Pyle's memoirs, and the experience of working with the enlisted men used in the film affected him profoundly. In 1948 Wellman made *The Iron Curtain* with Dana Andrews and Gene Tierney, an overtly anticommunist spy thriller set in Canada. *Battleground* (1949), starring Van Johnson and Ricardo Montalban, was followed by perhaps the poorest, and certainly the oddest, film of Wellman's career, *The*

Next Voice You Hear (1950), a surprisingly cheap MGM film in which the voice of God is heard on the radio. The film featured James Whitmore and the future Mrs. Ronald Reagan, Nancy Davis. By this point Wellman's career was winding down, and of his later films, only the commercial aviation drama *The High and the Mighty* (1954), produced by and starring John Wayne, and *Track of the Cat* (1954), which Wellman described as "a black and white film made in color," starring Robert Mitchum and Teresa Wright, compel attention.

Wellman's last feature was a nostalgic farewell to the two major loves of his professional life, filmmaking and flying. *Lafayette Escadrille* (1958), which Wellman also produced and co-wrote, starred Tab Hunter, the great Marcel Dalio (famous for his work in Jean Renoir's *Rules of the Game* [1939]), David Janssen, Clint Eastwood, and Wellman's son, William A. Wellman, Jr. In the early 1960s Wellman's old back injury worsened, and he was forced to endure a lengthy hospital stay, followed by a long convalescence at home. During this period he wrote his autobiography, *A Short Time for Insanity* (finally published in 1974), a bizarre and often hallucinatory account of his long career and of his herculean efforts to wean himself from the narcotic painkillers that had come to dominate his life. A second still unpublished volume of memoirs, appropriately titled *Growing Old Disgracefully*, was completed shortly before his death. As Wellman requested in his autobiography, his body was "cremated and emptied high above the smog—high enough to join a beautiful cloud—not one that brings a storm [but] one that brings peace and contentment and beauty."

Wellman's career was, in balance, peculiar. Obviously a driven man, he often would accept an indifferent project just to keep working. In the early part of his career he had little choice; working at Warner Bros. in the early 1930s was essentially akin to laboring on a factory assembly line. But even after his arrival as a first-rank director in 1937, Wellman continued to accept assignments that were transparently beneath his abilities. *The Ox-Bow Incident* (1943) is a fully accomplished piece of work; but *Buffalo Bill* (1944), *This Man's Navy* (1945), and *Gallant Journey* (1946) lack the fire and passion that made the best of Wellman's films so memorable. Yet within the confines of a studio system that was justifiably legendary for suppressing individual talent, Wellman made at least a dozen films of real brilliance, a remarkable accomplishment for any artist.

• Besides three volumes of memoirs, Wellman wrote the article "Director's Notebook—Why Teach Cinema?," *Cinema Progress* (Los Angeles), June/July 1939. He gave an interesting interview toward the end of his life in *Cinema*, July 1966. Of critical volumes on Wellman, worth reading are Frank T. Thompson's *William A. Wellman* (1983) and pertinent sections of Kevin Brownlow's *The Parade's Gone By* (1968). Articles about Wellman and his work include Lesley Brill, "Growing Up Gangster: *Little Caesar*, *The Public Enemy* and the American Dream," in *Hollywood: Réflexions sur l'écran*, ed. Daniel Royot (1984); Louise Brooks, "On Location with Billy Wellman," *Film Culture*, Spring 1972; Kevin Brownlow, "William Wellman," *Film*, Winter 1965/66; S. Eyman and Allen Eyles, "'Wild Bill' William A. Wellman," *Focus on Film* 29 (1978); J. Fox, "A Man's World," *Films and Filming*, Mar. 1973; John Gallagher, "William Wellman," *Films in Review*, May, June/July, and Oct. 1982; Richard Griffith, "Wyler, Wellman, and Huston," *Films in Review*, Feb. 1950; Keith A. Joseph, "Shifting Egos: Three Generations of *A Star Is Born*," in *Sex and Love in Motion Pictures*, ed. Douglas Radcliff-Umstead (1984); Gerard Langlois, "William Wellman 1896–1975," *Avant-Scène du Cinéma*, 1 Mar. 1978; H. F. Pringle, "Screwball Bill," *Collier's*, 26 Feb. 1938; Andrew Sarris, "Fallen Idols," *Film Culture*, Spring 1963; J. M. Smith, "The Essential Wellman," *Brighton*, Jan. 1970; and William Wellman 2nd, "William Wellman: Director Rebel," *Action*, Mar./Apr. 1970. A fascinating sketch of the director in midcareer can be found in *Current Biography: 1950* (1950), pp. 608–10. An obituary is in the *New York Times* 11 Dec. 1975.

WHEELER WINSTON DIXON

WELLS, Carolyn (18 June 1869?–26 Mar. 1942), author, was born in Rahway, New Jersey, the daughter of William Edmund Wells, a real estate and insurance salesman, and Anna Potter Woodruff. In her autobiography, *The Rest of My Life* (1937), Wells relates that at age three she read fluently and had begun writing poetry. At the age of six, scarlet fever left her partially deaf, a condition that frustrated her throughout her life. Although she graduated from high school as class valedictorian, she disliked school and refused to go to college; instead, Wells sought out private lessons from various authorities in subjects ranging from medieval history to botany. As librarian of Rahway's well-endowed library, she ordered all the books and magazines she wanted, especially in the field of belles lettres. Wells studied Shakespeare for "three blissful seasons" in Amherst, Massachusetts, where she met Emily Dickinson's sister Lavinia. Renaissance scholar William J. Rolfe, Wells's instructor and fellow lover of puzzles, encouraged her to write a book of charades, which she titled *At the Sign of the Sphinx* (1896). According to Wells, her more than 170 subsequent volumes—which included several other books of brainteasers and party entertainments—"mostly happened" in response to suggestions of fellow authors and publishers; she often wrote three or four books a year.

Throughout the 1890s Wells wrote humorous verse for "little magazines" and mass market journals, including the *Chap Book*, the *Lark*, the *Philistine*, the *Tatler*, the *Yellow Book*, the *Bookman*, the *Century*, *St. Nicholas*, and *Youth's Companion*. She published so frequently in *Life* that a reader jokingly asked, "Is Carolyn Wells a syndicate?" Wells's mentors during what she described as the "Nonsensical Nineties" were Oliver Herford, who illustrated her rhymes for *St. Nicholas* and shared her facility for writing limericks, and Gelett Burgess, editor of the *Lark* and author of the "purple cow" quatrain that Wells parodied. She became such a leading humorist that her name was incorporated into book titles, such as *The Carolyn Wells Year Book of Old Favorites and New Fancies for 1909*

(1908) and *Carolyn Wells' Book of American Limericks* (1925). Her *Abeniki Caldwell: A Burlesque Historical Romance* (1902) hilariously incorporates all the romance conventions, from a gallant Scottish hero to his beloved but aloof lady, Princess Berenice of Bois-Bracy: "Tall as an Amazonian goddess, yet not too tall to be called *petite*, her straight, arrow-like figure was full of graceful curves." Wells parodied Edward FitzGerald's immensely popular *Rubáiyát of Omar Khayyám*, while at the same time satirizing Americans' fascination with automobiles and card games, in her *Rubáiyát of a Motor Car* (1906) and *The Rubáiyát of Bridge* (1909). In *Ptomaine Street: A Tale of Warble Petticoat* (1921), she reacted quickly and comically to Sinclair Lewis's portrayal of Carol Kennicott in his bestselling *Main Street* (1920). She also achieved fame as an editor of comic works, including her lengthy *Outline of Humor: Being a True Chronicle from Prehistoric Ages to the Twentieth Century* (1923). Her most frequently reprinted books are two collections, *A Nonsense Anthology* (1902) and *A Parody Anthology* (1904).

Many of Wells's books are directed toward young readers. *The Jingle Book* (1899), the title of which pays homage to Rudyard Kipling's *Jungle Book* (1894), includes "An Alice Alphabet," inspired by Lewis Carroll, another of Wells's favorite writers of children's stories. Reacting to the demand for children's serial narratives, Wells wrote her "Patty," "Marjorie," and "Two Little Women" books for girls during the period when Edward Stratemeyer, using the pseudonyms Victor Appleton and Laura Lee Hope, published the Tom Swift and Bobbsey Twins series. More imaginative than her novels of youthful pastimes and small town family life are Wells's *Folly in Fairyland* (1901) and *Folly in the Forest* (1902), humorous fantasies whose wordplay, talking animals, and curious young heroine are obviously indebted to Carroll's pair of Alice books.

While Wells's humor literature is probably her best work, by the 1930s she had become known as the "Dean of American Mystery Writers" for her many novels in a genre that reflected her fascination with puzzle solving. Her suave detectives include the former movie actor Kenneth Carlisle, Alan Ford, Lorimer Lane, Pennington Wise with his gamine assistant Zizi, and Fleming Stone, who appears in about sixty of her eighty-two mystery books. Stone undertakes Wells's first case in *The Clue* (1909) and her last in *Who Killed Caldwell?* (1942). Dashiell Hammett, a pioneer of hard-boiled detective fiction, was highly critical of the formulaic nature of Wells's drawing room crimes. With their many pointed-weapon murders behind locked doors, her stories sometimes read like parodies of mysteries by Edgar Allan Poe, Anna Katharine Green, Arthur Conan Doyle, and other authors she admired. Wells's *Technique of the Mystery Story* (1913; rev. ed., 1929), is an extensive study of the genre. She collected some of her favorite short mysteries in *American Detective Stories* (1927), *American Mystery Stories* (1927), and *Best American Mystery Stories of the Year* (1931).

Wells wrote that she was "especially fortunate in the matter of friends," both at home and while on her frequent trips to England. Among the most "congenial spirits" was her husband, Hadwin Houghton, whom she married in 1918; they had no children. Houghton died in 1919, but Wells remained in New York, where she had moved after their marriage. Her autograph album was filled with drawings, verses, and signatures of visitors as diverse as Theodore Roosevelt (1858–1919), Mary Mapes Dodge, Charles Dana Gibson, and Mark Twain. Her large personal library contained volumes inscribed by George Ade, Kate Douglas Wiggin, Booth Tarkington, Edgar Lee Masters, Frances Hodgson Burnett, Woodrow Wilson, Mary E. Wilkins, and many others. Wells became a noted collector and early bibliographer of Walt Whitman's works. Although she said that "my literary output has come to be remarkable for quantity rather than quality," *Life*'s literary editor, Thomas L. Masson, writing in *Our American Humorists* (1922; rev. ed., 1931), called her "our chief woman humorist." Wells died in New York, five years after completing an autobiography that reveals her sensitivity to the changing literary fashions of a half century and records her success as an author and parodist of most of the popular genres of her lifetime.

• Ohio State University Libraries' Rare Books and Manuscripts Department, Columbus, Ohio, holds over thirty items of Wells's, dating from 1892 to 1940 and including photographs, greeting cards, pamphlets, and typescripts of three short pieces and eight of her later mystery stories. A partial list of works by Wells not mentioned in the text includes: *Idle Idyls* (1900), *A Satire Anthology* (1905), *The Emily Emmins Papers* (1907), *The Lover's Baedecker and Guide to Arcady* (1912), *The Re-Echo Club* (1913), *Such Nonsense: An Anthology* (1918), *The Book of Humorous Verse* (1920; rev. ed., 1936), *The Disappearance of Kimball Webb* (1920, under the pseudonym Rowland Wright), *The Omnibus Fleming Stone* (1923), *All at Sea* (1927), *The Umbrella Murder* (1931), *All for Fun: Brain Teasers* (1933), and *The Radio Studio Murder* (1937). Aside from her autobiography, the most complete introduction to Wells is Zita Zatkin Dresner's "Carolyn Wells" entry in the *Dictionary of Literary Biography*, vol. 11 (1982). A bibliography of over 170 books, divided by genre, appears in John M. Reilly, ed., *Twentieth-Century Crime and Mystery Writers* (1980). Paula Kepos ed., *Twentieth-Century Literary Criticism*, vol. 35 (1990), includes several excerpts from critics and reviewers of Wells's books, along with passages from her autobiography and a secondary bibliography. Obituaries are in the *New York Times* and the *New York Herald Tribune*, 27 Mar. 1942.

JOAN WYLIE HALL

WELLS, David Ames (17 June 1828–5 Nov. 1898), economist, was born in Springfield, Massachusetts, the son of James Wells, a struggling retailer, and Rebecca Ames. Wells was educated at Williams College, graduating in 1847, and at the newly opened Lawrence Scientific School, where he completed his studies in 1851. He then applied his educational background to the preparation of a series of manuals on topics in geology, chemistry, and general science that won an appreciative popular audience. In May 1860 he married Mary Sanford Dwight, with whom he would have one child.

Wells's career was fundamentally reoriented during the Civil War when he turned his attention to the fiscal problems facing the Federal government. His skills as a publicist and interpreter of empirical data had already been demonstrated. In a pamphlet titled *Our Burden and Our Strength* (published in late 1864), he deployed his skills to appraise the financial viability of the U.S. government in the face of the massive wartime accumulation of public debt, concluding that debt servicing would be manageable in light of the expected expansion in the wealth and tax-paying capacity of the American economy. Appearing at a time when the credit worthiness of the Union was in question, his findings were welcomed enthusiastically in Washington, and some 200,000 copies of the pamphlet were distributed in the United States and Europe.

In early 1865 Wells's newly acquired prominence as an economic analyst inspired President Abraham Lincoln and Secretary of the Treasury Hugh McCulloch to invite him to head a three-member national revenue commission. In the following year he was appointed as special commissioner of the revenue—a post created especially for him—for a four-year term. From this office, Wells produced a series of reports that were pathbreaking in their command of pertinent statistical details. But Wells was not content simply to mobilize and organize the "facts"; he also sought to reshape policy. With respect to internal taxes, he championed fundamental reforms in the system improvised during the Civil War, emphasizing elimination of excises on raw materials (on grounds that such taxes increased the costs of processors and compromised the competitive position of American producers) and significant reductions in the levies on alcoholic spirits (on grounds that excessive duties encouraged massive evasion and reduced the ultimate revenue yield). His recommendations on these points had significant impact on tax legislation.

Wells was not successful, however, in his efforts to reshape tariff policy. On this controversial matter, his own views shifted during his tenure as special commissioner of the revenue. The perspective he initially brought to this assignment had been heavily influenced by protectionist doctrines preached by Henry C. Carey. (Indeed, part of his optimistic reading of the debt-servicing capacity of the Federal fiscal system—as articulated in *Our Burden and Our Strength*—rested on a conviction that the nation's economic growth prospects would be enhanced by tariff shelters.) By 1868 Wells had reversed his earlier position. In his report for that year, he concluded that the tariff "as it now stands, . . . is in many respects injurious and destructive." Were the government to bend to the appeals of special interests for increased protection, such action would "aggravate the very difficulties under which the country now labors" and would "impair the revenues and hinder the return to specie payments." The correct course, as he then saw matters, was to move toward free trade (*Report of the Special Commissioner of the Revenue for the Year 1868*, p. 80). He held the protectionists responsible for sheltering inefficient producers at the expense of consumers, for padding costs of production and thus diminishing the nation's ability to export, and for generating needlessly high prices that retarded economic expansion.

Although Wells's espousal of free-trade doctrines was intellectually courageous, it denied him further influence in the official Washington of the Ulysses S. Grant administration. His ambition to become secretary of the treasury was frustrated. Even the post of special commissioner of the revenue disappeared in 1870 when its legislative authorization was not renewed. Shortly thereafter, he was appointed by the governor of New York to make recommendations on state and local taxation. The report of this commission, completed in 1871, was the first systematic investigation of this aspect of the public finances.

During the remainder of his career, Wells wrote prolifically about economic issues. He took it to be his charge to elevate the economic literacy of the public—and to win converts to the doctrines of free trade, sound money, and laissez-faire. These causes were to be advanced, both through his own pen and through his work with the Society for Political Education and the Free Trade League. One of his own pamphlets, a *Primer of Tariff Reform*, written as a catechism to explain "the subtleties and fallacies of the protectionists" to the average voter, was influential during Grover Cleveland's successful campaign for the presidency in 1884. Wells also sought to ensure that his support for economic investigation would outlive him. In his will, he endowed the David A. Wells Prizes to be awarded for excellence in economic research at Harvard University, but it was also in character for him to stipulate that "no essay shall be considered which in any way advocates or defends . . . the restriction of commerce in times of peace by legislation, except for moral or sanitary purposes; . . . or the impairment of contracts by the debasement of coin; or the issue . . . by government of irredeemable notes . . . as a substitute for money" (as quoted by Dorfman, p. 82).

In addition to his official reports, Wells's published works include *The Relation of the Government to the Telegraph* (1873), *The Cremation Theory of Specie Resumption* (1875), *Practical Economics* (1885), and *Recent Economic Changes* (1889). In 1874 he was made a foreign associate member of the French Academy to fill the chair vacated by the death of John Stuart Mill. Wells made no original contributions to economic theory, but his pioneering work in quantitative investigation has won the admiration of later generations of economists.

Wells was politically engaged throughout his adult life, though his partisan allegiances shifted. Embittered by his experience with the Grant administration, he abandoned the regular Republican party to support the Liberal Republican ticket in the election of 1872. In 1876 he identified himself as a Democrat, running unsuccessfully for a seat in Congress from Connecticut (as he was to do again in 1890). In June 1879 he married Ellen Dwight, younger sister of his deceased first wife. (The date of her death is unknown.) Wells died at Norwich, Connecticut, where he had maintained a residence since 1870.

• The private papers of David Ames Wells are housed in the Springfield Public Library, Springfield, Mass. Wells's work as special commissioner of the revenue is examined in depth in Herbert Roland Ferleger, "David A. Wells and the American Revenue System 1865–1870" (Ph.D. diss., Columbia Univ., 1942). Fred Bunyan Joyner, *David Ames Wells: Champion of Free Trade* (1939), provides a comprehensive treatment of Wells's life and career. Joseph Dorfman's comments in vol. 3 of *The Economic Mind in American Civilization, 1606–1933* (5 vols., 1946; repr. 1966), are useful in positioning Wells in relation to contemporary economists.

WILLIAM J. BARBER

WELLS, Dicky (10 June 1907–12 Nov. 1985), jazz trombonist, was born William C. Wells in Centerville, Tennessee, the son of George Washington Wells and Florence (maiden name unknown). Around 1917 Wells's family moved to Louisville, Kentucky, where he began studying music; at age thirteen, he was playing baritone horn in the Booker T. Washington Community Center band.

In 1923 Wells switched to trombone. He worked locally with Lucius Brown and Ferman Tapp until 1926, when he was hired by Lloyd Scott to join his Symphonic Syncopators in Springfield, Ohio. After some touring, the band went to New York in 1927 and worked at the Capitol Palace, the Savoy Ballroom, and other venues both in and out of New York through June 1929, when Lloyd's brother, saxophonist Cecil Scott, took over as the band's leader. After leaving Scott in mid-1930, Wells jobbed around New York, replacing J. C. Higginbotham in Luis Russell's band in the fall of 1931, then joining banjoist Elmer Snowden at Small's Paradise, where fellow sidemen included Roy Eldridge and Sid Catlett. While Wells was with Snowden, the band appeared in *Smash Your Baggage* (1933), a Vitaphone short. On leaving Snowden, Wells worked briefly with Russell Wooding at Connie's Inn and, from August 1932 to June 1933, was a featured soloist in the Benny Carter orchestra. A short engagement with Charlie Johnson at Small's preceded a June to December 1933 stay with the Fletcher Henderson band and an appearance at the Lafayette Theater with Chick Webb's orchestra.

Wells rejoined Carter's band in early 1934 to work at the Savoy and the Empire ballrooms. In September he returned to the Savoy and Connie's Inn with Teddy Hill. In the summer of 1937 he toured Europe with the Hill band, and, after playing dates in London, Manchester, and Dublin, he made the first records under his own name while in Paris. In July 1938 he joined Count Basie and remained with the band until early 1946, when he left because of illness. Opting to stay in New York for a while, Wells worked locally with the bands of Lucky Millinder, J. C. Heard, Willie Bryant, and Sy Oliver until the fall of 1947, when he rejoined the Basie orchestra. In January 1950 Basie disbanded, and Wells went with blues singer Jimmy Rushing into the Savoy for an extended stay. In October 1952 he began a European tour with trumpeter Bill Coleman, but the combination of extremely cold weather and his excessive drinking took a noticeable toll on both his health and his playing. When he returned to the States the following February he was still very ill, but by autumn he resumed regular work, this time with Lucky Millinder. A period of freelancing followed, during which he worked with Earl Hines, Buddy Tate, Buck Clayton, Max Kaminsky, Rex Stewart, Illinois Jacquet, and Red Prysock.

In early December 1957, as a member of Count Basie's All-Stars, he participated in the widely praised CBS telecast "The Sound of Jazz," as well as joining two Rex Stewart–led reunions of Fletcher Henderson alumni in November 1957 and August 1958. In the fall of 1959 and the spring of 1961 Wells toured Europe with Buck Clayton's All-Stars, a nine-piece group including former Basie sidemen Emmett Berry, Earle Warren, and Buddy Tate. Between these tours Wells worked in Tate's band at the Celebrity Club in Harlem. From October 1961 until June 1963 he toured with Ray Charles, and during the summer he played in Reuben Phillips's show band at the Apollo. In 1965 Wells returned to Europe to work as a featured soloist with Alex Welsh. On his return to New York, he resumed freelancing. In September 1967 he began working days for a Wall Street brokerage firm, but he remained active in music, touring Europe with Buddy Tate in late 1968 and appearing at the New Orleans Jazz Festival in June 1969 and the Newport Jazz Festival in July 1972 with Benny Carter's all-star big band. Before the 1971 publication of his autobiography, Wells had been mugged three times: twice in Brooklyn, while attempting to collect rental income on property he owned, and once near his home in Harlem. A fourth, even more brutal attack took place in 1975, but he survived a long coma and began playing again in late 1976 with Earle Warren and Claude Hopkins. His last noted appearances were with his own combo at the West End Café in 1981 and with Bobby Booker's Big Band at Smalls' Paradise in 1984. Suffering from a complication of ailments, in 1985 he was admitted to a rest home in New York, where he died.

Wells made his first records in January 1927 with Lloyd Scott and, although he had been influenced earlier by trombonist Jimmy Harrison, a youthful idol in Louisville and later a major voice in Harlem bands, it is clear from Wells's solos on "Symphonic Scrontch" and the November 1929 "In a Corner" and "Springfield Stomp" by Cecil Scott's Bright Boys that his was a new and independent voice. Further growth toward stylistic individuality is apparent on Luis Russell's August 1931 session, but his indisputable high points during this early period are on the April and May 1933 recordings of the Benny Carter Orchestra, under the leadership of British arranger Spike Hughes. On almost all of the fourteen titles recorded, Wells is at his most distinctive. Even in the company of such widely regarded jazz soloists as Carter, Henry "Red" Allen, and Coleman Hawkins, the trombonist emerges as a totally matured stylist, as inventive and emotionally moving as any of his better-known colleagues. He conducts himself with similar conviction on Fletcher Henderson's "King Porter Stomp" from August 1933 and on Horace Henderon's "I'm Rhythm Crazy Now" and "Minnie the Moocher's Wedding Day" from October, but his major opportunity occurred in the spring of 1937 while he was with Teddy Hill. Strikingly fluent solos on "My Marie," "A Study in Brown," and "King Porter Stomp" were followed in July with twelve small band performances recorded in Paris under his own name. Here he is at his best on "Between the Devil and the Deep Blue Sea," "Lady Be Good," and "Dicky Wells Blues." In the four years since the Spike Hughes recordings, Wells's style went from unbridled passion and restlessness, as evidenced in his pronounced vibrato and yearning declamations, into a more mellow, controlled virtuosity characterized by a broader tone and increased technical mastery.

Without question, Wells's most stylistically definitive work took place during his first years with Count Basie. Beginning in August 1938 he was featured on such groundbreaking records as "Texas Shuffle," "Panassié Stomp," "Taxi War Dance," and "Dickie's Dream," as well as several more on which he provided stirring backgrounds to Jimmy Rushing's vocals. Wells made his second appearance as a small band leader in December 1943, and on these records, in the company of Bill Coleman and Lester Young, he can be heard giving full rein to his unconventional ideas. Although evident in his solos on the big band records, the compact setting of the septet allowed him even more space to experiment with asymmetrical rhythmic phrasing, upper register glissandos, wide interval skips, and other devices uncharacteristic of the trombone. At this time Wells was also mastering diverse timbres, both with and without mutes and replete with burry sonorities and growling guttural moans. These he had used earlier in his obligatos behind Rushing, but here they are brought into prominence as integral elements in his jazz solos, particularly when he wished to express his humorous side. In March 1944 Wells also played an important role in two small band sessions under the group names of the Kansas City Seven and the Kansas City Six. Recorded within a week of each other, these dates feature Young but are equally rewarding for the contributions of Wells, Buck Clayton, and Coleman. From the mid-1940s on, Wells recorded prolifically with both big bands and jazz combos, the best of these under the leadership of Basie, Rushing, Clayton, Coleman, Rex Stewart, and Buddy Tate. In 1958 and 1959 he led fellow former Basie trombonists Benny Morton, Vic Dickenson, and George Matthews on sessions for the Felsted label; the resulting albums, *Bones for the King* and "*Trombone Four-in-Hand*," were among his personal favorites.

• The best account of Wells's career until the late 1960s is his autobiography, *The Night People: The Jazz Life of Dicky Wells*, as told to Stanley Dance (1971; repr. 1991). Admittedly, its chronology of earlier events is at variance with other sources, but it provides an insight into Wells not available elsewhere. In addition to a comprehensive artist discography by Chris Sheridan, its appendixes include André Hodeir, "The Romantic Imagination of Dickie Wells," a 1954 critical appraisal reprinted in Hodeir's *Jazz: Its Evolution and Essence* (1956). Bill Coleman, *Trumpet Story* (1991), is of special value since trumpeter Coleman and Wells worked together frequently from the late 1920s on for such bandleaders as Lloyd and Cecil Scott, Charlie Johnson, Benny Carter, Teddy Hill, and Sy Oliver, in addition to their shared recording and concert activities later. Further background is in Albert McCarthy, *Big Band Jazz* (1974); Walter C. Allen, *Hendersonia: The Music of Fletcher Henderson and His Musicians* (1973); Stanley Dance, *The World of Swing* (1974) and *The World of Count Basie* (1980); Count Basie, *Good Morning Blues*, as told to Albert Murray (1985); and Buck Clayton, *Buck Clayton's Jazz World* (1987). An extended obituary is in Graham Colombé, "Dicky Wells," *Jazz Journal International* 39 (Jan. 1986): 20. For additional discographical information, see Brian Rust, *Jazz Records, 1897–1942* (1982), and Walter Bruyninckx, *Swing Discography, 1920–1988* (12 vols., 1985–1988). An abbreviated biography is in John Chilton, *Who's Who of Jazz* (1985).

JACK SOHMER

WELLS, Edward Curtis (26 Aug. 1910–1 July 1986), aeronautical engineer, was born in Boise, Idaho, the son of Edward Lansing Wells, a weather bureau official, and Laura Long. He grew up with four sisters in a frugal middle-class household that emphasized learning, modesty, and moral education. When he was nine, the family moved to Portland, Oregon, where wells attended public schools. After two years at a nearby college, he transferred to Stanford University's engineering program, from which he received a B.A. in 1931 and, it was said, one of the highest grade averages to that time.

Wells, who had already had a summer job in 1930 with the Boeing Aircraft Company, received in 1931 an offer of a permanent post as a draftsman and engineer there. Believing that practical employment suited him far better than an academic or research career, he joined a fifty-person engineering department to work on military biplane designs. Except for one period in 1969–1970 spent as a visiting scholar at Stanford, Wells would be employed exclusively by the Seattle, Washington, airplane manufacturer. He married Dorothy E. Ostlund in 1934; they had two children.

One of Wells's earliest assignments was the design of tail surfaces for the Boeing 247, a revolutionary all-metal monoplane that was engineered by the risky method of simultaneously integrating numerous innovations. This became the method that Boeing and Wells frequently adopted in later designs. In 1934, although only in his mid-twenties, he was assigned to the preliminary design of a large four-engine bomber, the prototype B-17 Flying Fortress, which eventually became largely his project. In the 1930s, however, a series of problems caused the company to fall into near bankruptcy.

Under company president Philip G. Johnson, Boeing recovered while building huge numbers of the B-17 during World War II. This aircraft, the dominant U.S. heavy bombardment aircraft of the early war, was followed by another equally dominant design overseen by Wells, the B-29 Superfortress, which once again brought together such numerous state-of-the-art innovations as fuselage pressurization and a remote-control gun firing system. One such B-29, named the "Enola Gay," was used in the atomic bomb missions over Hiroshima and Nagasaki, Japan, that resulted in the Japanese surrender. The new design took the piston-engine bomber to near its practical limits.

Both bombers were major advances in size and sophistication, characteristics that became synonymous with Boeing's designs. By the end of the war, Wells, who, still in his early thirties, oversaw thousands of technical employees, had developed strong engineering management procedures. In addition, he was responsible for fifteen patents, mostly for mechanical and flight systems including landing gears.

Wells's successes were also Boeing's. In the postwar period, under president William M. Allen, Boeing was the first to build a swept-wing jet bomber and in the process established the standard configuration of large modern turbine aircraft. Its B-47 and B-52 bombers were major American weapon systems and pillars of the "balance of terror" that gave the Cold War much of its peculiar stability. And in extending the general design to a transport aircraft, Wells and his staff would affect lives everywhere through the creation in 1958 of the first successful civilian jet airliner, the 707.

This was not an unchallenged step. Enormous international and domestic industrial battles followed due to product competition for market leadership, requiring Wells and Allen to make their firm responsive to airlines. Wells's close rapport with civilian customers often resulted in confidence-building design improvements. From the 1950s onward, Boeing's 700-series (707, 727, 737, etc.) airliners dominated their market. Their success largely tied Boeing to world consumer prosperity and loosened the firm's connection with military conflict.

Described as a "courteous, soft-spoken man who continually deprecates his own contributions" while praising others (Boyne, p. 157), Wells was one of aviation's less visible giants. Still, many honors came to him, including the Sperry (1942), Guggenheim (1980), and Jannus (1985) awards, as well as selection to influential councils and boards. Over the years he enjoyed in his spare time boating, model trains, astronomy, and painting, and he became proficient in French, Italian, Portuguese, Spanish, and German. In 1972 he retired as senior vice president of Boeing but remained involved as a consultant and board member. He died in Bellevue, Washington.

• A biography is Mary Wells Geer, *Boeing's Ed Wells* (1992). See also Walter Boyne, *Boeing B-52: A Documentary History* (1981).

PAUL G. SPITZER

WELLS, Emmeline Blanche Woodward (29 Feb. 1828–25 Apr. 1921), suffragist and Mormon feminist activist, was born in Petersham, Massachusetts, the daughter of David Woodward and Diadama Hare, farmers. Marital relations were a defining characteristic of Emmeline's life. As a recent convert to the Church of Jesus Christ of Latter-day Saints (LDS church), she married at age fifteen fellow church member James Harris, also fifteen. By the next year, she had buried her first child and had been deserted by her teenage husband. Thereafter, Emmeline chose father figures as husbands. In 1845 she married Newel K. Whitney, a prominent Mormon bishop thirty-three years her senior, who was already the husband of two living wives. She wrote Whitney in 1847: "Like as a vine entwineth itself around an *aged* tree, so do my affections entwine about thy heart." They had two children before Whitney's death in 1850.

Emmeline then proposed marriage, a common practice in Mormon society, in 1852 to Daniel H. Wells. Wells, almost fourteen years her senior and already the husband of six living wives, married Emmeline six months later. Prominent in Utah civil office and in the theocratic Council of Fifty, Daniel Wells became a counselor to Brigham Young in 1857 and remained a "general authority" in the LDS church until his death in 1891. During her marriage to Wells, Emmeline had three children, published eloquent defenses of polygamy, and became a prominent Mormon suffragist.

Although Emmeline had met Joseph Smith shortly before his death in 1844, her life was more directly influenced by Brigham Young. He had performed her marriage to Whitney in 1845, while she was still legally married to James Harris. Known as the "American Moses," Young led Emmeline and other Mormon pioneers to Salt Lake City, Utah, in 1847. There Mormonism's "Lion of the Lord" performed the marriage ceremony for Emmeline and Daniel Wells in 1852. Her first marriage as a teenage bride was not legally dissolved until 1859, when Harris died. Young established the Mormon community of Utah as the first Anglo-American society where polygamy was the normative practice and ideal. As a result, Emmeline's status as a plural wife placed her among the elite of pioneer Mormon women. Her marriage to an LDS general authority put her within the inner circle of that elite.

However, because she shared her husband with his other wives in Utah, Emmeline Wells developed an extreme personal autonomy during his frequent absences. She taught this independence to her daughters and eventually promoted equality and autonomy among all Mormon women. During the first twenty years of her marriage and child rearing, Wells's extradomestic activities primarily involved teaching and ministering (often through faith healings) to other Mormon women. Her diaries reveal that, in part, she filled her days with activities to compensate for the emotional distance of her husband, and she frequently wrote of her longing for the romance of her first marriage and the nurturing love of Bishop Whitney.

Wells became assistant editor of the Mormon suffragist publication *Woman's Exponent* in 1875. A year later she editorialized, "Let women have all the same opportunities for an education, observation and experience in public and private" as men "on all general questions socially, politically, industrially, and educationally as well as spiritually." Her editorials ridiculed Victorian gender roles that forced a woman to be "a painted doll" or a "household deity." Instead, she insisted that every married woman must be "a joint-partner in the domestic firm."

Wells demonstrated this feminist philosophy in her own life. She served as the *Exponent* editor, owner, business manager, and publisher from 1877 to 1914. In 1878 she became a member of the territorial central committee of the LDS church's political party, the Mormon "People's party." That same year, her effort to be elected county treasurer failed because Utah territorial law did not allow women to hold civil office, even though at the time, approved Mormon candidates received 80 percent of election votes and Utah's women had had the franchise since 1870. After her frustrated candidacy in 1878, Wells repeatedly but unsuccessfully pressed Utah's federally appointed (non-Mormon) governors to approve legislation granting the territory's women the right to hold elective office. In 1879 she was among the first Mormon delegates at the convention of the National Woman Suffrage Association in Washington, D.C.

By the time Daniel Wells sought a closer relationship with Emmeline in the late 1880s, she was too occupied with feminist causes to offer him much time or attention. Her diary noted on 17 September 1890: "I had such a lovely letter from my husband & he said so many pleasant things, that in days past would have filled me with the most infinite pleasure, but now it is only like *dead sea apples*. . . . How strange that everything comes too late, when the desire to possess it has gone." A week later, LDS church president Wilford Woodruff published the Manifesto that officially ended plural marriages in Mormonism. As a result, some men, even a few general authorities of the LDS church, ceased living with their plural wives.

Daniel Wells died six months after this announcement, and later in 1891 Emmeline Wells became a founding member of the National Council of Women. That same year, she also helped draft the constitution for the International Press Federation of Women and became the first president of the Utah Women's Press Club. In 1892 she became the first president of the Reaper's Club in Utah, a women's organization that promoted reviews of current literature.

In 1895 Wells was among those who successfully lobbied for the inclusion of woman suffrage and women's right to elective office in the constitution for the proposed state of Utah (admitted to the Union in 1896). She was also an unsuccessful Republican candidate for the Utah state legislature that year. She regarded as the high point of her life her speech in Westminster Abbey on 1 July 1899 on "The History and Purposes of the Mormon Relief Society," which she delivered as a delegate from Utah at the International Council of Women in London. After attending the executive meetings of the National Council of Women for several years as a recording secretary, she was elected chair of its national Advisory Committee in 1913.

The LDS church rewarded Wells's feminist activism. In 1910 the church appointed her to the position of general president of its Relief Society, a Mormon women's organization that had been established in 1842. She also served as "presidentess" of the women who administered the "endowment," Mormonism's most sacred ordinances in the Salt Lake temple.

Praised by the Mormon *Relief Society Magazine* for her "fierce independence," Wells continued to serve as general president from 1910 until 1921, when the LDS church president denied her the life tenure of all other Relief Society general presidents in Utah. Devastated by her "release," she died three weeks later.

Nevertheless, this untiring Mormon suffragist had reached the pinnacle of Mormon women's authority. She also lived to see ratification of the U.S. constitutional amendment that gave the vote to women nationally. Her position as a nineteenth-century Mormon feminist was more uncompromising than that of the better-known Eliza R. Snow, and in feminist history, Emmeline B. Wells is the most significant early Mormon.

• Emmeline Wells's diaries are in the Archives Division, Harold B. Lee Library, Brigham Young University, Provo, Utah, and some of her correspondence can be found in the Newel K. Whitney Collection, also in the Lee Library. The most complete biography is Carol Cornwall Madsen, "A Mormon Woman in Victorian America" (Ph.D. diss., Univ. of Utah, 1985). Also important are Judith Rasmussen Dushku, "Feminists," in *Mormon Sisters: Women in Early Utah*, ed. Claudia L. Bushman (1976); Patricia Rasmussen Eaton-Gadsby and Judith Rasmussen Dushku, "Emmeline B. Wells," in *Sister Saints*, ed. Vicky Burgess-Olson (1978); Maureen Ursenbach Beecher, "The 'Leading Sisters': A Female Hierarchy in Nineteenth-Century Mormon Society," in *The New Mormon History: Revisionist Essays on the Past*, ed. D. Michael Quinn (1992); Madsen, "Emmeline B. Wells: 'Am I Not a Woman and a Sister?'" *Brigham Young University Studies* 22 (Spring 1982): 161–78, and "A Fine Soul Who Served Us: The Life of Emmeline B. Wells," *Journal of the John Whitmer Historical Association* 2 (1982): 11–21; and Vella Neil Evans, "Empowerment in Mormon Women's Publications," in *Women and Authority: Re-emerging Mormon Feminism*, ed. Maxine Hanks (1992). An obituary is in the *New York Times*, 27 Apr. 1921.

D. MICHAEL QUINN

WELLS, Frederic Lyman (22 Apr. 1884–2 June 1964), clinical psychologist and psychometrician, was born on Beacon Hill in Boston, Massachusetts, the son of Benjamin W. Wells, a professor of modern languages at the University of the South at Sewanee, Tennessee, and later a writer and editor in New York City, and Lena Lyman. Frederick, or Lyman as his family called him, received his earliest education in Europe under tutors at the Dritte Protestantische Volksschule in

Munich and at the University of the South Grammar School. He entered college at Sewanee when he was fifteen years old, but a year later he transferred to Columbia University, where he obtained an A.B. (1903) and M.A. (1904) in German philology. Coming under the influences of James McKeen Cattell, Robert Sessions Woodworth, and Edward L. Thorndike while at Columbia, Wells took his Ph.D. in Psychology (1906). His dissertation, on linguistic lapses, compared three syllable nonsense sounds with reproductions of what the subjects thought they had heard. He concluded that chaos is consistently translated into meaning but in ways idiosyncratic to the individual.

After a year of teaching at Columbia, Wells was appointed assistant in pathological psychology and director of the experimental laboratory at the McLean Hospital in Belmont, Massachusetts, where he was involved in introducing the techniques of experimental psychology into clinical psychiatry. His early research dealt with purely laboratory subjects, but he soon turned his attention to applied problems in clinical psychology and to mental testing, for which he is best known.

He appeared in the famous Clark University photo of 1909, along with Sigmund Freud, Carl Jung, William James, and others. This proximity to some of the greatest minds in psychiatry inspired Wells, and in addition to his experimental research, led him to become an interpreter of the ideas of Jung and the first to incorporate psychoanalysis into his clinical practice at McLean Hospital.

Wells remained at McLean until 1921, except during 1910–1911, when he worked under August Hoch at the New York Psychiatric Institute, and in 1917–1918, when, as an army captain, he supervised selection tests for the fledgling Air Service. In 1917 Wells was one of eight psychologists selected by the American Psychological Association in collaboration with the U.S. military to devise a standardized test that would differentiate the worst and the best recruits for military service. Wells's early study of psychological testing served him well, resulting in the Army Alpha and Army Beta tests of intelligence. He published his first book, the influential *Association Tests*, in 1911, co-authored with Robert S. Woodworth, followed by *Mental Adjustments*, his critique of dynamic psychology, in 1917. Also during this period, on 21 September 1915, Wells married Florence Gertrude Smart of Boston, an event reported in the *New York Times*. The couple had two sons.

In 1921 Wells became the chief psychologist at the Boston Psychopathic Hospital, where he remained until 1938. At the time he was also appointed instructor in experimental psychopathology at the Harvard Medical School. He took an active role in the affairs of the American Psychological Association as chairman of the Clinical Section in 1922 and was a member of the association's Council of Directors (1922–1924). He was also a member of the National Research Council (1925–1929). His major works during this period were *Pleasure and Behavior* (1924), an essay on the place of affect in a psychology of behavior, and *Mental Tests in Clinical Practice* (1927), a textbook of case studies and instructions on the administration of tests. In the early 1930s Wells became interested in the Rorschach Ink Blot Test and assisted Samuel Beck in drafting one of several methods still in use that were designed to systematically interpret a subject's responses to the tests. He also produced the widely used intelligence test, the Revised Army Alpha, in 1932.

In 1932 Wells was promoted to assistant professor of experimental psychopathology at Harvard Medical School and, in addition to his position at the Boston Psychopathic Hospital, was on the staff at the Boston City Hospital from 1935 to 1939. Thereafter, he was psychologist at the Massachusetts General Hospital from 1939 until his retirement in 1950. From 1941 to 1946 he served as a consultant to the Adjutant General's Office, where he assisted in developing the Army General Classification Test. He was a psychologist in the Department of Hygiene (the student health center) at Harvard University from 1941 to 1950, and with Jurgen Ruesch he published *The Mental Examiner's Handbook* (1945). The focus of his research during the 1940s was the normal personality and exceptional youth as part of the W. T. Grant Study.

In the final phase of his professional career, Wells held numerous posts of distinction in psychology. He was president of the Eastern Psychological Association (1939–1940), an officer in the American Association for Applied Psychology (1939–1940), twice president of the American Psychopathological Association (1942–1944 and 1946–1947), and a fellow in the American Association for the Advancement in Science. He was also a member of the American Board of Examiners in Professional Psychology (1947–1949), Boston Society of Psychiatry and Neurology, American Orthopsychiatric Association, American Academy of Arts and Sciences, Society for Research in Child Development, and New England Society of Psychiatry.

Affable, even-minded, and a pragmatist in the American tradition, Wells lived through most of the major events in the development of psychology as a modern science and profession. He made a number of important contributions to these developments; by the end of his career he had published more than 150 articles and four books. In 1958 he received a citation from the American Psychological Association for his contributions to the field.

After he retired in 1950, he turned his attention full time to the study of spiders, making several scholarly contributions to the literature of that subject, and to trekking outdoors with his beloved Appalachian Mountain Club. He also volunteered his time at the Metropolitan State Hospital in Waltham, and he returned to the McLean Hospital, where his career had begun. This time, however, it was to assist in any way he could in any chore that came his way, he said, "so long as its something that can be done in dungarees." He died at his home in Belmont.

• Wells's papers are held at the McLean Hospital Archives and the Harvard Medical School Archives. Obituaries are in the *American Journal of Psychology* 77, no. 4 (1964), and in the *New York Times*, 6 June 1964.

EUGENE TAYLOR

WELLS, Harry Gideon (21 July 1875–26 Apr. 1943), pathologist, was born in Fair Haven, Connecticut, the son of Romanta Wells, a wholesale druggist, and Emma Townsend Tuttle. After completing his high school's scientific curriculum in 1892, he matriculated at Yale University's Sheffield Scientific School, where he studied zoology and chemistry. In 1894 his father purchased a drugstore in Chicago, Illinois, that also housed the office of a surgeon, Edward W. Lee. Lee had gained notoriety in local medical circles by attempting to graft lamb and chicken skin on to humans to ameliorate large superficial skin defects. Wells spent the summer of 1894 accompanying Lee and his associates on house calls and assisting during experimental surgery; as a result of these experiences he decided to pursue a career in medicine. After receiving his Ph.B. from Yale in 1895, he enrolled in Chicago's Rush Medical College; he received the Benjamin Rush Medal for a paper on the thyroid gland and was awarded his M.D. in 1898.

Wells spent the next year as an intern at Chicago's Cook County Hospital and the following year as a fellow in pathology at Rush, which was now affiliated with the University of Chicago. In 1900 he supplemented his fellowship income with private practice, but he left both situations in 1901 to become an associate in pathology at the university. In 1902 he married Bertha Robbins, with whom he had one child. He received his Ph.D. in pathology from Chicago in 1903, based on his research concerning fat necrosis, the death of small, scattered areas in fatty tissue; he was then promoted to instructor, and in 1904 to assistant professor. He rose to associate professor in 1909 and full professor in 1913. He went to Germany in 1904 to do postgraduate research on the protein of horse hair at the University of Berlin with Emil Fischer, winner of the 1902 Nobel Prize for Chemistry for his work with purines, the biochemical end-products of nucleoprotein digestion.

After returning to Chicago in 1905, Wells embarked on several pioneering studies concerning the chemical changes that occur in disease. The two most important studies focused on the relationship between protein metabolism and autolysis, the self-digestion of tissue, and on metastatic calcification, the transfer of calcium from bone to soft tissue. These studies shed much light on the degeneration and death of tissue and served as an impetus to the nascent field of chemical pathology. In 1907 Wells furthered the development of this discipline by publishing *Chemical Pathology* (5th ed., 1925), which served for a number of years as the authoritative text on the subject. Although he was to devote much of his future research to studies of a similar nature, in 1908 he turned his attention to the chemical basis of immunity, particularly the role played by the chemical composition of protein as a cause of hypersensitization or allergic reaction. This line of investigation resulted in the publication of *The Chemical Aspects of Immunity* (1924; 2d. ed., 1929), which remained the most comprehensive treatment of this subject for a number of years.

In 1911 Wells became the first director of medical research at Chicago's Otho S. A. Sprague Memorial Institute. Under his direction the institute sponsored medical research in a number of fields, including cancer, diabetes, pediatrics, and tuberculosis. The most notable of these projects involved a long-term study of the genetics of cancer in mice, conducted by Maud Slye, which contributed to a decades-long running controversy concerning the inheritability of cancer. Perhaps the most disappointing project involved the treatment of tuberculosis by chemotherapy, a study conducted by Lydia DeWitt that lasted many years and ultimately failed to produce the desired result. However, the project resulted in the publication of *The Chemistry of Tuberculosis* (1923), which Wells coauthored with DeWitt and Esmond R. Long.

When the United States entered World War I in 1917, Wells was commissioned a lieutenant colonel in the U.S. Army and went to Rumania as a member of an international Red Cross commission charged with improving medical and hospital conditions. In 1918, after the commission was forced to leave that country, he went to France and took part in Red Cross activities while conducting research for the Army's Chemical Warfare Service. Following the cessation of hostilities in 1918, he went back to Rumania as commissioner of the Red Cross relief effort.

Wells returned to his positions in Chicago the next year and was made chairman of the university's department of pathology in 1925. Despite heavy administrative responsibilities he continued to conduct his own research on the chemical aspects of pathology and immunology until his retirement from both the university and the institute in 1940. He spent the remaining years of his life as pathologist at the Oak Forest (Ill.) Infirmary, a position he had held since 1928.

Wells served as president of the American Association for Cancer Research (1915–1916, 1919–1920), the American Association of Pathologists and Bacteriologists (1919), and the American Association of Immunologists (1923). He was on the board of editors of *Physiological Reviews* and *University of Chicago Monographs in Medicine*, and from 1915 to 1939 he was in charge of the pathology section of *Chemical Abstracts*. He also served as dean of medical work at the university (1904–1914), pathologist at Cook County Hospital (1906–1928), and member of the National Research Council's committee on medicine (1911–1931). He received the Order of the Star of Rumania in 1919 and was elected to membership in the National Academy of Sciences in 1925. He died in Chicago.

Wells was a pioneer in the field of chemical pathology. His research and administrative efforts contributed significantly to a better understanding of the chemical aspects of disease and furthered the growth of his discipline in the United States.

• A biography, including a bibliography, is Esmond R. Long, "Harry Gideon Wells," National Academy of Sciences, *Biographical Memoirs* 26 (1951): 233–63. The Sept.–Oct. 1941 issue of *American Journal of Pathology* consists entirely of articles written by Wells's former students in his honor. An obituary is in the *New York Times*, 27 Apr. 1943.

CHARLES W. CAREY, JR.

WELLS, Helena (c. 1760–c. 1824), novelist and advocate of improved education for women, was born in Charleston, South Carolina, the daughter of Robert Wells and Mary Rowand, who had emigrated from Scotland in 1753. She was educated at home by her father, a successful bookseller and newspaper publisher. According to Helena's older brother William Charles Wells, by 1775 Robert Wells "had become extremely offensive to the people of Carolina from his constantly maintaining the cause of royalty" in his newspaper. He consequently moved his family to London, his three daughters arriving there in 1777 and 1778. In the 1780s Helena Wells worked as a teacher and possibly a governess; for a few years beginning in 1789 she operated a London boarding school for girls in partnership with an older sister. Forced to abandon teaching because of poor health, she became a writer.

In two didactic novels, she championed well-bred young women of slender means and limited opportunities. Avoiding false sensibility, the self-disciplined heroines of *The Step-Mother* (1798) and *Constantia Neville, or, The West Indian* (two editions, 1800) rely upon their integrity and common sense. Rather than offend her benefactress Lady Glanvile by accepting young Edward Glanvile's proposal and so seeming to presume above her station, Caroline Williams marries a widower sea captain and, soon a widow herself, finds satisfaction as a stepmother, guiding her late husband's four daughters. In the second book, Constantia Neville shows that she can handle her own finances, talk intelligently in mixed company, and ward off unacceptable suitors until a man with the right qualities appears. The novel includes a defense of orthodox Christianity against deism and Unitarianism and an attack on the views of Mary Wollstonecraft; it is up to women to take pride in "protecting and supporting each other in what is laudable." Wells's Scottish sympathies are evident, and her close knowledge of the laws and customs of Jamaica suggests that she may have lived there at some time.

In *Letters on Subjects of Importance to the Happiness of Young Females* (1799), Wells addressed separate topics in each letter. In one she cautions against oversensibility; in another, against excessive novel reading: better a steady diet of classical epics and Tasso and Spenser than of novels like those of Frances Burney and Charlotte Smith, with whose implausible heroines young ladies may too easily identify. The last letter stresses the importance of proper English usage.

A serious work on education that Wells was planning about this time was delayed for almost a decade: Wells married Edward Whitford in 1801 and bore four children, becoming seriously ill after the birth of the last in 1806. In that year she sought assistance from the Royal Literary Fund, from which she had received ten guineas in 1801; but her claim was listed among others deemed "questionable," and further action on it is not recorded. In *Thoughts and Remarks on Establishing an Institution for the Education of Unportioned Respectable Females* (1809), she presented plans for a teacher-training school to be sponsored by the Church of England, somewhat on the model of Catholic convent schools (just before publication the words "an Institution" replaced "a Protestant Nunnery" in the title). Functioning with student participation in maintenance and payment according to their means, the school would provide sound academic training, proper health care, and spiritual guidance for a student body of 100 girls. The goal was for the graduates to enter the working world well prepared and with a strong sense of self-worth.

Although she had spent her youth in her native South Carolina, Helena Wells always considered herself an Englishwoman. After the publication of *Thoughts and Remarks*, which received little attention, she seems to have faded from public view until the appearance of her obituary in the *Gentleman's Magazine* in December 1824. She died in London.

• Some Wells manuscripts are in a collection at the South Carolina Historical Society in Charleston. A second edition of *The Step-Mother* appeared in Charleston in 1799, indicating that a transatlantic culture persisted despite revolutionary upheavals. The title page of *Thoughts and Remarks* indicates that the work is "by the Author of 'The Step-Mother' etc."; the author's preface is signed Helena Whitford. There is no biography, but family information can be found in the "Memoir," the last item in a collection of papers titled *Two Essays: One upon Single Vision with Two Eyes; the Other on Dew* [plus a Letter and several more papers] *by the Late William Charles Wells. With a Memoir of his Life, Written by Himself* (1818); Elisha Bartlett, *A Brief Sketch of the Life, Character, and Writings of William Charles Wells* (1849); and Frances M. Ponick, "Helena Wells and Her Family" (M.A. thesis, Univ. of South Carolina, 1975). Henri Petter considers Helena Wells's fiction in some detail in *The Early American Novel* (1971); brief comments are included in Patricia L. Parker's article on Helena Wells in *American Writers before 1800: A Biographical and Critical Dictionary*, vol. 3 (1983), and in the entry on Helena Wells in *The Feminist Companion to Literature in English* (1990). For a consideration of how her works reflect the values of a woman of her time and class, see David Moltke-Hansen, "A World Introduced: The Writings of Helena Wells of Charles Town," in *South Carolina Women Writers*, ed. James B. Meriwether (1979).

VINCENT FREIMARCK

WELLS, Horace (21 Jan. 1815–23 Jan. 1848), dentist and pioneer in the use of dental anesthesia, was born in Hartford, Vermont, the son of Horace Wells and Betsey Heath, farmers. Growing up in Westminster and then Bellows Falls, Vermont, where his father operated a gristmill, Wells began attending school in 1821. He attended a boys' private school in Hopkinton, New Hampshire, and subsequently attended academies in Amherst, Massachusetts, and Walpole, New Hampshire. When Wells was fourteen, his father died, and the following year his mother married Abiather Shaw. Wells moved with his mother to Shaw's home in Westmoreland, New Hampshire. The Shaws used part of their large home as a hotel for freight teams.

After 1830 Wells taught school while he decided what career to pursue. He considered the ministry, but for reasons that are unknown, decided instead to become a dentist. In the 1830s, entering this field required little training; the first dental school in the United States did not open until 1840.

In 1834 the only training Wells required was an apprenticeship, which he served in Boston under the guidance of an established dentist. It is not known with whom he worked. Upon completion of his training in Boston, Wells moved to Hartford, Connecticut, where he opened his own office on 4 April 1836.

In a letter to his sister, he described his first six months in Hartford as happy and profitable and told her that he had joined the church. Wells had many interests, and in letters expressed a desire to travel abroad and to "publish," by which he may have meant to write. Nevertheless, ill health began to hinder his ability to work. He reported in April 1837, "I have been unwell but am now nearly recovered." His letters of this period reflect a good deal on death (Archer, p. 92).

In 1838 Wells married Elizabeth Wales, daughter of Nathaniel Wales, a Hartford manufacturer, and in the same year published a small book entitled *An Essay on Teeth: Comprising a Brief Description of Their Formation, Disease, and Proper Treatment*. The following year the couple's only child was born. Wells also tried his hand at inventing and in 1839 took out a patent on a device for sifting coal ashes. In 1845 he patented a shower bath.

While early office records have not survived, the accounts of his practice for the years 1841 to 1845 clearly indicate that Wells was a reputable dentist. Among his patients were numerous respected Hartford families, including that of Connecticut governor William Ellsworth. In 1842 Wells had a house built for himself and his family at a cost of $4,000.

Wells is also known to have trained three apprentices: John Riggs, later a partner; C. A. Kingsbury, a founder of Philadelphia Dental College; and William T. G. Morton, the man traditionally given credit as the discoverer of dental anesthesia. In 1843 Wells set up a partnership with Morton in Boston. There is no evidence that he actually moved to Boston or set up practice there, but he appears to have gotten Morton started in practice and continued to instruct him. Wells and Morton dissolved the partnership in October 1844.

Wells's historical reputation, however, rests on an episode that began in 1844, when he happened on a means for eliminating the pain accompanying tooth extraction. Since 1798 the scientific community had been aware that nitrous oxide could relieve pain. Since 1840 Wells had shown interest in the possible use of nitrous oxide to deaden pain for dental patients. Popularly, however, nitrous oxide was known only for its intoxicating effects. When Gardner Q. Colton set up a public demonstration of the use of nitrous oxide in Hartford on 11 December 1844, he intended to entertain the public by revealing the giddy behavior that resulted from inhaling "laughing gas." Wells, however, attended the demonstration with the more serious purpose of improving his practice.

A member of Colton's audience, Samuel Cooley, volunteered to inhale the gas. While intoxicated, Cooley hit his shin on a bench. When the effects of the gas subsided, he and Wells noted that Cooley had felt no pain in his leg. Wells obtained a bag of nitrous oxide from Colton and, the next day, inhaled it himself in his office in the presence of his associate John Riggs, Cooley, and Colton. By their testimony, we know that Riggs then extracted one of Wells's teeth without causing him any pain.

After further experimentation, Wells informed Morton of the discovery. Morton helped Wells arrange a demonstration of his discovery for a class at Harvard Medical School. In the course of the demonstration, a volunteer was found who was willing to have a tooth removed while under the influence of nitrous oxide. However, the volunteer did appear to experience pain, perhaps because he had not inhaled a sufficient amount of gas. He cried out, and the demonstration was pronounced a "humbug affair" by the onlookers. Deeply stung, Wells returned to Hartford and suffered another bout of ill health, brought on, he said, by the failure of his demonstration.

The following year, William Morton, on the advice of Boston doctor Charles T. Jackson, successfully demonstrated the use of ether as an anesthetic for dental and medical surgery. Despite the fact that Wells referred to this as his "old discovery," Morton patented the discovery of ether as a dental anesthetic and sold the rights to it. This set off what Wells's wife termed the "gas war," and the conflict continues to this day over who legitimately earned the credit and the financial benefits of discovering anesthesia.

On 9 December 1846 Wells published his claim as the discoverer in a letter to the *Hartford Courant*. He said the same in a letter to Morton but added that he would not press any claim. Early the following year, however, having left his practice in the hands of a colleague, Wells sailed for Europe. In February and March 1847 he presented his claim as the discoverer of anesthesia to the Parisian Medical Society as well as the Academy of Sciences and the Academy of Medicine, both in Paris. It is not known if these presentations were his primary mission in Europe. He also appears to have purchased paintings for sale in the United States.

Upon Wells's return to the United States in March, he sought as many testimonials as he could to buttress his own claims. He immediately published a testament of his claim, entitled *History of the Discovery of the Ap-*

plication of Nitrous Oxide, Ether, and Other Vapors, to Surgical Operations. Later that year he left Hartford again for New York City, leaving his family in Hartford. The reason for this trip is also unknown.

In January 1848 he was jailed on charges that he had attacked a streetwalker. In jail, he took his own life while under the influence of chloroform, another gas with anesthetic properties. Among the letters he left was one to his wife, in which he wrote, "I feel that I am fast becoming a deranged man" (Archer, p. 139). He also indicated that he was destitute.

Horace Wells is today buried in Hartford's Cedar Hill Cemetery. While many honors have come to Wells posthumously, he received no financial benefit from his discovery, and historians have credited Morton as the legitimate discoverer of anesthesia for medical and dental practice. The facts show that Wells initiated the use of nitrous oxide for dental purposes and that Morton introduced the use of ether for dentistry and surgery (Richard J. Wolfe, personal communication).

• Collections of archival material on Wells may be found at the Museum of Historical Medicine and Dentistry, Hartford, Conn.; the Connecticut Historical Society, Hartford; the Connecticut State Library, Hartford; the Archer Collection in the Falk Medical Library, University of Pittsburgh; and the Francis A. Countway Library of Medicine, Harvard University. The major published source is Richard J. Wolfe and Leonard F. Menczer, eds., *I Awaken to Glory: Essays Celebrating Horace Wells And the Sesquicentennial of His Discovery of Anesthesia, December 11, 1844–December 11, 1994* (1994). A standard source of information on Wells is William Harry Archer, *Life and Letters of Horace Wells, Discoverer of Anesthesia* (1944), reprinted from the *Journal of the American College of Dentists* 11, no. 2 (June 1944). Also see Menczer, "Why Horace Wells—1985?" *Connecticut Medicine* 50, no. 2 (Feb. 1986): 105–7. Other articles by Menczer include "Dr Horace Wells: The Discoverer of General Anesthesia," *Journal of Oral and Maxillofacial Surgery* 50, no. 5 (May 1992): 506–9 (co-authored with Peter H. Jacobsohn), and "If Wells Were Alive," *Bulletin of the History of Dentistry* 39, no. 1 (Apr. 1991): 7–10.

SARAH H. GORDON

WELLS, Ida B. *See* Wells-Barnett, Ida Bell.

WELLS, James Madison (8 Jan. 1808–28 Feb. 1899), governor of Louisiana, was born on his family's plantation near Alexandria, Louisiana, the son of Samuel Levi Wells and Mary Elizabeth Calvit, planters. Orphaned at age eight, James was raised by an aunt and educated at St. Joseph's College in Bardstown, Kentucky, and Alden Partridge's military academy in Middletown, Connecticut. After attending the Cincinnati School of Law in Ohio and reading law in the offices of Charles Hammond, he returned to Louisiana and in 1830 decided to discontinue law and engage in planting and land speculation in Rapides Parish. In 1833 he married Mary Anne Scott. The marriage produced fourteen children. By the start of the Civil War his holdings included four cotton plantations along the Red River, a summer home in the pine hills, ninety-five slaves, and a thriving dairy trade. In the 1860 census, Wells's real and personal property were valued at $400,000 overall.

Despite his large slaveholdings, Wells was an outspoken opponent of secession. A lifelong Whig, he nonetheless campaigned for Stephen A. Douglas in 1860 on the grounds that the northern Democrat was the strongest Union candidate. Following the election of Abraham Lincoln, he organized the antisecessionist United Southern Action ticket in Rapides Parish. After Louisiana voted to secede from the Union, he campaigned against appropriations for military purposes and sponsored a pro-Union guerrilla group, led by his son Thomas Wells. During the first two years of the war, Wells lost 300 bales of cotton in an unexplained fire on his estate, was temporarily imprisoned by Confederate authorities, and upon his release was forced to go into hiding on his backwoods hunting preserve "Bear Wallow." When a Union army under Nathaniel Banks temporarily occupied the Red River region in 1863, Wells provided lodging and supplies to the Union troops, which led Confederate authorities to once again seek his arrest. He successfully evaded capture and eventually found sanctuary within Union lines.

In November 1863 Wells arrived in Union-occupied New Orleans. At the time, the Free State forces, around which Banks was attempting to organize a Unionist government, were fracturing into moderate and radical factions. Although his political views were unknown, Wells was seen as a man who could appeal to rural Unionist sentiment and was nominated by both groups as their candidate for lieutenant governor. In February 1864 the moderate candidate, Michael Hahn, was elected governor, and Wells easily won his own race. As lieutenant governor, Wells accompanied the Union army on its 1864 expedition into the Red River region, with an eye on engaging in cotton and sugar speculation. The expedition was a military fiasco, however, and most of Wells's property was destroyed during the Union retreat.

In March 1865 Hahn resigned the governorship to accept the U.S. Senate nomination offered by the state legislature. Succeeding to the governorship, Wells set himself to the task of building his own constituency. He recognized that without direct intervention by the federal government, a prospect less likely after Andrew Johnson assumed the presidency, the source of political power in Louisiana would rest with the men returning from the Confederate armies. To gain their support, Wells replaced several moderate Unionist officeholders appointed by Banks and Hahn with staunch conservatives, came out against extending suffrage to African Americans and using white tax dollars to support schools for blacks, and openly consulted with former Confederates. Wells's shift to the conservatives allowed him to overwhelmingly win election to the governorship in November 1865.

Relations between Wells and the former Confederates quickly deteriorated, however. During the next session of the state legislature, Wells vetoed several measures of major importance to the former Confederates and soon came to the realization that many of them remained bitter over the outcome of the war and hostile toward all Unionists. He subsequently began moving toward the more radical Unionists by appointing Republicans to state offices and cooperating fully with a Republican congressional committee investigating the New Orleans riot of July 1866, in which a meeting of Unionists of both races had been broken up and many people killed by New Orleans police with former Confederate backing. When the legislature convened in January 1867 to consider the Fourteenth Amendment, Wells urged ratification and openly reversed his earlier opposition to black suffrage. Outraged conservatives twice circulated memorials for Wells's impeachment. Wells was eventually forced out of office, but not by the conservatives. Disgusted by Wells's weakness during the New Orleans riot and his general lack of cooperation with the military authorities, most significantly over appointments to the levee board, General Philip Sheridan removed him from office on 3 June 1867.

Although Wells never again held elective office, he remained an important figure in Louisiana politics, serving on the returning boards responsible for canvassing the election returns in the controversial 1874 and 1876 elections. Republican victories in both elections once again made Wells a figure of controversy. He was particularly open to criticism because he had chaired both boards and, in what appeared to be a reward for his actions in 1874, had been appointed surveyor of customs for the port of New Orleans in 1875. In 1877 the state, under Democratic control, tried unsuccessfully to prosecute Wells and the other members of the board for perjury, forgery, and altering election returns. He subsequently returned to his post in New Orleans, which he held until 1880. Afterward Wells retired to the seclusion of his plantation home and spent his remaining years seeking reimbursement from the federal government for property lost during the war. He never regained his fortune and died at his home in Rapides Parish.

It is tempting to dismiss Wells as an opportunist primarily driven by personal ambition. Many of his problems were indeed of his own making, yet it must be noted that Wells held public office during an extremely difficult period in Louisiana history. Unionists, freedmen, and returning Confederates were all searching for their places in Louisiana and considering what their exact roles would be in the postwar order. As a man whose only real ideological commitment was to the Union and whose only outside guide was a continually shifting federal policy, Wells did his best to lead the new Louisiana. His failure in this endeavor is as much testimony to the confused upheaval that was Reconstruction as to Wells's own faults as a leader.

• A collection of Wells's papers is at the Louisiana State Museum Historical Center, New Orleans. Walter M. Lowrey, "The Political Career of James Madison Wells" (M.A. thesis, Louisiana State Univ., 1947), published in article form under the same title in *Louisiana Historical Quarterly* 31 (Oct. 1948): 995–1123, is the best study of Wells's life and career. See also G. M. G. Stafford, *The Wells Family in Louisiana and Allied Families* (1941). Wells figures prominently in all general studies of La. during Reconstruction. Joe Gray Taylor, *Louisiana Reconstructed: 1863–1877* (1974); Peyton McCrary, *Abraham Lincoln and Reconstruction: The Louisiana Experiment* (1978); and Joseph G. Dawson III, *Army Generals and Reconstruction: Louisiana 1862–1877* (1982), are good recent works on this topic. Obituaries are in the *New Orleans Daily Picayune* and the *New Orleans Times-Democrat*, both 1 Mar. 1899.

ETHAN S. RAFUSE

WELLS, Kate Boott Gannett (6 Apr. 1838–13 Dec. 1911), reformer, antisuffragist, and author, was born in London, England, the daughter of American-born Ezra Stiles Gannett, a minister, and Anna Tilden. Her father had gone to England with his wife to convalesce after suffering a nervous breakdown prior to Kate's birth. In July 1838 the Gannetts returned to Boston, where her father resumed his ministerial duties promoting good works among his large congregation. Kate established a close relationship with her father after her mother died when Kate was just eight years old. He instilled his high religious and moral values in his daughter, and they had an influential effect throughout her life, spilling over into her ideas and opinions on reform and suffrage.

Kate married Samuel Wells, an affluent Boston attorney, in 1863; they had three children. Although Wells valued her position in the home and opposed the new militant and aggressive woman she saw evolving, she believed women needed an outlet for free expression and should form their own opinions. She maintained that time was needed for women to balance "a profession and a home" and that women needed to react with "a calm, steady will" against the new assertive woman. In the meantime she advised women to "do something" and "be of worth to yourself."

She put her advice to work shortly after she joined the New England Women's Club. In 1874 she suggested that afternoon gatherings providing greater female interaction and participation be added to the program. This proved successful and gave the clubwomen an opportunity to speak about current issues and exchange ideas while retaining the "gentle female virtues" that Wells valued.

In the 1870s Wells funneled her energies into the Woman's Education Association of Boston, and in 1875 she became one of the first women elected to a seat on the board of the Boston School Committee. However, the following year the number of board members was reduced, and although three women won seats Wells lost hers. She continued to work for higher standards of education through the association, and she helped to promote the Harvard Annex in 1878.

Wells described women's placement on school boards as "natural and logical," stressing that success came through a willingness "at first to subordinate herself, until she has understood her new environment" and earned respect. Once accomplished, women could then show competency in areas of their expertise such as hospitality, development of hygiene, and enriching school studies. In 1888 her appointment to the Massachusetts State Board of Education, a position she held for twenty-three years, set Wells on a course to improve teacher education programs in normal schools, which were designed to prepare students for future teaching positions. She particularly focused attention on curriculum reform, especially at the Normal Art School in Boston. In addition to regular courses of history, mental philosophy, and teacher theory, Wells felt emphasis should be placed on quality, enthusiasm for teaching, and methods to instill a moral responsibility in children. After years of service in the education field Wells won recognition when in 1902 Wells Hall at the Framingham Normal School in Massachusetts was named for her.

Her interest in city reforms grew as large numbers of immigrants came to Boston, creating overcrowding and lower wages. In addition to her continuing alliance to the education field, Wells called for women to become involved in social agencies and the implementing of laws and to demonstrate to the public a need for a heightened sense of responsibility. For years she held the position of director of the Association for the Advancement of Women, a group that sought to organize clubs to discuss the problems of the cities. Employing a motto of All Girls Should Consider It Disgraceful to Be Idlers, the organization was well respected because it was moderately aligned.

Noting the importance of health and the need to educate working-class families on proper sanitary conditions, Wells became a leader in the Massachusetts Emergency and Hygiene Association in the 1890s. Staunchly working toward improvements for children's activities, she helped start the Boston playground movement in the 1880s, in an effort to provide children with a healthy, clean place in which to socialize.

Wells did not support suffrage but instead held to the old traditions of women's femininity and social graces, thinking the fight for suffrage made women too aggressive. Wells wrote that "restlessness" and "self-consciousness" had created many diverse interests that had directed women away from their primary concerns of the home. Her first public demonstration against suffrage occurred in 1884 when she appeared in front of the Massachusetts legislature protesting an annual woman suffrage petition. Her speech at the hearing led to her becoming one of the leading antisuffragists in the state. Although she realized that politics might be in women's future and believed that women should have an education, receive equal wages, and be able to have a profession, she also felt that women were already making strides without the vote. In her argument Wells stated that too few women had the degree of knowledge of politics necessary to make a rational vote and that most votes would be cast by "unintelligent and depraved women." To aid in the cause Wells advertised a petition against suffrage in the Boston *Herald* that had the signatures of many women and 140 prominent men.

Wells wrote many articles that appeared in numerous magazines. Her best known book, *About People* (1885), stressed the home atmosphere and exemplified her Unitarian views on the relationships between a variety of people, including husbands, wives, servants, and children. Her emphasis on a solid home life carried through in daily life, as many of her activities were based out of her home, where Wells held teas, receptions, classes, and discussions. An advocate of peace, a dedicated reformer for improvement in education, and a supporter of the beautification of the city, Wells won the respect of Bostonians, including the suffragists against whom she protested. Up until her death in Boston, Wells remained active, seeking to inspire women to function for their own greater good while maintaining their duty to family and home.

• Some information on Wells's youth can be found in a biography on her father by William C. Gannett, *Ezra Stiles Gannett* (1875). Wells's own views are best described in her writings: her forecast on women is in "The Transitional American Woman," *Atlantic Monthly* (1880): 817–23; for her stance on woman suffrage see "Address of Mrs. Kate Gannett Wells," *Woman's Journal* (16 Feb. 1884): 53; organizational activities and views are in "A Helpful Work," *Woman's Journal* (2 May 1891): 142, and "Women on School Boards," *North American Review* (Sept. 1905): 428–34; her religious convictions are affirmed in "Comments on Divorce," *North American Review* (Oct. 1901): 508–17. Wells also wrote two novels, *Miss Curtis* (1888), and *Two Modern Women* (1891). She is also mentioned in Ednah D. Cheney, "The Women of Boston," *The Memorial History of Boston*, ed. Justin Winsor (1880–1881); Susan B. Anthony and Ida Husted Harper, eds., *The History of Woman Suffrage*, vol. 2 (1902); Lillie B. C. Wyman and Arthur C. Wyman, *Elizabeth Buffum Chace* (1914); Elizabeth M. Herlihy, ed., *Fifty Years of Boston* (1932); and Arthur Mann, *Yankee Reformers in the Urban Age* (1954). Her stand on suffrage can be found in Thomas J. Jablonsky, *The Home, Heaven, and Mother Party: Female Anti-Suffragists in the United States, 1868–1920* (1994). Additional information on women's antisuffrage can be found in Jane Jerome Camhi, *Women against Women: American Anti-Suffragism, 1880–1920* (1994). Obituaries are in the *Boston Transcript*, 13–15 Dec. 1911, and the *New York Times*, 14 Dec. 1911. A death certificate is on file with Mass. Registrar of Vital Statistics.

MARILYN ELIZABETH PERRY

WELLS, Marguerite (10 Feb. 1872–12 Aug. 1959), social reformer, was born Marguerite Milton Wells in Milwaukee, Wisconsin, the daughter of Edward Payson Wells, a banker and politician, and Nellie Johnson. Wells was descended on both sides from seventeenth-century English settlers. One of her relatives, Thomas Welles, was a Connecticut colonial governor. Her early childhood was spent in the Dakota Territory, in Jamestown.

Growing up on the prairie, Wells was profoundly influenced by her father's political activity. Her community organized local and state government on the frontier, and she was impressed by democracy in action. Her interest in government deepened when her father was elected to the territorial legislature. Wells asked to attend an all-male party caucus, and her father agreed if she would disguise herself as a boy. Stirred by her successful disguise and excited by the events she witnessed, she composed a rhymed account of the event.

Wells was an avid student of government and politics. After passing an examination for teachers when she was fifteen, she became an instructor in a one-room Dakota schoolhouse during the summer. She then attended Miss Hardy's School in preparation for Smith College, where she enrolled in 1891. Winning distinction as a scholar at Smith, she received a B.L. in 1895. She maintained a lifelong association with Smith, first as a permanent trustee, a seat she held until 1930, and five years later as an honorary LL.D. recipient.

Wells taught for two years in New Jersey, then returned to her parents' home in Minneapolis. She spent nearly a decade traveling between Europe, where her sisters were educated, and Minneapolis to nurse her sick mother. A respected civic leader, Wells served as an officer on numerous community boards. In 1917, without warning, she resigned from every board she was on and offered her services to the Minnesota Woman Suffrage Association's headquarters. Not a proponent of causes, nonetheless she was convinced that the issue of suffrage should be resolved. Under the tutelage of Clara Ueland, Wells was a driving force in the final stages of the Minnesota suffrage struggle that successfully led to ratification of the Nineteenth Amendment.

In 1919 Wells attended the National American Woman Suffrage Association convention in St. Louis, Missouri. National president Carrie Chapman Catt proposed that the association form a league for the education of newly enfranchised voters. Catt envisioned a five-year, short-term time frame for the completion of this task, but Wells saw the fresh influx into the women's movement as a platform for positions in the U.S. government. The birth of the national League of Women Voters (LWV) in 1920 served as the catalyst for her thinking. For twenty-five years Wells devoted her tremendous energy to this organization, first as president of the Minnesota League from 1922 to 1932, simultaneously as a member of the national board, and, succeeding Belle Sherwin, as the national president from 1934 to 1944.

Seeking to educate LWV members in the vagaries of the government, Wells realized that as much could be learned through legislative failures as could be learned through its successes. The failure of the child labor amendment and the failure of the Sheppard-Towner Maternity and Infancy Act of 1921 convinced Wells that the public interest needed a voice, and she felt it her responsibility to help provide that voice.

Wells examined the role of women in politics in her 1929 article, "Some Effects of Woman Suffrage," in which she probed the importance of women voters, noting that a few women officeholders had won in local, state, and national elections. "Probably there is not one of them, even the least of the feminist among them, whose contribution is not somewhat colored by the fact that she is a woman, and newly enfranchised," Wells surmised. "They are so few, however, and so conspicuously in the public eye, that it is better not to try to analyze at present." According to Wells, women "who have advanced farthest in the present man-made political world have done so by dint of adaption." She noted that "it was too soon for women to influence organized political life" and admitted that possibly "infiltration will continue to be so gradual and the absorption so complete that the enfranchisement of women will result in no change at all in American political life" (p. 208).

Afraid that women's political opportunities could easily be lost, Wells urged women to form citizenship study groups and to join the LWV. She stressed that women could be effective molders of social welfare, political reform, peace programs, and social issues such as prohibition. In "Some Effects of Woman Suffrage," she claimed that woman's "bent for education, her aptitude for the long process of reform, her fresh interest in government for government's sake, her freedom from economic or party entanglements. . . . may bring into political life the very stimulus that, at the moment, it needs to turn it forward towards new successes by which to justify democracy" (p. 208).

At the 1934 national LWV convention, Wells was elected president. She was the third woman to hold that office and was considered a gifted organizer who decisively and confidently took action. During her term Wells encouraged members to "penetrate" political parties by attending meetings and communicating with leaders. Earlier, she had overseen the publication of the pamphlet *Know Your Parties* (1920–1924) to explain the structures and functions of the political system.

Interested in civil service and tax reform, Wells attacked political patronage. She demanded that civil service be a profession and spoke of the "meaninglessness of the political game." She urged LWV members "to preserve and purify the parties" and "find a way out of the dilemma over which good men were shaking their heads in despair." She informed members about world politics that affected the United States, and she promoted the League of Nations, protesting delays in ratifying it. When too few senators voted for the League of Nations, Wells issued a press release, explaining that voter ignorance was to blame: "Senators who understood the Court too well to fear it themselves apparently voted unfavorably out of deference to the fears aroused in the minds of their uninformed constituents" (Lall, p. 162).

Other failures to ratify amendments affecting women and children resulted in Wells's decision to select specific legislation and pursue political actions based on the realities of government. Noting that special-interest groups held power, she emphasized that the LWV should give voice to public concerns through intelligent, responsible, and disinterested community leaders. As democracies in Western Europe were threatened by fascism and totalitarianism during World War II, Wells suggested that the LWV educate American citizens about political conditions. Called the "architect of the league's philosophy of government," Wells wrote letters to LWV presidents that were published as her book *Leadership in a Democracy: A Portrait in Action* (1944), in which she urged league voters to take action instead of relying on the traditional study of political theory. "Americans do not understand democracy well enough," she lamented, exhorting educated voters to vote wisely. In *Citizens All*, fact sheets she distributed, Wells told LWV members that "by your faith and your works you may infuse thousands of individuals with a sense of deep personal responsibility for political order."

With the close of her presidency in 1944, Wells continued to strive for political change. Unfortunately, her changes were adopted gradually. Suffering from arteriosclerosis for several years, Wells died from pneumonia in Minneapolis. She was a driving force behind the national League of Women Voters and passionately believed that every woman should have the right to vote. She also believed that every vote counted. Unflagging in her enthusiasm and unswerving in her dedication, Wells was a major force in the woman suffrage movement of the United States.

• Wells's papers are in the Wells Family Papers, the Minneapolis League of Women Voters Papers, and the Minnesota Woman Suffrage Papers at the Minnesota Historical Society Archives at St. Paul; in the National League of Women Voters Papers at the Library of Congress; and in the Wells papers at the Schlesinger Library, Radcliffe College. See Wells's "Some Effects of Woman Suffrage," *Annals of the American Academy of Political and Social Science* 143 (May 1929): 207–16. An excellent account of the struggle for the vote is Louise M. Young, *In the Public Interest: The League of Women Voters, 1920–1970* (1989). Betty Lall, "The Foreign Policy Program of the League of Women Voters of the United States: Methods of Influencing Government Action, Effects on Public Opinion and Evaluation of Results" (Ph.D. diss., Univ. of Minnesota, 1964), describes how Wells and other women profoundly changed the rhythm of the male-dominated government.

MICHELLE E. OSBORN
ELIZABETH D. SCHAFER

WELLS, Mary Ann (7 June 1894–8 Jan. 1971), dance teacher, was born in Appleton, Wisconsin, the daughter of Charles Wells and Nell (last name unknown). Her parents' occupations are unknown. Her dance training included study with the noted ballet teacher Luigi Albertieri, who was at that time associated with the Chicago Opera. Wells's only performing experience was a brief stint with the Minnesota Stock Company.

At twenty-one she left for Seattle where she was engaged as the first ballet teacher at the Cornish School of Music. She remained there from 1916 to 1922, during which time she structured the ballet department and directed outstanding student performances. In 1916 she also married businessman A. Forest King; they had no children.

When Wells opened her own studio in 1922, its atmosphere was immediately established by a quotation from the poet Khalil Gibran, which hung on the wall: "If he is indeed wise, he does not bid you enter the house of his wisdom, but rather leads you to the threshold of your own mind. The teacher who walks in the shadow of the temple, among his followers, gives not of his wisdom but of his faith and his lovingness."

Despite her mysticism, further reinforced by membership in the I AM temple, whose tenets included strict vegetarianism, Wells's teaching was not in any way cultish. She was an inspirer rather than a stickler for technical finesse. Most important, she instilled in her students a deep love for dance in all its forms. By engaging guest teachers, she also saw to it that they were exposed to these forms.

Wells's studio was housed directly above the restaurant owned by the father of one of her most gifted students, Robert Joffrey, founder of the Joffrey Ballet. Other outstanding artists to emerge from her tutelage were Gerald Arpino, Martin Buckner, Richard Englund, Mary Heater, Frank Hobi, Louise Kloepper, Caird Leslie, Françoise Martinet, Marc Platt, Tommy Rall, and William Weslow. Of these, Arpino, Englund, Joffrey, and Platt became choreographers and company directors; Kloepper and Martinet became university dance department heads; after his dance career, Rall became an opera singer.

Severely diminished eyesight forced Mary Ann Wells to retire in 1958 after a 42-year teaching career whose open-mindedness and keen artistic sense were to remain with her disciples throughout their careers. Although she did not play a direct role in connection with the Joffrey Ballet, its eclectic style, which might be termed "American classicism," was a reflection of her philosophy. When she died in Seattle, the company's 1971–1972 season was dedicated to her memory.

• For information on Wells, see Nellie Centennial Cornish, *Miss Aunt Nellie: The Autobiography of Nellie C. Cornish* (1964). Obituaries appear in the *New York Times*, 12 Jan. 1971; the *Seattle Times*, 10 Jan. 1971; *Dance Magazine*, Feb. 1971; and *Dance News*, Feb. 1971.

DORIS HERING

WELLS, Samuel Roberts (4 Apr. 1820–13 Apr. 1875), publisher, was born in West Hartford, Connecticut, the son of Russell Wells, a farmer (mother's name unknown). Shortly after his birth the family moved to a farm near Little Sodus Bay on Lake Ontario in Wayne County, New York. Samuel was apprenticed to a tanner and currier, but, planning to study medicine at Yale, he pursued some preliminary work by reading medical texts.

On a visit to Boston in 1843, Wells attended lectures on phrenology by Orson Fowler and Lorenzo Fowler, and, convinced by the phrenological doctrine that the conformation of the skull indicated the nature and size of the mental faculties or characteristics, he determined to become a phrenologist. Phrenology was accepted during the early and mid-nineteenth century by some scientists who saw in it a reliable index to the workings of the mind, but, with the progress of exact science, phrenology was dismissed as a borderline pseudoscience. Wells, believing that phrenological examinations would help subjects know and improve themselves, abandoned his medical plans and the same year joined the Fowlers in their phrenological establishment in Clinton Hall, New York City. The following year he married Charlotte Fowler, sister of Orson and Lorenzo (no children were born of the marriage), and shortly thereafter became a member of the firm, restyled Fowlers and Wells.

Wells specialized in the publishing arm of the business. His list included phrenological handbooks by the Fowler brothers, a series of phrenological almanacs, and manuals on related reforms—vegetarianism, temperance, and water cure. Under Wells's aegis the publishing department of Fowlers and Wells claimed in time to have the largest mail-order list in New York with a market extending "from Nova Scotia to New Mexico, including the Canadas, and all the Territories on the American continent."

Despite some reluctance on Wells's part, Fowlers and Wells in 1855 advertised and placed on sale the first edition of Walt Whitman's *Leaves of Grass*. The following year the firm actually—albeit anonymously (that is, without citing the firm name on the title page)—published the second, expanded edition. At the same time, Whitman was employed by Fowlers and Wells as staff writer for their periodical, *Life Illustrated.*

With Orson Fowler's withdrawal, the firm was renamed Fowler and Wells. In 1854 it moved to 308 Broadway, New York City, and the publishing list under Wells's supervision was expanded with practical manuals on home- and self-improvement: *How to Write, How to Talk, How to Behave, How to Do Business* (all circa 1850; each went through several editions), some compiled by Wells himself. Books on physical health, sex education, and psychology as then understood (akin to magnetism and mesmerism) were strong features of a list that also offered works on social reform by such progressive thinkers as Albert Brisbane, Parke Godwin, Robert Dale Owen, and Horace Greeley.

While Wells directed the publishing division, his wife Charlotte supervised the business affairs of the office. She also encouraged publication of feminist books. Partly at her urging, the writings of Margaret Fuller were posthumously reprinted, and books on the nature and abilities of women by M. Edgeworth Lazarus, Marion Kirkland Reid, Thomas Wentworth Higginson, and Elizabeth Oakes Smith were added to the firm's list.

Between 1858 and 1860 Wells accompanied Lorenzo and Lydia Fowler on an extensive lecture tour through the United States and Canada. Between 1860 and 1862 they journeyed to England, lecturing and performing phrenological examinations, and by 1863 Lorenzo Fowler had established a branch office in London, where he took up residence with his family.

In August 1862 Wells became sole proprietor of the New York office. The firm, now simply S. R. Wells, moved to 389 Broadway, offering an exhibition hall for phrenological busts, casts, and skulls; a lecture room; and an examination room where Nelson Sizer now performed most of the phrenological examinations. The firm's analyses, many of which were based not on actual heads but on photographs, were published in the long-lived *Phrenological Journal* (1838–1911), now under Wells's editorship.

As publisher, Wells aimed at a mass audience. When offered a manuscript, he said, he considered two questions: Will it be useful? And can I afford it? He wrote of his profession: "To be a successful book-publisher one requires a rare combination of qualifications. A spirit of enterprise, tact, discrimination, a knowledge of human nature, a careful and continual study of the public tastes and wants, and a general knowledge of modern literature, are indispensable. . . . The publisher, who is generally also a seller of books, should have *a thorough knowledge of the wares in which he deals*" (Wells, *How to Do Business*, p. 87).

Wells, whose writings included *The Right Word in the Right Place* (1860), *New Physiognomy; or, Signs of Character* (1866), *Wedlock; or, The Right Relations of the Sexes* (1869), and *How to Read Character* (1868), continued to expand his publishing list with works on health reform, temperance and hydropathy, how-to manuals, "People's Editions" of English literary highlights, and the periodical *The Science of Health* (1872–1876).

In 1866 the American Institute of Phrenology was incorporated by the firm to offer courses on the so-called science of mind. The same year Wells, with a group of congressmen, joined the Union Pacific Railway excursion to the West. In 1870 he visited Salt Lake City, where he performed phrenological examinations, and in 1873, with his wife and a group of editors, he toured the Pacific Coast.

The panic of 1873 seriously affected Wells's business, which, in March 1875 moved to 737 Broadway, New York City. Shortly thereafter Wells succumbed to pneumonia and died in New York City. His widow announced that she would continue the concern and that the firm name would be changed to S. R. Wells and Company. Restyled Fowler and Wells with the brief re-entry of Orson Fowler, the business struggled against diminishing public interest in phrenological doctrine.

By the early twentieth century, when the firm no longer existed, Samuel Wells, whose achievement lay less in his phrenological insights than in his ability to sell phrenological publications to the public, was forgotten. Nonetheless, he had published books not only in the firm's specialty, but in a wide field of more or less related subjects, ranging from physiognomy and hydropathy to feminism and the relations of the sexes, from temperance to health, from business to etiquette, from literature and language to life in the West. Many of his publications reached a broad readership to whom they carried a doctrine that was optimistic, progressive, and affirmative.

• The Fowler Family Papers (including Wells's papers) are in the Collection of Regional History in Cornell University Library. Details of Wells's life and career are recorded in John D. Davies, *Phrenology—Fad and Science: A 19th-Century American Crusade* (1955), and in Madeleine B. Stern, *Heads & Headlines: The Phrenological Fowlers* (1971). See also the unattributed article "Fifty Years of Phrenology: A Review of Our Past and Our Work," *Phrenological Journal* 80 (Jan. 1885): 10–29. Obituaries are in the *New-York Daily Tribune*, 14 Apr. 1875; the *Phrenological Journal*, June 1875, and the *Science of Health*, June 1875.

MADELEINE B. STERN

WELLS, Seth Youngs (19 Aug. 1767–30 Oct. 1847), Shaker theologian, author, and educator, was born in Southold, New York, the son of Thomas Wells and Abigail Youngs. Little is known of Wells's early life. He attended high school, where he received a classical education, and studied bookkeeping at the Clinton Academy in East Hampton, New York, in 1788. He taught and served as a principal in the public schools of Albany, New York, and also taught at the Hudson Academy.

At the age of thirty the unmarried Wells converted to Shakerism, a celibate religious communal movement, and moved to the Shaker village of Watervliet, New York. In 1800 he was put in charge of recent Shaker converts, and he officially entered the leadership ranks as their elder in 1807.

Few Shakers received the level of formal education that Wells had, and the group eagerly tapped his abilities as a writer and intellectual. His talents were publicly displayed in 1808, when he became embroiled in a controversy surrounding the publication that year of *Testimony of Christ's Second Appearing*, a theological tome written by Shaker leaders in Ohio. The Central Ministry, the ruling body of the Shaker movement, approved of neither the *Testimony*'s frank exposition of Shaker theology nor the western Shakers' challenge to eastern intellectual dominance implied in the book's publication. In the ensuing debate, Wells emerged as one of eastern Shakerism's major theologians. His position was strengthened when he and Calvin Green, another prominent theologian, edited the *Testimony* for republication in 1810.

Wells continued his editorial work in 1816, when he and Rufus Bishop published an important collection of testimonies from the "first Believers," those who had personally known Ann Lee, the founder of Shakerism. Titled *Testimonies of the Life, Character, Revelations and Doctrines of Our Ever Blessed Mother Ann Lee, and the Elders with Her*, these stories provide some of the only information available about the life of Lee and the early movement. But Wells's greatest theological endeavor was completed in 1823, when he and Green published *Summary View of the Millennial Church*. Written in response to published attacks against the Shakers, *Summary View* offered readers "a plain and correct statement" of Shaker history and theology (p. iii). Wells and Green traced the progress of "the true spirit of christianity" from its origins in the "primitive church" to its ultimate manifestation in the Shaker movement (*Summary View*, p. 1).

Wells's work of this period shares one common theme—creating a usable past for the Shakers. He joined the Shaker movement in the midst of its evolution from a young, unformed religious group to an institutionalized religious sect. He aided this transition by giving the Shakers a historical grounding for their developing identity. Although the movement was relatively new (Lee came to America from England in 1774), Wells placed the Shakers within the larger context of Christian history, giving legitimacy to the movement. Even more important, Wells cast the emergence of Shakerism as providential, validating the Shakers' claim to be the true church.

Wells successfully filled his position as writer and theologian for the movement, but he was equally important for his role in Shaker educational reform. Because of his experience in the public schools, the Shakers appointed Wells superintendent of Shaker schools in Watervliet and Lebanon, New York, in 1821 and of all Shaker schools in 1832. During his tenure, Wells oversaw considerable changes in the Shaker system. Under his leadership the Shakers adopted the Lancastrian method of instruction, increased the number of subjects taught to the students, built separate schoolhouses, and developed an appreciation for formal education.

Wells's educational philosophy, which he set forth in an unpublished 1825 essay titled "A Few Remarks upon Learning and the Use of Books," emphasized "practical" over academic knowledge. "This life is but short at the longest," he wrote, "and ought not to be spent in acquiring any kind of knowledge which cannot be put to good use" (p. 12). He believed that one of education's primary goals was to inculcate morality in the students and emphasized the secondary role that education played in salvation. Wells avowed, "Since I first heard the gospel I have never believed that there was any more salvation in books than in linnen [*sic*] and cotton rags, or any other materials of which books are found" ("A Few Remarks," p. 1).

Despite Wells's protestations, he sometimes struggled with the anti-intellectualism of the Shakers. Because of his position as Shaker spokesman, he often read popular books on ecclesiastical history. Though his "natural disposition" was to read each book in its entirety, he consciously restrained himself, only reading those parts that pertained to his task at hand. He wryly mused that he had not read an entire history book since he joined the Shakers ("A Few Remarks," p. 2). Yet his attachment to books was strong; he could never bring himself to dispose of the French, Greek, and Latin texts of his youth that he brought with him when he joined the Shakers.

In October 1828 Wells moved to New Lebanon, where he lived the rest of his life. At the time of his death, he had become one of the most influential Shakers of his era. A prolific writer, his unpublished manuscripts cover a variety of subjects, from diet and health reform to the Jewish wars and pacifism, revealing a man deeply interested in the world around him. His theological writings provided the Shakers with the intellectual and historical underpinnings needed to create a strong sense of identity; these same works helped shape the world's view of Shakerism. As superintendent of schools, Wells created a viable educational system admired by many of the world's people. His accomplishments were enormous, yet a persistent underlying tension existed between the academic and scholarly nature of his pursuits and the Shakers' withdrawal from earthly vanities. In more ways than one, Wells's life reflected the constant struggle at the core of Shakerism—how to be in the world but not of it.

• Many of Wells's manuscripts are in the Shaker Collection of the Western Reserve Historical Society, Cleveland, Ohio, including "A Few Remarks upon Learning and the Use of Books, for Consideration of the Youth among Believers," 25 Apr. 1825, VII.B: 255. Also included in this collection is Calvin Green's "Biographic Memoir of the Life, Character, & Important Events, in the Ministration of Mother Lucy Wright," 1861, VI.B: 26, which contains a sketch of Wells's life. Wells's published works include *Millennial Praises* (1812), a compilation of Shaker hymns; with Green, *Testimonies Concerning the Character and Ministry of Mother Ann Lee and the First Witnesses of the Gospel of Christ's Second Appearing* (1827), a collection similar to the 1816 *Testimonies*; with Green, *A Brief Exposition of the Established Principles and Regulations of the United Society Called Shakers* (1830); under the pseudonym Philanthropos, *A Brief Illustration of the Principles of War and Peace* (1831); and *Thomas Brown and His Pretended History of the Shakers* (c. 1848). For a more complete list of Wells's writings, see Mary L. Richmond, *Shaker Literature: A Bibliography* (2 vols., 1977). Stephen J. Stein, *The Shaker Experience* (1992), discusses and interprets Wells's life within the context of his time.

SUZANNE R. THURMAN

WELLS-BARNETT, Ida Bell (16 July 1862–25 Mar. 1931), editor and antilynching activist, was born in Holly Springs, Mississippi, the daughter of James Wells and Elizabeth Warrenton, slaves. Son of his master, James Wells was a carpenter's apprentice and opened his own shop after emancipation. The eldest of eight children, Ida attended Rust College in Holly Springs until 1878, when a yellow fever epidemic killed her parents and one of her six siblings. Determined to keep her family together, Wells began teaching in surrounding areas. In 1881 she moved her youngest siblings to Memphis to live with an aunt and began teaching in nearby Woodstock.

While commuting, Wells was asked to leave the "ladies' car" and move to the smoking car, where all African Americans were expected to sit. She refused to leave, bit the conductor who tried to remove her, and then filed a successful suit against the railroad. Although the verdict was reversed by the state supreme court, her accounts of the case in a local black newspaper launched her journalism career. Teaching in the Memphis public schools from 1883 until 1891, Wells wrote articles for black newspapers around the nation under the pen name "Iola." In 1889 she became part owner and editor of the *Memphis Free Speech and Headlight*. Two years later the school board did not renew her contract after she wrote editorials critical of its actions.

Elected secretary of the black-run National Press Association in 1887, Wells became known as the "Princess of the Press" by her mostly male editorial colleagues. Many felt ambivalent toward this attractive young woman, whose writings were militant and uncompromising. In I. Garland Penn's *The Afro-American Press and Its Editors* (1891), fellow editor T. Thomas Fortune noted, "She has become famous as one of the few of our women who handle a goose-quill, with a diamond point, as easily as any man in the newspaper work. . . . She has plenty of nerve, and is as sharp as a steel trap." Never hesitant to criticize anyone, no matter how prominent, Wells collected enemies and suitors in almost equal numbers.

In 1892 Wells found a focus for her militancy following a triple lynching in Memphis. After three young black men opened the People's Grocery, a white competitor's resentment triggered a chain of events that led to their murders. Earlier lynchings had angered her, but the deaths of three friends brought the evil close to her. She had believed lynchings happened to innocent people but not to respectable ones. Turning the full force of her powerful pen against lynching, Wells attacked the premise that lynching was a necessary deterrent to black rapists. In May she wrote a *Free Speech* editorial in which she suggested that many rape charges arose from the discovery of voluntary sexual liaisons of white women with black men. While Wells was away, angry whites closed the newspaper office and ran her partner out of Memphis.

Afraid to return home, Wells settled in New York and began writing for T. Thomas Fortune's *New York Age*. In June the paper published a lengthy attack on lynching by the thirty-year-old exile. Reprinted as *Southern Horrors: Lynch Law in All Its Phases*, it became the first of several pamphlets on the subject. In it Wells argued that lynching was often used to counteract black achievement and had grown worse as African Americans became more educated and successful. Although raised in less than a third of all lynchings, charges of rape, she noted, "closed the heart, stifled the conscience, warped the judgment and hushed the voice of pulpit and press." Proclaiming "a Winfield rifle should have a place of honor in every black home," Wells asserted, "The more the Afro-American yields and cringes and begs, the more he has to do so, the more he is insulted, outraged and lynched."

After African-American women in New York gave Wells a testimonial dinner that raised about $400 for her crusade, she received dozens of lecture requests. On one visit to Philadelphia she met Catherine Impey, an Englishwoman who published the journal *Anti-Caste*. Early in 1893 Impey joined with Scottish author Isabelle Mayo to invite Wells to tour Scotland and England in the cause of antilynching. Following her first lecture the women organized the Society for the Recognition of the Brotherhood of Mankind, which invited Wells back the next year for a second tour.

The attention of the English press catapulted Wells to the leadership of the antilynching movement. She used all available platforms for her message. At the World Columbian Exposition in Chicago during 1893, she joined with the famous abolitionist Frederick Douglass and Chicago lawyer Ferdinand L. Barnett to circulate a coauthored protest pamphlet. Even after Wells married Barnett in 1895, she continued her activism. Assuming the editorship of her husband's newspaper, the *Chicago Conservator*, Wells-Barnett remained a militant voice, giving speeches, investigating lynchings, criticizing Booker T. Washington, starting organizations, and joining movements—while giving birth to four children.

Participating in the founding of such organizations as the National Association of Colored Women (1896), the Afro-American Council (1898), and the National Association for the Advancement of Colored People (1910), Wells-Barnett remained active in few. Her uncompromising attitude alienated many people and prevented effective membership in groups she did not lead. She personally founded the Ida B. Wells Women's Club in 1893; the Negro Fellowship League, a kind of settlement house for black men, in 1910; and the Alpha Suffrage Club in 1913. That year she desegregated a suffrage march in Washington, D.C., by slipping into the Illinois delegation at the last moment. In addition, from 1913 to 1916 Wells-Barnett served as an adult probation officer in Chicago. Always busy, she was active in the Republican party and, in the three years before her death, began her autobiography and ran for the state senate. For more than four decades Wells-Barnett's militant voice brought worldwide attention to the evil of lynching and influenced the course of American reform. She died in Chicago, Illinois.

• Wells-Barnett's papers are in the Regenstein Library at the University of Chicago. Her *Crusade for Justice: The Autobiography of Ida B. Wells* (1970) was edited by her daughter, Alfreda M. Duster. Her published writings are reprinted in *Selected Works of Ida B. Wells-Barnett*, ed. Trudier Harris (1991), and Mildred Thompson, *Ida B. Wells-Barnett: An Exploratory Study of an American Black Woman, 1893–1930* (1990). Some of her private writings are in *The Memphis Diary of Ida B. Wells*, ed. Miriam DeCosta-Willis (1995). See also Gail Bederman, "'Civilization,' the Decline of Middle-Class Manliness, and Ida B. Wells's Antilynching Campaign (1892–94)," *Radical History Review* 52 (1992): 5–30, and Linda O. McMurry, "Ida Wells-Barnett and the African-American Anti-Lynching Campaign," in *American Reform and Reformers*, ed. Randall M. Miller and Paul A. Cimbla (1996).

LINDA O. MCMURRY

WELLSTOOD, Dick (25 Nov. 1927–24 July 1987), jazz pianist, was born Richard McQueen Wellstood in Greenwich, Connecticut. His parents' names are unknown. His father, who worked in real estate, died when Wellstood was three. His mother, a graduate of the Institute of Musical Art (now Juilliard), was a church organist. Wellstood attended public schools in Greenwich and in Maine. He took piano lessons to age ten but thereafter was self-taught. Having won a five-year scholarship to the Wooster School in Danbury, Connecticut, he was performing there in a teenage canteen by 1944.

In 1945 Wellstood worked professionally at the Paddock Lounge in New York City, and he participated in jam sessions with a friend, clarinetist and soprano saxophonist Bob Wilber, who was a protégé of the legendary reed player Sidney Bechet. The following year he joined Wilber's Dixieland band, the Wildcats, and he accompanied Bechet at a jam session sponsored by Milt Gabler. In 1947 he recorded with Bechet as a member of Wilber's band in Chicago. From around March through 6 June 1948 he returned to Chicago to accompany Bechet at Jazz Ltd. in club owner Bill Reinhardt's band. He then joined Wilber's band at the Savoy Cafe in Boston. Apart from a period of work with Bechet at the Swing Rendezvous Club in Philadelphia in 1949, he played with Wilber until 1950, when trombonist Jimmy Archey took over the band. Wellstood remained a member, and in 1952 he toured Europe with Archey.

During the early 1950s Wellstood failed in an attempt to make the Olympic team as a cyclist. He married Flo (full name unknown) in 1952; they had four daughters. After a brief reunion with Bechet at the Bandbox in New York City in mid-August 1953, Wellstood joined trumpeter Roy Eldridge's group. While working in trombonist Conrad Janis's band from 1953 to 1960, Wellstood prepared for law school at New York University, studied at New York Law School, and ultimately passed the New York State bar exams, only to abandon this field after a brief and discouraging attempt to practice the law.

During these years Wellstood also played solo piano at Eddie Condon's club, and he began to work in many settings as a freelancer in the New York area. From 1957 to 1965 he appeared on and off at the Metropole club, playing with Eldridge—with whom he recorded the album *Swing Goes Dixie* in 1956—tenor saxophonists Coleman Hawkins and Ben Webster, trumpeters Red Allen and Wild Bill Davison, trombonist Vic Dickenson, clarinetist Buster Bailey, and other jazz notables.

Wellstood was the pianist on folk singer Bob Dylan's first album, released in 1962, and that same year he was musical director for two albums by the folk singer Odetta. From about 1962 to 1963 he worked at Nick's club, mainly in Davison's band, and in the latter year he joined Janis's Tailgate Five at the Actor's Studio in a production of *Marathon '33*, starring Julie Harris. Wellstood divorced in 1963. Late that year he worked as the house pianist for jam sessions at a lesser-known New York nightclub, Bourbon Street.

In 1964 he toured army bases in Greenland with trumpeter Carl Bama Warwick's band. From 1965 he worked alongside tenor saxophonist Charlie Ventura in drummer Gene Krupa's quartet, touring South

America and, in 1966, Israel. He also recorded as an unaccompanied soloist. In 1966 Wellstood moved to Brielle, New Jersey, and played locally at the Ferryboat in a band that included clarinetist Kenny Davern. He married Diane McClumpha in 1967; they had no children.

As rock music took over the market for jazz, Wellstood began working in the society dance band of Paul Hoffman. He remained with Hoffman until at least 1978, long after his jazz career revived. In 1970 he toured New England with New Orleans jazz musicians, including saxophonist Captain John Handy and trumpeter Punch Miller.

Wellstood made a series of consistently fine albums during the 1970s. These include the unaccompanied sessions *Alone* (1970–1971), *From Ragtime On* (1971), and *At the Cookery* (1975); as a bandleader, *From Dixie to Swing* (c. 1972); as a sideman with violinist Joe Venuti and tenor saxophonist Zoot Sims, *Joe and Zoot* (1974); and as coleader with bassist Peter Ind, *Some Hefty Cats!* (1977). Around 1975 he toured Europe for six weeks as a substitute for Ralph Sutton in the World's Greatest Jazz Band, but from 1974 he mainly worked as a solo pianist, whether giving concerts in Europe, playing in a New York jazz club, or supplying background music at a private party.

In the 1970s and 1980s Wellstood regularly participated in the Newport Jazz Festival in Rhode Island and its continuations in New York City. By 1978 he resided in Sea Girt, New Jersey. In this year he toured Europe on his own for six weeks, and he also worked in a duo with Davern. Wellstood was the pianist at Hanratty's, a New York bar, from 1979 to 1986. In 1981 he was heard on pianist Marion McPartland's public radio show; this hour of interviews and performances has been issued on CD as *Marion McPartland's Piano Jazz with Guest Dick Wellstood*. Wellstood worked as a lawyer for ten months in 1985. From 1986 to 1987 he was resident at Bemelman's, a lounge in the Carlyle Hotel. During the 1980s he also performed intermittently in duos with Davern and with pianist Dick Hyman. He died of a heart attack in Palo Alto, California.

Wellstood occasionally wrote reviews and record liner notes that are remembered mainly for his mocking wit and anti-intellectuality. Perhaps the most revealing example is "Waller to Wellstood to Williams to Chaos," which takes assorted swipes at the conventions of jazz literature, including an excessively overlong and undifferentiated alphabetical list of musicians with whom he had performed. Actively uninterested in teaching, Wellstood explained to writer Les Tomkins, "I played five years in a rhythm section with Pops Foster and Tommy Benford, and I played seven years with Panama Francis—with no bass player. . . . How do you teach *that* to somebody in your living-room in an afternoon?" (Mar. 1978, p. 7).

Together with pianists Sutton and Hopkins, Wellstood was among the best of those who kept the stride piano style alive, decades after James P. Johnson sparked its development. Perhaps more than any leading pianist of his era, he adhered to the required virtuosic left-hand technique, involving a slightly irregular striding motion between the instrument's low and mid-register. His forté was the music of Johnson and Fats Waller and, to some extent, Art Tatum, from whom he acquired a penchant for dramatic, hysterically fast passages of stride, but whose rhapsodic style of ballad playing he avoided.

In writings and interviews Wellstood offered a concise description of his stylistic development. He was devoted to traditional jazz in his first years of professional performance. He credited Eldridge with modernizing him, while noting the curious fact that Eldridge wanted him to supply a striding accompaniment underneath the trumpet's swing melody, rather than a looser and lighter chording more characteristic of swing piano playing. In the early 1970s, at the height of the rediscovery of Scott Joplin, Wellstood also began to perform classic ragtime piano solos, although admittedly he did not have a great feeling for the genre. From this same decade until his death he drew freely from the repertoire of ragtime and jazz, applying his pianistic method not only to Johnson and Waller's tradition, but also to the more modern sound of saxophonist John Coltrane's tortuous bop theme "Giant Steps" and composer Billy Strayhorn's ballad "Lush Life." Reviewing a performance during a British tour in 1976, writer Miles Kington called Wellstood "a one-man repertory company."

• Provocative quotations from Wellstood's writings are collected in French translation in *Le point du jazz*, no. 11 (June 1975): 72–75. Also notable among his publications are "Waller to Wellstood to Williams to Chaos," *Jazz Review* 3 (Aug. 1960): 10–11; a loving and reverent memory of his experiences with Bechet, "Walking with a King: A Memory of Sidney Bechet," *Down Beat Music '71* (1970), pp. 29–30; and musical commentary in the pamphlet accompanying the boxed LP set *Giants of Jazz: James P. Johnson* (1981). Surveys of his career and interviews of Wellstood are in Dan Morgenstern, "The Life-Flight of a Surrealistic Bent Eagle," *Down Beat* 34 (6 Apr. 1967): 22–24; Max Jones, "Wellstood: Barroom Blues," *Melody Maker* 49 (2 Feb. 1974): 51; Miles Kington, "Jazz in Britain: Dick Wellstood," *Jazz Journal* 29 (Mar. 1976): 16; Jones, "Wellstood in His Stride," *Melody Maker* 52 (12 Mar. 1977): 40; R. D. Johnson, "Many Faces of Wellstood," *Mississippi Rag* 6 (Dec. 1978): 10; and Les Tomkins, "Dick Wellstood," *Crescendo International* 16 (Jan. 1978): 10–11 and (Mar. 1978): 6–7. See also Whitney Balliett, *Jelly Roll, Jabbo, and Fats: 19 Portraits in Jazz* (1983); John Norris, "Dick Wellstood: Mister Stride," *Coda*, no. 220 (June–July 1988): 30; John Chilton, *Sidney Bechet: The Wizard of Jazz* (1987); and Bob Wilber, assisted by Derek Webster, *Music Was Not Enough* (1988). An obituary is in the *New York Times*, 27 July 1987.

Barry Kernfeld

WELSH, John (9 Nov. 1805–10 Apr. 1886), merchant, civic leader, and minister to Great Britain, was born in Philadelphia, Pennsylvania, the son of John Welsh, a merchant, and Jemima Maris. Although trained by his father, who specialized in trade with the West Indies, Welsh entered the dry goods business and became a partner in the firm of Dulles, Wilcox, & Welsh. In 1829 he married Rebecca B. Miller, with whom he had two children before her death in 1832. In 1838 he married Mary Lowber; they had nine children. After his father died in 1854, Welsh joined his brothers Samuel and William in the family sugar-importing firm. Welsh widened his business interests by investing in and becoming president, for one disastrous year, of the North Pennsylvania Railroad, which in July 1855 began a nineteen-mile run between Philadelphia and Gwynedd. In 1856 a careless conductor caused a collision on a North Pennsylvania excursion train carrying 500 Roman Catholic girls and boys from St. Michael's parish in Kensington. Thirty-nine children were killed and seventy-two were wounded. Deeply distressed, Welsh contributed $500 to a relief fund and gave up the presidency of the road.

Welsh, who was a member of the American (Know Nothing) party before becoming a Republican, was early involved in civic affairs. From 1855 to 1857 he served on the Philadelphia select council and then, because of his probity, chaired that city's sinking fund commission from 1857 to 1871. During the Civil War he organized Philadelphia's huge sanitary fair to raise funds for the Sanitary Commission, which aided and comforted sick and wounded Union soldiers. Welsh also was instrumental in convincing Philadelphia to adopt a more elaborate plan for Fairmount Park, and he served as a park commissioner, beginning in 1867 and continuing until his death.

Welsh made his greatest civic contribution on the 1876 Centennial Board of Finance. In 1871 Congress, to celebrate the first hundred years of American independence, authorized a commission (consisting of two members from each state and territory) to plan an international exhibition in Philadelphia under the auspices of the federal government, and the next year created the Centennial Board of Finance to raise the necessary capital for the exhibition. The leading spirit on the Board of Finance, Welsh had to raise funds to realize the elaborate plans for the exhibition's site in Fairmount Park. The federal government initially made no appropriation, and the panic of 1873 made fundraising difficult. After a long delay and prodding by President Ulysses S. Grant, Congress matched the $1.5 million appropriated by the state of Pennsylvania and the city of Philadelphia. The exhibition was an astounding success, and those grateful to Welsh for his crucial role presented him with a purse of $50,000 for a suitable memorial. He gave the money to the University of Pennsylvania, where he was a trustee, to establish the John Welsh Centennial Professorship of History and Literature.

A bizarre episode in 1877 led to Welsh's appointment as minister to Great Britain. After the loquacious Secretary of State William M. Evarts embarrassed President Rutherford B. Hayes by "gushing" in Senator J. Donald Cameron's presence that Pennsylvania was entitled to the British mission, Cameron engineered the recommendation for the post of his father, an enemy of both Hayes and Evarts. The next day the majority of the Pennsylvania congressional delegation insisted they were against Cameron's nomination, which they had recommended under duress. Hayes got out of the scrape with minimal damage by appointing Welsh, who was backed by Philadelphia businessmen. Despite his lack of experience in foreign affairs, no one, except a "shocked" Don Cameron objected to the appointment of Welsh, a proper Philadelphian of impeccable character.

While in London, Welsh arranged for the payment of the fishery award of $5.5 million by the United States to Great Britain and for the inconclusive international bimetallic currency conference called for by the 1878 Bland Allison Silver Coinage Act. A tall, distinguished-looking man with side whiskers, he was sufficiently wealthy to play the social role expected at the Court of St. James's, and in his travels he found England's cities, towns, and villages attractive. His sense of noblesse oblige, however, was disturbed by slums in the cities, by the small number of landowners in the country (2,184 men owned more than half the kingdom), and by drunkenness, "the besetting sin of the lower classes." Reflecting the interest of men of his stripe in civil-service reform, Welsh noted that there was "no such class here as office-seekers" and that elections were "conducted without their interference" (Willson, p. 371). To Hayes's regret, Welsh, who was suffering from bronchitis in the damp English winters, asked to be relieved after two years' service. On the day before Christmas in 1879, after his return to Philadelphia, Hayes and Grant used Welsh's home for a two-hour, private conference, during which Hayes tried without success to dissuade Grant from seeking to be nominated for a third presidential term. Continuing to serve as a trustee of the University of Pennsylvania, Welsh, who had become a strong advocate of higher education for women after visiting the women's colleges of Cambridge University, persuaded his fellow trustees to adopt in 1882 a resolution establishing a separate college for women at the University of Pennsylvania. Welsh died in Philadelphia.

• Welsh's papers are in the Historical Society of Pennsylvania. Brief sketches of his life are available in J. Thomas Scharf and Thompson Westcott, *History of Philadelphia, 1609–1884* (3 vols., 1884), and Beckles Willson, *America's Ambassadors to England (1785–1929): A Narrative of Anglo-American Diplomatic Relations* (1929). See also Erwin Stanley Bradley, *Simon Cameron, Lincoln's Secretary of War: A Political Biography* (1966); Nicholas Wainwright, ed., *A Philadelphia Perspective: The Diary of Sidney George Fisher, Covering the Years 1834–1871* (1967); Charles Richard Williams, ed., *Diary and Letters of Rutherford Birchard Hayes: Nineteenth President of the United States* (1922–1926); and Edward Potts Cheyney, *History of the University of Pennsylvania, 1740–1940* (1940). Obituaries are in the *Philadelphia Inquirer* and the *(Philadelphia) North American*, 12 Apr. 1886.

ARI HOOGENBOOM

WELSH, Lilian (6 Mar. 1858–23 Feb. 1938), physician, educator, and suffragist, was born in Columbia, Pennsylvania, the daughter of Major Thomas Welsh and

Annie Eunice Young. Her father served in the Mexican War in 1847, returned to civilian life, and then rejoined the military when the Civil War broke out. He had just risen to the rank of brigadier general, commanding a division of 4,500 men, when he took ill and died in 1863. Welsh graduated from Columbia High School at the age of fifteen as one of two young women making up the first graduating class. Between the years 1873 and 1881 she taught at the primary, elementary, and secondary levels and attended Millersville State Normal School in Pennsylvania and taught there. From 1881 to 1886 she served as the principal of Columbia High School. In 1885, finding no opportunities for women to advance their careers as superintendents of schools, she considered the two choices open to her for continuing her education: work for the A.B. at Bryn Mawr College, which had just opened that year, or proceed to the study of medicine for which at the time no college requirement was necessary. Interest in chemistry steered her on the latter course. She earned the M.D. from the Women's Medical College of Pennsylvania in 1889 and pursued her studies further by working toward a Ph.D. in chemistry at the University of Zurich in the hopes of becoming a research scientist. While in Zurich, she met Dr. Mary Sherwood, who was to be her lifelong collaborator, business partner, and faithful friend.

As Welsh was undertaking work on her dissertation, she had returned to Pennsylvania and secured a position as a physician in one of the few types of institutions that were hiring women at the time, the State Hospital for the Insane in Norristown, Pennsylvania. Sherwood had settled in Baltimore, where her brother was associated with Johns Hopkins University, and persuaded Welsh to join her there to begin a joint practice. Welsh moved to Baltimore in 1892, and though the two women were not very successful with their practice, their close association with physicians William Welch, Sir William Osler, and Howard A. Kelly and access to the "wards, clinics, the laboratories, the lectures, the courses, the libraries and societies of the Johns Hopkins Hospital" (*Reminiscences*, p. 47) made her and Sherwood feel that the years 1892–1894 were the most important in their professional lives.

Welsh's period of residence in Baltimore coincided with tremendous improvements in the availability and quality of education for women and girls there. The women's club movement in Baltimore was also gaining strength. Welsh quickly became an active member and officer of many clubs and associations organized to promote higher education for women, higher standards in education, and woman suffrage at a time when "the idea that women could have any direct interest in government, municipal, state or national, found scant consideration" (*Reminiscences*, p. 66). As chair of a committee of the Arundell Good Government Club in 1901, she oversaw the passing of a bill mandating school attendance, amidst great opposition.

The Evening Dispensary for Working Women and Girls in Baltimore was established in 1891. Welsh and Sherwood took over its management from 1892 to 1910, and both influenced its development and found their careers affected by their experiences there. They instituted prenatal and postnatal care, provided scientific care of women in childbirth, registered births, organized clean milk distribution, and more, besides providing a rare opportunity for women physicians to gain practical experience. Welsh was asked by Governor John Walter Smith of Maryland to serve as the lone woman on the Tuberculosis Commission in 1902, and she participated in the Maryland Tuberculosis Exhibition of 1904, which became a model for public health education nationally. Welsh also played a leadership role in public health campaigns combating venereal diseases and infant mortality.

In 1894 Welsh was invited to join the faculty of the newly established Women's College of Baltimore (later known as Goucher College) as professor of anatomy, physiology, hygiene, and physical training at a time when physical education and study of physiology for women was considered controversial. She spent five months in Sweden, Germany, and England, observing the training of teachers of gymnastics in preparation for the work, and instituted the European system at the Women's College. Shortening its title to the Department of Physiology and Hygiene, she designed the program with three subdivisions. Students were given physical examinations, assigned to gymnastics classes, and taught physiology and personal and public hygiene as an introduction to public health. According to the *Baltimore Sun* (7 Nov. 1954) on the occasion of the dedication of a building in her honor at Goucher, "In her three-fold capacity . . . she brought these three health services into a single effective organization which placed the science of preventative medicine in the college on a unique basis." Her work set the standard for combining these fields in other women's colleges.

In describing the primitive state of standards in secondary and postsecondary education in the United States in the 1870s, Welsh credited the "normal school movement," or teacher education, with the early high school instruction for girls in contrast to "finishing schools," the only alternative in education for girls of genteel families. Once women began to outnumber men in normal schools, and graduates began to demand collegiate training, many colleges and universities were opened to women.

Welsh's career at Goucher spanned the period of its birth as one of the pioneer colleges for women, through its early financial crises, to its establishment as one of the premier liberal arts colleges for women in the United States. She was such an integral part of the school's early development that she wrote her autobiography, at President William Westley Guth's wish, as an instrument in the school's fundraising effort. As significant were her contributions to the woman suffrage movement in Baltimore, to education for women, and to the promotion of the public health movement through preventive medicine and a greater appreciation of women's health issues. She retired in 1924 and remained active in her associations. She died in Columbia, Pennsylvania.

• Some records of Welsh's are in the Millersville State University Archives, the Archives and Special Collections on Women in Medicine at the Allegheny University of the Health Sciences (formerly Medical College of Pennsylvania), and the Goucher College Archives. The principal sources are Welsh's *Reminiscences of Thirty Years in Baltimore* (1925) and her introductory lecture of the Lilian Welsh Lectureship at Goucher College, "Fifty Years of Women's Education in the United States" (1923). Welsh also made several contributions to the *WMCP Alumnae Transactions* and the *Bulletin of the Women's Medical College of Pennsylvania*. The memorial pamphlet *A Tribute to Lilian Welsh* (1938) contains tributes from six women who were either her students or colleagues, four of them doctors. Her obituary in the *Columbia News*, 24 Feb. 1938, is in the Columbia Historical Preservation Society.

SUSAN KNOKE RISHWORTH

WELTFISH, Gene (7 Aug. 1902–2 Aug. 1980), anthropologist and human rights advocate, was born Regina Weltfish in New York City, the daughter of Abraham Weltfish, a lawyer involved in Tammany Hall politics, and Eve Furman. Weltfish spent the first ten years of her life with several other relatives in the apartment of her maternal grandparents. As the first grandchild of a successful Jewish immigrant couple, she was the focus of their attentions and hopes for much of her early life. Her grandfather hired a German governess to teach her German (her first language). Weltfish was bilingual as a child, switching from German to English with ease, acquiring French sometime later. Weltfish's family moved to a home of their own when she was ten years old. Her father died unexpectedly three years later without leaving a will. Her mother, a business-college graduate, was unable to make enough money to support them. Weltfish started working as a clerical assistant when she was fourteen, but she continued her education by attending night school, graduating from high school in 1919.

Weltfish worked her way through college, starting at Hunter, where she majored in journalism. After transferring to Barnard, she minored in philosophy and studied under John Dewey and Morris Cohen. In the 1924–1925 academic year she enrolled in an anthropology class with Franz Boas, who had as profound an influence on the course of her career as he did on her approach to anthropology. His charisma as a teacher persuaded her to switch to anthropology, and the entrées he would arrange for his promising student were to become the critical defining experiences of both her methodology and her approach to life and politics. In the same school year, her last at Barnard, she met Alexander Lesser, a fellow anthropology student, whom she married later in 1925. They had one child.

In 1925 Weltfish entered the Department of Anthropology as a graduate student at Columbia University to continue her studies with Boas, during the formative period of American anthropology. In the summer of 1928, at the urging of Boas, she went to Oklahoma to study and record the language of the Pawnee, a Caddoan language. At the time there were no thorough grammars of any language of the Caddoan family. Her acceptance by the group with which she studied made such an impact on her that she habitually addressed her small daughter with a Pawnee name that she gave her. She returned to Columbia in the fall and completed her Ph.D. requirements in 1929, submitting as her dissertation "The Interrelation of Technique and Design in North American Basketry," in which she asserted the primacy of artistic intent over material or tradition in the basketmaking she observed.

Weltfish's next five years were spent doing more field research, first another year with the Pawnee and later among other groups, including the Chitamacha, the Mescalero, the Jicarilla, the San Carlos Apache, the Rio Grande Pueblos, the Hopi, and the Cochiti. Various organizations sponsored her fieldwork, which concentrated on art forms. She received funding from the Columbia University Council for Research, the American Museum of Natural History, the Bureau of American Ethnology, the Smithsonian Institution, and the National Research Council, among others. The fieldwork resulted in a number of articles on Native American art forms, which were later synthesized in her book *Origins of Art* (1953). She also made two significant contributions to the understanding of the Caddoan languages, *Caddoan Texts: Pawnee, South Band Dialect* (1936), a bilingual compilation of folktales, and *Composition of the Caddoan Linguistic Stock* (1932), which she coauthored with her husband.

In 1935 Boas invited Weltfish to join the graduate faculty at Columbia University. She was asked to spend one-third of her time developing appropriate courses for the School of General Studies, a university extension program that served as an adult-education program and a source of enrichment courses for graduate students. Weltfish taught traditional anthropology classes and developed new ones, including one on race problems— one of the earliest recorded courses on this topic. She attracted a core of loyal students who expanded the demands for course offerings and provided the research and organization that convinced the board of trustees to meet the new demands. The university extension soon became a full college of the university—that is, it was authorized to grant a B.S. degree. It was during this period, in 1940, that Weltfish and Lesser divorced.

From 1939 to 1943 Weltfish worked with S. R. Powers from the Teachers College at Columbia to develop a curriculum for high schools on race and heredity to alleviate racial tension. In 1943 she wrote a pamphlet, *The Races of Mankind*, with Ruth Benedict as junior coauthor. The War Department selected the pamphlet to distribute to officers and instructors as a means of combating Nazi theories of racial superiority.

World War II depleted Columbia's faculty and students. Many of Weltfish's colleagues left to work in the Foreign Morale Analysis Division of the Office of War Information for the duration of the war. Weltfish met with an official of the Division of Psychological Warfare to ask what she could do to help in the war effort. He suggested that her fight against racism on the home front was more important than anything she could do in a government office.

Weltfish lectured about racial equality all across the United States, delivering as many as three hundred speeches in one year. She helped develop a conflict resolution committee and a community center in Morningside Heights, where Columbia University is located, a neighborhood then populated by blacks, new European immigrants, Puerto Ricans, Irish, and other ethnic groups. She worked with the Community Interrelations Division of the New York City Board of Education, the Chamber of Commerce, and other city agencies and neighborhood organizations. She wrote comic books and radio skits to speak to the children of the country in 1943 and 1944. She addressed the unique integration problems faced by Native Americans in two articles published in 1944.

During this entire time Weltfish continued to teach at Columbia University and publish scholarly articles on prejudice and on Native American culture. A synthesis of her involvement with the racial prejudice problem and her teaching responsibilities resulted in new courses in African anthropology that treated both ethnologically and historically the initial contact of Africans with the Americas.

At a time of great activity for the women's movement internationally, Weltfish found another forum to promote equality and human rights. In 1945 she was elected vice president of the Women's International Democratic Federation at a convention in Paris, and later she became president of a sister organization, the Congress of American Women. These groups argued for equal rights for women, improvements in the welfare of children, and world peace. Both organizations were critical of Harry S. Truman's policies, which they feared would lead to yet another war.

In 1944 Weltfish gained notoriety when the War Department announced it was discontinuing the distribution of the pamphlet *Races of Mankind* because some felt it represented northern blacks as more intelligent than southern whites. Weltfish argued, however, that the question at issue concerned the quality and content of education in two different geographical and economic areas and that the test scores from the two areas could not fairly be compared. The armed forces either ignored her explanations or failed to find them mitigating, and the pamphlet was censored in the armed forces libraries. Even so, it continued to be distributed in many countries and in various translations.

The postwar political climate was not friendly to a woman of Weltfish's beliefs. In 1946 Attorney General Tom Clark placed the Congress of American Women on the list of subversive organizations, stating that they were "composed of a hard core of Communist Party members and had a circle of close sympathizers." In 1952 Weltfish was interrogated by Senator Joseph McCarthy's Internal Security Committee about her political beliefs and her participation in the two women's groups in which she had held office. Her pamphlet was declared to be subversive material.

Five months later, Weltfish received notice that her untenured teaching position was being eliminated after seventeen years. Her department fought for her promotion to a tenured rank, but it was too late. Columbia University denied that her political actions were influential in her dismissal. In the student newspaper Weltfish attributed her fate to a "prejudice against women scholars."

In 1954 John Champe, who knew Weltfish at Columbia, invited her to the University of Nebraska in Lincoln to continue her research on the Pawnee in his anthropology laboratory. She supplemented and corroborated her 1930s fieldwork there until 1958, when she received a two-year grant from the Bollingen Foundation to work on her draft for *The Lost Universe* (1965), which was to become a classic in ethnography.

In 1961 Weltfish resumed her teaching career as an assistant professor at the Madison, New Jersey, campus of Fairleigh Dickinson University, and finally she was on a tenure track. By 1968 she was a full professor. Initially she taught courses not only in anthropology but in politics and sociology as well. As time passed, she developed a department of anthropology. She investigated other avenues for teaching. She initiated an international club, enrolled students in the National UN General Assembly program for colleges and universities, and started a program in regional history, archeology, and restoration projects. She stood in front of a bulldozer at one point to stop the destruction of an important archeological site. She worked on the improvement of public transportation for low-income people in Paterson, New Jersey. As she grew older, she developed a community center for senior citizens in Madison, and helped form one of the initial chapters of the Grey Panthers in New York City.

At the age of seventy, Weltfish encountered yet another prejudicial institutional obstacle to continuing her work, this time her age; she was forced to retire from her teaching position. In involuntary retirement, she taught part time at the New School for Social Research, the Madison School of Music, and Rutgers University, changing her specialization to gerontology. She continued teaching until she suffered a stroke in her Manhattan apartment; she died several days later at Roosevelt Hospital.

Stanley Diamond wrote in a festschrift for Weltfish: "Gene has refused to be determined by the limitations of her culture, or the routine expectations of her contemporaries. She has learned through disciplined self-examination and reflection (merging the personal and professional dimensions of the anthropological identity), what a human life in our time must be about, if it is to be more than a social reflex." Weltfish left a legacy in the people who were influenced by her teaching and in her efforts to make a better world by using knowledge and education "for the good of humanity and against the destructive forces of the world" (Weltfish, "Science and Prejudice," *Scientific Monthly*, Sept. 1945).

• Weltfish's papers, including her field notes and Caddoan linguistic material, are housed at the library of Fairleigh Dickinson University, Madison campus. For a comprehensive bibliography, see Stanley Diamond, ed., *Theory and Practice: Essays Presented to Gene Weltfish* (1980) or Ruth Pathé's biography in *Women Anthropologists: A Biographical Dictionary* (1988). The *Village Voice* of 15 Oct. 1979 ran an article about Weltfish's life, "Grandmother of Us All." The *New York Times* ran a front-page story on her dismissal from Columbia (1 Apr. 1952). An obituary is in the *New York Times*, 5 Aug. 1980.

RUTH E. BOETCKER

WEMYSS, Francis Courtney (13 May 1797–5 Jan. 1859), actor and theater manager, was born in London, England, the son of a British naval officer (name unknown) and his American wife (maiden name Courtney). Wemyss was schooled in Edinburgh, Scotland, and went into business with his mother's brother, but after quarreling with his dictatorial uncle, he abandoned commerce and became an actor. Wemyss joined a company at the Montrose Theatre in Scotland, debuting in 1814 as Young Norval in John Home's *Douglas* to little acclaim. He subsequently appeared in various provincial theaters with middling success. Then, at the invitation of the theatrical manager Robert Elliston, Wemyss debuted in London in April 1821 at the Adelphi Theatre as Sponge in *Where Shall I Dine?*

While Wemyss was appearing in London, an agent from the Chestnut (or Chesnut) Street Theatre in Philadelphia contracted him for an American engagement; Wemyss made his debut there in December 1822 as Vapid in *The Dramatist*. Other roles in Philadelphia during his first two seasons in America included Marplot (described as a good-natured, silly, and officious person) in *The Busy Body* and Rover in *Wild Oats*. In 1823 Wemyss married a Miss Strembeck, the daughter of the Philadelphia sheriff. Wemyss first appeared in New York City in September 1824 at the Old Chatham Theatre as Marplot.

William Warren, then manager of theaters in Philadelphia and Baltimore, asked Wemyss to travel to London to recruit actors for his company. Wemyss sailed for London in 1827 and returned to Philadelphia with what he termed "a whole ship load of actors." He was soon both acting and serving as stage manager at the Chestnut Street Theatre, and by January 1829 he had become co-lessee with Lewis T. Pratt, a theatrical speculator. They encountered a financial depression and barely managed to keep the theater open. In 1833 he expanded his operations to the management of the new Pittsburgh Theatre, a theater built according to his plans.

Wemyss continued his career in Philadelphia, taking over the Walnut Street Theatre in the fall of 1834. There he sought to take advantage of the growing interest in indigenous, rather than European entertainment. To this end, Wemyss first redecorated the theater with patriotic portraits and scenes, choosing an enormous American eagle as a symbol for the theater. He changed the name of the theater to the American Theatre and sought to attract middle- and lower-class audiences, in contrast to the Chestnut Street Theatre's more aristocratic clientele. Quarrels with the theater's stockholders, first about selling liquor in the lobby (Wemyss opposed the idea) and then about adding gas lighting, which Wemyss supported, led to the manager's departure from the theater before the 1840–1841 season opened.

In 1840 Wemyss became lessee of the Arch Street Theatre in Philadelphia, but he encountered financial difficulty and moved to New York to manage the National Theatre in April 1841. This theater burned later that year, probably as a result of arson. Wemyss commenced a season at the Front Street Theatre in Baltimore in September 1841, closing the next May after a weak season. He then left the theatrical profession for a time to sell, as he put it, "pills and periodicals," but returned to become the stage manager of William E. Burton's National Theatre in New York City. For the next few years he stage managed various theaters in the East and was at the Astor Place Opera House in May 1849, playing supporting roles for Macready, when the Astor Place Riot took place. This disturbance, which took the lives of twenty or thirty people, was stimulated by professional jealousy between Macready and Forrest. For the 1849–1850 season he managed P. T. Barnum's "lecture room," a hall that Barnum had converted to a theater, after which he returned to the National. By that time Wemyss was also giving acting lessons to young performers to supplement his income. In 1854 he managed the Bowery Theatre, and in 1855–1856 he played bit parts for Laura Keene, the owner and star of a New York City theater. Wemyss closed his career as stage manager at the Academy of Music in New York City in 1858–1859. He died at his home in New York City.

Although the theatrical profession held Wemyss in high regard for his good taste and professional integrity, his managerial successes were minimal, as was his impact as an actor. He founded a fund for indigent actors, one of the first such attempts to assist the profession financially, and he encouraged American playwrights more than most managers did at the time. Perhaps his greatest contribution to the American theater, besides editing sixteen volumes of the *Acting American Theatre*, is his detailed autobiography, *Twenty-six Years of the Life of an Actor and Manager* (1847) (also published in 1848 as *Theatrical Biography; or, The Life of an Actor and Manager*), and the *Chronology of the American Stage from 1752 to 1852* (1852), a valuable encyclopedia of theater personnel in the United States during the nineteenth century, including a brief essay on himself.

• The Hobitzelle Theatre Arts Library at the University of Texas lists Wemyss in its holograph file of dramatic performers. Wemyss's autobiography appeared under two titles: *Twenty-six Years of the Life of an Actor and Manager, Inter-*

spersed with Sketches, Anecdotes and Opinions of the Professional Merits of the Most Celebrated Actors and Actresses of Our Day (1847) and *Theatrical Biography; or, The Life of An Actor and Manager. Interspersed with Sketches, Anecdotes, and Opinions of the Professional Merits of the Most Celebrated Actors and Actresses of Our Day* (1848). Scattered references to Wemyss's life and career may be found in George C. D. Odell's *Annals of the New York Stage*, vols. 3–7 (1928–1931). His career at the Walnut Street Theatre is outlined in an essay, "American Theatre Company," by Mari Kathleen Fielder in *American Theatre Companies, 1749–1887*, ed. Weldon Durham (1986). A brief death notice is in the *New York Times*, 6 Jan. 1859.

STEPHEN M. ARCHER

WENDTE, Charles William (11 June 1844–9 Sept. 1931), Unitarian minister and author, was born in Boston, Massachusetts, the son of Carl Wendte, a painter of church frescoes, and Johanna Ebeling. Wendte's parents immigrated to the United States from Germany in 1842, settling in Boston. After the death of his father in 1847, Wendte's mother became a German tutor, and counted the Transcendentalist and abolitionist preacher Theodore Parker among her students. Parker's influence on the young Wendte was significant. Later Wendte served as minister at the Theodore Parker Memorial Church in Boston (1901–1905). In 1861 Wendte moved to San Francisco, where he was befriended by Thomas Starr King, the "apostle" of Unitarianism on the West Coast. Encouraged by King, Wendte abandoned a banking career in favor of ministry. He graduated from the Harvard Divinity School in 1869 and soon after accepted the pastorate of Fourth Unitarian Church in Chicago (1869–1875).

Over the course of his career, Wendte served seven congregations in all, including the Church of the Redeemer in Cincinnati (1876–1882), the prestigious Channing Memorial Church in Newport, Rhode Island (1882–1885), and First Parish, Brighton, Massachusetts (1905–1908). His pastoral successes and administrative skills brought Wendte to prominence within the denomination. From 1905 to 1915, Wendte was Foreign Secretary of the American Unitarian Association (AUA). He also served as president of the Unitarian Ministerial Union in 1915.

Although it has been described as a denomination largely restricted to the "neighborhood of Boston," Unitarianism managed to spread slowly westward throughout the nineteenth century. In 1885 Wendte was appointed superintendent of missions of the AUA for the Pacific coast states. He traveled throughout the region helping to plant new congregations and lecturing on behalf of the cause of liberal religion. Between 1886 and 1898, he held the pastorate of the First Unitarian Church, Oakland. In 1896 he married Abbie Louise Grant; they had no children. Wendte's autobiography offers vivid and often detailed accounts of the turbulent religious life of California during this period. In response to the various "cults and cranks" he encountered—as well as the efforts of orthodox Christian missions—Wendte proclaimed an alternative gospel of "religious enlightenment" in full accord with the findings of modern science and the new higher biblical criticism. He soon established a literary society in Oakland, inviting prominent "apostles of higher culture and social improvement" such as Harvard's John Fiske, William Alger, and Julia Ward Howe to give public addresses. A close association with Stanford University began when he invited President David Starr Jordan to give a series of lectures on the principles of Darwinian evolution. A tireless advocate of clerical education, Wendte also helped to found the Pacific Unitarian School for the Ministry (renamed the Starr King School for Religious Leadership). His pastorate at Unity Church in Los Angeles was less successful. An outspoken pacifist and critic of "yellow journalism," Wendte was publicly pilloried in the press for his opposition to the Spanish-American War and American colonialism. He returned to Boston in late 1898 after less than a year in southern California.

Wendte's work on behalf of religious liberalism also took him beyond the confines of American Unitarianism. He was a cofounder of the National Federation of Religious Liberals, serving as secretary of that organization from 1908 to 1920. The federation was an alternative to the more prestigious Federal Council of Churches from which Unitarians and other unorthodox liberals, including Reform Jews, felt excluded. Between 1910 and 1914 Wendte was also president of the Free Religious Association, established in 1867 by dissident Unitarians unhappy with the denomination's decision to include a generic Christian confession in its statement of purpose. Wendte's most ambitious and satisfying work, however, was his effort to establish an ecumenical organization to coordinate efforts for the spread of religious liberalism globally. In 1901 representatives from fifteen nations and twenty-one different religious communities attended the first meeting of the International Congress of Free Christians and Other Religious Liberals in London. Subsequent meetings were held in Amsterdam in 1903, Geneva in 1905, Boston in 1907, Berlin in 1910, and Paris in 1913. Plans for future meetings in Tokyo and Cairo were interrupted by the outbreak of World War I. Although the majority of participants were from Christian backgrounds, there was a significant participation by members of the Brahmo Samaj and other theistic societies in India. As executive secretary of the Congress until 1920, Wendte traveled widely throughout Europe, Egypt, Palestine, and Turkey to promote the Congress and its effort "to unite pure religion and perfect liberty" among liberal Jews, Muslims, Parsees, and "Bahaistis," as well as Christians. Inspired by the first World's Parliament of Religions in Chicago in 1893, Wendte saw the Congress as the harbinger of the "wider fellowship" of enlightened religions in the modern world. For his contributions to the cause of global liberalism, Samuel A. Eliot, former president of the AUA and cofounder of the Congress, described Wendte as "a citizen of the world" who "widened the horizons of men's thought and hopes" (Eliot, p. 248).

Wendte died in Berkeley, California. The work of the Congress continues under the auspices of the International Association for Religious Freedom, a Non-

Governmental Organization (NGO) attached to the United Nations. One of his most lasting contributions is his massive two-volume autobiography titled *The Wider Fellowship* (1927). Its judicious and comprehensive treatment of the major figures and events in the development of religious liberalism in the nineteenth and early twentieth centuries make it a most valuable resource for scholars. Indeed, one prominent contemporary considered it the work to be "the most important for Unitarianism in this country work since Channing" (Sunderland, p. 770).

• Wendte's most comprehensive statement of the essence of liberal religion came in his final book, *The Transfiguration of the Life By A Modernist Faith* (1930). The biography of his mentor, *Thomas Starr King, Patriot and Preacher* (1921), is perhaps his best literary work, providing insight into the development of nineteenth-century Unitarianism. His passionate pursuit of religious universalism is evident in the three volumes of proceedings published for the International Congress of Religious Liberals as *Freedom and Fellowship in Religion* (1907), *Proceedings and Papers* of the Fifth International Congress (1911), and *New Pilgrimages of the Spirit* (1921). The liberal ecumenism of the National Federation of Religious Liberals is well presented in the collections edited by Wendte, especially *The Unity of the Spirit* (1909) and *A World League of Nations and Religions* (1919). For the Free Religious Association he published *The Next Step in Religion* (1911), *The Promotion of Sympathy and Goodwill* (1913), and *World Religion and World Brotherhood* (1914).

Brief biographical sketches of Wendte can be found in David Robinson, *Unitarians and Universalists* (1985); Samuel A. Eliot, ed., *Heralds of a Liberal Faith*, vol. 4, *The Pilots* (1952); and J. T. Sunderland, "Charles William Wendte: An Appreciation of a Famous Liberal," *The Christian Register*, 8 Oct. 1931, pp. 769–70, 782. On Wendte's contributions to Unitarian missions, see Charles H. Lyttle, *Freedom Moves West: A History of the Western Unitarian Conference* (1952), and Arnold Crompton, *Unitarianism on the Pacific Coast* (1952). An obituary is in the *San Francisco Chronicle*, 10 Sept. 1931.

LAWRENCE W. SNYDER

WENTWORTH, Benning (24 July 1696–14 Oct. 1770), royal governor of New Hampshire, was born in Portsmouth, New Hampshire, the eldest son of Sarah Hunking and John Wentworth (1671–1730), lieutenant-governor of the province. The high social status of the Wentworth family resulted in his being placed fifth among twenty when he entered Harvard. He graduated in 1715, having established a new college record for fines and broken windows. After graduation Benning was employed in Boston by his uncle Samuel Wentworth, a prominent merchant. In 1719 he married Abigail Ruck, daughter of Boston merchant John Ruck; Increase Mather performed the ceremony. The young couple produced three sons in the early 1720s.

Wentworth's political career began the following decade. When his father died in 1730 Benning returned to Portsmouth, gained election to the assembly, and helped launch a campaign to embarrass the new governing authorities. The primary target was Richard Waldron III, councilor, provincial secretary, and chief supporter of Jonathan Belcher who served as governor of both Massachusetts and New Hampshire. Territorial ambitions heightened the resulting political conflict. Both Belcher and Waldron sought New Hampshire's absorption into the Bay Colony. Wentworth and his allies, on the other hand, wanted New Hampshire to be separated completely from Massachusetts, to have its size increased, and to be ruled by an independent governor. Hard-nosed politicking and good fortune produced a complete victory for the Wentworth group. Its leaders developed a close working relationship with John Thomlinson, an influential English merchant. The home government became indebted to Wentworth when for diplomatic reasons the Spanish government refused to permit payment for a load of timber Wentworth had shipped to the country. Thomlinson worked out a solution that gave New Hampshire the independent government it sought and compensated Benning Wentworth for his commercial loss by appointing him governor.

Wentworth remained in office from 1741 through 1767, longer than any other colonial governor. He did so in part because of Thomlinson's continuing support. Thomlinson was heavily invested in the mast trade with New Hampshire; Mark, Benning's brother, served as the primary transatlantic agent in the trade. Governor Wentworth bolstered his own political fortunes by an aggressive defense of the royal prerogative. He gained legislative support for military expenditures in the two separate colonial wars against the French. He beat back an assembly attempt to interfere with his right to determine which towns would have representation and to exercise a veto over the assembly choice of its speaker. The major constitutional confrontations of Wentworth's administration took place between 1748 and 1752, during which Wentworth kept the assembly either adjourned or suspended most of the time. By the end of the four years his antagonists, led by Waldron, had been completely defeated.

Wentworth's extended tenure in office also stemmed from his general popularity in New Hampshire. The popularity cut across class lines. Many provincial elite lived in the Portsmouth area and were relatives of the governor; he was one of fourteen children, most of whom married into prominent local families. Wentworth rewarded his relatives and other affluent provincial inhabitants with governmental and military appointments, wartime supply contracts, and, most important of all, land grants in the territory that constitutes present-day New Hampshire and Vermont. Wentworth also had ways of rewarding ordinary citizens. As surveyor general of the King's Woods—a position Thomlinson also obtained for him—he could have enforced laws limiting the harvest of New Hampshire's vast timber resources, but he never did. In addition Wentworth encouraged all interested men, not just the elite, to seek land grants. By the mid-1760s New Hampshire's governor and council had issued charters to over 180 townships, each with sixty to seventy individual proprietors. Such largess virtually eliminated complaints against Wentworth's administration.

Eventually, however, Wentworth encountered difficulties. Age and the accession of a new monarch in England eroded Thomlinson's effectiveness. One result was an administrative decision putting New Hampshire's western boundary at the Connecticut River and thus invalidating two-thirds of the town grants Wentworth had made. The constitutional crisis triggered by the Stamp Act of 1765 encouraged general opposition to royal government. In 1764 officials in Whitehall began looking for a gubernatorial replacement. Wentworth soon was forced to resign in favor of his nephew John Wentworth (1737–1820).

Benning Wentworth experienced far more disappointment in his personal than his public life. All three sons and Abigail died in the 1750s. As he aged Wentworth developed gout and became obese. In 1760 he married Martha Hilton, a young woman who served as his housekeeper. All the children of this union died in infancy. Moreover, the marriage scandalized the Portsmouth community and drove a social wedge between the governor and many of his relatives. In apparent response to criticism of the marriage, Wentworth rewrote his will, disinherited all his blood relatives, and left everything to Martha. He died in Portsmouth.

• Unpublished primary material is scattered among collections in several repositories including the Public Record Office in London, England, the Library of Congress, the New Hampshire Historical Society, the New Hampshire Records and Archives, the Massachusetts Historical Society, and the Newberry Library. The bulk of published Wentworth papers are in volumes 5–7, 10, and 18 of the *New Hampshire Provincial and State Papers* (1871–1890) and the *Massachusetts Historical Society Collections*, 6th ser., vols. 4, 6, 7, 9, and 10 (1886–1899). The longest biographical treatment is Clifford K. Shipton, *Biographical Sketches of Those Who Attended Harvard College*, vol. 6 (1942), pp. 113–33. The most detailed analyses of his governorship are Jere R. Daniell, "Politics in New Hampshire under Governor Benning Wentworth, 1741–1767," *William and Mary Quarterly*, 3d ser., 23 (1966): 76–105, and John F. Looney, "The King's Representative: Benning Wentworth, Colonial Governor, 1741–1767" (Ph.D. diss., Lehigh Univ., 1961). See also Jeremy Belknap, *The History of New-Hampshire* , vol. 2 (1791); Daniell, *Experiment in Republicanism: New Hampshire Politics and the American Revolution, 1741–1794* (1970); William Henry Fry, *New Hampshire as a Royal Province* (1908); and James K. Martin, "A Model for the Coming of the American Revolution: The Birth and the Death of the Wentworth Oligarchy in New Hampshire, 1741–1776," *Journal of Social History* 4 (1970–1971): 41–60.

JERE R. DANIELL

WENTWORTH, John (16 Jan. 1672–12 Dec. 1730), lieutenant governor of New Hampshire, was born in Portsmouth, New Hampshire, the son of Samuel Wentworth and Mary Benning, tavernkeepers. At his father's tavern in Portsmouth young John became acquainted with the political and commercial life of the province, of which the tavern was a center. In October 1693 Wentworth married Sarah Hunking, daughter of a Portsmouth sea captain active in provincial affairs. About the time of his marriage, Wentworth went to sea, eventually commanding a ship that carried pine masts for the Royal Navy from New Hampshire to England. In 1709 he bought the family tavern from his brother, elegantly refurbished it, and settled into a mercantile career.

In 1712, as a prominent wealthy merchant and innkeeper, well connected by marriage and known through his trading activities by mercantile interests in London, Wentworth received the royal appointment to the province council, an advisory body to the governor that also functioned as the upper house of the legislature, of which his father-in-law was already a member. A judgeship on the Court of Common Pleas, which he held in addition to being a councilor, followed in 1713.

During the first four decades of the eighteenth century New Hampshire shared a royal governor with Massachusetts while a lieutenant governor, appointed by the Crown, served as the governor's deputy for New Hampshire, and exercised gubernatorial authority while the governor was in Massachusetts, which was most of the time. Wentworth was appointed to this office in December 1717 following a rancorous dispute between his predecessor, George Vaughan, and Governor Samuel Shute. Through his social and business contacts, and especially through family alliances forged by the carefully arranged marriages of most of his and Sarah Hunking's fourteen children, Wentworth established a Portsmouth-based oligarchy that dominated provincial affairs until the American Revolution.

Around him arose a "Wentworth" or "New Hampshire" party devoted to three goals: achieving a favorable settlement of the long-festering dispute over the location of the boundary between the province and Massachusetts; advancing the interests of Portsmouth commerce; and in general resisting the dominance of Massachusetts over its much smaller neighbor and its encroachment into contested territory that included favorable township sites and valuable timberlands.

The crucial division between the "Wentworth" and "Massachusetts" factions in New Hampshire came with the appointment of Jonathan Belcher to the governorship in 1730. Responding to what he believed to be personal affronts, Belcher waged full-scale political warfare against Wentworth until Wentworth's death in Portsmouth. Belcher later resumed these attacks against Wentworth's son Benning Wentworth and his son-in-law Theodore Atkinson, who assumed the leadership of the opposition.

Primarily because of its valuable connections in London and their skill in behind-the-scenes imperial politics, the Wentworth party eventually prevailed, securing in 1741 a boundary dispute settlement advantageous to New Hampshire and the appointment of Benning Wentworth as royal governor of the province free from any ties to Massachusetts.

• Some John Wentworth papers can be found in the Wentworth manuscripts in the New Hampshire Historical Society,

Concord. His will is printed in *New Hampshire State Papers* vol. 32 (1914), pp. 378–81. Genealogical information can be found in John Wentworth, *Wentworth Genealogy*, vol. 1, (1878); in James Savage, *A Genealogical Dictionary of the First Settlers of New England* vol. 4 (1862), pp. 484–85; and in Sybil Noyes, Charles Thornton Libby, and Walter Goodwin Davis, *Genealogical Dictionary of Maine and New Hampshire* (1972), pp. 736–37. The standard early accounts of the political facts of Wentworth's career, from which at least the outlines of most modern treatments are derived, are in Jeremy Belknap, *The History of New-Hampshire* (1784–1831), and Thomas Hutchinson, *The History and Province of Massachusetts-Bay*, ed. Lawrence Shaw Mayo, vol. 2 (1936). Modern discussions include those in Charles E. Clark, *The Eastern Frontier: The Settlement of Northern New England, 1610–1763* (1970; repr. 1983); David E. Van Deventer, *The Emergence of Provincial New Hampshire, 1623–1741* (1976); and Jere R. Daniell, *Colonial New Hampshire—A History* (1981).

CHARLES E. CLARK

WENTWORTH, John (30 Mar. 1719–17 May 1781), judge, patriot, and first Speaker of the Revolutionary Congress of New Hampshire, was born in the part of Dover, New Hampshire, that in his lifetime became Somersworth (now Rollinsford), the son of Captain Benjamin Wentworth (occupation unknown) and Elizabeth Leighton. He was generally known as "Colonel John" or "Judge John," which distinguished him from his contemporary, political rival, and distant relative, Governor John Wentworth (1737–1820). Wentworth was left fatherless at the age of six and was supported by his paternal uncle Colonel Paul Wentworth. Upon his uncle's death, Wentworth inherited the homestead. He had little formal education, having never attended college or formally studied law. Yet he became a judge and a leader in town and provincial politics during the revolutionary era. As early as 1747 he was a selectman in Dover, became a provincial representative in 1749, and continued as one until Somersworth's separation from Dover in 1767, whereupon he became a representative from that town. He was elected Speaker of the house in 1771 and continued until the provincial assembly's dissolution in 1775.

In 1774 Wentworth was chosen Speaker of the First Revolutionary Congress and a member of the New Hampshire Committee of Correspondence. As Speaker, he signed the credentials for the first New Hampshire delegates to the Continental Congress and presided over the creation of new structures of government in New Hampshire. Because he was president of the provincial Committee of Correspondence and chairman of the Revolutionary Congress, all correspondence with other colonies was sent in his name, and all provincial addresses and proclamations were issued under his signature.

In January 1775, the provincial Congress issued an address, signed by Wentworth, that decried the abuses of the royal government and demanded resistance to those abuses, while also urging restraint and respect for traditional rights and personal property for all people, regardless of their politics.

When the Third Revolutionary Congress met in April of 1775, Wentworth's health had begun to fail, and he virtually retired from public life from this point. Nevertheless, when the old provincial assembly met for the last time in May 1775, Wentworth was again elected Speaker. Wentworth was appointed as a judge of the superior court by the next Congress, a post he held until his death.

Wentworth was married three times and outlived all of his wives. From around 1742 to 1750 he was married to Joanna Gilman, with whom he had four children; then from 1750 to 1767 to Abigail Millet, with whom he had eight children; and from 1768 to 1776 to the widow Elizabeth (Wallingford) Cole, with whom he had two children.

While not a major player in the Revolution nationally, Wentworth was representative of the grass roots supporters of the revolutionary cause. A leader on the local level, not involved with gaining and granting royal favors, he demanded respect for what he believed to be the natural rights of all men. Characteristic of the revolutionary era in New Hampshire, Wentworth was part of the movement away from government by royal beneficence and toward local control of politics and society.

• See John Wentworth, *The Wentworth Genealogy* (1870), which was privately printed in Boston; a copy is at the Strawbery Banke Museum, Portsmouth, N.H. The *New Hampshire Provincial Papers*, vols. 6 (1872) and 7 (1873), provide a selection of documents concerning political events of the revolutionary era. See also Jere Daniell, *Experiment in Republicanism* (1970), a political history of New Hampshire in the revolutionary era; Richard F. Upton, *Revolutionary New Hampshire* (1936), a civic history of New Hampshire from a late-nineteenth-century perspective; and Everett S. Stackpole, *History of New Hampshire* (1916), a standard reference source until the mid-1970s revival of New Hampshire history studies. For a more narrowly focused study, see Karen Andreson, "A Return to Legitimacy: The New Hampshire Constitution of 1776," *Historical New Hampshire* 31 (1976): 155–64.

GREGORY C. COLATI

WENTWORTH, John (9 Aug. 1737–8 Apr. 1820), colonial governor, was born in Portsmouth, New Hampshire, the son of Mark Hunking Wentworth, a merchant, and Elizabeth Rindge. John Wentworth inherited leadership of the Wentworth family oligarchy created by his grandfather Lieutenant Governor John Wentworth and his uncle Benning Wentworth, who served as royal governor for twenty-five years, longer than any other colonial governor in the history of Britain's North American colonies. Wentworth entered Harvard College at the age of fourteen. He graduated in 1755, along with classmate John Adams, with whom he remained friends for many years. Wentworth returned to New Hampshire to take up the mercantile trade, and he also acquired land in Wolfeboro in New Hampshire's interior.

By 1763 two developments conspired to send Wentworth to England. The Wentworth family control of the mast trade came under attack, and irregularities in the government of New Hampshire were bringing increasing scrutiny of Governor Benning Wentworth by authorities at Whitehall. Wentworth crossed the Atlantic and soon was in touch with persons indispensable in protecting Wentworth influence. Most important was a distant relation, Charles Watson-Wentworth, second marquis of Rockingham, who had inherited leadership of the Whigs in Parliament. Building on a common love of horses and a shared heritage, Wentworth became a close friend and confidant of Rockingham. Rockingham's importance for Wentworth became more pronounced later that year when King George III removed the Grenville ministry and called on Rockingham to form a new one. At the request of Rockingham, who was now first minister and was faced with growing unrest in North America over the Stamp Act, Wentworth wrote a long, detailed, and highly accurate description of all the colonies in America, including Canada and the West Indies. He emphasized the importance of the colonial trade to the mother country and decried measures that hindered commerce, such as the Stamp Act. Wentworth may have been the first to suggest its repeal to the Rockingham administration, which early in 1766 did so, against strong opposition in Parliament. The king, however, removed Rockingham, but before he left office Rockingham appointed Wentworth as the new governor of New Hampshire, to replace his uncle, and also made him surveyor general of the woods in America. In June 1767 Wentworth, at the age of twenty-nine, arrived in New Hampshire to take over the reins of provincial government.

Wentworth's primary goal was to make his province an economically contributing member of Britain's system of empire and thereby prove that, barring ill-founded and threatening measures such as the Stamp Act, the trade laws worked to the benefit of all. Toward that end he promoted settlement in the interior, the expansion of agriculture, and the building of roads to facilitate communication and shipment of products to Portsmouth, the province's only seaport, for export. Setting an example for interior growth, Wentworth undertook construction in Wolfeboro of his own country estate, which became one of the most elaborate in New England. Equally demanding of his time were the forests of northern New England and Canada, an important source of masts for British ships. As surveyor general, he personally roamed the woods on horseback, greeting new inhabitants and trapping violators of British mast law. Though an Anglican by birth and station, Wentworth diligently sought the relocation in New Hampshire of Eleazar Wheelock's Congregational Indian School, which led to the establishment in 1769 of Dartmouth College, a true feather in the governor's cap. Wentworth's marriage the same year to his young cousin Frances Wentworth Atkinson, whose husband, Theodore Atkinson, Jr., had died only ten days earlier, caused a minor stir. Only one of their children survived infancy.

In contrast to the hauteur projected by his uncle, Wentworth was eminently approachable. Youthful, energetic, and outgoing, he clearly had the common touch, something that served him well during the difficult times ahead. As did most royal governors, however, Wentworth sparred with the provincial assembly on numerous issues, in his case his salary, building roads, creating counties, and the royal prerogative generally. In 1768, when Boston merchants boycotted British goods bearing the newly created Townshend duties, the New Hampshire House voted to petition the king. Warned of British reprisals but not wishing to alienate provincial legislators, Wentworth surreptitiously suppressed the petition, a move that, when later discovered, cost him popularity within his province. Wentworth blamed the trouble on the heavy-handed enforcement of the customs commissioners in Boston, the British administration's lack of flexibility in allowing the colonial governors to take necessary steps to meet the peculiar circumstances of their colonies, and the insistent radical pressure of the Boston Whigs.

Wentworth's continued pressure for reversion of jurisdiction west of the Connecticut River from New York to New Hampshire placed him in a favorable light with the many New Hampshire grantees of land in that area. He could not, however, easily duck the charges of land grabbing and favoritism filed in England against him in 1772 by a disgruntled council member, Peter Livius. Though many of the accusations were exaggerations, Livius nearly secured Wentworth's dismissal before Rockingham's influence helped turn the case in the governor's favor.

Despite the furor aroused by the Boston Tea Party late in 1773, Wentworth managed to get tea landed in Portsmouth and reshipped without major incident in both June and September 1774. However, he could not prevent an extralegal provincial congress from choosing two delegates to the intercolonial congress called for Philadelphia in September. This was a blatant disregard of the royal prerogative and the first step in New Hampshire toward the creation of a government based on the sovereignty of the people. When Wentworth was discovered seeking carpenters in New Hampshire to help the British general Thomas Gage construct barracks for his troops in Boston, the long-favored governor was branded an "enemy to the community." In December 1774, four months before Lexington and Concord, two raids by New Hampshire citizens on Fort William and Mary in Portsmouth harbor disarmed the defending soldiers, hauled down the king's colors, and carried all the arms and ordnance into the interior. In May 1775, following a confrontation between the governor and the assembly over Wentworth's attempt to seat three newly elected members from previously unrepresented towns, an angry mob forced the governor and his family to flee their home and take refuge at Fort William and Mary under the protective cannon of the HMS *Scarborough*. When the ship sailed to Boston in August for reprovisioning, Wentworth had no choice but to leave with it.

Wentworth went to New York and in 1778 to England, where he waited futilely for a reconciliation between Britain and its American colonies. Following formal recognition of American independence in 1783, Wentworth traveled to Nova Scotia in his now much reduced capacity as surveyor general of his majesty's woods. In 1792, calling on the patronage of Lady Rockingham, he was appointed governor of Nova Scotia, a position he held until 1808. He became Sir John in 1795, when he was made a baronet by the king. Wentworth was the leader of the many Loyalists from all the colonies who made Nova Scotia their home. He pursued goals similar to those he had sought in New Hampshire, in particular the promotion of settlement and agriculture. As the Loyalist party declined in influence, he found himself at odds with the assembly over a question of prerogative. When the matter was referred to Great Britain, he found he no longer had friends in government, and he was replaced.

In 1810 Wentworth and his wife went to England to be with their son. Hounded by unscrupulous creditors in 1812, Wentworth was forced at the age of seventy-five to flee to Nova Scotia. He remained in Halifax until his death there.

Wentworth held equal affection for America and Britain and could not visualize a permanent separation of the two. His firsthand experience with the moderate Rockingham administration at the time of the Stamp Act led him to believe a solution to the British-colonial dispute could and must be found. As royal governor he did everything he could to make the system of empire work, though he was often opposed to British policies. When Wentworth was forced to leave America in 1778, he fully expected to return. In that sense he represented many colonists who never embraced Loyalism but who in the end were left with nothing else.

• Wentworth's original letterbooks are in the Public Archives of Nova Scotia, Halifax. Copies of the first three volumes covering his years as governor of New Hampshire are located at the New Hampshire State Archives, Concord. Much of his official correspondence is in the Public Record Office and the House of Lords Record Office, both in London. The Wentworth-Woodhouse muniments at the Sheffield Central Library, England, hold correspondence between Wentworth and the marquis of Rockingham. The fullest biography of Wentworth in New Hampshire is Paul W. Wilderson, *Governor John Wentworth and the American Revolution: The English Connection* (1994). See also Lawrence Shaw Mayo, *John Wentworth: Governor of New Hampshire* (1921). Wentworth's years in Nova Scotia are the subject of Brian C. Cuthbertson, *The Loyalist Governor: Biography of Sir John Wentworth* (1983).

PAUL W. WILDERSON

WENTWORTH, John (5 Mar. 1815–16 Oct. 1888), editor, congressman, and mayor of Chicago, was born in Sandwich, New Hampshire, the son of Paul Wentworth, a storekeeper, and Lydia Cogswell. His grandfather John Wentworth served in the Continental Congress and signed the Articles of Confederation. Young Wentworth attended first local public schools and then a series of private academies before entering Dartmouth College. After graduating from Dartmouth in 1836 he moved to Chicago, Illinois, where he gained employment as an agent for the *Chicago Democrat* and within a year became both editor and proprietor of the paper. He studied law at Harvard University in 1841 and was admitted to the Illinois bar upon his return, but politics was his first love.

Wentworth came by his vocation naturally—his father was an active local politician—and immediately established himself as one of the most outspoken western Jacksonians. He was particularly critical of banks and had a Locofoco's faith in hard money, and in 1843 he was elected to the House of Representatives, where he served four consecutive terms. He followed a consistent Democratic party line, deviating only on matters crucial to his own district. A rabid Anglophobe and an enthusiastic expansionist, he advocated the annexation of Texas and the Mexican War but was alienated by James K. Polk's surrender on Oregon and veto of the river and harbors bill. Wentworth's belief that the Polk administration was bending unduly to southern influence led him to advocate the Wilmot Proviso, but unlike other northern Van Burenite Democrats, Wentworth remained loyal to the party. He continued to emphasize traditional Democratic economic issues and to present himself as a champion of the cause of free labor against southerners and their doughface allies. Throughout the fight on the Compromise of 1850, Wentworth pressed for a free California, refused to accept either the Utah or New Mexico bills without the proviso, and opposed the fugitive slave law. When he was able to play a crucial role in gaining the charter for the Illinois Central Railroad, he wrote, "The long struggle is over. My ambition is more than realized."

His opposition to the Compromise of 1850 appeared to cut his ties with Stephen Douglas and the Democratic party, but Wentworth mended his political fences with the necessary pledges and his support of Franklin Pierce in 1852; after two years' absence, he was returned to Congress as a regular Democrat. He voted against the Kansas-Nebraska Act but silently acquiesced in the repeal of the Missouri Compromise. Wentworth's hostility to the Whigs, "temperance fanatics," and Know Nothings who made up the new party kept him from becoming a Republican until he was kicked out of the Democratic party and made the Fusion candidate for mayor of Chicago in 1857.

During his two terms as mayor (1858 and 1860), Wentworth established a fiscal policy of "retrenchment and reform," protecting the taxpayers from "the army of taxeaters," and successfully encouraged the awesome project of raising up the buildings of the city several feet and filling in underneath. While his opponents accused him of various forms of immoral behavior, he acted the part of the Puritan in both his destruction of the shantytown called the Sands and in the "sign raid" in which his police tore down overhanging signs and dumped onto the street merchandise that cluttered the sidewalks.

In 1861 Wentworth was appointed to the state board of education (1861–1864) and elected to the convention to write a new constitution for Illinois. The convention was controlled by Democrats, and the document they wrote—which included antibank provisions that reflected Wentworth's influence—along with their attempts to use the convention to govern the state, caused the Republicans to attack their work as treasonous and the product of Copperheadism. Yet Wentworth strongly backed the Abraham Lincoln administration on the war. He is best remembered for protecting the Copperhead Clement L. Vallandigham's right to speak while he was police commissioner in 1864 and then mounting the rostrum to defend the Union and attack the South's "unholy struggle for slavery."

In 1864 Wentworth campaigned vigorously for Lincoln and was himself elected for the sixth time to Congress, where he sustained the Radical Republican policy on Reconstruction, following the leadership of Thaddeus Stevens. But Wentworth retained certain economic outlooks from his Jacksonian past; he sought tariff reform and supported Secretary of the Treasury Hugh McCulloch's conservative monetary policy, breaking with the Greenbacker Stevens and the moderate leadership of the Republican party. But his personal behavior, which included excessive absences and heavy drinking as well as his compulsive "habit of playing the clown," allowed his old political enemies to conspire against his renomination.

After leaving Congress, Wentworth served a second term on the state board of education (1868–1872) and remained active in politics, but increasingly he focused his interest on his 5,000-acre breeding farm at Summit. He became exceedingly wealthy as Chicago's growth increased the value of the lots and farmland he accumulated during his years in the city. Eventually his daughter Roxanna moved to Chicago to live with him. Wentworth's marriage and personal life were unconventional. Although he had been raised as a Congregationalist, he was married in a Presbyterian church in Troy, New York, in 1844 to Roxanna Marie Loomis, the daughter of Riley Loomis, a wealthy upstate New York businessman. Subsequently they had five children, but John continued to live in Chicago hotels while Marie remained with her family in Troy until her death in 1870. Only one child, Roxanna, survived to adulthood, and she too stayed in Troy until 1872, when she joined her father.

In 1867 Dartmouth presented Wentworth with an honorary LL.D. degree that some disgruntled faculty and alumni believed came in exchange for his $10,000 gift to the college. In retirement he worked to preserve the history of his family and his adopted region through the state and local societies and wrote *Wentworth Genealogy* (1878) and *Congressional Reminiscences: Adams, Benton, Calhoun, Clay, and Webster* (1882). He had hoped to leave his many papers and extensive diary for future historians, but they were destroyed in the great Chicago fire of 1871.

"Long John" Wentworth, who stood 6′6″ and in his prime weighed more than 300 pounds, was the sort of colorful character that might have been created by a historical novelist seeking to portray a genial self-promoter who marched to his own drummer, yet retained the affections of the voters of Chicago and his northern Illinois district for three decades. A combative editorialist and debater who took forthright stands on the major issues of the day, Wentworth by the 1850s was a throwback to earlier times, representing a purer commitment to individual liberty and laissez faire capitalism than his businessmen enemies who thrived in the age of incorporation. He died in Chicago.

• For information on Wentworth, consult issues of the *Chicago Democrat* and the John Wentworth "Scrapbook" at the Chicago Historical Society. A biography is Don E. Fehrenbacher, *Chicago Giant: A Biography of "Long John" Wentworth* (1957). See also *United States Magazine and Democratic Review*, Apr. 1849; *Chicago Magazine*, Aug. 1857; *Biographical Sketches of Leading Men of Chicago* (1868); Alfred T. Andreas, *History of Chicago from the Earliest Period to the Present Time* (3 vols., 1884–1886); Theodore Calvin Pease, *The Frontier State, 1818–1848* (1918); Arthur Charles Cole, *The Era of the Civil War, 1848–1870* (1918); Bessie Louise Pierce, *A History of Chicago* (2 vols., 1937); Ann Steinbrecher Windle, "John Wentworth, His Contributions to Chicago," *Papers in Illinois History and Transactions for the Year 1937* (1938); Robert A. Smith, "The Wentworth Family," *Twenty-Ninth Annual Excursion of the Sandwich Historical Society, August 19, 1948*; and Stanley L. Jones, "John Wentworth and Anti-Slavery in Chicago," *Mid-America* 36 (July 1954): 147–60.

WILLIAM G. SHADE

WENTWORTH, Mark Hunking (1 Mar. 1710–28 Dec. 1785), merchant and politician, was born in Portsmouth, New Hampshire, the son of John Wentworth, a leading New Hampshire merchant and politician, and Sarah Hunking. As one of the younger sons of a burgeoning family, Wentworth was trained at home by his father to manage the family business, which specialized in the mast and lumber trade. After his father's death in 1730, Wentworth parleyed his £1,000 patrimony and a fortunate marriage alliance into an extraordinary mercantile career in overseas trade and commerce that saw him become Portsmouth's leading taxpayer by 1741. After his oldest brother, Benning Wentworth, became governor of New Hampshire in 1741 and surveyor general of the woods in 1743, the two men gained a virtual monopoly of the mast trade in the colony from which, through illegal manipulation of royal white pine law policies, Wentworth emerged as New England's "timber king," the richest man in New Hampshire throughout the 1750s and 1760s, the central economic figure in the Wentworth oligarchy, and a leader of Portsmouth's social aristocracy before the American Revolution.

The date of Wentworth's marriage to Elizabeth Rindge, the daughter of New Hampshire assemblyman and overseas trader John Rindge, is a mystery, perhaps because Elizabeth was only sixteen and pregnant at the time. They had a child (who died in infancy) baptized in the spring of 1733, which suggests that they married sometime in 1732. The couple had three other children. More importantly, in late 1731 John Rindge was chosen by the assembly to act as its agent in London regarding the boundary line dispute with Massachusetts. While in London during 1732–1733, he formed economic and political connections with John Thomlinson, a rising London merchant, and he let his new son-in-law, Wentworth, help run his business in Portsmouth. Wentworth invested in overseas trading ventures with his brothers, Rindge, brother-in-law Theodore Atkinson, and Thomlinson, and in 1738, when Thomlinson obtained a contract from the Royal Navy to supply it with masts, bowsprits, and other naval stores, he appointed Wentworth as his chief subcontractor in New England. The outbreak of European imperialistic wars from 1739 to 1748 and from 1754 to 1763 stimulated a remarkable demand for masts and naval stores. Large masts alone, which sold for £115 in 1740, increased in value to £190 by 1750 and to £218 by 1756. This development, coupled with his monopoly control over the mast trade gained after 1743, brought Wentworth great wealth.

Throughout the 1740s and 1750s, Wentworth, as the leading New Hampshire overseas trader, expanded his import-export activities beyond the mast and naval stores trade with England, sending lumber and fish to the West Indies and importing sugar, molasses, rum, and cotton wool. Moreover, in 1746 he became one of twelve Masonian proprietors who purchased the revived Mason claims in New Hampshire for £1,500, outbidding the New Hampshire General Assembly, and gained control of all lands within a radius of sixty miles westward of Portsmouth and the Merrimack River. Wentworth purchased two shares at £100 each; however, in 1750 he sold one of them to his brother-in-law, John Rindge. After quitclaiming all lands to the colonists in the existing settled towns, the proprietors over the next forty years established thirty-seven new towns, reserving lots for themselves in each town. Wentworth obtained at least 121 lots of varying sizes in these communities, and he paid much more attention to the meetings of the proprietors than to any other public or political activities. During the American Revolution the New Hampshire government seized many of these properties, but in the late 1780s Wentworth's estate received 8,740 acres of land from the state as a settlement of lawsuits with the proprietors. Besides these numerous grants, Wentworth purchased at least eleven valuable lots of land and buildings in Portsmouth and along the Piscataqua River and its tributaries between 1740 and 1763. The combination of his mast and naval stores monopoly, extensive landholdings, and expanding overseas trade made Wentworth the richest man in New Hampshire during the 1750s and 1760s.

Wentworth's political contributions were relatively modest. After a one-year stint as a Portsmouth constable in 1738, he avoided town politics. In 1751, as revenge against Wentworth's role in the Masonian purchase, Benning Wentworth blacklisted Mark from consideration for nomination to the New Hampshire Council. However, in 1759 Thomlinson obtained Mark's appointment to that body, where he served until the outbreak of war in 1775. He attended the council regularly through 1764, receiving numerous 500-acre grants (as did the governor and other councillors) in the new townships established along the Connecticut River, but he gradually lost interest in provincial politics, leaving such activities to Atkinson and his son, Governor John Wentworth, after 1767. He did hold a commission as justice of the peace from his son from 1767 to 1775.

Wentworth's socio-economic activities were far more significant than his political activities. He was a founder and ardent supporter of the Portsmouth Anglican Church from 1734 on. He helped found the Portsmouth Library Society in 1750 and was an active member of the town's Masonic lodge. During the 1760s he supported Eleazar Wheelock's Indian Charity School, which ultimately became Dartmouth College in 1769. He financed the building of significant houses in Portsmouth, two of which, "Wentworth Hall" (probably modeled after the "MacPhaedris House" across the street) and the "Wentworth-Gardner House" (built in 1761 and still standing), were outstanding and luxurious examples of Georgian architecture. At the same time he had a strong reputation as a man charitable to the poor and needy. Moreover, he acted as the central banker and employer for the Wentworth "clan" of family relatives, providing loans, mortgages, and jobs to his aristocratic connections. His social role was so powerful that in 1761 he almost single-handedly successfully vetoed the creation of a Portsmouth theater, which he saw as frivolous and worthless. Both of his sons attended Harvard College and then were brought into the family business, while his daughter Ann married an English military officer who settled in the colony.

The end of the French and Indian War, a devastating 1762 forest fire in the Piscataqua region, Thomlinson's declining health and influence in England, declining mast prices, and increasing competition for mast contracts along the Connecticut River and in Maine led to a gradual decline in Wentworth's economic fortunes. Even though he sent his son John Wentworth to England in 1763 to protect the family's business interests and though John was able to obtain commissions as governor and surveyor general in 1766, by 1769 Wentworth had lost the lucrative mast agency. By 1771 his overseas trade was reduced to sending a few vessels to the West Indies each year. After his son Thomas Wentworth died in 1768, Wentworth brought his young nephew, John Peirce, into his business. In the early 1770s Wentworth was paying taxes at the same level as most other well-to-do merchants in Portsmouth but was no longer its highest taxpayer.

The American Revolution and its aftermath brought tragedy to Wentworth. He had opposed the controversial British policies of the 1760s; but proud and supportive of his son John, the new governor, he became an enemy to policies that challenged royal authority, such as merchant nonimportation agreements, and he helped keep New Hampshire reactions to the Townshend Acts relatively innocuous. When violence and intimidation of royal officers became a significant problem in early 1775, Wentworth and other officials, friends, and relatives of the governor signed an agreement, the "Tory Association," to protect the governor and each other from mobs and unlawful attacks. By late August, with war in progress, both his remaining children, Governor John Wentworth and Ann Fisher, had fled the colony, and Wentworth would never see them or his grandchildren again. The war also destroyed his political and social status and reduced his economic fortunes further. He refused to sign the revolutionary government's loyalty oath, and, consequently, the government forbade him to leave the state. His son was proscribed as a Tory and never could return to New Hampshire. Moreover, because of hyperinflation and the high war taxes on his extensive unimproved western lands, Wentworth had to sell all of his trading stock. Yet he and Elizabeth survived relatively well economically by living off income from notes, bonds, and mortgages. When his son's huge estate at Wolfeborough (now Wolfeboro) was confiscated in 1778, Wentworth generously withdrew his £13,000 claim against it so that all other creditors could receive everything owed them. He endured the revolutionary years better than anyone else in the Wentworth oligarchy. After his death, his more modest estate was variously valued at approximately £16,000 and $40,000 and was ultimately (in 1803) divided among his grandchildren and Elizabeth's relatives.

• Manuscripts relating to Wentworth are in several repositories. The New Hampshire Archives at Concord have the Masonian papers, Peirce-Rindge papers, and transcripts of three volumes of John Wentworth's letterbooks, 1767–1778; the New Hampshire State Library at Concord has microfilm copies of the Portsmouth Town Records; the New Hampshire Historical Society at Concord has the Wentworth papers; the Portsmouth Athenaeum has the Peirce papers; the Massachusetts Historical Society at Boston has the Belknap papers; and the British Public Record Office in London has the New Hampshire Shipping Returns in CO5, 967–69. His will and inventories are at the Stafford County Courthouse in Dover, N.H., New Hampshire Probate Records, No. 5168. Published sources are in Nathaniel Bouton et al., eds., *New Hampshire Provincial and State Papers*, vols. 4–9, 18–19, and 29 (40 vols., 1867–1943). Short sketches of him are in Nathaniel Adams, *Annals of Portsmouth* (1825), and John Wentworth, *The Wentworth Genealogy* (3 vols., 1878). The best works placing Wentworth in historical perspective are Paul Wilderson, *Governor John Wentworth and the American Revolution: The English Connection* (1994); Jere R. Daniell, *Experiment in Republicanism: New Hampshire Politics and the American Revolution, 1741–1794* (1970); Joseph J. Malone, *Pine Trees and Politics: The Naval Stores and Forest Policy in Colonial New England, 1691–1775* (1964); Brian C. Cuthbertson, *The Loyalist Governor: Biography of Sir John Wentworth* (1983); and David E. Van Deventer, *The Emergence of Provincial New Hampshire, 1623–1741* (1976).

DAVID E. VAN DEVENTER

WENTWORTH, Paul (?–Dec. 1793), speculator and secret agent, was born probably on the island of Barbados, the son of William Wentworth, probably a sugar planter, and Elizabeth (maiden name unknown). Little is known about Paul's early life, but he was mentioned in his father's will of 23 August 1750. He appears to have been well educated with a special proficiency in languages. As a teenager he surfaced in New England with letters of recommendation that he presented to Samuel Wentworth of Boston and Mark Hunking Wentworth of Portsmouth, both merchants and brothers of Governor Benning Wentworth of New Hampshire. It is known that Wentworths had been living on Barbados since the 1670s, but they were not related to the New Hampshire clan. Nevertheless, the brothers accepted Paul as kinsman and helped establish him in the mercantile trade. He was taxed for occupancy of a pew in Portsmouth's Queen's Chapel in 1757, but he soon after moved to Surinam, where he was married, briefly, to a rich, childless widow. (Her name, the date of their marriage, and the number of their children, if any, are unknown.) On her death he inherited her substantial sugar plantation, "Kleinhope," located on the Demerara River. He was apparently living there in 1764, when he hired the young Edward Bancroft as a plantation doctor, but soon afterward he moved to England.

By 1766 Wentworth was well established in London and enjoying a large income derived from sugar profits, merchant trading, and stock market speculation, which necessitated extended business trips to the Continent. He never remarried, but his great Poland Street mansion and his later residence at Brandenburg House, "Hammersmith," were graced by a series of fashionable mistresses. His mistress in Paris was a Mlle Desmaillis. When in London, his hospitality was legendary; among his houseguests were Benjamin Franklin and John Wentworth, New Hampshire agent and the son of Paul's Portsmouth benefactor.

The two Wentworths quickly became close friends. When old Benning Wentworth was ousted from the New Hampshire governorship in 1766, he was succeeded by his ambitious nephew, Governor John Wentworth demonstrated his regard for Paul by securing the New Hampshire agency for him in 1769 and nominating him to the New Hampshire council in 1770, even though he lived in England. This colonial upper house was already packed with Wentworth's relations, but Paul never returned to Portsmouth to be sworn into office.

Paul Wentworth's goals in life were to become a member of the British House of Commons, to hold government employment, and to receive a title. Ambitious plans for a provincial, they could be achieved only through extraordinary service to the Crown, not by representing an increasingly recalcitrant New Hampshire assembly in a worsening colonial crisis. Accordingly, he declined to support a petition sent to the king by the First Continental Congress in 1774 on the convenient grounds that he could not act without instructions from the assembly. Shortly afterward, he resigned his position; he had, in fact, entered His Majesty's secret service two years before. He publicly demonstrated his true loyalties by opening his home to John Wentworth and his family after the governor was driven from New Hampshire at the start of the American Revolution. Paul later commented that the support of the impecunious Wentworths cost him from £500 to £600 annually. Meanwhile, with the war's expansion, his secret service duties became more onerous. Reporting to Sir William Eden, undersecretary of state and head of the secret service, at a salary of £500 per year and the promise of further honors to come, he was assigned to gather information at the French court and especially to spy on the American delegation at Paris.

Wentworth quickly became the most valuable of Eden's employees. He knew everyone worth knowing in Paris, spoke French fluently, and was an old friend of both Benjamin Franklin and Silas Deane, sent by the Committee of Secret Correspondence of the Second Continental Congress to promote the American cause with the French government. On Franklin's recommendation, Edward Bancroft of London, Wentworth's Surinam physician, was added to the Paris commission in the summer of 1776. In December of the same year, Wentworth was able to recruit Bancroft for the British secret service. Thereafter, Bancroft would operate as a double agent, but his services to Great Britain were far more significant than those rendered to the United States. Though Wentworth had some difficulty in managing Bancroft, the two shared an affinity for high living and stock manipulation. Eden deplored Wentworth's heavy spending, but, as the latter reminded him, "You encouraged me generally to take handsome lodgings, support them, take a mistress, induce intelligence, seduce it" (Augur, p. 135). When his expenses exceeded his salary, he cheerfully made up the difference. Afraid of detection, he changed living quarters frequently and used at least twenty aliases. He easily passed for a native in the French capital for, as Beaumarchais wrote to the comte de Vergennes, Wentworth spoke French, "as well as you do, and better than I" (Einstein, p. 16). His productivity earned Eden's complete trust but not that of George III, who, though keenly interested in espionage, nevertheless scorned an agent who was "a mere stock-jobber" and a "dabbler in the alley" (Einstein, p. 25).

Undoubtedly Wentworth's most important endeavor was his attempt to prevent a Franco-American alliance, which appeared extremely likely after the defeat of General John Burgoyne in the autumn of 1777. Though the king remained skeptical, by December 1774 Prime Minister Lord North had acknowledged the danger and agreed that the alliance might be thwarted by Wentworth's scheme to propose "a well-timed offer of indemnity and impunity to those Cromwells [of the Continental Congress]" coupled with a vague promise of American independence (Einstein, p. 29). Wentworth's terms, not all sanctioned by the ministry, included a wholesale bribery of the Congress through baronetcies, knighthoods, governorships, and even a loan of £30 million for economic development. Wentworth expected that George Washington, Franklin, John Hancock, and John Adams (1735–1826) would all eagerly accept peerages. Unfortunately, Wentworth had to wait six weeks for an interview with Franklin and other American commissioners, and the several meetings that were held were fruitless. Franklin and Deane refused to travel to London to negotiate, vetoed the discussion of "emoluments," and declined to negotiate on any grounds other than independence. Franklin asserted that his nation was prepared to fight for the next fifty years. Wentworth not only failed, but it is likely that his attempt to force negotiations may have precipitated the very alliance he was trying to prevent. The French ministry was aware of Wentworth's mission from the time of his arrival in Paris, and it had the promise of Franklin and Deane not to accept Wentworth's terms even before they met with him. On 7 January 1778, the day after their last meeting, Vergennes, representing the French government, pledged the anticipated alliance.

Wentworth continued his espionage efforts until the end of the American Revolution, but his usefulness decreased. He never received his coveted title, but in 1780 he was awarded a "safe" seat in the House of Commons by the Lord North ministry, which he held for only six weeks before a new general election drove him from office. Continuing his London stock speculation in the postwar years, he also revived his interest in New Hampshire. He presented expensive scientific equipment to Dartmouth College, where he was elected a trustee, and in 1786 published at his own expense the well-known Captain Holland map of the New England coast. In England, however, his reputation suffered. In 1790, suspected by the British government of intrigues with the French, he retired to his Surinam plantation, where he lived quietly until his death.

• What little is known of Paul Wentworth's early life can be found in John Wentworth, *The Wentworth Genealogy*, vol. 3 (1878); less familiar is his "Wentworth Genealogy: The Hitherto Unknown Councillor Paul," *New England Historical and Genealogical Register*, vol. 42 (1878), which traces Paul's Barbados roots. His personal papers have disappeared, but some of his secret service correspondence survives in Benjamin Franklin Stevens, comp., *Facsimiles of Manuscripts in European Archives Relating to America, 1773–1783* (1889–1895). His services as agent can be located in New Hampshire *Provincial Papers, Documents, and Records*, vol. 7 (1873). The John Wentworth Letter Books, 1767–1809, of the Public Archives of Nova Scotia includes some of the business papers of the two Wentworths, while Leonard Labaree and William B. Wilcox, eds., *The Papers of Benjamin Franklin*, vols. 21–25 (1978–1986), illustrate Wentworth's espionage activities. There is no biography of Paul Wentworth, but his career as secret agent is examined in some depth in Carl Van Doren, *Benjamin Franklin* (1938) and *Secret History of the American Revolution* (1941), Lewis Einstein, *Divided Loyalties: Americans in England during the War of Independence* (1933), and Helen Augur, *The Secret War of Independence* (1955). Finally, Samuel Flagg Bemis, "British Secret Service and the French-

American Alliance," *American Historical Review* 29 (Apr. 1924) remains the classic account of Wentworth's dramatic career.

GORDON E. KERSHAW

WENTZ, Abdel Ross (8 Oct. 1883–19 July 1976), Lutheran educator and clergyman, was born in Black Rock, Pennsylvania, the son of John Valentine Wentz, a farmer and storekeeper, and Ellen Catherine Tracy. He received his A.B. in 1904 from Gettysburg (then Pennsylvania) College and his B.D. in 1907 from the Lutheran Theological Seminary in Gettysburg. In the following three years he studied theology and church history at the Universities of Leipzig, Berlin, and Tübingen in Germany. In 1909 he was ordained into the Lutheran ministry. In 1914 he received his Ph.D. from George Washington University with a dissertation (subsequently published) on the German element in York County, Pennsylvania. He taught history and religion at Gettysburg College from 1909 until 1916 when he became the first professor of church history at Lutheran Theological Seminary, where he taught until his retirement in 1956. From 1956 to 1958 he taught church history at Lutheran Theological Southern Seminary in Columbia, South Carolina. In 1917 he married Mary Edna Kuhlman; they had three children.

Wentz wrote extensively. In 1923 he published the textbook *The Lutheran Church in American History*. It became the standard text in its field and was revised in 1955 as *A Basic History of Lutheranism in America*. By adapting for the Lutheran experience the dominant historiography of his day, Wentz provided a framework and a story with a widely influential interpretation that viewed America's Lutherans basically as birthright Americans, rather than primarily foreign-language immigrants, and compared church history to the major themes and periods of the broader American scene. He also produced several monographs, including *The Lutheran Church of Frederick, Maryland* (1938), *History of Gettysburg Lutheran Theological Seminary* (1965), and *Pioneer in Christian Unity: Samuel Simon Schmucker* (1967).

A popular teacher, Wentz served as librarian of the school and then as president from 1940 to 1951, during which time he increased enrollment and faculty and expanded the physical plant. He also broadened the curriculum, included women as tenured faculty, and encouraged married students to live on campus.

Wentz was a member of the American Bible Revision Committee and was one of the translators of the Revised Standard Version of the New Testament (1939–1962). Long an active member of the American Society of Church History, he served as secretary (1926–1931) and president (1931–1932). His 1931 presidential address, "Permanent Deposits of Sectionalism in American Christianity," became the first article in the first number of the periodical *Church History*. He was also secretary and treasurer of the American Association of Theological Schools in its formative years (1934–1946) and a member of its accreditation commission during the first sixteen years.

As a member of the United Lutheran Church in America, Wentz served on its national boards from 1918 to 1952. From 1918 to 1924 he served on the executive board for two terms. Then from 1932 until 1940 he was a member of the board of education. In 1940 he began twelve years of service on the board of foreign missions, serving as its president from 1942. He frequently served as parliamentarian at church meetings and was often consulted on constitutional matters.

Wentz served on the committee that planned the first assembly of the Lutheran World Convention, addressing that body in its closing ceremonies in 1923 at Eisenach, Germany. In the 1920s and 1930s and until its evolution into the Lutheran World Federation (1947), he served on its executive committee. He was also coauthor with Alfred Jørgensen and F. Fleisch of its publication *Lutheran Churches of the World* (1929). He drafted the constitution that was adopted in 1947 in Uppsala, Sweden, as the basis for the Lutheran World Federation and served as the federation's vice president until 1952. He also served on the Committee of Fourteen (1937–1948) that formed the World Council of Churches, successfully arguing that basic membership should be determined by denominational rather than geographic identity.

Following retirement, Wentz stayed at Gettysburg, researching and writing. He died in Rockford, Illinois.

• The bulk of the Wentz papers are in the archives of the Abdel Ross Wentz Library at the Lutheran Theological Seminary at Gettysburg. His papers pertaining to his work with the Lutheran World Convention and Federation and with the World Council of Churches are in the archives of the Evangelical Lutheran Church in America in Chicago, Ill. A detailed account of his life is in his *History of Gettysburg Lutheran Theological Seminary* (1965).

FREDERICK K. WENTZ

WERKMAN, Chester Hamlin (17 June 1893–10 Sept. 1962), bacteriologist, was born in Fort Wayne, Indiana, the son of John Carl Werkman, a businessman, and Ada Aliee Groves. He received his early education in the local public schools and graduated from Purdue University with a B.S. in 1919. He married Cecile A. Baker in 1913; they had one son. In 1918 he worked as an assistant bacteriologist for the U.S. Department of Agriculture's Bureau of Chemistry, and a year later he joined the staff of the University of Idaho's experiment station.

Werkman received his Ph.D. in 1923 from Iowa State College in Ames, where he worked his way through school as a graduate assistant and instructor in the Department of Bacteriology. After graduation, he accepted a position as assistant professor of microbiology at the Massachusetts State College and Experiment Station. In 1925 he returned to Iowa State College as an assistant professor in the bacteriology department and assistant chief in bacteriology at the

Iowa Agricultural Experiment Station. His research was recognized with promotions to associate professor in 1928, full professor in 1933, and chairman of the department in 1945. His special studies included bacterial physiology and antibiotics. Werkman's scientific reputation was known both nationally and internationally, and his peers considered him the "foremost bacteriologist" of his time.

Werkman's main interest was investigating cellular metabolism. One of his most significant scientific contributions was his discovery that heterotrophic organisms utilized carbon dioxide. His article "Vitamin Effects in the Physiology of Microbiology" (*Journal of Bacteria*, 1930) illustrates his results from studies with bacteria and the effects on mammalian tissue.

Werkman's studies of photosynthesis, the process by which green plants create food and "living matter" from air, soil materials, and water, changed modern theory on carbon dioxide and its effects on humans and the environment. In 1936, collaborating with his former student H. G. Wood, then a University of Minnesota professor, Werkman realized that when the body utilized carbon dioxide the gas was not poisonous. Their article "The Utilization of CO_2 in the Dissimilation of Glycerol by the Propionic Acid Bacteria" (*Biochemical Journal*, 1936) made a profound impact on previous bacteriology, botany, and medical research.

Werkman's carbon dioxide research resulted in the development and use of carbon 13 isotopes, a natural carbon found in plants and bodies, as tracer elements. When the tracer element was "followed," scientists could observe and analyze biological processes. Werkman's pioneering work in photosynthesis also revealed potential processes for artificially making food. A prolific researcher, Werkman prepared papers presented at the annual meeting of the Iowa Academy of Science as well as for national professional groups. In addition to bacterial physiology and cellular metabolism, he wrote about related aspects regarding food bacteriology, immunities, chemistry, and sanitation. His later studies expanded on microorganisms pathogenic in humans, acid-producing bacteria, and fermentation.

In 1930 Werkman and Ellis Fulmer published *An Index to the Chemical Action of Microorganisms on the Non-Nitrogenous Organic Compounds*. Listing references for the field of zymology, Werkman noted that microorganisms, including bacteria, yeast, and molds, were catalysts for chemical production in agricultural wastes. He emphasized, "One of the immediate needs in the fields of zymology is the development and consistent use of adequate analytical methods for the fermentation products."

Werkman's 1951 work, *Bacterial Physiology*, edited with University of Wisconsin professor P. W. Wilson, consists of chapters contributed by scientists at prestigious research universities. Encompassing current ideology, the book was written to incite researchers in the field of bacteriology. Werkman's desire was to centralize "fundamental knowledge" that would "provide the required background for critical reading of current literature through concise, authoritative discussions of specific topics" and highlight the "significance of bacterial physiology in the broader fields of general biology." He hoped the book would prove useful to researchers, teachers, and students in allied fields, such as veterinary medicine and zoology.

During his career at Iowa State, Werkman directed approximately fifty graduate students' research. He acted as major professor for at least twenty doctoral students, and many of his protégés secured important scientific positions with Werkman's support. Perhaps his most prominent student was Wood, who had assisted Werkman in his revolutionary carbon dioxide studies. In 1942 Wood won the Eli Lilly Award, honoring the young bacteriologist for his outstanding work. To help his students, Werkman prepared the *Laboratory Manual in General Bacteriology* with Eric B. Fowler in 1957.

In addition to publishing his scholarship, Werkman served as coeditor of *Advances in Enzymology and Related Subjects*. He was editor of the *Archives of Biochemistry* and for the *Proceedings of the Society of Experimental Biology and Medicine*, and he was assistant editor of *Biotek* and *Enzymologia*. In his lifetime Werkman published more than 280 articles addressing the cellular metabolism of bacteria.

Affiliated with numerous professional organizations, Werkman was a member of the Society of American Bacteriologists, the Biochemical Society, the Society of Experimental Biology and Medicine, and the American Society of Biological Chemists. He was invited to present papers at the International Congress of Microbiology in London and New York during the 1930s, serving as vice president of the section on chemical microbiology. The University of Wisconsin asked him to be a guest speaker at a symposium on respiratory enzymes in 1941, and in 1943 he toured as a lecturer for the American Chemical Society. During World War II, he aided the War Production Board's Division of Chemicals and Procurement.

Werkman was a fellow of the Iowa Academy of Science and a member of the National Academy of Science. The first Iowan to win the Pasteur Award, Werkman was named the most outstanding bacteriologist in the Midwest in 1951. He and his family were devout Catholics, and Werkman belonged to the Masonic order. He retired from administrative duties at Iowa State in 1957, remaining on the faculty to teach students and direct research. He died at Mary Greeley Hospital in Ames, Iowa.

The *Des Moines Register* printed an editorial praising Werkman for his dedication in acquiring and disseminating basic knowledge about plant and animal life. Acknowledging that Werkman was "not widely known in Iowa," the newspaper commented that "his work as teacher and researcher did not bring him to the attention of the public." The editor explained, "Werkman spent his career exploring areas that remain obscure to the public." His research was not in a glamour field like astronomy or rocketry, which were especially popular in the early 1960s. The editor commented that government funding and public accolades generally supported scientific applications for military and aerospace technology. "Let us remember the Werkmans who dedicate their lives to new knowledge in fields that have not caught the spotlight," the newspaper persuaded. "There is a danger that their basic proving of the unknown may be neglected in favor of work which can show immediate and profitable results."

• Clippings on Werkman are in Iowa State University's Special Collections. Several articles by Werkman are helpful in understanding his theories on bacteria, including "Microbiological Death Rates," *Proceedings of the Iowa Academy of Science* 34 (1928): 85–86; "Enzymatic Fixation of Carbon Dioxide in Oxalacetate," *Journal of Biology and Chemicals* (1943); and "Heterotrophic Assimilation of Carbon Dioxide," *Proceedings of the Fourth International Congress of Microbiology* (1943). A detailed obituary is "An Iowan Man of Science," *Des Moines Register*, 15 Dec. 1962.

ELIZABETH D. SCHAFER

WERNER, Heinz (11 Feb. 1890–14 May 1964), psychologist, was born in Vienna, Austria, the son of Leopold Werner, a manufacturer, and Emilie Klauber. In 1908 Werner enrolled in the Technische Hochschule for engineering training. The next year he transferred to the University of Vienna with an interest in musicology; later his interest shifted to philosophy and psychology. His earliest publications (1912, 1913) were in the areas of perception (research on the blind spot, for which he won the Trebitsch prize) and cognition (in which he focused on linkages between sensory-motor activity and conceptual thought). His Ph.D. dissertation in 1914 involved an integration of aesthetics with psychology. Werner spent one postdoctoral year (1914–1915) in the University of Vienna's Institute of Physiology. After a brief period of military service, he conducted research at the Psychological Institute at the University of Munich on such topics as the role of rhythmic factors on perception and invention of melodies in early childhood. Werner accepted a position as a research assistant in the Psychological Institute at Hamburg in 1917. In 1918 he married Jo Gervai, who was very much interested in aesthetics. In 1921, following publication of his first major work in language, *Die Ursprünge der Metapher* (1919), he was appointed as privatdocent in the philosophical faculty of the University of Hamburg.

At the University of Hamburg, his interests widened further, and he published works on the origins of the lyrik and physiognomics of language. His classic work in developmental psychology was first published in German in 1926 and appeared in English in 1940 under the title *Comparative Psychology of Mental Development*. In this work, Werner established his position that developmental conceptualization was applicable to various areas of the life sciences and was a mode of interrelating diverse fields of psychology. He viewed development as a framework for understanding and directing inquiry at the biological, psychological, and sociocultural levels to all aspects of existence in which mentality is manifested. Development was empirically investigated in the phenomena of ontogenesis, microgenesis, phylogenesis, neuropathology, and psychopathology and in the various levels of functioning (consciousness, reverie states, dreams) of the mature individual.

During his twelve years at Hamburg, he also published many articles on perception and language, and served as coeditor of the *Zeitschrift für Psychologie* and as director of the Psychology Laboratories. In July 1933, with the advent of Nazism, Werner left the University of Hamburg. He received an invitation to go to Holland and was permitted to leave on a temporary visa; while there he received an invitation from the University of Michigan and left for America in October 1933. During his three years at Michigan, he initiated studies on contour, metacontrast, and binocular disparity that had important impact in the field of perception.

Werner spent the year 1936–1937 as a visiting professor at Harvard, where he published a monograph on depth perception and a significant paper, "Process and Achievement," that focused on the need to analyze underlying process rather than achievement, which was currently stressed by the majority of researchers on mental testing. Following his year at Harvard, Werner activated a position offered earlier to him at the Wayne County Training School (1937–1942), where he conducted and collaborated on an extensive program of studies on endogenous and exogenous aspects of feeblemindedness. In this work, Werner's belief in the relevance of experimental analysis to practical clinical problems is most strikingly illustrated.

In 1942 his wife died. A year later, despite his worldwide reputation, he was offered and accepted an instructorship at Brooklyn College. Here he continued his work on the effects of brain damage. In 1945 he married the sister of his first wife, Erica Gervai, with whom he spent his remaining years. He had no children in either marriage.

In 1947 Werner was invited to Clark University as professor of psychology and education. In 1949, appointed G. Stanley Hall Professor of Genetic Psychology and chairman of the Department of Psychology, he initiated two major programs of research—on perception, with Seymour Wapner, and on symbolization, with Bernard Kaplan. Werner authored or coauthored numerous papers in the long-term research program in perception. His work on perception was characteristically broad. It ranged from more biologically oriented analyses (e.g., of blind spots and binocular perception) to those directed at more complex levels (e.g., intersensory phenomena, space orientation, and physiognomic perception). All of these aspects of perceptual phenomena were viewed in terms of organismic theory (e.g., Werner and Wapner's sensory-tonic field theory of perception). He coedited (with Wapner) *The Body Percept* (1964). The analysis of perception culminated in a study of age differences in the relations between body and object perception, which were interpreted in terms of organismic and developmental theory.

Werner published (with Kaplan) *Symbol Formation* (1963), which integrated approximately fifteen years of research. In this now classic work, Werner and Kaplan articulated an organismic-developmental theoretical framework that synthesizes diverse research (e.g., on the metaphor, expressive language, microgenesis, aphasia) and thereby provides a comprehensive understanding of thought, language, and symbolization in the progressive and regressive development of the human being.

Over the years at Clark, Werner received a number of honors in recognition of his outstanding contributions, including election as honorary member of Phi Beta Kappa at Clark (1956) and election to membership in the American Academy of Arts and Sciences (1957). In 1957 he was reinstated to the faculty of the University of Hamburg as Ordentlicher Professor Emeritus. In 1960, on the occasion of his seventieth birthday, a number of outstanding scholars contributed a Festschrift (*Perspectives in Psychological Theory*) in his honor.

In June 1960, after becoming professor emeritus at Clark, Werner became actively involved as chairman of the board of directors of the Institute of Human Development at Clark (founded by Werner in conjunction with Leslie Phillips and Seymour Wapner in 1957), which was renamed in 1965 in his honor as the Heinz Werner Institute for Developmental Psychology, and in 1986 as the Heinz Werner Institute for Developmental Analysis.

During his retirement, Werner continued his scholarly activity until his death in Worcester, Massachusetts. Werner's contributions in the areas of comparative developmental and organismic theory, perceptual experience, mental retardation and brain damage in children, and language and symbolization—recognized over the years by scholars in various subfields of psychology and diverse disciplines such as aesthetics, anthropology, biology, education, linguistics, and medicine—continue to speak to his ongoing role as a powerful contemporary thinker.

• Werner's publications are listed in a biography by Herman Witkin, "Heinz Werner: 1890–1964," *Child Development* 30 (1965): 309–28, and in the Festschrift for Werner, B. Kaplan and S. Wapner, eds., *Perspectives in Psychological Theory: Essays in Honor of Heinz Werner* (1960). A compendium and appreciation of some of Werner's main publications is found in S. S. Barten and M. B. Franklin, eds., *Developmental Processes: Heinz Werner's Selected Writings* (1978). For a tribute by a number of his students in the form of papers concerning the influence of Werner's comparative-developmental perspective on various aspects of contemporary psychology, see Wapner and Kaplan, eds., *Heinz Werner, 1890–1964: Papers in Memorium* (1966). For a brief obituary see Wapner and Kaplan's article in *The American Journal of Psychology* 77 (1964): 513–17.

SEYMOUR WAPNER

WERTENBAKER, Charles Christian (11 Feb. 1901–8 Jan. 1955), journalist and author, was born in Lexington, Virginia, the son of William Wertenbaker, an obstetrician and gynecologist, and Imogen Peyton. He attended public and private schools in Virginia and Delaware before entering the University of Virginia in the fall of 1919.

Uncertain of what he wanted to do with his life, Wertenbaker dropped out of college after his sophomore year and worked for a while at various jobs, including housepainting and merchant seafaring. Newspaper writing attracted him, and he spent a year as a reporter for the *Alexandria Gazette* and the *Washington Star* before returning to the university in 1923.

By the time of his graduation in 1925, Wertenbaker had written a comical and scandalous novel about university life called *Boojum*, which was published in 1928. He resumed his career as a journalist in the Washington area while writing a second novel in the same vein, *Peter the Drunk* (1929). Wertenbaker began contributing short stories to national magazines, including *The Saturday Evening Post*, which were later collected in the volume *Before They Were Men* (1931). During this period he also traveled extensively in Europe.

In 1931 Wertenbaker was hired by Henry Luce as a contributing editor of *Time*, and assignments took him on further travels in the United States and Europe. Two years later he joined the staff of another Luce publication, *Fortune*, and worked as a correspondent in Central and South America for three years.

Wertenbaker returned to *Time* in 1936 and remained on its staff for eleven years, serving successively as associate editor and foreign correspondent, foreign news editor, war news editor, chief military correspondent, head of *Time* and *Life*'s Paris bureau (1944–1945), and chief of European correspondents (1945–1946). During this time, in addition to his editorial responsibilities, Wertenbaker wrote and published books in varied genres, beginning with his autobiographical novel *To My Father*, which appeared in 1936. Five years later he published *A New Doctrine for the Americas*, an overview of international relations during the 1930s in the Western Hemisphere.

Heretofore Wertenbaker had enjoyed modest success as a writer but he was hardly well known. That status changed abruptly as a consequence of his coverage of the Allied D-Day invasion of Normandy in June 1944. In addition to his *Time* despatches, he quickly wrote a book-length account of the invasion that was paired with photographs by Robert Capa. Published a scant three months later, *Invasion* found a ready audience in a public eager to celebrate a dramatic turning point in a long and brutal war, and it was heralded by readers and critics alike for its stirring depictions of heroism.

Not long after publishing another novel, *Write Sorrow on the Earth* (1946), a fictionalized account of the French resistance, Wertenbaker concluded his career with the Luce empire early in 1947 to write fiction full time. Living alternately in the French Basque village of Ciboure, near St. Jean-de-Luz, and in a converted barn in Sneden's Landing, New York, overlooking the Hudson River, he produced two long novels in the last years of his life: *The Barons* (1950), the story of an American family of munitions manufacturers, and *The Death of Kings* (1954), a thinly disguised account of the early years of Time Inc. Both of them enjoyed modest success.

Wertenbaker was married three times. His first wife was Henrietta Hoopes, whom he wed in 1926; the couple had no children. Following their divorce in 1935, he married the writer Nancy Hale, by whom he had a son. They were divorced in 1941, and a year later he married his last wife, Lael Tucker Laird, also a writer; they had two children.

In the fall of 1954 Wertenbaker, at work on another book and anticipating greater literary success, was diagnosed with cancer and told that he had only a short time to live. Always a stylish man who was conscious of his public posture—his friend John Hersey once described him as presenting the "picture of a man who knew what he wanted from life and—far better—was getting it"—Wertenbaker resolved to die in stoic dignity amid the comfort of family and friends. Following surgery in New York he refused further treatment and returned to his home in Ciboure, where he kept a journal of his final weeks; it was published posthumously as *Sixty Days in a Lifetime* (1955).

The story of Wertenbaker's courage reached a wider audience two years later when his widow published *Death of a Man* (1957), her own admiring account of her husband's last days. It became a bestseller and is an early forerunner of what has become an established genre: death-and-dying literature that supports the rights of terminally ill patients to end their lives as they choose.

• Wertenbaker's manuscripts are at the University of Oregon Library. Biographical information on Wertenbaker can be found in *Sixty Days in a Lifetime* and *Death of a Man*. See also a review essay of *The Death of Kings* by Charles Lee in the *Saturday Review of Literature*, 16 Jan. 1954, pp. 14f; profiles of Wertenbaker are in the *New Yorker*, 26 Dec. 1953, pp. 28–30ff, and 5 June 1954, pp. 73–87; and Max Ascoli's memorial tribute, "Charlie Wertenbaker," in *The Reporter*, 27 Jan. 1955, p. 12. An obituary is in the *New York Times*, 9 Jan. 1955.

ANN T. KEENE

WERTENBAKER, Thomas Jefferson (6 Feb. 1879–22 Apr. 1966), historian and educator, was born in Charlottesville, Virginia, the son of Charles Christian Wertenbaker, a cigar manufacturer, and Francis Thomas Leftwich. He was educated at the University of Virginia: B.A. (1900), M.A. (1902), and Ph.D. in history (1910). His first career was in journalism, working as an editor for the *Baltimore News*, from 1905 to 1906. He again turned to editing, for the *New York Evening Sun*, from 1917 to 1923.

Wertenbaker, who would become one of the best-known American historians of the twentieth century, began his teaching career as an associate professor of history and economics at Texas A & M University from 1907 to 1909. He then returned to the University of Virginia, where in 1909–1910 he served as an instructor and put the finishing touches on his dissertation. In 1910 he was interviewed by Princeton University president Woodrow Wilson for a teaching job in the Department of History. Wilson hired Wertenbaker for $1,000 per year (he was elated with the position but disappointed with the salary). At Princeton, Wertenbaker moved through the professorial ranks to full professor, becoming in 1925 the Jonathan Edwards Professor of History, a chair he held until 1947, and serving as chairman of the Department of History from 1928 to 1936. He married Sarah Rossetter Marshal in 1916; they had one child.

Particularly interested in the early history of his native state, Wertenbaker wrote ten of his major scholarly works on Virginia. Beginning with his doctoral dissertation, which was published as "Patrician and Plebeian in Virginia: The Origins and Development of the Social Classes of the Old Dominion" in *Virginia under the Stuarts, 1607–1688* (1914), he plumbed the many original records of colonial Virginia in the Virginia State Library and during the summers of 1908–1914 in the British Public Records Office. He was instrumental in obtaining copies of these records for the Library of Congress, thus providing new opportunities for American colonial historical research. In his doctoral study he found that the colonial environment modified English social strata and created from largely lower working classes a uniquely American social structure; the Virginia aristocracy was not part of the English aristocracy. By closely examining Bacon's Rebellion in 1676 in Virginia in *Bacon's Rebellion* (1957), Wertenbaker defended the thesis of Philip A. Bruce that the rebellion was a precursor to the Revolution, and that Nathaniel Bacon was a "torchbearer" of democratic thought, who introduced the idea of popular sovereignty against injustice a century before actual revolution. He further argued that the years leading up to the Glorious Revolution were a "critical period" in which hard-won colonial liberties were tested by attempts of the British government to curb the powers of the House of Burgesses. The Glorious Revolution, Wertenbaker concluded in *Bacon's Rebellion*, was of more lasting importance in Virginia than in England.

Wertenbaker's other studies of Virginia ranged from urban development in Norfolk to describing the lifestyle of the tidewater plantations. In his classic work on the Puritans, *The Puritan Oligarchy* (1947), he rejected the terminology "theocracy" and "commonwealth," favoring instead "oligarchy," the rule of many by the few. He found that Puritanism had found a truer expression in Massachusetts than in Old England, and he reinterpreted New England's history accordingly. Later in his career, he used his considerable skills as Bicentennial Historian of Princeton University to write the official history of his institution. In *Princeton, 1746–1896* (1949), he affectionately recounted the pilgrimage of the university from a small college defending the reformed wing of American Calvinism to a progressive school that fostered scientific research and the interaction of scholarship and teaching. For many generations of university history students, *Virginia under the Stuarts* and *The Puritan Oligarchy* were required reading in the American colonial period. His overall thesis concerning the origins of American culture—outlined in *The Founding of American Civilization* (1938)—was that four factors shaped American civilization: foreign inheritance, local conditions, continued contact with Europeans, and the melting-pot phenomenon. He had the good fortune to publish broadly at a time when American historical literature was proliferating at a rapid pace.

Widely recognized for his scholarly contributions, Wertenbaker was a visiting professor at Georg-August Universität in Göttingen in 1931, the Harold V. Harmsworth Professor of American History at Oxford University in 1939–1940, the Anson G. Phelps Lecturer at New York University in 1942, a visiting professor in the American Institute at the University of Munich in 1950–1951, the Thomas Jefferson Research Fellow at the University of Virginia in 1954–1955, and the John Hay Whitney Professor at Hampden Sydney College in 1957–1958. He was awarded distinction by the New Jersey Historical Commission in 1963 for his history of the College of New Jersey. In 1947 he was elected president of the American Historical Association.

Possessed of an affable disposition and a natural sense of humor, Wertenbaker was a popular lecturer. He campaigned for a better understanding of American development, particularly for an improvement in the material well-being of the poorer classes of society. He frequently made reference to America's need to secure its economic place, while giving attention also to its cultural development. He died in Princeton, New Jersey.

• Wertenbaker's personal papers are collected at Princeton University. Among Wertenbaker's works not already mentioned in the text are *Patricians and Plebians in Virginia* (1910), *Planters of Colonial Virginia* (1922), *The First Americans, 1607–1690* (1927), *Stock-Taking of America 1687–1941* (1941), *The Old South: The Founding of American Civilization* (1942), *Father Knickerbocker Rebels: The Story of New York City during the Revolution* (1948), *The Golden Age of Colonial Culture* (1949), *The Government of Virginia in the Seventeenth Century* (1957), *Give Me Liberty: The Struggle for Self Government* (1958), and *The Shaping of Colonial Virginia* (1958). Obituaries are in the *American Historical Review* 71, no. 3 (Apr. 1966): 1542; *American Antiquarian Society* 76, pt. 2 (Oct. 1966): 221–22; and the *New York Times*, 23 Apr. 1966.

WILLIAM H. BRACKNEY

WERTHEIMER, Barbara Mayer (7 Nov. 1925–20 Sept. 1983), labor educator, was born in New York City, the daughter of Max Mayer, a surgeon, and Eleanor Sanford, a photographer, social worker, and dog breeder. She grew up on the Upper West Side and began her career in the labor movement upon graduation from Oberlin College in 1946. That year she married college classmate Valentin Wertheimer, who spent his life working for unions and in 1966 became a vice president of the Amalgamated Clothing Workers of America. They had two children.

From 1946 to 1958 Wertheimer worked for the Amalgamated Clothing Workers of America, first as an organizer, then as associate national education director, and finally as acting national education director. In that role she supervised education programs to train local union leadership. In 1960 she received an M.A. in adult education from New York University and between 1961 and 1966 worked as community services consultant to the New York State Division of Housing and Community Renewal, where her primary interest was training volunteer boards of directors of cooperative housing. In 1966 she began her association with Cornell University's New York State School of Industrial and Labor Relations as a senior extension associate teaching adult education students. It was at Cornell that she made her most lasting contributions to the field of labor education for women.

In 1972 the Ford Foundation awarded Wertheimer and her colleague Anne Nelson a grant to "study barriers that keep working women from participating more fully in the unions to which they belong." In 1975 they published *Trade Union Woman* based on survey data gathered from primarily blue collar unions in New York City. The material was organized into three sections: a survey of 195 locals, in-depth surveys of male and female members of seven locals, and interviews with union leaders. In addition to identifying sociocultural, job-related, and organizational impediments to women's mobility in unions, Wertheimer and Nelson found that "women members do not easily think of themselves or any woman as moving very far up the union leadership ladder." A large proportion of their female sample comprised the sole breadwinners in their families; the authors identified a strong desire of women, especially minority women, for educational programs and leadership training. Arguably the most influential of her three books, *Trade Union Woman* created a model that was followed by researchers elsewhere, and the baseline data in the study helped measure women's progress in unions during the next two decades.

Wertheimer's work on *Trade Union Woman* heightened her commitment to the advancement of working women. Having identified the barriers to women's advancement in trade unions, she devoted herself to addressing those problems. In 1972 she had become founding director of trade union women's studies at Cornell's labor relations school in New York with the help of an initial Ford Foundation grant. This leadership training program for union women included courses, conferences, and a reference center. A colleague noted that Wertheimer's curriculum seemed designed to train students for political activity beyond their unions. Indeed, a follow-up study by Ford showed that many graduates of the program became prominent in union offices as well as in community organizing. Her involvement in the program included administration and the teaching of such courses as women and union leadership, labor history, community skills and education methods, while she continued her research. In 1974 she was one of the founding members of Coalition of Labor Union Women (CLUW), which was designed to increase women's participation in union and political activities. The trade union women's studies program was copied by other universities and led to annual regional summer schools for women workers sponsored jointly by the AFL-CIO and the University and College Labor Education Association.

In 1977 she published *We Were There: The Story of Working Women in America*. Written in a lively, accessible style, the book advocated the addition of women to the mainstream of American history so that, for example, female "cooks, laundresses, secretaries, and scavengers of food" would be added to such historical tableaux as Valley Forge. A synthetic book, it was based on secondary sources, and some scholars found it disappointing. Wertheimer's goal, however, had been to inspire and empower working women, not to enter historiographical debates. She next wrote *Labor Education for Women Workers* (1981), a collection of twenty-three articles dealing with the "nuts and bolts" of creating programs for working women. The book was applauded by labor educators as a "solid resource" on a previously unexplored topic.

Described by one colleague as the "godmother of the women's trade union movement," Wertheimer was committed to making working women full partners in trade unions and to putting women's concerns on labor's agenda. She expressed her deep concern for social justice through her labor movement activities, her books, and her teaching. An intense woman partially driven by a need to prove herself, she was alternately kind and domineering toward her students. Her feminism was always apparent in her unfailing support for female colleagues in the male-dominated fields of labor education and the labor movement. She died of cancer in Lakeville, Connecticut.

• Wertheimer's papers can be found in the archives of the Martin P. Catherwood Library, Cornell University. Information in this essay is based primarily on interviews with Wertheimer's colleagues, friends, and family. An obituary is in the *New York Times*, 22 Sept. 1983.

ANN SCHOFIELD

WERTHEIMER, Max (15 Apr. 1880–12 Oct. 1943), psychologist and philosopher, was born in Prague, Bohemia, the son of Wilhelm Wertheimer, a business educator, and Rosa Zwicker. Wertheimer's father had become financially well off from the success of his private school for individualized instruction in business and accounting; he was also a government consultant (drafting the laws for warehouse practices in Austria-Hungary), was active in the International Order of Oddfellows (a philanthropic and benevolent organization), and was a prominent member of the Jewish community of Prague. His father's civic concerns and educational endeavours undoubtedly influenced Wertheimer during his early years, and his later development of Gestalt theory in part may have reflected the holistic orientation of Jewish cosmology. Wertheimer attended a Catholic elementary school and a municipal high school before enrolling in Charles University in Prague, primarily to study law, in 1898. He changed his studies to philosophy and psychology before transferring to the University of Berlin in 1901. In the spring of 1904 he went to the University of Würzburg, where he obtained his Ph.D. in psychology later that same year.

Between 1904 and 1910, fully supported by his father, Wertheimer worked at psychological and physiological institutes in Berlin, Vienna, Würzburg, and Prague, doing mostly follow-up studies to his doctoral dissertation on the detection of guilt with word-association techniques. In 1910 he undertook experimental studies on the perception of apparent motion at the Frankfurt Institute (soon to become the University of Frankfurt). These studies, published in 1912, became the basis of the new Gestalt school of psychology, a school which soon earned an international reputation, and of which Wertheimer, together with his main experimental subjects in those studies, Wolfgang Köhler and Kurt Koffka, were recognized as leaders. The studies demonstrated that the perception of motion is not the product of the total of individual stimulus elements, but that the visual perception of motion depends upon complex relational features of the entire pattern of visual stimulation. A major tenet of the Gestalt approach has been that a whole (such as perceiving a vertical line as oscillating horizontally) is not the sum of its parts (perception of the line in one position and then in another), nor simply more than the sum of its parts (sensation of the line in both positions plus perception of movement), but entirely different from a mere sum of parts (perceiving the dynamic whole of a single line moving back and forth in a particular manner). A whole (or "Gestalt") is usually such that its parts are not indifferent to each other; most natural Gestalten are integrated systems in which the characteristics of the whole determine the nature of the parts, and minute changes in one part of a dynamic Gestalt can yield dramatic changes in the whole itself (for example, pricking a soap bubble with a pin).

The Gestalt mode of thought, which Wertheimer had already hinted at in a paper on musicology in 1910 and in an article earlier in 1912 on the numerical thinking of natives in non-European cultures, was extended to an analysis of the organization of all of perception, to problem solving and thinking, to personality and motivation, and to social psychology by Wertheimer, Köhler, Koffka, and their students. The Gestalt approach eventually also was applied to epistemology, logic, and other fields of philosophy, and to the analysis of art as well.

Between 1912 and 1929 Wertheimer worked first at the University of Frankfurt and then at the University of Berlin. The Gestalt school became widely viewed as a major rival to the other dominant schools of psychology, such as structuralism, functionalism, psychoanalysis, and behaviorism. During World War I, Wertheimer, as a civilian working for the German military establishment, developed an underwater sound direction finder, a forerunner of sonar, which he, together with his collaborator, Erich von Hornbostel, patented in 1917.

In 1921, with several colleagues, Wertheimer established the journal *Psychologische Forschung* (Psychological Research), which served for decades as the main publication outlet for reports of research in the Gestalt tradition. In 1923, he married a student of his at the University of Berlin, Anna Caro. They had five children, one of whom died shortly after birth; they divorced in 1942.

Wertheimer was called in 1929 from Berlin to the chair in philosophy and psychology at the University of Frankfurt. By early 1933, concerned about the rise of the Nazi party, he went with his family to Marienbad, Czechoslovakia, to wait out developments. When the situation grew even more dim, he accepted a position in New York at the New School for Social Research. He and his family emigrated to the United States in September 1933. He soon heard that he was among the first wave of German university professors to be dismissed by the Nazi regime.

Wertheimer taught at the New School until his death. During the last decade of his life, he published articles providing a Gestalt perspective on such philosophical issues as the nature of truth, ethics, democracy, and freedom, and gave lectures on Gestalt theory at many educational institutions throughout the United States. Partly in cooperation with his friend Albert Einstein, Wertheimer was deeply involved in organized efforts to place refugee scholars from Europe in appropriate positions in the United States, efforts made especially difficult because of the Great Depression. He also completed a book on the Gestalt approach to creativity and problem solving, *Productive Thinking*, on which he had been working for decades and which was published posthumously in 1945. He died at his home in New Rochelle, New York.

A popular, dynamic lecturer, Wertheimer was a founder and proponent of a major school of psychology and philosophy that became a salient point of view in twentieth-century psychology. While that school, as well as its contemporaries, has begun to fade into history, the Gestalt orientation again became prominent during the 1970s and 1980s in the field of cognitive science in the writings of such individuals as Nobel laureate Herbert A. Simon.

• Wertheimer's papers are primarily in two locations. Those at the New School in New York when he died are in the Manuscripts and Archives Division of the New York Public Library, those that were at his home are at the Department of Psychology of the University of Colorado at Boulder. No book-length biography of Max Wertheimer exists, but brief biographical sketches of him, as well as characterizations of Gestalt theory, are in almost every general history of psychology that was in print during the second half of the twentieth century. A number of Wertheimer's more influential papers in English have been reprinted in Mary Henle, ed., *Documents of Gestalt Psychology* (1961), and some earlier articles (in abbreviated form, translated from the German) are in Willis D. Ellis, ed., *A Source Book of Gestalt Psychology* (1938). A complete list of Wertheimer's publications appears as an appendix to the enlarged edition of his *Productive Thinking* (1959; repr. 1982). Obituaries are in the *American Journal of Psychology* 57 (July 1944): 428–35, *Psychological Review* 51 (May 1944): 143–46, and *Social Research* 1, no. 2 (1943): 135–46.

MICHAEL WERTHEIMER

WERTMAN, Sarah Killgore (1 Mar. 1843–21 May 1935), attorney, was born in Jefferson, Clinton County, Missouri, the daughter of attorney and statesman David Killgore and his wife, Elizabeth (maiden name unknown). Raised in a pious Christian home, Killgore graduated in 1862 from Ladoga Seminary and then taught school in Clinton County, not far from her parents' home. In 1869, after years of conversations with her father, Killgore determined to act on her lifelong interest to study law. She enrolled at the Union College of Law in Chicago, Illinois, and transferred to the University of Michigan in 1870. In 1871 she became the first woman to receive the LL.B. from the Law School of the University of Michigan and the first to be admitted to the bar of the supreme court of the state of Michigan. However, three years of rigorous academic life took their toll on Killgore, and she spent the next several years in gradual recuperation before she regained her full health.

Killgore finally began her professional career in 1875 when she married attorney Jackson S. Wertman and joined his law office in Indianapolis. Excluded because of her sex from practicing before the bar in the state of Indiana, she helped her husband in his law practice by doing real estate law in his office. Like other nineteenth-century women lawyers who were married to lawyers, Wertman entered legal practice through marriage but remained in the private arena of the law office while her husband made public appearances in the courtroom. Moreover, Wertman believed in the virtue of this sexual division of labor. To her, it was all-encompassing, extending well beyond the physical boundaries of her law office to the realm of women's professional goals and principles. Wertman believed that women lawyers had a unique professional role, which was to elevate the legal profession beyond the "selfish aggrandisement" of so many male lawyers. In a letter to the Equity Club on 7 May 1888 Wertman wrote, "The wrecks of manhood strewn all along the shoals of this occupation tell plainly how much *principle* has been sacrificed for success." She called on women to lift "the profession to higher and nobler purposes." "Ours the part to give to the profession the love-lit hues of Christ's teaching so beautifully set forth in the 'Golden Rule'" (quoted in Drachman, p. 138).

The Wertmans moved to Ashland, Ohio, and started a family in 1878. Two of her three babies survived infancy, and Sarah Killgore Wertman, following her mother's example of domestic duty, left her legal career to assume the responsibilities of full-time child-rearing. When her son and daughter reached young adulthood, Wertman resumed her legal career. She was admitted to the Ohio bar in 1893 and returned to her practice as a real estate lawyer in her husband's law office.

The Wertmans followed their children to Seattle, Washington, and established a home there by 1905. Jackson Wertman reestablished his legal career in the new location, but Sarah Wertman chose not to continue hers. After the deaths of her husband and daughter, she lived her remaining years with her son's family. She kept an active interest in University of Michigan alumni affairs, and in 1928 she pledged financial support to construct a women's building on the campus in Ann Arbor. In her spare time she followed a heavy schedule of religious reading. She died in Seattle.

• A biographical sketch of Wertman as well as her Equity Club letter of 7 May 1888 are in Virginia G. Drachman, ed., *Women Lawyers and the Origins of Professional Identity* (1993). See also Frances E. Willard and Mary Livermore, eds., *A Woman of the Century* (1893); "First Woman Lawyer of Country Resides in Seattle," *Seattle Daily Journal of Commerce*, 6 June 1925; "Michigan's First Woman Lawyer," *Michigan Bar Journal*, 63 (1984): 448; and Donald Thompson, "Sarah Killgore Law Graduate," *Montgomery County Magazine*, Dec. 1988.

VIRGINIA G. DRACHMAN

WESCOTT, Glenway (11 Apr. 1901–22 Feb. 1987), author, was born in Kewaskum, Wisconsin, the son of Bruce Peters Wescott and Josephine Gordon, farmers. Because of a difficult early relationship with his father, who had difficulty accepting his son's homosexuality and artistic temperament, Wescott spent part of his high school years living with other relatives. He entered the University of Chicago in 1917 but left after a year and a half to begin a series of journeys that occupied him until 1933. Starting with a trip to New Mexico in 1919 to stay with the poet Yvor Winters, Wescott later left the Midwest to live in New York and Massachusetts; he then left the United States, living in England and Germany and in 1925 joining the expatriates in Paris, where he resided until 1933. During these years he supported himself as a private secretary, a companion to the publisher Monroe Wheeler, and as an author of poetry, fiction, travel writing, and numerous reviews for such little magazines as the *New Republic*, the *Dial*, *Poetry*, and the *Transatlantic Review*.

Although his early publications included two books of poetry, Wescott is known for his fiction, starting with *The Apple of the Eye* (1924), a three-part lyric novel set in Wisconsin and published when he was twenty-three. His first real literary success came with his Harper's Prize novel *The Grandmothers* (1927), a precise and intricate evocation of the Midwest, written from the point of view of a semiautobiographical character, Alwyn Tower. At the center of this book, published in England under its American subtitle, "A Family Portrait," are twelve depictions of individual members of the Tower family, described in almost photographic detail, which together form a group portrait of the Midwest and of America.

When in the next year Wescott published *Good-Bye Wisconsin* (1928), a collection of ten short stories and the title essay, he seemed to be heading for a major place on the American literary scene. By 1933, however, most of his early promise seemed wasted. His nonfiction books *Fear and Trembling* and *A Calendar of Saints for Unbelievers*, both published in 1932, had been condemned everywhere as failures; he had been parodied as the ineffectual character Robert Prentiss in Ernest Hemingway's *The Sun Also Rises*; and he had been described by Gertrude Stein in *The Autobiography of Alice B. Toklas* as having "a certain syrup but it does not pour."

Returning to the United States in 1933, he stopped publishing altogether until 1940, when his ballet libretto, *The Dream of Audubon* appeared. Living in New York City, Wescott sustained himself through the generosity of family and friends, sharing apartment space with his brother, Lloyd Wescott, Lloyd's wife, Barbara Harrison, as well as with Monroe Wheeler and George Lynes. His second major work of fiction, *The Pilgrim Hawk*, a novella, also appeared in 1940 and was well received for its polished language and understated tension. Again featuring Alwyn Tower as a narrator, this time writing from the United States about events that happened in Europe, *The Pilgrim Hawk* consists of a complex web of symbolic events, many involving falconry and the hawk of the title, whose attempts at escape reflect similar patterns in the interwoven lives of the three main characters.

In 1943 Wescott moved to family-owned land in New Jersey, where he lived for the remainder of his life, publishing a last novel, *Apartment in Athens*, in 1945 and little else except for essays, reviews, and introductions to collections he edited: *The Maugham Reader* (1950) and *Short Novels of Colette* (1951). In 1962 he published his last book, *Images of Truth*, a collection of personal essays, including long tributes to friends whose work he admired: Katherine Anne Porter, Colette, Isak Dinesen, and Thornton Wilder.

Although he wrote little else before his death in Rosemont, New Jersey, Wescott was an active literary figure, often appearing on radio and television programs, giving informal talks about the novel, serving on committees for the Authors' Guild, UNESCO, the Authors' League of America, and as president of the National Institute of Arts and Letters from 1959 until 1962.

Wescott was a classic minor figure in American literary history. Although his career spanned Imagist poetry, midwestern regionalism, and the expatriate movement, he is remembered only for *The Grandmothers* and *The Pilgrim Hawk*. Speculation about his failure to publish more fiction after 1945 (he is rumored to have written numerous unpublished novels) centers on his statement, "My talent has not seemed equal to my opportunities or proportionate to my ideas and ideals."

• See Sy M. Kahn's "Glenway Wescott: A Bibliography" in *Bulletin of Bibliography* 22 (1956–1959): 156–60. The only book-length studies are William H. Rueckert, *Glenway Wescott* (1965), and Ira Johnson, *Glenway Wescott: The Paradox of Voice* (1971). Obituaries are in the *New York Times*, 24 Feb. 1987, and *New Criterion*, May 1987.

TIMOTHY DOW ADAMS

WESLEY, Charles Harris (2 Dec. 1891–16 Aug. 1987), historian and educator, was born in Louisville, Kentucky, the son of Charles Snowden Wesley, an undertaker, and Matilda Harris, a seamstress and later a secretary. His father, who died in 1902, had worked in an "undertaking establishment under his stepfather who had a large funeral plant with a showroom, a chapel, embalming room and a stable for horses and carriages." Wesley's mother referred to his father as a "brilliant conversationalist." When he was a child his mother sang in the choir of Quinn Chapel African Methodist Episcopal Church. After his father's death Wesley's maternal grandfather became his "father figure." Wesley received his early education in Louisville. Around 1906, at age fourteen, he entered the Fisk Preparatory School, where he was active with the Fisk Jubilee Singers. Wesley appeared with this group at the 1911 World's Fair in Boston. In 1912 a recording of the group was made with Columbia Broadcasting Company, under the name of Aeolian Quartette, which included Roland Hayes. Three double-sized records were recorded. Music played a major role in Wesley's life; he sang in many church choirs that performed concerts while he attended Yale.

In his unpublished autobiography Wesley wrote, "I heard W. E. B. Du Bois deliver an address which has continued its echoes in my life and career. The title of this address was *Galileo Galilei*." It was delivered to the Fisk graduating class of 1908. He continued, "I had read *Souls of Black Folk* again and again, across my years, loved its balanced phrases, colorful writing, its argumentative expressions, and recognized no harmful effects on me or others."

In 1911 he received a bachelor of arts degree in classics with honors from Fisk University. That same year he enrolled in the Graduate School at Yale University at age nineteen. He wrote that his work in Negro history began with his graduate studies at Yale and that he had decided to prepare himself for college teaching; in 1913 he received a master of arts degree in economics. His courses in 1912–1913 were "Economics, the History of Economics, Corporation Economics, Value Prices and Distribution, Insurance and Science of Society," and he was a student in a Civil War and Reconstruction course. He wrote two theses, "The Rise of the Life Insurance Idea among Black Americans" and "The Struggle for the Recognition of Hayti [*sic*] and Liberia as Independent Republics." He wrote, "Through all of the past years of teaching and study there was one basic theme which remained with me. It was the history of the people who had come from Africa to the Americas. I had known that their written history was incomplete and I had also known that it should be written, printed, read and studied." Wesley was invited to join the Department of History at Howard University, and he accepted, becoming instructor in the teaching of history and modern languages. He completed postgraduate work at the Guild Internationale, Paris, in the summer of 1914. Later that year he married Louise Johnson in Baltimore; the couple had two daughters.

His earliest published articles included "The Teacher's Point of View in the Study and Teaching of History," which appeared in *Education* (34 [Apr. 1914]: 509–13); "Interest in a Neglected Phase of History," which was published in the *African Methodist Episcopal Review* (32 [Apr. 1916]: 263–68); "The Problem of Sources and Methods in History Teaching," which appeared in *School Review* (24 [May 1916]: 329–41); and "The Struggle for the Recognition of Haiti and Liberia as Independent Republics," in the *Journal of Negro History* (2 [Oct. 1917]: 369–83). Wesley wrote that this "was a first publication to appear on the subject of the recognition of these two black republics. Their effort to obtain recognition and acceptance as independent governments had no prior publication."

From 1913 to 1917 Wesley was instructor of the teaching of history and modern languages in the Teachers College at Howard University. He taught elementary and advanced French, modern European history, and literature of American history, with special lectures that considered the contributions of blacks to American civilization. He also taught courses in educational sociology, social problems of education, education and modern social problems, and rural social problems. In 1917–1918 he was assistant professor of history and in 1919–1920 associate professor of history at Howard University. In 1921 he was appointed professor of history and head of the department.

In 1916 he became a member of the Metropolitan African Methodist Episcopal Church and was invited to become the director of the choir. From 1918 to 1923 he was the pastor at Ebenezer AME Church in Georgetown, District of Columbia, although he was not an ordained minister. From 1923 to 1928 he served as pastor of the Campbell AME Church in Anacostia, Washington, D.C. In 1928 Bishop J. Albert Johnson made him the presiding elder of the church in the District of Columbia and nearby parts of Maryland.

Wesley attended Harvard University as an Austin scholar for the academic year 1920–1921 and received in 1925 the doctor of philosophy degree in history, becoming only the fourth African American to receive a doctorate from Harvard, following in the footsteps of W. E. B. Du Bois (1895), Carter G. Woodson (1912), and Alain Leroy Locke (1918). His Harvard dissertation, "Negro Labor in the United States, 1850–1925," was published in 1927 under the title *Negro Labor in the United States: A Study in American Economic History*. This work was received with great acclaim as a much-needed reference book on African Americans in the industrial United States. The *New York Times* wrote that the book made a valuable contribution to the economic history of the United States that will be useful to students of labor problems and economic development. In 1930–1931 Wesley was awarded a Guggenheim fellowship for a study of emancipation in the British West Indies from 1807 to 1838.

At Howard University from 1937 to 1938 Wesley was acting dean of the College of Liberal Arts and from 1938 to 1942 served as dean of the graduate school. In 1942 he was appointed president of Wilberforce University, "the premier and oldest institution of learning in America owned and operated by people of African descent." In 1947 the Ohio state trustees elected him president of the College of Education and Industrial Arts, which in 1951 became Central State College. Wesley wrote, "Thus we began a new college on an old campus. It was a college separated from Wilberforce University by a ravine." He remained there until his retirement in 1965.

In 1931–1940 Wesley served as general president of Alpha Phi Alpha fraternity. From 1950 to 1972 he was affiliated with the Association for the Study of Negro (now Afro-American) Life and History, which was founded by his friend Carter G. Woodson in 1915. He was the president from 1950 to 1965. Later he was appointed director of research and publications, and he was the executive director from 1965 to 1972. From 1931 to 1940 Wesley served as general president of Alpha Phi Alpha, and in 1953 he received a Phi Beta Kappa key. He received honorary degrees from fourteen colleges and universities.

Wesley authored and coauthored more than twelve books and monographs and published more than 125 articles in his lifetime. He updated *The Story of the Negro Retold* (1959) and *Negro in Our History* (1962), authored by Woodson. He wrote *The History of Alpha Phi Alpha: A Development in Negro College Life* (1929), the first book on any black college fraternity, published by Howard University Press. It was also the first appearance of a study of a selected group of African-American college men and the first comprehensive history of the oldest black college fraternity. The twelfth edition was printed in 1975. Other book titles include *Richard Allen: Apostle of Freedom* (1935), *The Collapse of the Confederacy* (1937), *The History of the Prince Hall Grand Lodge of the Free and Accepted Masons of the State of Ohio, 1849–1960* (1961), *Henry A. Callis* (1977), and *Prince Hall: Life and Legacy* (1983). He was also the editor in chief of the ten-volume set *The International Library of Negro Life and History* (1968). His last publication was *The History of the National Association of Colored Women's Clubs: A Legacy of Service* (1984). Wesley stated, "I wrote about Black History and pushed African History forward, for I knew that in the long run we would win and truth would conquer."

His wife died in 1973, and Wesley married Dorothy Louise Burnett Porter in 1979. They had no children together. The mayor of the District of Columbia declared 2 December 1981 "Charles H. Wesley Day." Wesley died in Washington, D.C.

Michael R. Winston, noted historian, eulogized Wesley as "one of history's great teachers. Not simply a teacher of history, but a man so gifted, so grounded, so centered in his spirit that he was of our time and all time."

• The majority of Wesley's papers, including his unpublished, unpaginated "Autobiography," are in the Dorothy Porter Wesley Archives at the Wesport Foundation and Gallery, Washington, D.C. For biographical information see Benjamin Quarles, "Charles Harris Wesley," *Proceedings of the American Antiquarian Society* 97 (1987): 275–79; Michael Winston et al., "The Life and Times of Charles Harris Wesley," *Boulé Journal* 51 (1987): 17–23, which is the cover story; Michael J. Price, "Charles Harris Wesley," *Sphinx* 68 (1982): 14–19, 21, 23, 24–28; "Charles H. Wesley," *Black Historian* (1971); James G. Spady, "Dr. Charles H. Wesley, Alpha Phi Alpha Fraternity and the Propagation of Black History," *Philadelphia New Observer*, 26 Feb. 1992; "Wesley Delivers Charter Day Address," *Hilltop*, 7 Mar. 1980; and "University's History Noted by Honored Educator," *Washington Afro-American*, 8 Mar. 1980. An obituary is in *Phylaxis News Quarterly* (Summer 1987): 3–4.

CONSTANCE PORTER UZELAC

WESSELHOEFT, Conrad (23 Mar. 1834–17 Dec. 1904), physician and educator, was born in Weimar, Germany, the son of Robert Wesselhoeft and Ferdinanda Emilia Hecker. His father, who became a physician after leaving Prussia, had been a lawyer in Weimar and an officer of the government. Robert Wesselhoeft's liberal principles and support for German unification resulted in his expulsion from Weimar, and he immigrated to the United States with his family in 1840, eventually settling in Cambridge, Massachusetts. Wesselhoeft's father and uncle William Wesselhoeft, M.D., founded the Brattleboro, Vermont, water cure establishment in 1846.

At the age of fifteen, Wesselhoeft was sent to Leipzig to acquire a classical education at the St. Thomas Gymnasium. Graduating at the head of his class, he returned to Cambridge upon the death of his father and soon after entered Harvard Medical School. Simultaneously, under the tutelage of his Uncle William, Wesselhoeft became interested in and began to study the principles and therapeutics of homeopathy. By this time, William Wesselhoeft had become one of Boston's leading homeopathic physicians, yet he shepherded his sons and nephews through Harvard's medical school for two specific reasons. He valued its scholarly curriculum in science and philosophy; and, assuming they would embrace homeopathy, he wished his young protégés to know all they could about the "errors" they would later oppose.

Popular in Boston and in most urban areas of the Northeast and Midwest at this time, homeopathy offered a comprehensive philosophy of healing and a therapeutic alternative to the prescriptions of large doses of noxious drugs so common to medical practice in the nineteenth century. Homeopathic physicians sought to cure disease by the administration of minute quantities of purified drugs that induced in the human organism symptoms or conditions similar to the disease itself. After much study and investigation of the theories of Samuel Christian Hahnemann, an early nineteenth-century German physician and the founder of homeopathy, Conrad Wesselhoeft became an enthusiastic advocate for, and occasional critic of, the new system of medicine.

After receiving an M.D. from Harvard in 1856, Wesselhoeft established a medical practice in Dorchester, Massachusetts, where he met and married Lily (Elizabeth) Foster Pope in 1863, they had one child. Within a few years the couple moved from the sparsely populated suburb to the city of Boston, where Wesselhoeft enlarged both his practice and his sphere of activity in homeopathic organizations.

Conrad Wesselhoeft's name soon became synonymous with the practice of homeopathy in New England, and he attracted such prominent patients as the Alcott family; Louisa May Alcott dedicated her last novel, *Jo's Boys* to Wesselhoeft, both her friend and longtime physician. Having developed a thriving medical practice in Boston, he worked tirelessly toward the establishment and success of homeopathic institutions there. He helped organize and served in the Boston Homeopathic Dispensary from its beginning in 1856 and was a longtime member of the medical staff of the Massachusetts Homeopathic Hospital, which he served as a trustee (1871–1900) and vice president (1901–1904). He was one of the founders of New England's first homeopathic medical college, at Boston University, in 1873 and served on its faculty throughout his professional career, first as professor of materia medica and therapeutics and later as professor of pathology and practice. He was also chairman of the consulting board of physicians and surgeons of the Westborough Insane Asylum in Westborough, Massachusetts.

His professional affiliations include founding member and past president of the Boston Homeopathic Medical Society, member and president (1872) of the Massachusetts Homeopathic Medical Society, and member and president (1879) of the American Institute of Homeopathy. He served as chairman of the Bureau of Materia Medica of the latter organization from 1866 to 1873 and from 1875 to 1877.

Although he was convinced of the superiority of homeopathy as a medical system, Wesselhoeft did not hesitate to expose and investigate what he considered its weaknesses. Perhaps spurred by his own careful translation in 1876 of Hahnemann's fifth edition of the *Organon of Rational Healing*, Wesselhoeft developed a keen interest in drug pathogenesy and through research sought to establish a scientific basis for the homeopathic knowledge of drug power. He was critical of associates who based their practice and opinions on untested hypotheses of Hahnemann or on their own limited experience. He advocated more rigorous methods in the proving of drugs for the homeopathic materia medica, including the comparison of accepted test results with control groups using placebos.

Wesselhoeft's many contributions to various homeopathic medical journals and his numerous scientific papers read before the American Institute of Homeopathy recorded his research into drug divisibility and potency and his interest in the accurate proving of drugs. Among the most important of these, *A Plea for a Standard Limit of Attenuated Doses* (1881) and "Demands of Modern Science in the Work of Drug Proving" (*American Institute of Homeopathy Transactions* [1891]: 513–30) were calls to his fellow homeopathic physicians to supplant accepted belief by the acquisition of sound knowledge through scientific means.

Wesselhoeft remained an outspoken critic of those homeopaths who were consumed with achieving and prescribing extremely high-potency remedies without paying equal attention to rigorously testing their efficacy. In "The Dose and Degree of Attenuation," a report he read as president of the American Institute of Homeopathy at its 1879 meeting, Wesselhoeft lamented that "the accurate proving of drugs has received but slight attention in comparison with the zeal displayed in the invention of new methods of attenuation" and warned that "unsubstantiated assertions of the superiority of highly potentized medicines" would contribute to inaccuracies of the materia medica. His conclusions regarding the limits of drug divisibility aroused vigorous opposition from many of his colleagues.

Despite the fact that Wesselhoeft's continuous questioning and testing of accepted knowledge cost him friendships and earned him the opposition of many in the homeopathic profession, it was largely through his efforts and direction that the institute undertook the considerable task of updating the homeopathic materia medica. Wesselhoeft was also coeditor of two major homeopathic publications that contributed to the knowledge of therapeutics: the *Cyclopedia of Drug Pathogenesy*, issued under the auspices of the British Homeopathic Society and the American Institute of Homeopathy from 1886 to 1891, and the *Pharmacopeia of the American Institute of Homoeopathy* (1897).

Intolerance of homeopaths by regular physicians was stimulated by the Consultation Clause of the Code of Ethics formulated by the American Medical Association in 1847, prohibiting consultation with "irregular" physicians. But by the end of the century, leaders in both the regular and homeopathic professions believed that the dictates of science rather than adherence to outworn ethical codes or dogmatic principles would direct medical practice. Wesselhoeft was convinced that carefully tested drugs applied according to the Law of Similars would be validated by modern science and urged both homeopaths and regulars to exhibit tolerance, respect, and better understanding of their respective schools of medicine. Only then, he said, would physicians reach the goal for which they were all striving—the cure of the sick.

A recognized leader and respected physician within the profession, Wesselhoeft was honored in Boston by colleagues throughout the United States on the occasion of his seventieth birthday. Nine months later, he died at his home in Newton Centre, Massachusetts.

• Much of Wesselhoeft's research, presented as scholarly papers at the annual meetings of the American Institute of Homeopathy, is reprinted in the *Transactions of the American Institute of Homeopathy* between 1867 and 1902. Included in this group are his reports as chairman of the Bureau of Materia Medica, Pharmacy and Provings. His *Reproving of Carbo Vegetabilis* (1877) made a case for the necessity of control tests in the proving of drugs. His books, pamphlets, and medical imprints are listed in Francesco Cordasco, *Homeopathy in the United States: A Bibliography of Homoeopathic Medical Imprints, 1825–1925* (1991), and Thomas Lindsley Bradford, *Homoeopathic Bibliography of the United States from the Year 1825 to 1891, Inclusive* (1892). Articles on his life and career appear in *The New England Medical Gazette*, Jan. 1905, pp. 25–32; *Hahnemannian Monthly*, Feb. 1905; *Transactions of the American Institute of Homoeopathy* (1905): 821–26; and *Medical Century*, May 1904. A short biography of Wesselhoeft that places him in the context of homeopathy in Massachusetts is in William Harvey King, ed., *History of Homoeopathy and Its Institutions in America*, vol. 3, pp. 159–93, and vol. 4, p. 403 (1905). For more detailed information on the Wesselhoeft family in Germany and their resettlement in the United States, see Thomas Lindsley Bradford, *The Pioneers of Homoeopathy* (1897).

ANNE TAYLOR KIRSCHMANN

WEST, Anthony (4 Aug. 1914–27 Dec. 1987), writer, was born in Hunstanton, Norfolk, England, the son of H. G. Wells, a novelist and journalist, and Rebecca West, a novelist and critic. Born out of wedlock, West remained with his mother throughout his infancy and adolescence. Wells, still married and the father of two sons, visited West sporadically. West attended several private schools. In 1936 he married the British painter Katharine Church, with whom he had a son and a daughter. He had aspired to be a painter, but by 1937 he determined on a writing career, instead, and began as a reviewer for the *New Statesman*.

West excited attention as a promising novelist when his first novel, *The Vintage*, won both the Eyre and Spottiswode Fellowship and the Houghton Mifflin-Esquire Award in 1949. Influenced by his mentor, the novelist Graham Greene, West probed in his second novel, *Another Kind* (1951), a vision of England as a great power in decline, vulnerable to antidemocratic forces. His heroes were latter-day romantic questers, self-questioning and guilty about their rejection of home, family, and other conventional values. As a character remarks to the hero of *The Vintage*: "You are too much the Byronic romantic figure. Who called on you to put yourself under a curse." This suspect romanticism evolved into melancholy characters who were unable to act decisively, and who had an air of what is called in *The Vintage* "Byronic pseudo personality."

West's personal life is crucial to an understanding of his writing and his theory of fiction. He never got over his childhood in England, where illegitimacy was still considered shameful and had to be concealed to protect both the child and his parents. In public Rebecca West camouflaged her identity as his mother, and even in private insisted that he call her "Auntie Panther," Panther being the nickname that Wells and her intimate friends used for her. Not until his late adolescence was West allowed to use the term mother. Wells, already embarrassed by public revelations of his affairs with other women and by the birth of an illegitimate daughter, visited his son secretly and did not invite him to his home until his wife died in 1927.

West blamed his mother more than his father for this tense state of affairs, believing that she was jealous of Wells and did what she could to keep father and son apart. This was the line he took in several essays and works of fiction after she refused, in 1949, to allow him to acknowledge himself as the son of Rebecca West and H. G. Wells on the jacket flap of his first novel. Wells had died in 1946, and West heaped all of his hurt feelings on his mother. This hostile view of her was shared by both of his wives. West's first marriage ended in divorce in 1952, and that year he married Lily Emmet, an American, with whom he also had a son and daughter.

West aimed to broaden the scope of his writing when he moved to the United States in 1950. There he became a prominent reviewer for the *New Yorker*, establishing a reputation as a formidable commentator on contemporary writing, exemplified in his collection *Principles & Persuasions: The Literary Essays of Anthony West* (1957). He also assessed the work of historical figures such as Winston Churchill, Chief Justice Charles Evans Hughes, and Florence Nightingale. But he is perhaps best known for his assaults on popular culture, avowing in the introduction to *Principles & Persuasions*: "The fact that many people enjoy pap, its softness, its blandness, and its digestibility, and that some people put a great deal of sincerity and intensity into making the best pap they can is beside the point—it is a weakening and debilitating form of food."

West's later work marked a return to literary themes and to the issues that had stimulated his decision to become a writer. *Heritage* (1955) is a thinly disguised novel about his unhappy upbringing and divided feelings about his famous parents. The novel, *David Rees, among Others* (1970), is a companion piece to *Heritage*, and *H. G. Wells: Aspects of a Life* (1984), completes West's trilogy about himself and his parents. The volume reflects his lifelong sorrow and bitterness about his illegitimacy and his parents' reaction to it. In *Mortal Wounds* (1973) West discussed literary figures such as Marcel Proust, George Sand, and Madame Anne-Louise-Germaine de Staël in order to elaborate his theory that fiction often is the author's way of taking revenge on those who have upset his or her life.

West's upbringing influenced not only what he wrote but also his view of literature. He treated his fiction and that of others as a species of autobiography and game playing, fully working out this theory in *Mortal Wounds* and pressing it with savage wit in *H. G. Wells: Aspects of a Life*.

A few years after the death of his mother in 1983, and just before he died at his Stonington, Connecticut, home, West admitted that he could not give up the struggle with the memory of his mother and father, remarking in *Publishers Weekly* (20 Apr. 1984) that "there was quite a richness in the conflict of personalities that I learned a good deal from."

West's novels were too fitfully produced and lacked the full-blown array of living characters required to make a lasting contribution to the genre. His work will be read more for its autobiographical value than its literary achievement. West is best remembered for his penetrating and witty essays in the *New Yorker*. His twenty-year presence in the magazine allowed him the opportunity to stamp his learned and shrewd sensibility on an era.

• Most of West's papers remain in the possession of his second wife. Some of his letters, however, are in the Rebecca West archive in the Beinecke Library, Yale University. West published *The Trend Is Up*, a novel, in 1960, and numerous magazine articles. His life and work are briefly discussed in Victoria Glendinning, *Rebecca West: A Biography* (1987), and in Carl Rollyson, *Rebecca West: A Life* (1996). An obituary appears in the *New York Times*, 28 Dec. 1987.

CARL ROLLYSON

WEST, Benjamin (Mar. 1730–26 Aug. 1813), astronomer and mathematician, was born in Rehoboth, Massachusetts, the son of John West, a farmer. His mother's name is not known. Not long after his birth, the family moved to Bristol, Rhode Island, where West worked discontentedly on the family farm. West attended the town school for only three months and took a course of navigation offered by Captain Woodbury, who waived his fees for the poor farm boy. Otherwise, West was self-educated, borrowing books from local parsons' libraries. In 1753 he married Elizabeth Smith; they had eight children. That same year West moved to Providence, Rhode Island, where he opened a private school, and then a dry-goods store that also sold books and was, by some accounts, the first bookstore in town. After nearly twenty years, his business failed and his effects were seized by creditors. His bankruptcy appears to have been a consequence of the depreciation of paper currency and the decline in transatlantic commerce just before the American Revolution. After his bankruptcy, some Bostonians offered to set him up in the book business again, but West doubted he could support his growing family this way. As a patriot, he chose to manufacture clothing for the American troops during the war. At war's end, he reopened his school in Providence.

What sustained West during the lean years of his business was the compilation of almanacs, beginning with one published in 1763 by William Goddard on Providence's first printing press. West explained that his purpose was to keep Rhode Island money in the colony by providing its citizens with an almanac that was published locally. With the 1764 issue, this work became known as the *New England Almanack*. West's astronomical calculations won wide acclaim for accuracy, and he contributed to almanacs published simultaneously for the meridians of Providence, Boston, and Halifax, Nova Scotia. As early as 1768, West borrowed the name "Isaac Bickerstaff" from a satire by Jonathan Swift making fun of John Partridge, a famous astrologer and author of a popular English almanac, and issued almanacs under this pseudonym. Although West contributed to perhaps as many as 200 almanacs between 1763 and 1806, his production is difficult to delineate. Sometimes he furnished calculations under different names to rival printers. Other works bearing his name or pseudonym were pirated.

Among his other scientific accomplishments, in 1769 West observed the transit of Venus, an event that was of use in determining the dimensions of the solar system. West used a three-foot reflecting telescope with adjustable cross hairs, a micrometer, and other refinements; a sextant; and two good clocks. The observations were financed by Joseph Brown, a businessman who pursued natural philosophy. Brown refused to pay for publication of the results until West inserted a long footnote praising Brown's genius. When West referred to Brown's "genius," he was being sarcastic, although it is likely that few readers understood this. For the most part, West left his meaning vague, but he did acknowledge Brown's mechanical skills and generosity in the cause of science. Copies of the pamphlet were sent to the Royal Society and the American Philosophical Society, which reprinted much of it in its *Transactions*. In 1781 West sent a paper on the extraction of roots of odd powers to the American Academy of Arts and Sciences and was elected a member. He communicated observations of comets to Harvard University professor John Winthrop as early as 1766 and discussed problems of natural philosophy and navigation with others.

West yearned to be appointed a science professor at Rhode-Island College (now Brown University), but he was twice passed over before achieving his goal, first in 1769 when the college named David Howell professor of natural philosophy and then in 1784 when Brown was asked to serve as professor of mathematics and astronomy. West was offered Brown's job in 1786, the year after Brown's death. Perhaps out of resentment or because of the meager salary, West did not assume his chair right away and in March 1787 became professor of mathematics at the Protestant Episcopal Academy of Philadelphia. As a teacher there, he was praised for doing away with the cudgel and for treating students as civilized gentlemen. In Philadelphia, he enjoyed the company of Benjamin Franklin and astronomer David Rittenhouse. Because his wife refused to leave Providence, West passed up a professorship of mathematics at King's College (now Columbia University) and returned to Rhode-Island College to begin his duties in 1788. In 1798 he was named professor of mathematics and natural philosophy. When his appointment was not renewed in 1799, West opened a school of navigation at his home. Between 1802 and 1813 he served as postmaster of Providence.

West received several honorary degrees and was a fellow of the American Association for the Advancement of Science. The Benjamin West named in the rolls of the American Philosophical Society was not he, however, but the artist who died in 1820. West was a member of the Pennsylvania Society for the Abolition of Slavery, despite living in Rhode Island where the slave trade flourished. His health deteriorated after the death of his wife in 1810, and he died in Providence three years later.

• Among West's more important works are *An Account of the Observation of Venus upon the Sun, the Third Day of June, 1769, at Providence, in New-England. With Some Account of the Use of Those Observations* (1769), which is partially reprinted in the *Transactions of the American Philosophical Society* 1 (1771): 97–105; "An Account of the Observations Made in Providence, in the State of Rhode-Island, of the Eclipse of the Sun, Which Happened the 23d Day of April, 1781," *Memoirs of the American Academy of Arts and Sciences* 1 (1785): 156–58; and "On the Extraction of Roots," *Memoirs of the American Academy of Arts and Sciences* 1 (1785): 165–72. West provided calculations for the *New England Almanack* (Providence: 1763–1781), *Bickerstaff's Boston Almanack* (Boston: 1768–1779, 1783–1793), *The North-American Calendar: or, The Rhode Island Almanack* (Providence: 1781–1788), *An Astronomical Diary* (Hartford and Boston: 1785–1797), *Town and Country Almanack* (Norwich, Conn.: 1795–1799), and *The Rhode Island Almanack* (Newport: 1804–1806), among others. For details, see Marion B. Stowell, *Early American Almanacs: The Colonial Weekday Bible* (1977). On West's life, see also "Biography of Benjamin West, LL.D. A.A.S., Professor of Mathematicks, Astronomy and Natural Philosophy in Rhode-Island College and Fellow of the Philosophical Society of Philadelphia," *Rhode Island Literary Repository* 1, no. 7 (Oct. 1814): 137–60; and Clifford K. Shipton, "Benjamin West," in *Sibley's Harvard Graduates*, vol. 12 (1962), pp. 220–26. A portrait is preserved at Brown University.

SARA SCHECHNER GENUTH

WEST, Benjamin (10 Oct. 1738–11 Mar. 1820), painter, was born in Springfield, Pennsylvania, the son of John West, an innkeeper, and his second wife, Sarah Pearson. Although both his parents had Quaker backgrounds and Springfield was a Quaker community, West was not himself a Quaker. As a boy he had some encouragement from an obscure English-born artist, William Williams, and from John Valentine Haidt, a German-born artist living in the Moravian community in Bethlehem, Pennsylvania. Shortly after 1750, primarily in Philadelphia but with periods in Lancaster, Pennsylvania, and in New York, West started to paint portraits, modeling them initially, it appears, on the example of Robert Feke and subsequently, and more obviously, on that of the peripatetic John Wollaston, who visited Philadelphia in 1752 and 1758. More original than West's portraits—and prophetic of his future activity as a history painter—is a *Death of Socrates* (private collection) painted in 1756, which he awkwardly adapted from an engraving by Hubert Gravelot in Charles Rollin's *Ancient History*. Sight of this painting supposedly prompted the Reverend William Smith, provost of the recently founded College of Philadelphia (now the University of Pennsylvania), to invite West to study with him and receive some elements of a classical education. West, however, was not a regular student at the college, and his overall education was thin.

In 1760 Smith arranged passage for West to Italy. In Rome the young American discovered a cultivated circle of connoisseurs, collectors, and artists, among them the German painter Anton Raphael Mengs, who was painting the first monuments of the nascent neoclassical style and who soon would be described by West as his favorite master. West's stay in Italy was plagued by ill health, but he did visit Florence, Parma, Bologna, and Venice in a course of study prescribed by Mengs, and he painted several copies, chiefly after old masters but including two after Mengs. He also painted a few portraits of American and English visitors to Italy.

Although West had initially planned to return to America from Italy, in the summer of 1763 he traveled via Paris to London. There, following the successful exhibition of three pictures at the Society of Artists (a precursor of the Royal Academy) in the spring of 1764, he made the decision to stay in England. His American fiancée, Elizabeth Shewell, joined him, and they were married in September 1764. Accompanying her on her voyage were West's father, who resettled in England, and her cousin, the painter Matthew Pratt, who became the first of West's American pupils. In London, where he remained for the rest of his life, West rapidly became magnet, model, and teacher for three generations of American artists who came to London to study under him, from Pratt and Charles Willson Peale in the 1760s to Charles Robert Leslie in 1811. Two of them, Gilbert Stuart and John Trumbull, worked for long periods as West's studio assistants in the 1770s and 1780s. West's only children, two sons, born in 1766 and 1772, also assisted their father in his later years.

West's output in England included numerous portraits, but he made his reputation as a painter of historical subjects. His first paintings to achieve major fame were *The Landing of Agrippina at Brundisium with the Ashes of Germanicus* of 1768 (Yale University Art Gallery) and *The Departure of Regulus from Rome* of 1769 (Royal Collection). Both show inspiring examples of virtuous behavior drawn from the history of ancient Rome, and both are painted in a severe, sober, dignified style reflecting contemporary art in Rome, particularly the paintings of Mengs and of the Scottish-born artist Gavin Hamilton, and, like their work, owing much to the influence of the great seventeenth-century artist Nicolas Poussin. With these works West established himself as the leading exponent of neoclassicism in England. At the time he was painting them, he was among the artists engaged in founding the English Royal Academy (officially established by royal command on 10 Dec. 1768), and these paintings, more than those of any of West's British contemporaries, represented the high-minded history painting, grounded in the classical tradition, that the academy would try to encourage. West's *Agrippina* was painted on commission for Robert Hay Drummond, the archbishop of York, who dictated its subject. Drummond arranged for West to show the picture to King George III, who promptly commissioned the *Regulus* and directed that it be exhibited in the first exhibition of the new Royal Academy in 1769. Subsequently almost all of West's important pictures appeared in the annual exhibitions of the academy, giving public visibility to a type of painting for which hitherto in England there had been virtually no patronage. To support a distinguished national school of painting, between 1768 and 1801 George III commissioned some sixty paintings from West, and in 1772 West became "History Painter to the King."

West's work for the king consisted of seven historical pictures (including the *Regulus*) painted between 1768 and 1773 and installed in Buckingham House (now Buckingham Palace); portraits of members of the royal family done between 1776 and 1783; biblical subjects on which he worked from 1779 until 1801 and which were intended for the royal chapel in Windsor Castle; an altarpiece and cartoons for stained-glass windows, which he started to design in 1782, for St. George's Chapel at Windsor; designs for allegorical panels celebrating British prosperity under George III, executed in *marmortinto* in 1788 on a ceiling in the no-longer-extant Queen's House at Windsor; and seven large pictures showing subjects from the reign of the fourteenth-century king Edward III, painted between 1786 and 1789 for the Audience Chamber in Windsor Castle. As this list suggests, classical subject matter constitutes only a small percentage of West's total oeuvre. As early as 1769 he began to work on a depiction of the death of General James Wolfe during the English victory over the French at Quebec in 1759. Archbishop Drummond and Sir Joshua Reynolds, the first president of the Royal Academy, both reportedly attempted to dissuade the artist from painting a picture in modern dress, but the completed picture shown at the Royal Academy in 1771 created a sensation and occasioned (in the words of Reynolds's recantation of his earlier objections) "a revolution in the art." Although it includes portraits of officers who served with Wolfe at Quebec and is thus partly an informal group portrait in the English tradition of the "conversation piece," it is essentially a history painting in the grand manner, albeit a modern one. West took extraordinary liberties with what was known to have actually transpired at Quebec to make the painting an "epic" (the word he used in justifying those liberties) celebration of the death of a modern hero, reminiscent not only of the deaths of classical heroes but also of the martyrdom of Christ, and in doing so he produced the forerunner of countless paintings of heroism and martyrdom from the American and French revolutions and the Napoleonic wars. The original picture (now in the National Gallery of Canada, Ottawa) was bought by Lord Grosvenor, who also purchased four paintings of seventeenth-century subjects by West to accompany it. George III, who initially rejected the picture because of the modern dress, subsequently commissioned a second version along with a pair of pictures of analogous heroic deaths in ancient Greece and medieval France to hang on either side of it. The engraving after the picture by William Wollett became one of the most commercially successful prints ever published.

Apart from a less successful *Death of Lord Nelson* of 1806 (Walker Art Gallery, Liverpool), West painted few obvious sequels to *The Death of General Wolfe*, and although he continued to paint subjects from history and indeed to paint all types of pictures, including landscapes and genre subjects, his chief later source was the Bible. During the 1770s and 1780s he received several commissions for altar pieces, including large paintings still in situ in the chapels of Trinity College, Cambridge, and the Royal Naval Hospital at Greenwich. In 1779 he started to work on what was supposed to be his magnum opus: a series of pictures, intended for the royal chapel in Windsor, devoted to the history of revealed religion from Genesis to the Last Judgment. At one point the program included thirty-six large paintings (measuring as much as 216 ×147 inches). West completed eighteen, all of which he exhibited at the Royal Academy; but plans kept changing; the project was never completed, and none of the pictures were ever installed at Windsor. Seven of them now belong to Bob Jones University in Greenville, South Carolina.

Following the death of Sir Joshua Reynolds in 1792, West became the second president of the Royal Academy. His tenure was a stormy one, and he was forced out of office for a year in 1805–1806 by a cabal led by his compatriot and erstwhile friend John Singleton Copley; nevertheless, he served for a total of twenty-seven years, longer than any other president in the academy's history. He was elected because of his close relationship with George III, the academy's patron, but the decade of the 1790s saw a weakening of West's royal ties, and in 1801 his royal commissions came to an end (starting in 1780 he received a royal stipend of £1,000 a year, which continued until the advent of the Regency in 1811). One reason for his loss of royal support was the deteriorating health of George III, who suffered his first mental crisis in 1788. Additionally, in 1794, while England was at war with revolutionary France and shortly after the death of Louis XVI on the guillotine, George III was said to be concerned about West's "democratic principles." Long before then, in 1775, West had written to Peale that prudence kept him from saying what he felt about the growing conflict between England and her American colonies. In 1783 he proposed and commenced painting a series of works depicting the great events of the American revolutionary war, an obviously promising subject for the painter of *The Death of General Wolfe* but not a prudent one for a member of George III's court. West dropped the idea (there is one unfinished work from the project, *Signing of the Preliminary Treaty of Peace in 1782*, in the Henry Francis Du Pont Winterthur Museum), but it came to fruition in a series of pictures begun in West's studio in 1885 by his pupil John Trumbull. Feelings engendered by the American conflict that West may not have acknowledged even to himself probably also underlay *Saul and the Witch of Endor* (Wadsworth Atheneum, Hartford), painted in 1777, in which a corrupt king hears of his impending defeat, and other similar Old Testament subjects from the same period.

As West's subject matter moved from Greek and Roman history to the Bible, the underlying messages also moved from celebration of philosophical and virtuous human behavior to the awe and terror of imperfect and impotent human observers before the visionary splendors and omnipotence of the Almighty. For such subjects he gradually replaced the earlier staid and disciplined style that had initially attracted George III with its polar opposite, a dramatic neobaroque manner. In the vocabulary of traditional art history, he went from neoclassicism to Romanticism. The best-known example of his later style is *Death on the Pale Horse*, a scene of visionary violence and destruction showing the four horsemen of the Apocalypse from the book of Revelation, which West first sketched in 1779 for the chapel at Windsor. He exhibited a drawing of the subject in 1784 (Royal Academy of Arts, London) and repeated the composition in 1796 in a large oil sketch (Detroit Institute of Arts). The oil sketch was followed by five further scenes from Revelation painted by West for William Beckford between 1796 and 1798. These works have been linked both with the chaos and warfare that followed the French revolution and with contemporary interpretations of the revolution as fulfillment of the prophecies of Revelation. With such paintings, the president of the Royal Academy and history painter to the king set an example for a true visionary, political radical, and opponent of the establishment, William Blake, who shortly after 1800 painted in watercolor an analogous series of scenes from Revelation.

In 1800 the Pennsylvania Hospital in Philadelphia asked West for the gift of a painting. He responded by painting a large *Christ Healing the Sick*, expanding a composition that he had sketched for Windsor. He completed it only in 1811 and then, instead of sending it to the United States, sold it to the British Institution, an organization dedicated to the creation of an English national gallery, for which West's picture was its first purchase (fifteen years later, when the present National Gallery came into being, the picture went there; West painted a second version for Pennsylvania). He sold it because he was offered 3,000 guineas, which was far more than anything he had been paid before and was widely reported at the time to be the most ever paid to any artist for a single work of art. West thereupon painted two even larger sequels: *Christ Rejected*, completed in 1814 (200 × 260 inches), and a final version of *Death on the Pale Horse*, completed in 1817 (176 × 301 inches), both of which now belong to the Pennsylvania Academy of the Fine Arts in Philadelphia. West did not sell the latter two but showed them in well-attended special exhibitions in Pall Mall (240,000 people are reported to have paid to see *Christ Rejected*). These late pictures essentially carried on the type of painting that West had started to paint for George III in 1779, and as art created for and paid for by the public, whose admission fees filled the monetary void left by West's loss of royal patronage, they fulfilled some of the ideals that had inspired that patronage. Their popularity was due, however, primarily to the renewed religious pieties of the early nineteenth century, not to their aesthetic qualities.

By all accounts, West's belief in his own genius never wavered. When offered a knighthood, he declined it, not out of modesty or on the basis of principle, but because he believed he deserved more: a hereditary peerage. After 1800, when he had become "the venerable West," he seems to have looked upon his life as the unfolding of predestined greatness, a view that underlies the near-mythic accounts of his early years that he provided the Scottish novelist John Galt for a two-volume *Life* published in 1816 and 1820. The exhibitions of his large late paintings were all accompanied by flurries of hagiographical exegesis, and after the artist's death in London in 1820, his sons displayed his works in a gallery, which became a popular tourist attraction, built for the purpose in the garden of his former home. Nevertheless, even the most generous assessment of West's output would describe it as uneven. He always had critics, and by the 1880s and 1890s there was widespread consensus that he was incapable of satisfactorily translating the vigor and intensity of his oil sketches, such as that for *Death on the Pale Horse*, into finished pictures. In colonial Pennsylvania he had no access to proper artistic training (despite his position at the head of the Royal Academy, he was not the product of an academy), and as a consequence he never overcame a stiffness in his figures, which is especially apparent in the over-life-sized scale of his late works. After 1800 his ambitions for a noble history painting in the manner of earlier painting no longer commanded the same respect as in the 1760s and 1770s, and as his art appeared ever more old-fashioned, it elicited the scorn of younger critics such as William Hazlitt, for whom, in 1816, West was "only great by the acre." Most cruelly, Lord Byron dismissed him as "the flattering, feeble dotard West, / Europe's worst dauber, and poor Britain's best." His reputation continued to fall through the nineteenth century and still has not fully recovered. Nevertheless, his central position in the histories of English and American art kept him from being forgotten. Since the 1960s art historians have increasingly acknowledged not only his historical significance but also the range of his ambitions over an exceptionally long and prolific career and the originality, interest, and quality of his best paintings.

• John Galt's two-volume *Life* (1816 and 1820), mentioned above, is the main source, but it must be read with some skepticism. Two long letters by West detailing his activity in Italy, 1760–1763, are published in E. P. Richardson, "West's Voyage to Italy, 1760, and William Allen," *Pennsylvania Magazine of History and Biography* 102 (1978): 3–26. A rich source for West's later life is the diary kept from 1793 to 1821 by his fellow artist Joseph Farington (26 vols., 1978–1984).

Robert Alberts, *Benjamin West: A Biography* (1978), is the only modern biography. Helmut von Erffa and Allen Staley, *The Paintings of Benjamin West* (1986), is a fully illustrated catalogue raisonné of the paintings. See also *Benjamin West: American Painter at the English Court* (1989), with text by Allen Staley, and Ann Uhry Abrams, *The Valiant Hero: Benjamin West and Grand-Style History Painting* (1985), an interpretative examination of his earlier career. Valuable considerations of specific dimensions of West's art and influence, both published as exhibition catalogs, are Dorinda Evans, *Benjamin West and His American Students* (National Portrait Gallery, Washington, 1980), and Nancy Pressly, *Revealed Religion: Benjamin West's Commissions for Windsor Castle and Fonthill Abbey* (San Antonio Museum of Art, 1983).

ALLEN STALEY

WEST, George (17 Feb. 1823–20 Sept. 1901), manufacturer and congressman, was born in Bradninch, Devonshire County, England, the son of George West, a paper manufacturer, and Jane (maiden name unknown). He briefly attended the local school and at age eleven went to work in a paper mill, perhaps that of his father. From ages fourteen to twenty-one he served an apprenticeship to a paper manufacturer, during which time he filled increasingly responsible positions. In 1844 he married Louisa Rose. They had six children.

West and his family came to America in 1849. He worked briefly at a paper mill in New Jersey and then moved to Tyringham, Berkshire County, Massachusetts, where he entered a writing-paper manufactory. There in 1850 he turned out the first machine-made watermark writing paper in the United States and also invented machinery for cutting watermarks in the center of sheets of paper. By 1853 he was in charge of the Russell mill, but a disastrous fire in the mill caused him to move in 1861 to Saratoga County, New York, where there was a flourishing paper-making industry.

In New York West shortly purchased the Empire Mill at Rock City Falls and subsequently bought or built seven additional mills along Kayaderosseras Creek for the making of manila (strong, light brown) paper, of which he became the largest manufacturer in the United States. Beginning in 1875 much of the product of his mills went into paper bags. With a daily capacity of three million bags, his bag factory was the foundation of his fortune. To market the bags, he set up a store in New York City, where the bags were printed to the customers' orders. At first dependent on imported raw materials for his mills, in the 1880s West established a wood pulp factory, supplied from the 8,000-acre spruce forest that he owned. He employed more than 400 men, women, and children in his various enterprises. When he sold his mills to the Union Bag & Paper Company in 1899, they brought $1.5 million.

Among West's other business interests were several mines in the western states. He was a member of D. S. Walton & Co., wholesale merchants of paper and paper boxes, and a director of the National Folding Box and Paper Co. Both firms were in New York City, where in his later years West spent much of his time. He had a large interest in the *Utica Herald* and the *Schenectady Union*. He was a founder and president of the First National Bank of Ballston and a director of the Franklin Bank.

A Republican, West served five terms in the New York state legislature, from 1872 through 1876. He was elected to Congress in 1880, was defeated for the seat in 1882, and was reelected in 1884 and 1886. He was a delegate to the Republican National Conventions in 1880 and 1884 and is reported to have been the New Yorker who suggested Benjamin Harrison for the presidency in 1888. As a lawmaker he supported government ownership of telegraph lines and railroads and advocated a protective tariff on both raw materials and manufactures, positions that reflected his experience as a businessman. Public ownership of communication and transportation lines, he believed, would free manufacturers from the excessive charges of monopolists. A protective tariff on raw materials shielded the manufacturer who produced his own such materials from domestic competitors who imported theirs, while a protective tariff on manufactures guarded the American processor from foreign competition.

West's philanthropic interests extended from Saratoga County to his native country. He contributed generously to the support of the village school in Bradninch and bought and operated a paper mill there to provide local employment. Closer to home he was for many years treasurer of the Round Lake Association, a summer colony a few miles south of Ballston Spa. In 1887 he donated the George West Museum of Art and Archaeology to the colony. In Ballston Spa, his principal residence, he paid half the cost of the Methodist church building and made a gift of a parsonage to the congregation. He died at Ballston Spa.

• There is biographical and occupational information concerning West in G. B. Anderson, *Our County and Its People: A Descriptive and Biographical Record of Saratoga County, New York* (1899); Edward F. Grose, *Centennial History of the Village of Ballston Spa, Including the Towns of Ballston and Milton* (1907); and Nathaniel Bartlett Sylvester, *History of Saratoga County, New York, with Illustrations and Biographical Sketches of Some of Its Prominent Men and Pioneers* (1878). See also the *Biographical Directory of the United States Congress, 1774–1989* (1989). Obituaries are in the *Ballston Journal*, 28 Sept. 1901, and the *New York Times*, 21 Sept. 1901.

IRENE D. NEU

WEST, James Edward (16 May 1876–15 May 1948), social worker and lawyer, was born in Washington, D.C., the son of James Robert West, a merchant who died around the time of the child's birth, and Mary Tyree, a seamstress. When West was six, his mother died, and he was sent to a local orphanage. The boy was frequently punished for laziness until it was recognized that he suffered from tuberculosis of the hip and knee. He spent two years in a hospital undergoing painful treatment and was then returned to the orphanage, still with a pronounced limp. His difficult early years helped shape his lifelong commitment to child welfare as well as his conviction that even the bleakest environment could be surmounted by strong character.

With the encouragement of one of his mother's friends, West developed a passion for reading. After graduating from Business High School in 1895, he worked first at the orphanage, then as bookkeeper in a bicycle shop, and next as a stenographer at the Young Men's Christian Association and the War Department. During these years West learned to walk without crutches. At the same time he began reading law in an attorney's office. He then entered the National University in Washington, graduating with both LL.B. and LL.M. degrees in 1901; he was admitted to the bar the same year. With the help of President Theodore Roosevelt, who became a close friend, West obtained a position on the Board of Pension Appeals and later served as assistant attorney in the Department of the Interior. In 1906 he opened his own practice, and the following year he married Marion Olivia Speaks. They had five children, four of whom survived infancy.

West continued to be concerned with child welfare. He organized a committee that persuaded Congress to create Washington's first juvenile court, and as director of the Washington Playground Association he helped establish the city's public playgrounds. In 1908, working through *Delineator* magazine (then edited by Theodore Dreiser), West and Dreiser launched a Child-Rescue Campaign that found homes for 2,000 dependent children who might otherwise have been sent to institutions. Soon after, President Roosevelt endorsed West's proposal for the first White House Conference on Children. West organized the meeting in January 1909 and helped frame its keynote statement: "Home life is the highest and finest product of civilization. Children should not be deprived of it except for urgent and compelling reasons." The conference's recommendation that poor parents be assisted to maintain their children at home helped set the stage for the passage of mothers' pension laws throughout the country in the following decade.

In 1911 West was chosen as the first executive director for the newly established Boy Scouts of America. The organization was struggling to define itself against several similar groups, but West managed to outdo his rivals. He persuaded several organizations to merge with the Scouts; others were driven into obscurity. "He was a real battler, and he could be ruthless," recalled Julian H. Salomon, an office boy during West's early years as head of the Scouts (Peterson, p. 54). As the Scouts grew, West emphasized symbols such as the uniform, the oath, and the merit badge that appealed to boys' sense of belonging. At the same time, he articulated an ideology that maintained an appealing balance between competition and cooperation, discipline and individualism. West was also a master of public relations. Americans were continually reminded that Scouts served their communities and their nation and that scouting taught boys to be patriotic, courteous, religious, and honest. At the same time, the complicated structure of troops and councils developed by West drew in thousands of adult volunteers who themselves became supporters and publicizers of the movement. Both West's idealistic belief in the power of character building and his organizational talent are suggested in his exhortation to his adult volunteers to "carry on as crusaders, with enthusiasm, with devotion, yes even with sacrifice if necessary, as those who are dedicated to a great cause."

Some early scouting leaders criticized West for devoting too much energy to fundraising and public relations. Ernest Thompson Seton, for instance, described West as a man "who has no point of contact with boys and who . . . has never seen the blue sky in his life." The British founder of scouting, Lord Baden-Powell, seconded some of Seton's observations. At the same time, other observers criticized the Scouts for being militaristic or too aggressively patriotic. Later critics would also note that the organization blended its idealism with an accommodation to established social patterns; southern troops often segregated or excluded blacks, while the organization sometimes had difficulty communicating with urban boys, especially the poor and the foreign-born. Scouting had enormous appeal in smaller towns, however, and the organization grew steadily; by 1919 it had a headquarters staff of 274 and an active membership of nearly 500,000 boys and adult volunteers. The development of Wolfcub packs (started in 1930) opened scouting to a younger age group, while *Boys' Life*, the Scout periodical, grew into the nation's largest circulation publication for youth.

West served on the International Scout Committee for many years and received awards from several foreign Scout organizations. He chaired a committee of the Conference on Mobilization for Human Needs called by Franklin D. Roosevelt in 1933, worked actively for the Reading Program for the Young of America, and wrote or cowrote several books for boys. He also participated in three more White House conferences on children, under Presidents Warren G. Harding, Herbert Hoover, and Franklin Roosevelt. He received many awards, including the gold medal of the National Institute of Social Sciences (1940).

On West's sixty-fifth birthday, in 1941, Roosevelt attributed to him "much of the credit for the effectiveness of Scouting in this country." By the time West retired two years later, the Boy Scouts had more than 1.5 million members of all ages; during his thirty years with the organization, it had served more than 10 million boys. He died in New Rochelle, New York, where he had lived since the 1920s. Scouting's main purpose, West once said, was "to create and maintain conditions so that boys intensely desire to become Scouts, and men of character are willing to give leadership." West was extraordinarily successful in achieving these goals, and in doing so he transformed the Boy Scouts from one of many youth groups into an American institution.

• Among the books that West wrote or co-wrote are *The Lone Scout of the Sky* (1928), *The Boys' Book of Honor* (1931, with Peter Lamb), *He-Who-Sees-in-the-Dark* (1932, with Lamb), and *The Scout Jamboree* (1934, with William Hillcourt). His *Making the Most of Yourself: The Boy Scout Trail to the Greatest of All Adventures* (1941) is a compilation of his editorials for *Boys' Life*, which he edited from 1922 to 1943. Regarding his career with the Boy Scouts, see David I. Macleod, *Building Character in the American Boy: The Boy Scouts, YMCA, and Their Forerunners, 1870–1920* (1983), Harold P. Levy, *Building a Popular Movement: A Case Study of the Public Relations of the Boy Scouts of America* (1944), Robert W. Peterson, *The Boy Scouts: An American Adventure* (1984), William D. Murray, *The History of the Boy Scouts of America* (1937), Edwin Nicholson, *Education and the Boy Scout Movement in America* (1941), and Boy Scouts of America, *Thirty Years of Service: Tributes to James E. West* (1941). See also Harold A. Jambor, "Theodore Dreiser, the *Delineator* Magazine, and Dependent Children: A Background Note on the Calling of the 1909 White House Conference," *Social Service Review* 32 (Mar. 1958): 33–40, and *Proceedings of the Conference on the Care of Dependent Children* (1909). A *New York Times* obituary appeared on 16 May 1948.

SANDRA OPDYCKE

WEST, Jessamyn (18 July 1902–23 Feb. 1984), author, was born Mary Jessamyn West near North Vernon, Indiana, the daughter of Eldo Roy West and Grace Anna Milhous. Her mother came from a well-established Quaker family, while her father, who farmed, studied law, and taught school, came from a poor, non-Quaker family. When Jessamyn was seven, her family moved to East Whittier, California, to be close to relatives who had moved there, and settled briefly on an orange ranch. Within two years her father bought a citrus grove in Yorba Linda and built the two-story house in which Jessamyn grew up. Their nearest neighbor was a quarter of a mile away, and relatives owned neighboring ranches. Yorba Linda at this time was in transition from sagebrush and brown hills to fruit orchards and grain ranches.

In 1914 the first public library opened in Yorba Linda. West would later say its opening marked the beginning of her "adult intellectual life." She read voraciously—John Fox and Gene Stratton Porter were favorites—kept a journal throughout her life, and recorded vocabulary words in a notebook. She attended Fullerton Union High School, which shared a campus and was affiliated with Fullerton Junior College. After graduation from high school, West attended Whittier College for one year. A composition teacher there used one of West's essays as an example of poor writing in front of the class, and a humiliated West briefly contemplated suicide. She transferred to Fullerton Junior College and then returned to Whittier College, where she received a B.A. in English in 1923.

That same year West married Harry Maxwell "Max" McPherson, the son of a Quaker family in Whittier. McPherson later served for many years as superintendent of the Napa Valley Unified School District, and was founder and first president of present-day Napa Valley College, and became professor of education at the University of California.

In 1924 West and her husband moved to Hemet, California, where she worked as a school secretary for one year and then for four years as a teacher in a one-room public school. In 1929 she attended Oxford University for a summer session and visited Paris.

After returning to the United States, West enrolled in graduate school at the University of California in Berkeley. In August 1931, just before taking her oral examinations for her doctorate, she experienced a tubercular hemorrhage and entered La Vina Sanatorium near Pasadena for care. This began a fourteen-year period of what she called her "horizontal life." After ten months her doctors sent her home to die. Her mother cared for her for six months, after which West improved enough to live with her husband in Yuba City, where he was a vice principal. Over the next seven years, as her husband became principal of different high schools, they moved successively to Mount Shasta, St. Helena, and finally Napa, where they settled for the rest of their lives.

West published her first short story, "99.6," about sanatorium life after her husband insisted she do so. It appeared in *Brown's Nutmeg* on 10 June 1939. In her subsequent stories and novels, she called on her own life growing up in southern California and her family's Indiana heritage. Her prose at its best is lyrical, witty, and technically proficient. She frequently used child and adolescent characters.

Most of West's early work was published in "little magazines" that paid nothing. In 1945, however, she published *The Friendly Persuasion*, a collection of stories about the Birdwell family in Indiana, stories loosely based on her great-grandfather Joshua Vickers Milhous, a nurseryman; his wife Elizabeth Price Griffith Milhous, a Quaker minister; and another grandmother, Mary Frances McManaman Milhous. The book was an immediate success and was quickly translated into five other languages.

In 1948 West wrote *A Mirror for the Sky*, an operetta about John Audubon, which was first staged in 1958 in Eugene, Oregon. Her first novel was *The Witch Diggers*, which came out in 1951, received good reviews, but did not sell well. *Cress Delahanty* (1953), a collection of stories about an adolescent girl, fared better. It received good reviews and was chosen as a Book-of-the-Month Club selection. West received the Indiana Authors' Day Award for her short-story collection *Love, Death and the Ladies' Drill Team*, written in 1955. Also in 1955 she worked in Hollywood on the script for *The Friendly Persuasion*, which became a movie classic. The film was directed by William Wyler, starred Gary Cooper, won an award at the Cannes Film Festival, and was nominated for an Academy Award for best picture of the year. West wrote of this filmmaking experience in *To See the Dream* (1957). Her other screenwriting work includes being sole writer of *Stolen Hours* and receiving partial credit for *The Big Country*.

Although West and her husband had no children of their own, during the early 1950s they welcomed a sixteen-year-old boy named Fred Oswald into their home so he could attend school. He lived with them for three years. Shortly thereafter, on a trip to Limerick, Ireland, in 1955, they met eleven-year-old Ann McCarthy and her thirteen-year-old sister Jean. Seeing the destitute conditions in which the girls and their family lived, West and her husband invited them to live with them and spent months making arrangements. Jean stayed for a short time, but Ann became their daughter.

West was awarded nine honorary doctorates and during the late 1940s and 1950s spoke about and taught writing. She lectured at the Bread Loaf Writers' Conference in Vermont and at Indiana University, Stanford, and the Universities of Washington, Utah, Colorado, Kentucky, and Redlands. She taught creative writing at Mills College and worked as writer in residence at Wellesley College and the University of Notre Dame.

In 1960 West traveled to Europe with her sister Carmen and published her second novel, *South of the Angels*. In 1963 Carmen committed suicide, and West's third novel, *A Matter of Time* (1966), was based on her death. In 1969 West published the bestselling *Except for Me and Thee: A Companion to "The Friendly Persuasion."* In all, she produced eight novels as well as autobiographical writings, including *Hide and Seek: A Continuing Journey* (1973), about her life in a trailer alongside the Colorado River; *The Woman Said Yes: Encounters with Life and Death* (1976), about the lives of her mother and sister; and *Double Discovery: A Journey* (1980), about her 1929 trip to Oxford and Paris. West's books have sold more than 6 million copies and have been translated into at least nineteen different languages. In 1982 West began suffering a series of minor strokes. She died in Napa.

• The major repository of West's papers is Whittier College. Other papers, many collected by Alfred S. Shivers for his book on West, can be found at Stephen F. Austin State University. Other published works by West not listed above include *The Reading Public* (1952), *Love Is Not What You Think* (1959), *The Quaker Reader* (1962), *The Chilekings* (1967), *Leafy Rivers* (1967), *Crimson Ramblers of the World, Farewell* (1970), *The Secret Look* (1974), *The Life I Really Lived: A Novel* (1979), *The Story of a Story and Three Stories* (1982), and *The State of Stony Lonesome* (1984). Shivers, *Jessamyn West*, rev. ed. (1992), is the most complete source of information about her life and work. Other sources include Ann Dahlstrom Farmer, *Jessamyn West* (1982), and Jennifer Chapman's interview with West in Marilyn Yalom, *Women Writers of the West Coast: Speaking of the Lives and Careers* (1983). Obituaries are in the *New York Times*, 25 Feb. 1984, and *Newsweek* and *Time*, 5 Mar. 1984.

ANN W. ENGAR

WEST, Joseph (fl. 1669–1685), mariner and three-time governor of South Carolina, was of unknown ancestry. Little is known of his life before 1669. In July of that year the Lords Proprietors of Carolina chose Joseph West to command their fleet about to sail from London with the first settlers from England bound for the southern part of their grant. The proprietors entrusted to West's care an expedition representing a large capital investment but failed to leave information about why they believed him capable of carrying out the mission. Moreover, no other sources have been uncovered that outline West's early career. In 1669 he styled himself "merchant of London." He was married to Joanna (maiden name unknown), who joined him in the New World. The couple left no offspring. He was probably a dissenter but of uncertain denominational affiliation. In his will recorded in 1691, he directed that his estate residue be given to London's Quaker poor. If a Friend at the end of his life, he was not one in the 1660s, serving in the Royal Navy under James Carteret, a son of one of the proprietors. West's association with the Carterets likely brought him to the attention of Lord Anthony Ashley Cooper (later the Earl of Shaftesbury), who was the prime mover of the proprietary in the late 1660s and 1670s. The earl became West's patron and supporter.

Following orders, West guided the vessels to Kinsale, Ireland, and on to Bermuda and Barbados. On reaching the Carolina coast in early 1670, he judged that the more northerly Charleston harbor area was safer from attacks by the Spaniards than the Port Royal destination chosen by the proprietors. West then put his settlers in the care of the governor-designate, William Sayle. Remaining in what was to become South Carolina, West made his mark as a proprietary appointee. He obtained land grants, but no record indicates he engaged in extensive planting. At first he was the proprietary's storekeeper, maintaining records of food and supplies advanced to settlers. He was also a member of the council. In late 1670, when Governor Sayle fell ill, he recognized that West was best fitted to succeed to the governorship. After Sayle died early the following year, the council chose West with the proprietary confirming his selection.

During his first term, Governor West demonstrated his common sense. Though bombarded from London with inappropriate advice about how to organize a new settlement, he focused on the colony's requirements for survival. He rationed food judiciously, and South Carolina never had a "starving time." He ordered that two acres of corn or peas be grown for every settler. Such an approach irritated the proprietors, who blamed West for failure to develop staples. They concluded in 1672 that Sir John Yeamans, a former Barbadian, would address their interests and do their bidding. West would revert to storekeeper, council member, and added responsibilities as register of writings.

The proprietors soon had multiple reasons to regret appointing Sir John. His major objective was to use his position to enhance his personal fortune. He built his export business to the West Indies by buying food grown locally and diverting labor from planting to harvesting timber. These policies dismayed the proprietors, who were forced to continue supplying the settlers with basic needs. By July 1674 they had had enough of Sir John, and they reinstalled West as governor.

Serving from 1674 to 1682, West never wavered from emphasizing security and self-sufficiency. In 1678 the town was shifted to Oyster Point, Charleston's present site, as a location easier to defend and better for commerce. West maintained peaceful relations with nearby Indian tribes, a requirement if a weak settlement were to survive and necessary to maintain a deerskin trade. He insisted on food crops and animal herds sufficient for local needs with an excess for export.

West's leadership created a subsistence-level but permanent colony, a situation that did not promote growth and the profits the proprietors sought. By the early 1680s most of the first proprietors had been succeeded by men who were more ardent in pursuit of their own interests. They accused West of dereliction of duty by failing to suppress clandestine trade with pirates and traffic in Indian slaves. They moved to find a more forceful governor who would develop the economy and enforce their directives. In May 1682 they replaced West with another Barbadian, Joseph Morton.

Once more the proprietors chose poorly. Morton did promote immigration from the islands, but he was unable to cope with the growing political factionalism in the colony. He was unable to collect quitrents on land granted or to adhere to proprietary rules for granting land. He was unable to stop illegal activities among settlers eager to conduct any kind of business for profit. With the colony in more turmoil than usual, the proprietary dismissed Morton in 1684. After the next appointee, Sir Richard Kyrle, died soon after arriving in the colony, the council turned to West, who was soon confirmed as governor by the proprietary.

West's third term was brief. He could satisfy neither proprietors nor settlers in the matter of land policy. He did battle with the Goose Creek men, a rising anti-proprietary faction, who made his life miserable as they did for a long succession of governors. Perhaps worn down by the constant strife, West resigned in the summer of 1685, abandoning the governorship of his own volition for the first time.

After resigning West may have remained in the colony for a few more years. As with his early years, almost nothing is known about the last phase of his life. Fragmentary evidence places him briefly in Massachusetts and residing in New York and suggests he died in the latter colony about 1691.

As governor for some eleven of South Carolina's first fifteen years, Joseph West accomplished much. He mediated between his proprietary masters and his people, who often held irreconcilable views. Despite being the middle man who displeased both sides on occasion, he retained the respect of both groups. Though the proprietors believed he should be doing better by them, they recognized he was honest, dependable, faithful, and possessed of administrative skills. Though the settlers were irked at proprietary policies he was obliged to implement, they knew him personally as a fair, prudent, reasonable man who had their best interests at heart. West deserves more credit than anyone else for establishing the settlement under challenging circumstances.

• West left no personal writings except for a few official letters and probate documents in various British and colonial record series. For an imaginative, yet plausible, assessment of the scanty evidence about West's career before 1669, see St. Julien R. Childs, "The Naval Career of Joseph West," *South Carolina Historical Magazine* 71 (1970): 109–16. This article also references almost all the primary sources and secondary works providing some information about West. His correspondence with the proprietors during the first years of settlement will be found in Langdon Cheves, ed., "The Shaftesbury Papers and Other Records Relating to Carolina . . . Prior to the Year 1676," *Collections of the South Carolina Historical Society*, vol. 5 (1897). A number of observations about West are included in the early volumes of the "Records in the British Public Record Office Relating to South Carolina, 1663–1782" (the first five volumes of this thirty-six volume set in facsimile were published, 1928–1947). This latter series is sometimes cited as "Sainsbury Transcripts."

The most probing and authoritative evaluation of South Carolina's early politics and West's role is the time-honored study by William J. Rivers, *A Sketch of the History of South Carolina to the Close of the Proprietary Government by the Revolution of 1719* (1856). While a few more facts about West have been uncovered since Rivers wrote, his interpretation of events has shaped the views of subsequent historians. Two more recent scholarly treatments provide perspective on West's career. As his title implies, M. Eugene Sirmans, *Colonial South Carolina: A Political History, 1663–1763* (1966), focuses on governmental affairs. Robert M. Weir, *Colonial South Carolina: A History* (1983), places politics within a broader context.

CONVERSE D. CLOWSE

WEST, Mae (17 Aug. 1893–22 Nov. 1980), stage and screen actress, was born Mary Jane West in Brooklyn, New York, the daughter of Matilda Delker Doelger, a corset and fashion model, and John Patrick West, a livery stable owner and heavyweight boxer. With the encouragement of her mother, she began an early show business career, winning an amateur night competition at the age of eight and acting in stock theatrical companies through her teens. As her comic and musical talents developed, she began appearing in musical reviews in New York, including *A la Broadway* (1911), *Vera Violetta* (1911), a Ziegfeld show entitled *A Winsome Widow* (1912), *Sometime* (1918), and *The Mimic World of 1921* (1921). During this same period West traveled on the vaudeville circuit, teaming for a while with the Girard Brothers and later with pianist Harry Richman, in addition to performing in her own solo acts. Receiving praise for her timing, mimicry, and comic gifts, West displayed an early penchant for the outrageous, introducing to Broadway audiences the controversial shimmy dance, which she learned from black nightclub patrons in Chicago.

Having refined the basics of her comic technique and theatrical style in vaudeville, West was able to make the transition to the legitimate stage, partly because of her talents as a writer of her own material. Although there is some question about how much work was contributed by collaborators and although she had to defend her authorship claims in several court cases, West certainly created in her plays the character that would become her trademark and possessed the power necessary to have the plays produced. After writing three unproduced plays—*The Ruby Ring* (1921), *The Hussy* (1922), and *Chick: An Unpublished Scandal* (1924)—West gained notoriety for her 1926 production of *Sex*, the somewhat melodramatic story of a prostitute with a heart of gold. After a successful run of almost a year, the show was raided by the police, who arrested West on morals charges. She was fined and served a short jail sentence. West's second play, *The Drag* (1927), dealt with the subject of male homosexuality and included an elaborately staged drag queen ball.

West returned to the stage for a production of her satire of beauty contests, *The Wicked Age* (1927), but it was her creation of *Diamond Lil* (1928), the play as well as the prostitute character, that would transform her from headline news to the status of a legend. Set in the Bowery with a colorful cast of gangsters, white slavers, politicians, and mission workers, the play showcased West's wisecracking sexual personae and musical talents as dance hall entertainer. Her next play, *Pleasure Man* (1928), again brought notoriety to her as a writer when it was raided by the police and closed after several performances. A backstage story of an actor-rogue who seduces innocent women and abandons them, the play included another drag ball scene. While waiting for the trial, West toured with *Diamond Lil*, wrote another play (*Frisco Kate*, 1930), which later formed the kernel of the movie *Klondike Annie*, and wrote a novel entitled *Babe Gordon*, which was translated to the stage as *The Constant Sinner* for a brief run in 1931. Though legal delays prevented her from reopening *Pleasure Man*, West continued to cherish the hope that it would someday be produced; she published a novelization of the play in 1975.

West began her film career in 1932 when her friend George Raft helped her get a small role as a wisecracking dame in his picture *Night after Night*. Her critically successful, energetic performance in an otherwise mediocre film provided her the opportunity to adapt *Diamond Lil* to the movies as *She Done Him Wrong* (1933). Replete with sexual innuendo and risqué banter, the popular film made West one of the most powerful women in Hollywood, brought about moral outrage that led in part to the creation of the industry's self-censoring Production Code, and made costar Cary Grant a leading romantic comedy star. For the next ten years, West concentrated on her film career, following her initial success with *I'm No Angel* (1933, also with Grant), *Belle of the Nineties* (1934), *Goin' to Town* (1935), *Klondike Annie* (1936), *Go West Young Man* (1936), *Every Day's a Holiday* (1938, her first box office failure), *My Little Chickadee* (1940, which teamed her with W. C. Fields), and *The Heat's On* (1943).

Controversy continued to surround her as she battled to preserve the raunchy humor of each film while under the close scrutiny of the Hollywood censors. A personal scandal erupted in 1935 when a Works Progress Administration worker accidentally discovered a record of West's 1911 marriage to vaudevillian Frank Wallace, who subsequently sued for community property rights from his now-famous wife. At first denying her failed, youthful marriage, West eventually admitted the truth and divorced Wallace in 1942. She never remarried, thinking marriage to be inconsistent with her freewheeling sexual screen personae (although she spent the last twenty-five years of her life with one male companion, Paul Novak). During this time West continued to offend the moral majority; as a guest on the popular "Chase and Sanborn Hour" radio show, West participated in an Adam and Eve sketch with Don Ameche and was effectively banned from radio for many years.

West returned to the stage in 1944 with her play *Catherine Was Great*, about the Russian empress. She toured England and the United States with a popular revival of *Diamond Lil* from 1947 to 1951. From 1954 to 1959 she developed a musical comedy nightclub act that featured herself (then in her sixties) surrounded by young bodybuilders. In the 1960s and 1970s West was rediscovered by a younger audience who appreciated her sexual frankness as well as her battles against the moral establishment. She recorded several rock and roll albums and appeared as a parody of her legend in *Myra Breckinridge* (1970) and *Sextette* (1978).

Building from a rich entertainment background in vaudeville and theater, West created a unique and enduring character in Diamond Lil, a character as powerful in the popular imagination as Chaplin's Little Tramp. Using the comfortable distance of the Gay Nineties, West showed depression-era audiences a supremely confident woman who could take care of herself in any situation. With a wisecracking wit, West waged war against hypocrisy, pretension, elitism, and sexual repression in her plots. She spun optimistic fantasies of self-reliance, survival, and eventual success, her character's struggles at times paralleling her own personal triumphs as demonstrated throughout her autobiography, *Goodness Had Nothing to Do with It* (1959). Through costuming, theatricality, and double entendre, West parodied sexual allure and Hollywood romance. She offended conventional audiences with her open enjoyment of sexual freedom and her defiance of sexual double standards. According to critic Parker Tyler, West's "sudden greatness was to have introduced a deliberately comic parody of the sex goddess. Her unique blend of sexiness and vulgar comedy, in other words, was the screen's first sterling brand of conscious sex camp" (*Sex Psyche Etcetera in the Film* [1969], p. 20). This campy, exaggerated style of humor, along with her early championing of controversial sexual issues, made West extremely popular with gay audiences. Credited with composing the most American aphorisms since Benjamin Franklin, West remains one of the most quoted women in history. Her famous quips include "When I'm good, I'm very good, but when I'm bad, I'm better"; "I used to be Snow White but I drifted"; "It's not the men in my life, but the life in my men that count"; "Too much of a good thing can be wonderful"; "Come up and see me sometime"; "Peel me a grape." West died in Los Angeles.

• West's extant play manuscripts are available for examination in the Library of Congress; many of her movie scripts exist in the University of Southern California Doheny Special Collections Library, the University of California at Los Angeles Theater Arts Library, and the Margaret Herrick Library of the Academy of Motion Pictures Arts and Sciences. A revised and enlarged edition of *Goodness Had Nothing to Do with It* was published in 1970. A collection of her witticisms, *The Wit and Wisdom of Mae West*, was edited by Joseph Weintraub in 1967. George Eells and Stanley Musgrove, *Mae West: A Biography* (1982), is a good account of her life. A detailed survey of her artistic contributions is contained in Jon Tuska, *The Films of Mae West* (1973). See also Carol Ward's *Mae West: A Bio-Bibliography* (1989) for extensive primary and secondary bibliography as well as summaries and reprints of major interviews. An obituary is in the *New York Times*, 23 Nov. 1980.

CAROL M. WARD

WEST, Nathanael (17 Oct. 1903–22 Dec. 1940), author, was born Nathan Weinstein in New York City, the son of Mordecai "Max" Weinstein, a builder, and Chana "Anna" Wallenstein. The families of both of West's parents were associated in the building trades in Lithuania, Russia, and both families immigrated together to New York City over a period of a few years in the late 1890s. In the then rapidly growing city, the families were successful in constructing large apartment buildings, so that West grew up in an affluent atmosphere. The arts were taken seriously; German and English rather than Russian or Yiddish were spoken; and similarly, Judaism was downplayed. West's family was anxious to be Americanized, but in many ways they felt superior to American culture, and this ambivalent attitude influenced West's attitudes and his writing. A family myth existed that they were related to the hero of Friedrich Schiller's play *Wallenstein*; as a young man West often wrote his name Nathaniel von Wallenstein Weinstein. In 1926 he legally changed his name to Nathanael West, using the Greek rather than the Hebraic spelling of his first name and claiming ironically that in his new surname he was literally following Horace Greeley's advice to Americans to "go West."

It was expected by the families that their children should enroll in good colleges, but the young West was less interested in high school classes than he was in attending movies and plays, doing his own reading in modern authors, going to museums, and plunging into the varied amusements of the city. Therefore he was faced with a dilemma: making little progress in passing academic subjects, he yet wanted to pass on to college. This led to his first creative act of self-definition and rebellion against conventional bourgeois values. By a complicated series of manipulations and outright fraud, he "created" academic transcripts that allowed him first to enter Tufts College, where he failed all his first-semester classes on account of nonattendance, and then to be admitted to Brown University as a second-semester sophomore.

At Brown University West spent his time, as his senior yearbook said, in "drawing exotic pictures [and] quoting strange and fanciful poetry." He also contributed two poems, a drawing, and an essay on Euripides to the college literary and humor magazines, and he made friends with three classmates who were later to make reputations as writers: S. J. Perelman, Frank O. Hough, and Quentin Reynolds. He even sketched out a few episodes of what was to become his first book. In addition, he attended enough classes to graduate from Brown in 1924 with a Ph.B.

Again West was faced with a conflict. His family expected him to assist in the construction business, but he was adamantly opposed to this idea. Thus, after a brief time working as a construction superintendent, he was allowed to go to Paris in the fall of 1926 to pursue a career as a writer or artist. However, due to the contraction in building in the mid-1920s, an early precursor to the Great Depression, West was called back from Paris after only three months there and obliged to take up jobs as assistant manager in family-owned hotels, first the Kenmore Hall Hotel on Twenty-third Street and then the Sutton Club Hotel on East Fifty-sixth Street.

For many reasons, this development, which was, on the surface, so unwelcome, was an important factor in West's literary career. First, working as a night manager gave him time to write. He published his first story, "A Barefaced Lie," in 1929 in the *Overland Monthly*, and he finished the novel that he had begun at Brown and had continued to work on in Paris. Published in 1931 by Contact Editions, which was famous for its stress on experimental writing, *The Dream Life of Balso Snell* took nearly six years to complete, despite its brevity. The unusual character of this satirical book is well suggested by an advertisement or manifesto that West wrote to promote it and to define his intentions. "English humor," he begins, "has always prided itself on being good natured and in the best of taste. This fact makes it difficult to compare N. West with other comic writers, as he is vicious, mean, ugly, obscene, and insane." However, he continues, West can be compared to the French dadaist and surrealist writers. The basic form of *The Dream Life of Balso Snell* is that of a journey, in which the antihero travels in "the swamps of [the] . . . mind," dreaming dream within dream. It parodies the Greek-Trojan epic; but ancient heroism is replaced by the foolish and bizarre, by self-deception and vagrant wandering. The book ends in a nocturnal emission. West's ambivalence toward art is evident: he elevates art to his central subject but also associates it with absurdity and pretentious illusion.

A second way in which his work at the hotel helped West was by introducing him to the sufferings of people in the early 1930s. He became interested in the dreams and desires of people in general. With the help of Lillian Hellman, he occasionally opened the letters of some of the down-at-luck residents, and he was profoundly moved by the reality of their misery. Through his friend Perelman, West gained access to the letters sent to a lovelorn columnist for the *Brooklyn Eagle*. These provided him with the idea for his second novel, *Miss Lonelyhearts* (1933), which many critics regard as his best work. West understood these letters to be a central expression of the bewildered fantasies of Americans during a time of great social and economic distress and psychological anguish. To provide a perspective on the letters' meaning, West invented a male lovelorn columnist, whom he named Miss Lonelyhearts, and his editor, Shrike, who scathingly satirizes Miss Lonelyhearts's wish to give meaning and comfort to his desperate correspondents. The book begins in comedy but, as Miss Lonelyhearts's predicament becomes clearer and clearer, moves toward despair; West described it as a "moral satire" in "the form of a comic strip." Miss Lonelyhearts describes his own moral transformation: "He . . . considers the job a joke, but . . . [eventually] he sees that the majority of the letters are profoundly humble pleas for moral and spiritual advice. . . . For the first time in his life he is forced to examine the values by which he lives. The examination shows him that he is the victim of the joke and not its perpetrator."

West had made the acquaintance, and earned the respect, of several important writers by this time, including Dashiell Hammett, William Carlos Williams, Edmund Wilson, and James T. Farrell; some of these took up residence, gratis, in the Sutton. Thanks to West's friends' help and aided by the author's growing underground reputation, *Miss Lonelyhearts* received remarkably good reviews, but his publisher went bankrupt just as they started to come in, and fewer than 200 copies were available for sale. West's reputation was established, but he was no further along in making writing a profitable career.

Very soon West began his third novel, *A Cool Million* (1934). This was conceived as a satire on the American dream of success—one of the most illusory and bitterly disappointing dreams during the depression. More personally, West's family's fortunes and his own had suffered considerable decline. As a child he had read Horatio Alger, and his parents had been inspired by the American Dream, but the success story was now thoroughly revealed as mythical. West's hero, Lemuel Pitkin, is a classic schlemiel, whose every effort at success is a failure. At the end of the book Lemuel is assassinated; only then does he become "successful"—as a martyr for the National Revolutionary party and its effort to deliver America "from sophistication, Marxism, and International Capitalism."

In the meantime, *Miss Lonelyhearts* was sold to Darryl Zanuck's Twentieth Century Pictures in 1933 and made into a movie titled *Advice to the Lovelorn*. West was hired at Columbia Studios in 1933, and from then to the time of his death he lived in Hollywood and worked in film, eventually being involved in the writing of some thirty movies, many unproduced. Intermittently he worked on many literary projects, but few were completed. He failed to get a Guggenheim fellowship for which he applied. With Joseph Schrank he coauthored a play titled *Good Hunting*; it received a Broadway production in 1938, but it closed after two performances. Film work seemed to be the only way that West could make a living by writing, and he returned to California.

But West's experience in Hollywood also gave him material for his best-known novel, *The Day of the Locust* (1939). While most Hollywood novels focused on movie stars or moguls, persons of power and wealth, West concentrated on a set designer, a group of minor film personages, and the large number of midwesterners who had followed a dream of excitement and fulfillment by coming to California. Tod Hackett, the main character, weaves his way along the seamy underside of Hollywood, among the confused, resentful people who have followed their dreams. He creates a prophetic painting called *The Burning of Los Angeles*, in which the "super-promisers" and their dupes are brought face-to-face apocalyptically. At the end of the novel, Tod is raving with pain and anguish. *The Day of the Locust* remains the best of the hundreds of Hollywood novels written before the 1970s. F. Scott Fitzgerald, who was himself working on *The Last Tycoon*, said that the novel had "scenes of extraordinary power."

On 19 April 1940 West married Eileen McKenney, the model for Ruth McKenney's bestseller, *My Sister Eileen* (1938). For almost the first time in his life West seemed to feel comfortable and satisfied in a relationship. Eileen even shared his love of fishing and hunting, which had long been activities of major importance for West. The couple was returning home from a hunting trip to Mexico on 22 December 1940, when, south of El Centro, California, West went through a stop sign and hit another car. Both he and his wife were thrown from the vehicle. Eileen died on the way to the hospital, and Nathanael died twenty minutes later, without treatment, in the hospital.

Posthumously, West's reputation continued to grow. Hardly known to the general public during his lifetime, he was praised in subsequent years as "the finest prose talent of our age" (William Carlos Williams) and as the author of "one of the three finest [American] novels of our century" (Stanley Edgar Hyman). He influenced many younger writers such as Thomas Pynchon and Flannery O'Connor. Many critics in England and America rank him among the greatest of twentieth-century American novelists.

• West's papers, including manuscripts, photocopied or mimeographed copies of screenplays, and tape recordings concerning his life, are in the Henry E. Huntington Library, San Marino, Calif.; the University of California, Los Angeles; and Brown University. The most complete biography is Jay Martin, *Nathanael West: The Art of His Life* (1970). See also Martin, *Nathanael West: A Collection of Critical Essays* (1971), which contains some of West's writings about his own work and an important essay by W. H. Auden, "West's Disease" (1957). Stanley Edgar Hyman, *Nathanael West* (1962), is brief but insightful. David Madden, *Nathanael West: The Cheaters and the Cheated* (1973), contains several interesting essays. A very helpful bibliography is Dennis P. Vannatta, *Nathanael West: An Annotated Bibliography of the Scholarship and Works* (1976).

JAY MARTIN

WEST, Roy Owen (7 Oct. 1868–29 Nov. 1958), Republican party leader and secretary of the interior, was born in Georgetown, Illinois, the son of Helen Anna Yapp and Pleasant West, an insurance salesman and lumber man. He obtained his early education in the Georgetown public schools. In 1890 DePauw University awarded him an A.B. and an LL.B., and he was elected to Phi Beta Kappa. In 1893 DePauw conferred on him an A.M.

Admitted to the bar in 1890, West began to practice law in Chicago. Three years later he became assistant county attorney, and the following year he took charge of the Cook County Tax Department. Elected city attorney of Chicago in 1895, he served for two years before winning election as a member of the Cook County Board of Review of Assessments, serving from 1898 to 1914. In 1898 West married Louise Augustus; they had one son.

For the next several decades West was almost equally active in law and politics. His firm represented a number of large corporations, including the Samuel Insull interests. West's career as a Republican party leader began in 1900, when he became a member of the Cook County Republican Committee, on which he remained until 1928. After his first wife died in June 1904, he married Louise McWilliams. They had one daughter. From 1904 to 1914 he served as chairman of the Illinois Republican State Central Committee, and he was committee secretary from 1924 to 1928. In 1920 he labored to secure the presidential nomination for Frank O. Lowden. His acquaintances in the party broadened as he attended the national conventions in 1908, 1912, 1916, and 1928.

Early in his career West formed a close association with Charles S. Deneen. He managed Deneen's gubernatorial campaigns in 1904 and 1908 and Deneen's election to the U.S. Senate in 1924. Together West and Deneen were credited with bringing about the resignation of William Lorimer from the Senate, when a state investigation and a Senate inquiry disclosed bribery in the Illinois state legislature's election of Lorimer. On 13 July 1912 the U.S. Senate adopted a resolution that corrupt methods and practices invalidated Lorimer's election. This action gave new life to a lingering Senate resolution in favor of the Seventeenth Amendment, providing for the direct election of senators.

West's activity in Republican politics brought him to Calvin Coolidge's attention. When Hubert Work, secretary of the interior, resigned in 1928, Coolidge appointed West to the vacant cabinet post. At that time West was Republican national committeeman from Illinois, vice chairman of the Finance Committee of the Republican National Committee, and a member of the party's executive committee. The appointment recognized West's decades of service to the party and was a boost to the Deneen wing in Chicago. West was appointed while the Senate was in recess.

Almost immediately opposition sprang up among Republican senators because of West's association with Insull, the utilities magnate. In 1926 West had testified before a Senate committee investigating a campaign contribution of $10,000 that Insull had made, and the investigation resulted in the rejection of Frank L. Smith as a senator from Illinois. When the Senate convened in December 1928, resistance to West's appointment increased among progressive Republican senators.

The Public Lands Committee held hearings on the appointment, interrogating West on his legal work for Insull, his ownership of Insull stock, and the Interior Department's recent activities concerning Insull interests. West testified that he had sold all his holdings in Insull enterprises, he and Insull disagreed on political matters, and the Interior Department's action had been carried out by the assistant secretary of the interior. Senator George Norris joined the opposition to West's confirmation. The Interior post had become a sensitive issue after the Teapot Dome scandal, and concern over power sites was growing. On 21 January 1929 the Senate in secret session voted 53 to 27 to confirm West's nomination. Incensed that West's supporters had resorted to a secret ballot, Norris denounced the proceeding as a further example of the degradation of the democratic process. He was instrumental in changing Senate rules to require that all business be in open session unless a majority vote in closed session determined that a nomination or treaty should be considered in secret.

West's nomination pointed to vital issues in the 1920s—financial contributions by interested persons, public power and conservation questions, undemocratic procedures, and the need for reform of these matters. During his brief tenure West wrote an annual report urging conservation of the nation's natural resources, linking conservation to the future industrial progress and prosperity of the country.

Only weeks after his confirmation, West's term ended on 4 March 1929. In December he declined the post of ambassador to Japan. He returned to his legal practice and involvement with DePauw University and the Methodist church, and he became the head of a conservative Cook County faction called the National Republican party. Retaining a lifelong attachment to his Methodist-affiliated alma mater, he served as president of the board of trustees from 1924 to 1950 and was responsible for raising over $10 million in contributions to the institution. In 1941 he accepted appointment as special assistant to the U.S. attorney general, serving until 1953 as a hearing officer in conscientious objector cases under the Selective Service Law. He died in Chicago. A party stalwart, never a candidate for state or national office, and "a skillful politician of the kid-glove type" (*New York Times*, 29 July 1928), he tended his party's machinery, promoted candidacies, and maintained a reputation untouched by the scandals that shadowed his party in the state and the nation.

• The Calvin Coolidge Papers, Library of Congress, have material related to West. His report is U.S. Department of the Interior, *Annual Report of the Secretary of the Interior, 1928* (1928). His confirmation hearing is U.S. Senate, Committee on Public Lands and Surveys, *Nomination of Hon. Roy O. West to be Secretary of the Interior*, 70th Cong., 2d sess., 12, 18, 19 Dec. 1928. See also the *Indianapolis Star*, 27 July 1928; the *New York Times*, 21 and 29 July 1928; and Richard Lowitt, *George W. Norris: Persistence of a Progressive, 1913–1935* (1971). Obituaries are in the *Chicago Tribune* and the *New York Times*, 1 Dec. 1958.

JAMES A. RAWLEY

WEST, Samuel (3 Mar. 1730–24 Sept. 1807), clergyman and author, was born in Yarmouth, Massachusetts, the son of Sackfield West, a physician, and Ruth Jenkins. During his infancy the family relocated to nearby Barnstable. While still a boy, Samuel displayed a definitive knowledge of the Bible and argued theological precepts so well that the local minister helped prepare him for Harvard College. At Harvard, West received the Fitch and Hollis scholarships, waited tables, and graduated with the class of 1754. After graduation he took a post as schoolmaster in Falmouth, Massachusetts.

West's career as a Congregational clergyman began in December 1757 when he was offered a trial position in Tisbury, Massachusetts. The Martha's Vineyard community was satisfied with his preaching and offered to make his post permanent, but West resigned from this pulpit in March 1759 because of its low salary terms. Afterward, he preached briefly in Plymouth before finally settling in 1760 in the town of Dartmouth (later incorporated as New Bedford), where he was ordained on 3 June 1761. In 1768 he married Experience Howland of Plymouth; they had six children.

Before, during, and after the American Revolution, West vigorously endorsed Whig principles and Federalist governmental concepts. He joined the Continental forces following the battle of Bunker Hill and served for several months as a chaplain. In late September or early October 1775, he helped decipher the traitorous coded letter of his Harvard classmate, Dr. Benjamin Church, in which Church had sent valuable intelligence information concerning General George Washington's military situation to the British. On 29 May 1776, he delivered the Election Day sermon before the Massachusetts legislature. In it, he denounced the king's ministry and staunchly endorsed the patriot revolt as the onset of the millennium. Three years later he was chosen to represent Dartmouth at the Massachusetts constitutional convention; he subsequently advocated ratification of the newly drafted state constitution in articles published in Boston newspapers. In 1788 West lobbied for adoption of the federal Constitution at the state's ratifying convention and personally called on his old Harvard classmate, Governor John Hancock, strongly urging him to support the work of the founding fathers in Philadelphia. In 1789 West's wife died. In 1790 he married a widow, Lovice (Lovisa) Hathaway Jenne; they had no children.

West was a founder of the American Academy of Arts and Sciences in 1780 and a member of the American Philosophical Society, but his most direct contribution to history stemmed from his religious pronouncements. West's sermons were often delivered from notes, and he disdained from resorting to grandiloquent or emotionalistic mannerisms in the pulpit. West's views, which were unusually outspoken, reflected increasing Arminian, anti-Trinitarian sentiments among New England's more liberal Congregational clergymen and, as such, were steps along the path to Unitarianism. In his theological writings he adopted an informal, rationalistic interpretation of the Bible; he questioned whether a Trinity could be positively deduced from the Bible or whether God had established the existence of sin, and he supported free-will concepts in his sermons as well as in his publications. In the latter respect, his *Essays on Liberty and Necessity; in Which the True Nature of Liberty Is Stated and Defended* . . . , first published in 1793 and enlarged in 1795, took issue with the divinely determinative and dogmatic viewpoints of the famed New Light revivalist minister Jonathan Edwards. West's *Essays* rejected several of Edwards's earlier theological arguments, including the revivalist's arguments that there was an unerring connection between the motives and actions of an individual. West also disputed Edwards's strict religious precepts by contending that God's presence is not the causal force for future events. West's more liberal, less dogmatic precepts served to widen divisions within New England's Congregational churches and to extend the openings for Unitarian beliefs in the region. On a different sectarian matter, the Dartmouth cleric, in a Dudlean Lecture to Harvard students, disputed the claims of Anglican clerics about the sole validity of apostolic succession for Episcopal bishops, thereby upholding the validity of Congregational or Presbyterian ordination.

West continued to preach in Dartmouth and the neighboring community of Fairhaven until his dismissal in 1803. Harvard University awarded him the Doctor of Sacred Theology degree in 1793. In his early career, he was evidently well respected by his parishioners despite a long-standing and popular reputation for absentmindedness. In addition to his religious interests, West also dabbled in fields such as anthropology, history, law, philosophy, science, and medicine. He even composed a work on the manufacture of porcelain. West's deteriorating memory, along with his increasingly intemperate habits, caused his dismissal from clerical duties. Afterward, he lived in relative obscurity with a son in Tiverton, Rhode Island, where he died.

• Manuscripts relating to West are in the Harvard University Archives and the Massachusetts Historical Society. West's other prominent publications include *An Anniversary Sermon, Preached at Plymouth, December 22nd, 1777* . . . (1778) and *A Sermon Preached Before the Honorable Council . . . May*

29th, 1776 (1776). There is no full biography of West. The best account of his life is a nine page study in Clifford K. Shipton, *Biographical Sketches of Those who Attended Harvard College in the Classes 1751–1755*, vol. 13 (1965). William B. Sprague, *Annals of the American Pulpit* (1865), offers a less lively and thorough, but still useful record of West's life. Secondary sources relating to this Massachusetts clergyman include Franklyn Howland, *A History of the Town of Acushnet [Massachusetts]* (1907); William J. Potter, *The First Congregational Society in New Bedford* (1889); and Letta B. Stone, *The West Family Register* (1928). Primary sources that mention West can be found in William Bentley, *The Diary of William Bentley, D.D., Pastor of the East Church in Salem Massachusetts* (1905–1914); *Records of the Town of Tisbury [Massachusetts]* (1903); Ezra Stiles, *The Literary Diary of Ezra Stiles* (1901); and Jonathan Edwards, *A Dissertation Concerning Liberty and Necessity, . . .* (1797).

SHELDON S. COHEN

WEST, William Edward (10 Dec. 1788–2 Nov. 1857), artist, was born in Lexington, Kentucky, the son of Edward West, a gunsmith and silversmith, and Sarah Creed Brown. West may have studied painting under George Beck, a landscapist and portraitist who settled in Kentucky prior to 1806, although there is no firm evidence of this. That he early showed an aptitude for painting and may have had lessons is demonstrated by his earliest known portrait, a likeness of his father painted about 1805. Although crudely painted, it is more accomplished than most itinerant portraits and appears to be an excellent characterization. His next known portrait, of Dr. Samuel Brown (c. 1805–1807) is slightly more accomplished. West family tradition holds that it was Brown who subsidized West's lessons with Thomas Sully. West arrived in Philadelphia, Pennsylvania, around 1808 and studied with Sully until the following year when Sully left for a two-year stay in London. From 1809 to around 1817 West maintained a studio in Philadelphia, but little is known of this period. He assisted Sully in painting a replica of Sully's 1815 portrait of Colonel Jonathan Williams.

At the beginning of 1817 West was in New Orleans, Louisiana, where he painted at least one portrait, of Julien de Lallande Poydras, a wealthy resident of the city. Some months later he moved to Natchez, Mississippi, where he painted several prominent citizens, including Joseph Emery Davis, the eldest brother of the future Confederate president, Jefferson Davis. Despite the affection he developed for Natchez and its inhabitants, West was determined to study in Europe. He evidently returned to Philadelphia and departed from there for Le Havre, France, in the latter part of 1819. Early the following year he arrived in Florence, Italy, where he studied and copied the Old Masters in the major Florentine collections. He also traveled to Leghorn, Italy, where he painted a portrait of Lord Byron (1822). The result was an appropriately romantic image of the poet, but his contemporaries held differing opinions as to the accuracy of the likeness; the portraits by British artists Thomas Phillips and Richard Westall are better characterizations. West also painted portraits of Byron's mistress, Teresa Gamba, Countess Guiccioli (1822) and his friends James Henry Leigh Hunt (c. 1824) and Edward John Trelawny, painted in 1829. In addition, West did a painting of Byron's visit in 1822 to the USS *Constitution* (c. 1822–1825), which is his only marine painting. (The *Constitution* was moored off Leghorn at the time.)

West moved in 1824 to Paris, where he did several portraits. He also painted his earliest known "fancy" picture, *The Muses of Painting, Poetry, and Music.* Washington Irving recorded visiting West in Paris in his journal under the date of 3 April 1825. Five weeks later the artist moved to London.

West spent a dozen years in Great Britain and painted many portraits there. His sitters included American banker and philanthropist Joshua Bates (c. 1830/1835) and English poet Felicia Hemans, whom he painted in 1827 and who became a close friend. According to West family tradition the artist, who never married, and Hemans, who was separated from her husband, were romantically involved. There is no certain evidence of this, but that they shared a deep friendship there can be no doubt.

West also painted a number of genre and literary pictures while living in England, among them *The Pride of the Village*, painted in 1830 from a story by Irving; *Annette Delarbre* (1831), which illustrates a scene from Irving's *Bracebridge Hall*; and *The Present* (1835), which shows a bride-to-be examining a gift of jewelry.

In the early 1830s West invested heavily in a pneumatic railway device invented by Jacob Perkins, but the venture failed, and he lost most of his money. In 1837 he decided to return to the United States to recoup his fortune. After an absence of eighteen years, he arrived in his native land that summer, choosing to settle in Baltimore, Maryland.

West established a studio on Baltimore Street and very quickly was painting the town's leading citizens. His sitters included Reverdy Johnson, Ellen Ward Gilmor, and John H. B. Latrobe (all c. 1837/1841). His Baltimore portraits represent his best work. They are distinguished by smooth modeling and a flair for catching something of the sitter's character while endowing that person with a romantic air. It was in Baltimore that he painted his best-known, and possibly his best, portrait: that of Robert E. Lee (Mar. 1838). The first portrait for which he sat, Lee is seen as a young, clean-shaven U.S. Army lieutenant, very different in appearance from the gray-bearded Confederate general of a quarter century later. Lee was said to be the handsomest man in the army; West's likeness bears this out. The artist also painted a companion portrait of Lee's wife, Mary, at the same time.

In 1841 West moved to New York City, where he painted portraits of the city's mercantile elite and distinguished visitors; he also traveled occasionally to Boston. Among those who sat for him during this time were Methodist minister and college president Stephen Olin (c. 1845); Warren Delano, grandfather of Franklin D. Roosevelt, whom West painted around

1845; historian William Hickling Prescott (c. 1844); and Abigail Brooks Adams, wife of Charles Francis Adams and mother of Henry Adams (1847). *The Confessional* (c. 1845/1850) was also executed during his New York period; it depicts a young woman confessing to an elderly priest in a room bathed in a soft light.

West painted relatively few portraits after 1850. The most impressive of these late works is a double portrait of Elizabeth Henrietta Young and Anna Elizabeth Mercer, painted around 1852, a smaller-than-life-size, double, seated full-length. In 1855 he moved from New York to Nashville, Tennessee, where most of his family lived. He resided with his sister Sarah West Woods, of whom he did a portrait not long after his arrival in Nashville; he also painted other relatives, including his nephew's wife, Laura Sevier Norvell, considered to be the best of his late portraits. He seems not to have painted anyone but family members while living in Nashville and eventually ceased painting altogether due to declining health. In April 1857 he wrote his friend Margaret Astor that he had "not taken my brush in my hand for five months" (Pennington, p. 43). He died in Nashville and was buried there in the family plot in the city cemetery.

West stands out from his contemporaries in several respects. He saw more of the world than many of them, traveling as far west as Mississippi and as far east as Italy. He was as comfortable in the best drawing rooms of London as he was on the frontier. He portrayed the leading political, literary, and social figures of his day and depicted individuals as disparate as Lord Byron and Robert E. Lee. His portraits invariably capture not only the personality and some of the character of his sitters but also something of the romantic age in which they lived.

• West's papers are owned by the Archives of American Art, Smithsonian Institution. Two self-portraits are known; one was painted about 1819, the other about 1835. The best account of West's life and career is Estill Curtis Pennington, *William Edward West, 1788–1857, Kentucky Painter* (a somewhat misleading title as West spent most of his life away from his native state), the catalog of an exhibition held at the National Portrait Gallery, Smithsonian Institution, 12 Apr.–16 June 1985 (and subsequently at the Lauren Rogers Museum of Art, Laurel, Miss., and the J. B. Speed Art Museum, Louisville, Ky.). There is a brief account of his career in Henry Theodore Tuckerman, *Book of the Artists* (1868), pp. 197–202.

DAVID MESCHUTT

WESTCOTT, Edward Noyes (27 Sept. 1846–31 Mar. 1898), author and banker, was born in Syracuse, New York, the son of Amos Westcott, a dentist, and Clara Babcock. Although his father was a prosperous and prominent citizen of Syracuse, serving as the first president of the New York State Dental Society and, during part of the Civil War, as mayor of his city, Westcott was unable to follow his desire to pursue a formal education and attend college. After finishing high school at the age of sixteen he took a job as junior clerk with the Mechanics' Bank of Syracuse. In 1866 he moved to New York City, where he worked for the Mutual Life Insurance Company for two years before returning to Syracuse to take a job as discount clerk with the Second National Bank. When that institution closed, he became a teller at the First National Bank and later a cashier with the banking firm of Wilkinson & Company. He married Jane Dows in 1874; the couple had three children.

Westcott was co-founder of Westcott & Abbott, a successful banking and brokerage firm, in 1880. The company was dissolved a few years later following the failure of Wilkinson & Company, with which it was allied, and Westcott took a position as registrar and financial consultant of the Syracuse Water Commission, then in the process of installing a new water supply system in the city. He served with distinction until 1895, when tuberculosis forced him to retire and, in hopes of improving his health, seek the pure air of the Adirondacks. He spent the summer of 1895 at Lake Meacham, New York, where he began to write the novel for which he became famous.

Though his health continued to deteriorate, Westcott worked steadily on the manuscript through the summer and completed the first draft during the winter of 1895 in Naples, Italy. Inspired by no very high literary ambitions, he wrote mainly to keep himself occupied. "It isn't a book yet, and I have not the smallest expectation that it ever will be," he reported in a letter to his daughter in August 1896. "The work has filled up a good many hours which would otherwise have been very dreary, and given me some amusement." Nevertheless he sent it to a publisher the next month. It was not accepted, and his carefully typed copy, given the name "David Harum" by the first publisher he tried, was offered to five other major houses before being accepted by D. Appleton & Company. Appleton's literary adviser, Ripley Hitchcock, wrote him in January 1898 of his firm's desire "to make David Harum's delightful humor known to the reading public." Hitchcock persuaded Westcott to rearrange the text and feature Harum as the focus of the story.

Westcott's novel was published as *David Harum: A Story of American Life* on 23 September 1898. It was an immediate popular success, exhausting six printings in twelve weeks and selling more than 400,000 copies within its first two years. It remained in print for over four decades, and by the early 1930s it had sold more than a million copies. Contemporary reviews were enthusiastic; the *Philadelphia Item* placed Westcott "as a humorist next to Mark Twain, as a master of dialect above Lowell, as a descriptive writer equal to Bret Harte." In 1900 Hitchcock adapted *David Harum* successfully for the stage, where it had a long run, and fifteen years later it was made into a silent movie. In 1934 Will Rogers played the title role in a popular talking film.

A happy blend of local color, romantic sentiment, genial humor, and vivid characterization, *David Harum* tells the story of a sharp-tongued small town banker in the fictitious upstate New York town of Homeville. Although he maintains a crusty manner and is a shrewd horse-trader, Harum is a secret philanthropist who helps a widow satisfy her mortgage and who furthers his assistant's romance. Some of his tart observations were to become proverbial: "'Bus'nis is bus'nis' ain't part of the Golden Rule, I allow, but the way it gen'ally runs, fur's I've found out, is 'Do unto the other feller the way he'd like to do unto you, an' do it fust'" (chap. 20); "They say a reasonable number of fleas is good for a dog—they keep him f'm broodin' on bein' a dog" (chap. 32); "The' ain't nothin' truer in the Bible 'n that sayin' that them as has gits" (chap. 35). Forbes Heermans describes David Harum in his introduction to the first edition as "a character so original, so true, and so strong, yet withal so delightfully quaint and humorous, that we are at once compelled to admit that here is a new and permanent addition to the long list of American literary portraits" (p. vii).

Westcott did not live to see his book in print; he died in Syracuse six months before its publication. Except for a few pamphlets on local political and financial matters, his only other literary efforts appeared posthumously. Two of his poems were published in *Harper's Magazine* in January 1900, and D. Appleton issued a short story of about 10,000 words, *The Teller*, with some of Westcott's letters, in 1901. Westcott was a respected figure in Syracuse, described by Heermans in a biographical essay in *The Teller* as "an intellectual leader in his native city" whose "fine courtesy was invariably a conspicuous part of his bearing" (pp. 106–7). Active in community affairs and the leading baritone in his church choir, Westcott wrote both the words and music of several songs that were published after his death, but it is for his bestselling novel *David Harum* that he is best known. Its place in the annals of American popular fiction as a portrayal of small-town life, and its influence on such later realists as Edgar Lee Masters, Sinclair Lewis, and Maxwell Anderson, give it historical stature above its modest claims as literature.

• A collection of manuscripts, letters, and material related to Westcott is in the Syracuse, N.Y., Public Library. Sketches of his life by his friend Forbes Heermans are in his introduction to *David Harum* (1898); the *New York Times Saturday Supplement*, 24 Dec. 1898; and Westcott's book *The Teller* (1901). An exchange of letters about the author and his book appeared in the *New York Times Saturday Supplement* from 22 Oct. 1898 to 23 Dec. 1899. See also the *New York Times Magazine*, 17 July 1938. For comments on the influence of *David Harum*, see Fred L. Pattee, *The New American Literature, 1890–1930* (1930), and Ima Honaker Herron, *The Small Town in American Literature* (1939).

DENNIS WEPMAN

WESTERGAARD, Harald Malcolm (9 Oct. 1888–22 June 1950), civil engineer and engineering professor, was born in Copenhagen, Denmark, the son of Harald Ludvig Westergaard, a professor of economics at the University of Copenhagen and an authority on mathematical statistics, and Thora Alvida Koch. Westergaard attended University of Copenhagen in 1906–1907 before moving to the Royal Technical College, where he earned a degree in civil engineering in 1911. From 1911 to 1914 he designed reinforced concrete structures, initially for the Danish government and later in Hamburg, Germany, and London, England. But during these same years he devoted time to graduate studies in Germany with Ludwig Prandtl at the University of Göttingen in the spring of 1913, and with August Föppl at the Technische Hochschule in Münich in 1914. He completed his dissertation in 1915 but, because of the war in Europe, did not receive his Doctor Ingenieure degree from Munich until 1925. Westergaard learned much from his German professors, who prepared him to approach engineering problems as exercises in applied mathematics.

Westergaard's life changed in 1914, when he was appointed a fellow of the American-Scandinavian Foundation, which sponsored students at U.S. universities. Westergaard was accepted at the University of Illinois, where he worked with A. N. Talbot on a Ph.D. in theoretical and applied mechanics. In 1916 he became the first recipient of that degree at Illinois and was invited to remain as an instructor in theoretical and applied mechanics. He then rose through the academic ranks, winning promotion to assistant professor in 1921, associate professor in 1924, and full professor in 1927. He became a U.S. citizen in 1920 and in 1925 married Talbot's daughter Rachel Talbot; the couple had two children.

According to one of his students, Nathan Newmark, Westergaard was aloof and had a reputation for absent-mindedness, sometimes driving to school and walking home, forgetting his car at the university. But he was a brilliant graduate instructor who demanded precision and style from his students, a reflection of his meticulous methods. Known as "The Great Dane" on campus, he affected the use of a cane, noting that "one should have an eccentricity to be remembered by" (Kingery et al., p. 10).

Newmark considered Westergaard's years at Illinois, during which he published most of his forty professional papers, to be his most productive. Westergaard had two main research interests: the design of reinforced concrete paving slabs and the stresses on dams. During the summers of 1923, 1926, 1928, 1929, and 1931 he worked for the U.S. Bureau of Public Roads to develop mathematical analyses of concrete pavements for roads and bridges, especially the problem of predicting pavement reactions to wheel loads. In 1923 and 1926 he served as a special analyst on the Stevenson Creek arch dam, an experimental design in California. In 1929–1930 he took a leave of absence from Illinois to become senior mathematician for the Bureau of Reclamation's Hoover Dam project and during subsequent summers was a consulting engineer there, calculating the stresses that Lake Mead, the world's largest man-made lake, would create on the ground. During the 1920s Westergaard also published several papers dealing with the effects of earthquake shocks on tall structures.

Through both his research and his instruction, Westergaard helped introduce engineering mechanics—a theoretical and mathematical European approach—into U.S. engineering. As another biographer commented, "Westergaard became an early, perhaps the earliest, exponent of the new school of thought which regarded engineering problems as problems in classical physics" (*Harvard University Gazette*, p. 80). This approach, which could also be called engineering science, used mathematics and physics to solve complex problems in areas such as vibrations and dynamics, where American engineers had not yet developed general solutions. Westergaard's contributions focused on understanding elasticity, the reaction of structural materials to loads and strains. He especially demonstrated this more sophisticated mathematical approach to engineering problems as a participant in the University of Michigan engineering summer school 1931, 1932, 1934, and 1936. Organized by Stephen Timoshenko, another European engineer, the Michigan program greatly expanded the familiarity of American engineering faculty and graduate students with the newer European approach to engineering.

Westergaard, like other engineering scientists of this period, most of them Europeans, was not a mere theoretician but was equally committed to solving problems in the real world. He therefore undertook professional design work that paralleled his academic research. In 1918 he consulted for the U.S. Shipping Board's Emergency Fleet Corporation on the design of reinforced concrete structures. His long-running studies for the Bureau of Public Roads later influenced state highway departments and BPR construction and design specifications. Moreover, his work on pavement eventually led him to study airport runways for the U.S. Air Force, and to examine tall buildings in Japan subject to earthquakes. In 1946 he considered ways to increase the capacity and security of the Panama Canal for the U.S. Navy.

In 1936 Harvard University invited Westergaard to become Gordon McKay Professor of Civil Engineering. At the time Harvard had initially approached him in 1935, internal politics and budgetary difficulties had intervened, and the University of Michigan then asked him to replace Timoshenko, who had moved to Stanford University. But when the Harvard job was reoffered in 1936, Westergaard turned down the Michigan offer and moved to Cambridge. He told Harvard president James B. Conant that he aimed to move the engineering school "along the lines of the science of engineering with special emphasis on the work of candidates for the higher degrees." In another note to new colleague Lionel S. Marks, he added that changes at Harvard, when combined with the emerging strong department of applied mechanics at Massachusetts Institute of Technology, "would make this neighborhood the real center for developments in Applied Mechanics in this country."

Westergaard's pursuit of this goal was deferred by his appointment as dean of engineering at Harvard in 1937, a post he held until 1946. The outbreak of World War II also forced adjustments, as Westergaard became involved in the military training programs that appeared on many college campuses, including Harvard. Westergaard also spent some time in a navy uniform during the war. After consulting on structural questions for the U.S. Navy's Bureau of Yards and Docks beginning in 1935, he had accepted a reserve commission as lieutenant commander in the navy's Civil Engineering Corps in 1936. Westergaard was promoted to commander in 1940 and served nine short tours of active duty totaling eighteen months between 1942 and 1946. On one tour, in 1945, he served as part of a mission to Japan to study the effects of nuclear blasts on buildings. After the war he turned to preparing a volume that brought together all of his work on elasticity. Unpublished at the time of his death, his only book, *Theory of Elasticity and Plasticity*, appeared posthumously in 1952.

Westergaard received recognition for his leadership role in engineering through the receipt of several awards. The American Concrete Institute presented him with its Wason Medal in 1921, while the American Society of Civil Engineers awarded him its J. J. R. Croes Medal in 1934 and its Thomas Fitch Rowland Prize in 1950. The latter was for a paper on formulas for stresses in airport runways. He was a member of a wide range of professional, engineering, scholarly, and honorary organizations. From 1938 to his death he was a trustee of the American-Scandinavian Foundation, the organization that had first enabled him to come to the United States, and chaired its scholarship committee. According to a student, he loved to walk, swinging his cane while lost in thought. He died in Cambridge, Massachusetts.

• Westergaard's professional papers and correspondence are in the Harvard University Archives. Biographical information is in the *American Philosophical Society Yearbook* (1950), pp. 339–42, and in R. A. Kingery et al., *Men and Ideas in Engineering: Twelve Histories from Illinois* (1967), pp. 9–10. Obituaries are in the *New York Times* and the *Boston Herald*, 24 June 1950, and *Harvard University Gazette*, 16 Dec. 1950.

BRUCE E. SEELY

WESTERMANN, William Linn (15 Sept. 1873–4 Oct. 1954), ancient historian and papyrologist, was born in Belleville, Illinois, the son of Louis Westermann, a store clerk, and Emma Tyndale. He attended the University of Nebraska from 1890 to 1896 (B.A., 1894; M.A., 1896). He returned to Illinois to teach Latin for three years at Decatur High School, but then revealed greater ambition by enrolling as a student of classical philology at the University of Berlin, in what he called the land of his ancestors. In Berlin and in Heidelberg, where he spent one semester, he studied with some of the leading classical scholars of the day, especially with Ulrich von Wilamowitz-Moellendorff and Hermann Diels, who were exacting masters. The product was the brief dissertation, "De Hippocratis in Galeno memoria quaestiones" (Berlin, 1902), notable for its incidental declaration that he was without religious faith.

On his return to the United States, Westermann became an instructor at the University of Missouri, where he was promoted to assistant professor in 1904 before moving in 1906 to the University of Minnesota. In 1908 he was appointed an associate professor of history at the University of Wisconsin, where he became a full professor in 1914. On 15 June 1912, he married Avrina Davies, with whom he had a son.

In 1918–1919 Westermann served as a "specialist on Western Asia" in the U.S. delegation to the Versailles peace conference, where he became acquainted with, among others, Lawrence of Arabia and Arnold Toynbee. He kept a diary, never published, which gives vivid impressions of many of the participants. In Paris in 1919 he met Michael I. Rostovtzeff, probably the most important ancient historian of his generation, who had left Russia after the revolution. The following year Westermann moved to Cornell, arranging that Rostovtzeff should succeed him at Madison, and in 1923 went on to Columbia University, where he remained until his retirement in 1948. The American Historical Association elected him as its president for 1944. Lesser appointments included a year as professor in charge of classical studies at the American Academy in Rome (1926–1927) and two periods at Farouk I University in Alexandria (1949, 1953–1954).

An internationalist in outlook, he helped to bring major foreign scholars to the United States, notably Rostovtzeff, Kurt von Fritz (1937), Elias J. Bickerman (1941), and Rafael Taubenschlag (1942). His most distinguished graduate pupil was Moses I. Finley.

Some time before 1914 Westermann turned his attention from Greek medicine and Greek institutions to the economic history of antiquity, and especially to the Greek papyri from Egypt, which had begun to bear ample fruit in the 1890s, because of the information they provided of daily economic transactions in the ancient world. He helped various American universities, especially Columbia, to acquire documentary papyri, and he edited or coedited a considerable number of such texts in the 1920s and 1930s. His work on inscriptional and papyrological documents was the distinctive mark of his magnum opus about Greek and Roman slavery, which was his greatest scholarly achievement. This began as the article "Sklaverei" (1935), commissioned by the authoritative *Real-Encyclopädie der classischen Altertumswissenschaft* on the advice of Rostovtzeff. It appeared in revised and expanded form as *Slave Systems of Greek and Roman Antiquity* (1955). The latter version had many technical flaws and received mixed reviews, but it attempts a very difficult task and has not been fully replaced. Westermann aimed at giving an account of slavery in its many forms in all the main regions of the Greek and Roman worlds for a period of well over a millennium. His very wide knowledge of the sources gives the work enduring value. His other major works were his coauthored edition of *Zenon Papyri: Business Papers of the Third Century B.C. dealing with Palestine and Egypt* (1934–1940), and his coauthored study, *Apokrimata: Decisions of Septimius Severus on Legal Matters* (1954).

Westermann's main achievement was to contribute to the understanding of the economic basis of Greek and Roman history. He and some of his contemporaries in the United States worked a quiet minor revolution in this respect, but they had few immediate successors.

• There are collections of Westermann's scholarly and professional correspondence in the libraries of the University of Wisconsin and Columbia University. A copy of his 1918–1919 diary is also at Columbia, and a one-page autobiographical statement appears in his dissertation on p. 52. Books not mentioned in the text are his textbook of ancient history (1912); with C. J. Kraemer, *Greek Papyri in the Library of Cornell University* (1926); *Upon Slavery in Ptolemaic Egypt* (1929); and, with C. W. Keyes, *Tax Lists and Transportation Receipts from Theadelphia* (1932). Obituaries are in the *New York Times*, 5 Oct. 1954, and in *Political Science Quarterly* 70 (1955): between pp. 480 and 481.

W. V. Harris

WESTERN, Lucille (8 Jan. 1843–11 Jan. 1877), actress, was born Pauline Lucille Western in New Orleans, Louisiana, the daughter of George Western, an actor and playwright, and Jane (maiden name unknown). Widowed when Lucille was a child, Jane Western was remarried to William B. English, whose name she took. Raised (and apparently financially exploited) by her mother and stepfather, Lucille and her younger sister Helen shared billing in "The Star Sisters," a child act that earned the girls considerable popularity. The Star Sisters toured, most often on the emergent New England circuit, and their act featured dance, comedy, and quick-change artistry. While still in her early teens, Lucille Western began to perform soubrette and juvenile roles in independent bookings, thus inaugurating her career in legitimate theater. (Helen Western, with whom Lucille is confused in some sources, pursued a brief stage career of her own, though less successfully.)

By the time she was twenty, Western had shifted from appearing in variety turns and juvenile roles to performing dramatic leads as a young tragedienne, specializing in the sentimental melodrama so beloved in mid-Victorian America. As one of the many "tragedy queens" (in Walt Whitman's descriptive terminology), Western won an immense following, playing tormented souls such as Lady Isabel/Madame Vine in the Tayleur-Wood *East Lynne*; Nancy Sykes in a popular adaptation of Dickens's *Oliver Twist*; the title roles in *Leah the Forsaken*, directed by Augustin Daly, and J. M. Weston's adaptation of Victor Hugo's *Lucretia Borgia*; and Mrs. Haller in the Benjamin Thompson version of Auguste von Kotzebue's *The Stranger*, perhaps the single most popular exemplar of this lachrymose genre. Such roles made Western a star while still in her early twenties. Joining forces with some of the major male leads of her time, including James A. Herne, James W. Wallack (the younger), and Edward L. Davenport, she toured constantly, playing star turns in virtually every major house in the country. During her prime, from c. 1863 until well into the

1870s, Western commanded an enormous following and salaries comparable to those paid to the biggest names of the day. It has been calculated that *East Lynne* alone brought her more than $250,000 over the course of her career. Western's somewhat prodigal lifestyle and poor choice of financial managers prevented her from attaining great wealth, but she remained economically comfortable throughout her short life.

Western possessed beautiful brunette hair, expressive though uneven features (her younger contemporary Clara Morris referred to "the inspired irregularity of Lucille's face"), and compelling gray eyes that she used to great effect in her many dramatically charged scenes of high passion (Morris, p. 126). She was noted for her volatile temperament and profound mood swings; her greatest successes were thought by some to have been achieved through natural extensions of her personality. Her acting was largely instinctive—untrained and often unrestrained—and she suffered from inadequate direction, such that her obvious natural talent went largely undeveloped. Western lacked "polish," as Morris notes, but nonetheless she possessed unquestionable power. A New Orleans press report of her performance of Nancy Sykes contended that her murder scene "sent ladies in the audience into fainting fits, and drove men from the theatre, so unable were they to endure the strain of her overwhelmingly realistic acting" (quoted in Kendall, p. 513). Morris also admits that she "knew how to interpret a woman's heart, even if she missed her best manner," observing further that "in all she did there was just a touch of extravagance—a hint of lawless, unrestrained passion" (p. 126).

Western literally devoted her life to the theater. Her 1859 marriage to James Harrison Meade of St. Louis lasted only a short time and produced no offspring, a source of considerable grief to Western. The couple eventually divorced (date unknown). (Some sources claim that she married Herne, with whom she toured extensively, but such was not the case.) Despite her personal disappointments, Western was a great success in her career, and she maintained an enthusiastic (though diminished) following until her death. Unquestionably, the vogue of sentimental melodrama and Western's identification with the female leads in these exercises in emotional extravagance served her well. Toward the end of her career melodrama became increasingly unpopular, and her stardom clearly waned. Nonetheless, at the time of her death Western was still very active in her career, despite failing health. She died of pneumonia in New York during an engagement at the Park Theater.

• There is no known repository of Western's papers. Most of the standard works on the nineteenth-century American stage treat aspects of her career, for example, Thomas Allston Brown, *History of the American Stage* (1870); Brown, *A History of the New York Stage* (1903); and George C. D. Odell, *Annals of the New York Stage*, vol. 7 (1931). Additional insights into her life may be gleaned from John S. Kendall, *The Golden Age of the New Orleans Theater* (1952); and Clara Morris, *Life on the Stage* (1901). Newspaper accounts, including obituaries, are in the New York *Clipper*, 20 Jan. 1877; the *New York Times*, 27 Feb. 1876 and 12 Jan. 1877; and the New York *Dramatic Mirror*, 23 Apr. 1898.

JAMES H. DORMON

WESTERVELT, Jacob Aaron (20 Jan. 1800–21 Feb. 1879), shipbuilder and marine architect, was born in Tenafly, New Jersey, the son of Aaron Westervelt, a shipbuilder, and Vroutie Westervelt; his parents were cousins. At the age of seventeen, Westervelt, following his father, served as an apprentice to Christian Bergh, a successful shipbuilder in New York City. After completing his training in 1820, Westervelt established a business in Savannah, Georgia, where he built several vessels. Returning to New York in 1822 at the invitation of his old boss, he became a partner in the firm of Christian Bergh and Company. Westervelt's timing could not have been better, for the age of the packet ship was dawning, and Bergh's firm, located on the East River in Lower Manhattan proximate to three other shipyards on the East River, would be the common birthplace of nearly 150 packets that would be built in New York in the next thirty years. In 1825 Westervelt married Elizabeth M. Thompson, with whom he had eight children. Two of his sons would join his firm in the late 1850s and take it over at his retirement.

Regularly scheduled transatlantic sailing lines were being established during these years, and both American and European shipping firms were seeking new ships to operate these lines. The American packet admirably suited this need. The new ships were roomy enough for both passengers and profitable cargo. They were also sturdy enough to withstand the heavy punishment of rugged seas in the westward passage where an ordinary ship would have been pounded apart.

Westervelt's packet ships became a major feature of this Atlantic trade in the 1820s and 1830s. While his vessels were to display no innovative features of design, they were noted for their seaworthiness and their economy of construction. His best-known packets in these years were the *Montana*, *Paris*, *France*, *Philadelphia*, and *Toronto*. They averaged about 600 tons to 700 tons with a 140-foot length and 32-foot beam. Durability rather than speed was the important feature. Thus an Atlantic crossing from New York to Liverpool took an average of twenty-four days with the return trip taking about thirty-six days. This sizable difference in time was due to the problem caused by wind direction across the Atlantic. Ships sailing eastward toward Europe were pushed along by the fairly constant force of winds called the Prevailing Westerlies. Because ships could not sail against these winds on the return trip, they were forced to head southward before crossing the ocean to pick up the Trade Winds, which blew in the opposite direction. This extra leg southward accounted for the time differential.

In 1837, after making a fortune in building ships, Westervelt traveled to Europe to study shipbuilding techniques in foreign yards. On his return to New

York City one year later he built two ships while in a brief partnership with Nathan Roberts. Then in 1841 he formed a partnership with William MacKay that was to endure for a decade. By 1847 Westervelt had launched forty-three ocean packets and seven coastal packets. In 1851 he began building on his own until he was joined in 1859 by his sons Daniel and Aaron; the three served as partners until Jacob Westervelt's retirement in 1868.

By midcentury when Westervelt was striking out on his own, major changes were taking place in maritime shipping. Steam was replacing sail power in the Atlantic trade, and a faster sailing-type vessel, the clipper ship, was about to dominate the Pacific region where, for the moment, few coaling stations were available. Westervelt's response to the challenge of steam was the construction in 1847 of the 1,700-ton *Washington* and the *West Point*. In the mid-1850s he completed the steam frigate *Brooklyn* for the navy. During the Civil War this vessel served as a major addition to Admiral David Farragut's fleet, where it played a significant role in the capture of the Confederate ports of New Orleans and Mobile.

But it would be the new clipper ship, rather than the steamship, that would capture Westervelt's attention. Gold discoveries in California in the late 1840s and then in Australia in the 1850s created an insatiable demand for the new fast-sailing ships. Westervelt responded with four clippers in 1851, the *N. B. Palmer*, *Eureka*, *Hornet*, and *Golden Gate*; two in 1852, the *Golden City* and *Contest*; and three in 1853, the *Golden State*, *Resolute*, and *Cathay*. In 1856 Westervelt took a break from his shipbuilding to make a 95-day trip around Cape Horn to San Francisco to test the sailing qualities of the clipper ship *Sweepstakes* that his sons had helped build. Although his clippers were of excellent quality, they were not the match of his closest rivals, William Webb and Donald McKay.

In addition to building ships, Westervelt was active in other fields. He became involved in politics, and as a member of the reform faction of the Democratic party he was elected mayor of New York City, serving one term (1852–1854). Any success against the powerful conservative machine forces opposing reform required the support of the city's new Know Nothing party. With that party's demise in the mid-1850s, both locally and nationally, the reform issue diminished, and the way was cleared for the emergence in the 1860s of the corrupt Tammany regime of William "Boss" Tweed.

Westervelt in the meantime moved in another direction. In 1870, just after his retirement, he was appointed superintendent of docks, and three years later he became president of the New York Dock Commission. His time as commission president was spent in efforts to strengthen New York's position in maritime trade. He died at his home on Grand Street in the East Broadway district of New York City.

• Biographical information concerning Westervelt can be found in William T. Westervelt, *Genealogy of the Westervelt Family* (1905). His shipbuilding achievements are well documented. His important role in New York shipbuilding operations is best seen in John H. Morrison, *History of New York Shipbuilders* (1909); G. W. Sheldon, "The Old Shipbuilders of New York," *Harper's New Monthly Magazine*, June–Nov. 1882, pp. 223–41; and Richard McKay, *South Street: A Maritime History of New York* (1934). Westervelt's fame in the construction of the clipper ship is clearly presented in four monographs, Octavius T. Howe and Frederick C. Matthews, *American Clipper Ships* (2 vols., 1967); Carl C. Cutler, *Greyhounds of the Sea* (1930); Arthur H. Clark, *The Clipper Ship Era* (1911); and Howard Chapelle, *History of American Sailing Ships* (1935). The story of America's loss of supremacy in shipping and shipbuilding, affecting Westervelt and his rivals in the 1850s, can be found in the *New York Times*, 4 and 24 Nov. 1858; 30 Apr. 1859; and 19 Sept. 1860.

WILLIAM L. CALDERHEAD

WESTINGHOUSE, George (6 Oct. 1846–12 Mar. 1914), inventor and manufacturer, was born in Central Bridge, Schoharie County, New York, the son of George Westinghouse and Emeline Vedder, farmers. In 1856 his father, blessed with mechanical aptitude, relocated the family to Schenectady, New York, where he formed G. Westinghouse & Company. The firm manufactured agricultural implements, and its machine shop provided young Westinghouse with his first opportunities for mechanical experimentation. Westinghouse divided his time between attendance at local schools and tinkering in his father's shop. He produced his first invention, a rotary engine, by the age of fifteen. With the outbreak of the Civil War in 1861, however, he followed the example of two older brothers and ran away from home to join the Union army. He briefly served with the Twelfth Regiment, New York National Guard, before his parents forced him, because he was still only fifteen, to return home. Finally able to sway his parents to his wishes, Westinghouse joined the Sixteenth Regiment, New York Cavalry, in 1863. He resigned from the army in December 1864 to join the Union navy, where he served as acting third assistant engineer aboard the USS *Muscoota*. Following the war's end, he returned to his father's plant in Schenectady.

With his military career over, Westinghouse wasted no time reestablishing himself in civilian life. He entered the sophomore class at nearby Union College in the fall of 1865 but dropped out shortly thereafter. The school's classical curriculum held little fascination for him. On 31 October 1865 he obtained his first patent for a rotary steam engine similar to his previous design, and later that year he patented a device for replacing derailed railroad cars. Sales of the latter invention were brisk, and he soon designed a reversible cast-steel frog, a device that prolonged the life of railroad track switches. His business arrangement, however, failed. The local partnership that he had formed to manufacture his inventions lacked sufficient capital, and Westinghouse also suspected his partners of cheating him. In the midst of these developments, in 1867 he married Marguerite Erskine Walker; they had one son.

Seeking greater horizons, Westinghouse relocated to Pittsburgh, Pennsylvania, in early 1868. On 13 April 1869 he patented the first of his many major innovations, the railroad air brake. The growth and development of the railroad industry at the time produced ever increasing amounts of railroad traffic, which created a demand for faster train speeds. Westinghouse's idea was hardly original; other inventors had produced similar devices as early as 1833. His invention, however, far surpassed previous designs in practicality and allowed either the engineer or the conductor to bring a speeding train to a quick stop. The device gained immediate acceptance in the railroad industry, and its impact was enormous. Trains traveled at higher speeds more safely than had previously been possible. On 28 September 1869 he formed the Westinghouse Air Brake Company to manufacture his invention, which he continued to perfect. He ultimately received more than twenty additional patents on the brakes.

While producing few original inventions in the course of his career, Westinghouse possessed a genuine talent for taking the ideas of others and making them practical. Having made a significant contribution to railroad safety with his air brakes, he next turned his attention to the problem of providing railroads with switching and signaling systems capable of handling the increased line traffic. Beginning in 1880 Westinghouse purchased patents for signal and interlocking switch systems and combined the best features of existing systems with his own innovations. He organized the Union Switch & Signal Company in May 1881, and his innovative system gained rapid approval within the industry.

Not yet fully occupied, Westinghouse accepted another industrial challenge. Although large deposits of natural gas had been discovered in the Pittsburgh area, an efficient and safe method of transporting the fuel had yet to be developed. Applying his mechanical acumen to the problem, Westinghouse devised a system that featured pipes of increasing diameters carrying gas at progressively lower pressures; this allowed gas to travel safely and with fewer leaks.

Westinghouse then embarked upon what would become his greatest achievement—resolving the so-called "war of the currents" in the favor of alternating electrical current. Although Thomas A. Edison had staked out a position as an industry leader in the field, his insistence upon the use of direct current electricity was problematic. Efficient electrical transmission demanded the usage of high voltages, and with direct current restrained to levels of 100 to 200 volts by safety requirements, its effective transmission range was minuscule. Westinghouse, learned that Lucien Gaulard and John D. Gibbs had in 1882 patented a "secondary generator" (better known as the transformer), and he cautiously investigated its possibilities. He hired talented engineers like Albert Schmid, O. B. Shallenberger, Nikola Tesla, and William Stanley to test a trial system in Great Barrington, Massachusetts, in late 1885. Encouraged by the results, he organized the Westinghouse Electric Company on 8 January 1886 and set out to conquer the market.

Resistance to the new form of transmission, however, was not long in coming. Industry leaders, including Edison, waged a loud campaign against the new development, alleging that it represented a hazard to the general public. Opponents of alternating current persuaded municipalities to outlaw high-tension wires over city streets and, in a masterful stroke of public relations, had New York State's electric chair fitted out with a Westinghouse generator. Despite the opposition, the advantages of alternating current soon made its use nearly universal, especially after Westinghouse created a brilliant display at the 1893 World Columbian Exposition in Chicago. Consisting of over 92,000 lamps and an electric kitchen, the presentation netted the firm a contract to build a huge hydroelectric power plant at Niagara Falls, New York.

The three 5,000-horsepower generators that Westinghouse Electric installed at Niagara Falls were the high point of the firm's development. Westinghouse constantly improved upon his creations and improvised new ones, and in the process he obtained some 361 patents in his lifetime. With the assistance of Shallenberger, he developed an induction meter to measure the amount of current received by customers in 1886. By 1889 the company operated around the globe and employed over 500,000 people and had concentrated a large part of its operations in the Turtle Creek valley east of Pittsburgh, where it established a company town called Wilmerding. An ideal community in many respects, the town was the most outstanding example of Westinghouse's benevolent employment practices. He developed a reputation for paying fair wages and providing generous benefits, and his workers responded by avoiding the labor strife that plagued many of Westinghouse's competitors. Conditions at Westinghouse were so good that labor leader Samuel Gompers said that more employers like Westinghouse would put labor unions out of business.

Westinghouse showed few if any signs of slowing down as the years passed. He returned to work with engines around 1895, when he learned of a new steam turbine developed by Englishman Charles Parsons. He purchased the American rights to Parson's design and installed test turbines in the Pittsburgh plant. By 1900 he had installed similar units in Hartford, Connecticut. Convinced of the potential of the design, Westinghouse also promoted its adaptation for nautical propulsion. The turbines, which generated effective power while occupying a fraction of the space of the more traditional reciprocating engines, became the predominant form of propulsion on the high seas by 1915.

Although highly profitable, Westinghouse's businesses faced considerable financial demands. Litigation, including patent infringement suits, was a costly drain on Westinghouse Electric, which was not immediately profitable and had to be supported by the air brake and switching firms. By 1889 Westinghouse had turned to local financiers for additional capital. Although Westinghouse Electric managed to carry a considerable amount of debt for many years, even surviving the aftermath of the panic of 1893, the panic of 1907 proved its undoing, and it was temporarily forced into receivership. Westinghouse managed to regain limited control of the company by 1908, but his powers were severely curtailed. In 1911 he retired from active management of Westinghouse Electric but remained involved with Westinghouse Air Brake and Union Signal & Switch. He received numerous awards during his lifetime and continued to experiment with turbines until his health broke in late 1913. He died in New York City.

Westinghouse made numerous contributions to the development of American transportation and industry. Although the unfortunate loss of control of Westinghouse Electric clouded his later years, his role in establishing the dominance of alternating current electricity was crucial, and his numerous mechanical improvements greatly facilitated the expansion and development of the American railroad system.

• Westinghouse's papers are at the George Westinghouse Museum in Wilmerding, Pa. He is the subject of numerous secondary accounts. Dated but still useful are Francis E. Leupp, *George Westinghouse: His Life and Achievements* (1918), and Henry G. Prout, *A Life of George Westinghouse* (1921). Among the best of the recent scholarship on Westinghouse are John H. White, *American Railroad Passenger Car* (1978); Mary Brignano and Hax McCullough, *The Search for Safety: A History of Railroad Signals and the People Who Made Them* (1981); and Thomas P. Hughes, *Networks of Power: Electrification in Western Society, 1880–1930* (1983). An obituary is in the *New York Times*, 13 Mar. 1914.

EDWARD L. LACH, JR.

WESTLEY, Helen (28 Mar. 1875–12 Dec. 1942), stage and film actress, was born Henrietta Remsen Meserole Manney in Brooklyn, New York, the daughter of Charles Palmer Manney, a drugstore proprietor, and Henrietta Meserole. She traced her lineage through her father back to the Huguenots and through her mother back to the Dutch. She claimed to have inherited her nature and strikingly handsome face from this mixture. While still a child she decided to pursue an acting career. In 1894 she entered the Brooklyn School of Oratory, where she tenaciously pursued her goal, a character trait for which she would be known throughout her life. She then attended Boston's Emerson College of Oratory (1894–1895) and the American Academy of Dramatic Arts in New York. She received a good dose of practical training while working for Rose Stahl in her touring stock company. She appeared with Stahl in her stage debut, when she was twenty-two, at the Star Theatre, 13 September 1897, in a comedy, *The Captain of the Nonsuch*. She continued her career, appearing in vaudeville and touring companies working the Mississippi River route, playing a wide variety of roles. This practical experience coupled with her professional training turned her into an actress of extraordinary ability, enabling her to play the strange characters for which she was sought after on stage and in film throughout her life. In 1900 she married Jack Westley, an actor. The marriage produced one child and lasted until their separation in 1912. During this period she was as tenaciously dedicated to her family as she later was to the ideals of an "art theater." In 1912 she cast off the role of domesticity and took on the role of bohemian, joining the ranks of the Liberal Club, the center of social life in Greenwich Village, where she rubbed shoulders with Susan Glaspell, Sinclair Lewis, and Theodore Dreiser. From the Liberal Club emerged the two important theater groups Westley was influential in forming: the Washington Square Players and the Theatre Guild. These two theaters greatly influenced the direction of American theater by raising the artistic standards of Broadway and film. With the Washington Square Players in 1915 she returned to the stage as the Oyster in *Another Interior*, a satire on Maurice Maeterlinck's *Interior*. In 1916 she acted with the group in *The Sea Gull*. She further demonstrated her range and versatility in the company's productions of plays by Henrik Ibsen, George Bernard Shaw, and Eugene O'Neill.

In 1918 Westley, Lawrence Langner, and Philip Moeller met to discuss an innovative idea for a new kind of theater. Their intention was to produce plays of high artistic merit, to spurn the character and commercialism of Broadway, and to establish an art theater that would produce intelligent plays that stirred the soul and gave beauty to the mind. Westley believed in the idea that a theater should produce not stars or personalities but plays, plays that showed the "mind of man and what his ego can, through its actors teach them to expect of people and life." It was her belief that "the popular play presents an actor, while the actor of the art theater presents a play." The New York Theatre Guild was founded in late 1918 with Westley as one of the six original members of the board of directors. She dedicated herself unselfishly to the Guild for more than fifteen years. It was at the Theatre Guild that Westley distinguished herself as one of the greatest character actresses in the United States, performing forty-six roles from shrew to seductress, genteel mother to child murderer, all distinctly different parts but all forceful women. "I have always liked a more forceful woman type," said Westley, "whether she be a force for good or bad. I have insisted that she have some strong strain in her make-up, a strong and passionate amorous strain." She was not interested in the size of the part and believed ardently in Stanislavsky's admonition that there are no small parts only small actors. Westley was a capable and passionate actress in whatever part she played. Among her varied roles were Dona Sirena in *The Bonds of Interest* (1919), Matryona in *Power of Darkness* (1920), Alice in *Dance of Death* (1920), Nurse Guinness in *Heartbreak House* (1920), Mrs. Muskat in *Liliom* (1921), Zinida in *He Who Gets Slapped* (1922), Mrs. Zero in *The Adding Machine* (1923), Mrs. Higgins in *Pygmalion* (1926), Mrs. Evans in *Strange Interlude* (1928), Mrs. Light in *Dynamo* (1929), and Mrs. Pesta in *The Camel through the Needle's Eye* (1929).

She went to Hollywood in 1934 to film *Moulin Rouge*. For the next eight years she portrayed creatures charming and odd, malevolent and repellent, in forty-one films and became affectionately known as the grande dame of stage and film. Among her film credits are *The House of Rothschild* (1934), *Death Takes a Holiday* (1934), *Roberta* (1935), *Showboat* (1936), *Heidi* (1937), *Rebecca of Sunnybrook Farm* (1938), *Alexander's Ragtime Band* (1938), *Sunny* (1941), and *My Favorite Spy* (1942), which she finished the year she died.

She appeared in films for RKO, United Artists, Warner Bros., Paramount, MGM, Universal, and 20th Century–Fox, leaving her time to appear only once on the stage, in 1939 in *The Primrose Path* at the Biltmore.

A handsome, mysterious figure, Westley was a "woman of vivid dark beauty, imagination and charm," as Langner recalled her. In his association with her in the Theatre Guild he came to respect her as "one of the most refreshing personalities in the theater as well as one of its most talented character actresses" and also as "one of the most original and delightful members of the board . . . who was possessed of a kind of impractical imagination which makes imaginative ventures practical." He credited her with the ability to go "always in the direction of greatness . . . her charm, vitality, and integrity in the selection of plays, her insistence that the board should produce only the finest, and her ability to evaluate the second rate and to distinguish it from that which was first rate, were invaluable to the board." Theresa Helburn described her as "an unforgettable woman, individual, striking and Bohemian" with a "theatrical appearance and manner." Carol Bird noted that there was something "distinctly exotic and baffling about her and she was never long divorced from her diversified and strange-women roles." Inquiring as to what was the most important thing in her life, Westley replied, "Love, love is the greatest thing in life."

After twenty-four years on the Theatre Guild board Westley resigned in 1942. After completing her last picture, she returned to New Jersey, ill with cardiovascular problems. Helburn observed that she managed her illness as if she were directing a play with herself in the lead role and her bedroom as the theater where she acted the last scenes of her life. She died at Jacques Lane Farm, Franklin Township, New Jersey. Ed Hogan said of her, "She was one of the rarest personalities I ever came across and I don't think she will really be dead until everyone who knew her is."

• A 1939 manuscript biography of Westley by Harry Brand, publicity director of RKO Studios, is in the library of the Academy of Motion Picture Arts and Sciences, Hollywood, Calif. For information on Westley see Lawrence Langner, *The Magic Curtain* (1951); Theresa Helburn, *A Wayward Quest* (1960); Walter Prichard Eaton, *The Theatre Guild: The First Ten Years* (1929); Carol Bird, "An Actress Who Plays Unusual Women," *Theatre Magazine*, Aug. 1922; "Adventuress with a Difference," *New Yorker*, 27 Mar. 1926; and profiles in the *Herald Tribune*, 15 Mar. 1942, and the *New York Times*, 12 Dec. 1937. Confusion over Westley's birth date is clarified through the death certificate, which gives the birth year as 1875. An obituary is in *Variety Weekly*, 16 Dec. 1942.

DIXIE SMITH

WESTON, Brett (16 Dec. 1911–22 Jan. 1993), photographer, was born Theodore Brett Weston in Los Angeles, California, the son of Edward Weston, a photographer, and Flora May Chandler. Edward Weston, who earned an international reputation for his soft-focus, pictorial-style portraits, made a bold move in the early 1920s by abandoning this technique. He ventured to Mexico in 1923 with his eldest son, Edward Chandler Weston, and experimented with subtle changes in his method of photographing nudes, still lifes, and natural forms. He returned to the United States at the end of 1924 but soon left again for Mexico, this time taking Brett with him. On this trip, which lasted several months from 1925 into 1926, Edward Weston further changed his style and began using the camera to produce sharper images. This change in his father's style affected Brett Weston's future as a photographer, for it was during this time in Mexico that he first became passionate about the craft and began taking pictures himself. He was still a boy, just thirteen years old, but he was afforded the use of his father's Graflex, a precision camera that cost $135. Edward Weston became mentor to his son, whose formal education ended after the sixth grade.

While in Mexico, Brett Weston studied his father's technique and offered variations on it, such as the substitution of glossy bromide paper for platinum matte paper. As Weston put it, "I was a pretty outspoken kid, you know, and he [Edward] was very responsive to what I said." Edward was more than responsive; he was impressed by his son's natural affinity for photography and said, "He is doing better at fourteen than I did at thirty. To have someone close to me, working so excellently, with an assured future, is a happiness hardly expected." This pride in his son's work led Edward in 1927 to include twenty of Brett's photographs in his show at the University of California at Berkeley and in 1928 to make him his professional partner in a portrait studio he opened in San Francisco. That same year Brett was given his first solo show by the Jake Zeitlin Gallery in Los Angeles. Of more importance to his career, however, he was invited, at age seventeen, to exhibit twenty of his photographs at the prestigious Film und Foto exhibition in Stuttgart, Germany. This exhibition, organized by the Deutsche Werkbund, a progressive art society, featured more than a thousand photographs that captured a functional understanding of the art of photography. Some of Weston's entries were reproduced in European magazines, thus gaining him an international reputation.

In 1929 Weston moved from San Francisco to Carmel, California. His father, having separated from Brett's mother (Edward's first wife), moved in with him soon thereafter. The two men continued to work together, sharing the responsibilities of the portrait business. In their spare time they explored Point Lobos, where according to historian Beaumont Newhall, they took some of their best photographs. They photographed driftwood, seaweed, and eroded rocks in close-up. They focused on the abstract patterns found in nature and produced photographs that emphasized texture and light.

In May 1930 father and son split amicably, Brett doing so to establish his independence. He set up his own portrait studio in Glendale, California. He used a 4″ × 5″ Graflex that his father bought secondhand in 1929, but for private work he had an 8″ × 10″—a gift from his mother. This became the camera he used most often.

In 1932 Weston was given his first major solo exhibition by the M. H. De Young Memorial Museum in San Francisco. Later that same year Group f/64, an informal art society founded by Ansel Adams and Willard Van Dyke and influenced by Edward Weston, asked him to contribute to their exhibition at the same museum. The group, named after the aperture setting on a camera lens that secures the greatest sharpness in the image, was comprised of photographers wanting to promote "straight" photography and protest against academic pictorialism. They also wanted recognition for West Coast photography similar to that achieved by Alfred Stieglitz in New York.

Like many fellow artists, Weston spent the depression years as an employee of the Works Projects Administration. In addition to being a photographer, he showed skill as a sculptor and worked as such on the Public Works of Art Project. He later served as supervisor of the photographic section of the Federal Arts Project, training and supervising the work of other photographers. During this time he married Elinore Stone, but the marriage lasted only two years. In 1935 Weston married cellist Cicely Edmunds, with whom he had his only child, a daughter. This marriage, too, ended in divorce, and Weston was married twice more: to Dody Warren in 1950 and Christine Goodwyn in 1970.

Beginning in 1941 Weston worked as a photographer for the Douglas and North American Aircraft corporations. He later worked at 20th Century–Fox as an assistant cameraman. In 1943 he joined the army and served three years, part of that time in New York City taking photographs. The assignments were routine, and Weston was left with much time to continue his personal work. He roamed the city, photographing places such as backs of buildings, alleyways, and other urban scenes away from the public eye. He photographed plant forms at the New York Botanical Garden in the Bronx and took pictures from rooftops and other high perches. "There are few people in these photographs," said Newhall, "but humanity is everywhere."

After his discharge from military service, Weston received a Guggenheim Fellowship that allowed him to travel from Texas to New York and all along the East Coast. Some of the photographs taken during this time are contained in two portfolios, *White Sands* (1949) and *New York* (1951). When he returned to California, Weston aided his father in the production of his *Fiftieth Anniversary Portfolio* (1952). Edward, who was then ailing from Parkinson's disease, could not print the photographs himself, so Brett handled the task, which involved gathering 12 pictures in an edition of 100. In addition to this massive project and with the help of his brother Cole and others, Brett also made prints of more than 800 of Edward's best pictures, assembling them in a special portfolio published in 1955.

Following his father's death in 1958, Weston traveled for the first time to Europe, photographing "whatever he found challenging in form and texture" instead of the famous sights and characteristic locales one might have expected. For example, rather than photographing London Bridge as a whole, Weston focused on a rusted, flaking patch of iron. After this successful trip, he returned to Europe in 1968 at the invitation of the West German government as part of a cultural exchange.

Weston spent much time during the 1960s and 1970s traveling throughout North America; in 1973 a grant from the National Endowment for the Arts enabled him to go on a working trip to Alaska. His work was influenced during this time by the new movements in painting, especially the work of abstract expressionists such as Willem de Kooning and Jackson Pollock. Although his subjects were found in nature, such as a glacier breaking up, they could be considered abstract. As Newhall said of Weston's work, "this combination of the abstract, in the emphasis upon form, and the sense of presence, in the rendering of light and substance, is something only photography can do."

In the 1980s Weston divided his time between Carmel and a home in Hawaii. His body of work continued to accumulate, and his last major project involved photographing the landscape and flora of the Hawaiian Islands. On his eightieth birthday Weston burned all but twelve of his negatives, much to the dismay of the photographic community. He strongly believed that the printing process was as important a part of the creative act as the subject matter, and therefore no one else would be capable of making the kind of print needed to express his vision fully. Weston died in Kona, Hawaii.

Weston's success as a photographer is demonstrated by the many exhibitions in which he participated, including more than 100 solo shows. At a time when few others thought to do so, he captured in his pictures harsh desert landscapes, decaying industrial sites, and other settings that seemingly were unaesthetic. He did not believe in manipulating the image through darkroom processing techniques such as double exposure or the use of filters, and he argued successfully that a photographer could create fantastic images through found objects in the natural world. Though his work is often compared to that of his father, Weston distinguished himself as an artist in his own right and further advanced the use of straight or pure photography.

• In the afterword of *Voyage of the Eye* (1975), historian and family friend Beaumont Newhall provides a good timeline of Weston's career up to the mid-1970s. This book also has a bibliography of articles on Weston and a list of his portfolios. Other photo collections include *Brett Weston Photographs*, with text by Merle Armitage (1956), and *Brett Weston: Photographs from Five Decades*, with text by R. H. Cravens (1980). Magazine articles include Lew Parella, "Brett Weston," *U.S. Camera* (1956): 238–43; Dody Weston Thomson, "Brett Weston, Photographer," *American Photography* 46, no. 9 (Sept. 1952); and Charis Wilson Weston, "Brett Weston: Photographer," *Camera Craft* 47 (Mar. 1940): 113–22. A motion picture documentary titled *Brett Weston: Photographer* was directed and distributed by Art Wright (1972; rev. 1974). An obituary is in the *New York Times*, 25 Jan. 1993.

DEBBIE GRIGGS CARTER
LISABETH G. SVENDSGAARD

WESTON, Christine (31 Aug. 1904–3 May 1989), novelist, was born Christine Goutière in Unao, India, the daughter of Georges Goutière, a lawyer, and Alicia Wintle. Georges Goutière's family were French indigo planters; Alicia Wintle was the daughter of an English army officer. Christine Goutière was taught mostly at home, learned to read at four, wrote stories at four and a half. Because of World War I and the danger of traveling, she was not sent to a Belgian convent for schooling as planned. She went instead to a convent school in the hills near her home. Miserable there, she kept running away and finally was withdrawn. Her education after that took place mainly in her father's law library, among his books. Except for short visits to England, she lived in India until she married Robert Weston, an American, in 1923 and they went to the United States to live in Maine. Robert Weston died in the early 1950s. Weston married Roger Griswold in 1960; he died in 1973.

Weston was awarded a Guggenheim Fellowship in 1940. *Be Thou the Bride*, her first novel, was published that same year. Although it received some negative reviews because of the darkness of the story, other reviewers commented on the power of Weston's prose, her ability to create characters, and her promise as a writer of narrative.

In *Indigo* (1943), the novel for which she is perhaps best known, Weston explored, through the lives of Jacques and his Indian friend Hyardal, the issues of race and the presence of the English in India. In a scene in which Jacques's mother, Madame St. Remy, the owner of an indigo farm, pays her workers, Weston delineated some of the problems caused by the colonization and exploitation of India:

> . . . men, women, and children, barefooted, their clothing splashed with the olive and orange and the final intense blue of indigo . . . arranged themselves in a semi-circle before Madame's table and there squatted, coughing, murmuring, exchanging glances and small signals of expectancy . . . there was nothing Madame St. Remy could do about that look in her labourer's eyes; there was nothing that the moneylender could do about it, for he too had to live, and it is never enough just to live . . . There were too many of them, too many just like them. . . . One's children took up the burden where one left off.

Indigo was praised for the richness of its setting, its nostalgic poignancy, its evocation of the culture of India. Speaking of the novel with *New York Times* critic Harvey Breit, Weston said, "I wrote that book almost from memory; I had been away twenty years, you know . . . You might say that it is an example of how important the impressions of childhood are."

Perhaps those childhood impressions and the desire to share them led to her next book, *Bhimsa, the Dancing Bear* (1945); her only children's book, it became a Newbery Honor book in 1946. Through the story of two boys who run away, one English, the other Indian, and the bear that accompanies them, Weston portrayed the beauty and freedom of India's wild places. *A Critical History of Children's Literature* (1953) speaks of the beautiful picture of India she painted and the magical quality of the story, explaining that "David . . . with Gopala and his wonderful bear . . . is rushing into the fulfillment of a dream that is common to children everywhere: the freedom to roam where they will, to eat what they will and to sleep when they will, to enjoy perfect, unchecked freedom."

The culture, traditions, and conflicts of India figure prominently in many of Weston's writings. In *There and Then* (1947), a collection of short stories, is "ample indication of her understanding of the Indian culture. Her imagination is caught up by folklore and philosophy of reincarnation of the soul. . . . 'The Mud Horse' and 'Roshan' are based on such beliefs" (Khattak, pp. 28–29).

Critic Joseph Hitrec linked Weston's name with that of British novelist E. M. Forster as novelists who "have contributed more to an understanding of India than all of the informative books of factual writers." Weston's novel *The World Is a Bridge* (1950), he says, shows "her sensitive appreciation of Hindu and Moslem at the moment when violence and passion were destroying the balance long maintained by the British Empire." Forster, in reviewing the same book, says Weston writes "seriously, carefully, compassionately . . . for those who are already emotionally involved in the country and love it."

Weston wrote more than thirty short stories, many published in the *New Yorker*; some are included in *Prize Stories* (1944), *Collier's Best* (1951), and *The Best American Short Stories* (1952, 1953, 1956). Among her other novels are *The Devil's Foot* (1942), *The Dark Wood* (1946), and *The Wise Children* (1951). She also wrote two nonfiction books, *Ceylon* (1960) and *Afghanistan* (1962). For the book jacket of Weston's last novel, novelist Pearl Buck wrote, "*The Hoopoe* [1970] is a sound and beautiful novel in the finest English tradition. The perception of the peoples on both sides of the world is sensitive and true. Perhaps only someone like myself can understand how strong the influence of Asia is, when it holds one's earliest childhood memories and experience. The longing, the need to return, are indeed all but irresistible."

Through her novels and stories Weston shared her appreciation and understanding of India, evoking the beauty of the country, the vastness of its problems, and the attempts at solutions. She died in Bangor, Maine.

• Additional biographical information can be found in Harvey Breit, "Talk with Mrs. Weston," *New York Times Book Review*, 16 Apr. 1950; this interview also appears in Breit, *The Writer Observed* (1956). For discussions of her work, see E. M. Forster, "A Novel of Changing India That Dramatizes Upheaval," *New York Times Book Review*, 26 Mar. 1950, and Joseph Hitrec, "Cameo of India," *Saturday Review of Literature*, 1 Apr. 1950. See also Zahir Jang Khattak, "British Novelists Writing about India-Pakistani's Independence: Christine Weston, John Masters, Ruth Prawer Jhabvala and Paul Scott" (Ph.D. diss., Tufts Univ., 1987). An obituary is in the *New York Times*, 6 May 1989.

BLANCHE COX CLEGG

WESTON, Edward (9 May 1850–20 Aug. 1936), electrical engineer, inventor, and industrialist, was born at Brynn Castle, near Oswestry, County Shropshire, England, the son of Edward Weston, a carpenter and mechanic, and Margaret Jones. When Weston was seven years old, his family moved to Wolverhampton, part of England's highly industrialized "Black Country." After his education in the town's grade schools, he attended St. Peter's Collegiate Institute. He studied chemistry and physics privately there with a fellow of the London Chemical Society, Henry A. Horton. Contrary to Weston's wishes, his parents insisted that he pursue a medical career. A three-year-long apprenticeship convinced Weston that medicine was not his field. In spite of his parents' bitter opposition, Weston abandoned that field of study in 1870 and went to London, intending to find work in a scientific field. When this hope proved futile, Weston disappointed his parents still more by leaving to seek opportunities in the United States.

Weston arrived in New York City in May 1870. After some weeks of searching, he found employment as a chemist with William H. Mardock & Co., a manufacturer of photographic chemicals. An explosion in this "factory," located in the basement of a four-story house, persuaded Weston to search for other employment opportunities. Soon he was working as a chemist and electrician for the American Nickel Plating Company. Over the next few years Weston would make substantial improvements in the electroplating process that became the basis of the modern art of depositing metals. In 1871 Weston married Wilhelmina Seidel, a young immigrant from the central German village of Blankenheim. They had two children.

Thinking that while working with stock tickers he could develop his ideas about batteries, Weston left the electroplating company to become a consulting expert to the Commercial Printing Telegraph Company. However, Weston was instead saddled with routine experimental work on telegraphy equipment, and he soon left the company, yearning for independence. After his 1872 resignation, Weston set up a photography studio in the front room of his apartment. His familiarity with photographic chemicals helped him to do a moderately good business but did not provide enough to support his family.

Late in December 1872 Weston started an electroplating business with George J. Harris. Putting to use Weston's numerous improvements, the firm made nickel plating its specialty, and business thrived. Weston, convinced that a dynamo would be a better source of power for electroplating than wet-cell batteries, set out to build one. Weston soon achieved his goal, building a compact, efficient dynamo with one field magnet and two armatures. In 1875 he moved his family to Newark, New Jersey, where he dedicated all his time to building dynamos. With the help of financial backers, on 10 June 1877 he formed the Weston Dynamo Electric Machine Company. Within the next few years he became the leading U.S. manufacturer of electroplating dynamos.

The late 1870s saw a great rush to develop a viable system of arc lighting. Charles F. Brush and Elihu Thomson had already made significant progress in the field by the time that Weston became involved in 1877, but Weston was not intimidated. By late 1879 he renamed his company the Weston Electric Light Company, and between 1880 and 1882 he took out thirteen patents on lamp mechanisms. Although Weston's work with arc lamps was fundamental and led to major technological advances in the field, it failed to equal the success of Brush's system.

In 1881 the United States Electric Lighting Company began buying up the stock of the Weston company, and it quickly absorbed it. Weston stayed on, serving as the consulting electrician and works manager for the company, which moved its base of operations to Weston's factory in Newark. The lighting of the Brooklyn Bridge, which was accomplished with Weston arc lamps and a Weston dynamo, was one of its first important contracts. As a consultant, Weston made a number of significant contributions to the incandescent electric light, including the "Tamidine," or "squirted," filament, which was patented on 26 September 1882 and was quickly adopted by the light industry. Also of importance was his thorium oxide "getter," which cleaned residual air and blocked gases from lamp bulbs while they were being exhausted.

On 1 July 1886 Weston resigned from the United States Electric Lighting Company after becoming increasingly dissatisfied with the company's operations. He outfitted a complete laboratory on his property and set to work with a vengeance on the development of electrical measuring instruments, often working fifteen to twenty hours a day. In December 1886 he produced the moving-coil voltmeter, which was granted a patent on 6 November 1888. To manufacture and market this invention, Weston founded his last company, the Weston Electrical Instrument Company.

After the first voltmeter was produced, the company rapidly expanded its line of instruments, making high-voltage voltmeters, high-capacity ammeters, and alternating current instruments of a similar design, for both portable and central power station uses. Weston's measuring devices were soon renowned for their accuracy and dependability. It was also during this time that Weston was granted a patent for a device that utilized solar energy to generate electricity.

In later years Weston received the Franklin Institute's Elliott Cresson Medal and Franklin Medal, the Society of Chemical Industry's Perkin Medal, and the American Institute of Electrical Engineers' Benjamin Lamme Medal, as well as several honorary doctorates. He stayed on as president of the Weston Electrical Instrument Company until 1924, when he relinquished his authority to his son, Edward Faraday Weston. Weston died at his home in Montclair, New Jersey.

Edward Weston's discoveries helped the fields of electroplating, arc lighting, and incandescent lighting to grow and develop. His Tamidine patent was sought by both the Westinghouse and Edison companies. Most important, however, was his manufacture of precise scientific instrumentation, which provided the groundwork for important developments in the electrical field.

• The Weston History of Science and Technology Collection, consisting of Edward Weston's extensive library, can be found in the New Jersey Institute of Technology's Robert W. Van Houten Library. David O. Woodbury, *A Measure for Greatness: A Short Biography of Edward Weston* (1949), provides an excellent overview of Weston's life and the time in which he lived. Also helpful is Harold C. Passer, *The Electrical Manufacturers, 1875–1900: A Study in Competition, Entrepreneurship, Technical Change, and Economic Growth* (1953). Also see the *New York Times*, 21 Aug. 1936, for Weston's obituary.

DANIEL MARTIN DUMYCH

WESTON, Edward (24 Mar. 1886–1 Jan. 1958), photographer, was born Edward Henry Weston in Highland Park, Illinois, the son of Edward Burbank Weston, a physician, and Alice Jeanette Brett. His mother died when he was four years old, and his older sister, May, assumed a maternal role. After she married, Weston continued to rely on her support and visited her at crucial times in his professional development, first in Tropico, California, in 1906 and later in Middletown, Ohio, in 1922. On the occasions of both visits his career in photography took special turns.

Two events prepared the way for Weston's choice of a life in photography: his father gave him a snapshot camera in 1902, and in 1903 he quit high school. His passion for photography dominated his interests, causing him to neglect school, as he recalled in an undated manuscript in the Weston archive at the Center for Creative Photography (CCP) at the University of Arizona: "I needed no friends now—I was always alone with my love—School was neglected—I played 'hookey' whenever possible—Zero weather found me wandering through snow-drifts—seeking the elusive patterns in black and white—which covered the ground—or sunsets over the prairie wastes—Sundays my camera and I would take long car-rides into the country around Chicago—always alone, and nights were spent feverishly developing my plates in some makeshift darkroom." Photographs made during this period (1903–1905), now in the collections of CCP, are his earliest surviving photographs of artistic merit.

Weston stayed with his sister in California from 1906 to 1908, holding various odd jobs and finally working door-to-door making and selling instant family portraits. He returned to Chicago in 1908 to learn the trade of portrait photography at the Illinois College of Photography. He finished the courses in six months but for unknown reasons was denied a degree. In 1909 he married Flora May Chandler, a grade-school teacher. They had four children, two of whom became recognized photographers.

From 1911 on Weston supported himself as a commercial photographer. As early as 1914, however, he decided to subjugate his means of making a living to his aspirations as an artist. He became a frequent prizewinner in the U.S. National Salon and the London Salon and was recognized as one of the best pictorialist photographers in the country by the Photographers' Association of America in 1916. In 1917 he was elected an acting member of the London Salon of Photography.

From 1915 to 1924 he reexamined his work and his honors: "I think success in the 'salons' got the best of me. Then articles by Rosenfeld, Tennant, Seligmann, about Stieglitz began to appear. Later by or about Paul Strand. These shoved me in the right direction. . . . That whole soft focus period in retrospect seems like a stage act; I even dressed the part: Windsor tie, green velvet jacket" (*Daybooks*, 3d ed., vol. 1, p. xviii).

Beginning in 1917 Weston began writing his *Daybooks* (later destroying nearly everything written before 1923), which continued until 1944. These writings chronicle his life, loves, philosophic beliefs, statements on the aesthetics of photography, and credo: "The approach to photography must be through another avenue, that the camera should be used for a recording of *life*, for rendering the very substance and quintessence of the *thing itself*, whether it be polished steel or palpitating flesh" (10 Mar. 1924, *Daybooks*, vol. 1, p. 54). The *Daybooks* provide much of the knowledge and understanding of his life and work; as critic Hilton Cramer noted in a review for the *Nation* in 1962, "There is no better way of grasping what lay behind Weston's struggle to achieve his purity of vision than to read his *Daybooks*."

Prior to 1921 Weston made a number of friends, including Imogen Cunningham, Margrethe Mather (with whom he shared a studio from 1912 to 1923), and Johan Hagemeyer, who introduced him to various aspects of the world of music and literature. As Weston moved to a more modernist style and away from the *japonisme* that dominated American pictorialism, these friends and the books on modern art he was reading caused him to renounce totally his earlier style. In 1920 he scraped the emulsion off old prizewinning negatives and used the glass to make a window.

The abundant literature that records Weston's life and work, including the *Daybooks*, exploits his numerous affairs with women, especially those who served as the subjects of his famous nude images. In most cases his affairs were notorious because, though he separated from Flora, they did not divorce until 1937. By then he had lived with at least three other women.

In 1921 Weston met Tina Modotti, a part-time actress, model, and photographer. A year later she arranged for an exhibition of his new "geometric" (cubist) photographs at the Academia de Bellas Artes in Mexico City. The response was enthusiastic. For the first time in his career his work was purchased by artists and collectors. He moved away from his commercial career and began to search out the leading proponents of photography as an art. In the process, he left his family and the professional life he had built up.

In 1922 Weston visited his sister and her husband in Middletown before going to Mexico with Modotti, his new love. May provided financial assistance for him to go to New York, where he showed his work to Clarence White, Charles Sheeler, and Alfred Stieglitz. Stieglitz reinforced the new, "straight" (meaning unmanipulated), avant-garde direction of Weston's work in their encounter but was critical of the majority of his photographs: "[He] discarded print after print, prints I loved. Yet I am happy, for I gained in strength, in fact strengthened my own opinion. I was ripe to change, was changing, yes changed, when I went to New York" (*Daybooks*, vol. 1, p. 4).

Weston and Modotti moved to Mexico in 1923. She introduced him to Diego Rivera and the other artists of the burgeoning Mexican Renaissance, who treated Weston as an artist of equal merit to their own aspirations and accomplishments. It was during the three years in Mexico (with a short return trip to the United States in 1925) that Weston produced a new way of photographing commonplace objects, such as his famous "Escusado," the commode in his apartment. He referred to this approach in selecting subjects in the same terms he used to describe some of the finest nudes of his career, which were also made in Mexico: "My excitement was absolute aesthetic response to form. . . . here was every sensuous curve of the 'human form divine' but minus imperfections" (*Daybooks*, vol. 1, p. 132).

Weston's stay in Mexico verified the direction he had begun before his visit to New York and Stieglitz in 1922. Regardless of subject matter, he sought out significant form in clear detail, precisely focused, in elegant natural light, as the most powerful statement of what he believed was the camera's greatest potential. He returned to Glendale in 1927 but restlessly opened a portrait studio in San Francisco with his son Brett in 1928.

In 1929 Weston settled in Carmel, California, remaining there the rest of his life, except for a short absence (1935–1937). He eventually eked out a modest living by operating a portrait studio part time in Carmel. By the year he moved there, his reputation had grown sufficiently that he was invited to select the American photographic contribution from the West for the International Deutschen Werkbund Exhibition, *Film und Foto*, in Stuttgart.

The period immediately after Mexico saw the introduction of Weston's renowned images of shells, peppers, and other objects. After arriving in Carmel he began exploring Point Lobos National Park, creating one of his most dramatic series of landscapes and rock forms.

At this time a brief but significant West Coast movement in photography, Group f/64, grew up around Weston. Led by Willard Van Dyke and including Ansel Adams, Imogen Cunningham, and other photographers, an informal association was formed to represent and promote aesthetic principles of unmanipulated, sharply focused image making not unlike what was being promulgated by Stieglitz and his circle on the East Coast. Weston, though initially a member of the group, withdrew from active involvement because he found some of what they advocated as too restrictive. The term f/64 represented an extremely small lens aperture, which provided sharp focus and great depth of field. The group's formation was a public statement about the members' move away from the then still dominant pictorialist salons of photography. The Group f/64 photographers organized a show of their works at the M. H. de Young Museum in San Francisco in 1932 at the peak of their involvement, but within a year or two they dissolved the group.

Sonya Noskowiak, a young photographer in the Group f/64, who modeled for Weston, lived with him and his sons from 1929 to 1934, providing a kind of stability for his life. She also introduced him to Charis Wilson, who became a new model. Weston eventually left Noskowiak for Wilson, marrying her in 1939; they had no children.

During their time in Santa Monica, Weston made a series of photographs of sand dunes and nudes of Wilson that sent his work in yet another direction. Landscape became a study in form like a nude, a shell, or a close-up of any object. In 1938 Weston moved back to Carmel and built a small house on property owned by his wife.

In 1937 Weston had been awarded the first Guggenheim grant to a photographer. The grant was renewed for a second year. Over the two years Weston and Wilson traveled thousands of miles throughout the West, producing at the conclusion of the grant *California and the West* (1940), with Weston's photographs and a text by Wilson. They divorced in 1946, after the onset of Parkinson's disease, which eventually claimed Weston's life.

In 1941 the Limited Editions Club commissioned Weston to make photographs to accompany a special edition of Walt Whitman's *Leaves of Grass*. The photographs had less unity than any previous series, yet many images rank among his greatest accomplishments. A retrospective exhibition was held at the Museum of Modern Art in 1946, organized by Nancy Newhall.

Owing to the advancing conditions of Parkinson's disease, by 1948 Weston could no longer spend hours in his darkroom making prints. His sons provided assistance in producing an important edition of his work, the *Fiftieth Anniversary Portfolio.* That same year he had a major retrospective exhibition in Paris at the American Embassy Annex. Between 1952 and 1955 Weston, his sons, and friends produced a major printing of his work in the form of eight sets of 832 prints. Weston died in Carmel.

The majority of photographers recognized for their historical contributions in the nineteenth century were inventors or innovators of the technology. Even artists like Julia Margaret Cameron, Henry Peach Robinson, and Oscar Gustav Rejlander, whose aesthetic contributions stand out, were dependent on technological variations, including the close-up and multiple printing. Only in the twentieth century have the majority of those recognized for photographic accomplishments received acclaim for their vision alone. Weston achieved such a place in the history of photography. He and Alfred Stieglitz represent the crucial influences that helped fine-art photography move from romantic pictorialism to modernism.

• Weston's papers, negatives, and the most comprehensive collection of his photographs are in the Center for Creative Photography at the University of Arizona. Important texts written by Edward Weston include *The Daybooks*, vol. 1, *Mexico* and *The Daybooks*, vol. 2, *California*, ed. Nancy Newhall (3d ed., 1973); and *Edward Weston on Photography*, ed. Peter Bunnell (1983). Merle Armitage, ed., *The Art of Edward Weston* (1932), was the first important monograph of Weston's photographs, with essays by leading artists and writers. Ben Maddow, *Edward Weston: Fifty Years* (1973), is an important monograph with a biographical text. James Enyeart, *Edward Weston's California Landscapes* (1984), provides a comprehensive look at Weston's landscape works; Charis Wilson, *Edward Weston: Nudes* (1977), furnishes a retrospective view of his nudes; and Beaumont Newhall, *Supreme Instants: The Photography of Edward Weston* (1986), is an important overview of his career and photographs. Amy Conger, *Edward Weston: Photographs from the Collection of the Center for Creative Photography* (1992), is the most complete reference and bibliographic source of Weston's life and work. An obituary is in the *New York Times*, 2 Jan. 1958.

JAMES ENYEART

WESTON, Edward Payson (15 Mar. 1839–13 May 1929), long-distance walker, was born in Providence, Rhode Island, the son of Silas Weston, a merchant, and Maria Gaines, a writer of popular romances. As a child, Weston moved with his family to Boston, where he attended public school. At age fourteen he was employed as a candy, magazine, and newspaper vendor on trains from Boston to Providence; a year later he worked the New York–Fall River Steamship Line. His first recognition as an athlete came in 1861 when he walked from Boston to Washington, D.C., in ten days to attend Abraham Lincoln's inauguration. The feat was publicized in newspapers and sporting journals, although he failed by one day to achieve his goal. He published an account of his walk in 1862 in a pamphlet entitled *The Pedestrian.*

Although Weston claimed Civil War service as a dispatch carrier, and later added that he was a spy, military records do not support his statement. He also said he was a runner and reporter for the *New York Herald* following the war.

In 1867 George K. Goodwin, a New York sportsman, wagered $10,000 with T. F. Wilcox that Weston could walk from Portland, Maine, to Chicago in twenty-six days. Weston's backer also bet that during the walk Weston would cover a hundred miles within a 24-hour period. However, if he failed to walk that distance in a single day, three-fifths of the bet would be forfeited. No event in American athletics until that time attracted so much attention from press and public. Daily newspaper reports appeared across the country, and people lined the route to cheer Weston on. As the walk progressed from town to town, he was met by crowds that followed him through the streets singing and cheering. He reached Chicago before the deadline, but he failed to win the 24-hour side bet.

The walk made Weston a national hero. He went on tour, demonstrating his technique before theater audiences. He was deluged with challenges for walking races, but he preferred to compete against the clock. In 1868 he demonstrated that he could walk a hundred miles within twenty-four hours by going from Walnut Creek, near Erie, Pennsylvania, to Buffalo, New York, arriving forty-seven minutes ahead of his time limit.

Soon Weston's record was eclipsed by others, but he went on to claim records for distances of 200, 250, and 300 miles. He introduced the six-day-go-as-you-please race in which the prize went to the runner who covered the greatest distance in 144 hours (later changed to 142 hours to avoid encroachment on the Sabbath). After being defeated by Daniel O'Leary in November 1875 in Chicago, Weston departed for England, where he soon became a popular sports figure. There, in January 1879, he claimed a record for walking two thousand miles. He won the Astley Belt, a gold and silver international championship prize in a six-day race in London in 1879, covering 550 miles within 142 hours. Responding to a challenge, he defended the belt in New York City that same year, but he finished sixth.

Weston faded from public view after his defeat, and he was seldom mentioned in sporting journals. Although he continued to make public appearances, lecturing on temperance and clean living and demonstrating walking techniques, he remained out of competition. Rediscovered by a new generation of newspaper reporters in 1906, he tried to repeat his earlier triumphs. He repeated the walk from Portland to Chicago, generating considerable attention. Sponsored by the *New York Times*, he set out on his seventieth birthday to walk from New York City to San Francisco, which he hoped to accomplish in a hundred days. He was accompanied by a team of reporters and photographers, who sent in daily accounts. He missed his goal by four days and seven hours, but a year later, without reporters, he covered the route in seventy days. His last great walk was from New York to Minneapolis in 1913 when he was seventy-four. Afterward he continued to make public appearances, lecturing on temperance and clean living in halls and theaters and demonstrating his walking technique, at local sports events.

In 1927 Weston was found dazed and helpless, wandering about the streets of New York. Anne Nichols, the author of the popular play *Abie's Irish Rose*, out of concern for the aging athlete, set up a trust fund for his care. Shortly thereafter, Weston was struck by a taxicab and spent his remaining years in a wheelchair. He died in Brooklyn. He had married Maria (maiden name unknown) sometime before 1879; they had at least three children. He was estranged from his wife at the time of his death.

• Weston's career as a professional walker from 1861 until 1880 was amply covered by the *New York Clipper*. His English period was detailed by English sporting journals, and these accounts were regularly reprinted in the *New York Clipper*. In the twentieth century he became a project of the *New York Times*, which chronicled his last notable feats in detail. He was also an expert publicist; at each of his great walking trials he sold pamphlets about his achievements. Obituaries are in the *New York Times*, 14 May 1929, and the *Brooklyn Daily Eagle*, 19 May 1929.

JOHN CUMMING

WETHERILL, Charles Mayer (4 Nov. 1825–5 Mar. 1871), chemist, was born in Philadelphia, Pennsylvania, the son of Charles Wetherill, a member of a prominent Philadelphia manufacturing family, and Margaretta Mayer. He was educated in private schools and in 1841 enrolled at the University of Pennsylvania, where he studied chemistry under Alexander Dallas Bache, who became his lifelong friend and patron. After his graduation in 1845, he spent a year at the chemical laboratory school of James C. Booth and Martin H. Boyé in Philadelphia and then went to Paris to the Collège Royal de France, where he worked in the laboratory of Theophile Jules Pelouze in 1846–1847 and attended lectures by Jean Baptiste André Dumas and Joseph Louis Gay-Lussac. From there he went on to the University of Giessen, attending the classes of Justus von Liebig, and received the Ph.D. there in 1848, having in the course of his education studied under the most eminent chemists of the day.

Following his return to Philadelphia, Wetherill opened a chemical laboratory and school and worked as a consulting analytical chemist and lectured at the Franklin Institute. The school did not flourish, unable to compete with that of Booth and Boyé, but as a result of his analytical activities, Wetherill published a number of papers and became well enough known in the scientific community to be elected to the American Philosophical Society in 1851 and to be awarded an honorary M.D. by the New York Medical College in 1853.

In 1853 Wetherill closed his laboratory to oversee the collection and exhibition of Pennsylvania minerals at the 1854 Crystal Palace Exposition in New York. In conjunction with this, he also prepared catalogs of the natural resources of Pennsylvania. His interest in this activity led him to decide to make a similar survey of the natural resources of the upper Midwest, and he spent several months of 1855 traveling through Michigan, Wisconsin, Illinois, Iowa, Minnesota, and North Dakota. It was toward the end of this trip that he met Mary C. Benbridge of Lafayette, Indiana, whom he married in 1857; they had at least one child.

After the publication of his account of his travels in an Austrian geological journal, Wetherill's ambition was to secure a faculty position at a major university. He turned to Bache for assistance but nothing satisfactory was available, and he became quite dispirited. Following his marriage, he moved to Lafayette and continued his independent chemical investigations, publishing monographs on local artesian waters, gas lighting, infant foods, and the manufacture of vinegar. He continued to seek an academic position, but as Bache pointed out, the onset of the Civil War had diminished both the population of college students and funds available for faculty positions.

In 1862, however, Bache recommended Wetherill for the position of chief chemist at the newly established U.S. Department of Agriculture. President Abraham Lincoln appointed him to this position in July and immediately gave Wetherill a special assignment. As the only chemist in the employ of a government bureau, he was apparently regarded as chemical adviser to the entire government. In April 1863 Lincoln again assigned him to a secret project in Philadelphia testing a new gunpowder formula. His repeated absence from his official duties aroused the anger of Commissioner of Agriculture Isaac Newton, who refused to pay Wetherill's salary for the period of his absence and who responded to Lincoln's intervention on Wetherill's behalf by firing Wetherill. Wetherill, fearful for his scientific reputation, appealed to his friends in Congress, who were able to exonerate him of any wrong-doing and restore his salary but were unable to secure his reinstatement as chief chemist. Wetherill was offered the position of chemist of the Smithsonian Institution by Joseph Henry. In this position, he continued his chemical investigations, the most substantive being a study of the problems of heating and ventilating the Capitol building.

Wetherill continued to search for an appropriate academic position. In 1866 he accepted the professorship of chemistry at the newly founded Lehigh University at Bethlehem, Pennsylvania. His first publication there was an outline of his lectures in chemistry. The chemistry courses that he designed were regarded by his colleagues at other universities as the most comprehensive in the United States at that time. By 1870 his reputation as an excellent teacher and administrator had grown so that he received offers of positions at several highly respected schools. In 1871 he chose to accept an appointment as head of the chemistry department at the new School of Science of the University of Pennsylvania. He began to draw up plans for the chemistry curriculum, but before he could take up his new position, he died unexpectedly of a heart attack at Bethlehem.

The importance of Wetherill as an American chemist is difficult to assess. He was a member of a prominent family that was profitably engaged in chemical manufacturing for several generations. He was educated by and a friend of the leading chemists of the mid-nineteenth century. He was a careful and accurate analyst, and as both a researcher and an educator, Wetherill was esteemed highly by his colleagues and students. During a period when chemical theory was in flux, however, he chose to hold to old ideas rather than to adopt new ones and died before he could see the ultimate triumph of those new theories. Admired and honored at the time of his death, his contributions have not withstood the test of time. He is probably best remembered as a scientific pioneer in government service and as an educator of subsequent generations of chemists.

• Wetherill's letters, papers, and other memorabilia are in the Edgar Fahs Smith Collection for the History of Chemistry at the University of Pennsylvania. Monographs that are available in major libraries include *Report on the Iron and Coal of Pennsylvania* (1854); *Report on the Chemical Analysis of the White Sulphur Water of the Artesian Well of Lafayette, Ind., with Remarks upon the Nature of Artesian Wells* (1858); *The Manufacture of Vinegar: Its Theory and Practice with Especial Reference to the Quick Process* (1860); *Artificial Lactation* (1860); *On the Relative Cost of Illumination in Lafayette, Ind.* (1860); *Report on the Chemical Analysis of Grapes, Submitted to Hon. Isaac Newton, Commissioner of Agriculture* (1862); *On a New Apparatus for the Determination of Carbonic Acid, and on Kemp's Thermostat* (1862); *A Brief Sketch of the Modern Theory of Chemical Types* (1864); and *On the Crystalline Nature of Glass* (1866). A biographical essay was written by E. F. Smith and originally published in the *Journal of Chemical Education* 6 (1929): 1076–89, 1215–24, 1461–77, 1668–80, 1916–27, and 2160–77. A bibliography is included in this essay. An obituary is in the Philadelphia *Public Ledger*, 7 Mar. 1871.

MARGARET JACKSON CLARKE

WETMORE, Alexander (18 June 1886–7 Dec. 1978), ornithologist, avian paleontologist, and museum administrator, was born Frank Alexander Wetmore in North Freedom, Wisconsin, the son of Dr. Nelson Franklin Wetmore, a general practitioner, and Emma Amelia Woodworth. As a boy, he walked to school in the town of Baraboo, which was six miles from his home. His interest in natural history, which dated from boyhood, was encouraged by his mother. For reasons of health, Emma Wetmore found it necessary to avoid the cold Wisconsin winters, and she often traveled further south with her son in tow. He spent his final year of high school in Independence, Kansas, graduating in 1905. The following summer he worked as a railway station night clerk.

From 1905 to 1910 Wetmore was an assistant in the University of Kansas Museum, except for one year (1909) when he performed similar duties at the Colorado Museum of Natural History. He joined the Bureau of Biological Survey in the U.S. Department of Agriculture as a field agent from 1910 to 1912, and, following his promotion to assistant biologist in 1913, he was sent to Washington, D.C., to study the eating habits of American birds. During the next ten years Wetmore developed his skills as an ornithologist while he completed graduate studies at George Washington University (A.M., 1916; Ph.D., 1920). In 1911 he traveled to the Caribbean and spent almost a year studying the bird life of Puerto Rico and neighboring islands. He subsequently went to Utah, where he looked into the reasons for the mortality of water birds in the vicinity of the Great Salt Lake. Part of 1920 was spent investigating birds from North America that spent part of their life cycles in Latin America. In 1923, on behalf of the Biological Survey and the Bernice Bishop Museum in Honolulu, Hawaii, he directed an expedition on the vessel *Tanager* in the central Pacific Ocean, where he explored bird and animal life on certain islands. In November 1924 Wetmore was named superintendent of the National Zoological Park in Washington, but he held this post less than four months.

In March 1925 Charles D. Walcott, secretary of the Smithsonian, elevated Wetmore to the post of assistant secretary with specific responsibility for the U.S. National Museum, a position that Wetmore would hold for two decades. In 1945 he succeeded Charles Greeley Abbott as secretary on the latter's retirement, and served in that capacity for seven years, retiring in 1952. A reserved, serious, but quietly effective leader, Wetmore essentially continued many of the traditions of his predecessors. Available funding was modest, particularly during the last dozen years of Wetmore's tenure at the Smithsonian. He was able to launch the National Air Museum (now the National Air and Space Museum) and the Canal Zone Biological Area (later the Smithsonian Tropical Research Institute). Wetmore consistently arrived early at his laboratory at the Museum of Natural History during his years as secretary, worked on one or another of his ornithological projects, and then put in a full day of administration. Following his retirement in 1952, Wetmore, appointed a Smithsonian research associate, continued to commute daily to his office at the National Museum of Natural History, carrying on with his ornithological research until several years before his death.

Wetmore contributed a number of important titles to the literature of scientific ornithology. These included *Observations on the Birds of Argentina, Paraguay, Uruguay, and Chile* (1926); *The Migration of Birds* (1927); *The Birds of Haiti and the Dominican Republic* (1931); *Fossil Birds of North America* (1931); and *The Birds of the Republic of Panama*, of which he completed three volumes between 1965 and 1972. This last work was the result of nearly twenty-five years of personal research begun in 1944. His Smithsonian colleagues completed and published the fourth and final volume in 1984. His *Systematic Classification for the Birds of the World* underwent four editions between

1934 and 1960. He also did much to promote the work of other scientists and naturalists, most notably Arthur Cleveland Bent's 21-volume series of studies dealing with the life histories of North American birds.

For forty-five years Wetmore was a trustee of the National Geographic Society, and a long-time member of the Society's Committee for Research and Exploration. From 1937 until 1974 he served as committee vice-chair and acting chair. He did not overlook the importance of less technical ornithological works for the general public. He edited and partly authored the society's *Book of Birds* (2 vols., 1937) and the two-volume set that superseded it nearly thirty years later, *Water, Prey, and Game Birds of North America* and *Song and Garden Birds* (1964–1965). The society honored his accomplishments with its Hubbard Medal in 1975.

Wetmore was personally responsible for adding more than 26,000 bird and mammal skins and 4,363 skeletons and anatomical specimens to the collections of the National Museum of Natural History. During his career he described and named 189 new species and subspecies of birds from North and South America. His scientific colleagues recognized Wetmore's achievements by naming fifty-six genera, species, and subspecies of animals (and one plant) in his honor during his lifetime. In addition, Wetmore Glacier in the Antarctic was named for him in recognition of his assistance in organizing the scientific program of the Ronne Antarctic Research Expedition in 1946–1948. On the occasion of his ninetieth birthday in 1976, S. Dillon Ripley, then secretary of the Smithsonian, observed of Wetmore's career, "Truly the incessant and intensive zeal which he has single-mindedly given to the study of birds over the years, often at very considerable personal expenditure in time and energy, will mark [his] career . . . as one of the most memorable in the entire history of American ornithology."

In 1940 Wetmore served as secretary-general of the Eighth American Scientific Congress, held in Washington, and in 1948 he was named Chairman of the Interdepartmental Committee on Research and Development by President Harry S. Truman. Wetmore's fourteen-man committee of federal government officials examined the means whereby scientific research efforts in the United States might best be coordinated.

Wetmore became a member of the American Ornithologists' Union (AOU) in 1908 and served as its president (1926–1929) and honorary president (1975–1978). In 1938 and 1950 he chaired the AOU's delegation to the International Ornithological Congress. He chaired the Union's Committee on Classification and Nomenclature, which brought the fifth edition of the *A.O.U. Checklist of North American Birds* to completion in 1957.

Actively interested in conservation issues, Wetmore was a member of the Advisory Committee of the International Committee for International Wildlife Protection, a member of the International Commission on Bird Preservation, and represented the United States in the Inter-American Committee of Experts on Nature Protection. He was the recipient of four honorary doctorates of science and the Geoffrey St. Hilaire Medal of the Societé Nationale d'Acclimatation of France (1927), among many other honors.

Wetmore was married twice. His first wife, Fay Holloway, whom he married in 1912, died in 1953. They had one daughter. Wetmore's second wife was Annie Beatrice "Bea" Thielen, whom he married in December 1953. He died at his home in High Point, Maryland.

• The Wetmore collection at the Smithsonian Institution consists of 237 boxes of correspondence, manuscripts, field notes, photographs, and other materials. Two useful biographical sketches are by S. Dillon Ripley and James A. Steed in National Academy of Sciences, *Biographical Memoirs* 56 (1987): 597–626; and by Paul Oehser in *Auk* 97 (July 1980): 608–15. There is a festschrift edited by Storrs Olsen, *Collected Papers in Avian Paleontology Honoring the 90th Birthday of Alexander Wetmore* (1976). See also Victoria Cooper and William E. Cox, *Guide to the Papers of Alexander Wetmore, c. 1948–1979 and undated*, Archives and Special Collections of the Smithsonian Institution, no. 11 (1990). An obituary appeared in *The Washington Post*, 9 Dec. 1978.

KEIR B. STERLING

WETTLING, George Godfrey (28 Nov. 1907–6 June 1968), jazz drummer, was born in Topeka, Kansas. His parents' names and professions are unknown. When he was fourteen Wettling moved with his parents to North Side Chicago, where he studied trap drums with Roy Knapp and heard some of the great jazz performers of his youth who moved through the clubs of the city's South Side. At age seventeen, while still in high school, he played dates with local bands such as those of Jack Chapman, Floyd Towne, and Eddie Niebauer. He soon graduated to the more professional touring bands of Art Jarrett, the Seattle Harmony Kings, and Paul Mares, making his first recording with the Mares group in 1935. His first notable professional break came later that year when he was hired for the highly touted U.S. Band from Britain fronted by Jack Hylton.

Moving his permanent home to New York City in 1936, Wettling played with a variety of bands that covered a broad spectrum of styles—small jazz combos as well as the big bands that made inroads with high school and college students throughout the country during the 1930s. He did residencies with Wingy Manone in New York City and Pittsburgh, followed by time with Artie Shaw's first band from 1936 to 1937, Bunny Berigan in 1937, Red Norvo's combo during 1937–1938, the Paul Whiteman orchestra between 1938 and 1940, Muggsy Spanier later in 1940, Joe and Marty Marsala during 1941, and the Ben Pollack band, organized in 1942, that was fronted by comedian Chico Marx.

In the early 1940s Wettling seems to have throttled back on his life as a traveling musician, opting for a sedentary life in his New York City home and work as a staff musician at ABC studios from 1943 to 1952, while still playing dates (some for which he was leader) with a variety of small bands in the city and its outskirts. His Chicago-style roots made painless his string of mergers with such artists as Eddie Condon (mostly at Condon's club in Manhattan), Yank Lawson (with whom he also made several recordings), Jimmy McPartland (at Metropole 54), and Our Dixieland Band (at Jack Dempsey's club). The steadiest professional affiliation from 1956 to 1959 was with Condon's group, which included a British tour in 1957. From 1959 he was essentially a freelance sideman, although he headed his own band for a short stay at the Gaslight Club in 1964.

A part of Wettling's time from 1947 was occupied with his second love, painting. He was a longtime friend of painter Stuart Davis, whose passion for jazz was the stimulus for several of his paintings, and jazz was the musical accompaniment to which he painted in his studio. Davis inspired Wettling's reciprocal interest and taught him enough painting basics to make him more than a "Sunday painter." Wettling showed his oils at one-man shows in Manhattan; two were used as album covers for recordings of the Condon and Sullivan bands. He also spent considerable time during his later years writing fiction as well as reportorial pieces, including a continuing drums column from 1939 into the early 1940s for the jazz periodical *Down Beat* and occasional book reviews for *Playboy*.

In addition to the inaugural session he did with Mares in 1935, Wettling made recordings with Shaw, Berrigan, Whiteman, Norvo, the Marsalas, McPartland, Jack Teagarden, and Billie Holliday. Few of these are of historical note, however, owing to Wettling's penchant for leaving bands before they recorded their best-known work. An exception is Berigan's great 1937 recording of *I Can't Get Started* (the second, big band version), in which Wettling provides the pushing ensemble backgrounds and occasional brush filigrees for soloists. His eclectic breadth, coupled with an innate sense of musical propriety, enabled him to excel with the big bands of his day as well as with the smaller Chicago- and New Orleans–style groups that dominated the final two decades of his career. The common characterization of Wettling, made by those who knew him and his work best, was the ultimate compliment: he was a drummer's drummer. He was not a colorful soloist in the mold of a Gene Krupa or a Buddy Rich. Known best for the talent and technique that enabled him to "kick" a band along with a forceful and precise beat, he also was valued highly by reed and brass soloists who benefited from his imaginative yet understated backgrounds for their own solos. He died of lung cancer in New York City and was buried in Chicago's Cedar Park Cemetery.

• Wettling can be heard on recordings with Bud Freeman on Commodore 513 (1938), with Ralph Sutton on Circle 413 (1952), and with Condon's band on World Pacific 1292 (1958). In-depth discussions of his career must be pieced together from passing remarks made in discussions of major jazz artists, although he is mentioned often in jazz chronicles of the twenties through the sixties, such as John Chilton, *Who's Who of Jazz* (1970), and Gunther Schuller, *The Swing Era* (1989). He appears in a group photograph of his jazz contemporaries in Frank Tirro, *Jazz: A History* (1977), p. 264. An obituary is in *Down Beat*, 25 July 1968.

WILLIAM THOMSON

WEXLER, Irving. *See* Gordon, Waxey.

WEXLEY, John (14 Sept. 1907–4 Feb. 1985), playwright, screenwriter, and short story writer, was born in New York City. His parents' names are unknown. Wexley helped his father in a roofing business and later worked at such odd jobs as waiter, bellboy, salesman, floorwalker, and stoker. A nephew of Maurice Schwartz, the celebrated Yiddish theater actor, he began his own career as an actor at age nineteen on the Yiddish theater stages. He spent some time as a small part actor with Eva Le Gallienne's Civic Repertory Company in 1926, but, recognizing that his talents as an actor were minimal, he soon turned his attention to writing for the stage. He became associated with the Washington Square Players and wrote numerous experimental one-act plays for them, including *Rules*, *The Machine Gun*, and *What Is Your Desire?* These, like the full-length plays he would later write, were inspired mostly by matters of injustice and social oppression.

Wexley's first full-length play is also his best remembered. *The Last Mile*, a tense three-act drama, was based on a short play by Robert Blake, a death row inmate (who was executed shortly after the publication of his play), called *The Law Takes Its Toll*. Blake's play had been published in H. L. Mencken's *American Mercury* magazine. Wexley expanded it and developed the characters. He succeeded in making a major, full-length drama about justice and social responsibility. While working on the play, he spent several weeks studying prison conditions at Sing Sing and at the state penitentiary in Joliet, Illinois. As with most of his other plays, Wexley depended significantly on dialogue taken from actual situations, striving in his work to create a pseudodocumentary style. The play is set on a death row at fictional Keystone State Penitentiary. The plot centers on John "Killer" Mears, a hardened and ruthless prisoner, who leads a daring revolt of his cellmates. The mayhem leads to the death of a guard and a harrowing stand-off between the inmates and the police. During the siege, the prisoners reveal their individual stories and ruminate on issues of crime and punishment before Mears is compelled to give in to prevent further deaths, even though he realizes it will mean his own death. Produced on Broadway by Herman Shumlin and directed by Chester Erskine, *The Last Mile* opened at the Sam H. Harris Theatre on 13 February 1930. It ran for 285 performances and made a star of the then little-known actor Spencer Tracy in the role of Mears (Clark Gable similarly found stardom playing the role in a touring production). Burns Mantle wrote that *The Last Mile* is "a tragedy so tense, so stripped of theatrical artificialities, and emotionally so moving that even calloused reviewers of plays were frank to admit its disturbing and unsettling effect upon their nerves." The play received considerable publicity and numerous performances in small theaters as well as college theaters. It was made into a movie in 1932 with Preston Foster as Mears and again in 1959 with Mickey Rooney in the part.

In 1931 Wexley's play *Steel* was produced. It involved a complex plot about labor unrest and agitation. His play *They Shall Not Die* (1934) was described by Brooks Atkinson in the *New York Times* as "a play of terrifying and courageous bluntness of statement." This work also caused considerable controversy for its frank depiction of the Scottsboro case, in which nine black youths in Alabama were charged with raping two white schoolgirls in what Wexley depicts as a gross miscarriage of justice. His *Running Dogs* (1938), produced off-Broadway, explored tensions between Chinese conservatives and Communists just prior to the 1931 Japanese invasion, but the play was not a success with either critics or audiences.

As a screenwriter, Wexley was applauded for two movies he wrote under contract for Warner Bros. The best of these was a taut melodrama, *Angels with Dirty Faces* (1938), which starred James Cagney. Benefiting from the gritty realism typical of Warner Bros. melodramas of the 1930s, *Angels with Dirty Faces* focused on the rise and fall of Rocky Sullivan, an appealing young hood played by Cagney, and his close relationship with a childhood pal who has become the neighborhood priest (played by Pat O'Brien). The priest struggles to keep the local kids (played by the Dead End Kids) in line, but they idolize Rocky and his exploits. When Rocky is sent to death row following a murder, the priest appeals to him to "die yellow" so the kids will not glamorize Rocky in death or the acts that put him on death row. Rocky vehemently resists but loses his bravado while walking the last mile; but neither the audience nor the priest is ever certain if Rocky really died "yellow." The film is regarded as a classic of its genre.

Wexley's other outstanding Warner Bros. screenplay featured Edward G. Robinson and Humphrey Bogart in *The Amazing Dr. Clitterhouse* (1938), which he wrote in collaboration with John Huston, based on a 1937 play by Barré Lyndon. This striking film, directed by Anatole Litvak, introduces Dr. Clitterhouse (Robinson), who is writing a book on criminals and their reactions to their crimes. He decides he must become a criminal to truly understand and observe their impulses and manages to become part of a gang led by Rocks Valentine (Bogart). After participating in various crimes, Clitterhouse attempts to leave the gang. However, Valentine wants to use Clitterhouse in a scheme to rob the doctor's rich friends. Instead, Clitterhouse becomes the last chapter of his own book when he poisons Valentine to stop him. Clitterhouse is ultimately acquitted when he insists that he was "sane" when he committed the murder. The jury believes that if he thinks so, he must be insane. At Warners, Wexley also contributed screenplays for *Confessions of a Nazi Spy* (1939), *Hangmen Also Die* (1943), and *The Long Night* (1947).

Wexley also wrote short stories and the critically applauded book *The Judgment of Julius and Ethel Rosenberg* (1955), which chronicled the lives of the couple who were tried and executed for treason in the midst of great controversy in 1953. The Rosenbergs were accused of giving American atomic secrets to the Soviet Union.

Wexley spent much of his later years lecturing, writing, and living quietly with his wife Katherine. They had one child, Thea. He died in Doylestown, Pennsylvania. Times and tastes had changed and to many critics he seemed to have failed to fulfill the promise of his work in the 1930s.

• For information on Wexley see Annie Laurie Farish, "A Legend of Sorrow: Odets and Wexley in the Thirties" (M.A. thesis, Mississippi State Univ., 1968), and Myron Matlaw, *Modern World Drama: An Encyclopedia* (1972). Obituaries are in the *New York Times*, 6 Feb. 1985, and *Newsweek*, 18 Feb. 1985.

JAMES FISHER

WEYERHAEUSER, Frederick (21 Nov. 1843–4 Apr. 1914), lumberman and capitalist, was born in Niedersaulheim, Hessen, Germany, the son of John Weyerhaeuser and Katherine Gabel, prosperous farmers. He completed his education at a local Lutheran parochial school by age fourteen. His father died in 1846, forcing Weyerhaeuser to work on his family's farm to help support his siblings and widowed mother. Weyerhaeuser came to the United States in 1852 at the age of eighteen. He had decided to leave Germany in order to escape that country's strict military requirements. Accompanied by his mother and sister, Weyerhaeuser settled in Erie County in northeastern Pennsylvania, where he first worked in a brewery, then for a local farmer. He remained in Pennsylvania until 1856, at which time he moved to Coal Valley, Illinois, becoming involved in the lumber, grain, and coal businesses. He married Elizabeth Sarah Bloedel, also from Niedersaulheim, in 1857; the couple has seven children.

In 1860, after forming a partnership with his wife's brother-in-law Frank C. A. Denkmann, Weyerhaeuser purchased at a foreclosure sale a sawmill located on a piece of land along the Mississippi River. During this time, logs for the Illinois mills flowed down the Mississippi, coming primarily from Wisconsin. While Denkmann managed the mill, Weyerhaeuser traveled to Wisconsin in order to buy tracts of yellow pine that grew in the valley of the Chippewa River. With this purchase, Weyerhaeuser and his partner joined with sixteen other lumbering firms to form the Mississippi River Logging Company, which employed nearly 20,000 workers. By 1870 Weyerhaeuser was elected president of the company.

Subsequent to this success, Weyerhaeuser started to make an even greater name for himself in the timber industry. In 1870 he owned a mere three mills; at that time he began leading numerous groups in investing in timberlands and sawmills located in Arkansas and Louisiana, and as he saw that new lumber opportunities were opening up in the West, he formed a land management company, the Weyerhaeuser Timber Company, headquartered in Tacoma, Washington. Additionally, beyond the formal confines of the corporation, he also became the head of what was commonly referred to as the "Weyerhaeuser Syndicate," an association composed of approximately one hundred wealthy partners with immense holdings in standing timber. Rather than developing logging operations on his own—a virtual impossibility given that nearly all viable streams were already occupied by other lumbermen—Weyerhaeuser, through the syndicate, began to acquire controlling interests in mills that were already in active operation, including the Bell-Nelson Mill Company in Everett, Washington. Eventually his domain stretched over 2 million acres of wooded land, and along with his associates he silently controlled some 15 billion feet of standing pine.

In 1879 Weyerhaeuser helped to organize the Chippewa Lumber and Boom Company, becoming its president. The mill, in Chippewa Falls, Wisconsin, was for many years the world's largest. It developed many new techiques for manufacturing and handling lumber, including the "brail" (a new type of river lumber raft for transportation purposes) in 1875. Chippewa Lumber was the first to use as many as five gangs of a hundred saws on a single floor. Weyerhaeuser relocated from Illinois to St. Paul, Minnesota, in 1891 but continued to buy up timber interests throughout the country. In 1896 he purchased the huge plant of the C. N. Nelson Lumber Company located on Lake Superior in Cloquet, Minnesota.

Weyerhaeuser's bold purchase strategies were not always met with approval. In 1900 he bought 900,000 acres in the remote Pacific Northwest from Northern Pacific Railway for a seemingly meager $6 per acre; the timber alone eventually would be valued at several thousand times that. However, at that time, many people in the industry suspected that Weyerhaeuser had finally gotten in over his head. "At the time the land was acquired it was a high-risk capital investment," said Charles Bingham, an executive in the Weyerhaeuser Timber Company. "Markets were uncertain and wildfire was rampant" (Dietrich, p. 126).

The risky investment panned out well for Weyerhaeuser, contributing to his becoming the world's biggest private timberland owner and earning him the moniker of "Lumber King." Neither his income nor his total accumulation of wealth was ever known with exact certainty, but some accounts estimated that he was worth as much as $30 million, thereby making him the richest private individual in the world in the early twentieth century. Despite his vast riches, though, he managed to live his life in relative anonymity, with most of the population never having known his name. He lived an isolated life, never attending public functions and remaining out of the political fray. His work was considered his only amusement.

Weyerhaeuser used to say of himself that he was one of the few wealthy men who came by his money honestly. "I think I have succeeded because I care more for my credit than for my clothes" (*New York Times*, 5 Apr. 1914). Although he had his critics—in his 1993 book *Showdown at Opal Creek* David Seideman wrote that "Weyerhaeuser, a loud voice against the so-called socialists defending the spotted owl, swilled at the federal trough long before smaller timber outfits struck it rich off national forests" (p. 50)—there is no disputing his business acumen. In the 1990s the company still carrying Weyerhaeuser's name controlled 13 million acres of timberland in the United States and Canada. Nor is there any question about the single-mindedness of his pursuit. It is believed that Weyerhaeuser's last words before his death in Pasadena, California, were a whispered, "Cut 'em low, boys, cut 'em low" (quoted in Dietrich, p. 41).

• The definitive work on Weyerhaeuser and his company is Ralph W. Hidy et al., *Timber and Men: The Weyerhaeuser Story* (1963). For further biographical information, see Frederick K. Weyerhaeuser, *Trees and Men: The Weyerhaeuser Story* (1951); William Dietrich, *The Final Forest* (1992); and David Seideman, *Showdown at Opal Creek* (1993). An obituary is in the *New York Times*, 5 Apr. 1914.

FRANCESCO L. NEPA

WEYERHAEUSER, Frederick Edward (4 Nov. 1872–18 Oct. 1945), business executive with the Weyerhaeuser Timber Company and its affiliates, was born in Rock Island, Illinois, the son of Frederick Weyerhaeuser and Elizabeth Sarah Bloedel. His father was the founder of the most prominent forest products company in the United States. A Phi Beta Kappa graduate of Yale University in 1896, F. E. (as he is identified in family biographies) immediately joined his older brother Rudolph with the Northern Lumber Company, a Weyerhaeuser-controlled firm that soon came to dominate lumbering activity in the countryside around Duluth, Minnesota. With a talent for efficient management and coordinated business effort that gained the attention of the Weyerhaeuser associates, the younger Frederick began his career purchasing timber stumpage for Northern Lumber and two other Weyerhaeuser mills in the vicinity.

Always on the financial and not the production end of the family's enterprises, F. E. and Edward Rutledge, a Weyerhaeuser associate, traveled to northern Idaho and purchased large tracts of low-priced timber in 1900. Two years later the senior Weyerhaeuser appointed F. E. to head a new Arkansas corporation, the Southern Lumber Company, part of the family associates' rapidly expanding business empire in the South. But it was in St. Paul, Minnesota, the central offices of the far-flung Weyerhaeuser enterprises since 1891, that F. E. best served the family's business interests. He married Harriette Louise Davis, daughter of a Michigan lumberman, in 1902; the couple raised three children.

The young Weyerhaeuser executive also proved astute in defending the company's interests against charges of monopoly practices. When critics charged Frederick Weyerhaeuser with monopoly landholding after the huge forest purchases from the Northern Pacific Railroad in 1900, F. E. advised the large-scale logging and milling of company timber, especially in the state of Washington where the largest holdings were located, to allay those suspicions. His recommendations spurred Weyerhaeuser directors to construct two state-of-the-art mills at Everett (1914) and Snoqualmie Falls (1917).

With the death of his father in 1914, F. E. quickly moved to the front as the financial manager of the family's welfare and its conveyer of tradition. Whereas the elder Weyerhaeuser managed business affairs through force of personality, the second-generation leaders adopted more formal management procedures. Among them, F. E. emerged as the person with the broadest perspective, the one with the most innovative managerial style, and, as such, the centerpiece of the new executive leadership. A man of intellectual depth and broad practical knowledge, he was instrumental in the establishment of the Weyerhaeuser Sales Company in 1916, a coordinated effort to eliminate competition among the Weyerhaeuser associates and to set common prices and selling policies. The Sales Company continued until 1959, when it became part of the Lumber and Plywood Division of the Weyerhaeuser Company.

Because of the difficulties of convincing individual company managers of the unified sales idea, F. E. withdrew from company business affairs and retired to southern California for a brief period. However, he returned to an active role in Weyerhaeuser business affairs in the mid-1920s when he was appointed vice president of sales operations. In addition to his work with the Sales Company, F. E. championed the creation of Weyerhaeuser Forest Products, a promotional vehicle of the Sales Company that was designed to serve as an advertising agency to push the company's trademark. Under the leadership of F. E. Weyerhaeuser, the company introduced its 4-SQUARE advertising program to provide a trademark and marketing acronym for select Weyerhaeuser lumber. Although he was far-sighted in most aspects of business enterprise, F. E. opposed plans to place the separate Weyerhaeuser associates together as one super company.

A modernizer in promoting forestry conservation, F. E. supported "practical" approaches to many measures important to lumbermen, including public and private cooperation in controlling forest fires and a yield tax on harvests in lieu of a fixed annual tax. Like other timberholders, F. E. wanted more attention given to the economic prerequisites of forest conservation. To promote that end, he was an enthusiastic supporter of the Clarke-McNary Act (1924), which provided for public and private support for controlling fires, and the McSweeney-McNary Act (1924), which established fourteen forest experiment stations nationwide.

F. E. showed an early interest in the economic aspects of sustained-yield forest management and listened to managers in the field who promoted progressive ideas like select logging. With the onset of the Great Depression, he participated in various voluntary schemes to control production but opposed federal efforts under the National Recovery Administration to impose production controls, minimum prices, and limits on the construction of new mills. At the same time, F. E. was a leader in the Weyerhaeuser move to purchase cutover timberland and to begin large-scale reforestation on the acquired properties.

Like most of his corporate peers, F. E. Weyerhaeuser held traditional and paternal attitudes toward labor. He opposed the recognition of labor unions and concessions or agreements with organized labor in the wake of strike activity. Yet with the onset of successful union organizing in the mid-1930, F. E. listened to realists among the Weyerhaeuser junior executives and accepted compromise and more amicable relations with organized labor.

But while he was a modernizer in the world of business and financial organization, F. E. remained a conservative person by temperament. He approved new technologies for production operations only when they proved feasible; his motto: "I would like to let the other fellow do the experimenting." But when younger managers confronted him with demonstrated proof of the profitability of innovative technologies, F. E. acquiesced. He showed a willingness to listen throughout his life and firmly believed in the art of the possible.

Frederick Edward Weyerhaeuser exercised his influence through the Weyerhaeuser Timber Company, originally incorporated in 1900 to control the vast properties being pieced together by the elder Weyerhaeuser. F. E. rose through the ranks from treasurer (1906–1928) and member of the board of directors (1906–1945) to vice president (1928–1934) and to president and chairman of the Executive Committee (1934–1945). His personal accomplishments include administering family and company affairs and the compilation of historical documents related to his father's achievements; at the time of his death in St. Paul, he was in the midst of discussions about a potential family biography. F. E. more than any of his siblings was a transitional figure between the first- and third-generation Weyerhaeusers.

• The key repository for primary materials related to the life of Frederick Edward Weyerhaeuser is the Weyerhaeuser Company Archives in Federal Way, Wash. The vast collection of correspondence and business records in the company archives provides information about the executive and leadership abilities of the various Weyerhaeuser family members. The standard published work on the history of the company is Ralph W. Hidy, Frank E. Hill, and Allan Nevins, *Timber and Men: The Weyerhaeuser Story* (1963). For a biography of a family member and family insights, see Charles E. Twining, *Phil Weyerhaeuser: Lumberman* (1985). An account of the Washington activities of the Weyerhaeuser Company for the first half of the twentieth century is Robert E. Ficken, *The Forested Land: A History of Lumbering in Western Washington* (1987).

William G. Robbins

WEYERHAEUSER, Phil (18 Jan. 1899–8 Dec. 1956), lumberman and corporation executive, was born John Philip Weyerhaeuser, Jr., in Rock Island, Illinois, the son of John Philip Weyerhaeuser, the president of the Weyerhaeuser Timber Company (WTC) from 1914 to 1928, and Nellie Anderson, a schoolteacher. His grandfather was Frederick Weyerhaeuser, founder of WTC and its first president. Phil attended Irving Public School in St. Paul, Minnesota, and the Hill School in Pottstown, Pennsylvania. In 1915 he entered Yale University, where he joined the Reserve Officers Training Corps and attained the rank of second lieutenant. During World War I he was assigned to Camp Jackson, South Carolina, and Camp Taylor in Kentucky. Soon after his 1920 graduation from Yale, Weyerhaeuser continued a family tradition by getting a job in the lumber industry in Washington State, studying under George Long, general manager of WTC, and learning timber cruising, log rafting, and other aspects of the industry.

In October 1921, Weyerhaeuser married Helen Hunt Walker in Seattle. They had five children, one of whom died in infancy. After marrying, the couple lived in Coeur d'Alene, Idaho, where Weyerhaeuser worked in the sales department of the Edward Rutledge Timber Company, becoming sales manager in 1922. In 1925 he took a job as general manager of the Clearwater Timber Company, and the couple moved to Lewiston, Idaho. As general manager, Weyerhaeuser supervised construction of the plant's sawmill and later was in charge of its operation. In 1931 Clearwater merged with the Potlatch Lumber Company and Weyerhaeuser's former employer, the Edward Rutledge Timber Company, to form Potlatch Forests, Inc., with Weyerhaeuser as president. In 1933 he moved to Tacoma to become executive vice president of the Weyerhaeuser Timber Company. He worked for the family firm for the rest of his life, becoming president in 1947 and serving in that capacity until his death.

On 24 May 1935 an emotionally grueling ordeal for Weyerhaeuser and his family began when his eight-year-old son George was abducted while walking home from school. Weyerhaeuser personally delivered the $200,000 cash ransom that the kidnappers demanded, and George returned home unharmed in one week. The three kidnappers were soon apprehended and sentenced to long prison terms, and more than three-quarters of the ransom money was eventually recovered. The incident was one of the most sensational kidnappings in American history, and the glare of publicity that accompanied it had a profound impact on Weyerhaeuser. Although he was touched by the thousands of letters and expressions of support that his family received, he was uncomfortable with the notoriety of the case and blamed the media for the surfeit of publicity. After the kidnapping, Weyerhaeuser, by all accounts a diffident and soft-spoken man, grew even more publicity-shy, resolving to shield himself and his family from the limelight; thereafter few details of his private life surface in the news.

As executive vice president of WTC and later as president, Weyerhaeuser fostered a significant change in the attitudes and practices of the lumber industry; biographers find little to criticize in his legacy. His vision and policies transformed not just the corporation he ran but the industry itself. As the *Time* magazine obituary observed, Weyerhaeuser "changed U.S. lumbering from a looters' pillage to a responsible industry." His emphasis on conservation was a salient example.

In the past timber companies descended on forests and quickly stripped an entire region clean. Trees were felled as minerals were mined, with little regard for preserving or renewing resources for the future. Beginning with his work at Clearwater and at Potlatch, Weyerhaeuser encouraged conservation and replacement of timber forests, and when he arrived at WTC in 1933 he and his brother Frank, the president of WTC, pushed to make these practices standard. Sensitive to criticism from the U.S. Forest Service that the timber industry acted in disdain of future resources and that the result would someday be a timber famine, Phil Weyerhaeuser supported long-range planning and argued that the country would never run out of wood. He advocated the concept of sustained-yield forestry, limiting cutting so that it struck a balance with growth. In 1934, under Weyerhaeuser's sponsorship, WTC implemented its first sustained-yield program under the Forest Conservation Code contained in the New Deal's National Recovery Act. In 1937 WTC inaugurated a national advertising campaign that touted the phrase, "timber is a crop," which embodied Weyerhaeuser's idea that trees, like crops, should be harvested but also replaced every year. The popular phrase became closely identified with the company and promoted its reputation as a champion of forest conservation. In 1938 WTC workers began to plant seedlings by hand in cutover areas where natural reforestation was impossible. Furthering the company's revolutionary efforts in conservation was the Clemons Tree Farm, which Weyerhaeuser helped to dedicate in 1941. It was the nation's first tree farm, where trees were raised and harvested on a rotation, allowing cuts to be made every year without worry of eventual depletion. The tree farm became a standard in the timber industry, and by the time of Weyerhaeuser's death there were 9,000 tree farms in the United States.

Weyerhaeuser also presided over a revolution in lumber manufacturing. Continuously critical of the enormous waste that occurred both in the harvesting of timber and in the manufacturing of lumber—for example, a considerable number of fallen trees were left behind on the forest floor, creating a fire hazard and impairing reforestation—Weyerhaeuser stressed the need to utilize more of each tree, an idea that he called "whole-log use." Speaking before the Forest Products Research Society in 1954, he declared, "In whole-log use, together with tree farming, lies the forest industry's practical answer to its critics and to skeptics who have cried 'Waste' and 'Timber Famine' in bygone days." In order to stretch the use of raw wood, Weyerhaeuser encouraged WTC to diversify its operations. In 1940 he got WTC involved in plywood manufacturing by gaining a controlling interest in the Washington Veneer Company of Olympia. The company also developed ways to use wood not suitable for lumber, and many mills began to operate exclusively on leftover wood. In 1948 WTC inaugurated a mill in Longview, Washington, that used Douglas fir sawmill residue to make bleached Kraft pulp, which was sold on the pulp market. WTC also built a plant at Klamath Falls, Oregon, to use overmature white fir to make hardboard, and a plant at Coos Bay, Oregon, to use Douglas fir planing mill shavings to make particle board. Likewise, WTC built plants to utilize bark, chips, and mill ends.

Increased research helped to pave the way for better utilization of forest products, and Weyerhaeuser pressed for more scientific study at WTC. In 1941 he became a member of the newly created Weyerhaeuser Development Committee, which coordinated research activities, and the following year the company established a research department.

Adhering to his conviction that the lumber industry involved more than just making lumber, Weyerhaeuser also invested considerable effort in improving WTC's public image and relations with communities. In 1937 he helped to produce a promotional film, *Trees and Men*, and in the same year WTC published a promotional pamphlet, *Timber Is a Crop*. In 1948 WTC's department of public information developed a press book to elucidate the company's strategies and goals. That year Weyerhaeuser also announced that WTC was establishing forestry scholarships at the University of Washington and at Oregon State University. In 1952 the Weyerhaeuser Foundation was established, dedicated to scholarship programs, charitable donations, educational workshops, and community projects. An avid hunter and fisherman, Weyerhaeuser encouraged WTC to open some of its lands for hunting and fishing. Under his direction the company also developed parks on its tree farms and sponsored a Christmas tree cutting on company lands. While Weyerhaeuser made few public speeches himself, when he did—usually informally before small groups—he came across as a sincere, unpretentious man who firmly believed in the principles he espoused and in the direction in which he wanted to steer the company.

In 1955 the State Department asked Weyerhaeuser to serve as a delegate to the United Nations Economic Commission for Europe Timber Committee, which met in Geneva, Switzerland. Also in 1955 the America Forestry Association also awarded him its Distinguished Service Award in Forestry. Weyerhaeuser died the following year of leukemia in Tacoma.

• The papers of John Philip Weyerhaeuser, Jr., are in the Weyerhaeuser Company Archives at corporate headquarters in Federal Way, Wash.; the company also maintains a number of short essays on his life. The Weyerhaeuser Business and Family Papers are kept at the Research Center of the Minnesota Historical Society. The *New York Times* gave extensive coverage of the kidnapping of George Weyerhaeuser; information on the kidnapping as well as on the FBI's investigation into the crime can be obtained from the Justice Department under the Freedom of Information Act. Charles Twining, *Phil Weyerhaeuser: Lumberman* (1985), contains an exhaustive record of his correspondences with family members. Information on Weyerhaeuser can also be found in Ralph Hidy et al., *Timber and Men: The Weyerhaeuser Story* (1963), and in "Lumberman of the Year . . . John Philip Weyerhaeuser, Jr.," *Crow's Lumber Digest*, 3 Jan. 1957. Obituaries are in *Newsweek* and *Time*, 17 Dec. 1956, and in the *New York Times*, the *Seattle Post-Intelligencer*, the *Seattle Times*, and the *Tacoma News Tribune*, 9 Dec. 1956.

YANEK MIECZKOWSKI

WEYL, Hermann (9 Nov. 1885–9 Dec. 1955), mathematician and mathematical physicist, was born Claus Hugo Hermann Weyl in Elmshorn (Schleswig-Holstein), Germany, the son of Ludwig Weyl, a bank director, and Anna Dieck. Weyl received his early schooling at the Gymnasium in Altona and in 1904 entered Göttingen University, where he was deeply influenced by the preeminent mathematician David Hilbert. His doctoral dissertation on integral equations, "Singuläre Integralgleichungen mit besonderer Berücksichtigung des Fourierschen Integraltheorems," was completed under Hilbert's direction in 1908. He remained in Göttingen as a privatdozent until 1913. Weyl followed his doctoral research with the work "Über gewöhnliche Differentialgleichungen mit Singularitäten und die zugehörigen Entwicklungen willkürlicher Funktionen" on the spectral theory of singular Sturm-Liouville problems, for which he would receive his habilitation and be eligible for a university professorship. This not only firmly established his reputation in mathematical analysis but was also of crucial importance in his later contributions to quantum theory.

In 1911–1912 Weyl lectured on the theory of Riemann surfaces, which led to his first book, *Die Idee der Riemannschen Flächen* (1913). This book not only succeeded in putting Bernhard Riemann's geometric function theory on a rigorous basis, but it also gave rise to numerous new topological notions, notably those of a two-dimensional differentiable manifold, a covering surface, and the duality between differentials and 1-cycles, which anticipated the more general concepts and results subsequently studied by algebraic topologists during the next two decades. Weyl's idea of a space also included the famous separation property later introduced and popularly credited to Felix Hausdorff (1914). If by some calamity Weyl's mathematical career had ended in 1914, the aforementioned material alone would have been sufficient to rank him as one of the most imaginative and talented mathematicians of his generation.

In 1913 Weyl married Helene Joseph, a well-known and talented translator of Spanish literature, with whom he had two children. That same year Weyl left Göttingen for a professorship at the Eidgenössische Technische Hochschule (ETH) in Zürich, Switzerland. His first year there coincided with the last year of physicist Albert Einstein's brief tenure at the school and occurred at a time when, together with Marcel Grossmann, Einstein was putting together the final formulation of general relativity. This prompted Weyl to turn his attention to differential geometry and relativity. This work had to wait, however, owing to his conscription into the German army in 1915. At the request of the Swiss government he was discharged in 1916 and returned to the ETH. He remained in Zürich, apart from 1928–1929, when he was a visiting professor of mathematical physics at Princeton University, until he returned to Göttingen as Hilbert's successor in 1930.

Weyl's ETH lectures in 1917 resulted in his second great work, *Raum, Zeit, Materie* (1918), the first comprehensive book-length presentation of Einstein's theories. Mathematically, this exposition was instrumental in setting forth the basic structure of higher dimensional differential geometry, and Weyl's achievement in this direction can be regarded as being a natural continuation of that first proposed in 1854 by Riemann. Weyl's approach was based on the seminal notion of a vector space, which was first introduced here in modern form. His exposition also included an intriguing blend of the philosophical aspects of the relation between geometry and physics. The book led Weyl to propose an enlarged view of geometry, and its later editions include his unified field theory of gravitation and electromagnetism. Historically, this was the first attempt to construct such a theory, and although it was to prove unsuccessful, its elegance and simplicity encouraged Einstein to seek other theories based on generalizing Riemannian geometry. Weyl's theory made use of the new principle of gauge-invariance (*Eichinvarianz*), the progenitor of the modern gauge theories, which are the paradigm of fashion in contemporary theoretical physics. By 1923 Weyl had given up hope for his theory, but he continued to be an active researcher and contributor to general relativity theories, producing the Bach-Weyl solution of Einstein's equations (1922) and the Weyl Principle in relativistic cosmology (1923).

The products of Weyl's early Zürich years also included a fundamental number-theoretic paper (1916) and the enunciation of the Weyl Problem on convex surfaces (1916), which was finally solved by Aleksei Pogorelov, Aleksander Aleksandrov, and Louis Nirenberg in 1951–1953, as well as his first incursion into the logical foundations of mathematics (1917). His study of the Helmholtz-Lie Space Problem (*Der Raum-Problem*) naturally led him into the theory of Lie groups and his profound study of the representation theory of semi-simple groups (1924–1926), which he personally regarded as his greatest single mathematical contribution. This work, which was done in friendly competition with Élie Cartan, has generated a major area of contemporary mathematics with Cartan and Weyl as its recognized architects. A paper written with F. Peter (1927) was noteworthy in establishing the possibility of carrying over classical analysis to compact topological groups. Weyl always felt that his Zürich years were the most creative and productive of his scientific career.

Although Weyl had played no role in the exploration of the old quantum theory, at the birth of the new quantum theory in 1926, he found himself in a unique position: his Zürich colleague Erwin Schrödinger was the creator of one version of it (wave mechanics), while his Göttingen friends Max Born, Werner Heisenberg, and Pascual Jordan had proposed a rival version (matrix mechanics). Weyl actively assisted both teams, and while he did not originate the group-theoretic approach he immediately perceived its importance for quantum theory. His Zürich lectures of 1927–1928 inevitably gave rise to his third major book, *Gruppentheorie und Quantenmechanik* (1928). In its second edition in 1931, on the basis of group-theoretic considerations, he made the observation that the new Dirac equation for an electron should also admit positively charged solutions having the same mass. Physicists, including Paul A. M. Dirac, were skeptical but subsequently won over when the positron was experimentally discovered in 1932. Thus group theory, previously irreverently known as *die Gruppenpest*, became an indispensable part of mathematical physics. Weyl attempted to carry the formalism of quantum mechanics over into general relativity—still an unsolved problem—but his results were nevertheless of significance. They include a quantum mechanical notion of gauge invariance and a new wave equation, the Weyl equation (1929), which despite its failure to be parity invariant, was found in 1957 to be applicable in Wolfgang Pauli's neutrino theory.

Upon the Nazi accession to power in 1933, Weyl returned to Princeton as one of the original members of the newly created Institute for Advanced Study. He became a naturalized U.S. citizen in 1939, was elected a member of the National Academy of Sciences in 1940, and was a foreign member of the Royal Society, corresponding member of the Académie des Sciences, and member of numerous other academies and societies.

The prewar Princeton years at the Institute for Advanced Study saw a continuation of his interests in forging new mathematical tools for physics, notably his work with Richard Brauer on spinors in n-dimensions (1935) and research preparatory to his last great book, *The Classical Groups: Their Invariants and Representations* (1939). During the war Weyl remained at Princeton but contributed to the war effort by turning his attention to the rigorous analysis of boundary layer problems in fluid dynamics (1941, 1942) and the theory of shock waves (1944, published in 1949). His work on potential theory (1940) and the theory of harmonic integrals (1943) provided fundamental contributions to classical analysis, and his critique of George D. Birkhoff's theory of gravitation (1944) was of importance in relativity theory.

The postwar years showed little diminution of Weyl's creative powers but were largely devoted to revisiting previously considered areas of research. This included the role of symmetry in quantum mechanics (1949), the translation and revision of his 1926 book, *Philosophy of Mathematics and Natural Sciences* (1949), which contained a masterful summary of his world view, and an excursion into game theory with an elementary proof of John von Neumann's minimax theorem (1950). He also produced a charming little book, *Symmetry* (1952), which he described as his "swan song" upon his retirement from the institute in 1951.

Weyl's wife died in 1948, and in 1950 he married sculptor Ellen Lohnstein Bär of Zürich; they had no children. After Weyl's retirement from the institute the couple divided their time between Princeton and Zürich. Weyl's final major intellectual effort was the rewriting of his first book, *The Concept of a Riemann Surface* (1955), which contained numerous improvements. He died in Zürich.

Weyl's contribution to twentieth-century mathematical and physical thought is unique and clearly marks him as one of the great men of our age. His work and interests were very broad and are singularly impressive in their depth and influence. His writing, in both German and English, has an unmistakable cadence and style that not only challenge the reader's ability but reveal the author's aesthetic sense and philosophical predilections. On more than one occasion he expressed his working credo of trying to unite the *true* with the *beautiful*, and he humorously said that, when forced to make a choice between the two, he was usually inclined to choose the latter. His writings, though not easy reading, provide a vivid image of the man and his profound belief in the harmony of Nature.

• Weyl's papers are in the Weyl Nachlass of the Wissenschaftshistorische Sammlungen in the ETH library in Zürich. A collection of nineteen of his publications, which he regarded of greatest significance for future work, appear in *Selecta: Hermann Weyl* (1956), and the four-volume *Gesammelte Abhandlungen* (1968), contains most of his published papers. A centenary volume, *Hermann Weyl 1885–1955*, ed. Komaravolu Chandrasekharan, contains three lectures devoted to his contributions and their influence on contemporary thought in mathematics and physics. In addition to the books previously mentioned, Weyl wrote about a dozen small booklets and sets of lecture notes, which often contain less formal presentations of his scientific work. Finally, several of his expository papers provide valuable insight into the man and his mode of expression. These include most notably his memorial tribute to Hilbert in the *Bulletin of the American Mathematical Society* 50 (Sept. 1944): 612–54; his Gibbs Lecture, "Ramifications, Old and New, of the Eigenvalue Problem," *Bulletin of the American Mathematical Society* 56 (Mar. 1950): 115–34; and "A Half-Century of Mathematics," *American Mathematical Monthly* 58 (Oct. 1951): 523–33. A discussion of his Zürich years can be found in Günter Frei and Urs Stammbach, *Hermann Weyl und die Mathematik an der ETH Zürich, 1913–1930* (1992). Two technical assessments of his work are in the *Biographical Memoirs of the Royal Society* 3 (1957) and *L'Enseignement Mathématique* 3 (July–Sept. 1957). An obituary notice is in the *New York Times*, 10 Dec. 1955.

JOSEPH D. ZUND

WEYL, Walter Edward (11 Mar. 1873–9 Nov. 1919), economist and writer, was born in Philadelphia, Pennsylvania, the son of Nathan Weyl, a wholesale milliner, and Emilie Stern. An excellent student, Weyl went through the Philadelphia public schools and earned a scholarship to the Wharton School of the University of Pennsylvania. In his senior year he won a prestigious national essay contest. At Wharton, Weyl came under the influence of the distinguished economist Simon N. Patten, who urged him to pursue graduate work in Europe. From 1892 to 1896 Weyl studied at the University of Halle and in Berlin and Paris. He then returned to the University of Pennsylvania, completed a dissertation on *The Passenger Traffic of Railways* (1901), and received a Ph.D. in economics in 1897.

Weyl later characterized the next ten years of his life as a time of "sheer drift." He taught a little, traveled widely, joined the settlement house movement, and worked for the federal government at both the Bureau of Labor and the Bureau of Statistics. In 1902 he enlisted on behalf of the coal miners in the great anthracite strike. This episode brought him into a warm and useful three-year association with John Mitchell, leader of the United Mine Workers (in 1903 Weyl ghost wrote Mitchell's *Organized Labor: Its Problems, Purposes, and Ideals*).

Weyl's marriage to Bertha Poole, a magazine journalist and social activist, in September 1907 transformed his life. The couple, who had first met at Jane Addams's Hull-House, moved to Woodstock, New York, settled down to a more disciplined, stationary, and regular existence, and were able to support themselves by writing for magazines; they had one child. Weyl published in many of the leading muckraking and popular journals of the day, including *Harper's*, *Saturday Evening Post*, and *Outlook*. He wrote articles on numerous topics—some of them chatty and light, others technical and academic—but was at his best in discussing railroads, labor problems, and immigration, areas in which his dexterity with statistics came most readily into play. His friend and colleague at the *New Republic*, the distinguished journalist Walter Lippmann, called him "by far the best trained economist in the progressive movement."

In 1912 Weyl supported Theodore Roosevelt for the presidency and published his most important and highly praised book, *The New Democracy*. A generally optimistic exploration of American life at the height of the Progressive Era, the book celebrated the democratic impulse in the social reform movement and argued that a "social surplus," a level of material prosperity comfortably above subsistence needs, gave the nation the chance to achieve greater social justice. Like other progressive theorists, Weyl lamented the excessive adulation of individualism (a residue, he thought, from frontier days), the near worship of the Constitution, and the fanatical insistence upon the untrammeled enjoyment of private property. He argued for more direct democracy, regulation of trusts by the central government, greater efficiency in business, and increased power for organized labor. An enthusiastic opponent of the privileged and powerful, Weyl nonetheless resisted the teachings of proletarian socialism. His desire for a middle ground between the economic theories of Adam Smith and Karl Marx led him to a hopeful faith in middle-class progressivism.

In September 1913 Herbert Croly invited Weyl to become one of the founding editors of the *New Republic*, a journal of progressive opinion that began publishing in November 1914. Specializing in economic questions but also branching off into political, cultural, and social topics, Weyl worked on the magazine until 1916. He then loosened his connection to it in order to work on a book. When the war came, Weyl produced two essays on foreign affairs: *American World Policies* (1917) and *The End of the War* (1918). He also helped to organize the quartermaster general's office in the War Department and later joined the Inquiry project, Colonel Edward House's ambitious attempt to enlist American experts in preparation for the Paris Peace Conference. He went to Versailles in early 1919 as a private observer of the peace conference.

Weyl was a man of exceptional gentleness and good humor—tolerant of differences, affable, gregarious, human, kindly. "He looked like a saint," wrote fellow economist Alvin Johnson, "and fundamentally was one." He died of cancer in a New York City hospital. In their issue of 19 November 1919, his former colleagues at the *New Republic* wrote: "His method was to comprehend, no matter where it led him. He asked questions and explained and always when he honestly could, he gave the benefit of the doubt."

• Two boxes of Weyl manuscripts covering the period from 1911 to 1920, including letters and a diary, are in the Rutgers Special Collections and Archives, at Rutgers University. The leading secondary work on Weyl is Charles Forcey, *The Crossroads of Liberalism: Croly, Weyl, Lippmann, and the Progressive Era, 1900–1925* (1961); also valuable are Forcey's "Walter Weyl and the Class War," in *American Radicals: Some Problems and Personalities*, ed. Harvey Goldberg (1957), and his introduction to the 1964 edition of *The New Democracy*. A collection of revealing personal reminiscences is Howard Brubaker, ed., *Walter Weyl: An Appreciation* (1922). An obituary is in the *New York Times*, 11 Nov. 1919.

DAVID W. LEVY

WEYMOUTH, Frank Elwin (2 June 1874–22 July 1941), hydraulic engineer, was born in Medford, Maine, the son of Andrew Jackson Weymouth and Charlotte Prudence Powers, farmers. Weymouth graduated from the University of Maine with a B.S. in civil engineering in 1896. His first job was with the City of Malden, Massachusetts, followed by a position in waterworks construction with the Metropolitan Water Board of Boston. After a brief stint as assistant city engineer with the City of Winnipeg, Manitoba, he joined the U.S. Isthmian Canal Commission in June 1899, surveying routes in Nicaragua for the proposed isthmian canal. There he worked with Arthur Powell Davis, with whom he formed a long professional association. He married Mary Maude Lane in 1900; they had no children.

In 1903 Weymouth joined the new Reclamation Service, formed out of the Geological Survey by the Newlands Act of 1902. The Reclamation Service held the responsibility for surveying possible locations for reclamation projects in the western states and territories. Irrigation and reclamation projects, flood control, hydroelectric power, and dam construction were all included in the Reclamation Service's agenda for reclaiming the arid West. Weymouth led field surveys and investigations for possible irrigation projects in North Dakota and Montana. In 1908 he was appointed supervising engineer for the Idaho District and oversaw construction of storage dams on the Snake River at Jackson Lake, Wyoming. His most notable assignment at this time was construction of the Arrowrock Dam on the Boise River in 1915, at the time the highest dam in the world.

Weymouth became chief of construction for the Reclamation Service in 1916. For the next four years he supervised all work undertaken by the service in the western states. Another promotion came in 1920 when he was appointed chief engineer, a post he held until 1924. During this time he pioneered in new methods of dam design and construction, most notably in what became Boulder Dam—since renamed the Hoover Dam—which, at 720 feet, would be more than twice as high as his Arrowrock Dam. Disputes over management of the Reclamation Service and its reorganization as the Bureau of Reclamation prompted Weymouth's resignation in 1924. He briefly held the job of president of the Brock and Weymouth engineering firm of Philadelphia, Pennsylvania. In 1926 he joined the J. G. White Engineering Corporation as chief engineer, supervising that firm's engineering work in Mexico. In the late 1920s Weymouth conducted extensive irrigation surveys throughout Mexico and supervised the planning and construction of canals and such dams as the Don Martin Dam and the Calles Dam.

Moving to Los Angeles in 1929, Weymouth began a long association with water agencies in southern California. After a brief stint with the Los Angeles Department of Water and Power, he became chief engineer of the Metropolitan Water District (MWD) of Southern California, and in 1931 he assumed the title of general manager as well. The MWD was a new agency, originally consisting of thirteen member cities, that wanted to tap the Colorado River as a source of municipal water. At the time the river, 300 miles from the MWD cities, had no storage facilities for diversion of water for domestic purposes. The cities would connect to the river by means of the Colorado River Aqueduct. The project presented major challenges to the MWD. Voter approval had to be secured to pay for the construction costs. The aqueduct would stretch across a vast desert about which little was known. Weymouth had already conducted feasibility studies for the aqueduct while working for the City of Los Angeles, and his estimates became the focus of the aqueduct bond campaign. On 29 September 1931 voters approved a $220 million bond issue by an impressive five-to-one majority for construction of the Colorado River Aqueduct.

The project was the last major effort of Weymouth's career. It took nine years to complete and was finished only a month before Weymouth's death. The development included the 242-mile-long main aqueduct, 150 miles of lateral canals, four main dams, and five pumping plants that lifted the water 1,600 feet from the river. Electrical power for the pumps came from Boulder Dam through 237 miles of high-voltage transmission lines. More than 100 miles of tunnels had to be dug. The desert presented a natural obstacle that had to be overcome by muscle and machine. At last, the Colorado River Aqueduct began delivering water to the MWD cities on 18 June 1941. Barely a month later Weymouth died in San Marino, California.

Throughout his career Weymouth was known as a dedicated professional who had few outside interests. His first wife died in January 1937, and in 1938 he married Barbara Turner; they had no children. He enjoyed reading for relaxation, his favorite subjects being biography and history. Other than this, he had no hobbies. Weymouth lived for his work. He brought reports home with him and spent hours going over them, checking every detail. At the professional level he avoided politics and political influence. He relied on his reputation for honesty and the quality of his work. He was also an excellent administrator who had a talent for hiring qualified people and supervising them well. His subordinates knew that their reports would be closely scrutinized for accuracy and attention to detail.

Early in his career Weymouth joined the American Society of Civil Engineers, first as an associate member on 4 September 1901; he became a full member on 5 February 1907 and was awarded honorary member status on 10 October 1938. He wrote a number of articles for engineering publications, especially the *American Society of Civil Engineers Proceedings*. His greatest achievement, the Colorado River Aqueduct, capped a long and distinguished career in civil engineering during an era of great constructions and technological change.

• Weymouth's main technical works are "The Proposed Colo. River Aqueduct and Metropolitan Water District," *American Society of Civil Engineers (ASCE) Proceedings* 56 (1930): 1283–89, and "Major Engineering Problems: Colorado River Development," *Annals of the American Academy of Political and Social Science*, Mar. 1930, supp. The most important sketch of Weymouth's life is the memorial in the *ASCE Transactions* 107 (1942): 1712–16. See also "Frank E. Weymouth," *Western Construction News and Highway Builder* 8 (Aug. 1933): 330. Obituaries are in the *New York Times* and *Los Angeles Times*, both 23 July 1941.

ABRAHAM HOFFMAN

WHALEN, Grover Michael Aloysius Augustine (2 June 1886–20 Apr. 1962), promoter, official greeter, and businessman, was born in New York City, the son of Michael Henry Whalen, a hauling contractor, and Esther De Nee. After graduating from DeWitt Clinton High School, Whalen attended Packard Business College. In 1904 he entered New York Law School while working part-time as a clerk in the John Wanamaker Department Store. After his father died in 1906, Whalen worked with his father's partner in their expanding hauling business. In 1913 Whalen married Anne Dolores Kelly; they had three children. The next year he sold his family's share in the hauling business and returned to Wanamaker's store. Soon his boss formed a Businessmen's League to help solve the city's problems and asked Whalen to become its secretary. In 1917 the Business League backed Democrat John F. Hylan, the successful candidate for mayor, and Whalen was given time off from Wanamaker's to serve as the new mayor's private secretary. In 1919 Whalen became the executive vice chairman of the Mayor's Committee for the Reception of Distinguished Guests, and he remained the city's official greeter until 1953, through seven mayoral administrations. From 1919 to 1923, as a member of the New York and New Jersey Bridge-Tunnel Commission, he improved the city's surface transportation with the first city-owned bus line. He was also the chair of the Board of Purchases from 1919 to 1924.

When Hylan left the mayor's office in 1924, Whalen returned to Wanamaker's, where he was general manager for the next decade. In December 1928 he took an eighteen-month leave from Wanamaker's to become police commissioner. In that post he founded the police academy, started a crime-prevention bureau, and boosted the department's flagging morale by raiding criminal hangouts and penetrating Communist cells with an undercover force. Beginning on 1 August 1933, as the New York administrator for the National Recovery Administration (NRA), Whalen supported the agency with speeches and the greatest parade in the city up to that time. On 15 January 1934 he left Wanamaker's and the NRA to become chair of the board of Schenley Distilling Corporation, where he remained until 1937. In that capacity he convinced Secretary of the Treasury Henry M. Morgenthau, Jr., to back federal legislation prohibiting the reuse or resale of liquor bottles. When passed, that law hampered illegal distillers from avoiding taxes and from passing off their liquors under the label of a legitimate distiller.

None of Whalen's other activities brought him as much renown as did his unpaid job greeting notables visiting New York City. Even Henry F. Pringle, a debunking contemporary writer who claimed that Whalen had ridden "to fame on a winning smile, irreproachable manners, and a meticulous attention to his wardrobe," admitted that he exhibited "a real flair for ceremonial" occasions and at times displayed "sheer genius" (Pringle, pp. 279, 283). For more than three decades Whalen's ticker-tape parades, staged when office workers filled the sidewalks during their lunch hour, made lower Broadway from Bowling Green to City Hall the "Canyon of Heroes." Whalen's contemporary, social historian Frederick Lewis Allen, stated that he had reduced "welcoming to a science" while raising "it to an art." When 1,800 tons of ticker tape whitened New York streets during Charles Lindbergh's welcome after his transatlantic flight, the parade became known as the Great Blizzard of June 1927. Decades later, when General Douglas MacArthur was recalled by President Harry S. Truman in April 1951, the general was greeted in New York with 2,850 tons of paper.

To celebrate the 150th anniversary of President George Washington's inauguration in New York City, Whalen suggested the 1939 to 1940 New York World's Fair. In addition, he headed the private corporation that organized it and named it "The World of Tomorrow." In June 1936, having raised most of the $155 million for the fair, Whalen used an ordinary spade to break ground for it in a stretch of Flushing Meadow, three and a half miles long, known as the Corona Dumps. What one associate called Whalen's "inability to recognize a stone wall" helped him surmount many difficulties in preparing for the fair's opening. Convinced by Whalen to make his planned around the world flight an advertisement for the fair, aviation pioneer Howard Hughes named his plane *New York World's Fair 1939* and carried letters from Whalen to the leaders of the countries he visited. Building the pavilions for the sixty countries, thirty-three states, and other organizations exhibiting at the fair gave jobs to many New Yorkers who had been without work during the depression, as did the local transportation projects planned in connection with the fair. Among these were the Bronx-Whitestone Bridge, La Guardia Airport, three expressways, a new line on one subway and a new station on another, and a new station on the Long Island Railroad.

The fair, as Whalen had planned, was "primarily a great theater," where "a thousand entertainments" delighted the nearly 45 million people who attended it. President Franklin D. Roosevelt's speech opening the fair on 30 April 1939 inaugurated the nation's regular television service. Elsie, the Borden cow, was born at the fair; visitors could watch the beating heart of a five-story-tall man; and long distance phone calls, placed free of charge, were tracked on a huge lighted map of the United States, while hundreds of people listened in. Excited visitors leaving General Motor's "Futurama" truly believed the inscription on their gift pens, "I have seen the future." Besides television, new products introduced included lucite, air conditioning, color film, and nylon stockings. Along with his greeting job, planning the 1939 New York World's Fair made Whalen "Mr. New York." Everywhere the fair was hailed as a great success, and few people seemed concerned that its revenue had only repaid forty cents of each dollar invested in it.

Whalen, who was active in the movement to make New York the world's fashion center, became in 1941 chair of the board of Coty, a cosmetic and perfume manufacturer, and the next year inaugurated the Coty American Fashion Critics' Annual Award for clothing design. Early in World War II he was appointed civilian adviser to the commanding generals of the Alaska Defense Forces and the Northwest Service Command, and in 1943 he became the head of New York City's Civil Defense Volunteers Office, which had 225,000 workers. In 1956 Whalen was made the president of a Detroit hardware firm, Trans Continental Industries, and the next year he became the president of the Fifth Avenue Association and helped plan its fiftieth anniversary celebration. He died in New York City.

• Some of Whalen's papers are in the Archives of the City of New York, references to him are in Columbia University's Oral History Collection, and material on him is in Columbia University's Rare Book and Manuscript Library. For Whalen's own story, see *Mr. New York: The Autobiography of Grover A. Whalen* (1955). For selections from Whalen's speeches boosting the NRA, see Hugh S. Johnson, *What the National Recovery Act Means to You* (1933). Views by contemporaries are in Frederick Lewis Allen, *Only Yesterday: An Informal History of the Nineteen-Twenties* (1931), and Henry F. Pringle, "Grover the Magnificent," *American Mercury* 17 (July 1929): 278–86. For evidence of the importance of the ticker-tape parade Whalen gave Lindbergh, see Howard F. McMains, "The Guest of the Nation: Politics and Charles Lindbergh's Return to the United States in 1927," *New York History* 66 (1985): 262–79. For more on the World's Fair, see David Gelernter, *1939: The Lost World of the Fair* (1995), and Helen A. Harrison, ed., *Dawn of a New Day: The New York World's Fair, 1939/40* (1980). An obituary is in the *New York Times*, 21 Apr. 1962.

OLIVE HOOGENBOOM

WHALLEY, Edward (1615?–1675?), regicide, was born in Nottinghamshire, England, the son of Richard Whalley and Frances Cromwell. As a second son, not destined to inherit the family estate, he was brought up to merchandise and became a linen draper. With his first wife, Judith Duffell, he had an unknown number of sons and daughters. These included his eldest son John and a daughter Frances, who married Major General William Goffe. With his second wife, Mary Middleton, sister of Sir George Middleton, he may have had a son, Edward.

About 1642 Whalley entered the Parliamentary army against King Charles I. He was one of the strongest supporters of his first cousin Oliver Cromwell. He became a major in Cromwell's regiment of cavalry in 1643 and distinguished himself in many battles and sieges, especially in the battle of Naseby in 1645. Army headquarters distrusted him because of his religious orthodoxy.

When troops seized Charles I in June 1647, Sir Thomas Fairfax, commander in chief of the New Model army, put Whalley in charge of the king. On 11 November Cromwell wrote Whalley to guard the king well because rumors were abroad that Levellers planned to assassinate him. Whalley showed Charles the letter to assure him that the officers had goodwill toward him. Charles escaped but left a note thanking Whalley for his courtesy.

On 6 January 1649 the House of Commons appointed Whalley a commissioner of the High Court of Justice established to try the king. By 26 January he was among the fifty-nine men who signed the death warrant against Charles I.

At the battle of Dunbar, 3 September 1650, Whalley contributed greatly to the complete defeat of the

Scots army. Cromwell rewarded him with the rank of commissary general and the command of four regiments of cavalry. Parliament gave him estates in Scotland worth £500 a year.

In 1655 Whalley was appointed major general in charge of the counties of Lincoln, Notts, Derby, Warwick, and Leicester. The twelve major generals each governed a section of England along Puritanical lines. Whalley closed alehouses, ejected scandalous ministers, and taxed cavaliers, or royalists.

Whalley represented Nottinghamshire in the two Parliaments called by Cromwell and served in the House of Lords in 1657. He was very zealous against the Quaker James Naylor, whom Parliament prosecuted for blasphemy for riding into Bristol on Palm Sunday in imitation of Jesus Christ's entry into Jerusalem. Otherwise, he took little part in debate.

After Oliver Cromwell's death in 1658, Cromwell's son Richard succeeded him as lord protector. The Long Parliament reassembled and took away Whalley's commission. They feared him as a relative of the protector and because of his influence with the army. Whalley's men, however, refused his orders to fight for Richard, who abdicated on 5 May 1659. When the army tried to seize power in October, they persuaded Whalley to meet with his old comrade, George Monck. The army hoped Whalley could secure a reconciliation with General Monck, who now supported Parliament against the military's attempted takeover. Monck, who was instrumental in reinstating members of Parliament whom Oliver Cromwell had purged, refused to deal with Whalley. The Stuart Restoration began the next spring when Parliament asked the exiled prince of Wales to assume the throne as Charles II.

Parliament insisted on capital punishment for those who had signed the king's death warrant. By the Bill of Attainder against the regicides, Whalley lost his estates in England and Scotland. He fled to America with Major General Goffe and Colonel John Dixwell, two other judges of the late king. Whalley and Goffe sailed from London under the names of Edward Richardson and William Stephenson. They arrived in Boston on 27 July 1660.

On 22 September 1660 the royal government issued a proclamation offering £100 to any who discovered either Whalley or Goffe in any British dominion and caused him to be brought in alive or dead. The fugitives settled in Cambridge, Massachusetts, and moved about freely for several months. On 22 February 1661 the council of Massachusetts Bay met to discuss how to protect them. On 26 February the refugees left for New Haven, where they hid in the house of Reverend John Davenport. Three weeks later, upon learning of the king's proclamation for their arrest, they began hiding in various towns, including Branford, Derby, and Guildford. They spent most of the summer in a cave formed by a pile of boulders. They next moved to Milford and conducted religious services for a few neighbors who visited them. On 5 September 1661 the royal commissioners of the united colonies published a declaration against harboring the fugitives but got no response.

In the autumn of 1664 Whalley and Goffe went to Hadley, Massachusetts, to the home of Reverend John Russell, pastor of the town church. They probably spent the rest of their lives at his house and at the home of Peter Tilton. In 1665 commissioners who had been sent to look into the government of the American colonies were ordered to search for the regicides. They had no luck.

In February 1665 Dixwell joined the Russell household for several years. Whalley and Goffe had visits from a few friends but otherwise had little outside contact. The leading colonists sent them presents, and Whalley's sister, Mrs. Jane Hooke, often sent money and clothing from England.

Goffe told his wife in a letter written in 1674 that her father was extremely ill. This letter is the last known reference to Whalley during his lifetime. The tradition at Boston, Barnstable, and New Haven was that one of the judges died at Russell's and was buried in his house. Historian Ezra Stiles believed it to be Edward Whalley.

Whalley was a conservative Puritan who wanted to reform the Church of England from within. He left no writings, but we may assume that he was literate, since the Puritans placed great stress on reading and interpreting the Bible for themselves. Although Whalley was prominent in the English civil wars, his personal role in American history was very slight. The protection he received from the American colonists points to antimonarchical attitudes and a sense of independence a century before the American Revolution.

• *Collections of the Massachusetts Society*, 3d ser., 1; 4th ser., 8 (1868), has copies of letters by Goffe and others that pertain to Whalley. The collections also contain papers of Governor Thomas Hutchinson, colonial governor of Massachusetts (1769–1774), in which may be found material pertaining to Whalley's exile in Massachusetts. Hutchinson, *The History of Massachusetts*, 3d ed. (1795), is available in microform, and his *History of the Colony and Province of Massachusetts Bay*, ed. Lawrence Shaw Mayo, vol. 1 (1936), is also a relevant source. Mark Noble, *Lives of the English Regicides* (1798), gives some biographical information from a royalist viewpoint. See also Ezra Stiles, *A History of Three of the Judges of King Charles I* (1794). Antonia Fraser, *Cromwell: The Lord Protector* (1974), provides much background information and contains several passages related to Whalley. Articles include Robert Patterson Robins, "Edward Whalley, the Regicide," *Pennsylvania Magazine of History and Biography* 1 (1877): 55–66; and Robins, "Notes and Queries," *Pennsylvania Magazine of History and Biography* 4 (1880): 258–60.

DIANNE JENNINGS WALKER

WHARTON, Anne Hollingsworth (15 Dec. 1845–29 July 1928), writer and historian, was born in Southampton Furnace, Pennsylvania, the daughter of Charles Wharton, a merchant in the iron trade, and Mary McLanahan Boggs. Wharton attended a private school in Philadelphia and there began the writing and research that constituted her lengthy career.

During the late nineteenth and early twentieth centuries, Wharton contributed articles and short stories on the customs and manners of colonial America to national magazines, the *Atlantic Monthly* and *Lippincott's* among them. Her earliest works were grounded in Wharton family legends of seventeenth- and eighteenth-century Philadelphia. For her first published book, *Genealogy of the Wharton Family of Philadelphia 1664 to 1880* (1880), Wharton worked with the archives of the Historical Society of Pennsylvania and records of the Philadelphia Friends Association. Privately published for distribution among family members, the genealogy became the foundation for much of her later writing.

By the 1880s Wharton was an honorary member of the Historical Society of Pennsylvania and a recognized specialist in Philadelphia history. In 1893, the same year in which she was appointed a judge of the Colonial Era Exhibit at the World's Columbian Exposition in Chicago, Wharton published the first volume of what was to become her most popular series, *Through Colonial Doorways*. In the preface, she wrote that "the revival of interest in Colonial and Revolutionary times has become a marked feature of the life of to-day. . . . Not only has a desire been shown to learn more of the great events of the last century, but with it has come an altogether natural curiosity to gain some insight into the social and domestic life of Colonial days."

Through Colonial Doorways offered contemporary readers sketches of the everyday life of a decidedly upper-class milieu. Wharton's publisher, J. B. Lippincott, packaged the text and its successor, *Colonial Days and Dames* (1895), in a deluxe boxed set featuring decorative gilding and illustrations. *Lippincott's* lauded the second volume as "even fuller in historic data and more sprightly in its fund of anecdote than its predecessor." In both works Wharton invited readers over the threshold of colonial mansions and into selected intimate spaces, providing along the way a detailed catalog of the material goods necessary for the furnishing of colonial revival homes. These two successful volumes were followed with *Heirlooms in Miniatures* (1897), *Salons Colonial and Republican* (1900), and *Social Life in the Early Republic* (1902). Although she published exclusively with J. B. Lippincott, Wharton was asked to contribute one volume, *Martha Washington* (1897), to the Scribner series "Women of Colonial and Revolutionary Times."

In the first decade of the twentieth century Wharton turned her literary attention to foreign landscapes. Drawing on her own travels for *Italian Days and Ways* (1906), *An English Honeymoon* (1908), and *In Chateau Land* (1911), she assembled bits of historical, literary, and art information and melded them into fictionalized travelogues. Written from the perspective of American tourists, Wharton's travel books were humorous; she satirized the adventures of American socialites abroad but also shaped the future itineraries of readers, offering instruction and suggesting sites of interest. Wharton returned in part to domestic subjects with *English Ancestral Homes of Noted Americans* (1915); using historical and genealogical lore, she traced the Washington, Franklin, and Penn families back to their transatlantic roots. With this text Wharton solidified Anglo-America's claim to the nation's increasingly contested culture. As a contemporary reviewer noted, Wharton reminded her selective readership of "the rock from which we were hewn and the pit from whence we were digged" (*Dial*, 1915).

Wharton's interest in memorializing the colonial past manifested itself in activities beyond literature. In the spring of 1891 she and other members of the Historical Society of Pennsylvania and "prominent" women of Philadelphia assembled to found the Pennsylvania Society of Colonial Dames. The newly organized group sought to form a national organization and ultimately succeeded in establishing the National Society of the Colonial Dames of America. Wharton was named the society's first official historian and held the post from 1898 to 1908. Perhaps the most notable event during Wharton's tenure as historian was the Colonial Dames' Commemorative Festival in Jamestown, Virginia. The Dames, both the Virginia chapter and the national council, were instrumental in erecting a suitable memorial to Jamestown colonists. Their efforts led to a reorganization of the island's ruins; the original church tower was repaired and a replica of the old church was attached to it.

With the exception of her travels abroad and research trips, Wharton lived most of her life in Philadelphia. She was witness to and participant in the city's decades-long theater of patriotic activity, from the laying of Independence Hall's cornerstone in 1874 to the hosting of the National Centennial in 1876. She died in Philadelphia, having never married.

An early advocate of historic preservation and an ardent colonial revivalist, Wharton helped shape a historical narrative that encouraged middle and upper classes to arrange about them vestiges of America's past—objects, architecture, books, and art works, both originals and reproductions. Her body of work included fifteen books and numerous articles and speeches. The appeal of her writing was lasting; at the time of her death eleven of her books were still in print. Her texts were part of a broader movement in America toward the invention of a useful history, one that would entertain and instruct while investing the country with a sense of national unity in the wake of immigration anxiety, labor unrest, political corruption, and racial discord.

• Wharton's papers, including a diary, research notes, and newspaper clippings, are at the Historical Society of Pennsylvania in Philadelphia. Wharton's other works include *A Last Century Maid and Other Stories for Children* (1896); *Genealogy of the Philadelphia Branch of the Damon Family of Massachusetts* (1896), jointly authored with Anne H. Cresson; *History of the National Society of the Colonial Dames of America* (1900), read at a meeting of the Dames' national board and reprinted for distribution among members; *Rose of Old Quebec* (1913); a short commentary in *American War Songs*, published by the National Society of the Colonial Dames of America (1925);

and *In Old Pennsylvania Towns* (1920), an amusing travelogue defining "quaint and unusual" destinations for automobile tourists. For information on the Colonial Dames, see Clarinda Huntington Lamar, *A History of the National Society of the Colonial Dames of America, from 1891 to 1933* (1934). An obituary is in the *New York Times*, 30 July 1928.

DEBORAH L. OWEN

WHARTON, Clifton Reginald (11 May 1899–23 Apr. 1990), Foreign Service officer, was born in Baltimore, Maryland, the son of William B. Wharton and Rosalind Griffin. He received an LL.B. cum laude from the Boston University School of Law in 1920 and an LL.M. in 1923 from the same institution. Wharton was admitted to the Massachusetts bar in 1920 and practiced law in Boston until 1924. In August 1924 he received a telegram appointing him as a law clerk in the Department of State. In 1924 he married Harriette Banks; they had four children before divorcing.

In January 1925 Wharton became the first black to take the new Foreign Service examination established by the 1924 Rogers Act, which had created a career Foreign Service based on competitive examinations and merit promotion. Only twenty candidates passed both the written and the oral parts of the examination. In March 1925 Under Secretary of State Joseph Grew wrote to a colleague that the twenty included "one negro, who will go at once to Liberia" (Calkin, *Women*, p. 72). Wharton later recalled that when he decided to take the Foreign Service exam, his prospective associates were not enthusiastic.

The lack of enthusiasm Wharton sensed also existed at the highest levels of the department. Following passage of the Rogers Act, the Executive Committee of the Foreign Service Personnel Board prepared a memorandum on how to avoid appointing women or blacks. One alternative suggested was an executive order stating that persons in those groups were not eligible to take the examination. Another was to rate such candidates so low that they could not achieve a passing mark. Secretary of State Charles Evans Hughes, however, emphatically rejected both alternatives.

Wharton was appointed a Foreign Service officer on 20 March 1925, and on 21 March he was assigned to Monrovia, Liberia. Blacks had been receiving diplomatic appointments since 1869, but such appointments were almost always to Liberia, Haiti, or small consular posts in tropical countries. Wharton was the first black in the new career Foreign Service, and his career followed the same pattern for more than half of his forty years in the Department of State.

Wharton was not sent to the new Foreign Service School for instruction as were the other new appointees. Department officials later informed him that this was because he was needed so urgently at his new post. Despite this urgency, however, they initially planned to send him and his wife to Liberia on a cargo ship. When Wharton said that he did not need the job that badly, the department officials relented and arranged for passage on an ocean liner and a passenger ship.

Wharton served as third secretary and vice consul in Liberia until December 1929. In June 1930 he became consul in Las Palmas in the Canary Islands. In July 1936 he returned to Monrovia on the first of three temporary assignments. He served alternately in Monrovia and Las Palmas until April 1942, when he was appointed consul in Antananarivo in the French island colony of Madagascar, where he also represented the wartime interests of Great Britain and Belgium.

In April 1945 Wharton was appointed a member of the U.S. maritime delegation at Ponta Delgada in the Portuguese Azores. In July of that year he became consul at Ponta Delgada, where he served for the next four years. In 1949 he married Evangeline L. Spears; they had no children. In October 1949 Wharton's career took a new path when he was named first secretary and consul in Lisbon, Portugal. In 1950 he became consul general at that post. From 1953 to 1957 he served as consul general in Marseilles, France.

When President Dwight D. Eisenhower offered him appointment as minister to Romania in February 1958, Wharton flew to Washington to talk to Deputy Under Secretary for Administration Loy Henderson to make sure that the appointment was based on merit, saying that if race were one of the criteria, he would not accept the appointment. Henderson wrote later that he had been glad to tell Wharton that "race had not been a factor" (Calkin, "A Reminiscence," p. 28). As minister to Romania, Wharton became the first black career Foreign Service officer to serve as chief of mission and the first black to serve as chief of mission in Europe. In 1959 he was promoted to career minister, once again the first black to achieve that honor.

Wharton became the first black ambassador to a European country when President John F. Kennedy appointed him ambassador to Norway on 2 March 1961. Democratic majority leader Mike Mansfield praised Wharton to the Senate as a "highly skillful, understanding and tactful diplomat" and quoted a *Washington Post* editorial looking forward to "a day when the appointment of a Negro so well qualified as Mr. Wharton will have ceased to be a novelty" (quoted in Calkin, "A Reminiscence"). While ambassador to Norway, Wharton also served as a delegate to the North Atlantic Treaty Organization (NATO) Ministerial Council meeting and as an alternate delegate to the sixteenth session of the UN General Assembly.

Wharton was a genuine pioneer, and his career was full of "firsts," including the first black to pass the Foreign Service exam, the first black chief of mission to a European country, the first black career minister, and the first black ambassador to a European country. Such achievements took not only superior ability but also great patience, tolerance, and persistence in the face of what was often blatant racial discrimination. For most of his career, Wharton had to fight against such discrimination alone. By the time he retired in October 1964, however, a sea change had occurred. Thanks partly to his achievements, Wharton inspired and helped to pave the way for professional careers in diplomacy for other blacks, who began to enter the

Foreign Service in ever increasing numbers during the 1960s. Wharton died in Phoenix, Arizona.

• Wharton left no papers or autobiography. The primary source of information concerning his career is Homer L. Calkin, "A Reminiscence: Being Black in the Foreign Service," *Department of State Newsletter* no. 198 (Feb. 1978): 25–28, which is based on an interview with Wharton. Calkin, *Women in the Department of State: Their Role in American Foreign Affairs* (1978), contains useful information about discrimination against women and blacks in the early years of the Foreign Service. David Trask, *A Short History of the U.S. Department of State, 1781–1981* (1981), provides context with a historical overview of the organization within which Wharton spent his career. Basic facts concerning Wharton's career are in the Department of State's annual *Biographic Registers* published during the years of his service. An obituary is in the *New York Times*, 25 Apr. 1990.

NINA DAVIS HOWLAND

WHARTON, Edith (24 Jan. 1862–11 Aug. 1937), writer, was born Edith Newbold Jones in New York City, the daughter of George Frederic Jones and Lucretia Rhinelander. To all appearances Edith Newbold Jones, as the youngest child of a well-to-do couple of fashionable old New York, led a privileged childhood and adolescence, which included winters in Paris, summers in Newport, Rhode Island, and the social season in New York, with its lavish balls and elegant dinners. But according to "Life & I," an unusually candid autobiographical fragment written in the early 1920s, Wharton's early years were anything but secure. She depicts herself as a deeply anxious child because of her cold and distant mother. As a bookish girl lacking in self-confidence, Wharton saw herself falling short of her mother's and her society's expectations for a young woman, whose purpose in life was to make a socially advantageous marriage. As Wharton saw it, Lucretia Jones thwarted her natural inclinations, depriving her of a regular supply of writing paper, accelerating the date of her debut (so that Wharton would have less time to read), and preventing an engagement with a man of Wharton's choosing. Wharton spent most of her early years retreating into the world of "making up," as she called her irresistible passion for telling stories, which prepared her for a career as a professional novelist and writer. By the time she was sixteen, Wharton had published several poems and had written a novel, *Fast and Loose* (first published in the Apr. 1978 issue of *Redbook*), to which she appended parodies of literary reviews.

In 1885 Edith Newbold Jones married Edward "Teddy" Robbins Wharton of Brookline, Massachusetts, who shared Edith's love of dogs, horses, and outdoor activity. The two, who remained childless, were poorly matched, however. Teddy had little understanding of and appreciation for his wife's intellectual life; Edith had little stomach for the social rituals in which the easygoing Teddy flourished. From the very start, their conjugal life was a disaster, with Edith blaming her mother for her sexual ignorance, which did "more than anything else to falsify & misdirect my whole life." Wharton could escape the constrictions of old New York only when the couple traveled in Europe each winter, where Wharton began to cultivate a circle of friends that included French writer Paul Bourget, art critic Bernard Berenson, and essayist Vernon Lee (Violet Paget). Her European travels were the basis for her early published work. Her first book, *The Decoration of Houses* (1897), written with architect Ogden Codman, was the result of her observation of European architecture and interior decoration; the essays collected in *Italian Villas and Their Gardens* (1904), *Italian Backgrounds* (1905), and *A Motor Flight through France* (1908) first saw publication as travel articles popular in magazines such as *Scribner's* and *Century*. Wharton's travel writings are noteworthy on several counts: she was one of the first writers to realize the potential of the automobile to change the face of travel; more important, she demonstrated an ability to capture local atmosphere, an extensive knowledge of history, art, and culture, and an exceptionally sensitive eye for detail and nuance.

At the same time she was writing her travel essays, Wharton was also publishing short stories, so much so that her publisher, Charles Scribner's Sons, proposed several collections of her fiction. These volumes—*The Greater Inclination* (1899), *Crucial Instances* (1901), and *The Descent of Man* (1904)—were delayed by a series of psychosomatic illnesses, most likely brought on by the frustration of her marriage to Teddy, a frustration heightened by her intellectual and professional growth as her circle of friends expanded and her confidence as a writer grew. The publication of her first novel, *The Valley of Decision* (1902), clearly reflects this confidence. A novel of *settocento* Italy, *The Valley of Decision* was favorably compared to George Eliot's *Romola*. It showcases Wharton's painstaking research and introduces a theme that dominates her subsequent fiction: striking a balance between the stability of tradition and the inevitability of change.

The Valley of Decision also brought Wharton to the attention of Henry James, a novelist whom she had long admired, but it was Wharton's next novel, *The House of Mirth* (1905), that solidified a vigorous friendship that flourished until James's death in 1916. This friendship, documented in Lyall H. Powers's *Henry James and Edith Wharton: Letters, 1900–1916* (1990), included frequent motor trips on the Continent and in the United States, shared acquaintances, and an amicable professional rivalry. James praised *The House of Mirth* as "altogether a superior thing"; more important, the 1905 novel, a popular and critical success, marked Wharton's debut as a talented and perceptive critic of American manners. *The House of Mirth*, with its strong naturalist overtones, chronicles the final years of Lily Bart, a young woman without parents or fortune, who must "barter" her beauty for an advantageous marriage. Her fine moral sensitivity, however, repeatedly gets in the way of social and practical expedience; the novel ends as she dies, alone and poor, in a boardinghouse. With this novel Wharton recognized, as she would note in her 1934 autobiography, *A Backward Glance*, that her true subject was the society of old New York and "its power of debasing people and ideals"; Wharton's best work is that in which she explores her ambivalence for old New York's continuity of tradition and its "frivolity."

Although Wharton invested in the construction of "The Mount," a mansion near Lenox, Massachusetts, completed in 1902 and incorporating the principles of design described in *The Decoration of Houses*, her interests increasingly lay in Europe, particularly in France. Included among Wharton's friends was an American-born journalist, Morton Fullerton, who wrote for British and French newspapers. By 1909 the two were involved in an affair (despite Fullerton's reputed engagement to his cousin Katherine Fullerton) that lasted two years. In this affair Wharton finally attained sexual fulfillment, which in turn enabled her to explore the darker sides of the human psyche. This exploration is evident in the highly popular 1911 novel *Ethan Frome*, which describes the love triangle of Ethan Frome, his wife Zeena, and his wife's cousin Mattie Silver, set in the winter isolation of aptly named Starkfield, Massachusetts. This novel presented a departure from Wharton's usual subject, the social elite of New York, as does the 1917 novel *Summer*, which Wharton herself characterized as her "hot Ethan." Also set near Starkfield, *Summer* recounts the sexual awakening of Charity Royall, who marries her guardian the lawyer Royall after Lucius Harney impregnates and abandons her.

Wharton's relationship with Fullerton and the mastery of her craft—by 1912 she was a well-regarded writer of fiction who commanded substantial prices for her work—further widened the gap between Wharton and her husband, who on his side contributed to the breakdown of the marriage by his own sexual escapades and by what Wharton perceived as increasingly erratic behavior. In 1913 Edith divorced Teddy, though she contributed to his medical expenses as his mental and physical condition deteriorated; he died on 7 February 1928. Wharton's divorce was clearly a watershed in her emotional life. She never remarried, though she did maintain a close friendship with Walter Berry, whom she had known since her teens, who frequently traveled with her, and whose death on 12 October 1927 she deeply mourned. Another watershed of sorts, World War I, occurred a year after her divorce. Wharton enlisted her pen in persuading the United States to come to France's aid. In *Fighting France* (1915), a series of essays based on her visits to the front lines, she wrote eloquently of her "vision of all the separate terrors, anguishes, uprootings and rendings apart . . . all the thousand and one bits of the past that give meaning and continuity to the present—of all that accumulated warmth nothing was left but a brick-heap and some twisted stove-pipes." She also worked tirelessly to help Belgian refugees, establishing schools and orphanages for them in Paris. King Albert of Belgium awarded her the Medal of Queen Elizabeth and named her chevalier of the Order of Leopold, while the French government recognized her work by making her a chevalier of the Legion of Honor and sending her to French Morocco to report on the efforts of General Hubert Lyautey to modernize the colony. *In Morocco* (1920), her last travel book, chronicles her travels through Morocco accompanied by Berry and includes vivid descriptions of religious festivals, colorful souks, and the harems, which she compared to ornate sepulchers.

While the 1910s were years of upheaval in Wharton's life, the same decade saw the publication of a series of masterpieces: *Ethan Frome*; *The Reef* (1912), a somewhat Jamesian analysis of a troubled relationship; *The Custom of the Country* (1913), a scathing critique of a predatory American girl and the society that spawned her; and *Xingu and Other Stories* (1916). With *The Age of Innocence* in 1920, a new note entered Wharton's fiction: mourning for "the old ways"—the decencies of life and the need for continuity and tradition—forever lost in the cataclysm of the Great War. The Pulitzer Prize–winning novel is Wharton's finest expression of her ambivalence over tradition and modernity. In telling the story of Newland Archer, who must choose between the stability of a safe marriage and the excitement of an affair, Wharton delicately balances the constricting power of convention with the bittersweet recognition that "after all, there was good in the old ways," particularly in contrast to the present, a "kaleidoscope where all the social atoms spun around on the same plane."

As Wharton surveyed her native land from the vantage point of France, she was increasingly dismayed by the rampant materialism and vulgarity of the 1920s. Her novels during this period—*The Glimpses of the Moon* (1922), *A Son at the Front* (1923), *The Mother's Recompense* (1925), *Twilight Sleep* (1927), *The Children* (1928), and *Hudson River Bracketed* (1929), as well as the four novellas collected in *Old New York* (1924)—condemn a society gone awry while attempting to come to terms with issues of the day such as eugenics, companionate marriage, and the culture of advertising. Critics maintained that by expatriating herself, Wharton had lost touch with what was admirable in American culture. Although her popularity declined throughout the 1920s and 1930s, Wharton's work continued to sell in spite of the economic depression and changing tastes in literature. An indication of Wharton's stature as a writer was the award of an honorary doctorate of letters from Yale University in 1923. She was the first woman Yale so honored, and the June ceremony in which she received the award was the occasion of her final visit to the United States.

From October 1933 to April 1934 the *Ladies' Home Journal* published a series of autobiographical essays by Wharton. These were later published as *A Backward Glance*. Wharton's autobiography recounts her childhood years of reading, describes her European travels, sketches her approach to writing (which she had discussed more fully in *The Writing of Fiction* in 1925), and paints affectionate portraits of her friends, with Henry James's being the most vivid. What is most notable about *A Backward Glance*, however, is what it does not tell: her criticism of Lucretia Jones, her difficulties with Teddy, and her affair with Morton Fullerton, which did not come to light until her papers, deposited in Yale's Beinecke Rare Book Room and Manuscript Library, were opened in 1968.

In her later years, after the war, Wharton devoted herself to writing; to renovating two residences in France, the Pavillon Colombe in Saint-Brice-Sous-Fôret and the Chateau Sainte-Claire in Hyères, on the French Riviera; and to gardening. Wharton's niece, Beatrix Jones Farrand, assisted her in the planning of the grounds at Pavillon Colombe and Sainte-Claire. Her final years were marked by the deaths of close friends and beloved dogs. Wharton died at Pavillon Colombe after a series of strokes. She is buried near Walter Berry in the Cimetière des Gonards at Versailles; her gravestone bears the epitaph she chose: *Ave Crux Spes Unica*.

In the years following Wharton's death, her novels and short stories continued to be read. Serious criticism and scholarship were sparked, however, by the opening of her papers in 1968 and the publication of two major biographies: R. W. B. Lewis's *Edith Wharton: A Biography* (1975) and Cynthia Griffin Wolff's *A Feast of Words: The Triumph of Edith Wharton* (1977). With these two works, coinciding with the growing interest in women's writing and women's studies, the fiction of Edith Wharton was recognized as a significant contribution to American literature. Although during her lifetime Wharton wrote numerous short stories, several volumes of travel essays, nonfiction, poetry, and an autobiography, her fame rests primarily on her novels, particularly those in which she examines and critiques American manners and culture. In her writing, Wharton exhibited that rare ability to combine artistic integrity with popular appeal. Her themes—the necessary price an individual pays to be a part of society, and the conflict between stability and change—continue to remain relevant to the American experience.

• The majority of Wharton's papers—notebooks, manuscripts, professional and personal correspondence, and photographs—is in the Yale Collection of American Literature, Beinecke Rare Book Room and Manuscript Library, Yale University. Diaries, some correspondence, and estate documents can be found at the Lilly Library, Indiana University: The Harry Ransom Humanities Research Center, University of Texas, Austin, holds Wharton's letters to Fullerton. Other major collections of letters are held by the William Royall Tyler Collection, Dumbarton Oaks, Washington, D.C., and by the Harvard Center for the Study of Renaissance Art at Villa I Tatti, Settignano, Italy. Additional letters are at the Robert Frost Library at Amherst College and at Harvard University's Houghton Library. The Scribners archive in the Firestone Library at Princeton University contains the largest collection of Wharton's correspondence with her publishers. In addition to those novels discussed above, Wharton wrote *The Fruit of the Tree* (1907), *The Marne* (1918), and *The Gods Arrive* (1932); *The Buccaneers*, uncompleted, was published posthumously in 1938. Novellas include *The Touchstone* (1900), *Sanctuary* (1903), and *Madame de Treymes* (1907). Wharton's short stories can be found in the two volumes of *The Collected Short Stories of Edith Wharton* (1968). See Wolff, *Feast of Words*, for a complete bibliography of her work, fiction and nonfiction, including reviews and essays. Lewis's and Wolff's biographies—the former a good source for the day-to-day details of Wharton's life, the latter an analysis of the relationship between Wharton's life and her writing—have been supplemented by two additional works. Shari Benstock, *No Gifts from Chance: A Biography of Edith Wharton* (1994), details Wharton's dealings with her publishers. Eleanor Dwight, *Edith Wharton: An Extraordinary Life* (1994), an illustrated biography, includes numerous photographs of Wharton, her friends, her homes, and her gardens. For bibliographies of secondary works, see Kristin O. Lauer and Margaret P. Murray, *Edith Wharton: An Annotated Secondary Bibliography* (1990), and regular updates in the *Edith Wharton Review*.

JUDITH E. FUNSTON

WHARTON, Greene Lawrence (17 July 1847–4 Nov. 1906), Disciples of Christ clergyman and missionary leader in India, was born in Bloomington, Indiana, the son of Stanfiel Wharton, an itinerant salesman and small farmer, and Ann Esther Berry. Wharton pursued undergraduate studies first at Southern Illinois College in Carbondale, Illinois, and finally received his undergraduate degree from Bethany College in Illinois in 1876. While still a student, he was ordained a minister of the Disciples of Christ church and from 1876 to 1882 was pastor of the Richmond Avenue Church of the Disciples in Buffalo, New York, one of the leading parishes of his denomination.

The Disciples of Christ maintained a popular, down-to-earth form of eighteenth-century Christian rationalism as well as an ethos of revivalism. But it had unusual features for American Protestantism: a ban on musical instruments in worship, a requirement for a weekly observance of Communion, and a restriction on all interchurch organizations and extraparochial agencies. Throughout the nineteenth century the Disciples were engaged in a heated debate on whether in fact their denomination should engage in foreign missionary activity. But when the Civil War ended, despite this debate and controversy, the Disciples were poised for their greatest half-century of growth and geographic expansion. Wharton symbolized, more than any Disciples of Christ leader in the second half of the nineteenth century, this commitment to foreign evangelism and expansion. He made India an example of what a missionary could accomplish if supported by extracongregational consortia.

In 1878 he married Emma Virginia Richardson. In 1882 they were appointed missionaries to India by the Foreign Christian Missionary Society of Cincinnati, Ohio, the first such Disciples consortium. They arrived in Bombay on 7 November 1882. Harda, in the center of India, became their headquarters, and from there the Whartons moved out to share the Disciples' faith with a variety of groups. In 1888–1889 they worked with the Gond and Kurku tribesmen of the Satpura mountains, and in 1890 Wharton was back in Bombay, working among the poor of the city.

Throughout his tenure Wharton and his wife were committed to founding schools, including a boys school at Harda in 1883, and in 1893 a training school for native missionaries who would fan out and establish their own centers on the subcontinent. In 1904 he helped found a Bible college at Jabalpur. He also made frequent trips to other parts of the English-speaking world to gain financial support for these enterprises: to Australia in 1889, to the United States in 1899, and to England in 1891.

Wharton's writings were all in the service of his evangelistic goals. In the 1880s and 1890s he wrote a series of tracts in Hindi that explained the Disciples of Christ interpretation of the Christian faith. In his tracts for the Indians the scheme of Christianity was reduced to a "five-finger exercise." The Gospel became something at once simple, rationalistic, and authoritarian. Here is Wharton's five-point summary:

1. Faith consists in accepting the proposition that "Jesus is the Christ."
2. If faith is genuine, repentance follows automatically, motivated by Christ's authoritative promises.
3. Baptism for the remission of sins is obedient response to Christ's command, making one's commitment complete.
4. The remission of sins is the fulfillment of God's promise.
5. His gifts are the Holy Spirit and eternal life.

This somewhat simplistic articulation of the Christian faith did not, in fact, appeal to the Indian population, and growth of the Disciples of Christ movement in India by the beginning of the twentieth century was minimal. In this endeavor, Wharton represents the last generation of a competitive denominational drive in foreign missions, an ecclesiatical parallel to imperialism, before the beginning of the modern ecumenical movement at the World Missionary Conference in Edinburgh, Scotland, in 1910. He died of pneumonia in Calcutta, India.

• A biography of Wharton is E. R. Wharton, *Life of G. L. Wharton* (1913); biographical sketches appear in *Christian Evangelist*, 15 Nov. 1906, and in *Missionary Intelligencer*, Dec. 1906, Jan. 1907. For a study of the Disciples of Christ see Winifred E. Garrison, *The Disciples of Christ: A History* (1948).

R. William Franklin

WHARTON, Joseph (3 Mar. 1826–11 Jan. 1909), industrialist, was born in Philadelphia, Pennsylvania, the son of William Wharton and Deborah Fisher, Quaker ministers of the Hicksite branch, the most liberal and least evangelical branch of Friends, as distinguished from the Orthodox branch. The family lived on wealth inherited from mercantile ancestors. Joseph, the fifth of ten children, was educated in private schools and by tutors. At the age of sixteen he began an apprenticeship in farming, a career favored by Hicksite Friends, but after three years he gave it up in favor of business. After a year of apprenticeship in accounting, he joined an older brother in Philadelphia in the manufacture of white lead for paint. Philadelphia was then the center of the nation's chemical industry, and Wharton took advantage of its resources to learn chemistry. In 1849 he left the manufacture of white lead and for the next five years engaged in brickmaking.

In 1854 Wharton married Anna Lovering, also a Hicksite. The couple had three children. In the same year he discontinued brickmaking and became a manager for the Pennsylvania and Lehigh Zinc Company, which operated mines a few miles south of the Lehigh River near Bethlehem, Pennsylvania, and had a factory in South Bethlehem for making zinc oxide, which because of its nontoxic quality was used as a substitute for white lead in making paint. By astute management he weathered the depression of 1857 for the company and then persuaded its directors to allow him to experiment with making metallic zinc, the manufacture of which, because of the peculiarities of the metal, were baffling refiners. Metallic Zinc, a necessary constituent of brass, was, because of its noncorrosive character, being used increasingly for roofing and packaging. By 1860 Wharton had succeeded and become the first person in the United States to have developed commercially profitable furnaces for refining metallic zinc. A rise in the price of zinc, occasioned by the need for brass in making shell casings for use in the Civil War, made Wharton wealthy, but he failed in attempts to control the company and in 1863 left the industry.

That same year, at the age of thirty-seven, Wharton began the mining and manufacturing of nickel. The Philadelphia Mint was looking for a domestic source of the metal in order to make small coins. A nickel-mining enterprise, the Gap Mining Company, owned deposits of ore in Lancaster County, Pennsylvania, and a refinery in Camden, New Jersey. Wharton bought the company and its assets, put his skills as a chemist and businessman to work, and at the end of five years had developed a commercially successful process for making nickel of high quality—and the "nickel" had joined America's family of small coins. A few years later he became the first person in the country to manufacture articles from pure malleable nickel. For almost twenty-five years Wharton had a monopoly over the nickel industry of the United States. He continued the business profitably even after others began exploiting the immense deposits of nickel ore in Canada and the island of New Caledonia in the South Pacific.

About 1865, when Wharton began making nickel, he also started investing in iron and steel and railroads. His principal venture in iron and steel at this time was with the Bethlehem Iron Company, a rolling mill controlled by managers of the Lehigh Valley Railroad as a source of iron and, from 1873, of steel rails. Within a few years Wharton became the principal stockholder and director of Bethlehem Iron. From that time on, he also bought the stocks and bonds of the Lehigh Valley and other railroads and used these as securities for his business dealings and as leverage to increase the sale of rails made by Bethlehem Iron.

In the late 1880s Wharton was one of the leaders in expanding the operations of Bethlehem Iron to include heavy forgings of armor plate and guns for the United States Navy. This made the company prosperous during the economically lean years of the 1890s and prepared the way for a change of name to Bethlehem Steel and the purchase of the company in 1901 by Charles M. Schwab.

Wharton's involvement with iron and steel included lobbying in Washington, D.C. From about 1873 until his death he was one of the principal lobbyists for the American Iron and Steel Association. "I do not believe there was any man who exerted such influence in Washington as your father did," wrote Andrew Carnegie to Mary Wharton Morris after her father's death. "He kept to the point and imprest Committee after Committee, until, under the mantle of temporary protection, the steel industry was able to stand alone, as it is today."

Politically, Wharton was a Republican and was friendly with most of the party's leaders, but he consistently refused to hold any elective office or to engage in any political activity that might take time away from managing his industrial enterprises.

Wharton never incorporated his nickel business. Frederick Voigt, foreman of the refinery, wrote

> Wharton personally managed and attended to the financial and commercial part of the business, including all office work, bookkeeping and correspondence, without assistance, except that which I could give. . . . How Mr. Wharton managed to get the utmost amount of work done in a given time is shown by his habit of putting his watch in front of him on the desk, while at work in the Camden office, and to mark on its face the last moment to which he could remain. (Wharton papers)

Wharton maintained much the same relationships with several other enterprises undertaken during the affluent years of his nickel business. These included farming in the Pinelands of southern New Jersey, fishing for menhaden off the Atlantic coast, and mining and refining magnetite iron ore in northern New Jersey.

Farming in the Pinelands was the earliest and most enduring of these other interests. The Pinelands, or Pine Barrens as they are also called, consist of marshes, poor sandy soil, and pine and cedar forests drained by several small rivers of pure water. Wharton began his acquisitions in the Pinelands in 1873 and continued them until he died, eventually acquiring a tract of about 150 square miles. Motivation for his initial interest in the Pinelands is unknown. He was probably acting on a personal whim. Most of the good timber had been logged off, and deposits of bog iron ore, which had supported an active industry for more than seventy-five years, were exhausted. He bought the land cheaply. One of his first projects there was an attempt to raise sugar beets—an unsuccessful venture. Later, he cultivated sweet potatoes and cranberries and experimented with scientific forestry. From about 1892 to 1902 he advocated piping fresh water of the Pinelands to Philadelphia and Camden—another unsuccessful endeavor. He made little if any money from ventures in the Pinelands, yet he continued buying the land. Many years after his death the state of New Jersey purchased the tract and reorganized it as the Wharton State Forest.

His interest in fishing for the menhaden—"mossbunkers," processed for oil and fertilizer—began in 1881. By 1907, when he terminated the business, he had a network of boats and processing plants along the coast from Massachusetts to Maryland.

Wharton's ventures in the magnetite iron deposits of northern New Jersey began with the acquisition of a furnace at Hackettstown in 1879. Over the next thirty years he bought other furnaces and iron mines, constructed several small railroads, and purchased coking coal lands in Pennsylvania and deposits of iron ore in New York. According to the newspaper *Iron Age*, he had by 1903 become the largest manufacturer of pig iron in the United States.

From about 1865 to the end of the century Wharton had many nonindustrial interests. He and Anna were active in the Hicksite Friends' Philadelphia Yearly Meeting and passed the months of summer in a residence called "Marbella" (later renamed Horsehead) on the southern tip of Conanicut Island in Narragansett Bay, Rhode Island. Wharton published papers on scientific subjects and in 1895 became the chairman of Harvard University's Committee of the Overseers to Visit the Chemical Laboratory.

He aided in establishing Swarthmore College and from 1883 until 1907 served as president of its board of managers.

Inspired by a belief that the country needed people formally educated for business, in 1881 Wharton endowed a school at the University of Pennsylvania, which he specified to be called the Wharton School of Finance and Economy. This was the first school of its kind in the United States. He later added to the endowment even though disturbed by some of the school's activities, especially those of its personnel in opposing his position in favor of high protective tariffs.

By the end of the century the good ore in the Gap Nickel Mine was exhausted. In 1902 Wharton sold the mine and the refinery to the newly formed International Nickel Company, of which he became a director.

He was then seventy-six years old, yet he had lost nothing of his vigor. He had earlier purchased the Southwestern Mining Company in southern Nevada and gold-bearing gravels in Boise County, Idaho. He now made trips almost every year to supervise work being done on these holdings with improved means for extracting gold. He wrote and published poetry and essays on scientific and religious subjects, maintained a dialogue with educators at Swarthmore and the Wharton School of the University of Pennsylvania, expanded his operations in New Jersey, and continued lobbying for the iron and steel industry. In 1904 he became president of the American Iron and Steel Association.

He was a pioneer in mining and manufacturing in an age when success depended in large part on an owner-manager's having a comprehensive and detailed knowledge of all aspects of his operations. By the time he died, this pioneering approach was giving way to specialized management aided by an industrial bureaucracy. At the same time, his emphasis on science and the need of formal education in business remained progressive. Wharton died at "Ontalauna," his home in the northern suburbs of Philadelphia.

• The Wharton papers are to be found in the Friends Historical Library of Swarthmore College. These papers include personal letters written by Wharton and his wife and several other members of the family and the account books, correspondence, and other papers concerning his industrial, commercial, scientific, and educational activities. The collection also has copies of articles about Wharton and Wharton's own publications. The Historical Society of Pennsylvania has manuscripts pertaining to Wharton, his family and ancestors, the Gap Mining Company, Joseph S. Lovering, the American Iron and Steel Association, and several other subjects pertinent to Wharton. A biography, W. Ross Yates, *Joseph Wharton: Quaker Industrial Pioneer* (1987), contains an annotated bibliography. Steven A. Sass wrote of Wharton's connections with the University of Pennsylvania in *The Pragmatic Imagination: A History of the Wharton School* (1982). Joanna Wharton Lippincott, at the time of her father's death, wrote a profile, *Biographical Memoranda Concerning Joseph Wharton, 1826–1909* (1909), which was privately printed and circulated. A copy may be found in the Friends Historical Library. An obituary is in *Iron Age*, 28 Jan. 1909, pp. 315–16.

W. ROSS YATES

WHARTON, Richard (?–May 1689), New England merchant and businessman, was born in England. Nothing is known of his parentage or early life. However, this relation of the wealthy and powerful Lord Wharton (Philip Wharton), a leading Dissenting and Whig politician, had no trouble marrying into the best New England families following his arrival in Massachusetts. Twice a widower between 1659 and 1672, he successively married Bethia Tyng (with whom he had three children); Sarah Higginson (with whom he had four children), the daughter of Salem's minister John Higginson; and Martha Winthrop (with whom he had four children), the daughter of Connecticut governor John Winthrop, Jr. The dates of his marriages are unknown.

Wharton came to public notoriety when he lost his license to practice law by too strongly contesting the will of the late governor Richard Bellingham, who died in 1672. Leaving most of his estate to encourage the ministry and preaching through various bequests, Bellingham was posthumously challenged by his son Samuel. Acting on his behalf, Wharton was disbarred for his vehemence but permitted to finish and win the case.

Thereafter, Wharton stuck to business and politics that could further his economic ends. With Fitz Winthrop and Wait Winthrop, grandsons of Massachusetts's first governor, he was involved in the Atherton Company, which sought to control a large block of land on the Connecticut–Rhode Island northern border and turn it into a proprietorship with manorial rents and privileges. The plan required that the land be given to sympathetic Connecticut rather than hostile Rhode Island. Despite efforts to bribe Lord Culpeper and Board of Trade member William Blathwayt with substantial shares in the company, this scheme came to naught when the royal governor of the Dominion of New England, Sir Edmund Andros, refused to sanction a grant based on dubious Indian purchases. Wharton's syndicated "million acre" purchase in the same region and an effort to start a colony at Casco Bay in Maine, independent of Massachusetts with a proprietary government, foundered for the same reason. Although authoritarian, Andros was incorruptible and as opposed to such land engrossment as were the Puritan magistrates of the first generation who favored small, democratic town grants.

Wharton was in Massachusetts to make money and obtain power. He shared these goals with the community of Anglicized merchants and land speculators that began to develop in the Bay Colony after the Restoration of 1660. Wharton became the leader of this group, which included many nonchurch members, and hence nonvoters, who could not hold public office under the Puritan regime. They hoped for a royal government that would institute a property rather than religious franchise, permit freedom of religion for Anglicans, as some of them were, and further their business schemes. For instance, during the 1673–1674 war with Holland, Wharton and his associates wanted to strike at the Dutch commerce of New York through privateering ventures, whereas the Bay Colony authorities preferred neutrality to ensure the flow of cheap goods with familiar commercial partners. Paradoxically, the Bay Colony looked more favorably on two of Wharton's ventures that did not pan out: his plans to develop production of naval stores and to organize a company for mining iron.

That Andros also approved of these last two schemes suggests the authorities had no trouble with Wharton when personal and public interests coincided. But Andros, installed in 1686 following an interim royal government under Joseph Dudley that Wharton and his fellows briefly controlled (1685–1686), was no more sympathetic to much of Wharton's and his associates' agenda than were the Puritans. He disapproved their land schemes and, to add insult to injury, imposed a tax on lands they (and everyone else) in Massachusetts legitimately owned. He enforced the Acts of Trade and Navigation, which limited much colonial commerce to the confines of the British Empire, far more rigorously than the Puritans. And he shot down a Wharton-led proposal that Massachusetts issue its own paper money to remedy a shortage of specie and a decline in trade.

Wharton thus found himself working in England with old Puritans such as Increase Mather to lobby King James II to remove Andros. Wharton returned for that purpose in 1687. They hoped, with some rational basis, that James would repudiate his governor's policies. However, the Glorious Revolution overthrew the king and installed William and Mary. Before he could commence lobbying anew, Wharton died in England, tired out with worry and excitement. Ironically, most of his vast projects had come to naught. He left little to his children: two daughters opened a small shop in Boston.

Wharton led and symbolized those men who came to New England not for God but for gold. A powerful if cantankerous personality, he sought to institute large-scale business enterprises in a land devoted primarily to farming. He inadvertently became a champion of religious and political freedom in the course of furthering his economic ends. Wharton did not live to see the triumph of his practices and ideas.

• Viola F. Barnes, "Richard Wharton: A Seventeenth-Century New England Colonial," Colonial Society of Massachusetts, *Publications* 26 (1924–1926): 238–69, is still the most thorough treatment of Wharton's career. See also Richard S. Dunn, *Puritans and Yankees: The Winthrop Dynasty of New England, 1630–1717* (1962), for important material. Primary materials may be found in Robert N. Toppan, ed., *Edward Randolph: Including His Letters and Official Papers* (7 vols., 1898–1909), and Charles M. Andrews, ed., *Narratives of the Insurrections* (1915).

WILLIAM PENCAK

WHARTON, Robert (12 Jan. 1757–7 Mar. 1834), merchant and mayor of Philadelphia, was born in Philadelphia, Pennsylvania, the son of Joseph Wharton, a merchant and landholder, and his second wife, Hannah Owen Ogden. One of eighteen children, he grew up on a large estate, "Walnut Grove," in the southern section of Philadelphia. Uninterested in education, he was apprenticed at age fourteen to a hatter but soon decided to learn the mercantile business instead from his half brother Charles. Becoming a flour merchant, "Bobby" later became a successful wholesale grocer. In 1789 he married Sarah Chancellor, daughter of William Chancellor and Salome Wistar. They had two sons, both of whom died young.

An ardent sportsman, Wharton was president of the Fox Hunting Club of Gloucester and governor of the Schuylkill Fishing Company, one of the most active gentlemen's groups in Philadelphia. He was also active in the militia, joining the city troop on 19 June 1798 and becoming a captain in 1803. (During the War of 1812, he briefly commanded the First Brigade of the Pennsylvania Militia, but because of his advanced age, he served as an honorary member of the troop when it was called into active service.)

With the formation of political parties in the 1790s, Wharton became a Federalist, attacking the Republicans as radicals inspired by the French Revolution. In 1792 he was elected a member of the common council, Philadelphia's governing body. In 1796 the governor of Pennsylvania appointed him an alderman; in this position he was involved in two major incidents in which he took the lead in suppressing acts of violence. In 1796 several hundred sailors from merchant ships in the harbor struck for higher wages and refused to allow ships in the port to leave. These actions terrorized the merchants along Delaware Avenue. Mayor Hillary Barker, too ill to deal with the situation himself, put Wharton in charge. With fifty constables, Wharton confronted the sailors, who were carrying clubs and knives. Although outnumbered, Wharton's men engaged in hand-to-hand combat with the sailors and subdued the rioters after Wharton grabbed a flag from the leader of the mob. One hundred sailors were jailed as a consequence of the action.

During the yellow fever epidemic of 1798, a riot broke out among the 300 inmates at the Walnut Street Jail; inmates trying to escape overpowered the jailers. With a small group of constables, Wharton held off the prisoners, personally killing two of them with musket shots. Wharton was attacked in the press for his actions and subjected to a grand jury investigation, but he was acquitted of all charges.

After Mayor Barker died on 25 September 1798, Wharton took over on an interim basis and then was elected mayor for the first time on 16 October. He served fourteen more one-year terms in this office, elected in 1799, 1806, 1807, and 1810, and from 1814 through 1819, and again from 1820 through 1824, giving him the longest tenure as mayor in Philadelphia's history.

During this period, the mayor of Philadelphia was elected by the common council, which chose from among the aldermen. The position had a few executive functions, but it was primarily a judicial office; it carried a salary of $2,000 a year, which was not unsubstantial. Perhaps the chief executive's most time-consuming task was as head of the Mayor's Court on which he sat as presiding officer along with the city recorder and at least one other alderman. Sitting almost daily, the court heard violations of municipal ordinances and ruled on seven to eight cases a day. Fines levied by the court composed a large part of city revenues.

As an executive, Wharton's primary activity was as the head of the constabulary, the area of government in which he was most interested. He helped to quell several riots and became known as a "man without fear." In 1814 he successfully persuaded the council to tighten the laws governing liquor and gambling, but he failed to get it to pass zoning legislation to restrict areas of the city for manufacturing. Wharton also failed to persuade the council to give constables more authority for maintaining law and order and thus reduce Philadelphia's reliance on citizen enforcement. Wharton unsuccessfully tried to change the manner in which the mayor was elected, proposing that the mayor be chosen from outside the council.

Perhaps Wharton's most lasting impact was his effort in 1816 to prevent the state from selling the land on which Independence Hall was built. Sale of the land to private parties would have resulted in the destruction of the hall. Wharton threatened to go to court to block the sale, but at the same time he began negotiating a purchase of the hall by the city to preserve it for posterity.

Because the mayor's role was largely judicial, Wharton had little involvement in the dramatic development of Philadelphia during his years in office. The population grew during his tenure from 75,000 to 150,000. Mayors would not begin to exercise any real power in Philadelphia until the 1854 charter, which consolidated Philadelphia with a number of surrounding townships and gave the city a real police force.

Wharton resigned as mayor in April 1824 because of poor health. But even his retirement did not go without incident. In 1829 a mob gathered outside his house to watch a fire in the neighborhood and attempted to intimidate him into supplying them with alcohol, but he refused, standing up to them. Five years later he died at his Philadelphia home.

• For contemporary materials, see Robert Wharton, "Civil Docket for 1808," located in the manuscript collection of the Historical Society of Pennsylvania along with a 13 Feb. 1816 letter from Robert Wharton to Thomas Fitting and W. C. Brenner's "Scrapbook," vol. 2. See also A. H. Wharton, *Genealogy of the Wharton Family* (1808); John Lowiar, *Ordinances of the Corporation of the City of Philadelphia* (1812); *Letter of Robert Wharton, Mayor, on City Police* (1814); and Henry Simpson, *The Lives of Eminent Philadelphians Now Deceased* (1859). An obituary is in *Poulson's American Daily Advertiser* (Philadelphia), 8 Mar. 1834.

HERBERT B. ERSHKOWITZ

WHARTON, Thomas, Jr. (1735–22 May 1778), merchant and president of Pennsylvania, was born in Chester County, Pennsylvania, the son of John Wharton, a saddler who served as county coroner from 1730 to 1737, and Mary Dobbins. He added "Junior" to his name to distinguish himself from his cousin, Thomas Wharton, Sr. (1731–1782). At age twenty Wharton served as apprentice to Reese Meredith, a wealthy Quaker trader, and soon emerged as a successful merchant in his own right. For a while he joined with Anthony Stocker in the firm Stocker & Wharton.

Wharton married twice. In 1762 he wed Susannah Lloyd, the daughter of Thomas Lloyd and Susannah Kearney, and this union produced five children. Susannah Wharton died in 1772, and in 1774 Wharton married Elizabeth Fishbourne, the daughter of William Fishbourne and Mary Tallman. The couple had three children. Wharton was born into a Quaker family but by the 1760s had left that faith. His first marriage was consecrated in an Anglican church. He continued his loose affiliation with Anglicanism, although not formally joining that church.

Before 1774 Wharton had a low profile in the revolutionary movement. He signed the petitions against the Stamp Act and Townshend Act and supported the boycotts of British goods, but so did almost all the merchants and shopkeepers in Philadelphia. Wharton was not a member of the various committees struck during 1765–1766, 1768–1770, or 1773. He did belong to the Society of the Sons of Saint Tammany, a patriotic club formed in 1772.

During 1774 and 1775 Wharton became increasingly prominent in the revolutionary movement. He served on several of the committees that guided the protests in Philadelphia, including the Committee of Nineteen (formed May 1774), the Committee of Forty-three (June 1774), and the First Committee of One Hundred (August 1775). Wharton was a valued member of these bodies because of his wealth, his firm commitment to the American cause, his administrative skills, and his ability to work with individuals of different persuasions and social classes. In June 1775 the assembly created a Committee of Safety to serve as the executive branch of government and oversee the defense of Pennsylvania. Wharton was a leading member of this body.

Wharton's willingness to support the new state constitution was the key to his continuing ascent. In no other state was the political revolution so thoroughgoing as in Pennsylvania. Artisans in the capital and western farmers gained an unprecedented measure of power. The new constitution, written in the summer of 1776, confirmed this shift. Representation was reapportioned; there was no upper house to check the assembly; and all voters had to swear an oath of loyalty to the new frame of government. Instead of a governor, there was a supreme executive council headed by a president. Overwhelmingly, upper-class patriots (for example, John Dickinson and Robert Morris) denounced the new charter. But not Wharton. He supported the state government during the months of transition. In July 1776 the revolutionary convention placed him on the Council of Safety, and in August he was chosen its president. Wharton worked closely with George Washington to strengthen the defenses of Pennsylvania when the British invaded New Jersey. In February 1777 Philadelphia voters chose him as their representative on the supreme executive council. He retained the backing of farmers and artisans because he was a wealthy merchant who accepted the new government. Morris and Dickinson bitterly opposed him on some issues, such as the state constitution, but cooperated with him on others, such as the defense of Pennsylvania.

Once the new state government was firmly established, the assembly and the supreme executive council in March 1777 elected Wharton president. Wharton was inaugurated in a lavish ceremony designed to reassure the citizenry about the strength of the new government. During the next fourteen months Wharton, along with the council, was extraordinarily busy. Defense was the first priority. As commander in chief of the Pennsylvania militia, Wharton helped organize the opposition to Sir William Howe's forces, which sailed up the Chesapeake and marched on Philadelphia. After Howe entered the capital in September 1777, Wharton moved with the council to Lancaster and continued to direct the Pennsylvania war effort. He also helped implement measures to regulate prices and prevent forestalling. He worked to reopen the courts, many of which remained closed because lawyers would not serve the new government. And Wharton took steps against suspected Tories. In September he ignored a writ of habeas corpus from Chief Justice Thomas McKean and approved the order to exile nineteen Quakers and two other individuals to Virginia. Included in the group was his cousin, Thomas Wharton, Sr.

Within the constitutionalist camp Wharton was a moderate. He told a friend that the new charter had "many faults which I hope one day to see removed; but it is true that, if the Government should at this time be overset, it would be attended with the worst consequences, not only to this State, but to the whole continent in the opposition we are making to the tyranny of Great Britain" (Armour, p. 209). His death in Lancaster from an attack of quinsy allowed Vice President George Bryan, who was more radical, to become acting president.

Wharton's death cut short a promising career. Because of his willingness to serve when many of his class would not, Wharton helped make certain that the new state government survived and that Pennsylvanians offered a spirited resistance to the British forces.

• Although Wharton apparently left behind no body of personal papers, his public career is well documented. See the Revolutionary Papers in the Pennsylvania Historical and Museum Commission, Harrisburg; *The Pennsylvania Archives*, 1st ser. (12 vols., 1852–1856), 2d ser. (19 vols., 1874–1890); *Minutes of the Supreme Executive Council of Pennsylvania . . .* (6 vols., 1853). Useful information about Wharton is provided in William C. Armour, *Lives of the Governors of Pennsylvania* (1872), pp. 192–210; Anne H. Wharton, "The Wharton Family," *Pennsylvania Magazine of History and Biography* 1 (1877): 324–29; and Anne H. Wharton, "Thomas Wharton, Junior," *Pennsylvania Magazine of History and Biography* 5 (1881): 426–39. On Wharton's career before independence (and the course of Pennsylvania politics), see Richard Alan Ryerson, *The Revolution Is Now Begun: The Radical Committees of Philadelphia, 1765–1776* (1978), and Marc Egnal, *A Mighty Empire: The Origins of the American Revolution* (1988). On his activities after independence, see Robert L. Brunhouse, *The Counter-Revolution in Pennsylvania, 1776–1790* (1942); and Thomas R. Meehan, "Courts, Cases, and Counselors in Revolutionary and Post-Revolutionary Pennsylvania," *Pennsylvania Magazine of History and Biography* 91 (1967): 3–34.

MARC EGNAL

WHARTON, William Harris (1802–14 Mar. 1839), lawyer, planter, and activist for Texas independence, was born in Albemarle County, Virginia, the son of William Wharton and Judith Harris. His father, who combined planting with milling and distilling, followed his lawyer brothers to Nashville, Tennessee, in the early 1800s. Both parents died in 1816, and William, his brother John Austin Wharton, and two sisters were raised by their uncle, Jesse Wharton, a prominent lawyer and briefly a U.S. senator. The uncle, a supporter of Andrew Jackson, encouraged his nephews to study law, and William attended the University of Nashville where Jesse Wharton was a trustee. Both William and his brother were admitted to the bar in Nashville.

William married Sarah Ann Groce in 1827, at her father's plantation near present-day Hempstead, Texas. They returned to Nashville, where their only child was born the following year. The Whartons moved to Mexican Texas in 1831 when Sarah's father, Jared E. Groce, the largest slaveholder in Texas, built them a comfortable plantation home at Eagle Island near the mouth of the Brazos River. Wharton represented the lower Brazos community at the Convention of 1832, a gathering of Anglo-Texans (illegal under Mexican law) wanting separate statehood for Texas and other reforms. Texas had been joined to its neighbor, Coahuila, in 1824 because both were underpopulated. Wharton presided at a second convention in April 1833 that sent Stephen F. Austin to Mexico City with petitions. Wharton personally preferred an independent Texas, but the majority of delegates voted to remain within the Mexican nation.

Wharton had no loyalty to Mexico in part because he had not applied for the standard headright of 4,406 acres having received 8,000 acres from his land-rich father-in-law. Moreover, Mexico's changing policies threatened to end slavery in Texas and to limit Anglo-American immigration, actions that threatened Wharton's rising fortunes. He also supported President Andrew Jackson's policy to acquire the eastern portion of Texas. Wharton aligned himself with Sam Houston, fellow Nashville lawyer and Jackson's protégé, who had recently settled in Texas and who favored an independent Texas. Wharton and his brother established a newspaper to oppose Austin and his conservative, nonconfrontational policy toward the Mexican government.

In mid-1835 debate over severing ties with Mexico resurged when President Santa Anna began centralizing the national government at the expense of states' rights. After a military incident at Gonzales in October 1835 between Anglo-Texan volunteers and a company of Mexican regulars, the Wharton brothers joined the volunteer army, where William served as judge advocate. Although both Whartons were chosen delegates to a third convention (called the Consultation) in November, only John attended the session. Again the demand for independence from Mexico was defeated by conservative delegates, but the Texans unilaterally organized a separate state for Texas and hoped for support from Mexican federalists who opposed Santa Anna. The Texan volunteers captured San Antonio in December 1835 and allowed the Mexican army to retreat to the Rio Grande.

Knowing that Santa Anna would launch an effort to reoccupy the old town, the provisional Texas government sent William Wharton and two other commissioners to the United States to raise money and volunteers to defend Texas. While the commissioners were absent, the Texans defeated and captured President Santa Anna at the battle of San Jacinto on 21 April 1836. John Wharton served there with distinction.

Elected to the first senate of the Republic of Texas in September 1836, William Wharton was named minister to the United States. In Washington, D.C., he worked to secure recognition for the new republic, which was granted on 3 March 1837. Texas's bid for annexation to the United States was defeated, however, and Wharton left for Texas. In April his vessel was seized by the Mexican Navy just off the mouth of the Brazos River and taken to Matamoros. John Wharton secured permission from Texas president Sam Houston to exchange Mexican officers captured at the battle of San Jacinto for his brother, but by the time he reached Matamoros, William had escaped and was en route to Texas.

William Wharton served in the senate of the Republic of Texas from 1837 to 1839. His promising political career ended tragically when he accidentally discharged a pistol while dismounting from his horse at the home of his brother-in-law, Leonard W. Groce, near Hempstead on 4 March 1839. The bullet penetrated his arm and chest and ten days later he died. His brother John had died the previous December.

Wharton was the first man of wealth and standing to publicly oppose Stephen Austin's conciliatory policy toward Mexico. Soon after his arrival in 1831, Wharton agitated Texans to cut their ties with Mexico in order to be joined to the United States. In 1837 he used his family connections and diplomatic skill to aid the young Republic of Texas to achieve independence and secure diplomatic recognition from the United States. His untimely death denied Texas his considerable skills. The state of Texas named Wharton County in honor of the brothers in 1846.

• Few Wharton papers exist except in official documents of the Republic of Texas, the published Stephen F. Austin Papers, and those of Sam Houston. Letters from Washington are published in George P. Garrison, ed., *Diplomatic Correspondence of the Republic of Texas*, American Historical Association, *Annual Report* for 1907, vol. 1 (1908). John H. Jenkins, ed., *The Papers of the Texas Revolution, 1835–1836* (1973), includes many references to Wharton, while Amelia W. Williams and Eugene C. Barker, eds., *The Writings of Sam Houston, 1813–1863* (8 vols., 1938, repr. 1970), has a few items. Barker, ed., *The Austin Papers*, contains a few pertinent documents, especially about the bad feeling between the Whartons and Austin; vols. 1 and 2 appear in the American Historical Association, *Annual Report* for 1919 (1924), and 1922 (1928); vol. 3 was published by the University of Texas (1927). Nineteenth-century Texas historians should be used with care, as should Groce family works such as Rosa Groce Bertleth, "Jared Ellison Groce," *Southwestern Historical Quarterly* 20 (1917): 356–68, and Sarah Wharton Groce Berlet, *Autobiography of a Spoon, 1828–1956* (1971), which give some genealogical details but are romantic family stories.

MARGARET SWETT HENSON

WHATCOAT, Richard (23 Feb. 1736–5 July 1806), bishop of the Methodist Episcopal church, was born in Quinton, Gloustershire, England, the son of Charles Whatcoat and Mary (maiden name unknown). (Their occupations are unknown.) Richard's parents were faithful members of the Church of England influenced by Samuel Taylor, their parish priest and an active leader in the new Methodist movement. While Richard was still young, his father's death left his mother to raise him and his four siblings. At thirteen he started an apprenticeship of eight years with Joseph Jones in Birmingham and Darlaston. Upon completion of his training, Whatcoat settled in Wednesbury, where he began to attend Methodist preaching services regularly.

On 3 September 1758, after several weeks of intense spiritual introspection, Whatcoat experienced conversion, which he described as follows: " . . . the Spirit [of God] did bear witness with my spirit, that I was a child of God. In the same instant I was filled with unspeakable peace and joy in believing: all fear of death, judgment, and hell, suddenly vanished" (Phoebus, p. 11). On 28 March 1761 he experienced what the Methodists called sanctification. He recalled: "Suddenly I was stripped of all but love. Now all was love, and prayer, and praise" (Phoebus, p. 12). Whatcoat was a respected meeting leader and steward in the Methodist society in Wednesbury.

In 1767 Whatcoat began to hold religious meetings near his home, at which he preached. Encouraged by the success of these meetings, he decided to enter the Methodist traveling ministry in July 1769. For the next fifteen years he was appointed to circuits of preaching places in England, Ireland, and Wales.

Methodist work in the United States flourished in the years following the Revolution. As a result, John Wesley, Anglican priest and founder of Methodism, formulated a plan to allow American Methodists to form their own church, a step he refused to grant British Methodists before his death in 1791. On 1 September 1784, assisted by Thomas Coke and James Creighton, both ordained priests in the Church of England, Wesley ordained Whatcoat and Thomas Vasey deacons and the next day ordained them elders, giving them authority to administer baptism and the Lord's Supper. Wesley then dispatched Whatcoat, Vasey, and Coke to America to lead Methodism in the New World. Whatcoat and his companions arrived in New York on 3 November 1784 and immediately initiated an itinerant ministry.

American Methodism, which had started about 1766, had grown from a handful of members to 15,000 in 1784. From 24 December 1784 until 2 January 1785 Whatcoat played an important role at the famous Christmas Conference in Baltimore, which resulted in the formation of the Methodist Episcopal church in America. At the conference Whatcoat assisted in the ordination of several men into the ministry, including Francis Asbury, who was also ordained superintendent of American Methodism at the conference.

In the succeeding years Whatcoat was an active preacher, presiding elder, and acknowledged leader of the Methodist Episcopal church. He traveled extensively and preached in various cities, towns, and rural regions of Maryland, Delaware, Pennsylvania, New York, New Jersey, Virginia, North Carolina, South Carolina, Georgia, and Kentucky.

Whatcoat became a center of controversy in 1787, when Wesley sent instructions to America with Coke directing the American Methodists to hold a conference in May and appointing Whatcoat a superintendent of the American work. The American preachers resented Wesley's autocratic order to elevate Whatcoat to the superintendency. When they gathered for the conference, they refused to follow Wesley's command, thereby canceling their earlier agreement to remain under Wesley's direction in all matters. The preachers may have felt that Whatcoat was not qualified for the office, or perhaps that his election would lead to Wesley's recalling popular Asbury to England. They chose not to select a new superintendent. Whatcoat continued his work as a presiding elder and traveling preacher.

At the General Conference of May 1800 in Baltimore, Whatcoat was elected American Methodism's third bishop. His episcopal duties included conducting numerous annual conferences along the eastern seaboard and as far inland as Tennessee and Kentucky. At these gatherings, often accompanying Bishop Asbury, Whatcoat preached with great success, assisted in the organization of Methodist work, and ordained men for the ministry.

The strain of age and the hardship of travel gradually took their toll on Whatcoat. He preached his last sermon at Milford, Delaware, on 8 April 1806. He died at the home of Richard Bassett, prominent Methodist and influential state and national politician, in Dover, Delaware, and was buried under the altar of Wesley Chapel in Dover. He never married. When Asbury received word of Whatcoat's death, he wrote in his journal, "A man so uniformly good I have not known in Europe or America" (Clark, vol. 2, p. 512).

Whatcoat was one of the more important leaders in early American Methodism. He impressed people with his piety, knowledge of scripture, commitment to the doctrines and principles of Methodism, and energy for the traveling ministry. Although he did not match the ability or fame of Coke and Asbury, he was highly respected among those who came under his influence and was an effective shepherd of the young American Methodist flock.

• Important primary sources regarding Whatcoat's life and work include Elmer T. Clark et al., ed., *The Journal and Letters of Francis Asbury* (3 vols., 1958), and William Phoebus, *Memoirs of the Rev. Richard Whatcoat* (1828). A more recent biography is Sidney B. Bradley, *The Life of Bishop Richard Whatcoat* (1936). Whatcoat's name appears in most of the histories of American Methodism.

CHARLES YRIGOYEN, JR.

WHEAT, Zack (23 May 1888–11 Mar. 1972), baseball player, was born Zachariah Davis Wheat in Hamilton, Missouri, the son of Basil C. Wheat, a farmer, and Julia Davis. The Wheats moved from a farm near Bonanza to Kansas City when Zack was fourteen. He first played semiprofessional baseball in 1906 for a team in Enterprise, Kansas, and went to Fort Worth for a few games in 1907. In 1908 and 1909 he played both at first base and in the outfield for teams in Shreveport, Louisiana, and Mobile, Alabama. On 29 August 1909, Brooklyn Dodgers' National League scout Larry Sutton signed him to a contract. He became the Dodgers' regular left fielder in August 1909 and remained in that position through the 1926 season. The 5′10″ Wheat, who batted left-handed and threw right-handed, weighed around 185 pounds during his career. He wore a size 5 ½ shoe, and because of his small feet he frequently suffered ankle injuries.

Known for his line drives, Wheat had 2,884 base hits, batting over .300 fourteen of his eighteen seasons; he hit 476 doubles, 172 triples, 132 home runs, had 1,261 runs batted in, and compiled a lifetime .317 batting average. A soft-spoken man, he was never ejected from a game. He once said that there was no sense in cursing an umpire since ejection usually followed, and he wanted to play nine innings or longer. Despite hitting .375 in both 1923 and 1924, he won only one National League batting title—in 1918 with a .335 average.

Wheat maintained that the greatest thrill of his career was having played in the 26-inning 1–1 tie between the Dodgers and Boston Braves in 1920. After his legs weakened, he was waived out of the National League, but was hired by Connie Mack in 1927 and batted .324 in a part-time capacity for the Philadelphia Athletics. He ended his baseball career the next year with the Minneapolis Millers of the minor league American Association. The consistent Wheat surpassed 200 hits in a season three times and played in more games (2,410) than any other Dodger of his era. He appeared in two World Series with Brooklyn in 1916 and 1920, getting nine hits and batting .333 in 1920.

Wheat owned a 162-acre farm near Polo, Missouri, until 1932 when depression conditions forced him to sell. Earlier, he had been a part-owner of a Kansas City, Missouri, bowling and billiards parlor. After selling his farm, he returned to Kansas City and soon joined the police force. In April 1936 he suffered serious injuries in a patrol car accident and retired from police work. Following doctors' orders, he settled on the Lake of the Ozarks at Sunrise Beach, near Versailles, Missouri, and operated a fishing camp there through the 1950s. He was elected to the National Baseball Hall of Fame and was inducted in July 1959, joining Ty Cobb, Frank "Home Run" Baker, Jimmy Foxx, Rogers Hornsby, and other baseball greats at a Kansas City Athletics' game held in his honor.

Wheat married Daisy Forsman in 1912 and had a son and a daughter. Always a popular player with the fans, he was described by Branch Rickey as the best outfielder to play for Brooklyn. Wheat was known as a deadly accurate thrower, feared by opposing base runners. His brother, Mack Wheat, also played seven years in the National League with Brooklyn and Philadelphia (1915–1921).

Wheat died in Sedalia, Missouri. Casey Stengel, a former Brooklyn teammate, summed him up: "One of the grandest guys ever to wear a baseball uniform, one of the best batting teachers I have seen, one of the truest pals a man ever had and one of the kindliest men God ever created."

• The Zack Wheat files are located at the National Baseball Library, Cooperstown, N.Y. Other Wheat family papers are in the possession of Maxine Tedlock, Wheat's grandniece. Biographical and career information on Wheat can be found in David L. Porter, ed., *Biographical Dictionary of American Sports: Baseball* (1987); *The Baseball Encyclopedia*, 9th ed. (1993); and Lowell Reidenbaugh, *Cooperstown: Where Baseball's Legends Live Forever* (1983). Obituaries are in the *New York Times*, 13 Mar. 1972, and the *Kansas City Star*, 13 Mar. 1972.

ARTHUR F. MCCLURE

WHEATLEY, Phillis (c. 1753–5 Dec. 1784), poet and cultivator of the epistolary writing style, was born in Gambia, Africa, probably along the fertile low lands of the Gambia River. She was enslaved as a child of seven or eight and sold in Boston to John and Susanna Wheatley on 11 July 1761. The horrors of the middle passage likely contributed to her persistent trouble with asthma. The Wheatleys apparently named the girl, who had nothing but a piece of dirty carpet to conceal her nakedness, after the slaver, the *Phillis*, that transported her.

The Wheatleys were more kindly toward Phillis than were most slaveowners of the time, permitting her to learn to read. The poet in Wheatley soon began to emerge. She published her first poem on 21 December 1765 in the *Newport Mercury* when she was about twelve. The poem, "On Messrs. Hussey and Coffin," relates how these two gentlemen narrowly escaped drowning off Cape Cod.

Much of her subsequent poetry deals, as well, with events occurring close to her Boston circle. Of her fifty-five extant poems, nineteen are elegies; all but the last of them are devoted to the commemoration of someone she knew personally. Wheatley herself and her career are the subjects of her last elegy. One possible explanation for her preoccupation with this genre may be that she recalled the delivery of oral laments by the women of her tribal group whose responsibility it was to make such deliveries.

In October 1770 Wheatley published an elegy that must be called pivotal to her career. The subject of this elegy is George Whitefield, evangelical Methodist minister, a close friend of Charles Wesley, and privy chaplain to Selina Hastings, countess of Huntingdon. During his career Whitefield had made seven journeys to the American colonies, where he was known as the "Voice of the Great Awakening" and as the "Great Awakener." Only a week before his death in Newburyport, Massachusetts, on 30 September 1770, Whitefield preached in Boston where Wheatley very likely heard him. As Susanna Wheatley regularly corresponded with the countess, she and the Wheatley household may well have entertained the Great Awakener. Wheatley's vivid, ostensibly firsthand account in the elegy, replete with quotes the minister is alleged to have spoken, may, then, have been based on actual acquaintance. Owing to this evangel's extreme popularity, Wheatley's deft elegy became an overnight sensation and was often reprinted.

It is almost certain that the ship that carried news of Whitefield's death to the countess also carried a copy of Wheatley's elegy. It was this elegy that brought Wheatley to the sympathetic attention of the countess. Such an acquaintance ensured that Wheatley's elegy was also reprinted many times in London, giving the young poet an international reputation. This acquaintance also ensured that Wheatley's *Poems on Various Subjects, Religious and Moral* appeared in print, not in Boston where the project was rejected for racist reasons but in London printed in 1773 by the English publisher Archibald Bell and financed by the countess.

Wheatley's support by Hastings and her rejection by white male-dominated Boston signaled her nourishment as a literary artist by a community of women. While Wheatley received encouragement for the writing of her poems by prominent men of Boston such as the ministers Mather Byles (nephew of Cotton Mather) and Samuel Cooper, she was taught to read the King James Bible by Susanna Wheatley and probably as well by her daughter Mary. In addition, Susanna promoted Wheatley's publication of her poems in local newspapers.

Wheatley displays in her poems a sophisticated classicism. She knew Latin well enough to craft the excellent epyllion (or short epic) "Niobe in Distress . . . " from book 6 of Ovid's *Metamorphoses*. Of Wheatley's twenty-two extant letters, seven are addressed to Obour Tanner, an African American who many have speculated may have been forced to make the journey of the middle passage with Wheatley; in any event, the intimacy of their relationship is self-evident from the tone and detail of Wheatley's letters to her (none of Tanner's responses are extant). Tanner must have been a close friend and probably a valuable counselor and confidante of the poet.

All these women (the countess, who encouraged and financed the publication of her *Poems*; Mary and Susanna Wheatley, who taught her to read and write; and Obour Tanner, who could empathize probably better than anyone with her condition as a slave) were much older than the poet and obviously nurtured her development. Their importance to Wheatley's development is virtually incalculable. It is not excessive to submit that without this community of women, Wheatley's poems may never have been printed. Although Anne Bradstreet's poems, Jane Turell's, and those of other women poets who preceded Wheatley were published by now, the publication of her poems through the efforts of women marks the first such occasion in the annals of American letters.

During the summer of 1773 Wheatley journeyed to England, where she assisted in the preparation of her volume for the press. While in London she enjoyed considerable recognition from such dignitaries as Lord Dartmouth, Lord Lincoln, Granville Sharp (who escorted Wheatley on several tours about London), Benjamin Franklin, and Brooks Watson, a wealthy merchant who presented Wheatley with a folio edition of Milton's *Paradise Lost* and who later became lord mayor of London. Wheatley was to have been presented at court when due to an illness of Susanna Wheatley, she was summoned to return to Boston in August. It is significant that sometime before 18 October 1773 Wheatley was granted her freedom, according to her own testimony, "at the desire of my friends in England" (*Collected Works*, p. 170). It follows then that if Hastings had not agreed to finance Wheatley's *Poems* and if the poet had not then journeyed to London, she probably would never have been manumitted.

When the American Revolution erupted, Wheatley's patriotic feelings separated her even more from the Wheatleys. After Susanna died on 3 March 1774, Wheatley's relationship with her Loyalist former master doubtless became strained. As her position in regard to independence has often been confused with the Loyalist position of John Wheatley and his son Nathaniel, her patriotism requires underscoring. Throughout her career she repeatedly celebrated American freedom, indeed rivaling Philip Freneau's claim to the title "Poet of the American Revolution." Her two most famous revolutionary war poems are "To His Excellency General Washington" (1775), which closes with the encomium "A crown, a mansion, and a throne that shine, / With gold unfading, WASHINGTON! be thine," and "Liberty and Peace" (1784), written to celebrate the Treaty of Paris and containing the forceful line "And new-born *Rome* [i.e., America] shall give *Britannia* Law."

Another misunderstood contribution of Phillis Wheatley is her attitude toward slavery. Because major statements Wheatley made attacking the institution of slavery were recovered only in the 1970s and 1980s, she was earlier thought to have ignored the issue. In February 1774, for example, Wheatley wrote to Samson Occom (recalling her first piece of writing to Occom in 1765): "In every human breast, God has implanted a Principle, which we call Love of Freedom; it is impatient of Oppression, and pants for Deliverance." This letter was reprinted a dozen times in American newspapers over the next twelve months. Certainly whites and blacks of Wheatley's time never questioned her attitude toward slavery.

Later in the same year Wheatley observed in a letter to John Thornton, the English philanthropist, "The world is a severe schoolmaster, for its frowns are less dang'rous than its smiles and flatteries, and it is a difficult task to keep in the path of Wisdom." This entire letter appears cast in the tone of the African American who has found her white would-be benefactor's motive to be less than philanthropic and indeed hollow or even destructive, much in the manner of the fictions of Langston Hughes, Richard Wright, and Ralph Ellison. In an elegy of July 1778 on the death of Major General David Wooster, who, according to Wheatley, "fell a martyr in the Cause of Freedom," Wheatley challenges the notion that whites can "hope to find / Divine acceptance with th' Almighty mind" when "they disgrace / And hold in bondage Afric's blameless race."

The year 1778 was a pivotal one for Wheatley. Soon after John Wheatley died, she married John Peters, a free African American who was a jack-of-all-trades, serving in various capacities from storekeeper to advocate for African Americans before the courts. But Wheatley's fortunes began to decline. In 1779 she published a set of "Proposals" for a new volume of poems, probably in an effort to mitigate her worsening poverty. While the "Proposals" failed to attract subscribers, they show that she had produced some 300 pages of new poetry since the publication of *Poems* six years earlier. The volume never appeared, and, sadly, most of its poems are lost.

Wheatley's final proposal for a volume of poems in September 1784 went virtually unnoticed. This volume, whose title was to have been *Poems and Letters on Various Subjects*, would have included thirteen letters to dignitaries such as Benjamin Rush, the earl of Dartmouth, and the countess of Huntingdon. Once having carried a reputation of such distinction that it earned her an audience with General Washington in March 1776, Wheatley and her newborn child died alone in a shack on the edge of Boston. It is believed she died as a result of an infection from the birth.

Wheatley's end, like her beginning in America, was pitiable. Yet this genius of the pen left to the country a legacy of firsts: the first African American to publish a book, the mother of African-American letters, the first woman writer whose publication was urged and nurtured by a community of women, and the first American woman author who tried to earn a living by means of her writing.

• For additional information on the life and work of Phillis Wheatley, see Arthur P. Davis, "Personal Elements in the Poetry of Phillis Wheatley," *Phylon* 13 (1953): 191–98, and Sondra A. O'Neal, "A Slave's Subtle War: Phillis Wheatley's Use of Biblical Myth and Symbol," *Early American Literature* 21 (1986): 144–65. For an in-depth look at her work, see William H. Robinson, *Phillis Wheatley in the Black American Beginnings* (1975), *Black New England Letters: The Uses of Writing in Black New England* (1977), and *Critical Essays on Phillis Wheatley* (1982), which he edited. John C. Shields assesses the poet in "Phillis Wheatley and Mather Byles: A Study in Literary Relationship," *College Language Association Journal* 23 (1980): 377–90, "Phillis Wheatley's Use of Classicism," *American Literature* 52 (1980): 97–111, "Phillis Wheatley's Struggle for Freedom in Her Poetry and Prose," in *The Collected Works of Phillis Wheatley*, ed. Shields (1988), "Phillis Wheatley" in *African-American Writers*, ed. Valerie Smith (1991), four essays in *Style: African-American Poetics* 26 (Fall 1993), and "Phillis Wheatley's Subversive Pastoral," *Eighteenth-Century Studies* 27 (June 1994): 631–47.

JOHN C. SHIELDS

WHEATON, Frank (8 May 1833–18 June 1903), Union general, was born in Providence, Rhode Island, the son of Francis Levison Wheaton, a doctor, and Amelia S. Burrill. After attending public schools in Providence, Wheaton enrolled at Brown University to study engineering. But in 1850, after only one year of college, he took a job as a surveyor with the Mexican-American Boundary Commission. Then, in 1855, he joined the First U.S. Cavalry and was commissioned a first lieutenant. His unit participated in Colonel Edwin Sumner's 1857 campaign against the Cheyenne Indians near the South Fork of the Platte River, and he was sent to Utah Territory in 1858 and to quell disturbances carried on by Mormons against federal authority.

Wheaton became a captain in the Fourth U.S. Cavalry on 1 March 1861 but four months later, after the outbreak of the Civil War, was appointed lieutenant colonel of the Second Rhode Island Infantry. On 21 July, immediately after the first battle of Manassas (Bull Run), Wheaton was promoted to colonel of the regiment, replacing Colonel John S. Slocum, who had been mortally wounded in the engagement. Wheaton commanded his regiment at Williamsburg, Mechanicsville, and Seven Pines and covered the retreat from Malvern Hill during the Peninsula campaign (May–June 1862). In August his regiment participated in General John Pope's Second Manassas campaign.

On 29 November 1862, in recognition of his conduct during the Peninsula campaign, Wheaton was again promoted, this time to brigadier general of volunteers. From this point on his brigade served with the Federal VI Corps, seeing service in the battles of Fredericksburg (Dec. 1862) and Second Fredericksburg (May 1863), during the Chancellorsville campaign (2–6 May 1863), and on the final day of fighting at Gettysburg (3 July 1863).

In the Overland campaign of spring 1864, Wheaton's brigade initially fought with General John Sedgwick's VI Corps at the Wilderness and Spotsylvania. After Sedgwick's death at Spotsylvania, he was replaced by General Horatio G. Wright, and Wheaton would serve under him for the duration of the war. Persevering through the savage fighting at Cold Harbor, Wheaton's brigade was among the initial troops to arrive at and assault Petersburg on 18 June. Shortly afterward Wheaton was given charge of the First Division of the corps. On 11 July his division, having been ordered from Petersburg to Washington, D.C., arrived at Fort Stevens to save the capital from an impending assault by Confederates led by General Jubal A. Early. Successful in this endeavor, Wheaton was awarded the rank of brevet major general. In the Shenandoah campaign (Winchester, Fisher's Hill, Cedar Creek), Wheaton originally commanded the First Brigade, Second Division, through September, then was promoted to command of the First Division. Wright said of his service, "A portion of the First Division, under Generals Wheaton and Mackenzie . . . behaved admirably in checking the enemy and giving time for the rest of the troops to take position [during the battle of Cedar Creek]." In December 1864 the VI Corps returned to the Petersburg front.

Wheaton's division, called out as support during the battle of Hatcher's Run (5–7 Feb. 1865), successfully carried the Confederate lines in the 2 April assault on Petersburg. His last engagement in the war was on 6 April, at the battle of Little Sailor's Creek, where his men captured most of Confederate general Richard S. Ewell's command. During the last year of the war Wheaton was cited for gallantry and meritorious service for his role in the battles of the Wilderness, Opequon, Fisher's Hill, and Cedar Creek (Middletown) and the capture of Petersburg. Other awards Wheaton received in recognition of his war service were an honorary A.M. from Brown University (1865) and a sword from the state of Rhode Island. He was mustered out of the volunteer service on 30 April 1866.

The following summer, on 28 July, he was appointed a lieutenant colonel of the Thirty-ninth Infantry in the regular army. Later, on 15 March 1869, he was transferred to the Twenty-first Infantry. During 1872–1873 he commanded the expedition against the Modocs at the lava beds in northern California. He was promoted in 1874 to colonel of the Second Infantry and eventually, in 1892, to brigadier general, U.S. Army. With the latter appointment he was assigned to command the Department of Texas. He received his final promotion, to major general, in 1897; he retired from the army on 8 May of that year.

The general made his final home in Washington, D.C., where he died, survived by his wife, the former Maria Cooper, and their two children. Maria Cooper Wheaton was the daughter of Confederate general Samuel Cooper and the niece of Virginia senator and diplomat James M. Mason. Wheaton was buried in Arlington National Cemetery.

As was true of many American men who came of age during the mid-nineteenth century, Frank Wheaton's life revolved around military service, with his greatest accomplishments taking place during the Civil War.

• In the years following Wheaton's service in the Civil War, a small publication was produced on the general's career, *Civil and Military Record of Frank Wheaton, Brevet Major General U.S. Army, Lieutenant Colonel Thirty-ninth U.S. Infantry* (1869). His early war services with his home state unit are discussed in Augustus Woodbury, *The Second Rhode Island Regiment: A Narrative of Military Operations* (1875). Likewise, *All for the Union: A History of the 2nd Rhode Island Volunteer Infantry*, ed. Robert Hunt Rhodes (1985), provides insights on the general from the diary of Colonel Elisha Hunt Rhodes. Wheaton's military promotions can be charted in Francis B. Heitman, *Historical Register and Dictionary of the United States Army* (1903). For brief summaries of Wheaton's life and military career see Brigadier General Elisha Dyer, *Annual Report of the Adjutant General of the State of Rhode Island and Providence Plantations, for the Year 1865* (1893), and Ezra J. Warner, *Generals in Blue* (1964).

CHRISTOPHER CALKINS

WHEATON, Henry (27 Nov. 1785–11 Mar. 1848), scholar, diplomat, and Supreme Court reporter, was born in Providence, Rhode Island, the son of Seth Wheaton, a prosperous merchant, civic leader, and later president of the Rhode Island branch of the Bank of the United States, and Abigail Wheaton (a cousin). Wheaton entered Rhode Island College (now Brown University) at age twelve, studied law at his father's urging, and graduated in 1802. After three years in the offices of Providence attorney Nathaniel Searles, he gained admission to the Rhode Island bar in 1805 at age nineteen. His father then sent him for a year abroad to become familiar with the languages, history, and literature of Europe. While in France and England, Wheaton studied civil law at Poitiers and attended the law courts, including the Court of Admiralty at Westminster. He returned to Providence in 1806, embarking on six years of law practice and increasing political involvement, including writings on local, state, national, and international affairs. In 1811 Wheaton married his cousin Catherine, the daughter of Dr. Levi Wheaton, his uncle and mentor. They had three children.

The Wheatons moved to New York City in 1812 to enhance his professional opportunities. During the required three-year waiting period for admission to the New York bar, Wheaton edited the *National Advocate*, a Tammany paper, writing often on international law and issues occasioned by the War of 1812. He also appeared as counsel on the federal circuit in Rhode Island and before the Supreme Court in Washington. In the process he struck up a warm friendship with Justice Joseph Story, who shared his interest in Republican politics, the creation of a comprehensive American jurisprudence, and maritime law (which Story, from the bench, would help greatly to expand). At Story's suggestion, Wheaton published his first book, *A Digest of the Law of Maritime Capture and Prizes* (1815).

In 1816, again with Story's support, Wheaton succeeded William Cranch as the Supreme Court's third Reporter of Decisions. The ablest of the early reporters (and a frequent advocate before the Court himself), Wheaton redefined the office and greatly improved the quality of the product. Unlike his self-appointed predecessors, Wheaton became reporter through selection by the Court, held an office recognized by law, and received a modest salary. He attended court sessions faithfully, reported arguments and opinions accurately, and published each volume within the year, thereby enabling bench and bar to know promptly the rulings of the nation's highest court.

In addition, aided occasionally (but anonymously) by Story, his roommate while in Washington, Wheaton enhanced his *Reports* with unprecedented annotations, elucidating particular points in opinions or exploring entire areas of developing law, and relying where appropriate on British and continental analogues. The resulting twelve volumes, spanning the epochal years from *Martin v. Hunter's Lessee* (1816) to *Ogden v. Saunders* (1827), became what one German writer called upon Wheaton's death "the golden book of American national law" In 1823 Wheaton himself was considered for appointment to the Supreme Court seat ultimately awarded to Smith Thompson.

By 1827 Wheaton's expertise in international law, standing at the bar and continuing political activities prompted President John Quincy Adams's offer of appointment as the first American chargé d'affaires to Denmark. Confident that sales of his *Reports* would supplement his diplomat's salary, Wheaton embarked on a career in foreign service that would span the administrations of Adams, Jackson, Van Buren, Harrison, Tyler, and Polk.

In Denmark Wheaton quickly demonstrated a natural aptitude for diplomacy. By 1830 he negotiated a treaty of indemnity to resolve the longstanding dispute concerning the seizure of neutral American vessels by Danish ships during Denmark's war with England twenty years earlier. In the same year his avid study of Scandinavian history and literature brought his election to the Scandinavian Society and the Icelandic Literary Society.

In late 1833, however, Wheaton took a leave of absence to return to the United States to assist Daniel Webster and Elijah Paine in pressing Wheaton's suit against Richard Peters, Jr., his successor as reporter to the Supreme Court, for allegedly infringing the copyright in Wheaton's *Reports*. Peters had destroyed the market for Wheaton's twelve volumes (and the earlier *Reports* of Dallas and Cranch) by producing cheaper, more compact volumes, omitting his predecessors' original contributions, and reproducing merely the Justices' opinions.

In a decision establishing the major contours of American copyright law, the Court in 1834 ruled against Wheaton. The decision established copyright in the United States as a limited monopoly recognized by law primarily for the benefit of the public rather than the author; required punctilious compliance with the statutory prerequisites to copyright protection, which the Court doubted Wheaton had accomplished; and held unanimously "that no reporter has or can have any copyright in the written opinions delivered by this court; and that the judges thereof cannot confer on any reporter any such right" (33 U.S. (8 Pet.) 591, 668). Wheaton's finances were seriously damaged, and his friendship with Justice Story dissolved.

Happily for Wheaton, his diplomatic career resumed triumphantly when President Andrew Jackson acceded to Prussia's request and appointed Wheaton chargé d'affaires to Berlin in 1835. Wheaton soon published his landmark treatise, *Elements of International Law* (1836). In the Advertisement to the first edition, he noted:

> The object of the Author in the following attempt to collect the rules and principles which govern, or are supposed to govern, the conduct of States in their mutual intercourse in peace and in war, and which have therefore received the name of International Law, has been to compile an elementary work for the use of persons engaged in diplomatic and other forms of public life, rather than for mere technical lawyers, although he ventures to hope that it may not be found wholly useless even to the latter.

The sagacity of Wheaton's learning and judgment concerning diplomatic affairs and relevant judicial opinions quickly proved his anticipations far too modest. *Elements of International Law* earned Wheaton, among contemporaries, deserved acclaim as the "chief modern expounder of the science of international law" (Hicks, p. 215). The work passed through several editions in his lifetime; was translated into French, Italian, Spanish, Chinese, and Japanese; and, edited by others, remained influential into the twentieth century. A companion work, *History of the Law of Nations in Europe and America* (1845), helped cement Wheaton's fame.

In 1837, the year following the first publication of *Elements*, President Martin Van Buren promoted Wheaton to envoy extraordinary and minister plenipotentiary. In that role he spent six years negotiating a treaty, hailed by European and American diplomats alike, to govern commercial relations between the United States and the states of the German *Zollverein*. Although signed by Wheaton on behalf of the United States in 1844, the treaty failed to be ratified in the Senate because of political and constitutional concerns. Wheaton resigned his diplomatic post at the request of President Polk in 1846. He returned home to widespread acclaim the following year, having accepted a lectureship in civil and international law at Harvard, which ill health prevented him from occupying. Wheaton died in Dorchester, Massachusetts, survived by his wife and three children.

Although his fame today is less than theirs, Wheaton's place among the giants of nineteenth-century American law and diplomacy is clear: "In jurisprudence, Marshall and Kent and Story and Wheaton, by judicial opinion or by written text, laid the foundations of American public and private law" (A. C. McLaughlin, in *Cambridge History of American Literature*, vol. 2 [1918], p. 71).

• Wheaton's papers are collected in the Pierpont Morgan Library in New York City. His life is the subject of one full-length biography, Elizabeth F. Baker, *Henry Wheaton, 1785–1848* (1937), and of numerous other treatments, including Edward Everett, "Life, Services and Works of Henry Wheaton," *North American Review* 82 (1856): 1–32; James Brown Scott, "Henry Wheaton, 1785–1848," in *Great American Lawyers*, ed. W. D. Lewis, vol. 3 (1907), pp. 241–85; and Frederick C. Hicks, "Henry Wheaton," in *Men and Books Famous in the Law* (1921), pp. 190–235. For an account of Wheaton's Reportership and battle with Richard Peters, Jr., in *Wheaton v. Peters*, see Craig Joyce, "The Rise of the Supreme Court Reporter: An Institutional Perspective on Marshall Court Ascendancy," *Michigan Law Review* 83 (1985): 1291–391.

CRAIG JOYCE

WHEDON, Daniel Denison (20 Mar. 1808–8 June 1885), Methodist Episcopal clergyman and theologian, was born in Onondaga, New York, the son of Daniel Whedon and Clarissa Root. During his earlier years he was a member of a Presbyterian Sunday school, although his mother and eldest brother were active Methodists. His father wanted him to become a lawyer and placed him under the instruction of Oliver C. Grosvenor in Rome, New York. When he was eighteen, Whedon entered the junior class at Hamilton College in Clinton, New York. After his graduation in 1828 he studied law with Judge Chapin in Rochester, New York, and Alanson Bennett in Rome. While in Rome he experienced conversion under the evangelistic preaching of Charles G. Finney and joined the Methodist Episcopal church, being drawn by its doctrine of free will that made salvation a possibility for all.

In 1830 Whedon was appointed teacher of Greek and mental philosophy at Oneida Conference Seminary in Cazenovia, New York. While teaching at Cazenovia, he received his license to preach and occasionally spoke to religious gatherings in the area. In 1831 he accepted a teaching position at Hamilton College, where he also completed his master's degree. In 1833 he became professor of ancient languages and literature at Wesleyan University in Middletown, Connecticut, where he taught for ten years. In 1834 the New York Methodist Episcopal Conference admitted him on a trial basis. Two years later he was ordained a deacon and admitted to full membership. He received ordination as elder in 1838.

Whedon's first significant publications were articles published in 1835 in *Zion's Herald* in which he attacked the radical abolitionist views of the Methodist Episcopal clergyman Orange Scott. Although Whedon believed that slavery was evil and admonished slave owners to emancipate their slaves, he criticized the bitter rhetoric and divisive agitation of northern extremists. On 15 July 1840, he married Eliza Ann Searles; they had five children.

Weary of the routine of the classroom, Whedon resigned his position at Wesleyan and became the pastor of Methodist churches in Pittsfield, Massachusetts, in 1843 and Rensselaerville, New York, in 1845. The pastoral ministry was neither challenging nor satisfying to Whedon. He returned to teaching in 1845 when he was named to the chair of logic, rhetoric, and philosophy of history at the University of Michigan. His opposition to the extension of slavery resulted in his dismissal from the Michigan faculty in 1851, so he opened a classical and commercial school in Ravenswood, Long Island, New York, in 1852. That year he attended the Methodist Episcopal General Conference in Boston, Massachusetts, having been elected the previous year a Michigan delegate. When the duties of the school proved too much for him, he served pastorates in New York City and Jamaica, New York, from 1854 to 1856.

The 1856 General Conference elected Whedon editor of the *Methodist Quarterly Review*, the denomination's chief theological periodical, a position he held for twenty-eight years. When he took up his editorial responsibilities, Whedon was one of the church's most competent and influential theologians and writers. Among his more important writings were *The Freedom of the Will as a Basis of Human Responsibility, and a Divine Government Elucidated and Maintained in its Issue with the Necessitarian Theories of Hobbes, Edwards, the Princeton Essayists, and Other Leading Advocates* (1864), in which he defended John Wesley's Arminian view of the freedom of the human will to respond to

God's offer of salvation, as opposed to the Calvinistic view that the human will is not free; and his *Commentary on the New Testament*, which appeared in five volumes between 1860 and 1880. He also edited a series of commentaries on the Old Testament. The commentaries incorporated the insights of modern biblical scholarship and were designed for popular reading and study. He died at the summer home of his son, Charles, in Atlantic City, New Jersey.

The predominant theme of Whedon's theology was moral responsibility. He believed that genuine responsibility presupposed freedom of the human will, a central tenet of Wesleyan theology. While Whedon's understanding of human freedom and moral living was similar to Wesley's view, Whedon's ideas are based much more on philosophical and psychological arguments. In emphasizing divinely aided human freedom and moral ability, he departed from Wesley's theology at many points, including the traditional emphases on the seriousness of human depravity and the necessity of Christ's atoning death.

Whedon was one of the most important figures in the Methodist Episcopal church in the nineteenth century. Southern Methodist theologian Thomas Osmond Summers claimed that Whedon was "the foremost theologian in America" (Scott, p. 187). His books and articles provided theological guidance and inspiration for a generation of Methodists.

• For biographical information see Whedon's *Essays, Reviews, and Discourses* (1887; repr., 1972), which also includes some of his most important essays on Methodist doctrine and polity. A collection of his earlier writings is *Public Addresses, Collegiate, and Popular* (1852). His theology is examined in Leland Howard Scott, *Methodist Theology in America in the Nineteenth Century* (1954).

CHARLES YRIGOYEN, JR.

WHEELER, Anna Johnson Pell (5 May 1883–26 Mar. 1966), mathematician, was born in Hawarden, Iowa, the daughter of Andrew Gustav Johnson and Amelia Friberg. Her parents were Swedish immigrants; Johnson's father, initially a farmer, worked later as a furniture dealer and undertaker in Akron, Iowa. Johnson obtained an A.B. degree from the University of South Dakota in 1903. There her talent for mathematics was recognized by one of her professors, Alexander Pell. Pell, a former Russian revolutionary whose real name was Sergei Degaev, encouraged her to pursue a mathematical career. She received A.M. degrees from the University of Iowa (1904) and from Radcliffe College (1905). Winning an Alice Freeman Palmer Fellowship from Wellesley College, she went to Göttingen University to study during 1906–1907. While at Göttingen, the lectures of David Hilbert, one of the driving forces in twentieth-century mathematics, turned her interest toward integral equations.

Pell's first wife died in 1904, and in July 1907 Johnson married Pell in Göttingen. The couple returned to the University of South Dakota but Alexander Pell soon resigned to teach at Chicago's Armour Institute of Technology. Anna Pell completed her doctoral studies at the University of Chicago in 1910, magna cum laude, under Eliakim Hastings Moore.

Pell's husband suffered a stroke in 1911, placing the burden of financial support on her. Her first full-time teaching position was at Mount Holyoke College (1911–1918), where she taught, did research, and took care of her ailing husband. In 1918 she went to Bryn Mawr College, where she remained, except for short periods, until she retired in 1948. At Bryn Mawr she continued to be active as a teacher and, later, as a chairperson as well as a researcher. Pell's husband died in 1921, and in 1925 she married Arthur Leslie Wheeler, a colleague, who became professor of Latin at Princeton University. Moving to Princeton, Anna Wheeler continued to lecture part time at Bryn Mawr College. She moved back to Bryn Mawr in 1932 after her second husband's sudden death.

In the early 1900s Hilbert's work and interest evolved around integral equations. These are equations in which unknown functions occur under integral signs. He attached a great deal of importance to this subject. Hilbert's interest inspired mathematicians throughout the world to pursue further investigations in this area. As the years passed, interest declined, and many of the results obtained passed into relative obscurity. An outgrowth of the work on integral equations was the development of a field in mathematics known as functional analysis, dealing with transformations, or operators, acting on functions.

Anna Pell Wheeler's research spanned this period when the study of integral equations per se was at its peak of popularity and functional analysis was in its infancy. Her work centered on integral equations and equations in infinitely many variables, extending and generalizing Hilbert's results. Particularly important was her investigation of biorthogonal systems of functions. More recently, these specialized systems have been found to be of use in numerical analysis, statistics, and applied mathematics. Wheeler applied them in her work on integral equations. She determined conditions under which solutions existed for linear integral equations and infinite systems of linear equations, finding expressions for such solutions. In 1927 she was invited by the American Mathematical Society to deliver Colloquium Lectures (an annual series) on quadratic forms in infinitely many variables (the only woman so honored until Julia Robinson in 1980).

Wheeler was active in the governance of the American Mathematical Society, serving on the Board of Trustees (1923–1924) and the Council (1924–1926). She also chaired the Philadelphia section of the Mathematical Association of America (1943–1944).

A fine teacher, Wheeler took a sincere interest in her students, helping them attain professional and personal fulfillment. Aware of the difficulties faced by women as mathematicians, she often took students to mathematical meetings, urging them to participate actively. Many of her students later became university professors and research mathematicians.

Wheeler tried to enhance the reputation of the Bryn Mawr College mathematics department. She advocated reduced teaching loads and encouraged her faculty in their research efforts. In 1933, after the rise of the Nazis to power, Wheeler was successful in attracting the noted German Jewish algebraist Emmy Noether to Bryn Mawr College.

Wheeler was a warm and modest person, mindful and considerate of others. She took pleasure in the outdoors, being a birdwatcher and wildflower enthusiast. Retiring in 1948, she retained her home in Bryn Mawr and her summer retreat in the Adirondacks. Despite arthritis attacks, she continued to attend mathematical meetings. She died in Bryn Mawr.

Wheeler was respected professionally during her lifetime. In *American Men of Science* (3d ed., 1921) her name is starred, indicating her prominence among American mathematicians. (Of 211 mathematicians ever starred, only three were women.) Honorary degrees were conferred on her by the New Jersey College for Women (1932) and Mount Holyoke College (1937). In 1940 she was among the one hundred American women to be acclaimed by the Women's Centennial Congress for succeeding in careers not open to women a century before.

• Bryn Mawr Archives contain a scrapbook of letters from colleagues and students compiled at Pell Wheeler's retirement. Church records of the Immanuel and Union Creek Lutheran churches in Akron, Iowa, contain vital statistics for Pell Wheeler's family. Invaluable information, both verbal and written, has been supplied by Jean Hoagland Owens (Anna Wheeler's niece), Ruth Stauffer McKee (a Bryn Mawr graduate who obtained her Ph.D. under Emmy Noether), and Mrs. David Roy (wife of the pastor of Immanuel and Union Creek Lutheran churches). Wheeler's doctoral thesis was published in two parts: "Biorthogonal Systems of Functions," *Transactions of the American Mathematical Society* 12 (1911): 135–64, and "Applications of Biorthogonal Systems of Functions to the Theory of Integral Equations," *Transactions of the American Mathematical Society* 12 (1911): 165–80. The Colloquium Lectures were abstracted by T. H. Hildebrandt: "The Theory of Quadratic Forms in Infinitely Many Variables and Applications," *Bulletin of the American Mathematical Society* 33 (1927): 664–65. Summaries of Pell Wheeler's life appear in *American Men of Science*, 9th ed. (1955), p. 2076; *Who's Who in America* (1950–1951), vol. 26, p. 2921; and Johann Christian Poggendorff, *Biographisch-Literarisches Handwörterbuch zur Geschichte der exakten Wissenschaften*, vol. 6, pt. 4, p. 2861. A detailed biography that includes a complete listing of her works was published by Louise S. Grinstein and Paul Campbell in *Historia Mathematica* 9 (1982): 37–53 as well as in *Women of Mathematics: A Biobibliographic Sourcebook* (1987), pp. 241–46. Alexander Pell's life in Russia is discussed in Von Hardesty and John D. Unruh, Jr., "The Enigma of Degaev-Pell," *South Dakota History, South Dakota Historical Society Quarterly* 3 (Winter 1972): 1–29, as well as in Adam Bruno Ulam, *In the Name of the People* (1977), pp. 380–89. For detailed surveys of integral equations, see Harold Thayer Davis, "The Present Status of Integral Equations," *Indiana University Studies* 13 (June 1926), study no. 70 (specifically, bibliography entries 76, 369–71, 464 and p. 14), as well as Ernst Hellinger and Otto Toeplitz, "Integralgleichungen und Gleichungen mit unendlichvielen Unbekannten," *Encyklopädie der Mathematischen Wissenschaften*, vol. 2, pt. 3 (1923–1927), pp. 1335–1597. Obituary references appear in the *New York Times*, 1 Apr. 1966, and the *Philadelphia-Evening Bulletin* 29 Mar. 1966. A description of the memorial service held at Bryn Mawr College as well as a photograph appear in the *Bryn Mawr Alumnae Bulletin* 47 (Summer 1966): 22–23.

LOUISE S. GRINSTEIN

WHEELER, Arthur Leslie (12 Aug. 1872–22 May 1932), classical scholar, was born in Hartford, Connecticut, the son of William Ruthven Wheeler, an artist specializing in children's portraits, and Emily Elizabeth Crego.

Wheeler received his university education at Yale, earning the B.A. degree in classics in 1893 and the Ph.D. in 1896 for a dissertation entitled "The Use of the Imperfect Indicative in Plautus and Terence." In 1894 he married May Louise Waters; they had one child. He remained at Yale as an instructor in Latin from 1894 to 1900. The bulk of his professional life was spent at Bryn Mawr, where he taught Latin from 1900 to 1925. For thirteen of those years (1907–1919) Tenney Frank was one of his colleagues in Latin, and together they helped establish Bryn Mawr's reputation for excellence in classics. In 1925, ten years after the death of his first wife, he married Anna Johnson Pell, a mathematician at Bryn Mawr, and was appointed professor of Latin at Princeton. Throughout his life he devoted much time to professional organizations, such as the American Philological Association and the Classical Association of the Atlantic States (president 1923–1924). In the spring semester of 1928 he gave the Sather lectures at Berkeley, a high honor.

Of Wheeler's professors at Yale, Edward P. Morris exerted the most influence on him. Wheeler's dissertation topic reflects Morris's interests in syntax and Latin poetry. His first articles, a series of studies on the use of the imperfect indicative, which appeared in *Transactions of the American Philological Association* (1899), *American Journal of Philology* (1903), and *Classical Philology* (1906), arose from his dissertation.

Wheeler's more mature work was on literary rather than linguistic topics. The pervading theme is the relationship between Latin poetry and its Greek antecedents. He explored this problem in three studies published in *Classical Philology* (1910 and 1911) on the *praeceptor amoris*, where he concluded that Latin elegiac poets seem to have borrowed the motif of erotic teaching directly from comedy rather than from some lost intermediary. This finding confirmed and helped establish the view, which still prevails, that Latin love elegy was not largely shaped by a corresponding body of Hellenistic elegy, now lost, but was essentially a Roman invention. In 1924 he published an edition of Ovid's *Tristia* and *Epistulae ex Ponto* in the Loeb Classical Library. The introduction is concise, useful, and judicious. When he died, of a cerebral hemorrhage in Princeton, he was preparing an annotated edition of Plautus's *Epidicus*, which was later completed and published by G. E. Duckworth (1940).

Wheeler is best known today for his Sather lectures, published posthumously as *Catullus and the Traditions of Ancient Poetry* (1934). Drawing inspiration from the recent publication of Ulrich von Wilamowitz-Moellendorff's *Hellenistische Dichtung* (1924), Wheeler set about mapping the extent of Catullus's indebtedness to his Greek and Roman predecessors in order to delineate more precisely the degree of his originality. He stressed Catullus's remarkable success in revitalizing an astonishing variety of Greek poetic genres by transposing them to a Roman setting and infusing them with immediacy and passion and, in particular, his role as forerunner of the Roman elegiac poets. More than fifty years later, though fashions in Catullan studies change rapidly, Wheeler's book remains an excellent introduction to the poet and is still in print.

Not a prolific scholar, Wheeler is admired today for his sound judgment and common sense. He demanded high standards of himself and of his students. In his memorial address Tenney Frank said of him: "Careless interpretation, slipshod thinking, fallacious logic, evasive statements and cloudy style were things that he abhorred, and his students soon learned that these had no place in his classroom."

• Letters to and from Wheeler are in the M. Carey Thomas archive at Bryn Mawr; see *Who Was Who in America*, vol. 1 (1897–1942), for basic biographical details. Obituaries are in the *New York Times*, 24 May 1932, and the *Bryn Mawr Alumnae Bulletin*, Nov. 1932.

DAVID A. TRAILL

WHEELER, Benjamin Ide (15 July 1854–2 May 1927), educator, was born in Randolph, Massachusetts, the son of Benjamin Wheeler, an austere and religiously conservative Baptist minister, and Mary Eliza Ide. The younger Benjamin was always proud of his New Hampshire inheritance and his New England upbringing. He was graduated Phi Beta Kappa in 1875 from Brown University, where he studied mathematics, physics, classics, and philosophy and was on the baseball team, rowed in his class crew, and was a member of the Alpha Delta Phi fraternity.

For the next few years Wheeler taught in the Providence high school while obtaining an A.M. from Brown (1878). He then taught Latin and Greek for another two years at Brown. His lifelong involvement in politics began in 1880–1881 with a year as a member of the Providence School Committee. To complete his education, Wheeler did what many of his ambitious contemporaries were doing: he went to study in Germany. He was accompanied by his new bride, Amey Webb, whom he married in 1881 and who proved to be, though tiny in stature and sometimes more than necessarily outspoken, a loyal companion and very capable partner in the scholarly and, later, public life he was choosing. They had one son, to whom they were devoted.

Traveling and studying at four universities in Germany, for which he acquired a great affection as well as respect, Wheeler received a Ph.D. summa cum laude in classical philology from the University of Heidelberg (1885). He returned to the United States to teach German at Harvard but was soon called to Cornell. From 1886 to 1899 Wheeler was professor of comparative philology and from 1888 also of Greek at Cornell. He also wrote and edited for scholarly journals and encyclopedias. His Ingersoll Lecture at Harvard was published as *Dionysos and Immortality* (1895); this and his *Alexander the Great: The Merging of East and West in Universal History* (1900), which was first published in serial form in *Century Magazine*, are his best-known writings. Wheeler often referred to the latter, written for a semipopular audience, as expressing his deeply held view of the world's "two halves"—the Orient and the classical West—brought together.

Wheeler, known affectionately at Cornell as "Benny Ide," was so popular a teacher that classes in freshman and sophomore Greek were doubled. He continued his enthusiasm for college sports: as a friend of the crew coach he was allowed in the coaching boat and was called by the student paper "the soul of the Cornell navy." Maintaining his interest and involvement in politics, Wheeler became, while in New York State, a constant correspondent of Theodore Roosevelt (1858–1919). His twelve years at Cornell, which Wheeler always looked back upon with enormous fondness, were interrupted only by a year of teaching at the American School of Classical Studies at Athens in 1895–1896. While in Greece, Wheeler officiated at the first modern Olympic Games.

Wheeler's scholarly reputation and his abilities as a leader, innovator, and energetic competitor earned him bids to several college presidencies before he was wooed for that position by the University of California in 1899. This university had been founded in 1868 as a Morrill Land Grant university with a small staff, no president, and a powerful but unpracticed board of regents composed primarily of political appointees. It was, however, endowed with a beautiful site overlooking San Francisco. By 1898 the struggling university, now with a faculty of 150 and a student body of 2,000, had had seven presidents, all of whom, except for Daniel Coit Gilman during his brief tenure (1873–1875), had been crippled by the barbarous antics of the students, the intransigencies of some faculty members, and above all a continuing tradition of regental governance. Thus, before accepting California's offer, Wheeler met and corresponded with various regents and received advice from David Starr Jordan of Stanford. Wheeler accepted the post in July after telling the regents that he intended to take control of the faculty and employees, appointments and dismissals included, and that he expected the regents to support him fully, at least in public. The regents were to refrain from dealing with the faculty over the president's head. These conditions were accepted and, during Wheeler's twenty years in office, were rarely abrogated.

Wheeler began his duties on 3 October 1899 and was met with a student rally on the campus. Here he gave a famous speech, encouraging the students to consider themselves part of a university "family," to love the university as a mother, to consider him a personal friend, to look for character in their teachers, and to realize that although much would be "pumped into" them, they would "pour most of it out again." He concluded with his most famous saying, which he later consciously took as a motto: "It has been good to be here."

Like Wheeler's first appearance, his first decade as president was a great success. He established a student-run disciplinary system and the foundations of an advanced form of student government that he designed himself. These were given concrete form in 1905 by the placing of a large golden *C* on the hill over the campus to mark the ending of the sometimes violent and injurious freshman-sophomore "rush." In athletics Wheeler encouraged enthusiasm and responsible behavior both inside and outside the stadium. At the same time, like President Jordan at Stanford, Wheeler considered the current form of collegiate football to be too brutal, and the two men abolished the game on their campuses, substituting English rugby as the chief intermural sport from 1906 to 1919, when student and alumni demand brought football back.

During his first decade at Berkeley Wheeler also recruited important faculty. He brought the historian Henry Morse Stephens from Cornell, where the two men had been close friends, and placed him in charge of the newly reorganized university extension program in 1902. Other prominent scholars brought by Wheeler, who himself did the high-level hiring, were Jacques Loeb in physiology, Adolph Miller in economics, Herbert Evans in anatomy, Gilbert Lewis in chemistry, Alfred Kroeber in anthropology, and many others in nearly every field. The Wheeler years were a time of expansion of existing disciplines, of frequent additions of new ones—some highly academic and some unashamedly vocational—and of seemingly little coercion from the president toward an emphasis on either research or teaching. Wheeler did, however, keep control of departmental staffing and salaries, and he even chose the members of academic senate committees himself. To one of his faculty he appeared "somewhat ruthless," but another considered him "the easiest person that I have ever worked with." Wheeler tried when he first arrived to protect from "decapitation" the older men "who deserve well of the university." He took an interest in faculty careers, helping some teachers move into administration.

One of Wheeler's first tasks was appointing a supervising architect to carry out the grandiose and comprehensive beaux-arts-style campus plan that had been adopted in 1899 after a worldwide competition sponsored by the wealthy patron and university regent Phoebe Apperson Hearst. Wheeler also had to find the funds to carry out the plan. The first task was fulfilled in 1901 by the choice of John Galen Howard, who until 1927 served the university as supervisor of the Hearst plan and designer of almost all of the more than thirty buildings erected during Wheeler's presidency. Addressing himself to the second task of raising money for the expansion of the university, Wheeler, with the cooperation of the regents, charmed, cajoled, and impressed the state legislature into providing the necessary funding.

Wheeler was tireless in his attention to the public image of the university: through contacts with the alumni, speaking tours, and appearances before legislative committees, he secured an extra provision of $100,000 in 1901. A gala reception on campus for the legislators in 1903 resulted in an extra appropriation of $25,000. He called upon the state again when the San Francisco earthquake of 1906 destroyed both teaching and endowment property. Wheeler also offered his boundless hospitality to Presidents Roosevelt and William Howard Taft, to famous college and university presidents and professors, and to other important politicians. All this effort enhanced Berkeley's image, increased Wheeler's popularity with the public, and earned him friends in high places so that between 1904 and 1908 he was invited to three university presidencies—at Illinois, the Massachusetts Institute of Technology, and Michigan. In 1909 he received the appointment of Theodore Roosevelt Professor at the University of Berlin.

Wheeler returned to California in 1910 to face a second presidential decade that was not as satisfying in terms of growth, glory, and accord. On the one hand, between 1910 and 1919 the John Galen Howard buildings continued to rise—including the enormous and stately Doe Library in 1911 and the equally impressive Wheeler Hall in 1917, along with other granite monuments of agriculture, law, chemistry, and physics. Decorative additions of a campanile and entrance gate were donated by Jane Sather, a competitor for Phoebe Hearst's role as the university's "Lady Bountiful" (both women received careful attention from Wheeler). On the other hand, this was a period of financial difficulties: deficits occurred in 1911–1913, and in 1914, happily, a needed bond issue was passed. Wheeler was greatly troubled by the approach of war, especially since in 1913 he had made his third trip to Germany, where he had meetings with the kaiser, whom he admired. Moreover, in 1916 Wheeler was forced to deal with the first signs of an academic senate revolt against presidential prerogatives.

The war itself meant new and wide responsibilities for Wheeler: male students were organized into military units; a preflight training school was established on the campus; faculty, staff, and women students were mobilized to serve in the war effort both on and off campus. Meanwhile, Wheeler was fighting to obtain a place for his twenty-two-year old son in military intelligence. In the midst of the wartime anti-German hysteria, which caused the dismissal of two professors, Wheeler was himself attacked for his previous friendship with the kaiser. The regents reacted in May 1918 by creating an advisory council of deans to "assist" the president and lessen public criticism.

This event, his age, now sixty-five, and real fatigue after twenty years of unceasing activity impelled

Wheeler to retire in July 1919. After a trip to Japan with a private delegation and attendance at both Republican and Democratic conventions, he and his wife settled in Berkeley close to the campus. Wheeler taught a course entitled "The Study of Human Speech" in 1921, continued to advise the new president, David Barrows, rode horseback, as he had ridden across the campus for years, and attended California football games. He died in Vienna.

Some contemporaries thought of Wheeler as austere, even forbidding in manner, but the picture that emerges from his correspondence is of a lively intelligence, an optimistic but never humorless attitude toward life, and a contagious enthusiasm for scholarship, sport, and California. He understood students because he had enjoyed being one himself; as a real scholar he knew how to hire good professors and to leave them alone to do their work. As a cosmopolitan "man of the world" and the best dressed of the college presidents, he could talk to the regents as one of them; perhaps because he was a philologist, he wrote and spoke plainly and convincingly. As he moved west, first to Ithaca and then to Berkeley, he "lost faith in the stiff schedules of the east" and very naturally adapted to democratic California. His gift for public speaking with a style perhaps homely, but never bombastic, gained him the allegiance of the California public. If Wheeler had a presidential fault, it was his lack of experience in business that made him uneasy with the new regime of the university comptroller.

Robert Sibley, alumni secretary for twenty-five years and one of Wheeler's greatest admirers, said of him that his "one great shortcoming was his somewhat deep antipathy to the fact that so many girls were on the Berkeley campus." In fact, there remains a puzzling ambivalence in Wheeler's attitude toward women's education. He often expressed a high regard for the civilizing influence of women in general and thought that "bachelors and clubmen are the bandits, guerrillas and outcasts"; on the other hand, he hated what seemed to him the frivolity and sheeplike behavior of the female students on campus—their having too many "teas and balls." He established the Department of Home Economics in 1916 in order to give female students the option of becoming employed as teachers. Some women faculty objected to this move, however, on the grounds that its goal contributed to the ghettoization of women.

Wheeler believed in democracy for the university students, for the United States, for Germany; he believed the aim of education was to create character; he believed in service. As an administrator he had a genius for putting these ideals to work in the planning of a great university in a state whose population tripled in size during his presidency. This, as a member of his faculty said, "takes skill and it takes nimbleness of mind, and I think it takes kindness, too" (Mitchell, p. 70).

• Wheeler's presidential papers are in the Bancroft Library of the University of California, Berkeley. The Bancroft also contains important oral histories of men and women who knew Wheeler: among them, Lucy Sprague Mitchell's *Pioneering in Education* (1962). There is no book-length biography of Wheeler; the introductory chapter in Monroe Deutsch, *The Abundant Life* (1926), a collection of Wheeler's speeches by a close friend, has a sketch of his life, and the chapter devoted to Wheeler in Verne Stadtman, *The University of California, 1868–1968* (1968), gives an excellent summation of his Berkeley career. An older history of the university, William Ferrier, *Origin and Development of the University of California* (1930), has material on Wheeler's years; Edward Slosson, *Great American Universities* (1910), has an incisive chapter on California; and Laurence Veysey's classic *The Emergence of the American University* (1965) treats Wheeler in the context of the beginnings of the modern university. For special aspects of Wheeler's career see Colin Wilson, "Benny Ide," *Cornell Alumni News*, Sept. 1979, pp. 30–33; Judith Robinson, *The Hearsts: An American Dynasty* (1991); and the chapter "Women at the University of California," in Lynn Gordon, *Gender and Higher Education in the Progressive Era* (1990).

CARROLL WINSLOW BRENTANO

WHEELER, Burton Kendall (27 Feb. 1882–6 Jan. 1975), senator and lawyer, was born in Hudson, Massachusetts, the son of Asa Leonard Wheeler, a cobbler, and Mary Elizabeth Tyler. Wheeler's ancestors had emigrated from England early in the colonial period. He worked his way through college, receiving his law degree from the University of Michigan in 1905, and began his law practice soon after in Butte, Montana.

Wheeler married Lulu M. White in 1907, and the couple had six children. His bright and feisty wife shared and reinforced Wheeler's often courageous political activism.

As a Democrat, Wheeler served one term in the Montana House of Representatives (1910–1912) and then was appointed by the Woodrow Wilson administration as U.S. district attorney for Montana from 1913 to 1918. With support from the reformist Nonpartisan League and opposition from the Anaconda Copper Mining Company, Wheeler lost his bid for the governorship of Montana in 1920 but won election as a Democrat to the U.S. Senate two years later. He served four terms in the Senate until defeated in the Democratic primary of 1946. The vice presidential running mate in Robert M. La Follette's (1855–1925) unsuccessful bid for the presidency on the Progressive third-party ticket in 1924, Wheeler was widely mentioned as a possible Democratic presidential candidate in 1940, had Franklin D. Roosevelt not run for a third term.

Wheeler was bright, quick, and scrappy. Politically he identified with western progressives, and in both Montana and in the Senate he battled on the side of farmers, workers, and small businesspeople against monopoly, big business, big finance, and big government. He mastered the legislative skills and developed into a powerful orator and a formidable adversary in debate. He never backed away from a fight for what he considered a worthy cause and was "about as easily cowed as a grizzly bear." He struggled against the Anaconda Copper Mining Company in Montana, against hysteria and intolerance during World War I, against Roosevelt's court-packing proposal, and against American involvement in World War II before the Japanese attack on Pearl Harbor. He did not discourage easily and could bounce back quickly after political reverses.

In the Senate Wheeler was a longtime member and later chairman of the Interstate Commerce Committee, in which capacity he worked for effective government regulation of railroads. Early in his Senate career he initiated steps that led to the ouster of President Warren G. Harding's attorney general, Harry M. Daugherty, for his role in the Teapot Dome scandal. In 1930 Wheeler was the first major Democrat to promote Roosevelt's nomination for president. Once elected President Roosevelt included Wheeler among the western progressives with whom he conferred in shaping his New Deal program. Wheeler spoke and voted for most of Roosevelt's liberal New Deal measures and led the fight for adoption of the administration's Public Utilities Holding Company Act of 1935. Though Wheeler had differed with the president on some issues, such as the need to inflate the currency, he campaigned for Roosevelt's election to a second term in 1936.

The senator broke sharply with Roosevelt, however, in 1937, when Wheeler led the fight against the president's "court-packing" bill on the grounds that it was a step toward dictatorship. Wheeler won that contest. Though Roosevelt never entirely forgave or forgot, Wheeler led the support for Roosevelt's Transportation Act of 1940 and cooperated on other legislative matters.

Until the European war began in 1939, Wheeler focused most of his legislative energies on domestic issues; indeed, he never served on the Foreign Relations Committee. During the early 1930s he favored diplomatic recognition of the Soviet Union, opposed military intervention in Nicaragua, and endorsed independence for the Philippines. Agreeing with other western progressives in opposing U.S. involvement in European affairs, he voted against the World Court in 1935 and for the neutrality laws of 1935–1937.

In 1940 Senator Wheeler became convinced that President Roosevelt was moving the United States toward unnecessary and unwise involvement in the wars raging in Europe and the Far East. Before Pearl Harbor the senator played an increasingly active leadership role in opposing President Roosevelt's aid-short-of-war foreign policies. In his most quoted statement, in 1941 Wheeler charged that the administration's lend-lease proposal was "the New Deal's triple 'A' foreign policy—it will plough under every fourth American boy." Senator Wheeler was also one of the leading speakers in 1941 at the noninterventionist America First Committee rallies all over the country.

After Pearl Harbor Wheeler supported America's war effort and even voted in 1945 for American membership in the United Nations—though he had grave misgivings. His unsuccessful noninterventionist activities before the war, however, had tarnished his reputation and led to his political demise the next time he faced the voters in 1946. Like other so-called "isolationists," Wheeler was accused unjustly of disloyalty and even of pro-Nazi sympathies. The campaign against him in the 1946 primary was particularly vicious, including publication of a book, *The Plot against America*, that was later condemned in a Senate inquiry as "one of the vilest, most contemptible, and obscene pieces of so-called literature ever to be published concerning a man in public office in the United States." By that time, however, the smears had accomplished their goal of putting Wheeler out of office.

After his senate career ended in 1947, Wheeler joined his son, Edward, practicing law in Washington, D.C., and spent summers at his lodge in Glacier National Park in Montana. He died at his home in Washington, D.C. To the very end, Wheeler was proud of his progressive crusades for the common people and of his battle against American intervention in World War II. He never recanted or retracted the views he had advocated so boldly over the course of a very long life.

• The Burton K. Wheeler Papers are in the Montana Historical Society, Helena, Mont., but the collection is thin and uneven in quality. Wheeler's autobiography, Burton K. Wheeler with Paul F. Healy, *Yankee from the West: The Candid Turbulent Life Story of the Yankee-Born Freewheeling U.S. Senator from Montana* (1962), is a lively, frank, and informative volume. Richard T. Ruetten, "Senator Burton K. Wheeler and Insurgency in the 1920s," in *The American West: A Reorientation*, ed. Gene M. Gressley (1966), ably treats Wheeler's role in the context of the western progressives during that conservative decade. An excellent dissertation on Wheeler's views and role in American foreign affairs is John Thomas Anderson, "Senator Burton K. Wheeler and United States Foreign Relations" (Ph.D. diss., Univ. of Virginia, 1982). For a scholarly study that covers Wheeler's relations with President Roosevelt see Wayne S. Cole, *Roosevelt and the Isolationists, 1932–45* (1983).

WAYNE S. COLE

WHEELER, Candace Thurber (24 Mar. 1827–5 Aug. 1923), textile designer and interior decorator, was born in Delhi, New York, the daughter of Abner Thurber, a dairy farmer, and Lucy Dunham. Educated at home and at the Delaware Academy in Delhi, she married Thomas M. Wheeler, a shipowner, on 28 June 1844 and lived in Brooklyn and New York City most of her life.

During the years when she was raising her four children, Wheeler traveled in the artistic circle of the Tenth Street Studio in New York. She received informal instruction in painting from Frederic Church, Sanford Gifford (1823–1880), and Albert Bierstadt at her country home, "Nestledown," near Jamaica, on Long Island. After seeing a display of English women's needlework at the 1876 Philadelphia Centennial Exposition, Wheeler, at the age of fifty, embarked on a career as a textile designer and a promoter of women in the decorative arts. Influenced by the burgeoning women's movement, she hoped to unite her interest in women's reform with her commitment to an artistic life. Thus in 1877 Wheeler established the Society of Decorative Art in New York to improve the artistic quality of American household decoration and to aid women in earning a living. The society was modeled on London's Kensington School, with the same prototype school, workshop, exhibition gallery, and sales outlet. Wheeler formed auxiliary committees to contract with manufacturers and importers, thus combining art, education, and industry under the society's aegis. As correspondence secretary, Wheeler helped organize a network of art societies all over the country, including groups in Chicago, St. Louis, Hartford, Baltimore, Detroit, and Charleston. In 1878 Wheeler resigned from the society and inaugurated the Women's Exchange as another outlet to promote the sale of women's artistic handicraft. Wheeler herself served as an inspiration to other women by winning a first prize for a portiere design in a Society of Decorative Art competition (1879) and a first prize in Warren, Fuller and Company's wallpaper design contest (1881).

Wheeler moved into the commercial sphere as cofounder of a household art journal, the *Art Interchange* (1878). As chairman of the committee on publications, she served as liaison to the publishers, writing articles and contracting known authors to contribute to the magazine. In 1879 Wheeler became a partner in Associated Artists, an interior decorating firm in New York begun by artists Louis C. Tiffany and Samuel Colman and woodcarver Lockwood de Forest. The firm's work included commissions for the Veteran's Room of the Seventh Regiment Armory (1879–1880), the stage curtain for the Madison Square Theater (1879), Mark Twain's Hartford House (1881), the Union League Club (1882), and four rooms in the White House (1882–1883). A suite of eleven tapestries commissioned by Cornelius Vanderbilt II was woven in 1882 after designs prepared by Wheeler's daughter, Dora, who had studied with William Merritt Chase. Candace Wheeler also designed embroidered tapestries for Ellen Terry and Lily Langtry, the English actresses. Her only church venture was ecclesiastical embroideries for the interior of the Church of the Divine Paternity on Fifth Avenue. As an inventor, Wheeler received patents for a new weaving process, called "needle woven tapestry," in England (1882) and in the United States (1883).

By 1883 the original Associated Artists had dissolved, but Wheeler retained the name when she began her own textile manufacturing firm, utilizing her needle woven tapestry and the expertise of a corps of women artisans in a workshop at 115 East 23rd Street in New York. Although running a commercial venture, Wheeler viewed needlework as art and felt that, for her artisans, "using a needle expresses . . . [what] the pencil or brush expresses for the painter" (*Art Amateur*, Feb. 1888, p. 71). She experimented with common material like denim and, following the example of William Morris, used native plants and weeds as design elements in her textile patterns. Many of her tapestries featured American themes—Minnehaha, for example, or heroines from Hawthorne—in an attempt to achieve "a distinct American embroidery type." Wheeler believed that "a colorgift belongs to us as a people" and contended that art as "a natural language to both sexes instead of one . . . [is] certain to show the wider range of feeling . . . in the race as a whole" (*Art Amateur*, Feb. 1888, p. 71). Thus her philosophy for American design was a protest of the gendering of art in society as it elevated aesthetics as a common national virtue. Besides working with her own firm, Wheeler contracted with fabric houses in New Jersey and with Cheney Brothers of Connecticut, a well known silk mill, to produce her designs on a variety of fabrics. In the 1880s Associated Artists expanded, as women artists in the firm designed wallpapers, and, by 1893, decorated entire interiors. Wheeler's main aim was "the conversion of the common and inalienable heritage of feminine skill in the use of the needle into a means of art-expression and pecuniary profit" (*Yesterdays*, pp. 211, 213). The firm remained in business until 1907, giving dozens of women the opportunity to earn a livelihood.

In addition to these endeavors, Wheeler was "adviser" of the Woman's Art School at the Cooper Institute, instructed at the Gotham Art School and at the New York Institute of Artist-Artisans, wrote numerous articles in journals, and was a member of the State Charities Aid Association in New York. Plans for a network of cooperative hotels for professional women never materialized, but Wheeler was elected director of the Bureau of Applied Arts for New York State, mounting the display of the state of New York for the World's Columbian Exposition in 1893. As president of Associated Artists, Wheeler was appointed color director of the Woman's Building at the exposition and designed not only the interior decoration, but also some of the furniture, which was produced by Associated Artists.

Apart from all of her public work, Wheeler planned and built for herself a mountain house, "Pennyroyal" (1883), near Tannersville, New York, in the Catskills. An artistic and literary group, the Onteora Club, which included such notables as Samuel Clemens, Richard Watson Gilder, Mary Mapes Dodge, and John Burroughs, grew up around Pennyroyal. At the age of eighty, Wheeler built "Wintergreen," a home near Thomasville, Georgia, where she lived during the winter months until her death.

Wheeler wrote prolifically until late in her life. These writings included articles on embroidery and design; a series of books on the decorative arts, *Household Decoration*, which she edited in 1893; *Household Art* (1893); *Principles of Home Decoration* (1903); *How to Make Rugs* (1908); *The Development of Embroidery in America* (1921); an autobiography, *Yesterdays in a Busy Life* (1918); and a book promoting corn as a national emblem, *Columbia's Emblem, Indian Corn: A Garland of Tributes in Prose and Verse* (1893). Wheeler also published poetry; a children's book, *Doubledarling and the Dream Spinner* (1905); and a garden book, *Content in a Garden* (1901). In her retirement years in Georgia, she designed art education curriculums for several southern colleges. She died in the Atelier Building in New York City.

Wheeler's public profile as a textile designer, entrepreneur, and author gave her a strong cultural presence. In 1888 one critic claimed that Wheeler's "pictorial needlework" pieces were "works of art . . . unsurpassed if not unequaled in modern times," extolling Wheeler as a "benefactor to her sex . . . while greatly develop[ing] the artistic taste of our country" (Bolton, pp. 181, 179). Wheeler had hoped to establish her own American School of Embroidery allied with America's commercial interests, but, by the turn of the century, her efforts were unsuccessful as decorating tastes shifted to more simple styles. Although relatively unknown today, Wheeler influenced both the decorative arts and women's reform during the last decades of the nineteenth century, achieving celebrity in her time as a successful designer and decorator.

• Source material on Candace Wheeler is in the E. Davis Gaillard Archives at the Onteora Club, Tannersville, N.Y., and at the Mark Twain Memorial Collection in Hartford, Conn. The reports of the Society of Decorative Art are at the New York Public Library. The best holdings of the *Art Interchange* are at Winterthur and the Library of Congress. No full-length study on Wheeler exists, but the best available information on her can be found in *In Pursuit of Beauty: Americans and the Aesthetic Movement* (1986); Madeleine B. Stern, *We the Women: Career Firsts of Nineteenth-Century America* (1974); and Kathleen D. McCarthy, *Women's Culture: American Philanthropy and Art, 1830–1930* (1991). Wheeler is mentioned in Anthea Callen, *Women Artists of the Arts and Crafts Movement, 1870–1914* (1979); Sarah K. Bolton, *Successful Women* (1913); S. R. Koehler, "American Embroideries," *Magazine of Art* 9 (1886): 209–13; Mrs. Burton Harrison, "Some Work of the 'Associated Artists,'" *Harper's New Monthly Magazine* 69 (1884): 344–51; and "The Associated Artists," *Art Amateur* 12 (1885): 38–40.

MARY W. BLANCHARD

WHEELER, Earle Gilmore (13 Jan. 1908–18 Dec. 1975), army officer, was born in Washington, D.C., the son of Clifton F. Wheeler, a dentist, and Ida Gilmore. While still in high school, Wheeler enlisted in the District of Columbia National Guard in 1924, rising to the rank of sergeant before entering the U.S. Military Academy in 1928. He graduated in 1932 and was commissioned a second lieutenant in the infantry. That year he married Frances Rogers Howell; they had one son.

Wheeler, known to his friends as "Bus," was initially assigned to the Twenty-ninth Infantry Regiment at Fort Benning, Georgia. Advanced to first lieutenant, he was a student at the Infantry School at Fort Benning from 1936 to 1937. After graduation, he served with the Fifteenth Infantry Regiment at Tientsin, China; Fort Lewis, Washington; and Fort Ord, California. In the academic year 1940–1941 Wheeler, recently promoted to captain, was a mathematics instructor at West Point, and during the summer and fall of 1941 he was an aide to the commander of the Thirty-sixth Division at Fort Sam Houston and Camp Bowie, Texas.

After the United States entered World War II in December 1941, Wheeler completed the accelerated course at the Command and General Staff School (later College) at Fort Leavenworth, Kansas, and served successively as a battalion commander in the 141st Infantry Regiment at Camp Blanding, Florida, operations officer of the Ninety-ninth Division at Camp Van Dorn, Mississippi, and beginning in May 1943, chief of staff of the newly activated Sixty-third Division at Camp Van Dorn. During the next year and a half Wheeler, with the rank of colonel, oversaw the division's training program, and in the final months of the war in 1945 he helped direct its operations in its drive across Germany to the Danube River.

Between 1945 and 1962 Wheeler rose to the rank of full general while holding a variety of assignments. These included tours as an instructor at the Field Artillery School at Fort Sill, Oklahoma; supply officer of the Western Base Section headquartered at Paris, France; staff officer with the U.S. Constabulary in Germany; student at the National War College; intelligence officer with the Joint Chiefs of Staff (JCS); deputy commander of the 351st Infantry Regiment at Trieste, Italy; readiness officer and later the assistant chief of staff for plans and operations of the Allied Forces Southern Europe; director of plans in the Office of the Deputy Chief of Staff for Military Operations; assistant deputy chief of staff for military operations; commander of the Second Armored Division and then the III Corps at Fort Hood, Texas; director of the Joint Staff of the Department of Defense; and deputy commander in chief of the U.S. European Command. In these assignments Wheeler impressed his superiors as a highly urbane, intelligent, and articulate officer who possessed outstanding administrative skills and understood the workings of the Washington bureaucracy. In October 1962 President John F. Kennedy appointed him army chief of staff.

As chief of staff, Wheeler worked to expand and modernize the army and established a good working relationship with Secretary of Defense Robert McNamara. In contrast to some of the service chiefs, who openly fought McNamara in a blustery manner over his attempts to impose civilian control over the services, Wheeler had a modest, low-key style that appealed to McNamara and Presidents Kennedy and Lyndon B. Johnson. Conscious of the politics of executive-legislative relations, Wheeler early showed his willingness to defer to civilian authority; he endorsed the controversial Nuclear Test Ban Treaty in 1963 even though it was opposed by many military men. Regarding Wheeler as a loyal "team player," Johnson in July 1964 appointed him chairman of the JCS, a job he held for six years.

In his new post Wheeler's primary concern was the Communist effort to take over South Vietnam. Like most of his colleagues in the Pentagon, he believed that a swift application of military power would stop the flow of men and supplies from North Vietnam into South Vietnam and force North Vietnam's leaders to cease their aggression against South Vietnam. During the first half of 1965, as Johnson escalated America's involvement in the war, Wheeler urged Johnson to declare a national emergency, mobilize the reserves, and go all out to win quickly through massive bombing of North Vietnam, the rapid buildup of American ground forces in South Vietnam, and offensive operations to destroy enemy main force units in South Vietnam and, if necessary, in neighboring Laos, Cambodia, and the panhandle of North Vietnam.

Johnson did not follow many of Wheeler's recommendations. He was concerned about possible Chinese intervention in the war and that the full-scale war envisioned by the JCS would create political problems at home, especially with the implementation of his Great Society social programs. Hence he relied primarily on his civilian advisers in the decision-making process and adopted a gradualist approach based on a limited bombing campaign against North Vietnam and a limited deployment of troops to South Vietnam for operations within South Vietnam. Furthermore, Johnson refused to mobilize the reserves, making it more difficult to fight the war while concurrently meeting America's global commitments. Johnson's decisions, particularly in regard to the air war and the reserves, dismayed the military, which harbored bitter memories of the frustrations of the Korean War with its limited objectives and restrictions on the use of force. But Wheeler, sensitive to the controversy aroused by General Douglas MacArthur's challenge to President Harry S. Truman's strategy for the Korean War, did not relish a confrontation with his civilian superiors and acquiesced without a protest or even forcefully indicating the military's fear that Johnson's approach would fail. Apparently, he thought that once Johnson was committed to the war, the military could chip away at his restrictions and get the strategic freedom it wanted.

Over the next two years Wheeler publicly supported Johnson's war policies and expressed optimism about the war's outcome. Privately, however, he complained about Johnson's gradualist approach and Johnson's failure to include him regularly in the Tuesday Lunches, where many of the most important military decisions were made by Johnson and his civilian advisers. Rather than formulate a military strategy in Vietnam that accommodated Johnson's restrictions, Wheeler and the JCS continued to urge Johnson to approve the stronger measures he had earlier rejected. Gradually, as the fighting intensified, Johnson lifted many of the bombing restrictions and sent more troops to South Vietnam. But continuing to rely primarily on his civilian advisers in the making of strategy, he still placed limits on the use of force.

By 1967 growing differences between the JCS and the Johnson administration over the war's conduct were severely straining civil-military relations. In August 1967 Wheeler, increasingly frustrated by his inability to get Johnson to change his strategy, briefly considered leading a revolt by the JCS against Johnson's war policies through a resignation en masse. Wheeler's nonconfrontational style kept him from such a direct challenge to civilian authority, however, and publicly he dismissed reports that the military and the Johnson administration were at odds over the war.

When the Communists launched the Tet offensive at the end of January 1968, Wheeler saw an opportunity to get Johnson to mobilize the reserves to reconstitute the strategic reserve, which had been severely depleted by Vietnam, and to lift all of the restrictions on American operations in Vietnam. At Wheeler's prodding, General William Westmoreland, the American commander in Vietnam, requested 206,000 additional troops, a step that would require the mobilization of the reserves. Westmoreland wanted to use the additional troops to take the initiative against the Communists through a move into Laos and the demilitarized zone between North and South Vietnam. But Wheeler, aware of Johnson's aversion to expanding the war, told Johnson that the troops were necessary to prevent a "tactical" reverse in Vietnam, believing that this prospect would finally force Johnson to give the military control of the nation's war policies. The request sparked a fierce debate over the future course of the American war effort, and in a rebuke to the military, Johnson at the end of March 1968 rejected any reserve call-up or expansion of operations. Johnson further decided to call a partial halt to the bombing and seek an end to the war through negotiations.

The failure of his gambit left Wheeler dispirited and somewhat embittered because he was convinced that the military would be blamed for the inevitable failure of the nation's civilian-directed strategy. When Richard Nixon became president in January 1969, Wheeler asked to retire, a request Nixon rejected with the promise that he would listen more seriously to the military than did Johnson. At Wheeler's suggestion, Nixon ordered the bombing of Communist santuaries in Cambodia. But Nixon was also committed to American troop withdrawals and a gradual winding down of American ground operations, a policy Wheeler came to endorse out of fear that the American army was beginning to disintegrate under the strain of Vietnam. By the end of 1969 Wheeler, whose health had been suffering for several years, was sharing many of his responsibilities with Admiral Thomas Moorer, chief of naval operations, and in July 1970 Wheeler retired. He died in Frederick, Maryland.

Wheeler represented a new type of JCS chairman. Unlike his predecessors, he was a politician of sorts who climbed the ladder largely through staff assignments rather than combat commands, demonstrating planning and administrative skills, an understanding of the complexity of national security problems in the nuclear age, and acceptance of civilian authority. Opposed to Johnson's war policies, he sought to change them; however, when he failed he refused to engage in public recriminations. In this respect, Wheeler reaffirmed the principle of military loyalty to civilian control. At the same time, his reluctance to confront Johnson vigorously with the military's conviction that the United States should go all out to win in Vietnam ensured the implementation of a strategy that ultimately proved both militarily and politically bankrupt.

• The National Archives has a collection of Wheeler's professional papers. Oral histories by Wheeler are in the John F. Kennedy Presidential Library, Boston, Mass., and the Lyndon B. Johnson Presidential Library, Austin, Tex. Wheeler's military career is summarized in Keeneth J. Zitzman, "Earle Gilmore Wheeler USMA 1932," in the West Point alumni magazine *Assembly*, Dec. 1976, pp. 8–9, 41–43. For Wheeler's chairmanship of the JCS see Robert Buzzanco, *Masters of War: Military Dissent and Politics in the Vietnam Era* (1996); George C. Herring, *LBJ and Vietnam: A Different Kind of War* (1994); H. R. McMaster, *Dereliction of Duty: Lyndon Johnson, Robert McNamara, the Joint Chiefs of Staff, and the Lies That Led to Vietnam* (1997); and Mark Perry, *Four Stars* (1989). An obituary is in the *New York Times*, 19 Dec. 1975.

JOHN KENNEDY OHL

WHEELER, Everett Pepperrell (10 Mar. 1840–8 Feb. 1925), legal and civil service reformer, was born in New York City, the son of David Everett Wheeler, a lawyer, and Elizabeth Jarvis. He attended the Free Academy, from which he graduated with honors in 1856, the youngest student in his class. This "People's College," which became the City College of the City University of New York, aimed to shape the character of its students and to train them for occupations in the workaday world. Throughout his life Wheeler remained attached to his alma mater and active on its committees. In April 1857 he became a law student in his father's office, and when he left shortly thereafter for Harvard Law School, he was "full of ambition and determined to become an advocate" (Wheeler, "Chapters," p. 21).

After securing his law degree in 1859, Wheeler returned to New York, where he worked in his father's law office and was admitted to the bar in 1861. He did not serve in the Civil War and in 1866 married Lydia Lorraine Hodges, with whom he had three children. She died in 1902, and in 1904 he married Alice Gilman. They had no children.

Combining "common sense, practical education and legal acumen," Wheeler "won and maintained" a "leading place at the Bar" (Bowker, p. 8). In 1869 he was asked by older colleagues to help form the first bar association in the country, which secured its charter in 1871. In February 1870 Wheeler joined a new law firm—Vose and McDaniel, which became McDaniel, Wheeler and Souther—where he specialized in patent and admiralty law and numbered among his clients the White Star steamship line and the Atlantic and Pacific Telegraph Company. Thanks to his practical and scientific training, Wheeler was extremely effective in the courtroom. He drew clear diagrams to help juries understand shipwrecks and used physics to explain a ship's motion and direction.

As Wheeler's practice increased, his interest in law reform grew. Throughout his career, primarily through bar association committees on the city, state, and national level, he helped develop the theory and practice of law and worked to maintain its ethical standards. He lectured in at least four law schools, published a number of books, and wrote numerous articles on law, history, economics, and politics. He was a member of the council of the American Bar Association from 1896 to 1905 and chaired its Committee on International Law, of which former President Benjamin Harrison was a member, as well as its Special Committee on Law Reform. He worked to simplify procedures and proposed laws to prevent delays and unnecessary costs. He also chaired the Committee on International Arbitration of the New York State Bar Association and was instrumental in making that bar association, in 1915 and 1916, one of the first organizations to propose an international court and police force.

A lifelong Democrat who never held elected office, Wheeler was a member of the Elevated Railroad Commission in 1875 and of the New York City Board of Education from 1877 to 1879. In February 1878 he was an incorporator of the Free Trade Club, and he was its president from 1883 to 1888. The club campaigned to lower the tariff for which it blamed bouts of overproduction, followed by the closing of factories, reduced wages, and strikes. To quiet protectionist attacks and to attract members interested in other political issues, the club reorganized in 1888 as the Reform Club "to promote honest, efficient, and economical government" (Wheeler, *Sixty Years*, p. 183).

Wheeler, who chaired the new club's Committee on Tariff Reform, represented it at a debate in Boston's Tremont Temple. The Reform Club published his speech, and he participated in several further debates during the presidential campaign. Although his hero Grover Cleveland, running on a low tariff plank, lost to the protectionist Republican Benjamin Harrison, Wheeler believed "that the persistent teaching of the truth . . . will . . . in the end bear abundant harvest" (*Sixty Years*, p. 222). In 1889 and 1890 the club polled 659,100 New York State voters and ascertained their party politics, occupation, opinion on the tariff, and veteran status. Meanwhile, the Reform Club published a semimonthly periodical called *Tariff Reform* and remained the national center for literature on that subject and on the gold standard. "Never was there . . . more successful political propaganda than that of the Reform Club," Wheeler later recalled (*Sixty Years*, p. 254).

Wheeler was active in the movement to make government service less corrupt, more efficient, and nonpartisan by adopting the merit system. When the first Civil Service Reform Association, which was formed in New York City in 1877, was reactivated three years later, Wheeler became the chair of its Executive Committee, a position he held until 1897. He served as its vice president (1903–1913, 1918–1925) and as its president (1913–1918). He was also on the association's legislative committee, which shaped the bill that in 1883 passed in Congress as the Pendleton Act.

The same year the federal law passed, Wheeler and reformer Edward M. Shepard—like him a Democrat and a graduate of City College—applied its principles to what Wheeler called "the first Civil Service Reform bill adopted by any State in the Union" (*Sixty Years*, p. 282). In 1884 he prepared reform rules governing city workers, and he implemented these rules as chair of the city Civil Service Commission, a position he held from 1883 to 1889 and from 1895 to 1898. Wheeler was also a council member of the National Civil Service Reform League from 1898 until his death. A firm believer in meritocracy, he was pleased that civil service reform associations had "done much to make democracy efficient" (*Sixty Years*, p. 313).

In 1891, two years after visiting Toynbee Hall, an early settlement house in London, Wheeler opened East Side House. With an average of 1,500 participants coming daily for programs and classes, it was one of the city's largest and most useful social settlements. From its founding until his death, Wheeler was either its headworker or its president. Encouraged by neighborhood involvement, the city established John Jay Park, a public bath, and a public library in the area. Paralleling and reinforcing his settlement work, Wheeler helped form a Christian Social Union "to bring educated men . . . into closer relations with the plain people" (*Sixty Years*, p. 474). His reform proclivities were heightened by his deeply religious convictions. He was an Episcopalian vestryman, active in his church's clubs and conventions.

In 1894 Wheeler ran unsuccessfully for governor as a Reform Democrat. That same year citizens—revolted by police corruption—held a mass meeting in Madison Square Garden. Determined to make a difference, they appointed a Committee of Seventy to oversee the cleanup of city politics. From his position on the Executive Committee of the Committee of Seventy, Wheeler was influential in the successful campaign of reform Republican mayoral candidate William L. Strong in 1894. The committee implemented reforms in the management of public schools, securing badly needed buildings and new, well-equipped high schools, and successfully agitated for improved piers and new water mains. But the state legislature blocked the committee's attempt to abolish the corrupt police board.

To involve more people in municipal reform, Wheeler and other concerned citizens in 1897 formed a Citizens' Union, whose Law Committee he chaired. The union aimed to secure a reform mayor for the enlarged city and collected 127,903 signatures favoring Seth Low. Although Low lost in a divided field, the Citizen's Union became "the moving spirit" of his victory in 1901. Although he worked to reform government, Wheeler challenged the right of women to participate in electoral politics. He worked tirelessly to prevent women from gaining the vote. From 1912 to 1918 he was president of the Association Opposed to Woman Suffrage, and in the eyes of the suffragists he was "the evil genius of the opposition" (Flexner, p. 301).

The "evil genius" was to many a good-tempered, resilient, persistent laborer for reform. Refusing to be intimidated or discouraged, Wheeler remained more actively involved in more reform organizations for longer periods than any other American of his generation. He died in New York City.

• Wheeler's extensive papers, including correspondence, legal papers, articles, and speeches, are at the New York Public Library. For his own writings on his life, see "Chapters from the Life of a Lawyer," "Autobiographical Chapter: Early Professional Life," *City College Alumnus* 13 (1917): 6–21 and 16 (1920): 10–22; *Sixty Years of American Life: Taylor to Roosevelt, 1850–1910* (1917); and *Reminiscences of a Lawyer: A Few Pages from the Record of a Busy Life* (1927). Among other books by Wheeler are *Modern Law of Carriers* (1890), *Real Bimetallism* (1895), *Daniel Webster: The Expounder of the Constitution* (1905), and *A Lawyer's Study of the Bible* (1919). For a short biography, see R. R. Bowker, "Everett Pepperrell Wheeler—'56," *City College Alumnus* 12 (1916): 5–12. For his hostility to woman suffrage, see Eleanor Flexner, *Century of Struggle: The Woman's Rights Movement in the United States* (1959). An obituary is in the *New York Times*, 10 Feb. 1925.

OLIVE HOOGENBOOM

WHEELER, George Montague (9 Oct. 1842–3 May 1905), army geographer, was born in Hopkinton, Massachusetts, the son of John Wheeler and Miriam P. Daniels. Two of his brothers moved to Colorado, and although George remained in Massachusetts, he was appointed to the U.S. Military Academy as the first cadet from Colorado. He graduated sixth in the class of 1866 and accepted a commission in the Corps of Engineers.

Wheeler served from 1866 to 1871 in California, working on coastal surveys and defenses. In 1869 General Edward O. C. Ord sent Wheeler on a reconnaissance throughout eastern Nevada. Wheeler reached the junction of the Virgin and Colorado rivers a month after John Wesley Powell's boats. Wheeler hired civilian topographers for another survey under Ord in 1870 but had to postpone the survey when funds were reallocated. With support from the military and business communities in California, Wheeler proposed to General Andrew A. Humphreys, chief of engineers, an 1871 survey of California, Nevada, and Arizona. This became the first survey after the Civil War in the tradition of the former Corps of Topographical Engineers (which had merged with the Corps of Engineers during the Civil War), with military leadership and civilian scientists and topographers. Wheeler explored Death Valley in midsummer and during the fall attempted to take boats up the Colorado River into the Grand Canyon. A capsized boat cost the expedition many records and specimens. They labored thirty-nine days to get upstream and floated back downstream in five days.

Following the 1871 survey, Wheeler developed a comprehensive plan to map west of the 100th meridian, "the main object of this exploration to obtain correct topographical knowledge of the country traversed." Officially designated the U.S. Geographical Surveys West of the 100th Meridian, the "Wheeler Survey" became one of four great federal surveys after the Civil War. While Clarence King was just completing his 1867–1872 fieldwork for the chief of engineers, Interior Department surveys under Ferdinand V. Hayden and Powell remained active. The other surveys had no military presence, but army officers commanded Wheeler's parties and performed much of the astronomy required for detailed surveying. Civilian topographers performed most mapping for Wheeler, and civilian scientists did pioneering studies in geology, botany, paleontology, and archaeology. Topographic emphasis also differentiated Wheeler from the other surveys' concentration on geology.

Wheeler's service in San Francisco introduced him to business leaders and the California congressional delegation, preparing him for the delicate annual task of guiding appropriations through Congress. During winters in Washington, D.C., Wheeler met Lucy Blair, a niece raised by Francis Preston Blair of the influential Blair family. Married in 1874, she strengthened the young lieutenant's access to capital society. They had no children.

Duplication of mapping in Colorado by the Hayden and Wheeler parties led to congressional hearings in 1874, where civilian geologists attacked Wheeler's mapping. Perhaps because President Ulysses S. Grant recommended consolidation under the army, Congress only called on all parties to exercise good judgment. The hearings, however, accelerated a change in focus for Wheeler's mapping. The 1869 and 1871 surveys were rapid reconnaissances covering vast regions; in early 1872 Wheeler filed mining claims in northwestern Arizona staked during this survey work. The 1872 and 1873 seasons marked a transition to the final phase (1874–1879), during which Wheeler's topographic mapping moved to a level of precision comparable with other contemporary surveys.

Renewed competition, fueled by desires of an expanding civilian scientific community to control government science, led Congress in 1878 to ask the National Academy of Sciences to consider government surveys. Accepting a report from a committee chaired by Professor Othniel C. Marsh of Yale, the academy recommended to Congress that federal surveys be consolidated, and in March 1879 Clarence King became director of the new U.S. Geological Survey.

Wheeler worked until 1889 completing office work for his survey, preparing a final report for publication, and attending the Third International Geographic Congress in Venice in 1881. He spent significant time on medical leave, and when he became the senior captain in the Corps of Engineers, he was medically retired in June 1888 rather than being promoted. Special legislation promoted him retroactively to major on the retired rolls.

The Wheeler Survey covered 359,065 square miles, one-third of the mountainous West, and published maps of 326,891 square miles at a cost of $618,644.05. He argued for complete topographic coverage with emphasis on "map delineations of all natural objects, means of communication, artificial and economic features, the geologic and natural history branches being treated as adjunctive" and promised complete coverage of the West by the late 1880s at scales of four and eight miles to the inch. The new U.S. Geological Survey did not resume a coordinated topographic mapping program, and complete national coverage at scales comparable to that undertaken by Wheeler was not achieved until the 1950s, ironically by the Army Map Service.

Wheeler was author or editor of 15 annual reports, 8 final reports, 16 miscellaneous publications, 50 topographic atlas sheets, 33 land classification sheets, 11 geologic sheets, and a total of 164 maps, published from 1872 to 1889. The most lasting contribution of the survey was probably the reconnaissance geology of Grove Karl Gilbert, who named the Basin and Range Province and recognized it as fundamentally different from the folded Appalachians. Timothy O'Sullivan created some of the finest photographs of the West for Wheeler.

Following his retirement, Wheeler was a private engineer and consultant in Washington and New York. His wife died in 1902, and his last years were marked by illness, lawsuits, and eviction for nonpayment of rent. He died alone in New York City.

Wheeler was the last army explorer of the American West, attempting to continue the work and traditions of the former Corps of Topographical Engineers. He viewed the goal of mapping to "furnish all the practical topographical information required by the Government and people in these thinly settled areas. With the necessary revisions, as slowly-increasing settlement shall demand, it becomes of permanent value." But the frontier was fading and with it the need for exploration; working scientists no longer needed army escorts, and the rising scientific class chafed under the leadership of junior military officers. Wheeler was left lamenting the shift in government mapping from providing practical final products to providing a base for scientific studies.

• The breakup of the papers of the Wheeler Survey is discussed by C. E. Dewing in "The Wheeler Survey Records: A Study in Archival Anomaly," *American Archivist* 27 (1964): 219–27. The largest remaining holdings are in RG 77 of the National Archives, with additional material in RG 57 (Grove Karl Gilbert's notebooks for 1871, with the best description of life during fieldwork), RG 92, Box 1230 (quartermaster general correspondence), and the Map Division, which has many draft and compilation maps. Yale University has a small collection of Wheeler Survey material, which includes a number of the most interesting materials, including many of the letterpress books that record the survey's official correspondence. The University of New Mexico and the University of Colorado have collections of notebooks, mostly data compilations of marginal interest. The Bancroft Library at the University of California at Berkeley contains a scrapbook that appears to be Wheeler's. Recent assessments of Wheeler's role in mapping the West during the 1870s and the creation of the U.S. Geological Survey include Richard A. Bartlett, *Great Surveys of the American West* (1962), William H. Goetzmann, *Exploration and Empire* (1966), and Mary C. Rabbitt, *Minerals, Lands, and Geology for the Common Defence and General Welfare*, vol. 1, *Before 1879* (1979). D. O.

Dawdy, *George Montague Wheeler: The Man and the Myth* (1993), presents some interesting records of mining activity by Wheeler. Obituaries are in the *New York Times*, 5 May 1905, and the *Army and Navy Journal*, 6 May 1905.

PETER L. GUTH

WHEELER, Hugh Callingham (19 Mar. 1912–26 July 1987), playwright, screenwriter, and mystery novelist, was born in Northwood, Middlesex, England, the son of Harold Wheeler, a civil servant, and Florence Scammell. His early education began at the Clayesmore School in Salisbury. Following his graduation from secondary school, he was admitted to the B.A. degree program in English literature at London University, from which he graduated in 1933. After completing his education, Wheeler immigrated to the United States in 1934, taking up residence in New York City. Two years later he entered the literary world with the publication of the first of a series of mystery novels, many co-written with Richard Wilson Webb.

Wheeler became a naturalized American citizen in 1942. With the onslaught of World War II, he enlisted in the U.S. Army and served as an army medic in the European theater, but his military career was short lived because of a minor eye ailment. He received an honorable medical discharge and returned to New York City.

From 1936 to 1965 Wheeler focused his literary career on writing thirty-six mystery novels. Nine were co-written with Webb under the pseudonym Q Patrick; nine were co-written with Webb under the pseudonym Jonathan Stagge; and seventeen Wheeler wrote alone under the pseudonym Patrick Quentin. In 1951 he published his only novel written under his own name, *The Crippled Muse*. In addition to writing novels he was also a major contributor of short stories and novelettes to popular mystery magazines under all three pseudonyms. Wheeler was a two-time winner of the Edgar Allan Poe Award from the Mystery Writers of America in 1963 and 1973.

But it is as a playwright for the musical theater, opera, and dramatic stage that Wheeler carved his career niche. Beginning in 1961 with a dramatic production at the Hudson Theatre, Wheeler's first stage play was *Look, We've Come Through!* It was largely dismissed by the New York theater critics. Undaunted, Wheeler followed up with the more successful (but, ultimately, financially disastrous) *Big Fish, Little Fish*, this time working for the American National Theatre Academy and presenting the play at the ANTA Playhouse in New York City later in 1961. Marilyn Stasio includes the text of the play in her anthology, *Broadway's Beautiful Losers* (1972).

Slightly "burned" by the reaction of the New York theater critics to his first two stage attempts, Wheeler took his third drama to the Walnut Street Theatre in Philadelphia. In 1964 his adaptation of a play by Hispanic playwrights Miguel Mihura and Alvaro de Laiglesia called *The Case of the Slightly Assassinated Wife* became *Rich Little Girl*. Directed by Noel Willman, the cast starred Jean Simmons, Larry Blyden, and Elizabeth Wilson. For Wheeler's last attempt at a stage drama he adapted a novel, Shirley Jackson's *We Have Always Lived in the Castle*. Presented at the Ethel Barrymore Theatre in 1966, the play was dismissed by the New York theater critics.

During the 1960s Wheeler came to the attention of composer Harold Arlen and lyricist Martin Charnin. They were attempting to develop a musical called *Softly* and needed a librettist. Wheeler signed on as librettist, but the musical lost its financial backers and was never produced. Wheeler would have to wait almost an entire decade before his career as a musical theater librettist would be recognized by the New York critics and the world at large. Producer/director Harold Prince and composer/lyricist Stephen Sondheim had acquired permission from film director Ingmar Bergman to adapt one of his romantic screenplays, *Smiles of a Summer Night*, into a stage musical. Wheeler was asked by Prince to adapt the screenplay, and the result was the highly successful *A Little Night Music* in 1973. Directed by Prince, the musical opened at New York's Shubert Theatre and won Wheeler the first of his three Antoinette Perry ("Tony") Awards for best musical. The production starred Glynis Johns, Len Cariou, and Patricia Elliot. Wheeler also adapted the musical for the 1977 film starring Elizabeth Taylor, Len Cariou, and Diana Rigg, also directed by Prince.

For Wheeler 1973 was a banner year in which he contributed the librettos for three popular musicals. Following on the heels of *A Little Night Music*, Wheeler was approached by director Gower Champion, who was attempting to bring the 1930s London musical *Irene* to the Broadway stage as a vehicle for screen actress Debbie Reynolds. With music by Harry Tierney and lyrics by Joseph McCarthy, Wheeler became coadapter with librettist Joseph (*Fiddler on the Roof*) Stein. Opening at the new Minskoff Theatre, *Irene* became an overnight success.

At the same time he was coadapting *Irene*, Prince asked Wheeler to rework the Lillian Hellman libretto for the 1954 Leonard Bernstein musical *Candide*, which Prince was mounting at the Brooklyn Academy of Music. With additional lyrics by Sondheim, Wheeler's new libretto was hailed by the critics as an improvement over the original, and the musical was soon transferred to the Broadway Theatre in Manhattan.

In November 1974 Wheeler was asked by Prince, who was directing a musical adaptation of the William Congreve play *Love for Love*, to contribute the book and lyrics. With music by Paul Gemingnani, the "play-with-music" had an unsuccessful run of only twenty-four performances at the Helen Hayes Theatre, opening on 11 November 1974. The cast included Glenn Close, John McMartin, Mary Beth Hurt, David Dukes, Charles Kimbrough, and Charlotte Moore.

September 1975 found Wheeler writing the libretto for an original musical with music by Louis St. Louis and lyrics by Wes Harris. Called *Truckload*, it opened (for previews only) at the Lyceum Theatre and was directed and choreographed by Patricia Birch, *A Little*

Night Music's choreographer. Shortly after the quick demise of *Truckload*, both Birch and Wheeler were asked by Prince to join his production team for an original Sondheim Japanese "kabuki" musical titled *Pacific Overtures*. Focusing on the Westernization of Japan, Wheeler joined librettist John Weidman in creating a panoramic documentary of feudal Japan's invasion by Western civilization. The musical opened at the Winter Garden Theatre in New York and received a mixed reception by the critics. Although it won the Drama Critics Circle Award for best musical of 1976, the production was a financial failure.

Three years passed before Wheeler wrote what most critics agree is his "musical theatre masterpiece." Sondheim had approached Prince with the idea of adapting Christopher Bond's melodrama *Sweeney Todd* for a stage musical, and Prince offered the project to Wheeler. Opening in March 1979 at the Uris (now Gershwin) Theatre in New York, *Sweeney Todd, the Demon Barber of Fleet Street* starred Len Cariou in the title role and Angela Lansbury as Mrs. Lovett. Both actors won Tony Awards for their performances, and the production garnered a total of eight Tony Awards, including best musical of 1979. In addition to the Tonys, the musical also won the Drama Critics Circle Award, the Drama Desk Award, and the Outer Critics Circle Award for best musical.

Shortly after completing his work on *Sweeney Todd*, Prince was contracted to direct a new production at the New York City Opera. *Silverlake*, adapted from Georg Kaiser's *Der Silbersee* (The silver lake), with music by Kurt Weill and lyrics by Lys Symonette, opened as part of the New York City Opera's 1980 repertory season at the New York State Theatre in Lincoln Center and starred Joel Grey. *Silverlake* is one of two opera librettos adapted by Wheeler; the other is a modern interpretation of *The Student Prince*.

In 1981 Wheeler was asked by film composer John Barry to contribute the libretto for a stage adaptation he and lyricist Don Black were planning of the Saint-Exupéry novel *The Little Prince*. The musical, *The Little Prince and the Aviator*, opened at the Alvin (now Neil Simon) Theatre in 1982 and closed after five performances.

Wheeler never saw his final musical libretto onstage, as he succumbed to "lung and heart failure" at the Berkshire Medical Center in Pittsfield, Massachusetts, following his hospitalization for pneumonia. But in November 1989 director Louis Burke brought the film adaptation of the Judy Garland classic *Meet Me in St. Louis* to the Gershwin Theatre stage. With music and lyrics by Hugh Martin and Ralph Blane, Wheeler had provided an updated libretto to showcase the film's well-known classic songs and additional songs and scenes written especially for the stage version.

Wheeler also had a fairly successful career as a screenplay writer in Hollywood. His first film screenplay, co-written with Peter Viertel, was *Five Miles to Midnight* (1963), directed by Anatole Litvak and starring Sophia Loren, Anthony Perkins, and Gig Young. Another screenplay, which Prince invited Wheeler to write for the film adaptation of the novel *The Cook*, by Harry Kressing, was titled *Something for Everyone*. It was directed by Prince for National General Films in 1970 and starred Angela Lansbury and Michael York.

Of the six screenplays for which Wheeler contributed the books, the best known is *Cabaret* (1972), directed by Bob Fosse and starring Liza Minnelli, Joel Grey, and Michael York. Co-written with Jay Presson Allen, Wheeler was responsible for the shooting script of the movie based on the Christopher Isherwood novel *Goodbye to Berlin*.

That same year, 1972, again working with co-writer Jay Presson Allen, Wheeler adapted the screenplay of Graham Greene's novel *Travels with My Aunt*, directed by George Cukor and starring Maggie Smith, Alec McCowen, Lou Gossett, and Cindy Williams. His final screenplay was *Nijinksky* in 1980, directed by Herbert Ross and starring Alan Bates, George de La Pena in the title role, Leslie Browne, and Jeremy Irons. Wheeler's only foray into the field of television was the teleplay for the 1972–1974 NBC series "The Snoop Sister," which starred Helen Hayes and Mildred Natwick as amateur spinster detectives.

Wheeler, who never married, lived for many years in Monterey, Massachusetts (where he later died), and in New York City at the Manhattan Plaza Apartments. Director Harold Prince best described Wheeler's contribution to the American musical theater and his place in its historical development: "Hugh was the best book writer I ever worked with. He had a terrifically sharp mind about the structure of how to write musical scripts. As a first-rate playwright, he was very quick and very even-tempered, both artistically and professionally, who did not begrudge the incursions of the musical form. . . . Hugh had a will of iron and a very acerbic sense of humor. He did not suffer fools gladly. . . . I miss him terribly."

• Wheeler's papers, including his notes, scripts, manuscripts, and unfinished librettos, are in a special collection at Boston University. James Vinson, ed., *Contemporary Dramatists* (1982), contains a useful review of *Big Fish, Little Fish*. Lesley Henderson, *Twentieth-Century Crime and Mystery Writers* (1991), includes a complete bibliography of Wheeler's written work. Obituaries are in the *New York Times*, 28 July 1987, and *Variety*, 29 July 1987.

EUGENE R. HUBER

WHEELER, John Hill (2 Aug. 1806–7 Dec. 1882), government official and writer, was born in Murfreesboro, North Carolina, the son of John Wheeler, a merchant and shipper, and Elizabeth Jordan. Wheeler graduated with distinction from Columbian College (later George Washington University) in 1826 and studied law at the University of North Carolina, where he received an M.A. in 1828, and with North Carolina's Chief Justice John Louis Taylor. He was admitted to the bar in 1828. Wheeler served in the North Carolina General Assembly from 1827 until 1830 and ran unsuccessfully for the U.S. House in 1830. In 1831 Wheeler raised a volunteer company from Hertford county that participated in the suppression of the Nat Turner rebellion. The following year he was appointed clerk of the Board of Commissioners to adjudicate the French spoilation claims. In 1837 he became the first superintendent of the U.S. branch mint at Charlotte, which had minted all U.S. gold coins until 1828 and much of it thereafter, but he lost the post in the Whig victory of 1840. Wheeler was elected North Carolina state treasurer in 1842 but was defeated in his bid for reelection. He later served in the North Carolina House of Commons from 1852 to 1854. Wheeler married Mary Elizabeth Brown in 1830; they had three children. She died in 1836, and in 1838 he married Ellen Oldmixon Sully, with whom he had two children.

The compiler of *Indexes to Documents Relating to North Carolina* (1843), Wheeler also wrote *Historical Sketches of North Carolina from 1584 to 1851* (1851), which reportedly sold 10,000 copies, and edited *The Narrative of Colonel David Fanning* (1861). He was a plantation owner, staunch advocate of slavery, and firm believer in America's manifest destiny to annex parts of Central America and the Caribbean. He was appointed U.S. minister to Nicaragua in August 1854. Wheeler angered many Nicaraguans when he hastily recognized the puppet government that North American filibuster William Walker (1824–1860) established under Patricio Rivas in 1855. Wheeler used his mission to support Walker's filibustering when he extended recognition without instructions from his government. Moreover, his class and racial views produced considerable tension between the Central American leaders and the U.S. government, and he was recalled in October 1856. Although Secretary of State William Marcy repeatedly requested his resignation, Wheeler used delaying tactics and excuses to postpone his resignation until March 1857, just prior to the end of the President Franklin Pierce administration. He worked in the statistical bureau in Washington until the start of the Civil War, when he returned to North Carolina but played no role in the conflict.

In 1863 Wheeler departed for Europe, where he intended to update and revise his *Historical Sketches of North Carolina*, but a subsequent volume or second edition was never published. He also wrote—but never published—a book-length manuscript with the title "Nicaragua, the Centre of Central America: Its Past History, Present Position, and Future Prospects" (Manuscripts Division, Library of Congress). Returning to Washington at the end of the war, he resumed his work in the statistical bureau and as a journalist and historian. In 1874 he published *The Legislative Manual and Political Register of the State of North Carolina*. He died in Washington, D.C.

Wheeler demonstrated the public dimension of U.S. expansionism, which has not been adequately recognized by historians who prefer to emphasize private filibusters like William Walker.

• Wheeler's papers are in the Manuscript Division of the Library of Congress and the University of North Carolina Library. His *Reminiscences and Memoirs of North Carolina and Eminent North Carolinians* (1884) also discusses his life. Various sketches of Wheeler's personal and public life include "John Hill Wheeler," in *Biographical History of North Carolina: From Colonial Times to the Present*, ed. Samuel A. Ashe and others (8 vols., 1905–1917), vol. 7, pp. 472–74; Benjamin B. Winborne, *The Colonial and State Political History of Hertford County, North Carolina* (1906); and Hugh Talmage Lefler and Albert Ray Newsome, *North Carolina: The History of a Southern State* (1963). Randall O. Hudson, "The Filibuster Minister: The Career of John Hill Wheeler as United States Minister to Nicaragua, 1854–1856," *North Carolina Historical Review* 49 (1972): 278–97, and Robert E. May, *The Southern Dream of a Caribbean Empire, 1854–1861* (1989), describe his activity in Nicaragua.

THOMAS SCHOONOVER

WHEELER, Joseph (10 Sept. 1836–25 Jan. 1906), army officer, was born in Augusta, Georgia, the son of Joseph Wheeler, a banker and businessman, and Julia Knox Hull, a daughter of General William Hull. Following his mother's death, Wheeler was sent north to live with relatives in Connecticut and attended the Cheshire Academy. In 1854 he won appointment to the U.S. Military Academy, West Point. A mediocre student, Wheeler graduated eighteenth in a class of twenty-two and was commissioned a second lieutenant on 1 July 1859. He subsequently attended the cavalry school at Carlisle Barracks, Pennsylvania, before being posted with the Regiment of Mounted Riflemen. He accompanied his unit to Fort Craig, New Mexico, and spent several months skirmishing with hostile Apaches. Despite his northern upbringing, the onset of the Civil War prompted Wheeler to resign his commission on 27 February 1861 and join the Confederate army. He became a first lieutenant of artillery on 3 April 1861 and performed garrison duty in Florida under General Braxton Bragg. Favorably impressed, Bragg used his influence to have Wheeler appointed colonel of the Nineteenth Alabama Infantry, Bragg's Army of the Mississippi, on 4 September 1861. In this capacity Wheeler distinguished himself at the bloody battle of Shiloh, 6–7 April 1862, and garnered additional praise by successfully covering the Confederate withdrawal.

In July 1862 Bragg appointed Wheeler commander of all cavalry in the Army of the Mississippi. The assignment was fortuitous, for Wheeler proved himself to be one of the hardest-riding and tactically astute troopers of his day. His brigade spearheaded Bragg's drive into Kentucky in August 1862 and fought well at the battle of Perryville on 8 October. For effectively covering another retreat, Wheeler received promotion to brigadier general. On 31 December 1862 he skillfully contested the advance of Union forces under General William S. Rosecrans at Stones River (Murfeesboro) and in January 1863 became major general, commanding all cavalry in the newly created Army of the Tennessee.

Wheeler fought conspicuously at the bloody battle of Chickamauga, 18–20 September 1863, and unleashed one of the most devastating cavalry raids of the war. Galloping through eastern Tennessee, his men inflicted 2,000 casualties and captured or burned more than 1,000 supply wagons while sustaining a loss of only 212 men. It was a masterstroke against Rosecrans's lines of communication and nearly destroyed his ability to resist. Bragg, however, was himself defeated at Lookout Mountain and Missionary Ridge in November 1863, and once again Wheeler covered a Confederate withdrawal.

Throughout most of 1864 Wheeler provided the most obstinate resistance to General William T. Sherman's advance through Georgia. He expertly covered the withdrawal of General Joseph E. Johnston's army from Chattanooga and repeatedly clashed with pursuing Union cavalry. Following the death of General J. E. B. Stuart in May, Wheeler became the Confederacy's senior cavalry officer. In July 1864 he heavily defeated a large Federal raiding column commanded by Generals George Stoneman, Kenner Garrard, and Edward M. McCook, capturing 3,200 prisoners in the process. As Sherman inexorably approached Atlanta, General John B. Hood dispatched Wheeler on large-scale raids against his supply lines. Between 10 August and 10 September Wheeler's troopers rode as far as central Tennessee and northern Alabama, destroying wagon trains and cutting railways. After Atlanta's fall, Hood marched his army north against central Tennessee, while Wheeler's corps deployed to contest Sherman's march to the sea and into South Carolina. Wheeler made lieutenant general in February 1865 and scored additional successes against Union cavalry. However, he had been criticized for failing to control his men during operations in Georgia and South Carolina and was placed under the command of General Wade Hampton for the remainder of the war. Shortly after Johnston's army surrendered, Wheeler was captured near Atlanta in May 1865.

Wheeler was briefly detained in Delaware before being paroled in June 1865. Soon afterward he moved to New Orleans and became a merchant. He married Daniella Sherrod Jones in 1866; the couple had seven children. In 1868 he moved to Wheeler Station (named in his honor) in northern Alabama and became a successful planter. Wheeler also read law and became an attorney as well as director of the Memphis and Charleston Railroad. He served briefly as a Democratic member of Congress in 1881–1882 but was unseated when a Greenbacker contested his election. He again served briefly in 1883 after winning a special election. Wheeler returned to the House of Representatives in 1885, beginning an unbroken tenure of fifteen years, during which he became ranking Democrat on the Ways and Means Committee. Congressman Wheeler, like many southern Democrats, opposed protective tariffs and backed the free and unlimited coinage of silver, but he also spoke for federal aid to education and sectional reconciliation. He became a symbol of national healing when, following the declaration of war against Spain in 1898, President William McKinley appointed him a major general of volunteers.

As a soldier, Wheeler had lost none of his dash. He accompanied General William R. Shafter's V Corps and commanded all cavalry forces engaged in the invasion of Cuba. On 24 June 1898 Wheeler launched a successful attack against Spanish forces at Las Guásimas and, though very ill, partook of the famous battle of San Juan Hill. Wheeler recovered sufficiently to participate in the closing phases of the Santiago campaign and subsequently commanded a convalescent camp at Montauk Point, Long Island. He was then ordered to lead an infantry brigade as part of the Philippine occupation in June 1899 but returned the following year. On 16 June 1900 Wheeler became a brigadier general in the regular army and took charge of the Department of the Lakes. He retired from the military on 10 September 1900 and pursued the quiet life of a historian. Wheeler died at Brooklyn, New York, becoming one of few Confederate veterans interred at Arlington National Cemetery.

Wheeler, who was known as "Fighting Joe," was one of the most active field commanders of the Civil War. A veteran of 200 major engagements, he was wounded three times, lost sixteen horses, and witnessed thirty-six staff officers fall by his side. In a military establishment renowned for superb cavalry leadership, his record is second only to Nathan B. Forrest in terms of successful small-scale actions. Wheeler crystalized his views on mounted warfare in the manual *Cavalry Tactics* (1863). Although he lacked the strategic acumen of Stuart and his performance during large-scale independent operations was unspectacular, in terms of raiding, screening, and covering the rear of a retreating force, Wheeler was unsurpassed by any other trooper, Union or Confederate.

• No single collection of Wheeler papers exists, but scattered materials can be accessed by consulting various volumes of the *National Union Catalog of Manuscripts Collections* (1959–). Among Wheeler's own works are *The Santiago Campaign* (1898) and the section on Ala. in Clement Evans, ed., *Confederate Military History*, vol. 7 (1899). Published letters are in *The War of the Rebellion: A Compilation of the Official Records of the Union and Confederate Armies* (128 vols., 1880–1901). Two standard, if dated, biographies are T. C. DeLeon, *Joseph Wheeler, the Man, the Statesman, the Soldier* (1899), and John P. Dyer, *Fightin' Joe Wheeler* (1941). His Civil War activities are amply covered in Lewis A. Lawson, *Wheeler's Last Raid* (1986); and David Snider and William Brookshear, "A Ride down the Sequatchie Valley," *Civil War Times Illustrated* 22 (1988): 32–39 and "The War Child Rides Again: Joe Wheeler at Stones River," *Civil War Times Illustrated* 14 (1976): 4–6, 8–10, 44–46. Materials relating to his later career are in William C. Dodson, ed., *Campaigns of Wheeler and His Cavalry* (1899), and Fitzhugh Lee, *Cuba's Struggle against Spain* (1899).

JOHN C. FREDRIKSEN

WHEELER, Royall Tyler (1810–9 Apr. 1864), jurist, was born in Vermont, the son of John Wheeler and Hannah Thurston. His family moved to Ohio, where Wheeler studied law and was admitted to the Ohio bar. In 1837 he moved to Fayetteville, Arkansas, and entered into a law partnership with William S. Oldham, who later became a justice of the Arkansas Supreme Court and a senator in the Confederate Congress from Texas. In 1839 Wheeler married Emily Walker of Fayetteville; they had three sons and a daughter.

The Wheelers relocated to Nacogdoches, Texas, in 1839, and Wheeler entered into partnership with Kendreth L. Anderson, vice president of the Republic of Texas. After serving one term as a district attorney, Wheeler was selected in 1844 as the district court judge for the Fifth District, which included most of eastern Texas. This position also entitled him to sit as a justice of the Supreme Court of the Republic; the court was comprised of the several district court judges sitting *en banc*, with a chief justice presiding. After Texas was admitted to the Union and the state government was organized in 1845, Wheeler was appointed as one of the first associate justices of the Texas Supreme Court. When the position was made elective, he was elected in 1851 and reelected in 1856. In 1858 Wheeler was selected as chief justice of the Texas Supreme Court, a position he held until his death.

As the clerk of the Texas Supreme Court noted, Wheeler was an "efficient special pleader, under the common law system. . . . " Perhaps because of this, Wheeler's written opinions as a justice include a significant number relating to civil procedure and sufficiency of evidence. In addition, he wrote extensively on criminal procedure, particularly on the sufficiency of indictments. In his first major opinion interpreting a provision of the state constitution, *Willie Dixon v. State of Texas* (1847), the court held that criminal fines were not to be considered debts; therefore, a defendant who failed to pay a criminal fine could be imprisoned without the state violating the constitutional provision against imprisonment for debt.

While most of the opinions decided during Wheeler's tenure on the Supreme Court were unanimous, Wheeler was recognized for the forcefulness of his dissenting opinions when he believed that the majority either did not follow precedent or should break with precedent. For example, in *Snoddy v. Cage* (1849), Wheeler dissented from the majority of the court in interpreting Texas's statute of limitations. Wheeler, in an extensive dissent, cited precedent from other states and England in arguing that the statute was improperly interpreted by the majority.

Wheeler is most noted for upholding the Confederacy's conscription law. The fundamental issue raised was one that has plagued American constitutional interpretation: should the constitution be read narrowly or broadly? In *Ex Parte F. H. Coupland* (1862), Coupland, a soldier in the Confederate army, sought a writ of habeas corpus alleging, inter alia, that he was improperly detained in the armed forces and that the "Conscript Law" was unconstitutional. By a two-to-one margin, the court upheld the law. In broadly interpreting the language of the Confederate constitution, the majority opinion of the court, written by Justice Moore, held that the conscript law was constitutional for two basic reasons. First, the "power to raise and support armies" was an express grant of authority to the Confederate Congress. There were no limitations, either express or implied, as to how the army may be raised. Second, even if there were no express grant of authority, Congress did have the authority "to make all laws which shall be necessary and proper for carrying into execution" the expressly enumerated powers. One of those powers was the right to make war—which requires an army, and which could be raised through the "necessary and proper" clause. Because he presided over the case in the lower court, Chief Justice Wheeler did not write the opinion of the court. However, Wheeler's concurrence in the case completely supported the reasoning in Justice Moore's majority opinion.

According to George Paschal, clerk of the Texas Supreme Court, unionist, and an erstwhile friend of Wheeler's, Wheeler suffered from depression over his responsibility in support of secession. As a result, he committed suicide in Washington County, Texas. Wheeler County, Texas, was created in 1876 and named in his honor.

Wheeler is best remembered as one of the first justices of the Texas Supreme Court and as a supporter of Texas secession. His continuing legacy is his concurring opinion in *Ex Parte Coupland*, which upheld the constitutionality of the Confederate "Conscript Law." Without a national supreme court, the Confederate government had to rely upon the support of the state judiciaries in upholding a law necessary to maintain the Confederacy's existence. Chief Justice Wheeler provided that support.

• There is no known collection of Wheeler's papers. For further information, see Jenette H. Davenport, *The History of the Supreme Court of Texas* (1917); James D. Lynch, *The Bench and Bar of Texas* (1885); George W. Paschal, *Texas* 28 (1882): 7; James W. Paulson, "The Judges of the Supreme Court of the Republic of Texas," *Texas Law Review* 65 (1986): 305; C. S. West, "Hon. Royall T. Wheeler," *Texas* 27 (1865).

MICHAEL POWELL

WHEELER, Ruth (5 Aug. 1877–29 Sept. 1948), nutritionist and educator, was born in Plains, Pennsylvania, the daughter of Jared Ward Wheeler and Martha Jane Evans. She was influenced by her Welsh grandfather, a minister concerned with feeding the poor. Wheeler's mother taught her to read, and she graduated from high school in West Pittston, Pennsylvania, to which her family had moved. Wheeler entered Vassar College and took remedial work in Latin and algebra before receiving her A.B. in 1899. She taught high school science and German in West Pittston and Saratoga Springs, New York. Beginning in 1905, she was a chemistry instructor for five years at Pratt Institute in Brooklyn. During this time, Wheeler became interested in home economics, a field undergoing professionalization and offering scientific opportunities for women.

Wheeler was a charter member of the American Home Economics Association when it was founded in

1908. She began graduate studies at Yale University in 1910, worked in the physiological chemistry laboratory with Professor Russell H. Chittenden, and earned a Ph.D. in 1913. Her dissertation was titled "Feeding Experiments with Mice." She also studied nutrition at Cornell University and the University of Chicago.

Wheeler had joined the faculty of the University of Illinois's Department of Household Science in 1912. She taught dietetics and nutrition classes and was promoted to the rank of associate professor by 1918. During World War I, Wheeler was appointed chair of the American Red Cross's national committee on nutrition (she continued to serve the organization until 1932). She focused on food conservation and healthy diets for civilians and soldiers. She also represented nutritionists at the National Research Council and was present at the 1917 conference that organized the American Dietetic Association.

In 1918 Wheeler accepted a position as department head and professor of home economics at Goucher College in Baltimore, Maryland. She strengthened the department and enhanced the popularity of nutrition studies. By 1921 she was named professor and head of the Department of Nutrition newly established at the College of Medicine of the University of Iowa in Iowa City. She was also chief dietitian of the university's hospitals, monitoring food service to patients and personnel.

At Iowa, Wheeler initiated a pioneering one-year master's degree course for dietitians that required an internship. Concurrently, as chair of the Educational Section and president of the American Dietetic Association (ADA), she promoted the establishment of professional standards. She recognized that dietitians came from a variety of backgrounds and underscored the need for regulated qualifications to enhance the profession's prestige and ensure competent practitioners. She introduced minimum educational standards for hospital dietitians in the 1924 "Outline for Standard Course for Student Dietitians in Hospitals."

In her 1925 presidential address, Wheeler urged members to survey hospitals and training programs. She stressed that "work so intensely concentrated as that in hospitals . . . demands in the dietitian such a breadth, sympathy, and mental outlook as are greatly helped by a broad and protracted education." The ADA approved her outline in 1927, requiring dietitians to earn a bachelor's degree in foods and nutrition and to undergo supervised training in an approved hospital for six months. Wheeler helped to create a centralized placement bureau for qualified members.

Wheeler also established the *Journal of the American Dietetic Association* despite low funds and resistance from members who believed that existing journals were sufficient and balked at the expense involved. She served on its editorial board and also wrote articles about nutrition and nutrition education for the *Journal of Home Economics*. She urged dietitians to share ideas and unify the profession. She supported instructive programs at the ADA section level. "Our aim is to stimulate growth of the profession, the Association and individual members," Wheeler stated, "not by plumpness, size, numbers of followers; not by stimulants giving apparent force, money power, rights, but by all nutrients balanced, good solid all-round growth with stability and endurance" (Barber, p. 39).

At Iowa, Wheeler insisted that her students strive for scientific accuracy, act professionally, and "prove that interns in nutrition are as indispensable to hospitals as other interns." She expected her students to assume the responsibilities and duties of career dietitians. She also initiated her most significant dietary research at Iowa. In "Food and Dietetics for Student Nurses," another outline that she produced in 1924, she was the first dietitian to emphasize the importance of normal nutrition for the sick. She insisted that patients should be fed vitamins and protein instead of undergoing corrective procedures such as starvation that would deny them necessary nutrients required to heal.

Wheeler expanded this argument in *Talks to Nurses on Dietetics and Dietotherapy* (1926), written with her sister Helen. In the book she claimed that nurses needed to understand how foods affected tissues and organs; the purpose of food components such as minerals, fats, and carbohydrates; and the relationship between diseases, metabolism, and digestion. She insisted that medical staffs and dietitians must cooperate to ensure the therapeutic effects of hospital diets. She also examined the dietary needs of patients from infants to the elderly and explored food-related conditions such as ulcers, gout, and diabetes. The book's vision for dietotherapy remained valid for many years as revealed by a latter-day nutritionist who claimed, "This book is twenty years old and its vitamins are out of date, but the philosophy is still sound" (*Journal of the American Dietetic Association* [Dec. 1948]: 1071).

In 1926 Wheeler published (with her student Edna Shalla) "A Nutritive Analysis of Hospital Food Bills" in the *Journal of the American Dietetic Association*, detailing her experiences with food administration at Iowa. Analyzing the food consumed and wasted by patients, Wheeler concluded that an "adequate general diet" is as "wise from an administrative standpoint as it is necessary from a nutritive one." She elaborated that "it minimizes the calculation of individual diets, furnishes a sound basis for the special diet system, and groups together foods which stimulate the appetite and at the same time furnish nutritive constituents in amounts which have been found necessary by experimental work" (p. 27).

Wheeler returned to Vassar in 1926 as a professor of physiology and nutrition. She also was a nutritional consultant for the New York City Presbyterian Hospital and a lecturer in Columbia University's medical department. In 1927 Wheeler published the *American Red Cross Textbook on Food and Nutrition: A Study of the Basis of Food Selection* (again collaborating with her sister), reiterating her opinions about the role of foods in health care. From 1928 to 1942 she also served as director of the Vassar Summer Institute of Euthenics, which were classes for social workers, teachers, and parents designed for the "improvement of human relations."

Wheeler was known for her optimistic attitude toward both peers and students. She bolstered dietitians' self-confidence and helped secure employment for them, personally notifying hospitals of capable nutritionists. She was a well-loved teacher who enthusiastically conveyed her professional ideals to her interns and staff. She maintained a careful balance between teaching, research, and food service.

A member of the American Society of Biological Chemists, the American Institute of Nutrition, and Sigma Xi, Wheeler was also a fellow of the American Association for the Advancement of Science. The ADA gave her an award in the 1940s for her service to the group and at its 1944 convention unveiled a plaque in her honor. She was also inducted into the organization's Hall of Fame. Dietitian Florence Smith called Wheeler the profession's "patron saint and guiding star" to whom she had often gone "for help and, sometimes, consolation." Perhaps Wheeler's empathy was strengthened by her devotion to the Episcopal church. She sang in the choir, taught Sunday school, and prepared students for confirmation.

Wheeler retired from Vassar in July 1944 as professor emeritus. She died in Poughkeepsie, New York, from an intestinal obstruction. One former student reminisced about Wheeler, "What one remembers most about her is her smile, not a perfunctory one, but always expressing a genuine feeling of friendliness."

• In addition to the works mentioned above, Wheeler published "Home Economics in the Woman's College," *Journal of Home Economics* 11 (1919): 375–80. See also her "Presidential Address," *Journal of the American Dietetic Association* 1 (Dec. 1925): 97–102. For further information on her contributions see "Ruth Wheeler," *Iowa Alumnus* 19 (Nov. 1921): 51, and Mary I. Barber, ed., *History of the American Dietetic Association, 1917–1959* (1959). Obituaries are in the *Journal of the American Dietetic Association* 24 (Dec. 1948): 1070–71, and the *New York Times*, 1 Oct. 1948.

ELIZABETH D. SCHAFER

WHEELER, Wayne Bidwell (10 Nov. 1869–5 Sept. 1927), prohibitionist and de facto leader of the Anti-Saloon League, was born near Brookfield, Ohio, the son of Joseph Wheeler, a farmer and cattle dealer, and Ursula Hutchinson. While working as a boy on the family farm, Wheeler's leg was injured by the hayfork of an inebriated hired hand. Young Wheeler also observed another inebriate frighten his mother and sisters. These events appear to have prompted his antipathy to alcohol. After graduating from high school, he taught school for two years and then entered Oberlin College, where he excelled in argument and debate.

After receiving his B.A. from Oberlin in 1894, Wheeler accepted employment as an organizer for the recently established Anti-Saloon League. While continuing this work full time, he attended Western Reserve Law School, which awarded him the LL.B. in 1898. He was promptly named attorney for the league, an organization to which he devoted the rest of his life.

Early in his career Wheeler exhibited a keen sense of politics and the use of power. He quickly developed a style of pressure politics that became known by both supporters and opponents as "Wheelerism." He became superintendent of Ohio for the league in 1903. His organizational skills and political success in engineering the reelection defeat of a prominent wet (antiprohibition) governor of Ohio dramatically increased his stature, and in 1915 he moved to Washington, D.C., where he could more easily wield important political pressure and influence.

Wheeler tended to present his views as the views of the league, when the organization often had either no view or a different view on the issue in question. Convinced of the importance of the cause of Prohibition for which he fought, he demanded hard work from himself and others in its furtherance. Frequently ignoring holidays, including Christmas and Easter, he expected others to do the same.

Even his love letters to his fiancée, Ella Belle Candy, typically contained observations on Prohibition along with professions of affection. After their marriage in 1901, their house became an extension of his office. The couple had three children, but everything in life, including his family, was subordinate to his Prohibition activities.

While he frequently claimed to have essentially written the National Prohibition Enforcement Act (Volstead Act [1919]), an assertion repeatedly denied by Congressman Andrew Volstead, it is clear that he was at least highly influential in the drafting of its contents, and he was continually called on to explain its complex provisions to Congress and others.

Many prohibitionists stressed the importance of education to bring about voluntary compliance, but Wheeler insisted on strict and vigorous enforcement as the proper course. He was a proponent of force, and "he desired the most severe penalties, the most aggressive policies even to calling out the Army and Navy, the most relentless prosecution" (Steuart, p. 14). The Prohibition Bureau added poisons to industrial alcohol to prevent its consumption as a beverage. Wheeler opposed the use of nonpoisonous denaturants such as soap or other harmless but noxious substances, arguing that "the government is under no obligation to furnish people with alcohol that is drinkable when the Constitution prohibits it. The person who drinks this industrial alcohol . . . is a deliberate suicide" (Herbert Asbury, *The Great Illusion: An Informal History of Prohibition* [1950], p. 279).

According to Wheeler's biographer, Wheeler wielded a great deal of power and influenced much legislation regarding Prohibition. He "was recognized by friend and foe alike as the most masterful and powerful single individual in the United States" (Steuart, p. 11). Even though the cause for which he labored so tirelessly would soon be overwhelmingly repudiated by the American people as a dismal failure, Wheeler never wavered in his Prohibition conviction and never rested in its pursuit. He died of exhaustion and kidney disease at his summer home at Little Point Sable in Michigan, while attempting to regain his strength to continue the fight.

At Wheeler's funeral, league orators carefully phrased their eulogies, reflecting a cleavage between his policies and those of the nominal leadership. No sooner was he in his grave than the league abandoned his policies in favor of those of his longtime rival Ernest Cherrington, who stressed the need for education to bring about voluntary compliance. Increasingly, league members openly criticized Wheeler's alignment with avowed racial and religious bigots, his advocacy of illegal actions in enforcing Prohibition, his deceptive practice of writing self-aggrandizing articles that he asked others to publish as their own, and his alienating, caustic personality. Yet he played a major role in making the league the first major political pressure group in the United States and, by sheer force of personality and unrelenting drive, made himself into one of the most powerful leaders and promoters of Prohibition in the country.

• Although his major publications number in the dozens, Wheeler's most important work is generally considered to be his *Federal and State Laws Relating to Intoxicating Liquor* (1921). A highly detailed biography is Charles M. Hogan, "Wayne B. Wheeler: Single Issue Exponent" (Ph.D. diss., Univ. of Cincinnati, 1986). Wheeler's former publicity secretary, Justin Steuart, wrote *Wayne Wheeler, Dry Boss: An Uncensored Biography of Wayne B. Wheeler* (1928), which, as evidenced by papers of the league, was not entirely uncensored. Broader treatments can be found in former Wheeler aide Peter Odegard's *Pressure Politics: The Story of the Anti-Saloon League* (1928) and K. Austin Kerr's *Organized for Prohibition: A New History of the Anti-Saloon League* (1985). An obituary is in the *New York Times*, 6 Sept. 1927.

DAVID HANSON

WHEELER, William Adolphus (14 Nov. 1833–28 Oct. 1874), lexicographer, bibliographer, and librarian, was born in Leicester, Massachusetts, the son of Amos Dean Wheeler, a Unitarian minister, and Louisa Warren. Having spent much of his youth at Topsham, Maine, Wheeler attended Bowdoin College, where he received an A.B. in 1853 and an A.M. three years later.

After receiving the bachelor's degree, Wheeler taught at Marlborough and Northfield, Massachusetts, and in 1854 became preceptor of Partridge Academy in Duxbury, Massachusetts. On 13 July 1856 he married Olive Winsor Frazar of Duxbury; they had six children. That same year, Wheeler relocated to Cambridge, Massachusetts, and assisted Joseph Emerson Worcester in the production of his *Dictionary of the English Language* (1860). In addition to providing editorial assistance on the dictionary, Wheeler contributed an appendix, entitled "Pronunciation of the Names of Distinguished Men of Modern Times."

For several years after his association with Worcester, Wheeler was employed as an editor by the Merriam Company during which time he supervised the publication of the new unabridged *Webster Dictionary* (1864) as well as a number of abridged editions. To the 1864 unabridged edition Wheeler contributed an "Explanatory and Pronouncing Vocabulary of Noted Names of Fiction, Including Also Familiar Pseudonyms Bestowed upon Eminent Men," which was published separately under a slightly different title in the following year.

In April 1868 Wheeler entered the service of the Boston Public Library and by the end of that year had assumed the dual duties of assistant superintendent and chief of the catalog department. During his tenure at the library he oversaw publication of the *Prince Catalogue* (1870), an inventory of a collection of books formerly owned by Rev. Thomas Prince and deposited in the library by the Old South Church to which the collection had been bequeathed, which had been prepared by his predecessor, William Everett Jillson. In addition, he completed work on the *Ticknor Catalogue* (1879), a description of a bequest of over 2,000 books, primarily on Spanish literature. Actual publication of this catalog did not occur until after Wheeler's death, a situation similar to that in which the *Prince Catalogue* had not been published until after Jillson's death.

Even more important than his work on these special-collection catalogs or on the annotated *Bulletin* of new books issued quarterly to supplement the library's book catalogs, however, was Wheeler's supervision of the creation of a general public card catalog in 1871 containing the holdings of the entire library, an innovation based on European models and similar to that which Harvard University had begun in 1862.

While working at the library, Wheeler continued his extracurricular literary pursuits. In 1869 he published his edition of *Mother Goose's Melodies*, a subject that had earlier involved him in a public dispute regarding the true identity of the real Mother Goose. Wheeler maintained that Mother Goose was a New Englander, Mistress Elizabeth Goose, a suggestion that has subsequently proven to have little merit (see *The Nation*, 8 Feb. 1866, pp. 179–80; *The Oxford Dictionary of Nursery Rhymes* [1952], pp. 37–39). In 1872 Wheeler published his edition of Gilbert Ashville Pierce's *The Dickens Dictionary*. It was during this very productive period that Harvard conferred an honorary master of arts degree on Wheeler in 1871.

When William Adolphus Wheeler died in Boston of typhoid pneumonia after a three-week illness, the trustees of the Boston Public Library resolved that the library "has lost an officer signally fitted by scholarly accuracy and thorough research for the special duties of his position" (*Superintendent's Monthly Report*, Oct. 1874). His obituaries emphasize that his productive career was cut short prematurely. At his death Wheeler left in manuscript form a still unpublished encyclopedia on Shakespeare. Two other works, *Who Wrote It?* and *Familiar Allusions*, were completed by his nephew, Charles G. Wheeler, and published in 1881 and 1882, respectively.

• In addition to the works mentioned above, Wheeler prepared the *Bowdoin College, Class of 1853: Chronological, Biographical and Statistical Record* (1873), coauthored *First Les-*

sons, in Reading (1866) and *A Manual of English Pronunciation and Spelling* (1861) with Richard Soule, and edited Charles Hole's *A Brief Biographical Dictionary* (1866). There is no full-length biography of William Adolphus Wheeler available. Nehemiah Cleaveland, *History of Bowdoin College* (1882), mentions Wheeler. Additional information, especially on his years at the Boston Public Library, is in Horace G. Wadlin, *The Public Library of the City of Boston* (1911), Walter Muir Whitehill, *Boston Public Library: A Centennial History* (1956), and in the *Annual Report* of the trustees of the Boston Public Library for the years 1869–1875. The most comprehensive obituaries are in the *Boston Evening Transcript* and the *Boston Evening Journal*, 29 Oct. 1874, and in the *Boston Daily Advertiser*, 30 Oct. 1874.

WILLIAM M. GREALISH

WHEELER, William Almon (30 June 1819–4 June 1887), nineteenth vice president of the United States, was born in Malone, New York, the son of Almon Wheeler, a lawyer, and Eliza Woodworth. His father died when William was eight years old, leaving Eliza and her three children all but destitute. A purposeful young man, William took advantage of the Franklin County district schools to gain a solid basic education. With the help of a small loan, he then attended the University of Vermont for two years (1838–1840) before returning to Malone without a degree, the victim of extreme poverty and eye afflictions. Those eye afflictions proved to be the first of several health-related crises that would affect Wheeler's career.

Back home, Wheeler taught and supervised schools, studied law, was elected town clerk, and became a successful lawyer. He married Mary King in 1845 and began four years of service as Franklin County district attorney in 1846. In 1850 he was elected as a Whig to the New York assembly, where he chaired the Ways and Means Committee. Faced with another health crisis, this time a chronic throat problem, Wheeler abandoned active courtroom pleading in 1853 and became counsel for a number of St. Lawrence Valley banking and railroad corporations.

An ardent opponent of slavery, Wheeler switched from the Whigs to the new Republican party in 1855. Elected in 1858 to the state senate, he became that body's first Republican president pro tempore. Elected in 1860 to the House of Representatives, Wheeler supported the Lincoln administration and pressed for emancipation through the early years of the Civil War but did not stand for reelection.

In 1867 a Republican majority elected Wheeler president of the New York state constitutional convention. In that capacity he first presided over inclusion of a Radical Republican amendment to guarantee racially equal suffrage in New York; then, sensing a sharp backslash on racial matters, he maneuvered successfully to keep the amendment off the 1867 state ballot. The latter effort failed as a political tactic, and the Republicans lost badly in the state elections of 1867, largely on the issue of racial equality. Wheeler, nonetheless, had gained a reputation as the sober broker of intraparty compromises and the honest engineer of careful retreats. A devoutly committed Congregationalist, his conspicuous religiosity and unswerving personal integrity no doubt helped him in this regard, for what might have seemed personally cynical or politically expedient in others apparently seemed less so in this rigorously upright man.

In 1868 Wheeler was reelected to Congress and in 1869 began serving the first of four consecutive terms in the House. Though almost never in the public spotlight, Wheeler exercised considerable influence as a chairman of key committees (including those on Pacific railroads, southern affairs, and appropriations), as an advocate of federal aid to education in the South, and as a scrupulously honest officeholder in an era known even by the flexible standards of the day for its loose public ethics. Wheeler was more adamantly opposed to the so-called "salary grab," an 1873 act in which Congress voted itself a retroactive pay increase, than any other Republican in the House. His one appearance in national headlines came as the head of a commission to sort out the chaotic political situation in Louisiana following the 1874 state elections. The "Wheeler Compromise" restored order among contending factions at the state level in 1875 and thereby bought the Republican party maneuvering time in that potentially explosive southern state. Wheeler's report criticized previous Republican policies in Louisiana, including the implementation of black suffrage without black education, and signaled the growing disinclination of the Grant administration to continue federal support for the remaining Reconstruction governments in the South.

The Republican National Convention of 1876 nominated Rutherford B. Hayes of Ohio for president of the United States. As a gesture to the New York delegation, many of whom had opposed Hayes, the convention encouraged the New Yorkers to suggest a vice presidential candidate. Subsequent commentators have indulged semihumorous speculations about the choice of Wheeler. Some have alluded to a perverse joke in which the New Yorkers were supposed to have advanced the most obscure candidate they dared, while others have quoted with glee a letter in which Hayes confessed to having no idea who Wheeler was. But the nomination was not a joke. Hayes's letter had been written well before the convention; indeed, Wheeler's name had come to Hayes's attention precisely because others, including the powerful general Philip Sheridan, were already pushing Wheeler as an ideal running mate: a healer of intraparty rifts, a former antislavery Radical now willing to conciliate the South on racial issues, and a personally ethical public citizen in an era plagued by abuses of office.

Wheeler accepted the nomination in a letter that implied the need for national Republicans to withdraw from southern entanglements. As things turned out in the disputed election of 1876, that was exactly the policy Hayes had to adopt in 1877. Once again Wheeler played a principal, if publicly invisible, role in extricating his party as gracefully as he could from earlier postwar positions that seemed to be costing it power. Negotiating and implementing those reorientations of

Republican party policy from 1867 to 1877 constituted his most lasting impact on American history.

A third and final health crisis beset Wheeler even as he assumed the vice presidency. Just prior to the national convention of 1876, his wife had died. The couple was childless, and Wheeler found himself alone in the capital, disliking the day-to-day duties of the vice presidency, and suffering from what would now almost certainly be termed serious depression. He became a close confidant of President Hayes, dined frequently at the White House, joined the president and his wife in the singing of hymns, and at least once took a short vacation with Lucy Hayes. Wheeler was otherwise reclusive. When the Hayes administration ended, Wheeler returned to Malone and locked himself into a retirement from which he never reemerged. His doctors attributed his death in Malone six years later to a brain disorder, which had made his final six months a wretched period of physical and mental deterioration. Wheeler bequeathed almost all of his modest estate to the home and foreign missionary boards of the Congregational church.

• Although no scholarly biography has yet been published, one of the popular biographies produced for the 1876 campaign was written by the notable American novelist William Dean Howells, *Sketch of the Life and Character of Rutherford B. Hayes. Also a Biographical Sketch of William A. Wheeler* (1876). Wheeler's activities in the New York state constitutional convention of 1867 are addressed in James C. Mohr, *The Radical Republicans and Reform in New York during Reconstruction* (1973) William Gillette, *Retreat from Reconstruction, 1869–1879* (1979), and Eric Foner, *Reconstruction: America's Unfinished Revolution, 1863–1877* (1988), place Wheeler's Louisiana compromise of 1875 in national context. The best source for Wheeler's life as vice president and his close relationships, both personal and political, with the Hayes family is President Hayes himself, *The Diary of a President, 1875–1881*, ed. T. Harry Williams (1964). Both the *New York Tribune*, 5 June 1887, and the *New York Times*, 5 June 1887, have lengthy obituaries.

JAMES C. MOHR

WHEELER, William Morton (19 Mar. 1865–19 Apr. 1937), entomologist, was born in Milwaukee, Wisconsin, the son of Julius Morton Wheeler, a land speculator and owner in a hide and leather business, and Caroline Georgiana Anderson, an English immigrant.

Wheeler developed an early interest in natural history, through exposure to the Natural History Society of Wisconsin and the Engelmann Museum in Milwaukee. The museum was associated with the German-English Academy, which Wheeler attended, and he graduated from its teachers' seminary in 1884. Milwaukee purchased a major collection of mounted specimens of mammals and birds and some invertebrates from Henry Augustus Ward in 1883 and, while helping Ward prepare this exhibit, Wheeler was offered a position at Ward's Natural Science Establishment in Rochester, New York. He worked there for a year and a half, identifying and cataloging birds, mammals, and many invertebrates.

Wheeler returned to Milwaukee in 1885 to teach at the German-English Academy and the public high school. At the Natural History Society he met Charles Otis Whitman, then director of the Allis Lake Laboratory in Milwaukee, who outlined a program of study in embryology for him. In 1887 Wheeler became director of the Milwaukee Public Museum, where his primary interest was insects, of which he devised educational exhibits. He published a few papers on insects, including his first on aspects of their embryology.

At Whitman's urging Wheeler entered the new Clark University in Worcester, Massachusetts, in 1890 for graduate studies. He began spending summers at the newly founded Marine Biological Laboratory in Woods Hole, Massachusetts, where he both assisted Whitman in teaching laboratory sessions and conducted his own researches. He was drawn more intensely into the expanding field of embryology and wrote his Ph.D. dissertation (1892) on the development of a grasshopper. It was later said to be "the most comprehensive treatment of insect embryology available in English at that time."

In 1892 Wheeler became instructor in embryology at the fledgling University of Chicago, where Whitman was chairman of the Department of Biology. The next year Wheeler visited Europe, where he spent six months at Würzburg, Germany, with Theodor Boveri, a professor of zoology and comparative anatomy. There he concentrated on embryology of a lamprey, which led to a long, carefully illustrated paper, "The Development of the Urinogenital Organs of the Lamprey" (1899). He then spent four months at the Zoological Station in Naples, Italy, and two months with Edouard van Beneden at the Zoological Institute in Liège, Belgium. On his return to Chicago in mid-1894 he taught courses in the comparative anatomy of vertebrates and in entomology. Wheeler became assistant professor at Chicago in 1896. His publications of this period were in cytology, morphology, embryology, and entomology.

Wheeler married Dora Bay Emerson in 1898; they had two children. The next year he became professor of zoology at the University of Texas in Austin. He taught most of the zoology courses and took a close interest in the department's few graduate students. He found laboratory facilities sparse, but a new subject that did not require much equipment and was rampant in his new locale drew his attention: ants. "I have taken to ants heart and soul, and find them more interesting than anything I ever studied before," he wrote to colleague E. O. Jordan in 1900. In Texas he ended his studies in embryology, maintained colonies of ants in the laboratory, and published about thirty papers on them.

In 1903 Wheeler accepted the position of curator of invertebrates at the American Museum of Natural History in New York. There he organized and arranged the Hall of Invertebrates, curated the large collections, and gave public lectures. He participated in field trips in the western United States and the Caribbean and visited European scientific facilities. In December 1906 he was one of the founders of the Entomological Society of America and became its second president a year later.

Wheeler accepted an appointment in 1908 at a new facility: Harvard University's graduate school of applied science, located at the Bussey Institute in West Roxbury, Massachusetts. He was professor of economic entomology and in 1915 became dean of the graduate school until 1929. A number of students who graduated from this school went on to significant careers in biology. They credited Wheeler with taking a keen interest in their work. From 1931 until his death he had an office in the Museum of Comparative Zoology at Harvard.

In 1910 Wheeler published his most significant work: *Ants, Their Structure, Development, and Behavior*, which was still acknowledged as a standard reference fifty years later. Wheeler's publications included descriptions of the various castes of members of ant colonies; accounts of the parasitic inhabitants of the colonies; habits; ecology; and detailed taxonomy. He identified specimens sent to him by scientists from all over the world and published regional accounts, which covered various parts of the United States as well as Japan, Cuba, Borneo, China, Belgian Congo, Canary Islands, Hawaii, and Oceania. As he said, "Ants are to be found everywhere." He adopted an unwieldy system of naming ants in five parts (genus, subgenus, species, subspecies, and variety), based on minor differentiation, with the result that many of his names have not been retained. Although unaware of the chemical substances that are now known to affect much of the behavior of social insects, Wheeler provided careful observations on an important group of animals and laid the groundwork for further studies. His overall interest was in tracing phylogenetic relationships.

Wheeler's publications totaled more than 450 titles. Among his nine books were *Social Life among the Insects* (1923) and *The Social Insects, Their Origin and Evolution* (1928), each resulting from a series of lectures and summarizing much of Wheeler's knowledge for a general audience. They brought out the point, for example, that colonies of social insects are "true organisms and not merely conceptual constructions or analogies." His most popular book, *Foibles of Insects and Men* (1928), presented scientific information while it drew often absurd analogies between insects and people. His final book, *Demons of the Dust* (1930), treated ant lions and worm lions that dig pits to trap ants.

In 1923 Wheeler visited Panama for the Gorgas Memorial Institute and then participated with Thomas Barbour and David Fairchild in establishing the Barro Colorado laboratory, a tropical research facility.

Wheeler was elected to the National Academy of Science in 1912 and received its Elliot Medal in 1922. He received the Leidy Medal of the Academy of Natural Sciences of Philadelphia (1931), the cross of the French Legion of Honor (1934), and a number of honorary degrees. He died in Cambridge, Massachusetts.

• Some of Wheeler's papers are at the University of Chicago, the American Museum of Natural History, and the Museum of Comparative Zoology. His family, however, retained much of his correspondence according to biographers Mary Alice Evans and Howard Ensign Evans, whose *William Morton Wheeler, Biologist* (1970), is a detailed account of his life and work that includes a bibliography. See also George Howard Parker's sketch in the National Academy of Sciences, *Biographical Memoirs* 19 (1938): 201–41.

ELIZABETH NOBLE SHOR

WHEELOCK, Eleazar (22 Apr. 1711–24 Apr. 1779), Congregational minister and educator, was born in Windham, Connecticut, the son of Ralph Wheelock and Ruth Huntington, farmers of old New England ancestry. Wheelock entered Yale in 1729, developed a reputation for both piety and scholarship, and graduated in 1733 having been awarded a prize for distinction in classics. After additional study at Yale he became, in 1735, pastor of the Second Congregational Church at Lebanon Crank (Columbia), Connecticut. He remained the pastor for thirty-five years even though relationships with his parishioners were often strained. Wheelock also managed a large personal estate of land acquired through inheritance, marriage, church settlement, and purchase.

Wheelock's historical reputation stems from a variety of activities related to, but separate from, his ministry. He became deeply involved in the Great Awakening as an itinerant preacher; an indefatigable evangelical, he delivered over 400 sermons in one twelve-month period during the early 1740s. Jonathan Edwards (1703–1758) encouraged his itinerancy; George Whitefield became a frequent correspondent. Wheelock's critics, including some of his own parishioners, considered him irresponsible, disruptive, and self-centered. At one point the Connecticut assembly temporarily released the Lebanon parish from its contractual obligations to Wheelock because of his frequent absence. Wheelock remained committed to evangelical preaching and "New Light" principles throughout his life but lost interest in itinerancy as the Great Awakening ran its course.

Meanwhile, Wheelock had begun to supplement his income by preparing scholars for college. The long-term thrust of his career as an educator was shaped by the unexpected arrival at his home in 1743 of a Christianized Mohegan Indian named Samson Occom. Occom asked to be instructed in the classics and proved such an apt pupil that Wheelock, always an aggressive opportunist, developed a plan to educate and Christianize large numbers of Indians. Young male Native Americans would be trained simultaneously to become schoolteachers, missionaries, and farmers and young female Native Americans to become their future wives. When sufficiently prepared these Christian Indian teams would return to their tribes to spread the word of God. Wheelock's enthusiasm for the idea soon produced results. Colonel Joshua More (or Moor) from neighboring Mansfield contributed land and buildings for what quickly became known as Moor's Charity School. The first Indians arrived in 1754.

The charity school remained in Lebanon for fifteen years. During that period Wheelock and his assistants instructed over forty male Indians as well as a lesser number of female Indians and male whites. More than a dozen Indian scholars at the school and eight additional white scholars served in the 1760s among Indian nations in the northeast, instructing and preaching to hundreds of natives. The bulk of the activity was among the Iroquois in central New York. Charitable organizations and provincial governments provided most of the initial funding. In 1765 Wheelock sent Occom to England on what proved to be an immensely successful fundraising mission. Soon thereafter, however, Wheelock became increasingly disillusioned with progress at Moor's. Defections from the school, misbehavior among those who remained, reversion of the supposedly converted to what Wheelock considered savagery, the total failure of his plans to train Indian women, tensions between white and native students, and, finally, withdrawal of support by the Iroquois and their mentor Sir William Johnson forced a change in plans.

The new plan was to concentrate on the education of white missionaries, to do this at an incorporated, degree-granting college, to abandon the experiment in training women, and to move to a new location where he could forget troubles with his parishioners. Funding would come from the monies raised by Occom, even though they were supposed to be used for the education of Indians. Wheelock would move the charity school, run it side by side with the college, and limit its enrollment to Indians. Wheelock chose Hanover, New Hampshire, as the new site because of its accessibility and the fact that in 1769 John Wentworth (1737–1820), the provincial governor, granted him the necessary charter of incorporation. Wheelock and Wentworth agreed to name the new institution after Lord Dartmouth, the English nobleman who served both as one of Wentworth's political patrons and head of the charitable trust controlling most of the money Occom had raised. In 1769 Wheelock asked to be relieved of his pastoral responsibilities to the Second Congregational Church, was granted formal dismission, and soon moved both family and scholars north to Hanover. He spent the last nine years of his life as president of both college and school. He also preached, farmed, served as local justice of the peace, raised money (the English trust was exhausted in 1774), and scrambled to keep the disruptions of revolution from destroying his new enterprise. Age and multiple responsibilities soon eroded Wheelock's health. He died in Hanover.

Wheelock married twice, the first time in 1735 to Sarah Maltby, a widow with three children; they raised three additional children before Sarah died in 1746. The following year he married Mary Brinsmead (d. 1783), by whom he had five additional children, including John (1754–1817), his successor as president of Dartmouth and Moor's Charity School.

• Most Wheelock manuscripts are in the college archives at Dartmouth and are conveniently indexed in *A Guide to the Microfilm Edition of the Papers of Eleazar Wheelock* (1971). Wheelock described his career as an educator in *A Plain and Faithful Narrative of the Original Design, Rise, Progress and Present State of the Indian Charity School at Lebanon in Connecticut* (1763) and eight subsequent narratives (1765–1775). James D. McCallum, *Eleazar Wheelock: Founder of Dartmouth College* (1939), is the only full-length biography. See also James Axtell, *The Invasion Within* (1985); Frederick Chase, *A History of Dartmouth College* (1891); Jere R. Daniell, "Eleazar Wheelock and the Dartmouth College Charter," *Historical New Hampshire* (Winter 1969): 3–44; James D. McCallum, *The Letters of Eleazar Wheelock's Indians* (1932); David McClure and Elijah Parish, *Memoirs of the Rev. Eleazar Wheelock* (1811); Leon B. Richardson, *History of Dartmouth College* (2 vols., 1932) and *An Indian Preacher in England* (1933); and Margaret Szasz, *Indian Education in the American Colonies, 1607–1783* (1988).

JERE R. DANIELL

WHEELOCK, John (28 Jan. 1754–4 Apr. 1817), college president, was born in Lebanon, Connecticut, the son of Eleazar Wheelock, a Congregationalist minister and founder of Dartmouth College, and Mary Brinsmead. After attending Yale for three years, he transferred to the newly established Dartmouth College in Hanover, New Hampshire, graduating in 1771 with an A.B. as a member of the first class of four students. He then served as a tutor at Dartmouth until 1774. In 1775 he served in the New Hampshire assembly and, with the onset of the American Revolution, joined the Continental army as a major in the spring of 1777. Promoted to the rank of lieutenant colonel in November 1777, he was serving on the staff of General Horatio Gates when he received word of his father's death on 24 April 1779. Named in his father's will as the new president of Dartmouth, Wheelock left the army and reluctantly assumed his new duties in October 1779.

The reasons for Wheelock's lack of enthusiasm were many. The college was in poor condition physically and financially. The war had depleted the supply of students and had also brought about food shortages and rampant inflation. Additionally, the college and the town of Hanover were in the center of a long political controversy between the states of New York and New Hampshire over the control of both Vermont and the territory east of the Connecticut River, of which Hanover was a part.

Undaunted by the multitude of problems faced by the college, Wheelock approached the presidency with vigor. In addition to his duties as president, he served as professor of history from 1782 to 1815 and as an instructor in natural and politic law from 1796 to 1815. Often stiff and pedantic in his dealings with others, he took his father's bequest of the college at face value. In response to student complaints about a lack of written rules, Wheelock set up a formal code of conduct for the students, whose numbers greatly increased during his administration. In the face of overwhelming financial difficulties, a new chapel and a main building, Dartmouth Hall, were built. The Medical School was founded in 1798, and the work of Moor's Charity School, an institution founded by his father for the education of Native Americans that was incorporated into the college in his father's will, was revived in 1800.

All of these advances required funds, and Wheelock left no potential sources unexplored in this regard. In 1783 he journeyed to Europe, visiting France, the Netherlands, and even England (where he met with the college's namesake, the earl of Dartmouth) to personally solicit funds, only to lose £5,000 (by his estimate) in a shipwreck on the return voyage. Funds were raised from individuals and two lotteries (Oct. 1784 and Sept. 1787) were authorized by the New Hampshire state legislature, with mixed results. The same legislature was the target of endless requests by Wheelock for funds. Land owned by the college was sold off at a shilling an acre, and the college rented some of its other properties. In spite of the paucity of funds, the first twenty years of the Wheelock administration were marked by growth in the college and relative tranquility within the administration. In 1786 he married Maria Suhm. They had one child.

About 1803, however, relations between Wheelock and the board of trustees began to show signs of strain. New members had replaced older men loyal to Wheelock's father, and Wheelock's brand of autocratic rule, another legacy of his father, began to wear thin. Matters came to a head over issues of religion and the president's and trustees' respective powers of appointment. The college church had been built in 1795, but it was not owned by the college. When Wheelock attempted to pass on user fees for the chapel to the students, the outcry was so great that the trustees revoked his order. Further controversy erupted when Roswell Shurtleff was appointed professor of theology and pastor of the church against Wheelock's wishes in 1804. The trustees later passed laws that restricted Wheelock's power, thwarting his efforts to forbid Shurtleff from preaching at the church, and he responded in May 1815 with the anonymous publication of *Sketches of the History of Dartmouth College and Moor's Charity School, with a Particular Account of Some Late Remarkable Proceedings of the Board of Trustees from the Year 1779 to the Year 1815*, which attacked the trustees in strong language, accusing them of subordinating college interests to their own religious prejudices (the board was becoming increasingly orthodox in its Congregationalism, while Wheelock was a somewhat more liberal Presbyterian), spending wastefully, and failing to fund the education of Native Americans at Moor's Charity School.

The public feud spilled over into the state's newspapers and then into the political arena, with Federalists supporting the trustees and Democrats supporting the president. In the late spring of 1815 Wheelock appealed for assistance directly to the state legislature, resulting in his removal from office on 26 August 1815 on charges of libel, usurpation of authority, and misuse of funds.

What followed was the academic equivalent of civil war. The 1816 election was dominated by the Democrats, whose legislative members promptly created Dartmouth University, with a new and enlarged set of trustees and Wheelock as president. The original trustees of Dartmouth continued to operate the college, and Wheelock, who had become ill, saw his son-in-law William Allen serve as acting president of the university. Wheelock died in Hanover while the two competing academic institutions were in parallel operation. The ensuing legal battle ultimately reached the U.S. Supreme Court, where in March 1818 the case, *Trustees of Dartmouth College v. Woodward, 4 Wheaton 518*, was won for the college and the original trustees by Dartmouth graduate Daniel Webster. The court ruled that a corporate charter was, in effect, a contract and could not, under the federal Constitution, be thereafter altered by state governments.

The early and real achievements of Wheelock were overshadowed by the famous proceedings of the Dartmouth College Case. Strong-willed and vain, his failure to adapt to the changed politics of college government resulted in a gigantic controversy that had profound legal implications for college-government relations and government-business relations throughout the United States.

• The papers of Wheelock are at Dartmouth College, Hanover, N.H. His career can be traced in most of the histories of Dartmouth. Some of the best are William Jewett Tucker, *My Generation* (1919), Wilder Dwight Quint, *The Story of Dartmouth* (1916), and Frederick Chase, *A History of Dartmouth College and the Town of Hanover, N.H., to 1815* (1891). See also Claude M. Fuess, *Daniel Webster* (2 vols., 1930), regarding the Dartmouth College Case. An obituary is in the *Portsmouth New Hampshire Gazette*, 15 Apr. 1817.

EDWARD L. LACH, JR.

WHEELOCK, John Hall (9 Sept. 1886–22 Mar. 1978), poet and editor, was born in Far Rockaway, Long Island, New York, the son of William Efner Wheelock, a physician, and Emily Charlotte Hall. Wheelock grew up in a Manhattan neighborhood and from the age of three until his death spent summers in a home that his father built on Long Island's South Fork in East Hampton with money earned in a flourishing medical practice. Wheelock's love of poetry was cultivated by his mother, who made him and his brother memorize a poem each week. The discipline also influenced his habits of composition; as an adult, he could recite by heart "most of classical English poetry" (Mitchell, p. 139) and composed and revised his poems in his head before setting down a final version on paper.

After graduating from the Morristown school in New Jersey, Wheelock matriculated at Harvard in 1904; there he met Van Wyck Brooks and Maxwell Perkins and with them was active in literary organizations—the Stylus Club and the *Harvard Advocate*. In 1905 Wheelock and Brooks privately printed an anonymous, brief volume of poetry, *Verses by Two Undergraduates*, which garnered few sales and no reviews.

The book was steeped in the rhetoric of British nineteenth-century poetry, and Wheelock was so influenced by Romanticism and Aestheticism that he convinced his father to finance a trip to London in 1906 so that he could meet Algernon Charles Swinburne. But once he arrived and had waited for days outside the poet's door, the shy young man could only summon courage enough to touch Swinburne's coat on the one occasion the poet passed by. Returning to Harvard, Wheelock went on to edit the *Harvard Monthly*, and he graduated in 1908 as class poet and a member of Phi Beta Kappa.

Succumbing to his father's insistence that he earn a doctorate, Wheelock left in 1909 to study at the University of Göttingen, Germany. Seeking uncollected folksongs for his thesis, he traveled through Germany and Hungary and also studied at the University of Berlin. But he was more devoted to writing poetry than to scholarship, and when he returned to the United States in 1910, Perkins, who was working in the advertising department at Charles Scribner's Sons, found him a job in the company bookstore, which Wheelock called "a Byzantine cathedral of books" (Berg, p. 10), on the first floor of the Scribner's building in New York City.

During his years as clerk and then manager at the store, Wheelock published five books of poetry, as well as *Alan Seeger: Poet of the Foreign Legion* (1918) and *A Bibliography of Theodore Roosevelt* (1920). His first book, *The Human Fantasy* (1911), was well received by critics, but reviews of subsequent volumes were increasingly mixed, for Wheelock, staunchly unaffected by the modernist movement, continued to base his lyrical, romantically nostalgic poetry on nineteenth-century models. His second book, *The Beloved Adventure* (1912), received the admiration of Sara Teasdale, who, after moving to New York in 1913, soon fell in love with him. Wheelock, however, loved another woman and could not fully return Teasdale's affection. But Teasdale's friendship with Wheelock remained close until her death in 1933, and their charged relationship inspired some of her best lyrics.

In 1926 Wheelock was promoted to junior editor at Scribner's, where, as senior editor Perkins's closest associate, he helped consolidate the firm's new reputation as a publisher of innovative modern fiction and assisted Perkins in working with writers such as F. Scott Fitzgerald, Ernest Hemingway, and Thomas Wolfe. He was also responsible for Scribner's fine poetry series and oversaw publication of books by Conrad Aiken, John Peale Bishop, Louise Bogan, and Allen Tate.

As an editor, Wheelock was known for his generosity, graciousness, high standards, and commitment to his authors' best interests. He served as director and secretary of the firm from 1932 to 1942, as treasurer from 1942 to 1946, and as assistant treasurer and assistant secretary from 1946 to 1957. After the death of Perkins in 1947, Wheelock edited and published his letters three years later in *Editor to Author: The Letters of Maxwell E. Perkins*; he also became senior editor.

Wheelock's most notable project in his last years at Scribner's was the Poets of Today series, an annual that published the first books of three poets together in one volume. Although the series, which ran from 1954 to 1961, was occasionally criticized for forcing comparisons between the three poets, it was praised for its excellent poetry, and it initiated the careers of twenty-four poets, including James Dickey, Donald Finkel, Louis Simpson, and May Swenson. Wheelock was also commended by reviewers for his introductions to the volumes, essays on poetry that he revised and collected in *What Is Poetry?* (1963).

The demands of Wheelock's duties at Scribner's limited the attention he could give to writing poetry; during his thirty-one years as editor, he published only three volumes of verse. He did, however, find the opportunity for marriage to Phyllis de Kay in 1940. (They had no children.) The emotional security his wife provided, along with time afforded by his retirement from Scribner's in 1957, initiated a new level of skill and sureness in his work. This ripening was praised by reviewers and helped earn him the 1962 Bollingen Prize for Poetry, which he shared with Richard Eberhart; the 1965 Signet Society Medal, from Harvard; and the 1972 Gold Medal of the Poetry Society of America. He was also a member of the National Institute of Arts and Letters, the American Academy of Arts and Letters, honorary consultant in poetry to the Library of Congress, and a chancellor of the Academy of American Poets.

Completing six more books of poetry before his death in New York City, Wheelock explored in lyrics and long meditative poems his "inner, subjective universe, the . . . complex of spirit, of feeling, of experience, which is an image of the objective universe" (*What Is Poetry?*, p. 62). The objective universe that he detailed in the late poems encompassed his domestic life with Phyllis and, above all, the East Hampton house and its surrounding woods and beaches. In love poems such as "Eight Sonnets" and blank verse meditations such as "Bonac," "Night Thoughts in Age," "Anima," "House in Bonac," and "The Part Called Age," Wheelock succeeded in his lifelong aim of "giv[ing] the world back to the maker of the poem, in all its original strangeness, the shock of its first surprise" (*What Is Poetry?*, p. 22). He accomplished this by stripping from his later poetry much of the abstraction and nineteenth-century rhetoric that characterized his earlier work and by writing about old age with moving directness, objectivity, and an intense wonder at the odd double consciousness of a present imbued with the past that the East Hampton house and landscapes evoked for him. Often criticized for his refusal to adopt modernist irony and experimentalism, Wheelock was also greatly admired for continuing to develop as a poet and for the new work's spare, conversational elegance and dignity of feeling.

• Wheelock's poetry manuscripts are housed in the Library of Congress; much of his correspondence can be found in the Scribner's archive at Princeton University. His books of poetry include *Love and Liberation* (1913), *Dust and Light* (1919), *The Black Panther* (1922), *The Bright Doom* (1927), *Poems 1911–1936* (1936), *Poems Old and New* (1956), *The Gardener and Other Poems* (1961), *Dear Men and Women* (1966), *By Daylight and in Dream: New and Collected Poems* (1970), *In Love and Song* (1971), *This Blessed Earth: New and Selected Poems* (1978), and *Afternoon: Amagansett Beach* (1978). He also translated *Happily Ever After: Fairy Tales Selected by Alice Dalgliesh* (1939), edited *The Face of a Nation: Poetical Passages from the Writings of Thomas Wolfe* (1939), and contributed to Scribner's *Dictionary of American History* (1940). Burroughs Mitchell discusses Wheelock's editorial career and late poetry in his memoir, *The Education of an Editor* (1980), and Charles Scribner, Jr., briefly comments on Wheelock's editorial temperament and achievements in *In the Company of Writers: A Life in Publishing* (1990). Information about Wheelock's supportive editing can also be found in Elizabeth Frank, *Louise Bogan: A Portrait* (1985). See also Van Wyck Brooks, *An Autobiography* (1965), for which Wheelock contributed the foreword; Wheelock's interview with William Cahill and Molly McKaughan in the *Paris Review* (Fall 1976): 161–72; Henry Taylor's "Letting the Darkness In: The Poetic Achievement of John Hall Wheelock," the *Hollins Critic* (Dec. 1970): 1–15; and the *New York Times* obituary, 23 Mar. 1978.

MEG SCHOERKE

WHEELOCK, Lucy (1 Feb. 1857–2 Oct. 1946), kindergarten educator and founder of Wheelock College, was born in Cambridge, Vermont, the daughter of Edwin Wheelock, a Congregational minister, school superintendent, and representative to the state legislature, and Laura Pierce, a teacher. She was educated in her mother's small school, at Underhill Academy in Vermont, and at the public high school in Reading, Massachusetts, where she lived with family friends. After graduation in 1874 she returned to Vermont to teach school briefly and then moved by herself to Boston to attend the Chauncy Hall School to prepare for admission to newly founded Wellesley College. A chance visit to the Chauncy Hall kindergarten inspired her with an immediate desire to work with young children and she decided to seek kindergarten training rather than attending college. Boston's well-known kindergarten advocate Elizabeth Peabody recommended she attend Ella Snelling Hatch's school, at which Peabody was a frequent lecturer, and personally signed Wheelock's diploma at the end of the year-long course.

After completing her training in 1879 Wheelock began teaching kindergarten at the Chauncy Hall School. Her excellence as a teacher attracted the attention of prominent educational reformer Henry Barnard, who asked her to translate Friedrich Froebel's autobiographical letters for publication in his *American Journal of Education* in 1880. This and other of Wheelock's translations appeared in Barnard's *Kindergarten and Child Culture Papers* (1884), and she and Barnard remained in close contact. She also became acquainted with Robert A. Woods, the crusading social worker, who asked her to help start a kindergarten in his settlement in Boston's South End, and with psychologist G. Stanley Hall, whose summer sessions on child study she attended at Clark University, along with other influential American kindergartners.

In 1888, the year public kindergartens were permanently instituted in Boston, the headmaster of the Chauncy Hall School asked Wheelock to begin a kindergarten training class. The one-year course became so popular that in 1893 she expanded it to two years, and in 1896 she left Chauncy Hall to direct her own Wheelock Kindergarten Training School in Boston. The school was known for its innovative vocational curriculum, which integrated kindergarten training with study of aspects of the arts and sciences related to teaching young children. A primary education course was added in 1899, a permanent campus begun in 1914, and a nursery education course initiated in 1926. By the end of 1939, when Wheelock retired, enrollment at the school, which soon became a chartered college, had reached more than 350 students.

In addition to her work as a teacher trainer, Wheelock was active in the kindergarten movement nationally. In 1892 she was elected to the committee of the National Education Association, out of which the International Kindergarten Union was formed, and became the union's second president, serving from 1895 to 1899. In 1903 she was appointed to the International Kindergarten Union's Committee of Nineteen, which she chaired for five years, during which time the group attempted unsuccessfully to arrive at a compromise between Froebel's original, German kindergarten pedagogy and Americanized versions influenced by G. Stanley Hall's child study movement and other forms of developmental psychology. At issue was whether kindergarten teachers should continue using prescientific, formalistic educational methods or adapt Froebel's ideas on the basis of more modern, experimentally derived psychological research. Wheelock took the middle ground and coauthored a "liberal conservative" report with Chicago Kindergarten College founder Elizabeth Harrison, who also favored gradualism in the evolution of kindergarten methods. Wheelock's allegiance to Froebel was evident in her organization of a pilgrimage in the summer of 1911 for some seventy American kindergarten teachers to Froebel's birthplace in Germany. The Committee of Nineteen's final report, three competing positions on curriculum that Wheelock helped to edit, appeared in book form as *The Kindergarten* (1913).

Wheelock was very interested in educating women to be better mothers and in extending kindergarten education to the children of the poor. She thought all women should be taught how to use kindergarten methods at home with their own children and thought all children, rich and poor, would benefit from kindergarten education. In 1899 she was appointed to the committee on education of the National Congress of Mothers, the forerunner of the National Congress of Parents and Teachers, and served as liaison between this group and the International Kindergarten Union and the National Education Association. She toured the South in 1916 as part of a "Mother's Crusade" for kindergartens and was the primary author, with Elizabeth Colson, of a book of advice, *Talks to Mothers* (1920). She helped organize free kindergarten programs for children in impoverished sections of Boston, beginning in 1895 with a kindergarten for African-American children at Hope Chapel under the auspices of Boston's Old South Church. She also worked to introduce kindergarten methods to Sunday school teachers and wrote columns in the *Congregationalist* and edited the *Kindergarten Children's Hour*, a journal for Sunday school teachers. She wrote words and music for a religious song book, *Songs for Children*, and was the author of many widely read moral tales for young children. She also translated some of the children's stories of Johanna Spyri, the author of *Heidi*, which were published as *Red Letter Stories* (1884) and *Swiss Stories for Children* (1887).

Lucy Wheelock was a moderating and modernizing force within the American kindergarten movement. At a critical time when some insisted on adhering rigidly to Froebel's methods and others criticized their dogmatism and lack of grounding in developmental psychology, Wheelock tried to maintain good relations between older and younger kindergartners and mediated between orthodox Froebelianism and experimentation. A believer in the efficacy of committees and organizations, she was a member of many groups, including the Woman's Educational and Industrial Union in Boston, the Ruggles Street Neighborhood House in Roxbury, the House of Good Will in East Boston, the Twentieth Century Club of Boston, the Woman's Republican Club, and the Educational Committee of the League of Nations. Never married, she died in Boston, leaving the training school she had successfully launched as one of the principal private colleges specializing in the education of young children.

• Lucy Wheelock's unpublished autobiography, "My Life Story," and papers are held in the Lucy Wheelock Collection in the archives at Wheelock College in Boston, Mass. There is also a "Biography Report" by Winifred Linderman in the Lucy Wheelock File at the Schlesinger Library on the History of Women in America at Radcliffe College, Cambridge, Mass. There is a biographical entry on her in Frances E. Willard and Mary A. Livermore, eds., *A Woman of the Century* (1893). Her work is discussed in Winifred E. Bain, *Leadership in Childhood Education* (1964); Evelyn Weber, *The Kindergarten: Its Encounter with Educational Thought in America* (1969); Elizabeth Dale Ross, *The Kindergarten Crusade* (1976); Michael Steven Shapiro, *Child's Garden: The Kindergarten Movement from Froebel to Dewey* (1983); Barbara Beatty, "'The Kind of Knowledge of Most Worth to Young Women': Post-Secondary Vocational Training for Teaching and Motherhood at the Wheelock School, 1888–1914", *History of Higher Education Annual*, vol. 6 (1986), pp. 29–50; and Elizabeth Ann Liddle, ed., *Wheelock College: One Hundred Years* (1988).

BARBARA BEATTY

WHEELWRIGHT, John (c. 1592–15 Nov. 1679), clergyman, was born in Lincolnshire, England, probably in the town of Saleby where his grandfather John Wheelwright and his father, Robert Wheelwright, were large landholders in the fen country. (His mother's name is unknown.) John Wheelwright was admitted to Sidney Sussex College at Cambridge University in 1611. There he first met Oliver Cromwell, who was a fellow student at the college. Wheelwright received his B.A. in 1615 and his M.A. three years later. In 1619 he was ordained as a deacon and priest at Peterborough.

Having inherited a substantial estate from his father, Wheelwright married Marie Storre, daughter of the vicar of Bilsby, in 1621. Following the death of his father-in-law in 1623, he succeeded to the Reverend Storre's position and remained in Bilsby for the next decade. Following the death of his wife at the birth of their third child late in the 1620s, Wheelwright married Mary Hutchinson in 1630. (This marriage is believed to have produced six children.) Mary's brother was William Hutchinson, whose wife, Anne Hutchinson, would play a large role in Wheelwright's later career.

Wheelwright, along with other Puritan clergymen, found that changes in the church made it extremely difficult to conform to the practices required by the bishops. He lost his living, however, not because of nonconformity but because he was convicted of simony in 1632. He seems to have already thought of emigration because in 1629 he had evidently purchased land in what would become New Hampshire (though the authenticity of the deed has been questioned by some scholars). He did not actually emigrate until 1636, the same year as William Hutchinson and his family.

When Anne Hutchinson accused the ministers of Massachusetts of preaching a covenant of works, she exempted John Cotton and Wheelwright from her criticisms. Because Wheelwright became identified with Hutchinson's teachings and was supported by her and her followers, John Winthrop and other members of the First Church in Boston opposed his appointment as a second teacher of the congregation. Wheelwright was, however, chosen to become pastor of a new church in Mount Wollaston (now Quincy) in 1636. Preaching on a colony fast day in January 1637, Wheelwright emphasized that justification was by faith alone and attacked the preparationist views held by many of his clerical colleagues. In the sermon he acknowledged that his views might produce "a combustion in the Church and common wealth." Though he later argued that the magistrates had read into his sermon a rebellious intent that was not his purpose, in the inflamed state of affairs it became the basis for Wheelwright being charged and convicted of sedition and banished from the Bay in November 1637. A few months later, Hutchinson likewise was banished.

Wheelwright spent the winter in the vicinity of Squamscot, New Hampshire, and in April 1638 purchased land from the Indians where his family and friends founded the town of Exeter and a church to which he ministered. There he remained until 1643 when, following the Bay Colony's annexation of the region, Wheelwright and other residents of Exeter moved to Wells, in Maine. There he exchanged letters with the Massachusetts authorities, expressing a spirit of submission, and in May 1644 the General Court lifted his banishment. Despite this, he wrote a defense of his position in response to what he felt were misrepresentations of his views contained in Winthrop's account of the Antinomian Controversy, *A Short Story*, which was published in England in 1644. In correspondence with John Cotton and in his *Brief and Plain Apology* (1658), he steadfastly refused to concede that he was an Antinomian and defended himself against those who had called his Calvinist orthodoxy into question.

In 1647 Wheelwright moved again, back into the Bay jurisdiction to become pastor of the church in Hampton, New Hampshire. In late 1655 or early the following year he returned to England, where Cromwell had become lord protector. Wheelwright renewed their acquaintance and wrote to his former congregation in Hampton assuring them of Cromwell's orthodoxy. There is no record of him having assumed a clerical post or being deprived of such following the Restoration, but in 1662 he returned to New England. He became pastor of a congregation in Salisbury, New Hampshire, and preached there until he died.

Wheelwright was involved in some of the pivotal events in the seventeenth-century history of English and American Puritanism but did not have a significant role in any episode other than the Antinomian Controversy, in which he always maintained that his position was misunderstood. That blight on his record undoubtedly kept him on the periphery of New England religious life. Wheelwright seems to have displayed considerable ability in meeting the pastoral needs of frontier congregations, but he aspired to act on a larger stage. He failed to find one in either England or America.

• Wheelwright's *A Sermon Preached at New England upon a Fast Day* (1867) was published over a century after its delivery. It is most accessible in David D. Hall, ed., *The Antinomian Controversy, 1636–38: A Documentary History*, 2d ed. (1990), which also includes other documents relevant to Wheelwright's treatment. *Mercurius Americanus* (1645), often attributed to Wheelwright, was most likely written by his son, then a Cambridge student. Wheelwright's actual answer to his critics was *A Brief and Plain Apology* (1658). Correspondence is included in Charles H. Bell, ed., *John Wheelwright: His Writings* (1876). A biography is John Heard, Jr., *John Wheelwright, 1592–1679* (1939).

FRANCIS J. BREMER

WHEELWRIGHT, William (16 Mar. 1798–26 Sept. 1873), entrepreneur, was born in Newburyport, Massachusetts, the son of Ebenezer Wheelwright, a successful merchant, and Anna Coombs. Wheelwright attended Phillip's Andover Academy from 1812 to 1814 before persuading his parents to allow him to go to sea. After only three years' experience, he commanded a merchant vessel to Rio de Janeiro on a prosperous voyage. In 1823, while captaining another vessel (owned by the grandfather of his future bride), he ran aground off the coast of Argentina.

In 1824 a new acquaintance befriended Wheelwright by sponsoring his travel to Valparaiso, Chile, as the supercargo of a merchant vessel. Wheelwright found conditions in Chile chaotic, and so he moved to the Ecuadoran port of Guayaquil, the thriving principal harbor of Gran Colombia (now Ecuador, Colombia, and Venezuela) and the most active port on the Pacific side of South America. He became a successful merchant and was soon named the first U.S. consul in Guayaquil. He wanted "peace and tranquility" for his business but blamed the ambition and intrigue of Simón Bolívar for generating problems in the region. In 1828 Wheelwright obtained permission to leave a vice consul in charge while he returned to Newburyport. The following year he married Martha Gerrish Bartlet, the daughter of Edmund Bartlet, allegedly the richest man in Newburyport. They had three children, two of whom died in childhood.

When Wheelwright and his family returned to Ecuador, he discovered that a partner had totally mismanaged his business; he lost all his property, valued at $100,000. In addition, during his absence, Ecuador had separated from Gran Colombia, leaving his business in the port of an unimportant country that had an uncertain economic and political future. He decided to move his family to Valparaiso, Chile, where business prospects had improved vastly.

In Chile Wheelwright initiated a series of public works projects. He organized a modern fire company. He introduced pure water delivered in iron pipes; gas lighting in Valparaiso and Copiapó, Chile, and Callao, Peru; and kilns for manufacturing bricks in Chile. As a seaman, he managed to have badly needed lighthouses and buoys built at many South American ports. The public improvements he pursued in Chile were models for similar projects elsewhere in South America.

About 1830 Wheelwright began a small packet ship service between Valparaiso and Cobija, Peru, but his first major success in transportation occurred in 1835, when he persuaded the Chilean government to grant him a ten-year exclusive privilege to establish steam navigation on rivers and in ports that were open to coastal commerce. He intended to establish a steamer service from Valparaiso to Panama that would reduce the need for cargo between the Pacific coast of South America and Europe to pass through the Straits of Magellan. He obtained steamship concessions from Bolivia and Ecuador that would tie them into his steamer service to the Panama isthmus. He needed three years to locate capitalists in London who would underwrite the venture. In 1838 the Pacific Steam Navigation Company (PSNC) was capitalized at £250,000 ($1,250,000). In late 1840 he arrived in Chile with two 700-ton steamers, *Chile* and *Peru*, which initiated the PSNC service. Wheelwright provisionally solved one major problem for his steamship company—cheap coal—by uncovering a site in south Chile with mediocre coal that served until a better source became available. The PSNC had a difficult first decade. It had large losses during the first five years, and when it finally turned a profit in 1848, the gain was only 2.5 percent. Before the PSNC could solicit a renewal of its ten-year lease, the California gold rush had produced so much traffic and commerce on the Pacific side of the New World that seven Chilean companies were formed to bid for the steamer concession. The PSNC lost its exclusive concession after only a few profitable years. Wheelwright severed his ties with the PSNC in 1855.

In the 1840s Wheelwright had turned some of his attention to railroads. In 1842 he had petitioned for a contract to build a railroad from Santiago to Valparaiso. The contract, much revised, was finally granted in 1849, but the money markets had turned bad, and he could not undertake the project. In 1849 he formed the Copiapó Railway Company to connect the silver and copper mining area of Copiapó with the port of Caldera. This railroad—one of the first in South America—began operating in late 1851. The 750,000 pesos (the peso was roughly equal to the dollar) was raised locally.

In 1850 Wheelwright also built South America's first telegraph line. In the mid-1850s, however, Chilean officials became less receptive to Wheelwright's projects. His success with the privately funded Copiapó rail line prompted the Chilean government to reconsider building the Santiago to Valparaiso railroad using private funds. Wheelwright, however, was excluded from any role in finalizing the plans for a project that he had proposed earlier. In the 1850s Wheelwright sought to construct a potable water supply for Valparaiso. His plans were not well received, and Joshua Waddington, a British merchant naturalized in Chile, actually received favored treatment to institute a water supply system. Wheelwright's disillusionment with the Chilean government's conduct in this project may have contributed to his decision to leave Chile. More important, however, was the poor reception in Chile for his proposal to build a transandean railroad connecting the port of Caldera with Rosario, Argentina, on the Paraná River.

In 1855 Wheelwright visited Argentina, where he obtained a concession to build a 250-mile section of the transandean line from Rosario to Córdoba in central Argentina. In 1860 he moved to Argentina. British capitalists supplied about $8 million, and this section was completed in 1870. About $30 million was raised in Britain to complete the transandean line, but when the Argentine government began diverting funds to naval and military expenditures, Wheelwright and his British partners ceased transferring the funds to Argentina. Wheelwright's last major project implemented the vision to build a port at Ensenada that would serve Buenos Aires, because the Plata River was too shallow and treacherous for large ships to pass to Buenos Aires. In December 1872 he completed the rail link between Buenos Aires and Ensenada.

Wheelwright's health deteriorated noticeably in early 1873, and so he left for England, but he died in London soon after arriving. His death was sincerely mourned in the southern cone of South America. From his earlier days in Chile, a portrait of Wheelwright hung in the Valparaiso Merchant's Exchange, and in 1876 the Valparaiso Board of Trade erected a statue in his honor.

• There is no known repository of Wheelwright's papers. Wheelwright published several works related to his enterprises: *Statements and Documents Relative to the Establishment of Steam Navigation in the Pacific* (1838), *Report on Steam Navigation in the Pacific, with an Account of the Coal Mines of Chile and Panama* (1843), *Observations on the Isthmus of Panama* (1844), and "Proposed Railway across the Andes," *Journal of the Royal Geographical Society* 31 (1861). Jay Kinsbrunner has described William Wheelwright's early business career in "The Business Activities of William Wheelwright in Chile, 1829–1860" (Ph.D. diss., New York Univ., 1964) and added to the story in his *Chile: A Historical Interpretation* (1973). Episodes of Wheelwright's life in South America are retold in Fessenden Nott Otis, *History of the Panama Railroad* (1867); Frank G. Carpenter, *The Tail of the Hemisphere: Chile and Argentina* (1923); and Henry Clay Evans, *Chile and Its Relations with the United States* (1927). Two older, but useful, biographies are Juan B. Alberdi, *Life and Industrial Labors of William Wheelwright in South America* (1877); and Frederic M. Noa, "William Wheelwright: The Yankee Pioneer in Modern Industry in South America," *Arena* 36 (Dec. 1906): 591–602, and 37 (Jan. 1907): 31–38. An obituary is in *The Times* (London), 27 Sept. 1873.

THOMAS SCHOONOVER

WHERRY, Kenneth Spicer (28 Feb. 1892–29 Nov. 1951), businessman and politician, was born in Liberty, Nebraska, the son of David Emery Wherry, a storekeeper, and Jessie Comstock. When he was eight months old, his family moved to Pawnee City, Nebraska, where his father opened a farm implement, furniture, and undertaking establishment. Wherry graduated from the University of Nebraska in 1914 and studied law and business at the Harvard School of Business Administration. He served in the Naval Flying Corps during World War I but did not go overseas. After reading law privately, he won admission to the Nebraska bar in 1931.

In 1915 Wherry joined the prospering family firm, which now included an auto dealership. He opened Ford showrooms in two nearby towns, became president of Wherry Brothers in 1927, and later boasted of being certified in undertaking in three states. He took a civic activist's role in such endeavors as the county fair board. In 1920 he married Marjorie Colwell; they had two children.

The Wherrys were Presbyterians and Republicans. Like his father, a five-term mayor, Wherry took avidly to politics. In 1928 he was elected both mayor of Pawnee City (serving until 1931) and to the first of two terms as state senator. He lost bids for the Republican nomination for governor in 1932 and U.S. senator in 1934.

Though initially close to George W. Norris's wing of the party and progressive on such issues as banking and aid to farmers, Wherry grew more conservative in the 1930s. Norris's refusal to advance his career may have prompted Wherry to shift allegiance. Additionally, if, as one journalist claimed, Wherry's primary (and far from unique) bugaboo was "remote bigness," by the late 1930s New Deal "big government" had increasingly come to fill that role.

In 1938 Wherry became mayor again and eventually served four terms. Chosen chairman of the state Republican party in 1939, he earned acclaim for his energetic electioneering. In 1942, as Republican nominee for U.S. senator, he won a three-way race, retiring Norris from public life. He was reelected in 1948.

Wherry espoused a fundamentalist Republicanism as a senator. He fought the New and Fair Deals with a conservatism often more obdurate even than that of Robert A. Taft. Reviling the Office of Price Administration's "totalitarian controls" and the harm they did farmers and small businessmen, he defended the latter's interests as a member of two special committees on small business. He later opposed the Brannan Plan, federal aid to education, public housing, and other trappings of what he deemed the "socialistic welfare state."

Wherry's chief legislative contribution was a 1947 law altering the presidential succession, as ordained in 1886, by interposing the Speaker of the House and president pro tem of the Senate between the vice president and the members of the cabinet. In a rare instance of agreement with Harry S. Truman, Wherry thought it more democratic to place the two legislative officers ahead of unelected presidential appointees in the succession.

An isolationist, Wherry opposed such foreign policies as aid to Greece and Turkey, the Marshall Plan, and NATO (North Atlantic Treaty Organization), warning that the Truman Doctrine portended "a perpetual state of war emergency and government by control and crisis." He thought air power ample to defend the free world. In 1951 he authored a resolution opposing Truman's plan to send troops to Europe until Congress had elaborated a policy on the issue, but a softer substitute was passed. Wherry was outraged by the firing of General Douglas MacArthur.

Wherry's energetic partisanship gained him the post of minority whip, despite his junior status, in 1944. He was elected minority leader in 1949. A roughhouse partisan orator, Wherry often pounded his chest with his fists to emphasize a point. Such noted "Wherryisms" as references to "Indigo China" and "opple amportunity" showed that his verve sometimes outpaced his syntax. He died in Washington, D.C., of lung cancer.

• The Wherry papers are at the University of Nebraska, Lincoln. Most thorough on Wherry is Harl Adams Dalstrom, "Kenneth S. Wherry" (Ph.D. diss., Univ. of Nebraska, Lincoln, 1965). Sketchier and more admiring is Marvin E. Stromer, *The Making of a Political Leader: Kenneth S. Wherry and the United States Senate* (1969). Also see Dalstrom, "'Remote Bigness' as a Theme in Nebraska Politics: The Case of Kenneth S. Wherry," *North Dakota Quarterly* (Summer 1970), and William S. White, "Portrait of a Fundamentalist," *New York Times Magazine*, 15 Jan. 1950, pp. 14ff. Glimpses of Wherry appear in Allen Drury, *A Senate Journal* (1963). An obituary is in the *New York Times*, 30 Nov. 1951.

RICHARD M. FRIED

WHETSOL, Arthur Parker (1905–5 Jan. 1940), jazz trumpeter, was born in Punta Gorda, Florida. He was known by the nickname Artie. He became Arthur Parker Schiefe when his widowed mother remarried "Elder" Schiefe, a Seventh-Day Adventist minister. His natural father's given name is unknown.

Whetsol's mother ran a boardinghouse in Washington, D.C., where he became a childhood friend of Duke Ellington and reed player Otto Hardwick. Whetsol and Hardwick attended Garnet Elementary School. Whetsol may have attended Armstrong High School, but he and Hardwick reportedly played in the Dunbar High School orchestra. From 1920 on he performed with Ellington, pianist Claude Hopkins, and the White Brothers, and in June 1923 he traveled to New York City to join Ellington, Hardwick, and others in the Washingtonians, led by banjoist Elmer Snowden.

Later that year Whetsol returned home, ostensibly to study medicine at Howard University. Writer Mark Tucker reports that no record of Whetsol exists at Howard, and hence nothing is known of his activities before rejoining the then-famous Ellington orchestra in 1928 as its lead trumpeter and a soloist. He is featured on "Black Beauty" (recorded in 1928); "The Dicty Glide" and "Stevedore Stomp" in the film short *Black and Tan* and on "Jungle Jamboree" (all from 1929); "Rocky Mountain Blues" and "Mood Indigo" (both 1930); "Black and Tan Fantasy" (1932); and "A Hymn of Sorrow" in Ellington's film *Symphony in Black* (1934). The victim of a brain tumor, Whetsol began to suffer mental problems in 1935. He returned to Ellington's orchestra until the autumn of 1936, when illness forced his retirement. He died in New York City.

Tucker republished a 1937 press release describing Whetsol as "very loyal . . . always on the job even when not well . . . intellectual . . . tender personality . . . a bridge fanatic." Ellington summarized Whetsol's stylistic contributions: "We paid quite a lot of attention to our appearance, and if any one of us came in dressed improperly Whetsol would flick his cigarette ash in a certain way, or pull down the lower lid of his right eye with his forefinger and stare at the offending party." He added that Whetsol's "tonal character, fragile and genteel, was an important element in our music."

We have nothing more than these sketchy references to Whetsol's life. Nonetheless, he is regarded by aficionados as a significant figure in early jazz, both for the unknown specifics of his contributions to the formation of Ellington's big band from childhood to the Washingtonians and for the well documented evidence of his having recorded more than 100 solos with that band in its prime. In helping to create perhaps the most satisfying integration of sweet dance music and hot jazz, Whetsol's function within the brass section was, as Ellington indicated, to offer the sweet component by playing in a pretty manner. A certain rhythmic stiffness prevented him from being considered among the great jazz soloists, but in the Ellington mix this same quality served as a foil for the raucous and swinging melodies of his colleagues, trumpeters Bubber Miley and Cootie Williams and trombonist Joe "Tricky Sam" Nanton.

• Useful information on Whetsol is in Harvey Pekar, "Arthur Whetsol," *Jazz Journal* 16 (July 1963): 19, 22; G. E. Lambert, "The Ellingtonians, 1: Arthur Whetsol," *Jazz Monthly* 10 (Apr. 1964): 16–17; Duke Ellington, *Music Is My Mistress* (1973); Albert McCarthy, *Big Band Jazz* (1974); John Chilton, *Who's Who of Jazz: Storyville to Swing Street*, 4th. ed. (1985); James Lincoln Collier, *Duke Ellington* (1987); Mark Tucker, *Ellington: The Early Years* (1991); and Tucker, ed., *The Duke Ellington Reader* (1993). Dick M. Bakker, *Duke Ellington on Microgroove*, vol. 1: 1923–1936 (1977), identifies Whetsol's recorded solos. For musical description, see two works by Gunther Schuller, *Early Jazz: Its Roots and Musical Development* (1968) and *The Swing Era: The Development of Jazz, 1930–1945* (1989).

BARRY KERNFELD

WHIFFEN, Blanche Galton (12 Mar. 1844–25 Nov. 1936), actress and singer, was born in London, England, the daughter of Joseph West Galton, a secretary of the London General Post Office, and Mary Ann Pyne, an opera singer. After the death of her father in 1851, Whiffen and her sister attended a boarding school in Gravesend, Kent, until 1857. They later studied at Mrs. Chapman's School in London and spent eighteen months at a school in St. Omer, France. Whiffen made her stage debut in November 1865 at London's Royalty Theater as Rosatinta the Fairy in the light opera *Prince Amabel*. She occasionally filled in as the opera's lead contralto. Whiffen then spent a brief period as a singer and actress with a stock company at Portsmouth and toured Scotland with the Pyne and Harrison Opera Company, which was run by her aunt, the noted singer Louisa Pyne. While in Scotland she became engaged to Thomas Whiffen (originally Whiffin), a tenor with the Pyne and Harrison company. The couple married in London in July 1868 and eventually had two children.

Immediately after her marriage Whiffen (who was still known professionally as Blanche Galton) and her husband embarked for New York as members of the Galton Opera Company, a small troupe organized by her mother. In August 1868 Whiffen made her American debut at Wood's Theater in Offenbach's *Marriage by Lanterns*. After playing at New York's Opera Comique and touring in both Philadelphia and New Orleans, the Galton company disbanded, but Whiffen and her husband soon found singing and acting parts at Lina Edwin's theater in Albany, as well as at the Adelphi Theater in Boston. In 1871 Whiffen toured alone with the Horace Lingard Company as a singer and performer in comedy sketches. In the summer of 1872 Whiffen and her husband reunited to appear in Offenbach's *The Grand Duchess* in New York. The Whiffens, who were competent character actors as well as talented singers, remained together to play for a season with the John Templeton Company in Key West, Florida (1872–1873), and to appear with the Lingard company in the New York and national tour engagements of *The New Magdalene* (1873–1874), a stage adaptation of a Wilkie Collins novel. Whiffen then spent several years touring both with and without her husband in the Templeton, Lingard, and James A. Herne companies.

In 1878 Whiffen returned to New York to play Buttercup in the original American production of Gilbert and Sullivan's *H.M.S. Pinafore*. Thomas Whiffen, who had been a close friend of Sir Arthur Sullivan in England, took the part of Sir Joseph Porter. After a lengthy run in New York, the Whiffens played in the Chicago production of *H.M.S. Pinafore*. In 1800 Whiffen and her husband also had supporting parts in Steele MacKaye's *Hazel Kirke*. The crowd-pleasing melodrama opened in the new Madison Square Theater and ran for 486 performances, the longest run of a nonmusical production up to that time. The great success of *Hazel Kirke*, in which Whiffen played a middle-aged woman, channeled the round-faced yet gaunt Whiffen into older woman roles, though she was still in her mid-thirties. After *Hazel Kirke*, Whiffen also began using the name Mrs. Thomas Whiffen instead of Blanche Galton.

Whiffen and her husband stayed on as permanent members of the Madison Square Theater stock company. Whiffen was the shrewish mother of Annie Russell in Frances Hodgson Burnett's *Esmeralda* (1881). She also appeared in Bronson Howard's *The Young Mrs. Winthrop* (1883), with a youthful Henry Miller, who became a close friend of Whiffen; *Alpine Roses* (1884), with Richard Mansfield; *May Blossom* (1884), an early success for playwright David Belasco; *The Private Secretary* (1884), a farce by William Gillette; and *Denise* (1885), with Clara Morris.

In the summer of 1886 Whiffen and her husband returned to England and tried to reestablish themselves in their native country by putting on performances of *Hazel Kirke*. The venture did not succeed, and they returned to New York in the fall of 1887. Whiffen, without her husband, joined the newly formed stock company at the Lyceum Theater, managed by Daniel Frohman. Among the plays in which she appeared are Henry De Mille and David Belasco's *The Wife* (1887), with Georgia Cayvan and Arthur Wing; Pinero's *Sweet Lavender* (1888), with Cayvan and Henry Miller; *The Charity Ball* (1889), also by De Mille and Belasco; *Merry Gotham* (1892), by Elizabeth Marbury; and Oscar Wilde's *An Ideal Husband* (1895). In 1897, while touring with the Lyceum Theater stock company in a repertory of plays starring James K. Hackett, Whiffen received word that her husband, who was visiting relatives in England, was ill with typhoid. She left the Lyceum company to be with him and arrived two weeks before his death.

Whiffen was one of the most highly regarded and busiest character actresses in the history of American theater. One of her greatest successes was her portrayal of Mrs. Mossop in Pinero's popular comedy *Trelawny of the Wells* (1898), starring Mary Mannering and Hilda Spong. After the demise of the Lyceum Theater stock company in 1899, Whiffen went to San Francisco in a repertory of plays with Henry Miller and Margaret Anglin. Returning to New York, she worked for producer Charles Frohman in Clyde Fitch's *Captain Jinks of the Horse Marines* (1901), a popular drawing room comedy that launched Ethel Barrymore as a star. Whiffen also appeared with Barrymore in *Cousin Kate* (1903).

Whiffen suffered a stroke in 1904 but returned to the stage as soon as she was physically able. She kept working to keep herself young in spirit and to avoid the inevitable drift into obscurity endured by even the most prominent performers after they retire. "I don't mind old age, but I shudder at the thought of being forgotten. The apathy of the public is ghastly. You are forgotten, and your place is usurped before you can realize how it all happened," she told the *New York Dramatic Mirror* (18 Jan. 1896). Notable plays in the later part of Whiffen's career include *Zira* (1905), with Margaret Anglin; William Vaughn Moody's landmark drama *The Great Divide* (1906), also with Anglin; *Hedda Gabler* (1906), with Alla Nazimova; *The Brass Bottle* (1910), with Richard Bennett; Victorien Sardou's *A Scrap of Paper* (1914), with John Drew and Ethel Barrymore; *The Goose Hangs High* (1924), a comedy by Lewis Beach; and an all-star revival of *Trelawny of the Wells* (1927), with John Drew and Wilton Lackaye. Her last new role was Aunt Lydia Lee in the musical *Just Fancy!*, which opened in October 1927 (illness forced her to leave the production in March 1928), and her final stage appearance came in a benefit performance of *Trelawny of the Wells* in 1930. Whiffen acted in one film, *Hearts and Flowers* (1914), and also performed in vaudeville. She died at her son's home in Montvale, Virginia.

• Clippings files on Whiffen are at the New York Public Library for the Performing Arts and the Harvard Theater Collection. *Keeping off the Shelf* (1928) is Whiffen's autobiography. See also "Mrs. Whiffen Looks Back on 91 Full Years," *New York Herald-Tribune*, 22 Mar. 1936. An obituary is in the *New York Times*, 27 Nov. 1936.

MARY C. KALFATOVIC

WHIPPER, William (1804?–9 Mar. 1876), businessman and moral reformer, was born in Lancaster, Pennsylvania, the son of a white merchant and his black domestic servant. Very little is known about Whipper's early life or education. In the 1820s he moved to Philadelphia, where he worked as a steam scourer. In March 1834 he opened a free labor and temperance grocery store next door to the Bethel Church in Philadelphia. Whipper supported the temperance movement. He condemned liquor for its destructive effect on Africa and believed that alcohol consumption induced Africans into selling their brothers and sisters to slave traders. As a supporter of the antislavery movement, he also kept a supply of abolitionist books and pamphlets on hand for customers.

In 1835 he moved to nearby Columbia, Pennsylvania, and formed a successful business partnership with the black entrepreneur Stephen Smith. Their eventual holdings included a lumberyard, a merchant ship on Lake Erie, railroad freight cars, and real estate in Pennsylvania and Canada. Smith and Whipper amassed considerable wealth and were classified among the country's wealthiest blacks in the prewar years. Whipper married Harriet L. Smith in 1836.

For more than twenty years Whipper operated a major underground railroad station. Columbia was a major port of entry for fugitive slaves from Virginia and Maryland. Whipper housed as many as seventeen slaves in one night, the next day sending them to Pittsburgh by boat or to Philadelphia by rail in the false end of a boxcar. He estimated that over a thirteen-year period he spent $1,000 annually aiding hundreds of fugitive slaves.

In the 1830s Whipper began to participate in the antislavery and black national convention movements. Although he was not noted for being a great speaker, he gained prominence as an intellectual and moral reformer. In 1832 he helped to lead a petition campaign against a Pennsylvania state measure that restricted immigration of blacks and enforced the 1793 Fugitive Slave Law. Whipper credited the abolitionist movement with giving blacks a heightened sense of self-respect. He felt that the crusade had a more powerful influence on black life than any other influences combined. As a moral reformer, he believed that the movement served as a check on the evil dispositions of blacks and inculcated moral principles.

In his earlier years, Whipper was known as a Garrisonian. As such he felt that political participation and physical resistance by blacks should not be encouraged. He opposed separatist action until blacks developed strong internal social bonds among themselves. In an 1849 letter to Frederick Douglass, Whipper asserted that blacks had no national existence as a people and therefore could have no national institutions. Further, blacks lacked a distinct civil and religious code that generally served as rallying and unifying points for other groups.

As an integrationist, Whipper opposed terms that designated race. Therefore, in 1835 he urged delegates at the annual convention of the Improvement of Free People of Color to adopt a resolution giving up the use of the word "colored." The convention chose to organize a society with no racial designation, calling it only the American Moral Reform Society (AMRS). At the first annual meeting of the society in 1835, Whipper was elected its secretary and the editor of its journal, the *National Reformer*. His ideology shaped the character of the organization. However, his opposition to racially separate organizations often infuriated those members who wanted the AMRS to address race-specific issues.

Whipper's initial views on the origin and nature of American racism were that prejudice occurred because of the condition in which blacks found themselves, not because of their skin color. If blacks were to overcome their condition they had to conform to white expectations. That is, blacks had to improve their mental, economic, and moral situations. This, he believed, would ultimately change the attitudes of whites about race.

Although he maintained a lifelong commitment to moral reform, Whipper began to question its antislavery value in the 1840s. He also tempered his opposition to racial separatism in the 1850s. At the 1853 black national convention, he helped draft a plan for the National Council of Colored People and accepted the necessity of separate black schools. Consistent with black abolitionist thought in the 1850s, Whipper abandoned the "condition" argument and increasingly blamed racism on white ignorance.

Although Whipper was for years a faithful opponent of colonization to Africa and a supporter of integration, he became more receptive to the idea of black emigration. He endorsed the African Civilization Society, an organization for which he served as a vice president (c. 1853–1854). He saw emigration as a rational response of people who were dispossessed and persecuted.

In 1853 Whipper visited Canada, where he purchased land on the Sydenham River at Dresden, Ontario. Several of his relatives emigrated, and he had plans to emigrate as well. However, those plans were interrupted by the start of the Civil War. During the war, Whipper promoted black enlistment in the Union army and later served as vice president of the Pennsylvania State Equal Rights League.

After 1865 Whipper conducted his lumber business with his nephew, James Purnell. He had been sole operator of the business since 1842 when his partner had moved to Philadelphia. In 1868 he moved to New Brunswick, New Jersey. Two years later he took a position as a cashier of the Philadelphia branch of the Freedmen's Savings Bank, returning in 1873 to reside in Philadelphia, where he died.

• Sterling Stuckey, comp., *The Ideological Origins of Black Nationalism* (1972), contains references to Whipper as well as three letters written by him in 1841. William Still, *The Underground Railroad* (1879), contains a brief biography, portrait, and autobiographical memoir of Whipper. Richard P. McCormick, "William Whipper: Moral Reformer," *Pennsylvania History* 43 (Jan. 1976): 23–46, provides a biographical study of Whipper. Jane H. Pease and William Pease, *They Who Would Be Free: Blacks' Search for Freedom, 1830–1861* (1974), contains several references to Whipper, particularly outlining his position as a moral reformer. C. Peter Ripley, ed., *The Black Abolitionist Papers*, vol. 3 (1985), contains a brief biographical sketch of Whipper as well as scattered references. He is also mentioned in volume four, in which there are letters from him to Frederick Douglass and Gerrit Smith. Benjamin Quarles, *Black Abolitionists* (1969), addresses Whipper's views on the antislavery movement.

MAMIE E. LOCKE

WHIPPLE, Abraham (26 Sept. 1733–27 May 1819), privateersman and naval officer, was born in Providence, Rhode Island. According to a family genealogy, he was the son of Noah Whipple and Mary (maiden name unknown); no official birth information is extant. After going to sea at an early age Whipple became associated with the Brown family in the West India trade. During the Seven Years' War Whipple served as a privateersman under the command of Esek Hopkins, whose sister Sarah he married in 1761. They had three children. He later commanded the *Gamecock*, a successful privateer out of Providence.

In 1772 Whipple led a party of Rhode Islanders in an attack on the British schooner *Gaspée*. The schooner had been patrolling Narragansett Bay on the lookout for smugglers, and its success made it a great nuisance to the merchants and seamen of Providence. With about forty men, Whipple, during the night of 10 June 1772, boarded and burned the schooner. The exploit made Whipple a hero in Rhode Island.

Whipple's reputation as a seaman, privateersman, and patriot made him the logical choice to command the two-vessel Rhode Island navy when it was formed in June 1775. After the Congress created the Continental navy, Whipple was commissioned in that force. His Rhode Island command *Katy* was also taken into the new navy and renamed *Providence*, with Whipple still in command. In November Whipple was given *Columbus* and joined Esek Hopkins in his attack on Nassau in March 1776. In 1778 Whipple took command of the *Providence*, which made a successful voyage to France to obtain valuable supplies of arms and uniforms.

Whipple's most famous wartime exploit occurred in July 1779. *Providence* was cruising in company with *Queen of France* and *Ranger* off the coast of Newfoundland. Early in the morning of 18 July through heavy fog they heard the sound of ship bells. Whipple soon realized that he had sailed into the British Jamaica fleet, sixty vessels heavily laden with cargo. The three American frigates cut out several prizes, seven of which they brought safely to Boston, where they were auctioned. The proceeds were divided between the captors and the Congress. It was the richest haul of the Revolution; Whipple and his crew shared nearly $1 million.

Toward the end of the war Whipple was sent to Charles Town (Charleston), South Carolina, to help defend it against British attack. When the city fell on 12 May 1780, he was taken prisoner. He was released on parole and never resumed his duties as a naval officer. After the war he returned to Rhode Island but in 1788 headed west and settled on a farm in Marietta, Ohio, with his family. Aside from a voyage to New Orleans and Havana in 1801 Whipple lived in Marietta, where he died.

• The Abraham Whipple Papers are located at the Rhode Island Historical Society in Providence. Other important manuscript items, including correspondence and reports, can be found in the papers of the Continental Congress at the National Archives. The most lengthy treatment of Whipple can be found in William James Morgan, *Captains to the Northward: The New England Captains in the Continental Navy* (1959). Whipple is also discussed in the standard histories of the Continental navy, including Gardner W. Allen, *A Naval History of the American Revolution* (2 vols., 1913), and William M. Fowler, Jr., *Rebels under Sail: The American Navy during the Revolution* (1976).

WILLIAM M. FOWLER, JR.

WHIPPLE, Allen Oldfather (2 Sept. 1881–6 Apr. 1963), surgeon and teacher, was born in Urmia, Persia (later Resaiyeh, Iran), the son of William L. Whipple, a Presbyterian clergyman, and Mary Allen. After spending his boyhood in the Near East, he entered Princeton and graduated in 1904. He then attended Columbia's College of Physicians and Surgeons and graduated with his medical degree in 1908, then interned for two years at Roosevelt Hospital in New York. He briefly joined the faculty of the Sloane Hospital for Women in New York, then in 1911 became a staff surgeon at Presbyterian Hospital.

In 1912 Whipple married Mary Neales; they had three children. In 1921 he was appointed Valentine Mott Professor of Surgery and director of surgical services at the Presbyterian Hospital. He held these positions with distinction for twenty-five years and trained more than 300 promising young surgeons during his tenure as chief of surgery.

In 1928 Whipple and Walter Palmer established the spleen clinic. There they accumulated valuable knowledge that resulted in innovative treatments of spleen and liver diseases. With talented physicians A. H. Blakemore, J. W. Rousselot, J. W. Lord, W. D. Thompson, and others, Whipple made numerous advances in understanding and managing splenic and hepatic disorders. These included the use of splenectomy in treating thrombotic thrombocytopenic purpura, the discovery of the role of intrahepatic and extrahepatic hypertension in Banti's syndrome, and the origination of the concept that it was a congestive condition rather than a primary spleenomegaly. To aid in the diagnosis he routinely measured the spleen and portal pressures and used portocaval shunts to treat portal hypertension.

Whipple also contributed to the management of pancreatic diseases. He pioneered operations to remove pancreatic tumors, which resulted in his recognition as the "father of pancreatic surgery." Based on his experience in the management of pancreatic tumors, Whipple defined the symptoms of hyperinsulinism, which later became known as Whipple's triad: spontaneously occurring hypoglycemia (low blood sugar), acute onset of the symptoms of severe hypoglycemia, and the relief of those symptoms by administration of glucose (sugar).

Prior to Whipple's work, the pancreas was forbidden territory to the surgeon because of the risk of shock, hemorrhage, sepsis, and jaundice. Whipple eradicated early objections to partial pancreatectomy by showing that, if one maintained a normal bile flow through the common bile duct, the remaining pancreas could be sewn into the small bowel and the function of the residual pancreas preserved.

After retirement Whipple spent the years between 1945 and 1951 reorganizing the training program at Memorial Hospital in New York. He also revised the medical program at the American University of Beirut in Lebanon. In World War II, Whipple served as a member of the National Research Council as well as a consultant for the Council of Great Britain in North Africa. He served as editor of *Nelson's Looseleaf Surgery* for twenty years and was an editorial board member for the *Annals of Surgery* between 1932 and 1946. In 1951 he was elected as a charter trustee at Princeton. The following year the Allen O. Whipple Society was established to honor distinguished contributors to surgery. He also received the Woodrow Wilson Award, the highest honor given to alumni by Princeton, and served as president of the American Surgical Association and the New York Surgical Society. He was also a fellow of the American College of Surgeons, the Royal College of Surgeons, and the New York Academy of Medicine. He died in Princeton, New Jersey.

Considered a gifted teacher and an innovative surgeon, Whipple made numerous contributions to the science of surgery and spent his entire life seeking new ways to heal his patients. One of his colleagues wrote, "His greatest contribution was his continued dedication to teaching, guidance, and encouragement of others," and this is surely evidenced by his work.

• The scanty information on Whipple that is available can be found in Fordyce St. John, "Allen Oldfather Whipple, 1881–1963," *Transactions of the American Surgical Association* 82 (1964): 471–72. See also "Allen Whipple Awarded Distinguished Service Medal," *American Medical Association Journal* (23 June 1951), and T. S. N. Chen and P. S. Y. Chen, *The Whipples and Their Legacies in Medicine, Surgery, Gynecology, and Obstetrics* (1993), pp. 501–6. Obituaries are in the *New York Times*, 17 Apr. 1963, and *Time*, 26 Apr. 1963.

DAVID Y. COOPER
MICHELLE E. OSBORN

WHIPPLE, Edwin Percy (8 Mar. 1819–16 June 1886), author and lecturer, was born in Gloucester, Massachusetts, the son of Matthew Whipple and Lydia Gardiner. When Whipple was eighteen months old, his father died of cholera, and his mother moved to Salem, Massachusetts, with her four young sons. Whipple attended school in Salem, took commercial courses, and graduated from high school in 1834. He clerked in Salem's Bank of General Interest and voraciously read books of literature and history in his spare time. In 1837 he moved to Boston, where he was a clerk and then the chief clerk for Dana, Fenno and Henshaw, a banking and brokerage firm. He continued to read widely and began to collect books. He also socialized and debated with fellow members of two Boston organizations, the Mercantile Library Association and the Attic Nights Club, the latter of which he helped found.

Whipple occasionally presented his writings before members of both groups. In 1840 he read his one and only poem at an association gathering. More important, he began to write essays of literary criticism. He anonymously published an uncharacteristically harsh piece (*Boston Notion*, 18 Dec. 1841) on Edgar Allan Poe, rebuking him for his subjective and dictatorial critical stance. Often unsigned, Whipple's earliest works, some of which appeared in the *Boston Times*, have never been completely identified and listed. His unusually perceptive essay on Thomas Babington Macaulay (*Boston Miscellany*, Feb. 1843) attracted considerable local notice and even a commendation from Macaulay himself. Whipple acutely analyzed works of literature as organic, stemming from the subject's personal life and feelings and possessed at their best of a living unity. This critical approach owes much to his appreciative study of the aesthetic theories of August Wilhelm von Schlegel and Samuel Taylor Coleridge. Their insights and those of other romantic European critics also inspired Ralph Waldo Emerson, Whipple's friend and one of his favorite authors. Whipple's regard for poetry as a splendid medium for the reform and inculcation of moral values is evident in his extensive review (*American Review*, July 1845) of *The Poets and Poetry of England in the Nineteenth Century*, Rufus Wilmot Griswold's influential 1842 book. Typical of Whipple's sentimental style is his lauding of Oliver Wendell Holmes's poetry for its "clear sweetness and skylark thrill." In his "British Critics" (*North American Review*, Oct. 1845), Whipple tempers his praise of British analysts of literature by labeling many of them too intense, and he voices his preference for Coleridge in "Coleridge as a Philosophical Critic" (*American Review*, June 1846).

Whipple discontinued work in the brokerage office in 1844 or 1845 and began to supervise the news office of the Merchant's Exchange Building, a post he held until 1860. In 1847 he married Charlotte B. Hastings; the couple had two children. His wife knew Holmes, whom Whipple was therefore able to meet and through whom he gained entrance into that influential man's circle of acquaintances. Whipple continued to publish short pieces, which he collected in *Essays and Reviews* (2 vols., 1848, 1849). This work was so popular that it went into a second edition in 1850 and enjoyed a twelfth edition in 1888. Beginning in the late 1840s he was a consultant for James Thomas Fields of the Boston publishing firm of Ticknor, Reed and Fields, and in that capacity was involved in the publication in 1850 of *The Scarlet Letter* by Nathaniel Hawthorne. Whipple tempered his generally favorable review of that novel (*Graham's Magazine*, May 1850) by deploring its morbidity. Possibly as a result, Hawthorne's next novel, *The House of the Seven Gables* (1851), the title for which Whipple had a hand in recommending, has a slightly lighter, more humorous tone. Hawthorne was so grateful for Whipple's perceptive review of it (*Graham's*, May 1851) that he sought his aid in revising *The Blithdale Romance* (1852), which Whipple's review (*Graham's*, Sept. 1852) praised for its organic unity. The publication in 1860 of *The Marble Faun* occasioned Whipple's partly negative general assessment of Hawthorne (*Atlantic Monthly*, May 1860) that Hawthorne regarded as "keen and profound."

Whipple was one of the original members of the Saturday Club, the famous literary dinner club established in Boston in 1855. He was also a popular lecturer and appeared on lyceum platforms from the early 1840s to the mid-1850s an estimated thousand times, traveling north as far as Maine and west into Ohio. He assembled six speeches in *Lectures on Subjects Connected with Literature and Life* in 1849 (expanded as *Literature and Life* [1871]) and six more in *Character and Characteristic Men* in 1866. Whipple was the official orator for Boston's Fourth of July celebration in 1850. Best among his formal platform appearances were his twelve Lowell Institute lectures in 1859, published in magazine form (*Atlantic Monthly*, Feb. 1867–Dec. 1868) and then as *The Literature of the Age of Elizabeth* (1869). In these pieces he especially lauded the plays of William Shakespeare for their range, display of tolerance, vividness, and organic unity. In 1872 Whipple became the literary editor of the *Boston Daily Globe*. He and his wife established an informal salon in their home, which his genial personality, gentle wit, and conversational ability, combined with his fame as a critic, made attractive.

Whipple was in ill health during his last ten years. His final writings are marked by continued critical conservatism. Whipple idolized Charles Dickens and George Eliot, about both of whom he wrote skillfully, but he did not like the new realists, many of whom were inspired by Walt Whitman. Whipple's most quotable judgment—that the *Leaves of Grass* poet had every leaf but the fig leaf—betrays his conservatism. He could not appreciate Whitman's more rugged forms of expression and more liberated embrace of subject matter. Publication of Whipple's *Works* (6 vols., 1885–1887) began shortly before his death, which occurred in Boston. Sadly, the book he is best remembered by, *Recollections of Eminent Men, with Other Papers*, was published posthumously (1887). Best among these essays, many of which first appeared in periodicals, are his favorable judgments concerning Louis Agassiz, Rufus Choate, Emerson, John Lothrop Motley, Charles Sumner, and George Ticknor. Another posthumous collection is his *American Literature and Other Papers* (1887). Of great value in it is "American Literature 1776–1876," a lengthy pioneering survey (*Harper's Magazine*, Feb. and Mar. 1876) displaying critical acumen in comments on Benjamin Franklin and Jonathan Edwards and in predicting fame for Mark Twain and Henry James. Time has passed Whipple by, but in the mid-nineteenth century he was surpassed only by Poe and James Russell Lowell as an informed, judicious, and comprehensive critic.

• Many of Whipple's papers are in libraries at Harvard University, the University of Illinois, the University of Virginia, and Yale University. Others are in the Boston Public Library; the Buffalo and Erie County Public Library, Buffalo, N.Y.; and the Historical Society of Pennsylvania, Philadelphia. Edward Waldo Emerson, *The Early Years of the Saturday Club, 1855–1870* (1918), has an evaluative chapter on Whipple's personality, ability, and limitations. Van Wyck Brooks, *The Flowering of New England, 1815–1865* (1936), briefly defines Whipple's personality and accomplishments. John McAleer, *Ralph Waldo Emerson: Days of Encounter* (1984), touches on Whipple's relationship to and opinions of Emerson. Obituaries are in the *Boston Transcript* and the *New York Times*, both 18 June 1886.

ROBERT L. GALE

WHIPPLE, George Hoyt (28 Aug. 1878–1 Feb. 1976), pathologist and medical educator, was born in Ashland, New Hampshire, the son of Ashley Cooper Whipple, a physician, and Anna Hoyt. His home was surrounded by lakes and mountains, and he spent a happy childhood filled with days of hunting, fishing, and camping, activities he continued to enjoy into his ninth decade.

Whipple was two when his father died. His mother, a well-read woman who sought the best educational opportunities for her son, enrolled him in 1892 in Phillips Andover Academy in Andover, Massachusetts. From there he went to Yale (1896–1900), where he met Lafayette B. Mendel, a young biochemist who loved research and took a personal interest in his students. Lacking the money to continue his studies after Yale, Whipple taught for a year at Dr. Holbrook's Military School in Ossining, New York.

At his mother's urging he then enrolled in Johns Hopkins Medical School, the nation's premier medical school. Upon his graduation in 1905, his other great mentor, William H. Welch, offered him a position as assistant in pathology.

During the nine years he stayed at Johns Hopkins, Whipple investigated the pathology of tuberculosis and pancreatic disease. His autopsy of a physician whose illness had baffled prominent internists led Whipple to publish a paper on intestinal lipodystrophy ("Whipple's disease"). In 1907 he left Hopkins for a year to join the pathology staff of Ancon Hospital in Panama. The position gave him the opportunity to study tropical diseases and led to an important publication on blackwater fever, a severe form or complication of malaria. The money he saved while working in Panama enabled him to do postgraduate study in Heidelberg and Vienna.

In 1914 Whipple accepted an invitation from the University of California at San Francisco to organize a new medical research institute established by the Hooper Foundation. Shortly before assuming this position he married Katharine Ball Waring of Charleston, South Carolina, whom he had met while he was in medical school; they would have two children. Whipple's new position carried with it a professorship of pathology, and in 1920 he became dean of the medical school at UCSF.

Soon after his move to California, Whipple began a study of the influence of food on blood regeneration in dogs (1915–1925). With the help of his able assistant, Frieda Robscheit-Robbins, Whipple withdrew blood from the dogs until he had induced anemia and then fed them different foods to see which ones were best in treating the kind of anemia that results from the loss of blood (secondary anemia). He found that liver was one of the best foods for the production of new, hemoglobin-filled red blood cells. This discovery gave George R. Minot (1885–1950), a Harvard hematologist, and his assistant, William P. Murphy, the idea of using a liver diet to treat pernicious anemia in humans, a previously incurable and fatal disease. For this work Minot, Murphy, and Whipple were awarded the 1934 Nobel Prize in medicine or physiology.

Whipple's work on blood regeneration was temporarily interrupted when he moved to Rochester, New York, where in 1921 he agreed to serve as dean of the proposed new medical school of the University of Rochester. It was to be established with a grant of $10 million from the General Education Board of the Rockefeller Foundation and local philanthropists. It took four years of hard work to get the Rochester School of Medicine and Dentistry started. Whipple recruited outstanding department chairmen, most of whom were still in the early stages of their scientific careers.

Whipple was industrious, frugal, and imperturbably calm. By insisting on economy and simplicity, he got all the buildings of the new medical school in Rochester built in less time and for far less money than had been projected. His biographer, and ex-pupil and colleague, George W. Corner, wrote that in dealing with students, Whipple "had learned from [Franklin P.] Mall not to spoon-feed medical students, from [William] Osler to treat them as if they were professional colleagues, and from [William H.] Welch not to despair of them."

Whipple retired as dean in 1953 at the age of seventy-five, but retained the professorship of pathology until 1955. His last and most sophisticated scientific study was of the body's methods for storing and releasing proteins, which he summarized in his only book, *The Dynamic Equilibrium of Body Proteins* (1956). He died in Rochester.

• A bibliography of Whipple's writings is found in George W. Corner, *George Hoyt Whipple and His Friends: The Life-Story of a Nobel Prize Pathologist* (1963). See also his "Autobiographical Sketch," *Perspectives in Biology and Medicine* 2 (Spring 1959): 253–89.

STUART GALISHOFF

WHIPPLE, Guy Montrose (12 June 1876–1 Aug. 1941), educational psychologist and editor, was born in Danvers, Massachusetts, the son of John Francis Whipple, a wounded Civil War veteran working as mail carrier, and Cornelia Eliza Hood, a schoolteacher who took up painting in her old age. He received an A.B. from Brown University in 1897, spent a year as assistant in psychology at Clark University, and in 1898 moved to a similar position at Cornell University. In 1901 he married Clarice Johnson Rogers; they had three sons. In 1925 he married Helen Davis, they had one son.

Whipple received his Ph.D. under. E. B. Titchener at Cornell in 1900, starting out in "pure" experimental psychology and contributing several pieces to its apparatus, such as the "Whipple Disk Tachistoscope" and a chronoscope. Soon, however, he began to move toward the application of psychology, especially to education. In 1906 he began work on what became one of his major contributions, the landmark *Manual of Mental and Physical Tests: A Book of Directions Compiled with Special Reference to the Experimental Study of School Children in the Laboratory or Classroom* (1910). The first edition of this work, which contributed much to the standardization of test administration, was followed by a two-volume second edition in 1914–1915. Whipple's interest in testing also led him to translate from the original German text William Stern's *Psychological Methods of Testing Intelligence* (1914), which introduced the new method of describing test results by means of the "Mental Quotient," later renamed the "Intelligence Quotient" by Lewis M. Terman. In 1914 Whipple was elected to the governing council of the American Psychological Association, where he introduced a resolution in the following year that the association discourage the administration of psychological tests by persons without psychological training. Although his proposal was adopted, this attempt to impose some control on the then mushrooming test usage was unworkable in the long run.

In 1914 Whipple moved from Cornell, where he had been assistant professor of educational psychology, to the University of Illinois, as associate professor of education. In 1917 he joined the unique new program in applied psychology at Carnegie Institute of Technology in Pittsburgh, replacing Walter D. Scott as acting director of the institute's Bureau of Salesmanship Research and becoming one of the first professors of applied psychology. After the outbreak of World War I he joined R. M. Yerkes and L. M. Terman on the famous Committee on Methods of Psychological Examining of Recruits at the Training School in Vineland, New Jersey. There he participated in the creation of the classic Army Alpha and Beta group intelligence tests. Subsequently, he participated in 1917 in the first trials of the new tests as chief examiner at Fort Benjamin Harrison, Indiana, and later that year, remaining a civilian, joined Yerkes's Division of Psychology in the Surgeon General's Office, U.S. Army, as advisory staff member.

After the war Whipple became professor of experimental education at the University of Michigan from 1919 to 1925. During that time he also served on the National Research Council and became a director of the National Intelligence Test, which, sponsored by the NRC as a civilian adaptation of the army intelligence tests, was used in the testing of millions of school children in the 1920s. He responded to the public attacks on intelligence testing then launched by journalist Walter Lippmann, philosopher John Dewey, and others by defending Lewis Terman's hereditarian views against fellow educational psychologist William C. Bagley's charges of "Educational Determinism" and against what he called Lippmann's "exhibition of stupidity."

Whipple had served from 1910 to 1920 as coeditor of the new *Journal of Educational Psychology*. Eventually editorial work became his main occupation, after he left academia in 1928 for reasons that are not entirely clear. From 1928 to 1937 he was the editor for elementary school books with Heath and Co., a major textbook publisher. He also served as secretary-treasurer of the National Society for the Study of Education and as editor of its yearbooks for more than twenty-five years, almost up to his death. In this capacity he organized the publication of two important yearbook volumes, in 1928 and in 1940, on the "Nature-Nurture" controversy and on the battle between the Stanford hereditarians and the Iowa Child Welfare Station environmentalists.

Whipple belonged to the second generation of American academics taking up the "New Psychology." His contributions to its development, for which he was "starred" in J. M. Cattell's *American Men of Science* of 1909, were in effect more methodological than substantive. The trajectory of his career is, if not quite representative, still noteworthy. After starting out, under Titchener's tutelage, in pure laboratory psychology, working on discrimination of tones and chords, he found himself fairly soon attracted to more applied problems. Gradually he moved away from psychology and, as Frank Freeman (1984) speculates, was perhaps pushed out by Titchener's intolerance to anything but "pure" science. By the 1930s he had even dropped his membership in the American Psychological Association and ceased publishing in its journals. He died in Clifton, Massachusetts, where he had spent the latter part of his life, not far from the Marblehead Yacht Club, which he had joined as charter member.

• A discussion of Whipple in the secondary literature is Frank S. Freeman, "A Note on E. B. Titchener and G. M. Whipple," *Journal of the History of the Behavioral Sciences* 20 (1984): 177–79. An obituary is by Christian A. Ruckmick, in the *American Journal of Psychology* 55 (1942): 132–34.

FRANZ SAMELSON

WHIPPLE, Henry Benjamin (15 Feb. 1822–16 Sept. 1901), Episcopal bishop and champion of Indian rights, was born in Adams, New York, the son of John Hall Whipple, a merchant, and Elizabeth Wager. Raised in a Presbyterian home, he studied in private schools supported by that denomination until he went to Oberlin College in 1838. Forced by poor health to leave the following year, Whipple spent the first decade of his adult life as an inspector of township schools and a militiaman and served for a year as secretary of the New York Democratic party (1847). He was also continuously associated with his father's mercantile activities. In 1842 he married Cornelia Wright; over the years they had six children. Whipple's wife belonged to the Episcopal church, as did his grandparents. This combination of influences helped him decide to become Episcopalian too and to seek the priesthood. Accordingly, he studied theology under William D. Wilson of Albany, New York, from 1847 to 1850. After ordination as deacon in 1849 and as priest in 1850 he was ready for an ecclesiastical vocation.

The first place where Whipple served as rector was Zion Episcopal Church in Rome, New York. His years there extended from 1850 to 1857, interrupted by one hiatus. Cornelia Whipple's persistent illness called for a warmer climate, and so from 1853 to 1854 the rector accompanied her south and conducted missionary work in St. Augustine, Florida. After further success in New York, he served briefly (1857–1859) as rector of the Church of the Holy Communion in Chicago, Illinois. There his energy, compassion for the working poor, and zeal to provide benefit of clergy for everyone in a large parish drew the attention of ecclesiastical superiors. In 1859 he was named the first bishop of Minnesota.

Minnesota had become a state less than a year before Whipple became bishop and still consisted largely of frontier expanses dotted by small settlements. After arriving at his diocesan headquarters in Faribault, Whipple threw himself into visitations and clerical surveys intended to expand Episcopal presence in the burgeoning territory. His travels were lengthy and arduous; his health remained precarious; his complaints were few. His work among white parishioners stimulated church growth, and over time he helped provide for continuing stable leadership by founding St. Mary's Hall, the Shattuck Military Academy, and Seabury Divinity School, all in Faribault. These successes notwithstanding, it was his work among Native Americans that made him internationally famous.

Missionary work among local native groups had already been inaugurated by pioneering evangelicals such as James L. Breck and Jackson Kemper. Their efforts took place principally among the Ojibway (Chippewa), who had originally inhabited approximately half of the state. Whipple strengthened these efforts, especially on the White Earth Reservation, and urged that men like Enmegahbowh and Good Thunder, local natives who fellow tribe members already trusted, be ordained deacons. Those natives and other converts accompanied the bishop on frequent visits to Indian churches, including those at Birch Coulee and Gull Lake. There they served as interpreters and as ad hoc pastors in their own right. By 1860 Whipple also instigated missionary outreach to the eastern Dakota, or Santee Sioux, the state's other major resident tribe. It was this contact that taught Whipple how the national government mismanaged its treaty obligations to native groups. By 1862 violent protest erupted among the Dakotas, and after Little Crow's War was quelled, Whipple proved instrumental in having the death sentence commuted for more than three hundred captives.

This intercession was not Whipple's first experience with governmental authorities. As early as 1859 he wrote President James Buchanan about suffering among the Indians, drawing his comments from his own direct observation. The following year he traveled to Washington, D.C., in order personally to urge federal authorities to protect natives from encroaching whites, prevent liquor traffic, provide adequate schools, establish decent reservations, and inspect agencies regularly to ensure compliance. These points became standard pleas, and for the next three decades Whipple waged a steady campaign through correspondence and lectures to achieve better treatment of native charges at the hands of businesspeople and politicians. His perennial efforts to reform Indian service made frontiersmen resent him, while eastern philanthropists applauded his service on treaty commissions and his advocacy of both civilization and Christianization for Native Americans. His reputation for opposing fraud and deceit gained him the nickname "Straight Tongue." Toward the end of his episcopate Whipple became honorary presiding bishop of the Protestant Episcopal church in 1897. A compelling orator, he was renowned on two continents for stirring sermons and addresses. After his first wife died in 1890, he subsequently married Evangeline Marrs Simpson in 1896. He died in Faribault after more than four decades of episcopal activity.

• The main depository of Whipple's papers, including correspondence, diaries, and notebooks, is housed under his name at the Minnesota Historical Society. Related materials are also housed there under the heading of the Minnesota diocese of the Episcopal church. Whipple's own publications are *Five Sermons* (1890) and *Lights and Shadows of Long Episcopate* (1899). There is information of some use in Lester B. Shippee, ed., *Bishop Whipple's Southern Diary, 1843–1844* (1937), and Phillips Endecott Osgood, *Straight Tongue: A Story of Henry Benjamin Whipple, First Episcopal Bishop of Minnesota* (1958). An obituary is in the *New York Times*, 17 Sept. 1901.

HENRY WARNER BOWDEN

WHIPPLE, Prince (fl. 1776–1783), revolutionary war soldier, was born to unknown parents in Amabou, Africa. When Whipple was about ten, his parents sent him to America with either a brother or cousin, ostensibly to be educated in the manner of Prince's older brother, who had returned from America four years before. Unfortunately, the captain of the ship on which the two boys traveled diverted to Baltimore, Maryland, and sold them into slavery instead.

Prince Whipple was purchased by William Whipple, a Portsmouth, New Hampshire, merchant. During the American Revolution, William Whipple was a member of the Continental Congress, a signer of the Declaration of Independence, and a captain and later a general in the New Hampshire militia. When his master periodically took the field in command of his New Hampshire troops between 1776 and 1779, Prince Whipple fought with him as his personal "body guard." Many army and militia officers brought slaves with them into the military service, and periodically slaves were even sent to serve in place of their masters in the enlisted ranks.

William Whipple emancipated Prince Whipple during the revolutionary war, at least partly in recognition of his bravery and military service. Though Prince Whipple served part of the war as William Whipple's property, he received the same freedom that most slaves who fought in the war gained either by running away or as a personal reward for service.

Legend has it that Prince Whipple is the black man in the famous nineteenth-century artistic depictions of George Washington crossing the Delaware River in the attack on Trenton, New Jersey, in December 1776. Thomas Sully, who painted the scene in 1819 for the state of South Carolina, depicted an African American on horseback at Washington's side, and Emmanuel Leutze in his 1851 painting showed an African-American man rowing Washington's boat across the frozen river. Prince Whipple sometimes served as an aide to General Washington. However, it is unclear whether Whipple was actually present at the crossing of the Delaware because William Whipple did not see most of his military action until later in the war. Regardless of whether or not the figure actually represents Prince Whipple, he did become a patriotic hero to nineteenth-century abolitionists, who believed he was the man the artists depicted. For example, in 1858 black abolitionists William Nell and Lewis Hayden included an engraving of Prince Whipple crossing the Delaware in an exhibit of revolutionary "relics" at Faneuil Hall organized in celebration of Crispus Attucks Day, an abolitionist festival that celebrated African Americans of the Revolution.

What is known for sure about Prince Whipple is that in November 1779, though he had probably already been personally emancipated, he petitioned the New Hampshire legislature along with nineteen other "Natives of Africa . . . born free," to have their freedom restored. Many African Americans realized the inherent contradictions between the principles of freedom upheld by the American Revolution and the continuance of slavery, and government petitions were one way they made their desire for freedom known. The New Hampshire petition used the language of the American Revolution and of natural rights to justify the emancipation of enslaved Africans, arguing, "The God of Nature gave them Life and Freedom, upon the Terms of the most perfect Equality with other men, That Freedom is an inherent right of human Species, not to be surrendered, but by Consent, for the Sake of social life; that private or public Tyranny and Slavery, are alike detestable to Minds conscious of the equal Dignity of Human Nature" (Kaplan and Kaplan, p. 29). Slavery was gradually phased out in New Hampshire during the 1790s.

After the war, Whipple returned to Portsmouth, New Hampshire, where he sometimes went by the name "Caleb Quotem." Nell records that Whipple married a woman named Dinah and had children before he died in Portsmouth at age thirty-two.

Whipple's enslavement, revolutionary war service, and subsequent emancipation demonstrate how the ideology of the American Revolution spawned the first antislavery efforts in America and how African-American males' military service buttressed their claims to be treated as free men. The visual image of Whipple as the noble black soldier became an icon of black independence to abolitionists in the mid-nineteenth century.

• The exact facts of Whipple's life are sketchy at best. Almost all that is known about Whipple rests on the information and local tradition recorded by William C. Nell in *The Colored Patriots of the American Revolution* (1855), the first important American work of black history. Another profile is in Bill Belton, "Prince Whipple, Soldier of the American Revolution," *Negro History Bulletin* 36 (1973): 126–27. Information about Whipple's petition to the N.H. legislature and his importance as a nineteenth-century symbol is in Sidney Kaplan and Emma Nogrady Kaplan, *The Black Presence in the Era of the American Revolution*, rev. ed. (1989).

SARAH J. PURCELL

WHIPPLE, Squire (16 Sept. 1804–15 Mar. 1888), civil engineer, was born in Hardwick, Massachusetts, the son of James Whipple, a farmer and owner of a small cotton mill, and Electa Johnson. Whipple attended school in Hardwick until 1817, when his family moved to Otsego County, New York. There he taught school for several years and attended Fairfield Academy. He entered Union College in 1829 for his senior year, graduating in 1830 with a bachelor of arts degree.

Whipple's early employment was typical of the engineering profession in the nineteenth century. In the 1830s he obtained a position with the Baltimore and Ohio Railroad, as a rodman and leveler. Later he was employed with Holmes Hutchinson in surveying boundaries required in the construction and maintenance of the Erie Canal. For one year, 1836–1837, Whipple was the resident engineer for the New York and Erie Railroad, until financial problems closed the road down. In 1837 he was self-employed manufacturing field instruments, including leveling instruments and transports. The same year he married Anna Case of Utica, New York; they had no children.

In 1840 Whipple received his first patent, for a canal boat scale that was built on the Erie Canal. The following year he received his first patent for a truss bridge design, for "independent cast-iron arch truss," commonly referred to as the Whipple bow-string truss. Using wrought iron for tension members, and cast iron for compression members, Whipple was among the early users of all-iron construction in the United States. Several bridges of this design, with spans from 70 to 100 feet, were built across the Erie Canal.

In 1847 Whipple published a pamphlet, *A Work upon Bridge Building Consisting of Two Essays, the One Elementary and General, the Other Giving Original Plans and Practical Details for Iron and Wooden Bridges*, the first work to use theories from structural mechanics to calculate the stress in trusses and among the earliest works of bridge design based on scientific principles. Although initially the pamphlet received little notice, it was updated several times, including an illustrated 1869 edition. In 1872 a publisher in Albany, New York, printed the work under the title *An Elementary and Practical Treatise on Bridge Building*. The final edition of this work was published in 1883. Other published works include the 1847 treatise "Way to Happiness," in which Whipple advocated a vegetarian diet, and a second bridge pamphlet, *The Doctrine of Central Forces, Illustrated without the Use of Calculus* (1866).

During the 1850s the partnership of S. and J. M. Whipple, one of the earliest bridge building firms in the country, built more than 100 iron bridges. Most of these bridges spanned the Erie Canal, but several Whipple bridges were also built on the New York and Erie Railway. Iron bridges, of all types, received a serious setback in 1852 when an iron bridge on the New York and Erie collapsed. Although the bridge design was considerably different from Whipple's, all iron bridges were removed from the New York and Erie line.

Since iron railroad bridges were capable of handling heavier loads and longer spans than wooden bridges, however, this episode only temporarily impeded their development. In 1852 Whipple built a bridge with new design specifications for the Rensselaer and Saratoga Railroad, near West Troy, New York. This design featured double intersecting pin-connected Pratt trusses and inclined end posts, with cast-iron top chords and lower chords of wrought iron. This "Whipple Trapezoidal Truss" bridge type became his most famous style. This design, along with its pin-connections, became part of the distinctive American railroad bridge style for the next fifty years.

In 1873 Whipple was involved in the creation of a lifting drawbridge, which he designed and built to cross the Erie Canal at Utica, New York. With the counterbalance provided by the bridge flooring, the span was lifted to allow passage of boats. About his bridge designs, Whipple wrote in the American Society of Civil Engineers' *Transactions* (1872), "If I have accomplished anything valuable in the way of advancing the science of Bridge Construction, it consists more in the introduction of proper dimensions and proportions of parts in the truss, than the discovery of any new combinations which can be recommended as absolutely the best for all occasions." Elected an honorary member of the American Society of Civil Engineers in 1868, he remained active in the organization, publishing papers and comments in its magazine, until his death in Albany, New York.

Over the four decades from 1840 to 1880, the development of the modern railroad bridge truss design was accomplished in the United States. Along with contemporaries Wendell Boleman and Albert Fink, Whipple was at the center of this achievement. By building bridges and sharing their theories with other professionals, Whipple and his contemporaries influenced the transition from craft-hand tradition in engineering to a more scientifically trained engineering profession. In a transitional period from wood to iron bridges, Whipple was a steadfast advocate of iron construction through the bridges he built in the field and his published works. He also promoted his bridges and aided the professional movement with his bridge analysis. Once called the "Father of American Metal Bridges," Whipple's work is still considered the beginning of American scientifically oriented bridge design.

• A memoir of Whipple was published in *Transactions of the American Society of Civil Engineers* (Dec. 1896). He also published articles on his bridge design, the lifting drawbridge, and letters defending his theories and designs in this journal in the 1870s and 1880s. He wrote an article on the Whipple Trapezoidal Iron Railroad Bridge published in *Engineering News* (1883). For studies of bridge development see, Theodore Cooper, "American Railroad Bridges," in *Transactions of the American Society of Civil Engineers* 21 (July 1889): 1–52; J. A. L. Waddel, *Bridge Engineering* (1916); Richard Shelton Kirby and Philip Gustave Laurson, *The Early Years of Modern Civil Engineering* (1932); and Llewellyn Nathaniel Edwards, *A Record of History and Evolution of Early American Bridges* (1959).

FRANCES C. ROBB

WHIPPLE, William (14 Jan. 1730–28 Nov. 1785), merchant and signer of the Declaration of Independence, was born in Kittery, then part of Massachusetts (now Maine), the son of William Whipple, a farmer and maltster, and Mary Cutt. As a child in a small town at the mouth of the Piscataqua River, Whipple received an elementary education and early became well acquainted with ships in the harbor served by the larger town of Portsmouth, New Hampshire, on the opposite bank. At an early age he went to sea, and by his twenties he was master of his own vessel engaging in commercial trade, including the slave trade, through the port at Portsmouth. As a result, he maintained household slaves throughout his life. In 1767 he married Catherine Moffatt. Although Whipple had already accumulated his own fortune, the couple settled in a house owned by her family, overlooking the Portsmouth harbor, where they had one child, who died in infancy.

Whipple, in association with most of the influential families of Portsmouth, expressed concern about British governance of the provinces. He was elected to represent Portsmouth in New Hampshire's extralegal Fourth Provincial Congress, which convened on 17 May 1775 and was in session when Royal Governor John Wentworth took refuge on a warship in the harbor that August. Whipple served also on the New Hampshire Committee of Safety, which effectively managed provincial government between meetings of the Congress. On 24 August 1775 the Provincial Congress commissioned Whipple colonel of its First Regiment of militia.

In January 1776 the new legislature, as established in New Hampshire's Plan of Government (the first such written plan, or constitution, in America, adopted by the Fifth Provincial Congress on 5 Jan. 1776), selected Whipple to be one of twelve executive councillors for the state. Later that month the legislature chose him to represent New Hampshire in the Continental Congress, then meeting in Philadelphia. Although one of the less vocal members of Congress, Whipple served on the Marine Committee, the Commerce Committee, the Secret Committee, the Board of War, and other bodies of Congress as well as voting for and signing the Declaration of Independence. Consistently through 1780 he was reappointed to the Continental Congress, but his service was interrupted by duties closer to home.

In June 1777 he was promoted to major general of the militia and was simultaneously appointed to serve as a justice on the court of common pleas for Rockingham County, which included Portsmouth and was the most populous of the state's five counties. Throughout the Revolution he held a commission as a justice of the peace and quorum throughout the state. In September 1777 General Whipple led his brigade to the vicinity of Albany, where he met with General Horatio Gates following the surrender of British forces at Saratoga. Gates appointed Whipple and General James Wilkinson to meet with General John Burgoyne's delegates in mid-October to conclude articles of capitulation by the British army. Whipple then commanded the force that brought the British prisoners back to Winter Hill near Boston. Before returning to Congress in 1778, he served at Concord in a convention that proposed a new state constitution and again led troops, in August, to support forces around Newport, Rhode Island. Whipple sat for the last time in Congress from November 1778 through September 1779.

In December 1779 Whipple took a seat in the state house of representatives and held office until that body appointed him an associate justice of the state superior court, requiring circuit duty throughout the year. He held the position until his death. From 1782 through 1784 he acted as financial receiver for New Hampshire, a position he is said to have found frustrating because more money went into privateering than into public coffers. Whipple suffered from seizures during his last years, but died suddenly of a heart condition at his home in Portsmouth. Reputedly, Whipple freed one of his slaves, Prince, for military service during the Revolution, and his other slave, Cuffee, upon his death.

Whipple achieved lasting respect by his adopted state for his service in Congress and in the military, but his early death precluded major tributes by the state to his memory.

• Evidence of Whipple's public service survives within many collections that include letters or papers to or from him, many of which are being published in the multivolume *Letters of Delegates to Congress*, ed. Paul Smith (1976–), and are available in other published editions of papers of the period. His state service can be followed in *The New Hampshire State Papers*, ed. Nathaniel Bouton et al. (40 vols., 1867–1940). His probate is on file with the Rockingham County Clerk of Probate in Brentwood, N.H. His life is treated in printed papers by Dorothy M. Vaughan, "This Was a Man," National Society of the Colonial Dames in the State of New Hampshire (26 Feb. 1964), and Joseph Foster, "William Whipple," *Granite Monthly* 43 (1911): 204–19. Because he signed the Declaration of Independence very brief sketches and anecdotal items abound.

FRANK C. MEVERS

WHISTLER, James McNeill (11 July 1834–17 July 1903), artist, was born James Abbott Whistler in Lowell, Massachusetts, the son of George Washington Whistler, a civil engineer, and his second wife, Anna Matilda McNeill. Between 1843 and 1848, the Whistler family lived in Russia, where Whistler's father was engaged on a railway project and where Whistler himself studied art with a student, A. O. Koritskii, and at the Imperial Academy of Fine Arts in St. Petersburg. After his father's death in 1849 the family returned to the United States. In 1851 Whistler entered the U.S. Military Academy at West Point, studying art under Robert W. Weir. Deficiencies in chemistry and discipline led to his expulsion in 1854. An interlude in the drawing division of the U.S. Coast and Geodetic Survey, Washington, D.C., provided training in etching, the basis of his future career. In 1855 he sailed for Europe to study art, and though he remained an American citizen, he never returned.

Whistler attended classes at the École Impériale et Spéciale de Dessin in Paris and at the studio of Charles Gleyre in 1856. He visited the Art Treasures Exhibition in Manchester, England, in 1857, forming a lifelong passion for the Dutch masters and Diego Velasguez. In the Musée du Louvre, he met Henri Fantin-Latour and through him, Gustave Courbet, the leader of the realists. Whistler's first important painting, *At the Piano* (Taft Museum, Cincinnati), showing his half-sister Deborah Haden and her daughter at Francis Seymour Haden's London house, was rejected at the Paris Salon in 1859, but admired by Courbet. Around this time Haden showed Whistler his Rembrandt etchings and urged him to work from nature.

In August 1858 Whistler's tour of northern France, Luxembourg, and the Rhineland resulted in *Twelve Etchings from Nature*, dedicated to Haden and printed with Auguste Delâtre's help in Paris. His etchings hung at the Salon and Royal Academy in 1859. The success of the "French Set" encouraged Whistler to move to London, where he began twelve etchings of the river. In 1862 Baudelaire praised Whistler's depiction of contemporary city life in the "Thames Set," which was published in 1871. Whistler was now established at the forefront of an etching revival.

However, his love of color, fame, and money drew him to painting. A heavily realistic oil, *La Mère Gérard* (private collection), was his first Royal Academy exhibit in 1861. His second exhibit there, in 1862, was *The Coast of Brittany* (1861, Wadsworth Athenaeum) painted from nature but with brighter colors and thinner paint. Whistler's red-haired Irish mistress, Joanna Hiffernan, posed in a Thames-side conversation piece, *Wapping* (National Gallery of Art, Washington, D.C.), begun in 1860 and exhibited successfully at the Royal Academy in 1864. Bought by Thomas Winans, it was one of the first Whistlers exhibited in New York (1866).

Hiffernan also posed in Paris in 1861 for *The White Girl* (National Gallery of Art, Washington, D.C.). Rejected by the Royal Academy in 1862 and the Salon in 1863, it was, with Manet's *Déjeuner sur l'Herbe*, the "succès de scandale" of the Salon des Refusés. Calling it a "Symphonie du blanc," Paul Mantz inspired its later title *Symphony in White, No. 1: The White Girl* (*Gazette des Beaux-Arts*, July 1863). Whistler adopted such nomenclature publicly for *Symphony in White, No 3* (Barber Institute of Fine Arts, Birmingham University) at the Royal Academy in 1867.

In 1863 Whistler moved to Lindsey Row, on the Thames in Chelsea, where his neighbors included the Pre-Raphaelite D. G. Rossetti. He maintained contact with continental Europe, traveling to Amsterdam in 1863, posing with Manet and Baudelaire for Fantin's *Hommage à Delacroix* in 1864 and working with Courbet at Trouville in 1865. In 1866, avoiding family and political problems (the arrest of a friend, the Fenian John O'Leary), he traveled to Valparaiso, painting his first night scenes, including *Nocturne in Blue and Gold: Valparaiso Bay* (Freer Gallery of Art).

In 1865, when the second "Symphony in White," *The Little White Girl*, was exhibited at the Royal Academy, Whistler met the English artist Albert Moore. Together they explored the ideals of "Art for Art's sake." Whistler began a series of paintings of classically draped women and flowers on a musical theme, now known as the *Six Projects* (Freer Gallery of Art) for the "Liverpool Medici," the shipowner F. R. Leyland. Leyland also bought *La Princesse du pays de la porcelaine* (Freer Gallery of Art), one of several oriental subjects starring Whistler's own porcelain. Its conspicuous signature possibly led Whistler to develop his famous butterfly signature from his initials "JW" in about 1869.

After 1870 Whistler abandoned the *Six Projects* for portraits and night scenes, thinly painted in ribbon-like brushstrokes, with thin washes of paint like glazes, in which detail was subordinated to mood and mass. Leyland in 1872 suggested the title "Nocturnes" for such moonlights as *Nocturne: Blue and Silver: Chelsea* (Tate Gallery).

In 1871 Whistler painted a deeply felt portrait of his mother, restrained in color and severe in composition, showing her seated in profile against the studio wall, which is decorated only with a framed etching and an embroidered curtain. His affection for his mother was concealed by the title, which stressed the somber color harmony. In 1872 this *Arrangement in Grey and Black* barely escaped rejection and was the last painting he exhibited at the Royal Academy, yet it entered the Musée du Louvre twenty years later and became one of the most famous of American portraits. Seeing it, Thomas Carlyle agreed to pose for a second *Arrangement in Grey and Black*, an impressive psychological study and the first of Whistler's paintings to enter a public collection (in Glasgow, Scotland).

Whistler had parted from Hiffernan, who helped look after his illegitimate son, Charles Hanson, who was born in 1870 and whose mother was apparently Louisa Fanny Hanson, the parlormaid. Maud Franklin became Whistler's model and mistress. She stood in for his portrait of Mrs. Frances Leyland, *Symphony in Flesh Colour and Pink* (Frick Collection, New York), in which every decorative detail, from rug to dress, was designed by the artist. Leyland backed Whistler's first one-man exhibition at a Pall Mall gallery in 1874, where these portraits hung with etchings and pastels.

Whistler worked on a decorative scheme for Leyland's London house at 49 Princes Gate from 1876 until 1877. The dining room, originally designed by Thomas Jeckyll, was transformed into an all-embracing *Harmony in Blue and Gold* based on peacock motifs, which far exceeded Leyland's wishes. He paid half the 2000 guineas asked, and Whistler lost a patron. The "Peacock Room" has been reinstalled at the Freer Gallery of Art.

Whistler collaborated with Edward W. Godwin on a stand at the Paris Universal Exposition in 1878, and he rashly commissioned Godwin to design the "White House" on Tite Street in London. As costs escalated, he pursued a lavish lifestyle, entertaining guests to Sunday breakfasts, becoming known as a dandy and wit. He also defended his aesthetic theories publicly. Writing to the *World* on 22 May 1878, regarding *Nocturne: Grey and Gold—Chelsea Snow* (Fogg Art Museum, Harvard Univ.), he explained: "my combination of grey and gold is the basis of the picture . . . the picture should have its own merit, and not depend upon dramatic, or legendary, or local interest."

In the former Grosvenor Gallery in London, he exhibited *Arrangement in Black and Brown: The Fur Jacket* (Worcester Art Museum), a refined portrait of Maud, "evidently caught in a London fog," as Oscar Wilde wrote flippantly (1877). The influential art critic John Ruskin reviled *Nocturne in Black and Gold: The Falling Rocket* (Detroit Institute of Arts), writing that he "never expected to hear a coxcomb ask two hundred guineas for flinging a pot of paint in the public's face" (*Fors Clavigera*, 2 July 1877). Whistler sued for libel, justifying the price: "I ask it for the knowledge I have gained in the work of a lifetime." He won the case, won derisory damages (one farthing) without costs, and published *Whistler v. Ruskin: Art and Art Critics*, his first brown paper pamphlet, in 1878.

The birth of a daughter to Maud in February 1879 compounded domestic problems. To raise money Whistler published etchings, including *Old Battersea Bridge* (Kennedy, no. 177), and helped by the printer Thomas Way, lithographs, such as *The Toilet* (Way, no. 6), a portrait of Maud. He painted expressive watercolors of Nankin porcelain for a catalog of Sir Henry Thompson's collection (1878). None of these measures sufficed. In May 1879 he was declared bankrupt, and his work, collections, and house were auctioned. He destroyed some paintings that he did not want to go to auction.

With a commission for a set of twelve etchings from dealers at the Fine Art Society in London, Whistler left for Venice, Italy. He stayed more than a year, producing fifty etchings and more than ninety pastels of back streets and canals, bead-stringers, and gondoliers. He joined Frank Duveneck and his students in the Casa Jankowitz, and he worked on etchings with Otto Bacher. Superb etchings like *Nocturne* (Kennedy, no. 184) were distinguished by a combination of delicate line with a surface tone of ink, producing effects akin to monotype.

In pastels like *The Zattere: Harmony in Blue and Brown* (Terra Foundation for the Arts) the subject was vignetted, or less detailed toward the edge of the sheet, brown paper complementing expressive line and jewel-like colors. Godwin noted that "the preciousness of the blue [was] created by the base of the brown" (*British Architect*, 4 Feb. 1881). These pastels had considerable influence on the Americans, particularly J. H. Twachtman, and on the Society of American Painters in Pastel founded in 1882.

Exhibited at the Fine Art Society in 1881, framed in three shades of gold, the room decorated in reddish-brown, greenish-yellow, and gold, the pastels were extensively reviewed. The etchings were shown in London in 1880 and 1883, and at Wunderlich's in New York in 1883 in an "Arrangement in White and Yellow," which greatly influenced later exhibition design. The catalog, designed by Whistler, maliciously quoted earlier reviews.

The first Venice set of twelve etchings was published in 1880 but printed by Whistler over twenty years. He printed the second set of twenty-six etchings (published by Messrs. Dowdeswell in 1886) within a year. Whistler etched but never published several later sets, including a "Jubilee Set" in 1887, a "Renaissance set" in France in 1888, and another "Renaissance set" in Amsterdam in 1889, which was "of far finer quality than all that has gone before—combining a minuteness of detail . . . with greater freedom and more beauty of execution than even the last Renaissance lot can pretend to" (letter to M. Huish, Glasgow Univ. Library).

In the 1880s Whistler traveled widely in England and continental Europe, and his work was exhibited in Europe and the United States. The first watercolor he exhibited in New York (at the Pedestal Fund Art Loan Exhibition in 1883) was *Snow*, painted in Amsterdam in 1882 (private collection). In 1884 he painted seascapes in St. Ives with his pupils, the Australian born Mortimer Menpes and the Englishman Walter Sickert. In 1885 he was in Holland arguing with W. M. Chase. Watercolors like *Variations in Violet and Grey—Market Place, Dieppe* (private collection) were shown beside those of the impressionists at the Galerie Georges Petit in 1883 and 1887. "His little sketches show fine draftsmanship," wrote Camille Pissarro in May 1887; "he is a showman, but nevertheless an artist" (J. Rewald, *Camille Pissarro, Letters to Lucien Pissarro* [1943]). He traveled between London, Paris, and Dieppe. In 1899 he painted Belle-Ile, and in 1900, with an American friend Jerome Elwell, he painted Domburg.

Whistler alternated between small paintings, only five by eight inches in size, and full-length portraits of actors and aristocrats, children and collectors. Edouard Manet introduced him to the art critic Théodore Duret, who agreed to pose, as an experiment, in modern evening dress, carrying (for color's sake) a pink cloak (Metropolitan Museum of Art, New York). Duret mediated between Whistler and the aristocratic Lady Archibald Campbell, who was refusing to pose, and thus saved *Arrangement in Black: La Dame au Brodequin Jaune*, for his retrospective at the Goupil Gallery in 1892 and the Chicago Columbian Exhibition in 1893 (Philadelphia Museum of Art).

Another *Arrangement in Black*, the portrait of the violinist Pablo de Sarasate on stage (1884), illustrated Whistler's views, as stated in his "Propositions," that flesh should be painted "low in tone" and that the model should "stand *within* the frame." Exhibited in London, Hamburg, Paris, and finally in 1896 in Pittsburgh, it was bought by the Carnegie Institute, the first American public collection to acquire his work. Exhibiting at international exhibitions in Antwerp, Brussels, Paris, Munich, Chicago, Philadelphia, Dublin, Glasgow, and St. Petersburg, he earned medals and honors.

In 1885 Whistler delivered the "Ten O'Clock" lecture in Princes Hall (published 1888), an eloquent exposition of his views on art and artists. Stéphane Mallarmé translated it into French and introduced Whistler to the symbolist circle in Paris. Extensive correspondence and subjects like *Purple and Gold: Phryne the Superb!—Builder of Temples* (Freer Gallery of Art) document their growing friendship.

In 1886 the Society of British Artists in London, in need of rejuvenation, risked electing Whistler as president. He set out autocratically to reform the society, revamping the galleries, designing a "velarium" (a sheet of thin material hung across the center of a room) to soften the light and direct it on the pictures, rejecting substandard pictures, and inviting foreigners like Waldo Storey and Claude Monet to exhibit. The society revolted, and he was forced to resign in June 1888.

Meanwhile, pastels, oils, drawings, and watercolors—like the atmospheric *Nocturne in Grey and Gold—Piccadilly* (National Gallery of Ireland) hung in three one-man exhibitions of *"Notes"—"Harmonies"—"Nocturnes"* at Messrs. Dowdeswell in 1884 and 1886 and at Wunderlich's in New York in 1889. This gave Americans like Howard Mansfield, Howard Whittemore, and Charles L. Freer their first chance to buy Whistlers.

In 1888 Whistler married Beatrice, the widow of E. W. Godwin; they moved to Paris in 1892. An artist and designer, Beatrice worked beside him, encouraging pastels and lithographs of young models, like the Pettigrew sisters. Some of his finest lithographs, like *The Duet* (Way, no. 64) of 1894, show Beatrice at home in 110 rue du Bac in Paris; the most poignant, *By the Balcony* and *The Siesta* (Way, nos. 122, 124), were drawn as she lay dying of cancer during his lithography exhibition at the Fine Art Society in 1895. She died in 1896. Her young sister, Rosalind Birnie Philip, became Whistler's ward and inherited his estate.

Whistler published a collection of letters, pamphlets, and "Propositions" on art, *The Gentle Art of Making Enemies* (1890; 2d ed., 1892). Each document includes one of Whistler's distinctive butterfly monograms drawn with a stinging tail. His *Eden versus Whistler: The Baronet and the Butterfly, a Valentine with a Verdict* (1899) recorded a lawsuit against Sir William Eden in 1898, which resulted in a change to French law giving artists control over their work.

In 1898 Whistler was elected first president of the International Society of Sculptors, Painters, and Gravers. Joseph Pennell, Whistler's friend and future biographer, was an active and argumentative committee member. Independent artists from Europe and the United States were invited to send work to their exhibitions in 1898, 1899, and 1900, but academicians—even J. S. Sargent—were discouraged. The exhibitions were sparely hung, coherent, and effective. Whistler's own exhibits were modest, fluidly painted panels like *Green and Silver—The Great Sea* (Hunterian Art Gallery) and severely geometrical shopfronts like *Gold and Orange—The Neighbours* (Freer Gallery of Art).

Whistler directed operations from Paris, where with the sculptor F. MacMonnies he supervised an academy at 6 Passage Stanislas run by his model, Carmen Rossi, from 1898 until 1901. American students included Carl Frieseke and the British painter Gwen John, who later posed for Rodin's memorial to Whistler (Musée Rodin, Paris).

By 1901 Whistler's health was failing. Convalescing, he filled books with sketches of Algiers and Corsica. His last portraits—of Freer, the gambler Richard Canfield (private collection), George W. Vanderbilt (National Gallery of Art, Washington, D.C.), and Dorothy Seton (*A Daughter of Eve*, Hunterian Art Gallery)—were painted with the forceful brushwork and thin paint, strong characterization, and subtle color that were typical of his work. In his last self-portrait (Hunterian Art Gallery) the pose was based on Velasquez's portrait of Pablo de Valladolid in the Prado. In 1900 it hung in the American section of the Paris Universal Exposition, but he reworked it until his death in London. Painted with nervous flickering brushwork, serious and introspective, it is a deeply moving work.

Whistler's influence on printmaking was particularly strong. He was one of the finest etchers of the century and a leading figure in the etching and lithography revival. His emphasis on the importance of color harmony, rather than subject, had a lasting influence, and the simplicity of his interior and exhibition designs had an immediate impact on both sides of the Atlantic.

• The major collection of Whistler's manuscripts and works of art is in the University of Glasgow, which received the bulk of his estate through his sister-in-law Rosalind Birnie Philip. The Centre for Whistler Studies at the University of Glasgow is preparing an edition of Whistler's 11,000 letters. The other principal collections are the E. R. and J. Pennell Collection in the Library of Congress and the Freer Gallery of Art, both in Washington, D.C. The principal bibliography is Robert H. Getscher and Paul G. Marks, *J. McN. Whistler and J. S. Sargent* (1986). Since then, important excerpts from writings by and about Whistler have been published by Robin Spencer, *Whistler: A Retrospective* (1989); Joy Newton, *La Chauve-souris et le papillon: Correspondance Montesquiou-Whistler* (1990); Nigel Thorp, *Whistler on Art: J. McN. Whistler: Selected Letters and Writings* (1994); and Linda Merrill, *With Kindest Regards: The Correspondence of Charles Lang Freer and J. McN. Whistler* (1995). The fullest biographies are by his fellow artists Elizabeth Robins Pennell and Joseph Pennell, *The Life of James McNeill Whistler* (1908) and *The Whistler Journal* (1921). Recent publications include Merrill, *A Pot of Paint: Aesthetics on Trial in Whistler v. Ruskin* (1992), and a readable biography, R. Anderson and A. Koval, *J. McN. Whistler: Beyond the Myth* (1994). Whistler's household is described by M. F. MacDonald, *Whistler's Mother's Cookbook* (1995) and *Beatrice Whistler, Artist and Designer* (1997). The illustrated oeuvre catalog are Thomas R. Way, *Mr. Whistler's Lithographs: The Catalogue* (1905); Edward G. Kennedy, *The Etched Work of Whistler* (1910); Mervyn Levy, *Whistler Lithographs: An Illustrated Catalogue Raisonné* (1975); Andrew McLaren Young et al., *The Paintings of J. McN. Whistler* (1980); and Margaret F. MacDonald, *J. McN. Whistler: Drawings, Pastels and Watercolours* (1995). Specialized books include Katharine A. Lochnan, *The Etchings of J. McN. Whistler* (1984); Robert H. Getscher, *J. A. McN. Whistler: Pastels* (1991); and Deanna M. Bendix, *Diabolical Designs: Paintings, Interiors, and Exhibitions of J. McN. Whistler* (1995). Major recent exhibition catalogs include Richard Dorment and Margaret F. MacDonald, *James McNeill Whistler*, with contributions by Nicolai Cikovsky, Jr., Ruth Fine, and Geneviève Lacambre, Tate Gallery, London; Musée d'Orsay, Paris; and National Gallery, Washington (1995–1996); Edgar Munhall, *Whistler and Montesquiou: The Butterfly and the Bat*, the Frick Collection, New York (1995); and J. F. Heijbroek and M. F. MacDonald, *Whistler and Holland*, Rijksmuseum, Amsterdam (1997).

MARGARET F. MACDONALD

WHITAKER, Daniel Kimball (13 Apr. 1801–24 Mar. 1881), editor and essayist, was born in Sharon, Massachusetts, the son of the Reverend Jonathan Whitaker and Mary Kimball. He was the grandson of the Reverend Nathaniel Whitaker (1732–1795), a prominent theologian who had helped found Dartmouth College. His early education came from his father, a noted Congregationalist minister and eminent scholar. He later entered Harvard College, where he was awarded a B.A. degree in 1820 and an M.A. in 1823. His thesis, "The Literary Character of Dr. Samuel Johnson," won him academic honors, as did his skills at oratory. He later studied theology and was licensed to preach, but his interests were already inclining toward journalism, and, while working on his master's degree, he edited the *Christian Philanthropist* in New Bedford.

A frail young man, Whitaker sought a warmer climate in the South. Accompanied initially by his father, he lectured and preached throughout several southern states and organized a congregation in Augusta, Georgia, before giving up his ministry to settle on a farm in the low country of South Carolina. His health gradually improved, and in 1828 he married a well-to-do widow, Mary H. Firth, and managed her rice and cotton plantation in St. Paul's Parish. During this ten-year period of his life, Whitaker resumed his interest in literary affairs and, increasingly, identified himself with the conservative politics of the Deep South planter class. He actively embraced John C. Calhoun's doctrine of nullification, or "state interposition," to safeguard the interests of the minority South and began to read law under the guidance of James L. Petigru, the leading attorney in Charleston. By the mid-1830s he had opened his own law office and built a fair-sized practice, won several highly publicized cases, and earned a reputation throughout the region as a public speaker.

His first love was journalism, however, and from his law office in Charleston in 1835 he began the *Southern Literary Journal and Monthly Magazine*, which he edited until 1837, and the *Southern Quarterly Review*, which he edited from 1842 to 1847. After the death of his first wife, Whitaker was married again in 1849; his second wife, also a widow, was Mary Scrimzeour Furman Miller, a writer of fiction and poetry and the daughter of Samuel Furman. Together they launched *Whitaker's Magazine: The Rights of the South*, an influential journal that reflected Whitaker's growing alienation from the Union. In the prospectus for *The Rights of the South*, he wrote:

> The South, as a portion of the American Union, has its rights, derived from the guarantees of the Federal Constitution. It also has the rights that belong to an educated and enlightened people. But it may be doubted whether, under the existing circumstances of the country, it enjoys and exercises either of these classes of rights to the full degree,—whether, in a word, the Union has accomplished as much for the Southern States as it was expected to achieve for them, when the National Government was formed. There are murmurs of dissatisfaction, loud and deep, heard on all sides of us, and it is more than suspected,—it is openly avowed, and generally believed—that the Union, as far as the great interests of the South are concerned, has, to a considerable extent, proved a failure.

Whitaker would later be associated with a number of other publications, notably the *New Orleans Monthly Review*, 1874–1876, but of all his editorships the *Southern Quarterly Review* was the most important. Between 1841 and 1861, Whitaker guided the *Review* to a position unique in the southern literature of the period. While he was a gifted and persuasive writer himself—Edgar Allan Poe once referred to him as "one of the best essayists in North America"—Whitaker was famous primarily for his sure-handed editing and for affording a viable outlet for writers of the region, especially women writers, who might never have been published otherwise. "The very name of Southern literature," Whitaker wrote in 1850, "is treated with contempt by our Northern brethren." In an effort to broaden the base of the *Quarterly Review* to include readers from the Southwest, Whitaker moved the editorial offices from Charleston to New Orleans. When the magazine ceased publication with the outbreak of the Civil War in 1861, Whitaker returned to Charleston.

For a time during the administration of President James Buchanan (1857–1861) Whitaker held a minor appointed position with the federal government in Washington, and during the Civil War he served in the Confederate Post Office Department and Quartermaster General's Department in Richmond. In 1866 Whitaker again moved to New Orleans, where he edited the *New Orleans Monthly Review*. He was involved with this publication and its successors, the *New Orleans Quarterly Review* and the revived *Southern Quarterly Review*, until 1880. His elegant writing style, his thoughtful analyses of political and social problems, and the wide range of his intellectual interests won him many admirers throughout his long professional career. In 1878 he became a Roman Catholic. Whitaker died while on a visit to Houston but was buried in New Orleans. He was survived by two sons from his first marriage and two daughters from his second.

• Many of Daniel Kimball Whitaker's political and journalistic views are outlined in his *Prospectus for the Rights of the South*, a pamphlet printed in 1850. Leonard Allison Morrison and Stephen Paschall Sharples, *The History of the Kimball Family in America*, vol. 1 (1897), details the lives of Daniel Whitaker as well as those of his illustrious father and grandfather. Edwin Lewis Jewell, ed., *Jewell's Crescent City Illustrated* (1873; rev. ed., 1874), covers Whitaker's New Orleans years, while the *History of South Carolina*, ed. Yates Snowden and H. G. Cutler (1920), authoritatively reports on Whitaker's life in the Charleston area.

RONALD TRUMAN FARRAR

WHITCHER, Frances Miriam Berry (c. 1812–4 Jan. 1852), author, was born in Whitesboro, New York, the daughter of Elizabeth Wells and Lewis Berry, an innkeeper. As a child, Miriam (as she was then known) exhibited a talent for language and drawing, memorizing poetry and sketching caricatures. Her education at the village academy was supplemented by lessons in French in which she became proficient. Her early talent for caricature and parody, which would later make her one of the first American female humorists, was unappreciated by her family and neighbors. She grew up as a lonely, withdrawn child who struggled with the doctrines of the local Calvinist church.

Miriam Berry found her first public in the Maeonian Circle, a social and literary group in Whitesboro, which she discovered sometime around 1838. To this group she read from her "Widow Spriggins" sketches, extended monologues in dialect that parodied the popular sentimental novel, especially Regina Maria Roche's *The Children of the Abbey* (1798). A number of these sketches appeared between April and August 1839 in the *Gazette*, Rome, New York's weekly newspaper, but the complete series was not published together until 1867, after her death. In 1846, using the pseudonym "Frank," Miriam Berry sent to Joseph C. Neal, editor of *Neal's Saturday Gazette and Lady's Literary Museum*, several monologues ostensibly from the perspective of "The Widow Bedott." Neal, himself a humorist, recognized the author's talent, printed the monologues, and encouraged her to write more. The Widow Bedott sketches, written in dialect and featuring misspellings and malapropisms, became part of the tradition of vernacular American humor that had been pioneered by Seba Smith and Augustus Baldwin Longstreet. The garrulous Widow reveals her husband-hunting proclivities and her consequent competition with other women; she satirizes religious hypocrisy, sentimental poetry, and the social-climbing tendencies of the growing middle class. The popularity of Berry's sketches brought her to the attention of Louis Godey, editor of *Godey's Lady's Book*. From 1847 to 1849 Godey published another series of Berry's humorous sketches titled "Aunt Maguire's Experience."

In 1847 Miriam Berry, then in her mid-thirties, married the Reverend Benjamin W. Whitcher, an Episcopalian minister, and the couple moved to Elmira, New York, where he had recently been offered a pastorate at St. Peter's Church. In Elmira, Frances Miriam Whitcher finished what would be known as *The Widow Bedott Papers*, published in book form in 1856, and the "Aunt Maguire" sketches, which were written in the form of letters. Although best known in her own time and today for such humorous works, she also wrote hymns and devotional poetry, some of which were published in *Neal's Saturday Gazette* and in *Gospel Messenger*, a newspaper published in Utica, New York. Like Fanny Fern (pseudonym of Sara Willis Parton) a decade later, Whitcher was adept at both satiric and pious styles, and among the works left unfinished at her death was a novel, *Mary Elmer*, written in the sentimental tradition that she had satirized in her "Widow Spriggins" sketches.

Piety and satire could coexist in Frances Miriam Berry Whitcher's imagination, but the combination caused problems in her personal life. The townspeople of Elmira, and particularly the members of the Reverend Whitcher's congregation, began to suspect that they were the models for some of Frances Whitcher's caricatures. Although her sketches were extremely popular with readers of *Neal's Saturday Gazette* and *Godey's Lady's Book*, her portrayals of gossipy, social-climbing members of the church sewing society and women who, like the Widow Bedott, affect piety in order to attract the attention of a widowed minister brought local accusations that she lacked the religious devotion required of a minister's wife. Such accusations culminated in the threat of a lawsuit against the Reverend Whitcher by a man who believed that his wife was the inspiration for "Mrs. Samson Savage," a character in Whitcher's "Aunt Maguire" series. Ultimately the Reverend Whitcher resigned his pastorate in Elmira, and his wife was later said to have remarked that it was "a very serious thing to be a funny woman." The adverse reactions of her neighbors was one of several reasons why Frances Whitcher abandoned her career as a humorist after her husband moved to a parish in Oswego, New York. In 1849 she gave birth to a daughter, Alice Miriam, and in 1850, having developed tuberculosis, she returned to Whitesboro, where she later died.

Despite the fact that her career was a short one, Frances Whitcher's work long remained popular. A collection of her Widow Bedott sketches, *The Widow Bedott Papers*, was published in 1856 and sold more than 100,000 copies during the ensuing decade. In 1867 the "Widow Spriggins" sketches, the unfinished novel *Mary Elmer*, and other uncollected works were published, with a long biographical introduction, under the title *Widow Spriggins, Mary Elmer, and Other Sketches*. The Widow Bedott proved to be her most enduring character. In 1879, more than twenty-five years after Frances Whitcher's death, David Ross Locke, who used the pseudonym "Petroleum V. Nasby," produced a dramatization based on the sketches, *The Widow Bedott; or, A Hunt for a Husband*, which toured widely featuring actor Neil Burgess in the title role.

Frances Whitcher's humorous writing is part of the tradition of vernacular humor that culminated in the work of Mark Twain and is also a critique of the social mores of the mid-nineteenth century, especially the attempt by residents of rural America to imitate the fads and fashions of urban centers. Although her work furthered such traditional stereotypes of women as the gossip and the husband-hunter, it did so with a consciousness of the socioeconomic pressures that caused women to compete for male attention and support. Frances Whitcher is thus a forerunner of many women writers who have criticized these pressures in their humor, including Fanny Fern, Marietta Holley, Anita Loos, and Judith Viorst.

• Whitcher's letters are in the manuscript collection of the New-York Historical Society in New York City. The only biography of Frances Whitcher is Linda A. Morris, *Women's Humor in the Age of Gentility: The Life and Works of Frances Miriam Whitcher* (1992). Brief biographical and critical sketches are in the following sources: Kate Berry, "Passages in the Life of the Author of Aunt Maguire's Letters, Bedott Papers, Etc.," *Godey's Lady's Book* 47 (July 1853): 49–55 and (Aug. 1853): 109–15, and the Introduction to *The Widow Spriggins, Mary Elmer, and Other Sketches* (1867).

NANCY A. WALKER

WHITCOMB, James (1 Dec. 1795–4 Oct. 1852), governor of Indiana and U.S. senator, was born in Rochester, Windsor County, Vermont, the son of John Whitcomb, a farmer and revolutionary war veteran, and Lydia Parmenter. In 1806 the family moved to a farm near Cincinnati, Ohio. James Whitcomb's love of books and disregard for farming caused his father to prophesy that his son would never amount to anything in life.

Although no records of his attending the university survive, numerous Hoosier biographers of Whitcomb have claimed that the future Indiana governor graduated from Transylvania University, Lexington, Kentucky, in 1819, working his way through school by teaching. After reading law in a law office, he was admitted to the bar in Fayette County, Kentucky, in March 1822. Two years later Whitcomb moved to Bloomington, Indiana, and established a private law practice, which he operated for twelve years. In 1826 Governor James B. Ray appointed Whitcomb as prosecuting attorney for the Fifth Judicial District. Beginning in 1830 Whitcomb was elected to six consecutive terms in the state senate, where he adamantly opposed the movement in the state for massive internal improvements. In 1836 the legislature passed the Mammoth Internal Improvements Act, which provided for the construction of canals and a railroad and for improvement of the state's roads. Whitcomb was one of only nine legislators who voted against the act.

In October 1836 President Andrew Jackson appointed Whitcomb as the commissioner of the General Land Office in Washington, D.C., a post Whitcomb held through the end of President Martin Van Buren's term. During his time in this office, Whitcomb taught himself to read both French and Spanish in order to read land grants printed in those languages. He returned to Indiana in 1841, establishing a successful law practice in Terre Haute. A leading figure in Democratic politics in the state, he cemented his popularity with party members during the campaign of 1843, when he wrote *Facts for the People in Relation to a Protective Tariff*, which argued strongly against the protective tariff. Selected by the Democratic State Convention in 1843 as the party's gubernatorial nominee, Whitcomb defeated incumbent Whig governor Samuel Bigger by approximately 2,000 votes, becoming the first Democrat to win that office in Indiana. Whitcomb was reelected in 1846, winning 64,104 votes to 60,138 votes for Whig candidate Joseph Marshall and 2,301 votes for Liberty party nominee Stephen C. Stevens. In 1846 Whitcomb married Martha Ann Renwick Hurst, who died a year later following the birth of the couple's daughter.

Whitcomb won his greatest fame and the gratitude of Hoosier voters during his terms as governor by settling the enormous state debts incurred with the collapse of Indiana's internal improvements system. In an 1847 arrangement brokered by the legislature and Charles Butler, a lawyer who represented New York and London bondholders, the state agreed to pay half of its internal improvement debt, which amounted to more than $11 million, and the other half was assumed by creditors in return for stock in the Wabash and Erie Canal. Also during the Whitcomb administrations the state improved its educational system and public charities, establishing its first mental health institution (Central State Hospital in Indianapolis), a school for the deaf, and the Indiana Institute for the Education of the Blind. When the United States declared war on Mexico in 1846, Whitcomb secured loans from the various branches of the state bank to finance the raising of troops for the conflict.

Along with politics, Whitcomb was active in numerous organizations, serving as vice president of the American Bible Society, one of the founders of the Indiana Historical Society, an active Freemason, and a member of the Methodist Episcopal church. Although he smoked and took snuff regularly, the farmer's son was known for being very economical with his time and money. An accomplished musician, Whitcomb composed numerous pieces for the violin and enjoyed hosting parties at the governor's mansion in Indianapolis.

In 1849 the Indiana General Assembly selected Whitcomb over incumbent Edward Allen Hannegan to serve in the U.S. Senate. Suffering from gravel, a disease that causes calculous masses in the kidneys and urinary bladder, Whitcomb played little role in Senate proceedings. He died following an operation in New York City.

• Whitcomb's papers as Ind. governor are in the Indiana State Archives, Indianapolis. His role in the settling of the state's debt is explored in Justin E. Walsh, *The Centennial History of the Indiana General Assembly, 1816–1978* (1987). See also James H. Madison, *The Indiana Way: A State History* (1986). Whitcomb's life and career are highlighted in Rebecca A. Shepherd et al., eds., *A Biographical Directory of the Indiana General Assembly*, vol. 1: *1816–1899* (1980); Jacob Piatt Dunn, Jr., *Indiana and Indianans* (1919); and W. W. Woollen, *Biographical and Historical Sketches of Early Indiana* (1883). An obituary is in the *New York Times*, 5 Oct. 1852.

RAY E. BOOMHOWER

WHITE, Albert Smith (24 Oct. 1803–4 Sept. 1864), jurist, congressman, and senator, was born in Blooming Grove, New York, the son of Nathan Herrick White and Frances Howell. His father was presiding judge over the Orange County court for twenty years. White graduated from Union College in Schenectady in 1822, then studied law in Newburgh, New York. He was admitted to the bar in 1825 and soon moved to Indiana, where he lived briefly in Rushville and Paoli. In 1829 he settled in Tippecanoe County and opened a law office in the town of Lafayette. He lived the rest of his life in Lafayette or on his farm in nearby Stockwell, of which he was a founder. In 1843 White and a member of the Randolph family of Virginia were married; they had two sons and two daughters.

During the Indiana legislative session of 1828–1829, White reported the proceedings for the *Indianapolis Journal*, the first such reporting in the state. For the next two years he was the assistant clerk of the Indiana House of Representatives, and from 1832 to 1835 he was its clerk. During these years he met many important men in the state, and these contacts were beneficial to his future political career.

In 1833 White's first try for a seat in Congress was unsuccessful. He lost to Edward Hannegan, a brilliant and eloquent campaigner. White, however, was considered the "superior of that erratic man in education, culture, and in most of the qualities which go to make up the successful man" (Woollen, p. 205). Four years later White was the successful man, when his district sent him as its Whig representative to the Twenty-fifth Congress. He did not actively take part in debates, but he served on the Committee on Roads and Canals. He was not a candidate for renomination in 1838.

In 1836 White was a presidential elector for William Henry Harrison. When the term of Indiana's U.S. senator, John Tipton, expired in 1839, White was one of three candidates to succeed Tipton. All three candidates were Whigs. White was finally elected by the Whig-controlled legislature on the thirty-sixth ballot.

White took his seat in the Senate at the beginning of the Twenty-sixth Congress in December 1839. He established his reputation as an antislavery person by opposing the annexation of Texas and every other measure that would have extended slavery. He was, however, a moderate and generally voted with the conservative Whigs, led by Henry Clay, to confine slavery to where it already existed. White served on the Committee to Audit and Control the Contingent Expenses, the Committee on Indian Affairs, and the Committee on Roads and Canals. He worked hard for the extension of the Wabash and Erie Canal and his influence was instrumental in securing land grants for this purpose. He declined reelection and left the Senate at the end of his term in 1845.

White resumed his law practice, but he soon turned to the business of building railroads. He became the first president of the Indianapolis and Lafayette Railroad, serving in this capacity until 1856, and he was also head of the Wabash and Western Railroad for three years.

In 1860 White was returned to Washington, this time as a Republican representative in the Thirty-seventh Congress. Because of his past experience in both the House and the Senate, he assumed a leadership role. On 7 April 1862 White offered a resolution to the House proposing a select committee to consider voluntary, gradual, and compensated emancipation of slaves in some states and the possibility of colonization of freed slaves. Subsequently, as chairman of the select committee, White reported to the House a proposal for the practical accomplishment of such a plan, and he analyzed the political and social problems of slavery and the advantages of colonization. These measures had the support of Abraham Lincoln. White pointed out to the southern members that, if they did not accept a plan for compensation of slaves, they would eventually lose the slaves without compensation. This happened shortly thereafter, when President Lincoln's Emancipation Proclamation took effect on 1 January 1863, freeing the slaves in the unconquered Confederacy.

White's position on emancipation cost him support among his Indiana constituents, and he was not renominated to Congress. When White left the House of Representatives, he was rewarded by President Lincoln with an appointment as one of three commissioners to adjust claims against the federal government by citizens of Minnesota and Dakota. These claims were for losses incurred during the Sioux massacre on the Minnesota frontier in August 1862.

When White completed that assignment, President Lincoln nominated him to a judgeship. Although some doubted the wisdom of the appointment because White had not practiced law for some time, he was confirmed on 18 January 1864 as U.S. judge for the District of Indiana. The appointment proved to be a short one. After only eight months on the bench, White died at his home in Stockwell. He was mourned by contemporaries as a scholar and jurist who brought erudition and dignity to the frontier Indiana political scene. His legislative reports were clear and thorough; his writings and speeches contained classical allusions and shied from demagoguery. White was not a charismatic politician; he was honest and courageous. Amidst the passion of slavery debates, he refrained from ideological oratory, earning respect for sincere suggestions for compromise.

• White's remarks as a congressman and senator are in the *Congressional Globe* for Mar. 1837–Mar. 1845 and Mar. 1861–Mar. 1863. William B. Woollen, *Biographical and Historical Sketches of Early Indiana* (1883), includes a chapter on White's professional and political careers with interesting detail. Woollen also describes White's physical characteristics and his intellectual qualities. An obituary in the *New York Times*, 11 Sept. 1864, highlights White's political career.

SYLVIA LARSON

WHITE, Alfred Tredway (28 May 1846–29 Jan. 1921), housing reformer and philanthropist, was born in Brooklyn, New York, the son of Alexander Moss White, a wealthy importer, and Elizabeth Hart Tredway. After earning an engineering degree from Rensselaer Polytechnic Institute in Troy, New York, in 1865, White returned to Brooklyn, worked in his family's Manhattan importing firm, and, beginning in 1867, taught in the settlement school started two years earlier by young people in the First Unitarian Church of Brooklyn. In 1869 he was asked by his pastor, Alfred P. Putnam, to superintend his church's settlement work. White's commitment to the welfare of immigrant children led him almost immediately to confront the appalling living conditions of the urban poor and to inaugurate the housing reform movement.

"I got a great deal more from this school than I ever gave to it," White testified at his settlement school's fiftieth anniversary. He then explained how visiting the homes of settlement children had interested him "in the housing question" and taught him "some very great lessons" (Hoogenboom and Hoogenboom, p. 8) Shocked to find that the death rate in tenements exceeded the general rate of population growth, White blamed housing and resolved to build healthy tenements. "Well it is to build hospitals for the cure of disease," he said, "but better to build homes which will prevent it" (Hoogenboom and Hoogenboom, p. 8). In 1872 White began to plan housing that would benefit low-income renters and earn a modest return for investors. Reading of Sir Sydney H. Waterlow's buildings and of other English housing-reform projects, White went to England to investigate them.

In 1877, with financial aid from his family, he completed the Home Buildings on the corner of Hicks and Baltic streets in Brooklyn. Like the White tenements that followed, these six-story, twin red-brick fireproof buildings, resembling Victorian castles, were "the most advanced tenement houses in the world" (Hoogenboom and Hoogenboom, p. 6). Their street-level stores were topped by apartments with sunlit rooms, private toilets, and balconies. Proving the slogan "Philanthropy and five percent" with his buildings, White urged other builders to follow his lead. On 29 May 1878 he married Annie Jean Lyman, a teacher in the settlement school who belonged to the prestigious Low family and became one of Brooklyn's "best known charity workers" (Hoogenboom and Hoogenboom, p. 11). They had two daughters, who also taught in the settlement school.

In 1878 and 1879, near his Home Buildings, White constructed the Tower Buildings, with approximately 170 apartments. In 1890, in the proximity of his other buildings but near the waterfront, he completed the nine Riverside Buildings. Featuring a total environment far in advance of its time, this project was White's greatest housing achievement. Besides a community bathhouse, it had its own park, playground, and music pavilion. With their buildings never occupying more than 52 percent of their lot, White projects, reformer Jacob Riis said, were "like a big village of contented people, who live in peace with one another because they have elbowroom" (Riis, p. 225). White, who built apartments and homes for more than a thousand families, was the first American to prove that good housing rented to those of limited means could be a profitable investment. As he had planned, his tenants' rents ($2.10 to $2.90 a week for a three-room apartment in 1893) earned him and his family 4.7 percent on their investment the first decade and 5.1 percent the second decade.

The outstanding success of White's housing experiments and the publicity he gave them through his writings and lectures helped enact the New York state tenement reform legislation of 1895. Under that legislation a new tenement could occupy no more than 65 percent of its lot unless the board of health granted a variance, which it frequently did. By 1900 White was a leading member of the New York State Tenement House Commission, and Theodore Roosevelt (1858–1919) visited his buildings and consulted him on housing reform.

Inspired by his church's work for immigrant children, White was not only in the forefront of the national movement to reform housing; he was in the vanguard of movements to improve education and to organize charity. Under his direction, the settlement school in 1876 moved into its own building, the Willow Place Chapel. That same year it started a kindergarten and with the help of Pratt Institute became a leader in the preschool education of children. This work was increased when a second building, Columbia House, was added in 1906. White also helped immigrant children through the Brooklyn Children's Aid Society, of which he was an early member. To cut down on infant mortality, which more than doubled in the city in July and August, in 1876 White established for the Children's Aid Society the Sea-Side Home on Coney Island—the nation's first facility where slum children could receive medical treatment and nutritious food in a vacation atmosphere. Later credited with halving Brooklyn infant mortality rates, White was also a founder of the Brooklyn Society for the Prevention of Cruelty to Children. In 1878, with Seth Low—who was Annie White's cousin and would become mayor of Brooklyn and of Greater New York—White founded the Brooklyn Bureau of Charities and during the next thirty years was either its president or its secretary.

White was also responsible for planning in 1893 Brooklyn's attractive and functional Wallabout Market (which lasted until the nearby navy yard expanded during World War II) and for making the Brooklyn Botanic Garden a reality in 1910. With the help of his family, he saw the developing garden through each financial crisis, giving it more than a million dollars. Among White's greatest enjoyments was searching for rare plants in their wild habitats, and he wanted to provide a similar experience for other Brooklyn residents. The first 120 acres of what became Brooklyn's Marine Park was given to the city by White and his friend Frederic B. Pratt, and in 1962 that park's northern area was named the Pratt-White Field.

White's philanthropy extended beyond Brooklyn. He believed that education and training were as necessary for the children of former slaves as for the children of immigrants. "Tuskegee Institute would not have been possible," Booker T. Washington stated, "had it not been for the encouragement and inspiration I received from Mr. White and his family" (Hoogenboom and Hoogenboom, p. 25). White was also a major supporter of Hampton Institute, where Washington was trained. After meeting Francis Greenwood Peabody in 1880, who had started a course at Harvard in social ethics, White endowed a Harvard chair in that field to teach young economists moral imperatives and young philosophers economic realities. Other schools soon patterned courses on the one taught at Harvard, and in this way White brought his progressive ideas to generations of students. Early in World War I White sent money to ravaged towns in Belgium and later helped Herbert Hoover's Commission for Relief in that country, for which White received the Belgian Order of the Cross. White was an original trustee of the Russell Sage Foundation, a charter member of Survey Associates, and a member of the first executive committee of the American National Red Cross. When White drowned, after falling through thin ice while skating on Forest Lake, near Ramapo Hills, New York, former president William Howard Taft lamented, "I don't know any other one in all that six millions of New York City who would leave such a void as he does."

• Material on White and his buildings can be found in the First Unitarian Church Collection, Brooklyn Historical Society, Brooklyn, N.Y., and in other papers there. For his own writings, see *Improved Dwellings for the Laboring Classes* (1879), "Better Homes for Workingmen" (prepared for the Twelfth National Conference of Charities, held at Washington, D.C., June 1885), and *Sun-Lighted Tenements: Thirty-five Years' Experience as an Owner* (1912). For writings on White by his contemporaries, see *Memorial Meeting: Alfred T. White, 1846–1921* (Brooklyn Academy of Music, 3 Apr. 1921); *In Memoriam, Alfred T. White* (Brooklyn Botanic Garden Record, July 1921); Robert W. de Forest, "Alfred T. White," *Survey*, 5 Feb. 1921; Francis Greenwood Peabody, *Reminiscences of Present-Day Saints* (1927); and Jacob A. Riis, *How the Other Half Lives* (1957). For modern assessments, see Olive Hoogenboom and Ari Hoogenboom, "Alfred T. White: Settlement Worker and Housing Reformer," *Hayes Historical Journal: A Journal of the Gilded Age* 9 (Fall 1989): 5–30; Olive Hoogenboom, *The First Unitarian Church of Brooklyn: One Hundred Fifty Years* (1987); and Joseph B. Milgram, *Alfred Tredway White* (1977). Obituaries are in the *New York Times* and the *Brooklyn Daily Eagle*, 31 Jan. 1921.

OLIVE HOOGENBOOM

WHITE, Alma Bridwell (16 June 1862–26 June 1946), evangelist and founder of the Pillar of Fire denomination, was born Mollie Alma Bridwell in Lewis County, Kentucky, the daughter of William Bridwell, a farmer and tanner, and Mary Ann Harrison. Raised a Methodist, Alma joined a local congregation at age twelve and underwent a conversion experience four years later in which she felt the call to preach. After attending the Female Seminary in Vanceburg, Kentucky, for a year, she enrolled at Millersburg (Ky.) Female College in 1880. After teaching school in Millersburg for a year, Alma accepted an aunt's offer to move to Bannack, Montana, a mining town seventy miles south of Butte. Between 1882 and 1886 she held a series of teaching positions. In 1887 she married Kent White, a young Methodist preacher from West Virginia, whom she had met four years earlier; they had two sons.

Marital problems soon surfaced, exacerbated by her husband's relationship with his mother and the fragile health of her infants. Depressed and feeling alone, she searched to understand her situation. When her younger son came down with pneumonia, White believed God healed him in response to her promise to preach despite any opposition she might face as a woman. Around the same period, she was convinced that she underwent the experience of "entire sanctification" that gave her not only a victory over personal sinfulness but a "holy boldness." Encouraged by her experiences, White participated in the 1894 camp meetings of the Colorado Holiness Association and subsequently led revivals in Colorado, Idaho, and Montana. In 1896 the Whites established an independent ministry known as the Pentecostal Home Mission in Denver. Soon thereafter, they began a newspaper, the *Pentecostal Mission Herald*, and opened a school for Christian workers.

From the beginning, Alma White was the dominant force. As she began to adopt a "come-outer" stance—the belief that established denominations were shot through with worldliness—her reluctant husband and most of the people associated with the mission followed her lead in leaving the Methodists. In late 1901 she and about fifty followers formally organized the Pentecostal Union church. The group gained a reputation for eccentric behavior and were dubbed the "Jumpers" by the Denver press for their exuberant worship and practice of "holy jumping." White was formally ordained a preacher within her new denomination in 1902.

In that year the Whites' Pentecostal Union church established a cooperative relationship and held joint meetings with the Burning Bush, a Chicago-based holiness sect. With Alma White as the main speaker, their revivals drew crowds in excess of a thousand in several cities. In 1904 she accompanied a Burning Bush party to England for a series of meetings. In 1905 arguments over a piece of New Jersey property led to a bitter split between the two groups and several attempts by the Burning Bush to take over the land and White's group.

In 1904 the Whites changed the name of their publication to the *Pillar of Fire* (POF), a name that became the unofficial designation of the group as well. By this time new branches of the church had begun in Omaha, Colorado Springs, Salt Lake City, and Los Angeles. In 1908 Alma White moved the group's headquarters and a newly created Bible school thirty miles west of New York City to the New Jersey farm she had dubbed "Zarephath." In the new setting, members assumed a more communal lifestyle with new recruits expected to give up their property upon joining the community. Like the Salvation Army, both men and women were required to wear distinctive uniforms to emphasize their nonconformity with the "world." White also began to teach that sex was appropriate only for procreative purposes, and by 1914 she had steered the group into vegetarianism.

While in Denver in early 1909, Kent White embraced Pentecostalism. His attempts to introduce glossolalia into the POF caused renewed strife in his marriage. Upset over his wife's refusal to follow his lead and harboring resentment for years of being overshadowed, Kent withdrew his membership in Pillar of Fire and left Alma. Devastated, but unquestionably in control, she led the POF in a militantly anti-Pentecostal direction. To solidify her standing, she was consecrated as bishop of the POF in 1918—the first woman bishop of any American denomination. In 1920 Kent attempted to gain control of the POF for the Pentecostal Apostolic Faith denomination. Risking unfavorable publicity Alma moved to save her church by initiating a divorce suit, citing desertion as just cause. While the judge dismissed the case on grounds that a mutual affection persisted between the Whites, the combination of legal proceedings and media coverage were enough to deter the Apostolic Faith from any further plans to take over the POF.

The group continued to grow over the next two decades, adding branches in San Francisco, Cincinnati, Brooklyn, and other cities while expanding the complex at Zarephath. In 1912 White established a grammar and high school there, and in 1921 the Zarephath Bible Institute became Alma White College. In 1920 the group opened Belleview High School in Denver and added a Belleview elementary school, college, and seminary in the following years. In 1928 the group initiated a foray into radio with the establishment of KPOF in Denver. Three years later, White orchestrated the purchase of WAWZ and began broadcasting a mix of her preaching and Bible teaching and sacred and classical music from Zarephath to the New York City area.

During the 1920s White began to turn more attention to national political and social issues, in the process fashioning a unique hybrid philosophy dictated by her own personal views, concerns, and prejudices. In 1922 she came into contact with the Ku Klux Klan and, finding its anti-Catholicism and general opposition to modernist theology in harmony with her nativist and fundamentalist leanings, lent her support to the organization. White spoke at numerous Klan rallies in New Jersey and the Midwest in the early and mid-1920s. The relationship endured through the decade with the POF being the only religious denomination in the United States to publicly endorse the Klan.

During this same period, White's ministry began to actively take up the cause of women's rights. A supporter of suffrage since the early 1900s, she was unalterably opposed to conventional Victorian views limiting women's sphere to the home. White joined forces with the National Woman's party during the 1920s and supported the Equal Rights Amendment, making the POF the first religious group to support the ERA. In 1924 she founded *Woman's Chains*, a predominantly political magazine that advocated women's involvement in the political process at all levels.

White's health began to deteriorate during the 1930s, but the reins of leadership remained firmly in her hands. She continued to comment on women's issues and current events both over the radio and in POF publications. Throughout, she continued her attacks on Catholicism and Pentecostalism. White died in Zarephath, New Jersey, and was succeeded by her son Arthur White.

Although the Pillar of Fire has never formally had more than a few thousand members, the importance of Alma White's vision of Wesleyan Methodist holiness teachings had a much wider influence through the distribution of the group's literature and the impact of radio. White is particularly important because of her position as an evangelical protofeminist in her rejection of traditional evangelical views of women's roles in the home, church, and society. In a more general sense, White's dual allegiance to the Ku Klux Klan and to the women's rights movement demonstrates the difficulty in stereotyping the political and social views of American evangelicals.

• The Pillar of Fire denomination and White's descendants retain possession of her published and unpublished writings, photographs, and other materials, much of it in Zarephath, N.J. She was the author of more than thirty books on various topics as well as numerous pieces in her denomination's periodicals, the *Pentecostal Mission Herald*, *Pillar of Fire*, *Women's Chains*, and the *Good Citizen*. Details on White's life are provided in her five-volume autobiography, *The Story of My Life and Pillar of Fire* (1935–1943). For White's views on Pentecostalism, see *Demons and Tongues* (1910); for her views of the Ku Klux Klan, see *The Ku Klux Klan in Prophecy* (1925), as well as the pages of the *Good Citizen*. In this latter connection, see also Kathleen M. Blee, *Women of the Klan* (1991), and Robert A. Goldberg, *Hooded Empire: The Ku Klux Klan in Colorado* (1981). Apart from her connections to the Klan, much of the scholarly assessment of White's religious career has centered on the feminist implications of her life. For example, see Nancy Hardesty et al., "Women in the Holiness Movement: Feminism in the Evangelical Tradition," in *Women of Spirit: Female Leadership in the Jewish and Christian Traditions*, ed. Rosemary Ruether and Eleanor McLaughlin (1979); Margaret Lamberts Bendroth, "Fundamentalism and Femininity: Points of Encounter between Religious Conservatives and Women, 1919–1935," *Church History* 61 (June 1992): 221–33; and Susie C. Stanley, "Empowered Foremothers: Wesleyan/Holiness Women Speak to Today's Christian Feminists," *Wesleyan Theological Journal* 24 (1989): 103–16. The most concentrated scholarly treatment of White's life is Stanley's compact but well-researched monograph *Feminist Pillar of Fire: The Life of Alma White* (1993). An obituary is in the *New York Times*, 27 June 1946.

LARRY ESKRIDGE

WHITE, Andrew (1579–27 Dec. 1656), Jesuit missionary and promotion writer, was born in London, England. The names and occupations of his parents are unknown. He matriculated at Douai College, France, in April 1593. After studying at other Catholic colleges, he returned to Douai, arriving on 4 June 1604, where he took vows as a priest in 1605. He then went to England, where, since the Gunpowder Plot had just been discovered, Catholic priests were being persecuted. Promptly arrested and imprisoned, White was banished from England on penalty of death. On 1 February 1607 he was admitted as a novitiate at Jesuit college of St. John's, Louvain, Belgium. In 1612 White returned to London as a Jesuit missionary. From then until 1633, he alternated between various teaching positions on the Continent and missionary posts in England.

Early in 1633, White wrote the first Maryland promotion tract, *A Declaration of the Lord Baltimore's Plantation in Mary-land, Nigh upon Virginia: Manifesting the Nature, Quality, Condition and Rich Utilities It Contayneth* (1633). White wrote a version in Latin as a report to the general of the Jesuit order and another in English as a promotion tract. Cecil Calvert, second lord Baltimore, read over the tract and probably made some suggestions. No doubt Calvert dictated the terms offered to the earliest settlers: Calvert would grant two thousand acres to every person who set out, properly equipped, with five able men. The heart of the tract described Maryland, reflecting the writings of Captain John Smith (1580–1631).

White sailed for Maryland with the first colonists, including two other Jesuits, on 22 November 1633. He wrote three accounts of the voyage, exploration, and first settlement of Maryland. The Latin version consists of White's report as superior of the Maryland mission to the Society of Jesus. An English version, written for the Calverts and their friends, was entitled "A Brief Relation of the Voyage unto Maryland." Governor Leonard Calvert enclosed it in a letter of 30 May 1634 to Sir Richard Lechford. The third and most widely circulated version was written as a promotion tract, *A Relation of the Successful Beginnings of the Lord Baltimore's Plantation in Maryland* (1634). It abbreviates the difficulties of the voyage over (given in detail in the other two versions), describes the country in glowing terms, and enlivens the descriptions with humorous comments and dialogue. White praised the Potomac River: "This riuer, of all I know, is the greatest and sweetest, much broader than the *Thames*; so pleasant, as I for my part, was neuer satisfied in beholding it." He described the American Indians' comments on the colonists' large ship, the *Ark*: "it was worth the hearing, . . . to heare what admiration they made at our ship; calling it a Canow, and wondering where so great a tree grew that made it." White dated the tract "From St. *Maries* in *Mary-land*, 27 May 1634." In London, Calvert added the "Conditions of plantation," the date 15 July 1634, and published it.

White also wrote the first five chapters of *A Relation of Maryland; Together with a Map of That Country, the Conditions of Plantation, His Magesties Charter to the Lord Baltemore* (1635), the third Maryland promotion tract. The first chapter tells in greater detail of the colony's exploration and settlement. The second describes the country; the third, the native commodities; and the fourth, the commodities "that may be procured in Maryland by Industry." Though these materials appeared in White's earlier *Successful Relations*, he expanded the information and organized it better. White also added a new subject (chapter five) devoted to the Maryland Indians. The Calverts appended the final two chapters in London: chapter six gave the new terms for the prospective colonists, and chapter seven contained practical information, such as a list of the provisions that a prospective colonist should take to Maryland.

White spent his time in Maryland learning the languages of the American Indians and teaching them Christianity. His greatest success occurred on 5 July 1640, when he baptized Chief Chitomachon (of the Conoy tribe), his wife, daughter, chief counselor, and the counselor's son. Seventeenth-century Jesuit literature celebrated the baptism, and an imaginative portrait of the ceremony appeared in Mathias Tanner, *Societas Jesu Apostolorum* (1694).

During the local colonial wars between the Royalists and Puritans, White and Father Thomas Copley were captured by Virginia Puritans in 1644 or 1645 and sent in chains to England, where they were tried for being priests in England. White was acquitted, arguing that he had been taken to England against his will. He was nevertheless imprisoned in Newgate until 7 January 1648, when he was released and ordered to depart England within fifteen days. While White was in jail, the fourth Maryland colonization tract appeared, *A Moderate and Safe Expedient to Remove Jealouses and Feares of Any Danger by the Roman Catholickes of This Kingdom* (1646). It urged that Roman Catholics should either be given religious freedom in England or else be allowed to emigrate to Maryland. White had written almost half of the pamphlet, entitled "Objections Answered touching Mariland," between 29 June and 3 July 1633, while he was working with Cecil Calvert preparing for the first voyage to Maryland. His section answered five objections that William Claiborne (c. 1587–c. 1677) had brought against allowing Catholics to emigrate to Maryland.

White arrived at Antwerp, Belgium, on 1 March 1648. The annual letter to the Jesuit general for 1649 reported that White was writing a "perfecta et exacta" history of the Maryland mission, but he probably never finished this first projected general history of Maryland. In Antwerp he influenced the Teresian nun Margaret Mostyn, who praised him for his piety and humanity in her autobiography. White returned to England about 1650. Though he repeatedly requested to be sent back to Maryland, he was refused, probably because of poor health and advanced age. He died in Hampshire, England.

• A few pages of prayers and of notes by White in Conoy (a branch of the Algonquian language, similar to Nanticoke and Narragansett) survive at the Georgetown University Library. White's Jesuit records are best studied in Thomas A. Hughes, *History of the Society of Jesus in North America* (4 vols., 1907–1910), and in Henry J. Foley, *Records of the English Province of the Society of Jesus*, vols. 1–7 (1875–1883). A biographical and critical study, together with a primary and secondary bibliography, is in J. A. Leo Lemay, *Men of Letters in Colonial Maryland* (1972).

J. A. LEO LEMAY

WHITE, Andrew Dickson (7 Nov. 1832–4 Nov. 1918), university president and diplomat, was born in Homer, New York, the son of Horace White, a businessman, and Clara Dickson. Vigilant lest their wealth spoil Andrew, the Whites emphasized the duty of every person to serve others. At his parents' request, he enrolled at Geneva College, a small Episcopalian institution near Syracuse. In search of a more challenging intellectual environment, he transferred to Yale in his sophomore year and completed his undergraduate degree in 1853. Uncertain about his vocation, White traveled to Europe, first as unpaid attaché to Thomas H. Seymour, U.S. minister to Russia, and then as a student in Germany, where in the heady atmosphere of *Lernfreiheit* and *Lehrfreiheit* he decided to become a scholar and teacher. Returning to the United States, he married his childhood sweetheart, Mary Outwater, in 1859; they had three children. In 1857, after receiving an M.A. from Yale, he accepted a position as professor of history and rhetoric at the University of Michigan.

White's six years at Michigan were an apprenticeship in the reform of higher education. A popular and respected teacher, White supported President Henry

Tappan's initiatives in nondenominationalism and free electives and observed at close range Tappan's struggles with the legislature, which led to the president's dismissal in 1863. By this time, with Tappan's difficulties in mind, White was already drafting plans for a privately endowed nonsectarian university to be established in New York, but he could not locate a benefactor to build it. White's tenure at Michigan coincided with the secessionist crisis and the Civil War. An abolitionist, he lectured on the evil of slavery to his classes, arousing the ire of many Ann Arbor residents. After the war began, White organized and drilled students, though he himself did not enlist and probably purchased a substitute. He also gained a small measure of fame as an essayist. In articles on Thomas Jefferson, Cardinal Richelieu, and Alexander II's freeing of the Russian serfs, he argued directly and through analogy that slavery guaranteed the spiritual and economic stagnation of a nation. White also traveled to England, where he urged the British government not to support the South.

When he returned to the United States, White was elected to the New York state senate, serving Onondaga County from 1864 to 1867. As chairman of the committee on education, which was responsible for allocating funds generated by the Morrill Land Grant, White met Senator Ezra Cornell. The two lobbied successfully to concentrate the Morrill money on one state university, which would provide instruction in agriculture and the mechanic arts. Supplemented by Cornell's gifts, the university bearing his name opened in 1868, with White as its first president. As the architect of Cornell University, White emerged as one of the dominant figures in late nineteenth-century higher education. His *Report on Organization*, presented to the trustees in 1866, constituted the educational blueprint for Cornell. Although he often emphasized the "Christian character" of Cornell and made attendance at chapel compulsory, White insisted, in spite of criticism, that the institution be nonsectarian, open to faculty and students regardless of their religious beliefs. He also sought equality among both students and subjects. Under his pioneering stewardship, Cornell became one of the first universities in the United States to institute coeducation and to treat science, agriculture, and the mechanic arts as disciplines worthy of study within the traditional liberal arts curriculum. Although White did not quite share Ezra Cornell's passion for the practical, he strongly supported courses in the applied sciences and social sciences. He believed, moreover, that students should have some latitude in selecting courses. Convinced that the system of free electives introduced at Harvard by Charles W. Eliot encouraged superficiality, White allowed students several course options, but once a selection was made (of a science curriculum, for example) all classes for four years were prescribed.

As an administrator, White's educational principles were tempered by pragmatism. When low salaries and the prospect of dreary winters in Ithaca made it difficult to attract first-rate faculty, White scored a public relations coup by enlisting as nonresident professors zoologist Louis Agassiz, poet James Russell Lowell, and editor George William Curtis to deliver one course of lectures a year at whatever length they chose. More importantly, assaults on Cornell as an "atheistic" university inclined White to retreat on occasion from nondenominationalism in an effort to promote harmony inside the institution and retain support from the legislature and the public at large. Thus, in 1877 he acquiesced to a demand from the board of trustees that Felix Adler (1851–1933), a prominent Jewish professor of comparative religion who had implied that Christianity was merely a sect, not be retained. Four years later, he agreed to the removal of professor of history William Channing Russel, who referred in class to the church as an institution rather than a divine establishment. Similarly, White modified his pledge to treat all students equally by requiring that female students live in dormitories, subject to the discipline enforced by an ever-present matron. If parents thought women were unsupervised, he argued, the experiment in coeducation would fail. Justifying his actions, White claimed that in the long run the "Cornell Idea" would triumph. In the roles of president and historian, White evinced a decided preference for evolution over revolution, implicitly repudiating the abolitionism of his youth. That universities throughout the United States borrowed from and built upon White's educational innovations bolstered his argument.

As a prominent intellectual and politically active Republican, White participated in reform causes, including the civil service movement, and several times considered running for Congress or governor. A restless man committed to public service, he took lengthy leaves of absence from Cornell to serve in diplomatic posts. In 1871 President Ulysses S. Grant appointed White, Benjamin Wade, and Samuel Gridley Howe U.S. commissioners to Santo Domingo. After a fact-finding tour the trio wrote an enthusiastic report that, at White's suggestion, stopped just short of recommending annexation. The Senate, which had defeated a treaty in 1870, took no action, and the issue faded away. In 1879 President Rutherford B. Hayes named White U.S. minister to Germany. Throughout this two-year post White's sympathy for German civilization shaped his reports to the State Department. He recommended that the United States not retaliate against the German ban on American pork and predicted that the German treaty of "friendship and commerce" with Samoa was not the first step toward colonialism. Most of White's duties, however, were social, and he was enormously popular with the cultural establishment of Germany.

In 1885 White retired as president of Cornell. His wife died in 1887, and three years later, after a stormy courtship, he married Helen Magill, the first woman to receive a Ph.D. in the United States; they had one child. The remainder of White's public life was spent in diplomatic positions. Although several times mentioned as a candidate for secretary of state, he never reached the level of policy maker. As minister to Russia from 1892 to 1894, he labored unsuccessfully to prevent an Anglo-Russian agreement that would shut the United States out of the seal trade in the Bering Sea. He also worked to ease the persecution of Jews in Russia, opposing an extradition treaty that required the return to Russia of anyone convicted or accused of an act of violence against the tsar or his family. In 1896 White began work as a member of the Venezuela Boundary Commission only to learn that the British had yielded and submitted the issue to arbitration. One incident marred an otherwise successful tour as ambassador to Germany from 1897 to 1902. White's conviction that the United States had no designs on Spanish colonies during the Spanish-American War may have encouraged a German initiative, soon abandoned, to control the Philippines. Chastised by the State Department, White was more prudent during the remainder of his tenure. Appointment as head of the U.S. delegation to the First Hague International Peace Conference in 1899 capped White's diplomatic career. Though participation was voluntary, the establishment of a permanent panel of arbitration portended, he believed, the use of rational discourse to settle international disputes.

White authored a number of historical studies, publishing his magnum opus, *A History of the Warfare of Science with Theology in Christendom*, in 1895. Part of the attempt to reevaluate Christianity in the light of biblical higher criticism, comparative mythology, and Darwinian science, this ponderously titled two-volume work aimed to dissolve a mass of theological dogma and to affirm rational, nonmythical religion and its absolute truths (primarily ethical imperatives like love of God and neighbor). Believing "warfare" between religion and science to be unnecessary, White wrote a paean to progress, his most cherished belief. *The Warfare of Science* chronicled the triumph of the heliocentric theory, prehistoric archaeology, comparative ethnology, meteorology, chemistry and physics, sanitary science, comparative philology, and evolution. But by placing Scripture in an evolutionary context, this work and other works of the late nineteenth century undermined its authority, also casting doubt on the divine inspiration of the moral maxims of Christianity. An immensely learned and influential book, the *Warfare of Science* had the effect of contributing to a spiritual crisis in the Gilded Age.

White's other works also addressed contemporary problems through historical analogy. To combat the threat of populism, for example, he reissued in 1896 *Fiat Money in France*, which argued that paper money inflation was a cancer "more permanently injurious to a nation than war, pestilence or famine." In 1910 White completed *Seven Great Statesmen in the Warfare of Humanity with Unreason*, a series of biographical sketches of Sarpi, Grotius, Thomasius, Turgot, Stein, Cavour, and Bismarck. These men, he argued, were united in a faith that evolutionary change was possible and therefore desirable, a theme that also pervades White's two-volume *Autobiography* (1905). A founding member and first president of the American Historical Association (1885), White was convinced that the historian's first duty was to illuminate the present with the light of the past. His career in educational administration, politics, and scholarship was an attempt to determine how much change was possible without disturbing the stability of society.

After his retirement as ambassador to Germany in 1902, White divided his time between travel in Europe and residence in Ithaca. The death of a daughter and the suicide of his son and grandson made his last years tragic. With the outbreak of war in Europe, moreover, White's faith in the power of reasoned diplomacy and the superiority of German culture was badly shaken. As one who had looked upon Germany as a second mother country, he found unbearable the sight of Cornell students drilling to fight the Huns. Characteristically, White adhered to his lifelong belief in progress, indulging in "vague hopes that all this present condition of things, involving as it does so distressingly the modern world, may in some way be only a dream." Three days short of his eighty-sixth birthday, White died in Ithaca, New York.

• Letters to and from White are in the Andrew D. White Papers, Department of Manuscript and Archives, Cornell University. See also Glenn C. Altschuler, *Andrew D. White—Educator, Historian, Diplomat* (1979). An obituary is in the *New York Times*, 5 Nov. 1918.

GLENN C. ALTSCHULER

WHITE, Anna (21 Jan. 1831–16 Dec. 1910), Shaker eldress, author, and songwriter, was born in Brooklyn, New York, the daughter of Robert White, a businessman and farmer, and Hannah Gibbs, an almoner (a distributor of goods to the needy) for the Quakers. White was educated at Mansion Square Seminary, a Quaker school, in Poughkeepsie, New York. When she was seventeen she learned the tailoring trade and helped her mother distribute alms from the Quakers to the poor of New York City. Her father had become a Shaker and divided his time between living with his natural family and residing with the Shakers. His decision to become a Shaker angered his wife and alienated all his children except Anna who also became interested. Every effort was made to dissuade her from Shakerism, and an uncle even proposed to settle $40,000 on her if she would give up thinking about it.

Despite the great efforts made to deter her, White made a three-month visit to the North Family of Shakers in New Lebanon, New York, during the summer of 1849. She formally entered the North Family on 16 October 1849, a date that she kept for the rest of her life as her real birthday. She also became a vegetarian, a practice that was beginning in the North Family. Soon after she came to the Shakers, she received the first of the scores of "gift songs" that she would get by inspiration from the spirit world during the next sixty years.

Though only a believer for six months and only nineteen years old, White was permitted to sign the 1829 North Family Covenant on 26 March 1850. This legal document, usually signed only by those twenty-one years or older, was a promise to live forever as a Shaker without compensation for work done while in the community. The fact that she signed it after so short a time and before her majority showed both her great fervor and the esteem in which the Shakers held her. Besides helping with the housework, which included "turns" at cleaning and cooking, she worked at knitting, spinning, weaving, and palmleaf work. By the mid-1850s she was appointed to care for female visitors and inquirers. These guests were housed in the second dwelling with White, who shared a room with them. In this way she cared for scores of visitors, including many young children, until January 1865 when she was chosen to assist Eldress M. Antoinette Doolittle as second eldress. The major duty of the second eldress was to care for the young sisters in the family. On 1 February, the day she took office, Minnie Allen was brought to the North Family to live. Minnie Allen, who became Catherine Allen, was White's first "girl" and became one of the leading figures in twentieth-century Shakerism.

White had the privilege of knowing those who remembered the "First Parents" and founders of Shakerism. Thus, as she instructed and formed future generations, she became a valued link with the past. As a member of the elders' lot with Frederick W. Evans, she came to share his passionate interest in reform movements. She shared her thoughts in "gift songs," poems, and essays. Many of these were published between 1871 and 1899 in *The Manifesto*, the Shaker newspaper.

In January 1887 White became the first eldress of the North Family, and she began a two-decade period of public lecturing, writing, and publishing. Her work falls into two categories: memorial books to recently deceased Shakers and essays on Shaker religious thought and reform. She also compiled a book of poems by the North Family Shakers and compiled two hymnals of Shaker music still used by the Shakers of today. Her crowning achievement was *Shakerism, Its Meaning and Message* (1904). Though "the work of reading, note-gathering, composing and transcribing" was done by Sister Leila S. Taylor, "the inspiration, direction, weighing of evidence and final judgment" were White's (*Memorial to Anna White*, p. 70). This book was the last comprehensive history of the Shakers written by Shakers and is still a classic reference work used by Shaker scholars. It includes a detailed history of Shakerism, a description of Shaker literature, and a statement of Shaker religious beliefs. The final chapter is a strongly worded appeal, "A Message to Shakers," which highlights White's view of contemporary Shaker society and her hopes for the future.

Unlike the vast majority of Shaker women, Anna White ventured out into "the world." For example, at the time of the Dreyfus affair in France, she coauthored an article entitled "The Shaker Sisters' Plea for Dreyfus." She proclaimed, "We shall continue to do violence by waging a more effective war, as only Peace people can do, against the baseness of inhumanity to man and to woman." Later she collected more signatures than any other woman in New York State for the petition for international disarmament and was consequently appointed vice president for New York of the Women's International League of Peace and Arbitration in about 1903. She was also a member of the National American Woman Suffrage Association and vice president of the National Council of Women.

The culmination of White's efforts was the Peace Conference held at Mount Lebanon on 31 August 1905. Hundreds of people from around the country gathered in the Shaker meetinghouse to hear a large number of peace advocates. White's speech on this occasion could be used to summarize her life: "No citizen is more thoroughly alive to the interests of state or nation, than are the Shakers." Following the conference, White and her associate eldress presented the adopted resolutions to President Theodore Roosevelt in Washington, D.C. During her final years, White became interested in Christian Science and claimed to be healed by its methods from a near fatal illness. Her account of this healing appeared in the *Christian Science Journal* (Dec. 1907).

White was the last full-time eldress of the North Family. When she died, a solid link with the earliest years of Shakerism was gone. As the best-known eldress and strongest reformer at Mount Lebanon, she tried to bring Shakerism into modern times. During her years as eldress, the North Family became the largest Shaker family at Mount Lebanon and thus ensured its survival as the last family of that society to close in 1947.

• White's correspondence can be found on microfilm at the Western Reserve Historical Society, Cleveland, Ohio; at the Hancock (Mass.) Shaker Village library; and at the Winterthur Museum and Library, Winterthur, Del. A complete and annotated bibliography of the works of Anna White is Mary L. Richmond, comp., *Shaker Literature* (1977). Included are these works: *Affectionately Inscribed to the Memory of Elder Frederick W. Evans* (1893); *Affectionately Inscribed to the Memory of Eldress Antoinette Doolittle* (1887); *Dedicated to the Memory of Sister Polly Lewis* (1899); *The Motherhood of God* (1903); *Mount Lebanon Cedar Boughs: Original Poems by the North Family of Shakers* (1895); *Present Day Shakerism* (1906); *To Our Well Beloved Mother in Israel, Eldress Eliza Taylor* (1897); *True Source of Happiness* (n.d.); *Vegetarianism among the Shakers* (n.d.); *Voices from Mount Lebanon* (1899), a paper read at the Universal Peace Meeting, Mystic, Conn.; and *Woman's Mission* (1891). White's two books of hymns are *Shaker Music: Original Inspirational Hymns and Songs of the Shakers* (1884) and *Original Shaker Music* (1893). See also Leila S. Taylor, *A Memorial to Eldress Anna White and Elder Daniel Offord* (1912), a full-length biography.

STEPHEN J. PATERWIC

WHITE, Benjamin Franklin (3 Feb. 1873–20 May 1958), harness horse racing driver, trainer, and owner, was born in Whitevale, Ontario, Canada, the son of a gristmill owner. Though expected to take over his father's business, White never finished high school. In 1888 he traveled to Markham, Ontario, where he drove his first race behind a mare belonging to his sister. In 1893 White took a job in East Aurora, New York, at C. J. Hamlin's famed Village Farm stable, a leading breeder of harness horses. Tutored by the noted trainer Edward "Pop" Geers, White served successively as a groom, rider, assistant trainer, and, finally, upon Geers's departure in 1903, head trainer. In 1906, in the final heat of the Futurity at Columbus, Ohio, White finished with The Abbe in 2 minutes, 10½ seconds, the first time a three-year-old stallion had beaten 2:11. White rode winners every single season for the next 37 years.

White went to work as trainer for Seymour Knox, who had acquired a number of Village Farm horses in 1905. Remaining with Knox until 1915, he also raced independently. That same year the Pasttime Stable employed White as a rider and head trainer. During the 1915 and 1916 seasons, White, already famous as "the colt wizard," drove Pasttime horses Lee Axworthy and Volga to big cash harness victories. White won every race during these two years, and Lee Axworthy's world record for the mile (1:58¼) stood until 1938 when it was broken by another White-driven horse, Rosalind. Though Pasttime Stable did not long survive, one of its owners, Frank Ellis, subsequently hired White as trainer.

During the harness racing glory days of the 1920s and 1930s, White became the greatest rider-trainer-owner in the sport's history. He won scores of races in these decades, including seven Kentucky Futurities, and set world records with horses such as Mr. McElwyn, Main McElwyn, and Sumatra. The most famous trotting horse championship in this period was the Hambletonian, for three-year-olds. White drove in 19 Hambletonians, winning four times. Driving his first in 1926, White's initial victory came in 1933 with Mary Reynolds. From 1935 to 1939, behind the bay filly Rosalind, White won race after race, including the Hambletonian in 1936. John Hervey, writing in *Hoof Beats*, called the 1936 Hambletonian "a summit of achievement" in the sport of harness racing. Two years later, the 65-year-old White brought Rosalind to perfect form with the world-record mile (1:56¾). Of 36 races, Rosalind won 24, placed in seven, and showed in one, making her the greatest moneymaking mare of her day.

Despite his advanced years and the physical demands of the sport, White continued to race—and continued to win—in the 1940s. He won his third Hambletonian in 1942, he and The Ambassador pulling off an upset. White's fourth Hambletonian victory occurred the next year, with Volo Song, remembered by harness racing greats Delvin Miller and Frank Ervin as possibly "the greatest trotter to ever come along." White competed in his final Hambletonian in 1949, at age 76.

White had married Sarah (maiden name unknown). In his later years, he operated a stable in Orlando, Florida, with his son, Gibson. White continued to train horses until shortly before his death in Orlando.

White had a superb soft touch with all horses. Total concentration combined with near perfect effort at spreading the strength and speed of his horse were White's strongest traits. Dubbed "the dean of drivers" by *Newsweek* (2 June 1958), White insisted that "just getting into a race is not everything. It's training these young horses and bringing them into bloom that counts." Unexcelled both as a trainer and a driver, White was elected to the Trotting Hall of Fame.

• Trotting horse journals and sportswriters described Ben White's exploits in detail. See, for instance, issues of *Hoof Beats*, Christmas 1933, Oct. 1936, and Dec. 1940; the *New York Times*, 17 Aug. 1933, 9 Aug. 1936, 13 Aug. 1936, 13 Aug. 1942, 12 Aug. 1943, and 15 Aug. 1943; and the *Canadian Sportsman*, 8 Dec. 1981. For White's role in the worlds of racing and training, see Frank A. Wrensch, *Harness Horse Racing in the United States and Canada* (1948), James C. Harrison, comp., *Care and Training of the Trotter and Pacer* (1968), and Philip Pines, *The Complete Book of Harness Racing* (1970). The story of Ben White, his son, and Rosalind is told for young readers in Marguerite Henry, *Born to Trot* (1950). Following his death, White's career was recalled in *Harness Horse*, 28 May 1958; the *Horseman and Fair World*, 28 May 1958; *Hoof Beats*, June 1958; *Newsweek*, 2 June 1958; and in an obituary in the *New York Times*, 21 May 1958.

JOHN LUCAS

WHITE, Bukka (12 Nov. 1909?–26 Feb. 1977), blues artist, was born Booker T. Washington White in Houston, Mississippi, the son of John White, a locomotive fireman, and Lula Davisson. He spent his early years on the farm of his mother's father, Punk Davisson, a landowner and fundamentalist church leader. Booker sang in church with his sister and received rudimentary guitar instruction from his father, who played guitar, mandolin, violin, piano, and saxophone.

When Booker was nine, his father bought a guitar for him, and the youngster was soon testing his musical skills at local house parties. In 1920 he hitchhiked about fifty miles west to live with an uncle, Alec Johnson, near Grenada, Mississippi. There and in Clarksdale, White heard a number of accomplished Mississippi Delta blues artists, Charlie Patton among them. "I tried to be a second behind old Charlie Patton," White said in later years.

In his early teens, White hopped a northbound freight train and wound up in St. Louis, where he did odd jobs around a roadhouse and took piano lessons. In 1925 he returned to Houston and married Jessie Bea. He combined farming and local performances until his wife died from a ruptured appendix in 1928. Over the next several years, he moved between St. Louis and Mississippi, working briefly with a traveling minstrel show. While living in Swan Lake, Mississippi, in 1930 he was contacted by Ralph Lembo, the owner of a furniture store in Itta Bena and a part-time talent scout for RCA Victor Record Company. On 26 May 1930 Lembo took White to Memphis where he recorded as many as fourteen blues and religious sides. Four titles were issued: "New Frisco Train" and "The Panama Limited," both train blues, and two religious songs, "Promise True and Grand" and "I Am in the

Heavenly Way." White returned to Mississippi, where he began performing in roadhouses with Alabama-born harmonica player George "Bullet" Williams.

In 1934 he married Williams's niece Susie Simpson and moved to Aberdeen, Mississippi, about thirty miles east of his birthplace. From 1935 to 1937 he was on the road, working various musical and nonmusical jobs including stints as a prizefighter and a Negro League baseball pitcher. On one visit to Chicago, White was introduced to Lester Melrose, a music publisher with an ear for blues. Under Melrose's auspices, White recorded two sides for American Record Corporation on 2 September 1937: "Pinebluff Arkansas" and the hit side, "Shake 'Em on Down." The record was released on Vocalion and two other labels, Columbia and Conqueror. White's given name was spelled "Bukka" on the record label, a phonetic debasement that stayed with him for the rest of his life. The record sold well enough for Melrose to seek a second session, but by then White was serving a two-year sentence in Parchman Farm, the notorious Mississippi Delta prison, for shooting a man during an altercation in Aberdeen. White said he spent much of his prison time playing music. On 24 May 1939 he was asked to perform for folklorist Alan Lomax, who had came to Parchman Farm to make field recordings for the Library of Congress. Although unhappy that Lomax wouldn't pay him, White recorded two songs, "Po' Boy" and "Sic 'Em Dogs On."

Released from prison later in 1939, he returned to Chicago for the long-delayed second recording session with Melrose. On 7 and 8 March 1940 White recorded twelve songs including "Parchman Farm Blues" and "Fixin' to Die Blues," for Vocalion and Okeh, accompanied by a washboard player, probably Washboard Sam. These recordings, for which he received $17.50 per side, were touted for a time as the last great body of "country blues." In the 1940s, though, they were regarded as anachronisms by many blues consumers, whose tastes were becoming increasingly "citified."

Following the 1940 session, White continued to travel back and forth to Mississippi, working briefly with a small band in Chicago. By 1946 he had split up with his second wife and had moved to Memphis, where he occasionally played with Frank Stokes and Memphis Willie Borum. During World War II he spent some time in the navy and recalled entertaining troops in Tokyo. After the war, he returned to Memphis, playing less frequently and finally drifting away from music altogether.

In 1959 blues researcher Samuel Charters mentioned White and his composition "Fixin' to Die Blues" in his book *The Country Blues*. The song was rereleased on the book's companion album, and three years later, folk guitarist Bob Dylan included the song on his debut Columbia album, bringing White to the attention of a growing blues revival audience.

Aided by a geographical reference in a song, researchers John Fahey and Ed Denson traced White's whereabouts to Memphis, and in 1963 they took White to California to perform and record for Fahey's Takoma label. Thus began the second stage of White's musical career.

Through the 1960s and early 1970s he performed for an avid new following, touring with the American Folk Blues Festival in Europe and Dick Waterman's Memphis Blues Caravan in the United States. His performance credits included the Newport Folk Festival in 1966 and a festival coinciding with the Olympics in Mexico City two years later. In the mid-1970s he returned to Memphis, where he later died. Some sources say he had several other significant relationships, probably common-law marriages, and he may have had as many as four children, but the paucity of legal records and the necessity of relying on imperfect recollection when reconstructing the life stories of folk artists makes it difficult to confirm these details.

White brought his blues to life with a percussive slide-guitar style and expressive, hard-edged vocals. He drew on personal experiences and observations to create blues poetry that conjured up images of rural Mississippi. In concert, he sometimes improvised new compositions, which he called "sky songs," saying he pulled them out of the sky. During a career that reached across six decades, White's music remained frozen in time. At least partly for that reason, his work did not influence the changing blues tradition. Still, because he remained so true to his musical heritage, White was one of the most successful revival artists.

• For historical details and interview materials, see Margaret McKee and Fred Chisenhall, *Beale Black and Blue: Life and Music on Black America's Main Street* (1981); Samuel Charters, *The Legacy of the Blues* (1975); and *Tom Ashley, Sam McGhee, Bukka White: Tennessee Traditional Singers*, ed. Thomas Burton (1981). This latter work contains one of the most complete recountings of White's life and art in an essay by F. Jack Hurley and David Evans.

For interviews with White, see Julius Lester, "Mister White Takes a Break," *Sing Out* 18, no. 4 (1968), and "The House Frolic: A Reminiscence by Booker White," transcribed by Stephen Calt, *78 Quarterly* 1, no. 8 (N.D.). To hear his music, try *The Complete Bukka White*, Columbia Legacy, CK 52782. For discographical information, see Robert M. W. Dixon and John Godrich, *Blues and Gospel Records: 1902–1943* (1982); Mike Leadbitter and Neil Slaven, *Blues Records, 1943–1970*, vol. 2 (1968); and *The Blackwell Guide to Blues Records*, ed. Paul Oliver (1989). An obituary is in *Living Blues* 32 (May–June 1977).

BILL MCCULLOCH
BARRY LEE PEARSON

WHITE, Canvass (8 Sept. 1790–18 Dec. 1834), civil engineer, was born in Whitestown, New York, the son of Hugh White, Jr., and Tryphena Lawrence, farmers. White began displaying his talent for innovation at an early age, building several domestic and agricultural implements that remained in use for many years on his family's farm. After a short exposure to learning in the local common schools, White entered the Fairfield Academy in 1803, where he studied mathematics, surveying, astronomy, chemistry, and mineralogy. After completing the academy coursework, he continued to study these subjects with Dr. Josiah Noyes of Clinton,

New York. At the age of seventeen he took a job as clerk in a local store. He remained there until 1811, when his health became unstable, and his physician recommended an ocean voyage to restore his health. White obtained employment overseeing the commercial concerns of a merchant vessel and set sail for Russia. After returning from his adventure, his health restored, White took up again his work in the store. There he remained until 1814, when he raised up a company of volunteers to fight in the war against Great Britain. He received a commission as lieutenant and took part in the assault on Fort Erie in Upper Canada, across the Niagara River from Buffalo. After the capture of the fort, White was severely wounded by a shell fired from the British redoubt half a mile away. He remained with his regiment until his term of service expired, and then he returned home and resumed his studies with Dr. Noyes.

In the spring of 1816 White requested a position in a surveying corps being put together by Judge Benjamin Wright. He was hired as an assistant to Judge Wright and surveyed the path for the Erie Canal west of Rome, New York. During this time he became acquainted with Governor DeWitt Clinton, who formed a very good impression of White's abilities. Governor Clinton, well aware that the knowledge of America's civil engineers was outdated, urged White to visit England in order to observe their canal systems and obtain state-of-the-art surveying equipment. In the autumn of 1817 White journeyed to Great Britain and made a thorough study of British canals, traveling more than two thousand miles on foot along the towpaths of England and Scotland. He returned the following spring, bringing detailed drawings of the most important features of the canals and the desired surveying instruments. The knowledge that White had gained made him invaluable as Wright's principal assistant in the building of the Erie Canal, and White soon grew to be the chief expert on canal lock design and construction.

In Britain White had investigated the composition of hydraulic cement, which was imported by the United States at great expense from England. He experimented with the varieties of limestone found in New York and discovered that limestone rock found near the route of the canal in Madison County could be made into a cement that was an equal to the imported hydraulic cement. He obtained a patent for this waterproof cement on 1 February 1820 and permitted its use in the construction of the Erie Canal after being promised by the canal commissioners that he would receive compensation both for its use and for his expenses and services while in Britain. In spite of the recommendation of Governor Clinton, the state legislature refused to fulfill the commissioners' promise. In all, about a half-million bushels of White's hydraulic cement were used in the construction of the Erie Canal, but not one penny of compensation was paid to White by either the state or the canal contractors. In 1821 he married Louisa Loomis; they had three children.

White left his position at the Erie Canal in 1825, succeeding Loammi Baldwin as chief engineer of Pennsylvania's Union Canal. In the summer of 1826 he fell into poor health while surveying the canal west of the Susquehanna River and was forced to resign from his position. During the time that White was chief engineer of the Union Canal, he was summoned to New York City to evaluate the city's supply of drinking water. His report led to great improvements in the city's water system. During this time he was also asked to take charge of the works of the Schuylkill Navigation Company after the sudden death of its chief engineer. He made a rapid survey of the canal route and of the company's plans, suggested alterations, and recommended a new chief engineer. He continued his connection with the company as a consulting engineer until the work was completed. At the same time he was the consulting engineer for the Delaware and Chesapeake Canal, the Windsor Locks on the Connecticut River, and the Farmington Canal constructed from New Haven to Farmington, Connecticut.

In the spring of 1827 White was hired by the Lehigh Coal and Navigation Company of Pennsylvania to act as the chief engineer of the Lehigh Canal. He brought it to completion in July 1829. In its day, the Lehigh Canal, which was massive for its time and was built with future developments in mind, was considered to be a very bold undertaking.

During the summer of 1825, White had been appointed chief engineer of the Delaware and Raritan Canal in New Jersey. He had promptly arranged for preliminary surveys to be taken. Work was discontinued late in the autumn of that year, after the surveying of about twelve miles of the canal route, and was not resumed until the spring of 1831. Many difficulties and obstacles were encountered in the construction of this canal, but all were successfully overcome. As the canal neared completion in the autumn of 1834, White's health had again declined. His physician advised him to go south to recover, and White set sail for St. Augustine, Florida. Within a month of arriving there, he unexpectedly died.

White's familiarity with state-of-the-art European canal engineering made him preeminent among his contemporaries in canal building. After his return from England in 1818, he had a better understanding of canal construction than any other man in the United States. In addition, his discovery of hydraulic lime near Chittenango, New York, is said to have reduced the cost of the Erie Canal by one-half to one million dollars.

• A collection of Canvass White Papers is in the Department of Manuscripts and University Archives at Cornell University, and White's diary is in the Special Collections Department, Alderman Library, University of Virginia. Charles B. Stuart, *Lives and Works of Civil and Military Engineers of America* (1871), provides an excellent summary of White's life. Henry Wayland Hill, *Waterways and Canal Construction in New York State* (1908), gives helpful information about White's work on the Erie Canal, as do N. E. Whitford in *His-*

tory of the Canal System of the State of New York (1906) and George E. Condon in *Stars in the Water: The Story of the Erie Canal* (1974). *History of the State of New York*, vol. 5, *Conquering the Wilderness* (1934), details how White went about developing the hydraulic cement.

DANIEL MARTIN DUMYCH

WHITE, Charles Abiathar (26 Jan. 1826–29 June 1910), geologist, was born in North Dighton, Massachusetts, the son of Abiathar White and Nancy Corey, farmers. In 1838 the Whites, like many other New England families, decided that their future lay in the West and moved to Burlington, Iowa Territory. After being educated in the local schools, White worked for many years as a mechanic. In 1847 he returned to Massachusetts, where he married Charlotte R. Pilkington in 1848; they had eight children. He and his wife returned in 1849 to Burlington, where he again worked as a mechanic.

White became fascinated, possibly as early as during his childhood, with the rich fossil beds found in the vicinity of Burlington. He may have met with scientists who encouraged him to pursue this interest during his stay in Massachusetts. In any event, he continued to develop his knowledge of local geology, zoology, and botany after his return to Burlington. He was undoubtedly encouraged by contact with such noted local geologists as Charles Wachsmuth and Amos Worthen as well as by the occasional presence of geologists Louis Agassiz, James Hall, and Fielding B. Meek, who were drawn to Burlington by its fossil beds. White's first scientific article, "Observations upon the Geology and Paleontology of Burlington, Iowa and Its Vicinity," was published in the *Boston Journal of Natural History* (vol. 7) in 1861.

Sometime in the 1850s, White began to study medicine in the office of a local physician, Seth S. Ransom. Medicine offered the most widely available scientific education at the time, as well as a means to earn a secure living. In 1862–1863, however, White interrupted this training to work on the New York Geological Survey under James Hall. State geological surveys offered young geologists unparalleled opportunities for field work and advanced training. But because careers in geology were uncertain, White returned to medical studies, first at Michigan State University and then at Rush Medical College in Chicago, from which he graduated with an M.D. in 1864.

White then moved to Iowa City, where he practiced medicine for two years. In 1866 he was appointed state geologist of Iowa. White ran the Iowa Geological Survey until the end of 1869, after which the state legislature cut off his funds. Because the earlier survey under Hall had concentrated on eastern Iowa, White's two volumes of reports described geological structure and evaluated the economic potential of the natural resources in the western part of the state. He correctly discouraged hopes of finding profitable deposits of oil or metals. Of greatest economic interest, he thought, were the state's extensive peat deposits, which could be used as fuel.

In 1867, a year after becoming state geologist, White received a concurrent appointment as professor of geology at the State University of Iowa in Iowa City. For the next six years, he was at one time or another professor of geology and other natural sciences as well as curator of the cabinet. In 1873 he left Iowa for Maine to become professor of natural history at Bowdoin College. Finding, however, that he preferred survey work to teaching, he became in 1874, while still at Bowdoin, paleontologist of explorations and surveys west of the 100th degree of longitude under Lieutenant George M. Wheeler of the U.S. Army Corps of Engineers. In 1875 White left Bowdoin for Washington, D.C., where he joined John Wesley Powell's survey of the Rocky Mountain region. In 1876 he moved to Ferdinand V. Hayden's geological survey of the territories and completed the paleontological work that Meek had left unfinished at his death that year. At the same time, he unofficially took up Meek's duties as head of the paleontological collection at the U.S. National Museum—a branch of the Smithsonian Institution and the repository for the collections of the various federal surveys and explorations. When Congress terminated Hayden's survey in 1879, White entered a salaried position as curator at the U.S. National Museum.

The year 1882 was a busy one for White. He headed the U.S. Department of Agriculture's commission on artesian wells in the Great Plains; he was asked by the National Museum of Brazil to report on the fossils collected by that nation's geological survey (the report was published in 1887); and he was hired as a geologist for the reorganized and consolidated U.S. Geological Survey under Clarence King. Despite this activity, he did not abandon the National Museum; instead, he exchanged his curatorship for an unpaid position as an associate in paleontology, a position he held for the rest of his life. He retired from the USGS in 1892 but continued to write on paleontology and other matters until his death in Washington, D.C.

White's published works exceeded 200 books and articles, which were primarily but not solely on paleontology. His scientific writing is most important for its descriptions of hundreds of new invertebrate specimens brought back by the various surveys. After his retirement he wrote more extensively on geological theory and the implications of Darwinian evolution for his science. White also wrote on a variety of nonscientific subjects, especially the early history of Iowa. Though residing in Washington, D.C., from 1876 until his death, he always considered himself a citizen of Iowa and was an early supporter of Charles Aldrich's efforts to found that state's historical department. He was an important and regular contributor to the *Annals of Iowa*, the state's historical journal, writing on such subjects as the American Indians and early white settlers of Iowa and he deposited his personal papers with the state's archives.

White's accomplishments as a scientist were widely acknowledged during his lifetime. He was a member of the American Association for the Advancement of Science and served as vice president for its section on geology in 1888; a member of the Biological Society of Washington and its president in 1883–1884; a founder of the Geological Society of America; and a member of the National Academy of Sciences, to which he was elected in 1889. His historical significance as a scientist stems from his work in invertebrate paleontology, his participation in several of the most important federal scientific organizations of the late nineteenth century, and, finally, his contributions to the history of Iowa.

• White's papers, including scientific correspondence from 1863 to 1901, are in the Iowa State Department of History and Archives, Des Moines. See also the T. W. Stanton Papers and the records of the U.S. National Museum, both at the Smithsonian Institution Archives. Some of White's more important works include White et al., *Report of the Geological Survey of the State of Iowa . . .* (2 vols., 1870); White, "Contributions to Invertebrate Paleontology," *Twelfth Annual Report of the U.S. Geological and Geographic Survey of Territories for 1878* nos. 2–8 (1883): 1–171; and White, "The Relation of Biology to Geological Investigation," in *Report of the U.S. National Museum for 1891–1892* (1893): 245–368. Principal sources for biographical information are William H. Dall, "Biographical Memoir," National Academy of Sciences, *Biographical Memoirs* 7 (1911): 225–43; Charles R. Keyes, "Life and Work of Charles Abiathar White," *Annals of Iowa*, 3d ser. 11 (1914): 497–504; and Marcus Benjamin, "Charles Abiathar White," *Science* 32 (1910): 146–49. Dall and Keyes both contain bibliographies, but the most comprehensive bibliography (in three parts) is in the *Bulletin of the United States National Museum* 30 (1885): 113–81; and the *Proceedings of the United States National Museum* 20 (1898): 627–42, and 40 (1911): 197–99. For an assessment of his contributions as a geologist, see George P. Merrill, *The First One Hundred Years of American Geology* (1924). An obituary notice by Marcus Benjamin is in *Science*, n.s., 32 (1910): 146.

DANIEL GOLDSTEIN

WHITE, Clarence Cameron (10 Aug. 1880?–30 June 1960), concert violinist and composer, was born in Clarksville, Tennessee, the son of James William White, a medical doctor, and Caroline Virginia Scott, an educator. His parents were originally "free Negroes" from Fayetteville, North Carolina, who migrated before the Civil War to Oberlin, Ohio, and then to Tennessee. Soon after the death of his father, White went to live with his grandmother and his grandfather John H. Scott, a harness maker and former abolitionist. White received his early education in Oberlin and Chattanooga. In about 1890 his mother married Dr. W. H. Connor, a medical examiner for the U.S. Government Pension Office, and the family moved to Washington, D.C., where White attended public schools. When he was eleven White began studying the violin with the celebrated violinist Will Marion Cook, and at age fourteen he took lessons with Joseph Douglass, a Howard University professor and the grandson of Frederick Douglass.

White worked as a bellhop in Cleveland, Ohio, to earn his tuition to Oberlin Conservatory, where he was admitted in 1896. He left in 1901, apparently without receiving a degree (evidence indicates that he returned to the conservatory in 1923 and again left for reasons unrelated to scholarship). White accepted a job teaching in a Pittsburgh school immediately following his departure from Oberlin in 1901; however, all salaries at the school were suspended after a month's time, and he was forced to return to Washington.

Shortly thereafter, White decided to move to Boston for further study. On the way, he briefly visited New Haven, Connecticut, and was enticed by a scholarship advertisement from Hartford College. Drawing on his thorough musical background and demonstrating commendable virtuosity, he won a scholarship for a year's study with Franz Micki, head of the violin department. The close proximity of New Haven to New York allowed White to perform at various concerts, one of which was held at the Manhattan Casino before an audience of 4,000. It was at that point that he felt that his concert career had been launched, "for my engagements came rapidly and I played in practically all the large cities east of Denver." After leaving New Haven in 1902, Boston became his headquarters.

In 1903 White was appointed director of the string department at the Washington, D.C., Conservatory of Music. He taught there and in the District of Columbia public schools for the next five years. Also in 1903 White traveled to England, where he met Anglo-African composer Samuel Coleridge-Taylor. Deciding to stay for a summer, White studied orchestration with Hubert Harrison, the conductor at the Coronet Theater. When he ran low on money, White returned to the United States and resumed his teaching duties. In late 1904 or early 1905 he married Beatrice Louise Warrick, a pianist; they had two children.

With support from concert singer-composer E. Azalia Hackley, who was studying and teaching in Europe, and several other benefactors such as Henry O. Tanner, White was able to travel to London in 1908, accompanied by his family, to resume musical study. During his two years there, he studied violin with the famous Russian violinist Michael Zacharewitsch, studied composition with Coleridge-Taylor, and performed as one of the first violinists in Coleridge-Taylor's String Players Club.

Around 1910, White returned to the United States with his family and once again settled in Boston, where he established a teaching studio, gave many concerts, continued composing, and performed in concert tours (including one to Oberlin in 1911). He also conducted the Victoria Concert Orchestra, a multiracial group of fifty-three musicians, in a series of successful concerts over seven years. White was appointed director of the West Virginia Collegiate Institute (now West Virginia State College) in 1924. His duties included teaching violin and conducting the Young Men's Glee Club, which made eight recordings and several radio broadcasts. Also performing frequently, he held the position until 1930, at which time he was awarded the Rosenwald Foundation fellowship for two years of European study. He studied violin with Raoul Laparra in Paris and completed an opera and a string quartet.

On his return to the United States in 1932, White succeeded R. Nathaniel Dett as music director at Hampton Institute in Hampton, Virginia. This appointment, he wrote, afforded him the "most excellent opportunities for development, especially in the field of Negro Music and in my individual work." At Hampton, he taught, performed, and conducted the choir until 1935, at which time he secured the directorship of music at the National Recreation Association in New York City, where he organized community music groups. In 1943, following the death of his first wife, White married Pura Belpré. He died in New York.

White was hailed by the New York *Amsterdam News* as "the most finished violinist his race has produced in America." He also attained distinction as a composer of neoromantic works that ranged from operatic and symphonic pieces to Negro spirituals. White had compositions published by Carl Fischer, the Boston Music Company, Theodore Presser, John Church, C. C. Birchard, Gamble Hinged, and Sam Fox. His output consists of pieces for violin, voice (some of which were performed by Marian Anderson and Roland Hayes), piano, orchestra, band, organ, chorus, and other vocal ensembles. His opera, *Ouanga* (1932), with a libretto by John Matheus, is based on the life of the Haitian slave insurrectionist Jean-Jacques Dessalines. The work, which was premiered by the H. T. Burleigh Music Association of South Bend, Indiana, in 1949, was awarded the David Bispham Memorial Medal, and notable performances were presented by the Dra-Mu Opera Company at the Philadelphia Academy in 1950 and by the National Negro Opera Company at the Metropolitan Opera House in 1956. His *Elegy* for orchestra won the 1953–1954 Benjamin Award for Tranquil Music, and excerpts of his *Bandanna Sketches* (1918) for violin were played by Fritz Kriesler and Zacharewitsch. Violinist Jascha Heifetz recorded his *Levee Dance* (1927), and leading symphony orchestras performed his *Pantomime*, his *Suite of Folk Tunes*, and arrangements of *Bandanna Sketches*. Other works include studies for violin technique, a string quartet, a violin concerto, *Five Songs* (1949), *Forty Negro Spirituals* (1927), and *Negro Rhapsody* for orchestra.

White also excelled as a conductor. Newspaper accounts note his "masterly touch" with the Hampton Institute Choir and his success with other ensembles in West Virginia, Boston, and Washington. In addition, he authored several articles for such publications as *Etude*, *Musical Observer*, and *Modern Quarterly*, mainly on the subject of "Negro Music" but also about Joseph White, the internationally renowned nineteenth-century Afro-Cuban violinist and court musician for the emperor of Brazil who had served as a model inspiration for White. White overcame many difficulties during the depression era to realize his goals of becoming a virtuoso, conductor, composer, and educator. He also succeeded in his aim "to show the Negro's contribution to American art."

• White's papers and music are in the New York Schomburg Library, the Oberlin Conservatory, the Howard University Moorland-Spingarn Room, and the Azalia Hackley Room in the Detroit Library. Some of his letters have been published in "In Retrospect: Letters of Clarence Cameron White in the Collections of the Music Division of the Library of Congress," ed. Wayne Shirley, *Black Perspective in Music* 10, no. 2 (Fall 1982). See also Vernon Edwards and Michael Mark, "In Retrospect: Clarence Cameron White," *Black Perspective in Music* 9, no. 1 (Spring 1981); Maud Cuney-Hare, *Negro Musicians and Their Music* (1936; repr. 1974); Eileen Southern, *Biographical Dictionary of Afro-American and African Musicians* (1982); and Hildred Roach, *Black American Music: Past and Present* (1992). Newspaper accounts of White's life and works are in the *Afro-American*, 18 Mar. 1933, *Musical Courier*, 1 Dec. 1950, *Reading Times*, 27 Nov. 1939, and *Washington Star*, 28 May 1933. Obituaries appear in the *New York Times*, 2 July 1960, and *Washington Post*, 3 July 1960.

HILDRED ROACH

WHITE, Clarence J. (7 June 1944–14 July 1973), bluegrass and country rock guitarist, was born in Lewiston, Maine, the son of Eric White. A musical family, the Whites relocated to Burbank, California, by 1954. When they were teenagers, Clarence and his brothers Roland (mandolin) and Eric, Jr. (fiddle), formed a band known as the Country Boys; they appeared on local TV and radio programs and at fairs, dances, and local bars and clubs. Banjoist Billy Ray Latham had joined the trio by 1958, and, soon after, bassist Roger Bush became a member. By the early 1960s Eric had dropped out of the band, now known as the Kentucky Colonels.

As one of the first bluegrass revival groups, and certainly one of the few on the West Coast, the Kentucky Colonels did much to spark interest in bluegrass and to revive the country music scene in the Los Angeles area, inspiring the growth of folk-rock and country rock. White, in turn, was influenced by the folk revival, particularly when he heard North Carolina–born guitarist Arthel "Doc" Watson play a concert at a local club, the Ash Grove. From that point, White adopted Watson's style of flatpicking fiddle tunes on the guitar, and his lightning-fast rendition of traditional melodies soon became a highlight of the group's performances. The Colonels recorded several albums for the small World Pacific label, with the most influential being the all-instrumental *Appalachian Swing* (1964), on which they were joined by fiddler Bobby Sloane and dobro player Leroy Mack.

When the group folded in 1967, White formed a country-rock band with several other West Coast session players called Nashville West. A year later White was invited to play on the Byrds' influential country-rock album, *Sweetheart of the Rodeo*. White joined the band full time in 1969, remaining with them through 1972. This later incarnation of the band featured bassist John York (who, in turn, was replaced by Clyde "Skip" Battin) and drummer Gene Parsons along with White. The band scored minor hits with "Ballad of Easy Rider" (1969), from the popular film of the same name; "Chestnut Mare" (1970); and "Just a Season" (1970). White's electric guitar prowess was demonstrated on the double album *untitled* (1970), half of which was recorded live. Although less successful than the mid-1960s lineup, this version of the Byrds remained a popular touring and recording band, and their country-rock style influenced the formation of other groups, including the Eagles, Poco, and Manassas.

In 1972 White returned to playing session work and his first love, bluegrass music. He began performing again with his brother Roland in a revitalized Kentucky Colonels, most notably playing an extended tour of Sweden. He also formed, with session mandolin player David Grisman, a short-lived "supergroup" called Muleskinner, which also included guitarist and singer/songwriter Peter Rowan, banjo player Bill Keith, and fiddler Richard Greene. The group performed on a public television special, "Father and Sons," along with bluegrass veteran Bill Monroe and recorded a single self-named album for Warner Brothers Records that helped spur the bluegrass revival. They also inspired Jerry Garcia (of the Grateful Dead) and Grisman to form another informal bluegrass band, Old and in the Way.

Tragically, White's new career was cut short when he was struck by a drunken driver while loading his instrument into the trunk of a car, following a late-night engagement at a bluegrass club near Palmdale, California. After his death, many more recordings of White, the Kentucky Colonels, and various other combinations featuring the guitarist were issued thanks to a revived interest in bluegrass music. Guitarist Tony Rice, a bluegrass player who dabbled in jazz, cited White as a major influence and even purchased and recorded with White's guitar in homage to the player. Rice later played in a variety of bluegrass settings as well as newgrass and string jazz, often working with White's crony, David Grisman. Many guitarists working in bluegrass or country show White's influence in their flatpicking style, ranging from Norman Blake to Marty Stuart and Ricky Skaggs. Roland White continued to perform bluegrass as a well-respected vocalist and mandolin player, first with banjo player Alan Munde and various supporting musicians in the group Country Gazette from about 1974 through the late 1980s and then with the Nashville Bluegrass Band, one of the most respected revival groups in the field.

• White's work with the Byrds is documented in the booklet accompanying the four-CD set of their recordings. An instruction book, *Clarence White: Bluegrass Guitar*, was published by Oak Publications in 1980 and includes transcriptions of many of his famous guitar solos, plus biographical and bibliographic/discographic information as of that date. *Appalachian Swing*, the Kentucky Colonels' best-known album, was reissued by Rounder Records (catalog number 31). Numerous other recordings have been reissued on the Sierra and Vanguard labels.

RICHARD CARLIN

WHITE, David (1 July 1862–7 Feb. 1935), paleobotanist and geologist, was born Charles David White in Wayne County, New York, the son of Asa Kendrick White and Elvira Foster, farmers. Throughout his professional career, White never employed his first name in publications nor was it used by his colleagues. White grew up on a farm just north of the Finger Lakes region of New York. A Dutch laborer on the farm interested him in plants. With the aid of a county scholarship and by teaching school, he was able to attend Cornell and graduate with a bachelor's degree in 1886. White's senior thesis on fossil plants from the Devonian period (413–365 million years ago) found around Ithaca, New York, included excellent drawings of specimens.

In the spring of 1886, primarily as a result of his artistic skill, he went to Washington, D.C., as a temporary draftsman-artist for Lester Ward, then paleobotanist of the U.S. Geological Survey. That fall White was given a staff appointment at $900 per year; he remained with the agency his entire life, although he received repeated offers of private employment from coal companies. With the assurance of government employment, in 1888 White married Mary Elizabeth Houghton, whom he had met at Cornell; they had no children.

Ward appreciated White's excellent drawings but encouraged him in the professional activities of compiling bibliographies and indexes of fossil plants. Within a few years, White had gathered sufficient information from the literature on the distribution of fossil plants to publish his first paper, "Carboniferous Glaciation in the Southern and Eastern Hemisphere," in the *American Geologist* (3 [1889]: 299–330). As additional data accumulated, including that from his own study (based on museum collections) of extinct floras from Brazil, he returned to this subject. Between this first paper and 1925, White wrote eight significant papers on the use of fossil plants to interpret past climates. His research highlighted the differences between the fossil floras of the southern hemisphere (combined with those of India) and those of the northern hemisphere. White's final major contribution to paleoclimatic interpretation, "Some Features of the American Permian," based on the Hermit Shale of the Grand Canyon and published by the International Geological Congress in 1934, emphasized the aridity of the late Permian climate.

White's first field study of fossil plants (*American Journal of Science*, Feb. 1890), determined that the fossils from Gay Head, Martha's Vineyard, Massachusetts, were mid-Cretaceous in age, older than had been generally assumed. Although White continued to study floras of the Mesozoic era, and took an 1897 trip with Robert Peary to Cape York, Greenland, where he collected more Cretaceous plants, his major research was in elucidation of the older Paleozoic era floras.

After several years spent arranging the collections in the United States National Museum and studying Pennsylvanian-age fossil plants collected by field parties working in Missouri, White was convinced that the assemblages of fossil plants could be used for stratigraphic purposes, that is, to accurately sequence rock strata from older to younger. To demonstrate that he could identify a group of fossils of a particular age in the field, White then worked from 1893 to 1895 with M. R. Campbell, a skilled field geologist, in the southern Appalachian coal regions. In the course of this work, he recognized that the two-mile-thick sequence of sandstone, shale, and coal in this region represented only the lower part of the Pennsylvanian System and not the entire system; this significant reinterpretation of the geology was contrary to prevailing opinion but has been accepted. This new information had major implications for reconstructing the geologic history of the Allegheny Plateau. It also had profound economic significance, since White's new correlation of coal seams led directly to the development of the important New River coal field in West Virginia. During the course of field work in Pennsylvania, White made a detailed study of geologic structures and found a significant extension of an anthracite coal deposit.

White's investigations of Permian and Pennsylvanian Paleozoic floras in Kansas (1903) led him to another geologic discovery. In identifying species of fossil plants collected in West Virginia and Ohio, and by correlating them to fossils from Kansas, White determined that they also were of Permian age. Up to that time, no rocks as young as Permian had been recognized in the eastern United States; this was another major contribution to the understanding of the geologic history of North America. White's studies of fossil floras and their relationship to stratigraphy resulted in several Geological Survey monographs and nearly eighty papers. He described, illustrated, and named more than one hundred new species of fossil plants.

Examination of Pennsylvanian-age coal seams led White to study the formation of coal. He produced convincing evidence that most coals were formed in situ, rather than transported, an issue of contention in the literature. He also showed that the grades of coal, ranging from lignite (relatively impure and soft) through bituminous to anthracite (relatively pure, hard), are related to the thickness of the overlying rocks: the greater the pressure, the harder the coal. These observations led to his fundamental work on the classification of coal; more than twenty-five of his papers deal specifically with coal. White's single most important contribution to economic geology was to determine a relationship between the degree of metamorphism of coals and the quality of oil in adjacent strata. From this relationship he derived a "dead line," beyond which metamorphism was too extreme for oil to be found in commercial quantities. His "carbon-ratio theory" (the degree of devolitization of a coal), first announced in 1915, was one of the building blocks in the study of the origin of petroleum; he elaborated on this theory in the last scientific paper he wrote, "Metamorphism of Organic Sediments and Derived Oils," *Bulletin of the American Association of Petroleum Geologists* (May 1935).

Although he continued his investigations of coal, in the early 1900s White became interested in the growing petroleum industry and ultimately wrote forty-five papers dealing with oil formation, its geologic and geographic occurrence, and oil reserves. In 1917 and 1919 he was the first to experiment with the use of gravity measurements to locate anticlines where oil was likely to accumulate. He also directed attention to observation of temperature gradients in wells as a prospecting tool for oil. White was among the first to estimate American petroleum reserves (1920), and on the basis of what was then known, he predicted an oil shortage in the near future. White's publications awakened the petroleum industry to the need to curtail wasteful drilling and pumping practices; his work also stimulated the search for oil reserves overseas. In 1920, in recognition of his work, the American Association of Petroleum Geologists awarded him an honorary lifetime membership.

In 1912, shortly after his election to the National Academy of Sciences, White was placed in charge of the U.S. Geological Survey's Eastern Coal Fields Section. In the fall of the same year, he was further promoted to chief geologist, succeeding Waldemar Lindgren. He served a decade in this position—a particularly stressful time because of the need for greatly increased mineral resources during the First World War. Under White's direction, economically valuable minerals, particularly potash, were located and oil shales were investigated as a potential source of gasoline. When the United States entered the conflict, he focused the resources of the Geological Survey on a search for petroleum.

White retired from the position of chief geologist in 1922, but much of his time was still devoted to advisory duties rather than research. He was chairman of the National Research Council's Division of Geology and Geography (1924–1927), and home secretary (1923–1931) and vice president (1931–1933) of the National Academy of Sciences. During his later years he was a research associate of the Carnegie Institution in Washington, D.C. From 1926 to 1930, with support from the institution, he was engaged in geologic and paleontologic study in several national parks and attempted to develop public education programs concerning scientific aspects of the parks. Partly as a result of his work in Grand Canyon National Park, he became interested in Precambrian stromatolites (fossil structures of unclassified biologic origin), a significant step back in time from his work on Paleozoic coal floras. White suffered a stroke in 1931, but he continued to work at his desk until the day before he died.

• White's official correspondence is scattered and no collection of personal correspondence is known to exist. Some of White's important publications not mentioned in the text are "The Stratigraphic Succession of the Fossil Floras of the Pottsville Formation in the Southern Anthracite Coal Field, Pennsylvania," *U.S. Geological Survey 20th Annual Report*, pt. 2 (1900): 749–930; "The Petroleum Resources of the World," *American Academy of Political and Social Science* 89, no. 178 (1920): 111–34; "Permian of Western America from the Paleobotanical Standpoint," *Pan-Pacific Science Congress, Australia, 1923 Proceedings* 2 (1924): 1050–77; and "Climatic Implications of Pennsylvanian Flora," *Illinois State Geological Survey Bulletin* 60 (1931): 271–81. The principal memorials and interpretations are W. C. Mendenhall, *Proceedings of the Geological Society of America* (June 1937): 271–92; H. D. Miser, *Bulletin of the American Association of Petroleum Geologists* 19 (1935): 925–32; and Charles Schuchert, *National Academy of Sciences, Biographical Memoirs* 17 (1936): 189–221. White's career with the U.S. Geological Survey may be traced through the history of the organization by M. C. Rabbit, *Minerals, Lands, and Geology for the Common Defence and General Welfare*, vol. 2: 1879–1904 (1980) and vol. 3: 1904–1939 (1986).

ELLIS L. YOCHELSON

WHITE, Eartha Mary Magdalene (8 Nov. 1876–18 Jan. 1974), social welfare and community leader and businesswoman, was born in Jacksonville, Florida, the daughter of Mollie Chapman, a former slave, and an unnamed prominent white man. She was adopted shortly after birth by freed slaves Lafayette White, a drayman and Civil War veteran, and Clara English, a domestic and cook. Lafayette White died when Eartha was five. Throughout her childhood Clara made Eartha feel as though God had chosen her for a special mission. Listening to stories of hardships that Clara endured as a slave and watching her mother's humanitarian contributions to Jacksonville's "Black Bottom" community convinced Eartha White that she too would someday make a difference in the African-American community.

When yellow fever struck Jacksonville in 1893, White went to New York City, where she attended Dr. Reason's school, Madam Hall's school to study hairdressing and manicuring, and Madame Thurber's National Conservatory of Music. During the 1895–1896 season, White toured worldwide with the Oriental-American Opera Company, the first black opera company in the United States. On a visit home she met James Lloyd Jordan, a railroad employee, and they planned to marry in June 1896, but one month before the wedding Jordan died.

After Jordan's death White quit the tour and returned to Jacksonville, determined to marry "the cause of Christ" and dedicate her life to helping others. Following her graduation from Florida Baptist Academy in 1897, she volunteered as a nurse caring for soldiers wounded in the Spanish-American War. In 1899 she taught blacks in a poor rural school and took a second job as a clerk of the Afro-American Life Insurance Company, becoming its first woman employee. She organized and spoke on behalf of the Colored Citizen's Protective League in 1900. In the same year White attended the first meeting of the National Negro Business League in Boston, where she met Booker T. Washington, who became a lifelong friend.

In 1901 a devastating fire struck Jacksonville, and White transferred to downtown Stanton School while helping the homeless find shelter. Reactivating interest in the Union Benevolent Association founded in 1885, she collected money to build the Colored Old Folks' Home, which was completed in 1902. In 1904 she started the Boys' Improvement Club, received a donation of land for a park, and used her own money to support recreational activities in the new park. She then successfully lobbied for a facility for delinquent girls.

In 1905 White started what she termed a "department store" on $150, and between 1905 and 1930 she owned a taxi service, an employment agency, a janitorial contracting service, and a steam laundry. After a business became profitable, White sold it, using the revenue from the sale to fund a new business. Eventually she received a real estate license, which enabled her to buy and sell property more profitably.

No task was beyond the scope of Eartha White. A respected citizen of Jacksonville, White's reputation grew, and men and women, black or white, counted on her expertise. Called to service during both world wars, White acted as director of War Camp Community Services and coordinator of recreation in Savannah, Georgia, in World War I; was the only woman delegate at the Southeast War Camp Community Service Conference; and attended a White House meeting of the Council of National Defense as the only black. An active Republican, White campaigned in her precinct, headed the Negro Republican Women Voters in 1920, and became the only woman member of the Duval County Republican Executive Committee.

The death of her mother in 1920 profoundly affected White. As a tribute to the woman who had been her inspiration, she founded the Clara White Mission in 1928. Modeled after Jane Addam's Hull-House, the mission became a refuge for blacks during the depression and a center for job training for the unemployed. People of all ages gathered to paint, play music, or join in recreational activities. As a resident herself, White oversaw daily operations. In one month alone more than 2,500 persons were fed. On Sundays she taught the Bible to prison inmates, a practice she continued for fifty years. The police often sent delinquent teenagers to her rather than to jail. As the energetic White saw the need for other services, she expanded into other avenues, founding a maternity home, a child placement center, a community center, and a tuberculosis rest home.

White always maintained that the color of a person's skin did not matter and that all men were made "out of the earth." A follower of the ideals of Booker T. Washington, she thought eliminating prejudice resulted from blacks improving themselves through education and success in establishing their own businesses. In 1941 continued job discrimination led her to join A. Philip Randolph in organizing a protest march on Washington. The march never materialized, but their proposed activities led to the creation of President Franklin Roosevelt's Executive Order 8802, which banned employment discrimination in defense industries and in the federal government, and to the establishment of the Fair Employment Practices Committee.

During World War II White joined the Women's National Defense Program as an honorary colonel, coordinated Red Cross activities, and became the only woman on the Interracial War Camp Community Service Conference. Energized by the people whom she helped, White's service to the community continued as she advanced into her seventies and eighties. In 1967 she took great pride in the completion of the 120-bed Eartha M. White Nursing Home for county and state welfare patients. Underwritten by White and grants from the federal government, the institution had facilities for physical therapy, occupational therapy, and recreational activities.

Honors bestowed upon White included the Good Citizenship Award in 1969 and the Lane Bryant Volunteer Award in 1970, and in 1971 the American Nursing Home Association gave her its Better Life Award. Two years later she received the Booker T. Washington Symbol of Service from the National Negro Business League. Despite confinement to a wheelchair, White never stopped lending a hand and remained active until her death in Jacksonville.

Known as Jacksonville's Angel of Mercy, Eartha White's remarkable vitality and unending devotion derived from her mother's example as well as her own religious philosophy, and a belief that "service is the price we pay for the space we occupy on this planet." Collecting donations of fruits and vegetables from farmers, trudging down country roads in her tennis shoes when called out on an emergency, or simply holding the hand of a person in despair filled White with a renewed purpose of doing "all the good you can . . . while you can!"

• White's documents and papers are located in the Eartha White Collection at the University of North Florida library; the Clara White Mission, Jacksonville, Fla.; and the Rollins College Archives, Winter Park, Fla. Especially valuable in the White collection is the typescript by Daniel L. Schafer, "Eartha White: The Early Years of a Jacksonville Humanitarian" (1976). Other sources offering details on White's life are C. Frederick Duncan, "Negro Health in Jacksonville," *The Crisis* (Jan. 1942); L. W. Neyland, *Twelve Black Floridians* (1970); Angela Taylor, "She's 94 and Still Busy," *New York Times*, 4 Dec. 1970; Fred Wright, "Eartha White, Florida's Rich, Black, 94-Year-Old Senior Citizen of the Year," *Floridian*, 1 Aug. 1971; Harold Gibson, "The Most Unforgettable Person I Have Met," *Reader's Digest*, 19 Dec. 1974; Charles E. Bennett, *Twelve on the River St. Johns* (1989); James B. Crooks, *Jacksonville after the Fire, 1901–1919* (1991); and Maxine D. Jones and Kevin M. McCarthy, *African Americans in Florida* (1993). Interviews with White in her later years appeared in the *St. Petersburg Times*, 1 Aug 1971; and the *New York Times*, 4 Dec. 1970. Obituaries are in the *New York Times*, the *Jacksonville Journal*, and the *Florida Times-Union*, all 19 Jan. 1974; and in the National Business League's *National Memo* (Jan. 1974).

MARILYN ELIZABETH PERRY

WHITE, E. B. (11 July 1899–1 Oct. 1985), writer, was born Elwyn Brooks White in Mount Vernon, New York, the son of Samuel Tilly White, an executive of a piano manufacturing company, and Jessie Hart, the daughter of painter William Hart. White grew up in Mount Vernon, a suburb of New York, and spent summers with his family in Maine. According to his recollection, his ambition to become a writer dawned at the age of seven or eight, and when he was nine, he won a prize from *Woman's Home Companion* for a poem about a mouse. His first published article, "A Winter Walk," appeared in *St. Nicholas* magazine in June 1911.

In 1917 he entered Cornell University and in 1918 enlisted briefly in the campus Student Army Training Corps. At the end of his junior year, he was elected editor in chief of the *Cornell Daily Sun* and for the next year wrote most of the newspaper's editorials, many of them supporting student self-government. Here he picked up his nickname, "Andy," a name jocosely bestowed on any student named White, after Cornell's president, Andrew D. White.

After his graduation in 1921, White spent a month or so at United Press in New York. Unhappy over the agency's disregard of accuracy, he moved to the American Legion News Service, then quit to join a friend, Howard Cushman, on a cross-country trek in a Model-T Ford dubbed "Hotspur." By this time his verses had started to appear in "The Bowling Green," the miscellany column conducted by Christopher Morley at the New York *Evening Post*. He started such a column himself at the end of his western trip when he paused at the Seattle *Times* to work through the next winter and spring.

Back in New York in 1923, he found a dull job at the Frank Seaman advertising agency and burned to enter the world of literary journalism that he saw exemplified in figures such as Morley, Don Marquis, Robert Benchley, and Ring Lardner. Gradually he began to make a name for himself over his signature initials, "E. B. W.," in contributions to the most prestigious of the scrapbook columns, Franklin Pierce Adams's "The Conning Tower," in the *World*.

Further opportunity appeared in 1925 with the founding of the *New Yorker*, a weekly magazine edited by Harold Ross. White made his first appearance in the magazine in its ninth issue—18 April 1925—with a parody, "A Step Forward," hypothesizing how advertising copywriters might describe the coming of spring. That summer he left the advertising agency and moved out of his parents' home to Manhattan. After a dozen contributions of short, deft essays and verse, the *New Yorker* offered him a job, and late in 1926 he joined its staff, an affiliation that was to last the rest of his life.

The young magazine's elastic organization offered White an opportunity to show his versatility. His first assignment was to edit the "newsbreaks," small items from the press to which he would append amusing comments; he edited the newsbreaks for fifty-five years. The categories he devised for newsbreaks became famous in their own right: "Neatest Trick of the Week," "Letters We Never Finished Reading," and "Funny Coincidence Department," the last for examples of plagiarism. He also wrote editorials in the

"Notes and Comment" section, features for "Talk of the Town," cartoon captions, verse, and summer theater reviews. In the summer of 1927 he produced for the magazine a series of promotional ads, parodying self-improvement advertising and illustrated with store-window dummies; reprinted, the ads became his first book, *Less than Nothing—or the Life and Times of Sterling Finny*. His second book, *The Lady Is Cold* (1929), reprinted his verses from the *New Yorker* and "The Conning Tower." The third was a parody of self-help manuals called *Is Sex Necessary?* (1929); it was written with James Thurber, a *New Yorker* colleague, and contained Thurber's first published drawings.

White had been hired by the *New Yorker* on the suggestion of Katharine Sergeant Angell, Ross's chief lieutenant and the fiction editor. She and White were drawn to each other despite her marriage and two children and his diffidence toward entangling relationships. In the summer of 1928 they kept a rendezvous in France and Corsica, and in 1929 she obtained a Nevada divorce. Without informing friends, they married on 13 November 1929 and were back at work the next day. They had one child, born in 1930.

Although White's first models were humorists, and the *New Yorker* of that era was suffused with humor, he resisted becoming known as a humorist. The publication in 1934 of *Every Day Is Saturday*, reprints of his previously unsigned editorials, stimulated the growth of his reputation as an essayist. But he was turned down when he asked Ross to let him sign his name to his comments. Such frustrations and the onset of illnesses and hypochondria led him to seek a leave of absence and then in 1938 a permanent move to North Brooklin, Maine, where the Whites had bought a forty-acre farm on Allen Cove. After reducing his obligations at the *New Yorker*, he contracted with *Harper's Magazine* to write a monthly signed column, "One Man's Meat."

His political commentary had usually been deft rather than trenchant, but his attitude became more earnest in the world crisis of the 1940s. He wrote a memorable column for *Harper's* attacking the moral neutrality toward fascism of Anne Morrow Lindbergh's *The Wave of the Future* (1940). After the United States entered World War II, he edited an ideological statement, *Four Freedoms*, for the Office of War Information. In 1943 he gave up the *Harper's* column (which was collected in two anthologies), returned to New York, and again concentrated on work at the *New Yorker*, in particular on promoting postwar world government. His editorials on this subject were collected in *The Wild Flag* (1946). A by-product of his return to the city was one of his best-known essays, "Here Is New York," first published in *Holiday* magazine for April 1949 and later that year issued as a small book.

To this point White had written primarily for limited numbers of magazine and book readers, but his audience expanded dramatically when he turned to writing for children. Years before, as a "bachelor uncle," he had read to his array of nieces and nephews his tales about a mouse with human parents. He completed a book about the mouse in 1945; it was published as *Stuart Little*. In less than three months, 100,000 copies were sold, and over the next thirty years its distribution grew to 2.5 million copies in English and many more in translation. Seven years later, *Charlotte's Web*, a story of a spider, Charlotte A. Cavatica, who saves her friend, Wilbur, a pig, attained even greater success—total sales of more than 5 million in English and a durable animated film (1973), which White disliked. Scott Elledge suggested the basis of the book's enduring appeal to both children and adults when he wrote that "few children's books have so clearly embodied a love that can cure fear, make death seem a part of life, and be strong without being possessive" (*E. B. White* [1984], p. 305).

In 1957 the Whites again abandoned New York for Maine. Over the next twenty years, his writing for the *New Yorker* gradually diminished in volume, and he undertook fewer new projects. One of the most notable was his refurbishing of *The Elements of Style*, originally written in 1918 by one of his Cornell professors, William Strunk, Jr. A guide to clarity and concision in writing, it was widely adopted as a textbook after its publication in 1959; he issued a revision in 1972. In 1970 he completed a third children's book, *The Trumpet of the Swan*. In 1976, when the Xerox Corporation initiated a plan to underwrite specific articles in magazines, much as television advertisers sponsor programs, White argued that such a practice, however well intended, would reduce editors' independence and become "an invitation to corruption and abuse." Persuaded, Xerox abandoned the project (*Columbia Journalism Review*, Sept.–Oct. 1976, p. 54). Starting in 1972 he worked with several editors to prepare selections from his letters (1976), his essays (1977), and his poems and sketches (1981). He collected many honors, which culminated in a special Pulitzer Prize in 1978 honoring his entire body of work. After Katharine White's death in July 1977, White continued to live in Maine, not far from their son. In his last year his abilities were diminished, and he was bedridden. He died at his home in Maine.

His death drew forth many tributes. William Shawn, Ross's successor at the *New Yorker*, praised White's literary style: "It was singular, colloquial, clear, unforced, thoroughly American and utterly beautiful." His stepson, Roger Angell, said at the memorial service, "Almost without our noticing it, he seemed to take down the fences of manner and propriety and pomposity in writing."

Yet through the years others noted the self-contained, even insular nature of White's work—an opus almost bare of literary allusion and moored in what William Dean Howells once called "the more smiling aspects of life." In the 1930s his friend Ralph Ingersoll implied that White's "gossamer" editorials irresponsibly ignored the Great Depression, and his editorials on world government were criticized by some as middle-class, nostalgic idealism.

Still, he was justly compared as an ironist to Montaigne and Henry David Thoreau, and his work has found an enduring audience. Russell Lynes aptly called him an "Eagle Scout of American letters": "Mr. White has won all the merit badges, his heart is pure, he can tie and untie complicated knots, and he knows the names and habits of beast and fowl and sprout and loves them all. He is consistently on the side of the angels but flies a little below them, kept airborne by a precious and incorruptible sense of the ridiculous" (*New York Times*, 26 Feb. 1984).

• E. B. White's papers are at the Cornell University Library, Ithaca, N.Y. Printed materials in the collection are cataloged in Katherine Romans Hall, comp., *E. B. White: A Bibliographic Catalogue . . .* (1979). His books, most of them reprints of previously published work, include *Ho Hum* (1931), a collection of newsbreaks; *Another Ho Hum* (1932); *Alice through the Cellophane* (1933); *Farewell to Model T* (1936); *The Fox of Peapack and Other Poems* (1938); *Quo Vadimus?* (1939); *World Government and Peace* (1945); *The Second Tree from the Corner* (1954); and *The Points of My Compass* (1962). William W. Watt and Robert W. Bradford compiled *An E. B. White Reader* (1966), and Rebecca M. Dale edited his *Writings from the New Yorker, 1927–1976* (1990). With Katharine S. White, White edited *A Subtreasury of American Humor* (1941). Besides Elledge's *E. B. White: A Biography*, information on White's career is available in Edward Sampson's brief *E. B. White* (1974); Linda H. Davis, *Onward and Upward: A Biography of Katharine S. White* (1987) and "The Man on the Swing," *New Yorker*, 27 Dec. 1993, pp. 90–194, a sketch of White in his later years; Isabel Russell, *Katharine and E. B. White* (1988); Dale Kramer, *Ross and "The New Yorker"* (1951); James Thurber, *The Years with Ross* (1959); Jane Grant, *Ross, "The New Yorker" and Me* (1968); Thomas Kunkel, *Genius in Disguise: Harold Ross of the New Yorker* (1955); Charles S. Holmes, *The Clocks of Columbus: The Literary Career of James Thurber* (1972); Brendan Gill, *Here at "The New Yorker"* (1975); and Burton Bernstein, *Thurber* (1975). Critical appraisals include Warren Beck, "E. B. White," *College English* 7 (Apr. 1946): 367–73; John Updike, "Remarks on the Occasion of E. B. White Receiving the 1971 National Medal for Literature, 12/2/71," in Updike's *Picked-Up Pieces* (1975), pp. 434–47; Eudora Welty, "Dateless Virtues," *New York Times Book Review*, 25 Sept. 1977, pp. 7, 43; Roger Sale, *Fairy Tales and After* (1978), pp. 258–67; Helene Solheim, "Magic in the Web," *South Atlantic Quarterly* 80 (Autumn 1981): 391–405; R. S. Platizky, "'Once More to the Lake': A Mythic Interpretation," *College Literature* 15 (1988): 171–79; and Peter Neufeld, ed., *The Annotated Charlotte's Web* (1995). An obituary by Herbert Mitgang appears in the *New York Times*, 2 Oct. 1985.

JAMES BOYLAN

WHITE, Edna Noble (3 June 1879–4 May 1954), home economics and child development educator, was born in Fairmount, Illinois, the daughter of Alexander L. White, a prominent local businessman, and Angeline Noble. The second of three children, White grew up in comfortable surroundings with her older sister and younger brother. Her father was a teacher and later a hardware dealer in the small village of Fairmount. Her mother was educated although not professionally employed.

By age twenty White had begun teaching, later attending the University of Illinois, where she earned her A.B. in home economics in 1906. In the next two years she taught at Danville (Ill.) High School and the Lewis Institute in Chicago. In 1908 she was appointed associate professor in home economics at Ohio State University and was promoted to full professor and head of the department in 1913. She was active in expanding the field beyond its sentimental tone and traditional focus on cooking, sewing, and housekeeping, adding a new emphasis on the scientific study of the child. In 1914 she collaborated on a nutrition textbook, *A Study of Foods*, with Ruth A. Wardall.

In 1917 and 1918, while still at Ohio State, White headed the food conservation efforts of the Food Administration in Ohio, the only woman to hold such a post during World War I. Her success in this role earned a commendation from Herbert Hoover, and in 1918 her peers elevated her to the presidency of the American Home Economics Association; she served until 1920.

In 1920 White accepted an appointment as the first director of the Merrill-Palmer School for Motherhood and Home Training in Detroit, a post she held until 1947. Lizzie Merrill Palmer, widow of Michigan senator Thomas W. Palmer, had left $3 million in her will for the establishment of a school for the promotion of the "functions and services of wifehood and motherhood." The male directors responsible for implementing this general mandate lacked any relevant experience. Their principal contribution, after an extensive search, was hiring White, who then enjoyed uncommon freedom in shaping the new institution. The school came to be known as the Merrill-Palmer Institute until its affiliation with Wayne State University in 1981.

The institute sponsored one of the first laboratory schools devoted to the systematic and scientific study of young children and parenting. White assembled a faculty from such fields as developmental psychology, sociology, social work, medicine, nutrition, and home economics. Using her academic contacts, she established cooperative programs in which visiting college students from numerous institutions could receive credit for one term of study (later expanded to one year, offering graduate credit). Most of the students were destined to be high school and college teachers, through whom White hoped to educate future parents. Groups of Merrill-Palmer students lived together with one or two staff members and combined academic pursuits with work in a nursery school White founded in 1922 to study children aged two through five. Later the institute broadened its focus to include the family as a unit and older children up to adulthood—producing some of the first longitudinal studies of children, in which height, weight, and other physical characteristics were tracked over time.

Much of White's reputation came from her involvement with the nursery school movement, beginning with her 1921 visit to British nursery schools, which served mainly poor children. Finding their methods effective, she applied them to a more diverse population of children in the United States and added the research component, making the Merrill-Palmer nursery school a laboratory for the study of child development. White conceived of early childhood education as the formation of physical habits (in sleeping, feeding, elimination, and exercise), mental habits (concentration, self-control, and self-reliance), speech development, and attitudes toward authority. She emphasized the educational value of life activities; in this she reflected the progressive education movement associated with John Dewey. During the Great Depression she chaired the National Advisory Committee on Emergency Nursery Schools, a New Deal program administered jointly by the Federal Emergency Relief Administration and the U.S. Office of Education. The program was created for poor children but also required that persons employed in these schools be unemployed persons eligible for relief; in two years the program increased the total number of American nursery schools more than sixfold.

By all accounts White brought extraordinary energy and enthusiasm to her work. She demanded interdisciplinary cooperation and continual experimentation and innovation from her faculty at Merrill-Palmer. She sponsored numerous publications and conferences and participated in dozens of national and local organizations, most notably chairing the National Council of Parent Education from its founding in 1925 to 1937. She was also an influential member of the National Nutrition Advisory Committee of the American Red Cross in the 1920s. As her reputation grew, she was named to the boards of numerous organizations, beginning long tenures with the Child Study Association of America in 1927, the International Federation of Home and School in 1929, the New Education Fellowship in 1931, the Agricultural Missions Foundation in 1932, and the National Conference on Family Relations in 1939. A colleague credited her with "breadth of vision" and "high executive ability safely balanced by a rich human understanding."

White's pace hardly slackened after her retirement from the Merrill-Palmer Institute. As a specialist in family and children's studies for the American Mission to Greece in 1947–1948, she helped organize programs in Greek universities. After her return she studied the part-time employment of women and coordinated a study of the problems of the aged for several Detroit institutions. Ohio State awarded the last of her four honorary degrees in 1947, when a former student remembered White as "an inspiring, dynamic teacher."

White never married. For much of her adult life she lived with her sister and helped raise two motherless nephews. She was an avid reader and traveler and owned a farm that she used as a retreat. She remained active until her death in Highland Park, Michigan.

Edna Noble White was a significant figure in making child development and the family the subject of scholarly research. Her early work in promoting the field of home economics was a prelude to her most important contribution, nurturing the Merrill-Palmer Institute from infancy to a robust maturity. Both the institution and its long-time director were well known and frequently consulted by a wide range of professionals in government and in the general area of human development.

• The richest source of materials about Edna Noble White and the Merrill-Palmer Institute is the Merrill-Palmer collection in the Walter Reuther Archives, Wayne State University. See also *Handbook for Leaders of Parent Education Groups in Emergency Education Programs* (1934) and *Emergency Nursery Schools during the Second Year, 1934–1935* (1935?). Representative shorter works include "Health Education of Very Young Children," *Public Health Nurse* 15 (Oct. 1923): 527–30; "Nursery Schools (United States)," in *Encyclopedia Britannica*, 14th ed., vol. 16 (1929), p. 643; "Parent Education in the Emergency," *School and Society* 40 (24 Nov. 1934): 679–81; "The Nursery School: A Teacher of Parents," *Child Study* 4 (Oct. 1926): 8–9; "The Objectives of the American Nursery School," *Family* 9 (Apr. 1928): 50–51; "The Role of Home Economics in Parent Education," *Bulletin of American Home Economics Association*, ser. 11, no. 2 (Jan. 1929): 1–3; and "The Scope of Parent Education in America," in *Towards a New Education*, ed. William Boyd and Muriel M. Mackenzie (1929). Dorothy Tyler, "A Study of Leadership in the Making of an Institution," *Social Forces* 10 (May 1932): 594–600, recounts White's efforts in developing the Merrill-Palmer program. Lawrence K. Frank, "The Beginnings of Child Development and Family Life Education in the Twentieth Century," *Merrill-Palmer Quarterly* 8 (Oct. 1962): 207–27, places White's work in the context of innovations elsewhere. Obituaries are in the *Merrill-Palmer Quarterly* 1 (Fall 1954): 3, and the *Detroit Free Press*, *Detroit News*, and *Detroit Times*, 6 May 1954.

ROBERT E. BUCHTA

WHITE, Edward Douglass (3 Mar. 1795–18 Apr. 1847), congressman and governor, was born in Maury County, Tennessee, the son of James White and Mary Willcox. In 1799 the family moved to St. Martin Parish, Louisiana, where his father became a territorial district judge after the Louisiana Purchase. Graduating from the University of Nashville in 1815, White studied law in New Orleans under Alexander Porter, a prominent attorney and future member of the Louisiana Supreme Court who would become his political patron and adviser. He eventually established his own practice in Donaldsonville, a small town at the juncture of the Mississippi River and Bayou Lafourche some fifty miles upstream from New Orleans.

After serving from 1825 to 1828 as New Orleans city court judge, White turned to sugar planting along Bayou Lafourche, but at Porter's urging came forward to bid for Edward Livingston's seat in the national House of Representatives in 1828. His youth and inexperience exposed him to taunts of callowness and impudence, but he soon demonstrated a mixture of talents and charm that was to make him a formidable candidate. Although technically a member of the Anglo-Saxon element of the state's ethnically oriented politics, his lifelong association with the Gallic community along Bayou Lafourche gave him a much wider acceptance among them than that generally accorded members of the "American" faction, a major boost to his candidacy. But his greatest political asset seems to have been a warmth and generosity of character that unfailingly won over even those at odds with him politically, though this winsome attractiveness had a dark underside of sometimes bizarre eccentricity and violence of temper, exhibited during the campaign when he had to be restrained from stabbing a jeering opponent. These strengths and the overconfidence of the lethargic and distant Livingston, together with the ponderable backing of Porter and the incumbent governor, Henry Johnson, gave him an unexpected victory.

A vigorous supporter of Henry Clay and the National Republican cause during his congressional tenure, White backed the Kentuckian's Compromise Tariff of 1833 despite its reduced protection of Louisiana's sugar industry. Any consequent damage to his political future diminished when the unity of the Louisiana Jacksonian party was shattered that year in a bitter struggle for ascendancy between Martin Gordon, the Democratic leader, and John Slidell, who had been expelled through Gordon's influence from his position as federal attorney in New Orleans. Exploiting this disarray in the enemy camp, White began campaigning for the Louisiana governorship in 1833, only momentarily sidetracked by injuries sustained in the explosion of the Red River steamboat *Lioness*. Despite the primacy of nullification, tariff policy, and the Bank of the United States as national political issues, the Louisiana election of 1834 almost completely ignored those themes in a preoccupation with personal vilification of the candidates and Jacksonian allegations that White was the creature and slave of "foreign interests" attempting to subvert the community. That charge stemmed from the continued close ties between White and Porter, an Irish immigrant. The election unleashed xenophobic passions that became the foundation of the state's Native American movement. White won the election handily, defeating Gordon's handpicked candidate, John B. Dawson, with better than 60 percent of the vote in a canvass that saw White sweeping all but one of the state's parishes south of the Red River, where the Clay and ethnic French faction had its greatest strength.

The first two years of his 1835–1839 administration were marked by a vigorous economic prosperity highlighted by the chartering of six new banks capitalized at $16 million, construction of the famed St. Charles and St. Louis hotels in New Orleans, and installation of the city's first gas lighting. On the educational and cultural side, in 1837 White signed the charter of the Medical College of Louisiana, the forerunner of Tulane University.

But as a consequence of the bitterness of the 1834 campaign, White's administration found itself mired from the beginning in an inescapable morass of controversy and strife. Accusations that his appointments favored the foreign faction continued to swirl around him, creating a climate of gloomy foreboding deepened by paranoid fears of abolitionists and slave insurrection that swept the state during the mid-1830s. In the midst of these anxieties came the terrible dislocations of the panic of 1837 and the complexities arising from the Texas independence movement and the Seminole War in Florida, which forced White into the unpopular position of having to suppress illegal enlistment by Louisianians in the Texas forces while attempting to fill the state's troop quotas in the fight against the Indians.

This accumulation of bitterness and acrimony, especially as reflected in the sharpness of ethnic division and an eroding of the status of the state's free persons of color flowing from the slave insurrection hysteria, so pained and saddened White that he left the governorship in 1839 with no reluctance. In 1838 he had rewon his old seat in Congress, where he served until 1843 as a member of the Whig party, working particularly to expand the U.S. branch mint in New Orleans and to increase commerce with Mexico. Losing his bid for reelection in the Democratic sweep of the state in the congressional canvass of July 1843, White retired from politics and settled at his plantation in Thibodaux, Louisiana, on the banks of Bayou Lafourche with his wife Catherine Sidney Lee Ringgold, daughter of Tench Ringgold, marshal of the federal district under Presidents James Madison and James Monroe, whom he had married in 1834. One of their five children, Edward Douglass White, Jr., became a member of the U.S. Supreme Court in 1894 and chief justice of the United States in 1910. Governor White died of "bronchial infection" in New Orleans and is buried in St. Joseph's Catholic Cemetery in Thibodaux.

Considerable confusion has clouded the proper spelling of the middle name of the two E. D. Whites, frequently given as "Douglas," an assumption not easily dispelled since both men consistently signed themselves simply as "E. D. White." Documents in the probate files of the chief justice, almost certainly known to members of the family, establish the "Douglass" form of the name.

• There is no extant collection of White manuscripts, and official records of early Louisiana state government are practically nonexistent except for printed journals of the legislature and court proceedings. Some materials relating to White's administration are available, however, in the Louisiana Civil Records Collection (1812–1858) of the Louisiana State Museum in New Orleans. The most comprehensive survey of his life and political career is found in Diedrich Ramke, "Edward Douglas [*sic*] White, Sr., Governor of Louisiana, 1835–1839," *Louisiana Historical Quarterly* 19 (1936): 273–327. A more recent evaluation is in Joseph G. Dawson III, ed., *The Louisiana Governors* (1990), pp. 113–18.

JOSEPH G. TREGLE, JR.

WHITE, Edward Douglass (3 Nov. 1845–19 May 1921), chief justice and associate justice of the U.S. Supreme Court and U.S. senator, was born in Lafourche Parish, Louisiana, the son of Edward Douglass White, a Louisiana lawyer, congressman, governor, and sugar planter, who died shortly after White's birth, and Catherine Sidney Lee Ringgold. White was initially schooled on his family's plantation and then at a series of Jesuit institutions—the Preparatory School of the Immaculate Conception in New Orleans, Mount Saint Mary's College in Maryland, and Georgetown College (now Georgetown University), which he entered in 1858.

In 1861 the sixteen-year-old White left Georgetown without a degree to fight for the Confederacy but did not enlist in the Confederate army until the following year. He entered as a private, but through family intervention he became a lieutenant. United States troops captured White after their victory at Port Hudson in July 1863. He subsequently referred to secession as a mistake. After the war he studied law with Edward Bermudez and was admitted to the Louisiana bar in 1868, and in 1874, at age twenty-nine, White won election to the Louisiana Senate. Five years later he was appointed to the Louisiana Supreme Court, but a new state constitution requiring that all state supreme court justices be at least thirty-five years old forced the 34-year-old White to leave his seat in April 1880. During the next decade he practiced law. His most notable accomplishment was arranging for the state-funded University of Louisiana, located in New Orleans, to become a private institution through a donation from Paul Tulane, for whom the new university was named.

In 1888 White helped spearhead an attack on the Louisiana lottery. Although the antilottery campaign led to his election to the U.S. Senate that year, White remained in Louisiana until 1891 to fight the lottery. Once he arrived in Washington, Senator White was a conventional Democrat, except when the policies of President Grover Cleveland threatened the economic interests—especially the sugar interests—of Louisiana. White happily supported Cleveland's refusal to annex Hawaii as both a rejection of imperialism and as a way to prevent domestic competition for Louisiana's sugar growers. In the Senate he successfully led the opposition to the Hatch anti-option bill, which would have prohibited various kinds of speculation in stock and commodities. He was also unyielding in his opposition to cutting the tariff on imported sugar, despite Cleveland's support for lowering the tax.

In July 1893 U.S. Supreme Court justice Samuel Blatchford of New York died. Cleveland nominated two eminent New York lawyers, but that state's powerful senator, David Bennett Hill, who wanted the seat for himself, blocked both nominations through senatorial courtesy. When a third candidate declined the office Cleveland surprised all observers by nominating White on 19 February 1894. Senatorial courtesy now worked in the nominee's favor, and the Senate immediately confirmed White. Some scholars have suggested that Cleveland nominated White to remove him from the tariff debates. If this was the president's motivation, it backfired because White did not immediately resign from the Senate. Instead, he remained there for another three weeks to continue fighting (unsuccessfully) against the reduction in the tariff on imported sugar.

The same year he joined the Court, White married Leita Montgomery Kent, the widow of a Washington attorney. Two decades earlier White had courted her, only to be spurned for the now-deceased Mr. Kent. When he joined the Court, the 48-year-old White was a formidable personality: cultured, fluent in French, wealthy, and something of a gourmet and a gourmand, weighing more than 250 pounds at only five-feet, ten-inches tall. He had a powerful voice, a full head of brown hair, and was a careful, stylish dresser. One scholar has noted that the "huge Louisianan looked almost like a late nineteenth century caricature of a senator, with long and thick hair ringing his florid oval face, pacing slightly, nervously, gently swinging a wide expanse of vest-covered torso around the ornate chamber" (Watts, p. 1638). He was one of four former Confederates (along with L. Q. C. Lamar, Howell Jackson, and Horace Lurton) to serve on the Court as well as a rare Roman Catholic on the high bench. In 1910 President William Howard Taft elevated White to chief justice. This was the first time a sitting justice had become the chief justice. (In 1795 President George Washington had attempted to elevate Associate Justice John Rutledge to chief justice, but the Senate did not confirm him.) Although Taft was a Republican and White a Democrat, party affiliation was less important than ideological outlook. White and Taft were ideologically similar: supportive of big business while hostile to both labor and social experimentation. As Justice Louis Brandeis later remarked, the men Taft appointed, including White, "*did* have certain views on property" (Bickel, p. 6).

In addition to his ideological views, White was an important stabilizing force for the Court, which in 1910 was aging and ineffective. The year before his elevation to chief justice, White privately urged the attorney general to avoid bringing any important cases before the Court because so many of the justices were either ill or senile. White believed nothing significant should be decided until the inevitable change of personnel occurred. Starting in 1909 the changes were swift. That year Justice Rufus Peckham died; in 1910 both Justice David Brewer and Chief Justice Melville Fuller died, and Justice William Moody, who had been too ill to sit in 1909, resigned. Justice John Marshall Harlan was nearly eighty, and, as most observers expected, he soon died, in 1911. Thus the elevation of the genial, conservative, and safe White made sense; at sixty-five, with seventeen years on the bench, he was experienced enough to provide institutional stability and yet young and vigorous enough to provide some leadership. Taft may also have had another agenda. Although president, Taft actually coveted the chief justiceship. Taft doubtless realized that he himself would still be young enough to become chief justice when White retired or died, which is what happened. When White died in 1921, President Warren G. Harding appointed ex-President Taft to succeed him.

Throughout his career White was a conservative supporter of the status quo, big business, racial segregation, and government suppression of labor, radicalism, and free speech. He generally opposed progressive economic regulations by federal or state legislatures. He opposed serious restrictions on large corporations and monopolies, unless the monopolies acted in truly outrageous fashion. He argued that the Sherman Antitrust Act should not be applied literally, but only within a narrow "rule of reason." In practice this meant that the Court would not support most antitrust actions brought by the national government. White was more concerned with the freedom of contract of the corporations than the harm to consumers from monopolistic practices. Thus, he voted with the majority to prevent the breakup of the sugar trust in *United States v. E. C. Knight* (1895) and dissented in *United States v. Trans-Missouri Freight Association* (1897), when a majority of the Court found that the price-fixing arrangement of a number of railroads constituted an illegal restraint of trade. Similarly, he dissented in *Northern Securities Company v. United States* (1904), protesting that Congress had no power to authorize the breakup of this large railroad monopoly. As chief justice he wrote the majority opinion upholding the government in *Standard Oil Company v. United States* (1911), which led to the breakup of that monopoly. However, the doctrine he set forth in that opinion—a combination of common law and the rule of reason—undermined the Sherman act by making it applicable only to a very small number of extremely powerful monopolies. White's opposition to an expansive interpretation of the Commerce Clause almost always benefited employers.

White generally opposed legislation, state or federal, that aided workers and labor unions. In *Howard v. Illinois Central Railroad and Brooks v. Southern Pacific Co.* (1908), which is popularly known as the *Employers' Liability Cases*, White wrote the opinion of the Court striking down a new federal law making railroads liable for injuries to their workers. The federal law altered the long-standing common law approach to on-the-job injuries, the "fellow servant rule." Under that rule employees were not allowed to sue their employers for on-the-job injuries but instead were only permitted to sue negligent fellow employees ("fellow servants"). White's opinion overturning this new law was a major blow to the welfare of railroad workers and a huge victory for the companies. In other labor cases White usually voted against workers. He voted with the majority in *Adair v. United States* (1908) to strike down a federal law that prohibited railroads from requiring employees to sign "yellow dog contracts"—contracts in which an employee promised not to join a union. Similarly, White joined the 5–4 majority in *Hammer v. Dagenhart* (1918) to strike down a federal restriction on child labor, and he dissented in *Bunting v. Oregon* (1917), which upheld a maximum-hours law that applied equally to men and women.

White did, however, side with labor and reform in two important early cases, but his reasoning and approach were nevertheless quite limited. In *Lochner v. New York* (1905) the Court struck down a law limiting the number of hours a baker could work as a violation of the "liberty" guaranteed by the Fourteenth Amendment. White dissented in *Lochner*, but it was not a rejection of substantive due process or an endorsement of social legislation to protect workers; rather, he believed that the New York law was a legitimate exercise of state "police power." He also joined the unanimous court in *Muller v. Oregon* (1908), which upheld an Oregon statute limiting the number of hours women could work in laundries. Once again, White saw state police power as legitimate, believing that the states had some power to regulate the workplace. This was, of course, the same kind of power that allowed states, in White's view, to segregate blacks. But his views of state police power in labor-related cases were quite limited and became increasingly narrow.

Unlike some of the most conservative members of the Court during his tenure, White believed the national government had broad taxation powers. He dissented in the income tax case *Pollock v. Farmers' Loan & Trust Company* (1895) and wrote the majority opinion in *McCray v. United States* (1904), upholding a federal tax on oleomargarine. He also did not actively oppose the development of new administrative agencies that implemented their own rules, leading to what is today known as administrative law. Thus in *United States v. Louisville and Nashville Railroad Company* (1914) and other cases White gave broad latitude to the Interstate Commerce Commission and other agencies.

White's most lasting contribution to constitutional law was the development of the "insular doctrine." In the *Insular Cases* (1901) White argued that constitutional protections and guarantees were not applicable to overseas U.S. possessions without explicit congressional approval. In the second insular case, *Dooley v. United States* (1901), White dissented, arguing that a tariff on Puerto Rican sugar remained applicable to the new American territory until Congress changed the law. In *Downes v. Bidwell* (1901) he concurred in the judgment of the Court, asserting that the Constitution did not "follow the flag" into new territories. White reaffirmed this position in a concurring opinion in *Hawaii v. Mankichi* (1903). By 1905 White's views had prevailed, as he wrote the opinion of the Court in *Rassmussen v. United States* that Alaska was not an incorporated territory. In a similar approach he wrote the majority opinion in *Lone Wolf v. Hitchcock* (1903), arguing that Congress was free to ignore Indian treaties and to govern Indian lands as it wished. Native peoples, like the residents of overseas possessions, had no rights that Justice White was ready to respect or protect.

In civil liberties cases White strongly supported federal power to suppress radicalism and labor activism. He voted to uphold all of the federal prosecutions of opponents of World War I. He wrote the opinion in *Toledo Newspapers v. United States* (1918) upholding a contempt citation for criticizing the federal district court. Oliver Wendell Holmes (1841–1935) and Brandeis, who had not yet articulated strong theories of freedom of the press, dissented from White's opinion. White dissented in *Gilbert v. Minnesota* (1920), a state prosecution of a radical, but not because he supported the idea of free speech. Rather, he thought the federal government should have sole jurisdiction in sedition cases.

White had conventionally racist views but was not an extremist. Although the moviemaker D. W. Griffith claimed White endorsed his racist movie, *The Birth of a Nation* (1915), and asserted that White had been in the Ku Klux Klan, there is no evidence to support either of Griffith's contentions. White generally supported the creation of a segregated society, voting with the majority in such cases as *Plessy v. Ferguson* (1896), upholding a state law requiring segregation on trains; *Williams v. Mississippi* (1898), allowing the virtual disfranchisement of all blacks in that state; and *Berea College v. Kentucky* (1908), permitting Kentucky to prohibit a private college from maintaining an integrated student body. On racial issues he stands in marked contrast to Harlan, the other southern justice on the Court from a former slaveholding family, who valiantly protested the evisceration of the Fourteenth Amendment and civil rights protections.

White did support civil rights in a number of cases, all but one of which were decided unanimously, suggesting not a change in behavior on his part, but rather the egregiousness of the statutes or behavior in question. White wrote the opinions in *Guinn v. United States* (1915), striking down Oklahoma's grandfather clause, and in a companion case, *Meyers v. Anderson* (1915), striking down a similar Maryland law. These opinions dealt with laws that so undermined the right to vote that the Court was unanimous in striking them down. White joined the unanimous court in *Clyatt v. United States* (1905) and *United States v. Reynolds* (1914), upholding convictions for violating antipeonage laws. The practices in both cases so blatantly violated the Thirteenth Amendment that even many southerners opposed them. White also joined the majority in *Bailey v. Alabama* (1911), which struck a blow at peonage. This was the only case involving race that was not unanimously decided in which White voted for civil rights. White was part of the unanimous court in *Buchanan v. Warley* (1917), striking down a law that prevented nonwhites from living in certain neighborhoods. This case had as much to do with property rights—which White always supported—as it did with civil rights, which he rarely supported.

These cases, while important landmarks in civil rights law, did not challenge racial segregation at the time or radically alter the status of southern blacks. In a sense, White's jurisprudence on race dovetails with his jurisprudence on antitrust. In antitrust cases he supported a rule of reason that allowed him to generally protect corporations from government regulation unless they acted in ways that he found outrageous. Similarly, White supported segregation, restrictions in voting, and other oppressions of African Americans as long as they were "reasonable," as he saw it.

Over his Court career White became increasingly conservative and moved from supporting some progressive measures, like wage and hour regulations, to opposing them. As such, White consistently rewrote congressional and state legislation, interpreting it to fit his own views. His rule of reason gutted the Sherman act and other progressive laws. Similarly, he reinterpreted or blatantly ignored the language of the laws and treaties leading to the United States' overseas empire in order to establish his doctrine that the Constitution did not follow the flag.

Personally charming, White was able to get along well with most of his colleagues. Indeed, in 1910 members of the Court asked President Taft to promote him to the chief justiceship. White was a hardworking justice. In his twenty-seven years on the Court he wrote 590 majority opinions, sixteen concurring opinions, fifty-three dissents, and twenty-two "statements." Despite his productivity, White was not a particularly efficient chief justice. He often delayed cases and had a slow, lackadaisical attitude toward the court calendar. He opposed plans to construct a building to house the Supreme Court and discouraged any efforts by the justices to lobby for legislation that would affect the Court.

His productivity and geniality contrast sharply with his general obscurity. At his death *The Nation* prophetically observed that "by reason of his striking personality and his lovable human traits, the late Chief Justice will for a while receive higher tributes to his judicial services than time is apt to confirm" (1 June 1921, p. 78). His modern biographer, Robert Highsaw, reached the same conclusion, asserting that he has been "virtually unrecognized" and has "receded into an ever darkening past appearing occasionally in the footnotes of legal periodicals, constitutional history, or brief sketches of Supreme Court justices." This is not surprising, as he was "no juristic stylist or felicitous phrasemaker," he used no "particular methodology," and had little reputation before he joined the Court. However, to a great extent White represented the era in which he lived and the Court on which he served. He shared the stage with some giants of American jurisprudence—Harlan, Holmes, and Brandeis—but for the most part White and his colleagues were dull, conservative in style, often reactionary in jurisprudence, and usually conventional in analysis of law and society. Thus, when White died in Washington, D.C., after unsuccessful bladder surgery, he was mourned and missed but quickly forgotten.

• The most important sources for White's career are the reports of the U.S. Supreme Court, vols. 152 (1894) to 256 (1921). Also useful are his opinions on the Louisiana Supreme Court, vols. 31–32 of Louisiana Annual Reports (1879–1880). White papers are in a number of collections involving other justices and contemporary politicians at the Library of Congress, the archives of Georgetown University, the Archdiocese of Baltimore, and the Edward Douglass White Memorial at Thibodaux, La. The best biographical sketches of White are Judith A. Baer, "Edward Douglass White," in *The Supreme Court Justices: A Biographical Dictionary*, ed. Melvin Urofsky (1994), and James F. Watts, Jr., "Edward Douglass White," in *The Justices of the United States Supreme Court*, ed. Leon Friedman and Fred L. Israel (1980), vol. 3, pp. 1633–56. Robert B. Highsaw, *Edward Douglass White: Defender of the Conservative Faith* (1981), and Sister Marie Carolyn Klinkhamer, *Edward Douglass White: Chief Justice of the United States* (1943), are two full-length biographies of White. Books covering his tenure on the Court include Owen M. Fiss, *History of the Supreme Court of the United States*, vol. 8: *Troubled Beginnings of the Modern State, 1888–1910* (1993); Alexander Bickel and Benno C. Schmidt, Jr., *History of the Supreme Court of the United States*, vol. 9: *The Judiciary and Responsible Government, 1910–1921* (1984); John E. Semonche, *Charting the Future: The Supreme Court Responds to a Changing Society, 1890–1920* (1978); and Loren P. Beth, *The Development of the American Constitution, 1877–1917* (1971). Obituaries are in the *Washington, D.C., Evening Star*, 19 May 1921, and in most major papers for that date and 20 May.

PAUL FINKELMAN

WHITE, Elijah (3 April 1806–3 April 1879), medical missionary, federal agent, and proponent of westward emigration, was born in Havana, now Montour Falls, New York, the son of the Reverend Alward White and Clara Pierce. His father and uncles were Methodist Episcopal itinerant preachers, and as a youth White was an activist in the local Methodist congregation, being especially interested in temperance. He became a doctor, possibly having studied in Syracuse. He married Sarepta Caroline Rhoode sometime before 1835.

In 1836 White responded to an announcement in the *Christian Advocate* that a doctor was needed to join Jason Lee's Methodist mission in Oregon. White volunteered, and in 1837 he, his wife, and his two sons sailed from Boston on the *Hamilton* to the Sandwich (Hawaiian) Islands with the "reinforcements." After four months in the islands, the group traveled on the *Diana* to Astoria (near the mouth of the Columbia River) and then on to the Willamette Valley.

White's stay in Oregon, from 1836 until 1841, is chronicled in his book *Ten Years in Oregon: Travels and Adventures of Doctor E. White and Lady* (1848). It was not a happy time: his two children drowned in separate accidents, and White chafed under Lee's authority and made complaints about Lee to the Mission Board. Eventually White underwent two church trials on charges of usurpation of authority while Lee was in the East, financial irregularities involving mission funds allocated without Lee's approval to White's hospital, and unprofessional conduct vis-à-vis his female (mostly Indian) patients. White was found guilty of all charges but one. He later appealed and made countercharges against Lee. White left Oregon without church permission and settled his family in Lansing, Tompkins County, New York, on land owned by his uncles then called White Settlement (now, Lansingville).

White's knowledge of the Pacific Northwest brought him to the attention of President John Tyler, and after a trip to Washington, White was appointed subagent to the Indians west of the Rocky Mountains, the first federal appointment in the Pacific Northwest, territory then claimed jointly by the U.S. and Great Britain.

In 1842 White set out for Oregon. From New York to Missouri he spoke frequently at public meetings of opportunities in the Pacific Northwest. These speeches are credited with arousing interest in the Oregon country and helping to create the great tide of westward emigration that began in 1843. In April 1842 White led the first emigrant train to Oregon, a party of 117 people including ten families, who took wagons as far west as Fort Hall, Idaho. White began as captain of the train, but after a month Langford Hastings was elected to that post. As they approached Fort Hall, twelve of the party went on ahead, leaving the slower members to bring up the wagons. At Fort Hall the wagons were abandoned because of the difficult terrain ahead, and the emigrants made their way by foot and with mules to Walla Walla and by boat along the Columbia River.

In Oregon White busied himself accumulating as much authority as possible. In 1842 he set up a code of laws for the Nez Perce that ignored the realities of tribal life by encouraging farming, designating a single chief, and detailing laws and punishments to control conduct. White advocated temperance and clashed with the liquor interests, leading to a near duel in 1844, and another in 1845, when William Holderness charged him with slander. White participated in the "Wolf Meetings," during which a "committee considered the propriety of taking measures for the civil and military protection of the colony," and in subsequent meetings during which a provisional government for Oregon was created.

In 1845 White returned east and resumed life in Lansing. He published his memoir *Ten Years in Oregon* while expecting another government appointment. This was quashed, however, by letters from enemies in Oregon complaining about him. Life as a rural doctor must have seemed tame; in 1849 White organized the Ithaca-California Mining Company and led fifty men as far as Salt Lake City. While the rest continued to California, White and his partner James D. Holman headed to the north shore of the mouth of the Columbia River, where he sold land in Pacific City, near present-day Ilwaco, Washington. White exaggerated the degree of improvement at Pacific City. Settlement of the area began and a hotel was erected, but during the Civil War the area was appropriated for Fort Canby and the civilian city died out.

By that time, however, White had left Washington Territory and settled in San Francisco, where he petitioned for a government appointment as Indian agent. Although he had some supporters whose letters he published in pamphlets championing his cause, a position never materialized.

White was joined in San Francisco by his wife, Sarepta, but in 1870 she divorced him and resettled in San Diego. White practiced medicine in San Francisco and attended the Howard Street Methodist Church, whose minister's authority he challenged. White again faced a church trial in 1868, this time for allegedly making improper suggestions to female patients, fondling his stepdaughter, and promoting immoral conduct.

White died in San Francisco. Physically brave, he crossed the continent three times. A promoter of western settlement, he led the first emigrant train across the Oregon Trail, aiding dreams of Manifest Destiny. As a government agent, he encountered difficult circumstances, but his lack of success was mostly due to his inability to get along with people and his overriding ambition. He challenged authority, believed fully in his own ability, and breached contemporary sexual morality.

• Unpublished material by and about White appears in the papers of the Office of Indian Affairs, National Archives; Oregon History Society, Portland, Oreg.; Oregon State Archives, Salem, Oreg.; University of Puget Sound Archives; Bancroft Library, University of California, Berkeley; Huntington Library, San Marino, Calif.; and Board of Missions Archive of the Methodist Episcopal Church in New York. For contemporary sources on White, see Miss A. J. Allen, comp., *Ten Years in Oregon: Travels and Adventures of Doctor E. White and Lady* (1848, 1850); *Christian Advocate Journal*, 2 Sept. 1836, 15 Mar. 1839, 10 Feb. 1841, and 3 Mar. 1841; and H. H. Bancroft, *History of Oregon*, vol. 1, *1834–1848* (1886). Additional autobiographical information appears in White's *A Concise View of Oregon Territory* (1846), *Testimonials and Records* (1861), and *A Vindication of Dr. Elijah White* (1868). R. J. Loewenberg has published two relevant studies: "Elijah White vs. Jason Lee: A Tale of Hard Times," *Journal of the West* 11 (1971): 636–62, and *Equality on the Oregon Frontier: Jason Lee and the Methodist Mission, 1834–43* (1976).

CAROL KAMMEN

WHITE, Eliza Orne (2 Aug. 1856–23 Jan. 1947), writer, was born in Keene, New Hampshire, the daughter of William Orne White, a Unitarian minister, and Margaret Eliot Harding, the daughter of portrait painter Chester Harding. By age eleven Eliza was already writing, composing historical romances that her mother praised. Her early years in Keene provided a fertile environment for White to soak up the New England local color that was later a prominent part of her fiction. Her years in Keene were relatively peaceful, but she did suffer from a bout of typhoid fever during her senior year in high school. After this experience, she spent 1872 at a boarding school in Roxbury, Massachusetts, but afterward returned home to her family. This quiet country existence changed in 1881, when her family moved to Brookline, Massachusetts, to the house where White was to spend the rest of her life along with Elizabeth Dundass, her housekeeper. The Boston environment would become the background for many of her adult and children's stories.

In 1890 White published her first novel, *Miss Brooks*, which contains many of the elements, such as a love affair, a spirited heroine, and detailed descriptions of New England social customs, that would appear later in the author's other novels and short story collections for adults. *Winterborough* (1892) is a similar novel, except that the setting is changed from Boston to a small town in New Hampshire, much like the one in which the writer grew up. These two novels, like White's others, show some strengths, such as her development of female characters, but are ultimately conventional works that conform to gender stereotypes.

White's largest claim to fame, however, was not her adult novels. It was her twenty-nine children's books, the first being *When Molly Was Six* (1894). The placid girls' stories that White recorded were based on her own experiences and are notable for the realistic children that she portrays. White wrote these novels all her life, not even slowing down when she became blind and deaf in 1915, and only stopping at age eighty-eight with the publication of *When Esther Was a Little Girl*. She died in Brookline, Massachusetts. She had never married.

In the years between the publication of *When Molly Was Six* and *When Esther Was a Little Girl* appeared many other children's books, including *A Little Girl of Long Ago* (1896), *A Borrowed Sister* (1906), *The Blue Aunt* (1918), *Tony* (1924), *The Adventures of Andrew* (1928), *Where Is Adelaide?* (1933), *Lending Mary* (1934), and *I: The Autobiography of a Cat* (1941). Of these works, *Lending Mary* is fairly typical. It focuses on the domestic adventures of Mary Starr, who is facing a month's stay away from her parents. During this time, little happens. Mary earns money to buy a birthday present, learns how to swim, goes out for the mail, listens to a radio, and visits tide pools, all small adventures that any child might have. The book is filled with minutiae about Mary's life; a typical chapter begins, "Sunday morning there were waffles for breakfast with maple syrup, and when she saw them Mary felt very hungry." Since nothing unusually exciting happens to Mary during her entire stay, the reader receives endless details about Mary's clothing, her meals, and her routine activities. Although this description does become dull, the book is not without its strong points. One strength of the story is that the author does not make Mary into a Pollyanna figure. Instead, Mary is sometimes considerate and kind, but, at other times, she is outspoken and rude, just like a real child might be. Another strength of White's writing is that she does not set her tales in a fantasy land. Instead, real life events happen, such as the depression in *Lending Mary* and World War I in *The Blue Aunt*. These intrusions, however, are brief and are never developed in great depth.

Although White had a long writing career and modest success during her lifetime, her work is largely forgotten, and her books now seem dated and old-fashioned. Her work is of interest primarily to the historian of children's literature or the scholar interested in New England regional fiction.

• Archival materials about White, including letters, can be found in the Houghton Mifflin Company Papers located at Harvard University. For an article about White's work, see Bertha Mahony Miller, "Eliza Orne White and Her Books for Children," *Horn Book Magazine* 31 (Apr. 1955): 89–102. A number of sources contain biographical sketches, including

The Junior Book of Authors (1934), *Twentieth Century Children's Writers* (1983), and the *Woman's Who's Who of America* (1914–1915).

SHERRIE A. INNESS

WHITE, Ellen Gould Harmon (26 Nov. 1827–16 July 1915), cofounder of the Seventh-day Adventist church, was born on a farm outside Gorham, Maine, the daughter of Robert Harmon, a farmer and hatter, and Eunice Gould. In the early 1830s Ellen and her twin sister, Elizabeth, moved with the Harmon family to nearby Portland, where they began their schooling. When Ellen was about nine years old, an angry schoolmate hit her in the nose with a rock, severely injuring her and virtually ending her formal education. The accident left her a self-described "lifelong invalid" seldom free from pain.

In 1840 the farmer-preacher William Miller visited Portland to warn residents of the impending end of the world, which he expected to occur in 1843. Ellen, a Methodist since birth, joined Miller's apocalyptic band, the leaders of which eventually settled on 22 October 1844 as the date for Christ's return to earth. His failure to show at the predicted time left Ellen and her fellow believers confused and bitterly disappointed. A short time later, while praying with friends for new light, seventeen-year-old Ellen received the first of her many "visions," which closely resembled the mesmeric trances of the time. Under the influence of the "Holy Spirit" she saw that 22 October 1844 had marked the beginning of the heavenly judgment, an event shortly preceding the second coming of Christ. Possessed of her new prophetic gift, she for a time fell in with a group of enthusiastic Millerites who engaged in crawling, foot-kissing, and rebaptising; but she soon adopted a more decorous lifestyle and denounced her former associates as fanatics.

In 1845 Ellen met a young Millerite minister named James White, who, believing her visions to be of divine origin, took it upon himself to accompany the young prophetess on her speaking tours. Criticism of their travel arrangements led to their marriage in August 1846. About this time the Whites began observing the seventh-day sabbath, and shortly thereafter Ellen received a vision validating this practice as the distinguishing mark of God's people. For several years they toured the Northeast preaching their millenarian and sabbatarian message, while James simultaneously served as his wife's editor, publisher, and manager. In 1852 the itinerants finally settled in Rochester, New York, but three years later they pushed westward to Battle Creek, Michigan. There in the early 1860s they organized their company of believers into the Seventh-day Adventist church. By that time Ellen had given birth to four children (all sons), the last of whom died in infancy.

Throughout the 1860s Ellen White focused much of her attention on matters of health. Since her childhood injury, she had endured almost constant physical and mental suffering, which she attributed either to God's efforts to preserve her humility or to Satan's efforts to kill her. In addition to various heart, lung, brain, and stomach ailments, she experienced frequent "fainting fits" and recurrent bouts of anxiety and depression. Repeatedly, she feared imminent death. During a vision in June 1863, she received divine validation of what popular health reformers had been teaching for decades: that illness resulted from violating nature's laws, from eating meat and other stimulating foods, consuming alcohol and tobacco, and patronizing drug-dispensing doctors. The restoration of health, she learned, would come by relying on natural remedies, especially the water treatments promoted by the advocates of hydropathy, a midcentury medical sect. In 1866 White opened her own water-cure establishment in Battle Creek, the Western Health Reform Institute, which, under her protege John Harvey Kellogg, became the flagship of an international fleet of Adventist sanitariums.

Beginning in 1872 White spent increasing amounts of time cultivating Adventism on the West Coast, on occasion working alone because of strains in her marriage. In the late 1870s, her dramatic daytime visions ceased, but she continued to receive heavenly messages in the form of dreams or "visions of the night." Following her husband's death in 1881, Ellen sank into a year-long depression, but her spirits revived when God announced in a dream that he had appointed her favorite son, Willie, to be her companion and counselor. Together mother and son carried the Advent message to Europe (1885–1887) and to Australia and New Zealand (1891–1900). In 1900 she returned permanently to the United States and purchased a small farm near Saint Helena, California, where she died. By the time of her death, her Seventh-day Adventist church had grown to over 136,000 members, who regarded her as "the Lord's messenger," no less inspired than the biblical prophets.

White wrote over a hundred books and pamphlets, as well as thousands of articles. Her publications covered a vast range of subjects, from biblical history and eschatology to masturbation and dress reform. Her most popular work, a devotional booklet called *Steps to Christ* (1892), sold in the millions. She repeatedly insisted on her independence from earthly influences and her dependence on divine illumination, but more recent scholarship has documented that she borrowed extensively from other authors and that her literary assistants provided more than routine editorial and secretarial help.

• There is no satisfactory biography of Ellen G. White. The most complete autobiographical account is *Life Sketches of Ellen G. White* (1915), prepared with the help of assistants. White's grandson Arthur L. White has written a hagiographic six-volume official biography, *Ellen G. White* (1981–1986). Ronald L. Numbers, *Prophetess of Health: Ellen G. White and the Origins of Seventh-day Adventist Health Reform* (rev. ed., 1992), offers a nonapologetic view of her health-related activities, supplemented by a psychological profile of the prophet, coauthored by Janet S. Numbers. The best introduction to White's domestic life is Ronald D. Graybill, "The Power of Prophecy: Ellen G. White and the Women Religious Founders of the Nineteenth Century" (Ph.D. diss., Johns Hopkins Univ., 1983). Jonathan M. Butler has explored her formative years and her eschatological views, respectively, in two articles: "Prophecy, Gender, and Culture: "Ellen Gould Harmon [White] and the Roots of Seventh-day Adventism," *Religion and American Culture* 1 (1991): 3–29; and "The World of Ellen G. White and the End of the World," *Spectrum* 10 (Aug. 1979): 2–13. Evidence of Ellen Harmon's participation in Millerite enthusiasm appears in an article in the *Piscataquis Farmer*, 7 Mar. 1845, discovered by Frederick Hoyt and reprinted in *The Disappointed: Millerism and Millenarianism in the Nineteenth Century*, ed. Ronald L. Numbers and Jonathan M. Butler (rev. ed., 1993). The Ellen G. White Estate in Silver Spring, Md., holds an extensive collection of White's letters and manuscripts, but restrictions govern their use. For guidance in using White's published writings, there is a splendid three-volume *Comprehensive Index to the Writings of Ellen G. White* (1962–1963), supplemented by an additional volume in 1992.

RONALD L. NUMBERS

WHITE, Emerson Elbridge (10 Jan. 1829–21 Oct. 1902), educator, was born in Mantua, Ohio, the son of Jonas White and Sarah McGregory. White attended rural schools in Portage County, Ohio, and then studied at Twinsburg Academy. In 1848 he entered Cleveland University as a student and later became an instructor in mathematics. He left in his senior year to become principal of Mount Union Academy; he also served as principal of a Cleveland grammar school. He resigned to become principal of Cleveland Central High School. In 1853 he married Mary Ann Sabin, with whom he would have five children.

In 1856 White was appointed superintendent of the public schools of Portsmouth, Ohio, and in 1860, not having been reappointed as superintendent, he opened a classical school there. A year later he moved to Columbus and purchased the *Ohio Educational Monthly*, which, under his leadership, became the foremost educational monthly of its kind in the United States and the official organ of the Ohio State Teachers Association. Through the influence of the journal, White became the leading figure in the Ohio school system. He subsequently founded, in 1870, the *National Teacher*, which was published in conjunction with the *Monthly*.

From 1863 to 1866 White served as state commissioner of common schools in Ohio and organized the state board of examiners, which provided financial support for county teachers' pedagogical institutes. In 1865 White codified the school laws of Ohio. In 1863 he became president of the Ohio State Teachers Association; in 1866, the National Association of School Superintendents; in 1872, the National Education Association; and, in 1884–1885, the National Council of Education, an organization he had cofounded. In a paper addressed to the National Superintendents Association in 1866, White advocated the establishment of a national bureau of education. Ohioan James A. Garfield, then a member of the U.S. House of Representatives, asked White to write the legislation that, in 1867, created the U.S. Bureau of Education. White gave up the *Monthly* in 1875 and served as president of Purdue University from 1876 until 1883, when he moved to Cincinnati to write and to lecture on school management and teaching. From 1886 to 1889 White served as superintendent of the Cincinnati Public Schools. Then, in 1891, he returned to his home in Columbus, where he continued to be an influential educational writer.

White's *School Management*, published in 1893, was a lengthy volume on the importance of school discipline, the development of character, and teacher training for school administrators and teachers. It represented an application to education of the management revolution then taking place in America, which promoted efficiency in the workplace. White believed that efficiency could be achieved in the school as in the workplace by instilling in young learners work habits such as regularity, consistency of effort, punctuality, and neatness. The volume covered educational issues ranging from the value of the graded classroom (in which students are divided by age groups, as in first grade, second grade, and so forth) to detailed descriptions of primary, elementary, and secondary classroom activities, such as lesson preparation and execution, testing, classroom discipline, supervisory oversight, and the development of individual subjects, including reading, spelling, and personal health. *School Management* also provided a blueprint for an era in which school attendance among a more diversified population of students was rising and school construction was accelerating to meet the increasing demand for classrooms. White was particularly troubled by smoking among young people and their lack of interest in reading books.

In *The Art of Teaching* (1901), a lengthy volume on pedagogy, White defined teaching as fundamental to the education of young people. For him, teaching, which involved three processes: drilling, testing, and instructing, activated students' mental power, increased their knowledge, and honed their skills. White's work addressed some of the controversies confronting education at the turn of the century, such as oral instruction versus book study and individualization of instruction versus the graded classroom—issues that would continue to be debated by educators over the course of the twentieth century.

Throughout the volume White admonished teachers and administrators to refrain from taxing what he viewed as the fragile physical condition of their pupils by overemphasizing the practice of requiring lessons to be prepared in writing, calling it "the foolish desire of elementary teachers to imitate university methods" (p. 163). On the matter of "cramming and other vicious methods of study," including rote learning and corporal punishment, White was equally critical of current school practices. In sum, *The Art of Teaching* was an enlightened appeal to a new generation of professionally educated teachers to provide a rigorous yet humane elementary and secondary education. Several of White's addresses—among them, "Moral Training in Public Schools," "School Administration in Cities,"

"The Country School Problem," "Election in General Education," and "The Duty of the State in Education"—were published and widely distributed by the U.S. Bureau of Education.

An active Presbyterian throughout his adult life, White was president of the board of trustees of Lane Seminary for many years and often represented his presbytery at the annual General Assembly. He also was a delegate to the Pan-Presbyterian Council in Edinburgh (1877) and in Glasgow (1896). White died at Columbus, Ohio.

• White was a prolific popularizer of late nineteenth-century educational ideas and pedagogy. His works include *A Class-book on Geography* (1863), *Bryant and Stratton Commercial Arithmetic* (1870–1886), *A New Complete Arithmetic* (1883), *Oral Lessons in Number* (1884), *School Reader* (1886), *The Elements of Pedagogy* (1886), *Revised School Records* (1886), *First Book of Arithmetic* (1890), *Moral Instruction in Public Schools* (outlines of a lecture presented to the Nebraska State Teachers Association on 1 Jan. 1891), *School Management* (1893), *Elements of Geometry* (1895), *School Algebra* (1896), and *The Art of Teaching* (1901). For many years after its publication in 1891, teachers in the Midwest used *White's New School Register Containing Forms for Daily, Term, and Yearly Records*. Also see E. E. White and Thomas Harvey, eds., *A History of Education in the State of Ohio* (1876), published by the Ohio Teachers Association Centennial Committee. Obituaries are in the *Cincinnati Enquirer*, 22 Oct. 1902, and the *Ohio Educational Monthly*, Nov. 1902.

ANTHONY PENNA

WHITE, Frances Emily (7 May 1832–29 Dec. 1903), medical educator and social critic, was born in Andover, New Hampshire, the daughter of Thomas R. White and Mary H. May, farmers. During White's childhood her family prospered and moved to the neighboring town of Franklin, a newly established mill center on the Merrimack River. White's father held several town offices and was regarded as an important member of the Congregational church. One of White's older sisters married Austin Pike, Franklin's leading attorney and later a U.S. senator. White, who never married, intermittently lived in the Pike household after her parents' deaths.

Little is documented in White's life between 1850 and 1870. She was not living in Franklin at the time of the 1860 census but returned at some point to be a schoolteacher. In 1870 she left New Hampshire to enroll at the Woman's (later, Women's) Medical College of Pennsylvania. Upon graduating in 1872, she was appointed demonstrator in anatomy and for four years was responsible for acquiring cadavers and supervising dissections. She also taught and experimented with electrotherapeutics and in 1875 was named to the staff of the Woman's Hospital of Philadelphia. In some ways, White typified the late nineteenth-century single American woman who came to medicine late in life because it was more lucrative than teaching. Many contemporaries regarded a medical career as particularly well suited to those possessing the feminine virtues, and the profession was then attracting a growing number of women regardless of age. In contrast to most women physicians, however, White did not remain in clinical practice.

In 1876 White became the first female professor of physiology at her alma mater. While Henry Hartshorne, her predecessor and mentor, had kept up with the latest European developments, his course consisted entirely of lectures. In contrast, White tried to recast physiology education at WMC in the mold of Michael Foster's teaching laboratory at Cambridge University, to which she paid several visits. Although she antagonized her students during her first year on the faculty (for having inserted tangential philosophical discussions into her lectures), she eventually developed a reputation as a nurturing, if rigorous, teacher. She was the first woman to be nominated for membership in the prestigious American Physiological Society and one of the first nominees to be turned down; her rejection was justifiable on the grounds given—that none of her publications was based on original research.

Much more than in advancing science, White was interested in participating in contemporary public debates about evolution and society. Her medical thesis of 1872 advanced notions about human social organization based on the cosmic evolutionary schemes of the English philosopher Herbert Spencer, and the largest number of her eighteen publications appeared in *Popular Science Monthly*, the semiofficial voice of Spencer's thought in America. She delivered a series of lectures on nerve physiology at the Wagner Institute, a mechanic's institute located not far from the Women's Medical College, and she encouraged the college to make its facilities available to the Women's Society for the Promotion of Physiology and Hygiene. She thought of herself as a broadly cultured person, often alluding to music or poetry in her popular expositions of evolutionary theory or human physiology.

White had an important relationship with fellow medical student Elizabeth C. Keller, a widow with three children. The two worked together at a dispensary in a Philadelphia slum neighborhood in the late 1870s, before Keller moved to Boston to establish a surgical practice. Financially secure, Keller contributed money and appliances for White's laboratory and may also have subsidized some of White's travels. When White, suffering from uterine cancer, left her teaching position in 1903 at the Woman's Medical College, she went to Boston to die at Keller's home.

The only formal women's organization that attracted White's attention was the Alumnae Association of the WMC, which she helped found in 1875 and whose resources she helped direct toward student needs. The importance of such an organization to her can be seen in the addresses she delivered at the college, in which she frequently discussed the place of women in medicine and the prejudices they faced. White succeeded in challenging some of the most conservative members of the male-dominated medical world to accept her presence and the presence of women in general. She often represented the Women's Medical College at meetings, and in 1890 she attended the World Medical

Congress in Berlin on behalf of the Philadelphia County Medical Society.

At least as significant to White as the alumnae association were mixed-gender lay organizations. She joined the Philadelphia branch of the Ethical Culture Society soon after it was founded in 1885 and lectured to it several times—once, before a contentious audience, in support of vivisection. In 1887 she also helped establish the Contemporary Club of Philadelphia, a monthly discussion group whose limited membership was drawn from Philadelphia's academic, professional, and business strata. Her presentations to the Contemporary Club reflected her belief that evolution was inevitably leading the human species to higher levels of morality and that the moral traits bred in women through sexual selection would naturally lead to equality between the sexes.

White had nothing to do with the organized woman movement, despite several shared concerns: access of women to the professions, the right of women to be able to live singly and support themselves, and the importance of improving women's health through hygiene, physical culture, proper dress, and knowledge of physiology. As a good Spencerian she was no suffragist, and she spoke against social and political movements that she perceived as trying artificially to accelerate natural processes. While White contributed to the development of both women's medical education and laboratory instruction in this country, her greater significance lies in her attachment to the thought of Herbert Spencer and her advocacy of women's rights based on Spencerian conceptions of human evolution. She was an optimistic, progressive, agnostic, middle-class intellectual woman who enunciated a particular interpretation of evolution theory within American culture.

• There exists no collection of White's personal papers. Her medical thesis and other manuscript materials associated with her studies and teaching at the Women's Medical College are in the Archives and Special Collections on Women in Medicine at the Medical College of Pennsylvania. Also deposited there is a typescript by Edward T. Morman, "Frances Emily White: A Spencerian Woman," which provides an expanded discussion of her life and several of her published works and is accompanied by a complete bibliography of her writings. White's writings on medical science, ethics, evolution, and the woman question include "Woman's Place in Nature," *Popular Science Monthly* 6 (1875): 292–301; "The Relations of the Sexes," *Westminster Review* 111 (1879): 153–60; "Is the Blood a Living Fluid?" *Medical Record* 23 (1883): 564–67; "The Evolution of Morals," *Open Court* 3 (1889): 1775–76, 1788–92; and "The American Medical Woman," *Medical News* 67 (1895): 123–28, and *The Woman's Medical Journal* 4 (1895): 239–46.

EDWARD T. MORMAN

WHITE, George (1890–10 Oct. 1968), dancer, actor, and producer, was born George Weitz in the slums of New York City's Lower East Side. Little is known of his parentage other than that his mother's first name was Lena. He started to work at a tender age as a messenger boy, but he also danced for small change in the music halls of the Bowery until he was seven, when his family moved to Toronto. Canada did not offer him opportunities to be around racehorses, so at the age of eleven he ran away from home and became a racetrack exercise boy and jockey, first in Buffalo, then Detroit. He bet the horses avidly for many years. It was at about this time that he took the name White.

White returned to New York and began his theatrical career as a song-and-dance man in burlesque at the age of fourteen. He continued learning his craft and discovering the tastes of audiences, acting in *The Echo* in 1910, *The Pleasure Seekers* in 1913, and, finally, appearing as a featured dancer in the Ziegfeld *Follies* of 1915.

In 1918 White began his producing career with a group of eight vaudeville-wheel show girls. Perceiving that audiences would happily pay to see any sort of theatrical arrangement of pretty girls in skimpy outfits, White launched his own revue, producing and also acting in the *Scandals of 1919*. His naively suggestive revues avoided the nudity of the *Earl Carroll Vanities*, which came later, and were less extravagant than the revues of Florenz Ziegfeld, who had launched the form in 1907. Ziegfeld's *Follies* dominated the scene before the arrival of *George White's Scandals*, which were so successful that White put together twelve more editions, sometimes taking in as much as $20,000 a week. Unlike his competitors, White did not look for investors to fund his shows. They were produced with his own money; consequently, he was in and out of bankruptcy.

White had a real knack for discovering talent, and between 1919 and 1932 many future stars of stage and screen appeared in his *Scandals*. George Gershwin composed a number for the 1920 edition, Helen Morgan sang in her first (and last) show for White, and Alice Faye, Eleanor Powell, Ann Miller, Dolores Costello, Ethel Merman, and Kate Smith all made their debuts in the *Scandals*. Although the show girls made the revues famous, such comic talents as W. C. Fields, Tom Patricola, Harry Richman, Rudy Vallee, Moran and Mack, and Willie Howard also were featured.

The revue achieved its quintessential form during this period, in no small measure through the work of White. In a revue there was no "book" or story, only a succession of musical numbers punctuated by comic routines. The performers were not the only successful mark of the *Scandals*. The songs they featured revealed White's ability to select and produce quality work. White's revues launched many pop standards, including "Somebody Loves Me," "Life Is Just a Bowl of Cherries," "The Birth of the Blues," and "The Thrill Is Gone." As a dancer, he helped popularize the Turkey Trot, and as a producer he promoted the Black Bottom and the Charleston, popular social dances of the period. On Broadway, White produced such hits as *Manhattan Mary* (1927) and *Flying High* (1930).

The stock market crash of 1929 and the resulting depression, together with changing theatrical tastes, brought an end to regular editions of the revues. However, the *Scandals* were so popular that White wrote, directed, produced, and acted in three movie versions: in 1934, 1935, and 1945. His film acting also included an appearance as himself in the 1945 movie *Rhapsody in Blue*, a screen biography of George Gershwin. The last full-scale *Scandals*, featuring Ann Miller and Ben Blue, played the Alvin Theatre in 1939.

White, an inveterate bachelor, moved to Hollywood in the 1940s in an effort to revive his career. Although he continued to turn out road shows and nightclub revues, he seemed to have lost his sense of innocent charm and tended toward burlesque. In 1942 he filed for voluntary bankruptcy. After recovering financially, in 1946 he was convicted of a hit-and-run accident in which a newly married couple were killed. He served eight and a half months of his one-year sentence. In the 1950s his career was still on the skids, but in 1963 he returned to New York in a financially successful vest-pocket edition of his *Scandals* at Jack Silverman's International Theatre Restaurant. White died five years later in New York City.

Together with Florenz Ziegfeld, Earl Carroll, and a few others, George White created a theatrical form that continues to fill nightclubs, casinos, luxury hotels, and cruise ships and that can still be seen on television variety shows, featuring sparkling song and dance, extravagant displays of feminine pulchritude, and the cream of comic routines.

• There is very little in print about George White, but a small volume entitled *Art Impressions of George White's Scandals* (1926) can be found in the University of Pittsburgh library. Most print information can be found in theatrical works under the heading of "revues." There is considerably more in the way of sound recordings accompanied by notes. Most of these include instrumental and vocal excerpts from a number of White's revues, performed in part by members of the original casts. A typical recording of this kind is *Music of Broadway: The Twenties* (1979), which includes excerpts from both the 1926 and the 1928 *George White Scandals*. An extensive obituary is in the *New York Times*, 12 Oct. 1968.

CARY GLASZ

WHITE, George Henry (18 Dec. 1852–28 Dec. 1918), lawyer and member of Congress, was born in Bladen County, North Carolina, the son of Mary (maiden name unknown) and Wiley F. White. With one grandmother Irish and the other half American Indian, White jocularly described himself as no more than "mostly Negro." Like most black boys in the antebellum South, he had little opportunity for education. A biographical sketch in the *New York Tribune* on 2 January 1898 put it, in graphic understatement, "His early studies were much interrupted because of the necessity he was under to do manual labor on farms and in the forests, and it was not until he was seventeen years old that his serious education was actually begun." After attending a combination of local schools, public and private, and saving up $1,000 from farm work and cask making, White enrolled at Howard University.

White graduated in 1877 and returned to North Carolina. He settled in the old coastal town of New Bern, where he quickly became active in local affairs. At various times he was principal of three black schools, including the state normal school, and read enough law with Judge William J. Clark to earn his law license. In 1880 he won a seat in the state house of representatives as a Republican. After an initial defeat in 1882, he was elected to the state senate and served in the legislature of 1885. In 1886, a few weeks before his thirty-fourth birthday, he won a four-year term as district solicitor for the Second Judicial District, defeating the black incumbent and a white Democrat. Reelected to this position in 1890, he was, according to the *New York Freeman*, the only Negro prosecutor in the country. White prosecuted superior court cases in a six-county area, and his ability was so marked that even his political opponents occasionally praised him. Some whites resented his "presumption" and his demand to be "mistered" like other attorneys, rather than be addressed by an unadorned last name, as was customary with educated African Americans.

In 1894 White moved his home from New Bern to Tarboro so he could seek the Republican nomination in the Second Congressional District, a gerrymandered district that had elected three black congressmen since 1874. The district convention "broke up in a row," however, with both White and his brother-in-law, Henry P. Cheatham, claiming to be the regular nominee. After arbitration by the Republican National Committee, White withdrew from the race, but Cheatham was defeated in the general election, thanks partly to Republican disunity. In 1896, after another tumultuous convention, White won the Republican nomination for Congress and defeated the Democratic incumbent and a Populist nominee. Despite a statewide white supremacy campaign in 1898, he was elected to a second term.

As the only black member of Congress, White believed he spoke for all the nation's black people, not just the voters of the Second District, and he was prepared to reply spiritedly to racist pronouncements by southern congressional colleagues. "How long must we keep quiet," he asked, "constantly sitting down and seeing our rights one by one taken away?" He introduced the first federal antilynching bill and denounced disfranchisement and vote fraud. He also used the patronage power of his office to secure government jobs for his constituents, including some twenty black postmasters.

White supremacy zealots gave Congressman White special prominence during their struggle to defeat the Republican-Populist "fusion" in 1898 and the subsequent movement to disfranchise North Carolina blacks. Under the editorship of Josephus Daniels, the *Raleigh News and Observer* pilloried White as a belligerent man eager "to invite the issue" of white against black. An incident at a Tarboro circus, in which White refused to surrender his seat to a white man, became an "outrage" to many Democratic journalists anxious to demonstrate the dangers of "Negro domination." In 1900, after White denied from the floor of the House that rape was the primary cause of lynching, noting as well that white men were guilty of abusing black women, Daniels fired off an editorial broadside, describing the "nigger Congressman" as "venomous, forward," and "appealing to the worst passions of his own race."

In fact, the prosperous, middle-aged black lawyer was not a fiery militant. Though some historians have portrayed White as "impetuous" or "vindictive," he was in fact a fairly conventional Republican politician, supportive of tariffs and imperialism and suspicious of civil service reform. On racial matters, he advocated caution and strict respect for the law among both black and white. In the climate of the turn of the century, however, he was considered radical merely for demanding, as he said in one speech, "all the privileges of an American citizen."

After the passage in 1900 of the state constitutional amendment disfranchising most black voters, White decided to leave his native state. "I cannot live in North Carolina and be a man and be treated as a man," he told a northern interviewer. In a widely noticed valedictory address during his final session of Congress, he offered the Negro's "temporary farewell to the American Congress," adding the prediction that "Phoenix-like he will rise up some day and come again."

Unsuccessful in seeking an appointive office, White practiced law, first in the District of Columbia, then in Philadelphia. He continued to support efforts to secure civil rights for African Americans, including lawsuits and organized protests through organizations such as the National Association for the Advancement of Colored People. An investor and visionary, he helped establish an all-black community called Whitesboro in the Cape May region of New Jersey.

White married twice, first to Fannie B. Randolph and, upon Fannie's death, to Cora Lina Cherry, daughter of Henry C. Cherry, a former legislator from Edgecombe County. White had one child in his first marriage and three children in his second marriage.

White was an active layman in the Presbyterian church and a leader among the Colored Masons. He died in Philadelphia.

• No collection of White's papers exists. A few manuscripts in his handwriting are preserved in the N.C. legislative papers and court documents of the Second Judicial District, available at the N.C. Department of Archives and History in Raleigh, and scattered letters. White's personality is revealed in his congressional speeches and in his testimony before the Industrial Commission, *Report of the Industrial Commission*, vol. 10, 1901. Useful biographical sketches of White are in the *New York Freeman*, 5 Feb. 1887; the *Raleigh Gazette*, 12 June 1897; D. W. Culp, ed., *Twentieth Century Negro Literature* (1902); Maurine Christopher, *America's Black Congressmen* (1971); and the *Dictionary of North Carolina Biography*, vol. 6 (1996). The article on White in the *Dictionary of American Negro Biography* (1982) exaggerates the importance of his post-1901 career. For his career in N.C. politics, see Eric Anderson, *Race and Politics in North Carolina, 1872–1901: The Black Second* (1981). Samuel Denny Smith's comments on White in *The Negro in Congress, 1870–1901* (1940) are unreliable.

ERIC ANDERSON

WHITE, George Willard (8 July 1903–20 Feb. 1985), geologist and historian, was born in North Lawrence, Ohio, the son of William Sherman White, a Congregationalist minister, and Ora Batavia Battin. His father treated him as an adult from an early age, involving him in the preparation of his sermons; this practice significantly shaped White's professional career. After graduating from Cambridge (Ohio) High School, White entered Otterbein College in Westerville, Ohio, completing his undergraduate degree in 1921. He then entered Ohio State University, from which he received his M.A. in 1925 and his Ph.D. in 1933.

After one year as an instructor in geology at the University of Tennessee (1925–1926), White was appointed an instructor in geology and zoology at the University of New Hampshire in 1926. He married Mildred Kissner in 1928; they had no children. She accompanied him on most of his travels, acting as his secretary and assistant. He remained at New Hampshire until 1941, advancing from instructor to professor. He was the acting dean of the Graduate School in 1940. In 1941 he was appointed professor of geology at Ohio State University, and in 1946–1947 he served as state geologist. He was chairman of the Ohio Water Resources Board in 1946–1947. In 1947 he became professor of geology and head of the Department of Geology at the University of Illinois-Urbana. In 1965 White gave up this position, becoming a research professor. He retired in 1971. From 1944 to 1946 and 1949 to 1976, he held a concurrent appointment with the Water Resources Division of the U.S. Geological Survey. He also consulted with the Ohio Geological Survey from 1972 to 1985.

White's reputation rests on important contributions in geologic research, historical scholarship, and academic administration. He was perhaps the first to adapt principles and methods of stratigraphy and petrography (as applied to the study of consolidated stratified rocks) to interpreting continental glacial deposits. He personally mapped and determined the stratigraphic extent and succession of Wisconsinan till deposits in Ohio and northwestern Pennsylvania. He was also responsible for sending University of Illinois graduate students on regional mapping projects covering most of the continental glacial deposits in the northeastern United States and from Alberta to Quebec in Canada. Because of such work, till stratigraphy and petrography became the dominant methods studying continental glacial deposits.

White's personal contributions to the history of geology include his numerous interpretations of pre-1800 literature of travel and exploration in the eastern United States, emphasizing accounts of geologic observations and discoveries. He published extensively on the history of investigations of continental glaciation in the United States. White also established and led a center of scholarship in the history of geology at the University of Illinois. In support of this, he assembled one of the world's most extensive collections of classic geologic literature for the university library. Most of these books were personally obtained during repeated visits—he went to sixty-seven different European book dealers in eight countries on one trip in 1967—and by correspondence with both European and American antiquarian book dealers over a period of thirty years. At the same time, he assembled a notable personal library of classic works.

White directed an acquisition program that built the University of Illinois Geology Library into one of the most comprehensive in North America. He also stimulated and facilitated translators of classic early geologic treatises, including A. V. Carozzi, Aurèle La Rocque, and Alexander M. Ospovat. In the course of this work, White discovered and purchased a copy of Abraham G. Werner's *Von den Äusserlichen Kennzeichnen der Fossilien*, containing Werner's notes for a second edition that never appeared, and gave it to Carozzi for translation; he also arranged for publication of the translation. In November 1966 White helped organize the International Commission for Study of the History of Geology (INHIGEO) and the History of Geology Section of the Geological Society of America.

On assuming the leadership of the Department of Geology at Illinois—when the once-strong department was in disarray and when the post–World War II academic expansion of American universities was just getting under way—White moved aggressively to organize a research group centered on Pleistocene geology, geomorphology, hydrogeology, and engineering geology. This group included G. Burke Maxey, Don U. Deere, Jack L. Hough, and Paul Shaffer. They operated in association with Morris M. Leighton, John Frye, and H. Bowman Willman of the State Geological Survey of Illinois, and they quickly came to dominate academic Pleistocene study and research. White also encouraged strong research programs in clay mineralogy, stratigraphy, paleontology and sedimentology, fields related to local concerns. Finally, he built an international reputation for the department through the annual appointment of young, active foreign visiting professors. These included Kingsley Dunham, Frank F. H. T. Rhodes, Rhodes Fairbridge, and Carozzi. White also personally recruited foreign graduate students on his travels, carefully assuring himself of their ability to "swim" in American culture and of their professional quality.

White edited the Hafner Publishing Company's series *Contributions to the History of Geology* from its inception in 1967 through 1972, selecting titles for reprinting, locating suitable volumes for photocopy, and writing critical introductions for each volume. White also edited John Playfair's *Illustrations of the Huttonian Theory of the Earth*, a facsimile of the 1802 edition, in 1956.

White was a councillor of the Geological Society of America from 1964 to 1966 and the president of the Geomorphology Group in 1958–1959. He was a fellow of the American Association for the Advancement of Science and its vice president in 1951. White also was an active fellow of the Geological Society (London). He was a charter member of the American Institute of Professional Geologists and an honorary member of the Society of Bibliography of Natural History (London). From 1967 to 1975 he was vice president for North America of the International Commission on the History of Geological Sciences, and he was chairman of the U.S. Commission for the History of Geology in 1974–1975.

White delivered the Annual History of Science George Sarton Memorial Lecture, titled *History of Very Early American Geology*, at the American Association for the Advancement of Science Annual Meeting in 1980. The History of Geology Division of the Geological Society of America granted its first History of Geology Award to White in 1982. White died in Champaign, Illinois.

• White's papers are at the University of Illinois Archives, Urbana, Ill. His publications include "The First Appearance in Ohio of the Theory of Continental Glaciation," *Ohio Journal of Science* 67 (1967): 21–217; "History of Investigation and Classification of Wisconsinan Drift in North-Central United States," *The Wisconsinan Stage*, Geological Society of America Memoir no. 136 (1973); and, with S. M. Totten, "Glacial Geology and the North American Craton: Significant Concepts and Contributions of the Nineteenth Century," in *Geologists and Ideas: A History of North American Geology*, Geological Society of America Special Centennial no. 1 (1986). These works summarize White's contributions to the history of continental glaciation studies. Also see White et al., *Glacial Geology of Northwestern Pennsylvania*, Pennsylvania Geological Survey Bulletin G-32 (1959), and White and Totten, *Glacial Geology of Northeastern Ohio*, Ohio Division of Geological Survey Bulletin 46 (1982), which summarize most of White's research in glacial geology. Basic sources of information include A. V. Carozzi, "Tribute to George White," in *Earth Science History* 2 (1983): 1–3, which includes a bibliography of White's publications on the history of geology; and J. S. Scott et al., "Memorial to George Willard White, 1903–1985," *Geological Society of America Memorials* 17 (1987). An obituary is in the *Champaign-Urbana News Gazette*, 22 Feb. 1985.

RALPH L. LANGENHEIM, JR.

WHITE, Harry Dexter (9 Oct. 1892–16 Aug. 1948), Treasury Department official and moving force in the establishment of the World Bank and International Monetary Fund, was born in Boston, Massachusetts, the son of Sarah Magilewski and Jacob White, Jews who had emigrated to America from Lithuania shortly before he was born. Following his graduation from high school, White worked in the family hardware business until World War I broke out, at which time he became a volunteer in the army. Commissioned as a first lieutenant, he served in France but did not engage in combat. Just before going overseas, White married Russian-born Anne Terry, who later became a successful writer of children's books. They had two daughters.

After leaving the army, White spent three years heading a variety of social services institutions before deciding to return to college in 1922. Having taken courses at the Massachusetts Agricultural College (now the University of Massachusetts at Amherst) in

1911 and 1912, he matriculated at Columbia University. After one year at Columbia, however, he transferred to Stanford University and studied economics. He was awarded a bachelor's degree in 1924 and a master's degree in 1925. He then attended Harvard University, where, under Frank W. Taussig's direction, he earned a doctorate in economics in 1930. Harvard University Press later published his dissertation as *The French International Accounts, 1880–1913* (1933). White taught at Harvard from 1926 to 1932 but was frustrated in his efforts to gain a permanent position.

In 1932 White moved to Appleton, Wisconsin, where he took a position on the faculty at Lawrence College. Two years later he accepted an invitation from Jacob Viner, a University of Chicago economist then working on a research project for the Treasury Department, to spend the summer in Washington examining monetary and banking policy. When the summer ended, he accepted a regular position as an economist in the Treasury Department. One of his first important assignments was to discuss with representatives of the British government an agreement for stabilizing exchange rates. His negotiations helped lay the groundwork for the signing by the United States, Great Britain, and France of the Tripartite Agreement of 1936. The accord was intended to end competitive currency devaluations and thereby increase world trade but stopped short of establishing fixed exchange rates.

Many of White's colleagues disliked his ambition and considered him hard to get along with, but Secretary of the Treasury Henry Morgenthau increasingly came to rely on him, especially on matters relating to international finance and trade. White also tried to use his position to advance the Keynesian idea that countercyclical budget deficits could serve as a remedy for the depression. However, on matters of fiscal policy he exercised little influence and was generally unable to shake Morgenthau's faith in the desirability of balanced budgets.

Well before the start of World War II, both White and Morgenthau concluded that Japanese and German aggression posed a threat to American security. As early as 1936, White helped to arrange a silver purchase agreement between the United States and China, in order to aid that nation in its impending confrontation with Japan. Once the Japanese launched their attack on China in 1937, White continued efforts to facilitate the flow of American aid to the Chinese.

White, however, considered Germany to be even more of a threat to American interests than was Japan. Several months before the signing of the Nazi-Soviet Pact of 1939, White proposed imposing economic sanctions on Germany and developing a new "arrangement" with the Soviet Union that would have been cemented by a $250 million loan to the Soviets. Even in May 1941, when the Nazi-Soviet Pact was still in effect, White continued to hope that the Soviets might be drawn into an anti-Nazi coalition, and that an accommodation with Japan might be worked out so that the United States could focus its attention on Germany.

Once the United States entered the war, White became Morgenthau's chief adviser on all issues relating to foreign affairs. Much of his time was taken up with overseeing American aid to the government of Chiang Kai-shek. Before the end of the war, however, White had come to the conclusion that such aid did little good because of the corrupt and ineffectual nature of Chiang's regime.

White became a key figure in the Treasury Department's planning for the postwar world. Nearly a year before Germany's surrender, Morgenthau assigned White the task of developing a plan to render postwar Germany politically and economically incapable of ever again making "the tools of war." In addition, both Morgenthau and White believed that a plan to partition and deindustrialize Germany would make constructive relations between the United States and the Soviet Union more likely. Morgenthau was even more draconian than White in his desire to destroy Germany's industrial capacity and pressed White to draft a proposal, which became known as "the Morgenthau Plan," that called for dividing postwar Germany into three separate states and returning the German people to a pastoral existence. President Franklin Roosevelt put forth the Morgenthau Plan for discussion at the Yalta Conference, but opposition from other members of the administration caused Roosevelt, and then President Harry S. Truman, to back away from the proposal.

Morgenthau also put White in charge of planning the creation of a new international monetary system to be implemented after the end of the war. White's work in this area had more impact than any other task he undertook during his career in government. He had begun studying the problem of stabilizing postwar currency exchange rates just days after the United States entered the war. His experience in the negotiations leading to the Tripartite Agreement of 1936 proved useful, but he considered that limited agreement to be inadequate as a model for the establishment of an international monetary system that would sustain postwar economic recovery and expand world trade.

By 1942 the "White Plan" had taken shape. It proposed establishing a "United Nations Stabilization Fund" and a "Bank for Reconstruction." Consisting of $5 billion in assets, the stabilization fund was intended to prevent the kind of economic warfare that plagued the world economy during the 1930s—especially currency devaluations and limits on currency exchanges—by making foreign currencies available to nations experiencing short-term difficulties with balance of payments. When formulating their own domestic monetary and fiscal policies, participating nations would be required to consider the concerns of other member states. White's plan called for the United States to contribute approximately 40 percent of the fund's assets. Since voting rights and the ability to draw from the fund would be based on the amount of reserves a nation made available to the fund, the United States would exercise great influence in the new organization. Moreover, the United States would have the only currency that could be converted to gold at a fixed rate. The "Bank for Reconstruction," with an investment of $10 billion, was to have the power to underwrite reconstruction loans made by private institutions and to provide direct loans with its own resources. The bank would also be able to issue currency. Subsequently, White broadened the charge of the bank to include making loans designed to support projects to stimulate long-term economic development.

In wartime Britain, John Maynard Keynes became the central figure in the British effort to plan for the development of a more stable system of international finance and trade. Because Britain would emerge from the war in worse shape economically than the United States, the "Keynes Plan" called for even more sweeping changes than did White's. In contrast to the White Plan, it did not establish for each participating nation set amounts for contributions or drawing rights. The "International Clearing Union" that Keynes envisioned was to operate without any tangible reserves, either currency or gold. Instead, it would serve as a central bookkeeping agency for international transactions that would allow member nations temporarily to overdraw their accounts up to an amount equaling a total of $26 billion. The extent to which a nation could utilize the right to balance its accounts in this way would depend on its prewar share of world trade. The Keynes Plan was thus not only much more favorable to Britain's interests than the White Plan; it also would have done more to foster an expansionary international monetary system. In addition, the Clearing Union would have had considerably less power than White's stabilization fund to intervene in the internal affairs of participating countries.

After two years of ongoing discussions between the United States and Britain, a United Nations conference on the international monetary system took place in July 1944 in Bretton Woods, New Hampshire. As in the previous bilateral discussions, White and Keynes played the leading roles at the Bretton Woods Conference. The plans for an International Monetary Fund (IMF) that emerged from the conference to some extent reflected Keynes's influence, but, on the whole, White's conception of the fund triumphed.

The IMF did not initially allow for the kind of overdrafts Keynes had proposed as a means of fostering world trade (though this would change in 1969), but White and the participants at Bretton Woods did agree to the establishment of larger IMF reserves ($8.8 billion) than White had originally suggested and to the reduction of the contribution of the United States from roughly two-fifths to one-third of the total amount. White was also forced to compromise with regard to the extent of the IMF's powers to police the domestic policies and to approve all currency devaluations of member states. On the other hand, Keynes failed in his efforts to write into the IMF charter the right of participating countries to make use of their drawing rights without any oversight. The British did win American assent to a "scarce-currency clause" in the charter, which recognized the possibility that nations with unfavorable trade balances and weak currencies might have to impose temporary restrictions on imports from creditor nations with trade surpluses. Such a clause was obviously designed to allow debtor nations to limit imports from the United States.

The Bretton Woods Conference also agreed to the establishment of an International Bank for Reconstruction and Development (World Bank) that was to operate with $10 billion of capital. However, the bank was granted narrower powers than White initially proposed. It could neither issue its own currency nor provide loans for a wide variety of long-term economic development projects.

The Soviet Union's participation in the Bretton Woods Conference pleased White, for he had long been eager to have Soviet involvement in the new international institutions to help foster continued Soviet-American cooperation once the war ended. To win Soviet approval for the Bretton Woods accords, White and Morgenthau agreed to assign the Soviet Union a bigger quota in the IMF than had been initially proposed in the White Plan. White also subsequently supported a $10 billion loan by the United States to aid the postwar reconstruction of the Soviet economy. In the end, however, Soviet suspicions of the West and the emerging Cold War conflict between the United States and the Soviet Union caused the Soviets to stay out of the IMF and the World Bank.

The United States did not ratify the Bretton Woods accords until the summer of 1945. Congressional approval came only after President Truman agreed to certain provisions that gave a cabinet-level committee some control over the American who would serve on the IMF's board of directors. In early 1946 White became the first American executive director of the IMF, which established its permanent headquarters in Washington.

Most nations in 1946 and 1947 experienced larger dollar shortages than White had expected. As a result, the IMF was unable to prevent many nations from imposing exchange restrictions and engaging in bilateral trade agreements. Not until the Marshall Plan went into effect did the postwar recovery in Europe begin to make major headway, thereby creating the conditions that allowed the IMF to function more along the lines that White had envisioned.

Senate confirmation of White's appointment to the IMF took place just before President Truman learned that White was the subject of charges implicating him in a Soviet espionage plot. In 1945 Elizabeth Bentley, who admitted to having been a communist agent and who later became a prominent informant for the Federal Bureau of Investigation (FBI), told the FBI that during the war White had passed on secret documents from the Treasury Department to agents working for the Soviet Union. In order not to interfere with an ongoing FBI investigation into possible Soviet espionage, Truman allowed White to remain in his position at the IMF until March 1947, when White resigned without fanfare.

On 31 July 1948, in testimony before the House Un-American Activities Committee (HUAC), Bentley made her charges against White public. However, she never claimed to have had any personal contact with White, and she had no evidence to the effect that White spied for the Soviets. On 3 August 1948 ex-communist Whittaker Chambers told HUAC that he knew White and believed that he was a long-time "fellow traveller," but Chambers made no claim at that time that White had been involved in espionage.

At the time of the HUAC hearings White was living in New York, where he worked as a private consultant. The previous September he had experienced a serious heart attack and had still not fully regained his health. Despite this fact, White immediately asked HUAC for a chance to rebut the charges made by Bentley and Chambers. In testimony to the committee on 13 August 1948, he proclaimed his innocence, stating that he had never been either a communist or a spy. Just days after appearing before HUAC, White suffered a second heart attack and died at his summer home near Fitzwilliam, New Hampshire.

Only after White died did Chambers for the first time tell the FBI that he had personal knowledge of White's involvement in a Soviet spy ring. White's innocence or guilt remained a source of ongoing controversy. In 1995 the National Security Agency released copies of decrypted Soviet cables, which American intelligence had intercepted during World War II as part of the Venona project, that seemed to confirm the charge that White had passed on information to agents of the Soviet Union.

Charges that White functioned as a communist agent are rather ironic given that his most important government service involved his role in the founding of the IMF and World Bank, institutions that became closely identified with post–World War II capitalism. There is no evidence that sympathy for the Soviet Union affected White's basic conception of these institutions; nor did the Soviet Union opt to participate in them. These institutions may not have been as successful as White had hoped they would be in encouraging the growth of world trade and economic development, but they have remained his most enduring legacy.

• White's papers are in the Princeton University Library. A smaller selection of letters, memoranda, and documents, taken from White's home several years after his death, were published by the U.S. Government Printing Office in 1956 as part of a volume entitled *Interlocking Subversion in Government Departments*. White's own writings, in addition to the book cited in the text, include three articles dealing with the postwar international monetary system: "Postwar Currency Stabilization," *American Economic Review*, Mar. 1943, pp. 382–87; "The Monetary Fund: Some Criticisms Examined," *Foreign Affairs*, Jan. 1945, pp. 195–210; and "The International Monetary Fund: The First Year," *Annals of the American Academy of Political and Social Science*, July 1947, pp. 21–29.

The most important work on White is David Rees, *Harry Dexter White: A Study in Paradox* (1973). Rees reached no definitive conclusion about White's possible role as a Soviet agent, but he acknowledged the plausibility of the charge. A good deal of useful information about White is in John Morton Blum, *From the Morgenthau Diaries* (3 vols., 1959–1967). Nathan I. White wrote a sympathetic account of his brother's life, *Harry Dexter White: Loyal American* (1956), that was privately published by White's sister Bessie. Athan Theoharis questions the charges of communism made against White in "Unanswered Questions: Chambers, Nixon, the FBI, and the Hiss Case," in *Beyond the Hiss Case, the FBI, Congress, and the Cold War* (1982). See also Charles L. Whipple, "The Life and Death of Harry Dexter White," a twelve-part series that appeared in the *Boston Globe* beginning 15 Nov. 1953.

LARRY GERBER

WHITE, Helen Constance (26 Nov. 1896–7 June 1967), novelist and educator, was born in New Haven, Connecticut, the daughter of John White, a railroad clerk and civil servant, and Mary Josephine King. When White was five years old the family moved from New Haven to Boston, and White attended Girl's High School and then Radcliffe College, where she received her B.A. in three years and her M.A. in the following year (1917). White then spent two years teaching at Smith College before deciding to pursue the Ph.D. in English literature at the University of Wisconsin at Madison. She completed her studies, receiving the Ph.D. in 1924, and quickly published her doctoral dissertation as *The Mysticism of William Blake* (1927). On the strength of that work she was awarded a Guggenheim Fellowship in 1928 and spent two years in England researching the material that became her next major scholarly work, *English Devotional Literature* (1931). White returned to Wisconsin and taught there for the rest of her life, becoming the first female full professor in the university's history (1936) and one of the first female chairs of the English department (1955–1958 and 1961–1965).

White's professional career epitomizes the single-mindedness that characterized academic women in the early years of this century. She never married. In addition to her teaching, scholarly publications, novels, and administrative work, she was a diligent joiner of professional associations. At various times she served as president of the University of Wisconsin Teachers Union, the national president of the American Association of University Women, the president of the local University Club, and a U.S. delegate to UNESCO meetings.

White's scholarly books—primarily studies of mysticism in a variety of British authors—now appear dated, but in their day they opened up new fields of inquiry. In addition to the two studies mentioned above, she also published *The Metaphysical Poets* (1936), *Social Criticism in Popular Religious Literature of the Sixteenth Century* (1944), *Changing Styles in Literary Studies* (1963), and a number of edited anthologies: *Victorian Prose* (with Frances A. Foster, 1930), *Seventeenth-Century Verse and Prose* (with Ruth Wallerstein and Ricardo Quintana, 1951), *The Tudor Books of Pri-*

vate Devotion (1951), *Prayer and Poetry* (1960), and the *Tudor Books of Saints and Martyrs* (1963).

White's scholarly works gained her a prominent status in the academic profession, but her wider fame came from her reputation as a historical novelist. She published six historical novels, each set at a crucial period in the development of the history of the Catholic church. These novels earned her a place in the Gallery of Living Catholic Authors, where she was feted as "a novelist of first-class importance" (Michael Williams, *Commonweal*, 19 Apr. 1933, pp. 694–95). Her first novel, *Watch in the Night* (1933), follows the career of a thirteenth-century worldly lawyer, Jacomo da Todi, who forsakes the world and becomes the Franciscan spiritualist Jacopone, "the wild man of God." The novel concerns his futile attempt to overthrow the corrupt Pope Boniface VIII. *Not Built with Hands* (1935) focuses on the meeting in 1077 of Henry IV of England and Pope Gregory VII at Canossa. The issue under debate was priestly celibacy, which the pope supported against the wishes of his priests and Henry. The pope was aided in his struggle by Matilda of Tuscany, who lost her husband and army in the ensuing battle. *To the End of the World* (1939) follows the struggle that a young French priest undergoes with his conscience during the French revolutionary period. *Dust on the King's Highway* (1947) concerns the conflict that develops between the missionary Franciscan friars in California and the secular Spanish government. *Four Rivers of Paradise* (1955) concerns the history of Honorius and his attempt to equate heresy with treason against the Roman state, whereas *Bird of Fire* (1958) traces the life of St. Francis of Assisi. All of White's novels follow the same basic pattern: a religious principle or objective is blocked by a secular or pragmatic concern, and the conflict temporarily defeats the spiritual forces of good. God always works in mysterious ways, however, and the spiritual ends up victorious in the end.

White's Catholic novels are not widely read today, even by Catholics. Although she was lauded in her own day, and although there were high hopes that she would be a pioneer in the new field of "Catholic culture," such a culture has not developed on a widespread basis despite the increasing numbers of university-educated Catholics who presumably would form a large audience interested in reading material with a decidedly Catholic viewpoint. The issues that White addresses in her novels—the futility of armed resistance to evil, the corruption of human institutions, the preferential option for the poor—are perennial concerns within the Catholic community. And White's novels do provide a revealing series of microcosmic examinations of these issues as they were worked out in specific historical periods. Their major weakness may have resulted from their sheer bulk and weight. Each book is discursive, with multiple narratives running in a manner that diffuses the main plot line. White's language was frequently commended by reviewers as a major strength in her writing, but just as often it was noted that the luxuriant details and extemporaneous tone undercut the focus and power of the piece.

White died in Norwood, Massachusetts. Her novels and scholarly studies have long been out of print, but she is important as a pioneering model of the female academic who produced such a massive body of work that even a male-dominated literary establishment had to take her seriously.

• White's personal and professional papers are held in the University of Wisconsin at Madison Library Archives. The most extensive discussion of White's career can be found in Toni A. McNaron, *The Purple Goddess: A Memoir of Helen Constance White* (1985). A valuable source on her teaching is the volume assembled by her former students Margaret Thoma, Mark Schorer, August Derleth, and Harold Latham, *Helen Constance White* (1942). Also see Austin J. App, "Contemporary Catholic Authors: Helen C. White, Scholar and Historical Novelist," *Catholic Library World* 11 (1939–1940): 195–202, for a valuable discussion of the novels within a Catholic context. Brief biographies appear in a number of sources: *American Women Writers*, vol. 4 (1982); *Famous Wisconsin Women*, vol. 6 (1976); *American Authors and Books*, 3d ed. (1972); Harry Warfel, *American Novelists of Today* (1976); *Book of Catholic Authors*, 3d ser. (1945); *Catholic Authors*, vol. 1 (1981); *Twentieth-Century Authors: A Biographical Dictionary of Modern Literature* (1955); *Contemporary American Authors: A Critical Survey and 219 Bio-bibliographies* (1970); *Contemporary Authors* (1969); *Who Was Who in Literature, 1906–1934* (1979); *Index to Women of the World from Ancient to Modern Times* (1970); and *Current Biography Yearbook* (1945). Her novels were widely reviewed at the time of their publications in journals like *Commonweal*, the *New York Times Book Review*, and *Catholic World*.

DIANE LONG HOEVELER

WHITE, Helen Magill (28 Nov. 1853–28 Oct. 1944), educator, was born in Providence, Rhode Island, the daughter of Edward Hicks Magill, an educator, and Sarah Warner Beans. Both her parents were Quakers and strong believers in women's rights and education for women, particularly in a coeducational setting. Her father tutored Helen until 1863, when she enrolled in the Boston Public Latin School, where he was a submaster and teacher of languages. Helen was the school's first and only female student and thus had difficulty making friends. She compensated by dedicating her childhood to her education.

In 1869, at age fifteen, Magill entered newly established, coeducational Swarthmore College, where her father had been named president. Believing that women could earn equality through academic accomplishments, she worked relentlessly to fulfill her parents' and her own expectations. She was once again socially isolated by her dedication to her studies and her awkward position as daughter of the college president. She preferred the long-distance companionship of Eva Channing, her lifelong correspondent. In 1873 she graduated second out of six in Swarthmore's first graduating class.

After two years of postgraduate study at Swarthmore, Magill entered the doctoral program at Boston University to prepare herself for a career as a university professor and classical scholar. She earned a Ph.D. in Greek in 1877, earning a place in history by becoming the first American woman to obtain a doctorate. However, she was not impressed by the rigor of her program at Boston University and tended to make light of her achievement. Seeking more rigorous classical training, she attended Cambridge University in England (1877–1881), where she was one of a small number of women students. The culmination of study at Cambridge was an honors examination, the tripos. Magill was ill when she took the examination and disappointingly finished in the third rank, the lowest passing rank. Although this did not reflect her true level of scholarship, the performance diminished her job prospects.

Magill returned to the United States in 1882 to accept a position as principal of the coeducational English Classical Academy in Johnstown, Pennsylvania. This proved to be an unsatisfactory experience, and she leaped at the opportunity, in 1883, to organize and administer the Howard Collegiate Institute in West Bridgewater, Massachusetts. This all-female preparatory high school was not in keeping with her ambitions in higher education, but she was attracted by the possibility that it might develop into the first true liberal arts college for women. Her father, who had a financial interest in the school, urged her to accept the position and to hire two of her sisters as teachers. She successfully launched the school, but she eventually alienated the school's trustees, in part because of her "unwomanly" assertiveness and lack of diplomacy. The personality conflict was exacerbated by the precarious financial condition of the school, which had the misfortune of being established at the same time as public high schools were emerging. Magill resigned in 1887 with her confidence shaken, her reputation compromised, her father in debt, and her sisters unemployed. She was fortunate to secure a teaching position at Evelyn College, the newly established women's college of Princeton University, but she was dismissed after a year because of her ill health and cutbacks in the faculty. After taking a year off, she unenthusiastically taught physical geography for a short time at a Brooklyn, New York, high school. In 1890, at age thirty-six, she chose to end her once promising career as an educator when she married Andrew Dickson White, a man more than twenty years her senior.

White, a Yale classmate of Edward Magill, was a prominent educator who had recently retired as president of Cornell University. Helen Magill had met him in September 1887 at the annual meeting of the American Social Science Association, at which she presented a paper entitled "Progress in the Education of Women," and they became regular correspondents. White credited her with helping him through the depression that followed the death of his first wife in 1887. Despite her career ambitions and her strong beliefs in the equality of women, Helen Magill White believed that wife and mother were the primary roles for women and that these could not be combined with a career. She nonetheless refused to be an acquiescent wife, as Andrew expected, and the clash of these strong-willed individuals produced a turbulent marriage. They also endured the infant deaths of two of their three children.

Andrew White was appointed minister to Russia in 1892, but the Whites found Russia culturally isolated and intellectually unsatisfying. He resigned his post in 1894. In 1897 President McKinley appointed him ambassador to Germany. The Whites were delighted by life in Berlin, probably the happiest period in their marriage. Helen White reveled in her role as a diplomatic hostess and was popular among the German social elite. After her husband retired at the end of 1902, the Whites spent the next two years in Alassio, Italy, before returning to settle in Ithaca, New York.

Following her husband's death in November 1918, White continued to live in Ithaca until the early 1930s, when she moved to Kittery Point, Maine, to be close to her sister Beatrice. She died there, after having been an invalid for ten years. Her life epitomized the conflicting public and private roles of college-educated women in the nineteenth century and the obstacles faced by those individuals who sought to move outside their socially dictated sphere.

• The Helen Magill White Papers, held by Cornell University, contain correspondence with her family, Andrew Dickson White, and Eva Channing. Cornell also has microfilm copies of her diaries, which she kept intermittently between 1867 and 1933. Her writings include "The Greek Drama" (Ph.D. diss., Boston Univ., 1877); "Women's Work in the Nineteenth Century," *The Independent*, 5 Oct. 1882; and *What Is a Collegiate Institute?* (1884). An excellent biography is Glenn C. Altschuler, *Better than Second Best: Love and Work in the Life of Helen Magill* (1990). Other useful sources are her daughter Karin White's papers, the microfilm edition of her diaries, and the papers of Andrew Dickson White, all held by Cornell. Also helpful are Edward H. Magill, *Sixty-Five Years in the Life of a Teacher, 1841–1906* (1907), and Andrew Dickson White, *Autobiography of Andrew Dickson White* (1905). An obituary is in the *New York Times*, 30 Oct. 1944.

PATRICK F. CALLAHAN

WHITE, Henry (28 Mar. 1732–23 Dec. 1786), Loyalist and merchant, was born in Maryland, the son of a British colonel. His parents' names are unknown. His father had immigrated to Maryland in 1712. White went to England for his education but then returned to America and settled in New York City. He flourished in the merchant trade during the French and Indian War, serving as a commissary for the British forces. In 1761 he married Eva Van Cortlandt. They had several sons.

In the years that followed the French and Indian War, White emerged as an important defender of the political status quo in New York. Although he joined with other merchants in objecting to the Stamp Act, he did so on economic grounds. He believed in constitutional theory that King George III and the British Parliament were indeed sovereign in all matters over the colonies. White was sworn in as a member of the New York Governor's Council on 8 March 1769 and served on that body until 1783. He was on friendly terms with Governor William Tryon, and, after the repeal of the Townshend Duties in 1770, he refrained from any further objections to British colonial policy. In 1773 White was named as one of the three New York City merchants to whom the tea brought by the East India Company was consigned. Consequently, he soon found himself in a predicament.

Even prior to learning that on 16 December 1773 the colonists in Boston had dumped tea into Boston Harbor, White and his two fellow tea agents had informed Governor Tryon they would not accept the tea, knowing the dangers they might face. White, one of his fellow tea agents, and another member of the Governor's Council made a secret agreement with the Sons of Liberty, under which the tea would be sent back to England. In a letter to Lord Dartmouth, Governor Tryon explained that only bayonets, muskets, and rifles could have persuaded the colonists to allow him to land the tea and that even then he could hardly be assured that the tea would be purchased and consumed. White had made the best of a dangerous situation, and he perhaps deserves some credit for the fact that New York escaped the type of turmoil that Boston experienced during the end of 1773.

Governor Tryon made White his personal agent and attorney before leaving for England in 1774. The start of the Revolution in April 1775 left White in a precarious position. Although he was not an obvious Loyalist, he came under suspicion because of a letter to him from Governor Josiah Martin of North Carolina. Martin asked White to provide a royal standard and supplies. Questioned by a committee of the New York Provincial Congress, White declared he had not sent the standard, and the committee was satisfied temporarily with his explanation. However, in May 1776 he became known to the Sons of Liberty as one of the "Odious Six," a group of English sympathizers consisting of White, Cadwallader Colden, Myles Cooper, James De Lancey, John Watts, and James Rivington. After his safety was threatened several times, White fled for England.

White returned to New York City in the autumn of 1776, following the capture of that city by a combined land and sea assault led by the brothers Sir William Howe and Lord Richard Howe. Governor Tryon, who had also returned to New York, wrote to Lord George German in England that White was "very usefull to me from his influence among the Citizens, in such regulations of Police as are left me in my restricted sphere of executive power" (*New York Colonial Documents*, vol. 8, p. 691). White was among the signers of the Loyal Address to the Howe brothers and was active in the Loyalist political affairs of the city during the years of occupation (1776–1783). The British Commissioners for Restoring Peace included White on a list of ten persons who might serve on an intercolonial council to govern America in the future.

As a result of these activities, White was named in the New York State Act of Attainder in 1779. His numerous properties were confiscated, and he was threatened with execution if he were captured within the state. Faced with this, White and his family accompanied the British troops when they evacuated New York City in 1783. The terms of his will, drawn up in London, indicate he was still a wealthy man at the time of his death in London.

White's life and career left a divided legacy. Clearly a man of moderation in public affairs and, it may be surmised, a true believer in the British imperial system, his actions caused him to become reviled in the city and state where he spent most of his life. It is possible that his association with Governor Tryon provided the means of his undoing. Tryon was greatly hated for his association with a series of particularly brutal military raids on civilian targets. During his sojourn in occupied New York City, White apparently acted in a conciliatory manner, but his associations with the British occupying forces made him a wanted man by the American patriots. Throughout White's story runs the element of tragedy, common to many of the Loyalists who tried to maintain their connections to both England and their home provinces.

• Few sources on White's life and career exist. E. B. O'Callaghan, ed., *Documents Relative to the Colonial History of the State of New York*, vol. 8 (15 vols., 1853–1887), and Lorenzo Sabine, *Biographical Sketches of Loyalists of the American Revolution* (1864), provide some information. See also J. A. Stevens, "Henry White and His Family," *Magazine of American History*, Dec. 1877; and Peter Force, *American Archives*, 4th ser., vol. 2 (1839).

SAMUEL WILLARD CROMPTON

WHITE, Henry (29 Mar. 1850–15 July 1927), diplomat, was born in Baltimore, Maryland, the son of John Campbell White, a wealthy landowner, and Eliza Ridgely. After the death of White's father in 1853, White's mother moved the family to "Hampton," a large plantation owned by his mother's family approximately twelve miles from Baltimore. In 1857 and 1858 White traveled with his mother in Europe, where he became familiar with European traditions and learned French and Italian. In 1865 White's mother married Thomas Hepburn Buckler, a Baltimore physician.

During the next five years, White spent most of his time in France, Italy, and Germany with his mother and stepfather. In 1870 they moved to England to avoid the turmoil on the Continent caused by the Franco-Prussian War. Though White hoped to attend Cambridge University, Buckler prescribed an outdoor education in hopes it would cure a pulmonary condition White had contracted. White, who had attended American and French private schools, was thus exposed to private tutors and a strict disciplinary code formulated by his mother, who repeatedly questioned him on the Bible and spoke to him in Italian. Although he visited the United States several times during the 1870s, he was more familiar with European customs, such as fox hunting, English society, and country houses, than with post–Civil War America.

In 1879 White married Margaret Stuyvesant Rutherfurd, daughter of Lewis Morris Rutherfurd, a noted astronomer. They had two children. In 1883 President Chester A. Arthur appointed White secretary of the American legation in Vienna to serve under Alphonso Taft, whose son William Howard Taft would be president of the United States. This position began White's long and distinguished diplomatic career. In Vienna White learned German and the intricacies of diplomacy.

Later in 1883 White was transferred to the second secretaryship in London, where his knowledge of British politics and society added immeasurably to his diplomatic role. He ultimately achieved the post of first secretary, serving under such distinguished American ambassadors as James Russell Lowell, Edward John Phelps, and Robert Todd Lincoln. In this capacity White helped to resolve Canadian fishing and sealing controversies. In 1887–1888 he represented the United States at the international conference in London for the abolition of sugar bounties. President Grover Cleveland, a Democrat, replaced White in 1893. During the Democratic administration White acted unofficially as Secretary of State Richard Olney's representative in the Venezuelan boundary dispute with Great Britain.

After the Republicans returned to the White House in 1897, White's career and reputation gained momentum. President William McKinley offered him the ambassadorship to Spain or his former job as first secretary in London. He chose the latter, serving eight years under Ambassadors John Hay and Joseph Choate, and once again his tact, skill, and ability won praise from British leaders. On various occasions White served as intermediary, interpreter, and acting chargé d'affaires. He helped settle the Alaskan boundary and paved the way for the abrogation of the Clayton-Bulwer Treaty of 1850, allowing negotiations that produced the Hay-Pauncefote Treaty of 1901, which secured exclusive U.S. control over an isthmian canal.

White advised Secretary of State Hay on the 1900 Boxer Revolt, an attempt by Chinese revolutionaries to expel foreigners from China. In addition, White corresponded with Hay on the Open Door policy, designed to secure equal commercial opportunity in China and avoid discriminatory tariffs and other commercial barriers by foreign powers in regions of China under their influence. Altogether White's views and guiding efforts helped to encourage and strengthen Anglo-American rapprochement. During his presidency, Theodore Roosevelt considered White the most useful person in the diplomatic corps.

In 1905 President Roosevelt appointed White ambassador to Italy. That year White also went to Rome as senior U.S. delegate to the International Conference on Agriculture. In 1906 he was the American representative to the international Algeciras Conference in Spain, which affirmed the independence and territorial integrity of Morocco and guaranteed equality of commercial opportunities. He realized that the door actually had not been opened in the way Roosevelt had desired, but it may have prevented war. In 1907 White became ambassador to France.

In 1909, for personal reasons, President William Howard Taft removed White as ambassador to France, immediately incurring the wrath of Roosevelt and Republican senator Henry Cabot Lodge of Massachusetts. White remained in Europe for some time thereafter and in 1910 accompanied former president Roosevelt to Germany and England. Later that year Taft asked White to head the American delegation to the fourth Pan-American Conference in Argentina and also in 1910 designated him as special ambassador to Chile for the celebration of the centenary of Chilean independence. Harboring no resentment toward the beleaguered president, White graciously accepted the assignments and once again performed valuable services.

White returned to the United States in 1911. He built a house in Washington and enjoyed the city's social life. He kept in close touch with the British ambassador to the United States and with leading members of Congress. He was in Germany on a personal visit in 1914 when war broke out in Europe.

The First World War and the making of the peace treaty tested White's shrewdness and capabilities as a diplomat. He was the Potomac regional director of the American Red Cross and president of the War Camp Community in 1917 and 1918. In November 1918, upon the conclusion of the war, President Woodrow Wilson, a Democrat, appointed White to the commission that accompanied him to Paris to negotiate the peace treaty. The president saw White as a moderate who had connections with the Central Powers as well as the Allied countries. Surprised by the offer, White dutifully accepted. He sailed to France, where Wilson conferred with the British, French, and Italian leaders on the terms to impose on the defeated Germany and its former partners. Wilson's direct participation in the Versailles conference angered some Republican members of Congress, who believed that he could have negotiated from a stronger position at home. Moreover, his decision not to include any prominent Republicans, such as former president Taft, resulted in partisan mistrust of what should have been a nonpartisan endeavor. Although a nominal Republican, White was not considered by the party's leaders to be in their political league. Yet Wilson's invitation to White demonstrated the confidence leaders of both parties had in him.

Although Wilson played the major American role in drafting the treaty, White's influence was keenly felt. He opposed the extraordinary demands of Italy, France, and Poland for territory and for continuing the French food blockade of Germany. He was also cognizant of the folly of the revenge that the victors tried to extract from Germany. After Wilson and Secretary of State Robert Lansing returned to the United States, White was acting chairman of the American delegation.

White's most useful service in 1919 was in attempting to convince opponents of the necessity of a League of Nations. Once opposed to the league himself, he was quickly converted by touring war-ravaged Europe and witnessing firsthand the plight of millions of people. He thus believed the league would prevent future hideous conflicts.

The issue of the League of Nations divided White and Senator Lodge. Objecting to many of Lodge's statements regarding the league, White contended that Lodge revealed a marked ignorance of the realities in Europe. White was more afraid of Germany's political and economic collapse than Lodge, and he contended that, without a league, nations would settle international disputes only through more warfare. White wanted Lodge to cable him as to the clarifying amendments the U.S. Senate would want attached to the covenant before ratifying the treaty by the constitutionally required two-thirds vote. Fearing a trick instigated by Wilson, Lodge refused to cooperate. In reality, White acted on his own, without consulting with the president.

The Senate's rejection of the peace treaty and the attached league covenant on three occasions in 1919 and 1920 profoundly disappointed White. He blamed mostly the Senate "Irreconcilables," who stubbornly refused to endorse the league in any form, but he also thought that Wilson was wrong not to accept the mild reservations, which in his opinion would not have altered the character of the league. In 1920 White accurately predicted that the treaty would be smashed by the American electorate in the presidential election, which was indeed won by Warren G. Harding of Ohio. The postwar isolationist sentiment in the United States further disheartened White.

White spent his final years encouraging the professional development of diplomacy as a career. During this time he was also a generous supporter of the National Episcopal Cathedral in Washington. In 1920, four years after the death of his first wife, White married Emily Vanderbilt Sloane, a daughter of William H. Vanderbilt, the wealthy railroad magnate and financier. White died at his summer home, "Elm Court," in Lenox, a small town close to Pittsfield, Massachusetts.

White was one of the most accomplished diplomats the United States has produced. Considered the dean of American diplomats, he held distinctly progressive and liberal opinions on international affairs and saw diplomacy as an art that allowed nations to help one another to mutual advantage. He believed a successful diplomat must understand the psychology of foreign peoples and must look at issues through their eyes and from their positions. White never engaged in any business except diplomacy and never held elective office, but he was always ready to serve the nation, regardless of which party controlled the executive branch.

• White's papers are in the Manuscripts Division of the Library of Congress and in the State Department Archives in Washington, D.C. Many of his letters are also in the collections of prominent contemporaries, including Theodore Roosevelt, William Howard Taft, and Woodrow Wilson in the Manuscripts Division of the Library of Congress and the Henry Cabot Lodge Papers at the Massachusetts Historical Society in Boston. The major biography of White is Allan Nevins, *Henry White: Thirty Years of American Diplomacy* (1930). An obituary is in the *New York Times*, 16 July 1927.

LEONARD SCHLUP

WHITE, Henry Clay (30 Dec. 1848–30 Nov. 1927), chemist and educator, was born in Baltimore, Maryland, the son of Levi Stratton White, a merchant, and Louisa Elvira Brown. After attending schools in Baltimore, White entered the University of Virginia. After receiving his B.S. degree in chemistry and engineering in 1870, he took employment with a local chemical firm and presented lectures at the Peabody Institute and the Maryland Institute for the Promotion of Mechanic Arts. In June 1871 White accepted appointment as professor of chemistry at St. John's College, in Annapolis, but he remained there for only one year, giving up the position in 1872 to join the faculty of the University of Georgia. In that same year he married Ella Frances Roberts; they had no children.

Although his duties varied over the years, White always retained the title of professor of chemistry during his fifty-five year association with the University of Georgia. When he arrived in Georgia, White found an institution that "did not [even] own a test tube." Within a short time, however, he succeeded in establishing "the first modern chemical laboratory South of Virginia." Aware of the importance of agriculture in the region, he turned his attention to research in agricultural chemistry, especially to analyses of the cotton plant, soils, and fertilizers, and he began to publish his studies in the proceedings of the Georgia State Agricultural Society. His investigations into the quality of fertilizers in 1873–1875 played a significant role in the establishment of the Georgia State Department of Agriculture in 1876.

During the next three decades White held a number of ancillary appointments, serving as chemist for the State Geological Survey from 1876 to 1878, as state chemist from 1880 to 1890, and as chemist (1888–1914) and vice director (1891–1912) for the Experiment Station in Georgia. A key figure in establishing the Experiment Station in 1888, White contributed a number of articles to its *Bulletin*. The original purpose of the Experimental Station was to find ways to improve crop production and to analyze the contents of commercial fertilizers. White's efforts in behalf of the state enhanced his reputation, and in 1888 a number of public leaders and several members of the University of Georgia Board of Trustees, including his friend, "New South" spokesman Henry W. Grady, considered him to be the best person to succeed the retiring chancellor of the university. Many of the older trustees opposed his appointment, however, because they viewed him as too liberal on social matters. It is likely that some of them also feared that White's open advocacy of the theory of evolution was distasteful to denominationalists, many of whom had been attacking the university for several years. Certainly, at least one member of the board, the bishop of the Episcopal Diocese of Georgia, was strongly opposed to the theory of evolution. In any case, White lost the contest by a single vote. Only two years later, however, the trustees appointed him as the president of the State College of Agriculture and Mechanic Arts, which was affiliated with the university. As president of the A & M College, White sought to improve the state of agriculture in Georgia by initiating "a system of Farmers' Institutes" to promote scientific agriculture and by advocating "village farming," which would concentrate farmers in small communities to allow for "intensive farming," "mutual assistance," and better "social intercourse." A considerable number of Georgia agriculturists opposed White's ideas, however, and they criticized him for his lack of practical experience. In effect, they wanted to turn the college into a professional school, and White had to ward off many attempts to sever ties between the college and the university. Through persistence and persuasion, White triumphed, and the A & M College was integrated fully into the university in 1906 as the College of Agriculture. White stepped aside as the chief administrator the next year.

Meanwhile, White was gaining national and international notice. Elected to membership in Britain's Royal Chemical Society in 1893 for his "meritorious services and contributions to science," he was a corresponding member of the British Association for the Advancement of Science and an honorary member of the Academy of Sciences of Belgium. He took an active part in the affairs of the American Association of Official Agricultural Chemists, the National Education Association, of which he served as vice president in 1898–1899, and, especially, the Association of American Agricultural Colleges and Experiment Stations, of which he served on the executive committee for sixteen years and as president in 1897–1898. As a national leader, White believed that he was showing his fellow southerners that they must rise above regionalism and view themselves as "citizens of a plural United States."

During the time that White was active in national affairs he published two important papers in the *U.S. Office of Experiment Stations Bulletin*. One was "The Manuring of Cotton" (33 [1896]: 169–96); the other, a series of dietary studies in north Georgia (1907). As a result of his professional service and his contributions to scientific agriculture, White received six honorary doctorates, the last in 1908, from Columbia University. After relinquishing his administrative post at the University of Georgia in 1907, White devoted his energy to teaching and research and to the work of national peace and arbitration conferences. Long interested in the peace movement, he had organized the Georgia Peace Society soon after joining the University of Georgia faculty. With the increasing threat of war in Europe, he became active in the national movement, and he presented addresses before the Lake Mohonk (N.Y.) Conference on International Arbitration in 1908 and 1912.

Upon completion of his fiftieth year of service at the University of Georgia in 1922, White delivered the commencement address, using the theory of evolution as a model for the development of the university. In fact, he was so committed to evolution that, in 1909, he had sponsored a meeting to commemorate the centennial of the birth of Charles Darwin, whom he considered to be one of the four greatest thinkers in the history of civilization. During his later years, White wrote several essays on general topics, including articles for *The Library of Southern Literature* and *The South in the Building of the Nation*. His last publication, in 1926, was a biography of Abraham Baldwin, founder of the University of Georgia. A widower for the last fourteen years of his life, he died at the home of a niece in Athens, Georgia.

Although not a prolific publisher in the field of chemistry, White did make several important contributions to agricultural chemistry, and he helped to give chemistry a prominent place in the curriculum of his institution. Certainly, he was the most noted scholar at the University of Georgia in 1900, having won national acclaim for his efforts to advance professionalism in agriculture and chemistry.

• In 1903 a fire destroyed most of White's personal papers, and only a small number of professional letters, notes, and addresses are extant for the period thereafter. The Henry C. White Papers are located in the Special Collections Department, University of Georgia Libraries, Athens. Useful for filling gaps are newspaper accounts, faculty minutes, board of trustees' minutes, and personal reminiscences, especially those of Thomas Walter Reed, "History of the University of Georgia" (typescript, Special Collections, University of Georgia Libraries); Robert Preston Brooks, *The University of Georgia under Sixteen Administrations, 1785–1955* (1956); and C. M. Strahan, "Dr. Henry Clay White: A Memorial Address," *Georgia Alumni Record* 8 (1928): 113–15, 120. Stephen J. Karina, "The University of Georgia College of Agriculture: An Administrative History 1785–1985" (unpublished manuscript, University Archives, University of Georgia Libraries), provides a full account of White's tenure as president of the State College of Agriculture and Mechanic Arts, but his characterization of White as elitist is questionable. W. H. Waggoner, *Chemistry at the University of Georgia* (1983?), sketches the growth of the chemistry department but provides no comparative framework. White's advocacy of the theory of evolution is discussed in Lester D. Stephens, "Henry Clay White, Darwin's Disciple in Georgia, 1875–1927," *Georgia Historical Quarterly* 78 (Spring 1994): 66–91. Indispensable for the contextual setting of White's service as a professor and administrator is Thomas G. Dyer, *The University of Georgia: A Bicentennial History* (1985). An informative obituary is in the *Atlanta Journal*, 1 Dec. 1927.

LESTER D. STEPHENS

WHITE, Henry Seely (20 May 1861–20 May 1943), mathematician, was born in Cazenovia, New York, the son of Aaron White, a mathematics teacher, and Isadore Maria Haight. White attended Wesleyan University, from which he received a bachelor's degree in 1882. Of his professors there, the astronomer John Monroe Van Vleck in particular influenced White's decision to pursue graduate training in mathematics in

Germany, the nation recognized as the leader in the field in the last quarter of the nineteenth century. White finally had the opportunity to pursue this course of study in 1887, after spending 1882–1883 at Wesleyan as assistant in astronomy and physics under Van Vleck, the next year as a mathematics and science teacher at the Centenary Collegiate Institute in Hackettstown, New Jersey, and three more years at Wesleyan, as tutor in mathematics and registrar of the university.

White traveled first to the University of Leipzig, where Norwegian mathematician Sophus Lie lectured on his evolving theory of Lie groups and where Lie's colleague Eduard Study offered a wide range of courses in geometry and algebra. Remaining in Leipzig through the summer of 1887, White ultimately decided to move on to Göttingen University. There, Felix Klein, one of the premier German mathematicians of the day, enjoyed marked success in training students at the research level. In particular, he attracted in the closing decade-and-a-half of the century a number of Americans, who, like White, returned to the United States with a strong sense of what constituted high-quality mathematical research and with a keen desire to see mathematics at that level supported at home.

White earned his doctorate under Klein in 1891 with a dissertation on the then popular topic of Abelian integrals. He had already returned to the United States in March 1890 to take a temporary position at the preparatory school attached to Northwestern University in Evanston, Illinois. Also in 1890 White married Mary Willard Gleason, with whom he would have three children. White became an assistant in pure mathematics at the recently opened Clark University in Worcester, Massachusetts, in the fall of that same year. Founded with a strong emphasis on graduate level instruction, Clark provided White with the opportunity to teach advanced courses in his principal areas of expertise, namely, algebraic and projective geometry as well as invariant theory. White had taught at Clark for two years, when he, like the majority of the faculty, left in the wake of a vote of no confidence in university president G. Stanley Hall.

Eliakim Hastings Moore, White's friend and the newly named acting head of the mathematics department at the incipient University of Chicago, tried unsuccessfully to get a position allocated to White at that new school. White instead became an associate professor in 1892 at Northwestern University, where he rose to full professor in 1894.

The thirteen years White spent in Evanston, Illinois, proved fruitful for him both mathematically and relative to the wider arena of the developing American mathematical research community. In 1893 he, together with Moore, Oskar Bolza, and Heinrich Maschke of the University of Chicago, organized the Mathematical Congress of the World's Columbian Exposition in Chicago, the first major mathematical meeting held on American shores. This event served to cement the commitment of American mathematicians to high-level mathematical research. White had also arranged for his adviser, Felix Klein, who had attended the fair as an official representative of the Prussian government, to give a series of lectures for two weeks following the congress's close. The so-called Evanston Colloquium brought together a core of specialists to hear the German master's overview of insights into the areas of contemporary mathematical research. White subsequently secured Macmillan and Co. to publish these lectures in 1894, producing a milestone in the publication of research-level mathematics in the United States.

The success of the Evanston event led White in 1896 to lobby the American Mathematical Society (AMS) for the creation of an annual society-sponsored colloquium, which would consist of a series of two-hour lectures over the course of a full week. In his view, these colloquia would serve to expose a fairly wide audience to a particular area of mathematical research at a high level and at a meaningful depth. The society agreed, and the first AMS Colloquium took place in September 1896. In 1903 White himself was chosen as one of the expert speakers for the Boston Colloquium, the first in the series to be published. On this occasion, White lectured on one of the topics of his ongoing research, curves on algebraic surfaces. Both the colloquia and the publications associated with them have continued into the 1990s.

White's contributions to the broader mathematical community included his service as an associate editor of the *Annals of Mathematics* from 1899 to 1905; as vice president and then president of the AMS in 1901 and 1907–1908, respectively; and as editor of the *Transactions of the American Mathematical Society* from 1907 to 1914. He held the latter two of these posts following his move, necessitated by his mother's illness in upstate New York, to become a professor and the head of the mathematics department at Vassar College in 1905.

White's Vassar years witnessed his continued interest in questions in algebraic geometry. For his various achievements in both research and the advancement of mathematics in America, White was starred in *American Men of Science* in 1906, a distinction conferred by his peers and reserved for those perceived to be at the top of their respective fields, and was elected to the National Academy of Sciences in 1915. He remained at Vassar until his retirement in 1936. He died in Poughkeepsie, New York.

As a researcher, White produced solid, but perhaps not spectacular, results. His impact on the mathematical scene resulted more from his organizational talents and his vision than from his mathematical achievements. In his foreword to White's autobiography, Arthur Coble wrote that "White was one of perhaps a dozen men who furnished the inspiration and set the pattern for the development of the present school of American mathematics."

• Archival material pertaining to White is at the University of Chicago; in the Klein papers at the Niedersächsische Staats- und Universitätsbibliothek in Göttingen; and at Vassar College. Among White's most important research publications are "Semi-combinants as Concomitants of Affiliants," *American Journal of Mathematics* 17 (1895): 235–65, and "Seven Points on a Twisted Cubic Surface," *Proceedings of the National Academy of Sciences* 1 (1915): 464–66; his colloquium lectures in *Lectures on Mathematics* (1905); and *Plane Curves of the Third Order* (1925). White's autobiography appeared as an "Autobiographical Memoir of Henry Seely White 1861–1943," National Academy of Sciences, *Biographical Memoirs* 25 (1947): 17–33. Raymond Clare Archibald published a biographical sketch in *A Semicentennial History of the American Mathematical Society: 1888–1938* (1938), pp. 158–61. Both of these articles include a photograph of White and his complete bibliography. For a sense of White's influential role in the early organization of American mathematics, consult Karen Hunger Parshall and David E. Rowe, *The Emergence of the American Mathematical Research Community (1876–1900)* (1994), particularly chaps. 7–9. An obituary of White is in the *New York Times*, 21 May 1943.

KAREN HUNGER PARSHALL

WHITE, Horace (10 Aug. 1834–16 Sept. 1916), journalist, was born in Colebrook, New Hampshire, the son of Horace White, a physician, and Eliza Moore. When White was four years old, his father led the family and other New Englanders to the Wisconsin frontier, where they founded the town of Beloit. After his father died in 1843, White was raised by his stepfather, Samuel Hinman, a stern Presbyterian deacon and trustee of Beloit College; White entered the college in 1849 and graduated in 1853.

According to White's own recollections, the advent of the Free Soil movement in 1848 made him determined to become a journalist so that he could fight against slavery. In 1853 he accepted a position on the *Chicago Journal* and reported the renewed sectional strife caused by the Kansas-Nebraska Act of 1854. His marriage in 1856 to Martha Root, daughter of a prominent abolitionist, encouraged his activist career. (They had no children.) As assistant secretary for the National Kansas Committee, he helped arm John Brown (1800–1859) and other militant free soilers in Kansas. In 1857 he returned to journalism with a new Republican newspaper, the *Chicago Tribune*, and became captivated by Abraham Lincoln. The two men often traveled together while White covered the Lincoln-Douglas debates in 1858 with a stenographic reporter for the state's leading Republican newspaper.

White stayed closely allied to Lincoln as a coauthor of his 1860 campaign biography and vowed to the new president that he and other young Republicans stood ready to "plunge into blood to the horses bridles" to defend the new administration. After the outbreak of hostilities, the *Chicago Tribune* made White its Washington correspondent. During his stay, he helped form the Independent News Room, a news agency that competed with the Associated Press. The resulting profits allowed him to become a minority stockholder of the *Chicago Tribune*.

In the spring of 1865 White returned to Chicago as editor in chief of the newspaper. His radicalism about abolitionism and prosecution of the war had led him occasionally to berate the cautiousness of Lincoln. White waged a steady, bitter fight against Lincoln's successor, Andrew Johnson, over the latter's conservative Reconstruction policies. At the apex of the clash between Johnson and the Radical Republicans, White's editorials threatened to make a "frog pond" of Mississippi and demanded universal male suffrage and direct congressional control of the former Confederate states.

Reconstruction carried White well beyond his earlier philosophic and social convictions. Although an abolitionist, he had never advocated voting citizenship for African Americans until the clash with Johnson, and by 1868 he began an ideological retreat that in less than a decade found him advocating a classical liberalism that denounced almost all governmental interference in society except the protection of private property.

In 1869 White's opposition to the protective tariff led him into another party conflict, this time with the Stalwarts, who supported President Ulysses S. Grant. The division eventually led White and other newspaper editors to sponsor the Liberal Republican rebellion of 1872. As free traders, they were embarrassed, however, by the party's nomination of the nation's leading protectionist, Horace Greeley, and their hands-off policy toward the South offered no answer to the Ku Klux Klan's renewed rampages. Grant's overwhelming reelection led a series of reversals for White. He lost a part of his fortune in the Chicago fire of 1871; his wife died in 1873; and in 1874 the declining revenues of the *Chicago Tribune* forced him to resign as editor.

Still moderately wealthy, White began a new life. In 1875 he married Amelia Jane McDougall, with whom he had three children. The next year he moved to New York City and linked the rest of his career to the financial empire of Henry Villard, his closest friend since the Civil War, when both worked as reporters in Washington. From 1876 to 1891, White helped to manage Villard's interests in railroad and steamship companies. In 1881 Villard also helped White reenter journalism by providing most of the money to buy both the daily *New York Evening Post* and the weekly *Nation* and also to hire Carl Schurz and Edwin L. Godkin to join White in an editorial triumvirate.

In 1883 personal quarrels led Schurz to resign. As coeditors, White and Godkin turned the *Evening Post* and the *Nation* into major journals of prevailing literary values and conservative laissez-faire opinion. Their independent, nonpartisan reporting also helped set new standards for American journalism. They attacked all political parties and took up leadership of the Republican independents known as the Mugwumps by exposing the political scandals of James G. Blaine and by backing the presidential campaigns of the Democratic candidate, Grover Cleveland.

The industrial and economic conflicts of the late nineteenth century led White to concentrate on monetary and banking issues. He marshaled support for Cleveland's repeal of silver coinage in 1893 and worked strenuously to defeat William Jennings Bryan in 1896 by writing a widely distributed booklet, *Coin's Financial Fool* (1895), to counter the famous Populist pamphlets of William "Coin" Harvey, who promoted the free coinage of silver at inflated prices. During the heated political debate, White also published his major work, *Money and Banking Illustrated by American History* (1895), which went through ten editions and became the standard textbook on the subject in American colleges until the 1930s.

After Godkin retired in 1899, White renewed the independence of his papers as he attacked the McKinley administration after it declared war on Spain in 1898 and seized control of Puerto Rico and the Philippines. Just as he had dubbed his erstwhile hero Grover Cleveland an "international anarchist" for his jingoism in the Venezuela crisis of 1895, White condemned American colonialism. The reentry of William Jennings Bryan as the Democrats' alternative in 1900 drove White back into the Republican camp. Immediately after the election, White tried to reorganize the Anti-Imperialists to demand total independence for the Philippines. Even after his retirement from the *Evening Post* in 1902, White maintained his opposition to U.S. policy as president of the Filipino Progress Association.

In 1908 White headed a New York state commission that called for reforms of the New York Stock Exchange. He also helped shape the historiography of the Civil War era by writing his memoirs of Abraham Lincoln and a biography of Lyman Trumbull, a former U.S. senator from Illinois. Both James Ford Rhodes and William A. Dunning drew heavily on White's praise of Lincoln's antislavery views and his condemnation of the Radical Republican policy of Reconstruction. White died shortly after being struck by an automobile in New York City.

• The principal collections of White's papers are in the Horace White Papers at the Illinois State Historical Society and the New-York Historical Society. See also John G. Sproat, *"The Best Men": Liberal Reformers in the Gilded Age* (1968), and Joseph Logsdon, *Horace White: Nineteenth Century Liberal* (1971). The extensive obituaries in the *New York Times*, 17 Sept. 1916, and especially in the *New York Evening Post*, 18 Sept. 1916, demonstrate his reputation in American journalism.

JOSEPH LOGSDON

WHITE, Hugh Lawson (30 Oct. 1773–10 Apr. 1840), U.S. senator and presidential candidate, was born in Iredell County, North Carolina, the son of James White, a militia officer, and Mary Lawson. Around 1784 White moved with his family to Fort Chiswell, Virginia, and in 1786 the family relocated to White's Fort, which became the town of Knoxville in 1791. Beginning in 1788 White studied classical languages with Rev. Samuel Carrick and law with Archibald Roane. Eventually he became private secretary to William Blount, the territorial governor of Tennessee, but in 1793 he left this position to participate in a campaign against the Cherokee Indians. After this service, and after a brief term as deputy clerk for Knox County, White spent eighteen months in Pennsylvania furthering his education; he received instruction first in mathematics from Robert Patterson in Philadelphia, then in law from James Hopkins in Lancaster. Upon his return to Knoxville in 1796, he was admitted to the bar and began a successful legal practice.

From 1801 through 1807 White served as a judge on the Tennessee Superior Court of Law and Equity. In 1808 he was appointed U.S. district attorney, but he resigned this position the following year. Shortly afterward he was elected judge of the Tennessee Supreme Court of Errors and Appeals, and he remained on the bench until 1815. Between 1812 and 1827 White served as president of the Bank of Tennessee; under his direction the bank never suspended specie payments, despite the financial panic of 1819. His political career, meanwhile, had begun with his election in 1807 to a term in the state senate, in which he took a leading role in the reorganization of Tennessee's land laws. White was again elected to the senate in 1817; in his second term he strongly supported an act imposing a prohibitive tax on banks operating in Tennessee without a state charter and also drafted an act that outlawed dueling in the state. In 1821 President James Monroe appointed White as commissioner to determine American claims against the Spanish government in Florida, while the next year the governor of Kentucky named him to a commission to adjust that state's military land claims with Virginia.

By the 1820s White was already well known as a personal and political friend of fellow Tennessean Andrew Jackson. When Jackson resigned from the U.S. Senate in 1825, the state legislature unanimously elected White to serve the remainder of the term; he was reelected, again unanimously, in both 1829 and 1835. Once in Washington, White displayed his opposition to the administration of President John Quincy Adams in a speech against American participation in the proposed Pan-American conference and through his advocacy of the reorganization of the national judiciary to provide easier access to courts in the western states. After his election in 1828 as Adams's successor, Jackson offered White a cabinet appointment as secretary of war, but White chose instead to remain in the Senate, where he served as president pro tempore from 1832 through 1835. As chairman of the Committee on Indian Affairs, White introduced into the Senate the bill that became the Indian Removal Act of 1830, and he loyally supported Jackson's administration through his vote in favor of the Force Bill in 1833, his opposition to federally funded internal improvements and protective tariffs, and his endorsement of the "war" against the Bank of the United States. He also favored the principle of distributing to the states the proceeds from the sales of public lands, while he encouraged legislation to facilitate the purchase of public lands by actual settlers.

In spite of his support of Jacksonian measures, White gradually became estranged from the administration. Despite Jackson's renewed offer in 1831 to appoint White his secretary of war, the senator perceived that he had little influence with the president. Thus he again declined Jackson's offer and followed a more independent course in the Senate. Although he supported Jackson's Force Bill, he also backed Henry Clay's compromise tariff, rather than the administration proposal, to resolve the nullification crisis of 1833. Moreover, White approved an 1833 bill "to enquire into the extent and operation of the constantly increasing patronage of the executive of the United States"; opposed the Expunging Resolutions, by which Jackson sought to remove a censure resolution from the Senate journal; and in 1836 allowed his name to be put forward as a presidential candidate against Jackson's known preference, Martin Van Buren. White's supporters presented him as the candidate most loyal to Jackson's original principles and the chief opponent of the president's attempt to "dictate" his successor to voters. One of three opposition candidates, White carried only Tennessee and Georgia and finished third in the electoral college. However, he ran strongly in the South, possibly because he was the only candidate who was also a slave owner; he carried 49 percent of the popular vote in the nine states where he was Van Buren's main rival.

White's resistance to executive dictation and usurpation continued after the election as his supporters became an integral component of the coalescing national Whig party. He opposed Van Buren's Independent Treasury proposal "principally upon the ground that it was putting the control of the whole moneyed capital of the country into the hands of the executive" (Scott, p. 221), and in 1837 he testified before a House committee that Jackson's administration "had attempted to influence public opinion in elections" (Scott, p. 294). After White had openly committed to supporting Henry Clay's presidential prospects, the Democratic-controlled Tennessee state legislature forced him to resign from the Senate in 1840 by passing a series of "Instructing Resolutions" requiring him to support Van Buren's administration. Shortly before his death in Knoxville, Whigs in Tennessee chose White to head the state electoral ticket for William Henry Harrison's 1840 presidential candidacy.

White had married Elizabeth Moore Carrick, the daughter of his former teacher, in 1798. They had twelve children before Elizabeth White's death in 1831. The following year White married Ann E. Peyton. Richard P. McCormick notes that White was "a petulant man, sensitive about his dignity and easily wounded in his vanity" (McCormick, p. 58). Nevertheless, his presidential candidacy provided an important development in the formation of the national Whig party. His strong showing in the South divided a solidly Democratic region, while his opposition to party discipline and executive "dictation" reflected a significant component of Whig political culture.

• A small collection of White's personal papers is in the William R. Perkins Library, Duke University. The most thorough source on White is Nancy N. Scott, ed., *A Memoir of Hugh Lawson White, Judge of the Supreme Court of Tennessee, Member of the United States Senate, etc. etc, with Selections from His Speeches and Correspondence* (1856), which was compiled by White's granddaughter and contains speeches and private papers that have since been lost. A biography is Lunia Paul Gresham, "The Public Career of Hugh Lawson White" (Ph.D. diss., Vanderbilt Univ., 1943), from which Gresham derived three articles: "The Public Career of Hugh Lawson White," *Tennessee Historical Quarterly* 3 (1944): 291–318; "Hugh Lawson White as a Tennessee Politician and Banker, 1807–1827," East Tennessee Historical Society, *Publications* 18 (1946): 25–46; and "Hugh Lawson White, Frontiersman, Lawyer, and Judge," East Tennessee Historical Society, *Publications* 19 (1947): 3–24. Biographical sketches are in Mary U. Rothrock, ed., *The French Broad–Holston Country: A History of Knox County, Tennessee* (1946); and Betsey Beeler Creekmore, *Knoxville* (1958). See also Richard P. McCormick, "Was There a 'Whig Strategy' in 1836," *Journal of the Early Republic* 4 (1984): 47–70; Jonathan M. Atkins, "The Presidential Candidacy of Hugh Lawson White in Tennessee, 1832–1836," *Journal of Southern History* 58 (1992): 27–56; and Atkins, *Politics, Parties, and the Sectional Conflict in Tennessee, 1832–1861* (1997). An obituary is in the *Nashville Republican Banner*, 15 Apr. 1840.

JONATHAN M. ATKINS

WHITE, Israel Charles (1 Nov. 1848–25 Nov. 1927), geologist, was born near St. Cloud, Virginia (present-day Monongalia County, West Virginia), the son of Michael White and Mary Ann Russell, farmers. The father was a leader in the small community, and he participated in the separation of West Virginia from Virginia in 1863. White attended school in a limited manner when teachers were available by local subscription. His brother much later said that White was a "studious boy and efficient in all of his work. From the age of eight or nine years he was a persistent collector of fossils" (quoted in Fairchild, p. 127).

White entered West Virginia University at Morgantown when it opened in 1867. He intended to become a physician but turned away from that profession after helping a doctor perform an autopsy. He continued at the university, where he was drawn into geology by John James Stevenson. White received an A.B. in 1872, and that same year he married Emmy (or Emily) McLane (or McClane) Shay, who died in 1874; they had one child. He received an A.M. from the same university in 1875. He then had one year of graduate work in geology with John Strong Newberry at Columbia University.

During the summer of 1875 White was a field assistant for Stevenson on the second geological survey of Pennsylvania, and in the summers from 1876 to 1883 he was assistant geologist on that survey. He completed eight carefully detailed studies on counties in northwestern and central Pennsylvania and wrote the reports on them during winter evenings.

In 1877 White became professor of geology at West Virginia University, where he was noted for conducting field trips for his students, an uncommon practice at that time. White married Mary Moorhead in 1878; they had five children.

In the summers from 1884 to 1888 White was assistant geologist for the U.S. Geological Survey. His studies were on the coalfields of his area, published as "Stratigraphy of the Bituminous Coal Fields of Pennsylvania, Ohio, and West Virginia" (*U.S. Geological Survey Bulletin* 65 [1891]).

White was the first to present the anticlinal theory of oil and gas accumulation, in which he proposed that oil and gas accumulate by gravity in arched (anticlinal) and domed sedimentary structures. He first had the idea in 1882 and published it in 1885 as "The Geology of Natural Gas" (*Science* 5: 521–22). Other geologists were not at first convinced of his idea. White credits geologist Edward Francis Baxter Orton with providing significant support for his theory in the reports of the Geological Survey of Ohio (vol. 6, 1888). Other geologists eventually accepted it, especially following White's longer discussion in 1892: "The Mannington Oil Field (W.Va.) and the History of Its Development" (*Bulletin of Geological Society of America* 3: 187–216). He himself used the concept to become wealthy by investing in oil and gas leases in West Virginia and Pennsylvania. He resigned as professor at West Virginia University in 1892 to pursue his business interests and geologic studies. For a number of years he was a consultant to various companies to examine potential oil prospects in the southern United States and Mexico, and he discovered some significant properties for them.

In 1897, while he was attending the International Geologic Congress in Russia, White was appointed state geologist for the newly established West Virginia Geologic Survey. He held this appointment until his death, working intensively but refusing a stipend after the first two years because he believed that he did not need it and that he could thus employ a larger staff. He supervised the preparation of a complete set of topographic maps of the state. He wrote five reports for the survey, on oil, gas, and coal, and he edited about thirty other reports by his assistants, often providing suggestions during their studies and their writing. His goal was to have the survey prepare geologic reports on every county in the state, and only one county was incomplete when he died.

From 1904 to 1906 White was chief of the Brazilian Coal Commission, which was seeking foreign capital for development of its coal resources. He made two long trips to southern Brazil, in primitive areas difficult of access, to determine the nature, extent, and quality of coal beds there. His report in 1907 was published in both English and Portuguese.

White was skilled in careful field studies and detailed summaries. His concepts of oil and gas accumulation were pioneering and proved to be sound. He published about 150 scientific papers, mostly on coal, oil, and gas, as well as a number of company reports. At the request of President Theodore Roosevelt, White addressed in 1908 the first White House Conference of Governors on "Waste of Our Fuel Resources" at its meeting to discuss plans for conserving natural resources.

White was an active participant in civic affairs and a generous benefactor to his city and to West Virginia University. He was a charter member of the Geological Society of America, serving as its treasurer from 1891 to 1907 and as president in 1920.

After the death of White's second wife in 1924, he married Julia Posten Wildman in about 1925; they had no children. He lived most of his professional life in Morgantown, West Virginia, and died in a hospital in Baltimore, Maryland.

• Significant publications by White other than those cited in the text include "Report on the Coal Measures and Associated Rocks of South Brazil," pt. 1 (1908), pp. 1–300 (published by Brazil); "The Coals of Brazil," Second Pan-American Scientific Congress, Washington, D.C. (1918); "Important Epochs in the History of Petroleum and Natural Gas," *Bulletin of Geological Society of America*, 32 (1921): 171–86. He published additional material on the anticlinal theory under the repeated title of "The Geology of Natural Gas" in *Petroleum Age* 5 (1886): 1263–67 and in vol. 1 of the West Virginia Geological Survey (1899), pp. 160–63, as well as "The Anticlinal Theory," *Report of Proceedings of American Mining Congress* (1917): 550–56. His citation to Orton is "Edward Orton," *American Geologist* 25 (1900): 197–210. Biographies of White are Herman L. Fairchild, *Bulletin of Geological Society of America* 39 (1928): 126–45, with bibliography; and Ray V. Hennen, *Bulletin of American Association of Petroleum Geologists* 12 (1928): 339–51, with bibliography.

ELIZABETH NOBLE SHOR

WHITE, James (1747?–14 Aug. 1821), pioneer, was born in Rowan County (now Iredell County), North Carolina, the son of Moses White and Mary McConnell, occupations unknown. Little is known of White's boyhood in colonial North Carolina. In 1770 he married Mary Lawson. They were the parents of seven children, the most prominent of whom was Hugh Lawson White, who became a bank president, a U.S. senator, and an unsuccessful Whig candidate for the U.S. presidency. James White was about thirty-two years old and had apparently received an adequate education when he joined the Continental army in 1779. He served until 1781, attaining the rank of captain of militia.

White's revolutionary war service entitled him to receive land in Tennessee, which was a part of North Carolina when the land grant act was passed in 1783. In August of that year White set out on an exploratory trip along the French Broad and Holston rivers seeking the most attractive land on which to settle. Accompanied by Francis Ramsey, who was a land surveyor, Robert Love, and others, White's party journeyed down the French Broad to its confluence with the Holston, forming the Tennessee River. There they first beheld the beautiful spot on which White later founded the city of Knoxville.

Returning to his home in North Carolina, White made preparations to move his family to the West. In 1784 they journeyed to Fort Chiswell in Virginia where he produced a crop and left his family while he prepared their future home. In 1785 they moved to a spot north of the confluence of the French Broad and the Holston rivers. There he became involved in the tangled affairs of the abortive state of Franklin. He was a delegate to the 1785 convention that drafted its constitution. He also became a warm personal friend of John Sevier, who was governor of Franklin and later first governor of Tennessee.

When North Carolina's opposition brought the dissolution of the state of Franklin, White returned to the future Knoxville site with James Conner, a friend of his youth. There they busied themselves felling trees, clearing land, and selling lots to settlers. White did find time to return to politics; in 1787 the people of Hawkins County elected him to the North Carolina House of Commons. He also served as a delegate to the constitutional convention at Fayetteville (N.C.) that ratified the U.S. Constitution.

White's cabin, which stood on White's Creek near its junction with the Holston, constituted one corner of White's Fort, which protected the settlement from marauding American Indians. It became a rendezvous for new settlers and other travelers since it was easily accessible by water and trails along the rivers, and it occupied a strategic position between settlements on the upper reaches of the Holston and Cumberland.

Meanwhile, William Blount, another North Carolina native who was governor of the Territory Southwest of the Ohio River (which included present-day Kentucky and Tennessee) and a good friend of White's, appointed him a justice of the peace and major of militia. In 1791 Blount made White's Fort the territorial capital and named it Knoxville in honor of General Henry Knox, who was then secretary of war. The town developed into a city, which was twice Tennessee's capital (1796–1812 and 1817–1818). When Knox County was created, White was made lieutenant colonel and commander of the county militia. As such, he directed the defense of Knoxville when Cherokee and Creek Indians were on the warpath in 1793.

As the senior justice of the peace, White was the presiding judge of Knox County. In 1796 he was a delegate to the convention that drafted the constitution of the state of Tennessee and was elected to the state senate. The following year he was elected Speaker of the senate, but he resigned his seat so that Blount could be elected to fill the vacancy. Blount had been expelled by the U.S. Senate after being accused of involvement in a plot to help the British seize Spanish Florida and Louisiana. Some historians say that White's motive in stepping aside was merely to demonstrate that Blount still possessed the confidence of the people of Tennessee. However, historian Thomas Perkins Abernethy said, in *From Frontier to Plantation in Tennessee*, that the evidence "strongly indicates" that White was acting as Blount's agent in his Tennessee explorations (p. 53). Whatever the answer, White was elected to the state senate again in 1801 and 1803 and served as its Speaker both times.

In 1798 Sevier appointed White as one of Tennessee's representatives in negotiations with the Cherokees on the Treaty of Tellico, which settled the boundary between the Cherokees and settlers. The appointment was in recognition of the important part White had played in Tennessee's Indian affairs. In the late nineties he was promoted to brigadier general of militia in the Hamilton District and participated in the Creek War of 1813, serving under General John H. Cocke.

Historian Samuel Cole Williams described White as a philanthropist who owned two grist mills "and in times of scarcity would give of their product to those of his neighbors who were in need" (p. 295). White was a Presbyterian and donated the land on which the First Presbyterian Church of Knoxville was built. He donated a city block to Blount College (later the University of Tennessee) and was one of the trustees named in its charter (1794). He died in Knoxville. Of him, Tennessee historian James Gettys McGready Ramsey wrote, in his *Annals of Tennessee* (1853), "to extreme old age, he retained the esteem and affection of his fellow citizens, and never had a stain on his unsullied good name" (p. 639).

• For primary sources on White, consult the Calendar of the Tennessee and Kings Mountain Papers in the Draper Collection of the Wisconsin State Historical Society.

For additional information see Samuel Cole Williams, *History of the Lost State of Franklin* (1924); J. T. Moore and A. P. Foster, *Tennessee, the Volunteer State* (1923); Edward W. Phifer, *Burke: The History of a North Carolina County* (1977); Carl Samuel Driver, *John Sevier, Pioneer of the Old Southwest* (1932); Thomas Perkins Abernethy, *From Frontier to Plantation in Tennessee* (1932); and James Phelan, *History of Tennessee: The Making of a State* (1888).

NOEL YANCEY

WHITE, James Clarke (7 July 1833–5 Jan. 1916), dermatologist, was born in Belfast, Maine, the son of James Patterson, a banker and merchant, and Mary Ann Clarke. White learned Latin and Greek from the local clergy. At the age of sixteen, he entered Harvard College, from which he received a B.A. in 1853. He then began studies at Tremont Medical School in Boston, Massachusetts. Like many "supplementary," non–degree-granting medical schools of the day, Tremont offered a three-month series of lectures each year; additional courses could be taken over the winter months at the individual's expense. After repeating the same lecture series over three consecutive years and additional clinical courses at Harvard, White earned an M.D. in the spring of 1856 from Harvard Medical School. Like many financially comfortable students of the time, White then chose to go abroad for additional clinical and laboratory experiences. Eschewing Paris at the advice of clinical medicine professor Calvin Ellis, White went instead to Vienna, the site of the latest clinical advances. In the year he spent there, he worked in the wards and made rounds with physicians Johann Oppolzer, Karl Sigmund, Josef Skoda, and Ferdinand von Hebra, from whom he gained valuable knowledge about dermatology and disease.

Following his return to Boston in 1857, White decided not to choose a specialty. Although still somewhat novel and contentious in the United States at this time, specialties were the norm on the Continent; those physicians returning from Paris, Vienna, and Berlin often aspired to a specialty practice. Entering a general practice, White engaged in neither surgery nor gynecology but concentrated more and more on the dermatological work he had observed in Vienna, particularly under Hebra. As he cared increasingly for people with skin problems, his practice grew both larger and narrower. In 1858 he was named to the staff at St. Vincent's Orphan Asylum in Boston. That same year, he became an assistant professor of chemistry at Harvard Medical School, an appointment he would hold until 1863. In 1860 he opened the first dermatology clinic in the United States with fellow dermatologist Benjamin Joy Jeffries. Named in 1863 a lecturer, along with writer and physician Oliver Wendell Holmes, in the Harvard Medical School's University Lecture Series, White chose to give six lectures on skin diseases. In 1865 he was named physician to outpatients at Massachusetts General Hospital, a position similar to one he had held at the Boston Dispensary since 1863. He married Martha Anna Ellis in 1862; they had three children.

Dermatology at this time had few practitioners, and its main diagnostic techniques remained observational. Although White's interests and expertise in dermatology were well known, he continued to teach chemistry and became an adjunct professor at Harvard Medical School in 1866. White lectured on physiological, toxic, and clinical chemistry until 1871, when he was offered the chair of the medical school's chemistry department. In 1870 dermatology was officially recognized as a department at Massachusetts General Hospital; White was named its chief and remained in the position for thirty-five years. When he turned down the chair in chemistry at Harvard Medical School, he was subsequently offered a chair of dermatology, the first such department in any medical school in the country. He held the chair until his retirement in 1902, when he was replaced by his physician son, Charles James White.

The elder White's service to Harvard Medical School was long and devoted. Dissatisfied with the existing system of medical education, White advocated reform in an effort to produce better-educated physicians. Medical education in the nineteenth century was still largely a proprietary venture, benefiting teachers more than students. Students purchased tickets to attend specific lectures from those offering instruction; the lecture course at Harvard ran for eight months rather than the usual three, but exams at the end of the third year were oral, and not much attention was given to student progress. White began his campaign of reform with an editorial in the *Boston Medical and Surgical Journal* in 1866. Honored with the opportunity to offer the introductory address to the entering class in 1870, during Charles Eliot's first year as president of Harvard, White again emphasized the need for a reformed regimen encompassing a three-year, nine-month course with written exams in each department, as well as entrance requirements. White's campaign was successful; the changes he advocated were implemented in 1871. On a national level, the improved standards for admission and coursework at Harvard Medical School had a significant effect. Harvard's student population did not decrease, as feared, but rather increased and became more competitive.

A pioneer in dermatology, White's achievements in the field surpassed even his accomplishments in medical education reform. One of the founders of the American Dermatological Association in 1876, White served as its first president from 1877 to 1887; he served a second term in 1897. In 1907 he was honored as the president of the Sixth International Dermatology Congress. His *Dermatitis Venenata* (1887) is a classic for the complete clinical picture of dermatological problems it described. The detail and depth in this book complemented White's lecture style, which emphasized clinical cases in addition to textbook learning. In his autobiography, *Sketches from My Life* (1914), White professed an interest in leprosy, although he did not specifically follow up on this in his research and professional life. White was coeditor of the *Boston Medical and Surgical Journal* from 1861 to 1867. He wrote eight books and chapters, as well as 125 medical papers, 94 editorials, 50 reviews, 22 papers on natural history, and miscellaneous communications that appeared in the *Boston Journal* and other journals.

White, who always enjoyed comparative anatomy and natural history, had recorded in his college diary early experiences of collecting flora specimens. In 1856 he joined the Boston Society of Natural History and was its curator of comparative anatomy from 1859 to 1869. He was elected a member of the American Academy of Arts and Sciences in 1866. A member of the Massachusetts Medical Society, he served as its librarian in 1860 and president in 1892. He was a corresponding member of the French and Argentinean dermatology societies and an honorary member of the Italian, London, Vienna, Berlin, and New York dermatology societies. He died in Boston.

From improving medical education to helping found the American Dermatological Association, White always strove to elevate the medical profession. A pioneer in dermatology, he set the course in his field for many years.

• White's patient records for the early years of his practice are at the Francis Countway Library, Harvard Medical School. His autobiography, *Sketches from My Life* (1914), is an important source. For more on White's role in Harvard Medical School's educational reform, see Henry K. Beecher and Mark D. Altschule, *Medicine at Harvard: The First 300 Years* (1977). The best and most complete obituary is in the *Boston Medical and Surgical Journal*, 20 Jan. 1916, which also includes a bibliography of White's writings.

GWEN E. KAY

WHITE, James Platt (14 Mar. 1811–28 Sep. 1881), physician, was born in Austerlitz, New York, the son of David Pierson White and Ann Platt. His ancestors came on the Mayflower; his grandfather fought in the American Revolution and his father in the War of 1812. In 1816 the family moved to East Hamburg, near present-day Buffalo. He was privately tutored and briefly attended Middlebury Academy in nearby Genesee County, teaching part-time to support his studies. He started to study law under his uncle, then in 1830 switched to medicine, apprenticing under two local physicians in Black Rock (now part of Buffalo). White also attended lectures at Fairfield Medical College and then moved to Jefferson Medical College in Philadelphia, where he graduated in 1834, after which he returned to the Buffalo area to practice and gradually began to specialize in obstetrics. He married Mary Elizabeth Penfield in 1836; they later adopted a nephew.

White was one of the founders of the medical department of the University of Buffalo in 1846; in fact, the medical department remained the only department in the university until well after the Civil War. Though Buffalo had a well-established medical community, only White and his colleague Austin Flint (1812–1886) were practicing in the Buffalo area. The two men recruited the other five faculty members from Geneva College. Each professor served as chair of a department although White himself as organizer did not do so at first, devoting his time more to the running of the medical school. His position came to be equivalent to dean, a title he held at the time of his death.

In 1847 he also became professor of obstetrics, and it was in this capacity that he first taught a course in what he called "demonstrative midwivery," in which approximately twenty senior students observed a real delivery. In January 1850 White persuaded Mary Watson, an unmarried 26-year-old expectant mother in residence at the Erie County Alms House, to move in with the janitor of the medical school and his wife for the last few days of her confinement. The janitor's apartment was in the basement of the building housing the medical school, and proximity was an important factor to White, along with the willingness of the janitor's wife to act as an aid and helpmate to the woman. During the next nine days each member of the class, under the supervision of White, was permitted to auscultate the fetal heart sounds, perform vaginal examinations, and observe the birth of the baby. For this Watson was paid $10.

Though this has come to be regarded as a pathbreaking effort to better acquaint medical students with both female anatomy and childbirth, the exposure of the woman's genitalia to students (and even to physicians) was regarded by many of his medical colleagues (as well as others) as obscene. As news of his demonstration became public it was much debated in both the medical and popular press, and an anonymous letter published 22 February 1850 in the *Buffalo Commercial Advertisers* accused White of committing a "gross outrage upon public decency" for his exposure of an unmarried pregnant woman to medical students. This was soon followed by another letter signed by seventeen Buffalo "medical gentlemen of the older and more experienced class" denouncing White's obstetric demonstration.

The medical faculty had prepared itself for controversy and even before White had moved the woman to the basement of the medical school had adopted resolutions in his support. They felt it was essential to protect White's reputation and that of the medical school and encouraged the county attorney to bring criminal libel proceedings against the physician most active in disseminating the anonymous letter and organizing the opposition, Horatio N. Loomis. Mary Watson testified at the trial that the money had not influenced her to participate in White's demonstration, but rather she did so because she thought she would get better medical care. Since there was no evidence that Loomis had written the anonymous letter, and in fact another physician testified at the trial that he had done so, Loomis was acquitted. It is generally believed, however, that the letter had been written at Loomis's instigation.

The trial achieved considerable press coverage, and there was more or less national discussion of White's actions. At least ten of the fifteen medical journals then known to be in existence came out in support of this method of teaching and delivery. One of the witnesses for White, a professor named Gilman from the College of Physicians and Surgeons in New York City, stated that although he had never delivered a woman exposed, he believed in the value of doing so, but indicated that he would hesitate to introduce it either into his practice or to his students because of the "hubbub it had kicked up." He felt that if he tried "demonstrative midwivery" in New York City, mob violence might ensue.

The recently formed American Medical Association set up an investigative committee concerned with the question, which gave its report at the 1851 annual meeting in Charleston, South Carolina. Though the committee found considerable advantages to demonstrative midwifery, it concluded that these were not of sufficient value to make it proper that women "in their hour of extremity" should be made the subject of a public exhibition. It also argued that the confidential relationship between the woman and her physician would be impaired by allowing students to participate in a delivery. Their report was adopted by the AMA.

Still the issue persisted, and though White himself did not repeat his course experiment, he sought other ways to give his students practical experience, something that became much easier with the growth of hospitals, particularly in the period after the Civil War. Physicians developed a working agreement to give medical attention to the poor in return for using them as a resource for medical instruction. In this White served as a pioneer and transition figure.

Following the trial White traveled in Europe, observing obstetrical and gynecological practices in Edinburgh, Paris, and Vienna. He made a second European trip in 1866 to keep further abreast of medical advances. In addition to his establishment of the concept of "demonstrative midwivery," White developed new techniques for treatment of chronic uterine inversion and was an expert in ovariectomies, performing over 100 of them. He also wrote on the use of obstetrical forceps and suggested several changes in their construction. Almost all of his writings appeared in the local Buffalo medical journal.

During the Civil War White served as government medical inspector on military hospitals in the West and Southwest. He was president of the New York State Medical Society in 1870 and first vice president in 1878 of the American Medical Association, which by that time had changed its stand. He was a founder of the American Gynecological Society in 1876 and was among the founders of most of the Buffalo medical institutions and civic groups of that time, including the State Lunatic Asylum (now Buffalo Psychiatric Center), the hospital of the Sisters of Charity, Buffalo General Hospital, the Young Men's Association (later the YMCA), the Academy of Fine Arts, and the Foundling Asylum. He died at his home in Buffalo.

• White's 1,070-volume private library was left to the University of Buffalo (now State University of New York at Buffalo), where much of it still remains, as do the Minute Books of the Medical Faculty. Among his more important articles are "Remarks on the Construction of Obstetrical Forceps with a Description of an Instrument," *Buffalo Medical Journal* 4 (1849): 715–21, and "Report of a Case of Inversion of the Uterus Successfully Reduced after Six Months," *American Journal of Medical Sciences*, n.s., 36 (1858): 13–24. His last case of an ovariotomy was reported by C. M. Daniels, "Report on Last Ovariotomy Performed by Professor J. P. White," *Buffalo Medical Journal*, n.s., 21 (1881): 159–60.

For the controversy over "demonstrative midwifery" see Virginia C. Drachman, "The Loomis Trial: Social Mores and Obstetrics in the Mid-Nineteenth Century," in *Health Care in America*, ed. Susan Reverby and David Rosner (1979), pp. 67–83. See also Frederick T. Parsons, *Report of the Trial, the People versus Dr. Horatio N. Loomis, for Libel* (1850; repr. 1974). For other biographical information see the obituary in *Buffalo Medical Journal*, n.s., 21 (Oct. 1881): 183–90; "Memorials: James Platt White," a pamphlet in the collections at the University of Buffalo; and Oliver P. Jones, "Our First Professor of Obstetrics: James Platt White," *Buffalo Physician* (Spring 1974): 42–47.

VERN L. BULLOUGH

WHITE, John (fl. 1585–1593), painter, was the second governor of the Virginia colony (in what is now North Carolina). Nothing is known of White's origins; however, he was born probably in England, perhaps in Cornwall, sometime between 1540 and 1550. White most likely was educated as a limner, or illustrator, and a John White, possibly the same, is listed in 1580 as a member of the Painter-Stainer's Company, a London guild. White may have traveled with Martin Frobisher's 1577 expedition to Baffin Island in search of a northwest passage to Asia as attested by his paintings of Inuits; however, these paintings are copies based on lost originals, probably by White but possibly by someone else.

The earliest definite record of White comes in 1585. White traveled to the Caribbean and North America as part of the attempt by Richard Grenville and Ralph Lane to colonize Roanoke Island, along the Outer Banks of present-day North Carolina, under the sponsorship of Sir Walter Raleigh. White served as the expedition's official artist and worked closely with writer Thomas Harriot to portray the colony's discoveries in watercolors as well as words. White's paintings provide some of the earliest graphic representations of southeastern Native Americans, in particular Carolina Algonquins, at the time of their contact with Europeans. The watercolors also capture the flora and fauna of eastern North Carolina and Puerto Rico, where the expedition stopped to resupply. In addition, White's watercolor maps give a good idea of the state of the ever-changing Outer Banks in the 1580s. It is unknown whether White returned to England in late August 1585 with Grenville or if he stayed on at Roanoke Island with Lane's colony until June 1586. White's name is not included in the list of Lane's colonists, but the sheer number of paintings White did of Roanoke Island subjects, as well as his close work with Harriot, who did remain until 1586, implies that he may have stayed on Roanoke Island longer than Grenville's two months.

Harriot's description of Roanoke Island's people and natural resources was published in 1588 as *A Briefe and True Report of the New Found Land of Virginia*. In 1590 the Flemish engraver Theodore De Bry reprinted Harriot's book in Latin, English, French, and German editions; to illustrate the book, De Bry made twenty-three engravings based on White's paintings. In order to turn White's watercolors into engravings, De Bry portrayed the Carolina Algonquins with European facial features and musculature similar to that in classic statuary. White's accurate watercolors thus became some of the most influential representations of Native Americans in sixteenth and seventeenth-century Europe, albeit in this modified form.

In 1587 Raleigh appointed White governor of a second colonization attempt. Unlike the previous attempt, this one had both men and women colonists, including White's son-in-law Ananias Dare and his daughter Ellinor White Dare. Nothing is known of White's wife. Leaving England on 26 April 1587, the colonists arrived on Roanoke Island on 23 July. Repairs to the houses left by the 1585 expedition were begun, and on 18 August Ellinor gave birth to White's granddaughter, Virginia Dare, the first child of English parents born in North America. On 27 August, two days after Virginia Dare's christening, White left for England to get supplies for the colony. However, war between Spain and England prevented White from securing a supply ship. Not until 1590 was White able to return to the Roanoke colony, and then only as a passenger on board a ship that formed part of a privateering fleet to the Caribbean. In August 1590 White was allowed ashore at Roanoke Island, but the colonists were not to be found, only the word "CROATAN" carved in capital letters on an entrance post to the colony's fort. By prearranged signal, the carving was meant to indicate that the colonists had left without being under duress for a nearby island peopled by Native Americans friendly to the English. Poor weather forced White's ship to give up the search for the "lost colonists" without going beyond Roanoke Island and to return to England.

Little is known of White following his fruitless search for the 1587 colonists. His accounts of the 1587 expedition and of his later attempts to find these colonists were published in Richard Hakluyt's 1589–1600 edition of *The Principall Navigations, Voiages, and Discoveries of the English Nation*. These accounts were sent to Hakluyt in 1593, along with a letter addressed from County Cork, Ireland. After that date, nothing more is known of White. In 1606 a Brigit White was named as executor to the estate of her brother, a John White "late of parts beyond the sea," but whether this John White was the painter and colonial governor is not known.

White's records of both the 1585 and 1587 expeditions have influenced history. His writings about the events surrounding the founding and disappearance of the 1587 colony helped instigate the mystery of the "lost colony," including the many myths and legends surrounding it. However, it is through his position as the official artist of the 1585 expedition that White has had his most pervasive influence. White's paintings, especially as engraved by De Bry, were copied and used to illustrate works about Native Americans throughout the seventeenth and early eighteenth centuries. They were inaccurately employed to represent Native Americans outside of eastern North Carolina, from those of western New York state to the Apaches of New Mexico. Even today White's paintings, both in their original form and through De Bry's engravings, are perhaps the most widely used pictures depicting Native North Americans at the time of European contact.

• All of White's surviving paintings are in the British Museum in London. The best reproductions of White's paintings as well as the most complete biography and assessment of White's importance to ideas about North America concerning ethnography, natural history, and cartography are in Paul Hope Hulton and David Beers Quinn, *The American Drawings of John White, 1577–1590, with Drawings of European and Oriental Subjects* (1964); however, because the 1964 work was published in a limited edition, Hulton, *America 1585: The Complete Drawings of John White* (1984), is also useful and more generally available. It contains much of the same biographical and historical material, some of it updated, though the reproductions are not quite as good. The best modern editions of White's writings from Hakluyt's *Principall Navigations* are in Quinn, *The Roanoke Voyages, 1584–1590: Documents to Illustrate the English Voyages to North America under the Patent Granted to Walter Raleigh in 1584* (1955). The best general history of the Roanoke Island colonization efforts, including White's role in them, is Quinn, *Set Fair for Roanoke: Voyages and Colonies, 1584–1606* (1985).

E. THOMSON SHIELDS, JR.

WHITE, John Williams (5 Mar. 1849–9 May 1917), classical scholar, was born in Cincinnati, Ohio, the son of the Reverend John Whitney White and Anna Catharine Williams. He received an A.B. (1868) and A.M. (1871) from Ohio Wesleyan University and taught Greek and Latin at Willoughby College (1868–1869) and Baldwin University (1869–1874) in Ohio. In 1871 he married Mary Alice Hillyer, with whom he would have four children. White spent part of 1871 in Germany and Greece. In 1873 he produced a well-received edition of Sophocles's *Oedipus Tyrannus*, and he was subsequently appointed tutor in Greek at Harvard College (1874). In 1877 he was awarded a Ph.D. and A.M. in classical philology in the fledgling graduate program there and was made assistant professor. Upon the death of Professor E. A. Sophocles, he became full professor in 1884.

While at Harvard, White published *An Introduction to the Rhythmic and Metric of the Classical Languages* (1878), an English translation of J. H. H. Schmidt's controversial *Leitfaden in der Rhythmik und Metrik der classischen Sprachen* (1869). He also edited or coedited many elementary Greek grammars and readers, and with L. Packard and T. D. Seymour he founded the College Series of Greek Authors (1879). His *First Greek Book* (based on Xenophon), published in 1896, dominated the American market for almost a century. White was a dynamic and exacting but gracious teacher, who, along with J. B. Greenough, broke with Harvard tradition to encourage the reading of extensive passages of ancient authors "at sight." He was also involved in introducing at Harvard in the 1880s courses in classical civilization that did not require a knowledge of Greek or Latin, and he initiated the systematic use of slides in the classroom there as well. His production of *Oedipus* (1881) was perhaps the first revival of a Greek play in the original language in the United States. An enthusiastic amateur athlete, White served on and chaired Harvard's first athletic committee (1882–1892). His most important student was James Loeb, who later founded the Loeb Classical Library.

Together with C. E. Norton and W. W. Goodwin, White helped found the Archaeological Institute of America (1879) and the American School of Classical Studies in Athens (1881). He was chair of the Managing Committee of the ASCSA (1881–1887), professor of Greek literature at the school in 1893–1894, and president of the AIA (1897–1903). Together with J. B. Greenough and F. D. Allen, he founded *Harvard Studies in Classical Philology* in 1890, and he served as one of its editors until 1898. He also served on the editorial boards of *Classical Quarterly* (1909–1917) and *Classical Philology* (1906–1916). He held honorary degrees from Cambridge, Harvard, Ohio Wesleyan, Princeton, and Wesleyan.

In the late 1890s, White began gradually to withdraw from official university duties. In 1909 he retired completely in order to devote himself to producing an exhaustive edition of Aristophanes, including a collation of all manuscripts and scholia. Before his death, however, he published only *The Verse of Greek Comedy*

(1912), which remains authoritative, and *Scholia on the Aves of Aristophanes* (1914), an exemplary edition. He died in Cambridge, Massachusetts.

• White published several articles on Greek metrics and textual matters. "The Manuscripts of Aristophanes," *Classical Philology* 1 (1906): 1–20, 255–78, remains a valuable introduction to the subject. Sources for White's life include Almira Larkin White, *Genealogy of the Descendents of John White of Wenham and Lancaster, Massachusetts 1638–1900*, vol. 2 (1900), pp. 503–4, 508; William Gardner Hale, *Classical Journal* 12 (1916–1917): 585–87 (with a photograph as frontispiece to the fascicle); J. R. Wheeler, *American Journal of Archaeology* II.21 (1917): 202–4; and George Henry Chase, *Harvard Graduates Magazine* 26 (1917): 42–44 (with photograph). Samuel Eliot Morison, ed., *The Development of Harvard University since the Inauguration of President Eliot, 1869–1929* (1930), pp. 33–63, esp. pp. 44–45, offers details of White's teaching and places him in the context of larger changes at the university. The 1881 production of *Oedipus* is documented by Henry Norman, *An Account of the Harvard Greek Play* (1882). White's association with the American School is discussed by Louis E. Lord, *A History of the American School of Classical Studies at Athens (1882–1942): An Intercollegiate Project* (1947), pp. 1–48 (with photograph). An obituary is in the *New York Times*, 10 May 1917.

S. DOUGLAS OLSON

WHITE, Josh (11 Feb. 1915–5 Sept. 1969), folk and blues vocalist and guitarist, was born Joshua Daniel White in Greenville, South Carolina, the son of Dennis White, a teamster and preacher, and Daisy Elizabeth Humphrey. The fifth of eight children born into a poor African-American family, White received little formal education. He later completed the sixth grade and may have attended high school for a time. As a child he was exposed to music through his mother, a leading singer in the church choir. At age seven he began to serve as "lead boy" (guide) for blind guitarists. His masters included John Henry Arnold, Blind Joe Taggart, and (possibly) Blind Lemon Jefferson. Watching these itinerant street musicians as he traveled throughout the South and to Chicago, White taught himself to play the guitar. In 1928 he accompanied Taggart at a recording session.

Discovered by a scout for ARC records (predecessor to Columbia Recording Company) at age fourteen, White released a series of "race" records, including "Low Cotton" and "Jesus Gonna Make Up My Dying Bed," in the early 1930s under the name Pinewood Tom (for blues) and Josh White, the Singing Christian (for spirituals). He moved to New York City and played at clubs, where his appeal to urban white audiences allowed him to survive the decline of "race" records. He broadcast regularly from 1932 to 1935 with the Southernaires on NBC radio. During the 1930s he performed solo, with the Josh White Singers, and with jazz and blues musicians such as Sidney Bechet and Bessie Smith. White married Carol Carr in 1934; they had four children.

By the early 1940s White was an established part of the folk music scene. He performed regularly with Leadbelly at New York City's Village Vanguard. He also played with Sonny Terry, Brownie McGhee, Woody Guthrie, and, occasionally, the Almanac Singers. He sang at Leadbelly's funeral in 1949.

White achieved a unique sound. Contemporaries reported being impressed by his clear diction and sonorous baritone. Though he sometimes sang a cappella, he usually accompanied himself, finger-picking a small-bodied rosewood guitar strung with heavy steel strings. He punctuated rhythmic chord patterns with virtuoso single-line riffs that employed bent notes, slides, and other blues techniques. Pete Seeger claimed that "guitar players all over the country imitated Josh's guitar styles," according to Dorothy Schainman Siegel in *The Glory Road*. White was so popular among players that a guitar company marketed an instrument under his name.

White's repertoire ranged from spirituals to bawdy blues and topical protest songs. In later years it expanded to include English, Irish, and Australian ballads. His bestselling single, "One Meat Ball," sold more than one million records. Many of his songs expressed his strong commitment to social reform. In the early 1940s he released two albums that featured antiracist blues and ballads.

Strikingly good-looking and able to project a warm personality onstage, White performed in a number of shows and revues. In 1939–1940 he played Blind Lemon Jefferson in the musical *John Henry*, starring Paul Robeson. He appeared again with Robeson in 1942 in the Langston Hughes operetta *The Man Who Went to War*. In the late 1940s he appeared in *Blue Holiday* (starring Ethel Waters), *A Long Way from Home*, and *How Long Till Summer*. He also appeared in two musical film shorts, *Tall Tales* (1940), with Burl Ives, and *To Hear Your Banjo Play* (1947), with Terry and McGhee. White had small parts in the films *Crimson Canary* (1945) and *Dreams That Money Can Buy* (1948) and a major role in *The Walking Hills* (1949).

White's career broke musical and social barriers. His tour with Libby Holman in the 1940s is identified as the "first mixed race duo" by *The Oxford Companion to Popular Music* (1991). He fused African-American and international folk genres in his own performances, and in the 1940s he toured with the Haitian dancer Josephine Prémice. He also privately helped other musicians; he cared for Big Bill Broonzy during that blues master's last illness.

President Franklin D. Roosevelt and his wife admired and befriended White; Eleanor Roosevelt became godmother to White's son. White performed at the inaugural balls in 1941 and 1945 and was the first African-American folk artist to give a command performance at the White House. During the war he went on a goodwill tour of Mexico (1942) and broadcast weekly for the Office of War Information.

In 1950 White accompanied Eleanor Roosevelt on a goodwill tour of Europe, during which he performed before capacity audiences. He interrupted the tour to return home to confront accusations that he was a communist. Although he appeared without subpoena before the House Un-American Activities Committee and denied supporting communism, his career suffered in the United States. He remained popular, however, in England, where he recorded in the 1950s, and in Scandinavia. During his 1951 tour of England, he broadcast on the British Broadcasting Corporation, and in 1961 he appeared on a series of British television shows.

With the folk revival of the 1960s, White enjoyed something of a comeback, with occasional television appearances and bookings at major clubs and folk festivals. In the summer of 1961 he suffered the first of four heart attacks. Despite declining health and injuries, he continued to perform, touring Canada, Australia, and England as late as 1966–1967. He died during heart surgery in Manhasset, New York.

According to writer Studs Terkel, "During the early 1940s Josh was one of the first voices . . . that brought folk music to big cities on records and radio stations." White's fusion of ethnically diverse vocal traditions helped legitimate the broad cosmopolitan interests of folk musicians in the 1960s. He influenced many performers, including Pete Seeger, and is said to have served as a model for Harry Belafonte. His acoustic guitar technique has rarely been equaled. White received an honorary doctorate of folk anthology from Fisk University in 1949. He is the subject of a play by Peter Link, "Josh the Man and His Music," which was produced in 1983 with his son Josh, Jr., playing his father.

• White's papers are still held by his family and Douglas Yaeger, the executor of his estate. A few items pertaining to White are included in the People's Song Library Collection at Wayne State University Archives of Labor and Urban Affairs in Detroit. A lengthy juvenile biography is by Dorothy Schainman Siegel, *The Glory Road: The Story of Josh White* (1982, repr. 1991). Other monographs containing important biographical information include *Josh White Sings: Music of the New World* (1961) and *Presenting Josh White: Troubadour of Work Songs, Blues and Ballads*, a program printed for a mid-1940s tour with an introduction by Alan Lomax.

White published an instructional guitar book, coauthored with Ivor Mairants, *The Josh White Guitar Method* (c. 1956). Songs that he wrote and performed are collected in *The Josh White Song Book* (1963), commentary by Robert Shelton, with music ed. Walter Raim; it also includes a discography. A list of White's major public appearances is in Sheldon Harris, *Blues Who's Who: A Biographical Dictionary of Blues Singers* (1978; 3d ed., 1985). An obituary is in the *New York Times*, 6 Sept. 1969.

MICHAEL H. HOFFHEIMER

WHITE, Katharine Sergeant (17 Sept. 1892–20 July 1977), fiction editor, was born in Winchester, Massachusetts, the daughter of Charles Spencer Sergeant, vice president of the Boston Elevated Railway Company, and Elizabeth Blake Shepley. White grew up in a prosperous family in Brookline. After her mother's death in 1899, she and her sisters were raised by their father and an aunt, Caroline Belle Sergeant, whom White came to regard as her mother. In 1910 White entered Bryn Mawr College—an unusual step for a woman of her generation, when fewer than 65,000 women attended colleges and graduate schools in the United States. She graduated fourth in her class in 1914, with a classical education and a sense of her own importance in the world that would direct her life and have a profound effect on the *New Yorker* magazine.

In 1915 she married Ernest Angell, a lawyer who became a key force in the American Civil Liberties Union. They lived first in Cleveland, then in New York, and had two children. (Their son, Roger Angell, became a *New Yorker* fiction editor in his mother's last years at the magazine and a writer celebrated for his baseball essays.) Until 1925 White worked at a variety of jobs—not of financial necessity, but from a personal need to work outside the home. She briefly embarked on a writing career with several articles for *Harper's Magazine*, the *Survey*, the *New Republic*, and the *Saturday Review of Literature*. Then, six months after the *New Yorker* was founded in 1925, she was hired by its rough-hewn, brilliant editor, Harold Ross, as a first reader of manuscripts. Realizing what he had in the cultivated and highly literate White, Ross almost immediately doubled her salary and gave her full-time work.

Editing, writing, sitting in on the weekly art meeting, working closely with the artists themselves, and almost single-handedly shaping the *New Yorker*'s advertising policies by urging high standards of integrity on Ross and the magazine's chief financier, Raoul Fleischmann, she quickly proved indispensable. She believed that all editors should also be writers, but it was as an editor that she fully realized her talents and felt most rewarded. She gave a seemingly limitless amount of attention to the writers she edited, from the big talents to the minor, making them feel mothered and invaluable. As a secretary of White's said later, "She knew the whole person, not just the manuscript in front of her." Sensitive to writers' feelings, yet sure of her own opinions, she was respected by such literary figures as Edmund Wilson and Vladimir Nabokov. She worked well with writers who developed a reputation for being difficult—John O'Hara, Alexander Woollcott, and James Thurber in the early years. Thurber described her as "the fountain and shrine" of the *New Yorker*.

As the *New Yorker* took shape as a unique literary magazine, and White became more involved with it, her marriage to Angell foundered. She complained of his infidelity and temper, he of her absorption in her work. In 1929 she took another step unusual for a woman of her time and background when she divorced her husband in Reno, Nevada. Three months later she married the quintessential *New Yorker* writer she had encouraged Ross to hire in 1926, E. B. White. He was seven years her junior and looked younger. Never married before, boyish and shy, he seemed an unlikely companion for the formidable, matronly, and austere-looking White, whose Roman profile and great knot of brown hair would be caricatured by the *New Yorker* artist Peter Arno.

Until her retirement in 1961, White worked at the *New Yorker* as an editor of fiction, fact, and poetry—

first under the direction of Ross, who appointed her the magazine's first Head of Fiction, then under Ross's successor, William Shawn. During her thirty-six years there she edited, nurtured, and fought for higher earnings for writers and poets as diverse as Nabokov, Jean Stafford, Clarence Day, John Updike, Marianne Moore, Nadine Gordimer, Frank Sullivan, Mary McCarthy, Louise Bogan, Nancy Hale, Edmund Wilson, and Janet Flanner, who called White "the best woman editor in the world." She campaigned hard for serious poetry, which Ross shunned in favor of light verse. "Numberless writers have written better because of what you were able to give them," Shawn later wrote her.

After her marriage to E. B. White—a remarkably close, compatible union that produced one child—White divided her time between their New York apartment and a saltwater farm in North Brooklin, Maine, where they later lived year-round. Together the Whites, who came to be perceived at the *New Yorker* as two halves of a whole, edited *A Subtreasury of American Humor* (1941).

In addition to her editing chores, White reviewed children's books for the *New Yorker* (1933–1948), writing with wit and conviction about the inferior quality of much of the published work. In 1958 she invented a new series for the magazine, "Onward and Upward in the Garden," unique, literate essays that combined reviews of seed catalogs with chatty and charmingly written memoir. She wrote the garden essays until ill-health forced her to stop in 1970.

Her life increasingly circumscribed by illness and other infirmities, White died in Blue Hill, Maine. "More than any other editor except Harold Ross himself," wrote William Shawn in the *New Yorker*'s obituary, "Katharine White gave *The New Yorker* its shape, and set it on its course."

• White's papers are at the Bryn Mawr College Library. Linda H. Davis, *Onward and Upward: A Biography of Katharine S. White* (1987), is the only biography. Other important sources are *Onward and Upward in the Garden* (1979) by Katharine S. White, with an introduction by E. B. White, and Scott Elledge, *E. B. White: A Biography* (1984). Obituaries are in the *New York Times*, 22 July 1977, and the *New Yorker*, 1 Aug. 1977.

LINDA H. DAVIS

WHITE, Leonard Dupee (17 Jan. 1891–23 Feb. 1958), political scientist and historian, was born in Acton, Massachusetts, the son of John Sidney White, a farmer, and Bertha H. Dupee. After receiving a B.S. in 1914 and an M.A. in 1915 from Dartmouth College, White enrolled in the doctoral program in political science at the University of Chicago and from 1915 to 1918 taught government at Clark University in Worcester, Massachusetts. In 1916 he married Una Lucille Holden, with whom he had one child. White returned to Dartmouth in 1918 as an instructor of political science before accepting an appointment at the University of Chicago in 1920. He received his Ph.D. the following year and was promoted to full professor in 1925.

White was a protégé of Charles Merriam, the enterprising academician who expanded Chicago's department of political science and assumed its chair in 1923. Merriam brought White into the department to develop courses in the field of public administration, which was emerging as a distinct discipline. White's *Introduction to the Study of Public Administration* (1926), the first textbook on the subject, went through three more editions (1939, 1948, 1955) and had a significant influence on the development of the field. The Social Science Research Council (SSRC) and the Local Community Research Committee, both Merriam creations in the early 1920s, and a Guggenheim Fellowship supported White's early research, which appeared as *The City Manager* (1927) and *The Prestige Value of Public Employment in Chicago* (1929).

During his first decade at Chicago, White chaired the public administration committee of the SSRC and served on the Chicago Citizens' Police Commission, and later, on the Chicago Civil Service Commission. The publication of *Trends in Public Administration* (1933) reinforced his reputation as a leader in the new field. A masterful survey of public policy and administration in the United States, the volume was one of the reports of President Herbert Hoover's Committee on Social Trends. Adding international comparison to his study of public administration, White studied in England in the late 1920s and published several volumes on crossnational themes, including *Civil Service Abroad* (1935), a collaborative effort involving several authors.

On Merriam's recommendation, White was appointed as the Republican member of the U.S. Civil Service Commission in 1934. White used the position to press for the professionalization of public service; he was instrumental in establishing the Junior Civil Service Examination, which opened up conduits between higher education and public service, and the Career Executive Program, which provided "in-service training" for public administrators. He returned to Chicago in 1937 but did not abandon civic commitments that sought improvements in public service. He was an influential member of the President's Committee on Civil Service Improvement (1939–1941), the loyalty review boards of the Civil Service Commission, and the task forces on personnel policy for the first and second Hoover Commissions on the Organization of the Executive Branch. During the 1930s he helped to organize the American Society for Public Administration, serving in 1940–1941 as the first editor of its *Public Administration Review*, and the Society for Personnel Administration. His election as president of the American Political Science Association in 1940 and of the American Society for Public Administration in 1947 testified to his achievements in scholarship, education, and public service.

On Merriam's retirement White assumed the chair of the political science department for eight years

(1940–1948). During this period he embarked on an ambitious four-volume history of the national government's administration, beginning with *The Federalists* (1948), which won the Woodrow Wilson Prize of the American Political Science Association. *The Jeffersonians* appeared in 1951, followed by *The Jacksonians* (1954), which won Columbia University's Bancroft Prize, and *The Republican Era, 1869–1901* (1958), which won the Pulitzer Prize for history. Retiring from active teaching in 1956, White was a coeditor of the papers of James Madison at the time of his death in Chicago.

White had a significant impact on three professional endeavors. Recognizing that "administration has become, and will continue to be the heart of the problem of modern government" (*Introduction to the Study of Public Administration*, p. viii), he provided guidance to the field at a critical juncture in its history and actively nurtured its evolution for three decades. In addition to the twenty-two books that he authored or edited, he and Jean Schneider, his research associate for two decades, produced countless articles and reports. Second, White contributed to the development of public personnel policy through his participation on civic commissions and his recommendations to several task forces.

Third, White pioneered the study of American administrative history. His approach to the subject, as with most of his scholarship, was descriptive in character and historical in method, although he had used social scientific techniques in his 1929 study of attitudes toward municipal employees. Throughout his career he viewed the emergence of public administration as an outgrowth of the expansion of government and recognized that the transformation of the federal system posed fundamental challenges to the delivery of public services. He returned to these questions at the twilight of his career in a set of brilliant lectures at Louisiana State University, published as *The States and the Nation* (1953), in which he presciently urged reforms such as block grants-in-aid to enhance the viability of state government.

• White's papers that relate to his membership on the President's Committee on Civil Service Improvement, the University Senate, and the Department of Political Science are located at the University of Chicago. Franklin G. Connor in *Personnel Administration* 21 (July–Aug. 1958), John M. Gaus in *Public Administration Review* 18 (Summer 1958), and the *Chicago Sun Times*, 10 May 1959, sketch White's life and career. Lynton K. Caldwell in the *American Political Science Review* 52 (1958): 838–42, and Herbert Storing in *Public Administration Review* 25 (1965): 38–51, appraise White's writing. For assessments of White's contribution to academic public administration see Caldwell, "Public Administration and the Universities," *Public Administration Review* 25 (1965): 52–60; Barry D. Karl, *Charles E. Merriam and the Study of Politics* (1974); and Frederick C. Mosher, *American Public Administration* (1975). *Good Government* (Mar.–Apr. 1958): 14–20, reviews White's impact on civil service. An obituary is in the *New York Times*, 24 Feb. 1958.

BALLARD C. CAMPBELL

WHITE, Leslie Alvin (19 Jan. 1900–31 Mar. 1975), anthropologist, was born in Salida, Colorado, the son of Alvin White, a civil engineer and farmer, and Mildred Millard. When White was five years old his parents divorced, and he was raised by his father, who in 1907 left a city job and bought a farm near Greeley, Kansas. Here in 1910 White saw Halley's Comet blaze across the sky, and he dreamed of becoming an astronomer or a physicist. In 1914 the family moved to a farm near Zachary, Louisiana, where White went to high school. After graduating in 1916, he held several jobs before enlisting in the U.S. Navy in 1918. During his tour of duty, White found that much that he had been taught about his society was "a gross distortion of reality," and in 1919 he entered college determined to discover "why *peoples* behave as they do." After two years at Louisiana State University, where he majored in history and political science, White transferred in 1921 to Columbia University, from which he received a bachelor's degree in psychology in 1923 and a master's degree in the same field a year later.

Although White took no courses from anthropologist Franz Boas while at Columbia, he did study anthropology under Boas's student, Alexander Goldenweiser, at the New School for Social Research, where he also took courses from the behavioral psychologist John B. Watson and the economist Thorstein Veblen. Finding that psychology did not provide the insights into the behavior of "peoples" he was seeking, White enrolled in the Department of Sociology and Anthropology at the University of Chicago in 1924. "I went to the University of Chicago," he later wrote, "to study sociology. I quit sociology because . . . it seemed to me all theory and little fact. I jumped out of the sociological frying pan into the fire of anthropology only to find that the anthropologists had plenty of facts but no ideas" (Barnes, *Essays*, p. xvii). White was to spend much of his professional career introducing "ideas" into anthropology.

In 1925 White undertook his first ethnographic field work, spending a few weeks among the Menomini and Winnebago peoples in Wisconsin. An extended field session the following year at Acoma Pueblo, New Mexico, supplied material for his doctoral dissertation.

Having earned a Ph.D. from Chicago in 1927, White accepted a curatorship at the Buffalo Museum of Science and an instructorship at the University of Buffalo. There he taught the same Boasian antievolutionism, which was consistently critical of nineteenth-century cultural evolutionism, that he had learned from Goldenweiser at the New School and from Edward Sapir at Chicago but soon found that his students resisted his teachings, forcing him to reexamine his own views on the subject. White soon found that evolutionism did indeed contribute substantially to an understanding of contemporary cultures.

Living near a Seneca Indian reservation, White felt compelled to read Lewis H. Morgan's *The League of the Iroquois* (1851) and then Morgan's major work, *Ancient Society* (1877), in whose pages he found cultural evolution, the process by which human societies have developed from the simplicity of the Lower Paleolithic to the great complexity of today, treated in a sympathetic and convincing manner. Over the years, he continued to study Morgan's works, eventually went on to edit Morgan's letters and journals, and in 1964 brought out the definitive edition of *Ancient Society*. By then he had gained recognition as the leading Morgan scholar in the world. White also began reading extensively in the works and absorbing the evolutionary ideas of anthropologists E. B. Tylor and Herbert Spencer.

In 1930 White left Buffalo to accept a position in the Department of Anthropology at the University of Michigan, where he taught for the next forty years. When he joined Michigan's department, White was its only full-time anthropologist, but by the time he stepped down as chairman of the department in 1957, it had grown to twenty members and had become one of the leading anthropology departments in the world. In 1931 he married former student Mary Pattison; they had no children.

White was a stimulating, effective, and popular teacher; his major undergraduate course, "The Mind of Primitive Man," commanded large enrollments. He was iconoclastic and tough minded in his views, which he expressed clearly and forcefully. His outspoken hostility toward orthodox beliefs, especially those of organized religion, brought him into conflict with several church groups on campus. But while his unpopular stands did not endear him to the university administration and his promotions were slow in coming, his position at Michigan remained secure.

Professionally, White's advance was also slow. As he began to expound his theories more freely, especially on cultural evolution, he came to be regarded as a maverick in anthropology. Strong opposition to his views led White to engage in polemics against a number of his professional colleagues, most notably Robert H. Lowie on the issue of diffusion versus evolution. The diffusionist argument was that by making a trait available to a society before it had managed to evolve it for itself, diffusion would obscure and even forestall the occurrence of any regular pattern of development. In a series of articles written mostly in the 1940s and 1950s, White set forth his ideas on cultural evolution with clarity and vigor. Though his theoretical position was often labeled "neoevolutionism," White rejected the term, maintaining that his brand of evolutionism "does not differ one whit in principle from that expressed in Tylor's *Anthropology* in 1881." White's fullest expression of his evolutionary views came in *The Evolution of Culture* (1959).

In an earlier book, *The Science of Culture* (1949), White had championed "culturology," the study of culture as a distinct and autonomous class of phenomena, independent of biology, psychology, and sociology. In his often-reprinted article "The Symbol: The Origin and Basis of Human Behavior" (*Philosophy of Science* [1940]: 451–63), White argued that the basis of culture was the uniquely human capacity to use symbols. Culture itself he defined as "a class of phenomena, comprising objects, acts, ideas, and attitudes dependent upon the use of symbols." An amplification of his views on culture was contained in "The Concept of Culture" (1959), an article described by anthropologist Ashley Montagu as "one of the most cogent clarifications of the meaning of the anthropological concept of culture to be found in any language." Besides arguing that culture was a domain of nature *sui generis* that needed to be studied by a separate science, White held that it constituted the most powerful set of determinants of human behavior.

Throughout the period that his views were being disputed, White was nevertheless recognized as a major force in American anthropology, and he was invited to teach, as a visiting professor, at several leading universities, including Yale (1947–1948), Columbia (1948), Harvard (1949), and Berkeley (1957).

Although slow in coming, professional recognition eventually followed. White's major honors included the Viking Fund Medal in General Anthropology in 1959 and election to the presidency of the American Anthropological Association in 1964.

After retiring from Michigan in 1970, White taught at Rice University, San Francisco State College, and the University of California at Santa Barbara, where he remained in residence until his death.

At the time White entered anthropology, the discipline was inhospitable not only to evolutionism but to theorizing in general. The narrow empiricism of Boas and his students placed a strong emphasis on ethnographic field work and shunned theory. Partly through White's efforts, anthropology moved away from descriptive particularism toward vigorous and wide-ranging theorizing. Along with Julian H. Steward and V. Gordon Childe, White was instrumental in creating a movement in anthropology that sought broad regularities in the development of cultures and the reasons for these. Toward this end, he stressed the dominant role played by the utilization of energy, formulating what came to be known as "White's Law," namely, "that culture evolves as the amount of energy harnessed per capita per year increases."

The leading cultural materialist of his day, White regarded culture as "a system that grows by increasing its control over the forces of nature." Among the factors that affected society, he saw technology—the means through which energy was applied—as the most important one, asserting that the type of social organization, art, and philosophy of a given cultural system will be determined by the underlying technology.

Although he stressed the importance of material conditions, White had little to say about environment. While acknowledging its significance in molding particular cultures, he held that in any formula dealing with the evolution of culture as a whole, environments could be averaged out and thus canceled from the equation. His materialist views were nevertheless quite compatible with the major premises of the cultural ecology approach. Indeed, White was an important influence on the "new archaeology" that arose in the 1960s and whose emphasis on "process" represented a blending of Whitean evolutionism and ecological determinism.

Though known primarily as a theorist, for more than thirty years White carried out extensive ethnographic field work among the Keresan-speaking pueblos of New Mexico. Out of this work came monographs on Acoma (1932), San Felipe (1932), Santo Domingo (1935), Santa Ana (1942), and Sia (1962). These were straightforward, factual accounts of American-Indian cultures and, unlike his theoretical writings, were well received by the profession.

White died at Lone Pine, California. At the time of his death he was still working on unpublished manuscripts, some of which appeared in print posthumously.

• White's letters, papers, and unpublished manuscripts are in the Bentley Library of the Michigan Historical Collections, University of Michigan, Ann Arbor. In addition to the works cited above, White's most important writings include *Ethnological Essays*, ed. Beth Dillingham and Robert L. Carneiro (1987), which contains almost all of White's articles on cultural evolution; "Ethnological Theory" in *Philosophy for the Future*, ed. R. W. Sellars et al. (1949); *The Ethnography and Ethnology of Franz Boas* (1963); and *The Social Organization of Ethnological Theory* (1966). White's *The Concept of Cultural Systems* (1975), appeared just after his death. Among White's numerous works dealing with Lewis H. Morgan, the most important are *Pioneers in American Anthropology: The Bandelier-Morgan Letters 1873–1883* (1940), and *Lewis Henry Morgan, The Indian Journals 1859–1862* (1959), both of which he edited, and "How Morgan Came to Write *Systems of Consanguinity and Affinity*," *Papers of the Michigan Academy of Science, Arts, and Letters* 42 (1957): 257–68.

The two major sources on White's life and career are Harry Elmer Barnes's "Foreword" to *Essays in the Science of Culture in Honor of Leslie A. White*, ed. Gertrude E. Dole and Robert L. Carneiro (1960), and Carneiro's chapter, "Leslie A. White," in *Totems and Teachers, Perspectives on the History of Anthropology*, ed. Sydel Silverman (1981). An evaluation of White's contributions to anthropology appears in Carneiro's entry, "White, Leslie Alvin," in the *Biographical Supplement* of the *International Encyclopedia of the Social Sciences* (1979). Interpretative essays on White's theoretical views include A. L. Kroeber, "White's View of Culture," *American Anthropologist* (1948), and Elvin Hatch's treatment of White in his *Theories of Man and Culture* (1973). Obituaries include those by colleagues Elman R. Service and Richard K. Beardsley, in the *American Anthropologist* 78 (1976), which also contains a complete listing of his publications.

ROBERT L. CARNEIRO

WHITE, Maunsel (c. 1781–17 Dec. 1863), commission merchant and entrepreneur, was born in Tipperary, Ireland, the son of Lawford White and Anne Maunsell. White's early years were typical of early Irish emigrants to America; despite his poverty, he came hoping for opportunity. Orphaned in Ireland at about age thirteen, he joined his older brother who had emigrated to Louisville, Kentucky. As a boy, White met Zachary Taylor, the future president, there, and the two became lifelong friends.

White learned the rudiments of the commission merchant business in Louisville and then took a flat boat downriver, arriving in 1801 in New Orleans, where he apprenticed in the same business with family friends. He spent a large portion of his small income learning the French language, and by 1809 he opened his own commission business. He became a commission merchant, building his business by exhibiting an unimpeachable trustworthiness in an industry vulnerable to chicanery.

As a Protestant who married into a prominent Creole family, White was atypical of antebellum Louisiana. His father-in-law, Pierre Denys de la Ronde, who owned one of the plantations where the battle of New Orleans was fought, was military commandant of New Orleans during the Spanish regime. He later attained the rank of general in the Louisiana militia. White married his daughter, Celeste, in 1812. Upon her death in 1822, White married her sister, Heloise, in 1824.

General Andrew Jackson, sent to New Orleans in 1814 to defend the city, met White, who was captain of a volunteer militia company he had personally outfitted and armed. White's company, part of the battalion of General Jean Baptiste Plauché, fought alongside Jackson. After the successful battle, Jackson was charged with contempt of court for ignoring a writ of habeas corpus issued by a local federal judge and for jailing the judge for violating Jackson's imposition of martial law during the crisis. The city's populace split over the issue, with Plauché's battalion vociferously supporting Jackson, who was fined $1,000.

After the English had withdrawn to Dauphin Island, Jackson sent White and Edward Livingston, Jackson's unpaid aide de camp and signer of the Louisiana Purchase, to arrange an exchange of prisoners and the reclamation of captured slaves. Through these interactions White became a lifelong friend of Jackson, later representing the sale of products of his plantation, "The Hermitage," through the port of New Orleans.

As an entrepreneur during New Orleans's antebellum boom period, White helped organize a development bank to finance the digging of the New Basin Canal connecting Lake Pontchartrain with the city's American sector (c. 1832). He was a founder of a bank that built the city's waterworks, and in 1834 he was an organizer of a bank that built the Exchange Hotel, later called the St. Charles, the largest in the South.

After the early 1840s, White spent less time with his business than with his sugar plantation, "Deer Range," in Plaquemines Parish. From there he was elected to the state senate, chairing the commission that handled the construction of the Gothic capitol at Baton Rouge in 1847.

White became a board member of the University of Louisiana (later Tulane University), which was established by the state in 1847. He donated property to fund a chair in business studies to be filled by J. B. D. DeBow, the first such endowed chair in America. Believing in the emphasis that *DeBow's Review* put on statistics and scientific improvements in farming, White backed the journal financially when it became strapped.

White was an early supporter of railroading. In 1836 he helped found the line that is now the St. Charles streetcar, and he helped to organize the New Orleans, Opelousas and Great Western Railroad, which was intended to extend to Texas. Antebellum Louisiana railroads were mostly short lines connecting plantations to the Mississippi, but White thought in larger terms, envisioning trunk lines and eventually a transcontinental railroad through the South. He chaired or attended many regional conferences whose purposes were to unify a southern railroad system.

About 1849 White introduced Tabasco peppers from Mexico at Deer Range, growing several acres. He gave some plants to fellow capitol commission member Daniel Avery for his plantation. Later, when the McIlhenny family married into the Avery family, the Tabasco sauce industry was born in Louisiana, an enterprise that eventually became known worldwide.

While he reputedly favored the renewal of the slave trade to provide labor for the agricultural South, White only bought slaves and refused to sell them because he did not believe in breaking up slave families. Ex-slave narratives gathered in the 1930s confirm his humane treatment of his slaves. He was also active in the American Colonization Society of Louisiana.

White was an ardent supporter of Stephen Douglas's candidacy for president, despite "The Little Giant's" advocacy of "Popular Sovereignty," which ran counter to southern hopes of extending slavery. White disliked the idea of breaking up the Union, but when the movement for secession came, White called upon "brave Louisianians" to defend the South. "With four to one against us [in 1815]," he said, "we won the victory at New Orleans. . . . Let the Abolitionists come." The war, he noted, "has been approaching for years, and if politicians had looked to any other interest but their own, this calamity might have been averted" (*New Orleans Daily Delta*, 3 Feb. 1861).

At the time of White's death in New Orleans, the Union was asunder, New Orleans had fallen to Admiral Farragut, and the South was headed for ultimate defeat.

White had seen the deficiencies of the South and tried to address them all. He observed the need for venture capital and established several banks; he foresaw the need for railroad growth and promoted trunk lines and a transcontinental route. Lack of education in the South was ameliorated by White's contributions to the University of Louisiana, especially the establishment of the first chair in business education in America. And his bailing out of *DeBow's Review* helped to continue the dissemination of information on farming, the South's largest industry. Except perhaps for slavery, White can be counted as a true visionary and progressive of the Old South.

• The best source on White is his letters, held in the Southern Historical Collection at the University of North Carolina. White is mentioned in Clement Eaton, *The Mind of the Old South* (1967), as an epitome of "The Commercial Mind." The events of the battle of New Orleans come largely from the newspaper *Louisiana Courier* during the period of martial law in early 1815. An account of White's activities in connection with the construction of the Gothic Louisiana state capitol is in Arthur Scully, Jr., *James Dakin, Architect: His Career in New York and the South* (1973), as is his connection to the Tabasco pepper story. Information on White's contribution to the University of Louisiana can be found in *DeBow's Review* (1847). White's railroad activities are in Merle Reed, *New Orleans and the Railroads* (1966). His treatment of his slaves can be found in Ronnie W. Clayton, *Mother Wit: The Ex-Slave Narratives of the Louisiana Writers Project* (1990), pp. 178–80.

ARTHUR SCULLY, JR.

WHITE, Minor (9 July 1908–24 June 1976), photographer and teacher, was born Minor Martin White in Minneapolis, Minnesota, the son of Charles Henry White, a bookkeeper, and Florence May Martin, a dressmaker. Beginning in 1916 his parents were separated a number of times; White remained with his mother and often resided at the home of her parents. His parents were divorced in 1929. White attended the Minneapolis public schools, graduating from West High School in 1927 with distinction in science and literature. He entered the University of Minnesota in 1927 and majored in botany. He also took courses in literature and poetry, taught by scholar and writer Joseph Warren Beach. It was during these years that White recognized his homosexuality, an aspect of his life that was reflected in his art. When, in 1931, he failed to meet the degree requirements, he left the university and became a houseman at the University Club. His employment allowed him the time to concentrate on writing poetry, his chief interest. After taking some night courses, he graduated from the university in 1934.

Having been introduced to early photographs and photographic processes by his grandfather and having learned the rudiments of technique by making photomicrograph slides for the botany department, White took up photography with serious intent in 1937. That same year he made his first landscape images in northern Minnesota. In the summer of 1937 he left Minneapolis and settled in Portland, Oregon. It was there that he began his photographic career, both as an artist and a teacher. In 1938 he became a creative photographer for the Works Progress Administration Art Program, documenting the historic nineteenth-century cast-iron facades and buildings that were being demolished along the Portland waterfront. His pictures were exhibited in 1939, and the exhibition toured various national WPA centers until 1942. White was also active in theater circles, making photographs of productions and actors. In 1938 he began teaching photography to young people at the local YMCA. In 1940 he was sent to La Grande, Oregon, to teach at the WPA art center; he subsequently became its director. In 1941 he returned to Portland, having decided to establish a photography business there. Not long after his return, in February 1942, he had his first one-man museum exhibition at the Portland Art Museum, and in April he was drafted into the army.

In 1943, while stationed in Hawaii, White was baptized into the Roman Catholic church. This marked the beginning of his interest in religious practices and in Christian mysticism. He photographed little during the war and saw service throughout the Pacific theater, participating in the invasion of the Philippines in 1944. White did write poetry during these years, completing three extended verse cycles. He was discharged late in 1945 and traveled to New York, where he enrolled in the Columbia University Extension Division to study art history with Meyer Schapiro. Around the same time he befriended Beaumont Newhall, curator of photography at the Museum of Modern Art, and Newhall's wife, Nancy. Under their tutelage White was brought into the mainstream photographic art community. As part of his study at Columbia, White completed his first writing on photography, a work eventually titled "Fundamentals of Style in Photography" that was influenced by Heinrich Wölfflin's *Principles of Art History* (1915). White's work was never published, but it served as the basis for most of his later writings on the critical and interpretative analysis of photographs.

In 1946 White was invited by photographer Ansel Adams to assist him on the faculty of the California School of Fine Arts in San Francisco. It was there that White truly began his teaching career, remaining on the faculty until 1953. He then moved to Rochester, New York, and took a position at the George Eastman House, a museum of photography at which Beaumont Newhall was curator. In 1955 White joined the faculty of the Rochester Institute of Technology (RIT), at first on a part-time basis. He began teaching full time in 1956, after he had resigned from Eastman House to concentrate on teaching. He remained at RIT until 1965, at which time he joined the faculty of the Massachusetts Institute of Technology (MIT). He was granted tenure in 1969 and taught at MIT until his retirement in 1974. In addition to teaching, White pioneered in the development of the workshop format, implementing such alternative educational programs for small groups of select students in his home and in an abbreviated format at sites throughout the country and under various organizational auspices. Throughout his life White continued with his own photography. Working always during the summer months, he also produced a major body of work throughout the year.

In 1952, together with a group of others interested in serious art photography, including Adams, Dorothea Lange, Barbara Morgan, and the Newhalls, White founded the magazine *Aperture* and became its first editor. The publication was to become one of the most influential forces in the field during the next twenty years, aiding in the dialogue about creative photography and encouraging the wider acceptance of the medium as one of the major art forms of the twentieth century. The majority of White's writing was done for *Aperture*, until he resigned his editorship in 1975. White wrote extensively in book form, completing three major manuscripts on the methods of creative photography and interpretation, including one titled "Canons of Camerawork," but none of his works were published. Although his photographic work was frequently included in exhibitions, and despite the fact that his pictures are represented in every major collection of photography internationally, he himself produced the first monograph on his photography. His *Mirrors Messages Manifestations* (1969) is an extended autobiographical sequence of images with poetic text. The work accompanied a retrospective exhibition of his photographs at the Philadelphia Museum of Art in January 1970.

White also curated numerous exhibitions, including a cycle of four between 1968 and 1974 at the Hayden Gallery of MIT. These exhibitions—"Light^7," "Being without Clothes," "Octave of Prayer," and "Celebrations"—reflected White's deep interest in the spiritual and extended the religious and esoteric aspects of photography that he championed. Each exhibition was accompanied by a catalog publication.

Throughout his life, White was interested in the study of comparative religions, including Zen and the Gurdjieff philosophy, and in astrology. He strived to attain monastic simplicity in his life, and he practiced meditation ritual; he incorporated all of these spiritual explorations into his teaching. White died in Boston, leaving no survivors.

White was one of the most important photographic artists active during the thirty-year period after World War II. He produced a unique body of imagery that derives its meaning from his interests in poetry and spirituality. In photographic terms he is a successor to Alfred Stieglitz; as a younger colleague, he should be considered in the company of Adams and Edward Weston. The two additional facets of White's career, while fundamentally related to his expressive work as an artist, are also independently significant. One is his work as a writer on photography and as the publisher of an important journal, and the other is his contribution as a teacher. Over a thirty-year period, beginning in 1946, he taught directly and influenced through lectures and workshops several generations of artist photographers, some of whom became leading photographers and teachers, including Robert Bourdeau, Paul Caponigro, Abe Frajndlich, Jerry N. Uelsmann, and John Upton. White's concern for fundamental spiritual values placed him within a certain arena of thought that was particular to the 1960s, but it had originated earlier in his life, and he maintained his beliefs in spite of changing public and artistic taste. In 1989 a retrospective exhibition of his work, drawn from his archive, opened at the Museum of Modern Art in New York and subsequently toured to museums in the cities where he had lived throughout his career.

• White's personal photographic archive, papers, library, and collection of original photographs are in the Art Museum, Princeton University. One of the most concise statements by White on his philosophy of photography is "Equivalence: The Perennial Trend," *PSA Journal* 29 (July 1969): 17–21; see also (coauthored with Walter Chappell) "Some Methods for Experiencing Photographs," *Aperture* 5, no. 4 (1957): 156–71. With Richard Zakia and Peter Lorenz White published a book of technical fundamentals, *The New Zone System Manual* (1976). Peter C. Bunnell, *Minor White: The Eye That Shapes* (1989), is the first book published after White's death to make use of the material at Princeton. It contains a comprehensive chronology, a selection of his unpublished writings, including early poetry and personal correspondence, reproductions of 295 photographs, and a complete bibliography. A lengthy interview appears in Paul Hill and Thomas Cooper, *Dialogue with Photography* (1979). Michael Hoffman, ed., *Minor White: Rites and Passages* (1978), begun before White's death, contains a biographical essay by James Baker Hall that is based, in part, on personal interviews. Mark Holborn, ed., *Minor White: A Living Remembrance* (1984), includes reflections by several of White's students and colleagues. For a broad assessment of White's work, including a specific study of *Aperture*, see Jonathan Green, *American Photography: A Critical History 1945 to the Present* (1984); see also Colin Westerbeck, "Beyond the Photographic Frame 1946–1989," in Sarah Greenough et al., *On the Art of Fixing a Shadow* (1989). Obituaries are in the *New York Times*, 26 June 1976; *Newsweek*, 4 July 1976; *Time*, 5 July 1976; and *Parabola*, Fall 1976.

PETER C. BUNNELL

WHITE, Paul Dudley (6 June 1886–31 Oct. 1973), physician, was born in Roxbury, Massachusetts, the son of Herbert Warren White, a successful general practitioner, and Elizabeth Abigail Dudley. He graduated from the Roxbury Latin School in 1904 and that fall enrolled as a freshman at Harvard College. After an undistinguished start, his course work improved substantially in his junior year, and he went on to graduate in 1908 with honors. In 1907, after only three years of college, he commenced the study of medicine at the Harvard Medical School, excelled in his academic performance, and received an M.D. in 1911, ranking second in his class and again receiving honors. This was followed by an eighteen-month internship in pediatrics and internal medicine at the Massachusetts General Hospital in Boston, during the course of which he and physician Roger I. Lee collaborated in developing a method to measure the clotting time of blood (soon known as the Lee-White Coagulation Time), which was widely used for the next fifty years. At the suggestion of David L. Edsall, chief of medicine at the hospital, this internship was followed by a year of training in cardiovascular physiology in London at the University College Hospital under the brilliant young investigator Thomas Lewis.

Returning from England in July 1914, White commenced a long professional life that, characterized by extraordinary energy and a broad array of activities, centered around the field of heart disease. Previously, patients with heart problems had been cared for entirely by general practitioners or nonspecializing physicians. White was a pioneer in deliberately limiting his practice and his research to heart disease and in the process demonstrated both success in acquiring new knowledge and in attracting patients. From a modest office at the Massachusetts General Hospital, as well as in its clinics (where he received no salary), he quickly became known for his personal charm, diagnostic acumen, good sense, and skillful handling of patients. He was soon widely sought as a consultant and was visited by notables from around the world who craved his evaluation. In 1924 he married Ina Reid, with whom he adopted two children.

The peak of White's influence as a practicing cardiologist was reached in September 1955, when, while vacationing in Colorado, President Dwight D. Eisenhower experienced an acute myocardial infarction and White was promptly called in as consultant. For many decades, the diagnosis of such a heart attack had been regarded with the greatest apprehension; patients so labeled were all too often expected to live brief lives of semi- or total invalidism. White, however, took an optimistic approach, based on his many years of observation of similar cases. He used the widely reported press conferences as a pulpit to preach the nature of the common heart attack and the potential in most patients for an excellent recovery and further useful living. President Eisenhower was told that he might seek a second term, which he did, and was reelected. This episode marked the apex of White's influence on the attitudes of both the medical profession and the public at large.

The Eisenhower illness demonstrated two related aspects of White's life—his role as a practitioner and consultant, and his contribution as a teacher. In his roles as both director of the Cardiac Laboratory and chief of the Cardiac Service at the Massachusetts General Hospital and as faculty member of the Harvard Medical School, he conducted an active clinical research program and trained a series of young doctors from all over the world, including medical students, hospital residents and fellows, graduate students, and practicing physicians, thus seeding many geographic areas with his young disciples. He exerted his influence through bedside teaching, seminars, lectures in which he exemplified the wise, experienced heart specialist, and his successful textbook, *Heart Disease*. First published in 1931, the work went through three more editions, a tribute to his lucid writing, his large fund of knowledge including medical history, and his many years of practice. With the passage of years, White's effectiveness extended increasingly to the public at large. Making astute use of the media, as in the Eisenhower illness, he became famous for his promotion of physical exercise as a means of maintaining good health and preventing or modifying the inroads of disease, for his stress on the importance for older individuals of continuing an active useful life and avoiding sloth, and for the validity and benefit of an outlook of optimism even in the presence of significant heart disease.

Also exceedingly active in clinical research, White produced more than 700 scientific papers, books, discussions, and reviews. Particularly noteworthy was his report with Louis Wolff and John Parkinson of a new syndrome (later shown by others to be due to conduction from the upper to the lower muscle masses of the heart via a by-pass tract often associated with rapid heart rhythms), and articles describing valuable new approaches to Da Costa's syndrome (also called neurocirculatory asthenia), chronic constrictive pericarditis, and pulmonary embolism. Most of the published papers were authored with one or more associates.

From the age of fifty-five on, White was increasingly involved in organizations devoted to the issues of heart disease, both in individual patients and as community problems. One of the founders of the American Heart Association in 1924, he served as its president in 1941–1942. In 1948 he became the first executive director of the National Advisory Heart Council and chief medical adviser to the new National Heart Institute, a position he held until 1957. He was second president of the International Society of Cardiology from 1954 to 1958 and was a founder and president of the International Society of Cardiology Foundation from 1957 to 1970. He especially relished his international associations in the belief that global scientific exchanges could promote better understanding between peoples and contribute to world peace.

White remained busy and productive with his multitude of interests until 1970, when he first experienced a heart attack. He developed major disability in May 1973 following a stroke and died in Boston.

His long, productive career demonstrated how, in the twentieth century, cardiology became an increasingly important clinical and research specialty, to which he, a major international leader, contributed as a gifted teacher, astute practitioner and consultant, and important clinical investigator.

• There are three principal sources of biographical material: White's brief autobiography, *My Life and Medicine* (1971); a series of short recollections by former colleagues and students appearing in the *American Journal of Cardiology* 15 (1965): 533–603; and the full-length biography by Oglesby Paul, *Take Heart* (1986). An obituary is in the *New York Times*, 1 Nov. 1973.

OGLESBY PAUL

WHITE, Paul Welrose (9 June 1902–9 July 1955), journalist and broadcast executive, was born in Pittsburg, Kansas, the son of Paul W. White, a stone contractor, and Anna Pickard. While in high school, he was a newspaper reporter for the *Pittsburg Headlight* and, after graduation, the *Salina (Kans.) Sun*. He studied journalism at the University of Kansas for a year and worked as telegraph editor at the *Kansas City Journal*. White moved to New York City in 1922, enrolling at Columbia University and earning a B.Litt. in 1923 and an M.S. from Columbia's School of Journalism in 1924. After brief stints with the *New York Evening Bulletin* and the *New York Sunday World*, White joined United Press in 1924 as a staff correspondent in New York City and later as a features editor.

In 1930 White moved to the fledgling Columbia Broadcasting System (CBS) as a news editor in the radio network's publicity department. Three years later he became vice president and general manager of the Columbia News Service, the network's news division. White's radio news operation became so successful that the American Newspaper Publishers Association in 1934 forced CBS to cut back news broadcasts by threatening to stop publishing network program schedules and press releases. As Columbia's director of public affairs, White, with the support of network vice president and former *New York Times* editor Edward Klauber, rebuilt the news department by relying on news analysis and live broadcasts of events from around North America and Europe.

As World War II approached, White organized exhaustive coverage of Germany's annexation of Austria and the Munich crisis in 1938. During the Munich crisis in September, CBS broadcast nearly forty-eight hours of live news coverage with 471 separate broadcasts. Following the outbreak of war in 1939 CBS became the leading source of war news from Europe thanks to correspondents such as Edward R. Murrow in London, William L. Shirer in Berlin, and Eric Sevareid in Paris and commentators H. V. Kaltenborn and Elmer Davis. White ran Columbia's war coverage from New York City, combining reports from overseas with studio commentary while seated at what he called his piano, an elaborate studio console that allowed him to speak with correspondents around the world and coordinate network broadcasts. "Paul was, I think, the first real managing editor the business ever had," Sevareid recalled. "He loved the thing, you know—the switching around the world. That was his news, what he called 'the fine careless rapture' of the business" (*Broadcasting*, 14 Sept. 1987). Although White appreciated the drama and emotion radio could evoke, he was also an outspoken advocate of objective news coverage. Unlike a newspaper, the network must take no editorial position. A Columbia news analyst, he wrote in a memorandum to his staff that was later published in the *New York Times* (20 Sept. 1943), must "inform his listeners rather than persuade them. . . . Ideally, in the case of controversial issues, the audience should be left with no impression as to which side the analyst himself actually favors." The network's war coverage won a Peabody Award in 1945 for distinguished news broadcasting.

White resigned from CBS in 1946 following a corporate reorganization that saw Murrow promoted to network vice president for news. White had been an adjunct faculty member at Columbia University's School of Journalism from 1939 to 1946 and in 1947 published *News on the Air*, a classic textbook of broadcast journalism that also outlines the growth of CBS news. In 1948 he returned to newspaper work as associate editor of the *San Diego Journal*. He joined KFMB radio and television in San Diego as executive news editor in 1951 and the following year coordinated the American Broadcasting Company's radio and television coverage of the Republican and Democratic nominating conventions. While at KFMB, he broadcast editorials on behalf of the station. In contrast to his previous stance, White explained, "We take very seriously our responsibility to inform the public through news programs, but we think objective news reporting is not enough—that interpretation is called for" (1 June 1951). The station, he said, would give those on the other side equal time for rebuttals, but "from now on, intends to speak its mind on public issues." When it was pointed out that his editorials marked a radical departure from his commitment to absolute neutrality at CBS, White observed that times had changed. During World War II, he wrote in a letter to *Newsweek* (12 Apr. 1954), "I also thought that Soviet Russia was a valuable ally, that nuclear fission was impossible, and that, after the war . . . steaks would be plentiful and cheap." He remained at KFMB despite declining health until a month before his death from the effects of several chronic conditions including heart disease, emphysema, and cirrhosis of the liver brought on by periods of heavy drinking. White was married three times. He wed Katherine E. Kennedy in 1925; they had one child before the marriage ended in divorce. White married Susan Taylor in 1936, and they had one child before that union, too, ended in divorce. He married for a third time, to CBS staffer Margaret Miller, in 1945.

White played a critical role in shaping both the style and substance of network radio and television news coverage. Columbia's "World News Round-Up," first broadcast under White's direction in 1938, set the pattern for future network news reports from CBS correspondents on the scene of major events; such news programs were introduced and set in context by a network announcer. White's insistence on factual reporting rather than persuasion parallels the trend toward objective journalism that had become dominant in major newspapers and wire services since the 1890s. While he was a veteran of newspaper and wire service journalism, White understood that radio news was heard, not read and urged his reporters to adopt a conversational, intimate style using closely observed details that would connect the listener to the event. White also understood that live radio broadcasts of important news events had an immediacy that newspapers could never match. CBS reporters took network microphones out of the studio and let listeners hear the sounds of events as they took place. Many of Murrow's famous 1940–1941 radio broadcasts from London featured the sounds of anti-aircraft guns or fire sirens, which helped bring the reality of modern warfare home to the American audience.

• Several important letters and memoranda by White are in the Edward R. Murrow Papers at Tufts University (also available on microfilm) and the Eric Sevareid Papers at the Library of Congress. For contemporary observations of the CBS news operation, see Elmer Davis, "Broadcasting the Outbreak of War," *Harpers Magazine* 179 (Nov. 1939): 579–88, and "Fine Careless Rapture," *New Yorker*, 20 Jan. 1940, p. 17. His career and often troubled relationship with Murrow are discussed in A. M. Sperber, *Murrow: His Life and Times* (1986); Joseph E. Persico: *Murrow: An American Original* (1988); and Edward Bliss, Jr., *Now the News: A History of Broadcast Journalism* (1991). Obituaries are in *Broadcasting*, 18 July 1955, p. 84, and *Variety*, 13 July 1955, p. 26.

TIM ASHWELL

WHITE, Pearl (4 Mar. 1889–4 Aug. 1938), actress, was born Pearl Fay White in Green Ridge, Missouri, the daughter of Edward Gilman White, a farmer, real estate and insurance agent, and county assessor, and Elizabeth G. House. Pearl, the youngest of five children, was two years old when her mother died. Her father later remarried, and the family moved to Springfield, Missouri, where Pearl attended grade school. Although she neglected her studies, she got by with her quick wit and acting ability. After only one year, White quit high school and about 1905 went to work for the Diemer Stock Company, which operated a theater and patent medicine business. She sold tickets and helped print the theater programs and medicine ads, and she played bit parts during the evening. Her good looks, sense of humor, and determination proved to be assets for her later career.

At age eighteen White left home and joined the Trousdale Stock Company. For the next two months she traveled with Trousdale, appearing in a four-act drama, "Broken Hearts," until he fired her, after which she traveled throughout Kansas and Oklahoma with various companies, playing in schoolhouses and opera houses. Occasionally she had neither work nor income. White married fellow actor Victor Sutherland in 1907 and divorced him seven years later. They had no children. In 1908, the Chicago firm of Rowland & Clifford gave her a lead role as "Jane Eyre," playing for three days at a theater in East St. Louis.

White had begun to lose her voice before her role in "Jane Eyre," after which she decided to seek work with movie companies, where the silent movies would put no strain on her vocal cords. About 1909 she found a job with Powers Studio in New York City. Director Joseph A. Golden needed a girl who could ride horseback, and he gave her a start in a fifteen-minute motion picture. She completed it in two days and made ten dollars. Between July 1910 and January 1911, White made five films for Powers Studio, including two literary classics, *The Count of Monte Cristo* and *The New Magdalene*. White later wrote, "I intended all the time to go back to the stage when my voice got all right." Her voice did improve but she had found a better job.

White was just what the French film company Pathé Frères was looking for. She spent a year with Pathé studios in New Jersey, making six films and becoming well known to theater audiences in the United States. She then joined Crystal Film Company, making a slapstick comedy each week. Between 1912 and 1914 she made more than 100 movies including *The New Typist, First Love*, and *Lizzie and the Ice Man*. To help establish her identity, her name appeared in the movie titles: *Pearl As a Clairvoyant, Pearl As a Detective, Pearl's Dilemma*, and *Pearl's Mistake*. By now, White wore a blond wig, which became her trademark.

White's big break came in 1914 when she starred in the famous silent movie serial *Perils of Pauline*, "the best-known disaster-play ever filmed." The serial—a huge box-office success—ended each episode with the pretty heroine in a perilous situation, hanging from a cliff or sinking in quicksand. The movie would be continued from that point. The audience could hardly wait until the next episode to see how White managed to escape. Unfortunately, during the filming of the series, White fell down some stairs and broke a vertebra in her back. Although she did not think it serious enough to require medical attention, it would cause severe back pain later in her life.

The filming of another Pathé serial, *The Exploits of Elaine*, purportedly earned White a salary of $10,000 a week in 1914. This film, better acted and directed than *Perils of Pauline*, made over a million dollars.

White then made two feature films, *The King's Game* and *Hazel Kirke*, followed by additional serials, *The Iron Claw, The Fatal Ring, The House of Hate, The Lightning Raiders*, and *The Black Secret*. By 1919, serials were extremely popular and were shown all over the world. Because of their silent nature they could be understood by all people.

White published her autobiography, *Just Me*, in 1919 (with the assistance of Robert W. Chambers). She wove a great deal of fiction into the book, making it unreliable but colorful reading.

During World War I White promoted the war effort and the sale of war bonds. One of her serials, *Pearl of the Army*, emphasized military preparedness, and it boosted morale on the homefront as well as the battlefront. In the movies, White's heroine's exploits proved that women could handle difficult situations and encouraged American women to take greater roles in winning the war. In 1919 she married co-star Wallace McCutcheon, Jr., a wounded war hero; they had no children. They divorced in July 1921, and McCutcheon later committed suicide. Some blamed White for this tragedy, and the guilt devastated her.

In 1919 and 1920 White starred in ten undistinguished Fox features such as *The Black Secret* and *The Thief*. She then went to Paris for performances at the Casina de Paris. Late in 1922 she returned to New York and made another serial, *Plunder*. White had become famous for her dangerous performances, but she suffered back pain from the injury sustained years earlier. By now her eyesight had begun to fail, probably the result of many years before bright floodlights. The studios in the past had hired doubles (usually slightly built men) to do some of her most dangerous scenes. One stand-in fell to his death in 1922 in front of a large crowd of spectators; the public was outraged that White did not do the scenes herself.

After completion of *Plunder*, White suffered a nervous breakdown. She became a devout Catholic and lived in seclusion in France. Once recovered, she starred in her last movie, *Terreur (Perils of Paris)*, made in France in 1923. In 1925 she performed on stage in Paris and London, frequented casinos, and became the owner of race horses.

White traveled around the world until her health deteriorated. Constant back pain caused her to resort to drugs and alcohol. She continued to live in France until her death of cirrhosis of the liver. White died in Neuilly and was buried in Paris. Two screen biographies with the same title, *The Perils of Pauline*, one starring Betty Hutton (1947) and the other Pamela Austin (1967), are based loosely on her life.

• Biographies of Pearl White include articles in Ephraim Katz, *The Film Encyclopedia* (1979); William H. Walter, "Springfield's Pearl White: Queen of Movie Serials," *Springfield Magazine*, Jan.-Oct. 1984; and Laurel E. Boeckman, "Pearl White," *Show Me Missouri Women: Selected Biographies*, vol. 1, ed. Mary K. Dains (1989). White's work is mentioned in numerous histories of the screen, including Deems Taylor, et al., *A Pictorial History of the Movies* (1943; repr. 1950), and Joe Franklin, *Classics of the Silent Screen* (1959). An obituary appears in *Springfield Leader & Press*, 4 Aug. 1938.

MARY K. DAINS

WHITE, Solomon (12 June 1868–Aug. 1955), Negro League baseball player and manager and chronicler of early "blackball" years, also known as "Sol," was born in Bellaire, Ohio, an industrial town across the Ohio river from Wheeling, West Virginia. Nothing is known of his parentage or early life. In 1883 White began his baseball career with a three-year stint with his hometown Bellaire Globes, an amateur white team barnstorming the Ohio Valley. In 1886 White moved to the Wheeling Green Stockings of the Ohio State League and, after an abortive seven-game 1887 season with the Pittsburgh Keystones of the National Colored League, he returned to the integrated Wheeling club, reportedly batting .370 for the remaining 52 games, including 84 hits and 54 runs. Meanwhile, segregationist practices solidified in major league baseball represented by Chicago star Adrian "Cap" Anson's July 1881 refusal to play against a team with a black player. In response, African-American players filled the rosters of integrated minor league teams and organized their own circuits and ball clubs.

In 1889 White began the year with Trenton in the integrated Middle States League. After 31 games and a .333 batting average, he joined the black New York Gorhams earning $10 per week. In 1890 White's Cuban Giants became the York (Pennsylvania) Monarchs moving as a team into the Eastern Interstate League, an integrated circuit. As the Monarchs' second baseman, his signature position, the right-handed White—at 5′9″ and 170 pounds—batted .356, fifth best in the league, with 84 hits and 78 runs. White's 1891 season was split between the Cuban Giants, soon bankrupt, and the New York Big Gorhams, representing Ansonia in the Connecticut State League, which folded by midsummer. The Big Gorhams became a touring team recording 100 wins and 4 defeats versus weak amateur and semiprofessional teams. At some point in the year White left to join the Harrisburg Giants, apparently taking other teammates with him and leading sportswriters to dub Harrisburg the "Polka-Dots." From

1892 to 1894 White labored for J. B. Bright's Cuban Giants, the Pittsburgh Keystones, the Black Boston Monarchs, and a Hotel Champlain team in upstate New York, where he also waited tables. In 1895 White played 10 games for Fort Wayne, Indiana, in the integrated Western Tri-State League, being paid $80 while batting .385 with 20 hits and 15 runs. When the league disbanded in June, White joined the Adrian (Michigan) Page Fence Giants, owned by a barbed-wire company, hitting .404 with 21 safeties and 15 runs in just 12 games. At the end of the season White entered Ohio's Wilberforce University as a theological student and began a four-year pattern of summer ball and winter school. In 1897 White moved to the Cuban X-Giants for three years. White returned in 1900 to the Page Fence team, which had now become the Columbia Giants of Chicago. In 1901 the Cuban X-Giants welcomed White back as second baseman and captain.

In 1902 White began his longest and most successful tenure in baseball as player-manager of the Philadelphia Giants. Recruited by owner H. Walter Schlicter, sports editor of the *Philadelphia Item*, White played shortstop and second base while guiding the Giants to a record of 81 wins and 43 losses. After claiming the "blackball" championship, White's Giants lost two postseason exhibition games to the American League Champion Philadelphia Athletics. In 1903, with salaries ranging from $60 to $90 per month, the Philadelphia Giants and the Cuban X-Giants joined the white Independent League. Before the 1904 season White's squad acquired pitching stars Rube Foster and Danny McClellan, left fielder Preston "Pete" Hill, and catcher George "Chappie" Johnson, becoming one of the great "blackball" teams of all time, even moving south to win Cuba's winter league title. The Philadelphia squad reached its peak in 1905, with a record of 134 wins and 21 losses, and in 1906 at 108–31, both times claiming the "blackball" championship.

White's greatest contribution to Negro League baseball and the sport in general was as author of *Sol White's Official Base Ball Guide* published in 1907. Providing information about the origins and evolution of Negro League baseball, White's unique chronicle profiles special contests, star players, managers, the Cubans, and the "Colored" game. While noting the difficulties faced by the "Colored player," White was optimistic that one day black players would walk "hand in hand with the opposite race in the greatest of all American games—baseball."

In 1910 White organized his own Brooklyn Royal Giants in the International League of Colored Baseball Clubs. The circuit did not last more than a few weeks, and manager White moved in 1911 to the New York Lincoln Giants, which folded by 4 July. Following one more ill-fated season in 1912 as manager of the Boston Giants, White's baseball career ended except for a few isolated responsibilities: secretary, Columbus, Ohio, club in the National Negro League (1920); manager, Fear's Giants of Cleveland, a black minor league squad (1922); manager, Cleveland Browns, Negro National League (1924); and manager, Newark Browns, Eastern Colored League (1926). White's remaining years are not well known. Apparently he lived in Harlem, where he died, and wrote a column of observation for the *Amsterdam News* and the *New York Age*.

• *Sol White's Official Base Ball Guide* (1907) has been reprinted by Camden House (1984). The most complete modern profile of White is in John B. Holway, *Blackball Stars, Negro League Pioneers* (1988). Also consult Robert Petersen, *Only the Ball Was White* (1970), James A. Riley, *The Biographical Encyclopedia of the Negro Baseball Leagues* (1994), and Jerry Malloy, "Solomon 'Sol' White," in *19th Century Stars*, ed. Robert L. Tiemann and Mark Rucker (1989), p. 136.

DAVID BERNSTEIN

WHITE, Stanford (9 Nov. 1853–25 June 1906), architect, was born in New York City, the son of Richard Grant White, a writer and music critic, and Alexina Black Mease, a poet. The family lacked funds to send him to college, and in 1870, having exhibited some artistic talent, White followed the advice of John La Farge and obtained a position with the architect Henry Hobson Richardson in New York. White's ability manifested itself in renderings and interior decoration, and he made contributions to a number of Richardson's important designs, among them Trinity Church (Boston, 1877), the W. W. Sherman house (Newport, R.I., 1874), and the Senate Chamber at the New York State Capitol (Albany, 1878). While with Richardson, White became a close friend of Charles F. McKim, who worked there until 1874. His other future partner, William R. Mead, worked in a nearby office. In 1877 White, McKim, Mead, and William Bigelow made a sketching tour of colonial buildings along the North Shore of Massachusetts. White also partook in the artistic high life of New York of the 1870s, becoming a member of the Tile Club and an intimate of young artists such as Louis Comfort Tiffany, Richard Watson Gilder, and William Merritt Chase. Among these, Stanford's friendship with the sculptor Augustus Saint-Gaudens stands out; they met in 1875 and soon thereafter started collaborating. In 1878 White made his first trip to Europe, traveling extensively and taking a memorable journey down the Loire Valley with McKim and Saint-Gaudens. On his return in September 1879, after thirteen months abroad, White accepted a position recently vacated by William Bigelow as a partner with McKim and Mead in New York.

McKim and Mead had been partners since 1877 and had already received a number of significant commissions; White added an important decorative and ornamental talent to the firm. From the mid-1880s to the 1910s, McKim, Mead & White was the most important architectural firm in the United States. It gained a reputation as a great training office where young architects could learn before setting out on their own. Among the many who passed through were Cass Gilbert, John Carrere, Thomas Hastings, H. Van Buren Magonigle, and Banister Fletcher. The firm's approximately one thousand commissions were concentrated in New York and the Northeast; however, they did design buildings for many other areas, and their influence was nationwide. It is difficult to separate the individual contributions of the partners before the mid-1880s. Beginning about 1886 direct attribution becomes more possible, since a single partner would take charge of a project as the complexity and scale of the buildings increased and the firm grew to over one hundred employees at times. However, collaboration continued among the partners. McKim tended to be the style setter and intellectual leader of the office as he searched for appropriate images for the new American civilization. Mead became the office manager, keeping projects on track and, as he once said, "keeping my partners from making damn fools of themselves" (Moore, p. 46). White tended to follow McKim's direction, but his designs generally were lighter, more colorful, and extravagantly ornamented.

McKim, Mead & White's work until the mid-1880s followed the lines set down by Richardson and McKim in the 1870s: adoptions of the vernacular-based early American colonial style of the seventeenth century and the contemporary English Queen Anne style exemplified by various shingle-covered houses in Newport from the early 1880s, the Newport Casino (1881), and the Charles Tiffany house (New York, 1885). Probably White was responsible for the elaborate library in the Colonial Chinese Chippendale style at the Sherman house (1880), the luminous dining room addition at Kingscote (1881), and the wealth of decorative detail on the Samuel Tilton house (1882), all in Newport.

By the mid-1880s McKim, Mead & White began to adopt more orthodox classical styles, such as American Georgian for the Henry A. C. Taylor house (Newport, 1885) and Italian Renaissance for the Henry G. Villard houses (New York, 1886). White's own particular taste became more evident in buildings such as Madison Square Garden (New York, 1891), which had a tower based on the Giralda in Spain and a profusion of multicolored terra-cotta ornament. Several church renovations illustrated White's collaborative abilities: the Church of the Ascension (New York, 1887), the chancel of which he decorated with the assistance of John La Farge, Louis Saint-Gaudens, and David Maitland Armstrong; and the chancel at St. Paul the Apostle (New York, 1890), with La Farge, Frederick MacMonnies, and Philip Martiny. White enjoyed color and exploited it in the Judson Memorial Church (New York, 1891), constructed of yellow and brown brick and pale yellow terra-cotta trim, and the Tessie and Herman Oelrichs house (Newport, 1902), built of white terra-cotta. Historical references in these buildings—Northern Italian Renaissance for the church and the Grand Trianon for the house—were obvious but never mere copies.

White fully subscribed to the American Renaissance, a self-conscious attempt to import the standards and products of Old World art to the New World. Architecturally, this meant classicism in one of its various national idioms. For instance, White argued that "all the Gothic, Semi-Gothic or Elizabethan styles, however beautiful they may be in themselves, are absolutely inappropriate in our time and country" (letter to Temple Emmett, 21 Jan. 1897, Avery Library). At times White closely studied older models, such as the Palazzo del Consiglio in Verona, on which the New York *Herald* Building (1893) was loosely based. In details he mixed the Italian Renaissance with bizarre novelties, such as twenty-six bronze owls, each four feet tall, with electric lights for their eyes. White utilized the red-brick and white-trimmed Georgian style for numerous buildings, such as the house for Thomas Nelson Page (Washington, D.C., 1897) and the Colony Club (New York, 1906). He was enamored of early American architecture and adopted forms such as the portico of Mount Vernon for the James L. Breese house (Southampton, N.Y., 1906). White also designed book and magazine covers, women's jewelry, and picture frames, and he continued to paint when time allowed.

White contributed to the civic embellishment of New York and other cities in a variety of ways, perhaps the most notable being his frequent collaboration with sculptors such as MacMonnies and Saint-Gaudens. He designed the setting and pedestals for many of Saint-Gaudens's important statues: the Admiral David Farragut (Madison Square, New York, 1881), the Standing Lincoln (Chicago, 1887), the Adams Memorial (Rock Creek Cemetery, Washington, D.C., 1891), and Peter Cooper (New York, 1897). In turn, Saint-Gaudens provided sculpture for some of White's buildings, such as the Diana for the tower of Madison Square Garden. White designed the temporary wooden arch for the celebration of the 1889 centennial of George Washington's inauguration. Its popularity led him to design a permanent triumphal arch based on the Arch of Titus. Embellished with the work of various sculptors, it was erected in New York City's Washington Square in 1895. On a larger scale, White designed the Bronx campus for New York University in 1894 and enclosed with buildings the University of Virginia's Lawn, along with restoring the Rotunda there after a fire in 1897.

After his marriage in 1884 to Bessie Smith of Smithtown, Long Island, White began to travel frequently to Europe and the Near East and also to purchase large quantities of art, furniture, and decorative elements of buildings. His yearly sweeps through European antique shops became legendary. Some of this material he used in his New York City house and also in his summer place at Smithtown, both of which gained reputations as showplaces. He also used these imports in various interior decorating projects, such as the William C. Whitney house (1893, 1896) and the Henry W. Poor house (1899), both in New York. White frequently acted as adviser and middleman for wealthy clients in their art purchases. In the mid-1890s he was instrumental in obtaining for Harrison McKeon Twombly (for whom he designed a country house) a set of the Barberini tapestries.

White's public and private life were inseparable. Known for his colorful dress, his bright red hair and mustache, and his imposing stature (6′2″), "Stanny" White became a fixture of New York's fast café society. He moved frenetically from designing to partying, frequently with the same individuals. With some of his artistic friends and clients White joined not just the more public clubs, such as the Century, Players, and the Metropolitan (for which he designed the club houses), but also private clubs, or hideaways, used for assignations. White enjoyed the theater and opera and frequently escorted young actresses and other women with whom he developed liaisons. His wife seemed oblivious to his infidelities. Their first child died within a year of his birth, and the second, Lawrence Grant White, he tended to ignore. Lawrence grew up to be an architect and joined the firm after his father's death.

White's self-indulgence cost him in several ways. His health suffered in the 1890s, and by the early 1900s he was frequently ill. Finances were a constant problem, and although he made considerable money through the firm and also in buying and selling art, he constantly needed more and ran up large bills on credit. He speculated frequently in stocks and lost great sums. His finances were in such disrepair that in mid-1905 White became a salaried employee of his firm and not a partner. His wildly erratic way of life ended in June 1906 with his sensational murder by Harry K. Thaw, who shot White three times as he was watching a musical at the roof theater of Madison Square Garden. Thaw's ostensible motive was that White and Thaw's wife, Evelyn Nesbit (a former chorus girl), had had an affair several years before the Thaws' marriage and that she had taunted her husband with accounts of White's attentions. The ensuing trial was a field day for the yellow press, and in subsequent years the murder has been replayed in numerous movies and "true-life" crime stories, becoming part of a national mythology.

Although White is probably chiefly remembered for this scandal, his talents as an architect were widely appreciated during his lifetime and in subsequent years. Known for his generosity and support of other artists, White was sometimes viewed as a modern renaissance man because of his various activities. His decorative talent and frequent use of Italian Renaissance motifs caused some of his contemporaries to nickname him "Cellini." He helped to create a type of interior in which art is part of the ambience. His particular talent was as an eclectic: he had the ability to choose various motifs and combine them into a harmonious whole. His utilization of the Italian Renaissance style was significant, but of more importance was his popularization of colonial American and English styles as appropriate to America.

• A large portion of White's personal and business papers are at the Avery Library, Columbia University. The McKim, Mead & White firm collection, including drawings, is at The New-York Historical Society. Three earlier books contain valuable material: Lawrence Grant White, comp., *Sketches and Designs by Stanford White* (1920); Charles Moore, *The Life and Times of Charles Follen McKim* (1929); and Charles Baldwin, *Stanford White* (1931; repr. 1976). The standard biography is Paul Baker, *Stanny: The Gilded Life of Stanford White* (1989). David Garrard Lowe, *Stanford White's New York* (1992), is too adulatory but good on architectural descriptions. Coverage of the firm's work can be found in *A Monograph of the Work of McKim, Mead & White, 1879–1915* (4 vols., 1915–1920; repr. as *The Architecture of McKim, Mead & White*, ed. Richard Guy Wilson [1990]). Studies of the firm's work are Leland Roth, *McKim, Mead & White, Architects* (1983) and *The Architecture of McKim, Mead & White 1870–1920: A Building List* (1978); Richard Guy Wilson, *McKim, Mead & White Architects* (1983); and the Brooklyn Museum (Richard Guy Wilson, Dianne Pilgrim, and Richard Murray), *The American Renaissance, 1876–1917* (1979). Important articles on McKim and the firm's work are Russell Sturgis, "The Works of McKim, Mead & White," Great American Architects Series, no. 1, *Architectural Record* (May 1895): 1–111, and Henry W. Desmond and Herbert Croly, "The Work of Messrs. McKim, Mead & White," *Architectural Record* 20 (Sept. 1906): 153–246.

RICHARD GUY WILSON

WHITE, Stephen Mallory (19 Jan. 1853–21 Feb. 1901), lawyer and U.S. senator, was born in San Francisco, the son of Irish immigrants William F. White and Fannie J. Russell. His father had been the publisher of a New York weekly newspaper before acquiring a farm in Santa Cruz, California. Though not wealthy, his father was freed from the need to work and instead became embroiled in Democratic politics. He had been a member of the California Democratic Central Committee before leaving his party and becoming a leader of the "country" faction of the Workingmen's party, which nominated him for governor in 1879. Influenced in part by his father's example, White equipped himself for a life in politics. After graduating from Santa Clara College (B.S. 1871), he studied law and was admitted to the bar in 1874. White then moved to Los Angeles, where he gained prominence as an attorney and launched a political career that would reflect the growing national importance of southern California. In 1883 he married Hortense Sacriste; they had four children.

Though he rose to national stature in the Democratic party, White had early and brief involvements with the Independent and Workingmen's parties in the 1870s. With but a few lapses, from this time on he supported political reform, restriction of Chinese immigration, and regulation of monopolies. After several unsuccessful campaigns for district attorney for Los Angeles County, he gained that office for the term of 1883–1884. In the latter year he was selected as chair of both the Los Angeles County Democratic Convention and the statewide Democratic convention. He was elected to the state senate in 1886 and during that same year chaired the Democratic state convention. White served as president pro tempore of the state senate in 1887, and when that body was not in session, he worked as legal counsel for the Southern Pacific Railroad with his law partner, John D. Bicknell. This business relationship with the railroad is hard to explain in any other way than opportunism, for White had been a leader since the early 1880s of a tentative coalition of southern California and interior Democrats who opposed the San Francisco Democratic machine and the Southern Pacific Railroad. In the summer of 1888 White ended his association with that railroad, most likely to avoid any conflict of interest when the state legislature reconvened in January 1889. Also in 1888, while chairing the Committee on Platform and Resolutions at the Democratic state convention, White was able to insert the first plank in a California platform calling for the direct election of senators. Several weeks later he served as a delegate-at-large to the Democratic National Convention in St. Louis, for which he was temporary chair.

White's greatest political ambition was to serve in the U.S. Senate. In 1890 he made his first bid for that office but withdrew from the contest when he ran into powerful opposition from George Hearst, owner of the *San Francisco Examiner*. Perhaps the key reason for Hearst's opposition was his alignment with the San Francisco, or "city," wing of the Democratic party, while White identified with the "country" faction, composed of farmers and Los Angeles businesspeople who blamed their economic problems on the Southern Pacific Railroad. Country Democrats charged the railroad with bribing the California legislature (and indirectly Congress) and called for the direct election of U.S. senators as one way of counteracting this influence peddling. After opportunistically aligning himself with Christopher A. Buckley, the San Francisco Democratic boss, in order to secure passage of legislation in the California senate in the late 1880s, White helped wrest control of the California Democracy from him in 1891–1892. This was a notable achievement. By a very narrow margin, 61 votes out of 119 cast, California's legislature elected White to the Senate in January 1893, making him the first southern Californian to be so honored and signaling a major victory for the Democracy's country faction. White's dissatisfaction with Grover Cleveland's handling of California patronage matters in 1884 and 1885 carried over into the beginning of his Senate term. White joined a group of senators, led by Arthur P. Gorman of Maryland, that made the Democratic president's dealings with the upper house troublesome, particularly when Cleveland tried unavailingly to secure greater reductions in the Wilson-Gorman Tariff of 1894. Supporting the free coinage of silver, White also opposed Cleveland's repeal of the Sherman Silver Purchase Act. However, he generally supported the president's foreign policies.

Of the many important issues before the Senate during the mid-1890s, White's greatest challenge was to prevent Collis P. Huntington and the Southern Pacific Railroad from building Los Angeles's deep-water harbor in Santa Monica, where the Southern Pacific would have had a monopoly on traffic. From 1893 to 1896 White led the successful effort to construct a federally funded harbor, free of Southern Pacific control, at San Pedro. At times he worked sixteen-hour days, buttonholing senators for support, perhaps shortening his life thereby. He was backed by Harrison Gray Otis (1837–1917), Republican publisher of the *Los Angeles Times*. Furthermore, White advocated railroad regulation (while privately condoning government ownership), antitrust, and protection for California commodities. He opposed going to war with Spain as well as the acquisition of overseas territory.

White's anti-imperialism remained consistent throughout his single term in the Senate, where he was a key leader among the opponents of empire. He warned his fellow senators in a speech on 21 June 1898, "The annexation of Hawaii will constitute the entering wedge for an imperialistic policy." White's major concern regarding Hawaii and Spain's insular possessions was that these territories were being taken without "the consent of the governed" in violation of the Declaration of Independence. A less-principled reason for his anti-imperialism was his objection to bringing into the Union what he regarded as inferior races. Such nativism was typical of California politicians of that era.

Until the middle of his Senate term, White maintained a lucrative law practice. A knowledge of Spanish aided him in handling land title cases. An authority on mining law as well as admiralty and international law, he had in 1889 represented California before the Supreme Court of the United States, successfully defending the constitutionality of the Scott Exclusion Act, which restricted the immigration of Chinese laborers to the United States. Wishing to increase his income by attending more to his law practice and business investments, White decided in 1896 not to run for a second term and made public his decision in February 1898.

From 1889 until his death White was a member of the Los Angeles Chamber of Commerce and a charter member and trustee of the Los Angeles Bar Association. In 1898 the governor appointed him to the Board of Regents of the University of California. In declining health, he died of what his doctors termed "gastric ulceration" in Los Angeles.

White's historical significance lies mainly in his serving as a precursor of California progressivism. By helping to undermine Buckley's machine and showing that the power of the Southern Pacific Railroad could be successfully challenged, White anticipated the reform impulse that swept the state in the early twentieth century. Known for his courage, intelligence, and commitment to the public interest, White was remembered by the citizens of Los Angeles, who erected a statue of him in the city bearing the inscription "the people's champion."

• White's papers are in the Borel Collection at the Stanford University Library Archives. A collection of White's major speeches is in Leroy E. Mosher, ed., *Stephen M. White: Californian, Citizen, Lawyer, Senator* (2 vols., 1903). For biographical data on White and his parents, see the *Los Angeles Times*, 22–23 Feb. 1901. The most comprehensive scholarly treatment of White's political career is Curtis E. Grassman, "Prologue to Progressivism: Senator Stephen M. White and the California Reform Impulse, 1875–1905" (Ph.D. diss., Univ. of California at Los Angeles, 1971). An older but still useful work, emphasizing political institutions, is Edith Dobie, *The Political Career of Stephen Mallory White: A Study of Party Activities under the Convention System* (1927). See also Peter T. Commy, *Stephen Mallory White* (1956). An obituary is in the *Los Angeles Times*, 23 Feb. 1901.

THOMAS J. OSBORNE

WHITE, Stewart Edward (12 Mar. 1873–18 Sept. 1946), traveler and writer of novels and short stories, was born in Grand Rapids, Michigan, the son of Thomas Stewart White, a millionaire lumberman, and Mary E. Daniell. He did not attend grammar school but was tutored at home and while traveling. Much of White's education was informal, secured on outings with his father, whom he revered as a model of the energetic outdoorsman, displaying vitality, virility, honesty, and good judgment.

White graduated from Central High School in Grand Rapids in 1891. While still a student, he had become an amateur naturalist, and he continued his field studies for two years in the Michigan woods after graduating. He wrote articles and a pamphlet on the birds of Mackinac Island that was published by the Ornithologists' Union. He gave his collection of bird skins to the Kent Scientific Museum in Grand Rapids. Later, he resumed his "birding" in the Carpenteria marshes near Santa Barbara, California, and even bought an adjacent beach, which he called Sandyland, to preserve it.

In 1891 White entered the University of Michigan, where he made Phi Beta Kappa, graduating in 1895 with a bachelor's degree in philosophy. In 1903 he earned his M.A. His father did not believe that he could make a living at writing, so White tried fitting himself for other vocations. He worked in a Grand Rapids meat packing plant for six months and as an accountant in his father's lumber office. He spent three months looking after a mine in South Dakota and prospecting in the Black Hills before enrolling in Columbia Law School in 1896.

At Columbia, White took a literary composition course. Professor Brandon Matthews urged him to write about what he knew. He sent a story, "A Man and His Dog," to *Short Story* magazine, which bought it for $15. *Munsey's Magazine* paid him $500 for serial rights to his first novel, *The Westerners* (1901). He left law school in 1897 to write book reviews, as well as publicity for McClung's Chicago bookstore.

The Westerners and *The Claim Jumpers*, also published in 1901, are melodramatic—and gruesome—westerns set in the Black Hills. Both were praised for their vigorous action and descriptive power, although London reviewers found the brutality of *The Westerners* to be morbid. The *Brooklyn Eagle* described the book as a "fine failure rather than a strong achievement." *The Claim Jumpers*, mock-heroic in tone, is better constructed and more readable and profits from the use of autobiographical material.

White spent the early winter of 1901 working as a lumberjack, writing from four to eight each morning. His most famous novel, *The Blazed Trail* (1902), became a bestseller. Much superior to its predecessors, it was a love story of a self-reliant man coming to terms with his environment. It was even something of a muckraking book. The author, though a lumberman, was also a conservationist who exposed the corrupt side of logging interests. (The novel was included in Gregg Press's 1968 series of *American Novels of Muckraking, Propaganda and Protest*.) The book was seen as the classic novel of logging and was still in print thirty years after publication.

In 1903 White joined his parents in California. He spent most of his life there in what he called "the lovely land." In 1904 he married Elizabeth Calvert Grant; the couple had no children. When Theodore Roosevelt toured Santa Barbara, White was the president's favorite escort. The two men became fast friends. Roosevelt considered White "the kind of young American who is making our new literature." White soon came to be seen as a (lesser) London, part of the "red-blood" school of writers that, besides Jack London, included Rex Beach and James Oliver Curwood. White served in World War I in the 144th Field Artillery, becoming a major.

At times compelling, White's writing relied too much on coincidence and the predictable characters of melodramatic "formula" stories. He substituted action and adventure for insightful characterization and exploration of the complexity of frontier life. Critic Lawrence Clark Powell observed that White wrote too much and said too little, at least to readers beyond his own time. At his best, while examining the frontier spirit, he was an imaginative writer with a zeal for verisimilitude, especially authentic historical and geographical depictions. He was elected to membership in the National Institute of Arts and Letters and the American Academy of Arts and Letters. In 1913 White was elected a fellow of the Royal Geographical Society for mapping German East Africa (Tanzania). White produced thirty-four volumes of fiction and twenty-four volumes of nonfiction; he also wrote two mysteries and several stories for juveniles. Four travel books, two novels, and a collection of stories are set in Africa.

White was a dedicated hiker, hunter, and horseman. He was an early supporter of conservation and served as special inspector for the Forest Reserve (1905–1906). *The Forest*, *The Mountains*, *The Pass*, *Camp and Trail*, and *The Cabin*, published between 1903 and 1912, are stories of summer outings with advice on camping. In 1929 he contributed the foreword to *Reminiscences of Outdoor Life* by William Kent, who gave Muir Woods to the nation. A grove of sequoias on California's Redwood Coast was named in honor of White.

Toward the end of his life White developed an interest in spiritual phenomena and psychic research, claiming to communicate with the dead, notably his late wife. White died in San Francisco. His writing experienced a mild revival of interest by the late twentieth-century reader—paperback reprints of *Arizona Nights*, *The Long Rifle*, *The Mountains*, *Camp and Trail*, *The Forest*, and four of his African books were in print.

• Most of White's personal papers perished in a fire in his Montecito home. Information about his life and works is in bits and pieces, found in articles in literary magazines like *Bookman* (May 1903, July 1910, Sept. 1913, Apr. 1914, Aug. 1921). For an appreciation, see Eugene F. Saxton, *Stewart Edward White* (1939), and Judy Alter, *Stewart Edward White* (1975), in Boise State University's Western Writers Series. A bibliography is G. Dale Gleason, *Twentieth Century Western Writers*, ed. Geoff Sadler, 2d ed. (1991), pp. 717–19. Lawrence Clark Powell's chapter on *Arizona Nights* in his *Southwest Classics* (1974) is excellent. Two unpublished works are rewarding, Edna Rosemary Butte, "Stewart Edward White, His Life and Literary Career" (Ph.D. diss., Univ. of Southern California, 1960), and Margery Stewart McCall, "The Life and Works of Stewart Edward White" (M.A. thesis, Lousiana State Univ., 1931). An obituary is in the *New York Times*, 19 Sept. 1946.

RICHARD H. DILLON

WHITE, Theodore H. (6 May 1915–15 May 1986), journalist and author, was born Theodore Harold White in Boston, Massachusetts, the son of David White, a lawyer, and Mary Winkeller. First- and second-generation Jewish immigrants, the Whites struggled financially. In 1931 White's father died of a heart attack, leaving the family without any source of income. It was to help support his mother, sister, and two brothers that, at sixteen, White first entered the world of journalism by selling newspapers to streetcar passengers.

Two years after graduating from Boston Latin School, White was awarded a scholarship and grant that allowed him to attend Harvard, where he studied Chinese history and graduated summa cum laude in 1938. White was awarded a Sheldon Traveling Fellowship upon graduation, enabling him to travel throughout Europe, the Middle East, and Asia. White expected to return home after eight months to pursue a doctorate. However, while freelancing in China, then under siege from the Japanese, he realized his future lay not in a university professorship but in journalism.

White covered East Asia for *Time* magazine until 1945, rising to chief of the magazine's China bureau. During this period White began a lifelong, if turbulent, friendship with *Time*'s cofounder and publisher, Henry Robinson Luce. He resigned from *Time* in 1946 after disagreeing with senior executives over his criticism of Chiang Kai-shek and the American-supported Nationalist Chinese government. Collaborating with former *Time* correspondent Annalee Jacoby, White wrote *Thunder Out of China* (1946), which became a Book-of-the-Month Club selection and was internationally controversial for asserting that the Nationalist government was inept and that China "must change or die" (p. 298).

Success followed the publication of *Thunder Out of China*, and soon White was offered positions as correspondent for the *Saturday Evening Post* and senior editor of the *New Republic*. He joined the *New Republic* in 1947 but resigned after only six months because he found the magazine's liberal dogma too restrictive. White remained a prolific reporter, freelancing for a number of prestigious periodicals and editing *The Stilwell Papers* (1948), the private writings of World War II general Joseph W. Stilwell. In 1947 White married Nancy Bean; they had two children. The couple moved to Europe, where White served as chief European correspondent first for the Overseas News Agency from 1948 to 1950 and later for the *Reporter* from 1950 to 1953. He analyzed Western Europe's dramatic postwar recovery in *Fire in the Ashes* (1953). Like *Thunder Out of China*, his new book quickly made the bestseller list. After publication of *Fire in the Ashes*, White returned to the United States and began to cover American politics initially for the *Reporter* and then for *Collier's*.

White's reputation as a liberal journalist proved troublesome during the McCarthy era. The magazine *Counterattack* listed him as a "known subversive," and because of this listing he was unable to appear as a guest or visitor on any CBS show. Things got more complicated for White in 1954, when he testified in the security hearings of John Davies, who was being investigated for communist connections. After questioning White about Davies, the committee brought accusations against White, charging him with trying to organize the black troops in the Burma Road for a revolt during the war. White denied the accusations. As a result of the hearing, according to White, his name was added to a list that put him under newly passed legislation known as "Limitations on Issuance of Passports to Persons Supporting the Communist Movements" and, on 5 October, his passport was confiscated. He met with a passport hearing officer the next morning and was able to get a two-month passport with limited travel to Germany, France, and England. On 23 December, three weeks after the full Senate had condemned the McCarthy hearings, White met with the passport officer again and was issued a clean passport without restrictions.

When *Collier's* folded in 1956, White turned to fiction, publishing *The Mountain Road* in 1958 and *The View from the Fortieth Floor* in 1960. His first novel was set amid the evacuation of American and Chinese forces from Liu-chou in 1944, while his second fictionalized his experiences at *Collier's*. Reviews for both novels suggested that journalism, not literature, was White's proper calling.

White returned to what he did best with the book for which he is best known, *The Making of the President, 1960* (1961). In following all seven of the major candidates for the presidency for more than a year, White assembled a mosaic of speeches, analyses of political strategies, and the mundane details behind each campaign's daily routine. White planned the Making of the President series to be a twenty-year project, and when he was unable to convince his longtime publisher, Sloane, that the project would be profitable, he switched to Atheneum and began following the candidates. *The Making of the President, 1960* was a tremendous success, quickly topping the national bestseller list and selling more than four million copies by the middle of the decade. Later adapted for television, "The Making of the President, 1960" brought White the Emmy Award in 1964 for best TV film in all categories. The first book in White's proposed series pioneered a new style of political journalism in which the reporter doggedly followed the candidates behind the scenes and brought their daily struggles, both personal and professional, to the forefront. "Somehow a presidential campaign was not really over," President Reagan later commented, "until Teddy's book was written."

The subsequent books in White's Making of the President series, after the 1964, 1968, and 1972 campaigns, failed to match the success of the first book. Although his experimental style had at first been the subject of general admiration and was the victim of frequent imitation, the later books disappointed reviewers, who criticized White's reverence toward those in power. Perhaps the most famous example of what critics saw as White's hero-worshipping appeared in his famous article for *Life* where, at Jacqueline Kennedy's insistence, he became the first journalist to portray the Kennedy administration as Camelot. White became disenchanted with his own approach to recording history after his failure, while constructing *The Making of the President, 1972*, to understand the ramifications of the Watergate scandal as it unfolded around him. Sensing that his "old ideas no longer stretched over the real world" (*In Search of History*, p. 3), White abandoned his pursuit of presidential campaigns to reexamine his experiences from the previous forty years. The result was his autobiography, *In Search of History* (1978).

In 1967 White was awarded an Emmy for Outstanding Achievement in Documentary Programming for writing "China: The Roots of Madness." His first marriage ended in divorce in 1971, and in 1974 he married Beatrice H. Hofstadter. White was working on a second volume of his autobiography when he died in New York City. In almost a half-century of writing about history and politics, White had become one of the most influential journalists of the twentieth century, earning more than twenty journalism awards, including the Pulitzer in 1962.

• White's papers are in the Houghton Library at Harvard. A critical analysis of White's journalism may be found in Joyce Hoffmann, *Theodore H. White and Journalism as Illusion* (1995). Thomas Griffith, *Harry and Teddy: The Turbulent Friendship of Press Lord Henry R. Luce and His Favorite Reporter, Theodore H. White* (1995), is the most thorough account of White's early career. For a view of White and other journalists following presidential candidates, see Timothy Crouse, *The Boys on the Bus* (1973). The Making of the President series comprises four volumes covering the 1960, 1964, 1968, and 1972 election campaigns and is complemented by White's last published book, *America in Search of Itself: The Making of the President 1956–1980* (1982). In addition to his two novels, White's fiction includes a play, *Caesar at the Rubicon: A Play about Politics* (1968).

PAUL SOGGE

WHITE, Thomas Willis (28 Mar. 1788–19 Jan. 1843), printer and publisher, was born in Williamsburg, Virginia, the son of Thomas White, a tailor, and Sarah Davis. His father enjoyed brief prosperity in Richmond before dying from yellow fever in 1796, leaving four children. Self-educated, White was apprenticed to William Rind and John Stuart, printers of the *Virginia Federalist*, and accompanied them to Washington, D.C., in 1800. Returning to Richmond in 1807, he helped produce newspapers published by his uncle, Augustine Davis, and by Samuel Pleasants. He was soon hired as a compositor by the *Norfolk Gazette and Publick Ledger*. In 1810 he left for Philadelphia with his bride, Margaret Ann (maiden name unknown), whom he had married in 1809. They had several children (exact number unknown) and remained in Philadelphia two-and-a-half years before moving to another printing business in Boston. He again returned to Richmond in 1817, established his own business, and began publishing plays and novels as well as parliamentary papers.

White's encouragement of Virginia authors led him in 1834 to attempt what he later called "a rash and perilous enterprize," a literary magazine in a region where no such venture "had been able to survive a sickly infancy." His *Southern Literary Messenger* was badly undercapitalized, and this led White to institute economies that weakened the journal. He claimed to be perpetually "hard-run" in money matters and "overwhelmed in debt." Nevertheless, in 1837 he boasted to his friend Judge Beverley Tucker that he did not "believe there is another man in the country who could have prosecuted the Messenger, as I have prosecuted it, during the two volumes which I have pulled it thro, but what would have sunk 5000 in the two years instead of $1800" (quoted in Jackson, p. 112).

While the monthly *Southern Literary Messenger* ostensibly gave a voice to a class of talented cavalier writers who had lacked only a journal on southern soil to publish their works, few had anything worth publishing when offered the opportunity. In fact, the leisured gentlemen of the plantations were, as a class, in eclipse as the result of laws against primogeniture. Nor did White have the funds to compensate any putative plantation poets. What limited resources he did have were sent to established writers in the North where, not incidentally, significant numbers of potential subscribers were to be found. White's prospectus for his publication, written just three years after the 1831 Nat Turner insurrection, alluded to an even deeper problem. Especially in the South, White wrote, the educated classes were "more engaged in the search after political truth, than in mere literary elegancies and refinements."

White's southern contributors came largely from the rising professional classes. U.S. Army subaltern Braxton Bragg, later an ill-fated Confederate general, was one such scribe. Sentimentalists abounded; an elegy for White's son, who died of cholera in 1832 at the age of nineteen, was published. But with Edgar Allan Poe's arrival as nominal editor in 1835, the journal began to change. As Poe saw it, Virginia was becoming a "bye-word for imbecility," and its cultural sloth would not be improved by mitigating or encouraging the inadequacies of its writers.

Poe's relationship with White was difficult. "He is," Poe said, "a character if ever one was." White's "wretched taste," from Poe's perspective, was the formidable obstacle Poe had to overcome in increasing circulation. Poe's journalism troubled White, who feared his editor was about to ignite a literary dispute with the North that the *Messenger* could ill afford. And "Little Tom," as Poe called White, could not tolerate Poe's fondness for liquor. "You have fine talents, Edgar—and you ought to have them respected as well as yourself," White admonished him. "Separate yourself from the bottle, and bottle companions, for ever." White dismissed Poe in 1837.

With Poe gone White resumed full editorial control of the magazine and tried to broaden its audience. He continued to publish a full range of literary material, including essays, reviews, poetry, translations, biographies, speeches, and legal commentaries. Yet in 1841, when sectional politics forced him to take an editorial position on the slavery question, White promised to make the journal "the medium for the defence and exposition of Southern interests and Southern rights."

By 1842 the *Messenger* had achieved a measure of respect throughout the United States and thus advanced the cause of southern literature. The Richmond printer, however, had little time left to enjoy his fame. In poor health since 1835, he endured the added burden of his wife's death in 1837. While at supper at the Astor House in New York in September 1842, he suffered a paralytic stroke. He died in Richmond. His journal continued publication after his death, finally expiring in the last year of the Civil War.

White's numerous letters suggest a determined, desultorily self-educated man of strong character and abundant energy who was fundamentally generous and personable. James E. Heath, the first editor of the *Messenger*, said of him: "I have known few men more disposed to cherish kindly and benevolent feelings towards their fellowmen." White's trials with Poe, his bumptious protégé, have tended to trivialize the publisher's place in antebellum American letters. Viewed as something of a comic foil to a belletristic genius, White usually is consigned to the footnotes of a famous man's story. But without White there would probably have been a different and perhaps a diminished Poe. When it served Poe to curry favor with White he judged him "exceedingly kind in every respect." Poe notwithstanding, White presided at great personal risk over a journal that survived where others had failed as it nurtured an inchoate American literature.

• Many of White's letters appear in James A. Harrison, *Life and Letters and Edgar Allan Poe* (1903), and William Doyle Hull, "A Canon of the Critical Works of Edgar Allan Poe with a Study of Poe as Editor and Reviewer" (Ph.D. diss., Univ. of Virginia, 1941). Other letters are located in the Pierpont Morgan Library in New York and in the archives of the Virginia Historical Society in Richmond. The earliest comprehensive primary source is Benjamin Blake Minor, *The Southern Literary Messenger, 1834–1864* (1905). In an excellent chapter on the *Messenger* in his *History of American Magazines* (1938), Frank Luther Mott traces Minor's information to the magazine's files and to John W. Fergusson, an apprentice, who worked for White when he began the publication and later became one of its publishers. Other useful references are David K. Jackson's *Poe and the Southern Literary Messenger* (1934), *The Contributors and Contributions to the Southern Literary Messenger, 1834–1864* (1936), and "Some Unpublished Letters of T. W. White to Lucian Minor," *Tyler's Quarterly Historical and Genealogical Magazine* 17 (1936): 224–43, and 18 (1936): 32–49. See also Edward L. Tucker, "'A Rash and Perilous Enterprise': The Southern Literary Messenger and the Men Who Made It," *Virginia Cavalcade* 21 (1971): 14–21; Robert D. Jacobs, "Campaign for a Southern Literature: The Southern Literary Messenger," *Southern Literary Journal* 2 (1969): 66–93; J. V. Ridgely, *Nineteenth-Century Southern Literature* (1980); David T. Dodd II, "The Southern Literary Messenger," in *American Literary Magazines: The Eighteenth and Nineteenth Centuries*, ed. Edward E. Chielens (1986); Kenneth Silverman, *Edgar A. Poe: Mournful and Never-ending Remembrance* (1991); and Michael Allen, *Poe and the British Magazine Tradition* (1969). An obituary is in the *Southern Literary Messenger*, Feb. 1843.

PAUL ASHDOWN

WHITE, Walter Francis (1 July 1893–21 Mar. 1955), civil rights leader, was born in Atlanta, Georgia, the son of George Washington White, a mail carrier, and Madeline Harrison, a teacher. His middle-class, African-American family took seriously its obligations to the black community, even though they all shared features and skin color that made them appear white. After graduating from Atlanta University in 1916, White worked for the Standard Life Insurance Company for almost two years.

When the Atlanta school board threatened to discontinue seventh-grade classes for black students (who already were barred from public high schools), White helped to mount a community protest and to found the Atlanta branch of the National Association for the Advancement of Colored People (NAACP). In 1917 James Weldon Johnson of the NAACP's headquarters staff came to assist the local effort and took an immediate liking to White and secured his appointment as assistant executive secretary in the NAACP headquarters in January 1918. White held that post until 1929, when he became the acting—and in 1931 the permanent—executive secretary.

White was an outgoing and energetic leader and exhibited a fierce attachment to the NAACP's program for racial justice. His Caucasian-like features facilitated his courageous investigation of over forty lynchings and numerous race riots. Given the widespread racism and hatred of the time, the NAACP could hardly reverse racial discrimination in education, housing, employment, voting, and public transportation. Instances of mob violence, however, forced some white Americans at least to realize the need for reform. Driving the message home with press releases, conferences, exhibits, and public rallies, the NAACP lobbied Congress for an antilynching law. White and Johnson, who became executive secretary of the NAACP in 1920, were central to this campaign. The antilynching bill passed the House of Representatives on three occasions (1922, 1937, and 1940) but failed in the Senate each time because of actual or threatened filibusters.

Along with his senior NAACP colleagues Johnson and W. E. B. Du Bois, White encouraged and promoted the careers of the black writers, artists, and performers of the Harlem Renaissance. Moreover, White was part of it himself as the author of two novels, *The Fire in the Flint* (1924) and *Flight* (1926), and the classic study of lynching *Rope and Faggot: A Biography of Judge Lynch* (1929), written while on a Guggenheim Fellowship.

When White assumed leadership of the NAACP in 1931, the depression had eroded membership fees and contributions. Furthermore, the association faced intense competition from the Communist Party–USA, which was competing openly with the NAACP for African-American support. The two organizations clashed publicly over the 1931 Scottsboro case, when both tried to secure the exclusive rights to represent the defendants in court. White's animus toward the party and its tactics never receded, and he maintained a relentlessly anti-Communist posture, especially during the Cold War of the late 1940s and the 1950s.

It was during the New Deal years, however, that White began allying the NAACP with other progressive forces in the quest for equal rights. The 1930 Supreme Court nomination of John J. Parker, who had made racist remarks early in his career, prompted White and the NAACP to join the American Federation of Labor in defeating the appointment. When the Senate narrowly rejected Parker's nomination by two votes, White's stature and that of the NAACP rose accordingly. During the 1930s White, as executive secretary, also oversaw the implementation of the NAACP's plan for systematic litigation against discrimination, a campaign formulated by the NAACP Legal Defense and Educational Fund, Inc., and executed in the courts by Thurgood Marshall. At the same time, White wed the association to a number of liberal, labor, ethnic, women's, church, and civil liberties organizations in a shared pursuit of social justice. This coalition flourished under his guidance and shaped the goals and strategies of the civil rights movement into the 1990s.

White had a global perspective as well. In 1921 he attended the Second Pan-African Congress in London, Brussels, and Paris, which put him in direct contact with black leaders from Africa, the Caribbean, and the United States. All his life he worked for greater home rule and economic investment in the Caribbean. During and after World War II, he was a steady advocate of independence for India. Anxious to investigate the treatment of African-American troops, he went to England, North Africa, and Italy as a war correspondent in 1944. His findings were published in *A Rising Wind* (1945). A similar trip took him to Australia, the Philippines, and the South Pacific in 1945. On his return, he served as a consultant to the U.S. delegation at the founding conference of the United Nations in San Francisco and the 1948 General Assembly sessions in Paris.

After World War II White used his weekly columns in the *Chicago Defender* and in several major metropolitan dailies to argue that the war against fascism and America's competition with the Soviet Union for Third World allies only underscored the urgency of racial justice at home. White's prescriptions included desegregation of the military, fair employment practices, elimination of poll taxes, antilynching legislation, and voting rights for the District of Columbia. He helped to convince President Harry S. Truman to endorse them during his 1948 campaign.

White's final years were busy but not problem-free. An autobiography, *A Man Called White* (1948), was well received, but while working on the book he suffered the first of several heart attacks. In June 1949 White and his wife of twenty-seven years, Leah Gladys Powell, with whom he had two children, divorced. His second marriage within a week to Poppy Cannon, a successful white public relations consultant and food editor, provoked a storm of protest, not the least among African-American journalists and some NAACP board members, who worried about middle-class sensibilities and the NAACP's reputation.

Matters within the NAACP were further complicated in the early 1950s by personality and policy disagreements between White and two colleagues, Roy Wilkins, the assistant executive secretary who succeeded White as executive secretary in April 1955, and Thurgood Marshall. These were reminiscent of the more public and explosive clashes that White had had with Du Bois in 1934 (over the latter's advocacy of a separate African-American economic system) and in 1948 (when Du Bois openly championed the third-party candidacy of Henry A. Wallace for president). Such conflicts with his NAACP associates added to White's reputation among detractors as arrogant and self-serving. White died in his New York City home. His sixth book, *How Far the Promised Land?*, appeared posthumously in 1955.

• White's papers and those of Poppy Cannon White are in the James Weldon Johnson Collection at the Beinecke Rare Book and Manuscript Library at Yale University. The files of the NAACP at the Manuscript Division of the Library of Congress are indispensable for any evaluation of White's career. No scholarly and comprehensive biography currently exists, but one may consult Poppy Cannon, *A Gentle Knight: My Husband, Walter White* (1956); Edward E. Waldron, *Walter White and the Harlem Renaissance* (1978); and Robert L. Zangrando, *The NAACP Crusade Against Lynching, 1909–1950* (1980). Helpful as well are E. J. Kahn, Jr., "Profiles: The Frontal Attack," *New Yorker*, 4 Sept. 1948, pp. 28–32 and

34–38, and 11 Sept. 1948, pp. 38–40 and 42–46. Nathaniel Patrick Tillman, Jr., "Walter Francis White: A Study in Interest Group Leadership" (Ph.D. diss., Univ. of Wisconsin, 1961). Obituaries are in the *New York Times*, 22 Mar. 1955; *Crisis*, Apr. 1955; and *Journal of Negro History* (July 1955). *Phylon: The Atlanta University Review of Race and Culture* published a series of eulogies in its Sept. 1955 issue.

ROBERT L. ZANGRANDO

WHITE, William (4 Apr. 1748–17 July 1836), Protestant Episcopal bishop, was born in Philadelphia, Pennsylvania, the son of Colonel Thomas White, a lawyer and surveyor, and Esther Hewlings. Raised in an affluent family well connected with upper-class Philadelphia, White graduated from the College of Philadelphia (now the University of Pennsylvania) in 1765. While at college, the young White settled on a ministerial vocation. After graduation, he studied theology with the college's provost, the liberal Anglican William Smith, and with both the rector and assistant at Christ Church, Philadelphia. With no Anglican bishop in the colonies, it was necessary for White to travel to England to obtain ordination, but because of his youth he was not ordained priest until 25 April 1772.

White returned to Philadelphia on the eve of the American Revolution and soon became identified as a moderate revolutionary who attempted to remain on good terms with the significant Loyalist element within his parish. Though appointed assistant minister of Christ Church on his return, the departure of the Loyalist rector left White that post in 1779, and he remained rector of the united parishes of St. Peter's and Christ Church until his death. He was also named chaplain to the Continental Congress and became friends with several leading patriots, including George Washington. He married Mary Harrison in 1773 and eventually fathered eight children.

Before the Treaty of Paris formally ended the war in 1783, White wrote *The Case of the Episcopal Churches in the United States Considered* (1782) out of his concern for the unity and future growth of Anglicanism in the new nation. In it White argued that the American church might proceed to ordain clergy without bishops if forced by circumstances to do so and that these ministers would have perfectly valid orders. White cited similar pragmatic views of the episcopacy articulated by the Anglican Reformers, but high church clergy in Connecticut and elsewhere, a group that stressed the formal, liturgical character of Anglicanism, disagreed strongly with White's proposal. With peace formally secured, the latter group sent Samuel Seabury to Great Britain as their nominee, and he returned in 1785, having been consecrated by Scottish bishops.

Consistent with his pragmatism and overarching concern for denominational harmony, White cooperated with Bishop Seabury and pushed organizational efforts forward with enthusiasm and skill. He was elected president of the first General Convention of the Protestant Episcopal Church, meeting in Philadelphia in 1785, and helped write the constitution of the revivified church. His draft was innovative, seeking to give a republican form to the church's governing institutions. White insisted, for example, that the laity be represented in a separate deliberative body. He also (with Smith) exercised an important influence on the American revision of the English prayer book.

Not surprisingly, White was elected bishop by the convention of the diocese of Pennsylvania in 1786 and managed to secure consecration by the archbishops of Canterbury and York and three other English bishops at Lambeth palace the following year. White went on to serve both his national church and his home parish. He was presiding bishop of the Protestant Episcopal church between 1795 and 1836. In his own diocese, he concentrated on Philadelphia and its environs but began to visit the more isolated western portions of the state later in his episcopate. As a public-spirited citizen of Philadelphia, he was second perhaps only to Benjamin Franklin. Among other things, White was president of the Philadelphia Bible Society, a key member of the American Philosophical Society, and one of the first to be involved in prison ministry in the city.

White's service to the national church included his work as both a popular religious author and a theologian. As presiding bishop, he penned all of the House of Bishops's pastoral letters himself and was the author of *Lectures on the Catechism* (1813). Probably his most substantial theological tome was *Comparative Views of the Controversy between Calvinists and the Arminians* (1817), in which he argued tenaciously that the formularies of the Reformed Church of England were not Calvinistic, contrary to the writings of John Overton and Augustus Toplady. Though by no means a Latitudinarian, White sought to build the American expression of Anglicanism on a moderately liberal sort of evangelicalism that eschewed the perceived excesses of both Calvinists and Arminians. Moreover, church historians have also long found his autobiographical *Memoirs of the Protestant Episcopal Church in the United States of America* (1820) to be an invaluable resource.

It would be difficult to overestimate the significance of White's part in the formative years of the Episcopal church. Admittedly, White was not a riveting preacher, and much of his published writing was dry and dispassionate in tone. He has also been criticized for not pursuing missionary work more strongly in the western part of his diocese. Nevertheless, he was a careful and insightful theologian and a gifted organizer imbued with a cooperative, irenic spirit. These were the qualities that made him an essential leader within the Episcopal church during some of its most difficult times. He continued to preach and administer his parish into his eighties, and his influence continued well after his death through those he had prepared for ministry, including John Henry Hobart and William Augustus Muhlenberg, among others. He has been justly called "architect of the Episcopal church." White died in Philadelphia.

• Some of White's papers are at Christ Church, Philadelphia, and at the Archives of the Episcopal Church in Austin, Tex.

Byrd Wilson, *Memoir of the Life of the Right Reverend William White* (1839), and Walter H. Stowe, ed., *The Life and Letters of Bishop William White* (1937), are classic sources. Also notable though dated biographies are Julius Hammond Ward, *The Life and Times of Bishop White* (1892), and William Wilson Manross, *William White: A Sketch of the First Bishop of Pennsylvania* (1934). Those interested in White's theology should consult Sydney Absalom Temple, *The Common Sense Theology of Bishop White: Selected Essays from the Writings of William White, 1748–1836* (1946), and note the critique by Manross, "Bishop White's Theology," *Historical Magazine of the Protestant Episcopal Church* 15 (1946): 285–97. Probably the finest study in this latter area is John F. Woolverton, "Philadelphia's William White: Episcopalian Distinctiveness and Accommodation in the Post-Revolutionary Period," *Historical Magazine of the Protestant Episcopal Church* 43 (1974): 279–96.

GILLIS J. HARP

WHITE, William Alanson (24 Jan. 1870–7 Mar. 1937), psychiatrist and mental hospital administrator, was born and raised in Brooklyn, New York, the son of Harriet Augusta Hawley and Alanson White, a businessman. By family tradition the Whites traced their ancestry to the Mayflower, and because the family summered in Massachusetts, White considered himself as much a New Englander as a New Yorker, attributing "a very definite streak of hyperconscientiousness" to his Puritanical roots. White also regarded himself psychologically as an only child because his only sibling, a brother, was ten years older.

White attended a private school in Brooklyn until his father's business faltered. Unable to afford a college education, he secured a scholarship to Cornell University at age fifteen by registering as seventeen. Having never finished high school, White failed entrance exams in algebra several times and never took enough courses in mathematics to qualify for graduation. Nevertheless, he still made the most of his years at Cornell, from 1885 to 1889. White's interest in psychology began during these years, stimulated in part by the teachings of Jacob Gould Schurman, professor of Christian ethics and mental philosophy. White experienced great religious conflict at the time as he listened to debates over evolution and the relation between science and religion. Robert Ingersoll's agnostic teachings had earlier set White in turmoil, and he was also impressed by the sermons on evolution of Henry Ward Beecher at Plymouth Church in Brooklyn, which the White family attended. White's reading of Herbert Spencer and his deepening engagement with psychology would eventually help him to resolve the debate in favor of science and allow him to relegate religion to "a human method of reacting."

Early on at Cornell White decided on a career in medicine. He served as a teaching assistant in anatomy and worked in the laboratory of Burt Green Wilder, professor of comparative anatomy of the brain. He took to the subject naturally in part because of childhood experience. A professor of surgery at Long Island College Hospital Medical School, just down the street from where White lived, had sometimes allowed him into the surgery and dissecting rooms. White entered medical school there in 1889 and received his M.D. in 1891. After a brief stint as a house surgeon and ambulance surgeon at two local hospitals, he returned to the Long Island College Hospital as an intern. In 1892 he secured an appointment as a physician at Binghamton State (mental) Hospital, where he stayed for the next eleven years.

During this period, White's career as a psychiatrist began to take shape. Shy yet sociable, he threw himself into the life of a mental hospital, becoming a constant presence on the wards, developing an appreciation of patients as individuals, and directing the musical choir, band, and orchestra. Because he had received no formal instruction in psychiatry, he spent spare hours reading widely in the social and behavioral sciences to develop guiding principles for understanding the mind. His first two professional papers, one on the physical basis of insanity and another on reforming criminals, both reflected the influence of Spencer's synthetic philosophy, which White felt held the key to every field of learning. Henry Buckle's *History of Civilization in England* and S. Weir Mitchell's *Evolution and Dissolution and the Science of Medicine* further disposed White toward a deterministic philosophy and a belief that mental events followed definite laws.

The most determinative event in White's own career at this time was his work with research psychologist Boris Sidis. After meeting Sidis on a visit to the Pathological Institute of the New York State Hospitals, White secured time off from Binghampton to help him formulate methods for the study of such phenomena as multiple personality, amnesia, and hypnosis. Exploring the "subconscious" of mental patients, he learned the rudiments of what would later be termed dynamic psychiatry. His collaboration with Sidis brought him newspaper publicity and resulted in a joint publication, "Psychopathological Researches: Studies in Mental Dissociation" (1902), a work that established White's scientific credentials. In 1903 President Theodore Roosevelt appointed White, a Republican, superintendent of the prestigious Government Hospital for the Insane, later renamed St. Elizabeths Hospital, in Washington, D.C., a post he held until his death.

White transformed St. Elizabeths into a leading center of psychiatric treatment, training, and research. He became interested in psychoanalysis in 1907 after meeting Carl Jung at a conference in Amsterdam. In 1914 White organized a psychoanalytic society at the hospital and appointed a full-time clinical psychiatrist to administer therapy. Edward Kempf, the first to hold this position, published the results of his psychoanalytic work at St. Elizabeths in his pioneering *Psychopathology* (1920), and Edward Lazell organized an early form of group psychotherapy in 1919. White also established in 1907 one of the first psychological laboratories in a mental hospital, under the guidance of experimental psychologist Shepherd Ivory Franz. The department Franz built trained a generation of psychologists and pathologists, including Grace H. Kent, Edwin G. Boring, Karl S. Lashley, and Nolan D. C.

Lewis. In 1920 White developed a department of internal medicine that was accredited by the American Medical Association for training interns. Here, for the first time in the Western Hemisphere, malarial therapy was introduced in 1922 to treat general paresis, a stage of syphilis.

White also instituted reforms to improve and individualize care. Despite the large size of the hospital—2,300 patients when he arrived, increasing to nearly 6,000 during his tenure—he sharply reduced the use of mechanical and chemical restraints. He promoted various forms of hydrotherapy to calm agitated and disturbed patients; greatly increased the proportion of unlocked wards; expanded facilities for entertainment, recreation, and occupation; introduced a beauty parlor and cafeteria for patients; and improved their circulating library. On humanitarian grounds, he opposed the use of lobotomy and other radical surgical procedures of the 1920s and 1930s. For White's numerous hospital reforms, as well as for his general emphasis on treating patients with kindness, understanding, and dignity, Karl Menninger credited him with helping "to revive what was essentially the old moral treatment" of the early nineteenth century.

White also took measures to widen the hospital's influence, particularly by strengthening its ties with federal agencies. By 1908 he had arranged to train personnel of the Public Health and Marine Hospital Service to detect insane immigrants at Ellis Island, and as early as 1909 he gave instruction in psychiatry to medical officers of the army and navy. After World War I the hospital instructed medical and social service personnel of the Veterans Bureau, and a three-year nursing school was begun in 1924. White and many staff members taught students from Georgetown University and George Washington University—he accepted professorships at both institutions shortly after coming to Washington—and also from the army and navy medical schools and Howard University.

Through his writings, publishing activities, and public lectures, White reached a still wider audience. Despite his administrative duties, he published nearly twenty books, more than 200 articles, and almost 400 book reviews. His impact on medical education and on the spread of modern ideas in psychiatry was considerable. *Outlines of Psychiatry*, his first book, became a basic text in medical school, undergoing fourteen editions between 1907 and 1935. *Diseases of the Nervous System*, a work he coauthored with New York neurologist Smith Ely Jelliffe, became a standard text that went through six editions between 1915 and 1935. In 1907 White and Jelliffe founded the Nervous and Mental Disease Monograph Series, which made European works such as Freud's *Selected Papers on Hysteria* (1909) available in English translation. In 1913 they launched the *Psychoanalytic Review*, the first English-language journal of psychoanalysis and a pioneering interdisciplinary venture that sought contributions from historians, anthropologists, and philosophers. Next to Abraham A. Brill, White and Jelliffe were the primary disseminators of psychoanalysis in the United States.

White also was a leader in applying psychiatry to a range of social problems. He wrote about prison reform, the insanity defense, mental hygiene, holistic medicine, industrial medicine, rehabilative medicine, medical education, sex education, drug and alcohol abuse, eugenics and heredity, and social psychiatry. For a lay audience he wrote *The Mental Hygiene of Childhood* (1919), *Thoughts of a Psychiatrist on the War and After* (1919), and *Crimes and Criminals* (1933). His commonsense approach, straightforward language, and progressive outlook made him a popular lecturer before medical societies, scientific associations, social workers, lawyers, ministers, and academics. With his protégé Harry Stack Sullivan, in 1928 and 1929 he organized two colloquia for psychiatrists and social scientists exploring the topic of personality and culture.

White took a special interest in forensic psychiatry. He wrote two books on the subject and testified for the defense in the 1906 trial of Harry K. Thaw for the murder of architect Stanford White and in the celebrated Loeb-Leopold case in 1924. He opposed capital punishment, favored indeterminate sentences, and advocated an end to the power of juries to decide questions of insanity in criminal cases. Although White ultimately hoped to replace legal notions of crime with medical ones, he spent many years fostering cooperation between lawyers and psychiatrists. He was the principal architect of a historic set of joint guidelines, issued in 1930, between the American Bar Association and the American Psychiatric Association on the use of psychiatry in the courts and prisons.

White served as president of the American Psychiatric Association, the American Psychoanalytic Association, the American Psychopathological Association, and the International Congress on Mental Hygiene and was active in many other professional organizations. Sullivan and other former colleagues at St. Elizabeths established the William Alanson White Foundation in Washington during White's lifetime; Sullivan also played a role, along with Erich Fromm and Clara Thompson, in founding the William Alanson White Institute in New York shortly after White's death. Both organizations evolved into influential training institutes.

In 1918, at the age of forty-eight, White married Lora Purman Thurston, widow of a U.S. senator. He became a stepfather to her daughter, but they had no children of their own. His wife helped him negotiate the social and political waters of the capital, but White remained "a slave to his Institution and to his professional goals," according to his good friend Jelliffe. White died at St. Elizabeths.

Although White embraced many elements of modernism, he was essentially Victorian—in his dedication to work, in his sexual life, and in his idealism. During an age of specialization, he remained a generalist: a brilliant synthesizer and an effective popularizer who encouraged various fields in their pioneering stages but made no genuinely original contributions himself. Nonetheless he was instrumental in forging the elements of a distinctive American psychiatry and in shaping its relations with medicine, law, the social sciences, and American culture.

• White's voluminous papers are located at the National Archives as part of the records of St. Elizabeths Hospital; much valuable material on White can also be found in the papers of his collaborator Jelliffe at the Library of Congress. Two autobiographical accounts are *Forty Years of Psychiatry* (1933) and *The Autobiography of a Purpose* (1938); the latter includes a comprehensive bibliography of his writings. Other major books by White include *Mental Mechanisms* (1911), *Mechanisms of Character Formation* (1916), *The Principles of Mental Hygiene* (1917), *Insanity and the Criminal Law* (1923), *The Meaning of Disease: An Inquiry in the Field of Medical Philosophy* (1926), and *Twentieth Century Psychiatry* (1936). A useful guide to White's life and work is the collection of essays in Arcangelo R. T. D'Amore, ed., *William Alanson White: The Washington Years* (1976). An excellent chapter on White's role in defining an "American School" of psychiatry appears in David Evans Tanner, "Symbols of Conduct: Psychiatry and American Culture, 1900–1935" (Ph.D. diss., Univ. of Texas at Austin, 1981). For an analysis of his views on psychiatry and the law, see Janet Ann Tighe, "A Question of Responsibility: The Development of American Forensic Psychiatry, 1838–1930" (Ph.D. diss., Univ. of Pennsylvania, 1983). See also John C. Burnham, "Psychiatry, Psychology, and the Progressive Movement," *American Quarterly* 12 (Winter 1960): 457–65; Nathan G. Hale, *Freud and the Americans: The Beginnings of Psychoanalysis in the United States, 1876–1917* (1971); and Barbara Sicherman, "The New Psychiatry: Medical and Behavioral Sciences, 1895–1921," in *American Psychoanalysis: Origins and Development*, ed. Jacques M. Quen and Eric T. Carlson (1979).

FRANK RIVES MILLIKAN

WHITE, William Allen (10 Feb. 1868–29 Jan. 1944), journalist and author, was born in Emporia, Kansas, the son of Allen White, a physician and merchant, and Mary Ann Hatten, a schoolteacher. A year later the family moved sixty miles southwest to the frontier village Eldorado (now El Dorado), where Allen White quickly became the leading citizen and most energetic booster; he was the town's mayor when he died in 1882. William Allen would emulate his father's absorption in community and civic life. He attended the College of Emporia in 1884, but, seeking a skill to help pay his way, he found a job as printer's devil for a local newspaper. Quickly graduating from compositor to cub reporter, White worked for newspapers throughout the rest of his university career, which included a second year in Emporia and four years at the University of Kansas. He left without a degree in 1890 to manage the *Eldorado Republican*.

Although he had been raised a Democrat by his father, his mother was a fervent Republican. As his newspaper work increasingly involved him in local politics, White gravitated toward the Republicans, who had dominated politics in post–Civil War Kansas. He demonstrated his loyalty to his new party in scathing editorial attacks on the growing Populist movement, labeling its leaders "ragged nobodies" and its economic programs "demagoguery." His work attracted regional attention, and in 1891 he was hired by the conservative Republican *Kansas City Journal*. When an editor mishandled his biggest news scoop, White switched to the *Kansas City Star*, a more commercially successful and politically independent newspaper published by William Rockhill Nelson: Traveling throughout Kansas to cover politics, he learned firsthand how the game was played at the state and regional levels.

Meanwhile, White aspired to be a man of letters as well as journalist, writing dialect poetry and short stories that were published in regional journals. He met Sallie Lindsay, a schoolteacher with similar literary interests, and they were married in 1893. Throughout the rest of his life, Sallie White was his foremost editor and adviser on all matters literary, political, and business. They had two children.

In 1895, following a career pattern typical for journalists of his day, White went into business for himself and bought his own newspaper, the *Emporia Gazette*. With a circulation under 500, it was a dilapidated and faltering business, but White was able to buy it for $3,000, all borrowed from local political allies. Over the succeeding decade he modernized and expanded the *Gazette*, making it the town's dominant newspaper through business acumen as well as journalistic skill. His success was made possible by the general prosperity of the country press at the turn of the century, brought on by increased advertising, rural free delivery, and rising agricultural prices. By 1910 the *Gazette* had a circulation of 3,500; in the 1940s it would reach 8,000.

White first gained national attention during the 1896 presidential campaign when his feisty anti-Populist editorial, "What's the Matter with Kansas?" was widely circulated by the Republican organization. The publicity brought him to the attention of editors of the popular mass-market magazines that had been launched in the 1890s, most prominently *McClure's Magazine*, edited by S. S. McClure. White's vivid, colloquial style and his ability to write knowledgeably about the inner workings of politics made him increasingly sought after. His first volume of short stories, *The Real Issue: A Book of Kansas Stories*, also appearing in 1896, prompted further commissions for fiction. Thus was launched a national career as writer and political commentator, which continued to develop parallel to his local career as editor, publisher, and community leader.

White's literary style was heavily influenced by then-current trends toward realism and naturalism, perhaps most prominent in *Strategems and Spoils: Stories of Love and Politics* (1901). But the stories collected in *The Court of Boyville* (1899) also displayed a taste for sentiment and nostalgia for childhood, and his whimsical celebration of small-town life in the stories comprising *In Our Town* (1906) anticipates Thornton Wilder.

On his first trip east in 1897, White met Theodore Roosevelt (1858–1919) and formed a friendship and political alliance that lasted until the latter's death.

White was one of Roosevelt's most ardent and loyal followers, and later attributed his conversion from conservative to progressive Republican to the older man's influence, but this shift was actually more gradual and was closely implicated with complex factional developments within Kansas politics. Nonetheless, he did emerge by 1905 as a leader of the new "insurgent" wing of his party, which sought regulation of railroads and other corporations that now seemed to endanger their small-town way of life.

As a national reform coalition crystallized, White skillfully used his connections with Roosevelt and his access to such national magazines as *McClure's* and the *Saturday Evening Post* to advance simultaneously his political agenda and his journalistic career. When a number of his close friends at *McClure's*, including editor John S. Phillips and writers Ida Tarbell and Ray Stannard Baker, left to publish their own reform-oriented magazine, *The American Magazine*, he joined them as associate editor. In a series of articles there, collected as *The Old Order Changeth: A View of American Democracy* (1910), White expressed his conviction that the myriad reform activities of the period were but one expression of the same "spiritual growth in the hearts of the American people." His best-selling novel *A Certain Rich Man* (1909) embodied much the same idea in the story of the life and redemption of a typical "malefactor of great wealth." When Roosevelt's bid for another presidential term was defeated at the 1912 Republic National Convention, White helped found the Progressive party. As a national committeeman, he struggled to build a viable political organization, but after the party dissolved in 1916, he returned to the Republicans.

Though initially reluctant to become embroiled in the European conflict, White became an enthusiastic supporter of all wartime programs once the United States entered World War I. His fund-raising activities on behalf of the Red Cross led to a tour of the battlefields in 1917, which prompted the publication of *The Martial Adventures of Henry and Me* (1918), a humorous but earnest effort to educate locally minded Americans about what he saw as the nation's new responsibilities as a world leader. White's emerging career as world citizen was solidified when he returned to Europe in 1919 to report on the Versailles Peace Conference for a newspaper syndicate, and he actively supported the League of Nations in the subsequent controversy over ratification of the peace treaty. In later years the Whites traveled throughout the world, including the Soviet Union in 1933. In 1930 Herbert Hoover appointed him to a committee to study conditions in Haiti, and the report's criticism of U.S. policy there helped spur development of Franklin D. Roosevelt's Good Neighbor policy toward Latin America.

In the twenties and thirties, White continued to publish widely in national magazines, but after the critical failure of his second novel, *In the Heart of a Fool* (1918), he stopped writing fiction. His numerous nonfiction works included several political biographies, the best of which was *A Puritan in Babylon: The Story of Calvin Coolidge* (1938). He had always criticized Coolidge's obeisance to the interests of the "benevolent plutocracy," but he saw in "the reaction of this obviously limited but honest, shrewd, sentimental, resolute American primitive to those gorgeous and sophisticated times" of the 1920s, a fitting symbol of America's transition from a rural to an urban society. Above all, his reputation as shrewd spokesman for the values of small-town, middle-class America continued to grow, prompting H. L. Mencken to dub him the "Sage of Emporia." As one of the founding judges of the Book of the Month Club from 1926 on, he sought to represent the tastes of "middlebrow" Americans. Collections of his influential *Emporia Gazette* editorials, prepared by journalism-school teachers in 1924 and 1937, helped shape a rising generation of professionally trained journalists. Nonetheless, he remained best known to several generations of Americans for "Mary White," his obituary tribute to his seventeen-year-old daughter who was killed in a horseback-riding accident in 1921. White's sincere but contained grief and his powerful evocation of her joyous and humane personality would stand as a shining rebuke to the sordid sensationalism of American journalism in the twenties. It was reprinted throughout the country, read on radio programs, and for decades thereafter appeared in hundreds of school textbooks.

Though he had supported suppressing the civil liberties of dissidents during World War I, White repented in the 1920s, becoming an ardent defender of the freedoms of speech and press. He was also influenced by his son, William Lindsay White, who attended Harvard College in the early twenties and whose experience his father recalled as "a liberal education for his parents too." In 1922 White clashed with Kansas governor Henry J. Allen, a close friend, over whether he had the right to publicly support striking local railroad workers. "To an Anxious Friend," an editorial defense of free speech, won the newly established Pulitzer Prize in 1923. In 1924 he ran for governor as an independent to protest the influence of the Ku Klux Klan in both parties in Kansas. Such principled stands were widely publicized in the national press and gained him the respect of urban liberals like Walter Lippmann and Oswald Garrison Villard, who praised him as a rare example of tolerance and humane values in conservative Middle America. But such causes were not necessarily popular at home: he failed to carry his own county in the 1924 election. Nor could his liberal friends comprehend White's immoderate attacks on Alfred E. Smith in 1928 or his continued loyalty to the Republican party even when Franklin D. Roosevelt carried the banner of reform to the Democratic party in the 1930s. Yet, however unfashionable or inconsistent it might seem to this younger generation of liberals, White remained committed to the more communitarian values of the Progressive Era, which included prohibition. He also delighted in the give and take of "practical politics" in Emporia and Kansas, where his power base inevitably rested with the Republican party.

White was a longtime admirer and supporter of Herbert Hoover, whom he considered the heir of prewar progressivism, but he sadly conceded Hoover a failure as president because of his inability to "dramatize his cause" to the public. Yet he had misgivings about the charismatic FDR and gave a mixed reception to the New Deal, supporting measures to regulate the economy and improve the lot of common Americans while repeating reservations about the increased concentration of power in the federal government. In 1936 he supported Kansas governor Alfred Landon, son of an old Progressive party ally, against Roosevelt, who responded by thanking White for his "support for three and a half years out of every four."

Like many Americans, White had been disillusioned by the results of America's involvement in World War I, and he watched with horror as a second international conflict began to build during the 1930s. But aroused by the Nazi invasion of Poland in 1939 and influenced by his son's experiences as a European war correspondent, he began to oppose the nation's policy of strict neutrality toward all belligerents. In 1940 White headed the bipartisan Committee to Defend America by Aiding the Allies, which attempted to persuade the public that increased military assistance to Britain would help stop German aggression without requiring outright American involvement. The committee's publicity and lobbying were instrumental in achieving the Lend-Lease Act in March 1941, although White resigned in January when it became clear that a majority of the committee considered intervention inevitable.

As the United States moved toward its second world war in his lifetime, White set out to write his autobiography, a project that he had taken up and abandoned several times. The work remained uncompleted at his death in Emporia. Edited by his wife and son, *The Autobiography of William Allen White* was published in 1946. Encompassing through his own experience the sweep of American history between the end of the Civil War and the 1920s and bemusedly surveying American "evolution" from frontier innocent to industrial giant, the work was an immediate best-seller and received the Pulitzer Prize for biography. An enduring classic of American autobiography, it was an effective capstone to a lifetime spent articulating the ideals of his place and time. For many Americans, White himself had become the embodiment, as *Life* put it in 1938, of "small-town simplicity and kindliness and common sense."

• White's many publications are included in the comprehensive *Bibliography of William Allen White*, prepared by the Kansas State Teachers College, now Emporia State University (1969). Extensive collections of White's papers are in the Library of Congress, the University of Kansas Spencer Research Library, and the William Allen White Memorial Library, Emporia State University. Among the many biographies of White, Walter Johnson, *William Allen White's America* (1947), focuses on his activities in national affairs; E. Jay Jernigan, *William Allen White* (1983), on his writing; and Sally Foreman Griffith, *Home Town News: William Allen White and the Emporia Gazette* (1989), on his roles as newspaperman and community leader.

SALLY F. GRIFFITH

WHITE, William Lindsay (17 June 1900–26 July 1973), journalist, was born in Emporia, Kansas, the son of William Allen White, the famous small-town editor of the *Emporia Gazette*, and Sallie Lindsay. For "Young Bill," growing up the son of William Allen White was both a privilege and a curse. As part of his father's busy life, he met presidents and governors, novelists and syndicated columnists, book publishers and Broadway actresses. But as he once observed, his father "was the best-known citizen of our state, far more in the limelight than any Governor or Senator, with the result it was impossible for me to lead a relaxed and normal life in my boyhood."

While a World War I army private at the University of Kansas, Bill convinced his father to let him accompany him to the Versailles peace conference, as a Red Cross second lieutenant. Fascinated by international politics and Parisian culture, Bill returned to the University of Kansas only to find campus life there a bore and, as a result, transferred to Harvard, graduating in 1924. He hoped to win a Rhodes scholarship, but his parents insisted that he return home to work on the family newspaper, eventually to take over as its managing editor.

Except for two vacation trips to Europe and occasional forays to New York City, he stayed in Emporia with the *Gazette* for ten years, writing many editorials attributed to his father. In 1931 in New York City he married Kathrine Klinkenberg, a fellow Kansan who had "escaped" to the East, where she worked for *Time* magazine. Kathrine soon found small-town Emporia unbearable, and her discontent whetted Bill's. Both felt even more dissatisfied after the state was rocked by a depression-bred school bond scandal perpetrated by the Whites' closest hometown friends, the bankers Warren Finney and his son Ronald.

In 1934 Bill and Kathrine left for Boston, where she sought better medical treatment for chronic gynecological problems. Away from the confines of Emporia and the *Gazette*, Bill started a novel about the Finney bond scandal, while at the same time sending back editorial copy. By the summer of 1935 both father and son realized he could not return to Emporia. Instead, he took a job in Washington, D.C., with a scholastic newsletter, the *Weekly Observer*. After three months Bill quit to join the *Washington Post*, but he lasted there only a short time. Following several months of joblessness and indecision, he and Kathrine moved in 1936 to New York City's Greenwich Village, where, with financial help from his parents, he continued to work on his novel.

In the fall of 1937 he landed a job with Henry Luce's *Fortune* magazine, but he lost it in April 1938, the same month Knopf published his novel *What People Said* to good reviews. Buoyed by that success, Bill tried his hand at magazine freelancing, then interested the *Des Moines Register-Tribune* syndicate in his daily column "Take a Look" appearing in the *Gazette*. His break came when his father's old friend "FPA" (Franklin P. Adams) took a vacation in August 1939 from his syndicated "The Conning Tower" column and suggested Bill's column as a replacement. When FPA returned, about twenty newspapers continued Bill's pieces. War in Europe was by then imminent, and Bill decided to cover it in his column.

In Berlin in November William Shirer asked him to substitute on CBS's "Today in Europe." Impressed, CBS hired him to cover the Finnish-Russian war as an addition to his syndicated commentary, now being carried by over forty newspapers. After leaving Finland, Bill continued to broadcast for CBS from points in Europe and then substituted for Edward R. Murrow in London. Afterward, CBS asked him to return to New York to work as the anchor for its European news programs. But his father, convinced that his son needed to stick with a project, persuaded the syndicate to pull Bill off a ship at Gibraltar and send him to Romania, where—so Secretary of State Cordell Hull had predicted in private—war would break out. There he found nothing but delays, and he returned to New York in May 1940 depressed, with newspapers canceling his now-erratic column.

In the fall of 1940 he quit the syndicate to sail as a stringer for John Wheeler's North American Newspaper Alliance aboard a lend-lease destroyer to embattled Britain. There he found and brought back to the United States a three-year-old war orphan, Barbara, whom he and Kathrine adopted, and who became the subject of his second book, *Journey for Margaret* (1941). His British stories so interested DeWitt Wallace of the *Reader's Digest* that he signed Bill on as one of his first roving editors. Bill kept that post the rest of his life, because it gave him an identity and an income separate from his father and the *Gazette*. Wallace also gave him the encouragement he needed; as a result, his next two books and his numerous war-effort reports were highly successful. For example, *They Were Expendable* (1942), the story of the PT Boat squadron that brought General Douglas MacArthur out of Bataan, became a Book-of-the-Month Club blockbuster and the first book officially designated "imperative" to the war effort by the Council on Books in Wartime.

But in 1944, just after his father's death, Bill took on a correspondent's job that changed his life. He accompanied Eric Johnston, president of the American Chamber of Commerce, to war-torn Russia and recorded his observations in the book *Report on the Russians* (1945). In it he satirized Russian society, criticized Soviet war efforts, and expressed doubts about Stalin's good faith and postwar intentions. As a result, the American-Soviet Friendship Council led a campaign of vilification that cost Bill many liberal friends and, for several years at least, his reputation as an objective reporter. But soon afterward, as a moderately conservative libertarian, he was elected to the executive board of the American Civil Liberties Union (1946–1955). Later he became an overseer of Harvard University (1950–1956).

After the war he continued to reside chiefly in New York City, working for *Reader's Digest* and running the *Emporia Gazette* as its absentee editor-publisher. For a decade his primary interest was in his *Reader's Digest* assignments, his best-known postwar piece being his book-length report about Korean MASH units, *Back Down the Ridge* (1953). After 1954, with Kathrine's help, he began monitoring the *Gazette* more closely, completely revamping its backshop and working with his staff on layout. Under his closer supervision, the *Gazette* won the prestigious Ayer Cup in 1960 as the best newspaper in the United States in typography and format. During the 1960s, though continuing to work on an occasional *Reader's Digest* assignment and living about half the year in New York City or traveling, he spent increasingly more time and effort in Emporia. During those years he proved himself an outstanding small-town editor. To his fellow townsmen, though, he was still "Young Bill" White to the day of his death in Emporia.

• Some of W. L. White's papers are held in the Kansas Collection of the Spencer Research Library at the University of Kansas; some are with his father's at the Library of Congress; some are still held by the family. Other books by him are *Queens Die Proudly* (1943), *Report on the Germans* (1947), *Lost Boundaries* (1948), *Land of Milk and Honey* (1949), *Bernard Baruch: Portrait of a Citizen* (1950), *The Captives of Korea* (1957), *The Little Toy Dog* (1962), and *A Report on the Asians* (1969). Biographies and significant secondary sources are lacking. Obituaries are in the 27 July 1973 issues of the *New York Times* and *Washington Post* and in the 6 Aug. 1973 issues of *Time* and *Newsweek*.

E. Jay Jernigan

WHITE EYES (c. 1730–1778), Delaware chief, also known as George White Eyes, Quequedegatha, Koquethagechton, Koguethagechton, or Kuckquetackton, was born a member of the Turtle clan. The circumstances of White Eyes's youth are unknown. In the 1760s he was living in a Delaware town at the mouth of Beaver Creek, a tributary of the Ohio River, where he evidently ran a tavern and operated as a trader. White Eyes became the leading councilor and spokesman of the Ohio Delawares and seems to have acted as principal adviser to the Delaware chief, Netawatwees. He moved with his people to the Muskingum Valley in the years before the American Revolution, where the Delaware capital was established at Goschachgunk or Coshocton, near the mouth of the Tuscarawas River. White Eyes was named chief by the Delaware Grand Council in 1774; the aging Netawatwees died while attending a council at Fort Pitt two years later.

White Eyes took the role of a mediator in intertribal and Indian-white relations. He supported Moravian missionaries in their work among his people and generally pursued policies of accommodation with white society. He advocated peace during Dunmore's War in 1774 and kept the Delawares out of the conflict.

When the Revolution broke out he endeavored to keep his people neutral. At the Treaty of Fort Pitt in 1775, when Iroquois delegates demanded that the Delawares take up arms for the British, White Eyes formally and dramatically asserted Delaware independence, casting off the lingering dominance that the Iroquois had claimed over them for generations. Most Delawares remained neutral, although some young warriors left to join the British and Edward Hand's infamous "squaw campaign" (in which militia murdered peaceful Delaware and Munsee Indians in 1778) offered considerable American provocation. Coshocton grew into a cluster of neutral villages in the midst of war.

Located in the strategic Ohio Valley, between the Americans at Fort Pitt and the British and their Indian allies close to Detroit, the Delawares came under intense pressure to abandon their neutrality. Especially critical was the Delaware need for trade goods and the American inability to match the British in supplying them. Captain Pipe and the Wolf clan displayed growing pro-British sentiments, but White Eyes leaned increasingly toward the Americans. He cultivated close diplomatic relations with George Morgan, the Indian agent at Fort Pitt, and kept him informed of developments in Indian country. In 1776 White Eyes accompanied Morgan to Philadelphia to establish formal diplomatic relations with the Continental Congress. He requested that a teacher and clergyman be sent to educate his people and received $300, plus two horses with saddles and bridles, in recognition of his peace-keeping efforts. White Eyes traveled extensively on diplomatic missions and accompanied William Wilson, congressional emissary to the Indian tribes, on his journey to Detroit in 1776.

In 1778 at Fort Pitt, White Eyes and the Delawares signed a treaty with the United States permitting the Americans to cross their lands and requesting that forts be erected to protect their villages. The treaty also contained a provision guaranteeing Delaware territorial rights and suggesting that the Delawares would at some future date head a separate Indian state, which would have been the fourteenth in the union. As Americans recorded and interpreted the treaty, it also committed the Delawares to an active alliance with the United States. Delaware representatives later claimed that they misunderstood the terms of the treaty and were deceived into making a military commitment when in fact they only offered to act as intermediaries with hostile tribes. George Morgan, who was not present at the signing, described it as a product of shady dealing.

White Eyes, however, undertook to carry out his commitment by acting as a guide across tribal lands and accompanied General Lachlan McIntosh's ineffective campaign against Detroit in 1778. He did not return. American reports said White Eyes died of smallpox, but it is probable that this claim was a cover-up for the murder of the chief by the American militia.

White Eyes's death at the height of his career, and George Morgan's resignation the next year, removed two key players in the struggle to keep the Delawares out of the British camp. More and more Delawares joined the Crown until, in 1780, Daniel Brodhead marched to Coshocton and burned it. Afterward, although a few Delawares under Killbuck took refuge with the Americans at Fort Pitt, most followed Captain Pipe and made common cause with the British. The peace-keeping diplomacy of White Eyes was in ruins, and his people followed the path taken by many of their neighbors.

• The best sources on White Eyes are the Lyman Draper Manuscripts of the Wisconsin State Historical Society, available on microfilm, and George Morgan's manuscript letterbooks at the Carnegie Library in Pittsburgh. A typescript of Morgan's 1776 letterbook is in the Pennsylvania Historical and Museum Commission. Pertinent documents from the Draper manuscripts and elsewhere are reprinted in Reuben G. Thwaites and Louise P. Kellogg, eds., *The Revolution on the Upper Ohio, 1775–1777* (1908) and *Frontier Defense on the Upper Ohio, 1777–1778* (1912). C. A. Weslager, *The Delaware Indians, A History* (1972), and Randolph C. Downes, *Council Fires on the Upper Ohio: A Narrative of Indian Affairs in the Upper Ohio Valley until 1795* (1940), provide background.

COLIN G. CALLOWAY

WHITEFIELD, George (16 Dec. 1714–30 Sept. 1770), Anglican evangelist, was born in Gloucester, England, the son of Thomas Whitefield and Elizabeth Edwards, innkeepers. While still in his teens Whitefield entered Oxford University and came under the influence of John and Charles Wesley. They persuaded him, following his graduation, to become a missionary to the American colony of Georgia. On 2 February 1738 the young minister, with the approval of the Georgia trustees and the Anglican hierarchy, sailed for Georgia aboard the *Whitaker*, carrying with him "upwards of £300 for the poor."

Following his arrival in the colony on 8 May 1738, Whitefield promoted piety and "won the hearts of his Hearers." He soon decided to establish an orphanage in Savannah and in September 1738 sailed back to England to raise money for that purpose and to take priest's orders.

In England Whitefield found himself popular with the masses, who flocked to hear his sermons. With one eye askew (prompting critics to call him "Dr. Squintum"), he was not an attractive man, but he possessed a compelling voice and such strong convictions that he moved his listeners to cry out for God's mercy. Among those impressed by Whitefield's ability to stir his auditors were the heralded English actor David Garrick and Benjamin Franklin (1706–1790). However, he was unpopular with many Anglican clergymen, whom he had criticized for allegedly not proclaiming the truths of the Bible and the Articles of the Anglican church. Some of these ministers labeled Whitefield an "enthusiast" (meaning one who believed he had direct revelations from God) and closed their pulpits to him. Despite this opposition the young evangelist secured priest's orders and collected about £1,000 for his orphanage.

After completing his mission in England, Whitefield returned to America, arriving in Philadelphia in November 1739. There he drew huge crowds, thus launching a preaching career that soon made him the most publicized man in America. He became the most visible awakener of the Great Awakening in America and perhaps the greatest religious orator of the eighteenth century. He carried the torch of revival throughout the colonies, bringing unity to the efforts of awakeners who had been on the scene before him.

For the next fourteen months Whitefield left his confining "parsonage of Savannah" and preached all over America, touring the middle colonies and New England extensively. In his own mind he enjoyed his greatest success and encountered his most bitter opposition in Charleston, South Carolina. There Commissary Alexander Garden, representative of the bishop of London and the highest ranking Anglican official in the Carolinas, accused Whitefield of violating "the canons and Ordination vow" and ordered him not to preach again in the Carolinas. When the brash, young evangelist gave that order no more notice than "a Pope's bull," Garden summoned him to an ecclesiastical court held at St. Philip's Church in Charleston on 15 July 1740. The evangelist appeared but denied the commissary's jurisdiction over him and appealed to England. No clear-cut disposition of the case was ever made, and Whitefield continued preaching when and where he pleased.

Although itinerating almost continuously from November 1739 to January 1741, Whitefield did establish his orphanage, "Bethesda," and placed Jonathan Barber, a follower from New England, and James Habersham, a young Englishman whom he had met on his first voyage to America, in charge of it. Critics contended that Barber and Habersham overemphasized spiritual matters and were too harsh in disciplining the children who took refuge at Bethesda. Whatever its faults, however, the orphanage provided its wards with food, clothing, shelter, and schooling, and eventually Bethesda gained acceptance in the colony. It became colonial Georgia's best and most lasting school. Seldom did Whitefield preach without seeking donations for his "poor orphans."

Having started his orphanage and having preached all over America, the evangelist was satisfied upon his departure for England in January 1741 that he had contributed substantially to God's work. Five more times—in 1744, 1751, 1754, 1763, and 1769—he returned to the colonies, and each time he drew impressive audiences, but on none of those visits did the excitement created by his discourses reach the feverish pitch it had in 1740. When not in America, Whitefield was somewhere else in the British Empire calling sinners to repentance and begging money for Bethesda. Whitefield married Elizabeth Burnell James in November 1741; their only child died in infancy. Apparently Whitefield's work left him little time for family life. Bethesda was always on his mind; he dreamed of adding to it a Christian academy and even a college. Although the academy became a reality, he was never able to secure a charter for a college. At the time of his death in Newburyport, Massachusetts, he was still talking about that dream. Whitefield asked that he be buried in Newburyport beneath the First Presbyterian Church (also known as the Old South Church), and that request was honored.

Long before his death Whitefield had become far less controversial than he had been during his early ministry. Because of his accusatory declarations, he had been considered a radical, but except for his steadfast insistence that the old Christian-nurture approach to salvation was inadequate, Whitefield was a conservative. Theologically he claimed to be a Calvinist and at the same time a faithful Anglican. Actually Whitefield adhered to a modified version of Calvinism, professing to believe in the doctrine of election while simultaneously asking sinners to "choose" salvation. Presumably Whitefield was unable to wrestle intellectually with theological subtleties and never really developed a systematic theology. Throughout his 34-year ministry he harped on original sin, justification by faith alone, and life in the hereafter, leaving theological discussion in most cases to those who were more comfortable with abstract reasoning. He possessed a sincere and simple faith, an ecumenical spirit, and the ability to capitalize on tensions between dissenters and established churches. He made dissent respectable and thus prepared the way for the multidenominational religious system that emerged in America following the Revolution.

• Important sources by Whitefield are *The Works of the Reverend George Whitefield, M.A.* (1771–1772); *Memoirs of Rev. George Whitefield*, ed. John Gillies (rev. ed., 1834); and *George Whitefield's Journals* (1960). Biographical studies include Joseph Belcher, *George Whitefield: A Biography with Special Reference to His Labors in America* (1857); Albert David Belden, *George Whitefield, the Awakener* (1930); Stuart Clark Henry, *George Whitefield, Wayfaring Witness* (1957); and Luke Tyerman, *The Life of the Rev. George Whitefield* (2 vols., 1876–1877). On Whitefield's activities in Georgia, see Reba Carolyn Strickland, *Religion and the State in Georgia in the Eighteenth Century* (1939), and Harold E. Davis, *The Fledgling Province* (1976).

DAVID T. MORGAN

WHITEHEAD, Alfred North (15 Feb. 1861–30 Dec. 1947), mathematician, logician, and philosopher, was born at Ramsgate on the Isle of Thanet in Kent, England, the son of Alfred Whitehead, an educator and a member of the Church of England clergy, and Maria Sarah Buckmaster. The young Alfred North Whitehead enjoyed the benefits of the exceptionally fine schooling available in the mid-nineteenth century to the gifted sons of families that, even though of modest means, were well connected within church and education circles. For his university preparation he was sent to the Sherborne School in Dorsetshire in southern England, where he easily absorbed the broad curriculum, participated in sports, and reached the pinnacle of student leadership, a position roughly analogous to being president of the student council in an American school.

Whitehead did his university-level work at Trinity College of Cambridge University, an institutional affiliation that was to last for approximately thirty years. He formally enrolled as a student of mathematics, and mathematics alone, in 1880, but as his reminiscences make clear, the general intellectual life of the university was wide and deep and he participated in it richly, engaging frequently in conversations on literature, religion, philosophy, and politics. In 1884, the year he both earned his first-class degree in mathematics and was elected a Fellow of Trinity College, he became a member of the Cambridge Conversazione Society, also known as "the Apostles." This society is described by Victor Lowe (1985) as "the most elite discussion club in the English-speaking university world." It is important to note that although Whitehead formally studied and taught only mathematics, he interacted intensely with first-class minds from a wide range of disciplines. Whitehead's intellectual exposure at Cambridge was far broader than one might infer from a knowledge of his formal studies, and Lowe has observed that "Whitehead's membership in the Apostles was the climax of his Cambridge education in the humanities," an education he was to draw on heavily in those later years when his interests became technically philosophical.

In 1890 Whitehead met and married Evelyn Willoughby Wade; they had three children. Though not an intellectual, she had presence, wit, and an ability to converse on issues of the day. Most significantly, she had taste, a well-developed aesthetic sense. "Wherever we went, my wife's aesthetic taste gave a wonderful charm to the houses, sometimes almost miraculously," Whitehead wrote in his Autobiographical Notes. In Whitehead's later thought the concept "beauty" became a technical term conveying some of his most important philosophical insights; his wife clearly nurtured and developed this dimension of his experience.

Whitehead was a reader for Trinity College of the examinations taken by incoming freshmen in 1890 who were candidates for scholarships. Bertrand Russell was one of those candidates. Whitehead thought, in Lowe's words, that Russell's papers "showed more ability than was indicated by a summing of the marks he made in them" and he succeeded in convincing his fellow readers that Russell should be admitted with a higher level of support than the numerical grades would have indicated. Russell did study with Whitehead, but the relationship was not close at that time. In 1895 Russell submitted a dissertation on the foundations of geometry as part of his quest to obtain a teaching fellowship at Trinity College. Whitehead was one of the readers and the evening before the fellowship winners were to be announced, a very nervous Russell visited the Whiteheads to try to pry out some information about how things were going. Whitehead would make no specific comment other than to criticize, rather severely, several of the points Russell had made. The now very anxious Russell learned the next day that he had indeed been elected a fellow of Trinity. Russell later wrote that Whitehead defended his conduct by saying, "it was the last occasion on which he would be able to speak to me as to a pupil, and that, after the praise that he knew I was to get, I might have paid too little attention to his entirely justifiable criticisms."

In the years that followed, Whitehead and Russell, now colleagues, each published books in mathematics that they both expected to be followed by a second volume: Whitehead *A Treatise on Universal Algebra* in 1898, and Russell *The Principles of Mathematics* in 1903. By the turn of the century the Whiteheads and the Russells ("Bertie" had married an American, Alys Smith, in 1894) had become close friends, to the point of even sharing living quarters in the second half of 1901 and part of 1902. In the summer of 1900 the four made a trip together to Paris, where the men attended both the First International Congress of Philosophy and the Second International Congress of Mathematics. In Paris Whitehead and Russell attended presentations by the famous Italian mathematician Giuseppe Peano, whose well-known axioms for grounding the arithmetic of the positive integers were being used by him, and others, for further research into the foundations of mathematics. Back in England both Whitehead and Russell, in playing with Peano's formulations, discovered that his principles taken jointly led to inconsistencies. In a letter to Russell pointing out some of these inconsistencies, Whitehead observed: "My belief is that the development according to his own principles is much more lengthy than the one he gives. I have been working at it in my intervals of leisure." The development turned out to be lengthy indeed! Under the impetus provided by the encounter with the work of Peano, Whitehead and Russell merged their projected second volumes into one monumental study of the foundations of mathematics, the production of which consumed the next decade and resulted in the publication (in 1910, 1912, and 1913) of their three-volume masterwork, *Principia Mathematica*.

With the bulk of the work on *Principia* completed by the end of 1909, Whitehead, in 1910, somewhat precipitously resigned his lectureship at Cambridge and moved to London. He had no academic post lined up when he moved and spent his first year in London writing his *Introduction to Mathematics*, a work commissioned by the Home University Library of Modern Knowledge. In 1911 he secured a position at University College, and in 1914 he was named to the chair of applied mathematics at the Imperial College of Science and Technology. Whitehead was heavily involved in educational politics during his affiliation with the University of London, serving as dean of the faculty of science, a member of the senate, and chair of the academic council. This day-to-day involvement with the practical dimension of education—especially his leadership, from 1919 to 1924, of the body that governed Goldsmith's College, which trained teachers—led him to think deeply about the character of the education being offered to the working classes. His thinking at the time is reflected in *The Organization of Thought* (1917) and *The Aims of Education* (1929).

During these London years (1910 to 1924) Whitehead's technical interests broadened from a concern with the foundations of mathematics to a concern with the foundations of science. It had originally been projected that Whitehead would write a fourth volume of *Principia Mathematica* that would deal with the foundations of geometry, a study that would build a bridge between mathematics and natural science. Such a volume was never published, though it has been surmised that materials perhaps initially intended for it cropped up in later books, particularly in part 4 of *Process and Reality*, which is titled "The Theory of Extension."

In 1915 Whitehead joined the aristocrat of philosophical discussion groups, the Aristotelian Society, and commenced years of intense discussions about epistemology and the philosophy of science with the best philosophical minds in England. The research conducted during this period culminated in three published volumes: *An Enquiry Concerning the Principles of Natural Knowledge* (1919), *The Concept of Nature* (1920), and *The Principle of Relativity* (1922).

Whitehead's contributions to the philosophy of science were admired by a number of people across the Atlantic and in 1924 he was offered a position in the philosophy department at Harvard University. That year he accepted a five-year appointment and moved to the new Cambridge across the Atlantic. The original appointment stretched on; Whitehead finally retired from Harvard in 1937 after thirteen years on the Harvard faculty.

The move to the United States coincided with an enormous expansion in the scope of Whitehead's philosophical interests. His work in the philosophy of science had removed mind from nature, had ignored the functioning of mind in nature, and at the time he was crossing the Atlantic he was coming to see that this bracketing out of mind was ultimately untenable. In addition, he was coming to recognize that Western philosophy since Descartes had continued to presuppose the scientific assumptions of the seventeenth century, assumptions hopelessly at odds with the revolution in scientific thinking of the late nineteenth and early twentieth centuries. These reflections were at the core of his next book, *Science and the Modern World*, published in 1925, which created a good bit of excitement in the intellectual community. The book described how, century by century, the developing Copernican/Newtonian scientific revolution generated a set of philosophical assumptions that were now completely outmoded and in desperate need of revision.

Science and the Modern World describes the problem clearly, but only adumbrates the way that Whitehead feels we need to respond to the problem. His full-blown response did not emerge until his philosophical magnum opus, *Process and Reality* (1929), substantive parts of which were delivered as the Gifford Lectures in the University of Edinburgh during the session 1927–1928. The book is very difficult to read, in large part because Whitehead was convinced that the conceptual framework of traditional philosophical analysis would hopelessly distort his ideas. Consequently, *Process and Reality* is laced with neologisms; it is written in a new philosophical language that the reader must master before it will give up its insights and wisdom. In 1966 Donald W. Sherburne published a monograph titled *A Key to Whitehead's Process and Reality*; this book contains a 43-page glossary and presents a substantial portion of the text, reorganized and interspersed with interpretive comment.

Process and Reality can be described as the construction and defense of a scheme of ideas that does justice to the richness and complexity of human being and exhibits human being as a part of nature. The seventeenth-century dualism of Descartes, by bifurcating existence into two separate substances, mind and matter, led to the tendency to bracket mind out of nature in subsequent philosophy of science. This procedure seemed plausible in an era that conceived of matter as inert, static, passive stuff. What Whitehead saw as philosophically important in the science taking shape in the nineteenth and twentieth centuries was a revolution in the understanding of matter—matter was no longer viewed as inert, but as dynamic and energetic, as equivalent to quanta of energy. In seventeenth-century understanding, energy was separate from, external to, matter, so Descartes was quite justified, but Whitehead saw that the new science rendered the Cartesian distinctions obsolete and opened the door for a philosophical description of reality that viewed the real as dynamic, active, and in process. In Whitehead's vision, appropriately labeled process philosophy, "mind" is not a separate substance apart from "matter," but is, rather, a sophisticated state of the underlying dynamic reality that emerges with the complexity generated by the thrust of evolution (another nineteenth-century notion unavailable to Descartes). The articulation and defense of these ideas is complicated, and though the result of the discourse in *Process and Reality* is uniquely Whiteheadian, there are affinities of thought with others also influenced by recent developments in scientific understanding, thinkers such as Henri Bergson, Pierre Teilhard de Chardin, and Maurice Merleau-Ponty.

In 1933 Whitehead published another major volume, *Adventures of Ideas*. It is a multifaceted work, but it can perhaps best be described as a philosophy of civilization. Early in the book Whitehead suggests that at any given time and place there are two types of forces driving the processes of social change: brute, senseless agencies of compulsion on the one hand, and formulated aspirations grounded in articulated beliefs on the other. Whitehead's symbols for these two types of forces in the classical world are Barbarians (brute compulsion) and Christianity (a system of beliefs and aspirations); for the Europe of a century ago, examples of these two types of forces would be, respectively, Steam and Democracy. Whitehead's interest in *Adventures of Ideas* is in articulated aspirations, in how their articulation is related to the conceptual possibilities bedded in the philosophical understandings available at the moment when they struggle for release and efficacy. Part 4 of *Adventures of Ideas* is where Whitehead articulates his vision of how his new philosophical conceptuality permits the formulation of cultural aspirations appropriate to our age, a vision couched in the meanings he gives to such concepts as Truth, Beauty, Adventure, Zest, and Peace.

During Whitehead's American years he published a number of other books that helped solidify his reputation as one of the leading philosophers of the twentieth century: *Religion in the Making* (1926), *Symbolism: Its Meaning and Effect* (1927), *The Function of Reason* (1929), and *Modes of Thought* (1938). The Whitehead volume in the Library of Living Philosophers appeared in 1941 and contained, in addition to his Autobiographical Notes, two articles titled "Mathematics and the Good" and "Immortality." For the remaining six years of his life his health was failing and he wrote very little. In recognition of his work in England he won election to the Royal Society (1903) and became a Fellow of the British Academy (1931); in recognition of his work in the United States he was elected president of the American Philosophical Association (1931).

Whitehead's influence has been most widely felt in the area of philosophical theology. Even though Whitehead described himself as an agnostic from the mid-1890s until the end of World War I, his philosophical turn in the 1920s brought with it an acknowledgment that his categoreal scheme required for its coherent completion the notion of God. (Victor Lowe has suggested that this reappropriation of divinity, while most certainly motivated by philosophical considerations, might have also been encouraged by the tragic death, in the closing months of the war, of the youngest of the Whiteheads' three children—Eric Alfred Whitehead was shot down in an aerial dogfight over France on 13 March 1918.) In the same way that St. Thomas used the philosophical categories of Aristotle to give meaning and grounding to the Christian tradition, so many contemporary Christian thinkers have been motivated to use Whitehead's metaphysics as the context to give new meanings and grounding to the notion of divinity, meanings felt to be compatible with twentieth-century understandings. Charles Hartshorne, John Cobb, Lewis Ford, Robert Neville, David Griffin, Schubert Ogden, Marjorie Suchocki, Rita Brock, and Catherine Keller are a few of the many contemporary theologians who have fleshed out in imaginative and creative ways the rather barebones notion of divinity found in Whitehead's own writings. Other scholars have been more interested in exploring the philosophical applications and possibilities of Whitehead's categories: Victor Lowe, Ivor Leclerc, F. S. C. Northrop, Nathaniel Lawrence, Donald W. Sherburne, Frederick Ferré, and George Allan, to name just a few.

Alfred North Whitehead was a quiet, modest, unpretentious man. Genuinely kindly in nature, his interest in developing the imagination and originality of his students led many of them to feel that they had a special relationship with this teacher. His concern to encourage independent and creative thinking made him a notoriously easy grader. He could be critical, but his criticism was so gentle, and so positive, that it was exhilarating rather than intimidating. Whitehead believed that it was much more important to develop one's own ideas creatively than to argue over details in a scholastic manner. Consequently, it was difficult to get him to answer his mail or engage in polemical confrontation; if attacked he would tend not to hear or to move obliquely to a new topic of conversation.

• Following Whitehead's directive, the bulk of his papers were destroyed shortly after his death; there exists, consequently, no significant collection of original papers. A Center for Process Studies housed at the School of Theology at Claremont, Calif., however, supports a library of Whiteheadiana, publishes the journal *Process Studies*, and sponsors research professorships and national and international conferences focusing on Whitehead's contributions to philosophy. Lucien Price, a newspaperman in Boston and a frequent guest at evening gatherings of students and distinguished visitors in the Whitehead home, has recorded his impressions of those occasions in a book titled *Dialogues of Alfred North Whitehead* (1954). Victor Lowe, *Alfred North Whitehead: The Man and His Work* (2 vols., 1985–1990), is the most complete account of Whitehead's life and contains excellent coverage of Whitehead's Cambridge, England, years, and of the relationship with Bertrand Russell. See chapter 7, "The Cambridge Apostles," in vol. 1 for an account of the Cambridge Conversazione society and the gifted persons from many different academic fields who shared membership with Whitehead. There are a number of editions of Whitehead's masterpiece, *Process and Reality*; persons interested in exploring this volume should be sure to get the corrected edition (1978), edited by David Ray Griffin and Donald W. Sherburne. A journal, *Process Studies*, has appeared quarterly since 1971 and is dedicated to articles focusing on ideas generated by Whitehead. There is a large secondary literature: two of the best introductory studies are Ivor Leclerc's *Whitehead's Metaphysics: An Introductory Exposition* (1958) and Victor Lowe's *Understanding Whitehead* (1962). A complete bibliography of Whitehead's writings can be found in the back of the second edition of the Library of Living Philosophers volume on Whitehead, *The Philosophy of Alfred North Whitehead*, ed. Paul A. Schilpp (1941; 2d ed., 1951).

DONALD W. SHERBURNE

WHITEHEAD, John Boswell (18 Aug. 1872–16 Nov. 1954), electrical engineer, researcher, and educator, was born in Norfolk, Virginia, the son of Henry Colgate Whitehead, treasurer of the Norfolk City Railway, and Margaret Walke Taylor. Whitehead's grandfather and great-grandfather were both mayors of Norfolk, and the family was socially and politically prominent in the southern Virginia area. Whitehead left Norfolk in 1889 at the age of seventeen to pursue his education at the Johns Hopkins University in Baltimore, Maryland.

At Johns Hopkins Whitehead enrolled in the undergraduate historical/political science program, originally intending to pursue a career in law. He chanced to take a physics course taught by Henry A. Rowland and became fascinated by the work he saw going on in Rowland's laboratories and decided to enroll in the program in applied electricity. The two-year program was offered through the Department of Physics and was taught by Louis Duncan. In 1893 Whitehead received a Certificate of Proficiency in Applied Electricity. (Johns Hopkins did not have an engineering school and did not offer a B.E. at the time.)

After receiving his certificate, Whitehead began his professional career in 1893 as an electrical engineer with the Westinghouse Electric and Manufacturing Company in East Pittsburgh. Westinghouse was involved in manufacturing generators and transformers to supply the Niagara Falls Power Plant, which was then under construction. Whitehead transferred to Niagara Falls in 1896 and spent a year working at the new plant.

In 1897 Whitehead returned to Johns Hopkins to continue his studies. He worked as an instructor in applied electricity and as an associate in the physics department while he completed his B.A. in 1898 and his Ph.D. in physics in 1902. Whitehead also worked at the U.S. Bureau of Standards as a laboratory assistant and was a research assistant at the Carnegie Institution in Washington, D.C., from 1902 to 1905. He married Mary Ellen Colston of Baltimore in 1903; they had three daughters. Whitehead founded the Baltimore branch of the American Institute of Electrical Engineers in 1904 and remained its chairman for twenty years. He was named an associate professor at Johns Hopkins in 1904 and a professor of applied electricity within the Department of Physics in 1910. In 1927 he represented the university as an exchange professor in France for six months.

Whitehead's insight and expertise were instrumental in the founding of the Department of Engineering at Johns Hopkins in 1912, which officially became the Johns Hopkins School of Engineering in 1919. The school came into being despite the opposition of many faculty members, who believed that Whitehead wanted to begin a trade school rather than the scholarly, research-oriented school that he actually intended. Whitehead realized that the school would have to begin at a high level or it would be doomed to failure and insisted on excellence from the beginning. He personally selected the first faculty, comprised of himself as professor of electrical engineering, Charles Tilden as professor of civil engineering, and Carl C. Thomas as professor of mechanical engineering.

Whitehead became the School of Engineering's first dean in 1919. In 1938 he was made director of the school and remained in that position until his retirement in 1942. The school offered both a four-year undergraduate curriculum in theoretical and functional engineering and a graduate center for research. The curriculum focused on fundamentals, as Whitehead believed this type of learning to be the best way to equip students with the skills necessary to conduct their own research. When planning the curriculum, he also drew heavily from his own educational experiences and from what he had observed in Rowland's laboratories.

Whitehead's students found him somewhat intimidating because of his brilliance, stature, and reserve. He demanded that students follow a dress code, and he insisted on punctuality. However, he was also fair and dedicated to the welfare of his students above all.

Research was an integral part of Whitehead's career. He performed pioneering investigations in the theory of dielectrics (nonconducting materials) and was also involved in research into high-voltage insulations. To aid this work he invented the Corona voltmeter, a high-voltage measuring device that established the principle that attributes of air were usable as standards for the measurements of high voltages. The device won for Whitehead the prestigious triennial prize of the Montefiore Foundation of Belgium in 1922, awarded to the best original research in the technical applications of electricity. Whitehead downplayed his accomplishment, stating that the device was "too expensive; nobody could afford to use it." In 1925 Whitehead again took the Montefiore Prize after discovering why high-voltage equipment used in heavy industry regularly broke down for no apparent reason. He traced the problem to ionization of air trapped within the high-voltage generator spirals. This caused chemical and heat effects, which damaged insulation and exposed equipment to shutdowns and short circuits. Whitehead also investigated ways of minimizing the effects of lightning on high-voltage power lines, as well as high-voltage underground cables, low-frequency insulation, and high-frequency dielectric heating. He authored four books, including *Lectures on Dielectric Theory and Insulation* (1927) and *Electricity and Magnetism; an Introduction to the Mathematical Theory* (1939), and wrote over 100 articles on subjects in his field.

Whitehead's expertise was widely valued. Several large railways engaged him as a consultant in their electrification projects. At the start of World War I, Whitehead was commissioned a major in the U.S. Army Corps of Engineers and worked on a submarine detection project. Whitehead was also an adviser to the navy during World War II and used his skills to develop ways of safeguarding American ships from magnetic mines. The air force enlisted Whitehead's help on electronics research projects, on which Whitehead continued to work even after his retirement in 1942.

Whitehead's career and research brought him several prestigious awards and honors in addition to the Montefiore Prizes. The University of Nancy, France, presented him with the Henry Dailme Medaille d'Honneur in 1927. He was awarded the Edward Longstreth Medal and the Elliott Cresson Gold Medal of the Franklin Institute for his work in dielectrics and high-voltage insulation. The highest award of the American Institute of Electrical Engineers, the Edison Medal, was given to him in 1942. The Johns Hopkins University named the Whitehead Hall science building in his honor in 1948. It was the first time a building on the campus had been named for a living person. Whitehead was a member of the National Academy of Sciences, Phi Beta Kappa, Tau Beta Pi, Delta Phi, the National Research Council, and the French Society of Electricians. He was a fellow of the American Association for the Advancement of Science, the American Physical Society, and the American Institute of Electrical Engineers. In 1933 he was elected president of the American Institute of Electrical Engineers. Whitehead died in Baltimore, Maryland.

• A small amount of Whitehead's correspondence is scattered throughout several collections of the papers of Johns Hopkins professors in the Department of Special Collections and Archives, Milton S. Eisenhower Library, the Johns Hopkins University. Much of this correspondence was written by Whitehead in his official role as the dean of the School of Engineering. Memorials include Henry L. Straus, "Dr. John Boswell Whitehead," *Johns Hopkins Alumni Magazine*, June 1948, p. 105, and William Bennett Kouwenhoven, National Academy of Sciences, *Biographical Memoirs* 37 (1964): 343–61, which includes a bibliography of Whitehead's publications. An obituary is in the *New York Times*, 17 Nov. 1954.

JENNIFER ALLAIN RALLO

WHITEHILL, Robert (24 July 1735–5 Apr. 1813), farmer and member of the House of Representatives, was born in Lancaster County, Pennsylvania, the son of James Whitehill, a blacksmith and farmer, and Rachel Cresswell. His father had migrated from Ireland in 1723. Robert Whitehill acquired 440 acres and erected the first stone house in Lowther Manor, Cumberland County. In 1758 he married Eleanor Reed; they had five sons and four daughters.

Whitehill defended colonial liberties on the Lancaster County Committee of 1774–1775 and in the Provincial Conference on 18 June 1776. He helped write the revolutionary Pennsylvania constitution of 1776. Whitehill served in the assembly in 1776–1778 and 1783–1787, on the Council of Safety from October to December 1777, on the Supreme Executive Council from late 1779 to 1781, and in the Council of Censors in 1783–1784. He opposed Republican efforts to revise the constitution of 1776.

At the Pennsylvania ratification convention of 1787, Whitehill systematically opposed and voted against adoption of the U.S. Constitution. On 12 December 1787 he proposed fifteen amendments to the Constitution, eight of which were later incorporated in the U.S. Bill of Rights. For example, Whitehill proposed that "the rights of conscience shall be held inviolable" and that the U.S. government could not interfere in a state's "preservation of liberty in matters of religion." He wanted guarantees of trial by jury, enumeration of an accused person's rights, and protection against excessive bail or fines, cruel or unusual punishment, and unwarranted search or seizure. Whitehill wrote, "The people have a right to the freedom of speech, of writing, and of publishing their sentiments, therefore, the freedom of the press shall not be restrained by any law of the United States." His proposals calling for restrictions on congressional power to tax, creation of a constitutional council to advise and assist the president, and limitations on treaty making and judiciary power were not incorporated into the Bill of Rights. Whitehill argued for a Bill of Rights on the grounds that some rights were included in the Constitution. Did that mean rights not mentioned were unprotected? He insisted, "Loss of liberty is the necessary consequence of a loose or extravagant delegation of authority."

Whitehill signed "The Address and Reasons of Dissent of the Minority," which summarized Antifederalist arguments against the Constitution. He participated in a movement to call a second constitutional convention, engaged in a petition campaign to have the assembly abrogate Pennsylvania's ratification, and promoted the Harrisburg convention of September 1788 that proposed amendments to the Constitution and selected candidates for office in the new government.

Whitehill participated in the Pennsylvania constitutional convention of 1790 but refused to sign the new state constitution, saying it too drastically revised the 1776 constitution, was too undemocratic, and gave too much power to the governor and the courts. The Pennsylvania constitution of 1776 eliminated the office of governor, rendered the judiciary subservient to the legislature, and placed virtually all governmental power in the hands of a unicameral legislature elected on a basis close to manhood suffrage. The Supreme Executive Council performed executive functions, and a Council of Censors had authority to review all phases of the operation of state government. The 1790 constitution, while not significantly restricting the suffrage, instituted a governor with appointive, pardoning, and veto powers; a two-house legislature; and an independent judiciary.

Whitehill held several other state and national offices. He served in the Pennsylvania House of Representatives in 1797–1801, the state senate in 1801–1805, and the U.S. House of Representatives in 1805–1813. Known as a firm Jeffersonian, he opposed excessive judicial power. As Speaker of the state senate, he presided over the impeachment trials of three Pennsylvania Supreme Court judges in 1805. In Congress he worked to limit the tenure of federal judges to a term of years. He wanted justices removable by the president on the joint action of the Senate and House in impeachment trials when a simple majority vote convicted them of charges. Whitehill died at Lowther Manor.

• Whitehill papers are in the Cumberland County Historical Society, Carlisle, Pa. Whitehill materials are in Merrill Jensen, ed., *Ratification of the Constitution by the States: Pennsylvania* (1976). A biography is Robert G. Crist, *Robert Whitehill and the Struggle for Civil Rights* (1958). See also Crist, ed., *Pennsylvania and the Bill of Rights* (1990). An obituary is in *Poulson's American Daily Advertiser*, 14 Apr. 1813.

RODGER C. HENDERSON

WHITEHILL, Walter Muir, Jr. (28 Sept. 1905–5 Mar. 1978), librarian and historian, was born in Cambridge, Massachusetts, the son of Walter Muir Whitehill, an

Episcopal priest, and Florence Marion Williams. Following graduation from Harvard College in 1926, Whitehill remained as a tutor in Harvard's Department of Fine Arts for two academic years. Spending summers in Spain, he began research on Spanish Romanesque architecture, which he continued during 1928–1929. Returning to Harvard in 1929, he earned an A.M. in fine arts, and in 1930 he married Jane Revere Coolidge; they had two children.

In June 1930 Whitehill returned to Spain, where he worked principally at Santo Domingo de Silos in the province of Burgos on the reconstruction of an eleventh-century church and on the history of the monastic library. Between 1930 and 1936 he spent part of each year at the University of London, where he superintended Spanish studies at the Courtauld Institute of Art and earned a Ph.D. in 1934. His *Spanish Romanesque Architecture of the Eleventh Century*, appeared in 1941. The Spanish Civil War delayed publication of his *Liber Sancti Jacobi—Codex Calixtinus*, until 1944. While in England he became a fellow of the Royal Society of Antiquaries and a member of the Royal Archaeological and Royal Anthropological Institutes of Great Britain.

Whitehill returned to Massachusetts during the spring of 1936 and was appointed assistant director of the Peabody Museum of Salem that autumn. There he immersed himself in maritime history while he endeavored to modernize the diverse collections of the century-old museum. Continuing what was to become a torrent of publications throughout his life, Whitehill cofounded in 1941 the *American Neptune*, a quarterly journal of maritime history, which he edited for its first decade.

During World War II, Whitehill was granted a leave of absence from the Peabody Museum to accept a commission in the Naval Reserve. Rising to the rank of commander, Whitehill served in the Office of Naval Records and Library under Commodore Dudley W. Knox, and as an assistant to Fleet Admiral Ernest Joseph King's flag secretaries, he drafted King's second and third reports on the accomplishments of the navy to the Secretary of the Navy. Though separated from active duty in 1946, Whitehill cherished and maintained his connection with the navy, first collaborating with King on a biography, *Fleet Admiral King, A Naval Record* (1952), and serving from 1952 to 1978 as a member of the Secretary of the Navy's Advisory Committee on Naval History.

In 1946 Whitehill became librarian of the Boston Athenaeum. Described by Harvard professor Barrett Wendell as "a retreat for those who would enjoy the humanity of books," this private library was an ideal place for a man of Whitehill's talents. Named its director in 1947, he remained there for twenty-seven years. During Whitehill's tenure, the Athenaeum grew from a local proprietary library to an institution of national repute and usefulness. It was among the first libraries to establish a conservation department, taking a leadership role in that field.

Whitehill's extraordinary range of interests, prodigious energy, efficiency, and amiability drew him into a remarkable number of Boston's learned societies and museums, in which he tended to rise to positions of leadership. His many offices included president of the Old South Association (1949–1978), vice president of the North Andover Historical Society (1949–1970), chairman of the council of historians of the Institute of Early American History and Culture (1955–1959), and trustee of the Museum of Fine Arts (1953–1978), the Peabody Museum of Salem (1950–1978), the Society for the Preservation of New England Antiquities (1949–1956), and the Thomas Jefferson Memorial Foundation (1956–1978). As editor of the Colonial Society of Massachusetts (1946–1978) he published sixteen volumes on Massachusetts history, with nine more volumes in various stages of completion at his death. He also took considerable interest in historic preservation and served on the board of the National Trust for Historic Preservation. He knew how to bring a politician, a businessman, and a preservationist to a table, give them a good lunch, and produce a constructive solution to whatever problem they faced.

On 13 September 1958 a group of historians, curators, editors, printers, publishers, booksellers, librarians, professors, and others gathered at Minot, Massachusetts, to honor Whitehill in a spontaneous outpouring of admiration and affection that became known as "The Glades Congress." In spite of the accomplishments that had prompted this tribute, Whitehill had not yet reached the full height of his career.

For much of the 1950s Whitehill maintained his ties with Harvard as a member of the faculty of the Peabody Museum of Archaeology and Ethnology and as Allston Burr Senior Tutor at Lowell House. He wrote extensively on Boston history, including *Boston Public Library, A Centennial History* (1956), and *Boston, A Topographical History* (1959). His sphere of influence remained concentrated in the Northeast with some connections as far south as Virginia until 1959, when he took a year's leave from the Boston Athenaeum to make a study of privately supported historical societies for the Council on Library Resources. His *Independent Historical Societies* (1962), together with the friendships that he made along the way, established Whitehill as a national figure. His knowledge of historical organizations combined with his skill in evaluating an individual's talents and his genuine enthusiasm for like-minded people made him something of a one-man employment agency. Many librarians and curators found their first jobs through a Whitehill connection.

Among the most significant of Whitehill's more than 650 publications were *Boston in the Age of John Fitzgerald Kennedy* (1966), and *Museum of Fine Arts, Boston, A Centennial History* (1970). He produced a steady stream of reviews and articles on subjects that ranged from "Gregorian Capitals from Cluny" to "Tutor Flynt's Silver Chamber-pot" to "The Apotheosis of the Codfish" to "The Function of a School Library." He also excelled in the genre of the short biographical essay. Many of these appeared in the proceedings of the learned societies to which he belonged, and a group of them were brought together in *Analecta Biographica* (1969). He was appropriately chosen chairman of the American Council of Learned Societies Committee on the *Dictionary of American Biography* from 1970 to 1978, for publication of supplements three through five. He died in Boston.

Whitehill's life was one of remarkable accomplishment in what Lyman Butterfield, editor in chief of the *Adams Papers*, described as "the advancement of the means, the amenities and the ends of humane learning." A tribute that pleased Whitehill as much as any is a bronze plaque set in Dock Square near Faneuil Hall that bears his likeness and the inscription, "He put pen to paper and preserved a city."

• Whitehill's papers are in the Massachusetts Historical Society, Boston. Biographical information may be found in the periodic reports of the Harvard Class of 1926. His bibliography was published in the *Bulletin of Bibliography* 30, no. 3 (1958), and reprinted with additions in "Walter Muir Whitehill," a retirement booklet published in 1974 by the Boston Athenaeum, where an addendum is on file. *Walter Muir Whitehill, A Record Compiled by His Friends* (1958), includes a chronology, a bibliography, a list of the organizations with which Whitehill was affiliated, and a poem by David McCord, "The Man with the Vellum Valise," which in twenty-five quatrains describes Whitehill and his manifold interests and activities. An obituary is in the *New York Times*, 6 Mar. 1978.

ELTON W. HALL

WHITELEY, L. A. (1823?–1869), newspaper writer and editor, was probably born somewhere in Kentucky. His first name may have been Lambert; his parents' names are unknown. Raised in Kentucky, Whiteley was an associate editor of the *Louisville Journal* and then owner of the *Baltimore Clipper* in the 1850s. After the Civil War began, James Gordon Bennett, owner of the *New York Herald*, invited Whiteley to run that paper's Washington bureau. Being in the North's center of power, and working for one of the nation's most influential dailies, Whiteley now had one of the most important jobs in journalism. He was a Democrat, and he shared many of the views of his boss, Bennett, who was staunchly antiabolitionist and sympathetic to proslavery arguments. Whiteley warned his boss that Abraham Lincoln's Emancipation Proclamation would bring down the government and that the aim of the abolitionists was "revolution, anarchy, and secession" (Whiteley to Bennett, 9 Sept. 1862).

Whiteley's relationship with the government he was covering reflected the era in which he lived. Journalists before and during the Civil War held various posts, often sinecures, in the government, and Whiteley had a $1,600-a-year clerkship in the Treasury Department. In a letter to Secretary of the Treasury Salmon Chase, Whiteley wrote, "I have never allowed it [newspaper work] to interfere with the performance of my official duty, but have devoted to it the rest of the 16 hours of each day not required in the auditors office." But the relationship was fraught with an inherent conflict of interest, as the rest of his letter shows: "It is not my intention that any of the correspondents under my charge shall make the correspondence a medium for the expression of sentiments obnoxious to the administration and I have always been anxious to . . . render my efforts useful to its members" (Chase Papers, 17 May 1862). In June 1863 Whiteley was ousted by Chase, who declared publicly that no newspaper reporter could hold a job in the Treasury Department.

As the *Herald*'s bureau chief and head Washington correspondent, Whiteley's main responsibility was getting war reports to the paper as quickly as possible. His challenge was to avoid War Department censorship and to "beat" the other dailies. As required by Secretary of War Edwin M. Stanton, War Department censors often made correspondents send their telegraph dispatches to Washington before sending them on to their papers. During the Peninsula campaign in 1862, for example, Whiteley complained to his editor, Frederic Hudson, that "not one word is allowed to go" (Starr, p. 116).

To circumvent Stanton's censors, Whiteley developed methods for getting news to the *Herald*. One was to transport letters by hand to New York, and the *Herald* staff had an army of reporters and messengers to achieve this aim. Although it was "beaten" by the *Tribune* and other newspapers during a number of battles, including Gettysburg and the Wilderness, the *Herald* frequently received the news first. Whiteley may have resorted to other means. In 1863 he told his editor that he would make every effort to get advance copies of official reports "even if it should be necessary to pay," suggesting that *Herald* staffers may very well have bribed officials (Whiteley to Hudson, 29 Nov. 1863). Indeed, Whiteley had a reputation for getting news that other reporters could not.

After the Civil War, Whiteley left the *Herald* to accept an editorship at the *National Intelligencer*, which once had been a Whig party organ but was now attempting to cover national politics in a nonpartisan way. The *Intelligencer*, after more than a half century of prominence, folded in June 1869. Within a month Whiteley, suffering from consumption, died in Washington, D.C.

Whiteley rose from relative obscurity as an antebellum newspaper editor to become a prominent journalist of the American Civil War. His importance as a war correspondent and bureau chief can be explained both by the eminence of the *Herald* and by his relationship with the national government. His attempts to gather news from a government of which he was a part, and his dubious methods of news gathering in the War Department, reflected both the changing role of the press and the straitened conditions of reporting amid Civil War censorship.

• What little information regarding Whiteley's life that has survived must be gleaned from his letters to and from the *Herald*'s Frederic Hudson and James Gordon Bennett and the secretary of the treasury, Salmon P. Chase (Library of

Congress). A few books discuss his wartime career, including J. Cutler Andrews, *The North Reports the Civil War* (1955); F. B. Marbut, *News from the Capital: The Story of Washington Reporting* (1971); Louis M. Starr, *Bohemian Brigade: Civil War Newsmen in Action* (1954); and Bernard Weisberger, *Reporters for the Union* (1977). For a brief discussion of the relationship between the War Department and the press during the Civil War, see David Mindich, *Edwin M. Stanton, the Inverted Pyramid, and Information Control* (1993). Two short obituaries in the *New York Times* and the *Washington* (D.C.) *Evening Star*, 21 July 1869, give brief sketches of Whiteley's life. Whiteley's name is spelled "Whitely" in many of the above sources, including the *New York Times* obituary.

DAVID T. Z. MINDICH

WHITEMAN, Paul (28 Mar. 1890–29 Dec. 1967), band conductor and showman, was born Paul Samuel Whiteman in Denver, Colorado, the son of Wilberforce James Whiteman, a public school music supervisor, and Elfrida M. Dallison, a vocalist. Whiteman was trained in music and the violin by his father and played first viola with the Denver Symphony Orchestra at the age of sixteen. He briefly attended the University of Denver and married Nellie Stack in 1908. The marriage was annulled in 1910, and Whiteman moved to San Francisco in 1912.

Over the ensuing years Whiteman alternated between orchestra performances, including a job with the San Francisco Symphony Orchestra, and playing the fiddle in saloons and restaurants. He heard jazz music for the first time in a bar on the Barbary Coast and was immensely influenced by it. He resigned from his Symphony Orchestra position in 1916 and made an unsuccessful attempt to make a living solely with jazz.

When the United States entered World War I, Whiteman enlisted in the U.S. Navy. He organized and lead a forty-piece marching band at the Mare Island (Calif.) Naval Training Station. After demobilization he organized a dance band that initially played at San Francisco's Fairmont Hotel and then at the Alexandria Hotel in Los Angeles, where he became a favorite of the movie community. He moved the band to the East Coast in 1920 for engagements at hotels in New Jersey and New York, as well as Broadway performances with George White's *Scandals* and the Ziegfeld *Follies*. Whiteman married showgirl Africa "Jimmy" Smith in 1921 but was divorced a few months later. His third marriage in 1922 was to dancer Mildred Vanderhoff (stage name "Vanda Hoff"). The couple had one child and were divorced in 1931.

Whiteman and his band began making recordings for the Victor Talking Machine Company in 1920 and produced several of the first million-seller hits, including "Whispering" and "Japanese Sandman" (1920). His 1926 recording of "Three O'Clock in the Morning" sold more than three million copies. Whiteman's recorded hits also included a number of classical works performed in dance tempo, including Rimski-Korsakov's "Song of India" and Massenet's "Meditations" from the opera *Thais*.

The Paul Whiteman orchestra toured England in 1923 and performed the first completely jazz symphonic concert at New York's Aeolian Hall on 12 February 1924. It featured George Gershwin on the piano for the debut of his "Rhapsody in Blue," which Whiteman had commissioned for the occasion.

It was around this time that Whiteman became known as "the King of Jazz," a nickname that he disclaimed. He did not present himself as a composer or performer of pure jazz; his forte was in the orchestration and performance of musical pieces that combined elements of jazz with traditional music of dance bands and symphony orchestras. In the words of music critic Deems Taylor, Whiteman took jazz "out of the kitchen and moved it upstairs into the parlor." He also employed notable jazz instrumentalists such as Bix Biederbecke, Jack Teagarden, and Bunny Berigan, as well as more traditional musicians like Jimmy and Tommy Dorsey and Benny Goodman. Rather than "King of Jazz," Whiteman preferred the nickname "Pops," given to him around 1929 by one of his singers, Mildred Bailey.

In 1926 Whiteman made another tour of England and coauthored, with Mary Margaret McBride, *Jazz*, a book that further popularized the music. By the mid-1920s he was one of the highest-paid musicians in the world. His 1925 income was $680,000. The onset of the Great Depression did not impede his growing income because he had made a successful transition into radio and motion pictures. He began live radio performances in 1928, and his first motion picture was titled *The King of Jazz* (1930). It also featured the movie debut of singer Bing Crosby, in a vocal trio called "The Rhythm Boys." Whiteman subsequently appeared in *Thanks a Million* (1935), *Atlantic City* (1944), *Rhapsody in Blue* (1945), and *The Fabulous Dorseys* (1947).

Whiteman also remarried in 1931. His fourth wife, movie actress Margaret Livingston, became his business manager. The couple adopted four children.

Whiteman's radio performance included shows on both the CBS and NBC networks. His live performances included a stint in Billy Rose's *Jumbo* (1936), and he increased his notoriety in 1935 by leading an orchestra performance in the Hippodrome Theater in New York City while astride a white horse. He would repeat this performance at musical fairs in the West, where it was very popular.

In 1940 Whiteman had a nervous breakdown, attributed to overwork. He dissolved his band and retired temporarily from the music world to his 400-acre farm in Stockton, New Jersey, where he raised cattle and show horses. He also wrote his second book, *How to Be a Bandleader* (1941).

A year later Whiteman returned to music. He began the radio program "The Philco Hall of Fame" in 1943 and became music director of NBC's "Blue Network," which later became ABC. Whiteman also pioneered in the broadcasting of recordings, rather than live performances, on radio shows, becoming the nation's first "disc jockey" in 1947. He also wrote *Records for the Millions: A Guide to Record Collecting* (1948).

After the introduction of television Whiteman made appearances on "The Dave Garroway Show" and other programs and hosted his own series, "Paul Whiteman's Goodyear Revue," on ABC. He was also a vice president of the ABC network from 1947 through 1955.

The advent of rock and roll in the 1950s made Whiteman's style of music appear dated and old-fashioned, and his popularity declined. He made several attempts to retire, punctuated by attempts at comebacks, including a 1960 performance conducting Gershwin music at the Lambertville (N.J.) Music Circus and a 1962 engagement in Las Vegas. He died at Doylestown, Pennsylvania, and was buried in Trenton, New Jersey.

• Whiteman's voluminous papers are in the Whiteman Collection, Stetson Hall, Williams College, Williamstown, Mass. The collection is described in I. Shainman, "The Whiteman Collection at Williams College," *Notes* (1956–1957). Compiled for the same collection is Carl Johnson, *Paul Whiteman: A Chronology, 1890–1967* (1977, rev. ed. 1979). A complete biography is Thomas A. De Long, *Pops: Paul Whiteman, King of Jazz* (1983), which is more revealing than Margaret Livington Whiteman, *Whiteman's Burden* (1933). See also Albert McCarthy, *Big Band Jazz* (1974); David Ewen, *All the Years of American Popular Music* (1977); George T. Simon, *The Big Bands* (1967); William H. Youngren, "Giving Whiteman His Due," *Atlantic*, July 1984, pp. 103–6; Brian Rust, "Paul Whiteman: A Discography I," *Recorded Sound* 27 (July 1967): 219–28; Rust, "Paul Whiteman: A Discography II," *Recorded Sound* 27 (Oct. 1967): 255–58; and Richard M. Sudhalter, *Bix: Man and Legend* (1974), for information on Whiteman. An obituary is in the *New York Times*, 30 Dec. 1967.

STEPHEN G. MARSHALL

WHITFIELD, James Monroe (10 Apr. 1822–23 Apr. 1871), African-American poet, abolitionist, and emigrationist, was born in Exeter, New Hampshire, the son of parents whose names are unknown. Little else is known of his family except that he had a sister, a wife, two sons, and a daughter.

A celebrated poet, Whitfield published two volumes of poetry, *Poems* in 1846 and *America, and Other Poems* in 1853, the latter launching his career as an abolitionist and emigrationist. Richard Barksdale and Keneth Kinnamon point out Lord Byron's influence on his poetry's "brooding melancholy and latent anger" but see his strong abolitionist protest as more important. His poem "America" voiced the paradox of America as he saw it: "a boasted land of liberty" and "a land of blood and crime." One of the most forceful writers and speakers for the abolitionist cause, Whitfield was seen by Frederick Douglass as unjustly "buried in the precincts of a barber's shop" by the "malignant arrangements of society," and Martin Delany appraised his potential to be the equal of John Greenleaf Whittier and Edgar Allan Poe (Miller, p. 138). Jane R. Sherman (p. 176) praises Whitfield as "outstanding [among nineteenth-century black poets] for his metrical smoothness and breadth of classical imagery" and his poetry as among the most robust and convincing of the time . . . describ[ing] the crippling of a creative soul by race prejudice."

Whitfield's life exemplifies the ambivalence of African Americans toward the emigration and abolitionist/civil rights movements of the nineteenth century as well as the frustrations of talented African Americans barred from the pursuits of higher education and creativity. On one hand he signed the 1853 Rochester Colored National Convention's "Address to the People of the United States" that called for whites to allow blacks full access to what Whitfield accepted as his "native land" in his poem "America" and that simultaneously accepted segregation. On the other hand, a few months later, he signed Delany's 1853 call for the National Emigration Convention and, in letters to the *Frederick Douglass Paper*, advocated emigration and the establishment of a black nation. As late as 1862 he, along with almost 240 blacks, petitioned Congress for funds to "promote the emigration of free colored resident natives of the United States to Africa or to the tropical regions of America" (Miller, p. 265).

Whitfield, along with James T. Holly and Martin Delany, became one of the most prominent supporters of nationalist emigration during the 1850s. Whitfield's letter to the *Frederick Douglass Paper* began the extended debate over the Rochester convention proposals and Delany's call for emigration. His exchanges with William J. Watkins, Douglass's associate editor, and subsequent letters from the public anticipated the death knell for a viable emigration movement. Whitfield argued the connection between blacks' acceptance of their separate position in U.S. society, from which they would advocate their right to full participation, and emigration, from which they could form a separate black nationality to both elevate the race and free the slaves. He saw his embracing of emigration as a logical extension of the Rochester convention and the National Council it had established, and he advocated the emigration of a few blacks to form a nationality where they "can help strike an effective blow against the common foe" (Sherman, p. 174) should efforts for equality in the United States fail. By raising the nationality issue, Whitfield and Delany drew negative responses from Canadian and U.S. blacks, who saw themselves as part of a nation already, and Douglass saw to it that his paper used its unprecedented influence to discredit the emigration movement. Nonetheless, Whitfield served as one of the five notable delegates to Delany's 1854 National Emigration Convention in Cleveland. That convention's constitution of the National Board of Commissioners was ridiculed by antiemigrationists (who were by far the majority) as an impracticable and foolish plan of political neophytes. The national black community met the plan with either indifference or ambivalence, except in Cincinnati, where leaders sought unsuccessfully to rally black support for emigration in opposition to white supporters of slavery and colonization. White colonizationists advocated removal of all blacks from the United States. Black emigrationists, on the other hand, advocated voluntary emigration and sought to maintain family and political ties with those remaining in the United States to advance the uplift of the race.

Although Whitfield and significant other nationalist-emigrationists did not attend the 1858 Chatham (Canada) convention, with its broadened platform and more inclusive title, the Association for the Promotion of the Interests of the Colored People of Canada and the United States, that followed the Cleveland convention, he remained active in the emigration movement until 1858. He signed a prospectus (published in the *Provincial Freeman*, 6 Dec. 1856) for a quarterly to publicize the nationalist-emigrationist cause, the *Afric-American Repository*. Whitfield edited the *Repository* for a year, publishing the first issue in July 1858.

Whitfield then moved to San Francisco and may have traveled to "tropical regions." Settling in California in 1862, he worked as a barber, briefly moving to Portland, Oregon, then to the towns of Placerville and Centerville in Idaho, before returning to establish a "hairdressing shop" in San Francisco. On New Year's Day on the fourth anniversary of the Emancipation Proclamation, Whitfield published *A Poem*, a history of the founding of America and of slavery and its effects. Whitfield dedicated this poem to Philip A. Bell, the editor of the *Elevator*, a San Francisco publication in which Whitfield published poems and letters from 1867 to 1870.

Whitfield, a Masonic grand master of California, died in San Francisco of heart disease. He ranks among the leading articulate and prescient nationalist-emigrationists who, sadly foreseeing the intractability of American racism, embraced America's highest ideals and argued vociferously against racism while simultaneously struggling to realize the dream of establishing a black nation to free the slave and uplift the race worldwide.

• According to Jane R. Sherman, "James Monroe Whitfield, Poet and Emigrationist: A Voice of Protest and Despair," *Journal of Negro History*, Apr. 1972, pp. 169–76, Whitfield's *America* may be found in the Buffalo and Erie County Historical Society, Howard University's Moorland and Spingarn Collection, and the New York Public Library's Schomburg Collection. The Bancroft Library, University of California, holds a copy of *A Poem* in Ezra Rothschild Johnson, *Emancipation Oration . . . and Poem. . . .* Floyd J. Miller, *The Search for a Black Nationality: Black Emigration and Colonization, 1787–1863* (1975), and Sherman provide citations for Whitfield's letters, calls, and minor poetic publications and place his poetic and political work in the context of the nineteenth-century nationalist-emigration movement. Vernon Loggins, *The Negro Author: His Development in America* (1931); Sterling Brown, *Negro Poetry and Drama* (1969); and Richard Barksdale and Keneth Kinnamon, *Black Writers of America: A Comprehensive Anthology* (1972), provide critical commentary. William H. Robinson, *Early Black American Poets* (1969), anthologizes selected works.

JOHNNELLA E. BUTLER

WHITFIELD, Robert Parr (27 May 1828–6 Apr. 1910), paleontologist, was born in New Hartford, New York, the son of English immigrants William Fenton Whitfield, a spindle-maker, and Margaret Parr. In 1835 the family moved back to England, where the boy learned reading, writing, and arithmetic in a Sunday school teaching facility and became an avid reader. In 1841 the family returned to the United States and finally settled in Whitestown (near Utica), New York. Whitfield had no further formal schooling and learned spindle-making from his father. He took a keen interest in natural history, collecting fossils from the local Paleozoic sedimentary formations and live mollusks from the streams.

Whitfield married Mary Henry in 1847; they had four children. At that same time he began working in Samuel Chubbuck's factory in Utica, which produced pumps, galvanic cells, generators, and similar equipment. There he learned drafting and detailed drawing, at which he became skilled, and he was named manager of the factory in 1849. In his free time, he prepared carefully drawn illustrations for his own natural history collection. He joined the Utica Society of Naturalists, which met weekly for lectures and exhibits of specimens.

Whitfield's drawing ability came to the attention of James Hall, state geologist of New York and director of the state museum. Whitfield began work for Hall in 1856 in Albany as an illustrator, first of crinoids from Iowa, where Hall was conducting a geological survey, and then of crinoids of New York, as Charles Abiathar White had just discovered many crinoid fossils in northern New York State. Whitfield collected for Hall in New York and in western states. In the New York museum he became acquainted with many of the leading scientists of that time and learned taxonomy.

The autocratic Hall published most studies by his group of assistants, collectors, and artists under his own name, so, while Whitfield was working for him, he was credited as the author of only a few papers co-authored with Hall, one of which was "Palaeontology," part two of volume four, *U.S. Geological Explorations of the Fortieth Parallel* (ed. Clarence King [1877]). Under Whitfield's name alone he described the fossils collected in 1875 in the Black Hills of Dakota Territory (the year after the discovery of gold there by prospectors accompanying Lieutenant Colonel George Armstrong Custer) in *Report on the Geology and Resources of the Black Hills of Dakota* (ed. Henry Newton and Walter B. Jenney [1880], pp. 325–468). He published "Descriptions of New Species of Eocene Fossils" (*American Journal of Conchology* 1 [1865]: 259–68) and his observations of the anatomy of the brachiopod *Atrypa* (*Twentieth Annual Report of New York State Museum* [1867], pp. 141–44). Primarily, he prepared thousands of drawings of invertebrate fossils—graptolites, crinoids, corals, brachiopods, trilobites, cephalopods, and others—for Hall's thirteen-volume *Palaeontology of New York* (1847–1894) and other publications by Hall for various state surveys. Whitfield's biographer John M. Clarke said that "many of these drawings were the most exact as well as the most highly finished illustrations of paleozoic fossils that had ever been published and were a noteworthy embellishment of the science."

In 1872 Whitfield began teaching geology at Rensselaer Polytechnic Institute in Troy, New York, where in 1876 he was named professor, a title "which he always thereafter rightfully cherished."

When the American Museum of Natural History was established in New York, its founder, Albert S. Bickmore, in 1877 purchased the invertebrate fossil collection of Hall, who had acquired 100,000 specimens by purchasing items himself beyond the means of the state funds that he oversaw. To tend the new collection, Bickmore employed Whitfield that same year as curator of geology and custodian of the collection of modern shells. Whitfield worked as curator, labeling and arranging specimens and continuing to draw illustrations of them, until his retirement in 1909. He also began describing specimens and from 1878 to 1908 published almost 100 papers, many of them in the *Bulletin of the American Museum of Natural History*, which he had helped to establish. These were primarily descriptions of fossil invertebrates in the museum's collections. Separately he published three volumes on fossil brachiopods, mollusks, and crustaceans of New Jersey as monographs of the U.S. Geological Survey (1885, 1892, 1894). Other papers by Whitfield were on collections of fossils from Ohio, Wisconsin, and the West Indies. Assisted by Edmund Otis Hovey of the geology staff of the museum, Whitfield published four especially useful papers under the title "Catalogue of the Types and Figured Specimens in the Paleontological Collection of the Geological Department, American Museum of Natural History" (*Bulletin of the American Museum of Natural History*, parts 1–4 [1898–1901]). A few of his papers were on vertebrate fossils, an early fossil scorpion, living mollusks, marine algae, birds, and the fruiting of the ginkgo tree.

At a time when scientific description of specimens was advancing at a rapid rate in the United States, Whitfield contributed significantly and accurately to the field of invertebrate paleontology, with outstanding illustrations. He was acknowledged as an expert in identifying fragmentary invertebrate fossils.

Whitfield sold his personal collection of fossil and recent specimens to the University of California, Berkeley, in 1886. He died in Troy, New York.

• Whitfield's archival records from 1896 to 1910 are at the American Museum of Natural History Archives; some correspondence between Whitfield and Hall is in the James Hall Papers in the Manuscripts and History Department of the New York State Library. Whitfield's publications on New Jersey invertebrate fossils were U.S. Geological Survey monographs, vol. 9 (1885), vol. 18 (1892), and vol. 24 (1894). Biographies of Whitfield are by "I. P. G." in *American Journal of Science* 19 (1910): 565–66; Edmund Otis Hovey in *American Museum Journal* 10, no. 5 (1910): 118–21; John M. Clarke in *Bulletin of Geological Society of America* 22 (1911): 22–32, with bibliography; and L. P. Gratacap in *Annals of New York Academy of Sciences*, vol. 20, no. 9, part 3 (1911), pp. 385–98.

ELIZABETH NOBLE SHOR

WHITING, George Elbridge (14 Sept. 1840–14 Oct. 1923), organist, teacher, and composer, was born in Holliston, Massachusetts, the son of Nathan P. Whiting and Olive Chase. He came from a musical household and received his first music lessons from his older brother Amos at the age of five. When only thirteen he played the organ in a concert in Worcester, and in 1858, while still in his teens, he succeeded Dudley Buck as organist of the North Congregational Church in Hartford, Connecticut. By this time he was studying with the distinguished recitalist George Washbourne Morgan of New York. In 1862 he moved to Boston, becoming organist first at Dr. Kirk's Church, and then at Tremont Temple. In 1863 he traveled to Liverpool to study with the leading English organ virtuoso, William Thomas Best, organist of St. George's Hall; upon his return to the United States he accepted the organist's position at St. Joseph's Church in Albany, New York. This was a large and prestigious church, and its choir boasted at least one opera diva, Madame Albani.

In 1866 Whiting returned to Boston, where he became organist of King's Chapel and, for one year, organist of Boston Music Hall, where he played the large new Walcker organ installed in 1863. He married Helen Aldrich in 1867; they had one daughter before Aldrich died in 1912. In 1874 Whiting went abroad again, this time to Berlin, where he briefly studied harmony and orchestration with Karl August Haupt and Robert Radecke. Returning in the fall of that year, he joined the faculty of New England Conservatory as professor of organ, but in 1879 Theodore Thomas persuaded him to accept a similar position at Cincinnati Conservatory. While in Cincinnati he gave many recitals on the large new organ in the Concert Hall there and performed at the May Festivals. He returned to New England Conservatory in 1882 and in the same year was hired as organist and choirmaster at Immaculate Conception Church, which had a large professional choir and a recital-quality Hook organ. He remained there until 1910, when the Papal *motu proprio* reforming Catholic church music put an effective end to the ostentatious "concert masses" upon which Whiting and his singers had built their reputation. In his autobiography, *Sharps and Flats in Five Decades* (1947), Father William J. Finn, founder of the Paulist Choristers, comments on Whiting's "unorthodox" harmonizations of Gregorian chant and describes his youthful delight at hearing a performance of Whiting's own *Echo Mass*, in which sections were assigned to a semichorus singing behind a screen.

Whiting continued in an active recital career, being much in demand for organ dedications, and in 1893 he gave three recitals at the Chicago World's Fair, along with such notables as Clarence Eddy and Alexandre Guilmant. In 1896 he was among the group of organists who founded the American Guild of Organists. He also distinguished himself as a teacher, counting among his pupils Henry M. Dunham, who would ultimately succeed him as organ professor at the conservatory; Charles H. Morse, later to become director of the musical department at Wellesley College and Dartmouth College; and the composer George Whitefield Chadwick.

Whiting had no small reputation as a composer himself, and Henry C. Lahee, writing in 1902, stated that "the reputation of Mr. Whiting as a composer is equal to that which he has earned as organist and teacher" (p. 273). He composed for a great variety of media, although his choral and organ compositions lead the list numerically. He wrote a *Mass in C Minor* for four soloists, chorus, orchestra and organ, which was performed at the opening of the new Holy Cross Cathedral in Boston in 1874, as well as several large-scale secular cantatas for similar resources, among them *The Golden Legend* and *The Tale of the Viking*. Other compositions include *Our Country* (a "choral march" written for the inauguration of President William Howard Taft in 1909), more than fifty songs, part songs, several orchestral works, three masses, a suite for cello and piano, a piano concerto, a number of recital and church pieces for organ, two organ instruction books, and anthems and services for church use, as well as organ accompaniments for several large choral works such as Rossini's *Stabat Mater*. Only Whiting's organ works seem to have stood the test of time; his shorter church pieces are still useful, and some of his well-crafted larger works have found their way into contemporary recitals and recordings.

Whiting died in Cambridge, Massachusetts.

• Several of Whiting's compositions in manuscript are found at the Boston Public Library. References to Whiting appear in a number of histories written early in the twentieth century, such as Louis C. Elson's *The History of American Music* (1904). His career is summarized in some detail in Henry C. Lahee, *The Organ and Its Masters* (1902), and a list of his earlier compositions appears in F. O. Jones, *A Handbook of American Music and Musicians* (1886). A series of articles by Whiting titled "Reminiscences of Organ and Church Music in This Country," appeared in *The Organ* 1, nos. 4–8 (1892); this Boston periodical has been reprinted by the Organ Historical Society (1994). An obituary is in *The Diapason* 14, no. 12 (Nov. 1923): 2.

BARBARA OWEN

WHITING, Lilian (3 Oct. 1847–30 Apr. 1942), journalist, essayist, and poet, was born Emily Lilian Whiting in Olcott, New York, the daughter of Lorenzo Dow Whiting, an educator and politician, and Lucretia Calista Clement, an educator. Her childhood was spent on a farm near Tiskilwa, Illinois. Both her parents were school principals in the area. Later, her father edited a local paper and served as representative and senator in the Illinois State legislature. Whiting was educated by her parents and tutors. "I do not remember learning to read," Whiting said, "I was simply steeped, always and naturally as the sunshine, in the literary atmosphere of our quiet country home. The poets were my playmates, so to speak, my companions, my perpetual delight" (Rittenhouse, p. 4). The chief furnishings of her home, she said, were books and periodicals. She called herself a "dreamy and rudimentary girl who perceived the world as reflected through the pages of books rather than from outer realities themselves, and who was prone to regard the land of dreams as the only one worth living in" (*The Golden Road*, p. 20). She read and reread the English classics, copying down passages that caught her attention, a passion that led later to her studies of the Brownings: *A Study of Elizabeth Barrett Browning* (1899) and *The Brownings, Their Life and Art* (1917).

In 1876 Whiting went to St. Louis, Missouri, where she began her journalistic career. She called this time the beginning of her "conscious life." It was in St. Louis that Whiting met and was influenced by a group of people, "idealists" she said, who had formed a philosophical club. She attended the lectures of Susan Blow, a member of the club active in the movement for progressive education of children. She listened to Dr. William Torrey Harris, founder of the club, and read his *Journal of Speculative Philosophy*. She heard, among others, Ralph Waldo Emerson and Bronson Alcott. Becoming deeply interested in philosophy, religion, and mysticism, she read Kant and Hegel and explored Transcendentalism. When two papers she had written on Margaret Fuller were published by the *Cincinnati Commercial*, Whiting traveled to Cincinnati, Ohio, and obtained a position on the staff of the newspaper. After a year there, she moved to Boston, Massachusetts, to become the art writer and, later, the literary editor for the *Boston Traveler*. In 1890 she became editor in chief for the *Boston Budget*, where she wrote editorials, literary reviews, and her "Beau Monde" column. Her optimistic view of the world was first expressed in this column and was continued in a three-volume series of essays *The World Beautiful* (1894–1896).

Whiting dedicated *From Dreamland Sent* (1895), a volume of poems, to Kate Field. The collection brought Whiting praise from Louise Chandler Moulton. Both women were important in her life. In her early days with the *Traveler*, Whiting had been assigned to interview Kate Field, an author, lecturer, and actor; the two became close friends. When Field died suddenly, Whiting wrote of her own mystical experience concerning her friend's death in *After Her Death: The Story of a Summer* (1897). Later she wrote *Kate Field—A Record* (1899). In 1909 she wrote another biography, *Louise Chandler Moulton, Poet and Friend*.

Beginning in 1896 Whiting traveled regularly to Europe for many years. Based on these trips, she wrote *The Florence of Landor* (1905), *Italy the Magic Land* (1907), *Paris the Beautiful* (1908), and *The Lure of London* (1914). Concerning North America she wrote *The Land of Enchantment: From Pike's Peak to the Pacific* (1906) and *Canada the Spellbinder* (1917). For many years Whiting wrote columns for newspapers extolling the wonders of Boston: "Crumbs of Boston Culture" for the *New York Graphic* and a series about Boston for the *Chicago Inter-Ocean*/*New Orleans Times Democrat*. These writings became the basis for *Boston Days, the City of Beautiful Ideals* (1902).

Though her books were criticized by reviewers as being rambling and unorganized, as Whiting herself admitted, they contain much interesting information about the multitude of people she knew and the places she visited. As her titles suggest, she found and shared the beautiful in everyone, in everything, in every place.

Whiting's interest in things seen and unseen led her to explore many different philosophies and religions, including Bahai, New Thought, and Theosophy. In the introduction to Victor Charbonnel's *Victory of the Will* (1899), Whiting wrote: "The discovery of the law of telepathy has contributed signally to the understanding of the conditions of spiritual life, and the consequent advancement of intelligent comprehension. . . . If thought has such marvelous power as this, shall it not flash from mind to mind across that gulf we call death?"

Several of Whiting's books reflected these interests, such as *The Spiritual Significance; or, Death as an Event in Life* (1900), *From Dream to Vision of Life* (1906), *Life Transfigured* (1910), and two pamphlets about Katherine Tingley, Theosophist. She was also a contributor to the *National Spiritualist* (Chicago) in her later years. Whiting, who never married, died in Boston.

• Correspondence from Whiting is in the Frank Addison Manny papers at the Bentley Historical Library, University of Michigan, Ann Arbor; the Cairns Collection of American Literature by Women Authors at the University of Wisconsin, Madison; and the Roberts Brothers Correspondence at Ohio State University, Columbus. Letters written to her are at the Boston Public Library. Whiting's *The Golden Road* (1918) includes information about her life from the time she was in St. Louis until 1918. Jessie Rittenhouse, *Lilian Whiting, Journalist, Essayist, Critic and Poet: A Sketch* (1900), contains appended comments on her works by various authors. See also B. O. Flower, *Progressive Men, Women, and Movements of the Past Twenty-five Years* (1914), pp. 179–80. Obituaries are in the *Boston Globe*, the *Boston Herald*, and the *New York Times*, all 1 May 1942.

BLANCHE COX CLEGG

WHITING, Sarah Frances (23 Aug. 1847–12 Sept. 1927), physicist and astronomer, was born in Wyoming, New York, the daughter of Joel Whiting, a teacher and principal, and Elizabeth Lee Comstock. A precocious child, Whiting was tutored by her father and started studying Greek at age eight and Latin at age ten. She often assisted even as a young child in preparing scientific experiments for her father's classes in physics. Whiting graduated in 1865 from Ingham University (named Ingham Collegiate Institute from 1841 to 1857) at LeRoy, New York. As one of about a dozen pre–Civil War colleges in the United States to grant degrees to women, Ingham University was chartered by the New York legislature in 1857 to grant degrees to women enrolled in a four-year course of study. After graduating at the age of eighteen, Whiting began her career in education by teaching classics and math there and later at the Brooklyn Heights Seminary for girls for about ten years.

While living in New York City, Whiting took advantage of many opportunities to visit exhibitions, check laboratories for new equipment in physics, and attend lectures by prominent scientists, such as British physicist John Tyndall. With this new information, Whiting infused her classes with enthusiasm for scientific discoveries and ingeniously devised demonstrations for her students by rigging equipment and improvising with materials she had at hand.

In 1876 Whiting was appointed professor of physics by Henry F. Durant, the founder of Wellesley College, the new college for women in Wellesley, Massachusetts, which had an all-woman faculty. In order to gain knowledge of how to use the laboratory method in teaching physics, she was allowed as a guest at the physics classes of Edward C. Pickering at the Massachusetts Institute of Technology for two years. At this time women were not allowed as regular students at MIT, but a few women like Whiting and Ellen Swallow (Richards) were granted this special allowance. Then in 1878 Whiting opened her own undergraduate teaching lab of physics, only the second such laboratory in the United States and the first for women. She had to convert the organ loft and garret on the fifth floor of College Hall for this new laboratory, which was equipped with some apparatus she herself designed and had local artisans make. Ordering equipment was a challenge since most scientific apparatus was manufactured in Europe by companies that did not send out catalogs. To find out what instruments to order, Whiting decided she needed to see firsthand the equipment in other college science laboratories. For this purpose, she traveled throughout New England, although she said that she "found it nerve-racking to be in places where women were really not expected to be, and to do things which women had not done before" (*Popular Astronomy*, p. 540). She was able to order the most up-to-date scientific equipment for the new women's college and told of her "keen delight in beginning with nothing and ordering and unpacking every book and piece of apparatus. Mr. Durant was with me when the first arrival, a spectroscope from Europe, was unpacked, and we were like children opening a Christmas Box" (Hackett, p. 44). She and Henry Durant helped found the Microscopical Society, which flourished until 1891.

Until she acquired an assistant in 1885, Whiting handled all the purchasing, conducting of experiments and demonstrations, and teaching and administration of the physics department—a formidable undertaking, as all juniors at Wellesley College from 1878 until 1893 were required to take physics. In 1880 she introduced the first course in astronomy at Wellesley, at first called "applied physics." For twenty years she taught astronomy without an observatory and with only a celestial globe and a four-inch portable Browning telescope. The generous monetary donation of her friend Mrs. John Whitin, a Wellesley trustee, made possible Whiting's dream of an observatory. The Whitin Observatory, built of white marble as a symbol reflecting the surnames of the women devoted to the project, was completed in 1900 through plans drawn up by Whiting, who then had to equip the new observatory. She purchased a twelve-inch Clark equatorial telescope as well as a six-inch Clark telescope, mounted equatorially, a Browning spectroscope, a Rowland concave grating spectroscope, a Howard sidereal clock, and complete apparatus necessary for her advanced students in physics and astronomy.

Whiting was unfazed by skeptics who did not believe laboratories and science were women's work. Sir William Crookes once asked Whiting, who had visited his laboratory in England, "If all the ladies should know so much about spectroscopes, who would attend to the buttons and breakfasts?" Whiting herself had no problem with juggling an active scientific career with a rich social life. She and Elizabeth P. Whiting, an unmarried sister, lived in dormitories on the Wellesley campus and were known for their gracious hospitality. They were the hostesses at College Hall and then were heads of Fiske Cottage. In 1906 they moved to the Observatory House, built adjacent to the Whitin Observatory, where they continued to hold receptions. Whiting inaugurated an annual party for Wellesley "granddaughters," the daughters of alumnae. In 1907 she presented forty-six daughters of graduates from the years 1875 through 1887.

Whiting spent her sabbaticals abroad in order to bring back knowledge of the most up-to-date advances in physics. In 1888–1889 she visited laboratories throughout Germany and England and was received by prominent scientists such as Lord Kelvin (William Thomson), Lord Rayleigh (John William Strutt), and William Ramsay. In 1889 she studied at the University of Berlin and returned to Germany in 1913 to attend the meeting of the International Solar Union in Bonn. In 1895, when American newspapers reported the discovery of X rays, Whiting immediately set up an old Crookes tube and took some of the first photographs in the United States of bones underneath flesh and of coins in a purse. In 1896–1897, the first year study was open to women at the University of Edinburgh in Scotland, Whiting worked there with leading physicist Peter Guthrie Tait. In 1905 she received an honorary doctor of science degree from Tufts University, in part to make up for the degree she was not granted earlier.

In 1912 Whiting retired from the physics department to devote herself solely to astronomy until her retirement in 1916 as director of the Whitin Observatory, a position she had held for twelve years. Her publications were mostly concerned with teaching rather than original research, and she included a series of valuable exercises honed from her many years of teaching and practical experience in her *Daytime and Evening Exercises in Astronomy* (1912). Whiting was a member of the American Astronomical and Physical Societies and, as a devout Congregationalist, strongly supported the Wellesley College Christian Association. She followed her students' lives with great interest and trained many young women for important careers. One famous student, Annie J. Cannon, who became an astronomer at Harvard College Observatory, said that Whiting was "always dignified, calm and well-poised," had a genius for friendship, and led a "singularly happy life." Whiting, who never married, spent her last years in the company of her sister Elizabeth and her dear friend and fellow professor emeritus, Louise Manning Hodgkins, in Wilbraham, Massachusetts, where she died. Whiting's lifelong commitment to teaching women physics and astronomy, her enthusiasm for the experimental method, and her establishment of the first physics laboratory for women in the United States helped generations of women practice and understand science. Through these accomplishments, Whiting stands as one of the pioneers of science education for women.

• Whiting's papers are in the archives at Wellesley College. Two books on Wellesley that have interesting anecdotes or details about Whiting's life are Alice Payne Hackett, *Wellesley: Part of the American Story* (1949), and Florence Converse, *Wellesley College: A Chronicle of the Years 1875–1938* (1939). Obituaries are in *Popular Astronomy* 35, no. 10 (Dec. 1927): 540, and *Science* (4 Nov. 1927).

JOANNE A. CHARBONNEAU

WHITLEY, Keith (1 July 1954–9 May 1989), country music singer, songwriter, and guitarist, was born Jackie Keith Whitley in Sandy Hook, Kentucky, the son of Elmer Jackson Whitley, an electrical contractor and oil well maintenance worker, and Faye Ferguson. Whitley, who was in the vanguard of the 1980s country music boom, was inspired to play music by his mother, who played guitar, banjo, and organ as a hobby, and his older brother Dwight, who played guitar and banjo semiprofessionally in local country music bands. Keith began singing at local shows by age four, learned to play guitar at age six, and first appeared on a radio show at age eight. He and Dwight later performed on regional live shows, radio, and television, first as the Whitley Brothers and later as members of the Lonesome Mountain Boys.

Whitley was heavily influenced by Lefty Frizzell, a popular country-and-western singer of the 1950s and 1960s with whom he was later compared, and the Stanley Brothers, major figures in the mountain folk music–influenced bluegrass genre. In 1969 Whitley met Ricky Skaggs, a fellow Kentuckian who also later became a country music star. They shared a love for the Stanleys and began performing together.

Whitley's and Skaggs's professional careers were launched in 1970 when Ralph Stanley was delayed in getting to a show in Kentucky and arrived to find the youngsters filling in for him. Stanley recognized their talents, and they soon joined his Clinch Mountain Boys band, at first during summer vacations from high school and later full time. (Whitley dropped out of high school after completing his junior year in order to concentrate on his professional career. He later completed his high school education by correspondence course.) The tightly blended trio of Whitley (melody lead), Skaggs (tenor harmony), and Stanley (high baritone harmony) rivaled the original Stanley Brothers band at its peak and created a sensation on the bluegrass festival circuit. Whitley and Skaggs recorded several albums as members of the Clinch Mountain Boys plus their own *Second Generation Bluegrass* (1972).

The young men left Stanley in 1972. For most of the next decade Whitley performed with pop music–influenced bluegrass bands: the Country Store (also known as the New Tradition) from 1973 to 1974, and J. D. Crowe & the New South from 1977 to 1982. With the latter, he toured the United States and Japan. However, in 1974 he returned to the Clinch Mountain Boys at Ralph Stanley's request (after the murder of lead singer Roy Lee Centers), staying into 1977.

In January 1983 Whitley moved to Nashville, Tennessee, the center of the country music industry. In 1984 he was hired as a songwriter by Tree Publishing Company (now Sony Tree) and signed an RCA recording contract; his first single, "Turn Me to Love" (featuring a harmony by rising female star Reba McEntire), was released that September. But his initial Nashville years were difficult ones. None of his first three singles was particularly successful, and in 1985 he was divorced from Kathi Littleton, whom he had married in 1979.

In 1985 Whitley recorded "Miami, My Amy," his breakthrough single, and the successful album *From L.A. to Miami*. In 1986 he began working with Garth Fundis, a record producer who gave him latitude to develop his own sound. That same year, Whitley married country music singer Lorrie Morgan; he adopted her daughter Morgan, and in 1987 their son Jesse Keith Whitley was born. In 1988 the title track from Whitley's album *Don't Close Your Eyes* became a major hit as did another selection, "When You Say Nothing at All."

Whitley acknowledged that he had long engaged in binge drinking in private, behavior that was exacerbated by feelings that he was unworthy of his success. Although he abstained from public drinking and tried to keep his problem under control, he died at his suburban Nashville home of an accidental alcohol overdose.

Whitley's popularity continued after his death. His recording of "I'm No Stranger to the Rain" was named 1989 single of the year by the Country Music Association (CMA). In 1990 "'Til a Tear Becomes a Rose" (a duet created by Lorrie Morgan overdubbing a harmony onto an existing recording by her husband) was named vocal event of the year by the CMA. Other posthumously issued Whitley performances were well received, including the singles "Brotherly Love" (a duet with Earl Thomas Conley) and "Somebody's Doing Me Right" and the album *Kentucky Bluebird* (all released in 1991).

Rooted in both the "classic country music" of the 1950s and 1960s and the bluegrass genre, Whitley contributed strongly to the neotraditionalism of the "new Nashville sound" of the 1980s and 1990s. Possessed of a high-quality voice, his impassioned yet understated deliveries evoked deep emotional responses in listeners. Whitley has been cited as an influence by Garth Brooks, Alan Jackson, Tracy Lawrence, Tim McGraw, and other successful country music singers who have followed him.

• Information has been drawn from Tad Richards and Melvin B. Shestack, *The New Country Music Encyclopedia* (1993); the biographical booklet included in the press kit for the RCA recording *Keith Whitley: A Tribute Album* (1994); Bob Artis, *Bluegrass* (1975); Neil V. Rosenberg, *Bluegrass: A History* (1985); and telephone interviews conducted by the author with Whitley's manager Jack McFadden, brother Dwight Whitley (who verified Keith's year of birth, which is frequently listed incorrectly as 1955), and mentor Ralph Stanley (1995). An obituary is in *Bluegrass Unlimited*, June 1989.

RICHARD D. SMITH

WHITLOCK, Brand (4 Mar. 1869–24 May 1934), novelist, reform mayor, and diplomat, was born Joseph Brand Whitlock in Urbana, Ohio, the son of Elias D. Whitlock, a Methodist clergyman, and Mallie Lavinia Brand. Known by his middle name from childhood, Whitlock grew up in a number of western Ohio communities where his father held pastorates. He graduated from high school in Toledo and accepted a job in 1887 as a reporter for the *Toledo Blade*. In 1891 Whitlock moved to Chicago, where he became a reporter for the *Chicago Herald*. The next year he married Susan Brainerd, who died only four months later.

While working for the *Herald*, Whitlock became an ardent supporter of John Peter Altgeld, the Democratic gubernatorial candidate who won a reputation as a radical because of his support for labor and his sympathy for persecuted anarchists. When Altgeld became governor in 1893, he rewarded Whitlock by securing him a clerkship in the office of the Illinois secretary of state. Whitlock's duties were light, and in his spare time he studied law with former governor John M. Palmer. Espousing the literary realism of novelist William Dean Howells, he also began writing short stories. In 1895 Whitlock married his first wife's younger sister, Ella Brainerd; they had one still-born child and another child who died shortly after birth.

In 1897 the Republicans regained power in Illinois, leaving Whitlock unemployed. He returned to Ohio, where he began the practice of law in Toledo. Moreover, he continued to write and in 1902 published his first novel, *The Thirteenth District*. It is the story of a young lawyer who is willing to sacrifice honor and decency for the sake of a seat in the U.S. House of Representatives. Howells lauded the novel as a "great, honest, powerful, story . . . the best political story I know." Whitlock's rendition of the congressional district convention remains one of the most vivid fictional accounts of the American political process.

Meanwhile, Whitlock was also becoming involved in Toledo politics as an ally of that city's great reform mayor, Samuel M. Jones. Sharing Jones's sympathy for the poor and his opposition to monopolistic public utilities, Whitlock assumed leadership of reform forces after the mayor's death in 1904. Elected mayor the next year, Whitlock served eight years as Toledo's chief executive, earning a national reputation as a municipal reformer equal to that of Jones.

As mayor, Whitlock's goal was the creation of a "free city." By this he meant a city free of interference by the rural-dominated state legislature and free of control by party machines or money-hungry public utility monopolies. But Whitlock's free city would also liberate its citizens from the stultifying restraints of modern industrial life and nurture individual creativity. At a conference of the National Municipal League, the Toledo mayor explained: "We want cities that will be filled with free civic spirit, expressing itself in artistic forms." Whitlock believed that "the great purpose of democracy" was "to let every man realize his own personality."

Though Toledo never became a city of liberated creative spirits, Whitlock was instrumental in securing a home-rule amendment to Ohio's constitution, thereby limiting state legislative interference in municipal matters. Moreover, after years of struggle he secured lower streetcar fares in the city. The local clergy, however, vigorously attacked Whitlock's lenient policy toward saloons and houses of prostitution. A bitter foe of narrow-minded, puritanical morality, Whitlock would not suppress working-class pleasures for the sake of sanctimonious clerics and their self-righteous allies.

While mayor, Whitlock also completed one of his most significant novels, *The Turn of the Balance*. Published in 1907, this work is a grim indictment of social inequality and the injustice of the American legal system. Its most memorable character, Archie Koerner, is a product of poverty who turns to crime and ends life in the electric chair. Of all his novels, *Turn* aroused the strongest public response, garnering accolades from foes of the existing criminal justice system and attacks from supporters of the status quo.

Despite his renown as a municipal reformer, Whitlock conceived of himself primarily as a literary figure, and after eight years as mayor he sought more time to write. By 1913 Democrat Woodrow Wilson was president, and Whitlock's friends lobbied to secure the novelist a well-paid diplomatic post with few duties. In response to these petitions, Wilson appointed Whitlock as minister to Belgium. Whitlock arrived in Europe in early 1914, but that same year his hopes for a leisurely life of writing were shattered when the German army marched into Belgium at the onset of World War I. Belgium and Whitlock became the focus of world attention. Remaining in Brussels after the Belgian government had fled, Whitlock kept the Belgians from starving by coordinating food relief efforts. Moreover, as the leading neutral diplomat in the occupied country, he sought to defend the rights of Belgian civilians and to curb the most oppressive policies of the German occupation authorities. Still devoted to the notion of the free city and the liberation of the individual personality, Whitlock now found himself in a captive nation, coping with a repressive army of occupation.

Shortly before U.S. entry into the war in April 1917, Whitlock left Belgium for France, where he wrote *Belgium: A Personal Narrative* (1919). According to historian Allan Nevins, this work was "a tremendously eloquent indictment of military tyranny; a scathing study of autocracy" (Nevins, p. lxiii). Acclaimed as one of the finest works on World War I, *Belgium* was both a critical and financial success.

After Allied victory in November 1918, Whitlock returned to Brussels, where he was greeted as a hero and heaped with honors. When the Republicans reentered the White House in 1921, Whitlock was forced to resign as envoy to Belgium. A bitter critic of the repressive policy of Prohibition, Whitlock was disillusioned with the United States and felt that Europe offered a more congenial environment for literary figures. Consequently, he chose to remain in Europe and for the rest of his life divided his time between Belgium and the French Riviera.

In 1923 his most distinguished novel, *J. Hardin and Son*, was published. It is the story of the puritanical J. Hardin and his son Paul who spends his life trapped in the grim, narrow Ohio town of Macochee. In the novel the suffocating spirit of Macochee stifles Paul Hardin's creative personality as effectively as the Germans had suppressed the freedom of the Belgians. To Whitlock's dismay, the book did not become a bestseller or capture the American imagination as did Sinclair Lewis's contemporary indictments of midwestern life.

A series of lesser novels followed, and in 1929 Whitlock published his much-admired biography of the marquis de Lafayette, *Lafayette*. It was his last notable work, however, for during the early 1930s Whitlock's health declined. He died in Cannes, France.

A municipal reformer, diplomat, and novelist, Whitlock achieved distinction in a number of fields. Throughout his adult life, he remained dedicated to the ideal of freedom for the individual and liberation of the creative personality. Small-town Ohio, industrial Toledo, and occupied Belgium were the cages that Whitlock experienced, and he sought the key to unlock each. He may never have found that key, but his idealism was an inspiration to his contemporaries, earning him an international reputation as a devotee of liberty and a defender of humanity.

• Whitlock's papers are in the Library of Congress. His most important letters were published in *The Letters and Journal of Brand Whitlock*, ed. Allan Nevins (1936). Whitlock's autobiography, *Forty Years of It* (1914), covers the first half of his life and emphasizes the figures who inspired him. Jack Tager, *The Intellectual as Urban Reformer: Brand Whitlock and the Progressive Movement* (1968), focuses on Whitlock's reform career, and David D. Anderson, *Brand Whitlock* (1968), concentrates on his literary achievements. Another biography is Robert M. Crunden, *A Hero in Spite of Himself: Brand Whitlock in Art, Politics, and War* (1969). A series of nine articles on Whitlock's life by Samuel M. Jones III are in *Northwest Ohio Quarterly* 31–33 (1958–1961). An obituary is in the *New York Times*, 25 May 1934.

JON C. TEAFORD

WHITMAN, Alden (27 Oct. 1913–4 Sept. 1990), journalist, was born in New Albany, Nova Scotia, Canada, the son of Frank S. Whitman, a teacher and farmer, and Mabel Bloxsom, a teacher who had been born in Connecticut. He moved to the United States with his parents in 1915 and was naturalized four years later. Whitman grew up in Fairfield County, Connecticut; after attending local schools he enrolled at Harvard, graduating in 1934.

Immediately beginning his career as a journalist, Whitman worked successively for the *Bridgeport Post-Telegram*, the *Bridgeport Herald*, and the *Buffalo Evening News*. In 1943 he joined the staff of the *New York Herald Tribune* as a copyeditor, remaining with that paper for eight years. During that time he wrote his first book, *Early American Labor Parties* (1944).

In 1951 Whitman became a metropolitan desk editor of the *New York Times*. He then settled into an unexceptional daily routine, editing stories about city events. Whitman's life was abruptly altered in 1956, however, when he was called before the Senate Internal Security Subcommittee and questioned about his activities as a former member of the Communist Party. Whitman acknowledged being a member of the party from 1935 to 1948, but when he refused to identify other party members he was cited for contempt. He was then convicted in a federal court of contempt of Congress in two separate trials. After he appealed and obtained a new trial, the case was dismissed at the request of the Justice Department in 1957.

Whitman continued his work at the metropolitan desk until 1964, when, at the suggestion of the metropolitan editor, A. M. Rosenthal, he was named the newspaper's chief obituary writer. For the next twelve years, until his retirement in 1976, Whitman wrote hundreds of advance obituaries of prominent people, traveling the world to interview them and achieving the recognition that had eluded him for much of his career.

Although newspapers and broadcasting networks had long kept obituaries of public figures on file in the event that they died close to a production deadline, these were usually cut-and-dried lists of dates and achievements, based on readily available sources. Whitman's innovation was the pre-death interview, during which he collected comments and observations from the subjects themselves on aspects of their lives and careers. Based on both printed sources and these interviews, he then created graceful essays that interwove the facts of his subjects' lives with quotations offering revealing glimpses of their characters. Whitman wrote with seeming objectivity, neither fawning nor vindictive, but readers attuned to subtlety readily discerned his attitude toward a subject.

Whitman's artful essays on politicians, entertainers, artists, musicians, and writers turned the obituary page of the *Times* into one of its most popular features. Among his diverse subjects were Joseph P. Kennedy, Helen Keller, Pablo Casals, Henry Luce, Elizabeth Arden, Albert Schweitzer, Haile Selassie, Bertrand Russell, and Charles Lindbergh. After interviewing Lindbergh in 1968, Whitman became a close friend and accompanied him on his travels in behalf of conservation during the remaining years of his life.

Whitman was highly successful in gaining access to his subjects, whom he approached initially through a carefully worded letter requesting an interview in preparation for a biographical essay; he never used the word "obituary," assuming—correctly—that his subjects would interpret his letter accordingly. He conducted interviews as informal discussions, asking questions from time to time as unobtrusively as possible while taking careful note of the subject's demeanor. Subjects were encouraged to speak candidly after being assured that their conversations would remain confidential during their lifetimes.

Whitman published two book-length collections of his essays, *The Obituary Book* (1971) and *Come to Judgment* (1980). In the introduction to *Come to Judgment*, he wrote that a good obituary was "a lively expression of personality and character as well as a conscientious exposition of the main facts of a person's life. A good obit has all the characteristics of a well-focused snapshot."

After retiring in 1976 Whitman retained the persona of a bon vivant and literary man-about-town that he had cultivated in his years on the obituary desk, attending readings and luncheons and contributing book reviews to the *Times*. In 1983 he edited a biographical dictionary, *American Reformers*. During his final years he was a consultant to the *Dictionary of American Biography* and to the Oral History Project at Columbia University. Whitman was also the author of a biography of Adlai Stevenson, published in 1965. He died of a stroke in Monte Carlo, where he had traveled with his wife to help celebrate the seventieth birthday of the *Times* food writer Craig Claiborne.

Whitman was married twice, though he managed to keep the name of his first wife, from whom he was divorced and by whom he had four children, out of all printed sources, including his own obituary in the *Times*. He married his second wife, Joan McCracken, an editor in the Style section of the *Times*, in 1960.

• Biographical information on Whitman is limited. See his obituary in the *New York Times*, 5 Sept. 1990 (correction, 26 Sept. 1990); see also entries under "Whitman, Alden," in *Contemporary Authors*, vols. 17–20 and 132, and *Contemporary Authors, New Revision Series*, vol. 29.

ANN T. KEENE

WHITMAN, Alice. *See* Whitman Sisters.

WHITMAN, Charles Otis (14 Dec. 1842–6 Dec. 1910), zoologist, was born in Woodstock, Maine, the son of Jacob Whitman and Marcia Leonard. His father did some farming and some carriage building, while both parents were motivated by a strong religious (Millerite) conviction that the world would end with the Last Judgment in 1843. When that did not occur, and with a young baby, the couple moved to Waterford, Maine. In 1861 they returned to Woodstock, built a carriage shop, and continued their strict worship as Adventists. Born on the eve of the frustrated Second Coming, Charles remained a disappointment to his father, and the two were never close. Whitman also diverged from his parents' extreme religious views. He revealed an early interest in natural history by collecting birds and raising pigeons.

Whitman received his B.A. from Bowdoin College in 1868, with a typical classical education. He taught high school at Westford Academy in Westford, Massachusetts, then at Boston's English High School until 1875. While in Boston, he met Harvard's charismatic naturalist Louis Agassiz and attended Agassiz's summer program at the Anderson School of Natural History on Penikese Island, Massachusetts, in 1873, and again in 1874 following Louis's death, under Agassiz's son Alexander.

This experience inspired Whitman to pursue further studies in natural history, for which he traveled to Leipzig in 1875. He remained there until 1878, when he received his Ph.D. for his embryological work on the leech *Clepsine* under Rudolf Leuckart. After a brief return to English High School, he turned down a research fellowship at the prestigious Johns Hopkins University to replace Edward Sylvester Morse in the chair of zoology at the Imperial University in Tokyo in 1879. There he trained some of Japan's leading embryologists until he left in 1882, largely because of disagreements with the rigid university bureaucracy.

Returning to the United States, Whitman stopped at the Stazione Zoologica in Naples. As the first American to visit, Whitman was invited by director Anton Dohrn to work at the exciting new research station for six months. He then went to Leipzig to write up the results of his Naples research for publication. He returned to the United States in the fall of 1882, hoping to secure a rare position in zoology.

Fortunately, Alexander Agassiz hired him as assistant in zoology at Harvard's Museum of Comparative Zoology from 1882 to 1886. There he served essentially as Agassiz's assistant, though he also pursued his own research. During that time, he produced a series of articles examining the latest microscopic techniques and equipment, summarized in a useful manual in 1885. He also married a zoologist who worked in Agassiz's private Newport Laboratory, Emily Nunn, though there is no evidence that they did any research together. They would have two sons.

Whitman preferred greater independence than Agassiz allowed, and he accepted the directorship of the new Allis Lake Laboratory in Milwaukee, Wisconsin, from 1886 to 1889. It was at this private laboratory started by Edward Phelps Allis that Whitman began to articulate his ideas about how biology should be organized with a combination of specialization and coordination of specialties. He persuaded Allis to start a new American publication for zoological research in 1887, the *Journal of Morphology*. With William Morton Wheeler, Whitman began the *Zoological Bulletin* in 1898 for shorter articles (after two volumes, renamed the *Biological Bulletin* and moved to the Marine Biological Laboratory).

By 1888 Whitman had had considerable experience in directing and organizing biological research. He was thus selected as the first director of summer activities at the Marine Biological Laboratory (MBL) in Woods Hole, Massachusetts, an institution he sustained through numerous severe financial crises. There he combined teaching and research, junior and senior scientists, and physiology and morphology (as the two recognized main branches of biology) into a community of researchers examining questions especially about the embryology and morphology of marine organisms. He withdrew from active administration of the MBL after 1903, handing over the directorship to his protégé Frank Rattray Lillie officially in 1908.

In 1889 Whitman also moved to Clark University to accept his first academic position as chair of the zoology department at the just-founded graduate research–oriented university. He attracted a group of outstanding researchers and continued his own embryological work there until political battles over who should have control over curricular and research matters at the university caused him and nearly half the faculty to leave in 1892.

Whitman, and much of his department, went to the new University of Chicago, which promised greater support for scientific research. There Whitman remained until his death. At Chicago he carried out his duties as zoology department chair but soon returned to his real love, birds. He took up his boyhood interest in pigeon behavior, which resulted in 1898 in a lengthy pioneering and influential paper, "Animal Behavior." In it Whitman argued that animal behavior is biological and instinctual rather than psychological or concerned with mind.

Whitman did not publish the bulk of his pigeon studies, which he carried out in coops in his own backyard, since the university never fulfilled his dream of developing a "biological farm" to raise such animals. Instead, he left the data and his partially developed interpretations for his students to publish posthumously. Whitman preferred to spend his time with his birds, and he withdrew increasingly from the university's administrative and teaching demands. His health began to fail. On 1 December 1910, when a sudden cold spell hit Chicago, Whitman worked outside in the wind to protect his pigeons. He slipped into a coma, caught pneumonia, and died five days later.

• A few of Whitman's papers are in the Whitman Collection in the Department of Special Collections of the Joseph Regenstein Library at the University of Chicago, and a few are at the Marine Biological Laboratory. In addition, the Stazione Zoologica in Naples has a few of his letters. Whitman's major works include "The Embryology of *Clepsine*," *Quarterly Review of Microscopical Science* 18 (1878): 215–315; *Methods of Research in Microscopical Anatomy and Embryology* (1885); "Animal Behavior," *Biological Lectures Delivered at the Marine Biological Laboratory* (1899): 285–338, repr. in Jane Maienschein, ed., *Defining Biology, Lectures from the 1890s* (1986), pp. 217–72; and *The Posthumous Works of Charles Otis Whitman* (3 vols., 1919). The major biography, including a complete bibliography, is Frank R. Lillie's biographical sketch in the *Journal of Morphology* 22 (1911): xv–

lxxvii. For discussion of the Whitman family's unusual religious views, see Philip Pauly, "From Adventism to Biology: The Development of Charles Otis Whitman," *Perspectives in Biology and Medicine* 37 (1994): 395–408.

JANE MAIENSCHEIN

WHITMAN, Charles Seymour (28 Aug. 1868–29 Mar. 1947), politician, was born in Hanover, Connecticut, the son of John Seymour Whitman, a Presbyterian minister, and Lillie Arne. He attended Williams College for one year and then transferred to Amherst, graduating with an A.B. in 1890. He supported himself by teaching Greek and Latin at the Adelphi Academy in Brooklyn, New York, while attending New York University, where he earned a bachelor of law degree in 1894. After working for a time as a lawyer, Whitman was hired by Republican mayor Seth Low for a job in the city corporation counsel's office. One of Low's final acts in office in December 1903 was to appoint Whitman a magistrate, the lowest city judicial office. In 1907 Whitman became chief of New York's Board of Magistrates. He fought the corruption that was then rampant in the New York City police department and enacted changes that prevented police from accepting bribes from bail bondsmen and proprietors of after-hours bars. Campaigning on the strength of this reform, he was elected New York County district attorney. In December 1908 he married Olive Hitchcock; she died in 1926. They had two children.

The Rosenthal murder case was the dominant event during Whitman's tenure as district attorney. Early in his time in office he established a friendship with a reporter for the *New York World*, Herbert Swope. Whitman leaked stories to Swope in exchange for positive coverage of the district attorney's office. In 1911 a police lieutenant, Charles Becker, who had been assigned to investigate illegal gambling operations, raided the establishment of Arnold Rothstein, a close friend of Swope's. In retaliation, Swope published an interview, which appeared on the front page of the *New York World* (14 July 1912) with a Lower East Side gambler, Herman Rosenthal, who accused Becker of accepting bribes to ignore the existence of certain gambling houses. Although Whitman at once publicly rejected Rosenthal's reliability as a witness, Becker's credibility was damaged. On 16 July, two days after the publication of the interview, four gunmen killed Rosenthal in Times Square. On hearing the news, Swope phoned Whitman in the middle of the night and persuaded him to go immediately to the police station and take charge of the case.

The case enhanced the careers of both Whitman and Swope. Whitman fed the reporter inside information on the investigation for the next three years and Swope attributed his later rise to editor to these scoops. Whitman made national headlines with his investigation. The story was on 75 percent of the front pages of the *New York World* for six months following the murder.

The four gunmen, known as Gyp the Blood, Whitey Lewis, Lefty Louie, and Dago Frank, were electrocuted after they admitted that they had been hired by gamblers who were enemies of Rosenthal. Four of the gamblers named by the killers were arrested and jailed, but they were subsequently granted immunity and released after agreeing to testify against Becker. On their testimony Becker was convicted of murder. The New York Court of Appeals threw out the conviction fourteen months later, citing obvious unfairness. Becker was retried, again prosecuted by Whitman, and again convicted. The same Court of Appeals that had thrown out Becker's first conviction upheld the second one, largely because of Whitman's increased political clout. Becker based his plea for either clemency or a stay of execution on evidence that came to light after his trial; several witnesses had changed their stories. By the time this appeal was heard, however, Whitman had become governor of New York as a Republican, elected in 1914. He denied the plea and Becker was electrocuted on 30 July 1915.

Many questioned the ethical propriety of allowing Whitman, who had prosecuted Becker, to judge his last appeal. Becker's wife placed a plaque that read "Charles Becker . . . Murdered by Governor Whitman" on his coffin, but it was quickly removed by order of the district attorney.

The remainder of Whitman's term as governor of New York was uneventful. Despite his strong support of the Anti-Saloon League, he was known to drink excessively, and this caused increasing public criticism. He was also attacked for allowing his overwhelming ambition for the presidency to cause him to neglect his gubernatorial duties. Al Smith, who defeated him in the 1918 race for New York governor, accused Whitman of "sitting in the Capitol at Albany with a telescope trained on the White House in Washington." Crushed by his electoral defeat, Whitman refused for several weeks to concede the election. He then retired from politics and returned to his law practice in New York City. In 1933 he married Thelma Somerville Cudlipp Grosvenor; they had two children. He died in New York City.

• Information on Whitman is in Charles Henry Farnam, *The Whitman Family in America* (1889). His involvement with Swope and with Charles Becker is detailed in Ely Jacques Kahn, *The World of Swope* (1965), Matthew and Hannah Josephson, *Al Smith: Hero of the Cities* (1969), and Andy Logan, *Against the Evidence* (1970). An obituary is in the *New York Times*, 30 Mar. 1947.

ELIZABETH ZOE VICARY

WHITMAN, Ezekiel (9 Mar. 1776–1 Aug. 1866), jurist and congressman, was born in Bridgewater (now East Bridgewater), Massachusetts, the son of Josiah Whitman and Sarah Sturtevant. After his father's death in 1778 or 1779 and his mother's subsequent remarriage in 1783, Whitman was raised by his uncle, the Reverend Levi Whitman of Wellfleet, Massachusetts. He received a rudimentary education at his uncle's insistence and entered Rhode Island College (now Brown University) in 1791. A lack of funds compelled him to leave school before the start of his senior year. He continued his studies, however, and in the spring of 1795 returned to the college, where he passed his examinations and graduated with his class. Although he considered joining a company of theatrical players or going to sea, Whitman eventually settled on a career in law, again at his uncle's urging. After spending 1796 in Kentucky settling an estate, he studied for the bar, first under Benjamin Whitman of Hanover, New Hampshire, and then with Nahum Mitchell of Bridgewater. In 1799 Plymouth County admitted him to the bar.

While studying with Mitchell, Whitman married Mitchell's sister, Hannah Mitchell, in 1799. They had three children. Whitman decided to take up his law practice in Turner, Maine (at this time still a district of Mass.). He stayed in Turner only briefly before moving to New Gloucester, Maine, where he remained until 1807. Whitman's law practice prospered, and he moved his family to Portland, Maine, in 1807. Among his peers in the legal profession, Whitman was known for being a direct speaker whose arguments were models of force and clarity. He also had a reputation for honesty and integrity.

Although the law remained Whitman's passion throughout his life, he also entered Maine's political arena. In 1806, even before he moved to Portland, Maine's political center, he ran unsuccessfully for the U.S. Congress. Once in Portland, he became a prominent member of the Federalist party and was elected to the U.S. House of Representatives in 1808. He served for two terms. After his service in Congress, Whitman returned to state politics, where he served on the Massachusetts Executive Council in 1815 and 1816.

The primary political controversy of Whitman's time was Maine's attempt to separate from Massachusetts. Separation was originally a cause supported primarily by Maine Federalists, who believed that the Massachusetts government did not understand Maine's concerns or needs. After the Jeffersonian revolution of 1800 and the rise of the Democratic Republican party, however, Federalists realized that separation from Massachusetts would place them in the political minority in Maine. They needed the strong support of Federalist-dominated Massachusetts. Although many deserted the cause of separation, Whitman remained a supporter, albeit a lukewarm one. The issue of separation faded into the background of state politics until the Democratic Republicans revived the issue for the same reason the Federalists had previously supported it, mainly that Massachusetts was too far removed from Maine to address adequately the concerns of the district.

Whitman stayed in the background of Maine's struggle for statehood during the movement's formative years (1805–1815). He did, however, tutor a future leader of the movement, Albion K. Parris. Whitman was a delegate at both of Maine's constitutional conventions, and the Federalists nominated him for president of the 1816 Brunswick convention. He was defeated by the leader of the separation movement, William King.

In 1817 Whitman returned to Washington, D.C., upon his reelection to the U.S. House of Representatives, but Maine's application to Congress for statehood propelled the region to the forefront of national politics. Missouri had also applied for statehood, sparking a controversy over the existence of slavery within the state and threatening to destroy national harmony. Through various congressional moves, southerners linked Maine's bid for statehood with Missouri's. Senators Jesse Thomas of Illinois and Henry Clay of Kentucky suggested a compromise. Maine would be admitted as a free state, and Missouri would be admitted as a slave state, but slavery would be prohibited from all future states north of 36° 30′. This plan became known as the Missouri Compromise.

Whitman and the six other delegates from Massachusetts who represented Maine were at the heart of this debate. Five of them, including Whitman, voted against the Missouri Compromise. To justify their action, which might have deprived Maine of independence, Whitman and his colleagues published an address in the *Portland Gazette* on 21 March 1820. This statement claimed that their opposition to the proposed compromise stemmed from the conviction that the South was engaging in political blackmail by linking the admission of the two states. To vote for the compromise would establish a dangerous precedent in national politics.

Despite the opposition of these five delegates, the Missouri Compromise was passed by both houses of Congress. Although popular opinion in Maine lay with those who supported the compromise, Whitman and three of his colleagues were reelected to the House of Representatives. During his tenure in Congress, Whitman gained notoriety for his attacks on General Andrew Jackson, then the governor of Florida. Jackson, Whitman argued, had abused his powers by interfering unduly with the judiciary in that territory.

On 1 June 1822 Whitman resigned from the House of Representatives after his former student, Governor Parris, appointed him a judge of the court of common pleas. He served as such until 1841, when he was appointed chief justice of the Maine Supreme Court. He resigned from this position on 23 October 1848 with his reputation for honesty and integrity intact. After his wife's death on 28 March 1852, Whitman returned to East Bridgewater, Massachusetts, where he died.

Although Whitman's role in Maine's separation from Massachusetts was a minor one, his position on the Missouri Compromise was a harbinger of things to come. He was certainly not the first to prophesize the danger of the growing sectional conflict, but his clear articulation of that danger in his 1820 address to the people of Maine encapsulates what would become the dominant view of the North over the next forty years. Whitman and his four Maine colleagues who voted against the compromise understood that the principle established by the act would have far greater significance than Maine's independence.

• Whitman published a commemorative address in *Celebration of the Two-Hundredth Anniversary of the Incorporation of Bridgewater, Massachusetts* (1856) and *Memoir of John Whitman and His Descendants* (1832). Details about Whitman and his career appear in many histories of Maine, including William Willis, *A History of the Law, the Courts, and the Lawyers of Maine* (1863); and Ronald F. Banks, *Maine Becomes a State: The Movement to Separate Maine from Massachusetts, 1785–1820* (1970), which explores the separation movement and the Missouri Compromise in great depth. For general information about Maine during this time period, see Richard W. Judd et al., eds., *Maine: The Pine Tree State from Prehistory to the Present* (1995). Studies of Whitman's family and their settlement in Bridgewater, Mass., are C. H. Farnam, *History of the Descendants of John Whitman of Weymouth, Massachusetts* (1889), and Nahum Mitchell, *History of the Early Settlement of Bridgewater* (1840). Obituary notices that fill many of the gaps in biographical details include *New England Historical and Genealogical Register*, Oct. 1866: the *Bangor Daily Whig and Courier*, 4 Aug. 1866; and the *Daily Portland Press*, 8 Aug. 1866.

ELIZABETH DUBRULLE

WHITMAN, Malcolm Douglass (5 Mar. 1877–28 Dec. 1932), tennis player, was born in Andover, Massachusetts, the son of William Whitman, a wealthy textile mill owner, and Jane Dole Hallett. As a youth, Mac Whitman played tennis regularly at the Longwood Cricket Club in Boston. He was educated at Roxbury Latin School and Hopkinson's School in Boston, and he graduated from Harvard University in 1899 with a B.A., cum laude, and from Harvard Law School in 1902.

In 1894 Whitman lost in the early rounds of his first tournaments, the Harvard Interscholastics and the Longwood Bowl open. But the following year he reached three finals and earned a national ranking of twenty-fourth. He lost in two of the finals to Leo Ware, who would defeat him five times altogether, three more times than any other player. Whitman improved during the next two seasons to rank eighth in 1896, when he won the Intercollegiate championship as a freshman, and seventh in 1897, the year he first attracted attention in the national championships by eliminating Bill Clothier and the Irish star, Harold Mahony, and, in the quarter-finals, forcing the English player Harold Nisbet to a 7–5 fifth set before losing to him. "Mac," as he was known to friends, became U.S. champion in 1898. During the season he lost twice to Ware but won five tournaments: Massachusetts State, Middle States, Longwood Bowl, New York State, and the nationals before falling to Dwight Davis, his Harvard teammate, in the Intercollegiate Championship. To capture the U.S. title, he downed George Wrenn, Clarence Budlong (after almost losing a five-setter on a soggy court), Ware, and Davis. America's two top players of 1897, however, were absent; Bob Wrenn and Bill Larned spent the 1898 season with Colonel Theodore Roosevelt's (1858–1919) Troop A in Cuba fighting Spanish forces.

Undefeated in 1899, Whitman won seven tournaments and lost only four sets all season. As standing-out champion, he defended four titles in challenge rounds: Middle States, Longwood Bowl, New York State, and the nationals, turning back Larned, Davis, Eddie Fischer, and Parmly Paret. He also won Massachusetts State, Canada, and Long Island championships, in each final vanquishing his erstwhile nemesis, Ware. Afterward, he with former Harvard teammates Davis and Holcombe Ward and entering freshman Beals Wright traveled to the Pacific states where Whitman defeated the best local players in team matches. Davis on this trip conceived ideas for international competition that resulted in his donating the Davis Cup. The United States won the initial cup tie from the British Isles, 3–0, at the Longwood Cricket Club during August 1900. The American Twist services of the Harvard men baffled the visitors; Whitman easily bested Arthur W. Gore, while Davis won his singles, and Davis-Ward triumphed in the doubles. In tournaments, Whitman played only in challenge rounds, losing his Massachusetts State title to Davis but successfully defending the Middle States and Longwood Bowl from Davis, the New York State from Hackett, and the Canada and U.S. championships from Larned. Preoccupied with law studies, Whitman passed up competition in 1901, but, strongly urged, he consented to play in the 1902 Davis Cup matches versus the British. First, he won the Nahant (Mass.) Invitation round-robin from Clothier, Ware, Wright, and others. Then in the cup tie he played in old-time form to defeat Dr. Joshua Pim and Reggie Doherty, four-time English champion. Larned beat Pim, and the United States won the tie, 3–2. At the 1902 nationals several weeks later, Whitman proceeded to beat Wright, Kreigh Collins, and Bob Huntington to reach the all-comers' final, but there he lost to Doherty in four sets.

After gaining admittance to the New York bar, Whitman entered his father's firm, the William Whitman Company, of Boston, a large textile holding company. Subsequently, he became its vice president and New York manager, president of Nashawena Mills, of New Bedford, Massachusetts, and director of other textile properties controlled by the Whitman concern. A tall, blond, handsome man, he married three times: first, in 1907, to Janetta Alexander McCook, who died in 1910; second, in 1912, to Jennie Adeline Crocker, a marriage ended by divorce in 1925; and third, in 1926, to Lucilla de Vescovi, a concert soprano, who survived him. He had two children by the first marriage, three by the second. He authored, in 1907, a genealogical monograph on the Whitman family; in 1924, *Fly Fishing Up to Date; or, The Evolution of a Fisherman (Cum Grano Salis)*; and, in 1932, *Tennis Origins and Mysteries*, a scholarly book about historical aspects of court tennis and lawn tennis. In late 1932 he suffered a breakdown, and because in delirium he threatened to kill himself, he was placed under psychiatric care and guarded. However, he eluded his nurses and jumped to his death from his New York City penthouse.

Whitman decided early that he needed to build a consistent all-court game without a weakness. After careful studies of mechanics and strategy and long, dil igent practice, he succeeded to a remarkable degree. A 6′2″ or 3″, 175-pound right-hander, he developed graceful, seemingly effortless ground strokes, slightly topped and controlled by sweeping free swings on each flank, taking balls low on the forehand and at medium height on the backhand. At net, he used height and long reach to advantage, volleying and smashing surely and effectively, but without extreme severity. His serves were slow, well-placed, and varied in pace and direction. On key points, he employed the famous reverse twist service he had invented. It broke sharply to the receiver's right and almost invariably won points. While his prime intent always was to reach an advantageous net position, he did not follow in on serve; he generally stayed at the baseline, carefully and accurately maneuvering opponents until he obviously controlled rests and could advance without fear of being passed. Contrasting the approaches of his two great contemporaries, Holcombe Ward observed, "Whitman . . . strives not to lose points; Larned, to win them; the result, Whitman has been the most consistent player, and the most reliable we have yet produced; Larned, the most dashing and brilliant." While Whitman preferred to concentrate on singles, he also played doubles well and won a score of doubles tournaments, including the 1898 Eastern championship with George Wrenn and the 1897 and 1898 Intercollegiate titles with Ware. Whitman, in 1955, was among the first group of players elected to the National Lawn Tennis (later, the International Tennis) Hall of Fame.

• There are no biographies of Whitman. Malcolm D. Whitman, "Net Play: A Determining Factor," in U.S. Lawn Tennis Association, *Fifty Years of Lawn Tennis in the United States* (1931), pp. 73–81, furnishes a self-description of his development of his style of play. Other evaluative descriptions of his style by contemporaries include Arthur S. Pier, "Some Tennis Champions," *American Magazine*, 70 (Apr. 1910): 466–76; E. C. Potter, Jr., *Kings of the Court* (1936), pp. 74–81; and Holcombe Ward, "American Methods," in *Lawn Tennis at Home and Abroad*, ed. A. Wallis Myers (1903), pp. 186–211. Obituaries are in *American Lawn Tennis*, 27 Jan. 1933, and the *New York Times*, 29 Dec. 1932.

FRANK VAN RENSSELAER PHELPS

WHITMAN, Marcus (4 Sept. 1802–29 Nov. 1847), medical missionary, was born in Rushville, New York, the son of Beza Whitman and Alice Green. When Whitman was seven, his father died, and his mother sent him to his father's family in Massachusetts. Although he returned home at least once, he lived in Massachusetts until he was eighteen. The five years he studied in Plainfield, Massachusetts, were particularly important, for during this period he experienced conversion and began to think about becoming a minister.

When Whitman returned to his family in Rushville, he found little support for his ambitions. While the Congregational church provided some outlet for his religious enthusiasm, Whitman spent the next three years in his stepfather's shoe shop and tannery. In 1823 he apprenticed himself to a local doctor. Two years later Whitman studied briefly at the College of Physicians and Surgeons of the Western District of New York and received his license. He practiced in Pennsylvania and Canada, returning to Rushville in 1830.

Still tantalized by thoughts of the ministry, Whitman decided to abandon medicine for the study of theology, but poor health terminated this effort. Resuming his medical practice, he earned an additional medical degree in 1831 and moved to Wheeler, New York, the next year. While following the rounds of a country doctor, he began to think about becoming a medical missionary.

Recommended in 1834 by Rushville's Congregational minister as "a regular bred Physician" with a "solid judicious mind" and "more than ordinary piety and perseverance," Whitman explored the subject with the American Board of Commissioners for Foreign Missions (ABCFM). Whitman and the board agreed that his health precluded an assignment in a warm climate, but when the board contemplated opening an Indian mission in Oregon Territory it selected Whitman to assist the Reverend Samuel Parker on his investigatory trip during the spring of 1835. Before setting out with Parker for the West, Whitman proposed marriage to Narcissa Prentiss in nearby Prattsburg. Missionaries were expected to have wives, and Narcissa was known to harbor missionary hopes. She immediately accepted his offer. They would have one child, a daughter who drowned at an early age.

Whitman and Parker traveled with the American Fur Company to its annual rendezvous (in present-day Wyoming). There Whitman met Flathead and Nez Percé chiefs who expressed interest in having missionaries settle among them. Instead of accompanying Parker west, Whitman returned home after the rendezvous, convinced of both the feasibility of the proposed ABCFM mission and of the ability of women to make the overland trip successfully. He was instrumental in gathering a missionary party for Oregon and ensuring that they met up with the American Fur Company caravan headed for the 1836 rendezvous.

In the fall of 1836 Whitman selected Waiilatpu on the Walla Walla River for his mission site. There bands of the Cayuse, one of the tribes that had invited the missionaries to settle among them, spent part of each year. By the early 1840s his hard work, energy, and determination to make the mission self-supporting had transformed the remote site into a flourishing farm with many improvements. Henry Gray, who accompanied the Whitmans west, recognized the qualities responsible for this material progress. Once Whitman was "fixed in the pursuit of an object," he would adhere "to it with unflinching tenacity."

Whitman's missionary work among the Cayuse took many forms. Although not ordained, he conducted services and provided religious instruction for the Indians. He also practiced European-style medicine and struggled to overcome the tribal reliance on *tewats* (medicine men). Teaching the Indians how to farm was also an important component of his mission. Like other missionaries, he hoped that once they realized they could support themselves by farming, the Indians would abandon their seminomadic life and be available for continuous religious instruction. In addition to these responsibilities, Whitman provided medical care for other missionary families in Oregon and for employees of the Hudson's Bay Company. He was often away from Waiilatpu for weeks at a time on mission or medical business.

The results of these efforts did not live up to the Whitmans' hopes. While many Cayuse adopted some Christian practices, such as attendance at Sabbath services, none converted to Christianity. Some became hostile to a religion that seemed harsh. And while visitors to the mission often were impressed by Indian agricultural progress, the Cayuse did not settle down at Waiilatpu.

Missionary work was hampered not only by Cayuse resistance to the sweeping cultural and religious changes desired by the Whitmans but also by serious disagreements and jealousy among the several members of the ABCFM Oregon mission. When the board learned of this divisiveness, it determined to make serious changes in the mission. In 1842 the mission received a letter ordering the Whitmans to leave Waiilatpu for the remote station of Tshimakain in Washington State and recalling another missionary couple. These directives prompted Whitman to hurry east in the fall of 1842. During his meetings with the board, he persuaded its members that significant progress had been made in overcoming personal and professional difficulties, and the board rescinded its orders. Whitman's trip east also included discussions with officials in Washington, D.C. These gave rise to the claim, probably untrue, that Whitman was instrumental in "saving" Oregon from British domination.

Whitman's return west coincided with the "Great Migration" of 1843, the decade's first great overland migration and the first to bring wagons successfully into Oregon Territory. His experience and trailbreaking abilities were invaluable and led some to characterize him as the real leader of the large American migration. With increasing migration during the 1840s, Whitman's attention shifted away from the Cayuse. An avid proponent of American settlement, he urged family and friends to come west and solicited the ABCFM to send committed evangelicals and clergy to the territory. By 1846 he had little time "for the more important spiritual part of our duty." Instead, much time and energy were spent in finding better routes for migrant travel and in assisting weary migrants at the mission and along the trail. The ABCFM became concerned that he was spending too much attention and energy helping whites rather than the Cayuse. Also during the 1840s the Cayuse sporadically indicated dissatisfaction with the missionary teachings and with the presence and growing number of white migrants. When Cayuse efforts to dislodge the Whitmans failed, they resorted to violence. Both Whitman and his wife as well as a number of white migrants wintering at the mission were massacred by the Cayuse in November 1847.

Whitman became almost a folk hero in the nineteenth century for his supposed role in saving Oregon from the British, for the real assistance he provided migrants, and for his missionary activities. Whitman College at Walla Walla was founded in memory of the missionary couple. In the twentieth century Whitman came to be seen as a more complex figure, his missionary work viewed as part of a broad American effort to extend white culture and values to nonwhite groups inside and outside the United States. A recognition of his evangelical vigor and zeal is essential to understanding his life's work, whereas an appreciation of Native-American culture helps to explain the misunderstandings and conflicts that limited his impact as a missionary.

• Important Whitman manuscript collections are housed in the Houghton Library at Harvard University, in the Beinecke Library at Yale University, and in the archives of the Whitman College Library. Many of Whitman's letters to the ABCFM board can be found in the three-volume collection *Marcus Whitman, Crusader*, ed. Archer Butler Hulburt and Dorothy Printup Hulburt (1936, 1938, 1941). Clifford M. Drury published other letters in *More about the Whitmans: Four Hitherto Unpublished Letters of Marcus and Narcissa Whitman* (1979). Drury provides a detailed account of Whitman's life in *Marcus and Narcissa Whitman and the Opening of Old Oregon* (1973).

Modern evaluations of the missionary's career and its significance include Johnathan H. Webster, "The Oregon Mission and the ABCFM," and Roderick Sprague, "Plateau Shamanism and Marcus Whitman," both in *Idaho Yesterdays* 31 (1987): 24–34 and 55–56, respectively; and Julie Roy Jeffrey, "Empty Harvest at Waiilatpu," *Columbia: The Magazine of Northwest History* 6 (1992): 22–32. Additional insights can be found in Jeffrey's *Converting the West: A Biography of Narcissa Whitman* (1991).

JULIE ROY JEFFREY

WHITMAN, Narcissa Prentiss (14 Mar. 1808–29 Nov. 1847), missionary, was born in Prattsburg, New York, the daughter of Stephen Prentiss, a carpenter, farmer, and sometime distillery, gristmill, and sawmill owner, and Clarissa Ward. Her mother's religious zeal, reinforced by periodic evangelical revivals, encouraged Narcissa's spiritual commitment. Narcissa Prentiss experienced an early conversion when she was eleven and joined the Prattsburg Congregational church. By fifteen she had resolved to become a missionary. She gained an appropriate education at Auburn Academy in Auburn and at Franklin Academy in Prattsburg, although she never graduated. Like many other future missionaries, she was active in benevolent organizations and taught school.

After hearing a lecture in 1834 on the need for missionaries for American Indian tribes beyond the Rocky Mountains, in 1835 Prentiss wrote to the American Board of Commissioners for Foreign Missions (ABCFM) to volunteer for a missionary post. Probably because she was single, the board did not respond. Only after Marcus Whitman, whom the board had appointed as a medical missionary for the proposed Oregon mission, suggested marriage, did Prentiss obtain a missionary assignment. The two were married in February 1836. The couple started almost immediately for their post. Neither of the Whitmans had detailed information about the tribes whom they hoped to convert or any special training for missionary work.

Their party, which included Henry Spalding and Eliza Spalding, who were also assigned to the Oregon mission, traveled with American Fur Company traders as far as that year's rendezvous site (in Wyo.); Eliza Spalding and Narcissa Whitman were the first white women to cross over the South Pass of the Rocky Mountains. From the rendezvous site, Hudson's Bay Company traders guided the missionaries to Oregon territory. The company's chief factor, John McLoughlin, welcomed the Americans at Fort Vancouver in early September. Eliza Spalding and Narcissa Whitman remained as guests while their husbands scouted for suitable mission sites. Finally, in December, Narcissa joined Marcus at Waiilatpu, located on a branch of the Walla Walla River about twenty-five miles from the Hudson's Bay Company's Fort Walla Walla.

Narcissa Whitman's missionary work among the Cayuse started almost at once with her attempt to teach them hymns, first in English and later in Nez Percé. She also began a school in her kitchen. Occasionally when Marcus Whitman was away on medical mission business, she conducted worship, a responsibility she found "almost insupportable." Generally, her missionary efforts suffered from her slow progress with the Nez Percé language. As late as 1839, she reported she could not "converse satisfactorily . . . hardly in the least degree." Perhaps a more serious obstacle was her general discomfort with the Cayuse and their culture. While she was not alone in her negative response to Indian life, her feelings contributed to her sense of isolation. She often described her situation as a lonely one, deep in the "thick darkness of heathendom."

Despite her misgivings about missionary work, both Whitman and her husband were initially hopeful about their missionary prospects. The Cayuse seemed attentive and interested in the Christian message. By 1839, however, the Whitmans began to realize that converting the tribe both to Christianity and to a settled way of life was a problematic goal. Some members of the tribe violently opposed what the Whitmans presented as the truth and made their dissatisfaction clear. Narcissa Whitman's growing disillusionment with the missionary enterprise deepened when her only child, a daughter, drowned in June 1839. The accident probably precipitated a physical and emotional breakdown. By 1840 Whitman's bad health kept her from many of her former missionary duties. While she continued to copy missionary materials, to study Nez Percé, and to do some teaching, she was never again very active among the Cayuse.

The Whitmans' lack of success in converting the Cayuse as well as problems among members of the ABCFM mission led Narcissa Whitman to a period of self-doubt and questionning. She seems to have experienced a second conversion in 1841. While her spiritual life deepened, she lost some of the buoyancy that had characterized her early years in the field.

Increasing white emigration to Oregon in the 1840s and her decision in 1844 to adopt the seven Sager orphans (who joined three mixed-blood children already in her household) provided her with the means to restructure her life. She energetically undertook evangelical work among the white emigrants, many of whom spent the winter at the mission, and also devoted herself to the care and spiritual development of her large family. Though she expressed regret that she had no time for the Indians, she was satisfied with her choice. As she told her mother, you "will see that my hands are usefully employed, not so much with the Indians directly, as my own family. . . . I have no cause to complain."

While Whitman was reshaping her own life during the 1840s, the Cayuse were becoming increasingly restive. Clearly perceiving the missionaries' sweeping religious and cultural objectives and worried about increasing white emigration, the tribe tried repeatedly to make the Whitmans leave the mission. When a measles epidemic proved more deadly to the Cayuse than to white residents at Waiilatpu, some members of the tribe decided to end the white presence. In the fall of 1847 Whitman and her husband as well as several others living at the mission were killed, and the mission was abandoned.

Narcissa Whitman's life reveals the impact of evangelical religion on antebellum women and some of the new opportunities that religious commitment offered white middle-class women. While her missionary work was unsuccessful (none of the Cayuse converted to Christianity), her efforts were part of a larger attempt to spread American and Protestant values around the world.

Assessment of the Whitmans and their endeavors has varied. Initially, a Methodist missionary and friend suggested that Narcissa Whitman was ill suited for missionary work and that the Indians found her proud and haughty. But very rapidly other members of the ABCFM Oregon mission, especially Henry Spalding, began a process of heroicizing both the Whitmans and their cause. This positive depiction of the Whitmans continued well into the twentieth century. With a revival of interest in both the missionary movement and evangelical religion and new scholarship on Native Americans, a reassessment of Whitman and her work began. As the dynamics of cultural and racial interactions were better understood, the clash of cultures became a more prominent theme of this narrative. Moreover, the relationship of the Oregon ABCFM mission to other missionary efforts within and outside of North America provided a broad context for understanding Whitman, her missionary vocation, and her achievements and failures.

• Unpublished archival materials include the records of the American Board of Commissioners for Foreign Missions at the Houghton Library, Harvard University; a large collection at the Beinecke Library at Yale University; and varied holdings in the archives of the Whitman College library. Many of Whitman's letters were published in the *Oregon Pioneer Association Transactions* (1891, 1893). Other primary sources can be found in Clifford M. Drury, *First White Women Over the Rockies* (1963), *More about the Whitmans: Four Hitherto Unpublished Letters of Marcus and Narcissa Whitman* (1979), and "The Columbia Maternal Association," *Oregon Historical Quarterly* 39 (1938):99–122. Drury also wrote an admiring account of the missionaries in his two-volume study, *Marcus and Narcissa Whitman and the Opening of Old Oregon* (1973). An interpretative biography of Whitman that attempts to place her efforts in a broad context is Julie Roy Jeffrey, *Converting the West: A Biography of Narcissa Whitman* (1991). Shorter studies by Jeffrey include "The Making of a Missionary: Narcissa Whitman and Her Vocation," *Idaho Yesterdays* 31 (1987): 75–85; "Narcissa Whitman: The Significance of a Missionary's Life," *Montana: The Magazine of Western History* 41 (1991): 2–15; and "Empty Harvest at Waiilatpu," *Columbia: The Magazine of Northwest History* 6 (1992): 22–31.

JULIE ROY JEFFREY

WHITMAN, Royal (24 Oct. 1857–19 Aug. 1946), orthopedic surgeon, was born in Portland, Maine, the son of Royal Emerson Whitman, a saddle manufacturer, and Lucretia Octavia Whitman, a member of another branch of the family. Whitman grew up on a family farm in Turner, Maine, under his mother's care and strict religious supervision. This strong religious upbringing later turned him permanently against formal religion in his life. He graduated from a high school in Auburn, Maine, and worked as a pharmacist while studying medicine as an apprentice for two years. He then worked his way through Harvard Medical School, from which he received an M.D. in 1882.

In the early 1880s Whitman served as a surgical intern in the Boston City Hospital and began to practice in Boston. Toward the end of the 1880s, he studied at Cook's School of Anatomy in London, England, and became a member of the Royal College of Surgeons in 1889. On his return later that year to the United States, he became assistant surgeon at the Hospital for the Ruptured and Crippled, where he remained for four decades. In 1886 Whitman married Julia Lombard Armitage; they had one child.

Throughout his professional career, Whitman was a consummate orthopedic surgeon and originated several methods of treatment that became standard. Having published observations on seventy-five cases of flat foot, he described in 1990 the rational treatment of this disorder to the orthopedic section of the New York Academy of Medicine. The metal plate used in the procedure is still known as the Whitman plate. In 1901 he described an astragalectomy operation for stabilizing the paralytic foot, particularly when there was a calcaneus deformity. Whitman's method for treating fractures at the neck of the femur, which he presented in 1904, produced such impressive results that it became a standard treatment. In 1921 he described a technique for reconstruction of an ununited fracture of the hip, a procedure that he had first performed in 1916.

An accurate and careful surgeon, Whitman was also an exacting teacher who was responsible, over the course of his career, for educating more than 140 residents. His textbook, *A Treatise on Orthopaedic Surgery* (1901), became the principal text in its field and went through nine editions.

Whitman's lucid descriptions and exacting surgical technique attracted many residents and students from all over the world. From 1889 to 1929 he served as adjunct professor of orthopedic surgery at the College of Physicians and Surgeons, Columbia University, and as professor at the New York Polyclinic Medical School. Among his honorary affiliations were a fellowship in the Royal Medical Society in England and membership in both the French Academy of Surgery and the German Academy of Natural Scientists. In 1895 he served as president of the American Orthopaedic Association. Whitman is credited with contributing to the establishment of operative surgery as a dominant feature of orthopedic surgery. He died in his home in New York City.

• For a biographical account of Whitman, see Sir D'Arcy Power and W. R. LeFanu, *Lives of the Fellows of the Royal College of Surgeons of England, 1930–1951* (1953). Fenwick Beekman, *Hospital for the Ruptured and Crippled: A Historical Sketch* (1939), provides information on his career. See also Alfred R. Shands, Jr., in *American Orthopaedic Association News* (Oct. 1970). Obituaries are in the *Journal of Bone and Joint Surgery* (Oct. 1946): 890, and *Journal of the American Medical Association* (Sept. 1946): 97.

SEYMOUR I. SCHWARTZ

WHITMAN, Sarah de St. Prix Wyman (5 Dec. 1842–25 June 1904), designer and fabricator of stained glass, bookcover designer, painter, and writer, was born in Lowell, Massachusetts, the daughter of William W. Wyman, a banker, and Sarah Amanda Treat of Boston. Immediately following her birth, in the wake of a financial scandal and legal trials involving her father, the family moved to Baltimore. The Wymans returned to Lowell in 1853, but throughout her life, Baltimore held a special place in Whitman's heart, and she returned regularly to her childhood home for family visits and Christmas holidays.

In Lowell, young Sarah was fortunate to have as her tutor the intellectually gifted Elizabeth "Lissy" Mason Edson, daughter of the rector of St. Ann's Episcopal Church. Edson introduced Sarah to the plays of William Shakespeare, the work of English historian Thomas Babington Macaulay, poetry, penmanship, and drawing. She taught her German and French and instilled in her an enduring love and appreciation for learning. The two women became and remained cherished friends.

In June 1866 Sarah Wyman married Henry Whitman of Boston, a Nova Scotia–born wool merchant. It was an unhappy, childless marriage, but it gave her the freedom to pursue a career in art. Once settled in Boston, Whitman entered the studio of William Morris Hunt, champion of the Barbizon school, teacher, and cultural arbiter; she studied with Hunt for three winter seasons (1868–1871). In 1870–1871 she also attended sculptor William Rimmer's classes in drawing and artistic anatomy. Four years later, in the summer of 1875, Whitman resumed her studies. Armed with letters of introduction from Hunt, she toured Italy and France, probably with Elizabeth Bartol, another former member of Hunt's class. Whitman twice returned to France, in the summer of 1877 and again late in 1878 or early 1879, to study with Hunt's former master Thomas Couture. Whitman's studies with Couture marked the end of her formal training. She revisited Europe many times but did not seek out other teachers. The influence of Hunt and Couture remained constant and strongest in her portraits, in the soft modeling of the figure, the shadowy harmonies of contrasting lights and darks, the broken brush work. The summer of 1877 was the defining moment for Whitman: it led to her decision to live "the life of an artist in the thick of conventional adjustments & demands," that is, regardless of the disapproval then ascribed to women who earned money from their art.

Despite her doubts, given her limited formal education and art training, Whitman's accomplishments were remarkable. A member of both the National Academy of Design (1877) and the Society of American Artists (1880), she began to exhibit almost yearly in New York and Boston. William Brownell, writing in *Scribner's* 1881, considered her to be "representative of the successful women-painters of Boston." Whitman's reputation as a celebrated painter of flowers, landscapes, and portraits led to her first one-woman exhibition of oil paintings in 1882 at Doll & Richards, one of Boston's most prestigious galleries, and possibly to a second exhibition there in 1883.

Whitman lived on Beacon Hill, and during this period she became closely associated with the circle of writers and artists gathered at 148 Charles Street, the home of Annie Fields and Sarah Orne Jewett. The bookcover design for *Verses* by Sarah Chauncey Woolsey (pseudonym Susan Coolidge), a close friend of Fields and Jewett, started Whitman in 1880 on a long career as a stylist and designer of trade bookbindings. She designed books for many of the writers who were welcome at Charles Street, among them, James Russell Lowell, Amy Lowell, Elizabeth Stuart Phelps, Harriet Beecher Stowe, and William Dean Howells. Whitman designed most of the bookcovers for Jewett, with whom she became very close and devoted. Jewett dedicated *Strangers and Wayfarers* to her in 1890.

Working chiefly for Houghton, Mifflin and Company, Whitman stripped away the fussy clutter of bookcover designs of the period and brought to her work a spare elegance that reflected the influence of Dante Gabriel Rossetti, James A. M. Whistler, and the growing popularity of Japanese fabric design. By 1887, with the publication of *The Vision of Sir Launfall* by James Russell Lowell, Houghton Mifflin began to capitalize on Whitman's name recognition as cover designer and began to feature her name prominently in their advertisements. By the mid-1890s Whitman was regarded as "the pioneer of designing for modern cloth covers," and her innovative designs ranked with those by William Morris, Walter Crane, Elihu Vedder, Stanford White, and others. Her distinctive lettering, an informal, vernacular style comparable to calligraphy, began to appear on almost every book issued by Riverside Press, a division of Houghton Mifflin noted for high standards of book form and printing. For the World's Columbian Exposition of 1893 Whitman designed the Houghton Mifflin book pavilion.

Whitman's other driving interest was stained glass. Although there is no certainty about how she began or with whom she studied, it can be safely assumed that it was with John La Farge, a former student and friend of Hunt's and in 1877 the chief muralist and designer of stained glass for Trinity Church in Boston. Whitman's first known, major commission, in 1884–1885, to design the stained glass windows of Central Church (now United Church of Christ, Congregational) in Worcester, Massachusetts, may have come on the recommendation of La Farge, who was then "too busy to give the matter proper attention." Whitman personally supervised the work, from the design of the windows to the drawings for the wall decorations (now lost) to the handpainting (now lost) of scrollwork on the spandrels of the arches of the nave. It was an ambitious design program, a bold amalgam of traditional and nonconventional forms and painterly, striking colors, recalling the interior enrichment of Trinity Church. In 1886–1887 she received her second major church commission, to design the windows, organ case, and painted decorations for the apse (the apsidal windows and decorations are now lost) in Christ Church, Andover, Massachusetts. This commission reflected Whitman's personal approach to stained glass and interior design: quieter, more graceful and harmonious, stylistically closer in feeling and aesthetic to the school of William Morris in England. Although Whitman never fully and properly praised La Farge as the key figure in her development as designer and fabricator of stained glass, his fundamental conceptions of form, space, painterly color, and tone remained basic to her work.

In the 1890s Whitman did some of her finest work in stained glass, windows she designed and made in the Lily Glass Works, the studio she established in 1887. Among her crowning achievements were the Elizabeth Robbins Memorial Window, St. Ann's Church, Kennebunkport, Maine (1892); the windows in the Fogg Memorial Building, Berwick Academy, South Berwick, Maine (1890–1894); the Bishop Phillips Brooks Memorial Window, Parish House, Trinity Church, Boston (1895–1896); and the Martin Brimmer Memorial Window (1895–1898) and Honor & Peace (1896–1900), Memorial Hall, Harvard University, Cambridge, Mass.

Through years crowded with major commissions and soaring success, Whitman continued to paint and to exhibit her work. She won an honorable mention in the Paris Exposition of 1889 and had a third, one-woman exhibition at Boston's St. Botolph Club, a prominent men's club with exhibition space newly opened to local women artists. Also in 1889 Whitman painted her first known mural, *The Heavenly Pilgrimage* (now in storage), for Central Church. Recognition of Whitman's varied career came in November 1892 with an exhibition at Doll & Richards that brought together all aspects of her art, including her bookcover designs and stained glass; in December the exhibition moved to Avery Galleries in New York. In addition to the World's Columbian Exposition of 1893, Whitman participated in the 65th Annual exhibition of the Pennsylvania Academy (1895–1896) in Philadelphia. She received another honorable mention at the Paris Exposition of 1900 and a Bronze Medal at the Pan-American Exposition held in Buffalo, New York, in 1901.

Despite the pressures of her work Whitman found time to explore other avenues of design: a silver goblet and pitcher (1892), a monument to Dr. Oliver Wendell Holmes (1895), a plaque for the Hemenway Gym at Radcliffe (1897), and the plaque over the entrance to the Isabella Stewart Gardner Museum in Boston (1900). She designed interiors for Radcliffe: Fay House (1885), Bertram Hall (1900), and Agassiz House (1902); the offices of Houghton Mifflin (1900–1901); and the Parkman School, Forest Hills (1903–1904). She also found time to compose sonnets, write about art history and bookcover design for young people, examine the nature of crafts, and promote the importance of art in the public schools.

Whitman's sense of social responsibility extended to the community. She taught Bible classes for thirty years at Trinity Church and during summers at Beverly Farms Baptist Church on the North Shore. She taught art at the School of the Museum of Fine Arts Boston and was the first woman member on the Council of the School (1885). Her commitment to education, especially for women, led to her early involvement in the founding of Radcliffe College (1886). At the turn of the century Whitman was active in the formation of the Boston Society of Arts and Crafts (1897), and she organized the Women's Auxiliary of the Massachusetts Civil Service Reform Association (1901).

It was at this time, in 1900, that years of neglect took their toll and that Whitman's health began to fail. At her death in Boston, she was mourned by a large circle of friends. William James summed up the sense of loss in a letter to his brother Henry, "She leaves a dreadful vacuum in Boston." In a memorial address, Justice Oliver Wendell Holmes spoke of her as "a woman worthy of public honor and loving pride." In the late fall of 1804 the Friends of Radcliffe College bought Whitman's last work in stained glass, made specially for the Louisiana Purchase Exposition, held that year in St. Louis, "in commemoration of her services to the college and to the community in which she lived." (First placed in the newly opened Agassiz House, it was moved in 1907–1908 to what is now the Schlesinger Library at Radcliffe College.) Whitman was honored also with a memorial exhibition of her stained glass and bookcover designs by the Boston Society of Arts and Crafts (1905); a memorial loan exhibition of her paintings at the Museum of Fine Arts (1906); a paten given by Trinity Church women's Bible class (1906); a stained glass window installed in the Parish House, Trinity Church (c. 1910); and by the naming of the Whitman dormitory at Radcliffe College (1912).

By the 1920s Sarah Wyman Whitman's reputation had waned as the large, admiring circle of friends and patrons died and was replaced by a newer generation of artists and collectors as well as newer, avant-garde styles and tastes. The taste for Barbizon painters and the historicism of William Morris, his associates, and the Arts and Crafts movement were superseded by French impressionism. Whitman's work came to be viewed as old-fashioned and of uneven quality, the result no doubt of her having undertaken too much in order to satisfy her patrons.

• A miscellaneous collection of Whitman's letters, recollections, and notes is in the Radcliffe College Archives, Schlesinger Library, Cambridge, Mass. Houghton Library at Harvard University has personal correspondence both to and from Whitman as well as business letters and advertisements of her work covering nearly twenty years. Letters that best reveal Whitman's personality are in the "Constantia" letters (1887–1902) in the Fonthill manuscripts at the Bucks County Historical Society, Doylestown, Pa., and in *Manibus O Date Lilia Plenis: Letters of Sarah Wyman Whitman* (1907), a posthumous tribute edited by Sarah Orne Jewett. Another collection of letters, located in the Archives of American Art, Smithsonian Institution (Reel D32), affirms the close friend ship between Whitman and Martin Brimmer, the first president of the Museum of Fine Arts Boston. Whitman's approach to art and her work can best be described in "William Morris Hunt," *International Review*, Apr. 1880, pp. 389–401, her emotional tribute to her late teacher; "Stained Glass," *Handicraft*, Sept. 1903, pp. 117–31; "Cups," *Handicraft*, June 1902, pp. 57–60; "The Memorial Windows at Trinity Church," *Church Militant*, Jan. 1901, pp. 8–12–16; and *Notes on an Informal Talk on Book Illustration Inside and Out . . .* (1894). Her concern for art education is discussed in *Notes of Three Composition Class Criticisms by Mrs. Henry Whitman, Mr. Arthur Dow, and Mr. I. M. Gaugengigi* (Boston Art Students Association, 1893); *The Making of Pictures: Twelve Short Talks with Young People* (1886); and "The Pursuit of Art in America," *International Review*, Jan. 1882, pp. 10–17. Martha J. Hoppin, "Women Artists in Boston, 1870–1900: The Pupils of William Morris Hunt," *American Art Journal* 13, no. 1 (Winter 1981): 17–46, is a significant source of information about the careers of Hunt's pupils. John Chapman, "Mrs. Whitman," in *Memories and Milestones* (1915), is an effusive essay that attempts to capture Whitman's personality. The stained glass windows in Memorial Hall at Harvard University caught the attention of Annie Fields, "Notes on Glass Decoration," *Atlantic Monthly*, June 1899, pp. 807–11, and Mason Hammond, *The Stained Glass Windows in Memorial Hall, Harvard University* (1978; rev. ed., 1983). Obituaries are in the *Boston Sunday Herald*, 26 June 1904, and the *Boston Evening Transcript*, 27 June 1904. The record of the memorial service held at the Beverly Farms Baptist Church on 17 July 1904 was published by Merrymount Press, Boston. The Women's Auxiliary of the Massachusetts Civil Service Reform Association (July 1904), the Public School Art League (Nov. 1904), the Museum of Fine Arts *Bulletin* (Sept. 1904), and the *American Art Annual* (1905–1906) were among the organizations that formally recognized her passing.

BETTY S. SMITH

WHITMAN, Sarah Helen (19 Jan. 1803–27 June 1878), writer and spiritualist, was born Sarah Helen Power in Providence, Rhode Island, the daughter of Nicholas Power, a prosperous merchant, and Anna Marsh. Her father, bankrupted by the adverse commercial consequences of the War of 1812, sailed in 1813 for North Carolina and the West Indies and was captured by the British. When released in 1815 he continued his life at sea until he returned home after a nineteen-year absence. Meanwhile, Sarah Power read widely as a child, lived with an aunt in Jamaica, Long Island, and attended a Quaker school there. On returning to Providence, she was placed in a private school where she learned to read French, German, and Italian and began to write poetry. In 1828 she married John Winslow Whitman, a well-connected Boston lawyer who was more active as coeditor of the *Bachelors' Journal* and the *Boston Spectator and Ladies' Album*. He also wrote gloomy verse and prose. The couple, who had no children, lived in Boston until his death in 1833.

Helen Whitman, as she preferred to be called, moved back to her family home in Providence, in which she lived with her domineering mother and which she made her residence for the rest of her life. Initially through her husband's editorial work, then later by herself, she became friendly with many members of the Boston, Providence, and New York City literati. They included Bronson Alcott, the reformer; Sarah Josepha Buell Hale, the editor and author; John Hay, then a Brown College student; Ralph Waldo Emerson; Anne Charlotte Lynch, the New York hostess and from 1855 the wife of Vincenzo Botta, a professor of Italian at New York University; Frances Sargent Locke Osgood, the poet; and John Neal, the lawyer, novelist, and editor. In 1829 Whitman published "Retrospection," her first poem, in *Ladies' Magazine*, edited by Sarah Hale. Thereafter, she steadily placed her verses in various women's magazines and gift books. She also wrote critical essays in praise of Emerson, Goethe, and Shelley as well as scholarly articles on religion and aspects of modern European literature. Her writings on spiritualism, appearing in the *New York Tribune* in 1851, caused much interest. For upward of forty years, Whitman maintained a literary salon frequented by important persons and made attractive by her charming appearance and stimulating conversation. From the security of a well-appointed home, she expressed her advocacy of communal living, educational reforms, free love, individual development and perfectibility, the values of mesmerism and mysticism, women's rights, and universal salvation.

Whitman's first collection of verse, titled *Hours of Life, and Other Poems*, appeared in 1853. Representative poems in it are "A Still Day in Autumn," "On a Statue of David," "Evening on the Mooshaussuck," and "The Past." All are gentle and sincere but unoriginal in content and style and not very daring. Thus, autumnal birds "[f]lit noiselessly along from spray to spray, / Silent as a sweet, wandering thought." David, at the climax of his challenge, "[g]lorying, . . . met the foe and won the immortal fight." The Mooshaussuck River's "silver tide / Reflects each green herb on its side." And the poet's past is replete with "bridal memories, long affied [i.e., betrothed] / To the dread silence of the tomb." She also included a few sonnets inspired by Elizabeth Barrett Browning and some earnest but uninspiring translations from German poets. Her contemporary popularity is indicated by the frequent reappearance of her best verse in anthologies edited by such respected men of letters as Rufus Wilmot Griswold, Evert Augustus Duyckinck and his brother George Long Duyckinck, Thomas Buchanan Read, and John Greenleaf Whittier. Her complete *Poems* (1879) added to her popularity but without displaying either new subject matter or innovative techniques.

Whitman is now remembered almost solely because of her friendship with Edgar Allan Poe. He was born on her birthday, six years later, and she was pleased that her maiden name, Power, contained all three letters of his last name. He was intrigued by her poetry and first saw her from a distance in Providence in 1845. Early in 1848, a year after his wife Virginia Clemm Poe died, Whitman addressed an unsigned poetic valentine to him (published anonymously in *New York Home Journal*, 18 Mar. 1848). Learning her identity, Poe responded by composing and privately sending her an unsigned copy of his "To—— —— ——." This poem, now called his second "To Helen" (to distinguish it from his 1831 poem titled "To Helen"), begins: "I saw thee once—once only—years ago." On 10 July he praised her poetry in his lecture "The Poets and Poetry of America." In the 29 July *New York Home Journal* her "Stanzas" (later titled "A Night in August") respond to his second "To Helen." The two then first met in Providence in September 1848. He proposed marriage later that month, but she declined. He published his second "To Helen" in the *Union Magazine* (Nov. 1848). She accepted his renewed proposal in November on condition that he stop drinking. But then, after agreeing in December to an immediate marriage, she rejected him a final time, because her mother disapproved of him and controlled the family finances. Although Whitman never saw Poe again after they parted on 23 December 1848, she addressed veiled expressions of devotion and hope to him in "Stanzas for Music" (*American Metropolitan Magazine*, Feb. 1849, retitled "Our Island of Dreams" in 1853) and in "Lines" (*Southern Literary Messenger*, June 1849). Poe died in October 1849.

For the rest of her life, Whitman vigorously defended Poe's reputation. Her "Lines" (*Graham's Magazine*, Nov. 1849, retitled "The Last Flowers" in 1853) memorialize his September proposal in a cemetery overlooking the Seekonk River in Providence and her rejection of him—once "the bright veil of phantasy was riven." She always considered Poe's "Annabel Lee" (*Southern Literary Messenger*, Nov. 1849) to be addressed to her despite Poe's calling its heroine a child and a maiden and also despite other claimants to the honor. When Griswold and others undertook to besmirch Poe's posthumous reputation, Whitman published *Edgar Poe and His Critics* (1860), a short but scholarly and perceptive defense. She also generously corresponded with more able scholars, most conscientiously with the British biographer John Henry Ingram, who were eager to explain Poe's personality and praise his extraordinary literary accomplishments. Whitman, whose mother died in 1858, died in Providence.

• Whitman's papers are in the Lilly Library, Indiana University, and the John Hay Library, Brown University. An early biography is Caroline Ticknor, *Poe's Helen* (1916). John Grier Varner, "Sarah Helen Whitman, Seeress of Providence" (Ph.D. diss., Univ. of Virginia, 1940), is a definitive biographical and critical study. Detailed treatments of Poe's relationship to Whitman and of her help to John Henry Ingram are John Carl Miller, *Building Poe Biography* (1977), and Miller, ed., *Poe's Helen Remembers* (1979). Howard Kerr, *Mediums, and Spirit-Rappers, and Roaring Radicals: Spiritualism in American Literature, 1850–1900* (1972), relates Whitman and Poe to the phenomenon of spiritualism. Emily Stipes Watts, *The Poetry of American Women from 1632 to 1945* (1977), criticizes Whitman's poetry for being too derivative of that of Poe and William Cullen Bryant in subject, theme, and diction. Jamie Kageleiry and Christine Schultz, "Quoth the Mother-in-law, 'Nevermore,'" *Yankee* 58 (Feb. 1994): 31, amusingly describe the Poe-Whitman romance and its being discouraged by Whitman's purse-proud mother. An obituary is in the *Providence Daily Journal*, 1 July 1878.

ROBERT L. GALE

WHITMAN, Walt (31 May 1819–26 Mar. 1892), poet, was born at West Hills in the town of Huntington, Long Island, the son of Walter Whitman, a carpenter and farmer, and Louisa Van Velsor. His ancestry was English and Dutch, mixed with Quaker stock. The second of eight surviving children, Whitman grew up in Huntington and Brooklyn, where his family moved when the poet was four years old and where his father was an unsuccessful house builder. Whitman received only an elementary school education and at the age of eleven was apprenticed first to a lawyer as a clerk and then to a printer from whom he learned that trade and was introduced to journalism. Between ages sixteen and twenty-one, he returned to the country hamlets of Long Island and taught school.

In 1841 he moved to New York City, working initially as a printer but ultimately as a journalist. His first important post was as editor of the *New York Aurora* in 1842. Throughout the 1840s he worked for more than a dozen New York City newspapers, including the *Brooklyn Daily Eagle*, where he was editor between 1846 and 1848. He also wrote and published many short stories and poems, conventional in concept and revealing little of what was to come in his literary career. Many of his short stories appeared in the *United States Magazine and Democratic Review*, which also published such writers as Nathaniel Hawthorne and Edgar Allan Poe. His longer prose included two temperance tracts, though one exists today only in fragments (and indeed may have never been completed). The other, *Franklin Evans; or the Inebriate* (1842), was a 60,000-word novel that was serialized in the fashionable *New World* and is said to have sold more than 20,000 copies. Whitman finished out the decade by working for the *New Orleans Crescent* in 1848; becoming founding editor of the *Brooklyn Freeman*, a "free soil" antislavery organ, in 1849; and writing for the *Daily Advertiser* in 1850.

Whitman may have had to quit the *Crescent* because of his moderate antislavery views. His position at the *Eagle* was abruptly terminated in part because of his disagreement with the newspaper's owners over the wisdom of the Wilmot Proviso, which stated that all territories had to be admitted into the Union as free soil states. The fact that he started a free soil paper in 1849 reinforces the conclusion that Whitman left his New Orleans post partly for political reasons. Generally, Whitman's position on slavery was that it was an evil, but so long as the Constitution made it legal, he believed that fugitive slave laws should be obeyed. He stated his views on slavery in a quasi-political treatise called *The Eighteenth Presidency!* written between 1854 and 1856; although it was put into proof sheets, it was never published in Whitman's lifetime. In his optimism for the power of American democracy, he hoped that the American people would voluntarily give up slavery rather than lose it through civil war.

Whitman is best known for *Leaves of Grass* (1855), a book of poems that went through six official editions and several more issues during his lifetime. He is considered America's Dante or its Homer because these poems present an epic of American life at mid–nineteenth century; they also set the standard for modern American poetry by introducing "free verse." Instead of poetry in the conventional meter of an artificial rhythm (e.g., iambic pentameter), Whitman's rhythm reflects the speech patterns and verbal pace of Americans and American life. The closest parallel in English literature is the "sprung rhythm" of Gerard Manley Hopkins. This comparison to the British poet, who was also a Jesuit priest, ends, however, with their similarity in experimental metrics.

Whitman's central theme is that the body is as good as the soul and that all of its parts and sexual acts are worthy of poetic celebration. His poems, especially the one ultimately titled "Song of Myself," focused the poetic eye for the first time on the common people as they pursued their daily occupations and dreams. Inspired by the writings of Ralph Waldo Emerson ("I was simmering, simmering, simmering," the poet is alleged to have declared, "Emerson brought me to a boil"), many of the poems in *Leaves of Grass* extend Emerson's proclamation in *Nature* (1836) that nature is the emblem of the soul and, hence, God. Rather than an emblem in the Kantian sense, nature in Whitman's estimate is the equal of the soul, and as a result all that comes under its rubric is a fit subject for poetry. Whitman was controversial throughout his lifetime because of *Leaves of Grass*, which was said by the critic E. P. Whipple to have every leaf except the fig leaf.

When Emerson first read *Leaves of Grass* in the summer of 1855, he wrote Whitman: "I greet you at the beginning of a great career, which must have had a long foreground somewhere, for such a start." That foreground is still largely a mystery to scholars, but what is known about Whitman in the decade preceding the publication of the first edition of *Leaves of Grass* is based largely on what the poet wrote about himself in diaries, newspaper articles, and autobiographical essays. It is not known, however, exactly when Whitman changed from a poet of conventional verse forms into the author of the strikingly original *Leaves of Grass*. One influence was the opera, especially Italian opera, which Whitman attended regularly in the 1840s and 1850s; it showed him the value of the human voice unfettered by rhyme and meter. Another influence was the King James Bible; its rhythms also suggested the need for more freedom in poetry. Because an important part of his literary message owes a debt to Emerson, scholars have pointed out that the young Whitman first heard Emerson deliver an early version of "The Poet" (1844) in 1842 in New York City. Whitman also speaks of having read Emerson's "Spiritual Laws" in 1848. Other sources suggest 1852 as the year Whitman began writing *Leaves of Grass* in earnest, but his own testimony suggests that he wrote most of the 1855 volume in 1854 and 1855. Whitman's activities during this period are poorly documented. Basically all that is known is that the poet operated a printing office and a bookstore in Brooklyn and speculated on the construction of houses there.

Legend has it that Whitman published the first edition of his book on 4 July 1855, as if to declare his independence from the literary conventions of his day, but the available evidence suggests that he issued the book on 5 July, having set much of the type for the text himself. The book, a thin quarto of ninety pages, was elaborately decorated in green with flowers and foliage, following (as historians later discovered) a trend in books of that period. It contained twelve untitled poems under the *Leaves of Grass* umbrella title, which alludes to the leaves of a book and the grass, which as part of nature was both democratic ("growing among black folks as among white") and divine ("a uniform hieroglyphic," or emblem, as all nature is in the transcendentalist belief of God). The longest and most important poem in the volume was "Song of Myself." Later divided into fifty-two sections, it opens with a celebration of the poet as representative of all humankind: "I celebrate myself, and sing myself, / And what I assume you shall assume, / For every atom belonging to me as good belongs to you." As these lines suggest, Whitman was breaking not only poetic conventions but grammatical ones as well (with the use of an adjective for an adverb in the third line). He believed that poetry was no longer to be found only in palaces and universities but in the workplaces of America and in the vernacular of its common people. As he wrote in his 1855 preface, "The Americans of all nations at any time upon the earth have probably the fullest poetic nature," and "the United States themselves are essentially the greatest poem." The key word in "Song of Myself" and the whole of the first edition is freedom—"nature without check with original energy." As emblems of God, all nature is good and will do good as long as it has the freedom to do so. Later Whitman was to modify this doctrine, but throughout his life he subscribed generally to this transcendentalist doctrine. The other great poems of the first edition are (as Whitman eventually titled them) "The Sleepers," "I Sing the Body Electric," and "There Was a Child Went Forth."

Whitman followed up this first edition the next year with an expanded one containing thirty-two poems, including the original twelve of 1855. Like the first, it was privately published, but it also had—like the first—the secret backing of the phrenological firm of Fowler and Wells. Whitman believed in phrenology to the extent that the movement encouraged good personal hygiene and physical exercise, because he saw a healthy body as the signature of a healthy soul. The second edition is viewed as something of a curiosity in the Whitman canon, not only for the awkward titles given to each poem, but for the fact that he adorned the spine of the volume with a phrase from Emerson's private letter to him ("I greet you at the beginning of a great career. R. W. Emerson"), making the New England bard ipso facto the endorser of a book of poems he had read only partially. Whitman also included an open letter to the "Master," thanking Emerson for his inspiration, and this set off a scandal of sorts among New England literati who could not accept the possibility that Emerson might endorse a poet whose poetry seemed like prose and whose themes were hardly material for the standard of the "evening lamp" or reading material for the family circle. The most important poem in the edition, however, remains among the poet's most admired: "Sun-Down Poem," later called "Crossing Brooklyn Ferry," which transcends time and space to give readers over the decades the sense that the poet is looking over their shoulders as they read.

Neither the 1855 nor the 1856 edition sold very well. Whitman realized the need for promoting a book, but his unauthorized quotations from the Emerson letter backfired. For the first edition, he even wrote three anonymous reviews of his book. These were the tricks of a journalist, a profession to which Whitman returned after publishing his second edition. He continued writing poems until 1857, when he became the editor of the *Brooklyn Times*, the last regular position he was to hold on a newspaper, and kept this position until 1859, when he was dismissed for an editorial he wrote calling for more sexual freedom for women. Whitman was the first American poet to call for the equality of men and women, though he valued mothers most of all and expected women to fulfill their maternal obligations. Even more important to him was sexuality, which he thought was hidden away from polite society as if it were sinful instead of the source of "nimbler babes," as he wrote in "Song of Myself." Something of a eugenicist, he later complained about the corsets that forced women's bodies into hourglass shapes, sometimes cracking ribs and often endangering their fecundity.

Documents from the late 1850s and certain poems in the third edition of *Leaves of Grass* (1860) suggest that Whitman underwent an emotional crisis in the years immediately preceding the Civil War. Today, more than a few critics suspect that Whitman was a homosexual, though there is no documentary evidence to support this claim. The idea is based mainly on inference from reading the "Calamus" poems, which were among the many new poems in the third edition, which contained 146 poems, including the thirty-two of the second edition that were revised, some extensively. In "Calamus" Whitman allegedly tells the "secret of [his] nights and days" seeking lovers. This volume also introduced the "Infans d'Adam" poems (afterward called "Children of Adam"), which celebrated heterosexual love, or sex often outside of matrimony; but "Calamus" focused on the "need for comrades." Whitman was probably celebrating the romantic concept of male friendship. Yet there is a strong emotional element in these sonnet-like poems suggesting the possibility of something more. Furthermore, the calamus root, a large aromatic root, has a phallic shape. When asked directly whether these poems celebrated homosexuality, however, Whitman vehemently denied it and claimed to have sired six illegimate children. Curiously, it was the "Children of Adam" poems that caused so much controversy in Whitman's lifetime and kept him from membership in the literary establishment of the day (though one wonders whether Whitman would have wanted membership), not the "Calamus" poems, which focused perhaps on the love that had yet to "speak its name" in the nineteenth century. Whitman never married.

The third edition of *Leaves of Grass* was the first to have a publisher other than the poet himself, the Boston firm of Thayer and Eldridge whose catalog contained mainly antislavery tracts. The edition is Whitman's most famous after the first and contains some of his greatest poems, including (using final titles) "Starting from Paumanok" and "Out of the Cradle Endlessly Rocking." The first of these is a more literal rendering of the spiritual autobiography in "Song of Myself" (paumanok is the American Indian term for "fish-shaped," referring to Long Island). The second was originally titled "A Child's Reminiscence" in the volume (it had yet another title in an 1859 magazine publication) because it is a meditation on lost innocence as it is realized at midlife ("A man, yet by these tears a little boy again"). The poet comes to realize that the freedom celebrated in his first edition and in "Song of Myself" is not altogether consistent with a way of coping with life's essential imperfection and that the duty of the poet is thus to sing of Love and Death, the common denominators of such imperfection. In a real sense, this poem about a man in crisis at midlife also suggests the crisis of poetry, that is, the power of its romantic illusions to overcome completely the fear of death.

Whitman had written his best poetry by 1860 and would never—with one exception—reach that poetic height again. Soon after the publication of the third edition, the Civil War broke out and essentially deprived the volume of a reasonable sale. Whitman's books would not sell well until the banning of his sixth edition in 1882 (discussed below), and in the case of the third edition of *Leaves of Grass*, the publisher also went bankrupt. The first two years of the war are fairly blank in the Whitman biography, but he surfaces again in the fall of 1862. His younger brother, George Washington Whitman, an officer in the Fifty-first Regiment of New York Volunteers, was reported in the New York papers to have been seriously wounded in the battle of Fredericksburg in December 1862. Whitman was dispatched to Washington, D.C., by anxious family members in Brooklyn to search for his brother in the more than forty wartime hospitals. Failing to find George there, he went to the battle site to find his brother only slightly wounded. He remained in camp with his brother's regiment for more than a week and then returned to the nation's capital, escorting a group of seriously wounded and dying soldiers. Once at his destination, he felt he could not return to civilian life in New York. He remained in Washington throughout the war and beyond, worked at various government jobs, and devoted himself to cheering up sick and wounded soldiers in the hospitals. This unselfish service earned him the titles of "wound dresser" and "the Good Gray Poet," but no government pension (which Whitman later said he would have refused anyway).

In January 1865 Whitman was appointed a clerk in the Indian Affairs Department in Washington. By spring, not long after the assassination of President Abraham Lincoln, he was fired from his government post on the orders of Secretary of the Interior James Harlan. The charge was that Whitman was the author of a "dirty book," *Leaves of Grass*. Actually, Whitman's dismissal was part of an efficiency campaign, but Harlan, formerly a professor of mental and moral science in Iowa, also objected strongly to Whitman's emphasis on the body in his poetry. Whitman was hired the next day, through the influence of his friend and fellow government worker William Douglas O'Connor, as a clerk in the attorney general's office, but this did not deter the fiery O'Connor (also a writer of short fiction and one antislavery novel) from penning his polemical 46-page pamphlet titled *The Good Gray Poet* (1866). Not only did O'Connor denounce Harlan as "Cato the Censor" and argue for the freedom of American letters, he also created the legend of Whitman as somewhat larger than life—an image embellished at the turn of the century by the poet's disciples, who viewed him as more of a prophet than a great poet. O'Connor later reinforced this impression in his short story, "The Carpenter" (1868), which features Whitman as a nineteenth-century Christ figure.

Although Whitman himself never publicly encouraged this kind of hero worship, his poetry and activities during the war as a psychological "nurse" to soldiers tended to support this picture. Many critics have pointed to the similarity of parts of "Song of Myself" with the Sermon on the Mount; moreover, the picture in that poem of the narrator washing the feet of the fugitive slave is similar to Christ's washing the feet of the apostles, and "To a Common Prostitute" recalls the encounter between Christ and Mary Magdalen. Yet an even more direct rendering of the Christ parallel is to be found in his wartime poems, *Drum-Taps* (1865), written throughout the war. The earlier ones, such as "First O Songs for a Prelude" and "Beat! Beat! Drums!" suggest the excitement felt by those on both sides of the conflict who believed the war would be won within months instead of years. As the war and the killing progressed and the nation felt the burden of its terrible losses, *Drum-Taps* took on a poignancy unparalleled in any other Civil War poems, including Herman Melville's *Battle-Pieces* (1865). Because Whitman had visited two battle sites immediately after their ceasefires (Chancellorsville and Fredericksburg) and had lived with the soldiers and witnessed the consequences of battle for several years, he was in a unique position to poeticize what he had seen. In "Vigil Strange I Kept on the Field One Night," the poet imagines himself speeding into battle, but the story line quickly gives way to the pathos of losing a "dear comrade." In "A Sight in Camp in the Daybreak Gray and Dim," that young soldier reveals "the face of the Christ himself, / Dead and divine and brother of all, and here again he lies."

Drum-Taps represents yet another shift in Whitman's poetry. In the first two editions, the focus was on the self and its transcendent powers; in the third edition—with such seashore poems as "Out of the Cradle" and "As I Ebb'd with the Ocean of Life"—the poet exchanged the representative ego for a recognition that life has its human limits that the poet must also celebrate, somehow exorcising the bad from the good. In his third phase, he shifts the attention from the self of the first editions to the Christ figure in others. This is brought to its richest fruition in Whitman's elegy for Lincoln, "When Lilacs Last in the Dooryard Bloom'd." What is remarkable about the poem is its revitalization of Whitman's original powers as a poet.

Drum-Taps, of course, stands among the nation's finest poems; yet in Whitman's canon the volume must take second place to the poems of the first three editions because the war poems lack the originality, intimacy, and spontaneity of such poems as "Song of Myself," "The Sleepers," "Crossing Brooklyn Ferry," the "Calamus" poems, and "Out of the Cradle." "Lilacs," however, recaptured these qualities by celebrating the plurality of the personal; out of the multifaceted figure of the slain president had come the rebirth of Lincoln enshrined as a symbol of America's greatness. This was but one of four poems Whitman wrote in honor of Lincoln; another, "O Captain! My Captain," was Whitman's only poem that was popular during his lifetime. When Lincoln was assassinated, Whitman withdrew *Drum-Taps* and added the Lincoln poems and fourteen others under the title *Sequel to Drum-Taps*.

With the war over, Whitman began to think of posterity, and to this end he persuaded the future naturalist John Burroughs to write *Walt Whitman as Poet and Person* (1867). He also began to rearrange his life's poetry in future editions, beginning with the 1867 or fourth and carrying through with the 1871 and 1881 editions, the last of which Whitman named as his definitive arrangement. He revised extensively and continued to write minor poems. The major additions to his canon during the last decades of his life are probably only "Proud Music of the Storm" and "Passage to India," which signal the final shift in the poet's theme—celebrating the spirit more than the flesh, or nature as a means of transcendence. The theme of "Proud Music of the Storm" is that poetry should discover a "new rhythmus" by "bridging the way from Life to Death." Earlier, Whitman had made poems out of the earth, so to speak; at this time of his life he sensed the overwhelming spirituality of the body he once held up as equal to the soul. The poet hears in sounds of sea and prairie storms "the hidden orchestras" that blend "with Nature's rhythmus all the tongues of nations." The ultimate unity of humankind suggests a return to its source in the mind of God. Not only do storms suggest this destiny, but technological facts do as well. In "Passage to India," the Suez Canal, the transcontinental railroad, and the transatlantic cable suggest a "passage to more than India!"

In 1873 Whitman suffered the first of a series of paralytic strokes. He moved to Camden, New Jersey, to live with his brother George and eventually lost his government job. In 1874 he published "Prayer of Columbus" in *Harper's Magazine*. Critics have seen Whitman's self-portrait in the description of Columbus at the end of his days as "A batter'd, wreck'd old man." He was afraid his poetry was being forgotten, and ever ready to promote himself and *Leaves of Grass*, in 1876 he planted an anonymous story in the *West-Jersey Press* that eventually touched off an Anglo-American debate, with the British accusing the Americans of ignoring their greatest poet. The exchange strengthened Whitman's reputation in England, where the poet and critic William Michael Rossetti had already published an expurgated edition of *Leaves of Grass* in 1868. Whitman's book was back in the national headlines in 1882 when the sixth American edition of *Leaves of Grass* was essentially "banned in Boston" (the first book to win that dubious honor). The Boston district attorney deemed much of the edition (containing such poems as "To a Common Prostitute" and "A Woman Waits for Me") pornographic and demanded excisions, which Whitman refused. There was even an attempt during the public debate, by vice hunter Anthony Comstock, to make it illegal to send Whitman's book through the U.S. mails. Whitman withdrew the book from his Boston publisher, only the second in the life of *Leaves of Grass*, and had the volume republished in Philadelphia, where, with sales fueled by the scandals, he reaped significant royalties for the first time.

After the war Whitman also turned to prose. *Democratic Vistas* (1871), initially a response to Thomas Carlyle's attack on democracy in the essay "Shooting Niagara: And After?" ultimately expressed the fear that America was becoming too materialistic and less spiritual; the theme reflected in part the scandals of the Ulysses S. Grant administration. *Specimen Days and Collect* (1882) contains autobiographical essays, reminiscences of the war, and a lifetime of miscellany. Besides new books and essays, he also published three supplements to *Leaves of Grass*. His reputation grew during his last years from uncouth poet to national curiosity, drawing in many admirers, including not a few eccentrics. Women wrote the aged and partially paralyzed poet, offering to have his child. The Canadian psychiatrist and theosophist Richard Maurice Bucke became the poet's first official biographer, publishing *Walt Whitman* (heavily revised by its subject) in 1883. Socialists such as Horace Traubel became his devoted disciples. The Englishwoman Anne Gilchrist uprooted her home and family and moved to Philadelphia to be near Whitman, whom she wanted to marry. When his brother moved away from Camden in 1884, Whitman purchased (with the profits from the Boston edition of his book) a small row house in the same working-class neighborhood in which he had lived since 1873. During his life in Camden, he received many visitors from both sides of the Atlantic, among them Oscar Wilde, Lord Houghton, Edmund Gosse, Henry Wadsworth Longfellow, and the painter Thomas Eakins. A Whitman fellowship was formed near the end of the poet's life, holding an annual birthday banquet even when the poet was too sick to attend. When he died in Camden, the fellowship published various editions of his work until it finally caught the attention of more objective critics and admirers, leading to Whitman's reputation, a century after his death, as one of the greatest American poets and the central one in terms of influence on twentieth-century American poetry.

• The bulk of Whitman's manuscripts and personal papers are in the Library of Congress and the special collections of the libraries of Duke University and Yale University. Richard Maurice Bucke et al., eds., *The Complete Writings of Walt Whitman* (1902), has been superseded by the series edited by Gay W. Allen and Sculley Bradley, *The Collected Writings of Walt Whitman* (1963–1984), comprised of Edwin H. Miller, ed., *The Correspondence* (6 vols., 1963–1977); Thomas L. Brasher, ed., *The Early Poems and the Fiction* (1963); Floyd Stovall, ed., *Prose Works 1892* (2 vols., 1963–1964); Harold W. Blodgett and Bradley, eds., *Leaves of Grass: Comprehensive Reader's Edition* (1965); William White, ed., *Daybooks and Notebooks* (3 vols., 1978); Arthur Golden et al., *A Textual Variorum of the Printed Poems* (3 vols., 1980); and Edward F. Grier, ed., *Notebooks and Unpublished Prose Manuscripts* (6 vols., 1984). Neither a comprehensive bibliography nor a volume on the poet's journalism is available; however, his career as a journalist is discussed in White, "Walt Whitman's Journalism: A Bibliography," *Walt Whitman Review* 14 (Sept. 1968): 67–141. For a general bibliography see Scott Giantvalley, ed., *Walt Whitman, 1838–1939: A Reference Guide* (1981); Donald D. Kummings, ed., *Walt Whitman, 1940–1975: A Reference Guide*; and the *Walt Whitman Quarterly Review*. The only concordance of Whitman's writings not keyed to *The Collected Writings of Walt Whitman* is Edwin H. Eby, ed., *A Concordance of Walt Whitman's "Leaves of Grass" and Selected Prose Writings* (5 pts., 1955).

Also see (listed chronologically) Cleveland Rodgers and John Black, eds., *The Gathering of the Forces* (2 vols., 1920); Emory Holloway, ed., *Uncollected Poetry and Prose of Walt Whitman* (2 vols., 1921); Clifton J. Furness, ed., *Walt Whitman's Workshop* (1928); Holloway and Vernolian Schwarz, eds., *I Sit and Look Out* (1932); Charles I. Glicksberg, ed., *Walt Whitman and the Civil War* (1933); Holloway and Ralph Adimari, eds., *New York Dissected* (1936); Clarence Gohdes and Rollo G. Silver, eds., *Faint Clews & Indirections* (1949); Joseph J. Rubin and Charles H. Brown, eds., *Walt Whitman of the New York Aurora* (1950); Jerome Loving, ed., *Civil War Letters of George Washington Whitman* (1975); Randall H. Waldron, ed., *Mattie* (1977); Loving, *Walt Whitman's Champion* (1978); and Dennis Berthold and Kenneth M. Price, eds., *Dear Brother Walt* (1984).

More than twenty biographies of Whitman have been published, beginning with Bucke, *Walt Whitman* (1883), through Philip Callow, *From Noon to Starry Night* (1992). The most comprehensive to date is Gay W. Allen, *The Solitary Singer* (1955); also see Roger Asselineau, *The Evolution of Walt Whitman* (2 vols., 1960, 1962), and Justin Kaplan, *Walt Whitman: A Life* (1980). Obituaries are in the *New York Herald*, the *New York Sun*, and the *New York Times*, all 27 Mar. 1892.

JEROME LOVING

WHITMAN SISTERS, a vaudeville team, was formed by the daughters of Albert A. Whitman, who served as bishop of the Methodist church in Lawrence, Kansas, and Atlanta, Georgia, and as dean of Morris Brown College in Atlanta. Mabel Whitman (c. 1880–1942), the eldest sister, was a singer who also handled bookings and managed the company. Essie Barbara Whitman (1881–7 May 1963) was a singer and comedian who designed and made costumes. Alberta Whitman (c. 1888–1964) was a singer, dancer, and comedian who composed music and acted as financial secretary. In their youth, the three sisters traveled with their father and sang in the churches where he preached. They received their music education through private study, at Morris Brown College, and at the New England Conservatory in Boston. Mabel and Essie performed professionally in the 1890s as the Daznette Sisters. When Alberta joined the act, they changed its name to the Whitman Sisters Company and toured the United States and Europe as jubilee singers. According to several sources, their mother and aunt (whose names are unknown) also sang with this company. In 1904, the sisters reorganized the company as the Whitman Sisters' New Orleans Troubadours, a vaudeville performing troupe, and launched themselves into show business careers, whereupon it appears that the Reverend Whitman disowned them.

After the death of the sisters' mother, about 1909, Alice Whitman (c. 1900–1970) was introduced into the family act as "Baby Alice"; and the troupe was then expanded into a production revue called simply the

Whitman Sisters. However, according to Clyde E. B. Bernhardt, who traveled with the Whitman Sisters show, "Alice was not a Whitman sister at all. They [were] billed as sisters, but Alice was actually Essie's daughter. I can tell that now because they all passed" (Bernhardt, 1986). Alice, a gifted singer and versatile dancer, became the show's dancing star and major attraction.

Although the sisters were fair-skinned and blonde—and claimed to be cousins of the renowned poet Walt Whitman—they were acclaimed as the "Royalty of Negro Vaudeville." During the 1920s and 1930s, the company played every major vaudeville house in the United States and Europe and was the leading attraction on the Theater Owners' Booking Association (TOBA) circuit. The two-hour production, which was revised every six weeks, was performed as a daily matinee and two nightly shows. The style of the show included a minstrel repertory with a fashion-modeling segment. At its peak, the troupe consisted of an eight-piece band, thirty-five performers, who were singers, dancers, and comedians, and a chorus line that featured Alice. Alberta composed the music and starred as a male impersonator, becoming famous as a high-stepping strutter. Essie, who played the role of an inebriated high-society woman, was famous for belting out "Some of These Days" in a powerful contralto. Mabel, who originally sang and played piano, became the only African-American woman to manage her own company at that time.

The Whitman Sisters show served as a training ground for many of the great African-American tap dancers. Alice's tapping style was thus influenced by many male dancers, including Bill Robinson, Eddie Rector, the Berry Brothers, Aaron Palmer, Bunny Briggs, the legendary dancer known as Groundhog, and Joe Jones of the Three Little Words. Billed as "Queen of Taps," Alice Whitman achieved a balance between strong tap technique and the accepted standards of femininity and became one of the first women to gain prominence in the male-dominated field of tap dance.

Alice was known as a great comedienne and a terrific time dancer. Her dance styles ranged from buck dancing, buck-and-wing, and rhythm tap to sand dancing, the cakewalk, and song and dance. She performed vernacular dances such as Ballin' the Jack, Walkin' the Dog, the Charleston, and the Shim-Sham-Shimmy. Many of Alice's routines were similar to those of Bill Robinson—in particular, the "Stair Dance." She was considered to be one of the best women tap dancers in the country; her tap work was clear and clean and equaled the work of the best male tap dancers, though her movements maintained a feminine style. She was flirtatious and alluring, emitting squealing noises as she danced and using shimmying movements that were sexually suggestive. She usually wore costumes consisting of flimsy, short dresses with fringe and bows that accentuated her movements. Alice and Alberta had a routine in which Alberta performed as "Bert," dressed in a man's striped jacket, pants, and shoes and wearing her hair cut short and slicked back; Alice wore a gown of satin and lace with a floppy, wide-brimmed summer hat. They sang songs such as "It Had to Be You" as they strolled about the stage and danced in a close embrace. They made a thoroughly convincing male-female couple.

In 1919, Alice married Aaron Palmer, who performed with the Whitman Sisters from 1910 until 1922, when the couple apparently separated. Wearing top hat and tails, Palmer had an act in which he sang, strutted, and performed a ballroom style of tap dance. In 1919, Alice gave birth to Albert Palmer, her only child, who performed under the stage name Pops Whitman from age four until his death in 1950. "Pops" performed in many partner acts, the most notable of which was "Pops and Louie," in which he was paired with Louis Williams.

After the Whitman Sisters disbanded in the 1930s, Alice performed in theater revues and nightclub shows, such as *Hot Chocolates of 1935* at Connie's Inn in New York City. Mabel toured and managed Pops and Louie until her death in 1942. During the 1920s, Essie maintained a Chicago residence while making costumes for the company and taking on occasional two-week engagements. In 1933, she retired from show business and became an evangelist. Alice and Alberta later joined Essie in Chicago, where they used their home as headquarters for entertainers who had performed with their troupe. The Whitmans remained in Chicago until their deaths: Essie in 1963, Alberta in 1964, and Alice in 1970. All were buried in Atlanta.

• For additional information, see Clyde E. B. Bernhardt, as told to Sheldon Harris, *I Remember: Eighty Years of Black Entertainment, Big Bands, and the Blues* (1986); Rusty E. Frank, *Tap! The Greatest Tap Dance Stars and Their Stories, 1900–1955* (1955); Jack Schiffman, *Harlem Heyday: A Pictorial History of Modern Black Show Business and the Apollo Theatre* (1984); Eileen Southern, *The Greenwood Encyclopedia of Black Music: Biographical Dictionary of Afro-American and African Musicians* (1982); and Marshall Stearns and Jean Stearns, *Jazz Dance: The Story of American Vernacular Dance* (1968).

CHERYL M. WILLIS

WHITMER, David (7 Jan. 1805–25 Jan. 1888), early Mormon leader, was born near Harrisburg, Pennsylvania, the son of Peter Whitmer, Sr., and Mary Musselman, farmers. When David was four the family moved to a farm in Fayette, New York, in a region known as the "burnt-over district," so named because of the waves of religious revivalism that swept through the area in the first few decades of the nineteenth century. Many members of the Whitmer family were caught up in this religious fervor. An acquaintance, Reverend Diedrich Willers, wrote in 1830 that during the preceding nine years the Whitmers had been followers of, successively, "the Methodists, Reformers, Presbyterians, Mennonites, and Baptists" (*New York History*, July 1973, p. 333).

David Whitmer's connection with the Mormon prophet Joseph Smith began in June 1829. His friend

Oliver Cowdery, a young schoolteacher, had been serving as secretary to Smith during the transcription of the golden plates that Smith claimed he had unearthed from a hillside at the direction of the angel Moroni. Whitmer visited the two and witnessed Smith translating "by the gift and power of God," his face thrust in a hat containing his "seer stone." Impressed by the meeting as well as by Cowdery's report that Smith had described Whitmer's journey there in detail before he arrived, Whitmer invited Smith, Smith's wife Emma, and Cowdery to stay at the Whitmer farm, where the translation of the Book of Mormon was completed.

A special revelation given through Smith to Whitmer in that month suggested that he was marked out for a special role in the new movement: "And behold, thou art David, and thou art called to assist" (*Doctrine and Covenants*, sec. 14). This role was soon made clear: he was to be one of three special witnesses to the truthfulness of the revelation, along with Cowdery and Martin Harris, another early disciple. In the Testimony of Three Witnesses, prefacing every copy of the Book of Mormon since its original publication, the three men declare, "with words of soberness, that an angel of God came down from heaven, and he brought and laid before our eyes, that we beheld and saw the plates, and the engravings thereon." A local newspaper, the *Palmyra (N.Y.) Reflector* reported in March 1831 that the witnesses differed in their accounts of the experience. Whitmer himself originally claimed that the plates he saw were lying in an open field. Near the end of his life he claimed that he and the others had seen "as it were a table with many records or plates upon it, besides the plates of the Book of Mormon" (Brodie, p. 78).

The Mormon church (originally the Church of Christ, later the Church of Jesus Christ of Latter-Day Saints) was established in the Whitmer home on 6 April 1830, with David Whitmer and his brother Peter among the six founding members. Whitmer also was married in this year; the couple had two children. The church was relocated to Kirtland, Ohio, early in 1831 at the invitation of the former Campbellite preacher Sidney Rigdon. Whitmer was critical of the hold Rigdon came to possess over Smith but with his brothers followed the church to Ohio. The next move was to a settlement near Independence, Missouri, intended to be "Zion," or the new promised land. But the Mormons in Missouri were isolated and marginalized from the Kirtland community. Persecution was also intense in Missouri, and Whitmer led a militia group that on one occasion clashed violently with local settlers. Eventually driven from Jackson County, the group settled in nearby Clay County, where Whitmer was made stake president, or community head, in July 1834. In October he returned to Kirtland, where he and Cowdery selected the first Quorum of Twelve Apostles of the church. He was also a witness to the ecstatic pentecostal experience at the dedication of the Kirtland Temple in March 1836.

By the following year the church was threatened by a serious financial crisis and by mounting dissension. Whitmer for a time supported a seeress in Kirtland who prophesied using a seer stone, in opposition to Smith's exclusive authority. He was reconciled with Smith, but not wholeheartedly. Along with Cowdery and others, Whitmer returned to Missouri, where the new settlement of Far West, in Caldwell County, had been established. By December 1837 a movement had grown up in Kirtland, led by Warren Parrish, to overthrow Joseph Smith and replace him with Whitmer. When Smith and Sidney Rigdon fled to Far West in January 1838 as a result of the failure of the church's bank, confrontation with the "apostates" and dissenters soon followed. Whitmer, his brother John, Cowdery, and others were harassed by the "Danites," a secret Mormon vigilante group, and were warned to leave the county. On 13 April 1838 he was formally excommunicated.

After his expulsion Whitmer moved with his wife and children to Richmond, Missouri, and settled down to life as a businessman and civic leader. He owned a livery stable, served on fair boards, was a member of the city council, and was once elected mayor. In 1867 he was recruited by members of a Mormon splinter group to serve as elder of a revived Church of Christ. Another "Whitmerite" sect was headed by his brother John, with his support. A year before his death in Richmond he published a memoir, *An Address to All Believers in Christ*, in which he reaffirmed his witness to the Mormon revelation but set out his differences with the Latter-Day Saints (LDS) church and cataloged what he saw as Smith's errors, such as the introduction of the doctrine of plural marriage.

Although he never reconciled with the LDS church, Whitmer to the end of his life consistently reaffirmed his testimony regarding the golden plates and the revelation of the Book of Mormon. He is thus regarded by Mormons as an enduring witness to the genuineness of the prophet Joseph Smith and his message.

• Latter-Day Saints church materials pertaining to Whitmer and his role in the founding of the church include *History of the Church of Jesus Christ of Latter-Day Saints. Period I. History of Joseph Smith, the Prophet, by Himself* (1902–1912). A briefer account is contained in Joseph Fielding Smith, *Essentials in Church History* (1950). A work of the LDS church, *Doctrine and Covenants of the Church of Jesus Christ of Latter-Day Saints* (1921), contains revelations regarding Whitmer, accompanied by informative notes. Material on Whitmer from a perspective critical of Mormon origins is found in Fawn M. Brodie, *No Man Knows My History: The Life of Joseph Smith*, 2d ed. (1971).

MICHAEL J. LATZER

WHITMORE, Frank Clifford (1 Oct. 1887–24 June 1947), chemist and educator, was born in North Attleboro, Massachusetts, the son of Frank Hale Whitmore, a sewing machine salesman, and Lena Avila Thomas. The family moved first to Williamsport, Pennsylvania, and then to Atlantic City, New Jersey, where Whitmore attended elementary and high school. His mother introduced him to the works of William Shakespeare and classical literature, interests he retained throughout his life. In high school, where he enrolled in the Latin-Scientific course to prepare for college, he acquired the nickname of "Rocky Cliff" from his middle name, Clifford. This was shortened to "Rocky," the name by which his friends addressed him throughout his life. Leading his class in both academics and athletics, he was captain of the track team and took four years of Latin and two of Greek in preparation for a career as a professor of classics. In 1907 he graduated as valedictorian and entered Harvard University on a scholarship.

Whitmore's father lost his money during the financial panic of 1907, and Whitmore had to work his way through Harvard in a variety of jobs, including night telephone operator. He did not take any chemistry courses until his sophomore year. During the summer of 1910 he served as college guide for visitors to Harvard and met his future wife, Marion Gertrude Mason, a student of chemistry at Radcliffe College. Deciding to make chemistry his life's work, he studied the subject exclusively during his senior year. He received an A.B. magna cum laude in June 1911 and became Professor Charles Loring Jackson's laboratory assistant until Jackson's retirement in 1912, whereupon he worked under future (1914) Nobel chemistry laureate Theodore William Richards and Elmer P. Kohler. He received an A.M. with highest honors in June 1912. During his graduate studies he supported himself by tutoring at an excellent salary at the "Widow" Nolan's school, which prepared well-to-do Harvard students for examinations. He received a Ph.D. in organic chemistry in 1914. That same year he married Mason, who helped him first in the laboratory and later in writing his books and articles. The couple had three sons and two daughters (one daughter died in infancy). All four children followed scientific careers.

As a graduate student Whitmore had decided on an academic career, but because he could earn much more as a tutor than as an instructor at any college, he devoted two years after receiving his doctorate to tutoring in order to accumulate enough money to support his wife and growing family. In 1916–1917 he was also a part-time instructor of organic chemistry at Williams College in Williamstown, Massachusetts. In 1917–1918, during World War I, he was an instructor of organic chemistry at the newly founded Rice Institute, in Houston, Texas, where he worked on toxic gases for the U.S. Army Chemical Warfare Service, of whose advisory board he later (1934–1940) became a member. Because the president of Rice would not purchase a set of the journal Liebig's *Annalen*, which Whitmore considered indispensable for research, Whitmore left in 1918 to become assistant professor of organic chemistry at the University of Minnesota. In January 1920 he became professor of organic chemistry at Northwestern University, where he soon became acting head (1924–1925) and head (1925–1929) of the chemistry department and began to attract the first of numerous graduate students in organic chemistry. Here he established his habit of rising as early as 3:00 A.M. to work in his office until a normal rising time, when he returned home to be with his family for several hours before returning to his regular office schedule.

In 1929 Whitmore became dean of the School of Chemistry and Physics at Pennsylvania State College (now Pennsylvania State University), a post that he held until his death. He was also research professor of organic chemistry from 1937 to 1947. At Penn State, with the help of Merrell Robert Fenske and Dorothy Douglas Quiggle, he built a chemical engineering and research program with special strength in petroleum cracking, Fenske's area of expertise, which made available high-octane fuels. Although Whitmore made numerous research contributions to various aspects of organic chemistry, he was most proud of his graduate program in chemistry, where enrollment increased during his deanship from eighteen to more than 100. During this period the college awarded 871 bachelor's, 383 master's, and 215 doctoral degrees in chemistry and chemical engineering.

While at Minnesota, Whitmore began his research on organic compounds of mercury. He not only prepared many new organic mercurials, but he also improved methods for preparing various types of organic mercurials and showed how they could be used to prepare other types of organic compounds. After he moved to Penn State he initiated research in the area in which he was a true pioneer, that of the reaction mechanisms of organic reactions—the pathways by which starting materials (reactants) react to form products. A detailed knowledge of such mechanisms is of great significance both to the theoretical chemist and to the synthetic chemist seeking better and cheaper procedures for preparing known and unknown substances.

In the field of mechanisms, Whitmore's 1932 electronic theory of molecular rearrangements was greeted with skepticism but was soon widely accepted. He postulated that rearrangements of neutral compounds to form other neutral molecules could involve unstable positively charged intermediates called carbonium ions (now called carbocations). Although then unknown, their existence has since been proven by nuclear magnetic resonance (NMR) spectroscopy and mass spectroscopy. Whitmore used his theory to predict and explain not only molecular rearrangements but also other reactions, such as elimination, addition, and substitution reactions, and the polymerization (bonding) of olefins (unsaturated organic compounds) to form polymers.

In order to establish his electronic theory on a firm experimental basis, Whitmore carried out research on almost every phase of the synthesis of aliphatic compounds (those containing only straight carbon chains). By improving known procedures and devising new ones, he prepared hundreds of new and complex alcohols and studied their dehydration products. He added greatly to knowledge of the Grignard reaction, a general method for the preparation of a variety of organic compounds. He devised improved procedures for the ozonolysis (oxidation by ozone) of unsaturated hydrocarbons (those containing double bonds) to elucidate the structure of the products of rearrangements. He prepared pure saturated and unsaturated hydrocarbons, corroborating their structures and properties. He also related the rearrangement of olefins in acid solution to the rearrangement involved in the dehydrogenation (removal of hydrogen) of alcohols.

A consultant to the U.S. government as well as private industry, during World War II Whitmore conducted pilot plant studies on the preparation of Research Department Explosive (RDX, formally cyclotrimethylenetrinitramine), which were used as the basis for one of the first plants for the production of this plastic superexplosive (the first hundred pounds of RDX were made in Whitmore's laboratory). He also contributed to wartime research on antimalarial drugs, penicillin, aviation fuels, lubricants, synthetic rubber, and organosilicon compounds used in the production of silicones. At the time of his sudden and premature death of coronary thrombosis in his home in State College, Pennsylvania, at the age of fifty-nine, Whitmore was planning a twenty-year research program on organosilicon compounds, which he intended to be the third major phase of his research career after his work on mercurials and hydrocarbons. For his wartime contributions, he was posthumously awarded the President's Certificate of Merit. Whitmore's first book, *Organic Compounds of Mercury* (1921), became its century's standard reference text. His second book, *Organic Chemistry* (1937), nearly three-fourths of whose 1090 pages were devoted to the new fields of aliphatic and alicyclic chemistry, was one of the most comprehensive textbooks of descriptive organic chemistry. Most of Whitmore's articles appeared in the *Journal of the American Chemical Society*, *Organic Syntheses*, and *Industrial and Engineering Chemistry*. A number of his reviews and articles about the profession appeared in *Chemical and Engineering News*. His posthumously published article "Alkylation and Related Processes of Modern Petroleum Practice" (*Chemical and Engineering News* 26 [8 Mar. 1948]: 668) summarized seven methods for producing carbonium ion intermediates. More than thirty of his 249 articles and one of his twelve patents for the synthesis of organic compounds were published after his death.

A modest, personable, and cheerful man well liked by students and colleagues, Whitmore was an indefatigable worker whose work habits may have contributed to his premature death. He served as a member of the editorial boards of *Chemical Bulletin* (1923–1928) and *Organic Syntheses* (1925–1947; editor in chief, vol. 7 [1927] and vol. 12 [1932]). His numerous honors included the William H. Nichols Medal of the New York section of the American Chemical Society (1937), the presidency of the ACS (1938), the Willard Gibbs Medal of the ACS Chicago Section (1945), and election to the American Philosophical Society (1943) and the National Academy of Sciences (1946). While ACS president, he visited and talked before each of its more than 100 sections. An inspiring teacher, effective administrator, and prolific researcher, Whitmore contributed to nearly every field of organic chemistry. His electronic theory of rearrangements, still valid today, not only explained a variety of known reactions but also predicted new ones, which he utilized in the synthesis of hitherto unknown compounds.

• No collection of Whitmore's personal papers exists, but several of his letters are in the Pennsylvania State University archives. Biographical articles on Whitmore include Carl S. Marvel, "Frank Clifford Whitmore 1887–1947," National Academy of Sciences, *Biographical Memoirs* 28 (1954): 289–311, which contains an autographed portrait and complete bibliography, and Frank Whitmore, Jr. (Whitmore's son), "Frank Clifford Whitmore 1887–1947," in *American Chemists and Chemical Engineers*, ed. Wyndham D. Miles (1976), pp. 506–7.

GEORGE B. KAUFFMAN

WHITMORE, William Henry (6 Sept. 1836–14 June 1900), antiquary, Boston historian, and genealogist, was born in Dorchester, Massachusetts, the son of Charles Octavius Whitmore, a businessman, and Lovice Ayers. Whitmore studied at the Boston Latin and English High Schools. He then joined C. O. Whitman and Sons, his father's commission merchant business.

Whitmore achieved distinction as an antiquary and Boston historian. He joined the New England Historic Genealogical Society in 1854, edited its *Register* in 1859–1860, served on its committee on publication, and was chairman of its committee on heraldry from 1864 to 1872. In 1858 he was a founder of the Prince Society, which published rare American works. He served as its recording and corresponding secretary and edited several of its publications. Elected to the Massachusetts Historical Society in 1863, he was active in its publications as well. In 1867 he was awarded master of arts degrees by Harvard and Williams. In 1874 he was elected to the Boston Common Council; he served almost uninterruptedly until 1886 and was president in 1879. In 1875 he became a record commissioner for the city of Boston, and in 1892 he was appointed city registrar. In 1879 Whitmore helped to found the Boston Antiquarian Club, later absorbed by the Bostonian Society. He was a trustee of the Boston Public Library in 1882–1883 and from 1885 to 1888. In June 1884 Whitmore married Fanny Theresa Walling Maynard; they had one son.

The bulk of Whitmore's scholarly activities were generated by his position as a commissioner and city registrar, or undertaken for the societies mentioned above. Chief among these is undoubtedly his contribution to the first twenty-eight volumes of *A Report of the Record Commissioners of the City of Boston* (1881–1884), which included Boston and Dorchester vital records, various port arrival data, lists of Boston taxpayers, and other information; *The Colonial Laws of Massachusetts* (3 vols., 1887–1890); *The Hutchinson Papers* (2 vols., 1865; repr. 1967), *John Dunton's Letters from New England* (1867), and *The Andros Tracts* (1868), all sponsored by the Prince Society; the "Diary of Samuel Sewall" (*Collections of the Massachusetts His-

torical Society 5–7 [1878–1882]); and *The Elements of Heraldry* (1866) and *The Heraldic Journal* (4 vols., 1865–1868), both sponsored by the committee on heraldry. Whitmore contributed three chapters to Justin Winsor's *Memorial History of Boston* (4 vols., 1880–1881) and compiled *A Handbook of American Genealogy* (1862), an early bibliography of published family histories, and *The Massachusetts Civil List . . . 1630–1774* (1870). Genealogical articles or monographs, many published in the *New England Historical and Genealogical Register*, cover the Whitmore, Hall, Temple, Lane, Reyner, Whipple, Quincy, Norton, Winthrop, Vickers (Vickery), Hutchinson, Oliver, Usher, Ayres, Elliot, Dalton, Batcheller, Belcher, Wilcox, Bigg, Foster, Stone, and Blake families. He wrote two versions of *The Original Mother Goose's Melody* (both 1889) and devised a diagram of pedigrees called "Ancestral Tablets," which was still sometimes used by genealogists in the late twentieth century.

In addition to antiquarian and historical activities, Whitmore was also largely responsible for the preservation of the Old State House and the location there of the Bostonian Society. Frequently ill in his last years, he was somewhat of a recluse, although he could also be an entertaining companion. Tenacious and politically astute in the fostering of antiquarian projects, Whitmore deserves enormous credit for preserving and publishing early Boston records, for saving the Old State House, and for improving standards of editing and bibliography. His heraldic and genealogical studies dispelled much myth, but the latter especially have often been superseded, notably with regard to English origins or to instances in which wills and deeds add further data. Whitmore was a leader in the first generation of American local historians and antiquaries—a group that founded societies, published prolifically, discovered and catalogued the early records of New England, and pioneered the new fields of genealogy, archival management, historic preservation, and public health statistics.

• There is no known collection of Whitmore's papers. Early twentieth-century sources provide some information: *New England Historical and Genealogical Register* 56 (1902): 67–69; *Proceedings of the Massachusetts Historical Society*, 2d ser., 15 (1901–1902): 96–104, which includes a list of Whitmore's works; and J. W. P. Purdy, *The Whitmore Genealogy* (1907), pp. 126–27. An obituary is in the *Boston Transcript*, 15 June 1900.

RALPH CRANDALL

WHITNEY, Alexander Fell (12 Apr. 1873–16 July 1949), labor leader, was born in Cedar Falls, Iowa, the son of Joseph Leonard Whitney, a farmer and part-time schoolteacher, and Martha Wallin Batcheller. Hoping to improve their meager fortunes, the Whitneys moved to a Nebraska homestead in 1880 but after four years returned to Iowa, where they settled on a farm in Cherokee. Whitney attended school only briefly, receiving most of his education at home. In 1888 he started working on the Illinois Central Railroad, selling newspapers for two years and then becoming a brakeman.

In 1893 Whitney married Grace Elizabeth Marshman, with whom he had three children. An accident at about the same time cost Whitney parts of two fingers on his left hand. After trying unsuccessfully to support his family as a painter and paperhanger he again found work as a brakeman. In 1896 he joined the Brotherhood of Railroad Trainmen (BRT) and less than a year later was elected president of his local. He chaired the grievance committee from 1901 to 1907 and also served for two years as one of the union's grand trustees. In 1907 he became a BRT vice president.

In 1909 the union elected a new president, William G. Lee, who held office for twenty years. Whitney ran against him several times unsuccessfully and clashed with him constantly. Although Lee's autocratic style and Whitney's ambition were important elements in the feud, their differences soon expanded to matters of policy. Like Lee, Whitney had long thought in traditional craft union terms, but spurred by the rivalry he became increasingly progressive in his views. He was among the first BRT officials to advocate the eight-hour day, won a BRT majority in favor of employer liability laws over Lee's objection in 1913, and in 1916 as a member of the National Labor Committee helped rally support for the Adamson Act, which made the eight-hour day for railroad workers a federal requirement. Whitney (again opposing Lee) also backed the unsuccessful Plumb Plan, which urged the government to continue managing the nation's railroads after World War I ended. In 1923 Whitney joined the executive committee of the Illinois Conference for Progressive Political Action (CPPA), a political coalition of socialists and labor representatives, and in the 1924 presidential election, while Lee supported Calvin Coolidge, Whitney backed the Progressive party candidate, Senator Robert M. La Follette.

Whitney's first wife having died in 1923, he married Dorothy May Rawley in 1927; they had no children together. In 1928 he finally managed to win the BRT presidency from Lee; he held the office for the rest of his life. He had barely settled in when the depression began, catapulting him into years of battles against the carriers' efforts to cut wages. Whitney ruled his union nearly as imperiously as Lee had, but his militance and his effectiveness in collective bargaining kept the rank and file loyal to him. He continued to be active politically during the 1930s and 1940s, enthusiastically supporting President Franklin Roosevelt's New Deal and serving on the Political Action Committee organized by CIO leader Sidney Hillman to coordinate labor support for Roosevelt's 1944 reelection campaign. Whitney also endorsed those in Congress whom he regarded as friends of labor. For instance, in 1940 he ran a series of full-page newspaper ads encouraging Missourians to reelect "our good friend" Senator Harry S. Truman; with Whitney's encouragement railroad unions contributed nearly two-thirds of the total amount raised by Truman's campaign. Four years later, Whitney and other labor leaders helped influence President Roosevelt to choose Truman for vice president.

Most American unions accepted wage controls and refrained from work stoppages during World War II, but many unions struck in 1946, among them the nation's twenty major railroad brotherhoods, which announced that they would walk off the job unless their demands were met. Truman, who had now succeeded to the presidency, met with the railway union leaders and persuaded eighteen of them to accept arbitration. The only holdouts were the heads of the two largest organizations: Alvanley Johnston of the Brotherhood of Locomotive Engineers (BLE) and Whitney. On May 23 these two unions struck, and rail traffic all across America came to a standstill. Two days later, while negotiations with Whitney and Johnston continued in a downtown hotel, Truman appeared before a joint session of Congress and asked permission to draft the strikers into the army. At that moment Truman was handed a message; the strike had been settled, on his terms. The hardship imposed by even so brief a railroad strike, combined with Truman's success in facing it down, helped set the stage for the passage in 1947 (over Truman's veto) of a bill explicitly designed to weaken labor's power: the Taft-Hartley Act.

Proclaiming "You can't make a President out of a ribbon clerk," Whitney vowed that he would spend every dollar in the BRT treasury to defeat Truman in the next election. He helped organize the Progressive Citizens of America but withdrew from the group when it chose Vice President Henry A. Wallace as its candidate. Truman's Taft-Hartley veto helped repair the breach, and after a visit to the White House in January 1948 Whitney told reporters that his "dear old parents" had taught him the virtue of forgiveness; furthermore, he said, "I have been a Democrat for years." He supported Truman's campaign that fall and died less than a year later at his home in Bay Village, Ohio, outside Cleveland.

Whitney's career spanned a remarkable era in American labor history. As a young man he embraced the traditional values of craft unionism, focusing more on mutual assistance than on bargaining with employers or influencing legislation. Over time, he came to adopt a much more assertive stance toward the carriers than his predecessors, and he also entered the political arena more aggressively, successfully trading labor's voting strength for the government's legislative protection. The limitations of that alliance were highlighted by his need to continue supporting Truman even after the defeat of 1946; yet the importance of government action in improving union wages, working conditions, and bargaining rights over the course of Whitney's career helps explain why he and many of his contemporaries chose the strategy they did.

• Accounts of Whitney's life appear in Walter F. McCaleb, *Brotherhood of Railroad Trainmen, with Special Reference to the Life of Alexander F. Whitney* (1936); W. G. Edens, *A. F. Whitney* (1947); and Gary Fink, ed., *Biographical Dictionary of American Labor Leaders* (1974). See also Philip Taft, *Organized Labor in American History* (1964), and Wellington Roe, *Juggernaut: American Labor in Action* (1948). For discussions of his union, see Joel Seidman, *The Brotherhood of Railroad Trainmen* (1962), and Fink, ed., *Labor Unions* (1977). References to his dealings with Harry Truman appear in Truman's own *Memoirs*, vol. 1 (1955), as well as in most Truman biographies; see, for instance, Jonathan Daniels, *Man of Independence* (1950); David McCullough, *Truman* (1992); and Robert H. Ferrell, *Harry S Truman: A Life* (1994).

SANDRA OPDYCKE

WHITNEY, Anne (2 Sept. 1821–23 Jan. 1915), sculptor and poet, was born in Watertown, Massachusetts, to Nathaniel Ruggles Whitney, Jr., a justice of the peace, and Sally Stone. Whitney's parents belonged to a liberal sect of the Unitarian church. Its doctrine professed the belief that men and women were created equal. Whitney was educated as a liberal thinker, believing in the equality of the sexes and the races and deploring oppression and injustice of any kind.

Whitney's early education was through private tutors and later at a private girl's school in Maine. As a young woman, she became acquainted with members of the Boston literary society and with such abolitionists as William Lloyd Garrison, Lucy Stone, Ralph Waldo Emerson, and Elizabeth Blackwell. Through their influence, Whitney became a protagonist of abolition and women's rights.

Beginning in the late 1840s, Whitney published poems in the *North American Review* and the *Atlantic Monthly* and thought she would devote her life to writing. However, at age thirty-four she began studying sculpture. Largely self-taught, she used her family members as models for her first works. Divided between the literary and visual arts, Whitney continued writing poetry, and in 1859 she published a volume of her poetry entitled *Poems*. The following year she entered her first exhibit at the National Academy of Design with a portrait bust of a child entitled *Laura Brown* (National Museum of American Art). It is unknown whether she continued to write poetry after this time.

Whitney's plans to go to Europe to study art were delayed by the moral demands of the Civil War. She continued art study in America by attending William Rimmer's anatomy lectures in Boston. While in Boston, Whitney sculpted two major works. *Lady Godiva* (private collection, Dallas), her first full-length marble sculpture, was based on Tennyson's poem (1842), but in Whitney's hands it became a symbol of personal sacrifice for public good. *Africa* (now destroyed) was a full-length reclining female figure representing the African continent awakening from slavery by the activities of the Civil War. *Africa* toured Boston and New York, along with *Lady Godiva*, and was hailed by the critics. "It was a masterly design," wrote Mary A. Livermore, "wrought out in a most triumphant manner. It imitates no model, followed no tradition, copied no antique, but was a fresh, original masterpiece of genius, contributed to the art and history of the time."

Whitney finally went to Rome, then a magnet for American sculptors, in 1867. Accompanied by her friend, the painter Adeline Manning, she ultimately made three trips to Europe between 1867 and 1875, working in Rome, Paris, and Munich. While in Rome, she became acquainted with other American artists including the American women sculptors Harriet Hosmer and Edmonia Lewis. In 1869 Whitney turned her sculpture to social commentary by modeling *Roma* (Jewett Art Center, Wellesley), a symbol of Rome's declined condition under the Papacy before the final unification of Italy.

Back in America in 1873, Whitney received the Massachusetts state commission for a full-length marble statue of the patriot Samuel Adams for Statuary Hall at the Capitol in Washington, D.C. She completed *Samuel Adams* in 1876, and soon thereafter Boston commissioned her to produce a bronze replica (1878) for Adams (now Dock) Square in front of Faneuil Hall. According to Lydia Maria Child and Mary A. Livermore, contemporary critics were impressed by the animated quality of *Samuel Adams*. In 1875 Whitney won an anonymous competition for a public statue of Charles Sumner, the abolitionist senator from Massachusetts. The jury later denied Whitney the commission when they learned that the model was designed by a woman and awarded the commission to the runner-up, Thomas Ball. After this disappointment and obvious injustice Whitney never entered another public competition.

The sources for Whitney's artistic training are uncertain. She does not appear to have studied with fellow sculptors; rather, the eclectic Whitney interacted with and gleaned from them elements of her choosing. Although her early work in marble shows the influence of the neoclassical style popular in Rome at the time, her later work in bronze reveals the study of the French Beaux Arts style with its emphasis on naturalism and the artist's individuality and spontaneity in the conception and execution of the work.

Beginning in 1893, Whitney lived on Boston's Beacon Hill with her longtime companion Adeline Manning. She continued to sculpt portraits and privately commissioned public works. More than half of Whitney's sculptures are portraits of individuals influential in the causes that she also championed. The final major work of Whitney's career was completed in 1902. The life-size bronze sculpture *Charles Sumner*, based on her original model of 1875, was erected in Harvard Square in Cambridge, Massachusetts, made possible by private subscription.

Whitney never married. Her later years were spent in Boston sculpting, holding salons for the New England literary and artistic world, and fighting for woman suffrage and other political causes. She died in Boston.

Whitney selected sculpture as a profession at a time when few women chose professions and even fewer chose sculpture. Due to its physical aspects, sculpture was viewed as an inappropriate art for women. An artistic forerunner of the period, Whitney was one of the first Americans to use the art of sculpture to inspire social reform. Her subjects were often symbolic of the injustices suffered by humans at the hands of humans. This included prejudices against class and race as well as gender.

• The Anne Whitney Papers in the Wellesley College Library contain the bulk of Whitney's letters, scrapbooks, diaries, and art works, as well as Elizabeth Rogers Payne's manuscript, "Anne Whitney: Nineteenth Century Sculptor and Liberal," written in 1971. Biographical sketches include those by Mary A. Livermore in *Our Famous Women* (1887) and by Harriet Prescott Spofford in *A Little Book of Friends* (1916). See also Mary A. Livermore, "Anne Whitney," *Perry Magazine* 5 (Feb. 1903): 240–43; and Elizabeth Rogers Payne's "Anne Whitney, Sculptor," *Art Quarterly* 25 (Autumn 1962): 244–61, and "Anne Whitney, Art and Social Justice," *Massachusetts Review* 12 (Spring 1971): 245–60. See also the catalog entry for Anne Whitney in Eleanor Tufts's *American Women Artists 1830–1930* (1987). Obituaries are in the *Boston Transcript* and the *Boston Herald*, 25 Jan. 1915, and in the *Boston Sunday Globe*, 14 Feb. 1915.

CHARLENE G. GARFINKLE

WHITNEY, Charlotte Anita (7 July 1867–4 Feb. 1955), social worker and political activist, was born in San Francisco, California, the daughter of George Whitney, an attorney and a California state legislator, and Mary Lewis Swearingen. U.S. Supreme Court Justice Stephen J. Field was an uncle. Whitney's socially prominent, affluent parents, who originally were from the East, sent her to Wellesley College in 1885. She graduated in 1889 with a B.S. degree but no clear vision of her future. After several unsettled years, in 1893 Whitney trained in the new profession of social work at the College Settlement in New York City. There, among New York City's poor immigrants, she developed a firsthand understanding of class differences and poverty. Returning to California in 1893 Whitney taught in private schools and opened a Boy's Club in the slums of West Oakland. For several years she worked as the first probation officer of Alameda County, California, and later was secretary of the Associated Charities of Oakland. Whitney's commitment to racial justice and woman suffrage emerged in the years after 1910: she became a charter member of the National Association for the Advancement of Colored People and headed the California College Equal Suffrage League. When women won the vote in California, Whitney was instrumental in refashioning the league into the California Civic League, an organization through which women voters sought to make their influence felt.

Whitney joined the Socialist party in 1914 after violent police action against striking migrant laborers at the Wheatland Ranch (Calif.) and the speeches of Elizabeth Gurley Flynn and Eugene Debs convinced her that liberal reform policies were inadequate to address the tension between capital and labor. The Socialist party appealed to Whitney because of its commitment to electoral politics and its openness to women members.

As a Socialist, Whitney opposed U.S. involvement in World War I. She fought for the free speech rights of members of the Industrial Workers of the World who were arrested and charged with sedition under wartime legislation barring opposition to the draft and other "disloyal speech." Her decision to join other members of the California Socialist party in forming a more radical Communist Labor party led to her arrest in November 1919 for violations of California's new criminal syndicalism act. She was found guilty of organizing and being a member of the Communist Labor party, a group said to advocate criminal syndicalism, and was sentenced to one to fourteen years in prison. While her 1927 appeal to the U.S. Supreme Court (*Whitney v. California*) was unsuccessful, it provided Justice Louis D. Brandeis the opportunity to file an eloquent concurring opinion that expressed his view of the First Amendment and the "clear and present danger" test. Governor Clement C. Young pardoned Whitney later that year, quoting Brandeis's opinion and citing the vagueness of the law under which she had been convicted.

Whitney continued to fight for civil liberties and racial justice, working for free speech and assembly through the International Labor Defense and joining in Negro Labor Council antisegregation sit-in demonstrations. She was an ardent legislative lobbyist on issues of social and economic justice and ran for several political offices on the Communist party ticket. In 1934, as Communist party candidate for state treasurer, Whitney garnered more than 100,000 votes. From the 1920s until the early 1950s, Whitney was also very active within the party, serving locally as a fundraiser and state chairwoman and as a member of the Communist party National Committee. At age eighty, Whitney was again challenged for her political beliefs when she was called before the Tenney committee, one of the first of the Cold War–era investigations. Whitney died at her home in San Francisco.

• Whitney's private papers apparently have been destroyed. Clipping files on Whitney may be found at the Oakland History Room, Oakland Public Library, Oakland, Calif., and at the C. C. Young Manuscript Collection, California State Archives, Sacramento. See also Al Richmond, *Native Daughter: The Story of Anita Whitney* (1942); Lisa Rubens, "The Patrician Radical: Charlotte Anita Whitney," *California History* 65 (1986): 158–71; Vincent Blasi, "The First Amendment and the Ideal of Civic Courage: The Brandeis Opinion in Whitney v. California," *William and Mary Law Review* 29 (Summer 1988): 653–97; and Philip B. Kurland and Gerhard Casper, "Whitney v. California," in *Landmark Briefs and Arguments of the Supreme Court of the United States: Constitutional Law*, vol. 25 (1975). An obituary is in the *New York Times*, 5 Feb., 1955.

JILL NORGREN

WHITNEY, Courtney (20 May 1897–21 Mar. 1969), army officer, was born in Takoma Park, Maryland, a suburb of Washington, D.C., the son of Milton Whitney, the director of the Bureau of Soils in the U.S. Department of Agriculture, and Annie Cushing Langdon. In May 1917 he enlisted in the District of Columbia National Guard as an infantry private. That August he was inducted into the army as a private first class, joining the Aviation Section of the Army Signal Corps, where he served until March 1918. He then received a second lieutenant's commission in the same unit and entered the Signal Corps Aviation School at Gerstner Field, Louisiana. Subsequently he was made an adjutant at Payne Field, Mississippi, and, beginning in February 1920, at the District of Columbia's Bolling Field, where he also held the posts of supply officer and commanding officer and was promoted in July of that year to first lieutenant. In 1920 he married Evelyn Ewart Jones; they had two children. While stationed at Bolling Field, Whitney studied law in the evenings at the National University in Washington, D.C., and earned an LL.B. in 1923.

In 1925 and 1926 Whitney was adjutant to the Sixty-sixth Service Squadron, Camp Nichols, in the Philippines, where he was also post and personnel officer of the Fourth Composite Group. He was then sent to Manila, where he served as assistant to the air officer of the Philippine Department. In 1926 he was made chief of the Publications Section, Information Division, attached to the chief of the Air Corps in Washington.

In 1927 Whitney resigned from the regular army and became a lawyer in Manila, where he had a lucrative practice and was an executive of several corporations. He renewed an earlier friendship with General Douglas MacArthur, who was commander of the U.S. Army's Philippine Department and an adviser to the Philippine government.

In September 1940 Whitney returned to active duty as a major in the Specialist Corps of the Reserve Officer Corps and a month later was appointed assistant chief of the Legal Division of the Army Air Corps Headquarters in Washington. From 1942 to 1945 he advanced from the rank of lieutenant colonel to brigadier general, and in February 1943 he was made assistant air judge advocate. In May 1943 Whitney was transferred to MacArthur's Southwest Pacific headquarters in Brisbane, Australia, and was named chief of the Regional Section of the Allied Intelligence Bureau in the Philippines. He actively promoted Filipino resistance and dispatched American personnel to train guerrillas. His office disseminated propaganda on mirrors, matchboxes, and cigarette packs, all bearing MacArthur's promise, "I shall return." Barring the Washington-based Office of Strategic Services from any role in the Philippines, Whitney ensured that only groups sanctioned by MacArthur operated in the region, and he disarmed the Communist-leaning Hukbalahop "Huk" movement. In November 1944 he was made chief of the Civil Affairs Section of the U.S. armed forces in the Pacific. In January 1945 Whitney assisted Filipino officials in restoring civilian government to their land.

By 1945 Whitney was MacArthur's chief confidant and was often perceived by the media as the general's alter ego. Though Whitney was highly esteemed by the commander, who appreciated his intellect and achievement, the short, portly Whitney was highly unpopular with much of MacArthur's staff, who saw him as pompous, opportunistic, aloof, and abrasive. His feud with Major General Charles A. Willoughby was legendary.

In late August 1945 Whitney moved to Japan with MacArthur, who had been appointed supreme commander for the Allied powers (SCAP). In December Whitney became chief of SCAP's Government Section, the most powerful of all occupation agencies, where he supervised Japan's demilitarization and democratization. Though a staunch conservative, Whitney acted pragmatically, relying heavily on his liberal assistant, Charles Kades. In January 1947, following Whitney's recommendation, MacArthur launched a purge of some 2,200 Japanese economic leaders.

Dissatisfied with Japanese efforts to draft a new constitution, Whitney assigned members of his Government Section to design one. After examining the constitutions of several major democratic governments, the task force devised a document in which the judiciary was independent of the executive, the emperor's authority was limited to persuasion, and war itself was declared "forever removed." Whitney also supervised political reforms within Japan, including the introduction of woman suffrage. According to *United States News*, Whitney was the second most powerful man in postwar Japan and the only one who could walk into the supreme commander's office without an appointment.

When the Korean War erupted in June 1950, Whitney was named military secretary of the United Nations Command, which MacArthur headed. He accompanied MacArthur on his trips to the front as well as to the Wake Island meeting with President Harry Truman on 15 October 1950 in which MacArthur assured Truman that the Chinese would most likely not intervene in the Korean War and would easily be defeated if they attempted to do so. When in April 1951 the president relieved MacArthur of his command in Korea, Whitney returned to the United States with MacArthur and immediately resigned from the army, holding the permanent rank of major general. "I preferred to walk the plank with General MacArthur," he later said.

MacArthur became a corporate executive in New York City, and Whitney served as his personal secretary, handling press relations. However, as Whitney lacked tact and patience, he was soon eased out of such responsibilities. He remained MacArthur's spokesman on a number of matters, especially those dealing with assertions of the Truman administration, and at one point he called the claim that MacArthur wanted to use the atomic bomb in Korea "fictional nonsense." MacArthur was appointed chairman of the board at Remington Rand in 1952, and Whitney was hired as his assistant. In 1956 Whitney published *MacArthur: His Rendezvous with History*, a eulogistic, detailed account of the general from his youth to his removal from command in 1951. Whitney also helped write MacArthur's own *Reminiscences* (1964). In 1961 Whitney accompanied MacArthur on a triumphal visit to the Philippines. In 1964 Whitney relocated to Washington, D.C., where he died.

• No Whitney papers per se exist, but the archives of the MacArthur Memorial, Norfolk, Va., show the prominent role Whitney played in MacArthur's life. A superior portrait of Whitney is in *Current Biography* (1951). Critical treatments of Whitney are in D. Clayton James's trilogy, *The Years of MacArthur*, vol. 1, *1880–1941* (1970), vol. 2, *1941–1945* (1975), and vol. 3, *1945–1954* (1985); and William Manchester, *American Caesar: Douglas MacArthur, 1880–1964* (1978). His obituary is in the *New York Times*, 22 Mar. 1969.

JUSTUS D. DOENECKE

WHITNEY, Eli (8 Dec. 1765–8 Jan. 1825), inventor and gun manufacturer, was born in Westboro, Massachusetts, the son of Eli Whitney and Elizabeth Fay, prosperous farmers. From boyhood Whitney had shown an exceptional mechanical aptitude for repairing such intricate things as violins and watches and for using all kinds of tools on his family's Massachusetts farm. To have spending money he made nails, hat pins, and walking canes. Finally realizing he would never amount to more than a clever mechanic without a college degree, he taught school long enough to pay his own way and at twenty-three years of age was admitted to Yale.

After graduating in 1792 he went south to take a tutoring job and stopped off at the cotton plantation of General Nathanael Greene's widow in Savannah, Georgia. She inspired him to design a machine to clean the tight-clinging green seeds from short-staple cotton, a process that took a slave an entire day to clean only a pound. Within a few days he made a contraption for forcing the cotton through a series of narrow slits. The crude machine was easy to build and simple to operate. According to the economist Tench Coxe the "gin" was the production equivalent of 1,000 slaves.

In partnership with Phineas Miller, the manager of the Greene plantation, Whitney set out to patent and market his invention, but it was widely pirated as most southern planters jumped into cotton cultivation, leaving the inventor broke and bitter. The cotton gin itself was a tremendous success, making cotton king in the South until the Civil War and stimulating the expansion of cotton manufacturing in New England. Once a luxury, cotton became the cheapest and most commonly worn cloth. Annual production rose from 2 million pounds to an average of 60 million pounds by 1805.

In 1798, six years after his invention of the cotton gin, Whitney offered to make the government thousands of muskets, although he had no prior gunmaking experience. Gunmaking in the Connecticut valley was then strictly a handicraft, slow and unsystematic. Without a vision of fathering what he called "an entirely new and different system of manufacture," Whitney certainly would never have dared to submit such a grandiose proposal. Disillusioned by interminable legal wrangling over the infringement of his cotton gin patent, the inventor decided never to seek protection again for the methods, tools, and machines he would create.

He wrote his good friend Oliver Wolcott, Jr., then secretary of the treasury: "I am persuaded that machinery moved by water . . . would greatly diminish the labor and facilitate the Manufacture of this Article. . . . There is a good fall of water in the vicinity . . . which I can procure, and could have works erected in a short time." Wolcott succeeded in getting Whitney a contract to produce 10,000 French-type muskets at $13.40 each. Twenty-seven other gunmakers also received contracts at the same time.

Actually, when he signed the contract, the 33-year-old Whitney had neither experience nor a factory site, workmen, tools, or machines. In September he bought 100 acres along the Mill River, where New Haven's settlers had put their first gristmill. An old, six-foot log dam provided a year-round waterfall. Timothy Dwight, then president of Yale College, wrote that "no position for a manufactory could be better. From the bleak winds of winter it is completely sheltered by the surrounding hills. . . . No place, perhaps, is more healthy; few are more romantic."

Whitney encountered difficulties in completing the purchase. Not until 1 November could he rebuild the dam and erect buildings, which he rushed to occupy before the onset of what proved to be a long and severe winter. On 13 January 1799 he could exult that "my building which is 72 feet long by 30 & 2 stories high is nearly finished!" Soon he added shops for storing wood, metals, and leather and for a trip-hammer served by a flume; to reduce the fire hazard he located across the river at the foot of Mill Rock the forging shop, with seven pairs of bellows and a cluster of storehouses.

Quickly Whitney recruited, mostly from Massachusetts, some fifty skilled hands. For those with families he built five handsome stone houses, and for the unmarried he ran a boardinghouse. A bachelor himself, he lived in a farmhouse opposite the mill across the Hartford turnpike, along with three nephews, a dozen apprentices, and servants. A stone store served the little community, which was paternalistic. Although his consuming passion for work left him no time for worrying about details such as churches or schools, Whitney did show an interest in training young men as mechanical apprentices. By 1803 his factory had become a landmark, and Whitneyville constituted one of the first manufacturing villages in the country.

Fourteen months after receiving his first contract, Whitney wrote Wolcott:

> One of my primary objects is to form the tools so the tools themselves shall fashion the work and give to every part its just proportion—which when once accomplished will give expedition, uniformity and exactness to the whole. . . . In short, the tools which I contemplate are similar to an engraving on copper plate from which may be taken a great number of impressions exactly alike.

By uniformity he meant a tolerance of about a thirty-second of an inch, far inferior to the rigid machine tolerances of modern metalworking. Because of the dearth of experienced workmen Whitney stressed that should the execution of his plan fail, each mechanic would have to form every part "according to his own fancy & regulate the size & proportion by his own Eye," thus resulting in nonconforming parts and requiring triple the number of hands.

Whitney's first innovation was probably a filing jig (a holding device) to secure the pieces of the musket accurately. After two years of delays and disappointments, at the end of which time he could deliver only 500 guns, he apparently had in operation, besides his forge, a trip-hammer, new-fangled jigs, and machines for drilling parts and boring barrels. Sometime between 1801 and 1807 his system came to fruition. He completed his first contract almost entirely with unskilled labor, while several other gun contractors, who depended wholly on skilled craftsmen, failed.

Part of the Whitney myth is that on one of his trips to Washington he gave a convincing demonstration to the secretary of war of his standard, machine-made parts by assembling ten muskets from a pile of parts scattered on the floor. The government arms inspector, Captain Decius Wadsworth, a frequent Whitney visitor and friend, claimed that Whitneyville outperformed the Springfield Armory with much less manual labor, and he had nothing but the highest praise for Whitney's ingenuity and integrity.

Timothy Dwight described the operations at Whitneyville as singular:

> In forming the various parts of the musket, machinery, put in motion by water, and remarkably well adapted to the end, is used for hammering, cutting, turning, perforating, grinding, polishing, etc. The proportions and relative positions of the locks are so nearly similar, that they may be transferred from one lock and adjusted to another. . . . By an application of the same principles, a much greater uniformity has also been given to every part of the muskets.

By 1815 Whitney's system had won widespread recognition in the United States.

Basic to the development of mass production has been the use of powered metalworking tools, especially the lathe and milling machine. Gunmaking involves more milling, or rotary cutting, than any other operation. Whether or not Whitney deserves credit for originating the milling machine is moot, but he did make valuable and original contributions to the history of machines and tools. He has been particularly cited for introducing the jig and the gauge (a measuring device). Both were undoubtedly crude but essential to making his system work. Using a gauge meant that the worker, even an unskilled one, could inspect a piece accurately and determine if it fell within the tolerance of allowable error. Although Samuel Bentham and Marc Brunel applied some of the principles of repetitive production and precision to pulley blocks for the British navy, they overlooked the vital element of limit gauges. Europe did not adopt the American gauging system until 1855. Other American gunmakers, however, were quick to follow Whitney's example. Even before the machine-tool industry was established, his ideas also influenced the perfection of textile machinery in New England—until midcentury the primary heavy-goods industry in the United States. Robert Fulton, who corresponded with Whitney, said of him: "Arkwright, Watt and Whitney were the three men that did most for mankind of any of their contemporaries."

A long memoir that Whitney prepared in 1812 for the War Department in support of an application for another contract for 15,000 firearms summarized twelve years of his creative thinking:

> This establishment was commenced and has been carried on upon a plan which is unknown in Europe, and the great leading object of which is to substitute correct and effective operations of machinery for that skill of the artist which is acquired only by long practice and experience. . . .
>
> Having actually made about 15,000 muskets, at least equal in quality to any that have been manufactured in this country (which is more than has been accomplished by any other individual in the United States) he feels himself warranted . . . in believing that the New Methods which he has invented of working metals and forming the several parts of a musket, are practically useful and highly important to his country.

Whether Whitney should be credited with the discovery of the interchangeability of machined parts, the basis of mass production, is surrounded by myth and controversy. Similar but less spectacular efforts had been tried in Europe, and other gun establishments such as the Springfield Armory and Simeon North's pistol shop in Berlin, Connecticut, were also responsible for innovations leading to that goal.

Not every historian accepts the priority of Whitney's methods. There was, for example, the earlier contribution along similar lines of Honoré Blanc, a gunmaker whose workshop Thomas Jefferson, while minister to France, visited in 1785. The alert Jefferson wrote John Jay that Congress might be interested in the Frenchman's method. "It consists," he said, "in the making every part of [the guns] so exactly alike, that what belongs to any one, may be used for every musket in the magazine."

There is no doubt that North's government contract was the first to specify interchangeability. Yet while North and his three sons were applying its principles in 1808, Jefferson's letter to Monroe indicates that Whitney, seven years earlier, had already invented molds and machines for fabricating uniform locks in his rifles. Also enhancing Whitney's claims were his national fame as the father of the cotton gin, his factory as the largest and best-equipped in the country, his help in getting two government armories on their feet, and North's relative anonymity. Moreover, Whitney influenced other pioneers who perpetuated, refined, and adapted ideas of uniformity and precision, especially Eli Terry on wooden clocks, Chauncey Jerome on rolled brass clocks, Samuel Colt on revolvers, and Elias Howe and Isaac Singer on sewing machines. Each of them, through the miracle of low-cost production, further helped to bring the luxuries of life within the reach of every consumer.

At the age of fifty-two, in 1817 Whitney married Henrietta Frances Edwards, with whom he had four children. On his death in New Haven he left a good-sized fortune of $130,000. His only son being very young, before his death he had directed his nephews, Eli and Philos Blake, to carry on the business and complete the third contract for 15,000 muskets. A decade later they departed, and the trustee of the estate, former governor Henry W. Edwards, took over until Eli Whitney, Jr., was ready to assume control in 1842, whereupon he enlarged the armory and increased employment to 200. The inventor of the revolver, Samuel Colt, contracted with him in 1847 to make the first 1,000 Walker guns for use in the Mexican War and undoubtedly adopted—and perfected—Whitney's techniques when he built the great Colt armory in Hartford. The Whitneyville armory generally flourished until its sale in 1888 to Winchester Repeating Arms of New Haven.

• The papers of both Eli Whitney and his son are on microfilm in the Yale University Library and at the Eli Whitney Museum in New Haven, Conn. Two biographies, which contain much valuable material but do not shed light on the Whitney myth of interchangeability, are Jeanette Mirsky and Allan Nevins, *The World of Eli Whitney* (1952), and Constance M. Green, *Eli Whitney and the Birth of American Technology* (1956). Reminiscences of Whitney are in D. Olmsted's *Memoir*, published in 1846. A more up-to-date account of the inventor and his work is Carolyn Cooper and Merrill Lindsay, *Eli Whitney and the Whitney Armory* (1980), published by the Eli Whitney Museum. The debunking of the Whitney myth has been handled well by Robert S. Woodbury, "The Legend of Eli Whitney and Interchangeable Parts," Massachusetts Institute of Technology, Publication 63 (1960); Edwin A. Battison, "Eli Whitney and the Milling Machine," *Smithsonian Journal of History* 1 (1966); and Robert B. Gordon, "Who Turned the Mechanical Ideal into Mechanical Reality?" *Technology and Culture* 29 (Oct. 1988): 744–78; and Gordon, "Simeon North, John Hall and Mechanized Manufacturing," *Technology and Culture* 30 (Jan. 1989): 179–88.

ELLSWORTH S. GRANT

WHITNEY, Gertrude Vanderbilt (9 Jan. 1875–18 Apr. 1942), sculptor and patron of the arts, was born in New York City, the daughter of Cornelius Vanderbilt II, considered the wealthiest man in the United States, and Alice Claypoole Gwynne. She was raised in a neo-Renaissance palazzo in her native New York City. She attended the Brearley School and became a debutante, as befitted her social position. Vanderbilt graduated in 1894 and married Harry Payne Whitney in 1896; they had three children. In 1900 she began to study sculpture privately with Hendrik C. Anderson. She sought instruction from Daniel Chester French and Augustus

Saint-Gaudens, but they both refused her as a student. At the Art Students League she enrolled in 1903 in sculpture classes with academician James Earle Fraser. In 1907 Whitney set up a studio in MacDougal Alley in Greenwich Village, and in adjoining quarters she often housed young artists. In addition to accommodations, Whitney offered these American artists gallery space for exhibiting their work and stipends for living expenses or travel abroad. She also established a spacious studio on the grounds of her estate in Westbury, Long Island. Her bohemian aspirations were far different from the reality of her life as a wealthy socialite.

When the pioneering exhibition of "The Eight" was held at the Macbeth Gallery in 1908, Whitney purchased four paintings for her collection. She was one of the first collectors to support early modernism in America. In 1913 she contributed funds for the Armory Show, which introduced modernism to the American public. Her financial contributions to the Society of Independent Artists (founded in 1917) helped encourage rebellion from academic art, for this organization favored nonjuried exhibitions. Fearing that her art would not be properly judged because of her social position, Whitney first exhibited her sculpture under an assumed name. After one of her marbles was noted with distinction at the National Academy of Design in 1910, she began to exhibit as Gertrude Vanderbilt Whitney.

In 1910 Whitney studied with Andrew O'Connor in Paris and received private criticism from Auguste Rodin, who had a profound effect on Whitney's early sculpture. *Spanish Peasant* (1911, Metropolitan Museum of Art) is an early example of Whitney's sustained involvement with life-size bronze busts. She conveys the strength and dignity of her subject: while her sitter remains anonymous, the fleshy mouth, strong chin, downcast eyes, and contemplative expression all bespeak a bold but sensitive individual. Whitney's naturalistic approach and quiet classicism derive from the Beaux-Arts tradition in which she was instructed. Rodinesque, however, is her technique of contrasting smooth and rough surface textures to create dramatic effects of light and shadow and to give the work a sensual, tactile quality.

The bronze *Caryatid* (1913, Whitney Museum of American Art) was originally executed in 1912 as a study for one of three standing nude figures that support the basin of a monumental fountain designed for the Arlington Hotel in Washington, D.C., and presented in 1931 to McGill University, Montreal. *Caryatid*—more properly called "atlantid" since it is a male figure intended as an architectural support—strongly indicates Whitney's indebtedness to Auguste Rodin. Like many sculptors of her generation, she assimilated the innovations of the great French master into her style and used them in varying degrees for her subsequent work. While using classical contrapposto, Whitney brought her sculpture into the Rodinesque sphere by the emphasis on light and shadow, which alternately masks and reveals the figure. Whitney also suggested physical force through the taut musculature of the arms, legs, and back. The *Arlington Fountain*, carved in marble, and featuring plants and fish along with three muscular figures, was shown at the 1915 Panama-Pacific Exposition in San Francisco.

Shortly after World War I was declared in Europe, Whitney founded a hospital in Juilly, France, for war victims. The months she spent in the war zone caused a major change in her work to a naturalistic style featuring subjects drawn from her immediate experience. Small bronzes of soldiers with war injuries were executed rapidly in a loose, impressionistic style, different from the academicism of her public monuments. Whitney was awarded a bronze medal at the Panama-Pacific International Exposition in 1915 and the Medal of the New York Society of Architects in 1922.

Whitney is best known for her monumental sculptures, such as the *Titanic Memorial* (1914, Potomac Park, Washington, D.C.), an eighteen-foot-high figure in pink granite posed with outstretched arms, soaring above a thirty-foot-wide stone bench decorated with dolphins. The public monument was not installed until 1931. The *St. Nazaire Monument* (1924) in France and *Buffalo Bill* (1924), a thirteen-foot rearing horse and rider for the Buffalo Bill Historical Center in Wyoming, are among her notable sculptures.

Throughout her life Whitney was instrumental in promoting young American artists because she believed in the creative talent of her countrymen. She formed the Friends of Young Artists in 1915 and the Whitney Studio Club in 1918. Located in a building adjoining her studio in Greenwich Village, the Whitney Studio Club provided opportunities for artists to socialize, draw from models, and exhibit their work. Whitney had purchased more than five hundred paintings and sculptures from various exhibitions, and these she offered to New York's Metropolitan Museum of Art in 1929. When her collection was refused, she determined to open her own museum, with Juliana Force as the first director. In 1931 Whitney established the Whitney Museum of American Art on Eighth Street, helping to promote modernism in America and counter charges of provincialism leveled at American art. She sought to exhibit the works of Americans abroad, and she established *Arts Magazine* to promote research on modern art. Whitney was a member of the National Academy of Design, the Association of Women Painters and Sculptors, and the National Sculpture Society. She died in New York City.

Gertrude Vanderbilt Whitney is remembered as the founder of the Whitney Museum of American Art in New York and as the patron of many early modernists in America. Her sculpture, including commissions for public monuments, was largely in the academic style prevalent in the early twentieth century and less progressive than the works of artists she supported. Renowned as an art collector and philanthropist, she had to struggle to be taken seriously as an artist.

• Extensive archival holdings for Whitney can be found in the Archives of American Art, Smithsonian Institution

(Whitney Museum of American Art / Gertrude Vanderbilt Whitney Papers, rolls 2356–75; 2888–89; 4861). A biography is B. H. Friedman, *Gertrude Vanderbilt Whitney* (1978). See Guy Pène du Bois, "Mrs. Whitney's Journey into Art," *International Studio* 76 (Jan. 1923): 351–54; Whitney Museum of American Art, *Gertrude Vanderbilt Whitney, Memorial Exhibition* (1943), with a foreword by Juliana Force; and Margaret Breuning, "Gertrude Vanderbilt Whitney's Sculpture," *Magazine of Art* 36 (Feb. 1943): 62–65. Also see Avis Berman, *Rebels on Eighth Street: Juliana Force and the Whitney Museum of American Art* (1990).

JOAN MARTER

WHITNEY, Harry Payne (29 Apr. 1872–26 Oct. 1930), financier and sportsman, was born in New York City, the son of William Collins Whitney, a lawyer and financier, and Flora Payne. As the first son of wealthy parents, Whitney attended the Groton School and graduated Phi Beta Kappa from Yale University in 1894. He studied law at Columbia University in 1895 and 1896, as well as under Elihu Root, but he neither graduated nor took the bar examination. Characterized by one professor as "one of the most brilliant students I have known," Whitney found that his law studies interfered with polo. In 1896 he married Gertrude Vanderbilt, later a sculptor of some acclaim, with whom he had three children. In 1902 Gertrude wrote in her journal of her husband, "His nature is a strong one and given to many impulses and combined with a brain of unusual activity he might live to do great things . . . He has known no discipline. Life has given him all he has asked of it from the beginning. Indulgent parents provided for every wish before it was uttered; it is most wonderful of all that he retains any strength."

Whitney joined his father in business. Representing his family's interest in the Guggenheim Exploration Company (Guggenex), he accompanied Daniel Guggenheim west in 1902 to explore for silver, copper, and lead for the smelting business. Whitney financed the building of the resulting Guggenex mines until the profitable firm disbanded in 1916. Assuming increasing responsibility within his father's banking, mining, real estate, and street railway businesses, Whitney served as a director of twenty companies. Following his father's death in 1904, Whitney inherited $10 million—half of his father's estate—and increased this fortune more than sixfold by the time of his own death. On his own, Whitney invested in the petroleum industry, including Mammoth Oil and Sinclair Oil, and in mining companies.

Despite his success in business, Whitney preferred to spend his time playing polo, yachting, and building a successful horse racing stable and breeding farm. Whitney first distinguished himself in the sports world as a five-time, ten-goal-handicap polo player—the highest rank in the sport. As captain he led the American team, also known as the "Big Four," to its first International Cup victory against the British in 1909, and again in 1911 and 1913. Under Whitney's direction, the team radically changed the sport by using the back as an offensive player, a strategy later adopted by the British and Argentine players. Polo historian Thomas F. Dale wrote of Whitney that "he was able to obtain a unity of purpose of action from his men which English leaders have so far often failed to do" (quoted in Bowmar, p. 189). When age and stiffness hampered his ability to play competitive polo, Whitney served as chairman of the executive committee (1923–1924) and member of the selection committee (1924) of the U.S. Polo Association.

Introduced to horse racing by his father, who had successful stables in America and England, Whitney helped out at sales, planned strategy, and oversaw the English racing stable from 1901 to 1903. With his friend Herman B. Duryea, he purchased in 1902 his first two-year-old, Irish Lad, from John E. Madden. Madden noted that "they were exceptionally keen observers—learned the ropes quicker than any men I ever knew. Harry Payne Whitney has few, if any, equals in this line (selecting horses)" (quoted in Bowmar, p. 184). When his father died, Whitney bought his horses.

Racing a full stable under his own name for the first time in 1905, Whitney earned more that year than his father's stable had ever won and placed second on the owners list with $170,447. The Whitney stable ranked first eight times and near the top consistently between 1905 and 1930. Whitney replaced Madden as top breeder in 1929 with $825,374—a record that stood until 1944. His horses won nearly $4 million (twice as much as any other owner), and he bred 140 stakes winners—more than anybody of his time. Among Whitney's leading stakes-winning horses were Burgomaster, John P. Grier, Whisk Broom II, Mother Goose, Whiskery, Equipoise, and Top Flight. In 1915 Regret became the first, and for sixty-five years the only, filly to win the Kentucky Derby. The aptly named Upset defeated the great Man O'War in 1919 for his only loss. From 1904 until his death Whitney leased Lewis S. Thompson's Brookdale Farm in Lincroft, New Jersey, for his training facility, and in 1916 he moved the breeding operation to Lexington, Kentucky. By that time he also maintained breeding facilities in England. Whitney served as vice president of the Saratoga Association for the Improvement of the Breed of Horses and as a director of the Westchester Racing Association. Whitney's major influence on horse racing was his emphasis on developing outstanding two-year-old thoroughbreds. According to turf historian John Hervey, Whitney's "paramount ambition was the production of brilliant two-year-olds, in which he won unequalled success" (Hervey, p. 164).

Whitney devoted considerable time to his own pursuits, to the exclusion of his wife and children. Their marriage became an impersonal arrangement in which he attended to his horses, polo, shooting, and business, while Gertrude developed her sculpting talents. One of the many interests the couple did not share was hunting. In 1922 Whitney bought "Foshalee," a quail plantation in Leon County, Florida, adjoining Lewis S. Thompson's "Sunny Hill." At the time he seemed to be ready for a quieter type of hunt than the Indian tiger shoots he liked in his youth. Whitney's dogs excelled in the Georgia-Florida Field Trials. At the time Whitney served as vice president of the Georgia-Florida Field Trial Club in 1925, his dog Lady won third place in the trials. Two of his dogs placed first and second in 1926 and 1928.

Whitney's charitable activity centered around New York City's Museum of Natural History, the New York Public Library, the Metropolitan Museum of Art, and the Whitney Art Museum, the latter having been established by his wife. During World War I he supported a French hospital, contributed $100,000 to the Red Cross, subscribed heavily to war bonds, donated to various war relief agencies, and subsidized the First Yale Unit (an aviation training program). He died of pneumonia at his New York City home, leaving $71 million to his wife and children.

• The Gertrude Vanderbilt Whitney Papers at the Whitney Museum of Art contain the only extant letters of Harry Payne Whitney. Edwin P. Hoyt, *The Whitneys: An Informal Portrait, 1635–1975* (1976); B. H. Friedman, *Gertrude Vanderbilt Whitney* (1978); and W. A. Swanberg, *Whitney Father, Whitney Heiress* (1980), provide insight into his business dealings and personal relationships. Dan M. Bowmar III, *Giants of the Turf; the Alexanders, the Belmonts, James R. Keene, the Whitneys* (1960); John Hervey, *Racing in America, 1922–1936* (1937); and Edward Hotaling, *They're Off! Horse Racing at Saratoga* (1995), discuss Whitney's contributions to horse racing. An obituary is in the *New York Times*, 27 Oct. 1930.

SUSAN HAMBURGER

WHITNEY, Hassler (23 Mar. 1907–10 May 1989), mathematician, was born in New York City, the son of Edward Baldwin Whitney, a judge, and Josepha Newcomb. Whitney was a grandson of philologist William D. Whitney and astronomer Simon Newcomb, both of whom were members of the National Academy of Sciences. Whitney received a Ph.B. in 1928 and a Mus.B. in 1929 from Yale University, before entering Harvard University for graduate studies in mathematics. There, as a student of George D. Birkhoff, he received a Ph.D. in mathematics in 1932, with the dissertation "The Coloring of Graphs." During 1930–1931 he was an instructor of mathematics at Harvard, and from 1931 to 1933 he was a National Research Council Fellow at Harvard and at Princeton University. He then returned to Harvard, where he was successively instructor (1933–1935), assistant professor (1935–1940), associate professor (1940–1946), and professor (1946–1952). From 1943 to 1945 he was a member of the Mathematics Panel of the National Defense Research Committee. In 1952 he joined the Institute for Advanced Study at Princeton, where he was professor of mathematics until his retirement in 1977 (he remained there as emeritus professor until his death). During 1951–1952 he was an exchange professor in France and Fulbright exchange professor at the Collège de France in 1957.

Whitney once characterized his research interests as "a search for inner reasons" of phenomena, in which he studied the situation from various viewpoints, made bold guesses, and then tried again and again. Using this methodology, he was remarkably successful both in producing new ideas that were to be of seminal value for future work and in discovering and proving major theorems in algebraic and differential topology. Indeed, it would be difficult to cite another topologist of his generation who was more influential and innovative in his contributions. His first research was in graph theory and was a byproduct of his doctoral work on the celebrated four-color problem. At the time this theory was in a nascent stage of development, and Whitney introduced many new tools that would prove to be of lasting importance. These included the notion of duality, which he showed could be used to characterize planar graphs (1933), and an abstract theory of linear dependence and independence, which led to the theory of matroids (1935). Many of these were later applied by others in combinatorics and in the theory of electrical networks. He also did early work on global analysis on properties of differentiable functions defined on closed subsets of n-dimensional Euclidean space (1934), and subsequently he investigated the singularities of mappings between such higher dimensional spaces (1944). These results were to be of importance in René Thom's catastrophe theory (1969).

Whitney's most famous work was connected with his founding of the theory of differentiable manifolds and its related machinery in algebraic and differential topology. Breaking new ground, he proved the famous Whitney theorems, that every n-dimensional differentiable manifold can be embedded in a Euclidean space of dimension 2n+1 and immersed in such a space of dimension 2n (1935, 1936). These results employed the notion of a tubular neighborhood, which has become a very useful modern differential topology. In 1935 he introduced the notion of "sphere spaces," which was later renamed "sphere bundles" (1940) and was a precursor of the contemporary theory of fiber bundles. Almost simultaneously, he was a codiscoverer, with Swiss topologist Eduard Stiefel, of the concept of characteristic classes. The Stiefel-Whitney classes (1935, 1936) were a major advance in the mathematical apparatus of algebraic topology, and Whitney contributed important duality and product theorems (1939). Every paper of his during the years from 1935 to 1940 contained important new ideas. These include the notions of the "cap" and "cup" products (1935), the "section" of a fiber bundle (1937), and an abstract theory of tensors based on the tensor product of abelian groups (1938). Much of this material was masterfully summarized in his survey paper "Topological Properties of Differentiable Manifolds" (1937) and his Michigan topology lectures "On the Topology of Differentiable Manifolds" (1940). During the early 1940s Whitney intended to write a book on fiber bundles, and he vigorously pursued this theory in friendly competition with the French school of Charles Ehresmann and J. Feldbau. This book was never completed, and the material finally received its definitive treatment in Norman Steenrod's classic book *The Topology of Fibre Bundles* (1951). After the war Whitney turned his attention to the interaction of algebraic topology with integration theory (1947). This was the topic of his address to the 1950 International Congress of Mathematicians and his first book, *Geometric Integration Theory* (1957). Later his interests shifted to complex global analysis, and this led to a second book, *Complex Analytic Varieties* (1972). Both of these volumes were notable contributions to the literature and offer a revealing glimpse of Whitney's originality and of his style in mathematical exposition. A few years before his retirement, Whitney became actively involved in mathematical education at the elementary school level. He gave a number of lectures on this topic, conducted summer courses for teachers, and on one occasion spent four months teaching pre-algebra mathematics to a seventh grade class of students.

Much honored during his lifetime, Whitney was elected a member of the National Academy of Science in 1945. He was colloquium lecturer of the American Mathematical Society in 1946 and served as its vice president from 1948 to 1950. He was an editor of the *American Journal of Mathematics* (1944–1949) and the *Mathematical Reviews* (1949–1954). He was a recipient of the National Medal of Science in 1976, a co-winner of the Wolf Foundation Prize in 1983, and winner of the Steele Prize of the American Mathematical Society in 1985. He was also president of the International Committee on Mathematical Instruction (1979–1982) and a foreign associate of the Académie des Sciences of Paris.

Whitney was married three times. In 1930 he married Margaret R. Howell, with whom he had three children. After their divorce, he married Mary Barnett Garfield in 1955; they had two children. This marriage also ended in divorce, and in 1985 he married artist Barbara Floyd Osterman; they had no children. He died in Princeton.

• An autobiographical sketch appears in Sybil P. Parker, ed., *McGraw Hill Modern Scientists and Engineers*, vol. 3 (1980), pp. 309–10. His personal reminiscences are related in "Letting Research Come Naturally," *Mathematical Chronicle* 14 (1985): 1–19; his reply on receiving the Steele Prize in *Notices of the American Mathematical Society* 32 (Oct. 1985): 577–79; and in "Moscow 1935: Topology Moving toward America," in *A Century of Mathematics in America*, pt. 1, ed. Peter Duren (1988), pp. 97–117. Many of his mathematical papers are included in the two-volume *Hassler Whitney: Collected Papers*, ed. James Eells and Domingo Toledo (1992). Whitney's work is discussed in Norman L. Biggs et al., eds., *Graph Theory: 1736–1936* (1976), and in Jean Dieudonné, *A History of Algebraic and Differential Topology: 1900–1960* (1989). An obituary is in the *New York Times*, 12 May 1989.

JOSEPH D. ZUND

WHITNEY, Helen Hay (11 Mar. 1876–24 Sept. 1944), sportswoman and philanthropist, was born in New York City, the daughter of John Hay, secretary of state to Presidents William McKinley and Theodore Roosevelt and ambassador to Great Britain, and Clara Louise Stone. Helen attended the elite Miss Masters' School in Dobbs Ferry, New York. After her graduation from this school, she wrote several volumes of poetry, including *Some Verses* (1898), *The Rose of Dawn* (1901), and *The Punch and Judy Book* (1906). These literary endeavors were immensely pleasing to her father, who sent her work to his publishing friends and was said to have shown more enthusiasm for her writing than he had for anything else in years.

In 1902 Helen married financier Payne Whitney; they had one son and one daughter. Their wedding ceremony was a major social event in Washington, D.C., with guests including President Roosevelt and his entire cabinet. Wedding gifts to the couple included a home on Fifth Avenue in New York City, a yacht, and numerous pieces of diamond jewelry.

With her husband, Whitney developed a lifelong interest in horse racing, which ultimately led her to become known as the "first lady of the American turf." Her purchase in 1909 of steeplechaser Web Carter began her establishment of Greentree Stable in Red Bank, New Jersey. By the 1920s this 150-acre facility was recognized as one of the country's most significant steeplechasing stables and one of the largest ever run by a woman in the United States. Known for its horses carrying pink and black silks, Whitney's stable was among the top money-winners in the United States for some twenty years. It achieved particular success in 1931 and 1942, when her horses won the Kentucky Derby and placed well in other races.

Whitney's interest in horse racing extended into the world of politics. She used her wealth and influence to fight the efforts of New York Governor Charles Evans Hughes to enact antigambling legislation in the state and also to fight in 1939 for the legalization of parimutuel betting. She was credited with bringing the support of many society women to the sport of horse racing and with leading the effort to raise money among turf patrons for war relief during World War II.

Whitney served as honorary vice president of the Horticultural Society of New York. She was also a major supporter of the New York Hospital and the Henry Street Settlement in New York City. Beginning in 1919 she held an annual Greentree Fair at her estate in Manhasset, New York, to benefit the Family Welfare Association of Nassau County and the New York Hospital. In 1930 she and her children gave a major gift to Yale University for the construction of a new gymnasium in memory of her husband, who died in 1927. Whitney died in New York City.

A woman who was born into immense wealth and prestige and married into even more, Whitney used her money and position to further the sport of horse racing and to support charitable causes. Her financial success with Greentree Stable placed her among the elite in horse racing and earned her stable the added distinction of female leadership.

• A lengthy entry on Whitney, including an artist's rendering of her, is included in the *National Cyclopedia of American Biography* (1947). Shorter but significant insights into Whitney's family life are found in Tyler Dennett, *John Hay: From*

Poetry to Politics (1934), and Richard Kluger, *The Paper: The Life and Death of the New York Herald Tribune* (1986). A detailed obituary is in the *New York Times*, 25 Sept. 1944.

DEBBIE MAULDIN COTTRELL

WHITNEY, James Lyman (28 Nov. 1835–25 Sept. 1910), librarian, was born in Northampton, Massachusetts, the son of Josiah Dwight Whitney and Clarissa James. After early schooling at home and in boarding school, he prepared at the Northampton Collegiate Institute for Yale College, from which he received a B.A. in 1856. As an undergraduate, Whitney served as assistant librarian, then as librarian, of the Society of Brothers in Unity. After graduating, he remained at Yale as Berkeley Scholar of the House until 1857, when he moved to New York to work at the Wiley and Halsted publishing house. A year later, he moved to Springfield, Massachusetts, where he worked as a bookseller for Bridgman and Company and became a book trader in his own business, Whitney and Adams. In 1865 Yale granted Whitney an M.A.

In 1868 Whitney moved to Ohio to become assistant librarian at the Cincinnati Public Library. The next year he began service at the Boston Public Library, with which he retained an association for the rest of his life. In 1874 he was appointed chief of the catalog department, and in 1899 he was made librarian. Although ill health forced his resignation in 1903, he remained at the library as chief of the department of documents and statistics, a less stressful position.

Whitney was considered a dedicated librarian and a companionable and tolerant friend who handled his responsibilities with ease. He compiled and edited the *Catalogue of the Spanish Library and of the Portuguese Books Bequeathed by George Ticknor to the Boston Public Library: Together with the Collection of Spanish and Portuguese Literature in the General Library* (1879) and prepared a guide to the library's catalogs (1880) and a catalog of bibliographies of special subjects in the Boston Public Library (1890). His other writings include an unpublished biography of his predecessor as library director, Justin Winsor (1898), and an index to the pictures and plans of library buildings found in the Boston Public Library (1899).

In 1876 Whitney praised the *Index-Catalogue of the Library of the Surgeon-General's Office* (now the National Library of Medicine) when it was introduced that year at the Conference of Librarians at the Historical Society of Pennsylvania in Philadelphia (*American Library Journal*, nos. 2–3 [30 Nov. 1876]: 122). This catalog had been prepared by Whitney's colleague John S. Billings as an "alphabetical and anatomical arrangement, preferring the single alphabet to separate catalogues of authors and subjects." At the same 1876 conference, the American Library Association was organized "for librarians to become acquainted with one another." Whitney, an ALA charter member, was appointed to the Committee on the Sizes of Books. In 1886 he was elected president of ALA's Publishing Section, the product of librarians' concerns that certain kinds of publications could be handled more effectively in published bibliographies than in the subject catalogs of individual libraries. He was also head of ALA's finance committee and ALA treasurer.

Whitney's greatest contribution to American librarianship was his support of the development of a more accessible library catalog system. In 1899 he issued a report that signaled the end of the full printed catalog in book form. In "Considerations as to a Printed Catalogue in Book Form for the Public Library of the City of Boston," part of the forty-seventh annual report of the Boston Public Library, he systematically presented reasons why that library should not print its full catalog. He reasoned that even if no entries were added for books received after printing had begun, it would take from sixteen to twenty years to complete the catalog, and the demand for copies would be minimal. During the latter part of the nineteenth century, librarians were looking for some technological development to support retention of a printed book catalog until the Library of Congress inaugurated its printed catalog card distribution system in 1901. The Library of Congress system made available sets of cards containing complete bibliographical information for all of its books. These could be purchased by any library that wanted them, revolutionizing and centralizing the cataloging process and allowing local libraries to put their books on the shelves much faster. Whitney enthusiastically supported the card system against much opposition that favored the traditional book catalogs. His visibility in the American Library Association gave his views great significance, and that system was eventually adopted.

Whitney, who never married, served as chair from 1879 to 1887 of the school committee in Concord, Massachusetts, where he was then living. He died at his home in Cambridge, Massachusetts.

• Material on Whitney in the Rare Books and Manuscripts Division of the Boston Public Library includes the Boston Public Library trustees' records, copies of his publications, and an unpublished 1909 autobiography, "Reminiscences of an Old Librarian." The American Library Association Archives, Champaign, Ill., has Whitney documents in the Annual Conference record series in its Attendance Registers (1890–1900), the Cumulative Attendance Registers (1876–1939), the Administrative and Fiscal Series records (1885–1927), the Membership Dues Accounts Journals (1876–1909), and the Edward G. Holley Scrapbook Collection, among other records. There is also a signed letter in the Barbara McCrimmon Autograph Collection. The Manuscript Division, Library of Congress, has Whitney material in the Whiting Griswold correspondence. An obituary is in the *New York Times*, 26 Sept. 1910.

MARTIN J. MANNING

WHITNEY, John Hay (17 Aug. 1904–8 Feb. 1982), financier, philanthropist, and sportsman, was born in Ellsworth, Maine, the son of Payne Whitney, a capitalist and philanthropist, and Helen Hay, at the time a poet. "Jock" Whitney graduated from Yale in 1926 and studied history and literature at Oxford for one year. His father's death in 1927 brought him home to assume control over the Whitney business interests in oil, tobacco, street railways, and real estate, worth cumulatively almost $179 million.

At an early age Whitney developed his lifelong interests in theater, film, journalism, and sports. He pursued his love of theater and film as an investor in Broadway shows and motion pictures. Between 1928 and 1948 he backed forty plays, including *Gay Divorcee*, *Charley's Aunt*, *Life with Father*, and *A Streetcar Named Desire*. Whitney did not simply invest his money but read scripts and participated in the casting of shows. He entered the motion picture business in 1933 as owner of Pioneer Pictures, which introduced Technicolor. Between 1935 and 1940 he was the New York–based chair of the board and East Coast manager handling the commercial end of Selznick International Pictures, which made ten films, including the hits *A Star Is Born*, *The Prisoner of Zenda*, *Rebecca*, and *Gone with the Wind*. He handled the bookings, advertising, and foreign distribution and, with David O. Selznick, acquired story properties and made major casting decisions. Not every play or film Whitney backed found box office success, but his $2 million investment in movies earned him a profit of $1.5 million by 1948.

Whitney was a member of the board of trustees for the Museum of Modern Art in New York City beginning in 1930. He began its film library after the museum put him in charge of soliciting films and money from the studios between 1935 and 1955.

With the advent of World War II Whitney sold his film interests and enrolled in officers' training. In the fall of 1940 he joined with Nelson Rockefeller to run the Motion Picture Division of the Office of the Co-ordinator of Inter-American Affairs to develop better relations with Latin America. Whitney received his commission as captain in the U.S. Army Air Force in May 1942 and progressed through the intelligence ranks to colonel. He was captured by and escaped from the Germans in France in 1944. This experience profoundly affected Whitney, and he resolved to channel his resources into three main streams—wise investments, philanthropy, and living well. Whitney's first marriage, to Mary Elizabeth Altemus in 1930, ended in divorce ten years later; they had no children. He married Betsey Cushing Roosevelt in 1942 and adopted her two daughters in 1949.

He created the John Hay Whitney Foundation in 1946 to "promote the development of knowledge and application thereof to the improvement of social welfare" by ameliorating the plight of the disadvantaged through funding humanities programs with $1 million each year. Rockefeller said Whitney "has always been on the constructive, liberal side of things and hasn't been afraid to say so" (Kahn, p. 72). Selznick told an interviewer that Whitney was "an extraordinarily able, well-balanced, objective, and conscientious man with a wonderful sense of obligation, both to his wealth and to the public interest" (Kahn, p. 110).

Founded concurrently with the foundation in 1946, J. H. Whitney & Company began with $10 million to invest in chancy enterprises with limited appeal to conventional sources of financing. One of the many successes was Minute Maid orange juice. The original 1946 investment had increased tenfold by 1980; much of the success has been attributed to Jock Whitney's insights into individuals and his knack for evaluating business prospects.

Twice Whitney chaired fundraising committees to elect Dwight D. Eisenhower president; Eisenhower often golfed and hunted quail on Whitney's "Greenwood" plantation in Georgia. Because of his marked shyness and mild stutter, Whitney reluctantly accepted the ambassadorship to the Court of St. James from 1957 to 1960. Whitney's only other diplomatic or foreign relations experience consisted of appointments to the Presidential Commission on Foreign Economic Policy to investigate tariff and trade programs in 1953 and as special ambassador with the U.S. delegation to South Korea in 1956. The diplomatic post to Great Britain afforded Whitney the opportunity to smooth Anglo-American relations and negotiate the West Indian American Defence Agreement, ratified in 1961. While in England, he became interested in the plight of the *New York Herald Tribune* and began investing in the Republican newspaper. He formed the Whitney Communications Corporation in 1958 to buy small weekly newspapers, magazines, and television and radio stations. Upon returning to the United States in 1961, Whitney assumed the role of publisher and editor in chief but failed to salvage the *Tribune*. After spending almost $40 million, he closed the paper in 1966 but converted the Paris edition into the successful *International Herald Tribune*.

Throughout his adult life, Whitney owned horses. He began playing polo in prep school and took up the sport seriously in 1929. His Greentree team won the U.S. open championship in 1935 and in 1936, when he attained a six-goal handicap. Whitney sold the horses in 1939 and retired from active participation. For his twenty-second birthday, Whitney had received two thoroughbreds from his father to start his own racing stable. Two years later he became the youngest member of the American Jockey Club. He began racing thoroughbreds in England in 1928. In America, Whitney kept his stable, Mare's Nest Farm, in Lexington, Kentucky. His mother brought him into a 30 percent partnership in Greentree Stable in 1942; after her death in 1944, Jock and his sister Joan Whitney Payson inherited the remainder of Greentree Stable on Long Island and Greentree Stud in Kentucky. Whitney then incorporated his stable into his 63 percent share of Greentree. He preferred to breed his own racers and bought breeding stock only at sales. Whitney and his sister produced the 1949 Horse of the Year, Capot; the 1953 Horse of the Year, Tom Fool; and the 1968 Belmont Stakes winner, Stage Door Johnny, among other numerous stakes-winning horses. Throughout Whitney's career in racing he thought of it as a sport rather than a business, a philosophy he frequently espoused as an officer of the New York Racing Commission and the Westchester Racing Association and, after 1934, as an executive of the American Thoroughbred Breeders Association. Whitney died at his "Greentree" estate on Long Island.

• Whitney's personal papers are at Yale University's Sterling Library. Papers from his ambassadorship are at the National Archives, RG 84 and RG 59. E. J. Kahn, Jr., *Jock: The Life and Times of John Hay Whitney* (1981), is a full-length biography. Whitney's involvement with publishing is documented in Richard Kluger and Phyllis Kluger, *The Paper: The Life and Death of the New York Herald Tribune* (1986); and his business dealings in the film industry are covered in David Thomson, *Showman: The Life of David O. Selznick* (1992). For his horse-racing interests see Robert V. Hoffman, "Famous Families in Sport: Part II, the Payne Whitneys," *Country Life*, May 1932, pp. 57–59, 76, 78; and Bernard Livingston, *Their Turf: America's Horsey Set and Its Princely Dynasties* (1973), pp. 59–73. An obituary is in the *New York Times*, 9 Feb. 1982.

SUSAN HAMBURGER

WHITNEY, Josiah Dwight (23 Nov. 1819–19 Aug. 1896), geologist, was born in Northampton, Massachusetts, the son of Josiah Dwight Whitney, a well-to-do banker, and Sarah Williston. He was the oldest of his father's thirteen children by two marriages. William Dwight Whitney, Sanskrit scholar and linguist, was a brother, with whom he was particularly close in his adult years. After attending the Round Hill School at Northampton and Phillips Academy at Andover, he entered Yale College, graduating A.B. in 1839. The Winter of 1839–1840 he spent in the study of chemistry with Robert Hare in Philadelphia. Thereafter, he went with introductions to the chemical laboratory of Charles T. Jackson in Boston and in 1840–1841 assisted Jackson in his geological survey of New Hampshire. In the summer of 1841 he studied law at Northampton and set out for the Harvard Law School but never entered.

With the aid of his father and advice of Jackson, Whitney, having decided on a scientific career, left in May of 1842 for travel and study in Europe. His three years there took him from Holland to Moscow and included periods of study at the École des Mines in Paris and the Collège de France, field work with France's renowned geologist and cartographer Élie de Beaumont, and analytical work in Karl F. Rammelsberg's chemical laboratory in Berlin.

Whitney returned from Europe in 1845. That summer he was a field geologist for the Isle Royale Copper Company in northern Michigan, again as a result of C. T. Jackson's help. By the end of the year he was heading back to Europe with commissions to investigate mining and cloth works in Germany. During this excursion Whitney spent time in the Berlin laboratory of Heinrich Rose, the eminent analytical chemist, and studied in Giessen with Justus von Liebig, who was then at the peak of his powers as a chemical theorist and laboratory director. He returned home in May 1847, by then one of the best-trained scientists in the United States.

Whitney soon became a first assistant on Jackson's U.S. Lake Superior survey. The primary purpose of the survey was ore exploration, but it also encompassed other geological and natural features of the region. As a result of criticisms of various aspects of the survey, Whitney and the other assistant, John W. Foster, resigned in spring 1849, but the outcome of a government investigation led to the retirement of Jackson and the assignment of the two assistants to complete the work. A synopsis of the study appeared in 1849, and the remaining field work was accomplished in 1850. Whitney established a private laboratory at Brookline, Massachusetts, and carried out the analysis and writing for the Lake Superior survey; the resulting reports (coauthored with Foster) on the copper lands (1850) and iron region (1851) were issued as congressional documents.

Whitney settled in Cambridge, and in the early 1850s was active as a consultant mining engineer. He traveled widely throughout the United States east of the Mississippi. Drawing on his wide experience, in 1854 he published a work on American ores that became the standard overview of the subject. His strict code of scientific ethics was a deterrent to his becoming involved as an owner in any of the mining properties he appraised. He also married Louisa (Goddard) Howe in 1854. They had one daughter.

From 1855 to 1858, Whitney was professor of chemistry at the University of Iowa, although his chief assignment was with the state geological survey. James Hall (1811–1898) was titular head of the survey, but the greater part of the work was Whitney's. During the second half of the 1850s, Whitney also was associated with the Wisconsin survey (with Hall) and the survey of Illinois. The work in all three states involved studies of the lead region. His home base in this period was at Northampton.

Interested in a California survey since the late 1840s, he gained an advantage when a sister, Elizabeth, took up residence there and her influential husband promoted the idea. Whitney is said to have drafted the bill that resulted in his appointment as California state geologist in 1860. His fourteen years in the position encompassed his most significant scientific work but also involved him in controversy.

Whitney assembled a notable staff, including first assistant William H. Brewer (a geologist and botanist), William Ashburner, Clarence King (who later became head of the U.S. Geological Survey), topographer Charles F. Hoffman, James G. Cooper as zoologist, and William M. Gabb, paleontologist. In addition to describing the geological aspects of the state, the survey published reports on ornithology and botany. Several persons not directly connected with the survey were called upon to contribute to this work. The survey gave experience to scientists who went on to other work in the West. It also developed a useful method of triangulation for mountainous regions that made more accurate topographical mapping possible. The method subsequently was adopted by other surveys. The apparent loyalty that Whitney gained from those directly connected with the survey, however, was not reflected in his more public relations. Although he had engaged in scientific investigation supported by commercial interests, Whitney's identification was with the advocates of basic science studies. This naturally conflicted with the seekers after gold and other natural resources in those early California days. The precariousness of the state's finances also contributed to the volatility of the situation, and at times Whitney borrowed funds from his father to support the survey. Whitney emphasized a survey that would characterize the general geological structure of the state, and the first publication was on paleontology (1864). Under criticism for not tending to economic interests, Whitney frequently responded insensitively, which only led to further trouble.

Whitney's personality was a major factor in the evolution of his career. What seems to have been a strain of natural irritability was combined with his defense of pure science and an unbending professional ethic. One aspect of Whitney's pique involved the wider scientific community. In 1864, chemist and geologist Benjamin Silliman, Jr., was in California working for commercial interests hoping to promote oil exploration. Silliman's optimistic report, after a rather superficial reconnaissance and a sample later determined to have been mixed with kerosene, conflicted with the Whitney survey's conclusion that production of a commercially viable illuminant from California petroleum was unlikely (though oil eventually became a significant enterprise there). The controversy that resulted, combined with Whitney's overly optimistic promises of what the survey would do, led to the suspension of the survey in 1868. It was given new life in 1870, but support came to an end in 1874.

Whitney was an incorporating member of the National Academy of Sciences (1863). In the mid-1870s he took what amounted to a prosecutorial campaign against Silliman to the academy, attempting to drive him from membership on the basis of several instances of what he considered unethical behavior, including the oil case. Interestingly, Whitney never personally studied the oil region in question. The academy finally concluded that such a normative proceeding against a member was not part of its prerogative. Whitney terminated his membership, as did his brother William.

Controversy followed Whitney in his arguments for the antiquity of humanity in the Pacific coast region. His theorizing was based on the Calaveras skull, which reportedly was found in a mine shaft in that county in 1866. Subsequent judgment labels the episode a hoax and Whitney a too-gullible protagonist.

During his term with the California survey, Whitney had collateral involvements in the state, including a period (1860–1865) as chair of a commission charged with drafting plans for a state university. He also served as head of a board of commissioners to manage Yosemite National Park. In 1869, as state geologist, he published a *Yosemite Guide-Book*. He maintained his connections with the East, however, and Harvard University appointed him to the new Sturgis-Hooper professorship of geology in 1865, a position he retained until his death. At the same time the School of Mining and Practical Geology was established at Harvard, of which Whitney became dean in 1868. In 1875 it was united with the university's Lawrence Scientific School. In 1869 he led a group of students on a summer of study and exploration in Colorado.

After the termination of the California survey, and a trip to Europe in 1874, Whitney settled more fully into his professorial duties. He was exempt from teaching introductory courses. After the mining school's closure, his chief affiliation in the university was with the Museum of Comparative Zoology. He continued work on material accumulated in California, producing notable publications on auriferous gravels and on climatic changes in past geologic eras. But a complete report for the survey never materialized.

Whitney was a member of the American Academy of Arts and Sciences, the Geological Society of London, and other scientific organizations. Mount Whitney, the highest mountain in the contiguous United States, was named for him. He was a serious book collector and much interested in music. Whitney died at Lake Sunapee, New Hampshire.

• Major locations for Whitney's papers are the Whitney family collection in the Yale University Library (where his extensive correspondence with brother William resides) and the Bancroft Library at the University of California, Berkeley. Brewster (see below) excerpts a number of Whitney's letters and on pp. 387–400 includes a bibliography of his major writings. These include *The Metallic Wealth of the United States, Described and Compared with That of Other Countries* (1854); as state geologist with the Geological Survey of California, *Geology.*, vol. 1, *Report of Progress and Synopsis of the Field-work, from 1860 to 1864* (1865); *The Auriferous Gravels of the Sierra Nevada of California* (1880); and *The Climatic Changes of Later Geological Times: A Discussion Based on Observations Made in the Cordilleras of North America* (1882). Edwin T. Brewster, *Life and Letters of Josiah Dwight Whitney* (1909), is the basic biography. The California story, including the protracted conflict with Silliman, is well and thoroughly told in Gerald T. White, *Scientists in Conflict: The Beginnings of the Oil Industry in California* (1968).

CLARK A. ELLIOTT

WHITNEY, Mary Watson (11 Sept. 1847–20 Jan. 1921), astronomer, was born in Waltham, Massachusetts, the daughter of Samuel Buttrick Whitney, a real-estate dealer, and Mary Watson Crehore. She graduated from Waltham High School showing a strong mathematical aptitude and attended an academy in her home town for a year. With her family's support of her excellent intellectual abilities, in 1865 she enrolled in the newly opened Vassar Female College (now Vassar College) in Poughkeepsie, New York. Having received advanced standing, she received her undergraduate degree in astronomy with honors in only three years, in 1868, as part of Vassar's second graduating class. She excelled in all subjects and was the best of Maria Mitchell's first class of six astronomy students, popularly called the Hexagon. She taught in Auburndale, Massachusetts, after graduation in order to be with her family after her father's death while continuing to pursue her study of astronomy and mathematics.

Whitney accompanied Mitchell and her female students to Burlington, Iowa, to observe a total eclipse in August 1869. Because she was a woman, Whitney could find no employment in astronomy. On Mitchell's suggestion, she studied celestial mechanics and quaternions with Harvard College mathematician Benjamin Peirce, although women were not allowed course credit at Harvard at the time. Whitney subsequently worked in the Dearborn Observatory in Chicago for several months, after which Vassar awarded her a master's degree in 1872 for her individual study.

Whitney studied mathematics from 1873 to 1876 at the University of Zurich, Switzerland, where her sister was a medical student, before returning to the United States to teach high school at her alma mater in Waltham, since no astronomy jobs were available to her. She accompanied the Vassar women on another eclipse expedition to Colorado in July 1878.

In 1881 Mitchell urged Whitney to return to Vassar to assist at the observatory. Whitney assumed the observatory directorship and astronomy professorship in 1888, after Mitchell's retirement, and remained there until 1910 when partial paralysis forced her to retire. Approximately two hundred astronomical plates of variable stars, comets, and asteroids imaged by Whitney and her collaborators remain in the Vassar collection. While at Vassar, she determined the longitude of the new Smith College Observatory and studied Nova Aurigae and other variable stars, as well as comets.

Whitney's research also included a collaboration with Jacobus C. Kapteyn in Groningen, Netherlands. She was part of the team effort of photography and astrometry of Kapteyn's "selected areas," which were fundamental to the understanding of the rotational kinematics of our Milky Way galaxy. Her arrangement with Columbia University to analyze photographic plates of star clusters taken by Lewis Rutherfurd prompted her to actively involve students in undergraduate research. Whitney was a prolific writer, especially for her day; she wrote or collaborated on seventy-five articles in professional journals, notably the *Astronomical Journal*, and oversaw the publication of more than a hundred articles of the Vassar College Observatory during her directorship.

Whitney was also a dedicated and popular teacher. Her student and successor as observatory director, Caroline Furness, remarked that Whitney "gave out such a bright glow that it brightened all who came within her sphere" and that "in discovering such talents [of her students] and in giving them preliminary training, Miss Whitney made a greater contribution to astronomy than any she had any conception of." Many of her students continued in astronomy careers. In 1906 she gave one of the first courses anywhere on variable stars. In addition to her mathematical astronomy courses, she designed astronomy courses for non-science students.

Whitney was a charter member of the American Astronomical Society in 1899 and was elected a fellow of the American Association for the Advancement of Science. She was active in supporting equality for women throughout her career, especially because she had had difficult experiences trying to find employment as an astronomer. Whitney was the first president of the Maria Mitchell Association in Nantucket, Massachusetts, which was established in 1902. When an observatory was built on the island in 1908, she helped raise funds to support a female research fellow. She was a founder and first president of the Vassar Alumnae Association and bequeathed $5,000 to Vassar in her will, to be devoted to pure research by women. She also helped the college purchase a comparator and a small telescope. Whitney died in her hometown of Waltham, Massachusetts.

• Whitney's life in the context of Maria Mitchell is discussed further in Dorrit Hoffleit, *Famous Students of Maria Mitchell* (1983). Further recollections of her life were reported by her student Caroline Furness in *Popular Astronomy* 30 (Dec. 1922): 600, and 31 (Jan. 1923): 25; in Frederick C. Pierce, *Whitney: The Descendants of John Whitney* (1895), and in C. F. Crehore, *A Genealogy of the Crehore Family* (1887).

DEBRA ELMEGREEN

WHITNEY, William Collins (5 July 1841–2 Feb. 1904), lawyer and public official, was born in Conway, Massachusetts, the son of James Scollay Whitney, a former brigadier general of militia, and Laurinda Collins. Whitney grew up in a comfortable middle-class atmosphere in the lower Berkshire Hills of western Massachusetts. His politically active father was a Democrat, and Whitney himself would never swerve from allegiance to the Democratic party. The family moved to Springfield, Massachusetts, in 1854 and six years later to Boston, where Whitney's father served briefly as collector for the port of Boston. Whitney graduated from Williston Academy and went on to Yale where he excelled in his studies and rowed on the crew team. He graduated with honors in 1863 and attended Harvard Law School for one year (1863–1864). Admitted to the bar in 1865, Whitney moved to New York City where he developed a law practice by 1867. Even in these early years, it was generally acknowledged that he displayed an unusual combination of energy and intelligence, traits that would serve him well in the years ahead.

In 1869 Whitney married Flora Payne, the sister of one of his Yale classmates and the daughter of Henry B. Payne. The wealth of his father-in-law permitted Whitney to live in a brownstone in New York City, and his connection with the Payne family opened many doors in the social and business communities of the city. The couple had five children, four of whom lived to maturity.

As early as 1870 Whitney spoke out against the "Tweed Ring" that had dominated the politics of New York for a decade. He ran for attorney general of New York State in 1872 but lost the election. In 1875 he was appointed corporation counsel for New York City with a salary of $15,000 (he was subsequently reappointed by two successive mayors). By the late 1870s Whitney had become an important presence in the politics of New York; he was on friendly terms with the Vanderbilt and Astor families. His social success would have been incomplete without the assistance of his wife; Flora Payne Whitney was a societal lioness who loved to give parties.

Whitney's political aspirations came closest to fruition in the 1880s. In association with Thomas Fortune Ryan and Peter A. B. Widener, he gained the franchise for the Metropolitan Railway in New York City, a victory that enabled him to eventually become wealthy in his own right. He became closely associated with Grover Cleveland, and in 1884 he served as one of the three chief architects (Arthur Pue Gorman and Daniel Manning were the others) of Cleveland's presidential campaign. Rewarded for his efforts with the post of secretary of the navy, Whitney and his wife went to Washington, D.C., in the spring of 1885.

A storm of protest erupted over Whitney's appointment. Some newspapers alleged that he was in the pocket of the New York City corporations, and many declared that he was not a fit appointee for the post. Although there may have been some truth to the first accusation, Whitney performed so admirably in his new position that few voices remained in opposition after one year's time. Whitney inherited a navy that had languished since the end of the Civil War; the efforts of his predecessor, William E. Chandler, had been real but limited in their effect, and when Whitney took office the U.S. Navy stood below the navies of most of the European powers and some of the Latin American nations. During four years as secretary, Whitney authorized the expenditure of $80 million in the process of adding 93,000 tons of shipping to the fleet. Five protected cruisers, the USS *Charleston*, *Baltimore*, *Newark*, *Philadelphia* and *San Francisco*, and two battleships, the USS *Maine* and *Texas*, were all built during Whitney's tenure. When he left office in March 1889, following President Cleveland's defeat in 1888, Whitney left a far stronger navy than the one he had found, one that would go on from this strength and that would fight and win the battles of the Spanish American War.

During the same four-year period (1885–1889) Whitney and his wife were the virtual arbiters of Washington, D.C., society. They renovated their new house in the capital for this purpose, adding a ballroom, and it was later estimated that 65,000 guests were entertained by the Whitneys during the Cleveland administration. The dashing couple did experience serious marital conflicts at the same time. Whitney was irritated by his wife's constant entertaining, and she suspected that he was involved with other women. One way the couple was able to smooth over such difficulties was to occupy different residences; they owned properties in Bar Harbor, Maine; Lenox, Massachusetts; New York City; and Washington, D.C.

Often referred to as a model Democratic party man, Whitney was urged by many leading members of the party to seek public office during the 1890s. He declined the invitations and devoted his attention to making money; his efforts with the Metropolitan Railway bore fruit, and he was able to gain a measure of financial independence from his father-in-law. Whitney remained interested in politics, and he was an inveterate adviser to presidential cabinets during the 1890s.

Flora Payne Whitney died from a heart ailment in 1893. Whitney soon experienced a severing of his ties with his father-in-law. In 1896 Whitney married a second time, to Edith Randolph. He bought a new, even grander home in New York City, but his wife died before she ever set foot in it.

Following the death of his second wife, Whitney spent a good deal of time racing horses, both in Saratoga, New York, and in England. One of his horses won the Derby in 1901. He also brought deer and antelope from Wyoming to his estate in Lenox. Whitney died in New York City, leaving at least ten residences and an estate valued at nearly $23 million.

Whitney's remarkable life and career come close to serving as a window into the societal world described in Edith Wharton's *Age of Innocence* (1920). His rise in the business and social circles of New York City came from two factors: his relentless ambition and his propitious marriage to Flora Payne. Striving always to be his own man, Whitney resented the influence of his father-in-law. As a public administrator, he excelled. The growth of the navy during his tenure in office was remarkable, and it was at least in part because of his efforts that the United States entered the twentieth century as one of the five great naval powers of the world. Whitney might well have sought other public offices; he chose instead to increase his wealth, perhaps because he perceived himself as poor compared to his wife's family. One of the most colorful characters of the Gilded Age in New York City, one of the greatest landowners among the unofficial American aristocracy, and one of the most influential businessmen-politicians of his era, Whitney stands as a splendid example of American society in the late nineteenth century, when Horatio Alger novels proclaimed that a poor man could become rich, but when reality demonstrated the crucial importance of social connections.

• Many of Whitney's letters are preserved in the Dorothy Whitney Straight Elmhirst Papers at Cornell University. Biographies of Whitney are Mark D. Hirsch, *William C. Whitney, Modern Warwick* (1948), and W. A. Swanberg, *Whitney Father, Whitney Heiress* (1980). See also Harry James Carman, *The Street Surface Railway Franchises of New York City* (1919); Allan Nevins, *Grover Cleveland, a Study in Courage* (1932); and W. H. Rowe, "The Turf Career of Hon. W. C. Whitney," *Outing*, July 1901. An obituary is in the *New York Times*, 3 Feb. 1904.

SAMUEL WILLARD CROMPTON

WHITNEY, William Dwight (9 Feb. 1827–7 June 1894), linguist, Sanskrit scholar, and lexicographer, was born in Northampton, Massachusetts, the son of

Josiah Dwight Whitney, a businessman and banker, and Sarah Williston. At age fifteen he joined the sophomore class of Williams College, graduating three years later in 1845 as the class valedictorian after having spent "no small part of his time . . . roaming over the hills and through the valleys, collecting birds for the Natural History Society," according to his autobiography (repr. in Silverstein, p. 1). This early interest in natural science was sustained throughout Whitney's life and played an important role in his approach to the study of language.

For three years Whitney worked as a clerk in his father's bank, spending his leisure time collecting plants and birds and studying modern European languages. In 1848 he turned to Sanskrit at the recommendation of his father's pastor, George E. Day, who was from 1866 a professor of Hebrew and then the dean of the divinity school at Yale. Whitney left the bank in the spring of 1849 and, with the second edition of Franz Bopp's Sanskrit grammar (1832) borrowed from his older brother Josiah's library, he continued his self-study of Sanskrit over the summer. During this period he also was a member of the U.S. Geological Survey of the Lake Superior Region, headed by Josiah, who would later hold the post of professor of geology at Harvard. In the autumn Whitney went to Yale for a year of postgraduate study with Edward Elbridge Salisbury, a professor of the Arabic and Sanskrit languages who had studied with Bopp in Berlin and who was the only trained orientalist in the United States until Whitney himself returned from three years of further study of Sanskrit in Europe in 1853. The following year Whitney assumed the professorship in Sanskrit at Yale, initially established and funded by Salisbury. In 1856 he married Elizabeth Wooster Baldwin; they had six children.

During his years in Europe, Whitney studied with several prominent German Sanskritists, including Rudolph Roth, with whom he coedited what became the definitive text of one of the oldest and most important Vedic scriptures, the Atharva Veda, published as *Atharva Veda Sanhita* (1856), after Whitney had copied the manuscripts available in Berlin and collated them with others in Paris, Oxford, and London. Whitney followed this work with numerous articles, editions, translations, and notes on various Sanskrit texts and treatises, several of which appear in his *Oriental and Linguistic Studies* (1874). But his most important work on Sanskrit was *Sanskrit Grammar, Including Both the Classical Language, and the Older Dialects, of Veda and Brahmana*, first published in 1879, with a second edition in 1889, and a formal supplement, *The Roots, Verb-Forms and Primary Derivatives of the Sanskrit Language*, in 1885.

The *Sanskrit Grammar* stood apart from other such work and has withstood the test of time. Rather than adopting the framework of traditional Indian Sanskrit grammarians or applying the comparative method then dominating European linguistic scholarship, Whitney went his own way, providing a descriptive account of the Sanskrit language that drew directly on recorded Sanskrit literature. This was very much in keeping with his overall view of language as a human institution and his unwillingness to generalize beyond the empirical data of extant texts. Indeed, it was precisely on this matter that he most disagreed with the ancient Sanskrit grammarians, arguing that their grammatical rules were too abstract and produced forms that never actually occurred in the texts; for him their accounts were thus lacking in "scientific truth." Yet, as familiar as Whitney was with the literature of Sanskrit, he could never achieve the insights of the native grammarians whose own knowledge—as for all native speakers of every language—went far beyond a corpus. While his reluctance to generalize the principles of the language beyond what he could observe directly was prudent, it was also overly cautious by the standards of a more modern linguistics that seeks such generalizations. However, the grammar that he produced remains an impressive monument to the power of empirical description.

By also refraining from the comparative study of Sanskrit with Greek, Latin, and other ancient languages, the aim of which is normally the determination of those changes that produced these languages from a common ancestor (the reconstruction called Proto-Indo-European), Whitney disengaged from the dominant, largely German comparative philology that constituted much of the linguistic work of his day. This is not to say that his work was not historical, however. Indeed, for Whitney all study of language was historical, for he believed that in the history of a language, its speakers, and their culture lay the explanations for why that language was what it had become. The *Sanskrit Grammar*, as its subtitle indicates, drew on texts that included both the classical language and the older dialects, and this enabled Whitney to show how the language had changed over the centuries. For example, in the chapter on aorist systems of the verb, Whitney provides counts of aorist forms in classical Sanskrit, demonstrating their infrequency in comparison to earlier texts where aorist formations are quite common. This use of frequency data has sometimes been referred to by twentieth-century commentators as "statistical."

Of broader interest are Whitney's two books on linguistic science, *Language and the Study of Language* (1867) and *The Life and Growth of Language* (1875), both aimed at a general educated readership. The former resulted from a lecture series first delivered at the Smithsonian Institution in March 1864 and then at the Lowell Institute in Boston in December 1864 and January 1865. It also served as the basis of Whitney's lectures in the science of language at Yale College. To dissuade Whitney from accepting an attractive offer made by Harvard in 1869, Salisbury, his former teacher and predecessor, added to his endowment, and his professorship at Yale was expanded to include comparative philology. As a result, Whitney decided to remain at Yale.

Whitney made considerable efforts to distinguish comparative philology, narrowly defined, from the new linguistic science that he saw as still taking shape, stating, "The former deals primarily with the individual facts of a certain body of languages, classifying them, tracing out their relations," while linguistic science "makes the laws and general principles of speech its main subject, and uses particular facts rather as illustrations" (*The Life and Growth of Language*, p. 315). For Whitney, human language was "in itself of a variety which is fairly to be termed discordance . . . a congeries of individual languages . . . [that] differ among themselves in every degree" (p. 3), so the general principles were not to be found in fundamental properties of linguistic structure. Indeed, Whitney did not see any human language as a system with its own internal structure and, therefore, cannot be considered a precursor to twentieth-century structuralism.

The general principles of language for Whitney were instead to be identified in processes of historical change as these were exemplified, specifically, in words: "the broad principles, the wide-reaching views, the truths of universal application and importance, which constitute the upper fabric of linguistic science, all rest upon word-genealogies," that is, upon the results of the study of etymology (*Language and the Study of Language*, p. 55). And etymological study, he concluded, would yield a single unilinear pattern of change in all human languages, the pattern being that of the Indo-European languages. Through etymology, "a chief portion of linguistic analysis" consisted of distinguishing roots from affixes, with the latter traceable back to independent roots as well, as with modern English forms such as *fearful* and *truthful, godly* and *lovely*, in which the suffixes derived historically from the roots *full* and *like*. Recognizing that not all modern words would yield to such analysis, Whitney applied the principle of uniformitarianism to maintain that since this pattern could be found in some modern forms, it was reasonable, indeed scientific, to conclude that other forms, whose history was obscure, could nevertheless have followed the same pattern.

Whitney's uniformitarianism surely relates directly to the influence of his geologist brother, Josiah, and his own early field experiences in geology, which in the nineteenth century made important use of the principle that all geological phenomena, past and present, may be explained as resulting from observable processes that have operated in a uniform manner across time. His extension of this principle to diachronic linguistics was an important contribution, although in the case of his theory of the development of languages from independent roots to later inflectional forms, he was misled by the narrow range of languages, all within the Indo-European family, with which he was familiar.

Although Whitney did cite Native-American languages from time to time in his general linguistic works, he conducted no fieldwork and relied here, as for languages of many other parts of the world, on accounts prepared by others. He erroneously believed that all Native-American languages were of "a single type or plan upon which their forms are developed and their constructions made, from the Arctic Ocean to Cape Horn," a type he called "incorporative or polysynthetic" and that he judged to involve "the excessive and abnormal agglomeration of distinct significant elements in its words . . . tedious and time-wasting polysyllabism . . . and what is of yet more importance, an unwieldy aggregation, verbal or *quasi*-verbal, is substituted for the phrase or sentence" (*Language and the Study of Language*, pp. 348–49). With such secondhand and faulty characterizations of Native-American languages, Whitney was to play no role in what became, under the leadership of anthropologist and linguist Franz Boas, a prominent topic of American linguistic work at the end of the nineteenth century and the start of the twentieth.

Whitney's professional involvement with modern languages arose initially from the need to supplement his Yale salary by giving private lessons and later by teaching classes at the Yale Sheffield Scientific School in German and in French. He published grammar books (1869, 1885), readers (1870, 1876), a dictionary (1877) for the former, and a grammar for the latter (1886); but all of these were pedagogical, as was his unremarkable *Essentials of English Grammar for the Use of Schools* (1877). His most important contribution to modern languages was his service as editor in chief of the ten-volume *Century Dictionary and Cyclopedia* (1889–1891), his most extensive but not his only venture in lexicography. He had earlier contributed to the 1864 *Webster's Dictionary of English*. Further, he provided the entire vocabulary of the Atharva Veda for the St. Petersburg, Russia, *Lexicon* of Sanskrit (1852–1875), coedited by Rudolph Roth and Otto von Böthlingk.

This latter work became the initial impetus for a decades-long public feud on matters pertaining both to Sanskrit and to general linguistics between Whitney and the European linguist Max Müller, a fellow of All Souls College, Oxford, who began by criticizing the Russian lexicon. Whitney in turn challenged Müller's *A History of Ancient Sanskrit Literature* (1859), attacking Müller for having "given too loose a rein to poetic fancy . . . when more exact scientific statement had been preferable" (rep. in *Oriental and Linguistic Studies*, p. 95). The arguments went on for years, with Whitney especially virulent in his denunciation of Müller's "metaphysical" belief in the identity of language and reason. Even as late as 1892 Whitney, nearly totally incapacitated by heart disease, published his final volley, *Max Müller and the Science of Language: A Criticism*.

Despite his disagreements with aspects of Müller's work and with a variety of linguistic principles in the works of well-known European scholars such as Wilhelm von Humboldt, Richard Lepsius, August Schleicher, and Chaim Steinthal, Whitney's work was generally well received abroad. His linguistic books were promptly translated into several European languages, circulated widely, and referred to in the publications and teachings of major European linguists such as Karl Brugmann, Jan Baudouin de Courtenay, F. F.

Fortunatov, and Ferdinand de Saussure. At home in the United States, Whitney was an influential builder of scholarly institutions, elected early in life to the American Oriental Society (1850) in which he held the offices of librarian (1855–1873), corresponding secretary and editor (1857–1884), and president (1884–1890). He also served as a cofounder and the first president of the American Philological Association (1869–1870), and he held membership in the Modern Language Association of America, the American Dialect Society, and the Spelling Reform Association. Whitney died in New Haven, Connecticut.

Although little in modern American linguistics can be traced or attributed uniquely to Whitney's work, his writings on general linguistics have continued to be regularly praised for their "sanity," a term reflecting his clarity of style, the care he took to provide examples drawn from actual language usage in support of thoughtful, empirically based statements, and his avoidance of the "metaphysical" mysticism of some of his contemporaries. The writing table at which he stood to prepare so many of his 360 books and articles was eventually obtained by the Linguistic Society of America, founded in 1924, and is passed on to each successive editor of that society's journal, *Language*, as an honor of the office.

• Correspondence to Whitney is held at the Yale University Archives. A brief autobiography was published in *Forty Years' Record of the Class of 1845, Williams College* (1885), which Whitney edited, and is reprinted in Michael Silverstein, ed., *Whitney on Language: Selected Writings of William Dwight Whitney* (1971). That volume also contains Silverstein's essay "Whitney on Language"; Roman Jakobson, "The World Response to Whitney's Principles of Linguistic Science"; an extended excerpt from *Language and the Study of Language*; and eleven articles representative of Whitney's linguistic work. For a complete bibliography of Whitney's writings, as well as the memorial tributes at the First American Congress of Philologists in Dec. 1894, see Charles Rockwell Lanman, ed., *The Whitney Memorial Meeting* (1897). See also Brigitte Nerlich, *Change in Language: Whitney, Bréal, and Wegener* (1990), and the substantial section on Whitney in Julie Tetel Andresen, *Linguistics in America, 1769–1924* (1990). A discussion of Whitney is presented in Craig Christy, *Uniformitarianism in Linguistics* (1983), and in E. F. K. Koerner, *Ferdinand de Saussure* (1973). An obituary is in the *American Journal of Philology* 15 (1894): 271–98, and is reprinted in Thomas A. Sebeok, ed., *Portraits of Linguists*, vol. 1 (1966).

JULIA S. FALK

WHITNEY, Willis Rodney (22 Aug. 1868–9 Jan. 1958), chemist and research director, was born in Jamestown, New York, the son of John Jay Whitney, the prosperous owner of a furniture manufacturing company, and Agnes Reynolds. Whitney's childhood in an industrial town in still lightly settled western New York enabled him to mix outdoor pursuits with summer factory work, scientific hobbies, and reading. He learned much natural history, the craft of chairmaking, and the use of the microscope. In 1890 he earned a B.S. in chemistry at the Massachusetts Institute of Technology (MIT) where an inspiring teacher, Arthur A. Noyes, helped him decide on a career as a researcher in physical chemistry. After a few years teaching at MIT, Whitney went to Germany to study physical chemistry under Wilhelm Ostwald at Leipzig, earning the Ph.D. in 1896.

Whitney returned to become an instructor in chemistry and to carry out some research on the corrosion of iron and the properties of colloids. In 1896 he turned down an opportunity to work for a pioneer in industrial chemistry, Arthur D. Little, but soon afterward did take on with Noyes a consulting project on reclaiming solvents for a photographic supply company in his hometown of Jamestown. Running the project as an independent venture, both he and Noyes netted in excess of $20,000. This experience might have been in his mind in 1900 when he received an offer to take on a research program three days a week for the General Electric Company, then an eight-year-old electrical manufacturing firm in Schenectady, New York. This opportunity had come at the urging of Charles Proteus Steinmetz, GE's chief consulting engineer, and was strongly supported by one of the company's founders, Elihu Thomson, a prolific inventor, and two other top executives.

Whitney accepted the offer, beginning work in December 1900 with three GE colleagues. For a year he spent the week teaching in Cambridge and weekends at Schenectady, but soon he was spending most of his time at GE. His initial challenge was a defensive one: to help GE protect its leading position in the manufacture and sale of electric lighting equipment, then threatened by improvements being developed mainly in Europe. However, in addition to this concrete goal, Whitney received authorization to devote part of the time of his staff (which quickly expanded beyond the original trio) to fundamental scientific research. This was a first in U.S. industry; previous U.S. laboratories had been limited to tasks such as invention, product improvement, chemical analysis, and materials specification and inspection.

In 1904 Whitney made his most important individual invention, the GEM lamp, an incandescent lamp of improved efficiency based on an improved method of processing the lamp's carbon filament. However, this invention was soon made obsolete by even better European lamps using metal filaments. To counter that development, Whitney first tried to adapt one of the best European ideas, which GE licensed. But he soon found that his efforts could be more productively devoted to managing the research efforts of others. Over the next five years, a laboratory team led by William D. Coolidge came up with a key invention, a process for producing the normally brittle metal tungsten in the form of thin, ductile wire. Tungsten filaments made by this Coolidge process have since remained in use as the light-giving elements in incandescent lamps.

This episode assured the survival of the GE Research Laboratory and set a pattern that persisted throughout Whitney's thirty-two years of directing it. He would be the inspirational leader, walking from room to room, asking his cheery question, "Are you having any fun?" and encouraging rather than overtly directing the researchers' work. This atmosphere proved to be extremely productive. Innovations that emerged during the Whitney era included major improvements in the vacuum tube that helped spur the first electronics revolution; the modern type of X ray tube; further efficiency-boosting improvements in incandescent lamps, such as the practice of filling the lamp with an inert gas to prevent material "boiled" off the filament from blackening the bulb; development of heat-resistant materials for appliance burners; pioneering power electronics components; and improvements in electrical generators. By 1929 the laboratory had a staff of more than 500.

While the lab focused primarily on applying science to the development of new products and processes, its original purpose of encouraging some pure research persisted. Irving Langmuir, a chemist who turned work on light bulbs into discoveries in the field of surface chemistry that won him a Nobel Prize in 1932, best exemplified the scientific payoff of Whitney's approach. He was one of a handful of first-rate scientists (others included Albert W. Hull, Saul Dushman, and Coolidge) who made GE the outstanding example of science in industry in the pre–World War II era.

Whitney accepted but did not seek public responsibilities, serving, for example, on the Naval Consulting Board during World War I. He traveled and spoke widely as an advocate of industrial and government support of research. His enthusiasm, warmth, and broad interests gained him many friends throughout industrial, governmental, and academic circles. His views on politics and economics were close to those of Herbert Hoover, whom he admired.

Whitney had married Evelyn Reynolds in 1890; they had one child, a daughter. The family lived on a farm outside Schenectady, where Whitney carried on natural history hobbies, such as studying the habits of turtles.

Whitney became a vice president of GE in 1928. The depression that began in 1929 seriously shook his confidence in what he had come to believe was an automatic machine of progress created by modern technology and industry. He sank into a deep personal depression and retired in 1932 as GE's director of research. Under a reduced work schedule his spirits improved, and he continued to carry out personal investigations of topics such as the use of radio waves to heat body tissues for medical purposes such as the relief of bursitis. He continued active work until 1954 and died four years later at his home in Schenectady. Whitney's methods of running a research laboratory have long since been superseded by the constraints of tight management control and global competition, but his demonstration of the value of salting "invention factories" with a bit of science has remained central to the mission of the corporate laboratories of the world's largest technology-based companies.

• Whitney's personal papers are in private hands; his laboratory notebooks are at the GE Research and Development Center, Schenectady, N.Y. Whitney is the subject of three biographies, John Broderick, *Willis Rodney Whitney* (1945); Virginia Westervelt, *The World Was His Laboratory* (1965); and George Wise, *Willis R. Whitney, General Electric, and the Origins of U.S. Industrial Research* (1985).

GEORGE WISE

WHITSITT, William Heth (25 Nov. 1841–20 Jan. 1911), Baptist historian, educator, and seminary president, was born near Nashville, Tennessee, the son of Rubin Ewing Whitsitt and Dicey McFarland, farmers in the Cumberland Valley. In 1861 he graduated with distinction (M.A.) from Union University in Murfreesboro. With the outbreak of the Civil War, Whitsitt enlisted in the Confederate army as a private and served first as a scout, then as a chaplain. He was captured and spent a year in federal prisons.

Following his military service, Whitsitt resumed his education, first at the University of Virginia, where he studied Latin, Greek and math, then at the Southern Baptist Theological Seminary in Greenville, South Carolina, under the tutelage of John A. Broadus (1867–1868). From 1869 to 1871 he studied abroad at the universities of Leipzig and Berlin, where he encountered the work of Richard A. Lipsius and L. F. K. Tischendorf and learned the historical critical methodology then popular in the German schools. Upon his return to the United States he served a few months in 1872 as pastor of the Baptist church at Albany, Georgia, after which he took up the chair in ecclesiastical history at Southern Baptist Theological Seminary, which since his departure in 1868 had relocated to Louisville, Kentucky. In addition to church history, Whitsitt taught polemical theology, biblical introduction, history of doctrine, and readings in German theological works. In 1895 he was elected president of the seminary, succeeding Broadus. With Florence Wallace of Woodford County, Kentucky, whom he married in 1881, Whitsitt had two children.

One of the first American and Baptist scholars to employ critical methodology to the study of general church history and Baptist history, Whitsitt had varied interests. In *Origin of the Disciples of Christ: A Contribution to the Centennial of the Birth of Alexander Campbell* (1887), he maintained that the Disciples of Christ—the denomination that ironically originated as a result of Campbell's struggles against denominationalism—was an offshoot of a Scottish sect, the Sandemanians. This assertion disturbed both Campbellites and many Baptist historians. More significantly, Whitsitt contravened important assumptions in Baptist denominational life. In an 1886 article for *Johnson's Universal Cyclopedia* he argued that believers' baptism had been restored by English Baptists in 1641, thus challenging the widely held belief in an unbroken succession of baptist practices from apostolic times. Whitsitt rushed to print several newspaper articles in order to lay first claim to these theories, as church historians Henry C. Vedder, Henry M. Dexter, and Albert H. Newman were each espousing similar views. In his *A Question in Baptist History* (1896), Whitsitt not only held that the earliest Baptists did not practice immersion, he also advanced the view that the venerable Roger Williams was not immersed.

Whitsitt's positions drew the wrath of scores of Baptist editors and pastors in the South. Those who held to a "Landmarkist" position—that the church is a body of immersed believers and that the Kingdom of God is composed of visible Baptist churches—rejected outright the seminary president's teachings. Among Baptist historians, however, the Whitsitt controversy laid to rest the adequacy of the Anabaptist Kinship Theory, which held that the Baptists, with ideas similar to those of the Anabaptists of the sixteenth and seventeenth centuries, were an outgrowth of the earlier movement, as well as the successionist argument for Baptist origins. For Whitsitt and several members of the seminary faculty, the larger issues raised by the controversy were recognition of the church universal and the freedom of a teacher to conduct honest research. In the few responses he made to his adversaries, he was judged to have lacked tact and sensitivity. In 1899 the trustees of Southern Baptist Seminary, concerned about dissension within the denomination and its negative effect on the school, requested the president's resignation, which he submitted. After a year's rest he was elected James Thomas Professor of Philosophy at Richmond (Va.) College, where he taught until 1910. Ever pursuing his appreciation of English Baptist history, Whitsitt suggested that a memorial window in honor of the preacher and author John Bunyan be placed in Westminster Abbey; this occurred in 1905. Whitsitt died in Richmond.

• Whitsitt's papers are at the Southern Baptist Theological Seminary in Louisville, Ky., and the University of Richmond in Richmond, Va. His other significant works include *The History of Communion among Baptists* (1880) and *Genealogy of Jefferson Davis and Samuel Davies* (1908). An important 1885 manuscript on the origins of the Mormons, which Whitsitt completed but which was never published, is deposited at the Library of Congress. Among the useful biographical studies are E. B. Pollard, "The Life and Work of William Heth Whitsitt," *Review and Expositor* 9 (Apr. 1912): 159–84; William Owen Carver, "William Heth Whitsitt: The Seminary's Martyr," *Review and Expositor* 51 (Oct. 1954): 449–69; and Rufus W. Weaver, "Life and Times of William Heth Whitsitt," *Review and Expositor* 37 (Apr. 1940): 115–32.

WILLIAM H. BRACKNEY

WHITTAKER, James (28 Feb. 1751–20 July 1787), early Shaker leader, was born in Oldham, England, the son of Jonathan Whittaker and Ann Lee. During his childhood Whittaker and his parents joined the Shaking Quakers, a charismatic religious society to which Ann Lee, the future founder of Shakerism and a distant relative of Whittaker's mother, also belonged. Whittaker's relationship to Ann Lee was complex. He thought of her as a physical mother—for reasons unknown she became his caretaker when he was still a boy—as well as a spiritual mother. During the 1770s Lee experienced a powerful vision and began teaching the group what she claimed God had revealed to her: sexual intercourse caused the fall of Adam and Eve; therefore, celibacy was essential for salvation. Whittaker was heavily influenced by Lee's ideas, and in 1774, when she sailed for America to take her message there, he and six other followers went with her.

During their first years in America these Shakers, as the group came to be known, plied their trades—Whittaker was a weaver—and kept to themselves. In 1780, however, having settled on land in Niskeyuna, New York, Ann Lee "opened" her message of salvation to the world. Large crowds soon congregated there to worship, their meetings marked by dancing, glossolalia (speaking in tongues), and other forms of ecstatic behavior. Whittaker, who was a powerful orator, spoke often at these gatherings, exhorting his listeners to renounce their "carnal" lives. Indeed, Whittaker was wholly absorbed by this aspect of Shakerism, and, though the Shakers remembered him as a loving and tender man, he could be abrasive and arrogant toward those who did not embrace a celibate life. This side of his personality is reflected in a letter that he sent to his family in England in 1785. Angry because they continued to live "in the flesh," he wrote, "Why tell ye me of your increasing and multiplying after the flesh? . . . I hate your fleshly lives, and your fleshly generation, and increasing, as I hate the smoke of the bottomless pit." As it stood, Whittaker considered his relatives "a stink in [his] nostrils" (Meacham, pp. 21–23).

Ann Lee soon put Whittaker's talent for fiery words to a constructive use, choosing him to serve as the main public speaker on a missionary journey that she and her brother William Lee were planning to conduct in New England. The three left Niskeyuna in May 1781 and made a fair number of converts in the places where they stopped. Their message, however, also antagonized people, and mob violence erupted frequently. In a particularly bloody incident at Harvard, Massachusetts, angry citizens of the town beat many of the Shakers, including Whittaker, whom they tied to a tree and whipped severely.

After the missionaries' return to Niskeyuna in September 1783, the spiritual fervor of worship meetings increased; it was during this period that some witnesses claimed that the Shakers danced in the nude. Scholars disagree on the veracity of these accusations, but the possibility remains that the Shakers did engage in nude dancing. According to Angell Matthewson, who left the Shakers in 1799, it was Whittaker who stopped the practice when he told Ann Lee, "If you ever make the people strip naked again, you shall see my face no more" ("Reminiscences," letter VII).

Whittaker's censure of Lee on the issue of nude dancing was indicative of his increasing authority among the Shakers. His position in the community did not go unnoticed by William Lee, who felt that Whittaker had usurped William's rightful place in the power structure. Ann Lee had presumably promised William while they were still in England that he would be second in command over the new group. Whittaker's superior leadership skills and his talent for proselytiz ing, however, made him a more suitable candidate for such a position, and Ann Lee increasingly turned to him for support.

William challenged Ann on the issue, and the dispute came to a head after their return from New England, but the problem resolved itself in 1784 with the deaths of both William and Ann. Whittaker, who was the logical successor, acceded to power. Because of his experience and his relationship with the Lees, most of the Shakers accepted his leadership.

Whittaker's ministry, though short, was both busy and productive. One of his first projects was a proposal to convert the world through a massive evangelistic effort. While this particular plan failed, Whittaker's management of the internal organization of the developing sect was successful. He oversaw the movement of the group's primary location from Niskeyuna to New Lebanon, New York, and the building of a meetinghouse there in 1785. Even more important, Whittaker envisioned a future for Shakerism in which the Believers separated from the world and lived communally. To this end he traveled continuously throughout New England, visiting every cluster of Shaker converts and encouraging them to form communities and share their possessions. It was on one of these trips that Whittaker became ill and died in Enfield, Connecticut, at the home of David Meacham, an American convert. Even on his deathbed Whittaker took the opportunity to exhort his followers: "My body is under great sufferings; but I feel my soul at peace with God and man. I have given you the gospel; now see to it, what kind of use you make of it. If you keep the gospel, the gospel will keep you" (Wells and Bishop, p. 378).

Whittaker played an important role in the early years of American Shakerism, serving as the transitional figure between Ann Lee, the charismatic founder of the movement, and Joseph Meacham, the American convert who was responsible for organizing the Shakers into the villages that became a hallmark of the sect. As one of the original English converts who had worked closely with Ann Lee, Whittaker possessed the necessary authority to keep the movement alive after her death. He labored diligently to promote the tenets of his faith, traveling continuously, maintaining frequent correspondence with both Shakers and non-Shakers, and laying the foundation for the communal organization that Meacham later utilized successfully. Thus, Whittaker played a pivotal role in the development of Shakerism from a loosely organized religious movement to an American sect.

• Whittaker's written legacy, though not extensive, is mainly in the form of letters. Correspondence with fellow Shakers may be found in the collections of Hancock Shaker Village, Inc., Pittsfield, Mass., and Case Western Reserve Historical Society, Cleveland, Ohio. The latter collection also contains Whittaker's "Last Will and Testament," 9 June 1787, I.A: 20. His non-Shaker correspondents include Henry Van Schaack, whose letters are located at the Emma B. King Library, Shaker Museum, Old Chatham, N.Y. Whittaker's letter condemning his natural family was published in [Joseph Meacham], *A Concise Statement of the Principles of the Only True Church, According to the Gospel, of the Present Appearance of Christ . . .* , (1790). The first published Shaker record of Whittaker's life is in Seth Wells and Rufus Bishop, eds., *Testimonies of the Life, Character, Revelations and Doctrines of Our Ever Blessed Mother Ann Lee, and the Elders with Her* (1816). Three other accounts of early Shakerism, written by men who left the society, include observations about Whittaker and his rise to leadership: Reuben Rathbun, *Reasons Offered for Leaving the Shakers* (1800); Thomas Brown, *An Account of the People Called Shakers* (1812); and Angell Matthewson, "Reminiscences in the Form of a Series of Thirty-nine Letters to His Brother Jeffrey," which is located at the New York Public Library. Recent books that include a discussion of Whittaker are Stephen J. Stein, *The Shaker Experience* (1992); Clarke Garrett, *Spirit Possession and Popular Religion* (1987); and Stephen Marini, *Radical Sects of Revolutionary New England* (1982).

SUZANNE R. THURMAN

WHITTAKER, Johnson Chesnut (23 Aug. 1858–14 Jan. 1931), military cadet and educator, was born one of a set of twins, on the plantation of James Chesnut, Sr., near Camden, South Carolina, the son of James Whitaker, a freedman, and Maria J. (maiden name unknown), a slave. His twin brother died from an accident at the age of thirteen.

Johnson Whittaker (he added the second *t* sometime later in life) spent his early years in slavery, his mother at times serving as personal slave to Maria Boykin Chesnut, the author of *A Diary from Dixie* (1905). His father had purchased his own freedom, but at the birth of the twins he refused responsibility for them and an older son because he insisted that never before had twins been born in his family.

With the coming of emancipation, Whittaker and his mother, both very light-skinned, took up residence in Camden, where she worked as a domestic and Johnson attended a freedman's school. After five years he began receiving special tutoring from a local black minister while he worked as a bricklayer's assistant. In 1874 he entered the University of South Carolina, briefly integrated during Reconstruction, in Columbia. He did so well during his two years there that one of his teachers, Richard Greener, Harvard's first black graduate, suggested him as a candidate for appointment to West Point. He entered the military academy in 1876 on the nomination of a local white Republican congressman, S. L. Hoze.

The man destined to become the military academy's first black graduate, Henry O. Flipper, was in his final year when Whittaker arrived. The two men shared a room because no white cadet would room with either of them. Flipper passed along his nonviolence philosophy, which Whittaker, who was deeply religious, accepted enthusiastically. Throughout his time at West Point, he responded to insults and total social ostracism with patience. He refused to allow any provocation to take his mind off his ultimate goal—graduation. When a white cadet struck him, for example, Whittaker did not fight back but reported the offender to academy authorities. As a result, West Point cadets labeled him a coward.

On 6 April 1880, as Whittaker slept alone in a two-man room, three masked men entered, dragged him out of his bed, lashed his legs to the bed's side, and tied his arms in front of him. They slashed his ear lobes, gouged his hair, and made him look into a mirror that they then smashed against his forehead. He later recalled hearing one say, "Let us mark him as we mark hogs down South." After they had completed their vicious work, the attackers warned Whittaker not to make any noise. "Cry out, or speak of this affair, and you are a dead man," they said, and also told him he should leave the academy.

The next morning, when Whittaker was absent from reveille, another cadet was sent to his room and discovered him unconscious, surrounded by large blotches of blood. West Point authorities quickly decided that he had mutilated himself to avoid final examinations two months later.

General John M. Schofield, the military academy superintendent, established a court of inquiry to begin meeting on 9 April. The board took more than 3,000 pages of testimony, some of it casting grave doubts on the West Point position. Nonetheless, it found Whittaker guilty of mutilating himself. Hoping to clear his name, Whittaker demanded a court-martial. A panel that began hearings on 3 February 1881 recorded 9,000 pages of testimony. After taking his June 1880 oral examinations, Whittaker was placed on leave. Meanwhile, O. O. Howard, the one-time head of the Freedman's Bureau, replaced Schofield as West Point superintendent.

Like the court of inquiry, the court-martial was a national cause célèbre. Three presidents (Rutherford B. Hayes, James A. Garfield, and Chester A. Arthur), army commanding general William T. Sherman, and the nation's major newspapers all followed these judicial proceedings closely. Former South Carolina governor Daniel Chamberlain and leading army lawyer Asa Bird Gardiner were on opposite sides in the four-month trial. Once again Whittaker was found guilty; his race continued to be the major determinant in the military court decision.

On 1 December 1881 the army's judge advocate general, D. G. Swaim, found irregularities and prejudice in the proceedings and overturned the decision. Benjamin Brewster, the attorney general, agreed on 17 March 1882, and five days later President Arthur officially threw out the guilty verdict. Whittaker was exonerated. That same day, however, Secretary of War Robert T. Lincoln, the Great Emancipator's son, issued an army special order discharging Whittaker from the military academy for failing an oral examination in June 1880. Whittaker was innocent of wrongdoing, but he was separated from the academy anyway.

Whittaker tried for several years to fight the dismissal, even going on a brief national speaking tour to drum up support. "With God as my guide," he said in his first speech, "duty as my watchword, I can, I must, I will win a place in life!" Unsuccessful in his efforts to reverse the dismissal, he moved back to South Carolina, where he became a teacher in Charleston and Sumter, a member of the South Carolina bar in 1885, and a lawyer and school principal in Sumter. In 1890 he married Page Harrison, the daughter of a white Sumter city employee and his black wife. They had two sons, one of whom became a college president.

In 1900 Whittaker became secretary of the college and principal of the academy at the Colored Normal, Industrial, Agricultural, and Mechanical College of South Carolina (now South Carolina State University) in Orangeburg. In 1908, because of a son's asthma, the family moved from Orangeburg to Oklahoma City, where they had to contend with nightly gunfire when they moved into a white neighborhood. Whittaker became a teacher at all-black Douglass High School and in the early 1920s became the school's principal. One of his students was the novelist Ralph Ellison.

In 1925, at the age of sixty-seven, Whittaker returned to the black college in Orangeburg, South Carolina, again as principal of the academy. He maintained his post until his death there, a revered teacher but unknown outside of his community. It was not until the publication of a book about him and a made-for-television motion picture that Whittaker received the lieutenant's bars denied him in the 1880s. On 24 July 1995 in a White House ceremony, President Bill Clinton presented to Whittaker's descendants a posthumous commission.

• No collection of Johnson C. Whittaker papers exists. The records of his court of inquiry and his court-martial are preserved in the Records of the Judge Advocate General (Army), RG 153, National Archives. The fullest account of his life and courtroom struggles is John F. Marszalek, *Court-Martial: A Black Man in America* (1972), reprinted in paperback with a new afterword as *Assault at West Point: The Court Martial of Johnson Whittaker* (1994). A made-for-television motion picture and a video about his court-martial are both titled *Assault at West Point* (1994). For a brief account of the trials, see Marszalek, "A Black Cadet at West Point," *American Heritage* 12 (Aug. 1971): 30–37, 104–6. For an account of the posthumous commissioning, see the *New York Times*, 25 July 1995.

John F. Marszalek

WHITTAKER, Robert Harding (27 Dec. 1920–20 Oct. 1980), ecologist, was born in Wichita, Kansas, the son of Clive Charles Whittaker, a zoology teacher, and Adeline Harding, an English teacher. Shortly after his birth the family moved to Eureka, Kansas, where his father entered the oil-drilling business. Robert Whittaker received his B.A. in 1942 from Washburn Municipal College in Topeka, Kansas. After graduation he enlisted in the U.S. Army Air Force and served in the United States and England as a weather observer and forecaster. After his discharge in 1946, he entered the University of Illinois and received his Ph.D. in zoology in 1948.

Whittaker's dissertation on vegetation analysis was a major contribution to the study of ecology. In the 1940s the structure of plant communities was explained by two competing theories. The "community" theory, first advanced by Frederic E. Clements in 1905, was that gradients, or sharply defined boundaries coinciding with elevation and topography, exist between competing species in a plant community. The "continuum" theory, put forth by Henry A. Gleason in 1926, denied that such gradients cause species segregation; instead, it held that species develop in accordance with their own genetic, physiological, and life-cycle characteristics so that they overlap with little regard for gradients. Because neither theory had been supported or disproved by experimental data, Whittaker selected a slope on the Tennessee side of the Great Smoky Mountains and conducted a statistical examination of the patterns and densities of the local vegetation. The results of his field study showed clearly that the distribution of plant species across environmental gradients varies considerably, that these gradients do not form the sort of boundaries that Clements had hypothesized, and that segregated communities of a particular species do not occur, as a rule. Published in 1956, the dissertation was hailed by one scholar as "probably the most important ecological paper of the present century" (Westman et al., p. 427).

In 1948 Whittaker became an instructor of zoology at Washington State College (later University of Washington). He continued to conduct gradient analysis, working in the Klamath and Siskiyou mountains. Although he was promoted to assistant professor two years later, in 1951 his teaching contract was not renewed because of budgetary constraints, and he left academia to become a senior scientist at the Aquatic Biology Unit of the Hanford Laboratories Department of Radiological Sciences in Richland, Washington, site of one of the United States' first nuclear power plants. In 1953 he married Clara Caroline Buehl, who died in 1977; they had three children.

In 1954 Whittaker returned to teaching as an instructor of biology at the City University of New York's Brooklyn College, eventually rising to assistant professor. While there, he became interested in measuring the amount of standing crop (biomass) and the rate of conversion via photosynthesis of sunlight into biomass (productivity) in forest communities at higher elevations. To accomplish this task he developed dimension analysis, in which logarithmic regressions are used to compute a tree's biomass based on its diameter at breast height and at total height, while the biomass of herbs and shrubs is calculated from the weight of samples of all plant parts. Most of the fieldwork that led to the development of this concept was done in the Great Smokies. He also collaborated with William Niering of Connecticut College on a gradient research project in the Santa Catalina Mountains in Arizona; the published results won them the 1966 Mercer Award of the Ecological Society of America.

In 1964 Whittaker left Brooklyn to work at the Brookhaven National Laboratory and Forest on Long Island, New York. Tired of living amid the urban sprawl of New York City, in 1966 he accepted an offer to teach at the University of California at Irvine. However, southern California was being developed so rapidly that two years later in 1968, Whittaker moved to rural upstate New York to join the faculty of Cornell University as a professor of biology in the Ecology and Systematics Section, a position he held until his death.

Cornell's congenial natural and intellectual setting reinvigorated Whittaker. In 1970 he published *Communities and Ecosystems* (2d ed., 1975), a basic textbook for the study of ecology that within ten years established him among the foremost ecological authorities. Whittaker at this time undertook to close the rift he had helped to create between the community and continuum schools. He delivered a paper at a symposium in Europe, the stronghold of the community school, that stressed what the theories shared. Whittaker's peace offering healed the hard feelings among ecologists and earned him the editorship of *Vegetatio*, a European ecology journal. As editor from 1973 until 1980, he took care to juxtapose in each issue articles espousing both the community and continuum points of view.

In 1979 Whittaker married Linda Olsvig; they had no children. He was elected to the National Academy of Sciences in 1974 and was also elected to membership in the American Academy of Arts and Sciences (1979), the British Ecological Society, and the Swedish Phytogeographical Society. He served as vice president of the Ecological Society of America (ESA) in 1971 and was serving as president of the American Society of Naturalists at the time of his death. In 1980 he was named an Eminent Ecologist by the ESA. He died in Ithaca, New York.

Whittaker contributed to science by seeking patterns that explained the structure of plant communities while at the same time acknowledging the difficulty of categorizing, classifying, and simplifying natural systems. He emphasized the interrelationships among plant communities and developed the theories and methodologies of gradient and dimension analysis with which these communities can be examined.

• Whittaker's papers are located in the History of Ecology Archives at the University of Georgia and in the Cornell University Archives. Of the many articles Whittaker wrote, the most frequently cited ones are "Allelochemies: Chemical Interactions between Species," *Science* 171 (1971): 757–90; "Gradient Analysis of Vegetation," *Biological Review* 42 (1967): 207–64; "Dominance and Diversity in Land Plant Communities," *Science* 147 (1965): 250–60; and "Evolution and Measurement of Species Diversity," *Taxon* 21 (1972): 213–51. Good biographies of Whittaker appear in R. K. Peet, ed., *Plant Community Ecology: Papers in Honor of Robert H. Whittaker* (1985), and Walter E. Westman et al., "Robert H. Whittaker," National Academy of Sciences, *Biographical Memoirs* 59 (1990): 425–44; both include complete bibliographies of his work.

CHARLES W. CAREY, JR.

WHITTELSEY, Abigail Goodrich (29 Nov. 1788–16 July 1858), journalist and editor, was born in Ridgefield, Connecticut, the daughter of Samuel Goodrich, a Congregational minister, tutor, and farmer, and Elizabeth Ely. She lived at home with her parents and nine siblings until her marriage in 1808 to Samuel Whittelsey, also a Congregational minister. The couple had seven children, five of whom survived to adulthood.

The couple moved to New Preston, Connecticut, where Samuel Whittelsey's parish was located and lived there for ten years. Then the family moved to Hartford when the reverend was appointed superintendent at the Connecticut Asylum for the Education and Instruction of Deaf and Dumb Persons (later the American School for the Deaf); Abigail Whittelsey served as matron there. In 1824 the Whittelseys moved to Canandaigua, New York, where they supervised the Ontario Female Seminary. About three years later they went to Utica, New York, and established a women's school there.

In 1833, while living in Utica, Whittelsey began editing *Mother's Magazine*, her first foray into journalism. The magazine was one of a handful of publications in the 1830s that glorified, celebrated, and promoted the domestic sphere for women. Whittelsey, a member of the Maternal Association of Utica, began editing the magazine in response to her organization's lament that no popular journals devoted themselves exclusively to the work of mothers. The first issue of the magazine, January 1833, set forward its editorial goals: "Its design is to embrace physical education, intellectual training, the culture of the affections, the nurture of the soul, all the bearings of maternal intercourse, from its earliest watch over the cradle-dream, to the full development of that mysterious being, whose destiny is immortality." Whittelsey also promoted the establishment of maternal associations similar to her own group in Utica. Thus the magazine flourished as a popularizer of mid-nineteenth century views on women's domestic and maternal roles.

When the Whittelseys moved to New York City in 1834, she took the magazine with her. Circulation rose to 10,000 by 1837, despite the appearance of rival publications such as the *Mother's Journal and Family Visitant*. When her husband died in 1842, Whittelsey continued editing her journal with the help of her brother-in-law, Darius Mead, also the editor of the *Christian Parlor Magazine*. Then, in 1848 Whittelsey had a falling out with the new owner, Myron Finch, when Finch bought the competing *Mother's Journal* and decided to merge the two magazines. Beginning in 1850 she published a new journal with the help of her son Henry. *Mrs. Whittelsey's Magazine for Mothers and Daughters* circulated for two years before publication ceased.

During its brief tenure the new magazine continued to promote Whittelsey's vision of woman as wife and mother. Sarah Josepha Hale, the editor of *Godey's Lady's Book* during the same period, described Whittelsey as a "gentle and persuasive" person of sound judgment. Her magazine relied on essays and articles from other writers and ministers to lay down guidelines for happy and successful motherhood. After the magazine ceased publication, Whittelsey retired from journalism and lived her remaining years in her daughter's home in Colchester, Connecticut, where she died.

Whittelsey was one of a handful of women writers and editors who established themselves in magazine editing during the 1830s, when newspaper editors went to great lengths to woo women readers (such as publishing a "Ladies" newspaper). Women were attracted, however, to the style and content of magazines, and many of these publications succeeded. While Whittelsey was never in the forefront of magazine circulation or prestige, her magazines found a successful niche and can be seen today as evidence of the importance of domesticity in the lives of nineteenth-century American women.

Whittelsey found a ready audience for her publication. Women who spent their days at home, free of domestic chores, turned to reading as a leisure activity. This, coupled with the nineteenth-century glorification of motherhood as a noble calling, led them to discover service magazines that focused on the responsibilities of running a household. Whittelsey's magazine was an early example of this niche publication phenomenon that continues today. Women hungry for advice and guidance as mothers naturally turned to Whittelsey's magazine and then to other women's publications that met these needs.

• Copies of *Mrs. Whittelsey's Magazine for Mothers and Daughters* and *Mother's Magazine* are at the New-York Historical Society. Biographical material on Whittelsey is in Charles B. Whittelsey, *Genealogy of the Whittlesey-Whittelsey Family* (1941). References to her magazines and other women's magazines in the nineteenth century are in Frank L. Mott, *A History of American Magazines*, vol. 2 (1938; repr. 1968).

AGNES HOOPER GOTTLIEB

WHITTEMORE, Samuel (27 July 1696–3 Feb. 1793), farmer and folk hero of the American Revolution, was born in Charlestown (now Somerville), Massachusetts, the son of Samuel Whittemore and Hannah (maiden name unknown), farmers. As a young man he served with a royal regiment, the King's Dragoons, and attained the rank of captain. Whittemore's military reputation led to his election to numerous town offices in Cambridge, where he owned a farm at Menotomy (now Arlington) on the Alewife Brook. He rose to be deputy sheriff of Middlesex County, in which capacity he struck his first blow for liberty.

In 1740 Whittemore ran afoul of the wealthy West India planter and merchant John Vassall, who lived in Cambridge and had been elected its representative to the Massachusetts House of Representatives the previous year. When Vassall lost the 1740 contest, Whittemore commented that his interest "attained its full growth suddenly, like Jonah's gourd, and as suddenly collapsed," adding that Vassall "was no more fit to discharge the said trust than the horse that he . . . rode on." Vassall, who spent a good deal of his life suing people on one pretext or another, sued Whittemore for £1,000 in damages, which the Middlesex County Court of Common Pleas refused to grant. Whittemore then countersued for £200 and won. According to local tradition, he served his warrant on Vassall "at his own table, while surrounded by a large and fashionable dinner party." Whittemore's dislike of Vassall typifies the resentment resident farmers of small towns surrounding Boston felt when wealthy merchants, seeking relief from the city's crime, disease, and taxes, moved to nearby communities in the 1730s and 1740s and expected deference on account of their wealth.

Whittemore lost none of his ire against intruders into his community as he grew old. When the British marched on Lexington and Concord in April 1775, he exhorted the local militia to stand bravely in defense of their liberties. "If I can only be the instrument of killing one of my country's foes, I shall die in peace," the 78-year-old farmer exclaimed. As the British retreated from their debacle at Concord toward Boston, Whittemore positioned himself behind a stone wall on his farm with a musket and pair of pistols, killing three redcoats. The enraged soldiers then charged him, shouting "kill the old rebel," stabbed him with their bayonets, shot him in the cheek with a musket, and left him for dead. However, he survived another eighteen years and, as his obituary noted, lived "to see the complete overthrow of his enemies and his country enjoy all the blessings of peace and independence."

Whittemore was married twice, first to a woman named Elizabeth (full name unknown), with whom he had ten children. His daughter Elizabeth married William Cutler and was reputed to have had thirty-six children with him before she died at the age of thirty-five in 1770, which is almost certainly an exaggeration. Whittemore's first wife died in 1764. Shortly thereafter he married Esther, the widow of both Thomas Prentice and Amos Muzzey. Whittemore died at his farm in Cambridge.

A stone marker honors "Uncle Sam" Whittemore at the site of his farm near the intersection of Alewife Brook Parkway and Massachusetts Avenue in Arlington. His tale illustrates the long lives, numerous progeny, and fierce devotion to liberty of the Minutemen of eastern Massachusetts, to whom in large part we owe both the independence of the United States and much of its population.

• Lucius C. Paige, *History of Cambridge* (1877), which includes the Whittemore genealogy, is the principal source of information on this obscure farmer. He is mentioned in Arthur B. Tourtellot, *Lexington and Concord: The Beginning of the War for America* (1959), and two works by David Hackett Fischer, *Growing Old in America* (1978) and *Paul Revere's Ride* (1994). An obituary is in the *Columbian Centinel*, 6 Feb. 1793.

WILLIAM PENCAK

WHITTIER, John Greenleaf (17 Dec. 1807–7 Sept. 1892), poet, abolitionist, and journalist, was born on his family's homestead near Haverhill, Massachusetts, the son of devout Quakers John Whittier and Abigail Hussey, farmers. Of slender build, Whittier was unsuited to heavy farm work, but the family's impoverished circumstances required it. Over the years the hard work permanently impaired his health, and he was prone to chronic severe headaches and other ailments throughout his life. Although he received only a limited formal education, from stories told by members of his household he absorbed the local folklore and history of the Essex County region that would later inform his poetry. A zealous reader, he perused the limited family library, studying the Bible, various biographies, *Pilgrim's Progress*, and John Woolman's *Journal* and other Quaker writings, and became a Quaker of profound conviction and acute social consciousness. When Whittier was fourteen, his teacher, Joshua Coffin, introduced him to the poetry of Robert Burns. He responded to Burns's poetic treatment of rural life and was inspired to begin composing his own verses. Milton was also an important early influence whom Whittier would later emulate as a poet of social conscience in his antislavery writings. Although his father discouraged poetry as a vocation, Whittier continued writing covertly, encouraged by his mother and sister.

In 1826, without his knowledge, his sister sent one of his poems, "The Exile's Departure," to the *Newburyport Free Press*, a paper edited by William Lloyd Garrison. Garrison published the poem and visited the Whittier farm to meet the nineteen-year-old lad, but he could not persuade Whittier's father to allow John to go to school to develop his genius. Garrison published several more of his poems that summer before going to Boston. The next year, 1827, the Haverhill Academy opened, and Whittier's local reputation earned him the invitation to compose an ode to mark the inauguration. He enrolled, and to pay his fees he made shoes and taught school in the off terms. In the two terms Whittier attended the academy (1827–1828), he published nearly 150 poems, mostly in newspapers and chiefly in the *Haverhill Gazette*, where the editor, Abijah Thayer, printed one of his poems weekly.

In 1829 Garrison secured for young Whittier the editorship of the political weekly *American Manufacturer* in Boston, where he quickly became an earnest and outspoken critic of Democrat Andrew Jackson and a supporter of Whig leader Henry Clay. This position introduced him to the realities of politics and political discourse, where he acquitted himself credibly enough to attract the notice of George D. Prentice, editor of the *New England Weekly Review*, and Nathaniel Parker Willis. Manifesting early the character of the ardent reformer he would later become, Whittier voiced his approval of the temperance movement, condemned slavery, opposed prison sentences for debt, denounced the excesses of Puritan Calvinism, and expressed support for the Unitarian movement, which shared with Quakerism the tenets of a benevolent God and the intrinsic merit of humankind.

His father's illness required his return to Haverhill in the summer of 1829. While Whittier was there, Thayer gave him the editorship of the *Gazette*. After his father's death the next year, and on Prentice's recommendation, he was made editor of the eminent *New England Weekly Review* and moved to Hartford, Connecticut; he was just twenty-three. In 1831 he published his first book of prose and verse, *Legends of New England*, which he soon realized was common; he tried to suppress it, offering five dollars a copy so he could burn it. His output of verse and prose for the paper in the form of editorials, book reviews, and sketches would have filled a large volume. Working too hard, he had a nervous breakdown in the fall of 1831. Taking a leave of absence, he returned home to Haverhill, where he wrote the long narrative poem *Moll Pitcher*. Reluctantly he resigned from the *Review* in 1832 when convalescence failed to restore his former vigor. Yet his public voice in political matters and support of Clay had earned him repute throughout New England, and it is likely he would have been successful in a bid for Congress in 1832 if he had met the minimum legal age of twenty-five.

Despondent over the headaches that interrupted his work and his lack of direction in life, Whittier reached a turning point in 1833. Garrison wrote asking him to join the fledgling abolitionist movement. Recognizing the risks—both northern and southern interests opposed abolitionism—he joined, believing such a course to be morally correct and socially necessary. In June 1833 he published the antislavery pamphlet *Justice and Expediency* and in December was a founding member of the American Anti-Slavery Society. He would later regard his signing of the Anti-Slavery Declaration of 1833 the most important thing he had done. For Whittier, there was a willful consecration of his art to the cause of abolition, as reflected in lines he later wrote about this decision, saying he

> Had left the Muses' haunts to turn
> The crank of an opinion-mill,
> Making his rustic reed of song
> A Weapon in the war with wrong.

In 1835 Whittier was elected to a term in the Massachusetts state legislature and continued his work against slavery. While lecturing in Concord, New Hampshire, he and British abolitionist George Thompson were attacked by a mob and narrowly escaped serious injury. In 1836 Whittier sold the farm and moved with his mother and sister Elizabeth to Amesbury and published the narrative poem *Mogg Megone*, a treatment of colonial Indian life. In 1837 the first collection of Whittier's poetry, *Poems Written during the Progress of the Abolition Question in the United States, between 1830 and 1838*, appeared in an unauthorized edition published by antislavery associates in Boston. Whittier corrected and expanded the collection, retitled it *Poems*, and published it the next year in Philadelphia. He had gone to Philadelphia to succeed Benjamin Lundy as editor of the *Pennsylvania Freeman*, and before the year was out he saw the newly erected Pennsylvania Hall, which housed the office of the paper, burned by an antiabolitionist mob. Whittier risked his life masquerading as one of the mob to save some of his papers from the flames. He returned to Amesbury to permanently settle there in 1840.

In the late 1830s the abolitionist movement, encountering intense opposition, became divided over tactics, and Whittier's strong belief in legislative procedures made him a founding proponent in 1840 of the Liberty party, affirming an ideological split with Garrison. Whittier published *Lays of My Home* in 1843, turning again to a regional emphasis in his poetry, but significant themes such as tolerance and brotherhood linked his homespun and antislavery writings. *Ballads and Other Poems* followed in 1844, and *Voices of Freedom*, his last collection of antislavery poems, appeared in 1846. In 1847 *The Supernaturalism of New England* was published, but harsh critical reception caused Whittier to suppress it. The same year he began his affiliation with the antislavery journal the *National Era*, where the majority of his material was published until 1857. His only novel, *Leaves from Margaret Smith's Journal*, was serialized in the *Era* in 1848–1849. Two collections of prose works from the *Era* were published in 1850 as *Old Portraits and Modern Sketches* and in 1854 as *Literary Recreations and Miscellanies*. *Songs of Labor* was also published in 1850; it contained "Ichabod," Whittier's protest of Daniel Webster's support of the Compromise of 1850, and one of his best poems. *The Chapel of the Hermits* appeared in 1853, followed by *The Panorama* in 1856, which included "The Barefoot Boy."

With abolitionism gaining popular support in the 1850s, Whittier's reputation improved. He joined other prominent New England writers such as James Russell Lowell, Henry Wadsworth Longfellow, Ralph Waldo Emerson, and Oliver Wendell Holmes in founding the *Atlantic Monthly* in 1857. Writing for the new magazine brought the New England materials again to the fore and resulted in the collection *Home Ballads and Other Poems* (1860). "Barbara Frietchie," the best of Whittier's patriotic poems, appeared in *In War Time and Other Poems* (1863).

The death of his beloved sister Elizabeth in 1864, the passage of the Thirteenth Amendment in 1865 ending slavery and his public cause, and the fact that he never married combined to direct Whittier's energies to reminiscent musings. The poem that resulted made him famous. *Snow-Bound* (1866), regarded as his masterpiece, is a subjective treatment of rural New England's early nineteenth-century domestic life. It portrays the members of Whittier's childhood household gathered at the hearth to wait out a large snowstorm. The poem was celebrated for its portraitlike quality of a vanished way of life, went through a number of printings, and secured Whittier financially. *The Tent on the Beach* (1867) was also a financial success. These works were followed by *Among the Hills* (1869), *Miriam and Other Poems* (1871), an edition of John Woolman's *Journal* (1871), *The Pennsylvania Pilgrim* (1872), *Hazel-Blossoms* (1875), *The Vision of Echard*

(1878), *St. Gregory's Guest* (1886), and *At Sundown* (1890). After *Snow-Bound* Whittier enjoyed increasing popularity until his death. His birthday had become the occasion of a number of public observances, and his eightieth birthday was celebrated nationally. He died quietly in Hampton Falls, New Hampshire. Of his literary generation, only Holmes survived him.

In 1888, as Whittier reviewed the proofs of the seven-volume edition of his collected works, he regretted the lack of polish displayed by many of his poems: "I am old enough to be done with work, only that I feel my best words have not been said after all." However, for Whittier and many of his generation, besides art, poetry served a significant social function. Thinking of future opinion, Whittier underscored what was primary: "What we *are* will then be more important than what we have done or said in prose or rhyme." He did not live to see the eclipse of his popularity. Modern readers largely reject the sentimentality that informs so much of his work. But Whittier was aware of both his limitations and his purpose, and if his poetry is read today more for its moral tone than its sentimental themes, Whittier himself would have believed that the better part.

• The largest collections of Whittier's manuscripts, papers, and letters are in the Essex Institute, Salem, Mass.; Harvard's Houghton Library; and the Haverford College Library. His collected works are in the Riverside Edition of *The Writings of John Greenleaf Whittier* (7 vols., 1888–1889) and in *The Letters of John Greenleaf Whittier*, ed. John B. Pickard (3 vols., 1975). Biographies include Samuel T. Pickard, *Life and Letters of John Greenleaf Whittier* (2 vols., 1894); Thomas Wentworth Higginson, *John Greenleaf Whittier* (1902); Albert Mordell, *Quaker Militant: John Greenleaf Whittier* (1933); John A. Pollard, *John Greenleaf Whittier: Friend of Man* (1949); Lewis Leary, *John Greenleaf Whittier* (1961); and Edward Wagenknecht, *John Greenleaf Whittier: A Portrait in Paradox* (1967). Other important sources are John B. Pickard, *John Greenleaf Whittier: An Introduction and Interpretation* (1961); Robert Penn Warren, *John Greenleaf Whittier's Poetry: An Appraisal and a Selection* (1971); Albert J. von Frank, *Whittier: A Comprehensive Annotated Bibliography* (1976); Jayne K. Kribbs, ed., *Critical Essays on John Greenleaf Whittier* (1980); and Earl A. Harbert and Robert A. Rees, eds., *Fifteen American Authors before 1900* (1984).

RANDALL CLUFF

WHITTREDGE, Worthington (22 May 1820–25 Feb. 1910), painter, was born Thomas Worthington Whitridge in Springfield, Ohio, the son of Joseph Whitridge, a sea captain from Rochester, Massachusetts, and Olive Worthington. According to his autobiography, Whittredge was a born trapper who acquired an early love of nature that never left him. Like most rural youths of the period, he had little formal education, and his father denied him the opportunity to attend high school in Springfield. As the youngest son, Whittredge was expected to remain on the farm and care for his elderly parents. Tales of New England, however, instilled in him a restless desire to escape the confines of the farm. When his unmarried brother returned home, he "seized the opportunity to announce that I was going away."

Although "the very word 'artist' was anathema" to his father, Whittredge went to Cincinnati in 1837 and apprenticed himself to his brother-in-law Almon Baldwin, a house and sign painter who took up portraiture and landscapes as well. Whittredge's autobiography includes an amusing account, related with considerable gusto, of how he learned his trade literally from the ground, having spent countless hours painting baseboards. It is not known how long Whittredge's apprenticeship with Baldwin lasted. The Cincinnati city directory listed Whittredge for the first time in 1838 as a portrait painter, but he soon took up landscapes, which he began exhibiting a year later. During this time he probably remained under the general care of his brother-in-law, who also seems to have acted as his agent.

Whittredge arrived in Cincinnati during its cultural heyday. Despite Frances Trollope's vitriolic account of life there, the "Queen City" was the cultural capital of the frontier, with well over 100,000 residents and ambitions of becoming the "Athens of the West." During the second quarter of the century, Cincinnati had a thriving cultural life dominated by a community of transplanted New Englanders, including an active body of Transcendentalists and a rival group of Presbyterians under the leadership of the Reverend Lyman Beecher, who together helped make the city a hotbed of social and religious reform. And in 1839 the Cincinnati Academy of Fine Arts finally opened after a decade of false starts. Though it provided no training, the academy helped promote the rapid growth of painting in Cincinnati by creating valuable exhibition opportunities, and the number of painters active in the city rose from nine to twenty in only two years. Nevertheless, local artists had to struggle to make a living and often became itinerants. Thus, in the summer of 1842 Whittredge set himself up in an abortive partnership in a daguerreotype studio in Indianapolis. Things went so badly that he had to be rescued from destitution and illness by the Reverend Henry Ward Beecher, whom he had known in Cincinnati.

After leaving Indianapolis, Whittredge went home to finish recuperating from his illness before returning to Cincinnati. In 1844 he joined forces with B. W. Jenks, an itinerant portrait painter from Kentucky who was active in Cincinnati at the time. Their partnership, patterned along the lines of the successful Waldo and Jewett firm in New York, took them to Charleston, West Virginia, but it dissolved in Jenks's alcoholism. Only upon his return to Cincinnati in 1845 did Whittredge decide to devote himself seriously to landscape. Along with William Sonntag and Robert Duncanson, he helped create a distinctive regional variation of the Hudson River school style over the next four years. Despite growing success, he suddenly decided in 1849 to go to Europe with the goal, unusual among American painters of the time, of improving his training. Like most other artists going abroad,

Whittredge financed his travels through commissions. His survival assured by an adequate supply of orders, he left Cincinnati in early May for New York, where he and fellow artist Benjamin McConkey boarded a ship for London.

After a visit to Belgium and several weeks of sketching along the Rhine, Whittredge went to Paris in September but could find no teacher or school of landscape that he cared for. By October he and McConkey decided to settle in Düsseldorf, then the art capital of Germany. They were taken under the wing of Emmanuel Gottlieb Leutze, the city's leading artist. In the hope of receiving lessons from Andreas Achenbach, Whittredge persuaded the artist's wife to rent out a small storage room in their attic. Whittredge soon assimilated the Düsseldorf landscape style, which had been established by Carl Friedrich Lessing and his pupil Wilhelm Schirmer. He immersed himself in the cultural life of the city and became acquainted with all the leading poets and musicians, particularly Robert and Clara Schumann.

In the spring of 1856 he decided to transfer to Rome out of a desire for further travel and adventure. Following a summer of sketching in Switzerland, he arrived in October in the Holy City, where he was joined by Albert Bierstadt and Sanford Gifford. His funds nearly depleted, he was compelled to paint standard academic scenes of the Roman Campagna and Swiss alps for American tourists as souvenirs of their European travels. He managed to compete successfully and extended his stay in Italy. Characteristically, Whittredge abruptly returned to the United States in the summer of 1859 out of simple homesickness. It was at this time that he changed the spelling of his last name from Whitridge to Whittredge.

After spending a month painting "a few sketches in Newport," Whittredge went to Cincinnati until after Christmas, but despite pleas from local patrons he settled in New York, where he rented quarters in the recently completed Tenth Street Studio Building. He was elected an associate member of the National Academy of Design in 1860 and formally instated as a full member two years later. In addition to being an honor that he treasured, election to the academy was virtually a prerequisite of success. There he formed a lifelong friendship with Asher B. Durand, the dean of the Hudson River school. Along with several other artists, Whittredge was soon invited to join the Century Association, which proved vital to his career. Besides giving him entrée to a wider circle of patrons, the club brought Whittredge into close contact with a group of intellectuals, notably the poet William Cullen Bryant.

Confronted by the unfamiliar terrain and light of the East Coast, and by the unprecedented variety of style and subject that characterized American landscape painting after 1850, Whittredge underwent a profound crisis, despite favorable notices. The way to adapt his European experience to the American scene was shown by friends he had made in Düsseldorf: Gifford, Eastman Johnson, and Bierstadt. His work from the early 1860s consists largely of forest interiors and autumnal landscapes. Of particular importance to the formation of his vision of the United States was the tour of the West he undertook in the summer of 1866 with General John Pope. The Rockies made a strong impression on him, and western scenes figure prominently in his work for the next ten years. His canvases during this time translate compositions he had painted in Europe into a distinctly American idiom. Whittredge married Euphemia Foote in Geneva, New York, in 1867; they had four children.

Accompanied by Gifford and John Kensett, he returned to Colorado in July 1870 to revisit some trees on the Cache la Poudre River he wanted to include in *Crossing the Ford (The Plains from the Base of the Rocky Mountains)* (Century Association, New York), his best-known work, which he completed that same year. This trip proved nearly as momentous as the first and resulted in a major change toward a greater pleinairism.

During 1870–1871 Whittredge was preoccupied with western scenes, but in 1872 he once again began to devote himself to traditional Hudson River subjects. At the same time, he resumed spending a part of his summers in New England, staying mainly in the house of his grand-uncle Dr. William Whittredge near Middleton, Rhode Island, across Newport on the Seconnet River.

The high point of Whittredge's career occurred during the years 1872 to 1876, when he assumed effective artistic leadership of the Hudson River school. In 1874–1875, a time of great turmoil, Whittredge was elected to two one-year terms as president of the National Academy of Design, many of whose members had become disenchanted; the academy was furthermore heavily in debt for the new building that had opened in 1866. At the urging of Parke Goodwin, Whittredge organized a loan exhibition of foreign art at the Philadelphia Centennial in cooperation with the Metropolitan Museum of Art, which he had helped found. He was also a member of the Centennial's Hanging Committee, along with J. D. Smillie, James Sartain of Philadelphia, and William Perkins of Boston, which nearly dissolved in rancor over Sartain's insistence at giving pride of place to European artists. After serving out his presidency of the academy, Whittredge remained active in its affairs for several more years. But although he had saved it from ruin, he could not restore the academy's luster. Nor was he able to stem the tide of Barbizon that soon engulfed the Hudson River school and transformed his own work as well.

The problems faced by Whittredge and the rest of the Hudson River painters resulted from a fundamental shift in taste in favor of European art. With his European experience, Whittredge was uniquely capable among his generation of adapting to Barbizon art. Torn between his Hudson River outlook and the Barbizon aesthetic, however, he found it difficult to reconcile the contradictions between the two seemingly incompatible schools. Whereas the second generation of Hudson River artists practiced a meticulous naturalism, Barbizon painters emphasized a more spontaneous approach. Realizing that he had to change his style without renouncing his artistic personality, he turned for his subject matter to Newport, which held deep personal associations that enabled him to achieve a new synthesis. In effect, Whittredge's Newport scenes of the late 1870s and early 1880s translate his mature Hudson River style into a Barbizon idiom based on the light-filled style of Charles-François Daubigny. Simultaneously, he built a house, "Hillcrest," in Summit, New Jersey, which inspired a return to the autumnal subjects traditional to the Hudson River school but treated now in a Barbizon style.

By the mid-1880s Whittredge's art began to decline, and he gradually retired as a professional artist, although he continued to paint actively and kept quarters in the Tenth Street Studio Building until 1900 in order to maintain contact with New York art circles. In 1889 he was asked to serve as president of the Committee of United States Artists to select works by artists living in America for the Paris International Exposition; the invitation recognized him as the dean of American landscape painters and acknowledged his many contributions to the National Academy of Design. His exact role remains unclear, but he seems to have played little part in the controversies that surrounded the jury process. At the exposition he was accorded an honorable mention.

Whittredge's efforts from the later 1880s reflect his demoralization over the eclipse of the Hudson River school and demonstrate a reluctant acquiescence to the predominant style of George Inness and his followers. Around 1890, however, Whittredge was revitalized by the rise of a new generation of American Barbizon painters born in the 1850s and for the most part trained abroad. Moreover, he soon became the only Hudson River painter besides Homer Martin to explore an impressionist style.

In December 1892 Whittredge went to Mexico with Frederic Edwin Church, who sought to alleviate the effects of his crippling rheumatism in the warm, dry climate. They remained there into late February 1893. Remarkably, Whittredge continued painting regularly for another ten years. In 1904 he was accorded a major retrospective exhibition by the Century Association. He spent the last decade of his life at his home in Summit, where he died.

• Principal works by Whittredge include *View of Cincinnati* (c. 1847, Worcester Art Museum, Worcester, Mass.), *View near Brunnen on Lake Lucerne* (1857, Brooklyn Museum of Art, Brooklyn, N.Y.), *View in the Ashocan Forest* (1868, Chrysler Museum of Art, Norfolk, Va.), *The Camp Meeting* (1874, Metropolitan Museum of Art, New York City), *Trout Brook in the Catskills* (1875, Corcoran Gallery of Art, Washington, D.C.), and *Seconnet Point* (c. 1880, National Museum of American Art, Washington, D.C.). For more information on his life and work, see *The Autobiography of Worthington Whittredge, 1820–1910*, ed. J. I. H. Baur (1942), and A. F. Janson, *Worthington Whittredge* (1989). A useful exhibition catalog is E. H. Dwight, *Worthington Whittredge: A Retrospective Exhibition of an American Artist* (Munson-Williams-Proctor Institute, 1969).

A. F. JANSON

WHORF, Benjamin Lee (24 Apr. 1897–26 July 1941), linguist, was born in Winthrop, Massachusetts, the son of Sarah Edna Lee and Harry Church Whorf, a commercial artist and theater buff who wrote librettos, designed sets, and enjoyed a broad spectrum of literary and artistic avocations. Benjamin was one of three talented brothers. John became a world-famous painter with a special reputation for water colors; Richard became a stage actor and later a motion picture and television director with successful films in mystery, comedy, and musical genres. Benjamin was the most studious of the three: he had a penchant for codes and chemicals. It became a family ritual to give him anagrams to decipher. His father provided him with a formidable chemistry set. Benjamin was an academic standout at Winthrop Public High School.

Whorf enrolled in the chemical engineering program at the Massachusetts Institute of Technology. While attending ROTC camp during the summer of his junior year, he incurred a mysterious illness; he may have had a nervous breakdown. In any case, the camp was his only exposure to the military. The illness delayed Whorf's educational progress slightly, but he graduated from MIT with a bachelor's degree in chemical engineering in the fall of 1919, shortly after the armistice was signed in Europe.

Whorf went to work for the Hartford Insurance Company—his first and only job. After some initial training, he was assigned to the fire insurance section. There he remained for the rest of his life, rising to the rank of assistant secretary of the company. Decades later, Hartford Insurance would broadcast television commercials touting its "preventive" fire inspection program, a plan devised by Whorf during the 1920s.

Whorf married Celia Inez Peckham in 1920 and settled in Hartford. The well-matched couple enjoyed a happy home life. They had three children.

Whorf regularly walked the four miles to work from his home in Wethersfield, with frequent side trips to the public library. As his intellectual horizons broadened, he made use of a privately endowed research institution, Hartford's Watkinson Library. A large, special collection of American Indian manuscripts attracted his attention, reigniting a boyhood interest in the exotic cultures described by William H. Prescott's three-volume *History of the Conquest of Mexico* (1843). He shared his initial findings in public "chalk talks" on the Aztec and Mayan Indians of Mexico to civic groups. But Whorf was no dabbler; not long after commencing his studies, he published papers on Aztec and Mayan. His knack for decoding puzzles proved especially useful. At an academic meeting in 1928, his translation of a previously undeciphered Aztec manuscript drew notice. A businessman had beaten the professors at their own game! His translation of an Aztec manuscript in 1929 drew further attention to the amateur linguist; as a result of these small triumphs, in 1930 Whorf won a Social Science Research Council fellowship to visit Mexico for firsthand study of Aztec and Mayan materials—where he deciphered stone ideographs. His paper "A Central Mexican Inscription Combining Mexican and Maya Day Signs" drew further attention to his skills and justified the fellowship as did a series of articles about the Mayan language written during the 1930s.

Whorf was not unlike other thoughtful people in the 1920s and 1930s in his concern about the conflict between science and religion; while he was a theist who believed in a living God, he was also a very modern man whose profession involved chemistry and technology. In response to the Scopes Trial of 1925, Whorf wrote a novel of ideas titled *The Ruler of the Universe*. The protagonist, a man of faith, learns that the scientific theories of quantum mechanics and relativity physics can be reconciled with the metaphorical language of Genesis. In this context, the command "Let there be light" is pregnant with meaning. On the dark side, the novel argues that modern man has misused—and, because of original sin, will continue to misuse—the fruits of science. Toward the end of the story, the world is destroyed by a runaway nuclear reaction at a weapons laboratory in the Rocky Mountains. Whorf's book closes with a lesson: modern man must come back to the Puritan synthesis of faith and reason, using his intelligence for constructive purposes—or suffer apocalyptic consequences. Letters in Whorf's files show that he hoped H. L. Mencken would attack the book; since Mencken lacked scientific training, Whorf predicted victory for himself in any ensuing debate. Unfortunately, no publisher took an interest in the novel and it was not published in his lifetime.

Whorf's research in language reflected his spiritual concerns. Some of his first readings in linguistics after college were in the writings of Antoine Fabre d'Olivet and F. Max Müller. From d'Olivet, Whorf gained the notion of "deep structure," a concept that would be vital to the American's "linguistic relativity" hypothesis. D'Olivet was no dry academic. He promised that such studies would shed light on universal problems of the human spirit. F. Max Müller was a Christian apologist to the late Victorians who promised that "language is not outside the mind, but is the outside of the mind. Language is very thought as thought is very language" (*Science of Thought*, p. 215). Following the tradition of Kant, as well as Ralph Waldo Emerson and other New England Transcendentalists, both linguists shared Whorf's antipathy toward Locke's notion that the mind at birth was essentially blank.

Early in his studies of language, Whorf was drawn to the work of Franz Boas and Edward Sapir, leading members of what became known as the American School of anthropology. Unlike British anthropologists such as Edward B. Tylor, who marked the progression of civilizations from animistic savagery to Western rationality, Boas and Sapir respected the integrity of other worldviews. Whorf was inspired by the Americans' notion that other cultures produced different, rather than inferior, insights.

In 1930 Whorf made a research trip to Mexico; during the following year, Sapir moved from the University of Chicago to Yale University. Whorf enrolled in Sapir's evening classes, to which he commuted by train from Hartford. As is often the custom with academic mentors, Sapir steered Whorf toward a topic of his own interest, the languages of the Indians of the American Southwest. By studying the content and structure of the American Indian languages—in particular, the languages of the Navajo and the Hopi—Whorf claimed to have gained a perspective on the limitations of the Western worldview. The West had been extremely successful in the sciences and in the manipulation of matter because of the ability of Indo-European languages to manipulate mass nouns. Recent discoveries of physics of that era were difficult to accept because of embedded linguistic resistances to new ways of thinking about time, space, and matter. In a late article, Whorf summarized his interpretation:

> We dissect nature along lines laid down by our native language. The categories and types that we isolate from the world of phenomena we do not find there because they stare us in the face; on the contrary, the world is presented in a kaleidoscopic flux of impressions which has to be organized in our minds—and this means largely by the linguistic systems in our minds. We cut nature up, organize it into concepts, and ascribe significance as we do, largely because we are parties to an agreement to organize it in this way—an agreement that holds throughout our speech community and is codified in the patterns of our language. (*Language, Thought, and Reality*, p. 214)

This is the "Whorfian hypothesis" in its most succinct formulation.

In his unpublished "Outline of the History of Linguistics," Whorf lamented the death of Sapir in 1939 because Sapir—according to Whorf—was about to make some kind of grand synthesis about the relationship among the three factors that so interested Whorf: mind, language, and reality. It seems quite clear that Whorf's own writings on this subject were attempts to formulate the synthesis his mentor had failed to achieve. According to Whorf, the structure of Western languages had helped Europeans to establish a sense of routine in the vast mysteries of time and space. (For example, Westerners break time into a series of units—such as months, years, decades, or what Whorf called "metaphorical aggregates"—whereas it is really a continuous flow.) Though Western people gained an inordinate ability to manipulate concepts, they lost a precious sense of wonder. In contrast, the Hopi seemed always in contact with the primary processes of nature. Because they used a language sensitive to levels of energy intensity, the Hopi communed with nature in a manner recommended implicitly by the new physics of Max Planck and Erwin Schrödinger. The science of linguistics could serve the West by restoring a sense of wonder; the results would be monumental, revolutionizing both science and religion. In 1941, just before his death, Whorf published a series of articles that are still read in linguistics classes today because of the colorful way they lay out his concept of "linguistic relativity."

Even after his fame as a linguist spread—bringing him offers of academic positions—Whorf remained in the business sector. He attended Chamber of Commerce meetings and was a regular lecturer to civic groups. He felt that university life would constrict his interdisciplinary interests—not to mention lead to a severe diminishment of his income. Whorf's health declined during the spring and summer of 1941 until he died from cancer at his home in Wetherford, Connecticut. Some of his most provocative articles had seen the light of publication before his death, but his voluminous diaries and notebooks reveal that he had so much more to offer.

Shortly after his death, Whorf's ideas were honored in a very popular book about language, S.I. Hayakawa's *Language in Thought and Action* (1941). (In an appendix, Hayakawa included one of the provocative late articles.) In 1968 Whorf's ideas were ridiculed by Max Black in *The Labyrinth of Language*, where he sardonically observed that the Whorf hypothesis would be of little use "until some other 'near genius' with a talent for exact thought, succeeds in deriving some reasonably precise hypothesis" (p. 94). Today, there is still considerable debate about the usefulness of the concept—although most linguists agree that the "weak form" of the hypothesis has merit—i.e., that the structure of language influences perceptions but does not completely determine them.

Very few will miss the affinities between Whorf's ideas about "deep structure" and the revolutionary work of Noam Chomsky during the 1960s. Chomsky culled from Wilhelm von Humboldt many of the ideas Whorf derived from Fabre d'Olivet and F. Max Müller. Von Humboldt even put forward what he called his "Weltanschauung hypothesis," the notion that worldviews of different peoples varied because of differences in the internal structure of their languages—an idea with a familiar ring to it, thanks to Whorf. Chomsky's *American Power and the New Mandarins* (1968) provides criticism of contemporary science along Whorfian lines—challenging not only the language and worldview of putative "experts" in social science but also impugning the motives of the "new mandarins." According to Chomsky—in words that echo Whorf's critique of social scientists in his polemical novel of the 1920s—"the cult of the expert is both self-serving, for those who propound it, and fraudulent" (*American Power*, p. 5).

Subsequent writings about Whorf fall into three categories. There have been a number of conferences to consider the validity of the Whorf hypothesis; certainly, this kind of debate should continue. A second spin-off of Whorf's work seems to be in the area of literary criticism where linguistics has been brought to bear by theorists who have asked fundamental questions about how we know what we know and whether we mean what we say. A third group of writings focuses on Whorf's purely descriptive (and nontheoretical) studies of Mayan, Navaho, and Hopi. His work reveals fascinating tensions in the American mind during the 1920s and 1930s, stress-points usually overlooked in the rush to discuss traditional "lost generation" figures in the literary and historical canon. It also seems clear that Whorf's ideas can only increase in importance for our multicultural future. Someday, should the quest for a "Puritan synthesis" of science and faith ever be revived, his most prized legacy might come back into focus.

• The Yale University Library now has a collection of Whorf papers, many of which were given to the school after Whorf's widow pruned through a much larger collection in her possession. Many of Whorf's major published and unpublished writings were collected by John B. Carroll in *Language, Thought, and Reality: Selected Writings of Benjamin Lee Whorf* (1956). A thoughtful conference examining the validity of "the Whorf hypothesis" is preserved in *Language and Culture*, ed. Harry Hoijer (1954). Another general study is Lee Penny, *The Whorf Theory Complex: A Critical Reconstruction* (1996). A literary theorist compares Whorf to the Russian critic Mikhail Bakhtin in Emily A. Shultz, *Dialogue at the Margins: Bahktin, and Linguistic Relativity* (1990). The quarterly *Et Cetera* is a general semantics publication that has taken a long-term interest in Whorf's ideas. Peter Rollins, *Benjamin Lee Whorf: Lost Generation Theories of Mind, Language, and Religion* (1980), is an intellectual biography based on manuscript, diary, and published materials.

PETER C. ROLLINS

WHYBURN, Gordon Thomas (7 Jan. 1904–8 Sept. 1969), mathematician, was born in Lewisville, Texas, the son of Thomas Whyburn and Eugenia Elizabeth McCleod, farmers. Whyburn studied chemistry as an undergraduate at the University of Texas at Austin and obtained a B.A. in 1925. With the encouragement of his calculus professor, R. L. Moore, Whyburn took Moore's advanced mathematics courses while continuing with chemistry. After earning an M.A. in chemistry in 1926, he obtained a Ph.D. from the University of Texas in 1927 in mathematics as Moore's third doctoral student. In 1925 he married a fellow student in Moore's courses, Lucille Enid Smith; they had one child. Whyburn continued as an adjunct professor in the mathematics department at Texas until 1929. When he was awarded a John Simon Guggenheim Memorial Foundation Fellowship for 1929–1930, he and his wife traveled to Vienna, Austria, and Warsaw, Poland, where he worked with the mathematician Hans Hahn. While there and during a visit to Warsaw the Whyburns met with a number of people who closely followed the works of Moore and his students in point-set topology and who themselves influenced the American school, such as Karl Menger, Bronislaw Knaster, Casimir Kuratowski, Stefan Mazurkiewicz, and Waclaw Sierpiński.

Whyburn taught at Johns Hopkins University, 1929–1934, and then was appointed professor of mathematics and chair of the department at the University of Virginia, where he stayed, apart from brief teaching engagements as a visitor elsewhere, until his death. His wife, who also taught in the mathematics department as a lecturer during this period, was a critical reader of many of Whyburn's writings in preparing them for publication. According to a memorial article written jointly by a Whyburn student, E. E. Floyd, and another Moore student, F. B. Jones, Whyburn was brought to Virginia to build up the mathematics department, which at the time lagged behind those of the University of Texas at Austin and Rice University in Houston among southern institutions. By the 1940s, with the help of additional new faculty members E. J. McShane and G. A. Hedlund, Whyburn had established at Virginia an equally distinguished program.

Whyburn won the Mathematical Association of America's Chauvenet Prize for excellence in mathematical exposition in 1938 for his paper "On the Structure of Continua." Though this topological subject can be presented in a very abstract and general fashion, Whyburn's review of recent results brought out its concrete visual character. In the last year of his life Whyburn had the honor of being invited, as one of six previous winners of the prize, to give a talk at the Chauvenet Symposium. He was invited to be the American Mathematical Society Colloquium speaker in 1940, and his lectures were published in book form as *Analytic Topology* (1942).

From 1942 to 1945 Whyburn served as a member of the War Policy Committee of the AMS, on which he supported the employment of mathematicians for teaching or for war-related research. From 1948 to 1952 he was a member of the editorial committee of the *Transactions of the American Mathematical Society*. In 1950 he helped to form the International Mathematical Union and throughout the 1950s served on various panels and committees of the National Science Foundation. He was elected to the National Academy of Sciences in 1951 and was elected president of the AMS for 1953–1954.

Whyburn further developed the subject to which he had been introduced by Moore, point-set topology, and published more than 140 papers in this field, centering on the structure of continua, the theory of curves, and continuous transformations. Much of his later work was compiled in *Topological Analysis* (1958). He adapted the teaching method that was successfully developed by his mentor and commonly referred to as the "Moore method." One of his twenty-five doctoral students, Edwin Duda, later prepared a book based on Whyburn's course notes, *Dynamic Topology* (1979), in which another of Whyburn's students, J. L. Kelley, described Whyburn's implementation of Moore's method in a course given in 1937–1938. Whyburn gave definitions of the key concepts, some examples and diagrams, and then theorems to be proven by the students without any additional help from texts or from each other outside the classroom. In the classroom Whyburn patiently listened to student presentations while he and other students offered critiques. Although Whyburn offered to give the proofs of any theorems that no student in the class could prove, Kelley states that this did not happen in his class. Students were quickly brought up to research-level discussions by this method, but its major risk, according to Kelley, was that a narrower range of material was covered than in the conventional lecture courses.

In 1966 Whyburn became the first member of the newly formed Center for Advanced Studies in the Sciences at Virginia while he continued as alumni professor of mathematics. The University of Virginia awarded him its highest honor, the Thomas Jefferson Award, in 1968. Although he suffered a heart attack in 1966, he continued teaching and doing research until his death in Charlottesville. Floyd and Jones described Whyburn as "a very private man . . . quiet and shy, and remarkably gentle with students and family. But in moments of administrative crisis, he could be extremely tough when he had to be."

• E. E. Floyd and F. B. Jones, "Gordon T. Whyburn, 1904–1969," *Bulletin of the American Mathematical Society* 77 (1971): 57–72, provides an account of his career and mathematical work and includes a bibliography. His many connections with the American Mathematical Society as well as his portrait are in Everett Pitcher, *A History of the Second Fifty Years, American Mathematical Society 1939–1988* (1988).

ALBERT C. LEWIS

WIBBERLEY, Leonard (9 Apr. 1915–22 Nov. 1983), journalist and author, was born Leonard Patrick O'Connor Wibberley in Dublin, Ireland, the son of Thomas Wibberley, a professor of agriculture, and Sinaid O'Connor, a teacher. Wibberley was the youngest of six children and describes his childhood as "fortunate." The family moved from Dublin to Cork, where, as Wibberley described in *The Shannon Sailors* (1972), "We lived in a house opposite the Common, which seemed always to be flooded with rainwater." With both parents involved in education, the house "was filled with books." Wibberley was taught in Gaelic until 1923, when the family moved to England. There Wibberley learned English and continued his education at Cardinal Vaughan's School in London, where he enjoyed studying Greek, Latin, and English literature. Wibberley once said that he was "three parts Irish, one part English" (Wakeman, p. 1545). This mixed heritage can be detected in the use of Irish legends and English folktales in his writing.

When his father died, Wibberley, at the age of fifteen, was obliged to leave school and earn his living. Wibberley's first job was as an apprentice and then a copy boy for the *Sunday Dispatch* from 1931 to 1932 and later the *Sunday Express*. He advanced to a reporter's job for the *Daily Mirror* in 1935–1936. During this time, fearful of being fired because of the unemployment rate in Great Britain, he quit his job and worked as a street fiddler, ditchdigger, dishwasher, and cook. Wibberley tired of this life and returned to Fleet Street as an assistant London editor of the Malayan *Straits Times* and the *Singapore Free Press*.

In 1936 a job as editor of the *Chronicle* took Wibberley to Trinidad. He also worked as editor of the *Trinidad Evening News* and for an oil company. From 1939 to 1941 he served as a lance bombardier in the Trinidad Artillery Volunteers, a local defense militia.

Wibberley came to the United States in 1943 to work for the Walsh Kaiser Shipyards of Providence, Rhode Island, builders of Liberty ships. He was in charge of employee relations. His next move was to New York City and back to the newspaper world as cable editor for the Associated Press from 1943 to 1944. Wibberley was New York correspondent and bureau chief for the *London Evening News* from 1944 to 1946. He left this post to relocate to the West Coast as editor of the *Independent Journal* in San Rafael, California, from 1947 to 1949. In 1948 Wibberley married Katherine Hazel Holton. They had two daughters and four sons.

From 1950 to 1954 Wibberley worked for the *Los Angeles Times* as a reporter and copy editor. During this time he published several books whose modest success enabled him to retire. As Ted Hines notes in the *Wilson Library Bulletin*, Wibberley's "twenty-five years of servitude to others was nearly up, so he quit his work to write full time" (p. 882).

Wibberley 's first book, *The King's Beard* (1952), was followed by over fifty books in the next decade. Using his own name and pseudonyms Wibberley wrote more than 100 books, including adult and children's fiction and nonfiction, verse, plays, and travel books. He also wrote short stories and a weekly column, "The Wibberley Papers," syndicated by the *San Francisco Chronicle*.

Wibberley said about his children's books, "It is for the child inside myself that I write my children's books, for that child lives on into my more sombre years. . . . You must write for the child that you are if you are going to produce a children's book of any worth" (Higgins, p. 1021). Noteworthy among his books for children are the four-volume life of Thomas Jefferson and the "Treegate" series. Wibberley began the Treegate series with *Johnny Treegate's Musket* (1959) and continued with other Treegate novels, historical fiction centering on the revolutionary war. The Jefferson series began with *Young Man from the Piedmont* (1963), followed by *A Dawn in the Trees* (1964), *The Gales of Spring* (1965), and *Time of the Harvest* (1966).

Wibberley's childhood affection for Robert Louis Stevenson's *Treasure Island* resulted in *Flint's Island* (1972), which details what happens to the "treasure not yet lifted" from the island. The book includes the return of Long John Silver, although Wibberley claims it is not a sequel to the Stevenson novel: "Who would dare such a thing?"

Under his pseudonym Patrick O'Connor, Wibberley wrote a series of children's stories about motor racing and a number of teenage mysteries. All the books written as Christopher Webb are for children. As Leonard Holton, Wibberley wrote adult detective novels, creating the character of Father Joseph Breder, a Los Angeles priest and amateur sleuth. All the books have an underlying spiritual theme and inspired the television series "Sarge." Thirteen one-hour episodes were televised in 1971, after a successful two-hour pilot film starring George Kennedy. Many of Wibberley's own interests are reflected in his books. In *A Problem of Angels* (1970) a rare Guarnerius violin provides a clue. Wibberley not only played the viola and the violin but also constructed these instruments.

Wibberley's most popular work is *The Mouse That Roared* (1955), a satire of 1950s geopolitics with a subplot of the Cold War and the escalating arms race. The novel is about the tiny duchy of Grand Fenwick, five miles long and three miles wide, with 6,000 inhabitants, which invades the United States. Fenwickians believe they have a justifiable reason for anger at the United States, since a California winery has been marketing a cheap copy of their only product, an outstanding wine, the Pinot Grand Fenwick, under the label Pinot Grand Enwick. But they want only to halt the production of the California wine and lose the war: "There is no more profitable and sound step for a nation without money or credit to take, than declare war on the United States and suffer a total defeat" (pp. 43–44). The United States always provides "most generously" for the countries it defeats in war.

Through a series of comic mishaps, the invading army of Grand Fenwick, with its twenty longbows (its weaponry is fourteenth century), wins the war by capturing the "Q" bomb and the scatterbrained scientist who developed it. The novel was made into a successful film in 1959, and the plot was rewritten for Peter Sellers to play three different roles: Grand Duchess Gloriana, Prime Minister Count "Bobo" Mountjoy, and Tully Bascomb. A sequel, *The Mouse on the Moon* (1962), was also made into a film in 1963. Other "mouse" novels are *Beware the Mouse* (1958), *The Mouse on Wall Street* (1969), and *The Mouse That Saved the West* (1981).

Wibberley was working on another novel, *Nightmare*, about a plot to dissolve Britain's House of Lords, when he died in Santa Monica, California.

A man with a variety of interests and many careers, Wibberley embraced the same diversity in his writing. He wrote for audiences of all ages in genres as diverse as fantasy, science fiction, biography, history, adventure, and romance. A man of candor and humor, Wibberley once remarked, "What do I think of myself as a novelist? I think I'm good—not brilliant but not mediocre either" (*Contemporary Authors*, New Revision Series, p. 597).

• Wibberley's manuscripts are housed at the University of Southern California, Los Angeles. A complete list of his works, excluding uncollected short stories and articles, is in James E. Higgins, "Wibberley, Leonard (Patrick O'Connor)," *Twentieth-century Children's Writers* (1995). Higgins also includes commentary by Wibberley about his writing. See also John Wakeman, ed., *World Authors 1950–1970* (1975) and *Contemporary Authors*, New Revision Series (1981). For biographical information and an assessment of Wibberley's writing, see Ted Hines, "Leonard Wibberley,"

Wilson Library Bulletin (June 1963): 882. *Something about the Author* (1986) has a lengthy article that includes not only biographical information but also commentary by Wibberley about his life and his books. Obituaries are in the *Los Angeles Times*, 24 Nov. 1983, and the *New York Times*, 25 Nov. 1983.

MARCIA B. DINNEEN

WICKARD, Claude Raymond (28 Feb. 1893–29 Apr. 1967), secretary of the U.S. Department of Agriculture and administrator of the Rural Electrification Administration, was born near Flora, Carroll County, Indiana, the son of Andrew Jackson Wickard and Iva Lenora Kirkpatrick, farmers. Raised on the farm established by his grandfather in 1840, Wickard graduated from Purdue University in 1915 with a bachelor of science degree in agriculture. He exhibited a zeal for the concept of scientific farming and, according to his biographer, Dean Albertson, "had a vision of future farmers being the economic, social, and intellectual equals of the city folks whom they fed" (p. 20).

Wickard commenced full-time farming at a propitious time, taking over management of the family farm as the European war increased demand for U.S. farm products. With commodity prices on the rise, Wickard seized the opportunity to expand and upgrade his corn-hog operation, which became Fairacre Farms. In 1917, when the United States entered the war, Wickard acquired an occupational deferment, and in 1918 he married Louise Eckert, with whom he had two daughters.

Things went well for the Indiana agriculturalist during the 1920s despite the depression that plagued most other farmers. Wickard inaugurated his own soil conservation program, turned Fairacre Farms into a model agricultural plant, and won statewide recognition for his successful, progressive farm practices. He took a leadership role in the rapidly growing Farm Bureau and was elected president of its Carroll County organization. By 1928 Wickard also was active in the Democratic party organization; in 1932 he won election to the Indiana State Senate.

At the end of the 1933 legislative session, Senator Wickard helped devise the first corn-hog program for the Agricultural Adjustment Administration (AAA). Subsequently, he accepted an invitation to go to Washington, D.C., to help implement that program, which had as its primary objective the establishment of production quotas to reduce the price-depressing surplus. Wickard became chief of the corn-hog section of the AAA in 1935 and eventually rose to become the director of the reorganized AAA's North Central Division.

Despite his proven loyalty and devotion to President Franklin D. Roosevelt's farm program and his popularity as a spokesman for the New Deal in the Midwest, no one was more surprised than Wickard himself when Secretary Henry A. Wallace asked this unassuming "dirt farmer" to be his undersecretary of agriculture. Wickard took office on 1 March 1940. Just six months later, after Wallace received the Democratic vice presidential nomination, Wickard became the twelfth secretary of the U.S. Department of Agriculture.

By that time the war in Europe was a year old and the problems facing the USDA were quite different than those it confronted during the depression. Secretary Wickard feared the loss of overseas markets and a resulting overproduction, and he worried that farmers would too quickly abandon New Deal farm programs. Initially he sought to quell the optimism engendered by expected wartime demand and was criticized for the slow pace of agriculture's mobilization. Soon, however, circumstances changed; as the administration's commitment to Great Britain stiffened, Wickard came to believe that increased hog production was necessary to help the British, to prepare this country for war, and to reduce the corn surplus. Thus, in December 1940 the secretary called on farmers to increase their pork and cattle marketings. He helped devise a strategy to utilize food resources for the benefit of the Allied nations and directed the USDA to begin stockpiling various commodities in anticipation of lend-lease demands. By mid-1941 he had launched the department's "production goals program."

Employing an embellished First World War slogan—"Food will win the war and write the peace"—Wickard boldly defended the administration's preparedness program while encouraging farmers to make necessary production shifts. Three months before the United States entered the war, the secretary warned farmers of the need to overcome the shortages in farm labor, new machinery, and fertilizer. "Enough of the right food is the rock-bottom essential to war-time production and morale and fighting ability," he proclaimed. "This is OUR war. It is perfectly plain now that it's Hitler or us" (*Vital Speeches* 7 [1941]: 764).

Before and after U.S. entry into World War II, Secretary Wickard worked to make sure that substantial lend-lease funds were earmarked for agricultural commodities. Several hundred million dollars worth of food was purchased for the British out of the first appropriation, and he guarded agriculture's interests in subsequent measures. At the same time, the secretary tirelessly championed higher farm prices as an incentive for the increased production. He believed the USDA should have control over farm prices and for a time was able to hold on to that authority and more as the president's designated food administrator.

To his credit, and in the face of growing criticism from other agriculturalists, Wickard never lost sight of the need to limit inflation. He preached "fair prices for farmers," which to him meant "parity prices"—a return on agricultural commodities providing a semblance of equality between what farmers received and the prices they paid for the goods and services they purchased. Secretary Wickard supported a loan rate of 85 percent of parity and a 110 percent parity ceiling. "I don't believe the average farmer wants his prices to go much above parity," he told a national radio audience on 3 November 1941. "Farmers know that they are in the minority. Without the help of other groups, far mers can't get legislation to protect their interests" (*Vital Speeches* 8 [1942]: 179).

Despite many positive trends and developments on the farm front, all was not well with the "thick-set, bronzed, good-humored" secretary with the "Indiana twang" (*Life*, p. 58). Wickard faced criticism from all sides throughout the war and was blamed, both fairly and unfairly, for many farm problems: inadequate storage facilities, farm labor shortages, rationing that limited the supply of critical machinery and spare parts, and the failure of American agriculture to attain "full production." Many officials, including those within the USDA, had long questioned Wickard's managerial proficiency; before war's end, it seemed their fears were not unfounded. As secretary of agriculture, Wickard simply "was administratively over his depth" (Albertson, p. 227).

By March 1943 the White House believed changes in the food program were called for and decided to appoint a separate war food administrator, creating what amounted to a dual-headed USDA. Wickard considered this "the worst blow" of his career, but he stayed on the job and cooperated fully with Chester Davis and, later, Marvin Jones, the new "food czars." The secretary's willingness to work with these unwelcome partners for the duration contributed greatly to the overall success of the wartime food program.

Wickard tendered his resignation soon after President Roosevelt's death, and on 22 May 1945 President Harry S. Truman accepted it, offering Wickard the opportunity to head up the Rural Electrification Administration (REA). Wickard immediately accepted the new assignment and served successfully as REA administrator until 1953, at which time nearly 90 percent of U.S. farms were electrified—up from 46 percent at the end of World War II. He then returned to his Indiana farm but remained politically active; in 1956 he made an unsuccessful bid for a seat in the U.S. Senate. Just over a decade later, Wickard was killed in an automobile accident near Delphi, Indiana.

Some of the agricultural problems experienced by the nation throughout the Second World War must be placed at the doorstep of the secretary of agriculture. Under Wickard's stewardship, however, the USDA could be justifiably proud of many accomplishments. The civilian population was educated to the importance of full participation in the nation's various wartime programs: food for freedom, victory gardens, food conservation, price controls, and rationing. Important progress was made, too, in the development of food preservation technology, farm fertilizers, insecticides, and hybrid seeds.

• Wickard's papers and diary are on deposit at the Franklin D. Roosevelt Presidential Library, Hyde Park, N.Y., and his reminiscences are a part of the Columbia University Oral History Project. Also important for his wartime career are the Records of the Office of Secretary of Agriculture, Record Group no. 16, National Archives and Records Service, Washington, D.C. See also Claude R. Wickard, "The Great Green Battle," *New York Times Magazine*, 9 Aug. 1942, p. 3; Wickard, "The Story of Meat and Rationing," *New York Times Magazine*, 20 Sept. 1942, p. 8; and "Again, 'Food Will Win the War' 'and Write the Peace,' adds Secretary Wickard," *Life*, 11 Aug. 1941, p. 58. A useful biography concentrating on Wickard's service at the head of the USDA is Dean Albertson, *Roosevelt's Farmer: Claude R. Wickard in the New Deal* (1961), which includes extensive quotations from the secretary's diary, correspondence, and interviews. The serious student will also want to consult Walter W. Wilcox's excellent study, *The Farmer in the Second World War* (1947), and Gladys L. Baker et al., *Century of Service: The First 100 Years of the United States Department of Agriculture* (1963). Obituaries are in the *New York Times* and *Washington Post*, both 30 Apr. 1967.

VIRGIL W. DEAN

WICKERSHAM, George Woodward (19 Sept. 1858–25 Jan. 1936), attorney, Republican party leader, and attorney general of the United States, was born in Pittsburgh, Pennsylvania, the son of Samuel Morris Wickersham, an inventor and businessman, and Elizabeth Cox. Raised by his maternal grandparents in Philadelphia after his mother died in childbirth and his father became absorbed in the iron and steel business, Wickersham grew up in privileged circumstances on the fringes of the city's social elite. His grandfather, for example, had helped found the Philadelphia Stock Exchange. Wickersham studied civil engineering at Lehigh University in the mid-1870s and caught the eye of one of the city's leading Republican politicians, Matthew Quay, who hired him as a secretary. Quay himself was moving rapidly up the political ladder from state treasurer to U.S. senator, chair of the Republican National Committee, and presidential kingmaker.

While learning political skills from Quay, Wickersham studied law with Robert McGrath, graduated from the University of Pennsylvania Law School, and was admitted to the state's bar in 1880. In 1883 he married Mildred Wendell; they had four children. The same year he joined the New York firm of Strong and Cadwalader (later Cadwalader, Wickersham and Taft), where, except for several interludes of public service, he remained a partner until his death.

On Wall Street Wickersham's legal reputation and income rose rapidly in the era of William McKinley and Theodore Roosevelt. His partners included Henry W. Taft, brother of the secretary of war and future president. Specializing in bankruptcies and corporate reorganizations, his clients included major transportation and manufacturing companies. Wickersham regularly socialized with important Republican leaders, especially Elihu Root, a leader of the New York bar, Roosevelt's confidant, and secretary of state. When William Howard Taft entered the White House in 1909, he tapped Wickersham to be his attorney general.

The central issue before the Department of Justice in the years 1909–1913 concerned the relationship between the federal government and corporate enterprises, a field that seemed especially ripe for resolution by someone with Wickersham's background. Federal policy remained in a state of confusion and conflict, especially with regard to the Sherman Antitrust Act of 1890, which prohibited combinations in restraint of trade and attempts to monopolize interstate commerce.

The Supreme Court remained polarized between those, like Justice Edward White, who believed the law banned only "unreasonable" restraints, and the followers of Justice John M. Harlan, who advocated a strict prohibition on all combinations. President Roosevelt, who revitalized the Sherman Act with successful suits against several railroad cartels and the meat packers, advocated strict federal regulation through a commission similar to the Interstate Commerce Commission. Leading members of Congress offered their own panaceas, some stressing further criminal sanctions, others backing a regulatory approach.

As the nation's chief law enforcement official and a former corporate attorney, Wickersham attempted initially to reconcile all these competing policy demands. He continued antitrust prosecutions against Standard Oil and American Tobacco while also advocating federal incorporation of big business and creation of a strong regulatory commission. He even told Congress that the federal agency should have the authority to fix prices, a proposal similar to that advanced by some corporate leaders and by Roosevelt himself when he challenged Taft on the Progressive party ticket in 1912.

Once the Supreme Court adopted White's interpretation of the Sherman Act in the Standard Oil and American Tobacco decisions of 1911, however, Wickersham jettisoned his flirtation with federal incorporation and regulation in favor of aggressive antitrust prosecution through the federal courts. To the astonishment and horror of Wickersham's former associates on Wall Street, he and Taft brought almost twice as many Sherman Act prosecutions in four years, a total of eighty-nine, as Roosevelt had filed in eight, including indictments against U.S. Steel, International Harvester, Alcoa Aluminum, and Burroughs Adding Machine. Frank Vanderlip, a prominent Wall Street banker, complained that Wickersham "has out-radicaled the radicals" and called him "the most feared member of the Administration."

Wickersham's unprecedented use of the Sherman Act alienated important sectors of big business and probably contributed to Taft's defeat in 1912. It also hastened the efforts of both business and government leaders to inject greater certainty and consistency into the rules of economic competition. The result was passage of the Clayton Act and the Federal Trade Commission Act early in the Woodrow Wilson administration. These statutes further refined the scope of illegal methods of competition and created a new federal agency to help police the marketplace.

Returning to New York after Taft's defeat, Wickersham resumed his legal practice and plunged back into state politics, serving in the convention called to revise the Empire State's constitution and later on a commission created by Governor Alfred E. Smith to restructure the state government.

The outbreak of war in Europe, U.S. intervention against Germany in 1917, and the fierce debate about the nation's future role in world affairs also brought Wickersham back into the arena of national politics. He aligned himself with the internationalist wing of the Republican party, which had supported the Allied cause before 1917 and which endorsed U.S. membership in an international security organization after the armistice. Joining with like-minded Republicans Taft, Root, and Charles Evans Hughes, Wickersham backed the nation's participation in the League of Nations with minor reservations, a position rejected by both Wilson and Republican isolationists, whose inflexibility doomed Senate ratification of the Versailles treaty and the league.

Wickersham continued to advocate a strong internationalist position for the United States during the next decade, a policy that often placed him at odds with the Republican party's leadership. He urged American membership in the World Court, for example, served on the League of Nation's committee to codify international law, criticized German reparations, and urged the United States to cancel war debts owed by its wartime allies.

Wickersham made his final contribution to public affairs between 1929 and 1931 as chair of the National Commission on Law Observance and Enforcement, appointed by President Herbert Hoover to investigate and make recommendations concerning the federal system of criminal justice. Soon called the Wickersham Commission, it issued more than a dozen detailed reports on every aspect of federal law enforcement but generated severe criticism because of its muddled discussion of the Eighteenth Amendment and the Volstead Act. On the one hand, Wickersham and his experts criticized enforcement of Prohibition as both a waste of federal resources and ultimately futile; at the same time, they urged its retention. Four years after the commission finished its work, Wickersham died in New York City.

If the American legal profession and the Republican party can be said to have had an official establishment in the years from President McKinley to the Great Depression, Wickersham can be said to have sat on its board of directors. In those years he made notable contributions to American law and politics in at least four areas: commercial law, enforcement of the Sherman Antitrust Act, international law, and criminal justice.

• Wickersham's extensive public and private papers are open to researchers in the Library of Congress. In addition to the massive fourteen volumes that constitute the *Report of the National Commission on Law Observance and Enforcement* (1929–1931), students of his life can read his *Changing Order* (1914) and *Some Legal Phases of Corporate Financing, Reorganization and Regulation* (1917). Important aspects of Wickersham's career are discussed in Deborah S. Gardner, *Cadwalader, Wickersham & Taft: A Bicentennial History* (1994); Henry F. Pringle, *The Life and Times of William Howard Taft* (2 vols., 1939); George E. Mowry, *The Era of Theodore Roosevelt and the Birth of Modern America* (1958); and Martin J. Sklar, *The Corporate Reconstruction of American Capitalism, 1890–1916* (1988).

MICHAEL E. PARRISH

WICKES, Lambert (c. 1742–c. 1 Oct. 1777), revolutionary naval hero, was born at "Wickliffe," on Eastern Neck Island, Kent County, Maryland, the son of Samuel Wickes, a colonial planter, and his first wife, whose name is not known. The details of Lambert Wickes's early life are unclear; what is certain is that he was trained for the sea. By 1770 Wickes was captain of the ship *Chester*, owned by Thomas Willing and Robert Morris, carrying cargo between the Chesapeake Bay and Tenerife. The *Chester* had been formerly under the command of Wickes's older brother, Samuel, a captain in the Caribbean trade from at least 1764. Presumably Wickes received at least part of his early seagoing experience aboard his brother's ships.

By 1774 Wickes was skipper of the ship *Neptune*, then in London ready to sail for the Chesapeake, when he discovered that a shipment of tea had been placed aboard his vessel in defiance of the colonies' nonimportation agreement. Wickes ordered the casks removed and sailed for home. The tea ended up on the *Peggy Stewart*, also bound for Maryland; both the tea and the ship were burned at the behest of a patriot mob in Annapolis. The following year, Wickes became captain and part owner, with Chestertown merchant James Ringgold, of the 300-ton ship *Ceres*.

In March 1776 Wickes was given command of the *Reprisal*, a ship with eighteen six-pound guns, then being outfitted as a warship by the marine committee of the Continental Congress. In just over a month, Wickes supervised the conversion at Philadelphia, gathered his 130-man crew, and was ready to join Captain John Barry on his expedition against British warships patrolling the colonial coast. A secondary mission was capture of British merchant vessels as prizes.

Wickes's first serious contact with the enemy occurred in late June 1776, when he was at Cape May in the company of three other continental vessels waiting to go to sea. On 28 June they were notified that the American brig *Nancy* was heading for the cape, followed by some thirty-two British men-of-war. At the urging of his younger brother Richard, third lieutenant of the *Reprisal*, Wickes gave him command of the boat sent out from the *Reprisal* to assist the brig. Crews from the American vessels managed to run the *Nancy* aground and off-load much of its valuable cargo of powder and arms under devastating fire from British barges. The Americans set a charge with the last of the powder aboard the *Nancy* and retreated. When the British boarded the brig, the powder blew, killing a number of men and destroying one of the British boats. The rest broke off the engagement. Lambert Wickes wrote his brother Samuel describing the events, saying, "The Loss on our Side was the Life of our dear Brother who was shott through the Arm and Body by a Cannon shott 4 or 5 Minutes before the Action ended. . . . we have this Consolation that he fought like a brave Man & was fore most in every Transaction of that Day."

Immediately after the burial of his brother, Wickes left for the French island of Martinico (later Martinique), with an American agent to the French aboard. The *Reprisal* approached the harbor at St. Pierre to find the British sloop of war *Shark*, with sixteen nine-pound guns, waiting. The engagement that followed, the first of the Revolution in foreign waters, ended when the French shore batteries fired against the already damaged *Shark*, forcing it to bear off. The incident began Wickes's involvement in the diplomatic tensions between the British and the French, tensions he would exacerbate over the next fifteen months.

Wickes returned to Philadelphia in September 1776 and received orders from the marine committee to outfit the *Reprisal* for a trip to Europe. He left on 27 October with Benjamin Franklin, whose mission was to negotiate a formal alliance with France against Britain. Leaving Franklin in France, the *Reprisal* set out into the English Channel, where the ship captured four merchantmen and the king's packet *Swallow*. Having disposed of the five ships in France, Wickes returned to L'Orient, on the French coast, for repairs, to find that the *Reprisal* was the subject of a furious exchange of letters in which the British ambassador David Murray, Lord Stormont, accused the French of harboring American pirates in disregard of the Treaty of Utrecht.

In May 1777 Wickes sailed from France with the brig *Lexington* and cutter *Dolphin* for an extended cruise into British waters. Circumnavigating Ireland, the squadron took eighteen prizes in eight days, running back to France only after they encountered the British man-of-war *Burford* with seventy-four guns. From the American standpoint, the voyage had been a grand success. The American agent at Nantes wrote Congress, "The little american Squadron under Commodore Wickes have made very considerable havoc on the Enemys Vessells in the Irish Channel, this has created an universal Terror in all the Seaports throughout Ireland and on that side of England and Scotland, . . . and [has] taught them to respect our naval Force."

Again Lord Stormont protested any French involvement with the American ships. Finally, with the prospect of being detained by a French government still unwilling to commit to war with Britain, Wickes requested leave to go home. The *Reprisal* sailed from St. Malo alone on 14 September 1777 to cross the Atlantic by the northern route. On about 1 October 1777, off Newfoundland, a storm swept over the ship, sinking it. Only the cook was rescued; the rest of the crew, including the captain, were lost.

It is not known if Wickes ever married or had children. In his short life, Wickes captured twenty-eight prize ships, enraged the British, and contributed his efforts to bringing the French into the war on the side of the former colonies.

• The standard source for the life of Wickes is William Bell Clark, *Lambert Wickes, Sea Raider and Diplomat* (1932), but the pamphlet by Norman H. Plummer, *Lambert Wickes, Pi-*

rate or Patriot (1991), adds more recent scholarship. Communications to and from Wickes may be found in William Bell Clark and William James Morgan, eds., *Naval Documents of the American Revolution*, vols. 4–9 (1969–1986), esp. vol. 5, which contains Wickes's letter of 2 July 1776 quoted above, and vol. 9, which includes the letter from Jonathan Williams, Jr., to the Committee for Foreign Affairs, 10 Aug. 1777, also quoted above. Details of the diplomatic furor surrounding Wickes's stay in France are summarized in Jonathan R. Dull, *The French Navy and American Independence* (1975). For a general picture of Wickes and his fellow captains in the service of the country, see Nathan Miller, "Chesapeake Bay Ships and Seamen in the Continental Navy," in *Chesapeake Bay in the American Revolution*, ed. Ernest McNeill Elder (1981).

JANE WILSON MCWILLIAMS

WICKLIFFE, Charles Anderson (8 June 1788–31 Oct. 1869), congressman, governor of Kentucky, and postmaster general of the United States, was born near Springfield, Washington County, Kentucky, the son of Charles Wickliffe and Lydia Hardin, farmers. Although he was from a large family of average means, Wickliffe had the opportunity of some formal education in public and private schools as well as from tutors. James Blythe, president of Transylvania University, offered him private instruction, and Wickliffe read law under the supervision of his cousin, Martin D. Hardin. In 1809 he was admitted to the bar and began a practice in Bardstown. There he acquired a solid legal reputation, great wealth, and a basis for a political career. With Felix Grundy, Ben Hardin, John Rowan, and others, Wickliffe became known as one of the "Bardstown Pleiades."

Wickliffe's support for the War of 1812 coincided with his election to the Kentucky House of Representatives in 1812 and 1813 from Nelson County. Enlisting as a private in a company organized by his brother, Martin H. Wickliffe, he soon became an aide to General Samuel Caldwell and was present at the battle of the Thames, where he claimed he helped identify Tecumseh's body.

Wickliffe married Margaret Cripps in 1813; they had eight children. By the late 1810s the Wickliffes were one of the leading families in Kentucky. Wickliffe's brother Robert (1775–1859) was reputedly the wealthiest man in the state. Charles acquired the nickname "the Duke" because of his wealth, standing, and haughty attitude. Wickliffe served as commonwealth attorney for Nelson County in 1816 and was elected to the legislature in 1820 and 1821. Sent to Congress in 1823, Wickliffe served until 1833. In Kentucky's fragmented politics, Wickliffe was of the Old Court faction opposed to relief bills and paper currency that victims of the panic of 1819 desired. In national politics Wickliffe promoted Andrew Jackson's political ascendancy. In the disputed election of 1824, Wickliffe willingly obeyed the will of the Kentucky legislature and defied Henry Clay by voting for Jackson. When the Jacksonians attained a majority, they rewarded Wickliffe with the chair of the Committee on Public Lands. In his last elections his margin of victory dwindled significantly. In 1831 he was unsuccessful in a bid for the U.S. Senate. At the same time that he was fighting off the Whig party at home, Wickliffe was becoming disenchanted with Jackson, especially with "Old Hickory's" veto of the rechartering of the Bank of the United States and his break with John C. Calhoun. Uncertain of success, Wickliffe declined reelection in 1833 and followed Calhoun into the ranks of Jackson's opposition.

To establish his new Whig credentials, Wickliffe returned to the Kentucky lower house from 1833 to 1835, serving as Speaker in 1834 and 1835. In 1836 he received the Whig nomination for lieutenant governor. Although victorious, Wickliffe ran far behind his party's gubernatorial nominee, which suggests persistent Whig distrust of Wickliffe. In September 1839 he became governor upon James Clark's (1779–1839) sudden death. In his short time as governor, Wickliffe urged an increase in taxes to pay off the state's debts, to fund internal improvements, and to advance education in the state. He had modest success in paying the interest on the state bonds but had inadequate funds to achieve his far-sighted goals. As an aspiring party rival to Clay, Wickliffe met frustration. The Whig gubernatorial nomination fell to Clay's ally, Robert P. Letcher. An open U.S. Senate seat also eluded him, and Wickliffe could not pry president-elect William Henry Harrison away from Clay in order to secure a cabinet position for himself.

John Tyler's (1790–1862) accession to the presidency, however, reinvigorated Wickliffe's career and foretold another partisan transition. Wickliffe joined Tyler's administration as postmaster general in October 1841 and would be the only cabinet appointee to remain until the end of Tyler's term. Wickliffe maintained a scrupulously honest department, gently encouraged postal reform and efficiency, and helped reduce postal rates. Many politicians recognized the similarity of interests among Tyler, Calhoun, and Wickliffe—all expansionists and all concerned with protecting southern slaveholders—and were not surprised by Wickliffe's return to the Democratic party in the early 1840s. Wickliffe and his family were also close personal friends of Tyler and Julia Gardiner Tyler, his new bride. In 1843 Wickliffe survived a personally motivated assassination attempt by a mentally disturbed individual.

Wickliffe shared Tyler's desire to annex Texas, and in the election of 1844, according to one Tennessee Democrat, "Wickliffe went the *whole hog*" for James K. Polk. Immediately after the inauguration, Polk sent Wickliffe along with Congressman Archibald Yell and Commodore Robert F. Stockton to the Texas Republic. Each agent urged Texans to accept annexation immediately, and in return the United States would recognize the Rio Grande not the Nueces River as the border with Mexico. They whipped up popular support for annexation, which overwhelmed the plans of Texas president Anson Jones and Sam Houston, who were more reluctant and wary. By promising the Rio Grande as a southern boundary this mission probably contributed to the outbreak of the Mexican War.

Wickliffe returned to Kentucky in 1845 and in 1849 was elected to the Kentucky Constitutional Convention. He was the most frequent speaker, defending the institution of slavery and helping to provide protection and funding for the public schools. Wickliffe was appointed to a commission in 1850 to codify and revise the statutes of Kentucky. Throughout the 1850s he continued his lucrative law practice in Kentucky.

There was no doubt in Wickliffe's mind that the Union had to be preserved. He supported the Crittenden Compromise and attended the Washington Peace Conference in February 1861. When public addresses failed to halt disunionist tendencies in his own state, Wickliffe participated in the secret process of supplying county militia with arms from the federal government. In June 1861 Wickliffe, a slaveholder and the Union candidate, won election to the Thirty-seventh Congress. He became increasingly upset with the Republicans and Abraham Lincoln's administration. He decried the southern "sectional politicians" and the abolitionists, who he felt were responsible for the conflict. He denounced as unconstitutional the Emancipation Proclamation, martial law, and the creation of black regiments. In the summer of 1863 Wickliffe campaigned for governor as a "peace Democrat." The Union army's intimidation of voters and candidates sympathetic to Wickliffe contributed to a lopsided loss. The military was not above simply striking names, including Wickliffe's, from the pollbooks. He was a vocal opponent of the war at the Democratic National Convention in Chicago in 1864.

Lame and nearly blind, Wickliffe practiced law until a few months before his death at his daughter's home near Ilchester, Maryland.

Wickliffe was a maverick in the antebellum political culture. His financial independence perhaps contributed to his independent political style. Opponents found him to be an ambitious political "trimmer," or as the editor of the *Louisville Courier* called him, "the Kentucky Talleyrand" and "pompous Charley." No doubt driven by personal ambition, Wickliffe behaved responsibly once in office. Pursuit of the greater good of society (excluding slaves) characterized his policies as governor, postmaster general, delegate to the state constitutional convention, and leader on the eve of secession.

• Wickliffe's gubernatorial papers are in the Kentucky Department for Libraries and Archives, and a small collection of papers is at the Filson Club, Louisville, Ky. Charles A. Wickliffe, "Tecumseh and the Battle of the Thames," *Register of the Kentucky State Historical Society* 60 (1962): 45–49, is a reprint of his Nov. 1859 letter to the *Bardstown Gazette*. No full-length biography of Wickliffe has been published, but of particular importance are Lucius P. Little, *Ben Hardin: His Times and Contemporaries* (1887); H. Levin, ed., *The Lawyers and Lawmakers of Kentucky* (1897); Jennie C. Morton, "Governor Charles A. Wickliffe," *Register of the Kentucky State Historical Society* 2 (1904): 17–21; Richard H. Collins and Lewis Collins, *History of Kentucky* (1882); G. Glenn Clift, *Governors of Kentucky, 1792–1942* (1942); and Lowell H. Harrison, ed., *Kentucky's Governors, 1792–1985* (1985).

For his tenure as postmaster general see Peter T. Rohrbach and Lowell S. Newman, *American Issue: The U.S. Postage Stamp, 1842–1869* (1984), and Norma Lois Peterson, *The Presidencies of William Henry Harrison and John Tyler* (1989). On his work for Polk in Texas see Charles Grier Sellers, *James K. Polk, Continentalist, 1843–1846* (1966).

M. PHILIP LUCAS

WIDDEMER, Margaret (30 Sept. 1884–14 July 1978), writer, was born in Doylestown, Pennsylvania, the daughter of Howard Taylor Widdemer, an Episcopalian minister, and Alice de Witt. Widdemer began composing poetry as a child by dictating lines to a "frustrated-author aunt," who would then write them down for her. The aunt taught her how to write, thus beginning Widdemer's education. Widdemer's grandmother, who had a broad knowledge of books and music, was her mentor; in *Golden Friends I Had: Unrevised Memoirs of Margaret Widdemer* (1964), Widdemer notes that she had "a dynamic clergy-man father who disapproved of public school for little girls, and had no money for private ones; and a possessive if devoted grandmother who had nothing to occupy a good mind, so pounced on me as a resident pupil whenever she could get me away from my mother."

Widdemer's only formal schooling—a year's course at the Drexel Institute Library School—led to a job at a rare-book store in Philadelphia, where she read English essayists and poets when she was not assisting such customers as Arnold Bennett and "one of the Stetson Hat Stetsons," whose hobbies included "planting" Young Men's Christian Associations all over the United States and collecting French pornography. She married Robert H. Schauffler in 1919, but the marriage quickly ended in divorce.

Success came early to Widdemer. Her first novel, *The Rose Garden Husband* (1915), was a bestseller, and during her twenties she published nine novels. Her poetry earned her even greater recognition: in 1917 she published her first volume of poetry, *The Factories and Other Poems*, and in that same year she received the Trimmed Lamp Prize for best lyric of the year. In 1919 her *The Old Road to Paradise* (1918) shared the American Poetry Society Prize with Carl Sandburg's *Cornhuskers*. In 1922 her book of parodies, *Tree with a Bird in It*, received the *Saturday Review of Literature* Award for Best Satire, and in that same year she received the Lyric West Prize for her poem "Hill Sunset," which contrasts the still moment when "The changing sunset burns to violet, / While the black boughs arch out across, clear cut and beautiful" with the poet's search for "crippled dreams." "Fiddler's Green," which describes the place "where the souls did be going that was too bad for Paradise and too charming for Hell," was awarded the English Poetry Society Prize for Best Ballad in 1926.

In addition to her novels and volumes of poetry, Widdemer also wrote children's books, including the "Winona" series (1915–1923), *Binkie and the Bell Dolls* (1923), *Prince in Buckskin* (1952), and *The Great Pine's Son* (1954). She also wrote poetry for children—"Lullaby" received the *Child Life* award for best poem of the year in 1937—and contributed numerous short stories, serials, articles, and poems to American and British periodicals. The range of periodicals in which she published—*Harper's*, *Ladies Home Journal*, *Saturday Review of Literature*, *Good Housekeeping*, *Atlantic*, *McCall's*, and *Yale Review*—shows Widdemer's versatility. The series of broadcasts she did on radio for the National Broadcasting Company, "Do You Want to Write?" was published in book form as *Basic Principles of Fiction Writing* (1953).

The Dark Cavalier: The Collected Poems of Margaret Widdemer (1958) reveals Widdemer's wide-ranging interests in both the subject matter and form of poetry: she employs a variety of traditional narrative and lyric forms to explore folklore, religion, mythology, character, and the natural world. In 1960 she received the Lyric Award for distinguished services to poetry.

Widdemer's avocational interests included folksinging and modeling clothes, but she devoted her life to writing and to organizations that promoted writing and supported writers. She was vice president of the Poetry Society of America, an executive board member of Pen and Brush, and a member of the Authors' Guild, the Browning Society, the Query Club, and the International Association of Poets, Playwrights, Editors, Essayists and Novelists. During the academic year 1943–1944 she was a lecturer on writing fiction at New York University, and she continued to lecture on fiction and poetry throughout the United States and at various writers' conferences, most notably at Bread Loaf. During World War II Widdemer served as chair of the National Unity Committee of the Writers' War Board, and from 1950 to 1965 she was assistant director for the Chautauqua Writers' Conference.

Widdemer's 1964 memoir recounts her participation in the literary circles of Greenwich Village in the 1910s and 1920s, "a warm, gay, angrily excited moment of change and discovery," and describes such writers as Elinor Wylie, Edwin Arlington Robinson, Edna St. Vincent Millay, Ezra Pound, Thornton Wilder, Sinclair Lewis, F. Scott and Zelda Fitzgerald, and Theodore Dreiser. The chapter on Dreiser exemplifies Widdemer's combination of insight and wit. Dreiser, she writes, "slowly and with pains, with detailed literalism, related what he saw . . . of lives and characters, filtered of course as all writing must be through his own personality." Widdemer first met Dreiser at a party she hosted, and she described him as "big and heavy, and slouched where he sat as only rangy men should. His face was big, too; heavy-featured; brown in a dusty sort of way. . . . I offered him a drink and he took it at one swallow. And, as if I had dropped a penny in the slot of his being, he fixed his eyes on me and said slowly in a deep voice 'What do you think of lust?'" Widdemer's answer: "'Why—why I am sure it is all right!'"

Widdemer published her last novel, *Red Castle Women*, in 1968, at the age of eighty-four; she died in Gloversville, New York, her home during the final years of her life. In Widdemer's obituary for the *New York Times*, C. Gerald Fraser describes her as "an unflinchingly independent woman who took pride in the fact that she had been educated at home, that she worked hard at her writing and that she had been writing practically all of her life."

• Widdemer's papers are in the Department of Special Collections, Syracuse University Library. A bibliography of Widdemer's writings is in *Contemporary Authors*, New Revision ser., vol. 4 (1989). An obituary is in the *New York Times*, 15 July 1978.

JUDITH E. FUNSTON

WIDDICOMB, John (4 Aug. 1845–5 Feb. 1910), industrialist, was born in Syracuse, New York, the son of George Widdicomb, an English immigrant and skilled woodworker (mother's name unknown). Little is known about John Widdicomb's youth; at age seven, his father apprenticed him into the cabinetmaking craft while living in Elbridge, New York. It is noteworthy that Widdicomb's experience began in a water-powered factory. At this stage of industrial history, the manufacturing process still required the use of highly skilled artisans. During his life many industries would introduce machines that would hasten the demise of skilled work. Widdicomb was among those who pioneered the use of these new machine-operated manufacturing techniques that both changed the structure of the workplace and mass-produced consumer durables.

The Widdicomb family moved westward across upstate New York, following established migratory patterns into Michigan, eventually settling in the city of Grand Rapids in 1856–1857. The family, now composed of four sons, found work in the door, sash, and millwork plant of Charles C. Comstock, one of the few firms to weather the panic of 1857. Although the national effects of the recession were short-lived, the lumber and furniture interests in Grand Rapids remained depressed until the start of 1860.

With the end of the recession, Comstock underwrote Widdicomb's father and brothers in a small, independent cabinetmaking venture. The firm failed, and without binding obligations to the family business, Widdicomb entered the Union army.

Widdicomb returned to Grand Rapids in 1865 after two years of military service and formed a partnership with his brothers to produce a variety of home furnishings. At the same time he lost a large sum of money in lumber speculation unrelated to the family business. Struggling to pay back his loans, Widdicomb developed a new product that netted him $20,000 more than he owed. He produced steel bedsprings that rapidly replaced the older rope mattress supports, and the great profit derived from his new product allowed him to expand the family business in new directions.

Widdicomb built a six-story brick factory in 1869, the largest plant in the city at that time. He then made a public offering of shares in the company in 1873 with a capital stock of $150,000. Over the next twenty years the firm prospered by meeting the needs of a growing urban and rural home-furnishings market. Going beyond a single-item manufacture of spindle beds, Widdicomb's company produced a more complete line of bedroom furnishings that were noted as "not the most costly furniture but the best in design, workmanship, finish and material that factory could provide" for the average consumer.

During the 1870s Widdicomb was critical in assuring that furniture-making became the dominant industry in Grand Rapids. Instrumental in founding the Board of Trade, Widdicomb became part of a citywide consortium with other manufacturers to control shipping and labor costs. He was innovative in distributing his products. He opened up retail and warehouse facilities in the larger cities and used photograph catalogs and traveling salesmen to spread his name among an increasingly comfort-conscious market. Widdicomb became prosperous in the period after the panic of 1873–1878. He noted in 1887 that business was so good "we would pay a man a premium who would tell us how to avoid a portion of the orders which are coming in upon us with a rush, and as for collections, we have more money than we know what to do with."

In dealing with employees, Widdicomb was paternalistic, always on the shop floor inspecting the work and occasionally advancing salary for a family emergency. Worker loyalty was very important to him and was reciprocated to some degree. The story circulated that while attending a religious revival one employee responded to the question "Do you want to work for Jesus?" with the laconic "I verk mit John Widdicomb!"

This attention to detail, worker loyalty, and intimate knowledge of production became valuable assets after the panic of 1893. Committed to plant expansion when the panic hit, his loans were called in earlier than expected. Unable to pay the debt, Widdicomb declared bankruptcy and ceded control of the company to receivers; these receivers knew little or nothing about the furniture industry, and conflict between them and Widdicomb increased to the point that he resigned in 1896. Shortly thereafter the firm ceased operations.

In 1897, with the economy improved, Widdicomb borrowed enough money to buy an older factory on the city's less desirable west side, moving himself and family to an adjacent house. The name of his wife, the date of their marriage, and the total number of their children (they had at least one son) are unknown. His willingness to work alongside a core of loyal employees and an improving national market brought success to Widdicomb again. In the years after 1898 he expanded production several times. After plant expansion he grossed more than $1 million by agreeing to manufacture tops and cabinets for the Singer Sewing Machine Company. Widdicomb found a growing market among the buyers of the sewing machines: middle-class women, tailors, seamstresses, and sweatshop owners. By 1906 Widdicomb employed almost 700 people in several plants throughout the city and in 1909 announced plans for even greater factory expansion with a new building to cost more than $750,000.

Widdicomb's obsession with building and maintaining his business left little time for any outside pursuits, either political or philanthropic. While giving money to several local hospitals, supporting the Second Street Methodist Church, and serving a short stint on the city's Board of Estimates to prepare annual municipal budgets, he shunned social or fraternal organizations, saying that he "did not have time to spare for such things."

Widdicomb died of a heart attack while at work. The business passed to his son, Harry, who lost control and ownership by the 1930s, although the Widdicomb name still exists today as a Grand Rapids company doing very expensive reproductions.

• Although the Grand Rapids Public Library has accessioned the John Widdicomb Papers, they generally have remained unused by scholars. Neither a systematic study of John Widdicomb's life and work nor the important influence his brothers played in helping one another develop the family businesses has yet been published. Contemporary impressions and facts about Widdicomb come from the professional business newspaper the *Michigan Tradesman*, 3 Aug. 1887, 29 May 1901, 13 Nov. 1907, and 9 Feb. 1910. Brief mentions of Widdicomb are in Z. Z. Lydens, *The Story of Grand Rapids* (1966), and Gordon Olson, *A Grand Rapids Sampler* (1992). Obituaries are in Grand Rapids newspapers, the *Evening Press*, 5 Feb. 1910, and the *Herald*, 6 Feb. 1910.

JEFF KLEIMAN

WIDENER, George Dunton, Jr. (11 Mar. 1889–8 Dec. 1971), horseman and philanthropist, was born in Philadelphia, Pennsylvania, the son of George Dunton Widener, a financier, and Eleanore Elkins. An heir to the family fortune amassed by his grandfather, Widener received most of his education privately from tutors and at the Delancy School in Philadelphia. He did not attend college. He married the former Mrs. Earl (Jessie Sloan) Dodge in March 1917; they had no children.

Shortly after his father and brother went down with the *Titanic* in 1912, Widener entered horse racing and breeding, largely through the influence of his uncle, Joseph Widener, one of the leading horsemen of his era. The first victory of a Widener thoroughbred came in 1916 when Columbine won the Walden Stakes at Pimlico. Over the course of his career, horses owned and bred by Widener and his wife won 1,243 races and more than $9 million in purses; the Wideners bred others that won 4,524 races and $16 million. Significant winners included High Fleet in the 1936 Coaching Club of American Oaks and five Futurities with St. James (1923), Jamestown (1930), Battlefield (1950), Jester (1957), and Bold Hour (1966). His most notable horse, Jaipur, won the Belmont Stakes in 1962. But even more gratifying than this long-sought victory was Ring Twice's triumph in the 1967 Widener Handicap, for it was the first time a family member owned a horse that won the race named for his uncle. Widener never entered his horses in the Kentucky Derby because he believed the 1¼-mile race was too strenuous for three year olds so early in the season. He condemned the use of Butazolidin and other painkilling drugs on horses and opposed night racing and off-track betting.

In the early 1920s Widener and Joseph Widener challenged the federal income tax code and won a landmark decision for horse breeders and trainers. The Wideners had deducted losses incurred in the operation of their stables since 1919. When the Bureau of Internal Revenue attempted to collect $403,000 in back taxes for the period from 1919 through 1922, the Wideners filed an appeal, arguing that their stables were a business, not a hobby. In 1927, after years of legal proceedings, the U.S. Board of Tax Appeals ruled in their favor, allowing Widener to reduce his tax liability for 1919 and his uncle to reduce his for the entire four years. This favorable ruling also enabled them to deduct additional operating expenses, which more than doubled the amount of their initial deduction. Two years later, a federal appeals court upheld the decision.

Widener held many executive and administrative posts in organizations devoted to horse racing, breeding, and the humane treatment of horses. After his election to the Jockey Club in 1916, he served as a steward, vice chair, chair for fourteen years, and then honorary chair. He also held executive positions in the Westchester Racing Association (the owner and operators of Belmont Park), the Greater New York Racing Association, the National Museum of Racing, the Horseman's Benevolent and Protective Association Charitable Fund, the American Thoroughbred Breeders Association, the Thoroughbred Club of America, and the Grayson Foundation of Lexington, Kentucky, which funded research on equine diseases. An innovative and influential administrator, Widener adopted policies that streamlined the registration of racing silks, initiated an annual conference at Saratoga to discuss issues and problems in the racing and breeding industry, classified blood typing of thoroughbred horses, established a school for racing officials, and developed advances in horse identification methods.

Widener was also highly active in civic, academic, and benevolent organizations, serving as a trustee of museums, art centers, hospitals, universities, and scientific institutions in Philadelphia, New York City, and Washington, D.C. His philanthropy extended beyond these organizations to churches, divinity schools, libraries, and community-based charities. Although he devoted most of his time and effort to racing, Widener also held directorships at the Land Title Bank and Trust, Philadelphia Traction Company, and the Electric Storage Battery Company.

Widener won recognition as Man of the Year from the Horseman's Benevolent and Protective Association in 1954, and he received the Guest of Honor Award from the Turf and Field Club in 1961. The following year he was honored for his contributions and services to thoroughbred racing by the Jockey Agents Benevolent Association, and in 1943, 1948, and 1956 he was honored by the New York Turf Writers Association as the individual who had done the most for racing. His highest honor was the Exemplar of Racing Award, bestowed on him in 1971 as its first honoree by the National Museum of Racing, Saratoga Springs, New York.

Commenting on his breeding and racing career, Widener observed, "I did not seek it, but once that was the fact, it seemed to be a useful and creditable way of life." He found his niche as a horseman and devoted his life to the turf and its improvement. He died at his estate, "Erdenheim Farm," in Chestnut Hill, Pennsylvania.

• Collected Widener papers are at the National Museum of Racing, Saratoga Springs, N.Y., which has a clippings file on his career. Coverage of his income tax case is in the *New York Times*, 13 Oct. 1927. His place in thoroughbred racing and breeding is discussed in Bernard Livingston, *Their Turf: America's Horsey Set and Its Princely Dynasties* (1973), pp. 110–16. Obituaries appear in the *Thoroughbred Record*, 18 Dec. 1971; the *Blood-Horse*, 20 Dec. 1971; and the *New York Times*, 9 Dec. 1971.

J. THOMAS JABLE

WIDENER, Harry Elkins (3 Jan. 1885–15 Apr. 1912), book collector, was born in Philadelphia, Pennsylvania, the son of George Widener, a financier, and Eleanor Elkins. Harry Widener had collecting in his blood; he once remarked of his family, "We are all collectors. My grandfather collects paintings, my mother collects silver and porcelain, Uncle Joe collects everything, and I collect books." He began collecting in 1905 while a student at Harvard. His earliest interest was in books illustrated by the nineteenth-century English artist George Cruikshank, whose work he encountered when researching costumes for Hasty Pudding Club productions at Harvard. Widener also began collecting first editions of the writers whose books he had read and liked, and one of his earliest collecting enthusiasms was for Robert Louis Stevenson.

Widener bought from many booksellers, particularly Luther Livingston and Bernard Quaritch, but he was most influenced by Abraham Simon Wolf Rosenbach. Rosenbach, who specialized in English literature, encouraged Widener to broaden his collection to encompass all the great books of English literature. In September 1906, as he began his final year at Harvard, Widener began purchasing Charles Dickens first editions and made his first non–nineteenth-century purchases, buying the folio works of Ben Jonson and Beaumont and Fletcher. In March 1907 he bought (with financial backing from his mother) the First Folio of Shakespeare, the centerpiece of any collection of English literature, paying the highest price a folio had ever brought.

Widener graduated from Harvard in 1907 and entered business with his grandfather and father, helping to manage the family's numerous investments. With an income of his own, he also began collecting more heavily. By 1910 he felt his collection sufficiently far advanced to publish (assisted by A. S. W. Rosenbach) a limited edition catalog.

In 1912 Widener went with his mother and father to Europe. While in London, he purchased a number of books, including the extremely rare 1598 edition of Bacon's *Essays*, which he took with him. The family embarked for Philadelphia on the ill-fated *Titanic*. Just before the ship sank, he said to his mother, "Mother, I have placed the volume in my pocket: little 'Bacon' goes with me" (Stevenson catalog [1913], intro.). Both Harry and George Widener were lost; Eleanor Elkins Widener survived.

In his will, Harry Widener left his collection to his mother, with the request that it be given to Harvard when a suitable accommodation for it could be found. The Harvard College Library collection had outgrown its building, and the college was actively seeking a donor for a new library. Eleanor Elkins Widener decided that not only would she finance the construction of a new building, she would make her son's collection what it would have become had he lived. In 1915 the Harry Elkins Widener Memorial Library opened, with Harry Widener's collection, enriched by his mother's additional acquisitions, installed in a separate memorial room.

Fellow collector A. Edward Newton wrote in *The Amenities of Book Collecting* that Harry Widener once told him, "I don't want to be remembered merely as a collector of a few books, however fine they may be. I want to be remembered in connection with a great library" (p. 352). The gift of his collection and the library built in his name ensured that he will be remembered; they form what is perhaps the greatest benefaction in Harvard's history and an invaluable resource for American scholarship.

• No major group of papers survives, although some letters are in the Widener collection at Harvard and in the archive of the Rosenbach Company at the Rosenbach Museum & Library in Philadelphia. A. S. W. Rosenbach compiled a five-volume catalog of the Widener collection, with a memoir; the individual catalogs are *A Catalogue of the Books and Manuscripts of Harry Elkins Widener* (2 vols., 1918), *A Catalogue of the Books and Manuscripts of Robert Louis Stevenson in the Library of the Late Harry Elkins Widener* (1913), *A Catalogue of the Writings of Charles Dickens in the Library of Harry Elkins Widener* (1918), and *A Catalogue of the Works Illustrated by George Cruikshank and Isaac and Robert Cruikshank in the Library of Harry Elkins Widener* (1918). A detailed account of Widener's last purchases, centering on the volume of Bacon's *Essays* lost on the *Titanic*, is found in Arthur Freeman, "Harry Widener's Last Book," *Book Collector* 26 (Summer 1977): 173–85.

LESLIE A. MORRIS

WIDENER, Peter Arrell Brown (13 Nov. 1834–6 Nov. 1915), financier and philanthropist, was born in Philadelphia, Pennsylvania, the son of John Widener, a brickmaker, and Sarah Fulmer. He received his early education at the Coates Street Grammar School, after which he attended Central High School. Dropping out after two years, Widener then took a job in his brother's butcher shop. Hardworking and industrious, he saved enough money to open his own meat-cutting business, which he then expanded into a chain of stores. He soon became involved in the newly formed Republican party, forging in the process an important connection with Simon Cameron, the boss of the state Republican party, who later served as secretary of war. Widener took time in 1858 to marry Hannah Josephine Dunton, with whom he had three sons.

After the outbreak of the Civil War, Widener received an extremely lucrative contract from Cameron—supplying mutton to all Federal troops within a ten-mile radius of Philadelphia—that netted him a $50,000 profit. Widener's rise to prominence in the local Republican party paralleled his business success; following the war he was elected to a series of minor offices, including a stint on the Philadelphia Board of Education from 1867 to 1870. In 1873 he received an appointment to fill the remainder of Joseph F. Mercer's unexpired term as city treasurer, and the next year he was elected to the post outright, serving one term. The position, which carried a high salary, added to Widener's wealth and prominence. His political career stalled in 1877, however, when he failed twice in his quest to be nominated, as mayor of Philadelphia and as state treasurer. After these setbacks Widener turned his attention permanently to the world of commerce, the arena in which he made his greatest mark.

As early as 1875 Widener had become intrigued by the profit potential of urban transit systems. The earliest systems consisted of horse-drawn trolleys that were slow, inefficient, and rarely profitable. Forming a partnership with William L. Elkins the same year, the two men took the lead in organizing the Continental Street Railway Company. They soon joined forces with William Kemble, another entrepreneur who was serving as the secretary of a rival firm, the Union Passenger Railway Company. Although the Union was one of the more successful of the transit firms then in operation, Kemble had labored in vain to convince his partners of the need for an integrated rail system in the city. Frustrated by the inaction of his partners, Kemble (who was also a bank president) joined forces with Widener and Elkins. The three well-connected entrepreneurs set out to take over the Union Company. Parallel lines were constructed and the Continental, by offering better service, soon made inroads into the Union's business. In 1880 they captured control of the Union and followed up on this success by capturing the West Philadelphia Company the next year. Offering free passenger transfers between lines, the combined systems by 1882 carried nearly 33 million passengers annually.

Widener and his partners took another step toward market domination in 1883 with the establishment of the Philadelphia Traction Company. This new firm served not only as a holding company for their other concerns (with the other companies leased to the new firm) but also became the means by which the three men sought to transform the routes into "traction" lines (which used underground steam-powered cables as a means of locomotion). Although an improvement over the horse-drawn trolleys, the new system was enormously expensive to build and was plagued by technical problems. The system, never perfected, was replaced by the cheaper and more efficient electrical power beginning in the early 1890s. The line continued to expand, and by 1895 ridership exceeded 100 million passengers annually. In an effort to complete the consolidation of their holdings, Widener and his partners formed the Union Traction Company in 1895, using the old method of leasing subsidiaries. After the turn of the century, Widener and his group formed the Philadelphia Rapid Transit Company and held a virtual monopoly on the city's traffic. During this period the partners were also heavily involved in establishing traction lines in Chicago, New York, Baltimore, and Pittsburgh. The growing position of dominance that the partnership enjoyed in Philadelphia came with a price, however—increased city involvement in the management of the firm. Hobbled by a fixed-fare system, the firm struggled to keep up repairs and maintenance, and with the added burdens placed on it by the panic of 1907 the company reached a new agreement with the city, and a reorganization ended the reign of Widener and his partners.

Given his wealth and power, Widener naturally became involved in a variety of other enterprises. He took an active role in the formation of the American Tobacco Company, serving on the board of directors for a number of years. He also served as a director of the New Jersey Central, Lehigh Valley, and Philadelphia and Reading railroads and maintained investment interest in a diverse group of firms that included U.S. Steel, Standard Oil, Philadelphia Land Title and Trust, and United Gas Improvement.

Wealth also led Widener, as it did so many of his position, into philanthropy. His activity in this area led to the opening of the Widener Memorial Industrial Training School for Crippled Children in 1906. A widely traveled and literate man, Widener donated to the city his Broad Street residence, which then became the Josephine Widener branch of the Philadelphia Free Library. A voracious art collector, his holdings included a large selection of Chinese porcelains as well as bronzes, tapestries, and a group of paintings that included Raphael's *Cowper Madonna* and Rembrandt's *The Mill*; they were also donated to the city after his death.

Widener was burdened by poor health in the last three years of his life, as well as by the loss of a son and grandson on the HMS *Titanic*. After a short illness he died at "Lynnewood Hall," his home in Elkins Park, Pennsylvania (a Philadelphia suburb).

Peter Arrell Brown Widener rose from humble beginnings to a position of wealth and power through his business activities. While involved in a number of businesses during his lifetime, his greatest legacy was the growth and development of public mass transit systems in the urban centers of the United States.

• No collection of Widener papers appears to have survived. Widener's life and career received attention in Charles W. Cheape, *Moving the Masses* (1980); Sam Bass Warner, *Private City* (1968); and Frederick W. Speirs, *The Street Railway System of Philadelphia* (1897). Obituaries are in the *New York Times* and *Philadelphia Public Ledger*, 7 Nov. 1915.

EDWARD L. LACH, JR.

WIELAND, George Reber (24 Jan. 1865–18 Jan. 1953), paleobotanist and vertebrate paleontologist, was born in Boalsburg, Pennsylvania, the son of Washington Frederick Wieland and Margaret Reber, farmers. Wieland was a student in the preparatory department of Pennsylvania State College (later Pennsylvania State University) in 1882–1883 and 1887–1888. He became a college-level student in 1888 and completed his B.S. in chemistry in 1893. During his college years he developed a lasting interest in the origin and evolution of flowering plants. Prior to his graduation, he taught in country schools and, from 1890 to 1892, in secondary schools in Tennessee. He married Edla Kristina Andersson in Nykoping, Sweden, in 1891; they had two sons. He studied geology at Göttingen, Germany, in 1894. For the next two years he taught in secondary schools in Lincoln, Nebraska, and Chester, Pennsylvania. In 1896 and 1897 he collected fossil reptiles for the vertebrate paleontologist Edward Drinker Cope and studied at the University of Pennsylvania. After Cope's death, Wieland accepted a fellowship at Yale University, working with Cope's bitter rival Othniel C. Marsh. In 1900 he completed his Yale Ph.D. in vertebrate paleontology with a thesis under Marsh on fossil turtles. From 1895 to 1902 he spent his summers engaged in fieldwork in the Black Hills of South Dakota, working with living and fossil plants and vertebrate fossils.

Wieland's first professional appointment was as a lecturer on paleobotany at Yale in 1906. He became a research assistant in 1920, and in 1924 he was appointed a research associate, with the rank of an associate professor. A close friend of Andrew Carnegie, he was among the first research associates appointed to the Carnegie Institution of Washington, D.C., and he received the institution's support for his paleobotanical research and publications from 1903 to 1933. He was also a staff paleontologist of the Geological Survey of Mexico in 1905 and 1906, describing the fossil cycads of Mixteca Alta in the state of Oaxca.

Under the influence of Cope and Marsh, Wieland investigated fossil vertebrates during the early portion of his career. His discovery and description of the world's largest turtle, *Archelon ischyros*, was perhaps the most memorable consequence of this work, although he published twenty-seven technical papers and monographs on vertebrates, including *Osteology of the Protostega* (1906) and *Armored Dinosauria* (1911). Wieland's reputation primarily rests on his work with fossil cycadeoids (ancestors of sago palms) and auricariaceans (ancestors of monkey puzzle trees). His systematic descriptions, based on special techniques he developed for the groups, provided the first comprehensive global account of these "difficult" fossil plants. His determination of the detailed morphology of fossil cycadeoid cones is the basis for understanding their evolutionary significance. In addition, Wieland collected literally tons of specimens, which, although he was unable to study or catalogue them fully, have been a continuing resource for subsequent investigators. Wieland's theory of the polar origin of flowering plants stimulated great interest when advanced but he did not further develop the idea, which subsequently was largely discredited. His ideas on the extinction of the dinosaurs and the relationships between gymnosperms and angiosperms were also significant in their time. Finally, his advancement of thin-section studies of silicified fossil plants constituted a lasting contribution to paleobotanical technique. In this work a specimen is cut, polished, mounted on glass, and ground so thin as to transmit light, permitting detailed examination of the plant's cellular structure. In all, Wieland published 103 articles and books on paleobotany and the evolution of plants. Some of his more important paleobotanical books are *Polar Climate in Time the Major Factor in the Evolution of Plants and Animals* (1903), *La Flora Liasica de la Mixteca Alta* (1914), *American Fossil Cycads* (2 vols., 1906, 1916), *New American Cycadeoids* (1921), *Antiquity of the Angiosperms* (1926), *A New Cycad from the Mariposa Slates* (1929), *Raumeria of the Zwinger of Dresden* (1934), *The Cerro Cuadro Petrified Forest* (1935), *Cycadeoid Types of the Kansas Cretaceous* (1942), *The Carpathian-Black Hills Cycadeoid Parallel* (1941), *Fossil Cycad National Monument* (1944), and *The Yale Cycadeoids* (1945).

Wieland enthusiastically promoted the establishment of the Fossil Cycad National Monument in the Black Hills near Minnekahta, South Dakota. He homesteaded 320 acres of fossil-bearing land there in 1916 to protect the fossils. In 1920 he persuaded the Harding Administration to accept the property as a national monument. Wieland then began a publicity and lobbying campaign to persuade the government to purchase additional land and to develop the park. He succeeded in obtaining Park Service support for two months of excavation by the Civilian Conservation Corps in 1935, during which they collected more than a ton of specimens. After failing to submit a scientific appraisal to the Park Service, he was refused further support. Thereafter, he was involved in a public quarrel with Secretary of the Interior Harold Ickes, but by late 1941 he managed to regain Ickes's support. World War II soon began and halted progress. Although Wieland continued working at the site and persisted in lobbying, the monument was never developed. It was disestablished in 1957. Wieland's extensive collections, including the Fossil Cycad National Monument fossils, remained largely unstudied at his death but were later catalogued in the Peabody Museum of Yale University.

Wieland was a member of the American Association for the Advancement of Science, the Paleontological Society, the Geological Society of America, the Botanical Society, the Geological Society of Mexico, the Bologna Academy of Sciences, the Wilderness Society, and the New York Academy of Sciences. He was an honorary member of the International Botanical Congress and of the Geological Society of India. He was awarded a gold medal when he delivered an address at the dedication of the Capellina Museum of Bologna, Italy; he also received the Archduke Rainer Medal in Vienna in 1914. Wieland died in West Haven, Connecticut.

• Collections of Wieland's personal papers and correspondence are in the Manuscript and Archives Division of the Sterling Library, Yale University; the Ralph W. Chaney Papers at the University of Oregon; in the Carnegie Institution; and in the Fossil Cycad National Monument file in the National Archives. Basic sources of information on Wieland include Carl O. Dunbar, *Report of the National Research Council, Committee on Paleobotany* (Mar. 1954); and Joseph T. Gregory, "George Reber Wieland," *News Bulletin, Society of Vertebrate Paleontologists* 39 (1953): 27. Henry N. Andrews, *The Fossil Hunters in Search of Ancient Plants* (1980), includes a brief evaluation of Wieland's professional activity and an illuminating personal vignette. An obituary is in the *New York Times*, 20 Jan. 1953.

RALPH L. LANGENHEIM, JR.

WIEMAN, Henry Nelson (19 Aug. 1884–19 June 1975), philosopher of religion and theologian, was born in Rich Hill, midway between Joplin and Kansas City, Missouri, the son of William Henry Wieman, a Presbyterian minister, and Alma Morgan. The first of eight children, young Wieman attended church in his childhood, but he often stayed at home with his infant siblings and read poetry: Longfellow, Byron, and Tennyson. He was not taught religion and never joined most young Presbyterians in memorizing the "Shorter Catechism," but Wieman recalled catching something by contagion from his parents, especially his mother, a woman of "profound piety and religious devotion," who moved with "invincible propulsion," like "a force of nature" (Wieman, "Intellectual Autobiography," p. 6, and "Theocentric Religion," p. 339). At fourteen he read John Fiske's *Destiny of Man* and absorbed its commitment to evolutionary science as a means of knowledge. When Wieman's family moved to California's San Joaquin Valley, he attended a preparatory school at Occidental College. There, at seventeen, he read Herbert Spencer's *Synthetic Philosophy* and found that it did not destroy his religious belief.

By 1903 Wieman returned to the Midwest to study at Park College in Parkville, Missouri. Until his senior year, he expected to be a journalist, following the career of an uncle who edited a small-town newspaper. Studying philosophy with Silas Evans and comparative religions with Joseph Ernest McAfee, however, Wieman suddenly realized that he wanted to devote his life to studying philosophy of religion. Evans introduced him to the work of Josiah Royce, who became a strong influence on his early thinking. After earning a B.A. in 1907, Wieman returned to California to enter the Presbyterians' San Francisco Theological Seminary. Never intending to become a minister, he recalled that "I was a rebel in the field all through my stay at the seminary" (Wieman, "Theocentric Religion," p. 343). In religious studies, Wieman remained committed to philosophical idealism and graduated with a B.D. in 1910.

When he graduated from seminary, Wieman won a traveling fellowship and went to Germany in 1910 and 1911. There he studied with Rudolf Eucken at the University of Jena and Wilhelm Windelband and Ernst Troeltsch at the University of Heidelberg. In Eucken he found "great enthusiasm and an inspiring personality" but no "clarification of ideas." Wieman was unmoved by Troeltsch's historical enterprise, he recalled, because "history cannot show us how to live." Windelband was a great "classifier and systematizer," he thought, but he achieved that "at the expense of depth and constructiveness" (Wieman, "Theocentric Religion," p. 343).

After returning to the United States, Wieman spent four years in the Presbyterian ministry, most of them at Davis, California. There he married Anna M. Orr; they became the parents of five children. At Davis, Wieman read the work of Henri Bergson, who directed his attention away from metaphysical idealism to process philosophy.

In 1915 Wieman entered graduate school at Harvard University to study philosophy. His two years of study with William Ernest Hocking and Ralph Barton Perry, he wrote, were "the greatest two years of my life. . . . The stimulus and clarification surpassed anything I had ever known." Hocking helped him to reinterpret Royce's idealism in terms of an "interpersonal creativity" and embodied a religious way of living "unsurpassed among living men," said Wieman ("Theocentric Religion," p. 344), and Perry introduced him to the problem of value and brilliantly exemplified accuracy, clarity, and precision of thought. Wieman received his Ph.D. from Harvard in 1917.

From 1917 to 1927 Wieman taught at Occidental College in California. There he produced his first two major books: *Religious Experience and Scientific Method* (1926) and *The Wrestle of Religion with Truth* (1927). Writing them under the stimulation of John Dewey and Alfred North Whitehead, Wieman attacked liberal religious idealism for locating religious authority in abstract ideals and depicting God and the world in comfortable terms. The facts of human experience, said Wieman, teach us that "this is not a nice world and God is not a nice God. God is too awful and terrible, too destructive to our foolish little plans, to be nice." The task of theology, he argued, must be to reconstruct a theocentric religious belief from an empirical analysis of the hard data of human religious experience.

As an important theological interpreter of Whitehead's thought, Wieman was invited to join the faculty of the University of Chicago Divinity School in 1927. After the death of his first wife in 1931, he married Regina Hansen Westcott in 1932. They had no children. During his two decades at Chicago, his more important books included: *Is There a God?* (1932), *Normative Psychology of Religion* (1935), *The Growth of Religion* (1938), and *The Source of Human Good* (1946). In these and other works, Wieman developed his theistic naturalism against three major influences in contemporary Protestant thought. In reply to theological personalists, Wieman denied that God could be understood as a person in any meaningful sense. In answer to the neo-orthodoxy of Karl Barth, he denied that God is supernatural. In the metaphysical mysticism of Paul Tillich, who identified God as the "ground of being" or "being itself," Wieman recognized a more kindred spirit. By his refusal to identify God with anything that exists, however, he said, Tillich reduced the divine to noncognitive symbolism. Against all of them, Wieman asserted that God is the nonpersonal, deeply immanental creative process that is "the source of human good." His theological position fixed Wieman's place as a founder of process theology in liberal American Protestant thought.

After his retirement from the University of Chicago in 1947, Wieman was divorced from his second wife and married Laura Wolcott Matlack in 1948. They had no children. He taught at the University of Oregon from 1949 to 1951, at the University of Houston from 1951 to 1953, and as an emeritus professor at Southern Illinois University after 1956. During these last years, his more important books included *Man's Ultimate Commitment* (1958) and *Intellectual Foundation of Faith* (1961). He eventually settled in and died at Grinnell, Iowa. As a philosopher of religion and theologian, Wieman continues to influence the thought of others who would interpret human religious experience in terms of an evolutionary process.

• Wieman's papers are at Southern Illinois University. "Autobiographical statements" are "not trustworthy," he admitted, but Wieman published two intellectual autobiographies: "Theocentric Religion," in *Contemporary American Theology*, ed. Vergilius Ferm (1932), pp. 339–52; and "Intellectual Autobiography," in *The Empirical Theology of Henry Nelson Wieman*, ed. Robert W. Bretall (1963), pp. 3–18. For a nearly complete bibliography of his published work, see Bretall, ed., *Empirical Theology*. Critical assessments of Wieman's theological enterprise include: Kenneth Cauthen, *The Impact of American Religious Liberalism* (1962); William R. Hutchison, *The Modernist Impulse in American Protestantism* (1976); William S. Minor, *Creativity in Henry Nelson Wieman* (1977); Creighton Peden, *Wieman's Empirical Process Philosophy* (1977); and Peden, *The Chicago School: Voices in Liberal Religious Thought* (1987). An obituary is in the *New York Times*, 21 June 1975.

RALPH E. LUKER

WIENER, Leo (28 July 1862–12 Dec. 1939), philologist, translator, and educator, was born in Bialystok, Russia (now part of Poland), the son of Salomon Wiener, a scholar and teacher, and Fredcrika Rabinowitch, who was descended from a distinguished rabbinic family. Wiener grew up in a multilingual environment congenial to his stunning linguistic abilities. Although Wiener had a French governess, his father insisted that German be spoken at home. Hebrew was cultivated as the traditional language of prayer, study, and

Jewish intellectual discourse, while Yiddish, Russian, and Polish were the vernaculars most commonly used in Bialystok.

Wiener studied at the Classical Gymnasium in Minsk (1873–1877) and Warsaw (1877–1879); he then enrolled as a medical student at the University of Warsaw (1879–1880). Unable to stomach the dissection of cadavers and the narrow nationalism of his Polish fellow students, Wiener moved to Berlin, where he matriculated at the Polytechnicum to pursue a degree in mechanical engineering (1881–1882). Revolted by "German philistinism, with its juxtaposition of science and beer," Wiener became a member of the Berlin Academic Vegetarian Society. He renounced meat, alcohol, and tobacco for the rest of his life and soon advocated "the formation of a vegetarian colony in the tropics."

In February 1882 Wiener was on his way to British Belize, with enough money to buy passage as far as New Orleans. During his voyage he acquired Spanish and English by reading grammar books and novels, but having developed a thorough dislike of a fellow colonist, he abandoned the idea of going to Belize. Although "the United States was not my objective point," Wiener recalled in 1910, "I was quite prepared to begin life here." He found work in a cotton mill, on a railroad construction site, and finally as a farmer in a dilapidated progressive commune in Cedar Valley, Kansas.

After a year on the farm, however, Wiener moved on to become a teacher in a country school in Odessa, Missouri (1883) and then in the Kansas City High School (1884–1892), where he taught languages and mathematics. Wiener's sociable disposition ensured that his linguistic talents and vast knowledge did not go unrecognized. In 1892 he was appointed to an assistant professorship in Germanic and Romance languages at the State University of Missouri in Columbia. In 1893 Wiener married Bertha Kahn, the daughter of German-Jewish immigrants who owned a department store in St. Joseph, Missouri. The couple had four children.

In 1895 after Wiener was forced out of his job at the University of Missouri, he took his family to Boston, correctly assuming that he would find a market there for his intellectual gifts. Through the staff at the Boston Public Library, Wiener met Francis James Child, a professor of literature at Harvard University, whom he helped to trace Scottish ballads through the South Slavic area, and Archibald Cary Coolidge, who supported Wiener's appointment to an instructorship in Slavic languages and literatures at Harvard in 1896. Wiener was promoted to assistant professor in 1901 and to full professor in 1911. He retired from teaching in 1930.

At Harvard Wiener's talent crystallized into scholarship. He edited and largely translated an *Anthology of Russian Literature from the Earliest Period to the Present Time* (1902–1903), translated *The Complete Works of Count Tolstoy* (1904–1905), wrote a monograph on *Lev N. Tolstoy* (1905), and published a bibliography of Tolstoy criticism (1905). When the World War I erupted in 1914, Wiener attempted to explain the mentality of the Russian people to Americans in his popular work *An Interpretation of the Russian People* (1915). In the same spirit he translated V. V. Veresaev's memoirs of the Russian-Japanese War of 1904–1905, *In the War* (1917). With the ascendancy of the Communist regime, Wiener lost interest in Russia. He wrote only one other book about the literature he loved, *The Contemporary Drama of Russia* (1924).

Wiener's contributions to Jewish studies, though smaller in number, are perhaps even more significant. In 1893 he published an article "On the Judeo-German Spoken by Russian Jews," in which he analyzed the linguistic elements of Yiddish. He went on to explore Yiddish literature in "Popular Poetry of the Russian Jews" (1898) and more fully in his groundbreaking study *The History of Yiddish Literature in the Nineteenth Century* (1899). He translated the work of the American-Yiddish poet Morris Rosenfeld in *Songs from the Ghetto* (1898) and wrote an introduction for English readers.

However, Wiener's linguistic interests ranged far. His articles include studies of Ladino (Judeo-Spanish), Maya language, Native American languages, medieval Latin, Medieval Arabic, Sumerian, and Egyptian. Toward the end of his life Wiener was familiar with some thirty languages. Steady employment enabled Wiener in 1903 to purchase a farm in Ayer, Massachusetts. There his old enthusiasm for tilling the soil reasserted itself. "To my father's dying day," Norbert Wiener observed in his memoirs, "he was more pleased by raising a better crop than his professional farmer-neighbors than he would have been by the greatest philological discovery."

In 1932 Wiener was injured in a car accident. He died of a stroke in Belmont, Massachusetts. His work combined prodigious research and scrupulous scholarship with informed guesswork. Wiener did not pursue philology for its own sake but thought it a useful tool in his true profession as cultural historian.

• Wiener's papers covering the years between 1880 and 1935 are in the Harvard University Archives. Norbert Wiener, *Ex-Prodigy: My Childhood and Youth* (1953), is a valuable source of information about Wiener's personality. A comprehensive modern assessment is Susanne Klingenstein, "A Philologist: The Adventures of Leo Wiener (1862–1839)," in her *Jews in the American Academy, 1900–1940* (1991). An obituary is in the *New York Times*, 14 Dec. 1939.

SUSANNE KLINGENSTEIN

WIENER, Norbert (26 Nov. 1894–18 Mar. 1964), mathematician, was born in Columbia, Missouri, the son of Leo Wiener, a professor of Slavic languages at Harvard, and Bertha Kahn. Wiener's career had its roots in his identity as a child prodigy. Between the ages of about seven and nine, he was educated in a program of home study designed and taught by his father, after which he enrolled in Ayer high school, from which he graduated at age eleven. Wiener entered Tufts College in the fall of 1906, where his main interests were philosophy, biology, and mathematics. He graduated as a mathematics major three years later in 1909 at age fourteen.

Wiener's first effort at graduate study was as a student of biology at Harvard University in 1909–1910. However, essentially because of his clumsiness in the laboratory, he abandoned this pursuit and moved on to Cornell University, where he studied philosophy in 1910–1911. Wiener returned to Harvard Graduate School in the fall of 1911, where he wrote a thesis in mathematical logic and was awarded a Ph.D. in philosophy in 1913 at age eighteen. Under a traveling fellowship awarded by Harvard for 1913–1914, Wiener went to Cambridge University in England to study with Bertrand Russell. There he read Albert Einstein's 1905 paper on Brownian motion, the irregular movement of small particles suspended in a fluid; this subject would underlie much of his lifetime scientific work. Following the extension of his traveling fellowship for another year, Wiener served as an assistant in the philosophy department at Harvard University during 1915–1916.

After spending a year as an instructor of mathematics at the University of Maine, Wiener spent the next two years in a series of nonacademic positions that included working on the ballistics staff of an applied mathematics group at the Aberdeen Proving Ground in Maryland.

Wiener's career-long association with the Massachusetts Institute of Technology began in 1919 when he was hired as an instructor there. He was promoted to associate professor in 1929 and to full professor in 1932. In 1919 the mathematics department was in a state of transition from a service department for engineers to a research-oriented department. Wiener's first few years at MIT were productive. He solved the important problem of integration in function spaces. His search for a relevant physical theory led him to the study of Brownian motion, for which he constructed a rigorous mathematical model. He developed axioms for a structure now known as a Banach space, and he worked for a short period in the area of potential theory.

Wiener was challenged by the electrical engineering department at MIT to provide a mathematical foundation for the methods being used in the field of communication theory. Wiener's solution lay in the development of his generalized harmonic analysis, which he obtained by expanding the classical theories of the Fourier series and integral.

Wiener traveled to Göttingen in the spring of 1926 as a Guggenheim Fellow. There his use of Tauberian theorems enabled him to close a gap in his generalized harmonic analysis and led to the development of a major work on Tauberian methods that had applications to number theory as well as to harmonic analysis. Wiener's major paper on generalized harmonic analysis was published in *Acta Mathematica* in 1930; his major paper on Tauberian theorems was published in the *Annals of Mathematics* in 1932.

During the period from 1927 to 1931 Wiener collaborated with Vannevar Bush on the development of the computer. Wiener wrote a supplementary chapter on Fourier methods for Bush's book on electric circuit theory, *Fourier Analysis and Asymptotic Series, Operational Circuit Analysis* (1929). Other work in this period included his collaboration with German mathematician Eberhard Hopf. The solution of a problem on the radiation of stars led to the so-called Wiener-Hopf equations, whose wide applicability extends to prediction theory and to filter problems that arise in radar design—topics of future interest to Wiener.

Wiener spent the year 1931–1932 in Cambridge, England, where he wrote the *Fourier Integral and Certain of Its Applications* (1933). After returning to MIT, he spent 1932–1933 working with English mathematician R. E. A. C. Paley on the design of electric circuits. Wiener's work on generalized harmonic analysis and the Tauberian theorems was recognized by the American Mathematical Society in 1933 when he shared its award of the Bôcher Prize in analysis. This led to the publication of his joint work with Paley, *Fourier Transforms in the Complex Domain* (1934). In 1934 Wiener was named to the National Academy of Sciences but resigned shortly thereafter in disgust at the campaigning that took place prior to the election of new members. In the late 1930s Wiener combined, improved, and extended the existing ergodic theorems, thus providing an important step in the formal development of statistical mechanics.

Following the outbreak of World War II and the subsequent involvement of the scientific community in war-related work, Wiener chose computers and prediction theory as his areas of activity. Wiener advocated the electronic binary computer as the machine that would provide the computational speed necessary for solving problems involving partial differential equations. By recommending that all necessary decision-making processes be built into the machine itself, together with the capability for the rapid erasure and replacement of stored data, Wiener articulated similarities between the machine and the human nervous system that anticipated his later work.

Wiener ultimately turned his attention to the design of fire control apparatus for antiaircraft guns and more generally to the subject of prediction theory. Here the basic problem was that of predicting the future position of an airplane based on its observed past positions. To this problem Wiener brought a statistical approach that entailed the solution of a Wiener-Hopf type of equation. His solution to the prediction problem could also be used to deal with the problem of noise (disturbance) in radar transmission by providing a method for the design of a filter for the successful separation of the noise from the message. The issue of control of antiaircraft machinery involved the method of negative feedback, by which the performance of a machine may be corrected by a motion in the opposite direction. The confirmation that human control also depended on feedback established yet another similarity between human and machine.

Wiener's first work in linear prediction and filtering, combined with his study of messages and their transmission, was presented in *Extrapolation, Interpolation and Smoothing of Stationary Time Series with Engineering Applications* (1949), commonly known as the "yellow peril" due to the color of the cover of its manuscript form. This work, completed in 1942 and extensively used by engineers, provides a statistical approach to communication theory. Further reflection on the common characteristics of the brain and the computer led Wiener in 1944 to convene a meeting of scientists at Princeton University, which he regarded as the birthplace of cybernetics—"the theory of communication and control in the machine and the living organism."

In *Cybernetics or Control and Communication in the Animal and the Machine* (1948), Wiener brought to the general community information on the statistical approach to prediction and communication theory and on the many analogies between the human nervous system and the computer. Wiener's work was a confluence of his interests in mathematics, engineering, biology, and philosophy. A more popular treatment of cybernetics appears in *The Human Use of Human Beings* (1950). Here Wiener asserts that society is defined by the content and methods of its communication systems, emphasizes the increasing importance of communication machines, and warns of the dangers of the exploitation of human beings in the face of new technologies.

Wiener foresaw the automatic factory as an inevitable consequence of the cybernetic revolution. His concern for its possible negative social impact led him to reflect on his responsibility as a scientist for the social consequences of his discoveries. He then took steps to engage labor and management in a planning process designed to avoid disastrous unemployment. He also took steps to discourage the use of his recent work on prediction theory for military purposes.

Unlike many of his scientific colleagues, Wiener did not participate in the development of the atomic bomb; and, in retrospect, he was happy not to have done so. He opposed the course of action that led to the bomb, for it created a new world that would exist thereafter under the threat of universal destruction. In his view, the need for secrecy required by possession of the bomb would not only be adverse to the nature of scientific activity but would also be impossible to guarantee.

The first volume of Wiener's autobiography, *Ex-prodigy: My Childhood and Youth* (1953), covers his life up to his marriage in 1926 to Margaret Engemann, with whom he had two children. The second and final volume, *I Am a Mathematician* (1956), focuses on his career from 1919 to 1954.

Wiener did further work in linear prediction and filtering between 1949 and 1959. His interest in nonlinear circuits led to *Nonlinear Problems in Random Theory* (1958). Following his retirement from MIT in 1960, Wiener remained active in the scientific and academic communities. One of his last publications, in 1963, concerned the use of random functions in quantum mechanics. He died in Stockholm during a visit there.

A mathematician motivated by problems having physical significance, Wiener brought together the abstract methods of pure mathematics with the practical concerns of science and engineering. His work on Brownian motion and integration in function spaces was both creative and visionary, owing to his foresight in the use of probabilistic methods, the future impact of his work on stochastic processes, and the many uses of the Wiener integral, as, for example, in quantum mechanics. Today mathematical physicists refer to Brownian motion as a Wiener process. Such processes provide a prototype for random fractals and are widely applicable, as, for example, in the study of stock market fluctuations.

Wiener provided a theoretical base for developments in science and engineering. His work on generalized harmonic analysis supplied the mathematics needed for a statistical understanding of concepts in optics and offered a useful tool for studying phenomena such as electric noise. He gave theoretical underpinnings to many later developments in communication engineering; in his work with Paley, he established the basic building block for the study of linear electrical networks.

Wiener provided a new basis for future research in potential theory and the Dirichlet problem. And his work on prediction theory had an extensive influence on that theory's later development.

Wiener's independent and unorthodox ways of thinking served to free him from viewing problems within the confines of any one discipline. In his consideration of the common issues of communication and control that arise in a variety of situations—human, machine, and social scientific—Wiener established himself as a multidisciplinarian par excellence. In cybernetics, Wiener brought together communication engineering, computers, and physiology in the investigation of communication problems. Cybernetics has stimulated research in areas such as biological regulation, brain waves, and prosthetic devices, and it has contributed to the development of cognitive psychology.

Wiener had a worldview consistent with his scientific approach. In *I Am a Mathematician*, he asserts: "The declaration of our own nature and the attempt to build up an enclave of organization in the face of nature's overwhelming tendency to disorder is an insolence against the gods and the iron necessity that they impose. Here lies tragedy, but here lies glory too."

• Wiener's papers are in the Institute Archives and Special Collections, MIT Libraries. All of his nonbook scholarly publications and his academic vita are included in Pesi Masani, ed., *Norbert Wiener: Collected Works* (1976). Biographical information, analyses of his contributions to mathematics and science, and a bibliography of his scholarly books and journal articles are given in *Bulletin of the American Mathematical Society* 72 (1966): 1–145. His mathematical work, together with that of others, is placed in a broad historical context in Dalton Tarwater, ed., *The Bicentennial Tribute to American Mathematics, 1776–1976* (1977). An obituary is in the *New York Times*, 19 Mar. 1964.

SUSAN WILLIAMSON

WIESNER, Jerome Bert (30 May 1915–21 Oct. 1994), electrical engineer, presidential adviser, and university president, was born in Detroit, Michigan, the son of Joseph Wiesner, a shopkeeper, and Ida Freedman. The boy grew up in Dearborn, Michigan, where he attended public schools and took an interest in electrical equipment, even creating a private telephone network with his friends. He entered the University of Michigan in 1933 and as an undergraduate became associate director of the campus radio broadcasting facility. After receiving a B.S. in both electrical engineering and mathematics in 1937 and an M.S. in electrical engineering in 1938, he continued with the radio service and with studies of acoustics. In 1940 he became chief engineer for the Acoustical and Record Laboratory of the Library of Congress. With folklorist Alan Lomax he recorded ethnic music in the southern and southwestern United States. Also in 1940, he married Laya Wainger; they had four children.

From 1942 to 1945 Wiesner was on the research staff of the Radiation Laboratory, which was established early in World War II at the Massachusetts Institute of Technology (MIT). He participated in the development of microwave radar and led the project that successfully created an airborne early warning radar system. In 1945 he spent a year at the Los Alamos (N.Mex.) Laboratory of the University of California, where he developed electronic components for atomic bomb tests at Bikini Atoll in 1946. For his wartime service he received the President's Certificate of Merit in 1948.

Wiesner returned to MIT in 1946 as assistant professor of electrical engineering, advancing to associate professor the next year. He also became assistant director of the college's Research Laboratory of Electronics, the successor of the Radiation Laboratory for basic research in electronics, physics, and communications. In 1950 he received a Ph.D. in electrical engineering from the University of Michigan and advanced to professor at MIT.

Wiesner became director of the laboratory in 1952 and oversaw the development of two systems of long-range communication that used ionospheric and tropospheric scattering. With other faculty members he updated the college's curriculum in electrical engineering to include many wartime advances. Drawn to the ideas of his colleague Norbert Wiener, the mathematician who established the discipline of cybernetics (communication and its control), Wiesner encouraged research in speech, hearing, vision, and neural systems. His interest in interdisciplinary uses, techniques, and problems of electronics and communication attracted to his laboratory many psychologists, physiologists, and other medical specialists, as well as physicists and engineers. In 1959 Wiesner became acting head of MIT's large department of electrical engineering.

Wiesner became a member of the President's Science Advisory Committee (PSAC) in 1957, when Dwight D. Eisenhower was president. At that time he strongly encouraged the development of ballistic missiles. He served on other government advisory units and was a participant in the Pugwash Group, which consisted of scientists concerned with relations between Western and Communist nations. In the late 1950s he became concerned with the environmental hazards associated with the production and testing of nuclear weapons. From that time on, Wiesner became active in efforts to control and limit nuclear arms and was noted as "remarkably gifted in his ability to elucidate complex issues and to explain the effects of policies and their technical and political consequences" (Gray, p. 293). In 1961 he presented his views in his book, *Where Science and Politics Meet*. That same year he became an adviser to President John F. Kennedy as special assistant to the president for science and technology. He was also head of the PSAC and, in 1962, head of the White House Office of Science and Technology. Among his accomplishments was preliminary work to ban all above-ground nuclear tests, which led to a signed agreement by the United States, Britain, and the Soviet Union in 1963. Wiesner played a role in the establishment of the Arms Control and Disarmament Agency, and he led efforts to restrict the deployment of antiballistic missile systems. With his MIT colleagues Philip Morrison and Kosta Tsipis, Wiesner published *Beyond the Looking Glass: The United States Military in 2000 and Later* (1993), in which the authors urged deep cuts in U.S. military expenditure and equipment.

Soon after Kennedy's assassination, Wiesner returned to MIT in 1964 to assume its highest faculty post, institute professor. He became dean of the School of Science that year and MIT provost in 1966. With Abram Chayes he published *ABM: An Evaluation of the Decision to Deploy an Antiballistic Missile System* (1969). Wiesner was appointed president of MIT in 1971. Under his leadership the college expanded its programs in humanities, creative arts, social sciences, and health sciences while maintaining its stature as a science and engineering center. A proponent of civil rights, Wiesner encouraged an increase in women and minorities in both the student body and the faculty. He retired as president of MIT in 1980 and resumed his professorship, in which position he emphasized science policy. The Wiesner Building at MIT was dedicated to him and his wife in 1985.

While president of MIT, Wiesner helped found the Massachusetts Science and Technology Foundation to advise the governor and other officials on scientific matters and to encourage industry. He continued as a consultant-at-large for the PSAC, was on the board of directors of the Public Broadcasting Service, and held other civic positions.

Among many honors, Wiesner was elected to the National Academy of Sciences in 1960 and to the National Academy of Engineering in 1966. From the latter he received the Arthur M. Bueche Award in 1985, and from the National Science Foundation he received the Vannevar Bush Award in 1992. The National Academy of Sciences awarded him its highest honor, the Public Welfare Medal, in 1993.

Wiesner was especially concerned with the impact of rapidly advancing science and technology and the potential for damage to the environment through the misuse of technology, and he wrote effectively on these concerns in various publications. He was respected by colleagues for his competence in science and administration, his modesty, and his humor. He died in Watertown, Massachusetts.

• Wiesner's personal and administrative records are in the Archives of the Massachusetts Institute of Technology. Biographical material includes a detailed anonymous sketch in *MIT Tech Talk* 39 (26 Oct. 1994): 1, 4–5; and Paul E. Gray, "Jerome Bert Wiesner," *National Academy of Engineering Memorial Tributes* 8 (1996): 290–95. Obituaries are in *New York Times* and *Washington Post*, both 23 Oct. 1994.

ELIZABETH NOBLE SHOR

WIGFALL, Louis Trezevant (21 Apr. 1816–18 Feb. 1874), U.S. and Confederate senator, was born Lewis Wigfall near Edgefield, South Carolina, the son of Levi Durand Wigfall and Eliza Thompson, planters. Both of Wigfall's parents had died by his thirteenth year, when he was left to the care of a guardian. He received private tutoring, then attended Rice Creek Springs School, a military academy near Columbia, South Carolina. In 1834 he enrolled at the University of Virginia and, after almost challenging a fellow student to a duel over a misunderstanding at a school dance, decided to return to South Carolina. He completed his education at South Carolina College in 1837. He found oration in the school's Euphradian Society more alluring than his regular classes, which he often skipped. A frequent visitor to off-campus taverns, Wigfall and several friends further defied the regimen of college life by spending three months in Florida in 1836 fighting in the Seminole Indian war. He rose to the rank of lieutenant, but years later he boldly called himself "colonel."

While in college Wigfall developed an interest in law and in 1839 returned to Edgefield to join his brother Arthur's thriving law practice. The realities of serving as a junior partner were dull to Wigfall; even he admitted the most he could realistically hope for was to "establish some reputation as a back-country lawyer." Wigfall had a penchant for making matters worse for himself. Not only had he squandered his $13,000 inheritance by 1839, but he had also incurred a sizable debt, in part by spending money on cards, horses, and prostitutes, and was well on the road to alcoholism. When he attempted to gain control of himself by abandoning his vices, he grew so depressed that once he contemplated suicide. Only a resumption of drinking and spending beyond his means seemed to help.

In 1841 Wigfall's prospects brightened when he married Charlotte Cross; the couple eventually had five children. Although Charlotte remained stoically by her husband, their marriage became embroiled in Wigfall's money problems. He was unaware of the extent of his previous debts, and after he arranged for the purchase of a home and furnishings for himself and his bride, Wigfall owed creditors $1,300—after spending every penny of Charlotte's that he had acquired in marriage. To add to their problems, their first child was born with a serious skin disease. The new father worked assiduously, riding the legal circuit through western South Carolina, but his income barely kept pace with his son's medical bills. In 1846 the Wigfalls lost their home, their furniture, and their four slaves in a sheriff's auction. Later the same year their eldest child died.

As Wigfall waded through personal crises, he began dabbling in politics. In 1840 he had teamed up with his best friend from college, John Manning, to edit the *Edgefield Advertiser*, using it as a campaign organ to support Manning's uncle, John Richardson, for governor and to attack his opponent, James H. Hammond. The heat of the election thrust Wigfall, who was already predisposed toward recklessness and violence, into a series of fights, challenges, and duels. At the center of all these incidents was a supporter of Hammond, Preston Brooks, who would later become famous for caning Charles Sumner on the floor of the U.S. Senate. Despising one another, Wigfall and Brooks engaged in a series of public insults and challenges. When Brooks's father, Whitfield Brooks, intervened on his son's behalf, Wigfall challenged the elder Brooks to a duel. He refused. In accordance with the code of honor, Wigfall began posting placards denouncing Whitfield Brooks as a coward. When two men tried to stop him, Wigfall shot and killed one and challenged the other to a duel. Wigfall and Preston Brooks finally dueled in late 1840. After missing with their first shots, Wigfall hit Brooks in the hip and Brooks shot Wigfall in the thigh. Wigfall never again engaged in an affair of honor, but his well-earned reputation for violence followed him forever.

Soon after his confrontation with the Brooks clan, Wigfall took on a greater challenge, the federal government. In 1844 he joined the ranks of the "Bluffton Boys," a group of young Carolinians under the leadership of Robert Barnwell Rhett. These men threatened nullification or secession under any one of three possibilities: repeal of the congressional gag rule that prevented discussion of abolition petitions, adoption of a new protective tariff, or failure to annex Texas. John C. Calhoun eventually smothered the Bluffton movement, but the episode whetted Wigfall's enthusiasm for politics, introduced him to other young men interested in establishing a southern nation, and helped focus his mind on Texas.

After the upheavals of violence, bankruptcy, and the death of his young son, Wigfall decided to move to Texas in 1846 and start his life over. He began going by "Louis" instead of Lewis, and some of his luck changed as well. He soon established himself as a lawyer in Marshall, and, while his financial situation improved markedly, he never lost his knack for borrowing money from friends and losing it in bad investments. In 1848, at a Galveston County Democratic meeting, Wigfall offered a resolution opposing the enactment of the Wilmot Proviso and the next year vowed secession as a recourse. Elected to the state assembly in 1850, Wigfall continued his efforts to radicalize Texas by supporting the stance taken by secessionists at that year's Nashville Convention and by attacking the moderation and Unionism of Senator Sam Houston. Wigfall later led an effort to have the legislature censure Houston for his opposition to the Kansas-Nebraska Act, which allowed slavery a chance to move north of the Missouri Compromise line, and joined those who opposed Houston's reelection at mid-decade. After Houston refused to meet Wigfall for public debate in 1857, Wigfall simply followed Houston everywhere he went, launching a verbal assault that infuriated the senator and contributed to his defeat. Wigfall won election to the Texas Senate the same year. There he supported efforts to revive the African slave trade and endorsed filibustering expeditions to spread slavery to Cuba, Mexico, and beyond. He proposed a bill that would have prevented manumission of slavery by will; although that bill was defeated in 1857, its idea was later incorporated into the new constitution of Confederate Texas. In the wake of John Brown's raid into Virginia in 1859 and growing anxiety among white southerners, the Texas assembly selected Wigfall to represent their state in the U.S. Senate.

Wigfall carried his campaign for secession to Washington, D.C. He chastised Republicans and Democrats, northerners and southerners, all who stood in the way of southern independence. He introduced no significant legislation or resolutions, but ferociously attacked Union-saving propositions by southerners like John J. Crittenden of Kentucky or Andrew Johnson of Tennessee. During a heated debate on disunion, Senator Zachariah Chandler of Michigan proclaimed that rather than reason with a secessionist he would prefer to move west and live among the Indians. The caustic Texan replied, "God forbid! I hope not. They have already suffered much from their contact with whites." When the Federal supply ship *Star of the West* failed in its efforts to provision Fort Sumter in 1861, Wigfall gloated, "Your flag has been insulted; redress it if you dare. You have submitted to it for two months, you will submit to it forever." As tensions mounted in Charleston harbor that April, Wigfall made a spectacular return to his native state. During the bombardment of Fort Sumter (and, according to one witness, under the influence of alcohol), Wigfall commandeered a small boat and had slaves row him to the Federal position. He entered an embrasure and personally demanded the fort's surrender. Regular military authorities under the command of General P. G. T. Beauregard completed the negotiations and Union withdrawal.

His notoriety in the Federal capital helped secure Wigfall's election to the Confederate senate immediately after Texas seceded. Military concerns riveted his attention throughout the remainder of his career. For much of 1861 he served simultaneously in the provisional congress and as a Texas and Confederate colonel, helping drill troops for battle and build a new government. By November 1861 Senator Wigfall was also a Confederate brigadier general.

At first a close friend and supporter of Confederate president Jefferson Davis, Wigfall quickly became a leading foe of the administration in the senate, partly because of his sympathy for General Joseph E. Johnston during his long and bitter feud with Davis, and partly because he used Davis as a scapegoat for southern military defeats. Despite their personal animosity, Davis could count on Wigfall to back all efforts to fortify the military. Wigfall supported conscription, expansion of the age limit to include soldiers from sixteen to sixty, and a bill in 1864 that allowed the government to take over all private railroads. The Texan always supported the administration's efforts to impress slaves but adamantly opposed arming and emancipating slave soldiers.

As the war wound down, Wigfall made a futile effort to reach Texas before its occupation by Union troops. He and his family then fled to London, where he languished with other former Confederate officials and resumed heavy drinking. He returned to the United States in 1872, living with family in Baltimore, Maryland, for two years before venturing back to Texas. Intending to go back to Marshall and resume his law practice, Wigfall died in Galveston of an undisclosed cause.

• Wigfall's papers are few. The two largest collections are in the Williams-Chesnut-Manning Papers at the University of South Carolina and the Wigfall Family Papers in the Library of Congress. Wigfall's legislative record is chronicled in the *Congressional Globe*, 36th Cong., 1st and 2d sess., 1860–1861, and *Journal of the Congress of the Confederate States of America, 1861–1865* (7 vols., 1904–1905). His daughter Louise Wigfall Wright published an interesting and useful memoir, *A Southern Girl in '61* (1905). A complete biography is Alvy L. King, *Louis T. Wigfall: Southern Fire-Eater* (1970), although it focuses primarily on his Confederate years. For that period also see William C. Davis, *"A Government of Our Own": The Making of the Confederacy* (1994), and George C. Rable, *The Confederate Republic: A Revolution against Politics* (1994). The fifth chapter of Eric H. Walther, *The Fire-Eaters* (1992), also discusses Wigfall. Obituaries are in the *Galveston News*, 19 Feb. 1874, and the *Charleston News and Courier*, 23 Feb. 1874.

ERIC H. WALTHER

WIGGER, Winand Michael (9 Dec. 1841–5 Jan. 1901), third Roman Catholic bishop of Newark, New Jersey, was born in New York City, the son of German immigrant parents John Joseph Wigger and Elizabeth Strucke. He attended the College of St. Francis Xavier in New York and St. John's College in Fordham, from which he received an A.B. in 1860. He then applied to be a seminarian for the archdiocese of New York.

However, his ill health caused him to be rejected by Vicar General William Starrs. Bishop James Roosevelt Bayley of Newark eventually accepted him and sent him to Seton Hall Seminary in South Orange and later to the Vincentian Collegio Brignole-Sale in Genoa. He was ordained a priest on 10 June 1865 by Archbishop Andre Charvaz of Genoa and returned to Newark in 1866. In 1869 he secured a doctoral degree from the Roman Sapienza University. Wigger was multilingual, direct in speech, yet capable of tact and diplomacy, and he developed a life-long concern for the poor. Between 1866 and 1881 he performed pastoral duties at St. Patrick's Cathedral in Newark, St. Vincent's Church in Madison, St. John's in Orange, and St. Teresa's in Summit, ultimately returning to Madison.

In 1880, when Bishop Michael Corrigan was transferred to New York, Wigger was designated his successor in Newark. He was consecrated by Corrigan on 18 October 1881 in Newark. As a German-speaking bishop, Wigger closely associated himself with the "Germanizers" in the American hierarchy. This group strongly resisted the assimilationist tendencies of the "Americanizers" (English-speaking bishops and priests) and advocated the retention of distinct ethnic parishes, the use of the German language, and the development of German Catholic schools and social welfare institutions as a way to preserve the faith of German immigrants. Wigger was associated with the work of the St. Raphael's Society, a protection agency for German immigrants, and its president Peter Paul Cahensly. Wigger was president of the New York branch of this society and helped found the Leo House in the Battery in 1889, a temporary shelter for newly arrived German immigrants. He was close friends with Cahensly, who drafted the famous "Lucerne Memorial," which asked for greater representation for various ethnic groups (particularly German speakers) in the American hierarchy and caused a great deal of consternation in the American church. Wigger was also active in the "Priester-Verein," an organization of German-speaking priests from around the nation, and kept up contacts with leaders of this group such as Henry Mühlsiepen, vicar general of St. Louis, and Peter Joseph Schroeder of the Catholic University. He did not support all the positions taken by the Germanizers. One notable exception was his strong advocacy of temperance, a position scorned by many ethnic Germans. Wigger was so firmly opposed to drinking that he even advocated denying Christian burial to unrepentant alcoholics. However, on other issues he vigorously defended the proponents of German ethnicity, especially when he believed their positions were misrepresented in Catholic press. Yet despite his strong commitment to preserving German ethnicity, Wigger worked harmoniously with the English-speaking priests and laity of his own growing diocese.

In Newark, Wigger was a staunch proponent of Catholic schools. Although he had opposed the convocation of the Third Plenary Council of Baltimore in 1884, he worked vigorously to implement its mandate that every parish have a Catholic school. He tried unsuccessfully to secure state aid for parochial schools in the 1892–1893 New Jersey legislature. He opposed legislation in 1893 that would have linked parochial schools with New Jersey's public school system in order to secure state funds for them. Wigger built churches, began a new cathedral, and accommodated the growing spectrum of ethnic groups taking up residence in his diocese by allowing a proliferation of ethnic parishes. He died in East Orange, New Jersey.

• Wigger's papers are in the Archives of the Archdiocese of Newark, located at Seton Hall University in South Orange, N.J. See C. D. Hinrichsen, "The History of the Diocese of Newark, 1873–1901" (Ph.D. diss., Catholic Univ., 1963); J. M. Flynn, *The Catholic Church in New Jersey* (1904); Joseph F. Mahoney and Peter J. Wosh, *The Diocesan Journal of Michael Augustine Corrigan, Bishop of Newark, 1872–1880* (1987); John Tracy Ellis, *The Life of James Cardinal Gibbons, Archbishop of Baltimore, 1834–1921* (2 vols., 1952); Colman Barry, *The Catholic Church and German Americans* (1953); and Robert Emmett Curran, *Michael Augustine Corrigan and the Shaping of Conservative Catholicism in America, 1878–1902* (1978).

STEVEN M. AVELLA

WIGGERS, Carl John (28 May 1883–27 Apr. 1963), physiologist, was born in Davenport, Iowa, the son of Jurgen Wiggers, a farm worker and later a manager of a social club, and Anna Margaretha Kundel. Wiggers attended the University of Michigan Medical School, which, at that time, required only a high school education for admission. Although initially intending to specialize in obstetrics and pediatrics, Wiggers was influenced by his experiences as a student of physiologist Warren P. Lombard and pharmacologist Arthur Cushny, in whose laboratory Wiggers learned the technique of anesthetizing animals before exposing their hearts and recording cardiac contractions. After receiving his medical degree in 1906, Wiggers was appointed instructor in physiology at the medical school. In 1907 he married Minerva E. Berry, a fellow medical student. The couple had two sons.

In 1905 Wiggers began the first of his extensive studies of the blood vessels and the hemodynamics of hemorrhage. His presentation on the innervation of the cerebral vessels at the annual meeting of the American Physiological Society led, at the suggestion of Johns Hopkins physiologist William Henry Howell, to a position as an instructor at Cornell University Medical School in New York City. Two years later he became assistant professor of physiology at the school. Working under nutrition researcher Graham Lusk, Wiggers continued his physiological studies on the circulatory system. Wiggers spent a year in Munich studying in the laboratory of Otto Frank, who was developing new instrumentation for quantitative readings of systolic and diastolic blood pressures. When Lusk suggested that clinical interest in cardiovascular research might be stimulated by a monograph summarizing how new methodologies and animal experiments complemented clinical observations, Wiggers published *Circulation in Health and Disease* (1915). Before American entry into World War I Wiggers joined other physiologists in studying the problem of shock. In 1918 he served as a contract surgeon at an army hospital in Lakewood, New Jersey. One aspect of Wiggers's war work was to assess cardiac fitness of recruits. He also supervised the electrocardiography unit and conducted research on the problem of the effort syndrome, a functional disorder of the heart.

In the fall of 1918 Wiggers accepted the professorship of physiology at Western Reserve University (later Case Western Reserve University) in Cleveland, Ohio, an appointment he retained until his retirement in 1953. At Western Reserve, Wiggers devoted much of his time to creating and adopting instruments for physiological research, which at this time had to be imported from Germany. He also continued the enlargement of the physiological laboratories and his own research program in cardiovascular physiology. As chair of the institutional committee on animal experimentation, Wiggers assumed responsibility for establishing reliable sources of animals, especially dogs, and for dealing with antivivisectionists. The dearth of American training programs for investigators in circulation research encouraged Wiggers in 1924 to begin offering such programs at Western Reserve. At the time of his retirement, 123 cardiovascular physiologists were identified as having been closely influenced by Wiggers in their professional training.

In the 1930s and 1940s, Wiggers and his associates conducted sustained research on cardiac resuscitation, the only American group to do so. In addition to his search for a "miracle drug" that could restore the beating of the heart, Wiggers investigated the efficacy of manual cardiac compression, together with electric defibrillation, to revive hearts that experienced rapid movements instead of the normal contractions. In 1947 Western Reserve surgeon Claude S. Beck reported the first successful practical application of Wiggers's research, the survival of a patient who received countershock after experiencing ventricular fibrillation during an operation. This report excited widespread interest in the resuscitation work of Wiggers and Beck. In addition to his studies of electroshock resuscitation, Wiggers conducted research on heart sounds, pulse pressures, and the dynamics of the atria and ventricles of the heart. His research also included clinical and experimental studies of the hemodynamics of valvular lesions, including mitral valve and aortic stenosis; high blood pressure; and hardening of the arteries. During World War II Wiggers developed a method for the standardization of experimental shock in dogs, which allowed investigators to compare tests of new therapeutic drugs and procedures.

A prolific writer, Wiggers published over 400 scientific articles and eight books, including an influential textbook, *Physiology of Health and Disease*, which was published in five editions from 1934 to 1949. A charter member of the circulation group of the American Physiological Society, Wiggers was elected president of the society in 1949. A member of the original advisory editorial board of the *American Heart Journal* (1925–1937), he served as the first editor of *Circulation Research*, founded in 1953 by the American Heart Association. The most prominent American cardiac physiologist in the first half of the twentieth century, Wiggers was elected to the National Academy of Sciences, and received, among many honors, the 1952 Gold Heart and 1955 Albert Lasker Awards from the American Heart Association. He died from a heart ailment in Cleveland.

• The Archives in the Historical Division of the Cleveland Medical Library Association has a collection of Wiggers's reprints and some correspondence. Wiggers's *Reminiscences and Adventures in Circulation Research* (1958) chronicles his experiences in research and teaching, and includes references to many of his scientific articles. The best source of biographical information is E. M. Landis, National Academy of Sciences, *Biographical Memoirs* 48 (1976): 363–97. Other sources include Harold Feil and James W. McCubbin, "Carl J. Wiggers, M.D., a Biographical Sketch," *Circulation Research* 6 (1958): 548–53; Louis Katz, "Foreword to Special Issue," *Circulation* 4 (1951): 483–84; and Walter C. Randall, "Carl J. Wiggers," *Physiologist* 21 (June 1978): 1–5. Also see W. Bruce Fye, "Ventricular Fibrillation and Defibrillation: Historical Perspectives with Emphasis on the Contributions of John MacWilliam, Carl Wiggers, and William Kouwenhoven," *Circulation* 71 (1985): 858–65.

SUSAN E. LEDERER

WIGGIN, Albert Henry (21 Feb. 1868–21 May 1951), banker, was born in Medfield, Massachusetts, the son of James Henry Wiggin, a Unitarian minister, and Laura Newman. After graduating from Boston's English High School in 1885, he went to work as a runner for J. B. Moors & Company and, eight months later, for another Boston bank, the National Bank of the Commonwealth, headed by his uncle. He rose to bookkeeper a year later. At twenty-three he became assistant to the national bank examiner in Boston. In 1892 he married Jessie Duncan Hayden, daughter of a Boston banker. They had two children. He was named assistant cashier of the Third National Bank of Boston in 1894, and from 1897 to 1899 he was vice president of the Eliot National Bank of Boston.

Wiggin left for New York in June 1899 to become vice president of the prestigious National Park Bank. He served simultaneously as vice president of two small Manhattan institutions, the Mutual Bank and the Mount Morris Bank.

On 9 February 1904 Wiggin was named vice president and director of Chase National Bank. Less than a quarter the size of National City Bank, Chase derived most of its deposits from out-of-town banks using its correspondent services. He cultivated commercial and industrial accounts, which grew 183 percent within a decade as financial institutions' deposits increased 115 percent. He invited leading businessmen to become Chase directors. In turn he sat on many corporate boards—fifty-three excluding Chase entities in the early 1930s—usually expecting these firms to maintain a deposit relationship with Chase.

Wiggin was the key Chase decision maker from January 1911, when he became president, until his retirement twenty-two years later. He "dictates the policies," the national bank examination report noted in 1928. Wiggin acknowledged only that Chase had been under his "general direction." In January 1918 Wiggin became chair. He subsequently had various official titles, ending his career as chair of Chase's governing board from 31 May 1930 until he retired on 10 January 1933. Chase's deposits soared from $91 million at the end of 1910 to $2.074 billion twenty years later, while capital and surplus increased from $13 million to $358 million. Recognizing that Chase was "in no small measure a monument to his energy, wisdom, vision, and character," a unanimous directorate voted him a lifetime annual retainer of $100,000.

Shareholders numbered twenty in 1904; 2,189 in 1921; 50,510 in 1929; and 89,000 by 1933. Wiggin valued widespread ownership as "an asset of good-will" for Chase.

By 1918, without a single merger, Chase had grown to be the fourth largest bank in the United States. Seven commercial bank acquisitions (1921–1930) greatly enlarged the institution, beginning with Metropolitan Bank's seven local branches (1921). Chase's first branches outside the city, located in Havana, Cristobal, and Panama City (1925), were acquired from American Foreign Banking Corporation. Offices in London, Paris, Berlin, and Rome were added from 1927 to 1929. The combination with Equitable Trust Company on 2 June 1930 made Chase the largest bank in the world for a time. It remained the largest in the United States until overtaken by California's Bank of America in 1946. Chase "is known in every town in the country and in a great deal of the rest of the world," a proud Wiggin told the Senate Banking Committee in October 1933. As of 1930 Chase had some 7,000 bank correspondents all over the United States.

Known as "the man with a million friends," Wiggin stood by his business customers. Paul Warburg noted that he "would never go back on a friend." His courageous and active role in the crisis that started in the fall of 1929 enhanced his already high standing. Chase made more than a quarter of the total increase in the stock exchange loans by all U.S. banks in the last week of October 1929. The long-term basis of Chase's policy in the crisis years 1907, 1914, and 1921, "that those times of bad business were temporary," proved beneficial to the bank.

Wiggin did not anticipate the "tremendous world collapse" of 1930–1931. "It was a mistake not being more cold-blooded and more harsh," he admitted in late 1933. He remained confident, though, that Chase would gain from not being as cruel as it might have been. Chase had to write down assets and reserve against losses in excess of $212 million, and book value per share shrank by 54 percent between 1929 and 1933. A share of Chase sold for 4.38 times book value at the peak in 1929 but was worth only 45 percent of book value in 1932.

Chase was the leading American bank lender to Germany, and 3.5 percent of Chase's total assets were in German credits at the end of 1931. Wiggin, the U.S. representative, chaired the ten-nation committee that in August 1931 arranged a six-month standstill agreement, which had to be extended several times. Columbia conferred on Wiggin an honorary doctor of laws degree in June 1932, recognizing his "noteworthy constructive service in studying and adjusting difficult and involved economic and financial international relations which are the legacy of the Great War." In June 1933 he made his sixth European trip in two years as representative of American bank interests.

Wiggin testified before the Senate Banking Committee investigating stock exchange practices in October and November 1933. The ordeal did not embitter him, according to Wiggin's daughter. Committee counsel Ferdinand Pecora excoriated him, "In the entire investigation, it is doubtful if there was another instance of a corporate executive who so thoroughly and successfully used his official and fiduciary position for private profit" (Pecora, p. 161). A few days after describing it to the committee, Wiggin terminated his retainer arrangement with Chase. In December 1933 Winthrop W. Aldrich told Pecora that, in the light of the revelations, Chase's directors now considered the December 1932 action to have been a mistake. Wiggin, while denying claims of improper management, paid Chase $2 million in settlement of a shareholder's suit. A senior executive at the time, Wiggin assumed sole responsibility for the losses consequent on the alleged negligence.

The so-called "anti-Wiggin provisions" of the Securities and Exchange Act of June 1934 (sec. 16[b]) dealt with practices brought to light by Pecora. Insiders were now liable to the issuing corporation for trading profits and were forbidden to sell short.

In the spring of 1934 Aldrich arranged for Wiggin to exchange his Chase stock for shares in the holding company owning American Express. That firm had become part of Chase Securities in July 1929. Chase was rebuffed when it sought to acquire American Express in 1946 and again in 1949. In 1949 Wiggin sold his 24 percent interest in American Express, stipulating that it would not be broken up or wind up owned by Chase. Wiggin died at his summer home in Greenwich, Connecticut. His two daughters inherited most of his almost $19 million estate.

A memorial resolution unanimously adopted by Chase's board (which included Aldrich) mentioned Wiggin's "sturdy integrity and homespun virtue." General Electric's Owen D. Young described him as "the most colorful and attractive figure in the commercial banking world" of his time.

• There is no known collection of Wiggin papers. Chase Manhattan archives have some file folders of printed materials. For more information on Wiggin see "Head of the World's Largest Bank," *Bankers Magazine*, Nov. 1930, pp. 637–40; Marjorie Wiggin Prescott, *New England Son* (1949); U.S. Senate, Committee on Banking and Currency, *Stock*

Exchange Practices: Hearings, pts. 5–7, 73d Cong., 1st sess., 1933–1934; Ferdinand Pecora, *Wall Street under Oath: The Story of Our Modern Money Changers* (1939); and Arthur M. Johnson, *Winthrop W. Aldrich: Lawyer, Banker, Diplomat* (1968).

BENJAMIN J. KLEBANER

WIGGIN, Kate Douglas (28 Sept. 1856–24 Aug. 1923), educator and novelist, was born in Philadelphia, Pennsylvania, the daughter of Robert Noah Smith, a lawyer, and Helen Elizabeth Dyer. Her father died when she was three, and her mother then settled in Maine, which became a favorite setting for Wiggin's fiction. Three years after her father's death, her mother married Albion Bradbury, a physician. Although Wiggin attended several schools during childhood and adolescence, much of her education was under her stepfather's tutelage.

When she was seventeen she followed her family to Santa Barbara, California, where her stepfather hoped to improve his health and to invest in real estate. However, he died in 1876, leaving the family money invested in land of declining value. In 1877, while searching for a means of earning a living, Wiggin found her calling in the educational theories of Friedrich Froebel, whose ideas had been embraced by several of the New England Transcendentalists. In Froebel's kindergartens, children were not subjected to rote and drill but engaged in voluntary cooperative play and learned to help each other while their instructors gave attention to the individual qualities of each child. After completing a training course she first operated her own school in Santa Barbara and then was selected to organize the Silver Street Kindergarten in the slums of San Francisco, the first free kindergarten in the western United States.

During the summer of 1879, in the process of consulting kindergarten specialists, she met several members of the Concord group, including Elizabeth Peabody, William Ellery Channing, Bronson Alcott, and Ralph Waldo Emerson. The following year in San Francisco she opened the California Kindergarten Training School, at the same time continuing to operate the Silver Street school and energetically promoting her cause in speeches and articles.

In 1881 she married Samuel Bradley Wiggin, a lawyer, and passed direct management of the kindergarten to her sister Nora Smith. However, she maintained a lifelong interest in kindergarten projects and continued to direct her training school until 1884, when she and her husband moved to New York. At this time the focus of her life began to change. In 1883 she had published *The Story of Patsy* and in 1887 *The Birds' Christmas Carol*, both of which made money for her educational projects. Both books were well received and Wiggin, almost reluctantly, began to think of herself as a writer. In her autobiographical *My Garden of Memory* she writes:

> I am not at all sure even now about the precise quality of such powers as I possess, although I am well aware of my deficiencies as an author. . . . I half believe that Nature intended me, not for a writer, but for a teacher. I could always teach a thing whether I knew it or not, and I think I might always have remained a teacher had not my nerves been worn threadbare by "pioneering." (p. 166)

Her husband's death in 1889 left Wiggin dependent on authorship. The books she produced in ensuing years have various themes and locations, but a frequent setting is Maine, and a frequent subject is the career of an economically disadvantaged child. Her most successful work, *Rebecca of Sunnybrook Farm* (1903), is the story of a Maine girl reared by aunts because of her parents' poverty. Although it is considered a children's novel, it has adult appeal. It presents a Maine culture realistically and avoids the sentimentalities and most of the improbabilities common to late nineteenth- and early twentieth-century works with similar plots. Biographer Helen Frances Benner's statement about Wiggin has a special application to this novel: "She was the first to portray realistically, yet with sympathetic humor, Maine inland village character" (p. 136).

In 1895 she married George Christopher Riggs, an importer. Wiggin had no children. During most years they spent spring in Europe, summer in Hollis, Maine, and winter in New York, where they entertained Mark Twain, William Dean Howells, Clyde Fitch, Richard Harding Davis, Hamlin Garland, Rudyard Kipling, Sir Henry Irving, Ellen Terry, and many others. In the midst of her literary activity, she collaborated with her sister Nora on a three-volume work based on her lectures at the Kindergarten Training School, published under the general title *The Republic of Childhood* (1895–1896). Her fiction became extremely popular, extending to editions in ten languages, and she was in great demand as a speaker, often appearing before high school fan clubs.

Throughout her life Wiggin maintained a demanding pace of writing, speaking, and organizing. She worked with groups as varied as the Dorcas club, a women's civic club, and the New York Kindergarten Association, of which she was vice president for several years and was honored in 1912 for twenty years of active service. In 1922 years of overwork resulted in failing health as she became ill on a voyage to England. She left London for a nursing home at Harrow-on-the-Hill, where she died. Most of her books are no longer read, but two of them, *The Birds' Christmas Carol* and *Rebecca of Sunnybrook Farm*, are still read by children. Of these, the latter especially deserves to survive as a work of artistic merit. In addition, the kindergarten movement that Wiggin sponsored became one of the foundations of education in our society.

• Collections of Wiggin's papers are at the New York Public Library, at Harvard, and at Dartmouth. Wiggin's publications not mentioned above include: *The Village Watch-Tower* (1895), *Nine Love Songs and a Carol* (1896), *The Old Peabody Pew* (1907), *Half-a-Dozen Housekeepers* (1903), *Robinetta* (1911), *The Romance of a Christmas Card* (1916), *The Writings of Kate Douglas Wiggin* (1917), *Ladies in Waiting* (1919),

Homespun Tales (1920), and *Love by Express* (1924). Her autobiography, *My Garden of Memory* (1923), is supplemented by Nora Archibald Smith's *Kate Douglas Wiggin as Her Sister Knew Her* (1925). A good critical biography is Helen Frances Benner, "Kate Douglas Wiggin's Country of Childhood," *University of Maine Bulletin* 58, no. 12 (1956), which comprises the entire issue. An obituary is in the *New York Times*, 25 Aug. 1923.

MARYJEAN GROSS
DALTON GROSS

WIGGINS, A. L. M. (9 Apr. 1891–7 July 1980), banker, businessman, and undersecretary of the U.S. Treasury, was born Archibald Lee Manning Wiggins in Durham, North Carolina, the son of Archie Lee Wiggins and Margaret London Council. A. L. M.'s father had just started a private heating and plumbing supply business at the time of his death, when Wiggins was less than a year old. Wiggins's mother did odd jobs—mostly sewing—to put her son through school. In the Durham city schools he acquired a love of poetry and learned to strive for excellence. It made such an impression on A. L. M. that he devoted several pages of his *Autobiography* (1969) to his time there.

At age thirteen Wiggins worked in an uncle's print shop and then found a job at American Tobacco Company. Eventually he learned to use calculating equipment and bookkeeping methods before interrupting his full-time employment for college at the University of North Carolina at Chapel Hill, where he managed the university's print shop and edited the college annual. He graduated in 1913, whereupon he moved to Hartsville, South Carolina, to work for Daniel R. Coker at the J. L. Coker and Company partnership. That firm included agricultural supply businesses, cotton buying and selling services, and seed supply. Wiggins participated in expanding the business, being named secretary and treasurer in 1918. A year later Coker assigned general management responsibilities to Wiggins, who held the position of vice president and managing director until 1947, when he became undersecretary of the Treasury of the United States. In 1915 Wiggins married Pauline Lawton, and they had four children. Both Wiggins and his wife were Baptists, and he contributed his service to Baptist organizations such as the Baptist Foundation of South Carolina.

Placing advertisements for the Coker business in the *Hartsville Messenger* revived Wiggins's interest in printing and publishing. He bought the *Hartsville Messenger* in 1921 after the newspaper had experienced difficulties associated with the agricultural depression of the early 1920s. Wiggins operated the paper at a loss for several years, finally turning a profit in 1927. As with his position at the Coker company, Wiggins disassociated himself from publishing to move to Washington in 1947. However, he never completely abandoned publishing; in 1951 he organized a new corporation, the Hartsville Publishing Company, to hold the assets of all his publishing and printing interests. Under his control, the *Hartsville Messenger* became the first weekly paper in South Carolina to feature a regular column on black affairs edited by blacks. Wiggins supported blacks throughout his career. For example, in the 1960s he led the financial community's support for desegregation.

Wiggins's greatest contribution came in the field of banking and finance, stemming from his formation of the Trust Company of South Carolina in 1919. The Trust Company ownership group also quickly acquired the Bank of Hartsville. With Wiggins as vice president and managing director, the banks immediately experienced the effects of the depression afflicting South Carolina's agriculture. Wiggins helped guide the bank through the 1920s when other institutions closed with regularity. Acquisition of the Bank of Hartsville gave Wiggins a position in both institutions, and in 1932 he became president of the Hartsville bank. That same year he was also a member of the Banking and Industrial Committee, a committee formed by President Hoover, with representatives from each state. He participated in the liquidation of several other local banks. Partly as a result of surviving the 1920s, Wiggins had the questionable honor of being named president of the South Carolina Bankers Association (SCBA) at the worst time in the state's banking history, 1931–1932. His activities involved coordinating federal and state programs and put him in touch with federal regulators. He chaired the Federal Legislative Committee of the American Bankers Association (ABA), for example, which spoke for bankers at congressional hearings. He received appointments to several regional and national committees and commissions, honing his political skills and broadening his experience in dealing with national issues. Wiggins was on the regional advisory committee to the Reconstruction Finance Corp. (RFC) from 1930 to 1946. In 1936, as chairman of the SCBA's legislative committee, Wiggins drafted the blueprint for reorganizing the state's banking department.

In his *Autobiography*, Wiggins correctly termed management of his bank as "progressive." He pioneered installment lending long before other institutions considered it fashionable. He also initiated "character" loans, based on need with no collateral.

Following his service as president of the SCBA, Wiggins was appointed to the Executive Council of the ABA, rising to the presidency in 1943. During his service on the council and as president, Wiggins worked with the Federal Legislative Committee of the ABA that helped shape New Deal banking legislation. He especially worked on two issues, federal subsidization of agriculture and socialization of credit. Wiggins helped shape ABA policy statements on the Farm Credit Administration and the Production Credit System, although, as *Barron's* noted, Wiggins was "no torch-totin' New Dealer" (1 Nov. 1943). Indeed, the plaque presented to him by the ABA after his presidency summed up his position: "Lee Wiggins, Country Banker."

Wiggins's experience in those national matters led the Harry S. Truman administration to name him undersecretary of the Treasury in 1947. In that capacity

Wiggins crafted a formula of assessing Federal Deposit Insurance Corporation fees to member banks for deposit insurance, which Secretary of the Treasury John W. Snyder accepted. As Wiggins explained in his *Autobiography*, "I did not go to the Treasury with any crusading mission. I only wanted to do a good, workmanlike job" (p. 131).

Wiggins resigned from Treasury in 1948, but not from public service. He worked from 1949 to 1953 as a special assistant to Secretary Snyder and from 1953–1955 under Secretary Gordon Humphrey. He worked for more than three years without compensation to reorganize the Bureau of Internal Revenue. In 1955 that appointment ended.

Wiggins returned to private business affairs, accepting a position as chairman of the Atlantic Coast Line Railroad and the Louisville and Nashville Railroad. He placed the roads on better financial footing and retired as chairman of both roads in 1961 to devote himself to Baptist and charitable work. Nevertheless, Wiggins was still known as the country banker when he died in Hartesville, South Carolina. A. L. M. Wiggins to the end was the "small town banker" made big—a self-made banker of national prominence whose only formal banking training was a correspondence course.

• In addition to South Carolina newspaper articles, material on Wiggins appears in *Autobiography of A. Lee M. Wiggins* (1969), which also contains excerpts of many of his speeches. Clippings of Wiggins's articles are in the Caroliniana Library, University of South Carolina. Wiggins also wrote *David R. Coker—A Great Man in My Life and in the Life of His Country* (1963) and made numerous addresses to the state assembly, to civic groups and, of course, to the South Carolina Bankers Association and the American Bankers Association, which retain copies of his official speeches. A general perspective on Wiggins and South Carolina banking appears in John G. Sproat and Larry Schweikart, *Making Change: South Carolina Banking in the 20th Century* (1990).

LARRY SCHWEIKART

WIGGLESWORTH, Edward (1693–16 Jan. 1765), educator and theologian, was born in Malden, Massachusetts, the son of Michael Wigglesworth, a minister, physician, and Puritan poet, and Sybil Avery Sparhawk or Sparrowhawk. His father, a Harvard graduate, was known principally for his popular, catechistic poem "The Day of Doom" (1662). Edward Wigglesworth received early training at the Boston Latin School, then matriculated to Harvard College, where he graduated in 1710. Between 1710 and 1720 he preached in a number of churches throughout the Massachusetts Bay Colony and worked briefly for both the school at Casco Bay Fort and the Boston Latin School.

In 1721 Wigglesworth returned to Cambridge to become Harvard's first Hollis Professor of Divinity, a chair established by college benefactor Thomas Hollis. Prior to offering him the position, however, the Harvard Board of Overseers required him to affirm his position as a proper representative of the orthodox faith. Wigglesworth's declaration of religious principles, which included his belief in the Holy Trinity and the doctrine of predestination, satisfied the Board of Overseers, who granted him the position on 24 January 1722. Over the next forty-one years, Wigglesworth's affiliation with Harvard College grew in a number of ways. In 1723 he declined the rectorship of Yale College, a position he would decline again in 1761. In 1724 he was selected as an overseer at Harvard, and in 1726 he married Sarah Leverett, the daughter of President John Leverett. Theirs was a brief, childless marriage, as Sarah died in 1727. Two years later Wigglesworth married Rebecca Coolidge; they had four children. In 1730 Wigglesworth received a doctorate in divinity from the University of Edinburgh, Scotland, and he served as the commissioner of London's Society for Propagating the Gospel among Indians until 1755. He spent the remaining years of his life in Cambridge at Harvard, teaching, preaching, and engaging in some of the most difficult religious and intellectual controversies of his day in spite of periods of frail health and a worsening hearing disability.

Wigglesworth's tenure as Hollis Professor of Divinity spanned a turbulent period for religion in New England. The changes in his personal religious viewpoints were representative of those of the Congregationalist orthodoxy throughout a period that saw the rise of revivalism, the Great Awakening, and the numerous battles over theological controversies that would indelibly alter the history of religion in New England. Wigglesworth was a harsh critic of the itinerant evangelical ministers, whose numbers rose during the Great Awakening. An "Old Light" and a prominent representative of the Harvard theological faction, he objected to the evangelicals' stress on emotions, preferring instead a religion that foregrounded reason and intellect, an approach evangelicals regarded as little more than a system of bloodless moralism. In particular, Wigglesworth took issue with George Whitefield, who, upon arriving in Cambridge in 1745, levied charges against Harvard for what he saw as the school's disproportionate focus on the minds of its students at the expense of any concern for their hearts. In *A Letter to the Reverend Mr. George Whitefield* (1745) and *Some Distinguishing Characters of the Extraordinary and Ordinary Ministers of the Church of Christ* (1754), Wigglesworth addressed the criticisms of Whitefield and decried the rise of the evangelical clergymen.

Throughout this period of controversy, Wigglesworth and the members of the Harvard orthodoxy proved themselves anything but intractable, significantly altering some of their previously held theological opinions. The changes evinced in Wigglesworth's sermons from earlier efforts, such as *A Discourse Concerning the Duration of the Punishment of the Wicked* (1729), through *An Enquiry into the Truth of the Imputation of the Guilt of Adam's First Sin* (1738), and culminating in *The Doctrine of Reprobation Briefly Considered* (1763), illustrate one of the changes in the Boston-based heterodoxy: the displacement of strict Calvinist doctrine and the gradual embrace of certain

Arminian principles. This shift in theology liberated individuals from a predestined sentence of "good" or "evil," thereby granting them a more active role in determining the status of their salvation. In 1756 Wigglesworth faced another controversy when Jonathan Edwards petitioned him to use his power as the Hollis Professor to refute the Arian views supported by individuals like Jonathan Mayhew. According to an Arian view of the godhead, Jesus was to be placed in a subordinate position to God. Those espousing this belief still regarded Jesus as divine, but their system disrupted the traditional Congregationalist view of the Trinity, which accorded equal status to a three-person god. Wigglesworth, seeking to avoid a public schism, decided that a personal response was unnecessary, advising the reissuance of a previously published English response to the controversy.

Wigglesworth continued to serve as a Harvard overseer throughout his lifetime and maintained his position as Hollis Professor of Divinity until just before his death, when the position was granted to his son Edward Wigglesworth. He died in Cambridge. His lengthy tenure at Harvard, one of the most important ministerial colleges of the time, during an era of such religious upheaval, placed Wigglesworth squarely in the center of various New England religious controversies. He stands, in many ways, as a representative of the change that transpired among those associated with the Harvard theological community. The combination of his more liberal stance on the Calvinist/Arminian question and his refusal to openly fight the Arian issue reflects the evolving principles of his milieu and, in many ways, anticipates the nineteenth-century flowering of Unitarianism.

• In addition to the works mentioned above, Wigglesworth produced a number of short works, most of them theological in nature, that are in the American Antiquarian Society's *Early American Imprints, 1639–1800* microform collection. The Harvard Archives and the Andover-Harvard Theological Library house print editions of some of these works. For a critical appraisal of these writings, see Rick W. Sturdevant, "Edward Wigglesworth," in *American Writers before 1800: A Biographical and Critical Dictionary*, ed. James A. Levernier and Douglas R. Wilmes (1983). Further biographical information about Wigglesworth and his role in the changing face of New England religious life is in Nathaniel Appleton, *A Faithful and Wise Servant Had in Honour . . . A Discourse Occasioned by the . . . Death of the Rev. Edward Wigglesworth* (1765), with a short biography appended; Charles Chauncy, "A Sketch of Eminent Men in New England," *Massachusetts Historical Society Collections*, ser. 1, 10 (1809); J. B. Felt, *Ecclesiastical History of New England* (1855); F. H. Foster, *A Genetic History of the New England Theology* (1907); Perry Miller, *The New England Mind: From Colony to Province* (1961); L. R. Paige, *History of Cambridge, Massachusetts* (1877), with *Supplement and Index* by M. I. Gazzaldi (1930); W. B. Sprague, *Annals of the American Pulpit*, vol. 1 (1857); and Conrad Wright, *The Beginnings of Unitarianism in America* (1955).

CHRISTOPHER GOODSON

WIGGLESWORTH, Michael (18 Oct. 1631–10 June 1705), Puritan minister and poet, was born in Yorkshire, England, the son of Edward Wigglesworth, a tradesman, and Esther (or Hester, maiden name unknown). In 1638 the Wigglesworths left Yorkshire and persecution for religion for Charlestown, New England, and subsequently for New Haven, where the family spent the winter in a basement and where Michael became ill. Physical debility remained and affected the minister-poet throughout his life. Wigglesworth was sent to Ezekiel Cheever for his formal education at the age of eight, but he returned after two years to assist his injured father on the farm. Proving himself unfit for husbandry, Wigglesworth was returned to Cheever in 1644, who prepared him to enter Harvard three years later. Initially preparing to pursue medicine, he experienced conversion after three and one half years at Harvard and decided to enter the ministry instead, remaining at Harvard as a tutor and fellow until 1654, at which time he was offered the pulpit in Malden, Massachusetts.

Unsure of his calling, Wigglesworth preached in Malden until the summer of 1655 but was unable to fully commit himself. During this period he kept his well-known diary, documenting spiritual uncertainties brought about by his illness, his sexual desires, and doubts over his calling. A recurrent nightmare recorded in the diary depicts God on his throne separating sheep from goats—a vision that produced terror he found difficult to overcome and that would become a dominant image of his first major poem. Later that year he married Mary Reyner, a cousin, and settled in Malden with his mother and sister, Abigail. Mercy, the couple's only child, was born in 1656. Wigglesworth was not formally ordained until 1657, and in 1658 his ill health prevented him from fulfilling all his obligations to the townspeople. Wigglesworth struggled against his own poor health and the pressure from the parish to perform his duties for several years, and in 1659 his wife Mary died, adding to his difficulties. In 1661, at odds with his congregation and concerned about his own and the community's spiritual state, he turned to the writing of *The Day of Doom*, a poem describing Judgment Day.

The Day of Doom, published in 1662, was an immediate success. The first edition of 1,800 copies sold out within one year and clearly appealed to the needs and fears of its Puritan New England audience. Writing what Cotton Mather would call "Truth's dressed up in a *Plaine Meeter*," Wigglesworth described the Last Judgment in frightening detail, relying upon familiar scriptural allusion and millennial fear. The edificatory poem was further enhanced by common meter and internal rhyme, making the poem easy to memorize, and many did memorize it. Although the poem has been regarded as rhymed religious abstraction and biblical paraphrase, in fact Wigglesworth's scriptural allusion and paraphrase synthesized fragments of the Bible into a new vision for New England. Whether as an articulation of popular anxiety or as edificatory poetry, the poem enjoyed significant and lasting popularity. A second printing followed in 1663 or 1664, and three English editions and two American editions were published before the end of the seventeenth century. Wigglesworth's last edition, in 1701, was followed by eight more editions in the eighteenth and nineteenth centuries.

After sending *The Day of Doom* to press, Wigglesworth treated his concern for the community in "God's Controversy with New-England," which was not published until 1873. Using the language of Isaiah and Deuteronomy, the poem calls upon New Englanders to consider their behavior in light of "the years of many generations," comparing his community to that of the Israelites and comparing the New England migration to the Exodus, typical Puritan motifs.

In September 1663 Wigglesworth left Malden for Bermuda to improve his health. He returned the following year to find that Malden had hired Benjamin Bunker as minister. Wigglesworth continued to serve the medical needs of the community and began to tutor local boys for Harvard. His health still uneven, in 1669 Wigglesworth composed *Meat Out of the Eater; or, Meditations Concerning the Necessity, End, and Usefulness of Afflictions unto Gods Children*, published in 1670. Unlike "God's Controversy with New-England," *Meat Out of the Eater* emphasizes the edification of individual souls. The poem consists of ten meditations and a concluding hortatory on the purifying nature of afflictions for the individual, and it combines biblical paraphrase and allusion in explaining the action of afflictions upon the soul. The poem, with its familiar and consistent short hymn meter, enjoyed some of the success of Wigglesworth's first book of poems; *Meat Out of the Eater* was printed four times during his lifetime and again in 1717 and 1770.

During the following decade, Wigglesworth's life changed little; suffering from ill health, he did not assume the pulpit despite the death of Bunker in 1670. In 1679 he caused some scandal by marrying his housekeeper, a much younger Martha Mudge, who bore six children. After the marriage, Wigglesworth found it necessary to offer his resignation as pastoral teacher in Malden because of the community's disrespect for his new wife—a resignation Malden ignored. Within two to three years, Wigglesworth's health improved remarkably, and by 1686, he assumed full responsibility as pastor-teacher in Malden. When Martha Mudge died in 1690, Wigglesworth continued in his duties as he was not able to do when his first wife died, and he became more involved in the affairs of New England, joining the "Cambridge Association" of Boston ministers concerned about the community's spiritual life. In 1691 he married Sybil Avery Sparhawk (or Sparrowhawk), who bore another child, Wigglesworth's second son. Until his death in Malden, Wigglesworth remained in Malden's pulpit and was active among the leaders of the bay colony.

As a writer of edificatory verse, Wigglesworth has no equal in early America, although he does not demonstrate the poetic sensibility of Anne Bradstreet or Edward Taylor. Despite this shortcoming, both *The Day of Doom* and *Meat Out of the Eater* demonstrate the Puritans' emphasis on theology in the conception of community and self.

• Wigglesworth papers, including a commonplace book, sermon notebook, and college notebooks, are held at the New England Historic Genealogical Society; other papers are found in the Collections of the Massachusetts Historical Society. Wigglesworth's diary is reprinted in Edmund Morgan's *The Diary of Michael Wigglesworth 1653–1657: The Conscience of a Puritan* (1946; repr. 1965). Two useful biographies are John Ward Dean, *Memoir of Rev. Michael Wigglesworth, Author of "The Day of Doom"* (1871), and Richard Crowder, *No Featherbed to Heaven: A Biography of Michael Wigglesworth, 1631–1705* (1962). Ronald A. Bosco has edited a scholarly edition, *The Poems of Michael Wigglesworth* (1989), that includes a thorough discussion of the poetry in the introduction. Also see Jeffrey Hammond, *Sinful Self, Saintly Self: The Puritan Experience of Poetry* (1993), which includes two important chapters on Wigglesworth's poetry and audience, and Alan H. Pope, "Petrus Ramus and Michael Wigglesworth: The Logic of Poetic Structure," in *Puritan Poets and Poetics: Seventeenth-Century American Poetic Theory and Practice*, ed. Peter White (1985).

RAYMOND A. CRAIG

WIGGS, Johnny (25 July 1899–9 Oct. 1977), jazz cornetist, bandleader, and promoter, was born John Wigginton Hyman in New Orleans, Louisiana, the son of a Mr. Hyman (given name unknown) and Alice (maiden name unknown). Both of Wiggs's parents sang, and his mother played piano. He attended LaSalle school. He started to play the mandolin in 1907, studying from an older cousin until he discovered that he could play anything he wanted by ear and quit taking lessons. In 1908 he heard a bottle man who "had a New Year's Eve noisemaking horn that had a brass reed and a wooden mouthpiece. . . . That man blew . . . the dirtiest blues sounds I have ever heard. Those sounds got into my ear and stayed there," he later told writer George W. Kay. Influenced by this experience, he bought a cornet at age ten.

When Wiggs was twelve his family moved to Ocean Springs, Mississippi, where his father bought a farm. As a young teenager he played violin with hillbilly bands. He also learned to read music for cornet and joined a brass band. In 1915 his father had a stroke. The family then moved back to New Orleans; Wiggs's father died soon afterward.

In 1916 Wiggs heard jazz cornetist Joe Oliver at a dance at the Tulane Gymnasium. Later he heard recordings by the Original Dixieland Jazz Band. The music of both had a great influence on Wiggs. Working by day, he attended night school, studying law at Loyola University. In 1919 he traveled to New York for the summer. He returned to Loyola, secured a job writing for the *New Orleans Item*, and then transferred to Tulane University to study journalism. One night, while in class, he got scooped by another reporter, and as a consequence he lost his job the next day and had to drop out of college.

Wiggs then went to work as a sailor, voyaging to England and then back to Charleston, South Carolina.

He then bicycled and hitchhiked to New York City. After a year of trying to learn the violin, he returned to New Orleans, took up the cornet again, and began working professionally.

Wiggs's first jobs were with little-known bandleaders like drummer Earl Crumb and His New Orleans Owls at the Grunewald Hotel, Norman Brownlee, Dee Laroque at Beverly Gardens, Happy Schilling, and Jimmy Maguire between 1924 and 1926. He also had an opportunity to record two titles in 1927 as the leader of John Hyman's Bayou Stompers. "Ain't Love Grand" and "Alligator Blues" follow in the mold of Frankie Trumbauer's contemporary Dixieland jazz recordings, in which wacky little excursions into dissonance add a mannered edge to an otherwise straightforward and tuneful context; not coincidentally, he greatly admired Trumbauer's famous cornetist, Bix Beiderbecke.

In 1927 Wiggs played with pianist Peck Kelley and guitarist Snoozer Quinn for a few weeks in a dance orchestra at the Washington Hotel in Shreveport, Louisiana. He then joined a vaudeville band on the Loew's theater circuit, touring the eastern states and Canada. Back home in 1928, he worked by day in Werlein's Music Store while playing at night with clarinetist Tony Parenti at La Vida Dance Hall; he recorded two titles with Parenti. By this time he had married Betty (maiden name unknown); they had two daughters.

Wiggs worked for a time as a freelancer and then spent a year and a half with Ellis Stratakos's Hotel Jung Roof Orchestra, from 1929 to 1930, recording two further titles (1929). He then rejoined Crumb's band at the Suburban Gardens and then quit playing professionally to major in music at Loyola while working at Werlein's. On the condition that he would finish his degree in music, he obtained a job teaching music in New Orleans elementary schools. He taught clarinetist Pete Fountain and trumpeter George Girard in public school and organized his own state band and orchestra.

Seven years later, still without a music degree and drinking heavily, Wiggs switched careers again, studying architecture and mechanical drawing at Tulane. He taught these subjects at Fortier High School in the early 1940s and two years later transferred to Warren Easton High School.

From 1946 to 1947, known now as Johnny Wiggs, he led a six-piece jazz band on WSMB radio in New Orleans. He adopted this new surname, Wiggs, so as not to offend the parish (county) school board, which disapproved of his playing "indecent" music, that is, jazz, while still teaching children. When the radio job ended, he began looking for a forum to support local jazzmen. In 1948 he helped found the New Orleans Jazz Club, serving as first president. He brought many jazz musicians out of involuntary retirement, sponsored concerts and parades, established the New Orleans Jazz Museum (acquired by the Louisiana State Museum in New Orleans in 1979), and started the Jazz Club Radio Show, which ran on station WWL for at least three decades.

Wiggs recorded regularly from 1948 to 1957. A representative sampling of his playing may be heard on the albums *Sounds of New Orleans, ii* (1950–1955) and *Johnny Wiggs and His New Orleans Kings* (1953), recorded with a local New Orleans Dixieland band that included such veteran players as trombonist Tom Brown, clarinetist Harry Shields, and banjoist Edmond Souchon. He retired from teaching architecture and mechanical drawing in 1960. From 1965 onward he performed regularly at Preservation Hall and also at private parties and New Orleans Jazz Club concerts. He recorded again occasionally between 1968 and 1974, including discs made during this period in annual performances at the Manassas Jazz Festival in Virginia. After performing at the New Orleans Jazz and Heritage Festival in 1974, he became ill. Suffering from angina and other problems, he retired from playing. He died in New Orleans.

Strictly as a jazz cornetist, Wiggs was not of considerable importance, being one of many players who ably followed the styles of Oliver or Beiderbecke. But his position as a professional and historically oriented jazz cornetist gave him the authority to take a leading role in the revival and preservation of jazz in New Orleans.

• Shortly before his death Wiggs gave a detailed autobiographical account in "Wiggs Self-Explained," *Second Line* 30 (Spring 1977): 3–13. See also a taped interview of 26 Aug. 1962 by William Russell, held in the William Ransom Hogan Jazz Archive at Tulane University, a summary of which was published in microform as *New York Times Oral History Program: New Orleans Jazz Oral History Collection of Tulane University*, no. 46 (1978), chap. 176. Also useful are Al Rose, "Both of . . . Johnny Wiggs," *Second Line* 2 (Sept.–Oct. 1961): 11–14, 24; Larry Borenstein and Bill Russell (text) and Noel Rockmore (paintings), *Preservation Hall Portraits* (1968); George W. Kay, "The Johnny Wiggs Story," *Jazz Journal* 23 (June 1970): 12–14; and Peter R. Haby, "Johnny Wiggs," *Footnote* (Oct.–Nov. 1977): 4–14, which includes a catalog of recordings. Rose Souchon and Edmond Souchon, *New Orleans Jazz: A Family Album*, 3d ed. (1984), and William Carter, *Preservation Hall: Music from the Heart* (1991), are good histories. An obituary is in *New Orleans Times-Picayune*, 14 Oct. 1977.

BARRY KERNFELD

WIGHT, Peter Bonnett (1 Aug. 1838–8 Sept. 1925), architect, was born in New York City, the son of Amherst Wight, a lawyer, and Joanna G. Sanderson. He attended public school and the Free Academy (later the City College of New York), receiving a bachelor of arts degree in 1855. Having pursued a classical course of study, Wight read widely on architecture with a concentration on John Ruskin, a proponent of the Gothic style. In school he met Russell Sturgis, who would become a later associate and important Ruskinian devotee himself. An accomplished draftsman, Wight spent a postgraduate year cultivating his drawing before apprenticing with New York architects Thomas R. Jackson and later Isaac G. Perry. In 1858 a family friend and real estate speculator, Josiah L. James, gave Wight an opportunity to go to Chicago,

Illinois, to design a building for himself and his partner George Springer. He was given office space with James and Springer's architects, Carter & Bauer, and there remodeled the Commercial Club, which burned in the Chicago fire of 1871.

In 1859 Wight returned to New York. In 1861, a virtual unknown, Wight won the competition to design the building for the National Academy of Design. Because of him the Academy introduced America to the Italian Gothic style. From 1863 to 1868 Wight shared office space and presumably was in practice with his former classmate Russell Sturgis. Together Wight, Sturgis, and others published the *New Path* (1863–1865), a journal dedicated to Ruskinian reform in the arts. In 1864 Wight received the commission to design the Yale School of Fine Arts, the first college art school in America. That year he married Mary Frances Hoagland; they had two children before the marriage ended. Two more commissions, the Brooklyn Mercantile Library (1867–1869) and the T. P. Jacob House (1866–1868) in Louisville, Kentucky, affirmed Wight's allegiance to the High Victorian Gothic style that he helped popularize in America. A member of the American Institute of Architects he, received a fellowship in 1866 and helped found the New York chapter in 1867.

In 1871 the great Chicago fire destroyed the city and cleared the way for a massive architectural rebuilding. Former co-worker Asher Carter, then of Carter and Drake, invited Wight to join in the city's reconstruction; thus Carter, Drake, and Wight was formed. The firm became Drake & Wight when Carter died two years later. Over the years the firm was prodigious in its efforts and was said to have built more than a mile of commercial frontage. Due to the vast rebuilding efforts, a great many architects passed through the doors of Wight's firm including John Wellborn Root and Daniel Burnham, who both left in 1873 to start their own practice. Toward the latter part of the decade, Drake and Wight dissolved their partnership and Wight was hired by the American Express Company to oversee the construction of their headquarters, which had been designed by H. H. Richardson. Upon completion, Wight was put in charge of all of their Chicago building operations. Around this same time, he began to be more active in the Chicago chapter of the American Institute of Architects.

It was also after the Chicago fire that Wight became interested in fireproofing, through improved methods of construction. He delivered speeches and published frequent articles on methods of fireproofing. With Drake, he invented a fireproof iron column, the first of many economical innovations in the field. By 1881 he had embarked on his second vocation by forming the Wight Fireproofing Company. The following year he married Marion Olney. His company specialized in hollow tile construction and terra-cotta cladding of metal beams. This venture lasted until 1891, by which time Wight could say he was responsible for fireproofing more than two hundred buildings. Unwilling to retire, Wight took on work at the World's Columbian Exposition in 1893, acting as an architect and design consultant for numerous private buildings on the grounds. From 1893 to 1895 he consulted on the design of elevated railroad stations in Chicago. As secretary-treasurer of the Illinois Board of Examiners (1897–1914), he played a crucial role in the passage of the 1897 law that required licensing by examination for all architects—the first of its kind in America. Wight also authored more than 125 articles throughout his career.

In 1918, at the age of eighty, Wight finally retired. He left Chicago and moved to Pasadena, California, where he died.

• Wight's scrapbook is in the Burnham Library of Architecture at the Art Institute of Chicago and includes papers, drawings, and photographs. Among Wight's books worth noting is his *National Academy of Design: Photographs of the New Building with an Introductory Essay and Description* (1866). Michael Thomas Klare, "The Life and Architecture of Peter Bonnett Wight" (M.A. thesis, Columbia Univ., 1968), has an excellent bibliography of Wight's periodical publications. See also Sarah Bradford Landau, *P. B. Wight; Architect, Contractor, and Critic, 1838–1925* (1981), which also has a list of Wight's articles.

AMY L. GOLD

WIGHTMAN, Hazel Hotchkiss (20 Dec. 1886–5 Dec. 1974), tennis player, teacher, and patron, was born Hazel Virginia Hotchkiss in Healdsburg, California, the daughter of William Joseph Hotchkiss, a ranch owner and cannery founder, and Emma Lucretia Grove. In poor health as a child, Hazel became robust and athletic playing baseball, cricket, and field sports with her older brothers Miller, Homer, and Marius, and her friends. In 1900 her father moved his office to San Francisco, California, and the family's residence to Berkeley, California, where his children played lawn tennis. Two years later her brothers took Hazel to watch the Pacific States (later Pacific Coast) championships in San Rafael, California. She thought a Sutton sisters baseline duel monotonous but, on a subsequent trip, thrilled to the spectacular volleying, smashing, and net attack of the brothers Samuel and Sumner Hardy, former Pacific champions. The youngsters played on the asphalt court at the University of California at Berkeley during early mornings; they later played on their home makeshift court, where erratic bounces on gravel forced them to volley constantly to sustain rallies. Wightman also practiced solo against a barn wall. Self-taught, she quickly mastered grips, strokes, footwork, and proper balance, and her forte as a net and overhead attacker was established early.

In December 1902 Wightman won the Bay Counties women's doubles tournament at Golden Gate Park in San Francisco. In 1904 she captured the California women's singles title and lost the Pacific States final to Florence Sutton. Two years later she captured the Pacific States crown and, for the first time, defeated a member of the Sutton family, Ethel Sutton Bruce. Wightman lost that championship in 1907 to May Sutton Bundy but did gain the California and Pacific Northwest titles before entering the freshman class at the University of California. She won eight 1908 singles competitions and lost only twice, to Florence Sutton and to May Sutton Bundy. Wightman's abilities so impressed visiting sportsman George Wright that he persuaded her parents to let her enter the 1909 U.S. women's championships at the Philadelphia (Pa.) Cricket Club. Agile, square-framed, and just 5′½″ tall, the right-handed Wightman exhibited extraordinary concentration. Uniquely among women, she smashed, volleyed, and net-rushed like a man and developed a sound all-court game, including accurate forehand and backhand chops and slices, well-placed sliced serves, and offensive lobs. Invariably she found and exploited opponents' weaknesses. Although Wightman was excellent in singles play, her special skills made her even better in doubles; and in mixed doubles she showed others by her example that women could be active, not passive, partners. Most conspicuously, she demonstrated that fierce competitors can maintain consistent, exemplary levels of good sportsmanship.

While in Philadelphia playing in sleeveless dimity dresses, Wightman captured three U.S. championships on the same day: singles, by routing defending titleholder Maud Barger Wallach; doubles, with Edith Rotch; and mixed doubles, with Wallace F. Johnson. After returning to California she won four singles tournaments but lost twice to May Sutton Bundy and once to Florence Sutton. She first beat May Sutton in April 1910 at Ojai Valley, California. She then repeated her U.S. championship triple, without dropping a set. Fatigued by the journey home, she immediately lost to Bruce but scored four more singles tournament triumphs and lost a close match to May Sutton at the Pacific championships.

After her graduation from the University of California, Hotchkiss won all her events at ten tournaments in 1911: ten singles, seven mixed doubles, and five doubles. That year she made her third consecutive sweep of U.S. titles, a feat never before accomplished but later equaled by Mary K. Browne and Alice Marble. She won the doubles with Eleo Sears and the mixed doubles with Maurice McLoughlin, and she defeated Florence Sutton, 8–10, 6–1, 9–7, to win the singles after surviving a match point against her. In other tournaments she defeated Florence Sutton four times. At Niagara-on-the-Lake, Ontario, Canada, Wightman played May Sutton for the first time outside California and on grass. Trailing 0–6, 1–5, Wightman finally adjusted to the heaviness of soggy balls on wet turf, and she ran off twelve consecutive games to conquer, 0–6, 7–5, 6–0. At the Longwood Cricket Club's women's tourney she swept three events, but more importantly she met George William Wightman of Harvard University, a mixed doubles first-round loser. They married on 24 February 1912 in Berkeley, resided in Brookline, Massachusetts, and had five children.

After her marriage Wightman resumed competition only intermittently. Members at Longwood, she and her husband won the 1913 mixed doubles; that year she won the doubles and singles there, beating Mary Kendall Browne, the new national champion. In 1915, weakened by recent diphtheria, Wightman nevertheless reached the U.S. women's final before bowing to Molla Bjurstedt, the newest champion. In three other 1915 tournaments she won one of three matches with Bjurstedt; afterward, while visiting in California, she captured her last Pacific States crown. In 1918, partnered with Irving C. Wright, she won the U.S. mixed doubles championship. The following year she regained her U.S. singles championship and won three more tournaments, including the U.S. indoor singles and doubles. Women's national rankings began in 1913, and Wightman ranked second in 1915 and 1918 and first in 1919.

Wightman and her husband also participated in non-playing roles. George, a lawyer, served the U.S. Lawn Tennis Association as its secretary in 1920, its vice president in 1923, and its president in 1924. Hazel organized and managed tournaments for youngsters and "ladies," the term she preferred to "women." She also encouraged and coached many girls who later became champions or near-champions, including Helen Wills, Helen Jacobs, Sarah Palfey, Marion Zinderstein, Margaret Blake, and Kay Hubbell. As chairman of the USLTA Women's Advisory Committee, Wightman changed the dates of the women's national championships from June to September, so as to climax the turf circuit season.

In 1919, following a suggestion from USLTA official Mike Myrick, Wightman had a silver vase inscribed "Challenge Cup—Ladies Team Match" and donated it as a prize for women's international competition. She hoped that the vase would be akin to the Davis Cup for men; however, at that time too few countries could field good women's teams, and thus the International Tennis Federation vetoed the idea. In 1923 Myrick and the USLTA inaugurated the new stadium at the West Side Tennis Club in Forest Hills, New York, with a team match between touring English women players and an American team captained by Wightman, with the vase as the prize. The Americans won, 7–0, with Wightman and Eleanor Goss each scoring one doubles point. The following year in England, the British triumphed, 6–1, with the Wightman-Wills pair tallying the lone U.S. point. Known as the "Wightman Cup," the event was held annually until 1989, when the U.S. Tennis Association discontinued it; the United States won the event fifty-one times to Great Britain's ten. "Mrs. Wightie," as she was familiarly known, captained thirteen American teams between 1923 and 1948; she also won three doubles matches and lost two in the event during the years 1923–1931. Although she wanted other countries to participate in the event, the British opposed the idea.

After the U.S. women's indoor championships were moved to Longwood Covered Courts in 1921, Wightman gained nine more doubles and five mixed doubles championships. She also secured the 1924 and 1928 U.S. outdoor doubles titles, with Wills, and the 1920 outdoor mixed doubles, with Johnson. In 1924 Wightman suffered a 0–6, 0–6 drubbing from Suzanne Lenglen at Wimbledon, but in Paris, France, she earned Olympic Games gold medals with Wills in doubles and with Dick Williams in mixed doubles. Appearing in the national singles championship for the last time in 1928, Wightman reached the quarterfinals, after beating her career archrival, May Sutton Bundy, 6–4, 11–9. Wightman and Bundy had tournament encounters, with Wightman winning three of them; they drew large crowds because of Northern California vs. Southern California sentiments, spirited play, and personal antagonisms. Wightman also won eleven U.S. women's veteran doubles titles from 1940 through 1954, the last when she was age sixty-seven. Altogether Wightman won forty-five U.S. championships and more than 140 tournaments.

During and after the 1920s Wightman accelerated her volunteer instruction programs for girls at schools, clubs, churches, and camps, both winter and summer. Dissatisfied with prevalent coaching methods and manuals of the day, she wrote *Better Tennis* (1933), in which she presented the basics in simple, direct terms—stressing balance, rhythm, and footwork—and tactics for playing doubles. The book also contains an appendix that tersely summarizes memorable points in slogans and a much-quoted alliterative alphabet, such as "Concentrate Constantly." Invitations to girls from California and other far places to be her house guests during Longwood tournament weeks became habitual.

Wightman and her husband divorced in 1940, and she moved to a large house in Chestnut Hill, Massachusetts. Because of her proximity to Longwood, she sometimes housed as many as fifteen women players at tournament time until the major women's events moved away after 1969. She converted her two-car garage into a teaching area and installed a bangboard there. Pupils and protégés also received her admonitions on sportsmanship, posture, appearance, clothes, grooming, and femininity, as she felt appropriate.

Wightman excelled at other racket sports as well. In badminton she was the 1938 U.S. mixed doubles runner-up, and in 1930 and 1931 she was the Massachusetts state champion in both women's and mixed doubles. She also finished runner-up in the 1930 national squash rackets singles championship and won a Massachusetts state table tennis singles championship.

The tennis journalist Axel Kaufman wrote, "There are none who have exerted more profound, dedicated and beneficial influence on the game than Hazel V. Hotchkiss Wightman." In 1940 the USLTA Service Bowl was donated to honor her example, and she, herself, was the honored recipient in 1940 and 1947. She was elected in 1957 to the National Lawn (later International) Tennis Hall of Fame. In 1973 Queen Elizabeth II made her an honorary Commander of the British Empire. Considered the "Queen Mother of Tennis," Wightman once reflected, "Tennis has never been a career in the sense of being my sole absorbing interest. My life has been full and happy, with tennis thrown in." For decades she devoted many hours weekly to the Red Cross, Boston Children's Hospital, and various civic pursuits. Her total concentration and boundless energy enabled her to control multiple activities zestfully and effectively. She died at home in Chestnut Hill.

• Wightman's scrapbooks and original memorabilia are in the International Collegiate Women's tennis archives at the College of William and Mary, Williamsburg, Va. Autobiographical material is in her book *Better Tennis*, pp. 3–31, as well as in her articles in U.S. Lawn Tennis Association, *Fifty Years of Lawn Tennis in the United States* (1931): "The Net Attack Invades Women's Tennis," pp. 137–40, and "The Women's International Trophy," pp. 179–82. Bud Collins and Zander Hollander, eds., *Bud Collins' Modern Encyclopedia of Tennis*, 2d ed. (1994), contains a comprehensive sketch, pp. 451–53, much general reference, and complete summaries of Wightman Cup matches, pp. 575–82. Pertinent artices include "The House of Hotchkiss," *American Lawn Tennis*, 15 Oct. 1911, p. 333; "A Winner of Championships," *American Lawn Tennis*, 1 Sept. 1926, pp. 420–21; Axel Kaufman, "Hazel Wightman, Woman of the Century, Wins Marlboro Award," *World Tennis*, Apr. 1960, pp. 22–26; Barbard Klaw, "Queen Mother of Tennis, an Interview with Hazel Hotchkiss Wightman," *American Heritage*, Aug. 1975, pp. 16–24, 82–86; Mike Lupica, "Those Good Sounds," *World Tennis*, Jan. 1975, pp. 58–61; Herbert Waren Wind, "Run, Helen," *New Yorker*, 30 Aug. 1952, pp. 30–49; and Wind, "From Wimbledon to Forest Hills—A Summer to Remember," *New Yorker*, 13 Oct. 1975, pp. 116–41. Obituaries are in the *Boston Globe* (by Bud Collins) and the *New York Times*, both 6 Dec. 1974.

FRANK V. PHELPS

WIGMORE, John Henry (4 Mar. 1863–20 Apr. 1943), law professor and treatise writer, was born in San Francisco, California, the son of John Wigmore, an Irish-born furniture maker and lumber merchant, and Harriet Joyner. Wigmore attended the Urban Academy, a private school in San Francisco, and then, at his mother's insistence, Harvard College, from which he graduated in June 1883. His mother was so intent on having him go to Cambridge that she moved the whole family with him. An older half brother remained in charge of the lumber business in California. After college, Wigmore returned to San Francisco for a year, working in the family lumberyard, taking an interest in urban reform politics, and resisting his mother's demands that he become an Episcopal priest. In 1884 he went back to Harvard to study law and received both an A.M. and an LL.B. in 1887. In 1886 he was one of the small group of students who founded the *Harvard Law Review*.

After law school, Wigmore remained in Boston for two years trying to establish a law practice, which he combined with journalism, ballot reform politics, and legal writing. He also occasionally worked as a researcher for the lawyer and jurist Louis Brandeis and for Justice Charles Doe of the New Hampshire Supreme Court. In 1889 Wigmore accepted appointment as professor of Anglo-American law at Keio University in Tokyo, Japan. On 16 September 1889, three days before leaving for Japan, he married Emma Hunt Vogl. They had no children.

Wigmore spent three years in Japan, teaching virtually the entire law school curriculum, studying Japanese legal history, and acting as a correspondent for several American newspapers. He left Japan in December 1892 and in January 1893 accepted an offer to teach at the Northwestern University School of Law in Evanston, Illinois. He began teaching in September 1893 and remained there for nearly fifty years, serving as dean from 1901 to 1929 and as emeritus professor from his formal retirement in 1934 until his death. He continued as dean during World War I, when he obtained an army reserve commission and was on active duty at the Judge Advocate General's Office in Washington from July 1917 to May 1919.

Wigmore is best known as a prodigious legal scholar. He was extraordinarily prolific in a variety of fields, ranging from torts and criminal law to air law and international law. The bibliography of his published writings contains more than 900 entries, including 46 books written by him and 38 edited works. He is most closely associated with the law of evidence. His magnum opus, *A Treatise on the Anglo-American System of Evidence in Trials at Common Law*, was originally published in 1904–1905 and comprised four volumes. He brought out a second edition in five volumes in 1923 and a third edition in ten volumes in 1940. The *Treatise* was an influential and authoritative work on the law of evidence, and it has a fair claim to be, in the words of Supreme Court justice Felix Frankfurter, "the greatest treatise on any single subject of the law" (Frankfurter et al., p. 443). The reach of Wigmore's scholarship was captured in 1934 by Robert T. Donley, who humorously remarked, "The amount of research, thought and physical labor which must have been necessary for the production of this [*Treatise*] and other works of Dean Wigmore is simply appalling: ample to have developed round-shoulders and quarrelsomeness in any dozen professors of law" (Roalfe, "John Henry Wigmore—Scholar and Reformer," p. 284).

Wigmore was also an energetic academic instructor who, in twenty-eight years as dean, transformed Northwestern from its modest beginnings into a premier law school. Taking a keen interest in the smallest details of the institution, he not only raised the money to construct the school's new buildings, opened in 1926, but insisted, against economy-minded trustees, on oak-paneled corridors lined with legal portraits he had chosen. He delighted in organizing exhibits of legal fiction, plays, and detective stories and wrote the words and music of the school song.

Using the "case method" as an academic lightning rod, Wigmore successfully drew competent students and outstanding faculty to his institution, continuously impressing upon his colleagues the importance of standardizing American legal studies. Although he advocated practical training in addition to academic training, Wigmore believed that scholarship was paramount to "field work," and consequently the most important requirement for individuals who entered a four-year law program was either a college degree or a minimum of three years of undergraduate study. During his tenure as dean, he saw to it that students enrolled at Northwestern received the widest and most innovative course selections available.

He was connected, often as founder, with many organizations and publication projects aimed at extending the outlook of lawyers beyond legal doctrine. He was a founder of the Chicago Legal Aid Society and started the first law school clinic at Northwestern around 1907. In 1909, to mark the school's fiftieth anniversary, he organized a National Conference on Criminal Law and Criminology, which led to the establishment of the American Institute of Criminal Law and Criminology, the *Journal of Criminal Law & Criminology*, and an important series of translations of foreign works of criminology, the Modern Criminal Science series (9 vols., 1911–1917), on which Wigmore did much of the editorial work. He was active in the Association of American Law Schools from its beginnings and undertook massive editorial assignments under its auspices. He was the driving force behind *Select Essays in Anglo-American Legal History* (3 vols., 1907–1909), the Modern Legal Philosophy series (12 vols., 1912–1923), the Continental Legal History series (10 vols., 1912–1928), and the Evolution of Law series (3 vols., 1915–1918).

Wigmore was a member of the National Conference of Commissioners on Uniform State Laws from 1908 to 1924 and from 1933 to 1943. In 1916 he became the second president of the American Association of University Professors. Active in the Chicago, Illinois, bar and the American Bar Association (ABA), he was instrumental in establishing the *American Bar Association Journal* in 1915, the ABA Section on Comparative Law in 1919, the ABA Section on Criminal Law in 1920, and the ABA Section on International and Comparative Law in 1934. He was a prime mover in organizing the American Judicature Society in 1916, the International Association of Penal Law in 1924, and the Inter-American Bar Association in 1940. A pioneer in air law, he founded the Air Law Institute at Northwestern in 1929 and the *Journal of Air Law* in 1930, and he played an important role in planning federal regulation of aviation in the 1930s.

During World War I he rose to the rank of colonel in the army and thereafter loved to be called "Colonel Wigmore." He was ferociously patriotic and intolerant of pacifists. He generally was regarded as a conservative and was perhaps the last man in Chicago to wear shirts with high collars and detachable cuffs. While active in the 1880s in the Cambridge Republican League, he actually was an independent in politics. He cast his first vote for Grover Cleveland and allowed in 1937 that, having voted for Franklin Roosevelt, he "might be rated a Democrat."

At the same time, Wigmore was an ardent internationalist, staunchly supporting the League of Nations and establishment of the World Court. His cosmopolitan outlook was enhanced by a remarkable facility for languages. Over the years he mastered many European languages as well as Japanese, Russian, and Arabic. He had a lifelong interest in comparative and historical studies and sought to stimulate the interest of the general public as well as lawyers in the law of other places and times. In 1928 he published a lavishly illustrated three-volume *Panorama of the World's Legal Systems* and in 1941 a worldwide anthology of trials called *Kaleidoscope of Justice*.

Wigmore died in a traffic accident in Chicago while returning home by taxi from an editorial meeting of the *Journal of Criminal Law & Criminology*, an ironic death for someone who had never owned an automobile. He was buried with military honors at Arlington National Cemetery. While his diverse achievements are usually remembered only by those connected with institutions he helped found, his name remains familiar to all American lawyers as practically synonymous with the law of evidence, on which he was the century's leading authority.

• Wigmore's papers are in the Northwestern University Law School Library. They include an unpublished manuscript, Albert Kocourek, ed., "Recollections of a Great Scholar and Superb Gentleman: A Symposium," which contains appreciations of Wigmore by thirty-five contemporaries. A complete bibliography of Wigmore's writings, with introductory comments by David S. Ruder et al., was published as "John Henry Wigmore: An Annotated Bibliography," in a special supplement to the *Northwestern University Law Review* 75, no. 6 (Feb. 1981): 1–123, and also contains a list of selected writings about Wigmore. This list omits, however, the appreciations by Felix Frankfurter et al., "John Henry Wigmore: A Centennial Tribute," *Northwestern University Law Review* 58 (1963): 443–64. The standard biography is William R. Roalfe, *John Henry Wigmore—Scholar and Reformer* (1977). See also Roalfe, "John Henry Wigmore—Scholar and Reformer," *Journal of Criminal Law, Criminology, and Police Science* 53 (1962): 277–300. For interesting recent reassessments of Wigmore, see William Twining, *Theories of Evidence: Bentham and Wigmore* (1985), and Paul D. Carrington, "The Missionary Diocese of Chicago," *Journal of Legal Education* 44 (1994): 467–518.

DONNA GREAR PARKER
EDWARD M. WISE

WIGNER, Eugene Paul (17 Nov. 1902–1 Jan. 1995), physicist, was born Wigner Jenö Pál in Budapest, Hungary, the son of Antal Wigner, the director of a leather tanning factory, and Erzsébet (maiden name unknown). Wigner graduated from the Lutheran Gymnasium in Budapest. He then attended the Technical University in Budapest (1920–1921) before transferring to the Technische Hochschule in Berlin. There he studied chemical engineering, receiving his diploma in chemical engineering in 1924 and his doctorate in 1925. His doctoral dissertation, on chemical reaction rates and the formation of molecules, was written under the direction of Michael Polanyi.

Wigner then returned to work briefly in his father's factory in Budapest before becoming a research assistant to Richard Becker at the Technische Hochschule in Berlin (1926–1927). He spent the year 1927–1928 in Göttingen as research assistant to David Hilbert; however, during this time Hilbert was ill, and Wigner interacted mainly with the nascent group of quantum theorists headed by Max Born and James Franck. These included Pascual Jordan, Walter Heitler, Victor Weisskopf, and John von Neumann. This period was of tremendous importance to his career because it gave him access to the early stages of the new quantum mechanics.

Wigner embarked on an ambitious program to rebuild all of theoretical physics on the basis of quantum theory. One of his first papers in this endeavor introduced the use of group theory in quantum mechanics (1927). Although Hermann Weyl is often thought of as the originator of group-theoretical methodology in quantum theory, Wigner's paper appeared several months before Weyl's work. In collaboration with von Neumann, in 1928 Wigner wrote three papers that applied group theory to the quantum theoretic treatment of angular momentum and reflection symmetry (now called parity). With Jordan, he extended the Pauli Exclusion Principle to fermions, incorporating a general method now known as second quantization (1928).

Wigner returned to the Technische Hochschule as an instructor (1928–1930) and then as an untenured professor (1930–1933). In Berlin he became acquainted with two young Hungarians, Leo Szilard and Edward Teller, who were to become lifelong colleagues and friends. Since his Berlin position was temporary, he accepted a visiting lectureship at Princeton University (1930), which subsequently was extended to a visiting professorship (1931–1936). He was appointed professor of physics at the University of Wisconsin (1937-1938). Wigner became a naturalized U.S. citizen in 1937. He returned to Princeton in 1938 as the Thomas D. Jones Professor of Mathematical Physics and held this position (with some leaves of absence) until his retirement in 1971. His visiting positions included those at the University of Leiden, as Lorentz Lecturer (1957); the University of Utrecht, as Kramers Professor (1975); and occasionally as visiting professor at Louisiana State University (1971–1985).

In 1931 Wigner published *Gruppentheorie und ihre Anwendung auf die Quantenmechanik der Atomspektren*, which belatedly appeared in English translation as *Group Theory and Its Application to the Quantum Mechanics of Atomic Spectra* (1959). It was intended for physicists, and unlike Weyl's more abstract treatise, *Gruppentheorie und Quantenmechanik* (1928, 1931), it was readily accessible to them. It also contained a useful analysis of the rotation group $SO(3)$, and the result now known as the Wigner-Eckart Theorem. He then turned his attention to the application of quantum and group-theoretic ideas to the theory of solids (now known as solid state physics), and to theoretical nuclear physics. There followed a flurry of papers that included the Wigner-Seitz cellular method and wave functions (1933); the first quantum mechanical description of the scattering of neutrons by protons (1933); an electron theory of metals (1934); the Wigner-Bardeen work function (1935); the Breit-Wigner resonance formula (1936); and his supermultiplet—the $SU(4)$ theory—and the notion of isospin (1937). Much of the methodology employed in the Wigner-Seitz papers is now recognized as the beginning of the many body theory. Next, in 1939, came Wigner's monumental memoir on the unitary representations of the inhomogeneous Lorentz group (known as the Poincaré group); in this he determined the possible representations that are of physical significance and indicated their interpretation in relativistic quantum mechanics. This broke new ground, both mathematically and physically, and included a definition of an elementary particle as an irreducible representation of the Poincaré group. Mathematically, it led to the recognition of the need for a complete analysis of the Lorentz group, which was provided by Valentin Bargmann (1947), and by the Russian mathematicians Izrael M. Gel'fand and Mark A. Naimark somewhat later.

The decade of the 1930s ended with a truly seminal paper on the reduction of Kronecker products of representations of simply reducible groups (1940). At the time Wigner's friends advised him that it was too esoteric and lengthy, so it was privately circulated and remained unpublished until 1965. Nevertheless, it contained an exhaustive discussion of the algebra of angular momentum in quantum theory, including the famous three-*j* symbols (also known as Clebsch-Gordan or Wigner coefficients), and the six-*j* symbols (now known as Racah coefficients). Many of the results contained in it were subsequently (and often incompletely) rediscovered by other researchers over the next two decades.

As events in Europe drifted toward war, Wigner had no illusions about the seriousness of the situation: as a teenager he had experienced the communist takeover in Hungary, and with the Nazi accession of power his nominal Berlin position vanished. He was interested in nuclear physics and was acquainted with the principal figures in the United States pursuing experimental work in this area. In the summer of 1939, alarmed by the recent progress in nuclear fission, he and Szilard acquainted Einstein with these developments and persuaded him to write the famous letter to President Franklin D. Roosevelt that ultimately led to the creation of the Manhattan Project and the atomic bomb. Wigner himself became active in this research as head of the Theoretical Section of the Metallurgical Laboratory at the University of Chicago (1942–1945). There, charged with the design of nuclear reactors to produce plutonium, he displayed his talents not only as a theoretician but also as a nuts-and-bolts engineer. His combined expertise in nuclear physics, mathematics, engineering, chemistry, and materials science was unique, and his contribution to the success of the project was second only to that of Enrico Fermi. Many of the standard techniques in the theory of reactors were due to him, and he was the holder of thirty-seven patents in reactor technology (1945–1947). He served as director of research and development at the Clinton Laboratories at Oak Ridge National Laboratory (1946–1947) and suggested the type of parallel plate reactor used in the *Nautilus*, the world's first nuclear-powered submarine.

Following the war Wigner remained actively involved in defense work, although he returned to his full-time duties at Princeton in 1947. His research included a resumption of his group-theoretical studies in quantum mechanics, as well as his *R*-matrix theory of nuclear reactions (1947), done in collaboration with Leonard Eisenbud. He served for two terms (1952–1957, 1959–1964) on the general advisory committee of the Atomic Energy Commission. He coauthored two books: *Nuclear Structure* (1958), with Eisenbud; and *The Physical Theory of Neutron Chain Reactors* (1958), with Alvin M. Weinberg. Both were very influential. In the 1960s Wigner became interested in civil defense and directed programs on it for the National Academy of Sciences (1963) and the Oak Ridge National Laboratory (1964–1965). He continued to serve in various governmental advisory roles until a few years before his death; he was a supporter of President Ronald Reagan's Strategic Defense Initiative. During his latter years he became deeply interested in the philosophical implications and physical interpretation of quantum mechanics, and his writings in these areas from 1952 to 1986 exhibit unusual clarity and insight.

In 1936 Wigner married Amelia Zipora Frank, a physicist, but she died in 1937. He married Mary Annette Wheeler, a physicist at Vassar, in 1941; they had two children. Following her death in 1977, he married Eileen (Pat) Hamilton. Wigner died in Princeton.

Wigner was much honored during his lifetime. He was elected a member of the National Academy of Sciences in 1945 and received the Presidential Medal of Merit in 1946. He also received the Franklin Medal (1950); the Fermi Award (1958); the Atoms for Peace Award (1960); the Max Planck Medal (1961); the Nobel Prize in physics, which he shared with Maria Goeppert Mayer and J. Hans Jensen (1963); the National Medal of Science (1969); the Albert Einstein Award (1972); the Wigner Medal (1978); and the Order of Banner of the Republic of Hungary with Rubies (1990) and the Order of Merit (1994) from the post-communist Hungarian government. He was vice president (1955) and president (1966) of the American Physical Society.

Wigner was one of the leading figures of modern physics; however, his talent lay not in making fundamental discoveries to change the course of physics, but in patiently solving difficult problems. Thus he contributed new approaches and methodology to theoretical physics. He was instrumental in establishing the use of group theory and symmetry principles in quantum mechanics; there his influence has become so pervasive that it is difficult to imagine what the subject would be like without such tools. His pioneering role in the development of nuclear technology on a sound scientific basis earned him the title, "father of nuclear engineering." In person, he was a quiet, modest, private man who delighted in his family and in science.

He was devoted to his students and supervised more than forty doctoral dissertations, and his presence greatly enhanced the Princeton physics program. He believed in the responsibility of physics to provide a living picture of the world and was deeply concerned over his participation in the development of nuclear weapons. However, he chose to express his views in his writings rather than a more public manner. Consequently, to the general public he remained virtually unknown, while to theoretical physicists he was a living legend. Following Fermi's death in 1954, Wigner gradually assumed the role of a sort of conscience of physics who rendered judgments on the soundness of new ideas. Various anecdotes, known as "Wignerisms," circulated about his comments; he characterized a result as "amusing" when it was correct and beautiful, and as "interesting" when it was wrong and messy.

• Eugene Wigner and Paul Szanton, *The Recollections of Eugene P. Wigner as Told to Andrew Szanton* (1992), contains valuable personal information. A comprehensive eight-volume edition of his scientific, historical, philosophical, and sociopolitical writings, *The Collected Papers of Eugene Paul Wigner*, has been published (vols. 1–3, 1992, 1993, 1995); each volume is arranged topically and is accompanied by an expert appraisal of Wigner's contributions in the various areas. Obituary notices of Wigner are in the *New York Times*, 4 Jan. 1995; *Notices of the American Mathematical Society* 42 (July 1995); and *Physics Today* 48 (Dec. 1995).

JOSEPH D. ZUND

WIKOFF, Henry (1811?–28 Apr. 1884), author, publisher, and impresario, kept the secret of his birthdate and parentage throughout his life. His guardian, Samuel Price Wetherwill, may have been his father; some contemporary accounts claimed he was the son of a Philadelphia doctor also named Henry Wikoff. Whatever the circumstances of his birth, money was available to provide Wikoff with a good education. He entered Yale in 1827 but was dismissed before he graduated. He eventually graduated from Union College in 1832. He also studied law and was admitted to the Pennsylvania bar in 1834.

Although he used his legal knowledge throughout his life, Wikoff did not practice law as a profession. In the 1830s he began his lifelong practice of shuttling between the United States and Europe, living on his ample inheritance. On one of his transatlantic crossings he met James Gordon Bennett, editor of the *New York Herald*. Their relationship undoubtedly contributed to the attention Wikoff's doings were soon receiving in the press. Bennett printed Wikoff's dispatches from Europe and covered even the social activities of the "Chevalier Wikoff" as news. Wikoff served as an attaché to the U.S. legation in London for one year (1836–1837) and during the 1830s and 1840s acted in unofficial diplomatic capacities for various British and French interests. He was particularly proud of his relationship with and service to the Bonaparte family. At the same time he participated extensively in the social and cultural life of England and France, maintaining a keen interest in the theater.

Wikoff arranged the London debut of American actor Edwin Forrest and in 1840, when the death of promoter Stephen Price seemed liable to cancel a planned New World tour of dancer Fanny Elssler, Wikoff stepped in to organize and manage it. Wikoff's relationship with the *Herald* ensured a positive advance press for the tour, and it was an immediate success. Everywhere they played, the company attracted crowds of patrons, including significant new audiences of middle-class men and, in some cases, their wives. The tour in many ways presaged P. T. Barnum's later promotion of Jenny Lind. However, by the end of nearly two years of constant travel the relationship between Wikoff and Elssler was strained, and it ended completely on their return to Europe. Wikoff refused to marry Elssler, and he also angered her by publishing over her name a series of "letters" on the tour that he had written. These *Letters and Journal of Fanny Elssler . . .* were first published in parts in a British periodical, *Fraser's Magazine*, and as a book in the United States (1845).

Wikoff returned for a time to the United States, where he briefly edited the *Democratic Review* and wrote *Napoleon Louis Bonaparte, First President of France* (1849). In 1851 he was again in London, as he described it, "on business at the foreign office" (this time for Lord Palmerston), where he remade the acquaintance of Jane Gamble. He had first met Gamble in the 1830s, and now he renewed the relationship with the help of the somewhat iconoclastic but socially influential Harriet Grote (whom Wikoff had met through Elssler). Before long, Wikoff and Gamble were engaged. Shortly before the wedding she changed her mind and left for Genoa. Wikoff followed, and in an attempt to salvage their relationship tricked Gamble into accompanying him to an apartment he had rented. Jane Gamble later complained to the British consul that Wikoff had detained her against her will, and he was arrested and jailed for about fifteen months.

On his release Wikoff determined to respond to the negative publicity the episode had evoked in American and European papers and wrote *My Courtship and Its Consequences* (1855). He brought his manuscript to J. C. Derby, a prominent publisher of popular nonliterary work, whose vigorous advertising campaigns Wikoff admired. The book was an immediate success; according to some reports it outsold the autobiographies of Barnum and Horace Greeley, which were published at the same time. Reviews stressed the good humor with which he told his tale. A few years later Wikoff felt ready to tell "the whole story," including the political intrigues he claimed were primarily responsible for the British consul's reluctance to intercede and prevent his incarceration. That book, *The Adventures of a Roving Diplomist* (1857), was not quite as successful as *My Courtship* but also enjoyed good sales.

In the 1860s Wikoff published a pamphlet on slavery in the United States, *Secession and Its Causes, in a Letter to Viscount Palmerston* (1861), and a short *Memoir of Ginevra Guerrabella* (1863). The memoir is a defense of the singer-actress's character in the face of negative publicity surrounding her somewhat confused marital status. Although Wikoff published the volume anonymously and does not directly refer to his own history, his experiences with an unfriendly press less than ten years earlier undoubtedly influenced the writing. Wikoff spent his last years primarily in Europe, publishing a volume of political commentary, *The Four Civilizations of the World* (1874), and another volume of memoirs, *The Reminiscences of an Idler* (1880). Other projects, including another volume of memoirs that would have extended his story beyond the 1840s, remained uncompleted at the time of his death in Brighton.

Wikoff was recognized by his contemporaries as a man of great ability but also as one whose lasting impact on his times and culture was reduced by the dissipation of his energies across so many projects, plans, and interests. Despite several acknowledged amorous relationships, he did not marry and left no recognized heirs.

• There are manuscripts at Union College and in the E. B. Washburne Collection at the Library of Congress. Duncan Crow's biography, *Henry Wikoff: The American Chevalier* (1963), provides a British interpretation; Allison Delarue, *The Chevalier Henry Wikoff* (1968), reflects Delarue's focus on dance history. *Fanny Elssler* (1970), by Ivor Guest, treats in depth Wikoff's relationship with Elssler. The pages of the *New York Herald* are rich in contemporary Wikoff material. Contemporary accounts do lean heavily on Wikoff's own writings, which, although they are written with self-deprecating charm, exaggerate his importance as a player on the political stage. Obituaries are in the *Herald* and the *New York Times*, both 3 May 1884, and the *Boston Daily Evening Transcript*, 5 May 1884.

JOANN E. CASTAGNA

WILBARGER, John Wesley (12 Mar. 1812–? Feb. 1892), farmer, minister, and author, was born in Bourbon County, Kentucky, the son of John Wilbarger and Anne Pugh, farmers. In 1823 the family moved to Pike County, Missouri, where he continued his schooling, fulfilling the desire of his frontier parents that he master the English language. There, he and Lucy Anderson were married on 26 May 1836, less than a month before the Battle of San Jacinto assured the independence of Texas.

Nearly ten years earlier John's eldest brother, Josiah Wilbarger, had moved to Texas and settled in Bastrop County, where he became a prosperous landholder, fearless frontiersman, and Texas patriot. In 1837, when Josiah and his wife visited Missouri, John and Lucy decided to return to Texas with them, where another brother, Matthias Wilbarger, already lived. Later their parents and several other siblings joined them to form a prominent pioneer family for whom, among other things, a county, a creek, and a road called the Wilbarger Trace were named. In Bastrop County, in Travis County, and, beginning in the early 1850s, in Williamson County, John and Lucy lived for the rest of their lives, with John working as a minister and a farmer who owned and traded land frequently. Their only child was born in 1844.

Of the Wilbargers' several claims to local fame, Josiah's story of surviving a skirmish with Comanches in 1833, in which he was seriously wounded, mistaken for dead, and scalped while still conscious, ranked first. It spread through the region and eventually beyond it, and following Josiah's death in 1845 from complications of the scalping wound that never healed, it helped to inspire John to write his book, *Indian Depredations in Texas. Reliable Accounts of Indian Fighters and Frontiersmen of Texas Battles, Wars, Adventures, Forays, Murders, Massacres, Etc., Together with Biographical Sketches of Many of the Most Noted Indian Fighters and Frontiersmen of Texas* (1889). John mentions his brother's story in his preface and makes it the second story he records, presenting himself not as a hero but as a faithful witness to the heroism of others. Finding "no one else" inclined to recover and preserve stories of the "perils and hardships" of the early settlers, he decided to write about the "fights and massacres" of which he had personal knowledge, to record those told by people whom he knew "to be trustworthy," and to collect those "written by others" he knew to be reliable.

Wilbarger clearly devoted much time and energy to the tasks of collecting, transcribing, and arranging the 246 stories in his book, hoping to make it both inclusive and detailed. The settings of fifty-three stories are specified by terms such as Panhandle, Canadian River, Skull Creek, Lavaca Bay, and Live Oak Bayou; 193 are set in one of sixty-one counties, ranging from Nacogdoches in the east to Kimble in the west, and from Goliad in the south to Wichita in the north. All but twelve stories are dated; 1821 is the earliest, and 1889 the latest. Despite his efforts at inclusivity, however, the stories are concentrated geographically and chronologically. Many occur in Central Texas, the region he knew best, including nineteen in Bastrop County and thirty seven in Travis County. Of 234 dated stories, 216 fall between 1830 and 1869, eight are from the 1820s, and eleven occur after 1870. It is surprising that the third highest concentration of stories, thirteen is from Grayson County, located in northeast Texas, several hundred miles from Wilbarger's home. But several Grayson stories—"Rev. Mr. Brown, a Methodist Preacher Who Don't Eat Chicken" and "First Camp Meeting in Grayson County," for example—suggest that Wilbarger combined his work as a minister with collecting stories. Further, he sometimes moved beyond his defined tasks in ways that make his book an important source of information about frontier folkways and attitudes about race, class, and gender—as seen, for example, in stories such as "A Comanche Princess," "The Italian Trader," "Riding Match between Rangers and Comanches," "Negro Turns White," and "White's Negro." For the most part, however, Wilbarger kept his task of contrasting the savagery of the Comanches with the courage and perseverance of the Texas pioneers clearly before him. Stories like his brother's also show that truth can be stranger than fiction, while others, like that of Matilda Lockhart, argue that Comanches are not only fierce but diabolical. Since for Wilbarger there is no doubt about whose side God is on, several stories feature miraculous escapes and deliveries. But they focus on pitting doomed resistance against heroic purpose.

In September 1855, about the time he began searching widely for stories, Wilbarger recorded in Williamson County, Texas, a simple last will and testament, leaving all his possessions to his wife. In it he notes, without describing it as a lesson of the frontier or tying it to the task that dominated much of his life, that it is seemly for people "to be prepared for sudden and instantaneous death." When, in February 1892, shortly after his death, his wife had his will probated, only 250 acres of land west of Round Rock, Texas, and the copyright of his book, estimated as being worth $2,000, were listed as inheritances.

• Since some accounts on the life and work of John Wesley Wilbarger are in conflict and in error, the best sources are census reports, tax rolls, and like records, which Philip Wright and Caroline Minter have helped search. See also Jane H. DiGesualdo and Karen R. Thompson, *Historical Round Rock, Texas* (1985), pp. 153–56.

DAVID MINTER

WILBUR, Earl Morse (26 Apr. 1866–8 Jan. 1956), church historian and seminary founder and president, was born in Jericho, Vermont, the son of LaFayette Wilbur, a lawyer and judge, and Mercy Jane Morse. After attending school in Jericho and Essex Classical Institute, he entered the University of Vermont in Burlington, graduating with an A.B. in 1886, the youngest member of his class. After a year of teaching in a private school in Fishkill on the Hudson, New York, he studied as a Congregationalist at the Harvard Divinity School, where he played the organ at regular services, receiving the A.M. and the S.T.B. in 1890. Wilbur became a Unitarian after Dean William Wallace Fenn, a Unitarian, gently helped him resolve his remaining questions about the doctrine of the Trinity. In 1890 he moved to Portland, Oregon, to serve as assistant minister to Thomas Lamb Eliot at the Unitarian Church of Our Father. Wilbur was ordained to the Unitarian ministry in Oakland, California, in 1892. In 1898 he married Eliot's daughter, Dorothea Dix, a second cousin of the poet T. S. Eliot; they had two children. He studied in Berlin and Oxford before settling down in Meadville, Pennsylvania, as minister of the Independent Congregational (Unitarian) Church and lecturer at the Meadville Theological School (which later moved to Chicago). In 1937 he wrote a biography of T. S. Eliot.

In 1904 funds were donated to establish the Pacific Unitarian School for the Ministry in Berkeley, California, of which Eliot became the founding dean in 1904 and president from 1911 to 1931. He gave courses in Unitarian history, out of which grew his major contributions to Unitarian historiography, and he held tenaciously to the single academic title of professor of homiletics and pastoral theology. He modeled the school more on the Harvard Divinity School than the Meadville Theological School, but he wished to correct what he considered an imbalance of emphasis he had experienced in Harvard's program. He therefore stressed practical preparation for the liberal ministry. At the same time, he built up the greatest collection of Unitariana in the New World. Unfortunately the collection was partly dissipated some time after the school was taken over by eminent domain by the University of California, relocated across its Berkeley campus on LeConte Avenue, and renamed the Starr King School for the Ministry in 1941.

During the years 1932 to 1934, a Guggenheim Fellowship and a grant from the Hibbert Trustees (England) allowed him to teach at Manchester College, Oxford, and to search for Unitariana there and throughout the European continent, where he learned Italian, Polish, and Hungarian as well as the more common research languages. His initial view of the Unitarian movement from the sixteenth century on had been reflected in *Our Unitarian Heritage* (1925), written for high school pupils. This volume of marked clarity in exposition of complex material prepared the way for his two-volume magnum opus, *A History of Unitarianism: Socinianism and Its Antecedents* (1945) and *A History of Unitarianism: In Transylvania, England, and America to 1900* (1952); the work remains the definitive comprehensive account in any language of European Antitrinitarianism from Spain to Ukraine. The first volume he dedicated to his son, Thomas Eliot, who had died at Stanford University in 1932, while Wilbur was on his Guggenheim fellowship in Eastern Europe.

Wilbur characterized the movement he chronicled as marked by three recurrent traits: freedom, reason, and tolerance, that is, freedom and rationality in the expression of religion and toleration of differences among exponents of religion and on the part of the civil government. In his exposition of Antitrinitarianism, he followed roughly the pioneer work of the Königsberg historian of Christianity, Friedrich S. Bock, in his two-volume *Historia Antitrinitariorum* (1774–1784). In this line, Wilbur translated Michael Servetus in *Two Treatises of Servetus on the Trinity* (1932) and published *Bibliography of the Pioneers of the Socinian-Unitarian Movement in Modern Christianity in Italy, Switzerland, Germany, Holland* (1950). Like Bock, he identified Antitrinitarianism as a consequence of the Reformation drive to return to the biblical sources (in impatience with the accumulated patristic, conciliar, and scholastic elaborations of dogma), making no attempt to establish any continuity with ancient Arianism and other theological formulations. Like Bock, too, Wilbur did not recognize the extent to which, among others, the Polish Brethren of the Minor Reformed schism passed through an Anabaptist, pacifist stage at Raków and elsewhere before accommodating to Faustus Socinus's more rationalist theological system, perfected in Basel, Kolozsvár, and Kraków, which eschewed baptism altogether. In carrying the account into the New World and particularly into New England, Wilbur saw almost no continuity between greater Boston Unitarianism, arising within the Arminianized sectors of the Standing Order of Massachusetts, and Polish-Netherlandish Socinianism, which he had so comprehensively chronicled in Europe. Wilbur died in Berkeley.

• His only surviving offspring, Elizabeth Nelson, encouraged him to prepare the charming work *A Few Extracts from a Long Ministry* (1957), which was privately printed posthumously. Further sources include Herbert McLachlan, "Earl Morse Wilbur: Scholar and Traveler," [British] Unitarian Historical Society *Transactions* 2 (1956): 315–17; Henry Wilder Foote, "Earl Morse Wilbur," *Yearbook of the American Unitarian Association* (1956); G. H. Williams, "Wilbur's Vision: Freedom, Reason, and Tolerance Reglimpsed," *Unitarian Universalist Christian* 42, no. 2–3 (1987): 43–62; and Lech Szczucki, "Earl Morse Wilbur (1866–1956)," *Odrodzenie i Reformacja w Polsce* (1958). Wilbur's manuscript translation of Stanisław Lubieniecki's *Historia Reformationis Polonicae* (1685) lay at the basis of G. H. Williams, ed. and annotator, *History of the Polish Reformation: Stanisław Lubieniecki and Nine Related Documents*, Harvard Theological Studies, vol. 36 (1993).

GEORGE H. WILLIAMS

WILBUR, John (17 July 1774–1 May 1856), Quaker preacher and leader of the conservative "Wilburites," was born in Hopkinton, Rhode Island, the son of Thomas Wilbur and Mary Hoxie. His parents were orthodox Friends who brought up their son in a strict Quaker environment; he was, in turn, "sober and religiously inclined from his youth." He received a common-school education and, as a young man, taught in the Rhode Island public schools. In addition, throughout his life he was an occasional land surveyor. He married Lydia Collins in October 1793, and together they had thirteen children. As he grew older, he became increasingly committed to the primitive form of Quakerism taught to him by his parents, remaining strict and conscientious. He was appointed to be an elder in the New England Yearly Meeting at the age of twenty-eight and was officially recorded as a minister of the Society of Friends at thirty-eight (1812). He was "a kindly man, of deeply affectionate heart, an able preacher of the old 'prophetic' type, rugged, unswerving in his moral integrity, a person who loved distinction but who would not yield an inch of his convictions for popular favor" (Jones, vol. 1, p. 511).

Wilbur considered the orthodox Quaker beliefs of George Fox to be the truest expression of the Christian faith. He was a model Friend who affirmed the orthodox Quaker faith and rejected the Hicksite innovations proposed by Elias Hicks in the 1820s. Hicks rejected the doctrines of Christ's substitutionary atonement and the bodily resurrection of Jesus and argued that the Inner Light was not the Holy Spirit or the continued presence of Christ but the native rational capacity of human beings. Wilbur relied on divine initiative and direction and dismissed the Hicksite innovations as a departure from historic Christian orthodoxy. The Hicksite schism split the Philadelphia Yearly Meeting in 1827–1828; divisions in other meetings followed.

Wilbur also rejected the evangelical innovations espoused by English Quaker Joseph John Gurney. Beginning in the 1820s Quakers began to resemble evangelicals as they participated in social reform movements, became politically active, and formed benevolent societies. Gurney elevated the role of the Bible in Quaker faith by arguing that the Holy Spirit's primary role was not primarily to impart religious knowledge through the Inner Light but to help Christians read the Bible correctly. In so doing, he emphasized the external authority of Scripture and downplayed the role of personal revelation, which had been a central feature of traditional Friends' spirituality.

Wilbur denounced the evangelical innovations of Gurney and his followers as departures from primitive orthodox Quakerism. From 1831 to 1833 he traveled among the Friends in Great Britain and Ireland preaching in support of an orthodox, quietist faith. He became convinced that evangelicals were displaying a "love of the world" and a "superficial, busy spirit" by becoming involved in social causes and leaving behind a focus on personal spirituality and the ministration of the Inner Light. In 1832 he published *Letters to a Friend on Some of the Primitive Doctrines of Christianity*, a series of letters he had written to George Crossfield. In these letters he detailed the dangers of evangelical innovations and outlined what he considered to be the essentials of the Christian faith, including the central role of the guidance of the Inner Light. In the final letter he detailed his orthodoxy with its affirmation of plainness and self-denial and its rejection of worldly temptations.

From 1837 to 1838 Gurney traveled throughout the United States on a preaching tour. His missionary sojourn to America was extraordinarily successful. Most Quakers welcomed him enthusiastically and adopted his evangelical brand of Quakerism, which aroused fresh interest in the Bible and encouraged new enthusiasm for religious work. Wilbur opposed Gurney publicly and spoke directly against him during and subsequent to Gurney's preaching tour. Factions formed, and the friction between evangelical and conservative Quakers increased throughout the 1830s and 1840s. By 1850 there were significant divisions in every yearly meeting. Although the conservatives, led by Wilbur, were present in every yearly meeting, evangelicals were in the majority in each one except the one in Philadelphia.

Most American Quakers resented Wilbur and his divisive preaching. The New England Yearly Meeting launched disciplinary proceedings against him in 1838 because he opposed generally accepted innovations proposed by Gurney. The meeting dissolved his monthly meeting in South Kingston, Rhode Island, and added its members to the Greenwich, Rhode Island, meeting. The Greenwich meeting, along with the larger body, disowned Wilbur and expelled him from membership in 1843. After several unsuccessful appeals to the yearly meeting, he and five hundred of his supporters separated in 1845 to form an independent yearly meeting. In 1845 he published *A Narrative and Exposition of the Late Proceedings of New England Yearly Meeting* . . . , a 355-page duodecimo defending himself and his beliefs. Those who followed Wilbur were popularly known as "Wilburites," and the larger body of 6,500 were popularly referred to as "Gurneyites." Officially, the smaller body was called the "New England Yearly Meeting of Friends," and the larger body was named "The Yearly Meeting of Friends for New England." Smaller-scale separations followed in New York, Ohio, and Pennsylvania. The Wilburite/Gurneyite schism, on the heels of the Hicksite separation (1828), deeply divided American Quakers and created a crisis of identity for the Society of Friends as it entered the second half of the nineteenth century. Wilbur died in Hopkinton, Rhode Island.

• In addition to Wilbur's works noted above, see also his *Journal of the Life of John Wilbur: A Minister of the Gospel in the Society of Friends* (1859). Archival manuscript sources on John Wilbur and the Wilburites are in Haverford College (Haverford, Pa.), Earlham College (Richmond, Ind.), and Swarthmore College, Swarthmore, Pa. At Haverford in particular there is an extensive collection pertaining to the Sheppard family in the United States that includes materials on John Wilbur and the Wilburite separation. There is no book exclusively on Wilbur; however, many books on Quaker history discuss the man and the movement at length. For a brief historical overview of American Quakerism, see "An Historical Summary," in *American Quakers Today*, ed. Edwin B. Bronner (1966). The best discussion of American Quakerism during the nineteenth century, including treatment of the Hicksite, Gurneyite, and Wilburite movements, is Thomas D. Hamm, *The Transformation of American Quakerism: Orthodox Friends, 1800–1907* (1988). Rufus M. Jones, *The Later Periods of Quakerism* (2 vols., 1921), also has a lengthy discussion of John Wilbur and his impact on the Society of Friends.

KURT W. PETERSON

WILBUR, Ray Lyman (13 Apr. 1875–26 June 1949), president of Stanford University and secretary of the interior, was born in Boonesboro (now Boone), Iowa, the son of Dwight Locke Wilbur, a lawyer and businessman, and Edna Maria Lyman, a teacher. In 1882 the Wilbur family moved from Boonesboro to Jamestown in the Dakota Territory and in 1887 to the new settlement of Riverside in Southern California, where Wilbur attended high school. In 1892 he entered Stanford University, where he majored in biology, began a lifelong friendship with Herbert Hoover, and met Marguerite Blake, the daughter of a San Francisco physician. He earned a B.A. from Stanford in 1896 and in 1898 married Blake, with whom he had five children. As a student, Wilbur became active in San Francisco Republican politics. He also spent his summers in the Arizona desert collecting specimens for the Stanford Natural History Museum. He remained an outdoorsman and a student of nature throughout his life.

In 1897 Wilbur received an M.A. in physiology from Stanford and two years later an M.D. from the Cooper Medical College of San Francisco. He was appointed assistant professor of physiology at Stanford in 1899 and, in 1911, dean of its newly established medical school.

In 1916 the university's trustees appointed Wilbur president of Stanford, a position he held until 1943. As president, in conjunction with the Academic Council, he organized Stanford's academic departments into schools. Between 1917 and 1926 the Schools of Biological Sciences, Social Sciences, Engineering, Education, Physical Sciences, Letters, Nursing, and Law and the Graduate School of Business were created in order to facilitate both administrative and educational goals. These included increasing research facilities, reducing class size, personalizing education, and achieving social progress by utilizing scientific principles, voluntarism, applied learning, and social service. Curriculum reform was accomplished with the introduction in 1916 of a grading system and in 1920 of the lower division general education requirement of ninety quarter units. Throughout his tenure Wilbur also promoted the enlargement of the Stanford Medical School in San Francisco, its free clinic, and the Nursing School. The Food Research Institute was established in 1921, and the Hoover Institute had its beginnings in 1919 with a bequest of $50,000 from Hoover to Stanford for a historical collection on the Great War, which in the 1940s was moved to the Hoover Tower. Wilbur's scientific and medical background persuaded him to see the university as the key to achieving social progress by utilizing the scientific methods of research and scholarship, as well as by offering a sound education to undergraduates. Throughout his tenure as president he urged the trustees and faculty to improve and expand graduate teaching and research in order to make Stanford a leading university.

During World War I Wilbur served on the California and the National Councils of Defense and was recruited by Hoover to serve as chief of the Conservation Division of the Food Administration. Wilbur traveled extensively, urging Americans to conserve food on a voluntary basis in order to avoid mandatory rationing. Both Wilbur and Hoover viewed voluntarism as essential to maintaining a democratic society during a time of crisis.

In 1928 Wilbur strongly supported Hoover's candidacy for president. With Hoover's victory Wilbur was appointed secretary of the interior. The philosophy that governed the Interior Department under Wilbur was decentralization and voluntarism, guided by the principles of scientific management. As secretary, he ended the awarding of leases to private oil companies of the governments' naval oil reserves in order to avoid another Teapot Dome scandal. In 1930–1931 he also helped to open up new oil fields in California's Kettlemen Hills, and in 1930 he succeeded in completing the negotiations among the various states for the Hoover Dam project, with California receiving over 60 percent of the power produced. For the next fifteen years he fought to keep "Hoover" as the official name of the dam, which was accomplished by an act of Congress in 1947.

Having grown up on the western frontiers of Dakota and California, Wilbur advocated developing local solutions to local problems and restoring some local control over the decision-making process of the Bureau of Reclamation projects. He also called for a reassessment of the Bureau of Indian Affairs policies. He was convinced that the existing reservation policy was making American Indians permanent dependents of the state, and he preferred instead a policy of independence and assimilation. He strongly opposed the creation of a centralized, federal Department of Education, insisting on local control of schools. He encouraged private donors, such as the Rockefeller Foundation, to help develop the National Park System.

Adhering to President Hoover's philosophy that social reform could best be obtained by the collective wisdom of experts and scientific managers, Wilbur chaired a number of national conferences and committees including the National Advisory Committee on Illiteracy (1930–1931) and the White House Conference on Child Health and Protection (1929–1931); in 1931 he cochaired the President's Conference on Housing.

As a close friend and ally of President Hoover, Secretary Wilbur loyally defended Hoover during the Great Depression, claiming that the depression was caused by international economic dislocations, political opportunism, and personal greed. By 1932 he was certain that the depression was just about over; he also believed that if the president had been given a cooperative Congress to work with, he would have solved the economic collapse. With Hoover's defeat in 1932 Wilbur returned to Stanford and resumed his duties as president of the university. During World War II he supervised the creation of the School of Humanities, the Hoover Library, and the Far Eastern Studies program. He retired in 1943 but remained at the university as chancellor until his death in Palo Alto.

During his last years he assumed an active role in the Institute of Pacific Relations, defending the Institute against charges of being pro-Chinese and pro-Communist and arguing that if men of good will could get together on a scientific basis the world would have a better chance of solving its problems. In describing his life he observed that he wanted to be remembered for his work as a physician, his service as president of Stanford University, and his role as a volunteer in public service.

• Wilbur's papers are in the Hoover Institution, the Stanford University Library, and the Lane Library of the Stanford School of Medicine. See also Edgar Eugene Robinson and Paul Caroll Edwards, eds., *The Memoirs of Ray Lyman Wilbur* (1960). An obituary is in the *Nation*, 30 July 1949.

JACK D. ELENBAAS

WILBURN, Virgil Doyle (7 July 1930–16 Oct. 1982), country performer and businessman, was born in Hardy, Arkansas, the son of Benjamin Elijah "Pop" Wilburn, a disabled World War I veteran and farmer, and Katie Maple Zieger. Wilburn's musical career began early when he joined older brothers Lester and Leslie, younger brother "Teddy," and sister Vinita in a family band. The family's farm provided little support and the father's war injuries made it difficult for him to hold a steady job. In 1937 Pop Wilburn saw a neighbor's family singing on the street in Hardy, Arkansas, and had the idea for the Wilburn Family band. With a mandolin, guitar, and fiddle ordered from a Sears Roebuck catalog the children practiced entertaining neighbors on a makeshift stage in their backyard.

On Christmas Eve of that year they traded money acquired from their beehive for a ride to Thayer, Missouri, eighteen miles across the state line to sing on the streets and to Hardy, Arkansas, to perform in stores. Merchants in Hardy provided the group with transportation and entered them in a radio station talent contest in Jonesboro, Arkansas, where the Wilburn Family took first prize. The family troupe played at livestock auctions, farm sales, schools, churches, and radio stations. The farm was mortgaged for $100 to purchase a car, and they traveled to Springfield, Missouri, for a contest on KWTO radio.

The family's big break came in 1940. They were performing at radio station WAGF in Dothan, Alabama when their father heard of a Birmingham contest and concert featuring several acts from the Grand Ole Opry, including Roy Acuff and Bill Monroe. The car blew a tire and they were too late to enter the contest, but their father positioned them at the side door of the venue, and Roy Acuff heard them singing as he was leaving. Acuff, touched by their rendition of "Farther Along," championed the group and told program manager David Stone at Nashville radio station WSM about them. Soon after, the family received a telegram inviting them to Nashville to audition for the Opry. The Wilburn Family was hired for the Opry and proved to be quite popular, but after six months they were released because the restrictions of child labor laws became too much for the Opry management.

The family continued to perform without Vinita, who had married. The brothers found work at KWKH in Shreveport and performed regularly on the *Louisiana Hayride*. In 1951 Doyle and Teddy were drafted into the army during the Korean War. For fourteen months they served in the army's Special Service unit entertaining troops in the United States and abroad.

After being discharged in 1953 the two formed a duo, The Wilburn Brothers, with the older brothers performing in the band. The Wilburns gained considerable exposure touring with Ernest Tubb, Webb Pierce, and Faron Young and by taking first place on "Arthur Godfrey's Talent Scouts" television show. Their duet with Pierce, "Sparkling Blue Eyes," was a hit, and he helped them get a recording contract with Decca in 1954. In 1955 the Wilburn Brothers charted with their own song, "I Wanna Wanna Wanna." On 10 November 1956 the Wilburn Brothers joined the Opry as full cast members for the thirty-first anniversary broadcast and had their first top ten hits, "I'm So In Love with You" and "Go Away with Me." They turned down "Heartbreak Hotel," written by good friend Mae Boren Axton before Elvis Presley recorded it.

The Wilburn Brothers continued to climb the charts throughout the 1950s, including two top ten duets with Ernest Tubb, "Mister Love" and "Hey, Mr. Bluebird." They had three major hits on their own in 1959, "Which One Is to Blame," "Somebody's Back in Town," and "A Woman's Intuition." In the late 1950s all four brothers founded the publishing company, Sure-Fire Music to handle not only their music but that of other songwriters and artists as well.

In the 1960s the Wilburn Brothers maintained their popularity as entertainers and were awarded a lifetime recording contract with Decca. In 1960 "The Best of All My Heartaches" hit Billboard's top thirty, and "Blue Blue Day" reached the top fifteen the following year. They had three top five hits in the 1960s, "Trouble's Back in Town" (which won *Cashbox*'s award for top country music record in 1962), "Roll Muddy River," and "It's Another World." Other songs charting in the top twenty during the 1960s were "Someone Before Me" and "I Can't Keep Away from You." In 1967 "Hurt Her Once for Me" stayed on the charts for a remarkable twenty weeks. They appeared on *American Bandstand* and *Jubilee U.S.A.* The Wilburn Brothers would never meet that level of success again with their recordings.

While Teddy was more involved in songwriting, Doyle Wilburn was something of a workaholic and was the driving force in their business ventures. They diversified within the music business and cofounded the booking firm Wil-Helm Talent Agency with fellow country performer Smiley Wilson. Wil-Helm became one of Nashville's primary booking agencies for many top stars, including Jean Shepard, Martha Carson, Slim Whitman, the Osborne Brothers, and Charlie Louvin. Perhaps their biggest star was Loretta Lynn.

Doyle Wilburn signed Lorretta Lynn to Sure-Fire Music when Lynn arrived in Nashville on her famous self-promotional trek across the country over his brother Teddy's objections that she sounded too much like Kitty Wells. Wilburn had Lynn record "Fool Number One" as a demo and tried to get her a recording deal. Owen Bradley, the famous producer and A&R man for Decca wanted the song for Brenda Lee but wasn't interested in the artist. Wilburn talked Bradley into giving Lynn a six-month contract in exchange for the song. He arranged for fifteen straight Opry appearances for Lynn, although this is disputed by Lynn in her autobiography. Sure-Fire Music published all of her compositions up until 1970, when Lynn and the Wilburns became engaged in a ten-year legal battle over Lynn's switching management companies.

From 1963 to 1974 "The Wilburn Brothers Show," their syndicated television show, sponsored by Garrett Snuff and Bull-of-the-Woods tobacco, was broadcast to more than one hundred cities and had over four million viewers. Country music scholar Bill C. Malone characterized the show by saying it "emphasized 'traditional' country music, humor, patter and advertisements. Each show preserved much of the flavor of early stage and radio performances and a large sampling of down-home traits that country music seemed to be in danger of forgetting" (Malone, p. 270). Loretta Lynn was a featured cast member for several years.

In the 1960s the Wilburn Brothers continued to have respectable record sales and toured extensively, performing in all fifty states and Australia. They starred for thirty-nine weeks on Roy Acuff's "Open House" television show in Australia. In 1967 their schedule reached its peak. The Wilburn Brothers spent 250 days that year touring, had over fifty recording sessions, hosted fifty-two weekly half-hour television shows, and appeared at the Opry for twenty weekend performances. On 3 February 1968 the Wilburn Brothers announced they were splitting up the road show. Teddy no longer toured, but the duo continued performing on their television show and at the Opry; they also kept recording. In the early 1970s Patty Ramey joined their band during her school vacations. Patty Ramey went on years later to establish success on her own as Patty Loveless. The Wilburn Brothers maintained their popularity even though their last charted song was "Arkansas" in 1972.

In 1972 Doyle Wilburn considered running for the U.S. Senate as an American party candidate. The Wilburns had campaigned for George Wallace in his gubernatorial races and in 1968 when he was the American party presidential candidate. Although Wilburn did not run, he remained interested in politics. In 1979 he was named to the national steering committee for then-presidential candidate George Bush.

Doyle Wilburn died of cancer in Nashville, Tennessee. The night before his death Doyle spoke to his brother Teddy from his hospital bedside and asked him to sing "Old Flames" onstage at the Opry. He died the next day, his death noted that evening by performers at the Grand Ole Opry on the fifty-seventh anniversary broadcast of the show. At their induction into the Opry in 1956, Doyle had commented from the stage, "Our hearts are here. We hope to help the Opry celebrate its sixty-second anniversary."

Wilburn met singer Margie Bowes at the Grand Ole Opry and they married in 1961. They had one daughter and later divorced.

Doyle Wilburn's career spanned many generations, and he established a presence not only as a performer but as a businessman in the music industry. The Wilburn Brothers were one of the last tradition-based brother harmony acts, although in their recordings they veered toward pop flavorings. Through their television show they promoted traditional country music. Although it ended bitterly, one of Wilburn's most significant accomplishments in country music was shaping Loretta Lynn's career.

• A good source for background on the Wilburn Family's beginnings is Chet Hagan's *The Grand Ole Opry* (1969). Dixie Deen's article "The Woman Behind the Man," *Music City News* 3, no. 10 (Apr. 1966), presents the Wilburn Brothers' career from their mother's perspective. Information on the Wilburn Brothers is interspersed within Bill C. Malone's classic treatment of the history of country music, *Country Music U.S.A.* (1985). A brief obituary is in *Billboard*, 30 Oct. 1982.

MARILEE BIRCHFIELD

WILCOX, Cadmus Marcellus (29 May 1825–2 Dec. 1890), soldier, was born in Waynesboro, North Carolina, the son of Reuben Wilcox and Sarah Garland, who moved to Tipton County, Tennessee, when Wilcox was two. After studying briefly at Cumberland College (now University of Nashville), in 1842 Wilcox entered West Point, where his classmates included George McClellan (1826–1885) and Thomas J. "Stonewall" Jackson. Graduating fifty-fourth in a class of fifty-nine in 1846, Wilcox went immediately to the Mexican War. Campaigning with the Fourth and Seventh Infantry Regiments at Veracruz, Cerro Gordo, Chapultepec, and Mexico City, he won a brevet for bravery and became aide-de-camp to Major General John Quitman. After garrison duty in Missouri (1848–1849, 1850–1851), a tour in Florida against the Seminoles (1849–1850), and garrison duty in Texas (1851–1852), Wilcox returned to West Point in 1852 as an assistant instructor of infantry tactics. In 1857 he began a two-year medical leave of absence, taking the opportunity to write *Rifles and Rifle Practice* (1859) and to translate from French *Austrian Infantry Evolutions of the Line* (1859). *Rifles and Rifle Practice* was considered the first work of its type in the United States, and its distribution throughout the army and adoption as a West Point textbook widely established Wilcox's reputation as a promising young officer.

Wilcox was in the New Mexico Territory as a captain of the Seventh Infantry when he learned of Tennessee's secession in June 1861. Resigning his commission to join the Confederacy, Wilcox became colonel of the Ninth Alabama in time to see action at First Bull Run (First Manassas) in July 1861. Promoted to brigadier general in October 1861, Wilcox took command of an Alabama brigade which he led through heavy action in the Peninsular campaign and the Seven Days battles in the spring and summer of 1862. In temporary command of three brigades at Second Bull Run (Second Manassas) in August 1862, Wilcox handled his increasing responsibilities efficiently, winning favorable notice from superiors in the aftermath of the Confederate victory. Missing Antietam because of illness and playing but a minor role at Fredericksburg, Wilcox spent the rest of late 1862 and early 1863 chafing for greater opportunities, as he watched many of his prewar comrades rise to higher positions in both the Confederate and Union armies.

At the beginning of the Chancellorsville campaign in 1863, Wilcox seemed again destined for the periphery, as his brigade guarded Banks' Ford on the Rappahannock River in the rear of Robert E. Lee's Army of Northern Virginia, well removed from the main action. However, on the morning of 3 May Wilcox, always an acute observer of his tactical situation, noted that the Federal pickets opposite his lines had donned their haversacks, indicating an imminent movement. Correctly surmising Federal intentions, Wilcox relocated his brigade to oppose the Union advance and at Salem Church fought a brilliant holding action for hours against heavily superior Federal numbers, allowing Lee to finish his "masterpiece" in routing General Joseph Hooker's Army of the Potomac before turning to defeat the new threat. Had Wilcox been less observant or skillful in handling his brigade on this day, Lee would have found himself facing almost certain destruction in the pincers of a numerically superior foe. Douglas Southall Freeman, Lee's chief biographer, asserted, "Cadmus Wilcox that day gave military history an example far outliving his time, of the manner in which one Brigade, courageously led, can change the course of battle and retrieve a lost day" (Freeman, vol. 2, p. 626). Unfortunately, despite a commendation from Lee himself, Confederate bureaucratic inefficiency delayed the promotion that Wilcox expected and had earned.

At Gettysburg on 2 July 1863, Wilcox led his brigade in a Confederate assault that temporarily broke the Union center, but a lack of adequate support forced him to relinquish this critical position. The next day Wilcox's brigade moved in support of "Pickett's charge," but the failure of Confederate First Corps commander James Longstreet to cancel Wilcox's advance after George E. Pickett's repulse resulted in what Wilcox considered useless casualties among his men and later led to Wilcox's embroilment in the postwar controversy over Longstreet's actions at Gettysburg.

Receiving his overdue promotion to major general in August 1863, Wilcox ably commanded a division through the bloody Wilderness, Spotsylvania, and Petersburg campaigns of 1864. Although involved in severe fighting and suffering heavy casualties, Wilcox held his division together, losing fewer men to desertion than other Confederate leaders. In the desperate struggles that accompanied Lee's attempts to elude Grant's pursuit after the fall of Richmond, Wilcox continued to lead his troops capably until the final surrender at Appomattox in April 1865.

After the war, Wilcox went briefly to Mexico with Joseph O. Shelby and other Confederates but soon returned to the United States. Settling in Washington, D.C., Wilcox, a lifelong bachelor, undertook caring for the widow and children of his older brother John Wilcox, a Confederate congressman from Texas who died in 1864. Declining commissions in the Egyptian and Korean armies in order to be near his family, Wilcox relied on the many friends he had made in both the North and the South before the war, among whom was

U. S. Grant, at whose wedding Wilcox had been groomsman in 1848. A succession of lower positions in the federal government culminated in Wilcox's appointment by President Grover Cleveland as chief of the Railroad Division of the General Land Office in 1888. Wilcox died in Washington, D.C. The wide respect he enjoyed throughout his life was evidenced by the fact that his pallbearers came from the ranks of both former Union and Confederate officers. His family posthumously published his *History of the Mexican War* in 1892.

Although not among the great captains of the Confederacy, Wilcox consistently proved himself a highly competent brigade and division commander. Though not brilliant, Wilcox's steadiness, initiative, dependability, and popularity among his men made him the type of subordinate upon whom Lee built a formidable reputation as a military commander.

• Wilcox's papers are in the Library of Congress; most of the 1,200 items are small, but the collection includes a scrapbook, Wilcox's manuscript account of the Richmond campaign, and Wilcox's manuscript of an autobiography. Other valuable primary sources exist, most notably George W. Cullum, *Biographical Register of the Officers and Graduates of the U.S. Military Academy*, 3d ed., vol. 2 (1891), and James D. Porter, *Tennessee*, vol. 8 of *Confederate Military History*, ed. Clement A. Evans (1899). Details of Wilcox's Civil War years are best found in *The War of the Rebellion: A Compilation of the Official Records of the Union and Confederate Armies*, ser. 1 (128 vols., 1880–1901), most significantly in vols. 12 (Second Bull Run), 25 (Chancellorsville, wherein one can find Wilcox's report, which Freeman says "ought to be read by every soldier who thinks he has an unimportant position in the face of the enemy"), 27 (Gettysburg), and 36, 40, 42, 46, and 51 (Richmond campaign). Reference may also be made to Robert U. Johnson and Clarence C. Buel, eds., *Battles and Leaders of the Civil War*, vols. 2, 3, and 4 (1887–1888). Those interested in Wilcox's role in the postwar controversy over Longstreet at Gettysburg should see Longstreet, "Lee's Right Wing at Gettysburg," and William Allen, "A Reply to General Longstreet," both in *Battles and Leaders*, vol. 3, and Wilcox's statements in the *Southern Historical Society Papers*, Sept. 1877. The best secondary source for Wilcox in the Civil War is Douglas Southall Freeman's three-volume history of the Army of Northern Virginia, *Lee's Lieutenants* (1942–1944). Obituaries are General Darius N. Couch in *Twenty-Second Annual Reunion of the Association of the Graduates of the United States Military Academy* (1891), and in the *New York Times* and the *Washington Post*, 3 Dec. 1890.

BROECK N. ODER

WILCOX, Ella Wheeler (5 Nov. 1850–30 Oct. 1919), poet, was born in Johnstown Center, Wisconsin, the daughter of Marcus Hatwell Wheeler, a farmer and music teacher, and Sarah Pratt. Encouraged by her mother and frustrated by the drabness and near poverty of her life in rural Wisconsin, she began submitting poetry to popular magazines in her early teens, at first unsuccessfully. She was interested in her own writing rather than in formal education, and her higher education consisted of an unhappy year at the University of Wisconsin, beginning in 1867.

By her early thirties Wilcox's work had appeared in various magazines, including *Peterson's Magazine*, *Waverly Magazine*, *Arthur's Home Magazine*, *Frank Leslie's Illustrated Newspaper*, *Frank Leslie's Popular Magazine*, and *United Monthly Magazine*. She had become a favorite in literary circles in Milwaukee, although she continued to share her parent's rural home until her marriage and had lived in Milwaukee only three months, editing and writing for a literary column in a trade journal. Her local popularity proved crucial when a Chicago publisher inadvertently made her famous by rejecting her *Poems of Passion* (1882) as immoral. A friendly Milwaukee newspaper broke the story, which then appeared in papers throughout the country. A group of supportive Milwaukee citizens gave her a testimonial and a gift of $500. Another Chicago publisher saw the obvious financial possibilities and published the book, which, understandably, was highly successful, selling 60,000 copies in two years.

Poems of Passion was in most ways similar to the poetry Wilcox was to produce throughout her career. Much of her work plays variations on the theme of love, and it is emotionally charged and vaguely erotic rather than specifically sexual. Although her work was titillating instead of outrageous, it must be remembered that late nineteenth-century American audiences were very easily shocked. The following from "A Woman's Love" in *Poems of Sentiment* (1892) is typical:

So vast the tide of Love within me surging,
  It overflows like some stupendous sea,
  The confines of the Present and To-be;
And 'gainst the Past's high wall I feel it urging,
As it would cry "Thou too shalt yield to me!"
. . . .
Yet though I love thee in such selfish fashion,
  I would wait on thee, sitting at thy feet,
  And serving thee, if thou didst deem it meet.
And couldst thou give me one fond hour of passion,
I'd take that hour and call my life complete.

The underlying morality is conventional. A guest may shock and anger a married hostess by telling her he is leaving because he is in love with her, but, nonetheless, he leaves. Women expect men to be philosophic about women's earlier involvements, but marriage remains the ideal. After Wilcox's marriage in the 1880s, there was a noticeable shift in her work from themes of unfortunate entanglements to those of happy marriages.

Although Wilcox was first of all a love poet, she was not exclusively so. Her works deal with social problems such as intemperance, with history, and with the various crises of life. She wrote fiction, including *Mal Moulée* (1886), *Perdita and Other Stories* (1886), *Sweet Danger* (1892), and *An Ambitious Man* (1896), and she wrote editorials for the *New York Journal* and *Chicago American*. Both her prose and poetry appeared in syndicated newspapers and in many magazines, including *Good Housekeeping*, *Ladies' Home Journal*, *Women's Home Companion*, *Munsey's Magazine*, and *Cosmopoli-*

tan. She expounded her theosophical doctrines in *The Heart of the New Thought* (1902) and *New Thought Common Sense and What Life Means to Me* (1908). The bulk of her more than twenty volumes, however, was poetry. A very large audience looked to her for comfort and wisdom.

Wilcox's primarily sympathetic biographer Jenny Ballou said, "She was not a minor poet, but a bad major one" (p. 98). It is perhaps more accurate to say that Wilcox had a mass following among the kinds of readers whose modern counterparts seldom read poetry. She flourished in an age when newspapers and popular magazines regularly published verse for the unsophisticated. Her readers learned that she understood their griefs, their bereavements, and the frustrations of their love lives. They were told to persevere in dull, unrewarding lives because all lives have divine purposes. They understood her concerns with the evils of prostitution and her coolness toward the woman's movement.

Wilcox's personal life was conventional. Her only serious premarital love interest was a correspondence with poet James Whitcomb Riley, which dissipated when they met and did not like each other. In 1884 she married Robert Marius Wilcox, a businessman who became an executive in a silver company. Their child, a son born in 1887, lived only a few hours. The Wilcoxes settled for three years in Meriden, Connecticut and then in New York City, spending their summers at a home in Short Beach, Connecticut. After some unsatisfactory experiences with the literary salon of Mrs. Frank Leslie, Wilcox established her own literary center in Short Beach where she could give scope to her flamboyant personality. The Wilcoxes were inveterate world travelers.

A year after her marriage, at the instigation of her husband, Wilcox began a study of theosophy. After her husband's death in 1916 she explored varieties of Spiritualism and became convinced that he communicated through a Ouija board. Following what she believed to be his instructions, she went to France in 1918 to aid the Allied cause. She left France in early 1919 for England, where she collapsed. Broken in health, she returned to Short Beach, where she died.

It is unlikely that Wilcox will ever be read again except as a literary curiosity. Never in her lifetime a success with critics, she became even more at odds with the critical standards of the modernism that triumphed with the war to which she was drawn. Her blithe demotic optimism and the simple, direct statement of her poetry and its awkwardness are the very antithesis of what the world was coming to prefer. But in her time she brought consolation to millions of people with her verse.

• Wilcox's papers are located at Columbia University, Harvard University, Princeton University, the New York Public Library, and the State Historical Society, Madison, Wis. In 1905 she published *The Story of a Literary Career*, which contains a description of her lifestyle by Ella Giles Ruddy. Editions of Wilcox's collected poems appeared in 1917, 1924, and 1927. She also published *The Worlds and I* (1918), which was autobiographical and addressed Spiritualism. Jenny Ballou, *Period Piece: Ella Wheeler Wilcox and Her Times* (1940), is an informal, subjective biography. An obituary is in the *New York Times*, 31 Oct. 1919.

MARYJEAN GROSS
DALTON GROSS

WILCZYNSKI, Ernest Julius (13 Nov. 1876–14 Sept. 1932), mathematician, was born in Hamburg, Germany, the son of Max Wilczynski and Friederike Hurwitz. The family emigrated to the United States when Ernest was a schoolboy and settled in Chicago. He returned to Germany to enter the University of Berlin, where he studied mathematics, physics, and astronomy, and earned his doctorate in 1897. His thesis, "Hydrodynamische Untersuchungen mit Anwendung auf die Theorie der Sonnenrotation" (Hydrodynamical researches with application to the theory of the sun's rotation), followed his publication of several expository articles on solar theory. One result of this work was a "fairly satisfactory" mathematical explanation of the observed decrease, from the equator to the poles, of the angular velocity of the sun's rotation. Wilczynski subsequently tried, although ultimately unsuccessfully, to apply his theory to phenomena associated with sunspots, Jupiter's spots, and nebulae.

On Wilczynski's return to the United States, he did not immediately secure an academic post but instead took a position as a computer at the Nautical Almanac Office in Washington, D.C., early in 1898. By the fall of that year, however, he had moved on to an instructorship in mathematics at the University of California in Berkeley, where Mellen Haskell and W. Irving Stringham were working to build up a research-oriented department. Wilczynski was promoted to the rank of assistant professor in 1902, spent the years from 1903 to 1905 abroad on a grant from the newly formed Carnegie Institution of Washington, and rose to associate professor in 1906. That same year, he began a term as chair of the San Francisco Section of the American Mathematical Society (AMS) and married Contessa Inez Macola of Verona, Italy, with whom he had three daughters. While at Berkeley, Wilczynski focused initially on research in the theory of differential equations suggested by his doctoral work in mathematical astronomy. He adopted a Lie-theoretic approach in his analyses, working out the interconnections between differential equations, their solutions, and their associated groups. This led him quite naturally into more geometrically flavored questions; his most significant mathematical work, on the projective differential geometry of curves and ruled surfaces, built precisely on this research on differential equations.

Between 1901 and 1905, Wilczynski published some ten papers and gave numerous talks on his developing theory in projective geometry. In particular, he spoke before an international audience at the third International Congress of Mathematicians in Heidelberg in 1904 and was honored as one of the AMS's Colloquium lecturers in New Haven, Connecticut, in 1906. The complete statement of Wilczynski's new ideas appeared in 1906 in his *Projective Geometry of Curves and Ruled Surfaces*, with which he presented a new method in geometry and, according to his student and biographer Ernest P. Lane, "established himself as the leader of a new school of geometers, which may be called the American school of projective differential geometers" (Lane [1936], p. 303). Given a configuration to be studied, his method hinged on working up the associated invariant theory and using that to interpret the configuration's underlying geometrical properties.

Following this flurry of research and its very favorable reception, Wilczynski accepted an associate professorship in 1907 at the University of Illinois, where he extended his earlier work in projective differential geometry to the theory of *partial* differential equations of curved and ruled surfaces. By 1910, these researches had resulted in "Sur la théorie générale des congruences" (On the general theory of congruences), which won a research prize awarded by the Académie royale de Belgique and which subsequently appeared in the academy's *Mémoires* in 1911. Wilczynski remained at Illinois until 1910, when he was offered and accepted an associate professorship at the University of Chicago to replace the late Heinrich Maschke.

Wilczynski's move to Chicago placed him in what was then the country's strongest research program in mathematics and at a center for activism within the broader mathematical community. Wilczynski participated in both aspects of this vibrant department, fruitfully pursuing his geometrical lines of inquiry and actively serving the professional community. From 1909 to 1925 he acted as an associate editor of the *Transactions of the AMS*; from 1910 to 1912 he was an elected member of the AMS's governing council; in 1914 he became full professor at Chicago and vice president of the American Mathematical Society; in 1914–1915 he chaired the society's Chicago Section; and he was a member of the Council of the Mathematical Association of America following its founding in 1915.

Wilczynski's tenure at Chicago also found him fully engaged in the department's instructional mission. At the undergraduate level, he published *Plane Trigonometry and Applications* (1914) and *College Algebra with Applications* (1916), both of which demonstrated "his fondness for the heuristic method of presenting a subject" as well as his "powers of elegant mathematical exposition" (Lane [1936], p. 317). At the graduate level, he directed twenty-five doctoral dissertations (from 1911 to 1924) in addition to a number of master's theses. Lane observed that "his friendly, kindly, and informal attitude toward his students did much to win their affection and loyalty. He believed that a student could do his best work when he was thoroughly at ease in the presence of the instructor" (Lane [1933], p. 8).

Wilczynski's contributions to American mathematics were amply rewarded during his Chicago years. He was elected fellow of the American Association for the Advancement of Science, and in 1919 he received perhaps his greatest honor, election to the National Academy of Sciences. That year also brought a shift in his research focus to the theory of functions of a single complex variable. In particular, in a two-part paper published in the *Journal de mathématiques pures et appliquées* in 1922 and 1923, he analyzed the projective differential properties of such functions, adapting his earlier invariant-theoretic results and techniques to complex-valued functions.

The year 1919 also witnessed the beginning of a marked decline in Wilczynski's health, however. While teaching during the summer quarter of 1923, "in the midst of a lecture, he realized that he could go no further and, with a simple statement to that effect, walked from his class-room, never to return, leaving his students amazed by the classic self-restraint with which he accepted his tragic fate" (Lane [1933], p. 7). He was officially relieved of his teaching duties in 1923, became professor emeritus in 1926, and died in Denver, Colorado.

• A collection of Wilczynski's papers is in the Department of Special Collections at the University of Chicago. On his life, see Ernest P. Lane, "Ernest Julius Wilczynski," National Academy of Sciences, *Biographical Memoirs* 16 (1936): 295–327, which includes a full bibliography and a list of his doctoral students; Ernest P. Lane, "Ernest Julius Wilczynski—In Memoriam," *Bulletin of the American Mathematical Society* 27 (1933): 7–14; and Gilbert Ames Bliss, "Ernest Julius Wilczynski," *Science* 76 (1932): 316–17. For a sense of the mathematical research community in which Wilczynski participated, see Karen Hunger Parshall and David E. Rowe, *The Emergence of the American Mathematical Research Community, 1876–1900: J. J. Sylvester, Felix Klein, and E. H. Moore* (1994), especially chapters 9 and 10. Raymond C. Archibald thoroughly documented Wilczynski's participation in the American Mathematical Society in *A Semicentennial History of the American Mathematical Society, 1888–1938* (1938; repr. 1980). An obituary is in the *Chicago Tribune*, 16 Sept. 1932.

LOREN BUTLER FEFFER
KAREN HUNGER PARSHALL

WILDAVSKY, Aaron Bernard (31 May 1930–4 Sept. 1993), college professor and administrator, was born in Brooklyn, New York, the son of Sender Wildavsky, a bookbinder and apartment manager, and Eva Brudnow. Both parents emigrated from the Ukraine as young adults.

At Brooklyn's Public School 89 and Erasmus Hall High School, Wildavsky had a modest academic record, but at Brooklyn College, where his college work was interrupted by service in the U.S. Army from 1950 to 1952, he blossomed in the classroom, graduating Phi Beta Kappa. A Fulbright scholar at the University of Sydney in Australia (1954–1955), he earned the M.A. (1957), followed by a Ph.D. (1959) at Yale, which was developing a reputation as an outstanding graduate program in political science.

Wildavsky then began teaching at Oberlin College. After four years, he moved in 1962 to the University of California at Berkeley. He spent the rest of his career there except for a brief period (1977–1978) as president of the Russell Sage Foundation and visiting appointments at other universities and research institutions, such as the Center for Advanced Study in the Behavioral Sciences at Stanford. At Berkeley he was chairman of the Department of Political Science (1966–1969), dean of the Graduate School of Public Policy (1969–1977), and, at the time of his death, Class of 1940 Professor of Political Science and Public Policy.

Wildavsky's stature was recognized in the many professional awards he received. He was a Guggenheim Fellow (1971), National Academy of Public Administration Fellow (1971), American Academy of Arts and Sciences Fellow (1973), and president of the American Political Science Association (1985–1986). He also served on the editorial and governing boards of several institutions. Within the fields of political science and public administration, he received prizes and awards given in the names of a half dozen of the most distinguished leaders in those disciplines.

Wildavsky's influence cannot be confined by any single category. Instead, he was a recognized intellectual lodestar in several sectors of political science. Among his first professional publications (originally a graduate school paper) was an elaborate critique of Maurice Duverger's *Political Parties* (1954), then considered to be the definitive treatise on the comparative study of political parties. Wildavsky's article demonstrated key flaws in Duverger's analysis.

In 1964 Wildavsky published with his graduate school friend and subsequent longtime Berkeley colleague Nelson W. Polsby *Presidential Elections: Strategies of American Electoral Politics*. Unlike most textbooks, this work had an immediate and long-term impact, not only on teaching about presidential elections, but also as a fresh and influential perspective on those processes. Eight editions quadrennially appeared before Wildavsky died. In focusing on voters' behavior as shaped by the rules regulating nominations and elections, the book explained why some candidates were successful and others were not, as well as why a perplexing institution like the electoral college was unlikely to be reformed.

With the publication of *The Politics of the Budgetary Process* (1964), Wildavsky made his mark in public policy and public administration. Appearing in several revisions, this book was the focus of numerous articles, conference panels, and symposia. It put the human factor into the budgeting process of the national government, stressing the incremental principle on which the process rested. A decade later, Wildavsky, with coauthor Hugh Heclo, published *The Private Government of Public Money*, an anthropological perspective on Great Britain's Treasury Department. These two books, along with numerous articles and additional books on governmental budgeting, made Wildavsky the doyen among social science experts on the subject.

If anything was more influential than Wildavsky's impact on understanding political parties and budgeting, it was his effort to explain the presidency. In an article, "The Two Presidencies" (1966), Wildavsky touched off a stream of scholarly argument and rebuttal by students of the presidency that continued into the 1990s. Put simply, he contended that Congress was more willing to support a president's efforts in foreign affairs than in domestic issues. He buttressed this view with roll call data. Despite criticisms and refinements of his formulation, the basic theme persisted as an insightful approach to presidential-congressional behavior. On a broader canvas, his analytic collaboration with Richard Ellis demonstrated that our ratings of American presidents were largely determined by their ability to confront effectively the challenges before them; some failed these tests and others did not face them.

In the early 1980s Wildavsky, once a deeply committed New Deal Democrat, changed his party registration to Republican. Among other factors, this change coincided with his increasing concern about the national debt and his criticism of the environmental movement. He insisted that his students, although not trained in the physical sciences, could effectively evaluate research studies by environmentalists. He considered those studies to be seriously flawed and motivated by an effort to impose an egalitarian ideology on public policy. This egalitarian threat was linked to a formulation of policy preferences that Wildavsky employed frequently in later publications. Instead of the conventional liberal versus conservative dichotomy, he suggested a tripartite division among egalitarians, hierarchists, and individualists, which postulated a more complex but realistic political arena.

The breadth of Wildavsky's publications was remarkable, including federalism, foreign policy, community power, policy analysis and implementation, cultural theory, the collapse of communism, the leadership roles of biblical figures, academic administration, risk analysis, natural resource policy, and the craft of scholarship. He wrote or coauthored more than forty books and published more than 200 articles, not counting those in newspapers.

Wildavsky's personal and professional lives were firmly interwoven. His hobbies were gardening and walking. The latter was often a continuation of his current research in which he mentally reworked the topic of the moment, frequently accompanied with gestures as he "revised copy." His office was cluttered with piles of books, files, and clippings, reflecting the scope of his intellectual interests and his proclivity to pursue several projects at a time. With colleagues and students, he could appear gruff, but behind that initial impression one found a generous, kind, as well as brilliant individual. His intellectual legacy was not restricted to his publications but extended to his direct personal influence on scores of graduate students and professional colleagues.

He married Carol Shirk in 1955; they had four children and later divorced. In 1973 he married Mary Cadman, who survived him.

• Wildavsky's creative process and the genesis of several of his publications are eloquently delineated in his *The Revolt against the Masses* (1971), a collection of several articles, including the critique of Duverger, written during the first decade of his professorial career. His style of scholarship and intellectual contributions are recounted in Nelson W. Polsby, "The Contributions of President Aaron Wildavsky," *PS* 18, no. 4 (Fall 1985): 736–45, which is reprinted in *Aaron Wildavsky 1930–1993* (1993). The latter contains the most extensive bibliography of Wildavsky's writings. Additional insight about his professional significance is found in L. J. Jones, "Aaron Wildavsky: A Man for All Seasons," *Public Administration Review* 55, no. 1 (Jan.–Feb. 1995): 3–16. *The Politics of Mistrust: Estimating American Oil and Gas Resources* (1981), coauthored with Ellen Tenenbaum, illustrates Wildavsky's talent in taking a major public policy and illuminating the difficulties in comprehending it. *The New Politics of the Budgetary Process* (2d ed., 1992) is his most mature examination of national budgetary matters. Three books completed just before he died are indicative of the prodigious scholarly range as well as his final assessments on these diverse topics: *Assimilation versus Separation: Joseph the Administrator and the Politics of Religion in Biblical Israel* (1993); with Max Singer, *The Real World Order, Zones of Peace/Zones of Turmoil* (1993); and *But Is It True? A Citizen's Guide to Environmental Health and Safety Issues* (1995). Obituaries are in the *New York Times*, 6 Sept. 1993, and *PS* 26 (1993): 820–21.

THOMAS P. WOLF

WILDE, Richard Henry (24 Sept. 1789–10 Sept. 1847), poet and scholar, was born in Dublin, Ireland, the son of Richard Wilde, an ironmonger and hardware merchant, and Mary Newett. His mother's family was prominent in linen weaving and dying. Wilde's father settled in Baltimore, Maryland, in January 1797. After the death of his father in October 1802, Wilde moved to Augusta, Georgia, where his older brother was established, and went to work in a store owned by Irishman Captain John Cormick. In 1803 Wilde's mother joined her sons and opened her own store, employing Wilde. Throughout his life, Wilde remained Roman Catholic, his mother always Anglican.

Reading for the law in 1808, Wilde was admitted to the bar in 1809. Although the practice of law offered him the livelihood he always needed, Wilde was never happy in the profession, noting, years later, to his good friend American sculptor Hiram Powers that the spirit of art always suffers in the presence of law and commerce. Despite his personal preference for art, Wilde nonetheless distinguished himself as a lawyer, serving as attorney general for Georgia from 1811 to 1813 and practicing before the U.S. Supreme Court in 1817. In 1815–1817 and 1827–1835 Wilde served as a U.S. congressman.

In 1819 Wilde married Caroline Buckle, a widow, with whom he had three children. She died in 1827, a loss from which he never fully recovered.

Wilde is primarily remembered as an early Romantic American fugitive poet or as a scholar in classical Italian studies. The Wilde canon consists largely of unpublished manuscripts. His earliest poetry cultivated a brooding, melancholic attachment to the past. Restless, doomed to feelings of alienation and isolation, Wilde's Byronic hero is the paradigm of protean southern poetry: a clearly British literary figure in the face of developing American literary nationalism.

As a semichivalric southern poet in the tradition of Moore and Byron, a poet who dedicated many of his verses to women, Wilde preferred subject matters that enabled him to pursue themes of time, including the preciousness and transience of the moment at hand, the exaltation or lamentation of women, or a retrospection for a happier, idealized past.

The most often anthologized Wilde poem remains "The Lament of the Captive," published pseudonymously in April 1819 in *Analectic Magazine*, Wilde not claiming authorship until 1834. Because the poem became so popular with the reading audience—it was plagiarized by Irish poet Patrick O'Kelley and translated into Greek by Anthony Barclay, British consul in New York City—Wilde himself was accused of having plagiarized the poem from Barclay's Greek translation. Barclay explained his role in the affair in the *New York Mirror* of 28 February 1835.

The poem is based in part on Wilde's brother James's recounting of his travels through Florida, a landscape known to Americans primarily through the rhapsodic travel descriptions of William Bartram. Believed to have been composed as early as 1813 or 1814 (Tucker, p. 98), the poem conveys a sense of loss in large part as a result of Wilde's mother's death on 21 July 1815 and James Wilde's death in a duel on 16 January 1815. The poem became the third stanza of the Florida canto of *Hesperia* (1867).

The theme of alienation—of separation from one's civilization, family, humanity—is passionately lyrical in the poem, a grieving intensified by the repetitive *o* vowel sound in the next-to-last line. Each of the three stanzas opens with a simile and the repeated *like*, and each continues with the notion of natural transiency implicit in images of falling rose petals, autumn leaves, and footprints on the Tampa shore.

Wilde's only published book of poetry, posthumously issued in 1867, was *Hesperia*, dedicated to Manfredina di Cosenza (Mrs. Ellen Adair White-Beatty, whom Wilde greatly loved). The Byronic travelogue, comparable to *Childe Harold*, was published at a point in cultural history when the vogue for such expansive, reflective romantic excursions was over.

Wilde hoped to create an American epic with *Hesperia*. He drew his title from *Hesperus*, Greek for *Venus*. Knowing that the Greeks called Italy, to the west of them, *Hesperia*, Wilde envisioned America as the West or the Hesperides. The four sections of the epic include Florida, Virginia, Acadia, and Louisiana, Wilde using the most ancient Spanish, English, and French maps for the expansiveness attributed to each of the four areas by cartographers. Written in the ottava rima of *Don Juan*, the poem employs the journey of Fitzhugh DeLancey, who develops an increasingly dark and melancholic mind as he broods on the world about him.

Two poems deserve special note. "To Lord Byron" appeared in the *Southern Literary Messenger* (1, no. 4 [Nov. 1834]). Written in the Petrarchan sonnet form, the poem attains a neat compression and a pleasant music, Byron being likened to the classical Tacitus.

"To the Mocking Bird" was included by Griswold in *Poets and Poetry of America* (1842) but had been published at least as early as 1836. One of Wilde's best poems, this Petrarchan sonnet is particularly strong in its use of conceits such as the traditional fool of comedy; Yorick, the traditional satirist; and the Abbot of Misrule. As Graber (1959) has observed, that objectification of the abstract is not generally characteristic of the poet's work.

On 1 June 1835 Wilde sailed to Europe, spending two years traveling through western Europe and settling in Florence in 1837. Like American artist and writer William Wetmore Story, he undertook the study of Italian literature. In Florence he befriended American sculptor Horatio Greenough, who was completing his statue of Washington for the Capitol rotunda, and Hiram Powers, an American sculptor who was making a reputation for his candid treatment of the human body. Wilde began his studies of Dante and Tasso, spending the nearly five years of his Florentine sojourn in the Medici archives, the public libraries, and the private library of the grand duke of Tuscany. His crowning achievement in art history was the discovery of the lost Giotto portrait of Dante beneath the whitewashed walls of the Bargello of the Podesta in Florence.

After Wilde reluctantly returned to America, he published his *Conjectures and Researches concerning the Love, Madness and Imprisonment of Torquato Tasso* (1841–1842). Wilde's major interest in the book was why Tasso went mad and why he was imprisoned. Robert Browning reviewed the work favorably in the *Foreign Quarterly Review*, and Longfellow reprinted portions of it in his *Poets and Poetry of Europe* (1845).

Wilde's Florentine period also served to produce two major unfinished, unpublished manuscripts, *The Italian Lyric Poets* and *The Life and Times of Dante*. The longest entries in the anthology were those on Petrarch, Boccaccio, and Tasso. Although Wilde only completed one of the two planned Dante volumes, his love of Dante may well have influenced his own poetry like "Lines for the Music of Weber's Last Waltz" (composed 5 Jan. 1835).

Despite his love of poetry and Italian culture, Wilde settled down to the tedium of his Georgia law practice in 1841–1842. Needing money, especially for the education of his sons, Wilde left for New Orleans in 1843 to practice law with Judah P. Benjamin and to pursue opportunities offered him by his friendship with William C. Micou. He became the first professor of law at the University of Louisiana (now Tulane). He died of yellow fever in New Orleans.

• No one institution has a major collection of Wilde's manuscripts. Ralph S. Graber, "The Fugitive Poems of Richard Henry Wilde with an Introduction" (Ph.D. diss., Univ. of Pennsylvania, 1959), and Edward Llewellyn Tucker, *Richard Henry Wilde: His Life and Selected Poems* (1966), are the most helpful treatments of Wilde's life. Graber gives the locations of Wilde's scattered manuscripts on pp. xix–xxxiii. The standard assessment of Wilde's place in southern literature is Jay B. Hubbell, *The South in American Literature* (1954). Extremely helpful commentary on Wilde's connection to Powers is in the two-part article by Nathalia Wright, "The Letters of Richard Henry Wilde to Hiram Powers," *Georgia Historical Quarterly* 45, no. 9 (1962): 296–313 and 417–37; his connection to Greenough receives similar treatment in Wright, "Richard Henry Wilde on Greenough's Washington," *American Literature* 27 (1956): 556–57.

George C. Longest

WILDER, Alec (16 Feb. 1907–24 Dec. 1980), composer and music arranger, was born Alexander Lafayette Chew Wilder in Rochester, New York, the son of George Wilder, a banker, and Lillian Chew. From his earliest years, Wilder seems to have been solitary, retiring, and inclined to periods of melancholy offset by bouts of capricious humor.

As an adolescent, Wilder admired the Isham Jones orchestra and Noble Sissle and Eubie Blake's all-black musical *Shuffle Along*. His early education took place in private schools. After graduating from Collegiate School, a New York preparatory school, he failed to pass the regents examination to enter Princeton University; he then took private lessons for a while with Herbert Inch and Edward Royce at the Eastman School of Music, in Rochester. For the most part, however, Wilder was musically self-taught. While attending Eastman he met some lifelong friends for whom he would write music featuring them and their instruments: Mitch Miller, then an oboist; John Barrows, a French hornist; and Jimmy Carroll, a clarinetist. (Later, in the mid-1930s, he would form the Alec Wilder Octet, consisting of oboe, harpsichord, clarinet, flute, bass clarinet, bassoon, string bass, and percussion.) He soon left Rochester and moved to New York City, where he worked for various musicians and music publishers as a songwriter and arranger of popular music. It was at this time that he shortened "Alexander" to the less formal "Alec," feeling that this name was more appropriate for popular music. A very private person, Wilder was wary of marriage and avoided calling attention to himself. For most of his adult life his chief residence was the Algonquin Hotel in New York City.

One of Wilder's earliest efforts in New York was the song "All the King's Horses," with lyrics by Howard Dietz, which he wrote for the 1930–1931 revue *Three's A Crowd*. Wilder was soon writing songs or arranging numbers for such noted singers as Mildred Bailey, Bing Crosby, Mabel Mercer, and Ethel Waters, and later for Perry Como, Frank Sinatra, Peggy Lee, and Judy Garland. Benny Goodman and Jimmy Dorsey played his works for swing band. Four of his best-received songs, among the hundreds that he wrote, were "While We're Young" (1934), "I'll Be Around" (1939), "It's So Peaceful in the Country" (1941), and "Blackberry Winter" (1976). Some lyrics were his own, but most came from Johnny Mercer, Arnold Sundgaard, and Loonis McGlohon. The music for Wilder's popular songs strikes the ear as subtly pleasing to the senses. His melodies unfold somewhat unpredictably, often with unconventional interval skips. Some phrase shapes are surprising. His harmony is always supportive and often piquant. His jazz-inspired, frequently sprightly rhythms are always attractive, as might be expected from a musician who also worked in the jazz world, supplying music to such performers as Gerry Mulligan, Stan Getz, and jazz pianist Marian McPartland, one of his special friends. In 1972, after collaborating with James T. Maher, he published his insightful, though idiosyncratic and highly personal, book, *The American Popular Song*.

In the 1950s, Wilder turned increasingly to composing art music, especially when the new rock music, toward which he was unsympathetic, began to dominate the popular music world. He had always loved the music of J. S. Bach, Gabriel Fauré, Claude Debussy, and Maurice Ravel, and his own style derived from the latter three, synthesized with the popular and jazz styles with which he was intimately acquainted. Curious and somewhat askew reinterpretations of Bach-derived counterpoint appear here and there. Wilder assumes a creative stance between the American vernacular and the artistic that seem altogether individual. Melody, harmony, and rhythm share similar characteristics with those of his popular songs, with added leavening from the French composers he admired. The music immediately delights and always entertains its audience. Fast movements sound high-spirited and scintillate with good humor; slow movements often sing sadly, even inconsolably. Unfortunately, other art composers and academics judged his music superficial, while most jazz musicians criticized him for forsaking his true calling.

His artistic efforts went mostly into writing chamber music and musical stage works rather than symphonic orchestral pieces. Wilder also composed over 100 art songs. A ballet, *Juke Box*, was completed in 1940. Among his few concert compositions for orchestra are an early *Symphonic Piece* (1929) and the later *New England Suite* (1950), *A Child's Introduction to the Orchestra* (1954), and the *Carl Sandburg Suite* (1960). For his musician friends he fashioned solo concertos for oboe, saxophone, trumpet, French horn, euphonium, and tuba, backed by chamber orchestra or wind ensemble. Wilder liked the less tightly bound structures of the suite, composing several for strings and still others that allowed solo spots to every instrument employed in the symphony orchestra, including guitar and saxophone. He also composed several works (1961–1971), each described as an *Entertainment*, for winds or chamber orchestra. Further, he dashed off sonatas, duets, trios, quartets, octets, quintets, and a nonet. Whimsical titles and subtitles were his hallmark, including such names as "It's Silk, Feel It," "Neurotic Goldfish," "The House Detective Registers," "Sea Fugue, Mama," and "The Amorous Poltergeist."

Starting in the 1950s, Wilder produced many stage works, most of them short, requiring only a few singers and instrumentalists and making modest technical demands on the performers. He composed the one-act *The Lowland Sea* (1952), a folk production, following it with the one-act *Cumberland Fair* (1953), an unrestrained frolic. One theater work, *Miss Chicken Little* (1954), is a delightful children's fable meant for television. A number of others also were primarily written for children, including *The Churkendoose* (1968) and *Racketty Packetty House* (1971).

Wilder received an honorary doctorate from Eastman as well as the Peabody Award and the Deems Taylor ASCAP Award. His significance as a popular-song musician is attested by his induction into the Songwriter's Hall of Fame in 1983, but his importance as a composer of art music has yet to be assessed. He died in Gainesville, Florida.

• Wilder's manuscripts, letters, papers, and poems will eventually be held in the Alec Wilder Archive, established in 1989 at the Sibley Musical Library of the Eastman School of Music. Valuable insights into the man are found in Alec Wilder, *Letters I Never Sent* (1975). He is memorialized by people who admired his person and artistry in Whitney Balliett, *Alec Wilder and His Friends* (1974), and in Nancy Zeltsman, comp. *Alec Wilder, an Introduction to the Man and His Music* (1991). Also useful is the entry "Wilder, Alec," in the *Current Biography Yearbook* for 1980. David Demsey and Ronald Prather have issued a basic *Alec Wilder: A Bio-Bibliography* (1992).

NICHOLAS E. TAWA

WILDER, Laura Ingalls (7 Feb. 1867–10 Feb. 1957), author, was born Laura Elizabeth Ingalls near Pepin, Wisconsin, the daughter of Charles Ingalls and Caroline Quiner, farmers. The Ingalls family moved frequently during her childhood, settling finally in De Smet, South Dakota. She attended school until 1882, when she received her teaching certificate, although she was under the legally required age of sixteen. After teaching briefly, she married Almanzo Wilder, a farmer, in 1885. They had two children, one of whom died in infancy. In 1894 the Wilders purchased a farm near Mansfield, Missouri, where they spent the remainder of their lives.

Wilder's career began as a journalist, most notably as the home section editor and columnist for the *Missouri Ruralist* from 1911 to 1927. In 1915, with her daughter, Rose Wilder Lane, she wrote a children's poetry column, "Tuck'em in Corner," for the *San Francisco Bulletin*. More magazine articles followed, including works for *McCall's* and *Country Gentleman*.

Little House in the Big Woods was the first book in Wilder's chronicle of her pioneer childhood. Before publication in 1932, it was selected as a Junior Literary Guild book. More books followed: *Farmer Boy* (1933), based on her husband's childhood on a New York farm; *Little House on the Prairie* (1935); *On the Banks of Plum Creek* (1937); *By the Shores of Silver Lake* (1939); *The Long Winter* (1940); *Little Town on the Prairie* (1941); *These Happy Golden Years* (1943); and *The First Four Years*, published posthumously in 1971.

The books are based on Wilder's life, and the characters in the stories—Ma, Pa, Mary, Laura, Carrie, and Grace—retain the names of the Ingalls family.

Wilder referred to herself in the third person while writing, perhaps to avoid the appearance of autobiography, for the books are not truly autobiographical. Many of the family's moves were deleted or compressed into a single relocation, and various adjustments were made to make the novels more satisfying.

Wilder eloquently stated in her 1937 Bookweek speech her reason for writing the Little House series: "I realized that I had seen and lived it all—the successive phases of the frontier, first the frontiersman, then the pioneer, then the farmers and the towns. Then I understood that in my own life I represented a whole period of American history." By sharing this unique perspective with young readers, she hoped they would be able "to understand more about the beginning of things, to know what is behind the things they see—what it is that made America as they know it."

The view that Wilder presented of the early pioneer landscape was not falsely romanticized, nor was it drawn overly harshly. Her exuberant portrayal often differs sharply from the grim images prevalent in adult fiction about the American frontier. A good portion of this divergence comes from her point of view as she captures the initial fear of a child transported from her home to an alien landscape. Not only is the physical environment different—the Big Woods have been replaced by open prairie—but the emotional environment has also suddenly shifted. Laura's extended family of grandparents, aunts, uncles, and cousins has been replaced by the very close circle of her immediate family. Wilder effectively depicts the initial distress and difficult interpretation, subsequent wary exploration and tentative knowledge, and final understanding and joyful acceptance as Laura and the prairie develop a symbiotic relationship that will carry her into adulthood.

As the series progresses, Laura becomes more and more comfortable with her surroundings, and the reader can measure her steps to adulthood through her coming to terms with her surroundings. This subtle signal of growth is enhanced by the increasing reading difficulty of each successive volume in the series.

As Wilder's childhood provided her with the framework of the books, so did her own child assist her in preparing the books. Rose Wilder Lane was an established journalist and novelist and eager to help her mother embark on a writing career. Questions have arisen about the nature of Lane's input into the Little House books. Her expertise served Wilder well as Lane helped her mother through the often tricky roads of writing novels. The editorial relationship was unusual: not only were Wilder and Lane parent and child—a pairing innately fraught with potential for disputes—but the child in this case was advising and leading the parent. This led to an impact more direct and, at the same time, more convoluted than in a usual writer-editor relationship. Essentially what Lane did was "pre-edit" the manuscript, helping her mother shape it.

Five of the books in the series were Newbery Honor Books: *On the Banks of Plum Creek*, *By the Shores of Silver Lake*, *The Long Winter*, *Little Town on the Prairie*, and *These Happy Golden Years*. In 1942 *By the Shores of Silver Lake* received the Pacific Northwest Library Young Reader's Choice Award. The American Library Association established the Laura Ingalls Wilder Award, which recognizes an author's or illustrator's enduring contribution to children's literature. Wilder was the first recipient of the award in 1954.

Devoted to her family, Wilder was a practical and modest woman with a quiet sense of humor. Her need to "see out loud" for her blind sister Mary when they were young forced Wilder to develop an acute awareness of beauty and an ability to express her appreciation of nature, traits that are evident in the Little House books. Wilder died in Mansfield, Missouri.

A television program, "Little House on the Prairie," and later "Little House on the Prairie: A New Beginning," appeared on NBC from 1974 to 1983. The programs were loosely based on the books and introduced another generation to the pioneer novels.

In 1994 HarperCollins Children's Books, publisher of the Little House books, embarked on an innovative marketing attempt to reach a wider audience with Wilder's stories. A series of picture books adapting chapters from the Little House series for younger readers was released. Additional titles for other age groups continue to be added in response to an ever-increasing demand for more Wilder-related information and stories.

Wilder's books have found appreciative audiences since they were written. (By 1994 more than 35 million copies were in print.) Children find themselves strongly identifying with Laura: a constant theme running through the letters Wilder received and the responses from current readers is "I wish I were Laura." Laura seems to embody the pioneer spirit that brought so many families west, and as a child, she is able to be cognizantly unaffected by the difficulties and hardships that drove so many of those same families back. Yet her struggles are those of universal childhood—of arguing with her sister, of getting lost, of disputes with classmates, and so on—all within the framework of absolute joy. Laura is a timeless spirit.

• The major manuscript and correspondence collection is in the Rose Wilder Lane Papers, Herbert Hoover Presidential Library, West Branch, Iowa. The University of Missouri at Columbia holds some manuscripts and correspondence. Extensive biographies are Donald Zochert, *Laura: The Life of Laura Ingalls Wilder* (1976), written for young readers, and William T. Anderson, *Laura Ingalls Wilder: A Biography* (1992), written for a more generalized audience. *On the Way Home: The Diary of a Trip from South Dakota to Mansfield, Missouri, in 1894* (1962) contains Wilder's journal entries and an introduction by Rose Wilder Lane. *West from Home: Letters of Laura Ingalls Wilder, San Francisco 1915*, ed. Roger Lea MacBride (1974), includes letters from Wilder and her daughter to Almanzo Wilder. *A Little House Sampler*, ed. William T. Anderson (1988), is a collection of short writings, many previously unpublished, by Wilder and her daughter. For a chronology of her life, annotated bibliographies, primary and secondary sources, and critical comment, see Janet

Spaeth, *Laura Ingalls Wilder* (1987). Fred Erisman, *Laura Ingalls Wilder* (1994), is a brief but thorough literary study. An obituary is in the *New York Times*, 12 Feb. 1957.

JANET SPAETH

WILDER, Raymond Louis (3 Nov. 1896–7 July 1982), mathematician and mathematical historiographer, was born in Palmer, Massachusetts, the son of John Louis Wilder, a printer, and Mary Jane Shanley. Wilder's original intention was to become an actuary. He entered Brown University in 1914, but his studies were interrupted by World War I, during which he served as an ensign in the U.S. Navy from 1917 to 1919. Returning to Brown, he received a Ph.B. in 1920 and was an instructor in mathematics in 1920–1921, before being awarded an M.S. (specializing in actuarial mathematics) in 1921. From 1921 to 1924 he was an instructor at the University of Texas, where he received a Ph.D. in mathematics in 1923. His dissertation "Concerning Continuous Curves" was written under the direction of Robert L. Moore, who produced some fifty doctorates, and Wilder, Moore's first doctoral student in Austin, is generally considered one of his most prominent students. In 1921 Wilder married Una Maude Greene; they had four children.

In 1924 Wilder became an assistant professor at Ohio State University. He then moved to the University of Michigan, where he spent the major part of his academic career, serving successively as assistant professor (1926–1929), associate professor (1929–1935), professor (1935–1947), and finally research professor (1947–1967). During this period he was also a member of the Institute for Advanced Study (1933–1934), a Guggenheim fellow (1940–1941, in Austin), a visiting professor at the University of Southern California (1947), a research associate at the California Institute of Technology (1949–1950), Henry Russel Lecturer at Michigan (1958–1959), Taft Memorial Lecturer at the University of Cincinnati (1958), and visiting research professor at Florida State University (1961–1962). The Russel Lectureship is the highest honor the University of Michigan bestows on its faculty members. Following his retirement from Michigan, he was a lecturer at the University of California at Santa Barbara (1970–1971) and subsequently a research associate at the institution from 1971 until his death.

Active in the work of the American Mathematical Society, Wilder was a member of its council (1935–1937), a semicentennial lecturer in 1938, colloquium lecturer in 1942, vice president (1950–1951), president (1955–1956), and Josiah Williard Gibbs Lecturer in 1969. He was also president of the Mathematical Association of America (1965–1966) and recipient of its Distinguished Service Award (1973). He was elected a member of the National Academy of Sciences in 1963. In 1975 the University of Michigan honored him by creating the R. L. Wilder Professorship of Mathematics.

Wilder's mathematical research may be divided into two periods. The first (1924–1930) was largely concerned with plane point set theory as practiced by Moore and his school. During this time "Texas-style" topology, created by Moore, was devoted to continuous curves and the theory of continua as part of the body of work called the Schoenflies Program, named for German mathematician Arthur S. Schoenflies. Wilder was extremely active in this area, and much of the resulting theory was influenced by his work. His dissertation (published in 1925) contained a new approach and was widely hailed. Later, he showed that one of the assumptions in Moore's first group of axioms was not independent (1928), and this led to a simplification that was subsequently adopted by Moore in his monumental book *Foundations of Point Set Theory* (1932). From 1930 to 1950 Wilder worked primarily on higher dimensional topology and the theory of topological manifolds, producing topological characterizations of the sphere, extensions of the Jordan-Brouwer Theorem, and investigations of generalized manifolds. Generalized manifolds had been introduced earlier by Eduard Čech and Solomon Lefschetz, but Wilder recognized that the manifolds offered a natural context in which to extend the Schoenflies Program to higher dimensions (1934). He dealt with this in his 1942 colloquium lectures and ultimately gave a full account of the new theory in the monograph *Topology of Manifolds* (1949), which was well received and represented a real advance in the literature of algebraic topology; it was reprinted in 1963 and 1982.

The second period of Wilder's mathematical work (1950–1982) was of an entirely different character. Long interested in various aspects of the foundations, history, and philosophy of mathematics, he apparently decided in the late 1940s to devote the major part of his research effort to this new enterprise. For some twenty years he had lectured at Michigan on the foundations of mathematics, and the success of his course (which appealed to both specialists and nonspecialists in mathematics) led him to prepare a textbook, *Introduction to the Foundations of Mathematics* (1952; 2d ed., 1965). This remarkable book was a lucid amalgam of foundations, history, and the philosophy of mathematics. Wilder then proceeded to elaborate his own approach to the cultural development of mathematics and in doing so broke new ground by employing the methods of cultural anthropology. Following the lead of anthropologist Alfred L. Kroeber, he sought to classify the forces responsible for the evolution of mathematics in terms of environmental stress (physical and cultural), hereditary stress, symbolization, diffusion, abstraction, generalization, consolidation, diversification, cultural lag, cultural resistance, and selection. Wilder's view presented in his *Evolution of Mathematical Concepts: An Elementary Study* (1969), was that mathematics is something man made and that the type of mathematics that man creates is as much a function of the time as of any other adaptive mechanisms. Above all, his work was an inquiry (above the individual level) into the ways in which mathematical notions originate and an attempt to determine those factors that encourage or discourage their development and dissemination. Although an example of Wilder's engaging and low-key exposition, the book had a mixed reception. Some mathematical historians welcomed it as an innovative departure from the usual chronological treatment, while others were hostile or politely silent. It was mistakenly regarded as a popular history of mathematics, whereas, in fact, the author's intent was to encourage people to reflect on the nature of mathematics in a new manner using the methods of anthropology. As he maintained, his approach was neither mathematics nor history but merely a way of looking at mathematics and its history. Continuing his inquiries, he produced *Mathematics as a Cultural System* (1981), which was more overtly anthropological, and less historical, in tone.

Wilder's work on the problem of understanding the nature of mathematics succeeded in taking a step beyond the ideas expressed by Henri Poincaré in his last essays and by Jacques Hadamard in his seminal *An Essay on the Psychology of Invention in the Mathematical Field* (1949). Ultimately the questions Wilder raised remain as open challenges to historical research, and while he demonstrated that a cultural anthropological approach is viable, it is perhaps less clear that it is the "correct" approach.

Wilder was a significant figure in the creation of an American school of topology. He was an inspiring teacher, who greatly contributed to the creation of a distinguished center of excellence at Michigan. He personally supervised twenty-two doctoral students, many of whom, including Leon W. Cohen and Thomas Brahana, became noted topologists; and through his classes and seminars he "discovered" several other noteworthy topologists, such as Norman E. Steenrod and Stephen S. Smale. The University of Michigan Topology Conference of 1940 was the first major American conference of its kind, and its proceedings, *Lectures in Topology* (1941), edited by William L. Ayres and Wilder, was very influential. Wilder was also a tireless supporter of American mathematical organizations and one of the founders in 1952 of the *Michigan Mathematical Journal*. In all his endeavors, he was an enthusiastic promoter of American mathematics with an unfailing eye for mathematical talent and an abiding passion for excellence in scholarship. He was a much beloved figure in the American mathematical community, and his friendship and support of his student was legendary. Wilder remained active until his death in Santa Barbara, California.

• The Wilder papers are held by the University of Texas at Austin as part of its Archives of American Mathematics. Samples of his mathematical style and taste may be found in his papers "The Sphere in Topology," *American Mathematical Society Semicentennial Publications* 2 (1938): 136–84; "The Cultural Basis of Mathematics," *Proceedings of the Sixth International Congress of Mathematicians* 1 (1950): 258–71; and "The Origin and Growth of Mathematical Concepts," *Bulletin of the American Mathematical Society* 59 (Sept. 1953): 423–48. For examples of his perceptive and cogent writing on the methodology of mathematics, see his "The Nature of Mathematical Proof," *American Mathematical Monthly* 51 (June–July 1944): 309–33; "Axiomatics and the Development of Creative Talent," in *The Axiomatic Method with Special Reference to Geometry and Physics*, ed. L. Henkin et al. (1959); and "The Role of the Axiomatic Method," *American Mathematical Monthly* 74 (Feb. 1967). One of his last papers, "The Mathematical Work of R. L. Moore: Its Background, Nature and Influence," *Archive for the History of Exact Sciences* 26 (Apr. 1982): 73–97, provides valuable insight into both Moore and his influence on Wilder's mathematical work. There is an interesting autobiographical sketch in Sybil P. Parker, ed., *McGraw Hill Modern Scientists and Engineers*, vol. 3 (1980), pp. 318–19.

JOSEPH D. ZUND

WILDER, Robert Parmalee (2 Aug. 1863–27 Mar. 1938), mission activist, was born in Kolhapur, India, the son of Royal Gould Wilder and Eliza Jane Smith, missionaries. His parents worked with the interdenominational American Board of Commissioners for Foreign Missions from 1846 to 1858, independently from 1861 to 1870, and with the Presbyterian Board of Foreign Missions from 1870 to 1875. Raised in the devout and multicultural environment of an American Protestant mission in western India and committing himself to missionary service at the age of ten, Wilder maintained an international perspective, an intense personal faith, and a commitment to Christian evangelism throughout his life. The family settled in Princeton, New Jersey, after 1875, and Royal Wilder began publishing the *Missionary Review* (later the *Missionary Review of the World*) there in 1878. Robert Wilder attended Princeton Preparatory School and Williston Seminary in Easthampton, Massachusetts, before entering Princeton College in 1881.

In 1883 his missionary commitment earned him—though he was still an undergraduate—an invitation to an Inter-Seminary Missionary Alliance summer conference, where he was inspired further by conservative Baptist mission and holiness advocate A. J. Gordon. He returned to Princeton to organize a college foreign missionary society. He left school in poor health in 1884 and worked on a Nebraska cattle ranch for three months. Returning to Princeton, he graduated in 1886. That summer he attended, at the insistence of Young Men's Christian Association organizer Luther Wishard, evangelist Dwight L. Moody's first conference for college students at Mount Hermon, Massachusetts. Wilder introduced missions as a conference theme and persuaded Moody to allow mission meetings and presentations by himself and Moody's friend Arthur T. Pierson. In the end 100 students committed themselves to becoming foreign missionaries. The "Mount Hermon Hundred" were followed by others, and the Student Volunteer Movement for Foreign Missions (SVM) was formally organized in 1888, with an executive committee chaired by YMCA representative John R. Mott. Dedicated to recruiting students as missionaries of their denominational agencies, the SVM borrowed the pledge it asked students to sign—"I am willing and desirous, God permitting, to become a foreign missionary" —from Wilder's Princeton society. Its famous watchword—"the evangelization of the world in this generation" —has been variously attributed to that society and to Arthur Pierson.

In eight months of 1886 and 1887 Wilder and John Forman visited 162 educational institutions and collected more than 2,000 student pledges, including 250 from women. Wilder entered Union Theological Seminary in New York City in 1887 and graduated in 1891, taking off 1888–1889 to visit colleges for the SVM again. He believed that seminary training was an asset to his work but thought he was more accessible to students as a layman and so never sought ordination. In 1891 he left for India, by way of Great Britain, as a missionary to students of the Presbyterian Board of Foreign Missions.

Wilder's visits to British universities culminated in the creation of the Student Volunteer Missionary Union of Great Britain and Ireland (SVMU) at an April 1892 meeting he chaired in Edinburgh. The previous summer he had left England for Norway in search of better health and in the process met Helene Olsson of Gjovik. The couple was married in Kristiania on 7 September and sailed for India on 25 November 1892; they would have four children.

Wilder worked with the Calcutta YMCA from July 1893 through 1894 and with educated Hindus in Poona in western India from July 1895 to March 1897. The next two years he spent in the United States—at the insistence of John Mott—working with the YMCA and SVM. Wilder returned to India in 1899 as college secretary of the YMCA International Committee and then national secretary of the YMCA of India, until poor health forced his resignation in 1903. After recuperation in Norway, a 1905 tour of British universities led to eleven years in various positions in the British Student Christian Movement and the SVMU as well as periodic work in Europe with the World Student Christian Federation.

Wilder moved to Norway when World War I began and in 1915 to London—where he worked with foreign students—and then back to the United States in 1916. Until 1919 he was secretary of the YMCA's Religious Work Department and in this capacity directed the Religious Work Bureau of the YMCA's National War Work Council once the United States entered the war. In September 1919 he became general secretary of the Student Volunteer Movement.

Both the SVM and the foreign mission movement within the mainstream American Protestant churches peaked in numbers in the early 1920s: more than 8,000 volunteers had become missionaries since 1888, and a third of the almost 1,800 missionaries who sailed in 1921 came through the SVM. Thereafter the movements declined in the face of growing nationalism overseas, conflict between theological liberals and fundamentalists at home, and the shift of much liberal interest from evangelism to interreligious dialogue and social reform. In 1920 John Mott resigned as chairman of the SVM executive committee after thirty-two years, depriving the SVM of his fundraising connections and ties with other student and ecumenical organizations. The movement was affected also by the rise of competing student groups and the demands of SVM students for greater control of the organization.

Widely known and liked by Christian students worldwide, Wilder worked hard to help the SVM face these challenges. He urged that social action be balanced with evangelism and endeavored to raise funds from an increasingly indifferent audience. The number of volunteers continued to decline, however, along with—from Wilder's perspective—the organization's original spirit and clarity of purpose. He resigned in 1927 to become, at age sixty-four, executive secretary of the Christian Council for Western Asia and Northern Africa (after 1929, the Near East Christian Council). This ecumenical organization had offices in Cairo, but Wilder traveled extensively, visiting missions and various Christian and other religious bodies in the region. He retired to Norway in poor health at the end of his second three-year term in 1933.

Wilder visited England in 1934 and British universities in 1935 under the auspices of the Intervarsity Fellowship of Evangelical Unions, conservative rival of the SVMU. He published a history of the SVM, *The Great Commission, the Missionary Response of the Student Volunteer Movements in North America and Europe: Some Personal Reminiscences*, and a collection of his student addresses, *Christ and the Student World*, in 1935. He continued to travel throughout Europe and to the United States and Egypt and spent winters in Oslo, Norway, where he died.

• Wilder's papers are in the library of the Yale Divinity School. The archives of the Student Volunteer Movement also are in the Yale Divinity School Library. See in addition the published reports of its quadrennial conventions. Wilder preferred speaking to writing. His other published works include *Studies on the Holy Spirit* (1913) and *The Student Volunteer Movement* (1935). Wilder's daughter, Ruth Wilder Braisted, wrote and the Student Volunteer Movement published the only biography to date, *In This Generation: The Story of Robert P. Wilder* (1941). YMCA activist and missionary G. Sherwood Eddy made Wilder the subject of one of his brief reflections in *Pathfinders of the World Missionary Crusade* (1945). The most comprehensive study of Wilder is unpublished, Matthew Hugh Kelleher, "Robert Wilder and the American Foreign Missionary Movement" (Ph.D. diss., St. Louis Univ., 1974).

Regarding Wilder's work for the SVM see John R. Mott, *History of the Student Volunteer Movement for Foreign Missions* (1892), *Five Decades and a Forward View* (1939), and *The Student Volunteer Movement for Foreign Missions*, vol. 1 of *The Addresses and Papers of John R. Mott* (1946); Clarence P. Shedd, *Two Centuries of Student Christian Movements: Their Origin and Intercollegiate Life* (1934); Clifton J. Phillips, "The Student Volunteer Movement and Its Role in China Missions, 1886–1920," in *The Missionary Enterprise in China and America*, ed. John K. Fairbank (1974), and "Changing Attitudes in the Student Volunteer Movement of Great Britain and North America," in *Missionary Ideologies in the Imperialist Era: 1880–1920*, ed. Toben Christensen and William R. Hutchison (1984); and Valentin Rabe, *The Home Base of American China Missions, 1880–1920* (1978).

Standard histories of the YMCA are C. Howard Hopkins, *History of the YMCA in North America* (1951), and Kenneth Scott Latourette, *World Service: A History of the Foreign Work and World Service of the Young Men's Christian Association of the U.S. and Canada* (1957). Obituaries include L. Delavan Pierson, "Robert P. Wilder and His Vision of White Harvest Fields," *Sunday School Times*, Apr. 1938, and tributes by Mott, Robert E. Speer, and other missionary leaders in "A Man Who Stirred the Student World," *Missionary Review of the World* 61 (May 1938): 226–29.

ROBERT A. SCHNEIDER

WILDER, Thornton (17 Apr. 1897–7 Dec. 1975), novelist and playwright, was born Thornton Niven Wilder in Madison, Wisconsin, the son of Amos Parker Wilder, a diplomat and editor of the *State Journal*, and Isabella Thornton Niven. As a young child, Wilder lived in Madison, but in 1906 his father became consul general in Hong Kong, and the family moved overseas.

Because of the volatile political situation, Isabella Wilder and the children returned to America after only a few months. Amos visited as often as he could, and in 1910, when conditions stabilized in Hong Kong, the Wilder family again settled there. Thornton attended the Kaiser Wilhelm School and then the China Inland Missionary Boys' School, where he briefly fancied becoming a missionary himself. When Amos Wilder's assignment ended in 1913, the family settled in Berkeley, California. After graduating from Berkeley High School, where he first showed his talent as both playwright and actor, Wilder first attended Oberlin College and then Yale, where he received a B.A. degree in 1920. William Lyon Phelps, a Yale professor and noted literary critic, called Wilder "a star of the first magnitude."

Since Wilder had no specific career plans in mind after graduation, his father made decisions for him. First, he sent his son to study archaeology at the American Academy in Rome for a summer. Amos then found him a job teaching French at Lawrenceville, a preparatory school in New Jersey. During this period, Wilder began working on the novel that would be published as *The Cabala* in 1926.

The Cabala draws upon Wilder's memories of Rome, but more significantly it sets forth some themes and techniques that appear in his subsequent fiction and drama. In *The Cabala*, two Americans, Samuele and James Blair, find themselves involved with a group of bored aristocratic Europeans. Samuele is a typical Wilder protagonist: innocent, intelligent, sensitive, moral, rational, and stable. These qualities endear him to other characters, who turn to him as confidant and adviser. James also serves as prototype for future characters; he is a Harvard graduate and a classical scholar, a young man who has been "frightened by life" and therefore turns to books for solace.

Like many of Wilder's subsequent books, *The Cabala* is written as a series of linked episodes that question the meaning of the good life. Wilder also explores the confrontation between Europeans and Americans. Unlike many of his generation, he did not feel the lure of Europe as a place of artistic inspiration. He preferred the United States, even if he had to work within the context of a Puritan heritage that other writers found constraining.

The Cabala received warm reviews, and Wilder was encouraged to pursue a literary career. His next work, *The Bridge of San Luis Rey* (1927), is similar in structure, but here Wilder uses as a setting eighteenth-century Peru. Five people die in the collapse of an ancient bridge, and Wilder's protagonist, Brother Juniper, searches for some meaning in the deaths. What, he asks, did these five people have in common? What can we learn from their lives? The book sets forth themes that recur in Wilder's fiction: love, brotherhood, tolerance, and faith. Its last statement applies to many of Wilder's works: "There is a land of the living and a land of the dead and the bridge is love, the only survival, the only meaning."

Wilder was unprepared for the acclaim that followed the publication of *The Bridge of San Luis Rey*. In the *New Republic* (28 Dec. 1927), Malcolm Cowley called the book "perfect in itself. . . . The texture is completely unified; nothing falls short of its mark; nothing exceeds it; and the book as a whole is like some faultless temple erected to a minor deity." The novel won a Pulitzer Prize.

Although Wilder returned to Lawrenceville, new opportunities quickly presented themselves. He completed a speaking tour of Europe and then accepted an invitation from his former Oberlin classmate Robert Hutchins to teach at the University of Chicago, where Hutchins had just become president. Wilder's light teaching obligations enabled him to continue writing intensely. *The Angel That Troubled the Waters and Other Plays* was published in 1928, but it did not attain the popularity of *The Bridge of San Luis Rey*. The plays, some of which were written during Wilder's days at Oberlin, were not meant to be staged. Wilder considered them similar to poetry in their distillation of themes and compression of events. Their one underlying theme was, he explained, "religious, but religious in that dilute fashion that is a believer's concession to a contemporary standard of good manners." For Wilder, "good manners" indicated that he, as a writer, must not make readers feel uncomfortable.

His interest in "dilute" religious themes recurred in his next novel, *The Woman of Andros* (1930), set in pre-Christian Greece. Chrysis, the central character, sees beyond her pagan society to a world that is enlightened by Christian values. She counsels the young people who gather around her to open their minds and hearts to these new ideas.

The Woman of Andros received mixed reviews. Henry Seidel Canby, writing in the *Saturday Review*, called the novel a masterpiece. But other critics wondered why Wilder could not respond to his own world and time: the United States struggling in a severe economic depression. Michael Gold, writing in the *New Republic* (22 Oct. 1930), called Wilder a "Prophet of the Genteel Christ" and criticized him for targeting a wealthy minority who wanted to cut themselves off from the realities of contemporary life. The article inspired a month of debate, with letters flooding the magazine's offices. Wilder, however, remained silent.

Yet his next novel, *Heaven's My Destination* (1935), responded to Gold's criticisms. George Marvin Brush, a salesman of religious textbooks, travels across depression-ridden America dispensing his ideas on morality and involving himself in an assortment of lives. George is self-righteous, naive, and often exasperating, but he gives Wilder a chance to make his own statement about the importance of literature in times of crisis. Although George becomes depressed by the people he meets and their living conditions, he never loses his optimism or his faith in humanity. Rather than treat current events as tragic, Wilder preferred to place them in long perspective, searching for meaning that transcends daily experience.

For Wilder, this search culminated in his most successful and enduring work, *Our Town*, performed in 1938, when the world again was facing devastation. Grovers Corners—modeled after Peterborough, New Hampshire, which Wilder had visited in 1924 when he worked at the nearby MacDowell Colony—emerges as an archetypal New England town, where the milkman makes his morning rounds, teenagers stop for sodas after school, and one Emily Webb marries a certain George Gibbs, dies in childbirth, and returns in spirit to relive a day of her life on earth. As Emily learns, human beings take for granted the important relationships in their lives. Wilder explained that he wanted to show "the life of a village against the life of the stars." His was the right message for the time. *Our Town* earned Wilder his second Pulitzer Prize.

For the next few years, interrupted only by travel for the government and work in military intelligence during World War II, Wilder devoted himself to writing plays. *The Merchant of Yonkers* (which he revised as *The Matchmaker* and which was later transformed into *Hello, Dolly!*) was produced in 1939. This farce, set in the late nineteenth century, did not have the impact of *Our Town* or of Wilder's next play, *The Skin of Our Teeth* (1942).

"It was written," Wilder said of *The Skin of Our Teeth*, "on the event of our entrance into the war and under strong emotion." Will humankind survive repeated violence? Wilder asks. In answer, he traces the history of humanity from the Ice Age to contemporary America. Wilder's playful indifference to time and place, his irreverence, and his ability to interweave deeply philosophical themes into a broad comedy set *The Skin of Our Teeth* apart from contemporary plays. This work earned Wilder his third Pulitzer Prize.

After the war, Wilder returned to fiction with *The Ides of March* (1948), whose protagonist is Julius Caesar, portrayed here as an exemplary statesman. Concerned with the notion of verisimilitude in fiction, Wilder attempted a new form for this novel: instead of constructing a chronological narrative, he presents this work as a series of fictionalized letters, diary entries, messages, and documents. By the time *The Ides of March* was published, Thornton Wilder was one of the most famous men of letters in the United States and was widely read abroad. Sometimes, however, he needed to withdraw from public life in order to write. He favored such retreats as the New England village of Stockbridge, Massachusetts, or the small town of Douglas, Arizona. He liked to work, he said, where he was unrecognized and could chat with the natives.

In these settings he produced several collections of plays: *Three Plays: Our Town, The Skin of Our Teeth, The Matchmaker* (1957), *The Drunken Sisters* (1957), "Plays for Bleecker Street" (three one-act dramas staged in January 1962 at the Circle in the Square on Bleecker Street in New York City), and *The Alcestiad, or A Life in the Sun* (1977); and two more novels: *The Eighth Day* (1967) and *Theophilus North* (1973).

Published when Wilder was seventy, *The Eighth Day* tells the tale of John Barrington Ashley, tried for the murder of a neighbor and found guilty. After being sentenced to death, Ashley escapes to Chile, leaving his wife and children in the town that rebuffs and ignores them. Five years later, new evidence proves Ashley innocent. The story of Ashley and his family during those five difficult years enabled Wilder to send his message to the world: all individuals must work together toward a common good; humility, tolerance, and generosity are benchmarks of civilization.

Wilder always was reluctant to write autobiographically. Although correspondences with his personal life appear in many works, these usually are superficial. In his last novel, *Theophilus North*, for example, Wilder created a character who has lived in China, attended Yale, and spent a summer in Rome; after teaching at a boys' preparatory school, he spends some time in Newport, Rhode Island, where he becomes involved in many people's lives. But Theophilus remains essentially one-dimensional because Wilder does not offer a psychological context for his behavior. In none of his works does Wilder make any allusion to his own homosexuality, and in fact he seems uncomfortable writing about sexuality at all.

Throughout his career, Wilder reminded his readers of the power of love and joyfulness, and cautioned them about the perils of the unexamined life. Because he worked to simplify complex philosophical themes, he has often been seen as derivative, even simplistic. Yet Wilder was deeply committed to literature as a powerful force in shaping ideas and behavior, deliberately writing for a large middle-class audience rather than academic or "literary" readers. He was a strongly inventive writer of serious, affecting works. If it sometimes disappointed him that critics did not accord him the respect they gave to some of his contemporaries—Hemingway, for example, or Faulkner—he always was gratified by the connection he felt with his readers. He believed that his works would endure and bring to readers his message of hope and his abiding faith in humanity.

Wilder died in Hamden, Connecticut.

• Most of Wilder's manuscripts and papers are in the American literature collection at the Beinecke Library, Yale University. Other collections with Wilder material are at the University of Virginia, Harvard University, and the University of California at Berkeley. Wilder's essays have been edited by Donald Gallup, *American Characteristics and Other Essays* (1979). Gallup also edited *The Journals of Thornton Wilder, 1939–1961* (1985).

Several biographies have appeared: Richard Goldstone, *Thornton Wilder: An Intimate Portrait* (1975); Linda Simon, *Thornton Wilder: His World* (1979); and Gilbert Harrison, *The Enthusiast: A Life of Thornton Wilder* (1983). Critical studies include Malcolm Goldstein, *The Art of Thornton Wilder* (1965); M. C. Kuner, *Thornton Wilder: The Bright and the Dark* (1972); and David Castronovo, *Thornton Wilder* (1986). Amos Niven Wilder assesses his brother's career in *Thornton Wilder and His Public* (1980).

LINDA SIMON

WILENTZ, David Theodore (21 Dec. 1894–6 July 1988), attorney general of New Jersey and prosecutor in the Lindbergh baby kidnapping case, was born in Dwinsk, Latvia, the son of Nathan Wilentz, a tobacco importer, and Bertha Crane. Wilentz was brought to the United States at age two by his parents, who settled in Perth Amboy, New Jersey. His father became a successful tobacco importer, selling leaf to local cigar makers. One of David's earliest jobs was delivering tobacco leaf by horse-drawn cart. He attended local public schools, graduating from Perth Amboy High School in 1912. Following graduation he worked briefly for the local Baker Asphalt and Paving Co., after which he began the journalistic phase of his career, working first as a copyboy and reporter and then succeeding soon-to-be-governor Harold Hoffman as sports editor for the *Perth Amboy Evening News*. During this time he commuted to New York to attend night classes at the New York Law School, from which he graduated in 1917. His studies were followed by service in the army during World War I, from which he received an honorable discharge as a lieutenant. In 1919 Wilentz married Lena Goldman. They had three children: Robert, who was chief justice of the New Jersey Supreme Court from 1979 until his death in 1996; Warren, who became managing partner of the Wilentz law firm; and Norma, who married Leon Hess, chairman of the Amerada-Hess Corporation and owner of the New York Jets football team.

Wilentz returned to Perth Amboy to establish a private law practice with his high school friend John E. Toolan, who would become a state senator, and he soon became deeply involved in Democratic party politics, guiding Democratic candidates for the first time in decades to election to city council in 1921 and to the Middlesex County Board of Freeholders in 1923. He was appointed city attorney of Perth Amboy in 1928 and in the same year became chairman of the Middlesex County Democratic party. By 1929 he had fielded a slate of Democratic candidates for county offices. In that year he utilized his legal knowledge and ties to local papers to organize a well-publicized investigation of the finances of the overwhelmingly Republican board of freeholders. Although no indictments were ever handed down, the audit suggested that there had been irregularities in the awarding of road contracts and that personalized fountain pens had been used as rewards for political contributions. This so-called Pen Scandal, along with the looming Great Depression, helped Wilentz wrench power from the Republicans and solidify control for the Middlesex County Democratic Organization, which faced no serious challenge over the next four decades.

This stunning political pendulum swing catapulted Wilentz to statewide prominence, and on 5 February 1934 he was appointed attorney general by Governor A. Harry Moore at the direction of Mayor Frank Hague of Jersey City. Sensitive to implications that he would be beholden to Hague, Wilentz asserted his independence and was reported in the *Central New Jersey Home News* in 1934 to have said: "I will accept it [the position] on one condition. If I take the office I will be no dummy. I will be the attorney-general. I have no political or other obligations to anyone and I will accept none imposed on me by anyone else."

It was as attorney general that Wilentz made the largest mark of his career, his prosecution of the Lindbergh baby kidnapping case. A young lawyer who had never before tried a criminal case, Wilentz plunged into this one with an energy and brilliance that later would earn him such descriptions as vicious, merciless, and ferocious. The defendant, Bruno Richard Hauptmann, was a German immigrant carpenter with a criminal record in his native land who spoke with an accent and maintained his innocence to the end. After having been picked up by the New York police in possession of marked bills from the ransom money, Hauptmann was extradited to New Jersey, where, in the Flemington courtroom, the trial began on 3 January 1935.

The atmosphere surrounding the trial was extraordinary, with prominent coverage in the press by notable reporters, such as Walter Winchell and Damon Runyon, as well as in newsreels. The local sheriff sold tickets for the galleries: $10 for the main floor, $5 for the balcony. The defense attorney described the proceedings as a "Circus Maximus." Wilentz, as prosecutor in the case, cut a dashing figure in his double-breasted suits and his trademark fedoras. He was also energetic—to the point of fault, some would contend—in his questioning of the defendant. Winchell commented in a 1935 broadcast, "The entire courtroom was kept on edge by the fury and fire of the prosecutor . . . Mr. Wilentz, it seemed to some of us, was representing civilization . . . And he was confronting the defendant with facts—hard, stubborn facts—which lies, lies, lies can not drown out" (Thomas, p. 212). A segment from the cross-examination illustrates Wilentz's power and style:

Q. You think you are a big shot, don't you?
A. No, should I cry?
Q. You think you are bigger than anybody, don't you?
A. No, but I know I am innocent.
Q. You are the man who has the will power, that is what you know, isn't it?
A. No. . . .

Q. No. Will power is everything with you, isn't it?
A. No, it is—I feel innocent and I am innocent and that gives me the power to stand up.
Q. Lying when you swear to God that you will tell the truth. Telling lies doesn't mean anything.
A. Stop that!
Q. Didn't you swear to untruths in the Bronx courthouse?
A. Stop that!
(Whipple, p. 66)

In his closing statement, Wilentz told the jury: "That's the type of man I told you about before that we are dealing with. Public Enemy No. 1 of the world! That's what we are dealing with" (Whipple, p. 549). Hauptmann was convicted eleven hours later and subsequently sentenced to death and executed on 3 April 1936.

Following the Lindbergh trial, Wilentz became increasingly influential in the state Democratic party. By 1940 only the Hague organization in Jersey City was more powerful. Mayor Frank Hague, who was reputed to have said "I *am* the law" in response to a question about the legality of one of his actions, was defeated by John V. Kenny in 1950 in part with help from Wilentz, who then became the prime mover in the National Democratic Club of New Jersey. From that time on, "the General," as he had been known since the days of the trial, was consulted by party politicos before they chose a nominee for any office; he was instrumental in the presidential delegate brokering at the national Democratic conventions and became a close adviser to Governors Robert B. Meyner, Richard J. Hughes, and Brendan Byrne. Yet at his funeral he was remembered by the people of his hometown as the "wonderful man" who "got my brother a job when he needed one. He didn't mind giving you a $5 bill—in those days that was like giving you $50" (*News Tribune*, 8 July 1988).

During much of his political career Wilentz was at the helm of Wilentz, Goldman, and Spitzer, the law firm he founded in Perth Amboy in 1950 that grew from six partners and one associate to a firm of 110 lawyers at the time of his death. The firm, despite a growing number of corporate clients, has maintained its focus as a plaintiff's law firm.

In recent years, and at many times during and following the Lindbergh kidnapping trial, doubts were raised about Hauptmann's guilt. The methods of evidence-gathering and the style of cross-examination used in the trial would not, perhaps, be allowed in a modern courtroom, but they were standards at the time. Wilentz, who died peacefully in his sleep at his home in Long Branch, New Jersey, at the age of ninety-three, never had second thoughts about his handling of the case that had made him famous. Pressured by a succession of unsuccessful lawsuits brought by the widow of Bruno Hauptmann, at the age of eighty-six he again recounted the details of the case with ease. In response to a reporter who referred to him as "the man who sent Hauptmann to the chair," he shot back, "First of all, I didn't send him to the chair. A jury did."

• Sidney B. Whipple, *The Trial of Bruno Richard Hauptmann: Edited with a History of the Case* (1937), is an important source for matters pertaining to the trial. George Waller, *Kidnap: The Story of the Lindbergh Case* (1961), remains one of the best secondary sources about the case. Bob Thomas, *Winchell* (1971), is a good source regarding Walter Winchell's reporting on Wilentz. Ruth Marcus Patt, *Uncommon Lives: Eighteen Extraordinary Jews from New Jersey* (1994), is a good source on Wilentz's life before and after the trial. Obituaries are in the *New York Times* and New Jersey papers such as the *News Tribune*, *Star-Ledger*, *Central New Jersey Home News*, *Asbury Park Press*, and *The Record*, 7 July 1988. Other articles of note appeared in *The Record*, 11 July 1988; *News Tribune*, 8 July 1988; and *Star-Ledger*, 24 July 1988. A compendium of articles is held by the Wilentz family.

JAMES R. WILENTZ

WILES, Irving Ramsey (8 Apr. 1861–29 July 1948), artist, was born in Utica, New York, the son of Lemuel Maynard Wiles, an artist, and Rachael Ramsey. The family soon moved to New York City, where Lemuel Wiles pursued his career as a painter. Irving was educated at home and at public and private schools. He learned to draw and to play the violin, becoming accomplished at both, and he combined his interests in art and ornithology by copying in watercolor the plates in John James Audubon's *Birds of America*. He completed his schooling at the Sedgwick Institute in Great Barrington, Massachusetts, in 1878.

Although Wiles considered becoming a physician, he also thought of taking up a career in art and studied with his father for a year. Lemuel Wiles then suggested that he take classes at the Art Students League before choosing which career to follow. Irving enrolled in 1879 and studied with William Merritt Chase, Thomas Wilmer Dewing, and J. Carroll Beckwith. Chase was the most important influence on Wiles, and the two men developed a close friendship that lasted until Chase's death in 1916. Believing he needed further study in Europe, Wiles went to Paris in 1882, where he attended the prestigious Académie Julian. He also studied with French painter Carolus-Duran, who had taught John Singer Sargent and Wiles's Art Students League instructor Beckwith. Lemuel Wiles came to visit in the summer of 1883, and father and son traveled through Italy.

Wiles returned to America in 1884 and opened his studio in New York City. Business was slow at first, and he painted a number of oils and watercolors on speculation. He exhibited two watercolors at the Salmagundi Club, where they were seen by the art editor of the *Century Magazine*, W. Lewis Fraser. Impressed, Fraser invited Wiles to illustrate articles for *Century*. Wiles spent the next ten years producing hundreds of illustrations in watercolor, wash, and ink for the magazine. He illustrated a wide range of subjects, from articles on travel to stories of romance, and his work also appeared in *Harper's* and *Scribner's* magazines. In 1894 he commented that he tried to divide his time equally between painting and illustrating: "I stay in it [illustration] because it means bread and butter. . . . Portrait painting is what I really delight in, but there is not enough of it coming my way to keep me busy" (quoted in *Bookbuyer*, Sept. 1894, pp. 387–88). He usually rendered his illustrations in colored washes, thinking it would adversely affect his sense of color if he always worked in black and white, as most illustrators did. Although best known for his oil paintings, he was equally skilled as a watercolorist and enjoyed working in that medium. Relatively few of his watercolors are located today; a good example is *Park Scene—Large Planted Jar* (c. 1888, Weatherspoon Art Gallery, Univ. of N.C., Greensboro). The handling is free and easy, and his mastery of the medium is evident. He was a member of the American Water Color Society and participated in its regular exhibitions for nearly twenty years. He also supplemented his income during this period by teaching. Every summer between 1889 and 1894 he and his father jointly ran the Silver Lake Art School, which the elder Wiles had founded in the late 1870s in upstate New York. During the winter Irving Wiles taught classes in his New York City studio.

In 1887 Wiles married Mary "May" Lee, a young woman he had known for several years. They had a daughter, Gladys, who, like her father and grandfather, became an artist.

In addition to his membership in the American Water Color Society, Wiles belonged to the Society of American Artists and the Society of Painters in Pastel. In 1889 he was elected an associate member of the National Academy of Design and in the same year won the academy's Thomas B. Clarke Prize for the best figure composition. The prize-winning picture, *The Sonata* (Fine Arts Museums of San Francisco), shows Wiles's wife seated at a piano and another young woman standing next to her, holding a violin. The elegant gowns they wear and the painting's mood of reverie are reminiscent of the work of Thomas Wilmer Dewing. Wiles was justly proud of the painting and exhibited it in 1893 at the World's Columbian Exposition in Chicago. Also in 1889 he painted perhaps the best of his early paintings, *The Artist's Mother and Father* (Corcoran Gallery of Art, Washington, D.C.), a double portrait of his parents. It is a sympathetic depiction of the couple, who are shown in near-right profile and lost in thought. The success of this and other paintings helped advance his career, and he was able to give up his illustration work by the mid-1890s.

Around this time he painted *Sunshine and Shadow* (c. 1895, Thyssen-Bornemisza Collection), in which a young woman (probably his wife) is seen in the foreground reading under the shade of a tree against a brilliant, sunlit background, and *Russian Tea* (c. 1897, National Museum of American Art, Washington, D.C.), an interior scene that makes effective use of color and unusual lighting effects. In 1900 he won the Shaw Prize of the Society of American Artists for *The Yellow Rose* (New York art market, 1988), a half-length painting of a young woman in a formal gown adjusting a yellow rose in her hair. *Her Leisure Hour* (c. 1925, National Museum of American Art) is a late example of this idealized feminine image.

Wiles had long been interested in painting portraits but had had only limited success in obtaining commissions. In 1901 actress Julia Marlowe asked him to paint her, and the result (National Gallery of Art, Washington, D.C.) received much attention and praise when it was shown in the following year's annual exhibition of the National Academy of Design. Marlowe is depicted at full length, seated, wearing a white gown, and gazing earnestly at the viewer. It is an elegant portrayal, reminiscent of the work of Sargent, and demonstrated to both critics and potential customers that Wiles was a portraitist of the first rank. Thereafter he did not lack for commissions. His most notable portraits include those of actress Mildred Morris (c. 1902, New-York Historical Society); engraver Henry Wolf (1905) and architect Arnold W. Brunner (1911) (both National Academy of Design, New York); William Jennings Bryan (1916, U.S. Department of State, Washington, D.C.); Admiral William Sowden Sims (1919, National Portrait Gallery, Washington, D.C.); pianist Maria Safonoff (1925, Mount Holyoke College Art Museum, South Hadley, Mass.); and art collector John Gellatly (1932, National Museum of American Art). His favorite sitters naturally were his wife, daughter, and parents. A bust portrait of Lemuel Wiles painted in 1904 (Metropolitan Museum of Art, New York) is particularly noteworthy. Two portraits of his daughter make for an interesting contrast. In *The Student* (1910, Corcoran Gallery of Art) she is shown in the act of painting, concentrating on applying her brush to the palette. In *Portrait in Black*, also known as *My Daughter Gladys* (1912, National Museum of American Art), she is presented as a woman of fashion, dressed stylishly in a black gown and hat and looking directly at the viewer.

Lemuel and Irving Wiles discontinued their summer art classes at Silver Lake after 1894 and began holding them a year or two later at Peconic, Long Island, on the North Fork across Peconic Bay from Shinnecock, where Chase conducted his summer art school. Irving Wiles eventually purchased property at Peconic and built a studio there. Wiles's proximity to Peconic Bay inspired him to paint many maritime subjects. In 1931 he executed *Quiet Water*, for which he won the National Academy's Palmer Prize, given for the best marine painting; it was the only academy award he had not already received.

Wiles traveled extensively, both in the United States and abroad. He and American artist William T. Smedley traveled to Holland in 1904, and Wiles visited Spain the following year, where he studied and copied paintings by Velásquez and Frans Hals. He journeyed to Italy in 1910 and, with his daughter, to England in 1912.

Wiles remained active until shortly before his death at Peconic. Advancing age caused him to paint fewer pictures after the 1930s. His work was not as fashionable as it had been, although there is little evidence of any decline in quality.

Irving Ramsey Wiles was one of the best figure painters in America in the late nineteenth and early twentieth centuries. His portraits, genre scenes, marine paintings, and watercolors attracted a great deal of acclaim when they were painted and are still justly admired. Theodore Dreiser acknowledged Wiles's talent and recognized the source of his inspiration when he wrote in 1898, "His art has originality . . . [and] he believes art should present only the beautiful" (*Metropolitan Magazine*, Apr. 1898, p. 359).

• Wiles's scrapbook (New York art market, 1988) and the transcript of an interview he gave to fellow artist DeWitt M. Lockman (New-York Historical Society) are both preserved on microfilm at the Archives of American Art. He painted a number of self-portraits throughout his career; two are owned by the National Academy of Design. A good account of his life and career is *Irving R. Wiles*, the catalog of an exhibition held at the National Academy of Design in 1988.

DAVID MESCHUTT

WILEY, Alexander (26 May 1884–26 Oct. 1967), U.S. senator, was born in Chippewa Falls, Wisconsin, the son of Alexander Wiley and Sophia Ekern, immigrant farmers from Norway. As a young man, the talkative, gregarious Wiley worked as a lumberjack. Drawn to religious themes, he studied for the Lutheran ministry at Augsburg College in Minneapolis from 1902 to 1904 before concluding that he "was too much of a loudmouth type to look and act like a minister."

Instead, in 1904 Wiley entered the University of Michigan Law School, then transferred to the University of Wisconsin, where he earned his LL.B. in 1907. He then established his practice in Chippewa Falls and served three terms as district attorney. As his practice flourished, Wiley purchased a dairy farm, became a bank director and business investor, served on the school board, and joined a variety of civic and masonic organizations. In 1909 he married May Jenkins, with whom he had four children. She died in 1948.

While Wiley lost heavily in the stock market crash of 1929, his growing social contacts pulled him into politics. Already known in Chippewa Falls for his Fourth of July oratory, he crisscrossed the state in the 1930s delivering inspirational talks. Wiley's rambling, cliché-filled rhetoric would become his personal trademark. While critics referred to him as unimaginative, his civic talks inspirited thousands and created a network of followers. In 1933 he was elected president of the Kiwanis International for the Wisconsin–Upper Michigan District. As the Republican gubernatorial candidate in 1936 against Progressive incumbent Philip La Follette, Wiley ran a credible second. In 1938 he easily won election to the U.S. Senate.

Wiley punctuated his Senate career with endless boosterism, back slapping, and joke telling. He sponsored Capitol Hill parties promoting the Wisconsin cheese industry, and in 1939 he even unveiled a bust of Vice President John Nance Garner carved from cheddar cheese. Wiley enjoyed the camaraderie of the Senate and published a small book, *Laughing with Congress* (1947), detailing humorous vignettes of the institution. Frequently characterizing the overweight Wiley as a buffoon, critics overlooked his shrewdness and hard work.

Wiley followed the foreign policy leadership of Michigan senator Arthur Vandenberg. Prior to American entry into World War II, Wiley staunchly opposed administration proposals such as the Selective Service Bill, lend-lease, the extension of draftees' military service, and the arming of merchant vessels. His adamancy reportedly prompted President Franklin Roosevelt to characterize him as "the dumbest man in the Senate." At the same time, however, Wiley supported other preparedness proposals and in February 1941 warned against the vulnerability of American forces in Hawaii. After the Japanese attack on Pearl Harbor, Wiley followed Vandenberg into internationalism. He voted for the Truman Doctrine and the Marshall Plan and supported American membership in the United Nations and the North Atlantic Treaty Organization.

When the Republicans won control of Congress in 1946, Wiley assumed the chairmanship of the Judiciary Committee. He worked effectively with the Harry Truman administration and established the tradition of consulting local bar associations on the qualifications of judicial nominees. Wiley supported the controversial Taft-Hartley Act of 1947, designed to curb the power of labor unions. He also maneuvered himself onto the highly publicized Kefauver Crime Committee and pressed for public hearings in Chicago prior to his successful 1950 reelection campaign.

With the death of Vandenberg, Wiley became ranking minority member and, from 1953 to 1955, chairman of the Senate Foreign Relations Committee. He supported President Truman's decision to employ American troops in the Korean conflict but opposed Truman's firing of General Douglas MacArthur as commander of Allied forces there. The administration named Wiley as a delegate to the Japanese Peace Conference in 1951 and to the United Nations General Assembly in 1952. Wiley enjoyed the attention paid to his speeches on foreign policy issues. He called for a cabinet-level secretary of peace, for American sponsorship of counterrevolutionary activities behind the iron curtain, and for dispersal of government activities outside of Washington to protect against a possible Soviet attack. In 1952 he married Dorothy McBride Kydd; they had no children.

Three of Wiley's positions brought him considerable grief. In 1952 he made a complimentary reference to Secretary of State Dean Acheson, a favorite target for right-wing Republicans. In response, the *Chicago Tribune*, which had many readers in Wisconsin, attacked the senator as a "Truman Republican and Acheson stooge." His support in 1953 of President Dwight D. Eisenhower's nomination of Charles Bohlen as ambassador to the Soviet Union and his opposition to the Bricker Amendment, designed to place limitations on the president's treaty-making authority, elicited even more extreme reaction. Wisconsin's other senator, Joseph R. McCarthy, attacked Wiley as "a bag of fetid air" and helped engineer his censure by the state Republican convention over the Bricker issue in 1953.

Wiley tried to distance himself from his junior colleague. He refused to serve on the Tydings Committee in 1950, which looked into McCarthy's original charges of Communist influence in the State Department. In 1953 he criticized McCarthy's attack on Britain's prime minister Clement Attlee. During the heated McCarthy censure debate of 1954, however, Wiley arranged through Secretary of State John Foster Dulles to be in Brazil. His evasion on the censure of McCarthy hardly ended Wiley's problems. In 1956 the Wisconsin Republican Convention, influenced by McCarthy, endorsed Representative Glen R. Davis, rather than Wiley, for the senatorial nomination. Wiley campaigned vigorously in the primary, drawing voters' attention to his success in obtaining legislation creating the St. Lawrence Seaway, which promised easier access to international markets for Wisconsin products. Running stronger than usual in Milwaukee, a center of Democratic strength, Wiley edged Davis in the primary and then captured a fourth term in the November election.

Although never closely identified with the Eisenhower administration, Wiley thought of himself as a "modern Republican," committed to enlightened internationalism and a modest welfare state. He generally favored civil rights but criticized the John F. Kennedy administration for its lack of aggressiveness toward Fidel Castro in Cuba. In 1962 he was defeated for reelection by Democratic governor Gaylord Nelson. Wiley died in a Christian Science sanatorium in Philadelphia, Pennsylvania.

• The extensive Alexander Wiley Papers are at the State Historical Society of Wisconsin in Madison. Oral history interviews with Wiley are at the Princeton and Columbia University libraries. Material on Wiley and McCarthy is in Thomas C. Reeves, *The Life and Times of Joe McCarthy: A Biography* (1982); David M. Oshinsky, *A Conspiracy So Immense: The World of Joe McCarthy* (1983); Richard Fried, *Men against McCarthy* (1976); and Robert Griffith, *The Politics of Fear: Joseph R. McCarthy and the Senate* (1970). Useful also are William Howard Moore, *The Kefauver Committee and the Politics of Crime, 1950–1951* (1974), and Duane Tananbaum, *The Bricker Amendment Controversy: A Test of Eisenhower's Political Leadership* (1988). Valuable contemporary articles are Hugh Morrow, "Big Wind from Wisconsin," *Saturday Evening Post*, 20 Oct. 1951, pp. 36–37, 97–98, 101–2; Edwin R. Bayley, "Wisconsin: The War against Eisenhower," *New Republic*, 6 July 1953, pp. 15–16; and Arnold Heidenheimer, "Wiley: Another Vandenberg?" *New Republic*, 2 June 1952, pp. 13–15. Obituaries are in the *New York Times* and the *Washington Post*, 27 Oct. 1967.

WILLIAM HOWARD MOORE

WILEY, Bell Irvin (5 Jan. 1906–4 Apr. 1980), historian, was born at Halls, Tennessee, the sixth child of Ewing Baxter Wiley, a farmer, minister, and teacher, and Anna Bass, also a teacher. Wiley developed an early interest in the Civil War, in large part from his family upbringing. Wiley once remarked that he "grew up with the Civil War" and learned of the pains and glories of war from his maternal grandmother, who often reminisced about the experiences of her husband, a Confederate veteran.

Wiley's parents encouraged each of their eleven children to obtain an education, and Wiley earned a bachelor's degree from Asbury College in 1928, a master's degree in English from the University of Kentucky in 1929, and a Ph.D. in history from Yale University in 1933. At Yale, Wiley worked with U. B. Phillips, a pioneer in the study of slavery. Phillips encouraged his industrious student to undertake a study of slaves during the Civil War, which Wiley later published as his first book, *Southern Negroes, 1861–1865* (1938). In *Southern Negroes* Wiley demonstrated what became the hallmarks of his scholarship: copious research, exacting prose, and penetrating analysis that was balanced and objective. Wiley's first book was notable not only because it focused on the war experiences of African Americans but also because it was critical of both the southern myth that slavery was a benign and benevolent institution and the northern notion that the war was fought to liberate slaves.

In 1934 Wiley accepted a position in the department of History at Mississippi State Teachers College at Hattiesburg (later the University of Southern Mississippi) and taught summers at Peabody College in Nashville. At Peabody Wiley met Mary Frances Harrison, whom he married in 1937. The couple had two children.

After obtaining a teaching position at the University of Mississippi in 1938, Wiley began a research project to fill a gaping void in Civil War historiography. Despite the Civil War's already legendary stature (or perhaps because of it), historians had largely ignored the experiences of the common soldier until Wiley published his pathbreaking book, *The Life of Johnny Reb, the Common Soldier of the Confederacy* (1943). Wiley took advantage of the countless diaries and letters that soldiers and relatives had written to recount the previously forgotten experiences of ordinary white southerners during the war. Wiley consulted tens of thousands of documents in writing his monumental study and portrayed the common rebel with empathy and respect. Wiley's work carefully uncovered the most mundane aspects of soldiers' lives, including the food they ate, the diseases they fell victim to, the debauchery that accompanied military life, and the drudgery and boredom that proved to be almost as formidable a foe as northern armies. Wiley concluded that the typical Confederate soldier was a middle-class, rural, yeoman, "lacking in polish, in perspective and in tolerance," but "respectable, sturdy and independent." Wiley had high praise for the courage and military prowess of the Confederate soldier, whose desperate battle against heavy odds was "an eternal monument to his greatness as a fighting man."

Wiley's career was interrupted by the Second World War, during which time he served as a staff historian for the army and wrote two workmanlike treatises on the organization and training of combat troops. Wiley served with distinction in the military, rising to the rank of lieutenant colonel before being discharged in 1946. That same year he moved to Louisiana State University, heading its history department until 1949.

With his sense of patriotism renewed by the war, Wiley embarked on a study of the Union fighting man, which he published as *The Life of Billy Yank, the Common Soldier of the Union* (1952). Not surprisingly, Wiley found that Yankee and Confederate soldiers shared many of the same qualities: both had a propensity toward licentiousness, both exhibited irrepressible humor amidst death and destruction, both possessed deep-rooted prejudices, both were generous toward those in need, and both had a deep devotion to home and family, which was often expressed in a mawkish sentimentality but could occasionally elicit moving and engaging prose. Neither soldier was braver than the other, and each had a profound sense of pride and duty that inspired them to conquer the fear of battle with a gallant disregard for death. Wiley's soldiers, of the North and South, were motivated primarily by love of country rather than by ideology. Wiley believed that the typical Civil War soldier had little or no interest in the philosophical aspects of the conflict but instead was motivated by more visceral concerns. Southerners fought to protect their homes from invasion and to preserve their cherished southern way of life (which included slavery); northerners fought to preserve the Union and the freedom that it entailed. Ordinary folk, according to Wiley, had generally comported themselves well during the war, enduring privations with the same patriotic sturdiness that had seemingly sustained the country during the Second World War as well. Both contemporary and subsequent historians recognized Wiley's two encyclopedic volumes on the "social history of men at arms" as a landmark achievement in Civil War historiography.

Wiley admired the virtues that he found in rebel soldiers, but he had no qualms about criticizing those who tried to use the mantle of the Confederacy to legitimize discrimination against black southerners. Wiley supported a campaign to desegregate the Southern Historical Association in the 1950s, and he regarded racial discrimination as "illogical, contrary to common sense, and indefensible." Candid and frank in his historical and political views, Wiley maintained that one of the basic problems with the modern South was that many of its residents had "not fully accepted the result of the Civil War."

Wiley's talents as a researcher were not wasted in the classroom. An extremely popular teacher, Wiley attracted record numbers of students to his southern history courses at Emory University, where he taught from 1949 to 1974. Wiley's dynamic and carefully crafted lectures, combined with his dutiful concern for students, made him an inspiring and memorable teacher. Wiley firmly believed that teaching and research complemented one another, and his distinguished accomplishments in both regards earned him numerous awards and honors, including five honorary degrees.

In retirement, Wiley published *Confederate Women* (1975), which developed from a series of lectures that Wiley had presented at the University of Tennessee in 1971. *In Confederate Women*, Wiley applied the same exhaustive research techniques that characterized his earlier scholarship to the lives and opinions of three aristocratic southern women and concluded that war had helped liberate white southern women from the bonds of patriarchy. The traditional focus and derivative nature of the book elicited mixed reviews from historians. After leaving Emory, Wiley continued to teach on a limited basis; he served as a visiting professor at the University of South Carolina, Tulane University, Agnes Scott College, and the University of Kentucky. Wiley died of a heart attack in Atlanta.

A prolific social historian, Wiley became the preeminent authority on the lives and experiences of ordinary Civil War era southerners, especially the common soldier. Although he studied mostly "plain people," his writings and lectures were anything but ordinary, capturing the drama and complexity associated with more traditional historical research. To Wiley history was not the explication of impersonal forces that swept individuals away in an overpowering current but rather the pageant of the lives of ordinary people who faced the exigencies of life with determination, fortitude, and beauty. "In my view the essence of history is people," said Wiley, "and in all of my writings I have tried to make human beings the focus or the center of my consideration." Few historians, before or since, have been able to portray the basic humanity of their subjects better than Wiley, whose work will surely endure.

• Wiley's personal papers are at Emory University. A nearly complete bibliography of Wiley's work, along with a useful survey of his career, can be found in James I. Robertson, Jr., and Richard M. McMurry, eds., *Rank and File. Civil War Essays in Honor of Bell Irvin Wiley* (1976). An insightful posthumous assessment of Wiley can be found in John Barnwell, "Bell Irvin Wiley," in *Twentieth-Century American Historians*, vol. 17 of *Dictionary of Literary Biography*, ed. Clyde N. Wilson (1983). Informative obituaries are in the *Atlanta Constitution*, 6 Apr. 1980, and in the *New York Times* and the *Washington Post*, both 7 Apr. 1980.

TERENCE FINNEGAN

WILEY, Calvin Henderson (3 Feb. 1819–11 Jan. 1887), school reformer, was born in Guilford County, North Carolina, the son of David L. Wiley and Anne Woodburn, prosperous farmers. After attending local schools and Caldwell Institute near Greensboro, Wiley graduated from the University of North Carolina in 1840. He studied law, was admitted to the bar, and settled in Oxford, North Carolina, where he began parallel careers as a lawyer and writer. Wiley soon shelved his legal practice and focused his attention on journalism and literature. Editing the *Oxford Mercury* from 1841 through 1843, he devoted much of the rest of the decade to researching, writing, and publishing two novels: *Alamance; or, the Great and Final Experiment* (1847) and *Roanoke; or, Where Is Utopia?* (1849). He also began work on the *North Carolina Reader*, which would become a standard school textbook after its publication in 1851.

Wiley's writings reflected his growing interest in the social and economic conditions of his state. He followed this interest into Whig politics and won election to the state house of representatives in 1850, convinced like many other members of his party that an activist government committed to internal improvements could promote progress and uplift. The key improvement, Wiley believed, would be universal schooling for white children. He quickly gained a reputation in the legislature as an advocate of common school reform, a cause he also advanced as associate editor in 1851–1852 of the *Southern Weekly Post* in Raleigh. He helped persuade the Democrat-dominated legislature to establish the office of state superintendent of schools, and on 1 January 1853 the 33-year-old Wiley became the office's first occupant.

As a result of his efforts and of the political and economic circumstances of his state, Wiley was able to build the most successful common school system in the antebellum South. Elsewhere in the region, state superintendents had to organize from the ground up, working first to get district trustees and county officials into place. North Carolina, by contrast, already had a bureaucratic educational structure, albeit a loose and decentralized one. Wiley also faced less opposition on the financial front than did his counterparts in other southern states because North Carolina had a fairly stable economy, a state literary fund, and a tradition of local taxation for education. Of all the South's school reformers, Wiley came closest to matching the accomplishments of Horace Mann in Massachusetts and Henry Barnard in Connecticut, northern reformers who kept in contact with Wiley and supported his efforts. Wiley, in fact, patterned his common school campaign after theirs. Like many school reformers in the North, South, and West, he was a true believer in the power of common schooling, regarding it as a panacea for the ills of state, region, and nation.

During his thirteen-year tenure as state superintendent, Wiley maintained a busy schedule of writing, speaking, touring, and generally politicking on behalf of common schools. Drawing on his journalistic background, he enlisted the North Carolina press in his campaign. He organized the Educational Association of North Carolina in 1856 and edited its *North Carolina Journal of Education*. Keeping in close touch with his former colleagues in the legislature, Wiley submitted *Annual Reports* describing the conditions he hoped to improve: district schools in "apparent chaos," teaching that was "extremely primitive," and a populace "tenacious of old habits, conservative to the point of stubbornness." His reports optimistically charted progress toward an "efficient" school system, an "elevated" teaching force, and the "general disappearance of all prejudices" against common schooling.

Rhetoric aside, North Carolina did take major steps toward establishing a viable state school system under Wiley's direction, even if he never completely overcame resistance to centralized control. Wiley persuaded county school boards to submit more complete annual reports, but those boards continued to allocate school funds as they saw fit. Wiley promoted teacher training and boosted teacher salaries to the top of the region—indeed, salaries of the small but growing number of female teachers ranked among the highest in the nation—yet county officials jealously guarded their right to issue teaching certificates to virtually anyone they deemed qualified.

What Wiley achieved by the outbreak of the Civil War was a state-subsidized system that enrolled about two-thirds of the white school-age population—the largest percentage in the region. In North Carolina as well as in other southern states, local officials continued the long-standing practice of allocating public funds to independent tuition-charging schools. These quasi-public schools, an integral part of the mid-nineteenth-century North Carolina system, symbolized the incomplete transition to state-regulated schools open to all children.

Although Wiley managed to keep the system open during the war, the Reconstruction government of North Carolina abolished his position in 1865, and he issued his final report in January 1866. Twice proposed as a candidate for superintendent of the reorganized state system, his connections to the prewar government prevented his regaining the office. He did become an advocate of tax-supported schooling for African-American children, a moderate stance in the context of the times.

Wiley devoted the remainder of his life to religious work. Appointed a general agent of the American Bible Society in 1869, he was also a licensed and ordained Presbyterian minister, although he never had a regular congregation. He spent his last years in Winston with his wife Mittie Towles, whom he had married in 1862, and their seven children. At his death in Winston he was serving as chair of the city school board.

Wiley's contemporaries regarded him as the leading school reformer in the region. Historians still recognize him as the antebellum South's most effective advocate of the educational mode of tax-supported, state-regulated common schools, which eventually won out in every region and became the forerunners of today's public schools.

• Wiley's papers are in the Southern Historical Collection of the University of North Carolina Library at Chapel Hill. Most accounts of Wiley and his work are old and uncritical. Among the more useful are Edgar W. Knight, *Public School Education in North Carolina* (1916); H. C. Renegar, *The Problems, Policies and Achievements of Calvin Henderson Wiley* (1925); Marcus Cicero Stephens Noble, *A History of Public Schools in North Carolina* (1930); and Charles William Dabney, *Universal Education in the South* (1936). Carl F. Kaestle's *Pillars of the Republic* (1983), a more recent and analytical study of common school movements throughout the nation, places Wiley's work in a broad context.

JOSEPH W. NEWMAN

WILEY, Harvey Washington (18 Oct. 1844–30 June 1930), chemist and pure food crusader, was born in Jefferson County, Indiana, the son of Preston Pritchard, a farmer, Campbellite lay preacher, and schoolmaster, and Lucinda Weir Maxwell. Harvey's attendance at Hanover College (1863–1867), from which he received the B.A. degree, was interrupted by service as a hundred-day volunteer (May–Sept. 1864) with the 137th Indiana Regiment in Tennessee. After a year of teaching and a summer's apprenticeship with a Kentucky physician (1868), Wiley attended Indiana Medical College (1869–1871), where he ultimately earned his M.D., simultaneously teaching at Northwestern Christian University (later Butler University) and the Indianapolis high school. He then taught chemistry at both his medical school and Butler. During 1872–1873 Wiley spent some months at the Lawrence Scientific School at Harvard University, adding a B.S. to his M.D. Wiley was appointed the first professor of chemistry at the newly opened Purdue University, from 1874 to 1883, and state chemist (1881). In 1878 Wiley observed at German universities and studied food chemistry at the German Imperial Health Office. Back at Purdue, his research in the chemistry of sugars and the adulteration of cane syrup led to his appointment as chief chemist in the U.S. Department of Agriculture in 1883.

Wiley was preoccupied with sugar research during his first decade in Washington, D.C. He presided over sorghum and beet sugar experiments, improving extraction techniques without reducing the nation's dependence on imports. However, this did not provide Wiley an adequate power base. He found survival for his division and fame for himself by assuming leadership in the pure food campaign, applying his scientific abilities to exposing adulteration and his political talents to achieving a protective law. In 1887 he published the first part of Bulletin 13, *Foods and Food Adulterants*; nine more parts followed in the next sixteen years.

A food and drug bill had been before Congress since 1879, and Wiley sought to create a coalition and public sentiment powerful enough to get a measure enacted. In 1898 he emerged as leader in a National Pure Food and Drug Congress, assembled to attempt reconciliation among conflicting segments of industry and state and federal officials. The next year Wiley became scientific adviser and principal witness for the first congressional committee to hold hearings on the food and drug bill. In 1902 Wiley began tests with human volunteers, the "poison squad," to determine the safety of chemical preservatives. Earlier, he had stressed the unethical nature of unlabeled artificial additives. His experiments persuaded him that preservatives posed health hazards.

In the new century, Wiley worked hand-in-glove with congressmen favoring a strong bill. He orchestrated lobbying efforts of state chemists, physicians, women's club members, reform-minded journalists, and segments of the food, drug, and liquor industries. Finally, public concern aroused by Upton Sinclair's novel *The Jungle*, alleging filthy conditions in meatpacking plants, triggered passage of the Food and Drugs Act in 1906.

The law gave Wiley's Bureau of Chemistry responsibility for investigating adulteration and misbranding of foods and drugs in interstate commerce and for relaying evidence of violations through the secretary of agriculture to the Department of Justice for prosecution in the courts. Wiley determined to give the law rigorous enforcement. This policy aroused the ire of affected agricultural and industrial interests, who brought pressure on Secretary of Agriculture James Wilson (1836–1920) and President Theodore Roosevelt. Both men came to distrust Wiley's science and sought to double-check his decisions with a Board of Food and Drug Inspection within the department and the Referee Board of Consulting Scientific Experts, chaired by the Johns Hopkins chemist Ira Remsen, advisory to the department. Although the Remsen board sometimes agreed with Wiley's rulings, its determination that sodium benzoate did not render food injurious to health led to continuing controversy. Other major disputes concerned blended whiskey, sulphur dioxide in dried fruits, and bleaching of flour. Although the law markedly improved the marketplace, strife dominated Wiley's attention and the headlines.

Recurring rumors predicted Wiley's resignation or firing. In 1911 departmental opponents sought to oust him, charging he had illegally overpaid a New York expert on crude drugs, Henry H. Rusby, for part-time work. President William Howard Taft eventually exonerated Wiley but did not discipline Wiley's enemies, so the chief chemist resigned in 1912, hoping to continue his pure food crusade as a private citizen. Moreover, he needed more income because in February 1911, at age sixty-six, he had married Anna Campbell Kelton, thirty-three, and the next year the first of their two sons would be born. In 1912, at twice his government salary, Wiley became director of the Bureau of Foods, Sanitation, and Health for William Randolph Hearst's magazine *Good Housekeeping*, a position he retained until the year of his death. Wiley also went on the lecture circuit. In the 1912 election, he opposed both Taft and Roosevelt and campaigned for Woodrow Wilson.

Although Wiley had chosen the dedicated Bureau of Chemistry officials who after his departure systematized regulatory procedures, he never believed that the law was being properly enforced. This judgment he rendered in a book, *The History of a Crime against the Food Law* (1929). Wiley wrote other important books: *Principles and Practice of Agricultural Analysis* (1894–1897), *Foods and Their Adulteration* (1907), *Beverages and Their Adulteration* (1919), and *Harvey W. Wiley:*

An Autobiography (1930). He served as president of the Association of Official Agricultural Chemists (1886), the American Chemical Society (1893–1894), and the United States Pharmacopoeia Revision Committee (1910–1920). He represented his country at international conferences.

Wiley died in Washington, D.C. A member of the Grand Army of the Republic from the time of its founding in 1866, he was buried with military honors in Arlington Cemetery.

• The Harvey W. Wiley papers are in the Manuscript Division of the Library of Congress. Department of Agriculture and Food and Drug Administration records in the National Archives in Washington, D.C., and in the Washington National Records Center in Suitland, Maryland, contain many relevant documents. Annual reports of the Bureau of Chemistry are useful; those for the years after the enactment of the 1906 Food and Drugs Act are collected in the Food Law Institute Series, *Federal Food, Drug and Cosmetic Law: Administrative Reports, 1907–1949* (1951). Besides Wiley's own autobiographical writings, the essential biography is Oscar E. Anderson, Jr., *The Health of a Nation: Harvey W. Wiley and the Fight for Pure Food* (1958). See also William Lloyd Fox, "Harvey W. Wiley: The Formative Years" (Ph.D. diss., George Washington Univ., 1960), and James Harvey Young, *Pure Food: Securing the Federal Food and Drugs Act of 1906* (1989).

JAMES HARVEY YOUNG

WILKE, Lou (10 Oct. 1896–28 Feb. 1962), athletic administrator, was born Louis Gustav Wilke in Chicago, Illinois, the son of Gustav Herman Wilke, a businessman, and Katherine Sutter. He grew up in Alva, Oklahoma, and attended Northwestern State College, located in Alva. He captained the basketball team, which was known as the "65 Inchers," because the team's average height was 5′5″. After leaving Northwestern State without a degree in 1916, Wilke coached football and basketball at Shattuck High School in Oklahoma in 1916–1917. He served with the American Expeditionary Force during World War I. In 1920 he received a bachelor of arts degree from Phillips University in Enid, Oklahoma, where he played basketball for two years.

In 1920 Wilke began his career in earnest when he coached football, basketball, and track at Nowata (1920–1926) and Bartlesville (1926–1928) high schools in Oklahoma. In 1923 he married Frances Maxine Watson; they had two children. In 1928 Wilke returned to Phillips University as director of athletics and coach of the football and basketball teams. Wilke directed the football team to two upsets over the University of Tulsa in 1928. His basketball teams also enjoyed success as they topped Amateur Athletic Union (AAU) powers such as the Wichita Henrys (1928) and the Kansas City Cook Paints (1928). In 1929 Phillips reached the quarterfinals of the prestigious national AAU tournament, then held in Kansas City.

Also in 1929 Wilke's career took a new direction when the Phillips Petroleum Company hired him to coach its AAU basketball team and to work in its marketing division. Although Wilke amassed a 98–8 record in two years with Phillips Petroleum, his teams failed to move beyond the second round of the national AAU tournament. Because of the Great Depression, Phillips suspended its basketball program after the 1931 AAU championships. While Phillips resumed its basketball program in 1936 and became one of the dominant AAU teams of the 1940s and 1950s, Wilke never coached another basketball game after the 1930–1931 season.

As a coach Wilke demonstrated motivational and organizational skills that served him well in both business and sports administration. Between 1931 and 1937 he performed various jobs for Phillips Petroleum in Enid, Tulsa, and Bartlesville, Oklahoma, and in Wichita, Kansas. Except for two years, 1945 to 1947, when the Phillips company transferred him back to Bartlesville, Wilke worked in Denver from 1937 to 1952. In 1952 Wilke returned to Bartlesville as the assistant sales manager of the oil company.

It was in Denver, however, that Wilke established himself as a force in the administration and promotion of amateur basketball. In 1935 Denver persuaded the AAU to move the national AAU basketball tournament to Denver, where it would remain through 1968, with the exception of 1949 when it was held in Oklahoma City. In Denver Wilke teamed up with Willard N. Greim, director of Denver Parks and Recreation and also a major figure in the administration of AAU sports, to direct the AAU tournament. Jack Carberry, the colorful sports editor of the *Denver Post* wrote that Wilke and Greim were very authoritarian and "ran the national AAU Basketball tournament as if it were a private franchise." In Denver the tournament was called the "Dribble Derby" and for a week teams such as the Denver Safeways, the Phillips 66 Oilers, Twentieth Century–Fox, the Oakland Bittners, the Peoria Caterpillars, and the Alpine Dairy battled for the national championship. Denver called itself the "capital" of American basketball. In a 1947 column, Carberry said that it was to "Wilke, as much as any other man, that Denver owes its spot in the basketball sun." Wilke also endeared himself to Denver sports fans by organizing a Victory League at the beginning of World War II for service teams and by supporting a variety of youth league programs. Because of his flamboyant personality and prominence in the sports and business communities, it was even rumored that Denver's mayor, Ben Stapleton, saw Wilke as a possible successor.

After World War II Wilke played a progressively more prominent role in national sports administration. In 1948 he was elected chair of the U.S. Olympic Basketball Committee and the manager of the 1948 U.S. Olympic basketball team, which won the gold medal in London, England. In 1952 Wilke again served as the chair of the Olympic Basketball Committee, and in 1956 he was the vice chairman of the U.S. Olympic Committee. Wilke was elected president of the AAU in 1953 and reelected to a second term in 1955. Wilke also served as vice president of the International Basketball Federation and was a member of its rules committee. In 1959 Wilke headed the U.S. delegation at the World Amateur Basketball Tournament in Santiago, Chile. The following year, Kenneth Wilson, president of the U.S. Olympic Committee, appointed Wilke the administrative committee chairman in charge of all sports of the U.S. Olympic team, which competed in Rome, Italy. In 1962 Wilke was involved in negotiations to resolve differences between the AAU and the National Collegiate Athletic Association (NCAA) over the procedure for selecting players to represent the United States in international competition. In the midst of these discussions Wilke died in Chicago while visiting friends.

From the 1920s until 1962, before professional basketball became a national and profitable form of entertainment, the most popular form of postcollegiate play west of the Mississippi River was supplied by the Amateur Athletic Union. Wilke was a tireless champion and organizer of amateur basketball who played a major role in making this brand of basketball possible. His negotiating skills made it possible for him to provide the AAU and the American Olympic movement with outstanding leadership. His peers regarded him as a man of integrity who was sincerely committed to the principles of amateurism. In 1983 the basketball community recognized his contribution to basketball by enshrining him in the Naismith Memorial Basketball Hall of Fame.

• The Naismith Memorial Basketball Hall of Fame, Springfield, Mass., has a file on Wilke. The most helpful sources on his life are columns and obituaries in the *Denver Post* and *Rocky Mountain News*, both 1 Mar. 1962. See also Jack Carberry, "Amateur Sport Loses a Champ," *Denver Post*, 4 Mar. 1962, which provides useful insights into Wilke's work and personality. Another obituary is in the *New York Times*, 1 Mar. 1962.

ADOLPH H. GRUNDMAN

WILKERSON, Vernon Alexander (21 Aug. 1901–24 May 1968), biochemist, educator, and physician, was born in Fort Scott, Kansas, and grew up in Kansas City, Missouri. His parents' names and occupations are unknown. After attending Sumner High School in Kansas City (1913–1917), he entered the University of Kansas, where he majored in chemistry and graduated with an A.B. in 1921. He stayed an additional year at Kansas before attending the medical school of the University of Iowa, Iowa City, where he earned the M.D. in 1925. During his medical studies, he listed his place of residence as Council Bluffs, Iowa. Next came a year of internship at Kansas City General Hospital No. 2, followed by a one-year appointment as house surgeon at Wheatley-Provident Hospital, also in Kansas City. These hospitals, located in a racially segregated city, served the African-American community exclusively and provided one of the few means available anywhere in the country for black medical graduates to acquire postgraduate training.

In 1927 Wilkerson returned to General Hospital No. 2 as assistant surgeon and simultaneously established himself in private practice, working within the local black community. In 1928 he married Vivian Cheatham, with whom he had three children. The marriage ended, and he later married Helen (maiden name and date of marriage unknown); they had no children.

Wilkerson was so highly regarded that in 1929 he became one of a select few invited by Numa P. G. Adams, the newly appointed and first black dean of the Howard University School of Medicine, to accept a fellowship to pursue doctoral studies with the expectation of returning to Howard to teach. This program, supported by the Rockefeller-funded General Education Board (GEB), was part of a larger campaign at Howard to upgrade the medical curriculum, train full-time teachers in the preclinical sciences, and provide better educational and research opportunities for promising black scholars.

Wilkerson was among the first five GEB Fellows. He registered at the University of Minnesota, while others variously attended the University of Chicago, University of Michigan, and Columbia University. His major was agricultural biochemistry; his minor, physiology. Working under the supervision of Ross Aiken Gortner, chief of the Division of Agricultural Biochemistry, he carried out a study of the forms of nitrogen in pig embryos at various stages of development. One of his conclusions was that mammalian embryos appeared to be governed more by their inherent chemical nature than by variations in maternal nutrition. The project became his doctoral thesis and was published in condensed form (with Gortner as coauthor) first as part of the journal series of the Minnesota Agricultural Experiment Station and then in *American Journal of Physiology*. Awarded the Ph.D. in 1932, Wilkerson was said to have been the first African American to earn a doctorate at the University of Minnesota. The dean of the graduate school called him "one of the most brilliant students to ever attend the University, [earning] one of the highest grades ever recorded in a Ph.D. examination."

Wilkerson arrived at Howard University in spring or summer 1932 to help build a biochemistry department to replace the old physiological chemistry program. He served as acting head until 1935, when his appointment became permanent. According to foundation officer Robert A. Lambert, the Howard administration was pleased with the way he and other GEB Fellows—Roscoe L. McKinney (anatomy), Arnold H. Maloney (pharmacology), Joseph L. Johnson (physiology), Hildrus A. Poindexter (bacteriology), and Robert S. Jason (pathology)—seemed "equal to their new responsibilities, though none of them was really adequately prepared to take over the headship of a department" (Records of the General Education Board, box 28, folder 261). In addition to administrative responsibilities, their teaching load was heavy. Wilkerson, assisted by two or three others, delivered lectures and organized laboratory sessions in general biochemistry for all medical and dental students, provided a basic course for students in the dental hygiene program, taught an upper-level course on blood chemistry, led a seminar, and supervised students doing advanced research.

Although this left little time for his own research, Wilkerson remained productive by working long hours into the night. He continued his work on embryonic growth and developed a new interest, the chemistry of human epidermis. He published eight papers in six years (1934–1939). All but two related to his skin research, which sought to define and analyze the distinctive chemical properties of the skin's outer layer. Later he investigated the viscosity of whole blood and blood plasma, as well as the possible relationship between certain lymphatic and plasma proteins. Highly regarded, especially in Europe, Wilkerson's research was often cited in the scientific and medical literature. He was elected to membership in the American Society of Biological Chemists in 1936 and served in 1944 as president of the International Society of Biological Chemists. He served on the Nobel Prize selection committee for medicine in 1952, the year Selman A. Waksman won the award for the development of streptomycin.

Wilkerson carried on his research against growing odds. His teaching load—already heavy—almost doubled during World War II when, for example, two medical classes graduated at Howard in 1944 (Mar. and Dec.). Furthermore, financial support was minimal. Lambert noted that the GEB fellows had felt "discouragement in not finding on their return [to Howard] the facilities for research which they had during their fellowship study." Although the Howard administration attempted to garner small grants for apparatus and supplies, Wilkerson spent much time and energy improvising equipment essential to his work. Such pressures, in addition to growing family responsibilities, likely played a part in his departure from full-time academics and return to private practice. In 1948 he resigned as Howard's biochemistry department head and opened the Medical Arts Building at 61 K Street, Washington, D.C., a practice catering primarily to the inner-city poor. He remained as part-time lecturer in biochemistry at Howard until 1966. He also served as consulting biochemist for Freedmen's Hospital from 1948 until his death in Washington, D.C.

• Materials on Wilkerson's education and career may be found in the Records of the General Education Board (1902–1964), Rockefeller Archive Center, Pocantico Hills, N.Y., especially box 28, folders 260–61, and box 29, folders 267–70. A version of Wilkerson's doctoral thesis was published under the title "The Chemistry of Embryonic Growth. III. A Biochemical Study of the Embryonic Growth of the Pig with Special Reference to Nitrogenous Compounds," *American Journal of Physiology* 102 (Oct. 1932): 153–66. The first of his skin studies was "Chemistry of Human Epidermis. I. Amino Acid Content of the Stratum Corneum and Its Comparison to Other Human Keratins," *Journal of Biological Chemistry* 107 (Oct. 1934): 377–81. For his blood and lymph work, see "Proteins in Chylous Ascitic Fluids and the Possible Relationship to the Origin of Plasma Proteins," *Federation Proceedings* (Federation of American Societies for Experimental Biology) 4 (Mar. 1945): 109. Copies of two biochemistry texts compiled by Wilkerson, *Biochemistry for Medical Students: Outline of Lectures and Questions* (1944) and *Laboratory Manual of Biochemistry for Medical Students* (1944), are preserved in the National Library of Medicine. The most complete biographical summary is the obituary in *Journal of the National Medical Association* 60 (July 1968): 344–45, which contains a fairly comprehensive bibliography of Wilkerson's scientific writings. See also *Crisis* 39 (May 1932): 163, and the *Washington Post* obituary, 27 May 1968.

KENNETH R. MANNING

WILKES, Charles (3 Apr. 1798–8 Feb. 1877), naval officer and explorer, was born in New York City, the son of John de Ponthieu Wilkes, a banker, and Mary Seton. He was educated in private schools and with tutors, concentrating on mathematics, scientific subjects, surveying, and navigation, though he studied languages and drawing as well. Determined to go to sea but at first denied a naval commission, Wilkes made three voyages as a merchant seaman between 1815 and 1818. He received his appointment as a midshipman in the U.S. Navy on 1 January 1818. Promotion to lieutenant came two days after his marriage to Jane Jeffrey Renwick on 26 April 1826. The couple had four children. On 12 March 1833 he reported for duty as head of the navy's Depot of Charts and Instruments. In August 1836 Wilkes traveled to England and France to obtain equipment, books, and maps for the recently authorized exploring expedition to the Pacific Ocean. He hoped to play a significant role in the expedition as he had "studied with this view ever since the first Expedition was talked of" (*Autobiography*, p. 324). Public criticism mounted as delay and disorganization stalled the expedition's departure. After several senior officers resigned from or refused the command, it was offered to Wilkes on 28 March 1838. His acceptance antagonized many because he was a junior officer.

Wilkes drastically reduced the number of civilian scientific personnel previously engaged, assigning the fields of astronomy, surveying, hydrography, geography, meteorology, and terrestrial magnetism to naval officers. The long-delayed expedition, one of the last under sail, departed on 18 August 1838. It rounded Cape Horn; crossed the Pacific surveying, charting, and exploring the Tuamotus, Tahiti, and Samoa; and reached Sydney, Australia, on 21 November 1839. Next probing Antarctic waters, Wilkes cruised 1,500 miles along an unbroken ice shelf, obtaining soundings of mud and rocks and sighting mountain peaks in the distance. He recorded the discovery of a continental land mass in his log on 19 July 1840. The U.S. claim to influence in the area is based on his sighting.

The expedition sailed via New Zealand and Tonga, reaching Fiji in May 1840. Work there produced the first comprehensive and reliable charts of the reef-strewn waters of the archipelago. The expedition arrived on 4 September 1840 in Hawaii, where all coasts and possible harbors were surveyed and charted and the interior explored. Wilkes called Pearl Harbor "the best and most capacious harbor in the Pacific" (*Narrative*, vol. 4, p. 179) if its entrance reef could be broached.

Arriving off the Oregon coast in April 1841, Wilkes found the mouth of the Columbia a difficult and dangerous harbor. He recommended emphatically in his reports that Puget Sound and the Straits of Juan de Fuca be retained in the ongoing border negotiations between the United States and Britain. In California, describing the potential for a large commercial harbor in San Francisco Bay, he emphasized the lack of Mexican government control of the area. The expedition left San Francisco on 1 November 1841, crossing the Pacific again via Hawaii, Manila, and Singapore to Cape Town. Charting, surveying, and scientific studies were conducted along the route. The voyage ended in New York in June 1842.

An impatient and imperious perfectionist, Wilkes required from his officers and crew the same diligence, proficiency, and meticulous attention to detail he demanded of himself. Reprimands were often delivered loudly and publicly. Several officers were relieved of duty, reassigned, or sent home. After the expedition's return this disaffected group brought eleven court-martial charges against Wilkes, ranging from abusive treatment of officers and men to false reports of sighting land in the Antarctic. The one charge upheld, giving a seaman more than the allowed number of lashes, resulted in a public letter of reprimand read aloud at the New York Navy Yard. Wilkes subsequently filed charges against those who instigated the court-martial. Several received sentences ranging from demotion in rank to discharge from the navy. Wilkes's reputation and that of the expedition were tainted by this public squabble.

Anti-Wilkes and antiexpedition forces in Congress combined to limit the publication of the expedition reports to 100 copies each. (Reports of explorer John Charles Frémont, Wilkes's contemporary, numbered 10,000 each.) Wilkes spent the next twenty years managing the publication of the expedition results. The first work produced was his five-volume *Narrative of the United States Exploring Expedition* (1845); followed by Horatio Hale's studies in ethnology; three volumes by James Dwight Dana covering zoophytes, crustacea, and geology; and seven other volumes by various authors. Four volumes exist in manuscript but were denied government funds for printing. Wilkes's wife died in 1848. In 1854 he married Mary Lynch Bolton, with whom he had one child.

The Civil War interrupted the printing of expedition results. In April 1861 Wilkes returned to sea duty and participated in the destruction of the Norfolk Navy Yard, the port from which his expedition had sailed twenty-three years before. While on blockade patrol in the *San Jacinto*, Wilkes seized two Confederate commissioners from the British steamer *Trent* in open waters, thwarting their mission to enlist support from France and England. He was acclaimed in Boston, New York, and Washington, D.C., as the "Hero of the *Trent*," but British anger subsequently forced President Abraham Lincoln to release the prisoners and apologize.

In July 1862 Wilkes took command of the James River Flotilla. His ships shelled Richmond from the James River, as part of General George McClellan's attack. On 4 August 1862 he was promoted to commodore. He became acting rear admiral on 15 September 1862 when he was assigned to the command of the West India Squadron. This wide-ranging fleet was charged with finding and sinking Confederate ships in the open seas. Resting, refueling, and gathering information in Caribbean ports, Wilkes stretched the bounds of other nations' neutrality. Finally he overstepped them by seizing a British mail packet in a neutral port. British indignation again descended on the United States. The ship was returned, its letter bags unopened, and Secretary of the Navy Gideon Welles relieved Wilkes of his command on 1 June 1863. Pressured to explain the navy's lack of success against the Confederate raiders, the secretary publicly blamed Wilkes. Wilkes wrote an angry reply, which several newspapers published before it reached Welles. On 27 February 1864 Welles brought charges against Wilkes for disobedience, insubordination, disrespect, refusal to obey orders, and conduct unbecoming an officer. Found guilty on all counts, Wilkes was suspended from active duty for three years, but on 30 December 1864 Lincoln reduced the suspension to one year.

Wilkes retired and on 6 August 1866 was promoted to rear admiral on the retired list. In June 1870 he returned to active duty to continue editing the expedition volumes. One volume on botany was published but never officially distributed. Congress in 1873 refused further funding for the publications.

Wilkes felt his government never truly appreciated his accomplishments as a naval officer or the work of the exploring expedition. "Time will do me full justice . . . and my narrative of the Expedition will remain a monument to my exertions," Wilkes wrote in his autobiography shortly before he died in Washington, D.C. He was buried in Washington's Oak Hill Cemetery. In 1909 his body was reinterred in Arlington National Cemetery.

His most important command, the U.S. Exploring and Surveying Expedition to the Pacific Ocean and South Seas, 1838–1842, represented the first governmental sponsorship of scientific endeavor and was instrumental in the nation's westward expansion. Specimens gathered by expedition scientists became the foundation collections of the Smithsonian Institution. Significant American contributions in the fields of geology, botany, conchology, anthropology, and linguistics came from the scientific work of the expedition. Wilkes's evaluations of his landfalls influenced later U.S. positions in those areas.

• Wilkes's papers are in the National Archives, RG 45, Wilkes Family Papers, Library of Congress, and in the Duke University Library. In addition to Wilkes's *Narrative* (republished in 1970 by the Gregg Press), accounts of the expedition are in George M. Colvocoresses, *Four Years in a Government*

Exploring Expedition (1852); and Jessie Poesch, *Titian Ramsay Peale and His Journals of the Wilkes Expedition* (1961).

For evaluation of the expedition, see Herman Viola and Carolyn Margolis, *Magnificent Voyagers: The U.S. Exploring Expedition, 1838–1842* (1985); William Stanton, *The Great United States Exploring Expedition of 1838–1842* (1975); and Harley Harris Bartlett, "Reports of the Wilkes Expedition and the Work of the Specialists in Science," *Proceedings of the American Philosophical Society* 82 (1940): 601–705. Daniel C. Haskell, *The United States Exploring Expedition, 1838–1842, and Its Publications, 1844–1874* (1942), is a dated but valuable guide to the official and unofficial publications of the expedition and its members, as well as other works that discuss it. It lists and gives the location of unpublished manuscripts and journals.

Published works covering Wilkes's entire career are scarcer. His *Autobiography of Rear Admiral Charles Wilkes, U.S. Navy, 1798–1877*, ed. William James Morgan et al. (1978), provides insight into his personality. Daniel Henderson's *The Hidden Coasts* (1953) is more objective. An obituary is in the *New York Times*, 9 Feb. 1877.

ROBERTA A. SPRAGUE

WILKESON, Samuel (1 June 1781–7 July 1848), shipowner, iron founder, and manufacturer, was born in Carlisle, Pennsylvania, the son of John Wilkeson and Mary Robinson, farmers. Samuel Wilkeson's early years, after only two weeks of formal education, were devoted solely to working on his father's farm. In 1902 at age twenty-one he left the family farm and married Jane Oram, who subsequently bore all of Wilkeson's six children.

Between 1802 and 1809, after trying his hand at farming in southeastern Ohio, Wilkeson entered the shipping industry and engaged in the Great Lakes trade. He sent glass, nails, and bar iron from Pittsburgh to Black Rock and Buffalo and brought back Onondaga salt through Lake Ontario. During the War of 1812 he built ships for the American navy. Accompanying the militia to defend Buffalo, he was a witness, in 1814, to the burning of the town by the British. In that year he moved his family to what remained of the village.

Wilkeson proceeded to become a forceful figure in the Buffalo community. In spite of the economic depression suffered in the aftermath of the War of 1812, he became a successful merchant and made a fortune in lumber and real estate. Later he built the first iron foundry in Buffalo and started the manufacture of steam engines, stoves, and hollow ware. He also built blast furnaces in Lake and Mahoning counties, Ohio.

Wilkeson had the forethought to realize that the single most important factor in changing Buffalo's isolation and economic downturn would be for the town to become the western terminus of the Erie Canal. Putting his own business aside for a time, he organized the effort to encourage that result. He raised the funds to dredge Buffalo Creek, organized the needed labor force, and invented a pile-driving system, adapting a cast-iron mortar from the War of 1812 as a hammer strong enough to drive wooden piles into the Niagara River to create a harbor. By 1821 the harbor was completed. Wilkeson petitioned the state legislature, and Buffalo, rather than Black Rock, was designated as the terminus for the Erie Canal, which opened in 1825.

In 1815 Wilkeson was elected justice of the peace, and in 1821 he was appointed judge of the Erie County Court of Common Pleas, a position he held for three terms. In 1824 he was elected to the New York State Senate, where he served for six years, and in 1836 he was elected mayor of Buffalo. For a brief time he was influenced by Charles G. Finney in the religious revival that swept across western New York in 1831, but shortly thereafter he returned to his Presbyterian church.

Judge Wilkeson supported gradual and compensated emancipation of the slaves and was an active member of the American Colonization Society, serving as its president for two years and as editor of the *African Repository*. He advocated the use of the proceeds of a protective tariff to compensate slaveowners for every slave who was freed. The ex-slaves were to be sent back to Africa. To support his intentions, he instituted trade with Liberia from Baltimore and Philadelphia.

After his first wife died, in 1820 Wilkeson married Sarah St. John of Buffalo. After her death, he married Mary Peters of New Haven, Connecticut, in 1837. In 1848, while on a trip through Tennessee to visit one of his daughters, Wilkeson became ill and died in Kingston, Tennessee, where he was buried. His gravestone, referring to Buffalo, reads, "He built the city by building its harbor." Reverend John C. Lord, in his eulogy for Wilkeson, stated that "His early identification with the interest of this city [Buffalo] is well known, and it will probably be conceded that to no man, living or dead, is Buffalo so much indebted for its rapid growth and present position as the Queen City of the great island seas of the North."

Samuel Wilkeson was a successful businessman and merchant who correctly anticipated the economic benefits of the Erie Canal, to New York State as well as to Buffalo. His devotion to the project of creating a harbor at Buffalo ultimately led to the booming success of that city.

• The Wilkeson Family Papers are at the Buffalo Historical Society. The nearest work to a complete biography is John C. Lord's 1848 eulogy, "'The Valiant Man': A Discourse on the Death of the Honorable Samuel Wilkeson of Buffalo," in *Sermons by Celebrated Clergymen*, comp. John K. Porter (c. 1852). Several histories of Buffalo contain extensive information on Wilkeson, including Mark Goldman, *High Hopes: The Rise and Decline of Buffalo, New York* (1983); J. N. Larned, *A History of Buffalo: Delineating the Evolution of the City* (2 vols., 1911); Henry P. Smith, *History of the City of Buffalo and Erie County* (2 vols., 1884); and the [unsigned] work commissioned by the *Buffalo Times*, *History of the City of Buffalo and Niagara Falls* (1896).

R. BETH KLOPOTT

WILKINS, Roy (30 Aug. 1901–4 Aug. 1981), civil rights organization executive, was born in St. Louis, Missouri, the son of William DeWitte Wilkins, a minister, and Mayfield Edmundson. His parents left Holly Springs, Mississippi, for St. Louis soon after their marriage in 1900 to seek refuge from threatened racial violence against his father. His mother died while he was still quite young, and her sister Elizabeth Edmundson Williams took Wilkins and his younger sister and brother to live with her in St. Paul, Minnesota. His aunt and her husband, Sam Williams, a sleeping-car porter, provided a stable home for the Wilkins children in an integrated, working-class neighborhood.

Wilkins attended the University of Minnesota, where he earned a bachelor of arts degree in sociology in 1923. He also took journalism courses and gained experience as a journalist by working on campus publications. He supported himself while in college by working as a redcap, a dining-car waiter, and a slaughterhouse laborer. In 1922 he became editor of the *Appeal*, a local black weekly newspaper.

After graduation Wilkins began work on 1 October 1923 as news editor of the *Kansas City Call*, a black weekly. He found black Kansas City, even with all of its problems, to be an exciting and colorful place. "White Kansas City," however, he recalled, "was an entirely different place, a Jim Crow town that nearly ate my heart out as the years went by." In Kansas City Wilkins became a fighter for African-American rights. He joined the struggle for better schools, for an end to discrimination in education, for an end to police brutality, and for the defeat of racist politicians. In 1929 he married Aminda "Minnie" Badeau, a social worker; the couple had no children.

In 1931 Walter White replaced James Weldon Johnson as executive secretary of the National Association for the Advancement of Colored People (NAACP). White offered his former position as assistant secretary to Wilkins, who on 15 August 1931 began a 24-year apprenticeship under White. In his autobiography, *Standing Fast* (1982), Wilkins said of his new job, "My new duties involved a little bit of everything—writing, lecturing, organizing new branches, raising money for a treasury that was always Depression-dry, running the office while Walter was touring around the country. For a while I even reviewed legal cases." He also continued to write a column for the *Call* and worked with W. E. B. Du Bois on the *Crisis*, the NAACP's magazine.

Wilkins's duties turned out to be quite diverse. He undertook his first major investigation in 1932 in connection with a report that the U.S. Corps of Engineers was exploiting African-American workers employed in building flood-control dams and levees in Mississippi. He volunteered to get eyewitness evidence of conditions. After Du Bois resigned from the NAACP, in addition to his duties as assistant secretary, from 1934 to 1949 Wilkins also edited the *Crisis*.

The Scottsboro incident, a famous case of the 1930s, occurred just as Wilkins joined the NAACP staff. At the time, White told him, "Roy, the Scottsboro Case is your baby." He was involved in this struggle with the southern system of justice and the machinations of the Communist party for nearly two decades. The case involved nine young black men accused of raping two white women in Alabama while hitching a ride on a freight train traveling from Chattanooga to Memphis. Although the evidence was less than compelling, eight of the nine Scottsboro Boys were sentenced to death, and one received a life sentence.

At this point both the NAACP and the International Labor Defense (ILD), a Communist organization, offered to defend the young men. Their parents accepted the ILD's offer. The case became a profitable venture for the Communist party with an estimated $1 million raised through an international propaganda campaign. But after successive trials the men remained in prison. In 1935 the NAACP and other civil rights organizations entered the case. Wilkins represented the NAACP on a Scottsboro Defense Committee. He said that they set out as quickly as they could "to save the boys from the Communists and the white juries of Alabama." This, however, was a long process. The last of the Scottsboro Boys was not freed until 1950. Wilkins tried to help the young men in finding employment as they were released from prison. The Scottsboro case was Wilkins's initial encounter in his long opposition to Communist involvement in the struggle for civil rights.

During World War II job discrimination, racial violence, and segregation in the armed forces became the major issues for the NAACP and other civil rights groups. The NAACP provided both staff and financial support for A. Philip Randolph's proposed March on Washington in 1941. Wilkins played a key role in these activities. During the Harlem riots in 1943 he joined White and New York City mayor Fiorello La Guardia in the streets in sound trucks urging rioters to calm down. In May 1945 Wilkins was a consultant to the American delegation at the United Nations charter conference in San Francisco. The next year he was diagnosed with colon cancer. After an operation and a period of recuperation, he returned to his NAACP duties.

Wilkins welcomed Harry Truman's ascension to the presidency in 1945. He had followed Truman's political career in Missouri and assessed him as having a border-state view on race. Wilkins said that although Truman did not believe in social equality, "No one had ever convinced him that the Bill of Rights was a document for white folks only."

White took a leave of absence from the NAACP in 1949, and Wilkins became acting executive secretary. During this period fair employment practices became the NAACP's priority. Wilkins chaired the National Emergency Civil Rights Mobilization, a movement made up of more than 100 local and national groups that sent 4,218 participants from thirty-three states to a march in Washington on 15 January 1950. This event served as a mass lobby for fair employment legislation and other civil rights bills. President Truman met with a delegation from the march. The mobilization led to greater cooperation among civil rights organizations through the organizing of the Leadership Conference on Civil Rights, which Wilkins chaired. When White returned in May 1950, the NAACP board of directors relieved him of some of his duties and named Wilkins the day-to-day administrator of the organization. After White died in March 1955, the NAACP board of directors unanimously named Wilkins to succeed him the next month.

The first decade of Wilkins's leadership was the NAACP's greatest period of accomplishment. The crowning achievement was the 1954 Supreme Court decision in *Brown v. Board of Education*. In spite of the Court's failure to order immediate integration of schools, the NAACP leadership remained optimistic that desegregation could be achieved. But the organization had not reckoned on the tenacious resistance African Americans would face in trying to desegregate southern schools. NAACP efforts were frustrated by legal tactics, such as "freedom of choice" plans, by violence, and by economic and other forms of intimidation carried out by the newly founded White Citizens Councils. Wilkins became highly critical of the failure of the federal government to enforce the *Brown* decision.

Even so, there were encouraging signs of progress coming out of Washington. Congress passed the Civil Rights Act of 1957, the first such measure in the twentieth century. Wilkins took little satisfaction in the new law because Title III, a provision allowing the Justice Department to sue in civil rights cases (including school desegregation), was stripped from the bill before it was passed. Still, he had worked hard to get the measure through Congress. Looking back on this experience in his autobiography, he concluded, "I still think I did the right thing. In the middle of the battle, Hubert Humphrey took me aside and said, 'Roy, if there's one thing I have learned in politics, it's never to turn your back on a crumb.' He knew what he was talking about. The crumb of 1957 had to come first before the civil rights acts that followed later." Wilkins, along with NAACP lobbyist Clarence Mitchell, played a major role in working with President Lyndon B. Johnson and in lobbying Congress to get the civil rights acts of 1964, 1965, and 1968 enacted. He was also a key figure in the 1963 March on Washington.

The years after 1955 were also years of challenge for Wilkins. The Montgomery bus boycott, the lunch counter sit-ins in Greensboro, North Carolina, and the Freedom Rides brought new leaders, new organizations, and new tactics to the struggle. In spite of the successes achieved by Martin Luther King, Jr., Wilkins remained steadfast in his belief that legal and political action and not direct action had to be the main thrust of the civil rights struggle. NAACP youth councils, however, were among the first groups to employ direct-action tactics. At the organization's 1960 convention, Wilkins paid tribute to the sit-in demonstrators. He said that these demonstrations had made "men and women of the Negro youths overnight." He continued, "It has electrified the adult Negro community with the exception of the usual Uncle Toms and Nervous Nellies. It has stirred white college students from coast to coast as they have not been stirred since Pearl Harbor." After the speech the young conventioneers hoisted Wilkins to their shoulders and paraded around the hall.

As time passed, however, Wilkins became increasingly alienated from proponents of direct action and from African-American youths as they turned increasingly to black nationalism. He chided King that his tactics had not desegregated anything. Wilkins believed that in spite of its popularity, direct action was of limited effectiveness and was inappropriate for application on a national scale. His alienation from young blacks, such as Stokely Carmichael, became complete in the mid-1960s when they embraced black power. Wilkins's keynote address to the 1966 NAACP convention dealt with this issue. His nephew, the journalist Roger Wilkins, at first persuaded him to tone down his attack on black power advocates, but he restored to his speech the line "Black Power means black death." In *A Man's Life* (1982), Roger Wilkins wrote, "I think that line more than any other made him the target of the black youth and radical communities."

Wilkins was subjected to attack both from outside and from within the NAACP. Militant groups invaded and took over his office, and a group was arrested for plotting to assassinate him. "Young Turks" within the NAACP called for a more militant course for the organization and called for his retirement. Wilkins understood the frustration that led to the urban violence in the 1960s, but he condemned that violence and favored the use of the military when necessary to quell it. As a member of President Johnson's National Advisory Commission on Civil Rights, however, he helped to draft the tough language in the commission's report that warned of the danger of the nation dividing into separate black and white societies. He was also disappointed that President Johnson virtually ignored the work of his commission.

Wilkins's final years as executive director of the NAACP were far from halcyon. He spent the 1970s trying to hold back the tide of reaction that came with the administrations of Richard Nixon and Gerald Ford. He criticized these presidents and white liberals for slowing the pace of desegregation and for their opposition to school busing. Simultaneously, he struggled against members of his board of directors who openly urged his retirement. Finally, in 1977, at age seventy-five, he handed over the organization he had served for forty-six years to Benjamin Hooks. Wilkins spent the remaining years of his life in New York City, where he died.

Roy Wilkins was not a complex person. As Melvin Drimmer so aptly stated in *Phylon* (June 1984), his "place in the civil rights pantheon does not owe to his role as a dreamer, intellectual, rebel, poet, philosopher, revolutionary, or spellbinder. He was not any of these. He was rather a phenomenon of the 20th century, the professional bureaucrat." Working quietly as a power broker with national leaders, Wilkins was a key figure in the dismantling of the major legal barriers to civil rights. He never wavered in his belief that the ultimate goal in the struggle for African-American freedom must be full integration into American society.

This belief was bolstered by his implicit faith in the Constitution and the American legal system. During the Vietnam War, the Black Power Movement, and the setbacks of the Nixon and Ford administrations, he never let the NAACP lose sight of the ultimate goal. The organization that he handed over to Hooks was still strong and capable of carrying on the struggle for African-American equality.

• The NAACP Papers are in the Library of Congress. Wilkins's autobiography, *Standing Fast: The Autobiography of Roy Wilkins* (1982), is an important source. See also Roger Wilkins, *A Man's Life: An Autobiography* (1982). Other biographies provide valuable insights on Wilkins. See Sheldon Avery, *Up From Washington: William Pickens and the Negro Struggle for Equality, 1900–1954* (1989), and Denton L. Watson, *Lion in the Lobby: Clarence Mitchell, Jr.'s Struggle for the Passage of Civil Rights Laws* (1990). Aspects of Wilkins's career are also treated in histories of the NAACP and of the civil rights movement. See Minnie Finch, *The NAACP: Its Fight for Justice* (1981); Benjamin Muse, *The American Negro Revolution: From Nonviolence to Black Power, 1963–1967* (1968); Edward Peeks, *The Long Struggle for Black Power* (1971); and John Dittmer, *Local People: The Struggle for Civil Rights in Mississippi* (1994). See also Melvin Drimmer, "Roy Wilkins and the American Dream: A Review Essay," *Phylon* 45 (June 1984): 160–63; James Farmer, "Secret Meeting of the Six Who Shaped the Movement," *Ebony*, Apr. 1985, pp. 108–10, 112–15; Charles Sanders, "A Frank Interview with Roy Wilkins," *Ebony*, Apr. 1974, pp. 35–42; and Watson, "Assessing the Role of the NAACP in the Civil Rights Movement," *The Historian* 55 (Spring 1993): 453–68. Obituaries are in *Time*, 21 Sept. 1981; *Newsweek*, 4 Jan. 1982; and *Ebony*, Nov. 1981.

ARVARH E. STRICKLAND

WILKINS, William (20 Dec. 1779–23 June 1865), businessman and politician, was born in Carlisle, Pennsylvania, the son of John Wilkins, a tavernkeeper, a merchant, and a member of the Pennsylvania constitutional convention, and Catherine Rowan. Once a captain in the Continental army, John Wilkins moved his family to Pittsburgh in 1783 and achieved social prominence there. Young William received enough preparatory education to enter Dickinson College. After a few years of study, he read law in the Carlisle office of David Watts, joined the Allegheny County bar in December 1801, and returned to Pittsburgh to begin a career. Requiring flexibility and mobility, the practice of law carried Wilkins on horseback throughout western Pennsylvania, sometimes as far north as Crawford County, and smoothed a future path to elective office. In 1815 he married Catherine Holmes, who died just a year later. In 1818 he married Mathilda Dallas, daughter of Alexander J. Dallas of Philadelphia. They had seven children.

Community involvement, legal skills, and family name hastened political notice in early nineteenth-century Pittsburgh. Wilkins and several others pooled their capital to form the Pittsburgh Manufacturing Company. In 1814 the Pennsylvania legislature agreed to charter the firm as the Bank of Pittsburgh, with Wilkins as president. During that prosperous time before the panic of 1819, Wilkins also served as president of the Monongahela Bridge Company, the Greensburg and Pittsburgh Turnpike Company, and the Pittsburgh Common Council from 1816 to 1819. In addition, Wilkins's roles as president of the Vigilant Fire Company, director of the Permanent Library Company, trustee of the Western University of Pennsylvania, commissioner of the Western Penitentiary, and an investor in the Ohio Navigation Company presented an unusually rich ledger of service to his city and region.

Well known in a state where business and civic connections signified fitness for office, Wilkins won election to the legislature as an anticaucus candidate in 1819. Though nominally a Federalist at that time, he was careful to link himself to other local factions—the so-called Independent and Patent Republicans—as well. In 1820 Wilkins resigned his legislative seat in favor of a post as presiding judge of the Fifth Judicial District in Pennsylvania. He advanced from there in May 1824 to the U.S. District Court for western Pennsylvania, where he remained until 1831. A pre-1820 critic of the legislative caucus system in Pennsylvania, elitist corruption in state politics, and the high costs of government, Wilkins displayed attitudes that connected him ideologically to the early Jackson movement. His early Federalist connections, however, made Wilkins's support of Andrew Jackson from 1824 on subject to nagging charges of opportunism. He tried in vain for Congress in 1826 and again, successfully, in 1828 but resigned before being seated, apparently for business reasons.

Wilkins's immersion in national politics started with election to the U.S. Senate in 1831, when he beat William Marks, also a Jacksonian Democrat from Pittsburgh but, unlike his foe, a member of the Masonic order. As an anti-Mason and a strong supporter of protective tariffs and the National Bank, Wilkins offers insight into the complex nature of Jacksonianism in Pennsylvania, where state economic interest was not always consistent with policy in Washington, D.C. Sensitive to the iron industry, manufacturers in the Keystone State espoused the protectionist philosophy identified more with Mathew Carey and Henry Clay than with President Jackson and his followers. Richard Rush of Pennsylvania, treasury secretary under John Quincy Adams and a strong tariff man himself, remarked ironically to Clay in December 1830 that Wilkins's election to the Senate "looks well for our cause." Wilkins was a notable delegate, one of roughly 500 representing thirteen states, to the influential New York Tariff Convention of 26–31 October 1831. An economic nationalist where Pennsylvania interests dictated, he also voted for the Bank Recharter Bill of June 1832, for Clay's Land Bill of that year, and in March 1834 for $300,000 to repair the Cumberland Road east of the Ohio River. Chair of the Senate Judiciary Committee that drafted the Force Bill, Wilkins vigorously defended Jackson's stance during the Nullification Crisis with South Carolina in 1832–1833. The Pittsburgh senator also supported the president's controversial decision to remove federal deposits from the

Second Bank of the United States, even though it rankled powerful constituents in Philadelphia. Publicly tightening his ties with Jackson, he enthralled the Senate in February 1834 with a dramatic withdrawal of support for Nicholas Biddle (1786–1844), president of the doomed bank.

Wilkins's confusing role in the presidential campaign of 1832 also mirrored sectional and ideological tensions within the Jacksonian ranks. While Democrats from the South and West shared little of the northeastern enthusiasm for manufacturing, Pennsylvanians clamored for greater sway in the party. With Jackson up for reelection in 1832 and his prospects of winning Pennsylvania in doubt, the state Democratic convention at Harrisburg nominated Wilkins instead of Martin Van Buren for vice president in March 1832. In the minds of Pennsylvania Jacksonians, Van Buren had come to symbolize New York's much-resented political domination of their state. With Wilkins receiving the state's thirty electoral votes for the second-highest office in the fall election, "Old Hickory" carried Pennsylvania along with neighboring manufacturing states New York and New Jersey. With the episode aggravating the old questions of Wilkins's loyalty to the Jackson party, the Pennsylvania senator's 1834 abandonment of Biddle's cause in favor of Jackson's looks partly to have been political fence mending.

As Van Buren's star rose, Wilkins's prospects as party leader faded. In June 1834 he resigned his Senate seat in favor of the unglamorous ministership to Russia, succeeding the colorful and diplomatically effective James Buchanan. Wilkins should have been less happy to arrive in St. Petersburg than Buchanan was to be leaving after three difficult years. With horrible weather, a constant threat of cholera, steady surveillance by Russian police, regular screening of mail, and an insulting salary, the minister had to make the best of deplorable circumstances. Even worse, the Russian food, according to Buchanan, tasted bad enough to "have repulsed a Delaware Indian." Czar Nicholas I's fear of the West and general distrust of republicanism tended to poison relations with the United States. Trying to supplement Buchanan's Commercial Treaty of December 1832, Wilkins's efforts to secure further trading concessions from the Russians proved fruitless.

Returning home in April 1836, Wilkins grasped the chance to reenter domestic politics. Though defeated for Congress in 1840, he succeeded two years later and served until February 1844, when President John Tyler (1790–1862) offered him appointment as the fourth secretary of war since the death of William Henry Harrison, Tyler's predecessor, from pneumonia in April 1841. Wilkins's quick Senate confirmation scarcely lessened the impediment of serving a president who operated with neither party nor coherent factions behind him. The appointment of a Pennsylvania Jacksonian was itself further evidence of an irrevocable break between Tyler and the Clay Whigs, a quarrel that had begun in the summer of 1841 and led to the resignation of the entire cabinet except for Secretary of State Daniel Webster. By 1844 Tyler's cabinet was predominantly southern, headed by John C. Calhoun as secretary of state. Wilkins, though out of place among states' rights men who opposed protective tariffs and strove to protect slavery, embraced the administration's proexpansion agenda, especially annexation of Texas.

In March 1845, with Tyler's presidency ended, the 65-year-old Wilkins found himself politically unattractive to the new James K. Polk regime. For a decade he retired to his opulent mansion, "Homewood," in eastern Pittsburgh. With political ambition stirring in him for the last time in 1855, he won a seat in the Pennsylvania Senate, served a single two-year term, and sponsored a bill to boost state liquor interests. The Civil War aroused Wilkins's ardent unionism of thirty years before. As an octogenarian major general of the Pennsylvania Home Guard, he spent his remaining days raising troops and reproaching the Confederacy. He died at Homewood.

• A small collection of Wilkins papers is in the Historical Society of Western Pennsylvania, Pittsburgh. A full biography of him is Sewell E. Slick, "The Life of William Wilkins" (M.A. thesis, Univ. of Pittsburgh, 1931). Valuable for his Pennsylvania background is James A. Kehl, *Ill Feeling in the Era of Good Feeling: Western Pennsylvania Political Battles, 1815–1825* (1956). His career in the Senate can be traced in Joseph Gales and William W. Seaton, comps., *Register of Debates in Congress* (1830–1834). Wilkins's brief service as minister to Russia is covered in John M. Belohlavek, *"Let the Eagle Soar!" The Foreign Policy of Andrew Jackson* (1985); and for his time in the Tyler administration, see Norma Lois Peterson, *The Presidencies of William Henry Harrison and John Tyler* (1989). Obituary notices are in the *Pittsburgh Evening Chronicle*, 23 June 1865; the *Pittsburgh Commercial*, the *Daily Pittsburgh Gazette*, and the *Daily Post* (Pittsburgh), all 24 June 1865.

JOHN R. VAN ATTA

WILKINSON, James (1757–28 Dec. 1825), soldier and intriguer, was born in Calvert County, Maryland, the son of Joseph Wilkinson and Betty Heighe, merchant-farmers. He spent his early years on his parents' farm, but his father died when he was seven, and his mother apprenticed him to a local physician, John Bond, to learn medicine. When Wilkinson was seventeen he went to Philadelphia to continue his medical training. In 1775 he completed his studies and opened a practice in Monocacy, Maryland. But his heart was not in it. While in Philadelphia he had been dazzled by the fervor of the growing revolutionary movement, avidly watching militiamen drill and listening to heated oratory against the "Intolerable Acts." He began to neglect his patients, concentrating instead on drilling with a volunteer corps of riflemen, and soon he had joined colonial forces investing Boston. An affable young man, he received attention from General Nathanael Greene, who appointed him an aide. He also became a friend of Benedict Arnold, and in 1776, as a recently promoted captain, he joined Arnold in Canada. Later that year he was advanced to the rank of major, and in January 1777 he caught the attention of General Horatio Gates, who appointed him to his staff as a lieutenant colonel. After Gates's triumph at Saratoga, Wilkinson took the news to Congress (though tardily), was brevetted brigadier general, and was appointed secretary to the Board of War. But his proclivity for self-promotion soon put him at odds with his erstwhile friends, and he fell out of favor with the field officers of the army. Quarreling with Gates, he fought a bloodless duel with his mentor. He resigned his brevet commission but soon secured the position of clothier general in George Washington's army. He was forced to surrender this office in 1781 when Congress discovered serious deficiencies in his accounts. In the meantime, he married Ann Biddle, the daughter of Quaker merchant John Biddle, who bore him three sons and with whom he lived happily until her death in 1807.

Furloughed in 1783, Wilkinson for a time tried farming in Bucks County, Pennsylvania, but his questing soul needed new outlets, and he looked toward Kentucky as the place to fulfill his destiny. Purchasing large landholdings near Lexington with money provided by his wife's family, he migrated there, established a general merchandise business, and began agitating for Kentucky statehood. He also became deeply involved in attempts to persuade Spanish authorities at New Orleans to open the Mississippi River to American trade. Soon a popular leader of malcontents against eastern politicians, in 1787 he turned to his own advantage the Kentuckians' anger because the Mississippi River was closed to trade and because they felt neglected and ignored by politicians in Virginia. That year he organized a trading voyage to New Orleans, where he convinced the Spanish governor, Rodríguez Esteban Miró, that he was willing and able to help Spain gain possession of Kentucky. As proof of this assertion, he swore an oath of allegiance to the Spanish king. Impressed by Wilkinson's bombast, Miró gave him unlimited trading permission and an annual pension of $2,000 for this service. Thus, Wilkinson began a profitable trade on the Mississippi River while at the same time agitating in Kentucky primarily for statehood rather than separation from the union. Through it all he somehow managed to stay in the good graces of Spanish authorities in New Orleans.

In 1791 Wilkinson was commissioned lieutenant colonel in the U.S. Army and ordered to battle Indians in the Northwest Territory. A year later, when General Anthony Wayne was named commander in chief of an army organized for that purpose, Wilkinson was promoted to brigadier general and made second in command. Over the next five years, both secretly and openly, he intrigued against Wayne to secure the latter's position, while at the same time he participated in Wayne's campaigns against the Indians and fought bravely at Fallen Timbers. In 1796, upon the death of Wayne, he took charge of the army but was refused promotion to major general. Still in the pay of Spanish officials, he continued to pass on intelligence to them in return for large sums in gold, but most of his information was of little value. He was transferred to the southern frontier in 1798 and seven years later was ordered to St. Louis to take possession of newly acquired Louisiana. As governor of Louisiana, he encouraged Zebulon Pike's explorations and dabbled in self-aggrandizing land schemes. Soon he was in correspondence with Aaron Burr, and although it is not clear just how deeply involved he was in the Burr Conspiracy, he seems to have known of Burr's intentions to separate the Mississippi Valley from the United States and in fact may have originated the idea. But when rumors of Burr's activities began circulating in the East, Wilkinson, to protect himself, exposed Burr's plans to President Thomas Jefferson. He also warned the viceroy of Mexico about Burr's schemes and then brazenly asked for payment in return for his services. Soon Burr was brought to trial on charges of treason; because neither he nor Wilkinson dared testify against each other, both escaped judgment. In 1811, as a result of his dealings with the Spanish in the West, Wilkinson was court-martialed by order of President James Madison; when he was acquitted for lack of evidence, the president approved the verdict "with regret."

At the outbreak of the War of 1812, Wilkinson was promoted to major general and put in charge of an attempt to invade Canada in 1813. Due to his own lack of vigor and the failures of others, he did not commence operations against Montreal until November, and the assaults were a fiasco. Relieved of command, he was court-martialed once more, by Secretary of War John Armstrong, who charged him with drunkenness and neglect of duty. Although acquitted, he was not returned to duty, and thus his military career was finished. After 1815 he composed his memoirs, three huge volumes of turgid, rambling self-justification that conceal more than they reveal about James Wilkinson. In 1816 he moved with his second wife, the "divine little Creole" Celestine Laveau Trudeau, whom he had married in 1810, to New Orleans, where he lived quietly for a time with her and beautiful twin daughters. Then, needing money, he traveled in 1822 to Mexico City in search of Texas land grants. There, three years later, alone and miserable, he died of gout.

During his lifetime, most of Wilkinson's contemporaries—especially those who had any extensive dealings with him—came to dislike him thoroughly. Anthony Wayne called him a "vile invidious man . . . as devoid of *principle* as he is of *honor* or *fortune*," and John Randolph, foreman of the grand jury that examined evidence of Wilkinson's participation in the Burr conspiracy, declared that the man was "a mammoth of iniquity . . . the most finished scoundrel that ever lived." It is curious that his strongest supporter was always Thomas Jefferson, who usually was a better judge of men. "He is 'the man whom the king delights to honor,'" said Randolph, and that was explanation enough for his continuing presence in public life, long after many others had turned against him.

• The largest collection of Wilkinson papers is in the Chicago Historical Society. Other substantial holdings are in the Library of Congress and the Historical Society of Pennsylvania. His *Memoirs of My Own Times* (3 vols., 1816) are essential but must be used with extreme caution. The most useful and scholarly biography is James Ripley Jacobs, *Tarnished Warrior: Major-General James Wilkinson* (1938). Other biographies are Thomas Robson Hay and M. R. Werner, *The Admirable Trumpeter: A Biography of General James Wilkinson* (1941), and Royal O. Shreve, *The Finished Scoundrel: General James Wilkinson* (1933). Thomas Abernethy, *The Burr Conspiracy* (1954), gives useful background on that subject, while the politicomilitary setting in the western lands is covered admirably by Richard H. Kohn, *Eagle and Sword: The Federalists and the Creation of the Military Establishment in America, 1783–1802* (1975). Wilkinson's relationships with two key actors in his life are described in Paul David Nelson, *General Horatio Gates: A Biography* (1976), and *Anthony Wayne: Soldier of the Early Republic* (1985).

PAUL DAVID NELSON

WILKINSON, Jemima (29 Nov. 1752–1 July 1819), sectarian religious leader, was born in Cumberland, Rhode Island, the daughter of Jeremiah Wilkinson and Amey Whipple, farmers. Her family was Quaker, and Wilkinson drew strength from Quaker principles. Her mother died when she was about twelve years of age, and this may have increased an already pronounced interest in religious topics. Little else is known of her childhood except that she read a great many Quaker works, writings on theology and history, and the King James version of the Bible. She also responded positively to the revivals that by her day were being referred to as the Great Awakening. When evangelist George Whitefield visited New England in the 1760s, Wilkinson became enthusiastic about intensified religious experiences, adding such interests to her already strong concerns about religion. But the fervent preaching and quickened spirituality varied considerably from Quaker standards, and her support of revivals eventually incurred a serious sanction. In August 1776 she was dismissed from the Society of Friends for attending meetings led by pro-revival New Light Baptists.

The shock of dismissal may have set Wilkinson on a course of religious innovation, but another experience two months later was of even greater importance. Ill with fever in October 1776, she became convinced that she had died and returned to earth for a second life. She declared herself to be God's special emissary, sent back to this world as a preacher. Thereafter she refused to recognize her legal name, insisting instead that others address her as the "Publick Universal Friend." This unique status became part of her persona for the next forty years.

During the American Revolution Wilkinson preached in Rhode Island, Massachusetts, and Connecticut. She attracted large crowds; some people were simply curious about her magnetic personality, and others were greatly impressed that a woman could stand before large audiences and deliver effective sermons. Wilkinson added to her striking presence by wearing distinctive clothing that resembled a priest's cassock. Men and women, rich and poor, were drawn to her preaching. By 1784 one notable convert was William Potter of Kingston, Rhode Island, who was so affected by the Publick Universal Friend that he opened his home to her, abandoned politics, and freed all his slaves. Traveling as far as Pennsylvania, Wilkinson developed a personal following. By the early 1780s congregations of Universal Friends emerged in Greenwich, Rhode Island, and New Milford, Connecticut. These groups were not formal churches but cliques dependent on a single personality. More important than biblical doctrine or ethical guidelines, membership rested primarily on Wilkinson's personal approval of applicants. "Ye cannot be my friends," she maintained, "except ye do whatsoever I command you."

In 1785 she conceived the idea of protecting her flock from worldly wickedness by removing to the unspoiled frontier. Within three years her people established the first American outpost west of Lake Seneca in central New York. When Wilkinson arrived there in 1790, the Friend's Settlement had a population of 260. But continual internal disputes over land titles induced the religious band to move. Final settlement began in 1794 in Jerusalem Township near Crooked (now Keuka) Lake in Yates County. The peaceable settlers helped open that section of territory and encouraged other pioneers to inhabit the land. Wilkinson owned no land herself, living modestly on a follower's estate until her death there more than two decades later.

Doctrines and practices among the Universal Friends were not extreme. Some controversies swirled about Wilkinson's own head, but it is impossible to sift reliable data from rumors intended to smear her reputation. Some orthodox, white, Protestant males, suspicious of any departure from their control, claimed that she indulged in sexual aberrations, while others accused her of messianic pretensions. We cannot say whether she was a deliberate charlatan who duped gullible disciples or a kindly pastor who genuinely cared for her followers. She preached only that people should forsake evil and prepare for divine judgment. Beyond urging others to follow the golden rule in daily affairs, she apparently made some attempts at faith healing, prophesying, and mystical interpretations of dreams. While enjoining pacifism and plain dress, she did not discourage people from saying that she was a messiah. She also encouraged celibacy as a higher state of grace, but married couples continued to function as families when they joined her group. They were less rigorous on this point than the Shakers, and there is no known contact between Wilkinson and Shaker founder Ann Lee. Despite the intensity of external controversies, those in the inner circles regarded Wilkinson as a friendly woman who taught simple biblical principles of virtue and justice. The group depended heavily on her personal charisma, however, and it disintegrated within two decades after the leader's death. She had never married or had children.

• Papers of Jemima Wilkinson, including correspondence, journals, and sermons, are housed at Cornell University. An early biography, though biased and inaccurate, is David Hudson, *History of Jemima Wilkinson, a Preacheress of the Eighteenth Century* (1821). A far more trustworthy and balanced account is Herbert A. Wisbey, Jr., *Pioneer Prophetess: Jemima Wilkinson, the Publick Universal Friend* (1964).

HENRY WARNER BOWDEN

WILKINSON, John (6 Nov. 1821–29 Dec. 1891), U.S. and Confederate naval officer, was born in Norfolk, Virginia, the son of Francis Coleman and Jesse Wilkinson, a U.S. naval officer. On 18 December 1837 Wilkinson was appointed a midshipman in the U.S. Navy, and on 10 February 1838 he was assigned to the USS *Columbia* at Norfolk, Virginia. His initial service was with the Brazilian squadron onboard the USS *Independence*, and he later saw service with the East Indies squadron. In September 1842 Wilkinson was ordered to the Naval School at Philadelphia for his midshipman examination and on 12 July 1843 was warranted a passed midshipman. After a brief tour of duty with the Coast Survey Office, Wilkinson was assigned to warships in the South Atlantic and the Pacific.

At the start of the Mexican War, in May 1846, Wilkinson joined the USS *Perry*. Assigned to blockade duty in the Gulf of Mexico, the *Perry* encountered a hurricane between Florida and Cuba that forced it to return to Philadelphia for repairs in December 1846. On 9 March 1847 Wilkinson became the acting master of the USS *Saratoga*. On 20 October 1850 he was promoted to warranted master, and on 14 February 1851 he was commissioned lieutenant.

Between 1852 and 1858 Wilkinson served with the Coast Survey Office and the Home Squadron, then in June 1859 he was assigned as the chief, Hydrographic Party, and given the command of the steamer *Corwin*. With this vessel he charted the waters of eastern Florida and the Bahamas. While serving with the Coast Survey Office, Wilkinson married Mary Blair Peachy in 1857. They had four children. Though not active in politics, Wilkinson remained loyal to Virginia, and with secession in the air, he tendered his resignation on 6 April 1861.

Upon leaving the U.S. Navy, Wilkinson offered his services to his home state and was appointed a lieutenant in the Virginia State Navy. His first assignment was to the defenses of Richmond at Fort Powhatan on the James River. Later he was transferred to Acquia Landing, Virginia, where he assisted in the construction of batteries overlooking the Potomac River. In June 1861 the Virginia state forces were absorbed by the Confederacy, and on 10 June 1861 Wilkinson was appointed a lieutenant in the Confederate navy. His experience with both warships and the Coast Survey made him a very valuable officer.

In early 1862 Wilkinson was assigned to the Confederate squadron at New Orleans, where he served as the executive officer of the unfinished ironclad *Louisiana*. The vessel was towed to a position on the Mississippi River next to Fort St. Philip, and Wilkinson was on board during the 24 April 1862 attack that found Flag Officer David Farragut running his flotilla past the Confederate forts and capturing New Orleans. During the battle the commander of the *Louisiana* was mortally wounded, and Wilkinson assumed command. He planned a sortie against Farragut's squadron at New Orleans, but after a mutiny within the fort's garrisons, the army commander was forced to surrender his position, thus removing the *Louisiana*'s base of operations. After setting the *Louisiana* on fire, Wilkinson, his crew, and other members of the naval squadron were taken prisoners. Wilkinson was eventually exchanged on 5 August 1862.

Upon returning to Richmond, Wilkinson was detached to the War Department and assigned to purchase a British-built blockade-runner. Running the blockade out of Wilmington, North Carolina, he eventually made his way to Great Britain, where he negotiated the purchase of the *Giraffe*, a Glasgow-based, luxury paddlewheel ferryboat. By November 1862 Wilkinson had supervised its conversion to a blockade-runner and had loaded the vessel with munitions and lithographic equipment. He successfully ran the vessel into Wilmington on 29 December 1862. The War Department renamed it the *Robert E. Lee* and retained Wilkinson as its commander. Over the next ten months, Wilkinson directed the *Robert E. Lee* on fourteen runs through the blockade.

Because of his success as a blockade-runner, Wilkinson was chosen to lead a mission designed to liberate Confederate prisoners held at Johnson's Island in Lake Erie near Sandusky, Ohio. Twenty-six officers were assigned to Wilkinson, and on 10 October 1863 Wilkinson and his party sailed out of Wilmington on board the *Robert E. Lee*. Wilkinson guided the steamer to Halifax, Nova Scotia, where he relinquished his command and disembarked with his raiders. Moving by separate routes, the men reassembled in Montreal, where plans were made to capture the Federal warship *Michigan* and use its guns to overpower Johnson's Island's garrison and free the prisoners. However, Wilkinson's design was soon discovered by both the Canadian and U.S. governments, and the attempt had to be abandoned.

Returning to Wilmington in early spring 1864, Wilkinson was attached to the naval squadron there and briefly commanded the ironclad *Raleigh*. On 11 March 1864 he was assigned to take command of Wilmington's Office of Orders and Detail. With more than seventy men under his control, Wilkinson was charged with setting up lights to guide vessels in and out of Wilmington, inspecting blockade-runners, aiding stranded vessels, and enforcing government regulations. He was also involved in planning an expedition designed to free Confederate prisoners at Point Lookout, Maryland. Set to sail from Wilmington in early July 1864, the raid was abruptly cancelled when it became known that the enemy had received word of its destination. On 2 June 1864 Wilkinson was made a first lieutenant in the provisional navy to rank from 6 January 1864.

At the end of September 1864 Wilkinson was ordered to take command of the CSS *Chickamauga*, a blockade-runner that had been purchased by the Confederacy and converted into a makeshift gunboat and commerce raider. Though Wilkinson was unimpressed with his vessel and vehemently opposed raids directed at the North's fishing and coastal vessels, he ran the ship out of Wilmington on the night of 28 October 1864 in conjunction with a second, similarly obtained and outfitted raider, the CSS *Olustee*. On his twenty-day cruise, Wilkinson burned or bonded seven vessels, the majority of which he described as "fishing craft manned by poor men." On 19 November he brought the *Chickamauga* safely back to Wilmington.

Though the raiders had been successful, Wilkinson immediately went to Richmond to argue against the use of such commerce raiders. Pointing out that the sorties resulted in a tightened blockade, he urged that the commerce raiders be removed from service. He returned to Wilmington with instructions to convert one of the vessels back into a blockade-runner. Since the *Chickamauga* was known to the British authorities in Bermuda, Wilkinson renovated the *Olustee*, formerly the *Tallahassee*, and appropriately renamed it the *Chameleon*.

In late December 1864, as the Union forces were pulling away from their first attempt to capture Fort Fisher, the main guardian of Wilmington, Wilkinson ran the *Chameleon* to Bermuda. By the time he returned to Wilmington with a load of provisions, he found the entrance to the port controlled by Federal warships. Later attempts to reach Charleston also failed, and Wilkinson was eventually instructed to sail the *Chameleon* to England and report to Confederate officials. On 9 April he arrived in Liverpool. The *Chameleon* and all other government property and assets were turned over to the proper authority, and when the Confederacy collapsed, Wilkinson found himself a man without a country.

Wilkinson never signed a surrender document, and possibly because he feared being accused of being a pirate for his service on the *Chickamauga*, he settled in Halifax, Nova Scotia, where he opened a small business. In 1874, after the general amnesty, he returned to Amelia County, Virginia, where he attempted a number of businesses. In 1877 he published *The Narrative of a Blockade Runner* about his Civil War experiences. Though flawed by some slips of memory, it is considered to be one of the finest accounts of blockade-running. Wilkinson died in Annapolis, Maryland.

• Important sources on Wilkinson include *The Official Records of the Union and Confederate Navies in the War of the Rebellion* (30 vols., 1894–1922); Chester G. Hearn, *Gray Raiders of the Sea* (1992); Thomas J. Scharf, *History of the Confederate States Navy* (1886; repr. 1977); and Stephen R. Wise, *Lifeline of the Confederacy: Blockade Running during the Civil War* (1988).

STEPHEN R. WISE

WILKS, Samuel Stanley (17 June 1906–7 March 1964), mathematical statistician, was born in Little Elm, Texas, the son of Chance C. Wilks and Bertha May Gammon, farmers. Until high school, he attended a rural one-room school where, in the seventh grade, his teacher was William M. Whyburn, who became a leading American mathematician. He attended high school in nearby Denton, skipping study hall in his senior year to take a mathematics course at North State Teachers College, from which he received his A.B. in 1926. He was a part-time instructor at the University of Texas 1927–1928, where he was taught by R. L. Moore and Edward L. Dodd and received an M.A. in mathematics in 1928. Accepting a fellowship at the University of Iowa, he began research in mathematical statistics under Henry L. Rietz and was influenced by E. F. Lindquist and was awarded a Ph.D. in 1931. As a National Research Fellow in mathematics, he conducted research in multivariate statistical analysis at Columbia University (1931–1932) and at University College of the University of London and the School of Agriculture of Cambridge University (1932–1933), where he was influenced by Harold Hotelling, Egon S. Pearson, and John Wishart, respectively. In 1931 he married Gena Orr of Denton; they had one child.

On his return to the United States, Wilks joined the faculty of Princeton University, an affiliation that continued until his death. Appointed an instructor in the department of mathematics in 1933, he was promoted to assistant professor in 1936 and to associate professor in 1938. In 1944 he was appointed professor of mathematics, to be effective upon his return to academic duties following World War II, and plans were made for him to head a section of mathematical statistics. From his first year at Princeton until his death, Wilks worked with the College Entrance Examination Board, and later the Education Testing Service, on the scaling and equating of achievement tests. He published a comprehensive report on this subject in 1961.

During World War II, Wilks was a member of the Applied Mathematics Panel of the National Defense Research Committee and directed the Princeton Statistical Research Group. After the war, he served on many National Research Council and National Science Foundation committees on the mathematical, physical, and social sciences. He was a charter member of both the Advisory Committee to the Division of Statistical Standards of the Bureau of the Budget and of the Army Mathematics Advisory Panel and was a member of the Scientific Advisory Board of the National Security Agency.

Wilks was also active in the social sciences. He was the representative of the American Statistical Association on the Social Science Research Council (1948–1952), and subsequently served as chairman of several of the council's key committees. He served on the board of trustees of the Russell Sage Foundation from 1953 until his death and on its executive committee from 1955.

Wilks will long be remembered for his contributions to multivariate statistical analysis. "Certain Generalizations in Analysis of Variance" (1932), written as a National Research Fellow at Columbia, established him as a world leader in mathematical statistics. This was one of the seven papers he published from 1932 to 1946 in which he found the likelihood ratio criteria for testing various null hypotheses about multivariate normal distributions and characterized the corresponding sampling distributions of the criteria. In five papers published from 1935 to 1946, he investigated likelihood ratio tests and related confidence interval procedures for a variety of other probability distributions. Responding to a need expressed by W. A. Shewhart, father of statistical quality control, Wilks laid the foundations of the theory of statistical tolerance limits in "Determination of Sample Sizes for Setting Tolerance Limits" (1941) and "Statistical Prediction with Special Reference to the Problem of Tolerance Limits" (1942). The latter was Wilks's first contribution to "non-parametric" or "distribution-free" methods of statistical inference, a branch of statistical theory and methodology of which he provided an extensive review in "Order Statistics" (1948).

Wilks was deeply interested in all aspects of statistical education. In "Personnel and Training Problems in Statistics" (1947), he outlined the growing use of statistical methods and the demand for personnel with statistical training and made recommendations that served as a guide in the rapid growth of university programs in statistics after World War II. In "Teaching Statistical Inference in Elementary Mathematics Courses" (1958), he urged teaching the principles and techniques of statistical inference to freshmen and sophomores and proposed restructuring high school curricula in mathematics and the sciences to include instruction in probability, statistics, and other modern mathematical subjects. Wilks collaborated with six others to write an experimental textbook, *Introductory Probability and Statistical Inference for Secondary Schools* (1957), and joined with Irwin Guttman in drafting *Introductory Engineering Statistics* (1965; 2d ed. 1971, with Guttman and J. S. Hunter) for undergraduate and engineering students.

Wilks's important publications include three holograph books (written entirely by himself): *Lectures . . . on the Theory of Statistical Inference . . .* (1937), the first book devoted to some of the revolutionary developments of the 1920s and 1930s; *Elementary Statistical Analysis* (1948; repr. with corrections, 1951), designed for undergraduates with a mathematics background and very probably the first carefully developed treatment of mathematical statistics requiring only one term of calculus; and *Mathematical Statistics* (1943; rev. 1962), an encyclopedic book that covers almost all of mathematical statistics in the text or through problems that expand its coverage.

Wilks was one of the founders of the Institute of Mathematical Statistics (1935). He was the first editor appointed by the institute when it assumed full responsibility for the *Annals of Mathematical Statistics* in 1938. During his twelve years as editor, Wilks guided development of the *Annals* from a marginal journal with a small subscription list to the foremost publication in the field, with worldwide circulation.

Wilks was president of the Institute of Mathematical Statistics in 1940 and its Rietz Lecturer in 1949. He was president of the American Statistical Association in 1950. He was elected to the American Philosophical Society in 1948, to the International Statistical Institute in 1951, and to the American Academy of Arts and Sciences in 1963. He was awarded a Presidential Certificate of Merit in 1947 for his contributions to antisubmarine warfare and to the solution of convoy problems, and that same year he received the Centennial Alumni Award of the University of Iowa. The Samuel S. Wilks Memorial Medal of the American Statistical Association has been awarded annually since 1964. Volume 36 (1965) of the *Annals of Mathematical Statistics* is dedicated to his memory and includes articles on various aspects of Wilks's work as well as a photograph of Wilks at his desk. Wilks died peacefully in his sleep at his home in Princeton, New Jersey.

• Wilks's papers (1940–1963) are in the library of the American Philosophical Society. They consist principally of working papers on matters requiring statistical analysis, letters, reports, and papers relating to professional organizations. Forty-eight of Wilks's technical papers are reprinted in T. W. Anderson, ed., *S. S. Wilks: Collected Papers—Contributions to Mathematical Statistics* (1967), preceded by Anderson's obituary of Wilks (repr. from the *Annals of Mathematical Statistics* 36, no. 1 [Feb. 1965]), which reviews his life and career and reviews the technical papers. The article on Wilks in the *Dictionary of Scientific Biography*, vol. 14 (1976), includes extensive bibliographies of his writings and secondary literature but fails to mention the informative obituary by E. S. Pearson in the *Journal of the Royal Statistical Society*, ser. A, vol. 127 (1964). The eight articles of the "Memorial to Samuel S. Wilks," *Journal of the American Statistical Association* 60, no. 312 (Dec. 1965), with photo portrait, provide further information.

A great deal of additional information on Wilks's family, the individuals who guided the development of his career, his Princeton appointment, and some of his students, is contained in Churchill Eisenhart, "Samuel S. Wilks and the Army Experiment Design Conference Series," in *Proceedings of the Twentieth Conference on Design of Experiments in Army Research, Development, and Testing, held at Fort Belvoir, VA, 23–25 October 1974* (U.S. Army Research Office Report 75-2, June 1975), a portion of which has been reprinted as "S. S. Wilks' Princeton Appointment and Statistics at Princeton before Wilks," in *A Century of Mathematics in America*, pt. 3, ed. Peter Duren (1989). An obituary is in the *New York Times*, 9 Mar. 1964.

CHURCHILL EISENHART

WILL, William (27 Jan. 1742–10 Feb. 1798), pewterer, was born in Nieuwied, Germany, the son of John (or Johannes) Will, a pewterer, and Johanna Judith (maiden name unknown). William came to the United States with his family in 1752; they settled in New York City. Will's brother Henry became an important pewterer in New York, and most authorities suggest that William was trained in Henry's shop. William Will probably moved to Philadelphia with another brother, Philip, also a pewterer, who was working in Philadelphia by 1763. He was certainly in Philadelphia by the time of his marriage there to Barbara Culp in 1764; they had three children. His first wife having died, in 1769 he married Anna Clampher, and they had four children.

Will was apparently highly respected by his fellow artisans, and he took an active part in the Revolution and in local politics in the 1770s and 1780s. In 1776 he organized "Captain Will's Company of Associates," an infantry company, and during the next few years he served as an officer or commander of the First Battalion, Colonel Jacob's Third Regiment, and the Third Regiment of Foot. In 1777 he was appointed one of the commissioners "for the Seizure of the Personal Effects of Traitors," and their duties were broadened the next year to cover forfeited estates as well as personal property. Also in 1778 the Pennsylvania Council named Will storekeeper for the Continental army in Lancaster. The next year he was named "Commissioner for Collecting Salt." He was elected high sheriff of Philadelphia in 1780, 1781, and 1782, and in 1785 he was elected a representative to the Pennsylvania General Assembly, a signal honor for a working craftsman. In 1788 Will lost a narrow and hotly contested election for sheriff and retired from public service. The next year he filed for bankruptcy and was forced to sell off a good deal of the extensive landholdings in Pennsylvania that he had acquired as investments since his arrival in Philadelphia. He died in Philadelphia, and his estate was valued at a modest £1,000.

During his pewtering career Will produced a large body of objects in a variety of forms in his shop on North Second Street, and he is generally considered to have been the most important and distinguished pewterer in eighteenth-century America. His work is characterized by excellent craftsmanship, stylishness, and a strong sense of design. Although his work is primarily in an Anglo-American mode, he occasionally incorporated elements from the Germanic tradition, and his work is more closely allied to that of contemporary silversmiths than is usually the case. Because he made many up-to-date forms, including pear-shaped teapots with cabriole legs and claw-and-ball feet, urn-shaped neoclassical coffeepots, and drum-shaped neoclassical teapots, Will must have owned an impressive stock of brass molds and acquired new ones in a timely fashion. His shop was robbed by the British during the Revolution, and Will's advertisement in *Dunlap's Packet* (Philadelphia) for 31 December 1778 noted that he had lost "Three Pewterer's Wheels with all the furniture thereto belonging, one pair of bellows, a number of hammers, steel and iron tools, an iron ingot and many other things for carrying on the pewterer's business."

Among Will's most distinctive objects are pear-shaped tankards in the baroque style, rare globular teapots with cabriole legs and claw-and-ball feet, and double-bellied sugar bowls in the rococo mode. Later in his career, probably after the Revolution, he adopted the neoclassical style and produced drum-shaped teapots and tall, urn-shaped coffeepots very reminiscent of silver forms. His elegant church flagons echo the Germanic taste in their slender baluster stems and bold spouts. Surviving objects and documents also indicate that he made an array of other, occasionally more mundane, forms as well, including plates, dishes, mugs, sugar bowls, cream jugs, salts, chamber pots, measures, bottles, inkstands, spoons, candlesticks, and "Ice Cream Moulds." About two hundred surviving objects by Will are known, marked with one or more of the extensive number of touchmarks that he employed. The Winterthur Museum near Wilmington, Delaware, has the most extensive collection of his work, but important examples are also in the collections of the Brooklyn Museum, Yale University Art Gallery, Metropolitan Museum of Art, and Philadelphia Museum of Art as well as the Presbyterian Historical Society and many other public and private collections.

Poulson's American Daily Advertiser (Philadelphia) for 14 February 1798 reported: "On Saturday morning departed this life after a lingering disposition which he bore with Christian fortitude, Col. William Will, in the 56th year of his age." His burial was "attended by the members of the German Incorporated Society and a very large number of respectable citizens." Ledlie Irwin Laughlin, the dean of American pewter scholars, observed, "William Will typifies all that is best in the history of American pewter. The surviving examples of his work are of a standard of quality as high as our pewterers ever attained, and he as a man exemplified . . . the spirit we admire, the spirit which carried an immigrant boy to the chief legislative council of his adopted state" (*Pewter in America*, vol. 2, p. 55).

• There is no known repository of Will's papers. Will's life is discussed most thoroughly in Ledlie Irwin Laughlin, *Pewter in America, Its Makers and Their Marks*, rev. ed. (3 vols., 1969). See also Suzanne Hamilton, "The Pewter of William Will: A Checklist," *Winterthur Portfolio 7*, ed. Ian M. G. Quimby (1972), pp. 129–60, which includes reference to 197 objects by Will along with illustrations of his marks and of selected examples of his work; and Hamilton, "William Will, Pewterer: His Life and His Work, 1742–1798" (M.A. thesis, Univ. of Delaware, 1967), which provides more biographical detail. For a summary of his career and illustrations of some of his finest work, see Charles F. Montgomery and Patricia E. Kane, eds., *American Art, 1750–1800: Towards Independence* (1976), pp. 221–25. The Decorative Arts Photographic Collection at the Winterthur Museum maintains a file on Will's work.

GERALD W. R. WARD

WILLARD, Daniel (28 Jan. 1861–6 July 1942), president of the Baltimore & Ohio Railroad, was born in North Hartland, Vermont, the son of Daniel Spaulding Willard and Mary Ann Daniels, farmers. His mother died when he was five; he then was reared by the extended Willard family, principally his father and grandparents. The Willards were devout Methodists, and religion was central to Daniel's early life; he was a teacher in the local Methodist Sunday school at the age of fifteen. An avid reader, he also taught in the local public school. In the fall of 1878 he enrolled at the Massachusetts State Agricultural College in Amherst, but eyesight problems forced him to withdraw during the spring of his freshman year.

Willard thereupon returned briefly to the family farm before taking a job with the railroad. He began his career as a track laborer on the Vermont Central in the summer of 1879. Over the next three decades he worked his way up through the ranks, serving in a variety of roles on six other railroads. Between 1879 and 1884 he worked as a locomotive fireman, engineer, and brakeman. During the next five years, while with the Minneapolis, St. Paul, & Sault Ste. Marie (Soo Line), he rose into management, eventually serving as superintendent.

In 1885 he married Bertha Leone Elkins; they had two children. Willard joined the Baltimore & Ohio (B&O) in 1899, serving for two years as assistant general manager of operations. From 1901 to 1904 he was vice president of operations for the Erie; he maintained that title when he moved to the Chicago, Burlington & Quincy. In this last job, Willard worked for the great railroad entrepreneur James J. Hill, expanding and substantially upgrading the Burlington route's property. His success in this endeavor established his reputation as an outstanding operations manager and led to the offer of the B&O presidency. Willard assumed that office in January 1910.

The B&O was burdened by obsolescent equipment and a generally inadequate physical plant; Willard was hired to bring the property up to modern standards. This he did over the next half-dozen years. New cars and locomotives were purchased, freight yards were expanded, tunnel restrictions were reduced, multiple tracking of lines was increased, and line straightening projects were completed. Just as important, though, were the steps that he was taking quietly in the realm of personnel relations. Willard had matured into a leader with genuine concern for his followers—an inclination made firm by his early career experiences (he had been a member of the engineers' union and had been unemployed for a time in 1884) and his religious convictions. (He was an active member of the theologically and socially liberal First Unitarian Church of Baltimore.) In the spring of 1916, capping a series of preliminary actions such as the organization of a network of employee safety committees, Willard established a company welfare bureau. A manifestation of "welfare capitalism," a movement of liberal Judeo-Christian roots intended to foster comprehensive employee well-being, the welfare bureau organized company sports teams, musical groups and activities, social events, and intellectual pursuits. It lasted in some form throughout Willard's tenure, and it probably was the most fully developed program of its kind in the railroad industry.

Willard was temporarily removed from direct management of the railroad when the federal government, acting through the wartime United States Railway Administration, assumed control of the rail industry in December 1917. While he retained the presidency of the B&O's corporate shell, his principal responsibility during World War I was the chairmanship of the industrial advisory commission of the Council of National Defense. When the war ended, and the company regained control of the railroad in March 1920, Willard faced the task of rebuilding a physical plant badly worn by heavy wartime use and insufficient maintenance. This was his paramount concern until the summer of 1922. In July of that year, the rail shopcrafts unions of the American Federation of Labor (AFL) went on nationwide strike, causing disruptions of varying degrees of severity throughout the industry. Willard led a conciliatory faction of his peers in settling the strike without breaking the AFL affiliates on their lines; in doing so he solidified his reputation among the unions, badly beaten by rail executives outside the Willard faction, as a decent and sympathetic manager.

The strike was disconcerting to Willard—so much so that it confirmed his initially tentative decision to implement the personnel program that became his greatest accomplishment: the B&O Cooperative Plan. Proposed to Willard by consultant Otto S. Beyer and William H. Johnston, president of the machinists' union, the Cooperative Plan set up a network of union-management cooperative committees within which union members might offer advice on lower-level management decisions. It promised benefits to the company in the form of improved efficiency and better services, and to the workers in the form of greater job security and improved working conditions (as well as greater respect). The program was highly successful, particularly in company shops, where it was first established in 1923–1924. A few other firms, both among the railroads and in other industries, adopted similar cooperative programs, but the B&O plan was the only one at a major American corporation to survive the depression. This presumably was because of Willard's dogged support of the program as a matter of principle.

The late 1920s and early 1930s were years of considerable public acclaim for Willard. His railroad's public image and the morale of its employees, enhanced by the company's centenary celebration (The Fair of the Iron Horse) in 1927, were at their highest levels ever. The esteem in which he was held by organized labor was probably unmatched by any other major corporate executive of the time; one of the many honors he received was a "Doctor of Humanity" award bestowed by union officials at a testimonial dinner in 1930. He was generally regarded as the senior statesman of the railroad industry; he personally negotiated the compromise wage settlement that averted a nationwide rail strike in 1932.

As the 1930s proceeded, the grim economic environment and health problems related to his advancing age constrained his effectiveness somewhat. But he still should be credited for two further achievements: the establishment of the B&O's Cooperative Traffic Program in 1933 and the passage of the Chandler Bill in 1938. The former, building upon the original Cooperative Plan, involved employees at all levels in soliciting new business for the company. The latter, the result of the high regard held for the steadfastly progressive Republican Willard by both parties in Congress, was an amendment to the Federal Bankruptcy Act, which allowed the B&O to restructure its debt and thus avoid receivership. In June 1941, with the company healthy again, B&O directors finally accepted Willard's long-offered resignation of the presidency. He remained board chairman a year longer, until his death in Baltimore. He was mourned on the B&O and in civic circles across the nation as a great and good business leader—a "Puritan liberal" of rigorous morality and uncommon empathy.

• Willard's correspondence is widely scattered; the largest known collections from his B&O years are in the Otto S. Beyer papers in the Library of Congress and the Harrington Emerson papers in the Pattee Library at Pennsylvania State University. His biography is Edward Hungerford, *Daniel Willard Rides the Line* (1938). An analysis of his management programs is David M. Vrooman, *Daniel Willard and Progressive Management on the Baltimore & Ohio Railroad* (1991). Discussions of Willard's presidency are contained in the principal B&O histories: John F. Stover, *History of the Baltimore & Ohio Railroad* (1987), and Edward Hungerford, *The Story of the Baltimore & Ohio Railroad* (1928). A collection of retrospective commentary on his life and career is the Willard memorial issue of *Baltimore & Ohio Magazine*, Aug. 1942.

DAVID M. VROOMAN

WILLARD, Emma Hart (23 Feb. 1787–15 Apr. 1870), educator and historian, was born in Berlin, Connecticut, the daughter of Samuel Hart and Lydia Hinsdale, farmers. She attended a district school and a new academy in Berlin, then two schools in Hartford to study art and fine needlework. Her father, a Jeffersonian and a Universalist, introduced her to dissent and began her education in philosophy. She also found mentors outside the family.

Willard began her rise as an educator before she finished her schooling. She taught the district school in Berlin in 1804, opened her own school for older children in 1805, and conducted the Berlin academy in 1806. With several invitations in hand, she served as female assistant in the academy in Westfield, Massachusetts, in the spring of 1807 before taking charge of the female academy in Middlebury, Vermont, that summer.

Founded seven years earlier, the Middlebury academy already had a regional following, and the move increased Emma's opportunities. She began experimenting with more stimulating methods of teaching than the rote memorization and recitation that were staples of the time. She also honed her political skills by guiding the school through denominational divisions in the town. In her free time she studied history and painting and mingled with the local elite. Friendship with John Willard, a physician turned Republican officeholder, led to their marriage in 1809. He was widowed with four children. They had a son, John Hart Willard, in 1810.

Willard set aside teaching after her marriage but continued her education. Through her husband's nephew, who lived with them while studying at Middlebury College, she developed an appreciation of collegiate studies and followed his work in geometry and philosophy. When the Vermont State Bank was robbed in 1812, her husband lost heavily due to his liability as a director. Two years later he accepted his wife's proposal for a girls' boarding school in their home. The immediate need was financial, but she also intended to offer a better education than was available elsewhere.

At first Willard offered only the customary curriculum of a female academy, but soon she advanced toward the collegiate level in mathematics, science, philosophy, history, and geography by developing lessons from her own studies. She did not, however, provide exactly what colleges offered to young men. She continued the art and music classes that were customary for girls but not boys and added exercise, rest, and recreation to preserve health and enthusiasm. On the other hand, she neither required nor offered classical languages, and there was no sequence of studies leading to a degree.

Willard cultivated a following by inviting prominent citizens to witness examinations, and boarding students carried her reputation across Vermont and the Hudson Valley. Once she had demonstrated her ability to offer advanced studies and her students' ability to learn them without becoming less suited for women's place in society, she was ready to expand. Her aim was the public funding accorded to many institutions for young men and boys. When plans fell through for a female seminary on the college grounds in Burlington, she sought patrons in New York.

Willard began lobbying in Albany by asking Governor DeWitt Clinton to support her ideas. With his endorsement, she published *An Address to the Public: Particularly to the Members of the Legislature of New-York, Proposing a Plan for Improving Female Education* (1819), a strongly argued discourse that she had been developing for several years. First she described the current weakness of female education and the triviality it fostered. Then she offered an alternative, adding scientific housekeeping to the Middlebury academy curriculum. Her final argument was that such a school was necessary to the well-being of the republic because it would prepare women to be better wives and mothers and also provide capable teachers who could be paid less than men.

The New York legislature responded by chartering the Academy for Young Ladies that Willard had already been invited to establish in Waterford and by making it the first female institution to share in the state lottery fund. This enabled her to expand enrollment and curriculum beyond what she had achieved in Middlebury, but the legislature twice failed to agree on a regular appropriation, and her supporters in Waterford would not continue paying her lease. The

Common Council of nearby Troy saw her frustration as their opportunity. They resolved in 1821 to raise $4,000 for a building, and she immediately established herself there. Dr. Willard was necessarily the proprietor because a married woman's business could only be conducted in her husband's name. He was also an active manager until his death in 1825.

The Troy Female Seminary prospered despite continuing rejection of Willard's petitions for legislative support. Enrollment increased from 90 in the first class to 340 in 1837, a third of whom were from other cities or states. Willard used her growing prosperity to admit some students whose families were unable to pay, on the understanding that they would reimburse her from their earnings as teachers. In 1837 she founded the Willard Association for the Mutual Improvement of Female Teachers to guide their development and broaden her influence. Many of the seminary's teachers were former students, although it was necessary to look further and pay more for experts in performance fields such as music and French. When Willard visited Europe in 1830, her reputation as an educator and her acquaintance with the marquis de Lafayette from his 1824 visit to Troy enabled her to mingle with leading educational reformers in France and England.

The course of study continued to expand. Willard herself enhanced the offerings in history and geography. Amos Eaton, senior professor at Troy's Rensselaer Polytechnic Institute, taught science from experiments and tutored Willard's sister, Almira Lincoln Phelps, until she and other female teachers were able to take over. Language electives were Spanish, French, and Latin. Mathematics, philosophy, and theology remained staples for advanced students.

The success of Willard's schools owed to her ability to help children understand what they were learning as well as to her special offerings for advanced students. She began reaching for a broader audience even while she was implementing her plan at Waterford and Troy. First she collaborated with William C. Woodbridge on *A System of Universal Geography on the Principles of Comparison and Classification* (1822), contributing the section on the ancient world, then produced *Geography for Beginners* (1826) on her own. Next she wrote *A History of the United States, or Republic of America* (1828) and *A System of Universal History in Perspective* (1835). All these books were distinctive for their use of maps, charts, and concepts in contrast to the emphasis on memorizing names, dates, and places in widely used texts of the day. They also encouraged readers to see the United States in the context of its historical development and in comparison with other nations.

By the mid-1830s Willard had fulfilled her original plan for the seminary and provided a model for other female institutions. If she had been able to garner adequate state support or endowment, she might have expanded it into a women's college. Instead, she gave herself more time to write books and train teachers by making her son the business manager and appointing his wife, Sarah Lucretia Hudson, vice principal.

In 1838 Willard stepped down as principal to marry Christopher C. Yates, a New York physician. She was hoping to reproduce the nurturing companionship of her first marriage, but his main interest was the fortune she had earned through her school and her books. They set up housekeeping in Boston, Massachusetts, with the idea that he would practice and she would write, but his financial demands were unceasing despite a prenuptial agreement placing her property in her son's hands. By the time Willard left him the following summer, Yates had received more than $5,000. He responded by denouncing her in the press.

Willard went home to Berlin, Connecticut, to restore her spirit and reestablish her respectability. Henry Barnard, recently appointed secretary of the Connecticut Board of Commissioners for the Common Schools, welcomed her help with his reforms. Elected superintendent of common schools in the Kensington section of Berlin, she quickly reshaped the curriculum, staff, and facilities. Plans for a state normal school under her direction came to nothing when Barnard's position was abolished after the 1842 election. In 1843 she successfully petitioned the Connecticut legislature for divorce from Yates.

Returning to Troy in 1844, Willard remained important to the seminary as inspiration and adviser, but her main interest was writing books. She revised her *History of the United States*, recast her world history as *Willard's Historic Guide to the Temple of Time* (1849) and *Universal History in Perspective* (1859), and wrote *Last Leaves of American History, Comprising Histories of the Mexican War and California* (1849). She lived for months in New York and Philadelphia to work closely with her publishers, engaged in pamphlet warfare with the author of a competing U.S. history, and defended her geography copyrights against the Woodbridge estate.

Willard wrote on other subjects from time to time. In the midst of putting her school on a better footing in 1820, she found time to contribute *Universal Peace to Be Introduced by a Confederacy of Nations* to the nascent peace movement, and she offered a similar plan in 1864. Her poems were printed in 1831 at the request of former students. In 1833 she published an essay on the philosophical concept of universal terms. Her theory that the lungs circulate the blood, published in 1846, received some respectful attention. She responded to the threat of secession in 1861 by pleading for compromise, and the following year she proposed in *Via Media* to regulate slavery as an alternative to abolition. Families would be kept intact, the slave market would be abolished, and slaves who were already behind Union lines could earn their passage to Liberia by serving in northern households for ten or fifteen years.

Willard's principal associations were with her family and former students. Her main organizing activity beyond her school was to encourage women to play a leading role in local school reform. Twice she made broad appeals for women's support: to raise money for a normal school in newly independent Greece in 1833 and to petition for compromise between North and South in 1861. Locally, she empaneled women as overseers in her schools but did not give them control, and she led occasional civic betterment efforts in Troy. Her principal friendships among prominent women of her time were with the writer Lydia H. Sigourney and the editor Sarah Josepha Hale. She was not intimate with other pioneers in female education, and she did not support the women's rights movement, although many of its leaders were educated on her model, and Elizabeth Cady Stanton studied at Troy. Willard was an active Episcopalian.

Willard is most remembered for launching the advanced studies for girls that equipped growing numbers of women for a larger role in society and laid the groundwork for full-blown women's colleges. This achievement owed not only to her formidable intellect and energy but also to her business acumen, political skill, and imposing personality and appearance. She was almost as important in her own time for her lively, expansive, and patriotic histories and geographies, which sold more than a million copies.

Crucial to Willard's legacy is the tension between the boldness of her pursuits and the conventionality of her arguments. It is tempting to suppose that she deployed conservative rationalizations to mask revolutionary purpose, but her patterns of thought and action are consistent in her private writings and her public ones. When she used conventional ideas about women in her bold *Plan for Improving Female Education*, she was satisfied that teaching girls geometry would more readily enlarge their capacities as wives and mothers than pave their way to trigonometry. When she worked through male politicians and eschewed any involvement in women's rights, she was content to exert her influence through persuasion. Her passion for the republic undergirded her regressive scheme to perpetuate slavery as well as her progressive proposal to educate girls. Willard died in Troy nine days after her last journal entry.

• The most important repository of primary sources is the Emma Willard School, Troy, N.Y. Its Emma (Hart) Willard Collection contains a wide range of manuscript and printed materials as well as photocopies of letters in other repositories. Its own archives include catalogs and memoirs by former students. The other major repository is the Amherst College Library, which holds the Emma Willard Family Papers, featuring her diaries, her letters to her son after 1838, and documents about her second marriage. John Lord, *The Life of Emma Willard* (1873), includes letters and other primary sources. Many printed sources are available in the *History of Women* (1975) and other microform series.

Alma Lutz, *Emma Willard, Daughter of Democracy* (1929), remains the principal biography; her *Emma Willard, Pioneer Educator of American Women* (1964), is an adaptation. See also Anne Firor Scott, "What, Then, Is the American: This New Woman?" *Journal of American History* 65 (1978): 679–703; Nina Baym, "Women and the Republic: Emma Willard's Rhetoric of History," *American Quarterly* 42 (1991): 1–23; and Daniel H. Calhoun, "Eyes for the Jacksonian World: William C. Woodbridge and Emma Willard," *Journal of the Early Republic* 4 (1984): 1–26.

SUSAN GRIGG

WILLARD, Frances Elizabeth Caroline (28 Sept. 1839–17 Feb. 1898), educator and international temperance leader, was born in Churchville near Rochester, New York, the daughter of Josiah Willard, a businessman and farmer, and Mary Hill, a schoolteacher. When she was two her father sold his substantial farm and business interests and moved his family to Ohio, where both parents studied at Oberlin College. In 1846 the family moved to Wisconsin, where Frances spent the rest of her childhood on their large frontier farm near Janesville. Except for brief stints in rural schools, Willard was tutored by her mother until 1857, when she studied for a year at Milwaukee Female College (later Milwaukee-Downer College) and then at North Western Female College (later part of Northwestern University), receiving a "Laureatte of Science" in 1859. In 1861 she was engaged to Charles Fowler, who became a prominent Methodist clergyman and educator, but they never married. Willard had several serious romantic relationships with men, but her primary emotional ties, although they seem not to have been explicitly homosexual, were to women: her mother and several colleagues and friends, especially Anna Gordon, her secretary and lifelong companion, and Lady Henry Somerset, a British temperance leader.

Willard's first career was in education. In spite of her father's disapproval, she taught in a rural school and an Illinois academy as a very young woman. She continued to teach in the 1860s at several academies and also wrote her first book, a eulogy of a sister who had died of tuberculosis in 1862. A two-year hegira to the British Isles, western Europe, Russia, and the Near East from 1868 to 1870, including some formal study at universities in Paris and Berlin, completed her education and prepared her for larger educational responsibilities. Upon her return, she became president of Evanston College for Ladies, the women's department of Northwestern. She might have continued to pursue an academic career had not Charles Fowler, her former fiancé, become Northwestern's president in 1871. Unable to share authority with Fowler, she resigned in 1873.

The temperance movement provided Willard with a new career. She astutely saw that the women's movement and women's concerns found real focus in the temperance crusade of 1873 and the organization of the Woman's Christian Temperance Union (WCTU) the next year. A moderate temperance adherent like most middle-class women of her time, Willard recognized that temperance was about to become the reform cause most attractive to women moving into public life and that there was room in the movement for creative leadership. Elected secetary of the national WCTU at its organizing meeting in 1874, she transformed that position into the life-force of the organization. A talented speaker and writer, she took to the hustings, wrote the letters and pamphlets, organized the locals, knew more women in the organization than anyone else, and in 1879 was elected president of what was already the largest women's organization in the country, with 27,000 regular members and another 25,000 in junior auxiliaries. For the next twenty years the WCTU grew in both numbers and breadth of concerns. Under Willard's leadership the union endorsed and actively promoted woman suffrage, the kindergarten movement, prison reform, the eight-hour day, model facilities for dependent and handicapped children, federal aid to education, and vocational training. On the state and local level its legislative accomplishments were considerable. Even before women received the vote the WCTU had successfully lobbied for an impressive body of legislation ranging from compulsory scientific temperance education to the raising of the age of consent.

Willard became a highly visible, much respected national leader. By 1890 she was as well known nationally as Eleanor Roosevelt was to be in the 1930s and 1940s. She used her fame not only to promote the temperance cause, but to further her increasingly sweeping ideas on social reform. For example, she allied herself with the Knights of Labor and advocated Christian socialism. She joined the Knights of Labor and supported labor's struggles for the eight-hour day. She played an important role in the Prohibition party in the 1880s, and, although unsuccessful, her attempt to merge the Prohibition party, the new People's party, and Edward Bellamy's Nationalists into a new third party in 1892 remained a goal she never relinquished. Willard devoted much of her time in her last years to the international scene. She organized and served as first president of the World WCTU. These broader duties and her friendship with Lady Henry Somerset kept her in England much of the time after 1892. Ill health plagued Willard in the 1890s, sapping her energies and limiting her activity. Consequently, strong challenges to her leadership developed in the American WCTU, but she was able to maintain control of the women's temperance movement until her death in New York City from pernicious anemia.

As leader of the first mass organization of American women, Frances Willard made an unrivaled contribution toward the movement of women into public life. She combined skillful leadership, broad social vision, and keen intelligence with those virtues so dear to the nineteenth-century middle class, devotion to home and family. She made much of womanliness, justifying attention to reform under the slogan "Home Protection" while simultaneously encouraging women to espouse a set of goals and activities that led them into legislative chambers, union halls, and a host of professions. She raised temperance advocates' awareness of larger issues and the possible political clout of women in a modernizing society. She was able to exploit the nineteenth century's devotion to woman's sphere to secure for women an increasingly powerful public role.

• Willard's papers are in the Willard Memorial Library, WCTU Headquarters, Evanston, Ill., and are available on microfilm as part of the *Temperance and Prohibition Papers* (1977), which also includes WCTU publications, scrapbooks, minutes, and other organizational records. Willard's autobiography is *Glimpses of Fifty Years* (1889). Also by Willard is *Woman and Temperance* (1883). A recent biography is Ruth Bordin, *Frances Willard: A Biography* (1986). See also Bordin, *Woman and Temperance: The Quest For Power and Liberty, 1873–1900* (1981; repr. 1990); and Mary Earhart Dillon, *Frances Willard: From Prayers to Politics* (1944). The most complete obituary is in the *Union Signal*, 24 Feb. 1898. See also the *New York Times*, 18 Feb. 1898.

RUTH BORDIN

WILLARD, Frank (21 Sept. 1893–12 Jan. 1958), cartoonist, was born in Anna, Illinois, the son of Francis William Willard, a dentist, and Laura Kirkham. Although his father wanted him to follow in his footsteps, Willard never finished high school. He left home at about the age of seventeen to join another youth in running a concession with a traveling carnival throughout southern Illinois. While his partner ran the hamburger stand, Willard played the horses, and they split the profits on both enterprises. The business collapsed one day when his partner "became interested in trains" (as Willard put it in *Comics and Their Creators* [p. 72]) and took all the receipts to California. Willard next took a position as a claim tracer with a Chicago department store and conned a friend into doing all the work by supplying him with lunch (sandwiches that Willard obtained free at a nearby saloon). At night, Willard attended classes at the Chicago Academy of Fine Arts.

In 1914 Willard decided to become a newspaper cartoonist after having sold an editorial cartoon on the outbreak of World War I to the *Chicago Tribune*. When the *Tribune* would not put him on full-time staff, he applied at the *Chicago Herald*, but since the paper already had an editorial cartoonist, Willard drew a comic strip, *Tom, Dick and Harry*. He was drafted into the American Expeditionary Force shortly thereafter. When the war ended, he became a staff artist for King Features Syndicate in New York, for which he eventually produced an undistinguished strip called the *Outta-Luck Club*.

One day in the spring of 1923 Willard settled an editorial dispute with his fists and was fired. When Joseph Medill Patterson, publisher of the *New York Daily News*, heard of the incident, he sent for Willard and offered him a job doing a new strip. The *Daily News* was the nation's first successful tabloid, and Patterson wanted a comic strip tailored expressly for his sensation-hungry readers. He wanted a strip about the low life of the city, about roughnecks and confidence men who made their way with their wits and pure gall in total disregard of the Puritan work ethic, books of etiquette, and every other refinement. Judging from what he had heard of Willard's character, Patterson thought the cartoonist would be able to produce just what he wanted. And that's what Willard did. The result was a classic comedy of conniving, brawling, uncouth social pretension: *Moon Mullins*.

Beginning 19 June 1923 the strip at first concentrated on the title character (named by Patterson, who seized on a nomenclature just then emerging on the social horizon in those early years of Prohibition: moonshine). A denizen of poolrooms and locker rooms and training camps, Moon was an unabashed freeloader, a con man, always on the lookout for a free lunch and a quick buck, and willing to let anyone take the risks but himself. He failed more often than he succeeded. His only redeeming quality was his endurance; he kept at it. Disappointed at the outcome of one con, he immediately went on to the next, not bothered one whit by failure. Moon's motives were undisguised by the usual veneers of civilization's respectable society. And he was entirely forthright. His honest embracing of his own self-interest was refreshing, and that was his charm.

Willard surrounded Moon with kindred souls: Lord and Lady Plushbottom (the former, a harmless, pompous sort; the latter, the erstwhile spinster Emmy Schmaltz, angular and vinegary owner of the boardinghouse where they all live) and rotund ne'er-do-well Uncle Willie McAshcan (always in need of a shave) and his slovenly wife Mamie, the cook. Moon's diminutive kid brother Kayo (who slept in Moon's bureau drawer) was the only realist (and he was a full-blown cynic).

As Stephen Becker says in *Comic Art in America*, the strip was "the greatest collection of social pretenders ever assembled. . . . The impulse is always upward—to fame, riches, dazzling lights. But the culmination is always a descent to reality, via the nightstick, the pratfall, or the custard pie. Always, earthly reality wins out over the ideal, the pretension; beef stew defeats poetry." John Lardner called the strip a "permanent monument" to an easier time when lower and middle classes overlapped. But it was also definitely lowbrow: "[In] their way of life, which was the natural way, for them, of attrition . . . if they had to choose between a necessity and a pleasure to spend a couple of bucks on, they invariably went for the pleasure. But the primary rule of their existence, and Willard never let them forget it, was that they did not have the couple of bucks."

Assisted almost from the beginning by Ferd Johnson, Willard drew in a gritty, crosshatched style that was perfectly in tune with the threadbare vulgarity of the strip's lower-class setting. A procrastinator of epic dimension, Willard postponed work on each week's batch of strips (six dailies and a Sunday page) until the last possible moment. Then he summoned Johnson, and the two would work straight through without break for the next thirty-six to forty-eight hours, then collapse for the next twenty-four.

Willard was married three times, but information on his first two wives and the number of his children, if any, is unavailable. Willard traveled around the country with the seasons to a succession of residences—Poland Springs, Maine; Los Angeles, California; Tampa, Florida; Greenwich, Connecticut—where he pursued his passion, golf, on every day of the week that he wasn't bent over his drawing board. Johnson and his wife faithfully followed Willard and his third wife, Marie O'Connell, to every new locale. When Willard died in Los Angeles, Johnson inherited the strip, which he continued for another thirty years.

• Biographical information on Frank Willard can be found in Martin Sheridan, *Comics and Their Creators: Life Stories of American Cartoonists* (1944), and in more extensive form in Clive Howard, "The Magnificent Roughneck," *Saturday Evening Post*, 9 Aug. 1947, pp. 20–21, 58–61. Stephen Becker provides the best appreciation of the strip in his *Comic Art in America* (1959). Several collections of *Moon Mullins* strips were published by Cupples and Leon (1923–1931), two of which have been reprinted in *Moon Mullins: Two Adventures* (1976). An obituary is in the *New York Times*, 13 Jan. 1958, and in *Newsweek*, 27 Jan. 1958, John Lardner pays tribute to Willard.

ROBERT C. HARVEY

WILLARD, James Field (30 Dec. 1876–21 Nov. 1935), educator and historian, was born in Philadelphia, Pennsylvania, the son of Edward Malon Willard and Elizabeth Prudence Field. After attending public schools in Philadelphia, he enrolled in 1895 at the University of Pennsylvania, from which he earned a B.S. in 1898. On a scholarship and then a fellowship, he did graduate work in history at the University of Wisconsin from 1899 to 1901, partly under the distinguished historian of the American West, Frederick Jackson Turner. Willard returned to the University of Pennsylvania as a doctoral fellow and received his Ph.D. in 1902, with the dissertation "The Royal Authority and the Early English Universities." He taught history with the rank of instructor at Northwestern University (1902–1904) and was a research fellow at the University of Pennsylvania (1904–1906). In 1906 he joined the history department of the University of Colorado, at Boulder, as an assistant professor. His paper "The English Church and the Lay Taxes of the Fourteenth Century" (*University of Colorado Studies* 4, no. 4 [1907]: 217–25) was his first published work in the field of his most consuming research interest. He was promoted to full professor and became department chairman in 1907. The following year he published "The Scotch Raids and the Fourteenth Century Taxation of Northern England" (*University of Colorado Studies* 5, no. 4 [1908]: 237–42). In 1912 Willard married Margaret Love Wheeler, with whom he had one child.

A dedicated and tireless teacher, author, and editor, Willard concentrated his research on English institutions, mainly those of the fourteenth century, and on the history of Colorado. Because of his location, Willard found it relatively easy to pursue research into local western history, a field in which he was a pioneer. Gathering source materials, he initiated the University of Colorado Historical Collections and edited several of its numerous volumes. For the American Historical Association, he compiled *Report on the Public Archives of Colorado* (1911) and *Report on the Archives of Wyo-*

ming (1915). He also edited *The Union Colony at Greeley, Colorado, 1869–1871* (1918) and coedited *Experiments in Colorado Colonization, 1869–1872; Selected Contemporary Records Relating to the German Colonization Company and the Chicago-Colorado, St. Louis-Western and Southwestern Colonies* (1926). In addition to articles for learned journals, he published *Colorado: Short Studies of Its Past and Present: The Gold Rush and After* (1927). He was the principal organizer of a symposium held in June 1929 at the University of Colorado, during which historians presented several papers that he coedited as the *Conference on the History of the Trans-Mississippi West* (1930).

In 1913 Willard gained international recognition when he published "Side-lights upon the Assessment and Collection of the Mediaeval Subsidies" (*Transactions of the Royal Society*, 3d ser., 7 [1913]: 167–89). It represented unusually painstaking work by an American in the difficult field of taxation in the Middle Ages. Beginning in 1923, he made himself responsible for reporting research work in annual bulletins he titled *The Progress of Medieval Studies in the United States and Canada*. Awarded a grant from the American Council of Learned Societies, Willard spent the years from 1931 to 1933 in England pursuing, among other topics, British governmental functions during the late thirteenth century and the early fourteenth century. He helped the Surrey Record Society in England with its *Surrey Taxation Returns* (1932) and coedited *An Index of British and Irish Latin Writers, A.D. 400–1520* (1932). In 1934 he published *Parliamentary Taxes on Personal Property, 1290–1334: A Study in Mediaeval English Financial Administration* (1934). His most substantial work, in 357 thoroughly documented pages, it was the result of research over a period of two decades, with his most concentrated labor being accomplished during three sabbaticals spent in England, often at various libraries and in public record offices. It caused his being elected honorary vice president of England's Royal Historical Society—a signal honor for any American scholar.

Willard persuaded more than twenty fellow medievalists, most of whom were his personal friends, to prepare a three-volume study of government during the first decade of the reign of King Edward III, which he considered such a "normal," strife-free period that the king's servants could govern without undue strains. At the time of his death Willard had edited the first volume of this proposed study. Titled *The English Government at Work, 1327–1336: Central and Prerogative Administration*, it appeared in 1940. He had also done editorial work on some of the later essays. Two of his colleagues, William A. Morris and William H. Dunham, Jr., saw the second and third volumes to completion by 1950. In his introduction to the third volume, Dunham praised Willard's generosity and cordiality and his lawyer-like determination to weigh evidence so as to produce veracious history rather than giving in to any inclination, continuing among some historians, toward romantic narrative.

Willard was regarded as both an inspiring and a demanding teacher and was especially successful with small, advanced classes. He was also a community leader. He enjoyed participating in sports until late in life he suffered the amputation of one leg. He and his wife were saddened by the early death of their daughter. He spent the summer of 1935 at the Henry E. Huntington Library, San Marino, California, studying manuscripts of the Battle Abbey Rolls for a listing of William the Conqueror's companions. That fall Willard died suddenly at his home in Boulder, Colorado. His *Colorado Gold Rush; Contemporary Letters and Reports, 1858–1859*, edited by Le Roy R. Hafen, appeared posthumously in 1941.

• Some of Willard's papers are in the University of Colorado library. A short biographical essay on Willard appears under "Personal," *American Historical Review* 41 (Jan. 1936): 401. Obituaries are in the *Boulder (Colo.) Daily Camera*, 21 Nov. 1935, and the *New York Times*, 22 Nov. 1935.

ROBERT L. GALE

WILLARD, Joseph (29 Dec. 1738–25 Sept. 1804), clergyman and college president, was born in Biddeford, Maine, the son of the Reverend Samuel Willard and Abigail Wright. During Joseph's infancy his father died, causing the family financial hardship. Before the age of twenty-one Joseph was thus obliged to make several coasting voyages as a seaman and to teach school. Samuel Moody, a schoolmaster in nearby York, noted his academic talents as well as his interest in medicine. Moody helped prepare Willard for college and arranged a scholarship for him at Harvard College, which Joseph entered in 1761. During his undergraduate career he served as a waiter, taught school in Lancaster, Massachusetts, and was "Scholar of the House," a student position responsible for determining the cause, and handling the repair of, any physical damage to students' rooms. He took his bachelor's degree in 1765, at which time he was also named college butler, a position that entailed managing the storeroom that held beer and other beverages and taking inventories of the college's utensils.

The year after his graduation Willard was appointed a tutor in Greek at Harvard. He also received his master's degree there and as a senior tutor became a member of the Harvard Corporation. His academic career was interrupted in 1772 when he was appointed associate minister of the First Church of Beverly, Massachusetts. He was ordained there the following November. On 7 March 1774 he married Mary Sheafe of Portsmouth, New Hampshire. They had thirteen children. During the American Revolution his support of the patriot cause was evident in his published pronouncements such as *The Duty of the Good and Faithful Soldier* . . . (1781), and *A Thanksgiving Sermon* . . . (1784) delivered in Boston the previous year following word of the Peace of Paris.

Willard's distinction increased when he became an incorporating member, corresponding secretary, and, afterward, vice president of the American Academy of

Arts and Sciences. His many erudite writings for the academy, particularly in astronomy and mathematics, added to his prominence, as did his correspondence with eminent scholars from as far away as St. Petersburg who were eager to learn of American writings in these fields. Willard's work for the academy also earned him membership in the Royal Society of England, the Medical Society of London, the Royal Society of Göttingen, the American Philosophical Society, and other scientific and philosophical organizations. Such growing distinction no doubt played a role in his return to academia. In December 1781, over a year after the resignation of President Samuel Langdon, Willard was officially inaugurated as president of Harvard College.

Willard's tenure at Harvard was marked by several significant achievements. The entrance requirements were raised; financial stability improved when the funding of the national debt (some of which debt securities the college owned) made up for those monies lost from diminished state support; substantial gifts were obtained for the college; a new, larger library was built; daily sermons were discontinued; the level of instruction was updated and broadened by introducing new studies and textbooks; and the Harvard Medical School was officially opened.

President Willard himself earned the respect, if not the affection, of both faculty and students as a result of his fastidious, even-handed, though often blunt, management of college activities. One Harvard man described him as "stiff and unbending, but conscientious and honest." His scrupulous attention to order and precedence may have helped reduce undergraduate disorder during his governance, but it also led many of the students to regard him as an austere, uncaring disciplinarian. John Kirkland, later Harvard president, declared that Willard was "reluctant to be too familiar with his best students for fear it could breed contempt." In fact, Willard was a concerned humanitarian who participated in benevolent religious organizations such as the Massachusetts Congregational Charitable Society and the Society for Propagating the Gospel among the Indians and Others in North America. He was moderately liberal in his personal theological beliefs, though in politics he supported the more conservative Federalist party tenets as did most wealthy and prominent people in eastern Massachusetts. Although Willard tried to avoid partisanship on political or religious issues, he showed his intense patriotic zeal during his involvement in several national observances; he wrote, for example, an "Ode for Independence" in 1793 to commemorate a Fourth of July ceremony and supervised the university's annual Washington's birthday celebrations.

Harvard's reputation grew considerably during Willard's presidency, and he received an honorary doctorate from his alma mater and Yale College. However, the sudden onset of a serious bladder disorder in the spring of 1798 brought an end to his administration the following year. Even though Willard's ailment grew worse, during his retirement he was still able to travel around the United States. Back in Cambridge he delivered a memorial eulogy in Latin for George Washington in February 1800. Willard died in New Bedford while on a journey to Provincetown, Massachusetts.

• The most useful manuscript collections relating to Joseph Willard may be found in the Harvard University Archives, the Massachusetts Historical Society, and the American Academy of Arts and Sciences. The best published biography to date of Joseph Willard is a thirteen-page essay by Clifford K. Shipton in *Biographical Sketches of Those Who Attended Harvard College in the Classes 1764–1767*, vol. 16 (1972). It is a charming, insightful, albeit limited, examination of Willard's career. Samuel Eliot Morison focuses on Willard's college presidency in *Three Centuries of Harvard* (1936). Other relevant published works dealing with Joseph Willard and his life and family include William Bentley, *The Diary of William Bentley, D.D. Pastor of the East Church in Salem Massachusetts* (1905–1914), *Massachusetts Historical Society Proceedings*, vols. 9 and 17, 2d ser. (1895, 1903); Charles H. Pope, ed., *Willard Genealogy* (1915); Edwin M. Stone, *History of Beverly Civil and Ecclesiastical from Its Settlement in 1630 to 1842* (1843); and Sidney Willard, *Memories of Youth and Manhood*, vol. 1 (1855).

SHELDON S. COHEN

WILLARD, Josiah Flint (23 Jan. 1869–20 Jan. 1907), author and journalist, was born Josiah Flynt Willard in Appleton, Wisconsin, the son of Oliver Atherton Willard, a Methodist minister and newspaper editor, and Mary Bannister. Willard spent his childhood in Evanston, Illinois, surrounded by a pious family increasingly dominated by female figures after his father's death in 1877. While he rejected their confining religious sentiments, Willard recalled lovingly the warm attentions of his family, including his paternal aunt Frances Willard, the temperance activist.

A lifelong bachelor, Willard never attained a permanent home. From an early age, he was by his own account obsessed with traveling and ran away often to the "disappearing and fading Beyond." He undertook his first such adventure at the age of four. As a teenager he spent one month in a reformatory for stealing a horse and buggy in Pennsylvania. This early habit foreshadowed his later wanderlust, which in turn provided the subject matter for much of his writing.

In 1884 Willard's mother departed for Germany to run a girl's school, and Willard was sent to a small college in Illinois. He spent two years there and never graduated. After some months of tramping about, taking odd jobs, committing petty crimes, and serving some time in jail for them, he departed for Germany as a ship hand. Willard arrived in Berlin in 1890 and, living with his mother, attended the University of Berlin until 1895. At Berlin he majored in political economy but tried to take advantage of his frequent travels around the continent by minoring in geography. While in Germany, he studied under some well-known academic figures, among them the cell pathologist Rudolph Virchow, from whom Willard gained a lifelong skepticism for the criminological theories of the day, especially those of the biologically determinist Italian school.

Willard began his publishing career in 1891 with an article titled "The American Tramp" in *Contemporary Review*, a participant-observer account of an eight-month-long trek with tramps. Like many critics of social unrest and indigence in late nineteenth-century America, Willard was fascinated with this group of outcasts, bereft of homes, employment, and community. Personally he was drawn to their lifestyle and clearly reveled in his time on the road. In his published work, however, he proved unsympathetic to his subjects, calling them "riff raff" and "parasites" and explaining their predicament in moral, individualistic terms. A critic in the *Nation* would later remark that "whatever his practices may have been, his ideas of morality were absolutely conventional" (*Nation*, 25 Feb. 1909, p. 190).

Encouraged by what he considered easy money for recounting his experiences, Willard published in quick succession a number of articles on tramps. While still a student in Berlin, he used the earnings from these early publications to tramp through southern Germany, Switzerland, and Italy. After completing his studies in 1895, he departed for Russia. Willard worked as a field hand on Leo Tolstoy's estate for some weeks and, to his delight, became acquainted with the writer and his family.

Willard returned to the United States to take up the writing profession seriously. Upon his arrival in New York in 1898, Willard was offered a job with the Pennsylvania Railroad police by officials familiar with his writing on tramps. Willard saw the position as an opportunity to interview tramps and gather material for his books. Based on these experiences, he published *Tramping with Tramps* in 1899 and *Notes of an Itinerant Policeman* in 1900. His final book on tramps was the novel *The Little Brother: A Story of Tramp Life* (1902).

Willard also wrote on other classic Progressive Era topics and anticipated many of the methods and themes of early twentieth-century "muck-raking" journalism. These works included *The Powers That Prey* (1900) and *The World of Graft* (1901), dealing with the criminal underworld and police corruption, respectively. Willard is generally credited with bringing the word "graft" into popular usage. As a chronicler of tramp life Willard was noteworthy for his direct experience, which gave his tales immediacy and color. Claiming the superiority of personal knowledge and direct experience, Willard distanced himself from sociologists and other academic commentators. His friend Alfred Hodder recounted Willard's "profound contempt for the books written by frock-coated gentlemen who have academic positions, and say 'sociology,' and measure the skulls and take the confessions of the vagrant in captivity."

Willard died in a Chicago hotel of pneumonia complicated by alcoholism. His brief life was peripatetic but produced a number of widely read studies of tramps in particular and the underside of late nineteenth-century America in general. He was noted as an ephemeral member of turn-of-the-century literary circles in New York City and London (for example, his name is mentioned as a London acquaintance of Gertrude Stein's in *The Autobiography of Alice B. Toklas*). His work on tramps, however, proved too impressionistic and judgmental to be of enduring value to social scientists of "underworld" communities.

• Willard left no papers. His unfinished autobiography, titled *My Life*, was published by his friends one year after his death and includes commentary by some of his contemporaries. In addition to the books mentioned above, Willard published a novel titled *The Rise of Ruderick Clowd* (1903). A comment on Willard's work on graft can be found in the *Bookman*, May 1903, pp. 219–23. A critical review of Willard's *My Life* by Stuart P. Sherman appears in the *Nation* 88, no. 2278 (25 Feb. 1909): 188–90. Obituaries are in the *New York Tribune*, 22 Jan. 1907, and the *Bookman*, Mar. 1907, pp. 9–11.

JULIA E. RODRIGUEZ

WILLARD, Samuel (31 Jan. 1640–12 Sept. 1707), Puritan clergyman and theologian, was born in Concord, Massachusetts, the son of Simon Willard and Mary Sharpe. Simon Willard was one of the town's founders and its first deputy to the Massachusetts General Court. From 1654 to 1676 he sat on the colony's Court of Assistants. Samuel Willard graduated from Harvard in 1659, and in the early 1660s he was granted an M.A.

In June 1663 Willard became pastor at the frontier community of Groton, Massachusetts, and was ordained on 13 July 1664 at the formal gathering of its church. The town itself was incorporated in 1665. Several weeks after his ordination he married Abigail Sherman, the daughter of Watertown's minister, John Sherman. In 1671 he became involved in a case of demonic possession. His careful record of observations and treatment of the victim, Elizabeth Knapp, although not published until 1868, is now a classic of New England witchlore. By the early 1670s some of his sermons were being published, a sign of prestige unusual for a young, frontier cleric.

In March 1675, early in King Philip's War, Groton was twice attacked and virtually destroyed. As refugees, the Willard family lived with relatives in Charlestown while Willard himself preached in various Bay-area churches. Late in 1676 Abigail died, leaving four children. On 31 March 1678 Willard was ordained as colleague to Thomas Thacher at Boston's Old South Church. At Thacher's death in October 1678 Willard became sole pastor of the church, one of Boston's most important congregations. On 29 July 1679 he married Eunice Tyng; the couple had fourteen children. His new father-in-law, Edward Tyng, was a prominent merchant and political figure.

A subtle but steady defender of orthodox Puritan theology, Willard nonetheless favored pastoral reforms such as easing church membership requirements, including the Half-Way Covenant proposals. He played an active role in the Massachusetts Reforming Synod of 1679, attempting to forge a moral and social reform program to perpetuate the colony's identity as a model Puritan community. During the 1680s he was among those clergy who advocated submission to English efforts to incorporate the colony more closely into the developing empire without compromising orthodoxy though adopting formal religious toleration. However, after the loss in 1684 of the Massachusetts Charter of 1629 and the establishment of the Dominion of New England in 1686 under Sir Edmund Andros, Willard found himself increasingly in opposition to what he and most New England leaders regarded as an authoritarian, even papist, state. Indeed, it was Old South Church that Andros appropriated for Anglican services, leaving Willard and his congregation to wait outside until worship according to the Book of Common Prayer was completed each Sunday. Andros's pressing of other royalist and Anglican ceremonial usages on the Puritans, together with arbitrary fiscal and judicial devices, alienated virtually the entire colony. Inspired by word of the Glorious Revolution in England, the Boston townsfolk initiated the overthrow of the Dominion in April 1689. Willard's role in the revolt, if any, is unknown.

Willard's most significant reaction to the crisis of the Dominion Era was to begin, in 1688, a cycle of Tuesday lectures on the Westminster Shorter Catechism, thus making him the first "catechism preacher" in New England on the pattern recently established among Calvinists in Scotland, Germany, England, and the Netherlands. His goal was to clarify and explicate the whole of Puritan theology more fully in the face of resurgent Anglicanism. The lectures continued almost until his death and were immensely popular with both laity and clergy. They were published posthumously in 1726 during another period of renewed Anglican competition as *A Compleat Body of Divinity*, by far the largest volume produced by a colonial press to that date. This work is also American Puritanism's only systematic theology.

Willard was, at Increase Mather's suggestion, made a Fellow of Harvard, one of eight who, together with the president and treasurer, constituted the governing board under the college charter of 1692. During the witchcraft crisis of that year, Willard was among the leading clerical critics of the court's use of spectral evidence and published his views in *Some Misallany Observations on . . . Witchcraft* (1692). Another sign of his importance as an intellectual leader in this crucial transition period was his 1694 election sermon, *The Character of a Good Ruler*, which attempted to meld the Puritan tradition of "godly magistracy" with the more secular realities of Massachusetts's government as a royal colony.

On 12 July 1700 Willard became vice president of Harvard, a post he retained until he resigned due to poor health in August 1707. For much of that period he, in effect, headed the college administration, while remaining pastor of Old South. Always concerned to maintain the quality and prestige of the clergy, he joined the Mathers in the unsuccessful attempt to organize a formal association of ministers and churches. Although the effort failed in Massachusetts, a similar movement in Connecticut led to the famed Saybrook Platform, which permitted ministers to discipline each other and their flocks collectively. In his publications, including a pamphlet against the Quaker reformer George Keith in 1703, Willard continued his lifelong campaign to defend the Puritan tradition while adapting it to changing cultural and political conditions. Soon after his resignation from Harvard, he died in Boston and was buried in the Old Granary Burial Ground.

In terms of both quality and number of publications, Willard was clearly one of the leading intellectuals of American Puritanism. His importance was well understood by his contemporaries and is reflected in the posts he held as well as in the popularity of his sermons and pamphlets.

• There are two modern biographies of Samuel Willard, Seymour Van Dyken, *Samuel Willard, 1640–1707: Preacher of Orthodoxy in an Era of Change* (1972), and Ernest Benson Lowrie, *The Shape of the Puritan Mind: The Thought of Samuel Willard* (1974). For an excellent sense of the context and significance of Willard's work, see Harry S. Stout, *The New England Soul: Preaching and Religious Culture in Colonial New England* (1986), and Stephen Foster, *The Long Argument: English Puritanism and the Shaping of New England Culture, 1570–1700* (1991). A convenient list of Willard's publications together with a critical introduction can be found in James A. Levernier and Douglas R. Wilmer, eds., *American Writers before 1800* (1983).

RICHARD P. GILDRIE

WILLARD, Simon (Apr. 1605–24 Apr. 1676), soldier, was baptized at Horsmonden, Kent, England, on 7 April 1605, the son of Richard Willard, a yeoman, and Margery (maiden name unknown). His father, who died in 1616, stipulated in his will that Simon should be apprenticed to learn a trade or business, but there are no records of Simon having done this. He must have had military training in England, for he was chosen in Massachusetts to drill the militia. Nor is there reliable information regarding his first marriage, said to have been to a Mary Sharpe, also of Horsmonden. He married twice in America. His second brief marriage, about 1650, was probably to Elizabeth Dunster, sister of the first president of Harvard College. His third marriage, about 1652, was to Mary Dunster, a relation of Elizabeth's. He had seventeen children.

Willard's documented achievements begin with his arrival in Boston, Massachusetts, in May 1634. Willard was a committed Puritan at the age of twenty-nine, a man who was willing to leave a comfortable life in England because he was convinced that he had a duty to help build a new society in the New World. He bought land in Newtown, the settlement that later became Cambridge, at that time planned as a garrison town against not the Indians but the French in Canada. It was almost immediately clear that invasion by the French would not be a problem, and Willard led others inland to found the town of Concord in 1635. He moved still further westward in 1659, helping to found Lancaster, and settled finally in the town of Groton, less than fifty miles west of Boston and on the edge of the frontier.

In all the towns he founded, he earned his living as a fur trader with the Indians, and by 1657 he and three other men owned the fur trade franchises on the Merrimack River. Willard and the other traders had contradictory relations with the Native Americans. On the one hand they wanted to keep open the lands where the Indians trapped the beaver that were the main staple of the fur trade. On the other hand they negotiated with the natives to buy land for European farmers, thereby moving the frontier further west and north. They encouraged the settlements of "Praying Indians" on the grounds that the acculturated natives would be loyal to the Europeans. At all times, Willard personally seems to have respected the dignity of the natives and chose to parley rather than fight whenever possible, but he was a professional soldier who could resort to force when necessary.

He also controlled settlement on the frontier. With other speculators he bought land and founded many townships, although he never lived on those properties. He devoted a great deal of time to public service for the towns where he made his home, serving on many town committees, particularly those dealing with boundaries and military matters. He served in the Court of Assistants from 1654 until his death, representing in turn Concord, Lancaster, and Groton. He also served as a justice on the northern frontiers in what are now New Hampshire and Maine. From 1653 on he was major of Middlesex, second in command of the militia for the colony. Willard showed his professionalism when, in 1654, he led troops against Ninigret, sachem of the Niantics in Connecticut. He chose not to waste his men, to parley rather than punish. The legislature in Boston far behind the lines was not pleased with his pacific solution.

Willard had a long relationship with Peter Bulkeley, the first minister of Concord, and through him with John Eliot, who of all the Puritan ministers was the most interested in the Native Americans. Willard and Bulkeley together made the arrangements for Eliot to learn the Algonquian language and to preach to the Indians. Willard worked with Daniel Gookin, also a soldier from Kent, who was in direct charge of the Praying Indian settlements. All of these men misread signs that the Puritan version of Christianity undermined the stability of Indian culture, that the settlers were pushing hard and fast onto Indian lands, and that the Indians were bound to resist.

The outbreak was lead by Metacomet (King Philip), chief of the Wampanoags, who was based at Mount Hope, at the top of Narragansett Bay in Rhode Island. Philip first tried to use the settlers against his hereditary enemies, the Narragansetts, on the western shore of the bay, but then, goaded by slights by the English, turned his efforts to planning a general uprising on the whole frontier. The war broke out in June 1675 in southeastern Massachusetts and Rhode Island.

In July Willard became involved, trying to defend the long frontier against Indians attacking the settlements from the west and north. Willard relieved Brookfield just as it was about to fall and spent the summer of 1675 shoring up garrison houses (there were no forts), patrolling with a few trained dragoons. Most of his soldiers were from the amateur militia, desperately concerned for their families and unwilling to venture beyond their own settlements. The war lasted through the winter and into the next spring. The frontier was driven back twenty-five miles as settlement after settlement was burned to the ground. Willard's own house in Groton was destroyed, but he arrived in force in time to save the inhabitants. He died of exhaustion in Charleston that April, worn out by exertions in the struggle.

Willard left no writings, no explanation of why he came to America or what he found to admire or detest of the Native American culture. He stands, rather, as one of the earliest examples of the frontier leader: soldier, magistrate, and fur trader. His career is echoed in those of hundreds of other immigrant Americans for the next 250 years.

• The standard biography of Willard, which reprints all the surviving documents, is Joseph Willard, *Willard Memorial* (1858; repr. 1913). Samuel A. Green, *Historical Sketch of Groton* (1894), discusses Willard's last years in Groton. Thomas Wheeler, "A Thankfull Remembrance of Gods Mercy to Severall Persons at Quabaug or Brookfield" (1676), reprinted in the collection *So Dreadfull a Judgment: Puritan Responses to King Philip's War* (1978), gives a vivid picture of the aged Willard rallying the settlers to their own defense. John F. Martin, *Profits in the Wilderness: Entrepreneurship and the Founding of New England Towns in the Seventeenth Century* (1991), gives an excellent account of the way the frontier was settled. Douglas Edward Leach, *Flintlock and Tomahawk: New England in King Philip's War* (1958), is the only modern account of that conflict. William Hubbard, *A Narrative of the Troubles with the Indians* (1677), covers the conflict from the Puritan point of view.

MARY RHINELANDER MCCARL

WILLARD, Solomon (26 June 1783–27 Feb. 1861), sculptor, architect, inventor, and educator, was born in Petersham, Massachusetts, the son of William Willard, a carpenter and joiner, and Katherine Wilder. After completing an apprenticeship with his father, Willard left for Boston in 1804 to find work as a carpenter. There he may have studied architectural drawing with Asher Benjamin, for whom he constructed the spiral staircase in the Exchange Coffee House in 1808. Willard carved capitals for Peter Banner in the Park Street Church in 1809 and for Charles Bulfinch in the Federal Street Church in 1810. Willard's first major sculptural achievement, created at a time when the art of sculpture was first becoming known in the United States, was a five-by-five-foot wooden spread eagle for the pediment of the Custom House, carved in 1810.

Willard's intellectual curiosity led him to study perspective drawing, figure carving, geology, chemistry, anatomy, and French. In 1809 he and four other artisans, including the housewright Ithiel Town, established the Architectural Library of Boston "for the encouragement of the Sciences—Architecture, Painting, and Sculpture." It was undoubtedly at the library that Willard began his lifelong association with the architect Alexander Parris. In 1810 Willard went to Richmond, Virginia, where Parris was overseeing the construction of the Mason and Bell mansions. Willard spent three months there, probably in his friend's employ. In Richmond, and on subsequent trips to Charlottesville, Washington, D.C., Baltimore, and Philadelphia, Willard came in contact with works by Thomas Jefferson, Benjamin Latrobe (1764–1820), and Robert Mills (1781–1855).

Willard was also a carver of ship figureheads, including a large portrait bust of George Washington for a 74-gun ship built in 1816 in Portsmouth, New Hampshire. This piece, the only figure carving of Willard's that is still in existence, is now located in the collection of the United States Naval Academy in Annapolis, Maryland. In 1817 the Washington Monument Association, intent on having a statue made of Washington, sent Willard to Richmond to make extensive studies of Jean Antoine Houdon's famous statue of the former president. Willard also made a plaster copy of the portrait bust, but it was destroyed during its return trip to Boston. Discouraged, Willard abandoned the project and turned to making architectural models.

At this time, Bulfinch was already engaged in building the United States Capitol, and Willard took this opportunity to seek a position as a figure carver. But because Italian sculptors, who were brought to the United States for that purpose, were already at work on the Capitol, Bulfinch encouraged Willard to make a model of the building instead. He completed the model but rejected Bulfinch's offer to do carvings for the ceilings of the congressional rooms. Already living in Baltimore, Willard meanwhile found employment carving architectural details for Maximilian Godefroy's Unitarian church. In 1818 Willard returned to Boston via Philadelphia and New York City. While in Philadelphia he met the wood-carver William Rush, who admired his drawing skills and encouraged him to continue wood carving.

Willard was soon in the employ of Parris, for whom he carved in stone the capitals for St. Paul's church and five panels for the David Sears Mansion. By the early 1820s Willard had established himself as an architect and worked closely with both Parris and Isaiah Rogers. Willard is credited with designing the Central Universalist Church of Boston (1822–1823), the Bank of the United States (1824), Boston's Purchase Street Church (1825–1826), the First Church in Salem (1826, with Peter Banner), the Norfolk County courthouse in Dedham (1825–1827), the Suffolk County courthouse in Boston (1835), the Quincy School (1842), and the Quincy town hall (1844). His studies in engineering and geology, and his knowledge of the work of Mills and Latrobe, produced a neoclassical style that was functional, strong, and monumental, although somewhat rigid in appearance.

Willard taught drawing, architectural modeling, physics, and chemistry privately in his studio, and in 1826 he became one of the founders and vice presidents of the Boston Mechanics' Institution, where young engineers and architects were able to take both practical and theoretical courses. He was also a life subscriber to the Boston Athenaeum, for which he made plaster models of the Parthenon and Pantheon. Around 1823 Willard invented, but did not patent, a hot-air furnace that he installed in the Old South Church and in St. Paul's. Bulfinch consulted Willard about heating the Capitol and the White House with such a system.

In 1825 the Bunker Hill Monument Association appointed Willard to be architect and superintendent of the famous 220-foot obelisk that towers over the Charlestown section of Boston. Although Horatio Greenough won the initial competition for the project, and despite the fact that Parris's name was placed on the cornerstone and that Robert Mills claimed the concept to be his, Willard actually executed the design and the construction. The monument is a testimony to Willard's engineering and organizational skills, as well as his knowledge, creativity, and ingenuity. He discovered the granite quarry in Quincy and oversaw the cutting of the stones, for which he designed mechanical devices. He also introduced a railway system—one of the first in the United States—to handle the transportation of the blocks. After several interruptions due to lack of funds, the monument was finally completed in 1843. He described the project in *Plans and Sections of the Obelisk on Bunker's Hill, with the Details of Experiments Made in Quarrying the Granite* (1843).

During the construction of the monument, Willard continued to design other buildings and monuments, including the Concord monument (1825–1836), the Franklin monument in the Granary Burying Ground (1827), and the Harvard monument in the Old Burying Ground in Charlestown (1828). Willard furnished granite blocks for many buildings, including Isaiah Rogers's Merchants' Exchange Company in New York (1836–1841) and Willard's own Merchants' Exchange in Boston (1841). In his later years Willard retired to a farm in Quincy, where he engaged in scientific farming and where he died. He never married.

• Letterbooks of Willard's dated 1831 to 1835 and 1836 to 1844, and papers on quarrying stone at Quincy and on other matters relating to the Bunker Hill Monument Association (1823–c. 1830), are in the Massachusetts Historical Society, Boston, Mass. Drawings for the monument are at the American Antiquarian Society, Worcester, Mass. William W. Wheildon, *Memoir of Solomon Willard, Architect and Superintendent of the Bunker Hill Monument* (1865), was written by a friend of Willard's soon after Willard's death and, as such, is a detailed and reliable source. Talbot Hamlin, *Greek Revival Architecture in America* (1944), is an assessment of Willard's architectural work as well as his relationship to other leading architects in early nineteenth-century Boston. Jack Quinan, "Some Aspects of the Development of the Architectural Profession in Boston Between 1800 and 1830," *Old Time New England* 68 (1977), also discusses the collaboration of these early architects. Edward Francis Zimmer, "Architectural Career of Alexander Parris (1780–1852)" (Ph.D. diss., Boston Univ., 1984), is an excellent recent study of Willard's relationship with Parris, and it settles some chronological discrepancies and explains some of Willard's travels. Zimmer's footnotes and bibliography on Willard are also important. Robert Alexander, *The Architecture of Maximilian Godefroy* (1974), discusses Willard's work on the Unitarian church in Baltimore and explores the possibility that Willard used some of Godefroy's motifs. Helen M. P. Gallagher, *Robert Mills* (1935), discusses the controversy over the design of the Bunker Hill Monument.

SYLVIA LEISTYNA LAHVIS

WILLCOX, Louise Collier (24 Apr. 1865–13 Sept. 1929), writer and translator, was born in Chicago, Illinois, the daughter of the Reverend Robert Laird Collier, a well-known Unitarian minister, and Mary Price. After her mother's death when she was seven, her father took her and a brother, Hiram Price Collier, to Europe to study there. Hiram later became a well-known author and the husband of Kassie Delano Robbins, an aunt of Franklin D. Roosevelt. Louise's education abroad in France, Germany, and England led to her proficiency in German and French, an accomplishment that resulted in her later career as a translator. During her years in Europe she was tutored privately and studied piano at the royal Conservatory of Music in Leipzig (1882–1883). Although not wealthy, her family was well connected, and she met some notable figures of the period including John Henry Newman, John Bright, and Joseph Chamberlain.

Back in the United States and faced with the prospect of making her own living, Willcox became a teacher in 1887 at Norfolk, Virginia's Leache-Wood Seminary, a leading cultural force for women in its area. She resigned to marry J. Westmore Willcox, a Norfolk attorney, on 25 June 1890. Although Norfolk remained her home for the rest of her life and she was considered a leading literary figure of Virginia, she made frequent trips to New York City in connection with her career as a writer and editor. She and her husband also traveled in Europe with their two children. A prolific contributor to magazines of the period, often writing on spiritual themes, Willcox was a manuscript reader for the Macmillan Company from 1903 until 1909 and for E. P. Dutton and Company from 1910 to 1917. She published columns, essays, articles, reviews, and poems in a variety of magazines, acting as an editorial writer for *Harper's Weekly* and *Harper's Bazaar* as well as being a regular staff writer for the *Delineator*. From 1906 to 1913 she served as a member of the editorial staff of the *North American Review*, where she wrote literary criticism and was involved in setting up a pioneer "Book of the Month" club.

Her books, some of which presented her mystical version of Christian thought, were well received. Her first book, *Answers of the Ages* (1900), an anthology edited with Irene K. Leache, contained quotations from famous people on the meaning of God and the soul. In 1909 a collection of her essays on varied topics such as books, friendship, and the outdoors appeared in *The Human Way*. The following year she published *A Manual of Spiritual Fortification*, a selection of English meditations and mystic poems from the thirteenth to the twentieth century. A 1924 anthology of verse, *The Torch*, was subtitled *A Book of Poems for Boys* and was dedicated to her grandson, but its contents were of equal appeal to girls.

Translation, however, became her chief occupation during the last phase of her career. Holding a preeminent position in the field, she translated books by leading French and German authors. They included Jean Giraudoux's *My Friend from Limousin* (1923); *Gold* (1924), a translation of Jacob Wassermann's *Ulrika Woytich; A Sentimental Bestiary* (1924) by Charles Derennes; *The Sardonic Smile* (1926) by Ludwig Diehl; and *The Bewitched* (1928) by J. Barbey d'Aurevilly. She was an honorary member of Phi Beta Kappa at the College of William and Mary. She died unexpectedly in Paris, apparently of a heart attack, while visiting her son.

A woman of great intellectual gifts, Willcox popularized a religious philosophy keyed to self-improvement in harmony with the Christian thought of the day. A typical comment from her work declared, "Mistakes may be the stepping-stones of the stairs up which we are climbing. Everytime we recognize one for what it is and call it a step instead of a goal, we move on" (*Delineator*, 14 Nov. 1914). In her magazine columns, she drew on her experiences as a wife and mother, often using them to frame a lesson that showed how personal sacrifice leads to redemption. Yet she did not subscribe to a facile optimism. In a column on 9 August 1913 marking the end of ten years as a weekly contributor to *Harper's Weekly*, she complained of editors who tried to make her message one of false cheerfulness. She also asserted that an "editorial ban" had made it impossible for her to state her true views on women's rights. They were, she said, that "the ultimate emancipation of women . . . must be for the betterment of the race. . . . Ultimately a society made of free men and women will make a higher civilization." Her career demonstrated the heights that could be reached by a literary woman of her day, but it also showed her perception of limitations.

• Little material exists on Louise Collier Willcox. Vera Connolly's "Louise Collier Willcox: Woman, Essayist, Philosopher," *Delineator*, 14 Nov. 1914, offers a journalistic profile. Some personal information can be obtained from Esther Willcox Putnam of Charlottesville, Va. An obituary appears in the *Norfolk Virginian-Pilot*, 14 Sept. 1929.

MAURINE H. BEASLEY

WILLCOX, Orlando Bolivar (16 Apr. 1823–10 May 1907), Union general, was born in frontier Detroit, the son of Charles Willcox and Almira Rood Powers (occupations unknown). He graduated from the U.S. Military Academy at West Point in 1847, eighth in a class of thirty eight, and arrived in Mexico City as a second lieutenant of the Fourth U.S. Artillery just as hostilities with that country ended. Over the next decade he served at garrisons in Florida, Kansas, Missouri, New Mexico, Texas, and in the East. In 1852 he married Marie Louise Farnsworth, a cousin of Colonel Elon Farnsworth of Gettysburg fame; the couple had five children. After a year's service in the last Seminole War, he resigned as a first lieutenant on 10 September 1857 and moved back to Michigan.

For the next four years Willcox practiced law with his brother in Detroit. At the outbreak of the Civil War he accepted an appointment as colonel of the First Michigan Volunteer Infantry, which he led into the first major battle at Manassas (Bull Run) on 21 July 1861. Severely wounded and captured there, he was imprisoned for just over a year; for about three months of that time he was kept in close confinement in retaliation for the treatment of Confederate privateers. Once released, he was commissioned a brigadier general from the date of Bull Run and assigned to the Ninth Corps under his friend and West Point classmate, Ambrose E. Burnside. Willcox took command of the First Division of that corps, leading it at South Mountain, Maryland, and at Antietam three days later. At neither battle did he particularly distinguish himself, but Burnside's elevation to command of the Army of the Potomac led to Willcox's temporary assignment as chief of the Ninth Corps. He commanded the corps at Fredericksburg, where he again failed to demonstrate more than plodding competence.

When the Ninth Corps was ordered to the Department of the Ohio, Willcox showed better promise in the quasi-political capacity of district military commander, first in central Kentucky and later in Indiana and Michigan. He exercised commendable restraint when faced with draft riots in Indiana in the summer of 1863. Returning to field command that fall, he resumed his lackluster performance. He held Cumberland Gap during the siege of Knoxville and returned to the Virginia theater with Burnside in the spring of 1864, taking the Third Division of the Ninth Corps. He served capably enough in the confused fighting at the Wilderness, but at Spotsylvania his delay in arranging artillery to cover an infantry attack cost valuable time for Burnside, who was under pressure from army headquarters to drive the enemy back. At Cold Harbor he again used so much time to post his guns that an adjoining division suffered severely and a planned attack had to be called off.

A court of inquiry investigating the disastrous 30 July assault on the Petersburg Crater found Willcox at fault for not supporting adjacent divisions sufficiently, though there seems to have been some internal army politics involved in that decision. He fared much better in operations against the Weldon Railroad in August, launching one particularly opportune counterattack, but at Poplar Springs Church ("Pegram House") on 30 September his performance was again mediocre. By the end of the war he was one of the most senior brigadier generals in active service, and he achieved the rank of major general only by brevet—albeit in both the volunteer and regular services.

Mustered out of the army on 15 January 1866, Willcox reverted briefly to his old law practice in Detroit. A few weeks later he was appointed U.S. assessor of Internal Revenue, but by the end of July he secured reappointment in the regular army as colonel of the Twenty-ninth Infantry. After three years of duty in Reconstruction Virginia, he spent more than four years in command of Alcatraz Island. Following a year's respite on recruiting service in New York, he returned to California and Arizona for another eight years. Finally promoted to full brigadier general in the fall of 1886, he retired on his sixty-fourth birthday. By this time his first wife had died, and he married Julia Elizabeth McReynolds Wyeth, a widow; they had one child. Early in his retirement he served as "governor" of the National Soldiers' Home in Washington. In 1905 he moved to Cobourg, Ontario, where he died.

• Willcox wrote of his best day of battle in "Actions on the Weldon Railroad," in *Battles and Leaders of the Civil War*, vol. 4, ed. Robert U. Johnson and Clarence C. Buel (1887–1888); and he recounted the final hours of John Hunt Morgan's Ohio raid in "The Capture," *Century Illustrated Monthly Magazine*, Jan. 1891, pp. 403–25. He also wrote two romances based on his prewar service on the frontier called *Shoepac Recollections—A Wayside Glimpse of American Life* (1856) and *Faca—An Army Memoir, by Major March* (1857). General Willcox's military service is detailed in George W. Cullum, *Biographical Register of the Officers and Graduates of the U.S. Military Academy at West Point, New York* (supp. 1910). Unit histories that deal with Willcox's service include Augustus Woodbury, *Major General Ambrose E. Burnside and the Ninth Army Corps* (1867), and Milton A. Embick, ed. and comp., *Military History of the Third Division, Ninth Corps, Army of the Potomac* (1913). Incidental modern comments on his wartime service include Richard J. Sommers, *Richmond Redeemed* (1981), William Matter, *If It Takes All Summer* (1988), and William Marvel, *Burnside* (1991).

WILLIAM MARVEL

WILLEBRANDT, Mabel Walker (23 May 1889–6 Apr. 1963), lawyer and assistant attorney general of the United States, was born in Woodsdale, Kansas, the only child of Myrtle Eaton and David William Walker, homesteaders and teachers. She spent her early years in prairie towns in Oklahoma and Missouri. In 1902 the family settled in Kansas City, Missouri, so that Mabel, who had been educated at home, could receive formal schooling. She entered Park College and Academy in 1906. Expelled the next spring for arguing with the president over the doctrine of the virgin birth, she joined her parents in Buckley, Michigan, where her father had opened a bank. She taught for two and a half years, then married Arthur Willebrandt, the high school principal, in 1910. In 1911, after moving to Tempe, Arizona, for Arthur's health, Willebrandt earned a diploma from the State Normal School.

Next, the Willebrandts moved to Los Angeles, where Mabel became principal of schools in Buena Park and South Pasadena. In 1912 she began night classes in law at the University of Southern California, paying tuition for both herself and her husband in the day program. She received an LL.B. in 1916 and an LL.M. the following year. Meanwhile, she separated from her husband in 1916; they would divorce in 1924. Unable to have a child after an early miscarriage, she adopted a two-year-old girl in 1925.

In 1916 Willebrandt became Los Angeles's first assistant police court defender; she represented more than two thousand women, mostly prostitutes. After being admitted to the bar in July, she began private practice with two male USC colleagues, founded the Women Lawyers' Club of Los Angeles County, and built a lively nationwide correspondence and local networks to challenge the "old boy" system in the courts. She also lobbied in Sacramento for a revision in the community property law expanding the rights of married women and widows.

Willebrandt's networking and reputation as a progressive Republican won the backing of Senator Hiram Johnson; in 1921 she was appointed assistant attorney general in the new administration of Warren G. Harding. At thirty-two, with five years' legal experience, she was the second woman to hold that position, and she remained the highest ranking woman in the federal government throughout the 1920s. She was responsible for cases involving Prohibition, income taxes, and federal prisons. Although she had not advocated prohibition before her appointment, enforcing it became her most challenging responsibility. Faced with smuggling, bootleggers, conniving local politicians, incompetent federal enforcement units, and public indifference, she became known in the press as "Prohibition Portia" and sought public support through lectures and magazine articles. Her division averaged more than fifty thousand prosecutions annually, winning highly publicized cases against the "Savannah Four," the "Mobile Six," and the "king of the Bootleggers," George Remus. The division also won appeals of the padlocking of New York speakeasies. Willebrandt herself argued more than forty cases before the Supreme Court and presented cases in federal district courts when congressmen or local political figures were on trial. As public support withered, however, she admitted feeling like the boy who stood with his finger in the dike, adding, "I've *prevented* floods of wrong things, but it's a wearing way to be a hero." She summed up her frustrations in *The Inside of Prohibition* (1929).

Willebrandt's most enduring contributions involved changes in the federal prison system. Using her network of women's clubs and other groups, particularly the Women's Joint Congressional Committee and the American Prison Association, she won authorization and appropriations for the first federal prison for women at Alderson, West Virginia, a model facility on the cottage plan; the federal reformatory at Chillicothie, Ohio, for first-time young male offenders; and the establishment of prison industries. She also cleaned up major scandals at Atlanta and Leavenworth prisons and secured the appointment of Sanford Bates, an innovative prison administrator, as director of the Bureau of Prisons.

Throughout the 1920s Willebrandt sought an appointment as the first woman to hold a seat on the federal district bench. She had shown her loyalty to the Republican party by going on the hustings in support of Prohibition and the party in 1922 and 1924. Instead of rewarding her with a judgeship, however, the party again called her to political duty. In 1928 she became the first woman to chair the credentials committee of the Republican National Convention, and that fall she stumped for Hoover. A political commentator for *Collier's* would conclude, "No other woman has ever had so much influence upon a Presidential campaign as Mrs. Willebrandt has had on this one." However, after she exhorted two thousand Methodist ministers in Ohio to support Hoover and Prohibition, Alfred E. Smith, the Democratic candidate, accused her of bringing religion into the campaign. The ensuing controversy ended her hopes for a judgeship, and she resigned in May 1929.

Building on Washington contacts and her expertise in federal tax law, Willebrandt developed a wide-ranging practice with offices in California and Washington. She won landmark cases in aviation and radio and later became the first woman to chair an American Bar Association committee, the Committee on Aeronautical Law. When the Federal Farm Board was created in 1930 she won major funding for an association of California grape growers, much to the consternation of the dries, who opposed support for a product that could be made into wine at home. She also represented Metro-Goldwyn-Mayer, Louis B. Mayer, and many MGM stars, including Jeanette MacDonald, Clark Gable, and Jean Harlow. For twenty years she represented the Screen Directors' Guild, winning its first victory against producers in 1938–1939 and drafting its controversial loyalty oath in 1950.

Willebrandt's health began to deteriorate rapidly in 1961 after suffering broken bones from a series of falls caused by unsteadiness from an ear operation. She died in Riverside, California.

• Willebrandt's papers are in the Library of Congress, including a long memoir on her work in the Justice Department in the Harlan Fiske Stone Papers. Dorothy M. Brown, *Mabel Walker Willebrandt: A Study in Power, Loyalty, and Law* (1984), is a full-length biography. Avery Strakosch, "A Woman in Law," *Saturday Evening Post*, 24 Sept. 1927; Anne Hard, "America's Portia," *New York Herald Tribune*, 1 July 1928; and John S. Martin, "Mrs. Firebrand," *New Yorker*, 16 Feb. 1929, provide contemporary assessments of her early career and political campaigns. Her work in prisons is described in Mary Belle Harris, *I Knew Them in Prison* (1936). Obituaries are in the *Los Angeles Times*, 8 Apr. 1963, and the *New York Times*, 9 Apr. 1963.

DOROTHY M. BROWN

WILLETT, Herbert Lockwood (5 May 1864–28 Mar. 1944), clergyman, orator, and biblical scholar, was born near Ionia, Michigan, the son of Gordon Arthur Willett, a farm machinery merchant, and Mary Elizabeth Yates, a schoolteacher serving as a nurse in the Union army. Formative in his choice of vocation were the memberships of both the Willett and Yates families in a Disciples of Christ congregation founded in the 1850s by evangelist Isaac Errett. Willett never attended public school. He studied under his mother's tutelage, memorizing large portions of the Bible and poetry, an accomplishment that later lent distinction to his public and academic addresses. In 1883 his Disciples heritage prompted him to attend Bethany College in West Virginia, the school founded by the denominational leader Alexander Campbell, where Willett obtained his B.A. in 1886 and M.A. in 1887. He married Emma Augusta Price in 1888; they had three children. After he had served churches in Ohio for three years, his yearning for higher education led him in 1890 to take a leave of absence to begin work on a B.D. at Yale Divinity School, where he was persuaded by William Rainey Harper to specialize in the study of the Old Testament and Semitic languages. Willett left Yale in 1891 to return to his pastorate, but at the end of two years he resigned his position. Urged by the indomitable Harper, who held out the prospect of a faculty appointment, Willett began work in the spring of 1893 in the Department of Semitic Languages and Literatures at the new University of Chicago, earning his Ph.D. in 1896. Inspired by the example of other faculty members, he did postdoctoral work at the University of Berlin in 1898–1899.

Willett's career choices were variations on the theme of Christian education, specifically preaching, lecturing, publishing, and teaching about the Bible. Although he claimed that his primary calling was to teaching, he was formally ordained as a Disciples of Christ minister in 1890 and served churches and preached frequently for sixty years. Willett commenced his ministerial duties in North Eaton and Dayton, Ohio, 1886–1893. In connection with his work at the Disciples Divinity House of the University of Chicago, he was appointed the first pastor of the Hyde Park (now University) Church of the Disciples, 1894–1897, and later served as minister at First Christian Church in Chicago, 1905–1908; Memorial Church of Christ (Baptist and Disciple), Chicago, 1908–1912 and 1914–1917; and Kenilworth Union Church in Kenilworth, Illinois, 1926–1940.

Willett began his career as an educator in 1881, when he obtained a public school teacher's certificate and taught in the Yates school district for two years. In 1893–1895 he held the nation's first "Bible chair" established at a state university, the University of Michigan at Ann Arbor, where he taught from October to April while concurrently doing graduate work at the University of Chicago during the spring and summer quarters. His career as a faculty member in the University of Chicago's Department of Semitic Languages and Literatures was highly unusual. On the one hand, the Old Testament exegetical and survey courses he conducted for college and graduate students satisfied a unique requirement in Harper's design of a university that was "Christian in the broadest sense of the term." Recognizing Willett's talents as a biblical educator, Harper heralded his protégé's considerable success as a popular lecturer in the university's beleaguered extension program, contractually granting him the unusual liberty to conduct classes on campus for two academic quarters in exchange for off-campus travel and lecturing. On the other hand, although he moved steadily up the ranks from an instructorship in 1897 to a full professorship when the department was reorganized in 1915, protracted absences on speaking engagements and his leading of overseas tours resulted in administrative and collegial friction that persisted up to his retirement in 1929. As a biblical scholar, he trod the path of a conscientious popularizer, expounding his often controversial vision of liberal biblical higher criticism in thirteen nontechnical books and hundreds of essays and editorials. Willett's forceful appeal as a public speaker and willingness to undertake the rigors of the lecture circuit made him a star attraction on the Lyceum, American Institute of Sacred Literature, and Chautauqua platforms, where his message of a Bible responsive to a commonsense scientific worldview and the evolving social realities of the early twentieth century drew record crowds. "His lectures, delivered without notes, were on outlines one could remember, and were phrased simply and fluently, with no tricks of speech or ornamentation, no gestures or vehemence, and yet at times with a high eloquence" (Percy H. Boynton, "Herbert Willett," *University of Chicago Magazine* [Apr. 1944]: inside front cover).

Willett's major legacy to Christian scholarship proved to be the creation in 1894 of the Disciples Divinity House of the University of Chicago, a fellowship foundation that has supported graduate study at the university's Divinity School for hundreds of Disciples of Christ students. Its association with the University of Chicago and Willett's growing national reputation maintained the idea of the denominational facility in the public eye, but strident interdenominational controversies over Willett's liberal approach to biblical scholarship and his inconsistency in pursuing capital endowments led to a deanship (1894–1921) marred by organizational stagnation.

Willett's lifelong commitment to Christian unity found expression in his editorial work for the *Christian Oracle* (1898–1899) and then from 1900 to 1908 for its successor publication, the *Christian Century*, a nondenominational Christian weekly. In 1908 he acted as a delegate for the Disciples of Christ at the founding of the Federal Council of Churches of Christ and served as executive secretary of the Western Section, 1920–1925. He was also instrumental in founding the Chicago Federation of Churches and held the office of president, 1916–1920. In 1937 he attended the ecumenical conferences at Oxford and Edinburgh as a delegate.

Willett died while delivering a series of Lenten lectures, "The Great Books of the Bible," in Winter Park, Florida. Through sermons, lectures, and the press and by founding the Disciples Divinity House of the University of Chicago, Willett's advocacy of Christian intellectual freedom and the value of an educated ministry significantly influenced the history of the Disciples of Christ in the first decades of this century.

• Most of Willett's notebooks, correspondence, and assorted memorabilia are in the archives of the Disciples Divinity House of the University of Chicago and the Disciples of Christ Historical Society, Nashville, Tenn. Bound photocopies of his unpublished autobiography, "The Corridor of Years," comp. and supp. Herbert Lockwood Willett III, his grandson, are also available in Chicago and Nashville. The autobiography of Herbert Lockwood Willett, Jr., "Further Corridors: An Autobiographical Family Record," which is housed in the Disciples Divinity House as a looseleaf photocopy, provides unique supplementary details of his father's career and family life. Records and papers chronicling his teaching career are in the Archives of the Oriental Institute of the University of Chicago and the Special Collections Department of the Joseph Regenstein Library of the University of Chicago. His most important books include *Our Plea for Union and the Present Crisis* (1901), *The Moral Leaders of Israel: Studies in the Development of Hebrew Religion and Ethics* (1916), *Our Bible: Its Origin, Character and Value* (1917), *The Bible through the Centuries* (1929), and *The Jew through the Centuries* (1932). Significant studies of Willett's career include a comparison of J. W. McGarvey and Willett by M. Eugene Boring, "The Disciples and Higher Criticism: The Crucial Third Generation," and a comparison of James Philip Hyatt and Willett by Leo G. Perdue, "The Disciples and Higher Criticism: The Formation of an Intellectual Tradition," both in *A Case Study of Mainstream Protestantism: The Disciples' Relation to American Culture, 1880–1989*, ed. D. Newell Williams (1991). The fullest bibliography of Willett's works is in Boring's study, pp. 68–70. A portrait of Willett painted in 1929 by Charles W. Hawthorne hangs in the Herbert Lockwood Willett Library of the Disciples Divinity House. Obituaries are in the *New York Times*, 29 Mar. 1944, and *Christian Century* 12 (Apr. 1944): 454–56.

STEVEN W. HOLLOWAY

WILLETT, Marinus (31 July 1740–22 Aug. 1830), revolutionary war officer and mayor of New York City, was born near Jamaica, New York, the son of Edward Willett, a tavern keeper, farmer, and teacher, and Aletta Clowes. In 1749 the family moved to New York City, where Edward Willett owned an inn that was popular with the city's elite. Marinus received instruction in catechism and probably also some schooling at Trinity Church. Nothing further is known of his formal education. He was apprenticed to cabinetmaker William Pearsee and later became a master craftsman.

Willett joined the New York militia and during the French and Indian War served as a second lieutenant on the expedition of General James Abercromby, which met disastrous defeat at Ticonderoga on 2 July 1758. He then served with Colonel John Bradstreet's force that captured Fort Frontenac on Lake Ontario on 27 August 1758. Too ill to participate further in the war, he resumed his association with Pearsee. In 1760 Willett married his employer's daughter, Mary Pearsee; they had one son.

From 1765 to 1775, along with Isaac Sears, John Lamb, and Alexander McDougall, Willett led the Sons of Liberty in New York City. He was involved in the riot with British troops on Golden Hill, New York City, 19 January 1770, and in mid-1775 led citizens in raids on British military storehouses and in seizing munitions from the troops of the small British garrison that evacuated the city.

Commissioned as a captain in the First New York Regiment on 28 June 1775, Willett joined American forces under the command of General Richard Montgomery in the Canadian invasion. When Montgomery's troops headed toward Montreal, Willett was left in charge of troops at St. Johns at the entrance of the Sorel (Richelieu) River. When the enlistments of his men expired, he returned to New York City. He commanded militia at the battle of Long Island on 27 August 1776 and assisted in evacuating George Washington's army from Brooklyn, Harlem Heights, and White Plains. Commissioned a lieutenant colonel on 21 November 1776, he joined Peter Gansevoort's Third Continental Regiment. At Fort Constitution, opposite West Point, on 23 May 1777, he led his troops out of that post to drive away a British landing party at Peekskill, New York.

In May 1777 Willett was ordered to Fort Stanwix at Rome, New York. With the fort invested by British troops in August, Willett and another officer slipped through enemy lines to get to Fort Dayton near Herkimer, New York, to secure reinforcements. It is said that the American Indians thought Willett had supernatural powers and dubbed him "the Devil." On 6 August 1777 Willett and 200 men sallied out of Fort Stanwix to rout a Tory-Indian force under Sir John Johnson. Willett accompanied Colonel Goose Van Schaick in his raids on the Onondaga Indian villages in April 1779, and he was with the Sullivan-Clinton expedition against the Iroquois in central and western New York in May–November 1779. Both ventures resulted primarily in the destruction of Indian villages and crops. On 1 July 1780 Willett was made a lieutenant colonel in the Fifth New York Regiment and a colonel in the same unit in November 1780. When the five New York regiments were consolidated into two, Willett left the Continental army. However, he soon accepted an appointment from Governor George Clinton to command, with the rank of colonel, New York levies and militia for the purpose of frontier defense.

With 400 men divided among forts at German Flats (Herkimer), Ballston, Catskill, and Canajoharie, Willett had charge of protecting 5,000 settlers in a 2,000-square-mile area. Learning that 300 Indians under the Tory John Doxtader had raided Currytown on 9 July 1781, Willett went in pursuit the next day. Catching up with the enemy at Sharon Springs Swamp and outnumbered two to one, Willett arranged his force in the form of a crescent and pressed against the enemy's flanks. Nearly entrapped, Doxtader's Indians fled. On 25 October 1781, near Johnstown, Willett routed a Tory-Indian force of 700. In pursuit on 30 October, Willett engaged the enemy's rear guard at West Canada Creek, between present-day Ohio City and Russia, New York. This action, in which the Tory leader Walter Butler was killed, marked the final large-size British foray on the New York frontier. In

February 1783 Willett and 500 snowshoers were headed toward British-held Fort Oswego when they learned of the British surrender. During his military service Willett had an illegitimate child.

On 30 November 1783 Governor Clinton ordered Willett and Colonel John Lasher to take charge of all confiscated Tory lands and properties in New York City until they could be sold by the legislature. Elected to the New York Assembly in late 1783, Willett instead served as sheriff of New York City and County from 1784 to 1788. He served a second term as sheriff from 1792 to 1796.

President Washington sent Willett on a special mission to the Cherokee and Creek Indian country in 1790. Willett persuaded the Creek chief, Alexander McGillivray, and nearly thirty other Creek leaders to accompany him to the nation's capital at New York City, where the Treaty of New York, the first treaty under the Constitution of the United States, was ratified in August 1790. Offered a brigadier generalship in the new federal army in April 1792, Willett declined because he thought the problems with Indians in the Ohio country could be solved without resorting to arms. Around 1790 he and his family moved into their new mansion, "Cedar Grove," on the East River. An anti-Federalist, he was defeated for election to the New York convention to ratify the Constitution in 1788. After the adoption of the Bill of Rights, he gave his approval to the new government, but in the 1790s he emerged as a leader among Governor Clinton's Republicans. His first wife died on 3 July 1793, and later that year he married Susannah Vardle (or Vardill). They had no children and divorced in 1799. About 1800 he married Margaret Bancker, who was thirty-five years his junior. They had five children.

In his seventies Willett became active in New York's volatile Republican politics. With DeWitt Clinton attempting to assume leadership of the party in place of George Clinton, who became vice president in 1805, Willett supported Aaron Burr. Willett was one of the "Martling men," so-called from a tavern where they met, who gained control of the Tammany Society in New York City. In 1807 Morgan Lewis, who was governor of New York and who wished to appease the anti-Clinton faction of the Republican party, named Willett mayor of New York City, replacing DeWitt Clinton in that position. Willett was removed when Lewis failed of reelection in 1808. As mayor, which also included being president of the city council and chief judge of the court of common pleas, Willett proved that he was not in his dotage, as many had thought.

Willett ran a poor third in the election for lieutenant governor in 1811. His last political activity was working for the election of John Quincy Adams in 1824 and 1828. Willett became quite wealthy through his mercantile store in New York City and his extensive landholdings, principally forfeited Tory estates he purchased at low prices. In spring 1830 Willett suffered a stroke and had only partially recovered at the time of his death at Cedar Grove. A newspaper notice of Willett's death reported that he had "distinguished himself by his bravery and good conduct in the war of the revolution" and "was a man of great integrity, frankness and decision of character in private life."

• Willett's papers are scattered among many collections, including the Schuyler papers and the Emmet and Tomilson collections, New York Public Library; the Horatio Gates Papers and John Lamb Papers, New-York Historical Society; the George Washington Papers, Library of Congress; the papers of the Continental Congress, National Archives; and *Public Papers of George Clinton*, ed. Hugh Hastings and J. A. Holden (10 vols., 1899–1914). Willett's own reflections on his military career and the Indian mission of 1790 are in William M. Willett, *A Narrative of the Military Actions of Colonel Marinus Willett, Taken Chiefly from His Own Memory, Prepared by His Son William M. Willett* (1831). Biographies are Howard Thomas, *Marinus Willett: Soldier/Patriot, 1740–1830* (1954); Daniel E. Wager, *Col. Marinus Willett, the Hero of Mohawk Valley* (1891); Frederick L. Bronner, "Marinus Willett," *New York History* 17 (1936): 273–80; Fred J. Cook, *What Manner of Men: Forgotten Heroes of the American Revolution* (1959); and John W. Caughey, *McGillivray of the Creeks* (1938; repr. 1959), which covers the Indian mission of 1790. For Willett and the war in frontier N.Y. see Robert B. Roberts, *New York's Forts in the Revolution* (1980); Barbara Graymount, *The Iroquois in the American Revolution* (1972); Don R. Gerlach, *Proud Patriot: Philip Schuyler and the War of Independence, 1775–1783* (1987); and William W. Campbell, *Annals of Tryon County; or, The Border Warfare of New York during the Revolution* (1831; repr. 1924). Jerome Mushkat, *Tammany: The Evolution of a Political Machine, 1789–1865* (1971), relates to Willett's political career. A death notice is in the *New-York Evening Post*, 23 Aug. 1830, and a long obituary is in the same newspaper on the following day.

HARRY M. WARD

WILLEY, Samuel Hopkins (11 Mar. 1821–21 Jan. 1914), minister, educator, and cofounder of the University of California, was born in Campton, New Hampshire, the son of Darius Willey and Mary Pulsifer (occupations unknown). After attending several academies in New Hampshire, Willey graduated from Dartmouth College in 1845. Raised in the Congregationalist church, Willey joined the New School Presbyterians while enrolled at the Union Theological Seminary in New York City. Upon his graduation in 1848, he became acting pastor of the Congregationalist church in Medford, Massachusetts, where on 30 November 1848 he was ordained as a Presbyterian minister.

Willey's travels between Congregationalism and Presbyterianism did not represent a crisis of faith, but were typical of the era. Nearly identical in terms of doctrine, the two denominations differed mainly on questions of church organization and governance. These differences had been put aside in the 1801 Plan of Union. Designed as a cooperative effort to promote their expansion across the American West, the Plan of Union permitted members of the two churches to form joint congregations and to select ministers from either faith.

The Plan of Union led in 1826 to the formation of the American Home Missionary Society, the frontier proselytizing arm of the Presbyterians and Congregationalists. On the day following his ordination, Willey accepted a commission from the AHMS to spread the gospel in the newly acquired territory of California. Together with three companions, Willey left New York in December 1848. At New Orleans, his party received news verifying earlier rumors regarding the discovery of gold in California. Finding himself suddenly in the midst of the California gold rush, Willey continued on to Panama, crossed the isthmus, and boarded the steamer *California* on its famous maiden voyage for the Pacific Mail Steamship Company. Arriving at the territorial capital of Monterey on 23 February 1849, Willey found the city rapidly losing its population to gold fever. Willey decided to stay, however, and soon became chaplain at the Monterey presidio. In 1849 he also organized a public school, serving as its only instructor, and that same year helped open a public library, California's first.

When delegates to the founding state constitutional convention assembled at Monterey on 1 September 1849, they chose Willey and Antonio Ramirez, a Catholic priest, to serve as chaplains. Alternating daily, the two clergymen shared their duties until the convention adjourned on 12 October. During the course of the convention, Willey married Martha N. Jeffers, another recently arrived American whom he had courted for four months. The couple had six children.

In May 1850 Willey moved to San Francisco, where he founded the Howard Street Presbyterian Church and became its first pastor. In August of the following year, he helped launch *The Pacific*, a weekly Congregationalist and Presbyterian newspaper. Willey served as an associate editor of the paper from 1851 to 1855.

Willey also became deeply involved in early efforts to establish public education in California. In April 1850 he traveled to San Jose in support of a successful effort to convince the first state legislature to enact a law providing for the incorporation of colleges. Later that year, he and John Pelton, an educator, led 100 children on a march through the streets of San Francisco to demonstrate the pressing need for schools in that frontier metropolis.

Joining forces with Henry Durant and other Congregationalist and Presbyterian leaders, Willey aided in fundraising and site selection for Contra Costa Academy in June 1853 and was elected president of its first board of trustees. Located in Oakland, the nondenominational private academy received a state charter and became the College of California in 1855. Willey remained on the board, serving as secretary. In February 1858 Willey headed a special committee that recommended relocating the college to a larger and more desirable site four miles north of Oakland. Later named by the trustees in honor of philosopher George Berkeley, the new site was formally dedicated by Willey, Durant, and the rest of the board at a ceremony held at Founders' Rock on 16 April 1860.

Nearly two years later, in March 1862, Willey resigned as pastor of the Howard Street church to become vice president and acting president of the college. Under his leadership, the trustees completed the acquisition of the new campus properties and laid out the townsite of Berkeley in accordance with Willey's College Homestead Plan. Conceived in 1864, the plan called for the subdivision and sale of town lots in order to create a new college community and to raise funds for the construction of the actual campus. Willey also organized the College Water Company to secure a reliable water supply for the new town and school.

Unfortunately, Willey was never able to place the college on a firm financial footing. Funding difficulties eventually forced him to support an effort to merge the College of California with a proposed state college. Taking advantage of federal support offered by Congress under the Morrill Act of 1862, the California legislature had authorized the establishment of an "agricultural, mining, and mechanical arts" college in March 1866. Proponents of a full-fledged public university then stepped forward with the merger plan. By October 1867 an agreement was reached by which the College of California became, in effect, the College of Letters for the new University of California, chartered by the legislature on 23 March 1868. After a one-year delay, instruction began at the university in September 1869.

Following the merger, Willey returned to the ministry as pastor of the Congregationalist church in Santa Cruz, over which he presided for ten years. In 1880 he became pastor of the Congregationalist church in Benicia, where he preached for another decade before returning to San Francisco in 1890 to accept the presidency of the Van Ness Seminary. After his resignation in 1896, Willey retired and moved to Berkeley, where he spent the remainder of his life.

A member of the Society of California Pioneers, Willey published numerous works on the history of California and American Protestantism. Among his most important books are *Thirty Years in California* (1879), *History of the College of California* (1887), *History of the First Pastorate of the Howard Presbyterian Church* (1900), *The Transition Period of California, from a Province of Mexico in 1846 to a State of the American Union in 1850* (1901), *American Congregationalism in the Nineteenth Century and Entering the Twentieth* (1902), and *Founders of the University* (1903).

• Willey's papers are plentiful but scattered. The library of the Graduate Theological Union (San Francisco Theological Seminary Branch) in San Anselmo, Calif., has a collection of Willey materials, as do the Pacific School of Religion and the Bancroft Library at the University of California, both in Berkeley. The latter also contains a great deal of Willey's correspondence. Two valuable collections of American Home Missionary Society materials that contain numerous letters written by Willey are housed at the Amistad Research Center, Tulane University, New Orleans, La.; and in the United Church of Christ archives at the Pacific School of Religion.

Clifford Drury, "Samuel Hopkins Willey: California's Pioneer Missionary and Educator," an unpublished typescript housed in Drury's papers at the San Francisco Theological Seminary in San Anselmo, is a full-length biography. The best published sources on Willey are brief biographical sketches by Rockwell Hunt in *California and Californians*, vol. 5 (1926), and *California's Stately Hall of Fame* (1950). See also Laurie Maffly-Kipp, *Religion and Society in Frontier California* (1994); William Ferrier, *Origin and Development of the University of California* (1930); Verne Stadtman, *The University of California, 1868–1968* (1970); and Miriam Drury, "The Jeffers-Willey Wedding," *California Historical Society Quarterly* 35 (1956): 11–21.

MICHAEL MAGLIARI

WILLEY, Waitman Thomas (18 Oct. 1811–2 May 1900), lawyer and U.S. senator, was born near what is now Farmington, West Virginia, the son of William Willey, Jr., and Sarah Barnes, farmers. Growing up in a log cabin on the trans-Allegheny frontier, Willey experienced the hardships of rural isolation, soon intensified by the deaths of his mother and sister. A stepmother, Mary McCormack, subsequently provided maternal affection. Receiving only eleven months of formal schooling during his boyhood years, he supplemented these meager opportunities with instruction from his father and was enrolled at Madison College in Uniontown, Pennsylvania, in 1827. He graduated four years later and prepared for a legal career by studying with attorneys Philip Doddridge and John C. Campbell in Wellsburg, Virginia (now West Virginia).

Willey was admitted to the Virginia bar after settling in Morgantown, a village on the Monongahela River. There, in 1834, he married Elizabeth Evans Ray, the daughter of a locally prominent family. The couple had seven children, all of whom survived to adulthood. Prospering through his law practice and investments in cattle and real estate, Willey also served (1841–1852) as clerk of court in Monongalia County and as the county's first superintendent of schools. A devout Christian, he was active in Morgantown's Methodist Episcopal church and gained a statewide reputation as a lecturer for the Sons of Temperance.

Eager to advance the economic interests of northwestern Virginia, Willey joined the Whig party and campaigned as a presidential elector for the William Henry Harrison–John Tyler (1790–1862) ticket in 1840. A decade later he served in the Virginia constitutional convention of 1850, where he championed white manhood suffrage, more equitable legislative representation for his part of the state, and reforms in courts and local governments. In 1859, as the nominee of the Opposition (i.e., Whig) party, he made an unsuccessful race for the office of lieutenant governor. During the presidential campaign of the following year, he was a delegate to the national convention of the Constitutional Union party.

Willey, who had previously owned (and manumitted) a family of slaves, had long opposed the abolitionist movement, and he viewed the triumph of Republican Abraham Lincoln in the 1860 presidential election as an unfortunate development. Nevertheless, as a delegate to the Virginia Convention of 1861, he joined the minority that voted against the secession ordinance, arguing that civil war would lead to the military devastation and political division of the state. After the decisive vote on 17 April, he left the convention, lamenting that the antisecessionist northwestern counties confronted the dire prospect of what he called "triple treason" (to Virginia, to the United States, and, potentially, to the Confederate States of America).

Seeking a way out of this dilemma, Willey attended a Unionist mass meeting at Wheeling in May 1861. There he joined Francis H. Pierpont and other moderates in opposing demands for the immediate creation of a separate state of "New Virginia," composed of the loyalist northwestern counties. Although sympathetic to this goal, the moderates believed that delay was needed in order to rally support and conform with the U.S. Constitution's requirements for such an endeavor. A month later—with Willey absent because of the fatal illnesses of his father and stepmother—a second convention in Wheeling established a Reorganized (i.e., pro-Union) Government for Virginia, preparatory to eventual statehood.

In July 1861 the legislature of the Reorganized Government elected Willey to fill the Virginia seat in the U.S. Senate formerly held by secessionist James M. Mason. Shortly thereafter the Senate (by a vote of 35 to 5) recognized Willey's right to the post, thus setting the stage for his greatest accomplishments. In May 1862 he informed his Washington colleagues that the Reorganized Government had consented to the creation of the state of West Virginia. Congressional approval was necessary, and in the debate over the proposed constitution of the new state, particular criticism was directed at the document's failure to abolish slavery. With considerable reluctance, Willey agreed to provisions (known as the "Willey Amendment" to the statehood bill) emancipating all blacks born in West Virginia after 4 July 1863 and freeing various categories of young slaves when they attained the age of twenty-one or twenty-five years. Approved by Congress and signed by President Lincoln late in 1862, the statehood compromise was confirmed when West Virginia voters overwhelmingly ratified the gradual emancipation program in a March 1863 referendum. The legislature of the new state promptly recognized Willey's services by sending him to the U.S. Senate in 1863 and reelecting him to a six-year term in 1865.

Willey's senatorial tenure—first as a representative of "Reorganized" Virginia and then of West Virginia—witnessed a significant evolution in his political views and allegiances. Initially hostile to abolitionism, he clashed with Republican lawmakers in 1861 and 1862 over such issues as war aims, the confiscation of rebel property, and the emancipation of slaves in Washington, D.C. As the bloody conflict between North and South continued, however, Willey recognized that the "peculiar institution" was doomed. Consequently, his ardent support for the Union led him inexorably into the Republican orbit. By 1864 he was endorsing Lincoln's reelection and calling for a constitutional amendment to destroy slavery throughout the United States.

After the Confederate collapse in 1865, Willey feared that southern sympathizers and erstwhile rebels might win control of West Virginia and perhaps attempt to reunite the state with the Old Dominion. Determined to forestall such a possibility, he endorsed efforts by West Virginia Republicans to disfranchise disloyal elements of the electorate. Although aligned with the conservative wing of the GOP in the U.S. Senate, he voted for the Civil Rights Act of 1866, the Reconstruction Acts, the Tenure of Office Act, the removal from office of President Andrew Johnson, and the Fourteenth and Fifteenth amendments. Nevertheless, Willey's opposition to the Freedmen's Bureau and to the Enforcement Acts of 1870–1871 attested to a lack of enthusiasm for important features of the congressional Reconstruction program. Republican policies, especially support for black suffrage, alienated many West Virginians, and the GOP lost control of the governorship and the state legislature in 1870. Effectually barred from reelection, Willey left the Senate at the end of his term in March 1871.

Returning to Morgantown, Willey resumed the practice of law. Still active in politics, he served in the state constitutional convention of 1872, defending black suffrage but also calling for congressional restoration of political rights for ex-Confederates. He supported Republican candidates at all levels and, in 1876, chaired the West Virginia delegation at the GOP National Convention. Although an abortive effort was made to return him to the U.S. Senate in 1887, he contented himself with a prolonged (1882–1897) stint as the clerk of Monongalia County. He died in Morgantown at the age of eighty-eight, having played a pivotal role in the establishment of the Mountaineer State.

• Willey's papers, including his diary, are at the West Virginia University Library. In addition to his many political speeches and articles in religious publications, he was the author of *A Sketch of the Life of Philip Doddridge* (1875) and "The Final Crisis in Our Struggle for Statehood," *West Virginia Historical Magazine Quarterly* 1 (1901): 20–24. His son, William Patrick Willey, provides information about him in *An Inside View of the Formation of the State of West Virginia* (1901), but the most thorough biographical treatment is Charles H. Ambler, *Waitman Thomas Willey: Orator, Churchman, Humanitarian* (1954). Richard Orr Curry provides additional insights into events and circumstances surrounding Willey's activities during the Civil War era in *A House Divided: A Study of Statehood Politics and the Copperhead Movement in West Virginia* (1964) and "A Reappraisal of Statehood Politics in West Virginia," *Journal of Southern History* 28 (1962): 403–21. See also Richard Lowe, *Republicans and Reconstruction in Virginia, 1856–70* (1991).

JAMES TICE MOORE

WILLIAMS, Alpheus Starkey (20 Sept. 1810–21 Dec. 1878), Union general, was born in Deep River, Connecticut, the son of Ezra Williams, a manufacturer who died when Williams was eight, and Hepzibah Starkey, who died when he was seventeen. Bequeathed the then considerable patrimony of $75,000, he attended Yale, from which he graduated in 1831, and then spent the next five years intermittently studying law while devoting most of his time to traveling in North America and Europe. In 1836, having nearly exhausted his legacy, he moved to Detroit, where he practiced law, engaged in banking and newspaper publishing, and served as probate judge of Wayne County (1840–1844), city recorder (1845–1848), postmaster (1849–1853), and as a member of the board of education (1856–1857). He also was active in volunteer military organizations, with the result that he became lieutenant colonel of the only Michigan regiment to serve in Mexico during the Mexican War. In the meantime, in 1839 he married Jane Larned Pierson, a young widow. Before her death in 1849, they had five children, two of whom died in infancy.

Upon the outbreak of the Civil War in April 1861, Williams, who had become president of the Michigan Military Board in 1859, was appointed brigadier general of state troops, in which capacity he conducted a "School of Instruction" at Fort Wayne for Michigan units and their officers. On 9 August 1861 President Abraham Lincoln commissioned him a brigadier general of U.S. volunteers, to rank from 17 May 1861. Assigned to Major General Nathaniel P. Banks's army, he commanded first a brigade then a division during Banks's unsuccessful campaign in the Shenandoah Valley of Virginia in the spring of 1862. His first display of an exceptional talent for combat leadership occurred on 9 August 1862 at the battle of Cedar Mountain, Virginia, during the Second Manassas campaign. There his division played the key role in blunting Thomas "Stonewall" Jackson's attack, in the process suffering and inflicting heavy casualties. Following this engagement Banks's forces became the XII Corps of the Army of the Potomac, and at the battles of South Mountain (14 Sept. 1862) and Antietam (17 Sept. 1862), Williams served as its acting commander, performing with notable skill on both fields, especially the latter, where his troops advanced farther than those of any other Federal unit. On 2 May 1863 he gained fresh laurels during the battle of Chancellorsville, when the XII Corps, thanks in large part to his initiative, prevented Stonewall Jackson's Confederates from fully exploiting their crushing flank attack upon the Union right, thereby saving the Army of the Potomac from potential disaster.

Williams's greatest and most crucial performance as a combat leader took place on 2–3 July 1863 at Gettysburg, where he again was acting commander of the XII Corps. On the afternoon of 2 July, having been ordered to bolster the Union left against a threatened Confederate breakthrough, he pulled his troops from their works on the Union right and successfully accomplished his mission. Then, on returning that night to his former sector, he discovered that a strong enemy force had occupied his empty trenches, putting itself in position to seize Culp's Hill, the loss of which would have led to Union retreat and probable defeat. Wisely refraining from a night attack, Williams waited until daylight, then mounted an assault that Edwin B. Coddington described as "well-conceived" and "efficiently executed," with the result that the Confederates were driven back and the danger to Culp's Hill eliminated.

Few northern generals contributed more to the Union victory at Gettysburg than Williams.

In September 1863 the XII Corps was transferred along with the XI Corps of the Army of the Potomac to Tennessee to reinforce the Army of the Cumberland after its defeat at Chickamauga (19–20 Sept. 1863). Once more commanding a division, Williams passed the ensuing winter and spring in the tedious but vital task of guarding the railroad between Nashville and Chattanooga. In April 1864 the XI and XII Corps were consolidated into what was designated the XX Corps, commanded by Major General Joseph Hooker, with Williams heading the First Division. During William T. Sherman's Atlanta campaign (May–Sept. 1864), Williams again distinguished himself, as his division repulsed Confederate flank attacks at Resaca on 14 and 15 May, helped beat back a frontal assault at Kolb's Farm on 22 June, and along with the rest of the XX Corps, held against a fierce onslaught at Peachtree Creek on 20 July. On orders from Sherman, who in spite of strong evidence to the contrary believed the enemy line was weak, Williams's division made a gallant but futile and costly frontal attack at New Hope Church on 25 May.

On 27 July, following Hooker's resignation out of personal anger against Sherman, Williams assumed acting command of the XX Corps, a post he held until superseded by Major General Henry W. Slocum a month later. Returning to his division, he led it into Atlanta on 2 September, after the Confederate evacuation. Williams concluded his Civil War career by participating in Sherman's "March to the Sea" from Atlanta to Savannah (Nov.–Dec. 1864) and through the Carolinas (Jan.–Apr. 1865). During these campaigns he again served for much of the time as acting commander of the XX Corps but did not have the opportunity to engage in any significant battle action. With the coming of peace, Williams for a while remained in the army as head of the Ouchita District of southern Arkansas and then early in 1866 resigned his commission to accept an appointment as U.S. minister to San Salvador, a post he held for the next three years. Returning to Detroit, in 1870 he ran unsuccessfully as a Democrat for the governorship of Michigan. In 1873 he married Martha Ann Conant Tillman; they had four children. In 1874 and again in 1876 he won election to the House of Representatives, where he was serving as chairman of the Committee on the District of Columbia at the time of his death there.

Known to his soldiers as "Old Pap," Williams was one of the best fighting generals in the Union army and deserved promotion to major general no later than 1862. Yet for a number of reasons, among them lack of political backing in Washington from Michigan's Republican senators, not until 12 January 1865 did Williams become a brevet major general, and that only because it would facilitate his role as a corps commander. While denied the rank due him, Williams unintentionally secured his lasting fame by the letters he sent to his daughters and various friends. Well written and frank, long extracts from these letters were published in 1959 and at once became a most valuable historical source that gives Williams a high status among all knowledgeable students of the Civil War.

• Williams's papers, which include diaries as well as letters, are in the Burton Historical Collection of the Detroit Public Library. Milo M. Quaife, ed., *From the Cannon's Mouth: The Civil War Letters of General Alpheus S. Williams* (1959), presents extracts from Williams's wartime letters and the basic facts about his pre- and postwar careers. The sole full-length biography of Williams is Jeffrey G. Charnley, "Neglected Honor: The Life of General A. S. Williams of Michigan (1810–1878)" (Ph.D. diss., Michigan State Univ., 1983), a work that, although it contains much useful information, is impaired by analytical shortcomings and an inadequate coverage of Williams's military operations during 1864–1865. For Williams's roles in the battles of Antietam, Chancellorsville, and Gettysburg and in the Atlanta campaign, see, respectively, Stephen W. Sears, *Landscape Turned Red: The Battle of Antietam* (1983); Ernest B. Furgurson, *Chancellorsville 1863: Souls of the Brave* (1992); Edwin B. Coddington, *The Gettysburg Campaign: A Study in Command* (1968); and Albert Castel, *Decision in the West: The Atlanta Campaign of 1864* (1992).

ALBERT CASTEL

WILLIAMS, Anna Wessels (17 Mar. 1863–20 Nov. 1954), public-health physician and bacteriologist, was born in Hackensack, New Jersey, the daughter of William Williams, a private-school teacher, and Jane Van Saun. She studied at home with her father and at the State Street Public School, where her father served as a trustee. Williams was excited by science when she first used a "wonderful microscope" at age twelve. She graduated from the New Jersey State Normal School in Trenton in 1883. She then taught for two years, earning money for medical school. Williams apparently was motivated to become a physician when her sister Millie almost died in childbirth (some sources suggest her sister suffered from diphtheria), and she vowed to discover an effective treatment. At first her religiously devout mother objected to her career goal, but Williams won her approval when she suggested that she would apply medicine to missionary work.

Williams received her medical degree from the Woman's Medical College of the New York Infirmary for Women and Children in 1891. An instructor in pathology at the New York Infirmary, she also worked in the children's clinic and "out-practice" and was an assistant to the department chairman of pathology and hygiene for several years. Next Williams undertook advanced studies in European universities in Vienna, Heidelberg, and Leipzig and interned at the Royal Frauen Klinik of Leopold in Dresden.

In 1894 Williams volunteered at the New York City Department of Health's diagnostic laboratory, the first municipal laboratory to apply bacteriology to public-health concerns. Her first publication resulted from her examination of bacteria in a box of cheese sent to the laboratory. She then pursued pioneering work to prevent and cure diphtheria, which had reached epidemic proportions among children in the United States. With laboratory director William Hallock

Park, Williams sought a more effective antitoxin. She isolated a pure culture, later named the Park-Williams No. 8 strain, from mild tonsillar diphtheria. She prepared a toxin and successfully immunized goats, sheep, dogs, and a cow. This strong strain was utilized to make a commercial toxin and was distributed free to poor patients in the United States and Great Britain.

Williams's antitoxin eradicated diphtheria almost completely. She published two articles with Park, who received the credit for discovering the bacillus; Williams claimed, "I alone was the discoverer, since I happened to find it while Dr. Park was on a vacation." She also investigated how slate pencils passed out in schools transmitted diphtheria when children placed them in their mouths.

Williams was appointed a full staff member in 1895. During the next decade she worked as an assistant bacteriologist, organizing staff members—many of them women—and insisting on teamwork to increase the laboratory's productivity and growth. She focused on securing preventative toxins for streptococcal and pneumococcal infections.

In 1896 Williams traveled to the Pasteur Institute in Paris, hoping to acquire a scarlet fever toxin. She was unsuccessful but returned home with a rabies virus culture. Williams had acted as an interpreter at the institute's hydrophobia (rabies) clinic and researched that disease. In New York she examined animals suspected to be rabid and attempted to expedite and improve rabies diagnosis. By 1898 she had produced a rabies vaccine that was widely used. Because many rabies patients died owing to the lengthy diagnosis period, Williams worked on a quicker test. She was the first researcher to understand that changes in brain cells revealed rabies. Williams cautiously waited to publish her results; an Italian doctor, Adelchi Negri, simultaneously made a similar discovery and quickly published it, resulting in the name "Negri bodies" for the diagnostic cells.

During the Spanish-American War Williams tried to develop a serum to combat pneumonia, using rabbits, horses, and sheep as subjects. When her brother fell ill, she temporarily resigned in 1899 and lived at Saranac Lake, where she attempted to continue her research. Discouraged, she wrote to Park to send her necessary equipment.

Returning to the New York Infirmary as a consulting pathologist, Williams in 1905 published a new method to detect Negri bodies, utilizing brain tissue stains. This test required only minutes instead of ten days and was used until it was improved in 1939. Subsequently Williams was appointed chair of the Committee on the Standard Methods for the Diagnosis of Rabies by the American Public Health Association in 1907.

Williams continued to collaborate with Park on problems in preventative medicine, fighting infectious diseases. They were coauthors of *Pathogenic Micro-organisms Including Bacteria and Protozoa: A Practical Manual for Students, Physicians and Health Officers* (1905), known as "Park and Williams" by readers; the book went through eleven editions by 1939. Williams sought better diagnosis and cure of venereal diseases, measles, smallpox, and poliomyelitis. Working with S. Josephine Baker, director of the Division of Child Hygiene, she revealed that impoverished city children's eye inflammations had been incorrectly diagnosed as trachoma.

Williams was president of the Woman's Medical Association in 1915, and during World War I she served on the Influenza Commission, conducting joint research to battle the 1918 influenza epidemic. At New York University she trained laboratory workers to detect meningococcal carriers in the military.

Williams and Park published *Who's Who among the Microbes* (1929), a pioneering work for general readers. As assistant director of the diagnostic laboratory beginning in 1905, Williams focused on studies of pathogenic bacteria that caused streptococcal infections. She developed several toxins during her career and published a monumental tome, *Streptococci in Relation to Man in Health and Disease* (1932). In 1932 she was the first woman elected as chair of the American Public Health Association's Laboratory Section.

Williams was forced to retire because of age in 1934. Two years later the New York Women's Medical Society celebrated her service to the community and female professionals. Government employment enabled Williams to achieve success as a female scientist, and she insisted that "without the aid of my associates, little of this work could have been accomplished." She died in Westwood, New Jersey.

• Williams's papers are at the Schlesinger Library, Radcliffe College, Cambridge, Mass. For biographical sketches, see "Dr. Anna W. Williams," *Medical Woman's Journal* 43 (June 1936): 160; and Esther Pohl Lovejoy, *Women Doctors of the World* (1957). Her most important work is described in David A. Blancher, "Workshops of the Bacteriological Revolution: A History of the Laboratories of the New York City Department of Health, 1892–1912" (Ph.D. diss., City University of New York, 1979). Williams is also mentioned in Wade W. Oliver, *The Man Who Lived for Tomorrow: A Biography of William Hallock Park, M.D.* (1941); and Elizabeth D. Robinton, "A Tribute to Women Leaders in the Laboratory Section of the American Public Health Association," *American Journal of Public Health* 64 (Oct. 1974): 1006–7.

ELIZABETH D. SCHAFER

WILLIAMS, Aubrey Willis (23 Aug. 1890–3 Mar. 1965), social worker and civil rights advocate, was born in Springville, Alabama, the son of Charles Evans Williams, a blacksmith, and Eva Taylor. Williams's paternal grandfather voluntarily freed his slaves in 1855, and the Civil War completed the ruin of the once-affluent family. When Aubrey was six months old, the Williamses moved to Birmingham but remained so poor that he and his six siblings had to quit school early and go to work. Aubrey left school at the age of nine, when he became first a delivery boy and then a department store clerk. He attended night classes when he could. A devout Presbyterian, like his mother, the young sales clerk was influenced by a

Presbyterian evangelist who preached to Birmingham's exploited mill hands and convict laborers. Williams often accompanied the preacher on his rounds and began teaching literacy classes for workers.

When he was twenty-one, Williams enrolled at Maryville College in Maryville, Tennessee, where he remained for five years. He intended to study for the ministry, but his religious faith had begun to wane, while his devotion to the Social Gospel waxed. In 1916 Williams transferred to the University of Cincinnati; however, because he was short of money and eager to get into the war, he left for Europe in 1917. He briefly manned a YMCA recreation center in Paris and then joined the French Foreign Legion. When the American army reached France in 1918, Williams switched to the Fifth Field Artillery. In 1919 he returned to the University of Cincinnati. Further erosion of his faith in a personal God, influence of his social science professors, and a part-time job with the Community Service Association cemented his decision to become a social worker rather than a clergyman. In 1920 Williams received his bachelor's degree and married Anita Schreck, a physical education teacher, with whom he had four children.

Williams moved to Madison in 1922 to become the executive secretary of the Wisconsin Conference of Social Work, a position he held for a decade. Under Williams's leadership, the conference convinced the state to enact advanced public assistance programs. During his Madison years, Williams displayed traits that became the hallmarks of his career: dedication to those at the bottom of the socioeconomic ladder, impatience with bureaucratic red tape, decisiveness, and an outspokenness that sometimes got him in political trouble.

With the nation reeling from the Great Depression, the Public Welfare Association, another private social service agency, employed Williams in 1932 as midwestern and southern field consultant for the Reconstruction Finance Corporation. Williams's job was to persuade state governors to apply for federal loans for unemployment relief, to help them set up state administrations to distribute the money, and to review the functioning of the organizations once in place. During 1932–1933, Williams almost single-handedly created relief administrations in Mississippi, Texas, and several other states.

In March 1933 Franklin D. Roosevelt greatly expanded the loans and added outright grants to the states under the newly created Federal Emergency Relief Administration (FERA), headed by social worker Harry Hopkins. Hopkins, who had heard of Williams's accomplishments, took him on first as an FERA field representative and soon as deputy administrator in Washington, D.C. Despite strains in their relationship—Hopkins was embarrassed by Williams's tendency to speak his mind regardless of consequences, and Williams disapproved of Hopkins's growing political ambitions—the pair became close friends and collaborators. Both passionate New Dealers and defenders of the underdog, they planned, sold Roosevelt on, and administered the Civil Works Administration (CWA), employing four million people through the winter of 1933–1934. Bitterly disappointed when the president terminated the program in April, they began pleading for and planning a more long-lasting replacement. In 1935 Roosevelt signed the $4.8 billion Emergency Work and Relief appropriation and established the Works Progress Administration (WPA), again with Hopkins at the helm and Williams as deputy. In addition, Williams took responsibility for the National Youth Administration (NYA), a division of the WPA.

Much of the day-to-day running of the massive federal jobs program fell to Williams, especially during Hopkins's illnesses; through his NYA work, Williams became close friends with Eleanor Roosevelt. Williams made another lasting friend out of his Texas NYA administrator, Lyndon B. Johnson.

Between 1935 and its demise in 1943, the NYA made it possible for over two million high school and college students to complete their education by paying them for in-school, part-time work. It provided another 2.5 million youths with vocational training and out-of-school employment. By 1939 Williams increasingly emphasized preparing young men and women for high-paying jobs in the booming defense industry. Williams, committed to equal opportunity, urged his state directors to place African Americans on projects and appointed the black educator Mary McLeod Bethune to the NYA staff to direct a special grant program for black students. Senator Burton Wheeler of Montana regarded the NYA as "the most constructive" of the New Deal relief programs, and a black newspaper editor wrote that its treatment of black Americans had been the fairest of any federal agency. Nevertheless, by 1938 Williams had become one of the New Deal's most controversial figures, anathema to conservatives, Republicans, and most southern Democrats.

His willingness to recognize and speak to the radical organizations to which some WPA and NYA workers belonged, such as the Workers Alliance and the American Youth Congress, brought charges that Williams encouraged Communists. The *New York Times* accused him of trying to "introduce a sort of socialism through the back door" because he maintained that Americans had "a right to work" and that "society as a whole has the responsibility of providing useful work at decent pay." Never a Marxist, Williams attributed his commitment to social justice to the teachings of Jesus, Thomas Jefferson, and Abraham Lincoln.

Because Williams had become so controversial, Roosevelt did not elevate him to head the WPA when Hopkins became secretary of commerce in December 1938. Instead, the president appointed the nonpolitical colonel F. C. Harrington, separated the NYA from the WPA, and left Williams in charge of only the former. Williams's reputed radicalism also entered into Congress's decision to terminate the NYA in 1943, despite the army's request that it continue training skilled defense workers. In 1945 the Senate refused to confirm Williams as director of the Rural Electrification Administration after his enemies, including Mississippi's senator Theodore Bilbo, again accused him of having communist sympathies and of influencing Roosevelt to establish the Fair Employment Practices Committee.

Williams returned to Alabama, purchased a journal called the *Southern Farmer*, later *Southern Farm and Home*, and attempted through it to promote New Deal liberalism and racial integration in the South. In 1948 he also became president of the Southern Conference Education Fund (SCEF), a small but militant civil rights group. Mississippi senator James Eastland subpoenaed Williams and other leaders of the SCEF to appear before the Senate Internal Security Subcommittee's 1954 hearings in New Orleans. Denouncing them as Communists, Eastland demanded the names of their contributors, which they refused to divulge. Fortunately, Williams's old friend, Senator Lyndon Johnson, persuaded the committee to cancel further hearings and quash its contempt citations.

This new round of charges against Williams, as well as his support for the 1955 Montgomery bus boycott led by Martin Luther King, Jr., resulted in a rapid decline in advertisers and subscribers for his farm journal, which ceased publication in 1959. Suffering from stomach cancer, Williams moved back to Washington, D.C., in 1963. There, he marched in the August civil rights demonstration and listened to King proclaim "I Have a Dream." It was a dream Williams had shared and worked for most of his life. Williams died shortly thereafter in his Washington home.

• The Aubrey Williams Papers are in the Franklin D. Roosevelt Library in Hyde Park, N.Y. These include an unpublished autobiography, "A Southern Rebel"; his private correspondence; and materials pertaining to the FERA, CWA, WPA, NYA, and SCEF. The records of the WPA and NYA in the National Archives in Washington, D.C., also give insights into his work in those agencies. Williams's views are presented in his writings, including "Twelve Million Unemployed: What Can Be Done?" *New York Times Magazine*, 27 Mar. 1938, and *Work, Wages, and Education* (1940). John Salmond, *A Southern Rebel: The Life and Times of Aubrey Willis Williams, 1890–1965* (1983), is an excellent, sympathetic biography. For further biographical information on Williams and a sampling of the conservative attacks against him, see U.S. Congress, Senate Committee on Agriculture and Forestry, *Hearings on the Nomination of Aubrey W. Williams to Be Administrator, Rural Electrification Administration*, 79th Cong., 1st sess., 1945; and U.S. Congress, Senate Subcommittee on Internal Security, *Hearings on Subversive Influence in the Southern Conference Educational Fund, Inc.*, 83d Cong., 2d sess., 1955. See also Richard A. Reiman, *The New Deal and American Youth: Ideas and Ideals in a Depression Decade* (1992). An obituary is in the *New York Times*, 5 Mar. 1965.

BARBARA BLUMBERG

WILLIAMS, Ben Ames (7 Mar. 1889–4 Feb. 1953), short-story writer and novelist, was born in Macon, Mississippi, the son of Daniel Webster Williams, a newspaper owner and editor, Ohio state senator, and U.S. consul, and Sarah Marshall Ames. His family moved to Jackson, Ohio, when Williams was a few months old, and, when he was fifteen, to Massachusetts, where he attended the Allen School in West Newton for a year. In 1905 he went to Cardiff, Wales, where his father had been appointed U.S. consul, and in the fall of the next year returned to the United States to enter Dartmouth College in New Hampshire.

During his teens Williams had worked on his father's newspaper, the *Jackson Standard Journal*, occasionally reporting local news, and after his graduation from Dartmouth with a B.A. in 1910 he took a job as a reporter for the *Boston American*. He stayed with it for four years, during which time he applied himself diligently to learning the craft of fiction. In 1912 he married Florence Trafton Talpey, with whom he had three children. His literary career was frustratingly slow in starting; he later calculated that he had written over eighty stories before he sold "The Wings of Lias" to *Smith's Magazine* in 1915. Further sales came gradually, and for the next two years he received more rejection slips than checks; but in time he mastered the formulas of popular adventure, mystery, and romantic fiction and began to publish regularly in pulp journals such as *All-Story Weekly, American Boy*, and *Popular Magazine*.

In 1916 Williams felt confident enough to resign from his newspaper job and become a freelance writer. Financial success came with the sale of a four-part serial, "The Mate of Susie Oakes," to the *Saturday Evening Post* in 1917. During the next two decades he published some 135 stories and 35 serials in the *Saturday Evening Post*, then America's highest-paying magazine for fiction, and he also appeared frequently in popular periodicals such as *Collier's, Liberty, Cosmopolitan, Redbook*, and *Blue Book*. By 1919 he was one of the most prolific and successful short-story writers in the country. That year he made 20 magazine sales, including 4 stories and an 8-part serial to the *Post*, and 2 of his tales were reprinted in anthologies. In 1926 the *Post* alone published 21 of Williams's pieces, and numerous others appeared elsewhere. About 125 of his stories were set in rural Maine, in the fictitious town of Fraternity, and Williams came to be identified with that state, where he and his family spent their summers. First introduced in the *Post* in 1919, his Maine stories were collected into a volume as *Fraternity Village* in 1949. Though praised for their psychological insight, accurate use of colloquial speech, and detailed descriptions of locale, Williams's short stories, of which he published nearly 500 in his lifetime, were regarded by many critics as weakly plotted, often sacrificing pace and tension for detailed characterization and local color.

Williams's serials began appearing as novels with *All the Brothers Were Valiant* (1919), a pirate tale described by the *New York Times* as "a yarn of adventure at sea that is as fresh and crisp, as clear and bright as a water color picture." That same year he published *Sea Bride*, another nautical romance that was compared with the work of Joseph Conrad. He published twelve reworked serials and collections of short stories before his first independently written novel, *Splendor*, which appeared in 1927. Placed in Boston in the late nineteenth and early twentieth centuries, this narrative of the life of a journalist was the first of many historical novels to come from his pen. In the 1940s Williams felt that he had "lost the touch" for short stories, whose constraints of length had begun to irk him, and he turned his attention almost exclusively to longer fiction.

Among Williams's historical novels, the best received was *House Divided* (1947), a massive tome of 1,514 pages that took him nearly twenty years to research and more than four to write. Set in the Civil War, in which his mother's uncle, James Longstreet, had served as a Confederate general, it detailed the effects of the conflict on the civilian populace. The settings of others included the Fiji Islands in the 1860s (*The Strumpet Sea* [1938]), Nantucket during the War of 1812 (*Thread of Scarlet* [1939]), the American Revolution (*Come Spring* [1940]), nineteenth-century Maine (*The Strange Woman* [1941]), the American labor movement in Ohio in the 1890s (*Owen Glen* [1950]), and New Orleans during the Reconstruction period, 1865–1874 (*Unconquered* [1953]). Perhaps his most popular novel was *Leave Her to Heaven* (1944), a grim account of a psychopathically possessive woman. Although described in the *New York Times Book Review* (11 Jan. 1944) as "unconvincing," "overlong," and "incredibly contrived," with characters "made, not born" and "a plot as bony as a shad," and by the *Springfield* (Mass.) *Republican* (11 June 1944) as "a dull book and a bad book," it remained on the bestseller list for months, appeared in many languages, and was made into a successful movie.

Williams was a modest man who never had any pretensions about his literary status but was proud of being a successful storyteller. "I had early proof that I possessed no inborn ability as a writer," he admitted to Robert van Gelder in 1943, and he explained that he had put off writing novels for so long because he doubted that he "could write anything so impressive as a book" (p. 20). The leisurely tempo and sketchy plots of his short stories went out of style, but many of his thirty-five novels remained long in print and continued to be enjoyed for their positive outlook, sympathetic understanding of the human personality, and energetic style. Describing himself in *Collier's* in 1949 as "a large, calm man who likes to write, and next to do anything out of doors so long as it has a purpose," he enjoyed riding and hunting and was competing in a curling match in Brookline, Massachusetts, when he suffered a heart attack and died.

• Letters, journals, and manuscripts of Williams are in the Colby College Library in Waterville, Maine; the Dartmouth College Library; and the Ohioana Library Association in Columbus. Biographical and critical material is in Florence Talpey Williams, "About Ben Ames Williams," *Colby Library Quarterly* 6 (Sept. 1963): 263–77; Joseph B. Yokelson, "Ben Ames Williams: Pastoral Moralist," *Colby Library Quarterly* 6 (Sept. 1963): 278–92; Richard Cary, "Ben Ames Williams and Robert H. Davis: The Seedling in the Sun," *Colby Library Quarterly* 6 (Sept. 1963): 302–27; Ben Ames Williams, Jr., "House United," *Colby Library Quarterly* 10 (Dec. 1973): 179–89; and Richard Cary, "Ben Ames Williams and the *Saturday Evening Post*," *Colby Library Quarterly* 10 (Dec. 1973): 190–222. Useful information is also included in Robert van Gelder, "An Interview with Mr. Ben Ames Williams," *New York Times Book Review*, 14 Feb. 1943, pp. 19–20, and *Writers and Writing* (1946); Harry R. Warfel, *American Novelists of Today* (1951); William Coyle, ed., *Ohio Authors and Their Books* (1962). See also *Collier's*, 28 May 1949, p. 10. An obituary is in the *New York Times*, 5 Feb. 1953.

DENNIS WEPMAN

WILLIAMS, Bert (12 Nov. 1874–4 Mar. 1922), and **George Walker** (1873–6 Jan. 1911), stage entertainers, were born, respectively, Egbert Austin Williams in Nassau, the Bahamas, and George Williams Walker in Lawrence, Kansas. Williams was the son of Frederick Williams, Jr., a waiter, and Julia Monceur. Walker was the son of "Nash" Walker, a policeman; his mother's name is unknown. Williams moved with his family to Riverside, California, in 1885 and attended Riverside High School. Walker began performing "darkey" material for traveling medicine shows during his boyhood and left Kansas with Dr. Waite's medicine show. In 1893 the two met in San Francisco, where they first worked together in Martin and Selig's Minstrels.

To compete in the crowded field of mostly white blackface performers, "Walker and Williams," as they were originally known, subtitled their act "The Two Real Coons." Walker developed a fast-talking, city hustler persona, straight man to Williams's slow-witted, woeful bumbler. Williams, who was light-skinned, used blackface makeup on stage, noting that "it was not until I was able to see myself as another person that my sense of humor developed." An unlikely engagement in the unsuccessful Victor Herbert operetta *The Gold Bug* brought Williams and Walker to New York in 1896, but the duo won critical acclaim and rose quickly through the ranks of vaudeville, eventually playing Koster and Bial's famed New York theater. During this run they added a sensational cakewalk dance finale to the act, cinching popular success. Walker performed exceptionally graceful and complex dance variations, while Williams clowned through an inept parody of Walker's steps. Aida Reed Overton, who later become a noteworthy dancer and choreographer in her own right, was hired as Walker's cakewalk partner in 1897 and became his wife in 1899. They had no children. The act brought the cakewalk to the height of its popularity, and Williams and Walker subsequently toured the eastern seaboard and performed a week at the Empire Theatre in London in April 1897.

Vaudeville typically used stereotyped ethnic characterizations as humor, and Williams and Walker developed a "coon" act without peer in the industry. For the 1898 season, the African-American composer Will Marion Cook and the noted poet Paul Laurence Dunbar created *Senegambian Carnival* for the duo, the first in a series of entertainments featuring African Americans that eventually played New York. *A Lucky Coon* (1898), *The Policy Players* (1899), and *Sons of Ham* (1900) were basically vaudeville acts connected by Williams and Walker's patter. In 1901 they began recording their ragtime stage hits for the Victor label. Their popularity spread, and the 18 February 1903 Broadway premiere of *In Dahomey* was considered the first fully realized musical comedy performed by an all-black company.

Williams and Walker led the *In Dahomey* cast of fifty as Shylock Homestead and Rareback Pinkerton, two confidence men out to defraud a party of would-be African colonizers. Its three acts included a number of dances, vocal choruses, specialty acts, and a grand cakewalk sequence. Critics cited Williams's performance of "I'm a Jonah Man," a hard-luck song by Alex Rogers, as a high point of the hit show. *In Dahomey* toured England and Scotland, with a command performance at Buckingham Palace arranged for the ninth birthday of King Edward VII's grandson David. The cakewalk became the rage of fashionable English society, and company members worked as private dance instructors both abroad and when they returned home.

Williams composed more than seventy songs in his lifetime. "Nobody," the most famous of these, was introduced to the popular stage in 1905:

> When life seems full of clouds and rain,
> And I am filled with naught but pain,
> Who soothes my thumping, bumping brain?
> Nobody!

The sense of pathos lurking behind Williams's plaintive delivery was not lost on his audience. Walker gained fame performing boastful, danceable struts, such as the 1906 "It's Hard to Find a King Like Me" and his signature song, "Bon Bon Buddie, the Chocolate Drop," introduced in 1907. During this period Williams and Walker signed their substantial music publishing rights with the black-owned Attucks Music Publishing Company.

Walker, who was more business-minded than Williams, controlled production details of the 1906 *Abyssinia* and the 1907 *Bandanna Land*. Walker demanded that these "all-Negro" productions play only in first-class theaters. His hard business tactics worked, and Williams and Walker played several theaters that had previously barred black performers. In 1908, at the height of their success, the duo were founding members of The Frogs, a charitable and social organization of black theatrical celebrities. Other members included composers Bob Cole and J. Rosamond Johnson, bandleader James Reese Europe, and writer/directors Alex Rogers and Jesse Shipp.

During the tour of *Bandanna Land*, Walker succumbed to general paresis, an advanced stage of syphilis. He retired from the stage in February 1909. Aida Walker took over his songs and dances, and the book scenes were rewritten for Williams to play alone. Walker died in Islip, New York.

Williams continued doing blackface and attempted to produce the 1909 *Mr. Lode of Koal* without Walker. His attention to business details languished, and the show failed. Williams's performances, however, received significant critical praise, and he gained stature as "an artist of pantomime" and "a comic genius." In 1910 he joined Florenz Ziegfeld's *Follies*. He told the *New York Age* (1 Dec. 1910) that "the colored show business—that is colored musical shows—is at the low ebb just now. I reached the conclusion last spring that I could best represent my race by doing pioneer work. It was far better to have joined a large white show than to have starred in a colored show, considering conditions."

Williams was aware of the potential for racial backlash from his white audience and insisted on a contract clause stating that he would at no time appear on stage with any of the scantily clad women in the *Follies* chorus. His celebrity advanced, and he became the star attraction of the *Follies* for some eight seasons, leaving the show twice, in 1913 and 1918, to spend time with his family and to headline in vaudeville. His overwhelming success prompted educator Booker T. Washington to quip, "Bert Williams has done more for the race than I have. He has smiled his way into people's hearts. I have been obliged to fight my way."

An Actor's Equity strike troubled Ziegfeld's 1919 edition of the *Follies*, and Williams, who had never been asked or allowed to join the union because of his African ancestry, left the show. In 1920 he and Eddie Cantor headlined Rufus and George Lemaire's short-lived *Broadway Brevities*. In 1921 the Shuberts financed a musical, *Under the Bamboo Tree*, to star Williams with an otherwise all-white cast. The show opened in Cincinnati, Ohio, but in February 1922 Williams succumbed to pneumonia, complicated by heart problems, and died the next month in New York City. In 1900 he had married Charlotte Louise Johnson; they had no children.

Although Williams's stage career solidified the stereotype of the "shiftless darkey," his unique talent at pantomime and the hard work he put into it was indisputable. In his famous poker game sketch, filmed in the 1916 short *A Natural Born Gambler*, Williams enacted a four-handed imaginary game without benefit of props or partners. His cache of comic stories, popularized in his solo vaudeville and Ziegfeld *Follies* appearances, were drawn largely from African-American folk humor, which Williams and Alex Rogers duly noted and collected for their shows. Williams collected an extensive library and wrote frequently for the black press and theatrical publications.

The commercial success of Williams and Walker proved that large audiences would pay to see black performers. Tall and light-skinned Williams, in blackface and ill-fitting tatters, contrasted perfectly with short, dark-skinned, dandyish Walker. Their cakewalks revived widespread interest in African-American dance styles. Their successful business operations, responsible for a "$2,300 a week" payroll in 1908, encouraged black participation in mainstream show business. The *Chicago Defender* (11 Mar. 1922) called them "the greatest Negro team of actors who ever lived and the most popular pair of comedy stars America has produced."

• For a sample of Williams's writing, see "Keeping up with the New Laughs," *Theatre Magazine*, June 1919, pp. 346–48. Williams and Walker are treated in several histories of Harlem and black Broadway with dubious accuracy. Nevertheless, see especially James Weldon Johnson, *Black Manhattan* (1930); Henry T. Sampson, *Blacks in Blackface: A Source Book on Early Black Musical Shows* (1980); and Allen Woll, *Black Musical Theatre—From Coontown to Dreamgirls* (1989). Eric Ledell Smith, *Bert Williams: A Biography of the Pioneer Black Comedian* (1992), is factually precise and includes an excellent annotated bibliography and an appendix of Williams's musical compositions. Mabel Rowland, *Bert Williams: Son of Laughter* (1923), includes tributes from several of Williams's contemporaries as well as a sampling of his comic tales, and Ann Charters, *Nobody: The Story of Bert Williams* (1970), contains an accurate discography. Obituaries for Walker and Williams are in the *New York Times*, 8 Jan. 1911 and 5 Mar. 1922, respectively.

THOMAS F. DEFRANTZ

WILLIAMS, Big Joe (16 Oct. 1903–17 Dec. 1982), blues musician, was born Joe Lee Williams in Crawford, Mississippi, the son of John Williams, a tenant farmer and sawmill hand, and Cora Lee Logan. Joe's mother, who was in her early teens, placed the youngster in the care of her father, Bert Logan, a musician who played accordion and guitar. Inspired by his grandfather and by a cousin, Jesse Logan, who also played guitar, Joe showed an early aptitude for the local vernacular music. He won a dance contest at age nine, crafted a one-string guitar called a "diddley bow," carved a cane fife, or "fice," as it was known locally, and often beat rhythm on a bucket for musicians at his grandfather's Saturday night suppers.

After an argument with his stepfather, an incident he later sang about in "Stepfather Blues," Williams decided to strike out on his own. Although it is not clear when this happened, Williams recalled decades later that he became "a walking musician, all down through that Delta and all through the hills—Vicksburg, Leland, Clarksdale, oh boy, all over there." Williams continued to lead an itinerant existence for the rest of his life.

His early travels, during the 1920s, took him throughout the South. Around 1930 he settled briefly in St. Louis, but by 1932 or 1933 he was traveling the South again, this time with a protégé, David "Honeyboy" Edwards. Throughout the depression, he relied on his rural audiences to meet his meager needs, traveling as a hobo and performing as "Poor Joe" or "Big Joe."

Williams made his first documented recordings after landing in St. Louis in the mid-1930s. At the time, he was playing at clubs, rent parties, and on the city's streetcars, working with well-known bluesmen such as St. Louis Jimmy Oden, Peetie Wheatstraw, J. D. Short (his cousin), and Charley Jordan. Through these contacts, Williams met Chicago-based music publisher Lester Melrose, who signed him to RCA Victor Record Company's subsidiary label Bluebird. On 25 February 1935 Williams went to Chicago for his first session. Six songs were issued, including "49 Highway Blues," "Stepfather Blues," and "Somebody's Been Borrowing That Stuff," with St. Louis guitarist Henry Townsend sitting in on the latter two.

That same year Williams returned to Chicago and, on Halloween, did a second session for Bluebird, accompanied by Townsend, one-string fiddle player Chasey Collins, and a washboard player called Kokomo. One of the four issued sides, "Baby, Please Don't Go," eventually became a blues standard.

On 5 May 1937 in Aurora, Illinois, Williams recorded with Robert Lee McCoy, better known as Robert Nighthawk, and harmonica virtuoso Sonny Boy Williamson, a trio often cited as the forerunner of the Chicago blues band sound of the late 1940s and 1950s. In Chicago on 27 March 1941 Williams had another Bluebird session, working with William Mitchell, who did a vocal imitation of a string bass. The session yielded another popular recording, "Crawling King Snake." After a final 1945 session, Williams ended his successful ten-year relationship with Bluebird.

Beginning in 1957 Williams was launched on a second career during which he was promoted as a folk blues artist. He recorded on Robert G. Koester's Delmar (now Delmark) label, collaborated with pianist Erwin Helfer on several singles released on Collector Jen, and in 1958 recorded for Delmar again. In 1959 and 1960, now married to Mary (maiden name and date of marriage unknown) and staying at what recording executive Chris Strachwitz described as a "dreadful flea-bag hotel" in Oakland, California, Williams made his LP debut on the World-Pacific album "Down South Summit Meeting" recorded with harmonica player Sonny Terry and guitarists Brownie McGhee and Lightnin' Hopkins. He also recorded for the Arhoolie label, owned by Strachwitz. His wife died in 1961; the number of their children, if any, is unknown.

Williams was among the first artists to reach out to new audiences during the so-called "blues revival." Harmonica player Charlie Musselwhite, a one-time Williams roommate, said Williams helped spark the revival that occurred in Chicago's North Wells Street nightclub district in the early 1960s:

> There was a little bar down the street called Big John's. They asked Joe to come down and play. They thought Joe was kind of like a folk singer. They didn't know what they were getting into. . . . Joe asked me to play with him and the place was packed. The crowd loved it. So they started booking other blues bands and then other clubs started having blues. (personal interview, 9 June 1990)

In New York Williams added to his folk blues credentials by playing with young Bob Dylan, jamming as Big and Little Joe. Through the 1960s and 1970s Williams recorded for various small independent labels and toured extensively in the United States and

Europe. In 1976 he performed at the Bicentennial Festival of American Folklife in Washington, D.C.

As failing health curtailed his travels, he returned home to Crawford, Mississippi. He died in Macon, Georgia, and ten years later was inducted into the Blues Foundation's Hall of Fame in Memphis, Tennessee.

Williams's music was distinctive partly because he played in open G, or Spanish, tuning, and partly because he played a guitar that he had customized by adding three strings, doubling the first, second, and fourth strings. He developed the most percussive guitar sound of any recording artist of his time—comparable to Charlie Patton, whom he claimed to have bested in a music contest once. With his gruff voice and intense, declamatory vocal style, Williams epitomized the country bluesman. Moreover, he made his mark on every major phase of blues history—in the rural South in the early years of country blues, in St. Louis when it was a blues center, in Chicago at the beginning of the golden years of Chicago blues, and in the blues revival. Despite a talent for fantastic invention—his claim, for example, that he was invisible on certain days—Williams became a valued oral historian of the blues during the last twenty years of his life.

• For historical details and interview materials, see Margaret McKee and Fred Chisenhall, *Beale Black and Blue: Life and Music on Black America's Main Street* (1981) and Samuel Charters, *The Legacy of the Blues* (1977). Michael Bloomfield gives a curious account of Williams during the folk revival in *Me and Big Joe* (1980).

For reprints of record notes, see Paul Oliver, *Blues Off the Record: Thirty Years of Blues Commentary* (1984). For discographical information, see Robert M. W. Dixon and John Godrich, *Blues and Gospel Records: 1902–1943* (1982); Mike Leadbitter and Neil Slaven, *Blues Records 1943–1970*, vol. 2 (1994); and *The Blackwell Guide to Blues Records*, ed. Paul Oliver (1989). For samplings of his music from different periods, try *Big Joe Williams: Early Recordings, 1935 to 1941*, Mamlish S3810; *Piney Woods Blues*, Delmark, DL-602; *Big Joe Williams: Nine-String Guitar Wizard*, Collectables, COL 5534; and *Big Joe Williams: Back to the Country*, Testament, TCD 5013. An obituary is in *Living Blues* 57 (Autumn 1983).

BILL MCCULLOCH
BARRY LEE PEARSON

WILLIAMS, Carbine (1901?–8 Jan. 1975), weapons inventor, was born David Marshall Williams in Godwin, North Carolina, the son of James Claud Williams and Laura Kornegay, farmers. He left school after the eighth grade and worked at a blacksmith's shop, spending his spare time making wooden guns. His father, unhappy that he had quit school so early, agreed to allow him to lie about his age and enter the U.S. Navy at age sixteen. When naval life did not suit him, his father managed to arrange an honorable discharge because of his age but promptly enrolled him at Blackstone Military Academy in Virginia in 1917. Although he worked hard and flourished at first under the daily military routine, he was expelled after one semester. When he returned home, he married Margaret Isobel Cook in August 1918; they had one son. He then took a job with the Atlantic Coast Line Railroad.

Williams soon dropped his railroad job to make bootleg whiskey, a financially rewarding occupation in the neighborhood of Fort Bragg. For several years he operated up to eight stills within three miles of his home without much interference from local law enforcement authorities. Then, on 21 July 1921, deputies raided one of his sites. In the ensuing gun battle, one deputy was shot to death and a warrant was issued for Williams's arrest. He hid in the woods for a night, then turned himself in to be tried for first degree murder. A hung jury prevented a death sentence and Williams pleaded guilty to second-degree murder. He was sentenced to thirty years in prison.

While incarcerated, Williams began sketching ideas for new rifles. He was placed in charge of the blacksmith shop and began, with the warden's permission, to build models based on his designs using junked auto parts. In an era when weapons were manufactured with precision machine tools, he constructed his own tools and did all the work by hand. He invented a new style of automatic rifle, faster than the Browning machine gun, that attracted media attention. His accomplishments and the interest exhibited by the military and weapons manufacturers aided his parole petition. On 29 September 1929 he was granted a full pardon. He returned to Godwin to set up his workshop.

By the time Williams left prison, he had built six guns featuring his two major innovations—the short-stroke and the moving-chamber principles. His short-stroke feature increased the firepower of a weapon by reducing the length of the part of the barrel that opened the breech mechanism. Previously the whole barrel moved backward several inches, but in Williams's guns a short sleeve was sufficient to work the breech mechanism. His moving chamber "floated" in the barrel and recoiled with the cartridge case when a shot was fired, thus providing enough power to work the bolt and the loading mechanism. This innovation obtained intense operating energy from a small cartridge and permitted the use of .22 caliber ammunition in machine guns. In 1932 Williams demonstrated his first new gun, a .35 caliber rifle, to the military. The Ordnance Department recognized the revolutionary character of his inventions and awarded him his first government contract that year. In 1940 he became famous almost overnight for the invention of the M-1 carbine, the lightweight .30 caliber semiautomatic rifle that replaced the Browning. Williams constructed the pilot model of this weapon in just thirteen days. The M-1 was used extensively in World War II and afterwards, and more than 8 million of them were produced. Historically, a carbine was a light rifle used by cavalry. In World War II the lightweight, long-range M-1 carbine replaced the automatic pistol as a defensive weapon for soldiers who manned large machine guns, trench mortars, and antitank guns. The M-1 also served an important role in training. Williams invented many other weapons, including the Colt .22 service ace pistol and the Winchester .22 caliber machine gun. In total he held over sixty patents.

During his career, Williams worked for the Winchester Arms Company, Colt Patent Firearms, and the Remington Arms Company. He developed weapons both for the military and for private gun enthusiasts. In 1941 Winchester convinced him to move to Connecticut to work in their plant. Williams could not always verbally express his technical ideas clearly, so the company hoped that close proximity to their engineers would facilitate product development. His tenure at the plant did nothing to accustom him to a corporate work schedule and rules, so he returned home and reverted to working independently. At other times during his career, however, he worked for periods of up to a year at other manufacturers, including Colt's Hartford, Connecticut, plant and the Springfield Armory.

After World War II Williams enjoyed a brief period as a public figure. In 1951 several popular magazines featured articles describing his colorful life, including one written by the prison warden who had given him permission to build gun models. The following year, MGM made a motion picture about his career titled *Carbine Williams*, starring James Stewart. After the premiere in Fayetteville, North Carolina, Williams toured the country to promote the film. His story was also told in comic book form. During this heady time, he appeared on the television program "We the People" and was interviewed numerous times on the radio.

Whether or not Williams was adequately compensated for his inventions is a matter of debate. Contrary to widespread contemporary belief that Williams earned a royalty for every M-1 carbine produced, his government contracts stipulated that royalty payments ceased after a specified number of guns had been manufactured. In 1948 the Internal Revenue Service sued him for back taxes in what became an important case in the legal distinction between ordinary income and capital gain. Williams won the case, although that legal decision did not settle the entire dispute in the eyes of the Treasury Department. The movie contract with MGM was lucrative, but Williams reputedly spent most of these earnings on high living on the West Coast. In short, although he earned and expended a great deal of money during his eventful life, he did not derive as much financial reward as other inventors with more business acumen.

After the excitement of Hollywood wore off, Williams returned to Godwin. For years he hosted hundreds of school children on visits to his famous shop. He also donated his workshop to the North Carolina State Department of Archives and oversaw its removal and installation in the North Carolina Museum of History. The resulting exhibit was dedicated in June 1971. Williams died in Raleigh, North Carolina.

• The book-length biography by Ross E. Beard, Jr., *Carbine: The Story of David Marshall Williams* (1977), excerpts and reproduces in facsimile many original documents relating to Williams's life and work. Articles written about Williams during his lifetime include H. T. Peoples, "Most Unforgettable Character I've Met," *Reader's Digest* 58, Mar. 1951, pp. 6–10; and J. Kobler, "Story of Carbine Williams," *Collier's* 127, 3 Mar. 1951, pp. 22–23. See also *Fawcett Movie Comics*, no. 19, Oct. 1952. Obituaries are in the *New York Times*, 9 Jan. 1975; *Newsweek*, 20 Jan. 1975; and *Time*, 20 Jan. 1975.

HELEN M. ROZWADOWSKI

WILLIAMS, Catharine Read Arnold (31 Dec. 1787–11 Oct. 1872), novelist and biographer, was born in Providence, Rhode Island, the daughter of Alfred Arnold, a sea captain, and Amey Read. Her mother died when Catharine was a child, and her father entrusted her upbringing and education to two of her aunts.

What little is known about her life comes from an autobiographical sketch she produced in the 1850s at the request of journalist Sidney S. Rider. The offspring of two families that had distinguished themselves in the revolutionary war and the granddaughter of Rhode Island attorney general Oliver Arnold, Catharine led a sheltered childhood. Her maiden aunts "lived in strict retirement," she said, and gave her a religious upbringing. Catharine left their household at age twenty-three, after the death of one aunt and marriage of the other. Her autobiography recalled years of troubles as she tried to adapt to the world without having much practical knowledge of it.

In 1824 she married Horatio N. Williams in New York City. The unfortunate match—she declined to give her husband's first name in her autobiography, describing him merely as a descendant of Roger Williams—ended after two years when Catharine fled with the couple's only child, a daughter. She obtained a divorce in Providence, tried her hand at being a schoolmistress, and then settled into a seventeen-year career writing poems, stories, and books. Their success and an inheritance from one of her aunts let her live comfortably for the rest of her life. Williams also adopted a son, but when she did this is not known.

Her first publication, *Original Poems, on Various Subjects* (1828) sold well enough through subscription to encourage further writings. She then produced a story, *Religion at Home* (1829), and the books *Tales, National and Revolutionary* (1830) and *Aristocracy, or the Holbey Family* (1832).

Williams never settled into or excelled in a single genre. She wrote not only poetry and novels but also biographies, histories, and the difficult-to-categorize but noteworthy *Fall River: An Authentic Record* (1833). The journalistic work examines the trial of the Reverend Ephraim K. Avery in the killing of the pregnant, unmarried Sarah Maria Cornell in Tiverton, Rhode Island, in December 1832. Readers unfamiliar with the case find Williams's account difficult to follow in places, as the author experimented with literary style, interrupting her fact-based story line with digressions and exhortations to the reader. While not an objective work, *Fall River* paints a lively picture of labor and injustice in Jacksonian America.

Williams considered her best work to be *The Neutral French; or, The Exiles of Nova Scotia* (1841), a novel she dedicated to Maine governor John Fairfield for his help in her historical inquiries. Williams also conducted research in Canada for the book. She believed it inspired Henry Wadsworth Longfellow's *Evangeline: A Tale of Acadie* (1847).

She traced her interest in history to the early influence of women in her life. In the preface to *Biography of Revolutionary Heroes* (1839), she recalled the time, as a young girl, when she saw a woman crying at the news of Louis XVI's decapitation. "I remember I left her, and went to look into the street to see if the men were crying, but to my surprise, not one appeared different from their usual manner," she wrote. "I saw several females that day and all appeared more or less affected. And though I did not exactly comprehend the services of the French monarch, yet from that time I conceived the highest respect for the feelings and opinions of women on those subjects, and imbibed a feeling of interest in the history of my country, which has never left me from that hour to this."

Williams considered herself a devout member of the Democratic party. Her political convictions included universal suffrage for men in Rhode Island and the end of flogging in the navy. Rider said Williams "is an inveterate Talker and is always ready to talk to any one as long as they will listen—she is deeply interested in politics."

She was unafraid to share her opinions. At a public dinner, an Englishman asked her how she could write historical biography, considering that "even your Aristocracy here, don't always know, who their grandfathers were." Williams replied that Americans had an advantage in such matters because the English aristocrats "don't often know who their Fathers were." Another time, Williams, an Episcopalian, told a Roman Catholic official at a reception that she hated "King Craft & Priestcraft."

After 1845 Williams stopped publishing. In about 1849, she traveled to Brooklyn, New York, where she took care of an aunt for three years. After her aunt's death, she lived in Johnston, Rhode Island, with her daughter, Amey. She traveled, wrote her autobiography, and died in Providence.

She wrote with more energy than grace. The didactic tone of her works was popular in the early nineteenth century, but her works—particularly *Fall River*—survive more as snapshots of her times than as lasting literary achievements.

• Other works by Catharine Read Arnold Williams include *Annals of the Aristocracy: Being a Series of Anecdotes of Some of the Principal Families of Rhode Island* (2 vols., 1843–1845), and the manuscript of a short story, *Bertha: A Tale of St. Domingo*. Five of Williams's short stories were reprinted in 1928 by Henrietta Palmer in *Rhode Island Tales*.

The autobiography Williams produced at the request of Sidney S. Rider, *Catharine R. Williams, Sketch of Her Life*, is at the John Hay Library at Brown University in Rhode Island. Rider's biography based on the manuscript is contained in *Biographical Memoirs of Three Rhode Island Authors*, Rhode Island Historical Tracts, no. 11 (1880), also in the library at Brown. Useful sketches can be found in the foreword to Palmer's book and the introduction to the 1993 reprint of *Fall River*. An obituary is in the *Providence Daily Journal*, 14 Oct. 1872.

MICHAEL S. SWEENEY

WILLIAMS, Channing Moore (18 July 1829–2 Dec. 1910), Episcopal bishop, was born in Richmond, Virginia, the son of John Green Williams and Mary Ann Cringan, farmers. He was named for Richard Channing Moore, the Bishop of Virginia and rector of the Monumental Church, Richmond, at the time of his birth. His father died when Channing was a boy, and when he was about nineteen he went to Henderson, Kentucky, to make money for his education. He attended the College of William and Mary for about two years and graduated in 1853. He graduated from the Virginia Theological Seminary, Alexandria, in 1855, and he and his classmate John Liggins were ordained deacons on 1 July 1855. In November 1855 the two sailed for Shanghai, the center of the Episcopal church's China mission field. Williams wrote, "We held service on deck every Sunday that weather permitted; tho' all officers and crew attended regularly still there is no evidence that any of them became savingly acquainted with the truth as it is in Jesus" (Minor, p. 3).

On 11 January 1857 William Jones Boone, the first missionary bishop of China, ordained Williams and Liggins to the priesthood. Williams's primary missionary activities were preaching and distributing books and pamphlets. He offered everyone separately bound books of Genesis, Exodus, the Gospels, and Acts. Those who requested more were given Revelation, a geography of the biblical countries, and a work on the doctrines of Christianity. "The Chinese consider themselves a superior race," wrote Williams, "contemptuous of everything foreign but with a high regard for books and learning" (Minor, p. 5). Williams and Liggins soon learned that the most effective preaching station was on the steps of the outer court of the temple of the favorite deity of the city. In this discovery they echoed St. Paul at the Areopagus in Athens.

Early in the seventeenth century the gates of Japan had swung shut to the rest of the world. The Japanese feared especially the intrusion that had been made by Christian missionaries, and for years Japanese who converted to Christianity were subject to the death penalty. Commodore Matthew Perry broke though the bamboo curtain in 1853, and on 4 July 1859 a treaty signed between Japan and the United States went into effect. On 14 February 1859 the Foreign Committee of the Board of Missions appointed Williams and Liggins, then in China, the first Episcopal missionaries to Japan. They were the first non–Roman Catholic missionaries to enter the Japanese field. At first the two missionaries did not practice a campaign of open evangelism because the Japanese were still wary of Christianity. Williams said: "One judge in Nagasaki proclaimed that he could tolerate anything save opium and Christianity" (Goodwin, p. 327). They did not do open Christian work but employed a method of indirect evangelization, such as selling historic, scientific, and geographical books, written in Japanese, that included Christian elements and references to the Bible. Gradually interest was aroused and copies of the New Testament were distributed. Soon after their arrival, Williams and Liggins began to hold services for the English and American merchants living in Nagasaki, and in 1862 Williams built a chapel for these nationals, the first non–Roman Catholic church to be built on Japanese soil.

On 17 July 1864 Bishop Boone died, and on 23 October 1865 the House of Bishops elected Williams the second missionary bishop of China, with jurisdiction over Japan. He was consecrated at St. John's Chapel, New York, on 3 October 1866.

From 1862 to 1871 Williams was the only Episcopal missionary in Japan; the history of the mission in Japan is the history of Williams's life. He concentrated on preparing books in Japanese and translating the Apostles' Creed, the Lord's Prayer, and the Ten Commandments. He had been in Japan for seven years before a single Japanese was baptized. In February 1866 he baptized a samurai of Hiogo.

Williams's first love was the Japanese people, and in 1869 he settled in Osaka to live. In 1873 he moved to Tokyo. He knew that he could not adequately care for Japan and China and for this reason petitioned the general convention to divide his jurisdiction. On 23 October 1874 the House of Bishops constituted Japan the Missionary District of Yedo. On that same day Williams relinquished China and became missionary bishop of Yedo (in 1893 changed to Tokyo).

One of Williams's major contributions to the Japanese was his work in education. In February 1874 he established a school for boys in Tokyo, which became St. Paul's School. Many of the Japanese who became Christians date the beginning of their faith to their time in this school. In July 1878 Trinity Divinity School, founded by Williams and members of the Church of England, opened in Tokyo to train native clergy. When it opened Williams was president and professor of New Testament. He also translated parts of the *Book of Common Prayer* into Japanese.

During Williams's episcopate there was an American Church in Japan and an English Church in Japan. On 3 May 1868, at a meeting of the English Church Missionary Society (CMS) in Osaka, it was proposed to combine the work of the CMS, the Society for the Propagation of the Gospel, and the American mission. Williams supported this merger, and the first General Synod of the Japanese Church met on 8 February 1887. This was the birth of the Nippon Sei Ko Kwai (the Holy Catholic Church of Japan).

On 18 October 1889 Williams resigned as bishop, but he continued to do missionary work in Japan. He retired to the United States in 1908 and died in Richmond, Virginia. He had never been married.

Williams was a leading missionary bishop, a translator of Christian literature into Japanese, a dedicated educator, and a tireless servant of the church. His work and ministry is commemorated on the Episcopal liturgical calendar on 2 December.

• Williams's papers are in the archives of the Episcopal church, Austin, Tex., and the archives of the Bishop Payne Library, Virginia Theological Seminary. Studies of Williams include Joseph Sakunshim Motoda, *The Life of C. M. Williams* (1914); Hisakazu Kaneto, *A Story of Channing Moore Williams, the Bishop of Yedo* (n.d.); and Maria Minor, *Channing Moore Williams: Pioneer Missionary in Japan* (1959). His ministry is discussed rather fully in William Archer Rutherford Goodwin, *History of the Theological Seminary in Virginia and Its Historical Background*, vol. 2 (1924). His work in China is noted briefly in Arthur R. Gray and Arthur M. Sherman, *The Story of the Church in China* (1913), and his work in Japan is discussed in Henry St. George Tucker, *The History of the Episcopal Church in Japan* (1938). Numerous appreciations and obituaries were published, but the most helpful is John C. Ambler, "An Appreciation of 'The Old Bishop,'" *The Spirit of Missions* 76 (Apr. 1911): 307–9.

DONALD S. ARMENTROUT

WILLIAMS, Charles David (30 July 1860–14 Feb. 1923), rector and bishop, was born in Bellevue, Ohio, the son of David Williams and Eliza Dickson. After graduating from Kenyon College in 1880 and studying for the ministry at Bexley Theological Seminary, both in Gambier, Ohio, Williams was ordained an Episcopal deacon in 1883 and a priest the next year. From 1884 to 1889 he served simultaneously as the rector of Episcopal congregations in Fernbank and Riverside, Ohio, and from 1889 to 1893 he pastored Trinity Episcopal Church in Steubenville, Ohio. In 1886 Williams married Lucy Victoria Benedict, with whom he had nine children.

In 1893 Kenyon awarded Williams an M.A., and he accepted a call as the dean of Trinity Cathedral in Cleveland. While ministering for thirteen years to this prominent congregation, he participated actively in community affairs, chairing the Municipal League of Cleveland, fighting to improve education and recreation in the city, and supporting the crusade of progressive mayor Tom Johnson against political graft and corruption. He also served as a chaplain in the Ohio National Guard from 1893 to 1896, two terms as president of the Cleveland Library board, and as president of the city's Hiram House Social Settlement. During these years he belonged to the standing committee of the diocese of Ohio and was a delegate to all the triennial general conventions of the Episcopal church. His religious and civic achievements led to his selection as the fourth Episcopal bishop of Michigan.

Consecrated bishop in 1906, Williams developed an international reputation as an orator, a social reformer, and an author. Motivated by the writings of Walter Rauschenbusch, he became a strong advocate of the Social Gospel. Along with Vida Scudder, a professor at Wellesley College, he led Episcopal efforts to apply biblical teaching to contemporary social problems. He attended the Lambeth Conference (a gathering of Episcopalians from around the world) in London in 1910 and 1920, served with the Red Cross in France during World War I, and was a member of the Interchurch World Movement commission that investigated conditions in the American steel industry in 1919–1920. As president of the Consumers' League, he helped to improve working conditions for women. In 1921 he visited England to study the relationship between the labor movement and the church, and he served as the president of the Episcopal Church League for Industrial Democracy. His sermons, preached throughout the country, sometimes attracted nationwide attention and frequently stirred controversy because of his social views. In numerous lectures, articles, and four books he argued that the church must help reform social structures and alleviate social ills.

In *A Valid Christianity for To-day* (1909), Williams contends that Christianity should be judged by its fruits rather than by its roots. What made the gospel significant, he insisted, was not whether its origins and traditions were authentic but whether its teachings were relevant to contemporary problems. He maintained that the Christian faith could still cleanse the human heart, meet the spiritual needs of individuals, invigorate ethical life, and provide a solid moral foundation for industrial, political, commercial, and social life. His most influential book, *The Christian Ministry and Social Problems* (1917), argues that ministers must be concerned with the moral implications of the fundamental economic problem that underlay all social problems—the distribution of wealth—and urged churches to create a just society, not merely dispense charity. In *The Prophetic Ministry for Today* (1921), the bishop repudiates the idea that the gospel should be "confined to individual or personal life" and excluded from the public realms of business, industry, society, and politics (p. 62). In this book and *The Gospel of Fellowship* (1923), Williams argues that, because God was building a kingdom in the world and his love and righteousness were to progressively reign in all human activities, Christian faith could not be limited to worship services, personal piety, spiritual experience, and individual conduct. In all four books the bishop maintains that Christians must labor to regenerate human hearts as well as to reshape social structures. They must strive to improve working conditions, provide a living wage, combat disease, upgrade education, and construct a less materialistic, more biblically based industrial, social, national, and international order. In their efforts to create a Christian civilization, ministers, Williams argued, must not be mere social critics or even social reformers. They must rather be prophets who focused on the vision of God's kingdom, not on the details of practical reforms, who dealt "with motives, not methods; principles, not policies; spiritual dynamics, not merely economic mechanics" (*The Prophetic Ministry for Today*, p. 126).

Williams strongly supported the single tax of Henry George (the idea that the only tax should be on land), defended the right of anarchist Emma Goldman to speak in Detroit, held up Germany in 1917 as a model of social cooperation, argued for amnesty for political prisoners throughout the world, and denounced America's commercial and industrial system as "practically heathen." Such positions led *American Magazine* to label him "an insurgent Christian" and an "intelligent radical." His "denunciations of social wrongs" and "stinging rebukes" of those "guilty of social injustice" coupled with his liberal theology made him some enemies, and in 1921 he offered to resign as bishop if his beliefs were judged to create too many problems for his denomination.

A tenacious and compassionate crusader for social justice, Williams helped to inspire Reinhold Niebuhr, then a young pastor in Detroit, and many other Americans to work for a better society. In *The Prophetic Ministry for Today*, he declares that a modern bishop was expected to be an efficient administrator, a shrewd businessperson, an enterprising executive, a peacemaker, a scholar, a preacher, a teacher, a leader, and a person of prayer. The bishop of Michigan might have been describing himself. Williams died in Detroit.

• Williams's papers are in the Bentley Historical Library at the University of Michigan. The most important articles Williams wrote are "The Final Test of Christianity," *McClure's*, Dec. 1905, pp. 223–28; "Men of Vision," *The Chautauquan* 49 (Jan. 1908): 170–83; "The Bible; Have We Lost It?" *American Magazine*, Apr. 1908, pp. 644–49; and "The Conflict between Religion and the Church," *American Magazine*, June 1911, pp. 147–52. For brief accounts of his life, see "Bishop Charles D. Williams," *American Magazine*, June 1910, p. 185; "A Bishop for the Common Good," *Hampton Magazine*, Apr. 1911, pp. 505–7; and two articles in *The Churchman*: "The Bishop Williams Dies of Apoplexy," 24 Feb. 1923, p. 23, and "Bishop Williams Mourned by Thousands," 3 Mar. 1923, pp. 30–33. For the Interchurch World Movement's investigation of the steel strike of 1919, see "Interchurch Report on the Steel Strike," *Outlook* 125 (11 Aug. 1920): 627–28; and S. A. Shaw, "Steel making," *Survey* 44 (2 Aug. 1920): 557–61. Obituaries are in the *New York Times* and the *Detroit Free Press*, 15 Feb. 1923.

GARY SCOTT SMITH

WILLIAMS, Clarence (8 Oct. 1898 or 1893–6 Nov. 1965), blues and jazz musician, publisher, and music producer, was born in Plaquemine, Louisiana (information on his parentage is unavailable). In 1906 his family moved to New Orleans. Williams's first instrument was the guitar, which he abandoned before he reached his teens to concentrate on the piano. Most of his learning was done by ear or by watching others, although he did receive eight lessons in the early 1910s, at the end of which he believed he knew all he needed to know about piano playing. At the age of twelve he left home to join Billy Kersand's traveling minstrel show as a pianist, master of ceremonies, dancer, and comedian. Williams spent most of his teenage years in the clubs of New Orleans' legendary Storyville district as a pianist and songwriter. During this time he met pianist and composer Jelly Roll Morton, who played an important role in transforming ragtime music into jazz and represented the main musical influence on Williams.

Williams's entrepreneurial skill and multifaceted musical talents exhibited themselves early in life. About the year 1915 he founded his first publishing company, which lasted for two years, with bandleader and songwriter Armand John Piron. Among the copyrights they handled were "Brownskin, Who You For" and Piron's oft-covered jazz classic "I Wish I Could Shimmy Like My Sister Kate." Williams formed his own jazz group that featured jazz soloists Bunk Johnson, King Oliver, and Sidney Bechet, and they toured the South in the mid-1910s. At nineteen he served as a musical director for Salem Tutt Whitney's *The Smart Set*, a black touring company that produced musicals. He also toured briefly in 1917 with blues songwriter-entrepreneur W. C. Handy.

At the end of World War I Williams moved to Chicago and attempted to take advantage of the local activity surrounding jazz music by opening a music store and publishing company on State Street. Williams peddled his compositions door-to-door and on street corners, from Texas to New York. He was one of the first African Americans to demonstrate his songs in five-and-dime stores, which were usually segregated. Despite extensive effort, the business failed. Not easily deterred, Williams relocated to New York City in 1919 and launched a publishing business that initiated his meteoric rise in the music business. That year Piron's "Sister Kate" marked its first significant commercial success. For the next two decades dozens of hit songs in the blues, jazz, and vaudeville genres emanated from the company, and most of them were credited to Williams.

Being in New York City, home of the major record companies, represented a boon for Williams. Spurred on by the unprecedented sales of Mamie Smith's "Crazy Blues" (1920, the first popular vocal recording by an African American), these companies were starting to realize the previously untapped financial potential of a popular-music market aimed at African Americans. Williams, with his combination of songwriting, publishing, bandleading, and piano skills, proved invaluable in their efforts to exploit this market. By 1923 Williams became manager of the Race Artists' Section of Okeh Records and remained in that position for eight years. He directed sessions for his own groups and for others, sometimes playing piano or singing. He often selected the material to be performed, much of which was published under his company's banner. Perhaps Williams's most valuable skill to these companies was his ability to spot emerging and important artists. Many jazz legends made early recorded appearances on Williams's sessions long before they were famous, including Bechet, Louis Armstrong, Bubber Miley, Coleman Hawkins, and Don Redman.

Williams proved instrumental in the first recordings of Bessie Smith, the bestselling blues artist of the 1920s. Frank Walker, the head of Columbia Records' "race" music division, recalled seeing Smith perform in Alabama in 1917 and six years later had Williams find her so that she could record for the company. Williams played piano and contributed two original songs to her first eight sides. One of them, "Baby Won't You Please Come Home" (1919), became a blues standard and one of Williams's most covered compositions. A bitter disagreement over a one-sided personal representation contract that Williams had Smith sign with him led to a divisive impasse between them, though they would be reunited in the recording studio in the late 1920s and early 1930s. In 1923 Smith's debut recording, "Down Hearted Blues," featured her joined only by Williams. His piano playing was not virtuosic, but he provided a bittersweet ambience that complimented the song and attractively lined the edges of Smith's vocal performance. It is no accident that a disproportionate amount of Smith's best sides are the relatively few times Williams was paired with her, including "Black Mountain Blues" (1930) and "Long Old Road" (1931). Williams's talents as a simple but effective accompanist were regularly heard alongside the rich array of 1920s female vocal blues talent, including Ethel Waters, Alberta Hunter, Victoria Spivey, and Sippie Wallace. However, the female vocalist most identified with Williams was Eva Taylor, whom he met as a result of his work as an accompanist. They married in 1921. Taylor's successful career endured longer than most black female vocalists of the period; she appeared on recordings and radio well into the 1930s. The biggest hits by the Williams bands of the 1920s (such as the Blue Five, Morocco Five, and Blue Seven) usually showcased Taylor's vocals on Williams's songs. Some examples are "Everybody Loves My Baby (But My Baby Don't Love Nobody But Me)," "Cake Walking Babies from Home" (both from 1925 and featuring Armstrong), and the suggestive "Shake That Thing" (1926). Many of the mid-1920s Blue Five recordings are now considered early jazz classics, especially "Texas Moaner Blues" and "Mandy, Make Up Your Mind," two tracks from 1924 that document Armstrong and Bechet's definition of the jazz solo. Williams's skill at maintaining a relaxed and friendly atmosphere in the studio encouraged artists to perform at their highest level. "He could somehow manage to get the best out of them, and to this day hasn't received the credit he really deserves," marveled Walker in a 1950s interview (Shapiro and Hentoff, p. 239).

Throughout the late 1910s and 1920s Williams contributed additional jazz and blues standards: "Royal Garden Blues," cowritten with the non-related Spencer Williams (1919); "Tain't Nobody's Business If I Do" (1922); "Gulf Coast Blues" (1923); "West End Blues" (1928); and what may have been his most financially successful composition, "Squeeze Me," written with Fats Waller in 1925. Some latter-day authors have accused Williams of claiming popular "unwritten" tunes of the day rather than composing his own and of taking credit for songs that he only helped promote. No conclusive evidence has been found on these charges, but such situations were not uncommon in the music business of Williams's era.

Williams was also part of an exclusive group of black artists (others included James P. Johnson, Willie "the Lion" Smith, and Waller) contracted to record piano rolls for the QRS Company in 1923. Beginning in 1926 Williams embarked on a moderately successful series of recordings that utilized novelty "washboard" instrumentation that musically and humorously straddled the line between the hillbilly and vaudeville genres. In 1927 Williams wrote the music for an unsuccessful Broadway production titled *Bottomland*.

After his position at Okeh ended, Williams concentrated on administering his publishing and continuing his songwriting. His appearances on recordings and his string of hit songs subsided during the 1930s. Throughout the 1930s and 1940s Williams acted as an agent for black recording artists, arranging recording sessions with major record labels. By 1941 he had ceased to record, and two years later he sold his publishing interests to the Decca Recording Company for a large sum. Afterward, Williams enjoyed a wealthy and private semiretirement as the proprietor of a hobby shop in Harlem. He died in New York City.

Williams played a significant role in enlarging the scope of the commercial possibilities for black music, which led to the rise of the African-American music market and the dominance of blues- and jazz-influenced music on American radio airwaves in the 1920s and 1930s. He was one of the first African Americans to wield real power in the music business as an entrepreneur, executive, and artist. Williams was one of the main progenitors of the recording and songwriting legacy of the opening decade of recorded jazz and blues—writing, cowriting, and recording many of the standards identified with the music for decades to come. Despite his many achievements, Williams told an interviewer in the 1960s that there was a significant amount of struggle involved as well. He called the blues a "mood" that represented a "carry-over from slavery—nothing but trouble in sight for everyone. There was no need to hitch your wagon to a star, because there weren't any stars. You got only what you fought for" (Patterson, p. 56).

• Tom Lord, *Clarence Williams* (1976), is a book-length biography. Two helpful biographical articles appeared shortly after Williams's demise, both titled "Clarence Williams" (see *Jazz*, Oct. 1966, pp. 26–27, and *Jazz Journal* (June 1966): 10–11). Arnold Shaw, *The Jazz Age* (1987), fits Williams's contributions as a songwriter and publisher into the context of the African-American music market in the 1920s. Interviews of the man are rare but can be found in the following sources: *Metronome*, Sept. 1923, p. 78; Nat Shapiro and Nat Hentoff, eds., *Hear Me Talkin' to Ya* (1955); and Lindsay Patterson ed., *The Negro in Music and Art* (1967). Two wildly varying accounts of Williams's role in the career of Bessie Smith are detailed in Chris Albertson, *Bessie* (1972), and in the Shapiro citation. There is a discography in Byron Rust, *Jazz Records, 1897–1942*, 4th rev. ed. (1978). An obituary is in the *New York Times*, 9 Nov. 1965.

HARVEY COHEN

WILLIAMS, Cootie (24 July 1910–15 Sept. 1985), jazz trumpeter, was born Charles Melvin Williams in Mobile, Alabama. His parents' names are unknown. When he was a small child, Williams's father, the owner of a gambling house, took him to hear a brass band, which the boy described as sounding like "cootie, cootie, cootie," thus giving rise to his lifelong nickname. His mother, who played piano and organ, died when he was eight, and he and his three brothers were raised by a live-in aunt. After two years studying piano and violin, at age seven he entered the school band, where he played drums, trombone, and tuba before ultimately settling on the trumpet, which he then studied with Charles Lipskin. At fourteen, he worked for a summer with Billy Young's Family Band, a traveling act whose youthful members included the later renowned Lester Young. That same year Williams met the clarinetist and saxophonist Edmond Hall, who was then playing in Pensacola, Florida. In 1924, when Hall was asked to join "Eagle Eye" Shields's Orchestra in Jacksonville, he accepted on the condition that the teenaged Williams would also be hired.

In late 1926 or early 1927 Hall and Williams left Shields and moved to Miami to work with the Alonzo Ross De Luxe Syncopators, a band that also traveled all over Florida and Georgia. While in Savannah in August 1927, the band was recorded, but for some reason Williams was not present at the session. When the records were released, though, they so impressed the manager of New York City's Roseland Ballroom that he hired the band to play at his Rosemont Ballroom in Brooklyn starting on 18 March 1928. However, the Syncopators apparently were not up to New York standards, and they were fired after only two weeks. By this time Ross had been replaced as pianist by Arthur "Happy" Ford, who, after termination of the Rosemont job, quickly found work for Williams and Hall in his quartet at a taxi dance hall (a dime-a-dance ballroom so named for the time-metered practice by which women collected tickets from their "suitors") called the Happyland. After hours Williams and Hall often went to jam sessions at Harlem's Band Box, where the trumpeter was heard by drummer Chick Webb, who in turn hired him for a job at the famous Savoy Ballroom. Williams worked with Webb for three weeks at the end of 1928 and then in January 1929 joined the Fletcher Henderson Orchestra as a temporary replacement for lead trumpeter Russell Smith. To Williams's understanding, he had been hired only for a brief tour, but immediately after the band returned to New York in mid-February to resume its regular stand at the Roseland Ballroom, Williams was invited to stay on as first trumpeter.

However, Williams had already been approached by Duke Ellington to replace Bubber Miley as featured soloist in his band. Albeit with mixed feelings over his obligation to Henderson, he accepted the offer and made his debut recordings with Ellington on 18 February 1929. Until this time Williams had been noted as a powerful, Louis Armstrong–inspired openhorn trumpeter, who rarely if ever played with a mute.

He had a large, full tone that projected itself easily whether playing lead or solo, but Ellington had something else in mind for his new acquisition. Miley, a virtuoso in his own right, was a specialist in the so-called "wa-wa" style of trumpet playing, a technique of plunger-muted guttural growling that he had mastered in his own unique fashion after having first been impressed by Johnny Dunn and King Oliver. Although Ellington never actually told the young, fat-toned trumpeter to imitate Miley, Williams nevertheless started experimenting with this new technique on his own, using his bandstand mate, trombonist Joe "Tricky Sam" Nanton, as his nightly exemplar. It was not until the recording of "Doin' the Voom Voom" on 10 September 1929, seven months after he had joined the band, that he can be heard growling, tentatively, on record. But only a few days later, on "Jazz Convulsions" and "Mississippi," he emerges as a convincing, full-fledged Miley disciple.

Williams stayed with Ellington for almost twelve years, appearing on hundreds of recordings and broadcasts with such outstanding fellow sidemen as Johnny Hodges, Barney Bigard, Harry Carney, Rex Stewart, Nanton, and Lawrence Brown. But the time came, in November 1940, when Benny Goodman, with Ellington's consent, asked Williams to join his band for a year. Realizing that his star trumpeter would receive even greater exposure by playing in the most successful white swing band of the time, Ellington not only gave his blessings but also helped negotiate a substantial raise in pay. Williams's first assignment was the now-historic sextet date of 7 November that produced "Wholly Cats," "Royal Garden Blues," "As Long as I Live," and "Benny's Bugle" with the nonpareil combination of Goodman's inventive clarinet, Georgie Auld's robust tenor sax, Count Basie's prodding piano, Charlie Christian's pacesetting guitar, and his own incendiary growl trumpet.

Williams was also featured on several of Goodman's big-band recordings, such as "Superman" and "Pound Ridge," but it is undeniably the sextet titles that offer the best evidence of his flawless skill in an improvising context. Goodman's work schedule was easily the equal of Ellington's during this busy prewar period, and Williams's reputation was at its peak. Earlier, on 16 January 1938, he had appeared along with Hodges and Carney as a featured Ellingtonian at Goodman's historic Carnegie Hall concert, and in both 1939 and 1940 he was voted in as a member of *Metronome*'s All-Star Band. He also won similar awards from *Esquire* in 1944, 1945, and 1946.

After his contract with Goodman expired in October 1941, Williams told Ellington that he was ready to come back, but his former leader encouraged him to take advantage of his new popularity and go out on his own. After a few months of preparation, on 1 April 1942 he recorded his first session as a big-band leader. Successful from the start, his orchestra enjoyed long residencies at the Savoy Ballroom throughout the forties, and at various times his personnel included future modern jazz and rhythm and blues stars such as Bud Powell, Eddie "Lockjaw" Davis, Charlie Parker, Pearl Bailey, Sam "The Man" Taylor, Eddie "Cleanhead" Vinson, and Willis "Gator" Jackson. But because of changing popular tastes, in 1948 Williams had to reduce his personnel at the Savoy to a sextet. When the 32-year-old ballroom was torn down in 1958, Williams disbanded and spent some time touring as a single. He then formed a quartet and worked at the Embers, the Round Table, and other venues. After a long hiatus from the studios, he started recording again in 1957 and in July 1958 appeared at the Newport Jazz Festival as a member of the Ellington Alumni All Stars. He toured Europe with a small band in early 1959 and recorded his last album as leader in April 1962. In July 1962 Williams rejoined Goodman for a short time and in a striking reversal of historical sequence then went back to the Ellington Orchestra in September, where he remained, except for a 1973 illness, through Ellington's death in May 1974. He continued to play under son Mercer Ellington's leadership into the next year. Williams spent his final years of activity touring Europe, during which time he recorded in Holland in 1976.

Although open-minded in his acceptance and encouragement of younger jazzmen such as Bud Powell, Charlie Parker, and Thelonious Monk, whose "'Round Midnight" he chose for his band's theme, as a trumpet stylist Williams was considered passé by the generation that had produced Dizzy Gillespie, Fats Navarro, and Miles Davis. But he was still capable of great playing, as is evidenced by his latter-day appearances with Ellington, where, unburdened by the responsibilities of leading a band, he was required only to exhibit his most unique attributes—his majestic, Armstrong-like open-horn tone, his inimitable mastery of the plunger mute, and those adroitly placed, dramatically shaded, massive blocks of sound that had always lent so much authority to his presence within the Ellington fold. A chronic sufferer of high blood pressure, Williams played only sporadically from 1976 on. He died in Jamaica, New York, and was survived by his wife, Catherine.

• Williams is often referred to in connection with the professional careers of Duke Ellington and Benny Goodman, his two most illustrious associations. Thus, Stanley Dance, *The World of Duke Ellington* (1970) and *The World of Swing* (1974); Gunther Schuller, *The Swing Era* (1989); Mark Tucker, ed., *The Duke Ellington Reader* (1993); Duke Ellington, *Music Is My Mistress* (1973); D. Russell Connor, *Benny Goodman: Listen to His Legacy* (1988); and Ross Firestone, *Swing, Swing, Swing: The Life and Times of Benny Goodman* (1993), all offer valuable information. Also important are Albert McCarthy, *Big Band Jazz* (1974); Walter C. Allen, *Hendersonia: The Music of Fletcher Henderson and His Musicians* (1973); Rex Stewart, *Boy Meets Horn* (1991); Manfred Selchow, *Profoundly Blue: A Bio-Discographical Scrapbook on Edmond Hall* (1988); and Lewis Porter, ed., *A Lester Young Reader* (1991); the last two contain material on the Young Family Band. See also interviews with Williams in *Storyville* 71 (June–July 1977): 170–74, and *Down Beat*, 4 May 1967, p. 20. Williams's recording career is covered thoroughly in Brian Rust, *Jazz Records, 1897–1942* (1978; rev. ed., 1982), and

Walter Bruyninckx, *Swing Discography, 1920–1988* (1989), while short biographical entries are in John Chilton, *Who's Who of Jazz* (1972), and Roger D. Kinkle, *The Complete Encyclopedia of Popular Music and Jazz*, vol. 3 (1974).

JACK SOHMER

WILLIAMS, Daniel Day (12 Sept. 1910–3 Dec. 1973), theologian, was born in Denver, Colorado, the son of Wayne Cullen Williams, a lawyer and judge, and Lena Belle Day. After graduating from the University of Denver (A.B., 1931), he earned degrees at the University of Chicago (M.A., 1933), Chicago Theological Seminary (B.D., 1934), and Columbia University (Ph.D., 1940). His doctoral dissertation was published the following year as *The Andover Liberals: A Study in American Theology*.

In 1935 he married musician Eulalia Westberg; they had no children. Ordained to the Congregational ministry in 1936, he served the First Congregational Church in Colorado Springs from 1936 to 1938. Then, after a year as instructor of religion and dean of the chapel at Colorado College, he taught Christian theology at Chicago Theological Seminary and the Federated Theological Faculty of the University of Chicago (1939–1954).

In 1947 Williams delivered the Rauschenbusch Lectures at Colgate Rochester Divinity School. They were published two years later as *God's Grace and Man's Hope*, a widely read book. In it, seeking a more adequate Christian philosophy of history, Williams criticized two major but conflicting theories of human destiny, both of which commanded sizable followings at that time, pointing out their strengths and limitations. One was liberal theology, that movement in modern Protestantism which endeavored to bring Christian thought into organic unity with the evolutionary view of reality and to bring about social reform through its vision of a better world, a goal that was believed to be both realizable and near. Williams criticized that position for expecting too much too soon and for oversimplifying the nature of progress in history because it did not take into sufficient account the fact and universality of human sin. The other theory he criticized stemmed from neo-orthodox theology, then growing in popularity, which sought to recover as the foundation of the Church and its gospel the central Reformation theme of justification by faith through the redemption wrought by God in Jesus Christ. Williams argued that this view neglected a fundamental Christian insight into the meaning of life within the grace of God and therefore put the love of God outside of history. In his effort to clarify a middle position between these two theories, because he believed that neither sufficiently recognized the redemptive as well as the creative activity of God, he contributed significantly to the shaping of process theology, which was influenced by the leading process philosophers, Alfred North Whitehead and Charles Hartshorne. As a process theologian, Williams used process thought, with its characteristic attention to empiricism, relationalism, and process in nature and history, to criticize contemporary culture from the perspective of biblical culture and to formulate a constructive theological position that avoided the weaknesses of both liberal theology and neo-orthodoxy. Williams and other process theologians believed that a Christian view of history must take full account of God as redeemer as well as creator and thus help persons to discern, by grace through faith, a direct experience of divine love and providence in human life and history.

A quite different type of book, *What Present-Day Theologians Are Thinking* (1952), a survey of the contemporary field of theology, was widely used as a college textbook as it went through several updated editions (an edition was published in England the following year as *Interpreting Theology, 1918–1952*). In it, Williams discussed the nature of the theological renaissance at midcentury (a time of renewal movements in conservative evangelical theology as well as increases in theological scholarship), paying attention to such topics as the Bible, Christian ethics and society, Jesus Christ in history and faith, and the nature of the church. In 1954 he was made a professor of theology at Union Theological Seminary in New York City; five years later he was promoted to the Roosevelt Chair of Systematic Theology, serving in that position until his death.

He was granted a year's leave at the outset, however, in order to serve as associate director of a study of theological education sponsored by the American Association of Theological Schools and financed by the Carnegie Corporation. With the director, Yale theologian H. Richard Niebuhr, Williams coedited *The Ministry in Historical Perspectives* (1956), in which eight theological educators surveyed various aspects of how historical forces have shaped the forms and practices of ministry from the primitive church to the present. The major report of the study was written by Niebuhr, Williams, and assistant director James M. Gustafson as *The Advancement of Theological Education* (1957). Based on thorough studies of selected representative Protestant theological seminaries in the United States and Canada, the book paid particular attention to the methods of theological education and made several significant recommendations, focused primarily on the education of parish clergy and calling attention to the emergence of the minister as "pastoral director" as a major finding of the study. Williams was primarily responsible for the chapters that discussed the work of theological faculties and the need for improvement in teaching, the principles and problems of the curriculum and its fields of study, and the patterns of theological teaching in classroom, field, and library.

Beginning his full-time teaching at Union in 1955, Williams continued to pursue his interest in process theology, finding it an informative framework for his long-standing explorations of the relationship between theology and psychotherapy. He traced similarities and differences in the use of language by psychologists and pastoral theologians, noting that while the former spoke of anxiety, egocentricity, acceptance, integration, freedom, and love, the latter talked of anxiety, sin, forgiveness, faith, freedom, and love. Analogies between the two terminologies fascinated him, specifically the similarity between "divine forgiveness" and "therapeutic acceptance." Williams chaired the faculty advisory committee for Union's program in psychiatry and religion, participated in teaching in that area, and was himself involved in some counseling as a teacher and minister. Much of what he had learned was stated in his Sprunt Lectures at Union Theological Seminary in Virginia in 1959, published two years later as *The Minister and the Care of Souls*.

Williams discussed his various other interests—for example, prayer, tradition, social action, the ecumenical movement, and human suffering—in assorted addresses and lectures, many of which were published as articles or chapters in books. He served terms as president of both midwestern and eastern divisions of the American Theological Society, and his theological writings were frequently cited by scholars. An active participant in denominational affairs, he represented the United Church of Christ, which his Congregational tradition helped to form by uniting with other Protestant denominations in 1957, on the Faith and Order Commission of the World Council of Churches from 1971 to 1973. Also, with his Union colleague Roger L. Shinn, he wrote *We Believe: A Commentary on the Statement of Faith of the United Church of Christ* (1966).

His most distinctive book, *The Spirit and Forms of Love* (1968; repr. 1981), which has been called the first systematic process theology, was a perceptive effort to interpret the meaning and truth of the Christian assertion that God is love. Williams drew not only on the work of Protestant theologians, including his teacher and former colleague Hartshorne, but also on Catholic writers, such as Pierre Teilhard de Chardin and Martin C. D'Arcy. He contended that to understand love in Western culture one must know its roots in the Jewish and Christian traditions and that love is spirit taking form in history as a creative power that participates in the life it informs. Analyzing the many forms of human love, including those linked with sexuality, the struggle for social justice, and the intellect, Williams did not hide his conviction that all such loves are subject to sin and self-centeredness. Neither did he obscure his belief that the fulfillment of human love depends on the mysterious action of God in reconciliation.

Williams did not simply talk about love in his theological writings; those close to him were aware that he tirelessly sought to embody his beliefs in the way he lived and worked. He somehow found time to listen to many of those who sought him out, including colleagues as well as ministerial and graduate students, even as he carried heavy teaching loads and committee assignments and accepted requests to lecture at many institutions. Mild mannered in speech, he could be gentle but incisive in criticism, and he had an ability to encourage others to do their best. At his death in New York City, many people paid tribute to a beloved teacher, colleague, and friend.

• Williams's papers are at the Center for Process Studies in Claremont, Calif. A festschrift, containing fifteen articles in his honor and concluding with an extensive bibliography by Jean C. Lambert, was published in the *Union Seminary Quarterly Review* 30 (Winter–Summer 1975): 69–229. Twenty of Williams's articles were collected and edited by Perry LeFevre in Daniel Day Williams, *Essays in Process Theology* (1985); the Lambert bibliography with some addenda conclude the volume. Stacy A. Evans selected from Williams's previously unpublished Armstrong Lectures at Kalamazoo College and from other of his writings relating to eschatology in editing Williams, *The Demonic and the Divine* (1990). An unpublished thesis that compares Williams with several of his contemporaries in process theology was written by Danny Lee Stewart, "The Nature of the Relationship between God and Man in the Theologies of Daniel Day Williams, Schubert M. Ogden, and John B. Cobb., Jr.: A Study in the Adaptability of Process Philosophy to a Christian Theism" (Ph.D. diss., Baylor Univ., 1977). An obituary is in the *New York Times*, 4 Dec. 1973. Brief tributes by those who knew him well appeared in the *Union Theological Seminary Journal*, Mar. 1974, pp. 3–15.

ROBERT T. HANDY

WILLIAMS, Daniel Hale (18 Jan. 1856–4 Aug. 1931), surgeon and hospital administrator, was born in Hollidaysburg, south central Pennsylvania, the son of Daniel Williams, Jr., and Sarah Price. His parents were black, but Daniel himself, in adult life, could easily be mistaken for being white, with his light complexion, red hair, and blue eyes.

Williams's father did well in real estate but died when Daniel was eleven, and the family's financial situation became difficult. When Williams was seventeen, he and a sister, Sally, moved to Janesville, Wisconsin. Here Williams found work at Harry Anderson's Tonsorial Parlor and Bathing Rooms. Anderson took the two of them into his home as family and continued to aid Williams financially until Williams obtained his M.D.

Medicine had not been Williams's first choice of a career; he had worked in a law office after high school but had found it too quarrelsome. In 1878 Janesville's most prominent physician, Henry Palmer, took Williams on as an apprentice. Williams entered the Chicago Medical College in the fall of 1880 and graduated in 1883. He opened an office on Chicago's South Side and treated both black and white patients.

Late in 1890 the Reverend Louis Reynolds, a pastor on the West Side, asked Williams for advice about his sister, Emma, who had been turned down at several nursing schools because of her color. As a result Williams decided to start an interracial hospital and a nursing school for black women. He drew on black and white individuals and groups for financial support. Several wealthy businessmen, such as meatpacker Philip D. Armour and publisher Herman H. Kohlsaat, made major contributions to the purchase of a three-story building at Dearborn and Twenty-ninth Street and its remodeling into a hospital with twelve beds. Provident Hospital and Training School Association was officially incorporated on 23 January 1891 and opened for service on 4 May of that year. The

Training School received 175 applicants for its first class, and Williams selected seven for the eighteen-month course.

Provident had both white and black patients and staff members, although the lack of suitably qualified black physicians led to some problems. Williams appointed black physicians and surgeons who had obtained their medical degrees from schools such as the Rush Medical College and his own alma mater and who, in addition, had suitable experience. However, he had to deal diplomatically with some leaders of the black community who were pushing the appointment of young George Cleveland Hall, who had a degree from an eclectic school and only two years of experience (mostly in Chicago's red light district). Hall (and his equally aggressive wife) never forgave Williams for this early judgment to oppose Hall's appointment.

The hospital soon became overcrowded, but many donations—again including major contributions from Armour and Kohlsaat—resulted in the construction of a new 65-bed hospital at Dearborn and Thirty-sixth streets. The new Provident opened in late 1896.

In 1893 a longtime Chicago friend of Williams, Judge Walter Q. Gresham, recently named secretary of state by President Grover Cleveland, urged Williams to seek the position of surgeon in chief at Freedmen's Hospital in Washington, D.C. This, Gresham pointed out, would bring Williams onto the national scene. Williams, believing that Provident was in good hands, finally agreed to Gresham's suggestion and in 1894 was appointed to Freedmen's where his predecessor, Charles B. Purvis, unhappy at being replaced and often with the aid of Hall, made life as difficult as possible for Williams.

Williams, nevertheless, accomplished much at Freedmen's. He reorganized the staff interracially, created an advisory board of prominent physicians for both professional and political help, and founded a successful nursing school. Williams also began an internship program, improved relationships with the Howard University Medical School, and helped establish an interracial local medical society.

Williams also worked hard on the national scene and became one of the founders of the National Medical Association in 1895. Because at the time the American Medical Association did not accept black physicians, such a national organization was a necessary part of the educational and professional growth for black health-care givers. In 1895 Williams turned down the presidency but did become vice president.

With the election in 1896 of a new U.S. president, the control of Freedmen's became involved in partisan congressional hearings. These were sufficiently upsetting for Williams, but then William A. Warfield, one of Williams's first interns at Freedmen's, accused his chief, before the hospital's board of visitors, of stealing hospital supplies. Although the congressional hearings came to no conclusion and the board of visitors exonerated Williams, he had become soured on Washington and resigned early in 1898.

In April 1898 Williams married Alice Johnson in Washington, D.C. The couple moved to Chicago, and Williams returned to his old office. There the Halls continued to undermine the Williamses' professional and social lives. Hall finally forced Williams to resign from Provident in 1912 because the latter had become an associate attending surgeon at St. Luke's Hospital and was, therefore, "disloyal" to Provident. That this was a trumped-up charge was apparent from the fact that, since 1900, Williams had regularly had patients in up to five other hospitals at the same time.

National recognition, however, counterbalanced such sniping; in 1913 Williams was nominated to be a charter member of the American College of Surgeons, the first black surgeon to be honored in this manner. At the board of regents meeting to act on this, a surgeon from Tennessee objected because of the social implications in the South. After vigorous discussion, during which it was pointed out that "if you met him [Williams] on the street you would hardly realize that he is a Negro," Williams was accepted.

As a surgeon, Williams is best known for his stitching of a stab wound to the pericardium of Jim Cornish, an expressman, on 9 July 1893. After Williams had realized that conservative care would not be sufficient for Cornish, he searched the medical literature for reports of surgery in this area. Finding none, he nevertheless decided to perform surgery. Cornish lived for fifty years after the operation. While strictly speaking not an operation on the heart itself, this was the first successful suturing of the pericardium on record.

Perhaps more important surgically was Williams's successful suturing of a heavily bleeding spleen in July 1902, one of the earliest such operations in the United States. Williams also operated on many ovarian cysts, a condition that had not been believed to occur in black women. In 1901 he reported on his 357 such operations, almost equally divided between black and white patients.

Well aware of the lack of training opportunities available to black surgeons in the South, Williams readily accepted an invitation near the end of the century to be a visiting professor of clinical surgery at the Meharry Medical College in Nashville, Tennessee. He spent five or ten days there without pay each year for over a decade. He began operating in a crowded basement room, but by 1910 growing financial support for the college programs resulted in a separate hospital building with forty beds. Williams also operated and lectured at other schools and hospitals in the South.

In 1920 Williams built a summer home near Idlewild, Michigan, to which he and his wife moved. There Alice died of Parkinson's disease a few years later, and Williams then succumbed to diabetes and a stroke.

Williams became known for his long and successful efforts for medical care and professional training for blacks, although much of his work was multiracial. His logically developed and pioneering surgery, especially on the pericardium and the spleen, increased the possibilities and scope of surgical action.

• There is no major collection of Williams's papers. His three main contributions to surgery are documented in his articles "Stab Wound of the Heart and Pericardium—Suture of the Pericardium—Recovery—Patient Alive Three Years Afterward," *Medical Record* 51 (1897): 437–39; "Penetrating Wounds of the Chest, Perforating the Diaphragm, and Involving the Abdominal Viscera; Case of Successful Spleen Suture for Traumatic Haemorrhage," *Annals of Surgery* 40 (1904): 675–85; and "Ovarian Cysts in Colored Women, with Notes on the Relative Frequency of Fibromata in Both Races," *Chicago Medical Record* 20 (1901): 47–57, with discussion by Dr. A. J. Ochsner summarized on pp. 100–101. The most complete biographical source is Helen Buckler, *Daniel Hale Williams: Negro Surgeon* (1954; 2d ed., 1966). A summary of his life and career is William K. Beatty, "Daniel Hale Williams: Innovative Surgeon, Educator, and Hospital Administrator," *Chest* 60 (1971): 175–82.

WILLIAM K. BEATTY

WILLIAMS, David Marshall. *See* Williams, Carbine.

WILLIAMS, David Rogerson (8 Mar. 1776–17 Nov. 1830), politician, planter, and textile manufacturer, was born on the family plantation, on the Pee Dee River near Society Hill, South Carolina, the son of David Williams, a well-to-do planter, and Anne Rogerson. The elder Williams died a few months before his son's birth and left an estate that had grown to some 4,300 acres and 70 slaves by David's sixteenth birthday. Growing up in Charleston, where his widowed mother settled, Williams experienced the powerful influence of Richard Furman, the renowned minister and a close family friend. Apart from Furman, the youngster's formal education consisted of preparatory schooling in Wrentham, Massachusetts, and, beginning in 1792, intensive study at Rhode Island College.

Williams withdrew from college after three years and read law. He gained admission to the Rhode Island bar in 1797 and began a practice in Providence that lasted three years. The year before he married Sarah Power of Providence, who gave birth to John Nicholas, Williams's only child to reach adulthood. Within the next few years Williams returned to his native South Carolina to settle family debts and assume his plantation inheritance in Darlington County. Law practice gave way in 1801 to the newspaper business. With coproprietors John E. McIver and, later, Peter Freneau, Williams edited a pair of Charleston newspapers, the *City Gazette* and the *Weekly Carolina Gazette*, until 1804. Seven years after Sarah's death in 1802, he married Elizabeth Witherspoon, with whom he had no children.

Journalism broadened Williams's awareness not only of issues related to cotton planting and the lack of adequate transportation to market but also of politics in the era of Thomas Jefferson, whose views he generally shared. In 1805 the Darlington district sent Williams to Washington, where he served until 1813, except for a one-term hiatus in 1809–1811. Passionate and moralistic, ultrasensitive to insult, and quick to defend the Palmetto State, Williams's character personified elements of South Carolina's defiance of northern power. Though at first opposed to commercial sanctions against the British, the Orders in Council in 1807 prompted his call for retaliatory action. He supported the embargo policy of 1807–1808, despite its harsh impact on South Carolina. With the failure of economic coercion, Williams joined the "War Hawks," a group of vociferous young congressmen, including Henry Clay and John C. Calhoun, who in 1812 campaigned for a war against the British. For Williams, as for most War Hawks, it was a war to defend national honor and to assert trading rights that should have been granted after the Revolution.

Chairman of the House military affairs committee until 1813, Williams joined the fight in person when he received a presidential appointment as a brigadier general in that year. The army took him north again, and he served at Fort George under General John Parker Boyd, then returned home before the battle of Lundy's Lane. After trying and failing to secure a command in the fighting against the Creek Indians in Georgia, in early 1814 Williams left the army.

South Carolina paid a high price for war, as investments plummeted, imports stopped, and its docks piled high with unsalable cotton and rice. At the urging of John Belton O'Neall, the legislature chose Williams as governor in December 1814. As in Congress, military preparedness jumped to the forefront of Williams's priorities for the state. Hit especially hard economically, the port of Charleston lay open to possible enemy attack. The new governor focused attention on its defense, inspecting fortifications, surveying breastworks, and reviewing soldiers. Anxious planters regarded Williams's revamped militia as a bulwark against potential slave insurrection as well. When both the war and his term in office concluded in 1816, the governor repaired to his Darlington district estate and reaped his considerable share of the cotton bonanza that lasted until the panic of 1819.

After 1815 Williams embraced the fervid states' rights views of Senator William Smith, rather than the nationalistic Calhoun-Lowndes program. While staunchly opposed to protective tariffs and the use of federal money for state roads and canals, Williams urged "keeping the manufacturer on the same footing as the agriculturist," and, while in the South Carolina Senate from 1824 to 1827, he supported ample state funding for internal improvements. He implored fellow planters to invest in manufacturing and liberate themselves from northern industrial domination, but mounting debts, scarce capital, the absence of managerial experience, and traditional southern contempt for manufacturing undermined Williams's economic hopes for his region. Though sympathetic with the antitariff movement, Williams recoiled from the radical nullifiers and aligned with the "Unionist" group, saying, "I fear that violence may bring our doctrine into disrepute." This shrinking from nullification as well as his continued loyalty to the Smith faction distanced Williams even more from the Calhounites, who dominated the state's politics after 1828. Early that year, stung by mounting criticism of his Unionist views, he chose against reelection to the state senate.

Practicing the economic philosophy he advocated, Williams presented the anomaly of a cotton planter/ manufacturer in a culture increasingly hostile to the Northeast. Influenced by early personal contacts in Rhode Island, by the experience of Jefferson's embargo and the coming war, and by the vulnerability of South Carolina to outside economic forces, Williams had founded a cotton mill on Cedar Creek in 1812. One of the few factories in the state, it employed slave labor, including slave children. In years of uncertain trade, plagued by three panics in fourteen years, Williams thrived on cotton bagging, coarse cotton cloth and woolens, twine, and rope for baling. Though mostly limited to a regional market, business success warranted dramatic expansion by 1829. A hat and shoe factory was added and so was production of cottonseed oil—a lower priced alternative to spermacetic varieties from New England. Williams sold stock in his enterprise to neighboring planters who, in turn, augmented his store of raw cotton, purchased goods, and provided surplus slaves for hire.

Always interested in transportation improvements, Williams assumed supervision of a bridge project at Witherspoon's Ferry over Lynch's Creek in the fall of 1830. On 16 November one of the massive timbers fell on him and crushed both his legs. For seventeen hours he lingered in unbearable pain. He was buried on the old family plantation overlooking the Pee Dee River. At his death, Williams owned 245 slaves, not counting the holdings of his second wife and those given to his son. At his peak he owned nine plantations, totaling some 12,950 acres.

• Williams's private correspondence and business records are in the David Rogerson Williams Papers and in the Williams-Chesnut-Manning Collection, both located in the South Caroliniana Library, Columbia. His record in the 9th, 10th, and 12th Congresses is easily traced in Joseph Gales and William W. Seaton, comps., *Annals of Congress, 1789–1824* (42 vols., 1834–1856). Vital studies of South Carolina politics during Williams's era include William W. Freehling, *Prelude to Civil War: The Nullification Controversy in South Carolina, 1816–1836* (1965), and Lacy K. Ford, Jr., *Origins of Southern Radicalism: The South Carolina Upcountry, 1800–1860* (1988). For a full-length biography see Harvey T. Cook, *The Life and Legacy of David Rogerson Williams* (1916). An obituary is in the *Charleston Courier*, 19 Nov. 1830.

JOHN R. VAN ATTA

WILLIAMS, Dick (29 Jan. 1891–2 June 1968), tennis player, was born Richard Norris Williams II in Geneva, Switzerland, the son of Charles Duane Williams, a lawyer, and Lydia Biddle White. His parents, who came from wealthy, elite families of Philadelphia, settled in Switzerland but retained U.S. citizenship. Richard was educated by tutors and frequently accompanied his parents to other European countries and to the United States. He began playing lawn tennis in 1903. Self-taught, he quickly mastered grips, strokes, and tactics, and he first competed in Swiss championships in 1905. During the next half-decade he learned to take groundstrokes on the rise and to volley expertly. He was soon able to cope with first-class players on various court surfaces such as the dirt surface of courts in Switzerland, the clay of the French Riviera, the wood of indoor courts in Paris, the cement of California, and the grass of the eastern United States. Constantly encouraged by his father, he improved markedly every year. He won the 1911 Swiss and French indoor championships and defeated the great European star William Laurentz in the latter.

In April 1912 Williams and his father embarked on the liner *Titanic*, which was bound for the United States. After the liner struck an iceberg and began to sink, Charles Williams was killed by a collapsing funnell. Dick Williams jumped into the ocean and clung to a water-logged raft for six hours before being taken aboard the steamship *Carpathia*. Taking a physician's advice, he saved his almost frozen legs from amputation by very painfully hobbling around deck for many hours to restore sufficient basic function to the limbs. Devastated by the loss of his father, he avoided willing discussion of the *Titanic* disaster for decades.

Concentrating on tennis during the summer of 1912, he teamed with Mary K. Browne to win the U.S. mixed doubles championship. That year he also won four of eight major singles tournaments, including the U.S. Clay Court championship. He surprised and delighted Americans by his all-court, attacking style and his obvious enjoyment of the game, and his record earned him a number-two national ranking. As planned by his father, he attended Harvard University and graduated in 1916 with a bachelor of science degree. Afterward, he entered the bond business in Boston, although independent wealth rendered employment unnecessary.

Williams reached his peak in singles play during his Harvard years. He defeated defending champions Maurice McLoughlin and Bill Johnston, both times as an underdog, to capture the 1914 and 1916 U.S. titles. After his 1914 victory he was ranked second that year below McLoughlin; this provoked controversy because, for the first time, an American citizen who won the U.S. championship was denied the top position. McLoughlin had won his Davis Cup matches against Australasia, while Williams had lost his. Williams also won the 1913 and 1915 Intercollegiate and the 1915 U.S. Clay Court championships. His wholesome demeanor and "wonderful touch, rhythm, and economy of movement" captivated spectators. He prized difficult strokes above victories, titles, and rankings. He "never won a point with a soft, easy shot when a hard, dangerous smash would do instead." His ever aggressive style frequently produced erratic results; he would encounter streaks of overwhelming success and spells of ineffectiveness, sometimes within the same contest.

During World War I Williams enlisted in the U.S. Army. Arriving in France as a second lieutenant of field artillery, he was assigned to Major General James S. Harbold's staff. In this capacity he served as liaison to the French because of his fluency in French and German. France awarded him their Legion of Honor and the Croix de Guerre for conduct in the second battle of the Marne. In 1919, having been discharged as a captain, he married Jean Haddock; they had two children before her death in 1929.

From 1919 through 1925 Williams ranked nationally, in singles, third, fourth, and sixth twice each as Johnston, Bill Tilden, and Vinnie Richards virtually monopolized the top ratings. His abilities in doubles before the war were unimpressive, but afterward they became exceptional. His doubles wins included Wimbledon in 1920, with Chuck Garland; U.S. championships in 1925 and 1926, with Richards; four Davis Cup challenge round victories, two with Richards, one with Tilden, and one with Watson Washburn; and the mixed doubles gold medal in the 1924 Olympic Games, with Hazel Hotchkiss Wightman. In 1964 George Lott, himself an outstanding doubles player, rated Williams and Richards the greatest team in tennis history. Williams also served as captain of the U.S. Davis Cup team from 1921 through 1926 and the 1934 team, which reached the challenge round. He continued playing in U.S. singles championships through 1935, and at age forty-six he won one more doubles tournament, the Pennsylvania State championship of 1936, with the 42-year-old Washburn.

Williams moved to Philadelphia during the 1920s and worked as a statistician for an investment firm. In 1930 he married Frances "Sue" Gillmore; they had two children. Considering patriotism more important than self-accomplishment, Williams donated all his trophies to a scrap metal drive during World War II. In 1957 he was elected to the National Lawn (later International) Tennis Hall of Fame. From 1943 to 1965 he was associated with the Historical Society of Pennsylvania as its director and librarian. He died in Bryn Mawr, Pennsylvania.

• Williams provided a description of his playing style, as well as some reminiscences, in "The Mid-Court Game," *Fifty Years of Lawn Tennis in the United States* (1931), pp. 154–59. A succinct review of his career is in Bud Collins and Zander Hollander, *Bud Collins' Modern Encyclopedia of Tennis*, 2d ed. (1994), pp. 100–101. Bill Talbert with Pete Axthelm, in *Tennis Observed* (1967), includes an objective description of Williams's style and a record of all his match scores in the U.S. men's singles championships. "America's First Ten Players in 1914," in *American Lawn Tennis*, Jan. 1915, pp. 532–33, provides an analysis of Williams's style. George Lott, "A Midsummer Night's Dream," *World Tennis*, Nov. 1964, judges Williams as a doubles player. Obituaries appeared in the *New York Times* and in the *Philadelphia Inquirer*, both 4 June 1968.

FRANK V. PHELPS

WILLIAMS, Donald Cary (28 May 1899–16 Jan. 1983), philosopher, was born in Crow's Landing, California, the son of Joseph Cary Williams, a rural contractor, and Lula Crow. After studies in English literature at Occidental College (B.A., 1922), and at Harvard University (A.M., 1924), he undertook the study of philosophy, first at the University of California at Berkeley, then at Harvard (Ph.D., 1928).

In 1928 he married Katherine Pressly Adams, with whom he had two children. The couple spent a year in Europe in 1928–1929, after which Donald began a long and distinguished career as a professor of philosophy, first at the University of California, Los Angeles, until 1939, and from that year until his retirement in 1967 at Harvard.

Williams's importance as a philosopher rests in large measure on his persistence with a style of philosophizing that remained unfashionable throughout most of his active years: at a time when English-language philosophy was dominated by pragmatism, positivism, and linguistic philosophy, each of which turns away from philosophy's classic ambitions to create a systematic epistemic and metaphysical vision, he sustained the classic outlook and aspiration. He continued to insist that philosophical issues are real questions, having genuine answers, and that mere analysis can constitute an evasion of the philosopher's main duty.

In accord with these convictions, Williams worked steadily toward the development of his own distinctive position: in metaphysics, he favored a materialist naturalism that confines reality to the spatiotemporal world, and he was an important advocate of the four-dimensional conception of this world.

In epistemology, convinced that prevailing skepticisms were debilitating errors, Williams adhered to a direct realist account of perception and a broadly empiricist view of the development and validation of scientific conceptions.

Williams's two major contributions to philosophy concern the fundamental constituents of being and the problem of induction. On the first of these, which he explored in "The Elements of Being," he advanced an account of things, and their properties, that takes as basic abstract particulars, or "tropes," which are particular cases of general characteristics, such as redness or roundness. Williams's focus was on the very instance of red occurring as the color of a particular rose at a specific location in space and time, or the very case of circularity presented by some particular coin in one's hand on a single, particular occasion.

From these tropes as fundamental building blocks —"the alphabet of being"—Williams held we can construct both familiar objects and their properties and quantities. Objects such as shoes and ships and lumps of sealing wax consist in what might be called compresent clusters of tropes—their shapes, sizes, temperatures, consistencies, and so on. Properties and quantities such as acidity and velocity, which are common to many objects, are so-called resemblance classes of individual tropes.

This elegant and economical base can be used in the construction of further categories, of events, processes, and causality. It can be of use in explaining our divided attitudes toward the same thing, which can be good in some respects (tropes), but not in others. The scheme makes explicit the complexity of the realities with which we are ordinarily in contact.

In regard to the problem of induction, Williams was almost alone in his time both in holding that the problem does admit of solution and in presenting his own. *The Ground of Induction* (1947) makes original use of results already established, whose significance he was the first to appreciate. Williams treats the problem of induction, the problem of generalizing beyond current evidence to the not-yet-observed, as a case of the problem of validating sampling techniques. Among any population (class of like items—penguins, for example) there will be a definite proportion having any possible characteristic: 100 percent will be birds, about 50 percent will be female, some 10 percent, perhaps, will be Emperor penguins, some 35 percent, perhaps, will be more than seven years old, and so on. This is the complexion of the population, with regard to femaleness and other attributes.

Now in the pure mathematics of the relations between samples and populations, Bernouilli had shown in the eighteenth century that, for populations of any size whatever, the vast majority of samples of 2,500 or more closely match in complexion the population from which they are drawn. If the population has 35 percent of penguins seven years old or more, well over nine-tenths of samples of 2,500 penguins will contain close to 35 percent seven years old or more. This is a necessary consequence. The vast majority of reasonably sized samples are *representative* of their population, that is, closely resemble it in complexion.

Williams noticed that resemblance is symmetrical. If we can prove, as Bernouilli did, that most samples resemble the population from which they are drawn, then the population's complexion resembles that of most samples. Our observations of penguins, for example, up to this point provide us with a sample. What can we infer about the population from which it is drawn? That, in all probability, its complexion is close to that of the sample. We *may*, of course, have an atypical sample before us. But with more than 90 percent representing the population fairly closely, the odds are against it.

Thus Williams assimilates the problem of induction to an application of the *statistical syllogism*. Just as, if *all S is P*, this present one *must* be P, so, if *95 percent of S is P*, this present one is *probably* P. Ninety-five percent of samples are closely representative, so the sample we have, where there are no grounds to think otherwise, is probably one of them.

So Williams championed a nondefeatist, rational, and realist philosophy, responsive to developments in the natural sciences, which, owing to a general revival of concern with classical issues in metaphysics and epistemology, has in the later years of the twentieth century come to be more highly regarded than it was during his own scholarly lifetime.

He retired from Harvard with his wife to their beloved California, where he died at his home in Fallbrook.

• The Donald Williams Papers are in the archives of Harvard University. In addition to *The Ground of Induction*, the most accessible collection of his important articles, including "The Elements of Being," is Harry Ruja, ed., *Principles of Empirical Realism* (1966). The theory of tropes is elaborated and defended in Keith Campbell, *Abstract Particulars* (1990), while the solution to the problem of induction is analyzed and endorsed in David C. Stove, *The Rationality of Induction* (1986).

KEITH CAMPBELL

WILLIAMS, Edward Bennett (31 May 1920–13 Aug. 1988), trial attorney, was born in Hartford, Connecticut, the son of Joseph Barnard Williams, a department store floorwalker, and Mary Bennett. Williams received a degree in 1941 from Holy Cross College in Worcester, Massachusetts, where he studied philosophy and debating and was first in his class. He was graduated from Georgetown University Law School, first in his class, in 1944. Williams began his legal career at the Washington, D.C., firm of Hogan and Hartson, where he spent four years as a defense attorney in personal injury lawsuits. In 1946 he married Dorothy Guider; they adopted three children.

In 1949 Williams established his own practice in Washington, specializing in criminal law. Within a few years he had become famous for representing prominent underworld figures, labor leaders, and public officials. By the time of Williams's death his firm, then known as Williams and Connolly, employed nearly one hundred lawyers.

During the early 1950s Williams handled a number of civil cases for Senator Joseph R. McCarthy of Wisconsin; later he defended McCarthy in the hearings that culminated in the senator's censure in 1954. During the same years that Williams was serving as counsel to McCarthy, he represented Hollywood writers and producers who had been summoned to testify before the House Un-American Activities Committee, which was investigating charges of disloyalty inspired in large measure by McCarthy's allegations of widespread domestic Communist subversion.

Williams won acquittals for prominent clients in many highly publicized and often sensational trials. In 1957, for example, he successfully represented Teamsters Union official James R. "Jimmy" Hoffa in a bribery case. In 1960 Williams defended the controversial New York congressman Adam Clayton Powell in a tax evasion case that ended in a hung jury. Also in 1960 he married Agnes Neill, his first wife having died the year before. Williams and his second wife had four children. In 1975 Williams obtained an acquittal for former Texas governor and former U.S. treasury secretary John Connally, who had been indicted on bribery charges.

Not all of Williams's cases were successful. His most notable loss occurred in a politically sensitive case in which Robert G. "Bobby" Baker, a former aide to President Lyndon B. Johnson, was convicted of fraud and tax evasion in 1967 and sentenced to prison in 1970 after exhausting a series of appeals. Even in this and other unsuccessful cases, Williams generally won high praise for his professional skills.

In defending clients, Williams was known for histrionic gestures. In cases in which the government had eavesdropped on his clients, for example, Williams would sometimes brandish wiretapping equipment in court or before the press. He was also known for his effective use of expert character witnesses. During Connally's trial Williams elicited testimony from a parade of notables, including presidential widow Lady Bird Johnson, former secretary of state Dean Rusk, former secretary of defense Robert S. McNamara, and evangelist Billy Graham. Although Williams also was a colorful and effective advocate before a jury, his success ultimately was based on intensive pretrial preparation, during which he would become almost wholly absorbed by his work for weeks at a time.

Both in and out of court, Williams often spoke out against what he regarded as unfair and illegal prosecutorial tactics, particularly wiretapping. He argued two significant cases in which the Supreme Court constricted the scope of permissible searches and seizures under the Fourth Amendment. Justice William Brennan described Williams as one of the two or three most effective attorneys he saw during his long tenure on the Court.

Although many of his clients were professional criminals, Williams wrote in his memoirs that the right to counsel "extends to every person charged with crime, no matter how socially or politically obnoxious he may be, no matter how unorthodox his thinking or his conduct, how unpopular his cause or how strongly the finger of guilt may point at him" (*One Man's Freedom*, pp. 24–25). He believed that a "lawyer is neither expected nor qualified to make a moral judgment on the person seeking his help" (p. 27).

Williams's work was highly lucrative, and he became one of the best-paid lawyers of his day. Arriving in Washington as a student with $12, his net worth was reputed to be $100 million when he died. His investments included a Washington hotel and professional sports teams. Williams owned the Baltimore Orioles professional baseball team at the time of his death, and he served for many years as president of the Washington Redskins football team.

An emotional and gregarious man, Williams relished his far-flung friendships with an incongruous group of people that included organized crime figures, sports stars, film celebrities, powerful publishers, leading federal jurists, and hierarchs of the Roman Catholic church. Fascinated by power and politics, Williams became known as one of the leading Washington "insiders" of his day and was an informal confidant of many leading political figures, including Presidents Gerald R. Ford and Ronald Reagan.

Williams's relations with Presidents Richard M. Nixon and Jimmy Carter were distant, however, and he incurred Nixon's special wrath for representing the Democratic National Committee in its 1972 lawsuit against Nixon campaign officials arising out of the burglary at the Watergate Hotel. In 1980 Williams led an abortive movement on the eve of the Democratic National Convention to deprive Carter of renomination.

Despite his interest in politics, Williams never served in public office. He turned down an offer from President Johnson to serve as mayor of Washington, and he rejected offers from Presidents Ford and Reagan to serve as director of the Central Intelligence Agency. From 1974 to 1977 he served as treasurer of the Democratic National Committee. Williams died in Washington after a thirty-year battle against cancer.

• Williams's only published book, *One Man's Freedom* (1962), is an account of his early cases and his reflections on criminal justice and the Bill of Rights. Robert Pack, *Edward Bennett Williams for the Defense* (1983), provides detailed accounts of the cases handled by Williams. Evan Thomas, *The Man to See: Edward Bennett Williams: Ultimate Insider; Legendary Trial Lawyer* (1991), gives a comprehensive account of Williams's career and a balanced personal portrait.

WILLIAM G. ROSS

WILLIAMS, Edward Thomas (17 Oct. 1854–27 Jan. 1944), missionary and diplomat, was born in Columbus, Ohio, the son of William Williams, a cooper, plasterer, and housing contractor, and Dinah Louisa Hughes. Although raised a Baptist, Williams was attracted to the Disciples of Christ and attended Bethany College, established to prepare students for the ministry. He was influenced by his teacher, Charles L. Loos, who became his father-in-law in 1884, when Williams married Caroline Dorothy Loos, with whom he would have two children. After graduating in 1875, Williams was ordained a minister, and for the next twelve years he served a number of congregations, including the leading liberal church in Cincinnati (1881–1887). Williams became a prominent Disciples exponent of reform Darwinism and doctrinal innovation, which brought him into conflict with the conservatives, who emphasized the denomination's dedication to primitive Christianity. An advocate of the social gospel, Williams in 1887 volunteered for missionary work in China.

Williams plunged into intensive study of Chinese and became very proficient. In his evangelical work in China he increasingly turned to missionary journalism, both as a prolific essayist and as editor of the *Chinese Christian Review* and subeditor of the *Shanghai Mercury*. His work afforded him an opportunity to resolve his growing religious doubts, which developed from reading about scientific explanations of the origins of life and comparative philosophy as well as his exposure to Chinese civilization and thought. The death of his wife in 1892 added to his crisis of faith. His marriage to Rose Sickler in 1894 (they would have two children) helped ease his transition from orthodox Christianity to Unitarianism. Williams resigned from the ministry and severed his remaining ties with the Disciples church in 1901, when he accepted the position of Chinese secretary at the American legation in Peking (Beijing).

Williams had already served as vice consul and interpreter for the U.S. consulate general in Shanghai (1896–1898). From 1901 until his retirement in 1918, Williams held a succession of increasingly influential diplomatic posts in China and at the State Department in Washington. He was soon recognized as America's leading expert on China and was considered "the mainstay of the Legation" by Minister William W. Rockhill, himself a China "hand" and authority.

Initially, Williams shared with many of the missionaries the view that the Chinese were immoral and degenerate; he also looked upon Japan as an appropriate tutor to bring China into the modern age. He soon became a great admirer of the Chinese and their civilization and a sympathetic friend who tried to help China avoid internal disintegration and protect its independence from the imperial powers, above all from Japan, which emerged as China's (and America's) most dangerous enemy. His prescription called for China to strengthen itself through a program of modern education, political reform, and economic development. The United States could provide moral and some material assistance, but above all it must avoid undermining China's own efforts. Over the years, he became more pessimistic about China's ability to save itself. "There are times when nations as well as individuals must be born again if they are to be saved," the former missionary wrote in 1928.

Following his tenure as Chinese secretary in Peking and a brief stint as consul at Tientsin (Tianjin) in 1908–1909, Williams was transferred to the State Department. As assistant chief of the Far Eastern Division, he became involved in the Taft administration's efforts, which he considered misguided, to implement Dollar Diplomacy in China. He was sent back to Peking as first secretary of the legation and served long stretches as chargé d'affaires (1911–1913). After briefing Paul S. Reinsch, the new American minister, he returned to Washington in 1914 as chief of the Far Eastern Division. He was initially encouraged by the Wilson administration's different approach toward China, especially its early decision to recognize the new Chinese Republic, and generally endorsed Reinsch's aggressive program to develop American concessions in China and defend Chinese integrity from Japanese encroachments. He was upset by the administration's initial lackadaisical response to Japan's Twenty-One Demands (1915). However, he then waffled on protecting newly won American concessions from the protests of the other powers and on Reinsch's campaign to get China into the First World War. Williams periodically considered a quid pro quo with Japan over China and authored the formula acknowledging Japan's "special interests" that was incorporated into the Lansing-Ishii Agreement (1917).

Frustrated and fatigued by these problems, Williams welcomed his appointment as Agassiz Professor of Oriental Languages and Literature at the University of California (Berkeley) and retired from the State Department in 1918. He was soon recalled to government service as technical adviser on Far Eastern matters for the American delegation to the Paris Peace Conference. Here he suffered his most humiliating defeat, when to save the League of Nations, President Woodrow Wilson agreed to transfer German rights in Shantung (Shandong) to Japan. Williams then advised the Chinese not to sign the Versailles Treaty and left Paris as quickly as he could, "ashamed to look a Chinese in the face." Williams subsequently testified against the peace treaty. Despite his vocal moral outrage, Williams was named as a special assistant to the American delegation to the Washington Conference on the Limitation of Armament, 1921–1922.

Despite his age, Williams flourished as a teacher and scholar. Until his retirement from his chair at Berkeley in 1927, he delighted in interpreting China to American students. In addition, from 1918 to 1939, he published more than a dozen articles and two major books that were designed to prepare the West to grapple with Chinese problems, which he considered among the most pressing difficulties facing the world. Williams died in Berkeley.

Williams personified the transition in the early twentieth century from the employment of missionary-interpreters and amateur political appointees to career professionals and the increasing bureaucratization in the State Department. He welcomed the change and, in the words of historian Dimitri Lazo, was America's "first professional China watcher." Williams was also present at the assertion of the Open Door policy and collapse of the old order in China. Although he was not captivated by the dream of a huge China market, Williams was prepared to defend America's legitimate commercial and investment interests. He also recognized, if he did not personally accept, the brutal realities of international politics in East Asia as well as the limited ability of the United States to use force in that region. He thereby reflected the dilemmas and contradictions in America's China policy.

• The E. T. Williams Papers, including a lengthy manuscript of "Recollections," are at the Bancroft Library, University of California at Berkeley. His diplomatic career may also be followed in the extensive State Department files, both RG 59 and RG 84, and the correspondence of Secretary of State William J. Bryan with President Wilson, 1913–1915, at the National Archives in Washington. Other relevant manuscript collections are the papers of Nelson T. Johnson, Robert Lansing, Breckinridge Long, Woodrow Wilson (Library of Congress); Charles L. Loos (Disciples of Christ Historical Society, Nashville); and Paul S. Reinsch (Wisconsin State Historical Society, Madison). Williams's major publications include "Chinese Social Institutions as a Foundation for Republican Government," *American Historical Association Report, 1916* 1 (1916): 421–43; *China Yesterday and Today* (1923); and *A Short History of China* (1928). The fullest study of his life and career is Dimitri Lazo, "An Enduring Encounter: E. T. Williams, China and the United States" (Ph.D. diss., Univ. of Illinois, 1977). For a sketch, see Essen Gale, "Edward Thomas Williams, 1854–1944," *Far Eastern Quarterly* 3 (1944): 381–83. Williams's career is also treated in the basic secondary works on Sino-American relations for the first three decades of the twentieth century, including Burton

F. Beers, *Vain Endeavor: Robert Lansing's Attempts to End American-Japanese Rivalry* (1962); Michael H. Hunt, *The Making of a Special Relationship: The United States and China to 1914* (1983); and Noel H. Pugach, *Paul S. Reinsch: Open Door Diplomat in Action* (1979). An obituary is in the *New York Times*, 29 Jan. 1944.

NOEL H. PUGACH

WILLIAMS, Eleazar (1789?–28 Aug. 1858), Native-American missionary and pretender to the throne of France, was born at Sault St. Louis, present-day Caughnawaga, on the south side of the St. Lawrence River opposite Montreal, Quebec, Canada, the son of Thomas Williams or Tehorakwanekin, a mixed-blood Indian, and Mary Ann Kenewatsenri, who was three-fourths Indian. Eleazar (or Lazare) Williams was the great-grandson of John Williams, a minister at Deerfield, Massachusetts, and the grandson of John Williams's daughter, Eunice Williams, who had been captured by Abenakis Indians in 1704 and later married an Indian of Caughnawaga. Williams probably was born while the family was on a hunting trip, and he was baptized by a Catholic priest in Whitehall, New York.

In 1800 Thomas Williams accepted the invitation of a relative, who was the wife of Nathaniel Ely, a deacon in the Puritan church, to bring his sons John and Eleazar to Longmeadow School in Longmeadow, Massachusetts, to be educated. Although John soon returned home, Eleazar remained. He served with the U.S. Army as a scout in upstate New York during the War of 1812. Following the Treaty of Ghent in 1814 Williams was appointed a lay reader and catechist to do missionary work among the Oneidas of New York by the Protestant Episcopal church. He built a small mission on the Oneida reservation from which he ministered to his followers. His greatest accomplishment was the simplification of the writing of the Mohawk language, which he reduced to eleven letters. Using his translations, he published a *Spelling Book in the Language of the Seven Iroquois Nations* (1813), *Good News to the Iroquois Nation* (1813), and *Prayers for Families, and for Particular Persons, Selected from the Book of Common Prayer* (1816), as well as a number of translations of church books.

Williams apparently had a scheme in which he would form an Indian confederation in the West of which he would be the leader. In 1821 he persuaded a number of his followers to migrate westward where he negotiated a treaty with the Menominee and Winnebago tribes near Green Bay, Wisconsin, for a new homeland along the Fox River north of Lake Winnebago. The move was endorsed by the Episcopal church, and in 1822 Williams led his Oneida band to their new home and opened a school for Indians in Green Bay. Williams's original group soon was joined by a number of Stockbridge, Munsee, and Brotherton Indians. At the school he met and married one of his pupils in 1823, a fourteen-year-old Menominee named Madeleine Jourdain. Later the marriage was sanctioned by the church, and she changed her name to Mary Hobart. At the time of their marriage, Madeleine was betrothed to another man, who was away on business when Williams asked her parents for permission to marry their daughter. As a part of his wife's dowry Williams was given a large tract of land along the Fox River. The couple had three children.

Williams spent much of his time recruiting converts. As a result he was frequently away from his church, and in 1830 he was replaced as its preacher. During the following two years Williams preached at Duck Creek, west of Green Bay; however, in 1832 he also lost this following. Having spent his personal fortune, Williams mortgaged much of his wife's property to maintain himself. They had a home at Little Rapids on the Fox River, but more often than not he was away. His behavior became erratic, and he lost many of his supporters and friends.

In 1839 Williams began to claim that he was the dauphin of France and heir to the French throne. According to Williams's supporters, after the execution of Louis XVI and Marie Antoinette in 1793 their remaining heir, the dauphin, who was eight years old at the time, was imprisoned in Paris. Contemporary accounts maintain that the dauphin was kept prisoner for two years until he died; however, Williams claimed that he somehow escaped and fled to the United States, after another child was substituted to deceive his jailers. Two years after Williams first made his claim, the son of Louis Philippe of France, Prince de Joinville, visited Green Bay. Williams claimed that the visit was to persuade him to abdicate the throne, but he refused the request. Williams's claim attracted the interest of several periodicals and journals, and in 1849 an anonymous article appeared in the *United States Magazine and Democratic Review* asserting Williams's claim. The article probably was authored by Williams, but it popularized his contention. In 1854 John H. Hanson's book, *The Lost Prince*, was published supporting Williams's claim as the dauphin of France.

Williams returned to the ministry in 1850 to preach to the Mohawk, or St. Regis, Indians at Hogansburgh, New York. During his later years he prepared a biography of his father, Thomas Williams, which appeared in 1859. He died at Hogansburgh. However, his assertion to the throne of France endured and was debated as late as 1890. In 1901 a novel, *Lazarre*, by Mary H. Catherwood was published based on Williams's life.

• Williams's papers are on file at the State Historical Society of Wisconsin. General accounts of his life may be found in Fred L. Holmes, *Badger Saints and Sinners* (1939), and T. Wood Clarke, *Emigrés in the Wilderness* (1941). His role in the migration of the Oneidas to Wisconsin is discussed in Francis Paul Prucha, *The Great Father: The United States Government and the American Indians* (1984). Glimpses of his early life can be found in John Y. Smith, *Eleazer Williams and the Lost Prince*, Collections of the State Historical Society of Wisconsin, vol. 6 (1908), and Lyman Copeland Draper, *Additional Notes on Eleazar Williams*, Collections of the State Historical Society of Wisconsin, vol. 8 (1908).

KENNY A. FRANKS

WILLIAMS, Elizabeth Sprague (31 Aug. 1869–19 Aug. 1922), social worker, was born in Buffalo, New York, the daughter of Frank Williams, a civil engineer and businessman, and Olive French, a former schoolteacher. Williams's interest in the settlement house movement began while she was a student at Smith College (B.S., 1891) and prompted her joining the newly founded College Settlement Association (CSA) in 1889. After graduation, she returned to Buffalo to help found a settlement house aided by the local Unitarian congregation to which she belonged.

As a CSA member, Williams received some professional support for her work in Buffalo, but the challenges of settlement work led her to pursue more formal training in the social sciences. In 1896 she moved to New York City to enroll at Columbia University, receiving an A.M. in 1897 and continuing to take courses at Barnard College for another two years. Seeking practical social service training, Williams joined the Rivington Street Settlement in New York as a resident in 1896 and was appointed head worker there in fall 1898. She remained at Rivington Street until 1919, except for a sabbatical year in 1911–1912 to open a settlement in the steel town of Lackawanna City, New York, a suburb of Buffalo.

As head worker at Rivington Street, Williams pursued the major reforms of the Progressive Era, notably efforts to improve the living and working conditions of the neighborhood's residents. A proponent of the idea that immigrants needed to be "Americanized," Williams developed a range of programs and activities to teach immigrants the responsibility and civic values necessary to function successfully as American citizens. Through group projects and club work, immigrants and residents participated in programs to promote education, housing, sanitation, health, labor reform, and recreation.

Under Williams's direction, life at Rivington Street revolved around clubs. Literary, social, and athletic clubs served as an acceptable alternative to the urban entertainments available to immigrant youth. Older residents joined clubs that developed vocational skills—sewing, cooking, woodworking—or intellectual interests—debating, reading, and music. Club membership provided immigrants with the opportunity to learn both the self-control and the spirit of cooperation necessary for becoming effective American citizens. Whether planning a social event or organizing a group discussion or athletic contest, membership in a club taught immigrants a set of American values and ideals Williams believed they did not learn in the tenement—a sense of order and the spirit of mutual respect. Her annual reports to the College Settlement Association regularly referred to her belief that clubs could serve as "small republics," teaching club leaders and members the practical measures and civic values of self-government. Williams further advanced her ideas and practice of club work through her own and residents' involvement in such associations as the local school board, the Charity Organization Society, the Consumers' League, the Public Education Association, the Outdoor Recreation League, and the New York Committee on Amusements and Vacation Resources of Working Girls.

Williams's pet project was "Mount Ivy," the settlement's summer home community, located in Rockland County, New York, which she founded in 1896. Vacationers lived in separate camps and cabins but came together to share common meals and recreation. In addition to providing a rural setting for immigrants to enjoy, Mount Ivy also became a site to further the Americanization agenda pursued at the Rivington Street Settlement. The cooperative nature and simple lifestyle of the summer communities were designed to reinforce the values of self-government and cooperation to which immigrants were exposed in the settlement's clubs and classes throughout the year.

In spring 1919 Williams left Rivington Street and joined several other Smith College women to do reconstruction work in Serbia. For two years she served as head of an orphanage in Veles, Serbia, learning the native language in order to better communicate with the children. The orphans responded to her warmth and dedication by calling her "Mother Elizabeth." In 1921 she returned to the United States with a two-year-old orphan girl she had adopted. The Serbian government assumed control of the orphanage and continued the social and educational programs Williams had introduced. She was posthumously awarded a Serbian royal decoration for her work.

Williams, who never married, died suddenly of cancer in New York City a year after her return from Serbia. A small group of devoted friends and colleagues rallied together to assume the responsibility for the care and education of her adopted daughter as a living memorial to Williams's years of dedicating her life to improve the lives of others. Williams's contribution to the settlement house movement was her development of club work as a means to inculcate the ideals and exercise of democratic citizenship. Through the use of recreational, educational, and vocational clubs, she experimented in working intensively with small groups of people in order to effect social and individual change, a model later adopted by professional social workers.

• The archives at Smith College have clippings from the *Smith Alumnae Quarterly*, 1912 through 1923, documenting Williams's activities as well as letters written to Helen Rand Thayer (Smith, 1884) describing her involvement in reconstruction work in Serbia. The most comprehensive survey of Williams's social settlement philosophy is in her annual contributions as head worker at the Rivington Street Settlement to the *Reports* of the College Settlement Association, 1898 to 1919. Information about her membership in the CSA and residency at Rivington Street before her appointment as head worker is also included in the *Reports*. Biographical data is in the *Bulletin of Smith College: Alumnae Biographical Register Issue, 1871–1935* and in Jean Fine Spahr, "Elizabeth Williams: In Memoriam," *Smith Alumnae Quarterly* 13, no. 1 (Nov. 1922): 32.

JANET E. SCHULTE

WILLIAMS, Ephraim (7 Mar. 1714–8 Sept. 1755), soldier, was born in Newton, Massachusetts, the son of Elizabeth Jackson and Ephraim Williams, substantial farmers. His father was the first of four householders to settle in the frontier town of Stockbridge, and after going to sea and visiting Europe as a youth, Williams moved there as well. The Williams family, headed by Ephraim's cousin Israel, "the Monarch of Hampshire County," replaced the Stoddard family as western Massachusetts's most prominent clan. Among the Williamses' enemies was the Reverend Solomon Stoddard's spiritual heir, the Reverend Jonathan Edwards, whom they successfully ousted from his pulpit in Northampton in 1751 and whom they unsuccessfully tried to prevent from coming to Stockbridge to serve as missionary to the American Indians still residing nearby. Edwards considered Ephraim Williams a bitter opponent, but a ring of truth sounds in the reasons Williams advanced for preferring a different missionary. He claimed Edwards was "not sociable, . . . a great bigot, . . . [and] an old man unlikely to learn the Indian languages."

Williams's principal career was as a soldier. During King George's War (1740–1748) he commanded Massachusetts's forts on the western frontier. Chief among them was Fort Massachusetts, from which he was absent when a force of nearly a thousand French and Indians attacked and destroyed it in August 1746. The fort was soon rebuilt, and in 1750 Williams received 190 acres of land adjoining it on the Hoosic River in what is now North Adams.

When the French and Indian War broke out (1754–1763), Williams was angered that he was not promoted. In March 1755 he wrote to assembly leader James Otis, father of the famous revolutionary, "I am insulted by my enemies. . . . To be promised a colonelcy and get a lieutenancy sinks my spirits." He was also depressed by the unfortunate way the war was going for the British. Predicting the ultimate conditions of victory, he considered it necessary for ten to twelve thousand men to launch a three-pronged invasion of Canada to divide the French forces. Meanwhile, "our country is lost, . . . it is on the brink of ruin."

Williams did not live to see things improve. He received his colonelcy, but his first active duty was to lead the vanguard of William Johnson's expedition against the French fort at Crown Point on Lake George in New York. On 8 September 1755, in company with the old Mohawk chief Hendrick, Williams was ordered to lead a scouting force of a thousand soldiers and two hundred Indians. Hendrick's comment on the unfortunate mission, "If they are to be killed, too many; if they are to fight, too few," is now a part of colonial lore. Marching through a ravine, the advance party was surprised by Baron Ludwig August de Dieskau and "doubled up like a pack of cards." Williams bravely led his men up the slopes and was killed almost instantly. A monument to his courage was erected on the site in 1854. Colonel Timothy Ruggles of Roxbury sarcastically informed General Johnson, "General, I hope the damnable blunder you have made this day may be sanctified to your spiritual and everlasting good."

Williams was described by contemporaries as a large, portly man, greatly esteemed by his soldiers and "affable" in all kinds of company. According to Ruggles, "He had a taste for books and often lamented his want of a liberal education." His love of learning appeared in the will he made before he embarked on his last campaign. Never married, he left his estate to start a free school in the West Township, where he held substantial land, provided Massachusetts successfully retained it in its border dispute with New York and also on the condition the town was named Williamstown. In appreciation of his services, the Massachusetts General Court obliged. However, instead of the modest academy he doubtless envisioned, the town, when it became more heavily settled by 1785, held a lottery and greatly added to Williams's bequest. In 1793 the present Williams College, named for this valiant if unlucky frontier fighter, was established.

• Wyllis E. Wright, *Colonel Ephraim Williams: A Documentary Life* (1970), contains all known, relevant documents and supplants Arthur Latham Perry, *Origins in Williamstown* (1897), and W. A. Pew, *Colonel Ephraim Williams: An Appreciation* (1919). Patricia J. Tracy, *Jonathan Edwards, Pastor: Religion and Society in Eighteenth Century Northampton* (1980), has material on the rivalry between the Williams family and Edwards.

WILLIAM PENCAK

WILLIAMS, E. Virginia (12 Mar. 1914–8 May 1984), teacher and artistic director, was born Ellen Virginia Williams in Stoneham, Massachusetts, the daughter of Charles F. Williams, an engraver and inventor, and Mary Virginia Evitts. Williams's passion for dance began at a very early age, when her parents took her to see vaudeville. She studied with some of the better-known teachers in her city, among them Dana Sieveling (whose name she later gave to one of her students, Earle Sieveling), Geraldine Cragin, and Miriam Winslow. Throughout her life, she remained an indefatigable learner and reader.

Because her parents did not approve of a professional dance career, Williams early went into teaching ballet. By the time she was fourteen, she was teaching dance in Melrose, a Boston suburb to which the family had moved. By the time she reached her twenties, she had developed her own dance schools in Malden, Melrose, Stoneham, and Wakefield.

In 1938 she married a dancer, Carl Richard Nelson; they had one child. In 1955 the marriage ended in divorce, and in 1957 she married her accompanist and musical adviser, Herbert Hobbs. They had no children.

Williams was an exceptionally gifted teacher. She could foresee the theatrical and artistic potential of a student and set that student securely on the right path. Her taste in music, costuming, and stagecraft was also sophisticated. In 1950 she opened the Boston School of Ballet, and her students began to be in demand as performers. She formed the New England Civic Ballet in 1958. The following year, the young company appeared in the first Northeastern Regional Ballet Festival in Scranton/Wilkes-Barre, Pennsylvania, and was immediately singled out as the finest company in the event, which included companies from all over the northeastern United States. The dancers appeared in the ballet *The Young Loves*, which revealed Williams to be a gifted choreographer.

George Balanchine, ballet master in chief of the New York City Ballet, early took an interest in Williams. In 1962, after seeing her company in another regional festival, he invited Williams to monthly private sessions with him. They discussed choreographic and teaching principles and formed a close artistic bond. As her company continued to develop, Balanchine was extremely generous in letting her have his ballets and his company members as guest artists.

In 1963 the Ford Foundation, with Balanchine and Lincoln Kirstein as advisers, announced its celebrated $7.7 million in grants to American ballet companies. Among the seven companies named to receive the grants was Williams's New England Civic Ballet, which then changed its name to Boston Ballet. The initial grant enabled the company to begin paying its personnel.

The company made its professional debut on 25 January 1966 at Boston's John Hancock Hall in a nicely balanced program consisting of Balanchine's *Apollo* and *Scotch Symphony*, Anton Dolin's staging of *Pas de Quatre*, and *Reflections* by the modern dance choreographer Norman Walker, with Walker and his partner Cora Cahan in the leading roles.

Williams was imaginative in her choice of repertoire. Her motive was not only to develop varied and stimulating programming but also to challenge her dancers as well as her choreographers. For example, choreographer Agnes de Mille was known for her dramatic ballets like *Rodeo* and *Fall River Legend*, both in the Boston Ballet repertoire, so Williams commissioned a nondramatic work from her, *Summer* (1975). Conversely, Choo San Goh was known for his abstract works, and so the last commission Williams made (it had its premiere shortly after her death) was Goh's first dramatic work, *Romeo and Juliet*. In the 1960s, when ballet companies shied away from modern dance choreographers, Williams acquired works from modern choreographers like Anna Sokolow, Merce Cunningham, Talley Beatty, Pearl Lang, and John Butler. Not that Williams wished to form a modern dance company; her deepest love was for classical technique.

A second Ford Foundation grant in 1966 enabled her to begin adding nineteenth-century classical ballets to the repertoire. Here, too, she challenged guest artists with unfamiliar roles. For example, in 1968 Violette Verdy and Edward Villella of the neoclassical New York City Ballet were featured in the Boston Ballet production of the Romantic classic *Giselle*.

By 1973 the company had grown to thirty-four dancers and had initiated its free summer performances at the Hatch Shell of the Charles River Esplanade. Other full-length ballets also began to enter the repertoire: *The Sleeping Beauty* in 1977, *Swan Lake* in 1981, and in 1982, *Don Quixote*, staged by Rudolf Nureyev and with him in the principal role. Unfortunately, Williams stopped creating ballets of her own, and so a sensitive, lyrical dimension was lost to the repertoire. Her interest in new choreographers remained steadfast. In 1979 she initiated the company's first National Choreography Showcase, also called the Vestris Prize Competition. It preceded other companies' showcases by about twenty years.

E. Virginia Williams had the stuff of which pioneers are made. Physically she was short and stocky, with piercing blue eyes and a prominent lower jaw. Her voice was high pitched, and her accent was pure suburban Boston. She was honest, direct, and uncompromising. Her passion for dance eliminated much else from her life, and yet she was deeply sensitive and affectionate. She was also plagued by overwhelming shyness. Like many groundbreakers, Williams worked with her hands as well as her head. She was an expert seamstress who could often be found sewing sequins on costumes minutes before performance. Her family-inherited love of the sea was constant; it even inspired one of her loveliest works, the pas de deux *Sea Alliance*.

In 1980 the company traveled to China. That same year, under pressure from an increasingly powerful board of directors, Williams named former ballerina Violette Verdy as associate director. While the two women were artistically well attuned, Williams chafed under the double yoke. In 1983 the board pressured her into retiring with the title of founder–artistic adviser. She died in Malden the following year.

• Articles on Williams include Doris Hering, "New England Civic Ballet . . . Sweet Compulsion," *Dance Magazine* 34, no. 4 (Apr. 1960): 52–55, 64; Iris Fanger, "Ballet," *Boston Sunday Herald Magazine*, 26 Feb. 1989; and Debra Cash, "Yankee Doodle Dandies," *Ballet News* 5, no. 11 (May 1984): 12, 17, 41. Among the most complete obituaries are those by Jeff McLaughlin in the *Boston Globe*, 9 May 1984, Iris Fanger in the *Patriot Ledger*, 10 May 1984, and Christine Temin in the *Boston Globe*, 13 May 1984.

DORIS HERING

WILLIAMS, Fannie Barrier (12 Feb. 1855–4 Mar. 1944), lecturer and clubwoman, was born in Brockport, New York, the daughter of Anthony J. Barrier and Harriet Prince, free persons of color. She graduated from the State Normal School at Brockport in 1870 and attended the New England Conservatory of Music in Boston and the School of Fine Arts in Washington, D.C. She then taught in southern schools and in Washington, D.C., for a short time. In 1887 Barrier retired from teaching to marry S. Laing Williams, a prominent attorney in Chicago. The couple had no children.

Williams became known for her club work and lecturing. Though many of her early lectures and written works supported the militant, egalitarian protest ideology of Frederick Douglass, she later became a staunch supporter of Booker T. Washington's accommodationist views, including his emphasis on industrial education and practical training. She encouraged employers to hire qualified black women for clerical positions and sought other job opportunities for blacks. She did not, however, reject the value of education beyond that of industrial training.

Williams's prominence arose from her efforts to have blacks officially represented on the Board of Control of the Columbian Exposition in 1893. She was able to persuade the board to include black affairs in the exhibits planned for the celebration. At the exposition, Williams delivered an address, "The Intellectual Progress of Colored Women in the U.S. since the Emancipation Proclamation," to an enthusiastic, integrated audience of the World's Congress of Representative Women. In this address, Williams dismissed the charges of sexual immorality among black women with the claim that continued harassment by white men was the source of the problem. She stated that after emancipation black women were quick and eager to "taste the blessedness of intelligent womanhood," and she urged white women who were concerned about morality to find ways to help black women.

In 1895 Williams was a state representative at the National Colored Women's Congress, which was convened by the Negro Department of the Cotton States and International Exposition in Atlanta, Georgia. In the same year, following an initial rejection, she became the first black woman admitted to the Woman's Club of Chicago. She was also the first black woman to be appointed to the Chicago Library Board, on which she served from 1924 to 1926.

Active in many community and civic organizations, she was a director of the Frederick Douglass Center, Chicago's first interracial organization, and a member of the Abraham Lincoln Center. She also worked with the Phillis Wheatley Home Association. She was a founding member of the National League of Colored Women in 1893 and served as president of the Woman's Council, which hosted the 1899 meeting of its successor, the National Association of Colored Women. She wrote a column about women's activities for T. Thomas Fortune's *New York Age* and the *Chicago Record-Herald*.

Williams's political activism, which began with the 1893 Columbian Exposition in Chicago, continued with the black women's club movement. She often spoke on the need for black women to emancipate their minds and spirits. In the speech "Club Movement Among Colored Women of America," she stated that "the struggle of an enlightened conscience against the whole brood of miseries [is] born out of the stress and pain of a hated past." Williams advocated feminist thinking through her efforts in the club movement. She noted that black women had reached an age in which they were moving beyond the patriarchal notion of women doing what men felt they ought to do. "In our day and in this country, a woman's sphere is just as large as she can make it." Williams's activism focused on the social condition of the entire race, which distinguished the black women's club movement from that of white women. She strongly supported education of black women in order to move them out of domestic work, where sexual harassment was so prevalent. She also advocated voting rights and equal employment opportunities.

Williams sought to combat and defy Jim Crow laws in whatever manner she could. She once used her light complexion and knowledge of French to ride in the white-only section of a southern train. She wrote in "A Northern Negro's Autobiography" (1904) that "[I] quieted my conscious by recalling that there was a strain of French blood in my ancestry, and too that their barbarous laws did not allow a lady to be both comfortable and honest."

Williams worked closely with Dr. Daniel Hale Williams in establishing the Provident Hospital in 1891. It housed the first training school for black nurses in Chicago, which she helped organize, and which was distinctive for its biracial staff of doctors. After her husband's death in 1921, Williams withdrew from many of her activities. She died in Brockport.

• Williams's political views are most clearly outlined in her address to the 1893 Columbian Exposition, which can be found in May Wright Sewall, ed., *World's Congress of Representative Women* (1894). Her "A Northern Negro's Autobiography" was published in the *Independent*, 14 July 1904. Further information can be found in J. W. Gibson and W. H. Crogman, eds., *Progress of a Race* (1903), which has a chapter on the development of the black woman's club movement written by Williams. Gerda Lerner, *The Black Woman in White America: A Documentary History* (1972), contains three of Williams's speeches and a short biography. August Meier, *Negro Thought in America, 1880–1915: Racial Ideologies in the Age of Booker T. Washington* (1963), explores the relationship between the Williamses and Booker T. Washington. See also J. E. McBrady, ed. *A New Negro for a New Century* (1900).

MAMIE E. LOCKE

WILLIAMS, Francis Henry (15 Apr. 1852–22 June 1936), physician, was born in Uxbridge, Massachusetts, the son of Henry Willard Williams, an ophthalmologist, and Elizabeth Dewé Williams. He received a B.S. in chemistry from the Massachusetts Institute of Technology in 1873 and spent the following year on a tour around the world, including a visit to Japan as a member of the astronomy team for the U.S. Transit of Venus Expedition. The transit of Venus across the face of the sun is a rare event that allows individuals to make astronomical measurements of the features of the sun. The 1874 expedition included Southern and Northern Hemisphere observation stations, including one in Nagasaki, Japan. Williams received an M.D. in 1877 from Harvard University and then continued his medical studies in Vienna and Paris. In 1879 he returned to Boston, where he became a practicing physician and a pioneer in the development of diagnostic radiology and radiation therapy.

Williams was a member of the faculty of Harvard Medical School from 1884 to 1891, teaching materia medica and therapeutics. At the Boston City Hospital he served as visiting physician (from 1896 to 1913) and senior physician from 1913 to 1930. Williams was one of the first physicians in Boston to give bedside clinical instruction to medical students. In 1892 he initiated bacterial examinations at the Boston City Hospital and in 1894 became the first in Boston to use antitoxin in the treatment of diphtheria. Williams married Anna Dunn Phillips of Boston, granddaughter of Boston mayor John Phillips, in 1891; they had no children.

Williams's major contributions to medicine and medical physics were in the use of X-rays. Within a few weeks of the discovery of X-rays by German physicist Wilhelm Konrad Roentgen in November 1895, Williams began using X-rays to study pulmonary tuberculosis and other thoracic lesions. Williams fluoroscoped his first patients at the Rogers Laboratory of Physics at MIT with the cooperation of Professor Charles R. Cross. He also collaborated with MIT staff members Charles L. Norton and Ralph R. Lawrence. The first X-ray picture published by Williams appeared in the *Boston Medical and Surgical Journal* (now the *New England Journal of Medicine*) on 20 February 1896. He gave a dramatic demonstration of the value of fluoroscopy for determining cardiac size before the Suffolk County (Mass.) District Medical Society on 25 April 1896. Williams subsequently established, unofficially, the X-ray department at the Boston City Hospital in May 1896 in the basement of the library building.

Among the devices Williams developed were lead diaphragms to improve the definition of the X-ray beam and avoid unnecessary X-ray exposure to the patient and physician. Williams remained concerned with radiation safety. The "Rollins box" was developed near the turn of the century with Williams's frequent collaborator William Rollins, a physician and dentist as well as a gifted inventor. It consisted of an X-ray tube in a wooden box lined with white lead. An opening in the box allowed the X-rays to pass through. This improvement in X-ray shielding was of great importance to patients and radiologists, and Williams was later to point out that the avoidance of "the very serious results that follow the use of X-rays in many other places, [which] involve the loss of finger, hands, arms, or even life itself is attributable to the use of simple and efficient means of protection which has been employed and advocated at this hospital" (Williams, *History of the Boston City Hospital*, p. 319). Later in his career he pointed out the dangers of radium and recommended the use of a shielding capsule, holding the radium at a distance from the physician, and protection of the patient's healthy skin with a sheet of lead foil. In 1902–1903 Williams also invented a device called a fluorometer, which was used to determine the quantity and penetrance of X-rays issuing from a tube via comparison to a radium sample. Williams felt that by means of his fluorometer the "amount and kind of X-rays desired can be measured and applied, and therefore a definite dosage can be used of the kinds of rays adapted to this special patient" (Williams, *History of the Boston City Hospital*, p. 322). Williams and Rollins also developed the "see-hear" device (1896). A fluorescent screen was combined with a rubber diaphragm connected to a stethoscope to allow evaluation of intrathoracic sights and sound simultaneously.

Williams worked under difficult conditions, carrying on his work at the Boston City Hospital before 1908 in a single, cramped room. In order to keep the static machines dry it was necessary to keep them warm, so during certain seasons of the year the temperature of the room ranged between 95° and 100°F.

Among the first uses of the X-ray was the location of foreign bodies, such as bullets and needles. Williams collaborated with his brother Charles Herbert Williams, an ophthalmologist, on a method of localizing foreign bodies in the eye by means of X-rays. Francis Williams also collaborated with Walter Bradford Cannon in some of the earliest studies to evaluate the status of the gastrointestinal tract by administering a dose of subnitrate of bismuth and obtaining an outline of the changing outlines of the esophagus, stomach, and intestines on a fluorescent screen. Cannon and Williams began doing radio-opaque gastrointestinal studies in humans in 1899. Williams also investigated the use of the x-ray for the identification of organs and conditions in the abdomen by inflating the intestine with air or by taking advantage of the fact that the lower gut was filled with gas. He conducted experiments to determine the radio-opacity of genitourinary calculi, a variety of body fluids, and the post-mortem appearance of healthy and diseased lungs.

Williams had a particular interest in the diagnosis of diseases of the chest. He and his associate and successor S. W. Ellsworth described the use of the X-ray for the evaluation of various conditions of the thorax. Williams also noted that in some diseases such as leukemia, the use of therapeutic X-rays was followed by a good initial response. He was quick to note, however, that "unfortunately these results do not appear to be permanent and it is a question whether this method can never be more than palliative in this disease; but if used it should always be with great care" (Williams, *History of the Boston City Hospital*, pp. 343–44).

Williams was probably the first physician to use radium therapeutically, late in 1900 or early in 1901, after his collaborator Rollins sent him a capsule containing a weak source of radium chloride with the suggestion that it might be used for therapeutic purposes. In 1903 Williams traveled to Europe and observed the use of radium for therapy. There he obtained 100 milligrams of radium bromide, which he subsequently used at the Boston City Hospital for the treatment of superficial epidermoid carcinoma, rodent ulcers, lupus vulgaris, breast cancer, eczema, psoriasis, keloids, and acne.

Williams was a prolific author whose writings appeared in a variety of medical journals. Among his most important contributions to the scientific literature was the publication of the textbook *The Roentgen Rays in Medicine and Surgery, as an Aid in Diagnosis and as a Therapeutic Agent* (1901), which was reissued in 1902 and in 1903. In 1935 he published a second volume, *Radium Treatment of Skin Diseases, New Growths, Diseases of the Eyes, and Tonsils.*

Williams was a fellow of the American Association for the Advancement of Science and the American Academy of Arts and Sciences. He was president in 1917–1918 of the Association of American Physicians and a member of the Massachusetts Medical Society, the American Medical Association, and the Société de Radiologie Medicale de France. He was a corresponding member of the K. K. Gesellschaft der Aertze and Wein and an honorary member of the American Radium Society, the American Roentgen Ray Society, and the Radiological Society of North America. Williams donated to the Roentgen Ray Society a card catalog to the work of more than 10,000 contributors to the radiologic literature, with abstracts. He was a life member of the MIT Corporation and a member of its executive committee for twenty-five years.

Williams died in Boston, having made a bequest of $100,000 to MIT with instructions for its investment. By 1971 the fund had exceeded $2 million.

• Williams describes his early work in the X-ray department at the Boston City Hospital in chap. 17 of *A History of the Boston City Hospital from Its Foundation until 1904* (1906), authorized by the hospital's trustees and edited by a committee of its medical staff; a copy of this book, as well as of Williams's definitive text, *The Roentgen Rays in Medicine and Surgery*, can be found in the Duke University Medical Center Library. He published "Reminiscences of a Pioneer in Roentgenology and Radium Therapy, with Reports of Some Recent Observations," *American Journal of Roentgenology* 13 (1925): 253–59. Detailed discussions, many with excellent illustrations, of Williams's life and contributions to radiology are in Otto Glasser, ed., *The Science of Radiology* (1933); E. R. N. Grigg, *The Trail of the Invisible Light: From Strahlen to Radio(bio)logy* (1965); Andre J. Bruwer, ed., *Classic Descriptions in Diagnostic Roentgenology*, vol. 2 (1964); and Ruth Brecher and Edward Brecher, *The Rays: A History of Radiology in the United States and Canada* (1969). A scholarly and literate biography of Williams is in Juan A. del Regato, *Radiological Oncologists: The Unfolding of a Medical Specialty* (1993). Percy Brown's summary of Williams's life and contributions to radiology is "Frances Henry Williams 1852–1936," in the *American Journal of Roentgenology and Radium Therapy* 36 (1936): 106–10. A shorter obituary is in the *Journal of the American Medical Association* 107 (1936): 145.

EDWARD C. HALPERIN

WILLIAMS, George Henry (26 Mar. 1823–4 Apr. 1910), attorney general and senator, was born in New Lebanon, Columbia County, New York, the son of Tabor Williams, a farmer and shoemaker, and Lydia Goodrich. Three years after his birth, his family moved to Onondaga County, New York. Williams attended local public schools and Pompey Hill Academy in Onondaga County. He read law under Daniel Gott and was admitted to the bar in 1844. Borrowing money from friends, he relocated that year to Fort Madison, Iowa Territory, where he practiced law and formed a partnership with Daniel F. Miller. Three years later he bought a newspaper, the *Lee County Democrat*, and changed its name to the *Iowa Statesman*, continuing as its owner until 1852. In 1847 he also won election as judge of the First Judicial District of the new state of Iowa, earning a salary of $1,000 per year. In 1850 he married Kate Van Antwerp. They had one child and adopted two other children before Kate died in 1863.

Williams held his judicial position until 1852, when he was a Democratic presidential elector for the national ticket of Franklin Pierce and William R. D. King. In 1853, upon the recommendation of Senator Stephen A. Douglas of Illinois, President Pierce appointed Williams chief justice of the territorial courts of Oregon, where Williams remained until 1857. One of his controversial decisions involved a free African American, Robin Holmes, who had sued his former owner, Nathaniel Ford, to obtain legal custody of his children. Williams, who opposed the extension of slavery into Oregon, ruled in favor of Holmes.

Although reappointed chief justice of the territory of Oregon by President James Buchanan, Williams resigned in 1857 to practice law in Portland, Oregon. While building his practice, he, in partnerships, formed a woolen manufacturing company, acquired the *Oregon Statesman*, and established the Oregon Printing and Publishing Company. In addition, Williams helped found Bethel College in Oregon and served on the board of trustees of Willamette University in Salem.

In 1857 Williams published his "Free State Letter" in the *Oregon Statesman*, contending that, from a practical standpoint, slavery in Oregon should be prohibited. This letter antagonized many of his proslavery Democratic friends. That same year he participated in the Oregon constitutional convention, and because of his judicial background, he was selected to chair the committee dealing with the judicial branch of government. Oregon entered the Union in 1859.

By 1860, as a Portland attorney, Williams was intensely interested in politics and the questions of slavery, states' rights, and secession. In 1860 he supported the presidential campaign of Douglas, a Democrat. A northern Democrat hostile to slavery, Williams chaired the Executive Committee of the Union State Convention at Eugene in 1862. Becoming increasingly dissatisfied with the Democratic party during the course of the Civil War and pleased with the policies of President Abraham Lincoln, Williams joined the Republican party in 1864. That year the Oregon state legislature elected him as a Republican to the U.S. Senate, where he served from 1865 to 1871. In 1867 he married Kate Ann Hughes Ivans George. They had no children.

Williams supported the Radical Republicans, including Representative Thaddeus Stevens of Pennsylvania, in attempts to impose a strict policy of Reconstruction on the vanquished South. He wrote the Reconstruction Act of 1867, which reorganized the Confederate states under military governors. His position on Reconstruction was further refined in a Senate speech on 4 February 1868. A member of the Joint Committee on Reconstruction and of the Senate Committee on the Judiciary, he opposed President Andrew Johnson. Williams introduced the Tenure of Office Act of 1867 to prohibit the chief executive from removing cabinet members and other civil officials without senatorial approval, fearing that the southern president might replace loyal Republicans appointed by Lincoln with former rebels. Congress passed this controversial measure over Johnson's veto. In 1868 Williams was one of the chief advocates of the impeachment of Johnson.

When Ulysses S. Grant became president in 1869, Williams quickly changed his attitude toward the presidency. He surfaced as one of Grant's strongest supporters in Congress. The president, who often called on Williams for advice, appointed the senator to the Joint High Commission to resolve various controversies between the United States and Great Britain. The negotiations, conducted in conjunction with Secretary of State Hamilton Fish, resulted in the Treaty of Washington of 1871, a diplomatic triumph of the Grant administration.

Williams failed to secure reelection to the Senate in 1870, but this defeat opened the door to another opportunity for the Oregon Republican. In 1871 Grant appointed him attorney general of the United States to succeed Amos Tappan Akerman. The Senate unanimously confirmed the appointment in January 1872, and Williams served until 1875. He traveled widely in 1872 to campaign for Grant, who won reelection as president. The attorney general enjoyed high popularity at the time and was mentioned in some circles as a successor to Grant.

In 1873 the death of Salmon P. Chase, chief justice of the U.S. Supreme Court, gave Grant an opportunity to choose the head of the nation's judicial body. After waiting nearly six months, Grant named Republican senator Roscoe Conkling of New York, who declined the honor. On 1 December 1874 the president surprised the nation by nominating Williams, who almost immediately came under attack. Many believed that the attorney general lacked the requisite judicial experience to warrant sitting in the chief justice's chair, and the New York Bar Association passed a resolution protesting his nomination on grounds of insufficient qualifications. Charges that Williams had used money from the contingent fund of the Justice Department for personal purchases and that he used government money to pay the wages of two servants spread across the nation's newspapers and were brought before the Senate Judiciary Committee. The *Oregonian* castigated Williams relentlessly.

Williams also suffered from the activities and reputation of his second wife, whose ambitious desire to dominate Washington society antagonized the wives of senators, cabinet officers, and the president. She had a penchant for vicious gossip and for flaunting her extravagantly furnished home on Rhode Island Avenue, where she held receptions in royal splendor, leading some critics to believe the stories regarding improper use of public funds. His wife's arrogance toward the wives of senators proved more detrimental than Williams's own lack of high judicial qualifications.

Fearing another publicized scandal, Grant urged Secretary of State Fish to meet with Williams and request his withdrawal. On 7 January 1874 Williams sent a letter to the president, in which he withdrew his name from consideration, citing the floodgates of calumny that had disparaged his abilities and reputation. A victim of political and personal intrigue by those who sought to humiliate his wife, Williams went down to ignominious defeat.

Williams practiced law in Washington for a short time before returning to his law practice in Portland. In 1876 the Republican National Committee dispatched him to Florida to help Rutherford B. Hayes carry the state in the presidential contest. Williams served two terms as mayor of Portland, from 1902 to 1905. In 1905 he wrote an article on his six years in the Senate that was published in the *Sunday Oregonian* in November and December. Three years later he published *Careers for Our Sons*. During the Progressive Era, Williams championed woman suffrage and the Oregon system of political reform and popular government. He died in Portland, leaving behind a political legacy that spanned a half-century. He was one of Oregon's most prominent politicians during the late nineteenth and early twentieth centuries.

• The George Henry Williams Papers are at the Oregon Historical Society in Portland and in the Territorial Government Papers at the Oregon State Archives in Salem. His letters are also scattered in the collections of various contemporaries, such as Ulysses S. Grant in the Manuscripts Division of the Library of Congress. Williams published *Occasional Addresses* in 1895. His speeches are in the *Congressional Globe* from 1865 to 1871. The major work on Williams is Sidney Teiser, "Life of George H. Williams: Almost Chief Justice," *Oregon Historical Quarterly* 47 (1946): 256–80, 417–40. See also E. S. Wood, *History of the Bench and Bar of Oregon* (1910). Obituaries are in the *New York Times* and the Portland *Morning Oregonian*, 5 Apr. 1910.

LEONARD SCHLUP

WILLIAMS, George Washington (16 Oct. 1849–2 Aug. 1891), soldier, clergyman, legislator, and historian, was born in Bedford Springs, Pennsylvania, the son of Thomas Williams, a free black laborer, and Ellen Rouse. His father became a boatman and, eventually, a minister and barber, and the younger Williams drifted with his family from town to town in western Pennsylvania until the beginning of the Civil War. With no formal education, he lied about his age, adopted the name of an uncle, and enlisted in the United States Colored Troops in 1864. He served in operations against Petersburg and Richmond, sustaining multiple wounds during several battles. After the war's end, Williams was stationed in Texas, but crossed the border to fight with the Mexican republican forces that overthrew the emperor Maximilian. He returned to the U.S. Army in 1867, serving with the Tenth Cavalry, an all-black unit, at Fort Arbuckle, Indian Territory. Williams was discharged for disability the following year after being shot through the left lung under circumstances that were never fully explained.

For a few months in 1869 Williams was enrolled at Howard University in Washington, D.C. But with an urgent desire to become a Baptist minister, he sought admission to the Newton Theological Institution in Massachusetts. Semiliterate and placed in the English "remedial" course at the outset, Williams underwent a remarkable transformation. He became a prize student as well as a polished writer and public speaker and completed the three-year theological curriculum in two years. In 1874, following graduation and marriage to Sarah Sterret of Chicago, Williams was installed as pastor of one of the leading African-American churches of Boston, the Twelfth Baptist. A year later he went with his wife and young son (their only child) to Washington, D.C. There he edited the *Commoner*, a weekly newspaper supported by Frederick Douglass and other leading citizens and intended to be, in Williams's words, "to the colored people of the country a guide, teacher, defender, and mirror." It folded after about six months of publication.

The West beckoned, and Williams moved in 1876 to Cincinnati, where he served as pastor of the Union Baptist Church through the end of the next year. Also engaged as a columnist for a leading daily newspaper, the Cincinnati *Commercial*, he contributed sometimes autobiographical pieces on cultural, racial, religious, and military themes. He spent what spare time he had studying law in the office of Judge Alphonso Taft, father of William Howard Taft. Even before passing the bar in 1881, Williams had become deeply immersed in Republican politics—as a captivating orator, holder of patronage positions, and, in 1877, an unsuccessful legislative candidate. In 1879 the voters of Cincinnati elected him to the Ohio House of Representatives, making Williams the first African American to sit in the state legislature. He served one term, during which he was the center of several controversies, ranging from the refusal of a Columbus restaurant catering to legislators to serve him to a furor in the African-American community over his support for the proposed closing of a black cemetery as a health hazard. Williams's effort to repeal a law against interracial marriage failed; he also supported a bill restricting liquor sales.

By this time, Williams had developed an interest in history. In 1876 he delivered an Independence Day Centennial oration titled "The American Negro from 1776 to 1876." While in the legislature, Williams made regular use of the Ohio State Library to collect historical information. After completing his stint as a lawmaker in 1881, he devoted his full attention to writing *History of the Negro Race in America from 1619 to 1880: Negroes as Slaves, as Soldiers, and as Citizens*. Based on extensive archival research, interviews, and Williams's pioneering use of newspapers, and published in two volumes by G. P. Putnam's Sons in 1882–1883, the work was the earliest extended, scholarly history of African Americans. Comprehensive in scope, it touched on biblical ethnology and African civilization and government but gave particular attention to blacks who served in America's wars. Widely noticed in the press, Williams's *History of the Negro Race in America* was, for the most part, well received as the first serious work of historical scholarship by an African American. Williams followed it in 1887 with another major historical work, *A History of the Negro Troops in the War of the Rebellion, 1861–1865*. Drawing on his own experiences (but also on the wartime records then being published for the first time), Williams wrote bitterly of the treatment of black soldiers by white northerners as well as by Confederates. Despite disadvantages, their conduct, in his opinion, was heroic, and he concluded that no troops "could be more determined or daring." Though not as widely heralded as his earlier volumes, *A History of the Negro Troops in the War of the Rebellion* was generally well reviewed by the white and black press. Williams also planned a two-volume history of Reconstruction in the former Confederacy, but he never went beyond incorporating some of the materials he had collected for the project into his lectures in the United States and Europe. In his writings and lectures, Williams expressed an optimism based on faith in a divine power that preordained events and enlisted adherents to assist in evangelizing the rest of the world's peoples.

Williams had begun to lecture extensively early in the 1880s and by the end of 1883 had returned to Boston where he practiced law. He later resided in Worcester and continued his research at the American Antiquarian Society. In March 1885 lame-duck president Chester Arthur appointed Williams minister to Haiti. He was confirmed by the U.S. Senate and sworn in during the final hours of the outgoing Republican administration, but before Williams could assume the post Democrat Grover Cleveland appointed someone else to it.

Ever restless and aggressively ambitious, Williams turned his sights toward Africa, already an occasional subject of his writing and public speaking. He attended an antislavery conference in Brussels in 1889 as a reporter for S. S. McClure's syndicate and there met Leopold II, king of the Belgians. In the following year, without the blessing of the king but with the patronage of Collis P. Huntington, an American railroad magnate who had invested in several African projects, he visited the Congo. After an extensive tour of the country, which took him from Boma on the Atlantic coast to the headwaters of the Congo River at Stanley Falls, he had a clear impression of what the country was like and why. Having witnessed the brutal conduct and inhumane policies of the Belgians, Williams decided to speak out. He published for circulation throughout Europe and the United States *An Open Letter to His Serene Majesty, Leopold II, King of the Belgians*, thus becoming a pioneering opponent of Leopold's policies and anticipating later criticisms of Europe's colonial ventures in Africa. Among the barrage of charges against the king was that his title to the Congo was, at best, "badly clouded" because his treaties with the local chiefs were "tainted by frauds of the grossest character." He held the king responsible for "deceit, fraud, robberies, arson, murder, slave-raiding, and general policy of cruelty" in the Congo. "All the crimes perpetrated in the Congo have been done in *your* name," he concluded, "and *you* must answer at the bar of Public Sentiment for the misgovernment of a people, whose lives and fortunes were entrusted to you by the august Conference of Berlin, 1884–1885." While the attack inspired denunciations of Williams in Belgium, it was little noted in the United States, though Williams had already written a report on the Congo for President Benjamin Harrison at the latter's request. A closer scrutiny of conditions in the Congo would come only after such "credible" persons as Roger Casement of the British foreign office and Mark Twain made charges against Leopold that echoed those of Williams.

Following his exploration of the Congo and southern Africa, Williams fell ill in Cairo, Egypt, after giving a lecture before the local geographical society (he had not been in robust health since being wounded in the army). Separated but not divorced from his wife, he subsequently went to London with his English "fiancée," Alice Fryer, intending to write a lengthy work on colonialism in Africa. There, tuberculosis and pleurisy overtook him, and he died in Blackpool. In the United States, his death was noted in the national media as well as in the black press.

To the end, George Washington Williams remained a difficult person to understand fully. To many on both sides of the racial divide he possessed a curious combination of rare genius, remarkable resourcefulness, and an incomparable talent for self-aggrandizement. Although Williams was justifiably chided during his lifetime for making inflated claims about his background, W. E. B. Du Bois did not hesitate to pronounce him, long after his death, "the greatest historian of the race."

• A small collection of Williams's letters and notebooks was in existence as late as the 1940s but has since disappeared. There are numerous Williams letters, however, in collections of other people's correspondence, including the George F. Hoar Papers at the Massachusetts Historical Society in Boston and the Collis P. Huntington Papers at the George Arents Library at Syracuse University. For a full-length treatment of Williams's life and career, see John Hope Franklin, *George Washington Williams: A Biography* (1985), which also reprints his *Open Letter* and several reports from Africa.

JOHN HOPE FRANKLIN

WILLIAMS, Gluyas (23 July 1888–13 Feb. 1982), cartoonist, was born in San Francisco, California, the son of Robert Neil Williams and Virginia Gluyas. His early education took place in Germany, France, and Switzerland. He attended Harvard University, where he served as art editor of the *Lampoon*, the campus humor magazine. One of the undergraduate contributors who submitted essays as well as drawings was Robert Benchley, and their acquaintanceship developed into a lifelong association. (Humorist Benchley would later maintain that Williams advised him to give up drawing and to stick to writing, thus setting his feet on his career path.) In 1911, after only three years, Williams graduated and went to Paris for six months to study life drawing.

On his return to the United States, he followed the example of his sister, Kate Carew, who drew cartoons for newspapers. After doing a daily comic strip for the *Boston Journal* for about three months, however, he decided this was not his forte and left to join the staff of the magazine *Youth's Companion*, where he shortly became head of the art department. While there, he also freelanced cartoons to various publications. His first significant sale was to Frank Casey of *Collier's*, who bought and published as a cover a Williams drawing that had been rejected by the weekly humor magazines *Life* and *Puck*. With that, he began selling his cartoons regularly to *Collier's*, and when Charles Dana Gibson bought *Life* in 1918 and hired Casey as art director, Williams became a steady contributor to *Life*.

Williams married Margaret Kempton in 1915, and by 1920 he felt secure enough as a cartoonist to give up his salaried position with *Youth's Companion* in favor of a full-time freelance career. In addition to cartooning for magazines, he wrote and illustrated a political spoof about "Senator Sounder" for *Life* and he did theatrical caricatures for the *Boston Evening Transcript*. These efforts brought him to the attention of William Randolph Hearst, for whom he worked briefly, traveling to Washington, D.C., to do political caricatures. He also illustrated *Of All Things* (1922), the first of the book collections of Benchley's humorous essays to which he contributed; this Benchley book was followed by another in each of the next two years and nine more over the next two decades. Williams's drawings of Benchley and his milieu so perfectly caught the mood of "the little man" encountering the humiliations and frustrations of life in the twentieth century that the cartoonist's work was often acclaimed as the best part of the books. In this collaboration, Williams found his métier, a subject and a treatment that were exactly attuned to his sensibility.

In 1924 Williams sold a single-panel daily gag cartoon series to Bell Syndicate, which distributed the feature nationwide for twenty-five years. The title of the feature varied with the subject, as did similar features by J. R. Williams and Clare Briggs. Whether called "Suburban Heights," "The World at Its Worst," "The Moment That Seems a Year," "Difficult Decisions," "The Neighborhood League," or any of a half-dozen other names, the cartoon focused on the minor crises and tepid tribulations of middle-class life in the suburbs of an America that was becoming increasingly urban. The cast was composed of mostly anonymous businessmen, housewives, and youngsters, but a comfortably portly fellow named Fred Perley was frequently the springboard to the day's chuckle. Williams explained his philosophy for the feature: "Two things I strive for in my cartoons: to bring the reader to smile at himself in the past or to make it easier for him when the incident happens in the future."

In addition to his cartoons, Williams produced illustrations for numerous books and advertisements.

Williams was soon also a regular contributor to the *New Yorker*, a sophisticated humor magazine that had been launched by Harold Ross in February 1925. Although Ross began soliciting cartoons from Williams almost at once, the cartoonist did not produce anything for the magazine until 1926. When Ross returned his first drawing with suggestions for improvements, Williams sent it back without making any changes, explaining to the editor that his method was understatement rather than slapstick and describing the difference. Ross reportedly revised his ideas about graphic humor as a result.

For most of his career, Williams lived in West Newton, a suburb near Boston, but he did his work at a studio in the city, to which he commuted, completing his weekly quota of cartoons in four mornings. At one o'clock every day, he returned to life in suburbia, pursuing such activities as cabinetmaking, sailing, billiards, reading detective stories, and playing bridge. The father of a son and daughter, Williams exemplified in many respects the kind of life his cartoons depicted.

For the *New Yorker*, Williams produced the full-page cartoons under a series of titles that typified his approach. Under the heading "Industrial Crises," for example, the cartoonist depicted the panic and dismay among company officials "the day a cake of Ivory sank at Procter & Gamble's" and the chagrin and consternation that prevailed around the boardroom table when "a director of the Diamond Match Company absent-mindedly lights his cigar with an automatic lighter."

Typically, a Williams cartoon was crowded with people, each a distinct individual doing something appropriate for the scene. In "Office Building Lobby," Williams showed a throng of businessmen rushing to enter or leave, one looking at his watch, another asking the elevator operator a question, yet another consulting the building directory, two people arguing, a man flirting with a woman, and so on. In "The Waiter Who Put a Check on the Table Face Up," an entire restaurant population, waiters and customers, looks aghast at the offending party—as does every member of the audience at a piano recital when a woman snaps her purse "during a pianissimo."

Williams sought to reveal the humor in ordinary life among ordinary people doing everyday things. In many of his earliest endeavors, he said he was inspired by the French cartoonist Caran d'Ache. In these, Williams filled a full page (or two) with a sequence of drawings depicting in pantomine an individual's growing frustration at performing some activity—a man struggling to remove a stubborn dandelion from his lawn, a father trying to read aloud to his son who fidgets in his lap and climbs all over him. Later, Williams reflected the influence of British cartoonist H. M. Bateman when he depicted the fate or faux pax of "The Man Who . . . " Both models are evident in "The Woman Who Suspects All Restaurant Glasses," a succession of pictures showing an imposing matron arriving at a restaurant table and then intently examining her water glass while a gathering crowd of observing waiters displays, first, increasing concern, then obvious relief when the glass passes inspection.

Williams soon honed his influences into his own brand of pawky humor, low-keyed and restrained, and evolved a distinctive graphic style that was the perfect complement to the comedy. His drawings, models of lucid simplicity, were precisely outlined with a sturdy, unvarying line and then starkly accented with solid, flat blacks. In both attitude and visual treatment, Williams's cartoons were so wholly unpretentious that they seemed the embodiment of only honest reportage on the human condition. Williams died in Boston.

• Most of the information about Gluyas Williams's life and career can be found in *Current Biography* (1946) and in an interview with Richard Marschall published in *Nemo: The Classic Comics Library* 3 (Oct. 1983). Among the books he illustrated are *Father of the Bride* by Edward Streeter (1948); *There's a Fly in This Room* (1946) and *Wrap It as a Gift* (1947) by Ralf Kircher; *How to Guess Your Age* (1950) by Corey Ford; *The Camp at Lockjaw* (1952) by David McCord; and the following by Robert Benchley: *Of All Things* (1922), *Love Conquers All* (1923), *Pluck and Luck* (1924), *The Early Worm* (1927), *The Treasurer's Report and Other Aspects of Community Singing* (1930), *From Bad to Worse* (1934), *My Ten Years in a Quandry* (1936), *After 1903–What?* (1938), *Inside Benchley* (1942), *Benchley Beside Himself* (1943), *Benchley—Or Else* (1947), and *Chips off the Old Benchley* (1949). Williams cartoons are collected in two volumes, *The Gluyas Williams Book* (1929) and *Fellow Citizens* (1940). *The Gluyas Williams Gallery* (1957) includes sample text and illustrations from several of the books on which the cartoonist collaborated and a few cartoons.

ROBERT C. HARVEY

WILLIAMS, G. Mennen (23 Feb. 1911–2 Feb. 1988), governor and diplomat, was born Gerhard Mennen Williams in Detroit, Michigan, the son of Henry P. Williams, the head of a pickle company and a realtor, and Elma Mennen, the daughter of Gerhard Mennen, who had founded the Mennen Company, manufacturer of toiletries. Nicknamed "Soapy," young Williams grew up in an advantaged Episcopalian and Republican home. After excelling at Salisbury (Conn.) Preparatory School, he enrolled at Princeton, where he earned varsity athletic letters and graduated Phi Beta Kappa in 1933. President of the Young Republican Club at Princeton, he campaigned for Herbert Hoover in 1932. Moved by his readings on the Industrial Revolution and its impact on the English working poor, however, Williams began to shift his allegiance to the Democratic party and soon enthusiastically endorsed the New Deal. Aiming for a career in politics, he entered the University of Michigan Law School, where he earned a J.D. in 1936. In 1937 he married Nancy Lace Quirk, a liberal social services student, with whom he had three children.

After working with the Social Security Board from 1936 to 1937, Williams was called back to serve as Michigan assistant attorney general by Governor Frank Murphy, his political mentor. In 1939 Williams became the executive assistant to Murphy, who had been appointed U.S. attorney general. When Murphy became a Supreme Court justice in 1940, Williams stayed on briefly in the Justice Department before shifting to the Office of Price Administration (OPA). From 1942 to 1946 he served in the U.S. Navy, working as an air combat intelligence officer in the Pacific, rising to the rank of lieutenant commander, and receiving a number of combat awards. He then returned as deputy director of the Michigan office of the OPA before becoming a partner in the Detroit law firm of Griffiths, Williams, and Griffiths in 1947. Later that year Williams accepted an appointment from Republican governor Kim Sigler to the state liquor control commission, a position that permitted him to travel widely in the state.

Backed by the Michigan Democratic Club, a new liberal organization created by his law partners, and the Congress of Industrial Organizations's Political Action Committee, Williams sought the governorship in 1948 on a nine-point platform of undiluted New Dealism. Calling for improvements in education, housing, veterans' benefits, unemployment compensation, roads, and farm support, Williams stressed his support for civil rights and advocated repeal of Michigan's restrictive "little Taft-Hartley" labor act.

After a narrow primary victory, Williams and his wife mortgaged their home and drove their own automobile throughout upstate Michigan, campaigning exhaustively in the state's rural, heavily Republican hamlets. His Republican family refused to contribute to his campaign, and he had inherited none of the Mennen fortune in 1948. The handsome, 200-pound Williams adopted a polka-dot green bow tie as his political trademark, called square dances, and developed an unpretentious, folksy approach to the electorate. The spectacle of the Princeton-educated patrician mixing so easily with ordinary voters brought derision from his critics. His supporters, however, compared him to Franklin Roosevelt. One newspaper editor concluded, "Soapy is part cornball, part egghead."

Williams easily defeated Governor Sigler, even though the Republican national ticket carried the state that year. Because Michigan held gubernatorial elections every two years, Williams campaigned almost continuously among the state's diverse population. Reelected five times, he called for an expansive government. While Williams's liberal-labor coalition readily gained control of the state Democratic party, Republican critics argued that United Automobile Workers President Walter Reuther "controlled" Williams. When Williams refused to extradite a union tough accused of violence in a major strike in Wisconsin, right-wing critics lambasted the governor as a stooge of labor leaders. Throughout his twelve years as governor, Williams battled with a Republican-controlled legislature over tax policy. Republicans advocated an increase in sales and use taxes, while the governor proposed corporate profits taxes and a graduated personal income tax. Stalemated, Michigan was unable to resolve the differences and faced bankruptcy in the late 1950s.

Williams emerged as a significant national leader, frequently mentioned as a possible presidential or vice presidential candidate in 1952, 1956, and 1960, despite his troubles in Michigan. As Republicans made gains nationally among African-American and white ethnic voters as well as among rank-and-file union members, Williams's supporters argued that he was uniquely positioned to reverse these changes. Southern segregationist Democrats, on the other hand, found Williams's labor record and advanced civil rights position unacceptable. Distracted by his state's economic problems in 1959, Williams decided not to contest Senator John Kennedy for the 1960 Democratic presidential nomination. At the convention he supported Kennedy but opposed the selection of Lyndon Johnson for the vice presidential nomination.

While he had hoped for a cabinet-level appointment, Williams settled for the new post of assistant secretary of state for African affairs. Barnstorming the African continent, he urged a policy of "Africa for the Africans." When white settlers objected, Williams explained that whites, too, had a place on the continent, so long as they expected no special privileges. In 1961 and 1962 Williams played a significant role in negotiating a settlement between the forces of the newly liberated Congo (Zaire) and the secessionist Katanga province. Williams's influence dissipated considerably under the Johnson administration, but he stayed on in the State Department until early 1966.

At that time Williams returned to Michigan to run for the U.S. Senate, but he faced a serious challenge for the nomination from Detroit mayor Jerome Cavanagh. While he defeated Cavanagh, Williams lost the general election to Republican incumbent Robert Griffin. From May 1968 to March 1969 he served as ambassador to the Philippines. In 1970 he won election to the state supreme court, where he concerned himself with establishing a uniform system of justice throughout the state. Williams served as chief justice between 1982 and his mandatory retirement in 1986.

Williams's enormous energy helped restructure the Democratic party and make it competitive in Michigan politics. While he served abroad during the 1960s, his inclusive political style and especially his staunch support of civil rights foreshadowed changes in the national party during the Johnson administration. Williams died in Detroit.

• The G. Mennen Williams Papers are in the Michigan Historical Collections at the University of Michigan in Ann Arbor. The State Department years are best covered by Williams himself in *Africa for the Africans* (1969). A useful early biography is Frank McNaughton, *Mennen Williams of Michigan: Fighter for Progress* (1960). Williams's perennial campaign manager, Helen Washburn Berthelot, provides her recollections in *Win Some Lose Some: G. Mennen Williams and the New Democrats* (1995). Dudley W. Buffa, *Union Power & American Democracy: The UAW and the Democratic Party, 1935–1972* (1984), is particularly rewarding on the liberal-labor alliance and the debate over taxes. Valuable personal material is in Richard Thruelsen, "When Michigan Woke Up He Was Governor," *Saturday Evening Post*, 2 Feb. 1949, pp. 26–27, 112–14; Beverly Smith, Jr., "Soapy, the Wonder Boy," *Saturday Evening Post*, 9 Nov. 1957, pp. 25–27, 136–38, 140; and "Michigan: Prodigy's Progress," *Time*, 15 Sept. 1952, pp. 26–29. The *New York Times*, 13 June 1986, has a brief biography occasioned by Williams's retirement. An obituary is in the *New York Times*, 3 Feb. 1988.

WILLIAM HOWARD MOORE

WILLIAMS, Hank (17 Sept. 1923–1 Jan. 1953), country songwriter, vocalist, and guitarist, was born Hiram Williams in Mount Olive, Alabama, the son of Elonzo Huble Williams and Jessie Lillybelle Skipper. His father was a strawberry farmer when Hank was born, although his usual occupation was that of an engineer on logging trains in the Chapman, Alabama, area. Williams spent his earliest years in and around the logging camps of south-central Alabama. Then, when he was six years old, his father went into a Veterans Administration hospital with a brain aneurysm, and his mother moved the family to Georgiana, Greenville, and then on to Montgomery in July 1937.

Williams had always showed an interest in music, and it was in Montgomery that his musical career began to take root. He worked the sidewalks, singing and selling bags of peanuts, entered talent shows, and played spots on local radio stations WSFA and WCOV. After he quit school in October 1939, he worked as an apprentice builder for a short period, then concentrated on playing beer joints and schoolhouse dates. From the beginning, he called his band the Drifting Cowboys.

Williams's major influences were country gospel music (he often cited "Death Is Only a Dream" as his favorite song) and Roy Acuff (whom Williams would have heard regularly after Acuff joined the Grand Ole Opry in 1938). Black rural string bands were another influence. Williams often said that he learned much of his music from an African-American street musician, Rufus "Tee-Tot" Payne, who worked the streets of Georgiana and Greenville, Alabama, when Williams was in his early teens. This blues influence can be detected in Williams's phrasing and occasionally in his choice of material. Williams was only nine years old when Jimmie Rodgers, who is generally cited as the father of country music, died, and although Rodgers exercised a profound influence on Ernest Tubb, Hank Snow, and others, he seems to have had very little influence on Williams. Western music, performed by musicians such as Gene Autry and the Sons of the Pioneers, also had very little impact on him, despite the fact that he named his band the Drifting Cowboys and outfitted them in western attire. His music remained rooted in mountain (or, as it was then called, "hillbilly") forms and rural blues.

Williams was declared unfit for military service during the Second World War because of a congenital spinal disorder, spina bifida occulta, although he worked for short periods in the Mobile, Alabama, shipyards. In December 1944 he married Audrey Mae Sheppard from Banks, Alabama, whom he had met when he was playing a medicine show in southern Alabama the previous year. In 1945 they moved into his mother's boardinghouse in Montgomery, and there he resumed his musical career. The couple would have one child, Hank Williams, Jr., who also would become a country star.

After the war, Williams quickly became the most successful country musician in the area. He was signed by the Nashville-based music publisher Acuff-Rose in September 1946 and in December made his first recordings under Acuff-Rose's aegis, for the New York–based Sterling Records. He made four records for Sterling. He was signed to MGM Records in March 1947 by Frank Walker.

During the late 1940s, Williams's "hillbilly" style was seen as a throwback to an earlier style of country music. The received wisdom in the music business was that such music was popular only in rural areas and that even there it was dying out. It appeared as though Eddy Arnold, Red Foley, and others were pointing the way forward with a relatively sophisticated blend of pop and country. Thus when Williams's "Move It On Over," issued in August 1947, became a hit, many in the trade press were surprised.

In August 1948 Williams moved from Montgomery to Shreveport, Louisiana, to work on the Louisiana Hayride, a Saturday night barn dance show that blanketed much of the eastern United States on the 50,000-watt radio station KWKH. Williams had tried to get on the Grand Ole Opry, the most successful radio barn dance, but he was already pegged as a problem drinker and had a reputation for unreliability.

After struggling for several months in Shreveport, Williams became the major star on the Hayride when he began featuring "Lovesick Blues" on his shows. After a ban on making records that had been called by the American Federation of Musicians as of January 1948 ended that December, Williams was called to Cincinnati for a recording session. There, on 22 December 1948, he cut "Lovesick Blues." Released in February 1949, it quickly became the bestselling country song of the year. In April 1949 Williams signed a management contract with Nashville promoter Oscar Davis, who landed him a spot on the Grand Ole Opry, starting 11 June 1949.

"Lovesick Blues" was not a blues or a country song, nor was it one of Williams's songs; it was a show tune that had first been recorded in 1922. Williams's second big hit of 1949, "Wedding Bells," was not an original song either. From late 1949, though, Williams began recording what were—to a great extent—his own compositions. Under the tutelage of his music publisher, Fred Rose of Acuff-Rose, Williams quickly evolved into the most accomplished songwriter in country music and the writer whose work has more or less defined the vernacular of contemporary country music songcraft. His melodies often impinged to a great extent on archetypes and folk-based tunes and often were litigiously close to other melodies not in the public domain, but his lyrics had a confessional quality that was quite new to country music. This became evident in songs such as "I'm So Lonesome I Could Cry," "Cold, Cold Heart," and "I Can't Help It (If I'm Still in Love with You)."

Shortly after arriving in Nashville, Williams departed on a USO-sponsored tour of American forces based in Europe and the Caribbean. He had gone at the servicemens' request, which indicated that his music was finding wider acceptance than many thought possible. He also went on Opry-sponsored tours across the entire United States and several parts of Canada as well. In part, the migration of southerners during the depression and the Second World War created a market for his music outside the South, but it was also undeniable that, despite the regionality in his voice and the barebones instrumentation he employed, his relatively unsophisticated music quickly found a broader market.

Country music usually had to be reinterpreted to reach the pop audience (for example, Bing Crosby recorded Al Dexter's "Pistol Packin' Mama," and Patti Page recorded Pee Wee King's "Tennessee Waltz" for the pop market). The first Hank Williams song to be reinterpreted or "covered" for the pop market was "Honky Tonkin'" in 1949 (by both Teresa Brewer and Polly Bergen), but the first one to find broad acceptance as a pop song was "Cold, Cold Heart," which became a major pop hit for Tony Bennett in 1951. From that point, virtually all of Williams's songs were reinterpreted for the pop market by other singers, such as Jo Stafford ("Jambalaya"), Guy Mitchell ("I Can't Help It"), and Tommy Edwards ("You Win Again"). Williams was ambivalent about the interest his songs was attracting, but that interest had a trickle-down impact on his own career. He was invited onto network television ("The Perry Como Show" in Nov. 1951 and "The Kate Smith Evening Hour" in Mar. and Apr. 1952) and received an invitation from the motion picture division of MGM to make full-length movies. He was also written up in mainstream magazines such as *Collier's* and even the *Wall Street Journal*.

Williams's success exacerbated problems that had plagued him since the late 1930s. He wrestled throughout his life with alcoholism and appeared to have a low threshold for stress. His drinking was essentially a response to the pressures of the business as well as to personal difficulties with his wife and the insistent back pain that resulted from his spinal condition. After he arrived at the Opry, Williams made good for several months on his promise not to drink, but his bouts of alcoholism grew increasingly frequent in late 1950 and throughout 1951.

Perhaps the high point of Williams's career came with the Hadacol Caravan in August and September 1951. The caravan was assembled by Dudley J. LeBlanc, a state senator from Louisiana, who had invented a patent medicine called Hadacol. The caravan was a promotional tool, and Williams played alongside several of the biggest stars of the day, including Bob Hope, Milton Berle, Carmen Miranda, and Rudy Vallee. In all major centers, Williams consistently outdrew the others and surprised both himself and his band with the depth and breadth of his popularity.

By late 1951 Williams had been fitted with a lumbrosacral brace to ease his chronic back pain, but—after a hunting accident in the fall of 1951—he finally acceded to surgery. The operation, carried out on 13 December 1951 at Vanderbilt Medical Center in Nashville, was not a success, and from that time Williams's back pain scarcely ever left him.

In January 1952 Williams's wife insisted that he move out of the family dwelling on Franklin Pike in Nashville, and Williams moved into a rooming house with country singer Ray Price. This robbed him of one of the few elements of stability in his life and started a precipitous personal and professional downslide.

The career pressures mounted early in 1952. Williams was flying from coast to coast to meet concert engagements. He was being offered songwriting assignments for Bing Crosby, among others, and was being pressured to perform in motion pictures and in Las Vegas. He became increasingly unreliable, and by June 1952 he had almost ceased performing. This was a source of intense annoyance to the Grand Ole Opry, and in August 1952 Williams was presented with an ultimatum: he would have to appear at two Opry-sponsored shows or risk dismissal. He did not appear and was dismissed on 13 August 1952.

Williams returned to Montgomery, and in September Fred Rose negotiated his return to the Louisiana Hayride. Williams relocated to Shreveport and one month later married Billie Jean Jones, who, it later transpired, had not yet received a final divorce from her first husband, Harrison Eshliman. Williams and Jones married first in a private ceremony in Minden, Louisiana, on 18 October 1952 and publicly twice in New Orleans the following day. Their brief union was childless.

In arranging for Williams's return to the Louisiana Hayride, Fred Rose had hoped that Williams would regroup and eventually return to Nashville. However, during the four months that Williams worked in Shreveport, he became increasingly reliant on narcotic painkillers that were administered by a quack doctor, Horace Raphol "Toby" Marshall, whom Williams engaged as his personal physician. Williams was also unable to curb his alcoholism by this point, so despite the fact that his recording of "Jambalaya (On the Bayou)" was the number one record on the country charts, he was so unreliable that he could only get work in beer halls within a day's drive of Shreveport.

His final tour was in mid-December 1952. He appears to have suffered a heart attack or to have overdosed early in the tour, though he rallied to complete it. His last show date was at the Skyline Club in Austin, Texas, on 18 December 1952. Immediately after completing the show, Williams returned to Montgomery intending to regain his health by resting. He had committed, however, to perform in Charleston, West Virginia, on 31 December 1952 and in Canton, Ohio, on 1 January 1953. Williams was driven from Montgomery but was unable to make the Charleston date because of bad weather, so his driver continued toward Canton. He died, apparently of a heart attack, in his limousine at an undetermined point between Knoxville, Tennessee, and Oak Hill, West Virginia, on New Year's Eve or early New Year's morning. He was pronounced dead in Oak Hill on 1 January 1953.

Williams's remains were returned to Montgomery. He left no will, and his estate has been subject to litigation ever since his death.

In part, Williams's sustained appeal has resulted from the manner in which he lived and died. His career would probably have suffered a serious setback when Fred Rose died in December 1954 and would probably have suffered a more serious setback in the wake of rock 'n' roll a year or two after that. As it is, he left a remarkably consistent body of work. He recorded just sixty-six titles under his own name (he also recorded recitations under the pseudonym "Luke the Drifter" and religious duets with his first wife, Audrey); of those sixty-six titles, thirty-seven were hits. More than once, Williams recorded three hits during a three- or three-and-a-half-hour recording session.

Williams's songs, like the best country music, flirted with the banality of the obvious while nearly always avoiding it. Arguably, no one met the challenge of writing country music as successfully as Williams, or managed to bring such a variety and universality to an inherently limited form. Williams's recordings sold well decades after his death; few have ever been out of print. The emotionality of his singing, which rarely sank to a level of mawkishness, has a patent sincerity that has endured to become the benchmark of honesty in country singing.

Songs are still written about Hank Williams, which suggests that the enigma of his short life still holds a powerful fascination. Arguably, he set the standard for country music on every level, including self-destruction.

• Williams himself is supposed to have written *How to Write Folk and Western Music to Sell* (1951), with Jimmy Rule, although he probably contributed little toward it. His mother, Mrs. W. W. Stone, together with Allen Rankin, wrote a posthumous memoir, *Life Story of Our Hank Williams "The Drifting Cowboy"* (1953). His fiddle player, Jerry Rivers, also wrote an anecdotal booklet, *From Life to Legend* (1967).

The first biography was Roger M. Williams's *Sing a Sad Song: The Life of Hank Williams* (1970); later, it was followed by Jay Caress's *Hank Williams: Country Music's Tragic King* (1979). George William Koon, *Hank Williams: A Bio-Bibliography* (1983), contains little that is new but codifies references to Williams.

The most recent biographies have been Lycrecia Williams and Dale Vinicur, *Still in Love with You* (1989); Arnold Rogers and Bruce Gidoll, *The Life and Times of Hank Williams* (1993); and Colin Escott et al., *Hank Williams: The Biography* (1994).

COLIN ESCOTT

WILLIAMS, Henry Willard (11 Dec. 1821–13 June 1895), ophthalmologist, was born in Boston, Massachusetts, the son of Willard Williams and Elizabeth Osgood. He attended the Boston Latin School and, after his parents' deaths, the Salem Latin School. Ill health forced him to suspend his education, and at age seventeen he began training as a merchant in the counting room at the Central Wharf in Boston. Williams was active in the antislavery movement and became the secretary and publishing agent of the Massachusetts Anti-Slavery Society. At the age of twenty-four he entered Harvard Medical School, and after two years there, he traveled to Europe to complete his medical education. His interest in diseases of the eye began in Paris, where he studied in the clinics of Sichel and Desmarres; he continued this pursuit in Vienna with Jaeger and Rosas, and finally in London with Dalrymple, Lawrence, Dixon, Critchett, and Bowman. Williams received his M.D. from Harvard in 1849. Williams married Elizabeth Dewe of London in 1848; they had two children. After her death he married Elizabeth Adeline Low in 1860, and they had seven children.

After beginning his medical practice in Boston in 1849, Williams soon limited his practice to ophthalmology, becoming one of the first full-time ophthalmologists in the United States. In 1849 he became a visiting district physician for the Boston Dispensary. In 1850 he was appointed instructor in the theory and practice of medicine at the Boylston Medical School, a position he held for five years.

In 1850 as well, Williams delivered to a class of Harvard medical students a course of clinical lectures on diseases of the eye; this was the first distinct ophthalmology course given in any American medical school. Williams then held no official appointment at Harvard Medical School. Later, however, he was made ophthalmic surgeon at the Boston City Hospital at its opening in 1864 and lecturer in ophthalmology at Harvard Medical School in 1866. Until 1866 the sites for instruction of medical students in ophthalmology in Boston were the Massachusetts Eye and Ear Infirmary, the Boston City Hospital, and two private medical schools, Tremont and Boylston. The faculty in the latter two schools consisted almost exclusively of Harvard physicians. As Williams's ophthalmic practice grew, he utilized his own patients and clinical experience for his lectures at Harvard as well as at the Boylston Medical School. In 1864 he was a founder of the American Ophthalmological Society; he served as its second president from 1868 to 1873. In 1871 Williams was promoted to professor of ophthalmology at Harvard Medical School and retained that position until 1891, when he retired in poor health.

When Boston City Hospital was founded, Williams was the sole specialist named to its thirteen-member staff. The hospital consisted of medical, surgical, and ophthalmology divisions, and Williams was assigned his own beds, operating room, outpatient clinic, and a special extern. Edward Reynolds and John Jeffries, cofounders of the Massachusetts Eye and Ear Infirmary, were also members of the board of consultation and gave strong backing to Williams and his new department. Williams published in the *Boston Medical and*

Surgical Journal (1865) two reports describing his department's work during its initial months. He retained his appointment as ophthalmic surgeon to the Boston City Hospital until 1891, twenty-seven years of active work.

In 1865 Williams won the Boylston Prize for an essay, "Recent Advances in Ophthalmic Science." Earlier publications in the *Boston Medical and Surgical Journal*—"Iritis—Non Mercurial Treatment" and two papers both titled "On the Treatment of Iritis without Mercury"—led to a marked change in the treatment of this disease, in which "thorough mercurialization" had previously been considered the first requisite. Williams's most important contribution to ophthalmology, however, was his introduction of the corneal suture for use in cataract extraction. This was first mentioned in his Boylston Prize essay, but a more complete account appeared in his "Cataract Extraction Operation" (*Archives of Ophthalmology and Otolaryngology* [1868]). Williams also published two important texts, *A Practical Guide to the Study of Diseases of the Eye* (1862) and *The Diagnosis and Treatment of Diseases of the Eye* (1881). A second, enlarged edition appeared in 1886. Williams died in Boston.

Williams in the course of his career treated many prominent patients, but the best-remembered is Annie Sullivan, a half-blind ten-year-old orphan who came under his care in about 1876 for treatment of advanced trachoma. Williams operated on Annie's eyes but could not restore her sight. Eventually she regained some sight, and she became the teacher of Helen Keller.

• The life and contributions of Williams are reviewed in Daniel M. Albert, *Men of Vision* (1994), and in H. K. Beecher and Mark D. Altschule, *Medicine at Harvard: The First 300 Years* (1977). Williams's use of the corneal suture in cataract surgery was chronicled by Charles Snyder, "The Singular Suture of Henry Willard Williams," *Archives of Ophthalmology* 70 (1963): 574–76. Obituaries appear in the *Archives of Ophthalmology* 24 (1895): 555–56; and in *Transactions of the American Ophthalmological Society* 7 (1894–1896): 479–96.

DANIEL MYRON ALBERT

WILLIAMS, Israel (30 Nov. 1709–10 Jan. 1788), provincial militia officer and public official, was born in Hatfield, Massachusetts, the son of William Williams, a minister, and Christian Stoddard. His maternal grandfather, the Reverend Solomon Stoddard, was known as the "pope" of the Connecticut Valley for his religious authority and influence. Like him, Williams would achieve military, political, and economic dominance that would earn him a double-edged label: "monarch" of the Connecticut River valley in western Massachusetts. The male members of the Williams family and their political and business associates in western Massachusetts were known as the "River Gods"—a hard-working, aggressive, tightly knit, local elite with political ties to the dominant Hutchinson-Oliver faction in provincial politics. By the 1750s Israel had become the preeminent River God.

After graduating from Harvard College in 1727 and receiving his M.A. in 1730, Williams married Sarah Chester of Wethersfield, Connecticut; they would have eight children. Her ample dowry paid for a spacious house in Hatfield, where he served as a selectman from 1732 to 1764. From 1733 to 1737 Hatfield sent him to the Massachusetts House of Representatives. The long trip to Boston interfered with his various business enterprises at home, and after being twice fined by the house for nonattendance, he declined legislative service for a decade. By this time he was prominent enough to receive repeated military, civil, and Indian affairs appointments from the legislature. As the official who admitted new residents to western towns and as the militia officer who settled Indian claims to frontier lands, Williams was well-situated to engage in land speculation. Named clairman, or clerk, by the proprietors of more new towns in the Connecticut River valley than he had time to serve conscientiously, he gained a local reputation for greed and self-promotion. As a merchant he controlled trade between these new towns and Boston, and as a manufacturer of linseed oil, he obtained a countywide monopoly over its production. During King George's War (1744–1748) he coordinated the defense of western Massachusetts, thwarting Sir William Pepperrell's efforts to drain off military manpower from Hampshire County and successfully demanding that Connecticut acknowledge Williams's authority over a fort Connecticut had constructed in New Hampshire.

In 1748 Williams returned to the Massachusetts legislature, which appointed him and his Harvard classmate Thomas Hutchinson to negotiate land cessions from the Penobscot Indians in Falmouth, Massachusetts. He energetically promoted himself as an expert on military administration and in 1754 secured a long sought-after post as commander of military forces in Hampshire County. He submitted to Governor William Shirley a well-conceived plan for provincial defense of the northern New England frontier, and Shirley put Williams in charge of building and administering a chain of forts from Fort Dummer, in what is now Vermont, to Sheffield in Berkshire County, Massachusetts. When the minister in Northampton, Massachusetts, Jonathan Edwards, prevailed on Connecticut to send troops for the defense of the town, Williams bridled at this intrusion on his authority. He compelled Connecticut to acknowledge his control of that colony's troops stationed in Massachusetts and forced a humiliated Edwards to request Williams's help in defending the Congregationalist mission from the Indians at Stockbridge. Like his grandfather Solomon Stoddard, Williams was an Arminian in theology, believing that good works prepare the soul to embrace salvation. Like other politically conservative Arminians during the Great Awakening, he regarded Edwards's revivalism as a threat to public order and social hierarchy. He considered the war with France a struggle to do God's will. In 1759 he pointed to "the very visible . . . hand of Heaven" in British victories, meaning not just the defeat of the Catholic French but also the perpetuation of the conservative Congregationalist elite as a stabilizing force along the western Massachusetts frontier (Shipton, pp. 312–13).

Appointed a justice of the peace in Hampshire County in 1736 and probate judge in 1764, Williams acquired a reputation for high-handedness on the bench, particularly in his treatment of Baptists in the town of Ashfield, Massachusetts. In 1762 a Baptist majority in Ashfield had designated its own minister, rather than a Congregationalist cleric, as the recipient of a public salary. As justice of the peace, Williams sought to deny the Baptist minister a clerical exemption from property taxes. As a member of the Massachusetts house of representatives in 1768, he pushed through a bill restoring the Ashfield pulpit to the Congregationalists.

Though an overseer of Harvard College, Williams became alienated from the institution in the 1750s, when his eldest son, John, was denied admission and his second son, William, was refused permission to take an unscheduled admissions examination. Both sons went to Yale. Believing in the need for a college in western Massachusetts, Williams saw to it that a bequest of his cousin Ephraim Williams became in 1762 the initial endowment for Williams College.

His abrasive personality and close friendship with Thomas Hutchinson exposed Williams to fierce antagonism during the pre-revolutionary controversy. Defeated for reelection to the house of representatives in 1769, amid charges that he and his son Israel, Jr., had violated the nonimportation agreement, he assessed the political situation with remarkable analytical skill: "I am as much for liberty, for supporting the rights of the colonies and for taking every prudent reasonable measure to maintain them, as any of my countrymen," he explained to Hutchinson in 1769, "but I differ . . . as to what they are, wherein they have been invaded, and . . . the methods of redress" (Shipton, p. 319). Hatfield returned him to the state house in 1771, but he left the legislature in disgust the following year.

On 30 August 1774 a Hampshire County mob confronted Williams and his crony John Worthington, both of whom had been appointed to the new royal council created by the Coercive Acts. Old habits of deference and the new spirit of rebellion hung in precarious balance. "The people kept their tempers," one Whig observer noted, "and [Williams] tried to harangue them in mitigation of his conduct" but realized, in the words of the same observer, that "the people were not to be dallied with" (Nobles, p. 167). He was jailed in February 1775 when he and his sons refused to honor the patriots' public day of prayer and fasting and again in May 1777 after the discovery and publication of his private correspondence with Hutchinson. In June of that year he made his peace with the Revolution after posting a £3,000 bond and guaranteeing his good behavior. By the time he died in Hatfield, following a fall down his cellar stairs, his neighbors had agreed to forget past political differences.

• Williams's papers are in the Massachusetts Historical Society, Boston. Clifford K. Shipton, "Israel Williams," *Sibley's Harvard Graduates*, vol. 8 (1951), pp. 301–33, is a masterful biographical sketch. Gregory H. Nobles, *Divisions within the Whole: Politics and Society in Hampshire County, Massachusetts, 1740–1775* (1983), Robert J. Taylor, *Western Massachusetts in the Revolution* (1954), William G. McLoughlin, *New England Dissent, 1630–1833* (1971), and Robert Zemsky, *Merchants, Farmers, and River Gods* (1971), set Williams in political and social context.

ROBERT M. CALHOON

WILLIAMS, James (1 July 1796–10 Apr. 1869), journalist and diplomat, was born in Grainger County, Tennessee, the son of Ethelred Williams and Mary Copeland, farmers. Though little is known about his early years, Williams was educated at West Point and thereafter joined the army, where he saw action in Florida during the Second Seminole War. He retired from the military in 1837 at the rank of captain and later that same year married Lucy Jane Graham. The couple had three children.

In 1841 Captain Williams founded the *Knoxville Post*, a fervent pro-Whig organ, which he edited for about two years. In 1843 he was elected to the Tennessee state legislature, where he served a one-year term as representative for Knox County. Williams became involved in several ventures that characterized the spirit of private enterprise and social reform associated with the Jacksonian Era. In 1850 Williams captained the steamboat *Chattanooga* and promoted commercial development along the Tennessee River. He was the founder of the Deaf and Dumb Asylum of Knoxville, and he, along with his brother William Williams (1810–1894), established the Tennessee River Mining, Manufacturing, and Navigation Company. Both of the Williams brothers successfully promoted the development of railroad lines in Tennessee, and in 1852 they established the Knoxville and Charleston Railroad Company.

After moving to Nashville sometime in the early 1850s, Williams published a series of essays on diverse political issues, such as internal improvements and the tariff, in the local press, and he signed these anonymously as "Old Line Whig." Becoming increasingly disenchanted with the antislavery position taken by many northern Whigs and their eventual movement into the newly founded Republican party, he broke with the party in the late 1850s and joined the Democratic party. In 1858 President James Buchanan offered him the position of U.S. minister to Turkey, and Williams served at Constantinople until the outbreak of the Civil War in 1861. In 1860 he toured Syria, Palestine, and Egypt as a minister plenipotentiary and negotiated agreements granting greater liberties to foreign nationals involved in civil litigation in these lands. His visit also inspired greater respect of the United States among people who heretofore had maltreated and threatened American missionaries visiting the region. When he resigned his position upon the election of Abraham Lincoln, many American nationals living in Turkey urged him to reconsider his decision in light of his earlier diplomatic accomplishments.

Williams returned to the United States in an effort to prevent secession or to avert war, but sensing the futility of such an eleventh-hour mission, he enlisted in the Confederate cause, ran the Union blockade, and returned to Europe in September 1861. On board the *Africa* bound for Liverpool, Williams began an earnest campaign "to secure the sympathy and engage the attention of most of the passengers" to support the southern cause (*Official Records of the Union and Confederate Navies*, vol. 2, p. 2). During the four years of the American Civil War, he became the Confederacy's most eloquent propagandist and served as a virtual minister extraordinary, assisting other southern diplomats in seeking supplies, loans, and especially European recognition of the Confederacy. In London he became a close associate of Henry Hotze, the Confederate propagandist who edited *The Index*, a prosouthern journal intended to generate support among the British middle and upper classes. In addition to essays that appeared in *The Index*, Williams also provided perhaps the most articulate rationale for southern belligerency in articles that appeared in the *Times* and the *Standard* by arguing that abolition should be gradual to avoid commercial disruption and cautious to avoid social unrest. Several of his essays were collected and published in Nashville in 1861 under the title *Letters on Slavery from the Old World*, and the book was reprinted in London under the title *The South Vindicated* (1862). Williams used this work to chide the Republican party for waging a war "to effect the extinction of slavery in the American Confederacy" (p. viii). Hotze used his business connections to have the work translated into German in order to disseminate prosouthern literature to a larger audience on the continent. Williams was invited to the German Confederation to make his case among its member states. In 1863 he published another work, *The Rise and Fall of the Model Republic*.

Williams worked closely with James Mason and John Slidell, the official Confederate diplomats assigned to London and Paris respectively, hoping to encourage recognition of the Confederacy by either of the major European powers. When Napoleon III conducted his misguided foray into Mexico aimed at placing the Austrian prince Maximilian on the throne there, it was Williams who met with the new Mexican emperor at Miramar, Argentina, to try to persuade Mexico to recognize the Confederacy. His mission failed in large measure because of Napoleon III's insistence that Mexico not enter into any diplomatic arrangements without the approval of the French government.

Williams lived out the remainder of his life after the Civil War in Wiesbaden (Hesse-Darmstadt) in the German Confederation. He died at Gratz, Austria.

• While no collection of Williams papers exists, some of his Civil War era correspondence can be found in the James Murray Mason Papers and the John T. Pickett Papers, both housed in the Library of Congress. See also F. L. Owsley, *King Cotton Diplomacy* (1931), and W. T. Hale and D. L. Merritt, *A History of Tennessee*, vol. 3 (1913). A small amount of military-related references to Williams are included in *The War of the Rebellion: A Compilation of the Official Records of the Union and Confederate Armies*, vol. 2, ser. 2 (128 vols., 1880–1901); *The Official Records of the Union and Confederate Navies in the War of the Rebellion*, vol. 2, ser. 3 (30 vols., 1894–1922); and House, 35th Cong., 2d sess., H. Exec. Doc. 68.

JUNIUS P. RODRIGUEZ

WILLIAMS, Jesse Lynch (17 Aug. 1871–14 Sept. 1929), short story writer, novelist, and playwright, was born in Sterling, Illinois, the son of Meade Creighton Williams, a Presbyterian minister, and Elizabeth Riddle. Williams was named for his grandfather, a well-known civil engineer and government director of the Union Pacific Railway. After attending Beloit Academy in Wisconsin, Williams went to Princeton University, where he received a B.A. in 1892 and an M.A. in 1895. At Princeton, Williams explored his interests in literature and drama by editing Princeton's *Nassau Literary Magazine* and cofounding the Triangle Club, an undergraduate dramatic society that staged musicals.

After graduating from Princeton, Williams worked as a journalist for the *New York Sun* from 1893 to 1897, was on the staff of *Scribner's Magazine* from 1897 to 1900, and finally returned to Princeton to edit the *Princeton Alumni Weekly* from 1900 to 1903. In 1898 he married Alice Laidlaw of New York, with whom he eventually had three children. After 1903 Williams devoted himself full-time to writing.

Williams's literary works roughly correspond with the chronology of his early career: college stories, journalism stories, and finally domestic fiction and drama. Williams's earliest works fall into the category of college stories. These include *Princeton Stories* (1895), *The Adventures of a Freshman* (1899), and *The Girl and the Game and Other College Stories* (1908). While *The Girl and the Game* was published ten years after the other two works and exhibits Williams's stylistic maturation, it is very similar to the others in setting and tone. All the college stories take place in the upper-class male world of the Ivy League university. The stories in Williams's first book, *Princeton Stories*, are often little more than anecdotes in which plot and character are never fully developed. Heavily colored with the slang of young male college students, most of the stories celebrate some aspect of college life (in fact, *Princeton Stories* is dedicated to the class of 1892). Usually the stories involve some sort of competition (either athletic or academic) in which the protagonist must face a complication before emerging ultimately victorious. While the stories in *The Girl and the Game* more self-consciously employ literary techniques, particularly in plot structure (forgoing chronological exposition in favor of structures designed to heighten tension), they share *Princeton Stories*' celebratory tone and emphasis on competition. The college stories are so deeply centered in the world they attempt to portray that they contain no sense of critical distance. In most of the stories it is difficult to distinguish the voice of the author from the voice of the immature narrator.

Like Williams's later college stories, his journalism stories, *The Stolen Story and Other Newspaper Stories* (1899) and *The Day Dreamer* (1906), are more skillfully crafted than his earliest collections of short stories. Both *The Stolen Story* and *The Day Dreamer* (a novel based on the most popular story in *The Stolen Story* collection) rely heavily on seamless exposition designed to build narrative tension and uncertainty to its fullest. Also, like Williams's college stories, the journalism stories contain no sense of authorial detachment. While this gives the stories a certain kind of authenticity, again it is limiting in that there is no narrative critical distance from which to view events and characters.

The most famous of the newspaper stories, "The Stolen Story," which was expanded into a novel (*The Day Dreamer*) and adapted into a four-act play (*The Stolen Story* [1906]), is illustrative of both Williams's detailed descriptions and his disappointing lack of thematic depth. The plot centers around Billy Woods, a young star reporter who is as noteworthy for his absentmindedness as he is for his journalistic skill. When Woods is finally fired from his job at *The Day* for missing a story, he is immediately hired by *The Earth*, a rival newspaper. Laden with the scoop of the year, Woods absentmindedly returns to his old desk at *The Day* to write the story. *The Day* staff successfully keeps Woods from realizing that he is writing for the wrong paper so that they can print the story in the next morning's news. There are a few tantalizing moments in the story that almost question the logic of the competitive journalistic world, but the story yields little more than a few moments of tension and a glimpse into the inner workings of a turn-of-the-century newspaper office.

The domestic novels and plays, which form the apex of Williams's career, retain the fascinating detail of his earlier works while adding thematic complexity. From 1910 to 1930 Williams published nine novels and plays, including *The Married Life of the Frederick Carrolls* (1910), a comedy about newlyweds coping with marital strife; *Remating Time* (1916), in which two couples exchange partners to illustrate the absurdity of divorce laws; and *She Knew She Was Right* (1930), a satire about a woman whose feelings for her husband become confused after the baptism of their child. In 1917 Williams was awarded the first Pulitzer Prize for drama for his three-act comedy *Why Marry?* (1917), an adaptation of his 1914 novel *And So They Were Married*.

A social satire in the mode of George Bernard Shaw, *Why Marry?* not only gives the reader a close look at one family's set of domestic arrangements but it stands back to analyze them. The play involves five related couples, all in various stages of marriage, including engagement, dissolution, and divorce. Unlike Williams's earlier works, *Why Marry?* takes women and women's roles seriously. Two of its central female characters, Lucy and Helen, respectively represent old and new womanhood. Lucy, who champions traditional roles for women, is deeply unhappy in her middle-class marriage. Helen, whom Lucy refers to as "a sexless freak with a scientific degree" (p. 13), is an educated woman who refuses to marry out of principle, even when she meets a man she loves. In one way or another, each of the characters in the play expresses discontent with some aspect of marriage. In the play's climactic scene, Helen and the man she loves are tricked into marrying at a family gathering where they intend to declare their decision to share their lives without marriage. Although Williams saves his lovers from impropriety with a fairly conventional resolution, he does not completely absolve the institution of marriage. The play ends with the lines: "Respectability has triumphed this time, but let society take warning and beware! Beware! Beware!" (p. 160). All of Williams's domestic works similarly grapple with intimate relationships and their link to society.

After winning the Pulitzer Prize, Williams's career soared. In 1919 he became an officer of the National Institute of Arts and Letters, in 1921 he was elected president of the Author's League of America, and in 1925 and 1927 he was a fellow of creative art at the University of Michigan. Williams died suddenly in Herkimer, New York, of heart disease.

While Williams's domestic plays and fiction are perhaps his most successful literary products and won him the greatest critical acclaim, his earlier works are valuable as well for the detailed look they give us into two turn-of-the-century male subcultures, the Ivy League college and the newspaper.

• The major repository of Williams's correspondence is the American Academy of Arts and Letters Library in New York. The Princeton University Library Department of Rare Books and Special Collections also houses some of Williams's correspondence as well as unpublished manuscripts and diaries. Additional correspondence can be found in the University of Virginia Library, the University of Iowa Special Collections Department, and the University of Texas Humanities Research Center. Williams's other major published works include *History of Princeton University* (1898); *New York Sketches* (1902); *My Lost Duchess* (1908); *Mr. Cleveland: A Personal Impression* (1909); *Why Not* (three-act comedy produced in New York in 1922 based on the novel *Remating Time*); *Not Wanted* (1923); *Lovely Lady* (three-act comedy produced in Washington, D.C., in 1925); and *They Still Fall in Love* (1929).

KELLY WILLIS MENDIOLA

WILLIAMS, Joe (1 Apr. 1886–12 Mar. 1946), baseball pitcher, was born on Baptist Hill in Seguin, Texas, east of San Antonio, to a black father (name unknown) and a Comanche mother, Lettie Williams. Williams began his baseball career in 1905, pitching for the San Antonio Broncos and reportedly winning 28 games while losing 4. Following a season with Austin and a record of 15–9, he returned to San Antonio from 1907 through 1909, amassing 72 wins and 18 losses. In 1909

Williams defeated the touring Chicago Leland Giants, considered one of the premier black teams and managed by "blackball" entrepreneur Rube Foster. Williams's obvious potential brought an invitation from Foster to move north with the Lelands and then pitch for Foster's Chicago American Giants.

Williams, nicknamed "Smokey Joe," "Cyclone" and "Strikeout," relied on his fastball to overpower hitters. Being 6′4″ and considered perhaps the hardest thrower in the Negro League, he has been favorably compared to his contemporary Walter Johnson (Holway, 1988, p. 62; Peterson, p. 216). Williams delivered his fastball from a no wind-up, overhand motion in a slow, deceptive manner that appeared to make his pitches explode past batters. In time, he developed intimidating sidearm and crossfire deliveries; as his career wound down, he devised a variety of "cuter" off-speed pitches and the craft to artfully spot the ball to a batter's weakness.

Williams began 1912 in the winter Cuban Leagues with 10 wins and 7 losses. Cuban league teams were integrated, with white major leaguers, Latin players, and black players. From 1912 through 1916 Williams's record in Cuba was reportedly 32–22. In the spring of 1912 the American Giants toured the West Coast with Williams, earning a 9–1–1 record against Pacific Coast teams. In the summer Williams jumped for $105 a month to the New York Lincoln Giants, founded in 1911 by white boxing promoters Jess and Rod McMahon. His teammates earned $40–$75. It was common blackball practice for players lured by better money offers to change teams, as player contracts were poorly written or simply ignored. In New York, "Cyclone" teamed with "Cannonball" Dick Redding to provide one of Negro baseball's most formidable pitching duos. Playing at Harlem's Olympic Field in New York City, the Lincoln Giants became a top-ranked team, black or white. On 24 October 1912 Williams made the most of his first opportunity against a major league team, defeating the National League champion New York Giants on a four-hit shutout. Two weeks later he duplicated the feat against the American League New York Highlanders.

As Williams continued his career, its success was often measured by game appearances against white major league opposition. In 1913 the touring New York Lincoln Giants reportedly built a record of 101–6 against other black teams and white semipro squads. Williams was 4–1 against major league all-star opponents, including victories over Hall of Fame pitchers Chief Bender and Grover Cleveland Alexander. Against Alexander, Williams hit a home run while striking out nine and giving up eight hits in a 9–2 victory. Bender was defeated on a three-hitter.

In 1914 Williams apparently split the season between the Lincolns and the Chicago American Giants, reportedly posting a 12–2 record in New York and finishing the year 41–3. Misfortune struck him in 1915 as he broke his arm and then a wrist. On his return Williams split with two major league squads, losing to the National League Giants before shutting out the league champion Phillies and striking out ten. From 1917 through 1919 the fireballer faced major league all-star squads eleven times, emerging with eight victories, including four shutouts, and two defeats. Among the losing pitchers were Bender, Giants Hall of Famer Rube Marquard twice, and baseball immortal Walter Johnson. One defeat for Williams was a 10-inning, no-hit, 20-strikeout effort lost on an error.

In 1922 Williams married Beatrice (maiden name unknown), a showgirl in Harlem and Broadway revues. They had one daughter. Soft-spoken off the field and with a signature cigar in his mouth, on the field he was an intense competitor, yet he was never known to argue with an umpire.

In 1922 Williams became manager of the Lincoln Giants, leaving after two years to join Nat Strong's Brooklyn Royal Giants. In 1924 Williams struck out 25 in a one-run, 12-inning loss to the Brooklyn Bushwicks, Strong's topflight white semipro team. In 1925, at age 39, Williams moved to the Homestead Grays of Pittsburgh for an eight-year stint, reportedly losing only five games during the first five years. Among his efforts were four wins, including two shutouts, over major league all-star squads in 1927. In 1930 the Grays barnstormed part of the season with the Kansas City Monarchs who transported their own lights, which provided barely enough illumination for night games. One evening in the dim shadows Williams fanned 27 Monarchs in a 12-inning shutout victory, giving up one single. The Grays also toured in 1930 with the New York Lincoln Giants, staging a 10-game series to determine the East's best blackball team, with the Grays winning six times. Williams lost two of three starts.

Williams retired after the 1932 season. His career record against major league squads was 22 wins, 7 losses, 1 tie; against Hall of Fame pitchers 8–2–1. Two of the losses were at age forty-five and two others by the score of 1–0. In 1952 Williams was named best blackball pitcher in a *Pittsburgh Courier* poll of African-American baseball veterans and sportswriters, beating Satchel Paige by one vote. Following his retirement, Williams tended bar in Harlem, hired, for the most part, to draw patrons and talk baseball. He died in New York City.

• One biography of Williams is John B. Holway, *Smokey Joe and the Cannonball* (1983). Shorter personal profiles appear in Holway, *Blackball Stars: Negro League Pioneers* (1988); and Robert Peterson, *Only the Ball Was White* (1970).

DAVID BERNSTEIN

WILLIAMS, John (10 Dec. 1664–12 June 1729), minister and author, was born in Roxbury, Massachusetts, the son of Samuel Williams, a shoemaker, and Theoda Park. Choosing a life path different from that of his father, he attended Harvard College and graduated in 1683. After two years of teaching school in Dorchester, he married Eunice Mather in 1688 and was ordained as the minister of Deerfield, Massachusetts, on 17 October of the same year. The couple had twelve children, ten of whom lived to maturity.

Deerfield was the most exposed frontier settlement in colonial Massachusetts. Williams thrived as the pastor there, gaining prominence as a minister and as a father of the settlement. By 1700 his reputation had spread throughout western Massachusetts, owing partly to his close relationship with Solomon Stoddard, the renowned autocratic minister of Northampton, who was Williams's stepfather-in-law. Williams was also known as one of the most stalwart defenders of the Protestant faith in the area, and his faith and perseverance were soon tested.

In 1702 Queen Anne's War, known in Europe as the War of the Spanish Succession, began, pitting Catholic France and Spain against Protestant England and the Netherlands. The effect in North America was a colonial war between Protestant New England and Catholic New France. On 29 February 1704 Deerfield was attacked by between 200 and 300 French Canadians and their American Indian allies, primarily of the Abenaki tribes. The town was taken over briefly by the French and Indians, who then took 109 prisoners, two-fifths of the town's population, northward. Among the captives were Williams, his wife, and five of his children.

Eunice Williams was killed by her Indian captors on the first day of the march. Having recently borne her last child, she was weaker than many of the other captives. The other captive members of the Williams family survived, but they did not remain together. Each family member was separated from the others and held by a different group of French and Indians. Williams feared greatly for the souls of his children, especially his seven-year-old daughter Eunice, who was held by a group of Mohawks.

Even as the prisoners crossed the border into French Canada, Williams never lost sight of his role as the "keeper of the sheep" in the "wilderness" of captivity. He retained a respected presence among the Deerfield captives as the spiritual leader of their group. Realizing his stature, his French captors took him to a château just north of Quebec City in order to isolate him from his fellow captives. Nevertheless, his captors permitted him to write letters, which proved to be the means of providing a sense of cohesion and leadership in the family. Through correspondence he was able to prevent his son Stephen from converting to Catholicism.

Following extensive communication between the French governor Philippe de Rigaud de Vaudreuil and Massachusetts governor Joseph Dudley, a prisoner exchange was affected in 1706. Williams, two of his children, and fifty-four other Deerfield captives sailed from Quebec City aboard the brigantine *Hope* on 1 November and arrived in Boston on 28 November 1706. After celebrations in Boston, Williams returned to Deerfield, arriving at the village on 28 December 1706. During the winter of 1706–1707 he wrote the story of his captivity, *The Redeemed Captive Returning to Zion* (1707), which achieved remarkable success: six editions were published in the eighteenth century and five in the nineteenth. Williams portrayed in unforgettable terms the sufferings of his parishioners and their steadfastness in the time of their captivity. The book was also intended as a warning: surely God would not have allowed the people of Deerfield to be defeated and captured had they not permitted a spiritual relapse among them. Because of its wide readership, *The Redeemed Captive* spread the theme of "declension," the belief held by many ministers of the time that the people of New England had become less God-fearing over time and therefore were vulnerable to evils of the kind that befell Williams and his family.

In March 1707 Williams preached a sermon in Boston, titled *God in the Camp*, that underscored the theme of declension and further established Williams as its spokesman. Within two years of his return to Deerfield, he had won renown throughout all of New England.

In the summer of 1711 Williams served as a chaplain to the failed Anglo-American attack on Quebec during which the English fleet lost seven ships on the rocks at the mouth of the St. Lawrence River and failed to strike a blow. He also went to Canada as a commissioner in a prisoner exchange (1713–1714), but he failed to achieve his fondest and most pressing hope: the release of his daughter Eunice, who had become known as Marguerite A'ongote in Kahnawake, a village of Mohawks near Montreal. She had married a Mohawk and was truly lost to Williams.

Until his last days, Williams strove to correct what he saw as the moral and spiritual laxity that was increasing in New England. In 1707 he married Abigail Bissell, a cousin of his first wife, with whom he had five more children. He died in Deerfield and was eulogized in the Boston newspapers as one of the important spiritual leaders of his time. He left an estate that included eleven separate plots of land, fifteen cows, ten horses, and two servants or slaves (an ambiguous distinction in colonial New England), a black and a mulatto. One-third of his property was left to his widow, and the remainder was divided among his children, who received £220 8d. each.

Williams's book about his captivity brought him fame among the churchmen of his generation and made him a standard-bearer for Protestantism in New England against the Catholic church and New France. As a keeper of the faith he rose from ministering to the Deerfield captives to witnessing to his compatriots throughout New England. Because of his unwavering belief in Protestantism, Williams was a powerful voice on behalf of the doctrine of God's grace, even as rationalism was beginning to erode the reliance on pure faith. *The Redeemed Captive* remained popular well into the nineteenth century.

• Williams's papers are preserved by the Pocumtuck Valley Memorial Association in Historic Deerfield, Mass. An in-depth study of Williams and his family in captivity is John Demos, *The Unredeemed Captive: A Family Story from Early*

America (1994). Other important studies are Richard I. Melvoin, *New England Outpost: War and Society in Colonial Deerfield* (1989); Emma Lewis Coleman, *New England Captives Carried to Canada* (2 vols., 1925); and George Sheldon, *A History of Deerfield, Massachusetts* (2 vols., 1895–1896; repr. 1983). Novelistic attempts to capture the drama of 1704–1706 are Mary P. Wells Smith, *Boy Captive of Old Deerfield* (1904) and *The Boy Captive in Canada* (1905).

SAMUEL WILLARD CROMPTON

WILLIAMS, John (28 Apr. 1761–12 Oct. 1818), writer, was born in London, England. The names and occupations of his parents are not known. An exceptionally bright child, Williams attended the Merchant Taylor's School, the master of which he satirized in a sharp epigram and was chastised for doing so. He was hired as a booksellers' hack, mainly to produce translations. He became a journalist in Dublin, Ireland, where he worked for the *Morning Herald* and the *Universal Register*. He was prosecuted in Dublin for writing an attack on the government. Returning to London, he wrote several plays and, as a venomous drama critic, became notorious in the theatrical world.

In 1789 Williams published an unimportant volume or two of poetry. He soon followed with a series of seven short pieces, under the pen name Anthony Pasquin. By far the best, and coming first, is *The Life of the Late Earl of Barrymore, Including a History of the Wargrave Theatricals* . . . (1793). Richard, earl of Barrymore, Viscount Buttervant, and Baron Barry, was a personal friend of Williams and evidently something of a patron. He was a colorful sportsman, benefactor, scholar, actor, host, gambler, and practical joker. He was killed in 1793, at the age of thirty-four, when a friend accidentally discharged a shotgun in his face. Williams's prose here is straightforward, moving, and often entertaining. The remaining six pieces, occasionally combining verse and prose, are uneven. *A Cabinet of Miscellanies* (1794) is a scorching poetic blast against the school Williams attended. *Shrove Tuesday, a Satiric Rhapsody* (1794) is a miscellany of didactic, autobiographical poems, one of which includes this line: "When Puberty had strung the leading nerve, / I twin'd the sacred Myrtle round my brow." *A Crying Epistle from Britannia to Colonel Mack* (1795) is an imaginary appeal for a hero to come save the realm, which is endangered by the spirit of rebellion. It contains this representative couplet: "Give every Sans Culotte a kick or knock; / To bring these Ruffians to Perdition's block." *Legislative Biography* . . . (1795) is a set of eighteen sketches, often elaborately bitter, of notable Britishers, and is avowedly intended as a companion to current Parliamentary reports. *The New Brighton Guide* . . . (1796) offers comments in favor of many activities, including women's liberation, and against others, including too much drinking, all in rollicking verse with footnotes in bloated prose. And *A Looking-glass for the Royal Family* . . . (1797) warns of a cabal against the princess of Wales, with incidental comments against prostitution and gambling.

Williams made the mistake of suing a bookseller by the name of Robert Faulder, lost his case, was himself prosecuted and fined, and was adjudged "a common libeler" in 1797. Either that year or the next, he migrated to the United States, where he continued his literary career, without ever sweetening his bitter, satirical style. It has been reported that he edited a newspaper in New York called the *Federalist*. In 1798 he produced a poorly regarded play titled *The Federal Oath; or, The Americans Strike Home*. He also asked William Dunlap, the New York painter, historical playwright, and theater owner, to help him gain employment in the theater. Dunlap, however, was unfavorably impressed with Williams to the point of loathing him and therefore offered no assistance. Williams worked as the editor of the short-lived *Columbian Gazette* in New York (1799, twelve numbers). In 1804 he edited the Boston *Democrat*, until he had an explosive dispute with his two partners over money. That same year he published his *Hamiltoniad*. Its amusing subtitle is *An Extinguisher for the Royal Faction of New-England, with Copious Notes . . . Being Intended as a High-heeled Shoe for All Limping Republicans*. The three-canto poem, mostly in heroic couplets, is marred by vitriolic, bombastic, anti-Federalist lines, discreetly labels objects of his satirical barbs as "John A——s," "Ot—s," etc., and ends with "A Federal Epitaph." The work is improved by extensive footnotes, many of which are quotations in Latin and French, while others print correspondence between Alexander Hamilton and Aaron Burr. In 1804 Williams also published *The Life of Alexander Hamilton*. In this example of fulsome rhetoric, he briefly praises the "address" and "gallantry" Hamilton displayed during the American Revolution but immediately goes on to deplore his subsequent militant, pro-British, anti-French policies. He calls *The Federalist*, the classic political document written by Hamilton, James Madison, and John Jay, "a work of much merit" that is flawed by "a tautological vein of expression." He ridicules "the Hamiltonian school of anglo-federalism," praises Thomas Jefferson for saving America, and too cursorily laments the duel in which Burr killed Hamilton—concluding that no "tumult of execration" should fall on the victor.

The only book by Williams published in England after his migration to the United States is *Dramatic Censor* (12 monthly parts, 1812); thus, in all likelihood he revisited the city of his birth in 1811 or so. He was chronically despised there. Robert Watt regarded him as "a literary character of the lowest description," while William Babington Macaulay likened him to a "polecat" and a "malignant and filthy baboon." Although it is not known whether Williams ever returned to England again, it is certain that he died of typhus fever, and in dire poverty, in Brooklyn. It is not known whether he ever married or had children.

• The very few extant Williams papers are at Columbia University, Duke University, Yale University, the Historical Society of Pennsylvania at Philadelphia, and the Library of Congress. In *Diary of William Dunlap (1766–1839)* . . . , ed.

Dorothy C. Barck (3 vols., 1930), Dunlap records his displeasure with Williams. Obituaries are in the *New York Evening Post*, 16 Oct. 1818; the *New York Columbian*, 17 Oct. 1818; and the *New York Advertiser*, 20 Oct. 1818.

ROBERT L. GALE

WILLIAMS, John (29 Jan. 1778–10 Aug. 1837), soldier, lawyer, and legislator, was born in Surry County, North Carolina, the son of Joseph Williams and Rebecca Lanier. He attended schools in his home county and studied law in nearby Salisbury. He moved to Knoxville, Tennessee, soon after the turn of the century and was admitted to the bar in 1803. Two years later he married Malinda Lawson White, a daughter of General James White and a sister to Hugh Lawson White, who became Williams's lifelong friend, an organizer of the Whig party, and a presidential candidate in 1836. Williams and his wife had ten children, six of whom lived to adulthood.

Williams was commissioned a captain of the Sixth U.S. Infantry in 1799, when war with France appeared imminent. He was serving as state attorney general when the War of 1812 began. He resigned, hastily raised a force of 200 mounted volunteers, and led them against the Seminole Indians in Florida. In June 1813 he became a colonel of the Thirty-ninth U.S. Infantry and fought under Andrew Jackson in the Creek campaign of 1813, participating in the battle of Horseshoe Bend.

Williams resumed the practice of law in Knoxville after the war ended. In 1815 he was elected to the U.S. Senate to complete the term of George W. Campbell, who had resigned to become secretary of the treasury. Two years later Williams was chosen without opposition for a full six-year term. As a member of the Senate, he fell in line behind Presidents James Madison and James Monroe and consistently supported western and southern interests. Primary among these issues were internal improvements, particularly the construction of turnpikes, and protection of slavery, including his support of the southern position opposing any restrictions on slavery in the Missouri admissions issue.

The Republican party, although dominant in Tennessee, was divided into factions. A group centering largely in Nashville and led by John Overton sought to perpetuate its control by capitalizing on Jackson's recently acquired military glory and reputation. Williams headed another strong faction that was based largely in Knoxville but also had support in Nashville. After the presidential election of 1820, Williams lost little time in making known his preference for William Crawford for president over Jackson. Although voting patterns later indicated that Jackson had wide appeal among the common voters in Tennessee, by no means did the general find universal support among men of position and status. Williams, especially, had differed with Jackson over various military matters during the War of 1812, and he apparently regaled voters from Knoxville to Washington with stories of his lack of confidence in the "Old Chief."

As the senatorial election of 1823 approached, the Overton group cast about in despair for a candidate who could beat Williams. Williams traveled Murfreesboro, the state capital, several days in advance of the vote and received tentative commitments from more than enough legislators to assure his victory. In desperation the Overton clique turned to Jackson as a viable contender, and on at least three separate occasions they rode to "the Hermitage" to persuade him. Finally, Jackson, who was never happy as a lawmaker, agreed, and he arrived in Murfreesboro only a few hours before the scheduled voting. Overawed by the presence of the Old Chief himself, seven of Williams's tentatively pledged supporters turned to Jackson, who won by a vote of 35 to 25. Williams never forgave Jackson or the perfidious legislators.

Stunned, Williams left immediately for Knoxville and announced his candidacy for the state senate from the Knoxville District. Defeated by a small majority, he accepted an appointment two years later as chargé d'affairs to the Federation of Central America. Unhappy in Guatemala, he returned to his home the following year. In 1827 he was elected to a term in the state senate, but he retired in 1829 and did not serve again. Assured by supporters that he could win the congressional seat from the Knoxville District without opposition, he nevertheless declined and resumed the practice of law.

Throughout his life Williams had many business and civic interests. For several years he served as a trustee of East Tennessee College (now the University of Tennessee) in Knoxville. Supportive of the development of railroads, he was a promoter and member of the board of directors of the Louisville, Cincinnati, and Charleston Railroad. An active Mason and churchman, he died at his home near Knoxville.

• For more information on Williams see Leota Driver Maiden, "Colonel John Williams," *East Tennessee Historical Society Publications* 30 (1958): 7–46; Robert M. McBride, ed., *Biographical Directory of the Tennessee General Assembly*, vol. 1 (1975); Robert E. Corlew, *Tennessee: A Short History* (1990); Marquis James, *The Life of Andrew Jackson* (1939); Harold D. Moser et al., eds., *The Papers of Andrew Jackson* (1980–1996); and Robert Remini, *The Life of Andrew Jackson* (1988).

ROBERT E. CORLEW

WILLIAMS, John Bell (4 Dec. 1918–26 Mar. 1983), politician, was born in Raymond, Mississippi, the son of Graves Kelly Williams, a druggist, and Maude Elizabeth Bedwell. Williams graduated from Hinds Junior College in 1936. After spending a year at the University of Mississippi, he returned home to study at the Jackson School of Law. In 1940 he passed the bar exam and went into practice in Raymond. He earned a pilot's license at Hinds Junior College and entered the the Army Air Corps in November 1941. While flying to North Africa in 1943, his plane, the *Johnny Reb*, crashed in British Guyana. Williams lost the lower portion of his left arm and mutilated one leg. He returned home in 1944 and was appointed prosecuting attorney for Hinds County. That same year he married Elizabeth Ann Wells, with whom he had three children.

In 1946 Williams ran for Congress, patterning his speaking style after Senator Theodore Bilbo, a racist demagogue. Arriving once at a rally and hearing Williams, Bilbo commented, "That boy knows the words, but he hasn't quite got the tune." Williams learned fast. Finding that if he adjusted the microphone with his metal claw when he stepped up to speak, it made a terrible noise, Williams incorporated the trick into his standard campaign performance to remind voters of his lost arm. Williams became the youngest U.S. representative in Mississippi history.

Williams entered Congress prepared to "go along" with the Democratic leadership, but as Harry Truman developed a civil rights policy, he turned on the president, beginning a career-long estrangement from his party. Early in his career he became a single-issue representative for segregation. Williams believed in the racial inferiority of black people and never ceased telling racist jokes. He visited Bilbo days before his death and presented an emotional defense of him in the House of Representatives. The Democratic party leadership in the House denied Williams the committee assignments that he sought; columnist Drew Pearson rated Williams an "unpromising freshman."

He spent his early years in Congress on the Post Office and the Civil Service committees. Then in 1951 he moved to the Interstate and Foreign Commerce Committee. In 1959 he became chairman of the Transportation and Aeronautics subcommittee, where he supported federal matching grants for state and local governments to modernize airports. He opposed federal spending in almost every other instance. He served on the committee for the District of Columbia and used his membership to promote criticism of school integration. He made one congressional trip to Europe and swore never to go again. He visited the Soviet Union on that same trip, and the experience confirmed his hatred of communism. He voted against virtually all foreign aid. With John F. Kennedy's election, Williams became further estranged from the White House.

Williams supported the Democratic presidential candidate only in 1952. In 1948 he walked out of the Philadelphia convention to protest Truman's civil rights platform plank. He supported the Dixiecrats and as a result lost his patronage. In 1954 he coined the phrase "Black Monday" to describe the Supreme Court's announcement of the *Brown v. Board of Education of Topeka* decision and endorsed the call for Mississippi to pass "acts of nullification." One colleague in the House of Representatives said Williams was like an owl in a Mississippi swamp: the more light you shine in his eyes "the blinder he gets." He supported the States' Rights ticket that fielded slates of unpledged electors in 1956. In 1960 he endorsed an independent electors scheme, and in the next election he supported Republican Barry Goldwater, appearing on television at a fundraising event. Finally his party had enough and stripped Williams of his committee seniority.

Williams knew an opportunity when he saw it, and, portraying himself as the victim of the liberal establishment, he ran for governor of Mississippi in 1967. He faced formidable opposition for the first time in his career. Ross Barnett, the governor who had refused to enroll the first black student at the University of Mississippi until forced, ran in the primary along with a "moderate" named William Winter. Williams claimed Barnett was a traitor who made a secret deal with the Kennedys, and he depicted Winter as an overt liberal. Williams defeated Winter easily in the second round. The Republican candidate accused Williams of believing "the world is flat and that the edge of the world is the Mississippi state line." Williams carried every county in the state, but the first black since Reconstruction was also elected to the Mississippi legislature in the same race.

Williams, Mississippi's last segregationist governor, presided over the integration of Mississippi's schools. When the courts ordered desegregation, Williams failed to provide any leadership. The most generous assessment of his role was that he did nothing to prevent integration. In 1970 he sent state highway patrolmen to Jackson State University's campus to control a demonstration by black students. When police fired at demonstrators, killing two young men, Williams supported the police and refused to participate in either a city or an FBI investigation.

Journalists counted Williams's response to hurricane Camille in 1969 as the high point of his administration. He went to the coast before the storm subsided and stayed there directing the state's resources and encouraging local leaders.

During Williams's governorship, the Democratic party refused to seat the regular Mississippi delegates at the national convention in 1968. Instead, the convention chose the biracial loyalist Democrats to represent Mississippi. Williams left office as a Mississippi Democrat rejected by the national party. In retirement, he supported Republican candidates, helping to establish the Republican party in Mississippi.

His aid in establishing a two-party system in Mississippi is Williams's most notable contribution to the state. As governor he established an office of federal-state programs to coordinate and administer the federal funds that poured into the state from antipoverty agencies, but he tried to veto programs such as Head Start. His racism, which made him popular with white voters, prevented his becoming an effective leader of a state moving toward an integrated society.

• Williams's congressional papers are in the Mississippi Department of Archives and History, Jackson. Hinds Community College houses clippings assembled by Williams's congressional staff covering his career through 1967. Sandra Vance, "The Congressional Career of John Bell Williams, 1947–1967" (Ph.D. diss., Mississippi State Univ., 1976), is a biography. An obituary is in the *New York Times*, 27 Mar. 1983.

DENNIS J. MITCHELL

WILLIAMS, John Elias (28 Oct. 1853–2 Jan. 1919), industrial mediator, was born in Merthyr-Tydfil, Wales, the son of John Elias Williams, a coal miner, and Elizabeth Bowen. In 1864 the family moved to Streator, a coal-mining town in central northern Illinois. Soon after their arrival in the United States, Williams's father was killed by a rock fall while on the job, forcing Williams to take a job as a miner. He mined coal in and around Streator from age thirteen until he was twenty-eight years old. During the summer, when most mines operated at half-time, Williams spent his free time educating himself and participating in study clubs. He became the secretary and check weighman of the first labor union in Streator. In 1877 he married Isabella Dickinson.

After Williams left mining he worked as the editor of the *Streator Independent-Times* and was gradually drawn into mediating conflicts between workers and mine owners in Illinois. In 1897, during a major strike by the United Mine Workers that shut down mines in six states, Williams organized the Business Men's Auxiliary League, which attempted to settle the dispute through cooperation between the union, the company, and the general public. Williams helped facilitate financial compensation for the widows and orphans of miners who were killed in the Cherry Mine disaster of 1909. His career as a professional industrial mediator began in 1910, when he became the official arbitrator between the United Mine Workers of Illinois and the Illinois Coal Operators.

Williams's success in the Cherry Mine settlement and his work as an arbitrator in the Illinois coal industry brought him renown as a pioneer in the emerging field of industrial labor relations. In 1913 he was hired by the Hart, Schaffner, and Marx company and the United Garment Workers union to serve as an impartial arbitrator presiding over a contract between the company and the union. The contract, signed after a long strike in 1910 and 1911 involving 10,000 workers, provided for an arbitration board for final, binding decisions on disputes between the company and union. Williams was chosen as the chairman of the board and served in that position until his death. It was in this capacity that Williams became a mentor to Sidney Hillman, a union leader who became the head of the Amalgamated Clothing Workers (ACW), helped found the Congress of Industrial Organizations, and then served as the leading labor representative on production boards during World War II. Under Hillman's leadership, the ACW followed Williams's idea that a strategy of continual, mediated negotiations between management and union representatives was preferable to strike actions taken by the union. Other, more militant unionists criticized this strategy as ultimately concessionary—without the strike weapon, they argued, unions would be left with little or no economic leverage in negotiations.

In 1913 Williams testified before the U.S. Commission on Industrial Relations on his theories of labor relations. He argued that the promotion of trade unionism was the most effective means of disciplining workers and bringing order to the social chaos caused by rapid industrialization. "Trade unionism is the greatest educational force that we have," he testified. "It is through their unions that men become intelligent in the things they need to know most. It is the best school of ethics we have. Even at its worst, it compels one man to subordinate his individual greed to the interests of the group" (Potofsky, pp. 11–12). Seeking an alternative to the revolutionary program of the Socialist party and the authoritarian rule of the unregulated industrial shop, Williams publicly argued that trade unionism, mediated collective bargaining, and industrial cooperation could bring about industrial democracy.

Williams introduced a number of devices into the field of industrial mediation. Most significantly, he devised a compromise between the union-only "closed shop" and the union-optional "open shop." His proposal of a "preferential shop" that allowed the company to give preference to union members in hiring and condoned laying off nonunion workers before union members was instituted in a number of industrial settlements.

Besides his work as an industrial mediator, Williams was active in a number of civic and religious organizations in Illinois. He served as president of the Illinois Unitarian Conference and acted as chairman of the Advisory Board of the Illinois Free Employment Agencies. During World War I he served as federal fuel administrator for Illinois. Williams died in Streator.

Williams is generally considered the father of the field of modern industrial labor relations. His innovative work as a mediator and his theories of industrial democracy defined the field that grew along with the development of industrial capitalism in the twentieth-century United States.

• Jacob S. Potofsky, ed., *John E. Williams: An Appreciation with Selections from His Writings* (1929), contains a biographical sketch by Earl Dean Howard and several comments on Williams by Hillman and officials from Hart, Schaffner, and Marx. For Williams's philosophy of industrial relations, see *Final Report and Testimony of the U.S. Commission on Industrial Relations* (1916). For information on Williams's relationship with Hillman, see Steven Fraser, *Labor Will Rule: Sidney Hillman and the Rise of American Labor* (1991).

THADDEUS RUSSELL

WILLIAMS, John Foster (12 Oct. 1743–24 June 1814), officer in the Massachusetts State Navy and the U.S. Revenue Cutter Service, was born in Boston, Massachusetts. The identities of his parents are unknown, although he is believed to be a descendant of Roger Williams.

A product of Boston's North End, Williams gravitated naturally to the sea. He entered the merchant service at age fifteen and within seven years was master of his own vessel. In between voyages to the West Indies and South America, Williams married Hannah Homer in 1774. The beginning of the revolutionary war a year later interrupted his thriving career as a merchant captain. In early 1776 Williams accepted a commission in the Massachusetts State Navy and received command of the twelve-gun sloop *Republic*. He completed only a single brief cruise in the *Republic*, however, and after a short stint in the slightly larger *Massachusetts* he took a leave of absence to try his luck at privateering. He made two voyages as a privateer, both of which ended with his ship being captured by the British. Fortunately for Williams, on both occasions he managed to secure his exchange. By the summer of 1778 he was back in Boston and more than ready to return to state service.

His next command was the sixteen-gun brig *Hazard*. Williams made several short cruises during the winter of 1778–1779, taking the *Hazard* as far north as Newfoundland before shifting his hunting grounds to the West Indies. While searching for prizes in the vicinity of St. Thomas, Williams gained his first real taste of battle, battering an eighteen-gun brig into submission after a short but spirited fight on 16 March 1779. His personal triumph, however, was soon overshadowed by the disastrous outcome of the Penobscot expedition in the summer of 1779. Williams in the *Hazard* accompanied the small fleet of state vessels, privateers, and transports that sailed into Penobscot Bay to destroy a British outpost recently established on the shore. When an enemy relief squadron subsequently appeared in the bay, the Americans panicked and scuttled their entire flotilla. Although Williams preferred to fight rather than flee, he reluctantly followed suit. After putting the *Hazard* to the torch, the ship's former commander and crew escaped into the Maine wilderness.

The fallout from the Penobscot fiasco in no way affected Williams. The Massachusetts General Court demonstrated its confidence in Williams by assigning him to the brand new, 26-gun frigate *Protector*, the largest vessel in the state navy. After taking a small sloop on his maiden voyage in the *Protector*, he encountered a more worthy adversary on his second cruise: the 32-gun privateer *Admiral Duff*. The two ships crossed paths on 9 June 1780 near Newfoundland. Squaring off at close range, they traded broadsides for more than ninety minutes before the *Admiral Duff* suddenly caught fire and exploded. A few weeks later Williams narrowly escaped from a British frigate after a running fight, but he was less lucky the following spring. On 5 May 1781, while escorting a prize in the vicinity of Block Island, the *Protector* fell victim to a pair of enemy frigates. Once more a captive of the Royal Navy, Williams was first sent to the prison hulk *Jersey* in New York and then transferred to Plymouth, England. He eventually gained his release and made his way back to Boston in time to take command of the privateer *Alexander* during the last year of the war.

Williams's fine wartime record secured his status as one of Boston's most respected mariners. When Alexander Hamilton sought experienced seamen to officer the newly created U.S. Revenue Cutter Service in 1790, Williams's name was immediately put forward by state officials. Williams was among the first ten revenue officers commissioned by George Washington in the spring of 1791 with the rank of master. Later that summer he assumed command of the cutter *Massachusetts* and took up his assigned station at Boston. While enforcing the revenue laws and thwarting smugglers was his primary mission, he was also called upon to perform other duties. He carried out surveys of Provincetown and Nantasket harbors and assisted colonial historian Jeremy Belknap in retracing the path traveled by George Waymouth in Maine. A man of diverse talents and intellectual pursuits, Williams was well suited to these different tasks. Despite going to sea at a relatively early age, he had still managed to acquire some formal schooling as a youth in Boston and was particularly well versed in mathematics. Williams demonstrated something of his versatility in 1792 when he devised a system for turning salt water into fresh. He reported the results of his experiments to the Boston Marine Society, which ordered his paper to be published in Boston's *Columbian Centinel* and in *Massachusetts Magazine*.

Williams's Republican sympathies deprived him of the chance to see action in the Quasi-War with France. Although some revenue officers and cutters were incorporated into the ranks of the U.S. Navy, Federalists considered Williams to be too much of a political risk. His advanced age was also cited as a mark against him, but the doubts about his vigor turned out to be more than a little premature. Williams remained active in the revenue service apparently until his death in Boston. Over the course of his long and eventful career at sea, Williams showed himself to be a resourceful leader and a consummate sailor. In particular, during the twenty-plus years he wore the uniform of a revenue officer, he set a standard of meritorious conduct that contributed greatly to the service's development.

• Biographical material on John Foster Williams is scanty. By far the most complete and self-contained account of his life is provided by an anonymous, four-part sketch published in the *Army and Navy Register* (2, 9, 16, and 23 June 1883). John A. McManemin, *Captains of the State Navies during the Revolutionary War* (1984), includes considerable information on Williams's exploits in the Massachusetts State Navy, while Irving H. King, *George Washington's Coast Guard* (1978), contains scattered details about his career in the revenue service. An obituary is in the *Columbian Centinel* (Boston), 25 June 1814.

JEFF SEIKEN

WILLIAMS, John Harry (7 July 1908–18 Apr. 1966), physicist, was born in Asbestos Mines (now Asbestos), Quebec, Canada, the son of Harry John Williams, a mining engineer, and Josephine Leonore Stockwell. When Williams was two years old, his family moved to Kelowna, British Columbia, where he attended public schools and developed his lifelong devotion to fishing, swimming, and other outdoor sports. His interest in science was stimulated by one of his high school teachers, and at the age of sixteen he received a scholarship and matriculated at the University of British Columbia in Vancouver. He received a B.A. with first-class honors in physics in 1928. That same year he married Vera Martin, a swimming teammate; they had three children.

Williams entered graduate school at the University of California in Berkeley in 1928 on a teaching fellowship and immediately began carrying out research. In 1930 he received an M.A. in physics and one year later, as a Whiting Fellow in physics, he received a Ph.D. with a dissertation on the determination of certain X-ray line widths in the uranium spectrum. By this time his adviser, Samuel K. Allison, had left Berkeley to accept a position at the University of Chicago. Williams's award of a National Research Council Fellowship enabled him and Allison to continue their collaboration in X-ray researches from 1931 to 1933. In the fall of 1933, after working during the summer as a writer for Science Service in Washington, D.C., Williams accepted a position as a research assistant to John T. Tate at the University of Minnesota. He was promoted to assistant professor in 1934 and associate professor in 1937—an unusually rapid academic advancement in those depression years.

After the momentus discoveries and inventions of 1932, Tate recognized that the emerging field of nuclear physics would become more and more significant as time went on, and he encouraged Williams to change the direction of his research to pursue this field. Tate led an effort to generate a proposal to the Rockefeller Foundation to construct a four-million-volt pressurized Van de Graaff accelerator for carrying out an interdisciplinary program of physical and medical researches. This proposal was funded in April 1937, and Williams, who was placed in charge of the design and construction of the machine, personally built much of the equipment and instrumentation. Three years later, with the accelerator in operation, Williams and his colleagues and students began to study the disintegration of various light nuclei with it.

On 19 January 1942 Williams received his U.S. citizenship and immediately began a program of neutron cross-section measurements that were an integral part of the atomic bomb project. The following year, in March 1943, he became one of the first scientists to arrive at the atomic research center in Los Alamos, New Mexico. There he was placed in charge of using Raymond G. Herb's two pressurized Van de Graaff accelerators (which had been moved to Los Alamos from the University of Wisconsin) to carry out similar measurements important for the bomb project. On 16 July 1945 Williams served as deputy director of the Trinity test; his Services Division constructed the large Alamogordo, New Mexico, site and provided its power, transportation, communications, and other facilities. In 1946 he played a key role in selecting the Bikini atoll for the first postwar bomb tests.

Williams returned to the University of Minnesota in April 1946 as a full professor of physics, supervised the remodeling of its accelerator, and resumed his research program, training a long list of graduate students in experimental nuclear physics. In 1949 he obtained the authorization and financial support of the Atomic Energy Commission to construct a new fifty-million-electron-volt (MeV) linear proton accelerator at Minnesota, which ultimately reached an energy of 68 MeV, the highest energy reached by a machine of its type in the world at the time.

But Williams's vision extended well beyond Minnesota. In the early 1950s he was a prime mover in establishing the Midwestern Universities Research Association, serving on its board of directors from 1955 to 1958 and as its president in 1956–1957. MURA's goal was to construct a new and still higher energy accelerator in the Midwest that would be competitive with those then in operation on the East and West coasts, and in pursuing this goal the organization came into conflict with the Argonne National Laboratory, which was operated by the AEC under a contract with the University of Chicago. The AEC appointed Williams to membership on a new policy advisory board for Argonne, and in this capacity he did much to mediate and mitigate the dispute. The AEC subsequently funded a new 12.5-billion-electron-volt accelerator at Argonne, while the MURA facility, which on the recommendation of a site-selection committee chaired by Williams was located in Stoughton, Wisconsin (near Madison), became a leading center of accelerator design and development. In 1965 Williams became the first president of the Argonne Universities' Association, Inc., which was charged with overall responsibility for the policies and programs of the Argonne laboratory.

Williams was universally respected for his fair-mindedness and statesmanship and in 1958 was asked to serve as director of the AEC's Research Division in Washington, D.C. A lifelong poker player who now had to swallow a reduction in salary to accept this position, he remarked that "Every so often you have to put some chips back in the pot." A year later President Dwight D. Eisenhower appointed him an AEC commissioner to fill the unexpired term of Willard F. Libby, who had resigned to return to academic work. Williams too was forced to resign this position after just one year, because of a recurrence of chest cancer, which had been first detected a decade earlier. In early 1960, after receiving treatment in Minneapolis and Washington, he was the AEC's main witness at congressional hearings to consider authorization for the construction of the Stanford Linear Accelerator.

Williams bore his disease, which had spread throughout his body and had left him weakened and often near death, with great courage and fortitude. He continued to teach at Minnesota and to serve on important local and national committees, and he refused to relinquish billiards, golfing, and fishing trips to Ontario, Canada, with a few close friends and colleagues. In 1959 he was elected a member of the National Academy of Sciences and in 1963, president of the American Physical Society. In 1964, as the culmination of years of planning and work by Williams and his colleagues, the AEC awarded funds to the University of Minnesota for the construction of a new twenty-million-volt Emperor Van de Graaff accelerator to be housed in a new building constructed on the east bank of the Mississippi River with funds from the state and the National Science Foundation. These facilities were dedicated as the John H. Williams Laboratory of Nuclear Physics on 3 May 1966, a few weeks after his death in Minneapolis.

• Unpublished material on Williams's life and work is preserved in the University of Minnesota Archives. The longest biography of Williams, which includes a bibliography of his writings, is Alfred O. C. Nier, "John Harry Williams, July 7, 1908–April 18, 1966," National Academy of Sciences, *Biographical Memoirs* 42 (1971): 339–55. Obituaries are Glenn T. Seaborg, *Physics Today* 19 (June 1966): 117–19, the *Minneapolis Star*, 18 Apr. 1966, and the *Minneapolis Tribune*, the *St. Paul Pioneer Press*, and the *New York Times*, all 19 Apr. 1966.

ROGER H. STUEWER

WILLIAMS, John Joseph (27 Apr. 1822–30 Aug. 1907), Roman Catholic prelate, and first archbishop of Boston, was born on the north end of Boston, Massachusetts, the son of Michael Williams, a blacksmith, and Ann Egan, immigrants from County Tipperary, Ireland. Williams attended the Cathedral School in Boston where he impressed Bishop Benedict Fenwick of Boston, who sent him to the Sulpician college in Montreal. Williams remained there from 1833 until his graduation in 1841, after which he was dispatched to St. Sulpice Seminary in Paris; there he was ordained to the priesthood, on 27 May 1845, by Archbishop Denis Auguste Affre. That same year he returned to Boston and was appointed to Holy Cross Cathedral as an assistant. In that capacity Williams favorably impressed Bishop John B. Fitzpatrick, who appointed him rector of the cathedral in 1855 and in 1857 transferred him to the pastorate of St. James Church in Boston and later that year appointed him vicar-general of the diocese. When Fitzpatrick's health began to fail, he designated Williams as his coadjutor with right of succession. The official notification (bulls) of appointment arrived from Rome only four days before Fitzpatrick's death. On 11 March 1866 Archbishop John McCloskey of New York consecrated Williams fourth bishop of the Boston diocese. In 1875, when Boston was elevated to the status of an archdiocese, Williams became its first archbishop.

In the four decades that Williams presided over Boston's Roman Catholic population, the once-sprawling Boston archdiocese had to be subdivided into smaller and more manageable jurisdictions: Springfield in 1870, Providence in 1872, Manchester in 1884, and Fall River in 1905. Williams presided over a period of tremendous upward mobility for the Irish and the inpouring of new Catholic immigrant groups from Europe and Canada. Williams welcomed and accommodated the burgeoning growth of New England Catholic life by building churches and creating social welfare institutions and parochial schools. He founded the first conference of the St. Vincent de Paul Society in New England and approved the creation of separate ethnic parishes for French-Canadians, Italians, and Portuguese. To staff these new institutions he welcomed religious communities of men and women, among them the Sisters of St. Joseph (1873), the Franciscan Sisters (1884), and the Marist Fathers (1883). In 1884 he opened St. John's Seminary in Brighton to train diocesan clergy.

A pastoral bishop, Williams was unambitious for higher honors and twice turned down a proffered honorary doctorate from Harvard. In the internal feuding between Americanizers and Germanizers at the end of the nineteenth century, Williams kept a characteristically low profile, supporting many of the more democratic, less hierarchical goals of the Americanizers while at the same time cultivating a friendship with Bishop Bernard McQuaid of Rochester, an outspoken opponent of some members of the Americanist faction. Williams also became a co-owner of the diocesan newspaper, the *Boston Pilot*, in conjunction with Catholic layman John Boyle O'Reilly; he remained co-owner until his death.

At the time of his retirement in 1906, Williams left behind a large, prosperous diocese with more than 600 priests and nearly one million Catholics. His successor, William H. O'Connell, would parlay this tremendous size and prosperity into a cardinal's hat for himself. Williams died in Boston.

• The Archives of the Archdiocese of Boston contains Williams's papers. See also R. H. Lord, *History of the Archdiocese of Boston* (3 vols., 1944); James O'Toole, *Militant and Triumphant* (1992); Donna Merwick, *Boston's Priests* (1973); and Daniel McClellan, "A History of the Catholic Charitable Bureau of the Archdiocese of Boston" (Ph.D. diss., Univ. of Notre Dame, 1984).

STEVEN M. AVELLA

WILLIAMS, John Sharp (30 July 1854–27 Sept. 1932), U.S. congressman and senator, was born in Memphis, Tennessee, the son of Christopher Harris Williams, Jr., a lawyer, and Anne Louise Sharp. His mother died in his early childhood at Memphis, and when his father, a colonel in the Confederate army, was killed in battle at Shiloh, his grandfather, John McNitt Sharp, took him to his home on a 3,000-acre plantation in Yazoo County, Mississippi. His grandfather, a Confederate officer, also died in the war, and his step-grandmother Sharp assumed the responsibility of rearing and educating him. After graduating from the Kentucky Military Institute in 1870, he enrolled for six months in the University of the South at Sewanee, Tennessee. In 1871 he transferred to the University of Virginia, where he studied three years in the liberal arts and became a Phi Beta Kappa scholar but avoided the necessary science courses to qualify for a degree. To broaden his horizon and prepare for a political career, he then spent two years in Europe at the University of Heidelberg in Germany and the College of France at Dijon, after which he returned to the University of Virginia and earned a law degree in 1876. He practiced law two years in Memphis before going back to the Mississippi hills to live on the Sharp plantation.

In 1877 he married Elizabeth Dial Webb; they had eight children. Over the next fifteen years, he supervised his planting interests and maintained a law practice in nearby Yazoo City.

At the age of thirty-nine, Williams launched a political career, during which he would serve sixteen years in the lower house of Congress (1893–1909) and twelve years in the U.S. Senate (1911–1923). In Congress, where he was quickly recognized for his intellect and debating skill, he took clear positions on the issues and responded to opponents so that both sides would appear together in the *Congressional Record*. He spoke out for the free, unlimited coinage of silver and an income tax and opposed imperialistic policies. A staunch advocate of a tariff for revenue only, he delighted reporters as he effectively "removed the hides" of the Republican proponents of high protective rates. Yet he also earned their respect by balancing his caustic rejoinders with wit and parliamentary courtesy. His Democratic colleagues elected him minority leader in 1903, 1905, and 1907, and in this position he transformed the party's disorganized, unruly membership in the House into a cohesive, disciplined unit. "By sheer force and merit," asserted the *New York Times* (3 Aug. 1907), "he . . . attained on the Democratic side in that body a leadership . . . not . . . equalled for many years."

In 1904 Williams served as temporary chairman of the Democratic National Convention and was pleased when his moderate views on financial and trade policies prevailed in the platform. Seeking to remove the party's negative image among businessmen and organized labor in the North and Midwest, he wanted it to adopt a constructive, progressive program that would attract independent voters. He also publicized these concepts in "What Democracy Now Stands For" (*Everybody's Magazine*, Feb. 1904) and "Why Should a Man Vote the Democratic Ticket This Year?" (*Independent*, 27 Oct. 1904). In 1908 he supported presidential candidate William Jennings Bryan, although he did not admire him and rejected his proposal of government ownership of railroads. Four years later, as an ardent booster of Woodrow Wilson for the party's nomination, he complained of "the mad antics of Billy Bryan at one end of the [party's] line and of New York plutocratic Democrats at the other end" and declared that neither extreme had any "common sense at all." "The country can never be right," he contended, "until we get rid of the idea of government in the interest of special privilege," and this, he thought, was impossible as long as Republicans, "whether . . . conservative, progressive, or what-not," held office (letter to Norval Richardson, 3 Jan. 1912).

In the senatorial primary race against Governor James Kimble Vardaman in 1907, Williams opposed Vardaman's proposal to repeal the Fifteenth Amendment, asserting that the South ought to focus on the vital economic issues of the day and "not occupy itself with 'baying at the moon,' or in a thing equally useless and much more dangerous" (letter to J. F. Gray, 10 Jan. 1907). *Collier's* (17 Aug. 1907) reported that Williams "shared the feelings of his neighbors on the race question . . . [but] had seen enough of other parts of the world . . . to look at that subject in its proper perspective." He believed in solving public problems along sensible and safe lines and spurned "demagogic claptrap" to catch votes. After his narrow victory over Vardaman and formal election by the Mississippi legislature, Williams completed his congressional term and went to his plantation to rest and read until the beginning of his Senate term two years later.

In the Senate, Williams became one of President Wilson's most loyal supporters in both foreign and domestic policy. In answering critics of Wilson's appointment of Louis D. Brandeis to the Supreme Court, he argued that he "would rather have a radical upon the Supreme Bench who would be sobered by his responsibilities than to have a conservative who would be made more conservative" by the same token (letter to Robert R. Reed, 5 Feb. 1916). After the *Lusitania* incident in 1915, he urged war against Germany, and in 1917 he accused those opposing war of "grazing" on the edge of treason. In March 1918, however, he denounced a proposal for universal military training as "a curse to civilization, to nationality, to progress, to humanity, and to education" (*New York Times*, 28 Sept. 1932). Williams also made "the most impassioned fight of his public career" for ratification of the League of Nations (Osborn, p. 360) and later pleaded for nonpartisanship in foreign affairs. In addition, he was strongly opposed to government bonuses to "able-bodied" veterans. Patriotism, he believed, should carry no price tag.

Although a strong defender of white supremacy, Williams never exploited the race issue for personal gain. According to his close friend in Mississippi LeRoy Percy, he had "a sublime egotism" that made him feel it was "not necessary . . . to trim his sails in order to catch popular breezes" (letter to Joseph W. Bailey, 10 Aug. 1915). Williams characterized himself as "a hail fellow, well met, never thinking about anybody's wealth, social position or anything of that sort" (letter to Lucile Banks, 18 Oct. 1918). In 1916 he was reelected to the Senate without opposition, and in 1922 he did not seek a third term.

Thomas Jefferson was Williams's "patron saint," and in 1912 he had delivered a series of lectures on Jefferson at Columbia University. These were published later as a book, *Thomas Jefferson, His Permanent Influence on American Institutions* (1913). Williams clung to the homespun democracy of the soil and urged the Jeffersonian standards of competency, faithfulness, and honesty in selecting public officials.

In March 1923 Williams retired to his Mississippi plantation, where he remained among family and friends, out of the limelight, and continued to read a book a day. He died at the plantation home built in 1835 by his grandfather.

With a touch of genius and Jeffersonian idealism, Williams's leadership in Congress and moderating influence in the Democratic party helped pave the way for a more viable two-party system, Wilson's presidential nomination, and the introduction of idealistic concepts into domestic and foreign affairs. A natural optimist with faith in mankind, he never forsook Wilson's ideals for world peace. "Men sometimes disparage idealists," Williams asserted, "but they are coarse grained jackasses who do so and do it because they are coarse grained. But the idealists point the way and cheer men's souls" (*New York Times*, 27 Mar. 1920).

• The largest collection of Williams's papers is in the Division of Manuscripts, Library of Congress. Other letters and typewritten copies of the Library of Congress collection are in the Williams papers at the University of Mississippi and the George Coleman Osborn Papers at the Mississippi Department of Archives and History (MDAH). The Lizzie McFarland Blakemore Papers (MDAH) and the Percy Family Papers (MDAH) also contain correspondence about him. Three articles by Williams appear in *Annals of the American Academy of Political and Social Science*: "Federal Usurpations," 32 (1908): 185–211; "Control of Corporations, Persons, and Firms Engaged in Interstate Commerce," 42 (1912): 310–30; and "'War to Stop War,'" 52 (1917): 178–85. He also wrote "The Democratic Party and the Railroad Question," *Independent*, 1 Mar. 1906, pp. 485–88, and "The Ties That Bind: Our National Sympathy with English Traditions, the French Republic, and the Russian Outburst of Liberty," *National Geographic Magazine* 31 (Mar. 1917): 281–86. The only complete biography is George Coleman Osborn, *John Sharp Williams: Planter-Statesman of the Deep South* (1943), but Harris Dickson, *An Old-Fashioned Senator: A Story-Biography of John Sharp Williams* (1925), is a biographical vignette. William F. Holmes, *The White Chief: James Kimble Vardaman* (1970), includes much information on his political career. See also Robert W. Watkins, "Personal Sketch of the Minority Leader in the House," *Harper's Weekly*, 25 June 1904, pp. 970–71, and Edward M. Kingsbury, "John Sharp Williams, Leader," *Bookman* 19 (Apr. 1904): 168–71, on his career as a congressman; Frederick Palmer, "Williams-Vardaman Campaign," *Collier's the National Weekly*, 27 July 1907, pp. 11–12, on his senatorial primary race; and Samuel Blythe, "The Gentleman from Mississippi," *Saturday Evening Post*, 22 July 1911, p. 19. Judson C. Welliver, "Leaders of the New Congress," *Munsey's Magazine*, Feb. 1913, p. 717, and Dewey W. Grantham, Jr., "Southern Congressional Leaders and the New Freedom, 1913–1917," *Journal of Southern History* 13 (1947): 439–59, on his senatorial career. An obituary is in the *New York Times*, 28 Sept. 1932.

THOMAS N. BOSCHERT

WILLIAMS, John Shoebridge (31 July 1790–22 Apr. 1878), civil engineer, magazine editor, and spiritualist, was born in Newport, Carteret County, North Carolina, the son of Welsh immigrant Robert Williams, a plantation and mill owner, and English immigrant Anne Shoebridge. His mother provided him with his earliest education.

After his family's financial fortunes declined from affluence to modesty during the 1780s and then to poverty during the years after his father's death in 1790, Williams and his family joined a large migration of North Carolina Quakers in 1800 to what became the Concord Quaker settlement in Colerain Township, Belmont County, Ohio. There he lived and worked with a brother-in-law on rented farmland and received a little more than a year of schooling that included instruction in surveying. At age twenty-one he began to teach at a school that Quakers of the area had set up for him near Barnesville, Ohio; he then moved on to teach in Redstone in western Pennsylvania. In 1813 Williams married one of his Barnesville students, Sarah Patterson, at the Stillwater, Ohio, meetinghouse; they had twelve children, ten of whom survived infancy.

Williams spent the remainder of the 1810s in Redstone, where he worked in an iron foundry. When the foundry suffered the financial effects of the panic of 1819, he returned to Ohio and within a few years established himself as a civil engineer for the federal government. In this capacity, he became a key figure in the development of the Ohio Valley transportation system. In 1824 and 1825, as the state of Ohio began the construction of a canal system, Williams surveyed the route of a proposed Chesapeake and Ohio canal. In 1826 he became an engineer for the National Road's Ohio segments, supervising from 1829 to 1835 the construction of the Maysville Road in Kentucky and becoming an acquaintance of Henry Clay. In 1835 Williams became the superintendent of the road between Covington, Ohio, and Lexington, Kentucky. Turnpike construction slowed, and his role in it stopped for a time after the panic of 1837, but his activity resumed in 1849, and he oversaw construction of several more roads connecting the Ohio River and Cincinnati with the hinterlands of Ohio, Kentucky, and Indiana.

Williams consistently remained at the leading edge of contemporary transportation technology. He was a pioneer in the construction of what were called "McAdamized" (graded) roads. He immediately sensed the potential importance of the railroad when it appeared during the 1830s and became an active and outspoken advocate of railroad construction. He gave well-received speeches throughout the region, in which he warned of the dangers of remaining dependent on turnpikes. He also surveyed several potential railroad routes and played a leading role in the construction of the region's first railroad, the Hanging Rock and Lawrence Furnace line.

Williams was also an active promoter of American history, especially the history of the West. He served as the first secretary of the Logan Historical Society of Ohio, which was established in 1841, and he edited its monthly magazine, *American Pioneer*, which was published in 1842–1843 and was one of the first purely historical periodicals in the United States. He devoted considerable effort to collecting material on the Indians and on the exploration and development of the nation, paying special attention to the Ohio Valley. In the *Pioneer's* opening issue (Jan. 1842), Williams expressed his hope that the journal would appeal to the "pioneer patriot," and its masthead proclaimed his dedication to "the truth and justice of history." As the secretary of the society and the editor of the *Pioneer*, he established relationships and friendships with several prominent regional figures of the day.

Religion was central to Williams's identity, and his religious experiences were turbulent. He left the

Quaker fold during the Hicksite schism of 1827, became affiliated briefly with the Swedenborgian Church of the New Jerusalem during the 1830s, and turned finally to spiritualism after it burst upon the national scene, particularly in the Northeast and the West, in the 1850s. He began to practice spiritualist mediumship in 1852 and published a number of pamphlets on his religious views in the years that followed. Williams maintained a detailed journal of his experiences and theological reflections and went on a speaking tour in the Northeast and the Midwest. He also established in 1852 a short-lived benevolent organization called the Society for the Protection of the Defenseless Oppressed.

Williams's activities as a spiritualist were heavily informed by personal tragedies that included the death of a disaffected daughter in 1846, a bitter separation and divorce from his wife in 1849, strained relationships with many of his children, and his retirement from business as he entered his sixties. Concerned that his paternal leadership and masculine identity had been compromised by these developments, he spent long hours in what he believed to be contact with his daughter's spirit, contemplated gender and family issues central to Victorian American culture, and published several pamphlets on these issues. In *The Key that Opens Heaven to Every Man* (1852), he defended traditional patriarchy and his interpretation of the Fourth Commandment against what he perceived as a democratic system of American family governance that increased the domestic power of women and children. He soon began to grow a beard, explaining in *An Address to the Officers and Citizens of the United States* (1854) that all fathers ought to grow beards as visible symbols of their patriarchal leadership. In 1858 Williams married Drusilla (maiden name unknown) in the ultimately unfulfilled hope of having more children and enacting his ideals of family order. After Drusilla's death in 1870, Williams spent his final years practicing mediumship and arranging for the preservation of his spiritual diary, which he hoped would be published. He died in Viola, Iowa.

• Williams's papers, including his spiritual journal, are at the State Historical Society of Wisconsin. His published works on spiritualism and religion include *A Synopsis of the Spiritual Experience of J. Shoebridge Williams, Medium* (1853), *Bible Proof of Spirit Intercourse* (1857), *Spiritual Manifestations* (1857), and *Nature and the Bible Have One Author* (1861). He also published *The Patriarchal Order; or, True Brotherhood* (1855), which describes his unhappy experience with a fraternal order of spiritualists called the Patriarchal Order. An unsigned, detailed account of his early life is "John Shoebridge Williams: Our Cabin; or, Life in the Woods," *American Pioneer* 2 (Oct. 1843): 435–59. His spiritualist mediumship is considered in Bret E. Carroll, "The Religious Construction of Masculinity in Victorian America: The Male Mediumship of John Shoebridge Williams," *Religion and American Culture: A Journal of Interpretation* 7 (Winter 1997): 27–60; and Carroll, *Spiritualism in Antebellum America* (1997). Brief obituaries are in the *Cincinnati Daily Gazette* and the *Cincinnati Commercial*, both 24 Apr. 1878.

BRET E. CARROLL

WILLIAMS, John Whitridge (26 Jan. 1866–21 Oct. 1931), professor of obstetrics, was born in Baltimore, Maryland, the son of Philip C. Williams, a prominent physician, and Mary Cushing Whitridge. In 1884 Williams entered Johns Hopkins University, graduating with a bachelor of arts degree two years later, and then attended the University of Maryland Medical School, receiving his M.D. in 1888. He spent the following year in Europe, studying pathology and bacteriology in Vienna and Berlin. In 1891 he married Margaretta Stewart Brown, the daughter of a U.S. Army general; they had three daughters.

In 1889 Williams returned to Baltimore to join Howard A. Kelly, professor of gynecology and obstetrics in the newly established Johns Hopkins Medical School. He worked as a voluntary assistant (resident), concentrating on gynecologic surgery and pathology. He then spent the 1894–1895 school year on sabbatical, studying obstetrics in Leipzig, Prague, and Paris. In 1896 he became associate professor of obstetrics. In 1899 he was offered the chairmanship at the University of Chicago Medical School. Kelly, recognizing what the loss of Williams would mean for Johns Hopkins and also wanting to concentrate more on gynecologic surgery, turned obstetrics over to Williams.

Thus, at age thirty-three, Williams became professor of obstetrics and obstetrician in chief of the Johns Hopkins Hospital, positions he held until his death. In 1909 he returned to Europe for a sabbatical in Heidelberg, where he worked in biological chemistry. An admirer of the German universities and their *Frauenkliniks*, in subsequent years Williams worked abroad almost every summer. Following the retirement in 1911 of William H. Howell, dean of the Medical School, Williams served as dean until 1923. Williams worked to develop the "full-time" system, whereby the clinical faculty were paid by the medical school to teach and conduct research, rather than relying on income from private practice. In 1919 the Department of Obstetrics became the first full-time department devoted to that field in the United States.

Williams's pedagogic convictions were drawn largely from his experience in European universities. Because of his concern with the deplorable state of obstetrical practice, he was intensely interested in medical education generally and the teaching of obstetrics in particular. Williams emphasized pathology and pathophysiology, since he believed that unless students were intimately acquainted with the structure of the reproductive organs and the pathology and biochemical alterations underlying complications of pregnancy and the puerperium they could not understand the subject. He was also a pioneer in requiring students to participate in obstetrical deliveries under supervision. Following the indictment of American medical schools by Abraham Flexner's 1910 report on medical education, Williams conducted a national survey on the quality of teaching in obstetrics and presented a number of recommendations to improve obstetrical teaching.

Recognizing the lack of an authoritative textbook, in 1903 Williams published his *Obstetrics: A Textbook for the Use of Students and Practitioners*, a work that went through six editions in his lifetime (6th ed., 1930). *Obstetrics* was unique in being the first American textbook to present the subject as an academic discipline and to emphasize the vast potential for research. Rather than a mere compilation of the writings of others, each chapter presented a thoughtful analysis of the subject. It also placed each subject in historical perspective, referencing classic contributions as well as the most recent advances in the field. Williams's book aroused great interest in research in reproductive biology and did much to help establish the specialty as a legitimate medical science.

Originally Williams had planned to concentrate on gynecologic pathology and wrote on several aspects of the pathology of female generative organs. However, following his turn to obstetrical subjects, he wrote on many aspects of infection in obstetrics, caesarean section, premature labor, and postpartum complications. In all, he published more than 130 papers, several of which were monographs 100 pages or more in length.

Among Williams's most notable contributions was his role in the popularization of prenatal care, considered by many to be one of the most important advances in obstetrics during the first half of the twentieth century. With his interest in pathology and bacteriology, Williams was concerned with the primary causes of maternal mortality: infection, hemorrhage, and toxemia of pregnancy. During the first decades of the century he worked with pediatricians, public health workers, and various women's groups in what became known as the infant welfare movement. In 1909 these groups established the American Association for Study and Prevention of Infant Mortality. As one of its founders, Williams championed the view that efforts to reduce infant mortality should begin before rather than after the baby was born.

Williams also advocated the concept of university women's clinics modeled after the German *Frauenkliniks*. Williams proposed that in addition to providing excellent clinical care, such women's clinics should have a major commitment to teaching and to clinical and basic laboratory research. He encouraged animal research to investigate anatomical, physiological, biochemical, and pathological problems, such as the causes of fetal abnormalities and the toxemias of pregnancy. Williams was one of the first to promulgate the idea that lessons learned from the laboratory should be applied to the management of pregnant women.

As chairman of obstetrics at the Johns Hopkins Medical School, Williams helped to train a generation of residents who went on to become department chairmen and leaders in obstetrics and gynecology in other medical schools. One of his precepts for such individuals was to write at least one first-rate paper a year. He was president of the American Gynecological Society (1914–1915) and was elected to honorary fellowship in the British (later Royal) College of Obstetricians and Gynecologists (1931).

Probably more than any other individual during the first part of this century, Williams established obstetrics as an academic discipline in the United States. A physician thoroughly familiar with European standards, he evolved a philosophy of education that has served as a model to the present day. Almost singlehandedly, he built a department that served as a training ground for several generations of leaders in American obstetrics and gynecology. His prodigious textbook has been published continuously since its first printing. Together with other leaders in the early days of the Johns Hopkins School of Medicine, Williams helped to create a milieu in which medical education was supreme and in which the care of patients was combined with scientific research and historical scholarship.

All of this, together with Williams's efforts to reduce infant and maternal mortality, was seen by his contemporaries as one of the highly praiseworthy crusades of his day. In many ways Williams's life was a crusade—one against ignorance and prejudice and for the development of obstetrics as a legitimate academic discipline, one to unite departments of gynecology and obstetrics, one to have full-time faculty in academic medicine, one for prenatal care of pregnant women, and one for lowering the death rates of infants and mothers. Alan Guttmacher concluded, "Perhaps his contributions to medicine will not be immortal, but the incomparable training he gave to us in the art of obstetrics and in 'the way of life,' will pass on through countless generations" (Guttmacher, p. 30).

Following the death of his wife in 1929, in 1930 Williams married Caroline DeW. Theobold Pennington. They had no children. Williams died in Baltimore, Maryland.

• Some of Williams's papers are in the Welch Library of the Johns Hopkins University School of Medicine, Baltimore, Md. For additional information on Williams, see A. F. Guttmacher, "Recollections of John Whitridge Williams," *Bulletin of the History of Medicine* 3 (1935): 19–30, and H. A. Kelly, "John Whitridge Williams (1866–1931)," *American Journal of Surgery* 15 (1932): 169–74. N. J. Eastman, "The Contributions of John Whitridge Williams to Obstetrics," *American Journal of Obstetrics and Gynecology* 90 (1964): 561–65; L. D. Longo, "John Whitridge Williams and Academic Obstetrics in America," *Transactions and Studies of the College of Physicians of Philadelphia* 3 (1981): 221–54; and J. M. Slemons, *John Whitridge Williams, Academic Aspects and Bibliography* (1935), discuss his contributions to medicine and medical education. Obituaries are in the *New York Times*, 23 Oct. 1931, and the *Baltimore Sun*, 22 Oct. 1931.

LAWRENCE D. LONGO

WILLIAMS, Jonathan (26 May 1750–16 May 1815), merchant, lay scientist, and first superintendent of the U.S. Military Academy, was born in Boston, Massachusetts, the son of Jonathan Williams, a successful merchant, and Grace Harris. His father provided him with the finest education then available. Following several terms at Harvard College, Williams ventured to London in 1770 to conduct family business and finish studying under the aegis of his great-uncle Benjamin Franklin. Franklin recognized potential in the young man, made him his private secretary, and immersed him in the scientific and philosophical circles of England. Williams parted company with Franklin following the onset of the Revolution in 1775 and took up residency in France. There, American commissioners appointed him their agent at Nantes for inspecting arms and supplies being shipped to America. In pursuing his duties Williams became embroiled in a contretemps with a drunken rival, Thomas Morris, and a congressional agent, William Lee. A formal investigation subsequently cleared Williams of corruption charges. He maintained business ventures in Europe until 1785 and then accompanied Franklin back to Philadelphia. Williams returned to Harvard to pursue science and philosophy, receiving his A.M. in 1787. He then settled in Philadelphia with his wife Marianne Alexander, whom he had married in 1779, and raised one son. Williams became a successful merchant like his father but never forsook his scientific interests. In July 1788 Franklin sponsored his membership in the prestigious American Philosophical Society and he became a lifelong member.

Franklin's tutelage indelibly impressed scientific research on Williams and, in 1799 he published the tract *Thermometric Navigation*, whose findings were long utilized. Other experiments subsequently appeared in the *Transactions* of the American Philosophical Society. Following Franklin's death in 1790, Williams delved into mathematics, botany, and medicine. He served as a judge in the court of common pleas in Philadelphia and also became highly regarded for his expertise in military affairs and fortification. On 16 February 1801 Williams fulfilled a longheld ambition by obtaining a major's commission in the Second Regiment of Artillery and Engineers from President John Adams. In this capacity he oversaw translation of two European treatises, *Elements of Fortification* (1801) and Kosciusko's *Manoeuvers for Horse Artillery* (1808). These efforts and his rise to the vice presidency of the American Philosophical Society brought Williams to the attention of another lay scientist, President Thomas Jefferson. Jefferson was then attempting to flesh out the army's cadre with scientifically minded officers and appointed Williams inspector of fortifications and superintendent of the military post at West Point on 14 December 1801. When Congress established the nation's first military academy there the following spring, he also assumed responsibilities as its first superintendent.

Williams, initially enthusiastic, grew disillusioned with his charge. The fledgling academy consisted of but ten cadets, was underfunded and poorly staffed, and lacked a meaningful curriculum. Furthermore Williams, though senior officer present, exerted little actual control over the garrison. Line officers refused to follow his orders on the archaic grounds that he could only command fellow engineers. When Jefferson failed to ameliorate these difficulties, Williams resigned on 20 June 1803. Before departing, however, he made a significant contribution to the intellectual life of West Point by founding the U.S. Military Philosophical Society. Williams intended it to function as a conduit for the latest European writing on military science and a vehicle to disseminate useful knowledge.

Fortunately for the academy, Jefferson persuaded Williams to reenlist as a lieutenant colonel of engineers on 19 April 1805, although only after his control of West Point had been assured. For the next five years he struggled to manage his intellectual enclave with minimal funding and political support, but he did manage to replace a classical curriculum with a modern one stressing scientific methodology. Williams was also responsible for the erection of fortifications around New York City, including Castle Williams on Governor's Island. When hostilities with Great Britain erupted in June 1812, he requested command of that post but was denied for conflicting authority between artillerists and engineers. Outraged, Williams resigned a second time on 31 July 1812 and became brigadier general of militia defending New York harbor. His service proved uneventful, but the exigencies of war forced the U.S. Military Philosophical Society to disband on 1 November 1813. On 15 August 1814 Williams's only son, Captain Alexander John Williams, a West Point graduate, was slain in the attack on Fort Erie, Upper Canada. Shortly before peace was concluded, Williams relocated to Philadelphia to supervise defensive preparations. He subsequently ran for Congress as a representative in 1814 but died in Philadelphia before taking his seat.

Williams's tenure as superintendent of West Point was an unhappy one, but his efficacy is clear. A scientist by training, he sought to imbue academy training with the educational and scientific precepts espoused by his mentor Franklin. Williams is directly responsible for modernizing the curriculum of the U.S. Military Academy and making it the first school of scientific engineering in the country. Throughout the War of 1812, no post designed by West Point graduates was captured by the enemy. After the war, this same cadre was responsible for erecting many of the nation's public works, including roads, canals, and lighthouses. Without Williams's unflinching emphasis on science and mathematics, it is unlikely such skilled leadership would have emerged when it did. Perhaps his legacy is best expressed by the motto of the U.S. Military Philosophical Society: *Scientia in Bello Pax*, "Science in war is the guarantee of peace."

• The principal collections of Williams's papers are at the Lilly Library, Indiana University, and the library of the U.S. Military Academy, West Point. Smaller but useful caches are at the American Philosophical Society and Historical Society of Pennsylvania, Philadelphia; the Clements Library, University of Michigan; the New-York Historical Society; and the Yale University Library. Panegyrical sketches are in George W. Cullum, *Campaigns of the War of 1812–1815* (1879), and James B. Longacre and James Herring, *National Pictorial Gallery of Distinguished Americans*, vol. 1 (4 vols,

1868). The best analysis of his efforts at West Point is Dorothy J. Zuersher, "Benjamin Franklin, Jonathan Williams, and the United States Military Academy" (Ph.D. diss., Univ. of North Carolina, Greensboro, 1974). Also useful are Sidney Forman, "The United States Military Philosophical Society, 1802–1813," *William and Mary Quarterly* 2 (July 1945): 273–85, and Arthur P. Wade, "A Military Offspring of the American Philosophical Society," *Military Affairs* 30 (Sept. 1974): 103–11. Finally, an excellent overview of the military in which Williams served is Theodore J. Crackel, *Mr. Jefferson's Army* (1987).

JOHN C. FREDRIKSEN

WILLIAMS, Joseph Leroy (4 Feb. 1906–1 July 1965), entomologist and medical practitioner, was born in Portsmouth, Virginia, the son of Wiley Louis Williams and Lille Golden. His father, a Pullman Service employee with little formal schooling, urged the importance of a good education on his seven children—all of whom pursued college studies after high school. Joseph, the eldest, attended Booker T. Washington High School in Norfolk. He had planned to follow his father into railroad work for a short time to earn money for college tuition, but was too young. Instead, he accepted a football scholarship to Morgan College in Baltimore, Maryland. In 1926, after a year at Morgan, he transferred to Lincoln University in Pennsylvania, graduating with an A.B. in 1929. In 1934 he married Carrie Pauline Watson, an educator who became dean of women at Cheney State College. They had three children.

Williams's early career plans involved the ministry. "I'm expecting," he wrote in his college application, "to become a pastor of a church." At both Morgan and Lincoln (historically black institutions), however, his interest in science was piqued by a series of enthusiastic teachers. After graduation he accepted an appointment as instructor in zoology and chemistry at Lincoln. He took summer graduate courses in biochemistry and other subjects at Harvard and Columbia prior to enrolling in the master's program in zoology at the University of Pennsylvania. In 1937 he was awarded the A.M. in zoology, writing his thesis on the mating habits of the Mediterranean flour moth, *Ephestia kuehniella*.

Williams pursued doctoral studies at the University of Pennsylvania under the guidance of Philip P. Calvert, an eminent entomologist. Within a short time he became an internationally regarded authority on the sexual behavior and reproductive organs of certain species of lepidoptera (butterflies and moths). Williams was the first American scientist to work in the zoological laboratories at University College, Southampton, England (summer 1939). His work appeared in the journal and proceedings of the Society for British Entomology and he was elected a fellow of the Royal Entomological Society of London in 1943. He also published articles in major American journals, including *Entomological News* and *Journal of Morphology*, and was a regular contributor in his specialty to *Biological Abstracts*. He was awarded the Ph.D. in zoology at the University of Pennsylvania in 1941; his thesis was titled "The Anatomy of the Internal Genitalia and Mating Behavior of Some Lasiocampid Moths."

Williams taught at Lincoln University for seventeen years, first as instructor (1929–1937) and then as assistant professor (1937–1941), associate professor (1941–1945), and professor (1945–1946). He also taught summer school at Hampton Institute (1942) and Howard University (1945–1946). One of his special interests was the quality of science education for African-American youth. Almost singlehandedly he infused new life into Beta Kappa Chi, an all-black science honor society. The society, founded at Lincoln in 1923 and incorporated in 1929, comprised eight college chapters by 1936 but quickly fell into decline. When Williams assumed the presidency in 1943, he established a periodical—*Beta Kappa Chi Scientific Society News-Letter* (later *Beta Kappa Chi Bulletin*)—as part of a larger effort "to stimulate our science students [and] to promote a coordinated progressive plan for science through our college faculty members." By 1944 an additional thirteen college chapters were organized. Williams served as national president of the society until 1946 and subsequently as treasurer (1946–1951). He was also active in other scientific organizations, notably as a member of the executive committee of the American Association of Scientific Workers, Philadelphia branch (1943–1944); the membership committee of the Academy of Natural Sciences, Philadelphia (1943–1946); and the charter group of the Lepidopterists' Society (1947).

A new phase of Williams's career opened when he earned the M.D. degree at Howard University in Washington, D.C., in 1948. He had served as consulting chemist at Frederick Douglass Memorial Hospital, Philadelphia (1935–1944), and at Mercy Hospital, Philadelphia (1942–1944), so this interest in medicine was not new. The shift of focus, however, resulted in a break with his earlier scientific work. Within seven years between 1938 and 1945 he had published eighteen research articles in the field of entomology. In 1945, when he entered medical school, he essentially dropped this side of his work, although he did publish two more papers on the internal genitalia of lepidoptera in 1947 and a brief note on Cape Cod locusts as late as 1958.

After earning his medical degree Williams returned to Philadelphia and interned at the new Mercy-Douglass Hospital (the two institutions merged in 1948), remaining there as house physician, assistant pathologist, and professor of biological sciences in the School of Nursing. He earned a certificate in cardiology at Hahnemann Medical College and Hospital in 1950, and pursued further graduate studies at the University of Pennsylvania (1955–1956). In 1953 he was appointed clinical assistant in medicine at Hahnemann in Philadelphia, rising later to the rank of senior instructor. He headed the Department of General Practice at Mercy-Douglass Hospital from 1957 to 1965. During the early 1960s, he was among a vocal group of physicians who, concerned over evidence that general practitioners were a rapidly dwindling constituency of the physician population, urged the national medical establishment to recognize "family practice" through the creation of a certifying board. The board was established in 1964, although family practice did not achieve official recognition as a primary medical specialty until 1969. Williams was a member of the so-called founder's group and was elected to a term as secretary on 9 August 1964. Earlier, he had served terms as secretary and vice president of the Pennsylvania Academy of General Practice. Williams died in Philadelphia of colon cancer.

• Copies of writings by and about Williams are preserved in the Archives, Langston Hughes Memorial Library, Lincoln University (Penn.). A file of correspondence (1938–1944) between Williams and his doctoral thesis adviser, Philip P. Calvert, is in the Archives, Academy of Natural Sciences, Philadelphia. Other useful biographical information is contained in articles on Williams's life and career by Marion I. Schmieder in *Entomological News* 79 (Nov. 1968): 260–64, and Leroy D. Johnson in *Beta Kappa Chi Bulletin* 24 (Oct. 1964): 24–25. Schmieder's account includes a list of Williams's publications in the field of entomology. For Williams's role in the revival of Beta Kappa Chi, see his article titled "Beta Kappa Chi: A Challenge Not to Be Ignored," *Journal of the National Medical Association* 37 (Jan. 1945): 25–27. Williams's doctoral thesis in the field of entomology was published in *Journal of Morphology* 67 (Nov. 1940): 411–37. Among his writings reflective of his later interest in medical services is "Physician Manpower Available for Family Practice in Philadelphia," *Philadelphia Medicine* 60 (18 Sept. 1964): 905–6.

KENNETH R. MANNING

WILLIAMS, Lucelia Electa (29 Feb. 1824–22 Dec. 1895), educator, was born in Deerfield, Massachusetts, the daughter of Artemas Williams and Amelia Arms, farmers. Details of her education are not known, but she taught in common schools throughout Massachusetts for two decades.

During the Civil War she joined the hundreds of northern teachers who volunteered to work in the schools established for the benefit of the freed slaves, beginning twelve years of service to African-American education on the southeastern seaboard. She served in Beaufort (on Port Royal Island), South Carolina, during her first year, in Petersburg and Richmond, Virginia, in 1865–1866, and in the District of Columbia the following year. In 1867 she and her sister went to Hampton, Virginia. There Williams played a leading role, with Samuel Chapman Armstrong, in the founding of Hampton Normal and Agricultural Institute in April 1868. She established the school's library, organized temperance and religious activities for the students, assisted with fundraising, and taught the normal (teacher-training) classes.

The Williams sisters were the institute's only teachers in its first year and a half. They taught Latin and algebra to at least one student and defended the right of black students to aspire to higher academic work, actions that put them at odds with Armstrong. He forced the Williams sisters out of Hampton after the 1868–1869 term, and official histories of the institution make no mention of them by name. In the next decade under Armstrong's leadership, Hampton emerged as the leading southern black institution dedicated to "industrial education," an educational philosophy eschewing traditional academic training in favor of manual training and habit formation.

In the fall of 1869 Lucelia Williams became the founding principal of Stanton Normal Institute in Jacksonville, Florida, named for Edwin Stanton, the Union secretary of war during the Civil War. Established initially by private northern philanthropy, the school was partially supported by state and county funds. Within a year Williams was teaching and superintending a student body of nearly 300 and a faculty of six women, including her sister. Over a period of seven years she increased the student body to more than 400 and put the institution on a sound financial footing, but in 1875 control of the school shifted to leaders of the Jacksonville black community. Under her leadership Stanton Normal Institute had become the first school to provide teacher training to black Floridians. It continued to serve as a segregated black school into the twentieth century under the leadership of such men as Daniel W. Culp and James Weldon Johnson, himself a graduate of Stanton.

When she was fifty-two, Williams returned to western Massachusetts with her sister. A year later, in 1876, they attempted to return to the South as teachers, but when they received no acceptable offers they retired to their family home. Williams died in South Deerfield, Massachusetts.

Williams's correspondence was always spare and businesslike. Her letters provide no personal insight whatsoever, as they strayed beyond business matters only when she felt it necessary to appeal to northern benefactors for support. Yet her few surviving letters and appeals provide glimpses of her thinking about the proper schooling for African Americans. Although Williams shared many of Samuel Chapman Armstrong's conservative racial views, she had a higher estimation of the intellectual needs and abilities of the freedpeople. She never spoke of her educational goals in political or social terms, or about the aspirations of the freedpeople for self-determination. Rather, her concern was to produce graduates who could serve as teachers and preachers to the freed slaves and who would bring conservative ideas of Christian "civilization" to their communities. Fundamentally, her commitment was to use black schools as a tool for the evangelization of the black South through Congregationalism.

• Letters and reports from Williams during her work among the freedpeople are in the American Missionary Association Archives, Amistad Research Center, Tulane University. No secondary sources have taken notice of her or her work. A brief obituary is in the *American Missionary* 50 (Mar. 1896): 89.

RONALD E. BUTCHART

WILLIAMS, Margery. *See* Bianco, Margery Winifred Williams.

WILLIAMS, Mary Lou (8 May 1910–28 May 1981), pianist, composer, and arranger, was born Mary Elfrieda Scruggs in Atlanta, Georgia, the daughter of Mose Scruggs and Virginia Winn. Her father left home about the time she was born; her mother remarried, to Fletcher Burley, and the family moved to Pittsburgh, Pennsylvania, when Mary Lou was four. She began to play the piano at about the same time, learning first from her mother and then from the many pianists who frequented the family's home. She learned to play ragtime, boogie-woogie, and blues, and her uncle and grandfather paid her to play their favorite popular and classical tunes. Her stepfather took her to play in local gambling halls and similar venues and to Pittsburgh theaters to see musicians like the pianist Lovie Austin. Neighbors invited her to play at parties, and she even performed for wealthy white families like the Mellons, thus earning the rubric "the little piano girl of East Liberty." At the age of twelve she sat in with McKinney's Cotton Pickers when the group passed through Pittsburgh. Though she studied music at Westinghouse Junior High School, it was these other experiences and the hours she spent listening to the recordings of Jelly Roll Morton, Earl Hines, and Fats Waller that provided her true music education.

By the age of fifteen, Mary Lou was on the road full time, playing with a small band that backed a vaudeville act known as Seymour & Jeanette. The baritone saxophonist John Williams was also in the band and befriended her, defending her right to play against managers and performers who objected to working with a woman. While on a gig in New York City, Mary Lou also played for a week with Duke Ellington's Washingtonians. John formed his own group, the Synco Jazzers, in 1925, and the couple married in 1926. The following year they moved to Oklahoma City, where John joined Terrence T. Holder's Dark Clouds of Joy Orchestra. Mary Lou continued to manage the Jazzers for a time.

In 1928 the Clouds of Joy settled in Kansas City, where Mary Lou played with Jack Teagarden, Art Tatum, Tadd Dameron, and even a teenage Thelonious Monk, firmly establishing her reputation. In 1929 Andy Kirk assumed leadership of the renamed Clouds of Joy Orchestra. Mary Lou first played with the group in 1930, as a last-minute substitute for regular pianist Marion Jackson during an audition for a record executive. The executive liked the group, but he was even more impressed with Williams and insisted that she play on the subsequent record date. She recorded six titles, four written wholly or partly by her. Though she was only nineteen and still an eclectic stylist, her solo on "Somethin' Slow and Low" showed that she had learned well the lessons of two of her chief models, Earl Hines and James P. Johnson. Her strong left hand could play a ragtime bass, boogie-woogie, or swing while her right hand added lovely melodies, sophisticated harmonies, or counterrhythms.

Williams traveled with the band to New York City in 1930 and made occasional special appearances with them; at times, she waited in the car outside, only coming in to play a popular boogie-woogie piece or two if the audience seemed receptive to a woman musician. She joined the band full time in 1931, soon supplying Kirk with a half-dozen arrangements a week, which were characterized by a unique "light, bouncy swing." Following Henderson and Ellington, she divided the orchestra into sections, contrasting brass with reeds and producing creative harmonies by combining instruments in various forms—placing a trumpet, for instance, among four saxes. Scores like "Mary's Idea," "Walkin' and Swingin'," and especially "Froggy Bottom" (1936) made the Kirk band one of the most popular of its era. Williams was also the group's star soloist, playing in a variety of styles: a Gershwinlike solo on "Gettin' Off a Mess"; modernistic, in-and-out-of-key playing on "You Rascal You" and "Mess-a-Stomp"; and old-fashioned, barrelhouse piano on "Little Joe from Chicago." She provided excellent support for other soloists and filled in creatively during ensemble passages. She was, in short, one of the great swing-band pianists. Her powerful rhythmic skills led her to be billed as "The Lady Who Swings the Band." While with Kirk she also did arrangements for Louis Armstrong, Benny Goodman, Earl Hines, and Tommy Dorsey. Two of her 1937 arrangements for Goodman, "Roll 'Em" and "Camel Hop," are particularly noteworthy.

In 1942 Williams left the band and formed her own small group in New York City with her second husband, trumpeter Shorty Baker, whom she had married by May of that year after a divorce from her first husband. She led an all-women group in 1945 and 1946 that included the talented guitarist Mary Osborne, and she worked as a staff arranger for Duke Ellington for a short time, writing the well-known "Trumpets No End" in 1946 and providing the Ellington band with fifteen arrangements. She made a series of recordings from 1944 to 1947 under a variety of names: "Mary Lou Williams and Her Chosen Five," with Frankie Newton on trumpet, Vic Dickinson on trombone, and Edmund Hall on clarinet; "Mary Lou Williams and Her Orchestra"; and a trio that included trumpeter Bill Coleman. In 1945 she wrote the *Zodiac Suite*, each section written in honor of a particular musician, and each evoking a different sound—the first, for instance, brings to mind Debussy, the second Ellington. Three movements from the suite were performed that year at Carnegie Hall by the New York Philharmonic Orchestra.

While much of her playing during this period was an adaptation of the boogie-woogie style for which she was best known, she also added dissonances, sophisticated rhythms, and tone clusters that reflected the more modern approach of the bop revolution. Indeed, she became an important figure in the bop movement, serving as mentor and friend to Thelonious Monk, Bud Powell, and Dizzy Gillespie. Compositions like "Froggy Bottom," "Roll 'Em," "What's Your Story, Morning Glory," and "In the Land of Oo-Bla-Dee," successfully integrated bop innovations into the swing style, and Williams contributed several scores to Gillespie's big band.

Frustrated by the commercialism of the music business, Williams moved to Europe in 1952, but there she also found her talents constrained by market demands. She retired from music in 1954 to pursue religious and charitable activities. Moving first to the French countryside and then back to New York City, she began a "street ministry" to musicians hurt by alcoholism, drugs, and illness. She converted to Catholicism in 1957. Her apartment became almost a rest home, complete with cots and a soup kitchen. She established the Bel Canto Foundation to help needy musicians, ran a thrift shop to raise money, and used the profits from her own record company, Mary Records, to support her work.

Encouraged by Gillespie, Williams resumed her career in 1957, appearing at the Newport Jazz Festival. By the early 1960s she was again composing prolifically, focusing in particular on religious themes. She wrote a choral hymn, "St. Martin de Porres," which won the Grand Prix—Academie du Disque Francais; a cantata, "Black Christ of the Andes" (1963); and three masses. The last of these, the "Music for Peace" mass (1970), was commissioned by an American priest in the Vatican, choreographed as "Mary Lou's Mass" by Alvin Ailey in 1971, and performed at St. Patrick's Cathedral in New York City and in many other churches worldwide. She conducted musical workshops in storefronts and on college campuses and appeared throughout the sixties and seventies in concert and on numerous radio and television shows, including "The Today Show," "Sesame Street," and "Mr. Rogers' Neighborhood." Concerned that young blacks seemed unaware of their own rich musical heritage, she became a proselytizer for jazz itself. In 1970 she recorded *The History of Jazz*, a commentary with musical examples, and repeated similar programs many times in concert. As her close friend Rev. Peter F. O'Brien later noted, "the American Black man, in the Spirituals, the Blues, and in Jazz, had created something new and unique. And the music was powerful, beautiful, full of love and healing to the soul" (O'Brien liner notes, *From the Heart* [1971]).

Throughout these years, Williams's playing remained based on a rock-steady rhythmic pulse and a driving sense of swing, decorated with lovely melodic ideas. She recorded a number of critically acclaimed albums, including *Zoning* (1974); *Live at the Cookery* (1976); *Free Spirits* (1976), a trio album that is perhaps the best of her later recorded work; *My Mama Pinned a Rose on Me* (1977), an album of mostly blues; and a solo recital in 1978 that covered the entire stylistic range of her playing. The title tune on *Free Spirits* contains some of her most powerful, modernist playing. Indeed, Williams remained drawn to adventurous, modern ideas; in 1977, she performed in concert with the avant-garde pianist Cecil Taylor. During the last decade of her life she was honored with a Guggenheim Fellowship (1972–1973) and from 1977 until shortly before her death was an artist-in-residence at Duke University, where she taught jazz history and led the jazz orchestra. She died at home in Durham, North Carolina. A month after her death, pianists and a big band performed several of her compositions in a tribute at town hall in New York City.

Williams was an important swing pianist who sought constantly to broaden her style, and she was open to all kinds of modernist musical expressions. Influenced by such musicians as Fats Waller, Art Tatum, Teddy Wilson, and Milt Buckner, she never abandoned the basic blues feeling that was at the core of her playing. Duke Ellington, in his book *Music is My Mistress* (1973), wrote that "Mary Lou Williams is perpetually contemporary. . . . Her music retains a standard of quality that is timeless. She is like soul on soul" (p. 169).

• For a brief overview of Williams, see Linda Dahl, *Stormy Weather: The Music and Lives of a Century of Jazzwomen* (1984); Len Lyons, *The Great Jazz Pianists, Speaking of Their Lives and Music* (1983); and Whitney Balliett, *American Musicians: Fifty-Six Portraits in Jazz* (1986). Gunther Schuller, *The Swing Era: The Development of Jazz, 1930–1945* (1989), offers a perceptive analysis of Williams's music. Also see the excellent summaries in Frank Tirro, *Jazz: A History*, 2d ed. (1993); Lewis Porter et al., *Jazz: From Its Origins to the Present* (1993); and Albert McCarthy, *Big Band Jazz* (1974). Max Harrison et al., *The Essential Jazz Records*, vol. 1, *Ragtime to Swing* (1984), has useful analyses of several of Williams's recordings. The eleven-part interview by M. Jones, "Mary Lou Williams: A Life Story," *Melody Maker* 30 (3 Apr.–12 June 1954) is invaluable. Equally essential are the extensive liner notes by Dan Morgenstern for the Smithsonian/Folkways reissue of the *Zodiac Suite*, with additional commentary by Williams herself and a brief, but useful, discography. An obituary is in the *New York Times*, 30 May 1981.

RONALD P. DUFOUR

WILLIAMS, Mary Wilhelmine (14 May 1878–10 Mar. 1944), historian, was born in Stanislaus County, California, the daughter of Caroline Madsen of Denmark and Carl Wilhelm Salander of Sweden (changed to Carl Williams after immigrating to the United States), farmers. Williams studied in public elementary and secondary schools in California and worked as a public school teacher for four or five years before earning her Ph.D. from Stanford University in 1914. Her dissertation, published in 1916 as *Anglo-American Isthmian Diplomacy, 1815–1915*, won the Justin Winsor Prize of the American Historical Association in 1914. After one year as an instructor of history at Wellesley College, she joined the faculty of Goucher College in Baltimore, Maryland, as assistant professor of history. She was promoted to associate professor in 1919 and full professor in 1920. She retired in 1940.

Although her travels through her parents' native Scandinavia produced two books, *Cousin-Hunting in Scandinavia* (1916) and *Social Scandinavia in the Viking Age* (1920), her primary scholarly interests remained inter-American relations and Latin American history. A pioneer in the development of the field of Latin American history in the United States, Williams served on the editorial board of the *Hispanic American*

Historical Review from 1927 to 1933 and was secretary of the Conference on Latin American History of the American Historical Association from 1928 to 1934. Her *People and Politics of Latin America* (1930) was considered a standard text on the subject for two decades. She also published a biography of John Middleton Clayton in *American Secretaries of State and Their Diplomacy* (vol. 6, 1928) and of the nineteenth-century Brazilian monarch Pedro II, *Dom Pedro the Magnanimous, Second Emperor of Brazil* (1937).

Williams was active in the feminist and pacifist movements and was a member of the Women's International League for Peace and Freedom and founder of the California chapter of the National Woman's party as well as editor from 1935 to 1936 of *Equal Rights*, an independent feminist weekly. She introduced a course at Goucher College on women in U.S. society in 1922 and successfully defended the relevance of the topic to the study of history when the course came under attack in the early 1930s. Her extensive travels included a tour of Latin America taken in 1926–1927 to survey educational opportunities for women in Latin America and to identify candidates for the American Association of University Women's Latin American fellowships. Upon her return Williams published accounts of her findings on education and civil rights for women and on women's philanthropic activities. Like most of her contemporaries, she believed that elites made history, and her research and observations focused mostly on prominent men or on activities of upper-class, mostly white *señoras* (using the Spanish term) in charity organizations and the woman suffrage movement. Unlike most of her contemporaries, Williams recognized the relevance of women's position in society to general social and political history. Herself a unitarian, she placed much of the blame for women's oppression in Latin America on the Catholic church.

In *The People and Politics of Latin America*, a special edition of which the U.S. government produced for its diplomats, Williams sought to improve relations between the United States and Latin America by increasing the understanding of Latin American perspectives on inter-American relations and explaining why its southern neighbors resented the United States. Although Williams was uncritical of many U.S. policies and business practices in Latin America and dismissed much Latin American ill-will toward the United States as the work of "propagandists," she acknowledged the validity of some Latin American complaints of U.S. "dollar diplomacy" and unjustified intervention during the pre–World War I era. Through her teaching and writing, Williams worked to increase respect in the United States for Latin American culture and for the political positions of Latin Americans toward their North American neighbor.

Beyond the walls of the university, Williams's expertise in inter-American diplomacy was recognized by the U.S. State Department and by Latin American governments. She was a member of various U.S. committees on Latin American affairs including the advisory committee of the "Brave New World" radio broadcast series for Latin America (1937–1938). She also assisted in the 1918–1919 Honduras-Guatemala boundary dispute as a historical, geographical, and cartographical expert commissioned by Honduras, and she was awarded a decoration from the government of the Dominican Republic for her work to increase inter-American understanding. This work included Williams's energetic promotion of intellectual and cultural exchange between the United States and Latin America, partly through her work on the U.S. National Committee on Inter-American Intellectual Cooperation and the U.S. State Department Sub-Committee for Exchange of Fellowships and Professorships. She was particularly keen on increasing fellowship opportunities for Latin American women to study in the United States. Convinced of the benefits of U.S. influence and institutions in what she considered "backward" nations of Latin America, she called for U.S. funding of schools established there by U.S. Protestant missionaries, suggesting that funds might come from "the great business establishments which have prospered through activities in Latin America." In her opinion, the influence of the schools and other U.S. institutions would not only improve the image of the United States but would provide Latin American nations with a model of the advanced society they should strive to emulate.

Despite her belief in the superiority of U.S. institutions to those of Latin America, Williams attacked popular U.S. views that inherent cultural or racial traits caused the "backwardness" of many Latin American nations, which she understood as a result of economic and historical circumstance. As a teacher, scholar, diplomatic consultant, and political activist, Williams fostered recognition of and respect for the historical experiences of Latin American peoples and of women in general decades before these experiences had been accommodated in mainstream scholarship in the United States.

After her retirement, Williams moved to Palo Alto, California, where she died of a stroke.

• Correspondence and other papers relevant to Williams's academic work are held at Goucher College. See also *Notable American Women, 1607–1950* (1971) and *Who Was Who among American Authors, 1921–1939* (1976). Williams published articles in various journals, including the *North American Review, South Atlantic Quarterly, Hispanic American Historical Review*, and the *Journal of the American Association of University Women*. Obituaries are in the *Hispanic American Historical Review*, Aug. 1944; the *New York Times*, 13 Mar. 1944; and the *Palo Alto Times*, 11 Mar. 1944.

SUEANN CAULFIELD

WILLIAMS, Michael (5 Feb. 1877–12 Oct. 1950), journalist, was born in Halifax, Canada, the son of Michael Williams, a sea captain, and Ann Colston. His father caught yellow fever in Central America in 1890 and died on the return voyage, leaving his mother with a heavily mortgaged home, six sons (Michael the oldest), and one daughter. She opened the home to boarders, and Michael, a promising student at St. Joseph's

College in New Brunswick, Canada, left school against the protests of his instructors and obtained work in a warehouse to help the penniless family. At nineteen he sought work as a writer in Boston, where Philip Hale published one of his stories. He secured work with the *Boston Post* but soon experienced the first of his lifelong periodic bouts with tuberculosis. After recovering in North Carolina he resumed newspaper work in New York, where he remained the next six years reporting for the *New York World* and the *Evening Telegram*.

In 1900 Williams married Margaret Olmstead. By 1904 tuberculosis again led to a move, to San Antonio, Texas, with his wife and two children. In 1905 he moved the family to San Francisco where he became a reporter for the *San Francisco Examiner*, progressing to city editor the next year. Falling into disfavor with his superiors, however, he quit after just six weeks in his new post and returned to New York, where as a freelance writer between 1907 and 1913 his short stories appeared in *Everybody's Magazine*, *McClure's*, *American Magazine*, *Harper's Weekly*, *Munsey's*, and *Good Housekeeping*. He and his family also lived for a year at Upton Sinclair's utopian experiment, Helicon Hall, in Englewood, New Jersey, until fire destroyed all his manuscripts and the family's possessions. In 1909 he shared the authorship of *Good Health and How We Found It* with Sinclair, but his health was a periodic problem throughout his life, and Williams joked of his "iron constitution, heavily beset with rust."

In 1913 in Carmel, California, Williams experienced a religious conversion to the Catholicism of his youth from which he had been estranged since age fourteen. He recorded this in his 1918 spiritual autobiography, *The Book of the High Romance*. Published by Macmillan, it went through fourteen printings until 1951. This book, and articles that Williams began to write for publications such as *Catholic World*, led to his employment as the assistant press director of the National Catholic War Council, based in Washington, D.C. He traveled to Rome to write about the conclave that resulted in the election of Pope Pius XI and produced the book *American Catholics in the War* (1921). In 1922, however, he left Washington for New York, with a goal of founding an intellectual Catholic weekly of comparable literary excellence to the *Nation* and the *New Republic*.

Williams successfully founded the distinguished Catholic journal *Commonweal*. Begun in 1924, it was established principally through his drive, determination, and fundraising efforts though he was always careful to give credit to the financially supportive group known as the Calvert Associates, named after George Calvert, Lord Baltimore, the Roman Catholic founder of Maryland. In two years of efforts, Williams raised more than $250,000. Among the project's initiators were historian Carlton J. H. Hayes of Columbia University; Father Lawrason Riggs, of the Washington banking family, who served as Catholic chaplain at Yale until 1943; and architect Ralph Adams Cram of Boston, who was not a Catholic.

Williams was selected as the first editor, quite an achievement for the largely self-educated writer whose formal schooling had been aborted at age thirteen. He also selected the name *Commonweal* for the journal, feeling that it was most indicative of its purpose as a Catholic review of literature, the arts, politics, and religion, published by Catholic laity. It was an immediate success in 1924, with the *New York Times* commenting that "suavity not ferocity marks *The Commonweal* style of exposition and argument, and it refrains sedulously from insult or denunciation of those disagreeing with its ideas." In 1938 Williams left the editorship as new owners, who disagreed with his support of Franco, came to *Commonweal*, which continued the intellectually serious, ecumenical, and admirable trajectory on which it had been launched. He died in Hartford, Connecticut.

Williams's founding of *Commonweal* is his most significant and enduring achievement. His several books are now mostly of historical interest. He was the preeminent Catholic journalist of his day and covered important church issues such as the election of Pope Pius XII for the *New York Times* after he left *Commonweal*. In addition to his physical problems he also battled psychological cycles described by one *Commonweal* colleague, Edward Skillin, as "manic-depressive." He also had problems with alcoholism. Nevertheless, this improbable mystic and practical intellectual had a life of remarkable achievement.

• Some of Williams's papers can be found at the U.S. Catholic Conference, Washington, D.C., in the Calvert Associates, the *Commonweal*, and the Michael Williams files; other existing papers are in the Reverend Peter Guilday Papers and the Monsignor John A. Ryan Papers at the Catholic University of America, Washington, and the John J. Raskob Papers at Eleutherian Mills Historical Library, Wilmington, Del. Other books by Williams include *The Little Flower of Carmel* (1925), *Catholicism and the Modern Mind* (1928), *The Shadow of the Pope* (1932), and *The Catholic Church in Action* (1934). A complete modern assessment is Robert Brooke Clements, "'The Commonweal,' 1924–1938: The Williams-Shuster Years" (Ph.D. diss., Univ. of Notre Dame, 1972). Rodger Van Allen, *The Commonweal and American Catholicism* (1974), offers some insight. An obituary is in the *New York Times*, 13 Oct. 1950.

RODGER VAN ALLEN

WILLIAMS, Nathaniel (25 Aug. 1675–10 Jan. 1738), physician and educator, was born in Boston, Massachusetts, the son of Nathaniel Williams, a deacon, and Mary Oliver Shrimpton. He entered Harvard College ranked ninth out of the sixteen students in his class and graduated in 1693. He took his master's degree at Harvard in 1698 and was ordained the same year. His first preaching assignment was in a non-conformist church in Barbados where he wed Anne Bradstreet (date unknown). Of their eight children, only two daughters reached adulthood. On 17 January 1700 Williams returned to Boston, where he was retained by several prominent families as a private tutor. By 1703 he had become assistant in the Boston Latin School, becoming its headmaster in 1708.

Although the exact years are unknown, Williams studied medicine under the tutelage of his reputable uncle, James Oliver of Cambridge. According to a reliable contemporary, throughout his medical career he read available texts and "Carefully compar'd them with his own Observations, made many Extracts from them, and wrote down the Circumstances of his own Experience in difficult cases, for his future guidance" (Prince, p. 27). An energetic, studious, and kind person, Williams's practice quickly grew to include some of the families he already served as a tutor or headmaster. His patients were of diverse backgrounds and for some years Boston appointed him physician for Native Americans; he also provided gratis care to the poor.

Williams seems to have joined some Boston physicians in forming an informal self-improvement association. Under the leadership of William Douglass, a recent immigrant from Scotland and the area's only practitioner with an M.D., in 1721 the group became known as the Club of Physicians. The formalization of their group was elicited by the great smallpox epidemic of 1721 and their concerns about the safety of the new technique of inoculation used by some local physicians. Williams found himself embroiled in a major urban crisis. While he favored inoculation, he believed that a survivor could also spread the infection. His role, and certainly those of Zabdiel Boylston, the principal proponent of inoculation, and Douglass, the principal opponent, in the debates reported by newspaper and broadside may have been caricatured in a 1722 pamphlet entitled *A Friendly Debate; or, A Dialogue between Academicus and Sawny and Mundungus*.

Williams survived these debates and in 1723 was offered the rectorship of Yale College but declined. Although he remained active in the Old South Church he rarely preached himself. In 1726 he became a member of Douglass's Physicall Club, a group that was starting to go beyond voluntaristic self-improvement toward formal regulation of the medical profession. Then in 1733, after twenty-five years as headmaster, he resigned from the Boston Latin School and soon organized his own private school, which he continued to operate for some years. His professional standing and well-known commitment to education made Williams a natural subscriber for Thomas Prince's *Chronological History of New England* (1736).

As a physician with both a college education and a medical apprenticeship and as a respected schoolmaster, Williams was a member of the medical and cultural elite of early eighteenth-century Boston. In an unprecedented display of professional cooperation among local physicians responding to the scarlet fever epidemic of 1735, he joined Douglass and others to create the first Boston Medical Society, which would after his death seek to secure legislation to regulate the medical profession. When he died there a few years later he was a well-respected Bostonian. In recognition of his contributions to the welfare of the Commonwealth, Thomas Prince edited and published *The Method of Practice in the Small Pox . . . Taken from the Manuscript of the Late Dr. Nathaniel Williams* (1752).

• Biographical information can be found in Thomas Prince, *A Funeral Sermon on the Reverend Mr. Nathaniel Williams* (1738), and Clifford K. Shipton, ed., *Sibley's Harvard Graduates*, vol. 4 (1933), pp. 182–85. Useful accounts of his historical context include Eric H. Christianson, "Medicine in New England," in *Medicine in the New World: New Spain, New France, and New England*, ed. Ronald L. Numbers (1987), and Philip Cash et al., eds., *Medicine in Colonial Massachusetts, 1620–1820* (1980).

ERIC HOWARD CHRISTIANSON

WILLIAMS, Otho Holland (Mar. 1749–15 July 1794), revolutionary soldier, was born in Prince Georges County, Maryland, the son of Joseph Williams and Prudence Holland. One year after his birth, his family moved to a homestead on Conococheague Creek, where he secured a good education. His father died when Williams was twelve, and a year later Williams began working in the county clerk's office in Frederick. Retaining this position until 1767, he then transferred to a similar job in the county clerk's office in Baltimore. He returned to Frederick in 1774 to embark upon a business career, but his efforts were short-lived. On 22 June 1775, at the outbreak of the revolutionary war, he joined the Frederick City Rifle Corps of Captain Thomas Price as a lieutenant and marched with his company to the siege of Boston. When Price transferred to Colonel William Smallwood's Maryland regiment in January 1776, Williams succeeded him as commander of the corps with the rank of captain. On 27 June 1776 Williams was promoted to major when the Virginia and Maryland riflemen were combined to form Colonel Hugh Stephenson's regiment. After Stephenson's death in August, Williams was given command of the regiment. Seriously wounded in the groin during the defense of Fort Washington on 16 November 1776, he was captured and released on parole in New York City. British authorities, suspecting that he was secretly passing on intelligence to General George Washington, threw him into military prison. He shared a cell with Ethan Allen and was not exchanged until 16 January 1778, by which time his health was permanently impaired by harsh treatment, unsanitary conditions, and inadequate food. During his captivity, on 10 December 1776, he was promoted to colonel of the Sixth Regiment of the Maryland line. Upon his release he joined his command in New Jersey and led it in the campaign of 1778. He enhanced his reputation as a fearless fighter in the battle of Monmouth on 28 June. For the next two years, he served with Washington's army in New Jersey and New York.

On 16 April 1780 Williams and his regiment marched from Washington's encampment at Morristown, New Jersey, for the Southern Department as part of a force under the command of General Johann Kalb. After Kalb was superseded by General Horatio Gates on 13 July, Williams was appointed deputy adjutant general of the southern army. Although he did not admire his new commander's military abilities, he served brilliantly during Gates's advance into South Carolina in the disastrous battle of Camden on 16 August and the subsequent American retreat to Hillsborough, North Carolina. In late August Gates reorganized his army, and Williams was given command of an amalgamated regiment of Maryland and Delaware Continentals. When General Nathanael Greene superseded Gates (much to Williams's delight) in early December, Williams was appointed adjutant general of the southern army and a month later was given command of the First Maryland Regiment. On 9 February 1781 he was put in charge of an elite corps of cavalry and light infantry, which General Daniel Morgan had declined to lead because of his health. With this body of men, Williams was ordered to protect the rear of Greene's army from a superior British force led by General Charles, Lord Cornwallis, as Greene retreated for the Dan River. Williams's instructions were to decoy Cornwallis away from the main army by marching toward Dix's Ferry on the Dan while Green made directly for Irwin's Ferry lower down. For five days, 10–14 February, Williams maneuvered in a cat and mouse game within sight of the enemy, then, learning that Greene had escaped, he quickly crossed the river himself. Although highly praised by both Greene and the British for his exploits, Williams had little time to savor his triumphs. On 22 February Greene recrossed the Dan to challenge Cornwallis, and Williams once more was in command of a force of cavalry and light infantry, with orders to shadow the enemy closely and provide intelligence. Over the next few days, he was engaged in constant small fights, such as Clapp's Mills on 2 March and Wetzell's Mills four days later. He played an important part in the battles of Guilford Courthouse on 15 March, Hobkirk's Hill on 25 April, and Eutaw Springs on 8 September, commanding a brigade of Continentals in all of these major engagements. He was particularly outstanding at Eutaw Springs, where he led a bayonet charge at a critical moment and won the praise of General Greene. Greene sent him to Congress with dispatches in the spring of 1782, and Williams was belatedly promoted to brigadier general on 9 May.

With the revolutionary war drawing to a close in early 1783, Williams sought new employment. On 6 January the government of Maryland elected him naval officer of the Baltimore District, a civilian post, and ten days later he resigned his commission. He left the military with a record as a fearless fighter who was practically unequaled in his ability to handle a rearguard action. In the 1780s he became a substantial Baltimore merchant. An ardent Federalist, he was elected in 1784 as assistant secretary general of the national Society of the Cincinnati, and he also served as vice president of the Maryland chapter. In 1786 he married Mary Smith, with whom he had four sons. In 1787 Williams founded the town of Williamsport, although he remained "dependant upon Government for employment." He played an important part in Baltimore's reception of Washington in April 1789, when the president was on his way to New York for his inauguration. In the same year he petitioned Washington for a job in the new federal government, and on 3 August he became collector of the Port of Baltimore, a position he retained until his death. He hoped for a time in 1792 to be elected governor of Maryland, but nothing came of it. That same year Washington reorganized the army and offered Williams the position of first brigadier general, deeming him "a sensible man, but not without vanity." As the president suspected, however, Williams's "delicate health" precluded his accepting the offer. In 1793 Williams traveled to Barbados, seeking a restoration of his declining strength. He died at Miller's Town, Virginia, on his way home. In his last years he enhanced his substantial reputation for military sagacity by inscribing *A Narrative of the Campaign of 1780*, published in 1822. This informative and well-written document has been much used and quoted by historians.

• Williams's papers are in the Maryland Historical Society, and they are described in *Calendar of the General Otho Holland Williams Papers in the Maryland Historical Society* (1940). Some letters are in the George Washington Papers, Library of Congress, and Letters from Maj. Gen. Nathanael Greene, Papers of the Continental Congress, No. 155, National Archives. Published correspondence is in *The Papers of George Washington: Presidential Series*, vols. 1–4, ed. Dorothy Twohig (1987–1993); *The Writings of George Washington, from the Original Manuscripts, 1745–1799*, vol. 31, ed. John C. Fitzpatrick (1939); and *The Papers of General Nathanael Greene*, vols. 6–7, ed. Richard K. Showman et al. (1991–1994). Williams's *A Narrative of the Campaign of 1780* is published in William Johnson, *Sketches of the Life and Correspondence of Nathanael Greene*, vol. 1, app. B (1822), and as an appendix in William Gilmore Sims, *The Life of Nathanael Greene* (1849). Williams's life is outlined in Osmond Tiffany, "A Sketch of the Life and Services of Gen. Otho Holland Williams," *Maryland Historical Society Publications* 2 (1851). For his relations with other officers, see Paul David Nelson, *General Horatio Gates: A Biography* (1976); Johnson's aforementioned *Sketches* (2 vols., 1822); Theodore Thayer, *Nathanael Greene: Strategist of the American Revolution* (1960); Thomas E. Templin, "Henry 'Light Horse Harry' Lee: A Biography" (Ph.D. diss., Univ. of Kentucky, 1975); and Charles Royster, *Light-Horse Harry Lee and the Legacy of the American Revolution* (1981). His role in the southern campaigns is described in Russell F. Weigley, *The Partisan War: The South Carolina Campaign of 1780–1782* (1970); Henry Lumpkin, *From Savannah to Yorktown: The American Revolution in the South* (1981); and John S. Pancake, *This Destructive War: The British Campaign in the Carolinas, 1780–1782* (1985).

PAUL DAVID NELSON

WILLIAMS, Paul Revere (18 Feb. 1894–23 Jan. 1980), architect, was born in Los Angeles, California, the son of Chester Stanley Williams, the owner of a small fruit business, and Lila Wright. Because of the death of his father in 1896 and his mother in 1898, Williams was raised by a friend of the family. He attended public schools in Los Angeles and graduated from the Los Angeles Polytechnic High School in 1912. Having made the decision to become an architect, Williams attended the Los Angeles School of Art and participated in the local atelier of the Beaux-Arts Institute of Design during the years 1912 through 1916. Supplementing this educational experience he then studied architecture (on a part-time basis) at the University of Southern California from 1916 through 1919. In 1917 Williams married Della Givens, with whom he had two children.

Either in late 1913 or early 1914 Williams entered the office of the highly successful planning and landscape firm of Wilbur D. Cook, Jr., and George D. Hall. This experience was followed by employment in the office of Reginald D. Johnson, where he was exposed to the world of upper-middle-class suburban and country houses. Finally, he was engaged as a designer by the large commercial firm of John C. Austin during the years 1920–1922.

In 1921 Williams obtained his license to practice architecture in California. The following year he established his own office. He had been given several commissions for large suburban houses by the Austin firm to help him to start his independent practice. The success of these first designs, together with his ability to work easily with clients, immediately established him as one of southern California's major designers of suburban and country houses.

As one of the country's most successful African-American architects, Williams was the first of his race to become a member of the American Institute of Architects (AIA), and he was first to be made a fellow of the AIA in 1957. He served on a variety of local, statewide, and national governmental planning and architectural boards. He was appointed in 1920 to the Los Angeles Planning Commission, in 1933 to the Los Angeles Housing Commission, and in 1953 to the Los Angeles Municipal Art Commission. On the state level he was appointed in 1947 to the California Redevelopment Commission and in the same year to the California Housing Commission. Nationally, he was named by president Calvin Coolidge to serve on the National Monuments Committee (1929) and by President Dwight D. Eisenhower to the National Housing Commission (1953).

The early 1920s designs of Williams indicate that he had absorbed with ease the lessons of planning, scale, and detailing one associates with the best of America's period revival architects in the 1920s and 1930s. In addition, he developed an impressive ability to site his buildings sensitively and to integrate them with the landscape. In the 1920s his own stylistic predilection, and that of his clients, ranged from the English Tudor to the Spanish Colonial Revival and the Mediterranean. Williams's ability to design in such a wide array of styles perfectly matched the eclectic architectural spirit in California and in the United States during these years.

Williams's first commission in the upper-middle-class suburban enclave of Flintridge was the rural English-inspired Louis Cass house (1922). This was followed by a succession of suburban and country houses: the Mediterranean-image Lon Chaney house in Beverly Hills (1929), the Anglo Colonial Revival pair of Banning houses in west Los Angeles (1929), the Spanish Colonial Revival James Degnan house in Flintridge (1927), and the extensive English Tudor country house for Jack P. Atkins in Pasadena (1929).

In the 1930s Williams turned toward Anglo Colonial, Regency, and French Provincial imagery for much of his domestic and even commercial designs. His E. L. Cord house in Beverly Hills (1931) exhibited a two-story "Southern Colonial" porch across its front, and the house for Jay Paley in Bel Air presents a delicately detailed version of the English Regency. After World War II Williams continued to produce similar Anglo Colonial–image houses supplemented on occasion by "soft" versions of modernist-image houses. His own house of 1951 in Los Angeles was modernist in style, though there were many elements in its plan and detailing that were quite formal. A similar modernism with a light touch marks the Robert Gildred house in Beverly Hills (1957) and the Desi Arnaz and Lucille Ball house in Palm Springs (1954).

In addition to his extensive residential practice, Williams designed schools, churches, clubs, hotels, and office buildings. These included the Spanish-image Drive-In Market in Santa Monica (1928) and the Modern/Regency Saks Fifth Avenue in Beverly Hills (1939). Other important nondomestic commissions were the Georgian/Regency Music Corporation building in Beverly Hills (1937), his extensive alterations and additions to the Beverly Hills Hotel (1947–1951, 1959), and his co-design of the flying saucer–theme restaurant building at the Los Angeles International Airport (1957–1961). Before World War II he participated in the federal government's public housing programs in several projects, including the Pueblo del Rio Housing Project in Los Angeles (1940). Although most of his work was done in California, he designed other buildings in Arizona, Washington, D.C., and in Colombia in South America. Williams died in Los Angeles.

During his long and active career Williams's work was widely recognized and well published in regional and national journals, but with the advent of modernism after World War II his later work tended to be ignored. In more recent years, with the development of a more sympathetic view of twentieth-century traditionalism, the quality of his architecture has returned him to the limelight.

• Williams's architectural records are housed in Los Angeles under the personal curatorship of his granddaughter Karen E. Hudson. Williams published two popular architectural-pattern books, *The Small Home of Tomorrow* (1945) and *New Homes for Today* (1946). His experience as an African American practicing architecture is revealed in two articles, "I Am a Negro," *American Magazine*, July 1937, pp. 59, 161–63, and "If I Were Young Today," *Ebony*, Aug. 1936, pp. 56–58. Williams's architecture was extensively published in such journals as *Architectural Digest*, *California Arts and Architecture*, *Architectural Forum*, and *Architect and Engineer*. For critical evaluations of his work see Anita Morris, "Recent Work of Paul R. Williams, Architect," *Architect and Engineer* 141 (June 1940): 19–42; Karen E. Hudson, *Paul R. Williams, Ar-*

chitect (1993); and Karen E. Hudson, *The Will and the Way: Paul R. Williams, Architect* (1994). His work of the 1930s is put into the architectural context of the time in David Gebhard and Harriet Von Breton, *L.A. in the Thirties: 1931–1941* (1975).

DAVID GEBHARD

WILLIAMS, Peter, Jr. (1780?–17 Oct. 1840), clergyman and abolitionist, was born in New Brunswick, New Jersey, the son of Peter Williams, a slave, and Mary Durham, a black indentured servant from St. Kitts. A patriot soldier during the American Revolution, his father was sexton and undertaker for John Street Methodist Church in New York City. In an unusual arrangement, the church in 1783 purchased him from his departing Loyalist master and allowed him to purchase himself over time, completing his freedom in 1796. A founder of the African Methodist Episcopal Zion church and a tobacconist and funeral home owner, he was a leader of the small black middle class in New York City.

Williams, Jr., was educated first at the African Free School and tutored privately by a white minister, Reverend Thomas Lyell, of John Street Methodist Church. He became involved in Sunday afternoon black congregations at Trinity Episcopal Church, and in 1798 he was confirmed by John Henry Hobart. Williams was licensed by the Episcopal bishop in 1812 when the fledgling black Episcopalian group elected him lay reader. In the next six years, Williams organized the congregation as a separate institution, acquired land, and constructed a church costing over $8,000, much of it contributed by wealthy white Episcopalians. In 1819 the new edifice was consecrated as St. Philip's African Church. The following year the wooden church burned down. It was fully insured, however, and a new brick church was quickly constructed. Baptismal rolls indicate that the church's membership included primarily black middle-class tradesmen and female domestics. Among the young candidates for baptism were future abolitionists James McCune Smith, George Thomas Downing, Alexander Crummell, and Charles L. Reason.

Williams was a significant figure in black New York politics. He published a speech he had delivered celebrating the close of the slave trade in 1808, *An Oration on the Abolition of the Slave Trade: Delivered in the African Church, in the City of New York*. He was a prominent member of the African Society for Mutual Relief, a benefit and burial organization. In 1817 he preached the funeral sermon after the death of his close friend, colonizationist Paul Cuffe.

Despite deep reservations about the white American Colonization Society, Williams remained open to the possibility of voluntary black migration out of the United States. He favored colonization to the black republic of Haiti and visited there in 1824. In 1830 he delivered a speech at St. Philip's for the benefit of the Wilberforce colony in Canada. He also helped John Russwurm emigrate to Liberia in 1829 under the aegis of the American Colonization Society. Williams increasingly believed, however, that blacks should remain in the United States to work for full citizenship. He eventually denounced the efforts of the American Colonization Society as racist.

Although Williams enjoyed equality in reform organizations, he was forced to accept an inferior status within the Episcopal church, where he finally advanced to priesthood in 1826. His mentor, Bishop Henry Hobart, counseled him not to seek representation for himself or St. Philip's at the diocesan convention, even though all white clerics and churches assumed this privilege. Williams nevertheless accepted these limitations.

Williams was ubiquitous in black reform efforts in the late 1820s and 1830s. He was cofounder in 1827 of *Freedom's Journal*, the first black newspaper. A staunch believer in black education, in 1833 he helped found the Phoenix Society in New York, which enabled poor blacks to attend school, encouraged church attendance, and established a library. Williams personally assisted several young blacks, including Alexander Crummell, and frequently wrote letters of recommendation to potential white employers. Very active in the early black national convention movement, Williams was inspired by the 1831 convention to attempt to establish a manual training college in New Haven, Connecticut (the attempt was unsuccessful).

In 1833 Williams became deeply involved in the American Anti-Slavery Society as one of six black managers. In 1834 he suffered terribly for his beliefs. During early July, white mobs, angered by abolitionist efforts and competition with blacks for jobs, and inflamed by rumors of interracial marriages, terrorized New York City blacks for three days. After hearing rumors that Williams performed an interracial marriage, a mob sacked and burned St. Philip's and its rectory. Rather than support and defend Williams, Bishop Benjamin T. Onderdonk demanded that Williams refrain from public abolitionist activity. Reluctantly, Williams acceded to Onderdonk's commands. In a moving statement, published in New York newspapers, he described childhood conversations with his father about his revolutionary war service. His father's words, he said, "filled my soul with an ardent love for the American government." Williams longed for the day when his brethren "would all have abundant reason to rejoice in the glorious Declaration of American Independence." He also expressed his lifelong love for New York City. Although his congregation supported him, acquiescence cost him much respect among younger, more militant black abolitionists. Williams continued to work for social reform and lead St. Philip's until his death in New York City.

• Williams's orations and two hymns are reprinted in Dorothy Porter, ed., *Early Negro Writing, 1760–1834* (1971). His response to Bishop Benjamin T. Onderdonk is reprinted in full in *Journal of Negro History* 11 (1926): 181–85. Additional material is available in C. Peter Ripley et. al., eds., *The Black Abolitionist Papers* (5 vols., 1985–1992), especially vol. 3. Biographical material on Williams can be found in B. F. DeCosta, *Three Score and Ten: The Story of St. Philip's Church* (1889).

GRAHAM HODGES

WILLIAMS, Robert (c. 1745–26 Sept. 1775), pioneer Methodist preacher, was born probably in England, but nothing is known about his parents or his birth. His first recorded appearance was as a young preacher in the open air at Whitehaven, a seaport in Cumberland, England, on Sunday 29 June 1766. As Methodist leader John Wesley reported on the event, "At one Robert Williams preached in the market-place to some thousands of people, all quiet and attentive." Later that year Wesley sent Williams to northeast Ireland to serve under James Rea, whom Wesley had urged to promote open-air evangelism, noting on 21 July that "Robert Williams . . . is usually a reviver of the work wherever he comes." On 2 May 1767 Wesley wrote to Mrs. Sarah Crosby about "an amazing increase of the work of God within these few months in the North of Ireland," praising the five preachers who labored there—including Rea and Williams—as "men devoted to God, men of a single eye, whose whole heart is in the work." In 1767 Wesley moved Williams on to Castlebar to work under William Penington, Wesley's favorite colporteur-preacher. Penington died later that year, but not before Williams learned from him the great value of distributing tracts and books wherever he preached.

On 5 May 1769 John Wesley was in Manorhamilton, County Leitrim. After encountering Williams again, he entered a warning note in his journal: "There was a general love to the gospel here till simple R[obert] W[illiams] preached against the clergy." By this time Williams seems to have heard of Wesley's publication of Thomas Taylor's appeal from New York on 11 April for "an able experienced preacher." In any event, he would surely have heard of the brief discussion of the matter at the 1768 English Methodist Conference. Toughened, but by no means disheartened, by his three years in Ireland, he offered his services for America. Although Williams was not the fully trusted senior preacher Wesley wanted for America, he accepted Williams's eager offer, provided that he could secure his own passage and would remain under the oversight of the two authorized preachers whom Wesley planned to send from the following conference.

Permission, no matter how conditional, was sufficient for Williams. He wrote to Thomas Ashton, a Dublin Methodist, who agreed to pay his passage and emigrate with him. In August 1769 they disembarked in Philadelphia and received a welcome there from the infant Methodist society, which paid Williams's shipboard and laundry expenses before setting him on his way to New York. With no senior British preacher yet available to supervise him, Williams exercised his own considerable initiative, heeding perhaps especially his training by Penington. He had brought many Wesley pamphlets, notably sermons and hymns. Speedily he gave Philadelphia printer John Dunlap the twenty-four pages of Charles Wesley's *Hymns for the Nativity of Our Lord*, an edition printed by William Pine of Bristol in 1762. The cost of printing 300 copies (surely by prior agreement) was registered in the old "Cash Book" still preserved in St. George's United Methodist Church, Philadelphia, on 7 October 1769—not far in advance of the book's projected use at Christmas.

This enterprise, begun during his first few weeks in America, was apparently for Williams the planned birth of what became the Methodist Publishing House. Undoubtedly he carried to New York in his saddlebags still other Wesley publications for him—or his successors—to expound or to sell for a few pence, thus building up, as Wesley so constantly urged, "a reading people." No one knows exactly how many Wesley books Williams published and sold. It appears likely, however, that the tangible extant evidence of ten Wesley items (usually in single copies, printed in 1769–1771 by John Dunlap, James Adams, and Isaac Collins) represented a larger publishing enterprise by Williams during his late twenties. Jesse Lee, the first historian of American Methodism, and one of Williams's converts, testified that he "had reprinted many of Mr. Wesley's books, and had spread them through the country, to the great advantage of religion" (p. 48).

Williams arrived in New York City early in September 1769 and remained in touch with the John Street society for two years, as evidenced by his many expenses noted in the account book there, stretching from September 1769 to August 1771. Here he arranged for the printing in October 1769 of the first American class-tickets (known as "love-feast tickets," securing admission to a popular Methodist ritual). With the arrival of Wesley's missionary Richard Boardman in New York at the end of October, Williams journeyed south to Baltimore (probably to assist the freelance Methodist preacher Robert Strawbridge) via Philadelphia, where Wesley's missionary Joseph Pilmore made his own initial assessment: "[Williams] came over to America about business [apparently his bookselling], and . . . Mr. Wesley gave him a license to preach occasionally under the direction of the regular preachers. During his stay in the city he preached several times, and seemed to have a real desire to do good. His gifts are but small, yet he may be useful to the country people, who are, in general, as sheep without shepherds" (pp. 25, 96). Later he was glad to welcome Williams to his Philadelphia pulpit.

When in 1771(?) Williams preached the first Methodist sermon in Norfolk, Virginia, he mounted the steps of the courthouse and gathered a crowd by singing the Wesley hymn "Come, Sinners, to the Gospel Feast," which had been published by Charles Wesley in *Redemption Hymns* (1747). Almost certainly Williams had arranged for James Adams to reprint these fifty-two hymns at Wilmington in 1770 and probably also Isaac Collins in Burlington, New Jersey, in 1771. In Virginia Williams attracted the attention of the Anglican Devereux Jarratt, in Bath Parish, Dinwiddie County; Jarratt later described Williams as "the first

Methodist preacher I ever conversed with, or saw, in Virginia, . . . a plain, simple-hearted pious man." Williams stayed with him about a week in March 1773 and preached several sermons in the parish. "I liked his preaching in the main very well," Jarratt reported, "and especially the affectionate and animated manner in which his discourses were delivered." The end of Jarratt's account is typical: "Mr. Williams also provided me with some of their books" (pp. 107–8).

During his first two years in America Williams was a tireless salesman of Wesley's books and Wesley's gospel along the eastern seaboard. That gospel, of course, was that human beings are sinful and need the salvation offered by their savior Jesus Christ, which is a free gift from God in response to their faith in Him, by which they might be given spiritual certainty, perfect love on earth, and perfect happiness in heaven. With the coming in 1773 of Thomas Rankin as John Wesley's "General Assistant," discipline was tightened. At the first American Conference that summer (as well as at the 1773 British Conference) Williams, stationed in Petersburg, Virginia, was officially recognized as one of the ten regular itinerant preachers in America. He acknowledged the unrest among his brethren about his printing and agreed with them that he should no longer reprint Wesley's works without the consent of both Wesley and his colleagues. The conference instructed him "to sell the books he has already printed, but to print no more."

Jesse Lee pictured Williams as "a plain, artless, indefatigable preacher of the gospel" who "proved the goodness of his doctrine by his tears in public, and by his life and conduct in private." Thirty-five years after Williams's death, claimed Lee, "The name of Robert Williams still lives in the minds of many of his spiritual children" (p. 43). He reportedly married and settled down ("located" in American Methodist parlance) in a home on the main road between Portsmouth and Suffolk, in Virginia, where he died. To Francis Asbury fell the task of preaching his funeral sermon on Thursday, 28 September 1775, and the chore of settling his estate, including the problems of his many Wesley publications. In preaching the sermon Asbury paid a magnanimous tribute: "Perhaps no one in America has been an instrument of awakening so many souls as God has awakened by him" (vol. 1, p. 164).

• The best edition of the British *Minutes of the Methodist Conferences* is that published in London by John Mason (1862), vol. 1; for early American Methodism see Jesse Lee, *A Short History of the Methodists* (1810; repr. in facsimile, 1974). Francis Asbury, *The Journal and Letters*, ed. Elmer T. Clark et al. (3 vols., 1958), is standard. Frank Baker, *From Wesley to Asbury: Studies in Early American Methodism* (1976), contains much original research. C. H. Crookshank, *History of Methodism in Ireland* (3 vols., 1885–1888), remains standard. Joseph Pilmore, *Journal*, ed. F. E. Maser and H. T. Maag (1969), is very valuable. For Williams's important contacts with Devereux Jarratt see the autobiographical *Life of the Reverend Devereux Jarratt* (1806). J. P. Pilkington, *The Methodist Publishing House*, vol. 1 (1968), contains valuable material, including illustrations, and incorporates much of the research of Leland D. Case. J. B. Wakeley, *Lost Chapters Recovered from the Early History of American Methodism* (1858), is an early treasure trove.

FRANK BAKER

WILLIAMS, Robert Ramapatnam (16 Feb. 1886–2 Oct. 1965), chemist and nutritionist, was born in Nellore, India, the son of Robert Runnels Williams and Alice Evelyn Mills, missionaries. His mother educated him at a Baptist mission in Ramapatnam. After an accident crippled his father, the family returned to the United States in 1896. Williams attended schools in Kansas and California before enrolling in 1905 at Ottawa University in Kansas. Two years later he transferred to the University of Chicago, where he received bachelor's and master's degrees in chemistry in 1907 and 1908, respectively. He met Augusta Parrish at Ottawa. They married in 1912 and had four children.

Following the acquisition of the Philippines by the United States in 1898, Williams felt that it was the responsibility of Americans to help Filipinos develop into free and responsible citizens. In 1908 he became a teacher there and in 1909, a chemist with the Bureau of Science in Manila. The bureau, a mix of American and Filipino scientists, sought to combat disease, the Philippines then having the world's highest mortality rate. Edward Vedder, an army doctor at the bureau, studied tropical diseases and brought Williams into his investigation of beriberi, a leading killer among infants and children. Vedder linked the disease to polished rice, a dietary staple prepared by removal of the husk and outer layer of natural rice. He found that an extract made from the polishings had antiberiberi activity and asked Williams to try to isolate the active agent. From 1910 to 1915 Williams devoted himself to the task. He prepared active concentrates and distributed these to health clinics, where they proved effective in overcoming beriberi. He could not, however, isolate the active agent from the heterogeneous mixture.

In 1915 Williams yielded to the desire of Filipinos to take over the bureau and returned to the United States, where he worked at the Bureau of Chemistry of the Department of Agriculture. After World War I he left government service for private industry, his salary being insufficient to support his wife and children. In 1919 he joined a small research laboratory at the Western Electric Company, a subsidiary of the Bell system. It grew in size and importance to become in 1925 the Bell Telephone Laboratories, with Williams as its chemical director.

During his Bell years, from 1919 to 1945, Williams independently continued his beriberi research in the garage of his New Jersey home with the help of Bell volunteers. In 1927 he was able to increase his effort with the first of annual $5,000 grants from the Carnegie Corporation. In 1928 Columbia University offered him laboratory space and the assistance of Columbia scientists. He now worked on a much larger scale, preparing extracts from tons of rice polishings. In 1933 he succeeded in isolating the pure, crystalline antiberiberi factor (vitamin B_1) and named it "thiamin." Between 1933 and 1936 the Williams group determined its composition and structure and achieved its synthesis. Greatly aiding him were a Bell chemical engineer, Robert Waterman, and the Columbia scientists Hans T. Clarke and Edwin Buchman. The Merck pharmaceutical company joined in the investigation, offering its laboratories and expertise for the animal testing and development of large-scale chemical operations.

Williams, Waterman, and Buchman received several thiamin patents in 1935 and 1936. Williams, who wanted the vitamin to be used to eradicate beriberi worldwide, found an organization suited to his goal in the Research Corporation (then in New York City, now in Tucson, Arizona), founded in 1912 to take over patents and fund scientific research from the royalties. Williams and his collaborators assigned all thiamin patents to the Research Corporation, which then created the Williams-Waterman Fund for the Combat of Dietary Diseases (WWF). The scientists were reimbursed for their expenses and received a portion of the royalties. In 1936 Merck received the first license for the commercial manufacture of thiamin; the licensing to other firms followed, creating competition and the consequent lowering of the vitamin's price.

In 1940 WWF had enough income to make its first grants. Clemson University became the initial recipient for its program to improve staple southern foods which targeted degerminated cornmeal and grits. Robbed of its nutrients, especially niacin, by milling, low-quality cornmeal had resulted in a high incidence of pellagra in the South. WWF enabled officials to travel throughout the countryside, visiting the thousands of small mills that processed corn and teaching millers how to enrich meal and informing consumers of the health benefits of using enriched products, while Clemson developed and installed an inexpensive automatic device in mills to blend enriched ingredients with the milled corn.

During World War II Williams was chairman of the Cereal Committee of the Food and Nutrition Board of the National Research Council and initiated the enrichment of white flour and bread as part of the wartime goal of national fitness. Most Americans preferred the nutritionally deficient white flour to natural, whole-grain flour. In 1941 the Food and Drug Administration required enrichment with the B vitamins and some minerals, and by the end of the war about 80 percent of white flour had been enriched. The program was not without controversy as some nutritionists maintained that people should consume natural foods rather than foods enriched with synthetic vitamins. Williams also encountered critics who asserted that it was he who was being enriched by the program. Deeply hurt by the accusation, he was able to convince some opponents through sworn testimony that he made no profit from cereal enrichment, donating anything above $15,000 in the annual royalties due him to the American Friends Service Committee for its humanitarian programs.

In 1945 Williams left Bell Labs to become director of grants for the Research Corporation. As income came to WWF from companies using the thiamin patents, it expanded its grants to nations in Asia, Africa, Latin America, and the Caribbean to combat vitamin and protein deficiency diseases. In the postwar years Williams visited every Asian country except communist China and North Korea. In 1946 he returned to the Philippines, where WWF funded an antiberiberi program in the Bataan province that succeeded in eradicating beriberi through the enrichment of rice. From 1948 to 1950 the death rate due to beriberi dropped from 254 persons per 100,000 to zero.

Williams retired in 1956. Among his honors was the establishment in 1961 of the Robert R. Williams Professorship at Columbia University and the construction in 1963 of the Robert R. and Augusta C. Williams Laboratories for nutrition research near Nellore, India. Williams died in his Summit, New Jersey, home. His strong religious and humanitarian beliefs were reflected in his serving as Sunday school teacher at his Baptist church in Summit, as a board member of the United Negro College Fund, and by his signing away the rights to a personal fortune to enable the income from his patents to be used for the eradication of disease.

• Williams's papers, in the Library of Congress, include diaries, correspondence, notebooks, speeches, writings, patents, and materials regarding his relations with the Research Corporation and Merck, the establishment of the Williams-Waterman Fund, and travels in Asia. His three books are the best sources for his career: *Vitamin B_1 and Its Use in Medicine* (1938), with Tom D. Spies; *The Williams-Waterman Fund for the Combat of Dietary Diseases: A History of the Period 1935 through 1955* (1956); and *Toward the Conquest of Beriberi* (1961). For a brief account of his beriberi research, see his "The Beriberi Vitamin," *Industrial and Engineering Chemistry* 29 (Sept. 1937): 980–84. Two good accounts of his life and work are Richard S. Baldwin, "Robert R. Williams (1886–1965)—A Biographical Sketch," *Journal of Nutrition* 105 (1975): 3–14, and Joseph W. Barker, "Robert Runnels [*sic*] Williams (1886–1965)," *American Philosophical Society Yearbook 1966*, pp. 206–9. On the Research Corporation, see "Science, Invention and Society, the Story of a Unique American Institution" (1972), a brochure available from the Research Corporation, describing the acquisition of the thiamin patents and the formation of the Williams-Waterman Fund. Obituaries are in *Chemical and Engineering News* 43 (25 Oct. 1965): 91, and the *New York Times*, 11 Oct. 1965.

ALBERT B. COSTA

WILLIAMS, Roger (1603?–1683), clergyman and founder of Rhode Island, was born in London, England, the son of James Williams, a merchant, and Alice Pemberton. His precise birth date is unknown, and his own references to his age throughout his lifetime are contradictory. During his teens, Williams experienced a spiritual awakening that moved him to join the ranks of Puritan dissenters who were voicing opposition to the ecclesiastical policies of the Church of England and King James I; his religious fervor, however, caused a falling out with his father, a stalwart supporter of the Anglican church.

Outside his family, he received attention and approval from one of England's most prominent jurists, Sir Edward Coke, who employed Williams by having him sit in the Star Chamber and take down sermons and speeches in shorthand. Recognizing Williams's capabilities, Coke obtained a scholarship for him and placed him in the Charterhouse school in 1621. Two years later Williams was admitted to Pembroke Hall, Cambridge, although his formal matriculation did not occur until after he had spent nearly a full year at the school. He received a bachelor of arts degree in January 1627, and he stayed at the college for about eighteen months longer, studying toward a master's degree. For reasons that are not known, he abruptly left the school without obtaining a graduate diploma sometime between December 1628 and February 1629.

In the winter of 1629 he accepted employment as family chaplain in the household of Sir William Masham in the parish of High Laver, Essex. Living at Masham's manor, Williams gained the acquaintance of influential members of several Puritan gentry families, including the Barringtons, Whalleys, Cromwells, and Winthrops. His radical religious views, however, were already setting him apart from the beliefs of many other Puritans. On his way to an important Puritan meeting in Sempringham in the summer of 1629, Williams rode in the company of two noteworthy ministers, Thomas Hooker and John Cotton, and boldly informed them of their error in using the Book of Common Prayer. Williams probably had not fully embraced the views of separatism, but he was on his way toward rejecting the elements of religious conformity that were to be found in both the Anglican church and among the church's dissenting Puritan congregations.

Although his living at the Masham estate was secure, Williams worried about the future and sought to chart a course that would satisfy his own ambitions. Sometime prior to the spring of 1629, he had thought about emigrating to New England; according to his own testimony, he had received a "call" to accompany other Puritan emigrés there, but he had turned it down. For a while, he saw his future in Essex, where he wooed Jane Whalley, the niece of the formidable Puritan matron Lady Joan Barrington. Lady Joan put an end to Williams's fantasy of marrying above his station, so he turned his attention to another young lady, Mary Barnard, a maid in the Masham household and a daughter of a Nottinghamshire minister. The courtship did not last long. Williams and Mary Barnard were married at the small stone church at High Laver on 15 December 1629. During their long life together, they brought six children into the world, all of whom survived into adulthood. Despite numerous occasions of hardship and privation, they overcame their adversities and enjoyed a very close and loving relationship.

A year after they were married, the young couple took ship from Bristol en route to New England. It is not certain why Roger and Mary Williams decided to quit the Old World and take their chances in the new, although Williams in later life claimed that William Laud, the Archbishop of Canterbury and fierce persecutor of Puritans, "pursued me out of this Land." It is unlikely, however, that Laud was waging a personal campaign against Williams, who was a relative unknown among the Puritan clergy; probably Williams regarded Laud's generally harsh policies toward Puritans as threatening enough. Williams also said many years after his emigration that he had longed to deliver the gift of Christianity to the Indians, but his career as a missionary never panned out because he personally lacked Christ's commission or any apostolic authority to perform conversions among heathens.

Williams and his wife arrived in Massachusetts Bay aboard the ship *Lyon* on 5 February 1631. John Winthrop (1588–1649), governor of Massachusetts Bay, praised Williams as "a godly minister," but Williams's godliness would soon become a severe test of strength and endurance to Winthrop and the other leaders of Massachusetts Bay. In Boston Williams was offered the position of teacher in the church, but he declined it, saying that he dared not "officiate to an unseparated people," by which he meant that the Boston Puritans were not as religiously pure as they might like to think, for they had failed to separate themselves fully from the Church of England.

Over the next five years, Williams's separatism would be a painful thorn in the side of the bay colonists. Even after Williams moved from Boston to Salem, and from Salem to Plymouth, and from Plymouth back to Salem, each relocation designed to avert confrontation with the authorities in Boston, he nevertheless found himself repeatedly at the center of controversy. As pastor of the Salem church, a position he officially occupied after the regular pastor died in the summer of 1634, Williams preached defiantly against the validity of royal land patents, oaths of submission to the colony, and the right of magistrates to punish breaches of God's first four commandments. After several unsuccessful attempts to silence him, the General Court finally lost all patience with him. In October 1635 the court voted to banish him from the colony. Williams fell ill, however, so the court delayed the enforcement of the sentence until the following January, when the magistrates dispatched a sheriff to arrest him and forcibly place him on board a ship bound for England. The court's plan failed, however, when Williams was warned of his arrest by Winthrop, who suggested that he flee to the Indian country near Narragansett Bay. He took Winthrop's advice, escaped from Salem during a raging blizzard, and followed the Indian trails to the village of Massasoit, a sachem of the Pokanoket Indians. There he spent the winter.

By banishing him from the colony, the General Court defined the course of the remainder of Williams's life. Actually Williams suffered gladly as a persecuted witness of Christ, for he believed that faith was truly forged by such suffering, but he also bitterly resented the harshness of the sentence that had been imposed on him. For the rest of his life, Williams bore the scar of the banishment like a soldier's wound, his own peculiar badge of courage. In his writings he never let his readers forget the misery he and his family had endured as a result of the banishment. Neither did he let his persecutors forget their despicable act of unkindness toward him.

As winter turned to spring in the year 1636, Williams was joined by several followers from Massachusetts and by his own family. On a parcel of land along the eastern shore of the Seekonk River, Williams and the others set about planting and erecting shelters. In short order, however, word arrived from Plymouth Colony warning the settlers that they were within the jurisdiction of the colony and must vacate the land immediately. Acquiring a gift of land from the Narragansett Indian sachems Canonicus and Miantonomo, Williams and his small party of friends crossed to the western bank of the Seekonk and established permanent homes at the headwaters of Narragansett Bay, a place Williams named Providence in recognition of "God's merciful providence unto me in my distress."

Reluctantly, Williams became a political leader of the fledgling community, struggling with the uncertainties of how best to organize the settlement into a functioning government. Before much could be accomplished, however, war broke out between the Puritan colonists and the Pequot Indians of Connecticut. Williams provided invaluable assistance to the military campaign against the Pequots by persuading the Narragansett Indians not to ally with their Connecticut brethren and by supplying the Massachusetts leaders with the authoritative intelligence of enemy plans and movements.

His relationship with the Narragansetts was built on an understanding of the important role that reciprocity plays in Indian culture. Williams became a true friend to the Narragansetts for two other reasons as well: he recognized that the survival of the English colonies required a policy of peaceful coexistence, and he firmly believed that the Indians should not be treated as savages but as members of the brotherhood of man. "Nature knows no difference," he wrote, "between European and American [Indian] in blood, birth, bodies, etc." His close ties with the Narragansetts, however, became another sore point in his dealings with Massachusetts. John Winthrop thought that Williams was naive about Indian treachery and that he preferred to accept the word of an Indian over that of a fellow Englishman. Sometimes Williams was the unwary victim of Indian deceit, but mostly he was a keen observer who could readily discern truth from falsehood.

There were other factors besides Williams's friendship with the Indians that kept Massachusetts at odds with him. Providence became a haven for other dissidents who sought to live beyond the jurisdictional reach of the Puritan colonies. Williams's own brand of religious thinking, especially his belief in the utter necessity of religious freedom (or "soul liberty," as he called it) and separation of church and state, became the hallmark of the Providence settlement. During the first few years of the community, the inhabitants decided that "no man should be molested for his conscience." Williams took personal advantage of this broad liberty. In 1639, having grown disenchanted with separatism, he embraced the Baptist faith long enough to help found the first Baptist church in America. Four months later he abandoned the Baptist congregation in Providence and left organized religion behind. For the rest of his life, he would pray with his wife, but in his heart he was a congregation of one.

By 1643 four different communities had been established around Narragansett Bay, all sharing similar origins as havens for the religiously oppressed and the politically unwanted. Their Puritan neighbors, watching the growth of the settlements from afar, realized that these heretical denizens built their homes on some of the richest land in southern New England. As a result, the Massachusetts authorities laid claim to the territory around Narragansett Bay in an effort to create a contiguous jurisdiction of Puritan colonies from Boston to Hartford. Perceiving the threat, the Narragansett Bay towns quickly dispatched Roger Williams to England to defend the sovereignty of the four disunited settlements. He did better than that. With the assistance of Sir Henry Vane the Younger and other prominent Roundheads, Williams obtained from Parliament a patent, dated 14 March 1644, that united the four settlements into the colony of Providence Plantations. Implicit in the patent was an endorsement of Williams's concept of soul liberty.

In England, Williams visited family and renewed old friendships with prominent Puritans. He spent a good deal of his time writing and seeing through press a number of publications, including his two most famous works; *A Key into the Language of America* (1643), a dictionary of the Narragansett Indian language and a commentary on the culture and customs of the southern New England Indians, and *The Bloudy Tenent of Persecution* (1644), a sweeping condemnation of Massachusetts's intolerance and a manifesto defending the right of each individual to decide, according to his own conscience, how best to worship God without interference from any civil authority. With another, a smaller publication, *Mr. Cottons Letter Lately Printed, Examined and Answered* (1644), Williams initiated a protracted debate in print with prominent Massachusetts clergyman John Cotton over the issues that had led to his banishment; he did so, however, in the context of the much wider religious debate transpiring in England over the question of individual sanctification.

With patent in hand, Williams returned to Providence in September 1644, hoping that fierce political rivalries and petty jealousies among the settlers of Narragansett Bay could be put aside so that the towns could organize a colony government. A central government was established, and Williams served for more than three years as chief officer of the colony, but the internal dissension within and among the four towns did not abate. Soon William Coddington, a leader of a political faction on Aquidneck Island, received a parliamentary commission making him governor of the colony for life. In 1651 Williams sailed for

England, accompanied by John Clarke (1609–1676), to challenge the Coddington claim and obtain a confirmation of the 1644 patent.

Williams's second mission to England was less successful than the first, although he was able to renew his pamphlet war with Cotton by publishing another spate of controversial writings, including *The Bloody Tenent Yet More Bloody* (1652), and to pass his time discoursing religion and politics with Oliver Cromwell and John Milton. He saw to it that Coddington's commission was nullified, but he could not get the affirmation of the patent that he so desperately wanted. In the spring of 1654 he returned to New England, leaving Clarke in London to carry on the colony's work.

Later that autumn Williams was elected president of Providence Plantations, but the colony was in almost complete disarray, torn asunder by factions and special interests that refused to work together in the name of the commonweal. In a land of his own creation, where individualism was valued above anything else, Williams realized that the duty of each citizen to his neighbors needed to be clarified. He did so in what has become his most famous letter, an epistle written to the town of Providence in January 1655. In the letter, Williams defended his belief that religion and conscience should not be restrained by civil supremacy, but he also recognized that individualism sometimes had to be restricted for the sake of the common good. In it, he compared society to a ship, where the captain's authority extended only to the actions of the crew and passengers, not to their religious beliefs. Nonetheless, captain, crew, and passengers all had to work together to keep the ship on course. Therefore, if any on board refused to help, "the commander or commanders may judge, resist, compel, and punish such transgressors, according to their deserts and merits."

Williams's letter did not stop the dissension in Providence or the colony as a whole. In fact, during the remainder of the 1650s strife over land and boundaries was added to the political conflict that already existed, in some cases grafting "land lust," as Williams called it, onto the contending political factions. Leading one particularly land-hungry group in Providence was William Harris, who believed that the boundaries granted to Williams by the Indians should be extended beyond their original limits. Williams refused. The dispute, which was personal as well as political, lasted until Harris's death in 1681, but the land controversy itself dragged on until 1712.

While not embroiled in the flames of religious and political contention, Williams spent his time raising livestock and trading with the Indians. He set up a trading post near Narragansett Bay and made the business into a prosperous concern; according to his own report, one year he earned £100, considerably more than he could have made as a vicar in England. Often he retreated to the solitude of his post, where he could avoid the din of controversy, cultivate his friendship with the Indians, and write windy letters to friend and foe alike. Although his friendship with John Winthrop foundered prior to the elder statesman's death in 1649, Williams enjoyed a very close friendship with Winthrop's eldest son, John Winthrop, Jr. (1606–1676), governor of Connecticut and a man with whom Williams shared many interests, religious and secular.

In 1663 Charles II granted John Clarke a charter for the colony of Rhode Island and Providence Plantations that explicitly extended "soul liberty" as a right to every inhabitant. Despite the liberality of the charter and its provisions that fostered a "lively experiment" in freedom, Rhode Island was mired in the strife that had plagued it from its earliest beginnings. Throughout the 1660s Williams withdrew more and more from the political scene, although he continued to hold minor offices in the colony and town governments. His withdrawal was partly caused by the political ascendancy of the Quakers, who first arrived in the colony during the mid-1650s. Even though he shrank from politics, he did not refrain from speaking his mind. The Quakers troubled him both politically and religiously, especially because he was convinced that they elevated themselves over Scripture and paid no heed to conventional manners and morality. In 1672 he debated the Quakers in Newport and Providence, and later he wrote a long account of his experience, *George Fox Digg'd Out of His Burrowes* (1676). His encounter with the Quakers was not his most glorious moment. In the debate he came perilously close to abandoning his cherished principle of soul liberty, although to his lasting credit he never tried to enforce any actual limitation on the Quakers' form of worship or personal behavior.

During the 1670s his dealings with the Narragansett Indians also took a turn for the worse. Canonicus and Miantonomo, the two sachems who had given him the Providence lands, had died in the 1640s, and their descendants—the new generation of Narragansett leaders—felt no special affinity for Williams or any white man. Over the years threats of war, expropriation of lands, and spreading white settlements had taken their toll on the Indian way of life. When King Philip's War broke out between the Puritan colonists and the Indians of southern New England in June 1675, Williams could not keep the Narragansetts from allying with Metacom (Philip), a Pokanoket sachem, and the other tribes that had taken up arms. Williams suffered another personal and diplomatic defeat in March 1676 when a band of Indians, including some Narragansetts, attacked Providence and burned his house to the ground as he was negotiating with Indian leaders on the outskirts of town. Eventually the blood that flowed in New England left an indelible stain. Williams himself joined a militia company and, after the war ended in the summer of 1676, participated with other Providence men in rounding up and selling Indian captives into slavery.

As one might expect, the last years of his life were not spent in quiet repose. Williams was an outspoken man, and he kept on writing and talking until the very end. Mostly he wrote about spiritual concerns, about matters of faith and soul, but he also became increasingly nostalgic in his later years, remembering the events and the people that had helped shape his life in New England. King Philip's War had nearly laid waste to Rhode Island, but as his own demise approached Williams remembered mostly the early days, the happy memories of his friendship with Canonicus and Miantonomo. His banishment from Massachusetts remained a bitter memory, an unhealed wound that he revealed time and time again. His neighbors had greatly different opinions of him. He was held in high esteem by some, but many regarded him as a busybody, a man who took himself far too seriously, and—in the words of William Coddington—"a mere weathercock, constant only in unconstancy." When Williams died between January and March 1683, he was buried with military honors in a grave located somewhere in the boundaries of his house lot in Providence. Eventually no one could quite remember where Rhode Island's founding father had been laid to rest, and he became a forgotten hero. Not until after the American Revolution did Williams begin to gain a historical reputation as a progenitor of religious liberty.

His faults were many, to be sure. Often he expressed himself with great modesty and pronounced deference, but he was just as frequently bold and rash. He was also argumentative, brutally honest, and charitably fair. The different sides of his personality made people reach startlingly opposite conclusions about him: he was a saint or the devil incarnate. He was, of course, neither of those things. Cotton Mather, the Puritan divine, called him quixotic and dangerous, but he also admitted that Williams had "the root of the matter" in him. Nor was Williams the weathercock that Coddington had claimed, for if anything it was his belief in his role as one of Christ's witnesses that kept him steady and surprisingly consistent throughout most of his life. Rather, Williams was a bellwether. He led his fellow Rhode Islanders into an uncharted territory where a strict "wall of separation" (the Jeffersonian phrase was Williams's own) divided church from state, and he showed them how to prosper without the fetters of conformity or coercion.

• Few of Williams's papers survive today; most can be found in Providence at the Rhode Island Historical Society, the Rhode Island State Archives, and Brown University. The largest collection of his extant letters is contained among the Winthrop Papers at the Massachusetts Historical Society in Boston. His surviving papers and polemical works have been published among several different primary works: *The Publications of the Narragansett Club* (6 vols., 1866–1874), reprinted with an additional volume as *The Complete Writings of Roger Williams* (7 vols., 1963); John Russell Bartlett, ed., *Records of the Colony of Rhode Island and Providence Plantations in New England* (10 vols., 1856–1865); Horatio Rogers et al., eds., *The Early Records of the Town of Providence* (21 vols., 1892–1951); Howard M. Chapin, ed., *Documentary History of Rhode Island* (2 vols., 1916); and Glenn W. LaFantasie, ed., *The Correspondence of Roger Williams* (2 vols., 1988). More books have been written about Williams than about any other American colonial figure born before Benjamin Franklin. The best modern biography is Edwin S. Gaustad, *Liberty of Conscience: Roger Williams in America* (1991), although two older works, by Samuel Hugh Brockunier, *The Irrepressible Democrat: Roger Williams* (1940), and Ola Elizabeth Winslow, *Master Roger Williams: A Biography* (1957), also should be consulted. Williams's theology and ideology are analyzed by two brilliant scholars of Puritanism in Perry Miller, *Roger Williams: His Contribution to the American Tradition* (1953), and Edmund S. Morgan, *Roger Williams: The Church and the State* (1967). A perceptive essay by Sydney V. James captures the essence of the man and his times, "The Worlds of Roger Williams," *Rhode Island History* 37 (1978): 99–109.

GLENN W. LAFANTASIE

WILLIAMS, Roger (27 July 1890–23 Feb. 1978), research chemist, was born in Pottsville, Pennsylvania, the son of Henry Laurens Williams and Catherine Ann Phillips. Williams's family moved to Nebraska in 1901, and from 1909 to 1911 he attended the University of Nebraska. He then transferred to the Massachusetts Institute of Technology (MIT) and earned his B.S. in chemistry in 1914. For two years he continued at MIT, studying with the eminent physical chemist Arthur A. Noyes. Williams married Cady W. Jennings in 1915; they had one child. After his marriage, Williams left graduate school and joined the Nitrogen Products Company of Providence, Rhode Island, as a research supervisor. This company was developing a process to fix nitrogen from the air into molecules such as nitric oxide or ammonia, which could be used to make explosives or fertilizer. Until 1913 most of the world's fixed nitrogen came from mineral deposits in the Atacama desert in northern Chile. Just as World War I was beginning, the German chemical company BASF developed a novel process to cause atmospheric nitrogen to react with hydrogen from coal to make ammonia, using very high pressure and a catalyst. Without this process the Germans probably could not have fought for four years. In the United States the federal government and several companies initiated research programs to develop similar processes. Du Pont, which was making enormous quantities of explosives for the Allied war effort, began to study the problem. Probably because of his work in this area, Williams received a letter from Du Pont offering him a job in early 1918. For the next six years Williams worked in Du Pont's central Chemical Department.

In 1924 Williams became the chemical director of a new Du Pont joint venture called Lazote Company formed with the French engineer Georges Claude and an American marketing company, National Ammonia. Its goal was to manufacture and sell ammonia using a process similar to the one developed in Germany. The next decade was an extremely trying one for Williams and his organization. The high-pressure technology required to make ammonia pushed beyond the limits of Du Pont's technical capabilities. By the time the large plant in Belle, West Virginia, was operating at capacity, the world market for ammonia collapsed; the large number of new plants led to oversupply. Williams then sought other products that could be made from the technologies used to make ammonia. He achieved a major success with a process for making methanol, then used as antifreeze for automobile radiators. His organization also developed other new products including an acrylic plastic that was trademarked Lucite. The big opportunity for Williams came in 1935 when Du Pont was developing processes to make the precursor chemicals for nylon. Williams seized the opportunity and became the supplier of hexamethylenediamine and adipic acid. In this way Williams's Ammonia Department—Du Pont had bought out the minority interests in Lazote in 1929—shared the phenomenal success of nylon beginning in 1940. During his tenure as chemical director of the ammonia enterprise, Williams was a very effective leader and built one of the most respected technical organizations in the company.

Williams's skill at managing challenging research and engineering activities led the Du Pont management to tap him to run the most difficult job the company had ever taken on: the design, construction, and operation of a facility to make plutonium for the Manhattan Project during World War II. When Williams began this work in 1943, plutonium had been produced only in minute quantities by cyclotrons. Using very sketchy data, Williams's group had both to design massive nuclear reactors that would convert uranium to plutonium and to develop chemical separation processes to purify the product. For safety and security reasons a site was chosen at Hanford on the Columbia River in eastern Washington. In addition to the actual plant, facilities to house, feed, and amuse 25,000 workers had to be constructed quickly in the remote area. Under Williams's direction, the construction of the plant moved ahead expeditiously and production of plutonium began in the fall of 1944. Enough plutonium was produced for the first nuclear test at Alamogordo, New Mexico, in July 1945, and the bomb was dropped on Nagasaki several weeks later. (The Hiroshima bomb used enriched uranium-235 separated from natural uranium in another massive plant at Oak Ridge, Tennessee.)

In June 1945 Williams was elected vice president, director, and member of the executive committee of the Du Pont Company. Part of his responsbility was oversight of Du Pont research, which expanded dramatically in the postwar era. Although his authority over the company's research programs was "advisory," he was able to convince others to follow his suggestions. He helped to orchestrate a major initiative in agricultural chemicals, which became one of the major growth areas for Du Pont.

In the postwar era when many Americans saw science as a panacea, Williams continued to take a balanced and commonsense approach. He believed that successful research programs had to be carefully evaluated and managed. However, he also believed that research, when intelligently pursued, was a powerful problem solver. All his career he combined a quiet yet effective style of leadership with sound technical judgment. For his accomplishments, he was awarded the prestigious Perkin Medal of the American Section of the Society of Chemical Industry in 1955. In that same year he retired from the executive committee of the Du Pont Company.

• There is some biographical material on Williams in Accession 1689 at the Hagley Museum and Library, Wilmington, Del. His career is also discussed in David A. Hounshell and John Kenly Smith, Jr., *Science and Corporate Strategy: Du Pont R&D, 1902–1980* (1988).

JOHN KENLY SMITH

WILLIAMS, Samuel May (4 Oct. 1795–13 Sept. 1858), Texas colonizer, city founder, and banker, was born in Providence, Rhode Island, the son of Howell Williams, a sea captain, and Dorothy Wheat. After local schooling, young Sam served around 1810 as an apprentice in his uncle Nathaniel Felton Williams's commission house in Baltimore, Maryland, and he soon journeyed as supercargo to Buenos Aires. Naval activities associated with the War of 1812 prevented his return to the United States until after 1815, allowing Williams time to master the Spanish language and culture.

Williams settled briefly in New Orleans, Louisiana, clerking in commission houses; but he immigrated to Austin's colony in Mexican Texas in May 1822. The following year he became Austin's assistant—writing deeds, keeping accounts, writing and translating Spanish documents, and acting as Austin's agent until the close of the colonial period in 1834. He also was secretary to the *ayuntamiento* in San Felipe, the seat of government for Austin's colony. When Austin was unable to take his seat in the state legislature of Coahuila-Texas in 1835, Williams served as his substitute. Williams accumulated eleven leagues (49,000 acres) of land as his reward for his various services at a time when Texas had a barter economy. In 1828 Williams married Sarah P. Scott in San Felipe and fathered nine children, five of whom reached adulthood.

In 1834 Williams became the junior partner, with Thomas F. McKinney, in McKinney & Williams, a newly formed commission house based in Quintana, Texas. The house was destined to become the foremost mercantile venture in Texas until its sale to Williams's brother Henry H. Williams in 1842. McKinney & Williams used its credit with merchants in the United States, including Williams's kinsmen, to help supply the Texas revolution against Mexican president Antonio López de Santa Anna in 1835–1836. The revolution led to the creation of the Republic of Texas in March 1836. Neither the Republic of Texas nor the state after annexation into the United States in 1846 was able to repay the $99,000 owed to the firm. Because of this debt, and to stimulate commerce during the specie shortage following the panic of 1837, the Republic of Texas allowed McKinney & Williams—which had relocated to the new city of Galveston Island in 1837—to issue circulating small bills. Because of Williams's financial connections, the Republic also sent him to the Atlantic seaboard to negotiate a loan based on Texas land scrip and also to contract for six naval vessels to defend Texas from Mexican raiders.

Williams returned to his new home in Galveston (a house museum in the 1990s) in 1839, on board the first of the vessels but without securing the loan.

Williams's neighbors elected him to represent Galveston in the Fourth Texas Congress in 1839, the first to meet in the new capital at Austin. There he worked for solutions for Texas's financial problems, but his petition to open a bank of issue failed amid Jacksonian era suspicions about banking and paper money. During his travels as agent for the Republic, Williams became a Freemason, which included initiation into the Royal Arch and Knights Templar orders; upon his return to Texas he organized Freemason chapters and served as presiding officer at the highest levels. Texas president Sam Houston, during his second term, sent Williams and George W. Hockley to the Rio Grande in 1843–1844 to arrange an armistice with Mexican commissioners. This endeavor failed in part because of Houston's diplomatic maneuvers favoring annexation, which resulted in a rift between Williams and Houston.

On 1 January 1848 Williams used his 1835 bank charter acquired from the legislature of Coahuila-Texas to open the Commercial & Agricultural Bank in Galveston. This was the first bank in Texas not associated with a commission house, and under the guidelines of its charter it could issue and circulate its own paper money. Banking enemies passed a bill on 20 March 1848 that prohibited such notes, punishable by a $5,000 fine for each offense committed within each 30 days; the attorney general filed suit against the bank in June, and the first arguments were heard in Galveston district court in the fall. However, Williams's friends and attorneys defended the bank, and C&A notes continued to circulate for the next decade. They were redeemable always at par in specie during the political and legal maneuvers between Williams's supporters and enemies. His enemies finally triumphed in 1859, six months after Williams died at his home in Galveston, when the Texas Supreme Court declared the C&A Bank unconstitutional.

Williams's contributions to Texas, besides being its first banker and a public servant, include his original handwritten deeds for Austin's colonists, which were preserved in the General Land Office of Texas. Moreover, his very large collection of personal papers detail his activities and those of his associates in business, land speculation, and public service.

• Williams's personal papers are in the archives of the Rosenberg Library, Galveston, Tex., and a published calendar and name index are available. A biography is Margaret Swett Henson, *Samuel May Williams: Early Texas Entrepreneur* (1976). A detailed description of his 1839 Galveston home and his cofounders of Galveston is Henson, *The Samuel May Williams Home: The Life and Neighborhood of an Early Galveston Entrepreneur* (1992), a booklet in a series about historic sites published by the Texas State Historical Association.

MARGARET SWETT HENSON

WILLIAMS, Smokey Joe. *See* Williams, Joe.

WILLIAMS, Stephen West (27 Mar. 1790–7 July 1855), physician, naturalist, and medical historian, was born in Deerfield, Massachusetts, the son of William Stoddard, a physician, and Mary Hoyt. Williams attended the local academy and at age eighteen began to study medicine with his father. While still a student, he sent Dr. Benjamin Rush in Philadelphia an account of the suicides of identical twins; Rush published the letter, with a commentary on hereditary insanity (*Medical Inquiries and Observations on the Diseases of the Mind* [1812], pp. 48–55). Williams attended the medical school of Columbia College in the winter of 1812–1813. Returning to Deerfield to practice, he spent his leisure in botanical excursions in western Massachusetts with geologist Edward Hitchcock and his own medical student Dennis Cooley. They located nearly 1,000 species, and Williams compiled his "Floral Calendar Kept at Deerfield, Massachusetts" (*American Journal of Science* 1 [1819]: 359–73). In 1818 Williams married Harriet Taylor Goodhue, daughter of Joseph Goodhue, an army surgeon stationed at Portsmouth, New Hampshire; they had four children, one of whom died in infancy.

Williams lectured on medical jurisprudence at the Berkshire Medical Institution from 1823 to 1831. He also lectured on that subject, as well as botany, materia medica, and pharmacy, at the College of Physicians and Surgeons in New York, 1828; Dartmouth Medical School, 1838–1841; and Willoughby University in Ohio, 1838–1840. His botanical lectures were illustrated with paintings and drawings made by his wife and daughter. He prepared *A Catechism of Medical Jurisprudence* (1835). Throughout his life he contributed articles on medicine, surgery, and botany to professional journals. He was a member of the Vermont and Massachusetts medical societies and of the Physico-Medical Society of New York and a corresponding member in 1843 of the National Institute for the Promotion of Science.

Always deeply interested in the region where his family had lived for more than a century and a half, Williams collected books and manuscripts on Deerfield and wrote and lectured on the history of the village. An unpublished paper on the history of the Indians of the Connecticut Valley won him election as an honorary member of the New-York Historical Society. He was also a corresponding member of the Royal Society of Northern Antiquaries of Copenhagen and of the New England Historic Genealogical Society. Historians Francis Parkman and William L. Stone both consulted him in their research on the colonial Indian wars.

Williams wrote *A Biographical Memoir of the Rev. John Williams* (1837), an account of his collateral ancestor's life, which included an edition of *The Redeemed Captive*, the clergyman's famous narrative of his captivity by Indians. He also compiled the full and detailed *Genealogy and History of the Family of Williams in America* (1847). Invited to give the annual address to the Massachusetts Medical Society in 1842, Williams spoke on "A Medical History of the County of Franklin" (Massachusetts Medical Society, *Medical Communications* 7 [1848]: 1–76). An excellent work of local history with much biographical material, the essay led directly to his undertaking the work for which he is best known.

American Medical Biography (1845) continued the earlier two-volume work of the same title by James Thacher of Plymouth, Massachusetts, published in 1828. In addition to its historical purpose, the book aimed to demonstrate that physicians, though moving in a "humbler sphere," were no less worthy of notice than clergymen, lawyers, and statesmen, who were "more prominent actors on the theatre of life" (*American Medical Biography*, p. xiv). Williams's book covered a shorter period than Thacher's (essentially the fifteen years since Thacher published), contained fewer entries (110 to 168), and drew most of its subjects from New England and New York state, while the older work was more nearly a national selection. With endorsements from Thacher, the editors of the *Boston Medical and Surgical Journal* and the *American Journal of the Medical Sciences*, and other physicians and historians, Williams assembled biographical memoirs from the journals in his own library and from professional friends and colleagues. He wrote more than a dozen of the sketches himself. The biographies ranged in length from less than a page to more than twenty pages for outstanding figures such as surgeon Philip Syng Physick. They were uneven in quality, and almost none was edited with any rigor. Like most of Williams's published writings, *American Medical Biography* was a compilation rather than an original and critical study. Sales were disappointing—in three months only three copies were sold in Philadelphia—and no second volume was published. Nonetheless, the volume is a useful source of information about physicians of the second quarter of the century.

Williams was active in professional affairs. He was a councillor of the Massachusetts Medical Society for thirty-three years, and he was the society's delegate to the first meeting of the American Medical Association in 1847. He compiled, at the association's request, a "Report on the Indigenous Medical Botany of Massachusetts" (American Medical Association, *Transactions* 2 [1849]: 863–927) and wrote the association's first report on medical biography, thus inaugurating its practice of collecting and publishing biographies of prominent deceased physicians. He took a leading role in establishing the Franklin County Medical Society in 1851. His presidential address in 1852, on medical improvements and discoveries of the past half-century, noted particularly the dissemination of knowledge through the increasing number of professional journals (*New York Journal of Medicine*, n.s., 8 [1852]: 153–86).

For many years Williams suffered from angina; it forced him eventually to give up surgery. For reasons of health, Williams left Deerfield in 1853 to live with his son Dr. Edward Jenner Williams in Laona, Winnebago County, Illinois. Although he was "highly delighted" by the upper Mississippi Valley and enjoyed inspecting Indian mounds and "ponder[ing] over" Pontiac's rebellion in Detroit, the move from his ancestral home with its many personal and professional associations was a wrenching experience. Nonetheless he found subjects to engross his interest. "Although old," he wrote a friend, "I am still active and perform as much mental labor now, perhaps, as at any former period of my life" (*Philadelphia Medical and Surgical Journal* 4 [1855–1856]: 95). He was elected a member of the Wisconsin Medical Society; he compiled "A List of the Principal Medical Plants Enumerated by Botanists, and Known to be Growing in Northern Illinois and Wisconsin" (*North-Western Medical and Surgical Journal*, n.s., 4 [1855]: 49–70), and a few days before he died was preparing a Fourth of July address for Laona.

Williams's published writings may be described as botanical and historical taxonomy, collecting and describing the essential facts and phenomena others would use for broader and synthetic studies.

• A collection of Williams family papers, mostly of earlier generations than Stephen W. Williams's, is in the New-York Historical Society. The principal biographical sources are a sketch by "Plutarch" in a series of biographies, "Distinguished Living Physicians," in *Philadelphia Medical and Surgical Journal* 1 (1852): 81–84, 97–100, 113–16; James Deane's memoir in *Boston Medical and Surgical Journal* 53 (1855–1856): 29–32; and the sketch by Williams's daughter Helen M. Huntington (based on Williams's manuscript autobiography) in New England Historic Genealogical Society, *Memorial Biographies* 2 (1881): 389–97. A few additional data are included by Walter L. Burrage in Howard A. Kelly and Walter L. Burrage, eds., *Dictionary of American Medical Biography* (1928). Some Williams letters and other manuscripts, owned by the Heritage Foundation and the Pocomtuck Valley Memorial Association, both of Deerfield, were used by Whitfield J. Bell, Jr., in "Lives in Medicine: The Biographical Dictionaries of Thacher, Williams, and Gross," *Bulletin of the History of Medicine* 42 (1968): 101–20.

WHITFIELD J. BELL, JR.

WILLIAMS, Tennessee (26 Mar. 1911–24 Feb. 1983), playwright, poet, and writer of fiction, was born Thomas Lanier Williams in Columbus, Mississippi, the son of Cornelius Coffin Williams and Edwina Dakin. The circumstances of Tom Williams's birth speak volumes about his parents' relationship. In 1909 Edwina Williams had returned to Columbus to live with her parents, an Episcopal rector and his wife, rather than live with her temperamental, hard-drinking husband. (C. C. Williams, a traveling salesman, usually stayed with them on weekends.) The model for many of her son's characters, Edwina Williams played the role of southern belle more than was necessary, even in Ohio where she spent much of her adolescence. She also apparently had a distaste for sex, and her denial of what her husband saw as his connubial rights was one of the greatest sources of marital discord, particularly when he found sexual release elsewhere. C. C. Williams came from a good Tennessee family but hardly acted the southern aristocrat. In addition to his turbulent relationship with his wife, C. C. did not care much for his firstborn, Rose (born 1909), nor Tom, his second, whom he called "Miss Nancy." His affection was saved for his third child, Dakin (born 1919). The happiest times of Tom's youth were spent in his grandparents' rectory. In many ways, the Reverend Dakin was the central father figure for the young man, taking him to New York and Europe. And his beloved maternal grandmother later paid for the completion of his degree at the University of Iowa.

In 1918 the family moved to St. Louis, where Cornelius was made a sales manager at the International Shoe Company. The family moved from apartment to apartment, and the children endured their parents' battles and suffered mockery in the midwestern city for their exaggerated southern mannerisms. Rose became victim to increasingly irrational, sometimes violent fantasies. Tom found an outlet for fantasies and social dysfunction through writing, which became a vocation by the time he was a teenager. His first short story, "The Vengeance of Nitocris," was published by *Weird Tales* magazine when he was sixteen. From that point, his vocation was to be a writer, particularly a poet.

Tom entered the University of Missouri in 1929, hoping to major in journalism. He was not a distinguished student and failed in the one course his father, a veteran of the Spanish-American War, cared about, military science. Williams's innate inability to organize any aspect of his life was bound to hinder his ability to conform to military discipline. After a third year of undistinguished grades, C. C. pulled his son out of university and put him to work in a menial position at the International Shoe Company. There is some question as to whether this was really a result of Tom's mediocre academic performance or a matter of financial necessity. Though C. C. did not lose his job, the depression had affected the family's finances, and C. C. was not a man to sacrifice his pleasures for his children. He did fund a course for his son at Rubicam's Business College (immortalized in *The Glass Menagerie*), hoping that practical stenographic skills would be more effective than training in journalism in helping him find a steady job.

The years between the University of Missouri and Williams's move to Iowa City (1932–1937) were crucial, if in a negative way, for the creation of the man and the writer. Tom was miserable at his agonizingly dull job and stayed up most of the night writing, which was both a passion and an escape. His extreme anxiety attacks, which had begun on a trip to Europe with his grandfather in 1928, became more frequent. One cannot precisely ascertain the extent to which these attacks were a result of his repression of his homosexual desire. Later Williams claimed, probably accurately, to have remained a virgin until he was twenty-seven. Whatever their cause, the panics remained with him throughout his life and sustained his extreme hypochondria. They also motivated the behavior of many of his characters, particularly the terrified women he created, from Laura Wingfield to Blanche Dubois to Alexandra del Lago. Surviving one's terrors in "monster country" is one of the central subjects of Williams's work. Tom's sister, Rose, was not so fortunate as to have a creative outlet for her "blue devils" (as Williams called his panics). By the early 1930s she had been institutionalized for her increasingly frequent psychotic episodes. In 1943, after years in a state institution with no improvement, Rose was subjected to a prefrontal lobotomy. Rose's experience would also find its way into Williams's work: for instance, the horror of Blanche Dubois's institutionalization in *A Streetcar Named Desire* and the terrifying prospect of Catherine's lobotomy in *Suddenly Last Summer* ("Cut that hideous story out of her brain").

Williams audited courses at Washington University from 1935 to 1937, but the most important events of those years centered on his newfound love of theater. He joined a St. Louis amateur theatrical group, The Mummers, for which he wrote his first plays. In 1937 Williams entered the University of Iowa, a center for the training of writers, and studied with two of the most important teachers of playwriting of the time, E. C. Mabie and Elsworth P. Conkle. Mabie referred to Williams as "that pansy" and gave limited support to the shy young man, but Conkle offered generous advice and moral support. At the same time, in St. Louis, The Mummers produced Williams's *The Fugitive Kind*.

After receiving his degree in 1938, Williams began the itinerant life he was to continue to his death and that he would project onto many of his characters. His first stop was New Orleans, a city he loved and with which he has been identified. In his first brief visit, he finally had his first homosexual experience (he had his first and last affair with a woman at Iowa). It was the beginning of a life of obsessive sexual promiscuity, which also defines many of his characters, from Blanche Dubois and Alexandra del Lago to Sebastian Venable, the sexually voracious poet in *Suddenly Last Summer*. His travels took him from New Orleans to a California chicken ranch, but the next few years would be characterized by wanderings back and forth across the country and into Mexico. Eventually, when he had some financial success, he would buy a house in Key West, Florida, which would be his "home base," but domestic stability was something Williams would always flee.

While Tom was traveling, the Group Theatre's literary manager, Molly Day Thatcher (wife of director Elia Kazan, who would later direct Williams's most successful plays and films), announced in 1939 that Williams had won a "special award" for his one-act plays, collectively titled *American Blues*. Thatcher placed Williams's work in the hands of agent Audrey Wood, who would lovingly guide the major years of his career. The Group Theatre comprised the most important theatrical figures of the time, and several of them, directors Kazan and Harold Clurman, producer Cheryl Crawford, actor Karl Malden, would figure prominently in Williams's career. Williams had given himself a new name, Tennessee, to launch him in New York and, because of restrictions on the Group Theatre's award, a new birthdate, 1914. (Biographical accuracy was never Williams's strong point.) Oddly enough, his pen name connected him with his Tennessee-born father with whom he always had a strained relationship, but the name also defined Williams as a southern writer like William Faulkner, Carson McCullers, and his namesake, poet Sidney Lanier.

In 1939, in Taos, New Mexico, Williams met Frieda Lawrence and began his devotion to the works of her late husband, D. H. Lawrence, who became his primary influence. Williams identified strongly with Lawrence's life story, and Lawrence's obsession with sex as the primary human motivation and his insistent sexual imagery also became the hallmarks of Williams's work. Williams's goal became that of translating Lawrence's vision to the American stage. The fascination of aristocratic women with the raw sexual energy of the working-class stud was the center of *A Streetcar Named Desire*.

Williams's career as a Broadway playwright was temporarily launched by a $1,000 grant from the Rockefeller Foundation and an option on his play *Battle of Angels* by the most-prestigious producing organization, the Theatre Guild; the play was to be directed by the distinguished British director Margaret Webster and to star Miriam Hopkins. The production was a fiasco and closed during its Boston tryout (Dec. 1940). The novice playwright had no idea how to revise the play, the director had no experience with contemporary American drama, and the producer's choice of prim Boston as the place to launch this Lawrentian, southern Gothic epic of sexual desire and violence was misguided. Typically, Williams later rewrote this work. Renamed *Orpheus Descending*, it had a short Broadway run in 1957 but was turned into a hit film, *The Fugitive Kind* (1959), starring Marlon Brando and Anna Magnani.

During the summer of 1940 Williams had one of his few love affairs, a fraught, short-lived romance with a bisexual Canadian dancer, Kip Kiernan, whom Williams met in Provincetown, Massachusetts, which even then was a gay Mecca. By this time, Williams's sexual and social identity was established. He had already formed a close friendship with writer Donald Windham, with whom he would collaborate on *You Touched Me!* (1946), a dramatic adaptation of a Lawrence short story. During the 1940s Williams also became close friends with a group of literary figures: Jane and Paul Bowles, Carson McCullers, and the playwright William Inge.

After years of wanderings and a brief stint as a contract writer for Metro-Goldwyn-Mayer (MGM), Williams achieved artistic and commercial success with his dramatization of his St. Louis years, *The Glass Menagerie* (1945). This often-revived play is typical of Williams's best work in the way it shapes personal experience into circumstances having universal resonance and combines muted comedy with convincing pathos. Although the picture of Williams's mother, who as Amanda Wingfield is the central character of the play, is not totally flattering, Edwina Williams was not only delighted with being immortalized on stage, she was also made rich by the fact that her son gave her one-half of the proceeds from the play during her lifetime.

Williams was a late bloomer, not finding success until his late thirties, but the next decade and a half were the peak years of his career. Not all of his plays during that period were successful, but he nonetheless established himself as one of America's major dramatists with *A Streetcar Named Desire* (1947), *Summer and Smoke* (1948), *The Rose Tattoo* (1953), *Cat on a Hot Tin Roof* (1955), *Suddenly Last Summer* (1958), *Sweet Bird of Youth* (1959), and *The Night of the Iguana* (1961). Moreover, Williams's name—and fortune—were made by hit film versions of these plays and other works, such as *Baby Doll* (adapted from the short play "Twenty-seven Wagons Full of Cotton"), *The Roman Spring of Mrs. Stone* (from his 1950 novel), and *The Fugitive Kind*. In addition he wrote in this period his best short stories (such as "One Arm," "Desire and the Black Masseur," and "The Mysteries of the Joy Rio"), many on homosexual themes, and two volumes of poetry. The stories often were the first presentation of material that would later find its way into the plays. His most successful stage productions and film adaptations were those in which he collaborated with director Elia Kazan (*Streetcar* [stage and screen], *Cat*, *Sweet Bird of Youth*, *Baby Doll*).

Williams's best works are brilliant poetic projections of his own obsessions. His greatest characters are eccentric outcasts usually because their sexual desires put them at odds with conventional society. "Desire" is the central word in Williams's work, but desire is not simply lust; it is a yearning to attain, through sex, some psychological and spiritual state that is always unattainable. "The opposite of death is desire," Blanche Dubois cries in *A Streetcar Named Desire*. When Williams's heroines and heroes yearn for "life," they mean a union of physical and spiritual fulfillment. It is apt that the object of desire of one of his heroes is named Heavenly (*Sweet Bird of Youth*). What leads to the often violent destruction of Williams's central characters is not merely the agents of social and sexual order, but a violent cosmology, most cogently defined in the imagery of *Suddenly Last Summer*, in which the vision of birds of prey rapaciously feeding on baby turtles in the Galapagos Islands becomes the face of God. Williams's plays are filled with violence—castration, cannibalism, various forms of physical and psychological mutilation—and in his best work it gives form to his lurid, highly personal vision of experience.

During the period from 1948 until the late 1950s Williams was sustained personally and professionally by his relationship with Frank Merlo. Williams's promiscuity was a bone of contention between them, and as his dependence on alcohol and a variety of drugs grew during the 1950s, his erratic wanderings around the world and his increasingly bizarre coterie of hangers-on strained his relationship with Merlo to the breaking point. They separated years before Merlo died of lung cancer in 1963, but the guilt and grief elicited by Merlo's death signaled the end of what was left of Williams's personal and artistic control. His dogged persistence at writing despite the commercial failures and critical brickbats was a heroic counterpart to the personal behavior, which reached its nadir when his brother had him institutionalized in 1969. The combination of drugs, most prescribed or injected by irresponsible doctors, and large amounts of alcohol led to intense paranoia and threats of suicide. However, the St. Louis sanatorium's draconian regime of total, immediate withdrawal from drugs led to two heart attacks and convulsions. Williams wrote his brother out of his will as soon as he was let out of the hospital.

Williams never stopped writing during the last two decades of his life, but the output was erratic and often incoherent. Many of his later plays were produced either on or off Broadway. *Small Craft Warnings* (1971) had a reasonable run off-Broadway, in part because Williams appeared in it on occasion, but those appearances were typical of the late Williams: he undermined his own play by forgetting lines and ad-libbing, thus sabotaging the performances of the other actors and the continuity of the play. Williams became a sad public figure, confessing his private life in his *Memoirs* (1972), his novel *Moise and the World of Reason* (1975), and numerous public appearances. His circle of friends was dominated by paid companions (he was terrified of being alone) and cynical parasites.

Yet there are moments of greatness in his uneven later work. The first version of *The Milk Train Doesn't Stop Here Anymore* (1963; rewritten and given a disastrous production, directed by Tony Richardson and starring Tallulah Bankhead, in 1964 and adapted into a miscast, grotesque film, *Boom* [1968]) contains a powerful depiction of the author's mental and spiritual state at the time. In 1995 it had a successful revival at the Citizen's Theatre, Glasgow, where actor Rupert Everett played Mrs. Goforth, the play's eccentric "heroine." In 1996 the same director revived Williams's most problematic play, *In the Bar of a Tokyo Hotel* (1969). It may be too facile to see the later works as the outpourings of a drug-addled mind and not consider that Williams was always a theatrical experimentalist at odds with the dominant mode of theatrical realism and that his later work moved beyond what conservative Broadway audiences and critics understood. Lyle Leverich claims rightly that Williams "was never able to reconcile the diametric pull in being both a poet *and* a playwright," and in the later works, the poet dominates. Coherent narrative was never Williams's forte, and in many of the later plays it does not even seem to be a concern. Along with Edward Albee and William Inge, Williams also was subjected to a barrage of homophobic criticism in the 1960s, which limited the chances of Broadway success. Williams's career was tied to the Broadway theater, which by the mid-1960s was no longer the center for serious drama in America. Because there was no Broadway audience for works like *The Red Devil Battery Sign* (1975) or *Clothes for a Summer Hotel* (1980) did not mean that they would not have earned an appreciative audience elsewhere. The later works deserve revival and study, but they simply are not the masterpieces Williams wrote before 1961.

Williams died in a New York City hotel room from choking on the plastic cap of a pill bottle. As the culmination of years of personal and artistic deterioration, his death was grotesquely apt. Yet he remains justly celebrated as a daring, poetic playwright who, at his best, could capture on stage a haunting personal vision. The power of his most-realized works has made them part of the standard repertory throughout the world. Williams is also one of twentieth-century America's most important sexual revolutionaries whose highly popular works stretched the boundaries of what could be shown and discussed on the stage and screen.

• The largest collection of Williams's papers, journals, and manuscripts is housed at the Harry Ransom Humanities Research Center at the University of Texas at Austin. Some of Williams's most revealing letters can be found in *Tennessee Williams's Letters to Donald Windham, 1940–1965*, ed. Donald Windham (1977). Several biographies have been published. The most exhaustive is the two-volume biography by the official biographer, Lyle Leverich, *Tom: The Unknown Tennessee Williams* (1995) and *Tennessee*. Donald Spoto's *The Kindness of Strangers: The Life of Tennessee Williams* (1985) is well written and generally reliable. Various family members, friends, and companions have written more subjective memoirs of varying reliability. See, for example, Donald Windham's scathing account of Williams's self-destructive later years, *Lost Friendships* (1989). The most reliable critical study is contained in volume two of C. W. E. Bigsby's *A Critical Introduction to Twentieth Century American Drama: 1900–1940* (1982). More contemporary interpretations can be found in David Savran's *Communists, Cowboys, and Queers: The Politics of Masculinity in Arthur Miller and Tennessee Williams* (1989) and John M. Clum's *Acting Gay: Male Homosexuality in Modern Drama* (1992). A good sampling of critical approaches to Williams's work can be found in *The Cambridge Companion to Tennessee Williams* (1997). An obituary is in the *New York Times*, 26 Feb. 1983.

JOHN M. CLUM

WILLIAMS, Tex (23 Aug. 1917–11 Oct. 1985), musician, was born Sollie Paul Williams in Ramsey, Illinois. His parents' names are unknown. Williams had polio as an infant, which left him with a slight limp. He learned to play the guitar at age five, and by the time he was age thirteen he had his own one-man band and vocal show, playing banjo and harmonica, on WJBL in Decatur, Illinois. Williams attended high school in Bingham, Illinois, and began touring through the United States, Canada, and Mexico with hillbilly and western groups during his teens. In Washington, D.C., Williams joined the six-piece Reno Racketeers, and they became his backup band when he moved to San Francisco.

In 1939 Williams moved south to Hollywood, where he continued to play country music and also began to appear in films, usually in the role of a band member; his musical and cinematic careers progressed side by side for the next decade. By 1940 Williams, who was calling himself Jack, had joined Cal Shrum's Rhythm Rangers, with whom he appeared in Tex Ritter's Monogram movie *Rollin' Home to Texas* (1945). A few years later he joined Spade Cooley's band as a sideman and lead vocalist and sang with the band on the Columbia Records hit "Shame on You," which went to number one on the country chart in 1945. The same year Williams appeared with Cooley's band in *Outlaws of the Rockies*, part of the Durango Kid series.

In 1946 Williams formed his own twelve-piece group, the Western Caravan. This band was one of many "western swing" orchestras popular in the 1940s, especially in California. Western swing had a silkier sound than most country music and, with its large lineups (the Western Caravan even included a harp at one point), was closer to pop music of the period. The Western Caravan's first release, "The Rose of the Alamo" (1945), sold 250,000 copies. In 1947 Williams, who was then known as "Tex," signed a contract with Universal-International to make a series of musical shorts. Fifteen two- and three-reel shorts were made, some of which were spliced together in 1950 and 1951 to make feature films, including *Tales of the West* (1950).

Capitol Records, then in its infancy, signed Williams and the Western Caravan in 1946, and the following year he had his first and most lasting hit: "Smoke! Smoke! Smoke! (That Cigarette)." A novelty song written with Merle Travis and featuring Williams half singing and half talking, "Smoke!" went to the top of the country and pop charts and was Capitol's first million-selling record. In the next three years, Williams had a string of hits on the country and pop charts, including "That's What I Like about the West" (1947), "Don't Telephone, Don't Telegraph, Tell a Woman" (1948), "Life Gits Tee-Jus, Don't It?" (1948), and "Bluebird on Your Windowsill" (1949).

These hit songs guaranteed the band's success, and the Western Caravan toured to packed halls and ballrooms around the country. In the late 1940s and early 1950s, the band performed five nights a week at the Riverside Rancho or at Williams's own club, Tex Williams Village, in Newhall, California. Williams and his band played on the leading radio and television shows, including the "Grand Ole Opry," "Gene Autry's Melody Ranch," "National Barn Dance," and "Midwestern Hayride." Williams also became the first president of the Academy of Country and Western Music.

In the 1950s, Williams recorded for Decca, and in the 1960s he had his own show, "Riverside Rancho," which was broadcast on NBC. In 1965, no longer able to work every night, Williams disbanded the Western Caravan. However, the same year he signed with Boone Records and recorded a few more midlevel hits, "Too Many Tigers" and "Big Tennessee." In 1968 he recorded a new version of "Smoke! Smoke! Smoke!" His last two top thirty hits were "The Night Miss Nancy Ann's Hotel for Single Girls Burned Down" (Monument, 1970) and "Those Lazy, Hazy, Crazy Days of Summer" (Granite, 1974), a song recorded by Nat King Cole in 1963. His last album, for the Garu label, was issued in 1981.

Williams was married to Dallas Orr, with whom he had one child. He died in Newhall, California.

• There are entries on Williams in Nick Tosches's *Country: The Biggest Music in America* (1977) and Barry McCloud's *Definitive Country: The Ultimate Encyclopedia of Country Music and Its Performers* (1995). An obituary is in the *New York Times*, 13 Oct. 1985.

BETHANY NEUBAUER

WILLIAMS, Thomas Harry (19 May 1909–6 July 1979), historian and biographer, was born in Vinegar Hill, Illinois, the son of William D. Williams, a school teacher, farmer, and lead miner, and Emma Necollins. After attending the common schools of Wisconsin, Williams earned his bachelor's degree from Platteville State Teachers College in 1931, his master's degree in 1932, and his doctorate in history in 1937 from the University of Wisconsin. He taught briefly at the University of Wisconsin and the University of Omaha. In 1941 he accepted a position at Louisiana State University, where in 1953 he was appointed to the Boyd Professorship of History, a post he held until he retired in 1979. He married Helen M. Jenson in 1937; they were later divorced. In 1952 he married Estelle Skolfield; they had one child.

Williams was a brilliant and prolific scholar. A revision of his doctoral dissertation was published under the title *Lincoln and the Radicals* (1941) and established him as a leading Civil War historian. For the first time, attention was given to the conflict between Lincoln and the Radical Republicans. Thereafter, the study of Lincoln biography and Civil War history was changed. Williams portrayed the figures of the Civil War in colorful language, which made the book popular, but he was criticized as a revisionist by the consensus historians for doing so.

In 1952 Williams published *Lincoln and His Generals*, which further enhanced his reputation as a Civil War historian and became a Book-of-the-Month-Club selection. His sparkling prose gained a nonprofessional readership as well as the respect of professional historians. He stressed that Lincoln was, indeed, a great war leader and that Grant was a better general than Lee. He also held that Lincoln was a better strategist than any of his generals and designated the Civil War as the first modern war. Subsequently, he published other articles and monographs in the field. Among these were *The Union Sundered* (1962), *The Union Restored* (1963), and two volumes of the writings of Lincoln: *Abraham Lincoln: Selected Speeches and Messages* (1957) and *Selected Writings and Speeches of Abraham Lincoln* (1963). He also contributed analyses such as *Abraham Lincoln: Principles and Pragmatism* (1953) and *Lincoln the Commander in Chief* (1957). In 1955 he published the biography *P. T. G. Beauregard: Napoleon in Gray*, which went through six editions. The flamboyant Beauregard may well have been Williams's favorite Civil War character. He also had an interest in

Rutherford B. Hayes that led to his publishing *Hayes of the Twenty Third: The Civil War Volunteer Officer* (1964) and *Hayes: The Diary of a President, 1875–1881* (1965).

Gradually, Williams shifted his interest to twentieth-century politics. Here he contributed two general volumes: *Trends in Southern Politics* (1960) and *Essays in Recent Southern Politics* (1970). Ultimately, his reputation for this period lay in his research on Huey Long. He edited *Every Man a King: The Autobiography of Huey Long* (1964) and wrote *The Gentleman from Louisiana* (1960) and *Huey, Lyndon, and Southern Radicalism* (1973). He became best known for his massive biography *Huey Long* (1969), which went through seven editions and in 1970 was given both the National Book Award and the Pulitzer Prize in History. At the time of his death Williams was working on a biography of Lyndon Johnson.

Williams was something of a pioneer in his work on Huey Long in that he used the method of oral history more widely than had any historian before him. Historians had long used eyewitness accounts as well as the testimony of persons close to the subject at hand. In fact, the method had been polished and made respectable by Allan Nevins of Columbia University a generation before Williams. But as Williams pointed out, although the method was not new, the technology of the tape recorder was, making widespread interviews possible. He also noted that oral history became essential as technology such as the telephone made letter writing less common. For his work on Huey Long he interviewed more than 300 people who knew the colorful politician.

Williams received many honors for his scholarship, including a Guggenheim Fellowship in 1957. He was also the Harmsworth Professor of American History at Oxford University in 1966–1967. His courses at Louisiana State University were always popular. Indeed the last undergraduate course that he taught before his retirement brought an enrollment of 350. At the end of each of his courses it was usual for the students to give him a standing ovation. He was the mentor for thirty-six graduate students who received the Ph.D. degree. He was president of the Southern Historical Association in 1958–1959 and of the Organization of American Historians in 1972–1973. He died in Baton Rouge, Louisiana.

Williams loved conversation that was an extension of his teaching. Whether in the departmental offices at Louisiana State, the corridors of hotels at national conventions of historical societies, or at social gatherings in his own home, he liked nothing so much as a good conversation. As befits a good historian, he loved to clear up fuzzy thinking whether of the undergraduate history major or the eminent colleague.

• Williams's collected papers are in the Department of Archives and Manuscripts of the Troy H. Middleton Library, Louisiana State University, Baton Rouge. See Peggy Ann Brock, "An Exclusive Interview with T. Harry Williams," *Writer's Digest*, Sept. 1970, pp. 26–27, 35–38; and Joseph G. Dawson, "Remembering T. Harry Williams," *Civil War History*, Sept. 1980, pp. 267–69. Obituaries are in the *New York Times*, 7 July 1979, the *American Historical Review* 85 (Fall 1980): 283–84, and the *Journal of Southern History* 55 (Nov. 1979): 635–37.

DONALD F. TINGLEY

WILLIAMS, Walter (2 July 1864–29 July 1935), founder of the world's first separate professional school of journalism, was born in Boonville, Missouri, the son of Marcus Williams, a contractor, pottery owner, and ferry operator, and Mary Jane Littlepage. Williams began his newspaper career as a printer's devil on the *Boonville Topic*. A graduate of the local high school at age fifteen, Williams gave the valedictory address. His formal education ended at that point. Within five years of graduating Williams was the local editor of the *Topic*. By 1884 he was editor of the competing *Advertiser*, and by 1889, at age twenty-five, he became the youngest president of the Missouri Press Association (MPA).

In late 1889 Williams moved to Columbia, Missouri, to take an editorial position on the *Herald*, "one of the largest and most influential journals in the West." He made numerous content and format changes and soon became part owner. Williams earned international recognition in 1904 when he was the superintendent of publicity in charge of the World's Press Parliament at the St. Louis World's Fair. This event attracted 5,000 delegates, including 300 newspapermen from Europe. All states as well as forty countries were represented. Later Williams presided over gatherings of the Press Congress of the World in Switzerland, Washington, D.C., San Francisco, Hawaii, and Mexico. He traveled the world, planting seeds of journalism education, especially in the Orient.

Williams's contacts through the state press organization and the World's Fair project made him one of the best known of Missouri's editors. He used his position to press for the establishment of a school of journalism in the state. Some opposition was voiced from traditionalists who believed one learned newspapering only in the backshop. Williams continued to preach to his fellow newspapermen the significance of their profession, one that "wielded influence on the destinies of the state" and could influence "the thoughts of people toward better government, cleaner being, and more active citizenship." In a world-famous creed, he stated, "I believe that the public journal is a public trust; that all connected with it are, to the full measure of their responsibility, trustees for the public; that acceptance of a lesser service than the public service is betrayal of this trust." He considered journalism to be patriotic and when it "succeeds best . . . fears God and honors man." He thought journalism should rank with the legal, medical, and educational professions, considering the writers' potential in reaching and influencing the public minds.

Throughout the planning stages for the school, MPA members were active. Several editors, including Williams, were on the university's board of curators as well as its executive committee, which made major decisions. Some journalism courses had been offered in 1877 and a series of newspaper topics had been presented in 1905–1906, but it was not until 14 September 1908 that the School of Journalism officially opened. Williams had accepted the deanship on 2 April 1908, with some reluctance; the pay, $3,300 a year, was less than his previous income. Williams's initial faculty, Charles Ross and Silas Bent, came from the press. Ross had worked for the *St. Louis Republic* and later joined the *St. Louis Post-Dispatch* and eventually became press secretary for President Harry Truman; Bent had been with St. Louis, Louisville, Chicago, and New York newspapers. Frank Lee Martin, who became the second dean in 1935, came from the *Kansas City Star*.

Williams's first curriculum included ten courses for sixty-four students. There were six women in the class, including Mary Paxton Keeley, who in 1910 became the first woman journalism school graduate. Williams's "History & Principles of Journalism" course, required of all students, continued to be offered, although under a different name, long after his death. Among other courses were newspaper administration, comparative journalism, newspaper making, advertising and publishing, copy reading, and newspaper correspondents. There was also a course in magazine making. Williams sought to acquaint students with the "languages" of other specialized professions. To that end, he had professors from other campus units provide lectures in their areas, such as law. Williams insisted the school be "coordinate in rank with the departments of Law, Medicine, and other Professional Schools." This separated the Missouri program from earlier ones in other schools—often they were departments, not schools, at times under control of an English department. Williams demanded that all students take 75 percent of their courses in the arts and sciences, creating the "Missouri Plan" that continues today.

Williams called for "adequate laboratory equipment for practical journalistic training." This included the student-produced newspaper, the *Missourian*, designed to serve not only the campus but the entire community. This set Missouri apart from programs that utilized only on-campus publications for laboratory training.

By 1910 Williams had established what became known as Journalism Week, a program that brought leading media personalities to the campus. In 1930 the school established its Medal of Honor to recognize achievement by media leaders as well as by periodicals and, in later years, radio and television personalities and stations.

In 1907 and again in 1926 Williams had been considered for the presidency of the University of Missouri and beginning in April 1930 served in that capacity while retaining the deanship of the School of Journalism. He knew the administrative role, having been on the board of curators for ten years and dean for twenty-two years. His appointment was "given general approval and wide publicity," although some noted he was the "only college president who never went to college."

Serving during the Great Depression, Williams nevertheless called for a campus building program, higher salaries to keep top faculty members, more efficiency and financial support for the university, and a spirit of cooperation and goodwill within the faculty, along with more student body loyalty to the institution and more alumni support. He turned to the press to inform the public about the needs of the university. In the midst of financial straits, Williams took a pay cut, from $12,500 to $10,000. He helped the School of Law establish a five-year program and pushed for the reinstatement of the School of Medicine curriculum. Calling on his own background, Williams urged more travel and study abroad for the faculty. He helped to establish a journalism school at Yengching University in China. He enjoyed athletics and supported the school's programs but objected to subsidizing them, a situation then becoming more widespread. He retired in 1935 due to ill health and later died in Columbia.

In 1892 Williams had married Hulda Harned, the daughter of a planter in the Boonville area. They had three children before her death. In 1927 Williams married Sara Lockwood, a member of the faculty; they had no children. Williams was described as a "devoted family man," active in the work of the Presbyterian church. He once taught what he claimed to be "the world's largest Bible class" and at times edited church publications.

Throughout his life Williams maintained close contacts with his former students, visiting many as he traveled about the world. Hundreds of them had gained editorial positions with many of the leading newspapers of the day. Williams's influence was spread about the media world by these students and by the thousands who have followed the Missouri Plan and his Journalist's Creed.

• Official records of Williams's career as dean and later president of the University of Missouri are in the institution's files in Columbia. Other materials are located in the Western Historical Manuscript Collection, Columbia. Telegrams, letters, and editorials were collected in book form, *In Memoriam, Walter Williams, 1864–1935*, as a University of Missouri Bulletin (1935). Williams edited *History of Northeast Missouri* (1913); *History of Northwest Missouri* (1915); and *Missouri: Mother of the West* (1930), with F. C. Shoemaker. He collected the talks presented at the Press Congress of the World meetings and published them in books. His Columbia newspaper, the *Herald*, and some of the Boonville newspapers are on file at the State Historical Society of Missouri in Columbia. Frank W. Rucker, a former student of Williams and later part owner of the *Independence (Mo.) Examiner*, wrote a biography, *Walter Williams* (1964). See also William H. Taft, "Establishing the School of Journalism," *Missouri Historical Review* 84 (Oct. 1989): 63–83, and *Missouri Newspapers* (1964). An obituary is in the *St. Louis Post-Dispatch*, 29 July 1935.

WILLIAM H. TAFT

WILLIAMS, Walter Long (26 Feb. 1856–23 Oct. 1945), veterinarian, scientist, and educator, was born on a farm near Argenta, Illinois, the son of Jackson Williams and Lavina Long, farmers. He attended Illinois Industrial University (now the University of Illinois at Urbana-Champaign) from January 1875 until June 1877. Studying in the School of Agriculture, he took veterinary courses for farmers taught by Frederick W. Prentice, and therein found his life's work. Leaving the university because he could no longer afford it, he worked on his father's farm until the fall of 1878, when he left to study at the Montreal Veterinary College (MVC). There he encountered Duncan McEachran, a pioneering veterinary educator, and William Osler, the professor of the institutes of medicine at McGill University, who taught MVC students pathology, physiology, and parasitology. From McEachran, Williams learned that veterinarians could be scientists; from Osler, he learned the importance of correlating clinical signs with pathological findings. In 1879 Williams received the MVC diploma and the Province of Quebec's silver medal for best performance in the written and oral examinations.

Williams returned to Illinois and established a practice in Bloomington, a center of draft horse breeding and sales. In 1886 he married Mary E. Wilkinson, with whom he would have five children. The horse industry was large enough to permit Williams to make a good living and varied enough for him to obtain in depth clinical experience. He focused on the scientific study of equine reproductive diseases. While in Bloomington, he was the first in North America to diagnose, dourine, an equine venereal disease, and he studied abortion in mares for the federal Bureau of Animal Industry. He also served as assistant state veterinarian (1874–1891).

In 1891 a severe illness forced Williams to retire from full-time practice. He then obtained a position teaching veterinary medicine to agricultural students at Purdue University in West Lafayette, Indiana. His stay there was short and unhappy because he felt that the faculty and students had too little interest in science and too much in football. Williams soon left West Lafayette, and in 1893 he began to teach at the newly founded Montana Agricultural College (now Montana State University) in Bozeman and to conduct research at the Montana Agricultural Experiment Station. Teaching undergraduates human anatomy and physiology as well as veterinary medicine, Williams enjoyed his new home and the opportunities to study unfamiliar types of animal diseases. He won over ranchers—at first skeptical of a white-coated Easterner—and the college's faculty and administration, but his accidental damaging of laboratory equipment outraged the director of the Experiment Station, and his forthright support of evolutionary theory alienated some citizens. As a consequence, Williams applied in 1895 for a professorship at the New York State Veterinary College at Cornell University, then being organized. His application was successful in spite of the fact he had neither a college nor a veterinary degree. In 1896, when the new veterinary college admitted its first students, he moved to Ithaca. He soon found that the Cornell faculty were as committed to teaching and to the study of animal disease as he was. A good relationship with his director and Cornell's tolerance of outspoken professors contributed to his productive and happy career there.

Despite chronic ill health and Ithaca's harsh winters, Williams taught, researched, and practiced at Cornell for fifty years. With director James Law, he introduced structured clinical teaching with active student participation into the North American veterinary school curriculum. Before that time veterinary students had received little clinical training beyond observing cases with their teachers (who were not paid to teach and had to practice as well) or with their hometown veterinarians. This was an economical way of teaching, but students graduated with a limited and unsystematic knowledge of clinical medicine. Williams, a salaried professor like the rest of the Cornell veterinary faculty, was not dependent on a veterinary practice to earn a living and had time to prepare clinics that taught students systematically and in depth. His energetic and enthusiastic instruction created a generation of clinical teachers and researchers at veterinary schools throughout the United States, Canada, and Europe.

As a veterinary clinical scientist, Williams had no peer in North America and perhaps not in the world, especially in regard to reproduction in horses and cattle. He conducted fundamental studies of such subjects as genital diseases, teratology (the study of fetal malformations), infectious abortion, and convulsions during birth or pregnancy. In addition to publishing scores of scientific articles, he synthesized his clinical experience and research in two textbooks, *Veterinary Obstetrics* (1917) and *Diseases of the Genital Organs of Domestic Animals* (1921), both of which found international audiences. Although his knowledge of the field was unequaled, it was his approach to animal reproduction that was original and that earned him international respect. An anonymous French reviewer of *Veterinary Obstetrics* noted that obstetrics for Williams and his school comprised not merely the diagnosis and treatment of accidents related to reproduction and birth, but also included pathology based on a thorough knowledge of anatomy and physiology. Although the complex science of equine and bovine reproduction was intrinsically interesting to Williams, he did not pursue science for its own sake. His work had, as he often pointed out, large economic consequences for the agricultural, meat-packing, and transportation industries.

At Cornell Williams invented an operating table with electrically driven positioning devices for large animals that eased the administration of anesthesia, reduced the risk of bruises and fractures, and improved the application of aseptic and antiseptic procedures. Veterinary schools, the U.S. Army, and many practitioners quickly adopted his design. Williams also invented a number of surgical techniques that became standard worldwide. Among them were operations for roaring (defective, noisy breathing in horses and mules) and for poll evil, a muscular inflammation of horses. Both techniques, easily learned by practicing veterinarians, restored valuable work animals to production and in some cases reduced their mortality.

Williams was president of the U.S. Veterinary Medical Association (now the American Veterinary Medical Association), the Illinois State Veterinary Association, and the New York State Veterinary Medical Society. He also became an honorary member of veterinary associations in France, England, and Sweden. For twenty-two years he was associate editor of *American Veterinary Review*, and for three the U.S. editor for the *Veterinary Journal* (London) (1906–1908). He also published more than 250 articles on the veterinary profession, education, and ethics. After his retirement in 1921 he remained active, publishing articles and revising his textbooks until he was eighty-seven. He died in Ithaca, New York.

• Papers relating to Williams are in the archives of Cornell University, Ithaca, N.Y., and of Montana State University, Bozeman. Representative publications are "Maladie du coit," *American Veterinarian Review* 12 (1888–1889): 295–302, 341–49, 402–10, 445–50; "The Therapeutics of Colic," *American Veterinary Review* 19 (1894–1895): 457–73; *Glanders*, Bulletin No. 4, Montana Agricultural Experiment Station (1894); "Clinical Observations on Roaring," *American Veterinary Review* 25 (1901–1902): 811–15; "Bovine Infectious Abortion: Some Laboratory Findings and Conclusions Which Puzzle the Practitioner," *Journal of the American Veterinary Medicine Association* 64 (1923–1924): 154–67; and "State Medicine and Free Veterinary Clinics," *North American Veterinarian* 21 (1940): 593–96. His iconoclastic memoir, "Recollections of and Reflections upon Sixty-Five Years in the Veterinary Profession," appeared in *Cornell Veterinarian* 35 (1945): 167–90, 231–69 and an obituary by J. N. Frost appeared in *Cornell Veterinarian* 36 (1946): 100–3. Ellis Pierson Leonard provides accounts of Williams's career at Cornell in *A Cornell Heritage: Veterinary Medicine, 1868–1908* (1979) and *In the James Law Tradition, 1908–1948* (1982). On Williams's scientific work see Leon Saunders, "From Osler to Olafson: The Evolution of Veterinary Pathology in North America," *Canadian Journal of Veterinary Research* 51 (1987): 1–26; Saunders, "In Ever Widening Circles: Osler's Influence on Veterinary Medicine in Sweden," *Canadian Veterinary Journal* 34 (1993): 431–35; and *A Biographical History of Veterinary Pathology* (1996).

PHILIP M. TEIGEN

WILLIAMS, William (June? 1727–27 Apr. 1791), novelist and painter, was baptized on 14 June 1727 in Bristol, England, the son of William Williams, probably a mariner, and Elizabeth (Belshire?). As a boy Williams attended the Bristol Grammar School, but his preferred classroom seems to have been a local artist's studio, where he began to develop his interest in painting as a profession. Williams's parents had more practical plans for their son, however, and when Williams was perhaps sixteen or seventeen years old, he was bound as an apprentice to a captain in the Virginia trade. This arrangement proved to be short lived. Dissatisfied with his appointed career, Williams abandoned his position at the earliest convenience and fled to the West Indies. Many years later the renowned artist Benjamin West, who knew Williams intimately, quoted him as saying, "After going the second voyage . . . when in Norfolk, in Virginia—to tell you the truth . . . I left the ship & sailed for the West Indies, where I hoped to be unknown, that I might work my way to some places—& accomplish my wishes as a Painter." West was of the impression that his friend "was shipwrecked, & thrown into great difficulties, but Providence . . . preserved him through a variety of dangers." Although no documentary evidence has surfaced to corroborate this version of Williams's sojourn in the West Indies, the fact that his novel *Mr. Penrose: The Journal of Penrose, Seaman* recounts vividly and with apparent fidelity to environmental details the adventures of a castaway on the Mosquito Coast suggests that Williams may indeed have based the novel on firsthand experience.

In 1747, after two to three years in the Caribbean (of which possibly one to two years were spent among the Rama Indians of Nicaragua), Williams journeyed to Philadelphia, where he earned his living as a painter of portraits, landscapes, and conversation pieces. There he met West, at that time a precocious nine-year-old boy. Williams, the first professional artist West had ever met, encouraged the boy's interest in painting; lent him some books about the Old Masters, including his own manuscript "Lives of the Painters"; and instructed him over the next decade in the art of painting. So significant an influence was Williams as teacher and mentor to his young protégé that West later remarked that he would not have become a painter had Williams not come to live in Philadelphia.

In addition to painting, Williams taught drawing and music in an evening school he established for the instruction of "polite youth." Somewhat later, in 1759, he painted scenes in the Southwark Theatre for the Hallam Company, managed by David Douglas, thereby becoming the first known professional scene painter in American theater. The versatile artist took up the pen as well as the brush during these years, composing poetry in addition to his biographical sketches of Old World painters. It was also most likely at this time that he began to write *Mr. Penrose*.

Shortly after settling in Philadelphia, Williams married "a respectable townswoman" (name unknown), with whom he had two children, but she died within a decade of marriage. In 1757 Williams reportedly wed Mary Mare, who added a third child to the family in 1759 (William Williams, Jr., also a painter), but she passed away four years later. In 1760 Williams journeyed to Jamaica and possibly Antigua, where he hoped to commission portraits from wealthy planters. The trip was apparently a success: during fourteen months in the West Indies he is thought to have executed some fifty-four paintings. After returning to Philadelphia Williams resumed his business of "painting in general" and again supplemented his income by teaching. Several of Williams's surviving canvases date from this period, including portraits of William, David, and Deborah Hall, children of David Hall, Sr., the printing partner of Benjamin Franklin. One of Williams's most profitable undertakings, however, was the painting and ornamentation of ships for Philadelphia shipbuilders Thomas Penrose and James Penrose, quite likely the namesakes of Williams's protagonist Lewellin Penrose.

By 1769 Williams had moved from Philadelphia to New York, where he continued to paint and teach as well as clean and restore paintings. Several portraits from this period survive, including those of Jacob Fox, John Wiley and his sisters, and Master Stephen Crossfield, as well as his striking *Imaginary Landscape*. With the economic recession of the prewar years Williams's business declined, however. The revolutionary war brought additional hardships, including the deaths in battle of Williams's two sons from his first marriage. (Although Williams was a Loyalist, his sons fought for American independence.) Bereft and financially insecure, Williams returned to England in 1776, accepting an offer of patronage from a gentleman in Bedfordshire (identity unknown). When his patron died after eighteen months of sponsorship, Williams found himself alone and lacking means of financial support. With only one friend in England, he paid a visit to his former pupil Benjamin West, by this time a prominent artist living in London. Williams declined monetary assistance from West but consented to work for him as a model. (A likeness of Williams appears in West's celebrated painting *Battle of La Hogue*.)

Williams moved to Bristol, England, about 1781 and once again set up business as a painter. Among his works from this period are a local river scene titled *Hotwells and Rownham Ferry* and a triptych representing the birth, death, and burial of Christ. Williams married a third time, but his new wife, a widow named Esther, died shortly thereafter. Impoverished and by this time quite elderly, the painter, desiring a "place to die in," sought assistance from Thomas Eagles, a wealthy Bristolian merchant and patron of the arts. Eagles befriended Williams, provided him with discreet but regular financial support, and eventually secured shelter for him at the Merchants' and Sailors' Almshouse of Bristol. Williams was a pensioner of this charitable establishment for five years, during which he continued to paint until his death in Bristol. His fascinating self-portrait dates from this period (intriguingly, X rays reveal that the palette and brush the subject holds are painted over an earlier depiction of book and pen), and he evidently worked on a painting, now lost, with a theme from *Mr. Penrose*.

Although Williams's work is not widely known, his contributions to the literature and art of the colonial period are substantial. Williams was one of the first portraitists in the American colonies, and his novel *Mr. Penrose: The Journal of Penrose, Seaman* is probably the first novel to be written in what would become the United States of America. Although only a small fraction of the more than 240 canvases Williams reportedly completed in the American colonies and West Indies have been identified, those that have been positively attributed to him bear witness to a significant artistic talent, characterized by a distinctive sense of theatricality and a penchant for fantastic, dreamlike landscapes. Williams's influence on American literature was minimal due to the fact that his novel was not published until 1815 and then only in England and in a completely restyled form. In fact, Williams was almost wholly unknown to literary scholars until the much belated publication of the original text of *Mr. Penrose* in 1969. As a result, literary critics and historians have only recently begun to appreciate the importance of this early American tale of a Welsh sailor, "accustom'd," as he says, "to all Vice except Murder and Theft," who learns compassion and tolerance among the natives of Central America.

• The manuscript of *Mr. Penrose: The Journal of Penrose, Seaman* is housed in the Lilly Library of the University of Indiana at Bloomington, which also contains some of Williams's correspondence and letters concerning the authenticity and publication of *Mr. Penrose*. David Howard Dickason, *William Williams: Novelist and Painter of Colonial America* (1970), is an important source of biographical information as well as criticism of Williams's literary and artistic works. One of Dickason's key sources of biographical data was a letter from Benjamin West to Thomas Eagles, published in *Winterthur Portfolio* 6 (1970): 128–33. E. P. Richardson offers another interpretation of Williams's life and work in "William Williams—A Dissenting Opinion," *American Art Journal* 4 (1972): 5–23. See also James Thomas Flexner, *First Flowers of Our Wilderness* (1947); William H. Gerdts, "William Williams: New American Discoveries," *Winterthur Portfolio* 4 (1968): 159–67; and Richardson, *American Paintings and Related Pictures in the Henry Francis du Pont Winterthur Museum* (1986).

SARAH WADSWORTH

WILLIAMS, William (18 Mar. 1731–2 Aug. 1811), Connecticut patriot and signer of the Declaration of Independence, was born in Lebanon, Connecticut, the son of the Reverend Solomon Williams, pastor of the First Church in Lebanon and Mary Porter. Solomon Williams was a prominent New Light, or supporter of religious revivalism. William Williams prepared for college by studying with his father and probably by attending Lebanon's grammar school. He received his A.B. from Harvard in 1751. He was granted an ad eundem A.B. from Yale in 1753 and an M.A. "in course" from Harvard in 1754. Williams studied theology under his father but by 1756 became a shopkeeper. Except for having a one-ninth share in Trumbull and Company, a partnership organized in 1761 to supply clothing and refreshments to Connecticut soldiers in the French and Indian War, his business activities were local in nature. Williams married Mary Trumbull, daughter of Governor Jonathan Trumbull (1710–1785), on 14 February 1771; the couple had three children.

Although a merchant by trade, Williams's true vocation was officeholding and public service. He filled a succession of parish, town, county, colony, and state offices for more than fifty years. Williams was elected Lebanon town clerk and treasurer in 1752, an office he held for forty-four years. He was selectman from 1759 to 1786. He joined his father's church in 1757, was chosen deacon in 1768, and held a number of parish offices. Between May 1757 and May 1776, when Williams was elected to the Connecticut Council, he represented Lebanon in the assembly thirty-four times. Because of his abilities, the support of Jonathan Trumbull, and his devotion to New Light politics, Williams quickly rose to a position of political prominence in the colony. He held the positions of justice of the peace from 1759 to 1768, and from 1780 to 1810; justice of the peace and quorum from 1769 to 1775; judge of the Windham County Court from 1775 to 1805; and judge of probate for the Windham District from 1775 to 1810.

From the outset of his political career, Williams identified with Connecticut New Lights. He was involved in an abortive attempt to remove Governor Thomas Fitch and his Old Light allies from the council in 1759, but the real opportunity to do so came with the Stamp Act crisis. Williams supported the goals and activities of the Sons of Liberty; drafted the resolves of the Connecticut lower house, which asserted that because "an act for raising money by duties or taxes . . . is always considered as a free gift of the people made by their legal and elected representatives," that the Stamp Act was "unprecedented and unconstitutional" (*Public Records*, vol. 12, pp. 423–24); and participated in the planning that led to the defeat of Governor Fitch and other supporters of parliamentary supremacy in the spring 1766 elections.

Williams was rewarded by his peers in the lower house by being elected clerk, a position second in importance in that body only to the Speaker, and major of the Twelfth Militia Regiment. He was subsequently chosen lieutenant colonel (May 1772) and colonel (May 1775). Williams held the position of clerk continuously from May 1766 to October 1774, at which time he was elected Speaker.

Williams played a critical role in Connecticut politics from the time of the Stamp Act until independence. After passage of the Townshend Acts, Williams strongly endorsed nonimportation and supported domestic manufactures. He also served as clerk of Connecticut's Committee of Correspondence, established by vote of the lower house on 21 May 1773, and published several patriotic addresses in Connecticut newspapers, bearing the signatures of "America," "Cato Americanus," "Amicus Patriae," "Americanus," and "A Friend to His Country."

Williams was Speaker of the lower house at the time of Lexington and Concord and took the lead in preparing the colony for the trials of war and in establishing a council of safety to assist the governor in directing the war effort when the General Assembly was not in session. One of the council's nine original members and clerk for its entire eight-year existence, Williams served without pay, drafted hundreds of acts and resolves, and represented Connecticut at meetings in Philadelphia in 1775 and 1776 to obtain reimbursement for the colony's war expenses. At the October 1775 session of the General Assembly, new delegates were chosen for Congress. Speaker Williams played a critical role in recalling Silas Deane and Eliphalet Dyer and was selected as one of two alternate delegates to the Continental Congress. After the Connecticut General Assembly voted to instruct its delegates in Congress to vote for independence, Williams drafted Governor Jonathan Trumbull's 18 June 1776 proclamation, which set forth the principles for which they were fighting and invoked God's aid in the struggle.

Williams remained at the center of the revolutionary struggle in Connecticut throughout the war but is best known as a signer of the Declaration of Independence. He signed the parchment copy of the Declaration on 2 August 1776 along with Roger Sherman and Samuel Huntington (1731–1796). Williams only reluctantly served in Congress and was a delegate of lesser importance. He was present in Congress from 28 July to 12 November 1776 and from 25 June to 2 December 1777. A parochial and intensely religious New Englander, Williams disliked New Yorkers, southerners, and the French; opposed mercantile interests; hated Philadelphia; and spent a good deal of time advancing the interests of his Trumbull in-laws. He believed that the defeats suffered by George Washington's army in New York were the consequence of God's anger and displeasure at a sinful people; worked successfully to secure Silas Deane's recall from France; supported the Articles of Confederation; and endorsed currency regulation and price controls. He was appointed to the Board of War, his only major committee assignment, in October 1777.

Back in Connecticut, Williams continued to serve conscientiously in the upper house and council of safety but broke with the Trumbulls and their merchant allies over the issue of price controls, which he supported and they opposed. Whether because of his attitude toward price controls or his close identification with vigorous prosecution of an unsuccessful war, he lost his seat in the upper house in 1780 and did not regain it until 1784. He ceased shopkeeping operations at the outbreak of the war and by 1782 his financial position was so poor that he petitioned the council of safety for rock salt for his family.

Williams had not, however, lost the trust of the freemen of Lebanon, and they returned him to the lower house every session between October 1780 and his reelection to the council. He served again as Speaker from May 1781 through October 1783. During the period of political turmoil of the 1780s Williams generally supported local interests in opposition to the Connecticut nationalists, who supported a strengthened central government. He opposed both half pay for Continental officers and commutation, although he supported the idea of a Continental impost. He distrusted the Society of the Cincinnati, believing that it was hostile to democracy, and opposed the nationalist proposal to sell Connecticut's western reserve in 5,000-acre tracts before it was surveyed. As a result he was burlesqued as "William Wimble" by the Connecticut Wits. Williams was one of Lebanon's two delegates to Connecticut's January 1788 ratifying convention. Violating the instructions from his town, he voted in favor of the new Constitution. The elderly patriot remained politically active until he resigned his council seat in 1803, but he retained his appointments as judge of probate and justice of the peace until one year before his death in Lebanon, Connecticut.

William Williams was an important political figure in Connecticut for more than forty years. He was deeply religious, honest, dedicated, and a sincere patriot, but also impetuous, tactless, and parochial. Born and raised in the turmoils of the Great Awakening, he viewed all aspects of life through New Light lenses. Never once during the long struggle against Great Britain did he doubt the justice of the American cause or waver in his devotion to duty. He labored at the center of the Revolution in Connecticut from his positions in the General Assembly, Committee of Correspondence, and council of safety. His service in Congress was undistinguished, but Williams was one of the pivotal figures of the revolutionary era in his home state.

• The papers of William Williams are widely scattered, but most are in several collections at the Connecticut State Library and Connecticut Historical Society in Hartford. The most important are the Governor Jonathan Trumbull Papers, Governor Joseph Trumbull Collection, William Williams Letters, and Connecticut Archives, Revolutionary War, 1st ser., at the Connecticut State Library; and Connecticut General Assembly Papers, William Samuel Johnson Papers, Jonathan Trumbull, Sr., Papers, Joseph Trumbull Papers, and Williams papers at the Connecticut Historical Society. Additional items of significance are in the Historical Society of Pennsylvania, New York Historical Society, New York Public Library, and Yale University Library. Additional Williams material can be found in J. Hammond Trumbull and Charles J. Hoadley, eds., *The Public Records of the Colony of Connecticut* (15 vols., 1850–1890); Charles J. Hoadley et al., eds., *The Public Records of the State of Connecticut* (15 vols., 1894–1981); and two newspapers, the *Connecticut Courant* (Hartford) and *New London Gazette*. For information on Williams's impressions of the General Assembly in 1757, see Sylvie Turner, ed., *Journal Kept by William Williams of the Proceedings of the Lower House of the Connecticut General Assembly* (1975). For his views on the Constitution, see Merrill Jensen, ed., *The Documentary History of the Ratification of the Constitution*, vol. 3 (1978), pp. 584, 588–90.

Biographical information about Williams is located in John Sanderson, *Biography of the Signers of the Declaration of Independence*, vol. 4 (1823), pp. 90–105; Clifford K. Shipton, *Sibley's Harvard Graduates*, vol. 13 (1965), pp. 163–74; Bruce P. Stark, *Connecticut Signer: William Williams* (1975) and "William Williams: Portrait of a Connecticut Patriot," *Connecticut Historical Society Bulletin* 40 (July 1975): 80–87; and Harrison Williams, *The Life Ancestors and Descendants of Robert Williams of Roxbury* (1934). The best general works on Connecticut during the revolutionary era are Richard Buel, Jr., *Dear Liberty: Connecticut's Mobilization for the Revolutionary War* (1980), and Oscar Zeichner, *Connecticut's Years of Controversy, 1750–1776* (1949).

BRUCE P. STARK

WILLIAMS, William Appleman (12 June 1921–5 Mar. 1990), historian, was born in Atlantic, Iowa, the son of William Carlton Williams, an aviator, and Mildrede Appleman, a public school teacher. When "Billy" was eight, his father died in an air crash during an army training exercise. He spent nearly all of his formative years in the Atlantic home of his maternal grandparents. A local basketball star (though only 5′10″), paper delivery boy, and jazz enthusiast, Williams later attributed his socialistic sense of community values to the ethos of this Iowa farming and commercial center.

In 1939 Williams entered Kemper Military Academy in Booneville, Missouri, on a basketball scholarship. Having aspired to a career in architecture, he accepted a nomination to the U.S. Naval Academy two years later with mixed feelings. After initial difficulties in Annapolis, he demonstrated excellent leadership skills and served as assistant editor of the academy's *Trident Magazine*, all the while preparing himself for war. Williams also, he often suggested later, "learned about power" at the academy. He graduated in 1944.

Williams volunteered for the Amphibious Corps and served fifteen months in the Pacific theater as executive officer of a small landing craft. There, for the first time, he read Marxist literature and radical novels. While at sea during the closing months of the war, he suffered a serious spinal injury, a source of increasing pain through the rest of his life. Transferred to Corpus Christi, Texas, he married a high school sweetheart, Jeannie Preston, in 1945 and quickly became involved in the civil rights movement, serving as editor of the newsletter of the local branch of the National Association for the Advancement of Colored People. Hospitalized for further back treatments, Williams—anxious to "figure out the way the world ticked" (*Visions of History*, p. 129)—applied to the University of Wisconsin for graduate study in history.

In Madison, Williams encountered the "Wisconsin School" of progressive historians. Tracing their roots back to Wisconsin native Frederick Jackson Turner and to the egalitarian spirit of "Fighting Bob" La Follette, these historians prized social and economic history over the intellectual history long considered the domain of the Ivy League, collected and delved into the common records of state historical agencies, and insisted on the importance of the westward movement in making America unique. They also shared the widespread popular revulsion at the First World War and nurtured a mounting suspicion of the leviathan national state as an agency of imperial aims. In many ways, Williams would bring their collective work to heightened levels of insight and political relevance. He was awarded a doctorate in 1950 after completing a study on the early decades of U.S.–Soviet relations, and in 1952 he began to teach at the University of Oregon.

Williams's first published work was *American-Russian Relations, 1781–1941* (1952), a brisk revisionist account that evoked Charles Beard's political legacy and the scholarly work of Williams's mentor, Fred Harvey Harrington. As in his controversial essays for the *Nation* magazine during the 1950s, Williams stressed that American interests in international economic expansion and in blocking potential competitors had been in place long before the Bolshevik Revolution and remained largely unchanged over time.

Though welcomed by many scholars as a "realist" antidote to Cold War rhetoric, Williams's book enjoyed only a limited circulation. However, Williams edited two subsequent volumes of diplomatic documents and studies by other historians—*The Shaping of American Diplomacy* (1956) and *America and the Middle East: Open Door Imperialism or Enlightened Leadership?* (1958)—that were widely used in diplomatic history courses in the later 1950s and the 1960s. In 1956 Williams divorced his wife and married Corinne Croft Hammer; they had two children, and Williams adopted three others from his second wife's previous marriage. In 1957 he returned to Madison to assume an associate professorship at the University of Wisconsin.

Williams's *The Tragedy of American Diplomacy*, first published in 1959 and later significantly revised, had, by contrast to his first works, an explosive effect among not only scholars but most careful observers of foreign affairs. Though historians were beginning to rebel against the "consensus" approach—which contended that Americans' shared values had muted social and political conflict—Williams argued that the course of American history had indeed been shaped by a certain consensus, at least with respect to the importance of expansion to the nation's well-being. The book followed the progress of an "Open Door imperialism" from the 1890s to the Cold War, illustrating the growth of an American empire premised on economic preeminence more than military conquest. While ostensibly anticolonial, the United States became a counterrevolutionary power, the nation's success in terms of empire involving a tragic subversion of its own ideals. The book inspired Adolph Berle to invite Williams to assist him on the Latin American desk at the Kennedy State Department, an offer Williams politely declined. On the other hand, rumors of a volume to follow prompted the House Committee on Un-American Activities to call Williams for questioning and even to attempt to subpoena the manuscript.

The Contours of American History (1961) lived up to its advanced billing. A sweeping account of U.S. history, it reached back farther than *Tragedy* in exploring the roots of American expansionism, beginning with the rise of a semi-independent mercantilist colony demanding its own right to empire. In Williams's view, the Founding Fathers had seen an ever-growing empire as the only means to avoid the internal crises that European societies perennially faced. They did not foresee the human toll as the mercantilist commonwealth gave way to the mass cupidity set loose by laissez-faire frontiersmen like Andrew Jackson. An antislavery crusade fought in alliance with mighty railroad companies had, in turn, accelerated the growth of a national state and a corporate order poised to act on a global scale. Neither radicals nor conservatives (with the possible exception of Henry Adams, one of Williams's favorites) had taken the measure of empire in the century after the Constitution's ratification or sensed the ways that the immense tragedy of the next century had already been set in motion. The corporate state constructed after 1890 by government, business, labor leaders, and large farmers not only undermined the laissez-faire individualism that Williams was suspicious of but also proved fundamentally hostile to the vision of a decentralized commonwealth of local communities that Williams treasured as the foundation of true democracy.

Traditionalists of the center and right, such as Arthur Schlesinger, Jr., and Oscar Handlin, greeted Williams's work with outright hostility. But for an emerging generation of antiwar graduate students (not only in history but other fields as well), his books became a touchstone of scholarly acuity and political idealism. Williams had explained—to their satisfaction at any rate—the roots of American involvement in Vietnam as well as the nation's attendant crisis of conscience. By the end of the 1960s, *Tragedy* was recognized by historians as one of the influential books on America's inflamed campuses.

Yet even before the widening of the war, Williams had set in motion scholarship that would outlast his personal study. In the eleven years after his return to Madison, he trained more than forty graduate students and taught thousands of eager undergraduates. Among those who counted themselves students or devotees were Gar Alperowitz, Walter LaFeber, Lloyd Gardner, Thomas McCormick, and a half-dozen others who, with Williams, drastically reshaped diplomatic history. Indeed, it was later said that every foreign affairs study after *Tragedy* and *Contours* was in some sense an attempt to deal with the "revisionist" thesis that Williams proposed and that others elaborated in tracing U.S. dealings with Asia, Africa, and Latin America. Japanese and German historians applied his lessons to their own nations, with much the same "revisionist" effect. Moreover, historians of U.S. westward movement acknowledged the impact of Williams's upending of familiar themes of democratic expansionism. In the work of John Mack Faragher, Patricia Limerick, and others, the continuously moving frontier of contest and conquest undid egalitarian hopes rather than realizing them.

Williams abandoned Madison in 1968 for Oregon State University. He divorced his second wife in 1970 and married Wendy Margaret Tomlin in 1973. None of Williams's subsequent books proved nearly so influential as *Tragedy* or *Contours*, although a series of essays published in the *New York Review of Books* and collected as a small work, *Some Presidents: Wilson to Nixon* (1972), had wide circulation. A last philosophical summation of themes, published in 1980 as *Empire as a Way of Life: An Essay on the Causes and Character of America's Present Predicament along with a Few Thoughts about an Alternative* (1980), was excerpted in the *Nation* and distributed to delegates at the Democratic National Convention. The same year, Williams became president of the Organization of American Historians. This estimable honor ironically made Williams the representative of a scholarly generation younger than himself, writing history quite unlike that which he had undertaken—more socially oriented, more interested in the lower classes, women, and nonwhites than in the upper-class *mentalité* of Williams's favorite characters. His earnest attempts at the helm of the OAH to create a national fund for historians (especially underemployed women and non-white scholars) and to open or at least preserve from destruction security files of the Federal Bureau of Investigation and State Department were only partly successful.

In declining health, Williams retired from Oregon State in 1986. He died four years later in Newport, Oregon, having left an indelible stamp on the writing of U.S. history.

• Williams's papers are held at the Kerr Library, Oregon State University, Corvallis. Other works by Williams include *The Great Evasion: An Essay on the Contemporary Relevance of Karl Marx and the Wisdom of Admitting the Heretic into the Dialogue about America's Future* (1964); *The Roots of Modern American Empire: A Study of the Growth and Shaping of a Social Consciousness in a Marketplace Society* (1969); and *America Confronts a Revolutionary World: 1776–1976* (1976). For a full analysis of his life and work, see Paul Buhle and Edward Rice Maximin, *William Appleman Williams: The Tragedy of Empire* (1995). Also useful are Lloyd C. Gardner, ed., *Redefining the Past: Essays in Diplomatic History in Honor of William Appleman Williams* (1986), and the reminiscences and interviews in Paul Buhle, ed., *History and the New Left: Madison, Wisconsin, 1950–1970* (1990), and Henry Abelove et al., eds., *Visions of History* (1984).

PAUL BUHLE

WILLIAMS, William Carlos (17 Sept. 1883–4 Mar. 1963), author and physician, was born in Rutherford, New Jersey, the son of William George Williams, a New York businessman of British extraction, and Raquel Hélène Hoheb, who was from Puerto Rico. William Carlos Williams spoke Spanish and French as well as English. From 1897 to 1899 he was schooled in Switzerland, with some time in Paris. In 1902 he graduated from high school in New York and was accepted into the dental school of the University of Pennsylvania, but soon transferred to the medical school. There began his long-lived friendships with Ezra Pound, H.D., and artist Charles Demuth. Because his mother was an artist, Williams tried painting. Between 1906 and 1909 Williams did internships at both the old French Hospital and Child's Hospital in New York, and at the same time courted Florence "Flossie" Herman, who promised to wait for him while he studied pediatrics in Leipzig.

After his study in Germany, Williams traveled in the Netherlands, France, England, and Spain. In 1910 he opened a private practice in Rutherford, New Jersey, and in 1912 he and Flossie married; they were to have two sons. Williams had published his first poetry collection, *Poems*, in 1909; in 1913 Elkin Mathews, Pound's publisher, published a second collection, *The Tempers*, in London.

New York was afire over the 1913 Armory Show of French and Spanish modern paintings, and Williams was restless as a general practitioner in New Jersey while the literary and artistic world hummed happily away in Paris. He worked harder at being a writer than he did at being a physician; he came to know the *Others* poets Alfred Kreymborg, Marianne Moore, Wallace Stevens, Marcel Duchamp, and Maxwell Bodenheim, as well as Edna St. Vincent Millay. His work appeared regularly in both Pound's and Amy Lowell's Imagist collections of poetry. His third volume, *Al Que Quiere!*—which reflected Williams's Spanish and Puerto Rican roots—was published in 1917. But few writers had a more intense understanding of what being "American" meant; like Gertrude Stein, Williams loved his country with the fascination of the partly disenfranchised. The death of his father in 1918 may have intensified his quest for place and belonging. Elusive, evanescent, his country remained poised just outside his possession, and his love of America became a pervasive theme in both his poetry and the fiction he began to write in the 1920s.

Experimentation had become a way of life for Williams as he crafted such seemingly casual poems as "This Is Just to Say" and "At the Ballgame." With Mina Loy he acted in one of Alfred Kreymborg's plays, and he wrote a play himself (*The Apple Tree*), though Kreymborg lost the only copy. After his experiences with theater, Williams's need to innovate spilled into prose with the important *Kora in Hell: Improvisations* (1920) and his editing of *Contact* with Robert McAlmon. Stressing the need to connect with the earth and the reality of life, the editors of the short-lived magazine insisted on art that stemmed from the mundane. Williams's montage of poems and prose titled *Spring and All* (1923) explored the ways real speech and events could become art, continuing some of the wry irony of his 1921 poetry collection, *Sour Grapes; The Great American Novel*, his comic parody of James Joyce's *Ulysses*, also appeared in 1923 as part of Ezra Pound's series of new writing. In 1924 Williams took a sabbatical year. Working in the New York Public Library for half the year, he wrote magnificent characterizations of figures from American history, *In the American Grain* (1925); he and his wife then traveled to France, leaving the children with friends. In 1926 his short poem "Paterson" won the *Dial* Award, but an out-of-court settlement regarding his story "The Five Dollar Guy," published in *New Masses*, in which he had called a fictional character by a real person's name, cost him $5,000.

Still restless, in 1927 Williams sent his wife with their two sons to Europe; while they were in school, she traveled and Williams later joined her. His encounters with James Joyce, Brancusi, Gertrude Stein, Pound, and others whetted his appetite for literary success, but he believed his route to fame lay in his American experiences. He published another prose-poetry mélange, *The Descent of Winter*, and in 1928 *A Voyage to Pagany*, a first novel as romantic as his first poems had been. The next year he translated the surrealist Philippe Soupault's *Last Nights of Paris*, and in 1930, with Richard Johns, edited the experimental magazine *Pagany*. Close on the heels of his immersion in French surrealism came his prominent place in Louis Zukofsky's "Objectivist" issue of *Poetry*, for which he won the Guarantor's Prize from that little magazine. In 1932 Williams's publications combined unpredictable and often comic surrealism in *A Novelette and Other Prose* with the stark accuracy of the Objectivists in *The Knife of the Times and Other Stories*. With novelist Nathanael West, he resumed publishing the magazine *Contact* for a three-issue run.

Concerned and saddened by the 1930s depression, which hit his blue-collar patients hard, Williams continued to publish incisive short stories in *New Masses*, *Anvil*, *Little Review*, and other left journals; these stories appeared in his 1938 collection *Life along the Passaic River*. Although Williams was writing more fiction than poetry, in 1934 Zukofsky published Williams's *Complete Poems 1921–1931*; in 1936 Williams's opera libretto, *The First President*, appeared, along with another poetry collection, *Adam & Eve & the City*. James Laughlin's New Directions Press, one of the few publishing houses interested in innovative work, published in 1937 *White Mule*, the first of what Williams would call his "Stecher" trilogy, fictions loosely based on his wife's relatives. This successful and very American novel about German immigrants' lives was followed in 1940 by *In the Money* and, in 1952, *The Build-Up*. Although in 1938 Williams's *The Complete Collected Poems* had appeared, he was thought of more frequently as a prose writer because of his visible, and political, fiction throughout the decade.

World War II and Williams's busy practice with civilian patients nearly brought his writing career to a halt. In 1944 he published a poetry collection, *The Wedge*, in which the anguish of his own weariness with trying to combine the careers of a literary man and a physician was evident.

Finally, in 1946 *Paterson* I, the first book of the epic poem he had been struggling to write for nearly twenty years, was published. In its totality, *Paterson* was in some ways an answer to T. S. Eliot's lament over the decline of values in twentieth-century mechanized culture. The doctor-poet persona of the poem, who is himself named Paterson and lives in the industrial town of Paterson, New Jersey, leads a normal life, sees normal happenings, and learns to live with philosophical and sexual freedoms. He may not like the behaviors of his "townpeople," but he at least gives them the right to decide what their behaviors will be. By concentrating on the dailiness of the poet's experience, using idiomatic language and the rhythms of speech in his poetry, Williams forced readers to see that their lives were poetic. A distinctive blend of prose excerpts and free-form poetry, Williams's work grew from what he had learned by reading Pound's *Cantos*, Hart Crane's *The Bridge*, and the work of Walt Whitman, H.D., John Dos Passos, and countless other American writers—always reacting spiritedly against Eliot's poetry of the 1920s. Happily, critics recognized *Paterson*'s worth as the expression of Williams's unique voice and vision.

In 1947 Williams gave a series of lectures and workshops on the art of the short story at the University of Washington, his first academic exposure. But years of struggle to keep two careers going had worn him out; in 1948 he experienced his first heart attack. That same year he nevertheless published the second volume of *Paterson, A Dream of Love* (a play), and several small collections of poems. In 1949 he published *Selected Poems* and *Paterson* III, along with the chapbook *The Pink Church*, which later provoked controversy because of its apparent association with communism, even though it was simply a poem about the human body. He won the Russell Loines Award and was made a fellow of the Library of Congress.

In 1950 Williams's writing career peaked: he was awarded the National Book Award for *Selected Poems* and *Paterson* III; he and Flossie spent time at the Yaddo artists' colony—his first leisure to write seriously in twenty-five years—and then took a reading tour along the West Coast. He published *Make Light of It: Collected Short Stories* and *Collected Later Poems (1940–1950)*, and began publishing with Random House, the first commercial publisher besides New Directions to handle his work. *Paterson* IV, *Autobiography of William Carlos Williams*, and *The Collected Earlier Poems* all appeared during 1951.

In March 1951, however, Williams had his first stroke and retired from medical practice, and in August 1952 he had another serious stroke. Controversy over his being named consultant in poetry to the Library of Congress—because of his own supposed associations with communism and his friendship with Ezra Pound, who had broadcast for the Fascists during World War II—led to his hospitalization for depression during part of 1953. Though he shared the Bollingen Prize for Poetry with Archibald MacLeish that year, he lost the coveted consultantship and felt that his character and his devotion to his country had been maligned.

Writing in what became known as the "triadic line," Williams published two collections of late poems, some of his best work. *The Desert Music* appeared in 1954, *Journey to Love*, which included the moving "To Asphodel," a love poem to Flossie, in 1955. He also published *Selected Essays* and a translation, done with his mother, of Don Francisco de Quevedo's *A Dog and the Fever* (1954). In 1955 he took another extensive reading tour. In 1957 John Thirlwall edited *Selected Letters*, and in 1958 he published *Paterson* V and a conversational bibliography, done with Edith Heal, *I Wanted to Write a Poem*.

In October 1955 Williams had his third, paralyzing stroke. Though he eventually taught himself to speak again and learned to type with his unparalyzed hand on an electric typewriter, his pace necessarily slowed. In 1959 he published *Yes, Mrs. Williams*, a biography of his mother, and participated in the successful off-Broadway run of his play *Many Loves*. Short stories collected in *The Farmers' Daughters* and plays collected in *Many Loves and Other Plays* appeared in 1961. He also survived another debilitating series of strokes. In 1962 New Directions published what would be Williams's last poetry collection, *Pictures from Brueghel and Other Poems* (including the triadic line work of *The Desert Music* and *Journey to Love*), the collection that won the 1963 Pulitzer Prize for poetry posthumously. Williams died in Rutherford.

No listing of Williams's work can do more than suggest the range, interest, and experimentation of his writing in the forms of fiction, drama, poetry, epic, essay, and sketch. Criticism suggests that he is more properly a postmodernist than a modernist, for Williams embodied the spirit of adventure and quest that was hardly anticipated in the weary angst of modernism as it was then defined. As if he were listening continuously to Pound's maxim, "Make it new," Williams drew his life in America in his poems' terse images: "a young horse with a green bed-quilt / on his withers shaking his head," "A big young bareheaded woman / in an apron," "Flowers through the window / lavender and yellow / changed by white curtains." He presented these images unapologetically. His purpose was not to point a moral or teach a lesson; rather, he wanted his readers to see through his eyes the beauty of the real. He was content to rest with the assumption that the reader could duplicate Williams's own sense of importance of red wheelbarrows and the green glass between hospital walls, and thereby dismiss the need for symbolism. As he said succinctly in *Paterson*, "no ideas but in things."

Just as Williams established new principles for the writing of poetry, so he revitalized American fiction. Much of his prose is carried through dialogue that makes Ernest Hemingway's seem contrived and redundant. Moving as far from literary convention as possible—most of his fiction is plotless—his prose was criticized by contemporaries for being artless, but later readers have found his emphasis on the basic elements of language, structure, and character essential to postmodernist work (the Minimalists, led by Raymond Carver, owe a great deal to Williams). "The Burden of Loveliness," "Jean Beicke," "The Use of Force," and other stories are often anthologized. The same kind of paring away of convention dominated his plays, whether in the fragmented forms of *Many Loves* or the more conventional *A Dream of Love*. A powerful agent once told Williams that she could not place his dramatic writing because it was so unconventional; that segment of his work has yet to be rediscovered. The writings of William Carlos Williams are a nearly inexhaustible reservoir of twentieth-century American themes and images, given expression through a voice unique in the history of literature.

• Williams's papers are housed primarily at the Beinecke Library, Yale University, and the Lockwood Memorial Library, SUNY, Buffalo. Bibliographical information appears in Emily Mitchell Wallace, *A Bibliography of William Carlos Williams* (1968); Linda W. Wagner, *William Carlos Williams: A Reference Guide* (1978); and chapters by Wagner on criticism of Williams's work in *Sixteen Modern American Authors* (rev. ed., 1973; vol. 2, 1990). Reed Whittemore, *William Carlos Williams: Poet from Jersey* (1975), was the first biography; Paul L. Mariani, *William Carlos Williams: A New World Naked* (1981), is an exhaustive, complete biography. Some private papers are sealed until 2013, fifty years from the poet's death, so biographical work may begin again at that time.

From the slow beginning of critical work on Williams—Vivienne Koch, *William Carlos Williams* (1950); Linda Welshimer Wagner, *The Poems of William Carlos Williams: A Critical Study* (1964); and Wagner, *The Prose of William Carlos Williams* (1970)—other works began the onslaught that led to the diverse kinds of helpful criticism Williams's work has prompted: studies such as Thomas R. Whitaker, *William Carlos Williams* (1968; rev. ed., 1989); James Guimond, *The Art of William Carlos Williams: A Discovery and Possession of America* (1968); James Breslin, *William Carlos Williams: An American Artist* (1970); Mike Weaver, *William Carlos Williams: The American Background* (1971); and Joseph N. Riddel, *The Inverted Bell: Modernism and the Counterpoetics of William Carlos Williams* (1974). Among the seminal studies of Williams's oeuvre are Stephen Tapscott, *American Beauty: William Carlos Williams and the Modernist Whitman* (1984); Anthony Libby, *Mythologies of Nothing: Mystical Death in American Poetry 1940–70* (1984); Bernard Duffey, *A Poetry of Presence: The Writing of William Carlos Williams* (1986); Kerry Driscoll, *William Carlos Williams and the Maternal Muse* (1987); Peter Schmidt, *William Carlos Williams, The Arts, and Literary Tradition* (1988); and Ann Fisher-Wirth, *William Carlos Williams and Autobiography: The Woods of His Own Nature* (1989).

LINDA WAGNER-MARTIN

WILLIAMS, William Sherley (3 Jan. 1787–Mar. 1849), fur trapper, trader, and guide known as "Old Bill," was born on Horse Creek in Rutherford County, North Carolina, the son of Joseph Williams and Sarah Musick, farmers. In 1794 Joseph Williams took his family west through Cumberland Gap, down the Ohio, to Whiteside Station, fifteen miles south of St. Louis. The following summer (1795), the family crossed the Mississippi into Spanish Louisiana and settled a Spanish land grant near Owen's Station (sixteen miles to the north of St. Louis). There, Williams acquired a frontier education augmented by his mother's tutoring and some formal learning. During his teenage years, Williams gained acceptance with the Big Hill band of the Osage. He learned their language, gained influence, married into the tribe (wife's name unknown), and lived among them for nearly a quarter of a century.

In the spring of 1812 Williams joined Captain James Callaway's Mounted Rangers assigned to patrol the region northeast of St. Charles during the War of 1812. He served only a year and then returned to the Osage. Williams became a valued interpreter who served the Fort Osage Indian agent and factor George C. Sibley from May 1817 to June 1818. In July 1821 his interpretive services were again called on for a factory substation (a satellite trading post of a larger post called the factory, which were all part of the government-run Indian trade system of the early 1800s) established near his Osage village. The following month missionaries arrived and Williams became a benefactor by furnishing them with information and services as interpreter and translator. Williams revealed his intellectual capacity by producing an Osage-English dictionary by the end of 1821.

Williams lost his job as interpreter when Congress abolished the factory system in 1822. He remained in the region as a licensed trader to the Osage and Kickapoos until the fall of 1824, when he headed for the Rocky Mountains. Williams, as a free trapper, set up camp near the Hudson's Bay Company's Flathead (Salish) House. He trapped the 1824–1825 winter season with one of William Ashley's brigades under Jedediah Smith's command. While hunting, Williams narrowly escaped being killed by the Blackfeet. It appears that about this time he acquired his nickname, "Old Bill."

By May 1825 Williams was back with the Osage but only for a short time. In August he left his Osage family for good when he joined the government expedition under Sibley—which was to survey and mark the trade road from Fort Osage to Santa Fe—as interpreter and hunter. The expedition arrived in Santa Fe in November, and Williams gained leave to pursue trapping along the Rio Grande. He returned to Taos in February 1826 but quickly headed to the Great Salt Lake region to join Ashley's trappers. Williams and his group trapped the Wind River Mountains and the Bighorn River to its mouth—the entire time being hounded by Blackfeet, who saw them as interlopers.

Williams returned to Santa Fe by late summer, and there he and Ceran St. Vrain received license from Mexican governor Antonio Narbona to enter the Gila River region. While out trapping, Williams was surprised by Apaches, who stripped him of everything. Without clothing, afoot, and without weapons, Williams trekked 200 miles back to Taos. At Taos he joined an expedition headed for the Green River for the fall 1827 hunt led by Sylvester S. Pattie and St. Vrain. En route Pattie died; the party experienced little success and returned to Taos in May.

Williams continued to work out of Taos and became well acquainted with the Utes and their country in the central and southern Rockies and with the plains regions of the Comanche. In November 1833 Williams was again north trapping the Green River, this time with Henry Fraeb's brigade of the Rocky Mountain Fur Company. Williams did well and returned to Taos, which seems to have become his home. There he took as wife a Mexican widow, Antonia Baca; they had one son.

In 1834 Williams organized a two-man expedition in company with Jesús Ruperto Valdez "Pepe" Archuleta, his camp keeper. The two left Taos in April and arrived in Albuquerque, where Williams assisted the missionaries in translating some Bible stories into Navajo. The two headed west through Hopi lands and the petrified forest and eventually came upon the Grand Canyon near Marble Canyon. They worked their way south and wintered at what became known as Bill Williams Mountain. They eventually crossed the Colorado and headed north, past the Great Salt Lake to camp near Lake Coeur d'Alene with a Hudson's Bay group. The two trappers crossed the Rockies via Bozeman Pass to the Yellowstone River, where they trapped the 1836–1837 season. They sold their furs at the rendezvous on Green River and then headed south for Bent's Fort, where Williams took charge of a Bent–St. Vrain wagon train that was headed to Santa Fe.

Williams continued to trap throughout the Southwest and the central Rockies. After arriving in Santa Fe he headed again for the Colorado, trapping it to its mouth. By the next summer (1838) he was again north at the rendezvous on the Popo Agie. Furs, however, were becoming scarce, so Williams embarked on a new line of work—the horse trade.

In 1840 Williams ventured to California, where he helped direct the acquisition of horses, once mission property but, since secularization, largely abandoned. The American party ran off about 1,200 horses from Mission San Luis Obispo and another 1,800 from San Gabriel Mission and herded the animals all the way to Bent's Fort in present-day Colorado. After delivering the horses to Bent's Fort, Williams, for the first time since his departure, returned to Missouri to visit his Osage family during the 1841–1842 winter.

The following spring Williams went to St. Louis, where he became partners with George Perkins in a trading venture to the Cheyenne and Sioux. The caravan traveled along the Oregon Trail, where they joined the Shoshoni in a battle against some Blackfeet. Williams continued to trap and trade the Rockies and even ventured as far west as Modoc country in California.

In 1845 Williams and Kit Carson served as guides to John C. Frémont's expedition from the Arkansas River to the Great Salt Lake. Williams left Frémont's expedition before it set out across the Great Basin. Williams participated in various trading ventures along the Santa Fe Trail and even served as a guide for Major W. W. Reynolds's campaign against the Apache. In November 1848 Williams was again acting as guide for Frémont, who was now on his fourth expedition. The expedition encountered great difficulties in crossing the central Rockies during the winter and became snowbound. Frémont dispatched Williams along with four other guides to the New Mexico settlements for help. En route, eleven men died and the others suffered terribly, and Frémont's entire operation proved a failure. After recuperating in Taos, Williams accompanied members of the expedition back to its abandoned winter camp to recover whatever they could. En route the party was attacked, and all, including Williams, were killed, likely by Utes.

William S. Williams stood six feet one and was sinewy and lean with red hair. A skilled mountain man with a sharp business sense, he was generally considered an honest man in his dealings. He possessed a gifted intellect, received some formal education, and even enjoyed the study of Greek and Latin. His vast wanderings mark him as one of the most, if not the most, traveled and knowledgeable mountain men involved in the American expansion into the Southwest, California, the Rockies, and the Great Basin.

• The most complete single volume on Williams is Alpheus H. Favour, *Old Bill Williams, Mountain Man* (1936; repr. 1962). A shorter biography on Williams, by Frederic E. Voelker, can be found in Le Roy Hafen, *The Mountain Men and the Fur Trade of the Far West*, vol. 8 (1972), pp. 365–94. Thomas M. Marshall discusses the Williams–St. Vrain partnership in "St. Vrain's Expedition to the Gila in 1826," *Southwestern Historical Quarterly* 19 (1916): 253–58. Williams's trapping activity in the southern Rockies and southern plains is discussed in Albert Pikes's personal narrative, *Prose Sketches and Poems Written in the Western Country (With Additional Stories)*, ed. David J. Weber (1967). Archuleta's narrative of his journey with Williams was first published in the *St. Louis Globe-Democrat*, 24 Dec. 1911. The best overall examination of the southwest fur trade and Williams's involvement in it is David J. Weber, *The Taos Trappers: The Fur Trade in the Far Southwest, 1540–1846* (1971).

S. MATTHEW DESPAIN

WILLIAMSON, Andrew (c. 1730–21 Mar. 1786), revolutionary war officer, sometimes known as "the Benedict Arnold of South Carolina," was born in Scotland and, while still a boy, immigrated to South Carolina with his parents, whose identities are unknown. By 1758 he appeared in the record as a backcountry "cowdriver"; two years later he was in partnership with John Murray in the firm of "Andrew Williamson and Company," which supplied livestock to British and American troops during the Cherokee War. Williamson also served as a lieutenant in the South Carolina provincial unit that accompanied British troops against the Indians in 1761. By the early 1760s, Williamson was a leading figure in the area around the little town of Ninety Six. His store supplied Indians and white settlers; his fields produced indigo as well as provisions; and his orchards yielded more than 3,000 bushels of peaches.

Having purchased his plantation from Murray, who called it "Hard Labor," Williamson renamed it "White Hall" and became a slaveholding backcountry squire. His wife, Eliza Tyler, who had been born in Virginia, brought marriage ties to another locally prominent family, the Hammonds. Like many other established men, Williamson had an affinity for, but did not join, the Regulator movement, an extralegal attempt by rising backcountry planters to impose law and order on the area. In 1768 he signed a petition to the legislature that voiced Regulator demands for improved roads, schools, churches, and courts of law. Although colonial authorities initially viewed the Regulators' activities as a challenge, the South Carolina assembly responded, albeit somewhat slowly, to the needs of the backcountry. Williamson could therefore become a member of the grand jury of a newly established circuit court that met at Ninety Six in 1774.

At the outbreak of the Revolution, Williamson quickly emerged as one of the most influential Whigs in the region. He was a member of the First and Second Provincial Congresses in 1775 and 1776 and a major of the local militia. In both capacities, he vigorously supported the Revolutionary Council of Safety's attempts to ensure the allegiance of his neighbors and the neutrality of the Cherokees. When fighting appeared imminent, he constructed a small fort at Ninety Six. Besieged by Loyalists for three days, during which the first casualties of the Revolution in South Carolina occurred, Williamson negotiated a truce on 21 November 1775. He then participated in the "Snow Campaign" that captured a number of Loyalists who had taken refuge in Indian country. During the summer of 1776 he led the South Carolina troops that, in connection with similar expeditions from North Carolina and Virginia, ravaged the Cherokee settlements. Meanwhile, the first of three unsuccessful campaigns against British Florida began. The ineptness of these annual attacks, which involved Continental troops and some of Williamson's militia, as well as Georgians, no doubt contributed to his refusal to accept orders from General Robert Howe, the Continental army officer who claimed overall command of the disastrous expedition in 1778. Still, Williamson was promoted to brigadier general of the militia and, as such, took part in the failed Franco-American attempt to recapture Savannah in October 1779. He also remained a member of the South Carolina General Assembly, to which he had been elected in 1776, and, he later maintained, willingly cooperated with Howe's successor as commander of the Continental army in the south, General Benjamin Lincoln, in military operations during late 1779 and early 1780. On 12 May 1780 British forces captured Charleston and Lincoln's 2,600 Continental troops. Some contemporaries believed that most South Carolinians would quickly capitulate. Williamson, however, tried unsuccessfully to rally his men in the vicinity of Ninety Six. He then surrendered to British authorities who, realizing that he was a man of influence, treated him well. He in turn tried to persuade his neighbors to abandon further resistance, but scattered testimony suggests that he remained ambivalent about his loyalties. In an attempt to help him resolve his dilemma, some of his old Whig friends kidnapped him. He refused to avail himself of the excuse that he had been coerced into renouncing his new allegiance and, soon after being released, appeared to opt for the British side by moving to the vicinity of Charleston, which was then under royal control.

Early in July 1781, while Williamson lived under British protection, a party of Whigs under Colonel Isaac Hayne again captured him—this time, it was said, to hang him as a traitor. Reacting quickly, British forces liberated Williamson, captured Hayne, and shortly thereafter hanged him. Hayne's execution became a cause célèbre, and Williamson inadvertently incurred much of the blame for it. Accordingly, when the general assembly confiscated the estates of prominent Loyalists in 1782, Williamson's was included. Several months later, General Nathanael Greene, who then commanded Continental forces in the south, informed the legislature that for some time, at considerable risk to himself, Williamson had supplied information to the American army. The assembly responded by reducing Williamson's penalty to a 12 percent amercement or tax on the value of his property. After his death (of natural causes) at his plantation in St. Paul's Parish, the *Charleston Morning Post* (22 Mar. 1786) published a gracious obituary, and his executors asked the assembly to remit the amercement. Another petition from his neighbors and old comrades in arms from the Ninety Six area supported this request, and in 1791 a committee of the senate recommended that his property be restored to his heirs, who included two sons and two daughters. Williamson remains a controversial figure, but recent historians have been sympathetic toward him. Perhaps, as one of them has suggested, he just could not make up his mind.

• Reputedly illiterate, Williamson nevertheless signed some letters in the Benjamin Lincoln Papers at the Massachusetts Historical Society. Additional Williamson correspondence can be found in Robert W. Gibbes, ed., *Documentary History of the American Revolution* (3 vols., 1855; repr. 1972), as well as in Philip M. Hamer et al., *The Papers of Henry Laurens* (1968–). Robert Davis, "Andrew Williamson," in *The Encyclopedia of the American Revolution*, ed. Richard Blanco (2 vols., 1993), provides an informed but unusually favorable assessment. See also Rachel Klein, *The Unification of a Slave State: The Rise of the Planter Class in the South Carolina Backcountry, 1760–1808* (1990).

ROBERT M. WEIR

WILLIAMSON, Hugh (5 Dec. 1735–22 May 1819), scientist and political leader, was born in West Nottingham, Chester County, Pennsylvania, the son of John Williamson, a clothier, and Mary Davison, who were of Scots-Irish Presbyterian descent. Hugh Williamson was educated in local academies in Chester County and in Newark, Delaware, and graduated in 1757 from the College of Philadelphia, now the University of Pennsylvania. Three years later the college conferred the A.M. degree on him. From 1760 to 1763 he filled a position as professor of mathematics at his alma mater. Intending to be a Presbyterian minister, Williamson studied theology and was licensed to preach, but ill health and doctrinal disputes in the church drove him from the clergy to pursue medicine. He left Philadelphia in 1764 for Europe, where he studied at the universities in Edinburgh, London, and Utrecht, completing the M.D. degree at Utrecht.

Williamson returned to Philadelphia to begin practicing medicine and to continue his scientific and mathematical research. Elected to the American Philosophical Society in 1768, Williamson was appointed the next year to a commission to observe the transit of Venus and Mercury across the sun. His subsequent publications reflected his diverse range of interests in the origins of comets, the effect of climate on diseases, and, in collaboration with Benjamin Franklin, the nature of electricity. His numerous articles won him recognition from the Royal Society in England and from Dutch scientific societies, and the University of Leyden granted him the honorary LL.D. degree.

On a trip to England in 1773 to solicit funds for the Newark Academy, Williamson, as an observer of the Boston Tea Party, was called to testify to the Privy Council, before whom he sympathetically described the growing rebellion in the colonies. His revolutionary ardor was reinforced by his friendship with Franklin, who was also in London. While in England, Williamson delivered a paper on electricity before the Royal Society and anonymously published a letter entitled *The Plea of the Colonies* (1775), which was designed to win support for the revolutionary movement among the English Whigs.

Upon Williamson's return to America in 1776, he went into the mercantile business with his younger brother John Williamson in Charleston, South Carolina, but he relocated to Edenton, North Carolina, where he practiced medicine and developed a profitable trade with the French West Indies. When he offered his services to the state as a physician, Williamson was appointed the surgeon general of North Carolina. His advocacy of inoculation for smallpox and strict sanitation practices in camp significantly reduced the number of troops dying from disease. As a field surgeon he went with the American army into South Carolina in 1780 and attended the wounded from both sides after the bloody battle of Camden.

Williamson's political career began at the end of the war in 1782 with his election to the state House of Commons from Edenton and to the Continental Congress from 1782 to 1785 and from 1787 to 1789. Thomas Jefferson described him as "a very useful member, of an acute mind, attentive to business, and of a high degree of erudition." Taking a Federalist position, Williamson was an advocate of a strong central government, and his "Letters of Sylvius" (*American Museum* [Aug. 1787]) were an effective analysis of the domestic economy, the federal debt, the problems of paper currency, the necessity for industrial development, and the need for an excise tax. In the federal Constitutional Convention of 1787, Williamson was the leading representative in his state's delegation, serving on more committees and speaking more frequently than any other delegate from the state. A spokesman for the rights of the larger states, he advocated representation by population and was against equal representation of the states in the Senate. Although personally opposed to slavery, Williamson served on the committee on the slave trade that accepted the compromise that continued the traffic for another twenty years. During the ratification fight in North Carolina, Williamson actively campaigned for the Constitution, arguing that it was "more free and more perfect than any form of government that has ever been adopted by any nation." Although ratification initially failed, Williamson was elected to the second state convention in Fayetteville in 1789, where the Constitution was approved, bringing North Carolina into the federal union. Williamson served in 1788 as the state's agent to the new federal government to settle North Carolina's financial accounts relating to the war, and until the state entered the union Williamson was North Carolina's representative to the United States. In 1787 he was named by the legislature to the first board of trustees of the University of North Carolina. Two years later he was elected a representative to the U.S. Congress, where he served two terms. In Congress Williamson was most active in his opposition to the Bank of the United States, the assumption of state debt by the federal government, the whiskey excise tax, and the Jay Treaty.

While in New York on government business, Williamson met Maria Apthorpe, whom he married in January 1789. They had two children. When he finished his second term in Congress, he moved to New York City in 1793 and returned to his first love, scientific research. In his latter years he published on an eclectic array of topics, including reptiles, lightning rods, pleurisy, the relationship of climate and disease, canals, and commerce. He was an early advocate of what would become the Erie Canal. His books were *Observations on the Climate in Different Parts of America* (1811) and *The History of North Carolina* (2 vols., 1812). In New York he was a founder of the Literary and Philosophical Society and a trustee of the College of Physicians and Surgeons of the University of the State of New York. Williamson also volunteered significant time and money to the orphan asylum, the humane society, and the city dispensary of the New York Hospital. His wife and children predeceased him, and Williamson died suddenly in New York while riding with his niece and heir, Maria Hamilton.

Described by the noted Italian sculptor Giuseppe Ceracchi as "the American Cato," Williamson, like his friend Benjamin Franklin, was a Renaissance man. As scholar, teacher, minister, scientist, physician, businessman, legislator, statesman, historian, and humanitarian, Williamson had few peers.

• Williamson's papers, which have been microfilmed, are in the Historical Society of Pennsylvania, Philadelphia. His official correspondence and papers have been published in Walter J. Clark, ed., *The State Records of North Carolina*, vols. 14–25 (1896–1906). Additional correspondence is in Don Higginbotham, ed., *The Papers of James Iredell* (2 vols., 1976); Griffith J. McRee, ed., *Life and Correspondence of James Iredell* (2 vols., 1857); and Alice B. Keith, ed., *The John Gray Blount Papers* (2 vols., 1952–1959). Biographical sketches are David Hosack, *A Biographical Memoir of Hugh Williamson, M.D., LL.D.* (1820); Stephen B. Weeks in *The Biographical History of North Carolina*, ed. Samuel A. Ashe, vol. 5 (1906), pp. 458–66; Burton Craige, *The Federal Convention of 1787: North Carolina in the Great Crisis* (1987); and John W. Francis, *Old New York or Reminiscences of the Past Sixty Years* (1866). Useful for background are Delbert H. Gilpatrick, "Contemporary Opinion of Hugh Williamson," *North Carolina Historical Review* 17 (1940): 26–36, and Louise I. Trenholme, *The Ratification of the Federal Constitution in North Carolina* (1932). Obituaries are in the *New York Evening Post*, 24 May 1819, and the *Raleigh Register*, 4 June 1819.

LINDLEY S. BUTLER

WILLIAMSON, Isaac Halsted (27 Sept. 1767–10 July 1844), attorney, governor, and chancellor of New Jersey, was born in Elizabethtown (later Elizabeth), New Jersey, the son of General Matthias Williamson and Susannah Halsted. Educated in local schools, Williamson did not attend college. He studied law with his brother Matthias, a well-known attorney, and was admitted to the bar in 1791. Williamson soon established a successful practice in Essex County and was recognized for his thoughtful and thorough grasp of the law. Lucius Q. C. Elmer, a contemporary of Williamson's, ranked him with George Wood and Richard Stockton as one of New Jersey's three most effective lawyers.

In 1808 Williamson married Anne Crossdale Jouet. They had two children. Never an active partisan, Williamson nonetheless associated with Federalists in Essex County. During the War of 1812 he broke with party leaders and supported the Madison administration as a "War Federalist." In 1815 he accepted a nomination for the legislature as a Democratic-Republican and gained election. In the legislature Williamson served on committees dealing with complicated legal issues, including imprisonment for debt and the status of free blacks. Williamson also worked on legislation regarding the granting of divorces, at that time a legislative prerogative.

When Governor Mahlon Dickerson was elected to the U.S. Senate in 1817, Williamson was chosen by the legislature to succeed him. Federalism was moribund, and most political maneuvering was personal and factional. As governor, Williamson stood above the fray, and for twelve successive years was easily reelected.

Williamson's main responsibility as governor, aside from making appointments to many state offices, lay in his service as chancellor and judge of the prerogative court of New Jersey. During his years as chancellor, Williamson prepared a new set of rules of procedure for the state's equity proceedings, one consequence of which was to channel new business to the court. Because there was no reporter, Williamson's decisions were never printed, but according to all testimony, he was a forceful and intelligent judge.

As governor, primarily because he was disinclined to political activism, Williamson did not play a significant role in lawmaking. He even dropped the traditional practice of delivering an annual message to the legislature, thus diminishing his already small influence in making public policy. Williamson did advocate state support for a Delaware and Raritan River canal. Although the project was not pursued during his governorship, it gained a charter in 1830 and was completed in 1834.

In the aftermath of the presidential election of 1824, partisan activity in New Jersey intensified. When the Jacksonians gained control of the state legislature in 1828, Williamson—who had supported John Quincy Adams in both the 1824 and 1828 presidential elections—was ousted as governor. From 1830 to 1833 Williamson served as mayor of Elizabeth, and in 1831–1832 he represented Essex County in the legislative council. In 1832, after Charles Ewing died of cholera, Williamson was offered appointment as chief justice of the state supreme court, but he declined on account of his age and his unwillingness to sacrifice his thriving law practice.

Williamson's final service to his state occurred at age seventy-seven, when he was elected to the state constitutional convention of 1844 and then unanimously elected convention president. In the convention Williamson favored strengthening the governorship by increasing the governor's term from one year to three and giving the governor veto power over legislation. Williamson fell ill during the convention and resigned his position. He died several weeks later in Elizabeth. His son Benjamin, a Democratic party activist, also made a name for himself as a lawyer, and was named chancellor in 1852.

• The most significant body of Williamson papers can be found in the Bureau of Archives and History, New Jersey State Library, Trenton, N.J. Small collections of Williamson material are located in the New Jersey Historical Society, and Special Collections, Rutgers University. There is no monograph on Williamson's career, but two short treatments are worthwhile: Lucius Q. C. Elmer, *The Constitution and Government of the Province and State of New Jersey* . . . (1872), pp. 173–83, offers insights into Williamson's character and legal career; Frank J. Esposito, "Isaac H. Williamson," in *The Governors of New Jersey: Biographical Essays, 1664–1974*, ed. Paul A. Stellhorn and Michael J. Birkner (1982), pp. 96–98, is helpful on his years as governor.

MICHAEL J. BIRKNER

WILLIAMSON, Sonny Boy (5 Dec. 1899?–25 May 1965), blues artist, was born Aleck Miller in Glendora, Mississippi, the son of Millie Ford, a sharecropper; his father's name is unknown. He grew up on a farm near Yazoo City, where his mother and stepfather, Jim Miller, moved when he was young. He began learning to play the harmonica, or mouth harp, around the age of five, supposedly performing religious music before switching to blues, and was playing at local parties as a teenager.

By his own account, Miller's career as a wandering musician began in 1928. Using the name Little Boy Blue, he ranged as far afield as New Orleans and became a familiar figure in Mississippi, Arkansas, and Tennessee, always recognizable by the heavy belt of harmonicas he wore around his waist. Throughout the 1930s he worked with many of the emerging blues artists of the day, among them Robert Johnson, Robert Junior Lockwood, Sunnyland Slim, and Howling Wolf. In 1937 Miller courted and married Howling Wolf's half sister, Mary, who was then living in Parkin, Arkansas.

In late 1941 in Helena, Arkansas, Miller began a career in radio. Ever the hustler, he talked his way into a regular time slot on a new radio station, KFFA. With Lockwood as his guitarist and Interstate Grocery as his sponsor, he broadcast blues on weekdays at lunchtime to promote his local club dates. One of the sponsor's products, King Biscuit Flour, provided the show's name, "King Biscuit Time," and the artists their name, King Biscuit Entertainers. With the addition of sidemen like Peck Curtis, Robert "Dudlow" Taylor, Pinetop Perkins, and Joe Willie Wilkins, the Entertainers soon became a full-fledged band. Featuring electronically amplified instruments, a first for radio listeners in the Mississippi Delta region, the show became so popular that the sponsor later marketed corn meal with Miller's picture on the label.

Although he was using the name Miller when he came to KFFA, he soon adopted the name Sonny Boy Williamson. It is possible he took the name to capitalize on the reputation of then-popular harmonica player and blues recording star John Lee "Sonny Boy" Williamson. Nevertheless, most blues artists agreed that Miller was the superior musician. Miller, according to Lockwood, "could play rings around little Sonny Boy—and every damn body else that was playing harp at that time." Miller went to his grave claiming to be the "original" and "only" Sonny Boy—although the name was just one of nearly a dozen he adopted during his career, including Alex Miller, Willie Miller, Sonny Boy Williams, Willie Williamson, Biscuit Miller, Footsie, and Goat.

Miller left KFFA in 1944 and resumed the life of a traveling musician and occasional radio artist. By the late 1940s, he had married again, this time to Mattie Lee Gordon (or Jones), and had settled in West Memphis, Arkansas.

Although Miller claimed to have recorded earlier, his first documented session took place in 1951 for the Trumpet label in Jackson, Mississippi. Starting with the hit "Eyesight to the Blind," he recorded for Trumpet until 1954 as both a featured artist and sideman—most notably on Elmore James's "Dust My Broom."

With the murder of John Lee Williamson in Chicago in 1948, Miller became the foremost Sonny Boy Williamson (although older musicians generally referred to him as Sonny Boy No. 2). Through his Trumpet recordings his name spread, and by 1953 he was beginning to work the Midwest, where he came to the attention of Chicago-based Chess Records. Chess, the major blues label of the time, bought his contract, and his first record on the subsidiary Checker label, "Don't Start Me Talking," rose to number 3 on the rhythm-and-blues charts. Despite several other hits in the late 1950s, he remained third in the Chess blues hierarchy behind Muddy Waters and Howling Wolf.

In his sixties, losing the support of his traditional audience, Miller turned his attention overseas, where he once again achieved stardom. Traveling on a passport issued to one "Sonny Boy Williams," he went to Europe in 1963 with the American Folk Blues Festival, staying on once the tour ended. In Europe he indulged his eccentricity, dressing as a banker in bowler hat and tails. Despite his temper and steady drinking, audiences from France to Poland embraced him warmly, particularly the British. Beginning in 1963 he did a number of European sessions, working with touring Chicago artists and with newcomers such as Britain's Eric Clapton. He also played with Brian Jones, Jimmy Page, and John Mayall, influencing a generation of young blues rockers who, in turn, brought their versions of the blues back to the United States during the so-called British Invasion of the 1960s.

Following his European successes in 1963 and 1964 Miller returned home to Helena in deteriorating health. He told KFFA he wanted his old job back, explaining that he had come home to die. After several "King Biscuit Time" broadcasts, he died in Helena and was buried in Tutwiler, Mississippi.

Much of what is known about Sonny Boy Williamson No. 2 seems contradictory. Fellow musicians described him as a con man and a hard taskmaster. Blues artist Eddie Burns said Miller had a temper so volatile that he once fired his whole band when it showed up late and provided a full evening's music and entertainment by himself. On the other hand, songwriter Willie Dixon, who traveled with Miller in Europe, said he was a "beautiful guy."

By any of his names, Sonny Boy Williamson No. 2 was one of the blues tradition's most influential and historically important artists. He participated in all major blues eras, right up to the blues/rock transition of the 1960s, and was the single most important blues radio personality ever, his programs inspiring countless other artists. The list of artists who played with him in the South, the North, and over the airwaves reads like a who's who of the blues, including B. B. King, Earl Hooker, Willie Nix, Fred Below, Willie Love, and Baby Boy Warren. And even though many older artists disapproved of the name he appropriated, they all acknowledged that Sonny Boy No. 2 was a great musician—a true original.

A commemorative marker was erected at his grave as a tribute in 1980, and that same year he was inducted into the Blues Foundation's Hall of Fame.

• For discographical information, see Mike Leadbitter and Neil Slaven, *Blues Records 1943–1966* (1968), and Paul Oliver, ed., *The Blackwell Guide to Blues Records* (1989). For general information see Oliver, *Blues Off the Record: Thirty Years of Blues Commentary* (1984); Sheldon Harris, *Blues Who's Who: A Biographical Dictionary of Blues Singers* (1979; repr. 1989); and Leadbitter, ed., *Nothing but the Blues* (1971). For more on his years with Trumpet Records, see Jim O'Neal and Amy O'Neal, "Living Blues Interview: Lillian McMurry," *Living Blues* 67 (1986): 15–28. For a discussion of KFFA and "King Biscuit Time," see Jim O'Neal's program notes to the "King Biscuit Blues Festival Program," pp. 19–24, and Hank Harvey, "Growing Up with the Blues," *Living Blues* 71 (1986): 25–29. For a sample of his music, try *Sonny Boy Williamson II: The Harp from the Deep South* (Blues Encore, CD52018); *Down and Out Blues* (Checker, CHD-9257); and *King Biscuit Time* (Arhoolie, 2020).

BILL MCCULLOCH
BARRY LEE PEARSON

WILLIAMSON, Sonny Boy (30 Mar. 1914–1 June 1948), blues harmonica player, was born John Lee Curtis Williamson in Jackson, Tennessee, the son of Rafe Williamson and Nancy Utley, occupations unknown. His father died shortly before he was born, and he was raised by his mother, who later remarried. As a boy, Williamson sang with a gospel quartet at Blair's Chapel CME Church on the outskirts of Jackson. When he was nine or ten, his mother gave him a harmonica, or mouth harp, as a Christmas gift, and he began teaching himself to play, starting with the gospel tunes he sang in church. At least two other Tennessee musicians later claimed to have known him then: John "Homesick James" Williamson, a guitarist from Somerville, said he and Williamson were boyhood friends, and James "Yank" Rachell, a mandolinist from Brownsville, claimed Williamson was a youngster riding a bicycle in Jackson when they met.

Though still in his teens, Williamson was anxious to work with Rachell at country dances. Reluctant at first, Rachell finally gave in, and the two became partners. Around this time, Williamson also met two other musicians from Brownsville: Sleepy John Estes, a country blues guitarist who often played with Rachell, and harmonica player Hammie Nixon, six years Williamson's senior and a major influence on his style. In various configurations, Williamson worked with these bluesmen, playing local suppers and juke joints, and by 1929 they were playing throughout Arkansas and Tennessee.

By 1930 Williamson was visiting Memphis, home to several noted mouth-harp players, including jug-band artists Will Shade and Noah Lewis, who had been an early influence on Nixon. In Memphis, Williamson, known by now as Sonny Boy Williamson, picked up repertoire and techniques from an informal group of jug-band and street musicians who played in Church Park and on the city's streetcars. He also began an association with Mississippi piano player Albert Luandrew, better known as Sunnyland Slim.

Through most of the 1930s Williamson commuted between the burgeoning blues centers in the North and his home in Jackson, where in November 1937 he married Lacey Belle Davidson, the coauthor of many of his compositions. It was Williamson's second marriage, though little is known about his first wife, Sally Mae Hunt. The number of his children, if any, is unknown.

A 1934 commute took Williamson to Chicago, where he met Big Bill Broonzy and other transplanted southern artists. In 1936 he was in St. Louis, forming harmonica-guitar trios with Robert Lee McCoy (better known as Robert Nighthawk), Big Joe Williams, and Henry Townsend, among others. A year later, pianist Walter Davis, who doubled as a scout for RCA Victor Record Company's Bluebird label, arranged a meeting with Chicago-based music publisher Lester Melrose. That led to a recording session on 5 May 1937 in Aurora, Illinois, featuring Williamson with guitarists Williams and Nighthawk. The session yielded a half-dozen sides, including the classics "Good Morning, Little School Girl," "Bluebird Blues," and "Sugar Mama Blues." Six months later, a second Aurora session, which included Walter Davis and Henry Townsend, produced another blues standard, "Early in the Morning." While staying with Townsend in St. Louis in 1937, Williamson began working again with Yank Rachell, his first partner. That laid the groundwork for a third recording session in Aurora on 13 March 1938, on which Big Joe Williams rounded out the group.

In 1939 Williamson sent for his wife and permanently moved to Chicago. Starting that year and continuing through 1947, Williamson had at least one recording session each year, except for a two-year break during World War II. He cut 120 sides, including classics such as "Sloppy Drunk Blues," "Checkin' Up on My Baby," "Hoo-doo Hoo-doo," and "You Better Cut That Out." The recordings from that period document a change in Williamson's music. He generally worked with a piano player—Walter Davis, Joshua Altheimer, Blind John Davis, Eddie Boyd, or Big Maceo. Guitarists included Big Bill Broonzy, Tampa Red, and, in a final session on 12 November 1947 for RCA Victor, Willie Lacey on electric guitar, an innovation Williamson had resisted, at least on recordings, up to that point. He used drummers Charles Sanders, Fred Williams, Armand "Jump" Jackson, and Judge Riley, and bass players such as Ransom Knowling and Willie Dixon. These sessions helped spur the evolving postwar ensemble sound that would be brought to fruition after Williamson's death by artists like Muddy Waters, who supposedly played guitar in Williamson's band from time to time after he first hit Chicago in 1943.

In 1946 Williamson and fellow southern blues artists Broonzy and Memphis Slim participated in a New York recording session set up by folklorist Alan Lomax. The session, now available as *Blues in the Mississippi Night*, yielded a combination of commentary and music describing blues in relation to the oppressive conditions faced by African Americans in Mississippi, content then considered so controversial that Lomax concealed the identities of the three artists with pseudonyms—"Sib" in Williamson's case.

During the 1940s Williamson also made his mark outside the recording studio. He was a regular in Chicago's open-air Maxwell Street Market. He worked top blues clubs such as Sylvio's and the Plantation Club and was considered by fellow musicians to be the most popular blues-band leader in Chicago. Sidemen included the cream of the city's blues talent.

Returning from a late-night engagement at the Plantation Club on 1 June 1948, Williamson was assaulted and robbed. According to legend, he managed to stagger home, where he awakened his wife, said, "Lord, have mercy," and died in her arms. His body was shipped to his home in Jackson for burial in the Blair's Chapel cemetery.

It should be noted that late in his career Williamson was known professionally as Sonny Boy Williamson No. 1, to distinguish him from Aleck Miller, an older, Mississippi-born harmonica player who assumed Williamson's name and was often referred to as Sonny Boy Williamson No. 2. Although No. 2 went to his grave claiming to be the original Sonny Boy, other artists of that era generally condemned him for trying to cash in on Williamson's name.

A highly influential artist, Williamson changed the way the harmonica was played by those who followed him, including his most famous protégé, Little Walter Jacobs. He exemplified a traditional black folk style in which the harmonica acted as a second voice, responding to the vocal phrasing, as opposed to the more melodic phrasing common to the string-band or jug-band tradition, and thus he brought the harmonica to the forefront as a lead instrument. As fellow bluesman Otis Spann told author Rick Milne in a 1960s interview, "The first Sonny Boy put the harp in the union. . . . Then the price of harps went up."

An accomplished vocalist with a distinctive, personable delivery, Williamson turned a supposed speech impediment into an attractive, even imitated, vocal style. As songwriters, he and his wife composed a remarkable number of blues that have become part of the traditional repertoire of Chicago artists. From country string band to jug band to acoustic piano-guitar-harmonica trios to the full amplified Chicago blues sound, Sonny Boy Williamson participated in the changing blues tradition as a shaping force, taking it from its rural roots to its urban flowering as the immediate forerunner of rock and roll.

• For discographical information, see Robert M. W. Dixon and John Godrich, *Blues and Gospel Records: 1902–1943* (1982); Mike Leadbitter and Neil Slaven, *Blues Records 1943–1970*, vol. 2 (1994); and Paul Oliver, ed., *The Blackwell Guide to Blues Records* (1989). For general information see Sheldon Harris, *Blues Who's Who: A Biographical Dictionary of Blues Singers* (1979); Mike Rowe, *Chicago Breakdown* (1973); and the collected records and recollections on file at the Jackson-Madison County Public Library, Jackson, Tenn. For a discussion of Williamson's style, see David Evans, "Goin' Up the Country," in *Nothing But the Blues*, ed. Lawrence Cohn (1993). For details of his death, see Leadbitter, ed., *Nothing But the Blues* (1971). For a personal reminiscence, see Big Bill Broonzy and Yannick Bruynoghe, *Big Bill Blues: William Broonzy's Story* (1992).

BILL MCCULLOCH
BARRY LEE PEARSON

WILLICH, August (19 Nov. 1810–22 Jan. 1878), military leader and socialist writer, was born Johann August Ernst von Willich in Braunsberg, East Prussia, the son of Johann G. N. W. von Willich, an army officer and civil official, and Fredericka Lisette Michalowska. (Some prominent Cincinnatians, Karl Marx, Friedrich Engels, and Willich himself on one occasion supported the claim that he was an illegitimate Hohenzollern.) After his father's death in 1813, August went to live with Friedrich Schleiermacher, a philosophy professor in Berlin, who had married the widow of Willich's uncle. At the age of twelve he attended cadet school and then the Royal Military Academy in Berlin, directed by Carl von Clausewitz, from which he was commissioned lieutenant and stationed in Westphalia.

Around 1845 Willich and Friedrich Anneke led a circle of army officers studying Hegel and "true socialism" from Ludwig Feuerbach and Moses Hess. After Anneke was dismissed from the army, Willich protested in an open letter to the king and resigned his commission as incompatible with human rights and dignity. Dropping the "von" from his name, he became a carpenter—parading with an ax on his shoulder in front of his former associates—and president of the Cologne Communist Association. At the outbreak of revolution in 1848, he led a demonstration at the Cologne city hall in the name of "the working class" and joined the insurgent forces of Hecker and Struve, leaders of the movement for a national republic. A year later, with Friedrich Engels as his adjutant, he commanded a *Handwerklegion*, the last unit forced off German soil. Engels found him to be "brave, cold-blooded, skillful" in battle but otherwise a "boring ideologist and true socialist."

In spite of differences, Marx and Engels brought Willich into the Communist League in London, the gathering place for the defeated revolutionists. Willich's strong personality and sharing of privation made him a leader. With Marx, Engels, Jules Vidil, leader of French Blanquists, and George Harney, revolutionary English Chartist, Willich signed an international call for "overthrow of all privileged classes and their subjection to the dictatorship of the proletarians by maintaining the revolution in permanence up to the achievement of communism, the ultimate organizational form of the human family." Late in 1850, with improved economic conditions, the league split. On one side, Willich and Karl Schapper, agreeing with Auguste Blanqui, inveterate French insurrectionist, demanded forceful revolution in Germany for "principle" and "action." On the other, Marx and Engels condemned such action as "idealistic," a form of "alchemy" ungrounded in economic development. In the feuding that followed, Marx accused Willich of aiding Prussian police. Willich said that Marx regarded workers as "zeros" and the Communist League as his personal property. Marx belittled Willich's military record and challenged his veracity in a taunting pamphlet, *Der Ritter vom edelmütigen Bewußtsein* (*The Knight of Noble Consciousness*), using Willich's alleged answers to forged letters Marx himself had initiated and guided in their writing by his young associate, Conrad Schramm, to ridicule "the great Field Marshall and Social Messiah" for seeking a ruthless military dictatorship. For Marx the communist movement should proceed by "education and gradual development." The bitterness on both sides, however, had disappeared when Willich later linked his socialism with Marx, and Marx expressed misgivings about his accusations and commended Willich's record in the American Civil War, "the best," said Engels, of all the Germans.

Emigrating to America in 1853, Willich worked in the Brooklyn Navy Yard and U.S. Coastal Survey and then became "responsible editor" (1858–1861) of the *Cincinnati Republikaner*, through which he developed his philosophical and social views well beyond his letter to the king. He considered Hegel "the greatest philosopher of the nineteenth century" and publicized Marx's "proofs" in economics of Hegel's "dialectical principle of the interconnection of events in history."

Willich's view of human nature and history reflected the influence of Ludwig Feuerbach, a prominent "Left-Hegelian." Through thought man is infinite, a "universal being" in Humanity, but in relation to body and senses man is particular, egoistic, and selfish. The whole of history, Willich held, should be viewed as the struggle of these opposites toward unity in a series of "necessary steps." Hence he attacked the Christian dualism of spirit and matter as bolstering the cleavage between government and people, capital and labor.

In a prominent review (June 1859)—one of the first published anywhere—of the *Contribution to the Critique of Political Economy* (1859), Willich quoted virtually all of Marx's classic statement of his philosophy of history in relation to Hegel. Willich shared Marx's labor theory of value and related ideas of exploitation and class struggle. Workers cannot receive the true value of their labor, Willich insisted, until they take the power of government and industry into their own hands "to establish on the economic field as well as on the political and religious, the principle of the republic, self-government and self-direction of the people." So, workers must immediately organize or join self-governing, democratic unions and then connect them in representative assemblies and a sovereign national assembly. Willich thus anticipated Marx's position of 1871 on the basis of socialism in workers' associations and cooperatives and also the continuing movement for "industrial democracy."

But Willich did not neglect immediate political action. Though not himself a candidate, his Labor Ticket for Cincinnati included future president Rutherford B. Hayes for city solicitor, and he urged support of the Republicans, with reservations, as clearly preferable to the "Slavo-Democratic" party. In 1860 he ardently championed John Frémont and Cassius Clay, as did Hayes. Disappointed in the "compromise" nomination of Abraham Lincoln, he nevertheless urged his readers to "battle for Lincoln" as "soldiers of freedom."

At the call for a German regiment to support the Union, Willich enlisted as a private, was immediately elected adjutant, and trained four companies of workmen in "undefiled High Dutch." By the war's end he had been breveted major general with a fighting record hailed as "the finest" and "brilliant," reflected in monuments naming him at Shiloh, Chickamauga, and Missionary Ridge. He had the affection of common soldiers because he treated them "like men, not dogs." In camp he would assemble his troops, address them as "citizens," and proceed to a lecture on socialism.

After the war Willich was elected auditor of Hamilton County on the Union (predominantly Republican) ticket. Caught by the patriotic feeling for Germany against France in 1870, he offered his military services in Berlin. When his offer was declined, he attended lectures at the university on economics, physics, and natural law. From Germany he returned to Ohio to spend his remaining years in the canal town of St. Marys. He actively participated in the Liberal Republican movement against "Grantism" and particularly its element surviving in a radical "People's Party," frequently addressed patriotic meetings and German-

American societies, and organized a Shakespeare Club that fathered St. Marys' public library. His large military funeral marked the passing in St. Marys of a beloved figure, a lifelong bachelor with candy in his pockets for children, of whom he said, "Alle amerikanischen Kinder sind auch meine Kinder" ("All American children are also my children").

• The complete run of the *Cincinnati Republikaner* under Willich's editorship is in the Midwest Interlibrary Center, Chicago, and on microfilm in the Cincinnati Historical Society. Charles D. Stewart, "A Bachelor General," *Wisconsin Magazine of History* 17 (1933): 131–54, is a general biography including reminiscences of Willich's last years but neglecting his socialism and philosophical views as found in his pamphlet *Im preussischen Heere!* (1848). Also see E. Czobel, "Zur Geschichte des Kommunistenbundes," *Archiv für die Geschichte des Sozialismus* 11 (1925): 300–332, and articles in *Cincinnati Republikaner, Organ der Arbeiter*, translated in L. Easton, *Hegel's First American Followers* (1966), pp. 312–30. Willich's relation to Marx is developed in Karl Marx, *Revelations Concerning the Communist Trial in Cologne*, Chap. 6 and postscript, ed. R. Livingstone (1971); Willich, "Dr. Karl Marx und Seine Enthüllingen," *Belletristisches Journal und New-Yorker Criminal-Zeitung*, 28 Oct. 1853, pp. 329–30; Marx, "The Knight of Noble Consciousness," in *Marx and Engels Collected Works*, vol. 12, ed. Jack Cohen et al. (1979), pp. 479–508; and Marx Letter (10 Feb. 1851) and "Röser's Evidence," *Marx and Engels Collected Works*, vol. 38, ed. Jack Cohen et al. (1979), pp. 284, 551. Details on Willich's Civil War record are in James Barnett, "August Willich, Soldier Extraordinary," *Historical and Philosophical Society of Ohio Bulletin* 20 (1962): 60–74, and W. Kaufmann, *Die Deutschen in Amerikanischen Bürgerkrieg* (1911), pp. 474–75.

LOYD D. EASTON

WILLIER, Benjamin Harrison (2 Nov. 1890–3 Dec. 1972), embryologist and educator, was born near Weston, Wood County, Ohio, the son of David Willier, a farmer and banker, and Mary Alice Rickard. His childhood and early experiences were those of a country boy in the fundamentalist society of mid-America. He entered the College of Wooster in Ohio in 1912 and graduated with highest honors in biology in 1915. He taught biology for one year at Wooster before beginning graduate research in the Department of Zoology at the University of Chicago in 1916. His academic work was interrupted in 1918 by a brief period of military service in Washington, D.C. He returned to Chicago in 1919 and married Helen Beatrice Shipman, a teacher and his former college biology laboratory partner; they had two children. He completed his graduate research at the university under the direction of zoologist F. R. Lillie and received a Ph.D. in zoology magna cum laude in 1920.

Willier joined the faculty of the University of Chicago as an associate in zoology in 1919 and became an instructor in 1920, an assistant professor in 1924, an associate professor in 1927, and a professor in 1931. In 1933 he was named professor of zoology and head of the Department of Biology at the University of Rochester in New York. In 1940 he moved to Baltimore, Maryland, where he served as chairman of the Department of Biology at The Johns Hopkins University until 1955. From 1940 to 1958 he was also Henry Walters Professor of Zoology; thereafter he remained in residence as professor emeritus until his death in Baltimore.

Willier's eminence as a scientist resides in his contributions to the field of experimental embryology, his outstanding ability as an administrator, and in the number of eminent scientists who studied under him. He first received recognition while an instructor at Wooster, where he had the opportunity to make microscopic serial sections of a human embryo that had been removed from a hysterectomy patient about seventeen days after fertilization. Wax-plate reconstructions of this embryo are preserved in the collections of the Carnegie Institution of Washington (the "Mateer Embryo").

Willier's doctoral thesis at Chicago contributed significantly to knowledge of the role of sex hormones in the embryonic differentiation of the sexual characteristics of the gonads. In cattle, a female born co-twin to a normal male is called a "free-martin" and usually is sterile. The gonads of vertebrate animals are bisexual in origin, regardless of their genetic sex, but in the free-martin the sex hormones of the male suppress the development of the female component of the gonad while promoting the growth and differentiation of the male component. Willier made a detailed analysis of the microscopic anatomy of free-martin gonads, demonstrating that the varying degrees of modification in the male direction are correlated with the timing and extent of shared blood circulation with the male.

At Chicago, Willier rapidly achieved wide recognition as a developmental endocrinologist. He devoted much of his attention to the role of sex hormones in the differentiation of reproductive organs in birds. He introduced the method of transplanting bits of tissue to the vascular chorioallantoic membrane of the chick embryo to determine effects of thyroid and gonadal grafts on the sexual differentiation of the host embryo. The same method of grafting was later used to test the ability of fragments of embryos to produce organ-specific tissues when isolated on the chorioallantois. This procedure enabled construction of fate maps for as yet undifferentiated regions of the early embryo.

At Rochester, Willier turned his attention to the origin of melanocytes, the specialized cells that contribute the pigmentary patterns of skin, feathers, and hair. By means of suitable grafting experiments that involved various breeds of chicks, other kinds of fowl, and mice, Willier and his associates showed for fowl that the genetic endowment of the melanocyte determines the color pattern that it can create, as modified by the growth rate of feathers, and by hormonal secretions of the host embryo. Willier continued this work at Johns Hopkins and saw it expanded to other kinds of problems by some of his students, notably by those working in the fields of immunology and pattern regulation.

At Hopkins, Willier was an outstanding organizer and administrator who clearly foresaw that the future of experimental biology lay in the investigation of the molecular events underlying the life process. Assembling a coterie of talented investigators and teachers, he created an intellectual atmosphere that has led to the recognition of the Hopkins biology department as one of the leading centers for research in molecular biology.

An exceptional teacher, Willier trained his doctoral students largely through the seminar method. He outlined topics of current importance, such as problems of fertilization, biology of sex, neuroembryology, and dependent differentiation. For each topic, he would prepare a critical literature list directed to key papers organized about selected subtopics. Students were challenged to report orally on their assigned papers, to recognize the pertinent data, to examine them critically, and to make significant interpretations and generalizations. Seminar performance was judged by peers and faculty, and a student's fate depended on his or her seminar performance. Typically, a newly arrived student was presented by Willier with an imposing stack of publications from his laboratory. Once these had been digested, the student was to return with an idea for research that would presumably contribute a significant advance to the field of embryology and was then left essentially alone, reporting to the "chief" when something of importance was found.

This preceptoral method proved highly successful. Willier sponsored a total of thirty-four doctoral candidates, and almost all produced significant theses and embarked on distinguished careers in embryology. Through the training of his students, Willier probably exerted a greater impact on the field of developmental biology than any other person of his generation. His students have achieved international recognition as teachers and investigators and have served as advisers to federal agencies, editors of significant journals in the field of embryonic development, chairs of distinguished departments of biology, officers of major professional societies, and members of the National Academy of Sciences.

In these activities, Willier's students have followed in his footsteps. He was, himself, honored by election to the National Academy of Sciences, the American Philosophical Society, and the American Academy of Arts and Sciences, among other distinguished bodies. He exercised numerous editorial responsibilities, served on many advisory boards, and enjoyed ancillary appointments in various educational institutions other than Hopkins.

• A selection of reprints of Willier's scientific papers is held in the library of the Marine Biological Laboratory, Woods Hole, Mass. A paper that best indicates the meticulous quality of Willier's scholarship is his "The Embryonic Development of Sex," in *Sex and Internal Secretions*, ed. E. A. Allen et al. (1939). Willier's biography of F. R. Lillie, "Frank Rattray Lillie, 1870–1947: A Biographical Memoir," National Academy of Sciences, *Biographical Memoirs* 30 (1957): 178–236, provides interesting clues to his own scholarly information. The definitive biography of Willier is R. L. Watterson, "Benjamin Harrison Willier, 1890–1972: A Biographical Memoir," National Academy of Sciences, *Biographical Memoirs* 55 (1985): 539–628. Appended to this memoir are complete lists of Willier's publications, his doctoral students, honors, editorial activities, and activities in various professional societies and organizations. A more concise biography is Watterson, "Benjamin Harrison Willier: 1890–1972: His life as an Outstanding Biologist, Embryologist and Developmental Biologist," *Developmental Biology* 34 (1973): f–1 to f–19.

JOHN W. SAUNDERS, JR.

WILLING, Jennie Fowler (22 Jan. 1834–6 Oct. 1916), evangelist, reformer, and church worker, was born in Burford, Canada West (present-day Ontario), the daughter of Horatio Fowler, a homesteader and participant in the Papineau Rebellion of 1837, and Harriet Ryan, the daughter of the founder of Canadian Methodism, Henry Ryan. The Fowlers settled in Newark, Illinois, following Horatio's expulsion from Canada after the failure of the rebellion. Jennie was a sickly child and largely self-educated. Her first job was as a school teacher in Illinois at age fifteen.

Raised Congregational, she converted to Methodism when she married William Crossgrove Willing, a Methodist minister, in 1853; they had no children. They saw their ministry as a partnership and operated that way throughout their lives, during which they served fifteen charges in Illinois and New York. The nineteenth century was a time of revivals that stressed conversion and sanctification. People accepted Jesus into their lives—their conversion—and then they strove to love God perfectly, to make their wills one with God's will, and to do and be what God wanted them to do and be. This was entire sanctification. The Willings believed in entire sanctification and claimed it for themselves. Willing attributed her untiring activities to this "perfect love."

Willing was committed to the work of the church. In the mid-to late 1800s women were involved in church work primarily through missionary societies. Their task was to send and support single women in the mission fields of India, Persia, and China. In 1869 Willing became one of the three first corresponding secretaries for the Woman's Foreign Missionary Society (WFMS) of the Methodist Episcopal church. Her job was to organize all the territory between the state of Ohio and the Pacific Ocean, which she accomplished. She resigned as corresponding secretary in 1883 but continued to write articles for the society's magazine, *The Heathen Woman's Friend*. She remained active in the WFMS to the end of her life.

Her lifelong commitment to women's education was beginning to be shared by society. In January 1874 she was appointed professor of English language and literature at Illinois Wesleyan University in Bloomington, Illinois, a post she held until resigning in November 1875. While she was teaching at Wesleyan, she became more fully involved in temperance work. She organized and was president of the Bloomington and the Illinois Woman's Temperance Leagues. It was under Willing's name that the call to organize the Woman's Christian Temperance Union was sent following her lectures on temperance at Chautauqua in 1874. In 1875 she became editor of the organization's first paper, the *Woman's Temperance Union*. In 1876 the name was changed to *Our Union*, and Willing stepped down to become a contributing editor.

Willing's concern for missions was an ever present one. She felt that the duty of spreading the word about Christ and bringing people into the assurance of God's salvation had been laid upon all but especially upon women. Willing saw that mission work needed to be done at home in the United States as well, but the WFMS could not spread itself any thinner. A new organization, the Woman's Home Missionary Society (WHMS) of the Methodist Episcopal church, was formed in 1880. Willing was not active initially in forming the WHMS but was appointed "general organizer" in 1884, the only salaried officer of the society. For the next two years, she traveled thousands of miles, organizing local societies all over the country. At the 1886 annual meeting of the WHMS, Willing moved that the position of general organizer be abolished and the care and development of local organizations be turned over to the conference secretaries. From 1886 until 1894 Willing served as the secretary of numerous of the society's bureaus. She also wrote for the society's magazine, *Woman's Home Missions*.

In 1895, after her husband died and with her own money, Willing opened the New York Evangelical Training School and Settlement House in the section of New York City known as Hell's Kitchen. There she combined all the causes that had gripped her soul and life. As an active settlement worker and evangelist, she could actively bring people to Christ and address the issues of temperance, poverty, and injustice that had so moved her from a young age. As the principal and teacher, she could direct the education of the young women who would enter the field with her. She could also preach and write. She furnished a monthly column to the *Guide to Holiness* and in 1898 was named a corresponding editor of that journal. When the *Guide* ceased publication in 1901, she carried her literary endeavours over to her own project. In 1903 the *Open Door* first appeared. At first a quarterly, it went bimonthly in 1909 and monthly in 1910. Extant copies of the *Open Door* end in 1911; it is not clear if the magazine continued past this date.

Little is known of the last five years of Willing's life. The Training School closed in 1910, when the property was torn down to build the Pennsylvania Railroad station. It is clear that she remained in New York City. She continued writing, though her output slowed considerably, and she remained active in her organizations until her death. She died in New York City.

Willing was a tireless writer, authoring seventeen books and hundreds of articles for numerous magazines and journals. She wrote on many subjects: missions, temperance, women's rights, education for women, theology, advice books on how to raise boys and on how to raise girls, anti-Catholic and anti-Mormon material, poverty, and women's role in the church. She was granted a license to preach in 1877 by her husband, who was a presiding elder in the Rock River Conference of the Methodist Episcopal church at the time. She lost it in 1880 when the General Conference of the church revoked the licenses of all women to preach. Nevertheless, she was in great demand as an evangelist around the country. She worked out of the Rock River Conference (Illinois) and, after she and her husband moved to New York City in 1889, the New York Conference.

The facts cannot recover the person who had such a great effect on so many lives. All reports about Willing testify to her enthusiasm, her eloquence and power as a speaker, her smile, her tireless zeal, and her dedication to the cause of Christ, as do her writings. She was a woman who traveled widely, taking three trips abroad as well as traveling extensively within the United States. Even though she was one of the most widely known women of her time, she has passed into what Horace Bushnell referred to as "dead history," the realm of those whose influence remains but are themselves little remembered. This is partly because the causes that she championed, such as missions, temperance, and the Christian Socialist movement, became less popular as decades passed. It is also because of her grass-roots organizing style, never letting an organization become identified with her, as did Frances Willard, but moving on once things were up and running. Her motto *Plus Ultra*—More Beyond—sums up her life and her work.

• There are no manuscript collections or gathered archival material. All her books are extant in at least one copy, and her articles can be found in the journals for which they were written. Joanne Carlson Brown, *'Til Heart Purity Rules the Land: The Life and Thought of Jennie Fowler Willing* (n.d.), provides a thorough look at Willing's life and work. Brief biographical sketches are included in Clara Chapin, *Thumbnail Sketches of White Ribbon Women* (1895); Phebe A. Hanford, *Daughters of America* (1882); Frances E. Willard and Mary A. Livermore, *American Women* (1897); Frances E. Willard, *Woman and Temperance* (1883); Matthew Simpson, *Cyclopedia of Methodism* (1881); and Ernest Cherrington, *The Standard Encyclopedia of the Alcohol Problem* (1930). See also Theodore Agnew, "Reflections on the Woman's Foreign Missionary Movement in Late Nineteenth Century American Methodism," *Methodist History*, Jan. 1968, pp. 3–16, in which Willing is one of the women considered. Obituaries are in the *New York Times*, 7 Oct. 1916, and the *Christian Advocate*, 9 Nov. 1916.

JOANNE CARLSON BROWN

WILLING, Thomas (19 Dec. 1731–19 Jan. 1821), merchant, political leader, and banker, was born in Philadelphia, Pennsylvania, the son of Charles Willing, a successful merchant and, later, mayor of Philadelphia, and Anne Shippen, granddaughter of Edward Shippen, the first mayor of Philadelphia. The Willings in 1740 sent young Thomas to England to be educated. He first went to school at Bath between 1740 and 1743 and then attended Robert Wheeler's school at Wells, Somersetshire. Willing went to London in September

1748 and for six months took courses in business at the Watt's Academy. The same year he began to read law at the Inner Temple.

After his return to Philadelphia in 1749, Willing worked in his father's countinghouse and in 1751 became a partner. Willing's father died in 1754, leaving him an inheritance of about £6,000. Willing took control of the business and with Robert Morris in 1754 established the partnership of Willing, Morris and Company. Willing helped to develop the firm into one of the most profitable businesses in the city. He purchased ships to transport merchandise, sold grains and household products to merchants in Maryland and Virginia, exported flour and lumber to European firms, and imported sugar, molasses, and dry goods. In 1763 Willing married Anne McCall. The couple had thirteen children, one of whom, Anne Willing Bingham, later became a ranking figure in Philadelphia society.

Willing in many ways provided leadership to colonial Pennsylvania and Philadelphia. In his role as assistant secretary to the Pennsylvania delegation at the 1754 Albany Congress he participated in the first intercolonial assembly. He was elected in 1755 to the common council of Philadelphia. Willing in 1758 was named as one of the Pennsylvania commissioners for trade with the western Indians; he held this position for approximately seven years and worked to obtain funding from the Pennsylvania assembly for commerce and forts. In 1760 Willing began thirty-one years of service as a trustee of the Academy and Charitable School of the Province of Pennsylvania (now the University of Pennsylvania). As one of five commissioners named in 1761 to oversee the surveying of the disputed Pennsylvania-Maryland boundary line, he helped to bring a resolution by agreeing to extend the boundary 230 miles westward. That same year he was appointed judge of the Orphan's Court of Philadelphia. In 1763 Willing was elected mayor of the city for one year. As mayor, he secured monies for the building of bridges and markets in the city. Between 1764 and 1767 he served in the provincial assembly. Willing resigned from the assembly in 1767 and was named that year as a justice of the Pennsylvania Supreme Court, a position he held for ten years.

In the same period, Willing became a conservative and a cautious supporter of the American protest against British colonial policy. He was the first person to sign the 1765 Philadelphia nonimportation resolutions, for he thought that the Stamp Act was unconstitutional under British law. During the early 1770s Willing continued to speak in favor of colonial rights. However, his English education, his Anglicanism, and his friendship with Pennsylvania's longtime proprietors, the Penns, predisposed him against radicalism. He opposed groups favoring revolution within Pennsylvania and separation from Great Britain.

Willing was named in 1774 as president of the first Provincial Congress of Pennsylvania, supporting its petitions to the British to restore the constitutional liberties of the colonies. He was elected in 1775 to the Second Continental Congress and cast his vote on 1 July 1776 against the resolution of Richard Henry Lee for independence, believing that America was not sufficiently prepared for war and that neither the Pennsylvania assembly nor popular sentiment had authorized a vote for separation. Willing was not selected for the new Pennsylvania delegation to the Second Continental Congress in 1776. He stayed in Philadelphia after British troops occupied the city but refused to take the oath of allegiance to George III.

Business opportunities doubtlessly warmed Willing's interest in the American Revolution. His firm aided the revolutionary cause between 1776 and 1780, while accruing profits to itself. Willing negotiated profitable contracts with the Committee of Secret Trade to acquire supplies needed for the war. Through an intricate network of agents, Willing purchased guns, bullets, blankets, and medicines for the revolutionary armies, paying for these items with American grains, rice, and tobacco. As a result of his business activities from the late 1770s to the 1790s, he derived a fortune of approximately $1 million.

Willing occupied significant positions of leadership in American banking in the quarter century after the Revolution ended. He was elected in 1781 as president of the Bank of North America, the first national bank. Willing in various ways made the bank profitable; he created adequate cash reserves, limited loans to thirty days, and developed a short term credit base. However, a bank war posed a threat to Willing's bank. Quaker merchants in Philadelphia established in 1785 the Bank of Pennsylvania to rival the Bank of North America, and William Findley and other rural legislators the next year protested in the state assembly against Willing's bank for failing to extend loans to farmers. Willing in 1786 successfully protected the Bank of North America. He maintained the monopoly of his bank in Philadelphia by selling its stock at the reduced price of $400 per share to leaders of the Bank of Pennsylvania, and he agreed to have his bank provide loans to farmers in the state.

Willing's bank, which also was rechartered in 1787, had attempted during the early and middle 1780s to deal with the problem of reducing the national debt. Along with Robert Morris, Willing believed that to curtail the debt and to restore the nation's economic productivity, the Bank of North America should circulate a national currency, make loans to the states, and issue and redeem notes. However, the bank by 1786 met with little success over the issue of the public debt; it encountered pressures about extending loans. Moreover, the states, which had rejected the proposals of Morris, began to flood the market with their own paper money.

Willing, who was a spokesman for the 1787 federal Constitution, became involved in the affairs of the first Bank of the United States. When the debate about this bank arose in 1791, Willing was perceived by Thomas Jefferson, James Madison, and other opponents of the institution as being a member of the Philadelphia moneyed group that well might come to dominate the affairs of the nation. Willing, whose contact with Alexander Hamilton was limited, did back his proposal for the creation of a national bank. Willing believed that the bank was needed in order to bring stability to the nation's finances and to stimulate the development of its business and manufacturing enterprises.

Following enactment of Hamilton's bank bill in 1791, Willing was appointed as president of the first Bank of the United States. That year he played an active role in selling out the bank's stock shares to private investors and the next year in issuing its notes, which would become an acceptable form of paper currency in the nation. Between 1792 and 1795 Willing approved $6.2 million of loans to the Treasury Department to pay off debts from the Revolution. After receiving a payment in 1797 for $4.4 million from Treasury Secretary Oliver Wolcott, Willing between 1797 and 1799 conducted less business with this government agency. In 1802 Willing received from Albert Gallatin, Jefferson's treasury secretary, funds to reduce even further the debt owed to the Bank of the United States. Between 1802 and 1806 Willing had much to say about the central bank's policies regarding deposits and loan requirements. Under his direction, the bank catered much more to businessmen than to government leaders and especially relied on the operations of its branch offices.

In 1807 Willing was stricken by a paralytic stroke that left him unable to speak. He consequently was constrained to resign his position as president of the bank. His health subsequently improved, but he never resumed his career in banking. Willing died in Philadelphia.

Willing contributed to business and banking during the eighteenth and early nineteenth centuries. He became one of the most eminent members of the mercantile aristocracy in eighteenth century Philadelphia, and his career illustrated the success of merchant capitalism in that city. Willing at first was a reluctant revolutionary, but he then rendered through his business activities assistance that was essential for victory during the War of Independence. Moreover, he promoted the growth of finance capitalism in America; Willing is known for adhering to conservative business practices, for helping to establish a workable monetary system, and for assisting in the improvement of the nation's credit rating. He also played a prominent role in extending banking services to major regions in the nation and in providing capital to the private sector as well as to the national government.

• T. W. Balch, *Willing Letters and Papers Edited with a Biographical Sketch of Thomas Willing* (1922), includes an autobiography, letterbooks, and drafts of some minutes of the board of directors of the Bank of the United States. Other pertinent primary materials about Willing can be found in the Gratz Collection of the Historical Society of Pennsylvania and in the Hamilton Papers in the Library of Congress. The only comprehensive biography is Burton Alva Konkle, *Thomas Willing and the First American Financial System* (1937). See also Balch, "Thomas Willing of Philadelphia (1731–1821)," *Pennsylvania Magazine of History and Biography* 46 (1922): 1–14. For his business activities consult Clarence L. Ver Steeg, *Robert Morris: Revolutionary Financier* (1954), and Thomas M. Doerflinger, *A Vigorous Spirit of Enterprise: Merchants and Economic Development in Revolutionary Philadelphia* (1986). Eugene R. Slaski, "Thomas Willing: A Study in Moderation, 1774–1778," *Pennsylvania Magazine of History and Biography* 100 (1976): 491–506, explains his conservatism during the Revolution. His leadership in banking is assessed in Bray Hammond, *Banks and Politics in America from the Revolution to the Civil War* (1957); E. James Ferguson, *The Power of the Purse: A History of American Public Finance, 1776–1790* (1961); and Richard Beeman et al., eds., *Beyond Confederation: Origins of the Constitution and American National Identity* (1987). Also see James Wettereau, "New Light on the First Bank of the United States," *Pennsylvania Magazine of History and Biography* 61 (1937): 263–85, and Edwin J. Perkins, *American Public Finance and Financial Services, 1700–1815* (1994).

WILLIAM WEISBERGER

WILLINGHAM, Robert Josiah (15 May 1854–20 Dec. 1914), Southern Baptist pastor and leader, was born in Beaufort, South Carolina, the son of Benjamin Lawton Willingham and Elizabeth Martha Baynard, plantation owners. His family moved to a second plantation near Albany in southwest Georgia just prior to General Robert T. Sherman's march north through South Carolina at the end of the Civil War. With the cessation of hostilities, the family returned to South Carolina. Willingham's public acceptance of Christianity occurred in 1867 during a protracted meeting in a country schoolhouse. He was baptized in a small creek near Concord Church, where his family worshiped.

In 1868, at the age of fourteen, he set off for the University of Georgia in Athens to study literature. There he played football and participated in debates. He interrupted his studies after two years so that he could assist his father, who had now moved to Macon, Georgia, as a bookkeeper in the family's cotton warehouse. Eventually he returned to the university and graduated in 1873 with high honors, receiving his master of arts degree and a medal in mathematics.

Following his graduation, Willingham moved to Macon, where he took a job as a teacher at the Macon High School. He married Corneille Bacon in 1874; they had at least six children. In the fall of 1874 he became principal of the high school. He also served as treasurer and Sunday school teacher at Macon's First Baptist Church. In 1877 he resigned his position at the school to pursue a career in law but in the meantime experienced a calling to Christian ministry.

Willingham was licensed to preach by the First Baptist Church of Macon on 19 December 1879, and leaving his family behind he moved to Louisville, Kentucky, to study at Southern Baptist Theological Seminary. After only a year in Louisville he returned to Georgia, where he was ordained and called to serve as pastor of three churches around Talbotton and Thomaston. He never completed his seminary education.

In October 1881 he left his three churches to move to Sardis Baptist Church in Barnesville. There he served as the first moderator of the Centennial Baptist Association and assisted the church in relocating its facilities.

In 1887 Willingham left Georgia to become pastor of the First Baptist Church of Chattanooga (1887–1891) and then the First Baptist Church of Memphis (1891–1893). He was also elected as Tennessee's representative to the Foreign Mission Board of the Southern Baptist Convention. He moved to Richmond, Virginia, in 1893 to assume the position of corresponding secretary of the Foreign Mission Board.

Under Willingham the board experienced steady growth in financial support, missionary appointments, and the opening of missions, including those in Argentina (1903), Macao (1910), and Uruguay (1911). He focused attention on the need for educational, medical, and publishing institutions as well as decent housing for missionaries, whose number increased from 92 to 298 during his tenure.

Willingham presided over the board's affairs in the aftermath of the U.S. victory in the Spanish-American War, when a spirit of unparalleled evangelical cooperation gripped American Protestants. He continued the board's participation in the Interdenominational Conference on Foreign Mission Societies of the United States and Canada, a precursor to the Federal (later World) Council of Churches. Its primary purpose was to provide counsel and suggest directions for the worldwide Protestant mission effort. Willingham regularly attended its meetings. He also encouraged the board to support the work of the Student Volunteer Movement and the Layman's Missionary Movement. Between 1910 and 1912 he developed principles of cooperation in foreign missions with the Northern Baptist Convention and the Baptist World Alliance.

Willingham's ecumenical spirit of cooperation with other denominations and his indefatigable support of the Southern Baptist world mission were his greatest contributions to the Southern Baptist Convention. He died in Richmond, Virginia.

• Willingham's papers, including his correspondence and sermons, are in the archives of the Foreign Mission Board of the Southern Baptist Convention in Richmond, Va. Willingham's daughter Elizabeth Walton Willingham has written *Robert J. Willingham: A Biography* (1917). See also William R. Estep, *Whole Gospel, Whole World: The Foreign Mission Board of the Southern Baptist Convention, 1845–1995* (1994), and Baker James Cauthen, ed., *Advance: A History of Southern Baptist Foreign Missions* (1970).

ROBERT N. NASH, JR.

WILLIS, Albert Shelby (22 Jan. 1843–6 Jan. 1897), lawyer, congressman, and diplomat, was born in Shelbyville, Shelby County, Kentucky, the son of Shelby Willis, a locally prominent physician, and Harriet Button. When Willis was seven, he and his widowed mother moved to Louisville, Kentucky, where he attended common schools and graduated first in his class in 1860 from Male High School. He taught school and attended law school, graduating in 1866 from the Louisville Law School. Because at twenty-two he was too young to enter the practice of law, Willis taught for another year before entering into a partnership with his stepfather, J. L. Clemmons, a prominent member of the Louisville bar.

A skilled debater known for his thorough preparation of legal cases, Willis soon became involved in local politics and was chosen to serve as a Democratic presidential elector in 1872. He won election to the office of commonwealth attorney for Jefferson County in 1870 and was reelected in 1874. In 1876 he was elected to the U.S. House of Representatives, where he served five successive terms (1877–1887), chairing the Committee on Rivers and Harbors from 1883 to 1887. In November 1878 he married Florence Dulaney; they had one child.

In Congress Willis labored to bring benefits to his district through legislation to improve the Louisville and Portland Canal and make it free to users; he also secured funding for a new post office and customhouse in his hometown. In 1886 Willis was defeated in a bitter primary in which he was accused of being too friendly to reform-minded Republicans on such matters as civil service reform and maintenance of the gold standard. In addition, his cosponsorship of the Blair-Willis Bill to provide federal funding for common schools was seen by his segregationist constituents as an attempt to provide for integrated education.

Willis returned to Louisville in 1887 following his failure to secure renomination for his congressional seat. He practiced law and engaged in various business ventures, including the founding of the Sun Life Insurance Company.

In September 1893 President Grover Cleveland appointed Willis envoy extraordinary and minister plenipotentiary to Hawaii. Following a coup d'état against Queen Liliuokalani, Sanford B. Dole headed a provisional government that sought annexation to the United States. Earlier that year Cleveland had withdrawn from the Senate a treaty of annexation negotiated by Secretary of State John W. Foster during the final weeks of the administration of Benjamin Harrison (1833–1901). Concerned about U.S. involvement in the revolution that had brought the provisional government to power, Cleveland had sent former congressman James H. Blount to Honolulu to investigate the situation. Upon his arrival, Blount ended a U.S. protectorate over the islands and wrote a report critical of the provisional government and of the Harrison administration, particularly the actions in support of the revolutionaries by Harrison's U.S. minister to Hawaii, John L. Stevens. Cleveland and Secretary of State Walter Q. Gresham accepted Blount's views. On 18 December, a month after Willis's arrival in Hawaii, the president publicly expressed his desire to see the queen restored and amnesty granted to the revolutionaries.

In Honolulu, Willis found himself in an extraordinarily difficult, if not impossible, position. Speculation about the Cleveland administration's policy had caused the provisional government to view Willis with suspicion. Thus, leaders of the provisional government were not entirely surprised when, on 19 December, Willis called upon them to vacate office and restore the queen and her administration. Dole declined to step aside and immediately prepared to defend his government against any possible intervention by the United States. Meanwhile, having been instructed by Gresham to urge the deposed monarch "to pursue a wise and humane policy," Willis discovered that the distraught queen was determined to behead the leaders of the provisional government. Seeking to bring about the restoration of the queen through negotiations, Willis managed only to embitter all sides. The Cleveland administration was not prepared to restore Liliuokalani by force and eventually accepted the situation in Hawaii. On 4 July 1894 the provisional government established the Republic of Hawaii. Willis, whose first months in Hawaii were filled with tension and anxiety, settled into more routine diplomatic chores, once it became apparent to all that he would not be implementing a policy to restore the monarchy. Frustrated over the collapse of his Hawaiian policy, Gresham, an ardent anti-imperialist who opposed the acquisition of insular possession, considered Willis an ineffective diplomat, and Willis seems to have perceived the policies of the secretary of state as overly idealistic and impractical. Nevertheless, Willis remained at his diplomatic post for three years, becoming a popular figure with Hawaii's pro-American political leadership and social elite. He died in Honolulu of pneumonia.

• The records of the provisional government are located in the Archives of Hawaii. Willis's diplomatic correspondence can be found in *Papers Relating to the Foreign Relations of the United States* (1894, app. 2; 1895; 1896; 1897). One volume of letters from Hawaii along with miscellaneous items is held in the library of the Filson Club Historical Society in Louisville. Biographical sources include J. J. McAfee, *Kentucky Politicians* (1896); *Biographical Directory of American Congress 1774–1989*; and H. Levin, ed., *The Lawyers and Lawmakers of Kentucky* (1897). See the Louisville *Courier-Journal*, 3–10 Oct. 1886, for details of Willis's campaign and defeat in the Democratic primary. The most thorough account of Willis's tenure in Hawaii is found in Charles W. Calhoun, "Morality and Spite: Walter Q. Gresham and U.S. Relations with Hawaii," *Pacific Historical Review* 52 (Aug. 1983): 292–311. Also see Donald Rowland, "The Establishment of the Republic of Hawaii," *Pacific Historical Review* 4 (Mar. 1935): 201–20; William A. Russ, *The Hawaiian Republic (1894–1898) and Its Struggle to Win Annexation* (1961); Merze Tate, *The United States and the Hawaiian Kingdom: A Political History* (1965); and Michael J. Devine, "John W. Foster and the Struggle for the Annexation of Hawaii," *Pacific Historical Review* 46 (Feb. 1977): 29–50. Obituaries are in the Louisville *Courier-Journal*, 16 Jan. 1897; the *Hawaiian Star* and *Evening Bulletin*, 6 Jan. 1897; and the Honolulu *Pacific Commercial Advertiser*, 7, 9 Jan. 1897.

MICHAEL J. DEVINE

WILLIS, Bailey (31 May 1857–19 Feb. 1949), geologist, was born at his parents' estate near Cornwall, New York, the son of Nathaniel Parker Willis, a journalist and poet, and his second wife, Cornelia Grinnell, whose uncle Henry Grinnell had supported several Arctic expeditions. When Willis was ten years old his father died and his mother, as he recalled in *A Yanqui in Patagonia* (1947), sensing "a tendency to dream" in her youngest son, decided that he should be educated as a scientist. In 1870 she took him to Europe and enrolled him in a German high school, where he studied for three years under "severe but salutary discipline." In 1874 Willis entered Columbia University School of Mines, graduated in 1879 with degrees in mining and civil engineering, and applied for work at the newly established United States Geological Survey (USGS).

Survey director Clarence King gave Willis an assignment as assistant to mining geologist and explorer Raphael Pumpelly, who was organizing an economic survey of the mineral industries for the United States Tenth Census. Pumpelly immediately sent Willis into the wilderness of the Lake Superior region and elsewhere to gather samples of iron ore. Although slight of build, Willis proved himself to be resourceful and hardy under the most difficult conditions. In 1881, when Pumpelly began a geological/geographical survey of the Northwest for the Northern Pacific Railroad, he hired Willis to search for coal in Washington Territory. Willis organized crews of woodsmen, who called him the "boy boss," investigated reports of coal, and began what were to become ongoing studies of the geology of Mount Rainier, the Cascade Range, and the northern Rockies. An ardent conservationist, he was active in promoting the establishment of Mount Rainier and Glacier National Parks.

In 1882 Willis married Altona Grinnell, with whom he had one child. After her death in 1896, he married Margaret Baker, daughter of anatomist Frank Baker, superintendent of the National Zoological Park in Washington, D.C. With his second wife he had three children, of whom two sons, Robin and Cornelius, became geologists.

In 1884, after the bankruptcy of the Northern Pacific's president and the end of Pumpelly's survey, Willis returned to the USGS. His first assignment from the new director, John Wesley Powell, was to investigate reports of coal on a Sioux reservation in North Dakota, where he diplomatically overcame the opposition of a leader who claimed to have killed Custer. He then served as assistant to Grove Karl Gilbert, succeeding him in 1889 as director of the Appalachian Division. During these years Willis began the field and laboratory work that brought him recognition as one of the country's leading structural geologists. He directed the detailed mapping of sections of the mountains in the southern Appalachians, and he tried to create in the laboratory the conditions that had caused folding and faulting. He layered various thicknesses of strata made of plaster of Paris, wax, and turpentine in a box, loaded the layers with shot to simulate the weight of overlying rock, and compressed the layers horizontally with a screw. The results of his investigations were published in his "Mechanics of Appalachian Structure" (USGS *Annual Report* 13, pt. 2 [1893]: 211–81), which was compared favorably to the work of Albert

Heim and other European geologists who had been studying the structure of the Alps.

In 1900 Willis participated in the reorganization of the USGS and at that time became head of the new Division of Areal Geology, responsible for investigations in stratigraphy, structure, and pre-Pleistocene geomorphology. In this capacity and as editor of the folios of the geological atlas of the United States, Willis helped to establish standards for geologic nomenclature and stratigraphic classification, a cause also being taken up by the International Geological Congress (IGC), whose meetings he often attended. His *Index to the Stratigraphy of North America* (1912) and his map of North American geology remained standard reference works for many years.

In 1903 and 1904 Willis took leave from the administrative duties at the USGS that were becoming burdensome to him to lead an expedition to China sponsored by the Carnegie Institution of Washington. Traveling through the northern provinces and down the Yangtze, Willis and his assistants studied the geomorphology, paleontology, and economic and structural geology of the region that had been investigated earlier by his friends and mentors Raphael Pumpelly and Ferdinand von Richthofen. He published the scientific results of this work in *Research in China* (1907) and later wrote a popular account of his travels, *Friendly China* (1949). From 1910 to 1914 Willis served as consulting expert to the Argentine government, exploring the mineral resources and irrigation potential of northern Patagonia.

In 1915 Willis resigned from the USGS to take a position as professor and chairman of the geology department at Stanford University. In California, where he continued to live after his retirement from Stanford in 1922, Willis became known as an earthquake expert, promoting better building safety codes, studying faults, serving as president of the Seismological Society of America, and publishing frequently on earthquakes in California, Chile, and the Middle and Far East. A firm believer in his own theories, he often traded "verbal punches" at scientific meetings with his counterpart at the University of California at Berkeley, Andrew C. Lawson. Students at Stanford and Berkeley long remembered the way Willis stood up to the crusty and argumentative Lawson, especially on matters relating to earthquakes (Waters, p. P66).

In 1929, after attending an IGC conference in South Africa, Willis traveled the length of Africa, accompanied by his wife and supported by the Carnegie Institution of Washington, to study the geologic structure of the deep rift valleys that bisect the East African plateau. His study convinced him that the valleys had not developed because of separation, as most geologists thought, but were the result of "ramping" caused by compression and vertical movement.

Willis became one of the most outspoken American opponents of the continental drift theories proposed early in the twentieth century by Frank Taylor, Alfred Wegener, and others. Willis's lifelong studies of the earth's structure and the forces that shape it had reinforced his belief in the permanence of continents, a view shared by many of his American contemporaries. As did other opponents, he pointed out that drift theory provided inadequate explanation for the forces or mechanisms by which continents were moved. His criticisms stimulated the search for such mechanisms, but he did not live long enough to see the new developments in oceanography and paleomagnetism and the rise of plate tectonics during the 1950s and 1960s that brought about the general acceptance of drift theory. Willis died in Palo Alto, California.

• Willis's papers are in the Huntington Library, San Marino, Calif. Additional material is in the Stanford University archives and in the Western History Research Center at the University of Wyoming. His accounts of his travels in Patagonia and China, as well as *Living Africa: A Geologist's Wanderings through the Rift Valleys* (1930), contain autobiographical material. Willis was a prolific writer, publishing more than 150 books and papers. His textbook *Geologic Structures* (1923) went into three editions; the second (1929) and third (1934) were in collaboration with his son Robin. A summary of his ideas about the formation and permanence of continents can be found in his presidential address to the Geological Society of America, "Continental Genesis," *Bulletin of the Geological Society of America* 40 (1929): 281–336, and in "Continental Drift, ein Märchen," *American Journal of Science* 242 (1944): 509–13. Other publications of continuing interest are "Stratigraphy and Structure, Lewis and Livingston Ranges, Montana," *Bulletin of the Geological Society of America* 13 (1902): 305–52; *Northern Patagonia* (1914); "Folding or Shearing, Which?" *American Association of Petroleum Geologists Bulletin* 11 (1927): 31–47; "Earthquakes in the Holy Land," *Seismological Society of America Bulletin* 18 (1928): 73–103; *East African Plateaus and Rift Valleys* (1936); and "San Andreas Rift, California," *Journal of Geology* 46 (1938): 1017–57.

Biographical sketches have been written by Aaron C. Waters, "Memorial to Bailey Willis," *Bulletin of the Geological Society of America* 73 (1962): P55–P72, which has the most complete bibliography; and Eliot Blackwelder, "Bailey Willis," National Academy of Sciences, *Biographical Memoirs* 35 (1961): 333–50.

MARGARET D. CHAMPLIN

WILLIS, Frances Elizabeth (20 May 1899–20 July 1983), diplomat, was born in Metropolis, Illinois, the daughter of John Gilbert Willis (profession unknown) and Belle Whitfield James. When Frances was six, her family moved to Memphis, Tennessee, and subsequently to Kenosha, Wisconsin. As an undergraduate at Stanford University, California, Willis majored in history and was a reader in political science. She graduated with a bachelor of arts from Stanford in 1920 and in 1923, after spending a year at the University of Brussels, was awarded her Ph.D. in political science by Stanford. Upon graduating, she taught history for a year at Goucher College, Baltimore, Maryland, and political science at Vassar College from 1924 to 1927. The desire to gain practical experience in government prompted Willis to switch careers in her late twenties. "I didn't want to just teach political science, I wanted to be part of it," she explained (*Los Angeles Times*, 23 July 1983). She took the Foreign Service exam and in

August 1927 became the third woman to enter the service. She later acknowledged that her teaching experience had provided her with "excellent mental discipline and training."

After completing the Foreign Service school in 1928, Willis became vice consul at Valparaiso, Chile, and three years later she acted at the same level in Santiago, Chile. In 1933 Secretary of State Henry Stimson received a message from Willis, who was then serving as third secretary in the U.S. legation in Sweden, that read: "The minister left last night. I have assumed charge. Willis." A perplexed Stimson asked, "Who is Willis?" (*Time*, 20 July 1953). With the minister and his key assistants absent from Stockholm, Willis had indeed taken charge and in doing so became the first woman in U.S. history to act as the chief of a diplomatic mission. In 1933 she was transferred to Belgium and Luxembourg, again serving as third secretary. Four years later Willis was promoted to second secretary before being posted in 1940 to Spain, where she served as second secretary and consul. She became first secretary in Madrid in 1943 and remained in the position until 1944.

In 1944, after spending sixteen years abroad, Willis returned to the United States, where she worked as assistant to the under secretary of state in Washington. In 1946 she became assistant chief of the Division of Western European Affairs, and from there she was transferred to London, serving as first secretary and consul between 1947 and 1950. With her appointment in 1951 as counselor of legation in Helsinki, Finland, she became the first woman in U.S. history to be promoted to Foreign Service officer class I.

In 1953, with twenty-six years of diplomatic experience behind her, Willis was appointed ambassador to Switzerland, making her the first female career diplomat in U.S. history to attain such a rank. She was also Washington's first ambassador to Switzerland, the United States having been represented by a legation previously. Two other women, Eugenie Anderson and Clare Boothe Luce, had been made ambassadors earlier, but theirs were political appointments. As one of her colleagues explained, Willis started "at the foot of the ladder [and] step by step she worked her way up the ladder, assuming increasing responsibilities with each step upward" (Heath, p. 1052).

On hearing of her nomination as ambassador to Switzerland, former under secretary of state Joseph Grew, under whom Willis served between 1944 and 1946, remarked, "Nobody could do a better job." However, not all agreed. One detractor accused President Dwight David Eisenhower of trying to "gratify the malicious desires of a few meddling feminists." The Swiss will "feel slighted by what they will consider as the small importance attached by the U.S. Government to the diplomatic post in Switzerland," argued another critic. In the view of some non-Swiss diplomats, Willis's appointment to a country where women did not have the vote would be seen as "a slap in the face" (*New York Times*, 16 Apr. 1953), but as the *New York Times* correctly predicted on 15 April 1953, "the business-like attitude of the Swiss [was] likely to ignore such reasoning."

On 11 August 1953 Willis was sworn in as "Madam Ambassador." Following the ceremony she stated: "I've never considered myself an unusual woman. What I've done, others can do, too"—that is, as long as they possessed the "necessary mental equipment," the ability to "deal effectively with other people," and excellent reporting skills (*Washington Post*, 11 Aug. 1953). The new ambassador arrived in Switzerland on 4 October 1953 and remained there until May 1957.

With her appointment as ambassador to Norway in May 1957, Willis became the first woman to serve as chief of mission at more than one post. From Norway she was posted to Ceylon (now Sri Lanka), where she served as ambassador from March 1961 until her retirement from the Foreign Service in September 1964. In addition to her other firsts, Willis was the first woman to be appointed as a U.S. ambassador in Asia.

Being "able to contribute to the solution of some of the big problems of the world—no matter how small that contribution might be" was what Willis found most appealing about a diplomatic career. The recipient of the American Woman's Association's 1955 Eminent Achievement Award, she was described as a "brilliant woman" possessing "extraordinary capacity and versatility" (Heath, p. 1051). In November 1973 the American Foreign Service Association honored her with the Foreign Service Cup for her "outstanding contribution to the conduct of foreign relations of the United States" (O'Neill, p. 91).

Upon leaving the Foreign Service in 1964, Willis moved to Redlands, California, where her family had lived since 1916. She said, "I've been so many things in different countries, but in Redlands I've never been anything but Frances Willis" (*Los Angeles Times*, 23 July 1983). Willis, who never married, died in Redlands.

• Willis left no personal papers. The White House Central Files at the Dwight David Eisenhower Library, Abilene, Kans., contain some material on her ambassadorships to Switzerland and Norway. The most useful information on her career is in *Current Biography* (1954), and E. Wilder Spaulding, *Ambassadors Ordinary and Extraordinary* (1961). Additional biographical material is in Homer L. Calkin, *Women in American Foreign Affairs* (1977); "Career Diplomat," *Independent Woman* 32 (Sept. 1953); "Career Women," *Time*, 20 July 1953; D. R. Heath, "Women in the Foreign Service: A Tribute to Ambassador Willis," *Department of State Bulletin* 33 (26 Dec. 1955); Lois Decker O'Neill, ed., *The Women's Book of World Records and Achievement* (1979); and Estelle Sharpe, "First Woman Career Ambassador Sworn In," *Washington Post*, 11 Aug. 1953. Obituaries are in the *Los Angeles Times*, 23 July 1983; the *New York Times*, 24 July 1983; and the *Washington Post*, 22 July 1983.

MAREE-ANNE REID

WILLIS, Nathaniel Parker (20 Jan. 1806–20 Jan. 1867), writer and editor, was born in Portland, Maine, the son of Nathaniel Willis, a journalist and editor, and Hannah Parker. In 1812 the Willis family moved to

Boston, where Willis's father established the *Boston Advertiser*, a religious newspaper in which Willis published his first poems. Educated at the Boston Latin School in Andover, and at Yale, Willis continued to produce poetry and achieved a national reputation after the publication of a collection entitled *Sketches* in 1827, the year of his graduation.

After Yale, Willis promptly returned to Boston and began a long career as a magazine editor in which he had an important role in shaping the literary tastes of an antebellum readership. Working at first for others, Willis quickly went on to establish his own magazine, the *American Monthly Magazine* (1829–1831). A regular feature of this magazine was a column in which Willis presented the imaginary routines of his editorial office, filled with such exotic objects as his reading passages from favored literary works to friends. This column set the tone for Willis's literary persona throughout his career—a dandified blend of aestheticism and dilettantism.

When failing circulation shut down the *American Monthly* in 1831, Willis moved to New York City, where he took up the position of co-editor with George Pope Morris of the *New York Mirror*. This began a lifelong editorial partnership between Willis and Morris. That same year Willis left for Europe as a correspondent for the *Mirror*. He spent five years there writing and sending back articles that he called "Pencillings by the Way" (collected as a book of the same title in 1835). These alternated between travel sketches from the Mediterranean to Scotland and gossipy descriptions of life among Europe's literary and social elite. The publication of these social profiles made Willis an enormously popular, if controversial, figure in the United States, but it angered some London elites, who felt he had taken advantage of social connections in reporting on their private lives. In 1835 he married Mary Stace, the daughter of an English general.

Willis returned to the United States in 1836, soon after the publication of *Inklings of Adventure*, a collection of short fiction that joined travel sketches to romance storytelling, linked together by a narrative persona similar to Irving's Geoffrey Crayon, named Philip Slingsby. This work characterized his fictional production throughout his career: short, sentimental stories that emphasized plot and locale, had little or no character development, and appealed to the growing urban readership of antebellum periodical literature. Willis pursued this new audience in a number of New York periodicals co-edited with Moore, which grew out of the *Mirror: Corsair* magazine (1839); the *New Mirror* (1843–1844), in newspaper format as the *Weekly* and *Evening Mirror* (1844–1846), and, finally, the *Home Journal* (1846–1864). As an editor, Willis employed both Walt Whitman and Edgar Allan Poe and wrote to refute Griswold's attack on Poe after his death.

In addition to editing, Willis also wrote for such other popular magazines as *Godey's* and *Graham's*, earning an annual income of $4,800 in 1842. While the bulk of Willis's literary production came first in periodicals, often later collected and published in book form, he also wrote two plays, *Bianca Visconti* (1839) and *Tortesa the Usurer* (1839), both historical romances performed on the New York stage. He published a novel, *Paul Fane* (1857), which is often seen as a precursor to the work of Henry James for its presentation of the American sensibility's encounter with Europe.

In 1845 Willis's wife died in childbirth, and he made a return visit to England and the continent with his daughter. In 1846 he married Cornelia Grinnell; they had four children. From 1851 to 1852 Willis was involved in the divorce trial of the famous actor Edwin Forrest, which led to his being assaulted by Forrest, accused of adulterous behavior with Mrs. Forrest, and charged with libel. In 1853 he established a country home on the Hudson called "Idlewild," from which he would address his later writings for the *Home Journal*. During the Civil War he lived in Washington, D.C., as the *Home Journal*'s correspondent. After a period of failing health marked by epileptic seizures and paralysis, he died at "Idlewild."

Willis's popularity and prominence in antebellum literary circles came under reconsideration even before his death. His lifelong interest in the social world of the wealthy caused many to see him as simply a literary man about town. In his *A Fable for Critics* (1848), Lowell described Willis as "the topmost bright bubble on the wave of the town." In 1854 his sister, Sara Payson Willis, who established her own successful literary career writing under the pseudonym "Fanny Fern," published the autobiographical novel *Ruth Hall*, in which the heroine-writer, desperate for money to support her family, is discouraged from pursuing a literary career by her vain and snobbish editor brother Hyacinth, an unmistakably critical portrait of Willis.

While American literary history came to remember Willis as a snob and a writer of trifles, his role in the development of a distinctly national literary culture and economy should not be overlooked. Throughout his career Willis took American social life as his subject and was a keen observer of the development of class experience in the antebellum era. Despite the fact that he focused on the world of America's economic elite, Willis explicitly allied the antebellum writer with his magazine audience, the new middle class. In the *New Mirror*, Willis asserted: "Part the extremes—widen the distance between wealth and poverty—and you make room for a *middle class* . . . Of this middle class, literary men are a natural part and parcel. So are many of the worthiest and most intelligent people of this country" (24 June 1843). Willis's work set a standard for American literary professionalism in the antebellum era and played an important role in nineteenth-century American literary culture.

• Willis's letters are in the Yale University Library, and a diary is in the public library of Morristown, N.J. The standard biography has remained Henry A. Beer's *Nathaniel Parker Willis* (1885). The most complete modern assessment is Cortland P. Auser, *Nathaniel P. Willis* (1969). For information on Willis's place in the development of American magazine culture, see Frank Luther Mott, *A History of American Magazines*, vol. 1 (1930) and vol. 2 (1938). For a view of Willis in relation to other major New York writers of the era, like Cooper and Irving, see Van Wyck Brooks, *The World of Washington Irving* (1944). On Willis's place in the literary conflicts of antebellum New York, see Perry Miller, *The Raven and the Whale* (1956).

JOHN EVELEV

WILLIS, Sarah Payson. *See* Fern, Fanny.

WILLIS, Victor Gazaway (12 Apr. 1876–3 Aug. 1947), baseball player, known as Vic, was born in Cecil County, Maryland, and completed high school in Wilmington, Delaware. His parents' names are unknown. He signed his first professional baseball contract in 1895 with Harrisburg in the Pennsylvania State League. In 1896 the handsome, 6′2″ right-handed pitcher won 10 games with Syracuse, New York, of the Eastern League. The following season at Syracuse, Willis earned 21 victories and an invitation to the Boston Beaneaters' National League spring training camp in 1898. Boston manager Frank Selee inserted Willis as his fourth starter in a starting rotation that already boasted outstanding holdovers Kid Nichols, Fred Klobedanz, and Ted Lewis from the 1897 pennant-winning team. The quartet accounted for 101 of the Beaneaters' 102 victories in 1898, with Willis winning 25 games. Making half of his starts in spacious South End Grounds in Boston, Willis compiled a 27–8 mark in 1899 and on 7 August tossed a 7–1 no-hitter against the Washington Senators. He often aided his own cause with the bat that year, as he hit .216, the only time in his major league career he reached the .200 level. Despite Willis's efforts, Boston was unable to capture a third consecutive pennant, settling for second place behind the Brooklyn Dodgers. In 1900 Willis married Mary J. Minnis. They had two children.

The National League underwent major restructuring in 1900. Four teams disbanded, reducing the league to eight franchises. The Boston lineup still included future Hall of Famers Jimmy Collins at third base and Billy Hamilton and Hugh Duffy in the outfield, and Beaneater defense was second to none. However, Willis, Nichols, and Lewis had off years. Willis's decline was the steepest; he won only 10 times in 27 decisions and compiled a 4.19 earned run average, the highest of his career.

Willis rebounded to win 20 games in 1901 and enjoyed his finest season in 1902. He led the National League with 19 losses but also led with 51 games pitched, 46 games started, 45 complete games, 410 innings, and 225 strikeouts. He won 27 games for a team that recorded only 73 victories.

Willis's final three years in Boston were spent laboring for weak teams that were at or near the bottom of the National League in batting and fielding. In 1903 his record fell to 12–18. Willis led the league with 39 complete games and 25 defeats in 1904, yet his 18 victories accounted for one-third of the team total. The 1905 Beaneaters, now known as the Braves, lost a staggering 103 games, and Willis was tagged with 29 defeats, long a modern major league record.

The Braves traded Willis to the Pittsburgh Pirates of the National League for infielder Dave Brain, pitcher Vive Lindaman, and utilityman Del Howard in 1906. From 1906 to 1909 Willis was a paragon of pitching consistency for the Pirates. He averaged 302 innings of work per season and compiled nearly the same won-lost mark each campaign, finishing 22–13 in 1906, 22–11 in 1907, 23–11 in 1908, and 22–11 in 1909. His ERA over the four years was a sparkling 2.08. Willis was comfortable in Pittsburgh's huge Exposition Park, where the center and left field fences were more than 500 feet from home plate, and three speedy outfielders, Fred Clarke, Tommy Leach, and Owen Wilson, covered its vast reaches. Willis's best pitch was a baffling curveball. In the 1909 World Series Willis hurled 6⅓ innings in relief against the Detroit Tigers in the second game. He started and lost the sixth game, but the Pirates prevailed in the seventh game to gain the World Championship.

In January 1910 Pittsburgh sold Willis's contract to the St. Louis Cardinals. Cardinal manager Roger Bresnahan employed him as a starter and reliever. Willis won nine and lost 12 and was released after the season.

Despite Willis's impressive career, few baseball fans have heard of him. Little is known of his life outside baseball. Disagreement remains over some of his yearly and career statistics. For example, various sources credit him with between 244 and 249 career wins. According to MacMillan's *Baseball Encyclopedia*, Willis pitched 513 games and 3,996 innings, completed 388 of 471 starts (among the highest totals in history), and won 248 games and lost 204. He was a 20-game winner in eight of his 13 major league seasons. Willis recorded 1,651 strikeouts and posted a 2.63 ERA. He hurled 50 shutouts, ranking him high on the all-time list. Willis was among the most durable hurlers of his day. Year after year he was among the league leaders in innings pitched, complete games, and strikeouts. He was inducted into the National Baseball Hall of Fame on 4 August 1996. After retiring from baseball, Willis operated a hotel in Newark, Delaware. He died in Elkton, Maryland.

• The National Baseball Hall of Fame Library in Cooperstown, N.Y., has a file on Willis. Shorter biographies are available in Brent Kelley, *100 Greatest Pitchers* (1988); David L. Porter, ed., *Biographical Dictionary of American Sports* (1983); and Michael Shatzkin, ed., *The Ballplayers* (1990). Complete statistical information can be found in Rick Wolff, ed., *The Baseball Encyclopedia*, 8th ed. (1990).

FRANK J. OLMSTED

WILLISTON, Samuel Wendell (10 July 1851–30 Aug. 1918), paleontologist and entomologist, was born in Roxbury, Massachusetts, the son of Samuel Williston, a blacksmith and farmer, and Jane Augusta Turner.

The family moved from Massachusetts to Manhattan, Kansas Territory, in 1857, as part of an antislavery effort by the New England Emigrant Aid Society. Although his father had little schooling, Williston developed an early interest in reading. Earning his own way, he attended Kansas State Agricultural College in Manhattan, where the professor of natural philosophy was Benjamin Franklin Mudge. "That my life has been devoted to natural science was largely due to his influence," said Williston in late life.

After receiving his B.S. in 1872, he studied medicine briefly with a local physician. Then, rather by accident, he joined a college friend to collect vertebrate fossils in western Kansas with Mudge, who had been retained for the task by Othniel Charles Marsh of Yale University. After a second summer of field work with Mudge, Marsh invited Williston to Yale in 1876. For nine years Williston assisted in the museum, preparing and describing fossils; during his assistantship he would make extended field trips to collect fossils for Marsh in remote parts of Kansas, Colorado, and Wyoming. Williston was at the sites in Colorado and Wyoming where large dinosaurs were discovered for the first time in the United States in 1877, and he shipped tons of fossil bones to Yale. He was a very good collector, and the technique of wrapping fragile bones in flour paste was of his devising.

Dissatisfied with Marsh's autocratic ways, Williston looked for other outlets while continuing to work in the museum. He earned an M.D. at Yale in 1880 and deliberately set out while in the field to become an expert on flies (Diptera), after abandoning his collection of beetles when he discovered that the coleopteran literature was already extensive. He married Annie Isabel Hathaway in 1881; they had five children.

During this time Marsh became much embroiled in a collecting and scientific feud with Edward Drinker Cope. Marsh's laboratory assistants became disenchanted with his preemption of their work under him as his own while Marsh raced to publish ahead of Cope. This led to Williston's resigning from Marsh's employ in 1885. That same year he received a Ph.D. in entomology from Yale. His dissertation on the Syrphidae was the first monograph on flies by an American. For several years he was unsure of his future; he taught anatomy at Yale, he tried to become a practicing physician, he carried out public-health programs in Connecticut, and he published considerably on Diptera. In 1888 he published the 84-page pamphlet *Synopsis of the Families and Genera of North American Diptera*.

In 1890 Williston accepted an offer to become professor of geology at the University of Kansas. His decision was partly because of his acquaintance with its chancellor, Francis Huntington Snow, who had a high regard for Williston's abilities in several fields. Williston conducted summer collecting trips in the productive Cretaceous fossil beds of western Kansas, in the South Dakota badlands, and in eastern Wyoming, and he published extensively. Recognized then and later as valuable contributions to paleontology were his papers for the newly established Geological Survey of Kansas in 1897 and 1898, on the Kansas Niobrara Cretaceous formation, the Kansas Pleistocene, fossil birds, dinosaurs, crocodiles, mosasaurs, and turtles.

For the World's Columbian Exposition of 1893 in Chicago, Williston prepared an exhibit of Kansas rocks and building stones. At the urging of Snow, he also helped to found the study of medicine at the University of Kansas and was the first dean of its medical school (1898–1902). He served on the Kansas Board of Health, which established registration of physicians in 1901. Students considered him an excellent teacher in his several fields of interest.

In 1902 Williston accepted a position at the University of Chicago as its only professor of paleontology. For a year he also had an appointment with the Field Columbian Museum, and later he also taught comparative anatomy at Rush Medical School. His primary research was on vertebrate fossils. He led collecting trips to Wyoming in 1904 and 1905 and then in 1908 turned his attention to the Permian red beds of Texas. These continental deposits of red sandstones and shales contain bones of an assemblage of amphibians and the earliest known reptiles. Williston's analyses of collections from there, by himself and others, were summarized in *American Permian Vertebrates* (1911) and a number of scientific papers. Williston's publications on Paleozoic amphibians and reptiles constitute his most significant contributions in paleontology. Colleagues acknowledged his competence in comparative anatomy and analyses of evolutionary adaptations of the animals that he described.

Throughout his professional years Williston continued his avid interest in flies. To him it was a relaxing hobby, for evenings at home or during school vacations, not a profession. In 1896 he issued an enlarged revision of his manual, and in 1908 he completed the third edition of *Manual of North American Diptera*. This was extensively illustrated with photographs and many of his own detailed line drawings. Recognized internationally as an expert, Williston often identified specimens of flies for other entomologists, and he contributed to publications published abroad, including in the West Indies and Central America.

Williston's first concern, in both paleontology and entomology, was classification. A student of his, E. C. Case, later recalled one of his precepts: "I don't care whether they are named or numbered, just so we know what we are talking about." In 1915 Williston was elected to the National Academy of Sciences. He died in Chicago.

• Williston's personal papers, some correspondence, and his autobiographical manuscript, "Recollections," are held by his grandson, George G. Shor, Jr. No collection of his professional papers is known. In paleontology Williston wrote *Water Reptiles of the Past and Present* (1914) as well as about 150 scientific papers; *The Osteology of the Reptiles*, edited by William King Gregory, was published posthumously (1925). In addition to the three editions of the manual on Diptera, Williston wrote about a hundred shorter papers on insects. Biographical accounts include E. C. Case, "Dr. Williston as a Teacher," *University Record* (University of Chicago), Jan. 1919, pp. 97–101; Richard Swann Lull, "Samuel Wendell Williston," *Memoirs of the National Academy of Sciences* (1924), pp. 114–41; Henry Fairfield Osborn, "Samuel Wendell Williston," *Journal of Geology* 26 (1918): 673–89; and Elizabeth Noble Shor, *Fossils and Flies* (1971), which has a complete bibliography.

ELIZABETH NOBLE SHOR

WILLKIE, Wendell Lewis (18 Feb. 1892–8 Oct. 1944), corporation lawyer and executive, politician, and civil rights activist, was born in Elwood, Indiana, the son of Herman F. Willkie and Henrietta Trisch. His father was a lawyer and local reformer, and his mother was one of the first female lawyers in Indiana. Willkie attended local schools and Indiana University, graduating in 1913. After teaching high school in Kansas (Sept. 1913–Nov. 1914), he returned to Indiana University to complete a law degree in 1916.

In 1918, while in military service, Willkie married Edith Wilk, a librarian. They had one child. In 1919 Willkie left the family law practice and moved to Akron, Ohio. He first worked in the Firestone legal department and then became a hard-working courtroom lawyer in a local firm. A very successful attorney, he also actively condemned the Ku Klux Klan and participated briefly in Democratic politics. In 1929 Willkie accepted an offer, with a salary of $36,000, to become a partner in the New York law firm of Weadock & Willkie. He worked exclusively as counsel to the Commonwealth & Southern Corporation, a public utility holding company. In 1933 he became president of the holding company.

Willkie's leadership of Commonwealth & Southern coincided with Franklin D. Roosevelt's New Deal. Key parts of New Deal reform were greater regulation of public utility companies and the further step of establishing the Tennessee Valley Authority (TVA) in direct competition to the utility system Willkie headed. Defending his corporate interests, Willkie by the mid-1930s had become one of the most effective critics of the New Deal. He employed an orthodox attack on New Deal liberalism and big government with a spirited defense of economic freedom and big business, all tied up with an engaging personality and powerful rhetorical skills.

Willkie's attack on Roosevelt's New Deal launched him into the political arena, though as a decidedly latecomer. Not until 1939 did he change his political affiliation from Democratic to Republican. The Republican party always resented the newcomer, which attitude was best captured by Indiana Republican senator James Watson, who told people that he didn't mind if the town whore joined the church but he didn't think she should lead the church choir the first week. Willkie's wide popular appeal among the American public and the party's lack of outstanding leadership forced the Republicans to accept this dark horse as their nominee in 1940. Less apparent but critical to his success at the Republican convention in Philadelphia was the strong support of eastern businessmen and publishers, particularly Russell Davenport, editor of *Fortune* magazine.

Willkie's nomination in Philadelphia and his notification speech in his Elwood hometown were the highlights of the campaign. The candidate and his loyal supporters expected a grand victory and worked energetically to mount a grassroots effort. They had strong support from the press, many of whom were captivated by Willkie's frank conversation and bantering style. To many Americans he conveyed a comforting sense of the ordinary midwesterner, with his tousled hair cut country style, rumpled suit, Hoosier accent, and careful poses on the Rush County farms he owned. All this was while he was, in fact, a wealthy New York corporate executive. This image led New Dealer Harold Ickes to refer caustically to Willkie as the "simple, barefoot Wall Street lawyer." Image was not enough. A combination of campaign disorganization, mixed messages, and Roosevelt's commanding political power led downhill to defeat.

Willkie was the most successful Republican presidential candidate in two decades of Democratic dominance of the White House. His political charm energized voters, particularly young voters. Roosevelt carried 38 states, 449 electoral votes, and 55 percent of the popular vote to Willkie's 10 states, 82 electoral votes, and 45 percent of the popular vote. It was better than the two previous Republican presidential candidates had done and better than the Republican candidate in the next two elections would do.

In many ways Willkie's most important contributions came after he lost the 1940 election. The first was in international relations. As war came closer to the United States, he actively supported Roosevelt's lend-lease program and deserved major credit for its passage, to the distress of his more isolationist Republican colleagues. He made a trip in early 1941 to war-torn England to give Winston Churchill and the British reassurance about the American loyal opposition. Most important, Willkie in 1942 took a trip around the world. Traveling in a converted military bomber, he logged 31,000 miles in forty-nine days as he visited with heads of state in North Africa, the Mideast, the Soviet Union, and China, including Charles de Gaulle, Joseph Stalin, Chaing Kai-shek, and Chou En-lai (Zhou Enlai). In addition, he visited ordinary people in shops, marketplaces, and farmhouses.

In April 1943 Willkie reported on this voyage of discovery in a short book titled *One World*. Within a year it sold two million copies. In plain and sprightly language he recounted his travels and his constant feeling "not of distance from other peoples, but of closeness to them." With bold assertions and ordinary details he illustrated that this world was small and near. He wrote that when a Russian woman cooked a meal for him in her farmhouse, he felt very much like he did back home in Indiana.

Willkie also argued that changes were coming. Above all, *One World* is an argument against imperialism and colonialism. Newly emerging peoples, in places later labeled "Third World," were preparing to challenge the dominance of Western civilization and Western empires, Willkie reported. They would demand self-determination and independence, and if the developed nations of the West repressed their freedom and opportunity, the "newly awakened people will be followers of some extremist leader," he warned. The postwar world had to be one in which equality and understanding crossed divisions of race, ethnicity, and culture.

In *One World* and in many other ways Willkie connected changes across the globe with necessary change at home. He came to focus on the secondary status of black Americans. As he circled the globe, he reported, "The maladjustments of races in America came up frequently." The rest of the world was watching the least complete page in America's democratic experiment.

In the early 1940s Willkie became one of the most passionate and public figures in the civil rights movement. Perhaps only Eleanor Roosevelt, among white Americans, did as much as this Republican businessman. He spoke to public audiences across the country, gave countless radio speeches, and wrote articles for *Look*, the *Saturday Evening Post*, and other magazines. He attacked segregation in the American military and in Hollywood films. As chairman of the board of 20th Century–Fox, he led the campaign to eliminate the offensive racial stereotyping that characterized nearly all films in which a black character appeared. Even though Willkie was opposed to big government, he advocated federal action to guarantee voting rights for all Americans, equal employment opportunities, and public housing. Among his closest allies was Walter White, head of the National Association for the Advancement of Colored People.

Just why and how Willkie emerged in this role of civil rights activist is unclear. Earlier he had shown signs of progressive liberalism, a favoritism toward the underdog, and a sensitivity to others. Certainly Willkie was a person capable of growth and change. He read incessantly, especially history, and he loved to talk to journalists, authors, and ordinary people. He was far from the old-guard traditionalist set in his ways.

A portion of Willkie's growth toward civil rights and a more internationalist outlook was the result of his relationship with Irita Van Doren, the book review editor of the New York *Herald Tribune*. Van Doren and Willkie became close intellectual and personal friends and eventually lovers. Their relationship led Willkie to a wider circle of friends among journalists and writers, to long weekend conversations, and to new books to read. Willkie's own world changed to encompass new commitments unusual for a Republican businessman. He attacked anti-Semitism as well as discrimination against blacks. He defended the individual liberty and right to citizenship of a Communist, William Schneiderman, in arguing his case before the Supreme Court.

Willkie's enlarged interests were far too liberal for the Republican party of 1944. Although he eagerly sought the presidential nomination that year, the party abandoned him emphatically. By that time some of its old guard hated him more than they did Roosevelt. After a disastrous showing in the Wisconsin primary, Willkie dropped out of the race. In the summer of 1944 talk spread of a new political realignment, a liberal party with Willkie and Roosevelt as central magnets, but political realities prevented serious steps in that direction. Willkie's death from a heart attack in New York City followed by Roosevelt's a few months later ended any speculation.

Willkie remains among the most loved and interesting losers in American presidential politics. His 1940 campaign is a classic dark horse, "outsider" campaign that reflects both the volatility of American politics generally and the peculiarities of that specific time. Perhaps more significant than that campaign is his life after defeat, when he developed his eloquent plea for global thinking and for civil rights for African Americans.

• Willkie's papers are in the Lilly Library, Indiana University, Bloomington. Also important are the Irita Van Dorn Papers in the Library of Congress. Willkie's own writings include *An American Program* (1944). His earlier publications and speeches are in *This Is Wendell Willkie* (1940). The most detailed biography is Ellsworth Barnard, *Wendell Willkie: Fighter for Freedom* (1966). More readable and up-to-date is Steve Neal, *Dark Horse: A Biography of Wendell Willkie* (1984). The essays in James H. Madison, ed., *Wendell Willkie: Hoosier Internationalist* (1992), are treatments of the major issues of his life by experts in the areas covered, including presidential politics, civil rights, and international affairs. A good account by a contemporary and friend is Joseph Barnes, *Willkie* (1952).

JAMES H. MADISON

WILLOUGHBY, Westel Woodbury (20 July 1867–26 Mar. 1945), political scientist and legal adviser to the Chinese government, was born a twin in Alexandria, Virginia, the son of Westel Willoughby, a lawyer and a judge of the Virginia supreme court, and Jennie Rebecca Woodbury. Willoughby completed the A.B. at Johns Hopkins University in 1888 and the Ph.D. in 1891. Work on his doctoral dissertation, titled "The Supreme Court of the United States: Its History and Influence on Our Constitutional System," was completed under the supervision of Herbert Baxter Adams. In 1891 he was admitted to the bar and practiced in Washington, D.C., alongside his father. He worked there until 1895, the year he joined the Department of Politics and History at the Johns Hopkins University. During this period, in 1893, he married Grace Robinson, of Dubuque, Iowa. They had two children. Her death in 1907 came at the most productive time of his career.

Realizing that the future of the discipline depended on the production of high-caliber Ph.D.'s, Willoughby in 1903 created the graduate department of political science at Johns Hopkins and encouraged young scholars to pursue the same high standards of scholarship and teaching he set for himself. In the same year, he played a leading role in founding the American Political Science Association (APSA) and thus helped to establish political science as an independent field of study. He served as president of the association in 1913 and edited its *American Political Science Review* for the first ten years of its existence (1906–1916). To this day his presence is still felt in the department. Hanging in the political science conference room (now in Mergenthaler Hall), reminding students of the tradition of excellence he established, is the portrait of W. W. Willoughby.

Willoughby trained a generation of students in the principles of constitutional and political theory. His teaching and writing reflected his interests in the general principles of government and in timeless theoretical issues, such as the nature of the state, sovereignty, and justice. Although his major works—*An Examination of the Nature of the State* (1896), *Social Justice: A Critical Essay* (1900), *The Constitutional Law of the United States* (1910), and *The Fundamental Concepts of Public Law* (1924)—helped to establish political science as a discipline distinct from history and economics and were core texts read in many early political science courses, most public law scholars today have traded in his insights and approaches for more sophisticated models.

Beginning in 1916, Willoughby acted as legal adviser to the Chinese government. After World War I and his tour of service in Peking (1916–1917), his interests turned toward international affairs. He advised the Chinese delegation at the Washington Conference on arms reduction (1921–1922) and at the Opium Conferences held in Geneva (1924–1925, 1931). In September 1931 he represented the Chinese delegation at the League of Nations in the Sino-Japanese controversy over Manchuria. These experiences led to several books—*Foreign Rights and Interests in China* (2 vols., rev. ed., 1927), *China at the Conference* (1922), *Opium as an International Problem* (1925), and *The Sino-Japanese Controversy and the League of Nations* (1935). Unlike his major works in American constitutional law and political theory, these books are still read and are regarded as useful sources for these international events.

In 1933 Willoughby retired from the Johns Hopkins University faculty after a long career as a distinguished teacher, prolific writer, and highly sought adviser of the Chinese government. Author of numerous books on political theory, constitutional law, and China's role in international affairs, Willoughby was truly "the dean of American political scientists," as James W. Garner anointed him in a 1937 festschrift essay. He died in Washington, D.C.

• What little remains of W. W. Willoughby's papers is within the papers of Herbert Baxter Adams and Frank Goodnow, found in the Milton S. Eisenhower Library, Special Collections, at the Johns Hopkins University. Books by Willoughby include his published dissertation, *The Supreme Court of the United States—Its History and Administrative Importance* (1891), as well as *Government and Administration of the United States* (1891), *Political Theories of the Ancient World* (1903), *The American Constitutional System* (1904), *Prussian Political Philosophy* (1918), *Constitutional Law of the United States* (3 vols., 1929), *The Ethical Basis of Political Authority* (1930), and *Japan's Case Examined* (1940). For a more detailed evaluation of his contribution to the field, see John M. Mathews and James Hart, eds., *Essays in Political Science in Honor of Westel Woodbury Willoughby* (1937), and William H. Hatcher, "The Political and Legal Theories of Westel Woodbury Willoughby" (Ph.D. diss., Duke Univ., 1961). Willoughby's obituary, written by Professor James Hart, a former student, is in the *American Political Science Review* 39 (1945): 552–54.

MICHAEL C. TOLLEY

WILLS, Bob (6 Mar. 1905–13 May 1975), fiddler and band leader, was born James Robert Wills near Kosse, Limestone County, Texas, the son of John Tompkins Wills, a migrant farmworker and farmer, and Emmaline Foley. When Wills was age eight, the family moved to Hall County in West Texas. The eldest son in a family that eventually included ten children, Wills worked in cotton fields to help support the family, attending school only through the seventh grade. Impressed by the African-American music that he heard in migrant farm camps, Wills later incorporated some of its features into his own work. He had begun to play professionally at an early age, providing mandolin accompaniment for his father, an accomplished fiddler who supplemented the family income by playing at dances.

In the early 1920s Wills drifted through various Texas towns, working on farms and in factories and playing fiddle at Saturday dances. In this period he developed the serious drinking problem with which he struggled for the rest of his life and that handicapped his career. His biographer, Charles Townsend, remarked that alcoholism "was probably the greatest tragedy of his life. . . . The really remarkable thing is how well he did in spite of it" (p. 25).

In 1926 Wills married Edna Posey. The following year they moved to Amarillo, Texas, where Wills attended barber school and took music lessons. The couple then moved to Roy, New Mexico, where Wills worked as a barber and organized a dance band. He and his wife subsequently returned to West Texas, moving to the town of Turkey near his parents' farm. They had a daughter in 1929.

Wills's career was given a boost in 1930 when he won a fiddle contest sponsored by radio station KFJZ in Fort Worth, Texas. By the early 1930s he was a full-time musician and enjoyed a growing regional reputation, playing with guitarist Herman Arnspiger, vocalist Milton Brown, and others on a WBAP radio show in Fort Worth and at dances in West Texas. From 1931 to 1933 Wills and the Light Crust Doughboys (named for their sponsor's product) broadcast a local radio program daily from Fort Worth. By 1932 the Doughboys had transformed the rural string-band sound by adding urbane vocals and a pronounced upbeat rhythm. The band's great popularity spawned numerous imitators.

After disagreements with the president of Burrus Mill, the band's sponsor, Wills moved to Tulsa in

1933 and formed Bob Wills and His Texas Playboys. The band broadcast daily on KVOO, a powerful Tulsa, Oklahoma, station, and was in great demand at dances throughout the region. Initially, the Playboys continued to employ acoustic instruments but acquired a more driving rhythm by employing bass, archtop guitar, banjo, and resonator guitar. Wills wasted little time in developing the "western swing" sound further, adding steel guitar and embracing elements of jazz—incorporating percussion and tenor banjo from Dixieland into the traditional western string-band instrumentation, employing blue notes, and even affecting a rural African-American accent in his distinctive vocal calls and hollers. By 1935 the Texas Playboys included Herman Arnspiger and Sleepy Johnson (guitar), Jesse Ashlock (fiddle), Leon McAuliffe (steel guitar), Tommy Duncan (vocals), Everett Stover (trumpet), Son Lansford (bass), Johnny Lee Wills (tenor banjo), Alton Strickland (piano), Zeb McNally (saxophone and clarinet), and Smokey Dacus (drums). In the late 1930s Wills added more of the brass and reeds common to the era's big bands. The Texas Playboys, in fact, became one of the largest dance bands of its day, appealing to an audience that was larger, younger, and more urban than those of standard string bands, with a diverse repertoire that included traditional fiddle tunes, western and folk pieces played by the string core of the band, and popular jazz and swing numbers.

Wills's own playing blended folk, blues, jazz, and classical elements to produce a distinct fiddling style that was characterized by strong tone and long bow strokes carrying a melody above driving rhythm. Wills surrounded himself with outstanding musicians and was not afraid to engage talented young players and fiddlers who were even more proficient than himself. He required players with strong solo skills who were able to improvise at length on the dance melody, and he encouraged them to create. Band members collaborated with Wills in composing and writing lyrics for particular songs and in forging the distinctive sound of western swing. McAuliffe's instrumental "Steel Guitar Rag" (1935) became one of the band's hits.

The evolution of Wills's best-known song, "San Antonio Rose," demonstrated his natural ear for combining sounds and fusing styles with strong popular appeal. He originally wrote it as a fiddle piece to accommodate local dance steps while playing with Mexican-American fiddlers in New Mexico during the 1920s. As his career developed, Wills retained the piece—then titled "Spanish Two Step"—in his band's repertoire. He recorded it as the string-band composition "San Antonio Rose" in 1938. In 1940, rescored for a big band, with violins removed and lyrics added, Wills recorded it as a swing tune renamed "New San Antonio Rose." This arrangement achieved instant popularity, and the next year Bing Crosby recorded a million-selling version. Though "New San Antonio Rose" became his band's only gold record, Wills recorded regularly from 1935 until his death. His sales of hit singles totaled in the millions. Discographies list scores of 78s and over ninety long-play albums.

By the late 1930s the Texas Playboys had become the most popular dance band in the Southwest, attracting thousands to their dances and enjoying a large radio audience. In 1939 they performed at the Oklahoma governor's inaugural ball. But by that time, Wills's alcoholism, which he had controlled through the years immediately preceding, once again resurfaced and his personal life suffered. His first marriage ended in 1935, and he was divorced four more times by 1941. In 1936 he married—and separated from—his music teacher, classically trained violinist Ruth Elain McMaster. The next year he married Mary Helen Brown; they divorced, remarried, and separated again in 1938. In 1939 he married Mary Louise Parker. They divorced two years later after the birth of a daughter. Finally, in 1942, Wills married Betty Anderson. This union lasted until Wills's death and produced four children.

In 1940 Wills played a supporting role in a Hollywood film, *Take Me Back to Oklahoma*, in addition to leading the string band that accompanied its star, Tex Ritter. The next year he appeared in *Go West Young Lady*, which starred Glenn Ford, and between 1941 and 1944 he played in eight westerns featuring Russell Hayden. His movie and music work, however, were interrupted in 1942, when he enlisted in the army. Discharged in 1943, he relocated in California and reestablished the Texas Playboys, playing daily lunch-hour broadcasts on radio station KMTR in Los Angeles and appearing at dances in the area. In 1944 he took the band on its first national tour. In the first years of the postwar period, they continued to produce hits; in 1947 alone Columbia released seventy records by the band. Wills began to appear in more extravagant western apparel and smoked a cigar on stage while playing. At the same time, the band's sound changed a bit. Wills trimmed the Playboys' horn section, allowing guitars and fiddles to return to the fore.

Convinced of the need to reestablish a regular circuit in a particular region, Wills relocated repeatedly in the late 1940s and 1950s, working out of Sacramento, California; Oklahoma City; Dallas; Amarillo; Tulsa; and Abilene, Texas. Suffering from the declining interest in dance and swing, Wills was also dogged by bad investments, mismanagement, and recurring bouts of drinking. From 1958 to 1961 he was featured at Las Vegas and Lake Tahoe night clubs.

Wills suffered serious heart attacks in 1962 and 1964. Although he sold his band's name and business in 1963, he continued to perform through the late 1960s. In 1968 he was elected to the Country Music Hall of Fame in Nashville; the next year, the governor and legislature of Texas presented Wills with a resolution recognizing his contribution to western swing music. The following day he suffered the first of a series of disabling strokes from which he never fully recovered. He slipped into a coma in 1973 and died two years later in Fort Worth.

By the time of his death, Wills's music was starting to appeal to a new generation of country and folk music fans. His early recordings began to be reissued. Though folk music purists once dismissed him because of his commercial success, because his influences included popular music sources, and because he studied briefly with classically trained violinists, Wills deserves credit for championing the fiddle throughout the jazz age and for popularizing a style that survived the decline of swing and of live radio. In his contributions to new band instrumentation, his fusion of styles and repertoires, and even his glitzy stage presence, he figured prominently as a forerunner of contemporary popular and country-western music.

• Papers and other Wills material are located in the Southwest Collection, Texas Tech University Library, Lubbock; and at the Bob Wills Museum in Turkey, Tex. Charles R. Townsend, *San Antonio Rose: The Life and Music of Bob Wills* (1976), contains a useful bibliography and also a discography and filmography by Bob Pinson. Townsend's research commenced before Wills's coma, and his work benefited from the cooperation of Wills and his family and contemporaries. An earlier biography is Ruth Shelton Knowles, *Hubbin' It: The Life of Bob Wills* (1938). Other works that include discussions of his life and music are Cary Ginell, with Roy Lee Brown, *Milton Brown and the Founding of Western Swing* (1994); Georg Hunkel, *Western Swing and Country Jazz: Eine Einführung mit Kurzporträts über Bob Wills und Milton Brown* (1983); Richard Kienzle, *Bob Wills* (1982) and *Papa's Jumping: The MGM Years of Bob Wills* (1985); Jimmy Latham, *The Life of Bob Wills: The King of Western Swing* (1974; rev. ed. 1987); and Al Stricklin with Jon McConal, *My Years with Bob Wills* (1976; 2d ed. 1980).

MICHAEL H. HOFFHEIMER

WILLS, Childe Harold (1 June 1878–30 Dec. 1940), metallurgist and automobile designer and manufacturer, was born in Fort Wayne, Indiana, the son of John Carnegie Wills, a railroad mechanic, and Angelina Swindell. Wills's mother named the boy after the hero of Lord Byron's epic poem *Childe Harold's Pilgrimage*, but throughout his life Wills detested his first name, always using just the abbreviation "C." and preferring to be called Harold.

When he was seven, Wills's family moved to Detroit, where he attended public schools and showed an aptitude for drawing cartoons. But work as a cartoonist offered an uncertain future, so Wills began to train as a machinist. From 1896 to 1899 he worked as an apprentice toolmaker for the Detroit Lubricator Company. During this time he attended night school to study metallurgy and chemistry. Wills's next job was in the engineering department of the Boyer Machine Company, the world's largest maker of adding machines (which later became the Burroughs Adding Machine Company), where he soon became a superintendent.

But Wills was attracted by automobiles, and in 1899 he met with Henry Ford, who was the superintendent of the Detroit Automobile Company. Ford could not match the $18-a-week salary that Wills was earning at Boyer, so Wills kept his full-time job and began to work part time as Ford's assistant, from 5:00 A.M. to 7:00 A.M. as well as during evenings, before and after his regular work hours. The two men labored in a cramped, unheated machine shop and took breaks to don boxing gloves and spar in order to keep warm. Wills had an enormous ability to work long hours, eating just a sandwich to sustain him during his labors. He had a fervently practical approach to automobile mechanics, a propitious attitude during the early days of the automobile industry, when trial-and-error experimentation was the best way to achieve results. Wills said he frowned upon textbooks because they contained information that was already outdated by the time they were published.

Wills helped Ford to develop the famous "Arrow" and "999" racing cars, which built Ford's reputation because of their success on the race track. In 1901 the Detroit Automobile Company was reorganized as the Henry Ford Company (which later formed the nucleus of the Cadillac Company), and two years later the Ford Motor Company (FMC) was incorporated. By this time Ford had substantial financial backing from Alexander Malcolmson, a wealthy Detroit coal dealer, and Wills had a contract to work full time for Ford. It was Wills who in 1906 designed the distinctive Ford script emblem that was used to identify the company throughout the twentieth century. Meanwhile, in 1903 Wills had married Mabel Preston; they had one son and two daughters.

Wills's role at FMC was as chief designer, engineer, and metallurgist. He had no official title at the company because Ford refrained from giving specific duties to his lieutenants, but he was unquestionably a prime force in the company and, additionally, the only man to receive part of Henry Ford's personal dividend (a 10 percent cut, in addition to his own salary).

Wills was Ford's indispensable man. The two men formed a seamless partnership, working so closely that contemporaries could not distinguish what one of them did and where the other took over. Wills played a large part, perhaps just as large as Ford did, in every major FMC car from the company's founding until 1919. Both men dreamed of mass producing a light, inexpensive, and dependable car for the average American, and it was Wills who gave discipline to Ford's often rough-hewn ideas and put the final design and production plans on paper. While the Model T was primarily the brainchild of Henry Ford, it owed much of its design and success to Wills. Wills conceived the Model T's pedal-operated planetary transmission—an idea that struck him as he lay in his bathtub, a morning ritual that became a vital part of his creative process. Wills, drawing on his metallurgical training, was also the major force behind the tough vanadium steel alloy in the Model T, an innovation that brought Wills international renown as a metallugist.

Wills was always striving for improvements and perfection, and in 1912, while Ford was away in Europe, he created a new, improved version of the Model T. But Ford was more stodgy than Wills and was hostile to changes in the original Model T design. When he returned he was so infuriated with Wills's surprise prototype vehicle that he smashed it to bits.

This incident was a harbinger of deep strains in Wills's relationship with Ford. Wills bristled under Ford's refusal to update his cars, and increasingly Wills's ideas cut against the grain of Ford's. Ford's domineering leadership became harder for Wills to take, and he particularly demurred at Ford's rough treatment of stockholders such as the Dodge Brothers, John and Horace. For his part, Ford grew to consider Wills intractable, and pointed to Wills's bathtub ruminations as an illustration of what he considered as haphazard work habits. The final break came on 5 March 1919, when Wills, along with his close associate and labor relations expert John R. Lee, resigned from FMC. Wills received a settlement from Ford totaling $1.6 million, and Ford was said to be relieved to be rid of his uneasy alliance with his chief engineer.

Wills was then forty years old, a millionaire, and free to pursue his creativity and drive for perfection. He wanted to build his own car, and together with John R. Lee, he purchased 4,400 acres about fifty miles north of Detroit along the St. Clair River. There they founded Marysville, a planned industrial community that Wills named after his second wife and that comprised businesses, utilities, homes, schools, and parks. Wills envisioned it as a thriving community that would allow workers to escape the unpleasant, teeming characteristics of city life.

Wills founded C. H. Wills & Company and named his new car the Wills Sainte Claire, after himself and the river. The Wills Sainte Claire A-68, which first appeared in March 1921, offered several innovations and reflected the exacting engineering and metallurgical standards that Wills had demanded. It was the first car to be made with molybdenum steel, a tough alloy that Wills had used during World War I in making Liberty airplane engines. Another notable feature was a white backup light that lit when the car was put in reverse. On the car's radiator was the Michigan Grey Goose, which was the car's symbol.

Wills wanted his V-8 car to be "ten years ahead of its time" and far classier than the utilitarian Model T, and in many ways it was. But Wills's relentless drive for perfection—his constant and meticulous improvements to the car—coupled with a weak postwar market for cars delayed production of the car for over half a year and raised its price. The company was already on weak financial footing because it had poured millions of dollars into the Marysville community, and the postwar depression only aggravated its cash shortage. From the outset the company was thus mired in financial difficulty, and annual production levels, which peaked at 2,840 in 1922, fell far short of the 10,000 per year that Wills had predicted. In 1922 the company went into a friendly receivership, and Wills temporarily lost control of the firm. But it was reorganized the following year as the Wills Sainte Claire Company, and Wills returned to the helm. The company limped along for a few more years and in 1927 shut down for good. In total, the firm had produced between 12,000 and 18,000 cars, but the venture had left Wills almost $4 million in debt.

Over the ensuing years Wills found various jobs and managed to pay off his debts. He conducted research in metallurgy and further enhanced his stature as one of the nation's foremost authorities in this field. He served as a consultant to the Timken Roller Bearing Company as well as the New Era Motors Company, which briefly made the Ruxton car. In 1932 Walter P. Chrysler hired Wills as a metallurgist. But for Wills it was a rude drop from his former heights: an erstwhile car company head who in his career had been earning as much as $2 million annually, Wills was now working for a $5,000 annual salary and shared an office with two freshman engineers. But Wills proved his salt at Chrysler, making recommendations that resulted in enormous savings for the company and developing innovations such as the Oilite bearing. Eventually Wills was rewarded with his own office and secretary, and he spent eight comfortable years at Chrysler. One of his last metallurgical endeavors was with amola, a steel alloy that he invented. His marriage to Mabel Preston had ended in divorce in 1913, and he later married Mary Coyne Pommerer; they had two sons. After leaving Marysville, Wills lived the last years of his life in Grosse Pointe, Michigan. He died at Henry Ford Hospital in Detroit.

Although Wills is less known or remembered than Henry Ford, he was no less important to the success of the Ford Motor Company. A brilliant metallurgist and engineer, he displayed an uncompromising drive for perfection and an uncanny ability to translate Ford's plans and sketches into production vehicles. While Wills's drive for perfection ironically hindered his own venture into automobile manufacturing, his contributions to the automobile industry generally and to the Ford Motor Company particularly were immeasurable.

• Of the thousands of Wills Sainte Claire automobiles built, only about seventy have survived, some of which are at various automobile museums in America. Wills's papers are at the Henry Ford Museum and Greenfield Village Archives in Dearborn, Mich. The National Automotive History Collection of the Detroit Public Library maintains a file on Wills. Two articles on Wills provide a good overview of his life: M. D. Henry, "Childe Harold Wills: A Career in Cars," *Automobile Quarterly*, Fall 1966, pp. 136–45; and Jack Woodward, "Childe Harold Wills," *Special-Interest Autos*, Aug.–Oct. 1977, pp. 30–33. Information on Wills with a special emphasis on the Wills Sainte Claire automobile, including technical specifications, can be found in Warren Fitzgerald, "Wills Sainte Clair," *Car Life*, Feb. 1967, pp. 45–50. A chapter on Wills is in Bryan Ford, *Henry's Lieutenants* (1993). Information on Wills can also be found in a number of books about Henry Ford and the Ford Motor Company. They include Allan Nevins, *Ford: The Times, The Man, The Company* (1954); Nevins and Frank Ernest Hill, *Ford: Expansion and Challenge, 1915–1932* (1957); and Keith Sward, *The Legend of Henry Ford* (1948). An obituary is in the *New York Times*, 31 Dec. 1940.

YANEK MIECZKOWSKI

WILLS, Harry (20 Jan. 1889–21 Dec. 1958), heavyweight professional boxer, was born Harrison Coleman Wills in New Orleans, Louisiana, the son of Strother G. Wills and Georgie B. Kenner. He grew up in New Orleans in an impoverished waterfront neighborhood and received little formal education. While in his teens, he worked as a stevedore and frequented horseracing tracks. He hoped to become a jockey but soon became too big. Eventually he found work on freighters, and it is believed that he was introduced to boxing during a long voyage abroad.

Wills returned to New Orleans, where he had his earliest recorded fight in 1910. By 1913 he was fighting such competent black heavyweights as Joe Jeannette and Jeff Clark. In May and June 1914 Wills gained attention by boxing Jeannette on even terms and beating the great Sam Langford in fights in which official decisions were not given. At 6′2″ and 220 pounds, Wills towered over Langford by six inches and outweighed him by thirty pounds.

In August 1914 Wills went to the West Coast, where he gained a series of wins, mostly over white fighters. He suffered the first major setback of his career in Los Angeles on 26 November 1914, when he was knocked out by Langford in fourteen rounds after earlier scoring eleven knockdowns. He returned to New Orleans in December but was beaten on points by Sam McVea.

Over the next several years, Wills fought Langford fifteen more times. In 1916 Langford again knocked out Wills, but Wills generally had the best of the series, and by 1918 Langford had ceased to be able to compete seriously with him. Wills also fought other good black heavyweights, including Sam McVea six times and Jack Thompson ten times. Indeed, all of Wills's opponents during the years 1915–1918 were black, and the overwhelming majority of all of his fights were with other black men. During these years, in reaction to the controversial black heavyweight champion Jack Johnson, promoters seldom matched black fighters with white fighters, and whites often "drew the color line," refusing to box black fighters. Wills's earnings from his boxing career were so small that he continued to work as a stevedore between fights, first in New Orleans and later in West Hoboken, New Jersey.

In 1917 Wills was stopped in two rounds by Battling Jim Johnson when he suffered a broken arm, but he easily won a rematch. Wills thereafter won all of his fights (either officially or, in the case of no-decision fights, unofficially by "newspaper decisions") until 1926 except for a 1922 loss to Bill Tate on a foul and a draw with Tate in a rematch. In 1920 he gained an important victory when he knocked out white heavyweight Fred Fulton, and in 1922 he knocked out a major black rival, Kid Norfolk, in two rounds.

In 1922 some of the influential New York sportswriters, especially George Underwood, boxing writer for the *New York Telegram*, and Nat Fleischer, editor of *The Ring* (a boxing magazine), called for the white heavyweight champion, Jack Dempsey, to defend his title against Wills. Although Dempsey and his manager, Jack Kearns, were willing to have the heavyweight title defended against Wills, Tex Rickard, the great fight promoter of the period, opposed it. Rickard had promoted the Jack Johnson–Jim Jeffries fight in 1910 and was blamed for the "humiliation" of the white race after Johnson defeated Jeffries. He feared race riots if another black became heavyweight champion and claimed that unnamed political forces did not want the fight. Even so, a contract was signed for a fight between Dempsey and Wills in July 1922 in New York, contingent upon a reliable promoter's being found to stage the fight within sixty days. Neither Rickard nor any other promoter came forward. In February 1923 William Muldoon, the chairman of the New York State Boxing Commission, stated that he would not permit a heavyweight title fight in New York because Americans were opposed to any person earning more for a few minutes' work than the president of the United States made for a full term. New Jersey was also mentioned as a possible site for a Dempsey-Wills fight, but the authorities would not allow it.

In 1924 Wills's reputation suffered somewhat when he was unable to knock out the much smaller Bartley Madden in a fifteen-round fight. Although hampered by an injured thumb, Wills decisively beat Argentine heavyweight Luis Angel Firpo in twelve rounds at Jersey City (newspaper decision) on 11 September 1924. After two impressive knockouts by Wills over white heavyweights Charley Weinert and Floyd Johnson in 1925, there was renewed pressure from sportswriters for a Dempsey-Wills fight. This led to an ultimatum to Dempsey by the New York State Boxing Commission that he would be barred from fighting in the state unless he fought Wills. Kearns refused to accept the Wills fight and Rickard refused to promote it, and instead a fight between Dempsey and Gene Tunney was arranged. The License Committee of the New York Boxing Board refused to allow a Dempsey-Tunney fight, but Rickard simply moved the fight to Philadelphia, where it occurred on 23 September 1926.

Paddy Mullins, Wills's manager, had turned down possible fights for Wills with Tommy Gibbons and Tunney, insisting that Wills would meet only Dempsey. Tunney, by defeating Gibbons, secured the match with Dempsey and won the heavyweight title. On 12 October 1926 Wills fought Jack Sharkey in Brooklyn and suffered a bad beating, losing every round until being disqualified in the thirteenth, thus ending his heavyweight title chances.

On 13 July 1927 Wills made an attempt to put himself back into contention for the heavyweight title by fighting a young Spanish heavyweight, Paulino Uzcudun, in Brooklyn. Wills's more clever boxing held his opponent at bay for a couple of rounds, but the aggressive Uzcudun scored a four-round knockout. Afterward Wills had only three minor fights, the last in 1932.

In 1916 Wills had married a former model and schoolteacher, Sarah (maiden name unknown), who proved to be a good manager of money and handled the family finances well. Eventually the couple bought six apartment houses in New York City, made their own home in one of them, and managed them for many years. Wills lived quietly with his wife in New York City until his death there.

Wills was both a hard puncher and a good orthodox boxer. He was more agile than most of his opponents and, unlike many tall heavyweights, was a good fighter at close quarters. He had the ability to tie up his opponents with one arm and flail away with the other, to good effect.

The probable outcome of the Dempsey-Wills fight that never occurred has continued to be a matter of debate. Although the consensus is that Dempsey would have won, there is no doubt that Wills was prevented from getting his well-merited opportunity by the prevailing racist fears. Always gentlemanly and affable, Wills was almost the opposite in personality from the controversial Jack Johnson and would have been a well-liked champion. It is probable that the unjust denial of a heavyweight title fight to Wills worked to the benefit of the next African-American heavyweight challenger to appear, Joe Louis.

Wills had approximately one hundred professional fights, winning almost half of them by knockout and most of the rest by decision (either official or in the opinion of newspaper reporters). He lost fewer than ten fights. He was elected to the International Boxing Hall of Fame in 1992.

• Wills's record appears most recently in the 1979 edition of *The Ring Record Book*, comp. Nat Loubet and John Ort. The main source of information on Wills is a brief biography by Nat Fleischer in *Black Dynamite*, vol. 5: *Sockers in Sepia* (1947). The circumstances that prevented a Wills-Dempsey fight are discussed in Randy Roberts, *Jack Dempsey: The Manassa Mauler* (1979); Nat Fleischer, *Jack Dempsey: Idol of Fistiana* (1929; reissued as *Jack Dempsey*, 1972), and Jack Dempsey and Barbara Piattelli Dempsey, *Dempsey* (1977). Helpful articles include Jersey Jones, "The Legend That Was Harry Wills," *The Ring*, Mar. 1959, pp. 30–31, 60; and Wills's challenge to Dempsey as reported by John B. Kennedy, "If Dempsey's Afraid Let Him Say So," *Collier's*, 20 Mar. 1926, pp. 11, 43. An obituary is in the *New York Times*, 22 Dec. 1958.

LUCKETT V. DAVIS

WILLSON, Augustus Everett (13 Oct. 1846–24 Aug. 1931), governor of Kentucky, was born in Maysville, Kentucky, the son of Hiram Willson, a lumberman and mill operator, and Ann Colvin Ennis. Willson spent his childhood in Covington, Kentucky, and in New Albany, Indiana, where the family settled in 1852. Orphaned at age twelve, he went with his younger sister and brother to live first with their grandmother in New York state and then with an older brother, Forceythe Willson, a minor poet, in Cambridge, Massachusetts. Through his brother young "Gus" came to know eminent literary figures such as Ralph Waldo Emerson, Oliver Wendell Holmes, Henry Wadsworth Longfellow, and James Russell Lowell. Willson enrolled in Harvard College in 1865, but his studies were interrupted during his sophomore year when Forceythe became terminally ill. Following his brother's death, Willson reentered Harvard while taking care of his younger siblings and received a baccalaureate degree in 1869.

After reading law in Boston for several months, Willson returned in 1870 to New Albany, where he lived for a time in the home of Congressman Michael C. Kerr, a future Speaker of the U.S. House of Representatives. Bearing a letter of introduction from Kerr, Willson secured a position in the Louisville law firm of John Marshall Harlan, who later pronounced him "one of the brightest young fellows I ever met." Although their daily association ended in 1877, when Harlan was named associate justice of the U.S. Supreme Court, the two men remained lifelong friends. In 1877 Willson married Mary Elizabeth Ekin; they had one child, who died in infancy.

Largely because of Harlan's influence, Willson became passionately active in Republican politics. Between 1879 and 1892 the party nominated him for office on five occasions: for the Kentucky Senate in 1879 and for the U.S. House of Representatives in 1884, 1886, 1888, and 1892. Never could he overcome the handicap of being a Republican in a predominantly Democratic state. For the next ten years he eschewed active candidacy for himself but continued to work tirelessly to build the Republican party throughout the state. In 1907, at age sixty, he received his party's nomination for governor, even though he had never held major appointive or elective office. He defeated his Democratic opponent, State Auditor Samuel Wilber Hager, after a campaign in which the temperance issue figured prominently. Willson garnered 214,481 votes to Hager's 196,428.

As governor Willson pledged to act swiftly and decisively to quell the civil unrest that had plagued the tobacco-growing regions of western Kentucky for more than two years. During the so called Black Patch War, independent growers attempted to curb the price-fixing ability of the "tobacco trust," led by the American Tobacco Company, that they insisted eliminated competitive bidding and set artificially low prices for tobacco. Growers established cooperatives in an effort to control the supply of tobacco. Such a scheme could work only if every producer in the region participated. When some growers refused to join in pooling their tobacco, "night riders" resorted to violence and intimidation, including lynchings, whippings, and crop burnings, to secure their compliance. In his inaugural address, delivered on 10 December 1907, Willson vowed to restore order to the region. "Upon all who break the law we covenant to impose punishment," he declared. "The protection of all who obey the law and the punishment of all who break it must be so quick, so sure, so severe that no one shall dare to take the risk." When his administration failed in its efforts at mediation among the growers, the American Tobacco Company, and local residents, Willson declared martial law in unruly areas and sent in the National Guard. Gradually, tensions in the area eased.

Throughout his term Willson faced an antagonistic Democratic majority in the general assembly. Partisan rancor, particularly over the liquor issue and the election of a U.S. senator in 1908, forestalled enactment of needed reforms in areas such as taxation and redistricting. Democrats also condemned Willson's pardoning of two men convicted and six others implicated in the 1900 assassination of gubernatorial claimant William Goebel.

Prevented by law from seeking a second term, Willson left office on 12 December 1911 and resumed the practice of law in Louisville. Three years later he secured the Republican nomination for the U.S. Senate but was defeated in the general election by his predecessor as governor, John Crepps Wickliffe Beckham. Willson never again sought elective office. He died in Louisville.

Willson is remembered as a well-intentioned public servant, committed to law and order and fiscal conservatism. By education, training, and temperament he was among the best prepared of Kentucky's governors. Regrettably, he had little opportunity in office to demonstrate his executive skills. As one sympathetic student of his career notes, "During his administration Governor Willson seemed always to be engaged in fighting over matters which he did not create and over which he had little or no control" (Foster, p. 87). Indeed, "throughout his entire term he was checked by a hostile Democratic legislature, with the result that his administration was barren of constructive acts" (Foster, p. 92).

• An extensive collection of Willson's correspondence, scrapbooks, and clippings is owned by the Filson Club Historical Society in Louisville. Robert K. Foster, "Augustus E. Willson and the Republican Party of Kentucky, 1895–1911" (master's thesis, Univ. of Louisville, 1955), is insightful. A discussion of his career and influence is in Thomas H. Appleton, Jr., "Augustus Everett Willson, 1907–1911," in *Kentucky's Governors, 1792–1985*, ed. Lowell H. Harrison. An obituary is in the *Louisville Courier-Journal*, 25 Aug. 1931.

THOMAS H. APPLETON, JR.

WILLSON, Meredith (18 May 1902–15 June 1984), lyricist/composer, conductor, and flutist, was born Robert Reiniger Meredith Willson in Mason City, Iowa, the son of John D. Willson, a lawyer and businessman, and Rosalie Reiniger, a teacher. Both of Willson's grandfathers were considered early settlers by more recent immigrants, adding to the family's local prominence. Meredith appeared in his mother's Sunday school musicals as early as the age of four and at twelve sang a solo as Don ("a shepherd") in the local production of his sister Dixie's musical, *The Blue Heron*. He studied flute, played in the high school band and orchestra and in local dance and theater bands, and wrote a graduation song for his class at Mason City High School (1919). In 1920 he married Elizabeth Wilson, also of Mason City.

Willson moved to New York City to study flute with the great Georges Barrère and enrolled at the Institute of Musical Art (after 1946 called the Juilliard School) from 1920 to 1921. That year Willson obtained his first steady professional work, as the principal flutist in John Philip Sousa's touring wind band. Three years later he joined the New York Philharmonic Orchestra as a flutist. He played under Willem Mengelberg, Wilhelm Furtwängler, and Arturo Toscanini between 1924 and 1929.

In 1928, while still on the orchestra's roster, Willson traveled to Seattle to conduct an outdoor concert series for Adolph Linden, a radio producer. He spent some time in Hollywood in early 1929 scoring music for the films *Peacock Alley* and *The Lost Zeppelin*. Later that same year he was hired as music director at radio station KFRC in San Francisco (1929–1932), conducting music for "The Blue Monday Jamboree" and other shows. He was promoted rapidly to the position of NBC's western division musical director (1932–1938), a job in which he developed (among other programs) a show called "The Big Ten," a precursor of the "Lucky Strike Hit Parade." His two programmatic symphonies were premiered by the San Francisco Symphony Orchestra in 1936 and 1940. He went to Hollywood to become music director (1937–1942 and 1945–1949) of a series of nationally broadcast radio variety shows sponsored by Maxwell House Coffee under various names ("Show Boat," "Good News," [cosponsored by MGM], and "Coffee Time"). At various times these shows starred Broadway veterans Frank Morgan and Fanny Brice (as "Baby Snooks"), Gracie Allen and George Burns (after World War II), and a continuing panoply of famous guests. Willson bridged the gaps between skits and commercials (occasionally acting in both), arranged and conducted light classics and popular songs, and created and conducted his own compositions. His theme song for the show, "You and I" (1941), topped the "Hit Parade" for a record nineteen consecutive weeks.

During this period Willson also orchestrated Charlie Chaplin's melodies for the acclaimed film *The Great Dictator* (1940) and composed the score for the fine screen adaptation of Lillian Hellman's play *The Little Foxes* (1941), starring Bette Davis. During World War II Willson served the Armed Forces Radio Service as music director ("I fought the entire war without leaving Hollywood") and composed a symphonic poem, *The Jervis Bay*, a 1942 memorial to the crew of an Australian freighter. He divorced his first wife in 1947 and married Ralina Zarova, an actress and singer, in 1948.

Willson achieved his greatest prominence in radio after the war, in the medium's declining years. He served as music director (1950–1952) of "The Big Show," the last great radio variety show before the hegemony of television was established, hosted by actress Tallulah Bankhead. Again Willson's theme song for the show, "May the Good Lord Bless and Keep You" (1950), became well known, selling more than a half million copies as sheet music in four months in 1951 during the Korean conflict.

Despite his willingness to try (in television pilots such as the "Meredith Willson Show" in 1949), he was unable to find an appropriate vehicle for transferring his popularity as a radio performer to the new medium of television. He became a celebrity disk jockey in 1953, offering entertaining and educational commentaries on classical compositions on "Meredith Willson's Music Room." As television continued to gain ground, Frank Loesser, among others, encouraged Willson to try writing a Broadway musical, whose genesis Willson said dated from the late 1940s.

For many years Willson had kept a picture over his desk of Mason City's first band, which he had joined at the age of ten. This boyhood memory became the inspiration for his most celebrated work, *The Music Man*, which defeated Leonard Bernstein's *West Side Story* for the Tony Award for best Broadway musical of 1957, and outran it, too, totaling 1,375 performances. Robert Preston starred on both stage and screen (1962) as Dr. Harold Hill, a fast-talking traveling salesman who falls in love with Marian, the librarian (played by Barbara Cook on stage, Shirley Jones on film). In the story, despite his inability to read music or play an instrument, Hill gives the young people of River City (and their parents) something to believe in: a uniformed marching band. The show also features a barbershop quartet, cast as members of the town's school board.

"Words holler at me. I mean they are more sound than symbol [to me]," wrote Willson in *But He Doesn't Know the Territory* (1959), his account of making *The Music Man* (Willson also wrote two other volumes of memoirs and a novel). The score included a number of Willson's distinctive rhythmic "raps," including the opening number, "But He Doesn't Know the Territory"; "Trouble (Right Here in River City)," with its ominous chorus of chanting townspeople; and "Pick a Little, Talk a Little," which is counterpointed with the popular song "Good Night, Ladies." Equally memorable are "sung" songs such as "Till There Was You," later recorded by the Beatles, among others. Sousa's influence is clear in "Seventy-six Trombones," which also serves as the basis of the waltz song "Goodnight, My Someone," a clever variant of the same melody. The lovers turn out to have been indeed singing the same tune when the two croon a duet synchronizing waltz with march.

Willson followed up *The Music Man* with a more modest hit, *The Unsinkable Molly Brown* (1960; 532 performances), about a miner's daughter who rises to wealth and fame, then survives the sinking of the ocean liner *Titanic*. The title role was played by Tammy Grimes onstage and by Debbie Reynolds in the film version (1964). His final Broadway show, *Here's Love* (1963; 334 performances), based on the Santa Claus film *Miracle on Thirty-fourth Street* (1947), features the song "It's Beginning to Look a Lot Like Christmas" (composed by Willson in 1951) and an excerpt from the African-American spiritual "Swing Low, Sweet Chariot" (with new lyrics) as musical reminiscence motives. His *Fourteen Ninety-one* (1969), a historical romance portraying Christopher Columbus as a heroic figure, was produced by the Los Angeles Civic Light Opera.

As his professional career waned, Willson's civic activities increased. In 1964 he bought and donated a large collection of popular music items (including sheet music, recordings, photographs, and concert programs) to the University of California at Los Angeles, now in the holdings of its Archive of Popular Music, founded in 1976. He wrote campaign songs for both Democratic and Republican presidential candidates ("Ask Not" for John F. Kennedy and "WIN WIN WIN" for Gerald Ford) and served on the Council on the Humanities during the Lyndon Johnson administration. In 1966 his second wife died, and in 1968 he married his former secretary, Rosemary Sullivan. Willson had no children with any of his wives. He died in Santa Monica, California. His third wife continued his philanthropy, making a major donation to his alma mater, Juilliard, in 1991; the school's new dormitory was named after him.

In addition to his diverse talents, Willson's strong rural roots served him well among the cosmopolites of Manhattan and Hollywood and helped him to speak vox populi to a mass audience after his switch from classical to popular music, making him "probably the most durable composer-conductor in radio" (*Time*, 14 May 1951). Yet Willson's music and words were perhaps most exceptional when they mordantly depicted small-town life in the Midwest, although his vision was not as cynical as Sinclair Lewis's in the novel *Main Street*. *The Music Man* did for Iowa what Oscar Hammerstein II and Richard Rodgers's romantic classic *Oklahoma!* (1943) did for that state, capturing a way of life that has become part of the myth of the American West.

• The bulk of Willson's personal papers and musical manuscripts remain in the possession of his widow; published scores of some musical pieces and some manuscript material from his Broadway shows are at the New York Public Library. Recordings of radio shows in which Willson performed are available at the Museum of Television and Radio in New York City, including "The Big Show" (1950), "Burns and Allen" (18 Sept. 1947), "Maxwell House Coffee Time," pt. 1 (5 Mar. 1942), and "Good News of 1938" (3 Mar. 1938). Willson's three volumes of memoirs are out of print, but copies are widely distributed in the United States. His *And There I Stood with My Piccolo* (1948) covers Willson's years in New York and Hollywood up to his second marriage; *Eggs I Have Laid* (1955) recounts a series of memorable and professional mishaps, such as the time Willson had to substitute for Frank Sinatra in a duet with President Harry Truman's daughter in a December 1950 live radio broadcast. *But He Doesn't Know the Territory* (1959) details the ten-year-long making of *The Music Man*. Willson's novel, *Who Did What to Fedalia?* was published in 1952. His musical compositions also include popular songs such as "Banners and Bonnets," "Chicken Fat," and "I See the Moon"; choral works, including *Song of Steel* (1934), *Anthem for the Atomic Age* (1950), *Ask Not* (1964), and *Mass of the Bells* (1970); orchestral works, including Symphony no. 1, *San Francisco* (1936); *O. O. McIntyre Suite* (1936); Symphony no. 2, *The Missions of California* (1940); *The Jervis Bay* (1942); and *Symphonic Variations on American Themes*.

Useful articles on Willson appear in Stanley Green, *The World of Musical Comedy* (1960; rev. ed., 1980); David Ewen,

Popular American Composers (1962; supp. 1972); and E. R. Anderson, *Contemporary American Composers* (1982). See also contemporary general periodical articles such as Dixie Willson, "The Man Behind 'The Music Man,'" *American Weekly*, 4 May 1958, pp. 15–16; Peter Waddington, "Meredith Willson: Young Man with Ideas," *Opera and Concert*, Sept. 1948, pp. 16–17ff; and numerous articles in the *Mason City Glove-Gazette* on Willson and members of his family, as well as related articles in John Dunning, *Tune in Yesterday: The Ultimate Encyclopedia of Old-time Radio, 1925–1976* (1976). An obituary is in the *New York Times*, 17 June 1984.

ANDREW BUCHMAN

WILLYS, John North (25 Oct. 1873–26 Aug. 1935), automobile manufacturer, was born in Canandaigua, New York, the son of David Smith Willys, a brick and tile maker, and Lydia North. Willys showed an early talent for business and, at the age of fifteen, persuaded his parents to allow him to buy half interest in a laundry in a nearby town. Within a year he sold his share of the laundry at a profit. He intended to study law, but the death of his father ended his formal education when Willys was eighteen years old. The failure of his next enterprise, a bicycle shop, taught him the peril of extending credit too generously. Willys then developed a successful retail and wholesale bicycle business. In 1897 he married Isabel Van Wie; they had one daughter.

As he told the story in later years, Willys saw his first automobile in Cleveland in 1899 and understood immediately how automobiles would devastate the bicycle industry. In 1901 he began selling Pierce-Arrow and Rambler automobiles on a very small scale.

Willys found it easier to sell cars than to get them from the manufacturers, and he decided to contract for the entire output of a factory and distribute cars wholesale. In 1906 he established the American Motor Car Sales Company in Elmira, New York, and undertook to sell all the vehicles made by the American and Overland factories in Indianapolis. Overland collapsed in the Panic of 1907, and Willys raised $10,000 in cash to pay immediate bills and persuaded creditors to wait for full payment. Meanwhile he used his marvelous salesmanship to raise more cash. He became president, treasurer, and sales manager of the company, and within a year restored Overland to profitability.

In 1909 Willys purchased the failing Pope-Toledo automobile works and moved the renamed Willys-Overland into its large factory in Toledo, Ohio. Production increased very rapidly, as Willys expanded the factory and purchased parts manufacturing companies, largely with money borrowed from Toledo and New York banks. From 1912 to 1918 Willys-Overland ranked second to Ford in output. Willys boasted of challenging the Model T with a better-equipped and more powerful Overland at a competitive price. Always more a salesman than an industrialist, Willys ambitiously expanded his efforts. The Willys-Knight offered the advanced Knight sleeve-valve engine, but it was an expensive automobile to manufacture. Willys-Overland became a major military contractor during World War I, turning out trucks and aircraft engines. To direct his grand plan of expansion into other industries, Willys moved to New York in 1918, leaving associates to manage the Toledo plant. A long and bloody strike at the plant the following year was broken by city police and federal court orders—Willys himself, however, had a reputation for good labor relations.

Willys-Overland was unprepared for the peacetime market in 1919. The new Willys Corporation, his personal holding company, was greatly overextended by the acquisition of the Curtiss Aeroplane & Motor Corporation and the Moline Plow Company, along with smaller firms in the United States and Great Britain. Early in 1920, Willys's bankers forced him to accept Walter P. Chrysler as vice president and general manager of Willys-Overland. Chrysler quickly cut costs and reorganized production, while Willys went on the road to inspire the dealers. "I've shown the boys I'm not dead," he explained, and sales improved rapidly. The Willys Corporation sold off its major assets and went into receivership, but Toledo bankers and a friendly judge made it possible for Willys to regain full control of Willys-Overland in 1922. That year Chrysler left to establish his own automobile company, taking a number of Willys-Overland engineers with him. The company still flourished, but Willys was now conservative in both design and financing, except for the Whippet, the nation's smallest four-cylinder car and at the time its least expensive six. Overland cars ranked third in sales for 1928, trailing Chevrolet and Ford. Willys sold his common stock holdings in Willys-Overland for $21 million in the summer of 1929, saying that he had achieved everything he could wish in business.

From March 1930 until May 1932 Willys served as ambassador to Poland. His service in Warsaw was successful and uneventful, cut short because he was needed in Toledo. Willys-Overland sales dropped drastically during the Great Depression, and Willys's exceptional sales talent was again called upon to rescue the company. Despite his best efforts, the firm went into receivership in February 1933. Now in poor health, Willys struggled to save the corporation with which he was so closely identified. Operating costs were cut, financing secured from Toledo banks and business leaders, and sales increased, but Willys did not live to see his success. He and Isabel divorced in 1934, and that same year he married Florence Dingler Dolan; they had no children. He suffered a heart attack in May 1935 but resumed working from his home in New York City, where he died from a stroke.

Willys, "J. N." to his friends, was always a salesman at heart, optimistic and energetic, hard at work two weeks before his death. Below average height, he was always well dressed. Aside from business, Willys was highly regarded as an art collector and owned a fine collection of Old Master paintings, tapestries, and furniture.

• There are no known collections of personal or business papers. There are extensive personal and corporate clipping files in the local history section of the Toledo Public Library and the National Automotive History Collection of the Detroit Public Library. The best account of his automotive career is Beverly Rae Kimes, "John North Willys: His Magnetism, His Millions, His Motor Cars," *Automobile Quarterly* 17 (3d quarter 1979): 296–321. A brief biography by George S. May appears in May, ed., *The Automobile Industry, 1896–1920* (1990). The rise and fall of Willys-Overland may be followed in John B. Rae, *American Automobile Manufacturers: The First Forty Years* (1959). B. C. Forbes devoted a chapter to Willys in *Men Who Are Making America* (1917, 1919), and there is a detailed account of his art collection in Ralph Flint, "John N. Willys Collection," *International Studio* (Feb. 1925), pp. 363–74. Detailed obituaries are in the *New York Times*, the *New York Herald-Tribune*, the *Toledo Blade*, and the *Toledo Times*, all 26 Aug. 1935.

PATRICK J. FURLONG

WILMER, Richard Hooker (15 Mar. 1816–14 June 1900), Episcopal bishop, was born in Alexandria, Virginia, the son of William Holland Wilmer, an Episcopal clergyman, and Marion Hannah Cox. William H. Wilmer was a leading evangelical within the Protestant Episcopal church who died when his son was eleven. Richard Wilmer graduated from Yale in 1836 and Virginia Theological Seminary in 1839. Bishop Channing Moore ordained him priest the following year in Monumental Church, Richmond. Wilmer married Margaret Brown of Nelson County, Virginia, in 1840, and all three of their children grew to adulthood.

Wilmer served several rural parishes in Virginia in the 1840s and 1850s and St. James's in Wilmington, North Carolina, between 1844 and 1849. With the onset of the Civil War in 1861, Episcopal dioceses in the South organized themselves into the Protestant Episcopal Church in the Confederate States and proceeded to consecrate new bishops. Thus, in 1862 Wilmer was consecrated second bishop of Alabama at St. Paul's Church, Richmond. Among the consecrators were leading evangelical prelates William Meade and John Johns. The new bishop worked hard during the war to minister to both soldiers and civilians in Alabama.

Wilmer gained notoriety in 1865 when he instructed his clergy not to use the set prayers for the president and those in civil authority while Alabama was under federal military rule. Union commander General George H. Thomas responded by closing Episcopal churches and severely restricting the ministrations of Episcopal clergy. Thomas's order, widely viewed as inappropriate, was revoked by President Andrew Johnson early in 1866. The incident made Wilmer popular among conservative whites who opposed federal Reconstruction measures in the coming years. Wilmer's reputation as a defender of the "Lost Cause" was assured by the publication of his sentimental, prosouthern account of the Civil War and Reconstruction, *The Recent Past from a Southern Standpoint: Reminiscences of a Grandfather* (1887).

As a bishop, Wilmer was conservative theologically but not acutely partisan. He took a moderate line in the battles between Low Church Evangelicals who sought to defend Anglicanism's Reformation heritage against High Churchmen influenced by the Tractarian movement in the Church of England. This conflict between Low and High Church parties was a central feature of the institutional life of the Episcopal church from the 1850s to the 1870s. Though his own family roots were clearly in the Evangelical tradition, Wilmer opposed those Evangelical advocates of prayer book revision who, during the 1860s, complained of "Romanizing germs" in the liturgy. For his part, Wilmer argued that the Book of Common Prayer was virtually flawless. Accordingly, he also criticized the actions of discontented Evangelicals when, in 1873, a few organized a separate Reformed Episcopal church. Yet, despite his differences with some over how to handle the perceived excesses of the Ritualists, Wilmer did rebuke those who adopted Roman Catholic forms indiscriminately. "It does not become one of our clergy," Wilmer chided, "to ape usages from alien communions" (Whitaker, p. 309). Accordingly, he issued a carefully worded pastoral letter to diocesan clergy in 1871 that attempted to circumscribe the boundaries of appropriate ceremonial action during worship. His concern to discourage what he viewed as extremism of any stripe is evident in his opposition both to the Anglo-Catholic James De Koven's election as bishop and later in his joining with Anglo-Catholics in refusing to confirm Phillips Brooks's election as bishop of Massachusetts. (Approval was needed by a certain number of dioceses to validate the election.) Wilmer's opposition to Brooks underlined his mounting concern over theological liberalism within the denomination. Because of Wilmer's health problems, a coadjutor was elected in 1890. Wilmer died in Mobile, Alabama.

Wilmer was a transitional figure, coming between the emphatically Evangelical churchmen of his father's circle and the liberal Low Churchmen of the early twentieth century. While he retained many of the beliefs of his father's generation of Evangelicals, Wilmer eschewed their partisanship and assumed a more centrist, though still conservative, doctrinal position within the Episcopal church. Moreover, outside his denomination, Wilmer became an important Christian apologist for the "Lost Cause."

• A few of Wilmer's letters and papers (mostly connected with the larger Wilmer family) may be found in the Skipworth-Wilmer Papers in the Maryland Historical Society Library and in the Biddle Family Collection in the Historical Society of Pennsylvania. Wilmer also authored *Guide-books for Young Churchmen* (1889) and *Convention Addresses, Pastorals, Sermons, etc.* (n.d.). The most detailed (though uncritical) biographical study is Walter C. Whitaker, *Richard Hooker Wilmer: Second Bishop of Alabama* (1907). Also useful is Gardiner C. Tucker, "Richard Hooker Wilmer, Second Bishop of Alabama," *Historical Magazine of the Protestant Episcopal Church* 7 (1938): 133–53. There is an entry on Wilmer in William S. Perry, *The Episcopate in America* (1895). Obituaries are in the *Churchman*, 23 June 1900, and the *Mobile Daily Register*, 15 June 1900.

GILLIS J. HARP

WILMER, William Holland (29 Oct. 1782–24 July 1827), Protestant Episcopal clergyman, was born in Kent County, Maryland, the son of Simon Wilmer and Ann Ringgold, probably farmers. Wilmer attended Washington College and then entered into mercantile business with his brother-in-law. Because of the then moribund state of the Episcopal church in Maryland, Wilmer affiliated with the local Methodist Society and organized prayer meetings in and around Chestertown. Soon, however, he became convinced of a call to the ordained ministry and, rather than remaining with the Methodists, prepared for ordination in the Protestant Episcopal church. Bishop Thomas J. Claggett ordained Wilmer deacon on 19 February 1809 and priest on 16 June 1810. Because of Wilmer's evangelical sympathies, there were murmurings of opposition to his ordination, but he managed to secure appointment to Chester Parish, Maryland. Wilmer was named to the Standing Committee of the Diocese of Maryland in 1811 and there witnessed the conflict between high church and evangelical forces over the election of a suffragan bishop. High church elements distrusted evangelicals as disloyal enthusiasts with Methodist leanings and feared their ascendancy in the Southeast. This battle, along with opposition from within his own parish, probably encouraged him to seek appointment elsewhere. Evangelicals were at this time becoming active in the neighboring diocese of Virginia, and one of their leaders, William Meade (a future bishop of Virginia), was then rector of Christ Church, Alexandria. Meade helped Wilmer obtain a call in 1812 from Christ Church's mission congregation, St. Paul's, Alexandria.

With his appointment to St. Paul's, Wilmer joined that group of evangelical clergy who were leading the institutional and spiritual renewal of the Episcopal church in Virginia. With the death of Bishop James Madison, Meade and Wilmer managed to revive the diocesan convention and, with others, succeeded in securing the election of the evangelical Richard Channing Moore as the new bishop in 1814. Wilmer himself was elected president of the standing committee of the diocese and was also active in national church affairs for many years. One of his longstanding concerns was theological education, and thus Wilmer founded in 1818 the Society for the Education of Pious Young Men for the Ministry of the Protestant Episcopal Church (later the Protestant Episcopal Education Society) and served as its first president. A year later he also began and edited for many years the *Washington Theological Repertory and Churchman's Guide*, the official organ of the society.

Wilmer's plans for ministerial education did not end there. At his behest, a chair of theology was set up at the College of William and Mary in 1821, but this proved a failure, as did an attempt a year later to establish a seminary in Maryland headed by Wilmer himself. The hopes of Wilmer and other evangelicals were realized finally in 1823 with the founding of the Protestant Episcopal Theological Seminary in Virginia. The seminary soon became a nursery for evangelicals within the Episcopal church in general and a key institution within the rising Evangelical party. Wilmer was appointed to the chair of systematic theology, ecclesiastical history, and church polity. Because his contribution to the work of the seminary was so valued, friends convinced him to turn down a call from the prestigious Monumental Church, Richmond, that came in 1826. But when William and Mary offered its presidency and the rectorship of Bruton Parish Church in Williamsburg that same year, Wilmer accepted.

Wilmer also contributed to the evangelical cause within the Episcopal church through his writings. Besides scores of contributions to the *Theological Repertory*, Wilmer also authored a popular instructional work for laymen, *The Episcopal Manual* (1815). The *Manual*'s subtitle described it as "intended to illustrate and enforce Evangelical Piety." As well, Wilmer's doctrinal exchange with a Roman Catholic priest that first appeared in the secular press was reprinted as *The Alexandria Controversy* in 1817.

Wilmer was married three times and fathered a total of eight children. His first wife, Harriet Ringgold, died childless. In 1812 he married Marion Hannah Cox, who died in 1821 after giving birth to their sixth child. He married Anne Brice Fitzhugh soon thereafter and had two additional children. Wilmer died in Williamsburg only months after taking up his appointment at William and Mary.

Wilmer played a crucial role in the evangelical revival in the diocese of Virginia and within the Episcopal church at large. Though best remembered as one of the founders of Virginia Theological Seminary and author of *The Episcopal Manual*, Wilmer was also a tireless parish priest and evangelist. Under his rectorship, St. Paul's, Alexandria, grew dramatically, and a large new church needed to be built in 1818. By the time of his death, he was widely expected to succeed Moore as bishop of Virginia. In churchmanship, Wilmer was a convinced evangelical, serious in manner but not contumacious in spirit. A friend and former classmate aptly characterized Wilmer as "Evangelical in his religious opinions and feelings; [and] belonging to that class of Divines then represented by those apostolical men—Moore, [Alexander V.] Griswold, [Charles P.] McIlvaine, and afterwards by Meade." Wilmer's death at a comparatively young age has probably kept him from attaining the recognition of these illustrious contemporaries.

• Some of Wilmer's papers are at the Maryland Diocesan Archives. A longer version of *The Alexandria Controversy* was published under the title *The Controversy between M. B. and Quaero . . . on Some Points of Roman Catholicism* (1818). The sympathetic assessment of a contemporary is in William Meade, *Old Churches, Ministers, and Families of Virginia* (1857), and Wilmer's son's memoirs are also informative, Richard Hooker Wilmer, *The Recent Past* (1887). Scholarly treatments of Wilmer are few. David Holmes, "William Holland Wilmer: A Newly Discovered Memoir," *Maryland Historical Magazine* 81 (1986): 160–64, contains a previously unpublished account of Wilmer's life and an excellent introduction that highlights Wilmer's larger significance. Also, John Booty, *Mission and Ministry: A History of Virginia Theological Seminary* (1995), discusses Wilmer's contribution to the institution's early years. Older secondary treatments that merit attention are William A. R. Goodwin, ed., *History of the Theological Seminary in Virginia and Its Historical Background* (2 vols., 1923–1924); William B. Sprague, ed., *Annals of the American Pulpit*, vol. 5 (1859), pp. 515–19; and Walter C. Whitaker, *Richard Hooker Wilmer: Second Bishop of Alabama* (1907), pp. 6–15.

GILLIS J. HARP

WILMOT, David (20 Jan. 1814–16 Mar. 1868), antislavery congressman, was born in Bethany, Pennsylvania, the son of Randall Wilmot, a merchant, and Mary Grant. Wilmot's mother died in 1820, and his father married Mary Carr. He was raised in comfort in rural Pennsylvania. Reading law in the office of George W. Woodward in Wilkes-Barre in the early 1830s, he settled permanently in Towanda in northern Pennsylvania. In 1836 he married Anne Morgan, with whom he had three children.

Wilmot's interest in politics soon surpassed his concern for his law practice, and he became active in the county Democratic party. A supporter of Andrew Jackson, he was even more devoted to Jackson's successor, Martin Van Buren. Disappointed when Democrats denied the latter the 1844 presidential nomination, Wilmot nonetheless loyally campaigned for the party's nominee, James K. Polk, and ran successfully for the House of Representatives.

In the Twenty-ninth Congress Wilmot at first was loyal to the Polk agenda, voting to admit Texas as a slave state in December 1845 and supporting the president's Oregon policy and, alone among Pennsylvania's congressmen, the Walker Tariff, which reduced duties. Yet the congressman drew a distinction between slavery in Texas, where it had existed when the region was an independent republic, and any territory acquired from Mexico. Polk's request in August 1846 for a $2 million appropriation with which to make peace with Mexico precipitated Wilmot's revolt. The young congressman insisted that "slavery should be excluded from any territory acquired by virtue of such an appropriation" (Going, p. 96). In an evening session, he managed to gain the floor and surprised party leaders by introducing an amendment to the special appropriation bill that became known as the Wilmot Proviso:

> That, as an express and fundamental condition to the acquisition of any territory from the Republic of Mexico, by the United States, by virtue of any treaty which may be negotiated between them and to the use by the Executive of the Moneys herein appropriated, neither slavery nor involuntary servitude shall ever exist in any part of said territory except for crime whereof the party shall be first duly convicted. (*Congressional Globe*, 29th Cong., 1st sess., p. 1217)

Its wording was taken from Thomas Jefferson's phrasing proposed for the Ordinance of 1784, which applied to western territories after the Revolution.

Whether or not Wilmot actually originated the plan has always been a subject of controversy. Several other northern Democrats, including Jacob Brinkerhoff of Ohio and Preston King of New York, shared Wilmot's intentions and had various reasons for being at odds with the Polk administration, not all of which involved slavery. A plausible case can be made that a group of congressmen collaborated on the plan and chose Wilmot as their mouthpiece precisely because of his previous loyalty to the administration and his lack of antislavery background. Nonetheless, the Pennsylvanian was a key promoter of the proviso, which passed the House before dying in the Senate in August 1846. In the next session of Congress, the battle over the proviso was renewed and intensified, and it soon became the dominant issue of the Polk administration, passing the House on several occasions but always failing in the Senate. Voting in both houses was largely on sectional rather than party lines, with most northerners in support and virtually all southerners opposed.

Wilmot's admirers consistently maintained that antislavery conviction was the chief motivating factor behind his championing of the proviso. Yet he had previously shown little concern over slavery-related issues. Significantly, though, Wilmot had distanced himself from the dominant wing of the Pennsylvania Democratic party, led by Polk's secretary of state, James Buchanan, who had blocked Senate confirmation of several appointees championed by Wilmot. Wilmot, accordingly, drew closer to the Van Buren faction of New York Democrats, the so-called Barnburners. It is likely that that group's alienation from and eventual break with the administration over its proslavery policies and its denial to them of patronage positions was a more important factor than the antislavery principle itself in leading Wilmot into opposition.

Wilmot joined with the Barnburners when they bolted the Democratic party in 1848 and helped organize the Free Soil party, which nominated Van Buren for president. Winning reelection to the House with Free Soil and Democratic votes, he made it clear that in advocating the containment of slavery he was more concerned with the interests of his white constituents than he was with the plight of blacks. Calling his proposal the "White Man's Proviso," he boasted that his purpose was to "preserve for free white labor a fair country, a rich inheritance, where the sons of toil, of my own race and own color, can live without the disgrace which association with Negro slavery brings upon free labor" (Going, p. 174).

When the Thirty-first Congress organized in December 1849, the tiny Free Soil faction held the balance of power and, by supporting Wilmot for the office, prevented the House from electing a Speaker for more than a month. However, he and his party could do little to prevent the passage of the Compromise of 1850, which repudiated the proviso in organizing the territory acquired from Mexico. With most Barnburners returning to the Democratic fold in surrender, Wilmot found himself denied renomination by the regular Democratic forces led by his old nemesis Bu chanan. Nonetheless, Wilmot loyally voted for Democrat Franklin Pierce for president two years later.

During the next decade Wilmot served as presiding judge of the Thirteenth Judicial District in Pennsylvania, but he remained politically active. Vehemently rejecting Stephen A. Douglas's Kansas-Nebraska bill, he abandoned the Democratic party and became one of the founders of the new Republican party. Helping to organize the initial national Republican meeting in Pittsburgh in February 1856, he chaired the platform committee of the Republican nominating convention in Philadelphia later that year. He vigorously campaigned for the party's nominee, John C. Frémont, and the following year ran unsuccessfully for governor. In both instances Wilmot was closely identified with the Republican position of preventing the expansion of slavery, a stance that, because of the influence of Buchanan, who was now president, was not as popular in Pennsylvania as in many other parts of the North. Wilmot's continued opposition to protective tariffs and the still-nascent state of the Republican party further weakened his candidacy.

At the Republican convention in Chicago in 1860, Wilmot supported Abraham Lincoln despite the candidacy of fellow Pennsylvanian Simon Cameron. Considered by Lincoln for a cabinet position, he instead was chosen by the legislature for a short Senate term (1861–1863). There his work was undistinguished and was characterized by loyal support of Lincoln's policies. Supportive of the numerous measures weakening slavery, he took special pleasure in the 1862 law that adopted the proviso's principle and banned slavery in all territories. At the conclusion of his Senate term Wilmot was appointed by Lincoln to be a judge on the newly created Court of Claims, on which he served until his death at his home in Towanda.

An effective and forceful speaker throughout his career, Wilmot was a man of little personal discipline. Overweight because of an excessive appetite for food and alcohol, he cared little about his personal appearance and preferred to follow a relaxed and disorganized lifestyle. His primary significance remained his commitment to the containment of slavery, a principle he first conceived out of loyalty to Van Buren but one with which he came to be identified as it became the backbone of the Free Soil and Republican parties.

• No Wilmot papers have survived, and the researcher is forced instead to turn to the collections of his political contemporaries and to the *Congressional Globe*, 29th–31st (Dec. 1845–Mar. 1851) and 37th (Dec. 1861–Mar. 1863) Congs., for his words. A highly laudatory biography is Charles B. Going, *David Wilmot: Free Soiler* (1924), which also includes numerous Wilmot letters and speeches. A more balanced account of Wilmot's role in the antislavery movement of the Democratic party is Chaplain Morrison, *Democratic Politics and Sectionalism: The Wilmot Proviso Controversy* (1967). Clark E. Persinger, "'The Bargain of 1844' as the Origin of the Wilmot Proviso," *Annual Report of the American Historical Association, 1911* (1913), pp. 187–95; Richard R. Stenberg, "The Motivation of the Wilmot Proviso," *Mississippi Valley Historical Review* 19 (1932): 535–41; and Eric Foner, "The Wilmot Proviso Revisited," *Journal of American History* 56 (1969): 262–79, discuss the issues of authorship and motivation of the Proviso.

FREDERICK J. BLUE

WILSON, Alexander (6 July 1766–23 Aug. 1813), ornithologist, was born in the Seed Hills of Paisley, Scotland, the son of Alexander Wilson, a weaver, and Mary McNab. He attended grammar school until age ten and then was sent to work, first as a herd boy and later as a weaver's apprentice. He became a journeyman weaver and a peddler of woven goods but hated the confinement of the weaver's life. In his free time he memorized poetry and took long walks in the countryside, developing a profound love for its birds, animals, and plants.

Determined to make a name for himself, Wilson also wrote poems, many on pastoral themes that reflected his passion for the natural world, some in Scottish dialect inspired by Robert Burns. Wilson's first volume of seventy-two poems was published in 1790, and a second edition appeared in 1791. Disturbed by the labor conditions imposed by many mill owners on their weavers, Wilson, sometimes relentless and unforgiving, wrote poetry championing the workers, including a satirical piece published anonymously in 1792. The target of the satire, a weaving manufacturer, sued him, and he was imprisoned for a number of months and forced to burn his poems publicly. Embittered by life in Scotland, Wilson immigrated to America, sailing on 23 May 1794 with his nephew William Duncan. Arriving on 14 July at New Castle, Delaware, Wilson and Duncan walked the thirty-five miles to Philadelphia, captivated by the new flora and fauna they encountered. After being hired by a Philadelphia copperplate printer, Wilson eventually found work as a weaver and peddler. He moved to different towns in New Jersey and eastern Pennsylvania, taking teaching jobs, reading to increase his knowledge of the subject matter, and, in his free time, surveying to earn extra money. He avidly explored the countryside and continued to write poetry. He developed a passion for American politics and had great admiration for Thomas Jefferson. On 4 March 1801, Jefferson's inauguration day, Wilson read his poem "Oration on the Power and Value of National Liberty" at the festivities held in Milestown, where he lived. He also wrote a song called "Jefferson and Liberty."

In the fall of 1801 Wilson moved to Bloomfield, New Jersey, where he taught school. But the salary was low, and Wilson, although hardworking and frugal, was unhappy, partly because of a thwarted love affair. (He would never marry.) In early 1802 he moved to Gray's Ferry, Pennsylvania, a town near Philadelphia, where he became a neighbor of the naturalist William Bartram. Bartram was maintaining his botanist-father's celebrated garden and was an expert in American bird life. In 1791 he had published a book describing his travels through the southeastern United States, which contained the most complete list to date of American bird species. Bartram owned a distinguished library that included several important ornithological works, among them the first major illustrated study of American natural history, published in London by the eighteenth-century British naturalist Mark Catesby. Avidly studying the books and discussing their texts and illustrations with Bartram, Wilson discovered numerous gaps in American ornithological knowledge. By 1803, after a walking trip the previous summer to the Finger Lakes region of New York State, he had resolved to publish his own *American Ornithology*, in spite of his lack of formal training in either natural history or bird illustration. He recorded his field observations and drew in pencil or ink the birds with which he was becoming familiar, discussed them with Bartram, and in the spring of 1804 sent him two groups of drawings to assess. Bartram generously shared his knowledge and encouraged Wilson to perfect his drawing. In June 1804 Wilson became a U.S. citizen, and in October he took a two-month walking trip to Niagara Falls to gather data for his book. During the trip he covered more than 1,200 miles, mostly on foot. On returning, he composed a poem called "The Foresters," based on his travels to the Finger Lakes and Niagara Falls, which was published in the *Port Folio*, a major Philadelphia literary magazine. He also sent two of his bird drawings, together with a drawing of Niagara Falls, to Thomas Jefferson and received a gracious acknowledgement.

Through Bartram, Wilson met Charles Willson Peale, the artist and founder of Philadelphia's famous natural history museum, which Peale gave Wilson permission to use as a studio and repository for his bird skins. Wilson asked his friend and fellow Scot, the engraver Alexander Lawson, for help in improving his drawing techniques and in learning how to engrave. Wilson's first drawings were hesitant, but, through his patience and perseverance, his style improved over time and ranged from vigorous to sensitively refined, subtle, and flowing.

Wilson moved to Philadelphia, where the publisher Samuel Bradford offered him the position of assistant editor of Abraham Rees's *New Cyclopedia*, which Wilson accepted in April 1806. He convinced Bradford to publish his *American Ornithology*, and Bradford agreed to underwrite an edition of 200 sets if Wilson enlisted that number of subscribers. By 7 April 1807 Wilson had issued a prospectus for the book and had 2,500 copies of it printed for potential subscribers. *American Ornithology* was originally planned as ten volumes—six for land birds and four for water birds—with ten color plates in each volume, to sell for $120 per set. Wilson immersed himself in learning about the birds and their environment, writing in the preface to his book that he wanted to free New World ornithology from "that transatlantic and humiliating reproach of being obliged to apply to Europe for an account and description of the production of our own country." To limit the expense of producing the book, Wilson reproduced the birds in groups, in the order in which he drew them rather than scientific order, accompanying each with detailed notes about the birds' physiology and habits. After making several drawings on a sheet, he cut them out and rearranged them into a pleasing composition. Unable to master the engraving process, Wilson asked Lawson to engrave his drawings, which artists then hand colored, using Wilson's original drawings and bird skins as models. Some of the engravings were also made by John G. Warnicke, George Murray, and Benjamin Tanner.

Wilson oversaw the entire production and was responsible for signing up all subscribers, a group that ultimately included Thomas Jefferson, Robert Fulton, Columbia and Dartmouth Colleges, and the Library of Congress. The complete work included essays on 293 birds, with 315 species depicted in the seventy-six plates. The first volume, with nine plates, appeared in September 1808. Immediately thereafter Wilson set out to seek subscribers in New England and New York State. He then traveled to Georgia, stopping first in Baltimore, Washington (where he visited President Jefferson), Richmond, and Charleston. In Savannah he met the Englishman John Abbot, an entomologist greatly interested in ornithology with a large collection of bird drawings, who became Wilson's ongoing correspondent and a vital source of specimens and information. The following year Wilson visited Florida.

The book's second volume, including fifty birds in nine plates, with accounts of forty-two species, appeared on 1 January 1810. Wilson then set out for Kentucky, Tennessee, Mississippi, and Louisiana to collect bird specimens and subscribers. He walked to Pittsburgh, where he bought an open rowboat, and on 23 February he embarked on the 720-mile trip to Louisville. He arrived in March, and on the nineteenth paid a visit to the young John James Audubon in his Louisville store. From there Wilson traveled on horseback to New Orleans, returning to Philadelphia by boat in the fall of 1810. In 1811 volumes three and four of his book were published, and volumes five and six in 1812. By 1813 volume seven was finished. Wilson decided to reduce the final number of volumes from ten to nine.

Exhausted by his labors, Wilson contracted dysentery and died, in Philadelphia, ten years after he conceived his project. He had nearly completed volume eight and had made some notes and drawings for volume nine. His friend George Ord, a businessman, naturalist, and writer, edited the eighth volume and did much of the writing for the ninth, subsequently publishing two revised editions. A continuation of Wilson's work was published by Charles Lucien Bonaparte between 1825 and 1833.

American Ornithology, a work of evident genius by a virtually self-taught author, represents the first scientific description and listing of American birds. It includes a number of species that Wilson found and named for the first time, among them various species collected by the Lewis and Clark expedition. Wilson's was the first American bird book with colored plates actually published in America. It depicted fully three-quarters of the bird species identified in America at that time—more than any previous work—and covered an unprecedented area of the eastern, southern, and western United States.

Although Wilson was not able to observe certain species in the wild and did not depict his birds in their natural habitat, his images are precise and lively and his written scientific information accurate, thorough, clear, and lyrical. Wilson did not gain financial reward from his work, and it was ultimately surpassed by Audubon's life-sized, and in certain ways more authentic, illustrations, but Wilson's book gained him the well-deserved title of the "father of American ornithology."

• Wilson's principal scientific publication is his *American Ornithology*, published in nine volumes (1808–1814). George Ord's condensed biography of Wilson appears in the ninth volume. A fuller biography of Wilson by Ord was published in 1828. The 1831 and later editions of *American Ornithology* include supplements by Charles Lucien Bonaparte. Wilson published his memoirs in 1831. The principal modern work on Wilson is *The Life and Letters of Alexander Wilson*, ed. Clark Hunter (1983). Other important works include Robert Cantwell, *Alexander Wilson: Naturalist and Pioneer* (1961), and Elsa G. Allen, "The History of American Ornithology before Audubon," *Transactions of the American Philosophical Society* 41, no. 3 (Oct. 1951): 387–591. A useful summary of Wilson's career appears in Martina R. Norelli, *American Wildlife Painting* (1975).

CAROLE ANNE SLATKIN

WILSON, Augusta Jane Evans (8 May 1835–9 May 1909), author, was born in Columbus, Georgia, to Matthew Ryan Evans and Sarah Skrine Howard. Although a charming gentleman and a devoted husband and father, Matt Evans was a rash land speculator who embroiled his family in financial difficulties. To help her daughter cope with an unsettled childhood, Sarah Evans told her stories of great writers, stimulated her interest in history and geography, and recited poetry to her. Augusta was a receptive pupil, and her photographic memory later enabled her to display remarkable erudition in her novels.

In 1845 Matt Evans declared bankruptcy and moved his family first to Houston, Texas, then to Galveston, and finally to San Antonio. However, by 1849 the Evanses were homesick for the South and feared trouble with Mexicans and Comanches; they decided to return east, settling in Mobile, Alabama. There misfortune beset them when a fire burned the house they were renting. Next, Matt became ill, losing his income. Hoping to alleviate her family's financial problems by earning money as a writer, Wilson (her eventual married name) undertook her first novel. Confiding only in her slave Minervy, who supplied oil for her lamp, she worked secretly on her manuscript each night until early morning. On Christmas Day, 1854, she presented her father with *Inez: A Tale of the Alamo*, honoring the soldiers who fought in the Texas War of Independence. The novel was published the next year by Harper.

During the 1850s Wilson questioned the tenets of evangelical Protestantism that her mother had taught her. However, after studying the works of Thomas Carlyle, Samuel Taylor Coleridge, Johann Wolfgang von Goethe, William Wordsworth, Alfred Tennyson, Ralph Waldo Emerson, Walt Whitman, and Herman Melville, among others, she returned to the orthodox Methodism of her youth, vowing to "combat scepticism to the day of my death, and if possible, to help others to avoid the thorny path I have trod ere I was convinced of the fallibility of human Reason." The first consequence of that vow was the highly autobiographical novel *Beulah*, which charts the heroine's metaphysical wanderings until she attains Christian peace. Published in 1859 by Derby and Jackson, *Beulah* was immediately successful, selling over 20,000 copies within the first year. Not only did the novel establish its author as a leading sentimentalist and enable her to purchase a house for her family, but it also brought her attention from a northern editor named James Reed Spaulding, who proposed to her in 1860. They became engaged, but sectional disagreements soon broke up the relationship.

After Abraham Lincoln was elected president in 1860, Wilson became a fervid southern propagandist, advising politicians and military leaders, publishing articles in support of the Confederacy, serving as a volunteer nurse, and establishing in Mobile an army hospital, which she named Camp Beulah. However, the most important of her wartime activities was writing *Macaria*, which was published in 1863 by West and Johnson in Richmond on coarse wrapping paper—the only material available at the time. Wilson also managed to smuggle by blockade runner a copy of her manuscript to her friend J. C. Derby, who arranged with J. B. Lippincott for a northern edition, published in 1864. Dedicated "To the Brave Soldiers of the Southern Army," *Macaria* celebrates the Confederate victories in the Civil War. With its idealized portraits of kind aristocrats and loyal slaves who protect their mistresses and follow their masters into battle, *Macaria* represents a southerner's response to Harriet Beecher Stowe's *Uncle Tom's Cabin*. So effective was the novel as propaganda that Union General G. H. Thomas forbade his troops to read it and burned copies that he confiscated. Southerners read *Macaria* eagerly. In fact, the legend arose that a Confederate soldier's life was saved when the book, which he had hastily put into his breast pocket upon being called to battle, stopped a bullet from piercing his heart.

At the end of the war, Wilson was again beset by family difficulties. The family was virtually destitute, her father's health was declining, and her favorite brother, Howard, had returned home from the war with a wound that left his arm and shoulder paralyzed. To raise money, she wrote another novel in the domestic sentimental tradition of *Beulah*. That novel, *St. Elmo*, published in 1866, became one of the bestselling books of the nineteenth century; indeed, it reached over one million readers within four months of publication. Clearly indebted to Charlotte Brontë's *Jane Eyre*, *St. Elmo* traces the career of the orphaned Edna Earl from her poverty-stricken childhood spent with her uneducated grandfather to her marriage to St.

Elmo Murray, a Byronic hero who, redeemed by Edna Earl's Christian love, repents of his wayward ways and becomes a minister. A major cultural phenomenon, the book inspired a "St. Elmo" punch, a "St. Elmo" cigar, and even a "St. Elmo" camellia. Steamboats, railway coaches, hotels, and several villages were named after it, while a number of children were christened for the hero and heroine.

In 1868 Augusta Evans married Colonel Lorenzo Madison Wilson, the owner of "Ashland," a beautiful estate only a quarter of a mile from the Evans home. Despite a 27-year age difference, Augusta and Colonel Wilson were extremely compatible. Together they turned "Ashland" into a showplace, renowned for its live oaks, azaleas, and camellias.

Although Augusta Evans Wilson had many household responsibilities, including helping to raise a stepdaughter, she still found time for her writing. In 1869 she published *Vashti; or, Until Death Us Do Part*, portraying the plight of a heroine trapped in a loveless marriage. Then, at the request of her husband, who was concerned that she was exhausting herself, she took a hiatus from writing. She completed *Infelice*, a melodramatic tale of a suffering actress, in 1875. Her seventh novel, *At the Mercy of Tiberius*, did not appear until twelve years later, for she began suffering from such severe bouts of hay fever that she was often unable to write or read for months at a time. Her favorite work, *At the Mercy of Tiberius*, focuses on a sensational murder trial during which it is revealed that there was no murder; the victim was electrocuted by a lightning bolt.

After her husband died in 1891, Wilson decided to close "Ashland" and reside with her brother Howard in a large house in Mobile. In 1902, despite failing eyesight and a weak heart, she surprised her readers with the publication of *A Speckled Bird*, depicting the downfall of a woman who becomes involved with labor protesters. Her final publication, appearing in 1907, was a small volume entitled *Devota*, in which a woman must decide whether to marry the governor of the state—a man she once rejected. Howard Evans died in 1908, and Wilson never fully recovered from her grief. She died in Mobile.

Wilson was one of the leading domestic sentimental novelists of the nineteenth century. Influenced by Charlotte Brontë, her fiction most often depicts orphaned heroines who suffer from a variety of tribulations yet eventually find happiness through intellectual stimulation, self-reliance, and love. Although Wilson addressed political and social concerns in her work, her primary motivation as a novelist was expressing her Christian faith. Her goal, as she defined it in a letter to her friend J. L. M. Curry, was to be "the humble instrument of doing some good, of leading some soul safely to God."

• Letters from Wilson are in the University of Alabama Library and in the Curry Papers in the Library of Congress. The Alabama Department of Archives and History in Montgomery contains files on her and her father. The major study of her life is William Perry Fidler, *Augusta Evans Wilson, 1835–1909: A Biography* (1951). Personal reminiscences include a sketch by her friend Mary Forrest in *Women of the South Distinguished in Literature* (1860) and an account by her publisher J. C. Derby in *Fifty Years among Authors, Books and Publishers* (1884). Among the best critical assessments are Alexander Cowie, *The Rise of the American Novel* (1948), and Jay Hubbell, *The South in American Literature, 1607–1900* (1954).

LYNNE P. SHACKELFORD

WILSON, Charles Edward (18 Nov. 1886–3 Jan. 1972), industrialist and government official, was born in New York City, the son of George H. Wilson, a bookbinder, and Hannah Rebecca Stiles, a cleaning lady. Wilson's father died when the boy was just three years old, leaving him and his mother in poverty. Growing up and attending public school in the notorious Hell's Kitchen quarter, Wilson sold newspapers and gathered clams from the East River to earn whatever he could.

By age twelve, Wilson felt embarrassed by his mother's labors to support him. Despite her protests, he left school and began work as a factory hand at Sprague Electrical at three dollars per week. He became close to the factory's superintendent, who encouraged energy and initiative in the boy. He took night courses in stenography and accounting and rose rapidly into positions of greater responsibility. He studied shop practice and physics at the Mechanics Institute, yet also found time to swim and box at the Young Men's Christian Association and to sing for the Oratorio Society. In 1903 the General Electric Corporation absorbed Sprague. Wilson was only sixteen years old, but he was already the plant's accountant. In 1907 he became assistant superintendent at $20 per week. That same year, on his birthday, he married Elizabeth Maisch. They adopted one child.

By 1914 the 28-year-old Wilson had wide experience in all aspects of electrical manufacturing. When GE–Sprague began producing switchboards and panels, he was made manager of sales, engineering, and production. In 1917 he was put in charge of the new GE plants at Kensington, Pennsylvania, and Maspeth, Long Island. Wilson impressed Gerard Swope, president of GE, who in 1923 appointed him managing engineer of the works in Bridgeport, Connecticut, which was gearing up for the production of electrical appliances. He supervised the design, manufacture, and sales of electric clocks, lamps, washing machines, irons, refrigerators, and air conditioners. In 1930 he rose to vice president of GE.

Wilson's first government post came in 1934 when he served as a deputy for the National Recovery Administration. He became frustrated, however, by the political constraints on the NRA's efforts at coping with the Great Depression and soon returned to GE with an abiding mistrust of labor unions, the New Deal, and government economic intervention generally. In 1937 he was elected to GE's board of directors and made executive vice president. When Swope retired in 1940, Wilson became president of the corporation at an annual salary of $175,000.

During 1940–1942 Wilson's national prominence grew as he successfully oversaw the great expansion of GE manufacturing operations prompted by military contracts. He also became widely known for his confidence in the production potential of American industry and for his views on how national industrial and economic planning was needed to help avoid a return to mass unemployment and depression once the wartime boom ended. But Wilson insisted that such planning be carried out by the private sector and that the role of government be minimized. "The Free Enterprise System," he warned, "will have to provide full protection, full employment, full distribution of goods and services, or step aside for government agencies."

In September 1942 President Franklin D. Roosevelt asked Wilson to take up a leading role in managing the nation's output of war materiel, which was then hobbled by supply bottlenecks and bureaucratic cross-purposes. Wilson eagerly accepted, saying, "It took me 40 years to climb to the presidency of GE and 40 seconds to step out." Taking a 90 percent salary cut, he was put in charge of production schedules at the War Production Board.

In this key post, Wilson's energy and aggressive executive style were quickly felt. He was known for his "five- to ten-minute conferences" and his ability to focus on the basics of the many bewildering problems he dealt with. He also became identified with the struggle to limit the influence of the armed forces over the wartime economy and to preserve the autonomy of private producers and suppliers in the military-industrial relationship. Wilson's success in this complex political and bureaucratic struggle added to his influence on the War Production Board, and in 1943 he became its executive vice chairman.

However, Wilson grew weary of controversy. He sought to resign his post when in mid-1943 President Roosevelt tried to offset the conflicts by establishing a competing oversight agency, the Office of War Mobilization. But FDR persuaded Wilson to stay on. Wilson's efforts were instrumental in the success of wartime military production, especially the rapid production of new warplanes. Finally, by September 1944 Wilson's effectiveness in Washington had become so compromised by public disputes among high government officials that he resigned and returned to the presidency of GE.

The disputes leading to Wilson's departure revolved mainly around the extent to which the war economy ought to be prepared for the war's end and reconverted for civilian goods production. To Wilson such planning seemed premature and did not adequately account for ongoing military demands on industry. He expected continuing threats to U.S. national security in the postwar years. Presiding in 1945–1946 over the Air Power League—a new lobbying group of air force supporters, officers, and manufacturers—Wilson advocated defense industry preparedness, especially in advanced aircraft and electronics production. Wilson received numerous honors for his wartime service, including the President's Medal of Merit, the Navy's Distinguished Service Award, and the Horatio Alger Award, given by the American Schools and Colleges Association.

Beginning in 1945, Wilson initiated a major corporate reorganization at GE, a decentralization of authority, planning, and management made necessary by GE's enormous size and involvement in thousands of product lines, ranging in complexity from light bulbs and electric blankets to jet engines and nuclear reactors. When Wilson left GE in 1950, the company was among the world's largest manufacturers, with 206,000 employees and 112 plants in more than 20 states.

The last years of Wilson's tenure at GE were also noted for a major alteration in the way the company related to its workers and their unions. Encouraged by Wilson and emulated by many other major corporations, the change was known as Boulwarism, after Lemuel R. Boulware, to whom Wilson delegated authority over the company's labor relations in 1947. During the war years Wilson had become disturbed by the growing strength of organized labor, especially the insistence by many labor leaders that they participate in company management and planning and that workers share more fully in corporate profits. This violated Wilson's sense of the rights of free enterprise and business prerogative.

Prompted by a series of strikes at GE plants in 1946, Wilson strove to counter the power of the United Electrical Workers. Boulwarism essentially meant a more unyielding posture in bargaining with union officials, and it included aggressive public-relations campaigns aimed at undermining workers' views of the legitimacy of union leaders and mobilizing their support for the company and the free-enterprise system. As a spokesman for GE, Ronald Reagan came to play a prominent role in this campaign, which succeeded in part because of how badly factionalized the union had become over the issue of communists among the leadership.

During the late 1940s Wilson served on the federal Labor-Management Panel, where he advanced his Boulwarized views on labor relations. He also served on the Pentagon's National Security Resources Board and the Universal Military Training Commission. Wilson's main public role during those years was as chairman of the Committee on Civil Rights, to which he was appointed by President Harry S. Truman. In 1947 the committee released its report, *To Secure These Rights*, which proposed aggressive federal action to eliminate racial segregation and discrimination. "The United States can no longer countenance these burdens on its common conscience, these inroads on its moral fiber," said the report, which became a major source of contention in the 1948 presidential campaign. It linked Wilson with postwar liberalism, despite his conservatism on labor matters and his listing as a Republican.

Policy at GE required executives to retire at age sixty-five, so Wilson had planned to leave in 1952. Truman, however, named him director of the Office of Defense Mobilization at the height of the crisis in Korea in late 1950. In this post Wilson held broad powers that he used to aid a steady increase in munitions output while restraining inflation and maintaining relative economic stability. But he was again at the center of political storms. His position became untenable once more when in 1952 he opposed Truman's takeover of the big steel mills to prevent work stoppages by the United Steelworkers.

Wilson resigned his war-mobilization post in March 1952 and became executive-committee chairman of W. R. Grace & Company, the international industrial and transport company with a strong presence in Latin America. He rose to chairman of the board in 1955 but retired in 1956. From 1957 to 1959 he was president of the People-to-People Foundation, an organization formed at the suggestion of President Dwight D. Eisenhower and dedicated to fostering international peace and understanding.

From 1958 until his death, Wilson worked as a business consultant and served as a public representative on the New York Stock Exchange. He chaired the industries committee of the Advertising Council, a private advocacy group that sponsored public advertisements aimed at confirming popular commitment to mainstream economic and social values.

Throughout his life Wilson was an active member of the Baptist church. He was popularly known as "Electric Charlie," to distinguish him easily from Charles Erwin Wilson, the president of General Motors. A resident of Scarsdale, New York, Wilson died in a hospital in the nearby town of Bronxville.

• For additional information on Wilson see Kent Sangendorph, *Charles Edward Wilson, American Industrialist* (1949); Thomas R. Brooks, *Toil and Trouble* (1971); Ronald Schatz, *The Electrical Workers* (1983); and *Current Biography*, Apr. 1943 and Feb. 1951. An obituary is in the *New York Times*, 4 Jan. 1972.

JACOB VANDER MEULEN

WILSON, Charles Erwin (18 July 1890–26 Sept. 1961), businessman and U.S. secretary of defense, was born in Minerva, Ohio, the son of Thomas Erwin Wilson, the principal of a local high school, and Rosalind Unkefer, formerly a teacher. In 1894 the Wilsons moved to Mineral City, Ohio, and ten years later to Pittsburgh. Charles Wilson graduated from the Carnegie Institute of Technology in 1909, having earned an electrical engineering degree in three years. After briefly working as a patternmaker and signing on with the local union, Wilson secured a spot as an apprentice engineer with Westinghouse Electric and Manufacturing Company in Pittsburgh. In 1912 he married Jessie Ann Curtis; the couple had six children.

In the same year as his marriage, Wilson developed an automotive starting motor. By 1916 he headed Westinghouse's production of electrical equipment for cars. During the First World War, he designed dynamotors and radio generators for military use. In 1919 Wilson hired on as chief engineer and sales manager for Remy Electric Company, a General Motors (GM) subsidiary in Anderson, Indiana, where his career took its turn away from engineering and toward management. He became factory manager in 1921 and Remy's general manager four years later. Remy merged with Delco of Dayton, Ohio, in 1926. With Wilson as president and general manager, Delco-Remy employed 12,000 workers and produced, among other things, auto parts and appliance motors.

In 1928 Wilson moved to Detroit to enter the management of Delco-Remy's parent, General Motors. As a vice president and special assistant to company chief Alfred P. Sloan, Wilson's special province was the corporation's parts and accessories subsidiaries. With his support, the company claimed a larger stake in the aircraft industry and played a pioneering role in diesel-powered railroading through establishment of its Electro-Motive Division. In 1934 Wilson joined GM's board of directors and five years later became executive vice president, exercising general oversight of the company's many operating divisions, which included but were hardly limited to familiar auto lines like Chevrolet, Cadillac, Pontiac, Oldsmobile, and Buick. He was elevated to acting president in 1940 and the following year was named president of GM, which then employed more than 200,000 workers in over one hundred plants.

In his twelve years at the company's helm, Wilson earned a prominent place in the history not only of General Motors but also corporate America (another Charles E. Wilson headed General Electric, so GM's president was tagged "Engine Charlie," and his opposite number was "Electric Charlie"). Wilson shepherded one of the nation's most significant producers of both consumer and military goods through World War II and the early postwar period and became an architect of a "social contract" that important corporate leaders worked out with labor.

Having succeeded to the presidency when William S. Knudsen went to Washington to oversee defense production, Wilson saw to it that GM performed a good deal of war work. The company retrained workers and retooled its plants, though it did not end civilian auto production until the federal government forced its hand in early 1942. Of the $13.4 billion worth of goods GM sold between 1942 and 1945, over 90 percent was for military use. Much of this was quite unlike what the corporation had produced during peacetime. It included not only tanks, armored trucks, and aircraft and their component parts, but also arms and ammunition. Eventually GM was producing, on schedule, more than $10 million worth of war matériel a day. The effort ruined Wilson's health (he thenceforth suffered from circulatory complaints), but shortly after the war ended, in addition to staying on as president, he replaced Sloan as GM's chief executive officer. He thereby superintended the massive reconversion to civilian production. By the end of the decade General Motors turned out more than six million cars and trucks annually, winning 43 percent of new car sales. The expenses of reconversion and resistance from within GM, however, defeated Wilson's plans to introduce a smaller, lighter, and more economical make of car.

In industrial relations, Wilson helped define a postwar order by which big business conceded both recognition and a fairly generous schedule of wages and benefits to unions in return for stability, predictability, and firm control over the processes of production. From the sit-down strikes of 1936–1937 through the end of his presidency, Wilson led GM in its bargaining with the United Auto Workers (UAW). He developed a genuinely respectful relationship with the UAW's Walter Reuther, whom he termed "the ablest man in American industry." Reuther in turn pronounced the corporate leader "a very decent, genuine human being." Even before the war, GM had essentially recognized the UAW as the bargaining agent for its hourly workers and given ground to the union in standardizing wages throughout the vast corporation. In 1948 Wilson introduced to heavy industry the cost of living adjustment (COLA), tying wages to government price indexes, and instituted regular hikes in pay to reward increased productivity. Under the 1950 contract with the UAW, dubbed "the Treaty of Detroit," Wilson led the auto industry by ushering in a pension plan for GM workers. Throughout, however, Wilson and GM refused to surrender the shop floor to the union, insisting upon maintaining management control over the details of production and the hiring, firing, and promotion of personnel. By stonewalling Reuther's efforts to win wage increases while maintaining wartime price controls, GM scuttled an attempt to benefit both workers and consumers at the expense of corporate profits.

In 1953 Wilson left GM to become one of the tycoons in Dwight Eisenhower's "eight millionaires and a plumber" cabinet. His tenure as secretary of defense, however, was considerably more checkered than his corporate career. He got off to a rocky start when he initially resisted demands that he divest himself of his large holdings in GM, then the nation's largest defense contractor. Asked at his confirmation hearings whether he could pursue the national good irrespective of its consequences for GM, Wilson, not in the habit of carefully considering his public statements, asserted his belief that "what was good for our country was good for General Motors, and vice versa." While some have argued that Wilson had intended to suggest by adding "and vice versa" that what was bad for the country was bad for GM, his contemporaries tended toward the more obvious extrapolation. Wilson was widely cited as declaring "what was good for General Motors was good for the country," and, indeed, he was chiefly remembered in later years for coining what was taken to be a defining catch phrase of the 1950s. Wilson's service, it turned out, was good for General Motors, as his "single-source" procurement policy directed Pentagon contracts toward the largest and, presumably, most efficient suppliers.

Appointed not as a policy maker but instead for his demonstrated skill in managing a vast organization, Wilson nevertheless did a good deal of the work in bringing Eisenhower's "New Look" before Congress and the public. Anxious to balance the budget, Eisenhower insisted on cuts in defense appropriations, chiefly by trimming spending on conventional forces while simultaneously expanding America's nuclear capability; "more bang for the buck," as the phrase went. Wilson oversaw a decided retreat from the higher levels of defense spending to which the Harry Truman administration had committed the nation, to shrinking the Pentagon staff and army and navy manpower while seeking to further the development of nuclear weaponry and strengthening the Air Force. Wilson succeeded in carrying several New Look defense budgets through Congress. By 1956, however, critics within the military and the Democratic party had become more outspoken in denouncing the New Look as a pound-foolish policy that undermined the nation's military power and flexibility. Yet while Wilson had to bear much of the abuse congressional Democrats dealt out on this score, within the administration he had come by this time to be seen as one who surrendered too easily to the armed services' pleas for more money.

For the most part Wilson kept his head amidst the fierce anti-Communists crusading of the early 1950s. He was party to the process by which physicist J. Robert Oppenheimer was stripped of his security clearance, but his spine stiffened during the army-McCarthy hearings, and he spoke up for a number of the Wisconsin senator's targets. Witch-hunts were not carried on at the Pentagon on the same scale as in some other executive departments. Wilson's foreboding with respect to American intervention in Southeast Asia proved as prescient as his earlier interest in smaller cars.

Wilson's government service did not long survive Eisenhower's first term. The president came to regard Engine Charlie as something of a motor mouth, and a distinctly impolitic one. In widely noted statements, Wilson appeared to compare the unemployed to pampered pets and the White House to a dung heap while suggesting National Guardsmen were draft dodgers. Curiously, if Wilson's distinguished business career had not schooled him in circumspection, neither did it seem to have fully prepared him to lead an enormous public agency. He made real efforts to streamline his department's operations, but Eisenhower apparently found Wilson lacking in initiative, even in the day-to-day management he had been expected to perform expertly, and too willing to shift decisions in that realm to the White House or to underlings.

Wilson, pleading fatigue, stepped down in October 1957. He thereafter tended to his dairy farm in Michigan, a cattle ranch in Florida, and a Louisiana plantation. He died in Norwood, Louisiana.

• The Charles E. Wilson Archives are housed at Anderson College in Anderson, Ind. E. Bruce Geelhoed, *Charles E. Wilson and Controversy at the Pentagon, 1953 to 1957* (1979), covers the Eisenhower years in detail. It should be supplemented by more general studies of the administration, which tend to treat Wilson more roughly, including Herbert Parmet, *Eisenhower and the American Crusades* (1972); Chester Pach and Elmo Richardson, *The Presidency of Dwight D. Eisenhower* (1991); and Fred Greenstein, *The Hidden-Hand Presidency: Eisenhower as Leader* (1982). See also Carl W. Borklund, *Men of the Pentagon: From Forrestal to McNamara* (1966). Useful material on Wilson's work at General Motors is in Alfred P. Sloan, *My Years with General Motors* (1964); Nelson Lichtenstein, *The Most Dangerous Man in Detroit: Walter Reuther and the Fate of American Labor* (1995); and Ed Cray, *Chrome Colossus: General Motors and Its Times* (1980). An obituary is in the *New York Times*, 27 Sept. 1961.

PATRICK G. WILLIAMS

WILSON, Dennis Carl (4 Dec. 1944–28 Dec. 1983), drummer and vocalist for the Beach Boys, was born in Los Angeles, California, the son of Murray Gage Wilson, the owner of a small heavy machinery company, and Audree Korthoff. The second of three Wilson children, he spent his childhood in Hawthorne, a middle-class suburb of Los Angeles, and was exposed to music at an early age by his father, an amateur musician. With his brothers, Brian and Carl, first cousin Michael Love, and friend Alan Jardine he helped form the Beach Boys, a band whose music forged a link between the simple guitar-and-vocals-based rock and roll of the 1950s and the more complex rock music that emerged in America and England in the 1960s.

Dennis was a sixteen-year-old student at Hawthorne High School in 1961 when he urged his older brother, Brian, to write a song about the new surfing craze sweeping the West Coast. Brian, who would write nearly all of the band's music until 1967, responded with "Surfin.'" It became a top-10 hit with Los Angeles radio stations and rose to number seventy-five on *Billboard*'s national charts. The song's content had inspired a record producer to dub the band "the Beach Boys," and it was as the Beach Boys the following year that they began recording for Capitol records, where they turned out a string of hits that reinforced their image as a group of clean-cut teenage males who enjoyed endless California summers full of surfing, beach parties, hot rods, and beautiful girls.

Although self-taught on drums and piano, Dennis did not play on "Surfin'" and had to overcome resistance from his brothers and father, the band's business manager, to stay in the band. His first vocal solo, "You're My Miss America," appeared on the band's first album, *Surfin' Safari* (Capitol 1808), in 1962. He supplied vocals for many other songs, but most of the percussion on Beach Boys albums was the work of studio musicians. Nevertheless, he toured as the Beach Boys' drummer and played an invaluable role as the band's sex symbol. The most handsome and athletic member of the quintet, he epitomized the spirit of eternal adolescence that suffuses the Beach Boys' music. He was also the only Beach Boy who surfed.

Brian Wilson's near-complete withdrawal from recording by 1968 encouraged other band members to take an active role in revamping the Beach Boys' sound. Dennis posted his first songwriting credits on the 1968 album *Friends* (Capitol 2895), for which he co-wrote five songs. He was given solo credit for three songs on the 1969 album *20/20* (Capitol 133), although one of these, "Never Learn Not to Love," had been written in collaboration with cult leader Charles Manson. Manson had moved into Dennis's home in the spring of 1968 after Dennis picked up two hitchhiking members of Manson's "family." Although he considered Manson a friend at first, and referred to him as his "wizard," he became frightened by Manson's eccentric behavior and demands for money and moved to a friend's house by the summer of that year. Manson tried to contact Dennis for help on the night of his arrest for the murders of Sharon Tate and Leno and Rosemary LaBianca in the fall of 1969. Death threats from Manson's followers kept Dennis from testifying against Manson at his trial.

The Beach Boys spent most of the next decade trying unsuccessfully to transform their image as anachronisms who had fallen out of touch with the changing youth culture. During this time, though, Dennis's career prospects flourished. In 1969 he became the second Beach Boy after Brian to record independently of the group, releasing the two-sided single "Sound of Free"/"Lady" in England. In 1970 the four songs he wrote for the band's album *Sunflower* (Brother-Reprise 6382) were singled out for praise by the critics. He contributed two songs each to *Carl and the Passions* (Brother-Reprise 2083) in 1972 and *Holland* (Brother-Reprise 2118) in 1973 and about the same time was cast for a small part in the cult film *Two-Lane Blacktop*.

Friction between band members increased during these years, leading to constant rumors that the Beach Boys were on the verge of disbanding. Speculation that Dennis was planning to leave to pursue a solo career was fueled with the release of his solo album *Pacific Ocean Blue* (Caribou 34354) in 1977. The album's twelve songs included soft ballads, rhythm and blues, pop anthems, and gospel-accented rockers that were praised in the leading music magazines for their variety and production values.

During these years Dennis endured great personal turmoil. In 1970 he divorced his first wife, Carol Bloom, whom he had married in 1965 and with whom he had a daughter. The same year he married Barbara Charren, with whom he had two sons before the marriage dissolved in 1973. Dennis and Karen Lamm were married in 1975, divorced in 1976, remarried in 1978, and divorced again in 1980. Although Dennis became the most outspoken of the Wilson brothers about his father's physical and emotional abuse during their upbringing and early years in the band, he was deeply depressed after Murray Wilson died in 1973.

Between 1978 and 1983 Dennis's performing became increasingly erratic, owing to his escalating use of drugs and alcohol. He entered the first of several detoxification programs in 1978. In 1981 he became romantically involved with Shawn Love, his second cousin and the illegitimate daughter of Mike Love. Bad feelings between Mike and Dennis became so intense that a mutual restraining order was issued to keep the two cousins from fighting onstage. Shawn bore Dennis a son in 1982. Dennis married Shawn in July 1983 but filed for divorce by November of that year.

Aggravation at Dennis's difficult public behavior led the other band members to ban him from playing several 1983 concerts and to threaten him with ejection unless he enrolled in a detoxification program. On 28 December 1983 his body was found submerged in thirteen feet of water in Marina del Rey, where he had spent the day drinking and diving into the 58-degree water. His death was officially ruled an accidental drowning, possibly related to drug and alcohol abuse. Ronald Reagan granted a special dispensation for Dennis's burial at sea. Dennis's troubled life and ironic death have been characterized by several writers as symbolic not only of the changing fortunes of the Beach Boys, but of the troubled youth culture their music helped to shape.

• There is no official biography of Dennis Carl Wilson. Christopher Connelly and Parke Puterbaugh wrote his obituary for the 2 Feb. 1984 issue of *Rolling Stone* under the title "Dennis Wilson's Final Wave" (p. 36). The most extensive coverage of Dennis Wilson's life to date appears in Steven Gaines's unauthorized biography of the Beach Boys, *Heroes and Villains* (1986). Gaines's book draws from a variety of secondary sources, including Tom Nolan's two-part *Rolling Stone* article "The Beach Boys: A California Saga," 28 Oct. 1971, pp. 32–39; 11 Nov. 1971, pp. 50–53; Michael Goldberg's gossipy account of Wilson's final days, "The Beach Boy Who Went Overboard," *Rolling Stone*, 7 June 1984, pp. 19–20, 22, 25–26; and the best analysis to date of the Beach Boys' impact on the 1960s youth culture, David Leaf's *The Beach Boys and the California Myth* (1978; rev. 1985). Dennis's acquaintance with Charles Manson and his "family" is described in Vincent Bugliosi, *Helter Skelter* (written with Curt Gentry, 1974). A sympathetic but honest portrait of Dennis Wilson and the Beach Boys is available in John Milward's *The Beach Boys' Silver Anniversary* (1985). A complete Beach Boys discography through 1983, including records of many unreleased Dennis Wilson tracks, is available in Byron Preiss's *The Beach Boys* (1978; rev. 1983). His relationship with his brothers is discussed in Brian Wilson's autobiography, *Wouldn't It Be Nice* (1991).

STEFAN DZIEMIANOWICZ

WILSON, Edith Bolling Galt (15 Oct. 1872–28 Dec. 1961), first lady, was born in Wytheville, Virginia, the daughter of William Holcombe Bolling, a circuit court judge, and Sallie White. Her father struggled as a lawyer and judge to provide a comfortable income for a large extended family after the Civil War. They had lost their plantation and slaves as a consequence of the war but retained some African-American "servants." The Bolling family proudly claimed ancestry back to the early Virginia colonist John Rolfe and his Native American wife Pocahontas.

Edith's father and grandmother, Mrs. Archibald Bolling, provided most of her education, although she attended boarding school for two years in the mid-1880s at Martha Washington College in Abingdon and at Powell's School in Richmond, Virginia. Her father also gave her religious instruction, and she joined the Episcopal church. Much later, after her marriage to President Woodrow Wilson, she attended the Presbyterian church.

As a young woman, while visiting her sister in Washington, D.C., Edith Bolling met Norman Galt. Initially, she was not interested in this somewhat older man, but after several years of courtship, they were married in 1896. He was the senior partner and eventual owner of his family's prominent jewelry and silverware business in the nation's capital. A few years after their marriage, the couple's only baby died soon after birth.

Norman Galt's death in 1908 gave his young widow new responsibilities and opportunities; Edith Galt entered the world of business. Assisted by Henry Christian Bergheimer, a longtime employee whom she named as manager, she operated the jewelry store for years. After Bergheimer's death, she sold the business to her employees. Her investments allowed a life of comfort and financial security. The first woman in Washington to own an electric car, she proudly drove it around the capital. Accompanied by family and friends, she traveled to Europe three times before the First World War. Later, she made seven more private trips to Europe and two to Asia.

Edith Galt's life changed dramatically in 1915, after she met President Wilson. Although Washington's social elite had frequented the family's jewelry store to make purchases, the Galts had not mingled among them, nor had she shown much interest in politics, including Wilson's election to the presidency in 1912. On only two occasions had Edith Galt even seen him from a distance.

Dr. Cary T. Grayson, the president's physician and one of her friends, played a central role in bringing Edith Galt and Wilson together. Grayson had introduced her to Helen Woodrow Bones, Wilson's cousin. On one rainy day in March 1915, as the two women returned to the White House for tea after one of their frequent walks, Wilson and Grayson arrived from a round of golf. A lonely man since the death in August 1914 of his first wife, Ellen Louise Axson Wilson, the president quickly fell in love with the vivacious Mrs. Galt. By the summer of 1915, he urged her to marry him without regard for the impropriety of a second marriage so soon after his first wife had died. Despite her initial reluctance, they announced their engagement in early October. Disregarding the potentially negative consequences for Wilson's reelection in 1916, of which his close friend and adviser Edward M. House and Treasury secretary William G. McAdoo had warned him, they were married in a private ceremony at her house on 18 December 1915.

Always dependent on the women in his life, Woodrow Wilson relied on his new wife for emotional support. The first Mrs. Wilson had fulfilled the same need, as had Mrs. Mary Hulbert Peck, a woman he had met in 1907 during a vacation in Bermuda. He told Mrs. Galt before their engagement about his unusual relationship with Peck and insisted that the relationship was only platonic. After their marriage, Edith Wilson facilitated her husband's exercise and recreation. She joined him in early morning golf, late afternoon automobile or horseback rides, and evening theater or family time at home.

President Wilson also depended on his second wife for political advice and assistance. Even before their wedding, he had discussed state papers with her. This practice continued throughout the First World War. When he traveled, she went along. She accompanied him in 1916 on speaking tours to convince the country to support military preparedness and to reelect him for a second term. No first lady had previously involved herself so deeply in the daily routine of the White House. She coded and decoded secret messages between the president and House, his personal envoy to Europe. Mrs. Wilson was constantly available to assist the president, while also serving as a wartime Red Cross volunteer. After the war, she urged him to attend the Paris Peace Conference and accompanied him to Europe in 1918–1919. She was still at his side, giving advice and encouragement, during his western tour in September 1919 to advocate U.S. membership in the League of Nations.

Following the president's stroke on 2 October 1919, Edith Wilson assumed an even more critical position in the White House. Most concerned about her husband's survival and recovery, she determined which matters were sufficiently important to bring to his attention. In so doing, she wielded real power in the White House, although she sought only to pursue his agenda. She conveyed his instructions to others in government.

During the fight over the peace treaty with Germany in 1919–1920, Edith Wilson helped her sick husband to resist the Senate's reservations to the League of Nations, in spite of her own view that he should accept them. She shared his antipathy toward the Republican leader in the Senate, Henry Cabot Lodge (1850–1924) of Massachusetts. Her personal animosity toward House, Secretary of State Robert Lansing, and even the president's private secretary Joseph P. Tumulty, further isolated President Wilson. She denied access to him by most advisers and officials, whom she distrusted. Her "stewardship" evoked controversy at the time and has among historians ever since. Nevertheless, because Woodrow Wilson had regularly conferred with her during his presidency, she was much better prepared for this task than most first ladies. Ironically, she abhorred advocates of woman suffrage yet wielded far more power than most women in American politics.

In March 1921 Mrs. Wilson began a new phase in her life. She moved from the White House with her ailing husband to their new home in Washington, D.C. Caring for him until his death in 1924, she continued thereafter to protect the president's legacy. She aided Ray Stannard Baker in collecting the Wilson papers for his authorized multivolume biography. Offering her own version of history in *My Memoir* (1938), Edith Wilson criticized House, Lansing, Lodge, Tumulty, and a host of others who, in her judgment, had betrayed or mistreated Woodrow Wilson. As she grew older, she maintained her keen interest in politics, attending Democratic political conventions, presidential inaugurations, speeches in Congress, and White House functions. Her marriage to President Wilson had permanently established Mrs. Wilson in the social and political elite of Washington, D.C. She continued in that role until her death at home on his birthday.

• The Edith Bolling Wilson Papers are located in the Library of Congress, Washington, D.C. Some of her correspondence with the president is in *The Papers of Woodrow Wilson*, vols. 31–64, ed. Arthur S. Link (1979–1991). Their personal letters in 1915 are available in *A President in Love: The Courtship Letters of Woodrow Wilson and Edith Bolling Galt*, ed. Edwin Tribble (1981). Biographies include: Alden Hatch, *Edith Bolling Wilson: First Lady Extraordinary* (1961); Ishbel Ross, *Power with Grace: The Life Story of Mrs. Woodrow Wilson* (1975); and Tom Shachtman, *Edith and Woodrow: A Presidential Romance* (1981). See also Judith L. Weaver, "Edith Bolling Wilson as First Lady: A Study in the Power of Personality, 1919–1920," *Presidential Studies Quarterly* 15 (Winter 1985): 51–76; and Lloyd E. Ambrosius, *Woodrow Wilson and the American Diplomatic Tradition: The Treaty Fight in Perspective* (1987).

LLOYD E. AMBROSIUS

WILSON, Edith Goodall (6 Sept. 1896–30 Mar. 1981), blues and popular singer, was born in Louisville, Kentucky, the daughter of Hundley Goodall, a schoolteacher, and Susan Jones, a housekeeper. She grew up in a mixed middle-class and working-class black neighborhood of small, neat cottages. Like many African Americans, she began singing in the church and community social clubs. She completed her elementary education but dropped out of school by age fourteen. Her first taste of performing in an adult venue came in the White City Park talent shows in Louisville.

Eventually, Edith Goodall teamed with pianist Danny Wilson and his sister, Lena, a blues singer. The trio performed in Kentucky and Ohio and, later, Chicago, where jazz was making inroads. Edith Goodall married the pianist around 1919. Danny Wilson had had some musical training, which enabled him to teach his wife how to use her voice; he also encouraged her to sing a variety of ballads, light classics, and blues. After performing in small clubs around Chicago for two years, the trio moved to Washington, D.C., in 1921. Their musical exposure in the nation's capital and in clubs around Atlantic City, New Jersey, helped prepare them for the much tougher competition of New York City.

Edith Wilson was appearing in the musical revue at Town Hall, *Put and Take*, when Columbia Records signed her in September 1921 as the label's first blues singer. Johnny Dunn's Original Jazz Hounds, with Danny Wilson on piano, backed her on the first release, "Nervous Blues," by Perry Bradford. From 1921 until 1925 Wilson recorded thirty-one vocals, most of them blues, but a few of them humorous novelties such as "He May Be Your Man (But He Comes to See Me Sometime)." (This song was among the most popular with Wilson's audiences during blues festivals in the 1970s.) Wilson's voice, a light, plaintive soprano, was more refined—some jazz critics termed it "citified"—than those of most blues singers. This was partly the result of the training she received from her husband, who advised her to continue expanding her repertoire. In all, she made about forty recordings during the 1920s.

Wilson's stage career received a boost when she toured briefly on the TOBA (Theater Owners Booking Association) circuit to promote her recordings. A fine comedienne, she was sought to play roles in shows that featured both comedy and singing. She appeared in Lew Leslie's first major venture in producing black shows at Manhattan's Plantation Room in 1922. Noted for her blues and for songs featuring double entendres, she also sang at the Cotton Club in Harlem.

Wilson's first trip abroad was with Leslie's *Dover Street to Dixie*, which starred Florence Mills and played London's Pavilion in 1923. A theatrical version of the revue, *Dixie to Broadway*, opened at New York's Broadhurst Theater in 1924, then toured until early 1925. Wilson and Doc Straine were partners from 1924 until 1926, with Wilson singing the blues as part of their comedy routine. They traveled on the Keith theatrical circuit and, according to press reports, were highly popular. They also recorded two comedy songs about a bossy woman. That personality often became a Wilson feature in her later Broadway shows. Subsequent revues in which she traveled abroad included *Chocolate Kiddies* and two more Leslie shows, *Blackbirds, 1926* and *Blackbirds of 1934*. Wilson was a quick study with languages. Her fluency enabled her to perform blues and popular songs in French and German as well as the languages of other countries where she appeared.

Wilson's versatility kept her in demand in revues in the United States and overseas throughout the 1920s and 1930s. Her vocal style easily adjusted to the changing tastes and big band arrangements of the swing years. During the 1930s she was featured on occasion with orchestras led by Cab Calloway, Jimmie Lunceford, Lucky Millinder, Noble Sissle, and Sam Wooding. Later, in 1945, she worked with Louis Armstrong in *Memphis Bound*, but the Broadway show, excepting her own performance, received poor notices.

At the end of the 1930s Wilson moved to Los Angeles and began a new phase of her career with a nonsinging role in the film *I'm Still Alive* (1940). She appeared in other movies, her most important part coming in the classic *To Have and Have Not* (1944) that starred Humphrey Bogart and Lauren Bacall. During the mid-1940s Wilson toured on the major Burt Levy and Orpheum circuits and served with the USO.

Wilson, who had been widowed in 1928, married her second husband, Millard Wilson, in 1949. They had no children. Eventually, they moved to Chicago and remained together until her death.

Wilson's career took a social and political twist when she was signed by the Quaker Oats Company to be the radio voice of its Aunt Jemima character for pancake mix commercials. The opportunity resulted from her portrayal of the Kingfish's wife on the "Amos 'n' Andy" radio show. In her Aunt Jemima role she toured on behalf of many charitable projects. Notwithstanding her charitable activities, however, black civil rights leaders and influential activists criticized her for what they saw as the exploitation of her talents to promote minstrel show stereotypes. She refused to give in to the pressure, insisting that her work was for good causes for which she was not being given proper credit. Wilson was dropped from the role in 1965, and eventually Quaker Oats bowed to criticism and retired the Aunt Jemima character.

Nearly seventy, Wilson resumed her singing career, performing regularly at clubs in the Chicago area. She appeared on local television shows and recorded an exemplary album for the Delmark label in 1976. At eighty, she was singing with the verve and sophistication that were hallmarks of her younger years. She performed in local and national blues and jazz festivals, including the 1980 Newport Jazz Festival, and made her final appearance on Broadway in a 1980 show, *Blacks on Broadway*, produced by Bobby Short. She died in Chicago, having remained a highly regarded performer to the end.

• Biographical information on Wilson can be found in Daphne Harrison, *Black Pearls: Blues Queens of the 1920s* (1988). The most comprehensive discography is John Godrich and Robert M. W. Dixon, comp., *Blues and Gospel Records, 1902–1942* (1969).

DAPHNE DUVAL HARRISON

WILSON, Edmund (8 May 1895–12 June 1972), writer and critic, was born in Red Bank, New Jersey, the only child of Edmund Wilson, a lawyer who served as state attorney general, and Helen Mather Kimball; both parents came from families with roots in upstate New York. Although the younger Edmund was influenced by his father's moral standards and Lincolnesque prose style, both parents were remote—his father absenting himself during long intervals of depression, his mother having lost her hearing.

When Wilson went to the Hill School, in Pottstown, Pennsylvania, at the age of thirteen, his mother grafted onto him the nickname "Bunny"; it clung to him the rest of his life. At the school, he formed strong attachments with teachers, especially Alfred Rolfe, a demanding and inspiring master of Greek. Entering Princeton in 1912, he developed a durable bond with Christian Gauss, professor of French and Italian literature, who became the mentor of his early adulthood. In his adolescence, Wilson was already pointing himself toward a literary career, editing and contributing to Hill School publications and, later, Princeton's *Nassau Literary Magazine* and reading voluminously in English and French.

After graduating in Princeton's class of 1916, Wilson worked briefly and uncomfortably as a reporter at the *New York Evening Sun*. With American entry into the Great War, he enlisted in an army medical unit and was sent to France in November 1917. There he served almost a year tending the wounded and sick before being transferred to the intelligence service and occupation duty in Germany. He returned to the United States in 1919, convinced that his army service had freed him of the constraints of the genteel society from which he had sprung and had prepared him by experience, diligent reading, and writing to take up the vocation of "literary worker."

From the beginning, his writing career was marked by productivity and variety rather than specialization, and he thus failed to establish a dominant reputation in any one form. He thought of himself primarily as a journalist, not in the news sense but in the essay tradition of George Bernard Shaw, H. L. Mencken, and James Huneker. "When I speak of myself as a journalist," Wilson observed, "I mean that I have made my living mainly by writing in periodicals" ("Thoughts on Being Bibliographed" [1943]). His first magazine position was at *Vanity Fair*, in New York, where he served two brief terms between January 1920 and mid-1923, the second as managing editor. He also served for a short time in 1921 as managing editor of the *New Republic*. The first book bearing his name was published in 1922: *The Undertaker's Garland*, a miscellany he compiled with his Princeton classmate the poet John Peale Bishop, contained fiction based on his war experiences. In 1924 the Provincetown Players presented in New York his play *The Crime in the Whistler Room*, which featured Mary Blair, whom he had married in 1923; they had one daughter. In 1927 he became an associate editor at the leading liberal weekly, the *New Republic*, writing primarily on literature. A novel, *I Thought of Daisy*, a chronicle of New York during what Wilson called "the drunken siesta" of the 1920s, appeared in 1929; it refracted the great romantic disappointment of his life, his vain wooing in 1920–1921 of the fickle Edna St. Vincent Millay. In 1929 his divorce from Mary Blair became final and the disarray of his life overwhelmed him; he had what he called "sort of a nervous breakdown" and stayed briefly in a sanatorium.

This interruption turned out to be little more than a pause. By fall 1929 Wilson was presenting in the *New Republic* the essays that constituted his first major book of criticism, *Axel's Castle* (1930), a study of the "symbolist" movement in modern literature as developed through T. S. Eliot, James Joyce, and William Butler Yeats as well as French writers. As the country sank into economic crisis in 1931, he transformed himself into a reporter on the road, traveling coast to coast; his observations of a disoriented nation appeared in *The American Jitters: A Year of the Slump* (1932). The depression also pushed him to the left politically. He thought of himself as a Marxist and wrote that he would vote for the Communists in the 1932 election, but he scoffed at the idea of joining the party. Before the end of the decade he condemned the Stalinist form of communism.

Wilson suffered a lasting personal shock in 1932 when his second wife, Margaret Canby, whom he had married in 1930, was killed in a fall. Although he did not stop writing, his next major project was slow to emerge. But by 1934 he had set himself on the course of becoming a historian on the grand scale, undertaking a tracing of the intellectual currents of two centuries that led ultimately to the Russian Revolution of 1917. He won a Guggenheim Fellowship that allowed him to travel in the Soviet Union in 1935 (from which he spun off a book of reportage, *Travels in Two Democracies*, published the next year). *To the Finland Station* (named for the climactic return of Lenin to Russia in 1917) was published in 1940; republished in 1972, it was hailed by Marshall Berman as "a work of the historical imagination at its most creative."

By 1940 Wilson found himself alienated from the *New Republic*, gave up editorial work there, and devoted himself for a time primarily to literary chores. He edited two volumes of the work of his recently deceased Princeton friend, F. Scott Fitzgerald, and assembled a widely used historical anthology of comment on American literature by its creators, *The Shock of Recognition* (1943). In 1943 he found a new magazine home at the *New Yorker*; he served as the weekly's literary editor for five years and was a frequent contributor of reviews and journalism thereafter.

His major piece of original writing in the 1940s was his second novel, *Memoirs of Hecate County* (1946), a series of tales taking place in New York City and upstate New York; its sexually explicit (but hardly prurient) passages, based primarily on an affair that Wilson had recorded clinically in his notebooks, led to local suppression of the book while broadening its audience. Earlier he compiled a volume of his literary criticism, *The Wound and the Bow* (1941), which centered on the theme of the psychic trauma that is a wellspring of creativity.

In middle age, Wilson's private life eventually settled, after further upheaval, into an enduring pattern. In 1938 he married a third time; his spouse was a younger writer, Mary McCarthy, who later portrayed him caustically in her novel *A Charmed Life* (1955). The troubled, even mutually abusive, marriage lasted eight years; the couple had one son. Soon after the divorce, Wilson married Elena Mumm Thornton, to whom he remained married the rest of his life; they had a daughter. He maintained two homes, a house in Wellfleet on Cape Cod, which he bought in 1941, and his family's old stone house in Talcottville, New York, which he inherited from his mother in 1951.

In the 1950s his work shifted onto a kind of double track. He continued his original work, most strikingly in his study *The Scrolls from the Dead Sea* (1955; updated and retitled *The Dead Sea Scrolls*, 1969). But he also began to repackage earlier writing, slightly revised, first in a collection from the 1940s, *Classics and Commercials* (1950), then from the preceding decades, in *The Shores of Light* (1952), *A Literary Chronicle: 1920–1950* (1956), and *The American Earthquake* (1958). The last of these collections, *The Bit between My Teeth* (1965), covered the years 1950 to 1965. Ultimately, at the age of seventy, he began the process of review once again, with an autobiographical volume, *A Prelude* (1967), which commenced the editing of his diaries, a task he did not live to complete; they were published posthumously for the years through the 1960s.

Always forceful, outspoken, and cantankerous, and (as he conceded) frequently bolstered by drinking, Wilson never surrendered retrospection. The last fifteen years of his life yielded some of his most highly praised and original work. *Apologies to the Iroquois* (1960) was a prescient study of the survival of American Indian culture in the twentieth century. The formidable *Patriotic Gore* (1962)—for which he prepared with one of his rare stops in academia, a Lowell lectureship at Harvard—disinterred and analyzed the literary remains and key figures of the American Civil War. Although he marked himself as a dissident with his extended essay *The Cold War and the Income Tax* (1963), he was awarded the Medal of Freedom by President John F. Kennedy; the honor did not keep him from becoming an early opponent of the war in Vietnam. His final major work, the melancholy *Upstate* (1971), presented his reflections on his readoption of the ancestral stone house in Talcottville and on the fate of the American republican tradition. Even before the book appeared, he had suffered a heart seizure and slight stroke. He died at Talcottville.

Eulogists and historians found him difficult to characterize precisely. Most frequently he was called, in eighteenth-century terms, a distinguished "man of letters," or even "the last American man of letters." But critics discounted somewhat his achievement in any given field and pointed out flaws—for example, his lack of attention to the most recent American writers. They paid tribute to him, however, as a critic who helped universalize literature, as a journalist of literary skill, and to a lesser extent as a writer of fiction, plays, and poetry of quality. It was suggested that he may ultimately be remembered in broader terms—as "a literary artist driven by historical imagination" or, as George H. Douglas writes, as "one of the most enlightening and original critics of American life," a twentieth-century successor to Alexis de Tocqueville and Henry Adams.

• Edmund Wilson's papers are in the Beinecke Rare Book and Manuscript Library, Yale University. Autobiographical sources include, in addition to *A Prelude* and *Upstate*, the series of notebooks and diaries edited by Leon Edel—*The Twenties* (1975), *The Thirties* (1980), *The Forties* (1983), and *The Fifties* (1986)—and *The Sixties*, ed. Lewis M. Dabney (1993). Elena Wilson edited his *Letters on Literature and Politics, 1912–1972* (1977); see also *The Nabokov-Wilson Letters*, ed. Simon Karlinsky (1979), recording the friendship and disputes of the two writers. Other works and collections include *Discordant Encounters* (1926), *Poets, Farewell!* (1929), *This Room and This Gin and These Sandwiches* (1937), *The Boys in the Back Room* (1941), *Note-Books of Night* (1942), *Europe without Baedeker* (1947; 2d ed., 1966), *The Little Blue Light* (1950), *Eight Essays* (1954), *Five Plays* (1954), *A Piece of My Mind: Reflections at Sixty* (1956), *Red, Black, Blond and Olive* (1956), *O Canada* (1965), *The Fruits of the MLA* (1968), *The Duke of Palermo and Other Plays* (1969), *A Window on Russia* (1972), and *The Devils and Canon Barham* (1973). Memoirs dealing with Wilson include those of his daughter Rosalind Baker Wilson, *Near the Magician* (1989); Richard Hauer Costa, *Edmund Wilson: Our Neighbor from Talcottville* (1980); Frederick E. Exley, *Pages from a Cold Island* (1975); Mary McCarthy, *Intellectual Memoirs* (1992); and Alfred Kazin, *New York Jew* (1978). John Wain, ed., *Edmund Wilson: The Man and His Work* (1978), also contains reminiscences. Biographical and critical studies include Sherman Paul, *Edmund Wilson* (1965); Charles P. Frank, *Edmund Wilson* (1970); Leonard Kriegel, *Edmund Wilson* (1971); George H. Douglas, *Edmund Wilson's America* (1983); David Castronovo, *Edmund Wilson* (1984); and Janet Groth, *Edmund Wilson: A Critic for Our Time* (1989). The most extensive bibliography is Richard David Ramsey, *Edmund Wilson: A Bibliography* (1971). Obituaries are in the *New York Times*, 13 June 1972, and the *New York Times Book Review*, 2 July 1972.

JAMES BOYLAN

WILSON, Edmund Beecher (19 Oct. 1856–3 Mar. 1939), cytologist, embryologist, and geneticist, was born in Geneva, Illinois, the son of Isaac G. Wilson, a lawyer and judge, and Caroline Clarke. In 1859 Isaac Wilson was appointed circuit judge in Chicago, and he and Caroline left their three-year-old child, "Eddy," with his maternal aunt, Mrs. Charles Patten, in Geneva. He viewed his childless aunt and her husband as a second set of parents.

During his childhood in Geneva, Wilson became intrigued by both natural history and music, interests his foster parents encouraged by providing a separate room for his numerous collectibles. At sixteen he replaced his older brother for a year as a teacher at a little one-room school house near Oswego, Illinois. This "grand experience," as he later described it, was not one he wanted to repeat. Indeed, he became even more inspired to go to college and become a scientist. Encouraged by his father, around 1872 he took a competitive examination for West Point, outscoring everyone else, but was unable to accept an appointment because he was under the legal age.

Following in the footsteps of his older cousin, Samuel Clarke, Wilson spent a year at Antioch College in Ohio and then a year at the University of Chicago preparing himself for the Sheffield Scientific School at Yale. He matriculated at Sheffield in 1875, received his bachelor's degree (Ph.B.) in 1878, and remained at Sheffield as a graduate student and assistant for another year. As his thesis for this degree, Wilson wrote two descriptive papers on the systematics of sea spiders (*Pycnogonida*).

Again influenced by Clarke, who was at this time a student at Johns Hopkins, Wilson left Sheffield for Hopkins. During his three years there, he studied under physiologist H. Newell Martin and morphologist William Keith Brooks, who continually pointed out the vast number of unsolved problems in contemporary biology. After completing his Ph.D. in 1881, Wilson went abroad, the trip financed by his older brother. At Cambridge, Leipzig, and Naples he met, and was influenced by, many important European experimental biologists.

When Wilson returned from Europe, he substituted for Clarke at Williams College (1883–1884), where he complained that he "had no time nor appliances for research, no scientific stimulus, no incentive for research" (Morgan, p. 320). Possibly because he was not involved in stimulating research during this year, he and W. T. Sedgwick spent this time working on a textbook, *General Biology*, which was published in 1886. This popular text synthesized contemporary ideas on the nature of life. The book was completed during a one-year position at the Massachusetts Institute of Technology (1884–1885).

Throughout his career, Wilson was concerned with the tendencies of biologists to form uncorroborated hypotheses. He was meticulous, sometimes even overly cautious, before he embraced his own results and those of his colleagues. Early in his career, Wilson decided on the problem that defined his life's work: how the development of the individual is determined within the germ cells. His first major published work, "The Development of *Renilla* [a colonial polyp]" (*Philosophical Transactions of the Royal Society of London* [1883]), was an excellent example of descriptive embryology and resulted from his Ph.D. dissertation.

After leaving MIT, Wilson taught at the newly established women's college Bryn Mawr, where he was in charge of the biology department for six years (1885–1891). In 1891 he was appointed to Columbia University, where his research output increased greatly. He produced important papers on *Lumbricus* (earthworm) embryology (1887, 1889, and 1890) and on the "cell lineage" of the marine annelid *Nereis* (1892, 1895, and 1898). By tracking the fate of individual cells (cell lineage), Wilson showed that triploblastic (three germ layers) organisms fall into two large groups according to the way in which they produce mesoderm. The two types of mesoderm formation, mosaic or spiral (annelids, arthropods, and mollusks) and radial (echinoderms, primitive chordates, and vertebrates), provided a way to establish homologies in early embryonic development.

Wilson's conclusions from *Nereis* carried him away from purely descriptive embryology. He began to see the importance of both comparative observational methods and experimental embryology. The European investigators whom Wilson had visited (Theodor Boveri, Hans Driesch, and Curt Herbst) convinced him of the importance of the experimental approach. The old controversy between epigenesis (development proceeds from an undifferentiated point) and preformation (all organs are originally present in the embryo) had its early twentieth-century counterpart in the controversy between Wilhelm Roux's "mosaic theory" (each cell has only one kind of determinant) and Hans Driesch's conviction, derived from experimentation, that all cells have a full complement of hereditary material. Although Wilson was cautious in his conclusion, he favored Driesch's ideas and the experimental approach surrounding them but without the mystery of an illusive, directive vital force.

Theodor Boveri, Wilson's former teacher, spurred his interest in cytology. Wilson gathered all of the material that he had collected on cells, merged it with a series of lectures he had given, and then published a landmark book, *The Cell in Development and Inheritance* (1896). This book went through three quite different editions and numerous printings. Dedicated to Boveri, it was a thoughtful, wide-ranging synthesis that emphasized that although the physical basis of heredity was located in the nucleus with the chromatin as its essential constituent, the cytoplasm's role in development must also be considered.

Wilson's family life was compatible with his career. In 1904 he married Anne Maynard Kidder, whom he had met at the Woods Hole Marine Biological Station. Their only child, Nancy Wilson, became a professional cellist, greatly pleasing her music-loving father.

From 1903 to 1912 Wilson studied chromosomes and their relation to heredity. His hypothesis that the chromosomes were the agents of heredity proposed in *The Cell* was confirmed by one of his graduate students, Walter S. Sutton, who demonstrated that the visible behavior of the chromosomes explained Mendel's first two laws of heredity, the law of dominance and recessiveness and the law of segregation. However, no evidence existed that a distinctive trait was carried on a specific chromosome. In 1905 Wilson and Nettie Maria Stevens independently provided evidence that sex was determined chromosomally. From 1905 to 1912 Wilson produced a series of eight papers, "Studies on Chromosomes," in which his ideas based on chromosomal sex-determination evidence were expanded.

During his later years Wilson became less convinced that the chromosomes alone determined heredity. He studied the seemingly independent replication of chloroplasts and mitochondria in the cytoplasm and concluded that the cytoplasm could affect the genetic potential in the nucleus. These ideas resulted in a major revision of *The Cell* in 1925.

When he died in New York City, Wilson was considered to be one of the most important cytologists of the twentieth century. The scope of his work was wide ranging. Always alert to new developments in his field, he synthesized his own research with the works of others, was an outstanding teacher, and published prolifically. A meticulous experimenter and observer, he was cautious about drawing unwarranted conclusions. To deal with uncertainty, Wilson adopted a cautious approach, hesitating to embrace a theory in which he could find exceptions. This hesitancy may be illustrated by his approach to the chromosomal sex-determination problem. In the third part of "Studies on Chromosomes," he still was hesitant about embracing completely a Mendelian interpretation of his results and was not prepared to accept the chromosomes totally and unequivocally as the determinants of sex. Cytogeneticist Thomas Hunt Morgan provided a most telling tribute when he stated that Wilson would be remembered "by his many friends as a reserved, cultured gentleman whose sincerity, judgment, and breadth of knowledge were shown by the perfection of his lectures and his scientific papers" (Morgan, p. 335).

• During his lifetime, Wilson published more than 120 items. The following publications, in addition to those specifically mentioned in the article, give an idea of the scope and importance of Wilson's work. "The Embryology of the Earthworm," *Journal of Morphology* 3 (1889): 387–462, and "The Cell-Lineage of *Nereis*. A Contribution to the Cytogeny of the Annelid Body," *Journal of Morphology* 6 (1892): 361–480, are characteristic of his early work. A beautiful atlas, crafted by Wilson and Columbia University photography instructor Edward Leaming, *An Atlas of the Fertilization and Karyokinesis of the Ovum* (1895), shows changes that occur during cell division and fertilization. "Studies on Chromosomes. I. The Behavior of the Idiochromosomes in *Hemiptera*," *Journal of Experimental Zoology* 2 (1905): 371–405, is the first of his eight papers on the inheritance of sex.

Because a full biography of Wilson has yet to be published, two biographical memoirs represent the best sources of information about his life, Thomas Hunt Morgan, "Biographical Memoir of Edmund Beecher Wilson, 1856–1939," National Academy of Sciences, *Biographical Memoirs* 21, pp. 315–342, and H. J. Muller, "Edmund B. Wilson—an Appreciation," *American Naturalist* 77 (1943): 5–37 and 142–72. The Morgan Memoir was condensed in *Science* 89 (1939): 258–59 and in the *New York Times*, 4 Mar. 1939, and contains a bibliography of Wilson's published works. Muller's memoir was later condensed in his introduction to the 1966 reprint of *The Cell in Development and Inheritance*. Jane Maienschein, in *Transforming Traditions in American Biology, 1880–1915* (1991), includes an excellent chapter on Wilson's work and a useful bibliography. An obituary is in the *New York Times*, 4 Mar. 1939.

MARILYN OGILVIE

WILSON, Edwin Bidwell (25 Apr. 1879–28 Dec. 1964), mathematical scientist, was born in Hartford, Connecticut, the son of Edwin Horace Wilson, a teacher and superintendent of schools in Middletown, Connecticut, and Jane Amelia Bidwell. Wilson pursued a broad course of study and graduated summa cum laude from Harvard with a bachelor's degree in mathematics in 1899. He then entered Yale University for graduate training in mathematics and physics and was the last student to work under the distinguished physicist Josiah Willard Gibbs. Gibbs's scientific style, which brought fresh mathematical techniques to important problems in physics and chemistry, had a strong influence on Wilson, instilling in him an appreciation for the applications of mathematics. Wilson's earliest major publication, *Vector Analysis* (1901), was a textbook presentation of Gibbs's lectures.

Wilson joined Yale's faculty as an instructor in mathematics in 1900 and received a Ph.D. in 1901. He spent much of the 1902–1903 academic year studying mathematics at the École Normale Supérieure in Paris. In 1906 he became an assistant professor at Yale but the following year accepted an offer to join the faculty of the Massachusetts Institute of Technology as an associate professor. He was named full professor there in 1911, and in 1917 he became professor of mathematical physics and head of the Department of Physics. Wilson remained department head until 1922, and from 1920 to 1922 he also served on an administrative committee of three faculty members who had charge of the affairs of the university between the death of President Richard Maclaurin and the appointment of Samuel Stratton. Wilson left MIT in 1922 to become professor of vital statistics at the Harvard School of Public Health, a position he held until his retirement in 1945. He married Ethel Sentner in 1911; they had two children.

Wilson's professional life was characterized by his extraordinarily wide-ranging interests, all stemming from a fundamental commitment to the application of mathematical reasoning to problems of significance. Beginning as a student of mathematics and mathematical physics, he made contributions to several areas of pure mathematics, including projective geometry, representation theory, and differential equations. In addition to numerous research papers, he published *Advanced Calculus* (1912), a comprehensive, modern text that was widely used in the United States for many years. Throughout his career, Wilson also taught and did research in several areas of physics; he was one of the first Americans to become engaged in relativity theory research, some of which was done jointly with renowned chemist Gilbert N. Lewis in 1912.

The successful flights of pioneer aviators Orville and Wilbur Wright in 1908 and 1909 helped to bring Wilson's attention to aerodynamics and its theoretical problems. His extensive study of the behavior of airplanes when subjected to wind gusts appeared as "Theory of an Airplane Encountering Gusts" (Report No. 1 in *First Annual Report of the National Advisory Committee for Aeronautics* [1915]), and in 1920 he published *Aeronautics*, one of the first graduate texts on the subject. With his move to the Harvard School of Public Health in 1922, Wilson began to pursue seriously an interest that had begun for him during World War I: the applications of statistics to public health issues. The numerous resulting publications documented his basic research in theoretical statistics, investigated particular epidemiological problems, and gave general prescriptions for the responsible use of statistical tools to analyze social and biological phenomena. He is credited with establishing, in 1927, the foundations for the confidence interval, a widely used and important concept in inferential statistics. Wilson is also recognized for his contributions to economics, which came largely through courses he taught in graduate statistics and mathematical economics for the Harvard economics department during the 1930s.

Beginning with its first issue in 1915 and continuing until his death, Wilson was the managing editor of the *Proceedings of the National Academy of Sciences*. During this remarkably long tenure, Wilson worked to maintain in the *Proceedings* a balance among the disciplines represented by the academy's membership, and to keep personal controversies off of its pages. Shortly before his death, he prepared *The History of the Proceedings of the National Academy of Sciences 1914–1963* (1966). Having been elected to the academy in 1919, he was also active in many of its committees and affairs.

Wilson's wide range of professional memberships and activities reflect his contributions to many disciplines and his strong sense of the importance of maintaining productive scientific communities and effective channels for scientific communication. In addition to holding memberships in the American Philosophical Society, the American Academy of Arts and Sciences, and the American Association for the Advancement of Science, he was among the early presidents of the American Statistical Association and the Social Science Research Council (both in 1929). He was also a member of the American Mathematical Society, the American Economic Association, and the American Society for the Control of Cancer, among others.

After his retirement from Harvard, Wilson spent 1945–1946 in Glasgow, Scotland, where he delivered the Stevenson lectures on citizenship. From 1948 until his death he served as a consultant and adviser on mathematical and physical sciences for the Office of Naval Research. He subsequently received the Superior Civilian Service Award from the chief of naval operations in 1960 and the Distinguished Civilian Service Award from the secretary of the navy in 1964.

The breadth of Wilson's contributions to research and teaching, and the depth of his commitment to such scientific organizations as the National Academy of Sciences led Wilson's peers to regard him as a "modern Renaissance man." Wilson remained active in scientific affairs until his death in Brookline, Massachusetts.

• Wilson's personal papers are in the Harvard University Archives, Cambridge, Mass. The Archives of the National Academy of Sciences has a collection of papers relating to Wilson's work on the *Proceedings*. The Niels Bohr Library of the American Institute of Physics in College Park, Md., has a collection of materials relating to Wilson's work on aeronautics. A complete bibliography of Wilson's works is included in the memoir by Jerome Hunsaker and Saunders Mac Lane in the National Academy of Sciences, *Biographical Memoirs* 43 (1973): 285–320.

LOREN BUTLER FEFFER

WILSON, Ellen Axson (15 May 1860–6 Aug. 1914), artist and first lady, was born Ellen Louise Axson in Savannah, Georgia, the daughter of Samuel Edward Axson, a Presbyterian minister, and Margaret Jane Hoyt. She was raised in Rome, Georgia, and in 1876 graduated from Rome Female College. Despite her talents, the lack of family funds forced her to defer plans to gain further education either as a teacher or as an artist.

In April 1883 Ellen met Woodrow Wilson during his visit to Rome to attend to family legal matters. Ardently pursued by him, she accepted his proposal of marriage in August 1883. After the death of her father by suicide in 1884, Ellen enrolled in the coeducational Art Students League of New York. After Woodrow Wilson received a faculty appointment at Bryn Mawr College, they married in 1885.

Like many middle-class women of the era, Wilson deferred her own ambitions for those of her spouse. After getting married, she abandoned her art and took principal responsibility for maintaining a household and raising three daughters. Despite attending a coeducational art school, she initially discouraged her husband from accepting the offer to teach at Bryn Mawr College. In her view, his talents would have been better applied to an all-male institution, and she supported his decision to break his contract with Bryn Mawr and accept a professorship at Wesleyan University in 1888. After he accepted a professorship at Princeton University in 1890, Wilson forged close ties with the community.

Extensive correspondence between the Wilsons indicates a warm and close relationship. They shared a passion for English literature, and Wilson had a decisive influence in expanding her husband's aesthetic tastes. According to the memoirs of Wilson's brother, Stockton Axson, she served as an important critic of much of her husband's early writings and was his trusted adviser. His memoirs also maintain that she, after learning of the extent of academic dishonesty at Princeton, encouraged him and a group of Princeton undergraduates to press successfully for the adoption of an honor code.

Wilson assumed a host of official duties entertaining faculty members and distinguished visitors after Woodrow Wilson became president of Princeton University in 1902. She devoted a great deal of energy to redesigning the gardens of "Prospect," the presidential home at Princeton. Active in the affairs of the Ladies Auxiliary, she headed a subcommittee that improved conditions at the campus infirmary. She remained a firm supporter of her husband's plan to recast Princeton into a more ecumenical and cosmopolitan university.

As her daughters grew older, Wilson resumed her interest in art. In the late 1890s she began to work again in crayon portraiture and branched into painting landscapes. In 1905 she summered with her family in an artist's colony in Old Lyme, Connecticut, and began to paint in oils. Several summer residences in this community had an important impact on nurturing her artistic career and exposing her to American impressionist painters.

Wilson supported her husband's decision to seek the governorship of New Jersey in 1910 and later the presidency of the United States in 1912. She played a key role in advancing his career by actively promoting a political friendship between him and William Jennings Bryan during the latter's visit to Princeton in 1911. Before the Democratic National Convention she campaigned with her husband in Georgia in order to highlight their ties to the state. During the presidential convention of 1912, when her husband was behind in the convention balloting, she convinced him to retract an earlier decision to withdraw from the balloting.

Wilson's art work received increasing public recognition in this period. In 1911 she began to enter juried art competitions under a pseudonym, and her landscapes won places at the Macbeth Gallery in New York, the Art Institute of Chicago, and the Pennsylvania Academy of Fine Arts. In 1913 she opened a one-woman show at the Arts and Crafts Guild in Philadelphia to raise money to support the Berry School in Georgia. As first lady she continued to paint, and she successfully entered a number of juried exhibitions under her own name.

In her role as first lady, Wilson proved to be a transitional figure. Like her predecessors, she directed the household affairs of the White House and participated in a range of receptions, dinners, and other official entertaining. Despite her short tenure as first lady and her reticent style, she attracted public attention for her efforts to promote better working conditions for federal employees and to ameliorate the poor housing conditions that existed in the alleys of the nation's capital. Named an honorary president of the National Civic Federation, she supported efforts of the Washington, D.C., branch to build low-cost housing. By using her access to the press, key congressional leaders, and administration officials, she provided the crucial impetus behind the passage of federal legislation that set minimum standards for alley housing in the District of Columbia. Her interest in the progress of the legislation continued even as she lay dying at the White House of Bright's disease.

Some historians have maintained that Ellen Wilson promoted the Wilson administration's decision to segregate federal government offices in 1913. Little evidence can be found to sustain this view, although it is clear that she joined her husband in accepting white supremacy and segregation. Although she was paternalistic in her outlook regarding the question of social issues and race relations, nonetheless her efforts to improve life for the residents of Washington's black community were courageous given the resistance that such initiatives faced from the Democratic party's southern constituency.

Ellen Axson Wilson defined her identity around that of her husband and her family. Although she remained ambivalent about whether women should be given the vote, her three daughters were committed suffragettes. Uncomfortable in the role of a public figure, she nonetheless proved adept at using her position as first lady to try to shape public policy to benefit the less fortunate.

• The bulk of Ellen Axson Wilson's correspondence is in the Woodrow Wilson Collections of the Library of Congress and the Princeton University Library. The memoirs of her brother Stockton Axson, *"Brother Woodrow": A Memoir of Woodrow Wilson* (1993), and her daughter Eleanor Wilson McAdoo, *The Woodrow Wilsons* (1937), are particularly useful for documenting the relationship between Wilson and her husband. *The Papers of Woodrow Wilson*, ed. Arthur S. Link et al. (1966–1994), have published all the known correspondence between the two. For an extensively documented biography, see Frances Wright Saunders, *Ellen Axson Wilson: First Lady between Two Worlds* (1985). For scholarly accounts that document the influence of Wilson on her husband's career, see Link, "*Wilson*," *The Road to the White House* (1947) and *Wilson: The New Freedom* (1956), as well as John M. Mulder, *Woodrow Wilson: The Years of Preparation* (1978). To place Wilson's role of first lady into a larger historical context, see Betty Boyd Caroli, *First Ladies* (1987; rev. ed., 1995). For a differing interpretation of Wilson's role in the decision to segregate federal offices, see Constance McLaughlin Green, *The Secret City* (1967). Obituaries are in the *New York Times* and *Washington Post*, 7 Aug. 1914.

G. KURT PIEHLER

WILSON, E. Raymond (20 Sept. 1896–27 June 1987), peace educator and lobbyist, was born Edward Raymond Wilson on Cloverdale Farm near Morning Sun, Iowa, the son of Charles Brown Wilson and Anna Jane Wilson, farmers. Wilson's parents were devout Presbyterians. After graduating from high school, Wilson worked full-time on the family farm for a year. He entered Iowa State College in 1916 but left to return to his family's farm when the United States entered World War I. Grounded in the prevailing "just war" view, Wilson enlisted in the navy in July 1918 and served in the Chicago area until he was mustered out the following December. He graduated from Iowa State in 1921 with a B.S. in animal husbandry, and he received an M.S. in vocational education in 1923. Wilson, who was president of the student Young Men's Christian Association at Iowa State in 1921, was increasingly challenged by the pacifist view, particularly as articulated by Christian writer Kirby Page at the 1923 Student Volunteer Convention in Indianapolis.

Wilson attended the Teachers College at Columbia University and earned an M.A. in religious education in 1925. While there he lived in the newly established International House, an experience that strengthened his views on peace and internationalism. While working toward his Ph.D (never completed) at Columbia, Wilson was awarded the first Japanese Brotherhood Scholarship. It enabled him to live, study, and travel for more than a year in Japan and Formosa (Taiwan) in 1926 and 1927. During this experience he formed a lifelong bond with the Japanese people and gained insight into the negative impact of the U.S. enactment of the 1924 Japanese Exclusion Act, as well as into Japan's imperial policies in Formosa and Korea, and later in Manchuria and China.

Wilson's intellectual and spiritual journey, which he called "From Gob in the Dry Land Navy to Ardent Pacifist," is described in his autobiography, *Thus Far on My Journey* (1976). His peace advocacy began in 1925 at Columbia, where he worked part-time to organize the Committee on Militarism in Education, which opposed compulsory military training in colleges and universities and all military training in high schools. After his experience in Asia, cut short by his father's final illness, Wilson spent two years farming with his brother in depression-torn Iowa. He rejoined the staff of the Committee on Militarism in Education in 1929 and worked for two years, first in Pennsylvania and then in New York and Iowa.

In 1931 Wilson went to work for the Quakers, a role that filled his remaining fifty-six years. He spent the first twelve years with the American Friends Service Committee (AFSC) and then served with the Friends Committee on National Legislation (FCNL) as its first executive secretary from 1943 to 1962. Thereafter he remained very active as an executive secretary emeritus.

As AFSC field secretary for three years, primarily in the Midwest, Wilson traveled tens of thousands of miles, speaking at hundreds of church, civic, and school gatherings on peace and disarmament issues. As educational secretary of AFSC's Peace Section, Wilson was the principal organizer and dean of eleven AFSC Institutes of International Relations, ten- to twelve-day events that gave educators, ministers, student leaders, and public opinion molders the opportunity to interact with speakers from a variety of political, economic, and religious points of view.

Wilson had married Miriam Davidson in 1932; they had two children. He and Miriam formally joined the Religious Society of Friends at Frankford Monthly Meeting, Pennsylvania, in 1936.

With Ray Newton, a colleague at AFSC, Wilson worked with the Emergency Peace Campaign in 1936 and 1937 to secure legislation assuring U.S. neutrality in future wars. The campaign organized thousands of meetings in forty-seven states and had active contacts in more than two thousand towns and cities. But with the rise of fascism and Nazism in Europe, support for American intervention grew. Wilson maintained his opposition to all war, as well as his support for a U.S. foreign policy based on strengthened international institutions, international disarmament, and freer and fairer trade. He played a leading role in the Friends War Problems Committee, which began meeting in July 1940 and focused on support for conscientious objectors and opposition to conscription. With the December 1941 Japanese attack on Pearl Harbor, the U.S. peace movement shrank to include only a handful of pacifists who opposed all wars, primarily on religious grounds, a group that counted Wilson among its stalwarts.

When FCNL began operations in November 1943, Wilson continued his extensive travels among Quakers, performing lobbying activities and winning acceptance for his patient willingness to listen to all views, his comprehensive understanding of issues, and his deep religious motivation. He frequently testified before congressional committees and participated in legislative strategy sessions on Capitol Hill. Wilson first lobbied for the rights of conscientious objectors and then supported postwar relief and the United Nations. During the late 1940s he organized opposition to legislation to establish universal military training, a proposal finally defeated on the House floor in March 1952. Throughout the 1950s he was a leading proponent of legislative and educational efforts to promote general and complete disarmament under effective international controls, a concept finally approved in the 1961 McCloy-Zorin agreement between the United States and the Soviet Union endorsed by the UN. Wilson was one of the earliest advocates of U.S. recognition of the People's Republic of China, a process begun by President Richard Nixon in 1971 and formally concluded in 1978. His background in agriculture made him a valued consultant on food for peace legislation to politicians such as Hubert Humphrey and George McGovern.

Wilson helped to found and lead two broad Washington coalitions, the National Civil Liberties Clearinghouse, organized in 1948, and the Disarmament Information Service, begun in 1957. An active member of the board of the National Council of Churches of Christ from 1963 to 1975, he criticized U.S. participation in the Indochina war and the international arms race, constantly urging his colleagues to assume greater leadership on public policy issues. He died in Sandy Spring, Maryland.

As a leader in the U.S. peace movement in the mid-twentieth century, Wilson challenged Quakers and others to become increasingly sophisticated and active in the political process. He had an uncommon faith in the ability of people to understand their best interests and to act on their highest ideals, if given the facts. His skills in coalition building, consensus seeking, and identifying specific, relevant steps to reach lofty goals won respect for the pacifist position among policymakers. "I know Raymond Wilson very well and warmly," Senator Humphrey commented at a 16 August 1961 Senate hearing. "I do not know what this country would be like . . . without organizations [like FCNL] and the spirit which motivates it" (Senate Foreign Relations Committee on Creation of a Disarmament Agency, p. 259).

• Wilson's papers are in the Swarthmore College Peace Collection. The records of FCNL, AFSC, and a number of the coalitions in which he participated are also located there. Wilson's *Uphill for Peace, Quaker Impact on Congress* (1975) and his autobiography, both of which are teeming with anecdotes, provide the best insight into his political and religious views. Wilson's whimsical commentaries on the human condition, given as messages in Friends Meetings, are found in *If Flowers Behaved Like Human Beings* (1981). Edward F. Snyder et al., *Witness in Washington: Fifty Years of Friendly Persuasion*, ed. Tom Mullen (1996), gives additional context regarding Wilson's leading role in FCNL. Obituaries are in the *New York Times* and the *Washington Post*, both 29 June 1987.

EDWARD F. SNYDER

WILSON, Francis (7 Feb. 1854–7 Oct. 1935), actor, was born in Philadelphia, Pennsylvania, the son of Charles Edwin Wilson and Emily Von Erdon. In his autobiography Wilson described his father as "an impractical man, never succeeding though always confident of success." The actor remembered his family, which numbered nine children, as lacking in financial stability but loving. Although his father was a Quaker and presumably a pacifist, he served as a soldier in the Civil War. At the early age of eight Wilson was drawn to the stage as, he felt, "an overdue protest against the solemn repression suffered by generations of [my] ancestors" (p. 33).

Wilson made his professional debut at the age of fourteen as one-half of a black-face song and dance team, Mackin and Wilson. It was at this time that the performer began to develop his penchant for detailed, graceful physical comedy, an attribute he would use repeatedly in operetta and straight plays. Although Wilson's first week's salary was a paltry five dollars, he and Mackin eventually commanded $150 a week each. The partnership lasted nine years as the duo toured in minstrel shows throughout America.

In 1877 the team broke up and Wilson was hired as a Utility Player at the Chestnut Street Theatre in Philadelphia for the low salary of fifteen dollars a week. During his second season he advanced from Utility to Second Low Comedy, but his hopes for a substantial pay increase were dashed when he was informed that he would receive only a five-dollar-a-week raise. Nevertheless, he found the switch from minstrelsy to drama to be an invaluable educational experience as he played in a range of Shakespearean plays, classical comedies, and dramas by authors of the time.

In 1880 Wilson requested and received his release from the Chestnut Street Theatre in order to play the role of the Baron in the new musical comedy *Our Goblins*, written by William Gill. When the play opened in New York at the Fourteenth Street Theatre, it was a huge success. Wilson's salary was raised to $100 a week. The actor bought a large interest in *Our Goblins* and took the play to San Francisco, where he expected it would be equally successful. However, the musical quickly failed, and he was soon back in New York penniless.

After unsuccessfully attempting to sing in Gilbert and Sullivan's *H.M.S. Pinafore* (for which his voice was not sufficiently trained) Wilson joined the McCaull Opera Company for several seasons. He first appeared with the company in *The Queen's Lace Handkerchief* (1882). He also performed Tremolini, the clown part in the *Princess of Trebizonde*; the minor monarch Sigismund in Strauss's *Prince Methusalem*; Balthazar, the tulip grower in *The Merry War*; and the pompous old military man, Von Folback, in *Falka*.

In 1885 Wilson left the McCaull Company to perform at Rudolph Aronson's fashionable Casino Theatre in New York City. After appearing in numerous operas and musical plays, including *Nanon*, *Amorita*, and *The Gypsy Baron*, he performed the part of Cadeaux in the tuneful *Erminie*. Ironically, Cadeaux, which was considered to be a secondary role, made the actor a star. The play opened on 10 May 1886 and ran a remarkable 1,256 performances on Broadway and on the road. In playing Cadeaux, the little knave who serves a rogue-hero, Wilson added touches of sympathy and wistfulness to a role that was usually interpreted merely as a blundering comic clown. In this way he made Cadeaux more human and compassionate.

Wilson's next role was as the Persian marriage-broker, the rascal Hoolagoolah, in *The Oolah*, which opened at the Broadway Theatre on 13 May 1889. During the 1890s the actor spent most of his stage time in musical plays, including *The Merry Monarch* (1890), *The Lion Tamer* (1891), and *Half a King* (1896). In 1896 he took a short hiatus from the musical stage when he toured major American cities as part of Joseph Jefferson's "all star" cast of Sheridan's *The Rivals*.

In the second half of this same decade Wilson unsuccessfully fought a bitter battle against the businessmen of the Theatrical Syndicate, a monopolistic booking association, and its attempts to take control away from individual theater companies, managers, and stars. Wilson, who was then an actor-manager, attempted to form an association with other actor-managers, but by 1899 he and most other stars had given in to the Syndicate. Although he failed, Wilson would use this experience later to create and lead the Actors Equity Association.

After appearing in *The Monks of Malabar* (1900), *The Strollers* (1901), and *The Toreador* (1902), the actor opted in 1904 to leave musical theater and focus on straight drama and comedy. Wilson tried to acquire suitable vehicles for his talent by entering into an association with theatrical producer Charles Frohman. His first attempt was in the comedy *Cousin Billy* (1904), a Clyde Fitch adaptation of the French play *Le Voyage de M. Perichon*. In April 1905 he appeared as the heroic priest in Lloyd Osbourne and Austin Strong's one-act drama *The Little Father of the Wilderness*. In 1906 he played the deceptive husband in the comedy *The Mountain Climber*, from the German *Der Hochtourist* by Graatz and Neal, and during the 1907–1908 theatrical season he acted the part of a modern knight in Harriet Jay's comedy *When Knights Were Bold*. Although his departure from musical theatre was successful overall, Wilson was not completely satisfied with the plays Frohman had procured for him.

In response to his personal frustration, Wilson wrote *The Bachelor's Baby* for himself. Since Frohman was cold to the idea of a comedy that focused on a hater of children who accidentally becomes guardian of a baby girl, the actor decided to produce the play himself with a minimal budget while Frohman was out of the country. The play opened on 28 April 1909 at a midweek matinee in Baltimore, Maryland, and became instantly popular. When it premiered in New York on 27 December 1909, the *New York Herald Tribune* termed it "a comedy that was filled with a note of unselfishness, of human sympathy and love that struck home to the heart." The play ran for three years, making Wilson and Frohman a small fortune. His second attempt at playwriting resulted in *The Spiritualist*, an immediate failure.

Wilson was a powerful political activist for his profession. Much of his time from 1910 to 1912 was spent writing, lecturing, and testifying before state legislatures on behalf of the National Alliance for Stage children, which sought to relax laws against child actors appearing on stage. He went on in 1913 to help found and become the first president of the Actors Equity Association, the professional stage actors union. He was an extremely active leader and in 1919 marshalled the first actors' strike against the Producing Managers Association. During this time most of the casts of Broadway's major productions walked out and stayed on strike through the summer. The strike was marked by peaceful public meetings and demonstrations that garnered the public's sympathy. In the end the actors' union triumphed over the producers and went on to build a powerful organization. In 1935 Equity president Frank Gilmore told the *New York Times*, "No man was more responsible for the success of the Actors Equity Association than Francis Wilson. . . . He was a notable actor, a fiery and logical speaker, and he was a man of independent means whose livelihood could not be destroyed by his assumption of the leadership of this movement" (8 Oct. 1935, p. 23). In 1921, once Equity was well established, Wilson retired as president but still remained involved in various union activities.

During the 1920–1921 season Wilson undertook a farewell tour of *Erminie* with his good friend DeWolf Hopper as his costar. After his retirement he continued to act in special productions, including the part of Bob Acres in *The Rivals* for the Players Club (1922) and the Equity Players (1923); the title role in *Rip Van Winkle* for the opening of the Repertoire Theatre in Boston (1925); and the lead in *The Little Father of the Wilderness* for the Players Club (1930).

An avid book collector, Wilson also wrote numerous biographies, including *The Eugene Field I Knew* (1898), *Joseph Jefferson, Reminiscences of a Fellow Player* (1906), and *John Wilkes Booth: Fact and Fiction of Lincoln's Assassination* (1929). His autobiography, *Francis Wilson's Life of Himself* (1924), is a charming account.

The actor was married twice. In 1881 he wed Mira Barrie of Chicago in 1881, and they had two children. His first wife died in 1915. In January 1917 Wilson married Edna Burns; they also had two children. The actor died at home at 24 Gramercy Park in New York City.

As a performer, Wilson was known for both his intellect and physical control. He was a short man with a long nose, rubbery legs, a pliable body, and an active, humorous face, and he manipulated all of these attributes to create memorable comic roles. He successfully sustained a career in various forms of theatrical entertainment, learning from each experience and building one success upon another. An astute businessman and leader, he fought not only for his own rights as a leading actor and manager but for those of the common actor.

• For insight into Wilson's acting see Acton Davies, "Francis Wilson," *Frank Leslie's Popular Monthly* (1883): 76–78. For a series of reports regarding Wilson's ongoing battle with the Syndicate see the *Dramatic Mirror*, Nov. 1897–Feb. 1898. An obituary is in the *New York Times*, 8 Oct. 1935.

PAUL MROCZKA

WILSON, Frank Norman (19 Nov. 1890–11 Sept. 1952), physician and electrocardiogram researcher, was born in Livonia Township, Michigan, the son of Norman Orlando Wilson and Mary Holtz, farmers. Wilson was raised only a few miles from the University of Michigan, where he was to spend most of his career. He attended the university as both an undergraduate (B.S.) and a medical student and received an M.D. in 1913. That same year he married Juel Mahoney, a music student at the University of Michigan; they had one child.

After graduation from medical school, Wilson took a position in the Department of Medicine at the University of Michigan. There he started work with the electrocardiograph machine, a device invented in 1902 by Dutch physician Willem Einthoven that recorded the electrical signals associated with the heartbeat. Wilson, who used it initially to explore the tracings that were generated by people with abnormal cardiac rhythms, such as those with abnormally fast or slow heartbeats, was not highly regarded by his colleagues for his interest in this seemingly obscure piece of machinery. When the chair of medicine, Albion Hewlett, left the University of Michigan in 1916, he helped Wilson secure a position at Washington University in St. Louis.

After the outbreak of the First World War, Wilson went to Colchester, England, to join a distinguished group of physicians working on an obscure disease known as soldier's heart, as well as several other names. The variety of names given to the disease reflected its rather nonspecific nature. Soldiers afflicted with the syndrome became breathless and diaphoretic and complained of chest pain, a set of symptoms sometimes difficult to distinguish from the (very natural) sensation of intense fear. More important than the scientific work that Wilson did were the contacts he made with other physicians, most notably Thomas Lewis. At that time the most well-known person working on the electrocardiogram, Lewis had conducted extensive studies on the instrument's findings, including the irregularly irregular rhythm known as atrial fibrillation. After returning to the United States, Wilson was recruited back in 1920 to the University of Michigan, where he spent the remainder of his career.

Wilson's work in Ann Arbor was ultimately aided by material conditions there. Early electrocardiogram machines were too cumbersome to move about, and patients were often too ill to travel to the machine. The new University of Michigan Hospital, opened in 1925, had special wiring installed so that people could have their electrocardiogram tracings made without leaving their hospital bed. A place in the hospital—the "heart station"—was set aside for work on heart diseases. In addition, Wilson was able to purchase in 1927 an electrocardiogram machine with a double-string galvanometer, an improvement on the original instrument. That same year he contracted a serious illness that required him to spend a prolonged convalescence in bed. He took advantage of that time to improve his mathematical skills for use in his study of the electrocardiogram.

Wilson's first major contribution to electrocardiography resulted from his work on an abnormal pattern of conduction of electrical impulses through the heart. Impulses normally pass down two collections of fibers, and if one of the passages is blocked, the condition is known as bundle-branch block. Through a series of experiments on a person whose heart had been surgically exposed, Wilson showed that the electrocardiographic pattern of what had previously been thought to be right bundle-branch block was, in fact, left bundle-branch block, and vice versa. This finding was of critical importance in establishing precise diagnoses that would enable accurate prognosis and, somewhat later, treatment.

Wilson used his mathematical readings to contribute to the technical means of taking an electrocardiogram tracing. Initial electrocardiogram tracings were made using three leads, which were connected to a person's hands and foot. Those leads recorded a potential difference between two points. Wilson worked out a means of recording the electrical activity at a single point that was unaffected by the activity at other parts of the body. This 1934 invention, which he termed the central terminal, became an integral part of the standard electrocardiogram. Wilson also played a major role in establishing how to place leads over the chest, which increased the diagnostic potential of the electrocardiogram tracing. He died at his family farm in Stockbridge, Michigan.

Wilson's work was among the first to meld basic scientific ideas with clinical practice. At Michigan he trained many people, including Paul Barker, Franklin Johnston, and Hans Hecht, who were later to become key figures in the development of American cardiology. The electrocardiograph machine, which occupied so much of his time and energy, became central to a whole new area of medical practice and subspecialization.

• Material relating to Wilson's career at the University of Michigan, including correspondence with university officials and research grant applications, and unpublished material from Wilson's family members is in the Michigan Historical Collections, Ann Arbor, Mich. Wilson's most important publications include, with Paul S. Barker et al., "The Excitatory Process Observed in the Exposed Human Heart," *Transactions of the Association of American Physicians* 44 (1929): 125–33; with A. G. Macleod and P. S. Barker, *The Distribution of the Currents of Action and Injury Displayed by Heart Muscle and Other Excitable Tissues* (1933); and, with F. D. Johnston et al., "Electrocardiograms That Represent the Potential Variations of a Single Electrode," *American Heart Journal* 9 (1934): 447–58. For a biographical sketch, a complete bibliography, and a collection of many of Wilson's most important publications see Franklin D. Johnston and Eugene Lepeschkin, eds., *Selected Papers of Dr. Frank N. Wilson* (1954). An extensive essay that places Wilson into the context both of medical science and of the University of Michigan and includes a guide to most of the relevant biographical sources is Joel D. Howell, "Frank Norman Wilson: Theory, Technology, and Electrocardiography," in *Medical Lives and Scientific Medicine at Michigan, 1891–1969*, ed. J. D. Howell (1993), pp. 101–27. Obituaries are in the *New York Times*, 12 Sept. 1952; *Circulation* 6, no. 5 (Nov. 1952): 641–42; and *Transactions of the Association of American Physicians* 66 (1953): 18–19.

JOEL D. HOWELL

WILSON, Hack (26 Apr. 1900–23 Nov. 1948), baseball player, was born Lewis Robert Wilson in Elwood City, Pennsylvania, the son of factory workers. Wilson lived with his father or family friends after his mother died when he was a young child. In 1910 he and his father moved to Edystone, Pennsylvania. Wilson left school at age sixteen to take a job at the Edystone Print Works. By this time his talent for playing baseball was becoming well known, and over the next few years he worked for a number of factories that sponsored semiprofessional baseball teams.

In 1921 Wilson's professional career began as a catcher with the Martinsburg, West Virginia, Blue Sox, a Class D minor league team in the Blue Ridge League. Following the advice of a major league scout, Wilson became an outfielder in 1922; the following year he was promoted to the Class B Portsmouth, Virginia, Truckers. After a successful 1923 season for Portsmouth, Wilson was sold to the New York Giants of the National League, then managed by John J. McGraw. He played briefly for the Giants at the end of the 1923 season, and he had a good year in 1924. However, in 1925 his offensive production slipped enough that he was farmed out to the Toledo Mudhens of the American Association. Left unprotected in the annual minor league draft, apparently as the result of a front office oversight, he was selected by the Chicago Cubs of the National League.

In six years with the Cubs, Wilson came into his own as a superb baseball player. He led the National League four times in home runs (1926, 1927, 1928, and 1930), and twice in runs batted in (1929 and 1930). His 1930 totals of 56 home runs and 190 runs batted in established longstanding National League records, and he was the first National League player to have had two consecutive seasons batting in more than 150 runs. He also led the National league in strikeouts in five seasons and in walks twice. He was not known for his defensive skills, but he led all National League outfielders in putouts in 1927.

Wilson played in the 1929 World Series, in which the Cubs faced the American League champion Philadelphia Athletics. Although he batted a superlative .471 in the series, he is better remembered for losing a fly ball in the sun in the seventh inning of the fourth game. His error enabled the Athletics to score ten runs in the inning, overcome an 8–0 Cubs lead, and win the game and, eventually, the series.

The 5′6″, 200-pound Wilson was known for his pugnacious manner both on and off the field. His nickname "Hack" first appeared in 1924, although its origins are unclear. The name may have been a shortening of Hackenschmidt, a great Russian strongman and wrestler of the day, or it may have derived from Hack Miller, a former outfielder and son of a circus strongman. Others claim that Giants manager McGraw coined the name, because Wilson looked to him like a "hack" or taxi. His late nights, frequent fights, and increasingly heavy drinking made him a disciplinary problem.

In 1931, after it became clear that he could not get along with the new Cubs manager, Rogers Hornsby, and that his skills had substantially declined, Wilson was traded to the St. Louis Cardinals. Before the 1932 season began he was sold to the Brooklyn Dodgers, where he played in 1933 and 1934. Released by the Dodgers in August 1934, he then played briefly for the Philadelphia Phillies. His career ended after 59 games with Albany, New York, of the International League in 1935. In his major league career of 1,348 games, Wilson hit .307, with 244 home runs and 1,062 runs batted in.

Wilson returned to Martinsburg, where he was a player manager of the Martinsburg Blue Sox, a semiprofessional team, through the 1936 season. With a friend, he established a business called the Recreation Center, which was a combined bar, café, and pool hall. He sold his interest to his partner after a year, and for the next several years he drifted around, drinking heavily, playing semiprofessional baseball, and holding menial jobs in various cities. In 1941 he began working for the Glenn Martin Company in Baltimore, an aircraft manufacturer, but within a year he was employed as a bartender. In 1948 he took a job with the Baltimore Park District, first as a grounds maintenance worker and later as a swimming pool attendant.

Wilson married Virginia Riddleberger in 1923; they had one son before they divorced in 1938. That same year he married Hazel Miller, who was institutionalized for an eating disorder in 1948. Wilson died in Baltimore from the effects of his alcoholism, impoverished and alone; the National League paid his funeral expenses. In 1979 Wilson was posthumously elected to the National Baseball Hall of Fame.

• The National Baseball Library, Cooperstown, N.Y., contains a clipping file on Wilson. Information on Wilson's career is in Ralph Hickok, *Who Was Who in American Sport* (1971); Warren Brown, *The Chicago Cubs* (1946); Jim Enright, *Chicago Cubs* (1973); and Lowell Reidenbaugh, *Cooperstown* (1983). A lengthy magazine article on Wilson is Mark Kram, "Why Ain't I in the Hall?" *Sports Illustrated*, 11 Apr. 1977, pp. 88ff. A useful source of limited accessibility is Clyde Partin, "Lewis Robert 'Hack' Wilson, 1900–1948," an unpublished paper presented at the annual meeting of the North American Society for Sport History in May 1977. Wilson's career statistics are in *The Baseball Encyclopedia*, 9th ed. (1993). An obituary is in the *New York Times*, 24 Nov. 1948.

JOHN E. FINDLING

WILSON, Halsey William (12 May 1868–1 Mar. 1954), bibliographer and publisher, was born in Wilmington, Vermont, the son of John Thompson Wilson, a stonecutter, and Althea Dunnell. An only child, Wilson lost both his parents to tuberculosis before he was three, and he spent his early childhood with his mother's parents, first in Shelburne Falls, Massachusetts, and later near Colrain. When Wilson was twelve, he went to live with an uncle on a farm near Waterloo, Iowa. After attending the preparatory academy associated with Beloit College, in Wisconsin, from 1883 to 1885, Wilson moved to Minneapolis, studying at the University of Minnesota intermittently from 1885 to 1892. Hardworking and energetic, he financed his educational pursuits in a variety of ways, including running a small printing operation from his room. In December 1889 he and his roommate formed a partnership to sell books to fellow students, a venture that proved to be so successful and time-consuming that Wilson discontinued his college studies to concentrate on managing and expanding the enterprise. He later purchased his partner's share of the bookshop with money inherited from his grandfather.

In 1895 Wilson married Justina Leavitt. Their only child, a son, died the day after he was born in 1897. By 1898 his thriving business had become the University Book Store, and Wilson, spurred by his need for a reliable and timely means of identifying new books, conceived the *Cumulative Book Index* (*CBI*). He and his wife compiled the early issues from their apartment, but he soon hired a full-time editor to oversee its production. Determined that each monthly issue of the *CBI* should cumulate the preceding ones, Wilson developed a process that would become a standard feature of his publications: saving and interfiling slugs of linotype to produce cumulative issues and volumes. Recognizing the need for a more extensive tool that would list all trade books currently in print in the United States, Wilson also developed the *United States Catalog*, publishing the first edition in 1899.

To promote the availability of his publications, Wilson attended meetings of librarians and booksellers, where he became aware of the lack of a current index to major magazines. Thus, in 1901 he introduced the *Readers' Guide to Periodical Literature*. First issued as a supplement to the *CBI*, this author and subject index to leading periodicals began to appear under its own title in just a few months. From the seven magazines indexed by the initial issue, the *Readers' Guide* expanded rapidly to include sixty-seven titles by 1905, when the first five-year cumulation was published. Covering the years 1900–1904, that volume exhibited the characteristics that were to become hallmarks of all Wilson periodical indexes: a dictionary arrangement, standardized subject headings, a system of cross-references, and a dedication to quality. Although Wilson initially set a flat subscription rate for the *Readers' Guide*, he later developed the service-basis method of charge, in which libraries paid according to the number of indexed periodicals that they actually received. He applied this unconventional method to other Wilson indexes as well, and he remained a strong proponent of the concept throughout his life, since it made these publications accessible to smaller libraries.

In 1903 Wilson incorporated his business as the H. W. Wilson Company, selling shares of preferred stock to employees, university faculty, librarians, and friends. Two years later, he launched the *Book Review Digest*, a compilation of excerpts from book reviews, to meet the demand from librarians for timely assessments of new publications. Later observing that he had been struck by an incurable malady called the "Bibliographic Urge," the indefatigable Wilson created other new publications in rapid succession. In 1907 both the *Readers' Guide Supplement* (later, the *International Index*, then *Social Sciences and Humanities Index*, before splitting into two publications) and the *Debaters' Handbook* series (later, the *Reference Shelf*) were introduced. The *Fiction Catalog* appeared in 1908, followed in 1909 by the *Children's Catalog*, marking the beginning of the Standard Catalog Series of selective, annotated bibliographies for smaller libraries. Wilson established yet another facet of his operation in 1910, creating the Magazine Department (later, Periodicals Clearing House), which offered a central source from which librarians could purchase back issues.

By 1913, when his firm had published nearly ninety titles and had grown to more than 100 employees, Wilson decided that it was imperative to be nearer the hub of the publishing world. Selling his bookstore, which had long subsidized his bibliographical ventures, he moved his publishing concern to White Plains, New York, where the *Industrial Arts Index* (which later split into the *Applied Science and Technology Index* and *Business Index*) was born in 1913, followed by the *Agricultural Index* (later, *Biological and Agricultural Index*) in 1916. In 1914 the company also created a house organ, the *Wilson Bulletin*, which evolved into the *Wilson Library Bulletin*, a highly regarded professional journal until its demise in 1995. Under the pseudonym Harold Workman Williams, Wilson himself co-compiled the *Toaster's Handbook*, an anthology of jokes, stories, and quotations, issued in three editions between 1914 and 1916.

When his company outgrew its quarters in 1917, Wilson relocated to the Bronx borough of New York City. He found time to write *The Bookman's Reading and Tools*, a guide for beginning booksellers, first published in 1925 and issued in a revised version in 1932, and he also played a significant role in developing the *Union List of Serials in Libraries of the United States and Canada* (1927), publishing both it and its 1943 successor on a nonprofit basis. In 1929 the Pennsylvania Library Association became the first of many organizations and institutions to honor Wilson, presenting him with a gold medal in recognition of his "services to American libraries." During the next two decades Wilson oversaw the inauguration of numerous new publications, including *Education Index* and *Art Index* (both begun in 1929), *Famous First Facts* (1933), *Junior Book of Authors* (1934), *Current Biography* (1940), and *Biography Index* (1946). In 1938 he initiated a service that provided sets of printed catalog cards for new titles likely to be included in the Standard Catalog Series.

Early in his career Wilson adopted a philosophy that placed professional service over profit making. This commitment did not go unrecognized, for, when it elected Wilson as an honorary member in 1945, the American Library Association observed that he had "conducted his bibliographic activities in the spirit of service rather than merely for commercial gain." Wilson received an Outstanding Achievement medal from the University of Minnesota in 1948, but perhaps his highest honor came in 1950, when the American Library Association presented him with the Joseph W. Lippincott Award for Outstanding Achievement in Librarianship.

In 1952 Wilson stepped down as president of the company, but he remained active as chairman of the board. When he died at his home in Yorktown Heights, New York, the H. W. Wilson Company, with 450 employees and sales of over two million dollars, was publishing more than twenty major indexes, in addition to a wide variety of general reference books. Following the death of Justina Wilson in 1955, the Wilsons' estate went to the H. W. Wilson Foundation, which had been established earlier to benefit former employees and which continues to fund library school scholarships and other library-related programs and projects.

With an extraordinary mixture of vision, vitality, ingenuity, and business acumen, Wilson had guided his company to become the preeminent publisher of indexes and bibliographic tools of the first half of the twentieth century. The extent to which he solicited cooperation, advice, and counsel from the library world was unprecedented, and he was an innovator not only in developing new reference sources and publishing technologies but also in adopting enlightened employment practices. From the very beginning he hired many more women than men, placing them in responsible positions as editors, indexers, and members of the board. In addition, he established a pension fund, employed the physically handicapped, and provided health insurance benefits and cumulative sick pay.

Contemporaries of Wilson invariably noted his kindliness, lack of pretentiousness, and penchant for puns. The significance of his contributions to the world of scholarship was aptly summarized by the American Library Association, which, on the occasion of the H. W. Wilson Company's fiftieth anniversary in 1948, approved a resolution recognizing Wilson for developing "the most important bibliographical enterprise ever conceived and brought to fruition by any one man."

• Very few of Wilson's papers are extant. The H. W. Wilson Company has only a single folder of his business correspondence. Letters from Wilson to R. R. Bowker concerning their efforts to avoid duplication in their publishing activities are in the Richard Rogers Bowker Papers, Rare Books and Manuscripts Division, New York Public Library, and in the files of *Publishers Weekly*, New York City. The Francis S. Chapin Papers in the University of Minnesota Archives contain several Wilson letters, as do the Theodore Wesley Koch Papers in the Bentley Historical Library, University of Michigan. In addition to the *Toaster's Handbook* and *The Bookman's Reading and Tools*, Wilson published a number of papers and articles pertaining to library-related issues.

Invaluable for basic biographical information about Wilson and its detailed account of the company's history is John Lawler, *The H. W. Wilson Company: Half a Century of Bibliographic Publishing* (1950), which includes a company bibliography. Also important for early company history is *A Quarter Century of Cumulative Bibliography: Retrospect and Prospect* (1923). For Wilson's views on his company's first fifty years, see his "Random Reminiscences," *Wilson Library Bulletin* 22 (June 1948): 779–83. Other useful articles pertaining to the company's history appear in that same issue. Providing a more recent perspective is Arthur Plotnik, "H. W. Wilson," in the *Encyclopedia of Library and Information Science* vol. 10 (1973), pp. 250–78.

The prestige that Wilson enjoyed during his lifetime and the unique niche that his company occupied during the first half of the twentieth century are reflected in Creighton Peet, "A Mousetrap in the Bronx," *New Yorker*, 29 Oct. 1938, pp. 25–28 (see also a letter correcting two "misstatements of fact," 12 Nov. 1938, p. 60), and Jack Harrison Pollack, "Giant of Bibliographers," *Saturday Review of Literature*, 3 Feb. 1951, pp. 32–34. Also useful for its personal insights is Howard Haycraft, "'Mr. Wilson'—An Informal Reminiscence," *Wilson Library Bulletin* 29 (Sept. 1954): 52–57. Obituaries are in the *New York Times*, and the *New York Herald Tribune*, both 2 Mar. 1954, and *Wilson Library Bulletin* 28 (Apr. 1954): 664–68.

MARIE C. ELLIS

WILSON, Harriet E. (c. 1828–c. 1863), writer, was born Harriet E. Adams, probably in Milford, New Hampshire, the daughter of parents whose names and occupations are not recorded. According to Wilson's autobiographical novel, *Our Nig* (1859), which simultaneously constitutes Wilson's claim to an identity as a fiction writer and provides a version of the facts of her life, her father was a free black artisan and her white mother was an occasional domestic servant. Wilson's formal education was apparently limited to a few years at a one-room country school.

Alfrado or Frado, the heroine of *Our Nig*, was abandoned by her mother and stepfather at the age of six. Margaretta Thorn, one of three friends who provided supporting biographical statements in an appendix to the novel, says Wilson was "taken from her home so young." Thorn also confirms the novel's description of the cruel people with whom Wilson was left and whose indentured servant (Thorn says, "indeed a slave in every sense of the word") she became.

Most of the text of the novel describes the unremitting labor, severe deprivation, and harsh treatment that Frado was accorded during the years of her servitude. The novel, however, also devotes a good deal of attention to the other members of the family who attempted to alleviate Frado's sufferings by assuring that she obtained the rudiments of an education, insisting, sometimes successfully, on better food and less vicious treatment of the young black girl. They also introduced her, by precept and example, to true Christianity, although neither the statements in the appendix nor the official documents that have been recovered can corroborate this kindness. Evidence of both secular and religious education may be seen, however, in her choosing to write her story at all and in the fact that her writing itself is grammatically correct and descriptively vivid, reflecting Wilson's familiarity with poets from Byron and Shelley to Eliza Cook and Thomas Moore, as well as with the Bible and traditional Protestant hymns.

In the novel, the efforts to help Frado were only partially successful, as demonstrated by her poor health once the period of indenture ended; her condition rapidly worsened, so that she was soon unable to continue working for her new, kinder employer. In the appendix, Thorn says that Wilson never "enjoyed any degree of comfortable health since she was eighteen years of age."

The character Frado spent several years as a public charge and working as a domestic when her health permitted. According to the statement in the appendix signed "Allida," Wilson, whose constitution was "greatly impaired" by "former harsh treatment," was eventually taken into the home of a poor woman in a Massachusetts town that was a center for the production, by hand-sewing, of straw bonnets. Both the move to Massachusetts and the straw-sewing work are also described in the novel. Allida's narrative refers to Wilson's benefactress as Mrs. Walker and calls the town W——. The towns of Westborough, Ware, Walpole, and Worcester not only qualify alphabetically but also were towns in which the straw hat industry was established. In *Our Nig*, Frado continued to work at straw-sewing, eventually surpassing her teacher in her expertise with the needle. Allida writes, "being very ingenious . . . [Wilson] soon acquired the art of making hats."

Both Allida's statement and Wilson's novel agree that their protagonist believed in her work in W—— and in her new home she had found her place in the world, and she was happy in it. At this point in both versions, a man who represented himself as a fugitive slave to dramatize the oratory of an itinerant abolitionist lecturer made his appearance in her life. Both the novel and the biographical appendix describe Wilson-Frado as falling in love with this man and marrying him. Historical records show that Harriet Adams was married to Thomas Wilson on 6 October 1851 in Milford, New Hampshire, by the Reverend Ephraim N. Hidden, a member of the Congregational clergy.

Thomas Wilson had abandoned his wife by the time their son, George Mason Wilson, was born in late May or early June 1852. In her novel, Harriet Wilson writes that the husband, Samuel, ran away, and she exposes him as a sham who had never even seen the South, much less been a slave who had escaped bondage. (In the marriage record, Thomas Wilson's home is listed as "Virginia.") Wilson's child was born at the Hillsborough County Farm, an institution for indigent members of the community, in Goffstown, New Hampshire.

Wilson's own husband, and her character's, returned and briefly supported his wife and child, but soon deserted them again. In the novel, he is killed off; in the actual 1855 census records, Harriet Wilson is listed as a widow. Wilson—and her widowed protagonist—tries to support herself and provide for her son. Although her wish was to make a home for him and educate him, he was consigned in both fact and fiction to a kindly, apparently white couple who rescued him from the county farm and took him to live with them.

Still in poor health, both Frado and Wilson live by manufacturing and marketing a home remedy. The nature of the remedy is not specified in the novel, but Allida says it was a formula for restoring graying hair to its original color. In the last pages of the novel, Wilson explains that writing her "autobiography," which she got (privately) printed, rather than being published by a commercial house, was intended to supplement these earnings. In a sense the novel was another kind of home remedy. *Our Nig* was copyrighted on 18 August 1859 and published on 5 September, thus making it the first novel published by a black person in the United States.

Wilson's son died in Milford, New Hampshire, on 13 or 15 February 1860, less than six months after the publication of the book whose material purpose was to earn money for his support. The novel thus did not succeed in its announced primary goal of enabling its author to care for her child. Although a death certificate exists for the boy, the only information about his mother's life after his death is her listing in the annual Boston directories for 1855 through 1863. She is presumed to have died in the 1860s.

By tracing Wilson's life through her novel, the reader can discern the relationship between the life story it narrates and the reasons for telling it. The novel is subtitled "Sketches from the Life of a Free Black, in a Two-story White House, North. Showing That Slavery's Shadows Fall Even There." So, although Wilson candidly announces that she is telling her story as a way of earning needed money, even the subtitle reflects a larger didactic purpose, one that, if low sales and absence of public attention are accurate guides, discomforted rather than enlightened the northern audience. The novel was obscure in its own time and was lost to literary history until it was rediscovered by Henry Louis Gates, Jr., in 1982.

In his introduction to the reprinted text (1983), Gates emphasizes the extraordinary act of will involved in claiming for herself the racist epithet "Our Nig" that is the book's main title. He summarizes the overall import of the novel:

Its presence attests to a direct relation between the will and being of a sort rarely so explicit. Harriet E. Wilson's project, as bold and as unsure as it promised to be, failed to allow her to regain possession of her son. In this sense, Mrs. Wilson's project was a failure. Nevertheless, her legacy is an attestation of the will to power as the will to write. The transformation of the black-as-object into the black-as-subject: this is what Mrs. Harriet E. Wilson manifests for the first time in the writings of Afro-American women.

• *Our Nig* (1859; reissued with an introduction by Henry Louis Gates, Jr., 1983) is the only known work of Harriet E. Wilson. The testimonial statements in the appendix, signed by "Allida," Margaretta Thorn, and "C. D. S.," corroborate parts of the novel. The official documents and records cited by Gates are, he says, sufficient to establish "her existence and her authorship . . . [but remain] frustratingly sparse." Although Wilson's name does not appear in most historical, literary, or bibliographical sources, Gates has found mentions of her or her novel in six sources: John Herbert Nelson, *The Negro Character in American Literature* (1926; repr. 1968); Herbert Ross Brown, *The Sentimental Novel in America, 1789–1860* (1940), in which it is implied that H. E. Wilson was a white male; Monroe N. Work, *A Bibliography of the Negro in Africa and America* (1928), where Wilson is again listed as white; James Joseph McKinney's dissertation, "The Theme of Miscegenation in the American Novel to World War I" (1972); Geraldine Matthews's bibliography, *Black American Writers, 1773–1949* (1975); and Carol Fairbanks and Eugene A. Engeldinger, *Black American Fiction: A Bibliography* (1978). Gates's essay, "Parallel Discursive Universes: Fictions of the Self in Harriet E. Wilson's *Our Nig*," in his *Figures in Black, Words, Signs, and the "Racial Self"* (1987), offers both a comprehensive critical interpretation of the text and a fourteen-page chart showing the parallels between Wilson's text and the documentary evidence about her life.

LILLIAN S. ROBINSON

WILSON, Harry Leon (1 May 1867–28 June 1939), novelist and playwright, was born in Oregon, Illinois, the son of Samuel Wilson, a small-town newspaper owner and editor, and Adeline Kidder. Wilson's early life provided the sort of grass-roots traditional American experience that emerged in his best fiction. A year after the death of his father in 1883, he moved to Topeka, Kansas, where he learned typing and shorthand as preparation for a secretarial position. He worked as a stenographer for the Union Pacific Railway in Omaha and in 1885 was promoted to the Denver office, which he left to work as a researcher—traveling about interviewing pioneers—for Hubert Howe Bancroft's *History of the Pacific States of North America*. In 1887 he moved to southern California to work on Bancroft's *Chronicles of the Builders of the Commonwealth*. In 1889 he returned to Omaha as secretary for the Union Pacific Railway.

During these years, Wilson wrote fiction, taking the stories in *Puck*, one of the nation's leading humor magazines, as a model. In 1892, after publishing frequently in *Puck*, he accepted a position as a reader, the beginning of a ten-year association with the magazine, where he rose to editor in 1896. In 1899 Wilson married Wilbertine Teters Worden, who divorced him in

1900 because of attentions he paid to a woman at yachting parties. Wilson's memories of this situation were so painful that his children did not even know of his first marriage until they began managing his affairs near the end of his life.

Tiring of his editorial duties, Wilson set out to write a novel that would give him financial freedom. He worked with the encouragement of Rose O'Neill Latham, a highly talented illustrator, whom he married as soon as *The Spenders* (1902) and its dramatic adaptation proved highly lucrative. They had no children. The Wilsons retired to "Bonnie Brook," the O'Neill family home in the Ozarks, where he wrote three moderately successful novels, *Lions of the Lord* (1903), *The Seekers* (1904), and *The Boss of Little Arcady* (1905). In company with Booth Tarkington and his wife, the Wilsons sailed for Europe in 1905, first settling in Capri and then in Paris. The popularity of the first of their dramatic collaborations, *The Man from Home* (1907), inspired them to write five more plays in the next three years.

Wilson's heavy drinking and irascibility strained his marriage to the breaking point, and he and his wife separated after returning to the United States in September 1907. In 1910 he established himself at "Ocean Home," near Carmel, California, where he did the work for which he became best known. Realizing that the trend in drama was toward realism, Wilson turned again to the novel. His *Bunker Bean*, serialized in the *Saturday Evening Post* in 1912 and published by Doubleday the following year, established him as a *Post* author. *Bunker Bean* was followed by *Ruggles of Red Gap* (1915), *Merton of the Movies* (1922), *Oh, Doctor!* (1923) and *Professor How Could You!* (1924). *Merton of the Movies* became a highly successful film in 1922 as did *Ruggles of Red Gap* in 1937.

Wilson's conservatism and populist social values found extraordinary skillful expression in his humorous novels. He won the respect of critics as different as H. L. Mencken and William Dean Howells. His most fundamental attitudes are expressed with only slight hyperbole by his creation, Ruggles, an English manservant converted to things American: "I mean to say, having frankly taken up America, I was at last resolved to do it whole-heartedly. If I could not take up the whole of it, I would not take up a part. Quite instinctively I had chosen the slogan of our Chamber of Commerce: 'Don't Knock—Boost; and Boost Altogether'" (*Ruggles of Red Gap*, p. 357).

In 1912 Wilson married Helen Cooke, the seventeen-year-old daughter of novelist Grace MacGowan Cooke. They had two children. The Wilsons separated in 1926 and divorced in 1928; Helen Wilson remained at Ocean Home and Harry Wilson moved to Portland, Oregon, where he remained until 1929, when he again occupied Ocean Home.

In 1932 an automobile accident left Wilson with a degree of mental impairment, including memory lapses and loss of concentration. He now wrote with great difficulty and his last book, *When in the Course*, was rejected by the *Saturday Evening Post* and published posthumously in 1940. In 1936 he began suffering from the series of strokes that led to his death. Wilson, who lost Ocean Home for financial reasons in 1939, died in Carmel.

Although Wilson was a highly skillful humorist, it is doubtful that he will ever again be widely read, for there is no longer an audience that appreciates his glorification of the average American. His biographer George Kummer says quite accurately,

> From time to time . . . Wilson wistfully dreamed of writing a novel that would place his name on the roll of the illustrious in literature, but whenever he began this masterpiece, it soon turned into something comical, and, like his hero, Merton Gill, he had to reconcile himself to being what God meant him to be—a comedian. As such he made the most of his talent. (pp. 151–52)

• Most of Wilson's papers are at the University of California, Berkeley, with smaller collections at Harvard, the New York Public Library, and Princeton. Other important plays Wilson wrote with Booth Tarkington are *Cameo Kirby* (1908), *Foreign Exchange* (1909), *If I Had Money* (1909), *Springtime* (1909), *Your Humble Servant* (1910), *Up from Nowhere* (1919), *Tweedles* (1923), and *How's Your Health?* (1929). In addition, Wilson's *Life* was the 1919 Grove Play of the Bohemian Club of San Francisco. Tarkington's summation is in the *Saturday Review of Literature*, 12 Aug. 1939, pp. 9–10. George Kummer, *Harry Leon Wilson: Some Account of the Triumphs and Tribulations of an American Popular Writer* (1963), is an attractive treatment of Wilson's life. An obituary is in the *New York Times*, 30 June 1939.

MARYJEAN GROSS
DALTON GROSS

WILSON, Henry (16 Feb. 1812–22 Nov. 1875), U.S. senator and vice president, was born in Farmington, New Hampshire, and christened Jeremiah Jones Colbath, the son of Winthrop Colbath, Jr., a laborer, and Abigail Witham. When he was ten his father arranged with a local farmer to take him as an apprentice for the next eleven years, an experience that left the young Jeremiah with a lifelong appreciation for the tribulations of working men. On his twenty-first birthday Colbath, apparently hoping to repudiate his poverty-stricken past, changed his name to Henry Wilson and left his home for Natick, Massachusetts, where he became a shoemaker. In New Hampshire he had had little time for school; in Massachusetts he was able to save enough money from shoemaking to attend local academies for about a year.

In 1840 he married Harriet Malvina Howe; they had one child. Also in 1840 he was elected to the lower house of the Massachusetts legislature, and from that time on he sacrificed everything for his political career, including his business. Although by 1847 Wilson employed more than one hundred workers, he had no intention of remaining a shoe manufacturer. Political opponents nicknamed him the "Natick Cobbler," an intended slur that he quickly turned to his advantage. Between 1840 and 1852 he was elected to the state legislature eight times.

A career in politics enabled Wilson to satisfy his powerful ambition. He reveled in the machinations involved in building coalitions and controlling elections, but he also became devoted to political activity because it offered him a means of fulfilling his strong commitment to social and moral reform. Wilson was a firm believer in the superiority of the northern free-labor economy that allowed men like himself to succeed through their own efforts, and he wanted to guarantee such opportunities for others. As a state legislator he supported public schools, temperance reform, a mechanic's lien law, a secret ballot, a reduction in the poll tax, and the abolition of imprisonment for debt.

The causes that dominated his political career, however, were the abolition of slavery and the establishment of equal rights for black Americans. A visit in 1836 to Washington, D.C., where he first witnessed slavery, left him with a strong revulsion against the institution. As a champion of free labor, he warned that the same prejudices of class and race that subjugated blacks could also oppress poor white workers. He became an abolitionist because, he concluded, the slaves were the most degraded and helpless victims of society. In the Massachusetts legislature he called for the elimination of segregated schools, the repeal of laws forbidding interracial marriages and barring blacks from the state militia, and the passage of a civil rights law.

Although Wilson was morally opposed to slavery, he also resented the political influence of the southern planters, whom he referred to as the "slave power," and endeavored to create an antislavery party capable of wresting control of the federal government from the slaveholders. In 1866 he contended that "I have always subordinated political organizations . . . to the overshadowing issues growing out of the existence of slavery, the domination of the slave power, and the rights and privileges of the African race" (*Congressional Globe*, 39th Cong., 2d. sess., p. 191). Initially he joined the Whig party, partly because it already controlled Massachusetts, but also because he believed it to be more antislavery than its Democratic rival. He became a leader of the Conscience Whigs, who urged their party to take a strong stand against slavery expansion; when it failed to do so, in 1848 he left the Whigs to help found the Free Soil party, which was dedicated to that end. From 1848 to 1851 he edited the Boston *Republican*, a Free Soil newspaper. In 1851 Wilson organized a coalition between Massachusetts Free Soilers and Democrats that elected Charles Sumner, a strong antislavery man, to the U.S. Senate. In 1854, following the collapse of the Free Soil party, Wilson joined the newly emerged Know Nothing or American party, swallowing his distaste for its nativist doctrines because he hoped to convert it to an antislavery organization. In 1855 the Know Nothing legislature elected him to the U.S. Senate, an office to which he would be returned three times.

Secure in his new post, and deciding that the Know Nothings were doomed, Wilson helped organize the Republican party and remained loyal to it for the rest of his life. The new party was strongly opposed to slavery expansion, and Wilson devoted every effort to helping it win control of the federal government. Because of his strong antislavery views and his efforts to keep slavery out of the Kansas Territory during the Kansas crisis of 1855–1858, Wilson could be regarded as a member of the radical wing of the Republican party. He also voted for proposals that would strengthen the North's free-labor economy, including land grants to railroads, tariffs for industry, fishing bounties for New England fishermen, and homesteads for western farmers. In 1860 he traveled thousands of miles and gave more than one hundred speeches for the Republican presidential candidate, Abraham Lincoln. When Lincoln's victory resulted in the secession of the southern states Wilson opposed efforts to resolve the crisis by compromising sectional differences over slavery in the territories.

After the Civil War began in 1861, Wilson, who served as chairman of the Senate Military Affairs Committee, drew on his considerable political and legislative skills to draft and secure passage of the Union's manpower procurement laws, including the 1862 Militia Draft Act and the 1863 Enrollment Act. In gaining approval for these measures, Wilson demonstrated his ability to compromise and balance competing views and interests. As the first federal conscription law, the Enrollment Act helped raise and organize the armies that fought from 1863 to 1865, but it contained enough concessions to state governors jealous of their prerogatives and to businessmen fearful of being drafted themselves or losing their laborers to the war to weaken opposition to it and facilitate its implementation.

Wilson also conducted an unremitting campaign to abolish slavery and to recruit black men into the federal forces. He constantly pressured President Lincoln to issue an emancipation proclamation and whenever possible used legislation to secure the same end. One of his proudest achievements was introducing a measure in 1862 abolishing slavery in the District of Columbia. His militia draft bill authorized the president to enroll blacks, including slaves, for military service. Later legislation he sponsored granted freedom to slaves inducted into the army as well as to their families and provided black troops with the same bounties and pay as whites. In addition, he and his colleague Sumner obtained legislation securing equal civil rights for blacks in the District of Columbia. Wilson also played a critical role in the creation of the Freedmen's Bureau, a federal agency charged with overseeing the welfare of the former slaves.

After the Civil War ended in 1865, the ensuing struggle over the status of almost four million freed slaves absorbed Wilson's political and legislative skills. He was horrified by the Black Codes that former Confederate states enacted in 1865 and 1866 to severely restrict the freedom of former slaves, and he warned that "the dark spirits of slavery still live." Although Wilson supported federal legislation protecting the civil rights of the freedmen, he was convinced that granting them suffrage was the best way to secure their equal treatment. Realizing that such action would be unpopular with most whites in both the North and the South, he was willing to limit voting to blacks who could meet property or literacy requirements or who had served in the Union armies.

After the Republicans increased their power in Congress in the 1866 elections, Wilson endorsed universal suffrage and played a major role in writing the Reconstruction acts that required southern states to enfranchise black males before being readmitted to the Union. In 1869 he failed to obtain a provision in the Fifteenth Amendment protecting black rights to elective office as well as to the vote; in 1871–1872 he backed Sumner's efforts to prohibit segregation in schools and public accommodations throughout the nation.

For his support of black enfranchisement, because he voted for the impeachment of Lincoln's successor, President Andrew Johnson, and for his resistance to the congressional Reconstruction program, Wilson was known as a Radical Republican. Unlike some Radicals, however, he did not advocate confiscation and redistribution of southern plantation land, and he revealed no vindictiveness toward former Confederates. Although he supported federal enforcement laws to protect black rights against white violence organized by the Ku Klux Klan, Wilson believed that if racial justice were to prevail in the South, whites would have to play a role in the process. To encourage them to do so, as soon as the war ended he sought the release of Confederate leaders from jail and he consistently opposed depriving them of the right to vote or hold office. As soon as Congress finished enacting its Reconstruction program in 1867, he left to tour the South, hoping to coax whites to ally with blacks in the Republican party; it was a goal he continued to pursue for the rest of his life.

Although Wilson spent much of his time in the Senate pushing for racial justice, he continued to advocate other reforms. He supported an eight-hour day for government workers, opposed the importation of contract labor, backed civil service reform, and endorsed woman suffrage and federal aid to education. In 1868 he worked hard to secure the election of Union general Ulysses S. Grant, the Republican presidential candidate, and in 1872 the Republican party rewarded him for his long service by nominating and electing him vice president on Grant's ticket. To his frustration, he had little influence on administration policies. Eager to establish his place in history, Wilson spent his last years writing his monumental three-volume *History of the Rise and Fall of the Slave Power in America* (1872–1877), which was almost completed when he died in the vice president's room in the U.S. Capitol. Because Wilson was personally involved in many of the events leading to the Civil War and gathered a tremendous amount of data in his books, they remain a useful source for historians studying the controversy over slavery.

A common man himself, Wilson was sensitive to the limitations public opinion placed on politicians, and his contemporaries frequently complained that he compromised principles to expediency. A Boston journalist who knew him well, William S. Robinson, observed that "hence he is a legislator easily moved from his position, but never from his purpose" (*Boston Commonwealth*, 28 Jan. 1865). In his two-volume *Reminiscences of Sixty Years in Public Life* (1902), Massachusetts Republican George S. Boutwell admitted that Wilson's "political career was tortuous" but contended that "in all his windings he was true to the cause of human liberty" (vol. 1, p. 79). Ultimately Wilson left a significant legislative record that demonstrated how the political process he manipulated could serve the nation's interest, especially by achieving justice for black Americans.

• Small collections of Wilson's papers are in the Library of Congress and in the Natick Historical Society Museum of South Natick, Mass. Besides the *Rise and Fall of the Slave Power*, Wilson's major writings include *Antislavery Measures of the Thirty-seventh and Thirty-eighth Congresses, 1861–1864* (1864) and *Reconstruction Measures of the Thirty-ninth and Fortieth Congresses, 1865–1868* (1868). On the preparation of his major work, see John L. Myers, "The Writing of the *History of the Rise and Fall of the Slave Power in America*," *Civil War History* 31 (1985): 144–62. Two modern biographies of Wilson are Richard H. Abbott, *Cobbler in Congress: The Life of Henry Wilson, 1812–1875* (1972), and Ernest A. McKay, *Henry Wilson, Practical Radical: Portrait of a Reformer* (1971). A useful collection of obituaries prepared by members of Congress who knew Wilson is in *Memorial Addresses on the Life and Character of Henry Wilson* (1876).

RICHARD H. ABBOTT

WILSON, Henry Lane (3 Nov. 1857–22 Dec. 1932), diplomat, was born in Crawfordsville, Indiana, the son of James Wilson, a congressman, soldier in the Mexican and Civil wars, and diplomat, and Emma Ingersoll. He graduated from Wabash College in 1879, read law in the office of McDonald and Butler in Indianapolis, and practiced briefly until 1882, when he became the owner and editor of the Lafayette, Indiana, *Journal*. In 1884 he married Alice Vajen; they had three sons. The following year Wilson moved to Spokane, Washington, where he practiced law and engaged in banking and buying and selling real estate. He prospered until 1893, when the financial panic and ensuing depression took most of his fortune.

An active member of the Republican party, Wilson first campaigned for his older brother, John Lockwood Wilson, a member of the House of Representatives and senator from the state of Washington. He supported the presidential aspirations of Benjamin Harrison and William McKinley. When in 1889 President Harrison offered Wilson the ministerial post in Venezuela—the post Wilson's father had occupied at the time of his death in 1867—Wilson declined. On 9 June 1897 President McKinley appointed him as minister to Chile, where he remained until 1904. While in Santiago his service was routine. He was critical of the

Chilean government's inflationary policies, closely observed possible violations of neutrality during the Spanish-American War, reported criticisms of the growing power and influence of the United States, and offered his country's good offices to settle a Chile-Argentine boundary dispute. In 1911 the University of Chile awarded Wilson a doctorate of philosophy, humanities, and fine arts for his labors while in that country.

Wilson's refusal in 1902 to accept a post in Greece temporarily angered President Theodore Roosevelt but did not prevent Wilson's appointment as minister to Belgium in 1905, after spending a few months in the United States observing, at Roosevelt's behest, public opinion and political trends in several key states during the election of 1904. The years in Brussels were quite uneventful for Wilson. He attended, as a guest, the Hague Conference on International Peace in 1907 and was one of two special U.S. representatives for the coronation of King Albert in 1909.

After William Howard Taft's election as president, Wilson was considered for ambassadorial posts in Russia, Austria, and Turkey. He preferred the ambassadorship in Mexico, to which he was appointed upon the urgings of Senators Henry Cabot Lodge (1850–1924) and Elihu Root. Wilson's service in Mexico, beginning in March 1910, was the most notable and controversial of his diplomatic career. He presented his credentials to President Porfirio Díaz, but a year later he was predicting the fall of Díaz in the face of a growing revolutionary movement. After the exile of Díaz and the inauguration of Francisco I. Madero, Wilson had little faith in the new president's ability to control Mexico and, as revolution spread, seemed obsessive in pressing him on reported violations of U.S. citizens' rights. After fighting broke out between government and rebel forces in Mexico City in February 1913, Wilson convinced the Taft administration to mobilize naval forces along the Mexican coasts and, on his own, joined in a call for Madero to resign. When General Victoriano Huerta, commander of the government forces, decided to betray the president, the general informed Wilson of his intent. A few hours after Madero's arrest on 18 February, the ambassador invited Huerta and anti-Maderista leader Felix Díaz to use the embassy for concluding an agreement allowing Huerta to become provisional president. Wilson urged Mexicans to back Huerta and urged the U.S. government to recognize the new regime. The Taft administration ignored the advice, particularly after the killings of Madero and his vice president, who were shot while reportedly attempting to escape. Concern for the fallen president's safety allegedly had brought only half-hearted diplomatic representations from the ambassador.

The question of recognition remained for the new Woodrow Wilson administration. Despite continued assertions by Ambassador Wilson that Huerta would preserve order and protect U.S. interests in Mexico, the new administration was not moved and within a short time had lost faith in Ambassador Wilson's reports. The president relied more on special emissaries, such as William Bayard Hale, whose reports were critical of the ambassador's actions during the Huerta-Díaz coup. The president recalled Ambassador Wilson under guise of consultation but with the purpose of removing him. Wilson left Mexico on 17 July 1913 and returned to Indiana; his resignation was announced on 4 August. The announcement explained that his resignation was solicited because of the ambassador's part in earlier stages of the Mexican Revolution, but rumor held that the reason was his continued advocacy of Huerta's recognition.

During World War I Wilson was president of the Indiana branch of the League to Enforce Peace. He resigned in January 1917 because he thought some of its leaders were advocating a world alliance as proposed by President Wilson in an address to the Senate on 22 January 1917 and probably because of growing political partisanship on the Republican side regarding league proposals after the president's endorsement. During the presidencies of Warren G. Harding and Calvin Coolidge, he remained active in business and served as counsel for U.S. oil interests in Latin America. In 1927 the former ambassador's memoir, *Diplomatic Episodes in Mexico, Belgium, and Chile*, in which he defended his activities in Mexico, was published. He died in Indianapolis.

• Wilson's dispatches and telegrams and State Department instructions to him are among the records of the Department of State, RG 59, National Archives. Selections of these documents are published in the *Papers Relating to the Foreign Relations of the United States* for the appropriate years and countries. Books and articles about Wilson almost exclusively concern his tenure as ambassador to Mexico, and most historical accounts of this ambassadorship are critical. These include Lowell L. Blaisdell, "Henry Lane Wilson and the Overthrow of Madero," *Southwestern Social Science Quarterly* 43 (1962): 126–35; Walter V. Scholes and Marie V. Scholes, *The Foreign Policies of the Taft Administration* (1970); Howard F. Cline, *The United States and Mexico* (1963); Peter Calvert, *The Mexican Revolution, 1910–1914: The Diplomacy of Anglo-American Conflict* (1968); Arthur S. Link, *Wilson: The New Freedom* (1956); and Edward I. Bell, *The Political Shame of Mexico* (1914). Obituaries are in the *New York Times*, the *Crawfordsville Journal and Review*, and the *Indianapolis Star*, all 23 Dec. 1932.

WILLIAM KAMMAN

WILSON, Henry Van Peters (16 Feb. 1863–4 Jan. 1939), biologist, was born in Baltimore, Maryland, the son of Samuel Augustine Wilson, a clergyman, and Sophia Ann Stansbury. His father was a circuit rider in Maryland, Virginia, and Pennsylvania, then served in churches in Baltimore and Washington, D.C., until he retired from active service in the ministry and became a postal inspector. Both parents encouraged reading and study.

After attending the Baltimore City College (essentially a high school), Wilson entered the new Johns Hopkins University in 1880, intending to study medicine. Instead he received his A. B. degree in 1883 and continued for one more year of undergraduate biology. He enrolled in the University of Maryland Medical School but left after a few weeks, then served for a year as private tutor in zoology to the manufacturer Edward Phelps Allis, Jr. Allis's enthusiasm for biological research led him to establish the Allis Lake Laboratory in Milwaukee (directed by Charles Otis Whitman) and to provide financial support for the *Journal of Morphology*.

The next year, 1885, Wilson began his graduate studies in zoology with the morphologist William Keith Brooks. He joined most of Brooks's other outstanding students, including Thomas Hunt Morgan, Ross Granville Harrison, and Edwin Grant Conklin, in the study of marine embryology. Wilson concentrated on coral and completed his dissertation, "On the Development of *Manicina areolata*," in 1888. After a year supported by an Adam T. Bruce postdoctoral fellowship, with which he began his marine studies on sponges in the Bahamas, Wilson spent two years as scientific assistant at the U.S. Fish Commission's facility in Woods Hole, Massachusetts. His *Embryology of the Sea Bass* (1891) from that period provides a classic study of vertebrate embryology, complete with excellent illustrations.

In 1891 Wilson moved to the University of North Carolina in Chapel Hill, where he remained active in teaching and research until his death. Although the university expected its faculty to pursue research, it provided relatively little support for it. Wilson's biographer, Donald Costello, sketches a dedicated, strong-willed professor making his way by foot through muddy streets to ill-equipped laboratories with very basic equipment. This was a small university just undertaking a significant expansion, and as head of the one-man biology department, Wilson carried a heavy load. He added to his responsibilities by teaching and carrying out research at the U.S. Fisheries Department marine station at Beaufort, North Carolina, which he and a colleague in geology helped to organize. Partly as a result of these conditions, Wilson had relatively few graduate students. In 1893 he married Edith Theresa Stickney, who died in 1900, leaving two daughters and one son. A sister helped with housekeeping at first, then Wilson's daughters took over; he lived alone after his children moved on.

Continued research trips to marine stations brought new research materials, especially among the lower invertebrates, and new studies of development, regeneration, and classification, so that Wilson maintained an active research career. He produced more than ninety articles, including "Observations on the Gemmule and Egg Development of Marine Sponges" (*Journal of Morphology* [1894]) and "On Some Phenomena of Coalescence and Regeneration in Sponges" (*Journal of Experimental Zoology* [1907]), despite his relative isolation and heavy teaching load. Undoubtedly his most important work, centered on the sponges, began in 1890 in the Bahamas. He carried out taxonomic study for ten years on the sponges collected during the *Albatross* Expedition and sent to him by Alexander Agassiz, and he reviewed the collection gathered by the Fish Commission off Puerto Rico in 1899.

This careful taxonomic and morphological study prepared Wilson to notice an unusual phenomenon in sponge cells. At the Beaufort research station he observed that sponges in sea water dishes had disaggregated into a number of cells, which then reaggregated. Experimentally, he squeezed cells apart and watched as they moved together to form new, small aggregates. A single cell could even undergo differentiation and develop as a new sponge. This provided an important research tool for studying separate cells, as well as powerful suggestions concerning the nature of differentiation and regeneration of cells.

Wilson played active leadership roles in many organizations, serving as president of the American Society of Zoologists (formerly the American Morphological Society) in 1911, of the Elisha Mitchell Scientific Society (1905–1906 and 1938–1939), and of the North Carolina Academy of Sciences (1912). He was active in the American Philosophical Society and was a charter member and council member of the American Association of University Professors. The National Academy of Sciences elected him a member in 1927. He became Kenan Professor at the University of North Carolina in 1917 and held that position until his death in Durham, North Carolina, although he retired as department head in 1935.

Wilson was a much-loved and respected leader in the community where he spent his entire career; his former students reported that he was affectionately known as "Froggy." The chancellor noted in 1939:

> All of us who studied under Dr. Wilson, who worked with him, or even knew him, had a profound reverences for his fearless, honest and skilful personality. We thought of him as a great teacher and we rejoiced in his distinction as a scholar. Above all, we enjoyed him. He loved Chapel Hill and the University. No one enjoyed more than he did the round of life among the faculty and students. He enjoyed particularly the enterprise and initiative of the students and was a sympathetic but shrewd observer of all they did. (quoted in Howell, p. 185)

• Wilson's papers are in the Southern Historical Collection and in other special collections at the University of North Carolina. A biography is Donald Paul Costello, National Academy of Sciences, *Biographical Memoirs* 35 (1961): 350–83. See also R. E. Coker, *The American Philosophical Society Yearbook 1939* (1940), pp. 470–82, and A. C. Howell, *The Kenan Professorships* (1956), pp. 185–89.

JANE MAIENSCHEIN

WILSON, Hugh Robert (29 Jan. 1885–29 Dec. 1946), diplomat, was born in Evanston, Illinois, the son of Hugh Robert Wilson, the head of a Chicago men's furnishing firm, and Alice Tousey. Raised in an upper class family, Wilson received his A.B. in 1906 from Yale University. From 1907 to 1910 he worked in the family business, which he did not find congenial, and decided that a diplomatic career might better serve his personality and ambition. While studying at the École Libre des Sciences Politiques in Paris (1910–1911) he acquired fluency in French but had received no diploma when he accepted a position as private secretary to Edward Morgan, then the American minister in Lisbon. In late 1911, after a short sojourn, he returned to Washington, D.C., where he both passed the Foreign Service exam and met his future wife, Katherine Bogle, whom he married in 1914. The couple had one child.

His first posting was as secretary of the American legation in Guatemala in 1912. Over the next two decades, he served in a number of diplomatic positions: secretary of legation in Buenos Aires (1914–1916), second secretary in Berlin (1916–1917), first secretary in Berne, Switzerland (1917–1919), counselor of the American embassies in Berlin (1920–1921) and Tokyo (1921–1923), chief of the Division of Current Information of the Department of State (1924–1927), and American minister to Switzerland (1927–1937).

It was in the latter post that Wilson experienced the most enjoyable and satisfying years of his diplomatic career. With great skill he reported on the activities of the League of Nations at Geneva, participated in the unsuccessful Geneva Naval Conference of 1927, the London Naval Conference of 1930, the Preparatory Commission on Disarmament, and the World Disarmament Conference of 1932–1934. He worked strongly to secure League support for Secretary of State Henry L. Stimson's nonrecognition doctrine following the Japanese occupation of Manchuria in 1931. Wilson's advice to his superiors on the use of economic sanctions "applied ruthlessly" against Italy after its invasion of Ethiopia was not followed by the Franklin Roosevelt administration, which did not cooperate in the sanctions efforts of the League of Nations.

Wilson, who believed that he was "happier in the field abroad" than entangled in the Washington bureaucracy, was appointed assistant secretary of state in August 1937. His tenure was short-lived as five months later President Roosevelt named him ambassador to Germany. Wilson was one of the first career Foreign Service officers to achieve ambassadorial rank. Throughout his career he was a proud and vocal supporter of professional diplomacy by career diplomats.

Wilson found dealing with Nazi Germany and Hitler a most difficult task. The ambassador clearly belonged to the camp who feared Bolshevik Russia more than Germany. At first he believed that Hitler's goals were limited, that Hitler had the support of the majority of Germans, and that the Versailles peace settlement of 1919 had left Germany with legitimate complaints, but the hatred for various groups within the Nazi movement appalled him. In November 1938, after only ten months, president Roosevelt recalled Wilson in protest against Nazi actions against Jews. Never allowed to return to Germany, he resigned in August 1939. After a short stint in the Department of State, he resigned from the Foreign Service on 18 November 1940.

Recruited by General William J. "Wild Bill" Donovan, Wilson served from 1941 to 1945 with the secret Office of Strategic Services. He later served the Republican party (1946) as chief of the Foreign Relations Section of the Republican National Committee. He died in Bennington, Vermont.

• Wilson's personal papers are at the Herbert Hoover Presidential Library in West Branch, Iowa. He wrote his recollections in *The Education of a Diplomat* (1938), *Diplomat between Wars* (1941), and *Diplomacy as a Career* (1941). His son, Hugh R. Wilson, Jr., using his father's papers, wrote *For Want of a Nail* (1959), *A Career Diplomat* (1960), and *Disarmament and the Cold War in the Thirties* (1963). See also Arnold A. Offner, *American Appeasement: United States Foreign Policy and Germany, 1933–1938* (1969). An obituary is in the *New York Times*, 30 Dec. 1946.

THOMAS H. BUCKLEY

WILSON, Jackie (9 June 1934–21 Jan. 1984), singer, was born Jack Leroy Wilson, in Detroit, Michigan, the son of Eliza Lee. Nothing is known about his father. Known as Sonny and described as "a tough street kid" at his mother's urging he began singing at the Russell Street Baptist Church, becoming a member of the Ever Ready Gospel Singers in his early teens.

The often-repeated tale that Wilson won the Detroit Golden Gloves is erroneous, but he did box briefly as a professional, posting a 2–8 record. While finishing Highland Park High School he sang with several spiritual-oriented groups and won several amateur contests at the Paradise Theater. Before he turned to the popular idiom, he wanted to be "the world's best known gospel singer," remembered his wife Freda. He never studied music but listened to a diversity of acts, including the Dixie Hummingbirds, the Mills Brothers, the Ink Spots, James Cleveland, Louis Jordan, and Al Jolson. Still billing himself as Sonny, Wilson recorded two singles in 1951 and garnered interest from several people in the music industry that December at a talent show staged by bandleader Johnny Otis.

Wilson's break finally came in early 1953, when an audition earned him a place in Billy Ward and the Dominoes. Clyde McPhatter, lead singer for the group, "was my man," remembered Wilson. "I fell in love with the man's voice." He "learned a lot from Clyde," including the "high-pitched choke" that became one of Wilson's trademarks (Shaw, pp. 442–43). The internship with his idol was brief, as McPhatter left after a few weeks to join the Drifters. At age eighteen Wilson became the featured vocalist. The group released its most successful record of his four-year tenure in April 1956, "St. Therese of the Roses," which rose to number thirteen on the pop charts.

By then Ward, "a strict disciplinarian," according to Wilson, but "a nice man," had molded his lead singer into a polished showman. In 1957 Detroit-based agent Al Green convinced Wilson to pursue a solo career. Green had recently met young songwriters Berry Gordy (who later founded Motown Records) and Roquel "Billy" Davis (whose pen name was Tyran Carlo), and that July Wilson recorded their composition

"Reet Petite." Green died while this minor hit was climbing the charts, and Nat Tarnopol, one of his assistants, took over as Wilson's manager.

"Reet Petite" launched Wilson as a solo artist, and over the next two years other Gordy-Carlo songs made him a star. "To Be Loved" (1958), "That's Why" (1959), and "I'll Be Satisfied" (1959) were all hits, and "Lonely Teardrops" (1958) reached number seven on the pop charts. It would become Wilson's signature number. Only in his early twenties, Wilson was already an amazing talent, "the epitome of natural greatness," according to Gordy. Producer Dick Jacobs remembered that at the first recording session, Wilson's near-operatic range left veteran musicians "slack-jawed and goggle-eyed in disbelief." "Jackie . . . opened his month," said Jacobs, "and out poured that sound like honey on moonbeams" (Pruter booklet).

But it was as a live performer that Wilson was becoming a legend. Splits, spins, and knee drops were an integral part of his incredibly athletic act, and Wilson was soon being billed as "Mr. Excitement." Handsome, confident, and flashy, he worked audiences into a frenzy, with women screaming and men agreeing that Wilson "was just as pretty as he thought he was."

Fan zealousness proved dangerous in 1961. A woman who claimed that Wilson would not speak to her in the lobby of his New York apartment building went to his room and shot him twice as he attempted to disarm her. He was hospitalized for a month, and one bullet, lodged one-sixteenth of an inch from his spine, had to be left in his body.

By this time Wilson's career had leveled off. He was still producing hits, but Gordy and Davis were no longer writing for him, and Tarnopol was encouraging him to record songs that would be popular with patrons of nightclubs such as New York's Copacabana and the Las Vegas casinos. Tarnopol, Wilson, Jacobs, and Brunswick Records have all been criticized for the choice of material, but at the time most of the major record companies were unsure of how to market their black acts to appeal to white audiences. Sam Cooke and Aretha Franklin experienced similar problems. Instead of broadening Wilson's following, Brunswick lost contact with his fan base, and in the mid-1960s he went three years without placing a song in the top forty of the pop charts.

"Yeah, it's true I've recorded some things you don't expect from an R&B singer," Wilson admitted. "But I don't know that I am an R&B singer." He was proud to "have been accepted by the white world" and saw merit in classically based arrangements such as "Alone at Last" and "Night." "Now they knew I wasn't just a screamer," he believed. "Some people say I'm a soul singer," Wilson continued, "but I've [also] got the gospel in me" (Shaw, p. 444).

A brief career resurrection began in late 1966 when Tarnopol paired Wilson with Chicago producer Carl Davis. "Whispers (Gettin' Louder)" put Wilson back on the charts, and 1967's driving "(Your Love Keeps Lifting Me) Higher and Higher" became the biggest hit of his career, topping the rhythm-and-blues charts and going to number six on the pop charts.

It would, however, be his last substantial hit. Wilson remained a popular live performer, but by the 1970s he was considered an oldies act. On 29 September 1975, while headlining a Dick Clark revue at the Latin Casino in Cherry Hill, New Jersey, Wilson suffered a massive coronary in the middle of "Lonely Teardrops." He was rushed to a local hospital, but oxygen deprivation during the twenty-five minutes that it took to get him stabilized left him brain-damaged and in a coma. After four months he regained consciousness but never the ability to speak or take care of himself. A series of New Jersey and Pennsylvania hospitals and nursing homes cared for him during his last eight years before he died of pneumonia in Mount Holly, New Jersey.

Wilson was married three times, although during court battles over guardianship his second wife claimed that they had never divorced. He wed Freda Hood in 1951 and had four children with her, fathered another child with 1967 bride Harlean Harris, and had two more children with Lennie "Lynn" Bell, whom he married in 1971. The murder of his eldest son in 1969 caused him great distress. This incident, a chaotic personal life, and his fading career intensified drug and alcohol use that ultimately led to his collapse.

Wilson's legacy, however, is not that of a fallen star living out his final days in nursing homes, beset with financial problems so great that money had to be raised for a gravestone. It is of the athletic and vocally gifted performer who influenced an entire generation of singers, beginning with early fan Elvis Presley and continuing on through Michael Jackson. According to Gordy, Wilson "set the standard I would be looking for in artists forever." When asked who stands out from his decades in the music business, Dick Clark replied that Wilson, who was elected to the Rock & Roll Hall of Fame in 1987, "heads the list. . . . In person or on record, there was only one Mr. Excitement" (Pruter booklet).

• The most complete sketch of Wilson is in the booklet accompanying *Jackie Wilson—Mr. Excitement* (1992), authored by Robert Pruter. This publication also has a discography of Wilson's singles and albums. Pruter, *Chicago Soul* (1990), includes a Wilson bibliography, as does B. Lee Cooper, "Jackie Wilson—Mr. Excitement? Mr. Musical Diversity? Mr. Song Stylist? or Mr. Stage Show?" *Popular Music and Society* 17 (Summer 1993). Berry Gordy's autobiography, *To Be Loved: The Music, the Magic, the Memories of Motown* (1994), contains a good account of Wilson's early years as a solo artist. The best of the few published interviews with Wilson appears in Arnold Shaw, *Honkers and Shouters: The Golden Years of Rhythm and Blues* (1978). Bill Pollack, "Jackie Wilson's Lonely Tears: The Medical, Legal, and Financial Tragedy of Mr. Soul," *Village Voice*, 14 Aug. 1978, details Wilson's problems after his collapse. Al Duckett, "Jackie Wilson: Lonely Teardrops and Endless Tragedy," *Sepia* (Jan. 1979), follows a similar trail; his two-part interview with Wilson's second wife, Harlean, is in *Sepia* (Apr., May 1979). First wife Freda, writing as "Mrs. Jackie Wilson," contributed "'It's Tough to Be the Wife of a Star'" to *Tan* (June 1961). Bob

Claypool, "Wilson Would Set the Stage on Fire," *Houston Post*, 28 Jan. 1984, remembers Wilson in performance. Pierre Daguerre, "Soul Portrait: Jackie Wilson discographie," *Soul Bag* [France] 98 (Mar.–Apr. 1984): 13–21, lists many European recordings of Wilson's work. His funeral was covered by Trudy S. Moore, "Jackie Wilson Mourned by 1,500 during Funeral at Baptist Church in Detroit," *Jet*, 13 Feb. 1984. The three-disc *Jackie Wilson—Mr. Excitement* (Rhino, 1992) is the best musical compilation, superseding the two-volume *The Jackie Wilson Story* (Epic, 1983, 1985). Although Wilson is best remembered as a live performer, little film of him in action exists. He appeared briefly in one feature-length movie, *Go, Johnny, Go!* (1958), singing his own composition "You Better Know It."

KENNETH H. WILLIAMS

WILSON, James (14 Sept. 1742–21 Aug. 1798), lawyer and jurist, was born in Carskerdo, near St. Andrews, Scotland, the eldest son of William Wilson and Aleson Lansdale, farmers. His parents, members of the Associate Presbytery, intended him for the ministry. In 1757, having won a competitive scholarship, Wilson entered the University of St. Andrews, an important center of the Scottish Renaissance. He enrolled at the St. Mary's College divinity school four years later but, because of financial problems caused by his father's death, withdrew and became a tutor in a gentleman's family. In 1765 Wilson began learning merchant accounting, then quickly changed plans. Financed by family loans and anxious to advance in the secular world, he sailed for America. In 1765–1766 he tutored in the College of Philadelphia (later the University of Pennsylvania) and also received an honorary M.A. He then applied to study law with John Dickinson (1732–1808) and financed his studies by obtaining a £500 loan from his cousin Robert Anna, a Presbyterian minister in Marsh Creek, Pennsylvania. Upon completing his work with Dickinson in early 1767, Wilson moved to Reading. His growing practice quickly marked him as a talented young man, and he was allowed to court Rachel Bird, a local heiress. Drawn by a generous offer of preferment extended by Judge John Armstrong, another Scot, Wilson moved to Carlisle in 1770. When he married Rachel in 1771, they settled in Carlisle where other prosperous Scots also befriended them. The first three of the couple's six children were born there between 1772 and 1777.

Wilson took a leading role in Pennsylvania's revolutionary movement. In 1774 he was elected to the Cumberland County Committee of Correspondence and represented the county in the first provincial convention. That same year, he updated a manuscript he had written in 1768 and had it published as *Considerations on the Nature and Extent of the Legislative Authority of the British Parliament*. This pamphlet emphasized a cardinal tenet of Wilson's judicial and political philosophy: "all power is derived from the people." Since the colonists were not represented in Parliament, it followed for Wilson that Parliament had no authority over them. The colonies were, he maintained, united with England only through the monarch, whose prerogative power could be blocked by the colonial assemblies.

This bold, prophetic pamphlet marked Wilson as a leading Whig. In 1775 he again attended a provincial convention and also joined in organizing the county militia. In May he was elected to the Continental Congress and served there until 1777. Recognized as a most able delegate, he sat on many committees and was especially important in formulating policies for dealing with Native Americans. However, Wilson resisted the colonies' push toward independence because he feared that it would undermine Pennsylvania's balanced government. Yet ultimately he voted for independence and signed the Declaration of Independence.

As a conservative revolutionary, Wilson belonged to the state's Republican party. It aimed to overthrow the radically democratic Pennsylvania constitution of 1776 that eliminated the office of governor, stripped the judiciary of its independence, and put virtually all political power in the hands of a unicameral legislature. Although Wilson believed that government must rest on the consent of the governed, he supported checks to thwart the unbridled will of the majority. These views, along with his ardent desire to acquire wealth, fostered his alliances with conservative and wealthy men in Philadelphia. Wilson moved his family there in 1778. He continued to support the independence effort; Rachel did too by garnering more money than any other member when the Ladies Association of Philadelphia canvassed the city to raise funds for the revolutionary troops. But Wilson soon incurred widespread enmity among revolutionaries by representing accused Tories. Worse yet in the eyes of many, Wilson had close political and socioeconomic ties to Robert Morris (1734–1806), who in 1779 was accused by price-regulating forces of waging economic war on the poor. In October, militiamen marching in support of popularly mandated price regulation exchanged deadly fire with people who had barricaded themselves in Wilson's home because they incorrectly believed the militia crowd planned to arrest Wilson. This noted event, dubbed the Fort Wilson riot, helped perpetuate the view that Wilson was an opportunistic supporter of aristocracy and an enemy of the people.

Wilson's involvement in numerous speculative schemes reinforced the negative image. From the early 1770s on, and especially after the war, he speculated in land, often joining other speculators, most notably in the Illinois-Wabash Company, which claimed vast areas of the western frontier. He became the company's president in 1780. He also planned a manufacturing empire. For example, in 1783 he and his brother-in-law, Mark Bird, attempted to turn their Delaware Iron Works into the country's largest producer of nails. Wilson became deeply involved in banking ventures in 1780 when he assisted Thomas Willing and Robert Morris, leading and enormously wealthy Republicans, in creating the Bank of Pennsylvania. In part due to local political opposition, the bank functioned only from July through September 1780, but it provided the model for creating a national bank. Wilson, working closely with Morris, who had become superintendent of finance, helped convince Congress to charter the Bank of North America, which opened for business in January 1782. Nationalism fueled Wilson's determined support of the bank, for he believed that a national bank and significant manufacturing ventures would facilitate the fledgling nation's rise to power. But personal considerations also mattered. Wilson was a subscriber of the Bank of North America; he was its lawyer and became a trustee in 1781. Equally important, the bank could and did provide Wilson with loans. Gambling that America's economy would continually expand, Wilson routinely borrowed to acquire land or land warrants before his earlier purchases had turned a profit. The same pattern held for his other major economic ventures. Already deep in debt, by the 1780s he routinely sought funds from various sources to keep his potential land and manufacturing empire alive.

When political conservatives gained support in Pennsylvania, they sent Wilson to the Confederation Congress. He served there in 1782–1783 and again from 1785 to 1787. His actions revealed a strong nationalist who wanted the Union to have a powerful central government. Wilson's significant *Considerations on the Bank of North America* (1785), written to defend the institution when it came under attack in Pennsylvania, illustrates his views. Some charged that Congress had no right to charter a bank. Wilson disagreed and asserted that Article 5 of the Articles of Confederation, which spoke of Congress being annually elected "for the more convenient management of the general interests of the United States," gave Congress chartering power. Using this logic of implied powers, the feeble Confederation Congress would have become enormously powerful. Wilson also advanced the idea of dual sovereignty between the central government and the states, which eventually became a feature of the U.S. Constitution. Although Wilson's defense reflected his economic nationalism, the continued existence of the Bank was also of personal import to Wilson: when he penned *Considerations*, he owed the Bank $30,000.

Having already ardently supported efforts to strengthen the Confederation government, Wilson attended the 1787 Constitutional Convention as an advocate of creating a strong national government. He sat on the Committee of Detail that turned the delegates' resolutions into an actual draft constitution and was a vocal member of the convention. Only Gouverneur Morris delivered more speeches. Scholars often rank Wilson's importance to the convention as second only to that of James Madison (1751–1836). Wilson joined with most other big-state delegates in fighting for proportional representation in both houses of Congress. As he had with the Articles of Confederation, Wilson maintained that implied powers were built into the proposed Constitution. In addition, while he supported the principle of judicial review, he also wanted the national government to be able to prevent the passage of any state bill, not just an unconstitutional one, that the national government considered improper.

Wilson was, in one sense, perhaps the most democratic of the framers. Arguing that "no government could long subsist without the confidence of the people," he vociferously asserted that the powerful governmental "pyramid" that the delegates were building should be given "as broad a basis as possible." For Wilson this meant that the proposed Constitution must be submitted to ratifying conventions selected by the people. It also meant that both houses of the Congress should be directly elected. Moreover, and on this Wilson stood virtually alone, it meant that the people should directly elect the president.

Although he articulated a democratic theory of government resting on the consent of the governed, Wilson did not necessarily believe that effective political power belonged in the people's hands. Despite his claim that "the difference between a mediate and immediate election was immense," he seemed willing to undercut his own emphasis on direct elections. When authorized to present a plan for directly electing the president, he proposed the kind of indirect election that, in time, evolved into the electoral college. He also said that, if necessary, senators could be selected indirectly by electors. Perhaps pragmatism pushed Wilson to adopt these accommodations to what James Madison called the filtering of the people's vote. However, Wilson stressed the direct election of senators rather than their possible selection by the state governments in part to strengthen the national government at the expense of the states. More significant, Wilson tempered his democratic theory by calling for provisions that would routinely allow a few officials to thwart the will of the majority. Perhaps thinking as well of his hatred for Pennsylvania's 1776 constitution and of the Fort Wilson incident, Wilson cited English history to support his claim that the legislature was more likely to behave tyrannically than a powerful executive. He argued that executive power should be lodged in one person possessing an absolute veto. When the absolute veto idea proved unpalatable to the delegates, Wilson and Madison repeatedly pushed for having the president and some of the federal judiciary form a council of revision. The council would review proposed bills and return unacceptable ones to Congress where larger majorities would be needed to pass them. So while Wilson insisted that the people should vote on establishing the government and should elect many of its officers, he championed a system that would incorporate strong checks on the majority's ability to direct government policy.

Wilson played a vital role in securing the ratification of the Constitution. In an October 1787 speech, subsequently extensively reprinted, he advanced what became the basic Federalist argument against adding a bill of rights to the Constitution. A bill of rights was unnecessary, he said, because the rights not specifically granted to the central government by the Constitution were reserved to the individual states. Then, as the only member of Pennsylvania's Constitutional

Convention delegation also elected to the state's ratifying convention, Wilson led the pro-Constitution forces. Having a two-to-one majority, they quickly ratified the Constitution on 12 December 1787. Wilson delivered a speech at the ratifying convention on the democratic nature of the Constitution that was afterward widely circulated. In 1789–1790 Wilson's role in constitution-making extended to the state level. He was the principal author of the Pennsylvania constitution of 1790 that replaced the radically democratic 1776 constitution. It called for a governor with a limited veto power, a bicameral legislature, and an independent judiciary. Once again, and here successfully, Wilson argued for allowing the citizens to elect the governor and both legislative houses directly. He also successfully supported continuing an extensive franchise. However, the 1790 constitution was merely proclaimed, not submitted to a popular vote.

Wilson came to see teaching as a way to attain the lasting fame he desired. At least two others had offered law courses in the colonies before him, but Wilson hoped that the law course the College of Philadelphia authorized him to teach would establish the foundation of the new nation's legal system. He was, after all, one of the most visible architects of the new national government. Although he taught a law course for a brief period in the fall of 1791, he delivered his only full course of lectures in the winter of 1790–1791. Wilson emphasized that the correct basis of law was "the consent of those whose obedience the law requires." He argued for accepting common law but insisted that it be an American common law rooted in the American experience. Wilson, who trained several lawyers, delivered no more than half the lectures he produced; moreover, he lacked the time needed to develop his analysis as thoroughly as he had intended. Nevertheless, these lectures represent his major written work and reveal his desire to build a fully formed American philosophy and system of the law.

Coveting the chief justiceship of the U.S. Supreme Court, Wilson had boldly written to President George Washington in 1789 and asked for the position. Washington offered it instead to John Jay (1745–1829), but did appoint Wilson as an associate justice. Wilson sought the chief justiceship in part because, much better than most of his contemporaries, he grasped the potential importance of the Supreme Court. However, the cases brought before the Court when he sat on it gave him scant opportunity to display his talents. In fact, the reports of all his Supreme Court opinions—which reveal that he firmly supported the principle of judicial review and a broad interpretation of the Constitution to augment the central government's power—comprise little more than twenty printed pages. Lasting fame as a legal scholar or jurist eluded him.

Questions about his economic speculations and his deepening financial difficulties probably undercut Wilson's quest for the chief justiceship. He was thought to be one of America's wealthiest men, but by the time his wife died in 1786 Wilson was badly overextended financially. Yet he continued to be a major land speculator and industrial entrepreneur. He contracted for the development of massive cloth and saw mills in a town he named Wilsonville. His sense of buoyant optimism extended to matrimony. In 1793 he married Hannah Gray, a Bostonian who was not yet twenty, and they had a child, Wilson's seventh, in 1796. But even before he married Hannah, generally hard economic times threatened to ruin him. In January 1794 the Bank of North America allowed Wilson to consolidate his debt into a $71,000 loan due in six months but informed him that he could have no more extensions. Despite repeated advice to trim his holdings, Wilson stubbornly clung to the hope that new loans and better times would keep him solvent. By the spring of 1797 he feared being seen in Philadelphia lest he be imprisoned for debt. Wilson could not, however, escape his creditors: he was imprisoned for debt in New Jersey in late 1797 and again in the spring of 1798 in Edenton, North Carolina. Broken in health as well as financially, Wilson died there as a result of a stroke. Despite his highly visible role in the American Revolution, his great significance in the creation and ratification of the U.S. Constitution, and the fact that he was a sitting member of the Supreme Court, Wilson's standing had sunk so low by 1798 that his death occasioned no significant public response. His body was not even returned to Pennsylvania; instead, a friend, Associate Justice James Iredell, arranged for burial in North Carolina. Considering Wilson's solid achievements as a "founding father," his often perceptive vision of what America would become, and his desire for lasting fame, it is ironic that his remains were not reinterred at Christ Church, Philadelphia, until 1906 and that it took yet another half century for the first major scholarly biography of him to appear in print.

• Wilson manuscript materials exist in a variety of historical archives and also in some private collections, but the principal collection is housed in the Historical Society of Pennsylvania (Philadelphia) as the James Wilson papers. Wilson's activities in the Federal Convention can be followed in Max Farrand, ed., *The Records of the Federal Convention of 1787* (4 vols., rev. ed., 1937). Bird Wilson's 1804 edition of his father's works, which emphasizes Wilson's law lectures, has been updated in a modern edition by Robert G. McCloskey, ed., *The Works of James Wilson* (2 vols., 1967). Scholars who have analyzed aspects of Wilson's thought include: Randolph G. Adams, ed., *Selected Political Essays of James Wilson* (1930); William F. Obering, *The Philosophy of Law of James Wilson* (1938); Geoffrey Seed, *James Wilson* (1978); Jennifer Nedelsky, *Private Property and the Limits of American Constitutionalism* (1990). See also John K. Alexander, "The Fort Wilson Incident of 1779" *William and Mary Quarterly* 31 (Oct. 1974): 589–612. McCloskey provides an excellent brief biography in his "Introduction" to Wilson's *Works*; so does Elizabeth K. Bauer in her *Commentaries on the Constitution 1790–1860* (1952), pp. 41–58. Burton A. Konkle did not complete his massive biography of Wilson but did publish a useful essay, *James Wilson and the Constitution* (1907). Lucien H. Alexander's *James Wilson, Nation-Builder* (1907) is lengthy but dated. The only modern scholarly biography is Charles P. Smith's quite sympathetic *James Wilson, Founding Father 1742–1798* (1956).

JOHN K. ALEXANDER

WILSON, James (16 Aug. 1836–26 Aug. 1920), secretary of agriculture, was born in Ayrshire, Scotland, the son of John Wilson and Jean McCosh, farmers. After immigrating to Connecticut in 1851, the family settled permanently on a farm in Tama County, Iowa, in 1855. Wilson attended public schools in the area and Iowa College (now Grinnell) but did not graduate. He began farming in 1861 and was elected to a series of local governmental offices as a Republican. He married Esther Wilbur in 1873; they had eight children.

In 1867 Wilson entered the Iowa legislature and, during his third term, in 1871, became Speaker of the house. In 1872 he was elected to the U.S. House of Representatives, where he served competently and was a member of the Agricultural Committee. After his second term, he returned to farming for five years. Wilson was again elected to Congress from Iowa's Fifth District shortly after beginning a term on the state Railway Commission. During this session of Congress, which began on 4 March 1883, in addition to the Agricultural Committee, he was a member of the Rules Committee. To distinguish him from Iowa's junior senator, who had the same name, Wilson was nicknamed "Tama Jim" after his home county.

Although Wilson's reelection was successfully contested, he managed to retain his seat almost to the close of the 1885 session. He once more returned to farming and began writing for various farm journals, including *Iowa Homestead*. In 1891 he was appointed a professor of agriculture at Iowa Agricultural College (now Iowa State University of Science and Technology) in Ames, director of the school's agricultural experiment station, and senior dean until 1897. In both positions he emphasized the need for scientific and practical education.

In 1897, to settle a dispute involving several prominent Iowa Republican leaders, President William McKinley appointed Wilson to be the nation's third secretary of agriculture. He served in the post under Presidents McKinley, Theodore Roosevelt (1858–1919), and William Howard Taft. Wilson was involved directly or indirectly in all important legislation related to agriculture in the period. As secretary he introduced various crops, such as Cuban and Sumatran tobacco, durum wheat, Swedish oats, Egyptian cotton, and mohair goats. Wilson was responsible for programs to eradicate ticks, fight the boll weevil, check hog cholera, and control bovine tuberculosis as well as offering instruction in the proper handling and preparation of milk. Moreover, to encourage more scientific farm practices, he increased the number of agricultural experiment stations across the United States, began farm demonstration work and cooperative extension work, and fostered home economics. He also promoted scientific fertilization through the Bureau of Plant Industry and helped improve the nation's roadways as part of the function of the department's Office of Public Roads. At the time of his death, the *New York Times* remarked, "We don't know anybody who added so much to the national wealth as Mr. Wilson did in his sixteen years" (28 Aug. 1920).

Wilson was a close associate of Gifford Pinchot, chief forester in the Agriculture Department. With his help, Wilson put additional public lands in forest reserve and developed afforestation and reforestation projects. He championed "rational use" of natural resources, that is, a reasonable use rather than strict preservation and replenishing them if possible. Wilson was a major force behind the 1908 Conference of Governors, the so-called White House Conference on Natural Resources. Every state governor and representatives of some seventy national organizations attended the meeting that Pinchot called "the most distinguished gathering on the most important issue ever to meet in the White House" (Smith, p. 124). At the time, Wilson was president of the American Forestry Association (1898–1908).

Wilson became involved in some memorable controversies. Along with President Roosevelt, he opposed Asiatic immigration into Hawaii, hoping to save the islands for white landowners. In 1905 he was forced to fire Edwin S. Holmes, a department statistician who prematurely gave crop reports to private speculators and manipulated crop figures in order to gain illegal profits. Wilson became involved in the Ballinger-Pinchot affair in 1910, when Pinchot said that he had received the secretary's permission to write Senator Jonathan Dolliver (R.-Iowa) a letter highly critical of Taft's commitment to conservation. Dolliver read the letter on the floor of the Senate. Wilson denied Pinchot's claim and, at Taft's instruction, dismissed his longtime friend.

In 1911 Secretary Wilson was responsible for charges filed against Harvey W. Wiley, chief chemist of the Department of Agriculture, ostensibly for paying pharmacologist H. H. Rusby twice the amount fixed by law for his services. Some suggest that the problem was Wilson's lack of support for enforcement of food and drug laws. Wiley had been a major factor in the passage of the Pure Food and Drug Law and the Meat Inspection Act of 1906 and was responsible for their enforcement. Ironically, he and Wilson had worked closely together investigating businesses involved in meat packing and food processing and had received accolades from Roosevelt for their work. An angry and discouraged Wiley retired in March 1912.

When a political split developed between Taft and Roosevelt in 1910, Wilson met with Roosevelt to encourage a reconciliation and assure the former president that Taft was following "Roosevelt's policies." It was of no avail; Progressive Republicans convinced Roosevelt otherwise. In 1912 Wilson remained loyal to the party's nominee and, after Taft failed to be reelected, returned to his home in Iowa.

Governor George W. Clarke of Iowa appointed Wilson to observe and report on agricultural conditions in Great Britain in 1913. He was elected president of the

National Agricultural Society and supported his former cabinet colleague Elihu Root for the Republican presidential nomination in 1916. Wilson spent his final years in retirement. He died in Traer, Iowa.

Wilson was an energetic worker motivated by his Presbyterian ideals. He successfully bridged the gap between practical farmer and man of science. An obituary writer said, "His friends boasted that it was he who changed the entire viewpoint of the farmers of the country by teaching them that farming is a science" (*New York Times*, 27 Aug. 1920).

• Letters to Wilson and information about him appear frequently in Elting E. Morison, ed., *The Letters of Theodore Roosevelt* (8 vols., 1951–1954). He is mentioned in Archibald Willingham Butt, *Taft and Roosevelt: The Intimate Letters of Archie Butt, Military Aide* (2 vols., 1930). Earley Veron Wilcox, *Tama Jim* (c. 1930), is an old biography. He is also discussed in Margaret Leech, *In the Days of McKinley* (1959); Page Smith, *America Enters the World: A People's History of the Progressive Era and World War I* (1985); and Henry F. Pringle, *The Life and Times of William Howard Taft: A Biography* (2 vols., 1939). Much useful information may be found in the *New York Times*, including his obituary on 27 Aug. 1920; and in the Department of Agriculture's yearbooks and annual reports, 1897 to 1913.

ROBERT S. LA FORTE

WILSON, James Falconer (19 Oct. 1828–22 Apr. 1895), U.S. congressman and senator, was born in Newark, Ohio, the son of David S. Wilson, a carpenter, and Kitty Ann Bramble. As a youth, Wilson served as an apprentice to his uncle, a harness maker, in order to support his widowed mother. He attended the local schools from time to time and later read law. Wilson married Mary Jewett in 1852; they raised three children. In 1853 the family moved to Fairfield, Iowa, where Wilson formed a law partnership with Daniel P. Stubbs.

Wilson entered politics in the turbulent 1850s. Opposed to the extension of slavery, he joined the Republican party in 1854 and was one of the founding fathers of that party in Iowa. He actively participated in the convention at Iowa City to revise the state's constitution in 1857, and during the next two years, he served in both houses of the Iowa General Assembly. In May 1860 Wilson, a supporter of Abraham Lincoln, attended the Republican National Convention, which nominated Lincoln for the presidency.

Wilson was elected to fill a vacancy in the U.S. House of Representatives in 1861. At the outbreak of the Civil War, he announced his opposition to secession and his support of Lincoln's policies to preserve the Union. As a member of the important Judiciary Committee, which he chaired for six of his eight years in the House, Wilson also promoted legislation for the civil and political equality of African Americans as early as 1861, when he advocated enfranchisement of African Americans in Washington, D.C. He was also an early advocate of amendments to the Constitution to abolish slavery, grant citizenship to former slaves, and permit black suffrage.

Lincoln's successor, President Andrew Johnson, faced impeachment proceedings in 1868. At first Wilson opposed impeachment, reminding colleagues that specific violations of the law were mandatory for an indictable offense. When Johnson formally removed Secretary of War Edwin M. Stanton, Wilson reluctantly changed sides. Failing to recognize that a presidential removal could pose political and economic dangers not only to the Republicans but also to the nation, Wilson, momentarily caught in the frenzy of the times, subordinated his usual discretion and moderation for a more radical stance. Helping to draft the articles of impeachment, Wilson introduced to the Senate the evidence gathered by the House, arguing that Johnson had disregarded his constitutional obligation to administer the acts of Congress, but the tally for conviction in 1868 fell one vote short of the necessary two-thirds. Later that year Wilson announced that he would not seek another term, emphasizing in a letter to an Iowa friend that he had "served my constituents and my country to the best of my humble abilities during a most troublous period of our national history."

Wilson maintained a close personal friendship with President Ulysses S. Grant but for various reasons declined to serve in the cabinet as secretary of state. Instead, he devoted his time primarily to his law practice in Iowa, but the former congressman did serve for six years as a government director of the Union Pacific Railroad. A vigorous promoter of the railroad, Wilson demonstrated his support by investing in the stock of Crédit Mobilier of America, which acted as the construction company for the Union Pacific Railroad. Wilson later denied charges that he had received payments from a "special legal expenses" fund from the controlling company. Because of the absence of substantiating evidence to prove any wrongdoing, Wilson salvaged his reputation during the scandals that plagued the Grant administration. Little damage was done to his reputation in Iowa.

Although without a political office, Wilson was an important force in Iowa politics. Persuaded by Republican allies, including Grenville M. Dodge and William B. Allison, to terminate his political retirement, Wilson in 1882 won election to the U.S. Senate and secured a second term six years later. Wilson's senatorial years lacked the achievements that had marked his earlier legislative role in the House. For one thing, certain outstanding issues, such as the antislavery crusade that had propelled him into the national spotlight, had been resolved by the 1880s. Second, Allison, the dominant voice of Iowa Republicanism, overshadowed Wilson, his loyal friend and junior colleague. Finally, Wilson's health was steadily declining.

Wilson's Senate speeches covered a variety of subjects, including presidential responsibilities, railroads, farmers, internal improvements, and supervision of federal elections. He helped to frame the Interstate Commerce Act of 1887, supported protective tariffs, and endorsed bimetallism. The senator also devoted time to important social issues. A teetotaler who belonged to the Sons of Temperance, he favored prohibition and worked to get such laws enacted in Iowa. In 1894 Wilson chose not to seek a third term. He retired to Fairfield, where he died one month after completing his senatorial service.

Several factors shaped Wilson's political career. Among them was the fact that he practiced politics in a one-party state. Despite intraparty wrangling over spoils in Iowa, he enjoyed political security and could count on the loyalty of manufacturers and farmers. Wilson intertwined the fortunes of the Republican party with his own during the period from 1861 to 1895. Although he participated in many important events, he sometimes seemed bored by lengthy debate and angered by legislative obstruction. As a senator, he warned of the dangers of arbitrary executive power and held a Whiggish view relating to constitutional restrictions on the chief executive. He possessed a strong sense of duty and yearned for responsible political positions. However, he often hesitated to test his ambition with the public and his Republican cohorts and, having been sent to Washington, longed for the tranquility of his Iowa home. He saw a nation in transition, moving away from its rural and agricultural past into a republic characterized by urbanization and industrialization. The Iowan was a highly moralistic person who fell victim at times to the political culture of the Gilded Age. Politically active in a post–Civil War era beset by a crisis of values, he was more inclined to conform than to criticize.

• Wilson left no large collection of personal papers. In 1956 librarians discovered approximately sixty letters and four scrapbooks of newspaper clippings at the Fairfield Public Library. The State Historical Society of Iowa microfilmed these items. Some Wilson letters are in the papers of Grenville M. Dodge, William B. Allison, James S. Clarkson, and Samuel J. Kirkwood at the State Historical Society of Iowa in Des Moines; the papers of Jonathan P. Dolliver at the State Historical Society of Iowa in Iowa City; and the papers of Abraham Lincoln, Ulysses S. Grant, and James A. Garfield in the Library of Congress. Wilson's speeches are in the *Congressional Globe* and *Congressional Record*. The most complete assessment is Leonard Schlup, "Republican Loyalist: James F. Wilson and Party Politics, 1855–1895," *Annals of Iowa* 52 (1993): 123–49. Material relating to Wilson is in Leland L. Sage, *William Boyd Allison: A Study in Practical Politics* (1956), and Stanley P. Hirshson, *Grenville M. Dodge: Soldier, Politician, Railroad Pioneer* (1967). Some biographical information is in Earle D. Ross, "James F. Wilson, Legalistic Free-Soiler," *Annals of Iowa* 32 (1954): 365–75. Obituaries are in the *Fairfield Daily Ledger* and the *Iowa State Register*, both 23 Apr. 1895.

LEONARD SCHLUP

WILSON, James Harrison (2 Sept. 1837–23 Feb. 1925), army officer and author, was born near Shawneetown, Illinois, the son of Harrison Wilson, a county official and farmer-rancher, and Katharine Schneyder. He attended McKendree College in Lebanon, Illinois, for one year to prepare himself for an appointment to the U.S. Military Academy. Entering West Point in 1855, Wilson graduated sixth in a class of forty-one cadets in 1860 and became a second lieutenant of engineers.

During the first two years of the Civil War, Wilson's talent and intelligence impressed his superiors. He served as an engineer officer on the staffs of Major General George B. McClellan (1826–1885), commander of the Union's Army of the Potomac in the Antietam campaign (Sept. 1862), and Major General Ulysses S. Grant, leader of the Army of the Tennessee in the campaigns for Vicksburg, Mississippi (summer 1863), and Chattanooga, Tennessee (Oct.–Nov. 1863). In October 1863 Wilson was promoted to brigadier general of volunteers.

Although he had not been assigned to mounted units before, Wilson used his friendship with Assistant Secretary of War Charles A. Dana to gain the office of chief of the Cavalry Bureau in Washington, D.C. Holding the post for only a few months (Feb.–Apr. 1864), Wilson revamped and reorganized the bureau, correcting defects in the army's system for procuring horses and demanding adherence to War Department regulations against fraud. Moreover, he acted to give the Union cavalry a new rifle over the objections of hidebound traditionalists who favored single-shot weapons. The controversial firearm was the seven-shot Spencer repeating carbine. This weapon greatly increased the firepower of mounted units. Having demonstrated exceptional administrative skills, Wilson gained an opportunity for field service.

In April 1864 Grant, then general in chief of Union forces traveling with the Army of the Potomac, assigned Wilson to command the Third Division of Major General Philip H. Sheridan's cavalry corps. Wilson adopted a tactic similar to that used by dragoons of having his cavalry units approach close to the enemy, dismount, and fight on foot with the increased firepower of the Spencer carbine. Previously, most Union cavalry units had been used in such traditional roles as screening an army's flank, guarding wagon trains, and conducting reconnaissance. In his first skirmishes with Confederate forces, Wilson suffered defeats and the embarrassment of losing his supply wagons. However, he soon acquitted himself well in a series of battles in Virginia, including Spotsylvania and Yellow Tavern (May) and Winchester (Sept.), where he achieved recognition as a field commander. These actions earned him promotion to brevet major general of volunteers and the posting as chief of cavalry in Major General William T. Sherman's Army of the Tennessee in the western theater.

In the Civil War's closing campaigns in the West, Wilson came into his own as a field commander. He reorganized his new corps by selecting new officers, reassigning officers, transferring units, rearranging unit organizations, and bringing together scattered units fulfilling a variety of duties. The battles of Franklin and Nashville (Nov.–Dec. 1864) tested the new organization. While in winter quarters, Wilson subjected his soldiers to a rigorous training regimen in dismounted tactics. The training paid off when Wilson persuaded Grant to authorize an independent spring campaign in the Lower South.

From March through May Wilson launched slashing attacks that cut across 500 miles of Alabama and Georgia, the heart of the dying Confederacy. His 14,000 cavalrymen devastated a wide swath of territory, destroyed hundreds of railroad cars and many miles of track, razed numerous factories, and burned depots filled with supplies. To top off the campaign, Wilson's forces defeated the redoubtable southern cavalry hero, General Nathan Bedford Forrest, at Selma, Alabama (2 Apr.), and on 10 May captured Confederate president Jefferson Davis, who had fled to Georgia.

After the Civil War, Wilson was lieutenant colonel of the new Thirty-fifth Infantry Regiment in the reduced peacetime army. Serving on detached duty with the engineers, he worked on various construction projects. He married Ella Andrews in 1866 and with her had three children. He resigned from the army in 1870. Working as a consulting engineer or administrator with several railroad companies, he eventually became president of the New York & New England Railroad. When the line became caught up in the rivalry between Cornelius Vanderbilt (1794–1877) and Jay Gould, Wilson left the firm and took up residence in Wilmington, Delaware, to write magazine articles and make various business investments.

At the age of sixty, Wilson requested a senior combat assignment with the army when the country went to war with Spain in April 1898. One of several Civil War veterans returned to active service, he was commissioned a major general of volunteers. He served with Major General Nelson A. Miles in a sideshow of the war, the Puerto Rico campaign (July–Aug. 1898). Remaining in the army, Wilson became a military governor of the Department of Matanzas in Cuba. An avowed expansionist, he attempted to use his political friends to gain the governor generalship of either the Philippines or Puerto Rico without success. Instead, he took the posting as second in command to Major General Adna Romanza Chaffee (1842–1914) in the Relief Expedition to suppress the "Boxer Rebellion" in China (July–Nov. 1900).

Wilson stepped out of uniform in March 1901 holding the rank of brigadier general in the regular army. During his long retirement, he wrote a detailed autobiography, *Under the Old Flag* (2 vols., 1912). He died at Wilmington, Delaware.

Wilson's youth and his exploits during the Civil War made him one of the Union's "boy generals," a sobriquet he shared with others, such as Miles and George A. Custer. Wilson's innovative administration of the Cavalry Bureau during the war demonstrated promise that might have benefited the postwar army. As a field commander, Wilson showed aggressiveness and skill as well as innovation in his use of cavalry as mounted infantry, rather like motorized infantry of a century later. Considered by some to be vain and pompous, Wilson nevertheless was an effective Civil War general who contributed significantly to the Union's victory.

• Wilson's papers are in the Library of Congress in Washington, D.C. A biography is Edward G. Longacre, *From Union Stars to Top Hat* (1972). See also James P. Jones, *Yankee Blitzkrieg: Wilson's Raid through Alabama and Georgia* (1976). Other treatments are Stephen Z. Starr, *Union Cavalry in the Civil War* (3 vols., 1979–1985), and David F. Trask, *The War with Spain* (1981). An obituary is in the *New York Times*, 24 Feb. 1925.

JOSEPH G. DAWSON III

WILSON, J. Finley (28 Aug. 1881–18 Feb. 1952), journalist and civic leader, was born James Finley Wilson in Dickson, Tennessee, the son of James L. Wilson, a preacher, and Nancy Wiley. He attended Fisk University in Nashville, Tennessee, although he did not graduate; afterward, he traveled the United States, living in Missouri, Wyoming, Utah, Colorado, Arizona, and Alaska, and worked in various jobs including miner, porter, waiter, and cowboy.

In 1903 in Denver and Boulder, Colorado, Wilson joined a lodge of the Improved Benevolent and Protective Order of Elks of the World, an organization that had been started by a black porter, Arthur J. Riggs, in Cincinnati, Ohio, in 1897 to provide charitable relief and social outlets for people of color.

Wilson began his career in journalism in 1905 as a reporter for the *Baltimore Times*. During his career, he edited the *Salt Lake City Plaindealer* and wrote for the *New York Age* as well as the *Harrisburg (Pa.) Advocate-Verdict*. He was instrumental in the founding of the *Norfolk Journal and Guide*. In 1920 he was elected vice president of the National Negro Press Association, and he became president the following year, subsequently serving in that office for three years.

While working as a journalist, Wilson also advanced through the ranks of the Elks fraternity. On 28 August 1922 he was elected Grand Exalted Ruler of the Improved Benevolent and Protective Order of Elks of the World, which he developed into one of the largest and most important African-American organizations in the country, expanding from 30,000 to 500,000 members in 900 lodges throughout the United States and foreign countries including England, Canada, Cuba, and Bermuda. Wilson married Leah Belle Farrar, of Richmond, Virginia, in 1924. They had no children.

This new Elks organization stood in distinction to the older, exclusively white fraternity known as the Benevolent and Protective Order of Elks. During the 1920s and 1930s, Wilson's so-called "Negro Elks," the Improved Benevolent and Protective Order of Elks of the World, or IBPOEW, attracted many members from the ranks of blue-collar workers as well as educated professional black men who came together in the fraternity to offer assistance to needy members and their families and to work toward improving living conditions for blacks.

Although white men were not admitted to Wilson's fraternity, he insisted that it welcome members of other ethnic minorities, including Japanese and Chinese, into its ranks. He said, "It behooved the black man to make friends with all the sons of men—and still further in view of the fact that our organization is based upon the Christian religion, it should be our slogan, 'whosoever will, let him come.'" During his nearly thirty-year tenure as Grand Exalted Ruler of the Elks, Wilson traveled the nation setting up new lodges; he was immensely popular and became known simply as "the Grand."

Under Wilson's leadership, the Elks worked for the cause of civil liberties and strove to improve health and education among minorities through concrete measures such as college scholarships and youth programs such as the Daughter Elks and the Junior Herd. The Elks fraternity gained a position of national political influence and provided social advancement as well as improved business contacts for individual members within their own communities. Because of Wilson's direction, Elks' parades in major U.S. cities came to be regarded as important social events, and those attending were edified by speakers such as well-known African-American figures W. E. B. Du Bois and Ralph Johnson Bunche.

Wilson personally visited public officials such as Tennessee governor Austin Peay in 1923 to establish open communication and secure fair legal treatment for his fellow "black Elks" when their efforts to expand their organization were being impeded by lawsuits from the "white Elks." Personally, Wilson was colorful and fearless. He once defended himself with a gun, refusing to be forced off a Pullman train because he was black.

In 1925 the Elks' Grand Lodge established as its official publication the *Washington Eagle*, of which Wilson was founder, editor, and publisher. Wilson also edited the *John Brown Reader* with his longtime friend and colleague, William C. Hueston, and established John Brown's Farm near Harpers Ferry, West Virginia, as a memorial to the great abolitionist.

At the Grand Lodge meeting of 1927 Wilson established the Elks' Commission on Civil Liberties and issued a call to seventy-five black fraternities throughout the country to gather in Washington, D.C., to discuss the problem of racism. In 1933 Wilson was elected president of the Colored Voters League of America.

At the Elks' Grand Lodge meeting in Indianapolis, Indiana, in 1933, Wilson reported on his activities, including raising money to help with the legal defense of several black youths who had apparently been falsely accused of raping a white girl in Scottsboro, Alabama. In his speech he said that he looked forward to economic recovery after the Great Depression, and he encouraged members to support black banking institutions and insurance companies. He also encouraged black Americans to participate in politics and to vote; he praised the policies of the "New Deal" and said that there must be a "comprehensive policy of financial rehabilitation of the colored race in America which is a part of the trunk-line program of the National Recovery Administration of Franklin D. Roosevelt."

In 1936 Wilson reported on the expansion of the fraternity into the southern states of South Carolina, Georgia, Louisiana, Texas, and Florida. He also emphasized the importance of physical exercise and athletics, introducing Elks member Jessie Owens as an example.

Wilson was often in the forefront of national debate over racial issues. He spoke eloquently against all forms of discrimination, including poll taxes, hate crimes by the Ku Klux Klan, lynching, and police brutality against blacks.

One of Wilson's most famous speeches, delivered at the National Baptist Convention in Cleveland, Ohio, in 1941, was also published as a pamphlet, *The Colored Elks and National Defense*. In that speech, which typified the way he spent his life dealing with such issues, Wilson stressed the need for higher living standards and better nutrition and housing among blacks, as well as equal employment opportunities and wages. He emphasized the need for better insurance and health care in addition to Social Security coverage for agricultural and domestic workers.

Wilson praised President Franklin D. Roosevelt's 1941 actions ordering an end to discrimination in defense-related industries and federal government employment. Wilson advocated the integration of the armed forces during World War II, and he urged blacks to get involved in civic and church groups as agents for social change and to contribute to the national defense effort by supporting the USO and by purchasing defense savings bonds. Denouncing prejudice and espousing patriotism, Wilson encouraged all Americans to work together to fight against the evils represented by both Nazism and racism; in the "National Defense" speech he said, "I have tried to show how these handicaps to equal citizenship rights affect not only the ability of our people to serve their country's cause, but as well holds back the real national unity which must exist if democracy is to triumph."

Wilson assumed leadership of the International Association of Colored People of the World in 1945, the year it was established. That same year, Wilson helped found the Federated Organization of Colored People, which took part in State Department meetings when the United Nations was formed. He served as a delegate to the World Conference on Human Rights in 1947.

Wilson traveled around the country for many years, often at his own expense, recruiting members for the Elks and rallying people to work for better living conditions in the inner cities and an end to discrimination. He was a powerful orator, but he also related well to individuals. He urged blacks to act within the law but strive to change and improve the legal system, to work diligently to improve their own physical and financial well-being, and to build bridges of understanding with other ethnic, religious, and political groups.

Because of his prominence as one of the most beloved and influential leaders in the black community, Wilson was respected by many national political figures who sought his counsel and endorsement, including President Roosevelt. He died in Washington, D.C.

Wilson was one of the most charismatic leaders of the black community in America during the first half of the twentieth century. Though he worked as a professional journalist for some years, he is best remembered for bringing the "Colored Elks" fraternity to national prominence as a respected voice for the disadvantaged; an early proponent of civil rights, he spread a message of peaceful, constructive engagement in society as the means of improving the quality of life among black people.

• Elks (IBPOEW) records are at their Grand Lodge Headquarters in Winton, North Carolina. Much information about his life is in Charles H. Wesley, *History of the Improved Benevolent Protective Order of Elks of the World, 1898–1954* (1955). Obituaries are in the *Washington Post*, 20 Feb. 1952; the *Negro History Bulletin*, May 1952; the *Chicago Defender*, 1 Mar. 1952; and the *Journal of Negro History*, July 1952.

BRUCE GUY CHABOT

WILSON, John (c. 1591–Aug. 1667), clerical leader of early Massachusetts, was born in Windsor, England, the son of William Wilson, a clergyman, and Isabel Woodhall, a niece of Archbishop Edmund Grindal. His father had served for a time as chaplain to Archbishop Grindal and at the time of John's birth was canon of Windsor. John Wilson was educated at Eton and in 1605 enrolled at King's College in Cambridge. There he was influenced by the preaching of various Puritan clergy and by reading the Essex preacher Richard Rogers's *Seven Treatises* (1604). He traveled to Dedham to hear Rogers preach and subsequently began to associate with the university Puritans, in particular the Reverend William Ames, a leader of the movement and a prominent figure in the university. Wilson's rooms at King's College became a center for Ames and other Puritans to confer, study scripture, and pray. He received his B.A. in 1610, at which time he left the university, his strong Puritan views precluding him from a fellowship at King's. He moved to London and studied at the Inns of Court for a year or more, during which time he made the acquaintance of William Gouge and other Puritan clergy in the city. He eventually returned to Cambridge, residing for a while at Emmanuel College until he received his M.A. in 1613. It is likely that he befriended John Cotton and Thomas Hooker at this time, if he had not earlier.

After a time of preaching in the homes of godly families, such as that of Lady Elizabeth Scudamore, he accepted in 1618 the post of lecturer in Sudbury, Suffolk, where he was close to the admired Richard Rogers. Wilson's preaching drew students such as Jeremiah Burroughes, William Bridge, and Thomas Goodwin (all later leaders of English Congregationalism) from Cambridge to Sudbury to hear him. Wilson was suspended for nonconformity a few times during the 1620s and in 1630 decided to join the emigration to New England.

Wilson became one of the founding members and the first pastor of the First Church of Boston in the Massachusetts Bay Colony. He made visits to England in 1631, 1634, and 1635 to settle his affairs there and to bring his wife, Elizabeth Mansfield (date of marriage unknown), to the colony. The couple had at least four children. John Cotton joined Wilson in the Boston ministry in 1633, accepting the post of teacher. The relationship between the two clergymen was temporarily strained by the Antinomian controversy when Anne Hutchinson, claiming to be a disciple of Cotton, made Wilson her primary target in arguing that the Bay Colony's clergy were preaching a covenant of works. Wilson was one of the leaders in condemning her views, urging her banishment from the colony, and seeing to her excommunication from the Boston church.

Though he served as a chaplain to Boston troops in the Pequot War of 1637, Wilson was known as one of the early advocates of efforts to convert the Indians. On one occasion he took the son of a Sagamore who had died of smallpox into his own home and under his protection.

Frequently overshadowed by the more famous Cotton, Wilson was a respected clergyman and a noted defender of Massachusetts orthodoxy. He was noted for the quality of his extemporaneous sermons and for preaching that dealt less with dogma and more with practical instruction for the Christian life. Throughout his career in England and New England he was a frequent traveler to hear neighboring clergymen preach on weekly lecture days. Perhaps after the Antinomian controversy he was reluctant to become engaged in dispute, but in the 1650s he became a fierce opponent of the Quaker missionaries who journeyed to New England. In the last years of his life Wilson sided with the supporters of the Halfway Covenant. He died in Boston.

Before coming to the colonies, Wilson wrote *A Song, or Story, for the Lasting Remembrance of Divers Famous Works* (1626), which was a verse commemoration of the defeat of the Spanish Armada, as well as *Some Helps to Faith* (1624) and *Zacheus Converted* (1631), which appeared in print after he had left England. In Massachusetts he published *The Day-Breaking . . . of the Gospel with the Indians* (1647) and *A Copy of Verses Made* (1658). Like much clerical poetry of the period, interest in his verse is based on the ideas expressed rather than the artistic presentation. One of his last sermons was published posthumously as *A Seasonable Watch-Word unto Christians* (1677).

Because Wilson published no systematic works and few of his sermons were recorded, he is now not as well known as many of his peers. In particular, Wilson's reputation has unfairly suffered because of the image painted of him by Anne Hutchinson and her Antimonian supporters. Wilson was noted for his hospitality and kindness. He was also one of the most learned and best respected of the clergymen of the founding decades and was one of the best connected with leaders of English Puritanism.

• There is no collection of Wilson manuscripts or correspondence. Cotton Mather included an extended appreciation of the man who baptized him in the *Magnalia Christi Americana*, bk. 3, pt. 1 (1702).

FRANCIS J. BREMER

WILSON, John (25 Dec. 1800–9 July 1849), concert and operatic tenor, was born in the Canongate of Edinburgh, Scotland, the son of John Wilson, a coach driver. His mother's name is unknown. At the age of ten he was apprenticed in the printing trade. He gave early indication of ability as a compositor; he was eventually engaged as a reader at the press of James Ballantyne, where he worked with many of the manuscripts of the novels of Sir Walter Scott. Wilson was apprenticed until the age of nineteen, but during this period he began to feel his lack of early education and applied himself to the acquisition of Latin, French, and—later—Italian. Wilson married in 1820, and he and his wife had six children. His wife's name is unknown.

Wilson had always been a passionate singer but did not show professional promise as a child. His early music education was under the tutelage of John Mather, who taught at the Edinburgh Institution, and Benjamin Gleadhill, who led a band in the Tron Church in Edinburgh. Gradually Wilson became more interested in the idea of music as a career, and he began to entertain the thought of attempting to find a job as a precentor in a church. He was an occasional choir singer in the parish church in Duddingston and periodically substituted when the precentor was absent. His first professional musical position was as a precentor of the Relief Church in Roxburgh Place. By this time his tenor voice had developed from the thin and husky voice of his youth; it had become rich and agreeable, although apparently of rather limited range. His singing began to attract attention, and in 1826 he was offered a precentor position in the new Church of St. Mary, located in a fashionable Edinburgh neighborhood. Wilson quickly became popular with the parishioners, many of whom hired him to teach singing to their children.

In 1827 Wilson, who was by then well established as a voice teacher, left the employ of Ballantyne. He continued to appear in concerts in Edinburgh and also continued his musical studies under the Scottish composer and teacher Finlay Dun. In June 1827 Wilson went to London for three months to study with Gesualdo Lanza, an Italian singing teacher. Under Lanza he learned a vocal technique of producing the chest voice (or *voce di petto*) that was superior to any technique hitherto practiced by singers in Edinburgh. As a consequence, when he returned home Wilson quickly acquired a large number of new pupils. During the late 1820s he taught voice and also continued with his job at St. Mary's. He returned to London twice more for study: in 1828 for three months of harmony tutelage with a Mr. (William?) Aspull and from the summer of 1829 until February 1830 for lessons with the Italian singing teacher and composer Domenico Crivelli.

Wilson made his operatic debut in Edinburgh in March 1830 as Henry Bertram in Henry Bishop's *Guy Mannering*. He was subsequently engaged at Covent Garden, where he made his London operatic debut on 30 October 1830 as Don Carlos in Richard Brinsley Sheridan's *The Duenna*, with music by Thomas Linley. He sang successfully in English opera at Covent Garden and Drury Lane until 1837; during the 1837–1838 season he performed at the English Opera House in such works as John Barnett's *The Mountain Sylph* and his own adaptation of Vincenzo Bellini's *La Sonnambula*. In 1838 Wilson and fellow Covent Garden singers Jane Shirreff and Arthur Seguin were recruited for operatic performances by the management of the National Theatre in New York, where they first appeared in the United States. Wilson made his American debut on 15 October 1838 with the stock company of the National in William Michael Rooke's *Amilie; or, The Love Test*. He subsequently spent twenty highly successful months in North America, performing in English opera and English adaptations of Continental opera with Shirreff, Seguin, and Anne Seguin (and for a while with a chorus from the National Theatre) in New York, Boston, Washington, Philadelphia, and Baltimore; Shirreff and Wilson also appeared in operas in Providence, Rhode Island, and Charleston, South Carolina.

Wilson was described in 1866 by the theater historian Joseph N. Ireland as of "fine, open, [and] manly countenance" (Ireland, p. 278). His voice, according to music biographers James D. Brown and Stephen S. Stratton, was "pure, sweet, vigorous, and highly cultivated" (Brown and Stratton, p. 452); a critic writing in the *Philadelphia National Gazette* on 15 January 1839 described it as "clear, rich, and fresh." During their time in North America, Wilson and Shirreff also made two extended concert tours: the first in the summer of 1839 and the second in the autumn and winter of 1839–1840. Wilson and Shirreff presented concerts comprised of operatic arias as well as traditional ballads and composed popular songs; they sang in both small towns and large cities in an area bounded by Detroit to the west, Montreal to the north, and Savannah to the south. Wilson probably acted in a managerial capacity on their concert tours; he apparently also assumed the role of ward for Shirreff. The two singers returned to London in May 1840. Wilson and Shirreff were the most successful English vocal stars to perform in the United States in the late 1830s and early 1840s; they helped to further cultivate the growing American taste for opera and as a consequence played an important role in the development of musical culture in this country during those decades.

Wilson was also one of the most successful performers of Scottish song and as such capitalized on an early nineteenth-century craze for national and "folk" tunes. In 1842 he published *Edition of the Songs of Scotland*, a two-volume compendium of piano/vocal arrangements of traditional tunes, many of which he sang in concerts and interpolated into operas. He also composed various popular songs and in 1825 published *A Selection of Psalm Tunes, Sanctuses, Doxologies, etc.* for the congregation of St. Mary's Church. Wilson was also very successful in his "Songs of Scotland" entertainments. These highly enjoyable performances incorporated singing, dialogues, and story telling into a unified whole; they were popular in both Great Britain and North America (especially on his second visit). He returned to North America for a second concert tour in 1849 but was stricken with cholera in Quebec City, Canada, where he died. In 1854 a group of Wilson's friends and admirers raised funds for the erection of a monument in his memory in the city of his birth. The obelisk stands today in the Dean Cemetery in Edinburgh.

• Biographical information about Wilson, especially about his early life, is difficult to find. The best sources of information are entries in three biographical dictionaries: John W. Moore, *Complete Encyclopedia of Music* (1854); James D. Brown and Stephen S. Stratton, *British Musical Biography: A Dictionary of Musical Artists, Authors, and Composers* (1897; repr. 1971); and David Baptie, *Musical Scotland, Past and Present* (1894; repr. 1972); and an essay by John Ballantine, "Memoir of the Late John Wilson," an appendix in an unpublished pamphlet, "Monument to the Memory of John Wilson" (1858), the only known copy of which is in the Edinburgh Central Library. A detailed examination of the Wilson/Shirreff tour of the United States is Katherine Preston, "The 1838–40 American Concert Tours of Jane Shirreff and John Wilson, British Vocal Stars," in *Essays in American Music*, vol. 1, ed. James Heintze (1994); further information about Wilson's American operatic activities is in Preston, *Opera on the Road: Traveling Opera Troupes in the United States, 1825–1860* (1993). Other information is in Joseph Ireland, *Records of the New York Stage from 1750 to 1860* (1866–1867; repr. 1968); George D. C. Odell, *Annals of the New York Stage*, vols. 4–5 (1927–1931; repr. 1970); and Francis C. Wemyss, *Twenty-Six Years of the Life of an Actor and Manager* (1847). There are brief obituaries in the *Times* (London), 31 July 1849, and the *Gazette* (Quebec), 9 July 1849.

KATHERINE K. PRESTON

WILSON, John Leighton (25 Mar. 1809–13 July 1886), missionary, was born in Salem, South Carolina, the son of William Wilson, a wealthy planter, and Jane E. James. Entering the junior class, Wilson graduated from Union College in Schenectady, New York, in 1829. After teaching school for a year, he entered Columbia Theological Seminary in South Carolina in 1831 and graduated with the first class matriculated at the institution in 1833. The popular swelling of religious activity after 1800, known as the Second Great Awakening, gave rise to a variety of ecumenical and voluntary missions societies. Having been raised on a plantation with more than two dozen slaves, Wilson became interested in missionary work in Africa as a result of watching an uncle preach to local slaves. This interest was enhanced also by his lifelong friendship with John B. Adger, a college classmate and fellow missionary. Wilson chose Africa, his friend later related, because "it had been a very much neglected portion of the world by Christian nations" and because Wilson believed that "America, and especially the South, owed it to Africa to send her the gospel" given that so many of "her children were held in bondage there."

After studying Arabic at Andover Theological Seminary for a summer, Wilson was ordained as a Presbyterian missionary in 1833. That same year Wilson made an exploratory voyage to western Africa to choose a site for that region's first mission station sponsored by the American Board of Commissioners for Foreign Missions (ABCFM). Upon his marriage to Jane Elizabeth Bayard in 1834, Wilson freed the thirty slaves he had inherited through marriage and paid for their colonialization in Liberia. Two young slaves, however, reportedly refused his offers of freedom, and his ownership of them became a source of controversy when abolitionist sentiment increased in the 1830s, especially in Boston where the ABCFM was located. In 1842 Wilson sent an emancipatory document from Africa to the slaves, who subsequently remained on the family farm as hired laborers. These complications led southerners to consider him "a rampant abolitionist" while Northern abolitionists denounced him as a "manstealer."

In 1834 Wilson established a mission station at Cape Palmas in Liberia, about 250 miles south of Monrovia, the site he had chosen during his first voyage. There he organized a church of some forty members, established a school for more than one hundred children, systematized the Grebo language to writing, composed a dictionary and grammar, and translated several Christian works and portions of the Bible into the indigenous language. In 1842 the Wilsons moved to the Gabon River, 1,200 miles southeast of Cape Palmas, where he opened a mission station among the Mpongwe. He again systematized the language to writing, created a grammar and dictionary, and translated several volumes. His fascination with the wildlife of Africa was related in his "Notice of the External Characters and Habits of Troglodytes Gorilla, a New Species of Orang from the Gabon River" (*Boston Journal of Natural History* [Dec. 1847]). He also secured and sent to the Boston Society of Natural History the first gorilla skeleton known to America.

Wilson criticized both American colonialist efforts in Liberia and French colonialist efforts in Gabon because of the impoverished condition they left the repatriated slaves. He also disapproved of the system of domestic slavery practiced by the Mpongwe. When the British Parliament debated withdrawing the British squadron on the western African coast, Wilson argued in an article published in *Colonial Magazine* (Sept. 1850) that the withdrawal would further encourage the slave trade. Lord Palmerston, a staunch abolitionist, had 10,000 copies of the treatise reprinted as *The British Squadron on the Coast of Africa* (1850) and republished it in *United Service Journal* and Parliament's *Blue Book*. Lord Palmerston told Wilson that the essay helped rally opposition to defeat the proposed withdrawal.

Wilson returned to the United States in 1852 because of poor health. The following year he became secretary of the (Old School) Presbyterian Board of Foreign Missions, located in New York City. He published *Western Africa; Its History, Condition, and Prospects* (1856), which was valued for not only its survey of African religions but also for its detailed account of the region's geography, history, and slave trade. At this time he also edited the *Home and Foreign Record* and contributed to *Southern Presbyterian Review*.

Although he was a sharp critic of slavery, when his native state led the South in secession in 1860, Wilson resigned his position with the Presbyterian Church U.S.A. and moved back to South Carolina. After the Presbyterian Church of the Confederate States of America (later the Presbyterian Church of the United States) was organized, Wilson coordinated the missionary efforts of southern Presbyterians throughout the world. He became the first secretary of the Executive Committee of Foreign Missions and, until 1872, was secretary of home missions. After the war he orchestrated the southern Presbyterian church's missions work from Baltimore; he also founded and edited the *Missionary*. Wilson retired in 1884 and with his wife operated a female seminary until his death in Salem, South Carolina.

Wilson freed his slaves and criticized both the slave trade and the practice of colonialization yet remained a loyal southerner during the Civil War. Wilson's life and work thus reveal the mixture of humanitarian, religious, and sectional motives that not only drove many American missionaries overseas but also the nation to war.

• Wilson's papers are held by the Presbyterian Church U.S.A., Department of History, Montreat, N.C.; the Presbyterian Historical Society, Philadelphia; the James Woodrow Papers, South Caroliniana Library, Columbia, S.C., and the American Board of Commissioners for Foreign Missions collection, Houghton Library, Harvard University. Wilson's diary for the year 1854 is in the archives of the Princeton Theological Seminary Libraries, Princeton, N.J. The best source for biographical information is Hampden C. DuBose, *Memoirs of John Leighton Wilson* (1895). For a biography by a contemporary Presbyterian see *The Presbyterian Encyclopedia* (1884). See also Henry H. Bucher, Jr., "John Leighton Wilson and the Mpongwe: The 'Spirit of 1776' in Mid-Nineteenth Century Western Africa," *Journal of Presbyterian History* 54 (1976): 291–315, on Wilson's mission to Liberia and Gabon and his assistance to the indigenous resistance to colonialism; and Arthur J. Brown, *One Hundred Years* (1936), and Ernest Trice Thompson, *Presbyterians in the South* (1963–1973), on his role in Presbyterian missions.

P. C. KEMENY

WILSON, Joseph Chamberlain (13 Dec. 1909–22 Nov. 1971), industrialist, was born in Rochester, New York, the son of Joseph Robert Wilson, an industrialist, and Katherine M. Upton. He was educated in the public schools of Rochester and after graduating in 1931 with honors from the University of Rochester went on to the Graduate School of Business Administration of Harvard University, receiving an M.B.A. with high distinction in 1933.

Returning to Rochester, Wilson joined the Haloid Company, a manufacturer of photographic paper and chemicals, as a $20-a-week assistant to the sales manager. He married Marie B. Curran in 1935; they had six children. Wilson's grandfather, also named Joseph Chamberlain Wilson, had helped found Haloid in 1906 but sold majority control to an investor in 1912. Wilson's father had been one of the original twelve employees of the company, working on photographic emulsions; by 1933 he was secretary-treasurer and general manager. Because of the high quality of its newly introduced Record Photocopy Paper, the firm did well during the depression of the 1930s. After the company in 1935 sold stock to the public to finance the purchase of the Rectigraph Company, which manufactured a photocopier using Haloid paper and chemicals, Wilson's father was able to take over control of the company, becoming president in 1936. Wilson followed in his father's footsteps, replacing him as secretary in 1936, becoming secretary-treasurer in 1938, and president and general manager in 1946, when his father moved up to chair of the board.

When Wilson took over active management of Haloid he knew his company could expect to see major competition develop in the photocopying market. Wilson and Haloid's research director, John Dessauer, searched for new technology in which the company might invest. The two were intrigued by a report of Chester Carlson's invention of "electrophotography," which used optical methods to form electrostatic image patterns on a metal plate that could then be transferred to dry paper. Carlson's first successful trial occurred in October 1938, but he could not interest anyone in his invention until 1944, when the Battelle Memorial Institute of Columbus, Ohio, a nonprofit research institution, agreed to try to perfect the process in return for control of his patents. Unable to get any major corporation to show interest in the patents, Battelle reluctantly agreed on 1 January 1947 to grant Haloid, a small company Battelle managers had never heard of before, limited rights to commercialize the invention. Not until 1956, after the institute had failed to arouse any interest from the many large corporations it approached, did Battelle grant Haloid complete control of the basic patents in return for 50,000 shares of Haloid stock.

Wilson effectively bet his company's survival on the effort to produce a commercially viable copier using this process, which he renamed xerography, after the Greek words for dry and writing, choosing Xerox as a trademark. The first version, introduced in 1950, was rejected by all who tried it as being too complicated; it took a skilled operator thirty-nine steps using three different machines to produce a copy. Not until a Battelle engineer discovered it made excellent paper master plates for offset printing did any limited revenue come in from xerography. More than thirteen years elapsed between Wilson's first investment in the Carlson patents and the successful introduction of an office copier. Research costs rose enormously for the small company. Wilson had difficulty sustaining the morale of his employees and resolving the doubts of his board of directors as he borrowed money and issued stock to meet mounting expenses. Between 1947 and 1960 Haloid spent some $75 million on xerography, about twice what it earned from its regular operations.

As costs mounted Wilson tried to induce major American corporations to join with Haloid in developing xerography but could find no takers. During the 1950s desk-top copying machines such as Eastman Kodak's Verifax and Minnesota Mining and Manufacturing's Thermo-Fax, costing $300 to $400, became widely used for their convenience, despite that they required special coated paper or wet chemicals and produced poor copies. When Wilson approached IBM the company asked a consulting firm to evaluate the market for desk-size machines costing perhaps a hundred times as much; the consultant concluded they would not be profitable because the total demand was no more than 5,000 units. In spite of this discouragement Wilson never lost confidence and continued to prepare for the introduction of his machine, buying up land cheaply far in advance of need and building a national direct-sales force with showrooms across the country. He had the company's legal counsel, Sol M. Linowitz, erect a wall of patent protection around xerography in Europe and Asia as well as the United States. In the early 1950s, well before he had an office copier to sell, Wilson began to look for overseas partners, but he had little success with major photographic or office machine companies. Only the Rank Organization, a British motion picture company, showed any interest in a joint venture, forming the Rank-Xerox Company in 1957. When Wilson turned his attention to Asia in 1962, it was easier to get the Fuji Film Company to join with Xerox. In 1958 he changed the company's name to Haloid-Xerox; in 1961 it became the Xerox Corporation.

The Xerox 914 copier, introduced in 1960, proved an instant success. Wilson's decision to lease the machines instead of selling them outright and to charge for the number of copies used made the copiers affordable. To bring the machines to the attention of potential users and to demonstrate ease of use, the company turned to television with a memorable commercial in which a little girl copied a document for her father and then produced a picture of her rag doll. The quality of its dry copies made on plain paper rendered all other office copiers obsolete. Use of the machines proliferated, and revenues from leasing poured in. *Fortune* magazine called the 914 "probably the single most profitable product ever manufactured in the U.S." (Oct. 1966).

In 1966 Wilson became chair of the board of Xerox and in 1968 handed over full day-to-day control to Peter McColough, his successor as president. The two directed the company toward a policy of diversification into the fields of education and computers, a strategy that proved very difficult for other Wilson successors to follow.

Wilson had always believed industrialists should be socially responsible, and he had been willing to contribute his time to educational and philanthropic institutions long before he had substantial money to donate. He served on the board of the Rochester Community Chest and headed several fundraising campaigns; he led fund campaigns for the University of Rochester and served as chair of the school's board of trustees. As he became a national figure he joined the board of trustees of the Carnegie Endowment for International Peace, the United Nations Association, and the Alfred P. Sloan Foundation. He helped found the Business Committee for the Arts and served on many state and federal commissions.

Wilson died of a heart attack in New York City while attending a luncheon given in his honor by Governor Nelson Rockefeller. When Wilson took control of Haloid it had net profits of $138,000 on sales of $7 million; in 1970 Xerox earned $187.7 million on sales of $1.72 billion. His leadership had transformed a small local company into a giant of world commerce. His machine helped transform the way the world communicated information, and added to the English language a new verb—to xerox.

• The Department of Rare Books and Special Collections, University of Rochester Library, has a collection of Wilson papers relating to his civic activities from 1960 to 1971. Wilson describes his business philosophy and activities in "The Product Nobody Wanted," in Sidney Furst and Milton Sherman, eds., *The Strategy of Change for Business Success* (1969), pp. 33–48. Much information about the man can be found in the memoirs of his associates and in books about the Xerox Corporation. Wilson is the dominating figure in John H. Dessaur, *My Years with Xerox: The Billions Nobody Wanted* (1971), and Sol M. Linowitz, *The Making of a Public Man: A Memoir* (1985). Chester Carlson has a brief tribute to him in *The Invention and Development of Xerox Copying* (1971), an edited typescript of a Dec. 1965 tape-recorded interview by Joseph J. Ermenc. Wilson is featured in Gary Jacobson and John Hillkirk, *Xerox: American Samurai* (1986), which includes a lengthy interview with his successor Peter McColough, and in Douglas K. Smith and Robert C. Alexander, *Fumbling the Future: How Xerox Invented, Then Ignored, the First Personal Computer* (1988). Wilson's continuing influence on the company is illustrated in the memoir of David T. Kearns, McColough's successor as president, *Prophets in the Dark: How Xerox Reinvented Itself and Beat Back the Japanese* (1992), with David A. Nadler. The impact of the Xerox copier is described in John Brooks, "Xerox Xerox Xerox Xerox," *New Yorker*, Apr. 1967, reprinted in his *Business Adventures* (1969), which also concludes with an interview with Wilson, and in David Owen, "Copies in Seconds," *Atlantic Monthly*, Feb. 1986, pp. 64–73. Obituaries are in the Rochester *Democrat and Chronicle* and the *New York Times*, both 23 Nov. 1971.

MILTON BERMAN

WILSON, Joshua Lacy (22 Sept. 1774–14 Aug. 1846), clergyman, was born in Bedford County, Virginia, the son of Henry Wright Wilson, a physician, and Agnes Lacy. His mother provided Wilson with his early education. After his father died from typhus or "camp fever" contracted while serving as an army surgeon in the Bedford militia during the revolutionary war, his mother remarried. In 1781 Wilson's new stepfather, John Templin, moved the family to Wilson's Station, Kentucky, a fort on the Salt River. Until he reached age twenty-two, Wilson lived the life of a frontier farmer. He then entered the Kentucky Academy in Pisgah, but he left after less than a year, continuing his education for the next two years under the tutelage of the Reverend William Mahon. He then worked as the principal of an academy in Frankfort, studying law in his free time, but he soon gave up both to study theology with the Reverend James Vance.

In October 1801 Wilson married Sarah B. Mackay; they had eight children. Licensed to preach by the Presbytery of Transylvania in 1802, he worked in churches in Bardstown and Big Spring. Ordained two years later, Wilson continued at his former churches and then became the pastor of the First Presbyterian Church in Cincinnati, Ohio, in 1808. An invalid all of his life because of an illness he contracted as a young man after diving into freezing water to save a drowning boy, Wilson often preached sitting down with his eyes closed. With Daniel Drake, Wilson helped found Cincinnati College in 1812, served on its board of trustees, and lectured there as a professor of moral philosophy.

As a traditionalist and staunch defender of Calvinist doctrine, Wilson was drawn into the factional controversy of the time. In 1801 the Presbyterian church approved the Plan of Union, an agreement created in response to the perceived duplication of missionary work by the Congregational and Presbyterian churches, especially in the frontiers of the northeastern states. Many small frontier communities had churches of both denominations but lacked a sufficient population to justify both. Because the two churches shared a Calvinistic doctrine and similar simple services, they agreed to combine missionary efforts and allowed congregations to be simultaneously affiliated with both denominations. This agreement fell apart in 1830 when Albert Barnes, a Congregationalist minister and revivalist, was censured by the Presbytery for "laxity of doctrine," thus violating the letter and spirit of the plan. In 1835, in the wake of the Barnes trial, Wilson, a strong opponent of the plan, prosecuted Lyman Beecher, a leader of the "New Church," as a heretic before the Presbytery and the Synod of Cincinnati. Although he had supported Beecher when he became the head of Lane Academy, the preacher's liberal views and revivalist leanings soon eroded any good will between the men. When the synod did not pass what he considered to be a harsh enough judgment on Beecher, Wilson appealed to the General Assembly of 1836. However, his appeal was withdrawn because an equivalent test case was already on the assembly's docket. The Plan of Union was officially repudiated in 1837, splitting the Presbyterian church into two schools, Old and New. The 1837 General Assembly abrogation was also effective retroactively and removed the four synods of Western Reserve, Utica, Geneva, and Genesee, which were originally organized under the Plan of Union. The members of these synods were primarily New Schoolers, and their removal seriously weakened the New School faction within the church.

The two branches disagreed on ideological issues and on how the church should manage its missionary efforts. One major point of theological contention was the intellectual balance between the ideas of humanity's inherently fallen nature and an individual's free will. The Old School argued that after the fall from Eden, humanity was essentially flawed and irredeemable without the grace of God. The New School emphasized every person's responsibility for his or her moral condition and the free will necessary in sin. In addition, the Old School objected to the extensions of Calvinism developed by Jonathan Edwards, Samuel Hopkins ("Hopkinsianism"), and Nathaniel W. Taylor ("Taylorism"), which became accepted parts of the New School's theology. They also disagreed strongly over the Plan of Union and the implications it had for the role of missionary work in the church and within a denomination. The Old School believed that the church was inherently a missionary society and should therefore directly control missionary efforts without recourse to interdenominational cooperations, like that set up by the Plan of Union, or nondenominational outreaches, like those of the American Education Society or the American Home Missionary Society.

Wilson, a firm supporter of the Old School, helped write the Western Memorial, which railed against the New School and its more liberal ideology. Wilson also preached against theaters, dancing, Roman Catholics, and Masons.

Wilson is best remembered for his writings and his work within the Presbyterian church. He founded and edited the religious newspapers the *Pandect* (founded in 1828; later the *Cincinnati Journal*) and the *Standard* (founded 1831) and was the associate editor of the *Presbyterian of the West*. He also published numerous polemical religious pamphlets, including *Episcopal Methodism; or, Dagonism Exhibited: In Five Scenes* (1811) and *Four Propositions against the Claims of the American Home Missionary Society* (1831). He was the first chairman of the board of trustees at Lane Theological Seminary in Jackson, Tennessee (1828–1830), and he served as a trustee of Hanover College (Indiana) from 1839 to 1844. Wilson died in Cincinnati.

• Wilson's papers are housed at the University of Chicago. See also R. L. Hightower, *Joshua L. Wilson: Frontier Controversialist* (1934); Robert Davidson, *History of the Presbyterian Church in the State of Kentucky* (1847); W. B. Sprague, *Annals of the American Pulpit*, vol. 4 (1858); and R. E. Thompson, *A History of the Presbyterian Churches in the United States* (1895). For details of Wilson's prosecution of Beecher, see Charles Beecher, ed., *Autobiography, Correspondence, Etc., of Lyman Beecher* (1864). For an overview of Presbyterian controversies of his time, see L. A. Loetscher, *A Brief History of the Presbyterians* (1978), or John T. McNeil, *History and Character of Calvinism* (1954). An obituary is in the *Cincinnati Morning Herald*, 15 Aug. 1846.

ELIZABETH ZOE VICARY

WILSON, Shadow (25 Sept. 1919–11 July 1959), jazz drummer, was born Rossiere Wilson in Yonkers, New York. Singer and bandleader Billy Eckstine said that Wilson's given name was Rossier Van Donnel, adding, "We called him Shad." Virtually nothing is known of Wilson's parents, early background, or personal life. Starting in 1935 he worked with the bands of Frankie Fairfax and Jimmy Gorham in Philadelphia. When the Gorham band moved to New York in 1938, leadership transferred first to pianist Bill Doggett and then to Lucky Millinder from May 1938 to early 1939, when Millinder declared bankruptcy.

Wilson played with the orchestras of Jimmy Mundy (1939), Benny Carter and Tiny Bradshaw (1940), and Lionel Hampton (1940–1941). According to pianist Sir Charles Thompson, Hampton "wanted the drummers to play a back beat [strong accents on the second and fourth beats] all the time, and that was bad for a pianist. Shadow Wilson joined and he wouldn't be influenced. He had a lot of will power. One time there was a move to fire him, but all the fellows liked Shadow so well and their sentiment was so strong that Lionel had to keep him. After Shadow left, there were never any great drummers with Lionel" (Dance, *Basie*, pp. 338–39).

Wilson joined Earl Hines's orchestra in 1941 and is remembered as one of Hines's finest drummers. Late in 1943 he was among nine of Hines's sidemen—including Billy Eckstine, Charlie Parker, and Dizzy Gillespie—who simultaneously gave notice, in part because they wanted to explore their own developing bebop style and in part because they were discouraged by Hines's undertaking yet another grueling tour of the South. Eckstine had scarcely begun organizing a new big band when Wilson was drafted in the spring of 1944. Somehow extricating himself from army duty, Wilson was a member of the big band of saxophonist Georgie Auld by September, when Jo Jones was drafted out of Count Basie's orchestra. Basie wanted to hire Wilson to replace Jones immediately; Wilson joined two months later, after fulfilling his commitment to Auld. Recordings with Basie demonstrate his ability to drive a big band; on "Queer Street" (1945) he is heard as a soloist.

Jones returned from the army in early 1946, and Wilson left Basie to play with tenor saxophonist Illinois Jacquet's group through 1947. During that year Wilson also took part in celebrated recording sessions with Tadd Dameron's sextet and with Thelonious Monk's quartet; the faster of two versions of Dameron's "Our Delight" demonstrates how well Wilson transferred his forthright, well-rehearsed big band style to a combo setting.

Wilson briefly returned to Basie's orchestra in 1948, and he played with Woody Herman's big band during 1949. He rejoined Jacquet (1949–1950) before touring in Erroll Garner's trio (1950–1952). A recording such as Garner's "Lover" (1950) demonstrates the subtle side of Wilson's musical personality: quiet but briskly energetic swing rhythms, meticulous accents coordinated with Garner's piano arrangement of the tune, and a brief flurry of snare drum soloing to end the piece. Drummer Kelly Martin reports that Wilson was an avid baseball fan, and whenever Garner's trio was in New York at the same time as the Yankees, Wilson would fake a hand injury and—without asking Garner—hire Martin as a substitute.

In 1951, during the course of Wilson's association with Garner, the drummer participated as a freelance player in a session with tenor saxophonist Eddie "Lockjaw" Davis, organist Bill Doggett, and bassist Oscar Pettiford. According to Davis, these were the first tenor and organ recordings, although the archetypal tenor-organ groups (with organ foot pedals replacing string bass and, optionally, with electric guitar added as well) had not yet evolved. Wilson again played with Jacquet's band (1952–1954), worked with Hines again in a seven-piece group (1954), and was part of the trio accompanying singer Ella Fitzgerald (1954–1955). During 1957–1958 he was a member of Monk's quartet with John Coltrane at the Five Spot in New York. Intermittently through the decade Wilson also worked with saxophonist Sonny Stitt, with whom he recorded. During this same period he also recorded with pianist Herbie Nichols, trumpeter Joe Newman, and saxophonist Lee Konitz.

According to trombonist Dickie Wells, "Before he died, Shadow Wilson told me that before he went with Basie he had one way of playing in mind—the latest thing, that was it! Then he got hungry and found out, and began playing with a beat to satisfy the band. He was very versatile and a good drummer, and he played for the musicians on the order of Big Sid [Catlett]" (Dance, *Basie*, p. 93). After stopping all work for several months because of illness, Wilson died of bronchial pneumonia in New York.

• Outlines of Wilson's career are found in standard jazz reference books, together with a paragraph of biography and appreciation in Ira Gitler, *Jazz Masters of the '40s* (1966), p. 190. Additionally, segments of his career may be pieced together from Billy Eckstine, "When Sarah Vaughan Began to Sing," *Melody Maker*, 21 Aug. 1954, p. 5, and "Leading My Outfit," 28 Aug. 1954, p. 13; Albert McCarthy, *Big Band Jazz* (1974); Stanley Dance, *The World of Earl Hines* (1977); Dieter Salemann, "Billy Eckstine Orchestra 1944–1947," *Le point du jazz*, no. 14 (1978): 57; Eileen Southern, "Conversation with . . . William Clarence 'Billy' Eckstine: 'Mr. B' of Ballad and Bop," *Black Perspective in Music* 7 (1979): 197; Dance, *The World of Count Basie* (1980); James M. Doran, *Erroll Garner: The Most Happy Piano* (1985); and Chris Sheridan, *Count Basie: A Bio-discography* (1986). An obituary is in *Jazz Magazine*, no. 52 (1959), p. 15.

BARRY KERNFELD

WILSON, Teddy (24 Nov. 1912–31 July 1986), musician, was born Theodore Shaw Wilson in Austin, Texas, the son of James Augustus Wilson, an English professor at Tuskegee Institute, and Pearl Shaw, the chief librarian at Tuskegee. Wilson grew up in Tuskegee, and as a teenager he heard early recordings by Louis Armstrong, Bix Beiderbecke, King Oliver, and other jazz pioneers. He also spent summer vacations with one of his mother's sisters in Detroit, where he heard groups like the Fletcher Henderson Orchestra. Wilson studied music at Tuskegee and at Talladega College, focusing on the piano but also studying the violin. After a year in college he spent his summer vacation in 1928 in Chicago, where his exposure to many jazz greats profoundly influenced him. His parents convinced him to stay in college another year, but the following summer he moved to Detroit to pursue his musical career. He worked with various territorial bands, and in Toledo, Ohio, he heard the great pianist Art Tatum for the first time and frequently played with him.

Tatum's complex harmonic improvisation had a strong impact on the young Wilson, whose own increasingly melodic playing also influenced Tatum. Wilson himself always focused on melody and rhythm above all. Tatum generally stayed close to the original melody of a tune while exploring its harmonic implications. Wilson, on the other hand, constantly invented his own melodies and rarely played anything the same way twice. He also played with more restricted dynamics, and his touch emphasized clarity and clear articulation. Above all, his playing was tasteful. He had no interest in calling attention to himself, a quality that made him the perfect ensemble player.

In 1931 Wilson moved to Chicago, where he came under the influence of Earl Hines. When Hines left his permanent position at the Grand Terrace ballroom to go on the road, Wilson filled in with Clarence Moore's band. He also played with Armstrong and Jimmy Noone. In 1933 the producer John Hammond heard Wilson on a radio broadcast with Moore's band and arranged for him to travel to New York to play and record with Benny Carter's group, the Chocolate Dandies. Hammond introduced him to Benny Goodman, who hired Wilson to join him and drummer Gene Krupa in the influential Benny Goodman Trio in 1936. The pianist became the first black musician to be publicly featured with a white group in the United States.

In one memorable year, 1935, Wilson played and recorded with a variety of artists, made his debut as a leader of his own instrumental groups and of recordings with Billie Holiday, and began to play with the Goodman trio. The recordings he made with Holiday are among his greatest achievements, his rhythmically steady Mozartian clarity serving as the perfect foil for Holiday's emotive, rhythmically free style in songs like "These Foolish Things." Wilson left Goodman in 1939 and led his own big band for a short time in 1939 and 1940, but he lacked the personal charisma and showmanship that was essential to success in such a venture. He thereafter concentrated on his work with small groups and as a soloist, occasionally rejoining Goodman to tour or record.

A series of recordings Wilson made in April 1941 are typical of his creative output during this period, particularly an extraordinary rendition of "I Know That You Know." In this up-tempo piece and in others, Wilson smooths out the powerful left hand of the stride style while playing lyrical single-note lines with his right hand and adding subtle dynamic shadings throughout. While he could provide a powerful sense of swing when the piece demanded (as in "Sailin'" with a Goodman septet), his playing was most notable for its beautiful delicacy and symmetry. Wilson later commented that the introduction of microphones liberated him, allowing him to introduce a much softer style than that favored by Fats Waller or Hines. Similarly, the "muscle" supplied by Goodman drummers like Krupa and the emotionality of singers like Holiday allowed Wilson to pursue a less visceral approach. And like many other jazz players of his era, Wilson was profoundly influenced by classical musicians, particularly Mozart. He often played classical music for his own pleasure, had a substantial record collection, and kept abreast of classical pianists' careers.

By 1942 only Tatum surpassed Wilson in influence among jazz pianists. And though Wilson made few creative advances for the remainder of his career, essentially ignoring the newer styles that appeared, he continued to play widely. He taught regularly at the Juilliard School of Music from 1945 to 1952 and there and at other colleges periodically thereafter. During the 1960s he played in Europe, Japan, South America, and Australia, and in the 1970s he appeared regularly at Michael's Pub in New York City and annually at the Newport Jazz Festival. His playing in these later decades was often routine and his repertoire rarely varied, but even at this "ordinary" level his style retained its remarkable, well-crafted sense of beauty.

Teddy Wilson epitomized urbane sophistication in both his playing and personal life. Performing with grace and subtlety, he refined Hines's complex cross-rhythms, Waller's powerful stride style, and Tatum's harmonic sophistication into a personal, instantly recognizable style. Though he rarely moved beyond the achievements of his early career, he remained one of the most subtly satisfying of jazz pianists, influencing Hank Jones, Jimmy Rowles, Tommy Flanagan, Dick Katz, and many other modern players.

Wilson was married four times and had five children. His first marriage was in 1931 to Irene Armstrong, a songwriter and pianist better known by her name from a later marriage, Irene Kitchings. They had no children and were divorced. Wilson then married Janice Carati, with whom he had his first child, a son. After their divorce he married Blanche Louth. They had two sons before their divorce. He married for a final time to Joanne Roberts, with whom he had a son and a daughter. Wilson died in New Britain, Connecticut.

• The best introduction to Wilson's music is in Gunther Schuller, *The Swing Era: The Development of Jazz, 1930–1945* (1989). Briefer, but useful, discussions can be found in Len Lyons, *The Great Jazz Pianists, Speaking of Their Lives and Music* (1983); Frank Tirro, *Jazz: A History*, 2d ed. (1993); James Lincoln Collier, *The Making of Jazz: A Comprehensive History* (1978); Nat Hentoff, *Jazz Is* (1976; repr. 1992); and Gary Giddins, *Rhythm-a-ning: Jazz Tradition and Innovation in the '80s* (1986). His work on records is treated in

Max Harrison et al., *The Essential Jazz Records*, vol. 1 (1984). An interview with Irene Kitchings that provides details of her marriage to Wilson is in Stanley Dance's *The World of Earl Hines* (1977), pp. 179–82. Obituaries are in the *New York Times* and the *Washington Post*, 1 Aug. 1986.

RONALD P. DUFOUR

WILSON, William Bauchop (2 Apr. 1862–25 May 1934), labor leader, U.S. congressman, and the first secretary of labor, was born in Blantyre, Scotland, the son of Adam Wilson, a miner, and Helen Bauchop. In 1870 the family moved to Arnot, Pennsylvania, where William began working in the coal mines at the age of nine. He received little formal education but read extensively, forming a boys debating club at the age of fourteen. In 1883 he married Agnes Williamson; they had eleven children.

As a young man Wilson worked as a farmer and railroad fireman as well as a miner. He joined a union at the age of eleven, became secretary of his local at age fourteen, and was eventually jailed, blacklisted, and evicted from his home because of his union activities. In 1890 he helped organize the United Mine Workers of America (UMWA) and was elected to its executive board. In 1899 he became president of UMWA District 2 in Pennsylvania and from 1900 to 1908 served as secretary-treasurer of the national union. During the strikes of 1899, 1900, and 1902 he raised money and supplied food and clothing for striking miners.

In 1906 Wilson was elected to the first of three terms in the U.S. House of Representatives. As a Democratic congressman elected from a working-class district in north central Pennsylvania, he was active in labor legislation, sponsoring an investigation of mine safety, serving on a special committee to investigate the growing use by employers of time-motion studies and pay incentives known as "scientific management," supporting the establishment of a Bureau of Mines, and sponsoring legislation regulating the working conditions of seamen in the merchant marine. In 1912 and 1913 he served as chairman of the House committee on labor.

In 1912 Republican Edgar R. Kiess defeated Wilson in his bid for a fourth term. But following Woodrow Wilson's victory in the presidential election and the creation of a Department of Labor in early 1913, William B. Wilson became the nation's first secretary of labor. In that position he was responsible for organizing the new department, keeping the Children's Bureau and the Bureau of Labor Statistics intact, splitting the old Bureau of Immigration and Naturalization into two separate agencies, and creating a Conciliation Service to mediate labor disputes and an Employment Service to match prospective employers with workers looking for jobs. During World War I he served on the Council of National Defense and was appointed war labor administrator. He also presided over a growing department, which came to include expanded Employment and Conciliation Services, a new Bureau of Industrial Housing and Transportation that provided housing for war workers, a Woman in Industry Service that monitored conditions of women in the workforce, and other services concerned with information, training, and working conditions.

At the end of the war Secretary Wilson served as president of the International Labor Conference in 1919 and as chairman of the Federal Board for Vocational Training in 1920 and 1921. He was appointed chairman of the second National Industrial Conference, which tried unsuccessfully to control a surge in postwar industrial violence. With the end of Woodrow Wilson's presidency, William B. Wilson resigned as secretary of labor and pursued mining and agriculture interests in Pennsylvania during the 1920s. In 1926 he ran unsuccessfully as the Democratic nominee for U.S. senator from Pennsylvania. He died on a train near Savannah, Georgia.

• The William B. Wilson Papers are in the Historical Society of Pennsylvania, Philadelphia. Other Wilson materials are in the Woodrow Wilson Papers in the Library of Congress and the General Records of the Department of Labor, Record Group 174, in the National Archives. A biography of William B. Wilson has yet to be published, but two books, Roger Babson, *W. B. Wilson and the Department of Labor* (1919), and John Lombardi, *Labor's Voice in the Cabinet: A History of the Department of Labor from Its Origins to 1921* (1942), focus on Wilson's tenure as secretary of labor and give brief accounts of his early life. Two modern scholarly studies of Wilson's years in the cabinet are John S. Smith, "Organized Labor in the Wilson Era, 1913–1921: Some Conclusions," *Labor History* 3 (Fall 1962): 265–86, and Melvyn Dubofsky, "Abortive Reform: The Wilson Administration and Organized Labor, 1913–1920," in *Work, Community and Power: The Experience of Labor in Europe and America, 1900–1925*, ed. James E. Cronin and Carmen Sirianni (1983). An obituary appears in the *New York Times*, 26 May 1934.

BRUCE I. BUSTARD

WILSON, William Lyne (3 May 1843–17 Oct. 1900), politician and educator, was born in Jefferson County, (West) Virginia, the son of Benjamin Wilson, a teacher and farmer, and Mary Ann Whiting Lyne. Wilson received a B.A. from Columbian College (now George Washington University) in 1860 and attended the University of Virginia (1860–1861). From 1861 to 1865 he served as a private in the Confederate cavalry. His diary from these years reveals Wilson as an effective, learned writer. In 1865 Wilson returned to Columbian College to teach Latin and study law. Three years later he married Nannie Judson Huntington; they had six children. Admitted to the bar in 1869, Wilson entered practice at Charles Town, West Virginia, in 1871. There he played an active role in the Democratic party, serving as city attorney and county superintendent of schools and running unsuccessfully in 1874 for state representative. In 1880 he represented West Virginia at the national convention and served as a presidential elector. His speeches that year, tinged with erudition, earned him renown as a scholar in politics, and two years later the Democratic Board of Regents appointed him president of West Virginia University. But he held that post for less than a year. In 1882 he won election to Congress, where he served for the next twelve years.

In the House of Representatives Wilson made his mark as an advocate of a reduced tariff. In his maiden speech on the subject, in support of a tariff-reduction measure sponsored by Ways and Means Committee chairman William R. Morrison, Wilson portrayed the high tariff as a tax not unlike the tyrannical exactions against which the American revolutionaries had rebelled. He believed that the protective tariff represented an unfair and burdensome levy against consumers, especially farmers and laborers, in the interest of manufacturers, and that it led to the creation of monopolies. At the same time, Wilson took care to exempt West Virginia coal and other products from his call for general tariff reduction. At heart a Jeffersonian, suspicious of government activism, Wilson opposed the 1886 Oleomargarine Bill designed to aid dairy farmers by taxing oleomargarine and other substitutes. Yet, unlike many Democrats, he supported the Blair Bill calling for federal aid to education, especially in the South. To Wilson, the Fifteenth Amendment entailed a national obligation to raise the newly enfranchised black voters to literate citizenship.

Applauding President Grover Cleveland's low-tariff message of December 1887, Wilson accepted membership on the powerful Ways and Means Committee. In the ensuing months he championed the Mills Tariff Bill, which aimed at a general reduction in customs duties. Denying Republican arguments that the protective tariff kept American wage levels from being undermined by "pauper" foreign labor, Wilson argued that the wages of American workers derived mostly from labor's relatively high productivity and the generally low cost of production in the United States. Although the Republican Senate defeated the Mills bill, Wilson emphasized these and other low-tariff arguments in a speaking tour during Cleveland's losing campaign for reelection in 1888 and in his campaign book, *The National Democratic Party: Its History, Principles, Achievements, and Aims* (1888). As the monopoly issue emerged in the late 1880s, Wilson denounced trusts as a principal evil spawned by the high tariff. He supported the Interstate Commerce Act and the Sherman Anti-Trust Act, yet considered extensive federal regulation improper. Instead he favored state control through corporate charters and franchises, plus a broadening of competition through freer foreign trade. As a member of the minority in the Fifty-first Congress, Wilson condemned the new House rules promulgated by Speaker Thomas Reed, charging that they allowed Republicans to pass unwarranted and unconstitutional paternalistic legislation. Most egregious of all to Wilson was the McKinley Tariff Act, which raised the average duty to a peace-time record high.

In 1890 Wilson and other Democrats campaigned hard against the McKinley Act and other elements of Republican activism, which resulted in a landslide victory for Wilson and his party in the national House. The following summer Wilson became editor of the tariff-reform section of the Democratic St. Louis *Republic*, writing seventy-eight articles for the paper by the close of the 1892 election campaign. That year he presided at the Democratic national convention and argued on the stump that a tariff for protection was not only bad policy but unconstitutional. In his own district he triumphantly defeated a challenge from free silver forces in part by raising the specter of a "force" bill allowing federal regulation of elections in the event of Republican victory. In the nation the Democrats took both House and Senate and returned Cleveland to the presidency. Wilson played a leading role in the new Democratic Congress. When the panic of 1893 moved Cleveland to call a special session, Wilson led the House effort to repeal the Sherman Silver Purchase Act of 1890. As Ways and Means Committee chairman he spearheaded the preparation of a tariff bill that lowered the average rate twenty percentage points below McKinley Act rates and greatly expanded the free list. Acquiescing in an income tax amendment, Wilson squired his bill to a comfortable passage in February 1894. In the Senate, however, protectionist interests succeeded in attaching hundreds of amendments that raised the average rate, and in taking scores of items off the Wilson bill free list. The emasculated Wilson-Gorman Tariff became law without Cleveland's signature.

The Democrats' seeming ineptitude in dealing with the post-panic depression led to a Republican landslide in the 1894 congressional elections, which swept Wilson from office. At Cleveland's behest, the ex-congressman became postmaster general in April 1895. Diligent but not terribly effective as an administrator, Wilson made modest steps toward improved postal management. His commitment to keeping government small, however, prevented his giving more than half hearted support to a trial of rural free delivery and fueled his resistance to postal telegraphy. Adamant against free silver, he condemned 1896 Democratic presidential nominee William Jennings Bryan as an apostle of socialism and anarchy. Declining to run against Bryan on behalf of the Gold Democrats, Wilson supported their nominee John M. Palmer (1817–1900). Upon leaving the cabinet he became president of Washington and Lee University, where, though in ill health, he mounted a fund drive aimed at building the school's faculty in economics and political science. Appalled by the McKinley Administration's off-shore expansionism, Wilson returned to the regular Democratic fold in 1900 to support Bryan on an anti-imperialism platform. Before the election he died of tuberculosis at his home in Lexington, Virginia.

• The principal holdings of Wilson's papers are in the West Virginia University Library and the Washington and Lee University Library. Wilson correspondence is also found in the papers of W. C. P. Breckinridge, William D. Bynum, Grover Cleveland, and Carl Schurz, all in the Library of Congress, and in the William F. Vilas Papers in the Wisconsin State Historical Society Library. The National Archives holds papers relating to Wilson's service in Congress, particularly House committee records, and his tenure as postmaster general. The standard biography is Festus P. Summers, *William L. Wilson and Tariff Reform* (1953). Summers also edited two volumes of Wilson's diary: *The Cabinet Diary of William L. Wilson, 1896–1897* (1957), and *A Borderland Confederate* (1962).

CHARLES W. CALHOUN

WILSON, Woodrow (28/29 Dec. 1856–3 Feb. 1924), the twenty-eighth president of the United States, was born Thomas Woodrow Wilson in Staunton, Virginia, the son of Dr. Joseph Ruggles Wilson, Presbyterian minister and director of the Augusta Female Seminary, and Janet Woodrow. Young Wilson was educated at home and developed close attachments to both parents, who instilled in him their Scotch-Irish and English heritage, Calvinist faith, and southern values. He later attended private schools.

The boy experienced the American Civil War and the postwar Reconstruction in the South. The Wilson family, although from the North originally, adopted southern ways. Dr. Wilson believed the Bible justified slavery. Although he welcomed African Americans in church, he kept them separate from the white congregation. He also helped divide southern from northern Presbyterians. In 1861, as pastor of the First Presbyterian Church in Augusta, Georgia, he organized a meeting to form the General Assembly of the Southern Presbyterian Church and served prominently as its clerk for thirty-seven years. He ministered to the Confederate army one summer as a chaplain and used the Augusta church as a temporary hospital for Confederate soldiers. In 1870 the family moved to Columbia, South Carolina, where Dr. Wilson became a professor at the Theological Seminary and pastor of the First Presbyterian Church. Young Wilson witnessed the war's devastation of the South even more here than he had earlier in Georgia. Like his father, he abhorred the participation of African Americans in the postwar Reconstruction governments and criticized universal suffrage as "the foundation of every evil in this country." He joined his father's church in 1873. Thereafter, Wilson's Calvinist faith sustained him during times of trial.

Wilson attended Presbyterian colleges away from home. In 1873 he entered Davidson College near Charlotte, North Carolina. Before finishing the academic year, however, the homesick student returned to his parents, who had moved to Wilmington, North Carolina, where his father had begun a new pastorate. After spending over a year at home, reading under his father's tutelage about such topics as Manchester liberalism, Wilson resumed his formal education in 1875 at the College of New Jersey in Princeton, a well-regarded school that attracted southern Presbyterians.

Princeton University, as the College of New Jersey was later named, provided the right environment for Wilson. Eager to learn about government, he studied history and politics. He also practiced the art of persuasion and leadership as an active member of literary and debating clubs, including the prestigious Whig Society. He organized the Liberal Debating Club and drafted its parliamentary constitution. Political theories of Edmund Burke and Walter Bagehot especially appealed to Wilson. Inspired by the British parliamentary tradition, Wilson began to regard himself as a future statesman. While an undergraduate, he wrote his first article, "Cabinet Government in the United States," which editor Henry Cabot Lodge published in the *International Review* (Aug. 1879). Wilson, who was elected editor of the *Princetonian* and secretary of the Football Association, played baseball for recreation. He graduated in the class of 1879.

After Princeton, Wilson went to the University of Virginia to study law and prepare for a career as a lawyer and politician. Here in Thomas Jefferson's Charlottesville, he joined the Jefferson Society, a debating and literary club. In 1880 he endorsed John Bright's liberal British critique of the southern Confederacy and affirmed a pro-Union, nationalist interpretation of the Civil War. He agreed with Bright that southern independence was a futile dream and union with the North was the South's best hope for prosperity. Discouraged and lonely during the fall of 1880, and complaining of a cold, Wilson left the university on Christmas Day and returned home. He continued to study law at home and in 1882 passed the Georgia bar exam.

Wilson set up a law practice in Atlanta, but he and his law partner, Edward Renick, attracted few clients and did not share in the city's thriving economy. In 1882, having little else to do, he testified before a federal commission in favor of tariff reduction, which he endorsed as the way to promote international trade and peace. Wilson's mother gave him some legal business concerning inherited family lands, which took him to Rome, Georgia, in 1883. There he quickly fell in love with Ellen Louise Axson, daughter of the town's Presbyterian pastor.

Yearning for marriage but recognizing that he could not afford a family, Wilson decided to change careers. Abandoning law in 1883, but not his ambition to become a statesman, he entered Johns Hopkins University to study constitutional and political history. Modeled on German higher education, Hopkins offered doctoral degrees. Wilson studied history with Herbert Baxter Adams, who had earned a Ph.D. at Heidelberg. Adams taught him the "germ theory" of history, emphasizing the Anglo-Saxon origins of American political institutions. Wilson also studied political economy with Richard T. Ely, who rejected laissez-faire economics and later advocated progressive reforms in Governor Robert M. La Follette's Wisconsin.

Wilson found German-style research in historical documents, as taught by Adams, exceedingly tedious. He confessed to Ellen Axson: "I have a strong instinct of leadership, an unmistakably oratorical temperament, and the keenest possible delight in affairs; and it has required very constant and stringent schooling to content me with the sober methods of the scholar and the man of letters." Reading what he enjoyed and using his own imagination, he wrote his first book, *Congressional Government* (1885), which Adams approved as a doctoral dissertation. Emulating Bagehot's realistic approach to British politics, Wilson portrayed how the U.S. Constitution actually worked in contrast to its framers' theories as expressed in the *Federalist*. In his view, congressional committees dominated the government behind closed doors at the expense of both public discourse and presidential leadership. In 1886 Johns Hopkins University awarded the Ph.D. to Wilson (making him the first U.S. president with an earned doctorate).

Wilson began teaching history and political science at Bryn Mawr, a Quaker college for women near Philadelphia, Pennsylvania. With the promise of steady income, he and Ellen Axson were married on 24 June 1885. Their family soon expanded with the birth of three daughters. Ellen Wilson devoted her time to the family and helped with research for her husband's next book, *The State* (1889).

In this textbook, Wilson affirmed his Social Darwinian belief in the "stronger and nobler races which have made the most notable progress in civilization." He attributed the progress of western civilization to the Aryan and Semitic races, which had transmitted their political ideas and habits through the history of the Greeks, Latins, Teutons, and Celts to the modern nations of western Europe and the United States. "The existing governments of Europe and America furnish the dominating types of today," he added. "To know other systems that are defeated or dead would aid only indirectly towards an understanding of those which are alive and triumphant, as the survived fittest."

Wilson's academic career took off. Unhappy teaching women, he left Bryn Mawr in 1888 to join the Wesleyan University faculty in Middletown, Connecticut. He hoped to shape the minds of young men, who would provide the nation's future leaders. Wilson welcomed the opportunity in 1890 to return to Princeton as professor of jurisprudence and political economy. A popular teacher and productive scholar, he gained further local and national recognition.

Wilson published extensively during his Princeton years. In *Division and Reunion, 1829–1889* (1893), he interpreted the Civil War and Reconstruction from a pro-Union and pro-white perspective. By this time, however, he had abandoned the germ theory and instead propounded his own frontier thesis to explain American history. Influenced by conversations and correspondence with historian Frederick Jackson Turner, Wilson now credited the frontier, more than the Anglo-Saxon heritage, with the rise of freedom and democracy in the New World. He also wrote books for profit. *George Washington* (1897) and *A History of the American People* (5 vols., 1902) provided extra income for his growing family and their new house.

In 1902 Princeton's trustees chose Wilson as president. His national prominence and leadership potential promised to raise the university's stature. Its first president without formal theological education, he nevertheless possessed strong Presbyterian credentials. But unlike some clergy who rejected modern science and embraced fundamentalist religious beliefs, Wilson espoused liberal Christianity. He identified with his uncle, James Woodrow, who had endured a trial in 1888 before the General Assembly of the Southern Presbyterian Church for teaching Darwinian science at Columbia Theological Seminary. Like his uncle, who left the seminary rather than change his views, Wilson saw no contradiction between modern science and religion.

As president, Wilson sought to improve Princeton's academic standing by instituting structural reform. Emphasizing scholarship, he established new departments and hired new faculty. With the trustees' approval in 1905, he recruited young faculty as tutors or preceptors. To stimulate intellectual activity and attenuate gradations of status among undergraduates, he attacked their exclusive eating clubs and proposed that students instead take meals in a residential quadrangle. Students as well as alumni criticized these reforms. Wilson also encountered resistance from the graduate dean, Andrew Fleming West, who pressed ahead with his own plans for a residential graduate college. Facing overwhelming opposition, Wilson's plan to replace the undergraduate eating clubs failed. Moreover, contrary to his advice, Princeton trustees in 1910 accepted a generous bequest that West had secured for the graduate college. Stubbornly refusing to compromise, he denounced this decision as a violation of both educational and democratic values. This further alienated the trustees, who welcomed his resignation later in 1910.

By this time, Wilson was running for governor of New Jersey. Democratic political bosses saw him as a candidate who might transcend the party's divisions, collaborating with them but also attracting support from those favoring progressive reforms. The bosses enabled him to win the nomination and the 1910 election. But Wilson soon distanced himself from them and presented himself as the people's advocate against special interests. He enhanced his progressive reputation by gaining the legislature's approval for laws guaranteeing an open political process, if only for white men, with direct nomination of candidates and honest elections. Other reforms attacked abuses of corporate capitalism by establishing workmen's compensation, regulating public utilities, and improving labor conditions for women and children. New Jersey continued, however, as a haven for corporations.

Wilson's reputation as a progressive governor improved his prospects for winning the Democratic presidential nomination in 1912. Encouraged by "Colonel" Edward M. House of Texas, with whom he formed a close friendship, and other Democrats who wanted to end Republican control of the White House, Wilson attracted nationwide support. He nurtured a closer relationship with William Jennings Bryan, who, despite losing presidential elections in 1896, 1900, and 1908, had transformed the Democratic party into a more progressive institution. In his Jackson Day address on 8 January 1912, Wilson, who had once criticized Bryan's agrarian radicalism, now praised him for steadfastly advocating democratic principles. Wilson's progressivism, like Bryan's, affirmed both continuity and change. They both advocated self-government by the people. Their common Presbyterian faith undergirded their calls for reform and their patriotism. "Let no man suppose that progress can be divorced from religion or that there is any other platform for the ministers of reform than the platform written in the utterances of our Lord and Saviour," Wilson affirmed in 1911. He identified the United States with Christianity: "America was born a Christian nation. America was born to exemplify that devotion to the elements of righteousness which are derived from the revelations of Holy Scripture."

At the Democratic party's convention in Baltimore in June 1912, no candidate initially commanded the two-thirds majority required for the nomination. Wilson's strategists, including William Gibbs McAdoo, hoped delegates would eventually vote for him after their first choices fell short. Bryan, who supported Champ Clark of Missouri, switched to Wilson. As prospects faded for Clark and Oscar Underwood of Alabama, others followed Bryan's example. Indiana's delegation, led by Governor Thomas R. Marshall, was one of the first to shift to Wilson, who eventually won the nomination; Marshall was selected to run for the vice presidency.

In the 1912 presidential election, Wilson faced William Howard Taft, the incumbent Republican president; Theodore Roosevelt, the former Republican president and current Progressive candidate; and Eugene V. Debs, the perennial Socialist nominee. The Republicans' split between Taft "conservatives" and Roosevelt "progressives" made it possible for Democrats to capture the White House. Wilson presented himself as the people's champion within the progressive tradition. But his concept of democracy was limited. Stockton Axson, his brother-in-law, observed: "His instinct for democracy involved the idea that, because a democracy is free, it is the more necessary that it be led. His faith in the people has never been a faith in the supreme wisdom of the people, but rather in the capacity of the people to be led right by those whom they elect and constitute their leaders." Wilson wanted to exclude women from public affairs, opposing their right to vote because their place was "in the home" and their involvement would produce "the unsexed, masculinized woman." He also favored Jim Crow laws that excluded African Americans from voting and other basic rights. Nor did he expect Native Americans to assimilate into the nation as citizens. Wilson did not promise equality and freedom for all Americans.

Wilson and Roosevelt, the two leading candidates, advocated different reform alternatives for dealing with America's industrial and agricultural problems. Wilson's New Freedom and Roosevelt's New Nationalism embraced democratic capitalism, but differed over the best means to preserve both equality of opportunity and efficiency within a modern corporate society. Wilson wanted to ensure the competitiveness of the free market so that opportunities would remain open for future individual entrepreneurs. Roosevelt, more accepting of large-scale organizations, preferred government regulation of monopolistic trusts so that the country would benefit from their efficient productivity. Wilson and Roosevelt agreed, in contrast to Taft, that reforms were needed to preserve the political and economic system and also protect it from Debs's "radical" socialist alternative. In the election on 4 November 1912, Wilson won 435 electoral votes to Roosevelt's 88 and Taft's 8, but not a majority of the popular vote. The solidly Democratic South helped its first native son since the Civil War to capture the White House.

After the inauguration on 4 March 1913, Wilson implemented his new concept of the presidency. In *Congressional Government*, he had regarded Congress as the dominant branch of the federal government, and the president as a mere administrator. Impressed with Roosevelt's use of presidential power, however, Wilson adopted a positive view of the office. In *Constitutional Government in the United States* (1908), he offered a new concept of presidential leadership. "The President," he proclaimed, "is at liberty, both in law and in conscience, to be as big a man as he can. His capacity will set the limit; and if Congress be overborne by him, it will be no fault of the makers of the Constitution, . . . but only because the President has the nation behind him and Congress has not." Now Wilson could put his ideas into practice.

Wilson wanted to enhance the presidency by establishing a direct link to the American people. He thought the president, as their spokesman, should be the preeminent leader of the democratic nation. Long convinced that the British parliamentary government was better than the American constitutional system, he exerted personal influence on the legislative branch in unprecedented ways. Rejecting the traditional republican understanding of separation of powers among the branches of government as an old Whig or Newtonian theory, he endeavored to establish executive control over both domestic and foreign affairs. He used an office at the Capitol to confer with members of Congress. The first president to hold regular press conferences, he sought to shape public opinion by managing news from the White House. Moreover, he delivered messages personally to Congress, reviving a practice that George Washington and John Adams had used on a few occasions. From Jefferson through Taft, other U.S. presidents had submitted only written messages. Wilson hoped to use his rhetorical powers to mold public opinion and thus to pressure representatives and senators to vote as he directed.

Wilson successfully used these techniques of presidential leadership to gain the adoption of his New Freedom agenda. He advocated three major reforms. The first was the reduction of import tariffs. Now that the United States had emerged as the world's leading industrial nation, he saw no reason to protect American manufacturing against foreign competition. A lower tariff, he thought, would encourage greater efficiency in U.S. factories, undermine the monopolistic trusts, stimulate international trade, and promote world peace. On 8 April 1913 Wilson appeared before a joint session of Congress to make his case. Oscar Underwood, chair of the House Ways and Means Committee, introduced a tariff bill that would lower duties by about one-fourth and add many items to the free list. His bill also included a new income tax to replace the anticipated loss of tariff revenue. Within a month the House voted for the bill. The Senate initially hesitated but eventually succumbed to Wilson's pressure through the Democratic caucus. On 3 October 1913 Wilson signed the Underwood Tariff Act.

Wilson turned next to banking and currency reform. After the panic of 1907, almost all bankers, businesspeople, and farmers agreed that the nation needed a more modern banking system. They did not, however, share the same views on what it should be. Republicans generally preferred a privately controlled central bank. Secretary of State Bryan and other progressive Democrats advocated a regional banking system with government control of the nation's currency. Wilson worked with Bryan, Treasury secretary McAdoo, and the chairs of the House and Senate Banking Committees, Carter Glass and Robert L. Owen, to craft a compromise, a new Federal Reserve System that would regulate the nation's money supply. This provided for regional banks under a single Federal Reserve Board that could control the issue of currency. On 23 June 1913 Wilson again appeared before Congress. Both the House and Senate eventually voted for his banking and currency reform. On 23 December 1913 the president signed the Federal Reserve Act.

Wilson turned finally to antitrust reform. On 20 January 1914 he appeared before Congress and requested further sanctions against monopolies. Samuel Gompers and the American Federation of Labor urged him to exempt organized labor from antitrust injunctions. As he wrestled with the complexities of enforcing antitrust laws against industrial corporations and labor unions, Wilson shifted toward Roosevelt's New Nationalism. On 26 September 1914 he approved the Federal Trade Commission Act, which created a new regulatory commission. On 15 October 1914 he also signed the Clayton Antitrust Act, which revised the Sherman Antitrust Act to specify more precisely the unacceptable practices in restraint of trade and to provide penalties and remedies for violations. This legislative compromise sharpened the distinction between legitimate and illegal corporate practices and partially exempted labor unions from injunctions.

By reforming the tariff, banking and currency, and antitrust laws, Wilson's New Freedom sought to preserve an open political economy for a new generation of Americans. Yet these reforms left women as well as racial and ethnic minorities on the margins. When a delegation of the National American Woman Suffrage Association, headed by Anna Howard Shaw, visited the president on 8 December 1913, he refused to support voting rights for women, claiming that he could not endorse this reform because he had not campaigned for it in the 1912 election. Wilson authorized racial segregation in federal executive departments, permitting the southern Jim Crow system to become the national practice. William Monroe Trotter and W. E. B. Du Bois, two prominent African Americans who had supported him in 1912, quickly became disillusioned. On 12 November 1914 Trotter led a delegation of African Americans to the White House to plead for the removal of racial barriers. Wilson told them that he thought black as well as white Americans benefited from separation between races. When Trotter challenged his advocacy of racial segregation and inequality, the president angrily ordered the delegation out of his office. He also approved discrimination against Asian immigrants and allowed an increasing number of American Indians to lose their land to white owners. There were limits to his New Freedom and his underlying concept of democracy.

In his family, Wilson experienced both joy and grief during the early White House years. Two daughters were married, and the third also left home to pursue a career. Wilson's greatest loss, however, was the death of his wife on 6 August 1914. Ellen Wilson had provided constant love and support, especially during his recurrent bouts of ill health. His stress manifested itself in perennial stomach disorders and hypertension. In 1896 he suffered the first of what were possibly several minor strokes. She nurtured him and encouraged him to take vacations in Great Britain and Bermuda. She also tolerated his close friendship with Mrs. Mary Allen Hulbert Peck, whom he met in Bermuda in 1907. Mrs. Peck's divorce in 1912 generated rumors during the presidential campaign about their intimate relationship, which he claimed was purely platonic. Soon after Ellen Wilson's death, the lonely president met Edith Bolling Galt, whom he married on 18 December 1915. Wilson's second wife, also a southerner, furnished the emotional warmth that he so desperately needed.

In international relations, Wilson derived his orientation from the history and political culture of the United States. At home and abroad, he believed that democracy required "progressive order." First in the New World and then in the Old, he wanted to manage change rather than suffer uncontrollable chaos or anarchy. He preferred reform to revolution. After Europe plunged into war in 1914, he applied to the Old World the vision of America's mission that he first offered to the Western Hemisphere. The rise of the United States in the global political economy and the collapse of Europe's balance of power, which the First World War clearly revealed, provided the conditions for his redefinition of America's global mission.

Beginning with a new Latin American policy in 1913, Wilson urged "the development of constitutional liberty in the world." Edward House encouraged him to negotiate a Pan-American treaty of nonaggression and political cooperation, starting with the ABC nations, Argentina, Brazil and Chile. The president maintained that this treaty, which provided mutual guarantees of territorial integrity and republican political institutions, would extend the Monroe Doctrine throughout the Western Hemisphere. At the Pan-American Scientific Congress on 6 January 1916, he called for "the ordered progress of society" in South as well as North America. The proposed treaty, he said, would provide a guarantee against both internal revolution and external aggression. Latin Americans, however, were alarmed by Wilson's Pan-Americanism, which evoked the danger of U.S. hegemony throughout the hemisphere. He eventually dropped the treaty in early 1917, but this failure did not discourage him from projecting the same idea of collective security onto the entire world.

While promoting Pan-Americanism, Wilson used military force unilaterally in the Caribbean and Latin America. The region's strategic importance for the United States increased with the 1914 opening of the Panama Canal. Despite his earlier denunciation of Taft's "dollar diplomacy," Wilson was eager to protect American economic interests. By fostering governments friendly to the United States, he sought to exclude European influence and impose American control in the region. He sent U.S. troops to occupy Haiti in 1915 and the Dominican Republic in 1916 to compel their leaders to establish "acceptable" governments and meet their financial obligations. Although Wilson promised constitutional liberty, his use of military force did not enable the United States to export its democratic political culture to these island nations. Military intervention did, however, consolidate U.S. hegemony in the Caribbean.

U.S. rivalry with Europe in Latin America became most intense during the revolution in Mexico, which caused Wilson more difficulty than any other foreign policy issue in the Western Hemisphere. Early in 1913, General Victoriano Huerta captured Mexico City, ousting Francisco Madero's revolutionary government. Madero was murdered during this counterrevolutionary coup. Refusing to recognize Huerta's new government, Wilson sought an acceptable alternative. He once remarked, "I am going to teach the South American Republics to elect good men!" Huerta turned to Europe to counter Wilson's plan to replace him through a democratic election. Failing to shape Mexico's politics by peaceful methods, Wilson resorted to military intervention. The occupation of Veracruz in April 1914, although timed to prevent the landing of a German ship with munitions and justified by the brief detention of U.S. sailors in Tampico, revealed his determination to remove Huerta. Unexpected Mexican resistance and U.S. casualties led Wilson to accept mediation by the ABC countries to end the crisis. Venustiano Carranza eventually replaced Huerta as Mexico's president, and Wilson recognized his government in October 1915. Yet Carranza, too, resisted American paternalism. He saw a threat in General John J. Pershing's punitive expedition into Mexico in March 1916 to capture Francisco "Pancho" Villa, a Mexican outlaw who had raided Columbus, New Mexico. Pershing's soldiers clashed with Carranza's troops as well as Villa's. Mexico turned to Germany for military assistance. In January 1917, hoping to divert the United States from Europe by embroiling it in a war with Mexico, German foreign secretary Arthur Zimmermann proposed a possible alliance against the United States. This ill-conceived German plan failed. British intelligence intercepted the Zimmermann telegram and gave it to Wilson. As the United States moved toward war against Germany in 1917, Wilson released the telegram. He also ordered Pershing's withdrawal from Mexico, which improved Mexican-American relations. But the episode left a legacy of distrust.

Although Wilson had sought to keep the United States out of the European war, his efforts were failing by early 1917. U.S. relations with Germany had deteriorated before the Zimmermann telegram. From the beginning, the Great War had threatened to entangle the United States in Europe despite Wilson's pursuit of neutrality, which he proclaimed on 4 August 1914. He wanted the United States to remain aloof from both the Allies (the British, French, and Russian empires, and later Italy) and the Central Powers (the German, Austro-Hungarian, and Ottoman empires). He appealed to American citizens to "act and speak in the true spirit of neutrality, which is the spirit of impartiality."

Recognizing, however, that the war might threaten U.S. interests, Wilson was anxious to negotiate a compromise peace. He offered U.S. mediation and authorized Edward House, who had been in Europe on the eve of the July 1914 crisis, to continue his efforts to resolve the Anglo-German rivalry. He sent House back to Europe in February 1915 to seek a settlement between the Allies and the Central Powers and thereby protect neutral rights. Germany's decision that same month to use submarines against Allied shipping, in retaliation against the British offshore blockade of German ports, underscored the urgency of House's mission. But by April, when he returned home, it was obvious that House had failed to achieve any reconciliation between the belligerents.

On 7 May 1915 a German submarine sank the British passenger liner *Lusitania*, killing 1,198, including 124 Americans. Wilson vigorously protested. When he refused to make a comparable protest against the British blockade of German ports, Bryan resigned as secretary of state, believing that the president was no longer pursuing impartial neutrality. Yet Wilson still intended to avoid war, proclaiming that the United States was "too proud to fight." Robert Lansing, Bryan's successor, also wanted to maintain U.S. neutrality, despite his belief that Kaiser Wilhelm II's Germany threatened all democratic nations.

Wilson endeavored both to keep the United States out of the European war and to protect its maritime and commercial rights. The potential contradiction between these goals reappeared when a German submarine sank the British ship *Arabic* on 19 August 1915, injuring two Americans. Wilson again issued sharp protests but refused to break diplomatic relations with Germany, as House and Lansing proposed. Germany ended the crisis by pledging to refrain from attacking passenger liners. In pursuit of neutrality, the president also pressed the Allies. On 21 October 1915 he denounced the British blockade, which restricted American access to the ports and markets of the Central Powers.

Wilson sent House back to Europe in early 1916 in search of peace. Neither Germany nor Great Britain and France welcomed House's vague proposals, and both sides resented American meddling in Europe. British foreign secretary Sir Edward Grey encouraged House to focus instead on plans for guaranteeing world peace after the war. While Grey wanted good Anglo-American relations, he hoped to prevent the United States from disrupting the Allied pursuit of victory. On 22 February 1916 Grey approved the House-Grey memorandum, which provided for Wilson to call a peace conference, with possible American mediation, if requested by the Allies. The Allies, however, never intended to invite the president to call such a conference or determine the conditions of peace with the Central Powers.

A new submarine crisis encouraged Wilson to continue searching for peace. On 24 March 1916 a German torpedo struck the English Channel steamer *Sussex*, injuring some Americans. Wilson denounced this violation of the *Arabic* pledge and demanded an unequivocal German promise to follow the cruiser warfare rules of international law. On 4 May 1916, rather than risk a diplomatic break at this time, Germany capitulated to the president's demand. In the midst of this crisis, Wilson pursued the idea of a future League of Nations, which Grey had encouraged. On 27 May 1916 the president announced his vision of collective security in an address to the League to Enforce Peace, calling for a new global community of democratic nations to preserve world peace and protect universal human rights.

The *Sussex* pledge effectively deprived Germany of the use of its submarines. Under these conditions, the United States experienced more difficulty with British maritime practices. In July 1916 Wilson protested British discrimination against American firms trading with the Central Powers. The British largely ignored this protest. Still, he seemed to have preserved U.S. neutrality, asserting the nation's rights while keeping it out of war.

Fortunately for Wilson, the 1916 presidential election came before the war in Europe shattered the illusion that the United States could remain at peace without sacrificing maritime and commercial rights. At the Democratic convention in St. Louis in June 1916 and during the subsequent campaign, Wilson benefited from his reputation as a consummate statesman who had kept the nation out of the Great War. The Republican party and its presidential nominee, Charles Evans Hughes, appeared more likely to entangle the United States in Europe's conflict. With the split between "conservative" and "progressive" Republicans having been substantially healed, Hughes obtained the support of Theodore Roosevelt. But because Roosevelt openly identified with the Allies, the endorsement suggested that Hughes's election might indeed result in war.

Before the 1916 election Wilson expanded his political base among progressive constituencies. He nominated Boston attorney Louis Brandeis, a trusted adviser who had helped define the New Freedom, to the Supreme Court. Confirmed by the Senate on 1 June 1916, Brandeis became the first Jew on the court. Wilson went beyond his New Freedom agenda to support reforms that the Progressive party had championed in 1912, hoping to attract Roosevelt's former constituency. On 17 July 1916 he signed the Federal Farm Loan Act, which provided credits to farmers. On 3 September 1916 he approved the Adamson Act, which guaranteed the eight-hour day to railway workers. Wilson's record of peace and progressivism enabled him to win a second term on 7 November 1916 by a narrow margin of 277 electoral votes to Hughes's 254. Wilson again carried most southern and western states but lost several eastern and midwestern states that had supported him in 1912.

After the election, Wilson made another attempt to stop the Great War. On 18 December 1916 he asked the belligerents to state their war aims. Minimizing differences between the Allies and the Central Powers, he urged both sides to resolve the conflict through compromise and then join the United States in a postwar international order of universal collective security. Both sides, however, shunned Wilson's peace initiative.

Persevering in his search for peace, Wilson developed the idea of a new world order. In his "peace without victory" address to the Senate on 22 January 1917, he proclaimed that "the nations should with one accord adopt the doctrine of President Monroe as the doctrine of the world: that no nation should seek to extend its polity over any other nation or people." This worldwide Monroe Doctrine in a postwar League of Nations, Wilson anticipated, would replace Europe's discredited balance of power and old alliances. "There must be, not a balance of power, but a community of power; not organized rivalries, but an organized common peace." This was his vision of a new "covenant" among democratic nations.

Germany's decision to begin unrestricted submarine warfare in February 1917 ended Wilson's pursuit of impartial U.S. neutrality. On 9 January, in a desperate attempt to win the war, Kaiser Wilhelm II had approved the new submarine policy. After the Germans announced their new submarine warfare, the president in early February broke diplomatic relations with Germany but still hoped to avoid war. But in mid-March 1917, when German submarines sank three U.S. ships, Wilson was forced to make a choice. No longer able to remain at peace and protect the nation's maritime and commercial interests, Wilson led the United States into the European conflict shortly after the inauguration of his second term. At a special session of the new Congress on 2 April 1917, denouncing Germany's autocratic government and its submarine warfare, he called for war to liberate all nations from this threat, including the Germans themselves. He proclaimed that "the world must be made safe for democracy." Four days later, Congress declared war against Germany.

As commander in chief, Wilson appointed Pershing to take charge of the American Expeditionary Force (AEF) in Europe. But the United States had prepared for a defensive war against Germany, not for fighting in Europe. Only after declaring war did Congress pass and Wilson sign, on 18 May 1917, the Selective Service Act giving the federal government the power to draft young men into the U.S. armed forces. The War and Navy departments, under Newton D. Baker and Josephus Daniels, respectively, created the AEF and transported it to France. The AEF required a year to organize and train before it began to make a significant military contribution to the war.

On the home front, the president exerted vigorous executive leadership. To manage public opinion, he established the Committee on Public Information under George Creel. Using the authority granted to him by Congress under the Espionage Act of June 1917, the Trading with the Enemy Act of October 1917, and the Sedition Act of May 1918, Wilson acted to silence radical critics of the war, such as Eugene Debs and the Socialist party. The Lever Act of August 1917 enabled Wilson to mobilize the economy by creating the Food Administration under Herbert Hoover and the Fuel Administration under Harry Garfield. To solve the transportation crisis, the president consolidated railroads under the Railroad Administration, which McAdoo managed in addition to the Treasury. In March 1918 Wilson placed Bernard Baruch in charge of the War Industries Board to harness key industries for wartime production. The National War Labor Board, under former president Taft and labor lawyer Frank P. Walsh, mediated labor-management disputes to prevent strikes. All these wartime measures gave the Wilson administration unprecedented powers over the daily life of Americans.

Russia's 1917 revolution seemed at first to justify Wilson's wartime crusade for democracy. The new provisional government, which he welcomed in March, promised to replace the czarist regime with constitutional liberty. But after the Bolshevik revolution in November, the president refused to recognize Vladimir I. Lenin's Soviet government. Rejecting its worldwide appeal for peace and revolution, Wilson on 8 January 1918 outlined his vision of progressive order in the Fourteen Points address to Congress. His plan called for open diplomacy, freedom of navigation and commerce, disarmament, national self-determination, and a postwar League of Nations. Wilson insisted that the Fourteen Points promised a new world order far superior to Lenin's socialism or communism. He also approved limited U.S. and Allied military intervention in northern Russia and Siberia in 1918, having convinced himself that this would help the Russian people resist their common German and Bolshevik enemies and remain with the United States and the Allies in the war. But revolutionary developments in Russia, as in Mexico, eluded Wilson's control.

On the western front, after Soviet Russia abandoned the war, the Central Powers threatened to defeat the Allies in 1918 before the United States could provide much relief. British and French forces absorbed the brunt of Germany's summer offensive before Pershing's AEF contributed decisively to the Allied victory. In October 1918, facing military defeat, Germany appealed to Wilson for peace on the basis of his Fourteen Points. He sent House to Europe to commit the Allies as well as Germany to these terms. On this basis, but with reservations, the victorious and defeated enemies concluded the armistice on 11 November 1918, ending the war.

Wilson participated personally in the Paris Peace Conference of 1919. Of the five great powers, only Great Britain, France and Italy were European; the United States and Japan came from outside. Russia was conspicuously absent. German delegates from the new Weimar Republic, which had replaced Kaiser Wilhelm II, arrived only after Wilson and Allied leaders prepared the peace treaty. Some new nations, such as Poland and Czechoslovakia, were welcomed, but others were not. Wilson applied the principle of national self-determination with caution against the defeated enemy. In the Jones Act of 1916, the United States had promised independence for the Philippines, but Wilson chose to postpone it. Likewise, he accepted continuing British rule in Ireland, Egypt, and India as well as French rule in Indochina. He recognized only the new nations that had been carved out of the defeated Central Powers in Europe.

At the heart of Wilson's peace program was the new League of Nations. He made drafting the covenant for this new international organization his top priority and insisted on its inclusion in the peace treaty. He and British prime minister David Lloyd George anticipated Germany's eventual membership in the league. Wanting an anti-German alliance instead, French premier Georges Clemenceau sought to restore Europe's balance of power. In collaboration with the British, Wilson succeeded at Paris in drafting the covenant as he desired. It promised both order and change in international relations. Article 10 offered a mutual guarantee of territorial integrity and political independence for nations in the new league, yet Article 19 anticipated future revision of the peace settlement. The covenant thus embodied Wilson's vision of "progressive order." On 14 February 1919 he presented it to the peace conference, stressing that "throughout this instrument we are depending primarily and chiefly upon one great force, and that is the moral force of the public opinion of the world." The president realized, however, that military force might be needed "if the moral force of the world will not suffice." He viewed the league as a practical way to reform the Old World on an ongoing basis.

Wilson compromised with the Allies in other areas to win their approval of the league covenant. He acquiesced in Clemenceau's request for continued U.S. and

Allied military occupation of the Rhineland. He and Lloyd George also approved separate guarantees of French security, promising to defend France against future German aggression. Wilson and Allied leaders also decided to disarm Germany, force it to relinquish some of its territory and all of its colonies, and require it to pay an unspecified amount of reparations. The covenant disappointed the Japanese because it did not affirm racial equality, a principle they had sought to add by amending the Anglo-American draft. To gain Japan's approval of the covenant after helping the British defeat this amendment, Wilson agreed with the Allied leaders to permit Japan to replace Germany in the Shantung province of China.

Germans almost universally denounced the peace treaty, which included the covenant, that their delegation received at Versailles on 7 May 1919. They claimed that it violated the Fourteen Points. Approving only a few concessions, the president joined the Allies and compelled Germany to sign the treaty on 28 June 1919.

On his return home, Wilson presented the treaty to the Senate. "We entered the war as the disinterested champions of right, and we interested ourselves in the terms of the peace in no other capacity," he asserted on 10 July 1919. Although the treaty embodied the Fourteen Points, "it was not easy to graft the new order of ideas on the old." Wilson called the League of Nations "not merely an instrument to adjust and remedy old wrongs under a new treaty of peace"; it was, he said, the "only hope for mankind." Affirming, moreover, that America's global mission was God-given, he concluded: "It has come about by no plan of our conceiving, but by the hand of God who led us into this way."

Once Wilson identified the Versailles treaty not only with his Fourteen Points but also God's will, he refused to compromise. He rejected all amendments and reservations to the treaty, firmly resisting efforts by Republican senators, and even some Democrats, to limit U.S. obligations in the postwar league. As Stockton Axson noted at the time, Wilson was "uncompromising, unforgiving, stubborn." The president's great foe in the treaty fight was Massachusetts senator Henry Cabot Lodge, leader of the Republican majority and chair of the Senate Foreign Relations Committee. It soon became apparent that the Senate would not approve the treaty without attaching strong reservations, if not amendments, to the ratification resolution. Wilson once more decided to appeal directly to the American people and in September 1919 went on a speaking tour of western states. Among other arguments, he advocated U.S. membership in the league so as to contain Bolshevism. Although Wilson contributed to the Red Scare—the grossly exaggerated fears of radical subversion at home as well as abroad—he failed to mobilize public opinion effectively against Lodge and the Republican-controlled Senate. During the western tour, Wilson's health collapsed. On 2 October 1919, back in Washington, he suffered a massive stroke.

With Edith Wilson's assistance, and that of his loyal private secretary Joseph P. Tumulty, the president managed to finish his term but could exercise only minimal leadership during the remaining months. While his cabinet members ran their departments largely on their own, he focused primarily on the treaty fight. After the stroke, Wilson rigidly adhered to his position on the Versailles treaty. Nebraska senator Gilbert M. Hitchcock, the Democratic minority leader, followed the president's direction. Together, they stopped Democratic senators from compromising with Republicans to win a two-thirds majority for the treaty with the Lodge reservations, thereby ensuring its defeat. When Wilson perceived that the cabinet was too independent, he forced Lansing's resignation as secretary of state on 12 February 1920 and replaced him with Bainbridge Colby, who faithfully maintained Wilson's uncompromising stance. The Senate rejected the treaty on 19 November 1919 and again on 19 March 1920, thereby preventing the United States from joining the League of Nations.

Wilson's techniques of presidential leadership were no longer effective. The president's physical incapacity was matched by his diminished political leverage. In the 1918 elections the Democrats had lost their majority in both the House and Senate, and now he experienced a strong backlash against his wartime powers. The postwar deregulation of production, prices, and wages resulted in high inflation and labor strikes in 1919, followed by recession in 1920. Adding to social unrest was the rapid demobilization of Pershing's AEF, an upsurge in urban race riots and rural lynchings directed against African Americans, and scapegoating of striking workers and socialists, who were crudely caricatured as the causes of postwar turmoil and anxiety. The Red Scare, nurtured by Attorney General A. Mitchell Palmer and other members of Wilson's cabinet, provided a rationale for repression. Outside Washington other politicians and industrialists also called for "law and order" to enable them to retain their control of the political economy. Given Wilson's neglect of postwar reconstruction at home and his attitude toward radical or marginal groups, he bore some responsibility for the lack of domestic comity.

American voters rejected Wilson's leadership and priorities in the 1920 presidential election. Though gravely ill, he had considered running for a third term to make it "a great and solemn referendum" on the League of Nations, but his closest associates forced him to abandon this foolish idea. The Nineteenth Amendment to the Constitution, which had just been ratified, extended voting rights to women in 1920. Although Wilson had finally, in 1918, endorsed woman suffrage as an essential wartime reform in his global crusade for democracy, this expansion of the American electorate did not help the Democrats. On 2 November 1920 Republican senator Warren G. Harding won a landslide victory over Democratic nominee James Cox, who had attempted to defend Wilson's legacy. The American people wanted less government at home and less entanglement abroad—Harding's "normalcy" instead of more Wilsonian reform.

Woodrow and Edith Wilson retired to their home in Washington on 4 March 1921. Having experienced both phenomenal triumphs and great failures, the former president lived there in relative obscurity. He reaffirmed his most basic beliefs in a final article, "The Road away from Revolution," in the *Atlantic Monthly* (Aug. 1923). To protect "modern civilization" against communist revolution, he urged Americans to draw on "the spiritual life" to reform capitalism and preserve democracy. He wanted to save "Christian civilization" in the United States by infusing it with "the spirit of Christ." He thought this nation, as "the greatest of democracies," should keep the world "safe for democracy." Although the United States had apparently repudiated his vision of America's global mission, Wilson remained faithful to the tenets of Wilsonianism—a progressive and peaceful world order with democracy and capitalism, national self-determination and collective security—which would shape much of American history throughout the twentieth century. He died at home in Washington.

• The Woodrow Wilson Papers are available at the Library of Congress, Washington, D.C. *The Papers of Woodrow Wilson* (69 vols., 1966–1994), ed. Arthur S. Link et al., are the best published collection of primary documents. *The Public Papers of Woodrow Wilson* (6 vols., 1925–1927), ed. Ray Stannard Baker and William E. Dodd, are still useful. For the perceptive views of Wilson's brother-in-law, see Stockton Axson, *"Brother Woodrow": A Memoir of Woodrow Wilson*, ed. Link (1993).

Biographies of Wilson include Link, *Wilson* (5 vols., 1947–1965); Edwin A. Weinstein, *Woodrow Wilson: A Medical and Psychological Biography* (1981); August Heckscher, *Woodrow Wilson: A Biography* (1991); and, especially good, Jan Willem Schulte Nordholdt, *Woodrow Wilson: A Life for World Peace* (1991).

For Wilson's early life, see Henry W. Brandon, *Woodrow Wilson: The Academic Years* (1967); George C. Osborn, *Woodrow Wilson: The Early Years* (1968); John M. Mulder, *Woodrow Wilson: The Years of Preparation* (1978); and Niels Aage Thorsen, *The Political Thought of Woodrow Wilson, 1875–1910* (1988).

For Wilson's presidency, in addition to vols. 2–5 of Link's *Wilson*, see John M. Cooper, Jr., *The Warrior and the Priest: Woodrow Wilson and Theodore Roosevelt* (1983), and Kendrick A. Clements, *The Presidency of Woodrow Wilson* (1992).

For Wilson's international leadership, see N. Gordon Levin, Jr., *Woodrow Wilson and World Politics: America's Response to War and Revolution* (1968); Lloyd C. Gardner, *Safe for Democracy: The Anglo-American Response to Revolution, 1913–1923* (1984); Klaus Schwabe, *Woodrow Wilson, Revolutionary Germany, and Peacemaking, 1918–1919: Missionary Diplomacy and the Realities of Power* (1985); Arthur Walworth, *Wilson and His Peacemakers: American Diplomacy at the Paris Peace Conference, 1919* (1986); Frederick S. Calhoun, *Power and Principle: Armed Intervention in Wilsonian Foreign Policy* (1986); Lloyd E. Ambrosius, *Woodrow Wilson and the American Diplomatic Tradition: The Treaty Fight in Perspective* (1987); and Thomas J. Knock, *To End All Wars: Woodrow Wilson and the Quest for a New World Order* (1992).

LLOYD E. AMBROSIUS

WILTZ, Louis Alfred (21 Jan. 1843–16 Oct. 1881), governor of Louisiana, was born in New Orleans, Louisiana, the son of J. B. Theophile Wiltz, a New Orleans merchant, and Louise Irene Villaneuva. Educated in the New Orleans public schools, Wiltz at age fifteen left school to begin his business career as a merchant. Although only eighteen when the Civil War began, he immediately enlisted in a New Orleans artillery battery as a private. His enthusiasm and family connections secured his election as captain of Company E of the Chalmette Regiment, which was ordered to Fort Jackson below New Orleans on the Mississippi River. According to official reports, he gave efficient and brave service. The fort surrendered in 1862 to Union forces under General Benjamin Butler and Wiltz was taken prisoner and paroled. He was later exchanged and saw service in the Mississippi Department as a provost marshal. Wiltz married Marie Michaella Gueriniѐre Bienvenu in 1862; they had seven children.

After the war Wiltz restarted his commercial career, first as an accountant in his uncle's commission house then as a partner. In 1873, when the house failed because of the panic, he entered banking. He also entered the political arena after the war, becoming a member of the parish and state central committees of the Democratic party. In 1868 he was elected to the legislature. While a legislator, he became a member of the New Orleans Common Council and a school director. He was defeated for election as mayor of New Orleans in 1870 before winning in 1872 and subsequently losing in 1874.

In 1874 Wiltz was again elected to the legislature, and he quickly emerged as a leader of the Bourbon-Lottery wing of the Democratic party. (This wing supported the restoration of the prewar ruling elite in Louisiana and the Louisiana lottery.) He is credited with orchestrating the 1874 conservative revolt in the Louisiana house against the Republicans then in control of the state government. His organizational skills allowed him to seize control of the house and win election as Speaker before the startled Republicans could react. The Republican governor, William Kellogg, used federal troops to expel the conservative Democratic members, and a political crisis in the state ensued. Anarchy in the state was prevented when a compromise, proposed by a congressional investigating committee, allowed the Democrats to gain control of the Louisiana House of Representatives and the Republicans to maintain control of the executive branch. Governor Kellogg, however, successfully prevented Wiltz from becoming Speaker. Nevertheless, the compromise began the end of Republican rule in Louisiana.

In the gubernatorial election of 1877, Wiltz, the acknowledged leader of the Bourbon-Lottery faction of the Democratic party, was pitted against Francis Nicholls, the leader of the antilottery Democratic forces. After four ballots Nicholls won the Democratic nomination. Although not a political ally of Nicholls, Wiltz was nominated for lieutenant governor, ostensibly to bind the two factions of the party together. Violence and intimidation by the "White League" against black voters ensured that Nicholls and Wiltz won a clear majority. The Republican-controlled election board overturned the election and awarded the governorship to the Republican candidate, Steven B. Packard, precipitating another political crisis. A period of dual governments arose, with the Republicans in control of the state house and the Democrats in the Odd Fellows' Hall. Nicholls and Wiltz undermined the Republican power base either by offering political deals to defectors or by outright intimidation to quit the Packard camp. When President Rutherford B. Hayes ordered the federal troops to their barracks as part of the Compromise of 1877, the Republican government collapsed, and the Nicholls-Wiltz administration took complete control of the state government.

Nicholls angered the Bourbon-Lottery wing by signing legislation outlawing the Louisiana lottery. When a constitutional convention was called in 1879, Wiltz served as president and used this position to undermine Governor Nicholls. The new constitution, adopted in September 1879, effectively shortened Nicholls's term by a year. Wiltz ran for governor under the provisions of the new constitution and was elected, marking the return to power in Louisiana of the merchant-planter class, whose reign would last into the twentieth century.

In his inaugural address, Wiltz suggested a number of proposals that were unusually liberal for the time. He proposed the creation of an agriculture and immigration bureau in the state government, the creation of a public board of health to fight epidemics in the state, a more humane method of execution than hanging, and state promotion of education. We will never know if they were really issues he was endorsing or merely political rhetoric, as none of these proposals were initiated before Wiltz died in New Orleans of tuberculosis.

• There is no known repository of Wiltz papers. For further information on Wiltz see Joseph G. Dawson III, *Army Generals and Reconstruction: Louisiana, 1862–1877* (1982); William Ivy Hair, *Bourbonism and Agrarian Protest: Louisiana Politics, 1877–1900* (1969); Stuart O. Landry, *The Battle of Liberty Place: The Overthrow of Carpetbag Rule in New Orleans, September 14, 1874* (1955); and Joe Gray Taylor, *Louisiana Reconstructed, 1863–1877* (1974). An obituary is in the New Orleans *Picayune*, 16 Oct. 1881.

ROY R. STEPHENSON

WIMAR, Carl Ferdinand (19 Feb. 1828–28 Nov. 1862), artist, was born in Siegburg, Germany, the son of Ludwig Gottfried Wimar, a scrivener, and Elizabeth Schmitz, a washerwoman. A few years after Carl's birth his father died, and his mother then supported the family. By 1835 she had remarried, and her new husband, a merchant named Matthias Becker, moved the family to Cologne. During the 1830s and 1840s, the economic hardship and social repression experienced by many Germans led to the first major wave of emigration to the United States. Becker moved to St. Louis in 1839, opened a public house, and by 1844 was joined by his family.

The Germans' fascination with the American West was nurtured by an extensive body of literature, the so-called *Wildwestgeschichten* (wild West stories), which were immensely popular. By the time he reached Missouri as an impressionable fifteen-year-old, Wimar's vision of the frontier was undoubtedly colored by his reading of romantic German novels. His stepfather's public house was situated next to the encampment for Indians who came to St. Louis to trade. According to early accounts, Wimar was enchanted by the Indians and was befriended by one, who taught him much about native life-style, culture, and customs.

Shortly after the family's arrival in St. Louis, Wimar was apprenticed to a local house and steamboat painter. Dissatisfied with that type of painting, Wimar switched to the studio of French émigré Leon Pomarede, a local painter and decorator. During his apprenticeship, Wimar assisted Pomarede on his vast Mississippi River panorama *Portrait of the Father of the Waters*. Wimar accompanied Pomarede on some sketching tours up the Mississippi River to prepare studies for the panorama. On one of the trips, Pomarede advised Wimar to adopt frontier subject matter and "follow it exclusively, as through it he might achieve a reputation that, in years to come when the Indians would be a 'race clean gone,' would increase to a peculiar brightness, not only in this country but on the continent" (William Tod Helmuth, *Arts in St. Louis* [1864], p. 89). This proved to be wise counsel.

After completing his apprenticeship, Wimar set up his own painting business in 1851 with a partner named Boneau. The success of this venture is not known, but Wimar's surviving canvases suggest that he painted primarily portraits and a few genre paintings derived from prints. The most ambitious and finest painting from this period is *Three Children Attacked by a Wolf* (c. 1851, Missouri Historical Society), which Wimar imaginatively adapted from a print after Thomas Gainsborough's *Two Shepherd Boys with Dogs Fighting*. In November 1851, shortly after opening his first studio, Wimar was inspired by the unveiling of Emanuel Leutze's monumental painting *Washington Crossing the Delaware* to travel to Düsseldorf, Germany, to study with Leutze and to create grand history paintings of the American West.

Arriving in early 1852, Wimar spent four years in Düsseldorf, learning the German academic painting style. He applied the techniques to frontier subjects, earning the appellation "the Indian painter." Informed more by romantic myths of the West than by reality, Wimar's paintings from his Düsseldorf period portray confrontation and conflict between the Anglo-European settlers and the Native Americans. His first major painting, *Abduction of Daniel Boone's Daughter by the Indians* (1853, Washington University Gallery of Art, St. Louis), depicts three Native Americans apprehending Jemima Boone, who is posed as Mary Magdalen at the base of the cross. Wimar's use of sacred symbolism conveys prevalent beliefs among Anglo-Europeans concerning captive women as Christian martyrs, Native Americans as promiscuous "pagans," and their roles in a religious justification for westward expansion. The painting is a barometer of mid-nineteenth-century social values, making it one of the most compelling captivity paintings in the history of American art.

During his final season in Düsseldorf, Wimar created his most ambitious and accomplished painting of his student years, *The Attack on an Emigrant Train* (1856, University of Michigan Museum of Art). The painting presents a wagon train moving furiously forward, fending off attacking Native Americans. A French author's wild west story inspired Wimar to compose a heroic image of Native Americans attempting to repel the settlers' inevitable progress across the frontier. Wimar's rendering of the scene was novel in conception and, following the mass distribution of a lithographic print of the painting, established the prototype for images of Indian attacks on wagon trains.

The academic training that Wimar received in Düsseldorf emphasized drawing directly from nature in preparation for finished paintings. Wimar realized that his epic paintings of the West were, thus far, imaginary compositions drawn largely from past art and literature. At the conclusion of four years of study, Wimar returned to St. Louis and decided to explore the Missouri River frontier "to collect the necessary studies" (letter, 17 July 1855) in pursuit of his quest to paint the American West.

Arriving home in the winter 1856–1857, Wimar sought passage on one of the steamboats traveling up the Missouri River deep into Indian territory. Unsuccessful at first, Wimar received permission to accompany government-sponsored expeditions in the summers of 1858 and 1859 to deliver annuities to the native tribes and to explore the upper reaches of the Missouri River. On these expeditions, Wimar sketched the landscape and its inhabitants in pencil, chalks, and oil. In addition, on the 1858 journey he took an ambrotype camera, becoming one of the first to photograph the Native Americans in this region.

Armed with sketches, artifacts, and memories of his adventures, Wimar embarked on a series of panoramic Missouri River paintings that demonstrated his new appreciation for Native American culture. He abandoned his fascination with themes of conflict and confrontation and created romantic paintings that recorded the quickly passing life, land, and culture of the inhabitants of the plains. In this series of paintings, Wimar combined a nostalgic myth of the West with realistic renderings of the landscape and the Native Americans. His dramatic images are among the last depictions of the Missouri River frontier before its mass settlement after the Civil War.

Wimar's signature painting, and one of the seminal paintings on the subject, is *The Buffalo Hunt* (1860, Washington University Gallery of Art). The painting presents an ethnographically accurate portrayal of Sioux Indians hunting buffalo. A lancer flanks the buffalo while the bowman aims his arrow for the buffalo's heart. In the foreground is a rock that resembles a gravestone, suggesting that the Indian nations would ultimately face the same deadly fate as the buffalo in the painting. In a subsequent version of *The Buffalo Hunt* (1861, Missouri Historical Society), Wimar replaced the gravestone-rock with a buffalo skull to reinforce his pessimistic message.

Critical and popular acclaim for *The Buffalo Hunt* catapulted Wimar into artistic success. At the pinnacle of his career, Wimar married Anna von Senden in 1861; they had one child.

Within months after the successful exhibition of *The Buffalo Hunt*, civic leaders awarded Wimar and his half brother August Becker the largest commission of his career to decorate the dome of the St. Louis Courthouse with murals. For this monumental project, Wimar drew upon his academic training to orchestrate a cycle of four lunettes depicting seminal scenes from St. Louis's historic past and conveying the city's aspirations for its future as the gateway to the West. Begun early in 1862, the courthouse dome and its decoration were intended to precede and rival the dome for the Capitol in Washington, D.C., thereby establishing St. Louis as a western counterpart to the nation's capital.

For his mural cycle, Wimar chose four subjects representing the different empires that had ruled the territory, and he placed them symbolically at the cardinal points in the dome. On the south, Wimar painted *De Soto Discovering the Mississippi*, portraying the era of Spanish exploration and colonization. On the east, Wimar created *The Landing of Laclede*, depicting the founding of St. Louis in 1763 by Pierre Laclede, who claimed the territory for France. On the north, Wimar painted *The Year of the Blow*, an image of the French and Indian Wars. Finally, on the west, Wimar created an image of the region's imperial vision of the future entitled *Westward the Star of Empire*. The mural depicts the Cochetopa Pass, through which the continental railroad would have passed if Congress had selected the middle route through St. Louis. Unfortunately for St. Louis, Congress decided upon the northern route only months before Wimar's mural was completed.

During the year that Wimar painted the courthouse murals, he suffered from tuberculosis. Early biographers record that he required assistants to lift him onto the scaffolds in order to execute the work. In November 1862, as he was completing the commission, Wimar collapsed and died in St. Louis. In his ambitious mural decoration, Wimar recorded for posterity the important role St. Louis played in the history of the region and the nation, along with its grand civic ambitions. In his tragically brief career, Wimar made an important contribution to American art as the last artist to record the Missouri River frontier before mass settlement, creating romantic historical images that continue to influence the American myth of the West.

• The Carl Wimar Papers, Missouri Historical Society, St. Louis, contain a large body of correspondence between Wimar and family members. Perry Rathbone, *Charles Wimar, 1828–1862: Painter of the Indian Frontier* (1946), is the first comprehensive book on Wimar. Rick Stewart et al., *Carl Wi-*

mar: Chronicler of the Missouri River Frontier (1991), is the most thorough monograph on Wimar and includes a critical analysis of his art.

JOSEPH D. KETNER

WIMMER, Boniface (14 Jan. 1809–8 Dec. 1887), the founder of Benedictine monastic life in the United States and the first archabbot of St. Vincent's Abbey in Latrobe, Pennsylvania, was born Sebastian Wimmer in Thalmassing, Bavaria, the son of Peter Wimmer, a tavern owner and farmer, and Elizabeth Lang. Sebastian Wimmer was born during the Napoleonic wars and at a time when German Catholic life in general and Benedictine monasticism in particular were undergoing a Romantic revival. He matriculated at the University of Munich (1827–1830), where he studied theology and where the German Romantic revival was in full swing. In 1831, after completing one year of studies for the priesthood at the Regensburg diocesan seminary, he was ordained. His bishop, Johann Michael Sailer, sent him to serve as a curate at the Marian shrine at Altötting in the diocese of Passau because the diocese of Regensburg had more priests than it needed.

Bishop Sailer discreetly invited some of his diocesan priests to join King Ludwig I's newly restored (1827) Benedictine monastery at Metten, Bavaria, and in 1832 Wimmer was one of the first to respond to the desperate need for monks, taking the name of Boniface. As a Benedictine monk, however, Wimmer served primarily in Augsburg and Munich, outside the Metten monastic walls. In the late 1830s and early 1840s, as vast numbers of German Catholics were emigrating to the United States, King Ludwig I established the Ludwig-Missionsverein (1838) to aid the emigrants, and the Bavarian church became actively concerned about the religious needs of the emigrants. In this context, Wimmer began to beg his superiors to allow him to establish Benedictine monastic life in the United States to support the German Catholics there. In 1845 he met a German priest, Peter Lemke, who had been serving German immigrants in Pennsylvania since 1834. Lemke offered Wimmer some land in western Pennsylvania on which to establish a monastery as a source of religious stability and a major missionary service to the German immigrants. In 1846, after some initial reluctance on the part of his religious superiors, he was allowed to go to Pennsylvania to establish a Benedictine mission at Carrolltown with four postulants and fourteen young laymen. Financial support for the endeavor came from the Metten monastery, King Ludwig, and the Ludwig-Missionsverein.

By 1847 the small Benedictine community was enlarged by more recruits from Metten and moved to church lands at St. Vincent's in Latrobe, Westmoreland County, Pennsylvania. In 1848 Wimmer built St. Vincent College and St. Vincent Seminary to educate young men for secular as well as religious careers. He also built a brewery at the monastery to help sustain monastic life and to provide beer for the monks and immigrants in the area. Bishop Michael O'Connor of Pittsburgh, an Irish-Catholic temperance advocate, was horrified by this development and asked Rome to force Wimmer to halt the brewery operation. The bishop also wanted more rigorous controls over Wimmer's relatively autonomous monastic operation within his diocese. O'Conner was unsuccessful, and Wimmer remained relatively free from episcopal control in continuing to develop monastic institutions. In 1852 he brought Benedictine nuns to Latrobe, and they very quickly began to establish other houses of Benedictine monastic life for women in other parts of the country. In 1855 the monastic community had grown to 150 members, and Pope Pius IX elevated it to the status of abbey, naming Wimmer abbot. In 1883, Wimmer was given the honorary title archabbot of St. Vincent's in recognition of his many establishments and his fathering of Benedictine life in the United States.

Wimmer was an activist, not a contemplative monk, who believed that building and extending monastic institutions and providing active missionary work in the United States was a way of preserving German traditions, ethnic solidarity, and religious integrity in a pluralistic country where disintegration and the centrifugal forces of pluralism and diversity were constant threats to German immigrants. By the time of his death at St. Vincent's Monastery in Latrobe, Wimmer had helped develop fledgling Benedictine houses at St. John's in Minnesota (1856), which in a century was to become the largest Benedictine monastery in the world; Newark, New Jersey (1857); Atchison, Kansas (1857); Covington, Kentucky (1858); Texas (1859); Alabama (1875); and North Carolina (1876). He established missions and staffed various parishes with Benedictine monks throughout the country where German immigrants had located. Following the *ora et labora* (worship and work) traditions of Benedictine life, the monasteries were constructed primarily in agricultural regions where the monks could farm to support their monastic way of life and their educational and missionary works. The Benedictines under Wimmer also developed missions to the Indians and founded a school of agriculture for Blacks on Skidaway Island near Savannah, Georgia. During his lifetime, Benedictine missionaries reached into twenty-five states, Canada, and Ecuador.

Wimmer was an impulsive, strong-willed, and energetic project maker, very much like the pragmatic and westward-minded Americans among whom he spent forty-one years of his life. His authoritarian style of leadership made his plans effective and efficient, but it also crushed those who held different views and made uncomfortable those who were more inclined to reflective examination and a contemplative monastic way of life. His 1857 dismissal of Mother Benedicta Riepp as the first superior of the Benedictine nuns illustrated the forceful and at times arbitrary rule that he exercised over the first Benedictine communities.

• Wimmer's unpublished letters and papers are located in the Archives of Metten Abbey, Metten, Germany; St. Vincent's

Archabbey, Latrobe, Pa.; Propaganda Fide, Rome; and various American diocesan and abbey archives. Published correspondence includes Giles P. Hayes, ed., "Early Bayley-Wimmer Correspondence (1854–1857)," *American Benedictine Review* 14 (1963): 470–93; Warren Murrman, "The Wimmer Correspondence: A Collection and a Project," *Benedictine Confluence* 6 (1972): 16–24; Willibald Mathäser, "Erzabt Bonifaz Wimmer im Spiegel seiner Briefe," *Studien und Mitteilungen* 60 (1946): 234–302; and Conrad Zimmerman et al., "Wimmer Letters," *Scriptorium* 17 (1958): 3–64, 18 (1959): 67–82, 19 (1960): 61–83. The most recent scholarly biography is Jerome Oetgen, *An American Abbot: Boniface Wimmer, O.S.B., 1809–1887* (1976). Joel Rippinger, *The Benedictine Order in the United States: An Interpretive History* (1990), gives a good introduction to Wimmer's impact on the development of Benedictinism in the United States. An obituary is in *Studien und Mittheilungen aus dem Benedictiner- und dem Cistercienser-Orden*, vol. 9 (1888).

PATRICK W. CAREY

WIMSATT, W. K. (17 Nov. 1907–17 Dec. 1975), literary scholar, was born William Kurtz Wimsatt, Jr., in Washington, D.C., the son of William Kurtz Wimsatt, a lumber dealer, and Bertha Stuart McSherry. He earned both B.A. (summa cum laude, 1928) and A.M. (1929) degrees at Georgetown University. From 1930 until 1935 he taught English and was department head at the Priory School in Portsmouth, Rhode Island. After a year of studying and teaching at Catholic University of America, he enrolled in graduate school at Yale in 1936 and received his Ph.D. in 1939. That same year he began teaching at Yale and continued there until his death. In September 1944 he married Margaret Elizabeth Hecht; they had two sons.

Wimsatt's academic specialty was eighteenth-century British literature, and his first scholarly book was *The Prose Style of Samuel Johnson* (1941). Much of the previous commentary on Johnson (such as that of Thomas Babington Macaulay) had been anecdotal and general, but Wimsatt's study was rigorously analytical and specific. His attention to Johnson's diction led to a second book, *Philosophic Words: A Study of Style and Meaning in the Rambler and Dictionary of Samuel Johnson* (1948). After identifying eighteenth-century sources for terms considered scientific or philosophical, Wimsatt examined variations in Johnson's usage of such language. In doing so, his goal was to provide a "biography or the history of Johnson's mind."

The Verbal Icon: Studies in the Meaning of Poetry (1954) contains two of Wimsatt's most famous essays, "The Intentional Fallacy" and "The Affective Fallacy," both co-written with Monroe Beardsley. In the first essay Wimsatt repudiates the theory of French critic Charles-Augustin Sainte-Beuve, who argued that a primary purpose of literary criticism was to reveal the author behind the work. According to Wimsatt, Saint-Beuve was guilty of the intentional fallacy, which confuses a poem (i.e., a literary text) with its origins and mistakenly regards the poet's statements of intent or other biographical data as important clues to the poem's meaning. The affective fallacy, as practiced by George Saintsbury and others, confuses a poem with its results and focuses therefore on the emotions produced in the reader rather than on the literary work. According to Wimsatt, one approach led to barren pseudo-objectivity, the other to fuzzy impressionism. In both cases, says Wimsatt, "the poem itself, as an object of specifically critical judgment, tends to disappear." If these essays indicate what a poem is not and describe two faulty approaches, a third essay in *The Verbal Icon* is Wimsatt's not entirely successful attempt to define the proper critical method. In "Explication as Criticism" he argues that the task of a critic is not merely to provide neutral explanation but to "unify understanding and value as much as possible" or "to make our understanding evaluative." Wimsatt's sustained argument for a focus on the text itself, rather than on its genesis or its emotional effects, provided the foundation for much of the formalist literary criticism prominent during the 1950s and 1960s.

Wimsatt's most notable scholarly achievement is *Literary Criticism: A Short History* (1957), identified in its day by the *New York Times Book Review* as "the standard work on the subject." Although Cleanth Brooks was his collaborator on this project, Wimsatt wrote the entire book except for the final section on twentieth-century criticism. Comprehensive in scope, the book offers especially perceptive comments on eighteenth-century writers like Samuel Johnson whose individuality transcends the neoclassical stereotypes often repeated by literary historians. In discussing the emergence of Romantic poetic theory, Wimsatt questions Wordsworth's notion that "natural language" of common people is more poetic than more elevated language of higher social classes.

During his last years Wimsatt's literary criticism became increasingly polemic. Earlier in his career he had vehemently disagreed with Aristotelian critics at the University of Chicago and had parodied R. S. Crane in an essay titled "The Chicago Critics." Wimsatt accused Crane and Richard McKeon of professing a pluralistic approach to criticism while actually practicing narrow dogmatism. According to Wimsatt, they turned "their backs on the whole modern critical effort to scrutinize the relation of poetry to the rest of life" and constructed instead a definition of poetry that was "strictly self-contained." In "Explication as Criticism" Wimsatt staked his own position midway between the extremes of didactic criticism and formal, stylistic criticism. In *Hateful Contraries: Studies in Literature and Criticism* (1965) Wimsatt defended orthodox literary and religious values against new modes of criticism influenced by the French structuralist school. In his final collection of criticism, *Day of the Leopards: Essays in Defense of the Poem* (1976), the title essay suggests that certain contemporary critics contributed to sacrilege and social disintegration by using literary texts and literary criticism as mechanisms for promoting individual political agendas. The book contains more reasoned responses to the criticism of I. A. Richards, Northrop Frye, and J. Hillis Miller.

Throughout his career Wimsatt worked extensively as an editor both of primary texts and collections of literary criticism. A significant achievement in the first category is *Boswell for the Defence, 1769–1774* (1959), one of several volumes in the Yale edition of James Boswell's private papers. Volumes of criticism edited by Wimsatt include *English Stage Comedy* (1955), *Explication as Criticism* (1963), *Versification: Major Language Types* (1972), and *Literary Criticism: Idea and Act* (1974).

During most of his tenure at Yale, Wimsatt was a fellow of Silliman College (1941–1975), and he served for several years on the board of editors supervising the publication of Boswell's journals. He was named Frederick Clifford Ford Professor of English in 1965 and Sterling Professor of English in 1974. He was president of the Connecticut Academy of Arts and Sciences, chairman of the English Institute, and a member of the executive committee of the Modern Language Association.

In addition to literature, Wimsatt's interests included Native American artifacts and chess, and in 1966 his book *How to Compose Chess Problems and Why* was printed privately. One of his final essays, published posthumously under the title "Vladimir Nabokov: More Chess Problems and the Novel," combined his vocation with a fervent avocation.

One of the most prominent literary scholars of his generation, Wimsatt provided valuable commentary on eighteenth-century British writers such as Pope, Johnson, and Boswell. As a theorist he questioned important assumptions about teaching literary history (with attention primarily to lives of writers and historical contexts) as opposed to literary criticism. His traditional views of the canon and of the moral implications of literature made him unsympathetic to critical approaches emerging during his final years. Wimsatt died in New Haven.

• Most of Wimsatt's papers and manuscripts are at the Yale University Library. A fuller treatment of Wimsatt's specific contributions to literary criticism may be found in Robert Moynihan, *Modern American Critics, 1920–1955*, vol. 63 of *Dictionary of Literary Biography* (1988). An obituary is in the *New York Times*, 18 Dec. 1975.

ALBERT E. WILHELM

WINANS, William (3 Nov. 1788–31 Aug. 1857), Methodist minister, was born in Chesnut Ridge, Pennsylvania, the son of Creighton Winans, a cobbler, and Susanna Hopkins, a weaver. Winans's father died in 1790, and his mother, a devout Methodist, struggled to provide for her five children. Seeking better opportunities for her family, Winans's mother joined the migration to the rich lands of Ohio in 1804. After a rebellious adolescence, he underwent a conversion in a Methodist church on Easter Sunday in 1807. Deciding to become a minister, he spent a year as an exhorter and was licensed to preach on 27 August 1808. In October he was admitted on trial to the Western Annual Conference of the Methodist Episcopal Church. After he served a two-year probationary period in Kentucky and Indiana, the conference admitted him as a full member. He volunteered for missionary labor in the Mississippi Territory and arrived there in December 1810.

Winans found Mississippi a rough and difficult frontier, and his labors yielded only modest results. From November 1813 to July 1814, he served as a missionary in New Orleans, after which he returned to Mississippi to continue his efforts to spread Methodism in the territory. In 1815 he left the itinerant ministry because of throat problems, married Martha DuBose (with whom he would have four daughters and two sons), and became the overseer of the DuBose family's small plantation near Centreville. Within a year this arrangement proved unsatisfactory because Winans refused to inflict corporal punishment on the DuBose slaves. His mother-in-law purchased nearby land for the young couple, on which Winans erected a log home and began to grow cotton with the aid of his seven slaves. During the next five years, he continued to preach locally and for a time taught school. In 1820 he returned to the itinerant ministry and a year later became the presiding elder of the Mississippi District, which then included Mississippi, Louisiana, Arkansas, and Texas. For the next thirty-four years, he frequently served as a presiding elder, although he was also often forced into temporary retirement due to ill health. Throughout the period he was the chief spokesman of Mississippi Methodists. A formidable debater, he represented them in every General Conference of the Methodist Episcopal Church from 1824 to 1844.

In addition to his ministerial duties, Winans became a leading proponent of the American Colonization Society. Like virtually all white southerners, he insisted that slaves could not be freed and allowed to remain among whites without damage to the social and political order. The colonization movement solved this problem by removing emancipated blacks from southern society and settling them in Liberia. Winans collected funds in Mississippi to support the society and defended it against attacks by suspicious slaveholders.

Although Winans had little formal education, he read widely and assembled a large library. His examination of younger preachers during their assigned course of study earned him a reputation as "the flint mill." He was a strong supporter of and trustee for Centenary College, a Methodist institution founded in 1841 in Brandon Springs, Louisiana. In 1846 and again in 1850, he traveled the region as the college's agent.

Within the Methodist Episcopal Church, Winans forcefully opposed abolitionism and defended the status quo on a variety of issues. At the 1836 General Conference in Cincinnati, Ohio, in a debate with abolitionist Orange Scott, Winans declared, "I am a slaveholder on principle." Southern Christians had a moral duty to own slaves for two reasons: to provide many slaves with pious masters and to convince suspicious masters that Christianity did not threaten their ownership of slaves. By allaying fears of abolitionism, Christian masters could enhance missionaries' ability to preach the gospel to the slaves of irreligious owners. At the General Conference in 1844, Winans led southern delegates in their defense of Bishop James O. Andrew, a southerner who had become a slaveowner through inheritance and marriage. Winans also served on the committee appointed to resolve the difficulty or to devise a way to divide the denomination. At the urging of southern delegates like Winans, the 1844 General Conference in New York City adopted a Plan of Separation, which effectively split American Methodism along sectional lines. Winans played a prominent role in both the organizing conference of the Methodist Episcopal Church, South, in Louisville, Kentucky, in 1845, and in the new denomination's first General Conference, in Petersburg, Virginia, the following year. Contrary to many southern Methodists' expectations, Winans was not one of the two new bishops chosen in 1846, although he remained a principal voice of southern Methodism for another decade.

In politics, Winans was a loyal member of the Whig party and had staunchly opposed Andrew Jackson in the 1820s and 1830s. In 1844 he was a strong supporter of Henry Clay and opened Whig rallies with prayer. His political involvement raised the ire of both Democrats and churchmen. Ignoring widespread popular concerns over mixing politics and religion, Winans ran for a seat in the U.S. House of Representatives in 1849. Refusing to campaign, he lost overwhelmingly to Albert Gallatin Brown, the incumbent and former two-term governor of Mississippi.

After his unsuccessful foray into politics, Winans settled into the role of patriarch of the Mississippi Conference. During the 1850s, he quietly supervised his plantation, preached occasional sermons, represented Mississippi Methodists at southern General Conferences in 1850 and 1854, and prepared a series of religious discourses, which were published in 1855. Winans died at his plantation, "Rural Retreat," in Wilkinson County, Mississippi.

Throughout his career, Winans stubbornly defended the southern attitude toward slavery within the Methodist Episcopal Church against abolitionist preachers from the North, preferring ecclesiastical division to continued bickering. However, in the political realm, Winans and other nationalist Whigs decried the growing sectionalism that threatened to destroy the nation. His success in helping to divide American Methodism into separate denominations unintentionally helped others, whom he opposed, divide the nation into warring sections.

• The Winans Collection at the Millsaps-Wilson Library in Jackson, Miss., contains several journals, hundreds of letters, and a manuscript autobiography, which chronicles his life to 1824. Several of his sermons and public addresses were published in pamphlet form. Winans authored only one book, *A Series of Discourses, on Fundamental Religious Subjects* (1855), a series of seventeen essays on a variety of doctrinal matters.

Rex Paxton Kyker, "William Winans: Minister and Politician of the Old South" (Ph.D. diss., Univ. of Florida, 1957), was the first scholarly biography. Ray Holder, *William Winans: Methodist Leader in Antebellum Mississippi* (1977), is a more readable study of Winans's life, but it lacks notes and provides only a brief bibliographical essay. For Winans's role in the slavery controversy in the Methodist Episcopal Church, see Donald G. Mathews, *Slavery and Methodism: A Chapter in American Morality, 1780–1845* (1965). Randy J. Sparks, *On Jordan's Stormy Banks: Evangelicalism in Mississippi, 1773–1876* (1994), places Winans in the context of antebellum evangelical culture in Mississippi.

DANIEL W. STOWELL

WINANT, John Gilbert (23 Feb. 1889–3 Nov. 1947), governor and ambassador, was born in New York City, the son of Frederick Winant, a real estate broker, and Jeanette Laura Gilbert. Winant grew up in a fashionable East Side brownstone, in a milieu of "politically conservative, upper middle class, protestant values and prejudices" (Bellush, p. 9), and attended private schools. He was not a good student but immersed himself in reading and was particularly influenced by Charles Dickens, John Ruskin, and Abraham Lincoln. He was sent to St. Paul's School in Concord, New Hampshire, from which he graduated in 1908, and then Princeton University. Shy and lacking self-confidence, he had difficulties with his studies at both and did not graduate with his Princeton class. The discerning rector of St. Paul's extended him an open invitation to join its staff in 1911. He taught that year, went back to Princeton in February 1912, and returned to teach at St. Paul's in September 1913. Winant became a beloved instructor of history and a trusted friend to his students. With them he worked to democratize student organizations, and from them he gained a sense of purpose for himself: to serve.

In Concord Winant began his political career, a vehicle for acting on behalf of those deprived of social justice. He challenged the state's two most powerful forces, reactionary politicians and industry (railroads and textiles). Although Winant was not favored by his Republican party leadership, he was elected to the New Hampshire House of Representatives for the 1917 term. Hoping to build on the progressive beginnings of former governor Robert Perkins Bass, he introduced bills to improve working conditions and extend suffrage to women. Although the bills failed to pass, Winant learned the legislative process and strengthened his own ideas of social justice.

Unaffected by either the isolationism or pacifism of contemporary progressives, Winant served in the American Expeditionary Force in France. He enlisted as a private in 1917, became commander of the Eighth Aero Squadron, and completed many dangerous missions over Germany. He was discharged as a captain in April 1919. That year he married New York socialite Constance Rivington Russell, with whom he had three children.

Winant returned to St. Paul's in 1919, but politics still beckoned. In January 1920 Winant ran for delegate to the Republican National Convention; he was defeated. That fall he won the Ninth District primary contest and then the election for state senator. Winant resigned from St. Paul's in 1921. He retired from the state senate after one term, but in 1923, in spite of a Democratic trend, he won another term in the lower house. In September 1924 he defeated the powerful Republican Frank Knox, publisher of the influential *Manchester Union*, for the gubernatorial nomination. New Hampshire chose Winant its governor that November. He had reached the top of the state's political ladder not by skilled oratory or appealing promises but as a compelling proponent of humanitarian concerns.

Then the youngest governor in the country, Winant drove himself mercilessly, being available to all who would speak with him. Struggling against the power politics of the standpat, old guard leaders in the legislature, he achieved success only on issues that avoided their opposition. When he was defeated for reelection in 1926, Winant went to Texas to recoup his finances. His lack of success there, followed by the Great Depression, contributed to financial indebtedness for the rest of his life.

In 1930 Winant returned to the governor's office, becoming the first New Hampshire governor to serve more than one two-year term. By the end of 1931 one-third of New Hampshire workers were unemployed, and Governor Winant quickly moved toward experimental governmental approaches to the Great Depression. For example, his "New Hampshire Plan" provided a four-day work week, with the fifth day's hours going to unemployed workers. In spite of the nationwide Democratic sweep in 1932, Winant was reelected, and even the *Manchester Union* commended him for his emergency relief programs. Winant was showing that state governments could assume responsibility in times of economic distress. When the federal government created the New Deal, New Hampshire was ready to cooperate.

Winant began to extend his interests nationally. He pushed for the formation of an interstate (New England, N.Y., and Pa.) compact on minimum wages, and he was the first governor to meet the federal enrollment quota for the Civilian Conservation Corps and to cooperate with the National Planning Board. Appointed by President Franklin D. Roosevelt, he headed a special board of inquiry to settle the 1934 nationwide textile workers' strike. This success brought him national acclaim and attention as a possible 1936 Republican presidential candidate. Although he was interested in the White House, Winant could not campaign against the president, for he stongly supported Roosevelt's New Deal. Winant also rejected a fourth gubernatorial term.

In 1935 President Roosevelt appointed Winant assistant director of the International Labor Organization (ILO), an autonomous agency of the League of Nations. With hopes for peace in Europe fading, the ILO was, as Winant explained, "the only official international agency through which governments, organized labor, and organized employers work . . . for the realization of social justice," and without social justice there could be no lasting peace (Winant, "The I.L.O. Looks Ahead," p. 173). After spending a few months in Geneva, Winant was summoned back to Washington by the president to head the newly created Social Security Board. He had helped draft Social Security legislation, and he was now needed to ensure the program's success. In 1936 Winant felt it necessary to resign to defend the Social Security Act against attack from Republican presidential candidate Alfred M. Landon. Winant then returned to the ILO in Geneva and in 1939 became its director. As German armies marched over Europe and Axis spies threatened the integrity of the ILO, Winant insisted the organization must plan for its postwar responsibilities as a "symbol" of cooperation, a "centre of information and of study, and an organ for action." With great difficulty, he moved the ILO headquarters out of war-torn Europe to Canada in mid-1940. In late 1940 Joseph P. Kennedy resigned as U.S. ambassador to the Court of St. James, and Winant replaced him in March 1941.

When President Roosevelt's appointment of Winant was announced, approval was widespread. The *London Times* stated that Winant was a man "fully awake to the tremendous moral and social issues of the conflict" and one in whom British "confidences can be placed unhesitatingly" (Bellush, p. 160). As ambassador, Winant was totally devoted to the British people and to their struggle against totalitarian forces. He was convinced of the need for closer cooperation between his country and Britain in concluding the war and constructing peace.

In bombed and devastated Britain, amidst air raids and the danger of invasion, Winant walked the streets, offering help and inspiring confidence. The English soon realized that their peril had become his peril. He talked with the people who, although they knew the United States was a friendly neutral, questioned America's reluctance to join them in the struggle against tyranny. He spoke with Prime Minister Winston Churchill on the same question. Refusing the elegance of the American ambassador's residence, Winant "lived in a small flat over the office. . . . The job called for twenty-four hour duty" (*Our Greatest Harvest*, p. 199). He was available to all who sought him at the Grosvenor Square embassy. He restricted his household to British wartime civilian rations, giving formal dinners only for General Dwight Eisenhower and for Eleanor Roosevelt. Instead of the luxurious embassy car, he used a small car or an army truck. Winant, who hated public speaking, was asked to speak all over Britain. In spite of a poor delivery, he won the hearts and minds of his audiences with the sincerity and sense of his messages, conveying the urgency of his main theme, American and British cooperation during the war and after.

Early in 1941 Winant signed the Anglo-American Leased Bases Agreement, implementing the first concrete assistance to England. He helped plan the 1943 Foreign Ministers' Moscow Conference, leading to the summit conference at Teheran, and he served on the European Advisory Commission (EAC), which eventually defined the Allied zones of postwar occupied Germany. Winant was involved with the EAC for the rest of the war. Constructing a just peace became the focus of his energies, and he realized that planning for postwar Germany was critical to a peaceful future. It was a nearly impossible task, taxing his mental and physical endurance.

When the work of the EAC was finished and when Roosevelt died, Winant could not envision a future direction for his services. He hoped to become secretary general of the United Nations, but when the United States was chosen as the site of the organization's headquarters, the top position could not go to an American. In 1946 President Harry Truman appointed him a representative to the United Nations Economic and Social Council, and this temporarily eased Winant's depression, but Truman replaced him at the Court of St. James with W. Averill Harriman. The editor of the *New Statesman and Nation* expressed England's regret at Winant's departure, stating that almost everyone in Britain knew his name and respected him as one of their sincerest friends and suggesting that his appointment was one of the best things President Roosevelt ever did.

On 1 July 1946 Winant delivered a memorial address for the late president at a joint meeting of the two houses of the U.S. Congress. In December he submitted his final resignation as a public servant, leaving his Economic and Social Council post, and turned to writing his memoirs. Fighting illness, financial problems, and mental exhaustion, he completed only one volume. A copy of this volume, sent by the publisher, was waiting for him at the Concord post office the evening Winant took his own life in his Concord, New Hampshire, home.

• Most of Winant's papers are in the Franklin D. Roosevelt Library, Hyde Park, N.Y. Many letters are in the Robert Perkins Bass Collection, Dartmouth College, Hanover, N.H. Telegrams from Geneva and London are in the National Archives and the State Department. *Our Greatest Harvest: Selected Speeches of John G. Winant, 1941–1946* (1950), conveys Winant's appreciation of America's responsibilities and his concern for international cooperation. *Letter from Grosvenor Square: An Account of a Stewardship* (1947), the only volume of his memoirs that Winant completed, covers the year 1941 and is a compelling account of his involvement with the British people. Winant's memorial of Roosevelt is in *Franklin Delano Roosevelt: Memorial Address Delivered before the Joint Meeting of the Two Houses of Congress as a Tribute of Respect to the Late President* (79th Cong., 2d sess., 1946, H. Doc. 770). Other Winant writings include "Civil Organization in Wartime Britain," *State Government* 16 (Apr. 1945): 85–86; "The Role of the Federal Government in Unemployment Compensation," *American Labor Legislation Review* 26 (Mar. 1936): 23–28; "Hopes of Millions Rest with U.S.," *National Municipal Review* 31 (Jan. 1942): 5–8; "The International Labor Organization in Time of War," *International Labour Review* 40 (Oct. 1939): 445–47; and "The I.L.O. Looks Ahead," *International Labour Review* 42 (Oct. 1940): 173–74. Bernard Bellush's scholarly biography, *He Walked Alone* (1968), includes a bibliography of primary sources and footnote citations of secondary sources. Ethel M. Johnson, "The Mr. Winant I Knew," *South Atlantic Quarterly* 48 (Jan. 1949): 24–41, is a more personal story. A long obituary is in the *New York Times*, 4 Nov. 1947.

SYLVIA B. LARSON

WINCHELL, Horace Vaughn (1 Nov. 1865–28 July 1923), geologist, was born in Galesburg, Michigan, the son of Newton Horace Winchell, a geologist, and Charlotte Sophia Imus. The family moved several times before 1872, when his father became professor of geology at the University of Minnesota and the state geologist. As a child, Winchell attended public schools in Minneapolis.

Winchell studied at the University of Minnesota for two years, then transferred to the University of Michigan, where he concentrated in the natural sciences, especially the courses taught by his uncle Alexander Winchell, also a geologist. During summers he was an assistant on the Minnesota geological survey, then under the direction of his uncle and his father. After receiving his A.B. in 1889, he was employed on that survey. In 1890 he married Ida Belle Winchell (daughter of Alexander); their only child died in infancy.

Winchell's first assignment for the Minnesota geological survey was to the Mesabi iron range in the northeastern part of the state, where recognition of iron ore was just beginning. Because the region was obscured by glacial drift, determining the subsurface geology was done primarily by means of exploring pits. In 1889 Winchell published "The Iron-Bearing Rocks of Minnesota" (*Bulletin of the Minnesota Academy of Sciences* 3 [1889]: 277–80) and with his father that year published "On a Possible Chemical Origin of the Iron Ores of the Keewatin in Minnesota" (*American Geologist* 4 [1889]: 291–300), in which they proposed that the cherty iron deposits of northern Minnesota were the result of chemical precipitation from ocean water. The younger Winchell said in a later interview that the idea was primarily his and that it "was ridiculed at the time" (quoted by T. A. Rickard) but that it later was accepted by geologists. The same two authors summarized their work in 1891 in "The Iron Ores of Minnesota" (Geological and Natural History Survey of Minnesota, *Bulletin* 6), in which they described the location and extent of the ores, presented geologic sections, and included a detailed bibliography on iron mining throughout the world and history. Production of iron ore at Mesabi began the next year, and the report proved very useful to companies that were interested in finding and producing iron. The younger Winchell predicted in 1893 that the Mesabi range might produce 500 million tons of iron ore, and that amount had been reached in 1919, by which time the range was producing more than half of all the iron ore mined in the United States. This source of iron was of considerable importance to American participation in World War I.

In 1893 Winchell worked for Minnesota Iron Company for a year, continuing to explore the state's iron deposits, and the next year formed a partnership in chemical analyses with F. F. Sharpless for about two years. He then continued alone as a consultant to individuals and mining companies.

In 1898 Winchell was employed by Anaconda Copper Mining Company in Butte, Montana, where, for it and its successor in 1900, Amalgamated Copper Company, he established a research staff of geologists and devised a system to portray the mine's geology on superposed transparent maps of the working levels. This type of presentation soon became a standard format in the industry. Winchell and others recognized that rich copper ores of two different ages existed in the mine. After considerable chemical experimentation, he concluded that some of the copper mineralization had formed secondarily when sulfur dioxide was present. Because his employer was engaged in a lawsuit (commonly called an "apex suit"), Winchell was not allowed to publish the results of his experiments until 1903 ("Synthesis of Chalcocite and Its Genesis at Butte, Montana," *Bulletin of Geological Society of America* 14 [1903]: 269–76), after two other geologists had published a similar idea separately. The court decision was in favor of Anaconda Copper Mining Company, primarily because of Winchell's expertise on the geology.

In 1906 Winchell resigned from Amalgamated Copper and for two years served as geologist for the Great Northern Railway Company in St. Paul, Minnesota. He looked for iron and coal deposits in the western United States and in Canada. He then relocated in Minneapolis and became a consultant, both examining mining prospects and serving as an adviser to companies in mining litigation. For various companies he traveled considerably in the mainland United States, to Alaska ten times, to Mexico, South America, and Europe frequently, and to Russia. From there, when the revolution began in 1917, he and his wife departed by way of Siberia. In his later years he devoted considerable time to urging revision of the laws regarding ownership of mineral properties in the public domain of the United States, but his recommendations were not adopted.

Winchell was one of the small group that established the Geological Society of America in 1888, and he served as its president in 1902. He was a financial supporter of the journal *American Geologist*, which had been founded in 1888 through his father's and uncle's efforts, and which stopped publishing in 1905. In the following year he supported the establishment of *Economic Geology* and was one of its associate editors for five years. He was also one of three American associate editors of the German journal *Zeitschrift für praktische Geologie* from 1896 to World War I. An active participant in the American Institute of Mining and Metallurgical Engineers, he was its president in 1919.

Colleagues recognized Winchell as the leading authority on geological interpretation of mining law, and they commented on his fairness and honesty. His early interest in the history of mining, when he prepared a bibliography for the report on the Mesabi range, continued throughout his life, and he obtained a valuable collection of books on the subject. He retired to California in 1921 and died in Los Angeles.

• Winchell's extensive library was given to the Engineering Societies Library of New York by his widow and the Anaconda Copper Mining Company. He wrote about 100 scientific papers. An interview with Winchell by T. A. Rickard, "Horace V. Winchell, Mining Geologist," *Mining and Scientific Press*, 15 Feb. 1919, pp. 211–19, gives useful biographical information. Memorials are Charles Keyes, "Horace Vaughn Winchell: Mining Geologist," *Pan-American Geologist* 40 (1923): 161–80, with bibliography; and James F. Kemp, "Memorial of Horace Vaughn Winchell," *Bulletin of the Geological Society of America* 35 (1924): 46–56, with bibliography. Obituaries are in the *Los Angeles Sunday Times* and the *Minneapolis Sunday Tribune*, 29 July 1923.

ELIZABETH NOBLE SHOR

WINCHELL, Newton Horace (17 Dec. 1839–2 May 1914), geologist and archeologist, was born in Northeast, Dutchess County, New York, the son of Horace Winchell and Caroline McAllister, both schoolteachers. After education at local public schools in Northeast and the academy in Salisbury, Connecticut, Winchell taught in local district schools near home. His restless, reform-minded father, having returned from a fruitless venture in the California gold fields, could not offer Winchell the financial support for college earlier afforded Winchell's brother Alexander. By the mid-1850s, however, Alexander had successfully established himself as professor of geology, zoology, and botany at the University of Michigan and offered his younger brother the opportunity to stay in Ann Arbor and to begin language and other preparation for college entrance.

Leaving behind an unhappy home situation, Winchell spent the years after 1857 alternatively teaching in local schools in Michigan, assisting his brother in laboratory preparations, and attending classes at the University of Michigan. He graduated in 1866 and took his A.M. in 1869. He spent the two years before taking his first degree as superintendent of schools in St. Clair, Michigan, and after graduation became superintendent of schools in Adrian, Michigan. In 1864 he married Charlotte (Lottie) Sophia Imus, who had taught at Albion Academy; they had five children, including two sons who also became geologists.

Pursuing geological interests with his brother, Winchell was officially appointed as assistant to the Michigan State Geological Survey for 1869–1870. He then investigated copper and silver deposits in New Mexico in late 1870 before joining the Ohio survey under John Strong Newberry for 1871–1872. Then, based on his growing reputation, he was named head of the newly organized survey of Minnesota in 1872 and remained in that position until 1900.

Following well-established traditions among programs elsewhere, he initiated mapping and surveys of geology as well as natural history. The state legislators monitored expenditures and activities as Winchell and his staff produced twenty-four *Reports*, ten *Bulletins*, and six *Final Reports* of the Minnesota Geological and

Natural History Survey by the end of the century. From 1872 to 1881 he was concurrently chair of geology and mineralogy at the University of Minnesota, where a contribution from John S. Pillsbury provided a magnificent sandstone building in 1889 to house the survey collections and to make them available to students. Winchell served as official curator until 1900. Occasionally he worked outside the state, as in the summer of 1874 when he was geologist on a military exploring expedition in the Black Hills of the Dakota territory under General George Armstrong Custer. Active in promoting the survey to local legislators and beyond the state's boundaries, Winchell exhibited Minnesota mineralogy at international congresses of geologists (Bologne, France, in 1881 and Zurich, Switzerland, in 1894) and at international expositions in New Orleans, Chicago, and St. Louis. He worked in the laboratory as well as in the field, and with his son Alexander Newton, Winchell wrote *Elements of Optical Mineralogy* (1909), a volume still used in revised editions.

Responsive to his legislative patrons, Winchell and his assistants produced special reports on the mineral and natural gas resources in the state. This work helped to make clear the extent of the iron ore deposits discovered in the Mesabi and Vermilion ranges as well as smaller iron ore deposits, building-stone resources, copper deposits, salt wells, water supplies, and coal beds. His detailed interpretation of the origin of the iron ores, arguing two distinct geological events, was in conflict with that of the U.S. Geological Survey; scientific disagreements reflected a more general tension between geologists in the state surveys and those in the federal service. The Minnesota survey staff also reported on ornithology, entomology, botany, and meteorology in its annual reports and bulletins. Because of the specifics of Minnesota topography, Winchell's research interests in glaciation and drift deposition were awakened early and persisted throughout his life. His observations about englacial drift at the boundary of retreating glaciers appeared in technical detail in annual reports and more descriptively in such journals as *Popular Science Monthly*.

Shortly after his arrival in Minnesota, he persuaded local physicians, professors, and others to form the Minnesota Academy of Natural Sciences and remained its most active member for over forty years. He was a fellow of the American Association for the Advancement of Science, a founding member of the Geological Society of America in 1889 (council member, 1892–1894; president, 1902), and active at national and international scientific meetings. Frustrated by John Powell's leadership of the U.S. Geological Survey and intellectual dominance in the field, Winchell founded and was managing editor of the *American Geologist*. This monthly magazine, published from 1888 to 1905 with the help of his wife, became an important outlet for state geologists, particularly those in midwestern and western states.

After completing the final report of the survey in 1900, Winchell turned his attention largely to archeology and history. An early geological study of the recession of the falls at Saint Anthony on the Mississippi River had indicated the last glacial period (ice age) had ended about 8,000 years earlier. Winchell had published a brief report on "Primitive Man at Little Falls" in 1877 and considered whether human habitation had preceded that glacial retreat. Utilizing a collection of aboriginal artifacts that J. V. Bower and others had deposited at the Minnesota Historical Society, Winchell considered again the timing and types of early human settlement along the Mississippi River and in the upper Midwest, particularly in relation to glacial intrusions. In 1906 he was placed in charge of the Department of Archeology at the historical society. In this capacity he edited and extended the notes of previous researchers on American Indian mounds and published in 1911 *The Aborigines of Minnesota*. He persisted in arguing, based on regional evidence drawn from geology and archeology and despite the skepticism of well-known archeologists, that humans inhabited North America during and perhaps before the last glacial epoch.

Winchell extended *The Winchell Genealogy* (1916) begun by his brother and enjoyed the professional and social status acquired by his children. He died in Minneapolis of complications following surgery in 1914. A nature walk along the western bank of the Mississippi River in Minneapolis and the Winchell School of Geology and Geophysics at the University of Minnesota commemorate his work on the state's geology and archeology.

• The bulk of the Newton Horace Winchell Papers are at the Minnesota Historical Society, although considerable material is in the segment of the papers relating to Alexander Winchell, which was transferred to the Bentley Historical Library, University of Michigan, Ann Arbor. Some field notebooks and Winchell's library are in the Department of Geology and Geophysics at the University of Minnesota. Employment and other records relating to Winchell's management of the facilities in Pillsbury Hall are in the archives of the University of Minnesota. A pertinent overview of his early scientific research is in N. H. Winchell, "History of the Geological Surveys in Minnesota," *Bulletin* 1 (1889): 3–25. Contemporary evaluations are found in "Memorial for Newton Horace Winchell," Minnesota Academy of Science, *Bulletin* 5 (July 1914): 69–116; two memoirs by Warren Upham in the *Bulletin of the Geological Society of America* 26 (1915): 27–46 and *Economic Geology* 11 (1916): 63–72; and John M. Clarke in *Science* 41 (1914): 127–30. Additional biographical material is in F. Garvin Davenport, "Newton H. Winchell, Pioneer of Science," *Minnesota History* 32 (1951): 214–25. An obituary is in the *Minneapolis Sunday Tribune*, 3 May 1914.

SALLY GREGORY KOHLSTEDT

WINCHELL, Walter (7 Apr. 1897–20 Feb. 1972), journalist, was born in the Harlem section of New York City, the first son of Jacob Winschel, a salesman, and Jennie Bakst, recent Jewish immigrants from Russia. The *s* in the family name was dropped when he was a boy. This was a troubled marriage; Walter and a younger brother were raised by relatives. He was a poor student and left school in the sixth grade. His most important classrooms were his neighborhood, where he was a newsboy and worked odd jobs, and the vaudeville circuit, which he joined before he was thirteen. In the Newsboy Sextette he sang with George Jessel and did mock battle armed with a rolled-up newspaper. Winchell added an *l* to his name because he liked the way it looked on a theatrical bill.

Winchell enlisted in the navy in World War I and married Rita Greene (sometimes spelled Green), his dance partner before the war, in 1919. They lived apart after 1922 and were divorced in 1928. There were no children. Winchell went through a marriage ceremony with June Magee, also a dancer, in 1923, although he was never technically married to the woman who was known to the world as his second wife. They had three children and took two Chinese children into their home. Winchell stepped into journalism by selling short items about show business to *Billboard*, and publication led to his first reporting job with *Vaudeville News*. He took his gossip column to Bernarr Macfadden's new tabloid, the *Evening Graphic*, in 1924 and jumped to William Randolph Hearst's entry in this field, the *Daily Mirror*, in 1929. His column "On Broadway," syndicated by King Features, appeared in more than 800 papers, and beginning in 1931 Winchell had a regular spot on network radio. By the end of the decade, he had enlarged his audience for gossip to more than a third of the nation.

The census returns of 1920 showed that the United States had become an urban nation; Winchell helped to create the folklore to accommodate this change. He celebrated the noise, glare, and even the smell of his beloved New York, and he claimed to know the secrets of the place. He had a police radio, a red light, and a siren on his car and cruised New York at night looking for excitement. To his audience, Winchell was a safe step outside all particular cultural traditions into an ersatz world where class, ethnic, and geographical boundaries had fallen and anyone could be in-the-know. In their Middletown study during the depression, sociologists Robert Lynd and Helen Lynd found that even the citizens of Muncie, Indiana, loved Winchell's patter.

A Winchell column, the writer Ben Hecht said, had the sound of a man honking in a traffic jam. Winchell was even less restrained on the air. "Good evening, Mr. and Mrs. North America and all the ships at sea. Let's go to press! Flash!" he shouted as his finger tapped a telegraph key. He read his copy at 200 words a minute in a gravelly voice against the gibberish of Morse code. This act, carried on network radio until 1956 and simulcast by the American Broadcasting Company on television for a time, created a durable image of the working press. In the 1930s Winchell played himself in several Hollywood films, and critic George Jean Nathan counted twenty-seven plays and forty-three movies modeled after Winchell in a four-year period. The "Untouchables" television series (1959–1963) linked this insistent, hoarse voice with the sensational stories of the interwar years.

Earlier gossip columnists had been marginal in the eyes of editors and the public, but Winchell made celebrity watching a central appeal of the press. When not cruising the city, he stationed himself in the most exclusive section of Manhattan's Stork Club, usually at table fifty, and extracted respect and information as a sort of toll from public figures who wanted good press. To keep secrets from him was to invite attack; indeed, patrons who did not greet him warmly were berated above the din of the restaurant. Winchell brought the world of entertainment and politics together in his chronicle of the city. He grasped that entertainers and politicians now shared a common ground of celebrityhood and needed him to advance. He plugged administrations in the same way he recommended plays, movies, and books. Franklin D. Roosevelt held private conferences with Winchell and valued his support in newspapers whose publishers opposed the New Deal. Winchell traded information with the Federal Bureau of Investigation, and his friendship with J. Edgar Hoover was cemented in 1939 when he arranged for the mobster Louis "Lepke" Buchalter to surrender to the director on a Manhattan street corner.

Because Winchell defended the New Deal and condemned prejudice, he earned respect from liberals. In their *Treasury of Great Reporting* (1947) scholars Louis L. Snyder and Richard B. Morris noted that Winchell had "a solid reputation as the reporter who had done more to rouse the conscience of America against intolerance and totalitarianism than any other journalist of his time." Loud, profane, and ruthless, Winchell was capable of fighting for causes that writers with better manners ducked. He was a particularly outspoken opponent of anti-Semitism. Winchell attacked Adolf Hitler in 1932 and risked his commercial success on the National Broadcasting Company with his persistent attacks on Nazi leaders. Winchell's impulses for social justice were at war with his temperament, however. He spoke up for civil rights and black celebrities, for example, yet waged a vendetta against African-American entertainer Josephine Baker after a misunderstanding at the Stork Club in 1951. Often Winchell relished a fight more than he cared about what he fought for.

Winchell saw Harry S. Truman as a provincial politician who could not wear the Roosevelt mantle. The new president invited the columnist to the White House to court him, but Winchell left feeling insulted. In the postwar era, Winchell found more friends in the American right. As a merchant of innuendo and shock, he warmed to the talk of conspiracies in the Cold War. Senator Joseph R. McCarthy's assistant, Roy Cohn, was in the columnist's circle at the Stork Club, and Winchell supported the senator's reckless pursuit of communists. This alienated many liberals in his core audience. More seriously, Winchell could not master the new sources of popular culture and was seen as a throwback, as in the ruthless, thinly veiled portrait of him in the film *The Sweet Smell of Success* (1957). Winchell fumbled as an arbitrator of celebrityhood, losing his radio program and most of the papers that had carried his column.

The journalist's retirement in 1969 was prompted by the suicide of his only biological son. Winchell died in Los Angeles of the disease he had fought for a quarter-century as founder of the Damon Runyon Memorial Fund for Cancer Research.

• Winchell clippings and annotated radio scripts are at the Billy Rose Theatre Collection, the New York Public Library. His correspondence was scattered in 1990 when Butterfield & Butterfield auctioned some 40,000 letters, including more than 600 from J. Edgar Hoover.

The definitive biography is Neal Gabler, *Winchell: Gossip, Power and the Culture of Celebrity* (1994). The book corrects many errors in the memoirs by Winchell's associates; in ascending order of completeness these are Ernest Cuneo (credited only with the introduction) and Walter Winchell, *Winchell Exclusive* (1975), Ed Weiner, *Let's Go to Press: A Biography of Walter Winchell* (1955), and Herman Klurfeld, *Winchell: His Life and Times* (1976). St. Clair McKelway, *Gossip: The Life and Times of Walter Winchell* (1940), is a harsh profile that originally appeared in the *New Yorker*. John Mosedale, *The Men Who Invented Broadway* (1981), is a dual biography with Damon Runyon. Michael Herr, *Winchell* (1990), is a novel that borrows the form of a screenplay to bring the journalist to life. H. L. Mencken, *The American Language*, supp. 1 (1945), records, with approval, Winchellese. For one of the encounters that made Winchell notorious, see Phyllis Rose, *Jazz Cleopatra: Josephine Baker in Her Time* (1989).

THOMAS C. LEONARD

WINCHESTER, Elhanan (30 Sept. 1751–18 Apr. 1797), clergyman and leading figure in early American Universalism, was born in Brookline, Massachusetts, the son of Elhanan Winchester, a farmer and shoemaker, and Sarah (maiden name unknown). Winchester had little formal schooling because of his family's economic circumstances. Yet, he was a gifted child who loved to read and had a near photographic memory.

Winchester's career must be understood against the backdrop of the transatlantic spiritual awakenings occurring before, during, and after the American Revolution. These years were filled with political and religious turbulence. The language of liberty, war, and frontier migration opened debate on the meaning of freedom, authority, and democracy. Americans began to experiment with new forms of organization and belief. In American religious life, ordinary people challenged the authority of the dominant Calvinist tradition, objecting to religious establishment, the doctrine of limited atonement, and a privileged, learned clergy. They demanded an unpretentious and lively leadership adept at the art of persuasion and intent on searching for the Divine in revivals, dreams and visions, and biblical prophecy.

Winchester thrived in this environment. He patterned his style and message after the "Grand Itinerant" George Whitefield and was an avid interpreter of biblical prophecy. Like Whitefield, Winchester was a remarkable orator, his preaching inspiring outpourings of religious sentiment wherever he went. He was able to mesh his humble background, religious enthusiasm, and lively mind with the desires of his audiences. He led common folk to faith and moved comfortably among the best religious minds of America and Britain.

Winchester began preaching in his father's home at the age of nineteen after his father was converted by Whitefield. Winchester did not stay long among the evangelical Congregationalists of his home town. His restless mind struggled to reconcile the Great Awakening's emphasis on the centrality of adult religious conversion and the Calvinist notion of predestination and infant baptism. In 1770 Winchester joined an Arminian Baptist fellowship, permanently rejecting the doctrine of infant baptism. At this time Winchester also renounced his Calvinism, a decision he would revisit several times in his life.

Winchester began his ministry as an itinerant pastor among the Arminian Baptist congregations of New England. In 1771 his preaching drew large audiences and started a revival from which the Rehoboth, Massachusetts, Baptist church was started. Winchester was ordained pastor of this church. Within a year of his ordination, Winchester again struggled with Calvinism—especially the issue of free will. This time he reconsidered the possibility that humans had the facility of mind and will to choose their own path to salvation. In short, he rejected Arminianism. When his views became public, he was asked to leave the Rehoboth church.

During the years 1772–1774 Winchester traveled among various Calvinistic Baptist congregations in New England. In 1774 he took a pastorate in Welch Neck, South Carolina. He remained pastor there until 1780 and threw himself into the work of revival. His church in South Carolina grew quickly with new converts, including African slaves from the surrounding plantations.

Winchester's writings against slavery gained him fame among northern abolitionists during the 1840s. During his southern travels, Winchester became convinced that slavery was an "abomination." He preached a 1774 sermon against the slave trade and published it as a pamphlet, *The Reigning Abominations*, in 1788. Winchester argued forcefully that slave holding and slave trading were evils that debased all involved and kept Africans and plantation owners from full fellowship with God. Winchester worked to convert slaves and their masters with no reported tension among his congregants.

The South Carolina pastorate was also a significant period for Winchester's intellectual development. In 1778 he read Paul Siegvolck's (pseudonym of George Klein-Nicolai) *The Everlasting Gospel*. The idea that an eternal punishment for sin was inconsistent with the idea of a merciful God who promises a salvation open to all appealed to Winchester as consistent with his reading of Scripture. He did not immediately embrace Universalism but struggled with Siegvolck's arguments for several years, taking the new ideas with him to the First Baptist Church of Philadelphia, one of the biggest and most prestigious churches in the young nation.

Winchester worried that the doctrine of universal salvation undermined the need for a transforming conversion experience, the belief in divine justice, and a warm evangelical piety. Nonetheless, through personal study and through his friendship with George de Benneville, an early Universalist living among the pietist German Dunker sect, Winchester embraced the doctrine. Winchester argued that Christianity promised the complete destruction of Satan and evil; therefore, all souls eventually would find their way to union with Christ and with God. This did not mean, however, that unrepentant humans would escape punishment for sin. Hell existed, and its purpose was to cause repentance. Some form of purgation would be experienced for an undetermined period of time. Christians, however, would be spared the worst of the purification process, perfecting a bond already begun at conversion. Winchester set out this position most fully in his *Dialogues on the Universal Restoration* (1788).

Winchester's position on universal salvation split his Philadelphia church. He eventually left, taking a majority of the old congregation. The new fellowship moved its services to the Hall of the University of Pennsylvania and called itself the Society of Universal Baptists. Winchester preached in Philadelphia from 1781 until 1787, earning great praise and the friendship of Benjamin Rush and other prominent Philadelphians. Rush, in particular, was enamored by Winchester's mind and his oratory. Remarking on one of Winchester's sermons, Rush found him "as usual, eloquent, Scriptural, and irresistible in his reasoning upon all subjects" (L. H. Butterfield, ed., *Letters of Benjamin Rush* [1951], p. 773).

Winchester left Philadelphia for London in 1787, feeling a call to proclaim the gospel in Britain. His oratory and writing gained him some attention in Britain, including friendships with Joseph Priestly and John Wesley. During his London sojourn, Winchester turned out most of his published works and hymns.

Winchester's private life was tumultuous and marked by extreme sadness. He was married five times and was a widower four times: his first wife was Alice Rogers; he then married Sarah Peck in 1776; Sarah Luke in 1778, and Mary Morgan in 1781. None of his eight children survived infancy. Winchester succumbed to tuberculosis in Hartford, Connecticut. He was survived by his fifth spouse, Martha Knowles.

Winchester was remembered by friends and colleagues as a scholar. John Redman, first president of the College of Physicians in Philadelphia, called him "our Theological Newton." By the end of his life, Winchester had mastered five languages and written numerous theological books, pamphlets, and hymns. Winchester was a remarkable orator, an early antislavery advocate, and a prominent pastor during the years of the American Revolution. He should be remembered as one of the most influential contributors to early American Universalism and as a man who embodied the religious and intellectual ferment of his time.

• Early manuscripts and letters from Winchester and early Universalism material can be found at the Universalist Historical Society, Andover-Harvard Library, Cambridge, Mass. Winchester's most accessible published works include *The Fate of Moses Unveiled by the Gospel* (1787), *A Course of Lectures on the Prophecies That Remain to Be Fulfilled* (4 vols., 1789), *The Restitution of All Things . . . Defended* (1790), *The Three Woe Trumpets* (1793), and *Ten Letters Addressed to Mr. Paine* (1795). Useful information on Winchester's career can be found in a number of sources, including Joseph Sweeny, "Elhanan Winchester and the Universalist Baptists" (Ph.D. diss., Univ. of Pennsylvania, 1969); Charles White Mc Gehee, "Elhanan Winchester: A Decision for Universal Restoration," *Annual Journal of the Universalist Historical Society* 1 (1959): 43–58; and Edwin Martin Stone, *Rev. Elhanan Winchester: Biography and Letters* (1972). For background on the origins of American Universalism see Russell Miller, *The Larger Hope: The First Century of the Universalist Church in America 1770–1870* (1979), and David Robinson, *The Unitarians and the Universalists* (1985). Two books essential for interpreting the part played by Universalists during the religious upheavals of the early republic are Nathan Hatch's prize-winning *The Democratization of American Christianity* (1989), and Stephen Marini, *The Radical Sects of Revolutionary New England* (1984).

SCOTT FLIPSE

WINCHESTER, James (6 Feb. 1752–26 July 1826), soldier, planter, and pioneer, was born in Carroll County, Maryland, the son of William Winchester, a surveyor, and Lydia Richards. As a youth he learned his father's trade and was widely respected for his skill and industry. He enlisted as a private in the Continental army in 1776 and rose to the rank of captain. Wounded, captured, and imprisoned briefly by the British, he served to the war's end and was a leader in the organization of the Society of the Cincinnati.

After the Revolution, Winchester and his brother George bought land in the Cumberland settlements north of Nashville in present-day Sumner County. Both moved to the Tennessee country by 1785 and immediately became active in frontier government and military service. George was ambushed and killed by Chickasaw Indians in 1794, but James prospered. He added to his land holdings, built mills, and established trade in tobacco and other products with merchants in New Orleans and several eastern cities. In 1802 he built a spacious home, "Cragfont," which was described by a contemporary as "the most elegant house west of the Appalachians."

Congress in 1790 established a territorial government for the "Southwest Territory" that would become the state of Tennessee in 1796. Winchester was chosen a member of its legislative council while also remaining active in the militia. Five years later, as senior colonel, he became commandant of the western segment of the territory, called the "Mero District." When Tennessee became a state he was promoted to brigadier general of the state militia and also in the same year became speaker of the state senate.

Meanwhile, Winchester had become involved in a romance with fifteen-year-old Susan Black, who had settled with her mother and brothers at nearby Bledsoe's Lick in 1786. Susan apparently lived with him as a common-law wife and in 1793 bore the first of their fourteen children. She and Winchester apparently were married in 1803, and in that year Winchester secured legislative legitimization of their four living children.

During the decade following Tennessee's admission to statehood, Winchester further expanded his landholdings, raised livestock, and operated mills, distilleries, and cotton gins. He remained active politically and supported the "War Hawks" in their interest of annexing Spanish Florida and parts of Canada. When Congress did not move swiftly enough to suit him, Winchester offered to raise an army of Tennesseans "looking to Canada."

In June 1812, much to Winchester's satisfaction, Congress declared war on Great Britain. Already, President James Madison (1751–1836) had appointed him brigadier general of the U.S. Army, which required his resignation from the state militia. For several months he was in charge of recruitment in the Ohio and Mississippi valleys and was stationed in Lexington, Kentucky. But in August, shocked by news of the fall of Detroit and the surrender of General William Hull's army, he assumed command of the Left Wing of the Army of the Northwest under General William Henry Harrison and marched toward the Michigan Territory. After winning several skirmishes along the route, Winchester's forces were surprised and overwhelmed near Frenchtown (where the Raisin River flows into Lake Erie) and surrendered. Winchester and his son Marcus, who accompanied him as an aide, were taken prisoner and held at Quebec for more than a year. Exchanged in April 1814, he returned home and was given a hero's welcome in Nashville and Gallatin despite his defeat and capture. A few months later he was placed in command of the Eastern Section of the Seventh Military District at Mobile, where he served until March 1815 under the command of Andrew Jackson. On 31 March 1815 he resigned his commission and a few weeks later returned to Cragfont.

Back home, Winchester wrote extensively in defense of his actions at the battle of River Raisin and continued also to engage in a variety of commercial enterprises. In 1818 he joined Jackson and John Overton in planning a city on the Mississippi River. They named the city Memphis—a name suggested by Winchester with the expressed hope that it would become what the ancient Egyptian city of Memphis had been to the Nile. His son Marcus played an important role in the city's founding and became its first mayor when it was incorporated in 1826, shortly before Winchester's death at Cragfont.

• Walter Durham's *James Winchester, Tennessee Pioneer* (1979) is the definitive work on the subject. Collections of Winchester's papers at the Jean and Alexander Heard Library and Archives, Nashville, and the Tennessee State Library and Archives in the same city give insight into his activities, as do the Draper manuscripts at the State Historical Society of Wisconsin in Madison.

Articles include Ward Allen, "Cragfont: Grandeur on the Tennessee Frontier," *Tennessee Historical Quarterly* 23 (1964): 103–20; David Edwin Harrell, "James Winchester, Patriot," *Tennessee Historical Quarterly* 17 (1958): 301–17; John DeWitt, "General James Winchester, 1752–1826," *Tennessee Historical Magazine* 1 (1915): 79–105, 183–205; and James E. Roper, "The Founding of Memphis, August 1818 through December 1820," West Tennessee Historical Society's Papers 23 (1969): 5–29.

ROBERT E. CORLEW

WINCHESTER, Oliver Fisher (30 Nov. 1810–11 Dec. 1880), small-arms manufacturer, was born in Boston, Massachusetts, the son of Samuel Winchester and Hannah Bates. The early death of Oliver Winchester's father left the family in financial difficulty, and at the age of seven he started working on a farm in the summer and attending school in the winter. At age fourteen he was apprenticed to a carpenter. After six years he purchased the remainder of his apprenticeship and moved to Baltimore, where he worked as a master builder. He married Jane Ellen Hope in Boston in 1834. They had two children.

In 1834 Winchester, who had previously clerked in retail stores, opened a men's clothing store in Baltimore that manufactured and sold its own shirts. He sold his retail business in 1847 and moved to New York, where he and his partner, John M. Davies, engaged in importing, jobbing, and the manufacture of men's shirts using a new method of cutting shirts patented by Winchester on 1 February 1848. The partners prospered and about 1850 moved their shirt factory to New Haven, Connecticut, with Winchester in complete charge of the operation. Within a few years he was able to invest some of the profits in the newly organized Volcanic Repeating Arms Company. In 1855 he was elected a director of the company. Soon after Winchester became a director, the offices and shops of Volcanic moved from Norwich to New Haven. Within a year Winchester and Nelson Gaston, president of the Volcanic company, were forced to advance personal funds to keep the firm in business. The loans were secured by mortgages, and following Gaston's death in 1856 Winchester purchased Gaston's mortgages and became the principal owner and president of the Volcanic Repeating Arms Company. In less than a year the other creditors forced the company into receivership. As holder of more than $40,000 in first mortgages Winchester received all assets. Winchester reorganized the firm as the New Haven Arms Co., with himself as president.

Winchester acquired a number of important patents and skilled gunsmiths in the acquisition of Volcanic, including Lewis Jenning's patent for the lever-action loading of a repeating rifle and the right to manufacture metallic cartridges using an early Smith & Wesson patent. Earlier, David Wesson, who had been superintendent of the Volcanic shops, had left to rejoin

Horace Smith in the production of revolvers under the name Smith & Wesson. Fortunately Wesson was replaced by Benjamin Tyler Henry, one of the most famous gunsmiths ever employed by Winchester. Henry's major improvement was a tube, nearly the length of the barrel, for holding cartridges, from which they could be received and propelled into the breech of the rifle. Although patented in 1860, it was two years later that actual production and sales of the Henry repeating rifle got under way. The Henry was probably the best and certainly the most popular rifle being produced, and in 1865 the Connecticut state legislature, by special act, honored Henry by changing the name of the firm to the Henry Repeating Arms Co. A year later the legislature again changed the name of the firm, this time to the Winchester Repeating Arms Co., and Oliver Winchester disposed of his interests in manufacturing men's shirts to devote all of his efforts to the firm.

The Henry repeating rifle, using an improved rimfire (instead of a center-fire) cartridge, although intended primarily as a sporting gun, was undoubtedly the finest military weapon available during the Civil War. Indeed, even though the federal ordnance department harbored a bias against repeating rifles until well after the Civil War, a great many Henry rifles were privately purchased and used by state troops. In 1866 Nelson King, who had succeeded Henry as superintendent of the factory, developed a gate for loading the magazine through the receiver, which corrected the problem of fouling the magazine through the open port of the Henry. In 1869 Winchester acquired the property and patents of the American Repeating Rifle Company, and a year later he purchased the Spencer Repeating Rifle Company. After making improvements in Benjamin Hotchkiss's bolt-action repeating rifle, for which Winchester purchased the patent rights in 1876, he added it to the Winchester line. A year before his death he acquired the rights to John Browning's original patent for a lever-action, falling-block mechanism, which was later incorporated into the Winchester single-shot rifle.

While Winchester himself developed several patents, his real genius lay in his ability to recognize the potential of the improvements of others and in attracting outstanding talent to work for the Winchester Repeating Arms Co. In addition, he had a keen understanding of the very diverse market for small arms. The Winchester custom shop could supply an almost endless variety of options to the customer. By the 1870s Winchester could boast that the Winchester rifle had "become a household word, a household necessity on our western plains, and mountains" (Madis, p. 638). A modern expert on small arms noted that "Winchester Rifles are a field into themselves" and that "some of the finest rifles ever made" were produced by the Winchester custom shop in the late nineteenth century (Fjestad, p. 1055).

In 1864 Winchester served as a presidential elector at large and cast his vote for Abraham Lincoln. Two years later he was elected lieutenant governor of the state of Connecticut. A man of considerable wealth, Oliver Winchester was an active philanthropist. One of his gifts to Yale University helped establish the Yale Observatory. He died in New Haven.

• There are no known collections of Winchester papers, but some factory papers are at the Winchester Museum, Cody, Wyo. George Madis, *The Winchester Book* (1961), is by far the best study of Winchester firearms. Madis has included biographical information as well as material on the manufacture of Winchester firearms. S. P. Fjestad, *The Blue Book of Gun Values* (1995), is an extremely useful guide to firearms. The *New Haven Evening Register*, 11 Dec. 1880, contains a long and thorough obituary.

JAMES D. NORRIS

WINCHEVSKY, Morris (9 Aug. 1856–18 Mar. 1932), Yiddish poet, editor, and one of the founders of the socialist *Jewish Daily Forward*, was born Lippe Ben-Zion Novachovitch in Yanovo, Lithuania, when it was part of Russia, the son of Sissel Novachovitch, who had no trade and worked odd jobs, and Golda (maiden name unknown), a storekeeper. Winchevsky once said he became a socialist "twenty-five years before my birth," referring to the execution of his grandfather by the Russians for participating in the Polish rebellion of 1831. At age eleven the Lithuanian Jew took the unusual step of entering government school and learning Russian fluently. Languages came easily to him. He went on to learn German and English and translated Victor Hugo's *Les Misérables* and Henrik Ibsen's *A Doll's House* into his native Yiddish.

Winchevsky lived for a while in Kovno and Vilna (later Vilnius) with his family before accepting a job as a bank clerk/interpreter in the inner Russian city of Orel. During his three years there, he read populist and revolutionary literature, including works by Mikhail Bakunin and Peter Lavrov. He began to develop a social consciousness and write social satire in Hebrew. In his unfinished autobiography, Winchevsky expressed surprise that Russian peasants he visited in Orel could not afford salt for their tasteless bread.

In August 1875, when the Orel bank closed, Winchevsky returned to Kovno. He began writing to Aaron Lieberman, a socialist. Lieberman began publishing, in Hebrew, *Ha-Emet*, the first Jewish socialist magazine, and Winchevsky contributed poems with a socialist flavor. His socialist orientation was cemented in 1877 when he took a job at a bank in Königsberg, Prussia, home of many Russian-Jewish students and Western socialist ideas. There he became editor of a Hebrew socialist monthly, *Asefat Hakhamim*, and wrote his first poem in Yiddish.

Arrested in November 1878, soon after Chancellor Otto von Bismarck's antisocialist laws took effect, he spent five months in prison and was expelled shortly after a friend posted his bail. Winchevsky traveled to Denmark and then to England, arriving in London on 23 March 1879. "I was struck by a singular sight," he said in a magazine article nearly three decades later. "Every restaurant in Whitechapel and every stand selling what the Russians called *morozhenoye* . . . carried the sign 'Ice Cream.' Not knowing a word of English, I read it in the Latin way, *Itze Creem*. 'How right Marx proved to be,' I mused. 'Even such a small seasonal industry as *morozhenoye* is already concentrated in one hand; *Itze Creem* must be a man of great wealth.'"

Winchevsky never met Karl Marx, who also was in London at the time, but he agitated for socialism. He wrote the constitution for the Jewish Workers Benefit and Educational Verein ("verein" means "society"). At the verein, he believed he was "going to his own people," and he began to write in Yiddish, the everyday language of European Jews. In 1884 he founded the first Yiddish socialist periodical, *Der Polisher Yidel* (The little Polish Jew). That summer he gained his pen name when he produced the first socialist propaganda booklet in Yiddish, called *Yehi Or* (the Hebrew words for "let there be light"). A series of dialogues in the booklet are written as if they occurred between two ordinary workers, Morris and Hyman. For literary effect, the former of the two was designated the author of the pamphlets, which were signed "Morris Winchevsky." Later, the man born Novachovitch would become almost exclusively identified with this nom de plume, although he legally changed his name to Leopold Benedict. In 1885 Winchevsky married Rebecca Harris; they had two children.

In 1889 Winchevsky published a prose series, *Der Meshugener Filozof* (The crazy philosopher). It blended pointed commentary about religion and capitalism with a sharp wit and a moral purpose. "Consider a pen," Winchevsky the philosopher wrote. "It comes new and shining into your hand. It gets blackened working for you. You let it rust. And when it is worn out and can no longer serve you, you discard it with scorn. Remarkable, is it not? A pen has about the same fate as a good servant of the rich, or as a laborer in a factory."

Winchevsky moved in 1894 to the United States, where his family joined him the next year. His popularity as a writer led New York socialists to seek him out, but more than once he would prove too independent for them. Although he nominally was a member of the Socialist Labor party and contributed to the *Adenblatt*, the first Jewish socialist daily, Winchevsky felt uncomfortable in New York under the autocratic, ideological leadership of the party's Daniel De Leon. A Boston Jewish faction of the party invited Winchevsky to edit a newspaper, and he accepted. The first issue of *Der Emes*, a family weekly that proclaimed its devotion to "literature and enlightenment," appeared 3 May 1895. In two months Winchevsky turned his paper into an anti–De Leon platform. Booted off the paper by Boston's socialists, Winchevsky toured the country to raise money for a new newspaper—one more open to a broad range of ideas than the *Adenblatt*. In 1897 he helped Abraham Cahan found the *Jewish Daily Forward*, the influential Yiddish voice of socialism in New York City. In 1902, 1907, and 1909 Winchevsky edited the socialist monthly *Zukunft* (The future), where he published the bulk of his memoirs. He remained independent enough to tell the *Forward* one year that its editorials were "silly."

Winchevsky was fond of socialist leader Eugene V. Debs, following Debs into the Social Democratic party, and he later joined the united Socialist Party of America. In the 1920s his political views turned toward the left. Winchevsky made a triumphal tour of Soviet Russia in 1924, where he was regarded as a pre-Marxist socialist.

He broke his leg one evening on a dark Moscow sidewalk, and the injury eventually disabled him. He returned to America in 1925 and spent his last years semiparalyzed, reading books and listening to New York Yankees baseball games on the radio. His death in New York produced a political clash as thousands of communists tried to turn his funeral into a propaganda parade. They were thwarted by Winchevsky's family and a less-radical socialist faction that rushed Winchevsky's coffin through the communist crowd to a nearly unattended burial.

Socialist poet Abraham Liessen, who wrote editorials for the *Jewish Daily Forward*, called Winchevsky "the first socialist writer of prose whose talented columns and precise polished short pieces have contributed to our press, grace, and style." Winchevsky sometimes is called "the grandfather" of Yiddish socialist literature, but his voice ranges beyond politics. His works are true-to-life. His feelings are humanitarian and universal, but his appeal is to the intellect. More detached than most poets from the raw fire of human emotion, his passion lies in marshaling the forces of argument. Consequently, some critics find his tone a bit cold.

• Winchevsky's manuscripts, archives, and unfinished English-language autobiography are at the Yivo Institute for Jewish Research in New York City. His collected works are in the ten-volume *Gesamelte Werk*, ed. Kalman Marmor (1927–1928). In 1919 Winchevsky collected his verse in *Lider un Gedichte, 1871–1910*, and his *The Crazy Philosopher* was reprinted in two volumes in 1920. Marmor's biography of Winchevsky appears, in Yiddish, in vol. 1 of *Gesamelte Werk*. A 35-page biographical sketch in English is in Melech Epstein, *Profiles of Eleven* (1965). Also helpful is a lengthy discussion of Winchevsky and the socialist press in Ronald Sanders, *The Downtown Jews* (1969). Sanders includes a few English translations of Winchevsky's poetry, as does Ruth Rubin, *Voices of a People: The Story of Yiddish Folksong* (1973). Also see N. B. Minkoff, *Pionern fun Yidisher Poezye in Amerike* (1956); Sol Liptzin, *Flowering of Yiddish Literature* (1963); and Joseph Klausner's massive Hebrew-language *A History of Modern Hebrew Literature* (1958), which devotes forty pages to Winchevsky. An obituary is in the *New York Times*, 20 Mar. 1932.

MICHAEL S. SWEENEY

WINDER, John Henry (21 Feb. 1800–6 Feb. 1865), Confederate general, was born at "Rewston Plantation," near Nanticoke, Maryland, the son of General William Henry Winder and Gertrude Polk. Winder entered the U.S. Military Academy on 5 August 1814; nineteen days later his father was totally humiliated at the disastrous battle of Bladensburg. Determined to remove this military stain from the family name, Winder entered the army as a second lieutenant immediately after graduation from West Point in 1820. Except for the years 1823 to 1827, when he left the service to marry Elizabeth Shepherd of Washington, Georgia, and attempted to manage his in-laws' plantation, he remained in the army until 1861. The death of his wife shortly after the birth of a son and bad luck in running the plantation convinced Winder that he had best rejoin the army. In 1830, while stationed near Wilmington, North Carolina, he married a widow, Caroline Ann Cox Eagles, who had a daughter, and they had two sons.

Winder served in North Carolina for most of the 1830s and 1840s except for duty during the Second Seminole War in Florida from 1836 to 1838. He saw combat in the Mexican War, was brevetted twice for bravery, and finished the war with the brevet rank of lieutenant colonel.

Promoted to the permanent rank of major in March 1861, Winder accepted it but decided that he could not remain in the service the following month. Winder was not an avid secessionist, although he did serve in the South for most of his career. He did not resign his commission even after the firing on Fort Sumter. Not until North Carolina and the rest of the Upper South announced for secession and a riot broke out in his hometown of Baltimore in April 1861 in protest of the passage of Union troops did Winder decide that he must resign. If he remained in the army he feared he would find himself arrayed against family and close friends in the field. One son remained a Union captain, while the two others became Confederate officers. Having made his decision to serve the Confederacy, Winder never faltered in his duty, a duty that made his name an anathema in the United States long after his death.

Since Winder was too old for field command, he was initially charged with keeping the peace and dealing with Union prisoners in and about Richmond. From this inauspicious beginning in 1861, his duties and responsibilities grew enormously. He was provost marshal general of Henrico County from 1862 to 1864 and ruled the Confederate capital with such rigor that the citizens called him a dictator and begged for his removal.

While Confederate civilians mourned their loss of liberties under his iron rule, they also accused him of treating Union captives too generously, a charge soon negated and rejected in the Union newspapers. In these organs, he would be routinely and systematically vilified as an inhuman monster who deliberately inflicted unimaginable cruelties on his helpless captives.

Winder was relieved of his Richmond command in May 1864 and sent south to take charge of new prisons then being constructed in Georgia and Alabama, the most notorious of which was Andersonville. When the prisoner exchange ceased in early 1864, thousands of Federal captives were poured into these unfinished confines, and the suffering was terrible by June of that year. Winder was made the commissary of Confederate prisons that November, a position that was long overdue, and he did improve the general conditions before his death by centralizing control over prison construction, dispersion of captives, and securing more provisions of every description.

Winder was not the cruel tyrant his accusers claimed, but neither was he the saint that later defenders alleged. His commands were among the most sensitive as well as the most publicized, North or South, and as conditions in the Confederacy deteriorated in 1864 and 1865, his situation became impossible. When the commissary system and the railroads failed, Union captives suffered and died by the thousands; it is difficult to believe that anyone, given Winder's predicament, could have done any better.

Winder died of a heart attack while inspecting the prison at Florence, South Carolina. He was buried in an unmarked grave in Columbia (the family feared his body might be desecrated by William T. Sherman's troops) until 1878, when his corpse was reinterred in the family vault in Baltimore. His subordinate, Captain Henry Wirz, who was in command of the stockade at Andersonville, was later judged to be a war criminal and was hanged, the only such casualty of the war. Had Winder not died of natural causes, he might have taken the place of this unfortunate officer.

• A biography (with bibliography) of Winder is Arch Fredric Blakey, *General John H. Winder, C.S.A.* (1990). Other sources of information include Emory Thomas, *The Confederate State of Richmond: A Biography of the Capital* (1971); William B. Hesseltine, *Civil War Prisons: A Study in War Psychology* (1930); and Ovid Futch, *History of Andersonville Prison* (1968).

ARCH FREDRIC BLAKEY

WINDER, William Henry (18 Feb. 1775–24 May 1824), lawyer and soldier, was born in Somerset County, Maryland, the son of William Winder, a merchant, attorney, and legislator, and Charlotte Henry. He received his primary education at the nearby Washington Academy and went on to study at the University of Pennsylvania. His graduation date cannot be determined, but in 1798 he developed an interest in politics and was elected to the state legislature as a Federalist. The following year he married his cousin, Gertrude Polk; they had one son. In 1802 Winder relocated to Baltimore, where he studied law with his uncle John Henry and then with Judge Gabriel Duval in Annapolis. That same year he was admitted to the bar and became one of the state's leading attorneys by 1812. Though a staunch Federalist, Winder was motivated by patriotism to support renewed conflict with England. Accordingly, on 16 March 1812 President James Madison appointed him lieutenant colonel of the Fourteenth U.S. Infantry, assigned on recruiting duty in Baltimore. Four months later, on 6 July 1812, he was promoted to full colonel and ordered north to join American forces on the Niagara frontier.

Winder's ensuing military career was active but inauspicious. On 28 November 1812, during General

Alexander Smyth's aborted offensives, part of Winder's regiment crossed the Niagara River and captured Fort Erie. Winder failed to cross himself with the balance of his unit owing to severe enemy resistance. Nonetheless, on 12 March 1813 he gained promotion to brigadier general. In this capacity he fought at the 27 May 1813 capture of Fort George, and his brigade participated in the pursuit of British forces. The enemy abruptly counterattacked at Stoney Creek on 6 June, and in the confused night fighting Winder and General John Chandler blundered into British lines and were captured. Winder remained in Canada nearly a year before parole was arranged, but during that time he negotiated an agreement for the repatriation of American prisoners. Winder was released in April 1814 and returned to Baltimore as adjutant general and inspector general of the army.

On 5 July 1814 Winder was nominated by President Madison to head the Tenth Military District and was tasked with defending Washington, D.C., and Baltimore. It had long been suspected that British forces operating in the Chesapeake Bay might attack the capital, but Winder, unsure of enemy intentions, made no effort to build fortifications or summon reinforcements. On 19 August 4,000 veteran British troops under General John Ross landed at Benedict, Maryland, and advanced on Washington. Winder, with scarcely 2,000 men of his own, marched to meet them but, concluding that they were too powerful to attack, fell back on Bladensburg. On 23 August he was joined by contingents of Virginia and Maryland militia, who swelled his ranks to nearly 7,000 poorly disciplined men. While Winder was trying to sort his force into three distinct lines, which proved mutually unsupporting, the British suddenly appeared and attacked. The disorganized Americans repulsed an initial onslaught, but a swift British counterattack, covered by Congreve rockets, started a panic. Winder tried to establish order, but his army melted away, and he abandoned Washington to the enemy, who burned it.

Immediately after the debacle, Winder made his way to Baltimore and played a minor role in repulsing the British there. In late September he reported back to the Niagara frontier, where he learned that a congressional committee was investigating his conduct at Bladensburg. Angered by the final report, he demanded a court of inquiry. The trial, headed by General Winfield Scott, exonerated Winder, and he resumed control of the Tenth Military District. He was honorably discharged on 15 June 1815 and resumed his law practice. Following two terms in the state senate, he died in Baltimore.

It is Winder's misfortune that he, an earnest soldier of modest abilities, is indelibly associated with one of the most disgraceful episodes of American military history. As a regimental and brigade commander he displayed a marginal competence, but the confusion and sheer numbers at Bladensburg overwhelmed him. His efforts were further undermined by his failure to construct fortifications or to dispatch parties to harass the enemy. Winder's deployment of his force in three disparate lines also contributed to the debacle. In fairness, his inability to command at Bladensburg was compounded by the presence of Secretary of War John Armstrong and Secretary of State James Monroe, who were also on the field issuing contradictory orders. Defeat in this instance had many fathers, but in view of Winder's handling of events and the dilatory pace at which they were conducted, he is at least partially culpable for the disaster.

• Winder's military correspondence is in RG 94, Records of the Adjutant General's Office, and RG 107, Records of the Secretary of War's Office, National Archives. A large selection of letters is at the Maryland Historical Society, and a single item regarding Stoney Creek is at the Manuscript Department, Boston Public Library. For published materials see William H. Winder, *Statement of Occurrences on the Niagara Frontier in 1812* (1829); "General Winder and the Capture of Washington," *Historical Magazine* 5 (Aug. 1861): 227–29; and Ernest A. Cruikshank, ed., *Documentary History of the Campaigns upon the Niagara Frontier* (9 vols., 1898–1906). Some family information is in "General William H. Winder," *General Magazine and Historical Chronicle* 21 (1919): 217–19. For analysis of his military activities at Bladensburg consult Eric M. Smith, "Leaders Who Lost: Studies of Command under Stress," *Military Review* 61, no. 4 (1981): 41–45; Neil H. Swanson, *The Perilous Fight* (1945); Walter Lord, *The Dawn's Early Light* (1972); and Joseph A. Whitehorne, *The Battle for Baltimore, 1814* (1997).

JOHN C. FREDRIKSEN

WINDING, Kai (18 May 1922–6 May 1983), jazz trombonist and composer, was born Kai Chresten Winding in Aarhus, Denmark. His parents' names are unknown. When he was twelve years old he immigrated to New York City with his family. Winding attended Stuyvesant High School, where he began playing the trombone.

Winding began playing professionally immediately after graduation from high school. In the late 1930s and early 1940s he played with the Sonny Dunham and Alvino Rey big bands, and from 1942 to 1945 he played in a U.S. military band while serving in the coast guard.

After World War II Winding played with the Benny Goodman band (1945 and 1946) and the Stan Kenton band (1946 and 1947). During this period he began experimenting with the emerging "bebop" style in jam sessions at Minton's Playhouse and Monroe's Uptown House in New York City. His early sound was distinctive for its coarse, biting tone, but as his career progressed, it smoothed into a rounder, more delicate tone. In 1947 he emerged as a prominent bebop trombonist when he was hired by Charlie Ventura to perform in a group that featured bebop. In 1948 Winding joined the Tadd Dameron band, which featured such prominent bebop artists as Fats Navarro, Milt Jackson, Kenny Clarke, and Miles Davis.

Winding left the Dameron group in 1949 and began performing in New York jazz clubs with a variety of artists, including Charlie Parker, Miles Davis, Thelonious Monk, Bud Powell, and Dizzy Gillespie. In the late 1940s and 1950s Winding performed on two

Miles Davis recordings, *Birth of the Cool* and *Cool Boppin'*, with Stan Getz on *Prezervation* and *At Carnegie Hall*, with Quincy Jones on *Strike Up the Band* and *Walking in Space*, with Charlie Parker on *Rara Avis/ Rare Bird*, and with Charles Mingus on several Debut Records recordings.

In 1954 Winding teamed with trombonist J. J. Johnson in an unusual two-trombone quintet that was known as Jay and Kai. The group toured for two years and recorded fourteen LPs, including the popular *Jay and Kai* (1954). Winding and Johnson gained renown for creating a crisp, agile bebop style for the trombone that was far different from the broad sound of trombones in swing bands. In 1956 Winding established his own septet consisting of four trombones, piano, bass, and drums.

In the 1960s Winding worked as music director for the New York branch of the Playboy clubs. In the 1970s he recorded, toured, and appeared with various groups, including the Giants of Jazz, the World's Greatest Jazz Band with Eddie Condon, the Lee Konitz band, and the Lionel Hampton band, and worked as a member of the staff band on the Merv Griffin television show. During this period Winding also worked frequently for studios on television and film scores. In 1980 he formed a two-trombone partnership with Curtis Fuller, which they called "Giant Bones." The pair toured together through 1981. In 1982 Winding appeared at the Kool Jazz Festival in New York and was reunited with Johnson at the Aurex Jazz Festival in Japan. Winding died in Yonkers, New York. He had been married three times—to Marie, Jean, and Eleanor (maiden names unknown)—and had four children.

Winding was one of the first prominent trombonists to incorporate the bebop style. His work as sideman was featured in some of the most important bebop bands of the 1940s and 1950s, and his work with Johnson still stands among the finest, most original trombone playing in jazz history.

• There are useful summaries of Winding's career in *New Grove Dictionary of Jazz* (1988) and Leonard Feather, *The Encyclopedia of Jazz in the Seventies* (1976). There is also a useful biographical interview in *Down Beat*, 7 Sept. 1978, p. 27. See also "Kai Winding Returns with New Partner," *New York Times*, 27 Nov. 1981. Obituaries appear in the *New York Times*, 8 May 1983, and the *Los Angeles Times*, 7 May 1983.

THADDEUS RUSSELL

WINDOM, William (10 May 1827–29 Jan. 1891), U.S. representative, U.S. senator, and secretary of the treasury, was born in Belmont County, Ohio, the son of Hezekiah Windom and Mercy Spencer, farmers. In 1837 he moved with his family from eastern Ohio to a Knox County farm in the central part of the state. Despite the preference of his Quaker parents that he become a farmer or a tradesman, he insisted on becoming a lawyer. His father supported his education at Martinsburg Academy in Martinsburg, Ohio, by mortgaging the family farm. After his formal schooling, Windom read law with Judge R. C. Hurd of Mount Vernon. He opened his practice in Mount Vernon after being admitted to the bar in 1850, and two years later, as a Whig candidate, he was elected Knox County public prosecutor. In 1856 he married Ellen Towne Hatch; they had three children.

In 1855 Windom and Daniel S. Norton, his law partner, moved to rapidly growing Minnesota Territory. Windom settled in Winona, a Mississippi River port and one of the territory's principal communities. While practicing law with W. Wheeler Sergeant and Thomas Wilson, he became active in Republican party politics. Although Democrats dominated Minnesota's first state election in 1857, Windom was elected to the Thirty-six Congress in the state's second congressional election. His House service extended through five terms, from 4 March 1859 to 3 March 1869. As the representative of strongly Republican southeastern Minnesota, Windom championed passage of the Homestead Act. He was also a staunch supporter of the Lincoln administration's Civil War aims and, after Lincoln's assassination, satisfied his Minnesota constituents by identifying with the Radical opposition to Andrew Johnson. During his second term he reflected the popular sentiment of settlers on the Minnesota frontier by urging harsh federal punishment of the Dakota (Sioux) following the Indian war of 1862. However, this position was not consistent with his later attitude toward Indians. While serving as the chairman of the Committee on Indian Affairs during his last three terms, he seemed to be genuinely concerned about the plight of Indians nationally and urged more humane treatment of them by the Bureau of Indian Affairs.

In 1868 Windom declined to run for a sixth term. It was widely assumed that he wanted more time to pursue business opportunities and to revive his senatorial aspirations, which were first revealed in 1865, when he sought the position won by his former Ohio colleague Norton. Windom knew Norton's reelection prospects were doomed after being censured by the Minnesota legislature for voting against the impeachment of Johnson. However, the senatorial position opened sooner than anticipated because of Norton's death, and Windom was appointed by Minnesota's governor to fill the vacancy. His service in the Senate began 15 July 1870. On 22 January 1871 the legislature chose someone else to complete the few remaining weeks in the Norton term and selected Windom for a full term.

During his first term in the Senate, Windom distinguished himself as the chairman of the special committee that considered ways to reform the nation's internal transportation system. The committee studied transportation routes to the seaboard during the Grange's antirailroad crusade, which caused a number of midwestern states, including Minnesota, to legislate railroad controls. As the principal author of the committee's report, Windom, long regarded as a railroad supporter, opposed federal government regulation of rates. To achieve reduced freight charges, which Windom held would benefit everyone involved in the marketing of commodities, the committee recommended that rates be lowered through competition, including the possible construction of some government-owned railroads and the use of federal funds to improve waterways. The committee also believed that the nation would benefit from the establishment of some federal bureau that would collect data, report periodically to Congress, and publicize rates. The Windom committee's report of 1874 was later thought to have helped prepare the way for the creation of the Interstate Commerce Commission in 1887.

Minnesota's senior senator and leading Republican, Windom was easily chosen for a second term in 1877. Influenced by a number of Minnesota newspaper editors, the Minnesota delegation to the Republican National Convention in 1880 nominated him for president, but he never garnered more than Minnesota's ten votes. At the zenith of his national stature, Windom resigned his Senate seat to serve as secretary of the treasury in President James A. Garfield's cabinet from March to November 1881. After Garfield's death, Windom resigned, and the state legislature restored him to the Senate. During his short tenure in the Treasury Department, he skillfully negotiated the refunding of about $636 million in government bonds at lower interest rates, which saved the government millions of dollars.

Windom assumed that he would be chosen easily for a third Senate term. However, in 1883 his opponents, including the wealthy and persuasive William Rush Merriam of St. Paul, managed to exploit his weaknesses. Arguing that he had become an easterner out of touch with Minnesota and that he had blocked the renomination of Congressman Mark H. Dunnell of Owatonna, who was popular with many younger Republicans and a likely competitor for his seat, they managed to choose a Stillwater lumber dealer in his stead. Miffed by this rejection, Windom moved to New York City to practice law and manage his considerable real estate and railroad holdings. He visited Minnesota only infrequently after 1883.

In March 1889 Windom was appointed secretary of the treasury by President Benjamin Harrison, a position he held until his fatal heart attack, which occurred in New York City immediately after he had addressed the New York Board of Trade and Transportation. He was highly regarded by the eastern business and banking community, which readily identified with his conservative fiscal policies and his consistent advocacy of high protective tariffs. While philosophically in favor of bimetallism, Windom sharply opposed the agrarian call for free and unlimited coinage of silver. In Minnesota his name is perpetuated by the city of Windom.

• The Minnesota Historical Society has a collection of Windom papers. For Windom's "Report of the Select Committee on Transportation Routes to the Seaboard," see 43d Cong., 1st sess., 1874, S. Rept. 307, Serial 1588. The definitive study of Windom is Robert S. Salisbury, "William Windom, the Republican Party, and the Gilded Age" (Ph.D. diss., Univ. of Minnesota, 1982). Aspects of Windom's career are covered in William Watts Folwell, *A History of Minnesota* (4 vols., 1921–1930). For detailed coverage of Windom's defeat in 1883, see H. P. Hall, *Observations* (1904). A biographical sketch and numerous excerpts from obituaries are in *Memorial Tributes to the Character and Public Services of William Windom Together with His Last Address* (1891). Obituaries are in the *Minneapolis Tribune*, the *St. Paul Pioneer Press*, and the *New York Times*, all 30 Jan. 1891.

William E. Lass

WINEBRENNER, John (25 Mar. 1797–12 Sept. 1860), founder of the General Eldership of the Churches of God in North America, was born in Walkersville, Maryland, the son of Philip Winebrenner, and Eve Barrick, farmers. Early in life Winebrenner determined to enter the Christian ministry; he studied at Dickinson College in Carlisle, Pennsylvania, before it closed in 1816. He then studied theology under Samuel Helffenstein of the Reformed church in Philadelphia, Pennsylvania (1816–1819). Winebrenner experienced an evangelical conversion on 6 April 1817. Helffenstein recommended Winebrenner for the open pastoral charge in Harrisburg, Pennsylvania, which included a generous stipend of $1,000 per year. Winebrenner was ordained 24 September 1820 at Hagerstown, Maryland, by the General Synod of the German Reformed church and a month later moved to Harrisburg. His pastoral care included Middletown, Schupps, and Wenrichs in Dauphin County and Schneblys across the Susquehanna River in Cumberland County. In 1822 he married Charlotte Reutter, who died in 1834. They had several children. In 1837 he married Mary Hamilton Mitchell; they had four children.

Winebrenner's ministry was characterized by a deep piety and evangelical zeal. Before Charles Finney perfected the "New Measures" characteristic of the Second Great Awakening, Winebrenner employed vivid techniques such as directive preaching (that is, preaching directly to individuals), outdoor preaching, protracted meetings, camp meetings, simultaneous prayers, and small group assemblies. He cooperated with local Methodists (sometimes to the neglect of his own charge) and practiced continuous evangelism. At length, his congregations rejected his style and were repulsed by his fraternization with lower classes. He was discontinued at the Harrisburg church on charges best described as extreme enthusiasm and insubordination and in 1828 was exscinded from the ministerial roster of the Reformed Synod of 1828.

Winebrenner turned to a self-defined ministry of renewal and held meetings in markets and other public places in villages throughout central Pennsylvania and central Maryland, notably in the German communities; he preached with ease in both English and German. He was rebaptized on Independence Day, 1830, in the Susquehanna River by a follower, Jacob Erb. This event caused a stir, and for a time Winebrenner was perceived to have Baptist leanings. In the summer of 1830 he organized a loyal following into a new reform group, which called itself the General Eldership of the Church of God. Winebrenner chose the terminology "Church of God" because he conceived of the local church on the New Testament apostolic plan (in which the Holy Spirit spontaneously gathers local congregations of believers), not as a human institution. In a famous exchange of letters with Winebrenner, German Reformed theologian John Williamson Nevin referred to Winebrenner's following derisively as "Winebrennerians," to which Winebrenner strenuously objected. In spite of denominational antagonisms, the sect spread to Ohio, Indiana, and the Midwest. In 1845 the name General Eldership of the Churches of God in North America was officially adopted.

Although his leadership was frequently in dispute, Winebrenner worked at being the principal theologian and organizer of the group. He emphasized biblical literalism, restoration of the primitive order of the church, and a pietistic rationalism. In the area of social reform, he gradually became an abolitionist. He lent editorial support to the colonization movement in the mid-1830s and came out in favor of antislavery in 1836. That year he was one of three organizers of the Harrisburg chapter of the American Antislavery Society. By 1838, however, he had backed away from the more extreme forms of abolitionism, in part because of the loss of subscribers to his paper and also his own financial reverses from experimenting with silkworm and sugarbeet cultivation, two efforts promoted by the antislave enthusiasts. Well into the 1850s he continued to advocate an antislavery position for his denomination.

Winebrenner was also involved in the peace movement, and during the Mexican War he wrote widely on the horrors of military conflict. Any manifest destiny of the United States, he believed, was spiritual rather than territorial. From the first issue of his paper, the *Gospel Publisher* (1835–1840), he also railed against intemperance and supported the passage of laws prohibiting the sale and use of liquor.

Winebrenner chose not to take a permanent charge in the Church of God; rather he served as a "preacher at large" or general missionary. To further supplement his income, he published two church papers and produced historical materials, hymnbooks, and a pocket German New Testament. In addition, he worked at various jobs including being the proprietor of a pharmacy and a failed horticultural experiment to sell mulberry trees to prospective silkworm cultivators. Following a prolonged illness, he died in Harrisburg.

• Winebrenner's personal papers are in the Lancaster (Pa.) Theological Seminary and the Winebrenner Theological Seminary, Findlay, Ohio. He edited the *Church Advocate* (1846–1857). He also contributed a major article to I. D. Rupp's *He Pasa Ecclesia* in 1844 and coauthored and published the next edition in 1848 with Rupp, *History of All the Denominations in the United States*. Among his other books are *A Compendium of the Heidelburg Confession* (1822), *The Truth Made Known; or, A Fair and Correct Account of Facts, Which Have Transpired in the German Reformed Congregation of Harrisburg since the Fall of 1822* (1824), *A Prayer Meeting and Revival Hymnbook* (1825), *Letter on Slavery* (1858?), and *Doctrinal or Practical Sermons* (1860). See also George Ross, *Biography of Elder John Winebrenner* (1880), and Richard Kern, *John Winebrenner: Nineteenth Century Reformer* (1974). For differing perspectives on Winebrenner, see John W. Nevin, *The Anxious Bench* (1844), and James I. Good, *History of the Reformed Church in the United States in the Nineteenth Century* (1911).

WILLIAM H. BRACKNEY

WINES, Frederick Howard (9 Apr. 1838–31 Jan. 1912), Presbyterian minister and prison reformer, was born in Philadelphia, Pennsylvania, the son of Enoch Cobb Wines, a minister and prison reformer, and Emma Stansbury. After attending Washington College in Pennsylvania, Wines enrolled in the Princeton Theological Seminary in 1857. Forced to leave because of illness, he traveled to St. Louis, Missouri, where in 1860 the American Sunday School Union granted him a license to preach. Wines served as missionary in Springfield, Missouri, until 1862 when he received a commission as a hospital chaplain in the Union army. During the Civil War, Wines was the chaplain in charge of refuges at Springfield, Missouri, and served in the battle of Springfield (8 Jan. 1863). In 1864 he returned to Princeton and his studies, finally graduating from the seminary in 1865. That year he married Mary Frances Hackney, with whom he had eight children. The couple moved to Springfield, Illinois, where Wines spent the next four years as the pastor of the First Presbyterian Church.

In 1869 Wines won appointment as secretary of the Illinois State Board of Public Charities. The board had oversight authority over Illinois's growing number of charitable and penal institutions. This career move came at a seminal moment in the development of America's penal history. Starting in the late 1840s the nation's penitentiaries and poor houses shifted away from their original reformatory emphasis and became largely custodial institutions emphasizing harsh corporal punishments, especially for criminal offenders. In the twenty years after the Civil War the country experienced the birth of its third penal system. The new penology stressed reform over punishment as the primary goal of incarceration and was characterized by the establishment of adult reformatories, parole programs, graded classification of convicts, and the application of new scientific practices, such as the extensive recording of case histories and the collection of a broad range of statistical information, in the treatment of criminals.

There were three areas in the new penal reform movement where Wines had a major influence. The first of these was in disseminating ideas developed by European reformers in the United States. In 1878 he served as the Illinois delegate to the International Penitentiary Congress in Stockholm, Sweden. Having forged links with Europe's premier prison reformers, Wines returned home a dedicated advocate of many of their programs. In a lengthy report made to the Illinois legislature, he urged the adoption of Sir Walter Crofton's Irish plan of classifying and grading felony convicts as well as pushing for a new type of treatment for the criminally insane based on the English cottage system, a plan for housing the insane in separate quarters according to the classification of their disease. Influenced by Wines's report, Illinois constructed the nation's first insane asylum based on the European cottage system in the late 1870s at Kankakee. Wines continued his association with leading European reformers throughout his career. In 1886 he founded the *International Record of Charities and Correction*, a journal dedicated to addressing the problems of crime, deviance, and poverty.

Wines's second area of influence came in his efforts in creating professional conclaves for prison reformers. In 1878 he helped found the National Conference of Charities and Corrections, serving as its president during the 1883 meeting in Louisville, Kentucky. As a member of the Illinois delegation, he attended nearly all the early meetings of the National Prison Association, which was founded in 1870, and helped revive it in the early 1880s, after it had disbanded. Wines served as the association's new secretary for four years between 1887 and 1890. In 1887 he also served as secretary of the newly formed Warden's Association for the Identification of Habitual Criminals. Wines continued his work with these organizations throughout his life. In 1909 he founded his second journal, the *Institution Quarterly*. His efforts in institution building not only led to the development of criminology as a scholarly field of inquiry but also helped new social-work and law-enforcement occupations establish professional standing.

Finally, Wines proved to be an instrumental figure in developing and applying new quantitative social science techniques to the study of crime and deviance. In early reports made as secretary for the Illinois Board of Public Charities and as a member of the Social Science Congress, which he helped to found, Wines utilized a range of new statistical methods in his analysis of the root causes behind deviant behavior. He ultimately embraced an understanding that biological or hereditary influences were primarily responsible for determining crime, poverty, and social disorganization. In 1880 he served as a special adviser to the U.S. Census Bureau, which issued the report *The Defective, Dependent, and Delinquent Classes of the Population of the United States* (1881). By the late 1890s Wines was one of the country's leading advocates and practitioners of employing quantitative techniques in the study of sociological data. In 1897 he was appointed assistant director of the twelfth census, which published the *Report on Crime, Pauperism and Benevolence in the United States* (1896). By the end of his life, Wines had dedicated himself to the use and application of social science data. In 1909 Wines returned to Illinois from Washington, D.C., where he had moved in the late 1890s, to take a job as statistician of the newly formed Board of Control. He died in Springfield, Illinois.

Wines's career mirrored the major reform currents and scientific practices of his day more than he influenced their development. In his major written work, *Punishment and Reformation: A Historical Sketch of the Rise of the Penitentiary* (1895), he advocated reform programs designed to inculcate middle-class values such as thrift, industry, and obedience to authority. This class tension inundated much of the late nineteenth century's penal reform movement. But by accepting the growing belief in social Darwinism and the deterministic philosophy of Cesare Lombroso in understanding criminal behavior, Wines also embraced the darker side of late nineteenth-century reform. While he never achieved the same renown as his father, Wines's long career proved that he was a man cut from the same cloth as his father.

• A large proportion of Wines's published writings and scholarly discussions are in the various transactions of the National Prison Association. In addition, Wines occasionally published various lectures he had given. In particular see *The County Jail System, an Argument for Its Abolition* (1877), *Provisions for the Insane in the United States* (1885), and *Conditional Liberation, or the Paroling of Prisoners* (1886). In *American Prisons* (1977), Blake McKelvey discusses elements of Wines's career. For biographical material on Wines, see the 31 Mar. and 31 Dec. 1912 issues of the *Institution Quarterly* and his obituary in the *(Springfield) Illinois State Register*, 1 Feb. 1912.

HENRY KAMERLING

WINFIELD, Hemsley (20 Apr. 1907–15 Jan. 1934), actor and dancer, was born in Yonkers, New York, the son of Osbourne Winfield, a civil engineer, and Jeraldine (maiden name unknown but perhaps Hemsley), an actress and playwright. Educated at public schools, Winfield showed an early interest in theater, perhaps prompted by his mother's involvement. In 1924 he received his first role in a major production, in Eugene O'Neill's *All God's Chillun Got Wings*, performed by the Provincetown Players and starring a rising Paul Robeson. Winfield acted in other productions in the 1920s but soon turned to producing and directing. In April 1927 he put on his own play, *On*. The play was not critically received, but its production is indicative of the growing little theater movement of the early twentieth century, during which community and small theaters attracted larger audiences and offered greater and more varied opportunities to aspiring actors, writers, and directors. Winfield continued in this arena in 1928 and 1929, directing different versions of the popular *Salome*—once even playing the role of Salome when his female lead failed to show up—and collaborating with his mother in a production called *Wade in de Water* in 1929. Around this same time he began taking dance lessons, and this led him to shift his attention from theater to dance.

On 6 March 1931 Winfield's newly formed dance company, the Bronze Ballet Plastique, performed at the Saunders Trade School in Yonkers in a benefit for the Colored Citizens Unemployment and Relief Committee. This was Winfield's first collaboration with African-American dancer Edna Guy who had received much of her training from Ruth St. Denis, one of the founders of concert dance in America. Guy and Winfield went on to create the New Negro Art Theatre Dance Group, which placed itself by name and mission in the artistic resurgence now known as the Harlem Renaissance. This urban literary and cultural movement promoted the arrival of the New Negro, who, up from the fields of the South, was discovering the freedom and sophistication available to blacks in the northern cities, especially New York, where economic and social opportunities beckoned.

It was within this highly creative and receptive environment that, on 29 April 1931, Winfield and Guy performed what they called the "First Negro Dance Recital in America." Playing to an overflowing audience in the theater at the top of the Chanin Building on Forty-Second Street, the innovative duo hoped to initiate a new tradition in African-American dance separate from the swing and jitterbugging that characterized Harlem's dance halls. Concert dance provided a new means of expression, one that was more profound than the entertaining theatrics of social dancing for which African Americans were thought to be naturally talented. Winfield and Guy sought to place African Americans within the emerging artistic movement of modern dance, which was then dominated by the austere and serious works of Martha Graham and Doris Humphrey. Influential *New York Times* dance critic John Martin, recognizing the value of their purpose, described the performance as the "outstanding novelty of the dance season." In a further exploration of Winfield's group, Martin called Winfield's choreography "crude" but supported his effort to establish an African-American tradition in concert dance that neither mimicked European traditions nor restricted itself to what short-sighted whites delimited as "Negro art" (*New York Times*, 14 Feb. 1932).

Throughout 1931 and 1932 Winfield and Guy performed this program of the New Negro Art Theatre Dance Group in settings around New York City. In December 1932 they were included in a large benefit for the Dancers Club, a newly founded organization to aid struggling dancers, at the Mecca Temple, where they performed alongside famous dancers Ruth St. Denis, Charles Weidman, and Fred Astaire. Soon after, Winfield received the opportunity to choreograph the opera *The Emperor Jones* at the Metropolitan Opera in New York. Dancing the role of the Witch Doctor, Winfield became the first African American to perform at the Metropolitan. His choreography and performance received praise for depicting authentic sounds and movement of the African jungle. He was thus fast accomplishing the establishment of a concert dance tradition for African Americans.

In October 1933 Winfield and noted African-American sculptor Augusta Savage led a discussion on the topic "What Shall the Negro Dance About?" at a forum sponsored by the Workers Dance League, an organization associated with the Communist party, held at the YWCA in Harlem on 138th Street. Fittingly, the forum recognized the social as well as artistic implications of African Americans producing their own art and also considered the political relevance of such actions. There is no evidence that Winfield was a member of the Communist party, but he was keenly aware of the injustices facing African Americans, and he used modern dance to promote new and broader perspectives of African Americans and their capabilities. Unfortunately for the movement he initiated, Winfield's artistic responses to the question "What Shall the Negro Dance About?" were cut short; soon after the forum, he died of pneumonia in New York City, at the tragically young age of twenty-six. He had never married.

Despite his premature death, Winfield had made startling progress. Others who had been inspired by him, in particular Edna Guy, took up his mission of creating an African-American concert dance tradition, and by the late 1930s African Americans, led by dancer-choreographers Katherine Dunham and Pearl Primus, were making significant contributions to concert dance.

• Little documentation of Winfield's life is extant outside of newspaper reviews and some programs in the repository of the Dance Collection of the New York Public Library. Two dissertations give an overview of his life: John O. Perpener III, "The Seminal Years of Black Concert Dance" (New York Univ., 1992), and Josephine Monica Nicholson, "Three Black Pioneers in American Modern Dance 1931–1945" (George Washington Univ., 1984). Lynne Fauley Emery, *Black Dance from 1619 to Today*, rev. ed. (1988), places Winfield within a longer tradition of African Americans in dance, as do Richard Long, *The Black Tradition in American Dance* (1989), and Edward Thorpe, *Black Dance* (1990). Obituaries are in the *New York Amsterdam News*, 17 Jan. 1934, and the *New York Times*, 16 Jan. 1934.

JULIA L. FOULKES

WINGFIELD, Edward Maria (fl. 1586–1613), first president of the council in Virginia, was born in Stoneley, Huntingdonshire, England, the son of Thomas Maria Wingfield and his wife, whose maiden name was Kerrye. Although the family was distinguished, little is known of Edward's early career. It is believed, however, that he, like many aspiring young gentlemen, served as an officer in English military expeditions to Ireland and the Netherlands. Edward and several other Wingfields sued in 1586 to become proprietors in a plantation then being established in the province of Munster in Ireland. The suitors, who were disappointed, claimed that they were then all captains in Ireland "and in the Low Countries." Since Wingfield's name does not appear on the military establishment for Ireland, it is likely that he was in the Netherlands at that time. He was definitely there soon after, because in 1588 he and Sir Ferdinando Gorges, the noted military and naval commander and later a promoter of American colonization, were prisoners at Lille.

Contact with Gorges may explain Wingfield's subsequent interest in America and why he was named a patentee in the first Virginia charter of 1606. He was the only one of the patentees who sailed for Virginia in the first expedition that departed London on 19 December 1606. Wingfield was also one of six appointed by the King's Council for Virginia to serve on the local council established to rule the infant colony in Virginia. The first duty of this colonial government was to choose a president for the colony, and Wingfield, who had only arrived on 26 April, was duly elected on 13 May 1607. His tenure was short, however, and punctuated by persistent challenges from fellow council members and by threats of rebellion and desertion from ordinary colonists, who were discontented because of insufficient food, rampant disease, and occasional attacks from the indigenous population. The extent of popular discontent within the colony made it possible for three of Wingfield's fellow councillors to depose him after he had served only four months. Wingfield was also dismissed from the council, imprisoned on a pinnace in the James River, tried for several misdemeanors, and fined £300. However, he was rescued from confinement and assured a hearing in England when Captain Christopher Newport reached Jamestown with a supply from England on 2 January 1608 and assumed effective government of the colony for the next several months. Newport's departure for England on 10 April 1608 provided Wingfield with a passage home. We can assume he composed his treatise, "A Discourse of Virginia," at this time to explain his period in office to the King's Council for Virginia. The "Discourse," which was not published until 1860, is an important source of information on the first year of settlement and serves as a vindication of his actions and as a corrective to the accounts compiled by his contemporaries, especially Captain John Smith, whom Wingfield believed to have been "the first and only practizer" of his dismissal from the presidency. The fact that no prosecution followed Wingfield's return to England suggests that he was believed innocent of any malfeasance, but the further fact that he was never sent back to Virginia suggests that the members of the King's Council considered him unsuitable, though not corrupt. The last that we know of Wingfield is that he was resident, presumably unmarried, at Stoneley in 1613.

What we learn of Wingfield's character from his brief moment in the public gaze, and particularly what is said of him by Smith, suggests that he was haughty and insecure when dealing with his fellow councillors. His lack of certainty when confronted with the novel circumstances associated with settling in an alien environment conveyed the impression that he was a weak ruler, but he did address the fundamental problem of procuring food from the native Americans of the area through negotiation. Wingfield also proved himself scrupulous, if unimaginative, in following the instructions of his superiors in London, and this trait also meant that he was more humane and compassionate in his dealings with the American Indians than his immediate successors proved to be.

• Wingfield's "A Discourse of Virginia" has been printed in full in *New American World: A Documentary History of North America to 1612*, vol. 5, ed. David B. Quinn (5 vols., 1979). Texts by Wingfield's contemporaries in Va. are in the same collection and in Philip L. Barbour, ed., *The Jamestown Voyages under the First Charter, 1606–1609* (2 vols., 1969). Critical comment on Wingfield's career in Va. is available in Barbour, ed., *The Complete Works of Captain John Smith* (3 vols., 1986). Minor details on his career can be pieced together from W. N. Salisbury, ed., *Calendar of State Papers, Colonial Series*, vol. 1: *1574–1660* (1860), and H. C. Hamilton, ed., *Calendar of State Papers, Ireland* (24 vols., 1860–1912). The context within which Wingfield worked in Va. can best be understood from Barbour, *The Three Worlds of Captain John Smith* (1964); Edmund S. Morgan, *American Slavery, American Freedom: The Ordeal of Colonial Virginia* (1975); Wesley Frank Craven, *The Southern Colonies in the Seventeenth Century* (1949); and Alden T. Vaughan, *American Genesis: Captain John Smith and the Founding of Virginia* (1975).

NICHOLAS CANNY

WINGFIELD, George (16 Aug. 1876–25 Dec. 1959), banker, miner, and businessman, was born in Cincinnati, Arkansas, the son of Thomas Wingfield, a cattle buyer and Methodist minister, and Martha Spradling. Wingfield moved with his family to Lake County, Oregon, where his father operated a cattle ranch. Wingfield received a formal education through eighth grade until he moved to Nevada in 1896. There, in the railroad town of Winnemucca, and later in the mining camp of Golconda, Wingfield engaged in a number of pursuits including working in local ranches, running mowing machines, and playing poker. He operated the California Saloon in Golconda and excelled at gambling in the game of faro.

In 1901 a silver strike in the town of Tonopah brought Wingfield to that area, using his faro skills to amass a stake in the Tonopah Club Saloon. He also had investments in local real estate, saloons, and the Riverside and Golden hotels in Reno. A year later he began work for a Winnemucca banker named George S. Nixon (elected U.S. senator in 1905). Wingfield and Nixon engaged in a number of business activities together, especially purchasing and trading shares in local mining stocks and lending to miners. By 1906 Wingfield had experienced enough success in his business ventures that he turned his back on gambling as a livelihood forever. Along with Nixon, Wingfield helped consolidate a number of Goldfield, Nevada, mining companies into one large corporation, Goldfield Consolidated Mines Company, with Wingfield as vice president. He soon had accumulated a fortune of between \$25 and \$30 million. In 1908 he married Maude Azile Murdoch, the daughter of a wealthy San Francisco banker. The couple moved to Reno in 1909 and later had two children.

Wingfield soon became so powerful that Governor Tasker Oddie offered him the Senate seat formerly held by Nixon when Nixon died in 1912. Wingfield refused, preferring to operate behind the scenes as a "kingmaker." The national press referred to him as "the cowboy who refused a toga." In reality, all he refused were the public trappings of power; he gained even more influence and authority by declining the position. His connections to wealthy and powerful people outside Nevada supported his statewide status, as did his extensive investments in the state. When outsiders often eschewed investing in Nevada, Wingfield did not hesitate to do so. Nevada politicians subsequently sought his blessing before seeking office.

Wingfield focused his energy on forming an extensive chain of banks. Nevada prohibited a single bank from operating multiple branches, so each bank Wingfield owned had to maintain independent liquidity and operations. His empire included the Carson Valley Bank, the Churchill County Bank, the First National Bank of Winnemucca, the Henderson Banking Company, John S. Cook & Company, the Riverside Bank, the Bank of Sparks, the Tonopah Banking Corporation, United Nevada Bank, and his flagship, the Reno National Bank. Wingfield's chain made more than 80 percent of the loans in Nevada and had more than 50 percent of the total deposits by 1930. The vast majority of the loans were on sheep ranches or mining operations.

Such economic power allowed Wingfield to work for a variety of public causes and on behalf of personal friends. His political influence also permitted him access to the state legislature for his own purposes. In 1927, in the case of a defalcation by the state treasurer, the state controller, and the cashier of the Carson City Bank, Wingfield persuaded the legislature to charge the bank only 30 percent of the state's losses, even though the cashier had issued bogus checks and made Wingfield personally liable for 100 percent.

A personal crisis came when Wingfield's marriage to Maude ended in 1929, and a year later he married Roxy Bigelow Thoma. His second marriage produced no children. The business crisis for Wingfield, however, came in November 1932, when his chain could not reopen after the governor declared an emergency bank holiday. Wingfield's banks had received loans from the Reconstruction Finance Corporation (RFC) totaling more than $5 million by 1932 to cover losses incurred in loans to sheep ranchers. Over the years Wingfield had continued to extend loans to ranchers in the face of plummeting wool prices. Convinced that he had good financial grounds to do so—the price of wool did eventually recover—and, more important, a moral commitment to the sheep rancher community, Wingfield placed his banks in jeopardy. The RFC loans carried relatively high interest rates, had short durations, and were published with the names of borrowers. None of those factors contributed to strengthening the Wingfield banks. Worse, Nevada's chain banking structure did not allow him to move funds quickly from solvent institutions to those in trouble, as branch banking laws would have allowed. In the past, consortia of out-of-state banks had extended loans to Wingfield in times of trouble; this time efforts to form such consortia failed. Evidence suggests that by 1932 California corporations were concerned about federal investigations that such a "bailout" might trigger, due to the restrictions against interstate banking and the sheer size of the problem, and thus they refused Wingfield's calls for help.

Wingfield proposed a reorganization plan, but all the depositors had to approve it, and Wingfield had made more than a few enemies. Enough "nay" votes were cast to destroy the reorganization attempt, and the fate of the Wingfield banks was sealed. Worse for Wingfield, his position as director in the banks and his personal liability in the national banks exposed him to huge losses. In 1935 Wingfield filed for bankruptcy. Retained as a manager of the Riverside Hotel and Hotel Golden by the Crocker First National Bank that had purchased them, Wingfield still drew a salary. Wingfield also remained the president of Goldfield Consolidated.

By 1936 Wingfield was on the mend. A friend had sought help from Wingfield in attracting investors to gold mines outside Golconda, Nevada, and for his efforts Wingfield received a one-third interest in a very profitable mine. Those mines switched to tungsten production during World War II and continued to bring in profits. In 1944 Wingfield repurchased Reno Securities Company after paying off its outstanding loans; he had lost the company a decade earlier to Crocker Bank and regaining control of it symbolized his financial recovery.

The multimillionaire had seen his fortune vanish, then rebuilt it. He engaged in horse breeding at Spanish Springs Ranch and continued to manage the Goldfield Consolidated Mines and the Getchell Mines. He died in Reno, Nevada. Nevada had lost a kingmaker and a dynamic entrepreneur devoted to building the state.

• Wingfield's papers are located at the Nevada Historical Society in Reno. C. Elizabeth Raymond has prepared a *Guide to the George Wingfield Papers* (1988) and has written the definitive biography of Wingfield, *George Wingfield: Owner and Operator of Nevada* (1992). Specific work on Wingfield's banking career appears in Lynne Pierson Doti and Larry Schweikart, *Banking in the American West from the Gold Rush to Deregulation* (1991); Clel Georgetta, *Golden Fleece in Nevada* (1972); Jerome E. Edwards, *Pat McCarran: Political Boss of Nevada* (1982); and Larry Schweikart, "A New Perspective on George Wingfield and Nevada Banking, 1920–1933," *Nevada Historical Society Quarterly*, Winter 1992. An obituary is in the *Reno Evening Gazette*, 26 Dec. 1959.

LARRY SCHWEIKART

WINLOCK, Joseph (6 Feb. 1826–11 June 1875), astronomer, was born in Shelby County, Kentucky, the son of Fielding Winlock, a lawyer and farmer, and Nancy Peyton. Educated at Shelby College, in Shelbyville, Kentucky, Winlock was appointed professor of mathematics and astronomy at his alma mater after graduating in 1845.

Early on, Winlock had demonstrated initiative, learning German and purchasing a set of the *Astronomische Nachrichten*, the world's leading astronomical journal, at a time when few Americans were aware of the great achievements of German astronomy. In 1851 he attended the Cincinnati meeting of the American Association for the Advancement of Science, where he met Benjamin Peirce, astronomy and mathematics professor at Harvard. Their meeting led to Winlock's appointment the following year as a calculator for the *American Ephemeris and Nautical Almanac*, then headquartered in Cambridge, Massachusetts. While in Cambridge, he married Isabella Lane in 1856; they had six children.

Winlock remained with the *Nautical Almanac* until 1857, when he received an appointment as professor of mathematics to the U.S. Naval Observatory in Washington, D.C. In 1858 he returned to the *Nautical Almanac*, this time as superintendent. He left the *Nautical Almanac* a second time, in 1859, to head the department of mathematics at the U.S. Naval Academy. In 1861 he returned to the superintendency of the *Nautical Almanac*, where he oversaw its publication for five years. In 1863 he was named one of the original members of the National Academy of Sciences. He was appointed director of the Harvard College Observatory and Phillips Professor of Astronomy in 1866 and professor of geodesy in 1868.

Winlock's appointment as director of the observatory had been delayed seven months by opponents on the Harvard Board of Overseers. His nomination was viewed by some board members as an attempt by Peirce, his mentor, to gain control of the observatory by indirect means. Peirce had failed in his effort to be named director in 1859, losing out to George Bond. Those who feared that Winlock's selection would result in a repudiation of the work of his predecessors William Cranch Bond and George Bond (Peirce and his friends had kept George Bond out of the National Academy of Sciences), however, were pleasantly surprised. Winlock proved to be generous to the memory of the Bonds, ensuring that many of their manuscript observations were published, even at the expense of publishing his own annual reports.

This self-effacement was characteristic of Winlock, who was more concerned with facilitating the work of others and the progress of astronomy than his own reputation or authority. Contemporaries described him as amiable but reserved, modest, and selfless. Charles Sanders Peirce, who made photometric observations for the Harvard College Observatory between 1872 and 1875, noted that Winlock had "very considerately abstained from all interference" in his work (*Annals of the Astronomical Observatory of Harvard College*, vol. 9 [1878], p. v). At a time in American astronomy when there was intense competition for observatory directorships, disagreements over the relative merits of practical, theoretical, and physical (astrophysics) astronomy, and clashes among strong egos, Winlock represented reconciliation, embracing all forms of astronomical research. He was a wise choice for such an important position in American astronomy.

One of Winlock's chief concerns was the upgrading of instrumentation. The new meridian circle he acquired for the observatory in 1870 from Troughton and Simms in London provided improved stability and precision of movement. It was used by Winlock and William A. Rogers in determining stellar positions for the international survey organized by the Astronomische Gesellschaft. Winlock's work with spectroscopes led to the development that same year of a mechanical method of recording spectral lines. He was also interested in solar photography and invented a fixed, horizontal long-focus telescope, which was used at Harvard from 1870 to make daily photographs. His apparatus was also utilized to record the 1874 transit of Venus.

While Benjamin Peirce was superintendent of the U.S. Coast Survey, Winlock was twice selected to lead Coast Survey observing parties. In 1869 he led a Coast Survey party to Kentucky to observe the total solar eclipse of 7 August. One of the results of this expedition was the finest photograph of the solar corona to date. On his second expedition for the Coast Survey, which he led to Spain to observe the total solar eclipse of 22 December 1870, he concentrated on spectroscopy and identified four bright lines in the light of the outer corona. Winlock died in Cambridge after a brief, unknown illness.

Winlock is an example of a scientist whose significance cannot be correlated to the length of his bibliography. His contributions to astronomy, and especially to the birth and early development of astrophysics, were much greater than his output of some two dozen published articles would indicate.

• Winlock's papers, including his manuscript annual reports, are in the Harvard University Archives. The American Philosophical Society possesses an important letterbook. Winlock is mentioned in the various histories of the Harvard College Observatory; the most insightful treatment is in Bessie Zaban Jones and Lyle Gifford Boyd, *The Harvard College Observatory: The First Four Directorships, 1839–1919* (1971). The fullest obituary is in the American Academy of Arts and Sciences, *Proceedings* 11 (1875–1876): 339–50.

MARC ROTHENBERG

WINN, Richard (c. 1750–c. Jan. 1824), revolutionary war soldier and congressman, was born in Fauquier County, Virginia, the son of Minor Winn, Sr., and Margaret O'Connor, farmers. The parents emigrated from Wales in the 1740s and changed their surname from Wynne to Winn. Richard Winn's education is unknown, but he gained a knowledge of mathematics. He followed his brother John to South Carolina in 1768 and worked as a surveyor for a while in the employ of a British company. As was customary, Winn received as a fee one-eighth of the land that he surveyed. Winn and his brothers John and William became large landholders in the Fairfield District of upper-central South Carolina. They owned a whole town named after them, Winnsboro. Besides surveying, Winn was a planter and engaged in merchandizing. He was appointed a justice of the peace in 1775. About the time of the outbreak of the revolutionary war (c. 1775), Winn married Priscilla McKinnie; they had eleven children.

A man of considerable physical prowess and self-confidence, Winn easily fitted into the role of militia leader during the war. On 18 June 1775 he was appointed a lieutenant in Colonel William Thompson's regiment of rangers. He first engaged in combat during summer 1776 against General Henry Clinton's expeditionary force in Charleston Harbor. Winn and his fellow marksmen on Sullivan's Island prevented British troops from wading through a narrow waterway to assist naval units in an assault on Fort Sullivan (shortly thereafter named Fort Moultrie) on the island. Unsuccessful in driving American defenders out of the harbor, the British troops and fleet returned to New York. In early 1777 Winn, now a captain, had command of a small detachment of troops at Fort McIntosh on the Satilla River in southeast Georgia. Attacked by Tory raiders and Indians, Winn held out for two days, 2–4 February 1777, before surrendering. He was allowed to go home on parole, but it is not known when or if he was ever exchanged for prisoners taken by Americans. Although Winn was engaged in training militia troops for combat, no evidence confirms that he was again active in the field until early 1780. After the fall of Charleston, 12 May 1780, the partisan war (Loyalist versus patriot forces) heated up in the Carolinas.

Winn, now a major, led a hundred men on 29 May 1780 to rout a band of Tories at Moberley's (or Gipson's) Meetinghouse on the Broad River. On 20 June 1780 Winn served in the militia force under General Griffith Rutherford that defeated Tories led by Colonels John Moore and Francis Locke at Ramsour's Mill, North Carolina. About this time British troops plundered and burned Winn's home in Winnsboro, driving off his wife and their two infant children. "When this was made known to me," he later recalled, "my answer was: it is no more than I expected."

In summer 1780 Winn was named a colonel, serving under the command of Thomas Sumter, militia brigadier general. On 12 July 1780 Winn led militia in the defeat of Loyalist troops commanded by Captain Christian Huck (Huyck) in York County, South Carolina. At the battle of Hanging Rock on 6 August 1780, lasting four hours, Winn and his troops, giving an Indian yell, charged up a hill against the enemy. Severely wounded, Winn refused to leave the field; he remarked to Major William R. Davie at the time, "Isn't this glorious?"

After recuperating from his wound in Charlotte, Winn was back in action for the engagement at Fishdam Ford, thirty miles northwest of Winnsboro, on 9 November 1780. Although the battle was a draw, Winn's marksmen took a heavy toll of enemy cavalrymen who rode up to campfires that Winn had abandoned. The last battle for Winn was at Blackstocks, South Carolina, on 20 November 1780, when Winn and his troops fought to a draw against Lieutenant Colonel Banastre Tarleton's famed legion of mounted Loyalist troops. In December Winn learned that his brother John had been sentenced to hang at Winnsboro, then the site of British headquarters. Winn sent word that he would retaliate by executing the first 100 officers and soldiers of the enemy who would come into his custody. This had the desired effect, and John Winn was pardoned. On 21 November 1783 Winn was elected a brigadier general by the legislature and in 1800 a major general of the Second Division of South Carolina militia, a position he held until he resigned in 1811.

From 1779 to 1786 Winn served in the South Carolina House of Representatives. He was elected lieutenant governor on 10 February 1785 but declined. In 1786 Winn was a commissioner for purchasing land and laying out the state capital at Columbia. On the private side, Winn lived the life of a planter and was part owner of a store in Winnsboro.

On 29 February 1788 the Confederation Congress elected Winn superintendent of Indian affairs for the Southern District. His primary duty was to work with one commissioner each from North Carolina, South Carolina, and Georgia to negotiate treaties, principally with the Cherokees and Creeks. Efforts with the Cherokees failed, but Winn presided over arrangements that resulted in the Treaty of New York with the Creeks in 1790. In that year the Indian superintendency was abolished, and the responsibilities were placed in the hands of William Blount, the governor of the new Southwest Territory.

Winn was elected as a Republican to the U.S. Congress in the 1790s, serving two terms, 4 March 1793–3 March 1797. Not strictly a partisan in politics, Winn often voted with the Federalists during his early congressional terms, but on the more important questions he sided with the Republicans. He supported commercial sanctions against Great Britain and congressional prohibition of French émigrés from using aristocratic titles in the United States. He was lieutenant governor of South Carolina from 1800 to 1802. In 1803 he was appointed to the U.S. Congress to complete the term of Sumter, who resigned to enter the U.S. Senate. Winn was subsequently elected on his own, serving from 24 January 1803 to 3 March 1813. In these years as a congressman, Winn voted for the Twelfth Amendment to the Constitution, reduction of the size of the navy, implementation of Thomas Jefferson's Embargo, and a declaration of war against Great Britain in 1812.

Experiencing some financial difficulty for having gone surety for others and wanting to duplicate his landholding success in South Carolina, Winn moved with his family in fall 1812 to the Duck River valley, Maury County, in Middle Tennessee, settling as a planter on a 5,000-acre tract. Winn died at or near the village of Winnsborough, Tennessee. In 1876 a Maury County committee located his grave, and the U.S. government provided a granite marker. The exact date of his death is disputed. One author of a biographical sketch says he died on 18 December 1818 (Williams), and another notes 19 December 1818 (Curry). Buford S. Chappell, who researched the local court records, however, has the last word: Winn made his will on 28 February 1818 in Maury County; "it was recorded on January 20, 1824, and he probably died closer to this later date."

• Although Winn seldom participated in debates, the records of his votes in Congress are in *The Debates and Proceedings in the Congress of the United States* (8 vols., 1849–1853). Two biographical sketches are J. L. M. Curry, "Richard Winn," *Publications of the Southern History Association* 2 (July 1898): 225–29, and Samuel C. Williams, "Major-General Richard Winn: South Carolinian and Tennessean," *Tennessee Historical Quarterly* 1 (1942): 8–20. Buford S. Chappell, *The Winns of Fairfield County: Colonel John Winn, William Winn, General Richard Winn* (1975), meticulously uses local records, notes Richard Winn's land transactions in S.C. and Tenn., and has genealogy. For Winn's military role in the Revolution, see Williams, ed., "General Richard Winn's Notes—1780," *South Carolina Historical and Genealogical Magazine* 43 (1942): 201–12, and 44 (1943): 1–10; Anne K. Gregorie, *Thomas Sumter* (1931); Robert D. Bass, *Gamecock: The Life and Campaigns of General Thomas Sumter* (1961); and Edward McCrady, *The History of South Carolina in the Revolution, 1775–1780* (1901). The Indian superintendency is treated in Walter Clark, ed., *The State Records of North Carolina*, vol. 21 (1903); John W. Caughey, *McGillivray of the Creeks* (1938); and *The Papers of John Steele*, ed. H. M. Wagstaff, vol. 1 (1924). Some comment on Winn's politics is found in Rachel N. Klein, *Unification of a Slave State: The Rise of the Planter Class in the South Carolina Backcountry, 1760–1808* (1990), and John H. Wolfe, *Jeffersonian Democracy in South Carolina* (1940).

HARRY M. WARD

WINNEMUCCA, Sarah (1844?–17 Oct. 1891), spokeswoman for the Northern Paiute, was born near the sink of the Humboldt River in western Nevada, the daughter of Winnemucca, a Paiute chief, and Tuboitonie. In 1857 Chief Truckee, her maternal grandfather, arranged for Sarah and her younger sister Elma to live in the household of his friend, Major William Ormsby, a Virginian who managed a stage line at Mormon Station (Genoa). The girls worked at domestic chores and helped serve passengers at his stage stop. They were also companions to Ormsby's only child, nine-year-old Lizzi. Here Sarah and Elma learned to read, write, and sing in English, picked up some Spanish phrases, and studied American history and the Bible. One year later the Ormsby family and the Paiute girls moved to Carson City, but in late September 1859 Sarah and Elma were suddenly called home by their father.

In 1860, upon the deathbed request of Chief Truckee, Sarah and Elma were sent to his California rancher-friends, who enrolled them at the Academy of Notre Dame in San Jose, a prestigious boarding school. After only three weeks, the Paiute sisters were dismissed because some of the white parents objected to the Indian girls going to school with their children. After they returned home, Sarah did housework for white families in Virginia City and spent some of her hard-earned money on books for her own education. In 1866 she went to live with her brother Natchez in the Pyramid Lake Reservation.

Sarah began to take an active interest in the plight of her people. She was frequently called upon by the army officials to act as mediator between her father and other Indians and whites. While working at Fort McDermit, Sarah met First Lieutenant Edward C. Bartlett, a handsome native of New York but an irresponsible drunkard. Because of Nevada's antimiscegenation law, they went to Salt Lake City to be married in 1871. Neither her father nor Natchez approved the union, and Sarah quickly came to realize that the marriage would not work because she could not prevent Bartlett from drinking away their money. She soon left him and went back to Fort McDermit. She married an Indian named Jones in 1873 without a formal ceremony, but this marriage was also short lived because she could not endure his gross mistreatment.

In 1875 Sarah went to Fort Harney in Malheur Reservations, Oregon, where her father lived. She gradually became convinced that her people fared better under the supervision of the military than under the Indian Bureau. Regular rations, clothing of better quality, and protection from white depredations far outweighed all the inconveniences. Samuel B. Parrish, who was appointed the agent for Malheur in 1874, was a rare exception. He put the Indians to work at agriculture, providing an incentive program, and also offered Sarah a position as interpreter and later as a teacher's aide. Parrish, however, was dismissed within a year and was replaced by William Rinehart, who altered Parrish's policy drastically.

Meanwhile, Sarah had fallen in love with another white man, Joseph Satwaller, a local resident, and in July 1876 she filed for a divorce from Bartlett, which was granted two months later. In November Sarah and Satwaller were married, but after a brief honeymoon she returned to Malheur to lodge a complaint against Rinehart, who had already fired her for writing letters against him. After staying at Malheur for a few weeks, Sarah joined her husband. They went to live at the Warm Spring Reservation, Oregon, but her new marriage ended within a year.

During the Bannock War of 1878, many Paiutes, who had been outraged by Rinehart's policy, left the reservation to join the hostile Bannocks. Sarah accepted a dangerous mission to penetrate the Bannock camp, locate the Paiutes, and persuade them to escape to Fort Lyon. She succeeded in slipping the Paiutes out only to be overtaken midway by the pursuing Bannocks. Half of the Paiutes were forced to return, but Sarah was able to bring several hundred, including her father, to the fort. This accomplishment so greatly impressed General Oliver O. Howard that he hired her as his personal interpreter and guide. Sarah also received a $500 reward.

When her position was abolished after the war, Sarah began to lecture in San Francisco and in Nevada, speaking against Indian agents and calling specifically for the resignation of Rinehart and the restoration of Malheur to the natives. She dramatized the horrors at Yakima Reservation and pleaded for the return of the Paiutes unjustly detained there. Sarah, lecturing in native dress and speaking eloquently without notes, quickly established herself as spokeswoman for her people. In January 1880 Sarah and others were summoned to Washington, D.C., to discuss the problems of the tribe with federal officials. In the end, they obtained a document from Secretary of the Interior Carl Schurz allowing the Paiutes in Yakima to return freely to Malheur, where each adult male was to receive 160 acres.

Sarah triumphantly returned to Nevada, but none of the promises materialized. Meanwhile, Rinehart initiated a campaign to discredit Sarah, sending many damaging letters to the office of Indian Affairs. Her short temper, occasional drunkenness and bad behavior, and three short marriages helped to fuel her opponents' attack.

In 1881 in San Francisco, Sarah suddenly married Lewis H. Hopkins, a Virginian five years her junior and an Indian Department employee. They announced their plans for a speaking tour to the East, but it was more than a year before they set out.

On 2 May 1883 Sarah made her first speech before a Boston audience, pleading the cause of Indian rights, pointing out the corruption of the agents, misappropriations, poor government policies, and the abusive missionaries. Sarah delivered nearly 300 lectures in Boston, New York, Baltimore, Washington, D.C., and other cities, continually speaking of inequities and calling for restoration of lands in severalty to the Paiutes. In Boston she became the protégée of Elizabeth P. Peabody, noted pioneer in kindergarten education, and her sister, Mary T. Mann, widow of Horace Mann, who encouraged Sarah to write her autobiography and offered to edit it. Sarah's book, *Life among the Piutes: Their Wrongs and Claims* (1883), is not only a story of her own life but a history of her tribe, demonstrating that the Paiutes were willing to coexist with the whites and pleading with Congress to restore land and rights to her people.

Lewis Hopkins fully supported his wife, helping her gather material for her book at the Library of Congress, sitting on the lecture platforms, and selling autographed copies of Sarah's book and picture. They agreed that most of the money should be reserved for the Paiute school she was planning. Hopkins suffered from tuberculosis, however, and his medical expenses combined with his penchant for gambling made him a serious financial burden. He soon departed, leaving his debts for her to pay. Since only a few hundred dollars remained, Sarah decided to go to her sister's home in Idaho, instead of returning to Nevada to face her people. When she eventually reached Pyramid Lake in August, she had only $50 remaining of the money she had earned in the East.

Sarah decided to build her school on Natchez's farm near Lovelock. She went on a fundraising tour to Reno, Carson City, and San Francisco, selling her idea, fully endorsed by Peabody, of creating a school taught by and for Indians, where they would not be separated from the Indian lifestyle and languages. By the summer of 1885 Sarah was teaching twenty-six Paiute children. The Peabody Indian School, as Sarah called it, attracted the attention of many white men in Nevada and in the East. Peabody continued to support the school, and Mary Mann left her small legacy to Sarah when Mann died in 1887. Within six months, however, the status of the school became precarious.

The Dawes Severalty Act of 1887 established an Indian school policy requiring children to attend English-speaking boarding schools, where the native languages were forbidden. When Sarah lost many of her students to the new boarding school in Grand Junction, Colorado, she and Natchez decided to turn their establishment into an industrial school. While Natchez promised to contribute forty acres of his land, Sarah made another trip to the East to convince federal officials to support their new plans, but she failed to gain the attention and recognition that she had enjoyed previously. Sarah, however, saw and reconciled with Hopkins, whom her friends, including Peabody, had been urging her to divorce.

They returned to Nevada together, but Natchez and his family were soon in dispute with Hopkins over the sale of some wheat. Hopkins also contributed to the collapse of the Peabody School in 1887 by spending the last of Sarah's school fund. Despite the great strain Hopkins had caused, Sarah had a special memorial card made for her husband with a sentimental poem in his memory when he died in October 1887.

During the last two years of her life, Sarah made several trips to visit her sister in Idaho, usually spending the summer there and returning to Nevada in the winter. Having contracted tuberculosis from her husband, she was chronically despondent. One evening Sarah and her sister were drinking chokecherry wine after dinner when Sarah suddenly gasped, collapsed, and died; the local undertaker ruled she had died of too much wine. Sarah Winnemucca had no children. She is remembered as one of the ablest and most energetic advocates for Indian rights.

• In addition to her book, Sarah Winnemucca wrote "The Pah-Utes," *Californian: A Western Monthly Magazine* 6 (1882): 252–56. Sarah Winnemucca's school for the Indians is discussed in detail in Elizabeth P. Peabody, *Sarah Winnemucca's Practical Solution of the Indian Problem* (1886) and *The Piutes: Second Report of the Model School of Sarah Winnemucca, 1886–87* (1887). Major secondary works include George F. Brimlow, "The Life of Sarah Winnemucca: The Formative Years," *Oregon Historical Quarterly* 53 (1952): 103–34; Gae W. Canfield, *Sarah Winnemucca of the Northern Paiutes* (1983); Catherine S. Fowler, "Sarah Winnemucca, Northern Paiute, ca 1844–1891," in *American Indian Intellectuals*, ed. Margot Liberty (1976); Katherine Gehm, *Sarah Winnemucca* (1975); Dorothy N. Morrison, *Chief Sarah: Sarah Winnemucca's Fight for Indian Rights* (1980); Elinor Richey, "Sagebrush Princess with a Cause: Sarah Winnemucca," *American West* 12 (1975): 30–33, 57–63; and Patricia Steward, "Sarah Winnemucca," *Nevada Historical Society Quarterly* 14 (1971): 23–38.

YASUHIDE KAWASHIMA

WINOGRAND, Garry (14 Jan. 1928–19 Mar. 1984), photographer, was born in the Bronx, New York, the son of Abraham Winogrand, a leather worker, and Bertha (maiden name unknown), a garment pieceworker. Winogrand hated school and joined the army in 1945 because a recruiting officer told him he could graduate five weeks early if he did so. For the next two years he was stationed in Georgia as a weather forecaster with the Army Air Force. Returning to his parents' home, Winogrand studied painting for a year at City College under the G.I. Bill, then enrolled at Columbia University. Finding that the darkroom was open twenty-four hours a day, he began taking photographs during the day and printing them most of the night. Within two weeks of this discovery, Winogrand stopped painting. In 1949 he continued his studies at the New School for Social Research, taking a class with Alexey Brodovitch, the famed art director of *Harper's Bazaar*, who was a leading proponent of the new, allusive style of photography, with its emphasis on intuition and perception rather than on craft and precise description.

In 1951 Winogrand signed a contract with an agency, Pix, Inc., in New York. While he did not get much work (he estimated that one year he made $61 with Pix), this arrangement gave him an office to go to, a darkroom to work in, and a place where he could talk to other photographers. He received his first editorial assignment that year from *Harper's Bazaar*. But he was barely making ends meet, and he did not like waiting around to receive assignments. Intensely interested in anything that moved, he began to take photographs at Stillman's Gym, at fight clubs around New York, and backstage at the ballet. Disgusted with his prospects at Pix, he moved to Henrietta Brackman Associates in 1954, and his pictures began to appear in *Collier's*, *Pageant*, and *Sports Illustrated*. In 1955 he was included in the Museum of Modern Art's The Family of Man show, his first public exhibition. In 1952 Winogrand married Adrienne Lubow, a dancer, with whom he had two children. After several periods of separation, they divorced in 1966, although the marriage had effectively ended in 1963.

The photography market was changing in the late 1950s, as television made photojournalism seem less relevant. Winogrand began doing advertising photography, which he continued for many years. He saw ads as similar to magazine photos, in that both aimed to manipulate an audience. He made his living in advertising through most of the 1960s, even though he was technically unprepared and fundamentally uninterested in it. The requirements of advertising photography, like clarity and focus, were not what Winogrand and many of his contemporaries were seeking in their own work.

Winogrand went through a personal crisis in the early 1960s. His marriage was ending, he feared losing his children, and the Cuban missile crisis made him acutely aware of how little control he had over his own life. During these years he took pictures constantly and obsessively, especially of women on the street, an activity he continued for the rest of his life. He also photographed people and animals in the Central Park Zoo. These pictures were collected into a book, *Animals*, in 1969. Reflecting on the period, he said he "began to live within the photographic process," and it was then that he arrived at his own style. He began to use a wide-angle lens and to frame his images more freely. In order to control the visual distortions of the lens, he tilted the camera, a trope that would become identified with his photography. In 1964 Winogrand was awarded a Guggenheim fellowship, and he traveled to the Southwest and California. Some of the pictures from this trip were shown in the Museum of Modern Art's 1967 New Documents show, which also included work by Diane Arbus and Lee Friedlander. One reviewer labeled this new work the "snapshot aesthetic," a phrase Winogrand considered idiotic. While his pictures had a casual-seeming fluidity, their compositions were actually complex and carefully contrived. Winogrand described his photographs as "an illusion of a literal description of a piece of time and space." After his return from the West, he spent the next five years photographing the urban carnival of Manhattan's streets. In 1967 he married Judy Teller, an advertising copywriter at Doyle, Dane, Bernbach. They separated in 1969, and the marriage was annulled a year later. They had no children.

In 1969 Winogrand won a second Guggenheim fellowship to record the "effect of the media on events." He felt that public occasions were increasingly created as much for the media to record as for the pleasure or ritual relief they supplied. For this project, which continued until 1973, he photographed marches, rallies, press conferences, games, strikes, art openings, and parades. Many of these pictures recorded the national struggles around the Vietnam War. In the late 1960s Winogrand also began to examine the relationship between the commercial work he performed in order to make a living and the work he pursued for himself. As a result, he decided to quit advertising photography and instead began teaching. A "talking lion" with great energy and warmth, he found that he loved to teach. He stressed to his students that photography was a bad career risk and that if they had real talent they would be better off working on their own rather than coming to his class. All he had to offer, he insisted, was honesty. Between 1967 and 1973 Winogrand taught at the Parsons School of Design, the School of Visual Arts, and Cooper Union in New York and at the Illinois Institute of Technology in Chicago. From 1973 to 1978 he taught at the University of Texas in Austin, and after he moved to Los Angeles in 1978, he taught at the University of California at Los Angeles. He also gave workshops and taught for short periods at other schools from 1971 until his death. Between his teaching and the sales of his prints, Winogrand generated enough income to live on. In 1972 he married Eileen Adele; they had one child.

Winogrand never seemed as engaged by Austin or Los Angeles as he had been by New York and its active street life, and his work reflected this. In Los Angeles he took photographs almost reflexively, often from his car, but he did not print or edit most of them. At his death approximately 300,000 negatives remained to be sorted. Without the discipline of printing, his technique deteriorated rapidly. He bought a larger view camera and talked about putting away his Leica, apparently aware that he had exhausted his old line of inquiry. In February 1984 Winogrand was diagnosed with inoperable gall bladder cancer. He sought treatment in Tijuana, Mexico, but died there shortly after checking into a clinic.

Critics of Winogrand's work describe it as impersonal and compassionless, and his photographs do often depict an estrangement from the world. He said he took pictures to find out what the things he was interested in would look like as photographs, and he insisted on their status as representations rather than reality. His deceptively casual framing and subject matter influenced a whole generation of American photographers, including Robert Adams, Lewis Baltz, and William Eggleston.

• The Center for Creative Photography in Tucson, Ariz., has a large collection of Winogrand's negatives, contact sheets, and work prints. Books by Winogrand not mentioned in the text include *Women Are Beautiful* (1975), *Public Relations* (1977), and *Stock Photographs: The Fort Worth Fat Stock Show and Rodeo* (1980). See also Helen Gary Bishop, "Looking for Mr. Winogrand," *Aperture*, no. 112 (Fall 1988): 36–59; Kenneth E. Silver, "The Witness," *Art in America* 76, no. 10 (1988): 148–57; and John Szarkowski, *Winogrand, Figments from the Real World* (1988). Obituaries are in the *New York Times*, 22 Mar. 1984, and *Aperture*, no. 95 (Summer 1984): 5.

BETHANY NEUBAUER

WINSER, Beatrice (11 Mar. 1869–14 Sept. 1947), librarian and museum director, was born in Newark, New Jersey, the daughter of Henry Jacob Winser, a journalist, and Edith Cox. Two months after his daughter's birth, Henry Winser left the *New York Times* for a twelve-year term as U.S. consul general at the court of the Duke of Saxe-Coburg; the family later returned to New York City.

During her childhood in Germany, Beatrice became fluent in German and French and grew to love books. In 1888 she enrolled in the Columbia College Library School. The next year she became a cataloger of French and German books at the recently established Newark Public Library. In 1894 she became assistant librarian and then temporary head librarian. Passed over for the directorship, she served as assistant to the new director, the dynamic John Cotton Dana, from 1902 to 1929. Stirred by his excitement for educating adults and children through wide circulation of books, Winser became an energetic and capable assistant who strongly supported his advocacy of library service to the city. They made it their objective to "put into the hands of all the people they could reach all the books they could read."

Dana had many ideas for promoting library service to all Newark citizens, and Winser had the talent and imagination to develop Dana's ideas and to handle the daily management of the library. They formed a remarkable partnership. Winser visited staff in the main library building and in the branches to identify improvements, note strengths and weaknesses, and listen to suggestions. She also supervised the details of staffing, budget, and acquisitions.

During World War I and in the postwar expansion that followed, Winser learned some hard lessons about library management. She dealt with increased demands for library services, planned new branches, acquired a bookmobile, and monitored an expanding acquisitions program. As Dana's health declined, Winser took on his responsibilities. She succeeded him as librarian after his death in 1929, becoming one of four women in that period to head a library in a large city. She proclaimed in the *Newark Sunday Call* (29 Mar. 1936), "A woman can make good at whatever she wants to do."

In 1936 Winser took a prominent role in opposing the appointment of Archibald MacLeish as librarian of Congress. She criticized his lack of professional training and experience and took the American Library Association (ALA) to task for its weak stand against the nomination. She also protested attempts by customs officials to censor books and publications, and because she feared political control, she opposed federal aid to libraries. These were courageous acts in that era.

During World War II the Newark Public Library's National Defense Center became a War Information Center, and borrowing privileges were extended to members of the armed services stationed in the city. Winser chaired the Wartime Council of Newark Libraries, coordinating library work for wartime needs, and established the Newark Victory Book Committee to provide books for camps and military installations. She also organized an arts and crafts program for soldiers at Camp Kilmer. Winser resigned as head of the Newark Public Library in 1942, charging interference by the trustees in the library's administration.

Beatrice Winser's other professional interest, the Newark Museum, was founded by Dana in 1909 to accommodate an exhibition of Japanese art in the Newark Library. The museum soon included exhibits and books in the fields of art, industry, and science. Winser supported Dana's belief in museums as "the handmaidens of our schools." She became assistant director and assistant secretary in 1915, a member of the board of trustees the following year, and, after Dana's death, director and secretary (1929). She stayed on as head of the museum until a few months before her death and continued the close working relationship between the museum and the library. In 1925 Dana and Winser began publication of *The Museum*, the monthly bulletin of the Newark Museum Association. As director, Winser supervised exhibits on American primitive painting (1930) and American folk sculpture (1931) and gave early support to an appreciation of American folk art with the exhibits *Aviation* (1932) and *Three Southern Neighbors: Ecuador, Bolivia, Peru* (1941), promoting the federal government's Good Neighbor policy. During the depression she instituted Sunday concerts and an adult art workshop.

Winser served Newark in still another capacity when she was appointed in 1915 on the Newark Board of Education, the first woman to serve on any local governing board. She resigned, however, after her plan to reorganize the school system and to limit the board's authority was defeated.

Winser was a member of the ALA Council of Fifty (1909–1912, 1930) and the organization's second vice president (1931). She was also a charter member (1890), president (1907–1908, 1921–1922), and honorary member (1930) of the New Jersey Library Association.

Winser enjoyed many interests outside the library and museum. She was director of the Northern New Jersey Sub-committee on Employment of Artists, Public Works of Arts Project (1934), and chair of its chapter (1935); a member of the Committee Directing Library Colony, Lake Placid, New York (1930–1931); secretary of the Newark Art Commission (1936); and a member of the New Jersey Commission on the New York World's Fair (1938), the Committee on Waste of Consumer's Interest of the Newark Defense Council (1941), and the Citizens Advisory Committee, Central Planning Board of Newark (1945). She also held memberships in many local associations and societies and was a trustee of Dana College (now the University of Newark).

Contemporaries viewed Winser as a commanding and energetic woman with a "strong voice, hearty laugh, [and] quick sympathy" who sometimes intimidated strangers. She established the Newark Museum and Library as integral components of a large modern city. She was one of the first female heads of a big city library in an era when men held most of the library directorships and she took professional stances that were not always popular. Her life epitomized the professionalization of librarianship. Winser died at her Newark home.

• The John Cotton Dana Papers in the Newark Public Library contain materials on Winser relating to library and museum business and a file on the Newark Museum; the library also has copies of Winser's library publications. The New Jersey Historical Society, Newark, has the Winser Family Papers (1806–1963), as well as correspondence on Winser in the Miriam V. Studley Collection, Mary Philbrook Papers, Joseph Bradley Papers, and the Federal Writers' Project (N.J.) Women's Archives. The John Cotton Dana Papers in the Woodstock, Vt., Historical Society, also contain information on Winser. The American Library Association Archives, Champaign, Ill., has documents on Winser in the transcripts of executive board proceedings. Her writings consist largely of papers and speeches given at conferences and reprinted in journals, joint compilations with John Cotton Dana, edited works, and staff bibliographies. See also Newark Public Library, *This Is to Be a People's Library* (1963).

See also *Dictionary of American Library Biography* (1978); Dorothy Heiderstadt, "Busiest Woman in Newark," *Wilson Library Bulletin* 16 (1942): 478; Marian C. Manley, "Beatrice Winser, Administrator and Friend," *Library Journal* 72 (1947): 1481; and a tribute by Edward A. Jewell in the *New York Times*, 27 Apr. 1947. An obituary is in the *New York Times*, 16 Sept. 1947, with an editorial on 18 Sept. 1947.

MARTIN J. MANNING

WINSHIP, Blanton (23 Nov. 1869–9 Oct. 1947), army officer and governor of Puerto Rico, was born in Macon, Georgia, the son of Emory Winship, a clothing merchant, and Elizabeth Alexander. Winship graduated from Mercer University in Macon in 1889 with an A.B., from McKay's Business College in Macon in 1890, and from the University of Georgia in 1893 with a law degree. From 1893 to 1898 he practiced law in Macon.

After the United States declared war against Spain in April 1898, Winship enlisted in the First Georgia Volunteers as a captain. Mustered out in November 1898, he was commissioned a first lieutenant in the Twenty-ninth U.S. Infantry in July 1899, and for the next two years he served in the Philippines during the insurgency. Mustered out in June 1901, Winship served briefly as a second lieutenant with the Artillery Corps, then accepted an appointment as a first lieutenant with the Sixteenth U.S. Infantry in November 1901. In January 1904 Winship transferred to the Judge Advocate's Department, which brought him promotion to major, and he held a variety of assignments with the army's legal arm. In 1906 he went to Cuba as judge advocate of the Army of Pacification. A principal member of the Advisory Law Commission, he worked for two years to revise Cuba's laws to insure peaceful elections, representative government, and an honest judicial and civil service. Winship was in the American expeditionary force that occupied Veracruz, Mexico, in 1914 and served as the officer in charge of the city's civil administration.

Following the entry of the United States into World War I in April 1917, Winship was promoted to the rank of lieutenant colonel and sent to France with the American Expeditionary Forces (AEF). There his assignments included judge advocate of the Forty-second and First Divisions, the I Corps, and the First Army and commander of the 112th and 110th U.S. Infantry regiments of the Twenty-eighth Division. While commanding the 110th Infantry in the Thiaucourt sector, he was awarded the Distinguished Service Cross (DSC) for gallantry in action in organizing and leading a party to assist a patrol threatened by a German attack on 9 November 1918. After the armistice, Winship was transferred to the Services of Supplies, where he became director general of the Army Claims Commission. In this post he oversaw the settlement of 100,000 claims against the army in a prompt fashion. Promoted to colonel in 1920, he served as judge advocate of the American occupation army in Germany. For the totality of his service during World War I, Winship was awarded the Distinguished Service Medal (DSM), making him one of only nine AEF officers to be awarded both the DSC and the DSM.

During the 1920s and early 1930s Winship held various military and diplomatic assignments. From 1920 to 1923 he was a member of the Reparations Commission, a League of Nations commission that was responsible for enforcing the provisions of the Treaty of Versailles that required Germany to pay reparations to the victorious allies. In 1925 he was a member of the military court that tried controversial air power enthusiast Brigadier General William L. Mitchell for publicly criticizing his superiors. Later Winship served as military aide to President Calvin Coolidge, as legal adviser to Governor General Henry L. Stimson of the Philippine Islands, and as the American member of the League of Nations Commission on Liberian Affairs. Finally, in March 1931 Winship was appointed judge advocate general of the army with the rank of major general, a post he held until his retirement from active duty in November 1933.

In early 1934 President Franklin D. Roosevelt named Winship governor of Puerto Rico. At the time, Puerto Rico was suffering from economic depression and years of American indifference. As a result, its political system was enflamed by nationalist sentiment. The half-year tenure of Winship's undignified and inept predecessor had been a fiasco, and Roosevelt believed that Winship was qualified to restore order to the island's political life and decorum to the governor's office. As governor, Winship advocated legislation to improve conditions for workers, lobbied Washington for higher quotas for the island's sugar producers, initiated a campaign to establish the island as a tourist center, and eventually advocated statehood as the answer to the island's economic and political problems. However, his autocratic style angered many Puerto Rican leaders. In addition, his conservative outlook, skepticism about a New Deal reform measure limiting land ownership to 500 acres, and reluctance to take orders from civilians often placed him at odds with his superiors in the Department of Interior.

Responding to the growing number of nationalist demonstrations and terrorist acts, Winship attempted to suppress all anti-American sentiment in Puerto Rico and strengthened the insular police force. In March 1937, when unarmed demonstrators in Ponce violated a prohibition against marches, police fired into the parade, killing seventeen and wounding more than one hundred. Winship exonerated the police and defended the actions of his administration. However, an American Civil Liberties Union investigation later placed some of the blame for the "Ponce massacre" on Winship's predilection to use the "mailed fist" in handling disturbances. In August 1938 Winship narrowly survived an assassination attempt by a band of dissidents, which left three bystanders dead and thirty others wounded. Winship resigned his governorship in the summer of 1939, leaving Puerto Rico's relations with the United States as strained as they had been when he was appointed.

During World War II, Winship returned to military service as coordinator of the Inter-American Defense Board, retiring finally in April 1944 as the oldest general on active duty. He was highly regarded as a military and "colonial" administrator. He died a bachelor in Washington, D.C.

• Winship's official papers are in the National Archives. For his military career see *Official Army Register* (1945) and Edward Martin, *The Twenty-eighth Division, Pennsylvania's Guard in the World War* (5 vols., 1923–1924). Thomas Mathews, *Puerto Rican Politics and the New Deal* (1960), critically discusses Winship's tenure as governor of Puerto Rico. See also Raymond Carr, *Puerto Rico: A Colonial Experiment* (1984); Robert Fernandez, *The Disenchanted Island: Puerto Rico and the United States in the Twentieth Century* (1992); and T. H. Watkins, *Righteous Pilgrim: The Life and Times of Harold L. Ickes, 1874–1952* (1990). An obituary is in the *New York Times*, 10 Oct. 1947.

JOHN KENNEDY OHL

WINSHIP, George Parker (29 July 1871–22 June 1952), librarian and bibliographer, was born in Bridgewater, Massachusetts, the son of Albert Ellis Winship, a teacher, minister, and editor, and Ella Rebecca Parker. After graduating from Somerville (Mass.) High School, he entered Harvard, where he received the A.B. in 1893 and the A.M. in history in 1894. During college he explored the rare holdings of the Harvard library and translated and edited Pedro de Castañeda's *Relación* of Francisco Vásquez de Coronado's expedition to New Mexico and the Great Plains. The Bureau of Ethnology of the Smithsonian Institution subsequently financed a trip to the area and in 1896 published his *The Coronado Expedition*.

In 1895, at the age of twenty-four, Winship was chosen over philosopher and historian John Fiske to be the private librarian of the Americana collection of John Carter Brown, then owned by Brown's widow. The collection went to Brown University in 1901, and the John Carter Brown Library opened in 1904, with Winship as its librarian, a post that he held until May 1915. In his twenty years of work with the John Carter Brown collection of Americana, Winship doubled its size from 15,000 volumes to more than 30,000. Winship also made the library internationally known, in part through his own bibliographical scholarship. His *Cabot Bibliography* (1900), with its combination of detailed description of the physical objects as well as their content, set a new standard for bibliographies. In 1912 Winship married Claire Bliven; they had three children.

In early 1915, Winship, after having been denied a salary increase in 1914, agreed, to the dismay of the Brown family and the university's president, to return to Harvard as librarian of the Harry Elkins Widener Collection, largely the personal library of Harry Elkins Widener, donated by his mother, Eleanore Elkins Widener. Winship was well prepared to head a collection focused on literature and plate books, for, from 1897, he had been advising Marsden J. Perry of Providence, Rhode Island, in his formation of various collections, including one of Shakespeareana (sold with Winship's help to the Philadelphia bookseller A. S. W. Rosenbach in 1919), and he had long been interested in the history of printing and in contemporary fine printing.

Correspondence with Eleanore Elkins Widener indicates that Winship may have had hopes of support in making additions to the collection. If so, they were dashed, but from the start, since Winship had an assistant, he was free to pursue activities aimed at making the collection visible in bookish circles. He did so through speeches, active involvement in the Bibliographical Society of America, and his own scholarly writing. He also offered in the Fine Arts Department a course on the history of the printed book.

The wider arena of the Harvard College Library also beckoned, as Winship noted in the printed class report of 1918:

> The Harvard Library has been, in the opinion of many who use it, the best students' library in the world. It is also a very great collection of rare and valuable books, which have never had the care and attention that they deserve. If this can now be given to them, and an increasing number of owners of precious volumes realize that their treasures will be appreciated, intelligently preserved for the delight of future book-lovers, and made available under proper restrictions and oversight for the use of investigators, the Harvard Library can confidently anticipate rivalling some day even the Bodleian at Oxford. Laying the foundations for such a future is what my present job calls for.

One such step was starting in 1920 *Harvard Library Notes*, which clearly aimed to encourage gifts.

Winship's expansion of his role may not have fit with Eleanore Widener's desire that her son's collection be "entirely independent of the Harvard College Library." Perhaps for that reason, though it cannot definitively be established, her discontent with Winship came to a head, which was expressed in a penciled note of 29 September 1925, in which she informed him that she would ask him to resign in six months. After a long anxious period, he was able to do so in order to take up the position of assistant librarian in charge of the Treasure Room, then the rare books and manuscripts collection of the Harvard College Library.

In his new position Winship continued his scholarship and writing and other forms of proselytizing for rare books, locally and even on a national level, as when he publicly supported acquisition of the Vollbehr Collection of incunabula by the Library of Congress. In 1927 he formed an important special friends organization, the John Barnard Associates, made up of students, faculty, and alumni, whose dinners at the Club of Odd Volumes and outings to the Winships' farmhouse on the Charles River, in Dover, were memorable bookish occasions. Part of the pleasure for Winship was in printing for the associates on his handpress. Teaching continued through the academic year of 1931 and was given up then perhaps because of health problems. Winship retired in 1937. Thereafter he was more productive as a scholar, giving the Rosenbach Lectures in 1940 and 1941 at the University of Pennsylvania and then turning them into books. (*Printing in the Fifteenth Century* [1940] and *The Cambridge Press, 1638–1692* [1945]). He died in Dover, Massachusetts.

Winship was a pioneer in devoting himself to a general rare book collection in a university setting. If his accomplishments did not match his dreams, they were nonetheless great. He produced a number of books and many articles, had a hand in numerous bibliographical projects, and played a significant role in a number of other institutions, including the William L. Clements Library; for his role in shaping the latter, the University of Michigan awarded him the Litt.D. in 1917. Perhaps, though, he accomplished even more through others who, coming under the influence of his prodigious learning and engaging personality, subsequently devoted their careers to libraries and books, especially Walter Muir Whitehill and Margaret Bingham Stillwell, or became major collectors and supporters of libraries, Arthur A. Houghton, Jr., Carl Pforzheimer, and Philip Hofer being three among the many who have, in fact, helped the Harvard Library to rival the Bodleian.

• Winship's papers from his Brown and Harvard Library work are in those institutions. In the papers in the Harvard University Archives are also a large number of letters from individuals prominent in the library world. Winship's most important works, in addition to those mentioned, are *Sailors Narratives of Voyages along the New England Coast, 1524–1624* (1905), *Gutenberg to Plantin, a Outline of the Early History of Printing* (1926), *John Gutenberg* (1940), and *Daniel Berkeley Updike and the Merrymount Press of Boston* (1947). Walter Muir Whitehill's memoir on Winship in the *Proceedings of the Massachusetts Historical Society, 1953–1957* 71 (1959): 365–75 is by someone who knew and admired him. Margaret Bingham Stillwell, *Librarians Are Human* (1973), contains much about Winship and also is by someone who came under his influence. An obituary is in the *New York Times*, 24 June 1952.

KENNETH E. CARPENTER

WINSLOW, Charles-Edward Amory (4 Feb. 1877–8 Jan. 1957), biologist and public health pioneer, was born in Boston, Massachusetts, the son of Erving Winslow, a merchant and publicist, and Catherine Mary Reingolds, an English actress. Hoping to pursue a career in medicine, Winslow began his undergraduate work in biology at the Massachusetts Institute of Technology (MIT) in 1894. There he studied under William Thompson Sedgwick, a leading innovator in the use of applied biology in public health research. Winslow was inspired by Sedgwick's commitment to public health, and after receiving his bachelor's degree in 1898 he decided to begin graduate work at MIT rather than apply to medical school.

During his graduate studies, Winslow became a member of the American Public Health Association, which Sedgwick had helped establish. Winslow's 1899 master's thesis concerning the role of temperature in disease transmission was published in the memoirs of the American Academy of Arts and Sciences in 1902, the same year he received his M.S. from MIT. He joined the MIT faculty as an assistant and then as an instructor of sanitary bacteriology later that year, continuing to work closely throughout with Sedgwick. In 1905 Winslow was promoted to assistant professor and biologist-in-charge of sanitary research. At the same time he headed the MIT sewage experiment station for the investigation and purification of Boston sewage. In 1907 Winslow married Anne Fuller Rogers, a fellow researcher who worked with him in the lab; they had one child. His wife eventually wrote most of his speeches, and the couple produced an extensive study of Coccaceae in 1908 in which they considered the principles of bacterial classification.

Winslow left MIT in 1910 for a temporary assistant professorship at the University of Chicago. He was required to teach university students but also gave public lectures on industrial hygiene and municipal sanitation.

Later in 1910 Winslow moved to the City College of New York as an associate professor of natural history. There he restructured the curriculum to include public health bacteriology. Concurrently, Winslow initiated several public health exhibits at the American Museum of Natural History in New York and served as the curator of public health there for the next five years. He began to give regular public lectures in New York City and continued to do so until his death. In 1914 he was named the director of publicity for the New York Department of Public Health; he also edited the "Health Hints" and "Health News" articles created by the department and published in daily and weekly newspapers. Winslow helped establish health education services in New York City, which focused on the importance of nutrition and adequate housing.

In 1915 Winslow was nominated to fill the position he would hold for the next thirty years. A Department of Public Health had recently been endowed at the Yale School of Medicine, and Winslow was appointed as the Anna M. Lauder Professor of Public Health and the first department chair. Unlike most medical school professors, Winslow did not possess a medical degree, but Yale Medical School officials believed that Winslow's training in bacteriology and public health would allow him to focus on disease prevention rather than treatment. At Yale Winslow created both a doctoral program, which required six to eight years of study, and a two-year course of study for the certificate of public health—a degree designed for students outside of the public health department as well as medical students in their second year. To increase access to public health studies, Winslow had his courses cross-listed so students from other departments could take them for credit. In 1923 he helped establish the Yale School of Nursing.

While chair of the Yale public health department, Winslow stepped up his national and international activities. In 1917 he embarked on the American Red Cross mission to Russia and acted locally in support of a bill to create the Connecticut State Department of Health. He was named the director of the League of Red Cross Societies in Geneva, Switzerland, in 1921. A longtime member, Winslow became president of the American Public Health Association in 1925 and worked successfully to get the first public housing act passed in New York. He served as a member of the League of Nations' National Health Care Committee from 1927 to 1930.

Through all of these efforts, Winslow had come to believe that health care distribution in the United States was poorly organized, inefficient, and even detrimental to public health. In 1927 he was instrumental in the organization of the Committee on the Costs of Medical Care (CCMC) and became the chair of its executive branch. The CCMC launched a five-year study of national medical care practices, costs, and areas for improvement. Based on this study's results, Winslow spoke out against the inequities of the American health care system. He became a vocal advocate for group practice and national health insurance, thereby alienating many physicians on the Yale faculty who staunchly opposed these measures.

During the CCMC study, Winslow concentrated his efforts within the Yale Medical School and revived his interest in sanitary bacteriology as director of the John B. Pierce Laboratory of Hygiene. In 1939 he became the first chair of the New Haven Housing Authority, which initiated the construction of 2,500 apartments for low- and moderate-income families and was active in the passage of the first federal public housing act. He became chair of the Committee on the Hygiene of Housing as well and devised a system of housing inspection for the city of New Haven that has since been modified for use in other cities.

Winslow served as an editor of the *American Journal of Public Health* in 1944 and became editor in chief of the *Journal of Bacteriology* and president of the Society of American Bacteriologists, which had been founded by Sedgwick. Winslow retired as professor emeritus at the Yale School of Medicine in 1945 but continued to give speeches, edit journals, and serve on international and domestic committees for public health reform until the time of his death in New Haven. Winslow was awarded the Leon Bernard Foundation Prize at Geneva in 1952 for his contributions in international public health. The Albert and Mary Lasker Award of the American Public Health Association was presented to Winslow in 1956, acknowledging his work in the United States.

Winslow was an activist and a scholar. He helped shape public health as an academic discipline and demonstrated the practical implications of studying disease prevention through his emphasis on community and clinical medicine, his attempts to restructure health care delivery systems to increase overall access to medical resources, and his commitment to housing reform.

• Most of Winslow's papers are in the manuscripts and archives collection at Yale University. His works include *The Systematic Relationships of the Coccaceae, with a Discussion of the Principles of Bacterial Classification*, with Anne Rogers Winslow (1908); *Evolution and Significance of the Modern Public Health Campaign* (1923); *The Conquest of Epidemic Disease* (1943); *Temperature and Human Life* (1949); and *History of American Epidemiology* (1952). The most informative biography on Winslow is Benjamin Olatunde Adeltola, "The Teachings of Charles-Edward Amory Winslow and Public Health Today" (master's thesis, Yale School of Epidemiology and Public Health, 1991). See also Arthur Viseltear,

"C-E. A. Winslow and the Early Years of Public Health at Yale, 1915–1925," *Yale Journal of Biology and Medicine* 55 (1982): 137–51. An obituary is in the *New York Times*, 9 Jan. 1957.

KRISTIN M. BUNIN

WINSLOW, Edward (18 Oct. 1595–8 May 1655), diplomat, author, and political leader, was born in Droitwich, Worcestershire, the son of Edward Winslow, a salt merchant, and Magdalene Oliver. Baptized on 19 October 1595, he was well educated at the cathedral school in Worcester. By 1617 he had joined John Robinson's separatist congregation at Leyden. There he married Elizabeth Barker, of Chattisham, Suffolk, in 1618. At the time he was apparently a printer associated with William Brewster.

In 1620 Winslow and his wife, with two servants, sailed on the *Speedwell* for America, transferring to the *Mayflower* when the former vessel was forced to turn back. Having invested £60 in the initial Plymouth venture, he was, and remained, among the wealthiest of the Mayflower Pilgrims. On arrival at Cape Ann in December he was in the exploratory party that selected the site at Plymouth Harbor for the new colony. Elizabeth Winslow died (apparently childless) in March 1621. Winslow then married Susanna (Fuller) White, a widow with two sons, in May 1621, thus celebrating the first marriage in Plymouth Colony. The couple had four children, two of whom lived to adulthood, including Josiah Winslow who later became governor of the colony.

Early in 1621 he helped negotiate the first treaty with Massasoit and the Wampanoags and was chosen envoy to the tribe for subsequent talks, thus inaugurating his important role in Indian affairs. In 1641, for instance, he arranged the purchase of the Rehoboth region, some eight square miles, from Massasoit. Also in the early 1640s he was among the organizers of the New England Confederation to shape a common diplomatic front for the Puritan colonies. His last published work, *The Glorious Progress of the Gospel amongst the Indians in New England* (1649), was largely a collection of letters from missionaries among the Indians supplemented by his observations on Native American religion and culture. This publication led to the London founding of the Society for the Propagation of the Gospel in New England, of which he was one of the incorporators.

Winslow's diplomatic and literary talents were more extensively used to defend Plymouth's and later Massachusetts Bay's interests in England. He, together with William Bradford, prepared a set of narratives on the founding of the colony that was printed in London in 1622 as *A Relation or Journal of the Beginnings and Proceedings of the English Plantation Setled at Plimoth in New England*, commonly called *Mourt's Relation*. In 1623 he made the first of several voyages to England, returning in March 1624 with the colony's first cattle. Later in 1624, while back in London to negotiate with merchant investors in the Plymouth Company, he had published *Good Newes from New-England*, a promotion tract that included not only a narrative of events to 1623 and a defense of the colonists' dealing with the merchants but also another account of the Indians, together with descriptions of soil, climate, and resources.

During another trip in 1627 he successfully defended Plymouth's expulsion of the "particulars," those who were not part of the Plymouth Company contract, and negotiated a new arrangement in which he and several others, called the "undertakers," personally assumed the colony's English debts in return for special trading privileges. In 1629 he replaced Isaac Allerton as the colony's official agent and during the 1630s made three more voyages to England to defend Plymouth's and Massachusetts Bay's land claims. In 1634, while engaged in one of these missions, he was imprisoned for four months at the insistence of Archbishop William Laud for officiating at marriages and "teaching" in the Plymouth Church as a layman.

When in residence at Plymouth, Winslow was equally active in the politics and economic development of the colony and region. He was a member of the Court of Assistants nearly every year from 1624, when the Court was formed, to 1646 and was elected governor in 1633, 1636, and 1644. In 1636 he helped codify the Plymouth laws and was keenly interested in making certain that the code, as well as decisions of the Plymouth courts, was consistent with English precedent. As he explained, "I have brought my owne booke of the statutes of England into our court, so that when wee wanted a law or ordinance wee might see what the statutes provided in that kind." He was also the main founder of Marshfield and its church in 1633, as part of his continuing interest in buying, selling, and developing landholdings. As one of the undertakers, he fostered investment and development in Maine and Connecticut as well. In June 1640 Winslow and William Bradford negotiated the Plymouth-Massachusetts Bay border with John Endecott and Israel Stoughton.

In 1646 Winslow went to England to defend Massachusetts Bay against charges of religious persecution and fraudulent economic dealings made by Samuel Gorton and Robert Child. Winslow never returned to Plymouth. In England he again wrote in pamphlets to garner public support for the New England Way. Soon after arrival he wrote *Hypocrisie Unsmasked* (1646) to justify the Bay Colony's proceedings against Samuel Gorton. Then in 1647 he penned *New-Englands Salamander Discovered* to answer *New-Englands Jonas*, a personal attack on Winslow written by John Child, Robert's brother. In 1651 he sat for a portrait in London, making him the only Pilgrim for whom we have a contemporary formal likeness.

Winslow's reputation as an advocate and negotiator led Oliver Cromwell in 1654 to appoint him English chairman of an Anglo-Dutch commission to assess claims from English ships that were destroyed by the Dutch navy in neutral Denmark during the First Anglo-Dutch War. Late that year he was made chief of five commissioners to command Cromwell's "Grand

Design" against the Spanish West Indies, which resulted in the conquest of Jamaica. Winslow envisioned English settlements, each with its own congregational establishment, on the New England pattern. He also insisted that private plundering be forbidden so that all profits from captures could go into the government's treasury to pay for the expedition and the envisioned settlements. This notion, of course, was virtually without precedent in conflicts in the West Indies. On the return voyage to England, Winslow, among many others, was ill with fevers. He died and was buried at sea. Winslow was, without question, one of the most influential and effective of the leaders of New England's first generation.

• Nathaniel B. Shurtleff and David Pulsifer, eds., *Records of the Colony of New Plymouth in New England* (12 vols., 1855–1861), is a primary source for following Winslow's activities. There is no modern biography of Edward Winslow. However, William Bradford, *Of Plymouth Plantation, 1620–1647*, ed. Samuel Eliot Morison (1952), is the prime contemporary account, besides Winslow's own works. Eugene Aubrey Stratton, *Plymouth Colony: Its History and People, 1620–1691* (1986), with its strong biographical emphasis, is an excellent modern source. To understand the political and diplomatic context of Winslow's career, see George D. Langdon, Jr., *Pilgrim Colony: A History of New Plymouth, 1620–1691* (1966).

RICHARD GILDRIE

WINSLOW, John (10 May 1703–17 Apr. 1774), colonial soldier, was born in Marshfield, Massachusetts, the son of Isaac Winslow, a farmer, and Sarah Wensley. John was born into one of the leading families of southeastern New England; both his great-grandfather, Edward Winslow (1595–1655) and his grandfather, Josiah Winslow, had been governors of Plymouth colony. Although Winslow was raised in comfortable circumstances, his education was no better than that of a typical farmer's son. In 1725 he married Mary Little, who bore him two sons. She died in 1744, and in 1766 he married Bethiah Barker Johnson.

Before his mid-thirties, he held positions of local leadership in the town, including serving as captain of the militia. In 1740 he became a captain in Gooch's American Foot, a regiment led by regular field officers, with companies commanded by provincial officers and manned by provincial troops. The regiment participated in the Cartagena expedition in 1741. Although the campaign was a disaster and half the men in his company died of disease, Winslow proved himself an able, popular officer. Through the patronage of William Shirley, the governor of Massachusetts, in 1744 he received a regular captaincy in the 22d Regiment of Foot in Jamaica. He soon exchanged this post for the command of a company in the 40th Foot Regiment, based in Nova Scotia. Winslow served there and in Newfoundland until 1751, when he exchanged with a captain of the deactivated 50th Regiment, which allowed him to retire on half-pay and return home to Marshfield. In 1751–1753 he represented the town in the Massachusetts House of Representatives.

In 1754 Governor Shirley put Winslow in charge of an 800-man expedition up the Kennebec River in Maine to counter suspected French influence, build forts, and scout out a potential invasion route into Quebec. Winslow called the expedition "a Wild Goose Chase in a Wild Wilderness," but he nonetheless used an account of the mission to lobby British authorities for a regiment of his own in the event of war in the colonies. He was disappointed in this ambition, but in 1755 Shirley, now commander in chief of North America, appointed him lieutenant colonel commandant of a New England provincial regiment raised for service in Nova Scotia. His regiment served with distinction in successful sieges of two French outposts, forts Beauséjour and Gaspereau, on the Chignecto isthmus, the neck of land that connects Nova Scotia to the Canadian mainland.

Almost immediately after the fall of Beauséjour and Gaspereau, Winslow quarreled over disciplinary issues with Lieutenant Colonel Robert Monckton, the regular officer in command of overall operations. Relations between the New England provincials and their regular-army superiors deteriorated so much during the summer that the Massachusetts assembly intervened to protect Winslow and his men from what the legislators believed was an abusive attempt to absorb the provincials into the regular army. Despite these tensions, Winslow served loyally, even in the detention and deportation of Acadian civilians—a task that he found "Very Disagreable to my natural make & Temper." The Acadians had lived as neutrals in Nova Scotia for nearly a half century after the British had conquered their homeland during Queen Anne's War. Colonial authorities justified the deportation in the name of military security but in fact used this as the excuse for making an immense land grab.

In November 1755 Shirley, now commander in chief in North America, recalled Winslow to organize an intercolonial expedition against Fort Saint Frédéric, the French stronghold at Crown Point on Lake Champlain. He was appointed as major general of a 7,000-man provincial force, marking the climax of his military service. However, at this time Shirley was replaced in command by John Campbell, the fourth earl of Loudoun, who insisted on integrating Winslow's army into the regular command structure. The provincials strongly resisted this plan out of fear that their enlistment contracts would be violated and they would be turned into regular troops. Their incipient mutiny left Winslow in the uncomfortable position of trying to explain the provincials' reasoning to Loudoun, who blamed him for their recalcitrance. After prolonged bickering the army was disbanded for the winter, having accomplished nothing.

The failed campaign of 1756 ended the military career of Winslow, one of colonial Massachusetts's most distinguished military leaders. He returned to Marshfield, which he again represented in the provincial legislature in 1757–1758 and 1761–1765. In 1766 he moved to Hingham, where he continued, as he had since 1757, to petition the British government for preferment and to speculate in Kennebec and New Hampshire lands. He died in Hingham before the War of Independence began.

• The major collection of Winslow's papers is in the John Winslow and Winslow family papers at the Massachusetts Historical Society in Boston. Winslow letters can be found in the Loudoun papers at the Henry L. Huntington Library in San Marino, Calif., and in the Treasury Board In-letters and Chatham papers at the Public Record Office in London. The most important published primary source by Winslow is the large, quasi-official diary and orderly book that he kept in 1755, "Journal of Colonel John Winslow . . . ," Nova Scotia Historical Society Collections, vols. 3 and 4 (1882–1885). Other significant documents in print include correspondence between Winslow and Shirley in Charles Henry Lincoln, ed., *Correspondence of William Shirley, Governor of Massachusetts and Military Commander in America, 1731–1760*, vol. 2 (1912), and a broadside poem by Abiezer Peck, "On the Valiant New-England General" (1756), in the microform edition of the American Antiquarian Society, pub., *Early American Imprints*.

There is no biography of Winslow. Secondary accounts that make substantial mention of his life include Stanley Pargellis, *Lord Loudoun in North America* (1933; repr. 1968); John A. Schutz, *William Shirley, King's Governor of Massachusetts* (1961); Fred Anderson, *A People's Army: Massachusetts Soldiers and Society in the Seven Years' War* (1984); Douglas E. Leach, *Roots of Conflict: British Armed Forces and Colonial Americans, 1677–1763* (1986) and *Arms for Empire: A Military History of the British Colonies in North America, 1607–1763* (1973); G. A. Rawlyk, *Nova Scotia's Massachusetts: A Study of Massachusetts–Nova Scotia Relations, 1630 to 1784* (1973); Lorenzo Sabine, *Biographical Sketches of Loyalists of the American Revolution*, vol. 2 (1864); and E. Alfred Jones, *The Loyalists of Massachusetts* (1930). For a French-Canadian perspective, see Paul Surette, *Petcoudiac: colonisation et destruction, 1731–1755* (1988).

FRED ANDERSON

WINSLOW, John Ancrum (19 Nov. 1811–29 Sept. 1873), naval officer, was born in Wilmington, North Carolina, the son of Edward Winslow, a merchant, and Sarah Ancrum Berry. At the age of fourteen, young Winslow was sent by his New England–reared father from North Carolina to Massachusetts to prepare for college. Deciding instead on a naval career, Winslow was appointed midshipman in the U.S. Navy at age sixteen. Over the next several years sea duty included long cruises in the Pacific, South Atlantic, and Mediterranean. In 1837 Winslow married Catherine Amelia Winslow, a Boston cousin; they had three children. A deeply religious Episcopalian, Winslow was inclined to emphasize the dark side of human nature. He became increasingly frustrated and resentful toward a profession he was convinced encouraged and condoned immoral behavior by officers and common sailors alike. He also developed an intense hatred of slavery. Despite his unhappiness and alienation from many of his associates, Winslow remained in the service and was promoted to lieutenant in 1839 and commander in 1855.

Winslow's assistance in putting out a fire aboard a British Cunard liner in Boston Harbor (27 Oct. 1841) earned him a commendation from Queen Victoria. Two years later, however, another fire destroyed his own ship, *Missouri*, at Gibraltar. During the war with Mexico, Winslow served aboard the *Cumberland* off Veracruz then briefly commanded the schooner *Morris* off Tampico. When a storm caused the *Morris* to strike a reef and sink, Winslow was rescued and brought aboard the *Raritan*. He shared a stateroom aboard that vessel with Lieutenant Raphael Semmes, who had also lost his ship during a storm. The two men had already become friends while serving aboard the *Cumberland*.

At the beginning of the Civil War, Winslow was inspector of the Second Lighthouse District at Boston. He shared the radical abolitionist view that President Abraham Lincoln should seize the opportunity to launch a crusade to end slavery. When the administration indicated that it would not pursue such a policy, Winslow made no effort to conceal his contempt for the president.

While commanding the armored gunboat *Benton* on the Mississippi in 1862, Winslow injured a forearm when a tow chain broke. Following a six-month leave of absence, he came down with malaria. Adding to Winslow's misfortune, he was passed over despite his seniority when command of the Mississippi Squadron went to Commander David D. Porter. Although promotion to captain came in July 1862, no assignment befitting Winslow's new rank was forthcoming. He continued to needle the administration over its failure to free the slaves, commenting after the Union defeat at Second Manasses (Bull Run), "I was glad of it. I wish they would bag old Abe."

In November 1862 Winslow was assigned command of USS *Kearsarge*, a third-class man-of-war. The assignment was clearly a signal that Winslow was out of favor with the administration. The *Kearsarge*, then in drydock at Cádiz, Spain, was involved in the search for Confederate commerce raiders. Winslow's zealous dedication to duty eventually cost him his sight in one eye, when he would not take time to have the neuralgic and infected eye treated by a specialist. In addition, he suffered from recurring chills and fever.

During several weeks of 1864 the *Kearsarge* blockaded the CSS *Rappahannock*, in drydock at Calais. On 12 June, at Flushing, Holland, Winslow received a telegram informing him that the Confederate raider *Alabama* had arrived at Cherbourg. Two days later the *Kearsarge* took a position off Cherbourg, outside the three-mile territorial limit. Winslow and the *Alabama*'s captain—Semmes—prepared for battle. Following orders, Winslow ignored Semmes's written challenge to fight, although he had every intention of engaging his adversary. Semmes was confident that his men were prepared and that the two vessels were evenly matched. He failed to consider the condition of his ship and the deterioration of his gunpowder after almost two years at sea.

On Sunday, 19 June 1864, Winslow's customary religious service aboard the *Kearsarge* was interrupted by the call that the *Alabama* was leaving port. Outside

French territorial waters, the two ships circled each other in an engagement that lasted just over an hour. The gunners of the *Kearsarge* proved far more effective than their adversaries, wiping out an entire gun crew and crippling the raider with deadly accuracy. Realizing the battle was lost, Semmes made a futile attempt to bring his doomed ship within the three-mile limit. Uncertain whether Semmes had actually surrendered, Winslow delayed rescue efforts until convinced that the *Alabama* was actually sinking. Semmes later criticized Winslow for the delay, also accusing him of continuing to fire after Semmes had raised a white flag and of "cheating" by concealing chain armor slung over the midsection of the *Kearsarge* with boards. He never would have fought, Semmes contended, had he only known about them. The charges that irked Winslow the most came from his own government. Navy Secretary Gideon Welles criticized him for Semmes's escape to England aboard the English yacht that had rescued him. An unsubstantiated rumor even concluded that Winslow had purposely allowed Semmes to get away in order to save a "friend" from being tried for piracy. Welles also reproached Winslow for paroling the prisoners he had rescued. However, despite Welles's official disapproval, the man responsible for the destruction of the South's most notorious raider became an instant hero. Congress voted Winslow a Resolution of Thanks, and his promotion to commodore was made retroactive to the date of the battle. To show its appreciation, the New York Chamber of Commerce presented Winslow with a gift of $25,000. Personally, Winslow attributed his victory to divine intervention.

Winslow spent the remainder of the war on shore duty, serving on the court-martial board that found Commodore Thomas T. Craven guilty of dereliction of duty for failing to engage the Confederate iron ram *Stonewall* off El Ferrol, Spain. Despite failing health, he commanded the Gulf Squadron, 1866–1867. In 1870 Winslow was promoted a rear admiral and given command of the Pacific Squadron, but his recurring chills and fever, plus blindness in one eye, finally forced him to resign. Although officially retired 19 November 1872, Winslow was continued on the active list by a special act of Congress. He died in Boston.

Although a competent and conscientious officer, Winslow was temperamentally unsuited for a naval career. Tactless and outspoken, he was intolerant toward those who could not measure up to his own lofty principles. Yet by being at the right place at the right time—Cherbourg on 19 June 1864—Winslow earned his place among the great sea captains.

• Winslow's Civil War reports are found in the *Official Records of the Union and Confederate Navies in the War of the Rebellion* (30 vols., 1894–1922). The only biography of Winslow is John M. Ellicott, *The Life of John Ancrum Winslow, Rear Admiral, USN* (1902). A chapter on Winslow is included in Jim Dan Hill, *Sea Dogs of the Sixties* (1935), and another is in Clarence Macartney, *Mr. Lincoln's Admirals* (1956). Of the numerous accounts of the *Kearsarge-Alabama* encounter off Cherbourg, see N. C. Delaney, "The End of the *Alabama*," *American Heritage*, vol. 23, no. 3 (Apr. 1972): 58–69, 102, repr. in Stephen W. Sears, ed., *The Civil War: The Best of American Heritage* (1991). An obituary is in the *Boston Transcript*, 30 Sept. 1873.

NORMAN C. DELANEY

WINSLOW, Josiah (c. 1629–18 Dec. 1680), governor of Plymouth Colony and commander in King Philip's War, was born in the town of Plymouth, the son of Edward Winslow and Susanna Fuller White. His was a politically and economically prominent Pilgrim family. Winslow's father was a member of the colony's Court of Assistants and occasionally governor during Josiah's earliest years. In the early 1630s the family moved to Marshfield; Edward Winslow was the town's main founder. Marshfield remained Josiah Winslow's home throughout his life. In the mid-1640s Winslow was among the first three American-born students to enroll at Harvard. Winslow did not take a degree, that being, according to custom, largely restricted to those pursuing ministerial careers.

In 1652 Winslow replaced his namesake uncle as captain of militia at Marshfield and was elected to the Court of Assistants, a post he held continuously until he was chosen governor in 1673. Around 1657 he married Penelope Pelham of Boston, whose father, Herbert Pelham, was Harvard's first treasurer and a member of the Bay Colony's Court of Assistants. Thus, before his thirtieth birthday he took his place as the leading citizen and proprietor of his town and began his long career within New England's military and political elite.

As magistrate for Marshfield late in 1657 he sent a constable to suppress a Quaker meeting, but generally Winslow favored limited toleration for dissenters and accommodation of English authorities unlikely to be sympathetic to the New England religious and political arrangements. His chief interests were in Indian and military affairs. In 1658 he became a member of the Supreme War Council, a committee of eleven authorized by Plymouth's General Court to impress manpower and supplies and to plan campaigns in time of war. That same year he was made a Plymouth commissioner to the United Colonies, a federation of New England settlements, a position he held until 1672. In 1659 Winslow was appointed commander of the colony's militia, replacing the redoubtable Myles Standish who had died in 1656.

In his capacity as militia commander, Winslow was sent in 1662 to meet Massasoit's son, Wamsutta, whom the English called Alexander, and to bring him to Plymouth to answer for violating a treaty by selling land to those not of the colony. There was controversy over whether Wamsutta came voluntarily, as Wamsutta claimed, or was coerced by Winslow. The results, in any case, were Wamsutta's submission to Plymouth's authority, the sale of the Pachade Purchase lands of the Middleborough region to Winslow and others, and the prevention of war. In 1671 Winslow led a similar expedition to Saconnet to convince the female sachem Awashunks and her followers to surrender their arms and maintain peaceful relations under Plymouth's loose hegemony. By 1674 the Plymouth government was confident enough of its position to lift the embargo against the sale of weapons and ammunition to neighboring tribes.

In 1673 Winslow was elected governor of Plymouth, the first American-born governor of an English colony in North America. He was something of a reformer. In 1674 he encouraged the founding of Plymouth's first public school. In 1676, near the end of King Philip's War, John Cotton, a leading Plymouth pastor, suggested convening the colony's clergy to consider reforms. The next year Winslow tried to call the clergy together, asking the churches by letter to consider, among other questions, the extent to which toleration ought to be granted to dissenters. Although some pastors and leading laymen did assemble, the meeting failed because of lack of attendance and popular interest. Meanwhile, the Bay Colony was able to hold its reforming synod of 1679, which did address many of the moral and social problems plaguing both colonies.

As the failure of the Plymouth synod indicates, the great crisis of Winslow's era as governor was King Philip's War and its aftermath. As attacks began in June 1675, Winslow mobilized the militia. By early November he personally took command of a United Colonies force for invading the Narragansett country. In mid-December he established headquarters at Wickford, Rhode Island, and made a bold march south. On 19 December 1675 he inflicted heavy casualties on the Narragansetts in the Great Swamp fight, which essentially broke the tribe's capacity for further resistance and virtually ended the war in that region. However, during the battle and even more during the forced march back to Wickford in severe weather, the English lost seventy men, a heavy blow to a colony that could, at best, field a militia of 1,200. The march was carried out against the advice of Benjamin Church, to whom Winslow, increasingly ill after the campaign, turned over active command in February 1676.

Plymouth was devastated by the war. The tax rate, for instance, increased tenfold. It was increasingly apparent that the colony would not long be able to maintain itself as a fully independent entity. Winslow's problem, which occupied him the rest of his life, was to gain the best possible accommodation within the evolving English imperial system. His best hope of avoiding merger with Massachusetts was a new royal charter defining Plymouth's borders including the lands around Mount Hope. When Edward Randolph, a crown agent, arrived in Plymouth in June 1676, Winslow either suggested or acquiesced to the idea of a royal governor-general for New England, a notion he later had to repudiate as a result of political pressure from his peers to maintain a united front against English attempts to interfere with colonial government. On a later visit he even had Randolph made a freeman of the colony so as to cultivate his support. Winslow thus made a most favorable impression on Randolph, who roundly praised him in contrast to the Bay's leaders. Winslow himself wrote to England in 1677 and 1679 explaining the colony's problems and asking for help. He was in the midst of these delicate maneuvers when he died at his estate, "Careswell" in Marshfield, almost five years to the day after the Great Swamp fight. In 1691 Plymouth was merged into Massachusetts under a new charter that created a royal government to replace the earlier corporate form.

• There is no modern biography of Josiah Winslow. The best source for following his career is Nathaniel B. Shurtleff and David Pulsifer, eds., *Records of the Colony of New Plymouth in New England* (12 vols., 1855–1861). See also Douglas Leach, *Flintlock and Tomahawk: New England in King Philip's War* (1958); Eugene Aubrey Stratton, *Plymouth Colony: Its History & People, 1620–1691* (1986); and George D. Langdon, Jr., *Pilgrim Colony: A History of New Plymouth, 1620–1691* (1966).

RICHARD GILDRIE

WINSLOW, Ola Elizabeth (5 Jan. 1885–27 Sept. 1977), author and educator, was born in Grant City, Missouri, the daughter of William Delos Winslow, a local banker, and Hattie Elizabeth Colby. She grew up in California and attended Stanford University, earning an A.B. in 1906 and an A.M. in 1914. She was an instructor at the College (now University) of the Pacific from 1909 to 1914. Then she joined the faculty of Goucher College, in Baltimore, where she was professor of English and head of the department (1914–1944), taught history as well, and was assistant dean briefly (1919–1921). She received a Ph.D. from the University of Chicago in 1922. Upon leaving Goucher, she became a professor at Wellesley College (1944–1950). While there, she was revered as a faculty oddity—walking across campus scattering birdseed and catnip, and with neighborhood children behind her. Her last teaching position was as a lecturer at Radcliffe College winter seminars (1950–1962). In her later years she enjoyed flower gardening and observing wildlife.

Winslow, who never married, combined teaching with scholarly research and travel, both for professional reasons and for pleasure. Her distinguished publishing record began with her doctoral dissertation, "Low Comedy as a Structural Element in English Drama from the Beginnings to 1642" (1926). She followed it with *Harper's Literary Museum: A Compendium of Instructive, Entertaining and Amusing Matter Selected from Early American Writings* . . . (1927), her compilation of pieces from seventeenth-, eighteenth-, and nineteenth-century books, broadsides, and newspapers, chosen not for literary merit but for fun and the light they shed on the past. Winslow next edited *American Broadside Verse* (1930). Reproduced in facsimile and carefully annotated, its 101 poems are so deplorably naive that they are entertaining, even as they record much of America's spiritual history and the evolution of its consciousness.

Then came Winslow's finest work: *Jonathan Edwards, 1703–1758: A Biography* (1940), for which she won the 1941 Pulitzer Prize in biography. It is the result of meticulous, often laborious research at several academic and governmental libraries in the United States and also in London. Winslow regards Edwards, the great New England Calvinist intellectual, as significant because he "had a determining part in initiating and directing a popular movement of far-reaching consequence [the Great Awakening], and . . . laid the foundations for a new system of religious thought, also of far-reaching consequence." Her book humanizes Edwards, often called austere and aloof, by probing and presenting him as a conflicted and tragic figure.

After Winslow retired from Wellesley in 1950, she moved to Sheepscot, Maine, where she lived in a farmhouse she restored and remained active in scholarship. Her *Meetinghouse Hill, 1630–1783* (1952) depicts the New England meetinghouse as the center and the setting of regional religious, social, and civil activities. She treats potentially dull material with confidence, sympathy, and gentle humor. She arouses reader interest in church interiors, hymn singing, and the occasional quirkiness of parishioners. *Master Roger Williams* (1957), which followed, is an informative, exciting portrait of a genuine American hero. Winslow skillfully presents the old England in which Williams grew up, properly leaves gaps in his life where details should not be guessed at, and shows how his writings reflect his personality and prove that his democratic principles are of abiding importance.

Winslow went to England for four months to prepare for her next biography—*John Bunyan* (1961). In it, she presents the historical, religious, and moral background of Bunyan's era, and his village and rural environment as well; she discusses his extensive minor works and builds skillfully to analyses of *Grace Abounding*, *The Pilgrim's Progress*, and *The Life and Death of Mr. Badman*. Her portrait is bulwarked, as usual, with extensive, detailed, but unobtrusive notes. Returning home, and to a secular American figure next, Winslow wrote *Samuel Sewall of Boston* (1964). By presenting the complicated life of this churchman, college leader, judge, magistrate, merchant, and military man, Winslow shows how rapidly second- and third-generation New England changed. Sewall's thoughts, whether accepted or opposed, had a significant impact on others of his era. Winslow relaxed with her next book, *Portsmouth: The Life of a Town* (1966). Written for juvenile readers, it tells how the New Hampshire town was founded in 1603 and grew into a bustling nineteenth-century seaport.

Finally came two serious books: *John Eliot: "Apostle to the Indians"* (1968) and *A Destroying Angel: The Conquest of Smallpox in Colonial Boston* (1974). Winslow's *Eliot* offers an enjoyable, meaningful biography of the democratic, humane missionary to the Algonquins, praises his translation of the Bible into their language, and discusses problems inherent in any cross-cultural living. Winslow's compact little book about smallpox dramatizes the 1721 epidemic by emphasizing the cooperation and animosity of three leading Bostonians: Dr. Zabdiel Boylston, who proposed inoculation; Dr. William Douglass, who condemned the procedure and campaigned against it; and Cotton Mather, who had a bomb thrown into his bedroom for favoring it. This last book by Winslow, published when she was eighty-nine years of age, shows no diminution of intellectual strength. She died in Damariscotta, Maine.

• An informative little entry concerning Winslow is in *Two Thousand Women of Achievement*, vol. 4 (1972). Following her retirement, *Time* included her in an "Education" column titled "Goodbye, Messrs. Chips," 3 July 1950, p. 59. Her obituary is in the *New York Times*, 3 Oct. 1977.

ROBERT L. GALE

WINSTON, Ellen Black (15 Aug. 1903–19 June 1984), public welfare administrator, was born in Bryson City, North Carolina, the daughter of Stanley Warren Black, a lawyer, and Marianna Fischer, who was trained as a schoolteacher. Ellen's parents were leaders in the small mountain community. Her father was president of the bank and chairman of the county school board. Her mother organized a local parent-teacher association and a women's club, and she founded the public library that bears her name.

Ellen graduated from Converse College, a Presbyterian affiliated institution in Spartanburg, South Carolina, receiving a B.A. in English in 1924. She began teaching in the public schools of Raleigh, North Carolina. There Ellen met her future husband, Sanford Richard Winston, an instructor in sociology who urged her to get an advanced degree. The couple was married in 1928; they had no children. In 1928 she received her master's and in 1930 her doctorate in sociology from the University of Chicago.

While Winston's husband received an appointment at North Carolina State University, where he remained throughout his working life, she continued in secondary education until 1934. She then began to apply her sociological training as the editor of a Works Progress Administration series that focused on rural economic and social problems. For the series she coauthored *Seven Lean Years* and *The Plantation South*. Winston returned to academia in 1940 as head of the Department of Sociology and Economics at Meredith, a women's college in Raleigh. Yet she maintained her Washington ties as a senior social scientist for the Farm Security Administration, a member of the technical committee on long-range work and relief policies for the National Resources Planning Board, and a consultant on statistics and research for the U.S. Office of Education.

In 1944 Winston was appointed commissioner of the North Carolina State Board of Public Welfare, a job traditionally reserved for a woman. Her responsibilities included the federal programs Aid to the Aged, Aid to Dependent Children (ADC, later Aid to Families with Dependent Children), and Aid to the Blind, which were authorized under the Social Security Act of 1935. After 1950 she also oversaw Aid to the Permanently and Totally Disabled. In addition, Winston was in charge of General Assistance and Workman's Compensation under state authority.

Winston's encouragement of social services to help recipients achieve a better home life within the constraints of the low assistance payments available in a poor agricultural state was notable in a region almost devoid of any services beyond financial assistance and child welfare. Though she remained a southerner who accepted racial segregation as a given, she broke up the separate committees, boards, and meetings that had previously existed. She also pushed successfully for increased recruitment of black social workers. And in emphasizing professional training, her actions were color blind.

Though small of stature, Winston was a well-groomed, imposing figure, with large dark eyes and a lively, intelligent expression. She conveyed a businesslike professionalism, expecting from others the high standards and long work days she demanded of herself. During her tenure as welfare commissioner in North Carolina, Winston emerged as a leader in national public welfare, serving from 1951 to 1953 as chairperson of the Committee on Public Welfare Policy of the American Public Welfare Association (APWA) and from 1957 to 1959 as president of APWA. As a member of the policy committee, she helped to develop a reform platform that presented social services as the preferred way to answer widespread criticism of the ADC program. Beginning in 1947 the media repeatedly charged that the ADC case load contained many ineligible adults who abused the system by false claims about lack of income, refusing to work, having repeated "illegitimate" children, and engaging in deviant behavior, such as drinking and brawling. In the 1960s the term "welfare mess" was introduced to sum up these problems.

The 1960 presidential election of John F. Kennedy ushered in a series of welfare reforms, culminating in 1962 with the passage of much-publicized public welfare amendments to the Social Security Act. In January 1963 the Welfare Administration was established within the new Department of Health, Education, and Welfare (HEW). Winston was appointed its head. In this capacity she administered, through the Bureau of Family Services, four public assistance programs that were financed by federal matching grants of state expenditures. Old Age Assistance, Aid to the Blind, Aid to Families with Dependent Children, and Aid to the Permanently and Totally Disabled came under her jurisdiction as they had in North Carolina. Child welfare services, such as foster care and health and rehabilitation programs for handicapped children were administered by the federal Children's Bureau, which was also placed in the Welfare Administration. In addition, three research-advocacy groups—the Office of Aging, the Office of Juvenile Delinquency and Youth Development, and the Cuban Refugee Program—became part of the Welfare Administration.

Unlike the publicists surrounding her, Winston never predicted that social services would provide a quick solution for the troublesome issues facing the AFDC program. She promoted and was relatively successful in introducing "long-run" reforms—research, professional training for social workers, and the employment of medical doctors and lawyers in areas such as certification for disability and legal procedures in child support enforcement. Winston used her position to persuade welfare directors to bring state standards into conformity with federal regulations and to speak out publicly for a federal mandatory floor under welfare grants. These honest convictions, together with her well-earned reputation as a workaholic, won Winston admirers but not necessarily friends.

When the welfare rolls increased more than 50 percent during the 1960s, the 1962 amendments were pronounced a failure by congressional leaders and by the advisory staff within HEW. In June 1966 John W. Gardner, the secretary of HEW, shelved a congressional mandate that called for continuing welfare reform. Winston resigned as commissioner in April 1967.

Joining her husband in Raleigh, Winston pursued a host of volunteer activities: president of the National Council for Homemaker–Home Health Aides Services (1970–1974); chairperson of the North Carolina committees for the 1971 and 1981 White House Conferences on Aging; and a prominent member of the International Council on Social Welfare during the 1970s. Also in that time she chaired the grants committee of the Silberman Fund, which supports the improvement of social work education and delivery of social services in the United States. Winston was also a member of the President's Citizens Advisory Council on the Status of Women in 1967–1968. Over the course of her career she received awards from the Department of Health, Education, and Welfare (1967); the North Carolina Federation of Women's Clubs (1977); and the American Public Welfare Association (1980). She died in Raleigh.

• Winston's papers are in the University of North Carolina at Greensboro. Official reports, letters, and memoranda covering her tenure as U.S. commissioner of welfare are in the National Archives (RG 47) and within records of the Social and Rehabilitation Service (RG 318). Many of Winston's public addresses are reprinted in conference proceedings such as the *Social Welfare Forum* (1959 and 1966) and in social welfare policy journals such as *Welfare in Review* 2 (1964); 3 (1965); and 5 (1967). Informed reminiscences of Winston are in interviews conducted by Blanche D. Coll with Robert M. Ball, 2 Feb. 1988; Wilbur J. Cohen, 18 Oct. 1985; and Elizabeth Wickenden (Goldschmidt), 28 May 1986, housed in the Oral History Collection, Butler Library, Columbia University. An interview with Winston conducted by Coll on 13 Sept. 1982 for the Women in the Federal Government project, Schlesinger Library, Radcliffe College, is a biographical record and is housed in the Schlesinger Library and the University of North Carolina at Greensboro. For a discussion of Winston's activities as commissioner of welfare, see Coll, *Safety Net: Welfare and Social Security, 1929–1979* (1995). An obituary is in the Raleigh *News and Observer*, 20 June 1984.

BLANCHE D. COLL

WINSTON, Henry (2 Apr. 1911–13 Dec. 1986), a leading figure in the Communist party of the United States for forty years, was born in Hattiesburg, Mississippi, the son of Joseph Winston, a sawmill worker, and Lucille (maiden name not known). Both of his parents were children of slaves.

The family moved to Kansas City, Missouri, after World War I. Winston dropped out of high school in 1930 and, unable to find a job, participated in demonstrations of the unemployed led by the Communist party (CPUSA). Impressed by Communist efforts to help the jobless and agitate on behalf of the Scottsboro Boys, six young African Americans from Alabama convicted of raping two white women in a trial permeated by racism, he first joined the Young Communist League in 1931 and the Communist party shortly thereafter.

Promising young black Communists were not common in the early 1930s, and Winston quickly ascended the party ladder. He moved to New York City soon after joining the YCL, and for the next two years he organized unemployed workers. In 1932 he was involved with the National Hunger March to Washington, D.C., and in 1933 he made the first of many trips to the Soviet Union. Elected to the National Executive Committee of the YCL in 1936, he served as the organization's national executive secretary from 1937 to 1942.

Enlisting in the U.S. Army in 1942, Winston (serving in Great Britain and France) was out of the country when Earl Browder, the party's general secretary, dissolved the CPUSA in favor of a political association in 1944. As a result, he was untainted by the political sin of "Browderism" when, in 1945, the Soviet Union signaled its displeasure with Browder's decision. When the long-time party leader refused to recant, he was removed from his position and expelled. In 1945, following Winston's release from the army and the party's reconstitution, he was appointed to the National Committee of the CPUSA. Two years later he was chosen as organizational secretary, making him one of the party's top leaders.

Winston was thus one of eleven party leaders arrested in 1948 and charged with violating the Smith Act, a sedition law passed by Congress in 1940. Tried on charges of conspiring "to teach and advocate the overthrow" of the U.S. government by "force and violence," Winston and the other defendants were convicted in 1949 after a rowdy trial in New York where Winston was one of several to draw contempt citations for his conduct.

The U.S. Supreme Court upheld the constitutionality of the Smith Act in *Dennis v. the U.S.* in 1951. Convinced that fascism was imminent in the United States, concerned that the party's leadership might never emerge from prison, and determined to preserve its top cadres, the CPUSA decided to organize an underground apparatus. Four of the Smith Act defendants, including Winston, jumped bail and went into hiding. Winston managed to evade an intensive FBI manhunt and remained underground for nearly five years. At first, he lived in Brooklyn. Early in 1952, he moved to the Chicago area, traveling disguised as a clergyman. He lived with sympathetic families, used false names, and tried to remain inconspicuous. Two of the fugitives were arrested by 1953. Winston and Gil Green, the other National Board member still at large, met occasionally to discuss party policy. During this period Winston wrote for the party press under the name Frederick Hastings.

As the issue of communism lost its potency, the fugitives began to discuss surrendering. In March 1956, with Joseph R. McCarthy censured by the U.S. Senate and their co-defendants emerging from prison, Winston and Green, the last remaining party leaders still in hiding, surrendered to federal authorities; in addition to the five-year sentence for violating the Smith Act, Winston faced an additional three years for jumping bail.

Sent to the federal penitentiary in Terre Haute, Indiana, Winston began to suffer from headaches and dizzy spells in 1958. Not until 1960 was he diagnosed as having a brain tumor. In February he was sent to Montefiore Hospital in New York; while the tumor was removed, he lost his sight. His illness and charges that federal authorities had mismanaged his health care led to a campaign for his release that drew support from such prominent anticommunists as Reinhold Niebuhr and A. Philip Randolph. President John F. Kennedy granted him executive clemency in June 1961. Following his release, Winston traveled to the Soviet Union for medical treatment and remained there until 1965.

Elected national chairman of the CPUSA in 1966, he remained in that position until his death. Although Winston was titular head of the party, Gus Hall, the general secretary, actually wielded more power (throughout the communist world, general secretaries usually were more important than chairmen). Within the CPUSA, it was Hall and not Winston who was the dominant party leader in an era in which the CPUSA retreated to the margins of American life. Winston, however, loyally supported Hall's attacks on party dissidents and any critics of the Soviet Union. Winston did play a leading role in the 1972 campaign to free Angela Davis, a prominent California Communist accused of providing guns used in a foiled prison escape that left four people dead, after her arrest on charges of murder, kidnapping, and conspiracy. Frequently honored by communist countries such as Mongolia, East Germany, and the Soviet Union, Winston died in Moscow, where he had gone for medical treatment. He was survived by his wife, Fern, and a daughter. A son died in 1983.

For almost thirty years, Winston was the most prominent black within the party leadership. In 1992 a group of dissidents in the Communist party, including many of its leading black members, revolted against Hall's leadership. Although sparked by the upheaval in the world communist movement and fueled by Hall's hard-line Marxism-Leninism, the revolt also included charges that, by failing to replace Winston with another national chairman, Hall had downgraded black issues and blacks themselves within the party. In death as well as life, Winston was an important symbol of the CPUSA's attempt to stress its biracial character.

• Information about Winston is scattered in a number of works on American communism. The most complete biographical sketch can be found in Maceo Dailey's entry in Bernard Johnpoll and Harvey Klehr, eds., *Biographical Dictionary of the American Left* (1986). Other sources include Joseph Starobin, *American Communism in Crisis, 1943–1957* (1972); Dorothy Healey and Maurice Isserman, *Dorothy Healey Remembers* (1990); and Gil Green, *Cold War Fugitive* (1984). An obituary is in the *New York Times*, 16 Dec. 1986.

HARVEY KLEHR

WINSTON, John Anthony (4 Sept. 1812–21 Dec. 1871), governor of Alabama, was born in the northern reaches of Mississippi Territory (later Madison County, Ala.), the son of William Winston and Mary Cooper, planters. Winston studied at La Grange College and at Cumberland College in Nashville. In 1832 he married Mary Agnes Walker; the couple had one daughter. Three years after his marriage, Winston became a black belt planter, establishing himself in Sumter County, Alabama. He eventually expanded his holdings of plantation property as far west as Texas and Arkansas, and by 1844 he was not only growing cotton but also dealing in it from a commission house he founded in Mobile. Winston owned at least ninety-eight slaves in 1850; his commission business survived emancipation.

Even before establishing his firm in Mobile, Winston had entered politics, being elected as a Democrat to the Alabama House of Representatives in 1840 and 1842. In the latter year his first wife died, and Winston married Mary Logwood. In 1843 he was elected to the state senate, over which he presided from 1845 to 1849, showing himself to be an ardent Jacksonian, hostile to banks and the paper money they circulated. In 1847 Winston gunned down his second wife's paramour. Authorities deemed the murder justifiable, and the blood on Winston's hands seems not particularly to have soiled his political prospects. He remained in the state senate until his election as governor six years after the killing. However, the failure of his second marriage, which formally ended in divorce in 1850, has been said to have embittered Winston. Certainly he proved to be a cold and sharp-tongued schemer in his political dealings. A member of Alabama's delegation to the 1848 Democratic National Convention, Winston clearly felt that a proper devotion to southern rights did not require him to fall in line behind the fire-eating agitator William Lowndes Yancey. Though instructed to require pledges from the national party of noninterference with slavery, Winston accepted nominee Lewis Cass and his doctrine of "squatter sovereignty," which would have permitted settlers to ban slaveholding in their respective territories. Two years later, however, at the first session of the Nashville Convention, Winston suggested that a government that would not safeguard slaveholders' rights was not worth preserving.

Elected governor in 1853 against a divided Whig opposition and a Union Democrat candidate, Winston became known not for the laws he ushered through the legislature but for his opposition to those the lawmakers tried to pass. He vetoed bills with gusto—not, as had traditionally been the practice in Alabama, because of their alleged constitutional defects, but because he straightforwardly opposed their intent. Most of the vetoed bills involved state subsidy of economic development, specifically the use of public funds to support railroad construction by private companies. Although he had not been a prominent opponent of public assistance for internal improvements, Winston became increasingly adamant in his refusal to draw the state further into debt for such purposes or to "take money from the people to lend to corporations, monopolies, or individuals" (Thornton, p. 327). Not simply stingy when it came to subsidizing private enterprise, he also vetoed a bill providing funds to complete the state insane asylum, but he supported a law that established the office of state superintendent of education, which began to lay the groundwork for a public school system.

Despite a widespread zeal for economic growth, Winston won many Alabamians over to his point of view. The nascent Know Nothing movement attempted to cultivate those opposing him on the railroad issue as well as those placing a premium on sectional reconciliation, but in 1855 voters reelected him by a healthy margin. Nonetheless, his popularity could not win him the U.S. Senate seat to which he aspired in 1857, when his second term as governor ended. His vetoes had not necessarily endeared him to the legislators responsible for electing senators, and many preferred to send to Washington someone more exclusively identified with sectional, rather than developmental, issues.

Still coveting a Senate seat, Winston endeavored in the following years to demonstrate both his orthodoxy with respect to slaveholders' rights and his party loyalty. At the abortive Democratic National Convention in Charleston in 1860, Winston insisted that the Alabama delegation act on its instruction (inspired by his rival, Yancey) to bolt if the national party did not embrace federal protection of slavery in the territories, even though he himself opposed the instruction and Yancey was inclined to compromise. Wishing "to force those who had brought the trouble from Alabama to stand by their work," Winston apparently intended to illustrate both Yancey's recklessness and his own faithfulness to Alabama party dictates (Thornton, p. 392). But rather than boosting Winston's fortunes, this strategy of calling Yancey's chickens home to roost helped to break up the convention and speed the party's decomposition. Winston did not immediately embrace secessionism, however, but instead supported the northern Democrat Stephen A. Douglas in the subsequent presidential election.

After civil war erupted, Winston traveled to the Virginia front as colonel of the Eighth Alabama Infantry. Pleading ill health, he resigned his command after the Confederates thwarted General George McClellan's

Peninsular campaign in the summer of 1862. He returned to his Alabama plantation. Winston reemerged on the public stage early in Reconstruction, serving in the state constitutional convention of 1865. The subsequent legislature elected him to the U.S. Senate, but like other white southerners whom the Congress deemed unreconstructed, he was denied his seat. In the wake of the 1867 Reconstruction Acts, Winston, a "straight-out" Democrat, opposed those proposing that his party undertake a "New Departure" by cultivating either black support or alliances with conservative white Republicans.

Winston died in Mobile. He had distinguished himself chiefly by what he could not abide—railroad bills, William Lowndes Yancey, and a "New Departure" in postbellum southern politics.

• Winston's official correspondence and some personal papers are at the Alabama Department of Archives and History in Montgomery. J. Mills Thornton III, *Politics and Power in a Slave Society: Alabama, 1800–1860* (1978), contains piquant analyses of Winston's personality and his political course. Useful information on various aspects of Winston's career is in William Warren Rogers et al., *Alabama: The History of a Deep South State* (1994); Michael Perman, *The Road to Redemption: Southern Politics, 1869–1879* (1984); and Thelma Jennings, *The Nashville Convention: Southern Movement for Unity, 1848–1851* (1980). An obituary is in the *Mobile Daily Register*, 22 Dec. 1871.

PATRICK G. WILLIAMS

WINTER, Alice Vivian Ames (28 Nov. 1865–5 Apr. 1944), writer and women's club leader, was born in Albany, New York, the daughter of Rev. Charles Gordon Ames and his second wife, Fanny Baker (Fanny Baker Ames), a social reformer. Her father was a missionary in California in the 1860s, then a pastor in Philadelphia and Boston. Her mother was a woman suffrage advocate and a founder and supporter of the charity organization movement. Her mother's marriage, Winter wrote, "was (as she once said to me of mine) one that increased her own liberty and personality" (letter dated 30 May 1943, Fanny B. Ames File, Schlesinger Library). During her youth in Boston Winter met with Transcendentalists and with suffragists Lucy Stone and Julia Ward Howe.

Winter attended the Pennsylvania Academy of Fine Arts and enjoyed painting all her life. She graduated from Wellesley College in 1886 and received the M.A. in 1889 in political science and Greek. After teaching for two years in the Boston school of Pauline Agassiz Shaw, she married English-born Thomas Gerald Winter in 1892. They moved to Minneapolis, where he became president of Winter-Truesdell-Ames Company, a grain elevator concern, and became wealthy from grain futures. They had two children. The household also included the orphaned niece and nephew of Thomas Winter.

Winter published two romantic novels, *The Prize to the Hardy* (1905) and *Jewel Weed* (1906). When her son died in 1907, she embarked on a lifelong career in women's voluntary organizations. She was the founder and first president (1907–1915) of the Woman's Club of Minneapolis. She joined the Daughters of the American Revolution and the American Association of University Women. She was the first president of the Minnesota branch of the League of American Penwomen (1927) and served as the first vice president in the national administration (1928–1930). She served on the Minneapolis Playground Commission and Minnesota Child Labor Committee and, during World War I, directed the Minneapolis chapter of the American Red Cross and the Woman's Committee of the Minnesota Council of National Defense.

Winter attended her first convention of the General Federation of Women's Clubs in 1914 and moved quickly up the ranks, chairing the Literature Department in 1916 and the Americanization Division in 1919. The following year she defeated antisuffragist candidate Georgie Bacon of Massachusetts, assuming the presidency of the one-million-member organization. Her four-year administration pushed her large constituency toward bold stands on public issues. She pressed for federal action in support of child labor laws, the Sheppard-Towner Maternity and Infant Care Act, and Indian welfare. She supported the Women's Joint Congressional Committee and moved her organization into a permanent national headquarters in Washington, D.C., for access to legislators she expected to lobby. In 1921 President Warren G. Harding appointed her to the advisory committee of the International Conference on Limitation of Armaments.

Winter wrote a monthly column on clubwomen's issues for the *Ladies' Home Journal* from 1924 to 1928 plus two works of nonfiction, *The Business of Being a Club Woman* (1925) and *The Heritage of Women* (1927), which won an award from the League of American Penwomen in 1928. In 1929 she and her family moved to Pasadena, California, where she became active in local civic programs. As director of the Public Relations and Studio Service Department of the Motion Picture Producers and Distributors of America, she served as a liaison between the Hollywood film industry and the wary consumer of films. For thirteen years she worked with the organization, founded by Will Hayes to encourage film production of a high moral standard and to censor questionable films. Having outlived her husband by ten years, she died in Pasadena. Her ashes were interred in Minneapolis.

Winter devoted her life to organizing women in their effort to gain a public voice for progressive reforms. Her success at publicizing the accomplishments and potential of women's clubs, streamlining club administration and efficient operation, expanding membership size and influence, and arguing for international harmony and cooperation was enormous. Her special stamp on women's voluntarism solidified a social force to be reckoned with.

• Winter materials are in the President's File, General Federation of Women's Clubs headquarters, Washington, D.C., and the Fanny B. Ames File, Schlesinger Library, Radcliffe

College. See also Mildred White Wells, *Unity in Diversity* (1953), pp. 83–87; Lillian E. Taaffe, "Alice Ames Winter," *Woman Citizen*, 31 May 1924, pp. 12–13, 29; Mildred Marshall Scouller, "Mrs. Thomas G. Winter," in *The Women Who Man Our Clubs* (1934), pp. 38–42; and "Mrs. Thomas G. Winter," in *Pasadena Community Book*, ed. William L. Blair (1943), pp. 453–54. An obituary is in the *Los Angeles Times*, 6 Apr. 1944.

KAREN J. BLAIR

WINTER, William (15 July 1836–30 June 1917), drama critic, was born in Gloucester, Massachusetts, the son of Charles Winter, a sea captain, and Louisa Wharf. Unsettled by the early death of his mother, Winter endured a "rough and neglected" childhood in the Boston area with relatives and an unsympathetic stepmother. At sixteen he graduated from high school but delayed enrollment in Harvard's Dane School of Law until 1856 for financial reasons and poor health. Although admitted to the Massachusetts bar upon graduation in 1857, Winter never practiced law and two years later moved to New York City.

Before leaving Boston, Winter had begun the career in literature and criticism on which he embarked in the fall of 1859. He had met Thomas Bailey Aldrich and established a lasting friendship with Henry Wadsworth Longfellow that bordered on fawning adoration. It was, in fact, Longfellow's letter to Henry Clapp, Jr., which helped influence that bohemian satirist to hire Winter to write for his short-lived *Saturday Press*. Hoping to gain fame as a poet, Winter arrived in New York with a law degree, some experience as a journalist, and two published volumes of poetry.

By mid-December 1860, Winter's career as a writer of quite savage satire came to an abrupt end when the *Saturday Press* ceased publication, but his friendship continued with the group of "bohemians" who congregated at Pfaff's Cafe on Broadway near Bleecker Street. Unemployed, Winter began to experience the financial difficulties which plagued him much of his life. In response, he borrowed money from his friends and accepted temporary work on the *New York Leader*, which he left in December 1861 to manage the dramatic department of the *Albion*, a British weekly published in the United States. In December 1860 Winter had married Elizabeth Campbell, a fiction writer who adapted plays for such actresses as Helena Modjeska and Minnie Maddern Fiske and enjoyed a brief career as an actress with the best American theater companies. They had four sons and a daughter. Writing as "Mercutio," Winter soon established himself at the *Albion* as a major drama critic, and in July 1865 became dramatic editor and critic for Horace Greeley's *New York Tribune*, where he was accepted as the most powerful theater critic in the United States for the next twenty-five years.

Winter remained with the *Tribune* until 1909, always attempting to fulfill an ambition to affect the future of theater in the United States, but during the last decade of the century the force of his criticism weakened. As a poet, Winter was flagrantly sentimental and romantic. As a critic, his conservative nature and moral bias prompted him to adopt the ethical standards of the "genteel tradition" of writers such as Edmund Clarence Stedman and Bayard Taylor. Seriously disturbed by the vulgar, Winter embraced the ideal, finding it mainly in the writings of Shakespeare, which became the standard by which he judged excellence. To his love of Shakespeare, his understanding of Aristotle, and his substantial knowledge of theater, Winter applied a layer of prejudice vividly expressed in vitriolic or kindly effusive opinions that were seldom at variance with the majority of his readers.

Frightening to the objects of his disdain, Winter's prejudices were also the reason for the decline of his reputation. Because he found moral weakness in Edwin Forrest, he judged his art to be tainted, and he largely ignored the actor. Generally, he did not like foreign actors, and he always praised Edwin Booth and Joseph Jefferson (1829–1905), whom he called "a poet among actors." He disliked realistic drama and did not believe that social problems were fit subjects for plays. Therefore, he could not abide the plays of George Bernard Shaw or Henrik Ibsen, whose work he described as "deadly pessimism." Modern historians have sometimes questioned Winter's evaluations because he openly placed his artistic integrity in jeopardy by borrowing money from actors he reviewed, establishing personal friendships with a number of theater people, accepting trips to London with Augustin Daly, and helping Lawrence Barrett revise George Henry Boker's *Francesca da Rimini* and then enthusiastically praising the results. Yet Winter insisted that he was a fair man, that he always presented the truth. And he argued his position with conviction before the New York Goethe Club in 1889, in an address titled "Relations of the Press and the Stage."

From the 1880s until his death, Winter published a substantial number of biographies (Jefferson, Booth, Ada Rehan, David Belasco), critical studies (Shakespeare), and staged reminiscences. At odds with modern theater, he complained that the theater had "fallen into the clutches of sordid, money-grabbing tradesmen who have degraded it into a bazaar." After he died (in New Brighton on Staten Island, N.Y.) and had long since been replaced in theater circles, he was remembered by another prejudiced writer, H. L. Mencken, as "the greatest bad critic who ever lived."

• Biographical information, letters, and scrapbooks on William Winter exist in the files of Robert Young, Jr., his great-grandson. Personal glimpses of Winter appear in his books of literary and theatrical reminiscences. See especially *Shadows of the Stage* (3 vols., 1892–1895), *Other Days* (1908), *Old Friends* (1909), and *The Wallet of Time* (2 vols., 1913). See also Caroline Ticknor, *Glimpses of Authors* (1922); J. B. Pond, *Eccentricities of Genius* (1900); Richard M. Ludwig, "The Career of William Winter, American Drama Critic" (Ph.D. diss., Harvard Univ., 1950); Daniel J. Watermeier, *Between Actor and Critic: Selected Letters of Edwin Booth and William Winter* (1971); Tice L. Miller, *Bohemians and Critics: American Theatre Criticism in the Nineteenth Century* (1981). An obituary is in the *New York Tribune*, 1 July 1917.

WALTER J. MESERVE

WINTERS, Yvor (17 Oct. 1900–25 Jan. 1968), poet and critic, was born Arthur Yvor Winters in Chicago, Illinois, but grew up in Eagle Rock, California, the son of Harry Lewis Winters and Faith Evangeline Ahnefeldt. In 1917 and 1918 he attended the University of Chicago, but in the fall of 1918 he was diagnosed with tuberculosis, for which he entered a sanatorium in Santa Fe, New Mexico. After his recovery he worked as a schoolteacher in the coal camps of Madrid and Los Cerillos, New Mexico. In 1923 he began attending the University of Colorado, earning a B.A. and an M.A. in romance languages in 1925. Between 1925 and 1927 Winters was an instructor in French and Spanish at the University of Idaho in Moscow. During this time, in 1926, he married Janet Lewis, later an accomplished poet and novelist. The couple had two children.

In 1927 Winters matriculated at Stanford University, receiving his doctorate in English in 1934. He taught at Stanford throughout his career, beginning as an instructor in English in 1928 and rising through the ranks to become a full professor in 1949. In 1961 he was named Albert Guerard Professor of Literature at Stanford, a position he occupied until 1966. After retirement he lived in Los Altos, California.

Winters's first book of poetry, *The Immobile Wind*, was published in 1921. These early poems display the influence of Native-American culture, which absorbed him while he recuperated from tuberculosis in New Mexico. Reflecting the Native-American belief in the manifestation of the spiritual in physical objects, he writes that "Specific things are the material image of art." His early imagist poems and experiments with free verse embody this concept and convey the concreteness and immediacy typical of more prominent imagist poets, such as H.D. and Ezra Pound. Winters's work during this period is characterized by a starkness of imagery and simultaneous breadth of suggestion, and much of it is undoubtedly a response to the poetry of Hart Crane, with whom Winters corresponded between 1926 and 1930. But in the later 1920s Winters abandoned this approach, turning toward a more controlled and technically regular style. In "The Extension and Reintegration of the Human Spirit" (1929) he writes:

> Technique, then, is . . . created by the spirit to make its boundaries more precisely . . . to differentiate itself a little more from "nature," from that which will eventually . . . absorb and destroy it. Technique so understood not only has a place in the moral system, it is the outer boundary of consciousness.

Beyond merely clarifying a matter of poetic taste, Winters here makes formal regularity a moral issue, and much of his later poetry reinforces this connection. This can be seen, for example, in "Orpheus" (1934), a poem with a carefully structured meter and rhyme scheme. The final stanza climaxes with an image of Orpheus dismembered, his excised tongue singing "unmeaning down the stream." In this finely turned classical image of the "natural" poet, Winters displays the intense control of his mature style. The regularity of meter and structure further reflect an apparent fear of the disorder represented by his earlier experimentations with free verse and imagist poetics, and by poets like Hart Crane, to whose memory the poem is dedicated. Crane's work had an early and powerful influence on Winters, and although personal and aesthetic differences put an end to their correspondence in 1930, Winters's dedication of this poem to Crane can be seen as a gesture of respect to the power of a poetic program with which he did not agree. It is Crane, we imagine, who in the poem's climactic line "sings," like the dismembered Orpheus, "unmeaning down the stream." This is the fate of poets who stray beyond "the outer boundary of consciousness." Winters continued to publish poetry throughout his life. His first volume of collected poems appeared in 1952, and a complete collection was published in 1978. Winters's career as a critic began in earnest in 1922 when he published a review of Edward Arlington Robinson's *Collected Poems* in *Poetry* magazine. Subsequently Winters published numerous critical articles and eleven book-length works of criticism, including *Forms of Discovery* (1967), his final work. Well respected for his published criticism, Winters also made a substantial impression on literate minds of his age through unpublished evaluations of the work of friends and students. "I can remember some of the revisions he suggested to me over forty years ago," Donald E. Stanford said, "and looking back at them I think he was right every time." Hart Crane once told Winters: "Believe me when I call myself most fortunate in having a reader who simply *gets* everything on the page!"

Winters's criticism is characterized by his insistence on the possibility of correct evaluation; he was a controversial academician who did not shrink from criticizing many poets, such as Milton and Tennyson, considered sacred by his New Critical contemporaries. In "A Cool Master" (1922), his review of Edwin Arlington Robinson, Winters praises Ralph Waldo Emerson faintly as "slight enough, but at his best a master" and characterizes Emily Dickinson as "a master of a certain dowdy but undeniably effective mannerism, a spinster who may have written her poems to keep time with her broom." Throughout his career Winters made harsh assessments of many popular contemporary poets as well, including Ezra Pound, whom he describes in *Forms of Discovery* (1967) as "a man who is deeply moved by the sound of his own voice," and William Carlos Williams, "a thorough bore in print, except on a few occasions."

The progress of Winters's career as poet and critic embodies a tension between the pull of modernism, with its dedication to structural innovation and skepticism of received forms of order, and a belief in the superiority of more conservative, tightly ordered forms of expression. This tension was already well defined by 1930 in "The Progress of Hart Crane," Winters's first published review of Hart Crane's epic modern poem *The Bridge*. Here Winters codifies his mistrust of the poetics of disorder, arguing that Crane's poems "illustrate the danger inherent in [his] almost blind faith in his moment-to-moment inspiration," danger that Winters blames on "the entire body of anti-intellectualist literature of our time."

This and later reviews led to a falling out between Winters and Crane and defined Winters's position regarding the modernist movement in general. Though Crane and other important modernist poets had an early and profound influence on Winters, his final attitude toward them was one of mistrust. Winters's criticism has since been condemned overly absolutist and impressionistic, but it remains important, like his poetry, for its unique perspective on the mainstream of the modernist movement.

• Although Winters destroyed most of his papers and correspondence, collections exist at Stanford and Princeton Universities. Under the conditions of his will, these papers have been available for quotation only since 1993, twenty-five years after his death. Winters's output as poet and critic was substantial. Books of poetry include *The Magpie's Shadow* (1922), *The Bare Hills: A Book of Poems* (1927), *The Proof* (1930), *The Journey and Other Poems* (1931), *Before Disaster* (1934), *Poems* (1940), *The Giant Weapon* (1943), *Three Poems* (1950), and *The Early Poems of Yvor Winters* (1966). Winters also contributed poetry to the *Kenyon Review Gyroscope*, *Poetry*, the *Sewanee Review*, and other publications. Winters's major critical works include *The Testament of a Stone, Being Notes on the Mechanics of the Poetic Image* (1927), *Primitivism and Decadence: A Study of American Experimental Poetry* (1937), *Maule's Curse: Seven Studies in the History of American Obscurantism* (1938), *The Anatomy of Nonsense* (1943), *Edwin Arlington Robinson* (1946), *The Brink of Darkness* (1947), *The Function of Criticism* (1957), *On Modern Poets* (1959), *The Poetry of W. B. Yeats* (1960), and *The Poetry of J. V. Cunningham* (1961). The most complete bibliographical source is Grosvenor Powell, *Yvor Winters: An Annotated Bibliography, 1919–1982* (1983).

Biographical information is available in rich if scattered detail in the *Southern Review* 17, no. 4 (1981); the entire issue is devoted to analyses of Winters's poetry, criticism, and life as an educator. Further biographical information may be found in David Levin, "Yvor Winters at Stanford," *Virginia Quarterly Review* 54 (Summer 1978): 454–73. A very useful guide to Winters's poetry is Elizabeth Isaacs, *An Introduction to the Poetry of Yvor Winters* (1981). A brief obituary appears in *Contemporary Authors* 25–28 R (First Revision Series).

DAVID LAWRENCE ARNOLD

WINTHROP, John (12 Jan. 1588–26 Mar. 1649), first governor and chronicler of Massachusetts-Bay, was born in Edwardstone, Suffolk, England, the son of Adam Winthrop, lord of Groton Manor, and Anne Browne. His early life befitted a scion of the aspiring lesser gentry: matriculation at Trinity College, Cambridge, in 1603; marriage in 1605 to Mary Forth (she died in 1615), a wealthy landowner's sole heiress (shortcircuiting his college career); subsequent advantageous matches to Thomasine Clopton in 1615 (she died a year later) and Margaret Tyndal in 1618; and responsibility for managing the family lands, culminating with his becoming lord of the manor by 1618. He also took up law, entering Gray's Inn at age twenty-five and sitting as a county justice at twenty-eight. By the late 1620s he had attained minor prominence in London legal circles, drafting bills for Parliament, winning appointment as common attorney to the king's Court of Wards and Liveries in 1627, and gaining entrance to the Inner Temple the next year. Business trips from Groton made him pine for Margaret, his helpmate, consort, and affectionate "freinde" (*Winthrop Papers*, vol. 1, p. 253); their correspondence reveals a profound mutual passion enhanced by faith that in loving each other they loved God best. At her death in 1647 he married Martha Coytmore, widow of a Charlestown merchant; she died in 1660. Winthrop fathered sixteen children, eight of whom died young; the achievements of John Winthrop, Jr., his firstborn, as governor of Connecticut, entrepreneur, technologist, and scientist solidified the family's prominence in New England.

Winthrop embraced Puritanism, a Reformed Protestant temperament stressing humans' innate depravity and the necessity of undergoing conversion, a psychologically intense "new birth" into salvation effecting Saints' (regenerates') vocation to God and empowering them to carry out His commands. Winthrop's scruples about sin, agitated spasmodically in adolescence, intensified under the preaching of Ezekiel Culverwell, rector of Great Stambridge, Essex. At nineteen Winthrop began recording his spiritual travails and continued intermittently for thirty years; in his "Christian Experience," a classic text of Puritan introspection penned on his forty-ninth birthday, he decried his transgressions, admitted his incapacity to amend them unaided, and celebrated Christ's free grace, recapitulating his conversion to fortify his campaign against iniquity in general and Anne Hutchinson, whose heresies were riving Massachusetts, in particular. Puritans channeled personal devotion into collective activity to purge England's church of "papist" habits and its society of moral decay. In Massachusetts Winthrop made creating a godly polity and protecting the true church paramount concerns.

Puritans interpreted mundane events as evidence of God's Providence, and like fellow Saints Winthrop in the 1620s construed multiplying signs of His controversy with England. Depression unhinged the economy, Charles I feuded with Parliament, Arminians spoke liberal theology in the king's ear, and their leader, Bishop William Laud, hunted nonconformists down. The economic tailspin depleted Winthrop's rents, enlarged his debts, and frustrated his ability to provide for his elder sons, now coming of age. More income vanished in 1629 when he either lost or quit his position at the Court of Wards. Personal reverses encouraged thoughts of emigration, but he cast them in the context of wider woes. "This lande growes weary of her Inhabitantes," he lamented; Catholic victories abroad threatened Protestants at home, but God may have preserved New England as "a refuge" from "the generall callamity." Passing there would spread the gospel, thwart the Jesuits, increase settlers' prosperity, build fresh congregations, and spurn Old England's corrupted "Fountaines of Learning and Religion" (*Winthrop Papers*, vol. 2, pp. 138–39). On 28 July 1629 Winthrop met with heads of the Massachusetts Bay Company to discuss settling a colony and transferring the patent to America, beyond the Crown's effective grasp. On 26 August he and eleven others signed the "Cambridge Agreement," pledging to establish a "plantation" provided the corporation's government moved with them. The Company agreed three days later and on 20 October elected him governor. Aboard the flagship *Arbella*, Winthrop and six others issued "The Humble Request" (7 Apr. 1630), declaring they did not separate from the English Church and imploring its prayers; by "church" they intended only Saints, not the entire parochial body. Four ships, carrying some 700 passengers, embarked the next day. Winthrop landed at Salem on 12 June. At some point he composed the lay sermon "A Modell of Christian Charity"; traditionally ascribed to the time at sea, it may well date from a communion service celebrated before the fleet departed. Adducing Matthew 5:14 to proclaim "that wee shall be as a Citty vpon a Hill," he rehearsed his vision of godly elders ruling a highly stratified community dedicated to the common good and pulsing with Christian love. By affirming that "the eies of all people are vppon vs," he was not, as some historians suggest, broadcasting New England's putative errand to erect a holy commonwealth others might model but, rather, invoking the world's witness to underline failure's cost: dealing "falsely" with "our god in this worke," he warned, would allow "enemies to speake euill" of His "wayes" (*Winthrop Papers*, vol. 2, p. 295).

The Massachusetts Bay Company's charter of 18 March 1629 conferred authority on magistrates—governor, deputy governor, assistants—and freemen—stockholders entitled to elect officers and convene with them in quarterly General Courts to pass laws. Winthrop won the governorship twelve times, serving in 1629–1634 (the first term was prolonged), 1637–1640, 1642–1644, and 1646–1649. His gentry status, piety, and self-possession drew others to his lead, yet his commanding mien and elevated view of magisterial prerogatives raised suspicions that he would make himself the state and resulted in the freemen periodically ostracizing him from the governorship. Yet he never slid far from the governor's right hand, serving as the deputy in 1636–1637 and 1644–1646 and as assistant in 1634–1636 and 1640–1642. His successful career, given an electorate who respected social prominence and a calling to administer God's laws while demanding their English rights and mistrusting rulers' inherent sinfulness, testifies to both his adroitness in accommodating popular pressures and the colonists' abiding trust that he possessed the "character of a good ruler."

Winthrop's political philosophy presumed the superior judgment of a small elite: "the best part is always the least," he argued, "and of that best part the wiser part is always the lesser" (*Winthrop Papers*, vol. 4, p. 54). In calling magisterial authority a divine ordinance and judges "Gods vpon earthe," he demeaned neither the freemen's privileges nor an individual's right to justice: the magistrate owed his position (if not its powers) to the voters, who could remove him, and a judge had to display God's "wisdome and mercye" in prescribing penalties (*Winthrop Papers*, vol. 4, p. 476). Magistrates exhibited the same infirmities as did any human beings, Winthrop acknowledged, but he preferred to risk hoarding power with a wise few than dispersing it among the self-interested freemen. Hobbling the magistrates would turn Massachusetts into a "meere Democratie," the "meanest and worst of all formes of Government," dissolving necessary distinctions between rulers and ruled (*Winthrop Papers*, vol. 4, p. 383).

During the settlement's first four years, Winthrop supervised the government's evolution from the organs of a mercantile corporation into the institutions of a self-proclaimed commonwealth. He was willing to expand popular privileges for pragmatic reasons—conducting the first General Court in America (19 Oct. 1630) as a mass meeting that extended freemanship to the majority of adult males, thereby attaching them to the colony's interests—but he more often hedged them in. The assembly that enfranchised 108 new freemen also ceded the assistants both legislative authority and sole right to elect the governor and deputy. In May 1631 the Court secured the Saints' control over the state by restricting freemanship to male church members. Winthrop and seven assistants lowered the quorum necessary to conduct business, and for the next three years he summoned only one Court annually instead of four. Winthrop made numerous decisions unilaterally, arguably to the colony's benefit. Plotting town sites, obtaining food, warning potential migrants to come adequately prepared, and even spending his own money for public supplies, he held Massachusetts together despite a few hundred deaths and ensured that the colony did not endure the "starving time" others faced.

Once provided with food and shelter, settlers disputed the magistrates' dominion. Watertowners petitioned in 1632 that the Court had taxed them illegally to pay for fortifying Newtown (Cambridge). Winthrop explained that the Massachusetts government was a parliament, not a self-perpetuating oligarchy, and the townspeople accepted his conclusion that, having elected representatives to the Court, they had duly consented to the levy. The next Court nevertheless restored the freemen's right to elect the governor and deputy, and authorized the appointment of men from each town to consult about raising public funds. That summer, Deputy Governor Thomas Dudley privately berated Winthrop for reasons both personal—he envied Winthrop's eminence—and political, alleging that Winthrop's judgments were too lenient and that his claim as governor to wield greater authority than did the assistants was unwarrantable. Winthrop refuted complaints of malfeasance and maintained that the charter granted him powers customary by common law, but the charges rang true for many voters. Before the Election Court of 1634, some freemen demanded to see the patent and accused him of abrogating their legislative rights. Winthrop temporized, offering to summon representatives annually to review existing laws and consult with the Court about assessments, but he yielded too little too late. On 14 May the freemen demoted him to assistant. The new Court reinstated quarterly meetings and commissioned each town to send deputies to the Court as the freemen's delegates.

A variant dynamic played out in Boston. The charter made no provisions for municipal jurisdictions, allowing them to grow according to local circumstances. Winthrop's prominence and friendly ties to many Bostonians made him their natural leader. The assistants appointed him one of the town's justices of the peace in 1630, and the next year, when he planned to relocate to the colony's proposed capital at Newtown, his neighbors successfully importuned him to stay. Winthrop's position combined the duties of an English justice of the peace with the status of a magistrate's; he tried criminal cases, determined suits, issued licenses, and regulated trade. Simultaneously, an informal town government that accrued powers delegated by the General Court coalesced from meetings of the Boston church. In 1633 William Coddington, himself an assistant, charged Winthrop with taking away inhabitants' "liberty" by unilaterally naming a committee to distribute town lands, but Winthrop pointed out that he had acted at residents' behest. By 1 September 1634, a standing committee of ten including Winthrop was managing Boston affairs, and in 1636 the General Court formally recognized town governments.

Winthrop never recovered the expansive authority he enjoyed before 1634. Thenceforth he always upheld the charter, but he continued to urge liberal magisterial discretion. A minor brouhaha ensued over the Court's creation in 1636 of a Standing Council elected for life to exercise ill-defined powers between Court sessions; fearing a closed oligarchy, the deputies in 1639 forced the Court to limit its powers. Winthrop accepted the restriction grudgingly, and his attitude fueled fears that he coveted a hereditary governorship. Magnified by some ministers, this disquietude helped oust him from the office in 1640. A more substantive issue involved the deputies' desire for a system of positive law to check the magistrates' judicial license. Laws, Winthrop argued, should emerge from precedents and acquit judges from rendering prescribed penalties, which could contravene both human justice and scriptural example. Massachusetts's statutes might cross England's, imperiling the charter; it would be better to base law on custom, unpleadable against the patent, than to devise a potentially unconstitutional code. The magistrates stalled, but the deputies insisted, and the Court approved a "Body of Liberties" in 1641. Winthrop thought this compilation sufficient, but Robert Child's charges that Massachusetts did indeed violate English law changed his mind. A new compilation, the "Laws and Liberties," appeared in 1648.

The struggle between magistrates and deputies intensified over whether the former could exercise a "negative voice," that is, veto the latter's actions. The issue climaxed in 1642 when the magistrates ruled that a contested sow belonged to Robert Keayne, a wealthy merchant previously fined for usury, blocking the deputies' determination for Goodwife Sherman. The decision spawned popular grumbles that the negative voice had hindered justice and deserved abolition. Winthrop justified the veto power in a treatise that also aspersed some of his opponents, for which remarks he apologized; subsequent efforts conveyed the case more diplomatically. "Defense of the Negative Vote" (1643) fixed that power as a fundamental part of the government, sanctioned by the charter and consonant with Scripture. In 1644 the Court divided assistants and deputies into separate houses, giving each a veto. Almost immediately, the deputies questioned the extent of the magistrates' authority between Court sessions and their judicial discretion in the absence of express law. The two sides submitted their quarrel to clerical mediation; in November 1644 the elders recognized that interim juristic power lay solely with the magistrates but allowed the deputies competence in other areas and recommended judicial discretion within prescriptively legislated bounds. This qualified support for the magistrates' pretensions deflated the deputies' drive for a select committee to govern between sessions, but the affair excited one last campaign against Winthrop and his views.

The deputies' carping about despotism drove Winthrop in July to circulate a "Discourse on Arbitrary Government." Defining "arbitrary" as a government where people neither chose the authorities set over them nor enjoyed the rule of law, Winthrop denied that either condition applied to Massachusetts, educing its patent, statutes, and history as evidence. The deputies hoped to censure the book. Failing that, they bided their time until they thought Winthrop had blatantly exceeded his authority. An occasion appeared the next spring. Acting as a justice of the peace, Winthrop bound over to the Court of Assistants some participants in a dispute concerning the captaincy of the Hingham militia. Eighty-one petitioners protested that by issuing warrants forcing some townspeople to answer charges and summoning others to appear in court he had infringed their liberties. Winthrop allowed the General Court to try him on a criminal complaint, and after it fully acquitted him, he improved the occasion by reminding the assembly that magistrates may err but that the people owe them obedience unless they willfully do wrong. For Winthrop the trial ended in at least partial political victory and personal vindication. Cognizant of his popularity, perhaps crediting his supposed tyranny less and their own accreted powers more, the deputies ceased their remonstrations for two decades. Returned to the governorship in 1646, Winthrop was continually reelected until his death.

Winthrop's economic dealings occasioned less discord. Believing that moral law should frame economic transactions, he accepted just price theory—a vendor should sell at a cost determined by communal consensus of an item's worth—favored wage limits, and condemned excessive profit-taking. But, against John Cotton, Boston's teaching elder, he approved commercial loans with interest if the borrower held means to repay. Acquisitiveness was not wicked if moderated, nor wealth achieved in one's calling improper, since it resulted from honest labor cultivating God's munificence in His service. Winthrop's own income came from his offices and estates. The Court extended him yearly salaries, but in turn he shared his pockets with the state; a committee appointed in 1634 to audit his public expenditures discovered the commonwealth substantially in his debt. He owned extensive lands on which servants raised crops and livestock but sold most of them in the early 1640s to liquidate a £2,500 debit incurred by his steward's defalcations, a financial embarrassment that helped coax him from the governorship in 1640. Voluntary contributions from friends, his church, and some of the towns helped him recover solvency. Besides agricultural ventures, Winthrop built the first ship in Massachusetts, operated a windmill and a weir, and invested in Narragansett lands.

Winthrop's concern that market operations would derange social relations if left unchecked by moral superintendence predisposed him to favor extensive governmental intervention in the economy. He aimed principally to preserve social order but additionally to facilitate appropriate enterprise and encourage growth. In the 1630s the General Court fought inflation with wage and price controls, which collapsed under the high demand for labor. To offset the depression induced by England's civil war in the 1640s, the Court passed anti-debt legislation and attempted to stimulate domestic production through grants, bounties, tax incentives, and monopoly privileges.

Church and state occupied separate spheres in seventeenth-century Massachusetts—ministers could advise but not sit on the General Court—yet they cooperated intimately to insure moral and political order. Magistrates had authority to punish religious error. Winthrop welcomed the responsibility and, in Roger Williams's case, exercised it judiciously. Salem's teaching elder, Williams challenged the validity of land titles held without the Amerindians' assent, denied the magistrate's right to punish offenses against the First Table (the first four commandments), refused communion with congregations he considered impure, and called Charles I a minion of Anti-Christ—a "strange boldnesse," Winthrop mused, and he pressed Williams to keep his opinions private (*Winthrop Papers*, vol. 3, p. 148). When Williams persisted, the General Court in October 1635 banished him as of the following spring, but he continued preaching nevertheless. In January the magistrates decided to ship him to England. Winthrop leaked their plans, allowing Williams to escape and earning his undying gratitude.

Winthrop displayed far less lenity toward Anne Hutchinson, the "*American Jesabel*" (*Antinomian Controversy*, p. 310) whose Antinomian posture that grace frees Saints from the moral law undermined the Puritan state's foundations. By denying that good works can witness to one's salvation, Hutchinson challenged the churches' ability to identify regenerates, thus exploding freemanship's religious rationale, and by insisting that orthodox doctrine devalued the Holy Spirit, she encouraged followers to denounce the colony's ministers for preaching a dead faith. Winthrop could do little at first. A founding pillar of the Boston church, he was isolated by its Antinomian majority, barely deflecting a motion to install Hutchinson's kinsman John Wheelwright as a second teaching elder. Elected deputy governor in 1636, Winthrop could not overrule Governor Henry Vane, an ardent Hutchinsonian. Frustration ended in 1637 when the freemen, in an election fraught with potential violence, returned him to command. Under Winthrop's aegis, a ministerial synod denounced Hutchinson's heresies, and the General Court expelled Wheelwright from the colony. That November, Winthrop presided over her climactic examination before the Court and pronounced its sentence of banishment; next March the Boston church excommunicated her. Winthrop understood her subsequent passage of a hydatidiform mole (a mass of cysts) as a "monstrous birth" providentially signifying her errors, his insensitivity to her human suffering betraying, perhaps, his horror at how great a threat to Massachusetts's social order she posed (Hosmer, *Winthrop's Journal*, vol. 1, p. 277).

The Antinomian controversy intensified efforts to quash dissent. In 1643 Winthrop dispatched soldiers to arrest Samuel Gorton, claiming jurisdiction over Gorton's settlement in Rhode Island and charging his adherents primarily with civil offenses. Their letters to the Court vented heresy, however, and on trial Gorton asserted a radical human divinity established by Christ's indwelling presence that freed true Christians from instituted authority. The Gortonists "could not write true English," Winthrop fumed, but did not balk at parsing difficult scriptures (Hosmer, vol. 2, p. 147). The assistants urged executing them for blasphemy, but the deputies demurred, so the Court sentenced them to chains and hard labor in several towns, only to find them attracting the townsfolk. Ultimately, the Court sent them away. Anabaptists fared no better. Appalled by their increasing number, the Court in 1644 decreed banishing anyone who persevered in condemning infant baptism or denying the magistrate's right to prosecute First Table offenses. Winthrop sympathized with a petition to repeal the law and pursued uniformity more temperately than did many magistrates. When the majority expelled a Captain Partridge and his family during winter even after he renounced some errors, Winthrop averred that "hospitality" and hope for further reformation ought to inspire "more moderation and indulgence of human infirmity." According to traditions current in the eighteenth century, he refused on his deathbed to sign an ejection warrant, insisting that "I have done too much of that work already" (Hosmer, vol. 1, p. 260, 177n).

Keeping the Holy Commonwealth's political and ecclesiastical arrangements Puritan meant holding England at bay. To Winthrop, the charter gave Massachusetts total sovereignty over its internal affairs while subscribing formal allegiance to England, a position he held against Crown and Parliament alike. Disturbed by reports that the Bay Colony had cast off England's church and law, Charles I in 1634 appointed Archbishop Laud chair of the Commission for Regulating Plantations. Massachusetts prepared to fight, and the Court named five commanders, including Winthrop, to lead troops should war ensue, but the commission had no resources to mount an invasion and instead took action against the charter. Winthrop evaded or ignored repeated requests to return the patent, even after the commission claimed to have condemned it. Procrastination worked. The commission's legal proceedings were faulty, and the agency collapsed in the civil war. The colonists' sympathies in that conflict lay with Parliament, but in England the spread of presbyterianism and widespread clamor for religious toleration exposed New England's exclusionary congregationalism to increasing criticism from erstwhile allies. Winthrop watched warily as Parliament created the Warwick Commission, which granted self-government to Roger Williams's plantation and recognized Gorton's title. He refused to concede Parliament any control over Massachusetts law, a stand tested in 1646 when Robert Child, a wealthy doctor, and six other Remonstrants petitioned the General Court to lift the religious restrictions on freemanship and to allow presbyterianism. Winthrop preferred to negotiate with them privately, but the Remonstrants appealed for Parliament to impose English law and liberty of conscience, forcing a confrontation. Winthrop detained Child just before he could leave for England, preferred new charges on the basis of documents discovered in Child's baggage, delayed trial until the Court dispatched an agent to England, and fined Child heavily before finally releasing him. By the time Child reached England, the Warwick Commission had already endorsed Massachusetts's authority. Uneasy about presbyterian influences on both sides of the Atlantic, the ministers applied to the Court for a synod to codify their ecclesiology. Against the deputies, Winthrop urged the Court's right to summon them; a compromise gave it power to "invite." The elders issued the "Cambridge Platform," a comprehensive statement of congregational church governance and discipline, in 1648.

Winthrop conducted a pragmatic diplomacy calculated to expand Massachusetts's territory and commerce. In 1643 Charles de La Tour, a claimant to the governorship of French Acadia, solicited aid against his rival Charles, Sieur d'Aulnay. Winthrop weighed the dangers of meddling in French affairs and consorting with "papists" against the possible benefits of trade, the risk of offending a possible enemy to the colony's shipping, and assurance in God's management of dealings even with Catholics before allowing La Tour to recruit men and supplies. Winthrop acted after consulting only a rump of the magistrates, a precipitousness he regretted when the expedition failed; the resulting outcry helped drop him to deputy governor in 1644. When d'Aulnay gained the upper hand, Winthrop opened relations with him. Toward the Dutch in New Netherland he proceeded guardedly, encouraging trade and protesting territorial encroachment in the Connecticut River valley.

Winthrop's course with Amerindians was complex. Like most seventeenth-century Europeans, he considered them cultural inferiors living at a primitive stage of civilization and lacking true religion—but he supported proselytizing efforts only when tribes submitted politically to Massachusetts. He attended some of John Eliot's earliest sermons to native audience, but Eliot's enterprise received little direct assistance from the General Court. Winthrop adopted the doctrine of *vacuum domicilium* to justify Massachusetts's territorial possessions—the Amerindians had a natural right only to such land as they could improve, and the colonists could take the rest. This theory, although defining "use" more narrowly than did the natives, did not extinguish their title. Winthrop negotiated the submission of several bands to Massachusetts's dominion, but in criticizing Acadian trading policy he called the Amerindians "a free people" whose commercial affairs the French should not limit (Hosmer, vol. 2, p. 326). He accorded independent tribes sovereignty and dealt with them as such, shifting alliances as bands came to support or inhibit the colony's interest. He accepted the Pequots' offer to trade with Massachusetts—at the cost of their becoming tributaries—but in 1637 committed the colony to helping Connecticut and Plymouth destroy the tribe, thereby encouraging both intercolonial cooperation and Massachusetts's claims in the Connecticut River valley. He defended a treaty with Miantonomo, sachem of the Narragansetts, in 1636, then connived at his assassination by Uncas, sachem of the Mohegans, in 1643 when the Narragansetts conspired against New England. This plot helped precipitate the Confederation of New England, an entente among Massachusetts, Connecticut, Plymouth, and New Haven. A leading advocate of intercolonial union, Winthrop signed the articles of confederation for Massachusetts with Dudley and served as president in 1643 and 1645.

Winthrop's most significant writing is his manuscript history of New England, unpublished until the nineteenth century. Begun probably as a sea journal to inform family and friends about voyaging across the ocean, and then continued as a chronicle of God's acts in New England, the "History" begins with the fleet weighing anchor on 29 March 1630 and concludes on 11 January 1649 with a providential review of recent drownings. In between, it provides indispensable commentary on New England's development. Scholars have read it both as an autobiography cataloging the spiritual advances of self and community and as a defense of Winthrop's administration. However construed, the document is fundamental for understanding the "Puritan experiment."

Contemporaries regarded Winthrop as the preeminent figure of early New England, and historians concur. The rapidity with which Massachusetts's political, social, and religious institutions cohered derives from numerous factors, but to the degree that individuals mattered, Winthrop was the person most responsible for ensuring the colony's survival, shaping its institutions, and securing its public order. That prominence has made him the first generation's representative figure and subjected him to caricature: Cotton Mather apotheosized him as "Nehemias Americanus" governing the erection of a new Jerusalem, but others have pilloried him for evincing a persecutory self-righteousness inimical to the tolerant, democratic, and secular society America became. The tendency to transform man into symbol is epitomized by incessant invocations of his identifying Massachusetts as a "city on a hill" in order to certify and exalt a special providence for the United States, whereas he employed the phrase in a far more limited sense. A realistic appraisal would assess him as having lived according to his culture's highest standards and governed arbitrarily but broad-mindedly. Ruthless in defending his ideal commonwealth—witness Hutchinson and Child—he ordinarily ruled with moderation and equity, for which other civil and ecclesiastical leaders sometimes upbraided him. His bankruptcy proceedings displayed both his personal integrity—he insisted on honoring every obligation though he might well have contested many—and the respect he earned even from opponents: Richard Dummer, a principal Hutchinsonian disarmed for his activities, gave Winthrop £100. Having mastered himself, he could master others; self-confident but not complacent, he set down in the "History" good deeds and misdeeds alike for humans and God to judge.

• The Massachusetts Historical Society has published the majority of its Winthrop manuscript holdings in the *Winthrop Papers, 1498–1649* (5 vols., 1929–1947), ed. Worthington Chauncey Ford (vol. 1), Stewart Mitchell (vol. 2), and Allyn B. Forbes (vols. 3–5); see Malcolm Freiberg, "The Winthrops and Their Papers," *Massachusetts Historical Society Proceedings* 80 (1968): 681–705. One should also consult Robert C. Winthrop, *The Life and Letters of John Winthrop* (2 vols., 1864–1867). Winthrop's manuscript history has been edited by James Savage as *The History of New England from 1630 to 1649* (2 vols., 1825; 2d ed., 1853) and by James K. Hosmer as *Winthrop's Journal "History of New England"* (2 vols., 1908); scholars use both. Also see "John Winthrop Writes His Journal," *William & Mary Quarterly*, 3d ser., 41 (1984): 185–212. Nathaniel B. Shurtleff, ed., *Records of the Governor and Company of the Massachusetts Bay in New England*, vols. 1–2 (1853), compiles the General Court's proceedings during Winthrop's lifetime. David D. Hall, ed., *The Antinomian Controversy, 1636–1638: A Documentary History* (1968; 2d ed., 1990), includes Winthrop's "A Short Story . . . of the Antinomians . . . ." The standard biography, very sympathetic, is Edmund S. Morgan, *The Puritan Dilemma: The Story of John Winthrop* (1958); see also James G. Moseley, *John Winthrop's World* (1992); Lee Schweninger, *John Winthrop* (1990); Samuel Eliot Morison, *Builders of the Bay Colony* (1930); and J. H. Twichell, *John Winthrop* (1891). On the Winthrop family see Richard S. Dunn, *Puritans and Yankees: The Winthrop Dynasty of New England 1630–1717* (1962), a counterpoise to Morgan, and Lawrence Shaw Mayo, *The Winthrop Family in America* (1948); see also Joseph James Muskett, ed., *Evidences of the Winthrops of Groton, co. Suffolk, England* (4 pts., 1894–1896). On Winthrop's spirituality, see Charles L. Cohen, *God's Caress: The Psychology of Puritan Religious Experience* (1986), and Daniel B. Shea, Jr., *Spiritual Autobiography in Early America* (1968). Virginia DeJohn Anderson, *New England's Generation* (1991), covers the Great Migration; for Winthrop in particular, see Darrett B. Rutman, *John Winthrop's Decision for America, 1629* (1975). For political developments in early Massachusetts, see Charles M. Andrews, *The Colonial Period of American History*, vol. 1 (1934); for their social context in Boston, Darrett B. Rutman, *Winthrop's Boston* (1965). Winthrop's political ideas receive attention in T. H. Breen, *The Character of the Good Ruler* (1970); Stephen Foster, *Their Solitary Way* (1971); M. Susan Power, *Before the Convention: Religion and the Founders* (1984); and Stanley Gray, "The Political Thought of John Winthrop," *New England Quarterly* 3 (1930): 681–705. On economic policy, see E. A. J. Johnson, "Economic Ideas of John Winthrop," *New England Quarterly* 3 (1930): 235–50, and Bernard Bailyn, *The New England Merchants in the Seventeenth Century* (1955). For the relationship of church and state, see Perry Miller, *Orthodoxy in Massachusetts 1630–1650* (1933), and David D. Hall, *The Faithful Shepherd* (1972); Philip F. Gura, *A Glimpse of Sion's Glory* (1984), details the sectarian critique. For Winthrop as Puritan historian, see Peter Gay, *A Loss of Mastery* (1966); as emblem of Puritan history, Sacvan Bercovitch, *Puritan Origins of the American Self* (1975).

CHARLES L. COHEN

WINTHROP, John (14 Mar. 1638–27 Nov. 1707), soldier and governor of Connecticut, known as Fitz or Fitz-John, was born in Ipswich, Massachusetts, the son of John Winthrop Jr. (1606–1676), governor of Connecticut, and Elizabeth Reade. In 1646 Winthrop and his family moved to New London, Connecticut, where he lived for most of his life. After two years of formal education he turned to farming and then went to England to serve in the English army (1658–1660), reaching the rank of captain. He participated in General George Monck's march from Scotland to London in 1660, which resulted in the restoration of King Charles II.

Upon his return to New London in 1663, Winthrop devoted himself to farming and land speculation. In the 1670s he and his common-law wife, Elizabeth Tongue, had their only child. Winthrop served after 1672 as captain of the New London County militia and in the Third Dutch War (1673–1674), in which he successfully led colonial forces on eastern Long Island. He also served two terms as a New London representative to the Connecticut General Court (1671 and 1678). After the Massachusetts charter was nullified by the British because the colony had failed to honor English law in full, Winthrop and his brother Wait Still of Massachusetts were named to the council of Joseph Dudley's interim Massachusetts government

(1686) and then to the council of Sir Edmund Andros's Dominion of New England (1686–1689), with Fitz-John representing Connecticut. In 1687 he was commissioned as a colonel and then as a major general in charge of the militias of Connecticut, Massachusetts, and the Narragansett Country. Although suspected of plotting the April 1689 overthrow of the Dominion of New England, Winthrop was not directly involved. He did not serve in the reconstituted Connecticut government although elected a magistrate in May 1689.

In August 1690 Winthrop led a colonial-Indian force from Albany against Montreal during King William's War (1689–1697). Neither his effort nor that of William Phips against Quebec was successful, and Winthrop was arrested for a short time by New York's revolutionary ruler, Jacob Leisler. In October 1690 Connecticut's General Court exonerated Winthrop of any charges of misadministration or disloyalty in the king's interests.

In September 1693 Winthrop was sent by the Connecticut government to England to present a petition seeking reinstatement of the Charter of 1662, which had been suspended during Connecticut's eighteen months in the Dominion of New England. Beset by internal conflict concerning whether or not Connecticut had acted legally in unilaterally reintroducing the charter in May 1689, as well as by the external efforts of the royal governors of Massachusetts and New York to control Connecticut, the government of the colony hoped Winthrop would regain Connecticut's corporate autonomy. During his stay in England (1693–1697), Winthrop was successful despite the volatile context of imperial war and the government's efforts to achieve more centralized control of England's colonies.

Returning to Connecticut a hero, Winthrop was elected governor in 1698 and served in that office until his death nine years later in Boston. While the colony was successful in obstructing three new imperial attempts to reorganize England's private colonies (1701–1706), Winthrop's long-standing legal problems over inheritance ironically led the two plaintiffs who had brought suit against him to appeal to English authority against the governor. These actions added some weight to the charges raised by the imperial-minded that Connecticut's practical independence was antithetical both to the rights of English colonists and the interests of England. Despite a partial victory for one of the plaintiffs, Winthrop was the ultimate victor, and through him, Connecticut. Thus, while Fitz-John Winthrop did not attain the colony-building stature of his grandfather John Winthrop (1588–1649), the first governor of Massachusetts, nor the scholarly, entrepreneurial, and political achievements of his father John, he served his adopted colony well, and he died a much beloved and revered figure.

• The bulk of the manuscript collection of the Winthrop family papers is located at the Massachusetts Historical Society in Boston. Many of these documents have been published in the society's *Collections* and *Proceedings*. Winthrop's governorship may be followed in the appropriate volumes in the Connecticut Archives at the Connecticut State Library in Hartford and in J. Hammond Trumbull and Charles J. Hoadley, eds., *Public Records of the Colony of Connecticut*, vols. 4–5 (1850–1890). The best biographical account of Winthrop is Richard S. Dunn, *Puritans and Yankees: The Winthrop Dynasty of New England, 1630–1717* (1962). Additional information may be gathered from Richard L. Bushman, *From Puritan to Yankee: Character and the Social Order in Connecticut, 1690–1765* (1967); Robert J. Taylor, *Colonial Connecticut, a History* (1979); and Richard R. Johnson, *Adjustment to Empire: The New England Colonies, 1675–1715* (1981).

THOMAS W. JODZIEWICZ

WINTHROP, John (8 Dec. 1714–3 May 1779), scientist, was born in Boston, Massachusetts, the son of Adam Winthrop, a merchant and judge, and Anne Wainwright. John was a fifth generation descendant of Governor John Winthrop. At age thirteen Winthrop entered Harvard, his social status acknowledged by being "placed" first in his class. Intellectual crosscurrents of Congregational theology, Newtonian science, and Enlightenment ideas left lasting impressions on him. Copious entries in his "Book of Extracts" from the classics, English writers, and poets reveal the breadth of his inquiring, ordered mind. Graduating in 1732, he plunged into further studies and received an A.M. in 1735.

In 1738 Winthrop became a candidate for the endowed Hollisian Professorship of the Mathematics and of Natural and Experimental Philosophy, to succeed Isaac Greenwood, who was dismissed by the Board of Overseers for "gross intemperance by excessive drinking to the Dishonor of God" (Overseers Records, vol. 1, p. 154, Harvard University Archives). Suspicions that Winthrop's religious beliefs were unorthodox were quieted. Rival Nathan Prince's objections that he "Knew no more of Philosophy than a Fowl" were ignored. Barely twenty-four years old, John Winthrop was ceremoniously installed on 2 January 1739, beginning a remarkable forty-year scientific career.

A disciple of Isaac Newton, Winthrop emphasized the discovery of natural laws. He was less interested than Benjamin Franklin in practical applications of science, far more in developing scientific understanding in his students and the public. His course, "Experimental Philosophy," was notable, introducing mechanics, optics, magnetism, and the laws of motion through lectures and experiments. In 1746 he made the first classroom demonstrations of electricity, and in the 1750s he lectured on fluxions (calculus). John Adams and Jeremy Belknap took extensive notes on his lucid lectures and were intellectually whetted by their experience. Benjamin Thompson (Count Rumford) vividly remembered Winthrop's felicitous explications, while Harvard president Samuel Langdon remarked that "he had the happy talent of communicating his ideas in the easiest and most elegant manner" (S. Langdon, *The High Value of a Great and Good Name* [1779], p. 18).

Imaginative, clear-thinking, and analytical, Winthrop was an unassuming person who could with equal ease discuss philosophical matters or oversee the delivery of milk to the college buttery from his small Cambridge farm. The Reverend Charles Chauncy expressed Bostonians' esteem for Winthrop, remarking that "none will dispute his being the greatest Mathematician and Philosopher in this Country" (Chauncy to Ezra Stiles, 6 May 1768, Stiles manuscripts, Yale University). Winthrop's international reputation was established through publications, largely by the Royal Society, on diverse topics such as planetary transits, the nature of comets and earthquakes, and the aberration of light.

Unexpectedly noticing a sunspot on the haze-shrouded sun in April 1739, Winthrop jotted in his notebook, "I plainly saw *with my naked eye* a very large and remarkable spot" (Winthrop Diary, Winthrop papers, Harvard University Archives). He studied the phenomenon with Harvard's eight-foot telescope, discovering several additional sunspots, and sketched their appearance. Briefly he added, "At night a considerable borealis" (northern lights), leaving uncertain whether he surmised the interrelationship of the two phenomena. In 1740 Winthrop observed a rare transit of Mercury across the face of the sun. He sent his meticulous observations to the Royal Society, since "Mercury had never as yet been seen entering upon or going off the Sun's Limb at his descending Node." With Harvard's 24-foot telescope and a borrowed watch, fortunately showing seconds, he produced a valid record that commanded attention (Royal Society, *Philosophical Transactions* 42 [1742/1743]: 573).

Ever alert to natural phenomena, Winthrop noted in his meteorological record that on 18 November 1755 "we were alarmed w[i]th a most terrible Earthquake" (Winthrop papers, Massachusetts Historical Society). He timed the shock at 4:23 A.M., although in his *Lecture on Earthquakes* (1755) he more precisely established that the earthquake had stopped his pendulum clock at 4:11 and 35 seconds. Winthrop's account to the Royal Society proved that "the first motion of the earth was . . . a pulse, or . . . an undulation," producing simultaneous horizontal and vertical movement, for its day a major seismological discovery (Royal Society, *Philosophical Transactions* 50 [1757]: 2). He further established the direction, duration, and epicenter of the quake. In a long lecture to the student body, he speculated that earthquakes were caused by chemical explosions within the earth, revealing the limitations of early seismological inquiry.

An incensed Winthrop plunged into a controversy with the prominent Boston minister Thomas Prince, who proclaimed that earthquakes were manifestations of God's wrath with sinful mankind and were attributable to an "Electrical Substance" spread by lightning rods. Irked by concepts that denied the primacy of natural causes, Winthrop vehemently attacked Prince, forcing him to retreat while a supporter gloated that he had "laid Mr. Prince flat on [his] back" (Jared Eliot to Ezra Stiles, Mar. 1756, Stiles manuscripts, Yale University). However much he proclaimed the dominance of natural laws, he privately acknowledged that the "terrifying phenomena" did have a "grand moral purpose" (Winthrop to Ezra Stiles, 17 Apr. 1756, Stiles manuscripts, Yale University).

The transit of Venus in 1761 gave an unusual opportunity to calculate the solar parallax, essential in determining the distance of Earth from the Sun and in verifying Newtonian hypotheses. In a vessel provided by Governor Francis Bernard and with instruments lent by Harvard, Winthrop sailed to St. John's, Newfoundland, to observe the planet's course on 6 June. Bedeviled by swarms of insects and threatening weather, Winthrop and his two student assistants made the only successful observations in North America. His account, *Relation of a Voyage from Boston to Newfoundland, for the Observation of the Transit of Venus, June 6, 1761* (1761), presents an intriguing narrative in addition to his mathematical calculations. Unable to arouse interest in an expedition to Lake Superior to view the 1769 transit and hindered by ill health, Winthrop was limited to calculations from Cambridge.

Long held in high esteem among scientists, Winthrop was elected a fellow of the Royal Society in 1766 through the aegis of his friends Ezra Stiles and Benjamin Franklin. Harvard had named him a fellow of the Corporation, while the University of Edinburgh awarded him an honorary LL.D. in 1771. Having presented Franklin with an honorary A.M. degree in 1753, Harvard conferred its first honorary LL.D on Winthrop in 1774.

On the death of president Edward Holyoke in 1769, Winthrop took over Harvard's administrative duties but refused the presidency because of chronic ill health. The abbreviated tenure of President Samuel Locke, accused of an affair with his housemaid, led to Winthrop's sudden election as president in 1774 and a second refusal.

During the revolutionary crisis of the 1770s, frequent meetings with John Adams, John Hancock, and Samuel Adams intensified Winthrop's opinion that "America [was] groaning under the hand of an oppressive power . . . the fate of millions is now at stake" (Winthrop to Richard Price, 20 Sept. 1774, "The Price Letters," Massachusetts Historical Society, *Proceedings*, 2d ser., 17 [May 1903]: 271). Elected to the Massachusetts-Bay Council in 1773, he served until Governor Thomas Gage rejected his reelection. Winthrop then became a member of the revolutionary Provincial Council, remaining in office until 1777. During the battle of Lexington-Concord in 1775 Winthrop removed to Andover the college library and scientific instruments that he had so painstakingly assembled after the disastrous 1764 fire in Harvard Hall.

Winthrop was married twice, first in 1746 to Rebecca Townsend, with whom he had five sons before her death in 1753. In 1756 he married Hannah Fayerweather Tollman; they had no children. Winthrop died in Cambridge, honored by students and colleagues for his intellectual achievements. Abigail Adams referred to the "inexpressible loss" to the college, while Mercy Otis Warren expressed the greater loss to Newtonian science in an ode in the *Boston Independent Chronicle*. The most renowned scientist of Colonial America next to Benjamin Franklin, Winthrop was distinguished for his contributions in astronomy, physics, and seismology.

• Manuscript materials relating to John Winthrop's Harvard career, both as an undergraduate and as Hollis Professor are in the Harvard University Archives, which has Winthrop's "Abstracts of Sermons at Harvard, 1728–29," his "Commonplace Book, 1728," and "Diaries and Notes." The Houghton Library, Harvard University, has several Winthrop letters, while the Winthrop papers, the Bowdoin-Temple Papers, and the C. Davis Papers at the Massachusetts Historical Society have additional information. Correspondence between Winthrop and John Adams has been published in Massachusetts Historical Society, *Collections*, 5th ser., 4 (1878): 288–313. Winthrop's scientific papers, contributed to the Royal Society, London, were published in the society's *Philosophical Transactions* between 1743 and 1774. Another Winthrop publication not mentioned above is *Two Lectures on Comets* (1759).

An essay by Clifford Shipton in *Sibley's Harvard Graduates*, vol. 9 (1956), pp. 240–64, is rich in biographical detail. Lawrence Shaw Mayo, *The Winthrop Family in America* (1948), presents illuminating aspects about the scientist's life. Winfred E. A. Bernhard, "Vita—John Winthrop," *Harvard Magazine* 93 (Sept.–Oct. 1990): 52, provides a brief sketch of his scientific and political role. It also includes a color reproduction of John Singleton Copley's portrait of Winthrop, the original of which is in the Winthrop House Library, Harvard University.

Winthrop's scientific career is analyzed in Raymond P. Stearns, *Science in the British Colonies of America* (1970). Interpretive articles include Frederick G. Kilgour, "Professor John Winthrop's Notes on Sun Spot Observations (1739)," *Isis* 29 (Nov. 1938): 355–61; Charles E. Clark, "Science, Reason, and an Angry God: The Literature of an Earthquake," *New England Quarterly* 38 (Sept. 1965), 340–62; and Louis Graham, "The Scientific Piety of John Winthrop of Harvard," *New England Quarterly* 46 (Mar. 1973): 112–18. Brooke Hindle, *The Pursuit of Science in Revolutionary America* (1956), places John Winthrop in the context of his times.

WINFRED E. A. BERNHARD

WINTHROP, John, Jr. (12 Feb. 1606 5 Apr. 1676), colonial governor of Connecticut and fellow of the Royal Society, was born at Groton Manor in Suffolk, England, the son of John Winthrop (1588–1649), the founder and governor of Massachusetts, and Mary Forth. He studied at Trinity College, Dublin (1622–1624) and at the Inns of Court (1625–1627) but received no degree. After serving in the English attack on La Rochelle and traveling to the Levant, he assisted his father in plans to move the family to the New World. Having supervised the family affairs for a year in his father's absence, Winthrop migrated to America with his new wife, Martha Fones, in 1631. During the next year he joined the Boston church. Though a Puritan, he was never noted for the expression of strong religious feelings. Winthrop was also admitted to freemanship in 1631 and was elected to the colony's Court of Assistants. He was one of the first settlers of Agawam (later Ipswich), and there his wife and infant daughter died in 1634. In 1634 he returned to England on family and public business. While there he agreed to settle a town at the mouth of the Connecticut River on behalf of the Puritan Lords Brook and Say and Seale. During this stay in England he married Elizabeth Reade, stepdaughter of the Reverend Hugh Peter.

During the next decade Winthrop occupied himself with the settlement of the town of Saybrook on the Connecticut River and the founding of another Connecticut town, New London. He continued to fulfill his public responsibilities in Ipswich and pursued attempts to develop a saltworks in Beverley and an ironworks at Saugus. He traveled to England in 1641–1642 to raise support for the ironworks and used the occasion to bring back additions to a library that then numbered close to a thousand volumes. His collection reflected his interests in religion, natural history, physics, mathematics, medicine, alchemy, and law.

In 1646 Winthrop moved to New London and made Connecticut his home for the rest of his life, though he continued to be reelected to the Massachusetts Court of Assistants until 1649. Winthrop was elected governor of Connecticut in 1657 and was returned to that office continuously until his death. Following the restoration of the Stuart monarchy in 1660, Winthrop was chosen to travel to England to seek a royal charter that would confirm Connecticut's existence. Friends in England, such as Samuel Hartlib, helped him secure the assistance of key government officials, and Winthrop was able to obtain a charter in 1662 that not only recognized Connecticut but incorporated the nearby New Haven settlements into the colony and provided a favorable border with Rhode Island. In 1664 Winthrop further advanced his interests with the English authorities by cooperating with the duke of York's expedition to conquer the Dutch New Netherlands colony. In the early 1670s he presided over changes in his colony's political procedures and revision of its law code. He was note for his moderation in treating Quakers and other religious dissenters. Winthrop was governor at the outbreak of King Philip's War in 1675 and was responsible for organizing the colony's early response.

While serving his colony's political needs, Winthrop also continued his interests in other areas. He was widely respected as a physician, and his medical notebooks and correspondence testify to his efforts to alleviate the sufferings of his fellow colonists. His emphasis on chemical treatments put him in the forefront of the medical practices of his day. These interests were part of his ongoing scientific curiosity. While in England he associated with a number of the leading scientific figures of the time, including Hartlib, Sir Kenelm Digby, and Robert Boyle. He moved readily among these and other promoters of an empirical approach to science who were based in London as opposed to the universities. In 1661 he was chosen a member of the association that in 1663 was chartered as the Royal Society, Winthrop being listed as one of the original fellows. As the first American fellow, Winthrop held an informal commission as the society's correspondent for North America. He received and disseminated reports from the society's secretary, Henry Oldenburg, and contributed observations on the natural history of New England. He was especially interested in telescope optics and sent reports of his astronomical observations to European friends. In the winter of 1671–1672 he donated a telescope to Harvard College. He continued to be interested in the mineral wealth of the region, but concluded that efforts to exploit it, such as his earlier ironworks, were premature. He was also noted for his interest in alchemy, and it has been suggested that he authored a number of noted alchemical studies under the pseudonym Eirenaeus Philalethes. Though he did not make any significant original scientific contributions, he effectively popularized and promoted scientific inquiry into the natural order.

Winthrop died in Boston, where he had gone to attend meetings of the New England Confederation. He was buried there alongside his father. Among his six surviving children, his son Wait-Still later served as chief justice of Massachusetts, and his son John "Fitz-John" Winthrop (1638–1707) was governor of Connecticut.

• Virtually all of the surviving correspondence of John Winthrop, Jr., along with his medical notebooks and other manuscripts, are in the Massachusetts Historical Society. Much of the correspondence has been published in the *Winthrop Papers* (6 vols., 1929–). Some correspondence that has not yet appeared in those volumes can be found in *Massachusetts Historical Society Collections*, 5th ser., 8 (1882): 3–177; and in Robert C. Winthrop, ed., *Correspondence of Hartlib, Oldenburg, and others of the Founders of the Royal Society with Governor Winthrop of Connecticut, 1661–1672* (1878). The standard biography is Robert C. Black III, *The Younger John Winthrop* (1966). See also Richard S. Dunn, *Puritans and Yankees: The Winthrop Dynasty of New England, 1630–1717* (1962). The claim that Winthrop was Eirenaeus Philalethes and a discussion of the works published by that author can be found in R. S. Wilkinson, "The Problem of the Identity of Eirenaeus Philalethes," *Ambix* 12 (1964): 24–43.

FRANCIS J. BREMER

WINTHROP, Margaret (1591?–14 June 1647), third wife of Governor John Winthrop (1588–1649) of Massachusetts, was born at Much (Great) Maplestead in Essex County, England, the daughter of Sir John Tyndal, a master in the Court of Chancery, and Lady Anne Egerton. Her early life is unrecorded, but she appears to have received the education deemed appropriate for a young Puritan gentlewoman of the period. Judging from the correspondence of her adult years, she was highly literate, well versed in theology, and skilled in the management of a complex household. Margaret Tyndal was twenty-five when her father was shot and killed by a disgruntled client on 12 November 1616, as he entered his chamber in Lincoln's Inn. Margaret's reaction to her father's violent death is unknown, but a letter from her brother Arthur to their mother Lady Anne Tyndal, days after the assassination, hints that the controversy raised by the murdering client had threatened family honor. Arthur Tyndal praised God "who hath wrought wounderously alreadie in stoppeing the mouthes of malicious and naughtie people," adding that, "All the graue examiners of that business proclaime my fathers integritie and say if it had been theire case they must haue been subiect to the pistol to, for they would haue donne as he did."

Within a year of her father's death, Margaret Tyndal was being courted by the twice-widowed John Winthrop, a lawyer, Puritan, and heir to "Groton Manor" in Suffolk County. Her family was initially apprehensive about the intended marriage, since the thirty-year-old Winthrop had not received title to his father's estate and his income was therefore limited. The Tyndals' objections evidently carried weight: Adam Winthrop gave over the lordship of Groton Manor to his son sometime before John's marriage to Margaret in 1618. Her dowry, which consisted of Tyndal lands, was substantial. As the young mistress of Groton Manor she was incorporated into the household of her parents-in-law Adam and Anne Winthrop, whom she addressed as father and mother. She also became a surrogate mother to her husband's four surviving children by his first wife, who ranged in age from three to twelve. Social life at Groton was typical of gentry hospitality. Both the Winthrops and the Tyndals had extensive kinship ties, and visits between friends and relatives were common.

On 24 March 1619, after forty hours of "sore travayle," Margaret Winthrop gave birth to the first of her five children, after which she nearly died of a fever. For the first twelve years of their marriage, John Winthrop was often absent from home for weeks at a time, while he served as a legal counsel in Parliament and then as a Common Attorney in the Court of Wards and Liveries. Like other women alone, Margaret Winthrop acted as a "deputy husband" in overseeing the estate and household. During these periods, she exchanged letters with her husband in which she often belittled her capabilities, as female decorum dictated, while in practice proving herself more than competent in fulfilling her domestic responsibilities. She shared with her husband the urgent mission of completing the minutiae of daily tasks as a religious duty. Writing to him in November 1627, she teasingly commented: "I haue many resons to make me loue thee whearof I will name to. first because thou louest god, and secondly because that thou louest me. If these to ware wantinge all the rest would be eclipsed, but I am a bad huswife to be so longe from them, but I must needs borowe a little time to talke with thee."

There were times when she exerted her authority. When John Winthrop considered moving the family to a London suburb where he could commute to the city via the Thames River, Margaret Winthrop and her mother scotched the plan, arguing that the river route was too dangerous. Yet the dangers of a trans-Atlantic voyage failed to dampen her enthusiasm for the planned Puritan migration to Massachusetts Bay.

In October 1629 the General Court of Massachusetts Bay Company elected John Winthrop governor. When he embarked for New England with the first wave of settlers in April 1630, Margaret Winthrop remained behind at Groton with her stepson John Winthrop, Jr. (1606–1676), and her two youngest children. Her correspondence of 1630–1631 focused on the detailed preparations for her own departure. When Boston minister John Wilson returned to England in 1631 for his wife Elizabeth, who was "more auerce then ever" to cross the Atlantic, Margaret Winthrop expressed a thinly veiled disapproval to John Winthrop, Jr., in May 1631: "I maruiell what mettall she is made on. shure she will yeald at last, or elce we shal want him [Wilson] excedingly in new england." Some days later she wrote that if Wilson stayed in England with his wife, "it will disharten many that would be wiling to goe." As for herself, she resolved "to goe for New England as spedyly as I can with any Convenience." Needing money, she set about collecting rents from the tenants at Groton, who complained "of the hardnesse of the times."

Margaret Winthrop's determination to have all of her children in New England overrode her husband's suggestion that the eighteen-month-old Anne might stay behind with his sister. "For our little daughter, doe as thou thinkest best," he wrote; "the Lord direct thee in it. if thou bringest her, she wilbe more trouble to thee in the shipp then all the rest." Margaret Winthrop traveled with her children in the company of John Winthrop, Jr., and his wife aboard the *Lyon*, which arrived at Boston on 2 November 1631. One week into the voyage, the baby Anne had died.

Life on the Massachusetts frontier brought new and familiar challenges. In November 1637, during the brutal Pequot War and the divisive Antinomian controversy, Margaret Winthrop once again corresponded with her husband across the relatively short distance between Boston and Newtowne (Cambridge) where he was presiding over the General Court's examination of their neighbor Anne Hutchinson. Writing from "Sad Boston" on 15 November, she sounded close to despair: " . . . sad thougts posses my sperits, and I cannot repulce them which makes me unfit for any thinge wondringe what the lord meanes by all these troubles amounge us. shure I am that all shall work to the best." Two days later, John Winthrop responded in kind: "I suppose thou hearest much newes from hence: it may be some greiueous to thee: but be not troubled. I assure thee thinges goe well, and they must needs doe so, for God is with us, and thou shalt see a happy issue." In fact, by 1642, life in Massachusetts seemed singularly blessed compared to the turmoil of civil war in England, "When I thinke of the trublesome times and manifolde destractions that are in our natiue contrye," Margaret Winthrop wrote, "I thinke we doe not pryse our happynesse heare as we haue ca[u]se."

In May 1647 a respiratory disease spread throughout New England, from which she died in Boston. As in life, Margaret Winthrop's historical identity has been defined by her role as the wife of Governor John Winthrop. Their correspondence has illuminated the Puritan ideal of companionate marriage. She was praised by her nineteenth-century biographer as "the emblem and personification of . . . the Puritan wife and mother" (Earle, p. 334); and by a twentieth-century historian as "one of the most appealing [women] in American history" (Morgan, p. 13). Unfortunately, this mystique has tended to obscure her leadership role and she deserves to be recognized among her contemporaries as a woman of social and religious authority.

• Winthrop's correspondence, including Tyndal documents, is published in the *Winthrop Papers*, Massachusetts Historical Society (5 vols., 1929–1947). See also John Winthrop, *The History of New England*, ed. James Savage (2 vols., 1825; repr. 1972). Of limited use is Joseph H. Twitchell, ed., *Some Old Puritan Love Letters: John and Margaret Winthrop, 1618–1638* (1893). For a nineteenth-century appraisal of her life see Alice Morse Earle, *Margaret Winthrop: Biography of a Puritan Woman* (1895; repr. 1975). The best biography of John Winthrop (in which Margaret is also discussed) is still Edmund S. Morgan, *The Puritan Dilemma: The Story of John Winthrop* (1958). For a comparative background on women in colonial New England see Laurel Thatcher Ulrich, *Good Wives: Image and Reality in the Lives of Women in Northern New England, 1650–1750* (1982). On the epidemic that led to her death, see Ernest Caulfield, "The Pursuit of a Pestilence," *Proceedings of the American Antiquarian Society, April 19, 1950–October 18, 1950* 60 (1951): 26–27.

BARBARA RITTER DAILEY

WINTHROP, Robert Charles (12 May 1809–16 Nov. 1894), representative and senator from Massachusetts, was born in Boston, Massachusetts, the son of Thomas Lindall Winthrop, a prominent merchant who was then serving as lieutenant governor, and Elizabeth Bowdoin Temple. A sixth-generation descendant of John Winthrop (1588–1649), the first governor of the Massachusetts Bay Colony, Winthrop was educated at private schools and at Harvard College. Active in the militia and in many social clubs, Winthrop studied law in Daniel Webster's office and was admitted to the bar in 1832. In 1831 he married Eliza Blanchard; they had four children. After his first wife's death in 1842 he was married twice more: to Laura Derby Welles from 1859 until her death in 1861 and to Adele Granger Thayer from 1865 until her death in 1892. Each of these women had one child from her first marriage.

In 1834 Winthrop was elected to the house of representatives in the Massachusetts General Court. He soon became known for his oratory and for his principled stand on public issues. That year, for instance, a mob burned the Ursuline Convent in Charlestown, Massachusetts, in an atmosphere of anxiety over growing Irish competition in the job market and rumors of Catholic dungeons and torture chambers on the convent grounds. Making no pretense of welcoming Irish immigrants, Winthrop disavowed violence and urged passage of a bill compensating the Ursulines for the destruction. The bill was defeated, but Winthrop's support of the measure did not undermine his standing with his own constituents. He was especially outspoken in his denunciation of Jacksonian policies and of Andrew Jackson, whom he branded a tyrant. In common with many other members of the new Whig party, Winthrop favored a protective tariff and vigorous promotion of internal improvements. After four years in the Massachusetts legislature, Winthrop was chosen as Speaker of the house. In 1840 he won a special election to fill a vacant seat in the U.S. House of Representatives but resigned early in 1842 to be with his dying wife. Later that year he won the regular election and served in the House until 1850.

Winthrop continued to be recognized for his oratory, particularly for speeches criticizing the gag rule, which required antislavery petitions introduced in the House to be tabled automatically; opposing the annexation of Texas; and calling for a negotiated settlement of the Oregon boundary dispute. However, as questions concerning slavery and westward expansion received increased attention, the Whig party began to split along sectional lines and also within Massachusetts and a few other northern states. Winthrop became a casualty of these splits. In 1844 the Tyler administration negotiated a treaty of annexation with the Republic of Texas. Massachusetts Whigs were against the treaty but began dividing into two blocs. When the treaty to annex Texas was defeated in the Senate, expansionists tried to gain their end through passage of a joint resolution before President John Tyler (1790–1862) left office on 4 March 1845. Winthrop made one of the great declamations of his career in an hour-long address critical of annexation. "I am against annexation now and always," he concluded, "because I believe it to be clearly unconstitutional in substance; because I believe it will break up the balance of our system, violate the Compromises of the Constitution, and endanger the permanence of the Union; and, above all, I am uncompromisingly opposed to the extension of domestic slavery, or to the addition of another inch of slaveholding territory to this nation." To appease southern Whigs, however, he also affirmed that Congress had no jurisdiction over slavery in the states. This stand placed Winthrop in the camp of the conservative or Cotton Whigs, whose leaders came from the merchant-manufacturing elite of the Bay State and were believed to be more interested in maintaining established social and economic links with southern colleagues than in taking moral stands. Their antagonists, who were called Conscience Whigs, included Charles Sumner, Charles Francis Adams (1807–1886), and John Gorham Palfrey, all one-time friends and associates of Winthrop.

The dispute among Massachusetts Whigs intensified the following year, when President James K. Polk called on Congress to recognize that a state of war existed with Mexico since American troops stationed along the Rio Grande had been unjustly fired on. Winthrop denounced Polk's war message but voted funds to support the troops. His equivocal stand subjected him to heated attacks from the Conscience faction, who found that his wealth and transparent ambition for national office made him a convenient target. "Blood! blood! is on the hands of the representative from Boston. Not all great Neptune's ocean can wash them clean," charged Sumner in the *Boston Courier*. The topic of whether slavery should be allowed in any territory acquired from Mexico soon replaced the war itself in public debate. Although Winthrop agreed with Conscience Whigs in opposing expansion and the spread of slavery, he continued to speak in less explicit terms in order to avoid antagonizing the important southern element in the party. For instance, in 1847 at the Springfield convention of Massachusetts Whigs, Winthrop helped defeat a motion introduced by the Conscience faction that the next presidential candidate of the Whig party should pledge adherence to the principles of the Wilmot Proviso, requiring Congress to ban the introduction of slavery in any land taken from Mexico.

That same year Conscience Whigs vowed to oppose Winthrop's candidacy for the Speakership of the House of Representatives in the Thirtieth Congress, 1847–1849. With support from both northern and southern Whigs, Winthrop won the position anyhow in a spirited contest, but the dispute among Massachusetts Whigs had gone too far to be resolved. Many members of the Conscience faction moved into the new Free Soil party during the campaign of 1848. Although Winthrop's performance in the key office of Speaker is generally considered to be both fair and able, he was criticized by both northern and southern extremists for some of his committee appointments. When the new Congress convened in December 1849, Democrats held the majority in the House, but their own factional strife gave Winthrop the opportunity to win a second term as Speaker. His bid for the post was thwarted when two Whigs from Georgia, Alexander H. Stephens and Robert Toombs, withheld their votes from him. Democrat Howell Cobb of Georgia prevailed.

In an age of polarizing political alignments, Winthrop continued to seek the middle ground. Even though he had always opposed the spread of slavery, Winthrop ended up supporting the Compromise of 1850, which admitted California as a free state but was ambiguous on the status of slavery in the remainder of the lands taken from Mexico. Earlier that year Winthrop had been named U.S. senator to fill the place vacated when Webster accepted the position of secretary of state. Winthrop hoped the Massachusetts legislature would then elect him to a full term but was again disappointed when a coalition of Democrats and Free Soilers voted the Senate seat to Sumner, perhaps the man Winthrop most despised. As a quid pro quo, Democrats would receive important state offices. Within a few months the coalition again cost Winthrop dearly. He came in first in the popular vote for the governorship but failed to gain a majority. The election then went to the legislature, where coalition votes gave the governorship to a Democrat as the earlier agreement had stipulated.

No longer comfortable amidst the political upheaval that saw old party affiliations crumbling and new ones being established, Winthrop decided not to seek office again. He declined an offer to head the Know Nothing ticket in Massachusetts, saying he had long opposed secret societies based on religion or race. Later, in the wake of the Nebraska Act, spokesmen for the new Republican party approached him about assuming a leadership position in Massachusetts. Even though he was only forty-five years old, Winthrop declined the offer, for the party was sectional in nature and headed by men whose words and deeds, he feared, would arouse alarm in the South. He lamented that there had never been a party "more pure, more faithful to the principles of the Country and the true principles of the Constitution" than the old Whigs. Although he continued to speak out on sectional issues, seeking compromise at all opportunities, he considered himself an independent and refused to choose between Democrats and Republicans in the new sectional political alignments that had emerged by the late 1850s. Instead, he supported Unionist elements, such as the American party in 1856 (believing that its presidential candidate Millard Fillmore was the least objectionable of the three main contenders for the presidency) and the Constitutional Union ticket in 1860. Early in 1861 Winthrop joined a delegation of Bostonians to bring to Congress a peace petition with more than 15,000 signatures. Once war began, he did attend patriotic rallies and spoke on behalf of the Union cause as often as his then poor health permitted. In 1864 he endorsed the Democratic presidential ticket headed by General George B. McClellan (1826–1885). Although the Democratic platform placed peace foremost, McClellan himself seemed to favor prosecuting the war, and Winthrop reasoned that a victory by McClellan would not mean disunion. On the other hand, he believed that the reelection of President Abraham Lincoln would prolong the war, since negotiations to end the conflict could not succeed as long as Republicans placed social revolution in the South ahead of the restoration of the Union. Winthrop had little to do with politics thereafter.

Winthrop remained active in public service. He spoke often at historical observations, such as the centennial of the Boston Tea Party in 1873, and at the invitation of both houses of Congress, he spoke on the 100th anniversary of the battle of Yorktown in 1881. From 1855 to 1884 he served as president of the Massachusetts Historical Society, providing the leadership that transformed the organization from a somewhat parochial body to one that merited the respect of the historical community throughout the United States. Winthrop had particular success in raising the funds needed to expand the society's holdings and to establish its own journal, the *Proceedings*. In 1861 he turned over to it a large body of Winthrop family papers relating to colonial Massachusetts, personally helped edit several volumes of letters, and wrote a life of his ancestor, the elder John Winthrop. He had earlier made an important donation of books to help establish the Boston Public Library. Winthrop was also president of the Boston Provident Association and chaired the Board of Trustees of the Peabody Education Fund. Founded in 1867 by Winthrop's friend George Peabody (1795–1869), the Peabody Education Fund allotted money to assist progress in the South by promoting the establishment both of common schools and of normal schools for the training of teachers. Winthrop Normal and Industrial School (now Winthrop University) in Rock Hill, South Carolina, was named for him. He died at his home in Boston.

Winthrop served only a decade in Congress, winning recognition for his oratory. He was also an able parliamentarian and served as Speaker of the House during the Thirtieth Congress. However, his consistent efforts to maintain the Whig party as an effective national organization left him isolated from many of his former friends and brought him increasing criticism as the party fractured first in Massachusetts and then nationally. Ill at ease in the new politics of the 1850s, the genteel Winthrop sought haven in philanthropy and in historical pursuits, where his achievements earned him much respect.

• The papers of Winthrop are a subset of the Winthrop Family Papers, 1544–1963, at the Massachusetts Historical Society in Boston. A single folder of Winthrop papers is in the American Antiquarian Society in Worcester, Mass. Many other Winthrop letters can be found in the collections of his political contemporaries, among them the Edward Everett Papers at the Massachusetts Historical Society. Many of Winthrop's public addresses have been compiled and published in Robert C. Winthrop, *Addresses and Speeches on Various Occasions* (4 vols., 1852–1886). Donald R. Kennon, ed., *The Speakers of the U.S. House of Representatives, 1789–1984* (1985), lists writings by and about Winthrop. Robert Charles Winthrop, Jr., wrote a study of his father's life, *A Memoir of Robert C. Winthrop* (1897). Numerous studies dealing with the political crisis of the 1840s and 1850s discuss Winthrop's political standing. Among the most useful are Frederick J. Blue, *The Free Soilers: Third Party Politics, 1848–1854* (1973); Kinley J. Brauer, *Cotton versus Conscience: Massachusetts Whig Politics and Southwestern Expansion, 1843–1848* (1967); David H. Donald, *Charles Sumner and the Coming of the Civil War* (1960); Frank Otto Gatell, *John Gorham Palfrey and the New England Conscience* (1963); William E. Gienapp, *The Origins of the Republican Party, 1852–1856* (1987); Thomas H. O'Connor, *Lords of the Loom: The Cotton Whigs and the Coming of the Civil War* (1968); and David M. Potter, *The Impending Crisis, 1848–1861* (1976). Arthur B. Darling, *Political Changes in Massachusetts, 1824–1848: A Study of Liberal Movements in Politics* (1925), and Ronald P. Formisano, *The Transformation of Political Culture: Massachusetts Parties, 1790s–1840s* (1983), differ on many points but are essential for understanding the political and social culture in which Winthrop made his career. Louis Leonard Tucker, *The Massachusetts Historical Society: A Bicentennial History, 1791–1991* (1996), is invaluable for understanding Winthrop's important contributions to historical scholarship. Obituaries are in the *Boston Evening Transcript* and the *New York Times*, 17 Nov. 1894.

LLOYD J. GRAYBAR

WINTHROP, Theodore (22 Sept. 1828–10 June 1861), novelist, was born in New Haven, Connecticut, the son of Francis Bayard Winthrop, a mercantile businessman, and Elizabeth Woolsey. He was of New England aristocracy, on his father's side a descendant of John Winthrop, the first governor of Massachusetts, and on his mother's a descendant of Jonathan Edwards, as well as seven presidents of Yale College. Winthrop graduated from Yale in 1848.

Winthrop pursued independent studies in the classics and spent a year in Europe, often hiking to improve his frail health. His letters described the culture and scenery rather than the political turmoil of the time. In New York City in 1851, he worked for the Pacific Mail Steamship Company. In 1852 he traveled again to Europe, arriving home ill but resolved to become an author.

The steamship company sent Winthrop to Panama in 1852 as a railway ticket clerk and occasional guard over gold shipments from California. Six months later he landed in San Francisco, where he quit the company and traveled through the Northwest and up the Columbia River. In August 1853 he began a horseback trek home across a dangerous continent, arriving in New York in November. His journals show that he had shed his tendency to morbid introspection. He captured his adventures among the Indians of Oregon in *The Canoe and the Saddle* (1862) and his dislike of the Mormons in *John Brent* (1862).

After a surveying expedition in Panama, Winthrop studied law in New York, passing the bar in 1855, but he practiced for only one year. He hiked the Maine woods and campaigned for Republican presidential candidate John C. Frémont in 1856. Although he began by writing poetry, in the late 1850s Winthrop honed a prose narrative style that gave "the impression of always relating what he has witnessed" (*Westminster Review*, July 1865). On Staten Island, he was a frequent guest of George William Curtis, who, as editor of *Harper's*, inhabited a cultural circle that included writers such as Horace Greeley and Herman Melville, but Winthrop avoided such associations. Outspoken, he delighted in belittling religion and other conventions.

Immediately after Fort Sumter was bombarded in April 1861, Winthrop volunteered for the Union army. He was called Major Winthrop, although there is no record of his appointment; as his sister, Laura Winthrop Johnson, recalled, he wrote that his rank "is, I suppose, Captain or Major" (pp. 289–90). On 10 June, in the first engagement of the Civil War, a botched campaign at Big Bethal, Virginia, Winthrop was shot and killed.

At his death only two of Winthrop's works had been published—a short pamphlet, *A Companion to "The Heart of the Andes"* (1859), on Frederic Church's painting, and the first of his war sketches, "Our March to Washington" (*Atlantic Monthly*, June 1861). "Love and Skates" had already been sold to the *Atlantic* (Jan.–Feb. 1862). His sister Laura and his friend Curtis published more of his works, which were initially reviewed as a duty to a fallen war hero but later enthusiastically received.

These posthumous works bear no discoverable evidence of progressive development. The sentimental, gothic *Cecil Dreeme* (1861), with its directionless young hero and descriptions of New York City, was the most immediately popular, but *John Brent* and *The Canoe and the Saddle* are superior to it because of their keen rendering of the American West. Winthrop's sense of the open western atmosphere was highly praised ("Native Element in American Fiction," *Century Magazine*, July 1883; Carl Van Doren, *The American Novel* [1921]). A reviewer of the military narratives in *Life in the Open Air* (1863) insisted, "We have seen nothing better of their kind" (*North American Review*, July 1863). Twentieth-century reviewers have seen homoeroticism in the male bonding scenes in *Cecil Dreeme* and *John Brent* (Robert Martin in *Hidden from History: Reclaiming the Gay and Lesbian Past*, ed. Martin Duberman [1989]).

The strength of Winthrop's western tales lies in their realism and enthusiasm. *John Brent* was one of the earliest authentic westerns, after Robert Montgomery Bird's *Nick of the Woods* (1837) and Caroline Kirkland's *A New Home—Who'll Follow?* (1839). Winthrop's weakness, in spite of much narrative action and description, is a stilted prose style that is often sentimental and pedantic. His characters are static, and his frontier heroes are idealized gentlemen who quote classical Greek authors and Tennyson. *The Canoe and the Saddle* does not escape this, but as a memoir without a character-driven plot, it remains a western classic alongside Francis Parkman's *The Oregon Trail* (1849).

Cecil Dreeme went through three printings in one week, and nineteen by 1866. *John Brent* had five in ten days, sixteen by 1866, and twenty-eight by 1899; it was republished in 1970. *The Canoe and the Saddle* had eight printings by 1866 and sixteen by the century's end; two reset editions were issued after 1900. His Maine adventures, told in *Mr. Waddy's Return*, were finally published in 1904 but only after severe editing.

Winthrop was a minor novelist and a keen observer whose works combined the romanticism of James Fenimore Cooper and Nathaniel Hawthorne with the realism of John William DeForest and, later, of William Dean Howells. Americans appreciated his "fashion of plain truth-telling in fiction, which nevertheless remembers that life has its color and romance as well as its dun tameness" (Charles Richardson, *American Literature* [1892]). English reviewers admired his "touch of nature" and "optimistic faith" (see Howells, *Criticism and Fiction* [1892]). Readers in the twentieth century have been less enthusiastic, impressed by his descriptions of the West but disliking his melodrama and florid language.

• Winthrop's manuscripts are held in the New York Public Library. Biographical details, including a discrepancy over his birthdate, are in George William Curtis's sketch in *Cecil Dreeme* (1861; also in *Atlantic Monthly*, Aug. 1861); Laura

Winthrop Johnson, ed., *Life and Poems of Theodore Winthrop* (1884); and Willard Martin, *Life and Works of Theodore Winthrop* (Ph.D. diss., Duke Univ., 1944). Early reviews appeared in *Knickerbocker Magazine*, Dec. 1861, and the *North American Review*, Apr. 1862; surveys of Winthrop's works are in *Atlantic Monthly*, Aug. 1863, and *Saturday Review of Literature*, 22 Sept. 1883. Publication details are listed in "More Facts about the Publishing of Theodore Winthrop's Novels," *Bulletin of the New York Public Library* (May 1965). Winthrop is featured in Alexander Cowie, *The Rise of the American Novel* (1948). Two excellent introductions are provided by Alfred Powers in *The Canoe and the Saddle* (1955) and H. Dean Propst in *John Brent* (1970). Elbridge Colby provides a comprehensive life and criticism in *Theodore Winthrop* (1965). An obituary is in the *New York Times*, 14 June 1861.

JOEL ATHEY

WINTON, Alexander (20 June 1860–21 June 1932), early automobile manufacturer, was born in Grangemouth, Scotland, the son of Alexander Winton, a manufacturer of farm implements, and Helen Fea. After attending elementary school in his birthplace and toiling as an apprentice in shipyards on the Clyde River, young Winton came to the United States. For a few years he worked as an engineer on an ocean vessel. In 1883 he married a fellow Scot, Jeanie Muir McGlashan, and soon settled in Cleveland, Ohio, where a brother-in-law was already situated. The couple had six children. While employed in Cleveland as the plant superintendent of a furnace company, the Phoenix Iron Works, Winton entered a new business—bicycles. At first simply operating a bicycle repair shop, by 1891 he was making them. His firm participated in the great bicycle boom of the 1890s, making as many as 5,000 or 6,000 per year at its peak, but it was surpassed by the output of the leading bicycle manufacturers in Cleveland, the Peerless and White companies. All of the major bicycle makers in Cleveland eventually moved into automobile manufacturing after the end of the bicycle boom in 1897, but Winton got behind the wheel first.

He had begun experimenting with gasoline engines in 1893 and by 1895 had put one on a bicycle. He progressed to a four-wheel gasoline car in 1896 (the same year Henry Ford made his first car in Detroit and Ransom E. Olds his first gasoline car in Lansing, Mich.), and in 1897 incorporated the Winton Motor Carriage Company. As a pioneer in the automobile industry, he could not simply buy and assemble parts bought from specialist firms but had to design and make them himself or special-order them from job shops. In the summer of 1897 Winton drove a two-cylinder, 1,800-pound motorcar from Cleveland to New York City. For fuel he obtained cleaning fluid from hardware stores along the route. This 800-mile, ten-day expedition over wretched roads was the first long-distance automobile trip in the United States, but it brought little of the publicity Winton sought.

In 1898 Winton began to market an improved one-cylinder model, selling twenty-two passenger cars at $1,000 each and eight delivery wagons. Winton had moved quickly into the new industry; Olds sold no more than six cars that year and Ford had not yet formed his first company. The momentum increased in 1899, especially after the Cleveland *Plain Dealer* newspaper sponsored a second trip to New York City in May, this time in five days and well chronicled in the daily press. Winton's demonstration of a horseless carriage's reliability encouraged potential buyers and potential manufacturers to take these machines seriously. He took advantage of the burgeoning interest to double his price to $2,000 and further promoted his cars in races and reliability trials. For a few years Winton was the leading U.S. manufacturer of gasoline automobiles, turning out 850 in 1903. However, in 1902 R. E. Olds had already taken the lead, making 2,500 Oldsmobiles that year in Lansing and Detroit. Nevertheless, it was a rugged two-cylinder Winton that completed the first transcontinental automobile trip in 1903. After Winton's first wife died in 1903, he married three more times, to La Belle McGlashan in 1906, with whom he had one last child, to Marion Campbell in 1927, and to Mary Ellen Avery in 1930.

Like most producers in this first generation of automakers, Winton preferred to make large, elaborate, and expensive machines. A skillful engineer, he bent his efforts toward technical improvements to his cars and engines rather than to improved production methods. Winton never entered the mass market to compete with the early Olds, Rambler, and Ford. He held several dozen patents for improvements on bicycles, engines, and cars, but he does not appear to have derived an income from them. His first patent on a motor vehicle, granted on 6 September 1898, covered all the running gear except the engine. It had a transverse drive shaft that turned a very complex transmission with two forward and one reverse gears, each with its own clutch. For cooling he used a ribbed water tank "so that the water seldom reaches a temperature of 212 degrees." His patent of 5 July 1904 covered a braking system that with different levers operated bands on both the inside and outside of the brake drums. His 1905 model mounted a six-cylinder engine, and in 1908 he began installing a compressed-air self-starter on his cars. Winton continued with this type of starter for several years until finally adopting the Kettering-type electric starter in 1915. By 1910 he was producing over 2,000 cars per year, selling them from $3,000 to $5,700 each, but his personal interest had shifted to large marine gasoline engines and then in 1912 to the new diesel types. He sold some of both kinds to the United States and other countries involved in the First World War.

After the conflict sales of Winton cars rose to 2,500 in 1920, then dropped sharply to 325 in the 1921 recession. Production in 1922 reached 690, but sales were difficult in the face of intense competition in the mid- and high-price ranges. In 1924 Winton motorcar production ceased and the auto plant was sold, but large gasoline- and diesel-engine operations continued, under the leadership of George W. Codrington. When General Motors decided to enter the diesel-engine business it found that the Winton Engine company was the outstanding diesel-maker in the United States. GM entered the diesel-engine business by buying Winton and another diesel-engine firm in 1930 and went on to great success manufacturing diesel-electric railway locomotives as well as smaller diesel engines for trucks, buses, and naval craft.

Winton's strength lay in innovation, with bicycles, gasoline automobiles, and diesel engines, not in mass production or mass marketing. He died in the Cleveland suburb of Lakewood.

• By far the fullest account of Winton's automobile manufacturing is in Richard Wager, *Golden Wheels* (1975; rev. ed., 1986). See also Alexander Winton, "Get a Horse," *Saturday Evening Post*, 8 Feb. 1930, pp. 39, 42, 143–44, and William G. Keener, "Ohio's Pioneer Auto Maker: Alexander Winton" (Columbus, Ohio) *Museum Echoes* 28 (Mar. 1953): 19–22. An obituary is in the *New York Times*, 23 June 1932.

JAMES M. LAUX

WIRT, William (8 Nov. 1772–18 Feb. 1834), attorney general of the United States and anti-Masonic candidate for president, was born in Bladensburg, Maryland, the son of Jacob Wirt, a Swiss tavernkeeper, and Henrietta (maiden name unknown). The youngest of six children, Wirt was orphaned by the age of eight and entrusted to the care of an aunt for his upbringing. Wirt worked hard to raise himself up from this inauspicious beginning. Much of his youth was spent in a succession of boarding schools in the Georgetown area. By the time Wirt was fifteen, the small inheritance left him by his parents was nearly exhausted. He spent the next few years earning a small livelihood as a private tutor but was ambitious and wanted to make more for himself. In 1792, after moving to Culpeper County, Wirt was admitted to the Virginia bar.

Wirt was reportedly not a studious and industrious lawyer and as his earliest biographer claimed, was far "more disposed to cultivate the congenial pleasures of good-fellowship, than to pursue, by any painful toil, the road to fame." Still, with Wirt's ample rhetorical talent and charisma, his practice thrived in Culpeper while he worked to extend his business connections into neighboring Albemarle County, home of some of Virginia's leading figures.

In 1795 Wirt married Mildred Gilmer, the daughter of George Gilmer, the close friend and personal physician of Thomas Jefferson. The couple had no children. This opportune marriage allowed Wirt access to the social world of the Tidewater elite, and he moved rapidly up the ladder of Virginia society. Enamored with the vibrant, intellectual culture of Jeffersonian Virginia, Wirt continued to hone his skills both for the legal and literary arenas. Wirt longed to be not only a lawyer of great repute but also to be known as a scholar and a gentleman. In September 1803 Wirt began to publish, in the Richmond *Argus*, a series of gossipy biographical sketches under the pen name "The British Spy." Ten years later, *The Old Bachelor* appeared, a collection of heartwarming if pedantic parables highlighting virtues such as piety, temperance, and self-control. In 1817 he completed his monumental biography of Patrick Henry, a highly uncritical evaluation of the career of Virginia's revolutionary hero.

The death of his wife in 1799 prompted Wirt's move to Richmond where, on Jefferson's commendation, he was elected clerk of the house of delegates. During this period, Wirt served as counsel in the sedition trial of James Callender, a vicious libeler who had run afoul of Federalist judge Samuel Chase in the wake of the passage of the Alien and Sedition Acts. Wirt and his associates lost the case, but their argument that the Sedition Acts were unconstitutional was immensely popular in staunchly Republican Virginia. In 1802 the house of delegates appointed Wirt chancellor of the Eastern District of Virginia, a position he accepted with some reluctance. One year later, newly remarried to Elizabeth Gamble and expecting their first of twelve children, Wirt resigned, pleading relief from the "iron hand of want" that gripped those who accepted the small salaries of state office.

Wirt was rocketed to national prominence as an attorney in 1807 for his conduct of the prosecution in the treason trial of Aaron Burr. In 1816 James Madison appointed Wirt U.S. district attorney for Virginia. One year later James Monroe appointed him attorney general of the United States, a position he held for twelve years, through both of Monroe's terms as well as through the troubled administration of John Quincy Adams.

Wirt's reputation as a lawyer increased during his time in Washington, so much so that in April 1826 Jefferson offered Wirt a chair in the College of Law and the presidency of the University of Virginia, an offer that came with a salary of $1,500 a year. Wirt turned down the offer in favor of "the more profitable labors of my profession." Wirt had a reputation for oratory, which was enhanced by the famous eulogy he delivered in the House of Representatives on the occasion of the deaths of John Adams and Jefferson on the Fourth of July 1826.

It was during his years of service with the national government that Wirt began to drift from the political ideals of Jeffersonian Virginia that had guided him through the earlier phases of his career. One of the most active members in a law profession that was being forced to come to terms with the legal necessities of a rapidly expanding, capitalistic society, Wirt became a strong defender of regulatory measures designed to curb the judicial and commercial practices of the states.

Wirt's political views were transformed by the social and economic changes of the antebellum period, particularly the development of a national market economy, and became free, in the process, of that hostility toward the exercise of federal authority that had so characterized the republicanism of Jefferson. In 1818 John Quincy Adams described Wirt as having "an excessive leaning to State supremacy." But by the mid-1820s Wirt had fully reevaluated his position on the proper relationship between the states and the federal government.

Chief Justice John Marshall was particularly influential in bringing about this transformation. Wirt appeared frequently before the Supreme Court, appearing in many of the most famous cases argued before the Marshall court: the Dartmouth College case, *McCulloch v. Maryland*, *Cohens v. Virginia*, *Gibbons v. Ogden*, *Brown v. Maryland*, and the first argument of the Charles River Bridge case. The precise logic and highly nationalistic tone of Marshall's opinions greatly impressed Wirt, who reportedly told his younger associates "to speak like Henry, to write like Jefferson, and to reason like Marshall."

Wirt's shift toward a nationalistic interpretation of the Constitution coincided with the rise of Andrew Jackson to prominence in national politics and with him, the emergence of a more populistic political culture. Wirt had in fact long distrusted "Old Hickory," and he quickly became active in the loose coalition of opposition politicians who were slowly coalescing into the National Republican party. Wirt found a welcome home among a group, peopled by conservatives like Henry Clay, Daniel Webster, Joseph Story, and John Sargeant, who shared his nationalistic leaning.

Wirt enlisted his considerable legal talent and courtroom eloquence in the anti-Jacksonian cause. He emerged as a champion of the Supreme Court at a time when a new breed of Democratic politicians and states' rights advocates were growing increasingly resentful of the broad powers exercised by the judicial branch. In early 1830, for example, Wirt served as counsel for New Jersey in that state's long-standing boundary dispute with New York, a case that foreshadowed the tendency of other states to disregard openly the rulings of the Supreme Court. Wirt similarly came to the defense in the impeachment trial of James H. Peck, a Missouri district court judge who had run afoul of state Jacksonians. In the Cherokee cases of 1831 and 1832, two Indian land rights cases that touched as well on the relation of the states to the federal government, the authority of the Supreme Court, and the inviolability of treaties made under authority of the Constitution, Wirt argued that Georgia's attempts to enforce its laws in the Cherokee Nation were unconstitutional. That Wirt won the case and Jackson chose not to enforce the decision only underscored Wirt's belief that Jackson posed a threat to constitutional government.

In October 1831 Wirt reluctantly accepted the nomination of the Anti-Masonic party for the presidency of the United States. While Wirt shared with his anti-Masonic supporters the belief that Jackson was a demagogic usurper who threatened the institutions of the country, he recognized that he had entered a contest that he could not hope to win; Jackson was simply too popular. Desponding for the Union, Wirt turned away from the arena of national politics and longed for a period before the government had become "a sepulchre full of corruption and proscription." Much of the nation did not share Wirt's concerns, and Jackson was overwhelmingly reelected in 1832. Wirt won only the seven electoral votes of tiny Vermont.

In his remaining years Wirt pursued his dream of establishing a colony of German immigrants on his lands in Florida. The result was an expensive failure. Wirt remained in the nation's capital, practicing law, until the end of his life. He died in Washington, D.C., after a short illness.

• Wirt's personal papers are in the Maryland Historical Society, Baltimore; this collection is also available in microfilm. Wirt's historical and literary writings are easily obtained and have been frequently reprinted. The most complete biography of Wirt is still John Pendleton Kennedy, *Memoirs of the Life of William Wirt* (2 vols., 1849). Joseph C. Burke discusses Wirt's legal career in "William Wirt: Attorney General and Constitutional Lawyer" (Ph.D. diss., Indiana Univ., 1965), and Anya Jabour provides some useful information in "Hearts Divided: The Marriage and Family of Elizabeth and William Wirt, 1802–1834" (Ph.D. diss., Rice Univ., 1995). Michael L. Oberg explores Wirt's political beliefs in "William Wirt and the Trials of Republicanism," *Virginia Magazine of History and Biography* 99 (1991): 305–26, but see also Marvin R. Cain, "William Wirt against Andrew Jackson: Reflection on an Era," *Mid-America* 47 (1965): 113–38. Also useful is William R. Taylor, *Cavalier and Yankee: The Old South and the American National Character* (1957), esp. chap. 2.

MICHAEL L. OBERG

WIRT, William Albert (21 Jan. 1874–11 Mar. 1938), school administrator, was born in Markle, Indiana, the son of Emanuel Wirt and Mary Elick, farmers. He graduated from DePauw University, Greencastle, Indiana, in 1898, then completed one year of graduate work. While still in school, Wirt served as superintendent of schools in tiny Redkey, Indiana, and after graduation he became superintendent in Bluffton, Indiana, where he introduced a broader curriculum, a more flexible class schedule, and better facilities. In 1900 he married Bertha Koch, with whom he had three children. With experience as educational innovator somewhat influenced by John Dewey and other progressives, Wirt in 1906 eagerly accepted the superintendent's position in Gary, Indiana, a new town being built adjacent to U.S. Steel's burgeoning mill on Lake Michigan. His wife died in 1917, and two years later he married Martha Ruth Jacques, a marriage that ended in divorce in 1926. After the divorce he married Mildred Harter (1927), with whom he lived until his death.

Wirt was able to create an innovative educational system in Gary, termed the work-study-play or platoon school plan. The plan, which attracted worldwide attention, had two central aspects that pertained to all elementary grades. First, because of a concern for efficiency, Wirt believed in maximizing school facilities by using all of the classrooms all of the time, including nights (for adults), weekends, and during the summer. Second, he expanded the curriculum to include manual training, recreation, nature study, daily auditorium activities (including public speaking, music lessons, and movies), and other subjects beyond traditional academic concerns. Moreover, the larger schools, starting in 1909, were organized as unit schools, containing all grades from kindergarten through grade twelve. By the 1920s about half of the city's students were attending these large unit schools, which included swimming pools, shops, specialized rooms, and other modern facilities. Unlike their contemporaries in other cities, Gary's elementary students throughout the day continually moved about their schools, from specialized classrooms (English, math, history) to the auditorium, to the gym, to the shops, to the outdoor gardens, and perhaps even to the swimming pool.

Wirt's achievements in Gary appeared to many journalists, educators, and social critics, including John Dewey and Randolph Bourne, to create a rich, exciting educational experience for the city's students, an increasing number of whom were from immigrant families. Wirt's growing fame led the New York City school board to hire him as an adviser (1914–1917) to design a few platoon schools, but local concerns, particularly the fear that the Gary plan was a capitalist plot to produce only industrial workers, stopped the program. Wirt disagreed with the slightly critical conclusions of the eight-volume Rockefeller-funded General Education Board survey of the Gary schools (1918). The authors believed the schools were somewhat inefficient and slighted academic skills. Nonetheless, by 1929 over 200 school systems across the country had organized platoon schools, and he was nationally respected as an educational innovator. Wirt's belief—shaped by his rural background—that schools should extend their reach into the lives of both children and adults in order to counter the negative aspects and influences of modern urban life was widely shared at the time.

Wirt's educational activities and fame declined during the 1930s, although in 1937 he published *The Great Lockout in America's Citizenship Plants*, a pamphlet summarizing his educational views. The title captured his belief that the limited programs of traditional schools discouraged student attendance and interest. Economic problems forced a temporary cutback of many Gary school programs early in the decade, but they were returned as he worked to keep the system intact. Nationally, however, the platoon school plan was now ignored, as educators struggled to pay bills and had little time for innovations.

A lifelong conservative Republican, Wirt became more involved with economic and political matters during the 1930s and soon attacked what he saw as the New Deal's creeping socialism. In 1934 he gained notoriety from two days of congressional hearings following publication of his pamphlet *America Must Lose—By a "Planned Economy," the Stepping-stone to a Regimented State*. Though he was praised by Republicans and others on the far right, he was attacked and lampooned by Democrats throughout the country. He also fell on financial hard times, as his numerous business ventures, including a local bank and car dealership, failed. In 1937, a new Democratic-controlled school board and the simultaneous revival of the Gary Teachers Union created local challenges to his power but not to his educational ideas. He died suddenly at home of a heart attack, after thirty-one years as superintendent.

Wirt was a creative educational leader who molded an innovative school system but whose national influence did not survive the 1920s. His rural, Protestant, Republican background was shared by the majority of school administrators during the early decades of the twentieth century, but he was certainly more creative than most. His eclectic educational plan drew upon a variety of newer programs and theories, which he crafted into the unique platoon school system. Though Wirt was genuinely eager to promote the welfare of children and the community through creating a stimulating, influential, healthy school environment, his aloof personality and elitist views created difficulties in both his family—two of his children had severe mental problems—and public life. Moreover, he early accepted the segregation of black students, a common policy in northern cities. Nonetheless, Wirt's platoon school plan should be considered a significant and influential educational reform during the first three decades of the twentieth century.

• The bulk of Wirt's papers are in the Lilly Library, Indiana University, Bloomington, and a somewhat smaller collection, along with allied sources, is in the Calumet Regional Archives, Indiana University Northwest, Gary. There are also some letters in the General Education Board papers, Rockefeller Archives Center, North Tarrytown, N.Y. Wirt's life is covered in Ronald D. Cohen and Raymond A. Mohl, *The Paradox of Progressive Education: The Gary Plan and Urban Schooling* (1979), and most extensively in Ronald D. Cohen, *Children of the Mill: Schooling and Society in Gary, Indiana, 1906–1960* (1990).

RONALD D. COHEN

WIRTH, Louis (28 Aug. 1897–3 May 1952), sociologist and university professor, was born in Gemünden, Germany, the son of Joseph Wirth, a cattle merchant and small-scale farmer, and Rosalie Lorig. As one of only some twenty Jewish families in the village, Wirth's parents had to depend on either a Protestant or a Catholic elementary school for their children's academic training. Louis and his siblings were sent to the Volksschule operated by Protestant evangelicals. He received religious training, however, in regular sessions with the village rabbi in the basement of the synagogue and through visits by an itinerant teacher of Hebrew. During a brief visit to Germünden in 1911, Isaac Lorig (one of four Lorig brothers, all of whom had emigrated to the United States) offered to take Louis and his older sister, Flora, back to America with him to receive the education few village children could receive at home.

In the United States, Louis and Flora went to live with another uncle in Omaha, Nebraska, where Wirth enrolled in public school, mastered written and spoken English, and eventually won a regional scholarship to attend the University of Chicago. Although he began college as a premedical student, he soon found his way into the Department of Sociology, where he came under the influence of a group of men—including Albion Small, W. I. Thomas, Ernest W. Burgess, and Robert E. Park—who would later come to be identified as the "Chicago School" and who would be credited with transforming American sociology from a speculative, exhortative, and ameliorative activity to an empirically based and theoretically oriented discipline. With only two minor interruptions (when he worked as a caseworker for the Jewish Charities of Chicago from 1919 to 1922 and, later, as an assistant and associate professor at Tulane University from 1928 to 1930), Wirth was to be associated with the Department of Sociology at Chicago for the rest of his life: he graduated with honors in 1919, received his master's in 1925 and his doctorate in 1926, was appointed to the faculty as an assistant professor in 1931, advanced to associate the next year, and became a professor in 1940.

The University of Chicago figured prominently in Wirth's personal life as well. He met his future wife, Mary L. Bolton, when both were undergraduates, and after their marriage in 1923 they moved to a small apartment close to the campus. Thirteen years later, with a household swollen by two growing daughters and numerous kinfolk (some of whom, at Wirth's urging and with his financial help, had fled an increasingly dangerous Germany), he still preferred crowded quarters close to campus to more spacious accommodations available at a greater distance. Many of his close friends were University of Chicago colleagues, including the sociologists Herbert Blumer, Everett Hughes, and Robert Park and the political scientist Charles Merriam.

Neither a prolific nor an especially seminal scholar, Wirth is often characterized as a carrier of the ideas of Robert Park rather than as a creator of his own, a characterization he seemed somewhat willing to accept. "No one is original," his students remember him saying. "The only person that claims originality is the one who has a poor memory for sources" (Salerno, p. 21). During his lifetime, he was probably best known in terms of academic work as the English translator (with Edward A. Shils) of Karl Mannheim's *Ideology and Utopia* (1936), which introduced the sociology-of-knowledge perspective to an English-speaking audience, and as the author of *The Ghetto* (1928) and "Urbanism as a Way of Life" (*American Journal of Sociology* 44 [1938]: 1–24). But he was also widely known as an effective and influential teacher; as a popularizer of social science scholarship (between 1937 and 1952 he acted as a panel member on sixty-two of the University of Chicago's "Round Table" radio broadcasts); and, especially, as an activist both in professional associations (for example, he served as president of the American Sociological Society in 1947 and was a founding member of the International Sociological Association, becoming its first president in 1950) and in community and governmental organizations. It is characteristic of his life and his career that on the day before his death he had traveled to Buffalo to give the keynote address at a conference on race relations and community living, where the theme of his talk was a plea for action on behalf of progressive social change. He died of a heart attack just minutes after leaving the platform.

Wirth's discomfort with scholarship for scholarship's sake and his deep commitment to progressive social action and policy-relevant research led him into numerous extra-academic involvements. He was a consultant to the National Resources Planning Board (1935–1943) and the regional director of its region four (1942–1943), a consultant to and later director of planning of the Illinois Post-War Planning Commission (1944), and a founder and president of the American Council on Race Relations. He was an active member of the National Resources Planning Board's Urbanism Committee and Urban Section, the Chicago-area Metropolitan Housing and Planning Council, the Public Administration Clearinghouse, and the American Society of Planning Officials. This record of activism has given him a strong living presence in the continuing debate over the appropriate loyalties and responsibilities of social scientists.

In the years since his death, Louis Wirth's name has been added to the Chicago School pantheon. He is identified as one of the important transition figures (others are Herbert Blumer and Everett C. Hughes), linking Thomas, Park, and others with the much larger generation that received doctorates from Chicago in the immediate postwar period, many of whom, including Reinhard Bendix, Erving Goffman, Joseph Gusfield, Morris Janowitz, and Ralph Turner, went on to become major figures within the discipline. Wirth provided a bridge between this postwar group and the Chicago faculty of the early 1920s. One of the more important and enduring elements of this transmitted mindset has to do with the relationship between theory and research. Wirth explained his own assessment of his contributions:

> In my work in theory, especially through my years of teaching it to graduate students, I have tried to emphasize that theory is an aspect of everything they do and not a body of knowledge separate from research and practice. By theory, I mean the definition of interests of scholars, the assumptions with which they start, the conceptual framework in terms of which they analyze their materials and the types of generalizations which they develop as they are related to other generalizations in the field as a whole of knowledge as a whole. (Odum, p. 230)

Wirth's identification as a member of the Chicago School is also based on the 1928 publication of his doctoral dissertation, *The Ghetto*, which is simultaneously a social history of the Jewish experience in ethnic enclaves and an insightful analysis of a type of urban residential pattern common to many subordinate groups. But it is as the author of "Urbanism as a Way of Life"—sometimes interpreted as a summary statement of the Chicago School's general perspective on cities—

that Wirth has remained best known. As one historian of the school has argued, "No other single paper has precipitated so much discussion, debate, and research in urban sociology as [this] article" (Kurtz, p. 63). "Urbanism as a Way of Life" is a complexly themed and richly textured work and the discussions and debates it engendered are equally so. But it is Wirth's characterization of the city as an alienating environment in which "contacts . . . are . . . impersonal, superficial, transitory, and segmental" that has received the lion's share of attention and that frames the argument about the nature of urban life that, within and beyond sociology, continues unabated to this day. Yet there is considerable irony in such a legacy, for Elizabeth Wirth Marvick has claimed that for her father "Gemünden . . . was always an exemplification of the narrowness and monotony of village life. In 'Urbanism as a Way of Life' . . . and other writings he was later to pay tribute to urban civilization, which he contrasted implicitly with the deficiencies of the rural setting" (pp. 333–34).

• Wirth's scholarly papers are in the Regenstein Library at the University of Chicago. Wirth's writings were collected in *Community Life and Social Policy*, ed. Elizabeth Wirth Marvick and Albert J. Reiss, Jr. (1956). Roger Salerno, *Louis Wirth: A Bio-Bibliography* (1987), is the most complete source for biographical information and for listings of works by and about Wirth, including tributes and obituaries. Howard W. Odum, *American Sociology: The Story of Sociology in the United States through 1950* (1951), contains biographical data and includes excerpts from an interview with Wirth. See also Marvick, "A Biographical Memorandum," in *Louis Wirth on Cities and Social Life*, ed. Reiss. (1964). An assessment of Wirth's sociological contributions may be found in Reinhard Bendix, "Social Theory and Social Action in the Sociology of Louis Wirth," *American Journal of Sociology* 59 (1954): 523–29. Both Lester R. Kurtz, *Evaluating Chicago Sociology: A Guide to the Literature, with an Annotated Bibliography* (1984), and Fred H. Matthews, *Quest for an American Sociology: Robert E. Park and the Chicago School* (1977), provide useful introductions to the work of the Chicago School of sociology and to Wirth's place within it.

LYN H. LOFLAND

WIRZ, Henry (25 Nov. 1823–10 Nov. 1865), the only Confederate officer executed as a war criminal, was born Hartmann Heinrich Wirz in Zurich, Switzerland, the son of Hans Caspar Wirz, a tailor, and Sophie Barbara Philipp. After completing elementary and secondary school at the lower Gymnasium in Zurich, Wirz wanted to study medicine, but family finances did not permit medical school. Instead, he received commercial training at a Zurich firm and then worked for one year in Torino, Italy. He was listed as a merchant and also assisted his father, who was custodian of the customhouse in Zurich from 1834 to 1852. In 1845 he married Emilie Oschwald; they had two children. Shortly after his marriage Wirz borrowed 4,200 Swiss francs and was not able to repay the loan on time. He was sentenced to four years in prison on 3 April 1847, but the court decided the following June that he could be freed if he agreed not to return to Zurich for twelve years. Wirz decided to emigrate, but his wife refused, and they divorced in 1853.

After a year in Russia, Wirz came to the United States in 1849 and worked at a factory in Lawrence, Massachusetts, for a short time. He was employed as a doctor's assistant at Hopkinsville, Kentucky, by 1853 and moved to nearby Cadiz in 1853 or 1854. In 1854 he married Elizabeth Wolf; they had one daughter. Wirz practiced homeopathic medicine in Cadiz for a year but moved to Louisville and became superintendent of a water cure establishment in 1855. There he met Levin A. Marshall, a planter from Natchez, Mississippi, who hired him to oversee one of his plantations for $300 per year plus a horse. Wirz ran Milliken's Bend plantation for Marshall as overseer/physician until the war came.

On 16 June 1861 Wirz enlisted in the Fourth Louisiana Infantry as a private but was promoted to sergeant the next year. He later claimed that he was severely wounded in the right arm at the battle of Seven Pines on 31 May 1862. Whether he was even at that battle is debatable, but he was injured sometime that year, losing the use of his arm and suffering great pain for the rest of his life. Promoted to captain, he was assigned to the staff of Brigadier General John Henry Winder, who put him in command of the Richmond military prison. Called "Dutch Sergeant" by the prisoners because of his accent, he was not unpopular with them at that time. In fact, when he was sent to the prison in Cahaba, Alabama, later in 1862, he was much esteemed by the inmates there; they petitioned to keep him in command, a rarity at any time.

Wirz went to Europe sometime in 1863 and traveled for the rest of the year. He may have been on official Confederate business, but he may simply have been seeking medical help for his wound. The Confederacy he returned to in February 1864 had fallen on hard times as he found out when Winder placed him in command of the stockade at the Andersonville, Georgia, prison in March of that year. The exchange of prisoners had ceased, and the overpopulated compound rapidly became a hell on earth for everyone there. The Confederacy was so short of the basic necessities that even Confederate troops in the field were near starvation. Prisoners ranked last in importance, and Wirz was lucky to be able to feed his charges anything at all. Food, medicine, housing, even water were in short supply by that summer. As Union prisoners died by the thousands, the northern press characterized both Winder and Wirz as "inhuman fiends" and "monsters."

The assassination of Abraham Lincoln further inflamed the North, already sickened and enraged over the prisoner issue, and the public demanded that someone pay for these crimes. Winder died of a heart attack on 6 February 1865, thus depriving vengeful Union authorities of any opportunity of trying him as a war criminal. That left Wirz, who was arrested in May 1865, still tending to the sick at Andersonville. The Wirz "trial" lasted for three months; he was charged with murder and abuse of prisoners and of conspiring with Jefferson Davis, James Seddon, and others to murder the prisoners en masse. Lies and distortions were accepted as fact, and Wirz was sentenced to hang "for impairing the health and destroying the lives of prisoners."

According to Andersonville quartermaster Richard Bayley Winder, an officer and gentleman highly respected for his veracity as well as for his untiring attempts to relieve the agonies of the inmates, shortly before he was to be executed Wirz was approached by a secret emissary from the War Department, who offered him a full reprieve if he would swear that Davis had headed a conspiracy to murder Union captives. Wirz indignantly refused, but as he was being conducted to the gallows at the Old Capitol Prison in Washington, D.C., he told the officer charged with hanging him, "I know what orders are, Major—I am being hung for obeying them."

Wirz was a controversial figure, as was John Winder. Both have been savaged as beasts, but both were trapped in an impossible situation. Winder praised Wirz as one of the few truly able and energetic officers on his staff, and Wirz did make every effort to improve conditions at Andersonville. He dammed the creek trying to collect clean water, built sinks, and practically worked himself to death during August 1864. His health was so bad that many suspected he might not live to the end of his trial.

There is no question that Wirz did not receive a fair trial. Testimony by men who were not even at Andersonville was routine, accusations that he committed murder when he was not even there were accepted as unimpeachable facts, and he was not allowed to have anyone testify for his defense. Still, Wirz was not a likable figure; by all accounts he was rough, profane, and hot-tempered, and no one could deny the horrors of Andersonville. That no one could have performed any better, given the low priority that both governments assigned to the care of captives, was overlooked; the North demanded that someone pay for these tragedies. So it was that Wirz, poor, friendless, and foreign-born, was sacrificed.

• A book about Wirz published in Switzerland is Jurg Weibel, *Captain Wirz, Eine Chronik: Ein Dokumentarischer Roman* (1991). For his trial see U.S. Congress, *Trial of Henry Wirz. Letter . . . Transmitting a Summary of the Trial*, 40th Cong., 2d sess., 1867–1868, Executive Doc.; and the *New York Tribune*, 11, 12, and 22 July 1865. Wirz is also discussed in Otis Futch, *Andersonville* (1968); Arch Fredric Blakey, *General John H. Winder, C.S.A.* (1990); and William Marvel, *Andersonville: The Last Depot* (1994).

ARCH FREDRIC BLAKEY

WISE, Carroll Alonzo (31 Oct. 1903–5 Nov. 1985), educator in the field of pastoral counseling, was born in Verona, Pennsylvania, the son of Edwin Alonzo Wise, a machinist, and Bertha Elmira Neely. He attended Ohio Wesleyan University and received a bachelor of arts degree in 1927. Graduate studies at Boston University resulted in a bachelor of sacred theology in 1930. That same year he married Addiene Gates, with whom he would have two children. In 1930–1931 he participated in the student training program at the Worcester State Hospital for the mentally ill in Worcester, Massachusetts. There he worked under the direction of Anton Boisen, a leader in the field of mental illness and of the movement toward clinical pastoral training, an aspect of theological education that involves direct contact with persons confined to a hospital or clinical setting in an attempt to aid the healing process. This experience stimulated Wise's interest in the relationship of religion and health. Awarded a Th.D. in 1935, his dissertation was entitled "A Study of the Religious Factors in Seven Cases of Mental Illness."

In 1931 Wise became chaplain at the Worcester State Hospital, a position vacated by Boisen, and he continued in this capacity until 1942. During these years he completed his academic studies while teaching at Boston University on a part-time basis and serving as a counselor at the Worcester YMCA and YWCA. From 1942 to 1944 he served as director of the Department of Religion and Health for the Toledo Ohio Council of Churches, following which he accepted a position as minister of counseling at the Hennepin Avenue Methodist Church in Minneapolis. In 1948 he received an appointment as professor of pastoral psychology and counseling at Garrett Biblical Institute (now Garrett-Evangelical Theological Seminary) on the campus of Northwestern University in Evanston, Illinois. Wise taught at Garrett for nearly twenty-five years, until his retirement in 1972.

Wise began his teaching career with nearly two decades of training and experience in hospital and parish-based counseling. Influenced by this background and by Anton Boisen, he emphasized the personal and practical aspects of pastoral counseling, the importance of the counselor-client relationship, and the ability of the counselor to "feel with" the person being counseled. In this connection he remarked that "our chief goal is not to change persons' values, but to value persons" (E. Brooks Holifield, *A History of Pastoral Care in America* [1983], p. 282).

Soon after his arrival at Garrett, Wise began what proved to be a lifelong collaboration and friendship with a local psychiatrist, Carl W. Christensen. In 1952 they initiated a series of seminars on psychology and religion attended by members of the Garrett faculty and local psychotherapists. Through these seminars, Wise put into practice his firm belief that psychiatry and religion offer similar insights into the nature of human illness and health and that each has "a unique contribution to make, neither of which can be made by the other" (*Psychiatry and the Bible*, p. 5). His continuing close association with the psychiatric community led to a focus on the mental health of ministerial students, and Wise therefore encouraged pastoral counselors to undergo therapy themselves. He initiated various clinical training centers, which functioned in close connection with the theory being taught in the classroom. Finally, in conjunction with Garrett and the graduate school of Northwestern University, he inaugurated a Ph.D. program in pastoral counseling beginning in 1963; it became one of the largest and finest in the country.

Eventually Wise came to the conclusion that while every parish pastor needed to acquire certain counseling skills, there was also a need for a highly specialized and professionalized ministry of pastoral therapy. His commitment to this then controversial stance led to his participation in the development of the American Association of Pastoral Counselors (AAPC) in 1964. From then on Wise became a leader of as well as apologist for this group of professional counselors, which functioned as a standard-setting and accrediting body for their specialized vocation. In 1965 he was elected vice president of the group and from 1967 to 1969 served as its third president. His leadership brought national credibility to the fledgling organization, and in 1967 he was granted the AAPC Distinguished Contributions Award.

Following his retirement from the Garrett faculty, Wise spent the year 1973 helping to supervise the clinical pastoral education program at the Lutheran General Hospital in Park Ridge, Illinois. He also helped organize a hospital-based outpatient pastoral counseling center at Lutheran General, later known as the Pastoral Psychotherapy Institute, and served as its first executive director. He continued to serve the institute as a consultant, supervisor, and teacher until shortly before his death in Glenview, Illinois.

Because of his stress on the practical, Wise was sometimes accused of being anti-intellectual, a charge without substance. His convictions were biblically and theologically grounded. For nearly two decades, from the early 1950s until the 1970s, he was one of the foremost intellectual exponents of pastoral counseling. E. Brooks Holifield, a respected historian of the subject, has named Wise as one of the four pastoral theologians (the others being Seward Hiltner, Wayne Oates, and Paul Johnson) who "assumed a position of intellectual leadership in the postwar renaissance" (*A History of Pastoral Care in America*, p. 275).

In addition to his legacy of teaching and writing, Wise carried out pioneering work in the establishment of pastoral clinical training programs. He was instrumental also in the creation of higher professional standards for those specializing in the area of pastoral counseling.

• The Carroll Wise Papers are in the library of the Garrett-Evangelical Theological Seminary in Evanston, Ill. Wise was the author of five major books: *Religion in Illness and Health* (1942); *Pastoral Counseling, Its Theory and Practice* (1951), *Psychiatry and the Bible* (1956), *The Meaning of Pastoral Care* (1966), and *Pastoral Psychotherapy: Theory and Practice* (1983). He also was a frequent contributor to the *Journal of Pastoral Care* and *Pastoral Psychology*. The best overview and assessment of his work is a book of essays in his honor, edited by James B. Ashbrook and John E. Hinkle, Jr., *At the Point of Need, Living Human Experience* (1988). A brief assessment of his life and work is David M. Moss, "Epitaph: Carroll Alonzo Wise, Symbol of Pastoral Care," *Pastoral Psychology* 34 (Spring 1986): 147–50.

PAUL KUENNING

WISE, Henry Alexander (3 Dec. 1806–12 Sept. 1876), congressman, governor, and Confederate general, was born on Virginia's Eastern Shore in Drummondtown (now Accomac), the son of John Wise, a Federalist lawyer and legislator, and Sarah Corbin Cropper. Orphaned in 1812–1813, he was raised by relatives and had few resources other than a small inheritance. He received only a meager education until his admission in 1822 to Washington College (now Washington and Jefferson College) in Pennsylvania, where he graduated with first honors in 1825. He attended Chancellor Henry St. George Tucker's lectures in Winchester, Virginia, and passed the bar in 1828. Wise married Ann Eliza Jennings that year. They had four children before her death in 1837.

Wise cast his initial ballot in 1828 for Andrew Jackson and honeymooned at "the Hermitage." He investigated business opportunities in Tennessee but returned to his large farm, "Only." In 1833 Jacksonians nominated him for a congressional seat held by a nullifier. Wise won a narrow victory after a duel with his opponent and then opposed Jackson on both the Force Bill and a national bank, the first signs of his political independence from any leader or party. Wise was ambitious but had no powerful family connections or fortune to back him. He was further handicapped by his political base on the isolated Eastern Shore, whose economy and politics were often more closely tied to Baltimore and Philadelphia than to Richmond. Geography as well as conflicting political beliefs and priorities pulled him in different directions. Wise was idealistic and ambivalent, quixotic and pragmatic. He stood for important principles at various points in his career but did so unpredictably and inconsistently. His critics and defenders have emphasized different sets of characteristics. A true measure of the man would take both into account, as well as his mercurial temperament. Wise was hardly alone in switching party allegiances; the same was true of Edward Everett, Alexander Stephens, Thaddeus Stevens, and many other politicians in nineteenth-century America. Craig M. Simpson suggests that Wise may have longed for a father figure. He did not follow any leader for long and was occasionally a party of one. His own father's position in the Revolution has been debated, and Wise knew of the rumors that he had been a Tory.

A powerful speaker, wise was reelected five times (1833–1844). Named chairman of the Naval Affairs Committee, he nevertheless, as a party maverick, enjoyed little legislative success. Influenced by the writings of James Madison on a national bank and other major issues, Wise was not one of the original states' righters, an Old Republican, but he was antiabolitionist, supporting the gag rule to prohibit the reception in Congress of antislavery petitions in a losing battle with John Quincy Adams. Wise attacked the peculiar institution but also defended slavery and especially his state and region against northern criticism. He was an early opponent of Martin Van Buren, Jackson's designated successor, preferring " 'any decent *white* man in the nation' " (Braden, p. 119). Wise objected to the New Yorker's institutional loyalty and political organization.

Attracted to Hugh Lawson White by 1836, Wise joined the Whigs and broke with Jackson but always respected him and in many ways tried to emulate his leadership. The choice of William Henry Harrison over Henry Clay by the Whigs in 1839 followed by Harrison's early death and the succession of John Tyler, split the party. In 1840 Wise married Sarah Sergeant, daughter of a wealthy Whig congressman from Philadelphia. They had ten children, three of whom survived infancy. Sarah died in childbirth in 1850. Of his fourteen children born in nineteen years, only seven survived.

Wise backed his fellow Virginian Tyler over Clay, who was now an enemy. He had shielded Clay's involvement in a controversial duel and worked hard to carry Virginia for the Whigs, but he found Clay unappreciative and as domineering as Jackson. Wise was the leader of "the Corporal's Guard," a minority between Whigs and Democrats who backed Tyler in the House, and the president rewarded him in 1844, making him minister to Brazil. Wise spent much of his time attacking American involvement in the African slave trade, which he opposed on humanitarian grounds but also because of what he saw as the hypocrisy of northern shipowners. That crusade destroyed his usefulness in Brazil, and he left in 1847 virtually persona non grata. He then worked to revive his farm and law practice. He had become wealthy by local standards but not by those of Virginia's mainland elite, and, as the owner of nineteen slaves, he was just below the traditional criterion for membership in the planter class.

Wise rejoined the Democratic party in 1848 as he was increasingly out of step with national Whigs. He hoped for a Senate seat in return for his oratorical powers and following within Virginia, but he tried to avoid open politicking and did not attend the Nashville Convention. Wise thought the Compromise of 1850 was a disaster for the South because it denied slavery in California, whose gold mines Wise had hoped would draw off most of Virginia's slaves. His enemies felt that he did not act on his convictions, and at times he seemed to endorse the compromise, perhaps hoping to be seen as a national rather than a sectional leader. Fire-eaters sensed that Wise was not one of them and possibly unsound on slavery, and they preferred his greatest Virginia rival, Senator Robert M. T. Hunter, as the successor to John C. Calhoun, denying Wise election to the Senate.

Wise's political views have been characterized as "pure Jacksonian Republicanism." Clement Eaton was probably the first modern historian to recognize his "genuinely progressive instincts" (Simpson, p. 80). He supported universal public education and school reform, inspired by northern leaders like Horace Mann. Wise dominated Virginia's constitutional convention of 1850–1851, reaching out to underrepresented voters in the western part of the state. Men beyond the mountains won more proportional representation and a narrow majority in the Virginia House of Delegates, though easterners retained three-fifths of the seats in the senate. Wise's marriage in 1853 to the sickly Mary Elizabeth Lyons, the sister of James Lyons, a prominent Richmond lawyer and local political power, produced no children but helped his political career. In his 1855 campaign for governor against the Know Nothings, Wise won more ballots than any other Virginia politician in the nineteenth century. His victory by a 10,000-vote margin was the first defeat for the American party and rallied Democrats elsewhere. As governor he tried various measures to revive Virginia, encouraging industry, trade, transportation, and education and winning the praise of such disparate figures as George Fitzhugh and Horace Greeley.

Wise opposed Stephen A. Douglas's Kansas-Nebraska Bill in 1854, perhaps because he doubted the wisdom of repealing the Missouri Compromise. An early supporter of James Buchanan's presidential aspirations, he broke with him over Kansas, allying with Douglas. He was one of a few leading southerners to reject the Lecompton constitution embraced by the administration. Despite his vilification in the South, he had ties to fire-eater William L. Yancey and was mentioned in the North as a presidential candidate, with strong support among Catholic immigrants because of his earlier fight against the Know Nothings. Wise is best known as the governor at the time of John Brown's raid on Harpers Ferry in October 1859, and the two men were much alike in some ways. Wise came to have a genuine admiration for the antislavery zealot. He considered sending him to a lunatic asylum to spare him, but that would have required a joint resolution by the legislature, a political impossibility. Wise thought Brown to be both sane and brave; his hanging gave him the death that Wise thought Brown wanted and had earned.

"Once a critic of the established Southern order, Wise had become part of that order by 1860" (Simpson, p. 220). He pursued the presidency in 1860 but was undercut in his own state by Hunter's maneuvers. He then supported Vice President John C. Breckinridge, a states' rights Democrat and one of four candidates. Abraham Lincoln won almost no votes in Virginia, and Douglas got only a few, but it was enough to enable John Bell, the Constitutional Union candidate, to carry Virginia. Though he held no office, Wise was crucial to his state's secession. He claimed to favor "fighting in the Union," urging his followers to arm themselves with pikes if need be, like Brown. At the Richmond convention in February–April 1861, a majority of the delegates were conditional Unionists. Wise represented Princess Anne County, near Norfolk, to which he had relocated from the Eastern Shore. He gave little overt support to the secessionists until April, when he organized a "People's Convention" to pressure the delegates. After Fort Sumter he ordered an assault on the Harpers Ferry armory and the Norfolk Navy Yard on his own authority, 16–17 April 1861.

Appointed a brigadier general in the Confederate army on 5 June 1861, Wise served to the end as one of the most notable "political generals" on either side. Having no military training, he failed in the Kanawha Valley campaign that summer and at Roanoke Island in February 1862. He spent the last year in the Petersburg trenches, helping save the city from the initial Union assault in June 1864, and performed well on the retreat to Appomattox. A picturesque figure at the surrender, Union officers noted his defiance, including his brother-in-law George G. Meade.

Wise was indicted for treason, but the charge was soon dropped. He never sought a pardon and signed many letters "prisoner of war." Allowed to practice law in 1866, he worked with his oldest surviving son, John S. Wise, until his death. He served on the Virginia-Maryland Joint Boundary Commission, 1871–1874, and won his last case, a contested election dispute, before a House of Representatives committee in 1876. Wise obscured his own secessionism after the war while celebrating slavery's destruction and glorifying the Lost Cause. He defended blacks and Republicans as Conservatives regained control in Richmond and Virginia in 1869–1870, although he scorned Horace Greeley and supported Ulysses S. Grant in 1872. Wise was extraordinarily close to his family, as devoted to them as they were loyal to him. His memoir of the Tyler administration, *Seven Decades of the Union* (1871), sold well after Reconstruction, though neglected by historians. Wise died in Richmond, and James Cardinal Gibbons of Baltimore, remembering Wise's fight against the Know Nothings, spoke at his funeral. Wise was the quintessential Virginian, widely loved and deeply hated. A man of many contradictions but, as Simpson calls him, "a Good Southerner," he had been true in his own mind to Virginia and his deepest principles, including independence, loyalty to state and family, and courage.

• The major holdings of Wise's papers are at the Virginia Historical Society and the Library of Virginia, both in Richmond; the Library of Congress; and the National Archives. Significant holdings are also at the Huntington Library, San Marino, Calif.; the American Antiquarian Society, Worcester, Mass.; and both Duke and Harvard Universities. Craig M. Simpson, *A Good Southerner: The Life of Henry A. Wise of Virginia* (1985), is perhaps the best biography of any nineteenth-century southern politician. The extensive bibliography covers the literature, including several journal articles by Clement Eaton, who also discussed Wise in his books on intellectual currents in the Old South: *The Freedom-of-Thought Struggle in the Old South* (1940; rev. ed., 1964) and *The Mind of the Old South* (1964; rev. ed., 1967). A grandson, Barton Haxall Wise, wrote a detailed and comprehensive biography, *The Life of Henry A. Wise of Virginia* (1899), although it lacks documentation. His son, John Sergeant Wise, an important Readjuster and Republican politician in postwar Virginia, wrote a fascinating memoir, *The End of an Era* (1899), much of it about his father. Waldo W. Braden, ed., *Oratory in the Old South, 1828–1860* (1970), has some descriptions of Wise. Charles Henry Ambler, *Sectionalism in Virginia from 1776 to 1861* (1910); Henry T. Shanks, *The Secession Movement in Virginia, 1847–1861* (1934); Ollinger Crenshaw, *The Slave States in the Presidential Election of 1860* (1945); and Ralph A. Wooster, *The Secession Conventions of the South* (1962), all devote considerable attention to Wise. The best modern general study is the multivolume work of William W. Freehling, *The Road to Disunion* (1990–). Douglas Southall Freeman included rich detail on Wise in *Lee's Lieutenants*, vols. 1 and 3 (1942, 1944), with citations to references in *The War of the Rebellion: A Compilation of the Official Records of the Union and Confederate Armies* (128 vols., 1880–1901) and other published sources on the war. Noah Andrew Trudeau, *The Last Citadel: Petersburg, Virginia, June 1864–April 1865* (1991), describes Wise at the beginning of the siege. Jack P. Maddex, *The Virginia Conservatives, 1867–1879* (1970), is the standard work on the strange coalition of ex-Whigs, Know Nothings, Democrats, and northern capitalists whom Wise fought until his death. Richard Lowe, *Republicans and Reconstruction in Virginia, 1856–70* (1991), is the best study of their antagonists.

MICHAEL B. CHESSON

WISE, Henry Augustus (24 May 1819–2 Apr. 1869), naval officer and author, was born in Brooklyn, New York, the son of Captain George Stewart Wise, a naval officer, and Catherine Stansberry. His father died in 1824, at which time Wise was taken into the household of his grandfather, George Douglas Wise, at Craney Island, near Norfolk, Virginia. On 8 February 1834 he entered the navy as a midshipman under the guidance of his guardian and cousin, Henry Alexander Wise, later governor of Virginia. Over the next few years Wise was educated in maritime matters by serving on board ships. Then he attended naval school at Philadelphia for two years, 1839–1840, achieving the rank of passed midshipman in the U.S. Navy on 16 July 1840. From 1840 to 1843 he served in the Depot of Charts and on other special-duty assignments. In 1844 he joined the *Plymouth* on the Mediterranean Station. After a year's duty on board the *Plymouth*, Wise was promoted to master on 31 October 1846 and was transferred to the razee *Independent*. During the Mexican War, 1846–1848, he was with the *Independent* on the Pacific Station, participating in naval warfare in the Gulf of California, at Mazatlán, and at La Paz. On 25 February 1847 he was promoted to lieutenant. Because he had learned Spanish at some time during his career, he was chosen to carry crucial messages from Mazatlán to Mexico City on one important occasion.

After the war, in 1850 Wise married Charlotte Brooks Everett, daughter of Edward Everett; they had four children. From 1850 to 1852 he served with the Coast and Geodetic Survey then spent two years on the frigate *Cumberland* on the Mediterranean Station. From 1855 to 1860 he was on ordnance duty in Boston and Washington, becoming an expert in gunnery and writing numerous papers on the subject. Seriously wounded in an accident, he recuperated in France and clandestinely gathered information on German ordnance research. In 1860 he was assigned to the U.S. Japanese Commission and sent to Japan. Through all these years, he was developing a second career as a writer of popular books, stealing time to compose them under the pseudonym Harry Gringo. Also, he was often on leave of absence from the navy for health reasons, and he availed himself of these occasions to travel and collect information for his writing. In 1849 he published *Los Gringos; or, An Inside View of Mexico and California, with Wanderings in Peru, Chile, and Polynesia*, wherein he related some of his Mexican War experiences. His second book, *Tales for the Marines* (1855), contained much autobiographical material on his early life in the navy. In 1857 he published *Scampavias: From Gibel-Tarek to Stamboul*; three years later a children's book, *The Story of the Gray African Parrot*; and in 1864, *Captain Brand of the "Centipede"*.

When the Civil War broke out in 1861, Captain Wise was torn between his loyalty to the U.S. Navy, which was his professional home, and to the state of Virginia, where he had grown up. He finally opted for the navy and ironically was almost immediately ordered to Portsmouth, Virginia, to destroy the Gosport Navy Yard, near his old home. Later attached to the steam frigate *Niagara*, he was in the first blockading squadron off Charleston, South Carolina, in 1861. On 16 July 1862 he was promoted to commander and ten days later appointed assistant chief of the Bureau of Ordnance and Hydrography under Rear Admiral John Dahlgren. He served in this bureau until January 1869, rendering valuable service and working himself so hard that he may have contributed to his death. On 25 June 1863 he was promoted to acting chief of the bureau when Dahlgren was ordered to sea, but Wise felt he should have been made chief. Secretary of the Navy Gideon Welles mused on 8 April 1864 that Wise was "almost insane for the appointment" and had been denigrating Dahlgren to achieve promotion. On 25 August 1864 Wise was appointed chief by President Abraham Lincoln, but the bad blood between him and Dahlgren continued. Later that year he and Dahlgren got into a controversy over gun casting, which led Welles to accuse Wise of being "meddlesome and perhaps unjust." Despite his difficulties with Dahlgren, Wise was highly regarded by powerful men in Washington, and he hobnobbed with Welles, Postmaster General Montgomery Blair, and various senators and congressmen.

On 29 December 1866 Wise achieved the rank of captain, his last promotion in the navy. He ran into difficulties with Congress in June 1867, when a committee was appointed to inquire into ordnance financial transactions. Although Secretary Welles considered the committee members "scoundrels," he nevertheless ordered Wise to cooperate with the investigation. Wise, who Welles described as "nervously excitable, and not over-profound and firm," was startled by Welles's lack of support, but the secretary believed that Wise, although incorruptible, was too friendly with some contractors. Welles was not certain as to how Wise would fare before the committee, for although he believed Wise to be brave and sagacious, he also thought him "mentally timid." In fact, Wise acquitted himself well, and nothing came of the investigation.

In 1868, for reasons of health, Wise resigned his position with the board and took medical leave from the navy. He was replaced by his nemesis, Dahlgren, who immediately implored Welles to convoke a committee to review Wise's record as chief of the Ordnance Bureau, in hopes of blackening his reputation. Welles refused to cooperate, for he correctly believed that Dahlgren was motivated by spite and was merely using him as a cat's-paw. Wise died in Naples, Italy, while seeking a restoration of his health.

• Wise's correspondence with his cousin, Governor Henry Wise of Virginia (1855–1859), is in the latter's papers, Library of Congress. His correspondence during the Civil War is in *The Official Records of the Union and Confederate Navies in the War of the Rebellion*, ser. 1, vols. 7–14, 20–25 (30 vols., 1894–1922). Edgar Thaddeus Welles, ed., *The Diary of Gideon Welles*, vols. 1–3 (1911), is invaluable. Howard K. Beale, ed., *The Diary of Gideon Welles* (3 vols., 1960), is another version. Edward W. Callahan, ed., *List of Officers of the Navy of the United States and of the Marine Corps, from 1775 to 1900* (1901), contains biographical information. For a genealogy, see Jennings C. Wise, *Col. John Wise of England and Virginia (1617–1695): His Ancestors and Descendants* (1918). Background on the Board of Ordnance is in Robert V. Bruce, *Lincoln and the Tools of War* (1956); and Warren Ripley, *Artillery and Ammunition of the Civil War* (1970). Background on the Union navy is in Richard S. West, *Mr. Lincoln's Navy* (1957); and James M. Merrill, *The Rebel Shore: The Story of Union Sea Power in the Civil War* (1957). Wise's testimony before the congressional committee is in an obituary in the *New York Daily Tribune*, 12 Apr. 1869. Another obituary is in the *Boston Advertiser*, 22 June 1869, reprinted in the *New York Times*, 23 June 1869.

PAUL DAVID NELSON

WISE, Isaac Mayer (29 Mar. 1819–26 Mar. 1900), rabbi and leader of American Reform Judaism, was born in Steingrub (now Kammeny Dvur), near Eger (now Cheb), in Bohemia, the son of Leo Weis and his wife Regina (maiden name unknown). Little is known of his early years. He grew up in poverty, and his father died when he was quite young. Thrown on his own resourcefulness at an early age, he studied at talmudic schools in Bohemia and Austria. He may have attended university lectures in Vienna, but he was not registered as a student.

One influence from his sojourn in Vienna was that of the Mendelssohnian Enlightenment, mediated through Hertz Homberg. A collaborator of Moses Mendelssohn's, Homberg was an enemy of Hasidism. This influence may be seen as the source of Wise's ready acquaintanceship with rabbinic texts, informed by the belief in reason as the basis of Judaism. Whether he was ordained to the rabbinate is uncertain, but in 1843 he was appointed a religious functionary in the Jewish community of Radnitz, near Pilsen. In 1846 he joined the stream of migrants to the United States, landing in New York on 23 July, 1846, after a sixty-three day journey from Bremen. Whether he migrated with the intention of acting as rabbi is uncertain, but soon after his arrival the opportunity arose for him to serve the Jewish congregation in Albany, New York, and he remained there until 1854.

The differences between the society that Wise had left and the one in which he now settled need no elaboration. What would be interesting to demonstrate is the transformation that these differences caused in Wise's personality. Thirty years after his arrival, Wise professed to have had a dream on shipboard, according to which the ship was driven onto the rocks, but he alone had the courage to stride forward, climbing the promontory in his way, despite the derision of opponents ("hollow-eyed, ghostly, grinning dwarfs") until he brought himself with his wife and children to safety. This statement appeared at a time when Wise's long cherished plans for the organization of American Jewry, apparently near fruition, seemed in danger of being thwarted by his opponents. When the vision of himself as the man of destiny first took shape in Wise's mind is uncertain, but his settling in America brought forth traits—abundant energy, boundless self confidence, and broad vision—of which his life in Bohemia had given no hint.

The Jewish congregation had been established in 1838 in Albany. Here, as elsewhere in the United States, the Jewish scene betrayed both expansion and confusion. The flow of immigrants from central Europe resulted in the formation of new congregations scattered over a broad expanse of territory; but there was no guidance to which the newcomers could turn when facing the problems presented by the freedom to which they had never been accustomed. It was an open society, the reverse of that which most had known in Europe. The members of these congregations took for granted the practice of Judaism as known in their home towns. In America different elements were thrown together, and conflicts between different local usages needed to be resolved. Religion was entirely voluntary, and congregations as well as individuals were free to follow their own devices. Above all, there was a change of language. The younger generation needed English teachers. There was no one to train and authorize rabbis and teachers and to discharge the responsibility of producing religious literature. To add to the dilemmas, a philosophy of Reform Judaism was emerging in Germany, and the confusion was intensified by the injection of ideological controversies.

Wise quickly grasped the needs of the New World. He brought about the changes that he thought were needed in his Albany congregation, but he also saw that only through a union of congregations could the problems facing the local units be tackled. On the theological questions, Wise was inclined to be equivocal. In his thinking, a union of congregations came first. This would set up a synod and tackle practical questions, such as the production of a prayer book. In 1848 he joined in an attempt to set up such a union preparing the manuscript of a new prayer book, but the attempt failed.

Wise's program offended many members of the Albany congregation, and to this was added opposition to his flirtation with reform. In 1850 the congregation resolved to discharge him, but Wise refused to acknowledge the validity of the resolution of dismissal, and the upshot was a fracas in the synagogue during the New Year services. Wise and his followers thereupon formed their own congregation, which he led until 1854, when he received a call to congregation B'nai Yeshurun in Cincinnati.

Cincinnati was then the "Queen City of the West" and brought Wise many personal contacts. He quickly came to dominate his own flock. A program of gradual reform was initiated, but Wise had his eye on wider horizons. In July 1854 he launched a weekly newspaper, *The Israelite* (later, the *American Israelite*), and scarcely had it taken off when he began a second weekly, *Die Deborah*, in German. He ceaselessly advocated a union of congregations that would publish a prayer book and authorize modifications in traditional practice and that would also undertake the training of rabbis. Likewise he attacked with relentless vehemence any denigration of the Jews or Judaism, and he repeatedly claimed that as the result of his lonely advocacy, Judaism had been "naturalised" in the American system, instead of remaining an outlandish sect.

For these enterprises Wise sought immediate action. He was the moving spirit in the convening of a conference of rabbis that met in Cleveland in 1855. He managed to secure adherence to a platform that it was hoped would be acceptable to Orthodox and Reformers alike and would be the basis on which a synod and a union of congregations would be established. At the same time he announced the formation of the Zion Collegiate Association, which was to be both a Jewish university and a seminary for training rabbis. Both efforts failed because the congregations were separated by great distances. They were concerned primarily with local problems, and among the rabbis ideological and personal differences arose.

In his effort for comprehensiveness, Wise was accused of sacrificing the ideals of reform, while the Orthodox still did not trust him because of his inclination to reform. At a personal level, people believed that he had a desire for personal aggrandizement. Violent controversies ensued in which Wise took a leading part. He showed himself "neither simple nor all of one piece. He was generous, charming, and able. He was a soaring visionary, but also an astute politician with a sense of reality and a lust for leadership; he was prepared to stoop in order to conquer, but he never lost sight of his goal." In the atmosphere leading up to the Civil War, efforts to unite the Jewish community received little support. Purporting to draw on authority conferred by the 1855 Cleveland Conference, Wise issued a moderately reformed prayer book (*Minhag America*) in 1857, but this too became the butt of controversy.

Impelling Wise was not only his understanding of the needs of the Jewish community but a fervent belief in the American system of government. He saw in it the consummation of the ideas first promulgated by Moses. Hence, the threatened break-up of the American union was to be avoided, and he mistrusted the Abolitionists because he thought they were bringing about that catastrophe and because he considered their evangelical Christianity a threat to Judaism.

Despite the difficult circumstances, Wise constantly propagated his ideas, and, once the Civil War had settled the issue of the nation's unity, he could more easily pursue his goals.

A number of rabbinic conferences intended to promote unity took place during the period from 1869; instead they generated an acrimony among the rabbis that mostly centered on Wise. However, in 1873 the Union of American Hebrew Congregations was established in Cincinnati with the fundamental limitation that the autonomy of individual members was not to be thwarted. In 1875 the Union established Hebrew Union College, with Wise as its president, and in 1883 Wise ordained its first quartet of rabbis. In 1889 the Central Conference of American Rabbis was formed, and Wise was elected president for life. He carried on his shoulders every aspect of the life of the college, and his success in filling many pulpits with his own disciples enhanced his position.

While Wise was conscious of the superiority of his program, he was an affable man, and this quality helped to spread his influence during his constant travels; he was always in demand to officiate in other congregations. He never revisited Europe and, differing from an influential section of Reform Jews, was firm in his belief that American Jewry must develop self-sustaining institutions.

None of the three organizations that acknowledged Wise's leadership used the label "Reform," an indication of the comprehensiveness that Wise was expecting. Nevertheless, comprehensiveness eluded his group. His own disciples accepted a radical Reform position, and Wise's own endorsement of the Pittsburgh Platform (1885) indicated a surrender to that viewpoint. Moreover, a second and larger community of East European Jews was expanding that had no place for Wise's moderate Reform position.

Wise was a prolific writer; history, theology, and Bible studies, as well as novels, flowed from his pen. However, none of his writings has proved to be of lasting interest. His prayer book, *Minhag America*, had a certain vogue but was superseded in 1894 by the *Union Prayer Book* (issued by the Central Conference of American Rabbis). Wise had urged a synod that would exercise authority, but it was not achieved. He had also sought a comprehensive American Judaism, but his organizations came to represent the Reform group only.

Derided by opponents as the "Western Pope" and rejected by some for his intellectual deficiencies, he was accepted as the patriarch of the American Rabbinate. Americans admired the "doer," and the worth of his program is visible in the success of his institutions.

Wise first married Theresa Bloch in 1844. They had four sons and four daughters, and she died in 1874. In 1876 he married Selma Bondi, with whom he had four children. Their daughter, Iphigene, married Adolph Ochs, who became the proprietor of the *New York Times*.

• Though material in print concerning Isaac Mayer Wise is abundant, little by way of personal correspondence has survived. The most comprehensive collection of material is in the American Jewish Archives, on the Cincinnati Campus of Hebrew Union College. Two autobiographical works are *Reminiscences* (1901), covering the years 1846–1857, and *The World of My Books* (1954).

Of the several biographies that have appeared, the first was by his grandson, Max B. May, *Isaac Mayer Wise, the Founder of American Judaism* (1916); another is Sefton D. Temkin's *Isaac Mayer Wise—the Shaping of American Judaism* (1993). The most extensive biography is James G. Heller's *Isaac M. Wise—His Life, Work and Thought* (1965), which includes a full bibliography and a list of Wise's writings. Michael A. Meyer's *Response to Modernity* (1988) discusses Wise in the context of the history of Reform Judaism, and Israel Knox's *Rabbi in America* (1957) analyzes Wise's intellectual postion.

SEFTON D. TEMKIN

WISE, John (baptized 15 Aug. 1652–8 Apr. 1725), clergyman and political controversialist, was born in Roxbury, Massachusetts, the son of Joseph Wise, a farmer and former indentured servant, and Mary Thompson. Despite his family's modest resources, Wise graduated from Harvard College in 1673. He then preached briefly at Branford, Connecticut (1675–1676), served as an army chaplain in King Philip's War, and moved to the parish at Hatfield, Massachusetts (1677–1680). In 1682 he settled at Chebacco, the second parish of the town of Ipswich on Massachusetts's north shore, where he was ordained in August 1683 and remained until his death. A minister was expected to work like any other farmer in his spare time, and Wise received an additional £20 per year if he provided his own wood and hay and kept the parsonage in good repair. A man of great stature and strength, Wise in 1678 married Abigail Gardner; they had five sons and two daughters.

Wise first achieved prominence when he led a delegation to Boston in August 1687 to protest the levying of a tax by Governor Sir Edmund Andros of the Dominion of New England, who ruled without a representative legislature. Wise argued, "The said act doth infringe their liberty as free English subjects of His Majesty by interfering with the statute laws of the land, by which it was enacted that no taxes should be levied upon the subjects without consent of an assembly." He was arrested along with five others for "excit[ing] and stirring up His Majesty's subjects to disobedience." Councillor and former governor Joseph Dudley may have responded to the Ipswich protest saying, "You have no more privileges left you, than not to be sold for slaves," and Andros himself "ridiculed" the idea that "Jack and Tom might tell the king what moneys he must have for the use of his government." Given this attitude, Wise's contention that "the laws of England follow us to the ends of the earth" fell on deaf ears. He was declared guilty by a packed jury, fined £50, sentenced to three weeks in jail, and his right to preach was suspended for a year. This ban was lifted when he paid his fine and back taxes and abjectly apologized. Yet neither Wise nor Ipswich had done more than yield to necessity. When the Dominion of New England was overthrown in 1689, Wise sued Dudley for denying him habeas corpus, and the town paid his fine. The town seal of Ipswich still reads, "The Birthplace of American Independence: 1687."

In July 1690 Wise accompanied Massachusetts troops on their ill-fated campaign to Quebec, where he not only executed "the pious discharge of his sacred office, but his heroic spirit and martial skill and wisdom did greatly distinguish him," according to soldier John White. Wise also led thirty-one of his congregation in petitioning for the release of people accused of witchcraft during the Salem trials of 1692, arguing that God may "sometimes permit Satan to [im]personate, dissemble, and thereby abuse innocents."

Wise's most important political writings, *The Churches Quarrel Espoused* (1710) and *A Vindication of the Government of New-England Churches* (1717), were contributions to a protracted battle in the early eighteenth century over the governance of New England's established Congregational church. Led by Cotton Mather and Increase Mather, the more conservative ministers sought to establish a Presbyterian church polity, in which consociations of clergy would rule on doctrine and the acceptability of neighboring ministers instead of the congregations themselves. They thereby hoped to avoid fiascos like the appointment of "liberal" Benjamin Colman to preach to Boston's Brattle Street Church in 1699. Wise, however, linked self-government in church affairs with civil autonomy:

> By the suffrage of our Nation, that Government which sensibly Clogs Tyranny, and Preserves the subject free from slavery, under the ambition of men of great Fortune and Trust, is the only gover[n]ment in the state to advance man's temporal Happiness; and we in the Country Honour the Resolve in Civil Affairs, and also affirm (upon great Experience) that such a Constitution in Church Government is (also) the only way to achieve Grace and man's Eternal Happiness. (quoted in Cook, p. 107)

Wise criticized the Mathers' proposed innovations as "the beggared prerogatives of clergymen" that "come so thick in this place, and smell so strong of the POPE'S cooks and kitchen, where his broths and restoratives are prepared, that they are enough to strangle a *Free-Born English-Man*."

Such vivid prose justifies Wise's place in American literature. "He stands almost alone among our early writers for the blending of a racy and dainty humor with impassioned earnestness" (Tyler, p. 114). However, it does not support claims that he was the first American democrat (Tyler, p. 115). Wise's defenses of traditional New England church and civil government only stood out among those of many of his contemporaries' for their stylistic flair. For that reason they were reprinted in Boston in 1772 as the colonial crisis worsened.

In the last decade of his life, Wise also took up the cause of a private land bank that would issue paper money to relieve Massachusetts's shortage of hard currency and economic woes. His two anonymous pamphlets of 1721, *A Word of Comfort to a Melancholy Country* and *A Letter to an Eminent Clergyman in Massachusetts Bay*, warned that, if a bank were not "speedily adopted," the "whole province" would be "in a flame." "Indeed, it is now confessed by all, except a few of the most screwing misers who are for no bank at all, but the clam bank." Massachusetts's Council condemned the pamphlet and its unknown author for using "vile, scandalous, and very abusive expressions which greatly reflect on His Majesty's government and the people of this province, and tend to disturb the peace." The affair soon blew over, but Wise continued to enter the public fray by supporting novelties in both the medical and musical worlds, such as smallpox inoculation and singing in the Congregational church using notes. Wise died in Ipswich.

Wise is remembered for his eloquent defense of American liberty and his exciting pamphlets. These so vividly stand out among his contemporaries' more pedestrian essays that historians have credited him with pioneering modern ideas as well as a modern style. Wise exemplified rather than innovated for the world of late seventeenth- and early eighteenth-century New England. Study of his participation in war, the Glorious Revolution, and political, ecclesiastical, economic, and cultural battles is an excellent way of tracing Puritanism's responses to a variety of challenges.

• Wise's works are available in Clifford K. Shipton, ed., *Early American Imprints* (1959) microfilm. His works on currency and politics are reprinted in Andrew M. Davis, *Colonial Currency Reprints*, vols. 1–2 (1910–1911), and Edmund S. Morgan, ed., *Puritan Political Ideas* (1965). George Allan Cook, *John Wise: Early American Democrat* (1952), is a full-length modern biography. See also Clinton Rossiter, "John Wise: Colonial Democrat," *New England Quarterly* 22 (1949): 3–22; Raymond P. Stearns, "John Wise of Ipswich Was No Democrat in Politics," *Essex Institute Historical Collections* 97 (1961): 2–18; and Richard M. Gummere, "John Wise: A Classical Controversialist," *Essex Institute Historical Collections* 92 (1956): 265–78. Still useful is Moses Coit Tyler, *A History of American Literature*, vol. 2 (1897).

WILLIAM PENCAK

WISE, John (24 Feb. 1808–29 Sept. 1879), balloonist, was born in Lancaster, Pennsylvania, the son of William Weiss (occupation unknown) and Margaret Trey. Educated in both German and English, the nationalities of his parents, he attended local schools and graduated from the Lancaster high school. Following the custom of the third generation in immigrant families of Lancaster County, he anglicized his last name. From his sixteenth to his twenty-first years, he was apprenticed to a cabinetmaker, and until 1835 he was a piano maker. Then, from 1836 to 1847, he worked for a firm that produced scientific instruments.

Later in life, he claimed that his almost lifelong interest in ballooning sprang from an article he read on the subject in a newspaper written in German. He was fourteen at the time. Not until thirteen years later, however, in the spring of 1835 when he was living in Philadelphia, did he decide to make his first balloon. As he claimed, he did so without ever having witnessed an ascension or having any practical knowledge of how a balloon was constructed. He studied the atmosphere and contemporary technology, making the balloon of domestic sheeting muslin rather than the superior but more costly silk. Instead of expensive dopes and varnishes, he used birdlime suspended in linseed oil to cover the muslin and make it leakproof. His first flight took place on 2 May 1835, carrying him from Philadelphia some nine miles to Haddonfield, New Jersey.

After several more flights in the muslin balloon, he attempted an ascent on 1 October 1835 in which his gondola hit the eaves of a two-story house, dumping him on the roof while the balloon continued on without him. "Thus ended," he remarked, "the experiments with a machine that had given me much more trouble than reputation as a skillful aeronaut."

It did not end his troubles. He acquired a silk balloon and launched it from Lancaster on 7 May 1836. He landed in Harford County, Maryland, about seventy-five miles away, after an uneventful flight, but as he emptied the hydrogen from the envelope, the gas remained close to the earth in the humid air and ignited from a lantern. Wise and several bystanders were severely burned. After this experience he temporarily abandoned ballooning and became an instrument maker.

He did not, however, give up on the visions he had developed for the future of aerial transportation. Neither could he forget the thrill of flight despite the dangers he had encountered. He was moved to return to flying by the death of Robert Cocking while the English experimenter was testing a new, inverted parachute. Wise believed Cocking's concept was sound, so on 18 September 1837 he ascended in a balloon from Philadelphia, dropping a dog in a regular parachute and a cat in the Cocking variety. Both landed safely, although the aeronaut was swept against a three-story building and had to exit the balloon through a window.

Experiencing problems with the varnish he was using, in 1838 the balloonist experimented with different substances and discovered that linseed oil by itself proved an adequate treatment for the envelope fabric. He designed his next balloon with a line that enabled him to release all the hydrogen. Taking off from Easton, Pennsylvania, on 11 August 1838, he intended to release the gas and show that the envelope itself would act as a parachute when empty. When he reached 13,000 feet, however, the expanding envelope pulled the line taut, and the gas rushed from the opening "with tempestuous noise," as he recalled. Nevertheless, the empty bag did serve as a parachute, according to plan. On 1 October of the same year, Wise successfully repeated the experiment under more controlled conditions.

He continued his flights and experiments, and by 1847 he had become a professional balloonist rather than an instrument maker. Living in Lancaster from 1848 to 1872, he seems to have earned his livelihood from crowds in the Northeast and Midwest who observed his flights and/or paid to ascend in a tethered balloon. He also sold new and used balloons to other aeronauts. He was married, but there appears to be no information about the date of the marriage or his wife's name; his son Charles E. Wise became one of his students in the art of ballooning. Charles made his own first balloon ascent on 3 September 1853, when he was 17 and went on to become a professional balloonist.

John Wise was among those who observed the effect of solar heating on a dark balloon. He was interested in science, especially meteorology, and he appears to have anticipated the much later discovery of the jet stream, while underestimating its altitude. In Wise's own lifetime, his major claim to fame was a flight he made with three other men, including one of his students, from St. Louis, Missouri, to Henderson, New York, on 1–2 July 1859. They covered a distance of over 800 miles, a world record that lasted several decades.

In 1871–1872 Wise served as librarian for the Franklin Institute in Philadelphia. He continued occasional balloon flights despite advancing age and was involved for a time in 1873 in what proved to be an abortive scheme for a flight across the Atlantic. On 28 September 1879, Wise ascended from St. Louis on what turned out to be his last flight. The balloon with Wise and a companion aboard was last seen from the southern shore of Lake Michigan at 11:30 that night. A body identified as that of the companion was later recovered from the lake. Wise's body was not recovered, but he was presumed to have drowned sometime the following day.

During forty-four years as a balloonist, Wise made 463 ascents. He was the most experienced and distinguished American aeronaut of his day, perhaps the greatest American balloonist of all time. According to the *Missouri Republican* of 6 October 1879, he did more than any other American to advance the cause of aerial navigation. Supplementing the influence of his many and notable flights were his writings, *A System of Aeronautics* (1850) and *Through the Air* (1873), as well as several articles for *Scientific American* in 1870 on ballooning and the use of balloons in meteorological research.

• On Wise's life and ballooning feats, see Pearl I. Young, "John Wise and his Balloon Ascensions in the Middle West," *Wingfoot Lighter-Than-Air Society Bulletin* (Oct. 1967): 2–6, and Tom D. Crouch, *The Eagle Aloft: Two Centuries of the Balloon in America* (1983). There is a biographical sketch in *Appleton's Cyclopedia of American Biography* (1900) that concentrates on his ballooning more than his life. For details of his longest flight, consult Wise's *Full Particulars of the Greatest Aerial Voyage on Record From St. Louis, Mo., to Adams, New York, in Nineteen Hours* (1859). Further information on

Wise appears in two folders of newspaper clippings and biographical sketches at the National Air and Space Museum in Washington, D.C., including information on a flight on which he carried the first stamped letters in a balloon on 17 Aug. 1859.

J. D. HUNLEY

WISE, John Sergeant (27 Dec. 1846–12 May 1913), lawyer, politician, and author, was born in Rio de Janeiro, Brazil, the son of Henry Alexander Wise, a former congressman from Virginia who was then serving as U.S. minister plenipotentiary to Brazil, and Sarah Sergeant. When Wise was less than a year old, his family returned to Virginia. He grew up on the plantations "Only," in Accomack County, and "Rolleston," in Princess Anne County, near the Chesapeake Bay. From 1856 to 1859, during his father's term as governor, John lived in Richmond. Educated in private schools, he developed a precocious interest in politics and military affairs.

With the outbreak of the Civil War, in which Wise's father served as a Confederate general, the family moved inland to Franklin County to escape invading Union troops. In September 1862 Wise commenced studies at the Virginia Military Institute (VMI) in Lexington. Slightly wounded at the battle of New Market, where the VMI cadet corps helped to repel a May 1864 Federal offensive, he subsequently abandoned classwork for service in the Confederate army. A brief stay with his father in the Petersburg fortifications was followed by appointment as second lieutenant in a reserve unit in southwestern Virginia, where he participated in efforts to apprehend deserters. Reassigned to forces defending the Richmond and Danville Railroad, he performed hazardous duty as a courier between President Jefferson Davis and General Robert E. Lee during the final days of the war.

A few months after the Confederate surrender, Wise, still only eighteen, enrolled at the University of Virginia in Charlottesville. He graduated from the School of Moral Philosophy in 1866 and from the School of Law the following year. He began practice as an attorney in Richmond in partnership with his father. In 1869 Wise married Evelyn Byrd Beverley Douglas; the couple had seven sons and two daughters.

Despite the pressures of his legal practice and burdensome financial obligations stemming from the debts of an improvident in-law, Wise became increasingly involved in Reconstruction Era politics. Neither Wise nor his father, who was anxious to make a comeback at the polls, initially supported black suffrage or the other concessions that Virginia's dominant Conservative (or Democratic) party had made to meet the requirements for the state's readmission to the Union. Additional frustrations arose from a failed bid to return the senior Wise to the governorship in 1873 and from a prolonged, futile struggle to weaken the power of railroad lobbyist Bradley T. Johnson in Richmond's Conservative organization. Despite these adverse circumstances, compounded by his father's death in 1876, Wise's prestige was on the rise. Governor James L. Kemper appointed him to the VMI Board of Visitors in 1876, and he was elected captain of the Richmond Light Infantry Blues, an elite militia unit, two years later.

Meanwhile, the ambitious young attorney was gradually being drawn into the orbit of political manipulator par excellence William Mahone, an erstwhile Confederate general and one of the state's foremost railroad executives. Mahone championed popular demands for partial repudiation of Virginia's $45 million public debt and, in spite of his unsuccessful drive for the Conservative gubernatorial nomination in 1877, emerged as leader of the Conservative party's so-called "Readjuster" wing, which won control of the legislature in 1879 and elected him to the U.S. Senate. Mahone then forged an alliance with national and state Republicans that enabled his adherents to rout the Conservative "Funders" (debt payers) in gubernatorial and legislative elections in 1881.

Despite misgivings about Mahone's financial radicalism, Wise, who had known and admired the general since the war, soon joined the inner circles of the debt revolt. He worked for Mahone as a floor leader at the 1877 Conservative State Convention and later helped to draft key repudiationist legislation. Wise ran unsuccessfully for Congress against his Funder cousin George D. Wise in 1880. Lambasted for betraying the Old Dominion's "honor," John Wise later exchanged fire with one of his critics in a bloodless duel. Named to the University of Virginia Board of Visitors in 1882 by Readjuster governor William E. Cameron, he received a more tangible reward for his services when President Chester A. Arthur appointed him federal attorney for the state's eastern district. He occupied the latter post for less than a year, during which he campaigned for and won Virginia's at-large seat in the U.S. House of Representatives. Serving in Congress from 1883 to 1885, he affiliated with the Republicans and denounced the violence and election fraud perpetrated by southern Democrats.

Wise's subsequent political career proved anticlimactic. In 1885, as dividing lines between the Old Dominion's Funders and Readjusters faded, he ran for governor on the Republican ticket. His Democratic opponent, General Fitzhugh Lee, won by a narrow, 16,000-vote margin amid GOP charges of ballot-box manipulation. Disillusioned by defeat, Wise became increasingly critical of Mahone's autocratic management of the state's Republican party. The ex-congressman shifted into open insurgency in 1888, when he led a rival slate of delegates to the Republican National Convention and successfully challenged the credentials of most of the regular "Mahoneites," a pyrrhic victory. With Mahone still dominating Virginia's Republican machine, Wise was now a political outcast.

Fortunately, Wise's law practice offered an alternative outlet for his energies. Representing the Sprague Electric Railroad and Motor Company, which had built Richmond's trolley system, he won a series of suits contesting Bell Telephone's claim to a monopoly of overhead lines for the transmission of electric power. Employed by Frank J. Sprague as general counsel, he moved with his family to New York City in September 1888 and retained his position when the Sprague interests were absorbed into the Edison Electric Company the following year. After establishing himself as a pioneer in electrical law, he resumed private practice in Manhattan during the mid-1890s, at first in partnership with Dallas Flanagan and then from 1898 to 1911 with his son Henry A. Wise.

Still active in politics, the transplanted southerner served as a New York delegate to Republican National Conventions in 1896 and 1900 and made several multistate speaking tours, the last in 1908, on behalf of GOP candidates. On a related note, he appeared before federal courts from 1902 to 1904 in a succession of unsuccessful challenges to Virginia's newly imposed voting restrictions on blacks and poor whites, traditional Republican constituencies.

Widely celebrated as an orator and raconteur, Wise also achieved considerable prominence as a man of letters. His articles, many dealing with antebellum and Civil War topics, appeared in such periodicals as *Century*, the *Atlantic Monthly*, and the *Saturday Evening Post*. More significantly, he authored two novels, *Diomed* (1897) and *The Lion's Skin: A Historical Novel and a Novel History* (1905), a thinly disguised autobiography; two volumes of reminiscences, *The End of an Era* (1899) and *Recollections of Thirteen Presidents* (1906); and one civics text, *A Treatise on American Citizenship* (1906).

An underlying theme of many of Wise's publications was his love for the Old Dominion—its people, its Confederate heroes, and its contributions to the national heritage. Ultimately, the pull of these ancestral ties put an end to his self-imposed exile in the North. In 1899 he purchased "Kiptopeke," an estate at the tip of Virginia's Eastern Shore, and spent much time there, especially after his health began to fail in 1907. He died at the residence of one of his sons near Princess Anne, Maryland. A talented, controversial man, his life as wartime Confederate and Gilded Age Republican, state debt repudiator and corporate attorney, Virginian and New Yorker contained more than its share of paradoxes.

• The Wise Family Papers at the Virginia Historical Society (Richmond) contain extensive material pertaining to John S. Wise, as does the William Mahone Collection at Duke University. Additional Wise papers are housed at the Virginia Military Institute and at the College of William and Mary.

Several of Wise's publications provide valuable information about his life. For a list of his numerous literary endeavors see Curtis Carroll Davis, "Wise Words from Virginia: Published Writings of John S. Wise, of the Eastern Shore and New York City," *Papers of the Bibliographical Society of America* 54 (1960): 273–85. Davis provides a sprightly overview of Wise in "Very Well-Rounded Republican: The Several Lives of John S. Wise," *Virginia Magazine of History and Biography* 71 (1963): 461–87. Also by Davis, see "A Brief for John Sergeant Wise," in *The End of an Era*, repr. (1965), pp. xvii–lxiii; "His Name Was Diomed," *Virginia Cavalcade* 10 (1960): 42–47, about Wise's innovative idea of a dog as the narrator/protagonist in one of his novels; and "The Small Bang at Bangs," *Virginia Cavalcade* 11 (1961): 4–9, focusing on Wise's activities as a duelist. The most comprehensive treatment of Wise's role in the state debt struggle is Otho C. Campbell, "John Sergeant Wise: A Case Study in Conservative-Readjuster Politics in Virginia, 1869–1889" (Ph.D. diss., Univ. of Virginia, 1979). An obituary is in the *Richmond Times-Dispatch*, 13 May 1913.

JAMES TICE MOORE

WISE, Stephen Samuel (17 Mar. 1874–19 Apr. 1949), rabbi, reformer, and Jewish communal leader, was born in Erlau, Hungary (near Budapest), the son of Aaron Weisz (later Wise), a rabbi, and Sabine de Fischer Farkashazy, the daughter of a baron. Aaron Weisz immigrated to the United States in 1874 and fifteen months later sent for his wife and children. The descendant of six generations of rabbis, Stephen Wise never considered any other career. He studied first with his father, then simultaneously at both the new Jewish Theological Seminary and Columbia University (graduating from Columbia in 1892). In 1893 he took his rabbinical ordination in Vienna from Adolf Jellinik, the renowned Jewish rabbi and scholar.

Upon his return home, Wise became assistant rabbi of the Conservative Congregation B'nai Jeshurun in New York City and entered on a pattern that would mark the rest of his life. In addition to his pastoral work, he lectured widely on both religious and secular topics, became involved in local reform movements, and began work on a doctorate in Semitics at Columbia University, which he completed in 1902. He also joined the new Zionist movement that had been established by Theodor Herzl; he was a founder of the Federation of American Zionists in 1898 and attended the Second Zionist Congress in Basel that year.

In 1900 Wise married Louise Waterman, with whom he had two children. He also accepted a call to become rabbi of the Reform Congregation Beth Israel in Portland, Oregon. Wise had grown increasingly frustrated with Jewish communal politics in New York and with the European Zionist leaders who treated American Zionists as good for little besides fundraising. He also wanted the opportunity to shape a synagogue to his own emerging views, and he could not do that in the established New York congregations. Wise stayed in Portland six years and converted Beth Israel into a flourishing institution with extensive educational and social work activities. He provided a "free pulpit" in which the rabbi was free to talk about any topic, religious or secular in nature. Although active in local progressive reforms, the "bishop of Oregon," as he was called, declined an offer to run for political office.

Confident of his own abilities, Wise returned to New York. He was invited to Emanu-El, the cathedral synagogue of American Reform, but when the trustees insisted that they retain final control over sermon topics, Wise publicly denounced their attitude and decided to form his own congregation. He began the Free Synagogue in 1907 and conducted services in Carnegie

Hall for nearly forty years, since there was never enough money to build an independent structure. Wise's oratorical skills filled Carnegie Hall every Sunday. Rabbinical students as well as students from major Christian seminaries attended to study his style. Between 1907 and the onset of World War I Wise built up the Free Synagogue, became involved in New York City reform, and began his long friendship with Rev. John Haynes Holmes, in which the two men blazed a trail of interfaith cooperation. Despite the enormous public demands on his time, evidence suggests that Wise never neglected his pastoral work, remaining accessible whenever congregants needed him.

When war broke out in 1914, Wise entered a new phase in his career. Although a pacifist, and originally opposed to American entry into the conflict, Wise eventually endorsed Woodrow Wilson's 1917 decision to join the Allies. During that summer he and his son worked at a Connecticut shipyard for $3 a day until his anonymity was blown by a telegram from the president. The greatest change came when Louis Brandeis assumed leadership of the American Zionist movement in August 1914 and named Wise one of his chief lieutenants. Wise now had a leader whom he admired, one whose philosophy of an Americanized Zionism fit in with his own beliefs. When the established American Jewish Committee tried to block the Zionists' work, Wise led the fight to create an American Jewish Congress that would provide a democratic forum for the community. After Brandeis was appointed to the U.S. Supreme Court in 1916, Wise and Julian Mack took over the leadership of the Zionist and Congress movements.

By the end of the war Wise was a figure of national reputation, a confidant of Woodrow Wilson, and a player in both national and international Jewish affairs. He had helped secure American endorsement of the Balfour Declaration and now went to Paris as part of the American Jewish delegation to lobby for international recognition of the Jews' right to re-create their ancient homeland in Palestine. He also met, and came to distrust, the European Zionist leadership headed by Chaim Weizmann. He believed that, despite American contributions to the cause, the Europeans nonetheless considered them second-class members of the movement. The tension led to a split in American Zionism in 1921, when Brandeis, Wise, Mack, and others resigned in protest against Weizmann's policies. Although Wise remained a devoted Zionist, during the 1920s he turned his energies to other tasks.

The American Jewish Congress had been conceived as a temporary wartime arrangement, but Wise made it an ongoing institution, a democratic alternative to the American Jewish Committee. Wise headed the Congress for all but two years until his death, and under his leadership it dealt not only with Jewish issues, but with humanitarian reform as well. It was one of the first white organizations to back civil rights for Negroes.

Unhappy with what he considered the reactionary attitude of Hebrew Union College, the official seminary for the Reform rabbinate, Wise founded the Jewish Institute of Religion in New York. The JIR curriculum, reflecting Wise's liberal views, required students to engage in social work as part of their training.

Together with John Haynes Holmes, Wise took on Tammany Hall and its darling, Mayor James J. Walker, founding the City Affairs Committee to expose political wrongdoing. Although some people believed it inappropriate for a rabbi or minister to be active politically, Wise saw his attacks on municipal corruption as part of a liberal ministry devoted to combating evil. No one would fault a cleric for working to aid those who were homeless or hungry; so, too, political corruption deprived people of their sustenance and dignity. Wise's political activity extended beyond attacks on wrongdoing; he also campaigned on behalf of candidates, such as his friends Alfred E. Smith and Fiorello La Guardia.

In 1929 riots erupted in Palestine, and the British government began a decade-long reconsideration of its Palestine policy. England had received the mandate over Palestine from the League of Nations on the assumption that it would help the Jews reestablish a homeland there. But Arab opposition to this policy led to a series of White Papers recommending that Britain abandon the Balfour pledge and limit further Jewish immigration to the Holy Land. Wise fought this policy throughout the 1930s. He and Jacob deHaas attacked it in a book, *The Great Betrayal* (1930), and Wise worked against it as president of the Zionist Organization of America during the mid-thirties. He and the other members of the Brandeis faction had returned to power after the Weizmann group, led by Louis Lipsky, had proved unable to sustain the movement. The decade brought not only British betrayal, however, but the rise of nazism in Germany.

Few people, Jews or otherwise, then recognized the danger that Adolf Hitler represented, but Wise saw it almost from the beginning. During the early 1930s his was often a voice crying in the wilderness about the Nazi danger to democracy as well as to the Jews. Those warnings did not endear him to the established Jewish leadership, who believed that quiet remonstrances to the State Department would be more effective in dealing with the Germans. They opposed Wise's demand for a boycott of German goods, claiming it would call too much attention to the issue, but Wise and the Congress pushed ahead, and the boycott seemed to force the Nazis to back down, at least temporarily.

There is a major debate over whether American Jews and the American government did all they could to save European Jews, first from Nazi persecutions in the 1930s, later from extermination in the wartime death camps, and Wise is a major focus of this debate. Although he had become estranged from Franklin D. Roosevelt during the Walker scandals, when Roosevelt had been governor of New York, Wise and the president reconciled by 1935, and from then on Wise gave Roosevelt his complete—and uncritical—support, campaigning for him in 1936 and lauding Roosevelt as a great friend of the Jews. At Wise's urging, Roosevelt interceded in 1936 to persuade Great Britain to keep the gates of Palestine open to further Jewish immigration. But Roosevelt's agenda in the 1930s concentrated on domestic economic recovery, and in the 1940s on winning the war, objectives in which Jewish problems played a minor role. He listened sympathetically to Wise but could—or would—do little that directly affected the terrible fate of European Jewry.

In January 1942 Hitler decided upon the "final solution" to the Jewish problem, and the Third Reich began the systematic roundup and murder of six million European Jews. Although the Nazis tried to carry out this extermination in secret, news of the mass killings reached Wise that summer, and he immediately went to the State Department. There, Sumner Welles asked him to keep the information quiet until the government had a chance to confirm the story. Wise agreed, and subsequently critics have attacked him for not going public immediately. Whether he acted wisely or not is debatable, but even if he had raised a public outcry immediately, it is unlikely that that would have dissuaded the Nazis from carrying out their murderous plans.

Wise has also been attacked for being too passive in his role as Zionist leader during the war, and for concentrating on securing Palestine as a postwar goal rather than fighting to save European Jews, when, actually, the Zionists were caught in a double bind. On the one hand, Britain in 1939 had effectively closed Palestine to further Jewish settlement, and the Zionists fought this policy publicly and through illegal immigration; on the other hand, Britain was struggling against Hitler, so fighting Great Britain meant playing into Nazi hands. This dilemma led Wise to take, for him, a somewhat cautious approach, and in the war years he concentrated on uniting all the Zionist factions; he and Chaim Weizmann, by now also an elder statesman of the movement, finally made their peace. But both were attacked by younger and more militant leaders such as David Ben-Gurion and Abba Hillel Silver, who wanted to push for a more aggressive policy against both the American and British governments. They all agreed on the goal, an independent Jewish state in Palestine, but their views on tactics nearly split the movement. By 1944 the militants had taken control and pushed both Wise and Weizmann aside.

After the war Wise suffered increasingly from poor health, but he did manage to bring some projects to conclusion. He finally secured enough funds for the Free Synagogue to erect its own building, although he did not live to see it completed. A new leadership at the Hebrew Union College made it possible for Wise to sign a merger agreement, bringing the Jewish Institute of Religion into the seminary and ensuring that its philosophy of a liberal pulpit would be part of the mainstream reform movement. The American Jewish Congress, which had operated on a shoestring for more than a quarter-century, finally achieved some stability, as did the World Jewish Congress, which Wise had founded to fight anti-Semitism in the 1930s. Most gratifyingly, he lived to see the establishment of the State of Israel and to receive one of the pens President Harry S. Truman had used in signing the American recognition of the new Jewish state.

Wise died in New York City. Fifty thousand people lined the funeral route from Carnegie Hall, where services had been held, to the Free Synagogue cemetery in Westchester County.

• The extensive Stephen S. Wise Papers are in the American Jewish Historical Society in Waltham, Mass., which also houses the records of the American Jewish Congress. His autobiography, *Challenging Years* (1949), written during his final illness, lacks analysis or introspection. Two volumes of his letters are in print, J. W. Polier and J. W. Wise, eds., *The Personal Letters of Stephen Wise* (1956), and Carl H. Voss, ed., *Stephen S. Wise: Servant of the People* (1969). The major biography is Melvin Urofsky, *A Voice That Spoke for Justice: The Life and Times of Stephen S. Wise* (1982), but see also Carl H. Voss, *Rabbi and Minister: The Friendship of Stephen S. Wise and John Haynes Holmes* (1964).

MELVIN I. UROFSKY

WISELY, William Homer (20 Oct. 1906–16 Nov. 1982), civil engineer and administrator, was born in Coulterville, Illinois, the son of William Homer Blanchard Wisely, a craftsman and building contractor, and Helena Burkhardt. During his youth, Wisely learned the construction trade working with his father and paternal grandfather, who were craftsmen and building contractors, responsible for the construction of many homes, churches, and other buildings in Illinois and Missouri. When school was in session, he lived at the family home in Coulterville; during summers, however, he lived with his father near construction locations and often in St. Louis, where other relatives had settled. During one summer in St. Louis he developed an ear infection after swimming in the Mississippi River which resulted in partial deafness in one ear. The family later moved to Rankin, Illinois, so that the athletic young Wisely could join better high school sports teams while he finished school. From 1924 to 1928 he attended the University of Illinois at Champaign-Urbana, where he earned the B.S. in civil engineering with an emphasis on water and public health. He returned to the school in 1940 and earned a professional degree in civil engineering in 1941.

In 1926, before finishing his college studies, Wisely started working at the Illinois State Water Survey as an engineering assistant. After graduation he began as an assistant in the Division of Sanitation Engineering, Illinois Department of Public Health, where he was to remain until 1940. Water and public health would become the mainstays of his career, in part motivated by his boyhood ear infection. He married Hazel Anne Steinberg in 1930, and they had two daughters.

In 1940 Wisely took the position of engineer-manager in the Urbana-Champaign Sanitation District and in 1941 became part-time secretary of the Federation of Sewage Works Associations, later the Water Pollution Control Federation. In 1943 he became full-time executive secretary for this organization, and the following year he assumed editorship of all federation publication; he continued in these positions until 1955. Wisely's stewardship was credited as a prime factor in the organization's growth, geographic spread, and broadening scope and influence. During this same period he was a special lecturer in engineering at the University of Illinois.

Wisely's success as an administrator and organizer made him a top candidate in 1954 for executive secretary of the American Society of Civil Engineers (ASCE), of which he had been an associate member since 1936 and member since 1944. He left the WPCF and assumed this post in 1955. Wisely's position with the ASCE was later renamed executive director.

Aside from managing the business office and professional staff of the ASCE, one of Wisely's roles, in large part shaped by him, was to represent the civil engineering profession to the public. He particularly emphasized professionalism, public service, engineering education, and a greater role for the civil engineer in planning, ecological assessment, public health issues, and management of public works projects, all areas to which he contributed. During the 1950s and 1960s, for example, ASCE committees participated in systematizing further improvements to the design and expansion of the national highway system. Wisely was spokesman for the civil engineering profession when it became the target of a sensationalized exposé of highway construction graft broadcast by David Brinkley of NBC in 1962. In this era Wisely began to emphasize high ethical standards and professionalism for all engineers and promoted a conception of engineering as public service. While with the ASCE, for instance, he served as the only engineer on the New York State Health Council.

Wisely and his colleagues in ASCE and the engineering profession observed with growing consternation the decay of the country's infrastructure, especially in urban areas. The urgent requirements of World War II in the 1940s had resulted in postponement of much necessary infrastructure maintenance. With the postwar construction boom, this unfortunate trend continued. As the 1950s progressed, the engineering community was alarmed that aging water and transportation facilities were becoming a major problem, but its recommendations for more durable but expensive solutions to the engineering needs of society were usually vetoed by politicians in favor of cheaper, short-term solutions, which frequently became more costly in the long run. The cumulative result of such policies only reached the public consciousness during the 1960s and henceforth became a nationally recognized problem. Through talks and articles in his role as ASCE executive director, Wisely played an important role in putting infrastructure issues on the public agenda.

Wisely was instrumental in developing the Outstanding Civil Engineering Award Program, an outgrowth of his earlier "Seven Civil Engineering Wonders" program of the 1950s. This award came to be recognized as the most prestigious in its field, and the yearly competition brought the profession increased visibility and favorable publicity.

Out of a perceived need for communication and cooperation among the national engineering societies in the late 1940s, the Conference of Engineering Societies of Western Europe and the U.S.A., known by the acronym EUSEC, was created in 1948. The ASCE was one of the charter organizations in this largely western European and North American federation. Wisely, as executive secretary of the ASCE, also became in 1956 general secretary of EUSEC, a post he filled until becoming chairman of the federation in 1961. While with EUSEC he coauthored the 1961 *Report on Education and Training of Professional Engineers*, the first comparative study of world engineering education.

Beginning in 1959, Wisely initiated an attempt to create a truly international engineering organization, a technical counterpart to the successful International Council of Scientific Unions, by persuading engineers throughout the world that such an engineering organization was possible and useful. In 1966, on the initiative of Wisely and other engineers in EUSEC, and with the support of the United Nations Educational, Scientific, and Cultural Organization, Wisely headed the organizing commission to establish this world engineering federation. UNESCO hosted the first constitutive meeting in Paris in 1966 and the first general assembly meeting in 1968. Once member organizations had approved the new organization's constitution and their membership, in 1968 the World Federation of Engineering Organizations was created. By design, EUSEC was disbanded in 1971 when the visibility and survival of WFEO had been clearly assured. Wisely served a four-year term on the executive committee of the WFEO, which has served to foster the exchange of engineering information, the furthering of engineering education and training, cooperation among engineering organizations, and the free exchange and free movement of engineers between countries. During much of this period (1965–1972), Wisely was also chairman of Union Panamericana des Associaciones des Ingenieros (UPADI), the pan-American engineering federation.

In late 1971 Wisely joined a delegation of congressmen and engineers led by U.S. senator Henry Bellmon to Egypt, which had broken off diplomatic relations with the United States during the June "Six Day" 1967 war with Israel. A central purpose of the trip was to assess the impact of the just completed Aswan High Dam located on the Nile River, one of the largest hydrological projects ever undertaken. The U.S. secretary of state, John Foster Dulles, had refused to finance the project in 1956, with the ultimate result that the Soviet Union provided major financial and engineering support for the duration of the project. America's exclusion from firsthand participation on the project had given rise to U.S. skepticism about the soundness or prudence of the enterprise. The American delegation's task in 1971 was to assess the engineering soundness of the dam and the impact of the Aswan Dam on the food, power, public health, and ecological situation of Egypt.

Wisely primarily assessed the public health and ecological impacts of the project. He evaluated concerns that the 300-mile lake of impounded water behind the dam would increase the incidence of malaria as a result of a proliferation of mosquitos and that the slower moving Nile River below the dam would increase the number and spread of a species of snail known to transmit schistosomiasis, also known as bilharzia or, snail fever. Through inspections, research, and interviews, Wisely verified that no increase in malaria had occurred. However, he found that schistosomiasis had increased with the increase in intensification of year-round irrigation, although not beyond what would be expected in a region where the disease had been endemic since ancient times. While it recognized some of the adverse consequences of the project, his overall assessment was generally favorable, as were those of the other engineers of the delegation.

During a career spanning six decades, Wisely advocated a broadening of the role of civil engineer, observing that the civil engineer was professionally positioned to respond to the growing public concern over conservation, ecology, and pollution issues. Wisely was part of a small community of engineers who fostered the development of environmental engineering as a distinct specialty allied with civil engineering.

Despite numerous offers of appointments at universities, Wisely continued in his role at ASCE until his retirement in 1972. After retirement, he served for several years as professor of engineering at the University of Florida and later as lecturer at the University of Virginia, and he continued speaking and writing on themes of professional responsibility, ethics, and engineering education.

Over the course of his career Wisely authored more than 125 papers, primarily in water pollution control and environmental engineering, and several books. To fill a gap in the historical and engineering literature, Wisely wrote *The American Civil Engineer* (1974), an account of the professional society and history of the civil engineer in the United States.

Wisely was a charismatic, natural, and person-oriented leader, much esteemed and honored by his peers. William N. Carey, a longtime ASCE officer, said of Wisely that "no one in a similar position in the profession has done more personally for his association. And I know of no one who has done more internationally in the interests and ideals of engineering." Wisely died in Charlottesville, Virginia.

Wisely was a member of Mu San, a national honor member of Chi Epsilon, honorary member of the Water Pollution Control Federation and the American Society of Civil Engineers, and a recipient of the Kenneth Allen Award and the Charles Alvin Emerson Medal. In his memory the ASCE established the William H. Wisely American Civil Engineering Award.

• The bulk of the Wisely papers, located at the University of Virginia, Charlottesville, relate to his directorship of the American Society of Civil Engineering. A memorial tribute, "William H. Wisely: 1906–1982," appeared in *Civil Engineering* 53 (Feb. 1983): 73–74. An obituary is in the *New York Times*, 18 Nov. 1982.

MARK R. JORGENSEN

WISLIZENUS, Frederick Adolphus (21 May 1810–22 Sept. 1889), physician and lay scientist, was born in Königsee, in the German state of Schwarzburg-Rudolstadt, the son of a Protestant minister. His parents' names are unknown. Orphaned at a very early age, he and two older siblings were raised in the home of their mother's brother and his wife. In 1828 he attended the University of Jena, where he studied medicine. He continued as a medical student at universities at Göttingen and Würzburg. At these universities Wislizenus was very active in the *Burschenschaft*, a student society favoring revolution to create a unified, constitutional Germany. He participated in a student-led revolt at Frankfurt am Main in 1833, which failed. He then fled to Switzerland, where he received his doctor of medicine degree from the University of Zurich in October 1833. He briefly continued his revolutionary proclivities after graduating, joining the small army of Italian nationalist Giuseppe Mazzini in his abortive attempt to stir rebellion in Italy early in 1834. Wislizenus left Switzerland shortly thereafter, fearing extradition to Germany. After a stop in Paris and observations at its hospitals, he embarked for the United States, arriving in New York in 1835. There he practiced medicine until 1837, when he moved to St. Clair County, Illinois, also home to other German exiles. Two years later he relocated across the Mississippi River to St. Louis, Missouri.

"Chained for several years to an exacting medical practice," Wislizenus wrote in his book, *A Journey to the Rocky Mountains in the Year 1839*, "in which I had tasted to the full the sorrows and pleasures of the active physician, I felt the need of mental and physical recreation." He decided on an exploring tour to the "far West, with its wilderness and its aboriginals," and during the spring and summer of 1839 he traveled the Oregon-California Trail with a small caravan of fur traders (Pratte, Chouteau & Co.), missionaries, and adventurers, the traders carrying goods destined for the annual rendezvous of trappers and Indians in the Rocky Mountains. His party arrived at the rendezvous site on the Green River in present-day Wyoming on 5 July. After a short stay, Wislizenus left with a group of Hudson's Bay Company men, Flathead Indians, and members of his original party, intent on reaching the Columbia River and then California before returning to Missouri by way of Santa Fe in New Mexico. At Fort Hall, on the Snake River in present-day Idaho, however, he gave up these plans and began his journey homeward. With mountain man Paul Richardson as guide, his small party traveled to the South Platte River, in present-day Colorado, and then proceeded southward to the Arkansas River. They continued down the Arkansas to Bent's Fort and traveled the Santa Fe Trail back to Missouri, Wislizenus arriving in St. Louis on 31 October. His account of his adventures was published in German in St. Louis the following year.

Wislizenus returned to his profession and "soon gained a lucrative practice, and was loved and respected as a physician" (Engelmann, p. 466). For several years he was a partner in medicine with George Engelmann, also a respected botanist, who encouraged Wislizenus's scientific pursuits.

In 1846 Wislizenus left his practice once again, this time to gather information on the geography and natural history of northern Mexico and California. Shortly after he started down the Santa Fe Trail in May, however, war broke out with Mexico. He accompanied a caravan of wagons belonging to trader Albert Speyer, who was transporting two wagonloads of arms and ammunition ordered by the governor of Chihuahua. The train was consequently pursued a considerable distance down the trail by a detachment of U.S. dragoons. At Santa Fe, Wislizenus obtained a safe-conduct pass from the New Mexican governor and then traveled south along the Chihuahua Trail, passing through El Paso del Norte and arriving in the city of Chihuahua on 24 August. Because of his gathering of plant specimens and other scientific data in and near the city, Wislizenus was suspected of being a spy. He was later refused permission to leave the state and was held along with several American merchants at the village of Cusihuiriáchic, approximately ninety miles to the west, until 3 March 1847, after U.S. troops under Colonel Alexander Doniphan had taken Chihuahua.

Abandoning his planned visit to California, Wislizenus took a position as assistant surgeon with Doniphan's force, traveling with the army on its return to the United States via Saltillo, Monterrey, Matamoros, and New Orleans, arriving in St. Louis in early July. Despite the various difficulties of the trip, he brought back much important information on the physical character of the Southwest and Mexico. His journal, along with his meteorological tables, maps, and a botanical appendix prepared from his specimens by Engelmann, was published by the U.S. Senate in 1848 as *Memoir of a Tour to Northern Mexico, Connected with Col. Doniphan's Expedition, in 1846 and 1847*.

In 1849 St. Louis suffered a deadly outbreak of cholera, and Wislizenus helped attend to the thousands afflicted. The following year, on 23 July at Constantinople, he married Lucy Crane, sister-in-law of the U.S. minister to Turkey, George P. Marsh; they had three children who survived to adulthood. In November 1850 he established his practice in Washington, D.C., and in 1851 traveled to California to examine its prospects as a new home. He decided to return to St. Louis, however, and moved his family there in 1852. He would be listed as a physician in city directories until his death there, although he lost his eyesight in later years. He continued his scientific pursuits during his medical career in St. Louis, helping to found the Academy of Science of St. Louis in 1856 and contributing several articles and meteorological data to its *Transactions*. His most important contributions to science and history, however, remain his observations on the Southwest made during the Mexican War as "one of the first scientific pioneers through a great part of that country," as he correctly wrote in *Memoir of a Tour*.

• A small Wislizenus manuscript collection is in the Missouri Historical Society, St. Louis; it contains mostly genealogical information and a typescript memoir written by Lucy Crane Wislizenus for her children in 1888. Wislizenus's given name has several variations in the historical record, his first name often being dropped. It fully appears on St. Louis legal documents, however, as that given here. Wislizenus's *A Journey to the Rocky Mountains in the Year 1839* first appeared in 1840 as *Ein Ausflug nach den Felsen-Gebirgen*. The English edition, published in 1912, contains a biographical sketch of Wislizenus by his son Frederick A. Wislizenus, who also performed the translation. His *Memoir of a Tour to Northern Mexico, Connected with Col. Doniphan's Expedition, in 1846 and 1847* can be found in 30th Cong., 1st sess., Sen. Misc. Doc. 26 (Serial 511). It and *Journey* have received modern reprintings. The best biographical treatment of Wislizenus is Douglas D. Hale, Jr., "Friedrich Adolph Wislizenus: From Student Rebel to Southwestern Explorer," *Missouri Historical Review* 62 (Apr. 1968): 260–85. See also G. J. Engelmann, "Frederick Adolphus Wislizenus," *Transactions of the Academy of Science of St. Louis* 5 (1886–1891): 464–68.

MARK L. GARDNER

WISNER, Frank Gardiner (23 June 1909–29 Oct. 1965), intelligence official, was born in Laurel, Mississippi, the son of Frank George Wisner, a lumber businessman, and Mary Gardiner. He graduated in liberal arts in 1931 from the University of Virginia, where he also secured his LL.B. three years later. In 1935 he was admitted to the New York bar. In 1936 he married Mary Ellis "Polly" Knowles; they raised four children. Wisner's father, troubled by the economic depression, now demanded that his only surviving son quit training as a sprinter with the American Olympic squad and start earning money with a Wall Street law firm. In this way Wisner—who in future years showed himself to be deeply sensitive to aspirational frustration—became an uneasy recruit to the capitalist system he was to spend his life defending.

Just before the Japanese attack on Pearl Harbor in 1941, Wisner joined the Office of Naval Intelligence. He later joined the Office of Strategic Services (OSS), the wartime intelligence agency established in June 1943. There he first worked for "X-2," the counterintelligence section, but in December 1943 he achieved a transfer to SI (Secret Intelligence/espionage) and a foreign posting to Cairo. In June of the following year he moved to another center of Middle Eastern intrigue, Istanbul, Turkey. His energy, organizational skill, and leadership qualities began to impress his superiors.

In the fall of 1944 Wisner experienced a formative trauma when he transferred to Bucharest, Romania. To appease the Red Army gathering along its border, Romania had just changed sides by declaring war on the Axis powers. But this was to no avail, and Wisner now witnessed the brutal Stalinization of the wavering country. He joined the small but influential band of Americans who predicted that the United States would soon have on its hands a dangerous new enemy, the Soviet Union.

At war's end Truman disbanded the OSS, and Wisner returned to Wall Street. He began to prosper as a senior partner in his firm and from the discovery of oil under his family's southern timber tracts. But in 1947 he became deputy assistant secretary of state for occupied countries, and within a year he found himself in charge of a quickly expanding section of the newly established Central Intelligence Agency (CIA).

The CIA's Office of Policy Coordination (OPC) conducted covert operations. For two years Wisner enjoyed an unusual degree of autonomy—assisted by his ability to persuade, to tell good stories, to socialize late into the night, and to play off one governmental department against another. He also was able to recruit large numbers of personnel. He secretly diverted Marshall aid funds into black propaganda (such as the forgery of documents that discredited the Left) designed to ensure conservative victories in the Italian and French elections. Exploiting Nazi contacts he had made in Bucharest, Wisner hired some of Hitler's former Eastern intelligence specialists with the object of conducting a clandestine war against the Soviet Union. One of these specialists, Reinhard Gehlen, became head of West Germany's postwar secret intelligence organization and, in that capacity, cooperated with Wisner and the CIA. In 1949 Wisner confidently organized the agency's first attempt to topple a foreign government, the communist dictatorship in Albania.

Betrayed by the British traitor Kim Philby, the Albanian coup failed, and Wisner now went through a frustrating period. General Walter Bedell Smith, director of the CIA from 1950 to 1953, complained that Wisner was deceitful, slow-witted, and vague. Smith blocked Wisner's plans for further covert action, demoralized him with vituperative outbursts, and effectively maneuvered to demote him.

The election of President Dwight D. Eisenhower and the appointment of Allen W. Dulles as CIA director in 1953 inaugurated the so-called "golden era" of CIA covert operations, promising a safer, nonnuclear way of resisting Soviet expansion. Wisner was not directly involved in all of the operations, taking little part, for example, in the agency's overthrow of the Guatemalan government in 1954. But, with his authority reestablished, now as the CIA's director of plans, responsible for both covert operations and espionage, Wisner continued to be an apostle for the "rollback" of communism in Europe.

Though Wisner's tasks included directing an espionage offensive, he failed to establish an American spy network in the Soviet Union. Gehlen's client West German organization was too thoroughly penetrated by Communist secret agents to be useful, and the Soviet Union was virtually an impenetrable society. However, the failure was not insurmountable because American intelligence had alternative technical means of assessing the nature of the Soviet threat. For the time being, moreover, Wisner's covert political operations seemed to shore up his agents' reputation for effectiveness.

Wisner's plans finally came to grief when Soviet tanks crushed the Hungarian uprising of 1956. Wisner believed that the CIA could have assisted the Hungarian freedom fighters. But Eisenhower vetoed this covert action, and the imperialist nature of the contemporary Anglo–French–Israeli attack on Egypt eclipsed any propaganda advantage that Wisner and his colleagues might have wrested from the situation. Bitter and demoralized, Wisner succumbed first to a liver infection, then to nervous tension. His drinking became problematic. Apparently restored to health by 1959, Wisner was posted to London as CIA station chief, but he ended up in the hands of English psychiatrists, and had to be brought home in 1962. He retired a sick man and in 1965, at his home in Galena, Maryland, committed suicide—a victim, according to his friends, of the pressures he had endured as a Cold Warrior.

As an intelligence officer, Frank Wisner had mixed success. As an exponent of confrontational anticommunism, he had few peers.

• Documents by and about Frank Wisner are in several collections in the Dwight D. Eisenhower Library, Abilene, Kans. Burton Hersh, *The Old Boys: The American Elite and the Origins of the CIA* (1992), is informative on Wisner's background and on his career with the OSS and CIA. Sallie Pisani, *The CIA and the Marshall Plan* (1992), explains how he financed his early covert actions on behalf of the CIA. Some of Wisner's career frustrations are illuminated in Ludwell Lee Montague, *General Walter Bedell Smith as Director of Central Intelligence, October 1950–February 1953* (1992). Obituaries are in the *New York Times*, 30 Oct. 1965, and the *Washington Post*, 31 Oct. 1965.

RHODRI JEFFREYS-JONES

WISNER, Henry (c. 1720–4 Mar. 1790), revolutionary powder maker and legislator, was born in Goshen, New York, the son of Hendrick Wisner and Mary Shaw, farmers. As a farm boy, Henry had little formal education, but his ability and energy led to local prominence as justice of the peace and as assistant justice of the Court of Common Pleas of Orange County in 1768 or 1769. He represented Orange County in the New York colonial assembly, 1759–1769, and in 1759 the assembly adopted his bill facilitating the drainage of the annually submerged marshes of the Wallkill River.

Opposing the colonial policy of the British Parliament, Wisner was a member of the Orange County Committee of Correspondence and represented Orange County in the First Continental Congress in 1774. There he opposed Joseph Galloway's conservative plan of union with Great Britain and signed the association for nonimportation of British goods. Wisner was elected on 4 May 1775 by a town meeting at Goshen to the New York Provincial Congress, where he served until 1777. The provincial congress chose him as a delegate to the Second Continental Congress, where he served from May 1775 to May 1777. He warmly approved the Declaration of Independence, was present when independence was adopted, and immediately wrote, "The question of independence has been put in Congress and Carried in the affirmative without one desenting vote" (Burnett, vol. 1, p. 525). Although Delaware delegate Thomas McKean later asserted that Wisner "voted" for separation, the claim that he was the only New York delegate to do so is quite tenuous. He no doubt expressed himself in favor of separation, but the colonies voted as units, and the New Yorkers, in obedience to their instructions, refrained from voting.

In the revolutionary war Wisner was a zealous and energetic patriot. Early in the war, when New York offered loans and bounties for the manufacture of gunpowder and firearms for the Continental army, Wisner volunteered his assistance. In 1775 he was making saltpeter and powder at his mill in Ulster County. He increased his output, erected two more mills in Orange County, experimented with ways of improving quality, wrote an essay on powder production, and offered to teach his techniques. He also manufactured spears, bayonets, and gun flints. Wisner served on committees to facilitate the securing of saltpeter, sulfur, lead, and flint; to maintain the roads through the passes of the Hudson highlands; and to set up post offices to help convey military intelligence between Albany and military headquarters in Fishkill. Having long been watchful for Tory activities, he represented Orange County in 1778 as one of the commissioners for detecting and defeating conspiracies in the state of New York.

As a lieutenant colonel in the Fourth Regiment of the Orange County Militia, Wisner corresponded frequently during the war with General George Clinton, who trusted and respected him. Occasionally Wisner acted on his own initiative, as in calling out Ulster and Orange county militiamen in 1778, but his alertness and timely action were endorsed by the provincial congress. Helping to construct defenses along the Hudson River, he mounted cannon and manned them at his own expense. In 1776 he served on a secret committee to explore the terrain of the Hudson highlands and cooperated in the laying of an ill-fated iron chain across the river to obstruct British navigation. After British forces captured Forts Montgomery and Clinton in October 1777, new defenses were required, and early in 1778 Wisner served on committees that visited the highlands, selected sites, and obtained workers and materials to build new fortifications. The result was the construction at West Point of Fort Arnold and its outworks, which proved effective.

In the New York Provincial Congress, Wisner was a member of the committee that framed the New York State Constitution in 1777. A moderate in political outlook, he voted against the indirect election of state senators by delegates. He supported John Jay's motion to prevent toleration of Roman Catholics in civil or military office unless they swore that no pope, priest, or foreign authority could absolve them from their allegiance to the state. When this restriction was rejected, Wisner seconded Jay's motion that liberty of conscience should not be construed as encouraging licentiousness or used to endanger the safety of the state.

From 1777 to 1782 Wisner represented the Middle District (Orange, Ulster, and Dutchess counties) in the first five sessions of the New York State Senate. After the war he probably retired to his farm, but in 1788 he was elected to the convention in Poughkeepsie that debated the U.S. Constitution. He voted with the Antifederalists against the Constitution, fearing that a strong federal government would weaken the states and fail to safeguard individual liberties.

Wisner was physically tall and vigorous. He married twice and had five children. His marriage to Sarah Norton in 1739 brought him a farm in Queens County, Long Island, but the center of his activities was in the Goshen area, where over the years he acquired hundreds of acres of land for himself and his sons. He also owned a few slaves. After his first wife's death, he married Sarah Cornell Waters, a widow, in 1769 and thereby acquired more land. He died near Goshen.

An early enthusiast for American independence and a member of the Continental Congress, Wisner won respect for his support of the Revolution in New York as a supplier of powder and other military necessities, as a participant in the erection of fortifications along the Hudson, and as an active member of the provincial congress.

• No large collection of Wisner papers exists. A few items are in the New-York Historical Society, including Wisner's interesting letter to George Clinton, 10 Mar. 1778. In the Goshen Public Library and Historical Society are several documents relating to Wisner's land dealings, an inventory of Wisner's property in 1788, and Clinton's letter to Wisner, 6 Feb. 1772. This letter is not included in Hugh Hastings and A. J. Holden, eds., *Public Papers of George Clinton* (1898–1904), which contain Wisner's wartime correspondence with Clinton. The *Journals of the New York Provincial Convention* (1842) throw light on Wisner's activities as one of its members. In Edmund C. Burnett, ed., *Letters of Members of the Continental Congress*, vols. 1 and 2 (1921, 1923), are letters of the N.Y. delegates. Wisner is briefly mentioned in the *Minutes of the Commissioners for Detecting and Defeating Conspiracies in the State of New York* (1909). For his participation in the defenses along the Hudson, see Edward M. Ruttenber, *Obstructions to the Navigation of Hudson's River; Embracing the Minutes of the Secret Committee Appointed by the Provincial Convention of New York, July 16, 1776* (1860). Three secondary works that present highly sympathetic accounts of Wisner are G. Franklin Wisner, *The Wisners in America and Their Kindred* (1918); and two brief accounts by Franklin Burdge, *A Memorial of Henry Wisner, the Only New Yorker Who Voted for the Declaration of Independence* (1878) and *A Second Memorial of Henry Wisner* (1898).

ROBERT ERNST

WISSLER, Clark (18 Sept. 1870–25 Aug. 1947), anthropologist, museologist, and psychologist, was born Clarkson Davis Wissler in Wayne County, Indiana, the son of Benjamin Franklin Wissler, a schoolteacher, and Sylvania Needler. From 1888 to 1893 he taught public school in Wayne County. He entered Indiana University in 1893, graduating in 1897 with a B.A. in psychology. He continued his work in psychology at Indiana, receiving his M.A. in 1899 while also teaching psychology at Ohio State. That year Wissler married Etta Viola Gebbart; they had two children. In 1901 he received his Ph.D. in psychology from Columbia University, where he had become well acquainted with Franz Boas, a professor headed toward preeminence in the field of anthropology.

In his early research in physical anthropology Wissler attempted to demonstrate that there are no statistically significant physiological differences between "normal" and "feebleminded" individuals. His work was strongly influenced by research that he and Boas had conducted in 1900 at Clark University in Worcester, Massachusetts. Their work at Clark had helped to establish the field of population dynamics, and it had been instrumental in correcting physiological concepts that were incorrectly based on a presumed automatic expression of inherited characteristics. Boas and Wissler had shown the more complex ideas at the root of population dynamics: the importance of individual differences in populations and the necessity of accounting for environmental influences on the expression of inherent characteristics.

Wissler served as Boas's assistant curator at the American Museum of Natural History in New York City from 1902 to 1905. Wissler also held a position as associate professor of anthropology at Columbia University from 1903 to 1909. Upon Boas's resignation from the museum in 1905, Wissler became curator of its department of anthropology, a position he held until his own retirement in 1942. In 1937 he was elected dean of the museum's scientific staff. Wissler also taught at Yale University from 1924 to 1940, working at the Institute of Psychology and becoming a professor of anthropology in 1931.

One of Wissler's major contributions was to elaborate Boas's basic theories of "areal culture" and "culture areas and complexes." An example of an areal culture is that of the Plains Indians: whether they have blood ties or not, all peoples in the region share basic cultural traits. According to Boas's "age-area" hypothesis, characteristic traits are evident most completely and elaborately in the groups that first receive them and that live at the core of a culture area. Wissler followed Boas's lead in organizing his museum exhibits along regional and ethnographic lines rather than by using more traditional typologies. Thus he abandoned the idea that a culture can be defined by merely putting a series of its tools or dwellings on display. Instead he focused on a particular area and the peoples who lived there to highlight common histories and cultural responses to specific ecological regional demands.

Wissler's field studies of the tribes of the North American plains were inspired by the culture-area concept. His research on the Blackfoot tribe, the most extensive part of his fieldwork, drew on his background in psychology, an approach that Boas had also favored in developing anthropology as an important discipline within American social science. Wissler presented clear psychological accounts of Blackfoot behavior and interpreted the tribe's customs and traditions in terms of psychology. In the process of seeking to define the ethos of the Blackfoot—that is, the essence of their cultural values—he shed light on their questioning of the warrior ideals held in reverence by other Plains Indians. His focus on diversity within a general cultural type illustrated how subtle ethnographic analysis could be. An entire generation of American anthropologists, including Ruth Benedict, was inspired by Wissler's work to examine the cultures of the Plains Indians, who for a time were the most widely studied of any tribal group.

To buttress his work on the Sun Dance and the impact that the spread of the horse to the Great Plains had on the culture of the Plains Indians, Wissler consulted historical records, thereby setting an example of considerable consequence in the development of American anthropology. But his brilliant documentation of the Sun Dance and the role of the horse underscores the absence of historical methods in his attempts to test the culture-area hypothesis, which were aimed at analyzing the clustering of traits in particular areas. To delineate a culture region, as he did in *The American Indian* (1917), he studied distinctive aspects of the physical environment and material culture (tools, ornaments, house building). Wissler's *Man and Culture* (1923) and *The Relation of Nature to Man in Aboriginal America* (1926) were intended to refine the culture-area concept.

Wissler was especially interested in diffusion, or the spread of cultural traits from one society to another and the relative age of traits in comparison with the breadth of their spread. He saw cultural spread as analogous to waves rippling out from the point where a stone has been dropped into water. According to Wissler, the wider the spread, the older the trait. Furthermore, it may be assumed that a trait originated where it is found most elaborated. Where it is least elaborated one can assume that it was only recently acquired. Thus Wissler reformulated Boas's age-area hypothesis: the age of a trait is reflected in the expanse of its spread in an area. From his point of view, there were no exceptions to the hypothesis. Yet it had little impact on the discipline of anthropology because he neglected to consider the possibility of a two-way movement of traits from groups on the periphery to groups closer to an area's center. The hypothesis was also flawed by Wissler's failure to tie it to historical methods.

With Boas, Wissler challenged the nativist beliefs that sprang up in reaction to the cultural clashes generated by World War I. He argued that scientific analysis did not validate innate racial differences—especially concerning intelligence—as many of his fellow scientists believed. Wissler's strong advocacy of environmental effects ("nurture" rather than "nature") has been a cornerstone of American anthropology ever since.

In 1919 Wissler became president of the American Anthropological Association and expanded its interests beyond a focus on Native Americans, encouraging the study of African, South American, Polynesian, and other societies and cultures. Throughout his career he did much to organize a vast amount of ethnographic material and popularize the culture concept in America. He died in New Haven, Connecticut.

• Some of Wissler's papers are at the American Museum of Natural History in New York City and Yale's Institute of Human Relations. Other writings by Wissler include *North American Indians of the Plains* (1912), *An Introduction to Social Anthropology* (1929), *Growth of Children in Hawaii, Based on Observations by Louis R. Sullivan* (1930), and *Indian Cavalcade; or, Life on the Old-time Indian Reservation* (1940). Two memorial notices are George Peter Murdock, "Clark Wissler, 1870–1947," *American Anthropologist* 50 (1948): 292–304, which provides an extensive bibliography, and Harry L. Shapiro, "Clark Wissler, 1870–1947," American Philosophical Society, *Yearbook* (1948): 300–302.

FRANK A. SALAMONE

WISTAR, Caspar (3 Feb. 1696–21 Mar. 1752), merchant and glass manufacturer, was born in Wald-Hilspach, Germany, the son of Anna Catharina and Hans or Johannes Caspar Wüstar. His father was the huntsman or forester to Carl Theodore, the elector of the Palatinate. Although he served as an apprentice in his father's trade for four years and worked in the forests for an additional two years, Wistar was drawn to the New World. He set off from Heidelberg to get to Rotterdam, and there he embarked for Philadelphia. He landed in Philadelphia in September 1717.

Nearly penniless when he arrived, Wistar worked briefly as a laborer before making brass buttons. He quickly achieved success. His buttons, guaranteed for seven years, became a staple in the garment trade and were especially useful for working-class clothing. In the 1720s he expanded his commercial interests to include extensive investments in real estate and importing German-made goods, among other businesses. By the 1730s he had become a wealthy and respected member of Philadelphia society. In 1725 Wistar became a member of the Society of Friends, perhaps in anticipation of his marriage in 1726 to Catharine Johnson or Jansen, a Quaker. They had four daughters and three sons.

In 1738 Wistar purchased land near Alloway Creek in Salem County, New Jersey, not far from Philadelphia. This land would become home to the first important American glass manufactory of the eighteenth century. Construction of the glasshouse began in 1739, and the factory opened late that year. The factory's location, on some 2,000 acres of wooded land with an excellent supply of sand and ready access to the commercial waterway, was especially propitious. Wistar supplied capital and business acumen to the project but apparently had no technical knowledge of glassmaking. To operate the factory, known as the United Glass Company or the Wistarburgh or Wisterberg Glassworks, he formed a profit sharing partnership, possibly at their initiative, with four recent German immigrant glassblowers, Martin Halter, Caspar Halter, John William Wentzel, and John Martin Griesmayer. They primarily concentrated on bottles and windowpanes in both colored and colorless glass but also produced some tablewares, such as tumblers, candlesticks, and covered bowls, in a Germanic style featuring threading and applied prunts and with decorative handles, finials, and bases. In addition, they made scientific glass, such as tubes, jars, and retorts, for Benjamin Franklin's scientific experiments. The Wistarburgh enterprise imported significant quantities of English glasswares for resale to the expanding local market. While Wistarburgh was in operation, Wistar continued to maintain his residence and retail shop in Philadelphia.

The Wistarburgh Glassworks was an economic success, remaining in business for nearly forty years. Its profitability contributed to Wistar's large estate, valued at his death at £26,667, a tremendous sum that did not include the value of his glassworks or real estate in New Jersey. His son Richard Wistar continued the glassmaking business at Wistarburgh until 1777, when it succumbed to economic pressures caused by the Revolution. When Richard attempted to sell the factory in 1780, he placed an advertisement in the 11 October *Pennsylvania Journal* describing it as

> The Glass Manufactory in Salem county . . . with 1500 Acres of Land adjoining. It contains two Furnaces, with all the necessary Ovens for cooling the Glass, drying Wood, &c. Contiguous to the Manufactory are two flatting Ovens in separate Houses, a Store house, Pothouse, a House fitted with Tables for the cutting of Glass, a stamping Mill, a rolling Mill for the preparing of Clay for making of Pots; and at a suitable distance are ten Dwelling houses for the Workmen; as likewise a large Mansion-house, containing six rooms on a Floor, with Bake-house and Washhouse: Also a convenient Store-house, . . . There are about 250 Acres of cleared Land within fence, 100 whereof is mowable meadow, which produces hay and pasturage sufficient for the large stock of cattle and horses employed by the Manufactory. There is Stabling sufficient for 60 head of cattle, with a large Barn, Granery and Waggon-house. The unimproved Land is well wooded, and is equal if not superior to any place in Jersey.

Wistarburgh did not sell, probably because it was offered during the revolutionary war, but its importance as America's first significantly successful glasshouse had already been attained. Eventually workers from Wistarburgh migrated to other parts of New Jersey, Pennsylvania, New York, and New England, spreading what collectors have called the "South Jersey" style.

• The Wistar papers at the Historical Society of Pennsylvania, Philadelphia, include a five-page autobiography in German detailing Wistar's early life. An early secondary work that touches on Wistar and his glass is Frederick William Hunter, *Stiegel Glass* (1914). Hunter's overambitious attributions to Wistar were corrected in George S. McKearin and

Helen McKearin, *American Glass* (1941), which suggests that much of this glass should be called "South Jersey type." The best modern scholarship on Wistar is Arlene Palmer, "Glass Production in Eighteenth-Century America: The Wistarburgh Enterprise," in *Winterthur Portfolio 11*, ed. Ian M. G. Quimby (1976), *The Wistarburgh Glassworks: The Beginning of Jersey Glassmaking* (1976), *The Wistars and Their Glass, 1739–1777* (1989), "Benjamin Franklin and the Wistarburg Glassworks," *Antiques* 105, no. 1 (Jan. 1974): 207–10, and "The Glassmakers of Early America," in *The Craftsman in Early America*, ed. Quimby (1984).

GERALD W. R. WARD

WISTAR, Caspar (13 Sept. 1761–22 Jan. 1818), physician and teacher, was born in Philadelphia, Pennsylvania, the son of Richard Wistar, a glass manufacturer, and Sarah Wyatt. The fifth of eight children, Wistar was raised in the Quaker religion and was educated as a youth at the Friends School at Fourth and Walnut streets, where he studied classical literature and languages under John Thompson. In 1777 the sixteen-year-old Wistar volunteered as a nurse at the battle of Germantown. Deeply affected by the suffering he witnessed there, he decided to pursue a career in medicine.

That same year Wistar apprenticed himself to John Redman, one of the city's most prominent physicians and a preceptor of a number of leaders of Philadelphia medicine, including John Morgan and Benjamin Rush. In 1779, his last year with Redman, Wistar was also apprenticed to John Jones, an eminent surgeon who had fled New York because of the British occupation. Wistar matriculated in the medical school of the University of the State of Pennsylvania in 1779 and received a bachelor of medicine degree three years later.

In 1783 Wistar went abroad for further medical education, though he had some difficulty receiving permission to do so from the Quaker Monthly Meeting because of his participation in a duel. After spending a year in England attending John Hunter's anatomy lectures and visiting hospitals, Wistar entered Edinburgh University's medical school. While in Edinburgh, he was twice elected president of the Royal Medical Society of Edinburgh, a student organization, and was also elected president of the Edinburgh Natural History Society. He received his medical degree from the university in 1786.

After a brief tour of the Continent, Wistar returned to Philadelphia in 1787 and commenced private practice, which soon became, through the valuable influence of relatives, friends, and former preceptors, one of the largest in the city. That same year he was appointed one of the physicians to the Philadelphia Dispensary and elected a member of the College of Physicians of Philadelphia and the American Philosophical Society. During the yellow fever epidemic of 1793, Wistar nearly succumbed to the disease while assisting Benjamin Rush in fighting the malady. His friendship with Rush was brought to an end, however, when Wistar rejected the former's drastic treatment of bleeding and purging. Wistar was appointed physician to the Pennsylvania Hospital in 1793 and remained on the hospital staff until 1810. In 1788 Wistar married Isabella Marshall, who died two years later. Wistar married Elizabeth Mifflin, the niece of Thomas Mifflin, a governor of Pennsylvania, in 1798; they had three children.

Wistar was associated with the medical school of the University of Pennsylvania for thirty years. In 1788 he succeeded Rush as professor of chemistry in the Medical Department of the College of Philadelphia. In 1792, when the college merged with its rival institution, the University of the State of Pennsylvania, to form the University of Pennsylvania, Wistar was elected adjunct professor of anatomy, midwifery, and surgery. After William Shippen's death in 1808, Wistar became professor of anatomy only, since midwifery and surgery had been separated from that chair a few years before, and he served the university in this capacity until his death.

Wistar was an extremely popular teacher. As his classes grew in size, Wistar purchased, at his own expense, gigantic models and drawings so that all of the students could follow his anatomical demonstrations. Eventually his anatomy courses became so popular that they had to be divided into sections. In 1811 the first volume of Wistar's two-volume *A System of Anatomy for the Use of Students of Medicine* was published; the second volume appeared in 1814. The first American textbook devoted to the subject, it was used in many of the country's earliest medical schools and went through nine editions. Beyond this textbook, Wistar added little to medical literature other than a few journal articles. He did, however, write several papers on paleontology, including an examination of the bones of the giant "Megalonyx" that Thomas Jefferson had deposited in the American Philosophical Society in 1797. Wistar's detailed report on the bones, which appeared in the society's *Transactions* in 1799, is considered the first technical study to be published by an American in the field of vertebrate paleontology.

Wistar was active in the affairs of the American Philosophical Society, succeeding his good friend Jefferson as president of that learned body in 1815. To combat the critics of vaccination, he was the moving force behind the founding in 1809 of the Society for Circulating the Benefit of Vaccination, which succeeded in vaccinating about 11,000 people by 1817. Although he was not a pious man, Wistar did adhere to the principles of the Society of Friends. This is apparent in his work with the vaccine society as well as in his opposition to slavery and his support of prison reform. He was a member of the Pennsylvania Prison Society and the Humane Society, and in 1813 he succeeded Rush as president of the Pennsylvania Society for the Abolition of Slavery. He was also sympathetic to the plight of Native Americans.

Portly, charming, and urbane, Wistar was popular with his professional colleagues and the literati of the city. While his family and friends tended to support the Federalist party, Wistar was a Jeffersonian Democrat. Because he had few enemies, Philadelphia Democrats urged him, unsuccessfully, to run for Congress.

Wistar's weekly soirées at his house were famous, and after his death, his friends continued these Saturday gatherings by forming the Wistar Association, which has continued to late in the twentieth century.

Several years before his death, failing health (he had suffered from heart disease during his later years) forced Wistar to curtail his medical practice. When he died in Philadelphia, the city's medical and scientific institutions temporarily suspended their operations. University of Pennsylvania medical students carried his coffin from the American Philosophical Society to his house, while members of the society and the university faculty marched behind. Wistar's only scientific contribution, a description of the sphenoid sinuses, was published in the *Transactions* of the American Philosophical Society in 1818. While his teaching career and textbook on anatomy are now forgotten, his name still lives on in the Wistar Institute of the University of Pennsylvania, which grew out of Wistar's private collection of anatomical specimens. It was founded by Wistar's great-nephew Isaac Jones Wistar in 1892.

• Collections of personal and family papers are at the American Philosophical Society, the College of Physicians of Philadelphia, and the Historical Society of Pennsylvania. William Tilghman, *An Eulogium in Commemoration of Doctor Caspar Wistar* (1818); David Hosack, *Tribute to the Memory of the Late Caspar Wistar, M.D.* (1818); and Charles Caldwell, *An Eulogium on Caspar Wistar, M.D.* (1818), are the best contemporary accounts of Wistar's life. William Shainline Middleton, "Caspar Wistar, Junior," *Annals of Medical History* 4 (1922): 64–76, is the only modern account of note. See also [Caspar Morris], "Caspar Wistar. 1761–1818," in *Lives of Eminent American Physicians and Surgeons of the Nineteenth Century*, ed. Samuel D. Gross (1861), pp. 116–38; George Gaylord Simpson, "The Beginnings of Vertebrate Paleontology in North America," *Proceedings of the American Philosophical Society* 86 (1942): 130–88; and Thomas Horrocks, "Thomas Jefferson and the Great Claw," *Virginia Cavalcade* 35 (1985): 70–79.

THOMAS A. HORROCKS

WISTER, Owen (14 July 1860 21 July 1938), author, was born in Germantown, Pennsylvania, the son of Dr. Owen Jones Wister and Sarah Butler. Considering that Wister was to secure his fame as the author of tales of the Wild West, it is ironic but nonetheless significant that both his background and education were distinctly eastern and patrician. His father, a successful physician, was the son of a distinguished Philadelphia family. His mother, an author and poet, was the daughter of Fanny Kemble, the celebrated Shakespearean actress, and Pierce Butler, himself grandson of the eighteenth-century Pierce Butler who had been the delegate to the Constitutional Convention from South Carolina. Young Owen was educated in private schools in Switzerland and England as well as in the United States.

Both at the exclusive St. Paul's School, in Concord, New Hampshire, which he attended from 1873 to 1878, and then at Harvard, Wister's chief interest was in music, although his social interests also took much of his time. While at Harvard, Wister was welcomed into the higher reaches of Boston society, and within Harvard itself he formed lifelong relationships through his clubs. His friendship with Theodore Roosevelt, an older classmate, would prove to be particularly rewarding and enduring.

Graduating *summa cum laude* from Harvard in 1882, Wister intended to pursue a career in music. To that end he returned to Europe. His compositions were approved by Franz Liszt, to whom he had secured an introduction through his grandmother Fanny Kemble. His studies were further encouraged by Antoine-François Marmontel and Ernest Guiraud, teachers to some of the most famous European composers. Wister's one-act comic opera, *La Sérénade*, was performed in Paris in early 1883, and he then commenced work on a longer opera, *Montezuma*.

Wister's relationships with his parents had been strained for some time, his mother being particularly critical and demanding and his father being suspicious of his son's ambitions. Later in 1883 Dr. Wister secured a position for his son in a Boston brokerage. Although he apparently almost immediately relented and agreed to support Owen's studies in Paris, Wister now abandoned music as a profession. For the rest of his life, however, he continued to compose music and to write music commentary. Back in the United States, he worked in Boston and then spent a brief time as a clerk in a Philadelphia law office. He had long suffered from varieties of ill health, including bouts of severe headaches and episodes of semiparalysis of the face. In the summer of 1885, on the advice of Dr. S. Weir Mitchell, and, accompanied by two of his mother's spinster friends, he took a trip to Wyoming for a rest cure.

That trip at once restored Wister's health and changed his life. ("I'm beginning to be able to feel I'm something of an animal and not a stinking brain alone," he wrote in his journal soon after his arrival at the ranch where he stayed.) At the end of the summer he returned east to attend Harvard Law School, from which he graduated in 1888. He then settled in Philadelphia, where he practiced law sporadically. Wyoming, however, had been an inspiration, and he returned to the West repeatedly, recording his encounters with cowboys and others, anecdotes he heard, and his observations of details of western life. In the fall of 1891, after his fifth summer in the West, he drew upon his notebooks for the first of his western tales, "Hank's Woman" and "How Lin McLean Went East," both published in 1892, the first in *Harper's Weekly* and the second in *Harper's New Monthly Magazine*. Henceforth writing became a daily occupation for Wister, and hereafter, although in fact from his midforties onward he would largely abandon specifically western themes, Wister would become famous for his western tales.

Like many of the stories, sketches, and essays to follow, the two early tales pointed to fundamental differences between western manners and assumptions on the one hand, and those of the traditional East on the other, leading sometimes to tragic consequences and sometimes to comedy. "Hank's Woman" is a somber story about a cowboy who has married a religious, tradition-bound Austrian maid-servant who had been abandoned in the West by her European employers. The union is unlikely from the beginning, and ends with the killing of Hank by his wife, followed by her own accidental death as she tries to dispose of the body. "How Lin McLean Went East" is a brief comic sketch in which the rapscallion gambling and womanizing cowboy Lin visits his successful businessman of a brother in Boston, who is embarrassed by his ways and his appearance, whereupon Lin returns to the West.

Wister combined and elaborated his various tales in *Red Men and White* (1896), *Lin McLean* (1898), and *The Jimmyjohn Boss* (1900), and the novel *The Virginian* (1902), which he dedicated to Theodore Roosevelt. *The Virginian*, with its lanky, competent, gentlemanly and soft-spoken but nonetheless ominous hero, proved to be the archetypal American western, while "the Virginian" himself became the basic model for the cowboy in fiction and film to come. In this original, however, he is a fairly complex character and not merely a wild man from the West. Wister comments at length on his aristocratic bearing. Moving through his various adventures, the Virginian is sometimes tender and is often shy. He is given to ironical joshing and sometimes to practical jokes, but at the same time he is so proud a man that he will kill rather than accept even a mild insult. Thus in the most famous line of dialogue in the novel, after the villain Trampas accuses him of cheating at poker saying, "Your bet, you son-of-a——," he draws his pistol and says, speaking gently but with the sound of death, "When you call me that, *smile*!" Near the end of the novel, moreover, in a famous duel scene, in fact he will kill Trampas. The novel was a great best seller both in its own day and subsequently. It was adapted to the stage, made into movies, and in the 1960s became the basis for a television series.

At the end of this archetypal western, the hero does marry the eastern schoolmarm, herself the daughter of a distinguished Vermont family with ancestry going back to Revolutionary days, and, far from riding off into the sunset, he becomes a rich and important man with a grip on many enterprises. Here, as in an 1895 essay written in collaboration with Frederic Remington, "The Evolution of the Cow-Puncher," Wister would seem to have been as much intent upon recovering supposedly lost values and character for the East as in portraying the West for itself. The Virginian is the appropriate mate for a descendent of a Revolutionary War hero. In the 1895 essay the cowboy is seen to be the true remaining Anglo-Saxon, "still forever homesick for out-of-doors," and a potential savior for an East that, in Wister's view, had been adulterated by new immigrants.

In 1898 Wister married a distant cousin, Mary Channing Wister, the great-granddaughter of William Ellery Channing (1780–1840). As might be expected given the social position which he occupied with his wife, Wister came to be ever more conservative in his views. He wrote one more novel, *Lady Baltimore* (1906), in which he expressed appreciation of the aristocratic society of Charleston, South Carolina, to which he himself had access as a descendent of Pierce Butler. His other writing ranged from a lengthy comic sketch *Philosophy 4* (1903), a baldly anti-Semitic tale about a couple of Harvard undergraduates, to *How Doth the Simple Spelling Bee* (1907), which attacked the simplified-spelling movement, to a brief three-act satire on Prohibition, *Watch Your Thirst* (1923). In 1904 he became vice president of an organization called the Immigration Restriction League. During World War I, he published *The Pentecost of Calamity* (1915), in which he attacked supposed German barbarism and urged American participation in the war. In *A Straight Deal, or The Ancient Grudge* (1920), he vehemently attacked supposed anti-British feeling in the United States, following that book however with a less angry *Neighbors Henceforth* (1922) in which he urged American cooperation with the Allies.

Wister also wrote accounts of three presidents: *Ulysses S. Grant* (1900), *The Seven Ages of Washington* (1907), and *Roosevelt: The Story of a Friendship, 1880–1919* (1930), although the last was as much about Wister himself as it was about Theodore Roosevelt. His collected works were published in a standard edition of eleven volumes in 1928.

A week after his seventy-eighth birthday, at his summer home in Saunderstown, Rhode Island, Wister was struck by a cerebral hemorrhage and died the next day. His wife had died in childbirth, in 1913. Wister was buried in Philadelphia, next to his wife's grave. He was survived by five of his six children.

• The primary collection of Owen Wister papers is in the Manuscript Division of the Library of Congress. Other letters and papers are in the Houghton Library of Harvard University and the American Heritage Center of the University of Wyoming. For Wister's journals see Fanny Kemble Wister, ed., *Owen Wister Out West: His Journals and Letters* (1958). Letters and documents are reprinted in Ben Merchant Vorpahl, *My Dear Wister: The Frederic Remington–Owen Wister Letters* (1972). Both books contain biographical essays. The most substantial biography of Wister is Darwin Payne, *Owen Wister: Chronicler of the West, Gentleman of the East* (1985). Earlier biographies are John L. Cobbs, *Owen Wister* (1984), and Richard W. Etulain, *Owen Wister* (1973), both of which have bibliographies. Important discussion of Wister's interest in the West along with that of other Eastern patricians is to be found in Edward G. White, *The Eastern Establishment and the Western Experience: The West of Frederic Remington, Theodore Roosevelt, and Owen Wister* (1968).

MARCUS KLEIN

WISTER, Sarah (20 July 1761–21 Apr. 1804), Quaker diarist and poet, was born in Philadelphia, Pennsylvania, the eldest child of Daniel Wister, merchant, and Lowry Jones. The Wister family was wealthy, and Sally, as she was called, was educated at the Quaker Girls School run by philanthropist Anthony Benezet. There she followed a progressive curriculum that fostered her lifelong love of writing. In 1777, the Wister family fled war-torn Philadelphia and took refuge with relatives in rural Gwynedd, Pennsylvania, until July 1778. During this time, Wister began keeping a journal addressed to her close friends Deborah Norris (who became the influential Deborah Norris Logan) and Sarah Jones. Called her "Revolutionary journal," this is Wister's best-known work. Like her other published writings, it appeared posthumously, and it was first excerpted by the historian John F. Watson for his voluminous *Annals of Philadelphia and Pennsylvania* (1830).

When Wister returned to Philadelphia, she renewed friendships interrupted by the war and spent time on family matters, good works, reading, and writing. She continued to make sporadic entries in her journal until 1781. Gradually, she evolved from the spirited, worldly extrovert so evident in the pages of her Revolutionary journal to the spiritual introvert reflected in her later poems and her devotional journal, kept from 9 June 1796 to 15 May 1797. The girl who delighted in fiction by Henry Fielding and Sophia Briscoe became the woman who studied philosophy, theology, and history by John Locke and Hannah More, among others. Wister did not marry. She was especially devoted to her mother, whose death on 15 February 1804 was a severe emotional blow. Wister herself died only two months later in Philadelphia; the exact cause is unknown.

Wister's Revolutionary journal provides rare insights into an eighteenth-century adolescent female sensibility. Wister responded privately to the political and social turmoil of the Revolution, documenting neither battles nor politics. The result is a journal with a distinctly female view of the Revolutionary aftermath. Wister displaces the disharmony of war with the harmony of friendship, reduces macrocosmic events to microcosmic ones, emphasizes continuity and normalcy in the face of widespread disruption, and chooses a witty, whimsical tone rather than a serious one. For example, in the following extract, she mocks Lieutenants Lee and Waring, two Virginia officers billeted at her aunt's farmhouse:

> Lee sings prettily and talks a great deal how good turkey hash and fried hominy is (a pretty discourse to entertain the ladies), extols Virginia and execrates Maryland, which by the by I provoked them to, for though I admired both Virginia and Maryland, I laughed at the former and praised the latter, ridiculed their manner of speaking. I took great delight in teasing them; I believe I did it sometimes ill-naturedly, but I don't care. They were not, I am certain, almost first-rate gentlemen (how different from our other officers). But they are gone to Virginia, where they may sing, dance, and eat turkey hash and fried hominy all day long if they choose.

In contrast to her lively Revolutionary journal, Wister's devotional journal documents a spiritual crisis during which she doubted her religious convictions. Never intended for publication, it charted her unresolved struggle between faith and despair and in this sense departed radically from many published Quaker autobiographies, which followed a fairly standard pattern of spiritual growth and strength. Wister's Revolutionary and devotional journals should not be seen as complete, edited, perfected texts. Instead, they should be seen as works in progress, written by a self in process, prose and person remaining unfinished.

Sarah Wister was also an accomplished poet. Her poems are primarily neoclassical, but a few show nascent romantic elements. She often signed her poetry "Laura," adopting the convention of a classical pseudonym, as did many eighteenth-century women poets. Wister's verses tend to be occasional and private. They are often addressed to specific recipients, including her physician and friend, the famous Benjamin Rush.

• Wister's Revolutionary journal is at the Historical Society of Pennsylvania; her devotional journal and correspondence from 1777 to 1779 are also housed there in the Wister family papers. Three letters from Wister to Benjamin Rush can be found in the Rush Manuscripts, Library Company of Philadelphia. Ten letters, thirteen poems, and other fragments by Wister are in the Eastwick Collection, American Philosophical Society, which also includes much other Wister family correspondence. See Kathryn Zabelle Derounian, ed., *The Journal and Occasional Writings of Sarah Wister* (1987); Kathryn Zabelle Derounian, " 'A dear dear friend': Six Letters from Deborah Norris to Sarah Wister, 1778–1779," *The Pennsylvania Magazine of History and Biography* 108 (1984): 487–516; and Steven E. Kagle, *American Diary Literature, 1620–1799* (1979).

KATHRYN ZABELLE DEROUNIAN-STODOLA

WITHERS, Frederick Clarke (4 Feb. 1828–7 Jan. 1901), architect, was born in Shepton Mallet, Somersetshire, England, the son of John Alexander Withers, a solicitor's clerk, and Maria Jewell, a tutor. In 1839 the Withers family moved to Sherborne, Dorsetshire, where Frederick completed his formal education at King Edward's School. His father apprenticed him in 1844 for a period of five years to Edward Mondey, a local architect and builder. Following his indentureship Withers entered the London office of Thomas Henry Wyatt, a respected ecclesiastical architect, who was committed to the Gothic Revival style of Augustus W. N. Pugin.

Andrew Jackson Downing was seeking professionally trained architects for his newly formed workshop and office in Newburgh, New York, when he visited London in 1850. He recruited Calvert Vaux, and they returned to the United States. Withers accepted employment with Downing late the following year and made the trip to America on his own in 1852. The young American firm was struck by tragedy in 1852, when Downing died suddenly in a Hudson River steamboat explosion. Vaux continued the practice with Withers for three years, at which time he went to New York City and Withers launched an independent career in Newburgh. The same year, 1856, Withers married Emily A. DeWindt, a relative of Downing's wife; they had three children. Up to this time Withers's career had been based on domestic designs that reflected Downing's ideas filtered through his own Gothic sensibility. Examples of these were the David M. Clarkson House (1856) and the Walter Vail House (1859), both in Balmville, a northern suburb of Newburgh. He received his first religious commission, of which there would be many, in 1857 for the First Presbyterian Church in Newburgh, New York. Reviews of the building were favorable, and Vaux included an illustration of it in the second edition of his *Villas and Cottages* (1864). The fledgling American Institute of Architects invited Withers to join in 1857, and the following year *The Horticulturist* published "A Few Hints on Church Building," in which Withers established his debt to Pugin and the English ecclesiological movement, which emphasized the historical and intellectual validity of medieval forms of church building and liturgy.

Withers volunteered for service in the Union army in August 1861 and was commissioned as a lieutenant in Company B of the First New York Engineers. Duty in Georgia proved detrimental to his health, and recurring illness forced his resignation in August 1862. He returned home, and in July of the following year his wife died. Withers left Newburgh for New York City, where he formed a new partnership with Vaux that lasted until 1871. In 1864 he married Beulah Alice Higbee, the daughter of the Reverend Edward Young Higbee, the assistant minister of New York's Trinity Church; they had eight children.

Following the Civil War Withers positioned himself as a proponent of the international Gothic movement associated with John Ruskin in England and Eugène-Emmanuel Viollet-le-Duc in France and helped establish the English High Victorian Gothic style in the United States. His designs for the Tioronda School in Beacon, New York (1865), and the Newburgh Savings Bank (1866), with their polychrome masonry, horizontal banding, and high roofs, were representative works in that style. Withers's brother, Robert Jewell Withers, a London architect, was his source for progressive English architectural thought, along with current British architectural periodicals and books. Withers inaugurated application of the style to American hospital design with the commission for the Hudson River State Hospital for the Insane in Poughkeepsie, New York (1867–1878). Despite his progressive reputation in the secular arena, Withers retained his role as a traditional Gothicist in church architecture. The First Presbyterian Church in Highland Falls, New York (1868), and St. Luke's in Beacon, New York (1869), are small parish churches that exhibit Withers's ecclesiological design principles.

In 1866 Edward Miner Gallaudet, president of the newly chartered Columbia Institution for the Deaf and Dumb (now Gallaudet College) in Washington, D.C., asked Frederick Law Olmsted and Vaux to prepare a master plan for the college. He hired Withers to design and construct the campus buildings (1866–1885), including Chapel Hall (1867–1871), the President's House (1867), College Hall (1875), a gymnasium, and three professors' houses.

For reasons unknown Withers withdrew from the American Institute of Architects in 1869 along with Vaux and Leopold Eidlitz, fellow Gothicists. Withers's career and professional standing were unaffected as the 1870s saw the publication of *Church Architecture* (1873), containing illustrations of his church designs from 1857 to 1873. The same decade he produced his most famous design, the Jefferson Market Courthouse in New York City (1874–1877). His conception for the Jefferson Market Courthouse, to include a courthouse, fire and bell tower, prison, and market, was preceded by, involved with, and survived the corrupt New York City politics of the time. Additionally, Withers designed the prestigious William B. Astor Memorial Altar and Reredos (1876–1877) in Trinity Church, New York City. This necessitated remodeling the chancel and included the erection of a one-story sacristy to the rear of the church.

The 1880s and 1890s exhibited a gradual reversal in Withers's successful career. His conservative competition design for the New York City Produce Exchange (1881) lost. He retained the high quality of work he was noted for, but he chose not to follow current architectural trends. His design for the Van Schaik Free Reading Room, Bronx, New York (1882), recalled earlier picturesque buildings, and the Queen Anne–style Frank Hasbrouck House in Poughkeepsie, New York (1885), was his last domestic design. In 1887 Withers formed a partnership with Walter Dickson, an architect from Albany, New York. The firm's most distinguished design of the decade was the Chapel of the Good Shepherd, Welfare Island (now Roosevelt Island), New York City (1888). Withers's unsuccessful competition design for the Cathedral of St. John the Divine in New York City (1889) was succeeded by his largest church design, Trinity Episcopal Church in Hartford, Connecticut (1891). Withers's last commission was the New York City Prison (1896). Once again embroiled in the municipal chicanery of Tammany Hall, Withers died at his home in Yonkers, New York, before the project was completed.

• Withers's own writings and illustrations include "A Few Hints on Church Building," *The Horticulturist* 13 (July 1858); *Church Architecture: Plans, Elevations, and Views of Twenty-one Churches and Two School Houses* (1873); and *Buildings Erected from the Designs of F. C. Withers, Architect* (1877). For the most comprehensive study of Withers's life and work see Francis R. Kowsky, *The Architecture of Frederick Clarke Withers and the Progress of the Gothic Revival in America after 1850* (1980). Withers's Newburgh years are mentioned in John J. Nutt, *Newburgh: Institutions, Industries and Leading Citizens* (1891), while designs from this period appear in Calvert Vaux, *Villas and Cottages* (1857). Obituaries are in the *New York Times*, 8 Jan. 1901, and the *American Institute of Architects Quarterly Bulletin* (Apr. 1901).

SUSAN WAGER SCHWARTZ

WITHERSPOON, John (5 Feb. 1723–15 Nov. 1794), Presbyterian minister, college president, and American patriot, was born in the village of Gifford in the parish of Yester, Scotland, eighteen miles east of Edinburgh Castle, the son of James Witherspoon, a minister of the Church of Scotland, and Anne (or Anna) Walker. At home Witherspoon was instructed in the New Testament and the hymns of Isaac Watts and early developed a facility for rapid, accurate memorization. He entered the University of Edinburgh when only thirteen and received a master of arts in February 1739. He then studied theology, was licensed to preach on 6 September 1743, and in January 1745 was called as minister of the Church of Scotland parish in Beith, Ayrshire. The next year he helped raise troops to fight against Charles Stuart, the Young Pretender, but rebel forces captured him when he went to observe the battle of Falkirk. He underwent a brief but harsh imprisonment in Castle Doune near Stirling that permanently damaged his nervous system. In 1748 he married Elizabeth Montgomery; they had ten children, five of whom died during childhood.

Witherspoon made his reputation as an effective polemicist for the Popular party in the Church of Scotland. Against the Moderates, who favored patronage for filling vacant pulpits and cosmopolitanism in politics and the intellect, Witherspoon's Popular party stood for the right of congregations to choose their own ministers and a more traditional Christian faith. In 1753 Witherspoon published a witty satire called *Ecclesiastical Characteristics* that purported to describe the convictions and actions of the Moderates. When preaching, for example, a Moderate always took his authorities "from heathen writers, *none*, or as few as possible, from Scripture." Fifteen editions of this work from printers in Edinburgh, Glasgow, London, Philadelphia, and Utrecht over the next several years made Witherspoon a celebrity. To this satire Witherspoon soon added other blows, including an attack on the Moderates' attendance at the theater and a treatise denouncing clerical meddling in public affairs. His rising reputation was confirmed by a move in June 1757 to the larger, more prosperous Laigh Kirk in Paisley, near Glasgow, where he enjoyed contact with cloth manufacturers trading in the colonies as well as promoters of the expanding Scottish immigration to North America.

American Presbyterians first came to learn of Witherspoon through his polemical writings and expositions of biblical themes. A few Americans also knew of a short essay in the *Scots Magazine* of 1753, in which Witherspoon asserted, "The ideas we receive by our senses . . . are exactly according to . . . real truth, which certainly ought to be the same with philosophic truth." These sentiments were close enough to arguments later advanced by Thomas Reid and other philosophers of "Scottish common sense realism" to at least partially justify Witherspoon's later claim to have anticipated the central principles of their work.

In 1766 the College of New Jersey (now Princeton University) found itself in need of a president. College trustees, mostly New Side Presbyterians who favored revival, were also hoping that someone from outside the colonies might help heal a schism with the Old Sides, who distrusted religious enthusiasm. The trustees, impressed with Witherspoon's wit, orthodoxy, and learning, made him their choice. He was receptive, but his wife had no interest in leaving Scotland. The trustees began making other arrangements. Benjamin Rush, the colonies' most assiduous networker, who was then studying medicine in Edinburgh, made an effective appeal during a visit to the Witherspoon home. Elizabeth Witherspoon relented, the trustees straightened out details, and, to great applause, the Witherspoons and their children arrived in Princeton on 12 August 1768.

From his new position as president of the one college in the colonies (and later the early United States) that served several regions, Witherspoon almost immediately began to exert an influence as educator, churchman, politician, and thinker. At the college he reorganized instruction around lectures, which was a novel pedagogical strategy. He traveled to New York, Philadelphia, Virginia, and New England to raise funds, recruit students, and cultivate goodwill. Within a year the college's endowment doubled to over five thousand pounds. Soon Princeton was attracting nearly as many students as Yale; in the five years before 1776, it produced more graduates (twenty-five per year) than ever before in its history. The revolutionary war, with Princeton a battle site and a depot for troops on both sides, crippled the institution so that enrollments did not climb to prewar levels again until the 1790s. But Witherspoon's sterling reputation guaranteed its survival.

Among the students Witherspoon was a respected, even beloved figure. His wife died in 1789, and when Witherspoon two years later, at sixty-eight years of age, married a 24-year-old widow, Ann Dill, students turned the occasion into celebration rather than farce. Two daughters were born in this marriage, only one of whom survived to adulthood. In an age of often extreme undergraduate rowdyism, Witherspoon maintained a well-regulated institution by following his own maxim, "Govern always but beware of governing too much."

Presbyterian hopes that Witherspoon could help unite the church's quarreling factions were more than fulfilled. Under his tenure, the proportion of Princeton students entering the ministry declined, but Witherspoon still trained most of the leaders who guided the church through the first quarter of the next century. His moderate evangelical theology and earnest desire to link Christianity with republican liberty won applause from New Sides and Old Sides alike. He was selected to serve on several of the committees that prepared the way for a national general assembly, which replaced the regional synod of New York and Philadelphia. When this general assembly met for the first time in 1789, the statement of principles introducing its form of government included a preamble written by Witherspoon that called "the rights of private judgment, in all matters that respect religion . . . universal and unalienable," and he was asked to preach the opening sermon.

Having opposed arbitrary ecclesiastical power in Scotland, Witherspoon wasted no time in revealing his political colors to Americans. As a result of Witherspoon's first tour to Virginia, the Orange County planter James Madison, Sr., sent his son and namesake, the future president, to Princeton out of admiration for Witherspoon's defense of religious liberty. At Witherspoon's second Princeton commencement in September 1769, the college awarded honorary degrees to John Dickinson and Joseph Galloway of Pennsylvania and to John Hancock of Boston, all of whom had won renown for defending colonial privileges against British impositions.

When New Jersey patriots began to organize, Witherspoon was at the forefront. In July 1774 he joined the Somerset County Committee of Correspondence. On 22 June 1776 he was selected by New Jersey as a delegate to the Continental Congress in Philadelphia. He arrived on the 28th and soon thereafter affixed his signature to the Declaration of Independence as the only clergyman to do so. He then served in the Continental Congress for most of the period until November 1782, with appointments to more than one hundred committees, including especially important work in negotiations with foreign powers and drafting the Articles of Confederation. During his period in Congress he also wrote pamphlets opposed to the issue of paper money and penned recantations for two printers, Benjamin Towne of Philadelphia and James Rivington of New York, who, for publishing Loyalist essays, had fallen afoul of Congress. The latter tracts once again illustrated Witherspoon's gift for satire but also showed how quick the defenders of liberty could be to silence those who questioned independence. After the war he was elected to the New Jersey legislature in 1783 and 1789, and in 1787 he was a member of the New Jersey convention that approved the Constitution.

From the beginnings of his instruction at the college, Witherspoon's lectures on moral philosophy linked notions of natural law, radical republicanism, and Christian virtue in a pattern that soon became common throughout the new country. In 1774 he published a newspaper essay that gave his views wider circulation. "We are firmly determined," he wrote, "never to submit to [Parliament's claim to full sovereignty], and do deliberately prefer war with all its horrors, and even extermination itself to slavery, rivetted on us and our posterity." When war came, he preached a memorable sermon on 17 May 1776, "The Dominion of Providence over the Passions of Men," which proclaimed God's ability to bring good out of the unrestrained excesses of British tyranny. When this sermon was published, Witherspoon added a forceful appeal to his fellow Scots to join the patriot cause.

A few college trustees, including the influential lawyer Elias Boudinot, were initially nervous about their president's political involvements, but soon all who backed American independence came to esteem his manifold contributions. John Adams, who knew Witherspoon from Congress as well as from hearing him preach on several occasions, called him "as hearty a Friend as any of the Natives [i.e., American-born]—an animated Son of Liberty." For their part, the British recognized him as a formidable foe. Jonathan Odell, an Anglican minister from Burlington, New Jersey, even turned the satirical methods for which Witherspoon was famous against the Princeton president in a bit of Tory verse:

Whilst to myself I've humm'd, in dismal tune,
I'd rather be a dog than Witherspoon.
Be patient reader—for the issue trust,
His day will come—remember, Heav'n is just.
(*Journal of Presbyterian History* 52 [Winter 1974]: 433)

As an intellectual guide, Witherspoon led American Protestants away from older formulas (including those of the great New England Congregationalist Jonathan Edwards, who ended his life while serving as Princeton's president in 1758) toward convictions more at home with the evangelicalism, the science, and the common-sense philosophy of the eighteenth century. In his philosophical and theological lectures, Witherspoon gave up the idealism of Edwards and Bishop George Berkeley as well as Edwards's theocentric ethics. In their place, he employed the age's new moral philosophy as propounded by the Scots-Irish thinker Francis Hutcheson, whom Witherspoon had scorned in Scotland as an ally of the Moderates. Following Hutcheson, Witherspoon taught that careful attention to the ordinary perceptions of ordinary people, that is, to "common sense," provided a solid basis for science, politics, ethics, and Christian apologetics. With these common-sense principles, he reassured Princeton students that reason did not contradict revelation. By so doing, Witherspoon gave up the intense God-consciousness that had driven Puritans like Edwards. In return, he secured a foothold from which to promote in his contemporary climate both Christian faith and general learning, both divinity and science, and both respect for Christian tradition and devotion to new ideals of liberty. Witherspoon's own writings were not brilliant, though his collected essays, sermons, and lectures were published in three editions in Philadelphia and Edinburgh during the early nineteenth century. Rather, the general intellectual strategies he offered statesmen like James Madison, a host of other officeholders in the new nation, and numerous Presbyterian clergy made him an important intellectual figure.

For all his bluff savoir faire, Witherspoon was a complex figure. Several historians have emphasized the seeming contradictions of his career. In Scotland he opposed rebellion, denounced Hutcheson, and attacked clergymen who took part in politics, while in America he supported the American Revolution, borrowed Hutcheson for his own lectures, and eagerly accepted political service in state and nation. Apparent contradictions, however, may reflect a more basic consistency. That consistency is found in his status as a clergyman from the outlying provinces and in his consistent theological tactics. As a man of the provinces,

Witherspoon's life in Scotland and America was defined by suspicion of the cultural center, whether intellectual hegemony of the Moderates or British political power, as well as by defense of local prerogatives in ecclesiastical, intellectual, and political arenas. As an evangelical clergyman in an era of great intellectual change, Witherspoon preached the Calvinism of his Presbyterian tradition while accommodating it to the common-sense Enlightenment philosophy that was coming to dominate intellectual discourse in the entire English-speaking world.

Witherspoon was a thinking activist. To Ashbel Green, his student and successor as Princeton president, he had "in promiscuous company . . . more of the quality called *presence*—a quality powerfully felt, but not to be described—than any other individual with whom the writer has ever had intercourse, Washington alone excepted" (*The Life of the Revd. John Witherspoon*, pp. 258–59). He died at his farm "Tusculum," just north of Princeton. As an American Founding Father as well as a central actor in the cultural life of two countries, Witherspoon remains a figure whose significance during his own lifetime was greater than the historical recognition he has received.

• A few Witherspoon manuscripts exist at Princeton University, the Library of Congress, and the Historical Society of Pennsylvania, but most are lost or destroyed. Ashbel Green, ed., *Works of the Rev. John Witherspoon* (4 vols., 1800; corrected ed., 1802), is solid though not critical. Jack Scott, *Annotated Edition of Lectures on Moral Philosophy by John Witherspoon* (1982), is helpful. L. H. Butterfield, ed., *John Witherspoon Comes to America: A Documentary Account* (1953), combines well-chosen texts with expert commentary. The essential biography is Varnum Lansing Collins's accurate and readable *President Witherspoon* (2 vols., 1925; repr. 1 vol., 1969). Green's biographical memoir was published by Henry Lyttleton Savage as *The Life of the Revd. John Witherspoon* (1973). James McLachlan et al., eds., *Princetonians: A Biographical Dictionary* (5 vols., 1976–1991), covering the period 1748 to 1794, contains much information on Witherspoon in relation to his students. His importance for America's revolutionary politics is well explored in Thomas Jefferson Wertenbaker, "John Witherspoon (1723–1794): Father of American Presbyterianism, Maker of Statesmen," in *The Lives of Eighteen from Princeton*, ed. Willard Thorp (1946); and Timothy M. Barnes and Robert M. Calhoon, "Moral Allegiance: John Witherspoon and Loyalist Recantation," *American Presbyterians* 63 (1985): 273–83. His place in American intellectual history is treated in Douglas Sloan, *The Scottish Enlightenment and the American College Ideal* (1971); Henry F. May, *The Enlightenment in America* (1976); Fred J. Hood, *Reformed America: The Middle and Southern States, 1783–1837* (1980); and Mark A. Noll, *Princeton and the Republic, 1768–1822* (1989). The most persuasive argument for continuity in his memorable career is provided by Ned C. Landsman, "Witherspoon and the Problem of Provincial Identity in Scottish Evangelical Culture," in *Scotland and America in the Age of Enlightenment*, ed. Richard B. Sher and Jeffrey R. Smitten (1990).

MARK A. NOLL

WITMER, Lightner (28 June 1867–19 July 1956), clinical psychologist, was born in Philadelphia, Pennsylvania, the son of David Lightner Witmer, a druggist, and Katherine Huchel. Witmer attended the Episcopal Academy in the Philadelphia area prior to entering the University of Pennsylvania in 1884. After receiving a B.A. in 1888, he taught for two years at the Rugby Academy in Philadelphia. Witmer finished his Ph.D. in psychology under Wundt at the University of Leipzig in 1892; it was officially awarded in 1893. Inspired by his university professor James McKeen Cattell, who had studied with German psychologist Wilhelm Wundt, Witmer served in the military during the Spanish-American War and headed a Red Cross unit in Italy during the First World War. In 1892 he joined the psychology faculty at the University of Pennsylvania where he remained until his retirement in 1937. In 1904 he married Emma Repplier; they had no children.

Trained as an experimental psychologist, Witmer successfully blended his experimental background with his interests in the applications of psychology to the study of intelligence, the gifted child, and the intensive treatment of childhood disorders. His chief contribution to the burgeoning child study movement was his founding of the first psychological clinic in the United States, at the University of Pennsylvania, in 1896. In its first decade, the clinic primarily served children with school-related learning problems such as speech, vision, and hearing defects, and other conditions. Mainly a training facility at the time, the clinic saw comparatively few cases. After 1907 the clinic expanded in scope to include subclinics for speech, vocational guidance, and college personnel. Its total number of cases reached almost 22,000 before the clinic was phased out in 1961.

Another notable contribution was Witmer's founding in 1907 of the first clinical psychology journal, the *Psychological Clinic*, which served as an outlet for many of his ideas and for case studies that were conducted in the psychological clinic. In its first issue, Witmer coined and described the term "clinical psychology," emphasizing the need to train practitioners to blend psychological knowledge with that from the related fields of pedagogy, sociology, and medicine and to contribute to the improvement of schooling and society. His ideas provided the bases for the practice of clinical psychology within an idiographic conceptualization of services as opposed to the growing interest in nomothetic conceptualizations, especially among those psychologists developing tests. Witmer intended the clinic and clinical psychology for the intensive study of an individual's abilities and disabilities rather than for the comparative relationship of an individual's abilities and disabilities to those of others.

Widely respected for his clinical judgment and case analysis skills, Witmer relied sparingly on normative psychological tests, which gained prominence during his career. Instead he preferred clinical judgment, one-to-one experience with clients, and the use of instruments and methods that he had developed. During the period from 1910 to 1918 he developed the Witmer Form Board and the Witmer Cylinders from adaptations of earlier tests by Édouard Séguin and Maria

Montessori. The primary forum for Witmer's ideas, the *Psychological Clinic*, ceased publication in 1935, probably because of Witmer's impending retirement and the increasing availability of related publications.

Witmer's training program in clinical psychology evolved with the operation of the clinic and was well established by 1907. His graduates became pioneers in areas that would be recognized today as clinical, consulting, industrial, and school psychology, student personnel work in higher education, school counseling, special education, and speech therapy. They included Edwin Twitmeyer, Morris Viteles, and Robert Brotemarkle. In addition to influencing several fields of application, his clinic served as a prototype for numerous early twentieth-century psychological clinics. Witmer also established a hospital at the university in 1907, and a residential school near Wallingford, Pennsylvania, in 1908, which reopened in 1921 as the Witmer School in Devon, Pennsylvania.

Witmer was active in several professional associations and received honors for his contributions. He was a charter member of the American Psychological Association (APA) from 1892 and president of the Pennsylvania Association of Clinical Psychologists in 1934–1935 and 1935–1936. In 1931 a book was dedicated to Witmer by his colleagues and former students on the thirty-fifth anniversary of the founding of the first psychological clinic. At the 1946 annual convention of the APA, the first fifty years of clinical psychology were acknowledged. Witmer's personality has been described as complex. He is reputed to have been pedantic by some, argumentative by others, forceful, dogmatic, and self-confident. He took intense interest in his students, clients, and colleagues and engendered a strong sense of respect in others. He died in Philadelphia.

Frequently recognized as the father of clinical psychology, Witmer also had a direct impact on the origins of school psychology and special education. His contributions to clinical psychology have not, however, enjoyed long-term recognition among applied and professional psychologists. His work strayed from the experimental psychology of the period, and he was critical of the rise of psychodynamic psychology and standardized intelligence testing. Renewed interest in his contributions are observable: in 1982 the *Journal of Consulting and Clinical Psychology* commemorated the seventy-fifth anniversary of the founding of the *Psychological Clinic*, and the centennial celebrations of the APA in 1992–1993 included historical testimony to his work. Witmer's conceptualizations and practices continue to be recognizable in professional psychology, and his notions of diagnostic teaching remain relevant in the fields of special education and school psychology.

• Case records of Witmer's psychological clinic are maintained at the Archives of the History of American Psychology, University of Akron. A summary description of the records appears in Murray Levine and Julius Wishner, "The Case Records of the Psychological Clinic at the University of Pennsylvania," *Journal of the History of the Behavioral Sciences* 13 (1977): 59–66. See also Robert A. Brotemarkle, ed., *Clinical Psychology: Studies in Honor of Lightner Witmer to Commemorate the Thirty-Fifth Anniversary of the Founding of the First Psychological Clinic* (1931), and Paul McReynolds, "Lightner Witmer: Little-Known Founder of Clinical Psychology," *American Psychologist* 42 (1987): 849–58. Obituaries are Robert I. Watson, "Lightner Witmer: 1867–1956," *American Journal of Psychology* 69 (1956): 680–82, and Simon H. Tulchin, "In Memoriam: Lightner Witmer, Ph.D. June 28, 1867–July 19, 1956," *American Journal of Orthopsychiatry* 27 (1957): 200–201.

THOMAS K. FAGAN

WITMER, Safara Austin (31 Jan. 1899–11 Sept. 1962), Bible college educator, was born in Grabill, Indiana, the son of Samuel Witmer and Ida (maiden name unknown), farmers. In 1907 the family moved to Fort Wayne, where Samuel Witmer found work as a carpenter. Witmer's parents were devout members of the Missionary Church Association (MCA), a Mennonite offshoot; after high school Witmer followed in the footsteps of his father and attended the MCA's Fort Wayne Bible School, where he trained for the ministry.

Witmer graduated from Fort Wayne in 1922. After a summer as an assistant pastor in a rural region of western Canada, he began work toward his B.A. at Taylor University in Upland, Indiana. While at Taylor he courted, via letter, Edith McLean, a Canadian student he had met while in Bible school. They married in 1924 and eventually had two children.

Soon after they were married the young couple headed for Colorado, where Witmer was to pastor a Mennonite Brethren in Christ church. Not long after arriving in Colorado he received a request from J. E. Ramseyer, president of Fort Wayne Bible School, to return to the school as an instructor. The couple packed up and headed back east. Save for a few brief interruptions, Witmer worked at his alma mater for the next thirty-four years. In that time he steadily made his way up the administrative ladder, while also pursuing further education. Witmer served as an instructor from 1924 to 1932, except for one year when he returned to Taylor to complete his B.A. in 1929. From 1932 to 1935 he pastored the MCA church across the street from the Bible institute. He then returned to the school as dean. He would hold this position until 1943, when he became an Air Force chaplain. In 1945 he was named president of Fort Wayne. He held this post for thirteen years, during which time he also completed an M.A. from the Winona Lake (Ind.) School of Theology and a Ph.D. (1951) in higher education from the University of Chicago.

As president of Fort Wayne from 1945 to 1958 Witmer made his own changes, including upgrading Fort Wayne's academic program and expanding the curriculum beyond Bible and evangelism-related courses. He succeeded in establishing a core of liberal arts courses that was required of all students in tandem with their religion major. He also moved Fort Wayne from simply being an institute that issued diplomas to being a four-year, degree-granting college. Under his leadership Fort Wayne expanded from one building to five and from 132 students to 312.

Witmer's devotion to the institute grew out of his passionate commitment to the idea of Bible school education. In his numerous speeches and articles on this topic Witmer asserted, as he noted in a 1955 address, that while "frequently regarded as inferior," Bible school education should actually "be given a place of pre-eminence" when compared with other forms of college education (*Beloved Educator*, p. 33). Bible school education, he maintained, was based on values; a Bible school consciously and consistently integrated God's truth with human truth, hence providing students with a coherent worldview. Witmer readily acknowledged that sometimes "Bible schools have been directed by men whose zeal and vision were most commendable but whose educational know-how was sadly deficient" (*Beloved Educator*, p. 39). However, he insisted that although these problems needed to be corrected, the enterprise must not be abandoned. As Witmer saw it, in a world desperately hungry for God's truth, Bible schools had a crucial mission: to educate students in the Bible (or a fundamentalist understanding of the Bible) and to train them for lives of Christian service.

Witmer was so dedicated to and so knowledgeable about Bible school education that he was known in some circles as "Mr. Bible College." Given this reputation and that his Ph.D. thesis dealt with accreditation agencies in higher education it was not surprising that in 1958 he was asked to serve as the first full-time executive director of the Accrediting Association of Bible Colleges (AABC). While this meant leaving his beloved institute, Witmer accepted the post because it gave him the opportunity to promote throughout North America Bible school education, which had continued its expansion. Under his leadership the AABC also conducted research into the nature and quality of Bible school education in the United States and Canada. Witmer's 1962 work, *Education with Dimension: The Bible College Story*, was the product of this research. In this book Witmer not only explained and defended the notion of Bible-centered schooling, but he also provided a roster of Bible schools in North America, with detailed information regarding enrollment and denominational affiliation.

In the same year that *Education with Dimension* appeared Witmer died in his hometown of Fort Wayne. Safara Witmer should be remembered as a tireless advocate of Bible school instruction, an educator who desired Bible schools to hold to their educational distinction while also striving for academic excellence.

• Besides *Education with Dimension*, four of Witmer's addresses on Bible schools, including "The Paradox in Bible College Education" (1955), are collected in *S. A. Witmer: Beloved Educator* (1970), published by the Accrediting Association of Bible Colleges. Witmer also wrote *The Galilean Fisherman: A Manual in Personal Evangelism* (1940), which went through numerous printings. Not much has been written about Safara Witmer. The best biographical source is Timothy Warner's brief introductory chapter in *Beloved Educator*. Jared Gerig's treatment of Witmer in *A Vine of God's Own Planting* (1980) is little more than a compressed version of Warner's essay. Perhaps most helpful is William C. Ringenberg, "A Brief History of Fort Wayne Bible College," *Mennonite Quarterly Review* 54 (1980): 135–55, which places Witmer's efforts in the context of the school he loved.

WILLIAM VANCE TROLLINGER, JR.

WITTENMYER, Annie Turner (26 Aug. 1827–2 Feb. 1900), philanthropist and temperance leader, was born in Sandy Springs, Ohio, the daughter of John G. Turner, a prosperous farmer, and Elizabeth Smith. Educated at a girls' seminary, she married a wealthy merchant, William Wittenmyer, in 1847, and in 1850 moved with him to Keokuk, Iowa. They eventually had five children, only one of whom survived to adulthood.

Her husband died in the 1850s, and Wittenmyer's energy, social status, and deep Protestant faith led her into local benevolent activity. Among other projects, she established a free school that ultimately enrolled around 200 underprivileged children. Within this school she also developed a Sunday school class, which in 1857 formed the nucleus of a new congregation, the Methodist Episcopal Church.

With the coming of the Civil War, Wittenmyer plunged into the task of providing relief—bedding, bandages, clothing, food, Bibles, and other essential items—to Iowa's soldiers. By May 1861 she had spearheaded the organization of the Keokuk Ladies' Soldiers' Aid Society, soon the premier relief organization in the state. As the society's corresponding secretary and later general agent, Wittenmyer coordinated the contributions of sister societies throughout Iowa; determined, through regular trips to often distant encampments, the needs of the soldiers; and kept Iowans informed, through letters published in local newspapers, of their duty to their fighting men. Believing in women's suitability for relief work, Wittenmyer successfully led an often acrimonious struggle against efforts to turn the society's functions over to a group of prominent men associated with the United States Sanitary Commission. In May 1864, having engineered an arrangement that retained for her female colleagues considerable bureaucratic power within a new compromise organization, Wittenmyer resigned from the Aid Society. With her now substantial reputation and hard-earned political savvy, she moved on to national wartime relief projects.

In her travels Wittenmyer had frequently met wounded and ill soldiers anxious about the future of their children. Deeply touched by these experiences, she conceived a plan to relieve the men's worries. Her Orphan Asylum Association oversaw the establishment of homes for children across Iowa. Its crowning success came just after the war's end, when Wittenmyer managed to acquire from the federal government a new but vacant cavalry barracks on thirty acres in Davenport, Iowa. It was valued at $46,000 and could house more than 600 children.

It was her "special diet kitchen" project that brought Wittenmyer national attention. Concerned about the poor quality and inappropriateness of the food being served to patients in the Union's military hospitals, she set about developing a comprehensive system for providing these men with the kind of diet she thought proper. She successfully lobbied the United States Christian Commission to underwrite the project and to name her supervisory agent for the diet kitchens. Throughout the remainder of the war she directed the installation of more than one hundred such kitchens, in which she employed about two hundred female managers ("These dietary nurses were *not cooks*," Wittenmyer insisted). Wittenmyer's kitchens issued at least two million rations through April 1865. As she wrote, "The kitchens . . . have the endorsement of the highest medical authorities—the grateful blessing of thousands, to whose restoration to health they have directly contributed" (*Under the Guns*, p. 261).

Once the war was over, Wittenmyer set about recasting her Civil War activities into a public career that lasted the rest of her life. In the immediate postwar period her name was closely linked with the emerging women's temperance movement. In 1874 the Woman's Christian Temperance Union (WCTU)—the first national women's organization in the United States—elected Wittenmyer its founding president, a position she held for the next five years, traveling extensively, speaking at temperance meetings around the country, attending large temperance conventions, and helping to organize twenty-three state auxiliaries. In 1882 she published a massive work on the movement, *The History of the Woman's Temperance Crusade*.

Wittenmyer had already written *Woman's Work for Jesus* (1873), a discourse on the role of women in the work of the Christian church, and a summons to action. It reflected her postwar involvement in what came to be known as the home missionary movement, the outreach of middle-class and elite women to the nation's underprivileged. In 1885 she published *The Women of the Reformation*, a series of sketches about women active in the sixteenth-century Protestant movement. *Under the Guns* (1895) was an account of her activities during the Civil War. She also edited and contributed articles to various magazines and newspapers.

Wittenmyer remained in active public service long after her departure from the presidency of the WCTU in 1879. A founding member of the Woman's Relief Corps (auxiliary to the Union veterans' association, the Grand Army of the Republic); she was its president in 1889. In 1892 her work with the WRC took her to Washington, D.C., where she spent five months lobbying successfully for a nurses' pension bill. By the time of her death in Sanatoga, Pennsylvania, Wittenmyer's leadership in various postwar benevolent enterprises had heightened her public and professional status and enhanced the national reputation she had initially garnered during the war.

In spite of her own very public life, Wittenmyer always maintained a vision of the role of middle-class women that was essentially conservative. As Frances Willard, Wittenmyer's successor to the WCTU presidency, later wrote, Wittenmyer believed firmly that "the vast amount of talent and energy brought into activity by the philanthropies of the war should be maintained on a Christian basis in the Church," rather than in what would soon become the postwar woman's rights and suffrage movement. Wittenmyer's own experiences in the war told her that a woman could acquire political influence without the exercise of the vote, and she eventually broke with the WCTU over the suffrage issue. She saw herself as occupying a middle ground between women who retreated to their traditional sphere and those who would fight to overcome women's "social disabilities" and stake "claims to political preferment."

• The primary extant archival materials consist of Wittenmyer's massive correspondence from her Civil War years, housed at the Iowa State Historical Society, Des Moines. Wittenmyer's memoir, *Under the Guns: A Woman's Reminiscences of the Civil War* (1895), is a moving account of her wartime service. Shorter contemporary treatments of her war work are in Linus P. Brockett and Mary C. Vaughan's chapter on Wittenmyer in their *Woman's Work in the Civil War* (1867), and Frank Moore's chapter on Wittenmyer's trusted assistant, Mary E. Shelton, in his *Women of the War* (1866). Earl S. Fulbrook, "Relief Work in Iowa during the Civil War," *Iowa Journal of History and Politics* 16 (1918), also speaks of Wittenmyer's wartime service. A recent scholarly treatment of Wittenmyer's war work is a chapter in Elizabeth D. Leonard, *Yankee Women: Gender Battles in the Civil War* (1994).

For material on Wittenmyer's postwar life and work, especially with the WCTU, see Frances Willard, *Woman and Temperance* (1883), and Wittenmyer's own *History of the Woman's Temperance Crusade* (1882). For sketches of Wittenmyer's life, see Ruth A. Gallaher, "Annie Turner Wittenmyer," *Iowa Journal of History and Politics* 29 (1931): 518–69; "Mrs. Annie Wittenmyer," *Annals of Iowa* (Jan. 1900): 276–88; and Tom Sillanpa, *Annie Wittenmyer: God's Angel* (1972).

ELIZABETH D. LEONARD

WITTKOWER, Rudolf (22 June 1901–11 Oct. 1971), art historian, was born in Berlin, Germany, the son of Henry Wittkower and Gertrude Anspach. Educated at the University of Munich and at the University of Berlin, where he studied under Adolf Goldschmidt, he received his Ph.D. in 1923. In that year, too, he took up his first professional appointment, at the Bibliotheca Hertziana in Rome. On 31 December 1923 he married Margot Holzmann, who was to be his wife and companion for the next forty-eight years, as well as his later collaborator. They had one son.

Wittkower's first decade as a scholar was spent at the Hertziana—as a research assistant from 1923 to 1928 and as a research fellow from 1928 to 1932. During this time he collaborated with Ernst Steinmann, the director of the Hertziana, on an important bibliography on Michelangelo (1927) and with Heinrich Bauer on a definitive catalogue of the drawings of Gianlorenzo Bernini (1931). He also published a number of articles on other Renaissance and Baroque topics, indicating at an early stage both the breadth and profundity of his learning and interests. In 1932–1933 he held an appointment as a lecturer at the University of Cologne; and in 1933, with the rise of Hitler, he emigrated to England with his family, making that the center of his activities for almost the next quarter century.

During this period he was a member of the staff of the Warburg Institute (1934–1956); coeditor of the *Journal of the Warburg Institute* and its successor, the *Journal of the Warburg and Courtauld Institutes* (1937–1956), both highly regarded; and Reader in the Classical Tradition in Art (1947–1949) and Durning-Lawrence Professor in the History of Art (1949–1956) at University College, University of London. He continued his impressive scholarship in Renaissance and Baroque art, but, inspired by his new country, he also turned to the study of English art and architecture and their relationship to Continental trends. Among his major contributions during these years were his collaboration with Fritz Saxl on *British Art and the Mediterranean* (1948) and his own epochal *Architectural Principles in the Age of Humanism* (1949) and *Gian Lorenzo Bernini, the Sculptor of the Roman Baroque* (1955). These were accompanied by books on the drawings of the Carracci family and of Nicolas Poussin, the latter in collaboration with Walter Friedlaender and Anthony Blunt, and a host of articles on symbols, iconography, proportion, perspective, Michelangelo, Bernini, Leon Battista Alberti, Giovanni Battista Piranesi, Andrea Palladio, and English Palladianism, with emphasis on Inigo Jones, Lord Burlington, and William Kent. In addition to his influence in scholarly circles, he also provided, through his *Architectural Principles*, an inspiration for architects, with his exposition of proportion in the Italian Renaissance encouraging such contemporary practitioners as Alison and Peter Smithson.

In 1954 and 1955 Wittkower was a visiting professor at Harvard University and in 1955–1956 at Columbia University. In 1956 he was appointed professor and chairman of the Department of Fine Arts and Archaeology (later changed to Art History and Archaeology) at Columbia, a post he held until 1968. During this time he built that department into one of the leading graduate training centers in the United States (and, indeed, the world) for the study of art history. A large number of his students there subsequently assumed teaching and research posts throughout the United States and abroad. His own scholarship continued to flourish, with perhaps his most significant publication being his definitive volume in the Pelican History of Art series, *Art and Architecture in Italy, 1600–1750* (1958). This was accompanied by *Born under Saturn* (1963) and *The Divine Michelangelo* (1964), both written in collaboration with his wife, Margot; a study of the dome of St. Peter's in Rome (1964); and articles on a whole range of topics from Renaissance and Baroque art in Italy to English Palladianism and the landscape garden. He was coeditor of the Studies in Architecture series from 1958 to 1971 and editor of the Columbia University Studies in Art History and Architecture from 1962 to 1971. In 1968 he was named the Avalon Foundation Professor in the Humanities at Columbia, and in 1969 he became emeritus.

His breadth of knowledge and his approach to art history were summed up in a lecture he presented at the Winterthur Museum in 1959, when he defined the subject of his studies as "first and foremost the *history* of artists and styles, of subject matter (i.e., iconography) and techniques; and the *history* of ideas and concepts underlying the works of art." Important to an art historian, in his view, were "the allied fields of antiquarianism, art criticism, art theory, and connoisseurship," but "he also needs the support of philosophy, semantics, psychology, and social studies. He will have to concern himself with minute facts as much as with the problems of methodology and terminology." All of this—and much more—were grist for his mill.

He received a great many honors in Italy, England, Germany, and the United States. A Guggenheim fellow in 1965, he was Kress Professor at the National Gallery of Art in Washington, D.C., in 1969–1970; Slade Professor at Cambridge University in 1970–1971; and a member of the Institute for Advanced Study in Princeton, a fellowship he had barely begun in the fall of 1971, shortly before his death in New York.

A protean figure in the field of art history, as well as a warm human being, Wittkower combined unbounded energy and a humanistic approach to scholarship with the transformation and revitalization of a major graduate department and the inspiration of a host of students and other scholars.

• In addition to the books listed above, many of Wittkower's articles and lectures have been collected and, where necessary, translated into English in a series of anthologies edited by his wife, Margot Wittkower, and others. These include *Palladio and English Palladianism* (1974), *Gothic versus Classic* (1974), *Studies in the Italian Baroque* (1975), *Allegory and the Migration of Symbols* (1977), *Idea and Image: Studies in the Italian Renaissance* (1978), *Sculpture: Processes and Principles* (1977), and *Selected Lectures of Rudolf Wittkower: The Impact of Non-European Civilizations on the Art of the West* (1989). Complete bibliographies of his writings to 1966 are contained in *Essays in the History of Architecture* and *Essays in the History of Art Presented to Rudolf Wittkower*, ed. Douglas Fraser, Howard Hibbard, and Milton J. Lewine (1967), with later writings appended to the obituary by Howard Hibbard in *Burlington Magazine* 114 (Mar. 1972): 173–77. Another significant obituary is Milton J. Lewine, *Art Journal* 31 (Winter 1971–1972): 236–37.

DAMIE STILLMAN

WITTPENN, Caroline Bayard Stevens (21 Nov. 1859–4 Dec. 1932), penal reformer, social worker, and philanthropist, was born in Hoboken, New Jersey, the daughter of Edwin Augustus Stevens, inventor, railroad manager, shipbuilder, and founder of Stevens Institute of Technology, Hoboken, and Martha Bayard Dod, social worker and founder of Holy Innocents Church, now All Saints Parish, Hoboken. Members of the Stevens family, established in Hoboken since the

1780s, were instrumental in developing the steamship lines and railroads of nineteenth-century America. The family tradition of philanthropy and personal involvement in helping others and her parents' example, especially that of her mother, was a major influence on the socially conscious activities and interests Wittpenn tirelessly exhibited during her adult life.

Wittpenn was educated by private tutors and also attended a school on the Isle of Wight, Great Britain. By assisting her mother in the organization of the local Industrial School for Manual Training and the Memorial Day Nursery while still a young adult, she helped many working women of Hoboken and New York. She was married to Archibald Alexander, a college professor, in 1879; they had one son. After her marriage ended in a traumatic separation in 1895, she became even more active in the social work of her earlier years. She became associated with approximately sixty social-service organizations and New Jersey institutions during her life. She was manager of the New Jersey State Home for Feeble-Minded Girls and Women in Vineland in 1897 and of the New Jersey State Village for Epileptics in 1902 and president of the New Jersey State Board of Children's Guardians in 1913.

Through her involvement with these social-service groups, Wittpenn became increasingly aware of the problems of disadvantaged people, including orphans, the indigent, those with disabilities, and especially women in prison. In 1903, because of her concern and interest, New Jersey governor Franklin Murphy appointed her to a commission to study the possibility of a separate prison for women. Prison reforms were enacted at that time, and these changes encouraged Wittpenn to take action by urging the creation of a separate institution for female offenders.

Archibald Alexander, Wittpenn's son, and a member of the New Jersey state legislature, introduced a bill in 1910 providing for a separate women's penal institution, and when the Clinton Farms Reformatory for Women (now the Correctional Institution for Women) was opened in 1913, Wittpenn became the first president of its board of managers. Alexander died of typhoid in 1912, and in 1915 Wittpenn donated the Chapel of the Good Shepherd at Clinton Farms in her son's memory. In 1915 she married H. Otto Wittpenn, whom she had supported as a reform mayor of Jersey City.

Wittpenn was known not only for penal reform but also as a distinguished public servant on both state and national levels. In the first decade of the 1900s, she was appointed assistant probation officer of Hudson County, New Jersey, a position she held until the end of her life. In 1910 she represented the United States at the International Congress of Family Education in Brussels, Belgium, and during World War I she led several Liberty Loan drives in New Jersey. When Woodrow Wilson was governor of New Jersey (1911–1913), he consulted Wittpenn about state welfare problems, and she was later appointed to the New Jersey Department of Institutions and Agencies during the administrations of governors Walter E. Edge (1917–1919) and Morgan P. Larson (1929–1932). During Wilson's presidency in 1918, Wittpenn was New Jersey's first National Democratic Committeewoman, and in 1929 President Herbert Hoover appointed her to represent the United States at the International Prison Commission in Switzerland. In addition to her other activities, Wittpenn was a trustee of the Stevens Institute of Technology for several years. On 10 June 1922, at the first commencement ceremony of the New Jersey College for Women, New Brunswick (now Douglass College of Rutgers, the State University of New Jersey), an honorary degree of doctor of laws was conferred on Caroline Bayard Wittpenn.

On 24 November 1932 Wittpenn was honored at a public celebration for her seventy-third birthday and a newspaper editorial described her as the "best-loved woman in New Jersey," not only for her long-term work as a leader of state correctional and welfare programs but also for her kind, empathic, and generous character. Wittpenn died in Hoboken only two weeks after the public birthday celebration, and more than one thousand people attended her funeral. In accordance with the custom of the Stevens family, she was buried in a wicker basket at Hoboken Cemetery, North Bergen, New Jersey.

Wittpenn was known for her benevolence and active participation in improving the lives of those in adverse circumstances and mainly for her achievements in penal reform, especially for women. She was eulogized in the *Nation* as the "foremost citizen of New Jersey." The article stated, "Never was there a woman of means who felt more keenly the responsibility that wealth should impose upon those who are advantaged by it to serve the public, not spasmodically, or when the drums are beating, but day by day, year in and year out." A resolution by the board of trustees of the Stevens Institute on 8 December 1932 states that she had a sense of responsibility for the young, the distressed, and the unfortunate and served them to the last days of her life.

• The New Jersey Historical Society, Newark, the Jersey City Public Library, and the Samuel C. Williams Library at the Stevens Institute of Technology, Hoboken, N.J., hold the Stevens's family information and artifacts. Scrapbooks at the Hoboken Public Library include information about the Stevens family, their home, Castle Point, historical background, and lists of descendants and achievements. See also Sadie Leinkauf, "Caroline Bayard Stevens Wittpenn," *New Jersey Club Woman*, Nov. 1940; "C. Wittpenn, Pioneer of Enlightened Penology," *Welfare Reporter* 2, no. 4 (Aug. 1947); John J. Heaney, *The Bicentennial Comes to Hoboken, 1976* (1976); and articles in the *Hudson Dispatch*, 3 Dec. 1932, and *Stevens Indicator*, Dec. 1932. Obituaries are in the *Jersey Journal* and the *New York Times*, 5 Dec. 1932; the *Newark Evening News*, 6 Dec. 1932; and the *Nation*, 21 Dec. 1932.

ANNA BRAHM KANE

WODEHOUSE, P. G. (15 Oct. 1881–14 Feb. 1975), writer and lyricist, was born Pelham Grenville Wodehouse in Guildford, England, the son of Henry Ernest

Wodehouse, a civil servant, and Eleanor Deane, an Anglican minister's daughter. Wodehouse grew up nearly parent-free, his elders posted to Hong Kong. From age two, "Plum" (the early elision of his first name) boarded in England with surrogate families or in schools. He wrote: "We looked upon mother more like an aunt. She came home very infrequently."

Undoubtedly influenced by these arm's-length years, Wodehouse began at five to create a written world. Although his famed comic writing was invariably dispassionate, Plum the lyricist proved playful and warmly sentimental. He professed himself quite happy at suburban London's Dulwich College, a secondary school where his contemporaries included C. S. Forester and Raymond Chandler. "Good at games," he was wise enough to be an underwhelming scholar.

Mark Twain claimed to have met all of his fictional characters while a cub steamboat pilot on the Mississippi; nearly all of Wodehouse's cast—and their values—hailed from Dulwich. He admitted as much about Stanley Featherstonehaugh Ukridge, a self-righteous cadger, and Psmith, "a compulsive mouther of stilted rhetoric." It is equally true of silly Bertie Wooster, in his twenties still food-fighting at his club. Rogues like Oofy Prosser were no more oddly named than real-life English public schoolboys, nor were the villages of Wodehouseland stranger than truth.

Wodehouse endured two years in a bank, placing eighty items, usually school-related, in magazines and newspapers before his novel *The Pothunters* (1902) was published. By twenty-two, he had published another novel, become a London columnist with a theatrical eye, and quit the bank. In 1904 he made his first New York visit, learning the gangland slang that formed a part of his verbal slapstick. He began explaining the United States to British readers. In 1906 he collaborated with American composer Jerome Kern on the jaunty, topical song "Mr. Chamberlain" for *The Beauty of Bath*, a London musical comedy.

Writing for stage and page, Wodehouse became a transatlantic commuter. He arrived in New York in August 1914, meeting Ethel Newton Rowley, a British widow. They soon married "with $100 between them." Isolated by World War I and rejected by both the British and U.S. military because of poor eyesight, Wodehouse became *Vanity Fair*'s drama critic. He adopted his wife's daughter and began to write for George Lorimer's *Saturday Evening Post*.

Over the next twenty-five years Wodehouse became one of the world's most popular and loved writers. He created a dotty English world for the *Post*'s readers. In "Something New" (1915) he invented Blandings Castle, inhabited by fusty Victorian Lord Emsworth and his prize-winning pig, butler, and foppish son. In "Extricating Young Gussie" (1917) were born the hapless, ingratiating Wooster and his impeccable gentleman's gentleman, Jeeves—a benign authority figure who would become not only a household word, but a dictionary entry.

In 1915 Kern introduced Wodehouse to librettist Guy Bolton, another transatlantic. Between 1916 and 1924, largely in the New York Princess Theater shows, these three transformed the stage musical on both sides of the ocean. Out went pseudo-operetta, the star system, and spectacle; in came ordinary people, integrated book and music, and "situation comedy."

Wodehouse's most famous lyric was "Bill," the gentle torch song that found its way into Kern's 1927 *Show Boat*, but it was his punning, allusive, rhythmically ingenious, wiseguy/innocent lyrics that changed the standard. A gardener would rhyme "greenfly and I'd" with "or cyanide." The queenly "Cleopatterer" got her way via her "wibbly, wobbly, wriggly dance." He loved place-names. Musicologist John McGlinn wrote: "In Wodehouse's world, Paradise . . . is a bungalow in Quogue, and you reach it by riding the Enchanted Train (aka the Long Island Rail Road)."

The Inimitable Jeeves (1923) eventually sold more than three million copies in the United States, leading to further Jeeves collections and novels. Lauded for perfect plotting, Wodehouse said: "My books are musical comedies without the music." A confirmed collaborator, he was yet bemused by his first joust with films in 1930, coining "yes men" and "nodders." He horrified investors and writers alike, revealing that in one Hollywood year he had earned $104,000 for doing virtually nothing. Critics warred over his work. In 1939 he received an honorary Oxford doctorate.

In 1934 the Wodehouses moved to Le Touquet, the English playground in France near Boulogne. In September 1939, after a confusion of broken-down motor vehicles, they failed to escape Le Touquet, and Plum wound up in a German prison camp, accompanied by the works of Tennyson. Bolton roused Americans to petition on his behalf. In 1941 he made five broadcasts to America from Berlin. In his *Jeeves* tales he had harpooned British Nazism; in these talks, using typical hypo/hyperbole, he showed his jailors as Wodehouseian buffoons. Typically, he seemed perhaps too apolitical; he was vilified in British propaganda broadcasts; for a time the British government appeared to believe him treasonous, although he was still being held in custody by the Germans.

The Wodehouses remained in Paris after the liberation in "preventive detention." Wodehouse wrote on. Cleared by the British and French governments, in 1947 he and his wife returned to the States, in 1952 again becoming Bolton's Long Island neighbors.

In 1953 came Wodehouse's epistolary autobiography, *Performing Flea* (a cheerful riposte to Sean O'Casey, who had called him "literature's performing flea"), and the next year his and Bolton's *Bring on the Girls*. In planning this joint theatrical autobiography, Wodehouse revealed his priority: "Even if we have to invent every line of the thing, we must have entertainment." In 1955 he became an American citizen. The *Jeeves* stories were successfully dramatized on British television in the 1960s and 1990s. Wodehouse was knighted in 1975, the year of *Jeeves*, a failed musical by Andrew Lloyd Webber and Alan Ayckbourn. The flow and quality of his work never diminished; at ninety-three he was awaiting the publication of a Blandings book. He had even taken another manuscript to the hospital with him. He died at a Southampton, Long Island, hospital.

As classic American musicals were reevaluated after 1985, Wodehouse's reputation grew. Gerald Bordman called him "the first truly great lyricist of the American musical stage, his easy, colloquially flowing rhymes deftly interwoven with a sunny wit." McGlinn concluded: "It may be Wodehouse's greatest gift as a lyricist that he is capable of retaining a true warmth and sincerity at the core of even his most frivolous lyrics . . . it seems that he really *believes* this stuff."

In all, Wodehouse produced a stream of comic novels and stories, articles and autobiographical works—nearly a hundred titles under his own name alone—lyrics or libretti for more than thirty shows, thousands of letters. When he was not writing, he was planning to write, or writing about writing, or reading Shakespeare and "bilge literature." He was a superlative craftsman.

Whether Wodehouse was an heir of Restoration comedy and Dickens or a repressed formulaic literary drone has provided much critical exercise. No one wrote better one-liners. The villainous Spode had "the kind of eye that can open an oyster at 60 paces"; an anti-heroine was "a soppy girl, riddled from head to foot with whimsy." In eras when public life is indistinguishable from farce, he seems timeless.

• Aside from Wodehouse's various autobiographies, including *Over Seventy* (1957), all of them more entertaining than strictly accurate, David A. Jasen's and Frances Donaldson's books are particularly useful. Jasen's include *P. G. Wodehouse: A Portrait of a Master* (1974) and *The Theatre of P. G. Wodehouse* (1979). Donaldson's *P. G. Wodehouse* (1982) was the authorized biography. She edited *Yours, Plum: The Letters of P. G. Wodehouse* (1990). Barry Phelps's *P. G. Wodehouse: Man and Myth* (1992) seeks to penetrate the unflappable personality and sheds light on Wodehouse the moneymaker. An earlier assessment of Wodehouse's craft was Richard Usborne's *Wodehouse at Work* (1961), updated to *Wodehouse at Work Till the End* (1977). Richard J. Voorhees wrote *P. G. Wodehouse* (1966) and contributed a fully detailed essay to the *Dictionary of Literary Biography*, vol. 34, *British Novelists 1890–1929, the Traditionalists.* Iain Sproat's *Wodehouse at War* (1981) is an invaluable insider's (Sproat was a member of Parliament) explanation of the British government's attitude toward the German broadcasts. Although no full-length collection or analysis of Wodehouse's lyrics exists, Benny Green's *P. G. Wodehouse: A Literary Biography* (1981) cites more lyrics than anyone else has done. Wodehouse is discussed in such histories as Gerald Bordman's *American Musical Theater: A Chronicle* (1992), theatrical biographies such as Bordman's *Jerome Kern* (1980), and autobiographies—Ira Gershwin's *Lyrics on Several Occasions* (1959)—as well as album notes accompanying recordings of musicals such as John McGlinn's for *Sitting Pretty* (1990). An obituary is in the *New York Times*, 15 Feb. 1975.

James Ross Moore

WODZIWOB (fl. 1870s), generally believed to be the original dreamer of the 1870 Ghost Dance, was actually only the most notable of the line of Northern Paiute prophets before Wovoka (1858?–1932). Wodziwob can probably be identified with Fish Lake Joe (1852?–1918?), whose birthdate was given as 1845 in the 1900 census, but as 1852 in the more carefully done census of 1910; nothing is known of his ancestry. The paucity of data and difficulties in integrating imprecise "oral history" with historical documentation lead to massive difficulties in interpreting the prophetic tradition of which Wodziwob was a part. In the 1930s Willard Z. Park's informants recalled four prophets who "announced the imminent return of the dead and held dances to facilitate the event," but of these Park named only Wovoka.

It seems that Wodziwob marked a decisive turn from prophecy connected to a program of warfare to one based exclusively on the destruction of whites by supernatural agency. It is not known if he claimed invulnerability and weather control powers, but Wovoka certainly did. Neither had been warriors; only after they had become prophets did either become a curing shaman, thus departing from the career pattern of the war shamans who seem to have been the first prophets. Park found that war shamans, having invulnerability and weather control power, were "considered great warriors" and never engaged in curing activities.

The Northern Paiute Ghost Dance tradition can be dated to the rise of self-proclaimed bullet-proof shamans during the Owens Valley War of 1860–1864, when the Owens Valley Paiutes of California attempted to halt the traffic through their land on the road from California to the new Nevada mines. They were aided by some of the linguistically distinct Northern Paiutes, especially, it seems, those called Mono Paiutes, from the vicinity of Mono Lake and northward toward Walker Lake, Nevada. The Mono Paiutes seasonally gathered in the vicinity of Walker Lake with the Northern Paiutes who lived there. It is erroneous, as some have done, to identify Wodziwob, whose age would have prevented him from being a captain ("chief"), with the Mono Paiute leader "Waugh-ad-zabo," known as having been active between 1862 and 1866.

The early newspaperman of Nevada Myron Angel wrote that the Northern Paiute "chief" Wahee, who had both bulletproof power and the ability to raise the dead, tried to entice the Walker River Paiutes to fight the whites near the beginning of the Owens Valley War. Wahee was killed by another Northern Paiute "captain" early in 1862. Circumstances suggest that Tavibo, Wovoka's father, was a successor to Wahee. There is no real evidence that Tavibo was involved with the Ghost Dance; only an inference from James Mooney's interview with Wovoka in 1891 suggests as much. Mooney learned that Tavibo "was not a preacher, but a [Paiute] 'captain,' a dreamer and invulnerable." And Wovoka was probably born in California, which would make the Owens Valley War the "big war" used to fix the date of his birth. This is the only satisfactory interpretation of the recent "oral history" account of the "internment" of Tavibo after a war, as reported by Michael Hittman.

Mooney was uncertain as to how his own information on Tavibo could fit in with other statements that he accepted. J. M. Lee, who had been special Indian agent in Nevada between 1869 and 1871, seems to have suggested that prophecy in the vein of the Ghost Dance had begun "in the earlier part of the sixties," and that only after a third attempt to gain real acceptance from the Walker River Paiutes—seemingly during Lee's Nevada residence—did the original prophet succeed. But, said Lee, the prophet soon died, and there were no more prophets until Wovoka appeared. The prophet who won over the Walker River Paiutes, according to Lee, was the "actual or spiritual" father of Wovoka. Adding to the confusion about the individuals involved, Mooney had the statement of Frank Campbell, the agency farmer and only resident government employee at the time, that the prophet "Waugh-zee-waugh-ber" began preaching at Walker River in 1872. Mooney therefore assumed that Wovoka's father was dead and that Waughzeewaughber was either the name of a disciple of the prophet reported by Lee or another name for Tavibo (thereby equivocally suggesting that Tavibo might be alive). This, however, wrote Mooney, "was not certain."

Here things stood until the field work of Cora Dubois in the 1930s. She concluded that the original Ghost Dance dream had come to Wodziwob "about 1869," the year that the transcontinental railroad was completed, for his dream had been that a train was coming to the Indians filled with manufactured goods. They must dance, he had said, to secure the arrival of the train. According to Dubois, this original dream was modified by Weneyuga (also called Frank Spencer), who was sent out to do missionary work by his headman Zonchen. It was Weneyuga, she reported, who had changed the message of the Ghost Dance to the destruction of the whites. Neither Weneyuga nor Zonchen can be identified in any documents.

A major difficulty with the Dubois Hittman interpretation is the claim that the Walker River Ghost Dance ceased during 1871. In fact, Wodziwob only emerged as the Ghost Dance prophet in late 1871, and his movement persisted at Walker River until at least 1875. The dance had spread well beyond the Great Basin by the spring of 1870, so there can be no doubt that an unknown prophet was at work in 1869, even if the first contemporary reference to him was in May 1871. Yet this prophet must have died in 1871.

When Wodziwob began preaching, there was an explosive growth in the movement. On 19 January 1872, Frank Campbell wrote the Indian agent of Nevada that the Indians had gathered in great numbers at Walker River because God was going to come to them. Some days later Johnson Sides, an extraordinarily well-informed Paiute who had just returned from Walker River, told the *Carson (Nev.) Register* that Wodziwob was "a mere boy; a small young man" who had been unremarkable until he began to make prophecies the previous fall.

A fuller understanding of the career of Wodziwob must await the identification of Zonchen and Weneyuga. There is now only suspicion that Zonchen was in fact Tavibo. And it is not clear if Zonchen and Weneyuga were cooperating or in competition with Wodziwob.

During 1873–1874 the Utah papers remarked on the activities of the "boy prophet" of Walker Lake. And Mooney's evidence suggests a continuation of those activities into at least 1875. By 1874 the Ghost Dance doctrine had reached the Lakota Sioux of the northern plains and the Kiowas of the southern plains. Although most of the California tribes that accepted the 1870 Ghost Dance rejected it in 1890, Wodziwob's teachings prepared the way for Wovoka's later teachings among the tribes of the plains. There is no evidence that after the 1870s Wodziwob ever returned to the Ghost Dance. Afterward, referred to as Fish Lake Joe, he was known as a powerful shaman who persisted in the "old ways" to the consternation of the Indian agents.

• There are no contemporaneously recorded words or songs of Wodziwob. The information on his doctrine is from Johnson Sides's account in the 31 Jan. 1872 issue of the *Salt Lake Daily Herald* (reprinted from an unlocated issue of the *Carson Register*), and Cora Dubois, "The 1870 Ghost Dance," *University of California Anthropological Records* 3, no. 1 (1939). The *Daily Herald* and other newspapers in the state have periodic references to prophetic activities in the Walker River country in 1873 and 1874. These reports can only be interpreted within the framework for Northern Paiute (Paviotso) shamanism supplied by Willard Z. Park, *Shamanism in Western North America* (1938). Myron Angel, *The History of Nevada* (1881), had wide personal knowledge of events in early Nevada but also seems to have made use of documents (apparently mostly newspapers) that have in part disappeared. James Mooney, "The Ghost Dance Religion," Bureau of American Ethnology, *14th Annual Report* (1896), is still an essential document for the life of Wodziwob, even if it introduced great confusion. Other key documents are the letter (#105) of C. A. Bateman in the 1872 *Annual Report of the Commissioner of Indian Affairs* and his unpublished letter of 19 Jan. 1872 in Letters Received, Nevada Agency, Bureau of Indian Affairs (now in the National Archives, Washington, D.C.). Michael Hittman, *Ethnohistory* 20, no. 3 (Summer 1973): 247–78, first identified Wodziwob as Fish Lake Joe. The Dubois-Hittman chronology of the 1870 Ghost Dance is, however, very erroneous. Nonetheless, Hittman's *Wovoka and the Ghost Dance* (1990) is a significant account of Taribo's internment. Research for this paper was made possible by grants from the Harry Frank Guggenheim Foundation.

MELBURN D. THURMAN

WOERISHOFFER, Emma Carola (Aug. 1885–11 Sept. 1911), social worker, was born in New York City, the daughter of Anna Uhl and German-born Charles Frederick Woerishoffer, a prominent Wall Street banker. Carola, as she was known, inherited a strong tradition of female social activism. Her maternal grandmother, Anna Ottendorfer, managed the liberal newspaper the *New Yorker Staats-Zeitung*, a job she took over in 1852 when her husband died. Carola's mother was also well known for her support of New York City charities, labor legislation, and a progressive income tax. Exposed to political activism and philanthropy as a child, Carola developed an early interest and commitment to social reform. After graduating from the stylish Brearley School in New York, Carola was admitted to Bryn Mawr College, where she prepared for a career in social work. According to an oft-repeated story, Carola had planned to attend Bryn Mawr ever since the age of nine, when she had seen a portrait of Bryn Mawr founder M. Carey Thomas and informed her mother, "When I grow up I am going to Miss Thomas' school."

At Bryn Mawr Woerishoffer developed a reputation for scholarship, athleticism, and high-spirited pranks. When a dispute arose about the strength of the college's fire safety nets, she settled the question herself by diving off the top of her dormitory into a net held by her friends. Woerishoffer's scholarship also made a strong impression on Bryn Mawr founder Thomas, who recalled that Woerishoffer's course of study—economics, philosophy, politics, psychology, and languages—was exactly what she would recommend as a preparatory course for social work.

After graduating in 1907, Woerishoffer assumed a prominent role in New York's circle of social workers and reformers. One of her first projects was participation in a 1908 Congestion Exhibit at the American Museum of National History, a project designed to inform New Yorkers about crowded and unhealthy conditions in poorer areas of the city. This early project brought her in contact with Florence Kelley, a founder of the National Consumers League, and Mary Simkhovitch, founder of Greenwich House, a settlement in downtown Manhattan where Woerishoffer became a resident and member of the Board of Managers. Woerishoffer, like many New York female activists, was deeply concerned about women's working conditions, and she became one of the founding members of the New York Women's Trade Union League (WTUL) in 1908. A year later Woerishoffer conducted her own personal study of working conditions in New York laundries by going undercover and taking positions in a dozen different businesses; she worked nearly every day for four months and then reported back to the National Consumer's League. Not only did Woerishoffer expose herself to the dangerous, brutally uncomfortable, fifteen-hour work days of New York laundresses, but Florence Kelley later recalled that the millionairess also resolved to live off only a laundress's salary for those four months. Woerishoffer conducted a similar investigation of suspicious employment offices by posing as an immigrant service worker and reporting to the Wainwright Commission, a New York state body appointed to study the need for workman's compensation and employer liability. In addition to her many social welfare activities, she served as a district leader of the New York Woman Suffrage Party.

As an executive member of the WTUL, Woerishoffer served as treasurer, worked in the union label shop, and did much of the unglamorous, routine work of the organization. She also actively supported the protests of local women workers. In 1909, when tens of thousands of New York City garment workers went on strike and hundreds were jailed, Woerishoffer appeared in court, put up $75,000 of real estate for bond, and announced her intention to stay in court until the strike was settled. In a style that became characteristic of her philanthropy, Woerishoffer rebuffed the New York newspaper reporters who were immediately captivated by the story of a millionaire heiress's coming to the aid of working class strikers. Instead, she remained behind the scenes and fed information on the strike to the papers, threatening to cut reporters off if they wrote about her rather than the strike. Soon after, Woerishoffer anonymously donated $10,000 to the WTUL for a permanent strike fund.

Like many progressive era reformers, Woerishoffer was especially interested in social research, planning, and legislation as the means to correct social ills. According to journalist Ida Tarbell, Woerishoffer was critical of attempts to use emotional "gush" to elicit sympathy for reform. She instead advocated using social science research and "cold figures" to win support for change. Although she ardently defended trade unions, Woerishoffer also became convinced that governmental regulation of wages and workplaces would be necessary to ensure fair and safe working conditions. To this end, she became involved in a number of public and private reform projects. For example, Woerishoffer became a board member of the Taylor Iron and Steel Company of High Bridge, New Jersey, because of the company's plans to build a model industrial village. In 1910 the New York State Association for Labor Legislation appointed Woerishoffer an investigator of working conditions for the Bureau of Industries and Immigration, a position that permitted her to pursue her commitment to legislative reform. Her duties as an investigator involved an arduous schedule of solitary travel through New York State's immigrant labor camps. According to Tarbell, everyone who knew Woerishoffer attested to the fact that she "overworked persistently," and it was on one such trip that she lost her life. In September 1911, on the way home from an inspection trip to Cannonsville, New York, Woerishoffer's car went over an embankment on a wet road. Woerishoffer died the next morning. A memorial service held for her at Greenwich house, which included tributes from Florence Kelley, Greenwich House residents, and her social work colleagues, attested to the esteem and respect she had earned among New York's reform society. Tarbell wrote of Woerishoffer: "twenty-six fuller years are rarely lived." At the time of her death, Woerishoffer left her largest legacy, a bequest of $750,000 to Bryn Mawr College. In accordance with Woerishoffer's lifelong commitment to social reform and welfare, the college placed the money into an endowment fund and used a portion of the income in 1915 to found the Carola Woerishoffer Graduate Department of Social Economy and Social Research, the first professional school of its kind and the first school in the United States to award a Ph.D. degree in social work.

• Woerishoffer's papers, which include a scrapbook of obituaries and pertinent articles and memorabilia from her college years, are housed in the Bryn Mawr college library. A memorial biography published by the class of 1907, *Carola Woerishoffer, Her Life and Work* (1912, repr. 1974), is also available at Bryn Mawr. Other useful sources include Mary K. Simkhovitch, *Neighborhood: My Story of Greenwich House* (1938), and Cornelia Meigs, *What Makes a College? A History of Bryn Mawr* (1956). An obituary by Ida M. Tarbell, "A Noble Life: the Story of Carola Woerishoffer," *American Magazine*, July 1912, pp. 281–87, provides a flattering portrait of Woerishoffer's life and also provides a sense of her colleagues' high regard. Numerous memorials paid tribute to Woerishoffer at her death, including an editorial in the *New York Times*, 15 Sept. 1911, and memorials in *Survey*, 30 Sept. 1911, and the *Bryn Mawr Alumnae Quarterly*, Nov. 1911.

MICHELLE BRATTAIN

WOLBACH, S. Burt (3 July 1880–19 Mar. 1954), pathologist and teacher, was born Simeon Burt Wolbach in Grand Island, Nebraska, the son of Samuel N. Wolbach, a banker and merchant, and Rosa Stein. He entered Harvard University, spent two undergraduate years in the Lawrence Scientific School, and graduated from the medical school with an M.D. in 1903. His postgraduate training in pathology was at the Boston City Hospital under Frank Burr Mallory and William T. Councilman. In 1905 he returned to Harvard Medical School as assistant in pathology under Councilman and served as pathologist to the Lying-In and Long Island Hospitals. In 1908 Wolbach succeeded Richard Mills Pearce as director of Bender Hygienic Laboratory in Albany, New York, and as adjunct professor and department head of pathology and bacteriology at Albany Medical College. From 1909 to 1910 he was at McGill and the Montreal General Hospital, but in 1910 he returned to Harvard, in Harold Ernst's Department of Bacteriology. Wolbach's first scientific paper had been written with Ernst ("Observations on the Morphology of Bacillus Tuberculosis from Human and Bovine Sources," *Journal of Medical Research* 10 [1903]: 313–33), and his early scientific interests were in both bacteriology and pathology. In 1914 Wolbach married Anna F. Wellington; they had three children. Their home was a country farm in Sudbury, Massachusetts, twenty miles west of Boston. Wolbach was devoted to the countryside, the woods, and his beloved horses, and his students remember his fresh boutonniere flower. In 1916 Wolbach became associate professor of pathology and bacteriology, and in 1922 he succeeded Councilman as Shattuck Professor of Pathological Anatomy and head of the pathology department at Harvard.

Wolbach's work in microbiology and the pathology of infectious disease laid many of the foundations of modern understanding of infections. He elucidated the etiology and pathogenesis of many infectious diseases at a time when the modern concepts of virus, rickettsia, bacterium, protozoan, and host-pathogen interaction were still forming. In 1920 he was appointed to the Typhus Research Commission to study that disease in Poland. Wolbach and John L. Todd, a McGill parasitologist, carried typhus-free lice with them for research on transmission. On the long voyage from Montreal to Warsaw, the lice were fed in special metal boxes strapped to the legs of Wolbach and Todd. The boxes had openings in the part next to the skin, so the lice could feed on the blood of the scientists—effective, but dangerous for the human participants. The work in Poland led to elucidation of the mechanism of transmission (by lice) and showed that *Rickettsia prowazeki* is the cause of typhus. Wolbach received the Order of Commander, Polonia Restituta, from the Polish government. Some years later, he summarized his work and current knowledge in "The Rickettsia and Their Relationship to Disease" (*Journal of the American Medical Association* 84 [1925]: 723–28) and thereafter turned his investigative attention to the study of vitamins, in insufficiency or excess. His work in this field, continued until the end of his life, included contributions to basic biology as well as to the understanding of human disease. Wolbach did much of this work as pathologist in chief at the Peter Bent Brigham and Children's Hospitals from 1922 to 1947, and he was consultant to several other hospitals in Boston. Wolbach and K. D. Blackfan published the first description of the pathology of cystic fibrosis of the pancreas, and of much of its pathogenesis, as "Vitamin A Deficiency in Infants: A Clinical and Pathological Study" (*Journal of Pediatrics* 3 [1933]: 679–706). Coppoletta and Wolbach's tables of normal organ weights remain, with few changes, the foundation of pediatric autopsy pathology (*American Journal of Pathology* 9 [1933]: 55–70).

Wolbach's commitment to the dissemination of new information is illustrated by his participation in the *Archives of Pathology and Laboratory Medicine*. He was on the founding editorial board, served for twenty-eight years until his death, and was coauthor (with P. R. Howe) of the inaugural paper "Intercellular Substance in Experimental Scorbutus [scurvy, a vitamin C deficiency state]" (*Archives of Pathology and Laboratory Medicine* 1 [1926]: 1–24). In 1940 the *Archives* honored him with a festschrift issue, and a magnificent portrait etching by Arthur Heintzelman was reproduced as frontispiece.

Wolbach encouraged his pupils and colleagues to develop special expertise in different fields, and so founded a generation of productive scientific pathologists who began the development of subspecialties in pathology. In 1947 he retired as Shattuck professor and from his hospital duties, becoming director of the Laboratories for Nutritional Research at Children's Hospital, where he worked until his death. He was succeeded as pathologist in chief at Children's Hospital by his protégé of twenty years, Sidney Farber. Wolbach's friends and pupils endowed a chair at Harvard, and in 1967 Farber became the first S. Burt Wolbach Professor of Pathology.

After his death at his home in Sudbury, his doctor wrote, "He accepted his illness as an opportunity to participate actively in the study and investigation of a neoplastic disease process. . . . No greater compliment can be paid to a teacher than to say that he made his life's last illness a philosophic and scientific lesson to his physicians and students" (J. Hartwell Harrison, memorial letter to Arthur T. Hertig, Wolbach Archive).

Wolbach's scientific contributions touched on so many fields that his work could be seen as unfocused. This is far from true: to Wolbach's eye, different problems and different methods of study all illumined basic principles. The principles unifying radiation biology, infectious disease, pediatric pathology, and vitamin research are those of all biology; Wolbach's insight preceded the discovery of the molecular mechanisms of those principles by two generations. The late twentieth-century growth in the knowledge of basic life processes, such as embryogenesis, neoplasia, and repair, affirmed Wolbach's insight summarized in his DeLamar Lecture at Johns Hopkins: " . . . all pathological processes subsequent to injury recapitulate normal events of growth" (*Science* 86 [1937]: 569–76).

An editorial on the occasion of Wolbach's death focused on " . . . what will remain of enduring value, his contributions to science. These were distinctive and important, both in actually adding to the body of scientific knowledge and in transforming pathology from an inert and descriptive science to one alive and replete with logic and reasoning" (*New England Journal of Medicine* 250 [1954]: 1010). Much of Wolbach's original scientific work has survived the scrutiny of passing decades, in fields as diverse as microbiology, pathology, and embryology. The pathologists and other scientists he trained, professors and department chairs in their time, passed his belief in scientific rigor and excellence to their own students. Wolbach's greatest memorial is the establishment of academic centers of training at the Peter Bent Brigham and the Children's Hospitals in Boston, which continue to produce leaders of American pathology.

• Wolbach's professional papers, memorials, and related correspondence are in the Wolbach Archive, Francis A. Countway Library of Medicine, Boston. A valuable source is Esmond Long, *A History of American Pathology* (1962). Walter Cannon's foreword to the Wolbach festschrift *Archives of Pathology and Laboratory Medicine* 30 (1940): 1–6, is a powerful personal view by a faculty colleague and friend. For an early paper that brought Wolbach favorable attention, see "The Pathological Histology of Chronic X-ray Dermatitis and Early X-ray Carcinoma," *Journal of Medical Research* 21 (1909): 415–50. On his contributions to pediatric pathology, see J. D. Hubbard, "S. Burt Wolbach, MD: 1880–1954," *Pediatric Pathology* 7 (1987): 507–14. The typhus work is described in S. Burt Wolbach et al., *The Etiology and Pathology of Typhus Being the Main Report of the Typhus Research Commission of the League of Red Cross Societies to Poland* (1922). The scientific foundation for early rickettsial research by Wolbach and others is reviewed in Victoria Harden, "Koch's Postulates and the Etiology of Rickettsial Diseases," *Journal of the History of Medicine and Allied Sciences* 42 (1987): 277–95. Wolbach's definitive paper on spotted fever is "Studies on Rocky Mountain Spotted Fever," *Journal of Medical Research* 41 (1919): 1–197. Harden discusses Wolbach's competitive spirit in *Rocky Mountain Spotted Fever: History of a Twentieth Century Disease* (1990). His work in microbiology is commemorated by Marshall Hertig in "The Rickettsia, *Wolbachia pipientis* (gen. et sp. n.) and Associated Inclusions of the Mosquito, *Culex pipiens*," *Parasitology* 28 (1936): 453–86. A perceptive note written at the time of Wolbach's retirement as Shattuck professor is E. C. Cutler, "Simeon Burt Wolbach—An Appreciation," *Harvard Medical School Alumni Bulletin* 21 (1947): 108–9. Memorial notices include S. Farber and C. L. Maddock, *Archives of Pathology and Laboratory Medicine* 59 (1955): 624–39; C. A. Janeway, *Transactions of the Association of American Physicians* 67 (1954): 30–35; Maddock and A. T. Hertig, *Harvard Medical School Alumni Bulletin* 28 (1954): 41–45; and S. Warren, *Journal of Pathology and Bacteriology* 68 (1954): 656–57, and *Laboratory Investigation* 3 (1954): 304. Wolbach's last public address (Alumni Day, Boston, 28 May 1952) is published as "The Glorious Past, the Doleful Present, and the Uncertain Future of Pathology," *Harvard Medical School Alumni Bulletin* 28 (1954): 45–48.

JEFFREY D. HUBBARD

WOLCOTT, Erastus (21 Sept. 1722–14 Sept. 1793), influential Connecticut political leader and judge, was born in Windsor, Connecticut, the son of Roger Wolcott and Sarah Drake. There is no information about Erastus Wolcott's early life and education.

The Wolcotts were a prominent family in one of the largest and richest towns in Connecticut. Roger Wolcott was second in command of the New England force that captured Louisbourg in 1745 and subsequently served as governor of Connecticut between 1751 and 1754. Erastus's brother-in-law, Matthew Griswold, was Connecticut governor from 1784 to 1786 and his younger brother, Oliver Wolcott (1726–1797), served as lieutenant governor of Connecticut from 1787 to 1795 and governor from 1796 to his death in 1797.

Erastus married Jerusha, daughter of John Wolcott, on 10 February 1746. They had seven children, five of whom survived him. He entered the General Assembly as representative for the town of Windsor in May 1758 and continued in that capacity, with one interruption, until March 1762. For the next six years he failed to be elected to the legislature because of a dispute within the town over dividing the section east of the Connecticut River, where the Wolcotts resided, from the older, western section. But during this interval the legislature continued to appoint him to committees charged with reviewing petitions to the Assembly, which acted as the colony's highest court of appeals. He finally returned as a representative of the newly created town of East Windsor in 1768 and his political career resumed its ascent. In 1772 he was listed among the top twenty candidates nominated for the Council of Assistants, the elite group of twelve men who advised the governor and served as the upper house of the legislature; in 1773 he was named to the colony's Committee of Correspondence, which in turn selected him as a delegate to the First Continental Congress (although he declined to serve); and in May 1776 he was elected Speaker of the Assembly, the lower house of the legislature.

As was commonplace at the time Wolcott had simultaneously risen through the ranks of the militia, making major in October 1762 and colonel in 1774. Immediately after Lexington and Concord he was commissioned with the Loyalist-leaning William S. Johnson to deliver a letter from Governor Jonathan Trumbull (1710–1785) to General Thomas Gage (1721–1787) inviting Gage to disavow any hostile intent toward the colonists. Subsequently he led a rotation of militia to Boston to reinforce George Washington's army in early 1776. In July he was given command of a regiment of state troops assigned the task of defending the New London area. In December 1776 he was made brigadier of the newly formed first militia brigade in which capacity he served largely as an able administrator, drafting, equipping, and marching men to reinforce both the state and continental forces. But from April to June 1777 he personally commanded a detachment from his brigade on the Hudson River.

Wolcott's principal interests remained political, and from May 1778 through March 1779 he served intermittently on the Council of Safety, the specially constituted committee that acted with Governor Trumbull to direct Connecticut's war effort. As the war dragged on, however, he turned critical of the way it was being conducted. In 1781 he resigned as brigadier of the first brigade and launched an assault on the inequity of the state's system of taxation, arguing that it unduly penalized stock raisers by overvaluing grazing land. In 1783 he supported the prominent Connecticut Loyalist Richard Smith before the legislature in Smith's bid to be readmitted to the state. These incidents suggest that Wolcott resented the social and political turmoil brought about by the war as much as the painful economic burdens it had forced upon Connecticut.

Wolcott's political star rose during the Confederation period because of his insistence that equity in taxation should take precedence over paying the debt. In 1784 the Assembly placed him on the Pay Table, a committee charged with "liquidating" the state's accounts, and he was elected an Assistant in the years 1786 through 1789. In addition, he was chosen to represent the state in the Continental Congress and the Philadelphia convention. But he consistently declined to serve outside Connecticut. By the late 1780s Wolcott had emerged as an influential champion of the state's interests against those of the continent. He believed that Connecticut was well in advance of most of the other states in contributing to the war effort and looked forward to a final settlement of accounts between the states to confirm Connecticut's creditor status. His family connections, legal knowledge, judicial stature, and reputation with the public all qualified him for the role of leading Antifederalist. But when elected to the state ratifying convention, he bowed to Federalist arguments that the Constitution and the continental impost it would facilitate favored the state's interest in an equitable funding of the war debt; he therefore joined the large majority that voted to accept the Constitution. His graceful accommodation to the new government was as important to its eventual establishment as the vigorous advocacy of its more vocal proponents.

In October 1789 Wolcott accepted appointment to Connecticut's superior court on which he continued to serve until he was forced to resign in 1792 because of ill health. Though he never attended college, Yale awarded him an honorary M.A. in 1790.

• Occasional correspondence of an official nature both to and from Wolcott can be found in the Jonathan Trumbull Papers and the Connecticut Archives Revolutionary War Series, both in the Connecticut State Library, Hartford. Wolcott's attacks on the equity of the state's tax system appeared in the *Connecticut Gazette*, 7 Sept. 1781–5 Oct. 1781 under the title "Strictures on the Present mode of Taxation in the State of Connecticut." Another newspaper series entitled "Revenue Laws" developing similar themes and advocating discrimination by the state against federal creditors appeared in the *Connecticut Courant*, 29 Jan. 1787–19 Feb. 1787 and was republished in several other state papers. His public career is best followed in J. H. Trumbull and C. J. Hoadly, eds., *Public Records of the Colony of Connecticut, 1636–1776* (vols. 11–15, 1850–1890); and C. J. Hoadly et al., eds., *Public Records of the State of Connecticut* (vols. 1–7, 1894–1948). David McClure, *A Sermon, delivered in East-Windsor, Connecticut at the interment of the Hon. Erastus Wolcott, Esq.* (1794), contains information about the family, as does Henry R. Stiles, *The History of Ancient Windsor* (2 vols., 1976).

RICHARD BUEL, JR.

WOLCOTT, Marion Post (7 June 1910–24 Nov. 1990), photographer, was born in Montclair, New Jersey, the daughter of Walter Post, a physician, and Marion Hoyt, a trained nurse. Marion and her sister, Helen, were to pursue parallel careers in photography, the latter never gaining the recognition eventually accorded her younger sibling. Marion's early education was sporadic; she attended Bloomfield High but then was sent to a private girls' school in Pennsylvania during her parents' separation and eventual divorce. Her mother, deemed an eccentric radical by her New Jersey neighbors, moved to the city to work for Margaret Sanger, a birth control advocate. By the time Marion was sixteen she was familiar with Greenwich Village life and had contacts in New York's theater and gallery world. She finished her education at Edgewood, a progressive school in Connecticut. There her talents were encouraged and she gravitated toward the school's philosophy of liberal coeducation. After graduation Marion taught at a progressive elementary school in New Jersey and attended classes at New York's New School for Social Research.

She used her mother's residence as a home base in Manhattan from which to pursue her increasingly diverse interests—modern dance, anthropology, and educational psychology. Her peripatetic education continued; she made it halfway to a bachelor's degree at New York University and taught at four different schools in quick succession before embarking on the trip that changed her life.

At age twenty-two, disillusioned by America's lingering social and economic crises, she joined her sister in Europe. She traveled first to Paris and Berlin—remaining to study dance for a few months—and arrived in 1933 in Vienna, where Helen was studying photography. Marion continued her pursuit of a child psychology degree and taught at a school for working-class children. As Hitler gained power she returned to the United States. At some point during her last days in Europe, with a tiny camera given to her as a gift, she took a set of pictures. Her sister's teacher, Trude Fleischmann, developed the images and offered Marion words of praise and encouragement.

She returned to New York City and began to teach again and do freelance photography. Relying upon friends in her Greenwich Village circle, she acquired jobs and experience. At age twenty-five she gave up teaching to pursue photography full time. New York in the mid-1930s contained a vibrant photography culture. Her exposure to the New York Photo League's conversations and criticisms led to her first significant assignment: still photographer on a film project in the Cumberland Mountains of Tennessee. In 1938, in part because of the quality of her work for this film, photographer Paul Strand gave her a letter of introduction to Roy Stryker, head of the New Deal's Farm Security Administration (FSA) Historical Section. The letter offered hearty praise: "she is a young photographer of considerable experience who has made a number of very good pictures on social themes in the South and elsewhere. . . . If you have any place for a conscientious and talented photographer, you will do well to give her an opportunity" (20 June 1938). Stryker offered her a trial position; she gave up the Philadelphia newspaper job that she had taken out of economic necessity and moved to Washington, D.C.

The historical section's tasks were twofold: to observe and document scenes of the country's deterioration and economic plight and to provide images that evidenced the success of the FSA's programs—housing projects, nutrition classes, and agricultural experiments. By its close in 1943 the agency had 130,000 images on file. She maintained an apartment in Washington, D.C. during her years of service but traveled extensively, most often in the South; she crisscrossed the Carolinas, West Virginia, Florida, Georgia, Louisiana, and Texas, making repeat visits to many areas. She spent a few months in New England and a few months in the West as well. Stryker recognized her capacity for social observation and gradually gave her more creative leeway. Her views of migrant worker housing, coal mining families, and plantation farming demonstrate her flair for capturing subtle shifts in class and race hierarchies. Her studies of New England architecture are clean and simple, yet reveal a bitterness in climate and attitude that lay beneath village surfaces.

Most difficult for Marion was her status as a female photographer. She was not the only woman employed in the field; Dorothea Lange, Margaret Bourke-White, and Louise Rosskam were also perfecting the use of a camera as a research tool. Marion was, however, one of the first female photographers to travel alone. She encountered suspicious glances, denials of lodging, and moments of defeat: "People often mistrust any young girl who drives alone around the country. . . . They become particularly suspicious if she goes out alone in the evening, since it is not customary in their town. They do not realize that I take photographs at night or that I wish to get a cross section of life in their town" (Hurley, p. 81). People she met often found it inconceivable that her seemingly glamorous job included exhausting labor.

By 1940 she was tired of the constant travel and disappointed in some of the FSA programs she was asked to photograph. In 1941, after a whirlwind courtship, she married Leon Oliver Wolcott, the Agriculture Department deputy director of war relations under Franklin Roosevelt and a widower with two young children. She continued briefly to work for the FSA but resigned in February 1942.

The Wolcotts settled outside of Washington, D.C.; in ten years time they owned three different farms. Marion Wolcott never returned to professional photography. In her words, she was busy trying to survive in wartime America with two children of her own plus the two she "inherited." After their last attempt at farming ended, the Wolcotts embarked on a thirty-year period of constant moves, both in the United States and abroad. Wolcott followed her husband through a series of State Department posts; she sometimes taught or gardened and occasionally photographed her temporary home communities—Iran, Pakistan, and Egypt. The Wolcotts retired to California after a last posting in India.

Historical interest in the work of FSA photographers and in the social conditions of 1930s America increased in the 1970s and Wolcott's images received new attention from scholars. Wolcott resumed her interest in photography for a short period of time, granting interviews with students and gallery owners. The first solo show of her work occurred in 1978 in California. By the 1980s her images were included in the collections of the Smithsonian and the Metropolitan Museum of New York, among others. In 1983 Wolcott witnessed publication of the first monograph of her photographs. Still, women photographers had work to do, as Wolcott reminded a 1986 audience: "Women have come a long way, but not far enough. . . . Speak with your images from your heart and soul" (Women in Photography Conference, Syracuse, N.Y.). Wolcott died at her home in Santa Barbara, California. In a relatively short professional career Wolcott produced a vast body of compelling photographs; as a participant in the largest photographic history project of the nation, she helped create the visual language that still symbolizes depression-era America.

• Marion Post Wolcott's FSA images are housed at the Library of Congress in the Division of Prints and Photographs. The entire FSA collection contains 80,000 images and is available on microfiche. Wolcott gave an interview four years before her death that is in the February 1986 edition of *Photo Metro*. There are two biographical sources of interest for

Wolcott: Paul Hendrickson, *Looking for the Light—The Hidden Life and Art of Marion Post Wolcott* (1992), relays the narrative of Wolcott's career through a collage of interviews, unpublished writings, and photographs; F. Jack Hurley, *Marion Post Wolcott—A Photographic Journey* (1989), offers a more straightforward chronicle of Wolcott's career, family life, and philanthropic ventures. For a general history of photography and the role women have played in the field, consult Naomi Rosenblum, *A History of Women Photographers* (1994). Alan Trachtenberg, *Reading American Photographs* (1989), provides a sophisticated analysis of the complex role of photographer and photograph in postdepression America and includes insightful treatment of the FSA and its staff. Wolcott's photographs have served as the basis of a myriad of exhibits; two exhibit texts of note are *Marion Post Wolcott*, Robert B. Menschel Photography Gallery, Syracuse, N.Y. (1986) and *U.S.A., 1935–1943*, Gallery Taube, Berlin (1976).

DEBORAH L. OWEN

WOLCOTT, Oliver (20 Nov. 1726–1 Dec. 1797), Connecticut governor and revolutionary patriot, was born in Windsor (now East Windsor), Connecticut, the son of Roger Wolcott, a judge, member of the Connecticut Council, deputy governor, and governor (1750–1754), and Sarah Drake. He graduated from Yale in 1747, was granted a captain's commission by New York governor George Clinton in January 1747, and served on the northern frontier against the French until the Treaty of Aix-la-Chapelle. He studied medicine with his brother, Dr. Alexander Wolcott, and moved to newly settled Goshen in northwestern Connecticut to practice. In 1755 he married Laura Collins. They had four children who reached adulthood, one of whom, Oliver Wolcott, Jr., served as secretary of the treasury and Connecticut governor (1817–1827).

Upon the organization of Litchfield County in October 1751, Wolcott moved to Litchfield and became a merchant. His father appointed him county sheriff, a position he held for twenty years. His family, the appointment to an important position at the age of twenty-five, and undoubted competence combined to make Wolcott's political ascent possible. He was elected deputy to the Connecticut General Assembly in 1764, 1767, 1768, and 1770 and was elected to the upper house or Governor's Council in 1771. Although not actively associated with either the Old Lights or New Lights, the two factions that vied for political control of the colony, his election to the upper house was only secured with the support of the predominant New Lights. He was chosen major of the Thirteenth Militia Regiment in 1771 and colonel of the Seventeenth Regiment in 1774; judge of probate for the Litchfield District in 1772; and judge of the Litchfield County Court in 1774. He served as county court judge until 1786 and probate judge until 1796.

Wolcott enthusiastically supported the American cause in the struggle for independence. He served as moderator of a 17 August 1774 Litchfield town meeting, which denounced the Intolerable Acts and promised "all reasonable Aid & Support" to their brethren in Massachusetts. He also served on Litchfield's Committee of Inspection and on the Litchfield County Committee of Safety. The outbreak of fighting brought an end to his mercantile career, and he noted shortly after the battles of Lexington and Concord, "With Regard to my own Business I have neither Time nor Opportunity" (Wolcott Papers, vol. 1, p. 270). In April 1775 Wolcott was one of nine persons designated as commissioners to supply Connecticut troops, and in July he was appointed one of five "Commissioners of Indian Affairs for the Northern Depart[men]t" (Burnett, vol. 1, p. 163) by the Continental Congress.

Wolcott had two careers during the war years, one of Connecticut's principal delegates to the Continental Congress and a militia officer. First elected in October 1775, he served in Congress 16 January–28 June 1776; 1 October 1776–2 May 1777; 16 February–9 July 1778; 29 November 1780–13 April 1781; 16 November 1781–29 April 1782; and 20 December 1782–11 April 1783. Despite extended periods of conscientious service, Wolcott was not a major figure in that body and rarely served on committees. According to Thomas Rodney, Wolcott was "a man of Integrity, is very candid in debate, and open to Conviction and does not want abilities; but does not appear to be possessed of much political knowledge" (Burnett, vol. 6, p. 19). He was, however, appointed a member of the Committee on Army Accounts in March 1783 and one of the commissioners who negotiated a peace treaty with the Iroquois at Fort Stanwix, by which the Six Nations ceded their claim to land west of the Ohio River.

An early supporter of American independence in Congress, Wolcott stated in February 1776, "Our difference with Great Britain has become very great. . . . What matters will issue in, I cannot say, but perhaps in a total disseverance from Great Britain" (Burnett, vol. 1, p. 356). Although he was absent from Congress in July 1776, he signed the parchment copy of the Declaration of Independence that autumn and the Articles of Confederation on 9 July 1778. He opposed half pay for officers in the Continental army but was on the other hand, perhaps reflecting his mercantile background, a strong supporter of stable currency, of Robert Morris as superintendent of finance, and of the continental impost. Throughout the war, Wolcott continued to be reelected to Connecticut's upper house and served on the Council of Safety (1780–1783), the body that directed the war effort when the legislature was not in session.

Wolcott saw extensive militia service during the American Revolution. When the equestrian statute of George III was torn down in New York City in late June 1776, Wolcott took the pieces to Litchfield and was responsible for converting them into 42,022 bullets. On 11 August 1776 Connecticut officials ordered him to march the Seventeenth Regiment of militia to New York and put it under Washington's command. The next day the Connecticut Council of Safety appointed him a brigadier general and put him in command of all the state's militia regiments sent to New York. During the summer of 1777 Wolcott forwarded reinforcements to the northern army. In September he "Marched with between three and four hundred of the Militia of his Brigade" northward and continued "in said Service Until the Surrender of Genl Burgoyne" at Saratoga (Wolcott Papers, vol. 1, p. 203). He was promoted to major general in command of all Connecticut militia in May 1779. During that summer he worked with limited success to defend the state's coastal communities from attack by "a Foe who have not only insulted every Principle which governs civilized Nations But by their Barbarities offered the grossest Indignities to human Nature" (Wolcott Papers, vol. 1, p. 240).

After the end of hostilities, Wolcott aspired to higher office. He was elected lieutenant governor in 1786 and succeeded to the governor's chair in January 1796 after the death of the incumbent Samuel Huntington. Like most of those who had extensive congressional service, Wolcott supported the federal Constitution, saying in October 1787 that the convention "attended to the great objects of rendering government efficient, yet capable of having its errors corrected without public disturbance" (Jensen, p. 358). He was chosen one of Litchfield's delegates to the Connecticut ratifying convention, where he spoke in support of and voted in favor of ratification. He served as a presidential elector in 1789, 1792, and 1796. Although he never considered himself a partisan politician, Wolcott strongly supported the new national government and grew increasingly hostile to the Republican opposition. He branded Citizen Edmond Charles Genet, the French minister, as "too abhorred a villain to have his name mentioned by any man of the least honor" and deplored the "determination" of the Jeffersonians "to gratify France with an administration which will accord with its wishes" (Gibbs, vol. 1, pp. 132, 397). In addresses to the general assembly in 1796 and 1797, Governor Wolcott gave cautious support to domestic manufactures and, in response to the "unprovoked Aggressions made under the authority of the French Nation," urged that the state militia be better equipped and trained (Hoadly et al., vol. 9, p. 456). Wolcott served as governor for less than two years before dying in Litchfield.

Wolcott was elected an honorary member of the Pennsylvania Society for Promoting Agriculture in 1785, was elected the first president of the Connecticut Society for Arts and Sciences in 1786, and was cofounder of the Hartford Woolen Manufactory. The town of Wolcott was named after him in 1796. Remembered as "a real and not a theoretic republican," Wolcott was not an important national figure, but he stood as one of the half-dozen most significant leaders of the independence movement in Connecticut and a central personality in state politics in subsequent decades.

• The major collection of Oliver Wolcott Papers is located at the Connecticut Historical Society in Hartford. They have been microfilmed, and the citations in the text refer to the film edition. Wolcott letters are also in George Gibbs, *Memoirs of the Administrations of Washington and John Adams, Edited from the Papers of Oliver Wolcott, Secretary of the Treasury* (2 vols., 1846); Edmund C. Burnett, ed., *Letters of Members of the Continental Congress*, vols. 1–3, 5–7 (8 vols., 1921–1936); and Paul H. Smith et al., eds., *Letters of Delegates to Congress, 1774–1789* (1976–). Additional published Wolcott material is scattered in such sources as Merrill Jensen, ed., *The Documentary History of the Ratification of the Constitution*, vol. 3 (1978); "The Huntington Papers," *Connecticut Historical Society Collections* 20 (1923); and "The Wyllys Papers," *Connecticut Historical Society Collections* 21 (1924). Further information is in several series of the Connecticut Archives, Connecticut State Library, most notably, Revolutionary War, 1st ser. J. Hammond Trumbull and Charles J. Hoadly, eds., *The Public Records of the Colony of Connecticut*, vols. 11–15 (15 vols., 1850–1890), and Hoadly et al., eds., *The Public Records of the State of Connecticut*, vols. 1–9 (15 vols., 1894–1991), are also useful. Secondary material on Wolcott is relatively sparse, but useful detail is in James E. Bland, "The Oliver Wolcotts of Connecticut: The National Experience, 1775–1800" (Ph.D. diss., Harvard Univ., 1970); Franklin Bowditch Dexter, *Biographical Sketches of the Graduates of Yale College*, vol. 2 (1896); Ellsworth S. Grant, "From Governor to Governor in Three Generations," *Connecticut Historical Society Bulletin* 39 (July 1974): 65–77; Robert C. Griffen and Mitchell R. Algre, *Wolcott Genealogy* (1986); John Sanderson, *Biography of the Signers of the Declaration of Independence*, vol. 3 (1823); and Samuel Wolcott, *Memorial of Henry Wolcott . . . and of Some of His Descendants* (1881). General works of importance include Richard Buel, Jr., *Dear Liberty: Connecticut's Mobilization for the Revolutionary War* (1980); Christopher Collier, *Connecticut in the Continental Congress* (1973); Larry R. Gerlach, *Connecticut Congressman: Samuel Huntington 1731–1796* (1976); and H. James Henderson, *Party Politics in the Continental Congress* (1974).

BRUCE P. STARK

WOLCOTT, Oliver (11 Jan. 1760–1 June 1833), secretary of the treasury and governor of Connecticut, was born in Litchfield, Connecticut, the son of Oliver Wolcott, a sheriff of Litchfield and a farmer, and Laura Collins. His father would be a signer of the Declaration of Independence and a governor of Connecticut. After studies at a local grammar school, young Oliver entered Yale College in 1773 and graduated in 1778. His only service during the Revolution was as a volunteer during two brief campaigns in 1777 and 1779. After studying law under the direction of Judge Tapping Reeve, he was admitted to the bar in January 1781 and soon thereafter moved to Hartford, where he obtained a clerkship with the Committee of the Pay-Table, the organization that administered the provincial government's finances. His ability and efficiency quickly attracted attention, and in January 1782 he was appointed a member of the committee. Two years later he and Oliver Ellsworth represented Connecticut in negotiations to settle claims of the state against the national government. In 1788 the Office of Comptroller of Public Accounts was established to replace the Committee of the Pay-Table and to reorganize the state's financial affairs, and Wolcott was its head. On 1 June 1785 he solidified his connection with the Connecticut elite by marrying Elizabeth Stoughton, with whom he had seven children; three died in infancy.

Despite initial reservations, Wolcott accepted the post of auditor of the federal Treasury in September 1789. During his service as auditor, he played a key role in the implementation of Alexander Hamilton's financial program. He quickly developed a close personal and professional relationship with Hamilton, who relied on Wolcott to handle much of the day-to-day business of organizing and administering the largest department in the federal government. In June 1791 Hamilton recommended Wolcott's appointment to comptroller of the treasury, and President George Washington made the appointment. Because of his efficiency in developing the plan for the organization of the Bank of the United States, Wolcott was offered the opportunity to serve as its first president, which he declined.

Upon Hamilton's resignation in January 1795, Washington selected Wolcott as Hamilton's successor. Wolcott shared his predecessor's commitment to a strong national government and the use of government power to promote industrial and commercial development. As secretary of the treasury, his main ambition was to perpetuate the programs and policies put in place by Hamilton, whom he continued to rely on for advice and counsel. However, among the factors prompting Hamilton's resignation was the Republican party's majority in the House of Representatives following the 1794 elections. Led by Albert Gallatin, the Republicans thereafter endeavored to assert greater congressional authority over government finances by curtailing the Treasury's discretionary authority over their management, mostly by making specific rather than general appropriations. This conflict persisted until the 1798 elections returned the Federalists to the majority.

Impressed by Wolcott's ability, John Adams kept him at the Treasury Department when he became president. It soon became clear, however, that Wolcott's primary loyalty was to Hamilton and the High Federalist faction rather than to Adams. Although he was able to avoid an open breach with the president, Wolcott nonetheless participated in efforts to promote Hamilton's policies and authority at the expense of Adams's. When it became clear that the High Federalists were maneuvering to replace Adams as their presidential candidate in 1800, Adams removed Secretary of War James McHenry and Secretary of State Timothy Pickering from the cabinet. Yet Wolcott, who had been equally active if not as openly so in the movement to dump Adams, was retained at the Treasury. He subsequently provided Hamilton confidential information about the administration that was published, against Wolcott's advice, in *Letter from Alexander Hamilton, concerning the Public Conduct and Character of John Adams, Esq., President of the United States* in October 1800. Federalists everywhere were appalled by the *Letter*'s harsh attacks on Adams and Hamilton's apparent willingness to expose divisions within the party to advance his own interests. By November Wolcott realized the effort to replace Adams with Charles Coatsworth Pinckney was doomed and tendered his resignation from the cabinet. Although an investigation by a House committee produced a favorable report on Wolcott's tenure at the Treasury, he left office under a cloud of suspicion over a fire at the Treasury on 20 January 1801. An investigation ultimately cleared him of any wrongdoing.

When the Judiciary Act of 1801 was passed, creating sixteen circuit courts, Adams appointed Wolcott to be judge of the second circuit. In March 1802, however, Congress repealed the act, and Wolcott left the employ of the federal government for good. Later that year a highly critical House committee report compelled him to publicly defend his administration of the Treasury, which he did in *An Address to the People of the United States* (1802).

Upon returning to private life, Wolcott settled in New York City and, although he did not provide any of the capital to set it up, became a managing partner of a commercial firm, Oliver Wolcott and Company, which he hoped would do extensive business with China. The company dissolved in April 1805, and Wolcott subsequently became a partner in the Litchfield China Trading Company, speculated extensively in land, served as president of the Merchants Bank, and pursued various other business ventures. In 1804 he served as a pallbearer at Hamilton's funeral and spent several weeks afterward managing his friend's estate. Although his attention was focused on his family and business affairs during the decade after he left federal office, Wolcott kept a close eye on national politics. In his correspondence with fellow Federalists, he was sharply critical of Thomas Jefferson and his policies, which Wolcott viewed as obstacles to economic development.

Wolcott joined the main board of directors for the New York branch of the Bank of the United States in 1810. After that bank's charter expired in 1811, he was a leading actor in the establishment in 1812 of the Bank of America, which he served as president until ousted from office by political opponents two years later. Wolcott settled in Connecticut in 1815 with the intention of dedicating himself to farming.

By the time Wolcott returned to Connecticut, he had begun to distance himself from his fierce Federalist partisanship, most prominently through his outspoken support for the James Madison administration during the War of 1812. In 1816 Wolcott returned to politics, running an unsuccessful campaign against the incumbent Federalist governor as the candidate of the American Toleration and Reform party, a coalition of Connecticut's anti-Federalist elements unified by their desire to end tax support for the Congregational church. One year later he was again the candidate of the Toleration and Reform Party and won election to the first of ten terms as governor of Connecticut. By 1819, he had dropped the Toleration and Reform label and become a member of the Republican party.

In 1818 he presided over the convention that drew up a new state constitution, which was adopted on 15 September 1818 and ratified by the voters one month later. He played a key role in the writing of the constitution, which provided for religious toleration, separation of church and state, expansion of suffrage, and explicit division of the government into three equal and independent branches. Wolcott was also successful in promoting reforms in the state's tax system. He was unable, however, to win support for his call for government assistance to foster economic development through state-funded internal improvements, subsidies to agriculture and industry, support for education, and stricter regulation of banking. Wolcott left the governorship when Republicans, disenchanted by his efforts to pursue an independent course, denied him renomination as their candidate for governor in 1826. After an independent bid for the governorship failed in 1827, he returned to New York City, where he died in 1833.

Wolcott was a committed nationalist and advocate of commercial development, and his ability and efficiency played a key role in the Washington administration's success in placing the new government on a sound financial footing. However, his participation in the effort to undermine Adams casts a shadow on the reputation of one of the most significant figures of the Early National Period.

• The Connecticut Historical Society possesses an extensive collection of Wolcott's papers and other primary source material related to his life and career. James Bland, "The Oliver Wolcotts of Connecticut: The National Experience, 1775–1800" (Ph.D. diss., Harvard Univ., 1970); Neil Alexander Hamilton, "Connecticut Order, Mercantilistic Economics: The Life of Oliver Wolcott, Jr." (Ph.D. diss., Univ. of Tennessee, 1988); and Frederick H. Schmauch, "Oliver Wolcott: His Political Thought and Role between 1789 and 1800" (Ph.D. diss., St. John's Univ., 1969), are informative. See also Alan W. Brownsword, "The Constitution of 1818 and Political Afterthoughts, 1800–1840," *Connecticut Historical Society Bulletin* 30 (1965): 1–10; Robert Jay Dilger, "Oliver Wolcott Jr.: Conspirator or Public Servant?" *Connecticut Historical Society Bulletin* 46 (1981): 78–85; George Gibbs, *Memoirs of the Administrations of Washington and John Adams. Edited from the Papers of Oliver Wolcott, Secretary of the Treasury* (2 vols., 1846); and Linda K. Kerber, "Oliver Wolcott: Midnight Judge," *Connecticut Historical Society Bulletin* 32 (1967): 25–30.

ETHAN S. RAFUSE

WOLCOTT, Roger (4 Jan. 1679–17 May 1767), colonial governor and literary figure, was born in Windsor, Connecticut, the son of Simon Wolcott and Martha Pitkin, merchants and farmers. The youngest of nine children, Wolcott was educated at home by his mother, then apprenticed to a clothing shop in 1694. He established his own clothier enterprise at age twenty. In 1702 he married Sarah Drake. They had fifteen children before her death on 21 January 1748. Wolcott purchased a large estate in Windsor in 1702 where, following the eighteenth-century pattern of Hartford-area merchant-farmers, he established both a clothing manufactory and a farm.

In 1707 Wolcott was elected Windsor town selectman. Through his admittance to the bar in 1709 and subsequent election to the Connecticut General Assembly as a deputy, Wolcott launched a 45-year political career characterized by plural officeholding and incremental advancement. Among his numerous offices were assistant to the general assembly (1714–1741); justice of the peace (1710–1721); judge of the Hartford County Court (1721–1732); judge of the Connecticut Superior Court (1732–1741); chief justice of the Connecticut Superior Court (1741–1750); deputy governor of Connecticut (1741–1750); and governor of Connecticut (1750–1754). Although his *Memoir* (1759) advocated service to the common good through the practice of what would today be called consensus politics over self-interested factionalism, Wolcott's career was marked by intense partisan politics of an ideological nature. In the 1720s he opposed proprietors of Windsor's common lands; in the 1730s proponents of the Saybrook Platform; and in the 1740s paper currency advocates. Opponents objected to his election as deputy governor in 1748, touching off a bitter power struggle between the assembly and governor. Wolcott's unsuccessful bid for reelection as governor in 1754 resulted from a controversy involving the disappearance of 400,000 Spanish-milled dollars from a disabled Spanish ship in New London. Although exonerated by imperial authorities in 1755, he retired from political life and devoted his remaining years to religious study. He died at his farm in Windsor, Connecticut.

Wolcott also distinguished himself through numerous military and literary accomplishments. In military affairs he rose during this period of imperial wars from Connecticut commissary in Admiral Sir Hovenden Walker's 1711 Quebec raid, to Windsor militia captain (1722), Hartford County regimental sergeant major (1724), and colonel in the First Regiment (1739). In 1745 Wolcott's military career reached its peak when he was appointed major general and second in command of New England forces during King George's War. He chronicled the famous siege of the French bastion at Louisbourg in his *Journal* (1745) and in an oft-quoted observation claimed that the victory resulted from the superiority of "free born" New England militia over French "mercenary" soldiers.

Wolcott's reputation as a writer rests primarily on his *Poetical Meditations* (1725), the sole verse publication before 1750 by a Connecticut author. The poems consist of biblical reflections. He also wrote a lengthy heroic narrative of early Connecticut, "A Brief Account of the Agency of the Honourable John Winthrop." Perry Miller dismissed the former works as "sad rubbish," yet more recent scholars have characterized them as an attempt to revive the unique imagery of classical Puritan poetry. The "Account" has earned Wolcott his greatest poetical acclaim. It is a distinctly American epic presaging the efforts of Joel Barlow, David Humphreys, and Timothy Dwight (1752–1817). Although much of Wolcott's prose was the product of ideological political battles, his *Autobiography* (1755), *Memoir* (1759), and "Narrative of the Second Church of Windsor" (ms., 1737?) show him as a late imperial public figure longing for an idyllic past when concern for the common good and Christian virtue triumphed over self-interest and materialism.

• The bulk of Wolcott's manuscripts and published works are presented in Albert Bates, ed., "The Wolcott Papers, 1750–1754," *Connecticut Historical Society Collections* 25 (1915), 26 (1916); "Journal of Roger Wolcott at the Siege of Louisbourg," *Connecticut Historical Society Collections* 1 (1860): 131–61; R. Wolcott, *Poetical Meditations* (1725); "Autobiography of Roger Wolcott," in Samuel Wolcott, *Memorial of Henry Wolcott* (1881); and "Memoir for a History of Connecticut," *Connecticut Historical Society Collections* 3 (1895): 321–36. No full-scale biography of Wolcott exists, but an overview of his public and literary achievements is offered in Albert Bates, "Sketch of Roger Wolcott," *Connecticut Historical Society Collections* 16 (1916): xxv–xxxv. Richard Bushman, *From Puritan to Yankee: Character and the Social Order in Connecticut, 1690–1765* (1970), and Robert Taylor, *Colonial Connecticut: A History* (1979), provide excellent, although contrasting, analyses of Connecticut during Wolcott's life. For conflicting views of Wolcott's literary prowess, see Jo Ella Ann Osborn Doggett, "Roger Wolcott's *Poetical Meditations*" (Ph.D. diss., Univ. of Texas, 1974); Perry Miller and Thomas Johnson, eds., *The Puritans*, vol. 2 (1938), pp. 551–52, 657–62; and William Otis, *American Verse, 1625–1807* (1909), pp. 14–17.

RONALD LETTIERI

WOLF, Emma (15 June 1865–29 Aug. 1932), writer, was born in San Francisco, California, the daughter of Simon Wolf, a Jewish pioneer in Contra Costa County, and Annette Levy. Both of Wolf's parents had immigrated to the United States from France. Her father died suddenly when she was only thirteen, leaving her mother to support her and her ten brothers and sisters. Wolf grew up in San Francisco and completed high school there. Her family was part of a close-knit Jewish community of upwardly mobile families, and Wolf remained close to her family throughout her life. She suffered from polio as a child and had a withered arm as a result. As a young woman she was active in a local Jewish literary club but later had to withdraw owing to increasingly fragile health, which forced her to spend her time indoors observing the world rather than actively participating in it. Although her siblings married into prominent San Francisco Jewish families, Wolf never married.

Wolf began writing at an early age, and her first story was published when she was only thirteen years of age; much to Wolf's dismay, the story was submitted secretly by a relative and was published without her consent. As she began to publish stories and novels, she developed a national reputation but was particularly celebrated in San Francisco as a local writer of great talent. In her memoir *My Portion* (1925), Wolf's childhood friend Rebekah Kohut remarks on Wolf's exceptional intelligence and memory. Kohut also describes the dilemma they shared as Jewish women coming of age in the late nineteenth century: whether to stand up for Jewish ideals or choose the easier path of "being like all the rest" (p. 62).

Wolf wrote five novels. All are set in California, and most take place in the wealthy San Francisco neighborhood of Pacific Heights. The novels center around the fate of young women resulting from their choices in love and marriage. *Fulfillment* (1916), Wolf's last novel, explores the options left to a young woman who, along with her sister, is left penniless after her parents' death. Whereas the sister chooses to engage in menial work to support herself, the heroine, Gwen Heath, rushes into marriage with an aristocrat whom she does not love. Wolf's heroines are usually extremely erudite, as is evidenced by Gwen's familiarity with classical literature and philosophy. In her critique of the limited choices available to women of that time, Wolf echoes other early feminist writers such as Charlotte Perkins Gilman and Mary Wilkins Freeman. What differentiates Wolf is both her belief in the power of love to conquer differences and overcome obstacles and her abiding attachment to the family and the Jewish community as a locus of support and morality.

Two of Wolf's novels, *Other Things Being Equal* (1892) and *Heirs of Yesterday* (1900), chronicle the dilemmas of Jews at the turn of the century who must decide what price they are willing to pay for assimilation and to what degree they wish to retain their Jewish history, culture, and values. In *Heirs*, a young Jewish doctor returning to San Francisco after having completed his studies in Europe tries to repudiate his Jewish heritage in favor of assimilation and social success among the local gentility. As he realizes the extent of anti-Semitism in the community, he remarks, "Apparently, practically, we present the magnificent spectacle of a country without racial prejudices. Individually, morally, . . . we are very wide of the mark" (p. 35). Wolf keenly perceived the implications of assimilation and wrote in *Heirs* of a future in "which [American Jews] having escaped from out their fastness, shall some day change [the prayer 'Hear, O Israel'] to 'Hear, O Humanity'" (p. 231).

During the last fifteen years of her life, Wolf was restricted to a wheelchair and was cared for by her mother and sister. She died in San Francisco, where she had spent her entire life.

Wolf's novels chronicle the rapidly changing world of the late nineteenth century, when immigrants poured into the United States and both Jews and women found themselves questioning the roles to which they had been relegated. Wolf's work merges the concerns of Jews and women, exploring the various options for both without imposing a definitive solution or settling for an easy answer.

• Wolf's other novels are *A Prodigal in Love* (1894) and *Joy of Life* (1896). Biographical information on Wolf can be found in Barbara Cantalupo, "Emma Wolf (1865–1932)," in *Jewish American Women Writers: A Bio-Bibliographical Sourcebook*, ed. Ann R. Shapiro (1994). An interview with Wolf by Helen Piper was published in the *San Francisco Chronicle*, 3 Dec. 1930. Wolf is mentioned in the context of other early American Jewish women writers in Diane Lichtenstein, "Fannie Hurst and Her Nineteenth Century Predecessors," *Studies in American Jewish Literature* 7, no. 1 (Spring 1988): 26–39, and is also considered in a critical context in Louis Harap, *The Image of the Jew in American Literature* (1974). An obituary is in the *San Francisco Chronicle*, 30 Aug. 1932.

SOPHIA B. LEHMANN

WOLF, George (12 Aug. 1777–11 Mar. 1840), congressman and governor of Pennsylvania, was born in Northampton County, Pennsylvania, the son of George Wolf, a German immigrant farmer, and Maria Margaretta (maiden name unknown). After attending Allen Township Classical Academy, where he studied the sciences, Latin, and Greek, he worked on his father's farm and then took a position as principal of his alma mater. He next obtained a clerkship in the prothonotary's office in Easton, Pennsylvania, and during that time he studied law under John Ross, a prominent local attorney. In June 1798 he married Mary Erb; they had nine children. The following year Wolf was admitted to the bar and soon enjoyed a successful practice.

In 1801 Governor Thomas McKean appointed Wolf as postmaster of Easton and later as Clerk of Northampton County's Orphan's Court, where he served until 1809. A Jeffersonian, Wolf had supported McKean's candidacy. In 1814 Wolf won election to Pennsylvania's lower house when Thomas J. Rogers resigned. When Wolf ran for the state senate in 1815, however, he was defeated. His timing was unfortunate because Pennsylvania's Democratic-Republican party experienced internal strife and split the Republican vote between Wolf and a rival. Wolf continued at his legal practice until 1824, when he won a seat in the U.S. House of Representatives. A popular candidate, he ran unopposed in the next two congressional elections. During this time he worked to encourage industrial expansion and supported internal improvements such as the Western National road in 1825 and government purchase of stock in the Chesapeake and Delaware Canal. He also gained a reputation as a diligent worker and a careful researcher. Acquaintances characterized him as one who was steady and firm in his convictions, not dominated by others.

In 1829 Wolf was elected to the governorship of Pennsylvania, and he resigned his house seat. He gained national attention when he moved the governor's office from his private residence to the state house—the first to do so—thereby making the state's chief executive more accessible to the public. Public improvements and education dominated his tenure. He found the state's finances in a muddled condition, the state suffering a burdensome debt. Credit had fallen to such a low rating that entrepreneurs declined to invest in public works. Wolf proposed new taxes to raise funds for paying off the interest on state loans and to complete improvement projects. He gained the confidence of the people and laid the foundation for renewed faith in state investments. Wolf's dedication to education gained him praise for "his early and manly advocacy" of a common school system in Pennsylvania. Addressing Pennsylvania's legislators, he declared that educational reform was a necessary and difficult task, but was of "intrinsic importance to the general prosperity and happiness of the people of the Commonwealth, to the cause of public virtue and of public morals" and the key to "the stability and permanency of our Republican institutions." The opponents of education, he averred, were "prejudice, avarice, ignorance, and error." An education bill, his special project, passed in 1834.

Wolf, a Freemason, won his second term as governor in a close election against the anti-Masonic candidate; but in 1835 his popularity declined, and he lost his bid for a third term. His refusal to succumb to a state legislative demand that he appear and answer questions before a house committee investigating Freemasonry in 1835 may have contributed to that defeat. He cited Pennsylvania's Declaration of Rights and insisted that "no human authority, can, in any case whatever, control or interfere with the rights of conscience" (Gerrity, p. 187). He set an example for others who were called but refused to testify; despite proposals to arrest the uncooperative persons, the sergeant-at-arms was finally instructed to release them.

While his Masonic affiliation may have played some role in his gubernatorial defeat, his involvement in controversy over President Andrew Jackson's veto of the bill to renew the charter of the Second Bank of the United States (BUS) probably contributed to that loss. Wolf, an early Calhounite, approved of Jackson's actions against South Carolina's Nullification Act in the 1832 tariff debate. However, he initially opposed Jackson's veto of the bank recharter bill. Wolf signed a resolution of support for the bank charter renewal, but later attacked the BUS with such vigor that pro-bankers decried his "vulgar abuse" of the BUS. Some questioned his political principles, saying that he feared Jackson's disapproval, but many Democrats entertained conflicting views over the bank charter. Whatever Wolf's political motivation, he retained Jackson's support, and the president appointed him as comptroller of the treasury in 1836, a position he held until 1838 when President Martin Van Buren appointed him collector of the Port of Philadelphia. Wolf served as port collector until his sudden death in Philadelphia.

• The George Wolf Papers are at the Historical Society of Pennsylvania in Philadelphia and at the Pennsylvania State Archives Building in Harrisburg. For information on Wolf, see William C. Armor, *Lives of the Governors of Pennsylvania* (1872); Clara A. Beck, *Kith and Kin of George Wolf* (1930); H. J. Steele, "The Life and Public Services of Governor Wolf," Pennsylvania German Society, *Proceedings*, vol. 39 (1930); Philip Shipley Klein, *Pennsylvania Politics, 1833–1848* (1958); "Papers of the Governors," *Pennsylvania Archives*, 4th ser., vols. 5 and 6 (1902); Frank Gerrity, "The Masons, the Antimasons, and the Pennsylvania Legislature, 1834–36," *Pennsylvania Magazine of History and Biography* 99 (1975); John M. Belohlavek, "Dallas, the Democracy, and the Bank War of 1832," *Pennsylvania Magazine of History and Biography* 96 (1972); and *Gales and Seaton's Register of Debates in Congress* (1824–1829).

MARION A. BROWN

WOLF, Simon (28 Oct. 1836–4 June 1923), lawyer and prominent Jewish American leader, was born in Hinzweiller, Bavaria, the son of Levi Wolf, an invalid who had been a teacher of Hebrew, and Amalia Ulman. The family immigrated to the United States in 1848, settling in Uhrichsville, Ohio, where the younger Wolf worked as a salesman and bookkeeper in a general merchandise store owned by his uncles. When his uncles left Ohio in 1855, Wolf became proprietor of his uncles' business. Two years later he married Caroline Hahn, with whom he would have six children. In 1892, the year after Caroline's death, he married Amy Lichtenstein. Deciding that a career in law was more promising than one in commerce, Wolf retired from business in 1859, read law, took a course of lectures at the Union Law College of Cleveland, was accepted into the Ohio bar on 19 July 1861, and practiced at New Philadelphia, Ohio, for one year.

In July 1862 Wolf moved to Washington, D.C., where he would live for the rest of his life. Frustrated in his efforts to obtain a government position, Wolf took up the private practice of law, became an active member of both the Jewish and German-American communities, and dabbled in politics as a partisan Republican. His prominence in the national Jewish fraternal organization, B'nai B'rith, and his membership on the Board of Delegates of American Israelites, which was charged with the protection of the rights of Jews both in the United States and abroad, quickly led to his assuming a role as the principal representative to the American government on matters of Jewish concern.

Wolf moved to solidify his interdependent positions as lobbyist for Jewish causes and as Republican party activist in the election of 1868. During the campaign an issue arose of Ulysses S. Grant having signed, in 1862, what to Jews was the "infamous" Order #11, which excluded all Jews as a class from the Department of the Union army of Tennessee, then commanded by Grant, on the grounds that Jews were engaged in cotton smuggling. The Democratic effort to attract Jewish voters by attacking Grant as an anti-Semite provided Wolf with an opportunity to prove his loyalty to the Republican party and to win favor with the nominee. Wolf's chosen role in these circumstances was to write a letter, first published in the *Boston Transcript* on 6 August 1868 and reprinted by several papers, that excused Grant's actions as the work of a subordinate unauthorized by the general, and to argue that a Jewish bloc vote did not exist and thus that any political appeal to Jews as Jews was futile.

Wolf was rewarded for his efforts when Grant appointed him recorder of deeds for the district of Columbia in 1869, by which time Wolf's claim to be the semiofficial representative of American Jews at Washington was recognized at the highest level of politics. President Rutherford B. Hayes, however, was pressured by temperance zealots to dismiss Wolf as recorder. Wolf submitted his letter of resignation in 1878 and Hayes appointed him a judge of the District of Columbia municipal court shortly thereafter. Thanks to the good offices of his friend Carl Schurz, Wolf was commissioned consul-general to Egypt, one of the most important diplomatic posts to be held by a professing Jew, by President Chester A. Arthur in 1881; he served in that post for one year.

As a lobbyist for Jewish interests Wolf cultivated contacts with government officials through several means, the most important of which were personal charm, flattery, and his willingness to take to the hustings in support of Republican candidates. Candidates welcomed Wolf's "speechifying," for he was a noted orator in a political age as reliant on the spoken as on the written word. His political contacts, especially with Republican presidents and congressmen from Ohio, gave him entrée to cabinet officers who directed immigration and foreign policy. These connections paid handsome dividends, for they permitted Wolf to act effectively in areas of concern to American Jews. On several occasions Wolf was able to assume a leadership role in convincing the U.S. government to take positions advocated by the American Jewish leadership. In 1870, partially thanks to Wolf's influence, Benjamin F. Peixotto was sent as consul to Bucharest with a mandate to protect Roumanian Jews. Wolf took an active part in convincing President Theodore Roosevelt (1858–1919) to submit a petition to the Russian czar Nicholas II protesting the Kishinev pogroms of 1903, and he was a major player in the long-term effort by American Jewry, which finally succeeded during the administration of William H. Taft, to have the United States abrogate the 1832 commercial treaty with Russia that had denied to American Jews the travel rights of other Americans. Wolf also became adept at resisting ever more stringent laws, rules, and regulations designed to limit the immigration of Jews from Eastern Europe. He frequently opposed restrictionist policies, won favorable rulings from government agencies and the courts, and successfully argued the cases of many individuals who were threatened with deportation.

As he grew older, Wolf found himself increasingly out of favor with the Jewish leadership concentrated in New York City represented by Jacob Schiff, Cyrus Adler, and Oscar Strauss who were associated with the American Jewish Committee (1906). These men, younger and wealthier than Wolf, were socially more at ease with the rich and powerful than was the Washington attorney. Consequently, on occasions when Wolf recommended compromise, the New Yorkers urged aggressive action, and Schiff and his allies came to view Wolf as little more than a self-serving political hack and an inadequate representative of American Jewish interests. Despite the growing distance between Wolf and the New Yorkers, he retained the good will of his brethren in B'nai B'rith (he served as president in 1904–1905) and was deservedly praised for the leadership role he took in the founding of the Atlanta Hebrew Orphan Asylum and the Baltimore Orphan Asylum and his continuous efforts on behalf of many charities both Jewish and nonsectarian.

In addition to his law practice and forays into politics, Wolf published several books, all of which, in one way or another, proclaimed the contributions that Jews had made to civilization in general and to American progress in particular. His most important publications were *The American Jew as Patriot, Soldier and Citizen* (1895) and an autobiography, *Presidents I Have Known from 1860 to 1918* (1918). He died in Atlantic City, New Jersey, but his funeral was held in Washington, D.C.

• Correspondence and unpublished essays and lectures are located in the Wolf papers at the American Jewish Historical Society on the campus of Brandeis University in Waltham, Mass., the American Jewish Archives, and the Library of Congress. See also Simon Wolf and Max J. Kohler, *Jewish Disabilities in the Balkan States* (1916); Simon Wolf, *Selected Addresses and Papers of Simon Wolf* (1926); and Esther L. Panitz, *Simon Wolf: Private Conscience and Public Image* (1987).

JOHN C. LIVINGSTON

WOLFE, Catharine Lorillard (8 Mar. 1828–4 Apr. 1887), philanthropist and art collector, was born in New York City, the daughter of John David Wolfe, a merchant and real-estate developer, and Dorothea Ann Lorillard. Wolfe experienced the stereotypical childhood of the very rich, including private tutors, fashionable parties, and family tours in Europe. Her interests appear to have included art, social life, fashion, foreign travel, and daily horseback riding in Central Park or near "Vinland," her Newport estate. At the death of her mother in 1866 she inherited part of the Lorillard tobacco fortune and began to collaborate with her father in his philanthropic endeavors. She may also have begun speculating in real estate. After her father died in 1872 Wolfe possessed a fortune estimated at $12 million. It is difficult to determine how she invested or managed her money; as a refined woman, she shunned publicity, and contemporary observers only recorded her activities that were deemed appropriate for women. As seen by contemporaries, her main interests were the Episcopal church, social life, travel, philanthropy, and art collecting. One obituary declared, "Miss Wolfe was a most quiet and unassuming person and had no eccentricities of habit or character" (*New York Times*, 5 Apr. 1887). Wolfe died in New York City of Bright's disease (kidney failure) complicated by pneumonia.

Among Wolfe's numerous philanthropic gifts and bequests, she was most generous to Grace Episcopal Church, with gifts of $250,000 and $350,000 in addition to regular support. Most of her philanthropy seemed intended to carry on her father's good works: she gave $100,000 to Union College in Schenectady, New York, and $200,000 to the American Museum of Natural History, which her father had helped to establish and of which he had been president when he died. Wolfe also evolved her own philanthropic campaigns. She financed numerous archaeological expeditions, including those that led to the excavation of Nippur in Iraq by the University of Pennsylvania soon after her death. Wolfe received greatest public approval, though, for her innovative support of the Newsboys' Lodging House and Industrial School, maintained by Charles Loring Brace's Children's Aid Society. At a time when comfortable New Yorkers felt increasingly threatened by the presence of thousands of homeless boys on city streets, the Lodging House became the principal—and best-publicized—means by which the wealthy deluded themselves that they were curing this ill. The *Times* (21 May 1880) celebrated Wolfe as the patroness of newsboys.

It was Wolfe's involvement with art, however, that gave her historical stature. She was the only woman contributor to the campaign that established the Metropolitan Museum of Art in 1870. She owned one of the largest and most valuable collections of paintings in New York, but one cannot easily assess her aesthetic tastes because it is possible that a cousin, John Wolfe, assembled her collection for her. The exact origin of her collection is not important; it is what she did with it that mattered. She owned representative anecdotal and landscape pictures by the same European masters found in prestigious collections assembled all over the United States after the Civil War, but unlike her fellow millionaires, Wolfe bequeathed her collection to the public through the Metropolitan Museum of Art. She also left the sum of $200,000 to the Metropolitan as the first permanent endowment fund for buying art at a major museum. The acclaim that greeted her bequest emphasized the social benefits of cultural philanthropy. Her bequest established a precedent that has ever since fueled the establishment and growth of American museums.

The popular subjects and styles of Wolfe's paintings lured to the Metropolitan unprecedented numbers of visitors, helping to expand the museum's constituency beyond the traditional circle of educated New Yorkers. For several decades following her death the Wolfe Collection was exhibited en bloc in separate galleries. Its popularity is attested to by an episode in which the characters in Edith Wharton's *Age of Innocence* (1920) deliberately avoid the Wolfe pictures while touring the museum.

After World War I, however, the critical establishment repudiated the popular and academic masters of the nineteenth century, and curators began dismembering Wolfe's collection; large sections of it were deaccessioned in auctions as late as 1956 and 1973. Proceeds of these sales, along with Wolfe's original cash bequest, allowed curators to acquire some of the Metropolitan's most prized paintings, including Winslow Homer's *The Gulf Stream*, Pierre Auguste Renoir's *Mme Charpentier and Her Children*, and Jacques-Louis David's *The Death of Socrates*. One hundred years of curatorial sales and acquisitions made the Wolfe Collection one of the most diverse in any American museum. Late in the twentieth century there was a scholarly rehabilitation of popular nineteenth-century art, and the museum again exhibited a number of the paintings that Wolfe owned, including her fine portrait by Alexandre Cabanel.

Wolfe was nearly forgotten after her death, but her example impressed women artists in New York, who in 1896 formed the Catharine Lorillard Wolfe Art Club at Grace Church. In 1925 the club was reorganized as a professional society, and after 1954 it attracted members from throughout the United States. Until the 1970s it sponsored annual exhibitions of art at unusual locales, like LaGuardia Airport, to fund travel grants for curators at the Metropolitan Museum.

• Information about Wolfe is in the archive, curatorial files, and library of the Metropolitan Museum. The one significant discussion during her lifetime of her art collection is Edward Strahan, *The Art Treasures of America*, vol. 1 (c. 1880), pp. 119–34. The fullest descriptive list is Metropolitan Museum of Art, *The Catharine Lorillard Wolfe Collection and Other Modern Paintings* (1895). The opening of the Wolfe Galleries at the Metropolitan is reported in *Harper's Weekly*, 19 Nov. 1887, pp. 843, 845, and the *New York Times*, 7 Nov. 1887. Wolfe is mentioned in Robert H. Bremner, *The Public Good: Philanthropy and Welfare in the Civil War Era* (1980), and Kathleen D. McCarthy, *Women's Culture: American Philanthropy and Art, 1830–1930* (1991). The Metropolitan's indebtedness to her is recounted in Gary Tinterow, *The New Nineteenth-century European Paintings and Sculpture Galleries* (1993), and Calvin Tomkins, *Merchants and Masterpieces: The Story of the Metropolitan Museum of Art* (1970). Prime sources on her life are the numerous obituaries and reports on her bequests that appeared 4–9 Apr. 1887 in the *New York Times*, the *Tribune*, the *Herald*, the *World*, and the *Sun*.

SAUL E. ZALESCH

WOLFE, Harry Kirke (10 Nov. 1858–30 July 1918), psychologist, was born in Bloomington, Illinois, the son of Jacob Vance Wolfe, a farmer, lawyer, and land commissioner, and Eliza Ellen Batterton, a college professor of mathematics. Wolfe was thirteen years old when his family moved to a farm near Lincoln, Nebraska. He graduated from the University of Nebraska in 1880 with a concentration in philosophy. After teaching in Nebraska public schools for three years, he enrolled at the University of Berlin to pursue a doctorate in the classics. There he encountered Hermann Ebbinghaus, whose pioneering studies on memory drew Wolfe to the fledgling science of psychology. In the fall of 1884 he enrolled at the University of Leipzig, where in 1886 he became the second American to earn a doctorate in psychology from Wilhelm Wundt, who is generally recognized as the founder of the science of psychology. Wolfe's dissertation, "On the Memory for Tones," was an unusual topic for Wundt's laboratory and clearly indicates the importance of Ebbinghaus's influence. When William James discussed memory in his *Principles of Psychology* (1890), he cited the work of only two researchers: Ebbinghaus and Wolfe.

Returning to the United States, Wolfe found employment as a high school principal in San Luis Obispo, California. There he met the physician Katharine Hermine Brandt, whom he married in December 1888; they had four children.

In the fall of 1889 Wolfe became assistant professor of philosophy and chair of the one-person department at the University of Nebraska, where he taught for twenty-one years. There he established one of the earliest of the American psychology laboratories (sources recognize it as the sixth, and one source as the first, American lab to be devoted solely to undergraduate training). The emergence of psychology laboratories in the United States at this time marked the separation of psychology from its parent discipline, philosophy, and the emergence of psychology as a science. Wolfe struggled to improve his laboratory with needed equipment and space, but the university administration rarely fulfilled his requests. Despite this lack of support he managed to create a viable laboratory to accompany most of his psychology classes by borrowing equipment from other departments, building some of the apparatus himself (including devices to measure color perception and sound intensity), and using his own money to buy needed materials. An exceptionally popular teacher, he had the fastest growing course enrollments of the university in spite of his reputation as a demanding instructor whose required laboratory hours exceeded the credit hours given for his classes.

Wolfe's influence as a teacher is evidenced in two surveys of the 1920s that asked psychologists where they were when they received their first inspiration to pursue psychology as a career. The University of Nebraska ranked third in both surveys, which reflected the large number of psychologists who had earned their baccalaureate degree with Wolfe. His undergraduates included three future presidents of the American Psychological Association—Walter Pillsbury, Madison Bentley, and Edwin Guthrie—all of whom, in a 1948 survey, named Wolfe (rather than their doctoral mentor) as the psychologist who influenced them most in their career. Wolfe influenced an unprecedented number of undergraduates to pursue advanced study: a recent biography of Wolfe cites twenty-two of his students who became prominent in psychology.

Wolfe's popularity did not prevent his dismissal from the University of Nebraska in 1897 following a dispute with the university's chancellor, who charged that Wolfe had meddled in the affairs of other departments. These charges likely stemmed from the attention that Wolfe had called to his meager departmental budget in relation to the larger budgets of other departments with far fewer students. After a year without employment he became superintendent of the public schools in South Omaha, Nebraska, for three years and then served the next three years as principal of Lincoln High School in Lincoln, Nebraska. In 1905 he became professor of psychology and pedagogy at the University of Montana. He held that post for only one year before a new chancellor at the University of Nebraska asked him to return.

Although he taught courses in philosophy, Wolfe principally emphasized psychology and pedagogy and involved his students in research projects. Most of these projects were in the field of child study, a movement begun by G. Stanley Hall in the 1890s that advocated the improvement of education and parenting by exhaustive studies of child behavior and mental processes. Wolfe was a popular lecturer at child study meetings in the Great Plains states and a principal figure in founding the Nebraska Society for Child Study. The great majority of his fifty-five published works are on child study, and most appeared in regional magazines for educators.

With the United States at war with Germany in the spring of 1918, the University of Nebraska found itself embroiled in a controversy that involved accusations of disloyalty in its faculty. One of eighteen Nebraska professors who were formally charged with transgressions such as not signing a wartime activity subscription card and not displaying a Red Cross emblem, Wolfe was acquitted at the hearings that were held that summer. A month later, he died, apparently of a heart attack, while visiting his brother in Wheatland, Wyoming.

Wolfe was arguably the most inspirational teacher of psychology of his generation. His laboratory, the key to his influence, was an avenue for demonstrating the phenomena and principles of psychology; its greater purpose, however, was to get students involved in research. As he wrote in an unpublished manuscript found in his collected papers, "[Research] is the sole method of growth." Mental growth came from questioning, working through complex problems, and self-initiated discovery. Wolfe's laboratory put his students inside psychology. Although he argued that the lecture was not an effective tool for learning, he was a masterful lecturer. One of his students wrote, "His classes were notoriously difficult; there was no room for the slacker there; but there was never an uninteresting lecture hour, and year after year the students filed in, willing to venture the work for the sake of the zest" (*Science* 48, pp. 312–13). In recognition of his influence as a teacher, the American Psychological Association's Division on the Teaching of Psychology established the Harry Kirke Wolfe Memorial Lecture in 1988, an invited lecture on teaching that is given annually at the APA convention.

• Wolfe's papers at the University of Nebraska Archives in Lincoln contain lecture notes, departmental annual reports, and some correspondence; those at the Archives of the History of American Psychology (Akron, Ohio) contain notebooks from his study in Germany, lectures, research reports, and correspondence. The only full-length biography is Ludy T. Benjamin, Jr., *Harry Kirke Wolfe: Pioneer in Psychology* (1991). An obituary is in *Science* 48 (1918): 312–13.

LUDY T. BENJAMIN, JR.

WOLFE, Linnie Marsh (8 Jan. 1881–15 Sept. 1945), biographer and librarian, was born in Big Rapids, Michigan, the daughter of Daniel Marsh and Flora Badger. Wolfe received an A.B. from Whitman College and an A.M. in English from Radcliffe College in 1907. She was also a graduate of the University of Southern California Library School. She taught briefly in the public school system in the state of Washington. Later she was a librarian for the public library system in Los Angeles, as well as for several Los Angeles high schools. She married Roy N. Wolfe in 1924; they had no children.

Wolfe's renown rests upon her study of John Muir (1838–1914), the California naturalist, geologist, and explorer who was largely responsible for instituting the U.S. National Parks System. Wolfe spent over twenty-two years studying Muir and was the secretary of the John Muir Association, which sponsored the centenary celebration of his birth in 1938. In the same year she edited *John of the Mountains: The Unpublished Journals of John Muir*. A number of volumes of his journals had already been published, so Wolfe edited only the most important of the remaining journals from his domestic travels. Because Muir tended to write in several notebooks simultaneously, Wolfe dated each entry by using his correspondence and travel itineraries. *John of the Mountains*, then, is not a straightforward reprinting of his journals; rather, it is an anthology of selected, edited, and chronologically arranged individual entries.

Based on her editing work and her previous studies of Muir, Alfred A. Knopf requested that Wolfe write a biography of Muir. The result was *Son of the Wilderness: The Life of John Muir*, published in 1945. Wolfe never knew Muir personally, but she drew upon all known sources of Muir's writing and conducted numerous interviews with his family, friends, and colleagues. She also traveled extensively, visiting Muir's former homes and retracing the routes of some of his trips. Wolfe worked particularly closely with Muir's two daughters, Wanda Muir Hanna and Helen Funk Muir. Perhaps as a result of this close collaboration, *Son of the Wilderness* avoids controversy. Wolfe discounts or ignores negative stories about Muir, dismissing rumors, for instance, that Muir himself had engaged in destructive logging practices before he began his public career as a conservationist. Instead, Wolfe attempts to integrate the story of Muir's personal life with that of his public life, to make him "more than a disembodied voice crying in the wilderness" (p. vii). To this end, Wolfe portrays Muir as warm and generous in his personal relationships, especially with his family, claiming that these "[have] been the subject of misrepresentation" (p. x), for his activities as a conservationist earned Muir many political enemies. Some, for example, characterized Muir as a fanatic, so obsessed that he valued wilderness preservation above the welfare of his own family. Through letters and family reminiscences, Wolfe successfully demonstrates that Muir was deeply devoted to his family and friends, who themselves supported his conservation efforts. The later sections of the biography, however, focus almost exclusively on Muir's activism in the western conservation movement and the fight to save the Hetch Hetchy Valley from construction. Wolfe spends little time discussing Muir as a writer. *Son of the Wilderness* was well received critically, and it won the Pulitzer Prize for biography in 1946. Wolfe did not live to receive this award, though, because she died in a Berkeley, California, nursing home shortly after the book's publication.

Wolfe's two works remain important in Muir studies. *John of the Mountains* contains the only published version of some of Muir's journals. Although other biographies of Muir have since been published, *Son of the Wilderness* was reprinted in 1978 and remains useful because of Wolfe's unlimited access to both his published and unpublished papers and her interviews with Muir's acquaintances.

• Wolfe's papers are interfiled with the John Muir collection in the Western Americana Collection at the University of the Pacific in Stockton, Calif. These papers are on permanent loan from the Muir family. Although many of Muir's papers are filmed, Wolfe's are not filmed and are available only on site. Included in the Muir collection are Wolfe's transcriptions of Muir's journals, letters, and manuscripts, and her preparatory materials for his biography and her edition of his journals. The collection also includes the typed manuscripts for both of her books as well as business papers and promotional materials related to these volumes. The Muir collection also includes a limited amount of Wolfe's personal materials, focusing on her correspondence from 1918 to 1945. The majority of this correspondence dates from 1930 to 1945, the period during which she was researching Muir, and concerns queries that she was making to people who knew him. An article containing biographical material is in the *New York Times*, 7 May 1946.

KAREN A. WEYLER

WOLFE, Thomas (3 Oct. 1900–15 Sept. 1938), author, was born Thomas Clayton Wolfe in Asheville, North Carolina, the son of William Oliver Wolfe, a stonecutter, and Julia Westall, the owner of a boardinghouse. Wolfe, who began reading voraciously in childhood, fed his appetite for literature at first-rate schools. Indeed, in the words of his Pulitzer Prize–winning biographer, David Herbert Donald, Wolfe received "the best formal education of any American novelist of his day." After attending public elementary school in Asheville, he was recruited into the newly founded North State Fitting School. Graduating with literary distinction in 1916, he followed his father's wishes and entered the University of North Carolina at Chapel Hill. A brilliant and extroverted undergraduate, he joined the Carolina Playmakers and studied under Frederick H. Koch, who inspired him to pursue a career as a playwright. After earning a bachelor's degree from Chapel Hill in 1920, Wolfe entered Harvard University and became a student in George Pierce Baker's "47 Workshop." In 1922 Harvard awarded Wolfe a master's degree in English.

Although Wolfe delayed his departure from Cambridge until late 1923 in order to continue studying playwriting under Baker, his efforts to become a dramatist met with failure. The plays he wrote at Harvard were improvements over juvenilia such as *The Return of Buck Gavin*, a folk play he had written at Chapel Hill and produced in 1919, yet neither *The Mountains*, staged at Harvard in 1921, nor *Welcome to Our City*, an overlong play about southern race relations, put on at the university in 1923, reached the commercial stage. (Nor did Wolfe's final play, *Mannerhouse*, about the ruination of a southern plantation family, written after he left Cambridge.) Critics have since agreed that he lacked the artistic control to write for the theater.

Wolfe's transformation into a novelist did not occur overnight. In 1924 he joined the English department of Washington Square College (part of New York University) and taught there until his resignation in 1930. Struggling to find his artistic voice, he also began making pilgrimages to Europe in order to write fiction. During the first of these trips, in 1925, he became romantically involved with a prominent Manhattan set designer named Aline Bernstein, whom he encountered on the voyage home. With the encouragement of Bernstein, who was married and nineteen years older, he started a novel, and by the spring of 1928 he had written a quarter-of-a-million-word work titled *O Lost*.

Wolfe drew the plot of *O Lost* from events in his life. Casting himself in the persona of Eugene Gant, an ingenious southern boy whose volatile home life paralleled his own, he gave each member of his large and troubled family a fictional counterpart. The novel included bald, if loving, portraits of Wolfe's alcoholic father, parsimonious mother, and idiosyncratic siblings. Although Maxwell E. Perkins, the famed editor at Charles Scribner's Sons, insisted on cuts in the novel before the firm published it as *Look Homeward, Angel: A Story of the Buried Life* (1929), Wolfe's rhapsodic meditations on solipsism remained. "Which of us," he asked in the epigraph,

> has known his brother? Which of us has looked into his father's heart? Which of us has not remained forever prison-pent? Which of us is not forever a stranger and alone?
>
> O waste of loss, in the hot mazes, lost, among bright stars on this most weary unbright cinder, lost! Remembering speechlessly we seek the great forgotten language, the lost lane-end into heaven, a stone, a leaf, an unfound door. Where? When?
>
> O lost, and by the wind grieved, ghost, come back again.

The novel culminates in the death of Eugene's brother, Ben, a character based on and named after Wolfe's favorite brother, who died in the Spanish influenza epidemic of 1918.

Although many of Wolfe's acquaintances and friends in Asheville were annoyed to discover that they had been caricatured in *Look Homeward, Angel*, critics praised the novel, in which Wolfe mimicked and satirized an array of literary styles. Named a Guggenheim Fellow in 1930, he returned to Europe to begin work on his next book. Ignoring protestations of love from Aline Bernstein, from whom he grew estranged as his literary ambition mounted, Wolfe instead devoted himself to the new project. For the next four and a half years, with the counsel and encouragement of Max Perkins, he struggled with a work that took on gross proportions. *Look Homeward, Angel*, Wolfe explained, was only the first of six novels in which he would trace the genealogy of an American family over several centuries. Yet by 1934, Perkins, who had grown frustrated by Wolfe's inability to complete the books he proposed, retrieved his enormous manuscript and published it in truncated form as a 900-page novel, *Of Time and the River: A Legend of Man's Hunger in His Youth* (1935). A sequel to *Look Homeward, Angel*, this newest work brought Eugene Gant through his study at Harvard and into his early years as a novelist in the making.

Wolfe did, within his brief career, produce a number of shorter works, although most, as Francis Skipp has demonstrated, were never conceived as such (Skipp, pp. xvii–xxvii). Wolfe's book-length projects yielded almost sixty short stories, fourteen of which Scribner's collected in *From Death to Morning*, also published in 1935. The most famous of these stories, "Only the Dead Know Brooklyn," tells of an encounter between two New Yorkers on a subway platform. The story is one of the best examples of Wolfe's exaggeration of regional dialect for the purpose of conveying character. "Dere's no guy livin'," observes his cynical narrator, "dat knows Brooklyn t'roo an' t'roo (only the dead know Brooklyn t'roo and t'roo), because it'd take a lifetime just to find his way aroun' duh goddam town (—only the dead know Brooklyn t'roo and t'roo . . ."

After the publication of *Of Time and the River*, the preface to which included fulsome thanks to Perkins, some critics accused Wolfe of being able to write only with help from his editors. In "Genius Is Not Enough," a famous review of Wolfe's memoir, *The Story of a Novel* (1936), Bernard DeVoto wrote that "such organizing faculty and such critical intelligence as have been applied to the book have come not from inside the artist, not from the artist's feeling for form and esthetic integrity, but from the office of Charles Scribner's Sons" (*Saturday Review of Literature*, 25 Apr. 1936). By 1937 Wolfe, who was increasingly preoccupied by such charges, fell out with Perkins. Insisting that the editor was not only dictating the form of his work but his politics, Wolfe left Scribner's for Harper & Brothers, where Edward Aswell became his new editor.

Throughout his career, Wolfe's obsessive personality traits both propelled and impeded his artistic growth. After reading from Wolfe's collected letters (published in 1956), Malcolm Cowley, who chronicled the adventures of Wolfe's "Lost Generation" cohorts, observed that Wolfe "had a single-minded ambition to eat the world and digest it into words; everything he touched had to be written down in words; and he saved the words in a big packing box that was like a miser's hoard. Much as he wanted to be famous, it gave him a trauma to lose the words, to have them printed in a book. After each book, he had a prolonged fit of depression that almost amounted to dementia" (*Selected Correspondence of Kenneth Burke and Malcolm Cowley*, ed. Paul Jay [1988], p. 329). Certainly Wolfe, who tended to work in manic fits, derived therapeutic benefits from his writing. Yet one of the most common criticisms leveled at him is that he had trouble separating his artistic goals from his all-consuming ego. Robert Penn Warren, the novelist and poet, once reminded Wolfe that "Shakespeare merely wrote *Hamlet*; he was *not* Hamlet" (*American Review*, May 1935).

While psychologists such as J. R. Morris have suggested that Wolfe suffered from "borderline personality disorder" or bipolar disorder (manic-depressive illness), biographer David Herbert Donald has adopted more of a Freudian perspective and, citing Wolfe's ambiguous relationship to his mother, has labeled Wolfe a narcissist. Nearly all observers agree that Wolfe's emotionally uninhibited behavior was self-destructive. A heavy drinker given to promiscuous behavior, he experienced severe alterations in mood and quarreled with practically everyone he knew. (His mutually debilitating affair with Aline Bernstein, who suffered similar emotional troubles, ended for good in 1932, although their agonized correspondence persisted fitfully for several more years.) Almost as often as Wolfe alienated his friends, however, his charisma won their affection. Intuitive and gregarious, he was capable of making penetrating insights into human character.

As Wolfe matured, he also attempted to forge a social conscience. While his work is marred by racist caricatures of African Americans and anti-Semitic depictions of Jews, and he has been criticized for promulgating ethnic and gender stereotypes, he grew increasingly interested in dramatizing the plight of the common person. Distressed by the abject poverty he observed in America during the Great Depression and horrified by the persecution of Jews he witnessed on a 1935 trip to Germany, he attempted to turn away from a literature of provincialism toward an art based on sociological insight. As his social concerns blossomed, he also gained a new self-knowledge. "And what had he learned?" he wrote during this period, in the manuscript that became *You Can't Go Home Again* (1940), ". . . He had learned that he could not devour the earth, that he must know and accept its limitations. He realized that much of his torment of the years past had been self-inflicted, and an inevitable part of growing up. And, most important of all for one who had taken so long to grow up, he had thought he had learned not to be the slave of his emotions."

Wolfe, however, never had the opportunity to transform his maturing world view into a more controlled artistic medium. In the spring of 1938 he presented Aswell with the manuscript of *The Web and the Rock* (1939), at that stage a fragmented autobiographical novel about the burgeoning social conscience of a dislocated southern author. Departing New York that May and delivering a speech at Purdue University, Wolfe afterward set out on a summer road tour of the western national parks. Following an excursion to Vancouver, British Columbia, he came down with pneumonia. The pulmonary illness irritated a tubercular lesion that erupted and caused a cerebral infection.

He succumbed after surgery at Johns Hopkins Hospital in Baltimore, Maryland.

While some of Wolfe's phrases have endured in the English language, his skill as a writer has been debated fiercely since 1929. Perkins's conviction that Wolfe was a major American novelist put Wolfe in the company of Ernest Hemingway and F. Scott Fitzgerald. Sinclair Lewis, winner of the Nobel Prize for literature, observed on reading *Look Homeward, Angel* that Wolfe could well become "one of the greatest world writers" (quoted in Donald, p. 248). Years later, however, the critic Harold Bloom wrote: "There is no possibility for critical dispute about Wolfe's literary merits; he has none whatsoever" (*New York Times Book Review*, 8 Feb. 1987). Hostility from academic critics such as Bloom has been exacerbated by questions that have emerged regarding the textual integrity of Wolfe's posthumous works. In 1962 Richard S. Kennedy revealed that Aswell edited Wolfe's remaining manuscripts with a distorted view of the author's intentions. Aswell made silent changes in many of the manuscripts he received from Wolfe and even wrote brief passages to bridge gaps in *You Can't Go Home Again*. Although readers may still purchase and read the posthumous novels as originally published by Harper's, scholars have questioned the propriety of Aswell's actions.

In spite of all of the controversy—and perhaps because of it—Wolfe's work remains secure in the canon of twentieth-century U.S. authors. Although he is best known for his accounts of both the small-town boosterism of the South and the urban anomie of the North, he was not content with his reputation as a regional, or even a representative American novelist. In the words of William Faulkner, Wolfe "tried to do the greatest of the impossible . . . to reduce all human experience to literature" (quoted in Donald, p. 354). Wolfe's prodigious knowledge of literature, drama, and poetry made him into a novelist with a style as eclectic and learned as that of James Joyce, who was one of the chief influences on his work. (Wolfe's fiction also drew from William Shakespeare, Samuel Taylor Coleridge, H. L. Mencken, and Sherwood Anderson.) While not as popular as the writings of the heavily romanticized authors who expatriated themselves in Paris during the 1920s, Wolfe's autobiographical and lyrical novels have outlasted many works of the era and are still read for their powerful representation of both the hopes and the failures of America during the New Deal.

• The William B. Wisdom Collection of Thomas Wolfe Papers, reposited in Harvard University's Houghton Library, contains Wolfe's manuscripts and the bulk of his correspondence. A selection, *The Letters of Thomas Wolfe*, was edited by Wolfe's literary agent, Elizabeth Nowell, and published in 1956. Suzanne Stutman edited the correspondence between Wolfe and Bernstein as *My Other Loneliness* (1983). In recent years, critics have begun reediting the complete body of Thomas Wolfe's works with a view toward recovering his original intentions. See, for example, Stutman, ed., *The Good Child's River* (1991), and Stutman and John L. Idol, Jr., eds., *The Party at Jack's* (1995). The most accurately edited collection of Wolfe's short stories is *The Complete Short Stories of Thomas Wolfe*, ed. Francis E. Skipp (1987). Wolfe's principal plays are available in several editions: *The Mountains*, ed. Pat M. Ryan (1970); *Welcome to Our City*, ed. Richard S. Kennedy (1983); and *Mannerhouse*, ed. Louis D. Rubin, Jr., and John L. Idol, Jr. (1985). Entertaining, but now dated, biographies are Nowell, *Thomas Wolfe: A Biography* (1960), and Andrew Turnbull, *Thomas Wolfe* (1968). The definitive biography is David Herbert Donald, *Look Homeward: A Life of Thomas Wolfe* (1987). Major critical works on Wolfe include Richard S. Kennedy, *The Window of Memory* (1962); John Lane Idol, Jr., *A Thomas Wolfe Companion* (1987); Leslie Field, *Thomas Wolfe and His Editors: Establishing a True Text for the Posthumous Publications* (1987); and Harold Bloom, ed., *Thomas Wolfe: Modern Critical Views* (1987). The best discussion of Wolfe's mental condition is "Diagnosing Thomas Wolfe" (1992), an unpublished paper by J. R. Morris, Regents Professor of Psychology, University of Oklahoma. A comprehensive listing of Wolfe sources is contained in Carol Johnston, *Thomas Wolfe: A Descriptive Bibliography* (1987). An obituary is in the *New York Times*, 16 Sept. 1938.

THOMAS A. UNDERWOOD

WOLFF, Irving (6 July 1894–5 Dec. 1982), physicist, was born in New York, New York, the son of Max Wolff and Julia Gutman. After attending the Ethical Culture School in New York, Wolff studied physics at Dartmouth College, graduating with a Bachelor of Science degree in 1916. As a member of the ski club at Dartmouth he developed an interest in the sport, which led him later to vacation in places with mountains and snow, such as Switzerland. Motivated toward a teaching career in his early years, he pursued graduate work in physics, serving simultaneously as an instructor at Iowa State College in 1919–1920 and then at Cornell University, from which he received a doctor of philosophy degree in physics in 1923.

After spending one year as a Hecksher Research Fellow at Cornell University, Wolff joined the Radio Corporation of America's Technical and Test Department at the company's Van Cortlandt Park Laboratory in New York City in 1924. His early research involved acoustics. In the late 1920s he developed the first beat-frequency audio signal generator, i.e., an oscillator that produced audible sound frequency signals by combining two higher-frequency signals so that their difference (the beat) was the audio frequency desired, and, with colleagues, introduced new approaches to test loudspeakers. In the 1920s he and his colleagues designed a popular magnetic loudspeaker, which had substantial sales during that decade. His group of engineers developed some of the first loudspeaker units installed in sound motion-picture studios, as well as the velocity microphone, which responds to the velocity rather than the pressure of the sound wave, and the volume-compensated gain control, which, since it provided higher gain for weaker signals and vice versa, became a widely used circuit element in radios in the 1930s.

In 1930 Wolff moved to Camden, New Jersey, as a physicist on RCA's research staff. His interests there included flying—he obtained his pilot's license in 1930—and work with high-frequency radiation generators, which were used in experiments on microwave radio reflection, now known as radar. In 1934 Wolff demonstrated his early radar equipment to the U.S. Army Signal Corps by locating and tracking a boat sailing a half mile offshore in New York Bay. The obvious military application of the tests prevented much publication in the open literature. Through the efforts of Wolff and his colleagues, RCA can be credited with the first application of radar principles to aviation, in tests performed with RCA's own airplane and aimed at collision-avoidance applications. The tests, begun in 1937, continued for several years and demonstrated the effectiveness of radar in determining altitude and the presence of other aircraft or hazards such as mountains, with sufficient warning to enable the aircraft to avoid collision. In 1938 the group also assisted in the first installation of radar equipment on naval vessels. Several important inventions resulted from this work, in particular the altimeter used in many military aircraft and assault drones during World War II, and automatic homing equipment used in guided missiles.

In 1941 Wolff married Consuelo Hope Hughes; they had one child. In 1942 Wolff's pioneering work was honored through his election to fellowship in the Institute of Radio Engineers, "for basic research in centimeter wave radio and for application of it to the development of navigation instruments." When RCA opened its fundamental research laboratories in Princeton, New Jersey, in 1942, Wolff moved there and became director of its Radio Tube Research Laboratory in 1946. In 1948 the U.S. Navy awarded him its highest civilian honor, the Distinguished Public Service Award for "one of the fundamental contributions to modern-day radar." RCA promoted him to director of research of the RCA Laboratories in 1951, and vice president for research in 1954. During that period Wolff participated in an expansion of the RCA Laboratories' staff, including the addition of physicists like himself who could contribute both to furthering basic research and to making major contributions to practical developments. In 1959 he retired from his position, although he provided continuing service to RCA as chair of its education committee from 1959 to 1962.

The Franklin Institute recognized Wolff's contributions with the award of the Elliott Cresson Medal in 1959, "in consideration of his many contributions to the science of electronics . . . and especially in view of his pioneering work in the centimeter wave field and his contributions to microwave radar development." Wolff was also honored through election to fellowship in the American Physical Society, the Acoustic Society of America, and the American Association for the Advancement of Science.

An example of a physicist who was a highly productive developer and inventor in electrical and electronic engineering, Wolff held about eighty U.S. patents, primarily in the fields of acoustics, optics, radio, infrared detection, radiofrequency heating, and radio signaling. As a research leader in the last decades of his career, he supported a modest growth in industrial basic research which could not be sustained in later years. After he left RCA, the Laboratories emphasized applied research and development and essentially eliminated support for internal basic research. In leading a research laboratory, Wolff had recognized that nurturing the creativity of the individual researcher was most likely to lead to productive applications for the organization. His successors, at RCA and at other electronic, communication-oriented research centers, instead emphasized product-oriented research programs, perhaps as a sign of a "mature" technology. Without an emphasis like Wolff's on the quality of the research staff, later, heavily supported applied work often lacked the creativity that had marked the output of the RCA Laboratories during his tenure there.

• Information about Wolff's life and activities can be found in several articles in RCA's David Sarnoff Research Center internal publication, *Radiations*: in a "Profiles" article in 1956 and in his obituary tribute in the issue of Nov.–Dec. 1982. His contributions to research and development in electronics are described in Orrin E. Dunlap, Jr., *Radio's 100 Men of Science* (1944). A newspaper obituary is in the *New York Times*, 8 Dec. 1982.

MAURICE GLICKSMAN

WOLFF, Sister Madeleva (24 May 1887–25 July 1964), educator and poet, was born Mary Evaline Wolff in Cumberland, Wisconsin, the daughter of August Frederick Wolff, a harness maker, and Lucia Arntz, a schoolteacher until her marriage. To her mother's influence, she attributed her Roman Catholic faith and to her father's fondness for poetry, her own love of language and literature.

She began her education at the University of Wisconsin in 1905 but transferred at the end of her first year to Saint Mary's College, Notre Dame, Indiana, from which she received the B.A. degree in English in 1909, a year after she entered the Congregation of the Sisters of the Holy Cross at Saint Mary's Convent. In 1914 she took final vows. She completed a master's degree in English at the University of Notre Dame in 1918 and a Ph.D. in English at the University of California at Berkeley in 1925, specializing in medieval literature. During 1933–1934, she completed a year of postdoctoral work at Oxford University, studying under C. S. Lewis.

As an undergraduate, Sister Madeleva began writing poetry, which she continued to do all her life. She published several collections of verse, most notably *Knights Errant* (1923), *Penelope* (1927), *A Question of Lovers* (1935), and *American Twelfth Night* (1955). Her collected poems, *The Four Last Things*, appeared in 1959. Her poetry, which combines spiritual and erotic elements, earned her a reputation as one of the foremost religious poets of her day. Even at the time of their publication, the collections were criticized as uneven in quality; nonetheless, reviewers hailed her as a successor to Christina Rossetti and Alice Meynell in the mystical quality of her verse.

For her scholarly studies, *Chaucer's Nuns* (1925) and *Pearl: A Study in Spiritual Dryness* (1925), Sister Madeleva also chose religious themes, drawing on her experience as a nun. John Livingston Lowes, her teacher at Berkeley, encouraged her to continue research in medieval English literature, which needed "interpreters with vision"; however, the Holy Cross order, recognizing her administrative talents, instead assigned her to various positions in its academies and colleges, first as principal of academies in Utah and California, then from 1926 through 1933 as founding dean and president of the College of Saint Mary-of-the-Wasatch in Salt Lake City, and finally as president of Saint Mary's College, Notre Dame, Indiana, a position she held from 1934 until her retirement in 1961.

As president of Saint Mary's College, Sister Madeleva gave shape to her own "idea of a university," where theology holds pride of place in the curriculum and the arts pervade the campus milieu. In 1944, to mark the centennial of the founding of the college, she instituted the Graduate School of Sacred Theology at Saint Mary's. At the time Catholic graduate schools of theology were closed to religious women and laypeople alike. The school became the model for Regina Mundi, a similar school for religious women opened in Rome in 1953, and for subsequent programs offered by universities across the country. When the school finally closed in 1967, it had conferred seventy-six doctorates and 354 master's degrees in theology.

Sister Madeleva also proved to be instrumental in starting the Sister-Formation Conference, which was focused on the professional preparation of teaching nuns. Working through the National Catholic Education Association in 1948 and for several years following, she led the way in planning the programs and procedures by which a generation of Catholic nuns would be trained for their roles as religious educators in parochial schools and parishes across the nation.

During her tenure as president, Sister Madeleva brought the arts to Saint Mary's and the local South Bend community, overseeing the construction of the O'Laughlin Auditorium and Moreau Fine Arts Center on campus, completed in 1955. The largest facility in the area, it made possible the staging of opera, musical, and theater productions, some of which attracted national attention. During her presidency, the enrollment of Saint Mary's increased from 250 women to more than a thousand. She improved campus facilities, enlarged and strengthened the faculty, instituted several professional programs, and revamped the liberal arts curriculum of the college by adding interdisciplinary programs, one centered on the trivium (logic, rhetoric, and grammar) and another on the study of Christian culture.

In her later years, Sister Madeleva became a spokeswoman for Catholic education and published several collections of essays and talks on the subject, among them *Conversations with Cassandra* (1961). Especially in the 1950s, when her fame was at its peak, she traveled widely to lecture on education and on poetry. Awards and honors piled up in her later years. She received numerous honorary degrees and awards for her contributions to Catholic higher education and her achievements in poetry, among them the Campion Award, given in 1959 by the Catholic Book Club, and the 1960 Spirit Award of Merit from the Catholic Poetry Society of America. In 1959, at the request of the Macmillan Publishing Company, she published an autobiography, *My First Seventy Years*.

Sister Madeleva's charm and wit secured for her scores of friendships. She formed long, close relationships with, among others, author and scholar C. S. Lewis, writer and diplomat Clare Boothe Luce and her husband, publisher Henry Luce, actress Helen Hayes, and fellow religious Thomas Merton. A self-proclaimed extrovert, she was also a perfectionist who worked long hours and pushed herself past exhaustion to collapse. Most of her poetry, she often declared, she wrote in bed, recuperating from fatigue.

Although her major contributions were in the field of education, in particular the education of women religious, Sister Madeleva's poetry, reprinted in 1986, still has the power to move. It speaks of the deep and passionate spiritual life of a woman who, as she writes in the poem "Penelope," lashed herself to Christ and bound him to her with "a lifetime of years."

Sister Madeleva died in Boston, Massachusetts. In her writing she often contemplated death, which, after birth and baptism, she considered to be the most significant event of life.

• The principal papers of Sister Madeleva Wolff are collected in the archives of the Cushwa-Leighton Library at Saint Mary's College, Notre Dame; in the archives of the Congregation of the Sisters of the Holy Cross at Saint Mary's Convent, Notre Dame; and in the Benjamin Lehman Papers and the Noel Sullivan Papers in the Bancroft Library of the University of California at Berkeley. Major works by Sister Madeleva, in addition to those mentioned above, include collections of poems: *A Child Asks for a Star* (1964), *A Song of Bedlam Inn* (1946), *Four Girls* (1941), *Christmas Eve* (1938), and *Gates* (1938); and collections of essays: *A Lost Language* (1951) and *Addressed to Youth* (1944). She also published various articles: "Dame Julian of Norwich," in *The Image of the Work: Essays in Criticism*, ed. B. H. Lehman et al. (1955); "Saint Hilda of Whitby," in *Saints for Now*, ed. Clare Boothe Luce (1952); "Theology for Sisters," in *Religious Community Life in the United States* (Proceedings of the Sisters' Section of the First National Congress of Religious in the United States, 1952); and "Religion in Education," in *"The Catholic Mind" Reader*, ed. Benjamin L. Masse, S.J. (1952). Biographical information can be found in Sister Mary Immaculate Creek, *A Panorama: 1844–1977* (1977), and Barbara C. Jencks, *The Sister Madeleva Story* (1961), and *Holy Cross Courier: Alumnae Quarterly of Saint Mary's College* 38, no. 2 (Summer 1964). The entire issue is devoted to Sister Madeleva. An obituary is in the *New York Times*, 26 July 1964, and in the *Catholic Poetry Society of America Bulletin*, July–Aug. 1964.

GAIL PORTER MANDELL

WOLFMAN JACK (21 Jan. 1938–1 July 1995), radio and television personality, was born Robert Weston Smith in Brooklyn, New York, the son of Weston Smith, a shoe salesman who in the 1940s was a writer and editor for *Financial World*, and Rosamund (maiden name unknown). Smith became captivated by the culture of African Americans when his father bought him a huge transatlantic shortwave radio that allowed him to tune in early 1950s disc jockeys such as Alan Freed and "John R" (John Richbourg), who pioneered the marketing of rhythm-and-blues music to white teenagers. Besides airing an interracially daring selection of music for their time, Freed and Richbourg's on-air patter built a simultaneous sense of community and abandon that comforted, defined, and electrified the growing legions of teenagers in the United States during the 1950s. Decades later, Smith would constantly cite these two men as the primary influence for the simultaneously raucous and companionable radio personality who would eventually be known as Wolfman Jack.

Smith began to follow in his idols' footsteps at the age of sixteen, when he landed his first job at WNJR in Newark, New Jersey. According to biographer Wes Smith, he sold advertisements for the station, "cleaned toilets, fetched hamburgers, and sneaked up on the microphone whenever there was no one there to bat him away." Three years later Smith established a mentor relationship with Richbourg, which landed Smith a job selling ads and spinning records as "Daddy Jules" at WYOU, a black station in Newport News, Virginia. During his tenure at the station, Smith, showing early signs of his talent for entrepreneurship, opened an interracial dance club, which inspired the local chapter of the Ku Klux Klan to burn a cross on his lawn on two separate occasions. Soon thereafter, the station owner ordered a withdrawal of all black music from WYOU airwaves, and Daddy Jules transformed himself into Roger Gordon, a mellow disc jockey spinning conventional and safe pop records by white artists. Eventually, Smith moved to KCIJ in Shreveport, Louisiana, another station that shackled his freewheeling musical and performing sensibilities.

Smith's most significant radio engagement, and the one that inspired the birth of his famed alter ego Wolfman Jack, began in 1960 at XERF, a border station located a few miles south of Texas near Ciudad Acuña, Mexico, whose monstrous signal (which would have been illegal in the United States) could be picked up as far away as the Soviet Union and New York City. "That station was so *strong* in those days, man," Wolfman Jack told *Rolling Stone* in 1970. "It came into *New York* like a local. 1570 [AM], 250,000 watts—that was a *mothah*. Birds used to fly around the station and *drop dead*, y'know." The border radio stations of the 1950s and 1960s, beaming a heady mix of experimental musical programming, controversy, and flamboyant on-air personalities, represented a rebellion against the restrictive American radio establishment. This independent medium proved to be the perfect staging ground for Wolfman Jack's lusty and rowdy admonitions, supported by an adventurous free-form multiracial melange of rhythm-and-blues, rockabilly, jazz, and rock 'n' roll music. His croak-like, leering howl of a voice usually graced the airwaves at about midnight: "Ah ya wit me out deah? Ah ya redeeh? 'Cause we gonna DO IT FAW YA, honey! We gonna blow ya min' babeh! . . . Oooooooowwww! . . . Squeeze my knobs!!! . . . Get nekkid!" After a half-dozen years of knocking around the radio business, Wolfman Jack finally found himself free to let loose, verbally and musically. His style provided a new direction for disc jockeys, served as an antecedent to the free-form and "shock" radio formats, and brought international attention to many important African-American artists who had previously found it difficult to garner airplay.

Because he ran the station's business affairs and took a 50 percent commission on ad and product sales (including aphrodisiacs, glow-in-the-dark Jesuses, roach clips, and other items that could not be sold over the air in the United States), Wolfman Jack became wealthy during his engagement at XERF. But the constant threat of violence from the allegedly corrupt and criminal group of Mexican investors that had previously owned the station eventually led Wolfman Jack to sell XERF in 1963, though his taped shows remained on the air at the station until 1964. During this period, in 1961, he married Lucy "Lou" Lamb, and they had two children. He also appeared on tape in the mid-1960s over border stations XEG and XELO and in 1965 took control of another border radio station, XERB in Rosarito Beach, so that he could be close to California, where he bought a house in Beverly Hills. By the early 1970s, when the Mexican owners of XERB raised the rent of the station considerably, Wolfman Jack lost the station and incurred huge debts.

In 1970 Wolfman Jack initiated a sixteen-year run of broadcasts for Armed Services Radio, appearing on tape and via syndication on 600 stations abroad, as well as on 1,453 stations in the United States. His popularity may have peaked with his appearance as himself in George Lucas's *American Graffiti*, a 1973 hit film and bestselling soundtrack that memorably chronicled teen life of the early 1960s. This exposure led to Wolfman Jack's nine-year position as host of "The Midnight Special," a late-night television show that spotlighted live popular-music performances. By this time Wolfman Jack had become an American icon of sorts, appearing on rock artists' records as a guest or as an inspiration for song tributes (the Guess Who's "Clap for the Wolfman" was a top-ten single in 1974). He served as a spokesman for numerous products in TV commercials and appeared on such prime-time television shows as "The Odd-Couple," "Wonder Woman," and "Battlestar Galactica."

The 1980s proved to be a less lucrative time for the Wolfman. He still hosted his syndicated program, though it claimed a smaller listenership, and maintained a long association throughout most of the decade with KRLA in Los Angeles. His 1984 attempt at Saturday morning children's TV programming ("Wolfman Rock TV") and a country-themed syndicated radio program both fell flat. However, just prior to his death from a heart attack at his home in Belvidere, North Carolina, Wolfman Jack appeared to be on a career upswing. His syndicated "oldies" show boasted an audience of seventy-nine stations nationwide, he had recently completed a nationwide promotion tour for his autobiography *Have Mercy! Confessions of the Original Rock 'n' Roll Animal*, and he had just signed a deal to host a country music radio show as well.

On the air as Wolfman Jack, Smith reached out to people emotionally while giving them plenty of classic rock and rhythm-and-blues music that inspired decades of dancing, laughing, cruising, and loving. His radio personality expressed a freedom that was undeniably American and redolent of the spirit of the popular music of his time. His philosophy in life seemed to mirror the philosophy he espoused on the air. In a 1970 interview during a guest spot on a San Francisco FM station he pronounced: "So what does it come to? Love, right? Love your brother, right? If you make money, too, that's great. If you don't make money, that's great, too. The important thing is, whatever you get into, to have that *fullness*, that—that *freedom of thought* . . . I never *work*, man. I *vacation* all the time. I'm *vacationin'* right now."

• The most complete biographies of Wolfman Jack are Wes Smith's essay in his book *The Pied Pipers of Rock and Roll: Radio Dee Jays of the 50s and 60s* (1989) and Wolfman Jack's breezy autobiography *Have Mercy! Confessions of the Original Rock 'n' Roll Animal* (1995), co-written with Byron Laursen. For background on the history and economics of the border radio phenomenon, consult Bill Crawford and Gene Fowler, *Border Radio* (1987). As one might expect, there are many entertaining interviews of the subject, including *Rolling Stone*, 1 Oct. 1970; *Billboard*, 15 Apr. 1972 and 17 Dec. 1994; and *Melody Maker*, 6 Sept. 1975. Obituaries are in the *Los Angeles Times*, 2 July 1995, the *New York Times*, 3 July 1995, and the *Washington Post*, 3 July 1995.

HARVEY COHEN

WOLFSKILL, William (20 Mar. 1798–3 Oct. 1866), frontiersman, trader, and rancher, was born in Boonesborough, Madison County, Kentucky, the son of Joseph Wolfskill, Jr., and Sarah Reid, farmers. In late 1809 the family moved to Boone's Lick, Howard County, Missouri. William was sent back to Kentucky in 1815 to attend school for two years and then returned to Missouri, where he remained. In May 1822 he joined William Becknell's second Santa Fe trade expedition. In New Mexico, Wolfskill and fellow Kentuckian Ewing Young trapped near the Pecos River until December 1822. The next year he trapped along the Rio Grande to Paso del Norte (present-day Juárez), and in 1824 he and a few friends headed up the Colorado and San Juan rivers, possibly being the first whites to pass through southern Utah. Because of a gunshot wound he received in 1823, he returned to Boone's Lick in June 1825 to recuperate. Home only a month, Wolfskill headed then to Louisiana and Texas, where he secured mules he drove to Alabama and sold for good profit. In 1826 he returned to Santa Fe, where he trapped and traded until 1827, when he returned to Missouri. In the spring of 1828 he bought a freight wagon and joined a wagon train heading for the Taos–Santa Fe region. Recognizing that he needed Mexican citizenship to continue and widen his business activities, especially into California, Wolfskill applied for Mexican citizenship in 1829. He officially became a Mexican citizen and a Catholic by fall of the next year.

Between 29 September 1830 and 5 February 1831 Wolfskill made his first trip to Mexican California and pioneered a new trail in the process. The trip took him in a westerly direction to the San Juan River, then near present-day Durango, Colorado. He crossed the Colorado River near present-day Moab, Utah, and arrived at Los Angeles in February. Trapper-trader George Yount accompanied the expedition and helped the group win the confidence of Indians in southern Utah, who allowed them safe passage through their area and the right to hunt game along the way. In California, Wolfskill and others constructed a sixty-ton, seventy-foot-long schooner that he dubbed *Refugio*, from which to hunt sea otter along the coast, a vocation he attempted for a short time. During 1833 he purchased land near Los Angeles, where he tended grapevines. He entered into a common-law marriage with María de la Luz Valencia; they had two children. In order to support his family Wolfskill took up carpentry, a trade he had learned in Missouri. As he became financially able, he bought more land and launched full time into growing fruits—including in 1841 one of the first orange groves in the region—and vegetables and experimenting with grapes produced for brandy and wine. He continued this enterprise until his death. In 1837 Luz Valencia left California with another man and left Wolfskill with the two small children. In 1841 Wolfskill married Doña María Magdalena Lugo, daughter of Don José Ygnacio Lugo and Doña Rafaela Romero, a prominent Mexican California family.

Acquiring land in the Sacramento Valley, where he helped one of his four brothers, John Reid Wolfskill, get started in agriculture, William Wolfskill became influential and, by the standards of the time, quite affluent. He and Magdalena had six children. Although he generally remained aloof from politics, he served briefly as a public administrator in Los Angeles from September 1865 until his death. He was very successful in growing oranges and in the introduction of the persimmon and the Italian chestnut to his region in California. During the 1860s his vineyards had an estimated 85,000 vines. After his death in Los Angeles, Wolfskill's sons continued the orchards. In 1880, when President Rutherford B. Hayes visited California, he traveled to the outskirts of Los Angeles to see some of the Wolfskill orchards and ranches. Wolfskill was a frontiersman and pioneer not only of the Santa Fe trade but also of California's production of fruits, vegetables, and wines.

• Little about Wolfskill has been published. For additional biographical details, as well as considerable information about California before it became part of the United States, see Iris W. Engstrand, *William Wolfskill, 1798–1866: Frontier Trapper to California Ranchero* (1965).

JOE A. STOUT, JR.

WOLFSON, Erwin Service (27 Mar. 1902–26 June 1962), investment builder and general contractor, was born in Cincinnati, Ohio, the son of Bernard Wolfson, a successful textile manufacturer, and Rose Service. As a youngster he was fascinated by the workings of early radios, cars, and other mechanical contrivances. He enrolled in the University of Cincinnati, intending to study engineering, but he soon switched to philosophy.

After graduation in 1924 Wolfson spent the summer vacationing in Florida, an occasion that altered his future plans. The prevailing building mania excited him, and, starting with an investment of $500, he earned a small fortune within two years by concentrating on the construction of small-sized homes, apartment houses, and office buildings and speculating in real estate. In 1926 the land boom collapsed, following a disastrous hurricane, and he lost everything.

Moving to New York City, Wolfson went to work for the Adelson Construction and Engineering Corporation and in his five years there advanced from a position as assistant timekeeper on a construction crew to secretary of the firm and executive assistant to its head, Abe N. Adelson, having been involved in directing the construction of more than twenty large office buildings and other commercial structures. From 1931 to 1936 he operated a general real estate and brokerage business under his own name. In 1936 he married Rose Fivars; they had two children.

Also in 1936 Wolfson joined with others in organizing the Diesel Electric Company, which contracted to furnish commercial structures with their own power plants. In 1937 Wolfson and a partner formed the Diesel Construction Company and began putting up their own buildings. Originally vice president of these firms, Wolfson became their president in 1952; they were soon merged into one. He next created the Wolfson Management Corporation to handle tenants seeking rental space in his firm's buildings. Following a 1957 redistribution of executive responsibilities, Wolfson was named board chairman of Diesel Construction; in 1959 he assumed the same position with Wolfson Management. In 1960 he was listed as owning 51 percent of Diesel Construction stock and 100 percent of the management firm's stock.

From the end of World War II to 1962 Wolfson and his firms participated, either as principal investor or as general contractor, in the construction of over sixty major structures throughout Greater New York, ranging from office buildings to department stores and apartment houses. Included among his clients were RKO Pictures, the National Broadcasting Company's studios, Bankers Trust Company, and Pan American World Airways. His firm was responsible for the Americana Hotel, which, at fifty-seven stories, became the world's tallest hotel upon its completion in 1962.

Despite his fame as one of the major forces behind the skyscraper building boom that altered the profile of Manhattan island after 1945, Wolfson had no formal training in how to practice the commercial or residential real estate business. His professional integrity and reliability more than compensated for such shortcomings. Colleagues and competitors credited his ascendancy to a mixture of personality and superb entrepreneurial instinct. After signing a legal commitment to construct a skyscraper, the Wolfson firm would complete it within a year of the groundbreaking. At the time of his death, he was universally acknowledged as New York City's leading builder.

Wolfson and his firms provided nearly 16 million square feet of office space in New York City, with the Pan Am Building (now the Met Life Building) symbolizing the epitome of his life's work. He developed the plans for its location and construction, just north of Grand Central Station, financed it with the aid of British capital, and had his own contracting firm build it. When completed in 1963 it became the world's largest office building, moving ahead of the Empire State Building in square footage. Because it was intended to serve over 25,000 persons, who would be accommodated by elevators moving at a speed of twenty-six feet per second, some city planners and architects criticized the proposed structure in its planning stages on both aesthetic and sociological grounds. John Ely Burchard of MIT called it "a monstrous denial of urbane urbanism," and Sibyl Moholy-Nagy of Pratt Institute predicted morning and evening rush-hour nightmares. Wolfson took the criticisms good-naturedly. In addition to retaining the services of two eminent architects, Walter Gropius and Pietro Belluschi, he removed 600,000 square feet from the original rentable space in the interests of elegance and design.

Alongside a professional career, Wolfson's life had a civic dimension. Between 1957 and 1961 he served as a member of the Westchester County Parkway Authority, and in 1961 he was appointed the county's park commissioner. Having great respect for education, Wolfson endowed a chair in philosophy at Brandeis University and served as a trustee or director for the New School for Social Research, Pace College, and the Technion-Israel Institute of Technology. He was vice president and president of the Academy of Religion and Mental Health and treasurer of the Hospital for Joint Diseases. He was active in the American Jewish Committee and the Federation of Jewish Philanthropies. He died in Purchase, New York.

With a reputation as a quiet, studious mover-shaker in the New York construction industry, Wolfson managed to accomplish much. On most working days, he busied himself with clandestine conferences that exercised his skills in bringing together diverse personalities responsible for huge outlays of funds, and he committed himself to meeting project deadlines. He saw himself as a seller of space, soliciting tenants for his edifices by competitiveness and bargaining. He was proud of being able to utilize, for his commercial buildings, the latest advances in office automation procedures and equipment and the appropriate space arrangements for clerical, administrative, and executive personnel. Near the end of his life, after having accumulated a personal fortune close to $18 million, he depicted the investment-building business as "no place for the unenterprising or the faint of heart."

• The most complete account of Wolfson's life is the obituary in the *New York Times*, 27 June 1962. The same newspaper has more than forty items on Wolfson from 1931 to 1962. Assessments of his business reputation and firms can be found in "Erwin S. Wolfson: Builder of Skylines," *Time*, 22 Feb. 1960, p. 92; "A One-Man Operation in an Organized World," *Business Week*, 10 Sept. 1960, pp. 110–12, 114, 116, 121–22, 124; and "Sky-High Deal for a Skyscraper," *Fortune*, Dec. 1960, pp. 140–43, 266–68, 271.

IRVING KATZ

WOLFSON, Harry Austryn (2 Nov. 1887–19 Sept. 1974), scholar of Hebrew literature and historian of philosophy, was born Zvi Glembotsky in Ostrin, province of Vilna, Russian Poland, the son of Mendel "Max" Glembotsky, an uncertified teacher of Russian, and Sarah Savitzky, later a shopkeeper. Mendel's brother Beryl Velvel in Cincinnati took the name Wolfson—"vel" is "wolf" in Yiddish—so the rest of the family became Wolfsons when they arrived in the United States. At the age of fourteen Harry was sent away from home to study, eventually at the famous yeshiva at Slobodka. In 1903 he immigrated to the United States.

Wolfson worked for a brief time in the garment industry in New York City, attended the Rabbi Isaac Elchanan Yeshiva, and in the spring of 1905 went as a Hebrew teacher to Scranton, Pennsylvania. Friends there urged him to enroll in American high school so that he could attend an American college. Wolfson entered Harvard in 1908, received the A.B. (1911), the A.M. (1912), and after two years in Europe on a Sheldon Traveling Fellowship, the Ph.D. (1915). Except for four months on limited service during World War I, the rest of his career was spent as a member of the Harvard faculty, first as annual instructor (1915), then as assistant professor, and from 1925 as Nathan Littauer Professor of Hebrew Language and Literature. He retired in 1958 but remained active as a scholar until shortly before his death in Cambridge, Massachusetts.

Harry Wolfson's undergraduate honors thesis was "Maimonides and Halevi: A Study in Typical Attitudes towards Greek Philosophy in the Middle Ages," a first attempt to treat Jewish philosophy as part of the western philosophic tradition. A study of medieval manuscripts for his dissertation on the fourteenth-century philosopher Hasdai Crescas made clear to him that the medievals were no mere compilers of ancient treatises but quoted the ancients in the course of commenting on and correcting their conclusions. Wolfson came thereby to understand that the medievals built philosophical systems that were continuous with the old. The first fruit of this insight was *Crescas' Critique of Aristotle: Problems of Aristotle's Physics in Jewish and Arabic Philosophy*. Because of the high cost of setting type in Greek, Hebrew, and Arabic, it remained in manuscript, stored in Wolfson's only fireproof cabinet, his refrigerator, until Lucius Littauer funded its publication in 1929.

With time on his hands following his demobilization from the U.S. Army in January 1919, Wolfson began writing about Spinoza, the seventeenth-century Dutch philosopher. Although Spinoza was regularly identified as an apostate Jew, his Jewishness was taken nonetheless as a mark of Jewish participation in the Enlightenment, thus of the potential modernity of the Jewish people as a whole. Wolfson's first efforts were directed at Spinoza's use of particular terms—the technique he had employed to understand the philosophy of Crescas. In the process he began to recognize that Spinoza, allegedly one of the facilitators of modern methods in philosophy, was in fact doing the same old business of commenting on texts and that Spinoza, allegedly the apostate, knew those texts exclusively from Jewish sources. Already by 1921, his working title for the project was "Spinoza, the Last of the Medievals: A Study of the *Ethica Ordine Geometrico Demonstrata* in the Light of a Hypothetically Constructed *Ethica More Scholastico Rabbinicoque Demonstrata*," but he published it as *The Philosophy of Spinoza: Unfolding the Latent Processes of His Reasoning* (1934). At least one reviewer complained with modernist possessiveness that Wolfson had tried to make a rabbi of Spinoza.

During this period Wolfson began to say that philosophy was a set of terms and a set of problems and the task of the historian was to examine the impact of terms on philosophical systems and the ways in which old terms were modified to fit new contexts; that philosophy through the seventeenth century was a dialogue engaged in by professionals who paid due respect to what their predecessors had said and meant (in contrast to contemporary philosophy, in which anyone could say anything and mean anything by it); and that it was a single dialogue carried on in four languages (Latin, Greek, Hebrew, Arabic) and from the perspective of three traditions (Christian, Jewish, Muslim). These were unacceptable observations during the mid-twentieth century, when the idea of a western intellectual tradition with no Jewish or Muslim participants, and no patterns of discontinuity, was dominant, both in the academy and out. As a result, Wolfson's detailed elucidations of the history of problems and of terms yielded his reputation as a "scholar's scholar," someone to be cited but not heard. His demonstration that ideas had histories (that is, that they underwent change) was ignored in favor of a "history of ideas" as the history of real things that recurred in the philosophy of every age, resulting in an unbroken tradition from Plato.

In the 1930s Wolfson outlined a series of volumes under the general title Structure and Growth of Philosophic Systems from Plato to Spinoza, but by the 1940s he began to focus more precisely on what happened when "philosophy" based on "logic" met "religion" based on "scriptural presuppositions" that were the axioms and postulates behind which reason could not look. This problem absorbed him for the remainder of his life and yielded magisterial studies of the philosophical bases of Jewish, Christian, and Muslim theology: *Philo: Foundations of Religious Philosophy in Judaism, Christianity, and Islam* (1947); *The Philosophy of the Church Fathers*, vol. 1, *Faith, Trinity, Incarnation* (1956); *The Philosophy of the Kalam* (1976); and *Repercussions of the Kalam in Jewish Philosophy* (1979). Sections of the originally projected volumes were published in journals or *festschriften* and are reprinted (as are all of his articles) in *Studies in the History of Philosophy and Religion*, edited by Isadore Twersky and George H. Williams (2 vols., 1973 and 1977). In addition, Wolfson published *Religious Philosophy: A Group of Essays* (1961) and was general editor of the "Corpus Averrois" project of the Medieval Academy of America. He left unpublished a critical edition of the text of Crescas's *Or Adonai*, based on his dissertation research, and the draft of the second volume of *The Philosophy of the Church Fathers*.

Through the Intercollegiate Menorah Association and its *Menorah Journal*, Wolfson participated actively in the early twentieth-century debate over the nature and future of Jewish culture in the United States. From 1915, moreover, he became in his own person an emblem of the possibility of integrating Jewish culture and Jewish learning into the secular universities, thereby into modern American culture more generally. His relative isolation at Harvard and in the profession, despite a growing scholarly and public reputation (he was featured on the cover of *Life* magazine as a symbol of the triumphant American scholarship of the 1950s), suggests that during his lifetime at least, Jewish culture and Jewish learning could be integrated into the secular universities most easily one person at a time.

• Wolfson's papers are in the Harvard University Archives. Additional material is in the Department of Archives and Rare Books, University of Iowa Library. A bibliography of Wolfson's writings through 1963, prepared by Leo W. Schwarz, is in American Academy for Jewish Research, *Harry Austryn Wolfson Jubilee Volume* (1965). Schwarz is the author of the only book-length biography, *Wolfson of Harvard: Portrait of a Scholar* (1978), which quotes extensively from Wolfson's work. Also of interest are Lewis S. Feuer, "Recollections of Harry Austryn Wolfson," *American Jewish Archives* 28 (Apr. 1976): 25–50; Isadore Twersky, "Harry Austryn Wolfson (1887–1974)," *American Jewish Yearbook* 76 (1976): 99–111; and two brief tributes by George Huntson Williams, "Harry Austryn Wolfson (1887–1974)," *Year Book of the American Philosophical Society* (1975), and "Harry Austryn Wolfson (1887–1974): At Home and Yet Homeless at Harvard," in *Profiles from the Beloved Community*, ed. Peter J. Gomes (1975). The mythic Wolfson appears most concisely in Israel Shenker, "Harvard's Resident Sage Marks 85th Birthday Today," *New York Times*, 2 Nov. 1972, and his obituary of Wolfson, *New York Times*, 21 Sept. 1974.

HENRY D. SHAPIRO

WOLFSON, Theresa (19 July 1897–14 May 1972), labor economist and educator, was born in Brooklyn, New York, the daughter of Adolph Wolfson and Rebecca Hochstein, both Russian immigrants who took in boarders to support their five-member family. Perhaps influenced by the radical political beliefs of her parents, Wolfson, after graduating from Eastern District High School, helped to establish a chapter of the Intercollegiate Socialist Society (precursor to the League for Industrial Democracy) while an undergraduate at Adelphi College, where she began her lifelong study of women, work, industry, and the economy.

Wolfson graduated from Adelphi with an A.B. in 1917 and then became employed by the Meinhardt Settlement House in New York City as a health worker. In 1918 she took a job as field agent and investigator for the National Child Labor Committee, which she held until the summer of 1920. During that time she met Iago Galdston, a medical student who eventually was hired by the International Ladies' Garment Workers' Union (ILGWU) to work at its Union Health Center, an organization with which Wolfson later was affiliated. Wolfson and Galdston were married soon after her departure from the National Child Labor Committee. She then entered Columbia University, where she studied economics and earned an M.A. in 1923.

While at Columbia, Wolfson became increasingly interested in studying the problems experienced by working women. In the years 1920 to 1922, through the New York Consumers' League, she promoted minimum wage legislation and the eight-hour day for women. Also during this period she investigated the working conditions of women in the ladies' garment industry for its Joint Board of Factory Control and later used the data she compiled to complete her master's thesis. Investigating working conditions and campaigning for protective legislation for women convinced Wolfson that organizing in a union was the best way for women to improve their situations. Acting on her convictions, she went to work for the Union Health Center of the ILGWU in 1925. Once in place as education director, however, Wolfson realized that very few women held leadership positions at the ILGWU, and her study of this phenomenon became the basis of her Ph.D. dissertation in economics (Brookings Institution, 1926).

Inspiring at least a generation of historians, Wolfson's dissertation, published as *The Woman Worker and the Trade Unions* (1926), broached new and perplexing questions about women and work:

> Has the trade union adjusted itself to meet the need of women workers? Have women workers, despite their traditional handicaps, adjusted themselves to fit into the trade union? . . . Can we make the trade union movement appreciate the importance of treating women members as workers, and considering their interests as identical with those of men? . . . Can we bridge that transition period from the point where women do one thing and are thought to be doing another, to the point where women work and have a recognized place which brings with it not only an increased pay envelope, but an assured economic position as well? (p. 25)

Wolfson contended that these questions could be answered only by examining what she called the psychology of women and the psychology of trade unions. The psychology of women, Wolfson said, was rooted in the mix of "tradition, environment, and race concepts" (p. 23) that had shaped the limited role of women in the labor force. Wolfson argued further that the customs, rituals, and traditions associated with unions had been created by working men and thus originated in the needs of men. It was the coalescence of the psychology of women and the structure of unions, Wolfson wrote, that kept women in low-paid, undervalued, nonunionized jobs.

Wolfson devoted her career to studying the economy, wage-earning women, and trade unionism in a lifelong effort to strengthen the labor movement and, as a result, benefit the lives of workers. She taught from 1928 at the Bryn Mawr Summer School for Women Workers, organized in 1921, which provided a forum for women workers and educators to share their knowledge of industry. Also in 1928 she began her more than forty-year career as professor of economics and labor relations at the Brooklyn branch of Hunter College (later Brooklyn College). Wolfson also taught office workers, running summer schools for white collar workers in the 1930s and 1940s. In 1935 she and Galdston, with whom she had had two children, were divorced, and three years later she married Brooklyn College colleague Austin Bigelow Wood, a professor of psychology.

As a member of the public panel of the War Labor Board from 1942 to 1945, Wolfson put her knowledge to practical use as increasing numbers of women worked at well-paid unionized jobs that had been vacated by men fighting in World War II. In 1943 she advocated that these women, referred to collectively as "Rosie the Riveter," be allowed to retain their positions after the men came home, thereby anticipating the postwar dilemma faced by employers and women. Following the war Wolfson took an important position with the American Arbitration Association, an organization concerned with resolving labor-management disputes. For her work with the association, Wolfson received the John Dewey Award of the League for Industrial Democracy in 1957.

Wolfson retired from Brooklyn College in 1967 but continued to teach at Sarah Lawrence College. She died in Brooklyn. Wolfson's important work as a teacher of labor relations and economics and as the author of various books and articles on these subjects offered her students as well as succeeding generations a better understanding of the economy, of union strategies for attaining economic security for workers, and of women's roles in unions and the economy generally.

• Wolfson's papers are held by the New York State School of Industrial and Labor Relations, Cornell University, Labor-Management Documentation Center, Martin P. Catherwood Library. Wolfson coauthored *Labor and the N.R.A.*, with Lois MacDonald and Gladys Louise Palmer (1934), *Frances Wright, Free Enquirer: The Study of a Temperament*, with Alice J. G. Perkins (1939), and *Industrial Unionism in the American Labor Movement*, with Abraham Weiss (1937). Among her published articles are "Where Are the Organized Women Workers?" *American Federationist*, June 1925, pp. 455–57; "Trade Union Activities of Women," American Academy of Political and Social Science, *Annals* 143 (May 1929): 120–31; "Industrial Unions in the American Labor Movement," *New Frontiers*, Feb. 1937, pp. 3–52; and, with Weiss, "Should White Collar Workers Organize?" *Independent Woman*, Nov. 1936, p. 356. An obituary is in the *New York Times*, 15 May 1972.

LISA W. PHILLIPS

WOLHEIM, Louis Robert (28 Mar. 1881–18 Feb. 1931), actor, was born in New York City, the son of Elias Wolheim, an unskilled laborer; his mother's name is not known. The family was poor, but Wolheim learned several languages while growing up. After graduating from City College of New York (1903), he earned a degree in mechanical engineering from Cornell (1906). He also had his nose broken three times while playing football for Cornell, badly disfiguring his face. He became known in Cornell as a heavy drinker, brawler, and glib spinner of stories about his adventurous youth.

After a brief period with an engineering firm in New York, Wolheim returned to Cornell to work toward a Ph.D. Meanwhile, he taught mathematics at Cornell Preparatory School, tutored college undergraduates in mathematics and physics, and clerked at the cigar counter of the Ithaca Hotel. The hotel was his hangout, and he is said to have tutored his undergraduates in its bar. In 1910 he left to do engineering work for an American firm in Mexico, but when revolution broke out there in 1912, he returned to Ithaca to work again as tutor and cigar clerk. In later years he concocted tall tales about his adventures in revolutionary Mexico.

About that time the independent filmmakers Theodore Wharton and Leopold Wharton began using the surroundings of Ithaca as settings for their films. Wolheim picked up extra money as an extra and bit player. Thus he met Lionel Barrymore, who had come to play the villain in a Wharton serial. The two became cronies and drinking partners. Barrymore soon realized that behind Wolheim's thuggish face was an intelligent man, and he persuaded Wolheim to leave his aimless life in Ithaca to go into film and stage work, saying, "Anyone with a mug like yours should use it. It would be your fortune" (*New York Herald Tribune*, 19 Feb. 1931). Wolheim moved to New York, viewed plays, and took voice and acting lessons. For several years Barrymore obtained bit parts in films for him and used him as an assistant director on one film.

Wolheim first acted on the stage as a minor villain in a play starring John Barrymore and Lionel Barrymore, *The Jest* (1919). Lionel Barrymore later recalled in his autobiography that Wolheim "took part in a battle in the third act, and made me look so good by losing that I won much more applause than I deserved." Wolheim went on to other small stage roles, such as a Mexican bandit chief in *The Broken Wing* (1920). He continued to take small movie parts, showing increasing stage presence. In D. W. Griffith's *Orphans of the Storm* (1921), he made a memorable brief appearance as the half-naked executioner. Two other small but telling film roles were with John Barrymore, in *Dr. Jekyll and Mr. Hyde* (1920) and *Sherlock Holmes* (1922). In 1921 he helped to adapt two plays, *The Claw* from a French original, and *The Idle Inn* from Yiddish.

Wolheim's breakthrough to prominence as an actor came when Eugene O'Neill chose him to play the lead in *The Hairy Ape* (1922). He portrayed a brutish stoker, Yank Smith, who goes berserk and is killed after an experience with a young society woman causes him to doubt his place in humanity. Reviews of the play were divided, but Wolheim's performance was unanimously praised. An interview in *Theatre* (Aug. 1922) showed both his acceptance of his ugliness and his buried intellect: "I have no illusions whatever about my face and form." He said he was content with meaty character roles, for "I believe the strong and ugly face, and the powerful physique—the Man of Iron type—is coming in to his own. I believe that we are going to have more plays with real power to them, and real ideas, and it necessarily follows that virile plays will call for virile types."

Wolheim was even more of a success in just such a virile play, *What Price Glory?*, in 1924. In this disillusioned look at soldiers in World War I, he portrayed the brawling, cynical, joking Captain Flagg. The *New York Times* reviewer said he acted "with a security and variety that I have never seen this actor achieve before, as well as with intelligence and a kind of husky wit" (6 Sept. 1924). Along with his two stage successes, he married the actress and sculptor Ethel Dane in 1923. The couple did not have any children.

Wolheim found that work on the stage was uncertain for him, despite praise for his acting, because he was hard to cast as anything but a menace, and those parts were not leads. Work was more plentiful for him in the movie studios. Continuing to make films during the runs of his plays, he quickly became a leading screen actor in thug roles. By 1924, the *New York Times* movie review of *The Story without a Name* (6 Oct.) reported, "Mr. Wolheim is as usual the acme of villainy" as a run-running pirate. He joked to one interviewer that he was identified with "genteel parts [such as] stokers, ship captains, roustabouts, and gang leaders" (*Theatre*, Jan. 1926). He also did well in a few movie roles with a comic dimension, such as *Two Arabian Knights* (1927). By the late 1920s Wolheim had moved permanently to Hollywood, where he found higher pay, regular hours, and a better climate.

Wolheim easily made the transition to talking pictures. The pinnacle of his screen career came in *All Quiet on the Western Front* (1930), in which he appeared as the brutally funny and tender German army veteran, Katczinsky, who shepherds his recruits through four years of World War I battles, only to die of a random bullet from an airplane while being carried to a hospital. Jack Spears described Wolheim's performance as "beautifully low-key . . . a disciplined one, shaded with the right proportions of sentiment, humor, irony, and buried bitterness, all of which were projected on his unique face" (*Films in Review*, Mar. 1972).

At the end of 1930 Wolheim was cast as the tough editor Walter Burns in a screen version of *The Front Page*. Preparing for the role, he dieted punishingly and lost twenty-five pounds in one month. He became seriously ill during production and had to leave the film after collapsing on the set. He was kept in the hospital for two weeks, then underwent an exploratory operation for appendicitis. The surgeons discovered cancer of the stomach. Weakened by the operation, he sank into a coma and died.

Though known as a carouser in his younger days, Wolheim lived quietly with his wife in Hollywood, enjoying the company of friends, shunning social life and publicity. In private life he was nothing like his hard-boiled screen image, but he could switch from dignified academic speech into underworld jargon, and though ordinarily soft-spoken he was reputed to have a caustic wit. He may have been less accepting of his lucrative ugliness than he claimed: he attempted to have his nose remodeled by plastic surgery in 1927, only to be stopped by a studio injunction. His place in film history is ensured by his classic performance in *All Quiet on the Western Front*.

• Materials on the life and career of Wolheim are in the Billy Rose Theatre Collection at the New York Public Library for the Performing Arts, Lincoln Center. A survey of his movie career is Jack Spears, "Louis Wolheim," *Films in Review*, Mar. 1972, pp. 158–76, including portrait and production stills. For information on his stage career, views, and personality, see two *Theatre* articles: Carol Bird, "Enter the Monkey Man," Aug. 1922, pp. 102, 120; and "Mirrors of Stageland," Jan. 1926, p. 12. Anecdotes of his Ithaca years are in Lionel Barrymore, *We Barrymores* (1951). Obituaries are in the *New York Times* and *New York Herald Tribune*, both 19 Feb. 1931.

WILLIAM STEPHENSON

WOLL, Matthew (25 Jan. 1880–1 June 1956), labor leader, was born in Luxembourg, the son of Michael Woll, the owner and operator of an iron foundry, and Janette Schwartz. The family immigrated to the United States in 1891, settling on the South Side of Chicago. Woll was educated at local public schools until he was fifteen and then was apprenticed to a photoengraver. In 1899 he married Irene C. Kerwin; they had two children. He attended the Kent College of Law, Lake Forest University, at night from 1901 to 1904. Although he graduated and was admitted to the bar, he never practiced because by then he had become active in the Chicago local of the International Photo-Engravers Union of North America (IPEU). When he attended his first IPEU convention in 1906 he was immediately elected general president, an office he held until 1929.

Woll soon formed a close association with Samuel Gompers, head of the American Federation of Labor (AFL), which helped him win growing influence within the labor movement. He joined the AFL delegation to the British Trades Union Congress in 1915 and 1916, directed the American Alliance for Labor and

Democracy organized by Gompers in 1917 to promote the entry of the United States into World War I, served on the War Labor Board during the war, and functioned as Gompers's assistant on the wartime Council of National Defense. He drafted the AFL's postwar program in 1918 and became the eighth vice president of the AFL (and therefore a member of the executive council) in 1919. He also headed the AFL Union Label and Service Trades Department for many years. In 1923 Gompers appointed Woll head of a committee to review the union's arrangements for members' death benefits. Woll's report led to the founding of the Union Labor Life Insurance Company in 1925, which gradually expanded to include casualty and health coverage and became one of the nation's most successful insurance firms. Woll served as president until 1955 and then was general executive chairman until he died. Although the firm was accused by some of pressuring employers and labor lawyers to enroll, it also served many union members and by 1955 claimed nearly 500,000 subscribers.

When Gompers died in 1924 many expected the AFL presidency to go to Woll, who had long been known as "the crown prince." But John L. Lewis, head of the largest AFL union, had not forgiven Woll for helping Gompers defeat him for president in 1921. Too controversial to win the office himself, Lewis forced through the election of his subordinate, William Green. Despite his defeat, Woll remained a loyal AFL officer, so active that in 1929 he gave up the presidency of the IPEU and became the first vice president of the AFL, he held this office the rest of his life, along with the editorship of the union journal *American Photo-Engraver*. At President Green's request he worked zealously to eradicate Communist influence within the AFL. Woll himself was passionately anticommunist. Indeed, he tended to attribute any criticism of established policies to left-wing influence; for instance, he resolutely insisted that the AFL had no power to control its member unions and dismissed investigations of even the most flagrant corruption as "communistic." He also opposed many liberal programs, like the labor policies of the New Deal.

Woll's anticommunism helped intensify his role in the 1935 split of the AFL and the Congress of Industrial Organizations (CIO), since he distrusted the strong left-wing influence in the CIO. In addition, Woll favored traditional craft unionism over the CIO's industrywide approach to organizing. Despite his outspoken opposition to the insurgents in 1933–1935, Woll acted as something of a mediator in the periodic efforts to heal the split after it occurred; observers differ about how neutral he really was, but there is no question that he was genuinely troubled to see this division in the labor movement.

As war clouds gathered during the 1930s, Woll helped to organize a committee to boycott German goods. He also represented the AFL at the International Federation of Trade Unions in 1937 and the International Labor Organization conference in 1938; although he was interested in world labor issues, his particular mission at these gatherings was to minimize participation by either the CIO or the Soviet Union. In 1943 Woll became chair of the AFL's new standing committee on foreign affairs, and a year later he was named president of the Free Trade Union Committee (FTUC), which was organized by the AFL as a counter to the other major international labor organization, the World Federation of Trade Unions, in which Communists played an important role. Under FTUC influence, trade union organizations from most democratic countries withdrew from the World Federation and founded a separate organization, the International Confederation of Trade Unions, in 1949.

Woll's first wife died in 1945; he later married Celenor Dugas; they had no children. During the postwar years Woll followed international labor affairs closely. He vigorously advocated the restoration of a democratic Germany to full international status; in 1953 he was granted the German Order of Merit. Although a devout Catholic and lifelong member of the Knights of Columbus, he urged the Vatican to discourage separate Catholic labor unions. He also remained active on scores of civic, charitable, and labor boards. Unpredictably, given his political history, he supported President Harry Truman's effort to pass national health insurance. In 1955 he participated in the negotiations that finally reunited the AFL and CIO, becoming one of the eight members of the new executive committee and also an AFL-CIO vice president. He died in New York City.

Woll's wing collars and frock coats as well as his elaborate style of oratory evoked a vanished era, yet he was a quick-witted and able organization man who managed to maintain a position in the forefront of the American labor movement for most of his adult life. His opponent Lewis dismissed him as "an insurance agent who used his position . . . to promote his insurance business," but both Woll's talents and his interests were considerably broader. Although the scope of his contribution was limited by his fierce devotion to the principles of craft unionism, affiliate autonomy, and anticommunism, these were principles shared by many of his contemporaries, and for them he proved an articulate and dedicated spokesman for more than half a century.

• Woll's correspondence can be found in the William English Walling Collection at the State Historical Society of Wisconsin; the office records of the CIO, 1950–1956, and the Selma Borchardt Collection, both at Wayne State University in Detroit, Mich.; and the American Labor Conference on International Affairs Collection at the Tamiment Institute Library at New York University. Woll wrote *Labor, Industry and Government* (1935), and, with William English Walling, *Our Next Step—A National Economic Policy* (1935). A biographical sketch appears in Gary Fink, ed., *Biographical Dictionary of American Labor Leaders* (1974). See also Charles A. Madison, *American Labor Leaders* (1950); Bruce Minton and John Stuart, *Men Who Lead Labor* (1937); Marc Karson, *American Labor Unions and Politics, 1900–1918* (1958); Bernard Mandel, *Samuel Gompers: A Biography* (1963); Edward Levinson, *Labor on the March* (1938); Walter Galenson, *The CIO Challenge to the AFL: A History of the American Labor Movement, 1935–1941* (1960); and Melvyn Dubofsky and Warren Van Tine, *John L. Lewis: A Biography* (1986). An obituary is in the *New York Times*, 2 June 1956.

SANDRA OPDYCKE

WOLLSTEIN, Martha (21 Nov. 1868–30 Sept. 1939), pediatric pathologist, was born in New York City, the daughter of Louis Wollstein and Minna Cohn, German-born Jews. She entered the Woman's Medical College of New York Infirmary in 1886 and received her medical degree in 1889. Drs. Elizabeth and Emily Blackwell had founded the school in the 1860s to give women medical training of superior quality. In 1899 the Woman's Medical College became part of Cornell University Medical School but continued to accept women students.

Wollstein interned at the Babies Hospital in New York City in 1890 and two years later was appointed its pathologist. Initially she studied malaria, tuberculosis, and typhoid fever. Early in her career, there were no facilities available for Wollstein to pursue her interests in experimental pathology. After Christian Herter, a pioneer in biological chemistry, personally financed the construction of a pathology laboratory at the Babies Hospital in 1896, however, Wollstein made a major contribution to pediatric pathology in her diagnoses of infant diarrhea in 1903. Physicians had attributed this condition to poor feeding practices until 1902 when Charles Duval, a pathologist at Tulane University Medical School, discovered Shiga bacilli in the stools of some infants with diarrhea. He also related infant diarrhea to a concomitant outbreak of adult dysentery. Wollstein added to Duval's work when she discovered a related dysentery bacillus in the stools of thirty-seven infants suffering from diarrhea. Simon Flexner, a distinguished pathologist, had isolated this bacillus when he studied dysentery in the Philippines. Wollstein's work attracted his attention, and in 1904 her expanded study was published by the Rockefeller Institute. Wollstein joined the Rockefeller Institute as an assistant in 1906 while continuing to work at the Babies Hospital.

At the Rockefeller Institute, Wollstein worked closely with Flexner, and in 1907 they undertook the first experimental analysis in the United States of polio. They attempted to infect monkeys with polio using the cerebrospinal fluid from human polio sufferers. Although their experiments were unsuccessful, they contributed to later, more successful research by Flexner and others on the pathology of polio in humans and monkeys.

Despite the failed polio experiments, Wollstein went on to achieve notable success in other research areas, especially in meningitis research. World War I induced outbreaks of cerebrospinal meningitis in army camps, which stimulated new research on serum therapy. Flexner had developed a serum for the disease as early as 1907, but treatment presented many difficulties. In 1918 Wollstein and her colleague, Harold Amoss, also an early collaborator of Flexner's on polio, developed a new method that allowed rapid preparation of a potent antimeningitis serum. Wollstein and Amoss also created a standardized protocol for serum preparation.

Although Wollstein was never elected to membership at the Rockefeller Institute, she was a diligent, careful worker and an imaginative, creative researcher. Although it was fairly easy for women to be appointed to the institute, few women advanced far in rank or achieved recognition at the institute. In fact, during its first fifty years, the institute gave full membership to only one woman, Florence Sabin, who is best known for her study of blood cells and lymphatics.

In 1921 Wollstein returned to the Babies Hospital and devoted the rest of her working career to pediatric pathology. Her work focused on congenital anomalies, childhood leukemia, hemolytic jaundice, tuberculosis, and influenza-induced meningitis. Her forty-three years of careful pathologic studies helped a significant number of physicians who trained at the Babies Hospital to make accurate diagnoses. In 1928 she was appointed head of the pediatric section of the New York Academy of Medicine and in 1930 became the first woman member of the American Pediatric Society. Wollstein was accepted by this group probably because pediatrics was considered a more appropriate field for women than was pathology, dealing as it does with cancer, tumors, and dead bodies.

Wollstein appeared to form no close bonds with either sex. Some considered her difficult to work with, and she had few known close friends. She retired in 1935 and moved to Grand Rapids, Michigan. She returned to New York in 1939 as a patient at Mount Sinai Hospital, where she died.

Wollstein's appreciation of the revolution in medical education that allowed her to earn a medical degree is evident in "The History of Women in Medicine," which she published in the *Woman's Medical Journal* in 1908. She published eighty scientific papers, and although she made distinguished contributions to pediatric pathology, only a handful of colleagues attended her funeral, and obituary notices were brief. A distinguished researcher, she was, sadly, little recognized by her colleagues.

• Wollstein's many scientific papers include, with Harold L. Amoss, "A Method for the Rapid Preparation of Antimeningitis Serum," *Journal of Experimental Medicine* (1 Mar. 1916); with Ralph C. Spence, "A Study of Tuberculosis in Infants and Young Children," *American Journal of Diseases of Children* (Jan. 1921); with F. H. Bartlett, "Brain Tumors in Young Children," *American Journal of Diseases of Children* (Apr. 1923); and "Studies on the Phenomenon of d'Herelle with Bacillus Dysenteriae," *Journal of Experimental Medicine* (1 Nov. 1921). Sources that are informative on Wollstein's contributions include Kate Campbell Hurd-Mead, *A Short History of the Pioneer Medical Women of America and a Few of Their Colleagues in England* (1933); Rustin McIntosh and Harold Faber, *History of the American Pediatric Society 1887–1965* (1966); and George W. Corner, *A History of the Rockefeller Institute, 1901–1953: Origins and Growth* (1964). See also the entry in Martin Kaufman et al., eds., *The Dictionary of American Medical Biography*, vol. 2 (1984). Obituaries are in the *New York Times*, 1 Oct. 1939, and in the *Journal of the American Medical Association* 113, no. 23 (2 Dec. 1939): 2075.

H. CLAIRE JACKSON

WOLMAN, Abel (10 June 1892–22 Feb. 1989), sanitary engineer, was born in Baltimore, Maryland, the son of Morris Wolman, a clothing manufacturer, and Rose Wachsman. He was raised in East Baltimore and attended public schools there. He then entered Johns Hopkins University, where he enjoyed debating, took the premedical course, and received his B.A. in 1913. While an undergraduate, in 1912 he collected water samples for the U.S. Public Health Service in the first thorough pollution survey of the metropolitan Potomac River. An older brother was a doctor, and the parents considered one doctor in the family enough, so they persuaded Wolman to take advantage of scholarship funds and enter the new engineering school at Johns Hopkins. As one of four students in the first graduating class, he received the degree of bachelor of science and engineering in 1915. While at the engineering school, he directed the construction of a sewage disposal plant at Springfield, Maryland.

From a college course in bacteriology, Wolman became interested in the safety of drinking water. With chemist Linn H. Enslow of the Maryland Department of Health, he developed a method of adding measured amounts of chlorine into drinking-water supplies at the filtration plants. Although chlorine and other substances toxic to disease organisms had been used in drinking water earlier, the amount used was inconsistent, so that the water was sometimes not adequately disinfected and at other times had an objectionable odor and taste. Wolman and Enslow based their measuring technique on bacteriological and other qualities of the water source ("Chlorine Absorption and Chlorination of Water," *Journal of Industrial and Engineering Chemistry* 11 [1919]: 206–13). Their procedure came into use in almost all U.S. cities and later in many other countries. It is credited with bringing about great reduction in deaths from cholera, dysentery, and typhoid fever.

In 1915 Wolman became assistant engineer for the Maryland Department of Health, advancing to chief engineer in 1922. In that position he helped to coordinate state projects in sanitary engineering, public works, and wildlife conservation. He edited *Manual of Water Works Practice* (1925) and *Solving Sewage Problems* (1926), for which he also wrote several chapters. With Arthur E. Gorman he wrote *The Significance of Waterborne Typhoid Fever Outbreaks* (1931). Also in 1931 he participated in developing the reservoir system for the city of Baltimore. While working for the Maryland department, he was a lecturer in sanitary engineering at the Johns Hopkins School of Hygiene and Public Health (1921–1927 and 1936–1937); he taught or lectured at other colleges at various times.

In 1937 Johns Hopkins University invited Wolman to become professor and chairman of sanitary engineering in both the Department of Civil Engineering and the School of Hygiene and Public Health. He accepted, while retaining his position with the Maryland Department of Health for two more years.

Wolman's primary concern was in public health issues. He devoted special attention to programs close to home, including agencies of the city and county of Baltimore and the Federal Emergency Administration of Public Works for Maryland and Delaware. In a broader framework, he was a consultant or adviser to the U.S. Public Health Service, the American Public Health Association, the Tennessee Valley Authority, the National Resources Planning Board, the Surgeon General of the U.S. Army, other military offices, the Atomic Energy Commission, the National Science Foundation, the U.S. Geological Survey, the Panel on Water Resources of the U.S. State Department, the United Nations (for water resources), the World Health Organization, and more.

During the 1930s Wolman led a movement for interstate groups to address regional problems of water resources. He advocated using the Potomac River as a national model for cleaning up pollution. As chairman of the Special Committee on Water Pollution of the Natural Resources Board of the Interior Department in 1938, he wrote a report on problems of pollution and suggested solutions. This led to the founding of the Interstate Commission on the Potomac River Basin in 1940, to which Wolman was promptly appointed by President Franklin D. Roosevelt. Wolman felt that this job was never completed owing to lack of the funds requested from Congress (*Potomac Basin Reporter*, 45 [1989]: 2). When New York City had water shortages in 1951 and 1965, Wolman, as a consultant, proposed that purified water from the Hudson River be used, and the city agreed. The success of this earned him the sobriquet "friend of the thirsty" from the *New York Times*. Through the years, he advised more than fifty nations on water treatment and on waste disposal.

After reaching emeritus status at Johns Hopkins in 1962, Wolman continued his extensive consulting and advisory service. He was elected to the National Academy of Sciences (1963) and the National Academy of Engineering (1965). He published about three hundred papers; a selection of them, edited by Gilbert F. White, was published as *Water, Health and Society* (1969).

For his contributions to safety in drinking water and public health, Wolman received many honors, including the Albert Lasker Special Award of the American Public Health Association (1960), the National Medal of Science (1975), the Tyler Ecology Award (1976), the Ben Gurion Award of Israel (1976), and the medal "Health for All by 2000" of the World Health Organization (1984). He was the first recipient of the Abel Wolman Award of Excellence of the American Water Works Association (1984). He was especially gratified by the renaming of the public works office building in Baltimore as the Wolman Municipal Building (1986).

In addition to his significant contributions to drinking-water safety, Wolman strongly advocated a national policy on water resources. In his later years he recommended that industry be required to remove the pollutants from its waste water. His firm belief was that no one should be exposed to health hazards by using water. He died in Baltimore, Maryland.

• Wolman's extensive archival records are in the Manuscripts and Special Collections of the Milton S. Eisenhower Library, Johns Hopkins University. An oral history elicited by Walter Hollander, Jr., was published as *Abel Wolman: His Life and Philosophy* (2 vols., 1981). Anonymous biographies are in *Johns Hopkins Gazette*, 28 Feb. 1989, p. 1, 3; *Potomac Basin Reporter*, Mar. 1989, pp. 1–2; and *Johns Hopkins Magazine*, Apr. 1989, p. 37. An obituary is in the *New York Times*, 24 Feb. 1989.

ELIZABETH NOBLE SHOR

WOLMAN, Leo (24 Feb. 1890–2 Oct. 1961), labor economist, was born in Baltimore, Maryland, the son of Morris Wolman, a contract tailor, and Rosa Yetta Wachsman, Jewish émigrés from Poland (then part of Russia). Leo had three brothers and two sisters, and, despite becoming poor in their teens, the Wolman children nevertheless went on to exemplify the adage of America as a land of opportunity. Leo became an internationally recognized expert on unionism and the labor market; Abel, a world renowned sanitary engineer; Samuel, a distinguished professor of medicine; and Morton, an insurance executive. In three years at Johns Hopkins University, Leo Wolman earned a B.A. in chemistry and was elected to Phi Beta Kappa (1911), and received a Ph.D. in economics (1914). In completing his Ph.D., he became trained in statistics, knowledge that would advance his work in government and applied research. As he pointed out in 1917, "Recognition is at last, if grudgingly, being given to the fact that discussions of the economic forces and tendencies are of great or little value in proportion as there exists some numerical measure of the strength or extent of these forces."

After completion of his academic work, Wolman taught at Johns Hopkins, Hobart College, the University of Michigan, Harvard University, and the New School for Social Research. Intermixed were appointments to the U.S. Industrial Relations Commission, for which he did the first study on the extent of unionism in the United States. During World War I, he served on the Council of National Defense and later became chief of production statistics of the War Industries Board. At the end of the war, he was appointed to the American Peace Mission in Paris. After returning to the United States, he joined the faculty of the recently established New School for Social Research and in 1920 became the director of research for the Amalgamated Clothing Workers Union, developing data and statistical and other information to undergird the union's proposals in collective bargaining. He was the first professional economist to serve a union. Shortly afterward, he joined the National Bureau of Economic Research, where he conducted research on labor for the rest of his life; he also served for some years as its director of research. He continued his work on labor at the bureau until illness incapacitated him in around 1959.

In 1927 prominent Zionist and anti-Zionist leaders jointly invited Wolman to be a member of the Joint Palestine Survey Commission. He reported on the state of industry and labor in the Mandate. (Palestine at that time was a British Mandate. Mandates were established by the League of Nations to govern a territory until it could become independent.) Wolman's report was important because it provided empirical support for the idea (and the Zionist ideal) that Jews could establish a modern community in Palestine. In 1930 he married Cecil Clark, daughter of Eugene B. Clark, founder and president of Clark Equipment; they had one child. In 1931, on the initiative of New York governor Franklin D. Roosevelt, Wolman was named chairman of the Interstate Commission on Unemployment Insurance. In that year, he left the Amalgamated to become professor of economics at Columbia University, where he remained until his retirement in 1958.

At the onset of the New Deal, Wolman was thrust into the conflict surrounding one of its major policies, the unionization of workers. In 1933 U.S. president Franklin D. Roosevelt appointed him chairman of the Labor Committee Advisory Board to the National Recovery Administration, and later a member of the tripartite National Labor Board (NLB). Until Senator Robert Wagner assumed the chairmanship of the NLB in 1933, Wolman was acting chairman. In 1934, at the insistence of President Roosevelt, Wolman accepted the chairmanship of the Automobile Labor Board. As chairman he faced the question of whether to grant exclusive representation to the union that won a majority vote. He decided to establish the principle of proportional representation. The unions strongly objected, demanding exclusive representation. When the National Labor Relations Act was passed in 1935, exclusive representation was adopted in the legislation, repudiating Wolman's position. His experiences at the Amalgamated and with government led Wolman to a turning point in his assessment of unionism and the role of public policy. His critique and analysis contributed to the 1947 (Taft-Hartley) reforms of the National Labor Relations Act of 1935. He explained that "because we call a movement a social movement, does it mean that we are prepared to see it converted into one great economic monopoly, and then say that, since we approve of this social objective, there is nothing we can do about the monopoly?" Specifically, Wolman attacked mass picketing, secondary boycotts, the closed shop, and other practices that he felt should not be tolerated just because they are "incident to a movement that may be otherwise socially desirable."

Wolman's research and teaching reflected his experience in government and unions. As a scholar who studied the union movement from both within and without, he observed the influence of the movement on public policy and, equally important, on the administration of labor laws, making him a rarity among labor economists. His former students and associates recognized Wolman for the unusual degree of realism and knowledge that he brought to the subject of labor. He contributed to establishing industrial relations as a subject worthy of major consideration in the academic world and in the world of affairs. At the National Bureau of Economic Research, colleagues at all levels found that his comments and advice influenced their thinking, analysis, and the presentation of their findings.

Wolman published two major books, *The Growth of American Trade Unions, 1880–1923* (1924) and *Ebb and Flow in Trade Unionism* (1936), and many shorter works on union membership. In addition, he published numerous articles on wages, hours, employment, and unemployment. He planned a final, comprehensive volume on unions, which, because of other interests and finally illness, he did not complete. Leo Troy finished the study, and the bureau published it in 1965.

Wolman served as a director or officer of many leading institutions, including the Amalgamated Bank, the Institute for Advanced Studies, the New School, the National Bureau of Economic Research, the Mutual Life Insurance Company, and the Clark Equipment Company. He also served as president of the American Association for Labor Legislation and the investment trust of the Amalgamated Clothing Workers Union, and vice president of the Academy of Political Science, and served as review editor for the journal of the American Statistical Association. He died in New York City.

As an accomplished pianist, Wolman had acquired a sensitivity that he demonstrated in his work. He was recognized widely as a labor economist unique in his breadth of view, and a scholar characterized by thoughtful judgments. Recounting Wolman's sincerity in scholarship, public policy, and public lecturing, John A. Krout, vice president of Columbia University, observed in his eulogy that "people who did not love the truth were never comfortable around Leo."

• Wolman's memoirs are recorded in the Columbia University Oral History Collection. His first book was *The Boycott in American Trade Unions* (1916). His most notable publications, produced at the National Bureau of Economic Research, include *Planning and Control of Public Works* (1930) and contributions to many other bureau books. Most significant was "Unemployment Insurance" in *Business Cycles and Unemployment* (1923). He also authored numerous bureau bulletins, primarily on the topics of wages and hours of work. Among Wolman's major articles in leading academic journals are "Collective Bargaining in the Glass Bottle Industry," *American Economic Review* 6, no. 3 (Sept. 1916); "The Theory of Production," *American Economic Review* 11, no. 1 (Mar. 1921); "The Turning Point in American Labor Policy," *Political Science Quarterly* 55, no. 2 (June 1940); and "The Area of Collective Bargaining," *Political Science Quarterly* 59, no. 4 (Dec. 1944). Papers presented to learned societies include "The Extent of Trade Unionism," *Annals of the American Academy of Political and Social Science* (Jan. 1917); "A Plan for State Labor Statistics," *Annals of the American Academy of Political Science* (May 1923); and "Wages and the Recovery of Business," *Proceedings of the Academy of Political Science* 14, no. 3 (June 1931). His service in government is represented in the *Final Report of the Automobile Labor Board*, with Nicholas Kelley and Richard L. Byrd, to the president of the United States, mimeo. (1935). An obituary is in the *New York Times*, 3 Oct. 1961.

LEO TROY

WONG, Anna May (3 Jan. 1907–3 Feb. 1961), actress, was born in Los Angeles, California, the daughter of Wong Om-tsing, a laundry operator, and Lee Gon Toy. She was given the name Liu Tsong ("Frosted Yellow Willow") by her mother. Wong received a public school education, devoting after-school hours to working in the family laundry and frequenting the local movie houses, where her aspirations for a screen acting career developed. Her first screen appearance was an unspectacular walk-on as one of a multitude of lantern-bearers in Alla Nazimova's *The Red Lantern* (1919). After several bit parts, she won national recognition in 1924 when she was cast as a slave girl in Douglas Fairbank's *The Thief of Bagdad*.

Wong presented a strikingly elegant image with high cheekbones, an ivory complexion, straight black bangs, and a haunting, remote gaze. But Hollywood's failure to promote racial minorities to true star status, plus the taboo against Asian/Caucasian union, relegated Wong to a series of supporting roles, while Caucasian actresses like Myrna Loy (*The Crimson City*, 1928), Luise Rainer (*The Good Earth*, 1937), and Dorothy Lamour (*Disputed Passage*, 1939) were made up for starring Oriental roles. Hollywood preferred to use Wong's talents as a coach and consultant, as Paramount Studio did in preparing Dorothy Lamour for her role in *Disputed Passage*.

Disillusioned with Hollywood's taboo against Asians in leading romantic roles—"There seems little for me in Hollywood," she said—Wong went in 1928 to Europe where she quickly became a celebrity both on-screen and off. During her three years abroad, she enjoyed star status, first in *Lied* (*Song*, 1928) in Germany, then in England, where she had her stage debut opposite Laurence Olivier in the London production of *The Circle of Chalk*. She also appeared in the film *Piccadilly* (1929), with Cyril Ritchard and Charles Laughton. She became fluent in both German and French; when *The Flame of Love* (1930) was being made with English, French, and German soundtracks, Wong was able to play her role as the head of a Russian dance company in all three languages. In Vienna she had a German-speaking role in the operetta *Springtime*, in which she also sang and danced. But her language fluency failed to broaden the stereotypical Asian roles for which she had become known.

Through the thirties, at the peak of her popularity, Wong was in demand for personal appearances as well as for stage and film roles on both sides of the Atlantic. In London she had an engagement at the exclusive Embassy Club and appeared in *A Study in Scarlet* (1933), *Tiger Bay* (1933), a new sound version of the stage and silent film favorite *Chu Chin Chow* (1934), and *Java Head* (1934). In 1936 she made her first trip to China, to visit her father's family.

In spite of the more favorable image of the Chinese in Hollywood films during World War II, Wong was limited to two undistinguished roles, in *Lady from Chungking* (1942) and *Bombs over Burma* (1942). Her film career by this time was virtually over. She made only three additional films: *Impact* (1949); *Portrait in Black*, which was billed as her comeback film in 1960; and *The Savage Innocents* (1961), in which she played a minor role. (It was not actually put into general release until after her death.)

In the 1950s Wong appeared in a number of television dramas, including a video version of W. Somerset Maugham's short story "The Letter" (1956) as part of "Producer's Showcase." Poor health and casting in secondary, sinister, or exotic television and film roles resulted in less frequent screen appearances. She never married, and she shared a home with her brother Richard in Santa Monica, where she died of a heart attack.

By the 1960s, Asian actresses like Nancy Kwan (*The World of Suzy Wong*, 1960), France Nuyen (*A Girl Named Tamiko*, 1962; *South Pacific*, 1958), and Miyoshi Umeki (*Sayonara*, 1957) were being accepted in starring roles. But three decades earlier, at the peak of her career, a reviewer for the *New York Times* (23 May 1937) wrote, "Madame Sun Yat-Sen is famous, but the most famous Chinese woman is still Anna May Wong, who is an American." But Wong was never "American" enough to allow her true star status, and in spite of her striking appearance and considerable talent, she was inevitably groomed by the industry to reinforce the image of the Asian woman as slave girl, Oriental siren, or dreaded "daughter of the dragon." The image is typified by a promotional ad for *Daughter of the Dragon* that describes her role of Ling Moy as "China's loveliest flower. A supple body of appealing grace. Lips like lotus petals—a heart that yearns for love. But sworn by a blood-oath to slay the men her father calls his enemies!"

• There is no full-length biography of Wong, but a detailed, short biographical piece appears in James Robert Parish and William T. Leonard, *Hollywood Players: The Thirties* (1976). A personal account by Conrad J. Doerr is in *Films in Review*, Dec. 1968, pp. 660–62. See also Mary Winship, "The China Doll," *Photoplay*, June 1923, p. 35; Beverley N. Sparks, "Where East Meets West," *Photoplay*, June 1924, p. 55; and "Pin-Up of the Past," *Films and Filming*, June 1971, p. 98. Obituaries are in the *New York Times*, the *New York Herald Tribune*, and the *Los Angeles Times*, 4 Feb. 1961.

RICHARD L. STROMGREN

WOOD, Abraham (c. 1615–c. 1681), organizer of the first English explorations to cross the Appalachian Mountains, arrived in Virginia as an indentured servant in 1620. Nothing is known of his childhood. Having served at least a part of his indenture on Samuel Mathews's plantation in the vicinity of Jamestown, Wood moved in 1636 to Virginia's southwestern frontier, the Appomattox River at what is now Petersburg. Initially leasing land, within three years the former servant owned 600 acres and employed servants of his own.

In the fall of 1644, after an Indian attack against Virginia's scattered tidewater settlements, the freemen of the frontier county of Henrico selected "Mr. Abra. Wood" as their representative to the colony's General Assembly. The assemblies of 1645 and 1646 ordered the construction of four frontier forts. The responsibility for building and manning Fort Henry, at the falls of the Appomattox River, was assigned to militia captain Abraham Wood.

After the English and the Indians had concluded a treaty in October 1646 transforming the Indians into tributaries, the Virginia Assembly conferred ownership of Fort Henry upon Wood. The treaty, having designated Fort Henry as one of only a few places where the tributary Indians could legally trade, brought Wood into regular contact with Virginia's Native Americans.

Wood's military, business, and leadership skills advanced him to a position of unrivaled prominence in his region. As colonel of the Henrico–Charles City militia after 1656, Wood was responsible for the defense of a fifty-mile stretch of exposed frontier. By the 1650s he was the owner of 1,557 acres as well as a leading figure in the Indian trade. After service as a justice of the peace, he represented Charles City County in the House of Burgesses and in April 1658 took a seat in the council. As a member of the council until his death, Wood remained one of the most influential men in the colony. During Bacon's Rebellion he was either ill or chose not to take sides. When Wood married and whom he married are unknown, but a daughter, Mary, survived him. It is probable that Wood died at what was long known as Fort Henry and is now Petersburg, Virginia.

Wood's most significant contribution to the development of colonial America was as a participant in and organizer of English explorations of the southern piedmont and the Appalachians. His goal, however, was not to open new lands so much as it was to discover an overland passage to the Pacific Ocean. Wood and others believed that the western ocean was just beyond the Appalachian Mountains. Wood informed an acquaintance that "I have been att ye charge to the value of two hundred pounds starling in ye discovery to ye south or west sea."

In 1650 Wood and Edward Bland led a seven-member expedition on a nine-day, 180-mile exploration of the region between modern-day Petersburg, Virginia, and Weldon, North Carolina. They returned convinced that they had barely escaped from an Indian conspiracy to destroy them. At mid-century the dangers of the frontier seemed so daunting that two decades passed before further attempts were made to explore the West.

In 1670, John Lederer, having received a commission from Governor Sir William Berkeley, undertook the first exploration from Virginia of the North Carolina piedmont. When Lederer returned to Virginia after a sixty-day, 400-mile journey, his first point of contact was Fort Henry. Carefully debriefing Lederer, Wood learned that the piedmont natives knew of two routes through the mountains leading to westward flowing rivers. At his own expense, Wood dispatched Thomas Batts and Robert Fallam in September 1671 to attempt the first English crossing of the Appalachian Mountains. Their objective, set by Wood, was the discovery of "the ebbing and flowing of the [tidal] Waters on the other side of the Mountains." Entering the mountains by way of the New River Valley, Batts and Fallam traversed southern West Virginia to modern Matewan on the Kentucky border, a point some 185 miles west of Fort Henry. Wood's agents discovered that, while men could pass through the Appalachians, the route was too rugged to be developed for commerce.

Two years later Wood dispatched James Needham and Gabriel Arthur to reconnoiter what the Indians spoke of as a more southerly passage "to the south or west sea." Accompanied by Indian guides, the exploring party entered the mountains near present-day Asheville, North Carolina, and emerged at modern Rome, Georgia. Arthur's account of his travels from Port Royal Sound to Mobile Bay, and from Florida's Apalachicola River to Kentucky's Big Sandy River, convinced Wood that the Pacific Ocean lay beyond reach. Although the Appalachians had been crossed twice, the western ocean had proved too distant and the obstacles to its discovery too numerous for Wood to finance continued explorations on his own. In 1674 he lamented that he had received "no incouragement att all" from other Virginians. Although his appeal for a wealthy English patron "to curb and bridle ye obstructers here" fell on deaf ears, Wood's efforts had provided colonial Englishmen with their first realistic view of the dimensions and geography of the American Southeast.

• The only significant surviving example of Wood's writing is a letter to John Richards of 22 August 1674, in which Wood recounts the story of the Needham and Arthur exploration. The letter, from the Shaftesbury papers, Public Record Office, London, is reproduced and analyzed in Clarence W. Alvord and Lee Bidgood, *The First Explorations of the Trans-Allegheny Region by the Virginians, 1650–1674* (1912). Alan V. Briceland, *Westward from Virginia: The Exploration of the Virginia-Carolina Frontier, 1650–1710* (1987), reinterprets Wood's motives and contributions.

ALAN V. BRICELAND

WOOD, Carolena (21 May 1871–12 Mar. 1936), farmer, relief worker, and reformer, was born at "Braewold," a farm in Mount Kisco, New York, the daughter of James Wood, a farmer, and Emily Hollingsworth Morris. The farm, which Wood ran for her father and her brother, was situated on "the Woodpile," as her extended clan of cousins called the hilltop of family homes. She took courses at the New York School of Social Work, and in 1891–1892 she wintered with her family in Dresden and traveled through Egypt and Palestine. In 1897 she was chosen to be a recorder at a quinquennial gathering of delegates from all the regional "yearly meetings" of "orthodox" Quakers (Christ- and Bible-centered, as compared with the more universalist "Hicksite" Friends). Her father presided as the conference set up the first permanent central Quaker federation, the Five Years Meeting. Wood took a keen interest in the United Society of Friends Women and coordinated its Quaker missions, also visiting and reporting on Quaker schools in Mexico in 1902.

In 1900 Wood and her father were with her sister Ellen as she died of typhoid on a vacation trip by freighter to Scandinavia. Wood took on Ellen's roles as a sewing instructor, as one of the Board of Managers, and, from 1905 through 1911, as head of the nursing program for the New York Colored Mission. This agency had been reshaped by the Wood and Underhill families from the famous African Sabbath School burned in the Civil War. Wood also became an active trustee of the Howard Orphanage and Industrial School in Manhattan and of Oakwood, a Quaker boarding school near Poughkeepsie, New York. At Braewold she taught her young cousins and served on the boards of the local Bedford Women's Reformatory and the garden club. She drove her Model T Ford to recruit members for her Croton Valley Study Club, which discussed national and world issues with the help of the League of Women Voters. Her lectures for Bible study groups included current historical scholarship that she had learned at the Union Theological Seminary.

Wood cared vitally about world peace and took part in founding the American Friends Service Committee, set up by Quakers in 1917 to allow conscientious objectors to do relief work in war zones in France. She had already volunteered to explore the possibility of postwar relief work in Germany when she attended with social activist Jane Addams the Conference of Women for Permanent Peace in Zürich in May 1919. There she collected data from the twenty-six German delegates concerning the appalling starvation that resulted from the still-continuing Allied blockade: 700,000 people had died and 35 percent of the chil dren had tuberculosis. She wrote back to the American Friends Service Committee that "the birth-rate is reduced one-half and it is well. This is a hard world into which to invite a new life to come. . . . They say again and again, 'we are hopeless'" (quoted in Rufus M. Jones, p. 259).

Wood arranged in Paris for passports and the purchase and shipping of food through Herbert Hoover, the Quaker director of all American relief programs in Europe. Wood, Addams, Alice Hamilton, and two British Quakers were the first civilians sent into Germany in June 1919. The group arranged with Wood's lawyer brother in New York to immediately raise $30,000 (the American Friends Service Committee eventually collected $3 million) to pay for food from various sources. Helped by the Dutch Alletta Jacobs and the Swiss Elisabeth Rotten, who was already in touch with British Friends, they negotiated with Allied and German officials for the feeding as of March 1920 of 615,000 German children from eighty-seven towns. They worked through a network of German teachers and church and social workers organized by Albert Levy and F. Siegmund-Schultze. Eventually about thirty Americans helped Germans for three years to provide up to a million daily meals for children and mothers.

Wood went on to Silesia and Poland to scout for similar relief programs, spoke on Quakerism in Berlin churches, and attended a week-long conference of Germans in Frankfurt-am-Main on educational reform in August 1919. Lewis Gannett of the Red Cross wrote that Wood "is doing well one of the most valuable services ever undertaken by the Society of Friends. . . . Her deep concern and her intensely and genuinely loving spirit singled her out." Wood cabled Philadelphia Friends to "send five workers with a speaking knowledge of German, real concern, good digestion, and a calm judgment. . . . Mere handworkmen are not necessary in a country which has thousands." In October 1919 she toured the American Midwest to describe Germany's needs. In 1920 she was put in charge of the program in southwest Germany, but she took time off for the first Friends World Conference in London.

In December 1927 Wood, John Nevin Sayre of the Fellowship of Reconciliation, and two other Quakers were asked by their organizations to travel for a "goodwill" mission of mediation through Central America, where U.S. Marines controlled Nicaragua and were involved in a civil war between Anastasio Samoza and Augusto Cesar Sandino's independence movement. The four went by United Fruit Company ship and railroad to and across Honduras and Guatemala during a military coup and an earthquake. When their party divided en route, Wood and Sayre went on by a mail boat, which sank in the Gulf of Fonseca. Transferring to a dugout canoe, they rejoined Jones and Russell in Nicaragua, hoping to persuade Sandino to accept the result of an election the United States had sponsored. Sayre and Jones rode by oxcart to visit Sandino's wife, but Sandino refused to meet them.

Late in 1929 Wood was asked by British and American Quakers to join five English and Irish Friends and Gilbert Bowles from the Quaker school in Japan for a trip across China to visit the Quaker schools, hospitals, and churches near Nanking and Chengtu to reevaluate missionary goals. Wood hoped the visit to Quaker missions could also serve as a peace mission between China, whose church and cultural leaders the Quakers met, and Japan, whose civilian leaders were open to mediation but whose army increasingly controlled Manchuria. (Army officers seized Manchukuo in September 1931, and the navy shelled Shanghai early in 1932.) Wood proposed a Quaker mediation and study center in Shanghai, but it was opened only after the Japanese had overrun all northern and central China in 1937.

Though "she seemed built for bounty and held nothing back," Carolena Wood everywhere "traveled light" in heart and baggage, with only a pair of durable gray corduroy suits and white blouses for all occasions. She never married and died of cancer at Braewold.

• Wood's papers are divided between the Archives of the American Friends Service Committee in Philadelphia and the family archive at Braewold, Mount Kisco, N.Y. Papers and Minutes of the New York Colored Mission are in the Yearly Meeting Archive, 15 Rutherford Place, New York City. Harry T. Silcock's extensive typed reports on the China mission are at the Friends Service Council in London. The feeding program in Europe is described in J. William Frost, "'Our Deeds Carry our Message': The Early History of the American Friends Service Committee," *Quaker History* 81, no. 1 (Spring 1992): 1–51; John Forbes, *The Quaker Star under Seven Flags, 1917–1927* (1962); Willis H. Hall, *Quaker International Work in Europe since 1914* (1938); Mary Hoxie Jones, *Swords into Ploughshares* (1937); Frank Surface and Raymond Bland, *American Food in the World War and Reconstruction Period* (1931); Rufus M. Jones, *A Service of Love in War Time* (1920); and Elbert Russell, *Elbert Russell, Quaker: An Autobiography* (1956).

HUGH BARBOUR

WOOD, Edith Elmer (24 Sept. 1871–29 Apr. 1945), public health activist and housing reformer, was born in Portsmouth, New Hampshire, the daughter of Horace Elmer, a naval officer, and Adele Wiley. As part of a military family, she lived around the United States and the world. She graduated from Smith College in 1890 and worked at the College Settlement in New York City. She married Albert Norton Wood, a naval officer, in 1893; they had four children. Before becoming involved in housing reform, Wood wrote fiction and travel books.

When her husband was stationed in Puerto Rico in 1906 she became active in public health issues. She organized and presided over the Anti-Tuberculosis League of Puerto Rico, serving as its honorary president from 1908. Realizing that tuberculosis could not be eradicated without improving housing conditions, she wrote a new housing code for San Juan, thus beginning her career as a housing reformer.

The Wood family returned to the United States in 1910 after her husband retired from the U.S. Navy. They eventually moved to Washington, D.C., where from 1913 to 1915 she was active in that city's reform movement against alley dwellings. Wood began to disagree with the accepted wisdom of New York State's Tenement House Commission, led by Lawrence Veiller, which advocated housing legislation and regulations to protect the community's health, welfare, and safety and argued that both landlords and tenants who were irresponsible created poor housing conditions that threatened the general health. Wood believed that the poor in Washington, D.C., had no alternatives to slum conditions. Evicting them because they lived in dwellings that did not meet code requirements was not the solution, she argued.

To gain the training necessary to become a professional housing reformer, Wood abandoned her literary career in 1914. She and her family moved back to New

York City in 1915 so that she could attend the New York School of Philanthropy (later, New York School of Social Work), from which she earned a diploma in 1917, and Columbia University, receiving an A.M. in 1917 and a Ph.D. in political economy in 1919.

Her dissertation, published as *The Housing of the Unskilled Worker* (1919), called for a national housing policy to provide low-cost housing; Wood believed that housing should be a public service, like utilities. Veiller's regulatory methods eliminated bad housing without providing incentives to build good housing because meeting code requirements increased construction costs. Housing problems, Wood argued, resulted from a breakdown in the country's industrial system, not moral problems among residents, and therefore were a matter of public policy. The U.S. Bureau of the Census did not collect statistics on housing conditions, but, using data on wages, housing costs, and the number of wage earners, Wood concluded that approximately one-third of the nation's residents lived in below-normal housing conditions.

While Wood enjoyed the support of professionals such as Carol Aronovici, Charles Ascher, Jacob Crane, Leon Keyserling, Elisabeth Coit, Mary Kingsbury Simkhovitch, Edith Abbott, and Lillian Wald, the real estate industry and those who followed Veiller preferred to rely on regulation and private funding to provide housing, abhorring the European model of government construction of housing units that Wood advocated. Her goal was realized partially with the passage of the Wagner-Steagall Housing Act of 1937, which legislated her plan of slum clearance and construction of the nation's first publicly funded housing units as replacements.

Wood monitored the nation's housing problems and advocated professional planning while based at her home in Cape May Court House, New Jersey, where she lived after 1919. She was a member of the American Association of University Women's national committee on housing (chair, 1917–1929), Regional Planning Association of America (officer, 1920s), National Public Housing Conference (vice president, 1932–1936; director, 1936–1945), National Association of Housing Officials (founding member, 1933), New Jersey State Housing Authority (commissioner, 1934–1935), and International Housing Association (executive committee, 1931–1937). Wood advised the housing division of the Public Works Administration (1933–1937) and the United States Housing Authority (1938–1942) and taught housing courses at Columbia University extension (1926–1930) and the Teachers College.

Wood died in Greystone Park, New Jersey. Shortly after her death, Nathan Straus, in a *New York Times* tribute, observed that Wood's "unique contribution [had been] to marshal facts and figures so as to show the cost of bad housing in crime, delinquency, infant mortality and warped human lives."

• Wood's papers are at Columbia University. She was listed in *Who's Who* in 1903 as a writer, and her early works include *Her Provincial Cousin: A Story of Brittany* (1893), *Shoulder-Straps and Sun-Bonnets* (1901), *The Spirit of the Service* (1903), and *An Oberland Chalet* (1910). In addition to *The Housing of the Unskilled Worker*, her housing publications include "Four Washington Alleys" (*The Survey*, 6 Dec. 1914, pp. 251–54), *Housing Progress in Western Europe* (1923), *Recent Trends in American Housing* (1931), *Slums and Blighted Areas in the United States* (1935), *Introduction to Housing: Facts and Principles* (1939), and *The Homes the Public Builds* (with Elizabeth Ogg, 1940). Her career as a housing reformer is best discussed in Eugenie L. Birch, "Edith Elmer Wood and the Genesis of Liberal Housing Thought: 1910–1942" (Ph.D. diss., Columbia Univ., 1976) and "Woman-Made America: The Case of Early Public Housing Policy," *Journal of the American Institute of Planners* 44 (Apr. 1978): 130–44. An obituary is in the *New York Times* 1 May 1945.

BARBARA J. HOWE

WOOD, Fernando (14 June 1812–14 Feb. 1881), mayor of New York City and congressman, was born in Philadelphia, Pennsylvania, the son of Benjamin Wood, a merchant, and Rebecca Lehmann. His father's business failures led to an insecure childhood. In 1821 the family moved to New York City, where Wood attended a private academy until age thirteen. Leaving home, he supported himself in New York and elsewhere with a variety of low-paying jobs. In 1831 the tall, handsome, well-mannered young man married Anna W. Taylor, the daughter of a moderately successful Philadelphia merchant. The following year the couple returned to New York City where, his father having died, Wood invested his wife's dowry in business ventures to support his wife, mother, and younger siblings.

Although even his most successful venture, a "grocery" that sold drinks to longshoremen, made little money, Wood found he could excel in politics. A member of Tammany Hall, the Democratic club, by 1835, Wood rose to prominence locally as the issue of government support for banks divided his party. Switching to the antibank position in the panic of 1837, Wood found in antibank Locofocoism a popular ideology (equal rights, hard money, and antimonopoly), a devoted working class constituency, and an opportunity to lead as he headed the movement that ousted probank Democrats from Tammany. He attended his first national Democratic convention in 1840 and was elected to the U.S. House of Representatives that fall. Meanwhile, however, his childless marriage ended in divorce in 1839.

In Washington, D.C., Wood spoke against Whig banking, tariff, and spending measures (while voting for expenditures that benefited New York), established friendships with southern politicians such as Henry Wise and John C. Calhoun (while simultaneously reporting to northern Democrats such as Martin Van Buren the political plans of the southerners), and helped Samuel F. B. Morse to get a subsidy for his telegraph. In 1841 he married Anna D. Richardson, with whom he had seven children before her death in 1859. Her father, a judge, brought him valuable upstate New York political connections.

Congressional redistricting and a switch to single member districts cost Wood his congressional seat in 1842. Needing to supplement his income from a chandlery business, he successfully sought from John C. Calhoun in 1844 the patronage post of dispatch agent in New York City for the State Department, which he held until 1847. In 1848 he used $3,500 of his wife's money as a down payment on land for a new home in the remote nineteenth ward. The transaction introduced him to the real estate market, the source of his large fortune. Within twenty years his original parcel was worth $650,000 and he was regularly buying, selling, subdividing, and leasing property throughout the rapidly growing metropolis. In 1848 Wood also persuaded his brother-in-law and some of his friends (on the basis of a forged letter) to invest in a shipload of goods to be sold to gold miners in California. The expedition was successful, but Wood exaggerated his costs when dividing up the profits, causing a lawsuit that eventually resulted in a judgment against Wood as well as useful ammunition for his political enemies.

The division of the Democratic party over slavery extension into the territories brought Wood back to politics after 1848 as a prospective peacemaker between factions. Winning the mayoral nomination in 1850, he was defeated in a general Whig sweep. In 1854, however, he won the office, was reelected in 1856, defeated in 1857, reelected in 1859, and defeated again in 1861. Facing a city bitterly divided along ethnic, class, religious, and racial lines, Wood prefigured later political bosses by striving to address urban problems by assuming personal control of municipal affairs.

Power, however, was not easily centralized. Wood himself headed a factionalized party in a state in which hostility toward urban immigrant populations was growing. His own limited powers were further constricted by a factionalized city council and an often Republican state legislature. Attempting to appeal to businessmen and reformers in his first term, Wood appeared to crack down on prostitution, gambling, and saloons and pushed for the building of Central Park and a municipal university. Responding to working-class Irish immigrants, however, he found ways to avoid enforcing state liquor laws, and during the panic of 1857 he recommended putting the unemployed to work for the city building and repairing public structures. Bridging class lines proved impossible. Wood's desire to control patronage and his ambitions for the governorship frightened similarly ambitious politicians in his own party who engineered his defeat in 1857. Wood responded by forming his own organization, Mozart Hall, in September 1858. Through this society, which he funded and directed, Wood asserted that his followers represented traditional Democratic principles abandoned by Tammany.

Republicans also feared Wood as a demagogue and sought to divert municipal patronage to their own hands by using their power in the state legislature to form metropolitan commissions to control New York City's police, supervise the wharves and piers, and even oversee the construction of a new city hall. Wood created his own municipal police force in opposition to the Metropolitans, and for a time both battled in the streets before the courts ruled against Wood and his force was disbanded. Wood's frustration with state government provides the context to understand his proposal in 1861 that New York City secede from the state and become a free city.

While never fully trusting him, prosouthern Democratic leaders at the national level, such as James Buchanan, angled for Wood's support in the 1850s. His prosouthern and proslavery associations identified him in many minds as a treasonous Copperhead during the Civil War, although after Fort Sumter he proposed a million dollar tax levy to raise troops for the war. Shortly before his mayorship ended in 1861, Wood married Alice F. Mills, the sixteen-year-old daughter of a wealthy retired merchant. They had nine children.

With enthusiasm for the war dwindling in heavily Democratic New York City, Wood became a Peace Democrat and won election to the U.S. House of Representatives in 1862. Failing to be reelected in 1864, he was returned in 1866 and served until his death in Hot Springs, Arkansas. Despite his lengthy congressional service, the minority status of his party during most of the sessions and his own uncompromising stands on low tariffs and hard currency limited his leadership role in Congress. He was chair of the Ways and Means Committee after 1877 but faced more defeats than victories in that position. Although a gadfly to Republicans in Congress and a hard worker on budget and tax bills, his real political contributions lay in his earlier organization of New York's immigrant population and experimentation with ways to address urban problems.

• Wood's papers are at the New York Historical Society and New York Public Library. The best biography is Jerome Mushkat, *Fernando Wood: A Political Biography* (1990). See also Samuel A. Pleasants, *Fernando Wood of New York* (1948). On specific episodes in Wood's life see James F. Richardson, "Mayor Fernando Wood and the New York Police Force, 1855–1857," *New York Historical Society Quarterly* 40 (1966): 5–40, and Tyler G. Anbinder, "Fernando Wood and New York City's Secession from the Union: A Political Reappraisal," *New York History* 68 (1987): 67–92. On Tammany see Leonard Chalmers, "Fernando Wood and Tammany Hall: The First Phase," *New York Historical Society Quarterly* 52 (1968): 379–402, and Chalmers, "Tammany Hall, Fernando Wood, and the Struggle to Control New York City, 1857–1860," *New York Historical Society Quarterly* 53 (1969): 7–33. An obituary is in the *New York Times*, 15 Feb. 1881.

PHYLLIS F. FIELD

WOOD, Frederick Hill (2 Jan. 1877–28 Dec. 1943), corporation lawyer, was born in Lisbon, Maine, the only child of Frederick Ansel Wood, a teacher, and Mary Calista Hill. Wood's paternal ancestor, Daniel Wood, had emigrated from England to Ipswich, Massachusetts in the mid-seventeenth century. When the Civil

War began, Wood's father served in the Union Army as a first lieutenant. In 1886 the family moved to Kansas, where their father continued teaching.

Wood attended the public schools of Kansas City, Missouri, and went on to the University of Kansas at Lawrence, where he received his B.A. in 1897 and an LL.B. from the Law School in 1899. In later years he confessed that while an undergraduate he had leaned toward a career in journalism, but his father dissuaded him from becoming a newspaperman. He later thought he had made a mistake, because the demands of a law practice never left him time to engage in public affairs.

Wood began the practice of law in Lawrence, Kansas, in 1899, and for the next two years he also taught at the university's Law School. In 1901 he moved back to Kansas City, where he was employed in the law office of Clarence S. Palmer until 1905. There followed a long period of service representing various railroads: from 1905 to 1910 he was general counsel for the St. Louis and San Francisco ("Frisco") at St. Louis; from 1910 to 1913 he was attorney for the Kansas City Southern at Kansas City; and from 1913 to 1924 he was general counsel for the Southern Pacific at New York City. To be general counsel of a major railroad in the period after the Civil War was to occupy a position of great prestige and an enormous salary. His work kept Wood constantly on the move, appearing in the courts of the states in which his companies operated or before the Interstate Commerce Commission (ICC) in Washington, D.C. Some of his cases were argued before the Supreme Court.

Of greater importance to the earning power of railroads during this period than any Supreme Court or Commerce Court cases was the investigation of freight rates conducted by the ICC in 1910 in litigation known as the Eastern and Western Rate Cases. Hearings continued throughout the fall and winter of 1910 1911. Wood represented the "Frisco" in the Western case, and Louis Brandeis, a Boston lawyer, was one of the principal attorneys for the opponents of rate increases. In its decision (22 Feb. 1911) the commission held that the carriers had failed to establish the necessity for higher rates in view of the liberal returns on investments received over the previous ten years.

After eight years of successful practice as a midwestern railroad lawyer, Wood moved to New York City in 1913, where he continued this work as general attorney of the Southern Pacific Railroad until 1924. In 1914 he married Margery Pearson, who had come to New York from Kansas City and had begun a successful career as a singer in musical comedy, which she gave up after their marriage. They had one daughter.

On 3 June 1924 Wood joined the Wall Street firm of Cravath, Henderson and de Gersdorff (after 1928, Cravath, de Gersdorff, Swaine and Wood). For nearly five years the firm's senior partners had been searching for the ideal corporate advocate to fill a senior position, but with no result. Their search ended when ICC Commissioner Mark W. Potter told Cravath that Wood, counsel for the Southern Pacific, was the ablest advocate before the commission. The firm's three senior partners went to Washington to listen to some of Wood's arguments and were so impressed that they invited him to become the fifth ranking partner. New partners in the Cravath firm were invariably chosen internally, unless there was some compelling requirement to look elsewhere. In the four decades from 1910 to 1950 there were only three exceptions to this policy: two of them were advocates—Walker D. Hines and Wood; the third was the senior tax law partner, Roswell Magill. The office work in litigation did not attain standards that were fully acceptable to Cravath until Wood joined the firm in 1924. In the years from 1928 to 1943, among all the partners there were only four litigators (Henderson, Magill, de Gersdorff, and Wood), and over those twenty years they were active in developing what became known as the "Cravath system."

Wood was forty-seven when he joined the Cravath firm. The embryo partnership established in the early part of the nineteenth century between William H. Seward, Lincoln's secretary of state, and R. M. Blatchford was the forerunner of the large Wall Street "law factory" that Wood joined. Originally based in Auburn, New York, the office, after Seward became a U.S. senator, moved to New York City in 1854. By then it was already actively engaged in corporation law and patent litigation. After the Civil War its corporate business expanded, and from 1880 on the firm became actively involved in finance, business mergers, advising railroads, stockholders' suits, and floating bond issues. By the turn of the century the partnership had become the very model of a Wall Street firm.

The Cravath firm pioneered in legal specialization. Prior to 1900 lawyers did virtually every kind of work, but gradually it became customary for partners as well as associates in all large law offices to specialize, giving most of their time to a single type of practice. Wood's work, begun earlier, had been largely limited to railroad cases and litigating valuation and recapture cases. It continued to take up much of his time after 1924. In some cases he acted only in an advisory capacity, while in others he took full responsibility, from hearings to decision. In all the years since 1895 the Cravath firm had not been without participation in railroad receiverships, reorganizations, or readjustments, except in 1903 and 1904.

The work Wood did after 1928 proved the validity of Potter's prediction to Cravath that he could handle any kind of litigation well. His reputation was by then firmly established for the thoroughness of his preparation, his shrewdness in cross-examination, and the effectiveness of his argument. The expanded opportunities that working in the Cravath firm provided gave wider scope for his talents, and he was soon regarded as one of the ablest trial lawyers in the country.

Wood outdid all his partners in the organization of his cases. On out-of-town trips for major arguments, he was accompanied by numerous assistants, all with bulky files crammed into suitcases. When the matter took more than a few days, he set up practically a branch office in his hotel, including filing cabinets, stenographers, and associates engaged in adjoining rooms. He worked with an intensity that was in keeping with the Cravath tradition, but he was usually able to arrange his cases so that after the major arguments he could take a short holiday to restore his equilibrium.

In much of the litigation during the New Deal, the clients of the Cravath firm opposed the government. From 1930 to 1945 the firm had as much business in the U.S. Supreme Court as any private law firm in the country. Wood alone made twenty-five arguments before the high Court. A faithful servant of his clients, he became known after 1933 as one of the most successful anti-New Deal lawyers in the nation. He saw through to its successful outcome a suit brought against Westinghouse Electric & Manufacturing Company by the government. When it was taken on appeal to the Supreme Court in *U.S. v. General Electric* (1926), the unanimous opinion affirmed the lower court decision upholding the company's selling system and patent license condition. The ruling was anathema to the Department of Justice from the day it was rendered, particularly after 1933. Not until 1937 and a new court majority did the department have much success in whittling down that case's previously accepted scope, and in distinguishing every case of patent license condition attacked before the Supreme Court as a violation of antitrust law.

Wood made the arguments in three important New Deal cases: the Gold Clause cases, the Schechter case, and the Guffey Coal Act case. In one of the Gold Clause cases, Wood and his client, the Baltimore and Ohio Railroad, challenged the constitutionality of the New Deal's gold policy. The railway retained the Cravath firm when a bondholder sued, seeking payment on a $100 bond coupon in current dollars, equivalent in value to that of 1930 gold coin. In all three lower federal courts the case was argued by Wood for the railroad, with de Gersdorff on the briefs, and in all three he won his case. The cancellation of the gold clauses in private contracts (e.g., railroad bonds) was narrowly upheld by the Supreme Court in a five to four decision (*Norman v. Baltimore and Ohio Railroad* (1935).

In 1935 the Schechter brothers, owners and operators of a kosher poultry processing business in New York, challenged the constitutionality of the live poultry code in the National Industrial Recovery Act (NIRA) in what became known popularly as the "sick chicken case." Wood joined their lawyer, Joseph Heller, in arguing the company's appeal to the Supreme Court. Just how the Cravath firm became involved in the case or what interests paid the fee for Wood's participation is uncertain, except that he was clearly enlisted to represent the interests of big business. According to one account, when the Supreme Court granted certiorari, the Cravath firm, because of the interest of its steel clients, arranged to cooperate with the Schechter counsel (Swaine, p. 557). The case was argued in the Supreme Court two weeks after the firm entered it. Wood and members of the staff worked day and night in preparation of the brief.

In his oral argument Wood said that a favorable decision on the NIRA would expand the scope of the Constitution's commerce clause far beyond the meaning given to it in 1787, or in the years until 1935. Such expansion would threaten the very continuation of the American system of government in any recognizable form. The poultry processing operation of the Schechters was no more subject to federal regulation than other forms of production which took place before commerce began. A unanimous Court agreed with the plaintiffs in *Schechter Poultry Corp. v. U.S.* (1935), and the NIRA fell to the judicial axe.

Wood maintained memberships in the American Bar Association, the New York State Bar Association, the Bar of the City of New York, the New York County Lawyer's Association, and Phi Beta Kappa. His clubs included the University, Piping Rock, Manhattan, Broad Street, Down Town Association, Blind Brook Country Club, and the National Republican Club. He was trustee for the Nightingale-Bamford School in New York City. For many years he served on the executive board and attended the functions of New York's Town Hall, Inc., and was active in the city's Practicing Law Institute. Wood died at his desk in his office at 15 Broad Street, New York City.

• For information on Wood and the Cravath firm, readers are indebted to one of its partners, Robert T. Swaine, the firm's historian, for his detailed account of the rise of one of the nation's oldest and most prestigious Wall Street offices, in *The Cravath Firm and Its Predecessors, 1819–1948* (3 vols., 1946–1948). See especially vol. 2, *The Cravath Firm Since 1906*, for biographical material on Wood. Some material on the firm's early history and the development of the "Cravath System" is in Lawrence M. Friedman, *A History of American Law* (1973). Wood's obituary is in the *New York Times*, 29 Dec. 1943.

MARIAN C. MCKENNA

WOOD, George Bacon (13 Mar. 1797–30 Mar. 1879), physician and medical author and teacher, was born in Greenwich, New Jersey, the son of Richard Wood and Elizabeth Bacon, farmers. In 1815 he received an A.B. degree from the University of Pennsylvania. He began his studies in medicine with Joseph Parrish of Philadelphia and attained M.A. and M.D. degrees from the University of Pennsylvania in 1818. Immersed in the classics, he enjoyed composing verse, in Latin as well as in English, and was familiar with German, French, and Italian. He was well traveled, in the states of Virginia and Pennsylvania especially, and in many of the countries of Europe, to which he made three trips, the last of over a two-year duration in 1860–1862. His journals show him to have had varied interests, among them geology, art, and viniculture.

With the help of his preceptor, Wood established a successful medical practice soon after he obtained his degree. He was an attending physician at the Pennsylvania Institute for the Deaf and Dumb from 1822 to 1844 and an attending physician at the Pennsylvania

Hospital from 1835 to 1859. During his tenure at the Pennsylvania Hospital his duties included giving clinical lectures, and he was noted for his attention to the techniques of auscultation and percussion. His eminence, however, derived from his teaching, writing, leadership in organizational activities, and philanthropy.

Wood's teaching career began as instructor in chemistry to Parrish's students and to ladies who came to Parrish's private office for such instruction. In 1822 he became professor of chemistry in the newly established Philadelphia College of Pharmacy, a post he held until 1831, when he transferred to the professorship of materia medica. In 1830 he joined Parrish in the latter's Philadelphia Association for Medical Instruction and remained with the association until it was dissolved in 1836. In 1835 he was appointed to the chair of materia medica and pharmacy (later materia medica and therapeutics) in the University of Pennsylvania, a position he held for fifteen years, until he became professor of the theory and practice of medicine. He retired from the University of Pennsylvania in 1860. Until 1855 he instructed private students in his office as well.

At the University of Pennsylvania, he introduced illustrations and demonstrations into his lectures on the materia medica. He exhibited living specimens of medicinal plants from many parts of the world that he had cultivated in his own conservatory and garden and maintained also a complete cabinet of mineral and other crude and prepared drugs that he exhibited. His lectures were described by Henry Hartshorne in his eulogy before the American Philosophical Society as "splendid, almost magnificent" and were said to add "more to the great reputation and large classes" of the medical department of the university than any other "portion of the curriculum." He carried this "ocular demonstration" (that is, the display of specimens or models) over into his lectures on the theory and practice of medicine—and was said to be the first in the country to do so. Models, castings, and drawings of various pathological lesions that he had collected in Europe formed what Squier Littell, his eulogist before the Philadelphia College of Physicians, called "a cabinet of morbid representations unique in this country." In 1855 and 1856, for example, he made three purchases of wax models from Guy's Hospital, London, totaling over $1,500.

Wood was a prodigious writer and early exhibited an interest in history and poetry, and even wrote a novel. The latter was never published, but a long poem entitled *First and Last, a Poem Intended to Illustrate the Ways of God and Man*, was published under a London imprint in 1860 and then under a Philadelphia imprint in 1864. It was published anonymously, his nephew Horatio C. Wood was to say, so as not "to blur his medical reputation." His historical writings—histories of the University of Pennsylvania, of the Pennsylvania Hospital, of Christianity in India, and of Girard College—were collected, along with an essay on temperance and a variety of other essays, in a volume called *Historical and Biographical Memoirs, Essays, Addresses, etc. etc.* (1859, 1872).

Wood's national and international reputation derived, however, from his involvement with the *United States Pharmacopoeia* and from his professional publications. In 1829, as a member of the College of Physicians committee on revising the pharmacopoeia, a committee on which he was joined by his close friend and collaborator, Franklin Bache, and by Thomas T. Hewson, he devoted all of his leisure time to the project. The resultant revision was published in Philadelphia in 1831. Reflecting the reputation of the members of the committee, it displaced a revision that had been published in New York in 1830. The Philadelphia revision became the basis for subsequent revisions, and Wood and Bache were the major figures behind the decennial revisions of the pharmacopoeia during their lifetimes. Wood was a delegate of the College of Physicians at the national pharmacopoeial convention that met in Washington, D.C., in 1830, vice president of the 1840 national convention and chairman of its committee on revision and publication, president of the national convention in 1850 and 1860, and chairman of the revision and publication committee in 1870. As an outgrowth of their pharmacopoeial work, Wood and Bache issued the *Dispensatory of the United States of America*, a massive work that provided details and commentary that the *Pharmacopoeia* studiously avoided. The *Dispensatory*, first published in 1833, went through fourteen editions in Wood's lifetime, each brought up to date and each considerably augmented. It became an indispensable tool for pharmacists and physicians and continued to be published, by a variety of authors, up until its twenty-seventh edition in 1973.

In 1826 Wood also was prominent in the establishment and editing of the *North American Medical and Surgical Journal*, a journal that lasted only six years. In 1847 he published his *Treatise on the Practice of Medicine* that went through six editions, the last in 1866. It was acclaimed at home and abroad, a London critic calling the 1852 edition "the best work on the practice of medicine in the English language . . . [others] are far behind." His *Treatise on Therapeutics, and Pharmacology or Materia Medica*, that was first published in 1856 and that reached a third edition in 1868, was also widely acclaimed. The importance of these publications is pointed up by their large sales. The lowest estimates of the sale of *Dispensatory* during Wood's lifetime was 120,000 copies; of the sale of the *Treatise on the Practice of Medicine*, 30,000; and of the sale of the *Treatise on Therapeutics*, 10,000.

The esteem in which he was held, and perhaps his own sense of noblesse oblige, placed Wood at the head of the intellectual and scientific life of Philadelphia. Elected a fellow of the College of Physicians in 1827, he was president of the college from 1848 until his death. Elected a member of the American Philosophical Society in 1829, he was its president from 1859 until his death. He was a member of the board of trustees of the University of Pennsylvania from 1863. He served as chairman of the Committee on the Medical

Department of the latter board. He took a leading role, as well, in several benevolent societies in Philadelphia, including Girard College and the Institution for the Deaf and Dumb. Wood was president of the American Medical Association in 1855–1856. He held honorary or corresponding memberships in the New York Academy of Medicine, the Massachusetts and Rhode Island medical societies, and in professional societies in Scotland, Ireland, France, Italy, Germany, and Russia. In 1858 the College of New Jersey (Princeton) bestowed an honorary doctor of laws degree on him.

In 1823 Wood married Caroline Hahn. It was a happy, although childless, marriage. Caroline was a Lutheran, and Wood, because he was married "out of meeting," was formally disowned by the Society of Friends with which the Wood family had long been associated. (He was, however, "buried in the silence of a Quaker burial.") Caroline brought with her a considerable dowry and was the sole heir of her wealthy father. Although Wood did not develop an especially remunerative medical practice, he did receive a respectable income from his teaching (for example, his net income from student fees for the academic terms 1857 and 1858 totaled over $6,000) and from royalties (one estimate was that the *Dispensatory* paid Wood and Bache $150,000). It was his wife's inheritance, however, that made him a man of considerable wealth.

His wealth permitted him to purchase materials for demonstrations in his lectures, to have a botanical conservatory, and to develop a cabinet of materia medica and a collection of pathological specimens. Foremost among his gifts was his funding, starting in 1866, of an auxiliary faculty of medicine at the University of Pennsylvania to be composed of five chairs: zoology and comparative anatomy; botany; mineralogy and geology; hygiene; and medical jurisprudence and toxicology. Each professor was to deliver not fewer than thirty-four lectures in the spring and was to receive $500 for his participation. Also starting in 1866 he gave the College of Physicians $500 annually so that the library might be kept open daily.

Wood died in Philadelphia. His will provided substantially for the continuation of both of these programs and made substantial bequests to the Pennsylvania Hospital for the establishment of the Peter Hahn Ward and to the American Philosophical Society for its building fund. In addition, he canceled a mortgage he held on the building of the College of Physicians and presented the library of the college all his medical books not already in the library. He left the University of Pennsylvania his collection of plants, specimens, and models; and he made bequests to at least fourteen Philadelphia charities.

Those who knew George Bacon Wood described him in such terms as "dignified and formal," "grave and sedate," "precise," "passionless and distant." His nephew, Horatio C. Wood, characterized him as "an aristocrat, exceedingly orderly, punctilious and polite." Those who knew him found "little of originality in [his] mental constitution . . . [and that] he was more inclined to deal with fact than with speculation." But his contemporaries agreed that he "was an uncommonly skillful teacher, an effective writer, and successful author."

• There are some Wood papers in the libraries of the American Philosophical Society and of the Historical Society of Pennsylvania in Philadelphia. The main and large body of Wood papers—among them casebooks, clinical notes, lists of students, lecture notes, correspondence, and, especially, diaries ("journals")—are in the Library of the Philadelphia College of Physicians. His bequests have been published in a pamphlet called *The Last Will and Codicils of George B. Wood* (n.d.). The major biographical accounts are those by W. S. W. Ruschenberger, "Obituary Notice," *American Journal of the Medical Sciences*, n.s., 78 (1879): 591–96; by Henry Hartshorne, "Memoir of George B. Wood, M.D., LL.D.," *Proceedings of the American Philosophical Society* 19 (1880–1881): 118–52; and by S. Littell, "Memoir of George B. Wood, M.D., LL.D." *Transactions of the College of Physicians of Philadelphia*, ser. 3, 12 (1881): xxv–lxxv.

DAVID L. COWEN

WOOD, Grant (13 Feb. 1891–12 Feb. 1942), artist, was born Grant DeVolson Wood on a farm near Anamosa, Iowa, the son of Francis Maryville Wood and Hattie D. Weaver. After his father died in March 1901, the family left the farm and moved to Cedar Rapids, where Wood lived throughout much of his life. In the summers of 1910 and 1911 he studied metalwork and jewelry making under the arts and craft designer Ernest A. Batchelder at the Minneapolis School of Design and Handicraft and Normal Art. Wood also took art classes at the University of Iowa, Iowa City, in 1911 and at the Art Institute of Chicago in 1913.

Wood referred to his life during the 1910s and 1920s as the "Bohemian years." He spent much of those two decades experimenting with painting styles and creating unusual sculpture and interior decorating designs before settling, by the end of the 1920s, on his popular regionalist style. Wood briefly served in the army during 1918, first at Camp Dodge outside of Des Moines, then in Washington, D.C., where he painted camouflage for artillery. Returning to Cedar Rapids, Wood taught art at grade and high school levels and received a number of private painting commissions, including a large triptych titled *First Three Degrees of Free Masonry* (1921) and an advertising mural titled *Adoration of the Home* (1921–1922).

Wood traveled to Europe, primarily Paris, three times between 1920 and 1926. In the autumn of 1923 he took a life study class at the Académie Julien in Paris, where fellow classmates called him "Tete de Bois" or Wooden-head. During the summer of 1926 Wood exhibited his impressionist-like paintings in the Galerie Carmine in Paris. After a disappointing showing at the gallery, he returned to Iowa, later writing that his return had been prompted by an epiphany of regionalist idealism: "I came back because I learned that French painting is very fine for the French people and not necessarily for us, and because I started to analyze what it was that I really knew. . . . It was Iowa. . . . I realized that all the really good ideas I'd ever had came to me when I was milking a cow" ("Artist's Odyssey," *Literary Digest*, 18 Apr. 1936).

As the de facto town artist of Cedar Rapids, Wood honed his painting and decorating skills with local commissions. His major patron, David Turner, owned a funeral parlor and decorated his business with the artist's work. Turner let Wood and his mother live in a studio apartment above the mortuary's garage. Wood turned the apartment, which he dubbed "5 Turner Alley," into a multipurpose dwelling—an art studio, a living space, and a tiny theater. Wood and Turner also tried to create a Latin Quarter in Cedar Rapids where artists and writers could congregate. Artistic activity in the town got a boost in 1928 when the American Federation of the Arts set up an experimental outpost there called the Little Gallery. Directed by Edward Rowan, the Little Gallery featured exhibitions by national as well as local modern artists and sponsored programs in dance, music, and literature.

Wood's regionalist style crystalized in 1927, the year he received a commission to design a stained glass window for the local Veterans Memorial Building. The physical qualities of stained glass necessitated a precise, flat style that was different from his earlier, much looser technique. The final design featured a large female figure of the Republic towering over six figures, each representing veterans of the nation's great wars. The lack of trained artisans in America prompted Wood to have the glass manufactured in Munich. While in Germany in the fall of 1928 he studied fifteenth- and sixteenth-century Flemish and German artists, such as Albrecht Dürer, Hans Holbein, and Hans Memling. The realistic yet decorative style of their paintings appealed to Wood, as did the inclusion of the artist's environment in each work—characteristics that became central to Wood's regionalist style. During his time in Germany Wood also appears to have been influenced by the contemporary realist style called Neue Sachlichkeit or New Objectivity. Although he never admitted to any such influence, his subsequent paintings share certain qualities with the German movement, in particular, their refined sense of realism, simplified and rounded forms, hard lines, and delineated colors used in portraits and landscapes.

Emulating the Flemish portraits he so admired, Wood began to paint his family and neighbors in their native surroundings on a monumental scale. Yet his choice of subject matter also represented Wood's reaction against the over-arching influence of Paris and New York on the art world. Searching for a purely American expression, he turned to several native sources, including American folk art, frontier photography, and Currier and Ives prints. As he explained to one interviewer: "Gradually as I searched, I began to realize that there was real decoration in the rickrack braid on the aprons of the farmer wives, in calico patterns and in lace curtains. At present, my most useful reference book is a Sears, Roebuck catalogue" (*Christian Science Monitor*, 26 Mar. 1932). Among the first works he painted in his new regionalist style were two portraits. The first, *Portrait of John B. Turner, Pioneer* (1928–1930), features the father of Wood's patron David Turner posed in front of an 1869 map of Linn County, Iowa. Turner is depicted as a stern man who has risen financially and culturally above the pioneer generation that immediately preceded him. *Woman with Plants* (1929) is a Mona Lisa–like treatment of Wood's mother; shown standing in front of rolling Iowan hills, she wears a simple black dress and a green apron with rickrack trim. The painting was accepted at the annual exhibition of American painting at the Art Institute of Chicago in fall 1929.

Wood's first regionalist style landscape, *Stone City* (1929), depicts a fictional scene of man, nature, and industry in harmonious coexistence. In truth, Stone City was a town that grew up around a limestone quarry and with the advent of cement manufacturing at the turn of the century went out of business. Instead of painting a deserted town (only a few farmers and stone workers still lived there), Wood depicted a community thriving among rolling hills, gumdroplike trees, and perfect rows of corn. Inspired by his early memories of farm life, Wood mostly ignored modern technology as well as contemporary realities. No gas engine tractors mar the countryside. No depression-era struggles appear in any of his works. Rather, paintings such as *Overmantel Decoration* (1930) and *Fall Plowing* and *Young Corn* (both 1931) glorify the supposed simplicity of earlier times.

In 1930 Wood created one of the most famous—and most parodied—icons of American art, *American Gothic*. The painting's two subjects, an Iowan farmer and his unmarried daughter, were modeled after Wood's dentist, B. H. McKeeby, and Wood's own sister, Nan Wood Graham. Many viewers imagined that the subjects were married, but Wood repeatedly said, to explain their apparent age difference, that they were a father and his spinster daughter. The two figures stand in front of a small white house that was inspired by a similar structure Wood had sketched in Eldon, Iowa. The original structure was built in the Carpenter Gothic style, which was popular in the Midwest toward the end of the nineteenth century. In the painting, Wood simply extended the distinct features of the building style—lean lines and elongated shapes—to his two subjects, creating a "Gothic" couple instantly recognizable as midwestern and old fashioned. The artist intended but never completed a companion painting of a mission bungalow and mission-type people, a painting that would emphasize the horizontal rather than the vertical. In the fall of 1930, *American Gothic* won the Norman Walt Harris Bronz Medal at the Art Institute of Chicago's forty-third annual exhibit of American paintings. The Art Institute bought the painting for $300, and it quickly gained notoriety beyond the city. Reactions were mixed. Some viewed the work as a humorously honest recording of contemporary midwesterners with Victorian-era attitudes. Others found the work to be a vicious satire of close-minded small town folk frankly suspicious of modern society and inventions. In response to the polarized interpretations of the painting, Wood told a reporter,

"These people had bad points and I did not paint them under, but to me they were basically good and solid people" (*Cedar Rapids Gazette*, 5 Sept. 1942).

Wood followed *American Gothic* with paintings that straddle the line between an honest reverence for American history and a satirical perspective on the country's valued myths. His *Birthplace of Herbert Hoover* (1931) trivialized the tiny cottage in which Hoover, the first president from Iowa, was born and which he had capitalized upon in his "humble beginnings" campaign. Wood's *Midnight Ride of Paul Revere* (1931), included at the forty-fourth annual exhibition at the Art Institute of Chicago, reduced the popular colonial hero to a tiny figure in a doll-like scene. Perhaps Wood's most vicious satire was his *Daughters of Revolution* (1932), which was displayed at the first Biennial Exhibit at the Whitney Museum of American Art in New York City. Some members of the Daughters of the American Revolution and American Legionnaires had objected to the German manufacture of Wood's stained glass window for the Veterans Memorial Building, causing the window to remain undedicated during Wood's lifetime. As Wood's retort, the painting portrays three tight-lipped women (whom Wood called "those Tory girls") standing, with tea cups in hand, before a reproduction of German artist Emanuel Leutze's famous painting *Washington Crossing the Delaware*.

In the summers of 1932 and 1933 Wood, along with Edward Rowan and Adrian Dornbush, an instructor from the Little Gallery, ran an art school in Stone City that was established to celebrate Iowa's and the Midwest's cultural identity. Students were encouraged to portray their local surroundings, and on the weekends the general public was invited to visit to see art exhibitions, sing folk music, and listen to famous Iowan poet Jay Sigmund read from his work. From January to June 1934 Wood served as state director of the Public Works of Art Project (PWAP) for Iowa. In this capacity he helped coordinate the dispersal of funds and the production of American-scene murals in public buildings. After the PWAP offices moved to Iowa City, Wood followed and in July 1934 became associate professor of fine arts at the University of Iowa. As a member of the faculty he helped to modernize the department's studio curriculum; although the chairman taught in the French academic tradition, Wood taught with more modern methods, with an eye for abstract movement and sometimes using photography as an aid. During his tenure the university established B.F.A. and M.F.A. degrees. He also complemented the English department, which already featured such regionalist writers as Frank Luther Mott, Paul Engle, and John T. Frederick.

While vacationing during the summer of 1934, Wood and poet Jay Sigmund were both involved in separate car accidents. Wood's involved his new car and a milk truck. These two incidents inspired his painting *Death on Ridge Road* (1935), which depicts a crash about to happen on an inclined two-lane highway; a limousine straddles the lane just having passed a Ford, and a large truck is coming up over the hill, headed straight toward the limousine. No fan of automobiles, Wood chose to depict the hazards of careless driving and the capability for destruction of these modern machines.

Regionalism became a household word after *Time* magazine devoted the lead article in its 24 December 1934 issue to the regionalist art movement. The regionalist triumvirate of Wood, Thomas Hart Benton, and John Steaurt Curry was featured prominently, as were other American-scene artists who had rejected abstraction in order to paint "what could be seen in their own land—streets, fields, shipyards, factories and those people of those places." The article proclaimed Wood "the chief philosopher and greatest teacher of representational U.S. art." (In 1940 he drew a portrait of Secretary of Agriculture Henry A. Wallace that was reproduced on the cover of *Time*.) In 1935 Wood, assisted by Frank Luther Mott, wrote "Revolt from the City," a regionalist treatise in which he argued that the depression was freeing American artists from the oppression of European- and New York City–based styles such as cubism and surrealism by spurring a deep self-reflection of one's own culture and background. Wood hoped that art centers such as the Stone City school would promote competition between artists from different regions of the country.

Also in 1935 Wood surprised many family members and friends by marrying Sara Sherman Maxon, a singer and actress. He had had few serious relationships with women, and Maxon was not only older than Wood, she was also a grandmother. The couple bought a house in Iowa City and lavishly entertained the many guest lecturers who visited the university, including Robert Frost and Carl Sandburg. The marriage was childless, however, and Wood and Maxon were divorced in 1939. The same year of his marriage, Wood was elected to the National Academy of Design and had two one-man exhibitions—at Lakeside Press Galleries in Chicago and at Feragil Galleries in New York City. He received a book contract from Doubleday to write his autobiography, to be titled *Return from Bohemia*, but it was never completed. For the cover, Wood created a self-portrait showing himself seated in front of an easel, with palette and brush in hand, surrounded by anonymous bystanders looking over his shoulder.

Toward the mid-1930s Wood favored illustration and printmaking over painting. During this period he drew scenes for Madeline Darrough's children's story *Horn's Farm on the Hill* and made nine illustrations for a limited edition of Sinclair Lewis's novel *Main Street*. Wood also created nineteen lithographs for Associated American Artists (AAA), a group that promoted American artists by selling original prints at modest prices (as low as $5 each) to the general public by mail order from its headquarters in New York City. In the late 1930s Wood received several honorary degrees, which he poked fun at—as well as himself—in his lithograph *Honorary Degree* (1937). The artist, depicted as short and plump, is shown receiving a diploma from two elongated effete types while standing in front of a Gothic church window.

Wood painted his last major satirical painting, *Parson Weems' Fable*, in 1939. The image shows Weems, who in 1806 published the anecdote of George Washington cutting down his father's cherry tree, pulling back a red curtain with cherrylike trim exposing a scene from the story. Curiously, Wood depicted Washington as a small boy but with an adult face—the same face as in Gilbert Stuart's famous portrait. Washington holds a hatchet in his hand and looks up to his father who holds the broken tree. As in his paintings about the DAR, Paul Revere, and Herbert Hoover, *Parson Weems' Fable* addresses Wood's interest in the confusion of fact and fiction in collective history. The creator of the fiction, Weems, is the most important figure, gazing to the viewer and pointing at his "creation." Wood's painting manages to keep the story current and interesting to contemporary viewers, while underlining the fact that it depicts a folktale and not an actual historical event.

In February 1940 Wood lectured throughout California and painted *Sentimental Ballad* on location at a Hollywood studio production of the film version of Eugene O'Neill's play *The Long Voyage Home*. A young John Wayne is one of the actors depicted as a group of drunk sailors singing an old ballad.

Criticized for painting from photos and for using a strict compositional grid in every painting in order to create a dynamic composition, Wood took a leave of absence from the University of Iowa in 1940–1941 amid controversy over his rigid teaching methods. Some critics even likened his subject matter to that popularized in Nazi Germany. In the fall of 1941, however, the university asked Wood to return to fill a special chair position as University Professor of Fine Arts, a token position meant to satisfy the demands of Wood and his supporters without further detriment to the art department. He completed several more prints as well as the self-portrait he had labored over for years (housed at the Davenport Art Gallery in Davenport, Iowa) before succumbing to liver cancer one day short of his fifty-first birthday. A posthumous retrospective was held in the fall of 1942 at the fifty-third annual Exhibition of American Painting and Sculpture at the Art Institute of Chicago.

Wood was a severe critic of the idea of "art for art's sake," and he struggled valiantly his entire life to maintain regionalism as a popular art form. As he once remarked, "Art isn't worth a damn if you can't make these people around here appreciate it" (quoted in Garwood, p. 151). During the late 1920s and early 1930s, Wood's painting and the regionalist style meshed with the national interest, coinciding as it did with the depression, isolationism, and New Deal populism; but by the late 1930s, an outward-looking public began to view regionalism as either hopelessly naive or suspiciously xenophobic. After World War II, abstract expressionism, which prized personal expression over populist themes, dominated the modern art movement. Surviving the demise of regionalism, *American Gothic* in particular has continued to be an extremely popular image that, especially through parody, has remained familiar to succeeding generations.

• Wood's letters, papers, and scrapbooks are in the Archives of American Art, Washington, D.C. Also at the Archives are the first chapters of his unfinished autobiography, which actually were written by Park Rinard. Biographical works include Darrell Garwood, *Artist in Iowa: A Life of Grant Wood* (1944), and Nan Wood Graham, with John Zug and Julia Jensen McDonald, *My Brother, Grant Wood* (1993). The best critical monograph is James M. Dennis, *Grant Wood: A Study in American Art and Culture* (1986); also see Wanda Corn, *Grant Wood: the Regionalist Vision*, exhibition catalog, Whitney Museum of American Art (1983), and Brady M. Roberts et al., *Grant Wood: An American Master Revealed*, exhibition catalog, Davenport Art Museum (1995). An obituary is in the *New York Times*, 13 Feb. 1942.

N. ELIZABETH SCHLATTER

WOOD, Horatio C., Jr. (13 Jan. 1841–3 Jan. 1920), physician, educator, and editor, was born in Philadelphia, Pennsylvania, the son of Horatio Curtis Wood, a successful businessman, and Elizabeth Head Bacon. His parents used "C" (without a period) as his middle name, a compromise between Curtis and Charles. That Wood was inconsistent in signing his name, and that one of his sons, who also had a distinguished career in medicine, was named Horatio Charles Wood, Jr., further confused the situation. Wood began his education at age four in a Society of Friends boarding school, and he continued at the Friends Select School in Philadelphia. He traced his initial interests in science to two sources. First, on a visit to the Philadelphia Academy of Natural Sciences in his early teens, Wood convinced the director, Joseph Leidy, to permit him to study the academy's museum and book collections firsthand. Second, his uncle, George B. Wood, was a well-known figure in medicine, and he imbued his nephew with an abiding interest in science and medicine.

Wood enrolled in the medical department at the University of Pennsylvania in 1859, and he graduated three years later. He interned at the Pennsylvania General Hospital and the Philadelphia General Hospital (Blockley), then entered the army, where he was an acting assistant surgeon. He returned to Philadelphia to begin a private medical practice after the Civil War. In 1866 Wood married Elizabeth Longacre, daughter of the chief coiner of the U.S. Mint at Philadelphia; they had four children who reached adulthood.

Most of Wood's income derived not from his private medical practice but rather from his work as a quizmaster, or private teacher, in the medical department at the University of Pennsylvania, where he offered instruction in medicine, therapeutics, and chemistry. The university recognized Wood's abilities in the natural sciences by awarding him the professorship of botany in the auxiliary faculty of medicine in 1866; his uncle tried unsuccessfully to discourage this pursuit. In 1875 Wood was named clinical professor of nervous diseases, and by 1877 he was also professor of materia medica, pharmacy, and general therapeutics.

By this time Wood had earned a wide reputation in several fields. His research in entomology attracted the attention of Louis Agassiz. Like Agassiz and other natural scientists of the time, Wood conducted expeditions to collect samples of flora and fauna, in his case to enhance the collections of the Smithsonian Institution. His first excursion took him to the Bahamas, and he later explored the mountains, valleys, and deserts of Texas and Mexico.

Wood also promoted reforms in medical education. The changes for which Wood lobbied at the University of Pennsylvania medical department, certainly a high-profile program at the time, had ramifications elsewhere. With Provost William Pepper and others, Wood effected curricular reforms at the medical department by expanding the terms, adding new science subjects prior to clinical study, and helping to establish a university-operated hospital to enhance clinical instruction without outside interference from municipal or other sources.

Among Wood's most significant contributions to medicine and science was his text, *A Treatise on Therapeutics: Comprising Materia Medica and Toxicology, with Especial Reference to the Application of the Physiological Action of Drugs to Clinical Medicine* (1874), which reached its twelfth edition by 1905. The therapeutic armamentarium, at least insofar as it was presented to American medical students, had been based primarily on empirical clinical observations. The *Treatise* was a pioneering book that systematically applied modern pharmacological principles—an experimentally based understanding of the physiological action of drugs—to therapeutics. Wood did considerable research in pharmacology, but he did not go so far as to establish it as a discipline in the United States; John Jacob Abel, the German-trained pharmacologist who studied briefly in Wood's laboratory, led that effort beginning in the 1890s.

Wood's editorial interests derived from his expertise in drugs and therapeutics. For example, he coedited *The Dispensatory of the United States of America* (*USD*) from 1883 to 1907, covering the fifteenth through nineteenth editions. The *USD*, which George B. Wood cofounded in 1833, was a detailed commentary on *The Pharmacopoeia of the United States* (*USP*), the most important compendium of drug standards in the nation; many pharmacists and physicians actually knew the *USP* only from the *USD*. In the 1870s and 1880s Horatio Wood edited three journals, *New Remedies*, *Philadelphia Medical Times*, and the *Therapeutic Gazette*. From 1890 to 1910 he headed the U.S. Pharmacopoeial Convention, an organization that established policies for the *USP*. During this period the *USP* evolved substantially; for example, it added assays for active ingredients in crude drugs, and in 1906 it became an official, legally recognized compendium for drug standards.

Wood was a prolific scholar, producing numerous monographs and scores of papers on neurology, botany, entomology, pharmacology, physiology, medical jurisprudence, medicine and therapeutics, and medical education. His most personally satisfying research projects concerned the nature of sunstroke, the physiological action of hyoscine (a derivative of a henbane alkaloid), the treatment of accidents incurred during anesthesia, and the physiological action of alcohol on the circulation. As a man of many interests, Wood was not atypical of nineteenth-century medical scientists, yet he made significant contributions to several fields. In American pharmacology in particular he is best seen as a transitional figure, between the empiricism and testimony that informed therapeutics and the materia medica before him, and the systematic development of experimental therapeutics as the basis of drug therapy that followed him. He died in Philadelphia.

• Selected unpublished documents—notes of Wood's lectures for the most part—are in the Library of the College of Physicians of Philadelphia. Correspondence documenting his work for the *USP* are in the *USP* Papers in the State Historical Society of Wisconsin, Madison. Late in life Wood wrote "Reminiscences of an American Pioneer in Experimental Medicine," *Transactions of the College of Physicians of Philadelphia* 3d ser., 42 (1920): 195–234. The same volume of the *Transactions* includes a number of memorial pieces on Wood's life by his students and colleagues. More objective is the biography by George B. Roth, "Horatio C Wood, Jr.," National Academy of Sciences, *Biographical Memoirs* 33 (1959): 462–84. The Roth article and an appendix to G. E. de Schweinitz, "Dr. H. C. Wood as a Medical Teacher," *Transactions of the College of Physicians of Philadelphia* 3d. ser., 42 (1920): 242–57, both have a complete bibliography of Wood's contributions.

JOHN P. SWANN

WOOD, James (12 Nov. 1839–19 Dec. 1925), Quaker leader and experimental farmer, was born in Mount Kisco, New York, the son of Stephen Wood and Phebe Underhill, farmers. The clan of fifty Wood and Underhill cousins had lived on neighboring farms or homes in Westchester County since about 1809. James Wood attended the Philadelphia Quakers' Westtown School and then went to Haverford College. In 1866 he married a Philadelphia Quaker, Emily Hollingsworth Morris, with whom he would have three children. In 1870 they moved into "Braewold," a Scottish-style stone house that was built to replace the one that had burned down a year before. The Woods' oldest daughter, Ellen, a nurse, was engaged to Quaker reformer Rufus Jones, but she died from typhoid before they could marry. The Woods' other children, Carolena Wood and L. Hollingsworth Wood, later became famous in Quaker service.

From Braewold Wood wrote and lectured about experiments in fodder-growing and horticulture but mainly introduced, bred, and sold Hampshire sheep and Ayrshire cattle. He became president of the Bedford Farmers' Club and the Hampshire-Down Breeders Association of America. Active in community life, in 1886 he ran for Congress from Westchester County as a Teddy Roosevelt Republican, and lost narrowly.

He also lobbied against the expensive widening of the Erie Canal in 1903. An avid reader, Wood served as an officer of the Westchester County Historical Society (president from 1885 to 1896) and reported on local history. He also wrote on prison reform and state care of the feeble-minded as Letchworth Village, a pioneering institution for the feeble-minded, was being organized. He was an executive committee member of the New York Prison Association, an organizer of the New York State Reformatory for Women at Bedford, and the president of its board from 1900 to 1916. He also was president of the Westchester Temporary Home for Destitute Children from 1881 to 1909. On the national level, he organized the New York State agricultural exhibit at the World's Columbian Exposition held in Chicago in 1893.

Wood was unashamedly religious. A member of the Westchester County Bible Society beginning in 1860, he was treasurer from 1878 to 1905 and president from 1905 to 1925. He was elected to the board of managers of the American Bible Society (ABS) in 1896 and served as its vice president in 1903 and as its president from 1911 to 1919, thereafter as president emeritus until his death. In 1910 he represented the ABS at the World Missionary Conference in Edinburgh, where he began a friendship with Henry Hodgkin, Quaker teacher from China. Wood traveled twice to San Francisco. During his 1914 visit he set up the Bible House, headquarters of the ABS in New York. In 1915, while traveling to San Francisco via the Panama Canal, he set up an ABS center in Cristobal for sailors on passing ships; once in San Francisco, he presided at the ABS-sponsored World's Bible Congress. Never "zealous for office," Wood was described as a "natural leader" who "presided with a perfect knowledge of the business . . . always controlling it, yet without the appearance of control" (ABS board of managers minutes, 1 July 1926).

Wood often traveled with his family, which suggests that Emily Wood, although she was often sick, shared her husband's interests. In 1881 they visited Moravian schools in Europe, and the entire family spent much of 1891–1892 in Dresden, where they learned German and studied art. While there, Wood arranged for Mark Twain to present a lecture in support of the Dresden American Church. From Germany the Woods traveled, via Greece and Egypt, to Palestine and Lebanon in order to visit Quaker mission schools at Ramallah and Brumana. Wood revisited Europe with members of his family five other times. In 1898 Wood traveled through Mexico and Cuba to visit new Quaker missions in those countries.

Wood's important role was as a leader in the formation of cooperative national organizations within the Society of Friends. Wood's Croton Valley Meeting was part of the countywide Purchase Quarterly Meeting, over which he presided as clerk from 1876 to 1881. He belonged in turn to the Yearly Meeting of the New York region, of which he was assistant clerk from 1875 to 1880 and clerk in 1882 and from 1893 to 1925. Although Quakers in these Meetings worshiped in silence, were pacifists, and referred to one another as "thee" and "thou," they belonged to the more Christ-centered, or Orthodox, branch of Quakerism, which had interacted with other Christians through revivals and Bible societies, particularly in the Midwest. Some members even accepted Methodist or Baptist doctrines about the sacraments and sanctification. To that time, Quakers had no central body and were not bound by any external authority.

A general conference held in Richmond, Indiana, in 1887 was attended by delegates from all the Orthodox Yearly Meetings and delegates from the corresponding Philadelphia, London, and Ireland Yearly Meetings. Wood, a New York delegate, was chosen chairman, and in that capacity he guided the group to accept the doctrinal declaration, drafted by J. B. Braithwaite of England, that allowed for pastors in some Meetings. Plans also were made to gather again every five years. Wood attended each session of the resulting Five Years Meeting, beginning in 1902; he presided as clerk in 1907, as he had over the 1897 preparative session, during which he also chaired the Committee on Constitution and Discipline, through which a framework for a new federation was set up. The three crucial elements of this federation were: a sharing of much of the Yearly Meetings' mission work; the publication of a common weekly journal, the *American Friend* (edited by Rufus Jones), the result of the 1894 merger of the *Friends' Review*, a staid Philadelphia paper, with an evangelical midwestern one, the *Christian Worker*; the integration of materials on Quaker practices and doctrines for a uniform book of discipline intended for all Christ-centered Yearly Meetings, which Wood and Jones hammered out at Mount Kisco. After several rounds of interaction with other Quakers, and the publication of several interpretative articles in the *American Friend*, Wood and Jones persuaded the 1902 session, and many of the member Yearly Meetings, to adopt their guide book.

In 1893 Wood served as the Quaker representative to the World's Parliament of Religions, which was held in conjunction with the World's Columbian Exposition. There he delivered an address, published as *Our Church and Its Mission*. It, along with *Distinguishing Doctrines of the Society of Friends*, which was presented at the 1898 session of Philadelphia Yearly Meeting, were Wood's best-known published writings. They combined basic Christian doctrines as expressed in Wood's lifetime with the particular Quaker doctrines regarding peace and the individual believer's direct inspiration by the Holy Spirit. Wood also had summarized Quaker history in a bicentenary address for New York Yearly Meeting in 1895, and he was a frequent contributor to the *Friends' Review* and its successor, the *American Friend* on topics then debated between Friends, such as the calling and role of pastors, biblical research, and the new openness of British Quakers to Hicksite Friends. Yet he also cared and wrote about the unity of truth and of the branches of Christianity.

Wood served on the board of Bryn Mawr College from 1898 to 1918 and as chairman from 1912 to 1916—until he clashed with Mary Cary Thomas over policy. He served as a board member at Haverford College from 1885 to 1919, and in 1898 he gave an address on "The Intimate Relation of Christianity and the Modern Scientific Spirit, and Haverford's Connection with These." Because of that address, his evidence of breadth of scholarship, Philadelphia "Orthodox" Friends did not have the suspicion of science that other evangelicals have sometimes shown. Wood died at Mount Kisco.

• Wood's letters and manuscripts are at Braewold. They include six undated lectures he gave at Haverford on various periods of American history. There is also a manuscript autobiography, "The Education of James Wood" (1924). See also *Proceedings of the General Conference of Friends . . . at Richmond, Indiana* (1887); Minutes of the Five Years Meeting sessions of 1902, 1907, 1912, and the conference of 1897; files of *Friends' Review* and *American Friend*; Thomas D. Hamm, *The Transformation of American Quakerism: Orthodox Friends, 1800–1907* (1988); Hugh Barbour et al., *Quaker Crosscurrents: Three Hundred Years of Friends in the New York Yearly Meetings* (1995); and the archives of the American Bible Society. Herbert Barber Howe, *Yorkshire to Westchester: A Chronicle of the Wood Family* (1948), helps with personal details.

HUGH BARBOUR

WOOD, James Frederick (27 Apr. 1813–20 June 1883), Roman Catholic bishop, was born in Philadelphia, Pennsylvania, the son of James Wood, an importer and auctioneer, and Anne Bryan. He was baptized on 11 October 1813 in the First Unitarian Church of Philadelphia. His early education began in a grammar school on Dock Street, Philadelphia. From 1821 to 1826 Wood studied abroad at a grammar school connected with St. Mary de Crypt, Gloucester, England. Back in Philadelphia, he received commercial training at a Mr. Sanderson's private school on Market Street.

In 1827 the family settled in Cincinnati, Ohio, where the young Wood worked as a bank clerk. He advanced to the post of cashier of Cincinnati's Franklin Bank. There he met and was befriended by John Baptist Purcell, Cincinnati's young bishop; on 7 April 1836 Purcell received Wood into the Catholic church. The next year Wood decided to study for the priesthood. He spent seven years at the Urban College of the Propaganda, Rome. There, on 25 March 1844, he was ordained to the priesthood by Giacomo Cardinal Fransoni. In October of the same year Wood was appointed assistant rector of the Cathedral of Cincinnati, where he served for ten years. Next he became the pastor of St. Patrick's Church, Cincinnati. Three years later Wood was appointed titular bishop of Antigonia and coadjutor with the right to succession to John Nepomucene Neumann of Philadelphia. Purcell consecrated him bishop on 26 April 1857 in Cincinnati's cathedral.

Bishop Neumann had not asked Rome for a coadjutor but rather that his diocese, which included all Pennsylvania, Delaware, and western New Jersey, be divided. For his part, Wood understood, wrongly, that Neumann intended to resign from the see of Philadelphia. Instead, Neumann entrusted Wood with the diocese's financial affairs, an arrangement that the coadjutor found most unsatisfactory. Nonetheless, Wood's early financial experience proved a boon. Under his watchful eye, the "Bishop's Bank," established in 1848 by Francis Patrick Kenrick, survived the financial panic of 1857. Several decades later, when the bank of his friend Purcell failed, Wood prudently decided to liquidate his as too risky a venture.

In 1864 Wood's expertise brought to completion the Cathedral of Saints Peter and Paul, which Kenrick had begun sixteen years earlier. In 1866 he laid the cornerstone for a seminary located on a large tract of prime property in Overbrook that he had had the foresight to purchase. St. Charles Borromeo Seminary received its first students in 1871.

After Neumann's sudden death in 1860, Wood became full administrator of the vast diocese. Eight years later the diocese of Philadelphia was divided and the additional sees of Wilmington, Harrisburg, and Scranton were established. In 1875 Philadelphia became a metropolitan see and Wood its archbishop.

Always devoted to the pope, Wood introduced the "Peter's Pence" collection in his diocese in 1860. Regularly thereafter he sent generous sums to Rome. While in Rome for the canonization of the Japanese martyrs in 1862, Wood was appointed an assistant prelate to the papal throne. Five years later he returned for the eighteenth, one hundredth anniversary of the martyrdoms of Saints Peter and Paul. Wood attended the opening of the First Council of the Vatican in 1869. On the jubilee of Pope Pius IX, he read an address as representative of the Catholic church in the United States. Forced to leave the council because of illness, Wood voted in absentia in favor of the doctrine of papal infallibility. On 16 December 1870 Wood called for a mass meeting in the Philadelphia cathedral to protest the Sardinian invasion of the papal states. In 1877 Wood was again in Rome for the celebration of Pius IX's fiftieth anniversary as bishop.

Affection for Rome was evident in Wood's enthusiasm and financial support for the American College founded in 1859 for ecclesiastical students from the United States. After Wood's appointment as secretary of the college's board of finance in 1866, he insisted that the institution's funds be invested and kept in America.

Though he would always abstain from politics, during the Civil War Wood cooperated with Governor Andrew G. Curtin's call for military chaplains and for nursing Sisters. Several times during the conflict, the bishop visited Satterlee Hospital, confirming and comforting the wounded soldiers there.

Wood had a stern side, too. A staunch opponent of all secret societies, he appeared markedly unsympathetic to Irish causes, reprobating all their political activities in the United States. Wood excommunicated Catholic members of the Mollie Maguires, those exploited coal miners whose frustrations eventually turned criminal. To his credit, Wood sent some $60,000 for Irish famine relief during the years 1880 to 1883.

Wood's solicitude for the abandoned poor, especially orphans, led him to enlarge St. Vincent's Home, found and manage the Catholic Home for destitute orphan girls, and found a House of the Good Shepherd. Among the religious communities he brought to his see were the Little Sisters of the Poor. To help provide for the religious and secular education of youth, he invited the Sisters of Mercy, the Sisters of Christian Charity, and the Oblate Sisters of Divine Providence, founded in Baltimore, Maryland, in 1829, to educate "young girls of color." Wood brought from England the Sisters of the Holy Child, founded by a native Philadelphian, Cornelia Peacock Connelly. He encouraged the Franciscan Sisters, who had been brought by Neumann, and helped establish the Sisters of St. Joseph in Chestnut Hill and the Sisters, Servants of the Immaculate Heart of Mary in their new home in Chester County.

For the last fourteen years of his life, Wood suffered from Bright's disease and chronic rheumatism, which relentlessly eroded his vigorous frame. At the time of his death in Philadelphia, 300,000 Philadelphia Catholics were ministered to by 260 priests in 127 churches, and 22,000 children attended 58 parochial schools. Other Catholic institutions included six orphanages, four hospitals, one widows' asylum, and two homes for the aged. These institutions were staffed largely by thirteen religious orders of Sisters, whose total membership numbered more than 1,000. In 1964 Archbishop Wood High School was dedicated in memory of Philadelphia's fifth bishop. Still, his episcopal accomplishments have been overshadowed by those of his immediate predecessors, Neumann, the saintly bishop, and Kenrick, the scholar bishop. The cathedral and the seminary stand as Wood's most enduring memorials.

• The Wood collection is housed in the Archives of the Philadelphia Archdiocesan Historical Research Center. Several early accounts of Wood include Richard H. Clarke, *Lives of the Deceased Bishops of the Catholic Church in the United States*, vol. 3 (1888), pp. 533–47, and, anonymous, "Most Rev. James Frederick Wood, D.D., Bishop and First Archbishop of Philadelphia," in *Lives and Times of Philadelphia's Archbishops: Nineteen Hundred and Eighteen* (1918). Though brief, the best biographical piece is Francis L. Dennis, O.S.A., "Most Rev. James Frederick Wood (1813–1883), the Fifth Bishop and First Archbishop of Philadelphia" (master's thesis, Catholic Univ. of America, 1932). Wood's nettlesome relationship with the Irish is documented in Thomas C. Middleton, D.D., O.S.A., "Some Memoirs of Our Lady's Shrine," *Records of the American Catholic Historical Society* 12 (1901): 273–77. For a frank discussion of his discontent as Neumann's coadjutor see Alfred C. Rush et al., "The Saintly John Neumann and His Coadjutor Archbishop Wood," in *The History of the Archdiocese of Philadelphia*, ed. James F. Connelly (1976). Connelly also includes Wood in his *St. Charles Seminary: Philadelphia* (1979). Obituaries are in the Philadelphia *Evening Bulletin*, 20 June 1883, and the Philadelphia *Catholic Standard*, 30 June 1883.

MARGARET MARY REHER

WOOD, John (c. 1775–15 May 1822), political writer and cartographer, was born in Scotland. Nothing is known of his parents. He spent much of his early life in France and briefly resided in Switzerland. Although particulars of Wood's education are not known, he had solid learning, excelling in mathematics. Back in Scotland in 1799, he was named master of the Academy for the Improvement of Arts in Scotland in Edinburgh, and he published *A General View of the History of Switzerland* (1799), which tells of his experiences in Switzerland during the French invasion of that country in 1798.

Wood traveled to the United States in 1800, first settling in New York City, where he tutored the sons and daughters of the local elite in Latin, Greek, and French. Aaron Burr's daughter, Theodosia Burr, was reportedly one of his pupils. Wood published *Letter to Alexander Addison, Esqr. . . . in Answer to His Rise and Progress of Revolution* (1801), which took to task the denunciations by Addison, an extreme Federalist and presiding judge of Pennsylvania's Fifth Judicial District, of political expression adverse to the government. Wood's writing talent attracted the interest of leaders of the Jeffersonian Republican party, and James Cheetham and David Denniston, publishers of the daily Republican newspaper, the *American Citizen*, sized up Wood for Thomas Jefferson. Wood, they said, "is a Good Mathematician, and ellegant drawer, and a Complete master of the Greek, latin, and french languages. But he has *no fixed principles in politics* and in every respect he is a man of Great indecision and versatility. . . . By profession he is a republican: in action *anything*" ("Letters of James Cheetham," 30 Jan. 1802, p. 53).

On 19 June 1801 Wood signed a contract with William Barlass and Matthias Ward, booksellers of New York City, to write for $200 a 500-page book on the presidency of John Adams. Pressed by a tight deadline, Wood made *The History of the Administration of John Adams, Late President of the United States* (1802) a mishmash of materials borrowed from William Duane's Republican newspaper, the *Aurora*, James Callender's *The Prospect before Us* (1800), and other writings along with "some occasional hints, received from gentlemen in New-York and Philadelphia" (Kline, vol. 2, p. 642). Wood's book contained thirty pages of "high elogium" on Aaron Burr. Advance copies revealed that the book was highly libelous and if offered to the public could backfire on the Republicans. Shocked at what he read, Burr arranged to buy the entire edition. When Burr did not complete payments, the book was released and referred to as "the suppressed history." Burr was accused of trying to appease the Federalists to enhance his own political future in New York. A vigorous pamphlet war ensued between the partisans of Burr and DeWitt Clinton, representing different factions of the New York Republican party. Cheetham published five anti-Burr pamphlets, to which Wood responded in writings defending Burr, namely *A Correct Statement of the Various Sources from Which the History of the Administration of John Adams Was Compiled and the Motives for Its Suppression by Col. Burr* (1802) and *A Full Exposition of the [DeWitt] Clintonian Faction and the Society of the Columbian Illuminati . . .* (1802). The whole controversy injured Burr's chances of winning the New York governorship in 1804.

Wood moved to Richmond, Virginia, where he became associated with another hack writer, Joseph M. Street. In early 1806 the men went to Frankfort, Kentucky, and in July 1806 started publishing the *Western World*, a rival newspaper of the *Kentucky Gazette* in Lexington. The *Western World* carried a series of articles exposing supposed treasonable activities of prominent Kentuckians in dealing with the Spaniards to separate Kentucky from the United States. Wood disavowed any responsibility for the printing of the "Spanish conspiracy" articles and blamed Street for not clearing them with him. Acting on advice from Henry Clay and others, Wood severed his partnership with Street and withdrew from his involvement with the *Western World*. Wood returned to Richmond, Virginia. In 1807 he published *Full Statement of the Trial and Acquittal of Aaron Burr*. His Kentucky experience having soured him on political advocacy, Wood renewed his scientific interests. In 1809 he published *A New Theory of the Diurnal Rotation of the Earth*.

In 1815 Wood settled on a farm near Lynchburg, Virginia, but soon tired of the rural life. The next year he answered an advertisement placed by Governor Wilson Cary Nicholas for someone to map the major rivers of Tidewater Virginia. Jefferson recommended Wood to the governor, saying, "[Wood] has had good experience in the works of the field. He is a great walker and probably equal to the bodily fatigue." Wood received the assignment and by the end of 1818 had mapped the Piankatank, James, Rappahannock, Potomac, Chickahominy, Pamunkey, and Mattaponi rivers. In April 1819 Governor James P. Preston named Wood surveyor general in charge of mapping each of the Virginia counties and preparing a Virginia state map. Wood directly supervised the mapping of the western counties beyond the Blue Ridge, leaving the rest of the counties to Andrew Alexander, George Wyche, and William H. Merewether. By February 1822 Wood had submitted ninety-six county maps, leaving those for only six counties unfinished. One difficulty in producing the state map was that Wood used a scale of 320 poles (or perches, each 16.5 feet) per inch for counties west of the Blue Ridge (including present W.Va.) and 200 poles per inch for the counties to the east. Wood's successor, Herman Boye, later corrected this deficiency. The state map, published in 1827, was 61.5 by 93 inches, engraved by Henry S. Tanner on nine plates. It was, as E. M. Sanchez-Saavedra notes, "the most elaborate state map produced in America before 1850." In May 1822, while in Washington, D.C., to correlate his findings with U.S. government maps, Wood became ill and returned to Richmond, where he died.

• Wood's correspondence is in the Preston Family Papers, Virginia Historical Society, Richmond; the Harry Innes Papers, Library of Congress; H. W. Flournoy, ed., *Calendar of Virginia State Papers*, vol. 10 (1892); and *The Papers of Henry Clay*, ed. James F. Hopkins, vol. 1 (1959), which has two letters from Wood to Clay. The controversy over Wood's book on the Adams administration as it relates to Burr and N.Y. politics is treated in the text commentary of *Political Correspondence and Public Papers of Aaron Burr*, ed. Mary-Jo Kline, vol. 2 (1983); Milton Lomask, *Aaron Burr*, vol. 2 (1982); [Worthington C. Ford?], "Letters of James Cheetham," *Proceedings of the Massachusetts Historical Society*, 3d ser., 1 (1908): 41–64; and Justin Winsor, ed., *Narrative and Critical History of America*, vol. 7 (1888). Temple Bodley, ed., *Littell's Political Transactions in and Concerning Kentucky* (1926; repr. 1971), and A. C. Quisenberry, *The Life and Times of Hon. Humphrey Marshall* (1892), analyze the *Western World* and the "Spanish conspiracy" imbroglio. Earl G. Swem, comp., "Maps Relating to Virginia in the Virginia State Library and Other Departments of the Commonwealth," *Virginia State Library Bulletin* 7, nos. 2 and 3 (Apr., July 1914): 41–263, lists and describes twenty-five of Wood's maps. For discussions of Wood as a mapmaker, see E. M. Sanchez-Saavedra, *A Description of the Country: Virginia's Cartographers and Their Maps, 1607–1881* (1975), and Virginia State Library and Archives, *A Sense of Place: Early Virginia Cartography* (1990), a brochure for an exhibition at the Virginia State Library, 25 May–20 July 1990. A death notice is in the *Richmond Enquirer*, 17 May 1822.

HARRY M. WARD

WOOD, John Stephens (8 Feb. 1885–12 Sept. 1968), U.S. representative, was born near Ball Ground in Cherokee County, Georgia, the son of Jessie L. Wood and Sarah Holcomb, farmers. Wood attended public schools in the rural town of Dahlonega, Georgia, and labored on the family farm. Earning income for college by working in a harness factory and teaching school, he attended North Georgia Agricultural College in Dahlonega and law school at Mercer University in Macon, Georgia. He played varsity baseball at Mercer University and received his LL.B. on 8 June 1910. He commenced practicing law in Jasper, Georgia, on 1 January 1911. In 1913 Wood married Margurete May Roberts. They adopted one child, born in 1918, before she died. In 1914 Wood moved to Canton, Georgia, where he served as city attorney, 1915–1916. Elected to the Georgia House of Representatives in 1917, Wood resigned to enter the U.S. Army Air Service as a cadet private. Returning to his law practice following World War I, he served as solicitor general of the Blue Ridge Judicial Circuit of Georgia, 1921–1926, and judge of the Superior Courts of the Blue Ridge Judicial Circuit, 1926–1931. In 1926 he married Louise Jones; they had three children.

In 1930 Wood challenged Thomas M. Bell, a U.S. House veteran of over a quarter-century and "dean of Georgia's Congressional delegation," and won election as a Democrat to the Seventy-second U.S. Congress. Conducting an intensive six-week campaign, he delivered eighty-eight speeches to audiences averaging more than five hundred people with some as large as 5,000. At the time of Wood's election, the Ninth Congressional District consisted of eighteen counties, "seven of which had no railroads, two of which had no telephones, and two no newspapers." The district was primarily agricultural with some marble and limestone quarries, cotton textile mills, and sawmills.

Wood was reelected to the Seventy-third Congress and served until 3 January 1935. While supporting the Norris–La Guardia Anti-Injunction Act, the Agricultural Adjustment Act of 1933, the Relief Act of 1933, and the repeal of Prohibition, he opposed the Farm Relief Bill of 1933. Following completion of his second term in Congress, Wood was defeated in his renomination bid and returned to Georgia to resume his law practice. In 1944 he was elected once again to the U.S. House of Representatives and served in the Seventy-ninth, Eightieth, Eighty-first, and Eighty-second Congresses (3 Jan. 1945–3 Jan. 1953).

Upon returning to Congress, the southern Democrat, according to the *Congressional Quarterly*, voted more frequently with Republicans than with his own party membership. He opposed measures he thought would expand the federal government at the expense of the states. He supported the Bretton Woods Agreement, the Trade Agreements Act, and joining the United Nations in 1945.

In July 1945 Wood resigned from the House Committee on Foreign Affairs to accept the chairmanship of the House Committee on Un-American Activities (HUAC). Created in 1938 as a temporary, special investigating committee under the chairmanship of Martin Dies (D.-Tex.), HUAC in 1945 became a House standing committee chaired briefly by Edward J. Hart (D.-N.J.). The committee's activities included exposing perceived Communists and their sympathizers in the federal government, American labor unions, and Hollywood; repelling subversive propaganda; and investigating groups that were possibly disseminating atomic bomb information to foreign powers. Some committee meetings were televised, and their activities attracted national attention. As the third chairman of HUAC, Wood announced he would not become involved in "whitewashing or witch-hunting."

Republicans gained control of Congress in 1946, and J. Parnell Thomas (R.-N.J.) replaced Wood as HUAC chairman. Wood remained on the committee with Congressmen Karl E. Mundt, John Rankin, and J. Hardin Peterson. They were joined by new members John McDonnell, Richard Vail, and Richard Nixon. Nixon dominated the investigation that led to the perjury conviction of Alger Hiss. Wood resumed the committee chairmanship when Democrats regained control of the House following the 1948 elections. As chairman, the mild-mannered Wood sought to curb some of the sensationalism of the committee's hearings by conducting fewer public sessions. He announced in January 1949 that radio recorders, newsreels, television, and news photographers would be banned from the committee's hearing room. With the investigations of the committee threatening the civil liberties of numerous citizens, President Harry S. Truman stated indignantly on 22 September 1948, "The committee is more Un-American than the activities it is investigating." President Ronald Reagan later wrote, "Some members of the House Un-American Activities Committee came to Hollywood searching more for personal publicity than they were for Communists." Reagan added, "Many fine people were accused wrongly of being Communists simply because they were liberals."

Wood also served on the House Committee on Education and Labor and played a prominent role in the preservation of the Taft-Hartley Act, a promanagement bill drafted primarily by House majority leader Charles A. Halleck (R.-Ind.). President Truman vetoed the measure, but his veto was overridden. In 1949 Truman tried to repeal the Taft-Hartley Act and restore the Wagner Act via the Lesinski Bill. Wood took the floor of the House, sided with Republicans, and lent his name to a proposal designed to maintain the Taft-Hartley Act. The Lesinski Bill was defeated 275 to 37.

Wood decided not to seek reelection to the House in 1952. Stating that he was "going to try to make a living," he resumed his law practice in Canton, Georgia. In 1955 President Dwight D. Eisenhower nominated him to serve on the Subversive Activities Control Board. U.S. Senate confirmation was denied admidst controversy over whether Wood had been a member during his youth of the Ku Klux Klan, a charge he firmly denied.

Wood died in Marietta, Georgia.

• Biographical information on Wood is in the Department of Records, State of Georgia, and the Georgia Department of Archives and History. See also Carl Beck, *Contempt of Congress: A Study of the Prosecutions Initiated by the Committee on Un-American Activities, 1945–57* (1959); *Biographical Information for the Department of Records of the State of Georgia*; Alistair Cooke, *A Generation on Trial: U.S.A. v. Alger Hiss* (1950); *Current Biography* (1949); Frank J. Donner, *The Un-Americans* (1961); Walter Goodman, *The Committee: The Extraordinary Career of the House Committee on Un-American Activities* (1968); "Under Fire," *New Republic* 122 (26 June 1950): 7; Telford Taylor, *Grand Inquest* (1955); State of Georgia, Department of Archives and History, *Georgia's Official Register* (1951–1952); Ronald Reagan, *An American Life* (1990); "The Congress," *Time*, 9 May 1949, p. 25; and "Goal for Labor: 15 More Votes," *U.S. News and World Report*, 13 May 1949, p. 15. Obituaries are in the *Atlanta Constitution*, 13 Sept. 1968, the *New York Times*, 14 Sept. 1968, and the *Washington Post*, 14 Sept. 1968.

HENRY Z. SCHEELE

WOOD, John Taylor (13 Aug. 1830?–19 July 1904), naval officer, was born at an army outpost, Fort Snelling (now St. Paul, Minn.), the son of Robert C. Wood, Sr., an army surgeon, and Anne Mackall Taylor, the eldest daughter of Zachary Taylor. Jefferson Davis's first marriage was to one of Taylor's daughters. Wood was therefore well connected, grandson of a president of the United States and nephew (by marriage) of the president of the Confederacy. Little is known of his early life and education.

Wood's training as a naval officer was a combination of classroom study and sea duty. In June 1847 he entered Annapolis Naval School for a preparatory course. After serving at the Brazil Station on the frigate *Brandywine* and in the Pacific Ocean on the ship-of-the-line *Ohio* during the Mexican War, he was warranted a midshipman to rank from 7 April 1847. Following five more months of instruction at the naval school in 1850, he served a tour of duty suppressing the slave trade off the African coast on the sloop-of-war *Germantown* and the brig *Porpoise*. Returning to the renamed U.S. Naval Academy in October 1852, Wood graduated second in his class on 10 June 1853.

The intervals at Annapolis continued through Wood's early career, for after he shipped to the Mediterranean aboard the sloop-of-war *Cumberland*, he returned to the naval academy as assistant commandant. He was commissioned a lieutenant as of 16 September 1855. In 1856 he married Lola Mackubin, daughter of George Mackubin, a prominent Maryland public official; they had eleven children. In June 1858 Wood again went to sea, this time as a gunnery officer on the steam frigate *Wabash*, the flagship of the Mediterranean Squadron. Back at Annapolis in 1860, he taught the theory of gunnery, seamanship, and naval tactics.

With the onset of the Civil War, Wood did not wish to move with the remnant of the naval academy to Newport, Rhode Island, because of his growing southern sentiment. On 21 April 1861, his "blood boiling over with indignation" at the Union occupation of Maryland, Wood resigned from the navy. Weeks later the navy dismissed him effective 2 April, which carried the odium of being set prior to the outbreak of hostilities at Fort Sumter. For the moment Wood retired to "Woodland," a small farm he had recently purchased outside Annapolis. He broke with his father, a loyal Union man, who became assistant surgeon general during the war. When, in the wake of the battle of First Manassas, Union troops in Maryland increased the arrest of local citizens suspected of disloyalty, Wood was at risk. He crossed the Potomac River and made his way to Richmond, where his uncle, President Davis, appointed him a lieutenant in the Confederate navy effective 4 October 1861.

Wood first saw duty with naval shore batteries on the Potomac River below Washington, D.C., which disrupted Union shipping on the river during the first year of the war. He then reported to the Aquia Creek Landing batteries, also on the Potomac. In January 1862 he transferred to the CSS *Virginia* at Portsmouth. He participated in the battle with the USS *Monitor* and affiliated actions on Hampton Roads from March to May as commander of the ironclad's aft gun crew. When Union troops approached Richmond, the *Virginia*'s crew destroyed the vessel and moved up the James River to Drewry's Bluff, where Wood, in command of sharpshooters along the riverbank, aided in repulsing the Federal flotilla on 15 May 1862. He was promoted to first lieutenant on 29 September 1862.

Wood now found his niche in the war. He considered battle essential both for morale within the navy and public support of the naval program. Since ship construction was slow, Wood turned to an older method of naval combat—the cutting-out expedition. In October he slipped out of Richmond with small boats on army wagons and a detachment of "picked men" on the first of his midnight raids. Launching his boarding cutters on the Potomac opposite Popes Creek after dark on 7 October, he captured and burned the transport schooner *Frances Elmore*. Wood next led a raid on the Chesapeake Bay, where during the night of 28 October, off Gwyn's Island, he captured and fired the merchant ship *Alleganian*.

Between raids Wood served as naval aide to President Davis. One of the few men to hold dual rank, Wood received the rank of colonel of cavalry effective 26 January 1863. This allowed him to more effectively serve as liaison between the army and navy and put him in the inner circle of the Confederate high command. He made inspections of ship constructions and naval defenses, offering valuable suggestions. Wood found staff duty dull, however, and in August led another Chesapeake raid. On the night of 22 August, off Stingray Point, he captured two Federal gunboats, the USS *Satellite* and the USS *Reliance*, after hand-to-hand combat. (Wood liked the honor of being the first onto an enemy deck.) He also captured the transport schooners *Golden Rod, Coquette*, and *Two Brothers* and eventually destroyed all five vessels.

Davis promoted Wood to commander effective 23 August 1863 for "gallant and meritorious service" in the Chesapeake expedition. After a period of staff duty, on the night of 1 February 1864 Wood captured and fired the USS *Underwriter* on the Neuse River at New Bern, North Carolina. After the action, Wood's boats bore the marks of enemy balls; the wooden pegs inserted averaged fourteen to each boat engaged. It was one of the most arduous cutting-out expeditions in naval history, especially in view of the intensity of enemy fire from shore, and Wood received official thanks from the Confederate Congress. Wood's next raid, during three weeks in August, was on the high seas, where as commander of the commerce destroyer *Tallahassee*, he captured thirty-three Union merchant vessels along the Atlantic Coast between Wilmington, North Carolina, and Halifax, Nova Scotia (16 burned, 10 scuttled, 5 bonded, and 2 released). On 10 February 1865 Wood was promoted to captain for the *Underwriter* capture and the *Tallahassee* cruise.

Wood evacuated Richmond with Davis's entourage on 2 April and was captured with Davis on 10 May near Irwinville, Georgia. Wood escaped, however, by bribing a guard and made his way to Florida, where he joined a small band of ex-Confederates for an adventurous journey to Cuba in one of the great escapes of the war. From Cuba Wood sailed to Halifax, Nova Scotia, where he became a commission merchant and lived out his life as an expatriate. He died in Halifax. Well known in his own day, the gentlemanly Wood was modesty personified but conceived and executed his plans with skill and courage. He was the South's greatest coastal raider.

• The John Taylor Wood Papers are in the Southern Historical Collection, University of North Carolina at Chapel Hill. Some of his wartime letters and reports are included in *The Official Records of the Union and Confederate Navies in the War of the Rebellion* (30 vols., 1894–1922) and *The War of the Rebellion: A Compilation of the Official Records of the Union and Confederate Armies* (128 vols., 1880–1901). For an informative account of Wood's exploits while guarding against the African slave trade aboard the *Porpoise*, see J. Taylor Wood, "The Capture of a Slaver," *Atlantic Monthly* 86 (1900): 451–63. Postwar articles by Wood dealing with some of his wartime exploits are incorporated into Royce Shingleton, *John Taylor Wood: Sea Ghost of the Confederacy* (1979). An obituary is in the Halifax *Morning Chronicle*, 20 July 1904.

ROYCE SHINGLETON

WOOD, Leonard (9 Oct. 1860–7 Aug. 1927), army officer and colonial administrator, was born in Winchester, New Hampshire, the son of Charles J. Wood, a physician, and Caroline Hagar. Following in his father's profession, Wood entered Harvard Medical School in 1880, finished his training there in 1883, receiving an M.D. in 1884, and assumed a position as intern at Boston City Hospital. Wood's persistent violation of a hospital rule prohibiting intern surgery led to his dismissal, revealing an early attitude toward authority and regulations that would later plague his military career.

The dismissal, and a somewhat unremunerative private practice in Boston, forced the young surgeon to consider other alternatives. Acting on a boyhood wish to enter West Point, he impulsively joined the Army Medical Department in June 1885. Assigned as military surgeon in the Department of Arizona at Fort Huachuca, in May 1886 he joined a special unit created by Commanding General Nelson A. Miles to run down a group of Apaches led by the redoubtable Geronimo. The unit chased the Indians through Arizona and deep into the rugged and searing Sierra Madre of Mexico, marching without rest throughout most of the summer and finally forcing Geronimo to surrender in September. Amid much opposition from those who thought a regular army officer should have been selected, Wood alone of all those involved in the chase received the Congressional Medal of Honor.

Following the capture of Geronimo, Wood served several pleasant years of post life in California under General Miles. While stationed at the Presidio he was promoted to captain and married Louisa Condit Smith, the legal ward of U.S. Supreme Court Justice Stephen J. Field; the couple had three children. In 1895, after a two-year tour in Georgia, Wood secured appointment as attending surgeon general at the War Department in Washington, D.C. Because he served as physician to some cabinet members and President William McKinley's invalid wife, he made additional contacts with influential figures. None, however, rivaled his friendship with Assistant Secretary of the Navy Theodore Roosevelt (1858–1919). When the nation went to war with Spain in 1898, the two enthusiasts of the strenuous life and American expansion used their influence to secure command of the First Volunteer Calvary Regiment, popularly known as the Rough Riders. Their military exploits in Cuba launched both men's meteoric rise to prominence, Roosevelt to the presidency, Wood to commanding general of the army.

Wood found his niche after the war as a talented colonial administrator. Appointed military governor of the Cuban province of Santiago late in 1898, he assumed command of the entire island within a few months. He immediately undertook economic, municipal and educational changes that resembled early American progressive reforms. A public works department initiated vast projects from dredging the Havana harbor to constructing hospitals and schools. He restructured municipal governments and created an American style public school system. Finally, he encouraged and supported with government funds the Walter Reed experiments that identified the cause of yellow fever. His aggressiveness in attempting to reform the Cuban society was and still remains highly controversial; some have seen it as evidence of benevolent colonial progressivism, others as a failed attempt to impose an American social and political system on a Latin culture. Whatever the case, his work conformed to the Republican administration's Cuban policy and captured the imagination of the American people.

By the time the United States returned the island to Cuban control in 1902, Wood had received a regular army commission as brigadier general and had become, in the eyes of many, the United States's foremost colonial proconsul. More importantly, by then his comrade in arms was in the White House. In 1903, President Roosevelt appointed him military governor of the Moro Province in the Philippines, a group of islands ruled by recalcitrant Islamic Malays. Wood's policy of subduing the Moros by military force led to several expeditions that culminated in a bloody battle in 1906 at Mount Dajo that left over 600 Moro men, women, and children dead or wounded. Only President Roosevelt's firm support saved Wood from the adverse publicity that ensued from this battle. Such support was not unusual; a few years earlier Roosevelt had promoted Wood to major general, making him one of the highest-ranking officers in the army. This controversial promotion over the heads of hundreds of officers led to Wood's selection as chief of staff of the army in 1910.

As chief of staff, Wood helped bring to completion progressive professional army reforms that had begun several decades earlier. After a bitter and protracted struggle, he deposed the adjutant general as the de facto head of the army and established the dominance of the chief of staff as intended by the act of 1903. Wood's victory was essential to the ultimate consolidation of military leadership in a general staff system that, along with other administrative reforms intended to ensure more efficient administration, served the War Department well when it began organizing the country's World War I Expeditionary Force.

Still, Wood left the chief of staff office in 1914 believing that in one area his efforts had fallen far short of creating a modern American army. Convinced that the United States would fight its future wars with citizen soldiers, he and Secretary of War Henry Stimson tried to establish a permanent reserve training system. Their efforts were thwarted by a budget-cutting Congress and professional officers who distrusted the idea of citizen soldiers. He decided to take the military issue to the American people, a decision that placed him at odds with the apolitical tenets of military professionalism. The outbreak of war in Europe gave Wood a sense of urgency about his cause. Taking advantage of his assignment as commander of the Department of the East, he exploited the mass media of the Northeast in support of military preparedness, making speeches and writing articles and letters spreading the preparedness doctrine. In addition, he persuaded the War Department to sponsor summer civilian training programs—the famous Plattsburg Camps—which he used both to popularize his concept of universal military training and to make converts to preparedness.

Wood's public behavior as a uniformed officer set him on a collision course with the Wilson administration, which initially opposed military preparedness as contrary to its neutrality policy. When the Republicans seized the issue as a way of opposing Woodrow Wilson, Wood found himself in a political struggle with his commander in chief. Public clashes between a determined president and an equally stubborn general pushed Wood to the brink of insubordination and created a serious civil-military crisis. Finding Wood's behavior to be short of a court-martial offense, Wilson administered an even more damaging punishment: he kept the ambitious general out of the war in Europe.

Wood's prophetic prewar preparedness proselytizing gave him a sizable public following. After the war, posing as a victim of partisan politics, he became a candidate for the Republican presidential nomination in January 1920. A stalemate at the convention eventually resulted in the nomination of Warren Harding. Although embittered by this defeat, Wood supported Harding's successful campaign, hoping to be appointed secretary of war. Instead Harding offered him the governorship of the Philippines, and Wood reluctantly accepted it.

In 1921 Wood began the last and, possibly, the stormiest and most controversial of his public endeavors. Committed to Philippine independence, the Wilson administration had passed the Jones Act, which promised independence as soon as a stable government could be established. By 1920 a native assembly and council governed the islands, reducing the governor general to a figurehead. Convinced the Filipinos were not ready for independence, the Republicans were determined to restore their former policy. Wood was more than anxious to secure that restoration but was confronted with a militantly nationalist Filipino leadership that refused to relinquish its newly acquired authority. He managed to bring greater financial stability to the islands and to secure some economic reforms, but his dogged attempt to reassert the authority of the governor general precipitated a contentious struggle that lasted throughout his term. Wood never finished his final task. He died while in Boston undergoing a brain tumor operation.

Wood played a significant role in shaping many of the United States's major developments in the early twentieth century: progressivism, expansionism and colonialism, military reform, preparedness and American intervention in World War I, and the election of 1920. He was particularly representative of an era that valued moral and physical strength. Although admired by his generation for his honesty, forthrightness, and his intense and vigorous approach to life, he fell short of greatness. Early in his career he developed a self-righteousness that made him intolerant of those who differed with him, a dangerous trait for one holding high military office, prompting him to violate the same principles of military professionalism he had worked hard to establish.

• The voluminous Leonard Wood Papers are located in the Library of Congress. The authorized biography is Hermann Hagedorn, *Leonard Wood: A Biography* (2 vols., 1931). The Hagedorn Papers in the Library of Congress contain valuable interviews with Wood's contemporaries. Jack C. Lane, *Armed Progressive: Leonard Wood* (1978), is a recent biographical study. Lane has also edited and introduced Wood's journal in *Chasing Geronimo: The Journal of Leonard Wood, May-September 1886* (1970). For Wood in the context of military professional reform see Russell Weigley, *Towards An American Army: Military Thought from Washington to Marshall* (1962), and Walter Millis, *Arms and Men: A Study in American Military History* (1956). Wood plays a large role in A. J. Bacevich, *Diplomat in Khaki: Major General Frank Ross McCoy and American Foreign Policy, 1898–1949* (1989), a study of Wood's principal aide and admirer.

JACK C. LANE

WOOD, L. Hollingsworth (14 Aug. 1873–21 July 1956), lawyer, Quaker, and social reformer, was born Levi Hollingsworth Wood in Mount Kisco, New York, son of James Wood and Emily Hollingsworth Morris, farmers. Wood was born and grew up in the family farm mansion, "Braewold" in Mount Kisco, and graduated from Haverford College in 1896. After graduating in 1899 from Columbia University Law School, he formed the estate law firm of Kirby & Wood in New York City.

Among Friends Wood served as assistant clerk for the New York Yearly Meeting of the "Orthodox," Christ-centered Quaker branch under his father, whom he succeeded as presiding clerk in 1926; he served in this capacity until 1931. Helen Underhill, of Jericho, Long Island, whom Wood married in 1915, had grown up among the more liberal "Hicksite" branch of the Society of Friends. Wood worked with committees of both Yearly Meetings for many years until the branches were reunited in 1955. Helen Wood died on 30 January 1924, and on 23 April 1925 Wood married Martha Trevilla Speakman at Swarthmore's "Hicksite" Meeting House. Their son James was born in 1927.

Wood's continuing concern for Quaker unity led to his becoming an executive committee member and treasurer of the joint national Young Friends Board from 1912 to 1917, overseeing international Young Friends conferences and pilgrimages and the work of traveling secretary Thomas E. Jones. Wood was among the founders and long a board member of the American Friends Service Committee and secretary of the Arrangements Committee for the 1917 Five Years Meeting of "Orthodox" Quakers. In 1920 he organized funding and the U.S. delegation to the first Friends World Conference in London. He chaired the Nominating Committee and was on the Executive and Publicity Committees of the second at Swarthmore and Haverford in 1937, writing its Interracial Justice Commission's epistle, *We Know Better but We Do Worse*.

Wood was led from one committee to another, through a network of lifelong ethical and social involvements. Wood described his commitment to issues of racial justice as "starting with a small mission class which developed into a debating society for young colored boys." He became "more and more focused on the problems which beset the Negro in our country" (quoted in Parris and Brooks, p. 70). He became secretary and then treasurer of the New York Colored Mission, led by his sister Carolena. For its Negro Fresh Air Fund and as chairman of the Central Bureau of Colored Fresh Air Agencies, he persuaded railroads to offer reduced fares; he also approached guest houses and camps regarding their whites-only practices. In the same years (1906–1916) he was legal adviser to Hope Day Nursery for Colored Children and was fundraising agent for Mound Bayou Oil Mill & Manufacturing Company, a black community cooperative in the Mississippi delta. As treasurer he was drawn into Frances Kellor's National League for the Protection of Colored Women, trying to stem the exploitation as prostitutes of black women who had come to the cities from the South. In 1911 this group merged with the Committee on Urban Conditions among Negroes and the Committee for Improving the Industrial Condition of Negroes in New York to form the National Urban League, as Wood renamed it, which focused on housing, job training, and work opportunities for men. Wood was secretary from 1913 and board chairman and president from 1915 through 1941. He found that he had to balance the need for training social workers from and for black southern communities, which was a focus of Fisk University, against the growing needs of black workmen migrating in the war years from the South to factories in New York, Detroit, and Chicago, which the National Urban League had tackled under General Secretary Eugene Kinckle Jones. In 1940 Wood supported the ailing Jones, with whom he had worked well to raise bitterly needed funds for the Urban League, against a potential successor, T. Arnold Hill, letting Jones turn over control to Lester Granger.

In 1917 Wood, called to be a trustee of Fisk University, found himself in the midst of fundraising efforts for the university and its Jubilee Singers. A student strike against President Fayette McKenzie resulted from a speech by W. E. B. DuBois to the students, faculty, and alumni on 2 June 1924. DuBois accused McKenzie of responding to white friends rather than to blacks. The trustees and an alumni committee heard grievances on both sides. After McKenzie's resignation in 1925, Wood shared in an extensive search for his successor, which led to a call to white Quaker professor Thomas Elsa Jones to become president (1926–1945). From 1908 Wood also served as a trustee of Penn School on St. Helena Island, South Carolina. He was called after World War I to be a trustee of other schools for blacks, including Cardinal Gibbons in Maryland, Southland in Arkansas, Happy Grove in Jamaica, and the Booker T. Washington Institute of Liberia. From 1928 to 1938 Wood and Urban League members and Westchester friends attempted a cooperative housing project for blacks in White Plains, New York, but under local opposition had to give up the project. From 1930 to 1952, Wood was also treasurer for the Thessalonica "American Farm School."

Peace was a second lifelong concern for Wood, secretary of the joint New York Yearly Meetings' Committee on Peace from 1908 to 1913. In 1910 the Yearly Meetings of all Quaker branches were invited to a conference, which set up a Peace Committee of the Associated Yearly Meetings. Their 1912 conference at Chatauqua stressed international arbitration and the demilitarization of the Panama Canal. Wood also became a key member of a Peace Association of Orthodox Friends in America, which held conferences for young Friends in 1910 and in 1915 as they faced conscription. As a member of the American League to Limit Armaments, Wood reached out to the nation, despite mixed support from President Woodrow Wilson, in a Campaign against the "Perils of Preparedness." His lively written attacks upon military "Dinosaurs" faced increasing opposition. The League broadened into the American Union Against Militarism, which held mass meetings in Broadway Tabernacle and helped defuse the crisis with Mexico. In 1916, under the pressures of armed conflict in Europe, forty pledged members and much of the "masthead" of the organization resigned. Once America was at war, conscientious objectors who had been drafted were imprisoned and brutally and often illegally treated. In response to these and other civil injustices, Wood became chairman of the Civil Liberties Bureau, which became the Civil Liberties Union after 1920. Its director, Roger Baldwin, was in prison, as were socialist pacifists like Norman Thomas. After the war Wood was treasurer of *The World Tomorrow*, the journal of the Fellowship of Reconciliation. The staid Quaker lawyer supported its later secretary, A. J. Muste, a Dutch-born pastor who became a Quaker during the war and a gifted labor organizer during the Lawrence textile strike. Muste established the Brookwood Labor College in Katonah near Mount Kisco, and Wood organized a Brookwood Association to own legally the property used by the cooperative of students and faculty. Muste joined Wood's Croton Valley Meeting but turned Trotskyite as Brookwood's faculty splintered over communism.

In the 1910s Wood turned his attention to the problems of immigrants. In 1911 he joined the North American Civic League for Immigrants and was asked to chair its Legal Affairs Committee, draft its constitution, bylaws, and working links to the Legal Aid Society, and join a panel to investigate the 1912 Triangle Shirtwaist fire. When Americans heard about British atrocities from Eamon DeValera and James Douglas, who were in the United States after the Irish uprising of 1916, the Committee of One Hundred on Conditions in Ireland was formed, and Wood was chosen one of ten commissioners to hold six hearings in Washington in 1920. Wood handled the expenses of those called to testify and the bulky correspondence related to the report. He also joined the Executive Committee of a (Quaker) Committee for Relief in Ireland, the Spanish Child Welfare Association during the Spanish Civil War, Eleanor Roosevelt's Good Neighbor Committee on the Émigré, and the International Rescue Committee.

Particularly during the depression years, Wood helped raise funds for Quaker-affiliated Guilford and William Penn Colleges, and for Haverford, on whose Board of Managers he served diligently from 1929 to 1952. He died in Mount Kisco.

• The papers of L. Hollingsworth Wood are cataloged and filed with manuscripts of the Quaker Collection, Haverford College Library. They were used in Guichard Parris and Lester Brooks, *Blacks in the City: A History of the National Urban League* (1971), and in Hugh Barbour et al., *Quaker Crosscurrents* (1995). See also Charles Chatfield, *For Peace and Justice: Pacifism in America, 1914–1941* (1971); Thomas E. Jones, *Light on the Horizon* (1973); Nancy J. Weiss, *The National Urban League, 1910–1940* (1974); and Peggy Lamson, *Roger Baldwin* (1976). Obituaries are in the *New York Times*, 23 July 1956; *Time*, 6 Aug. 1956; *Friends Journal* 2 (1956): 501; and *American Friend* 63 (1956): 267.

HUGH BARBOUR
DIANE P. ROFINI

WOOD, Mary Elizabeth (22 Aug. 1861–1 May 1931), library educator, was born in Elba, New York, the daughter of Edward Farmer Wood and Mary Jane Humphrey, farmers. Wood attended private and public schools, including the Batavia High School, but she acquired most of her knowledge through private reading and study. Between 1889 and 1899 Wood worked as the librarian of the Richmond Memorial Library, a public library in Batavia, New York.

In 1899 Wood left her job at the Richmond Library and sailed to China to visit her brother, Robert E. Wood, who had gone there one year earlier as a missionary for the Domestic and Foreign Missionary Society of the Protestant Episcopal Church. Wood spent her first winter in China cataloging the collection of the St. John's School Library in Shanghai. In the school year of 1900 Wood began teaching English in the Boone School in Wuchang, Hubei, where her brother was stationed.

Wood found plenty of work in China that occupied her enthusiasm and devotion. What began as a short visit turned into a thirty-year-long stay. During her stay, she accomplished three major projects that significantly affected the development of the library movement of China. Her first project, the founding of the Boone Public Library in 1910, gave China its first public library that provided free access and open stacks. Her second project, the establishment of the first library school of China in 1920, became not only the first but the only professional library school in China until the 1950s. Her final project, the campaign to use the Boxer Indemnity Fund to promote libraries and library education in China, resulted in the organization of the China Foundation of Culture and Education and the Library Association of China and provided additional financial assistance for the Boone Library School.

Wood's preparation for a new public library in China began as early as 1903 when she started to solicit contributions of books and funds from friends, public agencies, and religious groups. In 1906 she returned to the United States for a fundraising trip, which lasted eighteen months. During her trip she visited libraries and attended the 1907 American Library Association conference, campaigning for monetary and book donations for her library. In addition, she took special library training classes at the Pratt Institute in Brooklyn, New York.

The construction of a freestanding building for the Boone Library started in 1909. The library opened its doors to the public in 1910 with a collection of 3,000 volumes of books in Chinese and English. Wood and her Chinese assistant, Samuel T. Y. Seng, who had just graduated from the Boone School in 1910, were the first two full-time employees of the Boone Library.

Wood's next project was to establish a library school in China. While planning the new library school curriculum, she realized the need for trained staff to cope with the growing collection and services in the Boone Library. Wood encouraged two of her students, Seng and Thomas C. S. Hu, to go to the United States for library training. Seng studied at the library school of the New York Public Library between 1914 and 1917 and became the first Chinese student to receive formal library training from the United States. Hu studied at the library school of the New York Public Library from 1917 to 1919. The Boone Library School accepted its first class of students in 1920. Seng and Hu carried most of the teaching load during the early years, while Wood served as the superintendent of the school.

Wood's contribution to the development of Chinese libraries was greatly enhanced by Seng's consummate devotion to her. Seng made up for Wood's inadequacy in the Chinese language and related many of Wood's ideals and projects to the Chinese library community. Together Wood and Seng formed a powerful alliance for furthering their common goals.

Wood encountered discouragement and setbacks during her effort to develop the library movement in

China. The Boone Library drew smaller traffic than expected, and the library school attracted only six or seven students each year during the early years. Her priority in promoting public libraries and library education constantly clashed with the missionary goals of the Boone University, resulting in irreconcilable bitterness between the library school and the university. She eventually separated her library school from the university in 1929.

Wood's final project, campaigning for the use of the Boxer Indemnity Fund to promote libraries and library education in China, began in 1923. It produced significant results in the course of developing modern libraries in China. Wood circulated her petitions among high-ranking officials of the Chinese government to obtain endorsement. She made another trip back to the United States in 1924 to speak before congressional hearings when the bill on the use of the Boxer Indemnity Fund was being discussed in the U.S. Congress. She not only brought library awareness to the officials of both the U.S. and the Chinese governments but also successfully connected Chinese library professionals with the American Library Association, which resulted in a close cooperative relationship between the two for the following three decades. Wood, who remained unmarried, died in Wuchang, Hubei.

• Wood's personal papers are at the Episcopal Church Archives, Southwest Theological Seminary, Austin, Tex. Wood's testimony before the Congress is in U.S. Congress, House Committee on Foreign Affairs, *Chinese Indemnity: Hearings before the Committee on Foreign Affairs on H. J. Res. 201 to Provide for the Remission of Further Payments of the Annual Installments of the Chinese Indemnity*, 68th Cong., 1st sess., 31 Mar., 1 and 2 Apr. 1924. Wood's brother and her student Seng provided two brief but valuable biographical accounts of Wood: Robert E. Wood, "Reflections on My Sister," *Boone Library School Quarterly* 3 (Sept. 1931): 6–7; and Samuel Seng, "Miss Mary Elizabeth Wood: The Queen of the Modern Library Movement in China," *Boone Library School Quarterly* 3 (Sept. 1931): 8–13. A biography written by another of her students, Ch'iu K'aiming, is in *Notable American Women*, vol. 3 (1971). John H. Winklemen, "Mary Elizabeth Wood: American Missionary-Librarian to Modern China," *Journal of Library and Information Science* 8 (Apr. 1981): 62–76, provides a detailed insight into the controversies that led to the clash between Wood and the university administration of Boone University. Cheryl Boettcher, "Samuel T. Y. Seng and the Boone Library School," *Libraries and Culture* 24 (Summer 1989): 269–93, demonstrates the important impact Wood and her students had on the development of the modern library movement in China. An obituary is in the *New York Times*, 2 May 1931.

KUANG-PEI TU

WOOD, Mrs. John (6 Nov. 1831–11 Jan. 1915), actor and theater manager was born Matilda Charlotte Vining in Liverpool, England, the daughter of two actors, Henry Vining and a woman whose last name was Quantrell. After making her debut in 1841, Matilda Vining appeared in provincial theaters in England until she married John Wood, a fellow actor, in 1854 and both signed contracts to appear at the Boston Theatre, John acting low comedy and Matilda playing singing chambermaids. She debuted in Boston on 11 September 1854 as Gertrude in J. R. Planche's *The Loan of a Lover*. Two years later the couple made their New York debuts at the Academy of Music, she as Don Leander in *The Invisible Prince*. After that production she appeared at Wallack's Lyceum, from Christmas 1856 through late January 1857, earning plaudits for her portrayal of Minnehaha in Charles Melton Walcot's *Hiawatha*. In reference to this performance, theater chronicler George C. D. Odell later called Mrs. Wood "joyous" and "one of the most captivating burlesque actresses of all time."

Next the Woods traveled west, first to St. Louis, then to New Orleans, and finally to San Francisco. Their marriage strained, the couple separated in San Francisco, and she remained there to perform during the following season. Western American theater was then in its infancy, and Wood was one of the early female actor-managers in California. In 1859 she managed the Forrest Theatre in Sacramento and then the American Theatre in San Francisco.

In the autumn of 1859 Wood returned to New York, where she appeared in Joseph Jefferson's company at the Winter Garden. She spent the next four years acting in Boston, New York, New Orleans, and Philadelphia before taking over Laura Keene's theater in New York on 8 October 1863. (Wood's estranged husband had died five months earlier in Victoria, British Columbia.) She renamed Keene's theater the Olympic and spent the next three years as both its manager and its premiere attraction.

Best in comedy, especially in such roles as Lady Gay Spanker in *London Assurance*, Wood filled each season with an eclectic mix of farce, extravaganzas, and burlesque. Critics applauded the style and variety of her productions, which improved consistently over time. They continued to praise her acting as well. William Archer called her "irrepressible." According to the *Examiner* (12 Nov. 1870), "Fun never flags for a moment while Mrs. Wood is on the stage." Kate Reignolds-Winslow, meanwhile, dubbed her "the ideal soubrette and the best burlesque actress I ever saw." Wood was also an excellent judge of others' acting talent, and she gradually hired a first-rate company. Among others, she gave James Lewis and Mrs. G. H. Gilbert, both of whom would make names for themselves at Augustin Daly's Fifth Avenue Theatre, their first big breaks. Indeed, the Olympic was not simply a starring vehicle for its manager. The most popular play of the 1864–1865 season was a very successful revival of Dion Boucicault's *Streets of New York*, in which Wood did not appear.

In 1866, at or near the height of her popularity, Wood decided to return to England. There, from 1869 to 1879, she successfully managed the St. James Theatre, which formerly had been regarded as impossible to make profitable. Wood returned to the United States to appear with Augustin Daly's company for most of the 1872–1873 season but afterward never again appeared in New York. Instead she pursued success in her homeland, where she had a fruitful association with both the old and new Royal Court Theatres in London. At the old Court she performed in *The Magistrate* (1885), *The Schoolmistress* (1886), and *Dandy Dick* (1887). With Arthur Chudleigh she comanaged the New Royal Court Theatre from 1888 to 1891.

Wood's final performance was at the Drury Lane in 1905, when she appeared in *The Prodigal Son*. She died ten years later at her home, "Dilkoosha," on the Isle of Thanet in Kent. She had come from, and left, a theatrical family. One of her cousins, Fanny Elizabeth Vining, was married to American actor E. L. Davenport and was the mother of actress Fanny Davenport. Wood's only child, Florence, also pursued a stage career and married playwright Ralph Lumley.

A powerful, polished, and vivacious actress, Wood was small in stature and not conventionally beautiful, yet she managed to captivate audiences no matter what the play. As her contemporary Clement Scott wrote: "When Mrs. John Wood appears the whole theatre seems to be charged with electricity. She is a complete battery of electric sparks in herself. I do not care in what plays she appears in, Shakespeare or Sheridan, in a roaring farce . . . or a Drury Lane drama, Mrs. John Wood will be certain to hold the house" (p. 139).

Matilda Vining Wood joins Louisa Lane Drew and Laura Keene as a leading female theater manager of the nineteenth century. During a time when most working women were confined to low-paying powerless jobs and middle-class women stayed home, these women challenged expectations. They capitalized on their creative as well as managerial abilities to carve out positions of power for themselves within the business of theater. Like Drew and Keene, Wood was a forceful leader who spared no expense in developing her productions. She hired and fired actors when needed, managed the books, and maintained a long and varied career. Through all this, she maintained high spirits and a sense of style, possessing, according to Scott, "all the glow and style of the old school, with the polish, nature, and finesse of the new" (p. 138).

• Jane Kathleen Curry, *Nineteenth-Century American Women Theatre Managers* (1994), gives a good overview, and excellent context, for Mrs. Wood's work. Another good source is James H. Stoddart, *Recollections of a Player* (1902). Wood's U.S. career can be traced through George C. D. Odell, *Annals of the New York Stage*, especially vols. 6–9 (1931–1937). Also helpful are F. Jerome Hart and John Parker, eds., *The Green Room Book* (1907); Eugene Tompkins and Quincy Kilby, comps., *The History of the Boston Theatre, 1854–1901* (1908); John H. Barnes, *Forty Years on the Stage* (1914); Walter M. Leman, *Memories of an Old Actor* (1886); Clement Scott, *The Drama of Yesterday and Today*, vol. 2 (1899); and William Winter, *Vagrant Memories* (1915). A brief obituary is in the *Times* (London), 14 Jan. 1915.

CYNTHIA M. GENDRICH

WOOD, Natalie (20 July 1938–29 Nov. 1981), film actress, was born Natasha Gurdin in San Francisco, California, the daughter of Russian immigrants Nicholas Gurdin, an architect and film set designer, and Maria Kuleff, a ballerina and actress. She was taught to dance and was privately tutored from the age of six and grew up in Santa Rosa, California.

She first appeared on screen in a walk-on role at the age of five in Irving Pichel's *Happy Land* (1943). At the age of seven her name was changed to "Natalie Wood" by producers of Pichel's *Tomorrow Is Forever* (1946), in which Wood was given a substantial role alongside Orson Welles and Claudette Colbert. By 1946, at the age of eight, Wood was a rising child star with a salary of $1,000 a week. After being cast as a cute little girl in several insignificant films, she portrayed a savvy, inquisitive, questioning child who did not believe in Santa Claus in *Miracle on 34th Street* (1947). Wood's popularity as a child superstar never rivaled that of the multitalented Shirley Temple. Nevertheless, Wood's accomplishments were widely acknowledged. She won the Box Office Blue Ribbon for *Tomorrow Is Forever* (1946) and for *Miracle on 34th Street* (1947), the Most Talented Juvenile Motion Picture Star of the Year in *Parents Magazine* (1947), and Child Star of the Year from the Children's Day National Council of New York (1949).

Wood's image and career were boosted when her portrayal of James Dean's girlfriend in the teenage cult favorite *Rebel without a Cause* (1955) earned her an Academy Award nomination, and after James Dean's unexpected death that year movie magazines became obsessed with Wood and Sal Mineo, her costar in the movie. Wood's refreshing beauty, sense of vulnerability, and appearance of innocence appealed to audiences.

Movie critics and news reporters incorrectly linked Wood romantically with Elvis Presley, who had come to Hollywood in 1955 to star in his first film, *Love Me Tender*, and who Wood admitted sang "all the time" to her (*Tupelo Daily Journal*, 20 Sept. 1956). Although Wood stayed with Elvis in Memphis in October of that year, they were friends, not lovers. In 1957 Wood married actor Robert Wagner; they divorced in 1962.

In 1957, when Wood was chosen over Elizabeth Taylor and Audrey Hepburn to play the title role opposite Gene Kelly in Herman Wouk's *Marjorie Morningstar* (1958), her career as a superstar was secure, and she became the teenage girl in movies with whom peers could best identify. When she was cast opposite Warren Beatty in William Inge's *Splendor in the Grass* (1961) and earned an Academy Award nomination, critics who previously had thought her a frivolous actress took her work more seriously. In the film she portrayed a young woman emotionally distraught over the loss of a love. Wood starred as Maria in the box-office smash hit *West Side Story* (1961), though it was Marni Nixon's voice that audiences heard whenever Maria burst into song. Then came roles that included *Gypsy* (1962), as Gypsy Rose Lee; *Sex and the Single Girl* (1964); *The Great Race* (1965); *This Property Is Condemned* (1966); *Penelope*; and *Inside Daisy Clover* (1966). In 1963 Wood was nominated for an Academy Award for her performance in *Love with the Proper Stranger* (1963), after which the *Harvard Lampoon* initiated the annual "Natalie Wood Award" for the worst performance of the year by an actress.

Following a three-year absence from filming in Hollywood, in 1969 she married film producer Richard Gregson and earned $2 million for her role in *Bob and Carol and Ted and Alice*. After giving birth to a daughter, Wood divorced Gregson in 1972 and remarried Robert Wagner later that year. They had a daughter and co-owned a film production company.

In 1977 Wood's Emmy-nominated performance opposite Sir Laurence Olivier in the television production of Tennessee Williams's *Cat on a Hot Tin Roof* received critical acclaim, and her 1980 Golden Globe Award performance in NBC's five-hour production of *From Here to Eternity* overshadowed her role in *The Last Married Couple in America* (1980).

In November 1981 Wood's plans to begin rehearsals for the lead role in a Los Angeles stage production of *Anastasia* and to continue filming as the lead in the movie *Brainstorm* abruptly ended. She drowned while yachting at night with her husband in a cove near Santa Catalina Island off the coast of southern California. Medical examiners said that her death was accidental. Wood appeared in forty-five films and will be best remembered for her roles as an innocent ingenue.

• For a listing of Wood's films, see Ephraim Katz, *The Film Encyclopedia* (1979). Her relationship with Elvis Presley is discussed in Patricia Jobe Pierce, *The Ultimate Elvis* (1994), and rumors of their marriage are noted in the *San Francisco News*, 1 Nov. 1956, and the *Tupelo Daily Journal*, 11 Sept. 1956. An obituary is in the *New York Times*, 30 Nov. 1981.

PATRICIA JOBE PIERCE

WOOD, Robert D. (17 Apr. 1925–20 May 1986), network television president, was born in Boise, Idaho, the son of Raymond Dennis Wood, a pharmacist, and Euphrosyne Planck, a teacher. He was raised in Beverly Hills, California. He completed an enlistment in the U.S. Navy during World War II and earned a B.S. in business at the University of Southern California in 1949. Wood began his 27-year career with the Columbia Broadcasting System (CBS) that same year, working at KNX radio station in Los Angeles. He married Nancy Harwell in 1949; they had two children and were divorced in 1972. In 1955 Wood became vice president of the CBS television division, and in 1967 he was promoted to president of that division.

Though early American television was largely experimental, CBS quickly began to offer stiff competition against the rival National Broadcasting Company (NBC) in setting the pace for network programming. CBS's founder and president, William S. Paley, cleverly used tax incentives to lure big-name stars from radio, including Jack Benny, Edgar Bergen, and George Burns and Gracie Allen. By 1950 CBS was the top-rated television network on Sunday evenings. Later it dominated the television airwaves with highly rated quiz shows, including the infamous "$64,000 Question."

Even the ensuing television quiz show scandal could not dethrone CBS from its position as the top-rated television network. CBS became known as "the largest single advertising medium in the world," notes Robert Slater in his sixty-year chronicle of the network.

By the early 1960s network television programming had evolved much from its early, formative years. Dramatic anthologies and variety shows gave way to cheaper, formulaic fare, such as situation comedies and hour-long dramas. Though there were still the occasional news documentary and variety special, the television airwaves soon came to be dominated by the cacophony of laughter emanating from the inane antics of sitcom characters like CBS's Gomer Pyle, Lucy, and, most notably, the Beverly Hillbillies.

With the great success of the "Beverly Hillbillies" came more "rural" fare. CBS television came to be jokingly known as "the hillbilly network." However, it held fast to its top-ratings position with a strong lineup of new and old shows, including programs with loyal audiences, such as "The Ed Sullivan Show" and "Gunsmoke."

Even with such unprecedented triumph, both Paley and Wood realized that they could not afford to become complacent. CBS's audiences for many of its successful shows were loyal but aging. The widely diverse audience for popular programs such as the "Beverly Hillbillies" and "Green Acres" were not the kind of sophisticated and monied spenders that attracted big-ticket advertisers. The focus on demographics meant that how many people tuned in to a program became less important than who they were and how much money they had to spend on advertisers' products. Current programming, designed to attract the widest audience possible, did not hold an attraction for certain groups, including the increasing youth audience. Despite its top rating, if drastic changes were not made, CBS could soon find itself losing advertisers as well as viewership. These hard facts set Wood and Paley along a perilous path in 1970.

Other important issues made it clear to Wood that CBS had to change. American society had experienced much social and cultural upheaval during the 1960s. The evening news brought grim footage of Vietnam War death and carnage into the living rooms of American television viewers. African Americans fought against discrimination and women fought for equal rights. Americans watched in horror as the bodies of the murdered John F. Kennedy, Robert Kennedy, and Martin Luther King, Jr., were laid to rest. Black Panthers wielded machine guns and college students burned down their campuses in protest against the war. Like the post–World War II film industry, which was compelled to shift its plotlines from wartime escapism to darker, realism-based themes, American television, too, needed to reflect the needs and feelings of the current culture. Though the situation comedy and the hour-long drama would remain the primary forms of programming, both would need to shift away from "the consensual mood of the 1950's and 1960's" to a tone more abrasive and confrontational.

Wood realized that television programming at CBS needed to shift toward a hip, young, educated, and sophisticated audience interested in social issues. It would be a risky undertaking. How could CBS attract the audience of eighteen through forty-nine year olds that advertisers wanted without completely alienating the loyal viewership? How would it continue to succeed as a top-rated network?

A strategy was devised by Fred Silverman with the help of independent producer Norman Lear. Formerly the vice president in charge of program planning and development, Silverman became CBS television's chief programmer in 1970. Like Wood, Silverman had long felt that television programmers should abandon the old strategy of airing shows that appealed to the widest possible audience and instead focus on "a certain slice of the population," those who would be most willing and able to buy the advertisers' products. His views were considered radical by some, but at CBS he found an ally in Robert Wood.

Wood initiated a "clean sweep" of CBS programming. Successful shows like "Green Acres," "Ed Sullivan," and the "Beverly Hillbillies" were canceled. Banished were old favorites such as "Here's Lucy," "Gunsmoke," and "Red Skelton." Lear had purchased the rights to a hit British television show called "Till Death Do Us Part." In the American version, "All in the Family," he cast veteran actor Carroll O'Connor as the lovable but bigoted and totally outrageous Archie Bunker. CBS launched "All in the Family" "with trepidation." The program made its debut in January 1971. Paley regarded the concept, with its raunchy verbal sparring, racial epithets, and sexual innuendo as too risky. He was afraid that the show might alienate viewers and advertisers alike. But Wood and Silverman persisted. They worked hard to allay the fears of censors and advertisers. They cajoled producer Lear to eliminate a few of the more choice lines of dialogue. They prepared for an onslaught of negative press and angry phone calls. Though "All in the Family" was not an instant hit, within about a year it became the number-one watched television program.

More importantly, the success of "All in the Family" bred other shows, including some additional products of Norman Lear. These "spin-offs" included "The Jeffersons," "Maude," and "Good Times." Also full of irreverent humor, the show "M.A.S.H." was developed from a successful hit movie and made its debut in 1972. Equally groundbreaking was "The Mary Tyler Moore Show," featuring a single woman with a professional career. Cop shows interjected gritty, street realism in the form of "Kojak" and "Cannon." One of the key words to the success of these programs is "relevant." Indeed, this particular era of American television history is often referred to as "the era of relevancy."

Wood's legacy encompasses an important period in the history of CBS and in the history of American television. Through his leadership at the helm of CBS during a turbulent period of American cultural history, he ensured the fortunes of a television giant; at the same time, he helped to forge changes that significantly altered the tenor of prime-time television and the process of television network programming.

After twenty-seven years, Wood left CBS in 1976. He formed his own company, Nephi Productions, and later was appointed president of Metromedia Producers Corporation. He died in Santa Monica, California, and was survived by his second wife, Laura Rohrer.

• References to Wood are scattered throughout the following sources: Ella Taylor, *Prime Time Families: Television Culture in Postwar America* (1989); Eric Barnouw, *Tube of Plenty: The Evolution of American Television* (1982); Robert Slater, *This . . . Is CBS: A Chronicle of 60 Years* (1988); and Todd Gitlin, *Inside Prime Time* (1983). An obituary is in the *New York Times*, 22 May 1986.

PAMALA S. DEANE

WOOD, Robert Elkington (13 June 1879–6 Nov. 1969), army officer and businessman, was born in Kansas City, Missouri, the son of Robert Whitney Wood, a merchant, and Lillie Collins, a former schoolteacher. Wood's mother instilled in him a love of learning, and the young man hoped to attend Yale University, but his family could not afford an Ivy League education. Instead, in 1896 Robert entered the U.S. Military Academy at West Point, New York.

After he graduated in 1900, the army stationed Wood in the Philippines, where he fought Filipino rebels. Two years later, the army sent Wood back to the United States, first to Fort Assiniboine, Montana, then to West Point, where he taught French. There he met Mary Hardwick, whom he married in 1908; they had five children.

In 1905, bored with his duties as a language instructor, Wood applied for transfer to Panama, where he took part in the construction of the Panama Canal. He rose rapidly through the ranks and became a key aide to General George W. Goethals, director of the canal project. As chief procurement officer, Wood secured supplies from all over the world and provided food and housing for canal workers. He replaced advertised bidding with negotiated contracts, an innovation that ensured that supplies arrived on time. In appreciation of his work on the canal, Congress granted Major Wood an early retirement in 1915. During his ten years in Panama, Wood had gained valuable management experience; he later recalled that "I never loved a job like that Canal" (Worthy, p. 7).

Wood's managerial skills made him much sought after in the business world. The Du Pont Company hired Wood and placed him in charge of securing food and housing for the company's construction workers. But Wood knew that members of the Du Pont family would retain all top management positions; therefore, he left Du Pont to join General Asphalt Company as an assistant to the president in charge of production

When the United States declared war against Germany in April 1917, Wood volunteered for military service. He organized supply lines between the United States and France and within a year was promoted to brigadier general and acting quartermaster general of the army (hereafter he became known as "General Wood" among his friends and associates). In recognition of his accomplishments, Wood was awarded the Distinguished Service Medal.

After the war, Wood became merchandising vice president at Montgomery Ward, a large mail-order company. Drawing on his army experience, Wood had the company's buyers negotiate contracts with manufacturers on a cost-plus-profit basis. The new arrangement improved Ward's relations with its suppliers and helped the company weather the severe recession of 1920–1921.

Wood envisioned chain stores as the wave of the future. An avid reader of *The Statistical Abstract of the United States*, Wood knew that a growing number of Americans were leaving the countryside in search of higher wages in metropolitan areas. The mass-produced automobile was, in turn, creating millions of commuters who worked in the city but lived in the suburbs. He urged Ward executives to open suburban retail stores to capture part of this metropolitan market. But the president of Ward saw no need to venture into retailing when the company was doing quite well with mail order. This and other disagreements over company policy led to Wood's dismissal from the company in September 1924.

Julius Rosenwald, the president of Sears, Roebuck, recognized Wood's talent and appointed him vice president for factories and retail stores. Although Sears, like Ward, was a mail-order firm, the company backed Wood's retail store strategy; during the next three years, Sears dramatically increased its sales by establishing several hundred stores.

In January 1928 Wood became president of Sears, and he led the company for the next twenty-six years. (In 1939, having reached the company's mandatory retirement age of sixty, Wood stepped down as president but took over as chair of the board of directors, a position that allowed him to retain control of the company.) Wood opened stores at an even faster pace than before, and by 1931 retail trade accounted for half of company sales. During the 1930s mail-order sales declined, but the retail end of the business continued to grow, thus helping Sears to survive and prosper during the Great Depression.

During this time, Wood developed new markets. He made sure that the consumers who drove their cars to Sears could purchase automotive parts, service, and insurance. He also cultivated the undeveloped men's market. Urban department stores catered to women shoppers by carrying "soft" lines of goods (for example, apparel and jewelry). Sears found its niche in "hard" lines (for example, hardware and sporting goods), which appealed to men, and "big ticket" items (such as washers, dryers, and refrigerators) designed for the whole family.

Wood's personal beliefs led him to create a decentralized organization that became a model for other large corporations. Wood detested bureaucracy; he felt it was undemocratic, inflexible, and produced a demoralized work force. Therefore, he granted a large measure of autonomy to the company's territorial units and to its store managers. In so doing, he hoped to create what he called a "cooperative democracy." This flexible structure enabled Sears to quickly respond to changes in the marketplace.

Wood believed that a motivated workforce was the key to Sears's success. When asked by the president of Montgomery Ward why Sears was so much more successful than his own company, Wood replied: "I've got the men" (Worthy, p. 243). Wood recruited young, ambitious, hardworking individuals driven by the promise of promotion from within. Thus Sears became a vehicle of social mobility, allowing many employees to enter the middle class. At the same time, however, Wood squashed labor union attempts to organize Sears employees.

Because of its success, Sears became a target of the anti–chain store movement of the 1930s. Small business owners complained that chain stores were driving them out of business. Wood responded by displaying a sincere sense of corporate responsibility for the social welfare. Wood saw himself as a trustee for his customers, employees, stockholders, and the communities served by Sears. He urged his store managers to become active in civic affairs. His company's Agricultural Division acted as an extension service for farmers, while the Allstate Foundation (created by Allstate Insurance, a subsidiary of Sears) promoted automotive safety. Wood also developed profitable relationships with many small manufacturers; in fact, several large corporations—including Whirlpool, a maker of home appliances—grew to their present size in large part because of the business they did with Sears.

Wood's concern with social welfare carried over into politics. In 1932 Wood, a Republican, crossed party lines to support the candidacy of Franklin Roosevelt. Wood supported the New Deal and served as a charter member of the Commerce Department's Business Advisory Council, a group established to improve the Roosevelt administration's relations with business. But in the late 1930s Wood opposed Roosevelt's mobilization for war. As chair of the America First Committee, Wood played a leading role in the movement to isolate the United States from the war in Europe. However, after the Japanese attack on Pearl Harbor, Wood disbanded the committee and volunteered his services in support of the war effort. He assisted with the air force's supply operations and was awarded the Legion of Merit. After the war Wood became active in Republican party politics. In 1948 he served as a delegate to the Republican convention, where he tried to nominate Douglas MacArthur for president. Four years later he supported Robert A. Taft in his unsuccessful bid for the Republican presidential nomination. Wood also gave financial backing to several far-rightwing organizations and was a prominent supporter of Senator Joseph McCarthy.

At the end of World War II many business executives feared the country would fall back into an economic depression, but Wood anticipated a postwar boom. He opened more stores in the United States and expanded abroad into Latin America and Canada. The results were dramatic: in just ten years, company sales more than tripled, and Sears strengthened its position as the largest general retailer in America.

In 1954 Wood retired as chair of the board but continued on as a member of the board of directors. He remained active throughout the 1950s and handpicked the company's presidents. During the 1960s he became less involved in company affairs. In May 1968 he gave up his seat on the board. He died in Lake Forest, Illinois.

Toward the end of Wood's life Sears had become, in the words of *Fortune* magazine (May 1964), "the paragon of retailers. Sears is No. 1 in the U.S., and also No. 2, 3, 4, and 5." Yet, Wood was partly responsible for Sears' declining fortunes in the years after his death. The decentralized organization he created worked because Wood imposed discipline on the structure, but his successors lacked his authority. The corporate culture of Sears, which Wood dominated for so long, produced able followers but weak leaders.

Nevertheless, during his lifetime, Wood was unequaled in his mastery of marketing and management. During the thirty years that he ran the company, Wood transformed Sears, Roebuck, from a mail-order company into the largest retailer in the world. Sears was also a job machine: during Wood's years at the helm, the number of employees increased from 23,000 to 200,000, offering thousands of Americans an opportunity to enter the middle class. But it was Wood's civic-mindedness that elevated Sears to the status of a great American institution.

• Nearly all of Wood's papers are held by Sears, Roebuck, and Company. His published works include *Mail Order Retailing Pioneered* (1948) and *Monument for the World* (1963). Boris Emmet and John E. Jeuck, *Catalogues and Counters: A History of Sears, Roebuck, and Company* (1950), contains an early, but still useful, account of Wood's role in transforming the company into the nation's largest retail chain. See also Alfred D. Chandler, Jr., "Sears, Roebuck, and Company—Decentralization, Planned and Unplanned," chap. 5 in his *Strategy and Structure: Chapters in the History of the Industrial Enterprise* (1961), and Justus D. Doenecke, "The Isolationism of General Robert E. Wood" in *Three Faces of Midwest Isolationism*, ed. John N. Schacht (1981). For a full-length biography, see James C. Worthy, *Shaping an American Institution: Robert E. Wood and Sears, Roebuck* (1984). Worthy, a former employee of Sears, based his biography on company records, interviews with Wood's associates, and "The Reminiscences of General Robert E. Wood" (1961), a transcript of interviews conducted by the Columbia University Oral History Project. Also see Gordon L. Weil, *Sears, Roebuck, U.S.A.: The Great American Catalog Store and How It Grew* (1977), and Cecil C. Hoge, Sr., *The First Hundred Years Are the Toughest: What We Can Learn from the Century of Competition between Sears and Ward* (1988). Richard S. Tedlow takes a long view of Wood's accomplishments in "Bringing the Mass Market Home: Sears, Montgomery Ward, and Their Newer Rivals," chap. 5 in *New and Improved: The Story of Mass Marketing in America* (1990). Donald R. Katz describes how Wood's imprint on Sears negatively affected the course of the company after his death in *The Big Store: Inside the Crisis and Revolution at Sears* (1987). There is an obituary in the *New York Times*, 7 Nov. 1969.

JONATHAN J. BEAN

WOOD, Robert Williams (2 May 1868–11 Aug. 1955), physicist, was born in Concord, Massachusetts, the son of Robert Wood, a physician, and Lucy J. Davis. As a child Wood showed an interest in tinkering with things mechanical. Fire also fascinated him. The family lived next to a working factory, and the young Wood was able to persuade the foreman to give him pretty much the run of the place. Wood had a mischievous nature, which was to stay with him all his life, and this resulted in numerous childhood and adolescent pranks.

In spite of his creativity, or perhaps because of it, Wood did not do well in school. However, he managed to pass Harvard's entrance exam by extensive study on his own. He entered Harvard in 1887.

During his Harvard years, Wood was "a difficult problem to most of the faculty with whom he came in contact and conflict" (Seabrook, p. 28). One such conflict led to his first major publication, "Effects of Pressure on Ice," in the *American Journal of Science* (3d ser., 41, [1891]: 30–33). At the time, Harvard geologist Southgate Shaler was teaching that ice liquefied under high pressure and that this effect accounted for the ability of glaciers to slide across the land. Wood doubted this explanation. To test it, he used equipment in the factory near his parents' home to drill a hole in a large block of iron. The hole was filled with water, which was then frozen. Other factory equipment was then used to subject the ice to great pressure. The pressurized ice did not melt, conclusively showing that Shaler's theory was wrong.

While at Harvard, Wood took a psychology course from William James, the famous American psychologist and author of *Principles of Psychology* (1890), and became one of his research assistants. His job was to classify responses on a questionnaire that James had sent out regarding hallucinations. In the course of this work, Wood became interested in hashish-induced hallucinations. With James's tacit approval, he ingested a quantity of hashish, which resulted in the hoped-for hallucinations, including one in which Wood turned into a fox. Wood wrote up his experiences for James, who included the report in his *Principles of Psychology*. It was also published, in a slightly different form, in the 23 September 1888 issue of the *New York Herald*.

Wood graduated from Harvard in 1891 and went to Johns Hopkins University to pursue a Ph.D. in chemistry. As he progressed at Johns Hopkins, he became more interested in physics and less in chemistry. In 1892 he married Gertrude Ames, a once-removed cousin from the West Coast; the marriage produced four children. After the wedding he transferred to the University of Chicago, where he finished his research for the Ph.D. in chemistry in 1894. But that year the chemistry department added new requirements for the degree, requirements in areas in which Wood had no preparation. Thus, he never received his Ph.D. at Chicago. Instead, in the fall of 1894 he moved to Berlin, Germany, where he worked with the physical chemist Wilhelm Ostwald. Wood stayed in Berlin for two years, having many run-ins with the German police and government bureaucracy. During this period he published several papers, the most important being his work on temperature distribution in vacuum tubes.

Wood and his family returned to the United States in the fall of 1896, but he had no job. For a period he did unpaid research at the Massachusetts Institute of Technology. His first academic position came in 1897 when he was appointed instructor in physics at the University of Wisconsin in Madison. He remained there for four years. It was during his stay at Wisconsin that his reputation as a lecturer and master of classroom demonstrations, many of a pyrotechnic nature, began to develop. While at Wisconsin he invented what fast became the standard way of thawing frozen underground water pipes, by passing an electrical current through the pipes to heat them. It was also at Wisconsin that Wood became interested in physical optics, especially spectroscopy, the area in which he would specialize for the rest of his career. His greatest contribution to spectroscopy was the study of fluorescence in various gases. By shining a light of a specific wavelength through a gas, one obtains a series of bands called a resonance spectrum. This pattern varies as a function of the wavelength of the illuminating light. The results of experiments of this sort had profound implications for theories of the atomic structure of matter being debated at the time, especially Bohr's theory. It was for his work in fluorescence that Erwin Schrödinger nominated him, in 1927, for the Nobel Prize in physics. The prize that year went to others, and Wood never did receive a Nobel Prize.

Wood's interest was not limited to spectroscopy. His curiosity knew few bounds, and he was a brilliant and creative experimenter in many areas of physics, including atomic physics, ultrasonics, and photography using infrared and ultraviolet light.

After his four years at Wisconsin, Wood moved to Johns Hopkins University in 1901 as a professor of experimental physics. He spent the rest of his life there, retiring in 1938, thereafter having the title of emeritus research professor.

In 1904 Wood was instrumental in exposing the N-ray delusion that had swept physics laboratories in France. French physicist René Blondlot claimed to have discovered a new type of radiation, N-ray, that had various surprising properties. Researchers outside France could generally not replicate Blondlot's findings and a major dispute arose. (See Nye, "N-Rays: An Episode in the History and Psychology of Science," *Historical Studies in the Physical Sciences* 11, no 1 [1980]: 125–56, for a full discussion of this interesting episode.) Wood visited Blondlot's lab and observed the methods Blondlot was using. Wood found them to be totally inadequate to support the claims Blondlot was making. He published his observations in the 29 September 1904 issue of *Nature*, even then one of the leading scientific journals in the world. Although Wood did not mention Blondlot's laboratory as the source of his observations in his *Nature* article, everyone in the field knew whose lab he was talking about. His comments more or less ended the N-ray episode.

The case of the N-rays was not the only time that Wood was involved in what, for most working scientists, would be considered unusual investigations. He helped investigate several spiritualistic mediums, including the famous Eusapia Palladino and Mina Crandon Margery. In both cases his skills as an investigator led to the conclusion that the mediums were frauds. He also frequently aided the police of various cities in investigations of bombings and became quite well known to the public for this work, on more than one occasion being compared to Sherlock Holmes.

During World War I Wood served as a major in the Army Signal Corps. In this capacity he invented signal lamps that were great improvements over what had previously been used for communication between units on the battlefield. In World War II he acted as a consultant to the Manhattan Project.

Wood received numerous scientific prizes and honors. He was a member of the National Academy of Sciences. He was made a Fellow in the Royal Society, a most unusual honor for a non-British scientist, and received the society's Rumford gold medal.

• The major holding of Wood's papers, at the Niels Bohr Library at the American Institute of Physics in Silver Spring, Md., contains Wood family papers from 1838 to 1942 and includes correspondence between Wood and other physicists of the time. The Milton Eisenhower Library at Johns Hopkins University has a small collection of Wood's papers. Wood wrote two books in physics: *Physical Optics* (1907), which went through three editions, the last in 1934; and *Supersonics, the Science of Inaudible Sounds* (1939). He published two books outside his field as well: *How to Tell the Birds from the Flowers* (1907), a spoof on nature books for children, which went through nineteen printings; and a collaboration with Arthur Train on a novel that would now be classified as science fiction, *The Man Who Rocked the Earth* (1915). A sequel was published in *Cosmopolitan* some years later. A biography is William Seabrook, *Doctor Wood: Modern Wizard of the Laboratory* (1941). A shorter biography by G. H. Dieke appeared in *Biographical Memoirs of Fellows of the Royal Society* (1956): 327–45. Both biographies list Wood's numerous publications, which run well over 200.

TERENCE HINES

WOOD, Sally Sayward Barrell Keating (1 Oct. 1759–6 Jan. 1855), novelist, was born Sarah Sayward Barrell in York, Maine, the daughter of Nathaniel Barrell, a New Hampshire merchant, and Sarah (or Sally) Sayward. Born while her father was serving under General James Wolfe, who led the British attack on Quebec, Sally was raised in the home of her maternal grandfather, Jonathan Sayward of York, Maine, who served as a judge in the York Probate and Common Pleas Court and as a representative in the Massachusetts

General Court. Wood grew up among wealth and culture in a social circle that included such prominent families as the Wentworths and Pepperrells, but few specifics are known about her childhood, youth, or education.

In November 1778, at the age of nineteen, Wood married Richard Keating, a clerk in Sayward's office who was described by William Goold as a slightly older classmate of Wood's (pp. 403–4). Keating suddenly died of a fever in June 1783, leaving his wife responsible for their three children. From the time of her husband's death until October 1804, Wood lived as a widow in the home built for her by her grandfather, raising her children and writing the novels for which she is now primarily remembered. Both her social status and her comment in the preface to her first novel that her writing "soothed many *melancholy*, and sweetened many *bitter* hours" suggest that she wrote for self-satisfaction rather than out of financial need. All four of her novels were published anonymously, no doubt out of the recognition that novels, particularly domestic romances by female authors, were a suspect literary form in the early republic. Like other sentimental writers concerned about the respectability of their work, Wood sometimes claimed that her fiction was founded on fact.

Wood's first published novel was *Julia, and the Illuminated Baron* (1800), a romance of the Radcliffe type. Set in France during the French Revolution, the novel recounts the tribulations of a virtuous orphan named Julia who is abducted by Count de Launa, an atheist aristocrat and member of the Illuminati, a secret society credited with instigating the revolution. The novel celebrates middle-class virtues and critiques both the corruption of the ancien régime and the dangers of political revolution and social upheaval. *Julia* was followed by *Dorval; or, The Speculator* (1801), an early specimen of the confidence theme in American literature. *Dorval* is set in America and deals with a contemporary American historical event—Georgia land speculation. Wood's third novel, a domestic romance set in England and France titled *Amelia; or, The Influence of Virtue* (1802), perhaps most clearly reveals her conservative social attitudes. Narrated by an Englishman named Harley who visits America, *Amelia* depicts a neglected and abused but resiliently virtuous wife who prefers enduring her husband's adultery and raising his illegitimate child to the shame of divorce. Praising the protagonist, the narrator comments that Amelia "was not a disciple or pupil of Mary Woolstonecraft [*sic*] . . . She was an old fashioned wife and she meant to obey her husband: she meant to do her duty in the strictest sense of the word. To perform it cheerfully would perhaps be painful, but . . . it would most assuredly be best." Because such attitudes appear throughout Wood's work, Cathy N. Davidson has called Wood one of "the most consistently conservative of the sentimental writers" of her age (p. 128). Wood's last novel, *Ferdinand & Elmira: A Russian Story* (1804), is a complicated picaresque tale of triumphant virtue tracing the reunion of lovers separated during the French and Indian War.

Some aspects of Wood's career suggest a more independent spirit. She apparently was interested enough in the business of authorship to secure personally the copyright of *Dorval*. Moreover, Wood expressed considerable admiration for Judith Sargent Murray, an outspoken proponent of equitable female education. Wood dedicated *Julia* to Murray, praised Murray in *Dorval*, and used two mottoes of Murray's as chapter headings in *Amelia*. For the most part, however, Wood's views concerning both women and authorship were conventional. The contrast that Wood drew in the preface to *Ferdinand & Elmira* between herself—"a Lady of refined sentiments and correct tastes, who writes for the amusement of herself, her Friends, and the Public"—and "the common English Novelist, who works for a living similar to a Mechanic" suggests that she viewed her writing as an avocation to be subordinated to the more important duties of motherhood and wifehood. Voicing a similar sentiment in the preface to *Julia*, Wood insisted that she had neither "sacrificed [n]or postponed" her social or domestic responsibilities to write her novel. While such protestations of duty from female writers of the time are to be expected, Wood evidently found authorship incompatible with the demands of matrimony and family. Wood stopped publishing when she remarried but resumed her career during her second widowhood.

In October 1804 she married General Abiel Wood, a wealthy widower and prominent citizen of Wiscasset, Maine, where the couple resided until Abiel's death in 1811. Within a few years of his death, Wood moved to Portland, Maine, probably to live near or with her son, Richard Keating, who had become a ship captain sailing out of Portland. Sometime after 1815 Wood wrote a long domestic tale about a family destroyed by divided loyalties during the American Revolution titled "War, the Parent of Domestic Calamity—A Tale of the Revolution." In 1827 Wood published a volume of stories, *Tales of the Night*, which contained two long domestic narratives about Maine life, "Storms and Sunshine; or, The House on the Hill" and "The Hermitage; or, Rise of Fortune." Although Wood promised a second volume of tales in her preface, it never appeared. According to family legend, Wood destroyed manuscripts of some of her unpublished works on reading Sir Walter Scott's Waverly novels.

In 1829 or 1830 Wood moved to New York City, again to be near her son who was then sailing a ship out of New York. She remained in New York until her son's accidental death in January 1833, soon after which she moved to Kennebunk, Maine, to live with a granddaughter. While living in Kennebunk, Wood wrote two letters of family reminiscences and local history at the request of relatives. Nathaniel Hawthorne's *American Notebooks* of 1842 indicate his familiarity with these letters, which were first published in 1859 ("Recollections," p. 91). Wood died in Kennebunk.

Like many writers of the early republic, Wood championed the development of a native literary tradition and hoped to provide readers with moral instruction through her works. She was a competent author of domestic fiction. Her literary career remains of interest for many reasons, as reflections of changing social attitudes about female authors and the professionalization of authorship, as examples of the evolving novel genre in America, and as expressions of contemporary social and political attitudes and debates.

• Hilda M. Fife has located a poem by Wood in the Old Goal Museum in York, Maine, and asserts that descendants have additional letters by Wood. Almost all biographical information about Wood is derived from William Goold, "Madam Wood, the First Maine Writer of Fiction" in *Maine Historical Society Collections and Proceedings*, 2d ser., 1 (1890): 401–8. Charles E. Banks, *History of York, Maine*, vol. 1 (1931), pp. 375, 389–401, and Charles A. Sayward, *The Sayward Family* (1890), provide useful information about her family and social background. "War, the parent of Domestic Calamity—A Tale of the Revolution," ed. with an introduction by Fife, is in *A Handful of Spice: A Miscellany of Maine Literature and History*, ed. Richard S. Sprague (1968). Wood's letters of reminiscence, edited by Fife under the title "Madam Wood's 'Recollections,'" are in the *Colby Library Quarterly*, 7th ser., no. 3 (Sept. 1965): 89–115. For discussions of Wood's contribution to American fiction, see Henri Petter, *The Early American Novel* (1971), and Cathy N. Davidson, *The Revolution and the Word: The Rise of the Novel in America* (1986). Her obituary is in the Portland *Eastern Argus*, 9 Jan. 1855.

JEANNE M. MALLOY

WOOD, Smoky Joe (25 Oct. 1889–27 July 1985), baseball player, was born Howard Ellsworth Wood, in Kansas City, Missouri, the son of John F. Wood, a lawyer, and Rebecca Stephens. The family moved to Ouray, Colorado, by covered wagon. The future pitcher spent the journey playing with a baseball glove. Wood later said he remembered seeing stagecoaches drawn by six horses, guarded by men carrying rifles. In 1906 the Woods returned to Ness City, Kansas, where Joe pitched for the town amateur team and barnstormed with the Kansas City Bloomer Girls' club.

In 1907 Wood signed his first organized baseball contract with Cedar Rapids of the Three I League, but the club didn't have room for Wood, so he was given (not sold) to Hutchinson (Kans.) of the Western Association. Wood won 18 games for Hutchinson. He then pitched for Kansas City of the American Association in 1908 until the end of the season, when he was sold to Boston Red Sox and posted a mark of 1–1. Early editions of the *MacMillan Baseball Encyclopedia* reported Wood's first major league record as 1–12, but Wood's son Robert proved this incorrect and subsequent editions corrected the error. The statistic is important in considering Wood for the Hall of Fame. Wood was 11–7 and 12–13 in 1909 and 1910, and then in 1911 he won 23, lost 17, struck out a club-record 231, and pitched a no-hitter. He was called "Smoky Joe" after 1909, when Paul Shannon of the *Boston Post* noticed the young pitcher throwing batting practice and said, "This kid certainly throws nothing but smoke."

In 1912 the Boston Red Sox won the World Series, and Smoky Joe Wood had arguably the best year a pitcher ever had. He won 34 games (which led the American League) and lost five, for a league-leading .872 percentage, had a 1.91 earned run average, which trailed only Walter Johnson's 1.39, and struck out 258, which was second to Johnson's 303. Wood also hit .290, solely as a pitcher, with 13 doubles and 13 runs batted in. He won three games in the World Series against the New York Giants. That summer Johnson won an American League record 16 straight games. Wood then won 13 straight, which set up a confrontation on 6 September 1912 at Fenway Park. The papers ballyhooed the matchup of record holder and challenger like a prize fight, providing height, weight, arm span, and bicep and tricep size. Johnson was the bigger man at 6′1″, 200 pounds, while Wood was 5′11″ and 180 pounds. Fans stood behind ropes in the outfield and along the foul lines. Boston won 1–0 even though the Senators had men in scoring position in four different innings, including the ninth. Wood's streak also ended at 16 wins.

The 1912 World Series was as wild as any ever played. Wood won the opener, fanning 11; the last two strike-outs came with the tying run on third base in the ninth inning. He won game four, fanning 8 and driving in a run, but was hit hard in game seven. In the final game (the eighth played: there had been a tie), the Giants went ahead in the tenth. Wood pitched the last three innings, and the Red Sox won with an improbable rally that featured a dropped fly ball and a muffed foul pop-up. Christy Mathewson was the losing pitcher.

By age twenty-two Wood had accomplished everything a pitcher could. When Johnson was asked if he threw harder than Wood he replied, "No man alive can throw harder than Smoky Joe Wood." In 1913, in St. Louis, Wood slipped trying to field a bunt and broke the thumb on his pitching hand. He subsequently hurt his shoulder compensating for the injured thumb and never again pitched without severe pain. Wood described the next five years as a "nightmare." He continued to pitch, despite pain, and led the American League in ERA (1.49) while going 15–5 in 1915. He worked with a chiropractor and stretched his arm on a trapeze, but neither helped; he sat out the 1916 season.

In 1917 Wood made the Cleveland Indians as an outfielder, at the recommendation of Tris Speaker. In six years with the Indians, he compiled a .298 batting average, including a .366 in 1921 in 194 at bats. His overall career batting average was .283 with 23 home runs. He hit .286 in the 1912 World Series and .200 in the 1920 Series. Wood and Babe Ruth are the only players to both win a World Series game as a pitcher and then play outfield in another Series.

Wood became the baseball coach at Yale in 1923 and over twenty years posted a 303–241 record, for a winning percentage of .557. His teams were 24–23 against Harvard, 26–17 against Princeton, and won eight Big Three Championships and two (1932 and

1937) Eastern Intercollegiate League titles. Upon retirement, Wood was commended for his "molding of young men." In 1985 he received an honorary doctorate from Yale, making him the first baseball player to be so honored by an Ivy League university.

Wood had married Laura T. O'shea in 1913. The couple had four children, including Joe Wood, Jr., who played 60 games for the Detroit Tigers in 1943. Between 1943 and 1985 Wood owned a driving range in Los Angeles with his brother Pete. In 1947 he changed his name legally to Joe Wood. He never called himself, or signed autographs, "Smoky." Wood died in West Haven, Connecticut.

Should Smoky Joe Wood be in the Baseball Hall of Fame? His lifetime pitching record is 114–57 for a .671 winning percentage. This is comparable to all but a few Hall of Fame pitchers who won over 100 games. For many years the fewest wins by a pitcher not in the Hall for accomplishments at another position was 150 by Dizzy Dean. Years after his death the Old Timers' Committee had not selected Wood.

• The best portrait of Wood appears in an interview in Lawrence Ritter, *The Glory Of Their Times* (1966). The 91-year-old Wood is portrayed in Roger Angell, "The Seamless Web," in his *Late Innings* (1982). Wood's baseball record can be found in Joseph L. Reichler, ed., *The Baseball Encyclopedia*, 8th ed. (1990). Articles about him are Emil H. Rothe, "The Wood-Johnson Duel in 1912," in *Baseball Historical Review*, ed. L. Robert Davids (1981), and John Thorn and Mark Rucker, "The Joe Wood Scrapbook," a photographic essay in *The National Pastime* (1982). He is mentioned briefly in Bill James, *The Bill James Historical Baseball Abstract* (1988); Lloyd Graybar, "World Series Three Game Winners," in *The Baseball Research Journal* ed. L. Robert Davids (1982); and Timothy Mulligan, "Seventh Game Syndrome," in *The Baseball Research Journal*, ed. Clifford Kachline (1986). An obituary is in the *New York Times*, 29 July 1985.

LUKE SALISBURY

WOOD, Thomas Bond (17 Mar. 1844–18 Dec. 1922), Methodist missionary, educator, and social reformer, was born in Lafayette, Indiana, the son of Aaron Wood, a Methodist minister, and Maria Hitt. He entered Indiana Asbury (later DePauw University) and then Wesleyan University in Middletown, Connecticut, receiving an A.B. from both institutions. He earned an M.A. from both universities (Indiana Asbury, 1866; Wesleyan, 1867). During this time he taught German and natural science at Wesleyan Academy in Wilbraham, Massachusetts (1864–1867). The New England Conference of the Methodist Episcopal church licensed him to preach in 1865 and ordained him deacon (1867) and elder (1868). He married Ellen Dow in 1867; they had at least four children. He transferred to the North-West Indiana Conference, the conference of his father, where he served as president of Valparaiso College (1867–1869) before his appointment as a missionary to Argentina.

At Rosario de Santa Fe, Argentina, in 1870, Wood initially served the English-speaking congregation but within a year conducted services in Spanish, German, and Portuguese. A Protestant school for boys (Colegio Americano) was initiated, and at his urging the Women's Foreign Missionary Society of the Methodist Episcopal church appointed Cecilia Elena Guelfi as its first indigenous missionary. The government appointed him to the National College in Rosario, as school examiner, as a member of the local city government, and as president of the National Education Commission of Argentina. In 1873 he was appointed by President Ulysses S. Grant as U.S. consul in Rosario, serving until 1878. In 1875 he qualified to practice law in Argentina. From 1877 to 1881 he served in Montevideo, Uruguay, where he founded in 1877 *El Evangelista*, the first Spanish evangelical paper in the world, composed the handbook *Breves Informaciones* (1881), which explained Methodism, and jointly edited a Spanish hymn book for Protestant services. In 1884 he became director of a self-supporting Protestant day school in Uruguay and then returned to Argentina, where he was president of the Buenos Aires Theological Seminary (1889–1891).

As superintendent of the Western District of the South American Conference in 1892, Wood had responsibility for Methodist work in Peru, Ecuador, and Bolivia. In Lima, he was superintendent of the North Andes Mission, president of the Lima Theological Seminary, pastor of the English-speaking congregation, and with his daughter Elsie, he established the Callao high school for girls (Colegio America). The government of Ecuador commissioned him to establish normal schools and recruit teachers from the United States. In cooperation with Daniel Armand Ugon, a Waldensian minister, he opened a theological school in 1889 that became the first Protestant school in South America to award the bachelor's degree. He organized a chapter in Latin America of the Society for the Prevention of Cruelty to Animals and also founded a chapter of the Good Templars. In all of his work Wood promoted religious liberty. He was in the vanguard of the cause for legal civil marriage, public education, and social reform.

Wood was a delegate to the Methodist Ecumenical Conference in London in 1881. He expanded Methodism by helping to form the South American Conference (1893); the Western South American Conference (1898); the Andes Conference (1905); and the North Andes Mission (1910). He introduced Methodism in Panama, initiated the YMCA and the University Club for Americans there, and promoted education for the natives of the Canal Zone. Upon returning to the North Andes Mission, he served a second term as superintendent and president of the theological school. After a nervous breakdown, he returned to the United States in 1913 and retired in 1915. He died in Tacoma, Washington.

• There is a collection of Wood papers in the archives of DePauw University, Greencastle, Ind. Helpful works are Wade C. Barclay, *The Methodist Episcopal Church 1845–1939*, vol. 3 (1957); Harlan P. Beach et al., *Protestant Missions in South America* (1907); John T. Copplestone, *History of Methodist*

Missions: Twentieth-century Perspectives (1973); Paul E. Kuhl, "Gringo in the Andes: Thomas B. Wood and the Normal School System in Ecuador," *Methodist History* (16 July 1978): 197–217; John Lee, *Religious Liberty in South America* (1907); Barbara H. Lewis, ed., *Methodist Overseas Missions* (1953); Edward C. Millard and Lucy E. Guinness, *South America: The Neglected Continent* (1894); and Homer C. Stuntz, *South American Neighbors* (1916).

FREDERICK V. MILLS, SR.

WOOD, Thomas John (25 Sept. 1823–25 Feb. 1906), soldier, was born in Munfordville, Kentucky, the son of George T. Wood, an army officer, and Elizabeth Helm. Wood was raised at his parents' home in Kentucky. In 1841 he was appointed to the U.S. Military Academy at West Point, and he graduated as a member of the class of 1845. He stood in the upper half of his class and received a commission in the Corps of Engineers upon graduation.

In 1846 Wood joined General Zachary Taylor's staff and fought in the campaign against Mexico. Later that year he transferred to the cavalry branch and took an assignment to the Second Dragoons Regiment, a formation of mounted infantrymen. He received notice for his bravery under fire in the battle of Buena Vista (22–23 Feb. 1847), where he personally reconnoitered the Mexican positions. After the war he advanced in the peacetime army and served in a succession of cavalry postings on the frontier.

After the outbreak of hostilities in the Civil War in 1861, Wood assisted the state authorities of Indiana in organizing, training, and equipping volunteer regiments. On 11 October 1861 he was appointed brigadier general of volunteers and given command of a brigade of Indiana volunteers he had helped raise. In November 1861 he married Caroline E. Greer. They had no children.

In early 1862 Wood was given command of a division in the Army of the Ohio, then led by General Don Carlos Buell, and took part in the Union invasion of Tennessee. In February 1862 he participated in the capture of Nashville, Tennessee, the first Confederate state capital to fall to the Union army. He fought with distinction at the battle of Stones River (30 Dec. 1862–2 Jan. 1863), where he was wounded. The Army of the Cumberland (formerly the Army of the Ohio) repulsed Confederate general Braxton Bragg's strongest effort to clear the Union army out of central Tennessee.

In 1863 Wood's role in the battle of Chickamauga provoked fierce controversy in the Union high command. In October 1862 Abraham Lincoln had relieved Buell and replaced him with Major General William S. Rosecrans. On the second day of the battle, 20 September 1863, Rosecrans personally and vehemently ordered Wood to move his division, which Wood promptly did, even though it left more than a quarter-mile gap in the Union line. Confederate general James Longstreet's corps, on loan from the Army of Northern Virginia, attacked into this gap, cutting Rosecrans's army in two and threatening to destroy the entire army. Rosecrans was furious with Wood and blamed him for the blunder. General Ulysses S. Grant, however, saw the incident in a different light and chose, with the advice of Major General George H. Thomas, to keep Wood but relieve Rosecrans.

Wood repaid the confidence of Grant and Thomas in spectacular fashion during the attack on Missionary Ridge, the key to the Confederate defense of Chattanooga. On 25 November 1863, after William T. Sherman's flank attack on the Confederate entrenchments began to falter, Grant ordered divisions commanded by Wood and Philip Sheridan to launch a hasty attack at the base of the well-defended Confederate ridge line. In one of the most remarkable and heroic incidents of the entire Civil War, Wood's men disobeyed orders to halt after they overran the Confederate line and raced to the top of the hill, throwing the entire Confederate army into confusion and winning a victory that astonished Grant himself. It was, Wood later said, "the proudest, most exultant moment of my life" (Sword, *Mountains Touched with Fire*, p. 290). It was also a vindication of Wood's military prowess, which had been called into question ever since Chickamauga.

In 1864 Wood took part in Sherman's invasion of Georgia. He was wounded again, this time at Lovejoy's Station on 2 September 1864, but again refused to leave his command. After the fall of Atlanta his division accompanied General Thomas back to Tennessee to defend Nashville against John B. Hood's final offensive. Promoted to commander of the IV Corps, Wood participated in the defense of Nashville on 15 December 1864 and pursued the remnants of the Army of Tennessee after Hood was defeated. His contributions to this decisive Union victory earned him promotion to major general on 27 January 1865.

After the Confederate armies surrendered, Wood was assigned to military occupation duty in Mississippi, where he was departmental commander in 1865 and 1866. He was also appointed assistant superintendent of the Freedmen's Bureau for that state in 1866. Though he was considered by many to be an impartial administrator in a difficult situation. Wood did not care to be involved in the contentious politics of Reconstruction, and his war wounds prevented him from being assigned to more active duty with the frontier army. He therefore retired from the army on 9 June 1868 and lived the rest of his life in his wife's home town of Dayton, Ohio. His later years were spent as an active and enthusiastic officer in the Grand Army of the Republic, the Union veterans' organization, and he also served as a member of the board of visitors at the Military Academy. He died in Dayton.

Wood was a fierce, effective, and tactically capable battlefield commander for the Union in the Civil War. He led his soldiers from the front, as his repeated wounds attested, and they rewarded him with one of the most thrilling performances in the Civil War and U.S. military history—the heroic charge up Missionary Ridge. His quarrel with Rosecrans over the blunder at Chickamauga probably prevented his rise to higher command in the war, but he did not appear to brood over it, as many of his contemporaries often did.

• Two books by Wiley Sword treat the Army of the Cumberland in scholarly fashion and place Wood's career of 1862 to 1865 in the context of the military operations in Tennessee. His *Mountains Touched with Fire: Chattanooga Besieged, 1863* (1995) covers the Rosecrans-Wood controversy and also gives an exhaustive account of Wood's assault on Missionary Ridge in 1863. His *Embrace an Angry Wind: The Confederacy's Last Hurrah: Spring Hill, Franklin, and Nashville* (1992) gives a similar treatment of Wood's command of the IV Corps under Thomas and his role in the pursuit and destruction of Hood's army after the battle of Nashville.

JAMES K. HOGUE

WOOD, William Barry, Jr. (4 May 1910–9 Mar. 1971), physician, medical educator, and medical researcher, was born in Milton, Massachusetts, the son of William Barry Wood, Sr., a cotton broker, and Emily Niles. After graduating from Milton Academy, he spent a year at the Thatcher School in Ojai, California, and then entered Harvard College in 1928. His college career was extraordinary, both academically and athletically. While compiling a straight A record and achieving election to Phi Beta Kappa, Wood acquired ten major letters, three each in football, hockey, and baseball, and one in tennis. He was an all-American quarterback and was offered a position with the Boston Bruins professional hockey team. While in college, Wood did original research on the response of the white blood cells to vigorous physical exercise, using his teammates and himself as subjects. His honors thesis was published in a leading German physiological journal. He graduated summa cum laude in 1932. That same year he married Mary Lee Hutchins, who later became a biomedical scientist; they had five children.

After leaving Harvard, Wood entered the Johns Hopkins University School of Medicine, where again he compiled a superb academic record, recognized by his election to Alpha Omega Alpha Honor Medical Society. After receiving his M.D. in 1936, he served an internship and two years of residency on the Osler Medical Service of the Johns Hopkins Hospital and then spent a year as a National Research Council Fellow in the Medical Sciences in the Department of Bacteriology at the Harvard Medical School. His original intention was to work in the laboratory of the late Hans Zinsser, then the head of the department, but as Zinsser was in the advanced stages of a malignant disease, Wood joined the laboratory of John Enders, who some years later became a Nobel laureate. Wood and Enders developed a method of producing pneumococcal pneumonia in rats and studied the progression of the infection and the role of leucocytes in the recovery process. It was this study that underlay many of Wood's subsequent investigations.

Wood returned to Baltimore in 1940 as an assistant and then associate in medicine at Johns Hopkins. In 1942, at the age of thirty-two, he was invited to the Washington University School of Medicine in St. Louis, Missouri, to become the Busch Professor and chairman of the Department of Medicine. During his years in St. Louis, Wood attracted an outstanding group of faculty members to his department, and appointments to his house staff were among the most sought after in the nation.

Recognized as a superb clinician and teacher, Wood at the same time continued to be a productive investigator, pursuing studies of the mechanisms by which the body defends itself against bacterial infection. His work led him to delineate the process known as surface phagocytosis, whereby leucocytes engulf pneumococci. Subsequently, he turned his attention to the pathogenesis of fever—particularly the role of endogenous pyrogen—the study of which he continued for the remainder of his career.

In 1955 Wood returned to Johns Hopkins University as vice president of the university and the hospital and professor of microbiology in the school of medicine. In the following four years he played a key role in reorganizing the medical curriculum at Johns Hopkins and in addressing the increasing challenges facing academic medical institutions. Ultimately preferring to devote his time and energy to carrying on his investigative program, he stepped down in 1959 as vice president and became director of the Department of Microbiology, a post he held until his death.

Wood's outstanding work brought him membership in leading professional societies, including the Association of American Physicians, the American Society for Clinical Investigation, the Central Society for Clinical Research (all three of which he served as president), the American College of Physicians (Master), the National Academy of Sciences (councilor), and the Institute of Medicine at the National Academy of Sciences. In addition, he served on the Armed Forces Epidemiological Board and several of that board's commissions. For many years he was a trustee of the Rockefeller Foundation, served on the Board of Overseers of Harvard College, was a member of the President's Scientific Advisory Council, and was one of two U.S. members on the World Health Organization Committee on Research. He was invited to present named lectures at various universities and research institutions and received a number of honorary degrees and other awards, including the Kober Medal of the Association of American Physicians. During the course of his career, Wood published 132 papers (primarily in the *Journal of Experimental Medicine*), was coauthor of a major textbook in microbiology (*Microbiology* [1967], with B. D. Davis, R. Dulbecco, H. Eisen, and H. Ginsberg), and contributed to numerous other scientific monographs and textbooks.

Over the years, Wood continued to be an avid, albeit amateur, athlete, enjoying tennis, golf, and in his St. Louis years, he was an active participant in softball and touch football games with his house staff and fellows. Although he was abstemious in his habits, maintaining a youthful physique throughout his life, Wood was found in 1964 to have a myocardial infarction and continued to have symptoms of coronary disease until he died of a heart attack, while attending a dinner, in Boston, Massachusetts.

• Wood's Shattuck Lecture, "Studies on the Cause of Fever," *New England Journal of Medicine* 258 (1958): 1023, summarizes his early work on the subject. His monograph *From Microbes to Molecules* (1961), based on his Bampton Lectures at Columbia University, is an exemplary history of diphtheria and of its ultimate conquest as a result of scientific investigation. Additional information on Wood's life is given in "Presentation of the Kober Medal for 1971 to W. Barry Wood, Jr.," *Transactions of the Association of American Physicians* 84 (1971): 47–52; National Academy of Sciences, *Biographical Memoirs* 51 (1980): 387–418; "Memorial Service," *Johns Hopkins Medical Journal* 129 (1971): 113–20; and a VHS videotape in "The Leaders of American Medicine" series (1971), available at the National Library of Medicine, Bethesda, Md.

ROBERT J. GLASER

WOOD, William Burke (26 May 1779–23 Sept. 1861), actor and theater manager, was born in Montreal, Canada, the son of Thomizen English and her husband (name unknown), a goldsmith. Because of his Tory sympathies, Wood's father did not return to the United States until after the Revolution, when he settled his family in New York City. There, William received some private schooling and attended the theater, soon becoming apprenticed in various mercantile houses for seven years. Wood journeyed to the West Indies in the hopes of improving his health. He returned to Philadelphia in 1798 and, through connections of his father, joined the Chestnut Street Theatre Company as an assistant to comanager Thomas Wignell. Despite his sickly condition and faltering work as a performer, Wood gained the confidence of Wignell and his partner, Alexander Reinagle, and he became treasurer of the company at age twenty-three. Wignell sent Wood to London in 1803 to recruit new talent, and he returned successful. Following Wignell's death later that same year, Wood assumed increased managerial duties. In 1804 Wood married Juliana Westray, an actor in the company; there is no record indicating that they had any children. He became a full partner with William Warren, comic star of the Chestnut, in 1810 after the deaths of Reinagle and Wignell's widow.

For much of the next sixteen years of Warren and Wood's partnership the Chestnut was celebrated as the preeminent acting company in the new nation. In addition to its home in Philadelphia, the company performed in theaters in Baltimore and Washington. Warren planned the seasons and performed major comic roles while Wood handled financial affairs and the casting of plays. Wood also achieved a modest reputation as a performer for his witty intelligence in high comedy and his stolid decorum in the father-figure roles of melodrama. The company included actors from the Wallack, Burke, and Jefferson families, names that would dominate the American stage for generations. Although Wood treated the permanent members of the company with care, his oppressive paternalism drove away several junior members of the troupe and in 1824 forced the comic actor Francis Wemyss to accept an inferior line of business than the one he had contracted to perform. As before, the company looked to London for its theatrical fare, performing mostly Shakespearean tragedy, eighteenth-century comedy, and popular operettas and melodramas; new American plays were rare. Warren and Wood's partnership weathered the burning of the gas-lit Chestnut Street Theatre in 1820, which destroyed their stores of scenery and costumes, and the best collection of theatrical music in the United States.

Nevertheless, Warren and Wood dissolved their partnership in 1826. Wood had grown perturbed at Warren's subservient attitude toward theater stockholders. Wood tried to become sole manager, but Warren, with the support of the stockholders, bought him out on easy terms, allowing Wood and his wife to remain as actors in the company. In 1828 Wood, believing that the Chestnut could not survive under Warren, assumed management of Philadelphia's new Arch Street Theatre and assembled a promising company. Neither company proved successful, and by the end of the year Warren had retired as manager of the Chestnut, and Wood had closed the Arch. The high price of stars also contributed to the collapse of the companies. Before 1827 Warren and Wood had successfully insisted that stars appearing in Philadelphia take only half of the net profits of their performances. By 1828, however, Thomas A. Cooper, Edwin Forrest, and other stars were signing contracts ensuring them of half of the gross receipts, regardless of the gate.

Instead of pursuing other managerial positions, Wood joined the Walnut Street company in 1829 and performed with them until his retirement in 1846. He performed mostly secondary roles as a stock actor, including the Ghost in *Hamlet*, Banquo in *Macbeth*, and stern fathers in melodramas and farces. For his final benefit, he acted Sergeant Austerlitz in *The Maid of Croissy, or the Last of the Old Guard.*

Wood sought to remain faithful to the values of deference and duty he had learned as a young man. His response to the debacle of traditional management practices in the Philadelphia theater, recorded in his *Personel Recollections* (1855), reflects his stubborn attachment to managerial paternalism. Wood faults the "spirit of locomotiveness," the steam-driven power of the modern age that facilitated the travel of itinerant stars and allowed them to achieve a public fame out of proportion to their talent. Wood used his memoirs to blame the star system for mediocre performances by stock actors, negligent scenic effects, excessive benefits, newspaper puffing, and lack of variety in the theatrical season, allegations that simplified and exaggerated the effects of itinerant starring. In its place, Wood argued the return of managerial control over stars, and he advocated the passage of laws that would grant a theatrical monopoly to a single company within a given region.

Wood's managerial career coincided with the end of a period marked by local elite control of the American stage. City patricians in Philadelphia, as in New York and Boston, relied on managers like Wood to provide fashionable entertainment that legitimated the patrons' values and extended their influence over theatergoers of other classes. Itinerant stars, however, bypassed the regimen of company hierarchy, transcended local elite control, and appealed directly to the public. Many managers accommodated the stars' lust for fame and fortune, but Wood refused to reject the traditional practices in favor of the star system. He deferred to elite tastes throughout his acting and managerial career and his own paternalism toward his acting company reflected the values of his employers.

• On the Warren-Wood management of the Chestnut, see Charles Durang, *History of the Philadelphia Stage* (1868); Reese D. James, *The Old Drury of Philadelphia* (1932); and Francis Wemyss, *Twenty-Six Years of the Life of an Actor and Manager* (1847). Excerpts from reviews on Wood's acting performances may be found in William C. Young, ed., *Famous Actors and Actresses of the American Stage* (1975). For an interpretation of Wood's managerial career see Bruce A. McConachie, *Melodramatic Formations: American Theatre and Society, 1820–1870* (1992).

BRUCE A. MCCONACHIE

WOOD, William Madison (18 June 1858–2 Feb. 1926), textile manufacturer, was born in Edgartown, Massachusetts, the son of William Jason Wood, a mariner and ship steward, and Amelia Christiana Madison. Wood lived his first years on the island of Martha's Vineyard with his parents, who were immigrants from the Portuguese Azores. At the age of three, he moved with his family to the mainland city of New Bedford, Massachusetts, where he spent the rest of his youth. Life was a struggle for the family with ten children. Wood's father held a series of menial jobs, and his mother occasionally worked as a scrubwoman.

Wood's father died in 1870, so William had to leave school to help support his family. Andrew G. Pierce, a textile manufacturer and the treasurer of the Wamsutta Mills, had known the Wood family and gave the young boy a job in the counting room. In 1876 Wood traveled from southeastern Massachusetts for the first time to go to Philadelphia, Pennsylvania, where he secured office work. He returned to New Bedford later in the year to work for a banking firm, where he learned the skills of an accountant. He left New Bedford in 1880 for a position in nearby Fall River as a paymaster for a textile manufacturer, and he would remain in that industry for the rest of his life.

Wood moved to Lawrence, Massachusetts, in 1886 to assist the owner of the Washington Mills, Frederick Ayer, in reorganizing and managing his faltering operations. Wood soon evinced the industrial-managerial skills that had been pioneered by Andrew Carnegie, a man with whom he had much in common. The young Lawrence businessman became a master of cost accounting and had an uncanny ability to discern market conditions. He also chose his staff with great care and insisted on installing the most efficient machinery in his mills. Wood impressed not only Ayer but also his daughter Ellen Wheaton Ayer. They were married in 1888 and had four children. Through his marriage, Wood became part of one of New England's richest families.

Like many other industries in the 1890s, woolen textile manufacturing suffered from excess competition, and Wood looked toward the solution that many other industrialists were embracing—corporate consolidation. Wood and Ayer convinced the owners of seven other woolen mills to join them in creating the American Woolen Company in 1899. In 1905 Wood replaced the retiring Ayer as the president of American Woolen. The corporation became the largest woolen textile manufacturer in the world and, at its peak in the first half of the 1920s, had a total of some sixty mills and forty thousand workers.

A labor conflict produced the greatest controversy of Wood's career, as was the case with other industrialists such as Carnegie and George Pullman. In January 1912, Wood and other manufacturers cut wages in Lawrence in response to a new state law that reduced the number of hours that women and children could work. A largely immigrant work force, soon led by the Industrial Workers of the World (IWW), went out on strike. The bitter Lawrence strike, which lasted for over eight weeks before the workers won significant gains, ranked among the most famous labor conflicts of the early twentieth century.

In one of the most bizarre aspects of the strike, prosecutors in Boston indicted Wood for conspiracy to place dynamite at several locations associated with the strikers, in an attempt to discredit them. A jury cleared Wood of the charges.

In the years after the strike, Wood introduced many of the programs that were known as welfare capitalism. These included sickness and accident benefits for workers, as well as day care and summer camp programs for workers' children. Wood's oldest son, William, Jr., who had recently finished studying social issues at Harvard University, was the major influence in having his father embark on these programs. It is also possible that, like some other manufacturers who introduced such programs, the antiunion industrialist hoped to avoid labor organizing among his employees.

Another new departure for Wood and American Woolen was the building between 1919 and 1924 of the model Shawsheen Village in Andover, near Lawrence. Architecture had always interested Wood, and the model village, which cost $20 million, included housing for managerial and skilled staff, company headquarters, and a large factory. Wood's mansion was nearby. Most mill workers, however, were expected to take the trolley or train from Lawrence. The majority of the buildings were designed in Georgian or Colonial Revival style, and the historian Sam Bass Warner has suggested that Wood, like his fellow industrialist Henry Ford, who built the model Greenfield Village in Michigan, hoped to recreate a nostalgic past. Both men had of course done much to transform America from its supposedly idyllic past.

The last years of Wood's life were tragic. The federal government charged Wood in 1920 with war profiteering, but the charges were dropped. More significantly, a daughter died in 1918, and Wood's elder son was killed in an automobile accident in 1922. Wood was very close to his family, and the deaths had a devastating effect on his health and mental stability.

Furthermore, problems at American Woolen began to surface in the early 1920s. American Woolen had never been able to control the costs of raw wool from its suppliers around the world. On the demand side, the popularity of wool clothing was beginning to decline as a result of central heating, styling changes that favored lighter clothing, and the introduction of synthetic fibers. American Woolen mass-produced staple goods that were low-priced and could be manufactured more profitably in cheaper-cost areas of the country and eventually the world. Wood's autocratic style of managing the sprawling corporation became an increasing problem. The manufacturer himself noted: "I am a man that works alone, because I cannot work any other way" (Sumner, p. 208). The massive expenditure for Shawsheen Village also severely taxed the company. After a year in which American Woolen lost $6,900,000, Wood resigned as president in December 1924.

Having lost his life's work, two of his four children, and his health, Wood committed suicide on a remote road near Flagler Beach, Florida.

William Wood's life was emblematic of many of the myths and realities of late nineteenth- and early twentieth-century industrial America. His rise from an impoverished son of immigrants to one of the best-paid executives in America, in part through marrying the boss's daughter, echoed the Horatio Alger myth. He was one of the major figures in the great trust creation movement of the late 1890s and remained for several decades the leading figure in the woolen textile industry. He became the bête noire for the workers of one of the great labor struggles of the period. And finally, American Woolen's troubles at the end of his career foreshadowed the fact that the northern textile industry would soon become one of the first cases of the twentieth-century phenomenon of deindustrialization.

• Wood's life is fully treated in Edward G. Roddy, *Mills, Mansions, and Mergers: The Life of William M. Wood* (1982). Sam Bass Warner's "William Madison Wood" in his *Province of Reason* (1984) is a briefer and more critical study. Donald B. Cole discusses Wood's role in the life of Lawrence in *Immigrant City: Lawrence, Massachusetts, 1845–1921* (1963). Contemporary and flattering accounts of Wood's life include John Bruce McPherson, "William Madison Wood: A Career of Romance and Achievement," *Bulletin of the National Association of Wool Manufacturers* (Apr. 1926): 245–57, and Keene Sumner, "A Business Genius Who Has Done What Others Said Was Impossible," *American Magazine*, June 1923, pp. 16–17, 203–8. The most complete obituaries are in the *Boston Post* and the *New Bedford Evening Standard*, both 3 Feb. 1926.

THOMAS A. MCMULLIN

WOODBERRY, George Edward (12 May 1855–2 Jan. 1930), man of letters and teacher, was born in Beverly, Massachusetts, the son of Henry Elliott Woodberry, a shipmaster, and Sarah Dane Tuck. His first American ancestor was William Woodberry, who came to Salem, Massachusetts, from Somersetshire, England, in 1628 and was one of the founders of Beverly. Educated at Phillips Exeter Academy in Exeter, New Hampshire, Woodberry entered Harvard College and graduated in 1877 with highest honors in philosophy. He wrote that Henry Adams and Charles Eliot Norton "were all of Harvard to me, so far as 'education' went," with Adams the greatest intellectual force and Norton the greatest aesthetic one (*Selected Letters*, p. 207). Woodberry edited the *Harvard Advocate* and in 1876 began to contribute to the *Atlantic Monthly*. Noticed at Harvard not only for his literary talent but also for "decided opinions to which he gives free expression," as President Charles Eliot wrote a correspondent in 1876 (Doyle, p. 136), he was deprived of his part in the commencement exercises when his proposed address, "The Relation of Pallas Athena to Athens," deemed potentially offensive to some religious sensibilities, was removed from the program.

After graduation Woodberry was appointed professor of English and history at the recently established University of Nebraska, where he taught in 1877–1878 and, after a year in New York on the staff of the *Nation*, again in 1880–1882. During the next nine years—living mostly in Beverly except for two periods in Italy in 1885 and 1889 and one in Boston when he served as literary editor of the *Boston Post* in 1888—he was occupied with writing. He contributed regularly to the *Atlantic* and the *Nation* and produced four books, *A History of Wood Engraving* (1883), a result of his studies under Norton; *Edgar Allan Poe* (1885), which while critical of Poe presented more soundly researched information than any previous study; *The North Shore Watch and Other Poems* (1890); and *Studies in Letters and Life* (1890).

Established as a poet and scholar, Woodberry was appointed on James Russell Lowell's recommendation as professor of literature (a title changed in 1900 to professor of comparative literature) at Columbia University, where he enjoyed extraordinary success, being repeatedly voted the most effective and respected teacher by undergraduate and graduate students alike. His writing activity continued in several fields. An edition of *The Complete Poetical Works of Percy Bysshe Shelley* (1892) was followed by one (with E. C. Stedman) of *The Works of Edgar Allan Poe* (10 vols., 1894–1895). Two volumes of verse then appeared, *Wild Eden* (1899) and *Poems* (1903), and critical essays related to his teaching were included in *Heart of Man* (1899) and *Makers of Literature* (1900). In an important biography, *Nathaniel Hawthorne* (1902), Woodberry explored the relationship between image and idea in Nathaniel Hawthorne's fiction. Next, in *America in Literature* (1903, French translation 1909), he proved to be no literary nationalist, observing that "we have been deeply indebted for impulse and guidance, for outlook and method, for a thousand subtly shaping influences, to all the world beyond seas, where both thought and life are old" (p. 193).

This refusal to see the United States as unique was consistent with views he expressed in a course of lectures at the Lowell Institute of Boston in 1903, published under the title *The Torch: Eight Lectures on Race Power in Literature* (1905). Woodberry's concept of what he called "the race-mind" has nothing to do with ethnicity but everything to do with humanity itself and its spiritual potential; it was central to his teaching. For Woodberry, science had weakened traditional religious belief and made it impossible to invest nature with spiritual significance. But spiritual triumph could be achieved in the world of art and letters, the world that finally matters to the race-mind, the one stable thing that redeems history from meaninglessness. "Men, tribes, states disappear," Woodberry writes, "but the race-mind endures. A conception of the world and an emotional response thereto constitute the life of the race-mind and fill its consciousness with ideas and feelings . . . It contains all human energy, knowledge, experience, that survives. It is the resultant of millions of lives whose earthly power it stores in one deathless force" (p. 7). Individual cultures rise, crest, and fall, to be succeeded by others that in turn leave their own spiritual high-water marks in the form of enduring masterpieces, which enrich the consciousness of our common humanity. History is important, "yet to vary Aristotle's phrase—poetry is all history could never be." Elements of history "enter into the eternal memory of the race, and are there transformed, and . . . spiritualized. Literature is the abiding-place of this transforming power" (p. 41).

The happy and productive Columbia period ended when, while on a year's leave of absence in 1904, Woodberry resigned without explanation. Newly adopted regulations limited enrollment in his courses to students competent in two or more foreign languages; realizing that some professors were anxious to protect their own offerings in the English and foreign language departments, he evidently decided that "the work he most wanted to do was not wanted" (Doyle, p. 22). Never afterward accepting a permanent academic appointment, he continued to write in the privacy he increasingly sought in the Beverly house where he was born; the family home for generations, it was still occupied by his sister Sarah Caroline and his brother Francis, neither of whom, like Woodberry himself, ever married. He lived for a time in Italy and traveled in other parts of the Mediterranean world. Woodberry also had occasional returns to teaching as a visiting professor for a semester or shorter session—Amherst (1905), Cornell (1907 and 1908), Wisconsin (1914), and California (1918)—or as a guest lecturer—Johns Hopkins (1907), Bowdoin (1912), Brown (1914), and Kenyon (1914).

Three of Woodberry's books appeared in 1907, *The Appreciation of Literature, Great Writers*, and an important biography, *Ralph Waldo Emerson*. Most notably, in 1909 he published *The Life of Edgar Allan Poe*, a two-volume work, entirely new, superseding the 1885 volume. Highly readable, it has earned the enduring respect of scholars. Honors also came to Woodberry in these years. He was a founder of the American Academy of Arts and Letters in 1904 and thereafter a fellow as well as an honorary fellow of the Royal Society of Literature in England. He received several honorary degrees, including one from Harvard, his alma mater, which gave him special satisfaction. In 1911 a group of former students founded The Woodberry Society and invited him to address their first meeting. Woodberry took the opportunity to mark the hundredth anniversary of the birth of a lifelong hero; his statement of democratic principles and exhortation appeared a few months later as *Wendell Phillips: the Faith of an American*, the first of several Woodberry Society publications.

Woodberry continued to write in the idealistic vein of his 1890 work, *The North Shore Watch*, a long threnody on the closest friend of his youth, dead at twenty-three. *Ideal Passion* (1917) is a sonnet sequence that takes to an extreme his pursuit of the Platonic ideal, "By earthly things the heavenly pattern guessing" (Sonnet 40). At a time when there was an emphasis on making poetry new, innovative in form, and realistic in content, the book was received somewhat skeptically. Harriet Monroe found it "monastic" in suggestion, "the poet['s] life expurgated of all common things" (*Poetry*, Nov. 1917, p. 103), a reaction echoed nearly sixty years later in *A History of Modern Poetry* (1976). There, noting Woodberry's belief that "poetry softens, refines, and ennobles the soul" and "illuminates life from within the consciousness of the reader," David Perkins remarks that "Woodberry's own poetry refines 'life' until it evaporates" (vol. 1, p. 119). Another volume, *The Roamer*, containing much of the earlier work, appeared in 1920. The posthumously published *Selected Poems* (1933) was reprinted in 1977, but otherwise Woodberry's poetry went out of print. His essays were collected in six volumes in 1921–1922, and his prose was in print in various forms throughout the twentieth century.

In addition to establishing the Woodberry Society, his admirers honored him in life by naming for him an endowed lectureship in literature at Phillips Exeter and an ambulance unit on the battlefields of Italy; they also quietly provided an annual pension of $2,000 during many years as his income and health declined. After his death in the hospital at Beverly, his admirers were equally devoted to his memory, endowing an undergraduate Woodberry poetry prize at Columbia and the Woodberry Poetry Room at Harvard. Columbia University tendered permanent recognition in 1965 by establishing the George Edward Woodberry Chair in Literature and Criticism.

Trying to explain the impact Woodberry had on them, former students often mentioned that he taught more than literature; he taught them how to live. John Erskine wondered about the extraordinary influence of this "quiet person of less than average height, who wore thick glasses," whose "fantastic success in the classroom was not to be expected and it remains difficult to account for . . . He was a fascinating and noble teacher only because what he said to us was fascinating and noble. He always lectured on a high plane on the obvious assumption that for others as for himself the masterpieces of poetry and the deep things of life would be of consuming interest. His students responded to the generous compliment" (*The Memory of Certain Persons* [1947], pp. 90–91). Woodberry himself stated his aims very succinctly in the two-sentence preface to *Heart of Man*: "The intention of the author was to illustrate how poetry, politics, and religion are the flowering of the same human spirit, and have their feeding roots in a common soil, 'deep in the general heart of men.'"

• Many of Woodberry's papers are in Columbia University's Rare Book and Manuscript Library, which has more than 6,000 of his items, including letters, poems, and reviews as well as personal memorabilia. The Woodberry Poetry Room at Harvard contains about 1,500 letters written to him and thirty by him. Woodberry letters are also in the Oberlin College Library. For additional information, see Joseph Doyle, "A Finding List of Manuscript Materials Relating to George Edward Woodberry," *Papers of the Bibliographical Society of America* 46 (1952): 165–68.

Woodberry's own publications are exhaustively listed in Michael Winship, ed., *Bibliography of American Literature*, vol. 9 (1991), pp. 413–38. Many more items, including unsigned essays and reviews, can be found in Joseph Doyle, "George Edward Woodberry: A Bibliography," *Bulletin of Bibliography* 21 (1955): 136–39, 163–68, 176–81, 209–14.

There is no full biography of Woodberry, but there is highly detailed information in Joseph Doyle's dissertation, "George Edward Woodberry" (Columbia Univ., 1952), which describes the first thirty-six years of his life, charts his intellectual history to 1891, and includes full data about his movements, residences, and speaking and teaching engagements until his death. Woodberry's own essay "Taormina" in *Heart of Man* (1899) and his *North Africa and the Desert: Scenes and Moods* (1914) provide personal information in a meditative context, and his *Selected Letters* (1933), ed. Walter De La Mare, presents Woodberry mostly in his later years. John Erskine, *My Life as a Teacher* (1948), contains a chapter titled "Last Conversations with Woodberry."

Useful studies include Louis V. Ledoux, *George Edward Woodberry, a Study of his Poetry* (1917), and R. B. Hovey, "George Edward Woodberry, Genteel Exile," *New England Quarterly* 23 (Dec. 1950): 504–26. Considerations of Woodberry's place in American criticism are presented in John Paul Pritchard, *Criticism in America* (1956), and in John W. Rathbun and Harry H. Clark, *American Literary Criticism 1860–1905* (1979). A typically eloquent tribute by a former student is Joseph M. Proskauer, "The Greatest Teacher I Ever Knew: The Gospel of George Edward Woodberry," *Saturday Review of Literature*, 28 Oct. 1944, pp. 12–13.

An informative obituary is in the *New York Times*, 3 Jan. 1930.

VINCENT FREIMARCK

WOODBRIDGE, Frederick James Eugene (26 Mar. 1867–1 June 1940), philosopher and educator, was born in Windsor, Ontario, Canada, the son of James Woodbridge, a king's counselor, and Melissa Ella Bingham. Woodbridge's father, also publisher of the *Essex Journal*, moved in 1868 to Kalamazoo, Michigan, to administer the Michigan Asylum. His father wanted Woodbridge to pursue law, and Woodbridge always admired his father's practical and common-sense approach to matters. But while a college student at Amherst, philosophy professor Charles E. Garman's Socratic style left Woodbridge with a lifelong respect for the thinking mind that eventually turned him toward philosophy.

After he graduated from Amherst in 1889 with a B.A., Woodbridge attended Union Theological Seminary in New York, graduating in 1892. He spent the next two years as a Union Fellow studying philosophy at the University of Berlin. He returned for postgraduate study at Amherst, receiving his M.A. in 1898. While at Union Theological Seminary, Woodbridge had considered entering the Christian ministry and served as a lay reader at First Church. When asked later why he did not go into the ministry, he responded, "The Church had moved from the worship of God to the worship of welfare." Further, he did not believe he possessed a pastor's temperament, and he was increasingly attracted to a philosophical "Odyssey" of the mind and to teaching.

In 1895 Woodbridge married Helena Belle Adams, with whom he had four children. Friends and family alike came to expect any conversation with Woodbridge to become an occasion for challenge and instruction, albeit with good humor, simplicity, and his omnipresent pipe, tobacco, and matches. A grandson's questions about fractions, for example, were answered by breaking a match in half and then the half in half again.

In 1894 Woodbridge began his academic career at the University of Minnesota as an instructor of philosophy, and in 1895 he was promoted to professor. He left Minnesota in 1902 for Columbia University, where he was appointed the first Johnsonian Professor of Philosophy in 1904. That same year Woodbridge, Wendell T. Bush, and James McKeen Cattell founded the *Journal of Philosophy, Psychology, and Scientific Methods*—entitled *Journal of Philosophy* beginning in 1921. Under Woodbridge's leadership as coeditor, and through his own articles, the *Journal* shaped American thought by providing a forum for philosophical realism and pragmatism to challenge idealism.

From 1912 until 1929 Woodbridge served as dean of the graduate faculties of political science, philosophy, and pure science at Columbia. As dean, he played a major role in shaping Columbia University. He was respected for his wit and hard-headedness in matters of principle, a wit that could bite in defense of scholarly excellence. When a doctoral student requested release from his dissertation defense because of illness, Woodbridge studied the catalog and responded, "I'm sorry, but I find that we don't give degrees for appendicitis" (King et al., p. 320).

Woodbridge's knowledge of different disciplines enabled him to talk with faculty on their own terms. He possessed clarity of vision about what university and graduate studies should be, a diverse "society of scholars" united in their disinterested research and sharing of learning. He thought that instruction should aim at making teaching unnecessary by preparing students to enter this society and that it should free students from prejudicial interests, including those of their teachers, by placing them under the authority of the subject-matter that alone could guide inquiry.

Combining a realistic philosophy of education with practical realism, Woodbridge fully understood that realizing the ideal of a society of scholars at Columbia required taking into account historical and geographic factors, such as the American economic climate and the university's location in New York City. For Woodbridge, all administrative reform needed to respect two principles, historical-geographic or "natural" conditions and the institution's "ideal" vision for education.

Woodbridge's philosophy was expressed in a lively series of annual reports, especially those from 1922 to 1927, and in his *Contrasts in Education* (1929). In his reports he criticized confusing means with ideal ends; for example, when "getting an education" is emphasized over learning and research, institutions become degree factories; when study is highly departmentalized, it yields only a narrow specialty. In addition to Columbia, his counsel helped shape his beloved Amherst, where he served nineteen years as a trustee, was confidant to two presidents, and was offered, but did not accept, the presidency.

Woodbridge warned against teachers who "substitute evangelism for instruction," for they turn students into disciples, indoctrinated by and bound to their teacher's biases. According to Woodbridge, "in America we have been trying to teach men to be good instead of teaching them to be intelligent" (Wolfe, p. 36). In contrast, preparing students for disinterested inquiry might enable them to rise above their prejudices and passions and to practice the virtues.

In 1929 Woodbridge resigned as dean but continued as Johnsonian Professor until 1939. He also served as Roosevelt Professor in Berlin in 1931–1932. Woodbridge published less than his influence, insightfulness, and rich literary style warranted because of his administrative duties and practical interests. Nevertheless, he exercised great intellectual influence through the students he taught, including Morris Cohen, Sterling Lamprecht, John Herman Randall, Jr., and Herbert Schneider.

In his popular history of philosophy class at Columbia, his realistic approach made philosophy come alive as he helped students trace ideas from their origins in a philosopher struggling with historical conditions to their inevitable intellectual consequences. Woodbridge's lectures yielded compelling interpretations, such as that Plato was "the dramatist of ideas," an idea also presented in his controversial *The Son of Apollo* (1929, repr. 1990). Will Durant said of Woodbridge's "wonderful class," "we were listening not to a professor of philosophy but to philosophy itself" (Edman, p. 194).

Woodbridge died in New York City. As a memorial the Woodbridge Lectures began at Columbia University in 1943.

In his "Epilogue" to *Naturalism and the Human Spirit* (1944), Randall claimed that Woodbridge, even more than John Dewey, had shaped the realism and "fundamental naturalism" of American thought. Woodbridge's instruction led his students to develop realistic, antireductionist philosophical methods and to revive metaphysics after the manner of Aristotle's naturalistic and humanistic "first science."

For Woodbridge, realistic inquiry begins with the subject-matter as experienced and follows its lead rather than allowing assumptions to prejudice inquiry by, for example, reducing subjects' diversity or complexity. When inquirers investigate subject-matters, Woodbridge believed, they discover the subject's nature through its interaction with an environment of conditioning factors, including the presence of the human inquirer. The variety of potential subject-matters in their rich contexts of conditioning factors is what Woodbridge, drawing on Aristotle, called Nature. So, for Woodbridge, a general philosophical description of the arena of realistic inquiry yields a naturalistic metaphysics. And since the human inquirer is a significant factor in the context of every subject-matter being investigated, naturalism entails humanism.

According to Woodbridge, when the metaphysician investigates Nature, especially Nature revealed through human functioning, Nature is disclosed as a "visible world" by her spatial and luminous conditioning of human perception (*An Essay on Nature* [1940]), a "realm of mind" whose intelligible structure conditions human thought when thinking is effective (*The Realm of Mind* [1926]), and a historical realm whose "natural teleology" conditions the human use of time and narrative (*The Purpose of History* [1916]). Moreover, Nature is a "moral order" because she conditions the human pursuit of happiness by providing knowledge of how to realize ideals without prescribing which ideal to pursue; human effort is thus justified by faith, as in religious commitment, not by knowledge of Nature (*An Essay on Nature*).

Woodbridge called his brand of realism "naive" partly because it was antireductionist but also because he wanted to avoid epistemological assumptions, such as those of the modern critical tradition beginning with Descartes, that tend to promote skepticism regarding the reliability of inquiry. Even though Woodbridge endorsed the pragmatists' reliance on experience and inquiry, he was disappointed when they allowed problematic assumptions to divert them from fruitful inquiry and became ensnared in controversies over the nature of truth. According to Woodbridge, problematic epistemologies arise not because Nature is unresponsive to inquiry but because Nature does not respond to the human yearning for a justifying faith.

Perhaps Woodbridge would have had even more influence over the intellectual currents of the twentieth century if he had been more personally involved in the polemics of his time. But also, perhaps Woodbridge chose, because of his realism, to avoid getting entangled in intellectual trends. Woodbridge was committed to offering a theory of Nature unencumbered by modern assumptions. Thus, Woodbridge's philosophy provides a needed vision for the emerging postmodern era.

• An extensive collection of Woodbridge's unpublished papers is held at Columbia University Library; it consists of correspondence, diaries, essays, and lecture notes. Amherst College Library also houses collections of correspondence. Woodbridge's collection of essays, *Nature and Mind* (1937), contains a complete bibliography of his publications through 1936. Woodbridge lectures on Aristotle were edited by J. H. Randall, Jr., and published posthumously as *Aristotle's Vision of Nature* (1965). The most complete exposition of Woodbridge's thought is William Frank Jones, *Nature and Natural Science: The Philosophy of Frederick J. E. Woodbridge* (1983), which quotes liberally from his unpublished papers, includes his important criticism of pragmatism, and provides a bibliography of unpublished as well as published materials. Another treatment of Woodbridge's thought is Hae Soo Pyun, *Nature, Intelligibility, and Metaphysics: Studies in the Philosophy of F. J. E. Woodbridge* (1972). Summaries of Woodbridge's philosophy by scholars who knew him personally are Harry Todd Costello, "The Naturalism of Frederick Woodbridge," in *Naturalism and the Human Spirit*, ed. Y. H. Krikorian (1944), and Sterling P. Lamprecht, *The Metaphysics of Naturalism* (1967), on Woodbridge's realistic method. For a picture of Woodbridge as person, educator, and teacher, see Paul A. Wolfe, "Conversations with the Old Man," *American Scholar* 14 (1945): 33–44; Stanley King et al., "Frederick J. E. Woodbridge," *Amherst Graduates' Quarterly* 29 (1940): 315–25; and Irwin Edman, "John Dewey and Others," in *Great Teachers: Portrayed by Those Who Studied Under Them*, ed. Houston Peterson (1946). See C. F. Delaney, *Mind and Nature: A Study of the Naturalistic Philosophy of Cohen, Woodbridge, and Sellars* (1946), on Woodbridge's philosophy of mind, and William M. Shea, *The Naturalists and the Supernatural* (1984), on Woodbridge's views on faith. Helena Woodbridge Wolfe and Donald Bingham Woodbridge provided biographical information. An obituary is in the *New York Times*, 2 June 1940.

WILLIAM F. JONES

WOODBRIDGE, William (20 Aug. 1780–20 Oct. 1861), lawyer and politician, was born in Norwich, Connecticut, the son of Dudley Woodbridge, a merchant, and Lucy Backus. In 1791 the Woodbridges left Connecticut seeking new economic opportunities in Ohio. Five years later, William Woodbridge returned to Connecticut to attend Tapping Reeve's law school in Litchfield. Woodbridge spent three years at the academy. In 1806, already practicing law in Connecticut, Woodbridge married Juliana Trumbull, whom he had met in Litchfield; they had four children. The couple moved to Marietta, Ohio, where Woodbridge, a Federalist, entered public life. In 1807 he was elected to the Ohio Assembly. The following year he was appointed prosecuting attorney for Washington County; in 1809 he was elected to the state senate. He held the latter two offices until his departure for Michigan in 1815.

Shortly after Woodbridge made plans to move his law practice to Cincinnati, Michigan territorial governor Lewis Cass, a Woodbridge acquaintance, recommended to President James Madison that Woodbridge be named secretary of the Michigan Territory. As further inducement, Cass promised Woodbridge he could also be the customs collector for Detroit; the two appointments offered an annual income of $15,000. Woodbridge accepted, took the oath of office on 1 January 1815, and headed for Detroit.

Woodbridge found his early years as territorial secretary frustrating. Living conditions in Detroit, which had suffered the ravages of the War of 1812, strained his finances. More important, he disliked the ambiguity of his position. Woodbridge was an independent officer, yet he was often looked upon as the governor's personal secretary. When Cass was away, Woodbridge was expected to operate as superintendent of Indian affairs, but he had no authority over the agents of the Indian Department. These annoyances help explain why Woodbridge joined Cass in 1818 to lobby Congress to advance Michigan to the second stage of territorial development, which included a nonvoting delegate to Congress. Although the change of status was denied, Congress allowed Michigan a representative in Congress. On 2 September 1819 Woodbridge was elected Michigan's first congressman.

Woodbridge's one year in Washington proved disheartening. Away from his family, suffering from asthma, and generally ignored, Woodbridge became disgusted with Washington politics, and he characterized the capital as a "noisy, caballing, immoral & wretched place—the same selfishness, weakness, envy, malice, vindictiveness of feeling, low intrigue & every variety of folly and impotence which can be found in the cabin, the grog shop or the country village." Choosing not to seek reelection, Woodbridge returned to Michigan as territorial secretary, a position that he had retained with the blessing of Governor Cass and President Monroe when he was elected to Congress. In 1826 Woodbridge gave up the customs collector post; two years later he ended his tenure as secretary when, "in a surprise move," he was appointed to the territorial supreme court. Woodbridge attributed President Andrew Jackson's decision not to reappoint him to the bench when his term expired in 1832 to political expediency and especially to the actions of territorial governor George Porter, who, Woodbridge claimed, was "very capable of baseness and malignity."

Although residing in a predominantly Democratic territory, Woodbridge played a role in Michigan's drive for statehood. One of the few Whigs to attend the 1835 state constitutional convention, Woodbridge chaired the Committee on the Change of Territorial Government and was a member of the committees on the Judiciary and Boundaries. Woodbridge's most important work centered on the issues of executive power and enfranchising aliens. He favored restricting a governor to two consecutive terms and denying him the power to grant reprieves or pardons. He also opposed giving newly arrived immigrants the right to vote—allowing them, in effect, to reap "where they have not sown"—while denying suffrage to American women. As a conservative, Woodbridge supported a limited constitution, and when the final draft appeared "too loose in interpretation," he was one of only two delegates to vote against it.

Although he was Michigan's leading Whig, Woodbridge sought a state senate seat rather than higher office in 1837, and he was one of the few Whigs to survive a Democratic landslide that year. In the senate, Woodbridge chaired the Committee on State Affairs, "one of the most important committees in both houses." He argued for internal improvements supported by funds from the sale of federal lands and emphasized Michigan's right to tax such lands within its borders. The Committee on State Affairs also took positions on national issues. In March 1838 Woodbridge offered a resolution opposing the annexation of Texas. In that same year the committee recommended to Congress that it initiate gradual emancipation in the District of Columbia. On another occasion the committee "pledged support for any legislation that would bar a slave state from entering the Union."

In mid-1839 Woodbridge reluctantly agreed to run for governor on the Whig ticket. Woodbridge's campaign slogan of "Economy, Retrenchment, Reform" reflected the economic malaise and fiscal mismanagement attributed to the outgoing Democratic administration. On 4 November 1839 Woodbridge became Michigan's first and only Whig governor when he was elected with 52 percent of the vote. Woodbridge's one year as governor proved unsatisfying. The state's economic situation did not improve, Michigan's state and national lawmakers were at odds with each other, the federal government was unresponsive to Woodbridge's pleas, and the future was gloomy for the state's many internal improvement projects.

On 3 February 1841 Woodbridge was chosen by a faction of Whig legislators allied with Democrats to replace Democratic senator John Norvell. Critics complained Woodbridge ran away from Michigan's economic troubles, but in the U.S. Senate he worked hard for the state. He continued to lobby for Michigan's right to tax federal lands within its borders and urged the federal government to address needs in the Great Lakes, especially harbor improvements. On national matters, he supported higher tariffs and, contrary to the wishes of the Michigan legislature, opposed President John Tyler's "wild & dangerous scheme of annexing Texas," predicting it would only bring "great & lasting evil, especially a war with Mexico."

After leaving the Senate in 1847, Woodbridge retired from public life. Although he styled himself a recluse, he continued to express his opinion on public matters. The Compromise of 1850 was "a false gesture" to accommodate the demands of the South; the Kansas-Nebraska Act was the result "of the most stupendous corruptions" that "ever characterized" the legislation of this country; and the Dred Scott decision was a "degrading & disgraceful argument." With the outbreak of the Civil War, Woodbridge contributed monies to raising volunteers to put down the rebellion. Woodbridge died in Detroit.

• Woodbridge's papers are in the Burton Historical Collection, Detroit Public Library. A useful guide is *William Woodbridge Papers, Transcripts and Footnotes, 1763–1858*, 12 vols., ed. Milo M. Quaife. A biography is Emily George, *William Woodbridge: Michigan's Connecticut Yankee* (1979).

ROGER L. ROSENTRETER

WOODBRIDGE, William Channing (18 Dec. 1794–9 Nov. 1845), educator, was born in Medford, Massachusetts, the son of William Woodbridge, a clergyman and educator, and his second wife, Ann Channing. He was educated at home by his father (with the aid of tutors) as the elder Woodbridge moved his family successively to Middletown (1798) and Norwich (1801), Connecticut, and Newark, New Jersey (1804), where he conducted several private academies and encouraged the improvement of local common schools. The younger Woodbridge entered the freshman class at Yale College in June 1808 at the tender age of thirteen and a half. After his graduation with an A.B. degree in September 1811, he moved to Philadelphia (where his father had since relocated) and followed a course of independent study in biblical history and theology for nearly a year. He then became principal at the nearby Burlington (N.J.) Academy in July 1812 and remained in the position until November 1814. At that time, feeling the need for more formal education, he returned to Yale and attended lectures in anatomy, chemistry, and philosophy.

While at Yale, Woodbridge underwent a religious conversion, and in September 1815 he began formal theological studies under the direction of Yale president Timothy Dwight. His studies abruptly ended upon Dwight's death in January 1817 and Woodbridge, who harbored ambitions of becoming a foreign missionary, moved to Princeton, New Jersey, and entered the theological seminary there in July. Later that summer, however, he received an invitation to join the instructional staff at the newly founded American Asylum for the Deaf and Dumb in Hartford, Connecticut. Woodbridge agonized over his decision, but the success he encountered in teaching a local deaf girl offered encouragement in that direction, and he joined Thomas H. Gallaudet in the pioneering effort in early December 1817.

At Hartford, Woodbridge quickly gained acceptance among the student body, and his success at the school did not pass unnoticed; he turned down a lucrative offer to join the faculty of the College of William and Mary as professor of chemistry in November 1818. Unable to give up completely his interest in the ministry, he was licensed to preach by the North Association of Connecticut in February 1819. Occasional preaching at various churches around Hartford only added to his burdensome list of duties at the school, however, and under the added strain his health, never robust, collapsed in the summer of 1820. Seeking recovery, he sailed for southern Europe in October 1820 and spent eight months overseas.

Woodbridge made effective use of his time in Europe. He not only regained his health, but in the course of his travels throughout the southern part of the continent he gained valuable additional knowledge of the region's geography. He had taught the subject, which was barely addressed in the American educational system of the time, at Gallaudet's school and saw great promise in the field. Returning to Hartford in July 1821, he devoted the following three years to the production of suitable textbooks. *Rudiments of Geography, on a New Plan, Designed to Assist the Memory by Comparison and Classification*, his first effort, appeared later that same year. An immediate success, the book went through several editions. He also collaborated with another noted educator, Emma Willard, who had introduced the same subject at her Female Seminary in Troy, New York, in the production of *Universal Geography, Ancient and Modern* (1824). Their effort netted a reception that was perhaps too favorable; the two authors soon found themselves fighting numerous plagiarists. The combined strain of producing and then defending his work took its toll, and Woodbridge's health collapsed once again. He again left for Europe in 1824 and spent five years abroad.

Once again combining research and recuperation, Woodbridge traveled extensively throughout the continent. His first stop was England, where he arranged for the London publication of *Woodbridge's Geography* (1827) and visited two deaf and dumb educational institutions, where he introduced improvements in the curriculum. Despite occasional collapses in his health, he met with most of the leading educators of Europe, including Johann Henrich Pestalozzi and his disciple von Fellenburg, and also studied at length the school systems of Switzerland and the Germanic states. Returning to the United States in the fall of 1829, he immediately proceeded to Hartford, where he embarked on the next phase of his career—the improvement of the common schools.

Physically unable to resume either teaching or preaching, Woodbridge threw himself enthusiastically into the budding movement to improve American common schools. An active member of the Hartford Society for the Improvement of Common Schools, he also attempted to found a normal school in Hartford. Denied this opportunity by poor health and finances, he purchased (in August 1831) the *American Journal of Education*, a monthly journal, then edited by William Russell, that disseminated new educational ideas and concepts to its readers. After changing the name of the publication to the *American Annals of Education and Instruction*, Woodbridge moved to Boston and, with the help of his father and several other associates, proceeded to put his stamp on the publication.

Within the pages of the *Annals*, teacher training, technical and vocational education, and special education all received attention; Woodbridge himself penned "Sketches of the Fellenburg Institution at Hofwyl, in a Series of Letters to a Friend" (January 1831–December 1832), based on his three-month-long firsthand observation of von Fellenburg's institution. Woodbridge also advanced the cause of specialized topics, including the teaching of music within the common schools and the inclusion of the Bible among the list of literary classics. While well received, the *Annals'* existence was in constant jeopardy; many thought it too erudite, while others merely found its subscription price too steep. Woodbridge took time from his labors to marry Lucy Ann Read, herself a teacher, in 1832; the couple had two children. Under the strain of running the publication, his health collapsed again, and in October 1836 he returned to Europe. Editing his publication from afar, his health did not measurably improve, and his wife, whose health was also precarious, died in Frankfurt after joining him in Europe. Woodbridge returned to the United States in October 1841 and split his remaining years between Santa Cruz in the West Indies and Boston, where he died after a long decline.

Although largely forgotten today, Woodbridge deserves to be remembered for his efforts on behalf of primary education. His greatest contribution to the advancement of American schools was his role in initiating instruction in geography and in his advancement, through the pages of the *Annals*, of the theories of Pestalozzi.

• No organized collection of Woodbridge's papers appears to have survived; however, scattered correspondence can be found among the papers of Horace Mann and Walter Channing at the Massachusetts Historical Society in Boston and among the Lowell Mason Papers at the Yale University Music Library in New Haven, Connecticut. Little secondary information is available on his life and career; the best sources remain Franklin Bowditch Dexter, *Biographical Sketches of the Graduates of Yale College*, vol. 6 (1912), and William A. Alcott, "William Channing Woodbridge," *American Journal of Education* 5 (June 1858): 51–64. An obituary is in the *Boston Daily Advertiser*, 11 Nov. 1845.

EDWARD L. LACH, JR.

WOODBURY, Helen Sumner. *See* Sumner, Helen.

WOODBURY, Isaac Baker (23 Oct. 1819–26 Oct. 1858), composer and music educator, was born in Beverly, Massachusetts, the son of Isaac Woodberry, a merchant and justice of the peace, and Nancy Baker. From an early age Woodbury preferred this spelling of the family name. His forebears, in Massachusetts since 1624, were solidly yeoman and middle class. In 1828 his father died, and his mother managed the property and took in boarders to support her eight children. In 1832 Woodbury was sent to Boston where, contrary to his mother's wishes, he studied music under Lowell Mason and others. In 1838, with a small legacy, Woodbury spent a year in London and Paris completing his musical education under composer and conductor Henry Rowley Bishop, prominent baritone Henry Phillips, and Auguste Panseron, a professor of singing at the Conservatoire Nationale in Paris.

Returning to Boston, Woodbury taught music privately, conducted singing conventions, and played organ at the Franklin Street Church (Methodist). In 1842 he made his debut as a baritone soloist with Mason's Boston Academy of Music. In the same year he published his first book of hymn tunes, in collaboration with Benjamin Franklin Baker, president of the Music Education Society and music director of the Federal Street Congregational Church (Unitarian). Woodbury was thus aligned with the mainstream religious establishment and with the leading musicians and music educators of Boston; he soon earned an enviable reputation as a singer, choral conductor, and composer and editor of hymn tunes. The composer George F. Root, his fellow student in Boston, said in his autobiography *The Story of a Musical Life* (1891), "He was a most indefatigable student and worker. . . . He was very prosperous and very ambitious. . . . Mr. Woodbury was a genial, pleasant gentleman, and because he wrote only simple music, never was credited (by those who did not know him) with the musical ability and culture that he really possessed."

Apparently because of Mason's autocratic methods in operating the "American Musical Convention," the summer training course for music teachers, Woodbury and Baker in 1843 led a group who broke away to found the very similar "National Musical Convention." Woodbury traveled extensively, as far as Illinois and Mississippi, conducting musical conventions and promoting his growing list of publications—music textbooks and tunebooks. From 1847 he collaborated frequently with Thomas Hastings; through the 1850s he worked with Mason, William Bradbury, L. A. Benjamin, and others. As a convention conductor Woodbury was quite successful: in the second half of the decade, when conductors were usually paid between $25 and $100, Woodbury commanded $50 to $150. In 1855 alone, he traveled over 15,000 miles, conducting more than forty conventions in eleven states. In addition to his American travels, Woodbury visited Europe twice in the 1850s. In 1851–1852 he visited England, France, Italy, Malta, and Egypt; in 1857–1858, Germany, Egypt, and Malta. The letters he wrote during these trips deal primarily with scenery, morals, and the hazards of travel rather than with music. Woodbury entered journalism as corresponding editor of the *World of Music* (1846–1848); he edited the *American Musical Review* from 1850 to 1853 and the *New York Musical Pioneer* from 1855 to 1858. In these periodicals he published reviews, reports and comments from his travels, and hymn tunes and pasticcio oratorios.

In 1846 Woodbury married Mary Abigail Putnam in Salem, Massachusetts, with whom he had seven children. His base of operations fluctuated for several years: in 1849 he became organist and director of music of Rutgers Street Church (Presbyterian) in New York and moved his music teachers' convention there. In 1851 he built a summer home on Wenham Lake in Massachusetts. During this period his music was published in both Boston and New York. In 1855 he moved to Norwalk, Connecticut, commuting to New York as needed. He contracted tuberculosis in 1851; from 1856 his life was dominated by attempts to stay the disease, and both of his trips to Europe were for rest and cure, as was his trip to Florida during the winter of 1856–1857. Woodbury died of tuberculosis in Columbia, South Carolina. His body was returned to Norwalk for burial. Although his will provided for the endowment of a permanent conservatory of music in Massachusetts, the estate was insufficient.

Woodbury composed and wrote prolifically. In a span of sixteen years, he produced over 400 hymn tunes, some 140 songs for voice and piano, forty songs for vocal ensembles, and a few piano works. He wrote seven instrumental instruction books (piano, violin, flute, melodeon, voice) and one on harmony and composition. He composed or edited four cantatas, three oratorios, and one "musical drama," of which three are pasticcios and five are original compositions. He edited fifteen oblong tunebooks of sacred music and fourteen of secular and served as an editor of three musical magazines for a total of eleven years. His colleague T. J. Cook wrote in the *New York Musical Pioneer* (Jan. 1859), "Gentleness was the character of the man and of his music. His music came directly from his own heart, and went directly to the hearts of those who heard it. . . . [T]hat it was successful has been amply demonstrated by the millions of his works that have found their way to the various choirs and musical societies throughout the land."

Woodbury was an important figure in the development of middle-class music in nineteenth-century America. He was among the earliest Americans to go to Europe for musical study and among the earliest to attempt the founding of a conservatory in this country. He believed strongly in the value of music as a social and moral force and worked to enhance the public's musical appreciation and knowledge of music-reading. His hymn tunes were enormously popular for many years, and eighteen or twenty have remained in use throughout the twentieth century. His parlor songs, dealing with popular themes and subjects of the day, were widely disseminated and admired.

• Woodbury's papers deteriorated beyond use or preservation before 1953. The music library of the University of Missouri—Kansas City houses the remains of his personal collection. The Library of Congress contains most of his publications and four short songs in manuscript. The only full biography is Robert M. Copeland, "The Life and Works of Isaac Baker Woodbury, 1819–1858" (Ph.D. diss., Univ. of Cincinnati, 1974), which includes a bibliography of Woodbury's works. For more information on Woodbury, see also Frank J. Metcalf, *American Writers and Compilers of Sacred Music* (1925), and J. Vincent Higginson, "Isaac B. Woodbury (1819–1858)," *The Hymn* 20 (1969): 74–80.

ROBERT M. COPELAND

WOODBURY, Levi (22 Dec. 1789–4 Sept. 1851), politician and associate justice of the U.S. Supreme Court, was born in Francestown, New Hampshire, the son of Peter Woodbury, a farmer and merchant, and Mary Woodbury, a distant cousin of Peter Woodbury. After graduating with honors from Dartmouth College in 1809, he attended Tapping Reeve Law School in Litchfield, Connecticut (making him the first justice of the Supreme Court to study at a law school), and also read law with Boston judges Samuel Dana and Jeremiah Smith (1759–1842). He began his law practice in Francestown and Portsmouth, New Hampshire, in 1813. During the War of 1812 Woodbury became a leader in the local Republican party. He was author of the *Hillsborough County Resolves*, a set of resolutions defending President James Madison's (1750–1836) entry into the war with England and thus was one of the few New Englanders to favor the war.

By 1816 the Republican party controlled New Hampshire government, and Woodbury was rewarded for his party loyalty with the post of clerk of the state senate. The following year Woodbury's friend New Hampshire governor William Plumer appointed him to the state supreme court. In 1819 he married Elizabeth Williams Clapp and moved from Francestown to Portsmouth, where his home became a mecca for his political friends. Five children came of this marriage. His wife's father, Asa Clapp, was the wealthiest merchant in Portsmouth; he was a leader of the Republican party, and later of the Jacksonians, and used his political and financial power to aid his son-in-law.

In 1823 Woodbury was elected governor of New Hampshire. By all accounts his single term as governor was a failure; partisan bickering and his lack of a strong legislative policy ensured that he was ineffective. As he left office he wrote, "every public man in this country who has any kind of talent, or independence, or opinions of his own, must expect abuse and ingratitude." Although he failed to win a second term in 1825, he won a seat that same year to the state legislature, where after being elected Speaker of the house he became U.S. senator, a position he held from 1825 to 1831. President John Quincy Adams's (1767–1848) advocacy of expanded national powers forced Woodbury into the Jacksonian camp; in 1826 he attacked the bankruptcy bill as an invasion of states' rights. The same year he also opposed the judiciary bill, which expanded the size of the U.S. Supreme Court from seven to an unprecedented ten members. Now a Jacksonian, he became known as the "Rock of New England Democracy," serving on the commerce, navy, and agriculture committees. Woodbury declined a second term in the Senate, and President Andrew Jackson appointed him secretary of the navy in 1831.

During Woodbury's tenure at the Navy Department, from 1831 to 1834, the Bank War raged. Woodbury remained reticent about the bank issue as long as possible, but when the Senate refused to confirm Roger B. Taney as Jackson's secretary of the treasury, Jackson appointed Woodbury to the post, and the Senate confirmed him in June 1834. Now the financial crisis fell to Woodbury. Although he was not a strong opponent of the Bank of the United States, he was politically ambitious, and he acceded to Jackson's wishes, refusing to accept drafts from the bank in payment for debts owed the government and supervising the withdrawal of federal funds from the bank. Woodbury was unable to deal effectively with dozens of state banks during the escalating crisis of credit, and he failed to forestall the panic of 1837. His reputation suffered, and many of Jackson's advisers felt he should be relieved of his duties.

In 1838 Woodbury refused the position of chief justice of the Supreme Court of New Hampshire to remain secretary of the treasury during Martin Van Buren's presidency, retiring when Van Buren left office in 1841. The New Hampshire legislature reelected him U.S. senator the same year. During this term Woodbury supported the annexation of Texas as vital to the security of the Mississippi Valley. Although he said that he opposed slavery, he believed that only slaveholders could abolish the institution. In 1845 President James Polk offered him the position of minister to Great Britain, but Woodbury declined. Four months later Justice Joseph Story died, and Polk nominated Woodbury for his seat on the Supreme Court. Although twenty-three years had passed since Woodbury had sat on the bench or practiced law, the Senate confirmed him early in 1846.

The new justice joined the court at a time of tension and controversy regarding constitutional rights, federal-state relations, and slavery. Although Woodbury was not prosouthern or proslavery, he was a strong believer in restraining the federal government from interfering in the rights of the states. In his dissent in *Waring v. Clarke* (1847) he argued that his colleague Justice James Wayne was wrong in granting admiralty jurisdiction to a case involving a shipping accident 100 miles inland of New Orleans. The case should be one for the Louisiana courts, he argued, because "We ought to forbear interfering with what has been preserved to the States." However, he did not believe that the rights of individuals should be violated in the cause of states' rights. In one of his most important dissents, *Luther v. Borden* (1848), a case involving Rhode Island's "Dorr War," Chief Justice Taney held that federal courts could not interfere with the domestic affairs of the states. Although Woodbury concurred that the court should stay clear of political issues, and should not usurp the rights of the states, he felt that the institution of martial law in Rhode Island violated the constitutional rights of individual citizens and that the Supreme Court had the right to rule on the constitutionality of the Rhode Island statute that imposed martial law.

Woodbury wrote perhaps his most controversial decision in 1847 in *Jones v. Van Zandt*. The decision hinged on the constitutionality of the federal Fugitive Slave Act of 1793. Van Zandt's attorneys, William H. Seward and Salmon P. Chase, argued that the act was unconstitutional because higher moral law took precedence over the slave-catching statute. Woodbury rejected this argument, contending that the original compromises of the Constitutional Convention required the strict enforcement of acts giving slaveholders the right of rendition of their fugitive slaves. This decision made him popular in the South, and indeed some historians have suggested that his presidential aspirations may have influenced him to support constitutionalism and forbearance in sectional matters. He also supported the Compromise of 1850, including the new and stronger federal Fugitive Slave Act that was a part of the compromise, an unpopular stand for a New Englander. Had Woodbury lived, he might have been the Democratic nominee for president in 1852. He died in Portsmouth, New Hampshire.

Levi Woodbury's career shows him to have been a man of talent and ability, although his considerable political ambition made his antislavery convictions seem contradictory to his support of states' rights and his defense of the South on the slavery issue. Although he was far from dynamic, he was sound, temperate, and hard-working in a great range of political offices.

• There is an extensive collection of Woodbury's papers at the Library of Congress (in two series). A printed collection of importance is the three-volume *The Writings of Levi Woodbury* (1852). No published biography exists, but two doctoral dissertations are Vincent J. Capowski, "The Making of a Jacksonian Democrat: Levi Woodbury, 1789–1831" (Fordham Univ., 1966), and Philip D. Wheaton, "Levi Woodbury, Jacksonian Financier" (Univ. of Maryland, 1955). Donald B. Cole, *Jacksonian Democracy in New Hampshire, 1800–1851* (1970), while not a biography, covers Woodbury's career extensively.

JUDITH K. SCHAFER

WOODFORD, Stewart Lyndon (3 Sept. 1835–14 Feb. 1913), lawyer and diplomat, was born in New York City, the son of Josiah Curtis Woodford and Susan Terry. Woodford graduated from Columbia College in 1854. He studied law and was admitted to the bar in 1857. That same year Woodford married Julia Evelyn Capen; they had four children.

An early Republican, Woodford supported the election of Abraham Lincoln in 1860, and in 1861 Lincoln appointed him assistant U.S. district attorney for the Southern District of New York. Woodford enlisted in 1862 as a private in the 127th New York Volunteers, was elected captain, and was commissioned a lieutenant colonel. He participated in the defense of Washington and served as the military governor of Charleston and Savannah. He was brevetted brigadier general in May 1865.

Woodford was elected lieutenant governor of New York in 1866. Nominated for governor in 1870, he failed to win election. A candidate from Brooklyn, he was elected in 1872 to Congress. Woodford advocated sound money and the gold standard. He resigned his congressional seat in 1874 because of personal financial need. U. S. Grant appointed Woodford in 1877 to be U.S. district attorney for the Southern District of New York, an office he held until 1883. From 1883 to 1896 Woodford practiced law.

When William McKinley was elected in 1896, Woodford angled for a federal appointment, and in June 1897 McKinley selected him to be minister to Spain. His mission to Madrid lasted from September 1897 to April 1898. Lacking diplomatic experience and firsthand knowledge of Spain and its colony Cuba, where an insurrection had been underway since 1895, Woodford brought to the office pro-Cuban views and prejudice against Spain. He was loyal to the president and energetic in pursuing his policies. McKinley and Woodford set out to end the fighting in Cuba by freeing the island from Spanish colonialism. They expected that American intervention would be necessary to end the Cuban conflict. Spanish officials distrusted the McKinley administration and received Woodford coolly. The assassination of the Spanish prime minister in 1897 brought a change of government in Madrid, and when the new government offered political reforms to Cuba, Woodford hoped peace could be restored to the island without American intervention. The Cuban revolutionaries, however, rejected Madrid's reforms. After the American battleship *Maine* was mysteriously blown up in the Havana harbor in February 1898, war became more likely. Woodford erroneously believed that under increased American pressure the Spanish government would withdraw from Cuba rather than enter an unwinnable and potentially disastrous conflict. However, rather than bow to American terms, the Spanish government accepted war. During the war McKinley did not consult Woodford about Spanish politics and possible peace terms. When the war ended, Woodford resigned his diplomatic office.

Along with resuming his legal practice in New York City, Woodford became general counsel and director of the Metropolitan Life Insurance Company and the director of two banks. His first wife died in 1899, and he married Isabel Hanson the following year. Still active in Republican politics, he nominated Charles Evans Hughes for president in 1908. He died in New York City.

• "Recortes periodisticos de los diarios de Madrid," 10 volumes of scrapbooks of Spanish newspaper clippings covering Woodford's diplomatic mission to Spain, are in the Library of Congress. Woodford wrote two brief accounts of his mission to Madrid: "Introduction," in *The American-Spanish War: A History by War Leaders* (1899), and "McKinley and the Spanish War," in *Yearbook of the Oneida Historical Society* (1905). See also John L. Offner, *An Unwanted War: The Diplomacy of the United States and Spain over Cuba, 1895–1898* (1992). An obituary is in the *New York Times*, 15 Feb. 1913.

JOHN L. OFFNER

WOODFORD, William (6 Oct. 1734–13 Nov. 1780), revolutionary war general, was born in Caroline County, Virginia, the son of Major William Woodford, Sr., and his third wife, Anne Cocke, daughter of Dr. William Cocke, the secretary of the Virginia colony. Woodford grew up on his father's plantation, "Windsor" on the Rappahannock River, ten miles east of Fredericksburg. As did other sons of gentry in the Fredericksburg area, he probably received his education in one of several private schools and by tutors.

Woodford was made a captain in the Virginia militia in October 1755. Entering the French and Indian War in 1757, he accepted the lower rank of ensign in George Washington's Virginia Regiment. In 1761

Woodford was promoted to lieutenant. During the war Woodford served with Washington at Fort Loudoun and probably was with the regiment in the campaign led by General John Forbes in 1758 that compelled the surrender of Fort Duquesne. Woodford served in the Cherokee expedition of 1761, first under Colonel William Byrd and then under Lieutenant Colonel Adam Stephen. Woodford had the responsibility of bringing a delegation of Cherokees to Williamsburg to finalize a treaty. The House of Burgesses allowed him £30 for this duty.

In 1762 Woodford married Mary Thornton, daughter of Colonel John Thornton and Mildred Washington Gregory (George Washington's aunt). They had two children.

After his father's death in 1755, Woodford succeeded to the ownership and management of the Windsor plantation and other estates. He established a brewery in 1773. Woodford served as a vestryman and warden for St. Mary's parish. From 1764 to 1775 Woodford sat on the county court as a justice of the peace, and in 1771 won appointment as lieutenant colonel of the Caroline County militia. In August 1770 he was also elected an inspector by the Caroline County "Association," consisting of 348 persons, formed for the boycott of British goods in response to the Townshend duties, passed by Parliament in 1767.

As the colonies responded to the British Coercive Acts, Woodford was elected to the Caroline Committee of Safety on 10 November 1774 and had charge of soliciting provisions to be sent to the aid of the people of Boston. On 11 May 1775 Woodford was elected alternate delegate to the Third Virginia Convention as a substitute for Edmund Pendleton, who had been named a delegate to the Continental Congress. Woodford attended the convention, 17 July–9 August 1775.

Woodford's revolutionary war military career began when the Virginia Convention, on 5 August 1775, appointed him colonel and commander of the Second Virginia Regiment. Though three regiments were planned at the time, only the first two were established. Patrick Henry was appointed colonel of the First Regiment and commander of all Virginia's forces. Woodford resented being superseded by Henry, who had no prior military experience. In actuality, Woodford, who took to the field while Henry did not, became the acting commander of the Virginia army. George Washington wholeheartedly endorsed Woodford's military appointment and sent Woodford, in a letter of 10 November 1775, rules for an officer's conduct, upon request from Woodford—something Washington did for no other officer during the Revolution.

Woodford and his troops won what might be considered the first American victory during the war, repelling a land-sea attack by a force under Governor Lord Dunmore at Hampton, 24–25 October. Under orders from the Virginia Convention to recover Norfolk from the British, Woodford on 2 December took position at the west end of Great Bridge, on the South Branch of the Elizabeth River, twelve miles below Norfolk. Here he erected a semicircular breastwork in which he posted about twenty-five men; the rest of his troops were held in readiness to the rear. Dunmore had constructed a stockaded fort, with seven cannons, at the east end of the bridge. On 9 December British grenadiers rushed across the bridge, only to be cut down by Woodford's troops. Dunmore was compelled to evacuate the fort and take his motley force of regulars, Tories, and "Ethiopians" (African Americans) shipboard. Woodford commented that the battle of Great Bridge was "a second Bunker Hill, in miniature, with the difference that we kept our post and had only one man wounded in the hand." The British had over sixty casualties. Woodford's troops and those under Colonel Robert Howe (North Carolina regulars and three companies of Patrick Henry's First Regiment) captured Norfolk on 13 December. Subsequently Dunmore's fleet bombarded the town on 1 January 1776; with Woodford and Howe setting fire to Tory homes, four-fifths of Norfolk was destroyed.

Woodford was engaged in local defense of Virginia until after Dunmore left the colony in August 1776. Woodford had been appointed by Congress on 13 February 1776 as colonel of the Second Virginia Continental Regiment. Because Adam Stephen, a rival, was promoted to brigadier general on 4 September 1776, Woodford resigned from the service, but acting on advice from Washington, reclaimed his commission several months later. On 21 February 1777 he was selected last of ten colonels raised to the rank of brigadier general (behind two new Virginia generals, John P. G. Muhlenberg and George Weedon). Woodford commanded the Third Virginia Brigade, which joined Washington's army at Morristown, New Jersey, 20 May 1777.

Woodford distinguished himself at the battle of Brandywine, 11 September 1777. His troops fought heroically, the last to leave Birmingham Meeting House Hill, from where they had been able to stop the British advance, allowing American forces to regroup. Woodford was wounded in the hand, not returning to the army until 18 October. His brigade fought without him at the battle of Germantown on 4 October.

Like many of Washington's brigadiers, Woodford expected promotion to major general and division commander. It appears from remarks made by Adam Stephen that Woodford gave damaging testimony at the court-martial of Stephen, which ended with Stephen's dismissal as a major general from the army. Woodford in vain expected that he would succeed Stephen. Woodford also pressed Congress to reinstate his seniority in rank above Muhlenberg and Weedon. Congress revoked the commissions of Muhlenberg, Weedon, and Charles Scott. After a board of general officers voted that Woodford be restored to his seniority (with Muhlenberg, Scott, and Weedon ranking after him in that order), Congress issued new commissions on 19 March. Weedon, in disgust, was permitted retirement from the army.

On 28 June 1778 Woodford led his brigade at the battle of Monmouth and joined in the withdrawal of the army under General Charles Lee. Woodford and General Enoch Poor were ordered to skirmish with the flanks of the British army after the battle, but the enemy proved elusive. Woodford was a member of the court-martial for Lee, which lasted for twenty-six sessions from 15 July to 9 August. Except for October 1778–March 1779, Woodford stayed with Washington's army in New Jersey and above New York City. In December 1779 he and his brigade were ordered to join the Southern army under General Benjamin Lincoln. With 1,200 men—reenlistees and new volunteers—Woodford set out from Petersburg, Virginia, on 8 March 1780, and, covering 500 miles in twenty-nine days, went through the American lines at Charleston, South Carolina, on 6 April. With the surrender of Charleston on 12 May, Woodford became a prisoner of war. In declining health, he was sent to New York City and died there aboard the British prison ship *Packet*. Kentucky and Illinois have counties named after Woodford.

The full measure of Woodford's military ability is difficult to assess because his actual service was short. He demonstrated tactical skills at Great Bridge and courage at Brandywine. Washington on 12 November 1777 referred to Woodford as "an exceedingly good officer." He does not appear, however, to have inspired either his officers or men. Though for a while willing to put duty and country above honor, he was too attentive to his own reputation. One of his disgruntled sergeants jotted down in his order book: "Beau Woodford Commander of the Virga. Divis and the Damndest Partial Rascal on this earth without exception."

• Woodford correspondence is found in the George Washington Papers, Library of Congress, microfilm, and in printed editions of the Washington papers; in "The Letters of Col. William Woodford, Col. Robert Howe and Gen. Charles Lee to Edmund Pendleton," in *Richmond College Historical Papers*, ed. D. R. Anderson, vol. 1 (1915), pp. 96–163; and in the voluminous and rambling biography, Mrs. Catesby Willis Stewart, *The Life of Brigadier General William Woodford of the American Revolution* (2 vols., 1973). A biographical sketch is found in Marshall Wingfield, *A History of Caroline County Virginia* (1924), pp. 184–90. Robert L. Scribner and Brent Tarter, eds., *Revolutionary Virginia: The Road to Independence* (7 vols., 1973–1983), fully chronicles Woodford's role in repelling the British during 1775–1776. Samuel S. Smith, *The Battle of Brandywine* (1976), sizes up Woodford's participation in that engagement. Douglas S. Freeman, *George Washington*, vols. 3–5 (1951–1952), has some evaluation of Woodford. For Woodford's relations with other Virginia officers and some description of his military career, see Harry M. Ward, *Duty, Honor or Country: General George Weedon and the American Revolution* (1979), *Charles Scott and the "Spirit of '76"* (1988), and *Major General Adam Stephen and the Cause of American Liberty* (1989). Ivor Noël Hume, *1775: Another Part of the Field* (1966), discusses the revolutionary movement in Virginia, with attention to military development. Death notices appeared in the *Pennsylvania Packet, or General Advertiser*, 16 Dec. 1780, and the *Pennsylvania Gazette and Weekly Advertiser*, 20 Dec. 1780.

HARRY M. WARD

WOODHOUSE, James (17 Nov. 1770–4 June 1809), chemist, was born in Philadelphia, Pennsylvania, the son of William Woodhouse, a bookseller and stationer, and Anne Martin. Woodhouse entered the University of the State of Pennsylvania (now the University of Pennsylvania) in 1784 and received the degrees of B.A. (1787) and M.A. (1790). Working with Benjamin Rush at the same school, he earned the M.D. degree in 1792. Before he finished his medical degree, he acted as a surgeon's mate in the campaign against the Indians of the Northwest Territory. Medical training was a common preparation at that time for those interested in the sciences; the title of Woodhouse's doctoral dissertation suggests his attraction to chemistry—"On the Chemical and Medicinal Properties of the Persimmon Tree and the Analysis of Astringent Vegetables." This interest was confirmed by his founding (1792) of the Chemical Society of Philadelphia, an organization of which he was senior president until his death. The society numbered seventy members over its years, with one corresponding member, Elizabeth Fulhane, in England. It had its own laboratory and published pamphlets on analysis of minerals, ores, and soils.

In 1795 Woodhouse was named professor of chemistry at the University of Pennsylvania. There he had a small but well-equipped laboratory, from which he produced a remarkable number of research findings and publications in the few years that remained to him. A frequent visitor to his laboratory was Joseph Priestley, recently arrived from England. Woodhouse also visited Priestley's home in Northumberland, Pennsylvania. Priestley, discoverer of oxygen, was an adherent of the phlogiston theory, believing in the existence of a flammable principle contained in materials that burn; Woodhouse, however, had produced some of the most telling arguments and demonstrations against the phlogiston theory. He summarized these in a powerful address published in the *Transactions of the American Philosophical Society* (reprinted in abridged form in the *Journal of Chemical Education* 53 (1976): 414–17). After such presentations by Woodhouse and others, the phlogiston theory was effectively dead in the United States. Nonetheless, Priestley and Woodhouse continued to get along well on a basis of mutual professional respect.

Woodhouse's investigations included the production of metallic potassium by carbon reduction, reported in *Nicholson's Journal of Natural Philosophy, Chemistry, and the Arts* in 1808, the year after Humphrey Davy produced potassium by electrolysis; analytical determinations of mineral chemistry that demonstrated the basaltic composition of certain geologic formations; observations on reaction of metals with nitric acid; demonstration of the superiority of anthracite over bituminous coal for industrial purposes; studies of white (corn) starch and Polish (potato) starch, showing the greater utility of the former; and even a series of experiments in bread-baking. In 1802 he traveled to England and France, where he met Davy.

Woodhouse's teaching was influential but received mixed notices. Benjamin Silliman, who made a point of going to Philadelphia to study with him, noted his "florid face" and complained that he was "wanting in personal dignity"—he enjoyed the company of students after class. An anonymous commentator felt that he "lost much of his influence over his pupils, by neglecting the manner of communicating instruction." Students seemed to learn from him, though, and perhaps these criticisms merely reflect his departure from the professorial style of the time.

In 1797 Woodhouse published *The Young Chemist's Pocket Companion*, a book of chemical experiments somewhat ahead of its time: directed laboratory instruction was virtually nonexistent until well into the nineteenth century. He also edited American editions of James Parkinson's *Chemical Pocket-Book* (1802), Samuel Parkes's *Chymical Catechism* (1807), and the *Elements of Chemistry* (1807) of J.A.C. Chaptal de Chanteloup. His studies of plant chemistry produced *Observations on the Combinations of Acids, Bitters and Astringents* (1793) and *Experiments and Observations in the Vegetation of Plants* (1802).

Chemistry was then emerging as a science in its own right in Europe and America, and woodhouse was one of the few who helped to establish it as an academic and industrial study, and to instruct a generation of students in both the theory and the practice of the discipline. Woodhouse died of apoplexy in Philadelphia; some historians have speculated that his untimely death can be traced to a series of assays of the fuel values of various coals. These would have produced carbon monoxide, and in his ill-ventilated laboratory during the hottest summer Philadelphia had yet known, the conditions may have hastened his death. Woodhouse never married.

• Woodhouse's papers are held by the University of Pennsylvania. He is the subject of a book-length biography, Edgar Fahs Smith, *James Woodhouse, a Pioneer in Chemistry* (1918). An interesting series of articles on Woodhouse's synthesis of ammonia and potassium, as well as the phlogiston paper and the carbon monoxide speculation mentioned above, appeared in *Journal of Chemical Education* 4 (1927): 1515–21; 9 (1932): 1744–47, 1748–50; 41 (1964): 282–84; 53 (1976): 414–18.

ROBERT M. HAWTHORNE JR.

WOODHULL, Alfred Alexander (13 Apr. 1837–18 Oct. 1921), U.S. Army medical officer, was born in Princeton, New Jersey, the son of Alfred Alexander Woodhull, a physician, and Anna Maria Salomons. Woodhull received an A.B. degree from the College of New Jersey (Princeton University) in 1856 and an A.M. in 1859, at which time he also received an M.D. from the University of Pennsylvania.

For two years he practiced medicine at Leavenworth and then at Eudora, Kansas. After the outbreak of the Civil War he helped recruit a troop of mounted riflemen for the Kansas militia, receiving a commission as lieutenant. After passing the required entrance examinations, in September 1861 he entered the Union Army Medical Department as an assistant surgeon, serving in that capacity throughout the conflict. He was brevetted lieutenant colonel in 1865. When the war ended, he was assigned to the Army Medical Museum in Washington, D.C., where in 1866 he was promoted to captain. One of the first of his many publications was a catalog of the surgical specimens collected for the museum during the Civil War. While in Washington, he married Margaret Ellicott in 1868; the couple did not have children.

In 1868 the Surgeon General's Office published Woodhull's *Medical Report upon the Uniform and Clothing of the Soldiers of the U.S. Army*. This document, the first of many he wrote about hygiene and sanitation, emphasized the importance of different designs and weights of uniforms for various climates and seasons. It was highly critical of the uniform then prescribed for army troops, terming it "insufferable in the warmer months" in the South. Woodhull was especially critical of the use of clothing so thick and tight as to "hold the soldier in position."

Early in his career Woodhull became intrigued by the use of ipecacuanha, a root usually employed as an emetic, for less conventional medicinal purposes. In 1875–1876 he published in the *Atlanta Medical and Surgical Journal* a series of articles on diseases in which the new use of this drug might prove helpful, including dysentery, cholera, morning sickness, and malaria. These articles came out in book form in 1876 as *Studies, Chiefly Clinical, in the Non-emetic Use of Ipecacuanha: with a Contribution to the Therapeusis of Cholera*. His interest in yellow fever after an outbreak at Savannah in 1876 led him to write two articles on the disease, one of which appeared in 1877 in the *American Journal of the Medical Sciences* and the other in 1879 in the *Transactions of the American Public Health Association*.

Promoted to major in 1876, from 1886 to 1890 he taught military hygiene to line officers at the Infantry and Cavalry School at Fort Leavenworth. This was one of his most productive periods. In 1887 he received a Military Service Institution award for an article published in the institution's journal on the enlisted soldier. In 1889 he published *Provisional Manual for Exercise of Company Bearers and Hospital Corps*. Perhaps his most valuable publication, *Notes on Military Hygiene for Officers of the Line*, a textbook based on his classroom lectures, was recommended by the surgeon general for use in new courses not only at Fort Leavenworth but, also at West Point, New York, and Fort Monroe, Virginia. This volume, initially published in 1890, went into four editions, the last coming out in 1909.

In 1890 Woodhull was sent to England to study the British army's medical service. His work there in 1891 led to the publication of *Observations upon the Medical Department of the British Army* in 1894. In the same year he also became one of the first members of the recently founded Association of Military Surgeons. From 1892 to 1895 he commanded the Army-Navy Hospital at Hot Springs, Arkansas. During his assignment there, he was promoted to lieutenant colonel and received an LL.D. degree from Princeton University.

During and after the Spanish-American War, Woodhull's assignments further familiarized him with the medical consequences of extremely poor sanitation. In 1898 the secretary of war sent him to inspect Camp Thomas at Chickamauga, Georgia, where a typhoid fever epidemic was taking a high toll of recruits undergoing military training. In 1899 he was stationed as the chief medical officer of the Department of the Pacific in Manila, where centuries of poor sanitation had resulted in high disease rates.

By the time Woodhull was named director of the Museum and Library Division of the Surgeon General's Office in 1900, he had gained a reputation for his devotion to precise documentation of research and accuracy even in minor details. He was promoted to colonel shortly before retiring in 1901. Three years later he was awarded the rank of brigadier general, retired, by act of Congress.

After leaving the army, he returned to New Jersey, where he continued to write and teach. From 1902 to 1907 he lectured on sanitation and personal hygiene at Princeton. In 1902 he published the first of two articles on the use of ipecacuanha in treating dysentery and, in 1906, *Personal Hygiene: Designed for Undergraduates*, a manual for college students. In 1907 his article about hygiene and sanitation won the Seaman Prize of the Military Service Institution, which published it in its journal the following year. He died in Princeton.

Woodhull's military career spanned the period during which both scientific medicine and the public health reform movement were in their infancy. Although his intellectual curiosity led him to explore many topics, it was his expertise in public health that enabled him to contribute to a field of growing importance in the United States and the territories it acquired after the Spanish-American War. Although he did not gain prominence in the new world of scientific medicine, Woodhull played a significant role in an important era in the history of public health.

• There is no known collection of Woodhull's papers. See the annual reports submitted to the secretary of war by the surgeon general of the U.S. Army during the period of Woodhull's service. The most detailed information can be found in Irving A. Watson, ed., *Physicians and Surgeons of America* (1896). An obituary is in *Military Surgeon* 49 (1921): 711–12.

MARY C. GILLETT

WOODHULL, Nathaniel (30 Dec. 1722–20 Sept. 1776), revolutionary war officer and alleged martyr, was born in Mastic, Suffolk County, New York, the son of Nathaniel Woodhull, a farmer and landowner, and Sarah Smith. His great-grandfather, Richard Woodhull (or Wodhull), had emigrated from Northampton County, England, and by 1648 held extensive tracts of land in Setauket and Mastic on Long Island. The family's primary occupation was in agriculture, though Nathaniel's uncle, Richard Woodhull, was a merchant or importer who dealt in paints, shingles, and related commodities. Nathaniel's father, a second son, evidently received a smaller share of the family estates, but his mother was of a prominent and prosperous Suffolk County family, the Smiths of Smithtown.

Though little is known about his boyhood, later events suggest that Nathaniel was prepared to assume title to his father's estates and to engage in the management of agricultural lands. He showed an early interest in military activity. He joined the New York militia at an early age and by the age of twenty was promoted to the rank of major. In 1758, during the French and Indian War, he served in the Third New York Provincial Regiment in General James Abercromby's campaign against Fort Carillon (Fort Ticonderoga) and led the Third Regiment when it took part in Lieutenant Colonel James Bradstreet's capture of Fort Frontenac on Lake Ontario—a minor but brilliantly executed campaign. Promoted to colonel, he commanded the regiment in Jeffrey Amherst's successful campaign against Montreal in 1760. His journal of that campaign, printed in the *Historical Magazine* (Sept. 1861), is terse and undramatic except when describing agricultural lands.

Woodhull returned to farming and estate management at the end of the campaign. In 1761 he married Ruth Floyd, daughter of a prosperous Long Island family. The Woodhulls had one child. By the outbreak of the American Revolution he was one of the most prosperous landowners in Suffolk County. A county census of 1776 indicates that he held fifteen slaves, a number equaled by only one other resident.

After 1765, as the conflict between Parliament and the colonies arose and then intensified, Woodhull, a devoted Presbyterian, aligned himself with the Whigs. In 1769 he was elected to the colonial assembly from Suffolk County and served until 1775 when the New York Provincial Congress was created. He was elected to that body in May 1775 and was immediately selected as its president. In October the Congress appointed him brigadier general and commander of all militia forces in Suffolk and Queens counties.

With the outbreak of hostilities and the movement toward independence, Woodhull displayed some moderation. He favored a lenient policy toward Loyalists and, through design or accident, he did not sign New York's endorsement of the Declaration of Independence. He had family ties to both camps: his wife's brother William Floyd was a signer of the Declaration; his brother Jesse and his wife's brother-in-law Ezra L'Hommedieu were strong Whigs. But his first cousins, Edmund and Phineas Fanning, were militant Loyalists, and his wife was tied by marriage and friendship to Loyalist Thomas Jones and the Loyalist De Lancey family.

Woodhull was in Suffolk County on family business in August 1776 when British forces landed on Long Island. The New York convention ordered him to lead the Long Island militia in driving livestock out of the reach of the British army. He was thus at Jamaica on 27 August when the battle of Long Island took place.

His small company did not take part in the battle, but the next day he was captured by a roving unit of the Light Dragoons under Oliver De Lancey, Jr. Wounded, he was placed on board a prison ship and then transferred to a hospital at New Utrecht. A gangrenous arm was amputated, but he died there on 20 September.

Forgotten for decades, Woodhull became the subject of a patriotic ballad in 1821 and then of an extended historiographical dispute when local historians and others, relying on hearsay, declared that he was maliciously wounded after his capture for refusing to say "God save the king." This myth was perpetuated by a monument erected at Jamaica in 1904. Woodhull has also been accused, on equally uncertain evidence, of attempting to turn Suffolk County over to the British. It is probable that he was wounded in a normal act of war while being captured. It is also probable that without the myth and the historical dispute Woodhull would be remembered only as a passive member of the New York revolutionary legislature. His military and civil career, as reflected in official correspondence and contemporary testimony, is that of an ambitious and industrious man who had firm convictions but was not a zealot.

• The bulk of Woodhull's papers evidently were destroyed when the family home burned in 1784. A number of his official letters and related documents are published in *Journals of the Provincial Congress of the State of New York* (1842), *Calendar of Historical Manuscripts, Relating to the War of the Revolution, in the Office of the [New York] Secretary of State* (1868), and *Journal of the Votes and Proceedings of the General Assembly of the Colony of New York . . . 1766 to 1776* (1820). Family history and genealogy are presented in Anna M. Woodhull, "The American Family of Woodhull," *New York Genealogical and Biographical Record* 4 (1873): 54–61, and, incidentally, in William Q. Maxwell, *A Portrait of William Floyd, Long Islander* (1956). Thomas Jones, *History of New York during the Revolutionary War*, ed. Edward Floyd de Lancey (1879), provides additional family information and a discussion of Woodhull's death, as does Henry Onderdonk, Jr., *Revolutionary Incidents of Suffolk and Kings Counties* (1849). Two volumes by William H. W. Sabine—*Suppressed History of General Nathaniel Woodhull* (1954) and *Murder, 1776 & Washington's Policy of Silence* (1973)—include information on Woodhull's life before the Revolution but focus almost exclusively on the circumstances relating to his death and to the emergence of a quasi-mythical version of the event.

WENDELL TRIPP

WOODHULL, Victoria Claflin (23 Sept. 1838–10 June 1927), reformer and first female presidential candidate, was born in Homer, Ohio, the daughter of Reuben Buckman Claflin, a mill owner, and Roxanna Hummel. Woodhull's education was limited to three years of erratic instruction in Homer's Methodist church school. Her childhood was marked by financial and domestic instability, culminating in the destruction by fire of the family's mill. Townspeople, suspecting the impecunious and alcoholic Buck Claflin of arson for insurance fraud, drove the family from Homer and into several years of drifting from town to town.

Victoria's tumultuous home life was interrupted only briefly by her 1853 marriage to Canning Woodhull, a physician. The couple had two children before divorcing in 1865. After brief sojourns in Chicago and San Francisco, where she worked in the theater, Woodhull and her husband returned to the Claflins in Ohio in the mid-1850s. Joining her younger sister Tennessee Claflin, who had been supporting the family by traveling through the Midwest telling fortunes and selling her own healing elixir, Woodhull became a "medical clairvoyant," claiming to heal the gravely ill with her touch and presence. Woodhull's career as a clairvoyant made her a wealthy woman and was the beginning of an involvement with spiritualism that remained important throughout her public life.

In 1866 Woodhull married Colonel James Harvey Blood, a Union army war hero who had approached her for treatment. Until their 1876 divorce, Blood remained a major figure in the background of Woodhull's public career, managing her financial affairs, writing many of the words that appeared under her name, and introducing her to many of the reform causes that she was to advocate. The couple had no children.

In 1868 Woodhull and her sister Tennessee, with Colonel Blood and the Claflin clan in tow, moved to New York City in search of an introduction to railroad baron Cornelius Vanderbilt. A shared interest in clairvoyance provided the introduction; the romantic attentions of Tennessee probably secured Vanderbilt as the sisters' financial mentor. Woodhull's move to New York marked one of her periodic efforts to reinvent her public self. She gave up medical clairvoyance and cultivated a genteel air more suitable to her attendance at Vanderbilt's dining table. After following the financier's advice to a small fortune on the Gold Exchange in September 1869, Woodhull embarked on one of her female firsts as head of the brokerage firm of Woodhull, Claflin and Co.

Woodhull wrote later that her success on Wall Street was part of a farsighted strategy to "secure the most . . . prominent notice to the world" and advance her political and reform ambitions. She launched herself almost immediately into political life by announcing her candidacy for president of the United States in an April 1870 letter to the *New York Herald*. Capitalizing on the publicity generated by her financial dealings, Woodhull published under her name in the *Herald* a series of position papers written by Stephen Pearl Andrews. Andrews, a radical reformer, had become Woodhull's intellectual mentor and, like Blood, performed much of the behind-the-scenes work that shaped her public image. Intended to present Woodhull as intellectually fit for the male realm of politics, the articles stressed Andrews's vision of a "Pantarchy," a society in which property and children are overseen by a beneficent state and adults are free to live and, particularly, to love as they see fit. The articles were published in book form, under Woodhull's name, as *The Origins, Tendencies, and Principles of Government* in 1871.

Woodhull's presidential candidacy soon spawned its own promotional vehicle in the form of *Woodhull and Claflin's Weekly*, the first issue of which appeared in May 1870. Edited mostly by Andrews and Blood, the *Weekly* published articles on women's education and employment, opposed abortion, serialized a novel by Georges Sand, and promoted free love. Throughout the paper's six-year run, its main purpose was the advancement of Woodhull's political and reform ambitions. Its content changed with her needs. In the paper's early years it capitalized on Woodhull's reputation on Wall Street by publishing financial news. In later years it practiced an early form of muckraking by uncovering Wall Street fraud and scandal.

Foremost among Woodhull's reform ambitions were the rights of women. She saw herself as a "representative woman," an example to men of women's capabilities and a reminder to women of their sex's potential. Woodhull first attended a suffrage convention in 1869. In late 1870 she moved briefly to Washington, D.C., where she lobbied for woman suffrage, gaining the support of congressional insiders, most prominently Massachusetts senator Benjamin Butler. Succeeding where suffrage leaders such as Elizabeth Cady Stanton and Susan B. Anthony had failed, on 11 January 1871 Woodhull addressed the House Judiciary Committee on the suffrage issue. "Woodhull's memorial" was delivered on the day of a suffrage convention in Washington. Woodhull's wealth, her boldness, and her quick rise in New York brought her to the attention of Stanton, Anthony, and their allies and earned her an invitation to address the Washington convention. A speaking tour before large and enthusiastic crowds brought her widespread acclaim and further increased her prominence, securing her a dominant role at the May 1871 national suffrage convention in New York. Woodhull's fiery convention speech asserted the need for suffrage supporters to divorce themselves from ineffective and indifferent political parties in favor of their own leadership: "We mean treason; we mean secession. . . . We are plotting revolution."

In 1872, having generated enthusiastic support but failing in her efforts to involve suffrage leaders in the nomination of a "People's party" candidate for the 1872 presidential election, Woodhull organized her own convention, through which she was nominated for president by the newly formed Equal Rights party. The candidate continued to travel and speak, promoting broad humanitarian reform, including suffrage, labor reform, financial regulation, free love, and the benefits of spiritualism.

Just as Woodhull reached the height of her political prominence, however, her fortunes began to fade. Financial reverses undermined her ability to travel and publish and were compounded by the loss of Vanderbilt's support upon his remarriage. Domestic problems sapped her energy and damaged her reputation. Throughout her life Woodhull continued to house and support family members, including her parents and siblings and her alcoholic ex-husband, Canning Woodhull. The latter's presence in particular provoked a public scandal.

Woodhull's political status was particularly weakened by her flirtations with Marxism. She commonly linked the cause of labor reform with the cause of suffrage and, with her sister Tennessee, took up enthusiastic leadership of a women's section of the Marxist International Workingmen's Association. Turning against the financiers who had helped to make Woodhull, Claflin and Co. a success, the *Weekly* began to publish articles targeting corruption and the inequitable distribution of wealth. Ultimately, Woodhull's continued emphasis on individual liberty and her efforts to link spiritualism and communism alienated Marxists just as her attacks on capitalism alienated her supporters on Wall Street and in the press. With her wealth fading and her reputation tarnished, Woodhull was of little use to suffrage leaders, who worked to limit her influence in their ranks. Her prominent role in the 1870 and 1871 conventions was nearly ignored by the first historians of the suffrage movement.

By mid-1872 Woodhull found herself in difficult straits; publication of the *Weekly* had been suspended, and she and her children had been briefly homeless. Although her outspoken advocacy of free love at times generated support from the mainstream press and "respectable" reform leaders, the evidence of her unconventional private life seriously damaged her reputation. In seeking to redeem herself and gain new respect for her views, Woodhull incited one of the greatest scandals of the nineteenth century. Her target was the Reverend Henry Ward Beecher, perhaps the country's most revered religious leader. Beecher had been involved in an adulterous affair with a parishioner, Elizabeth Tilton. The affair was revealed to Woodhull by Stanton and confirmed during her own affair with Tilton's husband, Theodore. After failing to persuade Beecher to come forth in honest support of free love, Woodhull revealed his transgressions, first in a speech to the National Association of Spiritualists and then in the revived *Woodhull and Claflin's Weekly* (2 Nov. 1872). Woodhull condemned Beecher for his hypocrisy in failing to endorse free love, not for his adultery. The Beecher affair briefly boosted Woodhull's fortunes; although she was arrested twice for publishing her "obscene" exposé, the *Weekly* sold well for several months, and she was again in demand on the lecture circuit. Ultimately, Woodhull's ill health, declining sales, and the loss of major supporters like Andrews led to the demise of the *Weekly* in June 1876, marking the end of Woodhull's public career in the United States.

Renouncing free love and disassociating herself from spiritualism, Woodhull sailed for England in August 1877. Accompanied as always by her sister Tennessee, her children, and other family members, she continued to write, publish, and lecture in a mostly successful effort to create a respectable image and to squelch all evidence of her scandalous past. Her 1883 marriage to banker John Biddulph Martin completed her self-transformation. From 1892 to 1901 Woodhull and her daughter Zula Maud published the *Humanitarian*, a journal promoting eugenics and the gentility of Victoria Woodhull. After Martin's death in 1897, Woodhull retired into a respectable country widowhood, publishing a small newsletter and assisting in local philanthropy until her death in Tewkesbury, England.

Victoria Woodhull did not fulfill her loftiest ambitions for fame and social reform. She spent election day 1872 jailed over the Beecher affair and received no votes. Her brief dominance of two suffrage conventions both energized and divided the movement. Nevertheless, as the first female stockbroker, presidential candidate, and weekly newspaper publisher in the United States, and as uncompromising advocate of free love and sexual equality, she offered to both her contemporaries and posterity a foil to conventional models of nineteenth-century womanhood.

• A large collection of Woodhull's papers is held by Southern Illinois University, Carbondale. Additional collections are held by Columbia University, the New York Historical Society, the Boston Public Library, and Hamilton College in Clinton, N.Y. Woodhull's publications include *A Fragmentary Record of Public Work Done in America, 1871–72* (1887), *Stirpiculture; or, The Scientific Propagation of the Human Race* (1888), and *Humanitarian Government* (1890), as well as pamphlet versions of many of her speeches. Lois Beachy Underhill, *The Woman Who Ran for President: The Many Lives of Victoria Woodhull* (1995), is the most complete biography and has an extensive bibliography of secondary sources. Emanie Sachs, *The Terrible Siren: Victoria Woodhull* (1928), is a less balanced but important biography. Theodore Tilton, *The Life of Victoria Woodhull* (1871), is a highly sympathetic account written with considerable input from its subject. Spiritualism is examined in Ann Braude, *Radical Spirits: Spiritualism and Women's Rights in Nineteenth-Century America* (1989). For the Beecher-Tilton scandal, see Altina L. Waller, *The Reverend Beecher and Mrs. Tilton: Sex and Class in Victorian America* (1982). Woodhull's obituary is in the *New York Times* and *The Times* (London), 11 June 1927.

KATHLEEN FEENEY

WOODIN, William Hartman (27 May 1868–3 May 1934), business executive and secretary of the Treasury, was born in Berwick, Pennsylvania, a coal mining and iron manufacturing area. He was the son of Clemuel Ricketts Woodin and Mary Louise Dickerman. Since 1835 his family had been active in operating an iron forge in the region, and William Woodin was expected to follow in the family business. To secure a good education for Woodin, his father sent him to the Woodbridge School in New York City and then to the School of Mines at Columbia University. Woodin was restless, however, and left there in 1890 without earning a degree. In 1889 he had married Annie Jessup, which whom he would have four children.

Shortly after his marriage, Woodin entered his father's firm and learned the iron trade from the bottom up. For a short time he worked as an iron molder, but in 1892 he became superintendent of the plant. In the course of the ensuing decade, the company expanded into the manufacture of steel and the fabrication of railway equipment. As a result of corporate reorganization in 1899, Woodin was selected as president of the firm of Jackson and Woodin in Berwick. The following year his company merged with the much larger American Car and Foundry Company, and Woodin became a district manager. There he found greater opportunities and rose steadily through the ranks. By 1902 he was appointed a director and in 1916 reached the presidency. At that time he also served as chairman of the board of the American Locomotive Company and held seats on the boards of other companies in related industries.

Like many corporate executives of his era, Woodin had business contacts that led to his involvement in various charitable and philanthropic organizations. In the 1920s he was at times involved in public service. Governor Nathan Miller of New York appointed him state fuel director in 1922. He also became active in the Warm Springs Foundation in Georgia. It was in that capacity that Woodin first met Franklin D. Roosevelt, and the two became close personal friends. They shared many mutual interests. Roosevelt's father had been involved with railroads. Like Roosevelt, Woodin was an avid stamp collector. Indeed, he was also a collector of prints, art objects, and butterflies. His deep interest in American coins led him to compile a catalog with Edgar H. Adams, *U.S. Pattern—Trial and Experimental Pieces*, published by the American Numismatic Society in 1913.

When Roosevelt decided to reenter politics in 1928 and run for the governorship of New York as a Democrat, Woodin, although a Republican, served as one of his intimate advisers. As governor of New York, Roosevelt appointed him to a committee to revise the state's banking laws. Woodin continued to counsel Roosevelt during the next four years and worked quietly but energetically for Roosevelt's election as president in 1932. Many of his responsibilities revolved around fundraising for the Democratic National Committee. His successful efforts strengthened his bond with Roosevelt.

In selecting his new cabinet in 1933, President Roosevelt rewarded Woodin with an appointment as secretary of the treasury. Apart from personal friendship, Woodin projected an image of a conservative business executive from the ranks of big business. Such an image stood Roosevelt in good stead as he experimented with untried financial policies. In March 1933 Woodin supervised the closing of the nation's banks to avoid a general economic collapse and cooperated with the president in the gradual abandonment of the gold standard. He was carrying out Roosevelt's policy and oversaw its implementation. Much of the groundwork had been laid by Treasury Department officials during the Hoover administration, from October 1932 to February 1933. Although Woodin publicly affirmed his support of New Deal policies throughout 1933, because of his business background some members of Congress viewed him with suspicion amidst an atmosphere of great hostility toward Wall Street. His political position was further weakened when the Pujo committee, conducting a congressional investigation of bankers, disclosed that Woodin's name had appeared on a list of preferred customers at J. P. Morgan and Company, leading some congressmen in the fall of 1933 to call for his resignation. Nevertheless, Roosevelt continued to support him. But Woodin's health was rapidly deteriorating, and he decided to resign in December 1933. He died in New York a few months later.

Throughout his life Woodin had an abiding love of music. In his later years he received recognition as a prominent amateur composer and an accomplished guitarist. One of his compositions was the "Franklin D. Roosevelt March," which was played at the president's inaugural ceremonies on 4 March 1933. Other compositions included pieces for piano, "Raggedy Ann's Sunny Songs" and "Spring Is in My Heart Again," with words by John Mercer. In public life Woodin's achievements were limited. As secretary of the treasury he was faithful in implementing the Roosevelt policies during the first year of the New Deal and was recognized as a respected member of the inner circle of the president's advisers.

• The Franklin D. Roosevelt Papers, Hyde Park, N.Y., contain useful Woodin correspondence. A close view of his policies in the Treasury Department is provided by his undersecretary Henry L. Morgenthau in John M. Blum, ed., *From the Morgenthau Diaries, Years of Crisis, 1928–1938* (1959). Biographies of Roosevelt, such as Frank Freidel, *Franklin D. Roosevelt* (5 vols., 1952–1974), and Arthur M. Schlesinger, Jr., *The Crisis of the Old Order* (1955), include references to Woodin. For additional information see Charles Miller and John Chapman, "Woodin Notes: Avocations of a Financier," *Saturday Evening Post*, 14 Oct. 1933; Jules I. Bogen and Marcus Nadler, *The Banking Crisis: The End of an Epoch* (1933); and G. Griffith Johnson, *The Treasury and Monetary Policy, 1933–1938* (1939). An obituary is in the *New York Times*, 4 May 1934.

GERALD D. NASH

WOODING, Sam (17 June 1895–1 Aug. 1985), band leader and pianist, was born Samuel David Wooding in Philadelphia, Pennsylvania, the son of a butler and a laundress (names unknown). Wooding claimed that a performance by the African-American vaudeville comedy team Bert Williams and George Walker inspired his interest in music as a career. Although singing, playing piano, and even composing from an early age, Wooding did not receive formal musical training, in the form of private lessons, until after he graduated from South Philadelphia High School for Boys. Following a career as a band leader in Europe and the United States, Wooding enrolled in the University of Pennsylvania for further musical study, earning a B.A. in 1942 and an M.Ed. in 1945.

During World War I, Wooding played tenor horn from 1917 to 1919 in the 807th Pioneer Infantry Band, one of a number of all-volunteer black military bands that played in France as part of the morale effort. The Pioneer Band was led by Ziegfeld Follies arranger William Vodery, who would have been well acquainted with popular theatrical and syncopated dance music; however, Wooding stated that the band performed only military music and marches. After the war Wooding returned to Atlantic City in 1919 and organized his first band, the Society Syncopators. He went on to play piano and lead ensembles in clubs in Detroit and New York City by 1920, playing first in Barron's Club and then at the Nest Club in 1923. In July 1924 he and his group replaced Fletcher Henderson's band at the Club Alabam.

In 1925 the Russian impresario Leoni Leonidof signed Wooding and his band to accompany a black theatrical revue, *The Chocolate Kiddies*, destined for Berlin. Wooding and his ensemble were to supply all the music for the revue as well as perform. The ten-member group Wooding took with him included Tommy Ladnier, who had played trumpet with King Oliver, trombonist Herb Flemming, and Garvin Bushell on reeds. All of these performers have written memoirs of their time in Europe.

With a cast of forty singers and dancers, the revue provided German audiences with supposedly authentic depictions of African-American life in Harlem and on a southern plantation. The music consisted of four numbers by Duke Ellington and Joe Trent, other popular songs, works by Stephen Foster, traditional African-American spirituals, and even "jazzed-up" arrangements of concert music. Wooding's ensemble performed alone as the second act.

Although American jazz and dance music were quite popular in Germany, no band consisting entirely of American performers had appeared in Germany prior to the arrival of Wooding and his orchestra. The band proved to be the most successful part of the revue, receiving thunderous and enthusiastic response. Within six weeks of the revue's opening, Wooding had signed a recording contract with the German Vox label and recorded four tunes from the revue, becoming the first jazz ensemble to record in Europe. These recordings, available on a Biograph reissue, provide a good idea of the exuberant, though unpolished, quality of the young band. Wooding's arrangements are generally in the style of the "symphonic jazz" popularized by Paul Whiteman, whom Wooding admired, and they feature some notable solos by his sidemen.

Program listings from subsequent performances indicate that the group's repertory consisted of works ranging from early jazz standards like "St. Louis Blues" and "Memphis Blues" to *Rhapsody in Blue* and jazzy arrangements of Tchaikovsky's *1812* Overture, Sousa's "Stars and Stripes" march, and even operatic selections from Verdi, Wagner, and Gounod. Wooding's revue orchestra recorded again in Berlin in 1926 and gave several live broadcasts over the Berlin radio.

After the revue closed in Berlin, it toured for another year, playing dates throughout Germany, Eastern Europe, Scandinavia, Russia, Turkey, England, and Italy. Wooding left the revue in 1926, and he and his ensemble continued touring throughout Europe, Russia, and South America. Often the first African Americans their audiences had ever seen, the band experienced some racist press coverage. More often they met with initial curiosity followed by genuine enthusiasm and admiration. After returning to the United States in 1927, Wooding turned down a job at the then unknown Cotton Club, and instead chose to resume touring Europe. The band recorded both in Paris and in Barcelona in 1929, and finally disbanded in Belgium in 1931 as the worsening economic climate and political changes, especially in Germany, made it difficult to book performances.

After returning to the United States in 1932, Wooding resumed his career as a band leader, but given his unknown standing in his native country, he had difficulty finding a steady position. He returned to school at the University of Pennsylvania and founded the Southland Spiritual Choir and other vocal ensembles that toured the United States with some success throughout the 1930s and 1940s. He also worked for a time as a public school music educator and ran his own recording studio.

In 1953 he began performing with singer Rae Harrison, whom he married (date unknown) and for whom he composed songs. They had no children. They toured extensively throughout the world during the late 1950s and 1960s, resided in Germany for a time, and made recordings. By 1975, Wooding had returned to New York and organized another big band with the intention of performing his old arrangements along with new material that featured Harrison as lead singer. The ensemble performed until two years before Wooding's death in New York City. An earlier marriage, before 1925, to Ethel (maiden name unknown) produced one child who predeceased Wooding in 1980.

Although still little known in the United States, Sam Wooding achieved a remarkable number of firsts: he led the first American jazz band to play in Germany, to record in Europe, and to tour extensively. The band was notable as well for providing audiences throughout Europe, Scandinavia, and Russia with their first exposure to true American jazz.

• Wooding's earliest recordings with the Chocolate Kiddies ensemble as well as nine recordings made in Barcelona in 1929 and one recorded in Paris in 1963 have been reissued as *Sam Wooding and His Chocolate Dandies*, with helpful liner notes by Chris Albertson. Rae Harrison, Sam Wooding's musical collaborator and wife, donated their personal papers to the Schomburg Center for Research in Black Culture, New York City. The two boxes of material are available as the Sam and Rae (Harrison) Wooding Collection. Albertson interviewed Wooding in 1975 for the Smithsonian's Jazz Oral History Project; this interview has been transcribed and is available at the Smithsonian as well as the Rutgers University Institute for Jazz Studies. Wooding published at least two articles during his lifetime, "Musique de Jazz et Orchestre," *Music* 7 (Sept. 1931): n.p., and "Eight Years Abroad with a Jazz Band," *Etude* 57 (Apr. 1938): 233–34, 282, in which Wooding, then directing his Southland Spiritual Choir, disparages aspects of his earlier career. Chip Deffaa interviewed Wooding shortly before his death, and his subsequent two-part narrative based on the interviews provides a good overview of Wooding's life and career, "Sam Wooding: Jazz Pioneer," *Mississippi Rag*, June 1986, pp. 1–2, 4, and July 1986, pp. 6–8. John S. Wilson, in "Jazz Notes: The Big Band Carries On," *New York Times*, 8 June 1975, describes Wooding's return as a band leader. The brief article on Wooding in the *New Grove Dictionary of Jazz* (1988) provides a good bibliography of articles pertaining to Wooding's European career, especially those that appeared in the British journal *Storyville*. Garvin Bushell's memoirs, *Jazz from the Beginning* (1988), is dedicated to Wooding and features an extensive discussion of the European tour. Other memoirs by former band members are Herb Flemming, "Old Sam: The Man Who Brought Jazz to Europe," *Jazz Journal* 21 (1968): 8–10; and those of Tommy Ladnier found in Max Jones, "Ladnier—Better as a Storyteller," *Melody Maker* 43 (7 Dec. 1968): 8, and "Sam Takes Jazz to the Russians," *Melody Maker* 43 (14 Dec. 1968): 10. Susan C. Cook places Wooding and his European career into the context of Weimar culture in "Jazz as Deliverance: The Reception and Institution of American Jazz During the Weimar Republic," *American Music* 7 (Spring 1989): 30–47. The best obituary is in *Variety*, 7 Aug. 1985.

SUSAN C. COOK

WOODRING, Harry Hines (31 May 1887?–9 Sept. 1967), banker, governor of Kansas, and secretary of war, was born in Elk City, Kansas, the son of Hines Woodring, a grain dealer, and Melissa Jane Cooper. Being the youngest of six children and the only boy, Woodring grew up in an overprotected environment. Although a good student, he never graduated from high school, choosing instead to go to Indiana and live with an aunt so he could attend Lebanon Business University. After his return to Elk City in 1905, he worked as a bank cashier and four years later took a similar position in nearby Neodesha, Kansas. In 1918 he enlisted in the U.S. Army and was sent to Camp Colt, Pennsylvania. In October he completed officer's school and was commissioned a second lieutenant, in the tank corps, but the war ended before he could go overseas.

He returned to banking and in the early 1920s became director and major owner of the First National Bank of Neodesha. During that same period, he became active in numerous organizations, especially the American Legion, then one of the largest and most active political organizations in the United States. As state commander of the legion, he fostered friendships throughout Kansas and in 1930, just one year after selling his interest in the bank, ran for governor on the Democratic ticket. In a very controversial election, an independent candidate, John Brinkley, stole enough votes from the Republican incumbent, Frank Haucke, to enable Woodring to win by 251 votes.

As governor, Woodring performed much better than most people had expected. Faced with a house and senate controlled by the opposition and a citizenry racked by economic depression, he succeeded in pushing through important tax legislation, including a state income tax and property tax limitations. He successfully took on the powerful natural gas industry, bringing about significant rate reductions. An extensive public works program, centering on road construction, improved the transportation system and put many Kansans to work. The establishment of a Crippled Children's Commission put the state among the leaders in meeting the needs of the handicapped.

In 1931 Woodring was one of the first governors in the nation to support the presidential candidacy of fellow Democratic governor Franklin D. Roosevelt of New York. The next year Woodring ran for reelection against Republican Alf M. Landon and the independent Brinkley. This time Woodring came in second, as Landon out-polled him by fewer than six thousand votes. That same election day saw Roosevelt win the presidency of the United States, and four months later, on 6 April 1933, he rewarded the Kansan by naming him the assistant secretary of war.

Woodring instituted many positive changes in the way the army secured equipment and supplies, with his most impressive achievement being the institution of a system of competitive bidding, which made better products available at less cost. Always a supporter of air power, he championed and then approved the development of a four-engine bomber—the B-17. He was also instrumental in the formation of General Headquarters, Air Force, an organizational change that gave considerable autonomy to the Army Air Corps. A quick learner and effective orator, Woodring established himself with Congress and the press as a respected spokesman for the War Department.

In August 1936 Secretary of War George Dern died, and Woodring was given an interim appointment, which was made permanent in April 1937. His major contribution came in the complete revamping of the army's mobilization plans. By 1939 he and army chief of staff Malin Craig had in place the Protective Mobilization Plan, which provided for a 400,000-man force three months after mobilization began and a million-man force eight months after M-Day. While the plan was less ambitious than earlier versions, it was clearly workable, as became evident when the United States entered into the Second World War. As both assistant secretary and secretary, Woodring was a key figure in developing the nation's industrial mobilization plans. That the United States was able to mobilize so much of its industrial and manpower potential during the war was in large part due to his efforts. In April 1939 Congress approved the so-called Woodring Plan, which increased the authorized strength of the air corps from 2,320 to 6,000 aircraft.

Although an able administrator and leader of the War Department, Woodring came into increasing conflict with his assistant secretary of war, Louis Johnson, and his superior, President Roosevelt. Johnson openly sought the secretary of war position and continually undermined Woodring. The intense feuding between the top civilian leaders created an awkward situation for military leaders at the War Department. What led to Woodring's downfall was his difference of opinion with Roosevelt over whether surplus military supplies and U.S. military aircraft should be given to England to halt German military expansion in Europe. Roosevelt felt the aid should be extended, but the secretary felt that if the scarce military supplies were given away and Britain fell to the Nazi menace, the United States would then be vulnerable. Woodring became so obstructive that on 19 June 1940 Roosevelt fired him—the only cabinet member FDR fired in his thirteen years in the presidency.

After his dismissal, Woodring and his wife of seven years, Helen Coolidge, daughter of Massachusetts senator Marcus A. Coolidge, returned to Kansas with their three children. In 1946 and again in 1956 he sought, unsuccessfully, to win the governorship. In 1946 his son Marcus died of polio, and in 1960 his marriage ended in divorce. Financial problems also plagued him during these later years. He died in Topeka, Kansas, following a stroke brought on by burns he suffered in his home when his pajamas caught on fire.

That the U.S. Army, including the air corps, was able to mobilize so quickly and efficiently during World War II was in large part due to Woodring's contribution in the realm of industrial and military mobilization planning. His strong advocacy of air power helped the groundwork for the role that the air corps played during the war. His accomplishments are even more impressive when one considers the financial austerity and isolationism of the 1930s.

• Woodring's official correspondence as assistant secretary of war and secretary of war are in the National Archives, Washington, D.C., under War Department, Chief of Staff, 1936–1940; Supply Division, 1936–1940; and War Plans Division, 1936–1940, all in RG 165; and also under War Department, Secretary of War, General Correspondence, 1932–1942, RG 107. His personal papers are located in the Spencer Research Library, University of Kansas at Lawrence, while his official correspondence as governor is at the Kansas State Historical Society, Topeka. For details of his life, see Keith McFarland, *Harry H. Woodring: A Political Biography of FDR's Controversial Secretary of War* (1975). An excellent account of his years as governor can be found in Francis W. Schruben, *Kansas in Turmoil, 1930–1936* (1969). For his activities at the War Department, see Mark S. Watson, *Chief of Staff: Prewar Plans and Preparations* (1950), and Marvin A. Kreidberg and Merton G. Henry, *History of Military Mobilization in the United States Army, 1775–1945* (1955). An obituary is in the *New York Times*, 10 Sept. 1967.

KEITH D. MCFARLAND

WOODROW, James (30 May 1828–17 Jan. 1907), clergyman and scientist, was born in Carlisle, England, the son of Thomas Woodrow, a Presbyterian pastor, and Marion Williamson. His parents emigrated first to Canada and then, when Woodrow was nine years old, to Chillicothe, Ohio. From 1846 to 1849 he attended Jefferson College in Canonsburg, Pennsylvania, and graduated with honors. During the summer of 1853 he studied at Harvard with the renowned natural scientist Louis Agassiz and then joined the faculty of Oglethorpe University in Milledgeville, Georgia. In 1856 he received an A.M. and a Ph.D. from Heidelberg University, where he studied under Robert Wilhelm Bunsen, inventor of the Bunsen burner. In 1857 he married Felie S. Baker, daughter of a Georgia Presbyterian minister; they would have four children. After he returned to Oglethorpe in 1856, he studied theology and was licensed by the Hopewell Presbytery in 1859 and ordained a year later. In 1860 he was named the first Perkins Professor at Columbia Theological Seminary in Columbia, South Carolina—a chair created for the purpose of teaching the compatibility of scientific and religious truth. During the Civil War his scientific training made him valuable to the Confederacy as chief of the Confederate Chemical Laboratory, which extracted nitrate of silver from donated household silverware for cauterizing battlefield wounds. From 1861 to 1885 he edited the quarterly *Southern Presbyterian Review*, and from 1869 to 1872 and again from 1880 to 1891 he taught science at South Carolina College.

For three decades Woodrow stood at the center of a controversy among southern Presbyterians over evolution. The struggle began in 1860 when Professor Robert L. Dabney of Union Theological Seminary in Richmond, Virginia, warned that current textbooks on geology contained accounts of creation that contradicted Scripture. Woodrow rebutted Dabney with a series of articles in which he distinguished between biblical passages on God as creator of the universe, which were to be believed, and those touching incidentally on natural phenomena, which reflected the scientific knowledge of earlier times. Christians, he argued, were free to use scientific discoveries to supplement the biblical narrative. "Denying and decrying none of the shades of truth, heartily rejoicing in all," Woodrow exhorted his readers, "let [Christians] with renewed zeal hold up . . . the grace and truth . . . of . . . Jesus Christ."

His claim that truth had different shades cast a shadow of suspicion over Woodrow's orthodoxy. Obliquely accused by a trustee and officer of Columbia Seminary of "covertly" teaching evolution, Woodrow delivered a major lecture on the subject in 1884 in which he contended that "the Bible does not teach science, and to take its language in a scientific sense is grossly to pervert its meaning." He went further: "The more fully I become acquainted with the facts of [natural history], the more I am inclined to believe that it pleased God . . . to create . . . organic forms not immediately but mediately in accordance with the hypothesis of [Darwinian evolution]."

From 1884 to 1888 the southern Presbyterian church was wracked with controversy over Woodrow's views on evolution. At first the seminary trustees held that "there is nothing in the doctrine of evolution as defined and limited by [Dr. Woodrow] which is inconsistent with perfect soundness in the faith," but then, at the insistence of several synods, they asked him to resign. When Woodrow refused, the board, in 1884, stripped him of his duties as Perkins Professor. Tried by the Augusta Presbytery on heresy charges for teaching that "Adam was not made or created of the dust of the ground, . . . but of organic matter preexisting in the body of a brute," he was acquitted by a vote of 17 to 6. After that charge had been brought, but before the trial occurred, the General Assembly of the southern Presbyterian church declared Woodrow's teaching "repugnant to the word of God." In 1886 the seminary fired him.

After his dismissal, Woodrow remained active in the church as editor and publisher of the weekly *Southern Presbyterian* and in 1901 as moderator of the South Carolina Synod. In addition to teaching at South Carolina College, he served as dean from 1889 to 1891 and president from 1891 to 1897. He was also president of the National Bank of Columbia.

Although he was respected for his piety and dedication to his denomination, Woodrow came to represent what one critic called "vaunted liberality" in the church, which only "strict construction" served to "control." Maternal uncle of Woodrow Wilson, he was also an intellectual mentor to the future president, much as Wilson's father was his spiritual guide. Woodrow died in Columbia, South Carolina.

• Arthur S. Link, ed., *The Papers of Woodrow Wilson* (1966–1993), contains many letters by and about Woodrow. The major biographical study is Robert K. Gustafson, "A Study in the Life of James Woodrow Emphasizing His Theological and Scientific Views as They Relate to the Evolution Controversy" (Ph.D. diss., Union Theological Seminary, 1964). An obituary is in the *State* (Columbia), 17 Jan. 1907.

ROBERT M. CALHOON

WOODROW, Nancy Mann Waddel (1866?–7 Sept. 1935), author, was born Nancy Mann Waddle in Chillicothe, Ohio, the daughter of William Waddle, a physician, and Jane S. McCoy. Although she was not formally educated, she was tutored throughout her early life in the subjects of her choice. In 1891 she and her two sisters moved into a boardinghouse above their father's office in Chillicothe, and in 1896 she became the assistant editor of the *Chillicothe Daily News*. Her editorship, however, lasted only about a year. In 1897 she married James Wilson Woodrow, a mining engineer and distant cousin of Woodrow Wilson, and quit her job to accompany her husband on prospecting trips across much of the Midwest and West. After three years of travel, she apparently separated from her husband, moved to New York City, and began a writing career that would span the rest of her life.

Woodrow wrote thirteen novels, one play, and numerous short stories, poems, and articles over the course of her lifetime. She published all of these works under the name Mrs. Wilson Woodrow except for *A Leaf in the Current*, which was published under the name Jane Wade. In 1902 *Munsey's* published Woodrow's first article, "American Women in Husbandry," a piece influenced by her prospecting trips through the mountains of Colorado and Arizona. The following year her works appeared exclusively in *Cosmopolitan*: "A Woman of Fifty" in March, "Floral Head-dresses" in June, "The Art of Entertaining" in September, "The Fascination of Being Photographed" in October, and "The Appareling of a Pretty Woman" in November. These articles are significant in that they mark the beginning of the most fruitful period of her writing life. Between the years 1904 and 1913 Woodrow published four novels, *The Bird of Time* (1907), *The Silver Butterfly* (1908), *The Beauty* (1910), and *Sally Salt* (1912); a play, *The Universal Impulse* (1911); and more than thirty-six articles, short stories, and poems in magazines such as *The American*, *The Delineator*, *Good Housekeeping*, *Harper's*, *Lippincott's Monthly Magazine*, *McClure's*, and *Munsey's*.

By 1904 Woodrow began branching out to a wider audience and experimenting in various genres. Between 1905 and 1906 she wrote several satires on popular novels for *Life*, and a series of short stories for *Munsey's*. The stories in *Munsey's* are linked by a cast of recurring female characters that Woodrow describes in "Old Man Johnson's Successor" as "a little band, composing a rather unique sisterhood, differing widely in temperament yet drawn together by some sympathetic tie which in spite of occasional battle was yet cemented as to friendship." Woodrow affirms the importance of such "sisterhood" throughout much of her earlier work; however, it is most obviously present in this series. She writes in "The Soul Problem of Marthy Thomas" that "in sickness or in sorrow, women turn instinctively to one another, knowing that they will thus find the truest comfort, the completest understanding of their needs: in love, they must fly to the wilderness, for they stand alone, aloof, alien to feminine sympathy." Although Woodrow stressed the importance of a strong women's community, she does not advocate blind support for excessive weakness and dependence. In fact, she overtly criticizes women who act irresponsibly or insensibly. As Mrs. Nitschkan, the matriarch of the group, tells Marthy Thomas, her irrational behavior and her sentiments make her "ashamed of [her] sex."

Not only was Woodrow concerned with advocating strong bonds between and among women, she was also interested in challenging the strict gender roles that oppressed the women of her day. As Mrs. Nitschkan states in "The Soul Problem of Marthy Thomas," "If it's the Lord's work for a woman to set all day an' stick a needle in an' out of a piece o' goods, why, I'm boun to disagree with Him." Woodrow was concerned with challenging these roles, but she had no desire to disrupt them completely. In describing a Mrs. Evans in "Old Man Johnson's Successor," she wrote, "everywhere the evidences of her lack of conformity to village standards were accentuated by a certain precise formality of manner." In other words, she presented her model characters as striking a balance between reasonable nonconformity and "proper" behavior.

Woodrow's works continued to exhibit a concern with women's issues until she turned to writing mysteries. The first, *Burned Evidence* (1925), was followed by *Come Alone* (1929) *The Second Chance* (1931), and *The Pawns of Murder* (1935). Although Woodrow often dealt with women's issues in her short stories and articles, she did not follow a similar agenda in these mysteries. In *The Pawns of Murder*, Woodrow's last novel, the women are less sharp and witty than those who appear in her short stories. And unlike the women in the short stories who rely on each other for help and support, the women in this novel depend on the male characters to handle their problems and concerns.

Woodrow died in New York City of a coronary occlusion and chronic nephritis.

• In addition to Woodrow's works mentioned above, her novels include *The New Missioner* (1907), *The Black Pearl* (1912), and *Swallowed Up* (1922). For biographical information, see *Bookman*, Dec. 1912; *Reader*, Feb. 1906; and *The Biographical Cycclopaedia and Portrait Gallery with an Historical Sketch of the State of Ohio*, vol. 2 (1884) (on William Waddle). The Chillicothe Public Library is also a useful source of information. Obituaries in the *Chillicothe News-Advertiser*, 7 Sept. 1935, and in the *New York Times* and the *New York Herald Tribune*, both 8 Sept. 1935. The obituary from the *Chillicothe News-Advertiser* gives 1866 as Woodrow's year of birth; however, her death record from the New York City Department of Health gives her age as sixty-five.

KIMBERLY A. COSTINO

WOODRUFF, George Waldo (27 Aug. 1895–4 Feb. 1987), industrialist and philanthropist, was born in Atlanta, Georgia, the son of Ernest Woodruff, an eminent businessman and head of the Trust Company of Georgia, and Emily Winship. Woodruff attended Edgewood Avenue School and Tech High School in Atlanta. His studies at Tech High inspired Woodruff's mechanical interests, and he set his sights on attending the Georgia School of Technology, which he entered in 1913 as a mechanical engineering major. He lived at home while in college, commuting to and from school on an Indian motorcycle, which was his prized possession. Woodruff was fascinated by machines and enjoyed tinkering with his motorcycle and family cars.

After three years at Georgia Tech, Woodruff transferred to the Massachusetts Institute of Technology as a junior. But with U.S. entry into World War I in 1917, he returned to Atlanta after his first year at MIT and worked for the Emory Medical Corps, using a motorcycle with a sidecar to shuttle doctors and medical supplies around the Emory University campus and to and from Fort McPherson. After eight months of this work, he joined the Terry Shipbuilding Corporation in Savannah, where he worked as a draftsman.

In 1915, while a student at Georgia Tech, Woodruff had begun dating Irene King, and when the latter began school at National Park Seminary in Maryland they continued their relationship through correspondence. In 1918 the two were married in Atlanta and settled in Savannah. They had three children.

Marriage and success as a draftsman dissuaded Woodruff from returning to MIT in the fall of 1918, and he never finished college. Instead, he continued working for the Savannah shipbuilding concern, and after the war ended he returned to Atlanta to work as a draftsman for the Atlanta Steel Company. In early 1919 he became an engineer at the Atlanta Ice and Coal Company. After a year in this position, Woodruff became the Georgia service manager for the White

Motor Company upon the urging of his older brother Robert, who was a sales manager for White.

Woodruff held positions in numerous companies that his father controlled, including Atlantic Steel and Atlantic Ice and Coal, and more notably the Coca-Cola Corporation, the Trust Company of Georgia, and the Continental Gin Company. In 1919 Ernest Woodruff had led a business syndicate that arranged the purchase of Coca-Cola, already a multinational corporation with enormous success in both fountain and bottle sales. Although he never was an officer of the corporation, George Woodruff served in an advisory role as a director of Coca-Cola from 1936 to 1985 and sat on the corporation's executive, compensation, and finance committees. (Woodruff's brother Robert served as president of Coca-Cola from 1923 to 1939 and as chairman of the board from 1939 to 1942.) Woodruff also served on the board of directors of the Trust Company of Georgia, one of the state's largest banks.

Woodruff was most directly involved with the Continental Gin Company (CGC), the world's premier manufacturer of cotton gins. In 1926 Ernest Woodruff asked his son to help reorganize the Birmingham, Alabama, corporation, and George Woodruff and his family left Atlanta for Birmingham. Although he had never seen a cotton gin before, Woodruff's superb mechanical skills and business instincts enabled him to combine a knowledge of the cotton gin manufacturing process with deft management of the corporation. Beginning work at CGC as an assistant to the president, in 1930 Woodruff was elevated to president and four years later became chairman of the board. He sold CGC to Allied Products of Chicago in 1959.

In 1933 Woodruff moved his family to Daytona Beach, Florida. The move was motivated partly by a desire for a more temperate climate to alleviate the childhood illnesses of one of Woodruff's daughters, and partly by concern over the wave of kidnappings of children from celebrity families, including the notorious 1932 Lindbergh case. The success of Coca-Cola, Woodruff feared, had made his family similarly vulnerable. In 1940 Woodruff had a family vacation home built in Highlands, a mountain village in North Carolina. Called "Ruffwood" (a play on his surname), this summer home quickly became a favorite family resort. Woodruff was an active community booster in Highlands, serving as a trustee at the local hospital and donating funds to build a new community center. In 1985 Highlands recognized Woodruff's munificent support when it opened the George and Irene Woodruff Community Center.

In the mid-1940s the family moved back to Atlanta, where Woodruff was to remain for the rest of his life. Woodruff's brother Robert bought a house two doors away, and they remained neighbors until Robert's death in 1985. The two brothers were extremely close and throughout their lives communicated daily about family and business concerns.

As a director of the Georgia-based West Point Manufacturing Company, a textile concern, Woodruff scored a significant victory for the southern economy when in 1951 he led a fight to keep the company in Georgia after it had merged with the Boston-based Pepperell, Incorporated. Woodruff also helped install a southerner as president of the new merger and pushed for more Georgians on the corporation's board.

Throughout his life Woodruff's gifts to educational institutions were numerous and substantial. A notable beneficiary was Emory University, where Woodruff was on the board of trustees from 1951 to 1965 and was a trustee emeritus until his death. In 1979 Woodruff and his brother Robert gave the university a gift of $105 million, representing the remaining assets of the Emily and Ernest Woodruff Fund, which the two men controlled and which had been named for their parents. At the time, the donation was the largest single gift on record to an educational institution. Woodruff was also an active participant in an ambitious five-year fundraising campaign at Emory that began in 1979. In 1983 Emory opened a new $20 million athletic complex named the George W. Woodruff Physical Education Center. Also in 1983 Woodruff established two endowed professorships at Emory University, one in surgery and one in internal medicine. Woodruff and his wife also gave extensively to the Henrietta Egleston Hospital for Children, an affiliate of the Emory University School of Medicine, and in 1981 the hospital named its new George and Irene Woodruff Pavilion in honor of the couple.

Woodruff also served as a trustee at Georgia Tech for forty-four years and gave money to the school to expand and upgrade programs and physical plant. In 1984 the school opened a new dormitory, the George and Irene Woodruff Residence Hall, and the following year the university dedicated the George W. Woodruff School of Mechanical Engineering. Other institutions to which Woodruff made substantial donations included Mercer University, Agnes Scott College, the Rabun Gap-Nacoochee School (a private school in Georgia), and the Westminster Schools in Atlanta. Woodruff's support of Mercer allowed it to purchase and restore a Greek revival mansion, renamed the Woodruff House, which serves as the home for the university's Institute for Public Affairs.

In 1979 Woodruff's health began to suffer. He was plagued by meningitis, suffered a mild stroke, and underwent surgery to remove part of his colon. In 1982 his wife died. Although slowed by these setbacks, he still maintained an office at the Trust Company Bank of Georgia and went there on weekdays until the last year of his life. Woodruff died in Atlanta.

Woodruff made an enormous contribution to the South as a businessman and philanthropist. As head of the Continental Gin Company for more than three decades and as a member of the board of directors of several southern corporations, including the mighty Coca-Cola, he wielded a powerful influence in southern business and amassed a personal fortune. (In 1984 *Forbes* magazine estimated his wealth at $200 million.) As one of the greatest philanthropists of the South, Woodruff expanded the resources and facilities of many schools and hospitals. He was solicitous of institutions' needs and actively promoted the growth of institutions as well as supported existing programs. A modest man, he gave gifts quietly, often without disclosing the amounts publicly.

• A biography of Woodruff is Della Wager Wells, *George Waldo Woodruff: A Life of Quiet Achievement* (1987). Obituaries are in the *New York Times*, 6 Feb. 1987, and the *Atlanta Constitution*, 5 Feb. 1987.

YANEK MIECZKOWSKI

WOODRUFF, Hiram Washington (22 Feb. 1817–15 March 1867), trotting driver, was born in Birmingham, New Jersey, the son of John Woodruff. His mother's name is unknown. Hiram's father was a successful horse trainer, who built up a stable of horses and was moderately prosperous as the proprietor of several race tracks; his uncle George Woodruff was a notable rider and trainer of trotters. The second of four children, Hiram's three brothers also were horsemen. He had virtually no formal education. In 1836 he married Sarah Ann Howe; there were no children.

Horses were Woodruff's life. Apart from five years, 1845–1850, as proprietor of trotting tracks in New York City and Boston, his racing life was concentrated on driving. He was precocious as a driver, handling horses in trial heats by the time he was ten years old. He drove in his first trotting race for money at fourteen. At sixteen he drove in an important match race before a large crowd at the Union Course on Long Island, the premier race track of the day, and won. Small in stature but with remarkable stamina and strength, he early revealed coolness under pressure and an unequalled feeling for pace. He drove at all the important trotting courses in the Northeast, under all conditions and with all kinds of horses; he then rode in the Middle Atlantic states and on the newer trotting tracks of the Middle West. In a relatively few years he established his position as the leading sulky driver of his time; and, although often challenged by the numerous other fine drivers of the day, he defeated the efforts of his rivals to displace him from his position of dominance.

Woodruff's rise to eminence as driver coincided with the expansion of trotting in the 1820s and 1830s, when it became one of the major forms of sporting entertainment for rural and small-town America, in all regions of the nation. The establishment of trotting as a popular spectator sport necessitated the building of innumerable race tracks and stimulated improvements in training, handling, and equipment. Famous trotters became household names—Lady Suffolk ("The Old Grey Mare"), Dutchman, Flora Temple, Dexter—and Woodruff drove them all, his name synonymous with theirs for success. By the late 1850s people commonly spoke of this as a golden age of trotting, certainly as compared with the rudimentary status of the sport in earlier times.

The enormous growth of trotting was associated with the greater emphasis on speed over stamina. Woodruff presided over the lowering of the record for a mile from 2′40″ to 2′18″. Purses became larger, competition more intense. There was a growth in gambling, in irregular practices, and in various forms of cheating. In this context, Woodruff's unquestioned honesty as a driver was, as much as his technical skill, the basis for his towering reputation.

If he adapted to the new demands of trotting with seeming ease, he also resisted many of the values of the new trotting era. He left to posterity tangible evidence of his views as a sportsman in *The Trotting Horse of America: How to Train and Drive Him; with Reminiscences of the Trotting Turf*, which appeared posthumously in 1868 and went through many subsequent editions. Edited by and dictated to Charles J. Foster, an important sporting figure and editor, *The Trotting Horse* is a handbook of horse training as well as a brief history of the sport and of its most famous horses.

Paradoxically, in an age of speed Woodruff counseled patience in dealing with horses and men; he insisted that the driver must love his horse and gain its confidence, that half the horse's speed was in the driver's mind. Getting to know a horse properly took time. Woodruff urged the primacy of nature, not of human artifice and technique. He preached the superiority of slow growth: there should be no forcing of horses at too early an age, no overtraining, no use of the whip. Success, he insisted, came from inner discipline in the driver, not from his use of external force; it came from the intimate association of animal and man. His fame as a driver was based on his success, but his success rested on a kind of natural philosophy summed up in his motto, which captured with Yankee pithiness Woodruff's temperament, his values, and his racing strategy—"wait and win."

He died of "bilious fever" at his home at Jamaica Plains, Long Island.

• The indispensable biographical source is the sketch by Charles J. Foster, which prefaces *The Trotting Horse of America*. There is also a chapter about Woodruff in John Dizikes, *Sportsmen and Gamesmen* (1981).

JOHN DIZIKES

WOODRUFF, Wilford (1 Mar. 1807–2 Sept. 1898), fourth president of the Church of Jesus Christ of Latter-day Saints (LDS) and church prophet, was born in Farmington (now Avon), Connecticut, the son of Aphek Woodruff, a miller and farmer, and Bulah Thompson. His mother died when he was a year old, and Aphek Woodruff then married Azubah Hart. Educated at the Farmington Academy, Woodruff grew up in a family of local leaders and pillars of the Congregational church. His father, however, and some of his immediate family and one uncle left Congregationalism and became seekers, searching for a modern form of primitive Christianity. Woodruff himself became a dissenter and continued his religious quest while operating mills and farming in Connecticut and New York until his conversion to the LDS church in 1833.

At that time, tension was developing in western Missouri between Mormon migrants, who were mostly northerners, and the old settlers, who were mostly southerners. Disputes arose over Mormon religious beliefs and practices, over economic exclusiveness, and over LDS attitudes toward slavery and free blacks. Dissension between the two groups led to violent opposition to the Mormons and to their forcible expulsion from Jackson County by the southern majority. In early 1834, Joseph Smith (1805–1844), prophet and president of the LDS church, called for volunteers to form an expedition called Zion's Camp to help restore the homes and businesses of the Missouri Mormons. Woodruff joined the expedition, which arrived but failed to recover lands in Jackson County, and afterward served proselyting missions to Tennessee and Kentucky and to Maine.

In 1835 Joseph Smith organized the Council of the Twelve Apostles as a body second in authority to the First Presidency to assist in governing the church's proselyting mission. Called in 1838 to the Twelve, Woodruff spent the remainder of his life as a missionary, community leader, and spiritual guide. On a mission with others of the Twelve to England from 1839 to 1841, Woodruff converted hundreds of people, including several whole congregations of United Brethren, dissenters from the primitive Methodists. Returning to the United States, he served as a missionary and as business manager for a Nauvoo, Illinois, newspaper.

Sent with other church leaders to campaign for Joseph Smith in the 1844 presidential race, Woodruff and others in the Twelve learned of the Mormon prophet's murder while campaigning in New England. Returning to Nauvoo, the Twelve, under the leadership of Brigham Young, assumed the presidency of the majority of the Latter-day Saints. Following a bloody civil war in Hancock County, the Twelve led the Mormons to Utah beginning in 1846–1847.

Woodruff settled in Salt Lake City, where he assisted in building communities principally in the Salt Lake Valley, Rich County, and Cache County and in governing the LDS church. Serving as church historian, he collected documents and established archives for Mormon records. Deeply spiritual, he received numerous revelations that provided guidance for the community in their marriage relationships, personal salvation, and sacred ordinances. Operating farms and ranches, he promoted education and scientific and cultural societies while establishing contacts outside of Utah to facilitate agricultural development. Serving as president of the Deseret Agricultural and Manufacturing Society (1862–1877), he sponsored the importation of animals, seeds, plants, and machinery from the United States and Europe to develop the economy.

First married to Phebe Whittemore Carter (four children survived infancy) in 1837, Woodruff was subsequently married polygamously to Mary Ann Jackson in 1846 (one child survived infancy; they were divorced), Sarah Elinore Brown in 1846 (no children, also divorced), Mary Carolyn Barton in 1846 (no children, also divorced), Mary Giles Meeks Webster in 1852 (no children), Emma Smith in 1853 (six children survived infancy), Sarah Brown in 1853 (six children survived infancy), Sarah Delight Stocking in 1857 (five children survived infancy), and Eudora Lovina Young in 1877 (no children survived infancy; they were divorced). The divorces from Mary Ann and Eudora resulted from incompatibility; those from Sarah Elinore and Mary Carolyn resulted from Woodruff's belief that they had been unfaithful to him.

As a church leader he worked loyally with the First Presidency and others in the Twelve while introducing modifications that reiterated the need for love, family solidarity, and harmony. During the Mormon Reformation of 1856–1857, in which harsh teachings and elaborate catechisms called members to task for straying from church teachings, he served to mitigate some of the blunt preaching of other church leaders by emphasizing the need for love and concern. He served as president of St. George Temple, the first temple completed in Utah (dedicated 1877). In that role he received revelations that promoted for the first time vicarious temple ordinances for deceased men and women not related to Mormons—in particular, national and international political, literary, and scientific leaders. In the temple, living men and women act as proxies for dead persons by receiving baptisms, ordinations, and other sacred ordinances in the belief that the deceased will accept or reject them in the hereafter.

The 1860 victory of the Republican party on a platform calling for the eradication of the "twin relics of barbarism," slavery and polygamy, resulted in a series of laws attacking the LDS church. Passed in 1862, 1874, 1882, and 1887, these laws prescribed fines and imprisonment for polygamy, brought the Utah Territorial courts under closer federal oversight, and resulted in the confiscation of property belonging to the church. Because of the campaign to imprison Mormons who had married polygamously, Woodruff and others hid from U.S. marshals during part of the 1880s. While underground, Woodruff lived in Arizona and southern Utah, unable even to attend the funeral of his first wife in 1885.

Leading the church as president of the Council of the Twelve Apostles after the death of John Taylor (1808–1887) and the consequent dissolution of the First Presidency in 1887, Woodruff was called as president of the LDS church in 1889. Following the imprisonment of more than 1,000 Latter-day Saint men and a number of women for practicing polygamy and the confiscation of much of the church's property, Woodruff received a revelation directing the abandonment of plural marriage, which he presented to the church leaders and membership in September and October 1890.

Throughout his presidency he worked for accommodation with the rest of American society. Before he became church president the Mormons and others in Utah had separated into the People's (Mormon) and Liberal (non-Mormon) parties. In 1891 Woodruff divided the church membership between the two national political parties. In addition, he encouraged church members to renounce offensive doctrines, such as blood atonement, and to develop productive relationships with national and local business and political leaders. He died in San Francisco while visiting a non-Mormon friend and was buried in Salt Lake City.

Arguably the third most important LDS leader after Joseph Smith and Brigham Young, Woodruff was a transitional figure. At first helping to build the LDS community on a millennialist basis (expecting Christ to return soon to reign on earth for a millennium), after he became president he promoted accommodations that laid the basis for the church to become one of the largest American churches in the twentieth century. Deeply spiritual, he was also well-educated, intelligent, and personable. Establishing relationships with leaders outside the LDS community, he facilitated changes in Mormonism to retain the essential spiritual aspects of LDS life while accommodating the larger society on secular matters. In doing so, he strengthened Mormonism as a distinctive religious tradition within Christianity.

• The bulk of Woodruff's papers is located in the archives of the Church of Jesus Christ of Latter-day Saints in Salt Lake City. Other collections containing sizeable numbers of papers include the Utah State Historical Society, the University of Utah Library, and Brigham Young University Library. During his lifetime a number of sermons were published in *The Journal of Discourses* (26 vols., 1855–1886) and in the Salt Lake City *Deseret News*. Many unpublished sermons were collected in Brian H. Stuy, ed., *Collected Discourses Delivered by President Wilford Woodruff, His Two Counselors, the Twelve Apostles, and Others* (4 vols., 1987–1991). Previously unpublished revelations were published as *Unpublished Revelations of the Prophets and Presidents of the Church of Jesus Christ of Latter-day Saints*, ed. Fred C. Collier (1979). Excerpts from his journals, arguably the best and most complete of any nineteenth-century Mormon leader, were published during his lifetime in serial form and as a single volume, *Leaves from My Journal, Third Book of the Faith-promoting Series*, 2d ed. (1882). His complete diaries are published as *Wilford Woodruff's Journal, 1833–1898*, typescript edition, ed. Scott G. Kenney (9 vols., 1983–1985). Three biographies have been published: Matthias F. Cowley, *Wilford Woodruff: History of His Life and Labors* (1909; repr. 1964); Francis M. Gibbons, *Wilford Woodruff: Wondrous Worker, Prophet of God* (1988); and Thomas G. Alexander, *Things in Heaven and Earth: The Life and Times of Wilford Woodruff, a Mormon Prophet* (1991).

THOMAS G. ALEXANDER

WOODS, Charles Robert (19 Feb. 1827–26 Feb. 1885), soldier, was born in Newark, Ohio, the son of Ezekiel S. Woods, a farmer and general merchandiser, and Sarah Judith Burnham. Woods grew up on the family farm and received an education from local tutors. As an adolescent he was apprenticed to a cooper but found the trade unsuited to his interests. He subsequently was appointed as a cadet at the U.S. Military Academy and began his education there on 1 July 1848. He graduated twentieth out of forty-three in the class of 1852 and was assigned to the infantry. Lieutenant Woods served seven years in the West, where he engaged in minor skirmishes with American Indians. While on furlough in 1860, he returned to Ohio to marry Cecilia Impey.

After resuming active service, Woods filled the post of acting superintendent of the recruit station at Fort Columbus, New York. There he received orders to assemble a force and sail to the relief of the besieged garrison of Fort Sumter, South Carolina. With two hundred soldiers under his command, Woods left New York City on 5 January 1861 aboard the steamer *Star of the West*. On 9 January the vessel entered Charleston harbor and immediately received the fire of Confederate batteries on Morris Island. The vessel continued through the channel until enemy ships stood out to the attack. With no possibility of reaching Fort Sumter, Woods ordered the *Star of the West* turned about, and the steamer escaped to the open sea. This act, in coordination with the bombardment of the fort, was the first overt act of war by the Confederacy in what became the Civil War.

Woods returned to duty at Fort Columbus; he received promotion to captain on 1 April 1861. In October Woods went to Ohio, where he raised the Seventy-sixth Ohio Volunteer Infantry and was elected its colonel. The regiment would serve with him throughout his long war service. On 15 February 1862 Woods and the Seventy-sixth Ohio were exposed to the full fire of the enemy in the battle of Fort Donelson, Tennessee. At the battle of Shiloh, 6–7 April, the regiment participated in the movements of Major General Lewis Wallace's division. During May Colonel Woods led a brigade in Major General John A. McClernand's advance on Corinth, Mississippi.

Woods next saw duty on the Mississippi River. During August 1862 he commanded a mixed brigade of infantry, cavalry, and artillery that operated in conjunction with the Federal gunboat fleet. Utilizing river transports as its base, Woods's brigade attacked and destroyed enemy encampments, supply depots, and telegraph stations from Tallulah, Louisiana, to Bolivar, Mississippi.

Woods led the attack of the Seventy-sixth Ohio at the battle of Arkansas Post, 11 January 1863. Under his leadership the regiment advanced to within seventy-five yards of enemy rifle pits and silenced two enemy guns in its immediate front.

Assigned to Major General William T. Sherman's Fifteenth Army Corps, Woods saw lengthy action during the final campaign against Vicksburg, May–July 1863. On 15 May Woods's brigade destroyed a railroad bridge and foundries in Jackson, Mississippi. The brigade took its place on the extreme right of the Vicksburg siege line on 19 May and suffered moderate casualties in a charge against Confederate positions on 22 May. Following the surrender of Vicksburg, the brigade defeated an enemy force near Canton, Mississippi, on 17 July. Woods marched into Canton on the following day and destroyed railroad terminus facilities. He was promoted to brigadier general of volunteers on 4 August 1863.

Moving to the relief of Chattanooga, Tennessee, Woods led his brigade during the battle of Lookout Mountain on 24 November 1863. On the following day, Woods's was one of several brigades that blocked the path of Confederate retreat at Rossville, Georgia.

Woods led a division in the campaign against Atlanta, May–September 1864. His most important action took place when he led a successful attack to retake DeGress' Battery on the outskirts of Atlanta on 22 July. Woods remained with Sherman's army as it marched eastward to the sea and commanded the Federal forces at the battle of Griswoldville, Georgia, on 22 November 1864. He was campaigning with Sherman in North Carolina at the war's end and received a brevet promotion to major general on 13 March 1865 for gallantry and meritorious service in the battle of Bentonville.

A consummate and tireless soldier of pronounced physical strength, Woods left the volunteer service in 1866 to rejoin the regular army as a lieutenant colonel. He ended his active career fighting American Indians in Kansas. He was promoted to colonel on 18 February 1874 and retired the same year because of declining health. Woods then moved to Ohio to engage in farming. He died on his "Woodside" estate. His brother was William Burnham Woods, general and Supreme Court justice.

• Woods's personal papers are not known to exist in any archival collection. For biographical details see the Newark, Ohio, *Weekly Advocate*, 5 and 9 Mar. 1885. Woods's own reports are numerous and scattered throughout *The War of the Rebellion: A Compilation of the Official Records of the Union and Confederate Armies* (128 vols., 1880–1901). Battle narratives that indirectly touch on his war service are found in Robert U. Johnson and Clarence C. Buel, eds., *Battles and Leaders of the Civil War*, vols. 1, 3, and 4 (1884–1887).

HERMAN HATTAWAY
ERIC B. FAIR

WOODS, George David (27 July 1901–20 Aug. 1982), investment banker, was born in Boston, Massachusetts, the son of John Woods, a Boston Navy Yard workman, and Laura Rhodes. When Woods was age two, the family moved to Brooklyn, New York, where his father worked for the Brooklyn Navy Yard. Soon after, his father died unexpectedly. The Woodses were poor, so while attending grade school Woods swept neighborhood porches and stoops to help earn money for the family. Bright and hard working, he attended Brooklyn Commercial High School, where he served as president of the school bank. Eventually, family financial problems forced Woods to quit high school to support his mother and younger sister.

Armed with a letter of introduction from his high school principal, Woods secured a job as office boy with the New York Bond House of Harris, Forbes & Company, a leading issuer of utility bonds, in 1918. He continued his schooling in the evenings at the American Institute of Banking and at New York University. His rapid progress on his career path from office boy to vice president of Harris and Forbes was no surprise to friends and colleagues; Woods was a quick study, with a keen business mind and a likable personality. In 1928 the company sent Woods on his first international mission to Japan, organizing financing for Nippon Electric. He continued his meteoric advancement when the company merged to become the Chase, Harris and Forbes Corporation in 1930. By 1934 Chase, Harris and Forbes became First Boston Corporation, owing in no small measure to Woods's involvement in the takeover. In 1935 he married Louise Taraldson; they had no children. Woods's continuing success at First Boston was put on hold in 1942, and for the next three years he served with the U.S. Army in the General Staff Corps at the Pentagon as a buyer of supplies, eventually rising in rank to colonel.

After his return to First Boston Corporation in 1945, he successfully handled a number of high-profile stock issues, which helped earn him the position of chairman of the board in 1951. First Boston had handled bond issues for the International Bank for Reconstruction and Development, coincidentally headed by Woods's former colleague, Eugene Black. Since 1949 Black had served as the president of the World Bank, created in 1945 to provide investment capital for reconstruction of post–World War II economies for member countries. Following its early reconstruction focus, the Bank shifted its attention to aiding underdeveloped nations. Black greatly expanded the World Bank's role in assisting these underdeveloped nations and often consulted with Woods on the sale of World Bank bonds or asked for help on select projects. Black sent Woods, as an unpaid consultant, on projects in India (1952, 1954), Pakistan (1956), and the Philippines (1962). Woods also was the lead negotiator in resolving recompensation issues between Egypt and stockholders of the Universal Suez Canal Company following Egypt's seizure of the canal. With this string of successes it was no surprise that Black supported Woods as his successor after his retirement.

At President John F. Kennedy's personal request, Woods accepted the job of heading the World Bank. Kennedy stressed to Woods that efforts to build a lasting world peace were threatened by a growing economic gap between poor and rich nations. Kennedy's charge to Woods was to use the World Bank to bridge the gap between the poor and rich. Woods was elected president of the World Bank by the board of directors in 1962.

In this post Woods exercised his talents in international finance and banking. In one of his first speeches before a joint meeting of the World Bank and the International Monetary Fund, he focused on two primary problems in international development that the World Bank would seek to solve under his leadership. The first was the import-export imbalance caused by wide fluctuations in the price of raw materials; the second was the numerous and costly short-term debts incurred by underdeveloped nations, which prohibited them from borrowing for longer terms, as was necessary when financing industrial expansion. Woods recommended lengthening the term of loans to countries beyond twenty-five years and issuing loans for a wider range of projects. He also focused on grant loans to improve technical education, as well as financing for much needed agricultural programs.

Woods believed the Bank's role was to help nations develop through improved economic management. Loans, credits, economic studies, and technical assistance were all vehicles to achieve this objective. Hence, Woods strengthened the role of economic analysis in Bank operations. Moreover, Woods was convinced that the World Bank needed to work closely with borrower nations in the areas of technical assistance, fact finding, and problem solving to ensure that the objectives of the loans were being met.

In 1967 Woods reaffirmed his commitment to serve for only a five-year term as president of the World Bank. Convinced that Robert McNamara, then U.S. secretary of defense, would be the best person to succeed him, Woods aggressively encouraged McNamara's candidacy. McNamara was elected president of the World Bank and assumed his duties on 1 April 1968. Woods left behind a legacy that established the primacy of agricultural policy, heightened the importance of economic analysis in World Bank operations, and stressed freer access to loans by underdeveloped nations to stimulate their economies.

Woods remained active in the investment banking field. He rejoined the board of directors at First Boston Corporation in May 1968 and was employed as a paid consultant. He also rejoined the board of the New York Times Company, on which he had served since 1959. From 1968 to 1971 he served as chairman of the Henry J. Kaiser Family Foundation. New York governor Nelson A. Rockefeller appointed Woods chairman of the New York State Urban Development Corporation (UDC) in 1968. In 1969 he served as a member of the U.S. Presidential Mission to Latin America, and in the 1970s he served as president of the Foreign Bondholders Protective Council.

Throughout his life Woods was enthralled by the theater. He was a financial backer of Broadway productions such as *Dead End* and *Sailor Beware*. He was also treasurer and a member of the board of Ringling Brothers, Barnum and Bailey Circus. He served as a director at the Lincoln Center for the Performing Arts in New York City and as chairman of the board of the Repertory Theater of Lincoln Center.

Although a lifelong resident of New York City, he and his wife enjoyed traveling and spending time in their summer home in Portugal. Woods died in New York City.

With his ability and skill as a man of business, Woods made a lasting contribution in improving the economies of the underdeveloped nations of the world. His pragmatic approach to economic development was balanced by a keen sense of a broader mission. The World Bank, according to George Woods, was more than just a bank that lent money; it had the resources to provide economic opportunity for the less developed nations of the world. Woods set in motion a new direction for the World Bank by aggressively assisting nations in achieving economic growth and financial stability, which no doubt helped level the playing field in the global community for the remainder of the twentieth century. In turn, this assistance laid the foundation for more positive and cooperative relationships between nations in economic, diplomatic, and social contexts.

• Key materials on Woods can be found in the taped "Conversations with George Woods and the World Bank" in the archives of the California Institute of Technology and the World Bank. Interviews can also be found in the oral history section of the Butler Library at Columbia University. The definitive biography on the life and times of George Woods is Robert W. Oliver, *George Woods and the World Bank* (1995). Obituaries are in *Time*, 30 Aug. 1982, p. 92; and the *New York Times*, 21 Aug. 1982.

ROBERT W. SMITH

WOODS, Katharine Pearson (28 Jan. 1853–19 Feb. 1923), author, was born in Wheeling, West Virginia, the daughter of Alexander Quarrier Woods and Josephine Augusta McCabe. A bright, reflective child, Woods was educated in private schools in Baltimore and later at home by her mother after her father's death when Katharine was nine. During this period, Katharine and her mother moved to the home of her grandfather, Rev. James Dabney McCabe, who was the rector of St. James Church in West River, Maryland. There Katharine not only studied under her mother's tutelage, but grew interested in missionary and religious work, encouraged by her grandfather.

In 1867 Woods's family returned to Baltimore, where she continued her reading and reflection; she did not begin studying away from home again until 1873, however, because of her fragile health. She then enrolled at a private seminary run by a former pupil of Harriet Beecher Stowe, until she changed her life dramatically by becoming a postulant with the All Saints Sisters of the Poor at Mount Calvary Episcopal Church. As she became more involved in missions for social betterment at the convent, her spiritual experiences began to flower into a personal brand of Christian socialism that would mark all of her mission and literary work to come.

After completing her education, Woods taught at girls' schools for the next ten years (1876–1886), primarily in Wheeling, West Virginia, where she also began her early mission work among the workers. Woods's literary career also began to take root in these years. Her first publication was an account of a strike for work reform in Wheeling; she then wrote two sympathetic short stories about the exploitation of the region's nail workers there. Woods immersed herself in programs to combat labor injustice and joined the Knights of Labor in 1888 when she returned to Baltimore.

The same year, Woods read Edward Bellamy's utopian romance, *Looking Backward: 2000–1887*, a work that influenced science fiction writers, such as H. G. Wells. Socialist groups advocated Bellamy's principles of social reform to abolish poverty by replacing private capitalism with public financing. She published a laudatory article on him in the *Bookman* in July 1898. Around this time, she gained another mentor, Richard T. Ely, professor of economics at the Johns Hopkins University, who also professed Christian socialism. With the aid of these two men, Woods anonymously published her first novel, *Metzerott, Shoemaker* (1889). The book aroused immediate popular response and recounted her experiences among the working-class German immigrants around Wheeling. *Metzerott, Shoemaker* attempted to mediate a more balanced relationship between workers and the bourgeoisie through Christian compassion and sharing. The book shows the influence of Woods's favorite literary figure, George Eliot, and garnered much attention at the time, particularly among sociologists.

From 1889 to 1901 Woods experienced a period of immense creativity and literary popularity. In 1890 two more of her novels were published: *A Web of Gold* and *The Mark of the Beast*; both continued the reform themes found in *Metzerott, Shoemaker* and achieved similar success. Woods stressed that she wrote not for success or popularity but instead to aid working families in need by gaining popular support for a national platform for change. *From Dusk to Dawn* (1892) had a different focus; the novel preceded the Emmanuel Movement for faith healing, which Woods defined as finding for the body "a balance, an equilibrium of forces . . . an equilibrium more or less stable." In subsequent years, Woods went on to write primarily religious fiction, a very popular genre at the time. Her works included *John: A Tale of King Messiah* (1896) and *A Son of Ingar* (1897), both of which were drawn from Christian history and the Scriptures. Woods's final major work, *The True Story of Captain John Smith* (1901), was a historical novel, in which she recounted the founding of the Virginia colony and attempted to lionize the English explorer. Woods also published numerous short stories and poems. Her short stories are mostly religious in bent and unsuccessfully mix Christian mythology with her own fictionalized narratives; her poems like "Hold Me Not False," "A Twilight Fantasia," and "A Song of Love and Summer," though sometimes flawed frequently garnered public appreciation for her obvious devotion to the beauties of the natural world and the human spirit.

Woods spent most of the remainder of her life in Baltimore, participating in social and mission work through the Episcopal church. In an important paper read at the Woman's Literary Club in 1891, Woods advocated woman suffrage and brought about an interest in the cause among the women of her faith and city. She spent a year away from home doing factory settlement work in Boston, New York, Philadelphia, and Hartford, when she held a fellowship from the College Settlement Association from 1893 to 1894. She went on to publish a report of her investigations of labor conditions in the *Quarterly Publications* of the American Statistical Association in December 1895. Concurrently, she was also the head resident of the Hartford Social Settlement. From 1903 to 1906 Woods lived in North Carolina, where she worked as a missionary among the Appalachian mountaineers, but she eventually returned to Baltimore to her greatest love, teaching kindergarten at St. John's Episcopal Church from 1907 to 1911. In her later years, she assisted in founding the Psychological Club in Baltimore. Woods died in Baltimore.

In the years since Woods's death, her literary reputation has waned and little scholarly research has been done on her social work. She is best remembered for her novels, all highly moral or religious, which helped to encourage grassroots interest in social reform and economic change.

• No critical study of Woods exists and her novels are all out of print. There is also no collection of her papers. The best source for information about her life is in the *Library of Southern Literature* 13 (1907); 5979–99, which contains a biographical essay and a brief collection of Woods's poems and short stories. Other sources are also fairly dated. They include Hester Crawford Dorsey, "The Author of 'Metzerott, Shoemaker,'" *Lippincott's Monthly Magazine*, Sept. 1890; and Robert A. Woods and Albert J. Kennedy, eds., *Handbook of Settlements* (1911). Nelson R. Burr's biographical essay in *Notable American Women, 1607–1950*, vol. 3 (1971), pp. 656–57, is one of the best existing accounts of Woods's life and includes information gleaned from family members and the mother superior of the All Saints Sisters in Maryland.

ANNE M. TURNER

WOODS, Leonard (19 June 1774–24 Aug. 1854), Congregational minister and professor of theology, was born in Princeton, Massachusetts, the son of Samuel Woods and Abigail Whitney, farmers. As a child Woods preferred books and school to farm work. After a serious illness left him unable to do physical labor, Woods was allowed to study for college in preparation for a career in the ministry.

After rudimentary preparation in his home town, Woods entered Harvard in 1792 and graduated at the top of his class in 1796. During his years at Harvard Woods was heavily influenced by the rationalist writings of Joseph Priestley and his interest in the ministry waned. After graduation he continued his studies at Harvard while teaching school at Medford, Massachusetts. There he developed a friendship with a young pastor, the Reverend Joseph Russel, and the two spent many hours discussing religion and theology. As a result, Woods was converted in 1797, and his desire to enter the ministry was renewed.

Woods abandoned his teaching position to study theology with the Reverend Charles Backus in Somers, Connecticut, during the winter of 1797–1798. In the spring he was licensed to preach by the Cambridge Association and was ordained late in 1798 as the pastor at Newbury, Massachusetts. In 1799 he completed his study for the master's degree at Harvard and was married to Abigail Wheeler, daughter of the Reverend Joseph Wheeler; the Woods had ten children. Abigail Woods died in 1846, and Woods later married the widow of Dr. Ansel Ives; she outlived him.

Perhaps Woods's greatest contribution to American church history was his work in uniting the two warring Calvinist factions in the Congregational church in the early 1800s. Congregationalist theology of the day was based largely on the theology of John Calvin as modified by Jonathan Edwards. When Woods entered the ministry the Congregational church was split into three theological groups: two factions of Calvinists, Moderate or Old Calvinists and the Consistent Calvinists or Hopkinsians (named for their mentor, Samuel Hopkins), and a liberal faction, later known as Unitarians. Discontent among the three factions over the degree of Calvinism necessary to be called a Congregationalist simmered for nearly a generation until 1805, when the Unitarian Controversy, which led in 1825 to the creation of a separate Unitarian denomination, began.

Before 1805 each group of Calvinists had taken tentative steps to counter the growing liberal sentiment of many of the clerics in and around Boston. Both factions had founded organizations (the Massachusetts Missionary Society in 1799 by the Consistent Calvinists and the Massachusetts General Association in 1803 by the Moderates) and magazines (the Hopkinsian *Massachusetts Missionary Magazine* in 1803 and the Old Calvinist *Panoplist* in 1805) to counter liberal theology in the churches. When Harvard, which became a bastion of Unitarianism, appointed a liberal to the Hollis Professorship of Divinity in 1805, the Calvinist factions launched separate movements to lay plans for theological seminaries.

Well respected by the leaders of both the Moderate and Consistent Calvinists, Woods was in a unique position to bring about a reconciliation between the two factions, and he and Jedidiah Morse proposed a plan for union. Their plan found favor among the Moderates, but the Consistent Calvinists, led by the Reverend Samuel Spring, held out for greater assurance of theological purity. After many months of negotiations a compromise was reached in May 1808. The two movements joined together to establish Andover Theological Seminary, located at Andover, Massachusetts. The seminary was subject to the control of the Moderate Calvinist trustees of Phillips Academy but also came under the supervision of a board of visitors comprising Hopkinsians. It was further stipulated that each professor of theology should subscribe to the Westminster Shorter Catechism and a creed (Andover Creed) prepared by Spring. The union was completed with the merger of both magazines into a single publication in June and the appointment of Leonard Woods as the first professor of theology.

Woods served as the sole professor of theology for thirty-eight years. Although he was not given to brilliant or original thinking, Woods was nonetheless a competent and influential instructor. His style of teaching was cautious but thorough, delivered in a simple, clear manner. What he lacked in originality he made up for in kindness and compassion for his students. Aside from his teaching duties, Woods was extremely active in the vast network of religious voluntary societies that flourished in early nineteenth-century America. He served in positions of leadership on the boards of directors for the American Board of Commissioners for Foreign Missions, the American Tract Society, the American Education Society, and the American Temperance Society.

Woods also authored numerous theological books and essays. Of his many writings, two stand out as most significant. The pamphlets constituting the Wood 'n Ware Controversy (1820–1822) has been called the "best theological discussions of human nature in American church history" by the eminent church historian Sydney E. Ahlstrom. Initiated by Woods's appraisal of William Ellery Channing's manifesto-like Baltimore sermon (1819), Woods and Henry Ware engaged in a four-year, five-volume debate over the origin of sin and the basic nature of man, with Woods defending the Calvinists' insistence that the inherent depravity of man was part of God's divine plan for good in the world and Ware defending the Unitarians' view of the "essential sameness" between God and man and the impossibility of God creating sin for the good of mankind. This paper controversy marked the opening phase of the Unitarian Controversy, which, as previously noted, would rend the Congregational church in two.

The second dispute sprung indirectly from the first. Nathaniel W. Taylor, professor of theology at Yale University, reviewed Woods's defense of Calvinism and stated that Woods had set the cause of Calvinism back fifty years with his archaic defense of the doctrine of Original Sin. In the major work of his career, *Conico ad Clerum* (1828), Taylor argued that sin is man's free choice, not a result of the original sin of Adam. In *Letters to Taylor* (1830), Woods charged that Taylor's scheme denied the sovereignty of God by granting man an omnipotent power to choose a power that God could not override. As a result of the Taylor-Woods dispute, the Congregationalists of Connecticut divided into supporters and opponents of "Taylorism." The opponents, led by Bennett Tyler, eventually severed their ties to Yale and founded the Hartford Theological Seminary in 1834. It is a sad irony that the pivotal figure in preserving the unity of Calvinistic Congregationalists during the early days of the Unitarian Controversy would also be an important player in the fracturing of that unity in the 1830s.

Woods retired from Andover in 1846. He then spent the remaining years of his life in Andover writing a history of the seminary and compiling his lectures, essays, and sermons into a five-volume work. He died in Andover.

• Woods's letters can be found in the Syracuse University Library and in the Case Memorial Library of the Hartford Seminary Foundation. The bulk of his writings, sermons, and lectures are contained in *The Works of Leonard Woods* (5 vols., 1850–1851). Perhaps the most important literary contribution made by Woods was his *History of the Andover Theological Seminary* (1885). An appraisal of his theological views are contained in Frank Hugh Foster, *A Genetic History of the New England Theology* (1907); George Nye Boardman, *A*

History of New England Theology (1899); and H. Shelton Smith, *Changing Conceptions of Original Sin* (1955). The only full-length biographical study of Woods is by Edwards Amasa Park, *The Life and Character of Leonard Woods* (1880). Brief vignettes can be found in Williston Walker, *Ten New England Leaders* (1901), and William B. Sprague, ed., *Annals of the American Pulpit*, vol. 2 (1857).

DAVID B. RAYMOND

WOODS, Robert Archey (9 Dec. 1865–18 Feb. 1925), social reformer, educator, and writer, was born in Pittsburgh, Pennsylvania, the son of Robert Woods, a businessman and founder of the United Presbyterian Church in East Liberty, Pennsylvania, a section of Pittsburgh, and Mary Ann Hall. At age sixteen he entered Amherst College, where he met Charles Edward Garman, a friend of the great social psychologist-pragmatist William James. Garman became Woods's mentor, acquainting him with a philosophy known as "the Social Gospel." This philosophy suggested that positive social evolution could be facilitated in reform efforts by applying experimental psychology and sociological knowledge and principles and also by helping people find and maximize the use of their moral and spiritual selves. After receiving his undergraduate degree, Woods went on to attend Andover Theological Seminary, concentrating on sociology and economics. In the latter capacity, he spent some time in New York interviewing key labor leaders; he also visited the east end of London as a resident of Toynbee Hall, studying the efficacy of the settlement house as an instrument of social reform.

Sponsored by a fellowship from the seminary, Woods incorporated the results of his interviews, internship, and studies in a series of lectures, which he published in *English Social Movements* a year after his graduation from the seminary in 1890. In 1892, after he had spent a summer assisting a chaplain at the Concord Massachusetts Reformatory, Jewett Tucker, professor of economics and field instructor at the seminary, put him in charge of opening the Andover House, which Tucker had founded as a settlement house in Boston, and asked him to be the head resident. In 1895 Woods renamed it the South End House, with location, goals, and strategies that were different from those of the original Andover House and the seminary. It was established as a reform-oriented settlement house whose staff actually lived and worked among those whom they served. Although Woods married Eleanor Howard Bush in Cambridge in 1902, he remained head resident of the house. In that position he conducted social surveys, established the house as an internship setting for social work students from major universities, lectured, wrote, supervised social intervention, advised on social policy issues, organized and chaired national professional organizations on social work and social reform, and spearheaded community and neighborhood development efforts.

From this vantage point, Woods became the philosopher and strategist for the settlement house movement throughout the country, especially in poor urban areas. South End House, the first settlement house in Boston and the fifth one in the country, served as an exemplary and typical social science laboratory. In this context, Woods popularized the use of survey methodology in American social sciences, especially in the development of applied sociology to accomplish social reform. These efforts at reform developed in response to the widespread and intense social pathology that emerged in and around industrial urban areas in the late nineteenth and early twentieth centuries.

Woods felt that humanitarian efforts could be effective only if they were tempered with the rational goal of responding to documented need and eligibility. The result was that he refined the social survey and used it frequently to gather appropriate descriptive demographic data. He also used it as a necessary antecedent to the social intervention of the South End House. Reform-oriented governmental policy makers used the survey to collect descriptive data that could distinguish between the "deserving" and the "undeserving" poor in ways that he thought were more objective and could move social welfare from the private to the public sector.

He first demonstrated the use of the survey as early as 1898 in a pioneering study of a poor urban area, published as *The City Wilderness: A Study of the South End*; he used it again in a study of the north and west ends of Boston that provided the content for publication in 1902, *Americans in Progress*. From these studies Woods empirically validated his sociological theory, which posited that the neighborhood is the elemental social unit of which all larger social units, especially in urban areas, are composed. Woods felt that if a settlement house first built strength at the neighborhood level, this strength would resonate throughout urban America. The theory was explicated in detail in his 1923 book, *The Neighborhood in Nation-Building: The Running Comment of Thirty Years at the South End House*.

Wood lobbied for and was able to secure a wide range of public and private facilities and accommodations for numerous urban neighborhoods throughout Boston and other urban areas. These facilities and accommodations included parks, gymnasiums, day care, playgrounds, industrial schools, libraries, concerts, museums, literacy programs, alcohol prohibition programs, vocational and cultural arts programs, and monitoring and evaluation of social service programs. In fact, recreation and planning at the neighborhood level originated in Woods's settlement house. He advocated the standardization of the settlement movement throughout the country and the formulation of licensure procedures to determine the qualifications of those who practice social work. In this vein, in 1911 he organized the National Federation of Settlements, which was the precursor of the National Association of Social Workers, and served as its secretary and president until his death in Boston. Woods wrote *The Handbook of Settlements* (1911), *Young Working Girls* (1913), *The Settlement Horizon* (1922), numerous articles and monographs, and many presentations that gave impetus to the settlement movement, placing it in the forefront of social reform. Although his last publication, *The Preparation of Calvin Coolidge* (1924), shifted focus to a political campaign biography, it indicated the national level of Woods's influence, insight, and professional involvement.

• The Houghton Library of Harvard University Library in Cambridge, Mass., houses Woods's papers, including a wide variety of material. His ideas and his work are presented in *The Neighborhood in Nation-Building* and in *The Settlement Horizon* (1922). Woods also prepared the *Andover House Association Yearly Reports, 1892–1894* and the *South End House Association Annual Reports, 1895–1924*. Sam B. Warner, ed., *The Zone of Emergence* (1962), studies communities that surround the city and presents Woods's perspectives on urban situations. His wife Eleanor H. Woods, *Robert A. Woods: Champion of Democracy*, discusses her husband's work and ideas and prints excerpts from his correspondence and unpublished materials. An obituary is in the *Boston Transcript*, 19 Feb. 1929.

CLYDE O. MCDANIEL, JR.

WOODS, William Allen (16 Mar. 1837–29 June 1901), lawyer and jurist, was born in Marshall County, near Farmington, Tennessee, the son of Allen Newton Woods, a Presbyterian preacher and theological student, and (first name unknown) Ewing. Both his grandfathers had been wealthy slave-owning farmers; his father, an abolitionist, died when William was three months old. In 1844, when Woods was age seven, his mother married Captain John Miller, also an abolitionist. The family moved to Davis County, Iowa, in 1847. Miller died a few months after the move, leaving Woods, his two sisters, stepbrother, and mother to tend the farm. Woods was a voracious reader, and his love of learning led to success during his professional career. He attended a local school during the winter months in Iowa, working to earn money for his education at a mill, sawmill, gristmill, and brickyard, and eventually as a clerk in a village store. At age sixteen he enrolled as a student at the Troy Academy, Davis County, Iowa, and worked as an assistant teacher while taking classes.

In 1855 Woods enrolled in Wabash College in Crawfordsville, Indiana. He worked year round to pay for college, but by 1858 he ran out of money. He had inherited a female slave and her child when his father died, and he was urged to sell the child to pay for college. By 1858 the slave boy, chattel property under Tennessee law, was worth several hundred dollars. Woods, an abolitionist like his father, refused to sell the boy and instead had him brought north and freed. He then borrowed the money to finish college and graduated from the classics department at Wabash College in 1859.

Woods worked at Wabash College as a tutor for a year after graduation. In fall 1860 he began teaching at Marion, Indiana; the school dissolved, however, after the first Battle of Bull Run later that year. A staunch supporter of the Union, Woods tried to enlist in the Union Army in late 1860 but was rejected because of a foot injury. He then commenced privately studying law in Marion. In December 1861 he was admitted to the bar of the Grant Circuit Court, where he served as a deputy prosecutor, conducting criminal trials.

In 1862 Woods moved to Goshen, Indiana, where on 17 March he opened a law office. Bright and amiable, he enjoyed quick success as a lawyer. By 1866 the twenty-nine-year-old Republican was elected to the Indiana House of Representatives. He served one term (1867–1869) and, as a member of the Judiciary Committee, introduced several bills that became law. One bill established a new judicial circuit, to which Indiana's Republican governor Conrad Baker offered to appoint Woods as judge. Woods declined the offer, just as he later refused renomination for the state legislature or candidacy for Congress, even though his nomination and election were sure. In 1870 he married Mata A. Newton of Des Moines, Iowa; they would have two children.

After returning to his law practice in Goshen, Woods was elected judge of Indiana's Thirty-fourth Judicial Circuit (Elkhart and LaGrange counties) in 1873 and reelected without opposition in 1878. In 1880 the Indiana Republican state convention nominated Woods for justice of the Indiana Supreme Court. He was elected in October 1880 and sworn in on 1 January 1881, as Indiana's thirty-first supreme court justice.

In 1882 President Chester A. Arthur nominated Woods to be the U.S. district judge for the District of Indiana. At the time of his nomination, Woods was chief justice of the Indiana Supreme Court. On 8 May 1883 he resigned from the supreme court to succeed federal district court judge Walter Q. Gresham. Woods served as Indiana's federal district judge until 1892, when President Benjamin Harrison nominated him to become a judge on the Seventh Circuit Court of Appeals. On 17 March 1892 Woods took his seat on the circuit court in Chicago; he served there until his death in Indianapolis.

Woods sat as judge in several notable political cases. In the case *In the Matter of Simeon Coy and William F. A. Bernhamer*, Democrats criticized Woods for his construction of a statute in the trial of several parties who had conspired to obtain tally sheets containing the vote records in Indianapolis for the 1886 congressional election. The U.S. Supreme Court later affirmed Woods's construction of the statute.

United States vs. William W. Dudley involved a letter allegedly written by Dudley on stationery of the National Republican Committee and addressed to someone in Indiana, encouraging bribery at the polls. Pro-Democratic newspapers criticized Woods's construction of a statute and his instructions to the federal grand jury, which did not indict Dudley. The criticism prompted Woods to publish an elaborate statement of the facts and law in the case in a pamphlet that showed his construction of the statute was accurate and that his critics had overlooked an important U.S. Supreme Court case. Woods also asked Supreme

Court justice John M. Harlan to examine the legal authorities on which the grand jury instructions were based. Justice Harlan reviewed the legal authorities and wrote that Woods's ruling was in accord with Supreme Court precedent.

In *United States vs. Eugene Debs*, a case involving a violent labor strike in Chicago that interfered with trains carrying U.S. mail, Woods issued an injunction against the strikers. When the strikers violated the injunction, Woods ordered the imprisonment of labor leader Eugene V. Debs for six months. Imprisoning Debs generated so much criticism that Woods wrote an article, "Injunction in the Federal Courts," in the *Yale Law Journal*, defending the authority of federal judges to imprison those who violate federal court orders.

• Biographical sketches of Woods appear in Charles W. Taylor, *Biographical Sketches and Review of the Bench and Bar of Indiana* (1895), pp. 174–77; *Encyclopedia of Biography of Indiana* (1895), pp. 12–15; Will Cumback and J. B. Maynard, *Men of Progress* (1899), pp. 386–87; and Russel M. Seeds, *History of Republican Party of Indiana* (1899), pp. 204–8. *Memorial Meeting of the Bench and Bar of Indiana upon the Occasion of the Death of William Allen Woods* (1901), contains personal statements of eleven of Woods's professional colleagues. See also W. W. Thorton, "The Supreme Court of Indiana," *Green Bag* 4 (June 1892): 267; "Death of Judge Woods," *Indianapolis News*, 29 June 1901; and *Report of the Sixth Annual Meeting State Bar Association of Indiana* (1902): 223–26. Woods's pamphlet "The Dudley Case—Judge Woods in Support of His Interpretation of the Law with Indorsement by Justice Harlan and Correspondence with Ex-Senator McDonald and Judge Niblack" is held at the Indiana State Library, Indianapolis, Indiana.

BRIAN W. BISHOP

WOODS, William Burnham (3 Aug. 1824–14 May 1887), politician and U.S. Supreme Court justice, was born in Newark, Ohio, the son of Ezekiel S. Woods, a farmer and merchant, and Sarah Judith Burnham. Woods started his education at Western Reserve College in Hudson, Ohio, but moved on to Yale College, where he took his degree in 1845 with honors. After college he returned to Newark, Ohio, and learned law by clerking with a prominent local lawyer, S. D. King, with whom he entered into a partnership and to whom Woods credited much of his later success. In 1855 he married Anne E. Warner; they had two children. A Democrat before the Civil War, Woods entered politics when he was elected mayor of Newark in 1856; the following year saw him elected to the general assembly of Ohio. Biographers disagree on when, but it is clear that Woods made an impression in the Ohio assembly, since that body elected him its speaker perhaps as early as 1857 but certainly by 1858. Although reelected to the Ohio assembly in 1859, Woods lost his position as speaker due to the rise of the Republicans. As a prominent leader of the Democrats, Woods was torn between his heartfelt support for that party and his belief in the permanency of the Constitution and Union. Publicly, he strenuously opposed all Republican measures in 1860 and into 1861, including denouncing a million-dollar loan act to defend Ohio against southern aggression after the events at Fort Sumter, South Carolina. But privately, Woods worked in the general assembly to further the bill through the committee structure. On 18 April 1861, in a speech that brought him prominence and signaled the beginning of his switch to the Republican party, Woods called for the passage of the million-dollar loan and called on all Ohioans to join in defense of the nation. He concluded his speech that day saying "The Federal Capital must not be assailed.—In the defense of these we will spend our last farthing of treasure and our last drop of blood. Around our imperilled country we lock shields, and by her we will stand or fall."

Abandoning the Democratic party for the Republicans, Woods personally acted upon his own rhetoric by volunteering for military service. His brother, West Point graduate and distinguished Union officer Charles Robert Woods, organized the Seventy-sixth Ohio Volunteers, which Woods joined as a lieutenant colonel in November 1861. From that time through the end of the conflict (except for one three-month hiatus), Woods served with the Seventy-sixth. He saw combat at Fort Donelson, Shiloh, Chickasaw Bayou, Arkansas Post (where he was slightly wounded), Jackson, and Vicksburg. He rode with General William T. Sherman on his march to the sea, during which Woods commanded a division and served through the fall of Savannah and Raleigh and on to Washington. In 1863 Woods was promoted to colonel and served with such distinction that Generals Ulysses S. Grant, Sherman, and John A. Logan recommended him for promotion to brigadier general in 1865. When mustered out of service in February 1866, he was accorded the brevet rank of major general.

Instead of returning to Ohio, Woods settled in Alabama, a decision that continues to haunt him because of the "carpetbagger" label it earned him. He became a farmer, an investor, and once again an attorney. In 1868 he became the chancellor of Alabama and began to develop the expertise in equity issues for which he would be noted when he reached the Supreme Court. The following year, President Ulysses S. Grant appointed him to the Fifth United States Circuit Court of Appeals. Woods left Alabama and moved to Atlanta, where he was soon well liked and respected by the city's legal and business leaders. During his tenure on the circuit court, Woods worked hard and successfully to be a "good judge." He sought compromise with the southerners he encountered while maintaining and upholding national authority, and some evidence suggests that southerners appreciated his efforts.

No doubt the most important issue brought to Woods's circuit court was the *Slaughter-House Cases*, 1 Woods 21 (C.C.D. La. 1870). Decided with Associate Justice Joseph P. Bradley (on circuit), the case tested the issue of the reach and breadth of the Fourteenth Amendment. Bradley and Woods found that a state act that created a monopoly in the slaughterhouse business violated the privilege and immunities clause of the new Fourteenth Amendment and therefore was void. Three years later, a majority of the Supreme Court reversed this circuit court opinion in *The Slaughterhouse Cases*, 16 Wall. (83 U.S.) 36 (1873), with Bradley as one of the dissenters. Early on, Woods was willing to read the provisions of the Fourteenth Amendment broadly. During and after his tenure on the circuit bench, Woods collected, edited, and published four volumes of Fifth Circuit Court case reports, *Woods Reports* (1875–1883), which proved useful to the bench and bar then and to historians ever since.

In 1880 Justice William Strong resigned his seat on the U.S. Supreme Court. Justice Bradley switched his circuit assignment from the Fifth and took over Strong's Third. That move left open the Fifth Circuit. Woods's name arose to fill the opening because of his experience on the Fifth Circuit and because, after the contentious judicial appointment and hearings of John Marshall Harlan, the administration of Rutherford B. Hayes wanted an appointment that would cause little trouble. Appointed by President Hayes to the Supreme Court on 21 December 1880, Woods easily received Senate approval by a vote of 39 to 8; he took the oath of office on 5 January 1881 and began work.

Because Woods did not take a leadership position while on the Supreme Court and because of his conservative principles and his exercise of judicial restraint, Woods has generally received low marks for his short service. Yet from 1881 to 1886, when illness incapacitated him, he wrote 218 opinions, most of which dealt with workaday issues of the Court especially in equity law. An example of such a case is *Miles v. United States*, 103 U.S. 304 (1880), a longstanding controversy about the reach of the Revised Federal Statutes and the disposition of property under those statutes. Twentieth-century civil-rights historians have severely criticized Woods for his opinion in *United States v. Harris*, 106 U.S. 629 (1883), in which the Court limited the reach of federal power into areas of law enforcement that had traditionally been state-centered and state-controlled. Following the state-action rule established in *United States v. Cruikshank*, 92 U.S. 542 (1876), Woods held that only actions by the state, not private individuals, could be restricted by the federal Force Act (Ku Klux Klan Act) of 1871. Once again, the Court limited the reach of national power and national citizenship against the states and thereby left blacks vulnerable to white violence in their localities and without federal remedy; all in apparent contradiction of his Fifth Circuit Court decision in *Slaughter-House*. But while Woods limited federal power in *Harris*, he supported federal power in the other case for which he is most remembered. In *Presser v. Illinois*, 116 U.S. 252 (1886), he rejected the argument that individuals could carry arms as a federal right in defiance of the policies of a state.

In 1886 Woods was struck with an unspecified illness that prevented him from continuing his duties on the Court. He died in Washington, D.C., still a member of the Court. The limited research and sources available on this justice support Chief Justice Morrison Remick Waite's description of him as "an upright man and a just judge." Woods influenced the people around him and he responded with concern and dedication to his times and to his constituencies.

• Woods's papers, if they exist, have never been collected and scholars have written very little about Woods. See William B. Woods, *Cases Argued and Determined in the Circuit Courts of the United States for the Fifth Judicial Circuit* (1875–1883). Far and away the best and most thorough analysis of Woods remains Louis Filler's analysis in *The Justices of the United States Supreme Court, 1789–1969: Their Lives and Major Opinions*, vol. 2 (1969). A slightly more recent article that aids in an understanding of him is Thomas E. Baynes, Jr., "Yankee from Georgia: A Search for Justice Woods," *Supreme Court Historical Society Yearbook* (1978): 31–42. An important primary source on Woods is Whitelaw Reid, *Ohio in the War: Her Statesmen, Her Generals, and Soldiers* (1868). See also *In Memoriam*, 123 U.S. 761 (1887). An obituary is in the *New York Times*, 15 May 1887.

THOMAS C. MACKEY

WOODSMALL, Ruth Frances (20 Sept. 1883–25 May 1963), Young Women's Christian Association executive and international women's rights advocate, was born in Atlanta, Georgia, the daughter of the Reverend Harrison S. Woodsmall, a lawyer, and Mary Elizabeth Howes, an art teacher. She grew up in Indiana, then attended Franklin College and Indiana University and was awarded her bachelor's degree from the University of Nebraska in 1905. After receiving her master's degree in German from Wellesley College in 1906, she did additional graduate study at Columbia and the Heidelberg University in Germany. From 1906 to 1917 she taught English and German in high schools in Ouray and Pueblo, Colorado; Reno, Nevada; and Colorado Springs.

In 1916 Woodsmall took a year off to visit her sister, Helen Woodsmall Eldridge, in India, stopping also in Japan, China, and Southeast Asia. This trip lit the spark for her lifelong interest in the East. By the time she returned to Colorado Springs in 1917, the United States had entered World War I, and she became director of the YWCA Hostess House at Camp Pike in Little Rock, Arkansas.

Forerunners of the United Service Organizations (USO), YWCA Hostess Houses served as hospitality centers near army camps for women war workers, nurses, and visiting relatives of soldiers. In the summer of 1918 Woodsmall went overseas to establish a hostess house in Tours, France, and, after the war, in Coblenz, Germany. From 1919 to 1920 she worked in rehabilitation and refugee relief for the YWCA, touring the devastated regions of France to report on the postwar rehabilitation work of YWCA centers. She also studied emigration trends in Western Europe and surveyed employment, education, and social conditions of women in Central and Eastern Europe and the Near East, which led to the establishment of several new YWCA offices.

From 1921 to 1928 Woodsmall served as executive secretary of the YWCA in the Near East. Based in Istanbul, she supervised branches in Turkey, Syria, and Lebanon. In April 1923 she was appointed secretary of the YWCA Eastern Mediterranean Federation, extending her jurisdiction to Egypt and Palestine. Her 1925 study of social conditions and American philanthropic activities in the Near East eventually formed the basis for the Near East Foundation.

In 1928 Woodsmall received a fellowship from the Laura Spelman Rockefeller Foundation for a pioneering study, cosponsored by the American University of Beirut, of the changing status of Moslem women in the Near East, the Middle East, and India. Her report was later updated and incorporated into her book, *Moslem Women Enter a New World* (1936). From 1930 to 1932 she traveled to China, Japan, India, and Burma as a member of the Laymen's Foreign Missions Inquiry. She was also on its Fact Finding Staff to study women's interests and activities in India, and in 1931 she served on the Commission on Christian Education in Japan, a group made up of Japanese and American educators. Her accumulated research was published in her first book, *Eastern Women Today and Tomorrow* (1933), which focused on the position of women in China, Japan, India, and Burma and the role of Christian missions in effecting change.

Returning to the United States in 1932, Woodsmall spent the next three years as associate executive and interpreter of international affairs for the YWCA national board's foreign division in New York City. In 1935 she went to Geneva as the general secretary of the World's YWCA. As World War II escalated in Europe, the World's YWCA office was relocated to Washington, D.C. Despite the dangers, however, Woodsmall continued to travel in Europe, the Mediterranean region, and the Far East to maintain contact with YWCA centers and women's organizations that otherwise would have been cut off completely. In 1935 she studied the position of German women under Nazi rule; the result was an article in the *Forum* (May 1935). In 1942 she toured South America, making contacts with leading women in social work, child welfare, education, and business.

Woodsmall left her position as general secretary in 1948, and from 1949 until 1952 she served as chief of the Women's Affairs Section of U.S. High Commission of Occupied Germany (HICOG). As liaison between the Educational and Cultural Relations Division of the American Military Government and women's organizations in Germany, she worked to improve education, public health, and cultural, governmental, and religious affairs affecting women and to reestablish relations between American and German women's groups. For her work with HICOG, she was awarded the Commander's Cross of the Order of Merit of West Germany in 1952. Woodsmall continued to be involved with YWCA activities during this time and organized several international conferences. In 1947–1948 she went to China to organize the international council of the World's YWCA held in Hangchow. She was an adviser for the United Nations commissions on the status of women in Beirut, Lebanon, in 1949 and in Geneva in 1952. She was also a member of the United Nations Educational, Scientific, and Cultural Organization Working Party on the Equality of Access of Women to Education in Paris in 1951.

In 1954 Woodsmall was given the opportunity to do a follow-up study on her 1928 research for the Rockefeller Foundation. She returned to the Middle East to direct a survey of women in five Arab countries, sponsored by the International Federation of Business and Professional Women under a Ford Foundation grant. The results were published in her *Study of the Role of Women, Their Activities and Organizations in Lebanon, Egypt, Iraq, Jordan, and Syria* (1955). In 1956 she received a second grant from the Ford Foundation to complete a related study on Moslem women in the East and spent the next two years touring Turkey, Iran, India, Pakistan, Afghanistan, and Indonesia. Her accumulated research was published in her final book, *Women and the New East* (1960), focusing on women in public life.

Woodsmall, who never married, died in New York City. In a YWCA tribute she was remembered by friends and colleagues as someone who inspired trust and respect among people of all cultural and religious backgrounds, a woman who, as Lilace Reid Barnes put it, "was vital and unafraid. She assessed the difficulties and the dangers with clear sanity. They were there to be dealt with. But at the core of her being there was courage and love" ("Ruth Frances Woodsmall" [tribute], p. 9). Woodsmall's extraordinary career spanned two world wars and gave her the opportunity to work and study in countries rarely visited and often misunderstood by most westerners, during a time of tremendous upheaval. It was a period, as Woodsmall writes in *Eastern Women Today and Tomorrow* (pp. 86–87), "that has marked the awakening of women into social and national consciousness [and] has brought the realization of their international relationship." Woodsmall's international work was inspired by her dedication to improving the position of women and her unwavering conviction that women played a unique role in the quest for international understanding.

• Woodsmall's personal and professional papers (approximately forty linear feet dating from 1904 to 1963) are in the Sophia Smith Collection, Smith College, Northampton, Mass. The papers include diaries, correspondence, writings and addresses, research files, and interviews, surveys, and hundreds of photographs documenting women's lives and work around the world. Significant articles on her life and work include Anna Rice, "To Ruth Woodsmall: For Twelve Years General Secretary of the World's YWCA," *Women's Press*, Nov. 1947, pp. 19, 46; "Personalities and Projects: Social Welfare in Terms of Significant People," *Survey*, Mar. 1949; and "Ruth Frances Woodsmall" (tributes), *World YWCA*, 1964, pp. 1–11. An obituary is in the *New York Times*, 27 May 1963.

MARGARET ROSS JESSUP

WOODSON, Carter Godwin (19 Dec. 1875–3 Apr. 1950), historian, was born in New Canton, Virginia, the son of James Henry Woodson, a sharecropper, and

Anne Eliza Riddle. Woodson, the "Father of Negro History," was the first and only black American born of former slaves to earn a Ph.D. in history. His grandfather and father, who were skilled carpenters, were forced into sharecropping after the Civil War. The family eventually purchased land and eked out a meager living in the late 1870s and 1880s.

Woodson's parents instilled in him high morality and strong character through religious teachings and a thirst for education. One of nine children, Woodson purportedly was his mother's favorite, and was sheltered. As a small child he worked on the family farm, and as a teenager he worked as an agricultural day laborer. In the late 1880s the Woodsons moved to Fayette County, West Virginia, where his father worked in railroad construction, and where he himself found work as a coal miner. In 1895, at the age of twenty, he enrolled in Frederick Douglass High School where, possibly because he was an older student and felt the need to catch up, Woodson completed four years of course work in two years and graduated in 1897. Desiring additional education, Woodson enrolled in Berea College in Kentucky, which had been founded by abolitionists in the 1850s for the education of exslaves. Although he briefly attended Lincoln University in Pennsylvania, Woodson graduated from Berea in 1903, just a year before Kentucky passed the "Day Law," prohibiting interracial education. After college, Woodson taught at Frederick Douglass High School in West Virginia. Believing in the uplifting power of education, and desiring the opportunity to travel to another country to observe and experience the culture firsthand, he decided to accept a teaching post in the Philippines, teaching at all grade levels, and remained there from 1903 to 1907.

Woodson's world view and ideas about how education could transform society, improve race relations, and benefit the lower classes, were shaped by his experiences as a college student and as a teacher. Woodson took correspondence courses through the University of Chicago because he was determined to obtain additional education. He was enrolled at the University of Chicago in 1907 as a full-time student and earned a bachelor's degree, and a master's degree in European history, submitting a thesis on French diplomatic policy toward Germany in the eighteenth century. Woodson then attended Harvard University on scholarships, matriculating in 1909 and studying with Edward Channing, Albert Bushnell Hart, and Frederick Jackson Turner. In 1912 Woodson earned his Ph.D. in history, completing a dissertation on the events leading to the creation of the state of West Virginia after the Civil War broke out. Unfortunately, he never published the dissertation. He taught at the Armstrong and Dunbar/M Street high schools in Washington from 1909 to 1919, and then moved on to Howard University, where he served as dean of arts and sciences, professor of history, and head of the graduate program in history in 1919–1920. From 1920 to 1922 he taught at the West Virginia Collegiate Institute. In 1922 he returned to Washington to direct the Association for the Study of Negro Life and History full time.

Woodson began the work that sustained him for the rest of his career, and for which he is best known, when he founded the association in Chicago in the summer of 1915. Woodson had always been interested in African-American history and believed that education in the subject at all levels of the curriculum could inculcate racial pride and foster better race relations. Under the auspices of the association, Woodson founded the *Journal of Negro History*, which began publication in 1915, and established Associated Publishers in 1921, to publish works in black history. He launched the annual celebration of Negro History Week in February 1926, and had achieved a distinguished publishing career as a scholar of African-American history by 1937, when he began publishing the *Negro History Bulletin*.

The *Journal of Negro History*, which Woodson edited until his death, served as the centerpiece of his research program, not only providing black scholars with a medium in which to publish their research but also serving as an outlet for the publication of articles written by white scholars, when their interpretations of such subjects as slavery and black culture differed from mainstream historians. Woodson formulated an editorial policy that was inclusive. Topically, the *Journal* provided coverage in various aspects of the black experience: slavery, the slave trade, black culture, the family, religion, and antislavery and abolitionism, and included biographical articles on prominent African Americans. Chronologically, articles covered the sixteenth through the twentieth centuries. Scholars, as well as interested amateurs, published important historical articles in the *Journal*, and Woodson kept a balance between professional and nonspecialist contributors.

Woodson began celebration of Negro History Week to increase awareness of and interest in black history among both blacks and whites. He chose the second week of February to commemorate the birthdays of Frederick Douglass and Abraham Lincoln. Each year he sent promotional brochures and pamphlets to state boards of education, elementary and secondary schools, colleges, women's clubs, black newspapers and periodicals, and white scholarly journals suggesting ways to celebrate. The association also produced bibliographies, photographs, books, pamphlets, and other promotional literature to assist the black community in the commemoration. Negro History Week celebrations often included parades of costumed characters depicting the lives of famous blacks, breakfasts, banquets, lectures, poetry readings, speeches, exhibits, and other special presentations. During Woodson's lifetime, the celebration reached every state and several foreign countries.

Among the major objectives of Woodson's research and the programs he sponsored through the Association for the Study of Afro-American Life and History (the name was changed in the 1970s to reflect the changing times) was to counteract the racism promoted in works published by white scholars. With several young black assistants—Rayford W. Logan, Charles H. Wesley, Lorenzo J. Greene, and A. A. Taylor—Woodson pioneered in writing the social history of black Americans, using new sources and methods, such as census data, slave testimony, and oral history. These scholars moved away from interpreting blacks solely as victims of white oppression and racism toward a view of them as major actors in American history. Recognizing Woodson's major achievements, the NAACP presented him its highest honor, the Spingarn Medal, in June 1926. At the award ceremony, John Haynes Holmes, the minister and interracial activist, cited Woodson's tireless labors to promote the truth about Negro history.

During the 1920s Woodson funded the research and outreach programs of the association with substantial grants from white foundations such as the Carnegie Foundation, the General Education Board, and the Laura Spellman Rockefeller Foundation. Wealthy whites, such as Julius Rosenwald, also made contributions. White philanthropists cut Woodson's funding in the early 1930s, however, after he refused to affiliate the association with a black college. During and after the depression, Woodson depended on the black community for his sole source of support.

Woodson began his career as a publishing scholar in the field of African-American history in 1915 with the publication of *The Education of the Negro Prior to 1861*. By 1947, when the ninth edition of his textbook *The Negro in Our History* appeared, Woodson had published four monographs, five textbooks, five edited collections of source materials, and thirteen articles, as well as five collaborative sociological studies. Covering a wide range of topics, he relied on an interdisciplinary method, combining anthropology, archaeology, sociology, and history.

Among the first scholars to investigate slavery from the slaves' point of view, Woodson studied it comparatively as institutions in the United States and Latin America. His work prefigured the concerns of later scholars of slavery by several decades, as he examined slaves' resistance to bondage, the internal slave trade and the breakup of slave families, miscegenation, and blacks' achievements despite the adversity of slavery.

Woodson focused mainly on slavery in the antebellum period, examining the relationships between owners and slaves and the impact of slavery upon the organization of land, labor, agriculture, industry, education, religion, politics, and culture. Woodson also noted the African cultural influences on African-American culture. In *The Negro Wage Earner* (1930) and *The Negro Professional Man and the Community* (1934) Woodson described class and occupational stratification within the black community. Using a sample of 25,000 doctors, dentists, nurses, lawyers, writers, and journalists, he examined income, education, family background, marital status, religious affiliation, club and professional memberships, and the literary tastes of black professionals. He hoped that his work on Africa would "invite attention to the vastness of Africa and the complex problems of conflicting cultures."

Woodson also pioneered in the study of black religious history. A Baptist who attended church regularly, he was drawn to an examination of black religion because the church functioned as an educational, political, and social institution in the black community and served as the foundation for the rise of an independent black culture. Black churches, he noted, established kindergartens, women's clubs, training schools, and burial and fraternal societies, from which independent black businesses developed. As meeting places for kin and neighbors, black churches strengthened the political and economic base of the black community and promoted racial solidarity. Woodson believed that the "impetus for the uplift of the race must come from its ministry," and he predicted that black ministers would have a central role in the modern civil rights movement.

Woodson never married or had children, and he died at his Washington home; he had directed the association until his death. For thirty-five years he had dedicated his life to the exploration and study of the African-American past. Woodson made an immeasurable and enduring contribution to the advancement of black history through his own scholarship and the programs he launched through the Association for the Study of Negro Life and History.

• Two small collections of Woodson's papers exist at the Library of Congress Manuscript Division and the Moorland Spingarn Research Center at Howard University. Much archival material can be found in the papers of Woodson's contemporaries and in the records of organizations of which he was a member. Among Woodson's major works are *The Education of the Negro Prior to 1861* (1915), *A Century of Negro Migration* (1918), *A History of the Negro Church* (1921), *The Negro in Our History* (1922), *The Mis-Education of the Negro* (1933), and *The African Background Outlined* (1936). The only full biography of Woodson is Jacqueline Goggin, *Carter G. Woodson: A Life in Black History* (1993), although August Meier and Elliott Rudwick devote a chapter to Woodson in *Black History and the Historical Profession, 1915–1980* (1986).

JACQUELINE GOGGIN

WOODWARD, Augustus Brevoort (baptized 6 Nov. 1774–12 June 1827), jurist, was born Elias Brevoort Woodward in New York City, the son of John Woodward, a merchant and importer, and Ann Silvester. Early in the American Revolution, John Woodward's Tory landlord seized his shop and merchandise, and he never recovered financially. The family relied on the beneficence of his wife's brother-in-law, Elias Brevoort, who paid Augustus Woodward's tuition to Columbia College. After graduating in 1793, Woodward rejoined his family in Philadelphia, where he worked as a clerk in the Treasury Department. Two years later he moved to Rockbridge County, Virginia, where he taught school and read law; he also struck up a friendship with Thomas Jefferson.

In 1797, by which time he had changed his first name to Augustus, Woodward relocated to the District of Columbia, where he was admitted to the bar. The small size of the district's bar—eleven attorneys in 1802—enabled Woodward to build a lucrative practice. He represented clients in some of the capital's most notable cases, including his unsuccessful defense of the first person to be executed in the district, and his more successful appearance before a congressional committee to represent Oliver Pollock, who sought remuneration for his part in bankrolling the conquest of the Northwest Territory. During this time Woodward authored several political pamphlets espousing home rule for the District of Columbia, and in 1802 he was elected to Washington's first city council.

In 1805 President Jefferson nominated his friend as chief justice of the supreme court of the newly created Michigan Territory. Although the tribunal retained an atmosphere of frontier justice, with the judges often holding court in a local tavern, Woodward exerted his authority to formalize the substantive and procedural law of the territory. He declared that only the English common law, not the laws and customs of France or Canada, carried precedential weight. He employed his fluency in French to educate mostly French-speaking grand jurors on principles of Anglo-American due process. His *Laws of Michigan* (1806) codified the laws of the territory for the first time.

Some of Woodward's most important judicial opinions involved slaves who petitioned the court for freedom. The judge personally abhorred slavery, regarding it as "the greatest of the enormities which have been perpetrated by the human race" (quoted in Woodford, p. 86), but he felt constrained by federal law, which outlawed slavery in the Michigan territory but allowed British and French residents to keep slaves acquired before the American occupation. In the absence of positive law, however, Woodward found ways to enforce his personal views. In a case involving slaves who fled from Canada, for example, he granted their freedom because no treaty required their return.

In addition to his judicial duties, Woodward worked as a civic planner and promoter. Just before his arrival in Michigan the city of Detroit had been razed by fire, and Woodward was assigned the task of supervising its rebuilding. Drawing on discussions with Jefferson and Pierre l'Enfant about scientific urban planning, Woodward designed a modern city, although much of his plan was later abandoned. He invested extensively in property in the Detroit area, and he designed and developed the town of Ypsilanti. He wrote the legislation that established the University of Michigan.

Woodward's federal appointment imposed an additional duty on him. Under the act that created the territory, the territorial legislature was comprised of the governor, secretary, and supreme court judges of the territory. Woodward did not relish his legislative role, discouraged by the factionalism that prevented the governing body from enacting any major initiatives. As the territory grew, American settlers who were accustomed to electing their leaders blanched at the idiosyncratic form of government, and Woodward became a convenient scapegoat. Three times he lost elections for territorial delegate to Congress. Lawyers who coveted his position criticized his judicial abilities. In September 1823, after the judge staggered into his courtroom under the influence of ether, brandy, opium, and mercury prescribed for his typhoid fever, his opponents accused him of public drunkenness and judicial misconduct. Five months later President James Monroe declined to renew his appointment.

In August 1824, at the behest of Woodward's friends and in recognition of the judge's nineteen years of federal service, Monroe appointed Woodward to a vacancy on the recently established superior court for the middle district of the Florida Territory, seated in Tallahassee. With all of Florida's major commercial and population centers situated in other districts, Woodward found himself with little trial court business to conduct. But the act that created the Middle District had also authorized the fledgling territory's first appellate tribunal, and Woodward busied himself organizing the territorial court of appeals, comprised of the three superior court judges sitting *en banc*. The court held its first session in January 1825, satisfying territorial litigants who had decried the lack of appellate relief from adverse judgments in the superior courts.

Because his court was seated in the territory's capital, Woodward had jurisdiction over suits defining the powers of government. He found an ally in the territorial governor, William P. DuVal, and he issued rulings in important cases that enhanced DuVal's power. In one case, he ruled that to override the governor's veto required the vote of two-thirds of the Legislative Council's entire membership of thirteen, not simply two-thirds of those members present.

The most important cases considered by Woodward required him to resolve the conflicting claims of property-holders under the federal Preemption Act. The act gave settlers on public lands in Florida prior to 1825 the right to purchase those lands at favorable prices. Woodward typically ruled in favor of smaller landowners, claiming preemptive rights over the claims of large grant-holders. This tendency drew the ire of speculators, planters, and federal land commissioners, who accused the judge of ignoring evidence and granting claims for tracts smaller than Congress had authorized. Small farmers and land-holders, on the other hand, appreciated Woodward's willingness to protect the property rights of ordinary citizens.

By 1826 Woodward's health had deteriorated to the point that he needed assistance from his fellow judges to hold court. He died in Tallahassee, a lifelong bachelor. His career had seen its share of political controversy and political conflict, but he also had been instrumental in the establishment and operation of trial and appellate tribunals in two distinct territories. His judicial decisions touched on some of the leading social, political, and economic issues facing the nation. In his capacity as territorial judge, Woodward made lasting contributions to the development of territorial government in the United States.

• Woodward's papers are housed in the Burton Historical Collection of the Detroit Public Library. Clarence E. Carter, ed., *The Territorial Papers of the United States*, vols. 10, 11, and 23, is an invaluable source for official correspondence related to Woodward's duties as judge in Michigan and Florida. His judicial opinions are reprinted in William Wirt Blume, *Transactions of the Supreme Court of the Territory of Michigan, 1805–1836* (6 vols., 1935–1940). As a practicing attorney he circulated briefs to encourage public support for his clients; see especially *A Representation of the Case of Oliver Pollock* (1803). See also his political writings, such as *Considerations on the Government of the Territory of Columbia* (1802).

The standard biography of Woodward is Frank B. Woodford, Jr., *Mr. Jefferson's Disciple: A Life of Justice Woodward* (1953). Also useful are William L. Jenks, "Augustus Elias Brevoort Woodward," *Michigan History Magazine* 9 (1925): 515–46, and Timothy Frederick Sherer, "Judge Woodward and the Territorial Supreme Court," *Detroit in Perspective* 4 (1979): 1–15. On the Supreme Court of the Territory of Michigan, see William Wirt Blume, "Criminal Procedure on the American Frontier: A Study of the Statutes and Court Records of Michigan Territory, 1805–1825," *Michigan Law Review* 57 (1958): 195–256; and Blume, "Chancery Practice on the American Frontier: A Study of the Records of the Supreme Court of Michigan Territory, 1805–1836," *Michigan Law Review* 59 (1960): 49–96. On the territorial courts in Florida, see Walter W. Manley et al., *The Supreme Court of Florida and Its Predecessor Courts, 1821–1917* (1997).

ERIC W. RISE

WOODWARD, Calvin Milton (25 Aug. 1837–12 Jan. 1914), educational reformer, was born in Fitchburg, Massachusetts, the son of Isaac Burnapp Woodward and Eliza Wetherbee. His father, a Unitarian farmer and bricklayer, led a movement in 1845 to reform Fitchburg common schools by introducing graded schools and age grouping and by providing funds for teacher education. Calvin attended Fitchburg common schools and benefited directly from his father's educational activism. After high school Calvin attended Harvard College, during which time he also taught in various Massachusetts schools. He graduated in 1860 as a member of Harvard's "War Class," which would fight for the Union cause in the Civil War.

From 1862 to 1863 Woodward served as a captain in the Forty-eighth Massachusetts Volunteers, a special nine-month volunteer enlistment. His regiment traveled to Baton Rouge, Louisiana, and took part in the campaign to regain control of the Mississippi. Upon his return to Massachusetts in 1863, he married Fanny Stone Balch, sister of his best friend and fellow soldier, Eben Stone. They had three children. Woodward spent the rest of the war working as a principal and mathematics teacher at Brown's Classical High School in Newburyport, Massachusetts.

In 1865 Woodward and his family moved to St. Louis, Missouri, where he became the vice principal and a teacher of mathematics at the new academy at Washington University. Founder William Greenleaf Eliot envisioned a great western university that could adequately compete with the eastern colleges' classical curriculum. By recruiting graduates of the best eastern colleges as faculty members, Eliot managed to put his new institution on the academic map. He devised a faculty and institutional structure to achieve a transition from elementary and secondary schooling to college level. He created three departments—the collegiate, the practical (also called the O'Fallon Polytechnic Institute), and the academic—to meet the needs of students in the booming West for college-level, work-related, and secondary studies. These three departments evolved over the years into the classical curriculum, an engineering and technology program, and the elite Smith Academy.

Studies in the practical department included pure and applied math, science, literature, language, and drawing. Classes were held in the evenings for those who were employed. When Eliot and local schoolmen decided that the St. Louis Public Schools should run the O'Fallon Polytechnic Institute at the secondary level, they persuaded Woodward to direct this school in transition in addition to his role as vice principal of the academy. During this transfer, Woodward disagreed with the superintendent of public schools and another national education reform leader, William Torrey Harris, on resources for the school and its priority within the school system, prompting Woodward to resign from the directorship.

With his focus back on the university and the academy, Woodward became so successful in his teaching that the university promoted him to professor of geometry in 1869 and, a year later, dean of the polytechnic school, with an endowed chair of mathematics and applied mechanics. Woodward personally assisted James Eads in design and construction of the Eads Bridge, completed in 1874, and received a doctorate from Washington University for his thesis on the building of this unique structure. Woodward's career at Washington University continued to flourish along with the growth of St. Louis (which expanded from 78,000 in 1850 to 458,000 in 1890) and the institution. He also became dean of the engineering and architecture school, where he served from 1901 until his retirement in 1910.

Woodward also became a leading spokesman for an educational program and philosophy known as the Manual Training Movement. After his unsatisfying experience with Harris and the O'Fallon Polytechnic Institute, he originated and directed the St. Louis Manual Training School, which opened in 1880 at Washington University. Urban students' lack of knowledge for elementary use of tools appalled Woodward, who had grown up on a farm learning about tools as part of everyday life. After observing that students could not make basic models, he enlisted the aid of Noah Dean, a sailor, carpenter, mechanic, and war veteran, to open the school workshop to students. Woodward discovered that students who worked with their hands could conceptualize principles of physics and mechanics. Victor Della Vos of the Moscow Institute had introduced the Russian method of tool instruction at the Philadelphia Exposition of 1876.

Woodward and John Runkle of the Massachusetts Institute of Technology took these ideas as the basis for a new pedagogy of teaching engineering and science. Woodward argued that the classical tradition in American education had poisoned people against the whole idea of manual labor. He argued that *to know* and *to do* were equally valuable. His polytechnic students studied both theory and practice because he believed that students who were not trained to do anything were miseducated. Two other innovations he sponsored were laboratory work in which students used a hands-on approach in chemistry and fieldwork in which the city itself became a laboratory of economic and building activities. Students visited local steel works, lead mines, and factories. Graduates of Woodward's St. Louis Manual Training School and the university's polytechnic school went on to become engineers, doctors, architects, and other professionals, lending credence to Woodward's view that manual training developed both the hand and the intellect.

Woodward also pursued his own scholarship and community service. He served on the Board of Education for St. Louis schools from 1877 to 1879 and from 1897 to 1899 and as board president in 1899 and 1903–1904. Here again he crossed paths with Harris, a staunch defender of the classical curriculum. Harris and Woodward were the leading voices in national debates on manual training versus classical studies. Harris argued that manual training was too narrowly vocational and limited students' options. Although the manual training movement swept urban public schools in this country and England, Harris resisted it in St. Louis. Only after Harris left to become U.S. commissioner of education was Woodward able, as a school board member and president, to get manual training into the local public school system. On the school board, Woodward supported other educational innovations such as Susan Blow's initiatives to establish and expand the kindergarten movement in St. Louis schools. Woodward and Blow shared an interest in Friedrich Froebel's ideas on primary students' work with their hands. The American Association for the Advancement of Science, the St. Louis Academy of Science, the Board of Curators of the University of Missouri, and the North Central Association of Schools and Colleges provided forums for other community and professional service during Woodward's later career.

A cause for which Woodward is less well known was his advocacy of education for African-American males. A great turn-of-the-century debate involved Booker T. Washington and W. E. B. Du Bois, who disagreed about the education of African Americans. O. M. Wood, principal of L'Ouverture schools in St. Louis, applied Woodward's ideas for manual training to the education of his black students, combining skill development along with academic studies and reading clubs for boys and girls. In the debate between Washington and Du Bois over professional or industrial education for blacks, Woodward argued that both intellectual and manual training were needed, for all students. Woodward and his ardent supporter, industrialist Samuel Cupples, also led the St. Louis School Board to hire black teachers and administrators for "colored" schools. On the day of his death in St. Louis, Woodward was raising money for manual training scholarships for black youth.

• Many of Woodward's papers, including his thesis and several speeches, are in the Olin Library at Washington University in St. Louis, Mo. Woodward's many articles and publications include *A History of the St. Louis Bridge* (1881); *The Manual Training School* (1887); *Manual Training in Education* (1890); *What Shall We Do with Our Boys?* (1898); *Rational and Applied Mechanics* (1912); "At What Age Do Pupils Withdraw from the Public Schools," in *Report of the Commissioner of Education*, vol. 1 (1894–1895); and "Manual and Industrial Education in the U.S.," in *Report of the Commissioner of Education*, vol. 1 (1903). Useful information regarding Woodward's career is available in William Hyde and H. L. Conard, *Encyclopedia of the History of St. Louis*, vol. 4 (1899), and C. P. Coates, *History of the Manual Training School of Washington University* (1923). For his place in the history of manual education in the United States, see Charles M. Dye, "Calvin Milton Woodward: A Leader of the Manual Training Movement in American Education" (Ph.D. diss., Washington Univ., 1971), and Donald Yoder, "Calvin's Crusade: A Reassessment of Calvin Milton Woodward's School and Educational Ideas for School Reform in the United States" (Ph.D. diss., Univ. of Hawaii, 1994). An obituary is in the *St. Louis Post-Dispatch*, 12 Jan. 1914.

KATHLEEN S. BROWN

WOODWARD, Ellen Sullivan (11 July 1887–23 Sept. 1971), federal official, was born in Oxford, Mississippi, to William Van Amberg Sullivan, an attorney, and Nancy Murray. Her mother died from tuberculosis when Ellen was seven years old. She attended the Oxford Graded School and later Washington College, a private school in Washington, D.C., while her father served in the House of Representatives from Mississippi (1897–1898) and briefly as a U.S. senator (1898–1901). In 1901–1902 she attended Sans Souci, a female seminary in Greenville, South Carolina; her formal education ended at the age of fifteen. She returned to live in Oxford with her family until her marriage in 1906 to Albert Young Woodward, an attorney from Louisville, Mississippi. They made their home in Louisville and had one son.

As a young matron, Ellen Woodward participated in community activities, served actively in her Methodist church, and became a district and state leader in the Mississippi Federation of Women's Clubs. She managed her husband's successful campaign for election as a chancery judge and to the Mississippi House of Representatives. After his sudden death from a heart attack in 1925, she easily won the seat in a special election, becoming the second woman to serve in Mississippi's lower house. Duties on legislative committees on libraries, higher education, and eleemosynary institutions provided experiences in areas in which she would later work for women and children. She completed the term and declined to run for reelection in 1927.

Woodward became director of the women's program of the Mississippi State Board of Development (MSBD), a quasi-public agency created to boost the economic growth of the state. Her duties expanded when she became director later in 1927 of the Civil Welfare and Community Development arm of the MSBD and in 1929 when she became the MSBD executive director. From that office she directed a number of activities to accelerate Mississippi's industrial and commercial growth while continuing to work with clubwomen in projects such as the national Better Homes in America program, a voluntary program initiated under Secretary of Commerce Herbert Hoover to stimulate the renovation of homes to improve standards of living.

At the MSBD, Woodward made important contacts with prominent out-of-state public administrators who surveyed social and fiscal conditions in Mississippi for a Brookings Institution study undertaken in 1930 by a legislative-mandated research commission that appointed Woodward its executive secretary. In 1932, when federal funds became available to states for relief purposes, she became a member of Mississippi's first Board of Public Welfare. She directed the women's program in Mississippi under Herbert Hoover's President's Emergency Committee on Employment and his President's Organization for Unemployment Relief. Thus she gained experience in meeting the needs of the unemployed although funds were modest and programs restrained.

Woodward attended the 1928 Democratic convention as a delegate and in 1932 became Mississippi's Democratic committeewoman, a post she left in 1934 because she was appointed to federal office. Her energetic campaign in Mississippi for Franklin D. Roosevelt in 1932 brought her to the attention of Democrats who would fill positions in the new administration after Roosevelt's victory. In August 1933, Harry Hopkins, head of the new Federal Emergency Relief Administration (FERA), prompted by colleagues who had known Woodward's work in Mississippi, named her director of the new FERA Women's Division. At the height of the Civil Works Administration, which supplanted the FERA in 1933–1934, Woodward had 375,000 needy unemployed women at work on a variety of work relief programs despite the resistance of many male state directors to endorse work programs for women.

In 1935 Woodward became an assistant administrator of the new Works Progress Administration (WPA) and oversaw the work of 450,000 women on work relief at the zenith of the Women's and Professional Projects (WPP) division. Women worked on projects in sewing, gardening and canning, school lunchrooms, nursing, housekeeping, household training, library work, public health, museum work, research, and in other fields. All the WPP forty-eight state directors and seven regional supervisors were women. When Woodward became administrator as well of a group of WPA cultural projects known as Federal One that included the Four Arts projects (music, art, the theater, and writing), her division became responsible for the employment of about 750,000 persons.

When the Federal Theatre and Writers' Projects came under congressional scrutiny in 1938, Woodward defended them vigorously, but she was unable to respond satisfactorily to intemperate charges of the House Un-American Activities Committee that the projects were frivolous and disseminated communist propaganda. In December 1938 both Hopkins and Woodward left the WPA, and the WPP passed to Florence Kerr's direction.

In 1938 President Roosevelt named Woodward to fill a position on the Social Security Board left vacant at the resignation of Mary W. Dewson. Woodward promoted economic security and welfare for heretofore unprotected women and children. She spoke out for the extension of Social Security to domestic workers and farmers, for an end to unemployment insurance features that penalized women, and for Social Security personnel employment policies favorable to women. During World War II, she was prominent among Democratic women who advocated that more women be given policy-making positions in postwar planning. She herself became an adviser to the U.S. delegations at successive conferences of the United Nations Relief and Rehabilitation Administration between 1943 and 1946.

When the Social Security Board was abolished in 1946, Woodward became director of the Office of Inter-Agency and International Relations of the Federal Security Agency (FSA). Her continued advocacy of programs for women's and children's welfare included lobbying at the United Nations for an international children's fund. Her FSA office became a clearinghouse for the foreign exchange of United Nations fellows in social welfare and of exchange teachers between the United States and Great Britain. Woodward's office was subsumed under the new Department of Health, Education, and Welfare early in 1953. On 31 December 1953 she retired at age sixty-six.

Woodward remained active in women's organizations, the Democratic party, and her private charities until the early 1960s when arteriosclerosis confined her to her Washington apartment where she died. Her contemporaries and later historians have stressed the impact of her energetic work on behalf of women's social welfare and economic security during the Democratic administrations from 1933 to 1953.

• There are extensive Woodward papers in the Mississippi Department of Archives and History and a smaller collection in the Schlesinger Library, Radcliffe College. Other useful manuscripts are in the Eleanor Roosevelt, Harry Hopkins, and Mary W. Dewson Papers at the Franklin D. Roosevelt Library, Hyde Park, N.Y. Essential to understanding her work are the records of the WPA (RG 69) and the Social Security Administration (RG 47) in the National Archives. Woodward wrote no books, but she published many articles in the 1930s and 1940s in such publications as the *Social Security Bulletin*. *Holland's* published two informal biographical sketches of Woodward (Mar. 1936 and June 1944), and the

Democratic Digest frequently featured her between 1934 and 1946. Woodward is cited frequently in Susan Ware, *Beyond Suffrage: Women in the New Deal* (1981), and is a subject of Elsie L. George, "The Women Appointees of the Roosevelt and Truman Administrations: A Study of Their Impact and Effectiveness" (Ph.D. diss., American Univ. 1972). Martha H. Swain is the author of several articles on Woodward, including "ER and Ellen Woodward: A Partnership for Women's Work Relief and Security," in *Without Precedent: The Life and Career of Eleanor Roosevelt*, ed. Joan Hoff-Wilson and Marjorie Lightman (1984), and "'The Forgotten Woman': Ellen S. Woodward and Women's Relief in the New Deal," *Prologue* 15 (Winter 1983): 201–13. Obituaries appear in the *Washington Evening Post*, 24 Sept. 1971, the Jackson (Miss.) *Clarion-Ledger*, 26 Sept. 1971, and the Winston County (Miss.) *Journal*, 30 Sept. 1971.

MARTHA H. SWAIN

WOODWARD, George (22 June 1863–25 May 1952), political reformer and suburban real estate developer, was born in Wilkes-Barre, Pennsylvania, the son of Stanley Woodward, a judge, and Sarah Butler. Woodward grew up in an important local family whose ancestors had been civic leaders and elected officials since the seventeenth century, including three governors of colonial New England as well as George's paternal grandfather and namesake, who served as chief justice of the Pennsylvania Supreme Court.

Following his education at a local private academy, Woodward attended Yale College, receiving his degree in 1887. He spent a year pursuing postgraduate work at Yale's Sheffield School and then entered the University of Pennsylvania medical school, graduating in 1891. He practiced medicine briefly at New Haven, Connecticut, and then in Philadelphia but did not enjoy these experiences and shifted his attention to a variety of public health issues in the Quaker City, which eventually led to his career as a reformer of the Progressive Era and beyond.

Woodward's decision to settle permanently in Philadelphia stemmed from his marriage in 1894 to Gertrude Houston, the daughter of Henry Howard Houston, a wealthy entrepreneur and the creator of an early planned suburb in the Chestnut Hill section of Philadelphia that was initially called Wissahickon Heights. Gertrude's inherited wealth allowed Woodward to devote his life to political reform and to extending the suburban development in Chestnut Hill, which he renamed St. Martin's in 1906.

Although Woodward had adopted his family's devotion to the Democratic party, he soon became a Republican in Philadelphia, where the power of the city's Republican machine made political success virtually impossible for Democrats. Nevertheless, Woodward and many other well-to-do reformers in the region regarded themselves as "independent Republicans," who held the machine in utter disdain. As a reform-minded or progressive Republican, Woodward fought successfully in 1899 to clean up Philadelphia's polluted water supply. In 1911 he helped to elect the reform candidate, Rudolph Blankenburg, mayor of the city. Meanwhile Woodward became a champion of better housing. As a director and then president of Philadelphia's Octavia Hill Association during the early twentieth century, he supported the organization's impressive work to rehabilitate slum housing and rent it to the working poor at low rates. Woodward and the association also helped to secure the licensing and inspection of Philadelphia tenement houses in 1907.

At the same time Woodward became involved in a number of child welfare issues. In 1904 he organized and financed the Child Labor Association of Pennsylvania, a group that campaigned for the child labor laws that finally cleared the Pennsylvania legislature in 1915. From 1913 to 1927 he was president of the Children's Aid Society, an agency that raised money to buy clothing and food and to provide medical care for the children of impoverished families.

Woodward's growing interest in reform politics led him to run for the Pennsylvania State Senate in 1918. He served in that body for twenty-eight years—seven successive terms—before stepping down in early 1947. Throughout the 1920s he promoted schemes for more honest local government in Pennsylvania, including nonpartisan municipal administration and scientific investigation of legislative issues. In order to force suburbanites who worked in Philadelphia to contribute their fair share of taxes to city coffers, Woodward became the chief sponsor of the Philadelphia wage tax, the first such levy in the nation, enacted in 1938. It was also during the 1930s that he proposed, this time unsuccessfully, a merger of Philadelphia with the four surrounding Pennsylvania counties as a way of eliminating a wasteful duplication of services and of allowing the entire region to find common solutions to numerous problems that did not respect official boundaries.

Like many aging progressives, Woodward had serious misgivings about Franklin Delano Roosevelt and the New Deal. He believed that the New Deal seriously compromised states' rights and that it endangered free enterprise and private initiative. At the same time, Woodward did not underestimate the suffering of the Great Depression, and he contributed several hundred thousand dollars of his family's own money for private relief in Philadelphia. Beginning in 1932 Woodward published his political ideas and criticisms as a periodic leaflet, which he collected and issued in a hardbound volume at the end of each legislative session under the title *Pennsylvania Legislator*, the last appearing in 1945.

Woodward lived with his wife and five children in the Chestnut Hill suburb begun by his father-in-law. Beginning in 1904 and continuing into the mid-1930s, Woodward added approximately 180 residences to the 100 or so commissioned by Houston in the 1880s and 1890s. Like Houston, Woodward continued the family's practice of renting rather than selling these houses in order to control who moved into the development and to make sure that the properties were well tended. He also patronized the church, the cricket club, the local private schools, and the other institutions created by Houston or his heirs as part of their planned community in Chestnut Hill.

Woodward's participation in the development of Chestnut Hill was connected to his overall interest in housing and municipal well-being in general. He shared with many other progressives the idea that the city was a complex entity with many sections or organs, each of which contributed a unique aspect to the whole. Thus he saw no contradiction between providing expensive, architect-designed housing for the more prosperous residents of Chestnut Hill while supporting more basic accommodations for the working poor through the Octavia Hill Association.

Some of Woodward's contemporaries found him a bit eccentric. He wore golf knickers and knee stockings nearly everywhere, prompting a local journalist to describe Woodward as the "oldest senator in short pants." He also preferred to read by a kerosene lamp in his library at home and refused to own a gasoline-powered automobile, maintaining two aging electric cars up to the time of his death at his home in Chestnut Hill.

Woodward's career as a political reformer provides rich insights into the Progressive Era as well as into Pennsylvania (and Philadelphia) politics for several decades thereafter. But a growing interest in suburbs and their history makes Woodward's role as the succeeding developer of his family's planned suburb, Wissahickon Heights/St. Martin's, every bit as important as his many years in politics.

• Although correspondence and other manuscripts generated by Woodward apparently have not survived, he authored numerous publications. The most important of these is his autobiography, *Memoirs of a Mediocre Man* (1935). Woodward compiled two volumes of letters, *Family Letters and Proletarian Essays* (1937) and *Family Letters* (1946). There are also seven volumes of his *Pennsylvania Legislator* (1932–1945). All of these works were privately printed by Woodward himself. However, he also contributed a number of articles to important periodicals during the first decades of the twentieth century. The most complete biography of Woodward is in David R. Contosta, *A Philadelphia Family: The Houstons and Woodwards of Chestnut Hill* (1988), pp. 37–121 (included are photographs of Woodward and his suburban development and a bibliography of writings by and about Woodward). Also relevant to Woodward's life and work in the local community is Contosta, *Suburb in the City: Chestnut Hill, Philadelphia, 1850–1940* (1992), pp. 78–117. On Woodward's public career see Contosta, "George Woodward, Philadelphia Progressive," *Pennsylvania Magazine of History and Biography* 111 (July 1987): 341–70. Specific studies of Woodward's suburban developments in Chestnut Hill include Cynthia Ann McLeod, "Arts and Crafts Architecture in Suburban Philadelphia Sponsored by Dr. George Woodward" (master's thesis, Univ. of Virginia, 1979), and Mary Corbin Sies, "American Country House Architecture in Context: The Suburban Ideal of Living in the East and Midwest, 1877–1917" (Ph.D. diss., Univ. of Michigan, 1987), pp. 272–353.

David R. Contosta

WOODWARD, Henry (1646?–1686?), medical doctor and Indian agent, was perhaps from England or from Barbados, the origin of many Carolina settlers. His forbears and social background are unknown. The quality of his writing and the fact that he was addressed as "doctor" indicate a fair degree of education. Woodward was a young man when he went to Carolina. He had a talent for manipulating the tricky and multilingual relations that characterized this volatile region. His talent included the capacity to charm others and to deceive them. He became the deputy of the Carolina lords proprietors who, in their royal charter of 1663, held title to territory that overlapped Florida land claimed by the Spanish and inhabited by native groups wary of both sets of Europeans. Woodward accompanied Captain Robert Sandford on a 1666 expedition to explore the proprietors' new province and to find natives who would ally with them against the Spanish. Woodward stayed with the Guale people in Santa Elena (near Port Royal) in exchange for the cacique's nephew, whom Sandford took as an envoy to the English. The exchange of men in 1666 involved a formal ceremony of adoption for Woodward, who was given a field of corn as well as the cacique's niece to attend him. This arrangement was almost certainly a form of marriage, though it is not known if the couple had any children. Woodward was also delegated by Sandford to act as the sole "tenant-at-will" of the Carolina proprietors—the lone English possessor of the province.

Woodward used his time in Santa Elena to learn native languages and customs. Within two years, however, he was in St. Augustine, supposedly kidnapped by the Spanish, though it was also rumored that he had willingly gone to Florida and converted to Catholicism. When buccaneer Robert Searle raided St. Augustine in 1668, Woodward sailed with him and served as ship's surgeon on a privateer before being shipwrecked in Nevis. There, in 1668 or 1669, he married a woman known only as Margaret. They had no children. Woodward took passage back to Carolina with the colony's fleet in 1669. Margaret joined him by 1677, the year the couple claimed land in Carolina. When the Carolina colony came close to blows with the Spanish in 1670, Woodward acted as interpreter to the American Indians around Charles Town to gain their support. He also served in the governor's council.

At this point Woodward was both officially engaged as Indian agent for the proprietors and occupied with double-dealing. In July 1670 he took a daring journey northwest toward the Upper Creek territory and found what he thought might be Cofitachiqui, the splendid native town and province reported by Hernando de Soto in the previous century. Woodward wanted to go to England to report, privately, to the proprietors about Cofitachiqui. Governor Sir John Yeamans refused, because Woodward was "the only Person by whose meanes wee hold a faire and peacable Correspondence with the Natives" (*Collections of the South Carolina Historical Society*). Yeamans also hoped to coax information out of Woodward. In the spring of 1671 the proprietors rewarded Woodward with £100 for his explorations and overall value to the province.

He then undertook two secret missions. He was personal informant for proprietor Anthony Ashley Cooper (later the first earl of Shaftesbury), to whom he sent coded information about any gold or silver. At the same time, Woodward led a covert expedition into Virginia for Governor Yeamans to scout out promising trade with the natives.

Woodward's most significant achievement came in 1674, when he obtained a treaty with the Westo Indians. He had been ordered by Cooper to seek alliance with either the Westo or the Cusabo with the intention of using one against the other. In October ten Westo met Woodward at the head of the Ashley River and took him to their central town. There he negotiated a treaty of trade and alliance that accomplished several things for the struggling English colony. The treaty permitted English territorial expansion; it provided military stability that allowed economic development, especially for agriculture and ranching; and above all, it opened a trade with the Indians that provided opportunity for investment and accumulation of capital. Woodward received one-fifth of the trade's profits.

The treaty revealed, however, the instrumental view the English had of the natives. The Westo trade included traffic in Indian slaves, who were often obtained by intertribal warfare. Conflict among the natives mounted, especially once a proprietary treaty with the competing Cusabo was in place in 1677. Despite the proprietors' attempts to control the trade, Carolina's settlers encouraged Indian warfare. The situation degenerated into the 1680 Westo War, which ended the proprietary control over Indian policy, decimated the Westo people, and opened a violent spiral of war and trade in the region that continued through the American Revolution. Woodward was fined and censured by the proprietors for his participation in the Westo War.

Woodward had in the meantime concerned himself with private affairs. His wife Margaret evidently died, and in 1681 Woodward married Mary Godfrey Browne, daughter of John Godfrey, a member of Carolina's gentry. They had two sons and a daughter. Throughout the 1670s and 1680s Woodward acquired considerable land and seven African slaves, both of which were bases for permanent wealth in the plantation economy emerging along Carolina's coastline.

Woodward continued to play a role in frontier affairs. In 1682 he received an unprecedented commission to find a passage over the Appalachian Mountains. Three years later his peregrinations brought him near enough to Henry Lord Cardross's Scottish colony near Port Royal to be arrested for trespass. Woodward extricated himself and forged ahead to the Lower Creek towns on the Chattahoochee River, where he tried to undermine Spanish influence. The Creek welcomed English overtures, leading to open Anglo-Spanish conflict and a Spanish manhunt for Woodward. At one point in 1685, shortly before he fled an armed force, Woodward wrote a coolly defiant note in Spanish: "I am very sorry that I came with so small a following that I cannot await your arrival. . . . *Vale*" (Bolton and Ross, *Debatable Land*). By 1686, however, Woodward was ill. He traveled by litter back to Charles Town, accompanied by 150 Creek, who carried the furs and deerskins that were the basis of Anglo-Indian trade and Anglo-Indian tensions. Woodward died by the time his father-in-law's will was written in March 1690.

• Records relating to Woodward are in the Shaftesbury Papers and the State Papers at the British Public Record Office, Kew. Some Spanish accounts of his activities are in the Archivo General de Indias, Seville. The South Carolina Historical Society, Charleston, and the South Carolina State Archives, Columbia, contain records of Woodward's land, family, and political career. Many of the English records have been published in the *Collections of the South Carolina Historical Society*, vol. 5 (1897), and Alexander S. Salley, Jr., ed., *Records in the British Public Record Office Relating to South Carolina, 1663–1710* (1928). Secondary discussions of Woodward include Herbert E. Bolton and Mary Ross, *The Debatable Land: A Sketch of the Anglo-Spanish Contest for the Georgia Country* (1968), and Verner W. Crane, *The Southern Frontier, 1670–1732* (1956).

JOYCE E. CHAPLIN

WOODWARD, Joseph Janvier (30 Oct. 1833–17 Aug. 1884), U.S. Army medical officer, was born in Philadelphia, Pennsylvania, the son of Joseph Janvier Woodward and Elizabeth Graham Cox. He entered the University of Pennsylvania in 1850 and was granted an M.D. degree in 1853. He then practiced medicine in Philadelphia until 1861. During this early period of his career he also taught surgery at the University of Pennsylvania, gave private lessons in the uses of the microscope in pathology, and published the first of a number of papers on cancer.

Woodward entered the Union army in June 1861 as a contract surgeon. He ranked first among those taking the entrance examination for the Medical Department with him. He was commissioned as a first lieutenant in August 1861 and assigned to serve as regimental surgeon with an artillery unit. By this point he was married; although he married twice, the dates of the marriages are not known, nor is the name of his first wife, although this marriage produced at least one child. His second wife was Blanche Wendell.

Woodward served with the Army of the Potomac until May 1862 and took part in the first battle of Bull Run (First Manassas). Thereafter he was assigned to serve in the surgeon general's office in Washington, D.C. He soon earned the reputation of being an accomplished physician and a promising scientist, but a "terrible fellow in a controversy."

While serving in Washington, Woodward planned and supervised the construction of several military hospitals before being assigned to the newly created Army Medical Museum. There he joined other medical officers in collecting material that was used for the exhaustive *Medical and Surgical History of the War of the Rebellion*, which included a large volume that he edited, dealing with disease and its management in the Union army; the first part of Woodward's volume was published in 1870, and the second in 1879. In 1866 he was promoted to captain. His work led to an article, "On Photomicrography with the Highest Powers, as Practiced in the Army Medical Museum" (*American Journal of Science and Arts* 92 [Sept. 1866]: 189–95), the first of his many papers on this and related topics. Woodward became an internationally known authority in the new field of photomicrography and was elected to many scientific societies, including the Royal Microscopical Society of London, the National Academy of Sciences, the Association for the Advancement of Science, and the Washington Philosophic Society. He was promoted to major in 1876.

Woodward was able to read medical literature in many languages, and his detailed comments on the history of the treatment of the diseases that afflicted the Union army reflected the depth of his study in the history of medicine since the days of the Greeks. However, he ridiculed the notion that minute living organisms could cause disease, and this stance, just as the germ theory was gaining support in Europe, eventually jeopardized his reputation as a medical scientist. In "Typho-malaria Fever: Is It a Special Type of Fever?" (*Transactions of the International Medical Congress of Philadelphia* [1876], pp. 305–40), he insisted on the existence of a hybrid disease he named typho-malarial fever. This embroiled him in bitter controversy, and his concept of a disease that combined the symptoms of typhoid fever and malaria was eventually abandoned, despite early support from respected physicians.

In the spring of 1880 Woodward's health began to fail, leading him to take three months off from his duties to travel in Europe to recover from overwork; he returned to the United States in the fall of 1880. In 1881 he was elected president of the American Medical Association, the first military physician to receive this honor. In July, when barely recovered from serious injury resulting from a fall from his horse, he was called to the bedside of the dying president James A. Garfield. The treatment by Woodward and other physicians, which included probing the wound made by the assassin's bullet with unsterile instruments, inspired highly publicized controversy. The physicians were blamed not only for failing to heal the president but for actually contributing to his demise after more than two months of agony.

The emotional strain that resulted from Woodward's attendance on Garfield, when the physician was in a weakened condition both physically and mentally, led to a further deterioration in Woodward's health. In early 1882 an army medical examination revealed that he was "suffering from a severe form of nervous dyspepsia, with great prostration and mental depression," and he was again given permission to travel abroad for his health. More than two years of leave, both in Europe and in the United States, brought about little improvement in his mental status. Army records attribute Woodward's death in WaWa, Pennsylvania, to "injuries from a fall, received while laboring under aberration of mind incident upon the mental disorder, from which he had been so long suffering."

Woodward was endowed with many talents and an intense, almost frenetic energy but was cursed with fragile emotional health. Although his achievements were many, he was one of a dying breed of physicians who flourished before the age of scientific medicine. The vigor of his attacks on the germ theory, blame for contributing to Garfield's death, and his unstable temperament all played important roles in his life and death.

• A small collection of Woodward's personal papers is in Entry 561 (Personal Papers of Medical Officers), RG 94 (Records of the Adjutant General's Office, 1780s–1917), at the National Archives in Washington, D.C. The range of his interests is indicated by such publications as "On the Use of Aniline in Histological Researches with a Method of Investigating the Histology of the Human Intestine and Remarks on Some of the Points to Be Observed in the Study of the Diseased Intestine in Camp Fevers and Diarrheas," *American Journal of the Medical Sciences* 49 (1865): 106–13; "The Army Medical Museum of Washington," *Lippincott's Magazine of Popular Literature and Sciences* 7 (1871): 233–42; *Outlines of the Chief Camp Diseases of the United States Armies* (1863); *Report to the Surgeon General of the United States Army on Certain Points Connected with the Histology of Minute Bloodvessels* (1870); and *On the Structure of Cancerous Tumors and the Modes in Which Adjacent Parts Are Invaded* (1873). He was also among the signers of "Official Bulletin of the Autopsy on the Body of President Garfield," published in *Medical Record* 20 (1881): 364.

The most comprehensive account of Woodward's life and death by a contemporary is in John Shaw Billings, "Biographical Memoir of Joseph Janvier Woodward," National Academy of Sciences, *Biographical Memoirs* 2 (1886): 297–307. A brief discussion of Woodward's career is in Mary C. Gillett, "A Tale of Two Surgeons," *Medical Heritage* 1 (1983): 404–13, 466. Roberts Bartholow, *The Opinions, Past and Present of J. J. Woodward, in Respect of Typho-malaria and Some Other Subjects* (1878), provides a biased view of the typho-malaria controversy. Obituaries are in *Medical News* 45 (1884): 249–50; *Boston Medical and Surgical Journal* 111 (1884): 237; and *Journal of the American Medical Association* 3 (1884): 279–80.

MARY C. GILLETT

WOODWARD, Robert Burns (10 Apr. 1917–8 July 1979), chemist and educator, was born in Boston, Massachusetts, the only child of Arthur Chester Woodward and Margaret Burns, a native of Glasgow, Scotland, who claimed descent from the poet Robert Burns and named her son after him. His father died in the influenza epidemic of October 1918, when Robert was less than two years old. His mother remarried but was soon abandoned by her second husband, causing her to work long hours to support her son. Although Woodward grew up in straitened circumstances, he was sustained by a devoted mother to whom he was deeply attached. A precocious and lively child, he attended public school in the Boston suburb of Quincy, where he lived. At the age of eight he received a chemistry set, and he carried out elaborate experiments in his basement laboratory. He developed a deep, lifelong interest in mathematics and literature. A nonconformist who disdained school routine and discipline, he was described as "a hellion, . . . whispering in classes, blowing bubble gum, being the last one 'in' after recess, and pulling the little girls' long curls" (quoted in Todd and Cornforth, p. 630). Yet he graduated from high school in 1933 with an outstanding scholastic record and an unhealthy aversion to physical exercise, which he retained for his entire life.

At age sixteen, Woodward entered the Massachusetts Institute of Technology (MIT) with advanced undergraduate standing. The following year, in 1934, he published his first paper, "Precipitation of Barium in the Copper-Tin Group of Qualitative Analysis," with W. J. Hall (*Industrial and Engineering Chemistry, Analytical Edition* 6). At the end of the fall 1934 semester he was advised to withdraw from college. He spent a semester as an employee of the MIT Biology Department. Through the good offices of James Flack Norris, a professor of physical organic chemistry at MIT who recognized the signs of genius in the brash but extraordinarily self-assured youngster, he was permitted to re-enroll in the fall 1935 semester. He received a B.S. in 1936 only after a brief but intensive effort in the gymnasium to fulfill a graduation requirement. He received his Ph.D. in organic chemistry in 1937 at the age of twenty; his dissertation title was "A Synthetic Attack on the Oestrone Problem."

After an unsuccessful summer of teaching chemistry at the University of Illinois, where through his intelligence and impatience he alienated several of the leading organic chemists of the United States, in fall 1937 Woodward began work at Harvard University, where he remained for the rest of his career. He served first as Elmer P. Kohler's assistant under a postdoctoral fellowship (1937–1938), then was elected a Junior Prize Fellow of the Harvard Society of Fellows (1938–1940), which gave him complete freedom to study and to carry out research. He began to work out ingenious and increasingly plausible schemes for the total synthesis of complex natural products, but to bring these schemes to fruition was not possible for one person with no access to student collaborators. Therefore he resigned his fellowship in January 1941 to become instructor in charge of the advanced organic chemistry laboratory, where his enthusiasm soon attracted a large number of students who collaborated with him on research carried out largely outside regular working hours, at night and on Sundays. He became assistant professor in 1944, associate professor in 1946, professor in 1950, Morris Loeb Professor of Chemistry in 1953, and finally Donner Professor of Science in 1960, a position that allowed him to devote all his time to research.

During his long tenure at Harvard, Woodward attracted about 400 junior collaborators, most at the postdoctoral level, from all over the world. He also stimulated and to some extent directed research groups in various industrial companies for which he was a consultant. He had a long and close association with Swiss chemists, and although he did not accept offers to move to the Eidgenössische Technische Hochschule (Federal Institute of Technology, ETH) in Zürich, in 1963 the pharmaceutical firm of Ciba, Ltd. established alongside its Basel headquarters the Woodward Research Institute, where he directed part-time research workers on topics not unconnected with the company's interests but essentially of his own choosing. With his extraordinarily retentive memory, Woodward was able to direct simultaneously and in detail the work of many individuals. At the institute, which closed after Woodward's death, he directed a series of brilliant studies on cephalosporin antibiotics, work that he chose as the subject of his acceptance address for the 1965 Nobel Prize in chemistry, which he was awarded "for his outstanding achievements in the art of organic synthesis." By the time of his death he was generally regarded as the greatest figure in American organic chemistry.

The total synthesis or preparation by chemical means in the laboratory of a natural product—an extremely complicated molecule made by nature—was an enormous challenge that Woodward early made his primary research goal. In such syntheses every atom and every group of atoms must be placed in their proper positions. Thus organic synthesis is not only an exact science but also a fine art, of which Woodward was a consummate master. He deliberately chose synthetic problems that were generally regarded as virtually impossible and that had practical applications. When he joined the Harvard faculty, organic chemists were still using the same techniques of separation and purification of natural products that had been used at the beginning of the century. He was one of the major contributors to the instrumental revolution after World War II that extensively used instruments—including infrared spectroscopy and nuclear magnetic resonance spectroscopy as well as mass spectrometry, X-ray crystallography, and chromatography—in addition to classical chemical methods to identify and characterize substances and to solve problems in organic synthesis and structural determination that had been difficult or even impossible to solve previously. He developed stereospecific syntheses (producing one desired optical isomer from many possible ones) of molecules with many asymmetric centers, using new reactions and reagents and newly revealed mechanisms from physical organic chemistry to control the stereochemical courses of reactions. Such syntheses not only served to confirm the correctness of a structure and advance knowledge of the reactions and the chemical properties of the molecule but, in the case of substances of practical utility, they enabled the production of synthetic products that are cheaper than, more easily accessible than, or improvements on the naturally occurring products (in syntheses of substances that had medical uses but undesirable side effects, the structure could now be modified to reduce or eliminate such effects).

During World War II Woodward participated in war-related research on two drugs in short supply—quinine and penicillin, the first of the "wonder drugs" that were effective against previously incurable diseases and infections. Although neither project resulted in a synthesis that could be scaled up to produce quantities large enough to treat military and civilian populations, they led him to develop understandings and approaches that he used to meet future challenges, and they made his name and work known throughout the world. Because quinine has the property of polarizing light, Edwin F. Land of the Polaroid Corporation of Cambridge, Massachusetts, hired Woodward as a consultant in 1942 to discover new light polarizers to replace quinine, a task that Woodward quickly completed. Woodward then convinced Land to support his quest to synthesize quinine.

Since English chemist William Henry Perkin had failed to synthesize the antimalarial drug quinine in 1856, its synthesis had gradually become a Holy Grail sought by many organic chemists. On 10 April 1944, his twenty-seventh birthday, Woodward, along with new Harvard Ph.D. William von Eggers Doering, completed this successful synthesis, a theoretical and experimental tour de force, accomplished over a period of only fourteen months and involving twenty intermediate substances, each of which had to be carefully separated from by-products, which left smaller and smaller quantities to use as starting material in the next step of the multistep synthesis. No other synthesis leading only to quinine, rather than to quinine and some of its isomers, has yet been found.

From the time of his youthful quinine synthesis until his death, Woodward synthesized compound after compound of increasing complexity, becoming a legendary architect of molecules by creating structures correct in every detail, with the most economical use of time, energy, and molecular constituents. Although he would always follow up each novel or unexpected result, serendipity played little part in his syntheses, every step of which was meticulously planned in advance in the light of available knowledge of reaction mechanisms derived from his wide and voracious reading of the literature. Before beginning any laboratory work he often visualized the entire synthetic route through its numerous steps in the form of intermediates, stereochemical configurations, and rearrangements. In his words, "Synthesis must always be carried out by plan, and the synthetic frontier can be defined only in terms of the degree to which realistic planning is possible, utilizing all of the intellectual and physical tools available" (Todd and Cornforth, p. 633).

Woodward's achievements, which are unparalleled by those of any other organic chemist of the twentieth century, include the following total syntheses: patulin, an antibiotic derived from fungi (1950); the steroids cholesterol, involved in causing heart attacks (1951) and cortisone, used to treat arthritis (1951); lanosterol, a sterol occurring in wool fat and yeast (1954); lysergic acid, the pharmacological drug whose amides, including LSD, cause uterine contractions, hallucinations, and a type of gangrene called St. Anthony's Fire (1954); strychnine, the toxic alkaloid derived from the Indian plant *Strychnos nux vomica* (1954), for which Woodward had proposed the correct structure in 1948; reserpine, an alkaloid of great medical importance (1956) (the French firm Roussel-Uclaf used Woodward's synthesis of this compound to produce treatments for high blood pressure and nervous disorders); chlorophyll, the green leaf pigment ultimately responsible for almost all life on earth, a synthesis which took Woodward and seventeen postdoctoral students five years (1960) (Woodward had proposed a theory of chlorophyll's biogenesis—its production within the living organism—in 1953); the tetracyclines, a group of broad spectrum antibiotics previously produced by fermentation (1962); colchicine, an alkaloid, extracted from the autumn crocus, used to treat gout (1963); cephalosporin C, an antibiotic produced by the fungus *Cephalosporium* (1965); prostaglandin $F_{2\alpha}$, a physiologically active compound that affects the nervous system, circulation, reproductive organs, and metabolism (1973); and his most complex synthesis of all, vitamin B_{12}, which required more than a dozen years and an international collaboration with Albert Eschenmoser of the ETH in Zürich (1972). The synthesis of erythromycin A, the antibiotic used to treat Gram-positive bacterial infections and the last major achievement of Woodward's group at Harvard, required the efforts of nearly fifty chemists working for more than a decade. It was completed in 1980, after Woodward's death, by Yoshito Kishi, who had taken Woodward's place as principal investigator.

Woodward did not limit his work to syntheses. In the field of structural determination he was the first to propose and show the fused-ring structure of the penicillins (1945), and he established the structures of the broad-spectrum antibiotics terramycin and aureomycin in 1952 and the deadly poison tetrodotoxin of the puffer (*fugu*) fish, a delicacy that has caused numerous fatalities in Japan (1964). In 1952 he proposed the "sandwich" structure of the recently discovered bis(cyclopentadienyl)iron, an idea that initiated a new era in organometallic chemistry. He proposed the name "ferrocene" to emphasize the compound's similarity in reactions to benzene. He also developed interesting and fruitful ideas about synthetic activity in nature, the genesis of complicated molecules within the living organism.

In 1965, in what many regard as his most significant contribution to organic chemistry, on a par with August Kekulé's proposal of the cyclic structure for benzene, Woodward, together with future (1981) Nobel chemistry laureate Roald Hoffmann, proposed the principle of the conservation of orbital symmetry. This so-called Woodward-Hoffmann rule was used to predict and explain the course and stereochemistry of certain types of organic reactions. It profoundly changed the thinking of chemists and has remained the most frequently cited of Woodward's publications.

Woodward received more than twenty-six major medals and awards from eight countries, including the U.S. National Medal of Science (1964) and eight awards from the American Chemical Society. He was a member of the U.S. National Academy of Sciences and held honorary memberships in more than twenty-eight academies and learned societies from sixteen countries.

Woodward was a superb and captivating lecturer and showman. He eschewed slides, preferring to use chalks of various colors, which, coupled with his histrionic ability, gave his public lectures, invariably titled "Recent Advances in the Chemistry of Natural Products," the flavor of an evangelical gathering. He strove to make the length of his lectures legendary; a lecture at Karlsruhe was said to have lasted five hours and twenty minutes. An extremely hard worker, he continually cultivated an image of himself as a unique person indifferent, if not immune, to the problems of everday life. His changeless attire—a blue suit, white shirt, and light blue tie—were part of this image. He strove not only to excel in everything that he did but also to be recognized publicly as indisputably first in everything. His youthful brashness, conceit, and arrogance diminished as he matured, but his scorn for the pretentious and superficial remained. Although he had a sense of humor and could be the life of the party, he was a lone wolf and, despite his numerous collaborators, made few friends. A heavy smoker and drinker, he kept unusual hours and claimed never to have slept more than three out of twenty-four hours.

Woodward's passion for chemistry to the exclusion of almost everything else and his pursuit of it at all hours of the day and night were not conducive to domestic harmony. In 1938 he had married high school classmate Irja Pullman, with whom he had two daughters; they divorced, and in September 1946 he married Eudoxia M. M. Muller, with whom he had a daughter and son before divorcing again. Eventually, his lifestyle caught up with him; he died, alone and very lonely, at his Cambridge, Massachusetts, home of a massive heart attack.

Woodward made outstanding contributions spanning almost the entire range of theoretical and experimental organic chemistry and was universally acclaimed as the world's leading exponent of organic chemistry. He utilized and inspired others to utilize new instruments and physicochemical techniques to understand and synthesize complex natural products.

• Of Woodward's 196 publications, about eighty-five are full papers; the rest are preliminary communications, lectures, and reviews. Because the rate of his activity exceeded his ability to publish all experimental details, much of his achievement remains in the form of published lectures and short communications, and much is available only in dissertations and laboratory notebooks preserved at Harvard University along with Woodward's papers. His Nobel Prize lecture, "Recent Advances in the Chemistry of Natural Products," appears in Nobel Foundation, *Nobel Lectures: Chemistry 1963–1970* (1972), pp. 100–121. Biographical articles include Paul D. Bartlett and Frank H. Westheimer, "Robert Burns Woodward, Nobel Prize in Chemistry for 1965," *Science* 150 (1965): 585–87; Harry Wassermann, "Profile and Scientific Contributions of Professor Robert B. Woodward," *Heterocycles* 7, no. 1 (1977): 1–28; David Dolphin, "Robert Burns Woodward: Three Score Years and Then?," *Heterocycles* 7, no. 1 (1977): 29–35; Alexander Todd and John Cornforth, "Robert Burns Woodward, 10 April 1917–8 July 1979," *Biographical Memoirs of Fellows of the Royal Society* 27 (1981): 629–95 (with autographed portrait, detailed discussion of Woodward's work, and a list of his honors, appointments, and bibliography of his publications); Derek Barton, ed., *R. B. Woodward Remembered: A Collection of Papers in Honour of Robert Burns Woodward* (1982); Crystal E. Woodward, "Art and Elegance in the Synthesis of Organic Compunds: Robert Burns Woodward," in *Creative People at Work: Twelve Cognitive Case Studies*, ed. Doris B. Wallace and Howard E. Gruber (1989), pp. 227–53; Donald W. Landry, "Robert Burns Woodward, 1917–1979," in *Nobel Laureates in Chemistry, 1901–1992*, ed. Laylin K. James (1993), pp. 462–70; and Albert B. Costa, "Robert Burns Woodward, 1917–1979," in *American Chemists and Chemical Engineers*, ed. Wyndham D. Miles and Robert F. Gould, vol. 2 (1994), pp. 296–97. On 10 Apr. 1992, the seventy-fifth anniversary of Woodward's birth, the Beckman Center for the History of Chemistry opened its traveling exhibit, "Robert Burns Woodward and the Art of Organic Synthesis"; a copiously illustrated book of the same name, ed. Mary Ellen Bowden and Theodor Benfey (1992), contains a wealth of personal and scientific material. Short articles about Woodward in *Chemical and Engineering News* include Richard L. Demmerle, "Robert B. Woodward," 25, no. 30 (1947): 2137, 2179 (with cover picture); Anonymous, "Dragons Yet to Be Slain," 34, no. 4 (1956): 1566, 1568; Anonymous, "Woodward Receives SOCMA Medal," 40, no. 43 (1962): 106; Anonymous, "Syntheses, General Approach Bring Nobel Prize," 43, no. 44 (1965): 38–39 (with cover picture); Anonymous, "First Cope Award Goes to Woodward, Hoffmann," 50, no. 51 (1972): 20 (with cover picture); and D. Stanley Tarbell, "Woodward Advances Organic Synthesis," 54, no. 15 (1976): 121–22. One of the episodes of the three-part television miniseries, "The Nobel Legacy" (aired in May 1995 by the Public Broadcasting System), is devoted largely to Woodward's life and work and includes personal reminiscences by William von Eggers Doering, Roald Hoffmann, and others. An obituary is in the *New York Times*, 10 July 1979.

GEORGE B. KAUFFMAN

WOODWARD, Robert Simpson (21 July 1849–29 June 1924), geophysicist and foundation official, was born in Rochester, Michigan, the son of Robert Lysander Woodward and Peninah A. Simpson, farmers. Woodward was educated as a civil engineer at the University of Michigan, from which he was graduated in 1872. In 1876 he married Martha Gretton Bond; they had three children.

Woodward's considerable mathematical skills led him into a career as a classical Newtonian physicist, largely in the federal service, an atypical career for an engineer. For ten years after graduating from Michigan he was an assistant engineer on the staff of the Lake Survey of the U.S. Army Corps of Engineers. From 1882 to 1884 he served as an astronomer with the U.S. Transit of Venus Commission. Between 1884 and 1890 he successively occupied the posts of astronomer, geographer, and chief geographer with the U.S. Geological Survey (USGS). His most notable scientific contributions were made during his tenure with the USGS.

Woodward was part of the tradition of classical, mathematical physicists who saw the planet earth as the great object of study. In 1904 he asserted that "the earth is thus at once the grandest of laboratories and the grandest of museums available to man." To this laboratory and museum Woodward brought great skills in mathematics and an insistence on obtaining data of the highest precision in forms suitable for computation. Concerned with the gravitational effects of rock masses—particularly on isostasy, the equilibrium of the earth's crust as effected by gravity—Woodward considered thermal effects. This research was closely related to his experimental studies of how heat affected base bars and other instruments of precision. In 1887–1888 Woodward completed a series of papers that investigated the cooling of homogeneous spheres and the diffusion of heat in rectangular masses.

Perhaps Woodward's most consequential result was his challenge to physicist William Thomson, Lord Kelvin's work on the age of the earth. From thermodynamic data Kelvin had derived an age that did not allow for a time span that was long enough to effect evolution through natural selection. Woodward took issue also with Kelvin's "unverified assumption" of an initial uniform temperature and of a constant heat diffusiveness in the earth. Kelvin's data were based on continental land masses, and Woodward was skeptical that analogous results could be obtained for the entire planet. American geologists who were uncomfortable with Kelvin's constricted time frame used Woodward to support their opposition to it. Many felt vindicated by the later discoveries of natural radiation, which vitiated Kelvin's results.

Woodward worked for the U.S. Coast and Geodetic Survey from 1890 to 1893, when he was hired as professor of mechanics and mathematical physics at Columbia University. Surviving copies of his examinations (Columbia University Archives) indicate that he gave sophisticated, comprehensive lectures in the classical physics of that period. In 1895 Woodward was named dean of the College of Pure Science, a position he held until his departure from Columbia in 1904 to become president of the Carnegie Institution of Washington (CIW) in Washington, D.C.

The CIW had been founded by industrialist Andrew Carnegie in 1901, partly in reaction to turn-of-the-century laments about the inferior status of basic research in the United States. Carnegie was cool to the idea of creating a national university or an administrative entity to funnel research funds to existing institutions; instead, he favored finding exceptional individuals and supporting their research. Some of his advisors—notably, Woodward's predecessor and the first CIW president, Daniel Coit Gilman—disagreed with Carnegie on the issue of funding to institutions; in addition, there was much disagreement among the trustees on which subject areas to favor and on whether CIW should establish its own research laboratories and bureaus. Initially the new organization took Carnegie's lead: by the end of 1905, CIW had dispersed funds to 206 individuals in eighty-nine different institutions in forms now designated as fellowships and project grants.

Gilman retired in frustration over his differences with the other trustees, and Woodward succeeded him in 1904. By then, CIW had embarked on the formation of its own research installations, partly in response to recommendations made by Woodward as head of two advisory committees (geophysics and physics) formed by the trustees. Geophysics became a major area of concern, with the establishment of a research institute, but lack of a suitable "exceptional man" blocked the creation of a research institute in physics.

As president, Woodward supported full-time professional devotion to research and did not share the belief of many of his contemporaries that scholars should engage in both teaching and research. A product of the pregraduate school era, Woodward did not, like Gilman, cite the German university as the model to emulate; instead, he sought to pattern the CIW after the Royal Institution of London of Sir Humphrey Davy and Michael Faraday. As a veteran of federal service, Woodward saw Carnegie's gift as an opportunity to set up research establishments free from both applied pressures and the vagaries of congressional oversight. In a very methodical and shrewd manner, Woodward—over strong protests—largely dismantled the existing program of granting funds to individuals and substituted support for only a few well-established researchers, among them the great geneticist Thomas Hunt Morgan, whom CIW supported as a "research associate" for many years, even after Woodward's retirement. The education of neophytes and the support of untested investigators were left to other funding agencies.

Woodward concentrated on the institution's research laboratories and bureaus. The overwhelming majority were in the natural sciences, but some focused on history, economics and sociology, and archaeology in Central America. As a classical physicist of the nineteenth century, Woodward accepted without question a hierarchy of fields like that of French philosopher Auguste Comte, and he attempted to skew CIW funding accordingly. His bookish streak, however, led him to be more open-minded than other CIW officials in offering support to the humanities and social sciences, and as president he dispensed a number of grants to support research and publications in both areas.

Woodward stepped down from the presidency of CIW in 1920. He died four years later in Washington, D.C.

• The annual *Yearbooks* of the CIW from its founding to Woodward's departure are filled with valuable material bearing on both Woodward and the research culture of the United States in that period. The CIW archives contains no personal papers for Woodward as such, but its holdings are extensive and include more than strictly institutional records. A small amount of Woodward's correspondence is in the files of Presidents Seth Low and Nicholas Murray Butler in the Columbia University Archives. Items about Woodward are widely scattered among the personal papers of his contemporaries. The papers of James McKeen Cattell in the Library of Congress and those of T. W. Richard at Harvard University are especially valuable regarding Woodward's policies at CIW. The most extensive treatment of his tenure at CIW is "National Science Policy in a Private Foundation: The Carnegie Institution of Washington," reprinted in Nathan Reingold, *Science, American Style* (1991). A general discussion of the emergence of foundation support for research, including a discussion of Woodward, is Robert E. Kohler, *Partners in Science: Foundations and Natural Scientists, 1900–1945* (1991). For Woodward's scientific output, see F. E. Wright's memoir in National Academy of Sciences, *Biographical Memoirs* 19 (1926): 1–23, which includes a good bibliography.

NATHAN REINGOLD

WOODWARD, Samuel Bayard (10 June 1787–3 Jan. 1850), psychiatrist and asylum superintendent, was born in Torringford, Connecticut, the son of Samuel Woodward, a prominent physician, and Polly Griswold. Raised in a devoutly religious household, Woodward was influenced by the Second Great Awakening and a Protestantism stripped of its Calvinist pessimism. In Woodward's eyes the perfectibility of humanity was within reach; as free moral agents, human beings had the capacity to eliminate individual and social evils. The prerequisite for progress was knowledge of the natural laws that governed the physical world. Woodward's interest in the study of medicine may have developed because, in the early nineteenth century, this profession closely linked moral and physical concerns. After an apprenticeship in his father's office, he received a diploma from the Connecticut State Medical Society in 1809. In 1810 he opened a general practice in Wethersfield. By the 1820s he had become a leading figure in the state's medical establishment, serving as secretary of the State Medical Society and examiner at the Yale Medical School, which awarded him an honorary M.D. in 1822. In 1815 he married Maria Porter, with whom he had eleven children.

Woodward's interest in insanity seems to have originated when he saw several such patients in his private practice. Because of his interest, colleagues began to call on him for advice regarding the treatment of mental illnesses. In cooperation with several other physicians, ministers, and reformers, he became involved in a project to establish the Hartford Retreat for the Insane (later the Institute for Living). Opened in 1824, it was one of the nation's first private hospitals and a forerunner of the public mental hospitals that proliferated in the nineteenth century. Woodward was already experienced in the field when the trustees of the Worcester State Lunatic Hospital—an institution that owed its existence to Horace Mann—chose him as its first superintendent in 1833. During his tenure at Worcester from 1833 and 1846, he became nationally known and began to contribute to the broader development of institutional psychiatry and the state mental hospital.

An eclectic thinker, Woodward absorbed many of the newer concepts of insanity that were associated with such figures as Philippe Pinel and Samuel Tuke. He rejected supernatural explanations and insisted that insanity was a disease of the brain (the organ of the immaterial mind or soul). Also influenced by Lockean psychology and phrenology, he argued that insanity could be caused by individual violation of natural law as well as by the influence of social and cultural factors. His therapeutic views were equally eclectic. He tended to emphasize such somatic treatments as narcotics, stimulants, tonics, and a variety of drugs as well as baths. By restoring bodily health, these interventions set the stage for what in the nineteenth century was known as moral treatment. Moral treatment generally implied kind, individualized, directed care in a small hospital with occupational therapy, religious exercises, amusements and games, while it generally eschewed physical violence and the use of mechanical restraint. In brief, the new therapy was designed to create a healthy psychological environment.

Within a few years after his arrival in Worcester, Woodward had acquired a national reputation. He claimed to have cured as many as 80 or 90 percent of all recent cases (which at that time was defined as those who had been certified as insane for less than a year). Although in the 1870s Pliny Earle (1809–1892) attempted to demonstrate that Woodward's claims of high cure rates were exaggerated, there is evidence to suggest that his claims were not without foundation. An 1893 follow-up study of nearly 1,000 patients who were discharged as recovered found that about 58 percent were never again institutionalized—a record that compares favorably with the best of today's discharge rates. Woodward's annual reports received national publicity and served as a powerful lever to support the creation of a public mental hospital system. He was also one of the founders of the Association of Medical Superintendents of American Institutions for the Insane in 1844 (later the American Psychiatric Association) and was elected the association's first president. In that capacity he helped strengthen the growing public commitment to the institutional care and treatment of the mentally ill that would remain in place until the mid-twentieth century.

By 1846 Woodward found that he could no longer meet the varied responsibilities of administering a growing hospital and resigned his position. Shortly thereafter he moved to Northampton, where he lived until his death.

• The Woodward papers are at the American Antiquarian Society in Worcester, Mass. The Yale University Library contains a small collection, and the Worcester State Hospital is the sole repository of a three-volume typescript of his "Collected Writings." In addition to articles in the *American Journal of Insanity* and *Boston Medical and Surgical Journal*, Woodward provided extensive commentaries on the care and treatment of the insane in the *Annual Reports* of Worcester State Hospital from 1833 to 1845. An older biographical sketch is George Chandler, "Life of Dr. Woodward," *American Journal of Insanity* 8 (Oct. 1851): 119–35. A lengthy and more recent account is Gerald N. Grob, *The State and the Mentally Ill: A History of Worcester State Hospital in Massa-*

chusetts, 1830–1920 (1966), and a briefer one is in Constance M. McGovern, *Masters of Madness: Social Origins of the American Psychiatric Profession* (1985).

GERALD N. GROB

WOODWARD, Theodore (17 July 1788–10 Oct. 1840), physician, surgeon, and medical educator, was born in Hanover, New Hampshire, the son of Jonathan Woodward and Rebecca Smith (occupations unknown). In 1810 Woodward attended one course of medical lectures at Dartmouth and was given private instruction by his distant cousin Dr. Nathan Smith. Choosing not to stay at Dartmouth for the second course of lectures, which would have made him eligible for the M.D., Woodward went instead to Poultney, Vermont, to study with physician Adin Kendrick. After two years he moved to Castleton, Vermont, was admitted to the county medical society (then the equivalent of licensure), and began to practice. He announced a particular interest in surgery and was welcomed by local physician Selah Gridley, who practiced what would later be called internal medicine. As Woodward acquired a reputation as a skilled and successful surgeon, he and Gridley received more requests for instruction from prospective doctors than they could accommodate. In 1818 they and another physician, John Leconte Cazier, jointly founded the Castleton Medical Academy (later called the Vermont Academy of Medicine and, after 1841, the Castleton Medical College).

The demand for physicians in New England was increasing as population grew, and although there were many quacks and self-professed healers, the public desired properly educated doctors. Consequently, the number of medical schools in America grew from five in 1800 to twenty-two by 1830. All that was required to establish a medical school was a few professors, a place in which to lecture, and a charter authorizing the award of the M.D. Castleton, the first such school in Vermont, was privately owned by its professors and had received its charter by arrangement with nearby Middlebury College.

Like most medical schools of the time, Castleton was located in a small town. After a slow start, the academy, which was able to offer young Vermonters conveniently located medical instruction at less expense than if they traveled to Boston, flourished. Soon the college also attracted students from outside Vermont: Dr. Charles Caldwell of Transylvania advised prospective students to attend country schools as "the incentives to vice of all sorts are more numerous and powerful in large cities than in small ones" (quoted in *Medicine without Doctors*, ed. Guenter B. Risse [1977], p. 38). In the 1820s and 1830s, Castleton had more pupils and graduates each year than did Harvard, Yale, or Dartmouth. Its success can be credited largely to the reputation and popularity of Woodward. Cazier moved on in 1818 and the older Gridley relinquished his professorship in 1822. The remaining mainstay of the school, Woodward served as professor of surgery, obstetrics and diseases of women and children, trustee, secretary, and treasurer of the faculty, and registrar for about twenty years, during which time he continued his busy practice as the leading surgeon of the area. He married Mary Armington, with whom he had six children.

In the 1830s the medical scene in New England began to change. The combination of economic depression and overproduction of physicians (there were by then three medical schools in Vermont) led to more doctors than society could absorb, and young graduates had difficulty finding positions. Increasing competition for the shrinking pool of potential students led to a bitter public controversy between Woodward and Professor Benjamin Lincoln of the University of Vermont over alleged attempts to seduce enrollees by offers of bargain rates of tuition. Both the Burlington and Castleton schools temporarily suspended operations shortly thereafter, Castleton in 1838 and Burlington in 1836. Castleton reopened in 1840 and finally closed in 1854. Burlington was reactivated in 1853.

Around the age of thirty-three, Woodward had the first of a series of epileptic seizures. He was able for a while to remain active, but over a period of fifteen years his health and effectiveness slowly deteriorated, and toward the end of his life he became quarrelsome, demented, and paralyzed in both legs. He died in Brattleboro, Vermont. In retrospect it seems likely he suffered from a brain tumor of a type now called parasagittal meningioma.

• No published writings by Woodward have been found, and what is known about him is learned from some letters, the minutes and records of his school, the diary of a student, and a somewhat flowery obituary. Letters from Woodward to the *Vermont Statesman* are in Benjamin Lincoln, *An Exhibition of Certain Abuses Practiced by Some of the Medical Schools of New England* (1833). The definitive history of Castleton Medical College is Frederick C. Waite, *The First Medical College in Vermont* (1949). It includes the most complete biography of Woodward, pp. 41–45. See also M. Therese Southgate, "Castleton Medical College," *Journal of the American Medical Association* 204 (1968): 698–701; and Samuel Rezneck, "The Study of Medicine at the Vermont Academy of Medicine as Revealed in the Journal of Asa Fitch by Samuel Rezneck," in *Theory and Practice in American Medicine*, ed. Gert H. Brieger (1976). Speeches, catalogues, and the manuscript bylaws and journals of the academy from 1818 to 1847 are in the library of the Vermont Historical Society in Montpelier. An obituary by Joseph Perkins appeared in the *Boston Medical and Surgical Journal* 23 (1841): 349–52.

LESTER J. WALLMAN

WOODWORTH, Jay Backus (2 Jan. 1865–4 Aug. 1925), geologist, was born in Newfield, New York, the son of the Reverend Allen Beach Woodworth and Amanda Smith. He received his early education in a number of schools as his father was transferred from pastorate to pastorate. After graduating from high school in Newark, New Jersey, he was employed as a secretary at the New York Life Insurance Company offices in New York City and later moved on to become assistant manager of the Edison Illuminating

Company of Boston, Massachusetts. At the age of twenty-five he enrolled in Harvard University's Lawrence Scientific School. At Harvard he came under the influence of Nathaniel S. Shaler, who inspired him to pursue a career in geology and with whom he would collaborate in studies of bedrock geology. In 1893 he became an instructor in geology and in 1894 received a bachelor of arts with honors.

By 1901 Woodworth was an assistant professor and was well on his way to a productive career as teacher, researcher, and practitioner in the fields of geology and seismology. His geological investigations had begun with studies of glacial deposits in southeastern Massachusetts when he was a graduate student under Shaler's supervision, and his collaboration with Shaler would continue for a number of years, concluding with a summary report on the Triassic coal deposits of the eastern seaboard.

He served on various advisory boards of the Department of Geology at Harvard. From 1900 to 1908 he worked with the Geological Survey of New York, conducting investigations of Pleistocene and Holocene geology. In 1908, when one of his field course students, R. W. Sayles, gave Harvard its first seismograph, Woodworth established Harvard's seismological station, one of the earliest in the United States. Woodworth served as director and observer for the station until his death. In 1908–1909 he led the Shaler geological expedition to Brazil and Chile. In 1912 he was promoted to associate professor, and in 1918 he was accepted as a geologist in the U.S. Geological Survey and retained this affiliation for the remainder of his career.

Woodworth gave of his time and talents to a number of professional organizations, including the Geological Society of America, the American Academy of Arts and Sciences, the Meteorological Society of America, and the Boston Society of Natural History. During World War I he was a member of the Geology and Paleontology Committee of the National Research Council and chaired the council's subcommittee on the use of seismographs in war. In 1917–1918, as a first lieutenant in the Reserve Officers Training Corps, he taught military topography.

In 1891 Woodworth married Geneva Downs of Newark, New Jersey; she died in 1911. They had one child, a daughter. Woodworth died in Cambridge, Massachusetts.

Jay Backus Woodworth distinguished himself as a structural geologist, geomorphologist, and seismologist. His major areas of concentration were the Pleistocene (ice age) history of New York and New England and the regional geology of the middle and northern Appalachian Mountains. He was notable as a teacher of geology, particularly for his summer field course. His reputation as a seismologist rests primarily on his involvement in using seismographs to locate enemy artillery during World War I and his establishment and longtime operation of the Harvard seismological station. Late in his career, Woodworth developed a theory of how mountains were built, which postulated that a compressional episode of folding and thrust-faulting was followed by extension and block-faulting. This theory, published only as an abstract of an oral presentation, was developed further by his successors.

• A collection of Woodworth's papers can be found in the Harvard University archives. Woodworth's works include four pieces that appeared in U.S. Geological Survey publications, the first three of which he wrote in collaboration with Nathaniel S. Shaler: "The Glacial Brick Clays of Rhode Island and Southeastern Massachusetts," *Seventeenth Annual Report* (1896): 951–1004; "The Geology of the Narragansett Basin," *Monograph No. 33* (1899); "The Geology of the Richmond Basin, Virginia," *Nineteenth Annual Report* (1899): 285–515; and "The Atlantic Coast Triassic Coal Field," *Twenty-second Annual Report* (1902): 25–53. Other reports include "Geological Expedition to Brazil and Chile, 1908–1909," Museum of Comparative Zoology at Harvard College, *Bulletin* 56, no. 1 (1912), and "Cross Section of the Appalachians in Southern New England," Geological Society of America, *Bulletin* 34 (1923): 253–62. See also W. M. Davis and R. A. Daly, "Geology and Geography 1858–1928," in *The Development of Harvard University since the Inauguration of President Eliot, 1869–1929*, ed. Samuel Eliot Morison (1930), pp. 316–18. Memorials include Arthur Keith, "Memorial of Jay Backus Woodworth," Geological Society of America, *Bulletin* 37 (1926): 134–41, and R. W. Sayles, "Jay Backus Woodworth," *Harvard Graduates' Magazine* 24 (1926): 395–401. An obituary is in the *New York Times*, 6 Aug. 1925.

RALPH L. LANGENHEIM, JR.

WOODWORTH, John Maynard (15 Aug. 1837–14 Mar. 1879), physician and public health administrator, was born in Big Flats, New York, of parents whose names and occupations are unknown. After his family moved to Illinois, he attended the University of Chicago, where he studied natural history. He helped organize the Chicago Academy of Sciences in 1858 and was directed to establish a museum of natural history in 1859. In aid of that project, he went to the Smithsonian to study under Spencer Baird from 1859 to 1861. In that latter year he began the study of pharmacy by taking lectures at Rush Medical College in Chicago. Abandoning his plans to study natural history, Woodworth went on to receive a medical degree from the Chicago Medical College in 1862.

After graduation Woodworth immediately enlisted in the U.S. Army as an assistant surgeon. In 1863 he was promoted to the rank of surgeon, and then to medical inspector and ultimately medical director of the Army of the Tennessee. He was chief medical officer with General William Tecumseh Sherman in the famous march to the sea, supervising the care of over one hundred wounded soldiers. He received commendation for delivering all those men to Savannah alive, a feat he credited to following strict hygienic practices. Woodworth was mustered out a lieutenant colonel in 1865.

Upon discharge Woodworth traveled to Vienna and Berlin to enhance his medical training before returning to Chicago and setting up a medical practice in 1866. During the next five years he was attending surgeon to the Chicago Soldier's Home, became sanitary inspector to the Chicago Board of Health, and taught anatomy at the Chicago Medical College. In 1873 he married Maggie C. Hannahs; they had no children.

Woodworth's administrative skills had not been forgotten, however, and in 1871 the secretary of the treasury under Ulysses S. Grant appointed Woodworth as the first supervising surgeon general of the Marine Hospital Service. The service had been created by Congress in 1798 to provide health care for civilian sailors and was funded by a tax on seamen. Between 1798 and 1871 a total of thirty-one hospitals were built at a cost of over $3 million. However, a combination of graft, inept management, and natural disasters left only ten hospitals operative by 1869, when a congressional commission recommended that the service be reformed and organized for the first time under a central supervising officer. This was Woodworth's charge.

Woodworth used his military experience to organize a professional, centralized physician corps. Under the old system physicians attending the hospitals were chosen from the locality as a patronage appointment. No qualifications other than political favor were required. Woodworth set up an examination system for Marine Hospital Service employment and established a series of grades with promotion based on merit. Officers were sent to hospitals as needed and promoted to better places as openings and merit indicated. The physician's loyalty was to the service, and not to a particular town. Marine Hospital Service insignia and uniforms added to the militarization of the corps.

Woodworth's able administration put the service into the black by 1877, ending years of deficit spending. He closed hospitals that had been poorly placed, because of either an unhealthy environment or an inadequate need. Woodworth was a strong believer in sanitary science and was a founding member of the American Public Health Association in 1872. He studied current knowledge of hospital design and incorporated the latest knowledge of ventilation and sanitation into the new hospitals that were built. Woodworth particularly emphasized the pavilion plan, with ward "arms" branching off a central trunk, since it allowed for maximal air movement and light. Run by his newly created professional corps rather than local physicians with connections, these hospitals became models for their time of proper construction and administration.

Woodworth had ambitions for his service that extended beyond the administration of hospitals. He saw the service as ideally positioned to govern the quarantining of U.S. ports and felt that such a nationally run quarantine service would work much more efficiently than the patchwork of state quarantines to keep out cholera, yellow fever, and smallpox. By the 1870s most physicians believed that these diseases were spread by some sort of poison that could be stopped by sanitary measures—either general cleanliness of a community or the disinfection of a ship, or both. Knowing when to disinfect a ship depended on having accurate medical intelligence about the port of origin, information Woodworth claimed the existing networks of U.S. consuls could supply in a systemic fashion to a national agency. In a report on the cholera epidemic of 1873, Woodworth argued for the need of such a national body and volunteered that his service could do the job well.

Woodworth's lobbying efforts continued through the 1870s; and in the wake of the 1878 yellow fever epidemic, quarantine powers were briefly entrusted to the Marine Hospital Service, but without funding to execute them. In 1879 opponents from the American Public Health Association such as John Shaw Billings and James Cabell, who wanted a national public health organization independent of the Marine Hospital Service, won out. Woodworth died in Washington, D.C., shortly after the National Board of Health legislation was passed in early March 1879. (The cause of death is not clear.) His successors as supervising surgeon general were pleased to note the demise of the board in the early 1880s and the ultimate acquisition of quarantine and public health powers by the Marine Hospital Service, which evolved into the United States Public Health Service.

Woodworth was directly responsible for creating a medical corps of professional physicians whose national orientation raised them above politics and mediocrity. His vision of a federal public health service was the blueprint his successors followed in building the strong service that evolved in the twentieth century.

• Woodworth's Marine Hospital Service papers are preserved in Record Group 90 of the National Archives, Washington, D.C. From his first year as supervising surgeon general Woodworth issued an annual report to Congress that contains many of his own publications as well as reports from subordinates. He also published frequently in the American Public Health Association's *Reports and Papers*, including articles on "Hospitals and Their Construction," *Reports and Papers* 2 (1874–1875): 389–95, "The Safety of Ships and Those Who Travel in Them," *Reports and Papers* 3 (1875–1876): 79–84, and "Some Defects in the Immigration Service," *Reports and Papers* 1 (1873): 441–46. He wrote the introductory essay in the *Cholera Epidemic of 1873 in the United States*, a report to Congress published by the Government Printing Office in 1875. Ralph Chester Williams's, *The United States Public Health Service, 1798–1950* (1951), remains the best account of Woodworth's role in the service's history. An obituary by his successor as surgeon general is in the *Transactions of the American Medical Association* 30 (1879): 845–47.

MARGARET HUMPHREYS

WOODWORTH, Robert Sessions (16 Oct. 1869–4 July 1962), psychologist, was born in Belchertown, Massachusetts, the son of William Woodworth, a Congregational minister, and Lydia Sessions, a teacher of mathematics and mental philosophy and founder of Lake Erie College.

In his senior year at Amherst College, Woodworth encountered the study of psychology in a course from the philosopher Charles Edward Garman, who emphasized the role of science in the solution of philosophical problems. After receiving an A.B. from Amherst in 1891, Woodworth taught high school science at Watertown, New York (1891–1892), and mathematics at Washburn College in Topeka, Kansas (1893–1895). In 1895 he began the study of psychology with William James and philosophy with Josiah Royce and George Santayana at Harvard, from which he received an A.B. in 1896 and an M.A. in 1897. Following James's recommendation, Woodworth spent a year as a physiology assistant at Harvard. He accepted a fellowship in psychology at Columbia University, from which he received a Ph.D. in 1899 under the supervision of James McKeen Cattell. From 1899 to 1902, Woodworth taught physiology at Columbia and Bellevue Hospital Medical College. He spent the summer of 1900 doing research and teaching in Edinburgh, Scotland, and 1902–1903 in Liverpool, England, as assistant to and demonstrator for the noted physiologist, Sir Charles Sherrington. While in Liverpool, he married Gabrielle Schjöth; they had four children. In 1903 Cattell offered Woodworth an instructorship in Columbia University's psychology department, where he remained for the rest of his career and was made a full professor in 1909. After becoming professor emeritus in 1942, he continued to teach psychology at Columbia's School of General Studies until 1959.

Woodworth's dissertation research and early publications were on the control of muscular movement. Throughout his career his wide-ranging interests included reflexes, transfer of training, imageless thought, psychophysics, time perception, and psychological testing. His 1901 work on transfer of training was carried out in collaboration with his lifelong psychologist friend, E. L. Thorndike. The two concluded that transfer was unlikely except when the two tasks contained identical elements, thus contradicting the popular notion that the mind could be developed through "formal discipline."

At the 1904 World's Fair in St. Louis, Woodworth and assistants made anthropometric and psychometric assessments of 1,100 individuals in order to study "racial differences." Compared to many of his contemporaries, Woodworth was cautious about the interpretation of group differences in intelligence and other abilities. In 1910 he warned psychologists against overreliance on the use of group averages and urged the proper recognition of group overlap and within-group variation. In addition, starting in 1906, Woodworth created a battery of tests for basic abilities such as color-naming, form-naming, and logical relations, which were commonly known as the Association Tests. In 1917 the American Psychological Association commissioned him to develop a test of emotional stability in World War I recruits. This questionnaire, known as the Personal Data Sheet, was later used for civilian purposes and was an important forerunner of self-report personality tests.

Woodworth authored at least 246 books, articles, and reviews. His greatest influence on the trajectory of American psychology was undoubtedly through his books rather than his research papers. He helped revise George Trumbull Ladd's *Physiological Psychology* in 1911. Known as "Woodworth's Physiological Psychology," the revision was the standard text in the field for many years. His 1918 *Dynamic Psychology*, based on a series of lectures at the American Museum of Natural History, laid the groundwork for the study of motivation by separating psychological inquiry into questions of "how" (mechanism) and "why" (drives). He later came to describe his dynamic approach as a "Stimulus–Organism–Response" (or "S–O–R") model for psychology, a conceptualization that was widely used by later writers. His 1931 *Contemporary Schools of Psychology* (rev. 1948), provided a widely read summary of the major movements in the discipline. One of his two most influential books, his introductory text, *Psychology*, first appeared in 1921 and was revised in 1929, 1934, and 1940, and in 1947 with Donald Marquis. The first three editions sold over 400,000 copies. Translated into dozens of languages, the book was used around the world and served as a model for later introductory texts.

The book that most clearly influenced generations of new psychologists was Woodworth's *Experimental Psychology*, also known as the "Columbia Bible." Though formally published in 1938, mimeographed portions of the work had been used by Columbia students since about 1912. The "Bible" provided comprehensive, analytical summaries of all major content areas and methods of experimental psychology. The book also helped to define the nature and scope of experimental psychology by drawing a clear distinction between experimental and correlational research. Using terminology from his 1934 edition of *Psychology*, Woodworth defined "experiment" as manipulation of an "independent variable" while holding all other variables constant and observing the effect on a "dependent variable." This definition, which was probably taken from E. G. Boring's *Physical Dimensions of Consciousness* (1933), became the standard definition used in nearly all introductory and experimental texts by the 1960s. From this perspective, mental testing and individual differences were excluded from the experimental psychologist's domain. More important, cause and effect relations, the goal of the scientific enterprise for Woodworth, could only be discovered by active manipulation of the independent variable and not through correlational research. *Experimental Psychology* underwent two revisions and all three editions were widely used in many countries.

Woodworth also exerted a powerful influence through a variety of administrative positions. He was elected president of the American Psychological Association in 1914 and was actively involved in APA affairs and governance for decades. He served as president of the Psychological Corporation in 1929 and remained on its board of directors until 1960. While serving as president of the Social Sciences Research Council in 1931–1932, he helped lay the groundwork for the founding of the Society for Research in Child Development. He edited the *Archives of Psychology* from 1906 to 1948 and served on the editorial board of a number of major journals such as the *Psychological Bulletin*. His advice on what should be published and who should be hired was widely sought. In 1956 Woodworth was the first recipient of the Gold Medal of the American Psychological Foundation "for his unequalled contributions in shaping the destiny of scientific psychology." Boring described Woodworth as the fourth "dean" of American psychology, after James, Cattell, and Thorndike. Woodworth died in New York City.

Given the extraordinarily widespread use of his textbooks, Woodworth, more than any other author, taught psychology to the world. Through his texts, he promoted an antidoctrinaire, eclectic empiricism that encouraged and foreshadowed the diversity of modern psychology. He steadfastly rejected the notion that psychology should study only consciousness or only behavior, maintaining that psychology can and must study both. During the course of his career, APA membership rose from 127 in 1900 to nearly 20,000 members by the time of his death. Woodworth's career spanned the founding of American psychology and its emergence as a major feature of academia and American society.

• Woodworth's personal papers are in the Rare Book and Manuscript Library, Columbia University. The collection includes a large number of letters from the early 1900s to the 1950s. Some additional documents are in the Library of Congress. An autobiographical sketch appears in C. Murchison, ed., *A History of Psychology in Autobiography*, vol. 2 (1932), pp. 359–80. A bibliography of Woodworth's publications up to 1938 appeared in *Psychological Issues: Selected Papers of Robert S. Woodworth* (1939), and a supplementary bibliography from 1938 to 1959 appeared in the *American Journal of Psychology* 75 (1962): 690–92. For a collection of papers by his students that indicates the breadth of his influence, see G. S. Seward and J. P. Seward, *Current Psychological Issues: Essays in Honor of Robert S. Woodworth* (1958). For an analysis of Woodworth's dynamic approach to psychology, see E. Heidbreder, *Seven Psychologies* (1933). For a discussion of the influence of Woodworth's textbooks, see A. S. Winston, "Robert Sessions Woodworth and the 'Columbia Bible': How the Psychological Experiment Was Redefined," *American Journal of Psychology* 103 (1990): 391–401. Obituaries are in A. Poffenberger, "Robert Sessions Woodworth: 1869–1962," *American Journal of Psychology* 75 (1962): 677–89, and the *New York Times*, 5 July 1962.

ANDREW S. WINSTON

WOODWORTH, Samuel (13 Jan. 1785–9 Dec. 1842), playwright, poet, and journalist, was born in Scituate, Massachusetts, the son of Benjamin Woodworth, a farmer and revolutionary war veteran, and Abigail Bryant. As a boy Woodworth revealed a talent for writing poetry, but his father's farm brought in very little income, and consequently he was afforded almost no formal education. At age fourteen, however, he was placed in the home of the Reverend Nehemiah Thomas, who tutored Woodworth in English and Latin grammar and grounded him in the classics. Within a year Woodworth was apprenticed to the editor of the *Columbian Centinel*. Coincident to this he wrote poems for several Boston periodicals and edited a juvenile paper, the *Fly*, with future writer and actor John Howard Payne.

At the end of his apprenticeship in 1806, Woodworth embarked on a career in journalism that took him from Boston to New Haven to Baltimore and finally, in 1809, to New York. He settled there, and the next year he was married to Lydia Reeder. They had ten children. Woodworth continued his journalistic efforts in New York, publishing and editing several periodicals on a variety of subjects. He published a weekly paper called the *War*, covering the War of 1812, and during the same period he edited the *Halcyon Luminary and Theological Repository*, a monthly devoted to the Swedenborgian faith, of which he was an ardent follower. He focused on language and letters in several journals, including *Ladies Literary Cabinet*, a newspaper published during 1819; *Woodworth's Literary Casket*, a miniature magazine printed in 1821; and perhaps his most important journalistic venture, the New York *Mirror*, for years the city's leading literary periodical. Woodworth cofounded the *Mirror* with George P. Morris in 1823 but abandoned his editorial duties soon after its inception. Woodworth was adept at diagnosing public taste with regard to periodicals, but his ventures often failed because he did not possess the business sense necessary to implement his ambitious plans. In 1816 he tried his hand at writing a novel, producing a patriotic, romantic account of the War of 1812 titled *The Champions of Freedom; or, The Mysterious Chief*. He was also a prolific writer in other genres, publishing *Poems, Odes, Songs and Other Metrical Effusions* in 1818, and *Melodies, Duets, Trios, Songs, and Ballads* in 1826. His most famous song is "The Old Oaken Bucket," whose refrain "The old oaken bucket, the ironbound bucket, / The moss covered bucket which hangs in the well," remained popular well into the twentieth century. Woodworth wrote many poems and songs for the stage, beginning in 1818, when his "Funeral Ode on the Obsequies of Montgomery" was recited at the Pavilion Theatre in New York City. Other odes, songs, and addresses followed, including a recitation to honor the reopening of the Park Theatre in 1821.

Woodworth's first full-length stage production, a comic opera titled *The Deed of Gift*, was printed in New York and performed in Boston in March 1822. The story concerns two brothers, one cheated out of his father's estate by the other but saved by his resourceful sweetheart. Woodworth utilized songs, rural settings, and libertarian sentiments to convey his theme, but the piece proved largely unsuccessful. His second play, *Lafayette; or, The Castle of Olmutz*, premiered on 23 February 1824 in honor of George Washington's birthday and in anticipation of Lafayette's visit to the United States. This historical drama, about the attempts to rescue Lafayette from a German prison in 1792, was more successful than *The Deed of Gift*, and it was performed several times during the next few years. It is Woodworth's third work for the stage, however, that secures his place in American theater history. In *The Forest Rose; or, American Farmers*, first presented at the Chatham Theatre in New York on 6 October 1825, Woodworth refined his earlier attempt at comic, "pastoral" opera. He set fifteen songs to the music of John Davies and exploited the contrast between hard-working Americans and effete English, a popular theme in antebellum American drama. More important, he created the character Jonathan Ploughboy, whose type had been portrayed before but never with such success. This "Yankee" character is a naive American bumpkin, clumsy where any sort of finesse is called for but shrewd in business. Audiences most enjoyed Jonathan's gab, as when he examines his conscience about a purse he's been given: "Twenty-three dollars is a speculation that an't to be sneezed at, for it an't to be catch'd every day. But will it be right to keep the money, when I don't intend to do the job? Now if I was at home in Taunton, I would put that question to our debating society; and I would support the affirmative side of the question" (Moody, *Dramas*, p. 169). Several prominent actors, including George Handel Hill, Danforth Marble, and Joshua Silsbee, made Woodworth's Jonathan one of their signature roles and made *The Forest Rose* one of the most frequently produced dramatic works in antebellum America.

Just over a month after the successful premiere of *The Forest Rose*, another Woodworth drama, *The Widow's Son; or, Which Is the Traitor?*, opened at the Park Theatre. The play is a mixture of historical drama and Gothic romance; although the story of "Crazy Peg" Darby's spying for Washington during the revolutionary war presented fine dramatic material, the production ran only a few nights. In 1826 a play called *King's Bridge Cottage: A Revolutionary Tale* was printed, its author listed as "a Gentleman of New York." This piece, another patriotic drama filled with praise for Washington, is generally agreed to have been written by Woodworth. The play was not produced until 1833, when, after a seven-year hiatus from the stage, Woodworth returned in strength. Along with a single performance of *King's Bridge Cottage* on 22 February 1833 to honor Washington's birthday, three other Woodworth plays opened that season in New York. *The Cannibals; or, The Massacre Islands*, based on Woodworth's recent voyages to the Pacific Ocean, was not a success, despite spectacular elements that include a battle with cannibals and the eruption of a volcano. *Blue Laws; or, Eighty Years Ago*, a farce, opened at the Bowery in March and was repeated four times that season. Woodworth's last play, *The Foundling of the Sea*, was entered in a play contest sponsored by the famous Yankee actor George Handel Hill. The selection committee found no entry worthy of the prize, but Hill awarded the money to Woodworth and performed the piece several times in New York and Philadelphia.

In 1835 Woodworth contracted an eye disease, and in 1837 he suffered a paralytic stroke that severely damaged his nervous system. He died in poverty. An obituary in the *New York Herald Tribune* describes him as "a man of most amiable disposition, good qualities and high worth and integrity of character." Woodworth made his mark on the literary world with his periodicals and poetry and on the theater by popularizing the Yankee character, a favorite on the nineteenth-century American stage.

• Biographical information on Woodworth is available in the front matter of his *Poems, Odes, Songs and Other Metrical Effusions* (1818), and of his posthumously published *Poetical Works of Samuel Woodworth* (2 vols., 1861). See also Kendall B. Taft, "Samuel Woodworth" (Ph.D. diss., Univ. of Chicago, 1936). Critical assessments of Woodworth's dramatic works can be found in Oral S. Coad, "The Plays of Samuel Woodworth," *Sewanee Review* 27 (Apr. 1919): 163–75; Arthur Hobson Quinn, *A History of the American Drama from the Beginning to the Civil War* (1923); and Richard Moody, *America Takes the Stage: Romanticism in American Drama and Theatre 1750–1900* (1955). For his place as a writer of Yankee characters, see Francis Hodge, *Yankee Theatre: The Image of America on the Stage, 1825–1850* (1964). New York productions of his plays are chronicled in J. S. Ireland, *Records of the New York Stage from 1750 to 1850* (2 vols., 1867); and in G. C. D. Odell, *Annals of the New York Stage*, vol. 3 (1938). The most recent and complete commentary is contained in two books by Walter J. Meserve, *An Emerging Entertainment: The Drama of the American People to 1828* (1977); and *Heralds of Promise: The Drama of the American People in the Age of Jackson, 1829–1849* (1986). Five of Woodworth's plays are available in the microprint collection *Three Centuries of Drama: American*, and *The Forest Rose* has been anthologized in Moody, ed., *Dramas from the American Theatre 1762–1909* (1966). An obituary is in the *New York Herald Tribune*, 13 Dec. 1842.

JACK HRKACH

WOODWORTH-ETTER, Maria Beulah (22 July 1844–16 Sept. 1924), Holiness-Pentecostal evangelist and pastor, was born in New Lisbon (later Lisbon), Ohio, the daughter of Samuel Underwood, a farmer, and Matilda (maiden name unknown). Woodworth-Etter's early years were marked by personal struggle. One of eight children, she received no formal education. Her family joined the Disciples of Christ in 1854, and her father died two years later. In 1857, she professed conversion and expressed a call into church ministry. After a one-month courtship during or shortly after the Civil War, she married Philo Harrison Woodworth, an injured veteran. Settling near Lisbon, the couple farmed unsuccessfully. Five of their six children died by early childhood.

In the late 1870s and early 1880s, Woodworth's religious and vocational life changed dramatically. In 1879 she experienced a spiritual awakening at a Quaker service and immediately began to minister as an evangelist in her native Columbian County. She held many revivals and started a handful of churches. Although she officially joined the United Brethren Church around this time, her ministry in eastern Ohio transcended denominational boundaries. Several denominations, including the Methodists, offered her local parishes, but Woodworth preferred itinerancy. Thus, in 1884, she joined the Thirty-ninth Indiana Eldership conference of the Church of God, founded in

1825 by John Winebrenner, as an appointed Eldership evangelist. As she journeyed across Ohio and eastern Indiana holding revivals, her husband traveled with her, selling at the meetings refreshments and religious items, including Woodworth's photographs.

Woodworth's interdenominational services were characterized by shouting, dancing, loud preaching, lively singing, and fainting. Her teachings included the standard Holiness doctrines of salvation and sanctification and the revivalist tradition's emphasis on divine healing and a premillennial Second Coming. In 1885 her largest meeting during this period, in Alexandria, Indiana, attracted an estimated 25,000 people. The press usually provided ample coverage of her meetings. In May 1885 the *Indianapolis Times* described her during an interview: "She is not particularly intellectual, does not look like a fanatic and as a talker is coherent and evidently sincere."

From 1885 through 1889 Woodworth stormed through the Midwest with her evangelistic ministry. Sites of well-publicized revival included Hartford City, Kokomo, and Anderson, Indiana, and Springfield, Illinois. In addition to many small regional newspapers, media from Indianapolis, Cincinnati, Boston, and New York reported the developments of a growing constituency for "Virgin Maria," an affectionate appellation used by many of her followers. During these meetings, Woodworth developed a practice she described simply as "the power," a trance-like state, characterized by religious visions and voices, which often lasted for many hours. Woodworth herself often succumbed to "the power" during the services, standing motionless for an hour or more with hands raised. Such activities drew criticism from the churched and nonchurched alike, inspiring some to label her the "trance evangelist" and the "voodoo priestess."

Woodworth endured enormous personal and professional strain during her campaign in California during late 1889 and early 1890. Three major Oakland newspapers faithfully and contemptuously reported her activities. Near riots often accompanied her meetings, occasionally necessitating the intervention of police. In mid-December 1889 Philo's diminishing public role in his wife's ministry and her private accusations of his infidelity prompted him to leave her and to return to the Midwest, possibly never seeing her again. In January 1890 Woodworth publicly predicted the destruction of the cities of Alameda, Oakland, and San Francisco by means of a tidal wave and earthquake on 14 April of that year. Enormous public controversy followed. Woodworth departed for St. Louis four days before the date of the failed prophesy.

Extensive details of Woodworth's life and ministry are scarce after her departure from Oakland until about 1912. Her St. Louis meetings in mid-1890 attracted extensive front-page coverage from local newspapers. Two physicians unsuccessfully attempted to have the evangelist committed to an institution for the mentally ill; in extensive editorials, the secular press defended Woodworth's sanity. Around this same time, Philo repudiated his wife's ministry as a fraud. The couple divorced in Indiana in 1891. During the remainder of the 1890s and into the first decade of the twentieth century, Woodworth held successful revivals in scattered parts of the United States, especially Iowa, Missouri, Illinois, Indiana, and Ohio, but also in Colorado, Arizona, Florida, California, and Oregon. In 1902 she married Samuel Etter, a native of Hot Springs, Arkansas, who, ironically, was often too ill to attend the services of his healer-wife.

From 1912 to 1924 Woodworth-Etter concluded her career by joining the nascent Pentecostal movement, continuing an expansive evangelistic ministry across the United States and establishing a large church of her own in Indianapolis. It is difficult to determine exactly when she joined forces with the Pentecostal movement, started in 1901 in Topeka, Kansas, under Charles Fox Parham, and catapulted into international prominence in 1906 with the Azusa Street revival in Los Angeles led by William Joseph Seymour. By at least 1912, however, Woodworth-Etter was a main speaker at Pentecostal churches and camp meetings that featured the distinctive postconversion experience of the baptism of the Holy Spirit with the evidence of glossolalia, or speaking in unknown tongues. In 1912 she ministered at a Pentecostal church in Dallas, drawing thousands of Pentecostal pilgrims from America and abroad. In spring 1913 she played a prominent role in the high-water mark of the early Pentecostal movement, the Los Angeles World-Wide Camp Meeting at Arroyo Seco near Pasadena. From 1913 through 1918, Woodworth-Etter's evangelistic ministry expanded to include new venues, especially in the Northeast. Controversy and personal tragedy continued to follow her. In Framingham, Massachusetts, the evangelist endured a formal trial in the summer of 1913, accused of taking money under false pretenses. The State argued that she used hypnotism and offered no lasting cure; the judge ruled her innocent. In 1914, while Woodworth-Etter was in Philadelphia conducting a campaign, her husband died in Indianapolis.

By 1918, Woodworth-Etter sought to establish formally in Indianapolis a home church of support for her traveling ministry. She built a modest-looking sanctuary that seated five hundred. When not traveling, Woodworth-Etter ministered to the resident Pentecostal community and the frequent visitors who thronged her church, including Aimee Semple McPherson in October 1918. Her last major evangelical tour took place in 1922, when she journeyed from Dallas-Fort Worth through Evansville, Indiana, and her last revival was conducted in Toledo, Ohio, in January 1924. She died in Indianapolis.

Woodworth-Etter's significance is considerable. She was a widely recognized, albeit controversial, evangelist at a time when American Christianity overwhelmingly frowned on any such activities for women in the Church. She was perhaps the most popular female Protestant minister in the late nineteenth century and the best-known Holiness preacher to embrace the Pentecostal movement in the early twentieth century. Her life served as an inspiration for a later generation of female ministers such as McPherson and Pentecostal itinerants such as William Branham and Oral Roberts. And although not an intellectual force in shaping Holiness or Pentecostal doctrine, her pragmatic ministry helped to spread their respective distinct messages and to bridge those movements at the turn of the twentieth century.

• Most of Woodworth-Etter's writings—she wrote at least nine books—took the form of personal journals, which were updated occasionally and given new titles. *The Life and Experiences of Maria B. Woodworth* (1885 and 1888), *Trials and Triumphs of Mrs. M. B. Woodworth* (1886), *Life, Work and Experience of Maria Beulah Woodworth* (1894), *Acts of the Holy Ghost, or Life, and Experience of Mrs. M. B. Woodworth-Etter* (1912), *Signs and Wonders* (1916; repr. 1980), and *Marvels and Miracles* (1922) are important, lengthy primary sources. Many were widely read during her lifetime and translated into various languages. Her assistant, August Feick, published *Life and Testimony of Mrs. M. B. Woodworth-Etter* (1925), which contains portions of her previous works and an account of her last three years in the ministry.

Despite the attention of the press that she enjoyed in her own day, Woodworth-Etter has not attracted the same attention from modern scholars. The most complete biography, Wayne E. Warner, *The Woman Evangelist: The Life and Times of Charismatic Evangelist Maria B. Woodworth-Etter* (1986), is hagiographic in tone but contains a valuable chapter on her writings and a bibliography of all the extant works by Woodworth-Etter with their locations in the United States. See also George R. Stotts's essay, "Mary Woodworth-Etter: A Forgotten Feminine Figure in the Late 19th and Early 20th Century Charismatic Revival," presented to the History of Christianity section of the American Academy of Religion meeting in Washington, D.C. (26 Oct. 1974).

MICHAEL THOMAS GIROLIMON

WOODYARD, Sam (7 Jan. 1925–20 Sept. 1988), jazz drummer, was born Samuel Woodyard in Elizabeth, New Jersey. His parents' names are unknown. His father played drums on weekends. Woodyard quit school on his sixteenth birthday and began working nonmusical jobs while playing drums on Saturday nights. He married in 1942, and evidently he married again later in life, but details are unknown.

Woodyard toured in the rhythm-and-blues groups of Paul Gayten (1950) and Joe Holiday (1951), and he worked with jazz trumpeter Roy Eldridge in 1952. In 1953, while with Holiday again in Philadelphia, he transferred into organist Milt Buckner's trio, with which he remained into 1955. He then joined Duke Ellington's big band from July 1955 to November 1966, leaving only for brief periods in 1959 and 1965. Among his notable recordings are *Ellington at Newport* (1956), *Such Sweet Thunder* (1956–1957), "Mr. Gentle and Mr. Cool" on the album *Billy Strayhorn: Live!* (1958), and "La plus belle Africaine" on *Soul Call* (1966). He may be seen and heard drumming in two film shorts, both titled *Duke Ellington and His Orchestra*, produced in 1962 and 1965.

After working in a trio accompanying singer Ella Fitzgerald, Woodyard settled in Los Angeles. During the early 1970s he suffered from ill health, presumably a result of his alcoholism. He worked occasionally with trumpeter Bill Berry's band, and he played conga with the Ellington (1973) and Buddy Rich bands (1974). In 1975 he toured Europe and worked with pianist Claude Bolling's band. He was based in New York City in the late 1970s, and he performed at numerous jazz festivals. He recorded an album with a group of all-star jazz musicians, *Swingin' the Forties with the Great Eight* (1983). He died of cancer in Paris, France.

Woodyard is remembered especially for his contribution to Ellington's "Diminuendo and Crescendo in Blue" in a lengthy, cathartic, rhythm-and-blues oriented performance that was the sensation of the 1956 Newport Jazz Festival. He was a spongy drummer whose approach fit well into the loose-jointed rhythmic conception that governed Ellington's band during his membership. He also brought to the band an irrepressible enthusiasm that manifested itself not only in his swinging drumming, but also in episodes of uninhibited accompanimental shouting, grunting, and scat singing.

• For additional information see interviews by Stanley Dance, *The World of Duke Ellington* (1970; repr. 1981); and Claude Carriére, "Jam with Sam," *Jazz Hot*, no. 318 (July–Aug. 1975): 17–19. A description of his drum set is in Max Jones, "To a Drummer It's the Tone That Counts," *Melody Maker* 39 (7 Mar. 1964): 16. See also Duke Ellington, *Music Is My Mistress* (1973), and Mark Tucker, ed., *The Duke Ellington Reader* (1993). Obituaries are in the *New York Times*, 23 Sept. 1988, and *Jazz Journal International* 41 (Nov. 1988): 16.

BARRY KERNFELD

WOOL, John Ellis (29 Feb. 1784–10 Nov. 1869), major general of the U.S. Army, was born in Newburgh, New York, and orphaned at age four. Details about his parents are unknown. He was raised by his grandfather, James Wool, and bound over as an apprentice to a bookseller in Troy, New York. He married Sarah Moulton in 1810; it is not known whether they had children. In 1811 he began reading law in a Troy law office. His law studies were interrupted by the outbreak of the War of 1812. Wool organized a company of volunteers, and with the backing of New York lieutenant governor DeWitt Clinton, he obtained a commission in the regular army as a captain in the Thirteenth Infantry (dated from 14 Apr. 1812). Wool distinguished himself at the battle of Queenstown Heights (12–13 Oct. 1812), seizing and holding the heights on the Canadian side of the Niagara River with only 240 men, without support from the rest of the American forces in the battle, and suffering from serious gunshot wounds through both thighs. He was transferred and promoted to major of the Twenty-ninth Infantry on 13 April 1813. He fought at the battle of Plattsburgh (11 Sept. 1814), where he was awarded the brevet rank of lieutenant colonel "for gallant conduct."

After the close of the war, Wool remained with the army, and with the disbanding of many of the regiments raised for the war, he transferred to the Sixth Infantry on 17 May 1815. Already noted as a stickler for detail, he was named army inspector general on 29 April 1816 and promoted to the rank of full lieutenant colonel of the Sixth Infantry on 10 February 1818. Over the next three decades, Wool settled into a peaceful, unruffled routine, jogged only by the award of the brevet rank of brigadier general in 1826 "for ten years faithful service in one grade," a visitation of European military establishments in 1832, and participation in overseeing the removal of the Cherokees from their tribal homelands in Georgia to the Trans-Mississippi in 1836. He was finally promoted to full brigadier general on 25 June 1841.

The outbreak of the Mexican War in 1846 gave Wool his first chance for active combat duty in more than thirty years, and on 11 June he was assigned command of one of the four field forces (the others being commanded by Zachary Taylor, Stephen Kearny, and Alexander Doniphan) poised to invade Mexico. Wool's "Centre Division" of 3,400 men—composed of the Sixth Infantry, a company of the First Dragoons, Major J. M. Washington's battery of light artillery, and three volunteer regiments (the First and Second Illinois and the Arkansas Mounted Rifles)—moved out of San Antonio, Texas, on 25 September 1846, crossed the Rio Grande at Presidio de Rio Grande, and struck southward through Chihuahua to Parras, which Wool occupied on 5 December. Wool was then diverted eastward to Saltillo (which he entered on 22 or 23 Dec.) to rendezvous with Taylor's column and confront a Mexican army. Wool was responsible for choosing the ground on which Taylor and the American army received the Mexican attack at Buena Vista on 22 February 1847, and his "gallant and meritorious" handling of his division during the battle earned a vote of thanks and a ceremonial sword from Congress as well as a brevet promotion to major general. In the fall of 1847 Taylor turned responsibility for the occupation of Chihuahua over to Wool. Wool had already earned a reputation as "Granny Wool" for loving "pomp and pomposity," and he now earned an even harsher reputation for vigorously suppressing Mexican guerrilla action and for keeping his unruly American volunteers in line.

With the end of the Mexican War, Wool resumed his quiet peacetime assignments as commander of the Eastern Military District (1848–1853), the Department of the Pacific (1854–1857), and the Department of the East (1857–1861). On the basis of his Mexican War record, he was mentioned briefly as a possible Democratic candidate for the presidency in 1852, as a counterpoise to the Whig hero of the Mexican War, Winfield Scott, but the nomination instead went to another Democratic veteran of the war, Franklin Pierce. At the beginning of 1861 Wool was appointed one of New York's representatives to the abortive Peace Conference, and as a northern Democrat, he announced his intention to be "an independent member" of the conference "with an uncompromising determination to preserve the Union" and to avert the outbreak of the Civil War. The war came anyway, and Wool (as the fourth-ranking officer in the army and junior in years of service only to Scott) immediately moved the headquarters of the Department of the East from Troy to New York City, where he assumed responsibility for mobilization, war contracts, and supplies.

Wool's burst of activity was based on his assumption that he was the logical candidate for active command of the Federal army in the war. However, on 1 May 1861 Wool was reprimanded by Secretary of War Simon Cameron for exceeding his responsibilities, and it became quickly evident that Wool would be given no major field command. Instead, in August he was offered command of the Department of Virginia, which, since Virginia had seceded from the Union, consisted of little more than the Federal garrison at Fort Monroe, a toehold at the top of the James River peninsula.

Fort Monroe strategically dominated the James River, Hampton Roads, and the lower Chesapeake Bay. Wool immediately recognized it as "the most important position on the coast, from which the Southern States can be menaced and assailed more effectually than from any other." Finding only 800 men in the garrison and 200 shells for the fort's 32-pounder guns, he began bombarding Washington with requests for reinforcements. He also began undertaking small offensive operations in September and October 1861. The responsibility for mounting a major invasion of Virginia was given instead to the youthful major general George Brinton McClellan (1826–1885). A struggle for jurisdiction over Fort Monroe soon broke out, with McClellan insisting on control of Wool's garrison and Wool claiming independence from McClellan's command. When McClellan opened his campaign on the James River peninsula in the spring of 1862, Secretary of War E. M. Stanton and President Abraham Lincoln ordered Wool not to "hazard" McClellan's operations "by a technical adherence to the strict letter defining your geographical command." Since neither Stanton nor Lincoln entirely trusted McClellan, they allowed Wool to retain titular command at Fort Monroe, and on 6 April Stanton began inviting Wool to submit critical reports on McClellan's performance to the War Department. On 10–11 May 1862 Wool undertook an independent operation that recaptured the Norfolk Navy Yard. Stanton hailed the action as "among the most important successes of the present war" and arranged for Wool's promotion to full major general on 16 May.

McClellan eventually persuaded Lincoln that success in his Peninsular campaign was impossible with Wool in independent possession of Fort Monroe, and on 1 June 1862 Wool was relieved of command of the Department of Virginia (which now fell under McClellan's command). Stanton, however, placed Wool in charge of the Middle Department (running from eastern Md. to the Ohio River). Unhappily for Wool, the Confederates invaded Maryland in September 1862, once more bringing McClellan across his department and touching off the same conflicts over jurisdiction. McClellan single-handedly stripped Wool of command over Harpers Ferry after the garrison there tamely surrendered with no more than token resistance. McClellan arranged to have Wool censured by a military tribunal for having left Harpers Ferry inadequately prepared. Wool was relieved of command of the Middle Department on 17 December and given an indefinite leave of absence.

However, the next month Stanton once again came to Wool's rescue by offering him command of the newly reorganized Department of the East (comprising all of New England and N.Y. with headquarters in New York City). By now Wool, almost seventy-nine years old, was becoming less and less able to cope with the stress of wartime administration. When the New York City draft riots broke out (13–17 July 1863), Wool sent only token detachments to suppress the rioters and wasted precious hours and days quarreling with the military commandant of New York City, Brigadier General Harvey Brown, over jurisdictional questions. The riots were suppressed instead by elements of the Federal army hastily shipped from the war zone in Virginia. Humiliated at his own incapacity, Wool resigned on 18 July 1863 and on 1 August announced his retirement.

Wool lived out the rest of his days in Troy, where he was lionized as one of the town's most famous citizens. He campaigned incessantly for reinstatement and vindication for his conduct during the draft riots, but neither General Ulysses S. Grant nor Secretary Stanton heeded his demands. Nonetheless, General George G. Meade attended Wool's funeral in Troy as a representative of the army.

• The largest collection of Wool's papers includes over 10,000 items in the New York State Library, Albany, N.Y. Letters by Wool can also be found in several other manuscript collections, including the Charles Ellet and Lewis Cass papers at the University of Michigan; the Washington Townsend Papers at the Historical Society of Pennsylvania; for Mexican War–related items, the Hardin papers at the Chicago Historical Society; and in the C. N. Boyd, Emil Hurja, George Brinton McClellan, John Marston, and J. F. K. Mansfield collections at the Library of Congress. Wool's service in the Mexican War was observed and documented by Jonathan Buhoup, *A Narrative of the Central Division, or Army of Chihuahua, Commanded by Brig. Gen. Wool* (1847); and Francis Baylies, *A Narrative of Major General Wool's Campaign in Mexico, In the Years 1846, 1847 & 1848* (1851). Baylies's papers on Wool's campaign are housed in the Taunton, Mass., Library. More recent commentary on Wool's military service in Mexico is available in K. J. Bauer, *The Mexican War, 1846–1848* (1974); John M. Hunter, "General John E. Wool in Texas," *Frontier Times* 30 (1953); Harwood Perry Hinton, "The Military Career of John Ellis Wool, 1812–1863" (Ph.D. diss., Univ. of Wisconsin, 1960); as well as other general histories of the Mexican War. Wool's Civil War service can be easily traced through his published letters and reports in *The War of the Rebellion: A Compilation of the Official Records of the Union and Confederate Armies* (128 vols., 1880–1901) and also in Samuel Rezneck, "The Civil War Role 1861–1863 of a Veteran New York Officer, Major General John E. Wool," *New York History* 44 (July 1963): 237–57. Wool's clashes with McClellan are discussed in Rowena Reed, *Combined Operations in the Civil War* (1978). Wool has the distinction of being the first American general ever photographed on actual campaign: an unknown photographer made two daguerreotypes of Wool and his staff on a street in Saltillo in 1847. Both daguerreotypes are discussed in detail in M. A. Sandweiss et al., eds., *Eyewitness to War: Prints and Daguerreotypes of the Mexican War, 1846–1848* (1989).

ALLEN C. GUELZO

WOOLLCOTT, Alexander Humphreys (19 Jan. 1887–23 Jan. 1943), writer, was born at the Phalanx, a Fourierist commune at Red Bank, New Jersey, the son of Walter Woollcott, a ne'er-do-well businessman, and Frances Grey Bucklin, a daughter of the community's long-time leader. When he was a reporter on the *New York Times*, Alexander Woollcott impressed his editors as "a young man of refreshing enthusiasm, who daily rediscovered the obvious and importuned for space that he might present it properly" (24 Jan. 1943). Throughout his multifaceted career, both those who esteemed him and those who found him wanting pointed to the same traits. To the one, they were strengths; to the other, they were not inconsiderable flaws.

Woollcott had gone to the *Times* after graduation from Hamilton College in 1909. A member of Phi Beta Kappa, he edited Hamilton's literary magazine, founded a drama club, and acted in school plays, often taking female roles. He loved the school, promoted it shamelessly, and in 1924 was awarded a doctor of humane letters. Woollcott had wanted to be a journalist from childhood, and years later he could still think of "no trade that is as much fun as newspaper work and no job a newcomer finds so satisfactory as a reporter's" (*Letters*, p. 219). He became an excellent reporter with an eye for detail and the knack of telling a good story, but after a minor nervous breakdown he was given a job on the rewrite desk. In 1914 he was made drama critic—to his eyes, the ideal position.

Woollcott very early precipitated a year-long battle between the *Times* and the powerful producers Lee Shubert and J. J. Shubert when he panned as "not vastly amusing" one of the brothers' plays. The Shuberts barred Woollcott from their theaters, and publisher Adolph Ochs retaliated by refusing them advertising space. Ochs lost a court fight to win Woollcott admittance to Shubert theaters, but the Shuberts began sending him tickets again so that they could advertise in the newspaper. When the Shuberts presented Woollcott a box of cigars, he quipped: "The whole thing went up in a puff of smoke" (quoted in Teichmann, p. 73).

Woollcott went to France in 1917 as a private in an army hospital unit. Within a year he was promoted to sergeant and transferred to the new military newspaper, *Stars and Stripes*, staffed by a group of journalists who would gain postwar fame. Among them were the columnist Franklin P. Adams; sportswriter Grantland Rice; Stephen Early, later President Franklin

D. Roosevelt's press secretary; and Harold Ross, who would found the *New Yorker*.

Woollcott's bearing was most unmilitary. At 5′8″ he had ballooned to about 200 pounds (he would reach 240) and had taken on an appearance that delighted caricaturists throughout his life. He had a large head with a face of small, tightly clustered features above a billowing chin. His nose was short and beaked. His thin, down-curved mouth was accented by a narrow moustache. His eyes bulged behind the thick lenses of his round, horn-rimmed glasses. He had the soft puffiness associated with a lack of testosterone, possibly the result of what he called "that beastly complication" of a bout with the mumps when he was twenty-two.

Despite his corpulence, he went wherever necessary to get his stories, and his reporting, focusing on doughboys in the trenches, was considered among the war's best. His most memorable story was that of "Verdun Belle, a trench dog who adopted a young leatherneck, of how she followed him to the edge of the battle around Château-Thierry, and was waiting for him when they carried him out." It was poignant and compelling and widely reprinted. The writer and editor John T. Winterich, a friend since his *Stars and Stripes* days, said later the story supported Woollcott ever after, appearing below his signature "in virtually every American periodical except the *Wall Street Journal* and the *Harvard Alumni Weekly*" (*Adams*, p. 198).

Woollcott returned to New York following the armistice to become the city's most influential drama critic. "His style," wrote fellow critic George Jean Nathan in *The Magic Mirror*, "never strikes a mean; it is either a gravy bomb, a bursting gladiolus, a palpitating missa cantata, an attack of psychic hydrophobia, or a Roman denunciation, unequivocal, oracular, fat, and final." He took to his work a passion that Nathan characterized as "that of a small boy at his first circus." Other critics might cavil, but theatergoers read him and accepted his judgments, and Actors' Equity voted him "the most discriminating and stimulating" critic on Broadway in the 1927–1928 season. Among those whose careers he spurred were Eugene O'Neill, Katharine Cornell, Alfred Lunt and Lynn Fontanne, Fred Astaire, and the Marx Brothers. In 1922 publisher Frank Munsey enticed Woollcott to the *New York Herald*. But after Munsey moved him to the evening *New York Sun*, Woollcott jumped to the *New York World;* he believed that the only influential drama critics wrote for morning newspapers. In 1928 he left the *World* and gave up daily criticism.

Woollcott was known as much for his flamboyance as for his criticism, largely through his leadership of a group of wits, dubbed the Algonquin Round Table, who regularly gathered for lunch in the dining room of Manhattan's Algonquin Hotel and who played poker as the Thanatopsis Literary and Inside Straight Poker Club. Among them were such literary and theatrical figures as Dorothy Parker, Heywood Broun, George S. Kaufman, Marc Connelly, Robert Benchley, Ring Lardner, Noël Coward, and Harpo Marx. Although he could be "testy as a wasp and much more poisonous," as *Life* once reported (30 Oct. 1939), Woollcott seemed always surrounded by friends; he presided with what one guest described as "the spirit of a social director and the discipline of a lion tamer." (*Teichmann*, p. 168).

When Harold Ross established the *New Yorker* in 1925, Woollcott began writing occasional profiles and, beginning in 1929, a weekly column, "Shouts and Murmurs," a potpourri of anecdotes about the theater, books, his friends, and ghost and murder stories. His column became one of the most popular of the magazine's features, but dealing with him was a trial for his editors. He often tried to sneak into the column what one of them, Wolcott Gibbs, characterized in a *New Yorker* profile (1 Apr. 1939) as "smoking car anecdotes." What followed were great battles that ended with Woollcott tendering his resignation and having "to be won back with humble telephone calls and ardent letters." He stopped writing the column in 1935 after Ross proposed that it be printed only once a month.

Woollcott began performing on radio in 1929. He was CBS's "The Town Crier," forging a personal bond with his audience with his stories, reading poetry and talking about plays and books and people he knew. He gained a wide following, including an Alabama woman—he delighted in telling—who commented after one broadcast: "There's voodoo in his voice but glory in his tales." He also became a sought-after lecturer.

Woollcott tried both playwriting and acting, but with indifferent results. After a visit to the home of playwright Moss Hart, where he made himself an overbearing nuisance, he told Hart he would like to be written into a play as the central character. In telling Kaufman of the visit, Hart asked, "Suppose he'd broken his leg on the way out and I had to keep him there?" The question was the germ for the play *The Man Who Came to Dinner*, although Woollcott refused to play himself in the role of Sheridan Whiteside on Broadway or in the 1941 movie. He did take the part, however, in a West Coast touring company in 1940. Woollcott suffered a heart attack while on that tour, but by autumn he was again lecturing and broadcasting, and before the end of the year he was delighting audiences once more as Sheridan Whiteside.

His health declined sharply in 1942. He suffered another heart attack and endured an operation for gallstones. Still, he prepared an anthology for members of the armed forces and kept up his public appearances. Four days after his fifty-sixth birthday, while appearing on a CBS discussion program, he suffered a cerebral hemorrhage. He died that night at New York's Roosevelt Hospital.

Woollcott's work was not durable. With his reporter's talent and training, he was an engaging raconteur who related tales, however stale in other hands, with what a *New York Times* obituary writer called "a combination of keenness and sentiment." His work, however, had neither originality nor depth but was woven of emotion and what Woollcott himself conceded was "incurable triviality." In the end his greatest success was his own prominence as Alexander Woollcott, a role he played even to his dramatic collapse in the radio studio.

• Woollcott's papers can be found in the New York Public Library and the Houghton Library, Harvard University. *The Letters of Alexander Woollcott* were collected by Beatrice Kaufman and Joseph Hennessey (1944). His published works include *Mrs. Fiske: Her Views on Actors, Acting, and the Problems of Production* (1917), *Mr. Dickens Goes to the Play* (1922), and *The Story of Irving Berlin* (1925). His plays, both written with George S. Kaufman, are *The Channel Road* (1929) and *The Dark Tower* (1933). Woollcott collected his own writing in *The Command Is Forward* (1919), *Shouts and Murmurs* (1922), *Enchanted Aisles* (1924), and *Going to Pieces* (1928), *Two Gentlemen and a Lady* (also published as *Verdun Belle*) (1928), *While Rome Burns* (1934), and *Long, Long Ago* (published posthumously in 1943). He anthologized the prose and verse of others in *The Woollcott Reader* (1935), *Woollcott's Second Reader* (1937), and *As You Were* (1943). Samuel Hopkins Adams, *A. Woollcott* (1945), is an excellent biography, as is Howard Teichmann, *Smart Aleck: The Wit, World and Life of Alexander Woollcott* (1976). The Teichmann book is entertainingly written and filled with anecdotes told by persons who knew Woollcott; it also contains a bibliography. Also available is Edwin P. Hoyt, *Alexander Woollcott: The Man Who Came to Dinner* (1944). Critical works include Wayne Chatterton, *Alexander Woollcott* (1978), and Morris U. Burns, *The Dramatic Criticism of Alexander Woollcott* (1980). Both contain detailed bibliographies of Woollcott's work.

ALFRED LAWRENCE LORENZ

WOOLLEY, Celia Parker (14 June 1848–9 Mar. 1918), writer and Unitarian minister, was born in Toledo, Ohio, the daughter of Marcellus Harris Parker, an architect, and Harriet Maria Sage. Celia grew up in the small town of Coldwater, Michigan, where she was a member of the first graduating class of the Coldwater Female Seminary in 1867. The next year she married Jefferson H. Woolley, a dentist; their only child died of tuberculosis in his adolescence.

In 1876 the couple moved to Chicago, where Woolley began her writing career. For eight years between 1876 and 1888, she wrote a regular column, "Chicago Letter," as the Chicago correspondent for Boston's *Christian Register*. She also established close working relations with the Chicago-based Unitarian journal *Unity*, edited by Reverend Jenkin Lloyd Jones, who became her lifelong friend and associate. She worked on the editorial staff in some capacity, including occasionally serving as editor, from 1884 until her death. In these two publications she saw into print many of her stories, essays, and poems. She also published several short stories in *Lippincott's Magazine*.

Woolley participated actively as a member of several women's clubs and suffrage groups beginning in the 1880s. The Chicago Women's Club elected her president in 1888, and in 1894 she led a successful campaign to state in the club's bylaws that there could be no bar to membership on the grounds of race or religion. She was a founding member of the League of Religious Fellowship; founder and first president of the Political Equality League, whose purpose was to promote the political rights of women; and a member of Chicago's Fortnightly Club, promoting the intellectual advancement of women, and the literary Chicago Browning Society. Much of her club work involved studying and lecturing on literary figures. Two of her favorites were George Eliot, about whom she wrote a study pamphlet, and Robert Browning, about whom she coauthored a reader's handbook.

In addition to her club vocations, her journalism, and her women's rights activism, Woolley wrote fiction, publishing three novels between 1887 and 1892. Her first novel, *Love and Theology* (1887), later republished as *Rachael Armstrong*, addresses liberal religion and the role it plays in individuals' lives. The headstrong Puritan Rachael Armstrong confronts and attempts to reconcile herself with her fiancé's liberal Unitarian religion. Her second novel, *A Girl Graduate* (1889)—concerned primarily with issues of women's rights—tells the story of a young woman in a small midwestern town who undergoes several trials typical of her era: finding work as a schoolteacher, refusing the offers or advances of older men who want her as the mother of their children or a mistress, and coming to terms with liberal religion. She finally must give up her teaching career to care for her family. *Roger Hunt* (1892), her third novel, takes as its subject divorce, a major social issue by the end of the nineteenth century. Rather than a moral tract, however, the book is an exploration of the dilemma of individual versus social responsibility. Each of her novels received very mixed reviews, and evidently only *Love and Theology* sold well enough to merit several reprint editions.

After this flurry of publishing, Woolley devoted most of her energies to liberal religion. In 1894 she became an ordained minister in the Unitarian church, serving as pastor of a church in Geneva, Illinois, and later at the Independent Liberal Church on Chicago's North Side. Though she stepped down as a minister in 1896, she remained a member of All Souls Church in Chicago, sometimes occupying its pulpit and leading classes.

In 1903 Woolley published *The Western Slope*, narrating her personal history and recounting the religious and social movements of the preceding half century. In this work, she evaluates the progress made in the areas of religious expression, civil rights, and women's rights.

In 1904 Woolley founded the Frederick Douglass Center, an organization dedicated to helping inner-city blacks find meaningful work and decent homes in Chicago, and she moved from her suburban home to reside at the center. Woolley gained notoriety in the black community for her efforts "to promote a just and amicable relation between white and colored people" and for encouraging civil, political, and industrial equal opportunity, regardless of race. Her career as founder and director of the center is indicative of her lifelong desire to act on her beliefs. For the remainder of her life she continued to be active politically, especially in supporting the Progressive party; socially in club work and as a suffragist; and religiously. She died in Chicago. A prototypical Unitarian of her age, Woolley put her religious beliefs into practice in the community. Her life was also typical of an era that saw women discovering many outlets for creativity and professions outside the private sphere.

• Woolley's correspondence with Jenkin Jones is housed in the Meadville Lombard Theological Library at the University of Chicago; the Jones Collection at the University of Chicago Library contains some additional Woolley-Jones correspondence; and the Peace Collection at Swarthmore College houses some correspondence between Woolley and reformer Jane Addams. Catherine Hitchings wrote a brief profile on Woolley in the *Journal of the Universalist Historical Society* (1975). Obituaries are in *Unity*, 18 Apr. 1918; the *Christian Register*, 2 May 1918; and the *Chicago Tribune*, 10 Mar. 1918.

LEE SCHWENINGER

WOOLLEY, Edwin Dilworth (28 June 1807–13 Oct. 1881), merchant, business manager for Brigham Young, and Mormon bishop, was born in West Chester, Pennsylvania, the son of John Woolley, a farmer and schoolteacher, and Rachel Dilworth. Raised a Quaker (he spoke with "thees" and "thous" all of his life), Edwin Woolley was the eldest of seven children. His mother died when he was nineteen and his father when Edwin was twenty-five, and he was left with the care of his brothers and sisters. In 1831 he married Mary Wickersham, originally of West Chester. The next year Woolley, his wife, and his orphaned brothers and sisters moved to East Rochester, Ohio, Mary's home. In addition to farming, Woolley operated a general store. Discovering coal under his land, he also engaged in coal mining. A man of unflagging industry, Woolley prospered.

Impressed with Mormon missionaries and officials in 1837, Edwin was baptized a Latter-day Saint and was appointed to preside over the East Rochester branch of the church. He served a proselytizing mission in West Chester County and converted Edward Hunter, later the presiding bishop of the Mormon church.

With other Mormons, the Woolleys moved to Quincy, Illinois, in 1839 and in 1840 to Nauvoo, Illinois, where Edwin became a merchant. He often loaned money to Joseph Smith, a Mormon prophet, and helped to finance Mormon educational, proselytizing, and colonizing programs. Although Woolley went on short-term preaching missions on several occasions, he was in Nauvoo in June 1844 when Smith paid him a visit on the way to Carthage, Illinois, where Smith was murdered by a mob.

The Mormons left Nauvoo in 1846 and moved to Winter Quarters on the Missouri River in eastern Nebraska. After two years there as a storekeeper and supplier, Woolley and his family crossed the Great Plains in the summer and arrived in Salt Lake Valley in the fall of 1849.

After years of farming, livestock raising, and merchandising, Woolley was appointed business manager of Brigham Young's many enterprises. He supervised the clearing of roads, extracted lumber, constructed homes and other buildings, manufactured flour, operated a general store and meat market, and conducted various missions for the church. He was the lay bishop of the Salt Lake City Thirteenth Ward from 1854 to 1881, a member of the territorial house of representatives from 1851 intermittently to 1878, served several terms as Salt Lake County recorder, and helped organize the Deseret Telegraph Company and Zion's Cooperative Mercantile Institution (ZCMI). He died at his home in Salt Lake City.

Woolley was outspoken, practical, and devout in his religion. Entering into the institution of plural marriage, practiced at the time by many Mormons, he married, in addition to Mary Wickersham, Ellen Wilding (1843), Louisa Chapin Gordon (1845), and Mary Ann Olpin (1850). He was the father of twenty-six children, many of whom became Utah and Mormon leaders in the late nineteenth and early twentieth centuries. His granddaughter, Mary Ann Woolley Chamberlain, was the second woman in the United States to be elected mayor of a city: Kanab, Utah. Woolley's grandsons included J. Reuben Clark, Jr., ambassador to Mexico and counselor in the first presidency of the Latter-day Saints church, 1933–1961, and Spencer Woolley Kimball, president of the Church of Jesus Christ of Latter-day Saints, 1973–1985.

• The Edwin D. Woolley Papers are in the Latter-day Saints Church Archives, Salt Lake City. A full biography, with documentation from all available sources, is Leonard J. Arrington, *From Quaker to Latter-day Saints: Bishop Edwin D. Woolley* (1976). Shorter biographies are in Andrew Jenson, *Latter-day Saint Biographical Encyclopedia*, vol. 1 (1901), pp. 630–33; and Orson F. Whitney, *History of Utah*, vol. 4 (1904), pp. 282–85. Family history is told in Preston Woolley Parkinson, *The Utah Woolley Family* (1976). An obituary is in the *Deseret News*, 14 Oct. 1881.

LEONARD J. ARRINGTON

WOOLLEY, Helen Bradford Thompson (6 Nov. 1874–24 Dec. 1947), psychologist, was born in Chicago, Illinois, the middle of three daughters of David Wallace Thompson, an inventor and shoe manufacturer, and Isabella Perkins Faxon. Although the family was of modest means, all three daughters were sent to college to prepare for teaching careers. In 1893, after graduating at the head of her high school class, Helen Thompson entered the recently founded University of Chicago, where she was recognized as a brilliant student. While an undergraduate, she became acquainted with John Dewey, who was chair of the departments of pedagogy and of philosophy and psychology. Attracted to the work being done in psychology, she studied for a Ph.D. at the university after earning her Ph.B. in 1897.

The subject of Helen Thompson's dissertation research, which was carried out under the direction of James Rowland Angell, was mental differences in men and women. Her review of the literature on the topic, which was of intense popular interest at the time, revealed that while there was consensus with regard to the existence and general nature of sex differences—for example, that men are more active than women—there was no agreement on precisely what the differences were. Proposing to study the question through an empirical investigation, she devised and carried out a lengthy series of tests that she thought would resolve the issue. Designed to measure cognitive and motor abilities, sensory acuity, and emotional responsiveness, the tests required up to twenty hours of participation from each of her fifty subjects, half men and half women. In analyzing the results of her study, she did not find a clear-cut pattern of sex differences but rather a marked overlapping of the men's and women's performances. In the cases where sex differences were found, such as better developed motor ability in men and finer ability to discriminate among colors in women, Helen Thompson was inclined to see the differences as arising from social influences rather than as inborn sexual traits. In the report of her research, *The Mental Traits of Sex* (1903), she concluded that the slight differences between men and women that her experiments revealed could be attributed to the different training of boys and girls from infancy to adulthood rather than to innate sex differences.

Citing the differences in socialization of females and males as an explanation for observed sex differences in psychological characteristics did not originate with Helen Thompson. Rather, it represented a position commonly taken in feminist writing of that era—as well as more recently—to rebut the dominant view that essential differences existed in the psychological makeup of men and women. While Thompson's experimental findings contributed to the ongoing dispute, they did not lend themselves to broad generalizations about the differing psychological natures of men and women.

In 1900 Helen Thompson received a Ph.D. summa cum laude; Dewey and Angell agreed that her research was the best yet done in the department. She was the recipient of a traveling fellowship from the Association of Collegiate Alumnae and spent 1900–1901 in Europe, where she studied at the Sorbonne in Paris and the University of Berlin. From 1901 to 1905 she was director of the psychological laboratory and professor of psychology at Mount Holyoke College in Massachusetts.

In the summer of 1905 Helen Thompson traveled to Yokohama, Japan to marry Paul Gerhardt Woolley, a pathologist whom she had become engaged to several years earlier. Paul Woolley's work took the couple first to Manila in the Philippines, where he held a position as a bacteriologist and pathologist in the Bureau of Science and she was employed by the Bureau of Education as an experimental psychologist. They moved next to Thailand (then Siam), where Paul became director of the Government Serum Laboratory in 1906 and in 1907 became chief inspector of health. In 1907 Helen Woolley returned to the United States alone to give birth to the first of two daughters. Nine months later Paul Woolley rejoined his family, and after a brief stay in Omaha, Nebraska, they moved to Ohio, where he joined the University of Cincinnati medical school faculty. From 1910 until 1913, Helen Woolley also had an appointment at the University of Cincinnati as an instructor in philosophy. In 1911, however, she became director of the Bureau for the Investigation of Condition of Working Children, which involved her in longitudinal research comparing the mental and physical abilities of working children with those of children in school.

The state of Ohio had passed a pioneering child labor law in 1910 that required all children to complete at least the fifth grade before being allowed to leave school. Also in accordance with the law, schools were required to issue an employment certificate for any position that a child under the age of sixteen held. This legislation made it possible to keep track of children who left school to enter wage-earning occupations. M. Edith Campbell and E. N. Clopper, who had worked for the passage of the law, obtained pledges from private contributors to fund a five-year, comprehensive investigation of working children. The project involved not only the assessment of the physical and mental status of children from year to year and the collection of information on their work histories, home situations, and the social status of their families, but also the responsibility for issuing and recording employment certificates for all children in Cincinnati. As director of the Bureau for the Investigation of Condition of Working Children until 1914 and then as director of the Vocational Bureau of Cincinnati Public Schools from 1914 to 1921, Woolley and several staff members carried out what became a massive study of 1,500 children and their families, which was aimed at evaluating the effects of child labor. The findings were compiled in *An Experimental Study of Children* (1926), with Woolley as the sole author. She admitted that once the research had been completed it had become apparent that its initial aim could not be realized. That is, the results could shed little light on the effect of child labor because, from the outset of the study, those children who intended to remain in school scored higher on the physical and the mental tests than those who intended to go to work. Woolley concluded from this and other evidence that children who left school to go to work were, as a group, less physically and mentally able than children who stayed in school. Nevertheless, she recommended that compulsory education be extended to at least age sixteen to encompass the years of most rapid mental and physical development.

Woolley was active in a wide array of Progressive era reform and social welfare activities during her years in Cincinnati. She served on the board of the Cincinnati Community Chest and became a member of the National Child Labor Committee, the National Society of Charities and Corrections, and the Social Workers' Club of Cincinnati. She helped draft and lobbied for the Bing law, a revised compulsory school attendance and child labor law for Ohio, which was passed in 1921. A longtime member of the Ohio Woman Suffrage Association, she chaired in 1919 the Woman's Suffrage Committee of Greater Cincinnati.

In 1921 the Woolley family moved to Detroit, where Paul had accepted a new position. Helen Woolley found a position at the Merrill-Palmer School, first as research fellow (1921–1922), and then as assistant director and psychologist (1922–1926). There, in 1922, she organized one of the first nursery schools in the country to focus on the study of child development, a forerunner of what was to become a flourishing nursery school movement by the end of the decade. Woolley undertook intensive studies of the personalities of individual children in the school to remedy what she deplored as a lack of psychological knowledge about very young children and began to publish her findings in the form of case histories.

While at the Merrill-Palmer school, Woolley became an influential figure in the growing child development movement. Reportedly an excellent public speaker, she was much in demand as a lecturer for lay as for professional audiences. Her writing on topics in child development also found its way into popular magazines as well as scientific journals. After two years in Detroit, her husband developed tuberculosis and in 1924 moved for health reasons to California, where he remained until his death in 1932.

In 1925 Teacher's College of Columbia University offered Woolley the directorship of their newly established Institute of Child Welfare Research, which was modeled after the Merrill-Palmer Institute. She accepted this opportunity to advance her career, and for the first half of 1926 commuted between Detroit and New York to finish her work at Merrill-Palmer and to begin her new job at Teacher's College. Overwork combined with a series of personal traumas that included her husband's request for a divorce resulted in Woolley's hospitalization for exhaustion at the beginning of 1927. Subsequently, she became severely depressed and was actively suicidal for almost nine months. Recovering from the depression, she attempted to return to work, but other emotional problems continued to plague her and led to her dismissal from Teacher's College in 1930. Never fully recovered, she eventually went to live with her elder daughter Eleanor in Havertown, Pennsylvania, where she remained until her death.

Woolley's contributions to psychology were tragically cut short by the severe emotional disorders that beset her at the height of her career. As a psychologist, she produced a significant early study that challenged the then dominant view that there were clear-cut sex differences in mental abilities, directed a monumental investigation to evaluate the physical and mental effects of child labor, and did pioneering work in the psychology of early childhood development. As a feminist and social activist, she worked in the campaign for woman's suffrage, lobbied for the passage of compulsory education and child labor legislation, and gave her support to many other causes that promoted social welfare and social justice. One of the first generation of American women to earn a doctorate in psychology, Woolley embodied the Progressive era belief that knowledge yielded by scientific research could serve as a compass for societal reform.

• There are no collections of Woolley's personal papers. Her last major publication was a chapter titled "Eating, Sleeping, and Elimination," which she contributed to *A Handbook of Child Psychology*, ed. Carl Murchison (1931), pp. 28–70. A chronology of her life and a bibliography are in Murchison, ed., *The Psychological Register*, vol. 3 (1932), pp. 565–66. For a discussion of her life and work in the context of late nineteenth- and early twentieth-century women social scientists who studied sex differences see Rosalind Rosenberg, *Beyond Separate Spheres: Intellectual Roots of Modern Feminism* (1982).

LAUREL FURUMOTO

WOOLLEY, John Granville (15 Feb. 1850–13 Aug. 1922), prohibition advocate, was born in Collinsville, Ohio, the son of Edwin C. Woolley and Elizabeth Hunter. Woolley graduated from Ohio Wesleyan University in 1871 and earned a law degree from the University of Michigan in 1873. That year he married Mary Veronica Gerhardt of Delaware, Ohio, with whom he had three children, and soon launched a successful career as an attorney.

His first practice was in Paris, Illinois, where Woolley was elected city attorney. In 1877 Woolley moved to Minneapolis, Minnesota, and was elected prosecuting attorney for Minneapolis in 1881. But Woolley had become an alcoholic. In an effort to quit drinking, he moved to New York in 1886. Suicidal by 1888, he pledged abstinence, joined the Church of the Strangers, and took up reform as an active member of the Prohibition party.

Woolley's career as a reformer soon followed. He gained a reputation as a dynamic orator, first for the Prohibition party and later for the Anti-Saloon League. He combined a denunciation of the liquor traffic with a warm sense of concern for the alcoholic. Woolley argued that the saloon was the church's chief enemy. By 1889 he began delivering prohibition lectures combining those themes to thrilled audiences, and Woolley's service as a lecturer was soon in great demand. Woolley's popularity caused temperance reformer Lady Henry Somerset to invite him for a seven-month temperance tour of Great Britain in 1892.

Woolley's popularity also led him to leadership in the Prohibition party, the only party to advocate a ban on the business that supplied and sold alcoholic beverages. In 1898 he became coeditor with Samuel Dickie of the Chicago *Lever* and in 1899 the editor of the *New Voice* in New York. In this work, Woolley represented a particular faction. The Prohibition party argued that only its candidates, once elected, were sure to enforce prohibition laws. The party divided into "broad-gauge" and "narrow-gauge" factions over the question of whether or not to support other reforms, such as woman suffrage. Woolley was squarely in the "narrow-gauge" faction, not because he opposed other reforms, but from his conviction that only a single-minded focus on prohibition was the surest route to that most important reform. When the narrow-gauge faction took control of the party apparatus in 1900, Woolley became the party's presidential nominee and captured over 200,000 votes. Meanwhile Woolley was also moving from expressing opposition to new, nonpartisan pressure groups, the Ohio Anti-Saloon League, founded in 1893, and the American Anti-Saloon League, founded in 1895, which sought to promote the election of candidates regardless of party who supported restricting the liquor trades. Woolley's eventual conviction that prohibition might best be achieved through alliances between the party and other temperance organizations, especially the Anti-Saloon League, operating as pressure groups and not nominating candidates directly, earned him the animosity of the "broad-gauge" faction but endeared him to the Anti-Saloon League, which mushroomed as an organization after 1900.

Woolley spent the next years traveling and speaking around the world. During a vacation in Hawaii in 1907 the Anti-Saloon League commissioned him to form an organization there. Woolley also served as a cosuperintendent of the Wisconsin Anti-Saloon League in 1911–1912. But his most important work remained in persuasion and education. With William E. Johnson he collaborated on *Temperance Progress in the Nineteenth Century* (1903) and launched *The Standard Encyclopedia of the Alcohol Problem,* completed after his death by the Anti-Saloon League's publishing company. Woolley also published other volumes of his collected speeches and editorials.

In ill health and fatigued from his years of service, Woolley retired in 1921. His wife died shortly thereafter, and the grieving Woolley plunged into temperance work anew. The World League against Alcohol commissioned Woolley to study the alcohol problem in Europe. He died in Granada, Spain, having seen the United States pass the Eighteenth Amendment to the Constitution for which he had worked so long, a national amendment to outlaw the manufacture, distribution, and sale of alcoholic beverages.

Woolley's career had played no small role in generating popular enthusiasm for the prohibition reform. The enactment of Prohibition, the culmination of reform agitation over many decades, conformed to the then prevalent notion that an expansion of government authority would improve the lives of Americans and the quality of American society.

• There is no collection of Woolley's papers. Woolley's writings include *Seed Number One Hard* (1893); *The Sower* (1898); *Civilization by Faith* (1899); *The Christian Citizen* (1900); with Mary V. G. Woolley, *South Sea Letters* (1906); *Civic Sermons* (1911); and *The Call of an Epoch* (1921). Jack S. Blocker, Jr., *Retreat from Reform: The Prohibition Movement in the United States* (1976), discusses Woolley's career.

K. AUSTIN KERR

WOOLLEY, Mary Emma (13 July 1863–5 Sept. 1947), educator, feminist, and peace activist, was born in South Norwalk, Connecticut, the daughter of Joseph Judah Woolley, a Congregational minister, and his second wife, Mary Augusta Ferris. May, as she was called, spent a happy, nurturing childhood in New England, first in Meriden, Connecticut, and then, beginning in 1871, at her father's new pastorate in Pawtucket, Rhode Island. Reverend Woolley's attempts to combine religious and social work—whether in reaching out to factory workers or in challenging St. Paul's injunction of silence for women—profoundly influenced his daughter.

After attending a succession of small schools run by women and a brief stint at Providence High School, Woolley finished her secondary school training in 1884 at Wheaton Seminary in Norton, Massachusetts, and returned there to teach from 1885 to 1891. After a two-month tour of Europe in the summer of 1890, she planned to continue her education at Oxford University, but the president of Brown University, E. Benjamin Andrews, persuaded Woolley to become the first woman student at Brown. Beginning in 1890, she attended classes with men at the university while still teaching at Wheaton. When classes for women began in 1891, she assumed her place among the first female undergraduates at Brown. Woolley took her position seriously, telling her sister students, "It depends on us in a very large measure whether there is ever a woman's college in Brown." In 1894 she received her A.B. and in 1895 her A.M., with a thesis titled "The Early History of the Colonial Post Office."

In 1895 Woolley became an instructor in biblical history and literature at Wellesley College. Combining a dignified, regal bearing with a friendly and warm interest in people, "Miss Woolley," as she was known, quickly became popular with students and colleagues alike. She was made an associate professor the next year and a full professor in 1899. Woolley made major changes in the curriculum and also gained administrative experience as chair of her department. There she also began her lifelong relationship with Jeannette Marks, an articulate, vibrant twenty-year-old freshman.

In December 1899 Woolley was at a professional crossroads. While she was planning a year of graduate study to complete her Ph.D., her alma mater, Brown, wanted her to head its newly instituted Women's College. In addition, Mount Holyoke College offered her its presidency. Woolley accepted Mount Holyoke's offer and took office on 1 January 1901, becoming, at thirty-eight, one of the youngest college presidents in the United States.

At her inauguration, Woolley outlined her views on female education. Invoking the college's past emphasis on women's education in service to society, Woolley also firmly stated that the days were gone when education for women had to be justified on any other than intellectual grounds. Education, according to Woolley, was preparation for life in its broadest sense, and there were no limits to what a woman with a trained mind could do. If women had not distinguished themselves in some fields, it was simply because their training had not taken them there, "and the time seems not far distant when it will be conceded that the ability to master certain lines of thought is a question of the individual and not of sex."

Woolley's inaugural speech reflected one of the challenges facing the new president. As president of a women's college, she had to be a public advocate for the efficacy of female education. Throughout her 36-year presidency, one of the longest such tenures in educational history, she fought the prevalent prejudice of the time that contended either that young women were naturally unable to learn or that they undertook intellectual work at the risk of their health. As Woolley's influence in the academic community increased, she took a leading role in cooperative efforts among the women's colleges in the raising of funds, academic standards, and public consciousness. Woolley brought Mount Holyoke up to the level of the finest schools in the country by building a strong faculty and by attracting scholars from the best graduate schools with increased salaries, fellowships, and sabbaticals, which Woolley introduced in 1925. In ten years she had doubled the faculty and increased the proportion of Ph.D.s substantially.

Woolley also strove to improve the quality of the students, raising admission standards and introducing honors work and general examinations for seniors. The college expanded in other ways; the endowment grew from half a million to nearly five million dollars, and the campus acquired sixteen new buildings. Perhaps the most symbolically significant change lay in Woolley's abolition of the domestic work system, instituted by the school's founder, Mary Lyon. In 1837 Lyon required that students help perform cooking and cleaning duties for reasons of economy and exercise, and other seminaries for young women followed suit. By the turn of the century, only Mount Holyoke retained the system, which had modified into an exchange of duties for a tuition reduction, similar to modern work-study programs. Woolley regarded the system as old-fashioned and an obstacle to her quest to make the college intellectually equal to male institutions. She also firmly rejected trustee suggestions for the introduction of home economics into the curriculum.

Heavily influenced by her father's passion for social action, Woolley brought her progressive view of the world to the country college. She believed that in addition to academic training a college should instill in its students a lifelong sense of social responsibility. Woolley combined a commitment to biblical and religious scholarship with progressive religious thinking. Student clubs and service organizations flourished, drawing Mount Holyoke students into a world of interests broader than those of home and family, allowing them, as Woolley said, to be complete participants in "the great human circle."

During her presidency, Mary Woolley devoted her time to a multitude of organizations, embracing social reform of all kinds—suffrage, pacifism, and church matters. Whether as vice president of the American Civil Liberties Union defending Sacco and Vanzetti, hosting Susan B. Anthony at the college, or working for U.S. entry into the League of Nations, Woolley used her personal management style, which emphasized open discussion and compromise laced with humor, to change the world. She worked extensively with two presidents—with President Herbert Hoover on women's issues and with President Franklin D. Roosevelt on pacifism. A high-profile figure in the United States, Woolley reached international fame when President Hoover appointed her a delegate to the Conference on Reduction and Limitation of Armaments, which met in Geneva in 1932.

Woolley's outside activities did not please some of the trustees at Mount Holyoke. Though she remained to oversee the college's centennial in 1937, Woolley retired that year at age seventy-four. To her bitter disappointment, and in spite of heavy alumnae opposition, the trustees appointed a male successor, Roswell Gray Ham. Woolley was against a male president for a woman's college in principle; it implied, she said, that no qualified female candidate could be found, thus weakening the goals of a school devoted to preparing women for positions of responsibility and leadership. Woolley never returned to the Mount Holyoke campus.

Woolley's retirement years were active ones, full of speaking engagements, meetings, and conferences. On 30 September 1944 she suffered a cerebral hemorrhage, which left her partly paralyzed at the Westport home she shared with Marks. She spent the last three years of her life in a wheelchair, dictating letters and being cared for by Marks. She died in Westport.

On her death, one of Woolley's most illustrious students, Frances Perkins, social reformer and secretary of labor under Roosevelt, wrote to a former schoolmate: "Miss Woolley had a very remarkable career and as one looks at it, it seems strange that a young woman whose principal training had been that of a teacher should have been able to go so far, not only in academic life but in the public life of the whole country and international affairs." After fifty years, Perkins's conclusion still stands: "She was undoubtedly one of the most influential women in the world in her period. That influence, I think, was based upon her personality rather than upon her position and training" (letter to Helen High, 9 Sept. 1947).

With her commitment to the intellectual life, her belief in the individual's responsibility to society at large, and her deep religious faith, Mary Woolley inspired generations of young women to believe in themselves and to succeed in the world. By acting on her convictions and working tirelessly for peace and social justice, Woolley also showed the world that an educated woman's ability knew no bounds.

• An extensive collection of Mary Woolley's papers is in the Mount Holyoke College Archives. Though no biographies of her have been published in recent years, several older works offer intriguing portraits of Woolley by people who knew her: Frances Lester Warner, *On a New England Campus* (1937); Arthur C. Cole, *A Hundred Years of Mount Holyoke College*

(1940); and Jeannette Marks, *Life and Letters of Mary Emma Woolley* (1955). More recently, Anna Mary Wells, a Mount Holyoke alumna, published *Miss Marks and Miss Woolley* (1978), a study of the relationship between the two women. The most complete and insightful work on Woolley to date is Ann Karus Meeropol, "A Practical Visionary: Mary Emma Woolley and the Education of Women" (Ph.D. diss., Univ. of Massachusetts at Amherst, 1992). An obituary is in the *New York Times*, 6 Sept. 1947.

CATHERINE A. ALLGOR

WOOLLEY, Monty (17 Aug. 1888–6 May 1963), stage and screen actor and director, was born Edgar Montillion Woolley in the Bristol Hotel in New York City, the son of William Edgar Woolley, a Saratoga Springs, New York, hotel owner, and Jessie Arms. In his father's hotel, the celebrated and exclusive Grand Union, he met some of the most famous theatrical artists of the day, including Lillian Russell and Sarah Bernhardt. Along with his two older brothers, Woolley enjoyed a privileged upbringing that included a tour of Europe and the best schools. After attending the Mackenzie School in Dobbs Ferry, New York, Woolley entered Yale's class of 1911. At Yale, as Woolley later remembered, "he fell in with the set which owned pianos [and] studied wine lists . . . and he soon became the leader of a clique which dabbled in dramatics and profligacy" (*New Yorker*, 20 Jan. 1940, p. 26). At Yale he also formed a lifelong friendship with Cole Porter (Yale class of 1913). Although they were never lovers, Woolley and Porter were both homosexuals and shared similar interests in the arts and in social circumstances. Woolley's unashamed acceptance of his own sexual persona undoubtedly had a strong influence on Porter. Both developed a sense of humor about themselves, and their similar attitudes were simply another tie that bound the two friends closely together. As Charles Schwartz wrote in his biography of Porter, whenever Woolley's name was mentioned, Porter "would inevitably break into loud, affectionate laughter."

Woolley appeared in theater productions of the Yale Dramatic Association and was the group's president during his senior year. After completing his undergraduate degree, Woolley stayed on at Yale to earn an M.A. in 1912. After his years at Yale, Woolley went to Harvard and studied with George Lyman Kittredge, the Shakespearean scholar. In 1916 Woolley enlisted in the National Guard to serve in the Mexican border campaign, but he progressed no further than a remount station at Tobyhanna, Pennsylvania. He later served in France during World War I as a lieutenant on the general staff. While overseas he continued his friendship with Porter, who had moved to Paris, and their circle of expatriate friends included Howard Sturges, Archibald MacLeish, Elsa Maxwell, Elsie de Wolfe, and Linda Lee Thomas.

After the war, Woolley returned to Yale to join the faculty as a professor of English literature and director of college drama. His students at Yale included Thornton Wilder and Stephen Vincent Benét. After a number of years in teaching, Woolley resigned his post in 1927, when George Pierce Baker was brought in from Harvard to take over the Yale program. After a period of relative inactivity back in Saratoga Springs, and with the help of Porter, Woolley turned his attentions to acting and directing on Broadway.

Woolley acted in or directed several classic revivals before appearing in several musicals, including Porter's *Fifty Million Frenchmen* (1929), his first Broadway directorial effort. He also appeared in *The New Yorkers* (1930) and *Jubilee* (1935) and directed both. Despite the fact that *Jubilee* contained several great Porter songs, including "Begin the Beguine" and "Just One of Those Things," it was a flop. As a result, Woolley ended his directing career. Another reason for this was that Woolley was finding so much success as an actor. Among the best of his stage roles in this period was the Russian ballet choreographer in Rodgers and Hart's musical *On Your Toes* (1936), which was directed by George Abbott. This led to a two-year contract at MGM, where he appeared in secondary roles in over a dozen films, most notably *Nothing Sacred* (1937) and *Dancing Co-Ed* (1939). Woolley's social reputation as a wit and partygoer was thought to prevent critics, including perhaps himself, from taking his acting career very seriously. However, his return to the stage after his stint at MGM would provide him with the role of a lifetime.

Woolley's acerbic wit, Van Dyke beard (Porter nicknamed him "the Beard"), and privileged background served him well in his acting, especially in his most memorable role as Sheridan Whiteside, a character based on Algonquin Round Table wit Alexander Woollcott, in George S. Kaufman and Moss Hart's comedy, *The Man Who Came to Dinner* (1939). Woollcott (whom writer Kaufman referred to as "Louisa May Woollcott") had a reputation as a master of insult, so the role of Whiteside was rich in acerbic wisecracks delivered memorably by Woolley. The *New York Times* described his performance as "arrogant, waspish, murderously comic and strangely lovable." Woolley scored a significant personal success in the role, and the play was a long-running and much-revived hit. The role made Woolley a star and a well-known theatrical personality, but it also trapped him in similar (and often lesser) roles throughout the remainder of his career.

When Warner Bros. began to plan a film version of *The Man Who Came to Dinner*, there was some interest in casting fading screen legend John Barrymore as Whiteside. Woolley won the part, however, and costarred with Bette Davis, Ann Sheridan, Jimmy Durante, Billie Burke, and others. The film was released in 1942 to strong reviews and significant commercial success. Woolley's popularity in the role is evidenced by one incident in particular. When he agreed to act in a revival of the play at Cambridge, Massachusetts, in 1949, he arrived at the train station and was greeted by members of Harvard's Dramatic Club, faculty members, and even Radcliffe coeds, all wearing false beards. Of his famous beard, he himself wrote in the

New York Times in 1942 that it was "the historic trademark of genius. . . . Take the beards off Santa Claus and Bluebeard and what have you? Nothing but a pair of middle-aged, overstuffed bores."

Woolley devoted much of his professional time to screen work beginning in the early 1940s. He was nominated for an Academy Award as best actor for his strong performance in *The Pied Piper* (1942), in which he played an elderly, self-centered Englishman who reluctantly helps smuggle several children out of Nazi-occupied Europe. His best other role in this era was his critically praised performance as an alcoholic Shakespearean actor in *Life Begins at Eight-Thirty* (1942). Woolley also played himself in *Night and Day* (1946), a highly fictionalized movie biography of Cole Porter starring Cary Grant and Alexis Smith. Woolley's other screen credits, which became less frequent in the late 1940s, include *Since You Went Away* (1944), for which he received an Oscar nomination as best supporting actor; the lighthearted *When Irish Eyes Are Smiling* (1944); *Molly and Me* (1945), a comedy in which he costarred with British stage star Gracie Fields; *The Bishop's Wife* (1947), costarring Cary Grant and Loretta Young; *Miss Tatlock's Millions* (1948); and *As Young as You Feel* (1951). Regardless of the fate of the pictures themselves, Woolley's work in all of these films was praised, especially the last, which the *New York Times* described as "a vastly superior entertainment." Woolley also appeared in the musical *Kismet* (1955), but the experience was marred by heart problems that slowed his working schedule after this time.

Woolley was a popular guest on countless radio shows beginning in the late 1930s, and he spent a season as comic foil to legendary stage star Al Jolson on Jolson's radio program for Colgate. Later Woolley tried some television appearances, which he did not enjoy. As quoted in his *New York Times* obituary, Woolley recalled, "For five minutes on a Fred Allen show I rehearsed for nine or ten days. I was nervous and watched the clock constantly. I thought it was all terrible." From the mid-1950s, he significantly curtailed his working schedule. Never married, Woolley died in an Albany, New York, hospital of kidney and heart trouble, after several years of declining health. As he certainly would have forecast himself with considerable irony, Woolley's obituaries began by pointing out that he would be remembered for his stage and screen portrayal of Sheridan Whiteside in *The Man Who Came to Dinner*.

• For information on Woolley, see R. Baral, *Revue* (1962); *The Historical Register of Yale University, 1701–1937* (1939); R. Kimball, ed., *Cole* (1971); M. Meade, *Dorothy Parker* (1989); P. Michael, *Movie Greats* (1969); F. C. Othman, "The Beard That Talks Like a Man," *Saturday Evening Post*, 4 Sept. 1943, pp. 12–13; and Charles Schwartz, *Cole Porter* (1977). His obituary is in the *New York Times*, 7 May 1963.

JAMES FISHER

WOOLMAN, Collett Everman (8 Oct. 1889–11 Sept. 1966), airline pioneer, was born in Bloomington, Indiana, the son of Albert Jefferson Woolman, a college physics professor, and Daura Campbell. Woolman grew up in Champaign-Urbana, Illinois, where his father taught at the University of Illinois. C. E., as the son was known, entered the University of Illinois in 1908, then took time off to attend an international aviation meet in Rheims, France, in 1909.

Seemingly destined for a career in agriculture after receiving a degree in that field in 1912, Woolman took a job as staff entomologist with the Louisiana State University extension division. With the passage of the Smith-Lever Act of 1914 establishing a county extension service, he became one of the first county agents, based in Monroe, the seat of Ouachita Parish. He married Helen Fairfield, a schoolteacher, in 1916; they had two daughters.

Pioneering in one field led to pioneering in another. Woolman focused on the boll weevils' devastating effects on cotton in the Mississippi River Delta country. He was drawn to experiments conducted at the U.S. Department of Agriculture's Delta Laboratory near Monroe in the early 1920s, in which modified army planes sprayed cotton with a poisonous dust to kill the boll weevils. The experiments led to a commercial enterprise. Huff Daland aircraft manufacturers developed a crop duster, created a dusting division, and in 1925 hired Woolman to sell its services. While in South America for the dusting division, Woolman helped establish an American airline, Pan American–Grace (Panagra), there. When Huff Daland decided to eliminate the dusting division in 1928, Woolman persuaded some Monroe-area businessmen to join him in purchasing its assets. They established Delta Air Service in Monroe, managed by Woolman.

Reflecting Woolman's interest in airlines, Delta in 1929 added two small cabin planes to carry passengers between Monroe and Dallas. It proved an abortive beginning for the airline. Air mail revenue was essential for any airline's survival, but in 1930 Delta's bid for a Fort Worth–Atlanta postal contract failed. Delta reverted to being mainly a crop-dusting concern, surviving depression times only through Woolman's tight-fisted leadership.

Two factors brought Delta firmly back into the airline business. The Franklin D. Roosevelt administration, believing the previous Republican administration had illegally awarded air mail contracts, reshuffled the deck. At Woolman's prompting, Delta bid on and in 1934 received the Fort Worth–Charleston route. After nursing airline operations along, with airline revenues only slowly overtaking dusting operations, Woolman in 1941 convinced the directors to move Delta headquarters to Atlanta.

From Delta's beginning, Woolman had made a number of decisions that would contribute to its success. No opulent offices or fat salaries were granted, even for executives. The fleet had been carefully and prudently selected; only after the move to Atlanta did Woolman decide Delta could afford the great airliner, the DC-3. Further, all personnel had been inculcated with the idea that Delta was their extended family, with Woolman as the father figure; thus only the pilots felt need of a union.

World War II restricted all airlines in their civilian operations. During the war, Delta like others saw most of its aircraft and many of its personnel absorbed by or operating on behalf of the military. Woolman prepared Delta for postwar expansion. In August 1945 the Civil Aeronautics Board awarded Delta a Chicago-Miami route, and it was no longer simply a regional carrier.

Woolman knew, however, that Delta was not yet a major carrier. The immediate postwar era was difficult for airlines as they overexpanded and were forced to retrench. Woolman steered his company through this turbulence while looking for a sound merger. He found a candidate in 1951, the Memphis-based Chicago & Southern, whose mainly north-south route system from the Midwest to New Orleans fit well with Delta's primarily east-west system. The merger, when concluded in 1953, made Delta an international line, for C&S had several Caribbean routes.

Woolman was the chief executive officer, and his stamp was on the merged organization from the outset. Except for the pilots, the segments of C&S that had been unionized were no longer unionized. The extended family image was impressed on the newcomers, and Atlanta remained the headquarters. The C&S portion of the joint name was eventually dropped. Delta received not only equipment, routes, and an expanded rank-and-file, it gained able administrators such as legal expert Richard Maurer, whose expertise and experience strengthened the airline.

Other Woolman decisions contributed to Delta's becoming a major airline. He avoided strikes and legal entanglements, like those that chief rival Eastern encountered, by practices such as choosing to give flight training to flight engineers, thus giving them a chance to advance. Woolman moved Delta from piston planes directly to jetliners, avoiding the intermediate turbojets whose problems plagued Eastern. He also fended off Bible Belt criticism and elected to please a majority of the passengers by serving alcohol on Delta aircraft.

In the early 1960s two events, both under Woolman's leadership, signaled Delta's arrival as a major airline. In 1961 the Civil Aeronautics Board awarded Delta routes that connected the airline's previous westernmost terminus of Dallas–Fort Worth with the West Coast. Delta had bested Eastern among ten other carriers for the award. In 1962 Delta led the way among several carriers in blocking an Eastern–American Airlines merger, with Woolman coaching his legal chief Maurer behind the scenes.

Health problems beginning in the late 1950s and the death of his wife in 1962 combined to slow Woolman down. He had been the patriarch of the Delta extended family, but he had built and maintained an exceedingly able management team. In the last years that team subtly took over the running of Delta, for Woolman had no intention of retiring. Telling only his children and a few trusted others, he went to Houston for a heart aneurysm operation in September 1966. Woolman died in Houston.

• Woolman's business correspondence and some personal papers are located at Delta headquarters at Hartsfield International Airport, Atlanta, Ga. The principal published works containing information about Woolman are: R. E. G. Davies, *Delta: An Airline and Its Aircraft* (1990); W. David Lewis and Wesley Phillips Newton, *Delta: The History of An Airline* (1979); Lewis and Newton, "C. E. Woolman," in *The Airline Industry* (1992), a volume of the *Encyclopedia of American Business History and Biography*; Newton, *The Perilous Sky* (1978); and Carleton Putnam, *High Frontier* (1945). An obituary is in the *New York Times*, 13 Sept. 1966.

WESLEY PHILLIPS NEWTON

WOOLMAN, John (19 Oct. 1720–7 Oct. 1772), Quaker leader and pioneer abolitionist, was born in Northampton, near Mount Holly, New Jersey, the son of Samuel Woolman and Elizabeth Burr, farmers. His grandfather had been a proprietor of West Jersey, and his father was a candidate for the provincial assembly. Woolman's upbringing by intensely pious parents led to early religious experiences. His *Journal* (1774) tells of being deeply impressed while reading the Bible at age seven, of a mystical dream at age nine, and of one day boyishly throwing stones at a fluttering mother bird and killing her. He then felt compelled to kill her nestlings, terribly troubled by his own cruelty.

Beginning about age sixteen, Woolman experienced several years of struggle with "youthful vanities." He gradually forsook the companionship of his peers, eventually finding his spiritual bearings, saying, "While I silently ponder on that change wrought in me, I find no language equal to it nor any means to convey to another a clear idea of it. . . . My heart was tender and often contrite, and a universal love to my fellow creatures increased in me" (*Journal and Major Essays*, p. 29).

In 1741 Woolman went to live in nearby Mount Holly, where he tended store and kept books for a merchant. He began his public ministry at age twenty-two, when he gave a testimony that he immediately regretted in a Quaker meeting. He then learned to "wait in silence sometimes many weeks together, until I felt that rise which prepares the creature to stand like a trumpet through which the Lord speaks" (*Journal and Major Essays*, p. 31). In 1743 he made his first religious journey of two weeks to points in New Jersey, traveling as he almost always did, with a companion and after taking counsel with Quakers. In 1746 Woolman set up shop as a tailor, selling a few goods on the side. Within a decade he found merchandising too demanding and confined himself to employments that freed him for a traveling ministry—tailoring, surveying, conveyancing (drawing up deeds and leases), executing bills of sale, drawing wills, and cultivating his orchard. In 1749 he married Sarah Ellis and with her had two children, only one of whom survived infancy.

Woolman had early developed strong convictions about slaveholding. When his first employer asked him to write a bill of sale for a slave, Woolman complied with great reluctance, and soon thereafter he refused to write an instrument of slavery for a friend, although many Quakers held slaves. Asked to write a will in which slaves were bequeathed, his *Journal* comments that "as writing is a profitable employ, as offending sober people is disagreeable to my inclination, I was straitened in my mind; but as I looked to the Lord, he inclined my heart to his testimony, and I told the man that I believed the practice of counting slavery to this people was not right . . . and desired to be excused" (*Journal and Major Essays*, p. 46). In 1746 he traveled 1,500 miles in three months through Pennsylvania into Maryland, Virginia, and North Carolina, lodging often in slaveholding Quaker families. He "saw in these southern provinces so many vices and corruptions increased by this trade and this way of life that . . . in future the consequence will be grievous to posterity!" (*Journal and Major Essays*, p. 38). Upon returning Woolman wrote *Some Considerations on the Keeping of Negroes*, which was published in 1754 by the Philadelphia Yearly Meeting and was followed in 1762 by Part Second. In 1755 he composed an epistle to all Quakers in America, advocating the pacifist position. That same year his text, "An Epistle of Tender Love and Caution," urged individuals to refuse to pay taxes that had been levied principally to support war.

In 1758 Woolman's abolitionist views helped persuade the Philadelphia Yearly Meeting to take an official position that urged Quakers to emancipate their slaves. The order also arranged for "the visitation of slaveholders" and excluded any who bought or sold slaves from Quaker business. Throughout the years of Woolman's traveling, from Massachusetts to North Carolina, much of his ministry involved quiet but urgent counseling with slaveholding individuals and families.

Seeing how the Indians were exploited by rum sellers and traders and were losing their land with very small compensation, Woolman made a hazardous three-week journey in 1763 to a tribe in Wyalusing. Reflecting on the meaning of this journey he wrote in his *Journal*, "Love was the first motion, and then a concern . . . that I might feel and understand their life and spirit they live in, if haply I might receive some instruction from them, or they be in any degree helped forward by my following the leadings of Truth amongst them" (*Journal and Major Essays*, p. 127).

Woolman's concern for slaves and Indians was an expression of the fundamental conviction expressed in *A Plea for the Poor*, much of it written in 1763 and 1764 and published in 1793, after his death, that God's love creates "a desire to take hold of every opportunity to lessen the distresses of the afflicted and to increase the happiness of the creation. Here we have a prospect of one common interest from which our own is inseparable [so that] to turn all the treasures we possess into the channel of universal love becomes the business of our lives." Woolman's belief that luxury and surplus for some is only achieved at the cost of hardship and deprivation for others led him to emphasize simplicity and frugality; to travel on foot in some of his later journeys; to oppose lotteries, frivolous entertainment, and alcohol; and to give up in 1761 the wearing of dyed clothes. He likewise objected to extensive maritime trade because he felt it caused hardship on seamen and was largely concerned with the transportation of superfluities.

On 1 May 1772 Woolman embarked on a visit to England, arriving in London on 8 June. Four months later he died of smallpox in York. At sea and in England he wrote five short essays, including "On a Sailors Life," that were published in 1773.

Woolman's ministry had few marks of public success; his role in moving the Quakers away from slaveholding was probably most notable, along with his influence on later abolitionists. The effect of his personal ministry upon countless individuals cannot be measured. His *Journal*, however, had obvious influence: Henry Crab Robinson called it "a perfect gem . . . in a style of the most exquisite purity and grace" (quoted in J. G. Whittier's introduction to an edition of the *Journal* published in England), and William Ellery Channing pronounced it "beyond comparison the sweetest and purest autobiography" in English. His writings, especially his *Journal*, were even more popular in England than America and have proved to be a spiritual and moral treasure that have had a growing influence upon successive generations.

• A collection of Woolman papers is in Friends Historical Library at Swarthmore College. *The Journal and Major Essays of John Woolman*, ed. Phillips P. Moulton (1971), is the definitive edition and an indispensable guide to Woolman's writings and career. It includes the *Considerations on the Keeping of Negroes* and *A Plea for the Poor*, as well as several Woolman fragments and an account of his final illness and death written by those who cared for him. A select bibliography provides a critical introduction to the numerous editions of Woolman's writings, to the extant manuscripts, and to useful secondary sources, including Edwin H. Cady, *John Woolman* (1965); Paul Rosenblatt, *John Woolman* (1969); and Janet Whitney, *John Woolman: American Quaker* (1942). Valuable interpretations of Woolman are found in the 1871 introduction by John Greenleaf Whittier to an English edition of the *Journal* and in Douglas V. Steere's introduction to the *Journal* in his *Doors Into Life* (1948).

DAVID M. STOWE

WOOLMAN, Mary Raphael Schenck (26 Apr. 1860–1 Aug. 1940), educator and author, was born in Camden, New Jersey, the daughter of Joseph Schenck, a physician, and Martha McKeen. As a child Mary Schenck lived a privileged life. Because her father was a leading doctor in the community—he was far ahead of his time in the use of prophylactic measures and modern medical surgical methods—she had access to his vast library, and after showing scholarly promise she was sent to a private Quaker school in Philadelphia that trained young women from upper-class families in many subjects, including domestic arts. In 1883–1884 she continued her education at the University of Pennsylvania, where she studied history and languages.

In October 1882 Mary Schenck married prominent New Jersey attorney and state legislator Franklin Conrad Woolman. The union seemed to portend a continuation of her privileged existence, but over the course of their first decade together the family finances deteriorated after the death of her father and serious illnesses of both her husband and her mother. As a result Woolman became responsible for the management of their large house as well as the family's health care provider. She learned how to cook from a restaurant worker, how to take care of invalids at a local hospital, and how to create a household budget. She also became personally aware of how inadequately trained women were in financial matters. In 1891 Woolman was forced to sell her home in Camden and move the family to a boardinghouse in New York City. Living on the verge of bankruptcy, she was forced to take a job as a copy editor in order to stay economically afloat.

During this time Woolman also tried to find a position teaching languages but with the help of Franklin Baker, a fellow boarder, ended up following a different path. Baker, a faculty member of Teachers College at Columbia University, asked Woolman to critique a book on sewing instruction. Her review was harsh, and both Baker and the president of Teachers College were impressed with her analysis; therefore, they requested that she write her own views on the subject. The sewing manual she wrote de-emphasized the English style of fancy work, the educational method then in vogue. Instead of instructing students in the art of making fine stitches on small pieces of unbleached muslin, she stressed selecting the cloth for, figuring the cost of, and making practical garments. In addition, her teaching methods employed aspects of child psychology. These innovations were major breakthroughs in vocational education.

The sewing manual was a success, and in 1892 Teachers College appointed Woolman an assistant in the Department of Domestic Science. The following year, though lacking a college degree, she became an instructor of sewing. At the same time, she also took classes at the college and earned a diploma in 1895 and a B.S. in 1897. After receiving her bachelors degree, she was appointed adjunct professor of household arts education, and in 1903 she became a professor in the department. Always interested in the education of young women, Woolman organized the Department of Domestic Arts and initiated the study of textiles at Teachers College. By 1902 Woolman was the leading specialist in the study of textiles and clothing and in the methods of teaching those subjects on a scientific basis, and a group of prominent New Yorkers asked for her help in addressing the problems of working women. After carefully studying the city's needle trades industry as well as Europe's professional industrial schools for women, Woolman developed a plan for a girls' school to train women in the art of dress making and millinery and to become machine operators in the needle trades. The school, which opened in November 1902, was called the Manhattan Trade School for Girls. Woolman believed that young women should learn how to be good citizens; thus, general education courses, such as basic mathematics and English, which could provide common bonds among Americans, were stressed as well. The school's founding was a significant milestone in the education of working women because not only did it enable women to enter the needle trades industry at a living wage, it also offered advanced night courses for female factory workers to learn more about their particular trades, thereby equipping them with the necessary skills to advance in their chosen fields.

Until 1910 Woolman taught at both Teachers College and the Manhattan Trade School, but that year, after the trade school became part of the city school system, she returned to full-time teaching at Teachers College. In 1912 she left Teachers College to become head of the home economics department at Simmons College in Boston, where she was also appointed president of the Women's Educational and Industrial Union. While at Simmons Woolman gave students there the opportunity to pursue practical training in vocational education. She resigned both positions in 1914 and for the next two years was an educational lecturer for the Retail Trade Board of the Boston Chamber of Commerce. For several years afterward she lectured at various universities and colleges and for many years also served as chair of the Woman's Committee of the National Society for the Promotion of Industrial Education. In 1917 she was a driving force behind passage of the Smith-Hughes Act, which authorized federal financial assistance to vocational education.

In addition to lecturing, Woolman continued to advance her own education. In 1921 and 1926 she attended Radcliffe College, where she and Harvard economist Thomas Nixon Carver studied the textile industry. Their collaboration led in 1935 to the publication of the critically acclaimed *Textile Problems for the Consumer*. Although by then in her seventies, Woolman continued to lecture, write, and study until she was involved in an automobile accident that left her an invalid. She died five years later at her home in Newton, Massachusetts.

The author of and a contributor to several scholarly texts—including *A Sewing Course for Schools* (1900), *A Sewing Course* (1907), *The Making of a Trade School* (1910), *Textiles*, with Ellen B. McGowan (1913), and *Clothing: Choice, Care, and Cost*, ed. B. R. Andrews (1920)—Woolman was an excellent teacher whose influence in the areas of consumer education, the use of textiles, and the education of working women was felt throughout the world. She put the study of textiles on a scientific basis and had a lasting impact on Teachers College by almost single-handedly developing its domestic arts courses. Woolman is best known for her educational work in home economics, particularly vocational training, for which she became in essence national spokesperson for the movement.

• For an account of Woolman's life and professional accomplishments, in addition to articles in the standard biographical reference works, consult Anna M. Cooley, "Mary

Schenck Woolman: Personality and Interest," *Journal of Home Economics* 32 (Nov. 1940): 585–88, and Ellen Beers McGowan, "Mary Schenck Woolman: Contributions to the Teaching of Textiles and Clothing," *Journal of Home Economics* 32 (Nov. 1940): 588–89; also see the *Journal of the National Institute of Social Sciences* 11 (1926): 51–60. Woolman's family history can be found in George R. Prowell, *The History of Camden County, New Jersey* (1886), and *American Ancestry* 4 (1889). An obituary is in *School and Society*, 24 Aug. 1940, p. 124.

CECIL KIRK HUTSON

WOOLRICH, Cornell (4 Dec. 1903–25 Sept. 1968), writer, was born Cornell George Hopley-Woolrich in New York City, the son of Genaro Hopley-Woolrich, a civil engineer, and Claire Attalie Tarler. After his parents divorced, Woolrich spent his early years with his father in Mexico, before moving to New York City at the age of twelve to live with his mother. He attended Columbia University intermittently between 1921 and 1926 but never graduated. While at Columbia Woolrich began to write, and when his first novel *Cover Charge* was published by Boni & Liveright in 1926, he left Columbia and dedicated himself to writing full time.

Between 1926 and 1932 Woolrich published six novels, most of which can be classified as "Jazz Age" fiction in the manner of F. Scott Fitzgerald, who greatly influenced Woolrich. In 1930, while living in Hollywood, Woolrich met and married Violet Virginia "Gloria" Blackton, the daughter of a movie executive. The couple separated after three months, and Woolrich moved back to New York.

In 1932, after the family home was sold, Woolrich and his mother took an apartment together at the Hotel Marseilles in Manhattan. This would be Woolrich's home until his mother's death in 1957. A turning point in Woolrich's career came on 4 August 1934, when he published his first mystery story, "Death Sits in the Dentist's Chair," in *Detective Fiction Weekly*. Woolrich described this move from romantic to mystery fiction as "killing them dead now instead of marrying them off" (Nevins, p. 315), but there may have been a more profound reason for the switch. While living in Mexico with his father, the eleven-year-old Woolrich had had an epiphany that he describes in his autobiographical recollections, *Blues of a Lifetime:* "[I] knew I would surely die finally, or something worse. I had that trapped feeling, like some sort of a poor insect that you've put inside a downturned glass, and it tries to climb up the sides, and it can't, and it can't, and it can't" (p. 16).

This realization gave Woolrich a sense of "personal, private doom" (*Blues*, p. 16) that stayed with him for the rest of his life. Mystery fiction clearly gave Woolrich more freedom to explore this feeling of doom. Whatever the reason for the change, "Death Sits in the Dentist's Chair" was the first of more than 200 stories Woolrich would publish in a bewildering variety of pulp detective fiction magazines, and it was in this field that he would exert his greatest influence. In 1940 Woolrich published his first mystery novel, *The Bride Wore Black*. This story of an obsessed bride tracking down and killing the men she believes to be responsible for her husband's death exemplifies the bleak and violent nature of Woolrich's fictional world.

The Bride Wore Black was the first of six novels in the so-called "Black" series. Woolrich published some fifteen mystery novels in all during his lifetime, either under his own name or under the pseudonyms of William Irish or George Hopley. By the late 1940s Woolrich was recognized as among the best-known, most-influential, and most-successful writers of mystery fiction alive. Woolrich's achievements were recognized in 1948 when the Mystery Writers of America presented him with an Edgar award for his life's work. Ironically, the presentation of the award coincided with the end of Woolrich's most creative period. From this point on he wrote little new material, preferring instead to live on the large amounts of money derived from reprint rights of his earlier work.

In contrast to his professional success, Woolrich's personal life was extremely difficult. Woolrich was troubled for years by his homosexuality and was physically weakened by alcoholism, and his life was dominated by an unusually close attachment to his mother. Claire Attalie Woolrich made it impossible for him to develop a circle of friends or even to leave their apartment for very long. After her death Woolrich moved out of the Hotel Marseilles, but rather than feeling liberated he became progressively more reclusive and embittered. The extent of his decline was vividly illustrated in January 1968 when, having failed to seek medical treatment for a gangrenous leg, he had to have it amputated. By the time Woolrich died later that year in New York City, he had few family or friends to bid him farewell. He left his estate of some $850,000 to Columbia University for the establishment of a scholarship fund for journalism in his mother's memory.

In spite of Woolrich's low opinion of his own work, it secured an important reputation for him. Along with Dashiell Hammett, Raymond Chandler, and James M. Cain, Woolrich is regarded as one of the founders of the noir tradition of detective fiction. Unlike classical detective fiction, with its faith that the detective can restore order and rationality to a world disrupted by crime, noir detective fiction sees chaos and violence as an inescapable feature of modern life, especially of modern urban life. Woolrich's novels and short stories, with their tortured protagonists roaming through darkened cityscapes, desperately trying to avoid their doomed fate, express this world view perfectly. The following words from his 1948 novel *I Married a Dead Man* sum up the feelings of the archetypal Woolrich character: "I don't know what the game was. I only know its name; they call it life. I'm not sure how it should be played. No one ever told me. No one ever tells anybody. I only know we must have played it wrong. . . . We've lost. That's all I know. We've lost, we've lost" (p. 15).

• Woolrich's papers are in the Rare Book and Manuscripts Collection, Butler Library, Columbia University. His major novels include *The Black Curtain* (1941), *Black Alibi* (1942), *Phantom Lady* (1942), *Deadline at Dawn* (1944), *Night Has a Thousand Eyes* (1945), and *Rendezvous in Black* (1948). Two useful collections of his short fiction are *Nightwebs*, ed. Francis M. Nevins, Jr. (1971), and *The Fantastic Stories of Cornell Woolrich*, ed. Charles G. Waugh and Martin H. Greenberg (1981). Nevins's biography, *Cornell Woolrich: First You Dream, Then You Die* (1988), is both monumental and indispensable. An obituary is in the *New York Times*, 26 Sept. 1968.

DAVID SCHMID

WOOLSEY, Abby Howland (16 July 1828–7 Apr. 1893), social worker, educator of nurses, and author, was born in Alexandria, Virginia, the daughter of Charles William Woolsey, a merchant, and Jane Eliza Newton. She spent her early years in England, then in Boston, where her father prospered in the sugar-refining business and she attended the Misses Murdock's School. When, in January 1840, Woolsey's father died on the sinking steamer *Lexington* in Long Island Sound, Woolsey's mother moved the family to New York City. Abby attended the Rutgers Female Institute followed by a year of finishing school at Bolton Priory in New Rochelle, New York. She was an avid reader of Horace Greeley's *New York Tribune*, the works of Thomas Carlyle, Hannah More, and Thomas Macauley, and literature in French, German, and Italian.

Out of school, Woolsey was expected to perform a traditional woman's role in the domestic sphere. However, she disliked such tasks as canning and preserving, and she thought her family's life "consisted in too large a part in receiving friends, uncles, aunts, and cousins into their home, and returning these calls" (Austin, p. 12). She vowed early never to marry, was not overly concerned with her appearance, and devoted herself to the Dutch Reformed Market Street Church, to which her family belonged. Though she attended service three times on Sundays, recorded sermons with "her reflections on her own inner life and spiritual aspirations," taught Sunday school classes, and visited the sick, in her diaries she "reproached herself . . . for her failure to live a life of service to others . . . [and] thought she indulged too much in frivolous pursuits, which she admitted enjoying" (Austin, p. 14).

Accompanying her mother on a trip through the South, in February 1859 Woolsey witnessed a Charleston, South Carolina, slave auction, a spectacle that "perhaps no lady-resident of Charleston" had seen and that "strengthened her already marked abolitionist sentiments" (Bacon and Howland, vol. 1, p. 3). Once sectionalism erupted into the Civil War, she supported the war effort by joining New York women and physicians in founding the Woman's Central Association of Relief. The organization, established in 1861 under the leadership of Dr. Elizabeth Blackwell, distributed supplies and prepared nurses for work in army hospitals. On 9 June President Abraham Lincoln acknowledged the value of this service and established the U.S. Sanitary Commission of which the Woman's Central Association was considered an independent branch.

Woolsey's prewar job as assistant manager at the House of Industry (in which she trained seamstresses) prepared her for the demands of wartime. She organized women from New York City, Boston, and New Haven to make and collect shirts, pants, socks, slippers, handkerchiefs, and pillowcases for distribution to the growing number of army hospitals. Determined to provide relief when and where needed, Woolsey corresponded incessantly with her sisters Georgeanna and Eliza, nurses in army hospitals, to get firsthand news on the war and reports on specific supplies needed. On 19 May 1862 she asked them not to "be mealy-mouthed as to asking, or in mentioning quantities. . . . If all we can do is to *send* things for you to make useful, do let us send enough!" (Bacon and Howland, vol. 1, p. 363). When they informed her of the absence of chaplains in army hospitals, Woolsey, under the aegis of the WCRA, collected names of men interested in becoming army chaplains. Her sister Georgeanna wrote and obtained approval for the appointments from President Lincoln.

By the time Woolsey had closed down her relief operation on the day of Confederate general Robert E. Lee's surrender, 9 April 1865, she had raised a good deal of money and spent much of her own for purchasing supplies. In 1872 her sister Jane, the resident director of the Presbyterian Hospital in New York City, appointed her acting clerk. Together they organized the hospital's care system, and Woolsey filled in as executive officer when her sister Jane was hospitalized for rheumatic fever. After Woolsey resigned in 1876, she invested her time and energy in the New York State Charities Aid Association, of which she was a founding member. Her first assignment was to visit Bellevue Hospital, determine how to improve its care of patients, and develop a professional program to educate nurses for private and public hospital service. In 1873 the Bellevue Hospital Training School for Nurses was founded. Because of Woolsey's organizational experience, "clear thinking," and "good judgment," she was delegated to draft the organizational plan. Woolsey followed the principles of Florence Nightingale, who believed that a nurse's "whole training is to enable them to understand how best to carry out Medical and Surgical orders" and that nurses "must be, for discipline and internal management entirely under a woman, a trained Superintendent" (*A Century of Nursing*). As a member of the school's first managing committee and board of managers, Woolsey attracted applicants to the training school by writing newspaper articles in which she promoted the hospital program. Beginning with six pupils, by 1911 there were 913 graduates and 1,100 additional nursing schools established throughout the United States. Woolsey contributed to enlarging the "sphere of woman's usefulness" by making the occupation of nursing "a noble one."

In 1876 Woolsey went to Europe to observe and report on the nursing practices in the almshouses, hospitals, and charitable institutions of England, France, Germany, Switzerland, Russia, and Italy. She returned and on 24 May presented her report "Hospitals and Training Schools" to the New York Association. Referring to official documents in four languages, medical articles, statements by physicians, clergymen, journalists, and literary persons, Woolsey's report, published in 1876, established her as the "author of the ablest and most valued publications of her time on the subject of trained nursing" (Delavan, p. 123). She also published *Lunacy Legislation in England* (1884).

In 1887 Woolsey was made a life member of the New York Association and remained an active member until 1893. She lived with and cared for her sister Jane until Jane's death in 1891. Woolsey died at her home in New York City.

• The Woolsey family possesses Georgeanna Woolsey's "History of the Woolsey Family," a large manuscript, diaries of Abby Woolsey, 1849–1851, and various newspaper clippings. The papers of the U.S. Sanitary Commission are at the New York Public Library. A complete biography is Anne L. Austin, *The Woolsey Sisters of New York, 1860–1900* (1971). See also L. P. Brockett, *Famous Women of the War: A Record of Heroism, Patriotism, and Patience* (1894). For a detailed genealogical sketch of the Woolsey family see Eliza Woolsey Howland, *Family Records: Being Some Account of the Ancestry of My Father and Mother, Charles William Woolsey and Jane Eliza Newton* (1900), and for pre-eighteenth-century ancestors, "The Woolsey Family of Great Yarmouth and New York" in John Ross Delafield, *Delafield: The Family History*, vol. 2 (1945). Information on Woolsey's Civil War activities and correspondence is in Georgeanna Woolsey Bacon and Eliza Woolsey Howland, eds., *Letters of a Family during the War for the Union 1861–1865*, vol. 1 (1899); Katharine Prescott Wormeley, *The Other Side of War* (1889); and Frederick Law Olmsted, *Hospital Transports* (1863). For Woolsey's postwar activity see *A Century of Nursing* (1950), which contains "Hospitals and Training Schools" (Woolsey's report to the Standing Committee on Hospitals of the State Charities Aid Association of New York, 24 May 1876) and Florence Nightingale's "Historic Letter on the Bellevue School," from which Woolsey outlined the organization of the Bellevue nursing school, and "Founding of the Bellevue Training School for Nurses," chap. 6 of Elizabeth Christophers Hobson's *Recollections of a Happy Life* (1916). See also M. Adelaide Nutting and Lavinia L. Dock, *A History of Nursing*, vol. 2 (1907); Robert J. Carlisle, *An Account of Bellevue Hospital* (1893); and David Bryson Delavan, *Early Days of the Presbyterian Hospital in the City of New York* (1926). Reference to Abby Woolsey is made in the annual reports of the New York State Charities Aid Association from 1874 to 1893.

BARBARA L. CICCARELLI

WOOLSEY, Jane Stuart (7 Feb. 1830–9 July 1891), nursing administrator, philanthropist, and author, was born aboard the ship *Fanny* en route to New York from Norwich, Connecticut, the daughter of Charles William Woolsey, a merchant, and Jane Eliza Newton. The family lived in England for two years with her paternal grandparents, then settled in Boston, where her father's sugar-refining business continued to thrive and Jane and her sisters attended Misses Murdock's School.

After her father's unexpected death in January 1840 on the sinking Long Island steamer *Lexington*, her mother moved the family to New York City. Woolsey attended the Rutgers Female Institute, which was "designed to prepare teachers, and to provide young ladies with a good general background" (Austin, p. 9). During her year at the Bolton Priory finishing school in New Rochelle, New York, she attended public lectures on national affairs. Her poetry and comments on current events and literature in French, Italian, and German reveal a character brimming with wit and determination. In response to letters from her sisters during the Civil War she wrote, "All your details are very interesting. . . . Your *mémoires pour servir* may immortalize you yet." Religious devotion led to study at the Union Theological Seminary and to the founding with her sisters of the Church of the Covenant in 1862.

Woolsey read Horace Greeley's *New York Tribune* and books such as Frederick Olmsted's *The Cotton Kingdom* on the slave economy. She attended antislavery lectures given by Wendell Phillips and Henry Ward Beecher, but, unlike her older sister, Abby Woolsey, to Jane "preservation of the Union was of first importance" (Austin, p. 29). She claimed in an 8 August 1861 letter that "the war is worth what it may cost, although the end may be only—only! the preservation of the Government, and not, just now, the liberation of the slaves" (*Letters*, p. 1). Woolsey joined other prominent New York women in founding the Woman's Central Relief Association, and she helped Abby produce and distribute relief supplies for the Union army from their Brevoort Place home in New York City. When the association became a branch of the newly established U.S. Sanitary Commission, it organized the training and assigning of women nurses to army hospitals.

Woolsey was one of thirty nurses who rotated at the New England Rooms, a temporary war hospital in New York City. Of her experience she wrote, "A great many have died at the city hospitals, and a great many are still here, slowly going, or slowly recovering. We do what we can . . . but it is heart-breaking work; I feel as if I had been wrung out and dried; and how nobly the men behave!" (*Letters*, p. 372). Her warm presence was as meaningful to the patients as her nursing. One patient even wrote to a newspaper of her beauty and charming appearance.

In May 1862 Woolsey joined a committee to investigate conditions at the army hospital on Bedloe's Island, New York, and distributed oranges, jellies, and towels. Because surgeons at first resisted the presence of women in the hospitals, she was surprised in September to be given more responsibilities in her five months at the U.S. General Hospital at Portsmouth Grove, Rhode Island. When assigned in September 1863 to Hammond General Hospital in Point Lookout, Maryland, she vowed nurses would "be involved in no gossip or small quarrels" but would do their work "without partiality and without hypocrisy" (*Letters*, vol. 2, p. 548). Although the army paid the nurses, Woolsey promptly donated her wages to the hospital "in the name of those poor soldiers who shall enjoy the benefits of [the] gift" (*Letters*, vol. 2, p. 551).

With a talent for solving problems and an ability to act quickly, Woolsey was the ideal candidate for superintendent of the nursing and dietary departments at the large Fairfax Theological Seminary Hospital in Alexandria, Virginia. She recorded the complaints of wounded soldiers and their food preferences, observing that some "sick men began to mend on good food alone" (*Hospital Days*, p. 33). Woolsey returned to Fairfax after the funeral of her sister Mary in 1864 and stayed in her "poorly furnished little bedroom" (which she was "perfectly contented and happy with") until August 1865 (*Letters*, vol. 2, pp. 709–10).

After the war Woolsey compiled the notes she had taken while at Fairfax Hospital and printed *Hospital Days* (1868). Concerned for the future of the freed slaves, she opened the Lincoln Industrial School in Richmond, Virginia, and trained black women to make clothes for the poor. From 1869 to 1872 she headed, without compensation, the Girls' Industrial Department at the Hampton Normal and Agricultural Institute. Described by the founder, General Samuel Chapman Armstrong, as "wise," "true," "strong and faithful," Woolsey taught and supervised young black women in housework and needlework. Her favorite recreational activity was sailing her boat, *The Quakeress*. After she left in 1872, the year Booker T. Washington arrived, she remained involved in the school's progress, contributing scholarship money and encouraging friends to do the same.

When she accepted the position of resident director of the newly established Presbyterian Hospital in New York City, she chose her highly qualified sister Abby to design the organization of the hospital. Meanwhile she taught a corps of nurses "the basic principles of the art of nursing" (Austin, p. 125). Woolsey even raised funds for the hospital by publishing in daily papers unsigned human interest stories on the hospital and its patients. On leaving in 1876, she urged the staff to continue thinking of patients as guests and to treat the smallest task with utmost diligence.

For the remainder of her life she was an active member of the New York State Charities Aid Association, organized in January 1872 as a peacetime version of the Woman's Central Relief Association. As a member of the Subcommittee on the Insane, she reported on the needs and conditions of public institutions. Jane Woolsey, who never married, lived with Abby, who cared for her until she died in Matteawan, New York.

• Members of the Woolsey family possess Georgeanna Woolsey's "History of the Woolsey Family," the diaries of Abby Woolsey, 1849–1851, and newspaper clippings. For a full-length biography on the Woolsey sisters, see Anne L. Austin, *The Woolsey Sisters of New York, 1860–1900* (1971). For a genealogical history before the eighteenth century, see "Woolsey Family of Great Yarmouth and N.Y." in the appendix of John Ross Delafield, *Delafield: The Family History*, vol. 2 (1945). Post–eighteenth century genealogy of the Woolsey family can be found in Eliza Newton Woolsey Howland, *Family Records* (1900). Georgeanna Woolsey Bacon and Eliza Newton Woolsey Howland provide an intimate sense of the effect the Civil War had on the Woolsey family with *Letters of a Family during the War for the Union, 1861–1865*, vol. 1 (1899). Further reference to Jane Woolsey's contribution to the Civil War relief effort can be found in "The Misses Woolsey," in L. P. Brockett, *Famous Women of the War: A Record of Heroism, Patriotism, and Patience* (1894). To contextualize her involvement in nursing and hospitals, see M. Adelaide Nutting and Lavinia L. Dock, *A History of Nursing: The Evolution of Nursing Systems from the Earliest Times to the Foundation of the First English and American Training Schools for Nurses*, vol. 2 (1907), esp. chap. nine; Katharine Prescott Wormeley, *The Other Side of War* (1889); and Frederick Law Olmsted, *Hospital Transports: A Memoir of the Embarkation of the Sick and Wounded from the Peninsula of Virginia in the Summer of 1862* (1863). For Woolsey's postwar activities, see Edith A. Talbot, *Samuel Chapman Armstrong* (1904); Francis Greenwood Peabody, *Education for Life* (1918); David Bryson Delavan, *Early Days of the Presbyterian Hospital in the City of New York* (1926), and *Annual Reports* of the N.Y. State Charities Aid Association, 1874–1892.

BARBARA L. CICCARELLI

WOOLSEY, Melancthon Taylor (5 June 1780–18 May 1838), U.S. naval officer, was born in New York State, the son of Colonel Melancthon Lloyd Woolsey and Alida Livingston. Colonel Woolsey was an officer in the Continental army and the New York State levies during the Revolution and later was collector of the port at Plattsburg on Lake Champlain. The younger Melancthon attended Flatbush Academy, where he developed a competence in the French language. He gave up the study of law to accept a commission as a midshipman on 9 April 1800. Serving first in the West Indies during the naval war with France and then two tours in the Mediterranean in the war with Tripoli, in 1801–1803 and 1804–1807, he learned seamanship and earned the confidence of his superiors. He was appointed acting lieutenant in 1804 and received his commission as lieutenant on 14 February 1807.

In 1808 Woolsey began a long-term association with the Great Lakes when he was ordered to superintend the building of a large gunboat on Lake Ontario (as well as two smaller ones on Lake Champlain). He established his headquarters at Oswego, New York, where he supervised the shipwrights Henry Eckford and Christian Bergh in the building of the sixteen-gun brig *Oneida*, the first U.S. naval vessel built on the Great Lakes. Under Woolsey's command, the *Oneida* operated out of Sackets Harbor, New York, near the source of the St. Lawrence River, and opposite Kingston, Upper Canada, the base of the British naval squadron on Lake Ontario. On 5 June 1812 the *Oneida* seized the British merchant schooner *Lord Nelson* for violating the embargo. On 19 July, the United States having declared war on Great Britain, the British squadron of five vessels of war made an attempt against the *Oneida* and her prize anchored in Sackets Harbor. Woolsey, after failing to get the *Oneida* into open water, anchored again where the brig could rake the harbor entrance and placed the guns from her land side in a battery ashore. After an exchange of cannon fire lasting two hours, the British squadron retired.

In the autumn the Navy Department made Woolsey subordinate to Commodore Isaac Chauncey, whom they sent to superintend a major buildup of naval power on the Great Lakes. Retaining command of the *Oneida*, Woolsey participated in the attack on Kingston in November. He was promoted master commandant on 24 July 1813 and joined in assaults on York and Fort George. Transferred to command of the sixteen-gun *Sylph*, launched 18 August 1813, he took part in the American squadron's numerous encounters with the British squadron during August and September. In May 1814 the British, having gained temporary naval superiority on the lake, blockaded Sackets Harbor, preventing delivery from Oswego Falls of heavy guns and cables needed to complete ships for the American squadron. Woolsey led an expedition of nineteen boats to carry the guns and cables to a creek close enough to Sackets Harbor that they could be transported safely overland. On the morning of 29 May, concealed with its cargo up Big Sandy Creek, Woolsey's command, assisted by riflemen, cavalry, light artillery, and some warriors from the allied Oneida nation, ambushed the British expedition sent out to intercept them. Taken by surprise, the entire British force of some 180 men, two gunboats, three cutters, and a gig, having many killed and wounded, surrendered. With the guns and cables delivered for the newly launched ships, the Americans regained control of the lake. Woolsey commanded the twenty-gun brig *Jones*, one of the new vessels, until the close of the war.

Promoted to captain on 27 April 1816, Woolsey remained at Sackets Harbor, once more in charge of the station, until 1824. In 1825 and 1826, on the frigate *Constellation*, he cruised against West Indian pirates. He was in charge of the navy yard at Pensacola in 1827–1831, was commodore of the Brazil station in 1832–1834, and oversaw surveys of Chesapeake Bay in 1836–1837. A disease, perhaps a form of hepatitis, that he developed while in Florida worsened during the last-named service and, accompanied by edema, led to his death at Utica, New York. He had married Susan Cornelia Tredwell in 1817; one of their seven children, Melancthon Brooks Woolsey, became a naval officer.

"Commodore Woolsey was of the middle height, sailor-built, and of a compact, athletic frame," wrote James Fenimore Cooper, who served as a midshipman under Woolsey's command on Lake Ontario before the War of 1812 (Cooper, p. 144). In Cooper's account, Woolsey comes across as an accomplished sailor, physically strong and attractive, companionable, popular, and even-tempered. Energetic and levelheaded, he led more through good humor than through the exercise of discipline. During an exploration by boat of Lake Ontario when provisions ran out, for instance, he kept the hungry men in good spirits with his jokes. Cooper praised Woolsey's application of discipline, attributing to him the want rather of "the grimace than the substance of authority" (p. 145). Statistical analysis of the use of flogging in the early American navy, nonetheless, suggests that Woolsey was among the least successful commanders in keeping troublemakers from becoming repeat offenders, perhaps because of his favoring a relatively low number of lashes (McKee, pp. 241–45). Cooper called Woolsey "a pleasing mixture of gentleman-like refinement and seaman-like frankness" and noted his chivalry toward women. An incident when Woolsey was still a midshipman in the Mediterranean, recounted in *Naval Documents Related to the United States Wars with the Barbary Powers* (vol. 2 [1940], p. 387), illustrates the generous character for which he was known. When the wife of one of the petty officers on board the USS *Constellation* gave birth at sea, Woolsey arranged for the child's baptism and "provided a handsome collation of Wine & Fruit." In gratitude, the parents named the child after him. Woolsey is most notable for the able contribution he made to the U.S. Navy's struggle to maintain naval superiority on Lake Ontario during the War of 1812.

• Woolsey's official correspondence is in the National Archives, RG 45, in particular in the correspondence of the secretary of the navy. Published documentation of his War of 1812 experiences is in William S. Dudley et al., eds., *The Naval War of 1812: A Documentary History*, vol. 1, *1812*, and vol. 2, *1813* (1985–1992). Abstracts of his service record as well as correspondence concerning research on his family and his widow's pension application are in the ZB Collection, Operational Archives, Naval Historical Center, Washington, D.C. James Fenimore Cooper's biography of Woolsey, which includes Cooper's personal reminiscences of his former commander, is in *Lives of Distinguished American Naval Officers*, vol. 2 (1846), pp. 113–45. Useful information will be found in Benson J. Lossing, *The Pictorial Fieldbook of the War of 1812* (1868; facsimile repr. 1976), as well as other standard military histories of the War of 1812. Christopher McKee, *A Gentlemanly and Honorable Profession: The Creation of the U.S. Naval Officer Corps, 1794–1815* (1991), includes extracts from Woolsey's personal journal, 1801–1803 (in a private collection), as well as an analysis of his use of flogging.

MICHAEL J. CRAWFORD

WOOLSEY, Sarah Chauncy (29 Jan. 1835–9 Apr. 1905), author also known by the pseudonym "Susan Coolidge," was born in Cleveland, Ohio, the daughter of John Mumford Woolsey, a land agent, and Jane Andrews. She attended Mrs. Hubbard's Boarding School in Hanover, New Hampshire, concentrating on literature and history, followed by Hanover's Select Family School or "The Nunnery," as it was then called by the students and later by Woolsey in her fiction. According to Evelyn I. Banning, Woolsey was "uncommonly tall, a vigorous young woman with a sparkling personality, who laughed easily and talked well" (p. 54). In 1852 her father retired and in 1855 moved the family to New Haven, Connecticut, where her uncle Theodore Dwight Woolsey was president of Yale.

Woolsey befriended author Helen Hunt Jackson shortly after moving to New Haven. When the Civil War began, both Woolsey and Jackson volunteered at

New Haven's Knight United States General Hospital, where wounded soldiers were sent from the battlefields on hospital transports. Jackson, known as "H.H.," fictionalized their experiences mending linen and distributing supplies in her children's story "Joe Hale's Red Stockings" (*Scribner's Monthly*, 1878). After volunteering with cousin Jane Woolsey at a New York temporary army hospital, the New England Rooms, in September 1862, she, Jane, and Jane's sister Georgeanna became assistant superintendents of nurses at Lowell General Hospital in Portsmouth Grove, Rhode Island. Woolsey's "winning manners, her tender and skilful care of the patients, and her unwearied efforts to do them good, made her a general favorite" (Brockett, p. 342). In the spring of 1863 her family's fear of an outbreak of smallpox in the camp convinced Woolsey to return home.

After the death of her father and a trip abroad, in 1870 Woolsey and Jackson traveled to the mountain town of Bethlehem, New Hampshire, where Woolsey collected ferns and flowers to sketch or paint, composed poetry, and outlined her first book for children. *The New-Year's Bargain* is a collection of twelve stories, one for each month, redeeming a promise made to a little boy. Thomas Niles, the editor of Roberts Brothers of Boston who discovered Louisa May Alcott, published the book in the spring of 1871. The book received positive reviews in America and England, particularly from writer Jean Ingelow and poet Christina Rossetti. Furthermore, in Woolsey the publisher found a future editor and reader. "[Woolsey] had a good deal of discretion and skill as an editor, and her knowledge of books and her sense of literature constituted no small part of the capital of Roberts Brothers at the time when the imprint of that firm meant a certain individuality and distinction" (*Outlook*, 15 Apr. 1905, p. 924).

With their publication earnings, in 1872 Woolsey and Jackson left New York by train for San Francisco via Salt Lake City. Though Woolsey is never mentioned by name, Jackson writes of their experience in *Bits of Travel at Home*. Woolsey meanwhile established herself as a talented children's story writer, choosing the pseudonym "Susan Coolidge," because her younger sister Jane Woolsey Yardley had written under the pen name "Margaret Coolidge." Unlike Alcott's audience of "little women," Woolsey wrote for the preadolescent girl. Most of her fiction is based on the childhood she shared in the outdoors with her three sisters, brother, and an adopted cousin at the large Euclid Avenue family home in Cleveland. Fashioning the main character of *What Katy Did* (1872) after herself, Woolsey creates an "illusion of a free world of youthful experience, albeit a temporary one" in which adults do not interfere (Foster, p. 107). Unlike Woolsey who lost her father, the Carr children have experienced the death of their mother, whom Katy is expected to replace. Yet rather than entirely subordinate Katy to the ideal of woman as self-sacrificing and abnegating, Woolsey portrays her as defiant: "Katy's girlhood is . . . unrestricted, and she too enjoys an ethos in which the exercise of female energies is not necessarily viewed with abhorrence or wholly stultified by properties" (Foster, p. 109).

The book gained recognition, though not all laudatory. Mark Twain accused Woolsey of plagiarizing material from his *Innocents Abroad* for the journal of Katy's smallest sibling, Dorry. Woolsey's old friend Jackson, however, insisted in a 14 January 1873 letter to Charles Dudley Warner, the editor of the *Hartford Courant*, that the journal was based on one her late son Rennie had written when he was six. Woolsey wrote four additional Katy stories about the Carr children playing games, attending school, relating with friends and family, traveling, and marrying: *What Katy Did at School* (1874), *What Katy Did Next* (1886), *Clover* (1888), and *In the High Valley* (1890).

Woolsey published with Roberts Brothers until 1898, then with its successor, Little, Brown and Company. Her later work consists mainly of poetry and historical and travel sketches that appeared in *Outlook*, *Scribner's*, and *Woman's Home Companion*. Her poems were collected in three volumes: *Verses* (1880), *A Few More Verses* (1889), and *Last Verses* (1906), printed postmortem with an introduction by her sister Elizabeth Woolsey Gilman. Woolsey's adult works include a collection of historical sketches in *A Short History of the City of Philadelphia from Its Foundation to the Present Time* (1887), *Ballads of Romance and History, with Others* (1887), and *An Old Convent School in Paris, and Other Papers* (1895). She edited and abridged *Autobiography and Correspondence of Mrs. Delany* (1879), *The Diary and Letters of Frances Burney Madame d'Arblay* (1880), and *Letters of Jane Austen, Selected from the Compilation of Her Great Nephew Edward, Lord Bradbourne* (1892) and translated from French Théophile Gautier's *My Household of Pets* (1882) and Arnaud's *One Day in a Baby's Life* (1886).

Woolsey was known for her "marked individuality, delightful humor, conversational ability . . . and many intellectual resources" (*Outlook*, 15 Apr. 1905, p. 924). In addition to writing and painting flowers, she gardened and enjoyed hosting at the Newport, Rhode Island, home she and her sister Dora Woolsey, also unmarried, purchased in 1874. An accomplished cook, she contributed "A Group of Recipes from a New England Kitchen" to the *Century Cookbook*, edited by Mary Ronald. She died in Newport, Rhode Island.

• For Woolsey's family history, see Appleton's listing for Theodore Dwight Woolsey in *Cyclopaedia of American Biography* (1888), Franklin B. Dexter's listing for Woolsey's father in *Biographical Sketches of the Graduates of Yale College*, vol. 6 (1912), p. 614, and Gertrude Van Rensselaer Wickham, *The Pioneer Families of Cleveland* (1914). Woolsey's volunteer work during the Civil War is mentioned in Anne L. Austin, *The Woolsey Sisters of New York, 1860–1900* (971), and L. P. Brockett, *Famous Women of the War: A Record of Heroism, Patriotism, and Patience* (1894). Helen Hunt Jackson records her impressions of Bethlehem in "The Miracle Play of 1870, in Bethlehem, New Hampshire" in *Bits of Travel at Home* (1878). Woolsey's affiliation with Jackson is detailed in biographies of Jackson by Ruth Odell, *Helen Hunt Jackson* (1939), and Evelyn I. Banning, *Helen Hunt Jackson* (1973). For reference to Woolsey's publishers and her affiliation with her editors, see Raymond L. Kilgour, *Messrs. Roberts Brothers, Publishers* (1952), and letters in Little, Brown & Co. files at the Galatea Collection of the Boston Public Library and the Yale University Library. For a complete list of Woolsey's publications, see Ruth K. MacDonald's entry for Woolsey in the *Dictionary of Literary Biography*, vol. 42. Frances C. Darling provides an overview of Woolsey's career as "Susan Coolidge" in *Horn Book Magazine*, June 1959. For a critical reading of her stories for children, see Shirley Foster, "Susan Coolidge: What Katy Did," in *What Katy Read: Feminist Re-readings of "Classic" Stories for Girls* (1995). Obituaries are in the *New York Times*, 10 Apr. 1905, and *Outlook*, 15 Apr. 1905, p. 924.

BARBARA L. CICCARELLI

WOOLSEY, Theodore Dwight (31 Oct. 1801–1 July 1889), president of Yale College, was born in New York City, the son of William Walton Woolsey, a well-to-do hardware merchant, and Elizabeth Dwight. After the family moved to New Haven, the young Woolsey attended the Hopkins Grammar School and the famous academy at Greenfield Hill, Connecticut. At fifteen he entered Yale and graduated as class valedictorian in 1820.

Woolsey's search for a vocation was protracted. He first studied law in the Philadelphia law offices of his relative Charles Chauncey and then prepared for the ministry with studies at the Princeton Theological Seminary. After election as a tutor, he returned to Yale College in 1823 and completed his studies in its theological department under Nathaniel William Taylor. Not wishing to be ordained and enter the ministry, he went to Europe in 1827 for advanced study. In Paris he tried Arabic but then devoted himself to mastery of the Greek language and literature at various German universities.

Returning to New Haven in 1831, he became professor of Greek at Yale. As the preeminent Greek scholar in America, Woolsey published many translations. Through his works such as *The Alcestis of Euripides* (1834) and *The Antigone of Sophocles* (1835), an American collegiate audience learned of the latest German linguistic scholarship.

In 1846 the Yale Corporation elected him to the college presidency in recognition of his scholarship and the esteem in which his colleagues held him. Doubting his suitability for ordination to the Congregational ministry, a prerequisite for the position, he later yielded to persuasion. In the early to mid-nineteenth century, it was customary for college presidents to teach the senior class. So Woolsey relinquished his teaching of Greek and instituted courses in history, political science, and international law, for which he was prepared by his previous study of the law and his study of ancient history and cultures. His Yale lectures on international law and political science were published as *Introduction to the Study of International Law* (1860) and *Political Science* (1877). Both texts were important collegiate textbooks throughout the remainder of the century and remained in print until 1908 and 1905, respectively. *International Law* had both Japanese and English editions and is reputed to have been in use at Oxford.

When Woolsey introduced political science into the Yale curriculum, he divided into two halves the traditional moral philosophy course that Princeton president John Witherspoon had introduced to America in 1768. While Woolsey's colleague Noah Porter lectured on man's private duties in moral philosophy courses, Woolsey lectured on the citizen's duties in the public sphere in his political science classes. Woolsey's notes show that he was fully cognizant of contemporary European works describing the state as a product of historical development, and he adapted his view of the state as a means to accomplish God's ends to these new conceptions. While he argued that theories of rights and government developed over time, he proposed the state as means of moral improvement—God's means to do his appointed work in the world. The state permitted sufficient freedom for human self-development, restricted public behavior destructive of self-development, and established institutions to promote self-development. Thus, Woolsey especially favored the state as the sponsor of public education, for he thought that social and political improvement came only "from sentiments that grow up in individual minds." His vision of a positive moral state put him and his colleagues at Yale in favor of Whig, and later Republican, political theory and in opposition to Democratic theory. In the postwar years, he argued that the state could promote freedom by cultivating each person's "moral nature thorough the discipline of justice," contrary to British and American advocates of a liberalism that advocated a state with minimal powers.

While president, Woolsey attracted a remarkable group of scholars to Yale to enrich its curriculum and strengthen its academic presence. These included James Dwight Dana, geologist and mineralogist; George Park Fisher, church historian; Noah Porter, moral philosopher and psychologist; and William Dwight Whitney, Sanskrit scholar and philologist. While faculty size increased from 37 to 65, the student body also grew from 584 to 788. Under his leadership, Yale established the Sheffield Scientific School and its graduate school (1860) and granted the first Ph.D. degree in the United States in 1863. While Woolsey did not move fast or decisively enough to keep Yale at the forefront of educational change, it educated many late nineteenth-century university presidents, including such innovators and institution builders as Daniel Coit Gilman and Andrew Dickson White.

Woolsey believed that a scholar should influence a broad audience of educated men. To this end, in 1843 he and his Yale colleagues had founded the *New Englander*, a journal dedicated to disseminating their scholarly, political, and educational views beyond New Haven. For Yale graduates and Congregationalists in New England and areas of New England settlement, the *New Englander* carried the same importance as Boston journals such as the *North American Review* and the *Christian Observer* did for Harvard graduates and Unitarians. Of all public issues, Woolsey was most concerned with threats to the family and to the state. He published *Divorce and Divorce Legislation* (1869) and *Communism and Socialism in Their History and Theory* (1880), collections of articles from the *New Englander* and the *Independent* (a Congregationalist, free soil paper published in New York City with the largest circulation of any northern weekly newspaper), respectively.

After Woolsey's retirement in 1871, his scholarly record and knowledge of Greek earned him the presiding position on the New Testament subcommittee of the American Committee for the Revision of the English Bible. Woolsey continued to serve Yale as a member of its corporation. He spent his retirement years collecting his Yale lectures for publication, composing articles on timely subjects, and revising the New Testament. Augustus St. Gaudens completed a bust, and John F. Weir, director and professor in the Yale School of Fine Arts, a statue. Woolsey died in New Haven. He had been first married in 1833 to Elizabeth Martha Salisbury, with whom he had nine children. After her death, he had married Sarah Sears Prichard in 1854; they had four children.

Though Woolsey's contemporaries held his scholarship in international law and Greek in great esteem, historians have only recently begun to rediscover his influence. Contemporary educational historians stress the relationship between the evangelical commitment of scholars like Woolsey to their scholarly attainments and now realize the significant advances in American scholarship that occurred at Yale under Woolsey and his successor. Woolsey's influence has yet to be recovered by political scientists. They have assumed that Progressive-era scholars and politicians rebelled against theories of the negative state taught by Woolsey's maverick pupil William Graham Sumner. When historians recognize the antecedents of Progressive-era thought in Whig-Republican theories of a positive state, they will rediscover Woolsey's crucial place in American political thought.

• The major collection of manuscripts is in the Woolsey Family Papers, Yale University Library. For a study of Woolsey, see Louise L. Stevenson, *Scholarly Means to Evangelical Ends: The New Haven Scholars and the Transformation of Higher Learning in America, 1830–1890* (1986). Also see George Park Fisher, "The Academic Career of Ex-President Woolsey," *Century Magazine* 24 (1882): 709–17, and Woolsey's son Theodore S. Woolsey, "Theodore Dwight Woolsey," *Yale Review* (1912).

LOUISE L. STEVENSON

WOOLSON, Constance Fenimore (5 Mar. 1850–24 Jan. 1894), writer, was born in Claremont, New Hampshire, the daughter of Charles Jarvis Woolson, a businessman, and Hannah Cooper Pomeroy, a niece of James Fenimore Cooper. Woolson was only weeks old when three of her sisters died of scarlet fever. These circumstances may have exacted a price on the writer, causing her to see life as particularly fragile and childbearing and motherhood as situations fraught with pain. Although some evidence suggests that she had a crush on a Union officer during the Civil War, Woolson was never seriously romantically involved with anyone male or female, her closest associates being family members.

Woolson was reared in the burgeoning mercantile and cultural atmosphere of Cleveland, Ohio, where she attended the Cleveland Female Seminary. She completed her formal education at Madame Chegaray's School in New York City, which provided the model for the schoolgirl scenes in *Anne*, Woolson's first major novel. Before *Anne*, however, Woolson had published a prize-winning young person's novel, *The Old Stone House* (1872), under the pseudonym of Anne March, several travel narratives in the *Cleveland Daily Mail*, and some short fiction in the *Galaxy* and *Appleton's*. A handful of these early stories set in the territory bordering the Great Lakes were collected in *Castle Nowhere: Lake Country Stories* (1875), published by James Osgood. Woolson built upon her growing reputation with the publication of *Anne*, serialized in *Harper's New Monthly Magazine* (1880) and later appearing in book form (1882). A sentimental tale of a strong young woman who saves her lover by revealing the identity of the real murderer in a climactic courtroom scene, *Anne* eventually sold 57,600 copies. Close upon the heels of her first novel came the publication of Woolson's second collection of short fiction, *Rodman the Keeper: Southern Sketches* (1880). Although the volume, like *Castle Nowhere*, was to have appeared with an Osgood imprint, *Harper's*, which had published *Anne*, secured the rights to all of Woolson's work, both past and future. (Throughout her life Woolson felt a strong obligation to *Harper's*, even foregoing possibilities for improving the terms of her contracts with other publishing houses.)

After her father's death in 1869, Woolson and her mother wintered along the East Coast, in North Carolina and in St. Augustine, Florida. But when her mother died in 1879, Woolson moved to Europe, never to return to the United States. The following spring she met Henry James (1843–1916), and a great friendship was born that left indelible marks on both writers' works. The two writers dined together, visited museums, and discussed each other's literary efforts. One of Woolson's best-known short stories, "'Miss Grief'" (1880), recalls James in its narrative voice and in its subject, that of a writer's literary legacy.

Following her move abroad, Woolson wrote novels, short stories, travel narratives, and poetry from her temporary homes in various locales: Florence, Venice, and Rome (winters 1880–1883); Switzerland and Germany (summers 1880–1883); London and Warwickshire (1883–1886); Florence (1887–1889); Cheltenham, Gloucestershire (1890–1891); Oxford (1891–1893); and Venice (1893–1894). She also toured France (1879–1880), Greece (1889), and Egypt (1890). Her novels, however, were written with American backdrops. *For the Major* (1883), set in the Carolina mountains, features an aging matron who maintains a youthful appearance out of love for her increasingly senile husband. *East Angels* (1886) is named for the Florida orange plantation where Garda Thorne and Margaret Harold play out their drama of love, duty, and sacrifice. Woolson's next novel, *Jupiter Lights* (1889), again features two women, both of whom love an abusive ne'er-do-well, Ferdinand Morrison, whose final redemption is not entirely convincing. *Horace Chase* (1894), Woolson's last novel, presented a departure for the writer, whose primary concern was to present a believable male protagonist.

While writing the novels, Woolson was also working on two volumes of short stories set in Europe: *The Front Yard and Other Italian Stories* (1895) and *Dorothy and Other Italian Stories* (1896). The most provocative pieces in these last collections are the title story of the former volume, which features an exiled New Englander whose only dream, after a life of hard work and emotional abuse by her Italian family, is to have a front yard; and "At the Château of Corinne," in *Dorothy*, which presents the tale of an aspiring poet who must deny her art when she marries a decidedly unliberated man. These two collections and a book of travel sketches, *Mentone, Cairo, and Corfu* (1896), were published posthumously.

Evidence suggests that Woolson's death, caused by a fall from a window of her rented Venetian rooms, was a suicide. Although her life and works have been interpreted largely in terms of her relationship to her famous companion, Henry James, Woolson's oeuvre is currently regaining her reputation as a talented realist in her own right. Her fiction, especially her stories about women artists, has been widely praised, appearing in literary anthologies and as the subject of presentations at scholarly conferences. Those who read and teach Woolson hold her up as an exemplary writer and traveler, who, because of her traditional upbringing in a world that gendered public expression as masculine, lived in constant conflict with her own domestic and professional expectations.

• The most significant collections of Woolson's letters and other memorabilia are in the Mather Family Papers at the Western Reserve Historical Society, Cleveland, Ohio; the E. C. Stedman Manuscript Collection at Butler Library, Columbia University; the Hay Family Papers at Brown Library, Brown University; and the Woolson Collection at Olin Library, Rollins College, Winter Park, Fla. Four important letters from Woolson to Henry James are reprinted in Leon Edel, ed., *Henry James Letters*, vol. 3 (1980). The best recent reprint of some of her short fiction is *Women Artists, Women Exiles: The Short Fiction of Constance Fenimore Woolson*, edited and with a superb introduction by Joan Myers Weimer.

Books about Constance Fenimore Woolson include John D. Kern, *Constance Fenimore Woolson: Literary Pioneer* (1934); Rayburn S. Moore, *Constance Fenimore Woolson* (1963); Cheryl B. Torsney, *Constance Fenimore Woolson: The Grief of Artistry* (1989); and Cheryl B. Torsney, ed., *Critical Essays on Constance Fenimore Woolson* (1992). Obituaries and discussions of the circumstances of Woolson's death include Henry M. Alden's in *Harper's Weekly*, 3 and 10 Feb. 1894, and those appearing in the *New York Times*, 25, 27, and 28 Jan. and 1 Feb. 1894.

CHERYL B. TORSNEY

WOOLWORTH, Frank Winfield (13 Apr. 1852–8 Aug. 1919), retailer, was born in Rodman, Jefferson County, New York, the son of John Hubbell Woolworth and Fanny McBrier, farmers. At the end of 1858, his paternal grandfather sold the landholdings in Rodman where Woolworth's family lived and farmed, and Woolworth's father had to find a new home. By spring 1859 Woolworth's father had relocated his family to a farm near Great Bend, also in Jefferson County. Woolworth attended common schools in Great Bend, New York. When he was sixteen years old his mother paid for him to spend a few months studying commerce at a commercial college in Watertown, New York.

While he worked on the family farm until he reached age twenty-one, Woolworth also worked for two winters as an unpaid assistant at a general store in Great Bend owned by Daniel McNeill. In March 1873 Woolworth was offered a job on the farm of his uncle, Albon S. McBrier. However, Woolworth detested farmwork and did not accept the offer. Instead, he tried hard to find a job in the retail trade. Later in 1873 he succeeded in obtaining a six-month trial with the merchants Augsbury & Moore in Watertown, New York. His position was unpaid for the first three months, and during the second three months he received $3.50 a week—this was just sufficient to pay his board. When the six months were completed, Woolworth's remuneration was increased by fifty cents a week. At the beginning of his third year, Augsbury's interest in the store was acquired by Perry R. Smith, and the business became Moore & Smith.

In the fall of 1875 Woolworth was appointed senior clerk at A. Bushnell and Company, a dry goods and carpet store in Watertown. In 1876 Woolworth returned to his position with his previous employer. However, Woolworth's poor health forced him to take a prolonged period of unpaid sick leave and to return to his father's farm. While recuperating on the farm, Woolworth married Jennie Creighton, a 23-year-old seamstress from Picton, Ontario, Canada, in 1876. They had three daughters.

In 1877 he returned to Watertown as senior clerk with Moore & Smith. In the spring of 1878 he helped introduce a five-cent counter in the store: this was to prove a revolutionary new concept in retailing. This concept had been developed by a former salesman at A. Bushnell and Company. Woolworth saw its commercial potential and adapted it by displaying goods on counters so customers could select items themselves. This meant that there was no longer any requirement for skilled clerks in the stores that he was to open. Relatively well-paid clerks were to be replaced with low-paid young women, who, in the long run, were to be an important cost advantage in a business with very low profit margins.

On 22 February 1879 Woolworth opened his first "Great 5-Cent Store" in Utica, New York, with $350 worth of goods purchased with a note underwritten by his former employer, W. H. Moore. This store was unsuccessful because it was poorly located; it was closed after three months. However, in June 1879 Woolworth opened a second store in Lancaster, Pennsylvania, which was a success. By 1882 three out of Woolworth's first five stores had failed, due to an insufficient number of customers and a lack of buying experience; of the remaining two, one was a great success and the other only partially successful.

During the 1880s Woolworth expanded his business partly through the use of partners. In 1885 Moore—now sole proprietor of his business—was on the verge of bankruptcy. Woolworth helped Moore to save his business by assisting him in the establishment of a five-and-ten-cent store. By 1886 Woolworth controlled seven stores with various partners. Woolworth's business strategy had some similarities with the modern-day franchising concept because the use of partnerships helped to minimize his own personal outlay of capital. In 1886 his expanding business led to the establishment of an administrative and purchasing office in New York City.

In 1888 stress and overwork made Woolworth ill and this persuaded him to incorporate his business in order to insure its survival. However, it was not until 1905 that he finally formed F. W. Woolworth & Co. In 1890 Woolworth moved to Brooklyn, New York. During the 1890s the five- and ten-cent stores started to adopt a diamond with a "W" in the center as a trademark. The same decade also saw a considerable improvement in the terms and conditions of employment for the Woolworth staff. In 1896 Woolworth, in response to upward pressure on wages in the retail sector, introduced a Christmas bonus, one week's paid holiday per annum for those with service of six months or longer, and a minimum wage of $2.50 a week for the female clerks. In 1898 Woolworth expanded into New England with the purchase of a group of nine stores from E. P. Charlton.

During the 1890s Woolworth began a series of annual vacations to Europe. On his first vacation in 1890, he discovered that Germany had a comparative advantage over the United States in the manufacture of toys and Christmas decorations. As a result, he started to import large quantities of toys and decorations from Germany. During this visit to Europe Woolworth also discovered that the Austrian Kingdom of Bohemia would be a good source of cheap vases and glass goods. By 1911 Woolworth was purchasing three-quarters of all the Christmas tree decorations made in Germany for his stores. In his quest to keep costs as low as possible he began to purchase "German toys" made in Japan. By this time he was employing seven buyers in foreign countries to purchase, for example, china, toys, laces, and agate ware.

Woolworth's 1890 European visit revealed to him the potential for five-and-ten stores in Great Britain. However, his first foreign store was actually opened in Canada in 1897. It was not until 1909 that he founded his British store chain, F. W. Woolworth & Company Ltd. His first British store was opened in November 1909 in Liverpool. It was to be the first of many British stores.

In 1900 Woolworth began to adopt a uniform appearance for his stores, which now numbered fifty-nine. After some experimentation, he adopted a fast and brilliant carmine red for his store fronts and show windows. In 1901 he purchased a new thirty-room mansion on New York City's Fifth Avenue. The following year, he increased the minimum wage in his stores to $3 a week. In 1904 Woolworth acquired over forty stores in the Midwest, Pennsylvania, and Massachusetts, bringing the total number of stores in the Woolworth syndicate to 120. In 1912 Woolworth merged his stores with rival five-and-dime stores owned by Moore, C. S. Woolworth, F. M. Kirby, S. H. Knox, and E. P. Charlton, to form the F. W. Woolworth Co. The new company owned 596 stores. During the early part of the same year Woolworth had a nervous breakdown. In May he left New York City to spend six weeks taking the cure in the West Bohemian spa towns of Carlsbad and Marienbad. After a motor tour of Switzerland and France, he returned to New York City. But in October he was taken ill again and was sent on another vacation to Europe by his doctor. By the spring of 1913 Woolworth had recovered sufficiently to attend the opening of the new Woolworth building by President Woodrow Wilson on 24 April. The Woolworth Building was a skyscraper that had been commissioned by Woolworth in the spring of 1910. It was designed by the architect Cass Gilbert, was 787 feet tall, cost over $13 million to construct, and was self-financed by Woolworth.

World War I caused considerable disruption to Woolworth's business because he was cut off from his European suppliers. It proved difficult to find suitable American substitutes for much of his imported merchandise. Nonetheless the number of Woolworth stores continued to grow and by 1919 the company controlled 1,081 five-and-ten stores in the United States and Canada.

During the summer of 1919 Woolworth was taken ill with a number of maladies, including bad teeth. He refused to have his teeth treated and developed septic poisoning, which contributed to his death at his country home in Glen Cove, Long Island, New York. He left a net estate of $27 million. In addition to his share of the eponymous company, at the time of his death he was also one of the largest stockholders in the Broadway-Park Place Company—which owned the Woolworth Building and other New York City real estate—and in the Irving National Bank and Irving Trust Company.

Woolworth helped to develop mass retailing. His genius lay in successfully adapting new ideas rather than in innovation. However, he personally identified ways of reducing costs through the use of counter displays of goods and the importation of cheap goods that afforded him profit margins lower than those of his competitors.

• John K. Winkler, *Five and Ten: The Fabulous Life of F. W. Woolworth* (1941), is a biography of Woolworth. James Brough, *The Woolworths* (1982), is a narrative history of the Woolworth family. The following are popular accounts of the history of Woolworth's company: John Peter Nichols, *Skyline Queen and the Merchant Prince: The Woolworth Story* (1973); and Nina Brown Baker, *Nickels and Dimes: The Story of F. W. Woolworth* (1954). Information about Woolworth's career can be found in *Fortieth Anniversary Souvenir, F. W. Woolworth Company: 1879–1919* (1919); *1879–1929: Fifty Years of Woolworth* (c. 1929); *Celebrating 60 Years of an American Institution: F. W. Woolworth Co.* (c. 1939); *Woolworth's First 75 Years: The Story of Everybody's Store, 1879–1954* (1954). A feature article on Woolworth and his business can be found in the *New York Times*, 1 Jan. 1911. A report on the opening of the Woolworth skyscraper is in the *New York Times*, 25 Apr. 1913. An obituary is in the *New York Times*, 9 Apr. 1919.

RICHARD A. HAWKINS

WOOSTER, Charles Whiting (1780–1848), commander of the Chilean navy, was born in New Haven, Connecticut, the son of Thomas Wooster and Lydia Sheldon. As the grandson of General David Wooster, of revolutionary war fame, he had deep roots in New England and came from a family with a long tradition of service in maritime commerce and the military. He went to sea on a merchant vessel at the age of eleven and in the next decade learned the ways of seafaring and ocean-borne trade. Master of the ship *Fair American* by 1801, he was sailing on voyages as far as Surinam. In 1810 he married Frances Stebbins, with whom he had one child; six years later she died. In the War of 1812 he became a privateer, sailing the seas as commander of the *Saratoga* and capturing twenty-two prizes. One of these was the letter of marque *Rachael*, which he seized off La Guaira, Venezuela, on the Spanish Main, after a notable battle. In 1814 he was appointed captain, and later major, of a battalion raised to defend New York harbor in case of amphibious assault. He returned to peaceful pursuits in 1816, commanding the merchantman *Halcyon* on trading voyages between Philadelphia and Liverpool, England. In 1817 Wooster met the Chilean patriot José Miguel Carrera, who was in the United States recruiting sailors to fight in Chile's war of independence against Spain. Immediately, Carrera began to proselytize Wooster, mournfully describing Chile's unequal struggle against the mother country.

Wooster needed little encouragement to join the Chilean cause. He was at loose ends because of his wife's recent death, and also he was lured by the possibility of naval adventure. Hence, on 8 October 1817, he accepted a commission as captain in the Chilean navy and began outfitting in New York harbor a corvette brig, the *Columbus*, which he had purchased with his own money. He sailed on 28 November for Buenos Aires, Argentina, with a consignment of military matériel for the Argentinians, reaching that port on 4 February 1818. He departed Buenos Aires in late March and arrived at Valparaiso, Chile, on 25 April. After protracted negotiations, he sold the *Columbus* to the Chilean government. He officially took command of the ship, now renamed the *Araucano*, on 14 August but a month later transferred his flag to the frigate *Lautaro*, the second largest ship in the Chilean navy. He sailed from Valparaiso on 10 October as part of a squadron of three ships under command of Admiral Blanco Encalada. Eighteen days later this squadron forced the surrender of the Spanish frigate *Maria Isabel* in Talcahuano harbor, and Wooster was the first man to board the enemy vessel. For this action, he received adulation from Admiral Encalada in a highly publicized official report of the encounter, and he returned to Valparaiso on 17 November a hero. His pleasure in his newly acquired status was short-lived, for on 28 November British admiral Thomas, Lord Cochrane, arrived in Chile and assumed command of the navy. The admiral, who had a general aversion to Americans, took a particular dislike to Wooster and treated him with disdain. Consequently, Wooster resigned his commission, although he remained in Chile as a partner in a whaling enterprise while awaiting a chance to return to the navy.

In 1822 Wooster's fortunes reversed, for Cochrane resigned as commander of the Chilean navy, and on 18 March Wooster was appointed in his place, with the rank of post captain. He unsuccessfully assaulted the last remaining Spanish stronghold in Chile, the Chiloé archipelago, in April and in the following year made a successful cruise along the coast of Peru. In late 1825 he launched another attack on the Chiloé archipelago, sailing from Valparaiso on 27 November in the bark *Aquiles* with an army under the command of General Ramon Freire. He and Freire conducted a brilliant amphibious operation on 11 January 1826, routing the enemy on Chiloé. That same year Wooster successfully conveyed General Andrés Santa Cruz to Bolivia. For these and many other services, on 4 November 1829 Wooster was promoted to rear admiral by President Francisco Vicuña, who praised him for his valor, daring, courage, and constancy. In September 1835 Wooster retired from the Chilean navy with only a small pension but with the heartfelt gratitude of many Chilean leaders for his military contributions. Former president Francisco Antonio Pinto declared that Wooster had battled for Chile with "honor and constancy," and General Freire lauded him for his "generous services." He returned to the United States but was unhappy. After visiting New Haven, his birthplace, in 1837, he returned to Chile, where he lived until 1848. Learning that gold had been discovered in California, he traveled to San Francisco in hopes of making his fortune. He engaged in mining on the Yuba River but had no success. He died in San Francisco in extreme poverty, having been obliged in his last days to pawn his Chilean military decorations in order to eat.

• Primary materials on Wooster's life are in *Manifesto que da en su Despedida de Chile el Contra-Almirante D. C. W. Wooster*

(1836). His seizure of the *Rachael* is described in *Niles' Weekly Register*, 13 Jan. 1813. Short biographical sketches are in Narciso Desmadril, *Galeria Nacional ó Colleccion de Biografías y Retratos de Hombres Célebres de Chile*, vol. 2 (1854), and *Norteamericanos Notables en la Historia de Chile* (1953). David Wooster, *Genealogy of the Woosters in America* (1885), contains information on the family. Wooster's Chilean naval career is surveyed in Charles Lyon Chandler, "Admiral Charles Whiting Wooster in Chile," *Annual Report of the American Historical Association for the Year 1916* (1919): 447–56. For Cochrane's role, see Thomas Cochrane, Tenth earl of Dundonald (Lord Cochrane), *Narrative of Services in the Liberation of Chile, Peru, and Brazil . . .*, vol. 2 (1859), and Warren Tute, *Cochrane: A Life of Admiral the Earl of Dundonald* (1965). Background on the War of 1812 is in Theodore Roosevelt, *The Naval War of 1812 . . .* (1882), and Kenneth J. Hagan, *This People's Navy: The Making of American Sea Power* (1991).

PAUL DAVID NELSON

WOOSTER, David (2 Mar. 1711–2 May 1777), soldier and merchant, was born in Stratford (now Huntington), Connecticut, the son of Abraham Wooster, a mason, and Mary Walker. He received a bachelor's degree from Yale College in 1738. In May 1741 the Connecticut Assembly appointed him lieutenant of the armed sloop *Defence*, used to guard the colony's coastline. The following year he was made captain of the vessel.

In 1745 Wooster served as captain of one of Connecticut's eight companies in the successful siege of the French fortress of Louisbourg on Cape Breton Island. After its surrender he sailed to France with prisoners of war for exchange. From France he went to England where he was commissioned a captain in a newly established colonial regiment commanded by Sir William Pepperell. In 1746, shortly after returning to Connecticut, he married Mary Clap, oldest daughter of Yale College president Thomas Clap; they had four children, two of whom died in infancy.

Wooster settled in New Haven following service in Colonel Pepperell's regiment and began a prosperous business career as a merchant. There, in 1750, he organized the town's first Free Mason lodge and became its master.

In March 1756, during the French and Indian War, Wooster was appointed colonel of Connecticut's Second Regiment, which served at Crown Point, Fort Ticonderoga, and other military actions under Sir Jeffrey Amherst. During the war Wooster was selected as a deputy from New Haven to the Connecticut General Assembly.

Wooster continued his successful mercantile ventures, acted as a New Haven justice of the peace, and served the town in several administrative capacities until the outbreak of the American Revolution. In late April 1775 the Connecticut assembly appointed him major general of the colony's military forces and colonel of the First Regiment. In June he was ordered to New York City to command Connecticut First Regiment troops guarding that strategic seaport. That same month the Continental Congress made him brigadier general in the Continental army, and the following autumn he led Connecticut troops in General Richard Montgomery's capture of St. Johns and Montreal. After the failed American assault on Quebec (31 Dec. 1775) during which Montgomery was killed, Wooster, who had not participated in that attack, succeeded to the command of patriot forces in Canada.

In April 1776 he commanded the dispirited and weakened American forces outside Quebec. Wooster's informality with enlisted men undercut discipline; his arbitrary, restrictive, and religiously biased actions toward civilians outraged Canada's Roman Catholics; and petty jealousies involved him in divisive quarrels with younger generals, including Philip Schuyler and Benedict Arnold. He was replaced in command by General John Thomas, and congressional commissioners shortly thereafter declared him "totally unfit to command." Silas Deane, a congressional delegate from Connecticut, vilified him as an "old woman."

In June 1776 Congress recalled Wooster, but with assistance from John Adams (1735–1826) he was exonerated after a congressional investigation of his conduct. He retained his Continental army rank of brigadier general, and in October the Connecticut General Assembly named him major general and commander in chief of the militia.

When word of the Loyalist general William Tryon's move to raid Danbury reached New Haven on 26 April 1777, Wooster, along with Generals Benedict Arnold and Gold Silliman, marched to intercept the British force. The next day Wooster was mortally wounded at Ridgefield while attempting to rally his panicky militiamen. He died in Danbury. A monument to his memory was erected there in 1854.

• Major collections of documents by or about Wooster can be found in the Connecticut Historical Society and the Connecticut State Library in Hartford and in the Library of Congress. He is also frequently mentioned in Charles J. Hoadley, ed., *Public Records of the Colony of Connecticut*, vols. 12–15 (1881–1890). The best biographies are Henry C. Deming, *An Oration upon the Life and Services of Gen. David Wooster* (1854), and Franklin B. Dexter, *Biographical Sketches of the Graduates of Yale College*, vol. 1 (1885). See also David Wooster, *Genealogy of the Woosters in America Descended from Edward Wooster of Connecticut* (1885). For accounts of Wooster's most important campaigns, see James R. Case, *An Account of Tryon's Raid on Danbury in April 1977* (1927), and Robert M. Hatch, *Thrust for Canada: The American Attempt on Quebec in 1775–1776* (1979).

SHELDON S. COHEN

WORCESTER, Elwood (16 May 1862–19 July 1940), Episcopal clergyman and founder of the Emmanuel movement, was born in Massillon, Ohio, the son of David Freeman Worcester, an affluent businessman, and Frances Gold. He grew up in Rochester, New York. As a youth he felt a call to the ministry, for which he prepared at Columbia University (B.A., 1886), General Theological Seminary (1887), and the University of Leipzig (M.A. and Ph.D., 1889). At

Leipzig he absorbed both the pragmatic religious idealism of Theodor Fechner and the experimental psychology of Wilhelm Wundt.

In 1889 he served as superintendent of the Sunday school at St. Ann's Episcopal Church in Brooklyn, but in 1890, the year in which he was ordained to the diaconate, he became chaplain and professor of philosophy, psychology, and Christian evidences at Lehigh University in Bethlehem, Pennsylvania. He was ordained to the priesthood in 1891. In 1894 he married Blanche S. Rulison; they had four children. In 1894–1895 he served as the acting rector of St. John's in Dresden, Germany, before accepting in 1896 a position as rector of St. Stephen's Church, Philadelphia.

At St. Stephen's, Worcester met the neurologist S. Weir Mitchell, who encouraged him to think of ministerial counseling as a means of nurturing psychological as well as spiritual health. When he moved in 1904 to Emmanuel Church in Boston, Worcester enlisted local doctors to work alongside the ministers of the church, and within a year he and his colleague Samuel McComb joined Joseph Pratt of Harvard Medical School in applying the "law of suggestion" with small groups of indigent tuberculosis patients in the hope that psychotherapy, offered within the caring environment of the church, could aid in their recovery. In 1906 Emmanuel Church began to provide diagnostic sessions staffed by physicians, who referred some cases to medical doctors, others to the ministers at Emmanuel.

The Emmanuel movement began when other clergy adopted the techniques that Worcester and McComb recommended in *Religion and Medicine* (1908), written in consultation with Isador Coriat, an early Freudian at Worcester, Massachusetts, State Hospital. The three men drew on the writings of Sigmund Freud, William James, Morton Prince, and Pierre Janet to develop methods of psychotherapy—muscular relaxation, rhythmic breathing, visual imagery, and suggestion—that could tap the powers of the subconscious or unconscious (terms they used interchangeably). Deeply moved by William James's essay "The Energies of Men," Worcester thought that the therapeutic benefits of modern psychology could enrich the ministry of the churches. He thought that every minister practiced psychotherapy, whether intending to or not, and that pastors should be guided by modern psychological theories rather than by older traditions of spiritual counseling. For a time his ideas about how ministers might use therapeutic methods borrowed from physicians and psychologists spread from coast to coast, but by the 1920s the movement faded. In 1929 Worcester left Emmanuel Church to devote more time to counseling. He died in Kennebunkport, Maine.

As a liberal theologian, Worcester wrote on themes ranging from the question of the historicity of Jesus to the psychological benefits of religious commitment. He was a vigorous critic of Christian Science, which he believed to be unscientific and unacceptable to doctors. Although the Emmanuel movement faltered, Worcester is remembered today as a pioneer in what became a largely successful movement to ensure that theological education expose seminarians to research and theory in psychotherapy. His belief that the clergy should alter their methods of counseling in the light of new research in psychotherapy found wide acceptance during the resurgence of Protestant interest in pastoral counseling after World War II.

• Worcester's publications include *Religion and Life* (1914), *The Issues of Life* (1915), *Was Jesus an Historical Person?* (1927), *The Allies of Religion* (1929); *Body, Mind, and Spirit* (with Samuel McComb) (1931), *Life's Adventure* (1932), *Studies in the Birth of the Lord* (1932), and *Making Life Better* (1933). For information on Worcester's career, see E. Brooks Holifield, *A History of Pastoral Care in America* (1983). An obituary is in the *New York Times*, 20 July 1940.

E. BROOKS HOLIFIELD

WORCESTER, Joseph Emerson (24 Aug. 1784–27 Oct. 1865), lexicographer and author, was born in Bedford, New Hampshire, the son of Jesse Worcester, a schoolteacher and farmer, and Sarah Parker. In 1794 the family moved to Hollis, New Hampshire, where Worcester spent his teenage years doing farm work during the day and pursuing a course of reading at night. When he was twenty-one, Worcester enrolled in Phillips Academy in Andover, Massachusetts, and spent three months there as a member of the class of 1805. From 1805 to 1809 he continued to prepare for college and taught for at least two years in Salem, Massachusetts. At the age of twenty-five he entered the sophomore class of Yale University. He graduated in 1811 and returned to teaching secondary school in Salem.

While teaching in Salem, Worcester prepared his first book, *A Geographical Dictionary, or Universal Gazetteer; Ancient and Modern*. He had the book printed in Andover in 1817, but it was published and sold in Salem, where Worcester introduced it into the secondary school curriculum. Like his later works, his first book ran to many editions and gave rise to several related publications. In 1818 came *A Gazetteer of the United States, Abstracted from the Universal Gazetteer of the Author; with Enlargement of the Principal Articles*. A hallmark of Worcester's works is his careful acknowledgment of sources, but he also makes large claims for his own original research; in the gazetteer of 1818, for example, he claims to have "visited the greater part of the most considerable towns in the United States, and . . . corrected and enlarged his former information, by personal observation and inquiry." The academic nature of Worcester's interests is reflected in the gazetteer's special attention to centers of learning, including accounts of their curricula.

In 1819 Worcester moved to Cambridge, Massachusetts, which became his permanent place of residence and was the place of his death. In the same year he published *The Elements of Geography, Ancient and Modern, with an Atlas*. The work is divided into "mathematical geography" (the place of the earth in the solar system), "comparative geography" (tabular, comparative statistics), and "ancient geography."

There are appendices with a list of ancient empires, a pronouncing table of town names, questions for class discussion, and instructions for making maps. The second edition was published in 1822 in Boston, which then became the center both of Worcester's work and his influence. *The Elements of Geography* was followed by *Sketches of the Earth and Its Inhabitants* (1823), and *The Elements of History, Ancient and Modern, with Historical Charts* (1826). These charts are foldout chronologies, color-coded in aquatint. Both *Elements* were reprinted numerous times, revised, abridged, and published in part throughout the nineteenth century. Their publishers often boasted that they were "made use of in the examination of candidates for admission into the University in Cambridge" (that is, Harvard). While working on his geographical and chronological textbooks, Worcester produced a scholarly paper on demographics for the American Academy entitled "Remarks on Longevity and the Expectation of Life in the United States, Relating More Particularly to the State of New Hampshire, with Some Comparative Views in Relation to Foreign Countries" (1825).

In 1828 Worcester began his career in lexicography by editing a version of Samuel Johnson's *Dictionary*, "as improved by Todd, and abridged by Chalmers, with Walker's Pronouncing Dictionary combined." This was the year of Noah Webster's final and most important work, *An American Dictionary of the English Language*, and Webster's publisher convinced Worcester to make an abridgment. The work came out in 1829 and marked the beginning of what turned out to be a long and bitter conflict between two lexicographical camps. In 1830 Worcester published *A Comprehensive Pronouncing and Explanatory Dictionary of the English Language: With Pronouncing Vocabularies of Classical and Scripture Proper Names*. Many spelling books and elementary dictionaries were derived from this work and continued to appear in various editions throughout the century. Worcester's conservative, more British orthography brought him and his publishers into conflict as well as competition with the more reform-oriented Webster. Moreover, Noah Webster accused Worcester of plagiarism in a letter to the *Worcester Palladium* in November 1834. Worcester defended himself, and there was an exchange of letters between the two in that paper and in the *Christian Register* into early 1835. Worcester went so far as to suggest that in later editions Webster had borrowed material from Worcester's dictionaries. Hostilities did not reach their high point, however, until 1846 (after Webster's death), when Worcester published his more elaborate *Universal and Critical Dictionary of the English Language*. Financial competition was certainly the source of the dispute, but charges of plagiarism were again involved. Worcester's American publisher sold the stereotype plates of his work to H. G. Bohn, a British publisher, who took the liberty of altering the preface and reprinting the work with the new title, *A Universal, Critical, and Pronouncing Dictionary of the English Language, . . . Compiled from the Materials of Noah Webster, LL.D., by Joseph Worcester* (1853). The title contradicted Worcester's unaltered declaration in the preface that he had refrained from using Webster's work: the London papers quickly picked up the apparent fraud.

Embarrassed by this turn of events, Worcester collected numerous letters and pamphlets going back to the days when he agreed to abridge Webster's *American Dictionary*; he displayed these in a small book entitled *Gross Literary Fraud Exposed; Relating to the Publication of Worcester's Dictionary in London* (1853). Webster's publishers, George Merriam and Charles Merriam, replied in a book with the same title (1854), which includes grandiose eulogies for their late author. They compare Worcester's attacks on Noah Webster to those suffered by Samuel Johnson from the obscure James Thomson Callender, and they refute Edward Gould's characterization of Webster as a "plodding Yankee, ambitious to be an American Johnson," which had been cited, if not elicited, by Worcester's publishers. The battle went on for some years with efforts on both sides to bring proof of their dictionary's superior popularity in the form of testimonial letters from famous people, surveys of colleges, and reports of librarians about the relative use of the two books by readers.

About the time that he brought out the *Universal Dictionary*, Worcester's career seemed over because he was blinded by cataracts in both eyes. At last, painful and dangerous surgery saved his left eye, and Worcester went back to work. The culmination of his lexicographic efforts was *A Dictionary of the English Language* (1860). The preliminary matter is rich, including disquisitions on pronunciation, grammar, etymology, archaisms, Americanisms, a history of English lexicography, with an extensive bibliography, and a list of the principal scientific works consulted. The appendices include pronouncing lists of proper names, abbreviations, signs used in writing and publishing, and foreign phrases and quotations. The entries feature pronunciation, etymology, illustrative quotations, and a great number of pictorial illustrations. The illustrative quotations come predominantly from important, canonical writers, but some respectable journals and reviews are also represented. Borrowing from earlier dictionaries is evident, but the effort to acknowledge such borrowing is remarkably strong. Worcester was a more conservative lexicographer than Webster and less individualistic and expressive than either Webster or Johnson. However, his work is very sound in all departments, and it deservedly continued to be published throughout the century. The Webster line of dictionaries capitalized on the more famous name but surpassed Worcester only by incorporating some of his ancillary material, his judgments, and some of his techniques, including the widespread use of pictorial illustrations.

In addition to writing books, Worcester also edited *The American Almanac* from 1831 to 1841 and participated in several learned societies, including the American Oriental Society. He received honorary doctor of laws degrees from Brown and Dartmouth. His eulogists praise his temperance, diligence, and charity. In 1841 he married Amy Elizabeth McKean, daughter of a Harvard professor of rhetoric. He had no children, but he took an interest in his nine nephews and corresponded vigorously with them while they fought on the Union side in the Civil War.

• Although there are some letters and other documents at the Beinecke Rare Books and Manuscript Library, Yale University, the most important repository of Worcester's papers is the Massachusetts Historical Society, Boston. For an assessment of Worcester's place in the history of American lexicography see Joseph H. Friend, *The Development of American Lexicography, 1798–1864* (1967). The principal secondary sources used for this biography are Ezra Abbot in the *Proceedings of the American Academy of Arts and Sciences* 7 (1868); the biographical sketch in *A Dictionary of the English Language* (1878 and later editions); S. T. Worcester, "Joseph E. Worcester, LL.D.," *Granite Monthly*, Apr. 1880; and Jonathan Fox Worcester, *The Descendants of Rev. William Worcester*, rev. Sarah A. Worcester (1914). A good bibliography of Worcester's dictionaries can be found in *English Language Dictionaries, 1604–1900: The Catalog of the Warren N. and Suzanne B. Cordell Collection* (1988), but Arthur G. Kennedy, *A Bibliography of Writings on the English Language* (1927), is still best for tracing Worcester's other writings.

ROBERT DEMARIA, JR.

WORCESTER, Noah (25 Nov. 1758–31 Oct. 1837), clergyman and founder of the Massachusetts Peace Society, was born in Hollis, New Hampshire, the son of Noah Worcester, justice of the peace and a delegate to the convention drafting the first New Hampshire constitution, and his first wife, Lydia Taylor. The younger Noah received a rudimentary education through his sixteenth year when he became a fifer in the American revolutionary forces. Worcester saw action in both the battles of Bunker Hill and Bennington.

From 1778 to 1782 Worcester taught school in Plymouth, New Hampshire. On his twenty-first birthday, he married Hannah Brown; they had ten children. In 1782 the couple moved to Thornton, New Hampshire, where Noah farmed, taught school, worked as a shoemaker, and also served as justice of the peace, town clerk and selectman, and delegate to the state legislature. In 1786 he was licensed as a Congregationalist minister. The following year he was called as pastor of the church in Thornton, then a part-time position. His first wife died in 1797. In Thornton he married Hannah Huntington in 1798; they had no children. In 1802 Worcester became an agent of the New Hampshire Missionary Society, working throughout the state until 1810 when he took over for three years as minister in Salisbury, New Hampshire, while its pastor, his brother Thomas, recovered from a serious illness.

According to notes Worcester wrote that were used by Henry Ware (1794–1843) in compiling his *Memoirs of the Rev. Noah Worcester, D.D.* (1844), for many years he had doubts about the orthodox Christian understanding of the trinity, especially about equating Christ with God. Rather, because the New Testament referred to Christ as the Son of God, Worcester came to believe that whatever divinity Christ had was derived from God and not intrinsic. When he published three theological tracts explaining his views, *Bible News of the Father, Son, and Holy Spirit: in a Series of Letters* (1810), *Impartial Review of the Testimonies in Favor of the Divinity of the Son of God* (1810), and *Respectful Address to the Trinitarian Clergy* (1812), he found himself at the center of theological controversy in New England. Orthodox Congregationalists, especially those identified with Hopkinsian theology, suspected him of holding Unitarian views, and the Hopkinton Association of Ministers, to which Worcester belonged, adopted a resolution condemning his views. The controversy brought Worcester to the attention of William Ellery Channing (1780–1842), who invited Worcester to edit the newly founded Unitarian periodical, the *Christian Disciple* (later the *Christian Examiner*). Worcester accepted and in 1813 moved to Brighton, Massachusetts, to begin work.

Soon a more compelling passion gripped Worcester, the cause of pacifism. The War of 1812 between the United States and Great Britain, which was particularly controversial in New England, prompted Worcester to reflect on the nature and effects of war. Always gentle and serene in personal demeanor, in 1814 he published his reflections in a pamphlet entitled *Solemn Review of the Custom of War*. In it he argued that the violence and destruction wrought by war stood totally in contrast to the Christian ethic of love and that, consequently, all who regarded themselves as Christians should eschew war. He was particularly repulsed by what he called the "wanton undervaluing of human life" that accompanied war. Although Worcester continued his editorial work for the Unitarian movement, in 1815 he also became a founder of the Massachusetts Peace Society, was designated its secretary, and served as the first editor of its periodical, the *Friend of Peace*. In the wake of the War of 1812, the Massachusetts Peace Society was at the forefront of a popular crusade for the abolition of war and spawned numerous other state and regional peace societies, including the American Peace Society in 1828. In 1818 he surrendered editorial direction of the Unitarian *Christian Disciple* to his friend Henry Ware in order to devote full time to the peace movement and to editing the *Friend of Peace*. Worcester, who believed no war was justified, wrote many articles for that journal.

Retiring in 1828, Worcester resumed theological writing, producing *The Atoning Sacrifice a Display of Love—Not of Wrath* (1829), in which he advanced a common nineteenth-century Unitarian understanding of Christ's death as an example of the extent of God's beneficence to humanity rather than as a payment demanded for human sin. Other works from his retirement years include *Causes and Evils of Contentions Unveiled in Letters to Christians* (1831) and *Last Thoughts on Important Subjects* (1833). Worcester died in Brighton, Massachusetts.

• The Noah Worcester Papers are in the collection of the Massachusetts Historical Society. Letters and other primary documents are in the Cowler Family Correspondence, Columbia University; papers of Noah and Thomas Worcester, New Hampshire Historical Society; Austin Collection of Moses Brown Papers, Rhode Island Historical Society; and William Ellery Channing Papers, Andover-Harvard Theological Library. Worcester also wrote *Letter to the Rev. John Murray concerning the Origin of Evil* (1786), *Familiar Dialogue between Cephas and Bereas* (1792), *Solemn Reasons for Declining to Accept the Baptist Theory and Practice* (1809), and numerous sermons, tracts, and theological articles. Henry Ware, Jr., *Memoirs of the Rev. Noah Worcester, D.D.* (1844), is an uncritical appraisal. See also William B. Sprague, *Annals of the American Pulpit* (1865), for a brief discussion of Worcester. William Ellery Channing's eulogy for Worcester was published as *A Tribute to the Memory of the Rev. Noah Worcester, D.D.* (1837) and extracted in Ware's *Memoirs*. Also see S. A. Worcester, *The Descendants of Rev. William Worcester* (1914).

CHARLES H. LIPPY

WORDEN, John Lorimer (12 Mar. 1818–18 Oct. 1897), naval officer, was born in Westchester County, New York, the son of Ananias Worden (occupation unknown) and Harriet Graham. On 10 January 1834 he joined the navy as a midshipman and sailed three years with the Brazilian Squadron. Following two additional years aboard the Mediterranean Squadron, Worden attended the Naval School in Philadelphia and graduated a passed midshipman on 16 July 1840. He took assignment with the Pacific Squadron for the next two years and, from 1842 to 1844, served at the Naval Observatory. Worden became a lieutenant on 30 November 1846 and spent the Mexican War off the coast of California aboard the storeship *Southampton*. He subsequently cruised the Mediterranean with the frigate *Cumberland* and completed a second tour with the Naval Observatory from 1850 to 1852. Worden thereafter alternated between sea duty with the Home Squadron and land assignments at the New York Navy Yard until 1861.

The onset of the Civil War found Worden stationed at Washington, D.C., and he requested immediate duty. On 7 April 1861 he was ordered to Fort Pickens, Pensacola, with secret instructions for the squadron lying offshore. Worden fulfilled his mission, the post was reinforced and remained in Union hands, but while returning to the capital by rail he was apprehended near Montgomery, Alabama. He remained a prisoner for seven months before being exchanged, but the experience had so damaged Worden's health that he could not resume duty until April 1862.

When he recovered, Worden assumed command of John Ericsson's experimental ironclad warship *Monitor*. This was a low-slung, heavily armored steam vessel whose design precipitated a revolution in naval warfare. It was commissioned at Greenpoint, Long Island, on 25 February 1862, and Worden sailed it southward toward Hampton Roads, Virginia. The *Monitor* arrived on 8 March and prepared to engage the Confederate ironclad *Virginia* (ex-*Merrimac*), which had previously sunk two U.S. frigates. On March 9 the two vessels clashed in an epic confrontation. For two hours they exchanged gunfire at close range without materially damaging each other. Worden avoided several attempts by the *Virginia* to ram him, but he sustained eye injuries when a shell struck his pilothouse. He relinquished command to Lieutenant Samuel D. Greene, who ordered a temporary withdrawal. During this interval *Virginia* also retreated back into Norfolk, thereby ending the battle in a draw. Worden's actions, however, constituted a strategic victory for the United States, for they preserved the naval blockade of Norfolk and ensured the city's eventual surrender. Worden endured a long convalescence, but he obtained the Thanks of Congress and promotion to commander as of 12 July 1862. President Abraham Lincoln was so impressed by his performance that he paid the injured sailor a bedside visit.

Worden resumed active duty as commander of the new *Passaic*-class monitor *Montauk* in January 1863 and joined the South Atlantic Blockading Squadron of Admiral Samuel F. du Pont. On 27 January he demonstrated the capabilities of his vessel by dueling four hours with Fort McAllister near Savannah, Georgia. Despite forty-six direct hits, *Montauk* continued to function. Worden advanced to captain on 3 February 1863 and three weeks later destroyed the Confederate privateer *Nashville* under the guns of Fort McAllister. He subsequently participated in the blockade of Charleston, South Carolina, and distinguished himself in Admiral du Pont's unsuccessful attack of 7 April 1863, in which *Montauk* sustained fourteen more hits. Shortly after, Worden returned to New York and, with his firsthand knowledge, supervised the construction of new ironclads until 1866.

After the war, Worden commanded the *Pensacola* while part of the Pacific Squadron. On 27 May 1868 he rose to commodore and the following year received appointment as superintendent of the U.S. Naval Academy, Annapolis. For five years Worden implemented academic reforms, including stringent regulations against hazing, and was instrumental in founding the U.S. Naval Institute. Worden was promoted rear admiral on 20 November 1872 and commanded the European Squadron between 1875 and 1877. He then served as a member of the examining board at the academy and also president of the retiring board until his own resignation on 23 December 1886. By special act of Congress, Worden continued receiving the full sea pay of his grade for life. He died in Washington, D.C.

Worden was a quiet, competent professional whose fifty-five years of service exemplify the best of the "old Navy." Capable rather than brilliant, he handled himself well during the historic battle at Hampton Roads and in subsequent actions demonstrated the viability of new naval technology. Worden was also unique among contemporaries in exercising authority and discipline judiciously, thereby gaining the respect and affection of men under him. He is a significant naval figure whose career successfully straddled the transition from sail to steam and helped steer the service toward modernity. Worden married Olivia Taffey; they had four children.

• Worden's official correspondence is in the Navy Records, National Archives. Personal letters are in the Manuscript Division, Library of Congress; the Lincoln Memorial University Library, Harrogate, Tenn.; and the Long Island Historical Society, Brooklyn. Useful biographical sketches are in Clarence E. MacCartney, *Mr. Lincoln's Admirals* (1956), and R. Gerald McMurty, "The Life and Career of John Lorimer Worden," *Lincoln Herald* 51 (1949): 12–20. For the early phase of his Civil War career consult two articles by James P. Jones, "Lincoln's Courier: John L. Worden's Mission to Fort Pickens," *Florida Historical Quarterly* 41 (1962–1963): 143–53; and "John L. Worden and the Fort Pickens Mission," *Alabama Review* 21 (Apr. 1968): 113–32. Finally, ample coverage of his famous sea duel is in William C. Davis, *Duel between the First Ironclads* (1975); A. A. Hoeling, *Thunder at Hampton Roads* (1976); Roy P. Nichols, ed., *Battles and Leaders of the Civil War*, vol. 1 (1956), pp. 719–29; and Virgil C. Jones, *The Civil War at Sea* (1960–1961).

JOHN C. FREDRIKSEN

WORES, Theodore (1 Aug. 1859–11 Sept. 1939), painter, was born in San Francisco, California, the son of Joseph Wores, a merchant, and Gertrude Liebke. He was educated in public schools, and his early interest in art was encouraged by private art lessons. Wores was one of the first pupils to enroll in the newly founded San Francisco Art Association's School of Design in 1874. In June 1875 Wores traveled to Munich, where he prepared for entrance examinations to the Royal Bavarian Art Academy by studying with fellow San Franciscan Toby Rosenthal. Wores won several medals in academy art classes, culminating in 1878 with the school's most prestigious award, which entitled him to free studio space and models. During his student years he was drawn to the classes of Frank Duveneck, who surrounded himself with a number of American art students interested in learning less academic methods of painting. At the end of 1879 Wores traveled along with the "Duveneck Boys" when their mentor relocated his school to Florence, Italy. The group spent the next two years alternating their time between Florence and Venice, where Wores met James MacNeill Whistler, who encouraged Wores's interest in traveling to Japan.

Wores returned to the United States in the summer of 1881, showing his works in New York, Philadelphia, and then San Francisco, where he lived for the next three and a half years. Elected to membership in the Bohemian Club, he was selected by club members to paint a portrait (now lost) of visiting writer Oscar Wilde in 1882. Wores began his teaching career as the first instructor at the newly created San Francisco Art Students League, exhibited locally, and painted Chinatown genre scenes.

In March 1885 Wores arrived in Yokohama, Japan, the second American artist to visit the country since its opening to Western trade in 1854. He subsequently settled in Tokyo for the next two years. There he produced a large body of paintings of the Japanese going about their daily lives. While a resident in Japan, he met Ernest Fenollosa, the prominent Far Eastern specialist, and the artist John LaFarge, who arrived during the summer of 1885 for a brief visit. Wores was given the honor of painting a portrait of Ito, the prime minister of Japan, and the singular tribute of a one-person exhibition, arranged shortly before Wores returned to San Francisco in December 1887. His Japanese paintings received enthusiastic praise when shown in San Francisco, New York, Boston, Washington, D.C., Chicago, and London over the next four years, and they were purchased by prominent international collectors such as Thomas B. Clark and Henri, Prince de Bourbon.

During his stay in London, Wores wrote extensively and became a contributing staff member of the publication *Art Weekly*. Also at this time he was elected to membership in the Society of British Artists, the Royal Academy, and the New English Art Club, and he was a sought-after speaker on the culture and customs of Japan.

Wores made his second visit to Japan in the summer of 1892. In the next year and a half he produced more than 130 paintings and pastels on Japanese themes, including the work that he regarded as his masterpiece, *The Light of Asia* (1894, San Francisco Theosophist Society), a painting of the great bronze Daibutsu of Kamakura.

While Wores traveled variously to San Francisco, New York, Hawaii, Samoa, and Spain over the next decade, his works were shown in the Art Exhibition of the World's Columbian Exposition in Chicago (1893) and San Francisco's Mid-Winter International Exposition (1894), as well as in numerous one-person shows at the Bohemian Club in San Francisco and in solo and group exhibitions in New York, Washington, D.C., and Boston. Wores was painting in Los Angeles at the time of the great San Francisco earthquake in 1906; the ensuing conflagration destroyed his hometown studio and its contents.

From 1907 to 1913 Wores served as dean of the faculty and instructor at the San Francisco Art Association's School. His painting *The Lei Maker* (1902, Honolulu Academy of Fine Arts) won a gold medal at the Alaska-Yukon Pacific Exposition in Seattle, Washington, in 1909. The following year Wores married Carolyn Bauer in San Francisco; they had no children. The paintings of Wores's remaining years took as their themes local scenery such as the vast flowering fruit orchards of the Santa Clara Valley and Bay Area beaches as well as subjects painted in the Canadian Rockies and the southwestern United States. Major retrospectives of his work were staged at the Century Art Association in New York in 1918 and at Stanford University in Palo Alto in 1922. During the final decade of his career he was an active member of the conservative Society for Sanity in Art, founded in Chicago in response to modernist trends in American art.

Wores worked in a realist style throughout his long career. His earliest exhibited paintings resembled the dark Munich manner of his mentor, Duveneck. Wores's palette gradually lightened, largely in response to painting out-of-doors in Italy and on the California Coast. The term *impressionist* might readily apply to the style of his later paintings. His most acclaimed subjects were drawn from his two trips to Japan, where he recorded everyday vignettes of an age-old culture that was rapidly modernizing. During the 1920s and 1930s, Wores repeatedly painted the blossoming fruit trees in the orchards of the Santa Clara Valley. He died in San Francisco.

Wores's work remains important as a document of late nineteenth-century Japanese life viewed through the eyes of a Western painter. His reputation among turn-of-the-century American realists is secure. As a result of his teaching and involvement with arts organizations in San Francisco, during the first quarter of the twentieth century he influenced a number of regional artists to pursue an interpretation of local landscape and genre motifs.

• Wores recounted his adventures during his two trips to Japan in several articles published in popular periodicals at the end of the nineteenth century. Among them are "An American Artist in Japan," *Century Magazine*, Sept. 1889; "Japanese Artists," *London Art Weekly* (7 June 1890); "The Wistaria Shrine of Kameido," *Cosmopolitan*, May 1898; and "Japanese Flower Arrangement," *Scribner's Magazine*, Aug. 1899, pp. 205–12. Other discussions of Wores's Japanese-inspired works are the exhibition catalog *Theodore Wores: The Japanese Years* (1976), with an introduction by Joseph A. Baird, Jr., and *Theodore Wores: An American Artist in Meiji Japan* (1993), with an introduction by William H. Gerdts and an essay by Jan Newstrom Thompson. General information regarding Wores's peripatetic career may be found in Lewis Ferbrache, *Theodore Wores: Artist in Search of the Picturesque* (1968). Museums with collections of Wores's works include the Oakland (Calif.) Museum; the National Museum of American Art, Washington; and the Natural History Museum of Los Angeles.

JAN NEWSTROM THOMPSON

WORK, Henry Clay (1 Oct. 1832–8 June 1884), songwriter, was born in Middletown, Connecticut, the son of Alanson Work and Aurelia (maiden name unknown). When Henry was three, the family moved to Quincy, Illinois, primarily to aid the escape to Canada of runaway slaves. Aiding runaways led to Alanson Work's imprisonment from 1841 to 1845, leaving his family impoverished during these years. It was in Quincy that Henry Work received much of his formal education. His first powerful musical impression was gathered there as well, reportedly by being enthralled at a religious camp meeting by the forthright, ecstatic singing. In 1845, the family returned to Middletown, and Work was apprenticed to a print shop in Hartford. There he first began composing songs, not from any technical training beyond that gathered in singing schools, but from self-instruction and intuition. "We Are Coming, Sister Mary," published in 1853, was his initial success, made famous in performance by the renowned minstrel troupe of E. P. Christy. Work returned to Illinois in 1854 or 1855 to ply his trade in Chicago. He married Sarah Parker in January 1857, and they had four children. He continued to write popular songs suitable for either the parlor or the minstrel show stage.

With the outbreak of the Civil War, Work found a cause that compelled his creative energies. His first song about the conflict, "Brave Boys Are They" (1861), led Chicago-based publisher George F. Root (of Root & Cady) to employ him to compose for and edit their house organ, *The Song Messenger of the Northwest*. To mutual benefit, there followed a body of songs, always Unionist and often abolitionist, that was the most powerful and popular of the wartime period. Among them were "Kingdom Coming" (1861), "Uncle Joe's 'Hail Columbia!'" (1862), "Babylon is Fallen!" (1863), "Wake Nicodemus" (1864), and "Marching Through Georgia" (1865). "Kingdom Coming," a bitterly satiric song heard first in a minstrel show, became a rallying song for slaves behind Confederate lines; several Union soldiers reported being serenaded with the song as they occupied areas of the South. "Grafted into the Army" (1862), one of Work's few humorous songs, was about a malaprop-spouting Corporal Schnapps. His most successful song of the period, though, was not about the War at all. "Come Home, Father" (1864), one of only two temperance songs by Work, was performed countless times in the popular temperance play *Ten Nights in a Barroom*.

Work was most productive from 1861 to 1866, and many of the songs for which he was known were composed then. Although he published songs regularly from 1866 to 1869, they approached in neither number nor quality those of earlier in the decade.

In 1867 or 1868, Work moved from Chicago and joined in a Vineland, New Jersey, land speculation. By mid-1868, his life had known several tragedies, including the deaths of two of his children. At this time, too, his wife was so obviously crippled by hereditary mental illness that their separation was inevitable. She was taken to her family home in Massachusetts, while Work rented a room in Philadelphia. The two years there were among the most engaging of his life for him, mainly for the friendship he established with his landlord's daughter, Susie R. Mitchell, who became at the very least a romantic ideal for him. Their extant correspondence of over forty long letters chronicles many of the most important events in Work's life from that point.

In 1870 Work moved to Brooklyn, New York, and resumed typesetting for a living. His reasons seem to have been to remove himself from the immediate temptation of Mitchell, on the one hand, and to immerse himself in the charismatic teachings of theologian Henry Ward Beecher, on the other. His music turned toward the religious, as suggested by the cantata-like "Joy in Heaven! or, The Returning Wanderer's Welcome" of 1871. Work's spirits and songwriting during the mid-1870s were tied to the ups and downs of his generally proper and circumspect correspondence with Mitchell. In 1875 he seemed to have entertained some hopes of full disclosures of affection on both sides. Work himself believed this prospect responsible for another period of creative energy. He wrote to Mitchell in 1875: "I have just written three new songs—written them, not because I thought it was time to take up my pen again; that motive has been ineffectually appealing to me for years; but because, through a combination of circumstances I have heard a voice saying, 'Write!' . . . I say that I had written them: more accurately speaking, they wrote themselves; and songs that write themselves always sing themselves, or at least require to be sung but once before they attain a momentum sufficient to carry them forward." The most popular of these songs was "Grandfather's Clock," likely the best-selling American song of the period between the Civil War and the 1890s. Among Work's contributions evident here is the new musical importance of the chorus.

Mitchell finally was not swayed by Work's entreaties of affection; she married another in July 1877. This effectively marked the close of Work's career as a songwriter of importance, but for a benedictory "Farewell, My Loved One!," published in December that year. He moved to New York City and, according to his own confession, became "a hermit absorbed in his philosophical studies and mechanical experiments." In November 1882 he moved to Bath, New York, where he had a brief period of songwriting, to no great success. Work died of heart disease while visiting his mother in Hartford, Connecticut, in 1884.

Work's songs reflect a range of subjects and perspectives: patriotism, mourning, freedom, romantic love, loneliness, women's sphere, joy. Each approach was finely chiseled and much care was evidently lavished in composition. It typically took him from one to three weeks to write the lyrics to a song (which he did for all but two of his songs), compose the melody and harmony, and polish it. This deliberate pattern contributed to a canon of only seventy-eight songs, an unusually high percentage of which achieved popularity.

• The most important treatment of Work's life is found in Richard Snyder Hill, "The Mysterious Chord of Henry Clay Work," *Music Library Association Notes* 10 (1952–53): 211–25, 367–90. This article is based largely on the Work-Mitchell correspondence, which is preserved in the Library of Congress. One might wish also to consult Samuel Ward Loper, "The Life of Henry Clay Work" (1907; unpublished ms. on deposit at the Middlesex County, Connecticut, Historical Society). See also Dale Cockrell, "Henry Clay Work," *The New Grove Dictionary of American Music* 4 (1986): 563–64. Thirty-nine of Work's songs were collected by his nephew in a privately printed facsimile edition that has since been reprinted by Da Capo (1974). Among the best analyses of Work's music is that by Charles Hamm, *Yesterdays: Popular Song in America* (1979).

DALE COCKRELL

WORK, Hubert (3 July 1860–14 Dec. 1942), physician and secretary of the interior, was born in Marion Center, Pennsylvania, the son of Moses Thompson Work and Tabitha Logan Van Horn, farmers. He graduated from Indiana (Pa.) State Normal School, studied medicine from 1882 to 1884 at the University of Michigan, then transferred to the University of Pennsylvania, where he received an M.D. in 1885. He established a practice in Greeley, Colorado, then moved to Pueblo, where he founded the Woodcroft Hospital for mental illnesses in 1896. He directed this facility until 1917.

Work acquired his professional reputation as a clinician and psychiatrist, earning honorary degrees and holding memberships in scientific organizations devoted to his specialty. In the 1880s and 1890s he served with the Colorado State Board of Medical Examiners and acted as president of both the State Board of Health and the Colorado State Medical Society. In 1906 he began his first term as a delegate of the American Medical Association, becoming in 1916 the first chairman of the House of Delegates and in 1921 the president of the association. He joined the Army Medical Corps in 1917, serving as medical adviser to the provost marshal general. Work earned the rank of colonel and at the end of World War I entered the Army Medical Reserve.

Although noted for his efforts in medicine, Work gained national prominence as a political activist. His reputation as a stalwart Republican landed him the chair of the Colorado State Republican Convention and a delegate's position at the Republican National Convention in 1908. He was a member of the Republican National Committee from 1913 to 1919. His talents as a political organizer became well known, and he established a strong base of support among farmers during Warren G. Harding's 1920 presidential campaign. His success in this endeavor led Harding to appoint Work as first assistant to Postmaster General Will Hays in 1921 and to postmaster general after Hay's resignation in 1922. He held this post for over a year, gaining a reputation for efficiency and businesslike management. He instituted mail service reforms and proposed economizing measures, such as government ownership of Post Office buildings.

When the controversial Albert Fall resigned under pressure as secretary of the interior in 1923, Harding named Work as Fall's successor. Allegations of corruption, mismanagement, and inefficiency followed as details of Fall's involvement in the Teapot Dome scandal surfaced. Work set out to alleviate the department's internal turmoil and to restore its credibility. He reorganized daily operations, simplified policy, gained the support of his agency and staff, and sought efficiency through application of business methods. He wanted to move beyond the controversy between the East and the West over proper disposal of western resources by declaring an end to the era of exploitation of the public domain and heralding a new age of conservation. These actions improved the Interior Department's image and raised awareness of serious threats to the environment.

The Reclamation Service represented one of the more pressing problems of Work's administration. Flat agricultural markets in the 1920s made it difficult for water users to cover their obligations to the government. He replaced the agency's director and appointed a review committee. In August 1923 Work issued a memo, "The Tentative Policy of the Reclamation Bureau of the Department of the Interior," addressing the status of existing and contemplated projects. He proposed to reduce overhead through implementation of business accounting measures, subdivision of large farms, diversification of crops, establishment of new markets for farm produce, and informing water users that government water projects should be treated as interest-free loans. Regarding new reclamation project proposals, he cautioned planners to consider the ability of farmers to repay work, operation, and maintenance costs.

Work addressed several other issues during his tenure. Stock grazing on public lands emerged as a serious problem in the 1920s. Unauthorized and unrestricted grazing threatened to destroy rangelands. Work lobbied for more government control of range resources, called for stock raisers to help preserve grazing lands, and stressed the necessity of cooperation between industry and government. In response to public criticism over the Teapot Dome scandal, Work helped establish the Federal Oil Conservation Board in 1924 to improve practices and encourage cooperation between government and the oil industry. Work demonstrated concern for the preservation of scenic resources and development of the National Park Service, generating interest in setting aside new lands for parks, especially in the East, where few existed. He felt these areas should be preserved in a natural state for the purposes of "recreation, education, and scientific research."

Work also faced condemnation of the controversial Bureau of Indian Affairs. The General Allotment Act of 1887—designed to assimilate Indians by promoting private ownership of tribal land—had led instead to an erosion of the Indian estate (individual and tribal landholdings on and off reservations), impoverishment, health and education concerns, and an assault on Indian culture. Work supported enforcement of the legislation, stressing only that more care be taken in the removal of government trust restrictions on Indian allotments. However, persistent criticism of the Indian Bureau led Work to commission the Institute for Government Research to prepare a study of Indian affairs, economics, and social conditions. This survey, published in 1928, revealed the ineffectiveness of the Indian Bureau and recommended sweeping changes in policy and administration. Work left the Interior Department just after this report was issued and could not implement any of its recommendations. Serious Indian policy reforms did not occur until passage in 1934 of the Indian Reorganization Act.

Work resigned his Interior Department post in July 1928 to lead the effort to nominate Herbert Hoover (1874–1964) for the Republican presidential ticket. After this success, Hoover appointed Work to manage his election campaign as chairman of the Republican National Committee. Following Hoover's election victory, Work retired from politics at the age of sixty-nine and returned to Denver, Colorado, to practice medicine. His wife, Laura M. Arbuckle, whom he married in 1887 and with whom he had five children, had died in 1924, and in 1933 he married Ethel Reed Gano. Work died in Denver. He is buried at Arlington National Cemetery.

• Work's papers are in the Colorado State Archives, Denver; the Postmaster General Files, National Archives, Washington, D.C.; and the Speech and Office Files, Department of the Interior Records, National Archives, Washington, D.C. Other papers are in the Warren G. Harding Papers, State Historical Society, Columbus, Ohio; Calvin Coolidge Papers, Library of Congress; and Herbert Hoover Papers, Hoover Library, West Branch, Iowa. See also Eugene P. Trani, "Hubert Work and the Department of the Interior, 1923–1928," *Pacific Northwest Quarterly* 61 (Jan. 1970): 31–40; Eugene P. Trani, *The Secretaries of the Department of the Interior, 1849–1969* (1975); Von Gayle Hamilton, *Work Family History* (1969); Janet A. McDonnell, *The Dispossession of the American Indian, 1887–1934* (1991); Kenneth R. Philp, *John Collier's Crusade for Indian Reform, 1920–1954* (1977); and Donald C. Swain, *Federal Conservation Policy, 1921–1933* (1963). Obituaries are in the *New York Times*, 15 Dec. 1942; the *Journal of Nervous and Mental Disease*, 97 (1943): 382–83; and the *Journal of the American Medical Association*, 120 (1942): 1332.

JOHN W. HEATON

WORK, Monroe Nathan (15 Aug. 1866–2 May 1945), African-American sociologist, was born in rural Iredell County, North Carolina, the son of Alexander Work and Eliza Hobbs, former slaves and farmers. His family migrated to Cairo, Illinois, in 1866 and in 1876 to Kansas, where they homesteaded, and Work remained to help on the farm until he was twenty-three. He then started secondary school and by 1903 had received his master of arts degree in sociology from the University of Chicago. That year he accepted a teaching job at Georgia State Industrial College in Savannah.

Living in the Deep South for the first time, Work became concerned about the plight of African Americans, who constituted a majority of Savannah's population. In 1905 he answered a call from W. E. B. Du Bois to attend the conference that established the Niagara Movement, a militant black rights group that opposed Booker T. Washington's accommodationist approach to black advancement. While continuing to participate in the Niagara Movement, Work founded the Savannah Men's Sunday Club. It combined the functions of a lyceum, lobbying group, and civic club, engaging in such activities as petitioning the city government, opening a reading room, organizing youth activities, and conducting a health education campaign among lower-class African Americans. Quickly accepted into the city's black elite, he married Florence E. Henderson in 1904. Their marriage lasted until his death, but no children survived infancy.

In 1908 Work was offered a position at Washington's Tuskegee Institute in Macon County, Alabama. As an ally of Du Bois, Work found it difficult to accept the position, but he did. By 1908 he had begun to doubt the efficacy of protest. A streetcar boycott had not halted legalized segregation in Savannah and the Niagara Movement had failed to expand. Work had begun to see another way to use his talents on behalf of black advancement. He was not a dynamic speaker or a natural leader, but a quiet scholar and researcher. He believed that prejudice was rooted in ignorance, and this suggested reliance on education rather than protest. In a 1932 interview, Work declared that while still a student, "I dedicated my life to the gathering of information, the compiling of exact knowledge concerning the Negro." Disillusioned about the power of protest, Work believed that the resources and audience available at Tuskegee would allow him to make his skills useful: "It was the center of things relating to the Negro," he noted.

Although Washington had hired Work primarily as a record keeper and researcher for his own articles and speeches, Work used every opportunity to expand the functions of his Department of Records and Research. In 1908 he began compiling a day-to-day record of the African-American experience. His sources included newspaper clippings, pamphlets, reports, and replies to his own letters of inquiry. All were organized by category and date, providing the data for the *Negro Yearbook* and the Tuskegee Lynching Report, both of which began in 1912. Each year he distributed the Tuskegee Lynching Report to southern newspapers and leaders to publicize the extent and injustice of lynch law. Under his editorship, nine editions of the *Negro Yearbook* provided information on discrimination and black progress to educators, researchers, and newspaper editorialists. In 1928 Work supplied another valuable research tool with the publication of *A Bibliography of the Negro in Africa and America*. It was the first extensive, classified bibliography of its kind.

Work did not spend all his time compiling data for others; he was also a teacher, department head, crusader, and researcher. He published over seventy articles and pamphlets. His research usually highlighted either the achievements of Africans and African Americans or the obstacles to black progress. Earlier than most black scholars, Work wrote in a positive manner about African history and culture. In a 1916 article for the *Journal of Negro History*, he declared that "Negroes should not despise the rock from which they were hewn." Work also investigated African-American folktales and their African roots. Even before the Harlem Renaissance, Work celebrated the distinctiveness of African-American culture. His meticulous scholarship was widely recognized in the academic community. In 1900 he became the first African American to publish an article in the *American Journal of Sociology*; the article dealt with black crime in Chicago and pointed to the lack of social services for African Americans. In 1929 he presented a paper at the American Historical Association meeting.

Although Work eschewed protest when he left the Niagara Movement and went to Tuskegee, he remained a quiet crusader for change. Early in his career Work developed a special interest in black health issues. In Savannah he started health education programs through the churches. He encouraged Booker T. Washington to establish National Negro Health Week in 1914. Work organized the week for seventeen years before it was taken over by the United States Public Health Service. He was also deeply concerned with the problem of lynching, and he became active in a southern-based movement to eradicate the evil. Work's estrangement from Du Bois made cooperation with the National Association for the Advancement of Colored People's antilynching campaign difficult, but Work found allies in the Atlanta-based Commission on Interracial Cooperation and the Association of Southern Women for the Prevention of Lynching. The latter groups sought to change the South through education, while the NAACP sought change through legislation. Through his contacts in the antilynching campaign, Work became actively involved in numerous interracial groups in the South.

Monroe Work overestimated the power of education to eliminate prejudice, but his numerous articles and his quiet, dignified presence in biracial professional organizations and reform groups undoubtedly helped to dispel some of the southern white stereotypes of African Americans. He accepted the constraints required to work in the Deep South in order to use his abilities to change it. After his death, in Tuskegee, two of his protégés established the Tuskegee Civic Association, which brought majority rule and desegregation to Macon County. Monroe Work was one of the lesser-known figures who tilled the soil from which the civil rights movement sprouted in the 1950s and 1960s.

• Although Monroe Work spent most of his life preserving material on the African-American experience, very few of his personal papers survive. Those that remain are in the Tuskegee University Archives in Alabama. Full citations for Work's journal articles mentioned in the text are "The Passing Tradition and the African Civilization," *Journal of Negro History* 1 (Jan. 1916): 34–41, and "Crime among the Negroes of Chicago," *American Journal of Sociology* 6 (Sept. 1900): 204–23. Jessie P. Guzman had planned to write a biography of Work, and some useful materials, including a transcript of a 1932 interview of Work by Lewis A. Jones, are found in her papers at Tuskegee. She did publish "Monroe Nathan Work and His Contributions," *Journal of Negro History* 34 (Oct. 1949): 428–61, which contains references to some materials that no longer exist. Linda O. McMurry, *Recorder of the Black Experience: A Biography of Monroe Nathan Work* (1985), is the only book-length biography.

LINDA O. MCMURRY

WORKMAN, Fanny Bullock (8 Jan. 1859–22 Jan. 1925), travel writer and mountain climber, was born in Worcester, Massachusetts, the daughter of Alexander Hamilton Bullock, a Republican politician and one-term governor of Massachusetts, and Elvira Hazard. Her mother was one of three surviving children of Augustus George Hazard, wealthy landowner and cofounder of Hazard Powder Company (one of the most prominent manufacturers of gunpowder in the mid-nineteenth century). Raised in affluence, Fanny Bullock was privately tutored during her early childhood. As an adolescent, she completed her education at finishing schools in New York City, Paris, and Dresden.

She returned to the family home in Worcester at the age of twenty and met William Hunter Workman, a Yale-educated physician who was twelve years her senior. In 1881 she married Workman, with whom she had one child.

Like his wife, William Workman had studied abroad, and in 1886 the couple returned to Europe for a lengthy tour of Germany and Scandinavia. In 1889, suffering from an unspecified health problem, William retired from medical practice, and the Workmans moved to Germany. For most of the next decade, with their daughter in boarding schools, they traveled throughout Europe and around the Mediterranean. Both enjoyed mountain climbing, a pursuit that William had introduced Fanny to in New England. Together they scaled well-known peaks in the Alps. They also took up bicycling, especially in temperate areas such as Spain and northern Africa. These excursions provided material for the Workmans' first two travel books, *Algerian Memories* (1895) and *Sketches Awheel in Modern Iberia* (1897). Eight books would eventually appear under their names, although some critics have suggested that Workman was the actual author and her husband only a minor contributor.

In 1897 the Workmans shifted their attention to Asia and spent much of the next two years on bicycle tours through Ceylon, Java, Sumatra, French Indochina, and India. Although conditions were poor and the Workmans generally limited their travels to the cooler winter months, by 1899 they had traveled thousands of miles throughout many parts of the Indian subcontinent. The Workmans published their accounts of these journeys, centering on descriptions of historical Asian architecture, artwork, and culture, in *Through Town and Jungle* (1904).

With the help of paid guides and porters, in 1899 the Workmans began to explore and climb in the Himalayas. Both became fascinated with the Karakorum range, a region just becoming known to geographers at the time. For the next thirteen years, they would make the area their second home and mount seven separate major expeditions to chart its glaciers and peaks. Their five jointly written books on the Karakorum, including *In the Ice World of the Himalaya* (1900) and *The Call of the Snowy Hispar* (1910), constituted a valuable descriptive introduction to the area for European and American readers. Photographs taken by both Workmans illustrated the volumes. The accompanying maps and charts were subsequently criticized and revised in many respects. Although Workman and her husband were keen observers of meteorological conditions, glaciology, and the effects of high altitudes on human health and fitness, they were not trained surveyors. The inaccuracy of their maps resulted both from inadequate skill in some of the topographers they hired to accompany them and from the minimal time that the Workmans were willing to allocate to the tedious process of chartmaking.

Defining themselves as equal working partners, the Workmans generally divided the obligations of each expedition in half and then alternated their individual responsibilities from one trip to the next. Workman might conduct the scientific and physiological tests on a given journey, while William organized the expedition's supplies and supervised the workers; on the next trip, they would reverse the assignments. Equally adept at the scientific and logistic aspects of their treks, the Workmans also shared a tendency to treat their Asian workers with disdain and impatience. Subsequent explorers in the Karakorum reportedly found lingering resentment in many porters who had served the couple.

Although they usually climbed side by side, occasionally the conditions or their health precluded such partnerships. Thus, in 1906 Workman was not accompanied by William when she scaled Pinnacle Peak, part of the Nun Kun cluster of summits. With her guides, Workman calculated their altitude at 23,300 feet, a height that topped any reached by a woman to that date. Her record was challenged in 1908 by Annie Smith Peck, who claimed that she had reached 24,000 feet on a guided climb in the Andes. In response, Workman hired a team of surveyors to calculate the actual altitude of Peck's climb, and in 1911 they reported that Peck had reached a height of only 21,812 feet. Subsequent surveys in the Himalayas, after the Workmans' expeditions were completed, accurately revised the height of Pinnacle Peak to 22,815 feet, but Workman's record as a woman climber was still not broken until 1934. A comprehensive assessment of her accomplishments as a climber also includes the fact that she spent months at altitudes between 15,000 and 20,000 feet, enduring conditions of extreme cold without the aid of modern thermal clothing and camping equipment.

For her work, and often in partnership with her husband, Workman was honored by some of the most prestigious geographical and alpine clubs in Europe. She presented lectures to audiences in a number of major European and American cities. The Workmans retired to France after their last Himalayan trek in 1912, and Workman died in Cannes. Her will, which designated bequests from her personal estate, directed that donations totaling $125,000 should go to four major women's colleges. Those bequests (fulfilled after her husband's death in 1937), reflected Workman's lifelong dedication to feminist causes and woman suffrage. She presented herself as a strong-minded, proud, and tireless explorer and commented occasionally on the condescension that some male mountaineers exhibited toward her. Her ability to deviate from the standard gender roles of her time stemmed partially from her personal wealth; Workman's inheritance, as a granddaughter of Augustus Bullock, made the couple's expeditions possible.

• There is no known repository of Workman papers. Fanny and William Workman's other books are *Ice-bound Heights of the Mustagh* (1908), *Peaks and Glaciers of the Nun Kun* (1909), and *Two Summers in the Ice Wilds of Eastern Karakorum* (1917). An account of Workman's climb of Pinnacle Peak, with references to Annie Smith Peck's challenge to her record, is in "My Highest Ascent in the Himalayas," *Travel*, Mar. 1911, pp. 222–26. A report on Workman's commissioned survey of Peck's climb is in "Mrs. Workman Wins," *New York Times*, 26 Mar. 1911. The most comprehensive modern assessment of Workman's life is in Rebecca Stefoff, *Women of the World: Women Travelers and Explorers* (1992). See also Dorothy Middleton, *Victorian Lady Travellers* (1965), and Kenneth Mason, *Abode of Snow* (1955), for balanced examinations of the Workmans' expeditions. Lengthy memorial articles on Fanny Workman, published after her death, can be found in the *Alpine Journal* (London), May 1925, and *Appalachia* (Appalachian Mountain Club), June 1925. Information on her bequests to women's higher education is in "Fanny Workman's Will Aids Colleges," *New York Times*, 4 Feb. 1925. William Workman's obituary in the *New York Times*, 10 Oct. 1937, describes his partnership with his wife. An obituary of Fanny Workman is also in the *New York Times*, 24 Jan. 1925.

BETH KRAIG

WORMELEY, Katharine Prescott (14 Jan. 1830–4 Aug. 1908), Civil War relief worker, translator, and biographer, was born in Ipswich, Suffolk, England, the daughter of Ralph Wormeley and Caroline Preble. Wormeley's father was born in Virginia and raised in England, where he became a rear admiral in the Royal Navy. He married Preble in Boston then returned to Virginia to help found the College of William and Mary. From 1836 to 1847 the family lived in London, except for the years 1839–1842, which were spent in France and Switzerland. When her father died in 1852, Wormeley, her mother, and her siblings wintered in either Boston or Washington and lived the remainder of the year among the literary elite in Newport, Rhode Island.

Wormeley gained a sympathy for the poor and invalid from her father, which she channeled into volunteer relief work during the Civil War. Inspired by the formation in 1861 of a Woman's Central Association of Relief in New York and the U.S. Sanitary Commission, Newport women gathered at Wormeley's home to found the Women's Union Aid Society. As head of the society and associate manager of the New England Women's Branch of the Sanitary Commission, Wormeley organized supplies and aid for volunteer soldiers. When the need arose for army clothing, Wormeley hired local unemployed seamstresses by using donations to the society. "During the winter of 1861–1862 about fifty thousand army shirts were thus made, not one of which was returned as imperfect, and [Wormeley] was thus enabled to circulate in about one hundred families, a sum equal to six thousand dollars, which helped them well through the winter" (Brockett, p. 319). Her success earned her a government contract to continue the work from the U.S. Office of Army Clothing and Equipage.

In May 1862 Wormeley was invited by Frederick Law Olmsted, secretary of the Sanitary Commission, to volunteer on the first steamer used to transport wounded soldiers from the battlefields up the James and Pamunkey rivers to northern hospitals and their homes. Her job she discovered was to "attend to the beds, the linen, the clothing of the patients . . . to do all the cooking for the sick, and see that it is properly distributed according to the surgeons' orders; we are also to have a general superintendence over the condition of the wards and over the nurses, who are all men" (Brokett, p. 17).

Wormeley returned to Newport in August and on 1 September 1862 became lady superintendent of the Woman's Department of the Lowell General Hospital at Portsmouth Grove, Rhode Island, which was organized for convalescent soldiers. "Under her charge were the Female Nurses, the Diet Kitchens, and Special diet, the Linen Department, and the Laundry, where she had a steam Washing Machine, which was capable of washing and mangling four thousand pieces a day" (Brockett, p. 322). She requested as a staff member Georgeanna Woolsey, who had also been on the hospital transports, Georgeanna's sister, Jane Woolsey, their cousin Sarah C. Woolsey, and Harriet D. Whetten. Each was in charge of a ward, instructing nurses under them on how to clean linen, take notes of a patient's treatment, medicine, and diet, and, when necessary, arrange special diets assigned by the surgeon. According to Woolsey biographer Anne L. Austin, "In this organization Katharine displayed her usual ability to plan wisely, and her friends worked harmoniously with her. This was the first time that 'ladies' had been permitted to nurse in a U.S. General Hospital in such responsible capacities, and they regarded it as a rare opportunity" (p. 92). Wormeley stayed for little more than a year "carrying on the arrangements of her department with great ability and perfect success" (Brockett p. 322). In September 1863 she returned to Newport, where she was asked to write a history of the Sanitary Commission for the Boston Sanitary Fair. Entitled "The United States Sanitary Commission: A Sketch of Its Purpose and Work," Wormeley's document was considered "graceful in style, direct in detail, plain in statement and logical in argument. . . . It met with great and deserved success, and netted some hundreds of dollars to the fair" (Brockett, p. 323).

Wormeley continued volunteer work after the war and in 1879 founded the Newport Charity Organization Society. As secretary and general agent, she organized domestic classes for poor women of Newport and remained a district visitor and member of the governing board for fifteen years. In 1887 she founded the Girls' Industrial School at Newport, which offered classes in cooking, sewing, and household work. She maintained the school at her own expense for three years, at which time it was incorporated into the public school system. In 1888 the Massachusetts commandery of the Loyal Legion published her collection of letters, *The Other Side of War with the Army of the Potomac*, which she had written during the peninsular campaign in 1862.

In addition to excelling as a leader of charitable work, Wormeley was one of the best-known and prolific American translators from French. Her translation of Honoré de Balzac's *La Comédie Humaine* in forty volumes (1885–1896) became the standard edition.

Wormeley's "distinguishing characteristic," according to an obituary in *The Dial*, was "sympathy and appreciation: the ability to enter heartily into the spirit actuating other workers helped to make her the sympathetic and faithful translator she so abundantly proved herself to be." Her other major translations include six volumes of Molière's works (1897), Paul Bourget's *Pastels of Men* (1891), the works of Alexandre Dumas (1894–1902), *The Works of Alphonse Daudet* (1898–1900), *Memoirs of the Duc de Saint-Simon* (1899), *Letters of Mlle. de Lespinasse* (1901), *Diary and Correspondence of Count Axel Fersen* (1902), and Sainte-Beuve's *Portraits of the Eighteenth Century* (1905).

Appearing in *Putnam's Monthly* a month before her death, "Napoleon's Return from St. Helena," Wormeley's final publication, was her impression of the second funeral of Napoleon in Paris, which she had witnessed as a child. Wormeley died of pneumonia at her summer home in Jackson, New Hampshire.

• For information on Wormeley's family history see George H. Preble, *Genealogical Sketch of the First Three Generations of Prebles in America* (1868); *Recollections of Ralph Randolph Wormeley* (1879), a privately printed account of her father written by Wormeley and her two sisters; and articles focusing on her sister, Mary Elizabeth Wormeley Latimer, in *The Dial*, 1 Feb. 1904. Sources for her charitable work in Newport are in the *Annual Report of 1889–1890* of the Newport School Committee and at the Newport Historical Society. For a brief biographical sketch of Wormeley see F. E. Willard and M. A. Livermore, *A Woman of the Century* (1893). Wormeley's contribution to the Civil War relief effort is discussed in Anne L. Austin, *The Woolsey Sisters of New York 1860–1900* (1971), and Mary C. Vaughan and L. P. Brockett, *Famous Women of the War: A Record of Heroism, Patriotism, and Patience* (1894). Reference to her translations is in the *Bookman*, Jan. 1908. Obituaries are in the *Newport (R.I.) Daily News* and the *New York Times*, 6 Aug. 1908, and *The Dial*, 16 Aug. 1908.

BARBARA L. CICCARELLI

WORMELEY, Ralph (Apr. 1744–19 Jan. 1806), colonial councillor, Loyalist, and legislator, was born at "Lansdowne," Urbanna, Middlesex County, Virginia, the son of Ralph Wormeley, a planter, and Jane Bowles. Though identified throughout his life with "Rosegill," the Wormeley seat on the Rappahannock River, he was not born at the ancestral home, which was still occupied by his paternal grandmother. The Wormeley family, established in Virginia since 1635, was one of the few families in the colony that had maintained its wealth and aristocratic standing from the period prior to 1650 until after the American Revolution. Wormeley was the fifth of his name to be a member of the ruling order in Virginia.

Wormeley was taught by private tutors until 1757, when he was sent to Eton in England. At Eton he was a school fellow of Charles James Fox, with whom he maintained a lifelong friendship. In 1762 he entered the University of Cambridge as a fellow commoner of Trinity Hall, a college favored by law students and American colonials. Leaving Cambridge without taking a degree, he returned to Virginia in 1765.

Through his connections in England, Wormeley sought the post of comptroller of customs for the Rappahannock River. Because he was still in England, he was unable to begin his duties immediately, and his father was named to the post in 1765, though the older Wormeley had little interest in the office and was engrossed with horse breeding and agriculture. On returning to Virginia, the younger Wormeley, however, performed the duties of the comptrollership for his father until the office was abolished in 1776. In local affairs Wormeley was soon named to the positions traditionally held by the gentry, such as vestryman, church warden, and justice of the peace. Although his arrogance prevented election to the House of Burgesses from Middlesex, he fulfilled an early ambition by being named to the Governor's Council in 1771. While the council still included members of the most prominent Virginia families and helped bolster the position of the royal governors, its influence and power were waning on the eve of the Revolution. Wormeley, however, was an assiduous councillor who was often delegated to draft legislation, proclamations, and addresses, and by 1774 he aspired to become president of the council. His marriage in 1772 to Eleanor Tayloe of "Mount Airy" connected Wormeley with another well-established family of the Virginia aristocracy. From this marriage Wormeley had seven children.

In 1774 and 1775 the situation in Virginia was unfavorable for Wormeley's political ambitions. It is not surprising that Wormeley, owing to his ambition and temperament, family background, and English associations, was among the few Virginia aristocrats who sided with the mother country during the Revolution. While he never articulated a formal rationale for his Loyalism, he was a zealous monarchist and may be described as a conservative, court Whig who thirsted for position and influence. Although opposed on constitutional grounds to parliamentary taxation of the colonies, he had no stomach for rebellion or rule by the "licentious multitude." Yet he was unwilling to take an active role in opposing the Virginia revolutionaries unless Britain provided effective support for the friends of royal government in Virginia.

In the spring of 1775 Wormeley supported Governor Dunmore when Virginians protested the governor's surreptitious removal of gunpowder from the Williamsburg magazine. After Dunmore fled Williamsburg in June, Wormeley, though still abhorring rebellion, prudently retired as a "passive subject" to Rosegill. From Norfolk, Dunmore in March 1776 urged Wormeley and other Loyalists to join him in the Chesapeake. Writing to a friend on 4 April, Wormeley, expressing his disapproval of the revolutionary cause, demurred to Dunmore's request because of poor health and lack of resources though indicating his readiness to come if officially summoned and adequately supported.

His letter was intercepted and sent to Major General Charles Lee, who was then in Williamsburg attempting to strengthen defenses against British forces. Lee had Wormeley brought to Williamsburg and submitted the intercepted letter to the Committee of Safety. That body concluded that Wormeley, though "extremely inimical" to American rights and "ready to join the enemy" if circumstances were propitious, had not committed any offense under the law. He was then dismissed, after posting bond for £10,000, subject to further action by the Virginia Convention meeting of 6 May. Summoned by that convention, Wormeley was confined, and his case was referred to committee. Throwing himself on the mercy of the convention, Wormeley declared that he had never aided the enemy nor opposed any of the revolutionary measures. On 15 May the convention, however, approved the committee's recommendation that Wormeley, having asked for pardon and having "shewn great contrition for his unworthy Conduct," post bond of £10,000 and be confined to his father's estates in the Shenandoah Valley counties of Berkeley and Frederick, not to leave that region unless permitted.

Wormeley remained in easy confinement for two years, though he was sometimes harassed by lawless elements in the valley and was given official protection when requested. Excepting two younger brothers, James and John Wormeley, who served in the British army, most of his family remained at Rosegill during his confinement. Through the good offices of Mann Page, Wormeley's brother-in-law, the Virginia General Assembly permitted Wormeley's return to Rosegill, where he lived in retirement until the end of the Revolution. Despite the Loyalist sympathies of the Wormeleys, a British privateer raided Rosegill in June 1781 and carried off slaves and personal property worth more than £4,000. Even though the Wormeleys furnished supplies and horses when requisitioned for the American forces, their name was "ever joined to that of Tory" by Virginia patriots. After the British invasion of Virginia in 1781, Wormeley and his father were accused of discouraging the sale of supplies to American forces and of corresponding with the enemy. Governor Thomas Nelson in September 1781 ordered their confinement in Richmond, but they were released following the British surrender at Yorktown.

After the Revolution, Wormeley, although resented by many Virginians because of his Loyalist sympathies, was one of the few American Loyalists who recovered to some degree their leadership in community affairs. Having been a visitor of the College of William and Mary since 1775, he became rector in 1784 and presided over the visitors until 1788. During his tenure as rector, Wormeley sought, apparently without success, to obtain the transfer of the Robert Boyle endowment for the college from England to Virginia. In 1785 he was a delegate to the convention that organized the Virginia diocese of the Episcopal church and helped frame its rules of order, governance, and discipline.

In 1788 Wormeley returned to public life when he was elected to the Virginia House of Delegates from the county of Middlesex. Reelected in 1789 and 1790, he was active in committee work and was often designated to draft legislation. He allied himself with the movement for a stronger federal government and was named a delegate to the Virginia Convention of 1788, which ratified the new federal Constitution. As a gesture of respect he was nominated in late 1788 to serve in the expiring Confederation Congress but declined the nomination. Despite these evidences of public esteem, Wormeley's erstwhile Loyalism still aroused bitter feelings. When he was reappointed justice of the peace for Middlesex in 1788, a member of the Virginia Council of State feared that he would never be a friend either to the independence of the United States or to the republican form of government. By 1791 Wormeley's identification with the Federalist party had become a handicap, and he was defeated for reelection to the house of delegates. His defeat in 1796 as a Federalist candidate for the electoral college was the end of his public career. Increasingly dejected and pessimistic about the future of American society and politics because of the rise of Jeffersonian democracy, he privately questioned the morality and wisdom of republican government.

Ralph Wormeley's despondency in his later years stemmed in part from the serious decline in his family's wealth. Although the Wormeleys in 1788 ranked thirteenth among Virginians in wealth, with more than 15,000 acres of land and 325 slaves, they had lost more than £10,000 during the Revolution. The family was also burdened by long-standing debts to Virginia creditors and British merchants, which Wormeley was struggling to pay as late as 1797. Moreover, the yield of Wormeley's tidewater lands was reduced by soil exhaustion, and buyers for his valley lands were difficult to find. Despite agricultural experimentation and commercial ventures in the buying and selling of tobacco as a middleman, Wormeley was forced to change his lavish lifestyle. Until the end of his life, however, he continued to read widely and to buy the most recent British and American books and periodicals. Wormeley's collection of more than 1,300 volumes, which included nearly 700 titles, was probably the second largest library in Virginia at the beginning of the nineteenth century.

Wormeley's death in Middlesex County, Virginia, marked the passing of a period in the history of Virginia when the great aristocrats were the natural leaders. The inscription on his gravestone at Christ Church near Rosegill lauds Wormeley as "the perfect gentleman and finished scholar," a fitting epitaph for one who cherished the ideals of a vanished era.

• The two major collections of papers pertaining to Wormeley and his family are in the University of Virginia Library, Charlottesville, and the Virginia Historical Society Library, Richmond. State and county records relating to Wormeley are in original documents or microfilm copies in the Virginia State Library. Documents with explanatory notes concerning Wormeley's Loyalism are in Robert L. Scribner, ed., *Revolutionary Virginia, the Road to Independence* (7 vols., 1973–1983). A brief biographical sketch is in Lorenzo Sabine, *Biographical Sketches of Loyalists of the American Revolution with an Historical Essay*, vol. 2 (1864). A full account of his background and early career is Jonathan H. Poston, "Ralph

Wormeley V of Rosegill: A Deposed Virginia Aristocrat, 1744–1781" (M.A. thesis, College of William and Mary, 1946). Darrett B. Rutman and Anita Rutman, *A Place in Time, Middlesex County, Virginia, 1650–1750* (1984), and Jackson T. Main, "The One Hundred," *William and Mary Quarterly*, 3d ser., 11 (1954): 354–84, are perceptive studies of Wormeley's economic and social milieu. James LaVerne Anderson, "The Virginia Councillors and the American Revolution, the Demise of an Aristocratic Clique," *Virginia Magazine of History and Biography* 82 (1974): 56–74; Robert McClure Calhoon, *The Loyalists in Revolutionary America, 1760–1781* (1965); and John E. Selby, *The Revolution in Virginia, 1775–1783* (1988), are studies of the political setting in which Wormeley operated.

MALCOLM LESTER

WORMLEY, James (16 Jan. 1819–18 Oct. 1884), hotelkeeper, was born in Washington, D.C., the son of Pere Leigh Wormley and Mary (maiden name unknown). Both his parents were free people of color before their 1814 arrival in Washington, where his father became proprietor of a livery stable on Pennsylvania Avenue between Fourteenth and Fifteenth streets, near the famous Willard Hotel. Wormley's early life is obscure, but it is certain that he went to work at a young age as a hack driver for his father, whose business was thriving by the 1820s. Eventually Wormley bought a horse and carriage of his own and began to work independently. Wormley's exposure to the city's fine hotels and high society through his clientele, which inevitably included many prominent public figures, might perhaps have influenced his later vocation.

In 1841 Wormley married Anna Thompson; they had four children. In 1849 he left his home to join the multitude of prospectors who traveled to California during the gold rush. Shortly before or after this, he was engaged as a steward aboard the elegant riverboats that plied the Mississippi. Eventually Wormley returned to Washington, where he worked as a steward at the fashionable Metropolitan Club. On the eve of the Civil War, he opened a catering business at 314 I Street (near Fifteenth Street), next-door to a candy store run by his wife. By the mid-1860s he had expanded his business to include a restaurant at the same address. Wormley's restaurant attracted members of Washington's political elite, particularly the Radical Republicans. The patronage of such men as Senator Charles Sumner (after whom Wormley named one of his sons) and Henry Wilson (later vice president under Ulysses S. Grant) ensured the establishment's success.

The next step in Wormley's career entailed a brief absence from Washington and his family. In 1868 Reverdy Johnson, recently appointed ambassador to Great Britian, persuaded Wormley to accompany him to London as his personal steward. One of Wormley's tasks was the preparation of such exotic American dishes as diamondback terrapin (a turtle caught in Chesapeake Bay and the Potomac River), which Johnson was persuaded would do much to "warm up" the reserved British worthies he was required to entertain at embassy functions.

When Wormley returned to Washington, he lost no time in capitalizing on the enhanced reputation he had gained as a connoisseur of fine dining. Representative Samuel Hooper of Massachusetts agreed to buy a five-story building on the southwest corner of H and Fifteenth streets and rent it to Wormley when Wormley was unable to finance the purchase himself. In 1871 Wormley opened the hotel that soon made him famous.

Wormley's Hotel, which included as an annex the building that housed his old restaurant on the other side of the block, could accommodate 150 guests in the sleeping apartments of its upper four stories. The halls and corridors were wide, and the rooms were spacious and elegantly furnished. The dining rooms, on the ground floor, acquired a reputation for attentive service and an elaborate menu, and the bar in the basement, where patrons also found a first-class barbershop, was known for its outstanding selection of wines and liquors. The hotel boasted the latest innovations of the day, including elevators, telephones, and electric bells for room service. The parlors on the upper floors were also beautifully appointed. One of them, known as the Sumner Parlor, was decorated with furnishings from the house of Wormley's old friend Sumner, which Wormley purchased from the estate after Sumner's death. In 1876 the room rate at Wormley's was a competitive five dollars a day.

With Lafayette Square, the White House, and the Departments of the Navy and the Treasury all near at hand, Wormley's Hotel was ideally located to serve the congressmen, diplomats, and other politicians who already knew Wormley as a restaurateur. Among his long-term residents were Vice President Schuyler Colfax, Assistant Secretary of State John Hay, and Senator Roscoe Conkling of New York. The hotel was equally popular with foreign dignitaries. The German legation resided there during the 1880s, as did at various times members of the French and Chilean diplomatic corps. Wormley's also housed delegates to the Pan-American Congress in 1889–1890.

Wormley's acquired a small but significant place in American history in the aftermath of the disputed presidential election of 1876. A conference held at the hotel in February 1877 among representatives of Republican candidate Rutherford B. Hayes and a group of southerners led by Major E. A. Burke yielded the "Wormley Agreement," which became in turn the basis for the "Compromise of 1877." In effect, the southerners acquiesced to Hayes's accession to the presidency in return for the withdrawal of the northern states' military support for the remaining Reconstruction governments in the South. Wormley played no part in and likely had no awareness of these negotiations, whose outcome signaled the North's final abandonment of southern blacks to the ravages of southern reaction. It is no small irony, nonetheless, that the hotel in which these dealings took place was owned by one of the capital's most prominent African-American citizens at a time when the city was noted for the enterprise and brilliance of its black citizenry.

Wormley's hotel and catering business continued to prosper until his death in Boston. In an obituary, the *Washington Star* called him "one of the most remarkable colored men in the country" (18 Oct. 1884). The well-known black minister Francis Grimké remarked that Wormley "demanded respect from others and respected himself." A public school on Prospect Avenue between Thirty-third and Thirty-fourth streets, built in the year of Wormley's death and named in his honor, remained in service until the 1950s.

• No personal papers of Wormley or his family are extant. A biographical article is Charles E. Waynes, "James E. Wormley of the Wormley Hotel Agreement," *Centennial Review* 19 (Winter 1975): 397–401. Information is also in John Clagatt Proctor, "Figures of a Vanished Past Linked with 15th Street," *Washington Star*, 27 Dec. 1936; Carter G. Woodson, "The Wormley Family," *Negro History Bulletin* 11, no. 4 (Jan. 1948): 75–84; S. Hyman, "Washington's Negro Elite," *Look*, 6 Apr. 1965; Geneva C. Turner, "For Whom Is Your School Named?" *Negro History Bulletin* 23, no. 8 (May 1960): 185; and Gerri Major, *Black Society* (1976). Obituaries are in the Washington, D.C., *Evening Star* and the *Washington Post*, both 18 Oct. 1884.

JOHN INGHAM

WORTH, Jonathan (18 Nov. 1802–5 Sept. 1869), governor of North Carolina, was born in Center, North Carolina, the son of David Worth, a physician, and Eunice Gardner. Both parents were Quakers who had an aversion to war and believed in the virtues of education. Jonathan first attended the neighborhood school and received his only formal education through two and a half years of study at Greensboro Academy, which he left in 1823. After deciding to become a lawyer, he selected as his mentor the distinguished and influential Archibald De Bow Murphey, who advocated both internal improvements and public education. Early in 1825, after completing his apprenticeship with Murphey, Worth married his mentor's niece, Martitia Daniel, with whom he had eight children. He set up a law office in Asheboro, where he practiced from 1825 to 1860.

Worth's prominence derived primarily from his role as a politician, which began when he served in the state house of commons in the legislatures of 1830 and 1831. In those sessions he displayed a strong nationalism during the nullification crisis. After remaining out of politics for the rest of the 1830s, he reentered the legislature in 1840—this time as a senator—and worked out the administrative details of the state's first public school system, under which he then served as county superintendent of Randolph County for nearly twenty years. One of Worth's central views was that education and democracy were closely related. Like Thomas Jefferson, he believed in democracy with the understanding that any electorate should not be ignorant.

From 1841 to 1858 Worth again was out of political office, although he twice campaigned unsuccessfully for a seat in Congress, in 1841 and 1845. He was elected to the state senate in 1858 and again in 1860. Worth's primary interest throughout all of his terms in the state legislature was the development of transportation facilities, particularly those connecting the western part of the state with the coast. He was a devout, consistent Whig who fervently admired Henry Clay. His terms in the legislatures of 1858 and 1860 were undistinguished, but by the time of the latter session, he was strongly opposed to secession.

Worth believed that secession was "madness" and dreaded the possibility of civil war, but when President Abraham Lincoln called for troops to enforce federal laws in the South, Worth advocated raising troops in a mistaken effort to avoid war. In 1862 he agreed to serve as public treasurer in the administration of Zebulon B. Vance and moved his family from Asheboro to Raleigh.

At the Treasury Worth was skillful and fiscally conservative. He refused to issue more bonds and paper money than was absolutely essential, and he frequently urged the legislature to shift the burden of war finance from the state to the Confederacy. He often wrangled with Confederate officials about debts owed by the central government to the state for troops and war matériel. Although Worth favored taxation as the primary means of financing the war, the legislature insisted on selling bonds and printing Treasury notes. As the Union army of General W. T. Sherman approached Raleigh, Worth removed and protected successfully the state's funds and the public records, both of which he returned after the military threat ended. His last important function as public treasurer was to collect scattered state funds and property, especially large amounts of cotton and rosin, in the summer of 1865.

Worth was twice elected governor after the Civil War, the first time in December 1865 under President Andrew Johnson's plan for a quick "restoration" of the Union. During that term he worked hard to restore civil government, tried to clarify the new status of blacks, and attempted to restore peace between the Unionists and the secessionists. In 1866, running against William W. Holden, he was again elected governor, representing the conservative, anti-Radical prewar elite, many of whom were former Whigs. In his second term he continued to wrangle with Freedmen's Bureau officers, who he believed were illegally interfering in the state's affairs. He favored allowing blacks to testify in court but was opposed to black suffrage and, apparently, to public education for blacks. When the Reconstruction Acts placed the South under military rule, Worth opposed the Fourteenth Amendment but cooperated with the military in the processes of holding elections, in which blacks voted, and of writing the new constitution of 1868. In the first elections held under that constitution, Holden, the Republican candidate, was elected to replace Worth.

It is difficult to evaluate Worth's overall role in the political history of North Carolina. Before and even during the Civil War, he was devoted primarily to the Union in the sense that he preferred it to the Confederacy. After the war he wished to see the Union restored quickly, but his conservatism and his racism made it impossible for him to accept the rapid change that was occurring at the time. He is best characterized as "a gentleman of the old school."

In his personal affairs, Worth was a successful lawyer, a devoted and indulgent father, and above all a successful businessman. He owned several farms, fourteen slaves, a number of general stores, stock in early textile mills, and stock in the Cape Fear Navigation Company. He also served as president of the Fayetteville and Western Plank Road Company. His interest in and success at business enterprise strongly inclined him to the political tradition of Alexander Hamilton and Clay, because they promoted economic development rather than restricting it with regulations.

At his main profession, the law, Worth's career was successful but undistinguished. He frequently used the word "diffident" to describe himself and to explain his lack of oratorical distinction. In addition to his regular general practice, he served as clerk and master in equity of the Randolph County Court, a position that helped him to acquire numerous tracts of land. Plain in appearance, short in stature, honest in character, and moderate in almost everything, Worth represented both the best and the worst in the thought of his era. He died in Raleigh.

• Worth's papers are in the North Carolina State Archives, with smaller collections at the University of North Carolina at Chapel Hill and at Duke University. A published version edited by J. G. de Roulhac Hamilton, *The Correspondence of Jonathan Worth*, appeared in 1909. The standard biography, which contains an extensive bibliography, is Richard L. Zuber, *Jonathan Worth: A Biography of a Southern Unionist* (1965).

RICHARD L. ZUBER

WORTH, William Jenkins (1 Mar. 1794–7 May 1849), army officer, was born in Hudson, New York, the son of Thomas Worth, a master mariner, and Abigail Jenkins. He led an unremarkable early life, working as a clerk in an Albany wholesale firm until enlisting in the army during the War of 1812.

Worth received a first lieutenant's commission on 19 March 1813, soon joined the staff of Brigadier General Winfield Scott, and saw action in the northern theater of operations. His cool conduct under fire at the battle of Chippewa won for him a brevet promotion to captain on 5 July 1814, and a similar performance at the battle of Lundy's Lane three weeks later earned him promotion to brevet major. Seriously wounded at the latter battle, Worth recuperated for over a year before returning to duty in August 1815. He spent the next five years on recruiting duty with the Second Infantry Regiment.

Major Worth married Margaret Stafford in 1818; they had four children. Worth assumed the duty of commandant of cadets and instructor of military tactics at the U.S. Military Academy in the spring of 1820. Although he had no formal military training, his haughty demeanor instilled in the cadets a sense of honor and precision that many of them remembered for the rest of their lives. In December 1828 Worth left West Point and rejoined his regiment, the First Artillery, at Fortress Monroe, Virginia.

After a succession of assignments to various arsenals, and a promotion to major in the Ordnance Department in May 1832, Worth again faced the prospect of active field assignment during a short-lived revolution in Canada known as the Patriots' War. Considerable American sympathy for the rebels caused the War Department to dispatch General Scott to the border to enforce America's neutrality. Scott again called upon Worth to help, and the major's prompt attention to military matters as well as his appreciation of diplomacy—he shared sensitive information with his British counterpart to forestall violence—helped preserve U.S. neutrality and reduce the threat of open warfare along our northern border.

Worth became colonel of the newly created Eighth Infantry Regiment on 7 July 1838. After almost two more years of border duty, he and his regiment reported to Florida to battle Seminole Indians who had refused to accept the government's plan to send them west of the Mississippi River. He soon commanded all U.S. troops in Florida and pushed them relentlessly to find and defeat the Seminoles. Unlike his predecessors, he even campaigned in the hot summer months, eventually leading to the surrender of the larger hostile bands. In recognition of the good work that Worth did to bring this war to a conclusion in August 1842, President John Tyler awarded him a brevet to brigadier general to take effect on 1 March 1842.

In 1845 the United States proceeded with plans to annex the Republic of Texas, even though Mexico still considered it a Mexican province. General Worth received orders to take his regiment to Texas to join Brevet Brigadier General Zachary Taylor's force, which was there to defend the border against Mexican incursions. Upon arrival, Worth almost immediately became embroiled in a controversy over rank with Colonel David E. Twiggs. Twiggs claimed seniority and, therefore, the right to assume overall command in case Taylor became incapacitated, because he had held the rank of colonel longer than had Worth. Worth based his claim on his brevet rank. Commanding General Scott decided in favor of Worth, but President James K. Polk, upon receiving a petition signed by roughly half of the army officers in Taylor's command, overruled Scott in favor of Twiggs. Worth, feeling badly betrayed, tendered his resignation on 2 April 1846 and headed for Washington.

Word of the opening skirmish of the Mexican War reached Washington about the same time Worth did, and he hurriedly recalled his resignation and received orders to return to his regiment. Upon his return to the army, General Taylor assigned Worth command of the Second Brigade in the assault on Monterrey. According to most contemporary observers, Worth's skillful handling of this mission proved to be the key to American victory there and earned for him another brevet, to major general.

After service as military governor of Monterrey, General Worth joined General Scott for the amphibious landing at Veracruz and the subsequent march on Mexico City. As the Mexican position at Veracruz became more and more untenable, Scott appointed a three-man commission to secure the city's surrender. General Worth, having served on a similar commission at Monterrey, became the senior member, and the city capitulated a few days later.

On 15 May 1847 Worth led the advance of the army into the city of Puebla, promising civilian authorities that his men would respect all local laws. For the next two weeks he seemed constantly to be mustering his troops to respond to one vague rumor of enemy attack or another. None of these materialized, and the men grumbled about Worth's apparent timidity. When General Scott arrived with the bulk of the army, he criticized the indulgence Worth had shown local officials as well as his conduct of the occupation of the city. Worth demanded a court of inquiry, but the results went against him, and he was officially censured.

On 8 September 1847 General Worth's division spearheaded the attack on a suspected cannon foundry at Molino del Rey, just outside the Mexican capital. The American troops continued their unbroken string of military successes, but at a considerable cost in casualties. General Scott had authored the flawed battle plan, but he blamed Worth's conduct of the battle for the heavy American losses. Even though Worth's jealously guarded reputation was thus impugned, American newspapers began lionizing him for his bravery and field leadership. General Scott, believing that Worth (and others) had overstated their contributions to victory in letters to various newspapers, reminded the army that regulations forbade soldiers from writing descriptions of army movements for publication. General Worth believed that Scott had aimed this general reminder specifically at him even though he had not violated the rule, so he wrote to Scott for clarification. Not receiving what he considered an adequate answer from the general, Worth complained to the president that Scott had acted in a manner "unbecoming an officer and a gentleman." Charge followed countercharge thick and fast, until Scott had Worth and two other officers arrested, although they were soon released by presidential order. The petty bickering irretrievably shattered a friendship between Worth and Scott that had begun thirty-five years earlier.

After the Mexican surrender, General Worth received command of the Departments of Texas and New Mexico late in 1848. Asiatic cholera soon swept through his command, causing his death at his San Antonio headquarters. Fort Worth, Texas, and Lake Worth, Florida, are both named in his honor.

Worth was almost paranoid when it came to defending his reputation against real or imagined slights. Yet in spite of any shortcomings in his personality, he was the man who brought the costly Seminole Wars to an end, and his leadership at Monterrey may well have been the turning point of that war.

• Edward S. Wallace, *General William Jenkins Worth: Monterey's Forgotten Hero* (1953), is a full-length biography of General Worth. Wallace states that most of Worth's personal papers were destroyed, but small collections exist at the New-York Historical Society, the Chicago Historical Society, and the U.S. Military Academy Library. Occasional Worth papers also appear in the personal papers of contemporaries, such as the John Pollard Gaines Collection at the New York State Library in Albany and the James J. Duncan Papers at the U.S. Military Academy. Much can be learned from the biographies and autobiographical accounts of Worth's contemporaries, including Charles Winslow Elliot, *Winfield Scott—the Soldier and the Man* (1937); K. Jack Bauer, *Zachary Taylor: Soldier, Planter, Statesman of the Old Southwest* (1985); Ethan Allen Hitchcock, *Fifty Years in Camp and Field* (1909); Raphael Semmes, *Service Afloat and Ashore during the Mexican War* (1851); and Zachary Taylor, *Letters of Zachary Taylor from the Battle-fields of the Mexican War* (1908). Francis Paul Prucha, *Sword of the Republic: The United States Army on the Frontier, 1783–1846* (1969), chronicles most of the actions in which General Worth was involved.

JAMES M. MCCAFFREY

WORTHEN, Amos Henry (31 Oct. 1813–6 May 1888), geologist, was born in Bradford, Vermont, the son of Thomas Worthen and Susannah Adams, farmers. As a child he worked on the family farm and attended local schools during the winter. He completed his schooling at Bradford Academy from which he graduated when he was twenty years old. He married Sarah B. Kimball of Warren, New Hampshire, in 1834 and decided to move west. Like many of their fellow migrants, the Worthens chose to follow family members who had already migrated. Thus they moved briefly to Cynthiana, Kentucky, where one of Worthen's older brothers lived, and then to Cumminsville, Ohio, where Worthen taught school for a couple of years. In June 1836 they joined several members of Sarah's family already settled in Warsaw, Illinois, where, with only a brief interruption, they would live for the rest of their lives. They had seven children, six of whom lived to adulthood.

In partnership with one of his brothers-in-law, Worthen went into business, briefly as a forwarding and commission merchant before settling on dry goods. In 1842 business was so bad that Worthen moved his family to Charlestown, Massachusetts, where he spent two years before returning to Warsaw. Like many of his neighbors, Worthen blamed the economic success of the Mormons in nearby Nauvoo for his financial troubles, but he was primarily responsible for his own lack of success. Contemporaries commented on his lack of effort or enthusiasm for the store. Instead, geology was his great passion.

Soon after arriving in Warsaw, Worthen noticed that the rocks in the region were full of fossils and geodes, and he became enthralled with geology. He began collecting local fossils and minerals, studying them, and sending them to collectors and geologists elsewhere in exchange for information and specimens. N. W. Bliss, a nephew who moved to Warsaw in 1850, recalled that at that time Worthen "was still engaged in business but his store as well as his house was more of a stone shop than a dry goods shop and he evidently begrudged the time there spent waiting for or attending upon customers."

Worthen's scientific education was typical of the time. He had access to few books on the subject and learned primarily through his own exploration of the region, supplemented with (and to an extent, directed by) letters of instruction from more knowledgeable geologists. In 1851 he attended a meeting of the American Association for the Advancement of Science in Albany, New York, where he widened his circle of scientific contacts. Serious students of geology frequently sought employment on state or federal surveys where they gained valuable field experience and additional training. Thus, Worthen was following a well-trod path when he took temporary leave of his store in 1851 and signed on as assistant to Joseph Granville Norwood, the newly appointed state geologist of Illinois. He left Norwood in 1855 to work on the Iowa Geological Survey under James Hall. (That same year he abandoned the dry goods business and determined to make a living in geology.) Worthen worked for Hall for two years and contributed two chapters to the report of the Iowa survey.

Meanwhile, by 1854, Norwood had come under attack by the Illinois legislature. A house of representatives investigative committee gave him a favorable review, but he was still vulnerable to criticism because he had produced only three brief accounts (1851, 1853, and 1857) of the survey despite a legal obligation to issue reports annually. Illinois elected a Republican governor in 1858 who fired Norwood, a Democrat, using the survey's poor publication record as an excuse. Of three qualified candidates for the position, only Worthen was a Republican, and it is likely that he was selected for that reason.

Worthen ran the Illinois Geological Survey until its termination in 1875. Politically adept, he was aware of the legislature's interest in practical results so he focused on economic geology and paleontology. He justified paleontology because it would help identify which formations in the state were most likely to hold valuable mineral resources. Despite delays caused by the Civil War and inadequate funds, Worthen, employing more than twenty assistants, produced regular reports containing both detailed discussions of particular topics and a county-by-county survey of the state. The articles on paleontology, which contained descriptions of almost 1,500 species new to science, have been recognized as Worthen's most significant contribution.

By 1875 Worthen had published six volumes of reports, including descriptions of every county in the state. That year the legislature decided to terminate the survey. Worthen, however, was so committed to his work that he maintained the survey's collection and continued to work up its results even after his position had ended. Two years later the legislature created the State Historical Library and Natural History Museum and appointed Worthen curator. As such he had three jobs, manage the natural history museum, act as librarian of the state's historical document collection, and "perform the acts which are or may be required by law of the State Geologist." However, as there were still no funds for fieldwork, he was a geologist without a survey. With special appropriations from the legislature, he eventually published two more volumes of reports from the Illinois survey. The final one, published posthumously in 1890, was edited by his successor, Josua Lindahl. Worthen died in Warsaw.

In 1861 geologist Fielding B. Meek wrote, "Worthen makes no pretensions to a thorough knowledge of chemistry . . . but I do know there is no living man better acquainted with all the details of western geology than he is. This is, I mean, with the formations that occur in the western states" (Merrill, p. 382). In recognition of his contributions to geology, Worthen was elected to the National Academy of Sciences in 1871.

• The principal collection of Worthen correspondence is in the Joseph Granville Norwood Papers in the Illinois Historical Survey Collection, University of Illinois at Urbana-Champaign. Also see his letters in the records of the Illinois Natural History Society in the University of Illinois Archives. Principal biographical studies of Worthen (with bibliographies) are Charles A. White, "Memoir," National Academy of Sciences, *Biographical Memoirs* 3 (1895): 339–62; and N. W. Bliss and White, "The Private Life and Scientific Work of Prof. Amos Henry Worthen," *Geological Survey of Illinois* 8 (1890): appendix, pp. 3–37. The most recent and the most extensive scholarship on Worthen is Anne Marie Millbrooke, "State Geological Surveys of the Nineteenth Century," (Ph.D. diss., Univ. of Pennsylvania, 1981). Also see George P. Merrill, *The First One Hundred Years of American Geology* (1924).

DANIEL GOLDSTEIN

WORTHINGTON, Henry Rossiter (17 Dec. 1817–17 Dec. 1880), hydraulic engineer and manufacturer, was born in New York City, the son of Asa Worthington, a millwright, and Frances Meadowcraft. Worthington's youth was spent in an area of Brooklyn that was originally known as Williamsburgh. There his father and uncle, Anthony Worthington, established the Hope Flour Mill. It was presumed that young Worthington, as the only male child, would eventually assume the management of the mill. His interest in, and facility for, mechanics, however, led him in another direction.

Worthington grew up in an era of territorial expansion and burgeoning commerce. The state of New York in 1840 challenged engineers to devise a steam-powered canal boat in an effort to promote traffic on the recently opened Erie Canal. With his father's financial backing, Worthington successfully developed a barge propelled by paddle wheels. Positioning the wheels at the bow, he was able to eliminate much of the wash that otherwise would have tended to erode the canal banks. Despite his being recognized and rewarded by the state for his achievement, opposing and more conservative canal interests won out, and traffic was forced to revert to movement by mule or horse power.

Out of this project came what would be the first in a long line of steam-driven pumps, for which Worthington is best known. Steam-powered vessels needed to replenish the boiler water continuously, and contemporary practice called for the boiler feed water pump to be driven directly by the engine. As a result, the pump operated only when the engine was in motion. Although canal boats lay idle while they waited in and about the locks or for obstructions to be cleared, boiler water was nevertheless consumed. During these stopped periods, it was necessary to resort to a hand pump to replenish the boiler. To free the crew from the drudgery of pumping by hand, and enable them to go about other tasks, Worthington developed a direct-acting, steam-driven feed pump that operated independently and automatically. The volume of water remaining in the boiler regulated the pump's operation. Compact and relatively simple, the steam and pump cylinders were constructed in-line and connected by a common piston rod. By using this configuration, the need for a flywheel, crank, or beam, which until that time characterized pumping engines, was eliminated.

To exploit this revolutionary machine, Worthington joined William H. Baker in 1845 to form the firm of Worthington & Baker for the sole purpose of manufacturing steam pumps. One of the first important applications of the device was for marine use. On both merchant and naval vessels, pumps supplied water for boilers as well as for washing and fire protection. Improvements in valve design and efficiency led to compact, quiet operating equipment and a market that grew to include hotels, factories, refineries, ironworks, mines, and quarries, with the company gradually becoming international in scope.

In 1854, in the first of a long succession of municipal projects, Worthington designed and built three large direct-acting pumps for the Savannah, Georgia, waterworks. As a result of his sustained interest in all things hydraulic, in 1855 he patented (#13,320), and soon began manufacturing, one of the first practical water meters in the United States. In 1857, in what was perhaps the most significant development in steam-powered pumps, Worthington introduced the duplex direct-acting pump (patent #24,838). Although its predecessor, the single-acting pump, was widely used, it was somewhat uncertain in operation, and delivery could be uneven. These shortcomings were eliminated in the duplex. Composed of two pumps arranged side by side with the piston rod of each connected to the valve rod of the other, operation was certain and delivery almost constant. The resulting pump was perhaps the most widely used means for handling water by steam power.

The first compound—using high- and low-pressure steam cylinders—duplex direct-acting pump was installed at the Charlestown, Massachusetts, waterworks in 1863. By 1876 eighty municipal waterworks that used Worthington pumps of varying capacities had been installed in the United States. While additional pumping engines were sold abroad, other large units were installed domestically for mining and sewage pumping.

In a move that complemented his pump manufacturing business, he became associated with, and then president of, the Nason Manufacturing Company, also of Brooklyn. Organized in the mid-1840s, this company produced a complete line of steam engineering specialties, which included boilers, valves, and fittings as well as general supplies.

Although Worthington was recognized as one of the leading hydraulic engineers of his time, he had received no education beyond the New York public schools. His highly regarded professional standing resulted from knowledge he had gained through practical experience. For those interested in an engineering education, courses in engineering subjects simply were not available. Realizing the increasing need for individuals with formal training, Worthington joined other concerned individuals in 1854 to establish the Brooklyn Collegiate and Polytechnic Institute and served on its first board of trustees.

He took a similar interest in the professional standing of those who referred to themselves as engineers by lending his support to the establishment of an engineering society. In early 1880 he and a group of engineers formed an organization that was patterned after the American Society of Civil Engineers, which had been founded in 1852. The American Society of Mechanical Engineers was established to promote professionalism through education and the exchange of ideas. He declined an offer of the presidency but in April 1880, eight months before his death, he did accept the vice presidency.

Worthington died in New York City. Survivors included his wife, Sara Newton, whom he had married in 1839, and four children. Only his son Charles C. Worthington entered the hydraulic pump business and succeeded him in the company.

• Worthington left no manuscript collection. Thorough descriptions and illustrations of his inventions can be found in records of the U.S. Patent Office. An understanding of his technological contributions can be gained from an unpublished history of the Worthington Pump and Machinery Corporation, which is located in the Worthington Collection, Division of Engineering & Industry, National Museum of American History, Smithsonian Institution. Similar material is found in a company publication, *100 Years Worthington, 1840–1940* (1940). Worthington's 1873 comments on his first patent are reprinted in "Henry Rossiter Worthington and the First Direct-Acting Steam Pump 1817–1880," *Deane News* 3, no. 34 (1920): 397–99. *POLYMEN* 43, no. 1 (1967): 12–15, contains an unsigned article describing Worthington's efforts in founding the Brooklyn Collegiate and Polytechnic Institute. A discussion by R. H. Thurston of the founding of the ASME was published in the *Transactions of the American Society of Mechanical Engineers* (1880): 1–15. Obituaries are in *Engineering News*, 25 Dec. 1880; the *New York Times*, 18 Dec. 1880; and *Scientific American*, 1 Jan. 1881.

WILLIAM E. WORTHINGTON, JR.

WORTHINGTON, John (24 Nov. 1719–25 Apr. 1800), lawyer, politician, and Loyalist, was born in Springfield, Massachusetts, the son of John Worthington and

Mary Pratt. Graduating from Yale College in 1740, he remained as a dean's scholar and tutor from 1742 to 1743. For a short time, he studied law under Phineas Lyman of Suffield, Connecticut, then within the boundaries of Massachusetts. In 1744 he established his law practice in Springfield and for many years served as the Crown's public prosecutor in western Massachusetts.

Worthington was commissioned colonel of the South Hampshire Militia Regiment in 1748. Under his command detachments from the regiment cut a military road from Westfield to Albany in 1753. It was over this road that Henry Knox brought the cannon from Ticonderoga for the siege of Boston twenty-two years later. During the Seven Years' War, he played a leading role in raising and provisioning Massachusetts troops. Worthington held the post of colonel until the outbreak of the Revolution, when he was forced from public commissions because of his Tory sentiments.

In 1759 he married Hannah Hopkins, the daughter of Rev. Samuel Hopkins (1721–1803) of West Springfield. They had four daughters; one married Jonathan Bliss, another Fisher Ames. Hannah died in 1766, and in 1768 Worthington married Mary Stoddard, the daughter of Colonel John Stoddard of Northampton. Through successful land speculation and a successful law practice, Worthington became one of the wealthiest men in western Massachusetts. One of his real estate ventures led to the successful settlement of the town of Worthington, Massachusetts, named for him.

From the time he returned to Springfield from Yale, Worthington was increasingly active in local, regional, and colonywide politics. Beginning as a regular member of Springfield's board of selectmen, he often served as moderator of the town meetings. He was high sheriff of Hampshire County and represented Springfield at the Massachusetts General Court in almost every year from 1747 to 1774. In 1754, he was a delegate to the Albany Congress.

Locally, Worthington in his position as high sheriff was known to have "ruled with a rod of iron." His conservative political positions in the General Court gained favor from several Massachusetts colonial governors, and he served on the governor's council from 1767 to 1769. During the turbulent year 1774, he was appointed as a "mandamus councilor" by Governor Thomas Gage (1721–1787). This led to a dramatic and life-threatening confrontation from a Springfield mob. With Worthington and his family facing violence from the mob, he was forced to recant his loyalism and refuse his commission. He was rescued from the crowd by Jonathan Bliss of Wilbraham. In 1775, Worthington went with Moses Bliss to Philadelphia to escape further harassment, but this only led him closer to the crisis. He then planned to emigrate to Loyalist Nova Scotia but was prevailed upon by the Dwights, the Blisses, and other influential friends to stay in Massachusetts.

He eventually became reconciled to the patriot cause, even contributing funds to its militia. He renewed his local political involvement as early as 1778. Although he was soundly defeated by John Hancock (1736–1793) in the state's first gubernatorial election in 1780, his campaign represented one of the most remarkable political recoveries in the state's history.

Among Worthington's most significant contributions in his later years was as incorporator of the company that began building canals around the falls of the Connecticut River. He also belonged to the commission that settled the Massachusetts-Connecticut boundary in 1791. When he died in Springfield, he was the wealthiest man in western Massachusetts, with an estate valued at well over $120,000.

• The John Worthington Papers are housed at the Connecticut Valley Historical Museum Library and Archives, Springfield, Mass. For biographical information, see George Worthington, *The Genealogy of the Worthington Family* (1894); F. B. Dexter, *Biographical Sketches of the Graduates of Yale College*, vol. 1 (1885); George Bliss, *An Address . . . at Springfield . . . 1828* (1828); J. G. Holland, *History of Western Massachusetts*, vol. 1 (1855); and Mason A. Green, *Springfield, 1636-1886* (1888). See also John Worthington Probate File, Hampshire County Registry of Probate, Northampton, Mass.; 1800 Tax Valuation of Springfield, Office of the City Clerk, Springfield, Mass.; Thomas Warren, "Springfield Families" (4 vols.), Connecticut Valley Historical Museum; William Pencak, *War, Politics and Revolution in Provincial Massachusetts* (1981); and Robert J. Taylor, *Western Massachusetts in the Revolution* (1954).

JOSEPH CARVALHO III

WORTHINGTON, Thomas (16 July 1773–20 June 1827), entrepreneur, politician, and U.S. senator, was born near Charlestown, Berkeley County, Virginia (now Jefferson County, W.Va.), the son of Robert Worthington, a prominent planter, and Margaret Matthews, from Frederickton, Maryland, who was of Irish background. Orphaned by the age of seven, he received little formal education and in May 1791 went to sea for two years. On his return he farmed the Berkeley County estate, took up surveying, and bought up Virginia military land warrants that he located near Chillicothe in the Northwest Territory. In December 1796 he married Eleanor Van Swearingen of Shepherdstown, Virginia, herself an orphan with a rich property. The couple had ten children. In spring 1798 Worthington freed his slaves and moved his family to Chillicothe; they were joined by his brother-in-law and lifelong political ally, Edward Tiffin. Worthington rapidly prospered through farming, stockraising, milling, and shipping farm produce, while as a land speculator he owned 18,273 acres by 1800.

Immediately prominent among the Virginians concentrated near Chillicothe, Worthington was elected in 1798 to the Territorial Assembly, where he associated with the opposition to Governor Arthur St. Clair. Though Republican in outlook, Worthington secured appointment in 1800 as register at the Chillicothe Land Office from the Adams administration. Determined to end the arbitrary rule of an externally imposed chief executive, he joined fellow Republicans to overthrow the Territorial regime. Sent to Washington by a Chillicothe meeting in December 1801, he persuaded President Thomas Jefferson and the new Congress not only to defeat St. Clair's plans to delay statehood but also to pass an act enabling Ohio to proceed to statehood. In the constitutional convention of November 1802, Worthington worked to secure a highly democratic state constitution, his votes revealing little desire to insulate the institutions of government from popular control. For his efforts, he became known as the "father of Ohio statehood."

Regarded as Jefferson's main adviser on Ohio appointments, Worthington was elected U.S. senator in 1803. In Washington he advocated western interests, formally proposing in 1806 what became the Cumberland or National Road. He has commonly been regarded as the leader of the "Chillicothe Junto," though his command at state and local levels was often successfully challenged. In 1807 he retired from the Senate and accepted election to the state assembly, where he sided with those Republicans who objected to the principle of judicial review. Though no longer a legislator after 1808, he remained active in Chillicothe, the state capital, supporting the dismissal of presumptuous judges and, in 1809, joining the new Ohio Tammany Society, a bulwark of Democratic-Republican principles. In both 1808 and 1810 he ran unsuccessfully for governor, on the first occasion failing to unite the votes of the opponents of judicial review and on the second facing vehement criticism as the "Idol of Tammany." In December 1810 the Democratic Republicans in the assembly elected him—without his consent—once more to the U.S. Senate.

In Washington he chaired the Committee on Public Lands and was responsible for the creation of the General Land Office in 1812. As chairman of the Committee on Indian Affairs, he secured added protection for the Northwest frontier against Tecumseh's hostile Indian confederation. This awareness of Ohio's vulnerability persuaded Worthington to vote against war with Britain in June 1812, believing it irresponsible to undertake more than a purely naval war. He then actively supported the war effort, negotiating with the Indians, energizing the Ohio militia, and serving as chairman of the Senate Committee on Military Affairs. As a result, he received broad support for the governorship in 1814 and 1816, winning with more than two-thirds of the vote on each occasion.

As governor he preached the need for a public school system, internal improvements, penal and poor-law reform, and temperance, though little of his program was enacted during his governorship. By the end of his term in December 1818, Worthington had become too closely identified with banking interests, as a director of two Bank of the United States branches and an opponent of state taxation of BUS branches. Two months later he was defeated for the U.S. Senate; his hopes for federal office under the Monroe administration were disappointed; and he retreated to "Adena," his home one mile northwest of Chillicothe. "The most magnificent mansion west of the Alleghenies," designed by Benjamin Latrobe and built between 1805 and 1807, Adena stood on a "fine estate" of 800 acres, "all of it elevated table land" and very productive. Even British visitors called him "the squire," though in the hard times after 1819 he took the plow himself and personally directed his commercial ventures.

In 1821 Worthington returned to politics, serving three more terms in the Ohio house. In January 1822 he came within one vote of election to the U.S. Senate again, owing his defeat primarily to younger politicians who, according to a contemporary, thought him "a designing, artful, intriguing man, who sees his own interests at the bottom of every measure in which he engages" (*Trimble*, pp. 118–19). Appointed to the commission supervising the state's canal-building program, he was elected to the chair but was compelled to resign it after a year; his fellow commissioners thought him too eager to hand the business over to a private company and too partial in the selection of routes. Worthington was unhappy at the collapse of Republican party nominating mechanisms in the 1824 presidential election and retired from politics in 1825, unenthusiastically supporting the Adams administration as the only rallying point for western Republicans. Though still active in business and canal-building, Worthington increasingly suffered from a painful "bilious colic" and died in New York City while on a business trip.

Of Quaker background on his father's side, Worthington was a pious Methodist for most of his adult life, observing that church's strict moral code. He was a devoted family man. Always active and decisive, he could annoy people by his manner—superior, knowing, impatient, sarcastic, and (to some) not quite straightforward. John Quincy Adams thought him in 1805 a person of "plausible, insinuating address" who "has seen something of the world, and, without much education of any sort, has acquired a sort of polish in his manners, and a kind of worldly wisdom, which may perhaps more properly be called cunning." Others were more impressed by his discriminating mind, his influence, patriotism, energy, and commitment; and, with his obituarist, recognized his contribution to state and national development through "a career of extensive usefulness, and almost unequalled activity."

• The chief collection of Worthington papers is in the Ohio Historical Society, now microfilmed with Worthington papers from other collections; see Linda Elise Kalette, *The Papers of Thirteen Early Ohio Political Leaders: An Inventory to the 1976–77 Microfilm Editions* (1977). The Library of Congress, Manuscript Department, has his diary, while the Ross County Historical Society, Chillicothe, has an important and unmicrofilmed manuscript collection. The authoritative biography is Alfred Byron Sears, *Thomas Worthington, Father of Ohio Statehood* (1958). For sidelights, see Charles Francis Adams, ed., *Memoirs of John Quincy Adams* (1874–1877), vol. 1, p. 377, vol. 4, p. 136; Reuben G. Thwaites, ed., *Early Western Travels, 1748–1846* (1904–1907), vol. 10, pp. 70–71, vol. 11, pp. 179–82; and Mary M. Tuttle and Henry B.

Thompson, eds., *Autobiography and Correspondence of Allen Trimble, Governor of Ohio* (1909), pp. 118–19, 121–22, 135, 192. For an obituary, see the Chillicothe *Scioto Gazette*, 5 July 1827. Adena is now the property of the Ohio Historical Society and is open to the public.

DONALD J. RATCLIFFE

WORTMAN, Sterling, Jr. (3 Apr. 1923–26 May 1981), plant geneticist, was born Leo Sterling Wortman, Jr., in Quinlan, Oklahoma. There is little information available about his parents. Wortman graduated in 1943 from Oklahoma State University, majoring in agronomy. After completing his degree, he joined the Reserve Officers Training Corps and saw active duty in the Philippines and New Guinea in 1943. For his service in the Philippines during the Second World War he received the Medal of Merit from the Philippine government.

Having returned to civilian life, Wortman enrolled in the University of Minnesota and completed his M.S. in 1948 followed by his doctorate there in 1950. For these graduate degrees he concentrated his research on plant breeding and genetics as well as plant pathology. In 1949 he married Ruth Eleanor Bolstad, with whom he had four children.

In 1950 Wortman joined the Rockefeller Foundation. This foundation, incorporated in 1913 by John D. Rockefeller, Sr., to promote worldwide well-being, funded projects ranging from infectious disease control and agricultural experiments to world population control. When Wortman first joined the organization, he worked in Mexico trying to find ways to increase wheat production. His research colleague in Mexico was Norman Borlaug, who later won the Nobel Peace Prize in 1970. They ran experiments where they crossed native wheat varieties with hardy imported strains in an attempt to breed more resilient and higher yielding varieties. By 1965 these hybrids led to a more than threefold increase in wheat production in Mexico.

From 1955 to 1959 Wortman served as the head of the Department of Plant Breeding at the Pineapple Research Institute, a commercial operation in Hawaii. He took a four-year hiatus from this work to help establish, as assistant director, the International Rice Research Institute in the Philippines. This initiative was the first of ten such institutes set up in the world responsible for research that led to new, high-yielding grain varieties, which contributed to greater food production. When he returned to Hawaii in 1964–1965 it was as director of the Pineapple Research Institute.

Wortman went on, in the 1960s, to found the International Corn and Wheat Research Institute in Mexico. In 1966 he became director of agricultural sciences at the Rockefeller Foundation and four years later rose to the position of vice president of the foundation.

One of the great world concerns in the early 1970s was the food shortage in developing countries. Reserves in countries such as the United States had dropped dramatically through the 1960s, and many researchers tried to find solutions to stave off the crisis. These solutions included ideas on curbing population growth as well as trying to increase food production in the countries most affected. In a number of lengthy features published in 1974 in the *New York Times*, Wortman was often quoted. In one such article from 26 July 1974 Wortman noted, "I don't think there's any solution to the world food situation unless we get population stabilized. Those of us who have been working to increase the food supply have never assumed we were doing any more than buying time."

In August 1974 Wortman headed a group of American plant scientists, including Norman Borlaug with whom he had worked in Mexico, that made a month-long visit to China. The initiative was arranged by the Committee on Scholarly Communication with the People's Republic of China, the Social Science Research Council, and the American Council of Learned Societies. The group visited research centers and farms in and around Canton, Nanking, Peking, Shanghai, Sian, and Kirin Province north of Korea. When he returned, Wortman told the New York Times, "We were tremendously impressed everywhere we went with the high quality of Chinese farming. I came away feeling I'm going to worry less about whether China is able to feed her people or not" (7 Oct. 1974). This was heartening given that, at the time, China had almost 800 million people, or one-quarter of the world's population, within its borders. One area of concern the group discovered, however, was the need for more agricultural training and research in China. Most of the researchers the Americans met with, Wortman said, were sixty or older.

Taking advantage of his experience on world food production, Wortman was invited to participate as a panelist in a televised debate on U.S. food policy held 27 October 1974. To recognize his efforts in setting up a global network of agricultural research centers, Wortman was awarded the first Joseph C. Wilson Award in 1975. This $10,000 prize, first sponsored by Xerox Corporation, was for achievement in international affairs.

In March 1979, when the president of the Rockefeller Foundation, John H. Knowles, died, Wortman was appointed acting president. He saw the foundation through a period of some turmoil as representatives searched for a new leader. In fact, Wortman was one of four finalists for the position that eventually went to Richard W. Lyman, then president of Stanford University, in 1980. Wortman retired from his administrative duties that year, although he continued work as a consultant. Most of his time, however, was spent on research and international development issues.

In addition to his longtime service to the Rockefeller Foundation, Wortman was a member of the American Association for the Advancement of Science and the agricultural board of the National Academy of Sciences from 1967 to 1971. He served on the steering committee of the President's Study on Food and Nutrition and was an adviser to the National Science Foundation, Department of Agriculture, World Bank, and a number of independent research institutes. He was also a fellow of the Philippine Association for the Advancement of Science. Wortman coauthored *To Feed This World: The Challenge and the Strategy* with Ralph W. Cummings, Jr. (1978), and he authored a number of reports for the Rockefeller Foundation.

Wortman died in Greenwich, Connecticut, of cancer. He remains best known for his leading role in the Green Revolution, a term used from the 1960s to 1980s for the agricultural movement that tried to combat world famine.

• Significant archival material on Wortman is at the Rockefeller Archive Center, Tarrytown, N.Y. There is relatively little in the traditional reference texts on Wortman. He is listed in the 10th to 14th editions of *American Men and Women of Science* (1960 to 1979, respectively). Many of the key events of his career, including his visit to China and the search for a new president for the Rockefeller Foundation, are noted in articles in the *New York Times*, especially 27 Aug. 1974, 28 Oct. 1974, 16 Mar. 1975, 18 Oct. 1975, 15 Aug. 1979, 5 Dec. 1979, and 1 Jan. 1980. An obituary is in the *New York Times*, 27 May 1981.

MARIANNE FEDUNKIW STEVENS

WOVOKA (1858?–29 Sept. 1932), Northern Paiute prophet of the 1890 Ghost Dance, was the son of Tavibo, a shaman and headman who was involved in the 1870 Ghost Dance. Wovoka was commonly known as Jack Wilson. Although generally reported as having been born in the Walker River country, a 1910 census schedule lists California as his birthplace and his birthyear as 1858. A 1900 census schedule, however, gives Wovoka's birthplace as Nevada and the year of his birth as 1855.

Widespread hunger was being experienced by the Northern Paiutes when Wovoka's mother died and his father became involved with the Ghost Dance. The boy seems to have then set out on his own. He soon became associated with the family of Presbyterian rancher David Wilson of Mason Valley, whose brother had in 1865 discovered a rich mine at Pine Grove, not far to the south. Wovoka took the name Jack Wilson and maintained some relations with the David Wilson family for more than four decades. The name Wovoka ("chopper" or "cutter") shows that his primary work for the Wilsons was as a woodchopper. Sometime between about 1874 and 1879 (probably by 1875) he established his own household, but continued to work for the Wilsons, when he married the Northern Paiute woman Mary, who was about his own age.

David Wilson may have read the Bible to Wovoka, as white acquaintances later recalled, but the Christian elements of Wovoka's 1890 Ghost Dance cannot be ascribed to this source. Nor, until after he became prominent, is there evidence that Wovoka traveled beyond his home area, contrary to claims that he had early knowledge of Smohalla's religion of the Pacific Northwest.

The early 1870s were a time of "nativistic" religious ferment among the Indians of the Walker River country. The nativistic movements of the trans-Mississippi West had something of an accretional character, with each movement building on the heritage of the previous one. The 1870 Ghost Dance began as a "cargo cult," promising the arrival of a trainload of goods for the Indians. It later promised the destruction of non-Indians. Wovoka's own 1890 Ghost Dance was first directed toward curing the sick, but soon moved to a second stage very similar to the last stage of the 1870 movement. It is not known if Wovoka was actively involved in the 1870 Ghost Dance.

Sometime between 1875 and 1880 David Wilson purchased his brother's mine at Pine Grove. For the next three decades Wovoka appears to have maintained his summer residence in Smith Valley and to have worked for the Wilsons and others following the pinenut harvest and into winter, which was the season for woodcutting and flour milling for the whites. In January 1892 anthropologist James Mooney found Wovoka's camp at Pine Grove.

Wovoka seems to have dated his first revelation to the series of earth tremors ending in March 1888. At this time Wovoka fell down as if dead and was taken to heaven. God told him that he (Wovoka) had the power to control weather and do other things. God said there must be peace, that all men are brothers, that people must be good to one another, and that people must not steal, lie, swear, or drink liquor. Later God showed him all the people who had died (white as well as Indian), including his mother. God then told him that the people must dance often, four nights and five days (but some sources say five nights) each time—five being the Paiute sacred number—and God gave him five songs (apparently one song for each weather power).

The first putative Ghost Dances after Wovoka's earliest revelation took place in late January and February 1888 at Sodaville and the Walker River Reservation. It is uncertain if these were led by Wovoka. By December 1888, more than a week before the total eclipse of the sun on 1 January 1889, it was stated that the "Mason Valley Piutes [*sic*] are having big dances every night now." At this time Wovoka's message seems to have only concerned healing the sick. In 1887 the Northern Paiutes suffered the highest death toll from disease (scarlet fever, measles, and smallpox) in almost a quarter of a century, and the dances of early 1888 took place during a new smallpox scare.

Directly informed by Wovoka, Mooney called the prophet's vision during the eclipse of 1889 his "Great Revelation": When " . . . 'the sun died' . . . he fell asleep in the daytime and was taken up to the other world." The world, said God, was old and worn out and must be remade. The dead would come back to life; the earth would be enlarged to hold them by doing away with heaven, and the land would be extended into the Pacific Ocean. Volcanic eruptions and mud slides, which would build the new earth, along with floods and whirlwinds would kill the whites. The believers would escape by being taken up into a great cloud above Mount Grant. After a sleep or trance of four or five days, they would descend from the cloud with the Messiah and the revived dead to possess the new earth with its fresh supply of game. Not only must believers dance to ensure the return of the Messiah; they must even quit wearing the clothes of whites. After the world transformation, which would eliminate the whites, the sick would be well, the blind would see, and everyone would become young again.

Following his Great Revelation, Wovoka required that believers dance every three months. Each dance involved singing and dancing in a circle with clasped hands. The writer Dan De Quille believed that Wovoka fell into a trance of about an hour at each dance. When he awoke, he told of the vision he had experienced and then, pointing above, told the people to listen, for he could see and hear the dead above him. Then he called on the people to sing and dance again, until they too could hear and see the dead. Porcupine, however, makes it clear that Wovoka had trances only on the last night, but he erred in believing that Wovoka then claimed to be Christ.

The first demonstration of Wovoka's great powers came at the end of April and the beginning of May 1889. Wovoka brought rain to western Nevada, which had experienced a long drought. This demonstration convinced many skeptical Northern Paiutes and drew emissaries from other tribes. The actual appearance of the Messiah seems to have first been predicted for the winter of 1890–1891. According to Dan De Quille, the plan had been for all the believers to assemble at Mount Grant, but the migration was frustrated by the trouble at the Pine Ridge Reservation and the "Sioux outbreak." There are definite signs that the Ghost Dance was building to a crescendo in Nevada as the end of 1890 approached. Three large dances in the Western Shoshoni country, heavily attended by Northern Paiutes, and perhaps led by Wovoka, were held in November: at Raycroft Canyon, "near Belmont"; near Battle Mountain; and in Smoky Valley, between Austin and Belmont. The concluding dance, in Mason Valley, was attended by 1,600 people.

The scout Chapman interviewed Wovoka a few days later, just before a snow storm ended hope of the arrival of the Messiah. From this interview it is clear that Wovoka conceived of himself as the head of "confederated" tribes of believers. And while the Northern Paiutes north of the Walker River country were actively against him, those of Walker River were solidly in his favor.

By this time Wovoka was prosperous for a Northern Paiute. Although he had three (perhaps four) children with Mary, Wovoka took another, younger wife in November 1890, as befitting a prominent man. He was said to have two "ranches," one in Mason Valley and the other seemingly in Smith Valley, with much stock.

When the Messiah failed to appear before the first snow of the winter of 1890–1891, Wovoka was reported to have extended the time of the Messiah's coming to the spring of 1891. Likely the Bannocks, Kiowas, Arapahoes, and Sioux who met with Wovoka in early 1891 came to find out what had happened to the predicted Messiah. Some of these delegates went away convinced that Wovoka was a fraud, even though he had had a new, third revelation and a new song, from Esa (Wolf), the Northern Paiute culture hero, who would release the dead. Gradually, Wovoka pushed forward the time of the Messiah's appearance from early spring 1891 to mid-May, then June, and finally July. By August 1891 Wovoka had begun to leave open the date of the Messiah's coming.

Following the fighting at Wounded Knee, all the Northern Paiutes feared that the whites might begin a war with them. Wovoka's new revelation effectively defused the potentially explosive "anti-white" doctrines of the Great Revelation. From that time on, Wovoka told emissaries that they should farm and take up white ways when they returned home.

The third revelation appears in the "Messiah Letter" that Mooney printed. Taking up white ways was presented as a "temporary" expedient until the Messiah transformed the earth. Jesus was said to be already on the earth, but Wovoka did not know when the dead would come back. Although this breaks with the nativism of the Great Revelation, it does not necessarily modify the apocalyptic vision.

From the time of the Esa revelation up through 1893, Wovoka may have been more influential than ever. Even though the Sioux had been made to stop dancing by force of arms, and the Western Shoshonis were also said to have stopped, the Kiowas held their first Ghost Dance in the same year, 1891, that the Cheyennes and Arapahoes twice sent delegates to Wovoka. That fall, Caddos, Wichitas, and Delawares went to see Wovoka. From 1892 to 1894 more tribal delegations met with him. In the summer of 1894 the Kiowas again took up the Ghost Dance, in a gathering that was attended by several thousand Indians from all over Oklahoma.

Wovoka himself ended his connection with the Ghost Dance the next year. He had told a visiting delegation of Arapahoes in 1892 that he was "tired of so many visitors and wanted them to go home and tell their tribes to stop dancing." The death of Wovoka's son, the third to die in three years, evidently was a factor too. A June 1895 issue of a local paper reported, "The Indian Doctors tell Jack [Wilson] that he talks too much [and] that is the cause of [his sons'] death[s]." Witchcraft could harm his family even if the prophet was immune to it. The presumed source of this witchcraft must have been the Northern Paiutes toward Pyramid Lake, who feared his continuing influence. The tribes that kept dancing after Wovoka's retirement in 1895 did so for varying lengths of time, but after a while more of the tribes ceased to believe that the Messiah would return in the near future. Among some tribes, particularly the Caddo, the Ghost Dance became something of a tribal church, synthesizing some of the elements of Christianity and native beliefs. In some tribes, Ghost Dance leaders turned more and more to peyote at the expense of the Ghost Dance doctrine.

By February 1896 Wovoka was working at the ranch of D. C. Simpson in Smith Valley, and circumstances suggest that he was employed there until 1902 or later. Four more children were born to him between about 1897 and 1902. By 1906 he had begun working seasonally at the Wilson Nordyke flour mill.

Wovoka returned to preaching the Ghost Dance between 1904 and 1906, but very little is known of these activities. During that time, Arapahoes and Sioux visited him. After the tentative revival of the movement, old believers sent Wovoka periodical requests for medicinal assistance, sacred paraphernalia and paint, and items associated with his person, such as shirts and hats, often enclosing money.

During his 1910–1917 revival of the Ghost Dance, Wovoka first became politically active in the concerns of the Northern Paiutes. The earliest dance of the 1910 revival was held in May, just after the appearance of Halley's comet. Probably soon after this dance, Wovoka undertook a mission to the Wind River reservation. His break with the David Wilson family seems to have occurred early in 1912 but surely became final in 1916; it likely began with Wovoka's new concern with Northern Paiute activism. By 1912 the prophet had moved to the Indian settlement near the town of Mason and perhaps lived with or in the vicinity of his declining father.

No doctrinal statements survive from the 1910–1917 revival, but Wovoka's failure to burn his father's house and other possessions after his death shows that the prophet still held the views expressed in the Messiah Letter. In addition, it is known that Wovoka preached against peyote, after it became inescapably evident that peyote represented a challenge to Ghost Dance teachings.

The details of Wovoka's missions of 1916 and 1917 are not known. It appears that in 1916 he made two trips to the Wind River Reservation in Wyoming and on one or both trips went on to Oklahoma. Even fewer details of his 1917 mission are known. The 8 March 1917 issue of the *Colony Courier* (Okla.) noted that he had just made a "flying trip among Cheyennes and Arapahoes to try to do some Faith Curing among the sick."

When the United States entered World War I in 1917, any disturbance among the Indians was looked on as subversive, and Wovoka appears to have almost immediately halted his Ghost Dance involvement. The Yerington Indian Colony townsite was laid out in early 1918; not long afterward Wovoka moved there and erected a small frame house.

On the death of Mary's uncle, she inherited half of allotment number 65 on the reservation, which Wovoka began to farm in late 1921 or early 1922. He may have made final efforts toward reviving the Ghost Dance between 1923 and 1926, but there is no evidence of his missions during this time. A dance of "five nights" held in May 1926 at the colony may have been, however, a Ghost Dance.

Poverty marked Wovoka's last few years. Having managed to maintain a wagon and team of horses, he did occasional work for the government until at least 1931. In 1929 and 1930 his wife Mary was one of twenty-seven destitute Indians drawing rations at the reservation. Wovoka was given a "quantity of old Clothing" by the field matron in early January 1930, and a year later both he and his wife were among the sixty-eight people drawing rations. After Mary's death in August 1931, Wovoka continued to be carried on the rations roll for another year. The prophet himself became very ill in September 1932 and, after two weeks in the care of the agency doctor, died at his Yerington Colony, Nevada, home.

In the 1890s James Mooney said of the Ghost Dance, "The moral code inculcated is as pure and comprehensive as anything found in religious systems from the days of Gautama Buddha to the time of Jesus Christ." Mooney found the best assessment of the prophet and his religion in the words a Christian used to describe one of Wovoka's disciples: "He has given these people a better religion than they ever had before, taught them precepts which, if faithfully carried out, will bring them into better accord with their white neighbors, and has prepared the way for their final Christianization." Except for the ethnocentrism and Christian value judgments embodied in the remarks he quoted, Mooney's conclusions would still be adequate. Above all, Wovoka's syncretic religion offered Indians a means of accommodating themselves to a dominant alien society while preserving core Indian values.

Mooney, however, failed to recognize Wovoka's political message: the unity of Indian believers and Indian interests beyond the interests of tribalism. Wovoka's changes in doctrine reflect his assessments of the political realities facing the Indians of his times, and thus they illustrate his penetrating intellect and acute political understanding. After the failure of his universal message, twice modified, he recognized the potential value of local activism.

• The Bureau of Indian Affairs, Special Case 188, National Archives, Washington, D.C., includes virtually all the important letters received by the commissioner of Indian affairs on Wovoka's Ghost Dance movement. The Bureau of Indian Affairs, Letters Received series, Nevada Superintendency, contains material on Wovoka's people. The papers of the Carson School and Agency, the Reno Agency, and the Walker Lake School and Agency, plus the Dorrington papers, are in the National Archives, Pacific Sierra Region, San Bruno, Calif. Some valuable manuscript items are also in the Nevada State Historical Society (Reno) and the University of Nevada, Reno, Special Collections. The historical society holds the original letters to Wovoka between 1907 and 1911, published by Grace Dangberg in Bureau of American Ethnology, *Bulletin* 154:279–96, and in a more useful edition in the *Nevada Historical Quarterly* 11, no. 2 (1968): 1–53. Dangberg's original notebook and the Jennie Weir fieldnotes are also in the historical society collection.

The most useful newspapers for Wovoka's life are the *Walker Lake Bulletin* and the *Lyon County Times* of Nevada, but many sporadic items of value appear in a great number of 1890–1891 newspapers from all areas of the country. The most important single newspaper items are Dan De Quille's contributions to the *Salt Lake Daily Tribune*, 21 Dec. 1890, 18 Jan. 1891, and 1 Feb. 1891.

The biography by Paul Bailey, *Wovoka, the Indian Messiah* (1957), and his fictionalized *Ghost Dance Messiah* (1970) are in error at almost every point. Michael Hittman, *Wovoka and the Ghost Dance* (1990), is a study of Wovoka's life and summarizes the views of an ethnographer with long experience among Wovoka's people; a third of the book conveniently reprints many of the sources on the prophet. For information on the Northern Paiutes and the Ghost Dance, see Edward C. Johnson, *Walker River Paiutes: A Tribal History* (1975). For Wovoka's position as a shaman, see Willard Z. Park, *Shamanism in Western North America: A Study in Cultural Relationships* (1938). James Mooney's classic *The Ghost-Dance Religion and the Sioux Outbreak of 1890* (1896), based on his own fieldwork and study of Special Case 188, is still the most penetrating work on the movement and contains several important documents, including the Messiah Letter, the only extant letter known to have been dictated by Wovoka. Mooney's book, however, must be considered in light of later studies of the 1870 movement, beginning with Cora Dubois, *The 1870 Ghost Dance* (1939). The study of the manuscript and newspaper sources cited here was made possible by grants from the Harry Frank Guggenheim Foundation.

MELBURN D. THURMAN

WRAGG, William (1714–2 Sept. 1777), Loyalist and lawyer, was born in the South Carolina lowcountry, the son of Samuel Wragg, a merchant of Welsh background, and Marie DuBose, a Huguenot. Samuel Wragg and his brother Joseph Wragg became leading suppliers of slaves to South Carolina during the 1730s. Samuel, who operated the British side of the business from London, took his son to England for schooling in 1718; en route, they became captives of Blackbeard, the pirate, but soon were released. William attended Westminster School, St. Johns College of Oxford University, and the Middle Temple, from which he was admitted to the bar on 23 November 1733. He then practiced law in England and in 1740 married Mary Wood of St. Clement Danes, Middlesex. Ten years later Wragg's father died, and he returned to South Carolina to claim his inheritance. As the owner of at least three rice plantations, he gave up the practice of law.

Wragg's wealth and experience qualified him for public life, and the Crown appointed him to the royal council on 29 January 1753. Assertive and opinionated, he soon clashed with Governor James Glen. Glen's successor, William Henry Lyttleton, considered Wragg to be "an insolent and litigious spirit" who obstructed public business (Weir [1977], p. xvi). Lyttleton suspended him from the council and thereby dealt a blow to that body's prestige from which it never recovered; thereafter, South Carolinians of stature were loathe to accept a position in which they appeared to serve only on sufferance. The following year (1758), the voters of St. John, Colleton County (a coastal parish south of Charleston) elected Wragg to the Commons House of Assembly, and for the next decade Wragg continued to represent this area. Much of the time he found himself out of step with most of his colleagues. During the Gadsden election controversy in 1762, the House refused to conduct further business with Governor Thomas Boone, who had succeeded Lyttleton, because he had challenged its right to judge the qualifications of its own members; Wragg opposed such a drastic step. In 1765, when the Commons passed resolutions against the Stamp Act, Wragg alone dissented. And when the House voted to erect a statue to William Pitt as a gesture of thanks for his aid in obtaining repeal of that act, Wragg unsuccessfully sought to substitute a statue of the king. But his legal knowledge and experience still commanded respect among his colleagues, and in 1767 he chaired an important committee that recommended establishment of a circuit court system for the increasingly populous and turbulent backcountry.

The Commons' impending endorsement of the Massachusetts and Virginia resolutions against the Townshend Duties appears to have been too much for Wragg, and in 1768 he declined his reelection to the House. Adoption of a nonimportation agreement the following year produced a rash of polemics in the local newspapers; Wragg's essays denouncing the coercive elements of the embargo were among the pithiest of all local writings. His loyalty and legal background made him a logical choice for chief justice of the colony, but when in 1769 the Crown officials offered him the position—as well as reinstatement on the council—Wragg turned them down, partly because he appears to have considered himself too controversial a figure for the judicial post and partly because making "this sacrifice," as he triumphantly observed, was "the fullest confutation of every illiberal and malevolent suggestion" that he had supported the Crown in the hope of reward (Weir [1977], p. xxxi). Wragg's refusal to accept election to the Commons House in 1773 confirmed his retirement from public life. His first wife, by whom he had at least one child, had died in 1767, and Wragg married his double-first cousin, Henrietta Wragg, two years later; they had four children. However, politics soon complicated his domestic life, for in 1775 Wragg refused to sign another nonimportation agreement, the Continental Association. Revolutionary authorities accordingly placed him under house arrest. Banishment followed two years later when he would not swear allegiance to the new state. Sailing for England with his seven-year old son (his wife stayed behind), Wragg drowned when the vessel ran aground on the Dutch coast. His son survived.

Wragg's own words written years earlier during the first nonimportation crisis epitomized his life. "I have," he allowed, "pronounced an audible 'no,' when I intended not to say yea" (Weir [1977], p. 89). But a memorial tablet in Westminster Abbey bears a more innocuous epitaph, " . . . Strong natural Parts, improved by Education, together with Love of Justice and Humanity, Formed the compleat character of A Good Man."

• No substantial body of manuscripts pertaining to Wragg himself appears to have survived, though the South Carolina Historical Society holds Wragg family papers. Some of William Wragg's correspondence appears in "American Loyalists," *Southern Quarterly Review* 4 (1843), and his political polemics from 1769 are in William Henry Drayton, *The Letters of Freeman, Etc.: Essays on the Nonimportation Movement in South Carolina*, ed. Robert M. Weir (1977). See also George C. Rogers, Jr., "The Conscience of a Huguenot," Huguenot Society of South Carolina, *Transactions* 67 (1962): 1–11. Robert McCluer Calhoon, *The Loyalists in Revolutionary America* (1973); M. Eugene Sirmans, *Colonial South Carolina. A Political History, 1663–1763* (1966); and Robert M. Weir, *Colonial South Carolina: A History* (1983), discuss Wragg in context.

ROBERT M. WEIR

WRATHER, William Embry (20 Jan. 1883–28 Nov. 1963), petroleum geologist and federal administrator, was born at Munford Farm, near Brandenburg, Meade County, Kentucky, the son of Richard Anselm Wrather and Glovy Washington Munford, farmers. He attended local schools before going to Chicago, Illinois, in 1898 to live with an uncle and work in his grocery while attending South Chicago High School. With savings from eighteen months' employment with the Illinois Steel Company and a first-year scholarship, Wrather began training for the law at the University of Chicago in 1903. There geology professor Rollin D. Salisbury redirected Wrather to science. After receiving a Ph.B. in February 1908, Wrather began graduate study in geology and also continued working toward a law degree, although he did not complete the latter. He married Alice Mildred Dolling, a fellow student, in 1910. They had four children, but only two lived to adulthood.

Wrather later viewed the summer of 1907 as the turning point of his career. William H. Emmons, a young lecturer at Chicago who also served part time with the U.S. Geological Survey (USGS), suggested that Wrather join that agency. As an assistant packer and field assistant, Wrather aided USGS geologists in mapping the rocks, structures, and mineral resources of the Philipsburg reconnaissance-scale quadrangle near Butte, Montana, for a folio in the *Geologic Atlas of the United States*. The USGS offered Wrather a position in its new Land Classification Board, but he resigned and joined the petroleum industry.

A friend at the university who had left to work for the J. M. Guffey Petroleum Company (later Gulf Production) of Texas recommended Wrather to that firm. After a year as a roughneck and office trainee, Wrather scouted surface seepages, drilling operations, and oilfield development and provided liaison for land leasing by Guffey, mostly in the Gulf Coast saltdome province of Louisiana and Texas. Operating principally from Wichita Falls, he also conducted detailed geologic studies of areas in western Texas and eastern New Mexico. Finding that Guffey did not value geologically based prospecting, he left the company in 1916 and did two years of additional exploration in Texas under contract to Pittsburgh's Michael L. Benedum, Joseph C. Trees, and Foster B. Parriott. In 1918, after a number of promising prospects all tested dry, Wrather recommended that his employers drill a geologic structure that he had located and leased in Comanche County, Texas, some thirty miles from the nearest producing field. Contemporary oil entrepreneurs viewed the successful wells in what became the Desdemona field as "the greatest find in Texas since Spindletop" (Sam T. Mallison, *The Great Wildcatter* [1953], p. 291). When Tex-Penn Oil, the small company Benedum, Parriott, Wrather, and two colleagues formed to develop the new pool, merged with other firms in 1919 to form Transcontinental Oil, Wrather received about $750,000 for his share.

Wrather moved to Dallas and began independent consulting in petroleum and investigations of other minerals, both precious and base. Studies of oilfield production for the Internal Revenue Service led to his appraising during the 1920s and 1930s the reserves and value of many oil properties, fields, and companies, including Union and Texaco. In some of this work Wrather collaborated with Texas oil entrepreneur Everett L. DeGolyer, his friend and fellow bibliophile, history buff, and USGS veteran, who pioneered Amerada Oil's application of geophysical methods to find saltdomes. Wrather also discovered a second but much smaller oilfield in Limestone County, Texas, in 1926, examined oil prospects nationwide, and helped to defend the unitization, or efficient joint development of oilfields that cross boundaries of leases held by individuals or companies, in New Mexico and California.

During these years Wrather also participated significantly in national professional societies. In 1917 he helped to found the American Association of Petroleum Geologists (AAPG), serving as its president in 1922–1923. He championed the early applications of foraminiferan micropaleontology and stratigraphy in oil exploration. As chair (1923–1929) of the AAPG's committee on research, he arranged in 1924 for a critical and comparative study of the relation of oil accumulation to geologic structure by Amerada veteran Sidney Powers and others. The results appeared in 1929 as *Structure of Typical American Oil Fields*, two volumes of symposium proceedings edited by Powers. Five years later the AAPG published *Problems of Petroleum Geology*, a second anthology, begun by Powers and completed by Wrather and Frederick H. Lahee. Wrather also served as an officer of the American Academy of Arts and Sciences (treasurer, 1941–1943), the American Association for the Advancement of Science (treasurer, 1941–1945; executive committee, 1942–1943), the American Institute of Mining and Metallurgical Engineers (AIMME; president, 1948–1949), the Geological Society of America (councilor, 1928–1932; vice president, 1932, 1936), and the Society of Economic Geologists (president, 1934–1935). From 1926 to 1963 Wrather helped to edit *Economic Geology*. He taught sporadically—in the spring of 1922 at Chicago and between 1927 and 1935 at Northwestern, Southern Methodist, Texas, and Yale.

Wrather traveled extensively outside the United States during these decades. He was a National Research Council delegate to or a vice president of three International Geological Congresses (IGC): in Madrid

(1926), Pretoria–Cape Town (1929), and Moscow-Leningrad (1937). In connection with these meetings, he examined the geology and mineral deposits of more than a dozen countries in Europe, Africa, and Asia. His assessment of geologic structures in Romania in 1925 and 1930 led to the discovery of the Ceptura field.

After the United States entered World War II, DeGolyer and Wrather moved to Washington, D.C., for full-time government employment. In 1942 Wrather became associate chief of the Board of Economic Warfare's Metals and Minerals Division, charged with procuring foreign supplies of strategic minerals. Less than a year later President Franklin D. Roosevelt appointed and the Senate confirmed Wrather as the USGS's sixth director, the first to be chosen from outside the agency. Secretary of the Interior Harold L. Ickes gave Wrather six months to place his impress on the USGS, then loaned him to Roosevelt's new Petroleum Reserves Corporation to accompany an oil mission to the Middle East. From November 1943 to January 1944 DeGolyer, Wrather, and three colleagues estimated the Middle East's oil reserves to supply wartime needs, further U.S. interests there, and conserve American supplies. After assessing oilfields and geologic structures in Egypt, Iran, Iraq, Saudi Arabia, and adjacent smaller states, they predicted reserves sufficiently large to shift the "center of gravity of world oil production . . . from the Gulf-Caribbean area . . . to the Persian Gulf area" (*AAPG Bulletin* 28 [1944]: 919). Wrather also visited USGS operations in Alaska, Brazil, and Hawaii during 1946 and 1947. He led the U.S. delegations to the British Empire Mining Congress at London and Oxford in 1949, the Third World Petroleum Congress at The Hague in 1951, and the 1953 IGC in Algiers.

Wrather returned to Washington as the executive branch began planning to resume peacetime operations in an era of big government and an endless scientific frontier. In 1944 he appointed an assistant director, freeing his own time and skills for business with Congress, government bureaus, industry, and other organizations. Beginning in 1946 Wrather reorganized the USGS to incorporate recent scientific and technological advances and to respond to increased needs, especially those for economic and engineering geology for national defense in the growing Cold War and the Korean conflict. These hostilities restricted the USGS's program of long-term basic research, which Wrather and his newly created science advisory committee considered vital to the agency's success.

Wrather continued to reorganize USGS programs and operations. Supporting an Interior Department request to decentralize its bureaus, he expanded or opened centers of field operations in Denver, Menlo Park, and Rolla, but he created no regional directors and kept the division chiefs at the Washington headquarters. The agency completed its conversion to topographic mapping by an advanced and integrated system of photogrammetry and pioneered the use of helicopters in fieldwork. In 1953 the USGS was made responsible for the programming and coordination of all federal topographic-mapping activities. During Wrather's directorate new geobotanical, geochemical, and geophysical techniques, including an airborne magnetometer originally developed by the navy to hunt Axis submarines, revolutionized the search for new mineral deposits. The USGS increased its efforts to assess U.S. oil reserves to aid exploration, including, from 1953, the nation's Outer Continental Shelf, and the agency also expanded its search for radioactive raw materials. Wrather promoted increased cooperation between the USGS and the state surveys in mapping, geologic studies, and investigations of water resources.

Wrather was seriously ill during his later years, and progressive paraplegia led to total disability in 1955. Immobilized in a wheelchair and with failing sight, Wrather submitted his resignation to President Dwight D. Eisenhower a year later. Many institutions and societies had honored his contributions to the nation. The University of Chicago awarded him its Alumni Medal on the occasion of its fiftieth anniversary. He received the AIMME's Anthony Lucas Medal (1950), the John Fritz Medal (1954, given jointly by the American Institute of Electrical Engineers, the AIMME, the American Society of Chemical Engineers, and the American Society of Mechanical Engineers), and the AAPG's Sidney Powers Medal (1956). Mount Wrather, in the Directors Range of Antarctica's Thiel Mountains, also commemorates his contributions to earth science. Wrather, an avid photographer, was active in the Chevy Chase, Cosmos, and Explorers clubs, served as a member and officer of municipal and state art, archaeological, geographical, and historical organizations, and participated on committees and on the board of trustees of the National Geographic Society. He died in Washington, D.C.

• Wrather's public papers from his USGS years are in RG 57 (Geological Survey) at the National Archives and Records Administration's (NARA) Archives II facility in College Park, Md. NARA's RG 169 (Foreign Economic Administration) contains documents relating to Wrather's service on the Board of Economic Warfare; RG 253 holds the files of the Petroleum Administration for War. Wrather's letters to DeGolyer, 1916–1956, are in the E. L. DeGolyer, Sr., Collection at Southern Methodist University's Fikes Hall of Special Collections and DeGolyer Library in Dallas, Tex. *U.S. Geological Survey Bulletin* 746 (1923): 1153; 823 (1931): 75, 586, 685–86; 937 (1944): 1047–48; 1049 (1957): 1012; and 1195 (1965): 1762, list most of Wrather's publications. These citations also are available on CD-ROM as part of the American Geological Institute's "GeoRef" online bibliographical database.

Wrather left a personal "Reminiscences" of 265 typescript pages prepared at St. Petersburg Beach, Florida; the USGS National Center Library in Reston, Virginia, holds a copy. The 42-page transcript of Henry C. Carlisle's interview "Reminiscences of Wrather" (1961) is in Columbia University's Oral History Collection and is described in *Mining Engineering* (Apr. 1964): 58–61. Ellis W. Schuler wrote an appreciation of Wrather in *Bulletin of the American Association of Petroleum Geologists* 28 (1944): 444–45. Brief memorials by colleagues include Alan M. Bateman, *Economic Geology* 59 (1964): 195; Wallace E. Pratt, *Bulletin of the American Association of Petroleum Geologists* 48 (1964): 1733–38 (with bibliography); John E. Brantly, *Bulletin of the Geological Society of America* 75 (1964): P71–P75 (with bibliography); and Thomas B. Nolan, *Proceedings of the Geological Society of London for 1963–1964*, no. 1618 (1965): 121–22. Mary C. Rabbitt, "The United States Geological Survey: 1879–1989," *USGS Circular* 1050 (1989): 35–38, provides an internal assessment of Wrather's directorate.

CLIFFORD M. NELSON

WRAXALL, Peter (?–11 July 1759), secretary of Indian affairs, was born in Bristol, England, the son of John Wraxall, a merchant. His mother's name is not known. No record of his early formal education has been found. Although the Wraxall family were prominent members of the local community, the economic fluctuations pertaining to merchant endeavors encouraged young Peter to leave the area in the hopes of achieving a greater degree of personal success and prosperity. He apparently resided in the Netherlands for a time, where he became familiar with the Dutch language. He next visited Jamaica and finally settled in the royal province of New York.

As early as 1746, during King George's war in America, Wraxall's name appears on the muster rolls of the colony, which include the names of men from Long Island "ready and truly inlisted in Peter Wraxall's Company of Foot for the present expedition to Canada." The following year, returning to England on urgent private business, he was entrusted with a letter from the colonial governor to the under secretary at Whitehall. Wraxall was to gather information on the state of relations between France and England in North America as well as on transactions relating to civil and military matters and political factionalism in the province of New York. The confidence shown in Wraxall suggests that he was competent and respected in colonial matters and was supported by powerful political friends in the governor's circle. While still in England, he received a royal commission dated 15 November 1750 to the positions of secretary or agent for the government of New York to the Indians and also as town clerk of the peace and clerk of the common pleas in the county and city of Albany. When he returned to New York, however, Wraxall discovered that through either neglect or ignorance the governor had already appointed someone town clerk. In spite of years of legal appeals, this royal commission was never honored.

Wraxall was therefore constrained to content himself with the wider duties of Indian secretary. This position was of significant importance, however, as the last great struggle for empire in North America between France and England was about to take place. Pivotal to the success of both powers was the ability to court and maintain the affections of the Six Nations Confederacy of Iroquois, whose land acted as a barrier between New France and the British colonies of New York and Pennsylvania, and "all other Indians." With the Iroquois wavering in their loyalty to the British, the factionalized American colonies, recognizing their military weakness and lack of defense preparations, organized a meeting at Albany in 1754. The "Albany Congress" resolved little, but of vital importance was the introduction of Peter Wraxall to William Johnson, one of the most powerful and influential men in the royal province of New York. The two men shared a common interest in Indian relations and a common distrust of the Albany Indian Commissionaires, who were essentially a group of self-interested merchants and traders.

That same year Wraxall wrote *An Abridgement of the Records of Indian Affairs: Contained in Four Folio Volumes, Transacted in the Colony of New York, from the Year 1678 to the Year 1751*. The *Abridgement*, based on the records of conferences and transactions between the Indians and the magistrates of the city and county of Albany, consisted of both Dutch and English documents and focused on the importance of Indian relations and the incompetency and inefficiency of the Albany Indian commissioners, suggested a single Crown appointment for Indian affairs, and hinted that William Johnson would be eminently qualified for the position. The *Abridgement* was promptly sent to the president of the Board of Trade and Plantations in London, a personal friend of Wraxall's, who subsequently forwarded to the king a series of recommendations drafted by the board, which offered solutions relating to the American colonies and Indian relations. Many of these recommendations echoed or recited the suggestions put forward by Wraxall, and in particular the idea of consolidating Indian affairs under one appointed Crown official. The importance of Wraxall's *Abridgement* in the formulation of British Indian policy in North America remains debatable, but there is no question that his detailed compilation of events, astute observations, and carefully worded suggestions influenced the final outcome. In April 1755 a formal and centralized Indian policy was finally realized when Johnson was given "the sole Management and Direction of the Affairs of the Six Nations and their Allies."

The close association and mutual respect between Johnson and Wraxall was strongly evidenced by the appointment of Wraxall, also in mid-April 1755, as Johnson's permanent secretary, a position he held until his death. With the outbreak of the French and Indian War in America, Wraxall participated alongside Johnson in conducting the affairs of the Indians. At Mount Johnson, north of the Mohawk River, a grand council was held between 21 June and 14 July 1755 in which an agreement was reached "to renew, to make more strong and bright than ever the Covenant Chain of peace and friendship." The Iroquois, especially the Mohawks, were particularly pleased with Johnson and put their trust in the king of England. Yet, for the most part, the "western nations" from the Ohio Valley and Great Lakes supported New France throughout the final conflict.

In the late summer of 1755 Wraxall, employed as secretary, aide-de-camp, and judge advocate, accompanied Johnson on the expedition against the French stronghold at Crown Point on the west side of Lake Champlain. A battle was fought south of that place at Lake George on 8 September in which Johnson's colonials won a stunning victory over a formidable force of French regulars. As a result of their success, one of the few victories achieved by the British and colonials over the next few years, Johnson's prestige, power, and influence in the colonies became paramount. In the shadows, his contributions to the shaping of British Indian policy unnoticed and not acknowledged by the public or the press, loomed the dominant figure of Peter Wraxall.

In January 1756, at Johnson's request, Wraxall prepared an astute analysis of the recent events from the Indian perspective. Titled "Thoughts upon the British Indian Interest in North America," the work accurately assessed the Indian view, observing in part that "our Six Nations and their Allies, . . . look upon the present disputes between the English and French . . . as a point of selfish ambition in us both and are apprehensive that which ever Nation gains their point will become their Masters not their deliverers." He concluded this section in prophetic fashion by declaring that the Indians suspected that neither of the two imperial rivals intended to restore lands to the Indians or to recognise the First Nations as the true "Proprietors of the soil."

For the next three years Wraxall continued to serve and attend the major Indian conferences as Johnson's secretary for Indian affairs. His last record of an Indian council was dated April 1759. But his life after 1756 was quite uneventful. He largely withdrew from military field service. Ill health and his marriage to Elizabeth Stillwell in 1756 may have contributed to his change of lifestyle. For the last two years of his life, he and his wife lived quietly in the city of New York, where he died.

Peter Wraxall made an important contribution to the formulation and implementation of British Indian policy during a critical period in the eighteenth century. His *Abridgement* and "Thoughts" influenced the course of British Indian policy and Indian-white relations for several decades. He understood and appreciated the nature of Indian politics and foresaw the long and bitter struggle between Indians and whites over the right of soil and land claims.

• The most important and useful source for the study of Peter Wraxall remains Charles Howard McIlwain's edition of *An Abridgement of the Records of Indian Affairs: Contained in Four Folio Volumes, Transacted in the Colony of New York, from the Year 1678 to the Year 1751* (1915). In particular, McIlwain provides a lengthy introduction that offers details, analyses, and background information to the events germane to Wraxall. In addition, there is an abundance of correspondence and records relating to colonial matters and Indian conferences to and from Peter Wraxall, scattered throughout *The Papers of Sir William Johnson*, ed. James J. Sullivan (14 vols., 1921–1965), and E. B. O'Callaghan and B. Fernow, eds., *Documents Relative to the Colonial History of the State of New York* (15 vols., 1853–1887). Some standard secondary sources that provide background details on events pertaining to Wraxall include Milton W. Hamilton, *Sir William Johnson: Colonial American, 1715–1763* (1976), and Francis Jennings, *Empire of Fortune: Crowns, Colonies and Tribes in the Seven Years' War in America* (1988).

ROBERT ALLEN

WRENN, Robert Duffield (20 Sept. 1873–12 Nov. 1925), tennis player and administrator, was born in Highland Park, Illinois, the son of George Lawson Wrenn, a Chicago insurance executive, and Eliza Everts. His three brothers, Everts, Philip, and George Lawson, Jr., also played tennis competitively. In 1891 Wrenn won the first U.S. Interscholastic championship as a student at Cambridge Latin School, Cambridge, Massachusetts. That fall he entered Harvard University and immediately won the U.S. Intercollegiate doubles title with upperclassman Fred Hovey. He captured that doubles crown again in 1892 with Fred Winslow.

During the 1892 U.S. championship at Newport, Rhode Island, Casino, Wrenn upset Percy Knapp, a tournament favorite, in a match lasting more than four hours. In the semifinals Hovey eliminated him. The following year Wrenn won the all-comers tournament at Newport and overcame Hovey in the challenge round to become the first left-handed player to win the U.S. championship. He defended his title in 1894 by downing Manliffe Goodbody, a visiting Irish star, who had won the all-comers. Wrenn prevailed by keeping Goodbody in backcourt, by reaching the net position first, and by lobbing 130 times.

Tested best at Harvard for quickness of perception and readiness and accuracy of muscular response, Wrenn excelled at sports. During the fall of 1894 he quarterbacked the Harvard football team to win eleven consecutive games, nine as shutouts. Harvard then lost, 12–4, to Yale, in a contest so rough that a three-year rift in football relations resulted, and, injury-ridden, lost 18–4 to the University of Pennsylvania. Wrenn, as acting captain against Yale, introduced the onside kickoff: "Instead of kicking the ball far down the gridiron, Waters sent it rolling down the ground while Wrenn chased it. The second it fell across the ten-yard line, Wrenn fell on it" (Morris A. Beale, *The History of Football at Harvard 1874–1948* [1948], p. 101).

That winter Wrenn joined an ice hockey team of men from several eastern colleges that played against Canadian squads in Canada during Christmas vacation. In the spring of 1895 he played second base on the Harvard baseball team before graduating with a bachelor of arts degree. He did not turn to serious business pursuits for another five years.

Wrenn's 1895 tennis season began late because of Harvard's lengthy baseball schedule, and he won no tournaments and lost his national singles title to Hovey. He did win the Eastern and National doubles championships with Malcolm Chace, a hockey teammate of the prior winter. He fared better in 1896, winning the Longwood and the Canadian singles and regaining his U.S. title at Newport. "Redoubtable Bob" survived tenaciously to win by defeating his brothers (Everts and George), Dwight Davis, Pen Hallowell, Carr Neel, and Bill Larned, all in five-set, come-from-behind efforts. In the challenge round, he defeated Hovey, his persistent nemesis, also in five tough sets. The following winter, Wrenn played forward for the undefeated St. Nicholas Hockey Club of New York City. His St. Nicks teammates included Larned and Harry Slocum, U.S. lawn tennis champion of 1888 and 1889.

American tennis players were opposed in 1897 by British visitors Wilberforce Eaves, Harold Mahony, and Harold Nisbet. During team matches, Wrenn defeated Mahony twice and split encounters with Eaves and Nisbet. Eaves and Nisbet swept Americans aside at Newport to reach the all-comers final, which was won by Eaves. In the challenge round, Wrenn bested Eaves in what James Dwight, president of the U.S. National Lawn Tennis Association (USNLTA), called "a great match, won by good judgement, endurance, and great power of return."

During the Spanish-American War of 1898, Larned and Wrenn served together in Cuba as privates in Troop A of the First U.S. Volunteer Cavalry, U.S. Army, the "Rough Riders," commanded by Colonels Leonard Wood and Theodore Roosevelt. Wrenn and Larned contracted virulent fevers. Wrenn, who suffered typhoid malaria, did not resume competitive tennis until 1900. Still sub par, he was defeated decisively at Newport by his brother George.

In December 1900 Wrenn purchased a seat on the New York Stock Exchange for a then-record $50,500 price. Later, with his brothers George and Philip, he formed the stock brokerage firm of Wrenn Brothers and Company, of New York City and Boston, Massachusetts: Philip was based in Boston, while the other two remained in New York.

On the tennis courts, George and Robert Wrenn formed a doubles combination that ranked first nationally in 1902 and represented the United States in the 1903 Davis Cup challenge round doubles, losing to Reggie and Laurie Doherty of the British Isles. Wrenn also played in the Davis Cup singles, losing to both Dohertys but extending Reggie to five sets. Wrenn's tournament career ended then but not his tennis activity. He accepted appointment in 1901 to the executive committee of the USNLTA, was elected vice president of the association, 1902–1911, and president, 1912–1915. He resigned the office after his 1915 term but remained a member of the executive committee the rest of his life.

In 1905 Wrenn married Grace Stackpole Dabney, a niece of Richard Dudley Sears, the first U.S. lawn tennis champion. Grace Wrenn died the next year, shortly following the birth of their daughter. Wrenn maintained residence in New York City and in the exclusive Tuxedo Park, New York, community. For athletic recreation, he played rackets, and in 1907 he won the American Racquet doubles championship with Reginald Fincke. During World War I he worked for the Signal Corps in Washington, D.C., and later, as a major, commanded an air squadron. Ill health forced his retirement from business in 1922. Three years later, he died of Bright's disease in New York City.

As a player, Wrenn's tennis game differed markedly from that of his first-class contemporaries. His forecourt and backcourt strokes had accuracy but lacked style and severity, and his backhand was weak. His best shot was a high lob, which he used frequently. He became an outstanding champion, despite stroke deficiencies, because he was a great match player and a brilliant strategist, who possessed endurance, fleetness, and the desire and ability to run down and return every ball. Above all, he demonstrated an indomitable will to win, never stronger than when he trailed in important matches. He devised the center theory, a long-respected strategy that directed the player, when forcing the net behind serve or drive, to send the ball to the center of the opponent's backcourt, in order to cut down the angles of passage on either side. He was elected in 1955 to the National Lawn Tennis (later International Tennis) Hall of Fame. A bronze tablet, erected in his honor in 1926 at the tennis stadium in Forest Hills, New York, describes Wrenn as "Courageous in Competition—Gracious in Personality—Inspiring in Leadership."

• Frederick H. Hovey, "Wrenn Becomes Champion," pp. 53–57, and "Passing Shots Win a Championship," pp. 58–62, in U.S. Lawn Tennis Association, *Fifty Years of Lawn Tennis in the United States* (1931), describes three championships in which Wrenn played Hovey. Edward C. Potter, *Kings of the Court* (1936), pp. 65–70, summarizes Wrenn's playing performance during 1892–1897, his peak years. Arthur S. Pier, "Some Tennis Champions," *American Magazine* 40 (Apr. 1910): 466–76, analyzes the playing characteristics of Wrenn and his chief rivals. Obituaries are in *American Lawn Tennis* 18 (15 Nov. 1925): 537–38, and the *New York Times*, 13 Nov. 1925.

FRANK V. PHELPS